W9-CTD-463

PRAISE FOR
THE BANTAM NEW COLLEGE
FRENCH AND ENGLISH DICTIONARY

"It will fill a real need. There is nothing of the kind. It is really *good*, with current, sensible translations reflecting real American and French usage . . . Clever, imaginative and oh-so-true equivalents of idiomatic expressions . . . A dictionary to recommend to students!"

—Yvone Lenard, Associate Professor of French,
California State College

"Professor Steiner's work contains a great deal of practical information not to be found in the large, expensive dictionaries. The book reveals genuinely imaginative scholarship, and his handling of it is intelligent, concise and meticulously consistent. I intend to make it known to students of all levels."

—Wilson L. Frescoln, Chairman, Department of
Modern Languages and Literatures,
Villanova University

Comprehensive, authoritative and completely modern, THE BANTAM NEW COLLEGE FRENCH AND ENGLISH DICTIONARY is a landmark in foreign language reference works.

THE BANTAM NEW
COLLEGE DICTIONARY SERIES

Roger J. Steiner, Author

Roger J. Steiner, A.B., A.M., Ph.D., has done extensive linguistic research in France, where he has traveled widely and taught for two years at the University of Bordeaux. Now a member of the French faculty at the University of Delaware, he is the author of a book dealing with the origin and development of bilingual dictionaries. TWO CENTURIES OF SPANISH AND ENGLISH LEXICOGRAPHY (The Hague and Paris, 1970), and has contributed articles and reviews to learned journals.

Edwin B. Williams, General Editor

Edwin B. Williams, A.B., A.M., Ph.D., Doct. d'Univ., LL.D., L.H.D., has been Chairman of the Department of Romance Languages, Dean of the Graduate School, and Provost of the University of Pennsylvania. He is a member of the American Philosophical Society and the Hispanic Society of America and the author of the Holt SPANISH AND ENGLISH DICTIONARY, THE BANTAM NEW COLLEGE SPANISH AND ENGLISH DICTIONARY and many other works on the Spanish, French and Portuguese languages.

THE BANTAM NEW COLLEGE
FRENCH & ENGLISH
DICTIONARY

DICTIONNAIRE
ANGLAIS et FRANÇAIS
BY ROGER J. STEINER
University of Delaware

BANTAM BOOKS
TORONTO · NEW YORK · LONDON

THE BANTAM NEW COLLEGE
FRENCH & ENGLISH DICTIONARY

A Bantam Book / published April 1972

PRINTING HISTORY

2nd printing .... July 1973   4th printing .. December 1975
3rd printing .... January 1974   5th printing .... July 1976
              6th printing ... December 1977

ISBN 0-553-11692-4

Published simultaneously in the United States and Canada

PRINTED IN THE UNITED STATES OF AMERICA

CONTENTS

PREFACE

Inasmuch as the basic function of a bilingual dictionary is to provide semantic equivalences, syntactical constructions are shown in both the source and target languages on both sides of the Dictionary. In performing this function, a bilingual dictionary must fulfill six purposes. For example, a French and English bilingual dictionary must provide (1) French words which an English-speaking person wishes to use in speaking and writing (by means of the English-French part), (2) English meanings of French words which an English-speaking person encounters in listening and reading (by means of the French-English part), (3) the spelling, pronunciation, and inflection of French words and the gender of French nouns which an English-speaking person needs in order to use French words correctly (by means of the French-English part), (4) English words which a French-speaking person wishes to use in speaking and writing (by means of the French-English part), (5) French meanings of English words which a French-speaking person encounters in listening and reading (by means of the English-French part), and (6) the spelling, pronunciation, and inflection of English words which a French-speaking person needs in order to use English words correctly (by means of the English-French part).

It may seem logical to provide the pronunciation and inflection of English words and the pronunciation and inflection of French words and the gender of French nouns where these words appear as target words inasmuch as target words, according to (1) and (4) above, are sought for the purpose of speaking and writing. Thus the user would find not only the words he seeks but all the information he needs about them at one and the same place. But this technique is impractical because target words are not alphabetized and could, therefore, be found only by the

PRÉFACE

La mission essentielle d'un dictionnaire bilingue étant de fournir à l'usager des équivalences sémantiques, les constructions syntaxiques sont données à la fois dans la langue source et dans la langue cible dans les deux parties de l'ouvrage. En s'acquittant de cette mission, le dictionnaire bilingue doit viser six buts; c'est ainsi qu'un dictionnaire bilingue français et anglais doit donner: (1) dans la partie anglais-français, les mots français que la personne anglophone désire utiliser pour parler et pour écrire; (2) dans la partie français-anglais, les acceptions anglaises des mots français que cette même personne entend dans la langue parlée et rencontre dans la lecture des textes; (3) dans la partie français-anglais, l'orthographe, la prononciation figurée, l'inflexion des mots français et le genre des noms français indispensables à l'anglophone pour l'utilisation correcte de la langue française; (4) dans la partie français-anglais, les mots anglais que la personne francophone désire utiliser pour parler et pour écrire; (5) dans la partie anglais-français, les acceptions françaises des mots anglais que cette même personne entend dans la langue parlée et rencontre dans la lecture des textes; (6) dans la partie anglais-français, l'orthographe, la prononciation figurée et l'inflexion des mots anglais indispensables au francophone pour l'utilisation correcte de la langue anglaise.

A première vue, il paraît logique que la prononciation et l'inflexion des mots anglais et la prononciation et l'inflexion des mots français et le genre des noms français soient indiqués à la suite des traductions puisqu'on recherche ces traductions, selon (1) et (4) ci-dessus, pour parler et pour écrire. Ainsi, l'usager trouverait au même endroit, non seulement les mots qu'il cherche, mais également tous les renseignements dont il aurait besoin. Cependant, ce procédé n'est pas pratique parce que les traductions ne sont pas présentées dans l'ordre alphabétique et l'on ne pourrait les

roundabout and uncertain way of seeking them through their translations in the other part of the dictionary. And this would be particularly inconvenient for persons using the dictionary for purposes (2) and (5) above. It is much more convenient to provide immediate alphabetized access to pronunciation and inflection where the words appear as source words. Showing the gender of nouns takes so little space that this information is provided with both source and target words.

trouver qu'avec difficulté. Cela entraînerait surtout des inconvénients pour les personnes qui utilisent le dictionnaire dans les cas (2) et (5) ci-dessus. L'ordre alphabétique permet un accès immédiat et plus commode à la prononciation et à l'inflexion quand les mots se présentent comme mots-souches. Néanmoins, l'indication du genre des noms prend si peu de place qu'elle figure aussi bien après les traductions qu'après les mots-souches.

All words are treated in a fixed order according to the parts of speech and the functions of verbs, as follows: article, adjective, substantive, pronoun, adverb, preposition, conjunction, transitive verb, intransitive verb, impersonal verb, auxiliary verb, reflexive verb, impersonal reflexive verb, interjection.

Tous les mots-souches sont traités suivant un ordre fixe—selon les parties du discours et les fonctions des verbes —qui est le suivant: article, adjectif, substantif, pronom, adverbe, préposition, conjonction, verbe transitif, verbe intransitif, verbe impersonnel, verbe auxiliaire, verbe pronominal (réfléchi ou réciproque), verbe à la fois impersonnel et réfléchi, interjection.

Meanings with subject and usage labels come after more general meanings. Subject and usage labels (printed in roman and in parentheses) refer to the preceding entry or phrase (printed in boldface). However, when labels come immediately, i.e., without any intervening punctuation mark, after a target word. they refer to that target word and the preceding word or words separated from it only by commas, e.g.,

Les sens d'un mot suivis des rubriques qui indiquent le sujet ou l'usage du mot viennent à la suite des sens d'emploi normal. Les rubriques qui indiquent le sujet ou l'usage du mot (imprimées en caractères romains et entre parenthèses) s'appliquent au mot-souche ou à la locution précédente (imprimés en caractères gras). Cependant, lorsque la rubrique suit immédiatement la traduction. c'est-à-dire sans aucun signe de ponctuation, elle s'applique à la traduction elle-même ou aux traductions précédentes qui n'en sont séparées que par une virgule, par ex.,

---

optometrist [ɑp'tɑmɪtrɪst] *s* opticien *m*; optométriste *mf* (Canad)

English adjectives are always translated by the French masculine form regardless of whether the translation of the exemplary noun modified would be masculine or feminine, e.g.,

Les adjectifs anglais sont toujours traduits en français au masculin, quel que soit le genre des traductions des noms donnés en exemple et auxquelles ils se rapportent, par ex.,

---

close [klos] *adj* . . . ; (*friendship*) étroit; (*room*) renfermé

In order to facilitate the finding of the meaning and use sought for, changes within a vocabulary entry in part of speech and function of verb, in irregular inflection, in the gender of French nouns, and in the pronunciation of

Afin de faciliter le repérage de l'acception cherchée, les traductions sont groupées selon la partie du discours, la fonction du verbe, l'inflexion irrégulière, le genre du nom français, et la prononciation des mots français et des

French and English words are marked with parallels: ||, instead of the usual semicolons.

Since vocabulary entries are not determined on the basis of etymology, homographs are included in a single entry. When the pronunciation of a homograph changes, this is shown in the proper place after parallels.

Note, however, that plurals and words spelled with capitals are shown as run-on entries. They must be preceded by parallels only when there is a change in part of speech, in pronunciation, or in inflection.

Peculiarities in the pronunciation of the plural of nouns and of run-on entries are generally indicated, e.g.,

mots anglais. Ces groupes sont séparés par deux barres: ||, au lieu du point-virgule habituel.

Etant donné que l'étymologie n'entre pas dans la séparation des articles, tous les homographes sont incorporés dans le même article. Quand la prononciation d'un homographe change, cette prononciation figurée est placée entre crochets à la suite des deux barres ||.

On remarquera cependant que les pluriels et les mots qui commencent par une majuscule sont présentés parmi les locutions dans l'ordre alphabétique et ne sont séparés de celles-ci que par un point-virgule. Ils ne sont précédés des deux barres || qu'en cas de changement dans la partie du discours, dans la prononciation, ou dans l'inflexion.

Les caractéristiques spéciales de la prononciation du pluriel des noms et des locutions sont généralement indiquées, ex.:

mouth [mauθ] *s* (*pl* mouths [mauðz])
house [haus] *s* (*pl* houses ['hauziz])
œil [œj] *m* . . . ; **entre quatre yeux** [ãtrəkatzjø]
guet-apens [getapã] *m* (*pl* guets-apens [getapã])

Periods are omitted after labels and grammatical abbreviations and at the end of vocabulary entries.

Proper nouns and abbreviations are listed in their alphabetical position in the main body of the Dictionary. Thus **Algérie** and **algérien** or **Suède** and **suédois** do not have to be looked up in two different parts of the book. And all subentries are listed in strictly alphabetical order.

The feminine form of a French adjective used as a noun (or a French feminine noun having identical spelling with the feminine form of an adjective) which falls alphabetically in a separate position from the adjective is treated in that position and is listed again as a cross reference under the adjective.

Les points sont omis après les rubriques, les abréviations d'ordre grammatical et à la fin des articles.

Les noms propres et les abréviations se présentent toujours dans l'ordre alphabétique de la nomenclature du Dictionnaire. Par exemple, il n'est pas nécessaire de chercher **Algérie** et **algérien** ou **Suède** et **suédois** dans deux parties du livre. Toutes les locutions se présentent rigoureusement dans l'ordre alphabétique.

Lorsque la forme féminine d'un adjectif français ne suit pas immédiatement la forme masculine alphabétiquement (ou lorsqu'il s'agit d'un nom féminin français qui aurait une orthographe identique à la forme féminine de l'adjectif), et lorsqu'elle est prise substantivement, sa position comme mot-souche substantif est strictement alphabétique; mais un renvoi se trouve alors après le mot-souche adjectif.

cher chère [ʃɛr] *adj* . . . || *f* see **chère** || . . .
chère [ʃɛr] *f* fare, food and drink; . . .

The centered period is used in vocabulary entries of inflected words to mark off, according to standard orthographic principles in the two languages, the final syllable that has to be detached before the syllable showing the inflection is added, e.g.,

Quand les mots-souches sont des vocables à flexions, on emploie le point centré · pour séparer, selon les principes reconnus de l'orthographe des deux langues, la syllabe finale qui doit être détachée avant que la syllabe de la désinence ne soit attachée, ex.:

heu·reux [œrø] **-reuse** [røz]
satis·fy ['sætɪs‚faɪ] *v* (*pret & pp* **-fied**)

Since the orthographic break coming in French words (a) between the two l's of liquid l, (b) between s and c followed by e, i, or y, and (c) between the two elements of any double consonant pronounced as a single consonant does not correspond to the phonetic break, the centered period is used as usual but the full form of the inflected variant is shown, also with the centered period, and the full phonetic transcription of both forms is shown without a break, e.g.,

Puisque la séparation orthographique qui se trouve dans les mots français (a) entre les deux l de l'l mouillé, (b) entre s et c suivi de e, i, ou y et (c) entre les deux éléments de n'importe quelle consonne doublée prononcée comme simple consonne, ne répond pas à la séparation phonétique, on présente la forme entière de toute variante, imprimée également avec le point centré; et la transcription phonétique complète des deux formes se présente sans séparation, ex.:

(a) **merveil·leux** [mervejø] **merveill·leuse** [mervejøz]
(b) **évanes·cent** [evanesã] **évanes·cente** [evanesãt]
(c) **éton·nant** [etonã] **éton·nante** [etonãt]
     miel·leux [mjelø] **miel·leuse** [mjeløz]

Where the orthographic break, according to some authorities,* is not permitted, for example, between a y and a following vowel, the centered period is not used, e.g.,

Lorsque selon l'avis de certains spécialistes,* la séparation orthographique n'est pas permise, par exemple, entre un y et la voyelle suivante, on n'utilisera pas le point centré, ex.:

croyant [krwajã] **croyante** [krwajãt]
métayer [meteje] **métayère** [metejer]

* V. Maurice Grevisse, *Le Bon Usage*, 8th ed., 1964, §89, p. 52.

If the two components of an English solid compound are not separated by an accent mark, a centered period is used to mark off the division between them, e.g., **la′dy·bird′**.

Dans les cas où les deux éléments d'un mot composé anglais écrit comme mot simple, ne seraient pas séparés par un accent, on utilisera un point centré pour montrer la division entre les deux, par ex., **la′dy·bird′**.

Numbers referring to the model tables of French verbs (p. 7 ff.) are placed before the abbreviation indicating the part of speech. Numbers referring to the model tables of other French parts of speech (p. 21 ff.) are placed

Les numéros qui renvoient aux tableaux des verbes français à partir de la p. 7, précèdent l'abréviation qui indique la partie du discours. Les numéros qui renvoient aux tableaux des indications grammaticales des autres parties

after the French word on both sides of the Dictionary.

du discours, à partir de la p. **21**, sont placés à la suite du mot français dans chaque partie du Dictionnaire.

There are some French transitive verbs which, when used reflexively, take the reflexive pronoun in the dative. As reflexive verbs they may still take a direct object and may, accordingly, be translated by English transitive verbs. And they may in turn be used to translate English transitive verbs. This equation is shown on the French-English side after the abbreviation *ref* by the insertion of (with *dat* of *reflex pron*). It is not shown on the English-French side, as the abbreviation *tr* indicates unmistakably the syntactical relationship.

Il y a certains verbes français transitifs qui sous la forme pronominale régissent le pronom réfléchi comme complément d'attribution. Cependant, sous cette forme pronominale ils sont également transitifs et peuvent se traduire par des verbes transitifs anglais. Inversement, ces verbes pronominaux français peuvent traduire des verbes transitifs anglais. Cette équation est indiquée dans la partie français-anglais à la suite de l'abréviation *ref* par l'insertion de (with *dat* of *reflex pron*). Elle n'est pas indiquée dans la partie anglais-français, puisque l'abréviation *tr* indique nettement la relation syntaxique.

The author wishes to express his gratitude to many persons who helped him in the production of this book and particularly to Dr. Edwin B. Williams, whose efforts were unstinting in the attempt to make this a useful dictionary, to his dear wife Kathryn, whose patience carried through the ten years of research and compilation, and to René Coulet du Gard and to Claud J. Pujolle for their constant help, as well as to the following: Jean Béranger, Brigitte Callay, Paul Dumestre, Maurice Jonas, Marc and Philomena Lampe, Daniel Pralus, Wayne and Paule Ready, and André Vincent.

Labels and Grammatical Abbreviations
Rubriques et abréviations grammaticales

abbr abbreviation—abréviation
(acronym) word formed from the initial letters or syllables of a series of words—mot formé de la suite des lettres initiales ou des syllabes initiales d'une série de mots
adj adjective—adjectif
adv adverb—adverbe
(aer) aeronautics—aéronautique
(agr) agriculture—agriculture
(alg) algebra—algèbre
(anat) anatomy—anatomie
(archaic) archaïque
(archeol) archeology—archéologie
(archit) architecture—architecture
(arith) arithmetic—arithmétique
art article—article
(arti) artillery—artillerie
(astr) astronomy—astronomie
(astrol) astrology—astrologie
(aut) automobile—automobile
aux auxiliary verb—verbe auxiliaire
(bact) bacteriology—bactériologie
(baseball) base-ball
(bb) bookbinding—reliure
(Bib) Biblical—biblique
(billiards) billard
(biochem) biochemistry—biochimie
(biol) biology—biologie
(bk) bookkeeping—comptabilité
(bot) botany—botanique
(bowling) jeu de quilles, jeu de boules
(boxing) boxe
(Brit) British—britannique
(Canad) Canadian—canadien
(*cap*) capital—majuscule
(cards) cartes
(carpentry) charpenterie
(checkers) jeu de dames
(chem) chemistry—chimie
(chess) échecs
(coll) colloquial—familier
(com) commercial—commercial
comp comparative—comparatif
(comp) computers—ordinateurs
(complimentary close) formule de politesse
cond conditional—conditionnel
conj conjunction—conjonction; conjunctive—atone
(culin) cooking—cuisine
dat dative—datif
def definite—défini
dem demonstrative—démonstratif
(dentistry) art dentaire
(dial) dialectal—dialectal

(dipl) diplomacy—diplomatie
disj disjunctive—tonique
(eccl) ecclesiastical—ecclésiastique
(econ) economics—économique
(educ) education—éducation, pédagogie
e.g. par ex.
(elec) electricity—électricité
(electron) electronics—électronique
(embryol) embryology—embryologie
(eng) engineering—profession de l'ingénieur, génie
(ent) entomology—entomologie
(equit) horseback riding—équitation
(escr) fencing—escrime
f feminine noun—nom féminin
(fa) fine arts—beaux-arts
fem feminine—féminin
(feudal) feudalism—féodalité
(fig) figurative—figuré
(fishing) pêche
fpl feminine noun plural—nom féminin pluriel
fut future—futur
(game) jeu
(geog) geography—géographie
(geol) geology—géologie
(geom) geometry—géométrie
ger gerund—gérondif
(govt) government—gouvernement
(gram) grammar—grammaire
(gymnastics) gymnastique
(heral) heraldry—héraldique, blason
(hist) history—histoire
(hort) horticulture—horticulture
(hum) humorous—humoristique
(hunting) chasse
(ichth) ichthyology—ichtyologie
i.e. c.-à-d.
imperf imperfect—imparfait
impers impersonal verb—verbe impersonnel
impv imperative—impératif
ind indicative—indicatif
indef indefinite—indéfini
inf infinitive—infinitif
(ins) insurance—assurance
interj interjection—interjection
interr interrogative—interrogatif
intr intransitive—intransitif
invar invariable—invariable
(ironical) ironique
(jewelry) bijouterie
(journ) journalism—journalisme
(Lat) Latin—latin
(law) droit
(*l.c.*) lower case—bas de casse

xii

(letterword) word in the form of an abbreviation which is pronounced by sounding the names of its letters in succession and which functions as a part of speech—mot en forme d'abréviation qu'on prononce en faisant sonner le nom de chaque lettre consécutivement et qui fonctionne comme partie du discours

(lit) literary—littéraire

(logic) logique

m masculine noun—nom masculin

(mach) machinery—machinerie

(mas) masonry—maçonnerie

masc masculine—masculin

(Masonry) franc-maçonnerie

(math) mathematics—mathématiques

(mech) mechanics—mécanique

(med) medicine—médecine

(metallurgy) métallurgie

(meteo) meteorology—météorologie

mf masculine or feminine noun according to sex—nom masculin ou nom féminin selon le sexe

[for *m* & *f* see abbreviation following **(mythol)**]

(mil) military—militaire

(min) mining—travail des mines

(mineral) mineralogy—minéralogie

(mountaineering) alpinisme

(mov) moving pictures—cinéma

mpl masculine noun plural—nom masculin pluriel

(mus) music—musique

(mythol) mythology—mythologie

m & *f* masculine and feminine noun without regard to sex—nom masculin et féminin sans distinction de sexe

(naut) nautical—nautique

(nav) naval—naval

neut neuter—neutre

(nucl) nuclear physics—physique nucléaire

(obs) obsolete—vieilli, vieux

(obstet) obstetrics—obstétrique

(opt) optics—optique

(orn) ornithology—ornithologie

(painting) peinture

(parl) parliamentary procedure—usages parlementaires

(pathol) pathology—pathologie

(pej) pejorative—péjoratif

perf perfect—parfait

pers personal—personnel; person—personne

(pharm) pharmacy—pharmacie

(phila) philately—philatélie

(philos) philosophy—philosophie

(phonet) phonetics—phonétique

(phot) photography—photographie

(phys) physics—physique

(physiol) physiology—physiologie

pl plural—pluriel

(poetic) poetical—poétique

(pol) politics—politique

poss possessive—possessif

pp past participle—participe passé

prep preposition—préposition

pres present—présent

pret preterit—prétérit, passé simple

pron pronoun—pronom

(pros) prosody—métrique, prosodie

(psychoanal) psychoanalytic—psychanalytique

(psychol) psychology—psychologie

(psychopathol) psychopathology—psychopathologie

(public sign) affiche, écriteau

q.ch. or *q.ch.* quelque chose—something

qn or *qn* quelqu'un—someone

(rad) radio—radio

ref reflexive verb—verbe pronominal, réfléchi ou réciproque

reflex reflexive—réfléchi

rel relative—relatif

(rel) religion—religion

(rhet) rhetoric—rhétorique

(rok) rocketry—fusées

(rowing) canotage

(rr) railroad—chemin de fer

s substantive—substantif

(sculp) sculpture—sculpture

(seismol) seismology—sismologie

(sewing) couture

sg singular—singulier

(slang) populaire, argotique

s.o. or *s.o.* someone—quelqu'un

spl substantive plural—substantif pluriel

(sports) sports

s.th. or *s.th.* something—quelque chose

subj subjunctive—subjonctif

super superlative—superlatif

(surg) surgery—chirurgie

(surv) surveying—topographie

(swimming) nage

(taur) bullfighting—tauromachie

(telg) telegraphy—télégraphie

(telp) telephony—téléphonie

(telv) television—télévision

(tennis) tennis

(tex) textile—textile

(theat) theater—théâtre

(theol) theology—théologie

tr transitive verb—verbe transitif

(trademark) marque déposée

(turf) horse racing—courses de chevaux

(typ) printing—imprimerie

(U.S.A.) U.S.A., E.-U.A.

v verb—verbe

var variant—variante

(vet) veterinary medicine—médecine vétérinaire

(vulg) vulgar—grossier

(wrestling) lutte, catch

(zool) zoology—zoologie

PART ONE

French-English

French Pronunciation

The following phonetic symbols represent all the sounds of the French language.

VOWELS

SYMBOL	SOUND	EXAMPLE
[a]	A little more open than the a in English **hat**.	patte [pat]
[ɑ]	Like **a** in English **father**.	pâte [pɑt] phase [fɑz]
[ɛ]	Like e in English **met**.	sec [sɛk] fer [fɛr] fête [fɛt] aile [ɛl] parallèle [paralɛl]
[e]	Like a in English **fate**, but without the glide the English sound sometimes has.	été [ete] fée [fe] et [e] créer [kree]
[ə]	Like a in English **comma** or like o in English **pardon**.	le [lə] petit [pəti]
[i]	Like i in English **machine** or like e in English **she**.	si [si]
[ɔ]	A little more open and rounded than **aw** in English **law**.	donne [dɔn] joli [jɔli]
[o]	Like o in English **note** but without the glide the English sound sometimes has.	mot [mo] eau [o] faute [fot]
[u]	Like **u** in English **rude**.	sou [su] four [fur]
[y]	The lips are rounded for [u] and held without moving while the sound [i] is pronounced.	su [sy] sûr [syr]
[ø]	The lips are rounded for [o] and held without moving while the sound [e] is pronounced.	peu [pø] eux [ø] feutre [føtr]
[œ]	The lips are rounded for [ɔ] and held without moving while the sound [ɛ] is pronounced.	peur [pœr] seul [sœl]

NASAL VOWELS

To produce the nasal vowels, sound is emitted through both nose and mouth by means of a lowering of the velum. The orthographic **m** or **n** has no consonantal value.

SYMBOL	SOUND	EXAMPLE
[ɑ̃]	Like **a** in English **father** and nasalized.	en [ɑ̃] tant [tɑ̃] temps [tɑ̃] paon [pɑ̃]
[ɔ̃]	More close than **aw** in English **law** and nasalized.	on [ɔ̃] pont [pɔ̃] comte [kɔ̃t]
[ɛ̃]	Like e in English **met** and nasalized.	pin [pɛ̃] pain [pɛ̃] faim [fɛ̃] teint [tɛ̃]
[œ̃]	Like [œ] of French **bœuf** and nasalized. There has been a tendency in this century to assimilate the nasal sound [œ̃] to the nasal sound [ɛ̃], making **brun** [brœ̃] and **brin** [brɛ̃] sound much the same.	un [œ̃] parfum [parfœ̃]

3

DIPHTHONGS

The sounds [j], [ɥ], and [w] are used to form diphthongs.

SYMBOL	SOUND	EXAMPLE
[j]	Like **y** in English **year** or like **y** in English **toy**.	**hier** [jer] **ail** [aj]
[ɥ]	Like the letter **u** [y] pronounced with consonantal value preceding a vowel.	**lui** [lɥi] **situation** [sitɥasjɔ̃] **nuage** [nɥaʒ] **écuelle** [ekɥel]
[w]	Like **w** in English **water**.	**oie** [wa] **jouer** [ʒwe] **jouir** [ʒwir]

CONSONANTS

The speaker of French characteristically keeps the tip of his tongue down behind his lower teeth and arches the back of the tongue at the same time. Thus, sounds such as [t], [d], [n], [s], [z], [l], and [r] must in French be articulated with the tongue tip and blade in the proximity of the back surface of the teeth.

SYMBOL	SOUND	EXAMPLE
[b]	Like **b** in English **baby**.	**basse** [bɑs]
[d]	Like **d** in English **dead**.	**doux** [du]
[f]	Like **f** in English **face**.	**fou** [fu]
[g]	Like **g** in English **go**.	**gare** [gar]
[k]	Like **k** in English **kill**, but without the aspiration which normally accompanies **k** in English.	**cas** [kɑ] **kiosque** [kjɔsk]
[l]	Like **l** in English **like** or in English **slip**—pronounced toward the front of the mouth. Not like **l** in **old**.	**lit** [li] **houle** [ul]
[m]	Like **m** in English **more**.	**masse** [mas]
[n]	Like **n** in English **nest**.	**nous** [nu]
[ɲ]	Like **ny** in English **canyon** or like **ni** in English **onion**.	**signe** [siɲ] **agneau** [aɲo]
[ŋ]	Like **ng** in English **parking**.	**parking** [parkiŋ]
[p]	Like **p** in English **pen**, but without the aspiration which normally accompanies **p** in English.	**passe** [pɑs]
[r]	Sometimes the uvular **r** but for some decades now usually a friction **r** with the point of articulation between the rounded back of the tongue and the hard palate. It resembles the Spanish aspirate in **jota**, the German aspirate in **ach**, and the **g** in the modern Greek **gamma** more than it resembles the modern American retroflex **r**. The tip of the tongue must point down near the back of the lower teeth and must not move during the utterance of the French [r].	**rire** [rir] **caractère** [karakter] **roi** [rwa] **roue** [ru]
[s]	Like **s** in English **send**.	**sot** [so] **leçon** [ləsɔ̃] **place** [plas] **lassitude** [lasityd] **attention** [atɑ̃sjɔ̃]
[ʃ]	Like **sh** in English **shall** or **ch** in English **machine**.	**cheval** [ʃval] **mèche** [mɛʃ]
[t]	Like **t** in English **ten**, but without the aspiration which normally accompanies **t** in English.	**toux** [tu] **thé** [te]

4

SYMBOL	SOUND	EXAMPLE
[v]	Like v in English **vest**.	**verre** [vɛr]
[z]	Like z in English **zeal**.	**zèle** [zɛl]
		oser [oze]
[ʒ]	Like s in English **pleasure**.	**joue** [ʒu]
		rouge [ruʒ]
		mangeur [mɑ̃ʒœr]

FRENCH STRESS

Stress is not shown on French words in this Dictionary because stress is not a fixed characteristic of the pronunciation of French words. It depends on the position of the word in the sentence and it falls on the last syllable of the word that terminates a rhythmic or sense grouping unless the vowel of that syllable is a mute **e** [ə], in which case it falls on the immediately preceding syllable.

VOWEL LENGTH

Vowel length is not shown in the phonetic transcription of French words in this Dictionary because it, like stress, is not a fixed characteristic of the pronunciation of French words. The following vowel sounds in the positions indicated are long when stressed: 1) all when followed by [r], [z], [v], [ʒ], or [vr]; 2) all spelled with a circumflex accent and followed by a consonant sound; and 3) [ɑ̃], [ɔ̃], [ɛ̃], [œ̃], [ɑ], [o], and [ø] followed by a consonant sound. When these conditions are not fulfilled, all vowel sounds are normal in length (or sometimes they may be short in length, even when stressed, if followed by [k], [p], [t], [kt], [rk], [rp], or [rt]).

ELISION AND LIAISON

Elision and liaison are usually made with words beginning with a vowel or a mute **h**. Elision and liaison are made with some words beginning with **y**, such as: **yèbe, yeuse, yeux, Yonne,** and **York**.

However, there are words which begin with a vowel or an h with which elision and liaison are not made. Most of these words begin with **h**, called aspirate **h**, although it has not been pronounced for centuries. In this Dictionary these words are indicated by an asterisk placed before the opening bracket of the phonetic symbols, e.g., **hameau** *[amo], **onze** *[ɔ̃z], **a** *[ɑ], **s** *[ɛs].

TABLE OF FRENCH REGULAR VERBS

The letters standing before the names of the tenses in this table correspond to the designation of the tenses shown on the following page. The forms printed in boldface correspond to the key forms described likewise on the following page.

TENSE	FIRST CONJUGATION	SECOND CONJUGATION	THIRD CONJUGATION
inf	**DONNER**	**FINIR**	**VENDRE**
ger	donnant	finissant	vendant
pp	donné	fini	vendu
a) *impv*	donne	finis	vends
	donnons	finissons	vendons
	donnez	finissez	vendez
b) *pres ind*	**donne**	**finis**	**vends**
	donnes	finis	vends
	donne	finit	vend
	donnons	**finissons**	**vendons**
	donnez	finissez	vendez
	donnent	**finissent**	**vendent**
c) *pres subj*	donne	finisse	vende
	donnes	finisses	vendes
	donne	finisse	vende
	donnions	finissions	vendions
	donniez	finissiez	vendiez
	donnent	finissent	vendent
d) *imperf ind*	donnais	finissais	vendais
	donnais	finissais	vendais
	donnait	finissait	vendait
	donnions	finissions	vendions
	donniez	finissiez	vendiez
	donnaient	finissaient	vendaient
e) *fut ind*	**donnerai**	**finirai**	**vendrai**
	donneras	finiras	vendras
	donnera	finira	vendra
	donnerons	finirons	vendrons
	donnerez	finirez	vendrez
	donneront	finiront	vendront
pres cond	donnerais	finirais	vendrais
	donnerais	finirais	vendrais
	donnerait	finirait	vendrait
	donnerions	finirions	vendrions
	donneriez	finiriez	vendriez
	donneraient	finiraient	vendraient
f) *pret ind*	**donnai**	**finis**	**vendis**
	donnas	finis	vendis
	donna	finit	vendit
	donnâmes	finîmes	vendîmes
	donnâtes	finîtes	vendîtes
	donnèrent	finirent	vendirent
imperf subj	donnasse	finisse	vendisse
	donnasses	finisses	vendisses
	donnât	finît	vendît
	donnassions	finissions	vendissions
	donnassiez	finissiez	vendissiez
	donnassent	finissent	vendissent

MODEL VERBS

ORDER OF TENSES

(a) imperative
(b) present indicative
(c) present subjunctive

(d) imperfect indicative
(e) future indicative
(f) preterit indicative

In addition to the infinitive, gerund, and past participle, all simple tenses are shown in these tables if they contain one irregular form or more, except the conditional (which can always be derived from the stem of the future indicative) and the imperfect subjunctive (which can always be derived from the preterit indicative). Those forms are considered irregular which deviate morphologically and/or orthographically in root, stem, or ending from the paradigms of regular verbs which appear on page 6. The infinitive is printed in boldface capital letters. And the following forms are printed in boldface: (1) key forms (that is, irregular forms from which other irregular forms can be derived, but not the derived forms), e.g., **buvons**, (2) individual irregular forms which occupy the place of key forms but cannot function as key forms because other irregular forms cannot be derived from them, e.g., **sommes**, and (3) individual irregular forms which cannot be derived from key forms, e.g., **dites**. The names of the key forms and the forms derived from each of them are listed below.

KEY FORM	DERIVED FORMS
1st sg pres ind	2d & 3d sg pres ind & 2d sg impv*
1st pl pres ind	2d pl pres ind, 1st & 2d pl pres subj, whole *imperf ind*, 1st & 2d pl impv, & ger
3d pl pres ind	whole sg & 3d pl pres subj
1st sg fut ind	rest of *fut ind* & whole *conditional*
1st sg pret ind	rest of *pret ind* & whole *imperf subj*

* Some irregular verbs of the third conjugation which end in s, not preceded by d, in the *1st sg pres ind*, end in s also in the *2d sg pres ind* and the *2d sg impv*, and in t in the *3d sg pres ind*, e.g., **crains, crains, craint** and **bois, bois, boit**. And three verbs, namely, **pouvoir, valoir,** and **vouloir,** which end in x in the *1st sg pres ind*, end in x also in the *2d sg pres ind* and the *2d sg impv*, and in t in the *3d sg pres ind*, e.g., **veux, veux, veut**.

7

1st sg pres subj of **faire,**   rest of *pres subj*
   pouvoir, & **savoir**
1st sg pres subj of **aller,**   *2d & 3d sg & 3d pl pres subj*
   valoir, & **vouloir**

§1   ABRÉGER—abrégeant—abrégé   Combination of §10 and §38
   (a) abrège, abrégeons, abrégez
   (b) **abrège,** abrèges, abrège, **abrégeons,** abrégez, **abrègent**
   (c) abrège, abrèges, abrège, abrégions, abrégiez, abrègent
   (d) abrégeais, abrégeais, abrégeait, abrégions, abrégiez, abré-
        geaient
   (f) **abrégeai,** abrégeas, abrégea, abrégeâmes, abrégeâtes, abré-
        gèrent

§2   ACHETER—achetant—acheté
   (a) achète, achetons, achetez
   (b) **achète,** achètes, achète, achetons, achetez, **achètent**
   (c) achète, achètes, achète, achetions, achetiez, achètent
   (e) **achèterai,** achèteras, achètera, achèterons, achèterez, achè-
        teront

§3   ACQUÉRIR—acquérant—**acquis**
   (a) acquiers, acquérons, acquérez
   (b) **acquiers,** acquiers, acquiert, **acquérons,** acquérez, **acquiè-
        rent**
   (c) acquière, acquières, acquière, acquérions, acquériez,
        acquièrent
   (d) acquérais, acquérais, acquérait, acquérions, acquériez,
        acquéraient
   (e) **acquerrai,** acquerras, acquerra, acquerrons, acquerrez,
        acquerront
   (f) **acquis,** acquis, acquit, acquîmes, acquîtes, acquirent

§4   ALLER—allant—allé
   (a) **va,** allons, allez
   (b) **vais** [ve], **vas, va,** allons, allez, **vont**
   (c) **aille** [aj], ailles, aille, allions, alliez, aillent
   (e) **irai,** iras, ira, irons, irez, iront

§5A   ASSEOIR—asseyant—**assis**
   (a) assieds, asseyons, asseyez
   (b) **assieds,** assieds, assied, **asseyons,** asseyez, **asseyent**
   (c) asseye, asseyes, asseye, asseyions, asseyiez, asseyent
   (d) asseyais, asseyais, asseyait, asseyions, asseyiez, asseyaient
   (e) **assiérai,** assiéras, assiéra, assiérons, assiérez, assiéront
   (f) **assis,** assis, assit, assîmes, assîtes, assirent

8

§5B ASSEOIR—assoyant—**assis**
  (a) assois, assoyons, assoyez
  (b) **assois**, assois, assoit, **assoyons**, assoyez, **assoient**
  (c) assoie, assoies, assoie, assoyions, assoyiez, assoient
  (d) assoyais, assoyais, assoyait, assoyions, assoyiez, assoyaient
  (e) **assoirai**, assoiras, assoira, assoirons, assoirez, assoiront
  (f) **assis**, assis, assit, assîmes, assîtes, assirent

§6 AVOIR—ayant—eu [y]
  (a) **aie** [e], **ayons**, ayez
  (b) **ai** [e], **as, a, avons**, avez, **ont**
  (c) **aie, aies, ait, ayons, ayez, aient**
  (d) avais, avais, avait, avions, aviez, avaient
  (e) **aurai**, auras, aura, aurons, aurez, auront
  (f) **eus** [y], eus, eut, eûmes, eûtes, eurent

§7 BATTRE—battant—battu
  (a) bats, battons, battez
  (b) **bats**, bats, bat, battons, battez, battent

§8 BOIRE—buvant—bu
  (a) bois, buvons, buvez
  (b) bois, bois, boit, **buvons**, buvez, **boivent**
  (c) boive, boives, boive, buvions, buviez, boivent
  (d) buvais, buvais, buvait, buvions, buviez, buvaient
  (f) **bus**, bus, but, bûmes, bûtes, burent

§9 BOUILLIR—bouillant—bouilli
  (a) bous, bouillons, bouillez
  (b) **bous**, bous, bout, **bouillons**, bouillez, **bouillent**
  (c) bouille, bouilles, bouille, bouillions, bouilliez, bouillent
  (d) bouillais, bouillais, bouillait, bouillions, bouilliez, bouil-
      laient

§10 CÉDER—cédant—cédé
  (a) cède, cédons, cédez
  (b) **cède**, cèdes, cède, cédons, cédez, **cèdent**
  (c) cède, cèdes, cède, cédions, cédiez, cèdent

§11 CONCLURE—concluant—**conclu**
  (f) **conclus**, conclus, conclut, conclûmes, conclûtes, conclurent

§12 CONNAÎTRE—connaissant—**connu**
  (a) connais, connaissons, connaissez
  (b) **connais**, connais, connaît, **connaissons**, connaissez, **con-
      naissent**
  (c) connaisse, connaisses, connaisse, connaissions, connaissiez,
      connaissent

9

(d) connaissais, connaissais, connaissait, connaissions, connaissiez, connaissaient
(f) **connus**, connus, connut, connûmes, connûtes, connurent

§13 COUDRE—cousant—**cousu**
(a) couds, cousons, cousez
(b) couds, couds, coud, **cousons**, cousez, **cousent**
(c) couse, couses, couse, cousions, cousiez, cousent
(d) cousais, cousais, cousait, cousions, cousiez, cousaient
(f) **cousis**, cousis, cousit, cousîmes, cousîtes, cousirent

§14 COURIR—courant—**couru**
(a) cours, courons, courez
(b) **cours**, cours, court, **courons**, courez, **courent**
(c) coure, coures, coure, courions, couriez, courent
(d) courais, courais, courait, courions, couriez, couraient
(e) **courrai**, courras, courra, courrons, courrez, courront
(f) **courus**, courus, courut, courûmes, courûtes, coururent

§15 CRAINDRE—craignant—**craint**
(a) crains, craignons, craignez
(b) **crains**, crains, craint, **craignons**, craignez, **craignent**
(c) craigne, craignes, craigne, craignions, craigniez, craignent
(d) craignais, craignais, craignait, craignions, craigniez, craignaient
(f) **craignis**, craignis, craignit, cragnîmes, craignîtes, craignirent

§16 CROIRE—croyant—**cru**
(a) crois, croyons, croyez
(b) crois, crois, croit, **croyons**, croyez, croient
(c) croie, croies, croie, croyions, croyiez, croient
(d) croyais, croyais, croyait, croyions, croyiez, croyaient
(f) **crus**, crus, crut, crûmes, crûtes, crurent

§17 CROÎTRE—croissant—**crû, crue**
(a) croîs, croissons, croissez
(b) **croîs**, croîs, croît, **croissons**, croissez, **croissent**
(c) croisse, croisses, croisse, croissions, croissiez, croissent
(d) croissais, croissais, croissait, croissions, croissiez, croissaient
(f) **crûs**, crûs, crût, crûmes, crûtes, crûrent

§18 CUEILLIR—cueillant—cueilli
(a) cueille, cueillons, cueillez
(b) **cueille**, cueilles, cueille, **cueillons**, cueillez, **cueillent**
(c) cueille, cueilles, cueille, cueillions, cueilliez, cueillent

    (d) cueillais, cueillais, cueillait, cueillions, cueilliez, cueillaient
    (e) **cueillerai**, cueilleras, cueillera, cueillerons, cueillerez, cueilleront

§19 CUIRE—cuisant—**cuit**
    (a) cuis, cuisons, cuisez
    (b) cuis, cuis, cuit, **cuisons**, cuisez, **cuisent**
    (c) cuise, cuises, cuise, cuisions, cuisiez, cuisent
    (d) cuisais, cuisais, cuisait, cuisions, cuisiez, cuisaient
    (f) **cuisis**, cuisis, cuisit, cuisîmes, cuisîtes, cuisirent

§20 DÉPECER—dépeçant—dépecé   Combination of §2 and §51
    (a) dépèce, dépeçons, dépecez
    (b) **dépèce**, dépèces, dépèce, **dépeçons**, dépecez, **dépècent**
    (c) dépèce, dépèces, dépèce, dépecions, dépeciez, dépècent
    (d) dépeçais, dépeçais, dépeçait, dépecions, dépeciez, dépeçaient
    (e) **dépècerai**, dépèceras, dépècera, dépècerons, dépècerez, dépèceront
    (f) **dépeçai**, dépeças, dépeça, dépeçâmes, dépeçâtes, dépecèrent

§21 DEVOIR—devant—**dû, due**
    (a) missing
    (b) **dois**, dois, doit, **devons**, devez, **doivent**
    (c) doive, doives, doive, devions, deviez, doivent
    (d) devais, devais, devait, devions, deviez, devaient
    (e) **devrai**, devras, devra, devrons, devrez, devront
    (f) **dus**, dus, dut, dûmes, dûtes, durent

§22 DIRE—disant—**dit**
    (a) dis, disons, **dites**
    (b) dis, dis, dit, **disons, dites, disent**
    (c) dise, dises, dise, disions, disiez, disent
    (d) disais, disais, disait, disions, disiez, disaient
    (f) **dis**, dis, dit, dîmes, dîtes, dirent

§23 DORMIR—dormant—dormi
    (a) dors, dormons, dormez
    (b) **dors**, dors, dort, **dormons**, dormez, **dorment**
    (c) dorme, dormes, dorme, dormions, dormiez, dorment
    (d) dormais, dormais, dormait, dormions, dormiez, dormaient

§24 ÉCLORE—éclosant—**éclos**
    (a) éclos
    (b) éclos, éclos, **éclôt, éclosent**
    (c) éclose, écloses, éclose, **éclosions, éclosiez**, éclosent
    (d) missing
    (f) missing

§25 ÉCRIRE—écrivant—**écrit**
- (a) écris, écrivons, écrivez
- (b) écris, écris, écrit, **écrivons**, écrivez, **écrivent**
- (c) écrive, écrives, écrive, écrivions, écriviez, écrivent
- (d) écrivais, écrivais, écrivait, écrivions, écriviez, écrivaient
- (f) **écrivis**, écrivis, écrivit, écrivîmes, écrivîtes, écrivirent

§26 ENVOYER—envoyant—envoyé
- (a) envoie, envoyons, envoyez
- (b) **envoie**, envoies, envoie, envoyons, envoyez, **envoient**
- (c) envoie, envoies, envoie, envoyions, envoyiez, envoient
- (e) **enverrai**, enverras, enverra, enverrons, enverrez, enverront

§27 ESSUYER—essuyant—essuyé
- (a) essuie, essuyons, essuyez
- (b) **essuie**, essuies, essuie, essuyons, essuyez, **essuient**
- (c) essuie, essuies, essuie, essuyions, essuyiez, essuient
- (e) **essuierai**, essuieras, essuiera, essuierons, essuierez, essuieront

§28 ÊTRE—étant—été
- (a) **sois, soyons, soyez**
- (b) **suis, es, est, sommes, êtes, sont**
- (c) **sois, sois, soit, soyons, soyez, soient**
- (d) **étais, étais, était, étions, étiez, étaient**
- (e) **serai**, seras, sera, serons, serez, seront
- (f) **fus**, fus, fut, fûmes, fûtes, furent

§29 FAIRE—faisant—**fait**
- (a) fais, faisons, **faites**
- (b) fais, fais, fait, **faisons, faites, font**
- (c) **fasse**, fasses, fasse, fassions, fassiez, fassent
- (d) faisais, faisais, faisait, faisions, faisiez, faisaient
- (e) **ferai**, feras, fera, ferons, ferez, feront
- (f) **fis**, fis, fit, fîmes, fîtes, firent

§30 FALLOIR—missing—**fallu**
- (a) missing
- (b) **faut**
- (c) **faille**
- (d) **fallait**
- (e) **faudra**
- (f) **fallut**

§31 FUIR—fuyant—fui
- (a) fuis, fuyons, fuyez
- (b) fuis, fuis, fuit, **fuyons**, fuyez, **fuient**

    (c) fuie, fuies, fuie, fuyions, fuyiez, fuient
    (d) fuyais, fuyais, fuyait, fuyions, fuyiez, fuyaient

§32 GRASSEYER—grasseyant—grasseyé
(regular, unlike other verbs with stem ending in **y**)

§33 HAÏR—haïssant—**haï**
    (a) hais [ɛ], haïssons, haïssez
    (b) **hais** [ɛ], hais, hait, **haïssons**, haïssez, **haïssent**
    (c) haïsse, haïsses, haïsse, haïssions, haïssiez, haïssent
    (d) haïssais, haïssais, haïssait, haïssions, haïssiez, haïssaient
    (f) haïs, haïs, haït, **haïmes, haïtes**, haïrent

§34 JETER—jetant—jeté
    (a) jette, jetons, jetez
    (b) **jette**, jettes, jette, jetons, jetez, **jettent**
    (c) jette, jettes, jette, jetions, jetiez, jettent
    (e) **jetterai**, jetteras, jettera, jetterons, jetterez, jetteront

§35 JOINDRE—joignant—**joint**
    (a) joins, joignons, joignez
    (b) **joins**, joins, joint, **joignons**, joignez, **joignent**
    (c) joigne, joignes, joigne, joignions, joigniez, joignent
    (d) joignais, joignais, joignait, joignions, joigniez, joignaient
    (f) **joignis**, joignis, joignit, joignîmes, joignîtes, joignirent

§36 LIRE—lisant—**lu**
    (a) lis, lisons, lisez
    (b) lis, lis, lit, **lisons**, lisez, **lisent**
    (c) lise, lises, lise, lisions, lisiez, lisent
    (d) lisais, lisais, lisait, lisions, lisiez, lisaient
    (f) **lus**, lus, lut, lûmes, lûtes, lurent

§37 LUIRE—luisant—**lui**
    (a) luis, luisons, luisez
    (b) luis, luis, luit, **luisons**, luisez, **luisent**
    (c) luise, luises, luise, luisions, luisiez, luisent
    (d) luisais, luisais, luisait, luisions, luisiez, luisaient
    (f) archaic

§38 MANGER—mangeant—mangé
    (a) mange, mangeons, mangez
    (b) mange, manges, mange, **mangeons**, mangez, mangent
    (d) mangeais, mangeais, mangeait, mangions, mangiez, mangeaient
    (f) **mangeai**, mangeas, mangea, mangeâmes, mangeâtes, mangèrent

§39 MAUDIRE—maudissant—**maudit**
- (a) maudis, maudissons, maudissez
- (b) maudis, maudis, maudit, **maudissons**, maudissez, **maudissent**
- (c) maudisse, maudisses, maudisse, maudissions, maudissiez, maudissent
- (d) maudissais, maudissais, maudissait, maudissions, maudissiez, maudissaient
- (f) **maudis**, maudis, maudit, maudîmes, maudîtes, maudirent

§40 MÉDIRE—médisant—**médit**
- (a) médis, médisons, médisez
- (b) médis, médis, médit, **médisons**, médisez, **médisent**
- (c) médise, médises, médise, médisions, médisiez, médisent
- (d) médisais, médisais, médisait, médisions, médisiez, médisaient
- (f) **médis**, médis, médit, médîmes, médîtes, médirent

§41 MENTIR—mentant—**menti**
- (a) mens, mentons, mentez
- (b) **mens**, mens, ment, **mentons**, mentez, **mentent**
- (c) mente, mentes, mente, mentions, mentiez, mentent
- (d) mentais, mentais, mentait, mentions, mentiez, mentaient

§42 METTRE—mettant—**mis**
- (a) mets, mettons, mettez
- (b) **mets**, mets, met, mettons, mettez, mettent
- (f) **mis**, mis, mit, mîmes, mîtes, mirent

§43 MOUDRE—moulant—**moulu**
- (a) mouds, moulons, moulez
- (b) mouds, mouds, moud, **moulons**, moulez, **moulent**
- (c) moule, moules, moule, moulions, mouliez, moulent
- (d) moulais, moulais, moulait, moulions, mouliez, moulaient
- (f) **moulus**, moulus, moulut, moulûmes, moulûtes, moulurent

§44 MOURIR—mourant—**mort**
- (a) meurs, mourons, mourez
- (b) **meurs**, meurs, meurt, **mourons**, mourez, **meurent**
- (c) meure, meures, meure, mourions, mouriez, meurent
- (d) mourais, mourais, mourait, mourions, mouriez, mouraient
- (e) **mourrai**, mourras, mourra, mourrons, mourrez, mourront
- (f) **mourus**, mourus, mourut, mourûmes, mourûtes, moururent

§45 MOUVOIR—mouvant—**mû, mue, mus, mues**
- (a) meus, mouvons, mouvez
- (b) **meus**, meus, meut, **mouvons**, mouvez, **meuvent**

14

   (c) meuve, meuves, meuve, mouvions, mouviez, meuvent
   (d) mouvais, mouvais, mouvait, mouvions, mouviez, mouvaient
   (e) **mouvrai**, mouvras, mouvra, mouvrons, mouvrez, mou-
       vront
   (f) **mus**, mus, mut, mûmes, mûtes, murent

§46 NAÎTRE—naissant—né

   (a) nais, naissons, naissez
   (b) **nais**, nais, naît, **naissons**, naissez, **naissent**
   (c) naisse, naisses, naisse, naissions, naissiez, naissent
   (d) naissais, naissais, naissait, naissions, naissiez, naissaient
   (f) **naquis**, naquis, naquit, naquîmes, naquîtes, naquirent

§47 NETTOYER—nettoyant—nettoyé

   (a) nettoie, nettoyons, nettoyez
   (b) **nettoie**, nettoies, nettoie, nettoyons, nettoyez, **nettoient**
   (c) nettoie, nettoies, nettoie, nettoyions, nettoyiez, nettoient
   (e) **nettoierai**, nettoieras, nettoiera, nettoierons, nettoierez,
       nettoieront

§48 PAÎTRE—paissant—pu

   (a) pais, paissez
   (b) **pais**, pais, paît, **paissons**, paissez, **paissent**
   (c) paisse, paisses, paisse, paissions, paissiez, paissent
   (d) paissais, paissais, paissait, paissions, paissiez, paissaient
   (f) missing

§49 PAYER—payant—payé

   (a) paie or paye, payons, payez
   (b) **paie**, paies, paie, payons, payez, **paient** or
      paye, payes, paye, payons, payez, payent
   (c) paie, paies, paie, payions, payiez, paient or
      paye, payes, paye, payions, payiez, payent
   (e) **paierai**, paieras, paiera, paierons, paierez, paieront or
      payerai, payeras, payera, payerons, payerez, payeront

§50 PEINDRE—peignant—**peint**

   (a) peins, peignons, peignez
   (b) **peins**, peins, peint, **peignons**, peignez, **peignent**
   (c) peigne, peignes, peigne, peignions, peigniez, peignent
   (d) peignais, peignais, peignait, peignions, peigniez, peignaient
   (f) **peignis**, peignis, peignit, peignîmes, peignîtes, peignirent

§51 PLACER—plaçant—placé

   (a) place, plaçons, placez
   (b) place, places, place, **plaçons**, placez, placent
   (d) plaçais, plaçais, plaçait, placions, placiez, plaçaient
   (f) **plaçai**, plaças, plaça, plaçâmes, plaçâtes, placèrent

§52 PLAIRE—plaisant—plu
- (a) plais, plaisons, plaisez
- (b) plais, plais, **plaît**, **plaisons**, plaisez, **plaisent**
- (c) plaise, plaises, plaise, plaisions, plaisiez, plaisent
- (d) plaisais, plaisais, plaisait, plaisions, plaisiez, plaisaient
- (f) **plus**, plus, plut, plûmes, plûtes, plurent

§53 PLEUVOIR—pleuvant—plu
- (a) **pleus, pleuvons, pleuvez** (fig & rare)
- (b) **pleut, pleuvent**
- (c) pleuve, pleuvent
- (d) **pleuvait, pleuvaient**
- (e) **pleuvra, pleuvront**
- (f) **plut, plurent**

§54 POURVOIR—pourvoyant—pourvu
- (a) pourvois, pouvoyons, pourvoyez
- (b) **pourvois**, pourvois, pourvoit, **pourvoyons**, pourvoyez, **pourvoient**
- (c) pourvoie, pourvoies, pourvoie, pourvoyions, pourvoyiez, pourvoient
- (d) pourvoyais, pourvoyais, pourvoyait, pourvoyions, pourvoyiez, pourvoyaient
- (f) **pourvus**, pourvus, pourvut, pourvûmes, pourvûtes, pourvurent

§55 POUVOIR—pouvant—pu
- (a) missing
- (b) **peux** or **puis**, peux, peut, **pouvons**, pouvez, **peuvent**
- (c) **puisse**, puisses, puisse, puissions, puissiez, puissent
- (d) pouvais, pouvais, pouvait, pouvions, pouviez, pouvaient
- (e) **pourrai**, pourras, pourra, pourrons, pourrez, pourront
- (f) **pus**, pus, put, pûmes, pûtes, purent

§56 PRENDRE—prenant—pris
- (a) prends, prenons, prenez
- (b) prends, prends, prend, **prenons**, prenez, **prennent**
- (c) prenne, prennes, prenne, prenions, preniez, prennent
- (d) prenais, prenais, prenait, prenions, preniez, prenaient
- (f) **pris**, pris, prit, prîmes, prîtes, prirent

§57 PRÉVOIR—prévoyant—prévu
- (a) prévois, prévoyons, prévoyez
- (b) **prévois**, prévois, prévoit, **prévoyons**, prévoyez, **prévoient**
- (c) prévoie, prévoies, prévoie, prévoyions, prévoyiez, prévoient
- (d) prévoyais, prévoyais, prévoyait, prévoyions, prévoyiez, prévoyaient
- (f) **prévis**, prévis, prévit, prévîmes, prévîtes, prévirent

16

§58 RAPIÉCER—rapiéçant—rapiécé   Combination of §10 and §51
- (a) rapièce, rapiéçons, rapiécez
- (b) **rapièce**, rapièces, rapièce, **rapiéçons**, rapiécez, **rapiècent**
- (c) rapièce, rapièces, rapièce, rapiécions, rapiéciez, rapiècent
- (d) rapiéçais, rapiéçais, rapiéçait, rapiécions, rapiéciez, rapiéçaient
- (f) **rapiéçai**, rapiéças, rapiéça, rapiéçâmes, rapiéçâtes, rapiécèrent

§59 RECEVOIR—recevant—**reçu**
- (a) reçois, recevons, recevez
- (b) **reçois**, reçois, reçoit, **recevons**, recevez, **reçoivent**
- (c) reçoive, reçoives, reçoive, recevions, receviez, reçoivent
- (d) recevais, recevais, recevait, recevions, receviez, recevaient
- (e) **recevrai**, recevras, recevra, recevrons, recevrez, recevront
- (f) **reçus**, reçus, reçut, reçûmes, reçûtes, reçurent

§60 RÉSOUDRE—résolvant—**résolu; résout** (invar)
- (a) résous, résolvons, résolvez
- (b) **résous**, résous, résout, **résolvons**, résolvez, **résolvent**
- (c) résolve, résolves, résolve, résolvions, résolviez, résolvent
- (d) résolvais, résolvais, résolvait, résolvions, résolviez, résolvaient
- (f) **résolus**, résolus, résolut, résolûmes, résolûtes, résolurent

§61 RIRE—riant—**ri**
- (f) **ris**, ris, rit, rîmes, rîtes, rirent

§62 SAVOIR—sachant—**su**
- (a) **sache, sachons, sachez**
- (b) **sais**, sais, sait, **savons**, savez, **savent**
- (c) **sache**, saches, sache, sachions, sachiez, sachent
- (d) savais, savais, savait, savions, saviez, savaient
- (e) **saurai**, sauras, saura, saurons, saurez, sauront
- (f) **sus**, sus, sut, sûmes, sûtes, surent

§63 SERVIR—servant—servi
- (a) sers, servons, servez
- (b) **sers**, sers, sert; **servons**, servez, **servent**
- (c) serve, serves, serve, servions, serviez, servent
- (d) servais, servais, servait, servions, serviez, servaient

§64 SORTIR—sortant—sorti
- (a) sors, sortons, sortez
- (b) **sors**, sors, sort, **sortons**, sortez, **sortent**
- (c) sorte, sortes, sorte, sortions, sortiez, sortent
- (d) sortais, sortais, sortait, sortions, sortiez, sortaient

§65 SOUFFRIR—souffrant—**souffert**
- (a) souffre, souffrons, souffrez
- (b) **souffre**, souffres, souffre, **souffrons**, souffrez, **souffrent**
- (c) souffre, souffres, souffre, souffrions, souffriez, souffrent
- (d) souffrais, souffrais, souffrait, souffrions, souffriez, souffraient

§66 SUFFIRE—suffisant—**suffi**
- (a) suffis, suffisons, suffisez
- (b) suffis, suffis, suffit, **suffisons**, suffisez, **suffisent**
- (c) suffise, suffises, suffise, suffisions, suffisiez, suffisent
- (d) suffisais, suffisais, suffisait, suffisions, suffisiez, suffisaient
- (f) **suffis**, suffis, suffit, suffîmes, suffîtes, suffirent

§67 SUIVRE—suivant—**suivi**
- (a) suis, suivons, suivez
- (b) **suis**, suis, suit, suivons, suivez, suivent

§68 TRAIRE—trayant—**trait**
- (a) trais, trayons, trayez
- (b) trais, trais, trait, **trayons**, trayez, traient
- (c) traie, traies, traie, trayions, trayiez, traient
- (d) trayais, trayais, trayait, trayions, trayiez, trayaient
- (f) missing

§69 TRESSAILLIR—tressaillant—**tressailli**
- (a) tressaille, tressaillons, tressaillez
- (b) **tressaille**, tressailles, tressaille, **tressaillons**, tressaillez, **tressaillent**
- (c) tressaille, tressailles, tressaille, tressaillions, tressailliez, tressaillent
- (d) tressaillais, tressaillais, tressaillait, tressaillions, tressailliez, tressaillaient
- (e) **tressaillirai**, tressailliras, tressaillira, tressaillirons, tressaillirez, tressailliront, or **tressaillerai**, tressailleras, tressaillera, tressaillerons, tressaillerez, tressailleront

§70 VAINCRE—vainquant—**vaincu**
- (a) vaincs [vɛ̃], vainquons, vainquez
- (b) vaincs, vaincs, vainc, **vainquons**, vainquez, **vainquent**
- (c) vainque, vainques, vainque, vainquions, vainquiez, vainquent
- (d) vainquais, vainquais, vainquait, vainquions, vainquiez, vainquaient
- (f) **vainquis**, vainquis, vainquit, vainquîmes, vainquîtes, vainquirent

§71 VALOIR—valant—**valu**
- (a) vaux, valons, valez
- (b) **vaux**, vaux, vaut, **valons**, valez, **valent**

(c) **vaille** [vaj], vailles, vaille, valions, valiez, vaillent
(d) valais, valais, valait, valions, valiez, valaient
(e) **vaudrai**, vaudras, vaudra, vaudrons, vaudrez, vaudront
(f) **valus**, valus, valut, valûmes, valûtes, valurent

§72 VENIR—venant—**venu**
(a) viens, venons, venez
(b) **viens**, viens, vient, **venons**, venez, **viennent**
(c) vienne, viennes, vienne, venions, veniez, viennent
(e) **viendrai**, viendras, viendra, viendrons, viendrez, viendront
(f) **vins**, vins, vint, vînmes [vɛ̃m], vîntes [vɛ̃t], vinrent [vɛ̃r]

§73 VÊTIR—vêtant—**vêtu**
(a) vêts, vêtons, vêtez
(b) **vêts**, vêts, vêt, **vêtons**, vêtez, **vêtent**
(c) vête, vêtes, vête, vêtions, vêtiez, vêtent
(d) vêtais, vêtais, vêtait, vêtions, vêtiez, vêtaient

§74 VIVRE—vivant—**vécu**
(a) vis, vivons, vivez
(b) **vis**, vis, vit, vivons, vivez, vivent
(f) **vécus**, vécus, vécut, vécûmes, vécûtes, vécurent

§75 VOIR—voyant—**vu**
(a) vois, voyons, voyez
(b) **vois**, vois, voit, **voyons**, voyez, **voient**
(c) voie, voies, voie, voyions, voyiez, voient
(d) voyais, voyais, voyait, voyions, voyiez, voyaient
(e) **verrai**, verras, verra, verrons, verrez, verront
(f) **vis**, vis, vit, vîmes, vîtes, virent

§76 VOULOIR—voulant—**voulu**
(a) veux, voulons, voulez
(b) **veux**, veux, veut, **voulons**, voulez, **veulent**
(c) **veuille**, veuilles, veuille, voulions, vouliez, veuillent
(d) voulais, voulais, voulait, voulions, vouliez, voulaient
(e) **voudrai**, voudras, voudra, voudrons, voudrez, voudront
(f) **voulus**, voulus, voulut, voulûmes, voulûtes, voulurent

GRAMMATICAL TABLES

§77 **le** *art def* the. The following table shows the forms of the definite article, the combination of **le** with **à** and **de**, and the combinations of **les** with **à**, **de**, and **en**.

		masc	*fem*
	sg	le; l' before a vowel or mute h	la; l' before a vowel or mute h
	pl	les	les
with à	sg	au; à l' before a vowel or mute h	à la; à l' before a vowel or mute h
with à	pl	aux	aux
with de	sg	du; de l' before a vowel or mute h	de la; de l' before a vowel or mute h
with de	pl	des	des
with en	pl	ès, e.g., **maître ès arts**	ès, e.g., **docteur ès lettres**

§78 **lequel** *pron rel* who, whom; which ‖ *pron interr* which, which one. The following table shows all the forms of the word **lequel** and their combinations with the prepositions **à** and **de**.

		masc	*fem*
	sg	lequel	laquelle
	pl	lesquels	lesquelles
with à	sg	auquel	à laquelle
with à	pl	auxquels	auxquelles
with de	sg	duquel	de laquelle
with de	pl	desquels	desquelles

The forms combined with **de** and used as relative pronouns sometimes mean: whose, e.g., **l'étudiant avec la sœur duquel j'ai dansé** the student with whose sister I danced

§79 **dont** *rel pron* of whom; of which; from which; with which; on which; at which; which; whose. The relative pronoun **dont** may be: a) the complement of the subject of the dependent verb, e.g., **cette malheureuse dont la jambe droite était brisée** that wretched woman whose right leg was broken; b) the complement of the object of the dependent verb, e.g., **sa grande chambre dont on avait fermé les volets** his large bedroom the shutters of which they had closed;

c) the complement of the verb itself, e.g., **les termes dont il se servait** the expressions which he used.

If the antecedent is one of point of origin, **d'où** is used, e.g., **la porte d'où il est sorti** the door from which he went out, unless the point of origin is one of ancestry or extraction having to do with a person, e.g., **la famille distinguée dont il sortait** the distinguished family from which he came.

The relative pronoun **dont** cannot be the complement of a noun which is the object of a preposition but must be replaced by a form of **lequel** combined with **de** (see §78), or by **de qui**, e.g., **l'étudiante avec le frère de laquelle** (or **de qui**) **j'ai dansé** the student with whose brother I danced.

§80 quel *adj* what; what sort of; which; what a, e.g., **quelle belle ville!** what a beautiful city!; **n'importe quel** any || *adj interr* what, e.g., **quel est le but de la vie?** what is the purpose of life?; who, e.g., **quel est cet homme?** who is that man? || *adj indef*—**quel que** whoever, e.g., **quel que soit l'homme** whoever the man may be; whatever, e.g., **quelles que soient les difficultés** whatever difficulties there may be; whichever, e.g., **quel que soit le pied sur lequel il s'appuie** whichever foot he leans on. The following table shows all the forms of the word **quel.**

	masc	*fem*
sg	quel	quelle
pl	quels	quelles

§81 quelqu'un *pron indef* someone, somebody; anyone, anybody; **quelques-uns** some; any, a few. The following table shows all the forms of the word **quelqu'un**.

	masc	*fem*
sg	quelqu'un	quelqu'une
pl	quelques-uns	quelques-unes

§82A ce *adj dem* this; that; **ces** these; those. The following table shows all the forms of this word.

	masc	*fem*
sg	ce; cet before a vowel or mute **h**	cette
pl	ces	ces

This word has two meanings as exemplified by the following example:

cet homme this man; that man

However, the particles **-ci** and **-là** are attached to the noun modified by the forms of **ce** to distinguish what is near the person speaking (i.e., the first person) from what is near the person spoken to (i.e., the second person) or what is remote from both (i.e., the third person), for example:

> **cet homme-ci** this man (*not that man*)
> **cet homme-là** that man (*not this man*)
> **cet homme-là** that man (*yonder*)

---

§82B ce *pron dem*

  it, e.g., **c'est un bon livre** it is a good book;

  he, e.g., **c'est un bon professeur** he is a good professor;

  she, e.g., **c'est une belle femme** she is a beautiful woman;

they, e.g., **ce sont des élèves** they are students

---

§83 celui *pron dem* this one; that one. The following table shows all the forms of the demonstrative pronoun with their translations into English.

	masc	*fem*
sg	**celui** this one; that one; he	**celle** this one; that one; she
pl	**ceux** these; those	**celles** these; those

This word in all its forms is generally used with a following **de** or the relative pronouns **que** and **qui**:

> **celui de**
> **celle de** ⎫
> **ceux de** ⎬ 's, e.g., **celui de Marie** Mary's
> **celles de** ⎭

celui que he whom; the one that; the one which ⎫
celle que she whom; the one that; the one which ⎬ whomever;
ceux que those whom; the ones whom; the ones which ⎬ whichever
celles que those whom; the ones whom; the ones which ⎭

celui qui he who; the one that; the one which ⎫
celle qui she who; the one that; the one which ⎬ whoever;
ceux qui those who; the ones who; the ones which ⎬ whichever
celles qui those who; the ones who; the ones which ⎭

§84 celui-ci *pron dem* this one; he; the latter. The particles **-ci** and **-là** are attached to the forms of **celui** to distinguish what is near the person speaking (i.e., the first person) from what is near the person spoken to (i.e., the second person) or remote from both (i.e., the third person). The following table shows all the forms of this word with particles attached and with their translations into English.

	masc	*fem*
sg	**celui-ci** this one	**celle-ci** this one
	celui-là that one	**celle-là** that one
pl	**ceux-ci** these	**celles-ci** these
	ceux-là those	**celles-là** those

The forms of **celui-ci** also mean the latter; and the forms of **celui-là**, the former, e.g., **Henri était roi et Catherine était reine. Celle-ci était espagnole et celui-là anglais**. Henry was a king and Catherine was a queen. The former was English and the latter Spanish. (The English word order requires the inversion.)

§85 Disjunctive personal and reflexive pronouns.

This table shows all the forms of the disjunctive personal and reflexive pronouns with their translations into English.

moi	me; myself; I	**nous**	we, us; ourselves
toi	you, thee; yourself	**vous**	you; yourselves
lui	he, him, it; himself	**eux**	they, them *masc*; themselves *masc*
elle	she, her, it; herself	**elles**	they, them *fem*; themselves *fem*
soi	oneself; himself, herself, itself	**soi**	themselves

A) The disjunctive personal pronouns are used:
1) as the object of a preposition, e.g., **Jean a été invité chez elle** John was invited to her house; e.g., **il est très content de lui** he is very satisfied with himself
   Disjunctive pronouns especially as objects of prepositions rarely stand for things. Prepositional phrases which would include them are generally expressed by y (see §87), e.g., **je m'y suis avancé** I walked up to it, as contrasted with **je me suis avancé vers lui** I walked up to him; or are expressed by one of the adverbs **là-dessus, là-dessous, là-dedans**, etc., e.g., **voilà mon nom; écrivez le vôtre là-dessous** there is my name; write yours under it, as contrasted with **il n'a pas d'argent sur lui** he has no money with him.
2) after the preposition **à** in phrases which are used to clarify or to stress the meaning of a conjunctive personal pronoun, e.g., **il lui a parlé, à elle** he spoke to her (or, he spoke to *her*)
3) after the preposition **à** in phrases which are used to clarify the meaning of a preceding possessive adjective, e.g., **son chapeau à elle** her hat
4) as predicate pronouns after the verb **être**, especially after **c'est** and **ce sont**:

c'est moi	it is I	**c'est nous**	it is we
c'est toi	it is you, it is thee	**c'est vous**	it is you
c'est lui	it is he	**ce sont eux**	it is they *masc*
c'est elle	it is she	**ce sont elles**	it is they *fem*

5) after **que** (than, as) in comparisons, e.g., **nous y allons plus souvent qu'eux** we go there more often than they; e.g., **nous y allons aussi souvent que vous** we go there as often as you
6) when the verb is not expressed, e.g., **qui a fait cela? Lui** who did that? He did

24

7) to stress the subject or object of the sentence, e.g., **lui, il a raison** he is right
8) in compound subjects and objects, e.g., **lui et moi, nous sommes médecins** he and I are doctors
9) when an adverb separates the subject pronoun from the verb, e.g., **lui toujours arrive en retard** he always arrives late
10) after **être + à** to contrast ownership, e.g., **ce stylo est à lui mais ce papier est à elle** this pen is his but this paper is hers.

B) The disjunctive indefinite reflexive pronoun **soi** corresponds to **on** and is used mainly as the object of a preposition, that is, according to A, 1 above, e.g., **on doit parler rarement de soi** one should seldom talk about oneself. But it may also be used in the predicate after the verb **être**, according to A, 4 above, e.g., **on a plus confiance quand c'est soi qui conduit** one has more confidence when it is oneself who drives.

§86 The following table shows all the forms of the intensive personal pronouns. They are made by combining the disjunctive personal pronouns with the forms of **même**.

moi-même	myself; I myself	**nous-mêmes**	ourselves; we ourselves
toi-même	yourself, thyself; you yourself	**vous-même**	yourself; you yourself
		vous-mêmes	yourselves; you yourselves
lui-même	himself; he himself; itself		
elle-même	herself; she herself; itself	**eux-mêmes**	themselves; they themselves
soi-même	oneself; itself		
		elles-mêmes	themselves; they themselves

§87 Conjunctive personal and reflexive pronouns.

person	1 subject	2 negative	3 direct & indirect object	4 direct object	5 indirect object
1	je (j')—I		me (m')—me, to me; myself, to myself		
2	tu—you, thou		te (t')—you, to you; thee, to thee; thyself, to thyself		
3	il—he; it elle—she; it on—one, they		se (s')—himself, herself, itself, oneself; to himself, to herself, to itself, to oneself	le (l')—him; it la (l')—her; it	lui—to him; to her
		ne (n')—not §90B			
4	nous—we		nous—us, to us; ourselves, to ourselves		
5	vous—you		vous—you, to you; yourself; yourselves, to yourselves		
6	ils—they elles—they		se—themselves; to themselves	les—them	leur—to them

This table shows all the forms of the conjunctive personal and reflexive pronouns with their translations into English and their positions (reading horizontally, not vertically) with respect to each other and with respect to the verb; and in negative declarative sentences. All of the elements in this table except the verb and pas and personne (and the other negative words listed in §90) are unstressed.

In affirmative and negative interrogative sentences, the subject pronouns in column 1 are placed after the verb or auxiliary in column 8 and attached to it with a hyphen. A t, preceded and followed by hyphens, is intercalated between third-singular forms ending in a vowel and the subject pronoun. The interrogative forms of the first singular present indicative whose final sound is a nasal vowel or a consonant are not used, while those whose final sound is an oral vowel are, e.g., **où vais-je?** where am I going?; e.g., **que dirai-je?** what shall I say?. And the ending **-e** of the first singular

my friends; my men; **les siens** his folks, his family; his friends; his men; her folks, etc.; c) **faire des siennes** (coll) to be up to one's (his, etc.) old tricks.

§90 The adverb **ne** is a conjunctive particle, that is, it always precedes a verb and, like conjunctive pronouns, is unstressed. Because of its weakness, it is generally accompanied by another word, which follows the verb (or auxiliary) in most cases, is stressed, and gives force or added meaning to the negation, e.g., **il n'est pas ici** he is not here.

A) The following table shows **ne** with the various words with which it is associated. (For more detail, see each expression under the second word in the body of the Dictionary, e.g., s.v. **aucun**; e.g., s.v. **aucunement**; etc.)

ne . . . aucun	no, none; no one, nobody	**ne . . . ni . . . ni**	neither . . . nor
ne . . . aucunement	by no means	**ne . . . nul**	no, none
ne . . . brin (archaic)	not a bit, not a single	**ne . . . nullement**	not at all
ne . . . davantage	no more	**ne . . . pas**	not, no
		ne . . . pas un	not one
ne . . . goutte (archaic)	not a drop, nothing	**ne . . . personne**	no one, nobody
		ne . . . plus	no more, no longer
ne . . . guère	hardly, scarcely; hardly ever	**ne . . . plus jamais**	never any more
		ne . . . plus que	now only
ne . . . jamais	never	**ne . . . point**	not, no, not at all
ne . . . mie (archaic)	not a crumb, not	**ne . . . que**	only, but
ne . . . mot (archaic)	not a word, nothing	**ne . . . rien**	nothing

B) The position of **ne** in the sentence is that of column 2 of **§87.** The position of **pas** and all the other like words, with the exception of **aucun, ni . . . ni, nul, personne,** and **que** is that of column 9. The position of **aucun, nul, personne,** and **que** is that of column 11. And the position of the first **ni** of **ni . . . ni** is that of column 11 unless the past participle is one of the correlatives, in which case its position is that of column 9.

Aucun, nul, pas un, personne, and rien may be used as subjects of the verb; they then precede **ne** and the verb, e.g., **personne n'est ici** no one is here. And **aucun, nul,** and **pas un** may be used as adjectives in the same position, e.g., **nul péril ne l'arrête** no danger stops him.

Usually when an infinitive is in the negative, **pas** immediately follows **ne,** e.g., **il m'a dit de ne pas y aller** he told me not to go there; e.g., **il regrette de ne pas me l'avoir dit** he regrets not having told me it.

C) The adverb **ne** is often used without **pas** or a similar word with the verbs **bouger, cesser, oser, pouvoir,** and **savoir,** e.g., **je ne saurais vous le dire** I can't tell you. And it is not translated (1) with a compound tense after **il y a . . . que, voilà . . . que,** and **depuis que,** e.g., **il y a trois jours que je ne l'ai vu** it is three days since I saw him or

29

(2) with the verb of a clause introduced by a) **à moins que, avant que, empêcher ... que,** and **éviter ... que,** e.g., **à moins que je ne sois retenu** unless I am detained; b) **si** meaning unless, e.g., **si je ne me trompe** unless I am mistaken; c) a comparative + **que,** e.g., **vous étiez plus occupé qu'il ne l'était** you were busier than he was; d) a verb or expression of fear such as **avoir peur que, craindre que, redouter que,** e.g., **je crains qu'il ne soit malade** I am afraid that he is sick; e) a negative verb or expression of doubt, denial, despair such as **ne pas désespérer que, ne pas disconvenir que, ne pas douter que, ne pas nier que,** e.g., **je ne doute pas qu'il ne vienne** I do not doubt that he will come.

§91 *adj & adv comp & super* The comparative of superiority of adjectives and adverbs is formed by placing **plus** before the positive, e.g., **heureux** happy, **plus heureux** happier. The superlative of superiority of adjectives and adverbs is the same as the comparative, e.g., **heureux** happy, **plus heureux** happier and happiest. It is to be observed that the superlative is generally used in both French and English with the definite article or the possessive pronoun, e.g., **le plus heureux** the happiest, **son plus heureux** his happiest.

Some adjectives and adverbs have irregular comparatives and superlatives.

	ADJECTIVES		ADVERBS
positive	*comp and super*	*positive*	*comp and super*
bon good	**meilleur** better; best	**beaucoup** much	**plus** more; most
mauvais bad	**pire** worse; worst	**bien** well	**mieux** better; best
petit small	**moindre** lesser, less; least	**mal** badly	**pis** worse; worst
		peu little	**moins** less; least

30

FRENCH—ENGLISH

A

A, a [ɑ], *[ɑ] *m invar* first letter of the French alphabet

à [a] *prep* to, into; at; by, e.g., **à l'année** by the year; from, e.g., **arracher à** to snatch from; in, e.g., **à l'italienne** in the Italian manner; on, e.g., **à temps** on time; with, e.g., **la jeune fille aux yeux bleus** the girl with the blue eyes

abaisse-langue [abɛslɑ̃g] *m invar* tongue depressor

abaissement [abɛsmɑ̃] *m* lowering; drop; humbling

abaisser [abese] *tr* to lower; to humble || *ref* to go down; to humble oneself; to condescend

abandon [abɑ̃dɔ̃] *m* abandon; abandonment; desertion; neglect

abandonner [abɑ̃dɔne] *tr* to abandon; to forsake; to give up || *ref* to neglect oneself, become slovenly; **s'abandonner à** to give way to

abasourdir [abazurdir] *tr* to dumbfound, flabbergast; to deafen

abasourdis·sant [abazurdisɑ̃] **abasourdis·sante** [abazurdisɑ̃t] *adj* astounding

abâtardir [abɑtardir] *tr* to debase || *ref* to deteriorate, to degenerate

abâtardissement [abɑtardismɑ̃] *m* debasement; deterioration, degeneration

abat-jour [abaʒur] *m invar* lampshade; eyeshade, sun visor; skylight

abats [aba] *mpl* giblets

abattage [abataʒ] *m* slaughtering (*of animals*); felling (*of trees*); demolition (*of a building*); bag, bagging (*of game*)

abattant [abatɑ̃] *m* drop leaf

abattement [abatmɑ̃] *m* dejection, despondency; prostration; tax deduction

abatteur [abatœr] *m* slaughterer; woodcutter; **abatteur de besogne** hard worker

abattis [abati] *m* felling (*of trees*); clearing (*of woods*); (mil) abatis; **abattis** *mpl* giblets; (slang) arms and legs

abattoir [abatwar] *m* slaughterhouse

abattre [abatr] §7 *tr* to pull down, to demolish; to fell; to slaughter; to overthrow; to discourage; to shoot down, to bring down (*a bird, airplane, etc.*); to lay (*dust*); (cards) to lay down (*one's hand*) || *ref* to abate, subside; to be dejected; to swoop down; to pounce; to crash (*said of airplane*)

abat·tu -tue [abaty] *adj* dejected, downcast

abat-vent [abavɑ̃] *m invar* chimney pot

abbaye [abei] *f* abbey

abbé [abe] *m* abbot; abbé, father

abbesse [abes] *f* abbess

a b c [abese] *m* (letterword) ABC's; speller

abcès [apsɛ] *m* abscess

abdiquer [abdike] *tr & intr* to abdicate

abdomen [abdɔmɛn] *m* abdomen

abécédaire [abesedɛr] *m* speller

abeille [abɛj] *f* bee

abêtir [abetir] *tr* to make stupid || *intr & ref* to become stupid

abhorrer [abɔre] *tr* to abhor

abîme [abim] *m* abyss; depth

abîmer [abime] *tr* to spoil; to damage || *ref* to sink; to be sunk; to get spoiled

ab·ject -jecte [abʒɛkt] *adj* abject

abjurer [abʒyre] *tr* to abjure

abla·tif -tive [tiv] *adj & m* ablative

aboiement [abwamɑ̃] *m* barking; yelp, cry, outcry

abois [abwa] *mpl* desperate straits; **aux abois** at bay; hard pressed

abolir [abɔlir] *tr* to abolish; to annul

abomination [abɔminɑsjɔ̃] *f* abomination

abondamment [abɔ̃damɑ̃] *adv* abundantly

abondance [abɔ̃dɑ̃s] *f* abundance, plenty; wealth; flow (*of words*); **parler d'abondance** to ad-lib

abon·dant -dante [dɑ̃t] *adj* abundant, plentiful; wordy

abon·né -née [abɔne] *mf* subscriber; season-ticket holder; consumer (*of gas, electricity, etc.*); commuter (*on railroad*)

abonnement [abɔnmɑ̃] *m* subscription

abonner [abɔne] *tr* to take out a subscription for (*s.o.*) || *ref* to subscribe, take out a subscription

abord [abɔr] *m* approach; **abords** outskirts, surroundings; **d'abord** at first; **d'un abord facile** easy to approach; **tout d'abord** first of all

abordable [abɔrdabl] *adj* approachable, accessible; reasonable (*price*)

abordage [abɔrdaʒ] *m* (naut) boarding; (naut) collision

aborder [abɔrde] *tr* to approach, to accost; to board; to collide with, run afoul of || *intr* to land, to go ashore

aborigène [abɔriʒɛn] *adj & m* native, aboriginal

abor·tif -tive [tiv] *adj* abortive

aboucher [abuʃe] *tr* to join; to bring together || *ref* to have an interview

aboutir [abutir] *intr* to end; to come to an end

aboutissement [abutismã] *m* outcome, result

aboyer [abwaje] §47 *intr* to bark; to bay

abracada·brant [abrakadabrã] **-brante** [brãt] *adj* amazing, breath-taking

abra·sif [abrazif] **-sive** [ziv] *adj & m* abrasive

abrégé [abreʒe] *m* abridgment, summary

abrégement [abreʒmã] *m* abridgment

abréger [abreʒe] §1 *tr* to abridge; to shorten, curtail

abreuvage [abrœvaʒ] *m* watering

abreuver [abrœve] *tr* to water; to soak; to overwhelm, to shower || *ref* to drink

abreuvoir [abrœvwar] *m* drinking trough, watering trough, horsepond

abréviation [abrevjɑsjɔ̃] *f* abbreviation; abridgment, curtailment

abri [abri] *m* shelter, refuge, cover; air-raid shelter; **à l'abri de** protected from

abricot [abriko] *m* apricot

abricotier [abrikɔtje] *m* apricot tree

abri-promenade [abriprɔmnad] *m* hurricane deck, shelter deck

abriter [abrite] *tr* to shelter, protect, shield, screen || *ref* to take shelter

abroger [abrɔʒe] §38 *tr* to abrogate, repeal

a·brupt -brupte [abrypt] *adj* abrupt, steep; rough, crude; blunt

abru·ti -tie [abryti] *adj* sottish

abrutir [abrytir] *tr* to brutalize; to besot; to overwhelm

abrutis·sant [abrytisã] **abrutis·sante** [abrytisãt] *adj* stupefying; deadening

absence [apsãs] *f* absence

ab·sent [apsã] **-sente** [sãt] *adj* absent; absent-minded || *mf* absentee

absenter [apsãte] *ref* to absent oneself, be absent, stay away

abside [apsid] *f* apse

absinthe [apsɛ̃t] *f* absinthe, wormwood; absinthe (*liqueur*)

abso·lu -lue [apsɔly] *adj* absolute

absolument [apsɔlymã] *adv* absolutely

absor·bant [apsɔrbã] **-bante** [bãt] *adj* absorbent; absorbing || *m* absorbent

absorber [apsɔrbe] *tr* to absorb, to soak up; to eat up; to drink || *ref* to become absorbed, be deeply interested

absoudre [apsudr] §60 (*pp* **absous, absoute**; no *pret* or *imperf subj*) *tr* to absolve; to forgive; to acquit

abstenir [apstənir] §72 *ref* to abstain, refrain

absti·nent [apstinã] **-nente** [nãt] *adj* abstinent; abstemious || *mf* moderate eater or drinker

abstraction [apstraksjɔ̃] *f* abstraction; **faire abstraction de** to leave out, to disregard

abstraire [apstrɛr] §68 (no *pret* or *imperf subj*) *tr* to abstract || *ref* to become engrossed

abs·trait [apstrɛ] **-traite** [trɛt] *adj* abstract

abs·trus [apstry] **-truse** [tryz] *adj* abstruse

absurde [apsyrd] *adj* absurd

absurdité [apsyrdite] *f* absurdity

abus [aby] *m* abuse

abuser [abyze] *tr* to deceive || *intr* to exaggerate; **abuser de** to take advantage of, to impose upon; to indulge unwisely in || *ref* to be mistaken

abu·sif [abyzif] **-sive** [ziv] *adj* abusive, wrong

acacia [akasja] *m* locust tree; **faux acacia** black locust tree

académicien [akademisjɛ̃] *m* academician

académie [akademi] *f* academy

académique [akademik] *adj* academic

acagnarder [akaɲarde] *tr* to make lazy || *ref* to grow lazy; to lounge

acajou [akaʒu] *m* mahogany; mahogany tree; **acajou à pommes** (bot) cashew

acariâtre [akarjɑtr] *adj* grumpy

acca·blant [akablã] **-blante** [blãt] *adj* overwhelming

accabler [akable] *tr* to overwhelm; to weigh down

accalmie [akalmi] *f* lull, standstill

accaparer [akapare] *tr* to corner (*the market*); to monopolize

accéder [aksede] §10 *intr* to accede; to acquiesce; to have access

accéléra·teur [akseleratœr] **-trice** [tris] *adj* accelerating || *m* accelerator

accélérer [akselere] §10 *tr, intr, & ref* to accelerate

accent [aksã] *m* accent; **accent de hauteur** pitch accent; **accent d'insistance** emphasis; **accent d'intensité** stress accent; **accent tonique** tonic accent

accentuer [aksãtɥe] *tr* to accent || *ref* to become more marked

acceptable [aksɛptabl] *adj* acceptable

acceptation [aksɛptɑsjɔ̃] *f* acceptance

accepter [aksɛpte] *tr* to accept || *intr* **accepter de** to agree to

acception [aksɛpsjɔ̃] *f* sense, meaning; preference, partiality

accès [aksɛ] *m* access; outburst; (pathol) attack, bout; **accès aux quais** (public sign) to the docks

accessible [aksesibl] *adj* accessible; susceptible

accession [aksesjɔ̃] *f* accession

accessit [aksesit] *m* honorable mention

accessoire [akseswar] *adj* accessory || **accessoires** *mpl* accessories; (theat) properties

accident [aksidã] *m* accident; unevenness (*of ground*); (mus) accidental

acciden·té -tée [aksidãte] *adj* rough, uneven; bumpy (*road*); eventful (*life*); (coll) wrecked (*car*) || *mf* (coll) casualty, victim

acciden·tel -telle [aksidãtɛl] *adj* accidental

accidenter [aksidãte] *tr* to make uneven; to vary; to injure

accise [aksiz] *f* excise tax

acclamer [aklame] *tr* to acclaim

acclimater [aklimate] *tr* to acclimate || *ref* to become acclimated

accolade [akɔlad] *f* embrace; accolade; (mus, typ) brace

accoler [akɔle] *tr* to hug; to join side by side; to couple (*names*); (typ) to brace

accommo·dant [akɔmɔdɑ̃] **-dante** [dɑ̃t] *adj* accommodating, obliging

accommodation [akɔmɔdɑsjɔ̃] *f* accommodation

accommodement [akɔmɔdmɑ̃] *m* settlement, compromise; arrangement

accommoder [akɔmɔde] *tr* to accommodate; to conciliate; to arrange (*furniture*); to prepare (*food*)

accompagna·teur [akɔ̃paɲatœr] **-trice** [tris] *mf* accompanist

accompagnement [akɔ̃paɲmɑ̃] *m* accompaniment

accompagner [akɔ̃paɲe] *tr* to accompany

accom·pli -plie [akɔ̃pli] *adj* completed; polished; accomplished

accomplir [akɔ̃plir] *tr* to accomplish; to complete; to fulfill (*a promise*) ‖ *ref* to come to pass

accomplissement [akɔ̃plismɑ̃] *m* accomplishment, performance

accord [akɔr] *m* accord, agreement, consent; harmony; settlement, bargain; (mus) chord; (mus) tuning; **d'accord** in accord; **d'accord!** O.K.!, check!; **d'un commun accord** by common consent

accordage [akɔrdaʒ] *m* tuning

accordéon [akɔrdeɔ̃] *m* accordion; **en accordéon** squashed; accordion-pleated

accorder [akɔrde] *tr* to grant; to reconcile; (mus, rad) to tune ‖ *intr*—**accorder à qn de** to allow s.o. to ‖ *ref* to harmonize; to tally; to agree

ac·cort [akɔr] **ac·corte** [akɔrt] *adj* sprightly, engaging (*e.g., young lady*)

accoster [akɔste] *tr* to approach ‖ *intr* to dock, to berth

accotement [akɔtmɑ̃] *m* shoulder (*of a road*)

accoter [akɔte] *tr* to shore up ‖ *ref* to lean

accouchement [akuʃmɑ̃] *m* childbirth

accoucher [akuʃe] *tr* to deliver ‖ *intr* (*aux:* ÊTRE) to be confined, be delivered ‖ *intr* (*aux:* AVOIR)—**accoucher de** to give birth to

accou·cheur [akuʃœr] **-cheuse** [ʃøz] *mf* obstetrician

accouder [akude] *ref* to lean on one's elbows

accoudoir [akudwar] *m* armrest

accouple [akupl] *f* leash

accouplement [akupləmɑ̃] *m* coupling; **accouplement consanguin** inbreeding

accoupler [akuple] *tr* to couple; to yoke; to bring together for breeding; to link; (elec) to hook up ‖ *ref* to mate

accourir [akurir] §14 *intr* (*aux:* AVOIR or ÊTRE) to run up

accoutrement [akutrəmɑ̃] *m* togs, get-up

accoutrer [akutre] *tr* to rig out ‖ *ref* to dress ridiculously

accoutu·mé -mée [akutyme] *adj* accustomed; **à l'accoutumée** as usual ‖ *mf* regular customer; frequent visitor

accoutumer [akutyme] *tr* to accustom ‖ *ref* to become accustomed

accouvage [akuvaʒ] *m* artificial incubation

accouver [akuve] *tr* to set (*a hen*) ‖ *intr* to set (*said of a hen*) ‖ *ref* to begin to set

accréditer [akredite] *tr* to accredit; to win a hearing for; **accrédité auprès de** accredited to ‖ *ref* to gain credence or favor

accréditeur [akreditœr] *m* bondsman

accroc [akro] *m* tear (*in a dress*); (fig) snag, hitch

accrochage [akrɔʃaʒ] *m* hanging; hooking; clinch (*in boxing*); collision; (mil) encounter; (rad) receiving; (coll) squabble

accroche [akrɔʃ] *m* hanger

accrocher [akrɔʃe] *tr* to hang, to hang up; to hook; to catch; (mil) to come to grips with; (rad) to pick up; (coll) to buttonhole ‖ *ref* (coll) to come to blows; to cling; to catch; to get caught

accroire [akrwar] (used only in *inf* after *faire*) *tr*—**faire accroire** (with *dat*) to make (*s.o.*) believe ‖ *ref*—**s'en faire accroire** to get a swelled head

accroissement [akrwasmɑ̃] *m* growth; accumulation (*of capital*); increment

accroître [akrwatr] §17 (*pp* **accru;** *pres ind* **accrois;** *pret* **accrus,** etc.) *tr* & *ref* to increase

accroupir [akrupir] *ref* to squat, to crouch

accu [aky] *m* storage battery

accueil [akœj] *m* reception, welcome

accueil·lant [akœjɑ̃] **accueil·lante** [akœjɑ̃t] *adj* hospitable, gracious

accueillir [akœjir] §18 *tr* to welcome; to honor (*a bill*)

acculer [akyle] *tr* to corner

accumulateur [akymylatœr] *m* storage battery

accumuler [akymyle] *tr, intr,* & *ref* to accumulate

accusa·teur [akyzatœr] **-trice** [tris] *adj* incriminating ‖ *mf* accuser

accusatif [akyzatif] *m* accusative

accusation [akyzɑsjɔ̃] *f* accusation; charge

accu·sé -sée [akyze] *adj* marked; prominent (*features*) ‖ *mf* defendant ‖ *m* acknowledgment (*of receipt*)

accuser [akyze] *tr* to accuse; to acknowledge (*receipt*)

acerbe [asɛrb] *adj* sour; sharp; caustic (*remark*)

acé·ré -rée [asere] *adj* keen (*edge*); sharp (*tongue*)

acétate [asetat] *m* acetate

acétique [asetik] *adj* acetic

acétone [asetɔn] *f* acetone

achalander [aʃalɑ̃de] *tr* to attract customers to ‖ *ref* to get customers

achar·né -née [aʃarne] *adj* fierce; relentless (*pursuit*); inveterate (*gambler*); bitter (*enemy*); **acharné à** bent on, set on

acharnement [aʃarnəmɑ̃] *m* fiĕrceness, fury; stubbornness; eagerness

acharner [aʃarne] *tr* to set, to sic (*dogs*); to bait (*a trap*) ‖ *ref* to fight bitterly; **s'acharner à** to work away at; to be bent on, to persist in; **s'acharner contre** to attack fiercely; **s'acharner sur** to light into; to swoop down upon; to bear down on; to be dead set against

achat [aʃa] *m* purchase; **achat à terme** installment buying; **aller aux achats** to go shopping

ache [aʃ] *f* wild celery

acheminement [aʃminmɑ̃] *m* forwarding; progress

acheminer [aʃmine] *tr* to direct ‖ *ref* to proceed

acheter [aʃte] §2 *tr* to buy; **acheter à** to buy from; to buy for; **acheter de** to buy from; **acheter pour** to buy for

achèvement [aʃevmɑ̃] *m* completion

achever [aʃve] §2 *tr* to complete; to finish off, kill ‖ *intr* to end; to be just finishing ‖ *ref* to come to an end

Achille [aʃil] *m* Achilles

achoppement [aʃɔpmɑ̃] *m* obstacle; impact

achopper [aʃɔpe] *intr & ref* to stumble

achromatique [akrɔmatik] *adj* achromatic

acide [asid] *adj & m* acid; **acide phénique** carbolic acid

acidité [asidite] *f* acidity

acidu·lé -lée [asidyle] *adj* acid; fruit-flavored

aciduler [asidyle] *tr* to acidulate

acier [asje] *m* steel; (fig) sword; **acier inoxydable** stainless steel

aciérie [asjeri] *f* steelworks, steel mill

acmé [akme] *f* acme; (pathol) crisis

acolyte [akɔlit] *m* acolyte; accomplice

acompte [akɔ̃t] *m* installment; deposit, down payment; **acompte provisionnel** payment on estimated income tax

Açores [asɔr] *fpl* Azores

à-côté [akote] *m* (*pl* -côtés) sidelight; path (*beside road*); kickback

à-coup [aku] *m* (*pl* -coups) jerk; **par à-coups** by fits and starts

acoustique [akustik] *adj* acoustic, acoustical ‖ *f* acoustics

acquéreur [akerœr] *m* buyer

acquérir [akerir] §3 *tr* to acquire, to get

acquiescement [akjesmɑ̃] *m* acquiescence

acquiescer [akjese] §51 *intr* to acquiesce

ac·quis -quise [aki] [kiz] *adj* established ‖ *m* know-how

acquisition [akizisjɔ̃] *f* acquisition

acquit [aki] *m* receipt; **pour acquit** paid in full

acquit-à-caution [akitakosjɔ̃] *m* (*pl* acquits-à-caution) permit to transport in bond

acquittement [akitmɑ̃] *m* acquittal

acquitter [akite] *tr* to acquit; to receipt (*a bill*); to pay, discharge ‖ *ref* to pay one's debts; **s'acquitter de** to fulfill, to perform

âcre [ɑkr] *adj* acrid

acri·nieux [akrimɔnjø] **-nieuse** [njøz] *adj* acrimonious

acrobate [akrɔbat] *mf* acrobat

acrobatie [akrɔbasi] *f* acrobatics

acropole [akrɔpɔl] *f* acropolis

acrostiche [akrɔstiʃ] *m* acrostic

acte [akt] *m* action; bill; act; certificate, deed; **acte de présence** personal appearance; **acte de vente** bill of sale; **actes** minutes; **faire acte** to make a declaration; **prendre acte** to take minutes

acteur [aktœr] *m* actor

ac·tif -tive [aktif] [tiv] *adj* active; full (*citizen*) ‖ *m* credit side (*of an account*); assets; (gram) active voice

action [aksjɔ̃] *f* action; share (*of stock*); **action de grâces** thanksgiving

actionnaire [aksjɔner] *mf* stockholder

actionner [aksjɔne] *tr* to actuate; to drive; to sue

activer [aktive] *tr* to activate; to hasten ‖ *ref* to hasten

activité [aktivite] *f* activity; active service; **en pleine activité** in full swing

actrice [aktris] *f* actress

actuaire [aktɥer] *mf* actuary

actualisation [aktɥalizasjɔ̃] *f* modernization

actualiser [aktɥalize] *tr* to modernize, to bring up to date

actualité [aktɥalite] *f* present condition; **actualités** current events; newsreel; **d'actualité** newsworthy

ac·tuel -tuelle [aktɥel] *adj* present, present-day, current

actuellement [aktɥelmɑ̃] *adv* now, at the present time

acuité [akɥite] *f* acuity

adage [adaʒ] *m* adage

Adam [adɑ̃] *m* Adam

adapta·teur [adaptatœr] **-trice** [tris] *mf* adapter ‖ *m* (mov) adapter

adaptation [adaptasjɔ̃] *f* adaptation

adapter [adapte] *tr & ref* to adapt

addenda [adɛ̃da] *m invar* addendum

addi·tif [aditif] **-tive** [tiv] *adj & m* additive

addition [adisjɔ̃] *f* addition; check (*for a restaurant meal*)

additionner [adisjɔne] *tr* to add up; to add; to dilute, mix

adénoïde [adenɔid] *adj* adenoid

adent [adɑ̃] *m* dovetail

adepte [adept] *mf* adept

adé·quat [adekwa] **-quate** [kwat] *adj* adequate

adhérence [aderɑ̃s] *f* adherence; traction; (pathol) adhesion

adhé·rent [aderɑ̃] **-rente** [rɑ̃t] *adj & mf* adherent

adhérer [adere] §10 *intr* to adhere; to stick; **adhérer à la route** to hold the road

adhé·sif [adezif] **-sive** [ziv] *adj & m* adhesive

adhésion [adezjɔ̃] *f* adhesion

adieu [adjø] *m* (*pl* adieux) farewell ‖ *interj* adieu!, bon voyage!; good riddance!; **sans adieu!** see you later!

adja·cent [adʒasɑ̃] **-cente** [sɑ̃t] *adj* adjacent

adjec·tif [adʒɛktif] **-tive** [tiv] *adj & m* adjective

adjoindre [adʒwɛdr] §35 *tr & ref* to join

ad·joint [adʒwɛ̃] **-jointe** [ʒwɛ̃t] *adj & mf* assistant, stand-by

adjudant [adʒydɑ̃] *m* warrant officer; sergeant major; (pej) martinet

adjudication [adʒydikɑsjɔ̃] *f* auction; awarding (*of a contract*)

adjuger [adʒyʒe] §38 *tr* to adjudge, award; to knock down (*at auction*)

admettre [admɛtr] §42 *tr* to admit

administra·teur [administratœr] **-trice** [tris] *mf* administrator, director

administration [administrɑsjɔ̃] *f* administration; **administration des ponts et chaussées** highway department

administrer [administre] *tr* to administer

admira·teur [admiratœr] **-trice** [tris] *mf* admirer

admira·tif [admiratif] **-tive** [tiv] *adj* admiring; amazed

admiration [admirɑsjɔ̃] *f* admiration; wonder

admirer [admire] *tr* to admire; to wonder at

admissible [admisibl] *adj* admissible; eligible

admission [admisjɔ̃] *f* admission; (aut) intake

admonester [admɔneste] *tr* to admonish

adolescence [adɔlesɑ̃s] *f* adolescence

adoles·cent [adɔlesɑ̃] **adoles·cente** [adɔlesɑ̃t] *adj & mf* adolescent

adonner [adɔne] *ref* to devote oneself; **s'adonner à** to give oneself up to

adopter [adɔpte] *tr* to adopt

adop·tif [adɔptif] **-tive** [tiv] *adj* adopted; adoptive

adoption [adɔpsjɔ̃] *f* adoption

adorable [adɔrabl] *adj* adorable

adora·teur [adɔratœr] **-trice** [tris] *mf* adorer; worshiper

adoration [adɔrɑsjɔ̃] *f* adoration

adorer [adɔre] *tr* to adore, worship

adosser [adɔse] *tr*—**adosser q.ch. à** to turn the back of s.th. against ‖ *ref*— **s'adosser à** to lean back against

adouber [adube] *tr* to dub

adoucir [adusir] *tr* to soften ‖ *ref* to soften; to grow milder

adrénaline [adrenalin] *f* adrenalin

adresse [adrɛs] *f* address; skill, dexterity; neatness; expertness, expertise; **adresse particulière** home address

adresser [adrese] *tr* to address ‖ *ref* to apply

Adriatique [adriatik] *adj & f* Adriatic

a·droit [adrwa] **-droite** [drwat] *adj* adroit, clever; neat

aduler [adyle] *tr* to adulate

adulte [adylt] *adj & mf* adult

adultère [adyltɛr] *adj* adulterous ‖ *m* adultery; adulterer ‖ *f* adulteress

adultérer [adyltere] §10 *tr* to adulterate; to falsify (*a text*)

adulté·rin [adylterɛ̃] **-rine** [rin] *adj* born in adultery

advenir [advənir] §72 (used only in *inf*; *pp*; 3d *pers sg & pl*) *intr* (*aux*: ÊTRE)

to come to pass; **advienne que pourra** come what may

adventice [advɑ̃tis] *adj* adventitious

adverbe [adverb] *m* adverb

adversaire [adverser] *mf* adversary

adverse [advers] *adj* adverse; opposite (*side*)

adversité [adversite] *f* adversity

aérer [aere] §10 *tr* to aerate; to ventilate; to air

aé·rien [aerjɛ̃] **-rienne** [rjɛn] *adj* aerial ‖ *m* elevated railway

aéro [aero] *m* airplane

aérodynamique [aerodinamik] *adj* aerodynamic; streamlined ‖ *f* aerodynamics

aérogare [aerogar] *f* air terminal

aéroglisseur [aeroglisœr] *m* hydrofoil

aérogramme [aerogram] *m* air letter

aérolite or **aérolithe** [aerolit] *m* meteorite, aerolite

aéronef [aeronɛf] *m* aircraft

aérophare [aerofar] *m* air beacon

aéroport [aeropɔr] *m* airport

aéropor·té **-tée** [aeropɔrte] *adj* airborne

aéropos·tal **-tale** [aeropɔstal] *adj* (*pl* **-taux** [to]) air-mail

aérosol [aerosɔl] *m* aerosol

aérospa·tial **-tiale** [aerospasjal] *adj* (*pl* **-tiaux** [sjo]) aerospace

A.F. *abbr* (**allocations familiales**) family (social security) allotments

affable [afabl] *adj* affable

affadir [afadir] *tr & ref* to stale

affaiblir [afeblir] *tr & ref* to weaken

affaire [afer] *f* affair; job; business; trouble; (law) case; (coll) belongings; **affaire à saisir** bargain; **affaire d'or** (fig) gold mine; **affaire en instance** unfinished business; **affaires** business; **bonne affaire** bargain; **cela fait mon affaire** that is just what I want

affai·ré **-rée** [afere] *adj* busy, bustling

affairiste [aferist] *m* slicker, operator

affaissement [afesmɑ̃] *m* sagging; cave-in, collapse

affaisser [afese] *tr* to weigh down; to depress ‖ *ref* to sag; to cave in, to collapse

affaler [afale] *tr* to haul down ‖ *ref* to drop, sink, flop

affa·mé **-mée** [afame] *adj* famished, starved

affamer [afame] *tr* to starve

affectable [afɛktabl] *adj* impressionable; mortgageable

affectation [afɛktɑsjɔ̃] *f* affectation; assignment; allotment

affec·té **-tée** [afɛkte] *adj* affected; assigned

affecter [afɛkte] *tr* to affect; to assign; to assume (*various shapes or manners*) ‖ *ref* to grieve

affec·tif [afɛktif] **-tive** [tiv] *adj* affective, emotional

affection [afɛksjɔ̃] *f* affection; mental state; disease, affection

affection·né **-née** [afɛksjɔne] *adj* loving, fond, devoted

affectionner [afeksjɔne] *tr* to be fond of || *ref* to become attached

affectueusement [afektɥøzmɑ̃] *adv* affectionately

affec·tueux [afektɥø] **-tueuse** [tɥøz] *adj* affectionate

affé·rent [aferɑ̃] **-rente** [rɑ̃t] *adj* due, accruing

affermer [aferme] *tr* to lease, to rent

affermir [afermir] *tr* to strengthen, harden || *ref* to become stronger, sounder

affichage [afiʃaʒ] *m* billposting

affiche [afiʃ] *f* poster, bill; (theat) playbill

afficher [afiʃe] *tr* to post, to post up; to display; (theat) to bill || *ref* to seek the limelight; **s'afficher avec** to hang around with

afficheur [afiʃœr] *m* billposter

affi·lé -lée [afile] *adj* sharpened; sharp (*tongue*) || *adv*—**d'affilée** in a row

affiler [afile] *tr* to sharpen, to whet; to hone, to strop; to set (*a saw*)

affi·lié -liée [afilje] *adj* & *mf* affiliate

affilier [afilje] *tr* & *ref* to affiliate

affiloir [afilwar] *m* sharpener; whetstone; hone, strop

affiner [afine] *tr* to improve; to refine; to sift || *ref* to improve; to mature, ripen

affinité [afinite] *f* affinity; in-law relationship

affirma·tif [afirmatif] **-tive** [tiv] *adj* & *f* affirmative

affirmer [afirme] *tr* to affirm || *ref* to assert oneself; **s'affirmer comme** to take one's place as

affixe [afiks] *m* affix

affleurer [aflœre] *tr* to level; to come up to the level of || *intr* to come to the surface

affliction [afliksjɔ̃] *f* affliction

affli·gé -gée [afliʒe] *adj* sorrowful

affli·geant [afliʒɑ̃] **-geante** [ʒɑ̃t] *adj* sorrowful (*news*)

affliger [afliʒe] §38 *tr* to afflict || *ref* to grieve, to sorrow; **s'affliger de** to sorrow for

affluence [aflyɑ̃s] *f* crowd

af·fluent [aflyɑ̃] **af·fluente** [aflyɑ̃t] *adj* & *m* tributary

affluer [aflye] *intr* to flow; to throng, crowd, flock

afflux [afly] *m* afflux, flow; rush

affo·lé -lée [afɔle] *adj* panic-stricken

affolement [afɔlmɑ̃] *m* distraction, panic; infatuation; unsteadiness (*of a compass*)

affoler [afɔle] *tr* to distract, to panic; to infatuate; to disturb (*compass*) || *ref* to be distracted; to stampede; to become infatuated; to spin (*as a compass*)

affran·chi -chie [afrɑ̃ʃi] *adj* emancipated; postpaid || *mf* freethinker

affranchir [afrɑ̃ʃir] *tr* to emancipate, free; to pay the postage for

affranchissement [afrɑ̃ʃismɑ̃] *m* emancipation; payment of postage; cancellation (*of mail*); **affranchissement insuffisant** postage due

affres [afr] *fpl* pangs

affrètement [afretmɑ̃] *m* chartering (*of a boat*)

affréter [afrete] §10 *tr* to charter (*a boat*)

af·freux [afrø] **af·freuse** [afrøz] *adj* frightful

affront [afrɔ̃] *m* affront

affronter [afrɔ̃te] *tr* to confront; to face

affût [afy] *m* hunting blind; mount (*for cannon*); **être à l'affût de** to lie in wait for

affûter [afyte] *tr* to sharpen

afin [afɛ̃] *adv*—**afin de** in order to; **afin que** in order that, so that

afri·cain [afrikɛ̃] **-caine** [ken] *adj* African || (*cap*) *mf* African

Afrique [afrik] *f* Africa; **l'Afrique** Africa

agacement [agasmɑ̃] *m* irritation, annoyance

agacer [agase] §51 *tr* to irritate, annoy; to tease; to set on edge

agape [agap] *f* agape; **agapes** banquet

âge [ɑʒ] *m* age; **d'un certain âge** middle-aged; **quel âge avez-vous?** how old are you?

â·gé -gée [aʒe] *adj* old, aged; old, e.g., **âgé de seize ans** sixteen years old

agence [aʒɑ̃s] *f* agency, office, service, bureau; **agence de location** rental service; real-estate office; **agence de voyages** travel bureau; **agence immobilière** real-estate office

agencement [aʒɑ̃smɑ̃] *m* arrangement; furnishing (*of a house*); construction (*of a sentence*); **agencements** fixtures

agencer [aʒɑ̃se] §51 *tr* to arrange

agenda [aʒɛ̃da] *m* engagement book

agenouiller [aʒnuje] *ref* to kneel

agent [aʒɑ̃] *m* agent; policeman; **agent comptable** accountant; **agent de change** stockbroker; **agent de location** realtor

agglomération [aglɔmerasjɔ̃] *f* agglomeration; metropolitan area; built-up area

agglomé·ré -rée [aglɔmere] *adj* compressed || *m* briquette; adobe

agglomérer [aglɔmere] §10 *tr* & *ref* to agglomerate

aggraver [agrave] *tr* to aggravate || *ref* to become more serious

agile [aʒil] *adj* agile, nimble

agilité [aʒilite] *f* agility

agio·teur [aʒjɔtœr] **-teuse** [tøz] *mf* speculator

agir [aʒir] *intr* to act; to take action || *ref*—**il s'agit de** it is a question of

agis·sant [aʒisɑ̃] **agis·sante** [aʒisɑ̃t] *adj* active

agissements [aʒismɑ̃] *mpl* machinations

agita·teur [aʒitatœr] **-trice** [tris] *mf* agitator (*person*) || *m* stirrer

agi·té -tée [aʒite] *adj* restless; rough (*sea*)

agiter [aʒite] *tr* to agitate; to stir; to wave; to discuss || *ref* to move about

a·gneau [aɲo] *m* (*pl* **-gneaux**) lamb

agnostique [agnɔstik] *adj* & *mf* agnostic

agonie [agɔni] *f* agony, death throes

agrafe [agraf] *f* clasp, pin; paper clip; staple (*for papers*); belt buckle; snap, hook; (med) clamp

agrafer [agrafe] *tr* to clasp, pin; to buckle; to snap; to hook; to fasten, to clip; to staple; (med) to clamp

agrafeuse [agraføz] *f* stapler

agraire [agrer] *adj* agrarian

agrandir [agrãdir] *tr* to enlarge || *ref* to grow, become larger

agrandissement [agrãdismã] *m* enlargement

agréable [agreabl] *adj* agreeable, pleasant; neighborly

agréé agréée [agree] *adj* approved || *m* attorney

agréer [agree] *tr* to accept, approve; veuillez agréer l'expression de mes sentiments distingués (complimentary close) sincerely yours || *intr* (with *dat*) to agree with, to please

agrégat [agrega] *m* aggregate

agrégation [agregasjɔ̃] *f* aggregation; admittance (*as a member of an organization*); competitive teacher's examination

agré·gé -gée [agreʒe] *adj* aggregate || *mf* one who has passed his *agrégation*

agréger [agreʒe] §1 *tr* to attach, to add || *ref—*s'agréger (à) to join

agrément [agremã] *m* approval; pleasantness; pleasure, pastime; agréments adornments

agrès [agre] *mpl* rigging; gym equipment

agresseur [agresœr] *adj & m* aggressor

agres·sif [agresif] **agres·sive** [agresiv] *adj* aggressive

agression [agresjɔ̃] *f* aggression; (law) assault

agreste [agrest] *adj* rustic, rural

agricole [agrikɔl] *adj* agricultural

agriculture [agrikyltyr] *f* agriculture

agrumes [agrym] *mpl* citrus fruit

aguerrir [agerir] *tr* to season, inure || *ref* to become seasoned, inured

aguets [age] *mpl* watch, look-out; être aux aguets to be on the look-out

agui·chant [agi/ã] **-chante** [/ãt] *adj* alluring || *adj fem* sexy

ah [a] *interj* ah!; ah çà! now then!

ahu·ri -rie [ayri] *adj* dumfounded

ahurir [ayrir] *tr* to dumfound

ahurissement [ayrismã] *m* stupefaction

aide [ed] *mf* aid, assistant, helper || *f* aid, assistance, help; aide sociale welfare department

aider [ede] *tr* to aid, help; aider + *inf* to help to + *inf* || *intr* to help || *ref—*s'aider de to use

aïe [aj] *interj* ouch!

aïeul aïeule [ajœl] *mf* grandparent || *m* grandfather || *m* (*pl* aïeux [ajø]) ancestor || *f* grandmother

aigle [egl] *mf* eagle; aigle de mer eagle ray; aigle pêcheur, grand aigle de mer osprey, fish hawk; grand aigle spread eagle

aiglefin [egləfɛ̃] *m* haddock

ai·glon [eglɔ̃] **-glonne** [glɔn] *mf* eaglet

aigre [egr] *adj* sour, tart, bitter; harsh (*voice*)

aigre-doux [egrədu] **-douce** [dus] *adj* bittersweet

aigrefin [egrəfɛ̃] *m* crook

aigre·let [egrəle] **-lette** [let] *adj* tart

aigrir [egrir] *tr* to turn (*s.th.*) sour || *intr & ref* to turn sour

ai·gu -guë [egy] *adj* sharp; acute; shrill, high-pitched || *m* (mus) treble

aigue-marine [egmarin] *f* (*pl* aigues-marines) aquamarine

aiguille [eguij] *f* needle; peak; spire (*of steeple*); hand (*of clock*); (rr) switch

aiguiller [eguije] *tr* to switch, shunt || *ref* to be switched, shunted

aiguilleur [eguijœr] *m* (aer, rr) towerman

aiguillon [eguijɔ̃] *m* goad; sting

aiguiser [eguize] *tr* to sharpen; to whet (*appetite*)

ail [aj] *m* (*pl* ails or aulx [o]) garlic

aile [el] *f* wing; flank (*of army*); fender (*of auto*); brim (*of hat*); blade (*of propeller*); vane, arm (*of windmill*); aile en flèche (aer) backswept wing

aileron [elrɔ̃] *m* aileron

ailleurs [ajœr] *adv* elsewhere; d'ailleurs moreover, besides; from somewhere else; par ailleurs furthermore

aimable [emabl] *adj* kind, likeable; voulez-vous être assez aimable de will you be good enough to

aimant [emã] *m* magnet

aimanter [emãte] *tr* to magnetize

aimer [eme], [eme] *tr* to love; to like; to like to; aimer à to like to; aimer bien to like, to be fond of; to like to; aimer mieux to prefer; to prefer to

aine [en] *f* groin

aî·né -née [ene] *adj & mf* elder, eldest, oldest; senior

aînesse [enes] *f* seniority

ainsi [ɛ̃si] *adv* thus; ainsi de suite and so forth; ainsi nommé so-called; ainsi que as well as; ainsi soit-il amen

air [er] *m* air; look, appearance; air de famille family resemblance; avoir l'air de to seem to; en l'air empty, idle (*threats, talk*)

airain [erɛ̃] *m* brass; bronze

aire [er] *f* area; threshing floor; eyrie; aire de lancement launching pad

airelle [erel] *f* huckleberry; blueberry

aisance [ezãs] *f* ease, comfort

aise [ez] *adj—*bien aise glad, content || *f* ease; aises comforts; à son aise well-to-do

ai·sé -sée [eze] *adj* easy; natural; well-to-do

aisément [ezemã] *adv* easily

aisselle [esel] *f* armpit

ajonc [aʒɔ̃] *m* furze

ajou·ré -rée [aʒure] *adj* openwork, perforated

ajourer [aʒure] *tr* to cut openings in

ajournement [aʒurnəmã] *m* adjournment, postponement; subpoenaing; rejection (*of a candidate*)

ajourner [aʒurne] *tr* to postpone; to subpoena; to reject (*a candidate in an examination*)

ajouter [aʒute] *tr* & *intr* to add ‖ *ref* to be added

ajus·té -tée [aʒyste] *adj* tight-fitting

ajuster [aʒyste] *tr* to adjust; to arrange; to fit; to aim at

ajusteur [aʒystœr] *m* fitter

alacrité [alakrite] *f* gaiety, vivacity

alambic [alãbik] *m* still

alambi·qué -quée [alãbike] *adj*. finespun, far-fetched

alanguir [alãgir] *tr* to weaken ‖ *ref* to languish

alar·mant [alarmã] **-mante** [mãt] *adj* alarming

alarme [alarm] *f* alarm

alarmer [alarme] *tr* to alarm ‖ *ref* to be alarmed

alba·nais [albane] **-naise** [nez] *adj* Albanian (*language*) ‖ (*cap*) *mf* Albanian (*person*)

albâtre [albɑtr] *m* alabaster

albatros [albatros] *m* albatross

albi·geois [albiʒwa] **-geoise** [ʒwaz] *adj* Albigensian ‖ (*cap*) *mf* Albigensian

albinos [albinos] *adj* & *m* albino

album [albɔm] *m* album; scrapbook

albumen [albymen] *m* albumen

alcali [alkali] *m* alkali

alca·lin [alkalɛ̃] **-line** [lin] *adj* alkaline

alchimie [alʃimi] *f* alchemy

alcool [alkɔl] *m* alcohol; **alcool à friction** rubbing alcohol; **alcool dénaturé** denatured alcohol

alcoolique [alkɔɔlik], [alkɔlik] *adj* & *mf* alcoholic

alcôve [alkov] *f* alcove; **d'alcôve** amatory, gallant

ale [ɛl] *m* ale

aléa [alea] *m* risk

aléatoire [aleatwar] *adj* risky; aleatory

alène [alen] *f* awl

alentour [alãtur] *adv* round about ‖ **alentours** *mpl* neighborhood

alerte [alert] *adj* & *f* alert; **alerte aérienne** air-raid alarm

alerter [alerte] *tr* to alert

alésage [alezaʒ] *m* bore (*of cylinder*)

aléser [aleze] §10 *tr* to ream; to bore

ale·zan [alzã] **-zane** [zan] *adj* chestnut (*colored*)

algarade [algarad] *f* altercation

algèbre [alʒebr] *f* algebra

Alger [alʒe] *m* Algiers

Algérie [alʒeri] *f* Algeria

algé·rien [alʒerjɛ̃] **-rienne** [rjen] *adj* Algerian ‖ (*cap*) *mf* Algerian

algé·rois [alʒerwa] **-roise** [rwaz] *adj* of Algiers; Algerian ‖ (*cap*) *mf* native of Algiers; Algerian

algues [alg] *fpl* algae

alias [aljɑs] *adv* alias

alibi [alibi] *m* (*law*) alibi

alié·né -née [aljene] *adj* alienated; insane ‖ *mf* insane person

aliéner [aljene] §10 *tr* to transfer, alienate ‖ *ref* (with *dat of reflex pron*) to alienate (*s.o.*); (with *dat of reflex pron*) to lose (*e.g., s.o.'s sympathy*)

alignement [aliɲmã] *m* alignment

aligner [aliɲe] *tr* to align; **aligner ses**

phrases to choose one's words with care ‖ *ref* to line up

aliment [alimã] *m* aliment, food; **aliments** (*law*) necessities

alimentaire [alimãter] *adj* alimentary; subsistence, e.g., **pension alimentaire** subsistence allowance

aliment·:tion [alimãtasjɔ̃] *f* nourishment; supplying; feeding (*a fire, a machine*)

alimenter [alimãte] *tr* to nourish; to supply; to feed (*a fire, a machine*)

alinéa [alinea] *m* indentation (*of the first line of a paragraph*); paragraph

aliter [alite] *tr* to keep in bed ‖ *ref* to be confined to bed

alizés [alize] *mpl* trade winds

allaiter [alete] *tr* to nurse

al·lant [alã] **al·lante** [alãt] *adj* active ‖ *m*—**allants et venants** passers-by; **beaucoup d'allant** (coll) a lot of pep

allé·chant [aleʃã] **-chante** [ʃãt] *adj* enticing, tempting

allécher [aleʃe] §10 *tr* to allure

allée [ale] *f* walk, path; going; **allée et venue** comings and goings; **allée** 1

allégeance [aleʒãs] *f* allegiance; lightening (*of care*); handicapping (*of a race*)

alléger [aleʒe] §1 *tr* to lighten; to alleviate, mitigate, relieve

allégorie [allegɔri] *f* allegory

allègre [allegr] *adj* lively, cheerful

alléguer [allege] §10 *tr* to allege as an excuse; to cite (*an authority*)

Allemagne [almaɲ] *f* Germany; **l'Allemagne** Germany

alle·mand [almã] **-mande** [mãd] *adj* German ‖ *m* German (*language*) ‖ (*cap*) *mf* German (*person*)

aller [ale] *m* going; go; **aller (et) retour** round trip; round-trip ticket; **au pis aller** at the worst ‖ §4 *intr* (*aux*: ÊTRE) to go; to work, function; (with *dat*) to suit, fit, become, e.g., **la robe lui va bien** the dress becomes her; **aller** + *inf* to be going to + *inf*, e.g., **je vais au magasin acheter des souliers** I am going to the store to buy some shoes; **allez!, allons!, allons donc!** well!, come on!, all right!; **allez-y doucement!** take it easy!; **ça va?, comment allez-vous?** how are you? ‖ *ref*—**s'en aller** to go away ‖ *aux*—**aller** + *inf* to be going to + *inf* (to express futurity), e.g., **il va se marier** he is going to get married

allergie [allerʒi] *f* allergy

aller-retour [aleratur] *m*—**faire l'aller-retour** to go and come back

alliage [aljaʒ] *m* alloy

alliance [aljãs] *f* alliance; marriage; wedding ring; **ancienne alliance** Old Covenant; **nouvelle alliance** New Covenant

al·lié -liée [alje] *adj* allied (*by treaty*); united (*in marriage*) ‖ *mf* ally; kin, in-law

allier [alje] *tr* to ally; to alloy ‖ *ref* to become allied, to ally oneself

alligator [alligatɔr] *m* alligator

allô [alo] *interj* hello!

allocation [allɔkɑsjɔ̃] *f* allocation, allotment; **allocations familiales** family (social security) allotments

allocution [allɔkysjɔ̃] *f* short speech

allonger [alɔ̃ʒe] §38 *tr, intr,* & *ref* to lengthen

allouer [alwe] *tr* to allow, allocate

allumage [alymaʒ] *m* lighting; switching on (*of a light*); kindling (*of a fire*); ignition

allume-feu [alymfø] *m invar* kindling

allumer [alyme] *tr* to ignite; to light (*a cigarette*); to light up (*a room*); to put on, switch on (*a light; a radio; a heater*); to provoke (*anger*) || *ref* to go on (*said of a light*); to light up (*said of eyes*); to catch fire

allumette [alymet] *f* match; **allumette de sûreté** safety match

allumette-gaz [alymetgaz] *m* pilot light

allumeur [alymœr] *m* ignition system; **allumeur de réverbères** lamplighter

allumeuse [alymøz] *f* (coll) vamp

allure [alyr] *f* speed, pace; gait, bearing, aspect; **à l'allure de l'escargot** at a snail's pace; **à toute allure** at top speed

allusion [allyzjɔ̃] *f* allusion

almanach [almana] *m* almanac; yearbook

aloès [alɔɛs] *m* aloe

aloi [alwa] *m* legal alloy; quality; **de bon aloi** genuine

alors [alɔr] *adv* then; **alors même que** even though; **alors que** whereas

alose [aloz] *f* shad

alouette [alwet] *f* lark, skylark; **alouette sans tête** rolled veal

alourdir [alurdir] *tr* to weigh down, to make heavy || *ref* to become heavy

aloyau [alwajo] *m* (*pl* **aloyaux**) sirloin

Alpes [alp] *fpl*—**les Alpes** the Alps

alphabet [alfabe] *m* alphabet

alpinisme [alpinism] *m* mountain climbing

alpiniste [alpinist] *mf* mountain climber

alpiste [alpist] *m* birdseed

alsa-cien [alzasjɛ̃] **-cienne** [sjen] *adj* Alsatian || *m* Alsatian (*dialect*) || (*cap*) *mf* Alsatian (*person*)

alté-rant [alterɑ̃] **-rante** [rɑ̃t] *adj* thirst-provoking

altération [alterɑsjɔ̃] *f* alteration, falsification; deterioration; heavy thirst; (mus) accidental

altérer [altere] §10 *tr* to alter, falsify; to ruin (*one's health*); to weaken, impair; to make thirsty || *ref* to undergo a change for the worse; to become thirsty

alternance [alternɑ̃s] *f* alternation; (agr) rotation

alterna-tif [alternatif] **-tive** [tiv] *adj* alternative; alternating; alternate || *f* alternative, dilemma; alternation

alterne [altern] *adj* alternate (*angles*)

alterner [alterne] *tr* to rotate (*crops*) || *intr* to alternate

al-tier [altje] **-tière** [tjer] *adj* haughty

altitude [altityd] *f* altitude

alto [alto] *m* alto; viola

altruiste [altruist] *adj* & *mf* altruist

aluminium [alyminjɔm] *m* aluminum

alun [alœ̃] *m* alum

alunir [alynir] *intr* to land on the moon

alunissage [alynisaʒ] *m* landing on the moon

alvéole [alveɔl] *m* & *f* alveolus; cavity; cell (*of honeycomb*); socket (*of tooth*)

amadou [amadu] *m* punk, tinder

amadouer [amadwe] *tr* to wheedle

amaigrir [amegrir] *tr* to emaciate; to make thin || *ref* to grow thin

amalgame [amalgam] *m* amalgam

amalgamer [amalgame] *tr* & *ref* to amalgamate

aman [amɑ̃] *m*—**demander l'aman** to give in

amande [amɑ̃d] *f* almond; kernel; **amande de Malaga** Jordan almond

amandier [amɑ̃dje] *m* almond tree

a-mant [amɑ̃] **-mante** [mɑ̃t] *mf* lover

amareyeur [amarejœr] *m* oysterman

amariner [amarine] *tr* to season (*a crew*); to impress (*a ship*)

amarre [amar] *f* hawser

amarrer [amare] *tr* & *ref* to moor

amas [ama] *m* mass; heap; cluster (*of stars*); **amas de neige** snowdrift

amasser [amase] *tr* to amass; to gather || *intr* to hoard || *ref* to pile up, to crowd

amateur [amatœr] *adj* amateur || *m* amateur; (coll) prospective buyer

amatir [amatir] *tr* to mat, dull (*metal or glass*)

amazone [amazon] *f* amazon; horsewoman; riding habit; **monter en amazone** to ride sidesaddle || (*cap*) *f* Amazon

ambages [ɑ̃baʒ] *fpl* circumlocutions; **sans ambages** without beating around the bush

ambassade [ɑ̃basad] *f* embassy

ambassadeur [ɑ̃basadœr] *m* ambassador

ambassadrice [ɑ̃basadris] *f* ambassadress; wife of ambassador; emissary

ambiance [ɑ̃bjɑ̃s] *f* environment, milieu; atmosphere, tone

ambidextre [ɑ̃bidekstrə] *adj* ambidextrous || *mf* ambidextrous person

ambi-gu -guë [ɑ̃bigy] *adj* ambiguous || *m* ambiguousness; buffet lunch; odd mixture

ambiguïté [ɑ̃biguite] *f* ambiguity

ambi-tieux [ɑ̃bisjø] **-tieuse** [sjøz] *adj* ambitious

ambition [ɑ̃bisjɔ̃] *f* ambition

amble [ɑ̃bl] *m* amble

ambler [ɑ̃ble] *intr* (equit) to amble

ambre [ɑ̃br] *m*—**ambre gris** ambergris; **ambre** (**jaune** *ou* **succin**) amber

ambulance [ɑ̃bylɑ̃s] *f* ambulance

ambulan-cier [ɑ̃bylɑ̃sje] **-cière** [sjer] *mf* ambulance driver or attendant

ambu-lant [ɑ̃bylɑ̃] **-lante** [lɑ̃t] *adj* ambulant || *m* railway mail clerk

ambulatoire [ɑ̃bylatwar] *adj* ambulatory; itinerant

âme [ɑm] *f* soul; spirit, heart, mind;

core (*of cable*); bore (*of cannon*); web (*of rail*); sound post (*of violin*); **âme damnée** evil genius; **rendre l'âme** to give up the ghost

améliorer [ameljɔre] *tr & ref* to ameliorate, to improve

amen [amen] *m invar* Amen

aménagement [amenaʒmɑ̃] *m* arrangement, equipping; preparation, development (*of land*); adjustment (*of taxes*); **aménagements** furnishings

aménager [amenaʒe] §38 *tr* to arrange, equip; to remodel; to parcel out; to grade (*a roadbed*); to feed (*a machine*); to harness (*a waterfall*)

amende [ɑmɑ̃d] *f* fine; forfeit (*in a game*); **faire amende honorable** (coll) to apologize

amendement [amɑ̃dmɑ̃] *m* amendment; fertilizer

amender [amɑ̃de] *tr* to amend; to manure ‖ *ref* to mend one's ways, to amend

amène [amen] *adj* pleasant

amener [amne] §2 *tr* to bring; to lead; to bring on; to furnish (*proof*); (naut) to lower; **amener pavillon** to surrender ‖ *ref* (coll) to arrive; **amenez-vous!** (slang) get a move on!

aménité [amenite] *f* amenity; **aménités** cutting remarks

amenuiser [amənɥize] *tr* to whittle ‖ *ref* to be whittled down

a·mer -mère [amer] *adj* bitter ‖ *m* bitters; seamark; gall (*of animal*)

améri·cain -caine [amerikɛ̃] *adj* American ‖ *m* American English ‖ *f* phaeton; bicycle relay ‖ (*cap*) *mf* American (*person*)

américanisme [amerikanism] *m* Americanism; American studies

Amérique [amerik] *f* America; **l'Amérique** America

amerrir [amerir] *intr* to land, alight on water

amerrissage [amerisaʒ] *m* landing (on water); (rok) splashdown; **amerrissage forcé** ditching; **faire un amerrissage forcé** to ditch

amertume [amertym] *f* bitterness

améthyste [ametist] *f* amethyst

ameublement [amœbləmɑ̃] *m* furnishings; furniture, suite

ameublir [amœblir] *tr* (agr) to soften, to mellow (*soil*)

ameuter [amøte] *tr* to rouse (*the pack*) ‖ *ref* to riot

a·mi -mie [ami] *adj* friendly ‖ *mf* friend ‖ *f* mistress

amiable [amjabl] *adj* amicable; **à l'amiable** privately, out of court

amiante [amjɑ̃t] *m* asbestos

amibe [amib] *f* amoeba

ami·bien [amibjɛ̃] **-bienne** [bjen] *adj* amoebic

ami·cal -cale [amikal] *adj* (*pl* **-caux** [ko]) amicable ‖ *f* professional club

amidon [amidɔ̃] *m* starch

amidonner [amidɔne] *tr* to starch

amincir [amɛ̃sir] *tr* to make more slender, to attenuate ‖ *ref* to grow thinner

ami·ral [amiral] *m* (*pl* **-raux** [ro]) admiral

amirale [amiral] *f* admiral's wife

amirauté [amirote] *f* admiralty

amitié [amitje] *f* friendship; **amitiés** (complimentary close) cordially yours; **faites mes amitiés à** give my regards to; **faites-moi l'amitié de** do me the favor of

ammo·niac -niaque [amɔnjak] *adj* ammoniacal ‖ *m* ammonia (*gas*) ‖ *f* ammonia (*gas dissolved in water*)

amnésie [amnezi] *f* amnesia

amnistie [amnisti] *f* amnesty

amnistier [amnistje] *tr* to amnesty

amoindrir [amwɛ̃drir] *tr* to lessen ‖ *ref* to diminish

amollir [amɔlir] *tr & ref* to soften

amollissement [amɔlismɑ̃] *m* softening

amonceler [amɔ̃sle] §34 *tr* to pile up, to gather ‖ *ref* to pile up, to gather; to drift (*said of snow*)

amont [amɔ̃] *m* upper waters; **en amont** upstream; **en amont de** above

amorçage [amɔrsaʒ] *m* baiting; priming

amorce [amɔrs] *f* bait, lure; fuse, percussion cap; beginning; leader (*of strip of film*); (mov) preview

amorcer [amɔrse] §51 *tr* to bait; to prime; to entice; to begin

amorphe [amɔrf] *adj* amorphous

amortir [amɔrtir] *tr* to absorb (*shock*); to subdue (*color; pain; passions*); to damp (*waves*); to amortize

amortissement [amɔrtismɑ̃] *m* absorption (*of shock, sound, etc.*); amortization

amortisseur [amɔrtisœr] *m* shock absorber

amour [amur] *m* love; love affair; **premières amours** puppy love ‖ (*cap*) *m* Cupid

amou·reux -reuse [amurø] *adj* amorous; loving; fond, devoted; **amoureux de** in love with ‖ *m* lover ‖ *f* sweetheart

amour-propre [amurprɔpr] *m* (*pl* **amours-propres**) self-esteem; vanity

amovible [amɔvibl] *adj* removable; detachable; (jur) revocable

ampère [ɑ̃per] *m* ampere

ampèremètre [ɑ̃permetr] *m* ammeter

amphibie [ɑ̃fibi] *adj* amphibious, amphibian ‖ *m* amphibian

amphibien [ɑ̃fibjɛ̃] *m* amphibian

amphithéâtre [ɑ̃fiteatr] *m* amphitheater; auditorium (*with raised seats*)

amphitryon [ɑ̃fitrijɔ̃] *m* host at dinner ‖ (*cap*) *m* Amphitryon

ample [ɑ̃pl] *adj* ample; long (*speech*); liberal (*reward*)

amplifica·teur [ɑ̃plifikatœr] **-trice** [tris] *adj* amplifying ‖ *mf* exaggerator ‖ *m* amplifier; (phot) enlarger

amplifier [ɑ̃plifje] *tr* to amplify, to enlarge

amplitude [ɑ̃plityd] *f* amplitude

ampoule [ɑ̃pul] *f* ampule; (elec) bulb; (pathol) blister

ampu·té -tée [ɑ̃pyte] *mf* amputee

amputer [ɑ̃pyte] *tr* to amputate; to cut (*an article, speech*)

amuïr [amyir] *ref* to become silent

amuïssement [amyismɑ̃] *m* (phonet) silencing

amulette [amylet] *f* amulet

amure [amyr] *f* tack (*of sail*)

amuse-gueule [amyzgœl] *m* (*pl* **-gueule** or **-gueules**) (coll) appetizer, snack

amusement [amyzmɑ̃] *m* amusement

amuser [amyze] *tr* to amuse; to mislead || *ref* to have a good time; to sow one's wild oats; **s'amuser à** to pass the time by; **s'amuser de** to play with; to make fun of

amygdale [amigdal] *f* tonsil

an [ɑ̃] *m* year; **l'an de grâce** the year of Our Lord

anacarde [anakard] *m* cashew nut

anachronisme [anakrɔnism] *m* anachronism

analogie [analɔʒi] *f* analogy

analogue [analɔg] *adj* analogous; similar

analphabète [analfabet] *adj* & *mf* illiterate

analphabétisme [analfabetism] *m* illiteracy

analyse [analiz] *f* analysis; **analyse des renseignements** data processing

analyser [analize] *tr* to analyze

analyseur [analizœr] *m* analyzer, tester

analyste [analist] *mf* analyst

analytique [analitik] *adj* analytic(al)

ananas [anana] *m* pineapple

anarchie [anarʃi] *f* anarchy

anarchiste [anarʃist] *mf* anarchist

anathème [anatem] *m* anathema

anatife [anatif] *m* barnacle

anatomie [anatɔmi] *f* anatomy

anatomique [anatɔmik] *adj* anatomic(al)

ances·tral **-trale** [ɑ̃sestral] *adj* (*pl* **-traux** [tro]) ancestral

ancêtre [ɑ̃setr] *m* ancestor

anche [ɑ̃ʃ] *f* (mus) reed

anchois [ɑ̃ʃwa] *m* anchovy

an·cien [ɑ̃sjɛ̃] **-cienne** [sjen] *adj* ancient, old, long-standing; antiquated; antique || (when standing before noun) *adj* former, previous, old; retired (*businessman*); ancient (*Greece, Rome*) || *mf* senior (*in rank*); oldster; **les Anciens** the Ancients

anciennement [ɑ̃sjenmɑ̃] *adv* formerly

ancienneté [ɑ̃sjente] *f* antiquity; seniority (*in rank*)

ancre [ɑ̃kr] *f* anchor; **ancres levées** anchors aweigh

ancrer [ɑ̃kre] *tr* & *intr* to anchor || *ref* to become established

andain [ɑ̃dɛ̃] *m* swath; row of shocks

andouille [ɑ̃duj] *f* (coll) fool, sap

andouiller [ɑ̃duje] *m* antler

âne [ɑn] *m* ass, donkey

anéantir [aneɑ̃tir] *tr* to annihilate; to prostrate || *ref* to disappear; to humble oneself (*before God*)

anéantissement [aneɑ̃tismɑ̃] *m* annihilation; prostration

anecdote [anegdɔt] *f* anecdote

anémie [anemi] *f* anemia

ânesse [ɑnes] *f* she-ass

anesthésie [anestezi] *f* anesthesia

anesthésier [anestezje] *tr* to anesthetize

anesthésique [anestezik] *adj* & *m* anesthetic

anesthésiste [anestezist] *mf* anesthetist

anévrisme [anevrism] *m* aneurysm

anfractuosité [ɑ̃fraktɥozite] *f* rough outline (*of coast*); ruggedness, cragginess

ange [ɑ̃ʒ] *m* angel; **ange gardien, ange tutélaire** guardian angel; **être aux anges** to walk on air

angélique [ɑ̃ʒelik] *adj* angelic(al)

angélus [ɑ̃ʒelys] *m* Angelus

angine [ɑ̃ʒin] *f* tonsillitis, quinsy; **angine de poitrine** angina pectoris

an·glais [ɑ̃gle] **-glaise** [glez] *adj* English; **à l'anglaise** in the English manner; **filer à l'anglaise** to take French leave || *m* English (*language*) || (*cap*) *m* Englishman; **les Anglais** the English || *f* Englishwoman

angle [ɑ̃gl] *m* angle; corner

Angleterre [ɑ̃gləter] *f* England; **l'Angleterre** England

angois·sant [ɑ̃gwasɑ̃] **angois·sante** [ɑ̃gwasɑ̃t] *adj* agonizing

angoisse [ɑ̃gwas] *f* anguish

anguille [ɑ̃gij] *f* eel; **anguille de mer** conger eel

angulaire [ɑ̃gyler] *adj* angular

angu·leux [ɑ̃gylø] **-leuse** [løz] *adj* angular, sharp

anicroche [anikrɔʃ] *f* (coll) hitch, snag

ani·mal **-male** [animal] (*pl* **-maux** [mo]) *adj* animal || *m* animal, brute, beast; (coll) blockhead

ani·ma·teur [animatœr] **-trice** [tris] *adj* animating || *mf* animator, moving spirit; master of ceremonies; **animateur de théâtre** theatrical producer

animation [animasjɔ̃] *f* animation

animer [anime] *tr* to animate; to encourage || *ref* to become alive, liven up

animosité [animozite] *f* animosity

anion [anjɔ̃] *m* anion

anis [ani] *m* anise

annales [anal] *fpl* annals

an·neau [ano] *m* (*pl* **-neaux**) ring

année [ane] *f* year; **année bissextile** leap year; **année de lumière** light-year; **bonne année** Happy New Year

année-lumière [anelymjer] *f* (*pl* **années-lumière**) light-year

annexe [aneks] *adj* annexed || *f* annex

annexer [anekse] *tr* to annex

annexion [aneksjɔ̃] *f* annexation

annihiler [aniile] *tr* to annihilate

anniversaire [aniverser] *adj* & *m* anniversary; **anniversaire de naissance** birthday

annonce [anɔ̃s] *f* announcement; advertisement; (cards) bid; **petites annonces** classified ads

annoncer [anɔ̃se] §51 *tr* to announce; to advertise || *ref* to augur; to promise to be

annonceur [anɔ̃sœr] *m* advertiser

annoncia·teur [anɔ̃sjatœr] **-trice** [tris] *adj* betokening, foreboding || *m* harbinger

annoter [anɔte] *tr* to annotate

annuaire [anɥer] *m* annual, yearbook, directory; catalog, bulletin (*e.g., of a school*)

an·nuel -nuelle [anɥel] *adj* annual

annuité [anɥite] *f* annuity

annuler [anɥle] *tr* to annul

ano·din [anɔdɛ̃] **-dine** [din] *adj & m* anodyne

ânon [anɔ̃] *m* foal of an ass

anonner [anɔne] *tr* to recite in a stumbling manner

anonymat [anɔnima] *m* anonymity

anonyme [anɔnim] *adj* anonymous; incorporated; (fig) colorless, drab ‖ *mf* unidentified person

anor·mal -male [anɔrmal] (*pl* **-maux** [mo]) *adj* abnormal ‖ *mf* abnormal person

anse [ɑ̃s] *f* handle; **faire danser l'anse du panier** to pad the bill

antagonisme [ɑ̃tagɔnism] *m* antagonism

antan [ɑ̃tɑ̃] *m* yesteryear

Antarctique [ɑ̃tarktik] *adj & m* Antarctic ‖ *f* Antarctic (*region*); **l'Antarctique** Antarctica

antécé·dent [ɑ̃tesedɑ̃] **-dente** [dɑ̃t] *adj & m* antecedent

antenne [ɑ̃ten] *f* antenna (*feeler; aerial*); outpost (naut) lateen yard; **porter à l'antenne** to put on the air

antépénultième [ɑ̃tepenyltjem] *adj* antepenultimate ‖ *f* antepenult

anté·rieur -rieure [ɑ̃terjœr] *adj* anterior; former; previous, preceding; earlier; front

antériorité [ɑ̃terjɔrite] *f* priority

anthologie [ɑ̃tɔlɔʒi] *f* anthology

anthropoïde [ɑ̃trɔpɔid] *adj & m* anthropoid

anthropophage [ɑ̃trɔpɔfaʒ] *adj & mf* cannibal

antiaé·rien [ɑ̃tiaerjɛ̃] **-rienne** [rjen] *adj* antiaircraft

antialcoolique [ɑ̃tialkɔɔlik] *adj* antialcoholic ‖ *mf* teetotaler; temperance worker

antibiotique [ɑ̃tibjɔtik] *adj & m* antibiotic

antichambre [ɑ̃tiʃɑ̃br] *f* antechamber, anteroom

antichar [ɑ̃tiʃar] *adj* antitank

anticipation [ɑ̃tisipɑsjɔ̃] *f* anticipation; **anticipations** prophecies (*of science fiction*); **d'anticipation** science fiction (*stories, films, etc.*); **par anticipation** in advance

antici·pé -pée [ɑ̃tisipe] *adj* anticipated, advanced, ahead of time; premature (*e.g., death*)

anticiper [ɑ̃tisipe] *tr* to anticipate; to advance ‖ *intr* to act ahead of time; **anticiper sur** to encroach on; to pay ahead of time; to spend ahead of time

anticléri·cal -cale [ɑ̃tiklerikal] *adj* (*pl* **-caux** [ko]) anticlerical

anticonception·nel -nelle [ɑ̃tikɔ̃sepsjɔnel] *adj* contraceptive

anticorps [ɑ̃tikɔr] *m* antibody

antidéra·pant [ɑ̃tiderapɑ̃] **-pante** [pɑ̃t] *adj* nonskid ‖ *m* nonskid tire

antidéto·nant [ɑ̃tidetɔnɑ̃] **-nante** [nɑ̃t] *adj & m* antiknock

antidote [ɑ̃tidɔt] *m* antidote

antienne [ɑ̃tjen] *f* antiphon, anthem; **chanter toujours la même antienne** to harp on the same subject

antigel [ɑ̃tiʒel] *m* antifreeze

antigi·vrant [ɑ̃tiʒivrɑ̃] **-vrante** [vrɑ̃t] *adj* deicing, defrosting ‖ *m* deicer

antigivre [ɑ̃tiʒivr] *m* deicer, defroster

Antilles [ɑ̃tij] *fpl* West Indies

antilope [ɑ̃tilɔp] *f* antelope

antimite [ɑ̃timit] *adj* mothproof ‖ *m* moth killer

antimoine [ɑ̃timwan] *m* antimony

antip..rasite [ɑ̃tiparazit] *adj* (rad) static-eliminating ‖ *m* (rad) static eliminator; insecticide

antipathie [ɑ̃tipati] *f* antipathy

antiquaire [ɑ̃tiker] *m* antique dealer

antique [ɑ̃tik] *adj* antique, classic; old-fashioned ‖ *m* antique

antiquité [ɑ̃tikite] *f* antiquity; **antiquités**.. ntiques

antisémite [ɑ̃tisemit] *adj* anti-Semitic ‖ *mf* anti-Semite

antisémitique [ɑ̃tisemitik] *adj* anti-Semitic

antiseptique [ɑ̃tiseptik] *adj & m* antiseptic

antiso·cial -ciale [ɑ̃tisɔsjal] *adj* (*pl* **-ciaux** [sjo]) antisocial

antispor·tif [ɑ̃tispɔrtif] **-tive** [tiv] *adj* unsportsmanlike

antithèse [ɑ̃titez] *f* antithesis

antitoxine [ɑ̃titɔksin] *f* antitoxin

antitranspirant [ɑ̃titrɑ̃spirɑ̃] *m* antiperspirant

antonyme [ɑ̃tɔnim] *m* antonym

antre [ɑ̃tr] *m* den, lair; cave

anxiété [ɑ̃ksjete] *f* anxiety

anxieux [ɑ̃ksjø] **anxieuse** [ɑ̃ksjøz] *adj* anxious, worried

aorte [aɔrt] *f* aorta

août [u], [ut] *m* August

A.P. *abbr* (**assistance publique**) welfare department

apache [apaʃ] *m* apache, hoodlum

apaisement [apezmɑ̃] *m* appeasement

apaiser [apeze] *tr* to appease ‖ *ref* to quiet down

apanage [apanaʒ] *m* attribute

aparté [aparte] *m* stage whisper, aside; **en aparté** privately

apathie [apati] *f* apathy

apathique [apatik] *adj* apathetic

apatride [apatrid] *adj* stateless ‖ *mf* stateless person

apercevoir [apersəvwar] §59 *tr* to perceive ‖ *ref* to notice; to realize; **s'apercevoir de** to notice, realize, be aware of

aperçu [apersy] *m* glimpse; view, look; outline

apéri·tif [aperitif] **-tive** [tiv] *adj* appetizing ‖ *m* appetizer

aperture [apertyr] *f* (phonet) aperture

apesanteur [apəzɑ̃tœr] *f* weightlessness

à-peu-près [apøprɛ] *m invar* approximation, rough estimate

apeu·ré -rée [apœre] *adj* frightened

aphorisme [afɔrism] *m* aphorism

aphrodisiaque [afrɔdizjak] *adj & m* aphrodisiac

aphte [aft] *m* mouth canker, cold sore

apiculteur [apikyltœr] *m* beekeeper

apiculture [apikyltyr] *f* beekeeping

apitoiement [apitwamã] *m* compassion

apitoyant [apitwajã] **apitoyante** [apitwajãt] *adj* piteous, pitiful

apitoyer [apitwaje] §47 *tr* to move (*s.o.*) to pity || *ref*—**s'apitoyer sur** to feel compassion for

ap. J.-C. *abbr* (**après Jésus-Christ**) A.D.

aplanir [aplanir] *tr* to even off; to iron out (*difficulties*)

aplatir [aplatir] *tr* to flatten || *ref* to go flat; to grovel

aplomb [aplɔ̃] *m* aplomb; hang (*of gown*); (coll) cheek, rudeness; **aplombs** stand (*of horse*); **d'aplomb** plumb; steadily

apocalyptique [apɔkaliptik] *adj* apocalyptic

apocryphe [apɔkrif] *adj* apocryphal || **Apocryphes** *mpl* Apocrypha

apogée [apɔʒe] *m* apogee

Apollon [apɔllɔ̃] *m* Apollo

apologie [apɔlɔʒi] *f* apology

apophonie [apɔfɔni] *f* ablaut

apoplectique [apɔplektik] *adj & mf* apoplectic

apoplexie [apɔpleksi] *f* apoplexy

apostille [apɔstij] *f* endorsement

apostiller [apɔstije] *tr* to endorse

apostolat [apɔstɔla] *m* apostleship

apostrophe [apɔstrɔf] *f* apostrophe; sharp reprimand

apostropher [apɔstrɔfe] *tr* to apostrophize; to reprimand sharply

apothicaire [apɔtikɛr] *m* apothecary

apôtre [apotr] *m* apostle; **faire le bon apôtre** to play the hypocrite

apparaître [aparɛtr] §12 *intr* (*aux:* AVOIR or ÊTRE) to appear, come into view; to become evident

apparat [apara] *m* pomp, ostentation

apparaux [aparo] *mpl* rigging

appareil [aparɛj] *m* apparatus, machine, appliance; apparel; radio set; airplane; pomp, show, display; camera; telephone; (archit) bond; **à l'appareil!** speaking!; **appareil à sous** slot machine; **appareil plâtré** plaster cast

appareiller [apareje] *tr* to prepare; to bond (*stones*); to pair, match; (naut) to rig || *intr* to set sail

apparemment [aparamã] *adv* apparently

apparence [aparãs] *f* appearance

appa·rent [aparã] **-rente** [rãt] *adj* apparent

apparenter [aparãte] *tr* to relate by marriage || *ref* to become related

apparier [aparje] *tr* to pair off, to match

apparition [aparisjɔ̃] *f* apparition; appearance

apparoir [aparwar] (used only in: *inf;* 3d *sg pres ind* **appert**) *impers*—**il appert de** it follows from; **il appert que** it is evident that

appartement [apartəmã] *m* apartment

appartenance [apartənãs] *f* appurtenance

appartenir [apartənir] §72 *intr*—**appartenir à** to belong to; to pertain to || *impers*—**il appartient à qn de** it behooves s.o. to || *ref* to be one's own master

appas [apa] *mpl* charms; bosom

appât [apa] *m* bait

appâter [apate] *tr* to lure; to fatten up (*fowl*)

appauvrir [apovrir] *tr* to impoverish || *ref* to become impoverished

ap·peau [apo] *m* (*pl* **-peaux**) decoy; bird call

appel [apɛl] *m* call; appeal; summons; roll call; ring (*on telephone*); (mil) draft; **appel interurbain** long-distance call; **appel nominal** roll call; **faire l'appel** to call the roll

appe·lant [aplã] **-lante** [lãt] *adj* appellant || *mf* appellant || *m* decoy

appelé [aple] *m* draftee

appeler [aple] §34 *tr* to call; to name; to summon; to subpoena; to require; to call up, to draft || *intr* to call; to appeal (*in court*); **en appeler à** to appeal to || *ref* to be named, e.g., **elle s'appelle Marie** she is named Mary, her name is Mary

appendice [apɛ̃dis] *m* appendix

appendicectomie [apɛ̃disɛktɔmi] *f* appendectomy

appendicite [apɛ̃disit] *f* appendicitis

appentis [apãti] *m* lean-to

appesantir [apzãtir] *tr* to weigh down; to slow down (*e.g., bodily activity*); to make (*a burden*) heavier || *ref* to be weighed down; **s'appesantir sur** to dwell on, to expatiate on

appétis·sant [apetisã] **appétis·sante** [apetisãt] *adj* appetizing, tempting

appétit [apeti] *m* appetite

applaudir [aplodir] *tr* to applaud; **applaudir qn** to commend, applaud s.o. for || *intr* to applaud; **applaudir à** to approve, commend, applaud || *ref*—**s'applaudir de** to congratulate oneself on, to pat oneself on the back for

applaudissement [aplodismã] *m* round of applause; **applaudissements** applause

applicable [aplikabl] *adj* applicable

application [aplikasjɔ̃] *f* application

applique [aplik] *f* appliqué; sconce

appli·qué **-quée** [aplike] *adj* industrious, studious; applied (*science*)

appliquer [aplike] *tr* to apply || *ref* to apply; to apply oneself

appoint [apwɛ̃] *m* addition; balance; aid, help; **faire l'appoint** to have the right change

appointements [apwɛ̃tmã] *mpl* salary

appointer [apwɛ̃te] *tr* to point, sharpen; to pay a salary to

appontage [apɔ̃taʒ] *m* deck-landing

appontement [apɔ̃tmã] *m* jetty (*landing pier*)

apponter [apɔ̃te] *intr* to deck-land

apport [apɔr] *m* contribution

apporter [apɔrte] *tr* to bring

apposer [apoze] *tr* to affix; to insert (*a clause in a contract*)

appréciable [apresjabl] *adj* appreciable

appréciation [apresjɑsjɔ̃] *f* appreciation, appraisal

apprécier [apresje] *tr* to appreciate

appréhender [apreɑ̃de] *tr* to apprehend; to be apprehensive about

appréhension [apreɑ̃sjɔ̃] *f* apprehension

apprendre [aprɑ̃dr] §56 *tr* to learn; **apprendre à vivre à qn** to teach s.o. manners; **apprendre q.ch. à qn** to inform s.o. of s.th.; to teach s.o. s.th. || *intr* to learn

appren·ti -tie [aprɑ̃ti] *mf* apprentice; beginner, learner

apprentissage [aprɑ̃tisaʒ] *m* apprenticeship

apprêt [apre] *m* preparation, finishing touches; **sans apprêt** unaffectedly

apprêter [aprete] *tr & ref* to prepare

apprivoi·sé -sée [aprivwaze] *adj* tame, domesticated

apprivoiser [aprivwaze] *tr* to tame; to contain (*sorrow*) || *ref* to become tame; to become sociable

approba·teur -trice [tris] *adj* approving || *m* (slang) yes man

approbation [aprɔbɑsjɔ̃] *f* approbation, approval, consent

appro·chant -chante [aprɔʃɑ̃] [ʃɑ̃t] *adj* similar || **approchant** *adv* thereabouts

approche [aprɔʃ] *f* approach

approcher [aprɔʃe] *tr* to approach; to draw up (*e.g., a chair*) || *intr* to approach; **approcher de** to approach, approximate || *ref* to approach, to come near; **s'approcher de** to approach, to come near to, to go up to

approfon·di -die [aprɔfɔ̃di] *adj* thorough, deep

approfondir [aprɔfɔ̃dir] *tr* to deepen; to go deep into, get to the bottom of

appropriation [aprɔprijɑsjɔ̃] *f* appropriation; adaptation

appro·prié -priée [aprɔprije] *adj* appropriate

approprier [aprɔprije] *tr* to fit, adapt || *ref* to appropriate, preempt

approuver [apruve] *tr* to approve, to approve of

approvisionnement [aprɔvizjɔnmɑ̃] *m* provisioning, stocking; **approvisionnements** supplies

approvisionner [aprɔvizjɔne] *tr* to provision, to stock || *ref* to lay in supplies

approxima·tif [aprɔksimatif] **-tive** [tiv] *adj* approximate

appui [apɥi] *m* support; endorsement

appui-bras [apɥibra] *m* (*pl* **appuis-bras**) armrest

appui-livres [apɥilivr] *m* (*pl* **appuis-livres**) book end

appui-main [apɥimɛ̃] *m* (*pl* **appuis-main**) maulstick

appui-tête [apɥitet] *m* (*pl* **appuis-tête**) headrest

appuyer [apɥije] §27 *tr* to support; to prop; to rest, lean; to endorse (*a candidate*); **appuyer le doigt sur** to push (*a button, a lever, a switch*) with the finger || *intr*—**appuyer sur** to lean on; to press (*a button*); to move (*a lever*); to pull (*a trigger*); to bear down on (*a pen or pencil*); to stress (*a syllable*) || *ref*—**s'appuyer sur** to lean on; to be based on; to rely on; (slang) to put up with

âpre [ɑpr] *adj* harsh, rough; bitter; greedy (*for gain*)

après [apre] *adv* after, afterward; behind; **après que** after || *prep* after; behind; **après Jésus-Christ** (ap. J.-C.) after Christ (A.D.); **d'après** after, from; by, according to

après-demain [apredəmɛ̃] *adv & m* the day after tomorrow

après-guerre [apreger] *m & f* (*pl* **-guerres**) postwar period

après-midi [apremidi] *m & f invar* afternoon

âpreté [ɑprəte] *f* harshness; bitterness

à-propos [aprɔpo] *m* ◊pportuneness, aptness

apte [apt] *adj* apt; **apte à** suitable for

aptitude [aptityd] *f* aptitude; proficiency

apurement [apyrmɑ̃] *m* audit, check

apurer [apyre] *tr* to audit, to check

apyre [apir] *adj* fireproof

aquafortiste [akwafɔrtist] *mf* etcher

aquaplane [akwaplan] *m* aquaplane

aquarelle [akwarel] *f* watercolor

aquarium [akwarjɔm] *m* aquarium

aquatique [akwatik] *adj* aquatic

aqueduc [akdyk] *m* aqueduct

aquilin [akilɛ̃] *adj masc* aquiline

aquilon [akilɔ̃] *m* north wind

ara [ara] *m* (orn) macaw

arabe [arab] *adj* Arabian, Arab || *m* Arabic; Arab (*horse*) || (*cap*) *mf* Arabian, Arab

arachide [araʃid] *f* peanut

araignée [areɲe] *f* spider; grapnel; **araignée de mer** spider crab; **avoir une araignée dans le plafond** (coll) to have bats in the belfry

aratoire [aratwar] *adj* agricultural

arbitrage [arbitraʒ] *m* arbitration

arbitraire [arbitrer] *adj* arbitrary || *m* arbitrariness, despotism

arbitre [arbitr] *m* arbiter; arbitrator; umpire, judge; **libre arbitre** free will

arbitrer [arbitre] *tr & intr* to arbitrate; to umpire

arborer [arbɔre] *tr* to hoist (*a flag*); to show off (*new clothes*)

arbouse [arbuz] *f* arbutus berry

arbousier [arbuzje] *m* arbutus

arbre [arbr] *m* tree; (mach) arbor, shaft; **arbre de Noël** Christmas tree; **arbre généalogique** family tree

arbris·seau [arbriso] *m* (*pl* **-seaux**) bushy tree

arbuste [arbyst] *m* shrub

arc [ark] *m* bow; arch; (elec, geom) arc

arcade [arkad] *f* arcade, archway

arcanes [arkan] *mpl* mysteries, secrets

arcanson [arkɑ̃sɔ̃] *m* rosin

arc-boutant [arkbutɑ̃] *m* (*pl* **arcs-boutants**) flying buttress

arc-en-ciel [arkɑ̃sjel] *m* (*pl* **arcs-en-ciel** [arkɑ̃sjel]) rainbow

archaïque [arkaik] *adj* archaic
archaïsme [arkaism] *m* archaism
archange [arkɑ̃ʒ] *m* archangel
arche [arʃ] *f* arch (*of bridge*); Ark
archéologie [arkeɔlɔʒi] *f* archaeology
archéologue [arkeɔlɔg] *mf* archaeologist
archer [arʃe] *m* archer, bowman
archet [arʃɛ] *m* bow
archétype [arketip] *m* archetype
archevêque [arʃəvɛk] *m* archbishop
archiduc [arʃidyk] *m* archduke
archipel [arʃipel] *m* archipelago
archiprêtre [arʃipretr] *m* archpriest
architecte [arʃitekt] *m* architect
architecture [arʃitektyr] *f* architecture
archives [arʃiv] *fpl* archives
arçon [arsɔ̃] *m* saddletree
Arctique [arktik] *adj & m* Arctic || *f* Arctic (*region*)
ardemment [ardamɑ̃] *adv* ardently
ar·dent [ardɑ̃] -dente [dɑ̃t] *adj* ardent; burning; bright-red (*hair*)
ardeur [ardœr] *f* ardor; intense heat
ardoise [ardwaz] *f* slate
ardoi·sier [ardwazje] -sière [zjɛr] *adj* slate || *m* slate-quarry worker || *f* slate quarry
ar·du -due [ardy] *adj* steep; arduous
arène [aren] *f* arena; sand; (fig) arena; arènes arena, coliseum, amphitheater
arête [aret] *f* fishbone; beard (*of wheat*); angle, ridge
argent [arʒɑ̃] *m* silver; money; argent comptant cash
argenter [arʒɑ̃te] *tr* to silver || *ref* to turn silvery (*i.e.*, gray)
argenterie [arʒɑ̃tri] *f* silver plate, silverware
argentier [arʒɑ̃tje] *m* silverware cabinet; (hist) Treasurer
argen·tin [arʒɑ̃tɛ̃] -tine [tin] *adj* silvery (*voice*); Argentinian || (cap) *mf* Argentinian (*person*) || l'Argentine *f* Argentina
argile [arʒil] *f* clay
argot [argo] *m* slang; jargon, cant
argotique [argotik] *adj* slangy
arguer [argɥe] (many authorities write: j'arguë, tu arguës, etc.) *tr* to argue, imply; arguer de faux to doubt the authenticity of (*a document*) || *intr* to draw a conclusion; arguer de to use as a pretext
argument [argymɑ̃] *m* argument
argumentation [argymɑ̃tasjɔ̃] *f* argument
argumenter [argymɑ̃te] *intr* to argue
argus [argys] *m* look-out, spy; price list, book (*e.g., for used cars*); argus de la presse clipping service
aria [arja] *m* (coll) fuss, bother || *f* aria
aride [arid] *adj* arid; (*subject, speaker, etc.*) dry
aridité [aridite] *f* aridity; (fig) dryness, dullness
aristocrate [aristokrat] *adj* aristocratic || *mf* aristocrat
aristocratie [aristokrasi] *f* aristocracy
Aristote [aristot] *m* Aristotle
arithméti·cien [aritmetisjɛ̃] -cienne [sjen] *mf* arithmetician

arithmétique [aritmetik] *f* arithmetic
arlequin [arləkɛ̃] *m* goulash; wrench || (cap) *m* Harlequin
armateur [armatœr] *m* ship outfitter; shipowner
armature [armatyr] *f* framework; keeper (*of a horseshoe magnet*); (mus) key signature
arme [arm] *f* arm; weapon; arme blanche cold steel; steel blade; armes portatives small arms; faire ses premières armes to make one's début
armée [arme] *f* army
armement [arməmɑ̃] *m* armament; fire power; (naut) outfitting
armé·nien [armenjɛ̃] -nienne [njen] *adj* Armenian || *m* Armenian (*language*) || (cap) *mf* Armenian (*person*)
armer [arme] *tr* to arm; to cock (*a gun*); to reinforce (*concrete*); armer chevalier to knight || *ref* to arm oneself, to arm
armistice [armistis] *m* armistice
armoire [armwar] *f* wardrobe, closet; armoire à pharmacie medicine cabinet; armoire frigorifique freezer
armoiries [armwari] *fpl* arms, coat of arms
armoise [armwaz] *f* sagebrush
armorier [armɔrje] *tr* to emblazon
armure [armyr] *f* armor; (tex) weave
aromatique [arɔmatik] *adj* aromatic
arôme [arom] *m* aroma
aronde [arɔ̃d] *f* swallow
arpège [arpɛʒ] *m* arpeggio
arpent [arpɑ̃] *m* acre
arpentage [arpɑ̃taʒ] *m* surveying
arpenter [arpɑ̃te] *tr* to survey; (coll) to pace (*the floor*)
arpenteur [arpɑ̃tœr] *m* surveyor
ar·qué -quée [arke] *adj* arched, bowed; cambered (*beam*); hooked (*nose*)
arquer [arke] *tr* to arch, to bow || *ref* to arch, to be bowed
arraché [araʃe] *m* (sports) lift
arrache-clou [araʃklu] *m* (*pl* -clous) claw hammer
arrache-pied [araʃpje] *adv*—d'arrache-pied at a stretch, without stopping
arracher [araʃe] *tr* to dig up, uproot, tear out, pull out; to wheedle (*money; a confession*); arracher q.ch. à qn to take away, snatch, or pry s.th. from s.o.; arracher q.ch. de q.ch. to pull s.th. off, from, or out of s.th.; to strip s.th. of s.th.; arracher qn à to deliver s.o. from (*evil; temptation; death*); arracher qn de to make s.o. get out of (*e.g., bed*) || *ref* to tear oneself away
arra·cheur [araʃœr] -cheuse [ʃøz] *mf* puller || *f* (mach) picker
arraisonnement [arezɔnmɑ̃] *m* port inspection
arraisonner [arezɔne] *tr* to inspect (*a ship*)
arrangement [arɑ̃ʒmɑ̃] *m* arrangement
arranger [arɑ̃ʒe] §38 *tr* to arrange; to settle (*a difficulty*); to fix (*to repair; to punish*) || *ref* to be arranged; to get ready; to agree
arrérages [areraʒ] *mpl* arrears
arrestation [arestasjɔ̃] *f* arrest

arrêt [are] *m* stop; stopping; arrest; decree; **arrêt complet** standstill; **arrêt facultatif** whistle stop; **mettre aux arrêts** to keep in, to confine to quarters

arrê·té -tée [arete] *adj* stopped, standing; decided, fixed || *m* decree; authorization; (com) closing out (*of an account*); **arrêté de police** police ordinance; **prendre un arrêté** to pass a decree

arrêter [arete] *tr* to stop; to arrest; to fix (*one's gaze*); to settle, decide upon; to hire, engage; to point (*game, as hunting dog does*) || *intr* to stop; to point (*said of hunting dog*) || *ref* to stop; **s'arrêter à** to decide on; **s'arrêter de** + *inf* to stop + *ger*

arrhes [ar] *fpl* deposit, down payment

arriération [arjerasjɔ̃] *f* retardation

arrière [arjer] *adj invar* back, rear; tail (*wind*) || *m* back, rear; stern; **à l'arrière** in back; astern; **en arrière** backward; **en arrière de** behind || *adv* back

arrié·ré -rée [arjere] *adj* backward; delinquent (*in payment*); back (*pay, taxes, etc.*); old-fashioned || *mf* backward child || *m* arrears; back pay; back payment; backlog

arrière-boutique [arjerbutik] *f* (*pl* -boutiques) back room (*of a shop*)

arrière-cour [arjerkur] *f* (*pl* -cours) backyard

arrière-garde [arjergard] *f* (*pl* -gardes) rear guard

arrière-goût [arjergu] *m* (*pl* -goûts) aftertaste

arrière-grand-mère [arjergrãmer] *f* (*pl* -grand-mères) great-grandmother

arrière-grand-père [arjergrãper] *m* (*pl* -grands-pères) great-grandfather

arrière-pays [arjerpei] *m invar* back country

arrière-pensée [arjerpãse] *f* (*pl* -pensées) mental reservation, ulterior motive

arrière-plan [arjerplã] *m* (*pl* -plans) background

arriérer [arjere] §10 *tr* to delay || *ref* to fall behind (*in payment*)

arrière-train [arjertrɛ̃] *m* (*pl* -trains) rear (*of a vehicle*); hindquarters

arrimage [arimaʒ] *m* stowage; docking (*of space vehicle*)

arrimer [arime] *tr* to stow

arrimeur [arimœr] *m* stevedore

arrivage [arivaʒ] *m* arrival (*of goods or ships*)

arrivée [arive] *f* arrival; intake; (sports) finish, goal; **arrivée en douceur** (rok) soft landing

arriver [arive] *intr* (*aux:* ÊTRE) to arrive; to succeed; to happen; **arriver à** to attain, reach; **en arriver à** + *inf* to be reduced to + *ger*

arriviste [arivist] *mf* upstart, parvenu

arrogance [arɔgãs] *f* arrogance

arro·gant -gante [arɔgã -gãt] *adj* arrogant

arroger [arɔʒe] §38 *ref* to arrogate to oneself

arrondir [arɔ̃dir] *tr* to round, round off, round out || *ref* to become round

arrondissement [arɔ̃dismã] *m* district

arrosage [arozaʒ] *m* sprinkling; irrigation; (mil) heavy bombing

arroser [aroze] *tr* to sprinkle, to water; to irrigate; to flow through (*e.g., a city*); to wash down (*a meal*); (coll) to bribe; (coll) to drink to (*a success*)

arro·seur [arozœr] *-seuse* [zøz] *mf* sprinkler (*person*) || *f* street sprinkler

arrosoir [arozwar] *m* sprinkling can

arse·nal [arsənal] *m* (*pl* -naux [no]) shipyard, navy yard; (fig) storehouse; (archaic) arsenal, armory

arsenic [arsənik] *m* arsenic

art [ar] *m* art; **arts d'agréments** music, drawing, dancing, etc.; **arts ménagers** home economics; **le huitième art** television; **les arts du spectacle** the performing arts; **le septième art** the cinema

artère [arter] *f* artery

arté·riel -rielle [arterjel] *adj* arterial

artériosclé·reux [arterjosklerø] *-reuse* [røz] *adj* & *mf* arteriosclerotic

arté·sien [artezjɛ̃] *-sienne* [zjen] *adj* of Artois; artesian (*well*)

arthrite [artrit] *f* arthritis

artichaut [artiʃo] *m* artichoke

article [artikl] *m* article; entry (*in a dictionary*); **à l'article de la mort** on the point of death; **article de fond** leader; editorial; **article de tête** front-page story; **articles divers** sundries

articuler [artikyle] *tr* & *ref* to articulate

artifice [artifis] *m* artifice; craftsmanship

artifi·ciel -cielle [artifisjel] *adj* artificial

artificier [artifisje] *m* fireworks maker; soldier in charge of ammunition supply

artifi·cieux [artifisjø] *-cieuse* [sjøz] *adj* artful, cunning

artillerie [artijəri] *f* artillery

artilleur [artijœr] *m* artilleryman

arti·san [artizã] *-sane* [zan] *mf* artisan, artificer || *m* craftsman

artiste [artist] *adj* artistic; artist, of art, e.g., **le monde artiste** the world of art || *mf* artist; actor

artistique [artistik] *adj* artistic

ar·yen [arjɛ̃] *-yenne* [jen] *adj* Aryan || (*cap*) *mf* Aryan (*person*)

as [as] *m* ace; **as du volant** speed king

A.S. *abbr* (assurances sociales) social security

a/s *abbr* (aux bons soins de) c/o

asbeste [asbest] *m* asbestos

ascendance [asɑ̃dɑ̃s] *f* lineal ancestry; rising (*of air, of star*)

ascenseur [asɑ̃sœr] *m* elevator

ascension [asɑ̃sjɔ̃] *f* ascension; **Ascension** *f* Ascension Day

ascèse [asɛz] *f* asceticism

ascète [aset] *mf* ascetic

ascétique [asetik] *adj* ascetic

ascétisme [asetism] *m* asceticism

aseptique [aseptik] *adj* aseptic

Asie [azi] *f* Asia; **Asie Mineure** Asia Minor; **l'Asie** Asia; **l'Asie Mineure** Asia Minor

asile [azil] *m* asylum, shelter, home

aspect [aspɛ], [aspɛk] *m* aspect

asperge [aspɛrʒ] *f* asparagus; **des asperges** asparagus (*stalks and tips used as food*)

asperger [aspɛrʒe] §38 *tr* to sprinkle

aspérité [asperite] *f* roughness; harshness; gruffness

asphalte [asfalt] *m* asphalt

asphyxier [asfiksje] *tr* to asphyxiate || *ref* to be asphyxiated

aspic [aspik] *m* asp

aspi·rant [aspirã] **-rante** [rãt] *adj* aspirant, aspiring; suction (*pump*) || *mf* candidate (*for a degree*) || *m* midshipman

aspirateur [aspiratœr] *m* vacuum cleaner; **aspirateur de buée** kitchen fan

aspi·ré -rée [aspire] *adj & m* (phonet) aspirate

aspirer [aspire] *tr* to´ inhale; to suck in || *intr*—**aspirer à** to aspire to

aspirine [aspirin] *f* aspirin

assagir [asaʒir] *tr* to make wiser || *ref* to become wiser

assail·lant [asajã] **assail-lante** [asajãt] *adj* attacking || *mf* assailant

assaillir [asajir] §69 *tr* to assail, to assault

assainir [asenir] *tr* to purify, to clean up; to drain (*a swamp*)

assainissement [asenismã] *m* purification; draining

assaisonnement [asezɔnmã] *m* seasoning

assaisonner [asezɔne] *tr* to season, to flavor

assas·sin [asasɛ̃] **assas·sine** [asasin] *adj* murderous || *m* assassin

assassinat [asasina] *m* assassination

assassiner [asasine] *tr* to assassinate; (coll) to bore to death

assaut [aso] *m* assault

assèchement [asɛʃmã] *m* drainage, drying; dryness

assécher [aseʃe] §10 *tr* to drain, to dry up

assemblage [asãblaʒ] *m* assemblage; assembling (*e.g., of printed pages*); (woodworking) joint, joining

assemblée [asãble] *f* assembly, meeting

assembler [asãble] *tr* to assemble || *ref* to assemble, convene, meet

assener [asne] §2 *tr* to land (*a blow*)

assentiment [asãtimã] *m* assent, consent

asseoir [aswar] §5 *tr* to seat, sit, place; to base (*an opinion*) || *ref* to sit down

assermen·té -tée [asɛrmãte] *adj* under oath

assertion [asɛrsjɔ̃] *f* assertion

asser·vi -vie [asɛrvi] *adj* subservient

asservir [asɛrvir] *tr* to enslave; to subdue (*e.g., passions*) || *ref* to submit (*to convention; to tyranny*)

asservissement [asɛrvismã] *m* enslavement; subservience

assesseur [asɛsœr] *adj & m* assistant; associate (*judge*)

assez [ase] *adv* enough; fairly, rather; **assez de** enough; **en voilà assez!** that's enough!, cut it out! || *interj* enough!, stop!

assi·du -due [asidy] *adj* assiduous; attentive

assidûment [asidymã] *adv* assiduously

assié·geant [asjeʒã] **-geante** [ʒãt] *adj* besieging || *mf* besieger

assiéger [asjeʒe] §1 *tr* to besiege

assiette [asjɛt] *f* plate, dish; plateful; seat (*of a rider on horseback*); position, condition; **assiette anglaise, assiette de viandes froides** cold cuts; **assiette au beurre** (fig) gravy train; **assiette creuse** soup plate

assignation [asiɲasjɔ̃] *f* assignation; subpoena, summons

assi·gné -gnée [asiɲe] *mf* appointee; **assigné à résidence** permanent appointee; **assigné intérim** temporary appointee

assigner [asiɲe] *tr* to assign, allot; to fix (*a date*); to subpoena, summon

assimilable [asimilabl] *adj* assimilable; comparable

assimilation [asimilɑsjɔ̃] *f* assimilation

assimiler [asimile] *tr* to assimilate; to compare; to identify with || *ref* to assimilate

as·sis [asi] **as·sise** [asiz] *adj* seated, sitting; firmly established || *f* foundation; stratum; **assises** assizes

assistance [asistãs] *f* assistance; audience, persons present; presence; **assistance judiciaire** public defender; **assistance publique** welfare department; **assistance sociale** social service

assis·tant [asistã] **-tante** [tãt] *adj* assistant || *mf* assistant; bystander, spectator; **assistante sociale** public health nurse

assister [asiste] *tr* to assist, help || *intr*—**assister à** to attend, be present at

association [asɔsjɑsjɔ̃] *f* association; (sports) soccer; **association des spectateurs** theater club

asso·cié -ciée [asɔsje] *adj & mf* associate

associer [asɔsje] *tr* to associate || *ref* to go into partnership

assoif·fé -fée [aswafe] *adj* thirsty

assolement [asɔlmã] *m* rotation (*of crops*)

assombrir [asɔ̃brir] *tr & ref* to darken

assom·mant [asɔmã] **assom·mante** [asɔmãt] *adj* (coll) boring, fatiguing

assommer [asɔme] *tr* to kill with a heavy blow; to beat up; to stun; (coll) to heckle; (coll) to bore

assommoir [asɔmwar] *m* bludgeon; (coll) gin mill, dive, clip joint

Assomption [asɔ̃psjɔ̃] *f* Assumption

assonance [asɔnãs] *f* assonance

assor·ti -tie [asɔrti] *adj* assorted (*e.g., cakes*); well-matched (*couple*); stocked, supplied (*store*); to match, e.g., **une cravate assortie** a necktie to match

assortiment [asɔrtimã] *m* assortment; matching (*of colors*); set (*of dishes*); platter (*of cold cuts*)

assortir [asɔrtir] *tr* to assort, match;

to stock ‖ *ref* to match, harmonize; **s'assortir de** to be accompanied with

assoupir [asupir] *tr* to make drowsy, to lull; to deaden (*pain*) ‖ *ref* to doze off; to lessen (*with time*)

assoupissement [asupismã] *m* drowsiness; lethargy

assouplir [asuplir] *tr* to make supple, flexible; to break in (*a horse*) ‖ *ref* to become supple, manageable

assouplissement [asuplismã] *m* suppleness, flexibility; limbering up; relaxation (*of a rule*)

assourdir [asurdir] *tr* to deafen; to tone down, muffle

assouvir [asuvir] *tr* to assuage, appease, satiate; to satisfy (*e.g., a thirst for vengeance*)

assouvissement [asuvismã] *m* assuagement, appeasement, satisfying

assujet·ti -tie [asyʒeti] *adj* fastened; subject, liable ‖ *mf* taxpayer; contributor (*e.g., to social security*)

assujettir [asyʒetir] *tr* to subjugate; to subject; to fasten, secure ‖ *ref* to submit

assujettis·sant [asyʒetisã] **assujettis-sante** [asyʒetisãt] *adj* demanding

assujettissement [asyʒetismã] *m* subjugation, subduing; submission (*to a stronger force*); fastening, securing

assumer [asyme] *tr* to assume, take upon oneself

assurance [asyrãs] *f* assurance; insurance; **assurances sociales** social security

assu·ré -rée [asyre] *adj* assured, satisfied; insured ‖ *mf* insured

assurément [asyremã] *adv* assuredly

assurer [asyre] *tr* to assure; to secure; to insure ‖ *ref* to be assured; to make sure; to be insured

astate [astat] *m* astatine

aster [aster] *m* (bot) aster

astérie [asteri] *f* starfish

astérisque [asterisk] *m* asterisk

asthénie [asteni] *f* debility

asthme [asm] *m* asthma

asticot [astiko] *m* maggot

astiquer [astike] *tr* to polish

as·tral -trale [astral] *adj* (*pl* -**traux** [tro]) astral

astre [astrə] *m* star, heavenly body; leading light; **astre de la nuit** moon; **astre du jour** sun

astreindre [astrɛ̃dr] §50 *tr* to force, compel, subject ‖ *ref* to force oneself; to be subjected

astrologie [astrɔlɔʒi] *f* astrology

astrologue [astrɔlɔg] *m* astrologer

astronaute [astrɔnot] *mf* astronaut

astronautique [astrɔnotik] *f* astronautics

astronef [astrɔnef] *m* spaceship

astronome [astrɔnɔm] *mf* astronomer

astronomie [astrɔnɔmi] *f* astronomy

astronomique [astrɔnɔmik] *adj* astronomical

astuce [astys] *f* slyness, guile; tricks (*of a trade*)

astu·cieux -cieuse [astysjø] [sjøz] *adj* astute, crafty

atelier [atəlje] *m* studio; workshop

atermolement [atermwamã] *m* procrastination; extension of a loan

athée [ate] *adj* atheistic ‖ *mf* atheist

athéisme [ateism] *m* atheism

Athènes [aten] *f* Athens

athlète [atlet] *mf* athlete

athlétique [atletik] *adj* athletic

athlétisme [atletism] *m* athletics

Atlantique [atlãtik] *adj* & *m* Atlantic

atlas [atlɑs] *m* atlas ‖ (*cap*) *m* Atlas

atmosphère [atmosfer] *f* atmosphere

atome [atom] *m* atom

atomique [atomik] *adj* atomic

atomi·sé -sée [atomize] *adj* afflicted with radiation sickness

atomiser [atomize] *tr* to atomize

atone [aton] *adj* dull, expressionless; drab (*life*); (phonet) unaccented

atours [atur] *mpl* finery

atout [atu] *m* trump; **sans atout** no-trump

atrabilaire [atrabiler] *adj* & *mf* hypochondriac

âtre [ɑtr] *m* hearth

atroce [atrɔs] *adj* atrocious

atrocité [atrɔsite] *f* atrocity

atrophie [atrɔfi] *f* atrophy

atrophier [atrɔfje] *tr* & *ref* to atrophy

atta·chant [ata/ɑ̃] **-chante** [/ɑ̃t] *adj* appealing, attractive

attache [ata/] *f* attachment, tie; paper clip; (anat) joint; **attache parisienne** paper clip

attachement [ata/mã] *m* attachment

attacher [ata/e] *tr* to attach; to tie up ‖ *intr* (culin) to stick ‖ *ref* to be fastened, tied; **s'attacher à** to stick to; to become devoted to

attaque [atak] *f* attack; (pathol) stroke; **attaque brusque** or **attaque brusquée** surprise attack; **attaque de nerfs** case of nerves

attaquer [atake] *tr* & *intr* to attack ‖ *ref*—**s'attaquer à** to attack

attar·dé -dée [atarde] *adj* retarded; behind the times; belated, delayed ‖ *mf* mentally retarded person; lover of the past

attarder [atarde] *tr* to delay, retard ‖ *ref* to be delayed; to stay, remain

atteindre [atɛ̃dr] §50 *tr* to attain; to reach ‖ *intr*—**atteindre à** to attain; to reach; to attain to

at·teint [atɛ̃] **at·teinte** [atɛ̃t] *adj* stricken ‖ *f* reaching; injury; **hors d'atteinte** out of reach; **porter atteinte à** to endanger; **premières atteintes** first signs (*of illness*)

attelage [atlaʒ] *m* harnessing; coupling

atteler [atle] §34 *tr* to harness; to hitch; to couple (*cars on a railroad*) ‖ *ref*—**s'atteler à** (coll) to buckle down to

attelle [atel] *m* splint; **attelles** hames

atte·nant [atnã] **-nante** [nãt] *adj* adjoining

attendre [atɑ̃dr] *tr* to wait for, await; to expect ‖ *intr* to wait ‖ *ref*—**s'attendre à** to expect; to rely on; **s'attendre à** + *inf* to expect to + *inf*; **s'attendre à ce que** + *subj* to expect (*s.o.*) + *inf*, e.g., **s'attend à ce que je lui raconte toute l'affaire** he expects me to tell him the whole story; **s'y attendre** to expect it or them

attendrir [atãdrir] *tr* to tenderize; to soften || *ref* to become tender; to be deeply touched or moved

attendrissement [atãdrismã] *m* softening; compassion

atten·du -due [atãdy] *adj* expected || **attendus** *mpl* (law) grounds || *adv*—**attendu que** whereas, inasmuch as || **attendu** *prep* in view of

attentat [atãta] *m* attempt, assault; outrage (*to decency*); offense (*against the state*)

attente [atãt] *f* wait; expectation

attenter [atãte] *intr*—**attenter à** to attempt (*e.g., s.o.'s life*); **attenter à ses jours** to attempt suicide

atten·tif [atãtif] **-tive** [tiv] *adj* attentive

attention [atãsjõ] *f* attention; **attentions** attention, care, consideration || *interj* attention!, be careful!

attention·né -née [atãsjɔne] *adj* considerate

atténuation [atenɥasjõ] *f* attenuation

atténuer [atenɥe] *tr* to subdue, soften (*color; pain; passions*); to attenuate (*words; bacteria*); to extenuate (*a fault*) || *ref* to soften; to lessen

atterrer [atere] *tr* to dismay

atterrir [aterir] *intr* (*aux:* AVOIR or ÊTRE) to land

atterrissage [aterisaʒ] *m* landing; **atterrissage forcé** forced landing; **atterrissage sur le ventre** pancake landing

attestation [atestasjõ] *f* attestation; **attestation d'études** transcript

attester [ateste] *tr* to attest, to attest to; **attester qn de q.ch.** to call s.o. to witness to s.th.

attiédir [atjedir] *tr & ref* to cool off; to warm up

attifer [atife] *tr & ref* to spruce up

attirail [atiraj] *m* gear, tackle, outfit; (coll) paraphernalia

attirance [atirãs] *f* attraction, lure, attractiveness

atti·rant [atirã] **-rante** [rãt] *adj* appealing, attractive

attirer [atire] *tr* to attract || *ref* to be attracted; to attract each other; to call forth (*criticism*)

attiser [atize] *tr* to stir, stir up, to poke

atti·tré -trée [atitre] *adj* appointed; regular (*dealer*)

attitude [atityd] *f* attitude

attrac·tif [atraktif] **-tive** [tiv] *adj* attractive (*force*)

attraction [atraksjõ] *f* attraction; **les attractions** vaudeville

attrait [atre] *m* attraction, attractiveness, appeal; **attraits** charms

attrape [atrap] *f* trap; (coll) trick, joke

attrape-mouche [atrapmuʃ] *m* (*pl* **-mouche** or **-mouches**) flypaper; Venus's-flytrap

attrape-nigaud [atrapnigo] *m* (*pl* **-nigauds**) booby trap

attraper [atrape] *tr* to catch; to snare,

trap; to trick || *ref* to trick each other; to hang on

attrayant [atrejã] **attrayante** [atrejãt] *adj* attractive

attribuer [atribɥe] *tr* to ascribe, attribute; to assign (*a share*) || *ref* to claim, assume

attribut [atriby] *m* attribute; predicate

attribu·tif [atribytif] **-tive** [tiv] *adj* (gram) predicative

attribution [atribysjõ] *f* attribution; assignment, assignation

attris·té -tée [atriste] *adj* sorrowful

attrister [atriste] *tr* to sadden || *ref* to become sad

attrition [atrisjõ] *f* attrition

attroupement [atrupmã] *m* mob

attrouper [atrupe] *tr* to bring together in a mob || *ref* to flock together in a mob

au [o] §77

aubaine [oben] *f* windfall, godsend, bonanza

aube [ob] *f* dawn

aubépine [obepin] *f* hawthorn

auberge [oberʒ] *f* inn; **auberge de la jeunesse** youth hostel

aubergine [oberʒin] *f* eggplant

auburn [obœrn] *adj invar* auburn

au·cun [okœ̃] **-cune** [kyn] *adj*—**aucun . . . ne** or **ne . . . aucun** §90 no, none, not any || *pron indef*—**aucun ne** §90B no one, nobody; **d'aucuns** some, some people

aucunement [okynmã] §90 *adv*—**ne . . . aucunement** not at all, by no means

audace [odas] *f* audacity

auda·cieux [odasjø] **-cieuse** [sjøz] *adj* audacious

au·deçà [odəsa] *adv* (obs) on this side; **au-deçà de** (obs) on this side of

au-dedans [odədã] *adv* inside; **au-dedans de** inside, inside of

au-dehors [odəɔr] *adv* outside; **au-dehors de** outside, outside of

au-delà [odəla] *m*—**l'au-delà** the beyond || *adv* beyond; **au-delà de** beyond

au-dessous [odəsu] *adv* below; **au-dessous de** under

au-dessus [odəsy] *adv* above; **au-dessus de** above

au-devant [odəvã] *adv*—**aller au devant de** to go to meet; to anticipate (*s.o.'s wishes*); to court (*defeat*)

audience [odjãs] *f* audience

audio-fréquence [odjofrekãs] *f* audio frequency

audiomètre [odjometr] *m* audiometer

audi·teur [oditœr] **-trice** [tris] *mf* listener; auditor (*in class*); **auditeur libre** auditor (*in class*)

audi·tif [oditif] **-tive** [tiv] *adj* auditory

audition [odisjõ] *f* audition; public hearing; musical recital

auditionner [odisjɔne] *tr & intr* to audition

auditoire [oditwar] *m* audience; courtroom

auditorium [oditɔrjɔm] *m* auditorium; concert hall; projection room

auge [oʒ] *f* trough

augmentation [ɔgmɑ̃tɑsjɔ̃] *f* augmentation; raise (*in salary*)

augmenter [ɔgmɑ̃te] *tr* to augment; to increase or supplement (*income*); to raise (*prices*); to raise the salary of (*an employee*) || *intr* to augment, increase; **augmenter de** to increase by (*a stated amount*)

augure [ɔgyr] *m* augur; augury

augurer [ɔgyre] *tr & intr* to augur

auguste [ɔgyst] *adj* august

aujourd'hui [oʒurdɥi], [oʒordɥi] *m & adv* today; **d'aujourd'hui en huit** a week from today; **d'aujourd'hui en quinze** two weeks from today

aumône [omon] *f* alms; **faire l'aumône** to give alms; **faire l'aumône de** (fig) to hand out

aumônier [omonje] *m* chaplain

aune [on] *m* alder || *f* ell

auparavant [oparavɑ̃] *adv* before, previously

auprès [opre] *adv* close by, in the neighborhood; **auprès de** near, close to; at the side of; to, at the side of; to (*a king, a government*); with; compared with

auquel [okel] (*pl* **auxquels**) §78

auréole [ɔreɔl] *f* aureole, halo

auréomycine [ɔreɔmisin] *f* aureomycin

auriculaire [ɔrikyler] *adj* firsthand (*witness*); auricular (*confession*) || *m* little finger

auricule [ɔrikyl] *f* auricle

aurifler [ɔrifje] *tr* to fill (*a tooth*) with gold

aurore [ɔrɔr] *f* aurora, dawn

ausculter [ɔskylte] *tr* to auscultate

auspice [ɔspis] *m* omen; **sous les auspices de** under the auspices of

aussi [osi] *adv* also, too; therefore, and so; so; **aussi . . . que** as . . . as

aussitôt [osito] *adv* right away, immediately; **aussitôt dit, aussitôt fait** no sooner said than done; **aussitôt que** as soon as

austère [ɔster] *adj* austere

Australie [ɔstrali] *f* Australia; **l'Australie** Australia

austra•lien [ɔstraljɛ̃] **-lienne** [ljɛn] *adj* Australian || (*cap*) *mf* Australian

autant [otɑ̃] *adv* as much, as many; as far, as long; **autant de** so many; **autant que** as much as, as far as; **d'autant** by so much; **d'autant plus all the more; d'autant plus** (or **moins**) **. . . que . . . plus** (or **moins**) all the more (or less) . . . as (or in proportion as) . . . **more** (or less); **d'autant que** inasmuch as

autel [otel], [otel] *m* altar

auteur [otœr] *adj*—**une femme auteur** an authoress || *m* author

authentifler [otɑ̃tifje] *tr* to authenticate

authentique [otɑ̃tik] *adj* authentic; genuine (*antique*); notarized

authentiquer [otɑ̃tike] *tr* to notarize

auto [oto], [oto] *f* auto

auto-allumage [otoalymaʒ] *m* preignition

autobiographie [otobjɔgrafi] *f* autobiography

auto-buffet [otobyfɛ] *m* drive-in; curb service

autobus [otobys] *m* bus, city bus

autocar [otokar] *m* interurban bus

autochenille [otoʃənij] *f* caterpillar (*tractor*)

autochtone [otokton] *adj & mf* native

autoclave [otoklav] *m* pressure cooker; autoclave, sterilizer

autocopie [otokɔpi] *f* duplicating, multicopying; duplicated copy

autocopier [otokɔpje] *tr* to run off, to duplicate, to ditto

auto-couchette [otokuʃɛt] *f*—**en auto-couchette** piggyback

autocrate [otokrat] *mf* autocrat

autocratique [otokratik] *adj* autocratic

autocritique [otokritik] *f* self-criticism

autocuiseur [otokɥizœr] *m* pressure cooker

autodétermination [otodetɛrminɑsjɔ̃] *f* self-determination

autodidacte [otodidakt] *adj* self-taught || *mf* self-taught person

autodrome [otodrom] *m* race track; test strip

auto-école [otoekɔl] *f* (*pl* **-écoles**) driving school

autogare [otogar] *f* bus station

autographe [otograf] *adj & m* autograph

autographie [otografi] *f* multicopying

autographier [otografje] *tr* to duplicate

autogreffe [otogref] *f* skin grafting

auto-grue [otogry] *f* (*pl* **-grues**) tow truck

autoguidage [otogidaʒ] *m* automatic piloting

auto-intoxication [otoɛ̃tɔksikɑsjɔ̃] *f* autointoxication

automate [otomat] *m* automaton

automation [otomɑsjɔ̃] *f* automation

automatique [otomatik] *adj* automatic || *m* dial telephone

automatisation [otomatizɑsjɔ̃] *f* automation

automatiser [otomatize] *tr* to automate

automitrailleuse [otomitrɑjøz] *f* armored car mounting machine guns

autom•nal -nale [otomnal] *adj* (*pl* **-naux** [no]) autumnal

automne [oton], [otɔn] *m* fall, autumn; **à l'automne, en automne** in the fall

automobile [otomobil], [otomɔbil] *adj* automotive || *f* automobile

automobilisme [otomobilism] *m* driving, motoring

automobiliste [otomobilist] *mf* motorist

automo•teur [otomotœr] **-trice** [tris] *adj* self-propelling, automatic || *m* self-propelled river barge || *f* rail car

autonome [otonom] *adj* autonomous, independent

autonomie [otonomi] *f* autonomy; cruising radius, range (*of ship, plane, or tank*)

autoplastie [otoplasti] *f* plastic surgery

autoportrait [otopɔrtrɛ] *m* self-portrait

auto-propul•sé -sée [otoprɔpylse] *adj* self-propelled

autopsie [otopsi] *f* autopsy

autopsier [otopsje] *tr* to perform an autopsy on

autorail [otɔraj] *m* rail car
autorisation [otɔrizasjɔ̃] *f* authorization
autoriser [otɔrize] *tr* to authorize || *ref* —s'autoriser de to take as authority, to base one's opinion on
autoritaire [otɔriter] *adj* authoritarian, bossy
autorité [otɔrite] *f* authority
autoroute [otɔrut] *f* superhighway
auto-stop [otɔstɔp] *m* hitchhiking; faire de l'auto-stop to hitchhike
auto-stop·peur [otɔstɔpœr] -stop·peuse [stɔpøz] *mf* (*pl* -stop·peurs -stop·peuses) hitchhiker
autostrade [otɔstrad] *f* superhighway
autour [otur] *m* goshawk || *adv* around; autour de around; about
autre [otr] *adj indef* other; autre chose (coll) something else; nous autres we, e.g., nous autres Américains we Americans; vous autres you || *pron indef* other; d'autres others; j'en ai vu bien d'autres I have seen worse than that; un autre another
autrefois [otrəfwa] *adv* formerly, of old; d'autrefois of yore
autrement [otrəmɑ̃] *adv* otherwise
Autriche [otriʃ] *f* Austria; l'Autriche Austria
autri·chien [otriʃjɛ̃] -chienne [ʃjen] *adj* Austrian || (*cap*) *mf* Austrian
autruche [otryʃ] *f* ostrich
autrui [otrɥi] *pron indef* others
auvent [ovɑ̃] *m* canopy (*over door*); flap (*of tent*)
aux [o] §77
auxiliaire [oksiljer] *adj* auxiliary, standby; ancillary || *m* (gram) auxiliary || *f* noncombatant unit
aux·quels -quelles [okel] §78
aval [aval] *m* lower waters; en aval downstream; en aval de below || *m* (*pl* avals) endorsement
avalanche [avalɑ̃ʃ] *f* avalanche
avaler [avale] *tr* to swallow || *intr* to go downstream
ava·leur [avalœr] -leuse [løz] *mf* swallower; avaleur de sabres sword swallower
avaliser [avalize] *tr* to endorse
avance [avɑ̃s] *f* advance; en avance fast (*clock*)
avan·cé -cée [avɑ̃se] *adj* advanced; overripe; tainted (*meat*)
avancement [avɑ̃smɑ̃] *m* advancement
avancer [avɑ̃se] §51 *tr, intr, & ref* to advance
avanie [avani] *f* snub, insult; essuyer une avanie to swallow an affront
avant [avɑ̃] *adj invar* front || *m* front; (aer) nose; (naut) bow; d'avant previous; en avant forward; en avant de in front of, ahead of || *adv* before; avant de (with *inf*) before; avant que before; bien (or très) avant dans late into; far into; deep into; plus avant farther on || *prep* before; avant Jésus-Christ (av. J.-C.) before Christ (B.C.)
avantage [avɑ̃taʒ] *m* advantage; (tennis) add; avantages en nature payment in kind
avanta·geux [avɑ̃taʒø] -geuse [ʒøz] *adj* advantageous; bargain (*price*); becoming (*e.g., hairdo*); conceited (*manner*)
avant-bras [avɑ̃bra] *m invar* forearm
avant-cour [avɑ̃kur] *f* (*pl* -cours) front yard
avant-coureur [avɑ̃kurœr] (*pl* -coureurs) *adj masc* presaging (*signs*) || *m* forerunner, precursor, harbinger
avant-goût [avɑ̃gu] *m* (*pl* -goûts) foretaste
avant-guerre [avɑ̃ger] *m & f* (*pl* -guerres) prewar period
avant-hier [avɑ̃tjer], [avɑ̃jer] *adv & m* the day before yesterday
avant-port [avɑ̃pɔr] *m* (*pl* -ports) outer harbor
avant-poste [avɑ̃pɔst] *m* (*pl* -postes) outpost; avant-postes front lines
avant-première [avɑ̃prəmjer] *f* (*pl* -premières) review (*of a play*); premiere (*for the drama critics*); preview
avant-projet [avɑ̃prɔʒe] *m* (*pl* -projets) rough draft; draft (*of a law*)
avant-propos [avɑ̃prɔpo] *m invar* foreword
avant-scène [avɑ̃sen] *f* (*pl* -scènes) forestage, proscenium
avant-toit [avɑ̃twa] *m* (*pl* -toits) eave
avant-train [avɑ̃trɛ̃] *m* (*pl* -trains) front end, front assembly (*of vehicle*)
avant-veille [avɑ̃vej] *f* (*pl* -veilles) two days before
avare [avar] *adj* avaricious, miserly; saving, economical || *mf* miser
avarice [avaris] *f* avarice
avari·cieux [avarisjø] -cieuse [sjøz] *adj* avaricious
avarie [avari] *f* damage; breakdown; spoilage; (naut) average
avarier [avarje] *tr* to damage; to spoil || *ref* to spoil
avatar [avatar] *m* avatar; avatars vicissitudes
avec [avek] *adv* (coll) with it; (coll) along, with me, etc. || *prep* with
aveline [avlin] *f* filbert
ave·nant [avnɑ̃] -nante [nɑ̃t] *adj* gracious, charming; à l'avenant in keeping, to match; à l'avenant de in accord with || *m* (ins) endorsement
avènement [avenmɑ̃] *m* Advent; accession (*to the throne*)
avenir [avnir] *m* future; à l'avenir in the future
Avent [avɑ̃] *m* Advent
aventure [avɑ̃tyr] *f* adventure; à l'aventure at random; aimlessly; d'aventure by chance; la bonne aventure fortunetelling; par aventure by chance
aventurer [avɑ̃tyre] *tr* to venture || *ref* to take a chance; s'aventurer à to venture to
aventu·reux [avɑ̃tyrø] -reuse [røz] *adj* adventurous
aventurier [avɑ̃tyrje] *m* adventurer
aventurière [avɑ̃tyrjer] *f* adventuress
avenue [avny] *f* avenue
avé·ré -rée [avere] *adj* established, authenticated
avérer [avere] §10 *tr* to aver || *ref* to prove to be (*e.g., difficult*)

avers [aver] *m* heads (*of coin*), face (*of medal*)

averse [avers] *f* shower

aversion [aversjɔ̃] *f* aversion

avertir [avertir] *tr* to warn; **avertir qn de** + *inf* to warn s.o. to + *inf*

avertissement [avertismɑ̃] *m* warning; notification; foreword

avertisseur [avertisœr] *adj masc* warning || *m* alarm; (aut) horn; (theat) callboy; **avertisseur d'incendie** fire alarm

a·veu [avø] *m* (*pl* **-veux**) avowal, confession; consent; **sans aveu** unscrupulous

aveu·glant [avœglɑ̃] **-glante** [glɑ̃t] *adj* blinding

aveugle [avœgl] *adj* blind || *mf* blind person; **en aveugle** without thinking

aveuglement [avœgləmɑ̃] *m* (fig) blindness

aveuglément [avœglemɑ̃] *adv* blindly

aveugler [avœgle] *tr* to blind; to dazzle; to stop up, to plug; to board up (*a window*) || *ref*—**s'aveugler sur** to shut one's eyes to

aveuglette [avœglet] *adv*—**à l'aveuglette** blindly

aveulir [avølir] *tr* to enervate, deaden || *ref* to become limp, enervated

aveulissement [avølismɑ̃] *m* enervation

aviateur [avjatœr] *m* aviator

aviation [avjasjɔ̃] *f* aviation

aviatrice [avjatris] *f* aviatrix

avide [avid] *adj* avid, eager; greedy; voracious; **avide de** avid for

avidité [avidite] *f* avidity, eagerness; greed; voracity

avilir [avilir] *tr* to debase, dishonor; (com) to lower the price of || *ref* to debase oneself; (com) to deteriorate

avilis·sant [avilisɑ̃] **avilis·sante** [avilisɑ̃t] *adj* debasing

avilissement [avilismɑ̃] *m* debasement; (com) depreciation

avi·né -née [avine] *adj* drunk

aviner [avine] *tr* to soak (*a new barrel*) with wine || *ref* (coll) to booze

avion [avjɔ̃] *m* airplane; **avion à réaction** jet; **avion de chasse** fighter plane; **avion long-courrier** long-range plane; **en avion** by plane; **par avion** air mail

avion-cargo [avjɔ̃kargo] *m* (*pl* **avions-cargos**) cargo liner, freighter

avion-taxi [avjɔ̃taksi] *m* (*pl* **avions-taxis**) taxiplane

aviron [avirɔ̃] *m* oar; **aviron de couple** scull

avis [avi] *m* opinion; advice; notice, warning; decision; **à mon avis** in my opinion; **avis au lecteur** note to the reader; **changer d'avis** to change one's mind

avi·sé -sée [avize] *adj* prudent, shrewd; **bien avisé** well-advised

aviser [avize] *tr* to glimpse, descry; to advise, inform, warn || *intr* to decide; **aviser à** to think of, look into; to deal with || *ref*—**s'aviser de** to contrive, to think up; to be on the look-out for; **s'aviser de** + *inf* to take it into one's head to + *inf*

aviso [avizo] *m* dispatch boat, sloop

avivage [avivaʒ] *m* brightening; polishing

aviver [avive] *tr* to revive, to stir up (*fire; passions*); to brighten (*colors*); (med & fig) to open (*a wound*)

av. J.-C. *abbr* (**avant Jésus-Christ**) B.C.

avo·cat [avoka] **-cate** [kat] *mf* lawyer; advocate; barrister (Brit); **avocat du diable** devil's advocate || *m* avocado

avoine [avwan] *f* oats

avoir [avwar] *m* wealth; credit side (*of ledger*) || §6 *tr* to have; to get; **avoir . . . ans** to be . . . years old, e.g., **mon fils a dix ans** my son is ten years old; **avoir beau** + *inf* to be useless for (*s.o.*) to + *inf*, e.g., **j'ai beau travailler** it is useless for me to work; for expressions like **avoir froid** to be cold, **avoir raison** to be right, see the noun || *intr*—**avoir à** to have to; **en avoir à** or **contre** to be angry with || *impers*—**il y a** there is, there are, e.g., **il n'y a pas d'espoir** there is no hope || *aux* to have, e.g., **j'ai couru trop vite** I have run too fast

avoisiner [avwazine] *tr* to neighbor, to be near

avortement [avɔrtəmɑ̃] *m* abortion; miscarriage

avorter [avɔrte] *intr* to abort; to miscarry

avorton [avɔrtɔ̃] *m* runt; (biol) stunt

avoué [avwe] *m* lawyer (*doing notarial work*); solicitor (Brit)

avouer [avwe] *tr* to avow, to admit; to claim, to acknowledge authorship of || *ref* to be admitted; **s'avouer vaincu** to admit defeat

avril [avril] *m* April

axe [aks] *m* axis

axer [akse] *tr* to set on an axis; to orient

axiomatique [aksjomatik] *adj* axiomatic

axiome [aksjom] *m* axiom

axonge [aksɔ̃ʒ] *f* lard

ayant-droit [ejɑ̃drwa] *m* (*pl* **ayants-droit**) claimant; beneficiary

azalée [azale] *f* azalea

azimut or **azimuth** [azimyt] *m* azimuth

azote [azɔt] *m* nitrogen

azo·té -tée [azote] *adj* nitrogenous

Aztèques [aztɛk] *mpl* Aztecs

azur [azyr] *adj* & *m* azure

azyme [azim] *adj* unleavened || *m* unleavened bread

B

B, b [be] *m invar* second letter of the French alphabet

baba [baba] *adj* (coll) flabbergasted, wide-eyed ‖ *m* baba

babeurre [babœr] *m* buttermilk

babil [babil], [babi] *m* babble, chatter; **babil enfantin** baby talk

babillage [babijaʒ] *m* babbling

babil·lard [babijar] **babil·larde** [babijard] *adj* babbling ‖ *mf* babbler ‖ *f* (slang) letter

babiller [babije] *intr* to babble, to chatter

babine [babin] *f* chop (*mouth*); **s'essuyer or se lécher les babines** to lick one's chops

babiole [babjɔl] *f* (coll) bauble

bâbord [babɔr] *m* (naut) port, portside; **à bâbord** port; **bâbord armures** port sail

babouche [babuʃ] *f* babouche, slipper

babouin [babwɛ̃] *m* baboon; pimple on the lips; brat

bac [bak] *m* ferryboat; tub, vat; box, bin; tray (*for ice cubes*); drawer (*of refrigerator*); case (*of battery*); (slang) baccalaureate

baccalauréat [bakalɔrea] *m* baccalaureate, bachelor's degree

bacchanale [bakanal] *f* bacchanal

bâche [baʃ] *f* tarpaulin; hot-water tank

bache·lier [baʃəlje] **-lière** [ljɛr] *mf* bachelor (*holder of degree*) ‖ *m* (hist) bachelor (*young knight*)

bâcher [baʃe] *tr* to cover with a tarpaulin

bachique [baʃik] *adj* bacchanalian, bacchic; drinking (*song*)

bachot [baʃo] *m* dinghy, punt; (coll) baccalaureate

bachotage [baʃotaʒ] *m* (coll) cramming (*for an exam*)

bachoter [baʃote] *intr* (coll) to cram

bacille [basil] *m* bacillus

bâclage [baklaʒ] *m* blocking up (*of harbor*); (slang) botching (*of work*)

bâcle [bakl] *f* bolt (*of door*)

bâcler [bakle] *tr* to bolt (*a door*); to close up (*a harbor*); (coll) to botch, to hurry through carelessly

bâ·cleur [baklœr] **-cleuse** [kløz] *mf* (coll) botcher

bacon [bakɔ̃] *m* bacon

bactéricide [bakterisid] *adj* bactericidal ‖ *m* bactericide

bactérie [bakteri] *f* bacterium; **bactéries** bacteria

bactériologie [bakterjɔlɔʒi] *f* bacteriology

ba·daud [bado] **-daude** [dod] *mf* rubberneck, gawk, idler

badauder [badode] *intr* to stand and stare

badigeon [badiʒɔ̃] *m* whitewash

badigeonner [badiʒone] *tr* to whitewash; (med) to paint (*e.g., the throat*)

ba·din [badɛ̃] **-dine** [din] *adj* sprightly, playful, teasing ‖ *mf* tease ‖ *m* (aer) air-speed indicator ‖ *f* cane, switch

badinage [badinaʒ] *m* banter; **badinage amoureux** necking

badiner [badine] *intr* to joke, to tease; to trifle, to be flippant

badinerie [badinri] *f* teasing; childishness

bafouer [bafwe] *tr* to heckle, to humiliate

bafouiller [bafuje] *intr* (coll) to stammer, mumble, babble

bâfrer [bafre] *tr & intr* (slang) to guzzle

bagage [bagaʒ] *m* baggage; **bagages** baggage, luggage; **bagages non accompagnés** baggage sent on ahead; **menus bagages** hand luggage; **plier bagage** to pack one's bags; (coll) to scram; (coll) to kick the bucket

bagarre [bagar] *f* brawl, row, riot; **chercher la bagarre** (coll) to be looking for a fight

bagarrer [bagare] *intr & ref* to riot; (coll) to brawl, scrap, scuffle

bagar·reur [bagarœr] **bagar·reuse** [bagarøz] *mf* (coll) rioter, brawler

bagatelle [bagatel] *f* trifle, bagatelle; frivolity ‖ *interj* nonsense!

bagnard [baɲar] *m* convict

bagne [baɲ] *m* penitentiary, penal colony; (nav) prison ship; (slang) sweatshop

bagnole [baɲɔl] *f* (slang) jalopy

bagou [bagu] *m* (coll) gift of gab

bague [bag] *f* ring; cigar band; (mach) collar, sleeve; **bague de fiançailles** engagement ring

baguenauder [bagnode] *intr* to waste time, to fool around ‖ *ref* (coll) to wander about

baguer [bage] *tr* to band (*a tree*); to baste (*cloth*)

baguette [baget] *f* stick, switch, rod; baton; long thin loaf of bread; chopstick; **baguette de fée** fairy wand; **baguettes de tambour** drumsticks; **mener qn à la baguette** (coll) to lead s.o. by the nose; **passer par les baguettes** to run the gauntlet

baguier [bagje] *m* jewel box

bahut [bay] *m* trunk, chest; cupboard; (slang) high school

bai baie [be] *adj* bay (*horse*) ‖ *f* bay; berry; bayberry; bay window

baignade [beɲad] *f* bathing, swimming; swimming hole, bathing spot

baigner [beɲe] *tr* to bathe; to wash (*the coast*) ‖ *intr* to be immersed, to soak ‖ *ref* to bathe; to go bathing

bai·gneur [beɲœr] **-gneuse** [ɲøz] *mf* bather; vacationist at a spa or seaside resort; bathhouse attendant ‖ *m* doll

baignoire [beɲwar] *f* bathtub; (theat) orchestra box

bail [baj] *m* (*pl* **baux** [bo]) lease; **passer un bail** to sign a lease; **prendre à bail** to lease

bâillement [bajmɑ̃] *m* yawn

bailler [baje] *tr*—**vous me la baillez belle** (coll) you're pulling my leg

bâiller [baje] *intr* to yawn; to be ajar, to be half open

bail·leur [bajœr] **bail·leresse** [bajərɛs] *mf* lessor; **bailleur de fonds** lender

bailli [baji] *m* bailiff

bailliage [baja3] *m* bailiwick

bâillon [bajɔ̃] *m* gag, muzzle

bâillonner [bajone] *tr* to gag; (fig) to muzzle

bain [bɛ̃] *m* bath; **bain de soleil** sun bath; **bains** watering place, spa; bathing establishment; **être dans le bain** (coll) to be in hot water

baïonnette [bajɔnɛt] *f* bayonet

baiser [beze], [beze] *m* kiss ‖ *tr* (vulgar) to have sex with; (archaic) to kiss

baisoter [bezote] *tr* (coll) to keep on kissing ‖ *ref* (coll) to bill and coo

baisse [bɛs] *f* fall; **jouer à la baisse** (com) to bear the market

baissement [bɛsmɑ̃] *m* lowering

baisser [bese] *m* lowering; **baisser du rideau** curtain fall ‖ *tr* to lower; to take in (*sail*) ‖ *intr* to fall, drop, sink ‖ *ref* to bend, stoop

baissier [besje] *m* bear (*on the stock exchange*)

bajoue [baʒu] *f* jowl

bal [bal] *m* (*pl* **bals**) ball, dance; **bal travesti** fancy-dress ball

balade [balad] *f* stroll; **balade en auto** joy ride

balader [balade] *ref* to go for a stroll; **se balader en auto** to go joy-riding

bala·deur [baladœr] **-deuse** [døz] *adj* strolling ‖ *mf* stroller ‖ *m* gear ‖ *f* cart (*of street vendor*); lamp with long cord

baladin [baladɛ̃] *m* mountebank, showman; oaf

balafre [balafr] *f* gash, scar

balafrer [balafre] *tr* to gash, to scar

balai [balɛ] *m* broom; **balai à laver** mop; **balai de sorcière** witches'-broom; **balai électrique** vacuum cleaner; **balai mécanique** carpet sweeper; **donner un coup de balai à** to make a clean sweep of (*s.th.*); to kick (*s.o.*) out

balai-éponge [balepɔ̃ʒ] *m* (*pl* **balais-éponges**) mop

balance [balɑ̃s] *f* balance; scales; **faire la balance de** (bk) to balance

balancement [balɑ̃smɑ̃] *m* swaying, teetering; (fig) indecision, wavering; (fig) harmony (*of phrase*)

balancer [balɑ̃se] §51 *tr* to balance; to move (*arms or legs*) in order to balance; to balance (*an account*); to weigh (*the pros and cons*); to swing, rock; (coll) to fire (*s.o.*) ‖ *intr* to swing, rock; to hesitate, waver ‖ *ref* to swing or to seesaw; to sway, rock; to ride (*at anchor*)

balancier [balɑ̃sje] *m* pendulum; balance wheel; pole (*of tightrope walker*)

balançoire [balɑ̃swar] *f* swing; seesaw, teeter-totter; (slang) nonsense

balayage [baleja3] *m* sweeping; (telv) scanning

balayer [baleje], [baleje] §49 *tr* to sweep, to sweep up; to sweep out; to scour (*the sea*); (telv) to scan

balayeur [balejœr] **balayeuse** [balejøz] *mf* sweeper, scavenger ‖ *f* street-cleaning truck

balayures [balejyr] *fpl* sweepings

balbutiement [balbysimɑ̃] *m* stammering, mumbling; initial effort

balbutier [balbysje] *tr* to stammer out ‖ *intr* to stammer, to mumble

balbuzard [balbyzar] *m* osprey, bald buzzard, sea eagle

balcon [balkɔ̃] *m* balcony; (theat) dress circle

baldaquin [baldakɛ̃] *m* canopy, tester

Baléares [balear] *fpl* Balearic Islands

baleine [balɛn] *f* right whale, whalebone whale; whalebone; rib (*of umbrella*); stay (*of a corset*)

baleinier [balenje] *m* whaling vessel

baleinière [balenjɛr] *f* whaleboat; lifeboat

balisage [baliza3] *m* (aer) ground lights; (naut) buoys

balise [baliz] *f* buoy, marker; ground light, beacon; landing signal

baliser [balize] *tr* to furnish with markers, buoys, landing lights, beacons, or radio signals

balistique [balistik] *adj* ballistic ‖ *f* ballistics

baliverne [balivern] *f* nonsense, humbug

balkanique [balkanik] *adj* Balkan

ballade [balad] *f* ballade

bal·lant [balɑ̃] **bal·lante** [balɑ̃t] *adj* waving, swinging, dangling ‖ *m* oscillation, shaking

balle [bal] *f* ball; bullet; hull, chaff; bale; (tennis) match point; **balle traçante** tracer bullet; **prendre** or **saisir la balle au bond** to seize time by the forelock

ballerine [balrin] *f* ballerina

ballet [balɛ] *m* ballet

ballon [balɔ̃] *m* balloon; ball; football, soccer ball; round-bottom flask; rounded mountaintop; **ballon d'essai** trial balloon

ballonner [balone] *tr*, *intr*, & *ref* to balloon

ballot [balo] *m* pack; bundle; (slang) blockhead, chump

ballottage [balota3] *m* tossing, shaking; second ballot

ballotter [balote] *tr* & *intr* to toss about

balnéaire [balnear] *adj* seaside

ba·lourd [balur] **-lourde** [lurd] *adj* awkward, lumpish ‖ *mf* blockhead, bumpkin ‖ *m* wobble

balte [balt] *adj* Baltic ‖ (*cap*) *mf* Balt

Baltique [baltik] *f* Baltic (*sea*)

balustrade [balystrad] *f* balustrade, banisters

balustre [balystr] *m* baluster, banister

bal·zan [balzɑ̃] **-zane** [zan] *adj* white-footed (*horse*) ‖ *f* white spot (*on horse's foot*)

bambin [bɑ̃bɛ̃] **-bine** [bin] *mf* (coll) babe

bambo·chard [bɑ̃boʃar] **-charde** [ʃard] *adj* (coll) carousing ‖ *mf* (coll) carouser

bamboche [bɑ̃bɔʃ] f (slang) jag, bender
bambocher [bɑ̃bɔʃe] intr (coll) to carouse, to go on a spree
bambo·cheur [bɑ̃bɔʃœr] **-cheuse** [ʃøz] adj (coll) carousing ‖ mf (coll) carouser
bambou [bɑ̃bu] m bamboo
ban [bɑ̃] m ban; cadenced applause; **ban de mariage** banns; **convoquer le ban et l'arrière-ban** to invite everyone and his brother; **mettre au ban de** to banish, to ban
ba·nal -nale [banal] adj (pl **-nals -nales**) banal, trite, commonplace ‖ adj (pl **-naux** [no] **-nales**) (archaic) common, public, in common
banaliser [banalize] tr to vulgarize, to make commonplace
banalité [banalite] f banality; triteness
banane [banan] f banana
bananier [banaje] m banana tree
banc [bɑ̃] m bench; shoal; school (of fish); pew (reserved for church officials); (hist) privy council; **être sur les bancs** to go to high school
bancaire [bɑ̃ker] adj banking, of banks
ban·cal -cale [bɑ̃kal] adj (pl **-cals -cales**) bowlegged, bandy-legged
bandage [bɑ̃daʒ] m bandage; bandaging; truss; tire (of metal or rubber)
bande [bɑ̃d] f band; movie film; recording tape; cushion (in billiards); wrapper (of a newspaper); **bande magnétique** recording tape; tape recording; **bande sonore** or **parlante** sound track; **donner de la bande** to heel, to list; **faire bande à part** to keep to oneself
ban·deau [bɑ̃do] m (pl **-deaux**) blindfold; headband; bending (of a bow); **bandeau royal** diadem; **bandeaux** hair parted in the middle
bander [bɑ̃de] tr to band, to put a band on; to bandage; to blindfold; to bend (a bow); to put a tire on; to draw taut ‖ ref to band together; to put up resistance
banderole [bɑ̃drɔl] f pennant, streamer; strap (of gun)
bandière [bɑ̃djer] f battle, e.g., **front de bandière** battle front
bandit [bɑ̃di] m bandit
bandoulière [bɑ̃duljer] f shoulder strap, sling; **en bandoulière** slung over the shoulder
banlieue [bɑ̃ljø] f suburbs; **de banlieue** suburban
banlieu·sard [bɑ̃ljøzar] **-sarde** [zard] mf suburbanite (especially of a Parisian suburb)
banne [ban] f awning (of store)
ban·ni -nie [bani] adj banished, exiled ‖ mf exile
bannière [banjer] f banner, flag
bannir [banir] tr to banish
bannissement [banismɑ̃] m banishment
banque [bɑ̃k] f bank; **banque des yeux** eye bank; **banque du sang** blood bank; **faire sauter la banque** to break the bank
banqueroute [bɑ̃krut] f bankruptcy (with blame for negligence or fraud)

banquerou·tier [bɑ̃krutje] **-tière** [tjer] adj & mf bankrupt (with culpability)
banquet [bɑ̃ke] m banquet
banqueter [bɑ̃kte] §34 intr to banquet
banquette [bɑ̃ket] f seat (in a train, bus, automobile); bank (of earth or sand); bunker (in a golf course); **banquette arrière** back seat; **banquette de tir** (mil) emplacement for shooting; **jouer devant les banquettes** to play to an empty house
ban·quier [bɑ̃kje] **-quière** [kjer] mf banker
banquise [bɑ̃kiz] f pack ice
banquiste [bɑ̃kist] m charlatan, quack
baptême [batem] m baptism; christening; **baptême de la ligne, baptême des tropiques** or **du tropique** polliwog initiation
baptiser [batize] tr to baptize; to christen; (slang) to dilute (wine) with water
baptis·mal -male [batismal] adj (pl **-maux** [mo]) baptismal
baptistaire [batister] adj baptismal (certificate)
baptiste [batist] mf Baptist
baptistère [batister] m baptistery
baquet [bake] m wooden tub, bucket; (aut) bucket seat
bar [bar] m bar; (ichth) bass, perch
baragouin [baragwɛ̃] m (slang) gibberish
baragouiner [baragwine] tr (coll) to murder (a language); (coll) to stumble through (a speech) ‖ intr (coll) to jabber
baraque [barak] f booth, stall; shanty, hovel
baraterie [baratri] f barratry
baratin [baratɛ̃] m (slang) blah-blah, hokum
baratte [barat] f churn
baratter [barate] tr to churn
Barbade [barbad] f Barbados; **la Barbade** Barbados
barbare [barbar] adj barbarous, barbaric, savage ‖ mf barbarian
barbaresque [barbaresk] adj of Barbary
barbarie [barbari] f barbarity, barbarism ‖ (cap) f Barbary
barbarisme [barbarism] m barbarism (in speech or writing)
barbe [barb] f beard; bristle; whiskers (of an animal); barbel; **barbes vane** (of a feather); deckle edge; **faire q.ch. à la barbe de qn** to do s.th. right under the nose of s.o.; **rire dans sa barbe** to laugh up one's sleeve; **se faire la barbe** to shave ‖ interj—**la barbe!** shut up!
bar·beau [barbo] m (pl **-beaux**) cornflower; (ichth) barbel; (slang) pimp
barbe·lé -lée [barbəle] adj barbed ‖ **barbelés** mpl barbed wire
bar·bet [barbe] **-bette** [bet] mf water spaniel
barbiche [barbiʃ] f goatee
barbier [barbje] m barber
barbillon [barbijɔ̃] m barb
barbiturique [barbityrik] m barbiturate
barbon [barbɔ̃] m (pej) old fogy

barboter [barbɔte] *intr* to paddle (*like ducks*); to wallow (*like pigs*); to bubble (*like carbonated water*); (coll) to splutter; (slang) to steal

barbo·teur [barbɔtœr] **-teuse** [tøz] *mf* (slang) muddler ‖ *m* duck; wash bottle ‖ *f* rompers

barbouiller [barbuje] *tr* to smear, blur; to daub; (coll) to scribble; **barbouiller le cœur à** to nauseate

barbouil·leur [barbujœr] **barbouil·leuse** [barbujøz] *mf* dauber; messy person; scribbler

bar·bu ·bue [barby] *adj* bearded

bard [bar] *m* handbarrow

bardane [bardan] *f* burdock

barde [bard] *m* bard ‖ *f* blanket of bacon

bar·deau [bardo] *m* (*pl* **-deaux**) shingle; lath

barder [barde] *tr* to carry with a handbarrow; to armor (*a horse*); to blanket (*a roast*)

bardot [bardo] *m* hinny

barème [barem] *m* schedule (*of rates, taxes, etc.*)

baréter [barete] §10 *intr* to trumpet (*like an elephant*)

barge [barʒ] *f* barge; haystack; godwit, black-tailed godwit

barguigner [bargiɲe] *intr* to shilly-shally, to have trouble deciding

bargui·gneur [bargiɲœr] **-gneuse** [ɲøz] *mf* shilly-shallyer, procrastinator

baricaut [bariko] *m* small cask, keg

baril [baril], [bari] *m* small barrel, cask, keg

barillet [barije] *m* small barrel; revolver cylinder; spring case

bariolage [barjɔlaʒ] *m* (coll) motley, mixture of colors

bario·lé ·lée [barjɔle] *adj* speckled, multicolored, variegated

barioler [barjɔle] *tr* to variegate

bariolure [barjɔlyr] *f* clashing colors, motley

bar·man [barman] *m* (*pl* **-men** [men] or **-mans**) bartender

baromètre [barɔmetr] *m* barometer

barométrique [barɔmetrik] *adj* barometric

baron [barɔ̃] *m* baron

baronne [barɔn] *f* baroness

baroque [barɔk] *adj* & *m* baroque

barque [bark] *f* boat

barrage [baraʒ] *m* dam; barrage, cordon (*of police*); tollgate; barricade, roadblock, checkpoint; (sports) playoff

barre [bɑr], [bar] *f* bar; crossbar (*of a t*); tiller, helm; bore (*tidal flood*); **barre de justice** rod to hold shackles; **barre du gouvernail** helm; **barres** (typ) parallels; **jouer aux barres** to play prisoner's base

bar·reau [baro] *m* (*pl* **-reaux**) bar, crossbar, rail; rung (*of ladder or chair*); (law) bar

barrer [bare] *tr* to cross out, strike out, cancel; to cross (*a t; a check in a British bank*); to bar (*the door; the way*); to block off (*a street*); to dam (*a stream*); to steer (*a boat*)

barrette [baret], [bɑret] *f* biretta; bar; slide; pin

barreur [barœr] *m* helmsman

barricade [barikad] *f* barricade

barricader [barikade] *tr* to barricade

barrière [barjer] *f* barrier; gate (*of a town; of a grade crossing*); tollgate; neighborhood shopping district

barrique [barik] *f* cask; hogshead, large barrel

barrir [barir] *intr* to trumpet (*like an elephant*)

barrot [baro] *m* beam (*of a ship*)

baryton [baritɔ̃] *m* baritone; alto (*saxhorn*)

baryum [barjɔm] *m* barium

bas [bɑ] **basse** [bɑs] *adj* low; base, vile; cloudy (*weather*) ‖ (when standing before noun) *adj* low; base, vile; early (*age*) ‖ *m* stocking; lower part, bottom; **à bas . . . !** down with . . . !; **bas de casse** (typ) lower case; **bas de laine** nest egg, savings; **en bas at** the bottom; downstairs ‖ *f* see **basse** ‖ **bas** *adv* softly; down, low

ba·sal ·sale [bazal] *adj* (*pl* **-saux** [zo]) basic; basal (*metabolism*)

basalte [bazalt] *m* basalt

basa·né ·née [bazane] *adj* tanned, sunburned

basaner [bazane] *tr* to tan, to sunburn

bas-bleu [bɑblø] *m* (*pl* **-bleus**) bluestocking

bas-côté [bakote] *m* (*pl* **-côtés**) aisle (*of a church*); footpath (*beside a road*)

bascule [baskyl] *f* scale; rocker; seesaw

basculement [baskylmɑ̃] *m* rocking, seesawing, tipping; dimming

basculer [baskyle] *tr* to tip over ‖ *intr* to tip over; to seesaw, rock, swing; **faire basculer** to dim (*the headlights*)

bas-dessus [badəsy] *m* mezzo-soprano

base [bɑz] *f* base; basis; **à la base at** heart, to the core; **de base** basic

base-ball [bezbol] *m* baseball

baser [bɑze] *tr* to base; to ground, found (*an opinion*) ‖ *ref* to be based

bas-fond [bafɔ̃] *m* (*pl* **-fonds**) lowland; shallows; **bas-fonds** dregs, underworld; slums

basilic [bazilik] *m* basil

basilique [bazilik] *f* basilica

basin [bazɛ̃] *m* dimity

basique [bazik] *adj* basic, alkaline

basket [basket] *m* basketball

basoche [bazoʃ] *f* law, legal profession

basque [bask] *adj* Basque ‖ *m* Basque (*language*) ‖ *f* coattail ‖ (*cap*) *mf* Basque (*person*)

basse [bɑs] *f* shoal; tuba; (mus) bass; **basse chiffrée** (mus) figured bass

basse-contre [bɑskɔ̃tr] *f* (*pl* **basses-contre**) basso profundo

basse-cour [bɑskur] *f* (*pl* **basses-cours**) barnyard, farmyard; barnyard animals; poultry yard

bassesse [bɑses] *f* baseness; base act

basset [base] *m* basset hound

bassin [basɛ̃] *m* basin; dock; artificial lake; collection plate; pelvis; **bassin**

de lit bedpan; **bassin de radoub** dry dock; **bassin hygiénique** bedpan

bassine [basin] *f* dishpan

bassinoire [basinwar] *f* bedwarmer

basson [basɔ̃] *m* bassoon

baste [bast] *m* ace of clubs; saddle basket ‖ *interj* enough!

bastille [bastij] *f* small fortress

bastion [bastjɔ̃] *m* bastion

bastonnade [bastɔnad] *f* beating

bas-ventre [bavɑ̃tr] *m* abdomen, lower part of the belly

bât [ba] *m* packsaddle

bataclan [bataklɑ̃] *m—tout le bataclan* (slang) the whole caboodle

bataille [bataj], [bataj] *f* battle, fight

batailler [bataje], [bataje] *intr* to battle, to fight

batail·leur [batajœr] **batail·leuse** [batajøz] *adj* belligerent ‖ *mf* fighter

bataillon [batajɔ̃] *m* battalion

bâ·tard [batar] **-tarde** [tard] *adj & mf* mongrel; bastard ‖ *m* one-pound loaf of short-length type of bread ‖ *f* cursive handwriting

bâtar·deau [batardo] *m* (*pl* **-deaux**) cofferdam, caisson

ba·teau [bato] *m* (*pl* **-teaux**) boat; **bateau automobile** motorboat, motor launch; **bateau à vapeur** steamboat; **bateau à voiles** sailboat; **bateau de guerre** warship; **bateau de pêche** fishing boat; **bateau de sauvetage** lifeboat; **monter un bateau à qn** (slang) to pull s.o.'s leg; **par** (le) **bateau** by boat

bateau-citerne [batositern] *m* (*pl* **bateaux-citernes**) tanker

bateau-feu [batofø] *m* (*pl* **bateaux-feux**) lightship

bateau-maison [batomezɔ̃] *m* (*pl* **bateaux-maisons**) houseboat

bateau-mouche [batomuʃ] *m* (*pl* **bateaux-mouches**) excursion boat

bateau-pompe [batopɔ̃p] *m* (*pl* **bateaux-pompes**) fireboat

batelage [batlaʒ] *m* lighterage; juggling; tumbling

batelée [batle] *f* boatload

bateler [batle] §34 *tr* to lighter ‖ *intr* to juggle; to tumble

bateleur [batlœr] **-leuse** [løz] *mf* juggler; tumbler

bate·lier [batəlje] **-lière** [ljɛr] *mf* skipper ‖ *m* boatman; ferryman

batellerie [batɛlri] *f* lighterage

bâter [bate] *tr* to packsaddle

bath [bat] *adj* (slang) A-one, swell

bâ·ti -tie [bati] *adj* built; **bien bâti** well-built (*person*) ‖ *m* frame; basting (*thread*); basted garment

batifoler [batifɔle] *intr* (coll) to frolic

bâtiment [batimɑ̃] *m* building; ship

bâtir [batir] *tr* to build; to baste, to tack ‖ *ref* to be built

bâtisse [batis] *f* masonry, construction; building, edifice; ramshackle house

bâtis·seur [batisœr] **bâtis·seuse** [batisøz] *mf* builder

bâton [batɔ̃] *m* stick; baton; staff, cane; rung (*of a chair*); stroke (*of a pen*); stick (*of gum*); **à bâtons rompus** by fits and starts; impromptu;

(archit) with zigzag molding; **bâton de reprise** (mus) repeat bar; **bâton de rouge à lèvres** lipstick; **bâton de vieillesse** helper or nurse for the aged; **mettre des bâtons dans les roues** to throw a monkey wrench into the works

bâtonner [batɔne] *tr* to cudgel; to cross out

bâtonnet [batɔne] *m* rod (*in the retina*); chopstick

battage [bataʒ] *m* beating; threshing; churning; (slang) ballyhoo

bat·tant [batɑ̃] **bat·tante** [batɑ̃t] *adj* beating, pelting, driving, swinging (*door*) ‖ *m* flap; clapper (*of bell*); **à deux battants** double (*door*)

batte [bat] *f* mallet, beater, dasher, plunger; bench for beating clothes; wooden sword (*for slapstick comedy*); (sports) bat; **batte de l'or** goldbeating

battement [batmɑ̃] *m* beating, beat; throbbing, pulsing; clapping (*of hands*); dance step; wait (*e.g., between trains*)

batterie [batri] *f* (elec, mil, mus) battery; train service (*in one direction*); ruse, scheming; **batterie de cuisine** kitchen utensils

batteur [batœr] *m* thresher; (sports) batter; **batteur de grève** beachcomber; **batteur de pieux** piledriver; **batteur électrique** electric mixer

batteuse [batøz] *f* threshing machine

battoir [batwar] *m* bat, beetle (*for washing clothes*); tennis racket

battre [batr] §7 *tr* to beat; to clap (*one's hands*); to flap, flutter; to wink; to bang; to pound (*the sidewalk*); to search; to shuffle (*the cards*); **battre la mesure** to beat time; **battre monnaie** to mint money ‖ *intr* to beat ‖ *ref* to fight

bau [bo] *m* (*pl* **baux**) beam (*of a ship*)

baudet [bode] *m* ass, donkey; stallion ass; sawhorse; (slang) jackass, idiot

baudrier [bodrije] *m* shoulder belt

bauge [boʒ] *f* lair, den; clay and straw mortar; (coll) pigsty

baume [bom] *m* balsam; (*consolation*) balm

ba·vard [bavar] **-varde** [vard] *adj* talkative, loquacious; tattletale ‖ *mf* chatterer; tattletale; gossip

bavardage [bavardaʒ] *m* chattering; gossiping

bavarder [bavarde] *intr* to chatter; to gossip

bava·rois [bavarwa] **-roise** [rwaz] *adj* Bavarian ‖ (*cap*) *mf* Bavarian (*person*)

bave [bav] *f* dribble, froth, spittle; (fig) slander

baver [bave] *intr* to dribble, to drool; to run (*like a pen*); **baver sur** to besmirch

bavette [bavet] *f* bib

ba·veux [bavø] **-veuse** [vøz] *adj* drooling; tendentious, wordy; undercooked

Bavière [bavjɛr] *f* Bavaria; **la Bavière** Bavaria

bavocher [bavɔʃe] *intr* to smear

bavochure [bavɔʃyr] *f* smear

bavure [bavyr] *f* bur (*of metal*); smear

bayer [baje] §49 *intr*—**bayer aux corneilles** to gawk, to stargaze

bazar [bazar] *m* bazaar; five-and-ten; **tout le bazar** (slang) the whole she-bang

béant [beɑ̃] **béante** [beɑ̃t] *adj* gaping, wide-open

béat [bea] **béate** [beat] *adj* smug, complacent, sanctimonious

béatifier [beatifje] *tr* to beatify

béatitude [beatityd] *f* beatitude

beau [bo] (*or* **bel** [bɛl] *before vowel or mute h*) **belle** [bɛl] (*pl* **beaux belles**) *adj* beautiful; handsome; **bel et bien** truly, for sure; **de plus belle** more than ever; **il fait beau** it is nice out, we are having fair weather; **tout beau!** steady!, easy does it! || (*when standing before noun*) *adj* beautiful; handsome; fine, good; considerable, large, long; fair (*weather*); odd-numbered *or* recto (*page*) || *mf* fair one; **faire le beau, faire la belle** to strut, swagger; **to sit up and beg** (*said of a dog*); **la belle** the deciding match; **la Belle au bois dormant** Sleeping Beauty || **beau** *adv*—**il a beau parler** it is no use for him to speak || **belle** *adv*—**la bailler belle** (slang) to tell a whopper; **l'échapper belle** to have a narrow escape

beaucoup [boku] §91 *adv* much, many; **beaucoup de** much, many; **de beaucoup** by far

beau-fils [bofis] *m* (*pl* **beaux-fils**) son-in-law; stepson

beau-frère [bofrɛr] *m* (*pl* **beaux-frères**) brother-in-law

beau-père [bopɛr] *m* (*pl* **beaux-pères**) father-in-law; stepfather

beau-petit-fils [bopətifis] *m* (*pl* **beaux-petits-fils**) son of a stepson or of a stepdaughter

beaupré [bopre] *m* bowsprit

beauté [bote] *f* beauty; **beauté du diable** (coll) bloom of youth; **se faire une beauté** (coll) to doll up

beaux-arts [bozar] *mpl* fine arts

beaux-parents [bopɑ̃rɑ̃] *mpl* in-laws

bébé [bebe] *m* baby

bec [bɛk] *m* beak; nozzle, jet, burner; point (*of a pen*); (mus) mouthpiece; (slang) beak, face, mouth; **avoir bon bec** to be gossipy; **claquer du bec** (coll) to be hungry; **clore le bec à qn** (coll) to shut s.o. up; **tomber sur un bec** (coll) to encounter an unforeseen obstacle

bécane [bekan] *f* (coll) bike, bicycle

bécarre [bekar] *m* (mus) natural

bécasse [bekas] *f* woodcock; (slang) stupid woman

bécas•seau [bekaso] *m* (*pl* **bécas•seaux**) sandpiper

bec-de-cane [bɛkdəkan] *m* (*pl* **becs-de-cane**) door handle; flat-nosed pliers

bec-de-corbeau [bɛkdəkɔrbo] *m* (*pl* **becs-de-corbeau**) wire cutters

bec-de-corbin [bɛkdəkɔrbɛ̃] *m* (*pl* **becs-de-corbin**) crowbar

bec-de-lièvre [bɛkdəljɛvr] *m* (*pl* **becs-de-lièvre**) harelip

bêche [bɛʃ] *f* spade

bêcher [beʃe] *tr* to dig; (slang) to run (*s.th.*) down, to give (*s.o.*) a dig

bê•cheur [beʃœr] **-cheuse** [ʃøz] *mf* (coll) detractor, critic; (slang) stuffed shirt

bêchoir [beʃwar] *m* hoe

bécoter [bekɔte] *tr* to give (*s.o.*) a peck or little kiss on the cheek

becqueter [bɛkte] *tr* to peck at; (coll) to eat || *ref* to bill and coo

bedaine [bədɛn] *f* paunch, beer belly

bédane [bedan] *m* cold chisel

bé•deau [bədo] *m* (*pl* **-deaux**) beadle

bé•douin [bedwɛ̃] **-douine** [dwin] *adj* Bedouin || (*cap*) *mf* Bedouin (*person*)

bée [be] *adj*—**bouche bée** mouth agape, flabbergasted || *f* penstock

beffroi [befrwa] *m* belfry

bégaiement [begɛmɑ̃] *m* stammering, stuttering

bégayer [begeje] §49 *tr & intr* to stammer, stutter

bègue [bɛg] *adj* stammering, stuttering || *mf* stammerer

bégueter [bɛgte] §2 *intr* to bleat

bégueule [begœl] *adj* (coll) prudish || *f* (coll) prudish woman

béguin [begɛ̃] *m* hood, cap; sweetheart; (coll) infatuation

béguine [begin] *f* Beguine; sanctimonious woman

beige [bɛʒ] *adj & m* beige

beignet [bɛɲe] *m* fritter

béjaune [beʒon] *m* nestling; greenhorn, novice, ninny

bêlement [bɛlmɑ̃] *m* bleat, bleating

bêler [bele] *intr* to bleat

belette [bəlɛt] *f* weasel

bel•ge [bɛlʒ] *adj* Belgian || (*cap*) *mf* Belgian (*person*)

Belgique [bɛlʒik] *f* Belgium; **la Belgique** Belgium

bélier [belje] *m* ram; battering ram

belière [beljɛr] *f* sheepbell

bélinogramme [belinɔgram] *m* Wirephoto (*trademark*)

bélinographe [belinɔgraf] *m* Wirephoto transmitter

bélître [belitr] *m* scoundrel

belladone [beladɔn] *f* belladonna

bellâtre [belɑtr] *adj* foppish || *m* fop

belle-dame [bɛldam] *f* belladonna

belle-de-jour [bɛldəʒur] *f* (*pl* **belles-de-jour**) morning glory

belle-de-nuit [bɛldənɥi] *f* (*pl* **belles-de-nuit**) marvel-of-Peru

belle-d'un-jour [bɛldœ̃ʒur] *f* (*pl* **belles-d'un-jour**) day lily

belle-fille [bɛlfij] *f* (*pl* **belles-filles**) daughter-in-law; stepdaughter

belle-mère [bɛlmɛr] *f* (*pl* **belles-mères**) mother-in-law; stepmother

belle-petite-fille [bɛlpətitfij] *f* (*pl* **belles-petites-filles**) daughter of a stepson or of a stepdaughter

belles-lettres [bɛlletr] *fpl* belles-lettres, literature

belle-sœur [bɛlsœr] *f* (*pl* **belles-sœurs**) sister-in-law

belliciste [belisist] *mf* warmonger

bellígé·rant [beliʒerã] **-rante** [rãt] *adj & m* belligerent

belli·queux [belikǿ] **-queuse** [kǿz] *adj* bellicose, warlike

bel·lot [belo] **bel·lote** [belɔt] *adj* pretty, cute; dapper

bémol [bemɔl] *adj invar & m* (mus) flat

bémoliser [bemɔlize] *tr* to flat (*a note*); to provide (*a key signature*) with flats

ben [bɛ̃] *interj* (slang) well!

bénédicité [benedisite] *m* grace (*before a meal*)

bénédic·tin [benediktɛ̃] **-tine** [tin] *adj & m* Benedictine || (*cap*) *f* Benedictine (*liqueur*)

bénédiction [benediksjɔ̃] *f* benediction; manna from heaven

bénéfice [benefis] *m* profit; benefit; benefice; parsonage, rectory; **à bénéfice** benefit (*performance*); **sous bénéfice d'inventaire** with grave reservations

bénéficiaire [benefisjɛr] *adj* profit, e.g., **marge bénéficiaire** profit margin || *mf* beneficiary

bénéficier [benefisje] *intr* to profit, benefit

benêt [bənɛ] *adj masc* simple-minded || *m* simpleton, numskull

bé·nin [benɛ̃] **-nigne** [niɲ] *adj* benign; mild, slight; benignant, accommodating

béni-oui-oui [beniwiwi] *mpl* yes men

bénir [benir] *tr* to bless, to consecrate

bé·nit [beni] **-nite** [nit] *adj* consecrated (*bread*); holy (*water*)

bénitier [benitje] *m* font (*for holy water*)

benja·min [bɛ̃ʒamɛ̃] **-mine** [min] *mf* baby (*the youngest child*) || (*cap*) *m* Benjamin

benne [bɛn] *f* bucket, bin, hopper; dumper; cage (*in mine*); **benne preneuse** (mach) scoop, jaws (*of crane*)

be·noît [bənwa] **-noîte** [nwat] *adj* indulgent; sanctimonious || (*cap*) *m* Benedict

benzène [bɛ̃zɛn] *m* (chem) benzene

benzine [bɛ̃zin] *f* benzine

béquille [bekij] *f* crutch

béquiller [bekije] *intr* to walk with a crutch or crutches

bercail [bɛrkaj] *m* fold, bosom (*of church or family*)

ber·ceau [bɛrso] *m* (*pl* **-ceaux**) cradle; bower; **berceau de verdure or de chèvrefeuille** arbor

bercelonnette [bɛrsəlɔnɛt] *f* bassinet

bercer [bɛrse] §51 *tr* to cradle, rock; to beguile; to assuage (*grief, pain*) || *ref* to rock, swing; to delude oneself (*with vain hopes*)

ber·ceur [bɛrsœr] **-ceuse** [søz] *adj* rocking, cradling || *f* rocking chair; cradle song, lullaby

berge [bɛrʒ] *f* bank, steep bank

berger [bɛrʒe] *m* shepherd; shepherd dog

bergère [bɛrʒɛr] *f* shepherdess; wing chair

bergerie [bɛrʒəri] *f* sheepfold; pastoral poem

berle [bɛrl] *f* water parsnip

Berlin [bɛrlɛ̃] *m* Berlin; **Berlin-Est** East Berlin; **Berlin-Ouest** West Berlin

berline [bɛrlin] *f* sedan (*automobile*); berlin (*carriage*)

berlingot [bɛrlɛ̃go] *m* caramel candy; milk carton

berli·nois [bɛrlinwa] **-noise** [nwaz] *adj* Berlin || *mf* Berliner (*person*)

berlue [bɛrly] *f*—**avoir la berlue** (coll) to be blind to what is going on

Bermudes [bɛrmyd] *fpl*—**les Bermudes** Bermuda

bernacle [bɛrnakl] *f* (orn) anatid; (zool) barnacle

berne [bɛrn] *f* hazing; **en berne** at half-mast

berner [bɛrne] *tr* to toss in a blanket; to ridicule; to fool

bernique [bɛrnik] *interj* (coll) shucks!, heck!, what a shame!

berthe [bɛrt] *f* corsage; cape

béryllium [beriljɔm] *m* beryllium

besace [bəzas] *f* beggar's bag; mendicancy

besicles [bəzikl] *fpl* (archaic) spectacles; **prenez donc vos besicles!** (coll) put your specs on!

besogne [bəzɔɲ] *f* work, task; **abattre de la besogne** to accomplish a great deal of work; **aller vite en besogne** to work too hastily

besogner [bəzɔɲe] *intr* to drudge, slave

beso·gneux [bəzɔɲǿ] **-gneuse** [ɲǿz] *adj* needy || *mf* needy person

besoin [bəzwɛ̃] *m* need; poverty, distress; **au besoin** if necessary; **avoir besoin de** to need; **si besoin est** if need be

bes·son [besɔ̃] **bes·sonne** [besɔn] *mf* (dial) twin

bestiaire [bɛstjɛr] *m* bestiary

bes·tial -tiale [bɛstjal] (*pl* **-tiaux** [tjo]) *adj* bestial || *mpl* see **bestiaux**

bestialité [bɛstjalite] *f* bestiality

bestiaux [bɛstjo] *mpl* livestock, cattle and horses

bestiole [bɛstjɔl] *f* bug, vermin

bê·ta [beta] **-tasse** [tas] *adj* (coll) silly || *mf* (coll) sap, dolt

bétail [betaj] *m invar* grazing animals (*on a farm*); **gros bétail** cattle and horses; **menu bétail** or **petit bétail** sheep, goats, pigs, etc.

bête [bɛt] *adj* stupid, foolish || *f* animal; beast; **bête à bon Dieu** (ent) ladybird; **bête de charge, bête de somme** pack animal; **bonne bête** harmless fool

bêtifier [betifje], [betifje] *tr* to make stupid || *intr* to play the fool, to talk foolishly

bêtise [betiz], [betiz] *f* foolishness, stupidity, nonsense; trifle; **faire des bêtises** to blunder, do stupid things; to throw money around

béton [betɔ̃] *m* concrete; **béton armé** reinforced concrete

bétonner [betɔne] *tr* to make of concrete

bétonnière [betɔnjɛr] *f* cement mixer

bette [bet] *f* Swiss chard; **bette à carde** Swiss chard

betterave [betrav] *f* beet; **betterave sucrière** sugar beet

beuglement [bøgləmɑ̃] *m* bellow, bellowing, lowing

beugler [bøgle], [bœgle] *tr* (slang) to bawl out (*a song*) || *intr* to bellow (*like a bull*); to low (*like cattle*)

beurre [bœr] *m* butter; **faire son beurre** (coll) to feather one's nest

beurrée [bœre] *f* slice of bread and butter

beurrer [bœre] *tr* to butter

beur-rier [bœrje] **beur-rière** [bœrjer] *adj* butter || *m* butter dish

beuverie [bœvri] *f* drinking party

bévue [bevy] *f* blunder, slip, boner

biais [bje] **biaise** [bjez] *adj* bias, oblique, slanting; skew (*arch*) || *m* bias, slant; skew (*of an arch*); **de biais** or **en biais** aslant, askew

biaiser [bjeze] *intr* to slant; (fig) to be evasive

bibelot [biblo] *m* curio, trinket, knickknack

bibeloter [biblɔte] *intr* to buy or collect curios

bibe-ron [bibrɔ̃] **-ronne** [rɔn] *adj* addicted to the bottle || *mf* heavy drinker || *m* nursing bottle

Bible [bibl] *f* Bible

bibliobus [bibliɔbys] *m* bookmobile

bibliographe [bibliɔgraf] *m* bibliographer

bibliographie [bibliɔgrafi] *f* bibliography

bibliomane [bibliɔman] *mf* book collector

bibliothécaire [bibliɔtekɛr] *mf* librarian

bibliothèque [bibliɔtɛk] *f* library; bookstand; **bibliothèque vivante** walking encyclopedia

biblique [biblik] *adj* Biblical

biceps [biseps] *m* biceps

biche [biʃ] *f* hind; doe; **ma biche** (coll) my darling

bicher [biʃe] *intr*—**ça biche!** (slang) fine!, it's fine!

bichlamar [biʃlamar] *m* pidgin

bichof [biʃɔf] *m* spiced wine

bi-chon [biʃɔ̃] **-chonne** [ʃɔn] *mf* lap dog

bichonner [biʃɔne] *tr* to curl (*one's hair*); to doll up || *ref* to doll up

bicoque [bikɔk] *f* shack, ramshackle house

bicorne [bikɔrn] *adj* two-cornered || *m* cocked hat

bicot [biko] *m* (coll) kid (*goat*); (pej) North African, Arab

bicyclette [bisiklɛt] *f* bicycle

bident [bidɑ̃] *m* two-pronged fork

bidet [bide] *m* bidet; nag (*horse*)

bidon [bidɔ̃] *m* drum (*for liquids*); canteen, water bottle

bidonville [bidɔ̃vil] *m* shantytown

bidule [bidyl] *m* (slang) gadget

bief [bjef] *m* millrace; reach, level (*of a stream or canal*)

bielle [bjɛl] *f* connecting rod, tie rod

bien [bjɛ̃] *m* good; welfare; estate, fortune; **biens** property, possessions; **biens consomptibles** consumer goods; **biens immeubles** real estate; **biens meubles** personal property || *adv* §91 well; rightly, properly, quite; indeed, certainly; fine, e.g., **je vais bien** I'm fine; **bien de** + *art* much, e.g., **bien de l'eau** much water; many, e.g., **bien des gens** many people; **bien entendu** of course; **bien que** although; **eh bien!** so!; **si bien que** so that; **tant bien que mal** so-so, as well as possible || *interj* good!; all right!; that's enough!

bien-ai-mé **-mée** [bjɛ̃neme] *adj & mf* beloved, darling

bien-dire [bjɛ̃dir] *m* gracious speech, eloquent delivery; **être sur son bien-dire** to be on one's best behavior

bien-di-sant [bjɛ̃dizɑ̃] **-sante** [zɑ̃t] *adj* smooth-spoken, smooth-tongued

bien-être [bjɛ̃nɛtr] *m* well-being, welfare

bienfaisance [bjɛ̃fəzɑ̃s] *f* charity, beneficence

bienfai-sant [bjɛ̃fəzɑ̃] **-sante** [zɑ̃t] *adj* charitable, beneficent

bienfait [bjɛ̃fɛ] *m* good turn, good deed, favor; **bienfaits** benefits

bienfai-teur [bjɛ̃fɛtœr] **-trice** [tris] *mf* benefactor || *f* benefactress

bien-fondé [bjɛ̃fɔ̃de] *m* cogency

bien-fonds [bjɛ̃fɔ̃] *m* (pl **biens-fonds**) real estate

bienheu-reux [bjɛ̃nœrø] **-reuse** [røz] *adj & mf* blessed

bien-nal **-nale** [bjennal] *adj* (pl **-naux** [no]) biennial || *f* biennial exposition

bienséance [bjɛ̃seɑ̃s] *f* propriety

bienséant [bjɛ̃seɑ̃] **bienséante** [bjɛ̃seɑ̃t] *adj* fitting, proper, appropriate

bientôt [bjɛ̃to] *adv* soon; **à bientôt!** so long!

bienveillance [bjɛ̃vejɑ̃s] *f* benevolence, kindness

bienveil-lant [bjɛ̃vejɑ̃] **bienveil-lante** [bjɛ̃vejɑ̃t] *adj* benevolent, kindly, kind

bienvenir [bjɛ̃vnir] *intr*—**se faire bienvenir** to make oneself welcome

bienve-nu -nue [bjɛ̃vny] *adj* welcome || *m*—**soyez le bienvenu!** welcome! || *f* welcome; **souhaiter la bienvenue à** to welcome

bière [bjɛr] *f* beer; coffin; **bière à la pression** draft beer

biffer [bife] *tr* to cross out, to cancel, to erase; (slang) to cut (*class*)

biffin [bifɛ̃] *m* (slang) ragman; (slang) doughboy, G.I. Joe

bifo-cal -cale [bifɔkal] *adj* (pl **-caux** [ko]) bifocal

bifteck [biftɛk] *m* beefsteak

bifurquer [bifyrke] *tr* to bifurcate, divide into two branches || *intr & ref* to bifurcate, fork; to branch off

bigame [bigam] *adj* bigamous || *mf* bigamist

bigamie [bigami] *f* bigamy

bigar·ré -rée [bigare] *adj* mottled, variegated; motley (*crowd*)

bigar·reau [bigaro] *m* (*pl* **-reaux**) white-heart cherry

bigarrer [bigare] *tr* to mottle, to variegate, to streak

bigarrure [bigaryr] *f* variegation, medley, mixture

bigle [bigl] *adj* cross-eyed ‖ *m* beagle

bigler [bigle] *intr* to squint; to be cross-eyed

bigorne [bigɔrn] *f* two-horn anvil

bigorner [bigɔrne] *tr* to form on the anvil; (slang) to smash

bi·got [bigo] **-gote** [gɔt] *adj* sanctimonious ‖ *mf* religious bigot

bigoterie [bigɔtri] *f* religious bigotry

bigoudi [bigudi] *m* hair curler, roller

bihebdomadaire [biebdɔmadɛr] *adj* semiweekly

bi·jou [biʒu] *m* (*pl* **-joux**) jewel

bijouterie [biʒutri] *f* jewelry; jewelry shop; jewelry business

bijou·tier [biʒutje] **-tière** [tjɛr] *mf* jeweler

bilan [bilɑ̃] *m* balance sheet; balance; petition of bankruptcy; **faire le bilan** to tabulate the results

bilboquet [bilbɔkɛ] *m* job printing

bile [bil] *f* bile; **se faire de la bile** (coll) to worry, fret

bi·lieux [biljø] **-lieuse** [ljøz] *adj* bilious; irascible, grouchy

bilingue [bilɛ̃g] *adj* bilingual

billard [bijar] *m* billiards; billiard table; billiard room

bille [bij] *f* ball; ball bearing; billiard ball; marble; log; **à bille ball-point** (*pen*)

billet [bijɛ] *m* note; ticket; bill (*currency*); **billet à ordre** promissory note; **billet d'abonnement** season ticket; **billet d'aller et retour** round-trip ticket; **billet de banque** bank note; **billet de correspondance** transfer; **billet de faire-part** announcement, notification (*of birth, wedding, death*); **billet de logement** billet; **billet doux** love letter; **billet simple** one-way ticket

billette [bijɛt] *f* billet

billevesée [bijvəze], [bilvəze] *f* nonsense

billion [biljɔ̃] *m* trillion (U.S.A.); billion (Brit)

billot [bijo] *m* block, chopping block; executioner's block

biloquer [bilɔke] *tr* to plow deeply

bimen·suel -suelle [bimɑ̃sɥɛl] *adj* semimonthly

bimes·triel -trielle [bimɛstriel] *adj* bimonthly (*every two months*)

bimoteur [bimɔtœr] *adj* twin-motor ‖ *m* twin-motor plane

binaire [binɛr] *adj* binary

biner [bine] *tr* to hoe; to cultivate, to work over (*the soil*) ‖ *intr* to say two masses the same day

binette [binɛt] *f* hoe; (hist) wig; (slang) phiz

bineur [binœr] *m* or **bineuse** [binøz] *f* cultivator (*implement*)

binocle [binɔkl] *m* lorgnette

binoculaire [binɔkylɛr] *adj* & *f* binocular

binôme [binom] *adj* & *m* binomial

biochimie [bjɔʃimi] *f* biochemistry

biographe [bjɔgraf] *mf* biographer

biographie [bjɔgrafi] *f* biography

biographique [bjɔgrafik] *adj* biographical

biologie [bjɔlɔʒi] *f* biology

biologiste [bjɔlɔʒist] *mf* biologist

biophysique [bjɔfizik] *f* biophysics

biopsie [bjɔpsi] *f* biopsy

bioxyde [bjɔksid] *m* dioxide

bipar·ti -tie [biparti] *adj* bipartite

bipartisme [bipartism] *m* bipartisanship

bipartite [bipartit] *adj* bipartite; bipartisan

bipède [biped] *adj* & *mf* biped ‖ *m* pair of legs of a horse

biplan [biplɑ̃] *m* biplane

bique [bik] *f* nanny goat

bir·man [birmɑ̃] **-mane** [man] *adj* Burmese ‖ (*cap*) *mf* Burmese (*person*)

Birmanie [birmani] *f* Burma; **la Birmanie** Burma

bis [bi] **bise** [biz] *adj* gray-brown ‖ [bis] *m*—**un bis** an encore ‖ *f* see **bise** ‖ bis [bis] *adv* twice; (mus) repeat; **sept bis** seven A, seven and a half ‖ bis [bis] *interj* encore!

bisaïeul bisaïeule [bizajœl] *mf* great-grand-parent ‖ *m* great-grandfather ‖ *f* great-grandmother

bisan·nuel -nuelle [bizanɥel] *adj* biennial

bisbille [bisbij] *f* (coll) squabble

biscaïen [biskajē] **biscaïenne** [biskajen] *adj* Biscayan ‖ (*cap*) *mf* Biscayan (*person*)

biscor·nu -nue [biskɔrny] *adj* misshapen, distorted

biscotin [biskɔtē] *m* hardtack

biscotte [biskɔt] *f* zwieback

biscuit [biskɥi] *m* hardtack; cracker; cookie; unglazed porcelain; **biscuit soda** soda cracker

bise [biz] *f* north wind; (fig) winter; (slang) kiss

bi·seau [bizo] *m* (*pl* **-seaux**) bevel, chamfer; **en biseau** beveled, chamfered

biseauter [bizote] *tr* to bevel, chamfer; to mark (*cards*)

biser [bize] *tr* to redye ‖ *intr* to blacken

bi·son [bizɔ̃] **-sonne** [zɔn] *mf* bison, buffalo

bisque [bisk] *f* bisque

bisquer [biske] *intr* (coll) to be resentful

bissac [bisak] *m* bag, sack

bisser [bise] *tr* to encore; to repeat

bissextile [bisɛkstil] *adj* bissextile, leap, e.g., **année bissextile** leap year

bissexué bissexuée [biseksɥe] *adj* bisexual

bissexuel bissexuelle [biseksɥɛl] *adj* bisexual

bistouri [bisturi] *m* scalpel

bistournage [bisturnaʒ] *m* castration

bistre [bistr] *adj invar* soot-brown ‖ *m* bister, soot-brown

bis·tré -trée [bistre] *adj* swarthy

bisulfate [bisylfat] *m* bisúlfate
bisulfite [bisylfit] *m* bisulfite
bitter [biter] *m* bitters
bitume [bitym] *m* bitumen
bitumer [bityme] *tr* to asphalt
bitumi·neux [bityminø] **-neuse** [nøz] *adj* bituminous
bivouac [bivwak] *m* bivouac
bivouaquer [bivwake] *intr* to bivouac
bizarre [bizar] *adj* bizarre, strange
bizutage [bizyta3] *m* (slang) initiation, hazing
bizuth [bizyt] *m* (slang) freshman
blackbouler [blakbule] *tr* to blackball; (coll) to flunk
bla·fard [blafar] **-farde** [fard] *adj* pallid, pale, wan; lambent (*flame*)
blague [blag] *f* tobacco pouch; (coll) yarn, tall story, blarney; **blague à part** (coll) all joking aside; **faire une blague** (coll) to play a trick; **sale blague** (coll) dirty trick; **sans blague!** (coll) no kidding!
blaguer [blage] *tr* (coll) to kid; **blaguer qn** (coll) to pull s.o.'s leg || *intr* (coll) to kid, to tell tall stories
bla·gueur [blagœr] **-gueuse** [gøz] *adj* (coll) kidding, tongue-in-cheek || *mf* (coll) kidder, joker
blai·reau [blɛro] *m* (*pl* **-reaux**) badger; shaving brush
blâmable [blɑmabl] *adj* blameworthy
blâme [blɑm] *m* blame; **s'attirer un blâme** to receive a reprimand
blâmer [blɑme] *tr* to blame; to disapprove of
blanc [blɑ̃] **blanche** [blɑ̃ʃ] *adj* white; blank; clean; sleepless (*night*); expressionless (*voice*); **blanc comme un linge** white as a sheet || *m* white; blank; white meat; white man; white goods; chalk; bull's-eye; **à blanc** with blank cartridges; **blanc de baleine** spermaceti; **blanc de chaux** whitewash; **en blanc** blank; **en blanc et noir** in black and white
blanc-bec [blɑ̃bɛk] *m* (*pl* **blancs-becs**) (coll) greenhorn, callow youth
blanchâtre [blɑ̃ʃɑtr] *adj* whitish
blanchir [blɑ̃ʃir] *tr* to whiten; to wash or bleach; to whitewash; to blanch (*almonds*) || *intr* to blanch, whiten; to grow old
blanchissage [blɑ̃ʃisaʒ] *m* laundering; sugar refining
blanchisserie [blɑ̃ʃisri] *f* laundry
blanchis·seur [blɑ̃ʃisœr] **blanchis-seuse** [blɑ̃ʃisøz] *mf* launderer || *m* laundryman || *f* laundress, washerwoman
blanc-manger [blɑ̃mɑ̃ʒe] *m* (*pl* **blancs-manger**) blancmange
blanc-seing [blɑ̃sɛ̃] *m* (*pl* **blancs-seings**) carte blanche
bla·sé -sée [blaze] *adj* blasé, jaded
blaser [blaze] *tr* to cloy, to blunt
blason [blazɔ̃] *m* (heral) blazon
blasonner [blazɔne] *tr* (heral) to blazon
blasphéma·teur [blasfematœr] **-teuse** [tøz] *adj* blasphemous, blaspheming || *mf* blasphemer
blasphématoire [blasfematwar] *adj* blasphemous
blasphème [blasfɛm] *m* blasphemy

blasphémer [blasfeme] §10 *tr & intr* to blaspheme
blatte [blat] *f* cockroach
blé [ble] *m* wheat; **blé à moudre** grist; **blé de Turquie** corn; **blé froment** wheat; **blé noir** buckwheat; **manger son blé en herbe** to spend one's money before one has it
bled [blɛd] *m* (coll) backwoods, hinterland
blême [blɛm] *adj* pale; livid, sallow, wan; ghastly
blêmir [blemir] *intr* to turn pale or livid, to blanch; to grow dim
blennorragie [blenɔraʒi] *f* gonorrhea
blèse [blɛz] *adj* lisping || *mf* lisper
blésement [blɛzmɑ̃] *m* lisping
bléser [bleze] §10 *intr* to lisp
bles·sé -sée [blese] *adj* wounded || *mf* injured person; victim; casualty
blesser [blese], [blɛse] *tr* to wound; to injure
blessure [blesyr] *f* wound; injury
blet blette [blɛt] *adj* overripe || *f* chard
blettir [bletir] *intr* to overripen
bleu bleue [blø] (*pl* **bleus bleues**) *adj* blue; fairy (*stories*); violent (*anger*); rare (*meat*) || *m* blue; bluing; bruise; sauce for cooking fish; telegram or pneumatic letter; (coll) raw recruit, greenhorn; **bleu barbeau** light blue; **bleu marine** navy blue; **bleus** coveralls, dungarees; **passer au bleu** to avoid, elude (*a question*); **petit bleu** bad wine
bleuâtre [bløɑtr] *adj* bluish
bleuet [bløɛ] *m* bachelor's-button
bleuir [bløir] *tr & intr* to turn blue
bleu·té -tée [bløte] *adj* bluish
blindage [blɛ̃daʒ] *m* armor plate; armor plating; (elec) shield
blin·dé -dée [blɛ̃de] *adj* armored; armor-plated; (elec) shielded || *m* (mil) tank
blinder [blɛ̃de] *tr* to armor-plate; (elec) to shield
bloc [blɔk] *m* block; blocking; tablet, pad (*of paper*); (elec, mach) unit; **à bloc tight**; **en bloc** all together, in a lump; **envoyer** or **mettre au bloc** (slang) to throw (*s.o.*) in the jug; **serrer le frein à bloc** to jam on the brakes
blocage [blɔkaʒ] *m* blockage, blocking; lumping together; rubble; freezing (*of prices; of wages*); application (*of brakes*)
blocaille [blɔkaj] *f* rubble
bloc-diagramme [blɔkdjagram] *m* (*pl* **blocs-diagrammes**) cross section
bloc-moteur [blɔkmɔtœr] *m* (aut) motor and transmission system
bloc-notes [blɔknɔt] *m* (*pl* **blocs-notes**) scratch pad, note pad
blocus [blɔkys] *m* blockade
blond [blɔ̃] **blonde** [blɔ̃d] *adj* blond || *m* blond || *f* see **blonde**
blondasse [blɔ̃das] *adj* washed-out blond
blonde [blɔ̃d] *f* blonde; blond lace; **blonde platinée** platinum blonde
blon·din [blɔ̃dɛ̃] **-dine** [din] *adj* fair-

haired ‖ *mf* blond ‖ *m* cableway; hopper for concrete; (obs) fop

blondir [blɔ̃dir] *tr* to bleach ‖ *intr* to turn yellow, become blond

bloquer [blɔke] *tr* to blockade; to block up; to fill with rubble; to jam on (*the brakes*); to stop (*a car*) by jamming on the brakes; to pocket (*a billiard ball*); to run on (*two paragraphs*); to tighten (*a nut or bolt*) as much as possible; to freeze (*wages*)

blottir [blɔtir] *ref* to cower; to curl up

blouse [bluz] *f* smock; billiard pocket

blouser [bluze] *tr* to deceive, take in ‖ *intr* to pucker around the waist ‖ *ref* to be mistaken

blouson [bluzɔ̃] *m* jacket

blouson-noir [bluzɔ̃nwar] *m* (*pl* **blousons-noirs**) juvenile delinquent

blue-jean [bludʒin] *m* blue jeans

bluet [blye] *m* bachelor's-button; (Canad) blueberry

bluette [blyet] *f* piece of light fiction; spark, flash

bluffer [blyfe] *tr & intr* to bluff

bluf·feur [blyfœr] **bluf·feuse** [blyføz] *mf* bluffer

blutage [blytaʒ] *m* bolting, sifting; boltings, siftings

bluter [blyte] *tr* to bolt, to sift

blutoir [blytwar] *m* bolter, sifter

B.N. *abbr* (**Bibliothèque Nationale**) National Library

boa [bɔa] *m* boa

bobard [bɔbar] *m* (coll) fish story, tall tale

bobèche [bɔbɛʃ] *f* bobeche (*disk to catch drippings of candle*)

bobine [bɔbin] *f* bobbin; spool, reel; (elec) coil; **bobine d'allumage** (aut) ignition coil

bobiner [bɔbine] *tr* to spool, wind

bocage [bɔkaʒ] *m* grove

boca·ger [bɔkaʒe] **-gère** [ʒer] *adj* wooded

bo·cal [bɔkal] *m* (*pl* **-caux** [ko]) jar, bottle, globe; fishbowl

boche [bɔʃ] *adj & mf* (slang & pej) German

bock [bɔk] *m* beer glass (*half pint*); glass of beer; enema; douche

boëte [bwet] *f* fish bait

bœuf [bœf] *m* (*pl* **bœufs** [bø]) beef; head of beef; steer; ox; **bœuf en conserve** corned beef

boggie [bɔʒi] *m* (rr) truck

bogue [bɔgi] *f* chestnut bur

Bohême [bɔɛm] *f* Bohemia; **la Bohême** Bohemia

bohème [bɔɛm] *adj & mf* Bohemian (*artist*) ‖ *f*—**la bohème** Bohemia (*of the artistic world*)

bohé·mien [bɔemjɛ̃] **-mienne** [mjɛn] *adj* Bohemian; gypsy ‖ (*cap*) *mf* Bohemian; gypsy

boire [bwar] *m* drink; drinking; **le boire et le manger** food and drink ‖ §8 *tr* to drink; to swallow (*an affront*) ‖ *intr* to drink; **boire à la santé de** to drink to the health of; **boire à (même)** to drink out of (*a bottle*); **boire comme un trou** to

drink like a fish; **boire dans** to drink out of (*a glass*)

bois [bwa], [bwa] *m* wood; woods; horns, antlers; **bois de chauffage** firewood; **bois de lit** bedstead; **bois flotté** driftwood; **bois fondu** plastic wood; **les bois** (mus) the woodwinds

boisage [bwazaʒ] *m* timbering

boi·sé **-sée** [bwaze] *adj* wooded; paneled

boiser [bwaze] *tr* to panel, to wainscot; to timber (*a mine*); to reforest

boiserie [bwazri] *f* woodwork, paneling, wainscoting

bois·seau [bwaso] *m* (*pl* **bois·seaux**) bushel

boisson [bwasɔ̃] *f* drink, beverage; **boissons hygiéniques** light wines, beer, and soft drinks

boîte [bwat] *f* box; can; canister; (slang) joint, dump; **boîte aux lettres** mailbox; **boîte de nuit** night club; **boîte d'essieu** (mach) journal box; **boîte de vitesses** transmission-gear box; **boîte postale** post-office box; **en boîte** boxed; canned; **ferme ta boîte!** (slang) shut up!; **mettre en boîte** to box; to can; (slang) to make fun of

boiter [bwate] *intr* to limp

boi·teux [bwatø] **-teuse** [tøz] *adj* lame, limping; unsteady, wobbly (*chair*) ‖ *mf* lame person

boî·tier [bwatje] **-tière** [tjer] *mf* box-maker; mail collector (*from mailboxes*) ‖ *m* box, case; kit; medicine kit; (mach) housing; **boîtier de montre** watchcase

boître [bwat] *f* fish bait

bol [bɔl] *m* bowl, basin; cud; bolus, pellet

bolchevique [bɔlʃevik] *adj* Bolshevik ‖ (*cap*) *mf* Bolshevik

bolcheviste [bɔlʃevist] *adj* Bolshevik ‖ (*cap*) *mf* Bolshevik

bolduc [bɔldyk] *m* colored ribbon

bolée [bɔle] *f* bowlful

bolide [bɔlid] *m* meteorite, fireball; racing car

bombance [bɔ̃bɑ̃s] *f* (coll) feast; **faire bombance** (coll) to have a blowout

bombardement [bɔ̃bardəmɑ̃] *m* bombing; bombardment

bombarder [bɔ̃barde] *tr* to bomb; to bombard; (coll) to appoint at the last minute

bombardier [bɔ̃bardje] *m* bomber; bombardier

bombe [bɔ̃b] *f* bomb; **bombe à hydrogène** hydrogen bomb; **bombe atomique** atomic bomb; **bombe glacée** molded ice cream; **bombe volante** buzz bomb; **faire la bombe** (slang) to go on a spree

bom·bé **-bée** [bɔ̃be] *adj* convex, bulging

bomber [bɔ̃be] *tr* to bend, to arch; to stick out (*one's chest*); **bomber le torse** (fig) to stick one's nose up ‖ *intr & ref* to bulge

bon [bɔ̃] **bonne** [bɔn] *adj* §91 good; **à quoi bon?** what's the use?; **sentir bon** to smell good; **tenir bon** to hold fast

|| (when standing before noun) *adj* §91 good; fast (*color*) || *m* coupon; **bon de commande** order blank; **pour de bon** or **pour tout de bon** for good, really || *f* see **bonne** || **bon** *interj* good!; what!

bonace [bɔnas] *f* calm (*of the sea*)

bonasse [bɔnas] *adj* simple, naïve

bon-bec [bɔ̃bɛk] *m* (*pl* **bons-becs**) fast talker

bonbon [bɔ̃bɔ̃] *m* bonbon, piece of candy

bonbonne [bɔ̃bɔn] *f* demijohn

bonbonnière [bɔ̃bɔnjɛr] *f* candy dish; candy box

bond [bɔ̃] *m* bound, bounce; leap, jump; **faire faux bond to** to miss an appointment; **faux bond** misstep

bonde [bɔ̃d] *f* plug; bunghole; sluice gate

bon-dé -dée [bɔ̃de] *adj* crammed

bondir [bɔ̃dir] *intr* to bound, to bounce; to leap, to jump; **faire bondir** to make (*s.o.*) hit the ceiling

bondissement [bɔ̃dismɑ̃] *m* bouncing, leaping

bondon [bɔ̃dɔ̃] *m* bung

bonheur [bɔnœr] *m* happiness; good luck; **au petit bonheur** by chance, at random; **par bonheur** luckily

bonheur-du-jour [bɔnœrdyʒur] *m* (*pl* **bonheurs-du-jour**) escritoire

bonhomie [bɔnɔmi] *f* good nature; credulity

bonhomme [bɔnɔm] *adj* good-natured, simple-minded || *m* (*pl* **bonshommes** [bɔ̃zɔm]) fellow, guy; old fellow; **bonhomme de neige** snowman; **Bonhomme Hiver** Jack Frost; **faux bonhomme** humbug; **petit bonhomme** little man (*child*)

boni [bɔni] *m* bonus; discount coupon; surplus (*over estimated expenses*)

bonification [bɔnifikasjɔ̃] *f* improvement; discount; bonus; advantage

bonifier [bɔnifje] *tr* to improve; to give a discount to

boniment [bɔnimɑ̃] *m* sales talk, smooth talk

bonimenteur [bɔnimɑ̃tœr] *m* huckster, charlatan

bonjour [bɔ̃ʒur] *m* good day, good morning, good afternoon, hello

bonne [bɔn] *f* maid; **bonne à tout faire** maid of all work

bonne-maman [bɔnmamɑ̃] *f* (*pl* **bonnes-mamans**) grandma

bonnement [bɔnmɑ̃] *adv* honestly, plainly

bonnet [bɔnɛ] *m* bonnet; stocking cap; cup (*of a brassiere*); (mil) undress hat; **bonnet d'âne** dunce cap; **bonnet de nuit** nightcap; **gros bonnet** (coll) VIP

bonneterie [bɔnɛtri] *f* hosiery; knitwear

bon-papa [bɔ̃papa] *m* (*pl* **bons-papas**) grandpa

bonsoir [bɔ̃swar] *m* good evening; (coll) good night

bonté [bɔ̃te] *f* goodness; kindness

booster [bustœr] *m* (rok) booster

borborygme [bɔrbɔrigm] *m* rumbling (*in the stomach*)

bord [bɔr] *m* edge, border; rim, brim; side (*of a ship*); **à bord** on board; **à pleins bords** overflowing; without hindrance; **à ras bords** full to the brim; **être du (même) bord de** to be of the same mind as; **faux bord** list (*of ship*); **jeter par-dessus bord** to throw overboard

bordage [bɔrdaʒ] *m* edging (*of dress*); planking (*of ship*)

bordé [bɔrde] *m* border, edging

bordée [bɔrde] *f* broadside, volley; (naut) tack; **bordée de bâbord** port watch; **bordée de tribord** starboard watch; **courir une bordée** to go skylarking on shore leave; **tirer une bordée** to jump ship

bordel [bɔrdɛl] *m* (vulgar) brothel

borde-lais [bɔrdəlɛ] **-laise** [lɛz] *adj* of Bordeaux || *f* Bordeaux cask || (*cap*) *mf* native or inhabitant of Bordeaux

border [bɔrde] *tr* to border; to hem; to sail along (*the coast*); **border un lit** to make a bed

borde-reau [bɔrdəro] *m* (*pl* **-reaux**) itemized account, memorandum

bordure [bɔrdyr] *f* border

bore [bɔr] *m* boron

boréal boréale [bɔreal] *adj* (*pl* **boréaux** [bɔreo] or **boréals**) boreal; northern

borgne [bɔrɲ] *adj* one-eyed; blind in one eye; disreputable (*bar, house, etc.*) || *mf* one-eyed person

borne [bɔrn] *f* landmark; boundary stone; milestone; (elec) binding post, terminal; (slang) kilometer; **bornes** bounds, limits

bor-né -née [bɔrne] *adj* limited, narrow; dull (*mind*)

borner [bɔrne] *tr* to mark out the boundary of; to set limits to || *ref* to restrain oneself

bosquet [bɔskɛ] *m* grove

bosse [bɔs] *f* hump; bump; (coll) flair

bosseler [bɔsle] §34 *tr* to emboss; to dent

bossoir [bɔswar] *m* davit; bow (*of ship*)

bos-su -sue [bɔsy] *adj* hunchbacked || *mf* hunchback; **rire comme un bossu** to split one's sides laughing

botanique [bɔtanik] *adj* botanical || *f* botany

botte [bɔt] *f* boot; bunch (*e.g., of radishes*); sword thrust; **lécher les bottes à qn** (coll) to lick s.o.'s boots

botteler [bɔtle] §34 *tr* to tie in bunches

botter [bɔte] *tr* to boot, to boot out; **cela me botte** that suits me || *ref* to put on one's boots

bottier [bɔtje] *m* custom shoemaker

Bottin [bɔtɛ̃] *m* business directory

bottine [bɔtin] *f* high button shoe

boubouler [bubule] *intr* to hoot like an owl

bouc [buk] *m* billy goat; goatee; **bouc émissaire** scapegoat

boucan [bukɑ̃] *m* smokehouse; (coll) uproar

boucaner [bukane] *tr* to smoke (*meat*)

boucanier [bukanje] *m* buccaneer

boucharde [buʃard] *f* bushhammer

bouche [buʃ] *f* mouth; muzzle (*of gun*); door (*of oven*); entrance (*to subway*); **bouche close!** mum's the word!; **bouche d'incendie** fire hydrant; **bouches mouth** (*of river*); **faire la petite bouche à** to turn up one's nose at

bouchée [buʃe] *f* mouthful; patty; chocolate cream (*candy*)

boucher [buʃe] *m* butcher ‖ *tr* to stop up, to plug; to wall up; to cut off (*the view*); to bung (*a barrel*); to cork (*a bottle*); **bouché à l'émeri** (coll) completely dumb ‖ *ref* to be stopped up

boucherie [buʃri] *f* butcher shop; **boucherie chevaline** horsemeat butcher shop

bouche-trou [buʃtru] *m* (*pl* -**trous**) stopgap

bouchon [buʃɔ̃] *m* cork, stopper; bob (*on a fishline*); **bouchon de circulation** traffic jam

bouclage [buklaʒ] *m* closing of circuit; (mil) encirclement

boucle [bukl] *f* buckle; earring; curl; (aer) loop; **boucler la boucle** to loop the loop

boucler [bukle] *tr* to buckle; to curl (*the hair*); to lock up (*prisoners*); to put a nose ring on (*a bull*); **boucler son budget** (coll) to make ends meet; **la boucler** (slang) to shut up, to button one's lip ‖ *intr* to curl

bouclier [buklije] *m* shield; **bouclier antithermique** heat shield

bouddhisme [budism] *m* Buddhism

bouddhiste [budist] *adj* & *mf* Buddhist

bouder [bude] *tr* to be distant toward ‖ *intr* to pout, sulk

bou·deur [budœr] -**deuse** [døz] *adj* pouting ‖ *mf* sullen person

boudin [budɛ̃] *m* blood sausage; **à boudin** spiral

boudiner [budine] *tr* to twist

boue [bu] *f* mud

bouée [bwe] *f* buoy; **bouée de sauvetage** life preserver

boueur [bwœr] *m* garbage collector; scavenger

bou·eux [bwø] **boueuse** [bwøz] *adj* muddy; grimy; (typ) smeary

bouf·fant [bufɑ̃] **bouf·fante** [bufɑ̃t] *adj* puffed (*sleeves*); baggy (*trousers*)

bouffe [buf] *adj* comic (*opera*) ‖ *f* (slang) grub

bouffée [bufe] *f* puff, gust

bouffer [bufe] *tr* (slang) to gobble up ‖ *intr* to puff out

bouf·fi -**fie** [bufi] *adj* puffed up or out

bouffir [bufir] *tr* & *intr* to puff up

bouffissure [bufisyr] *f* swelling

bouf·fon [bufɔ̃] **bouf·fonne** [bufɔn] *adj* & *m* buffoon, comic

bouffonnerie [bufɔnri] *f* buffoonery

bouge [buʒ] *m* bulge; hovel, dive

bougeoir [buʒwar] *m* flat candlestick

bougeotte [buʒɔt] *f* (coll) wanderlust

bouger [buʒe] §38 *tr*—**ne bougez rien!** (coll) don't move a thing! ‖ *intr* to budge, stir

bougie [buʒi] *f* candle; candlepower; spark plug

bou·gon [bugɔ̃] -**gonne** [gɔn] *adj* grumbling ‖ *mf* grumbler

bougran [bugrɑ̃] *m* buckram

bou·gre [bugr] -**gresse** [grɛs] *mf* (slang) customer; **bougre d'âne** (slang) perfect ass ‖ *m* (slang) guy; **bon bougre** (slang) swell guy ‖ *f* (slang) wench

bougrement [bugrəmɑ̃] *adv* (slang) awfully, darned

bouillabaisse [bujabɛs] *f* bouillabaisse, fish stew, chowder

bouil·lant [bujɑ̃] **bouil·lante** [bujɑ̃t] *adj* boiling; fiery, impetuous

bouilleur [bujœr] *m* distiller (*of brandy*); boiler tube; small nuclear reactor

bouilli [buji] *m* beef stew

bouillir [bujir] §9 *tr* & *intr* to boil; **faire bouillir la marmite** (coll) to bring home the bacon

bouilloire [bujwar] *f* kettle

bouillon [bujɔ̃] *m* broth, bouillon; bubble; bubbling; cheap restaurant; **à gros bouillons** gushing; **boire un bouillon** (coll) to gulp water; (coll) to suffer business losses; **bouillon de culture** (bact) broth; **bouillon d'onze heures** poisoned drink; **bouillons** unsold copies, remainders

bouillonnement [bujɔnmɑ̃] *m* boiling; effervescence

bouillonner [bujɔne] *tr* to put puffs in (*a dress*) ‖ *intr* to boil up; to have copies left over

bouillotte [bujɔt] *f* hot-water bottle

boulanger [bulɑ̃ʒe] *m* baker ‖ §38 *intr* to bake bread

boulangerie [bulɑ̃ʒri] *f* bakery

boule [bul] *f* ball; (slang) nut, head; **boule d'eau chaude** hot-water bottle; **boule de neige** snowball; **boule noire** blackball; **boules** bowling; **en boule** (fig) tied in a knot, on edge; **perdre la boule** (slang) to go off one's rocker; **se mettre en boule** (coll) to get mad

bou·leau [bulo] *m* (*pl* -**leaux**) birch

boule-de-neige [buldəneʒ] *f* (*pl* **boules-de-neige**) guelder-rose; meadow mushroom

bouledogue [buldɔg] *m* bulldog

bouler [bule] *tr* to pad (*a bull's horn*) ‖ *intr* to roll like a ball; **envoyer bouler** (slang) to send (*s.o.*) packing

boulet [bulɛ] *m* cannonball; (coll) cross to bear

boulette [bulɛt] *f* ball, pellet

boulevard [bulvar] *m* boulevard; **boulevard périphérique** belt road

boulevar·dier [bulvardje] -**dière** [djɛr] *adj* fashionable ‖ *m* boulevardier, man about town

bouleversement [bulvɛrsmɑ̃] *m* upset

bouleverser [bulvɛrse] *tr* to upset; to overthrow

boulier [bulje] *m* abacus (*for scoring billiards*)

bouline [bulin] *f* (naut) bowline

boulingrin [bulɛ̃grɛ̃] *m* bowling green

bouliste [bulist] *mf* bowler

boulodrome [bulɔdrɔm] *m* bowling alley

boulon [bulɔ̃] *m* bolt; **boulon à œil** eyebolt

boulonner [bulɔne] *tr* to bolt ‖ *intr* (slang) to work

bou·lot [bulo] **-lotte** [lɔt] *adj* (coll) dumpy, squat ‖ *m* (slang) cylindrical loaf of bread; (slang) work

boulotter [bulɔte] *tr* (slang) to eat

boum [bum] *interj* boom!

bouquet [buke] *m* bouquet; clump (*of trees*); prawn; jack rabbit; **c'est le bouquet** (coll) it's tops; (coll) that's the last straw

bouquetière [buktjɛr] *f* flower girl

bouquin [bukɛ̃] *m* (coll) book; (coll) old book

bouquiner [bukine] *intr* to shop around for old books; (coll) to read

bouquinerie [bukinri] *f* secondhand books; secondhand bookstore

bouqui·neur [bukinœr] **-neuse** [nøz] *mf* collector of old books; browser in bookstores

bouquiniste [bukinist] *mf* secondhand bookdealer

bourbe [burb] *f* mire

bour·beux [burbø] **-beuse** [bøz] *adj* miry, muddy

bourbier [burbje] *m* quagmire

bourbillon [burbijɔ̃] *m* core (*of boil*)

bourde [burd] *f* (coll) boner

bourdon [burdɔ̃] *m* bumblebee; big bell; (mus) bourdon; **avoir le bourdon** (slang) to have the blues; **faux bourdon** drone

bourdonnement [burdɔnmɑ̃] *m* buzzing

bourdonner [burdɔne] *tr* (coll) to hum (*a tune*) ‖ *intr* to buzz

bourg [bur] *m* market town

bourgade [burgad] *f* small town

bour·geois [burʒwa] **-geoise** [ʒwaz] *adj* bourgeois, middle-class ‖ *mf* commoner, middle-class person; Philistine; **gros bourgeois** solid citizen ‖ *m* businessman; **en bourgeois** in civies ‖ *f* (slang) old woman (*wife*)

bourgeoisie [burʒwazi] *f* middle class; **haute bourgeoisie** upper middle class; **petite bourgeoisie** lower middle class

bourgeon [burʒɔ̃] *m* bud; pimple

bourgeonnement [burʒɔnmɑ̃] *m* budding

bourgeonner [burʒɔne] *intr* to bud; to break out in pimples

bourgeron [burʒərɔ̃] *m* jumper, overalls; sweat shirt

bourgogne [burgɔɲ] *m* Burgundy (*wine*) ‖ (*cap*) *f* Burgundy (*province*); **la Bourgogne** Burgundy

bourgui·gnon [burgiɲɔ̃] **-gnonne** [ɲɔn] *adj* Burgundian (*dialect*) ‖ (*cap*) *mf* Burgundian

bourlinguer [burlɛ̃ge] *intr* to labor (*in high seas*); (coll) to travel, to venture forth

bourrade [burad] *f* sharp blow; poke

bourrage [buraʒ] *m* cramming; **bourrage de crâne** (coll) ballyhoo

bourre [bur] *f* stuffing, animal hair

bour·reau [buro] *m* (*pl* **-reaux**) execu-tioner; torturer; **bourreau des cœurs** lady-killer; **bourreau de travail** glutton for work

bourrée [bure] *f* fagot of twigs

bourreler [burle] §34 *tr* to torment

bourrelet [burlɛ] *m* weather stripping; roll (*of fat*); contour pillow

bourrer [bure] *tr* to stuff, cram; **bourrer de coups** to pummel, slug; **bourrer le crâne à** (coll) to hand (*s.o.*) a line, to take (*s.o.*) in ‖ *ref* to stuff

bourriche [buriʃ] *f* hamper

bourrique [burik] *f* she-ass; (coll) ass

bour·ru -rue [bury] *adj* rough; grumpy; unfermented (*wine*)

bourse [burs] *f* purse; scholarship, fellowship; stock exchange, bourse; **bourse du travail** labor union hall; **bourses** scrotum

bourse-à-pasteur [bursapastœr] *f* (*pl* **bourses-à-pasteur** [bursapastœr]) (bot) shepherd's-purse

boursicaut or **boursicot** [bursiko] *m* little purse; nest egg

boursicoter [bursikɔte] *intr* to dabble in the stock market

bour·sier [bursje] **-sière** [sjer] *adj* scholarship (*student*); stock-market (*operation*) ‖ *mf* scholar (*holder of scholarship*); speculator

boursoufler [bursufle] *tr* to puff up

bousculer [buskyle] *tr* to jostle

bouse [buz] *f* **bouse de vache** cow dung

bouseux [buzø] *m* (slang) peasant

bousillage [buzijaʒ] *m* cob (*mixture of clay and straw*); (coll) botched job

bousiller [buzije] *tr* (coll) to bungle; (slang) to smash up ‖ *intr* to build with cob

boussole [busɔl] *f* compass; **perdre la boussole** (coll) to go off one's rocker

boustifaille [bustifaj] *f* (slang) feasting; (slang) good food

bout [bu] *m* end; piece, scrap, bit; **à bout** exhausted; **à bout de bras** at arm's length; **à bout portant** point-blank; **à tout bout de champ** at every turn, repeatedly; **au bout du compte** after all; **bout de fil** (telp) (coll) ring, call; **bout de l'an** watch night; **bout d'essai** screen test; **bout d'homme** wisp of a man; **bout filtre** filter tip; **de bout en bout** from start to finish; **montrer le bout de l'oreille** to show one's true colors; **rire du bout des dents** to force a laugh; **sur le bout du doigt** at one's fingertips; **venir à bout de** to succeed in, to triumph over

boutade [butad] *f* sally, quip; whim

bout-dehors [budœr] *m* (*pl* **bouts-dehors**) (naut) boom

boute-en-train [butɑ̃trɛ̃] *m invar* life of the party

boute-feu [butfø] *m* (*pl* **-feux**) firebrand

bouteille [butej] *f* bottle; **bouteille isolante** vacuum bottle

bouteiller [buteje] *m* (hist) cupbearer

bouterolle [butrɔl] *f* ward (*of lock*); rivet snap

boute-selle [butsɛl] *m* boots and saddles (*trumpet call*)

boutique [butik] *f* shop; stock, goods; workshop; set of tools; **boutique cadeaux, boutique de souvenirs** gift shop; **boutique de modiste** millinery shop; **quelle boutique!** (coll) what a hellhole!, what an awful place!

boutiquier [butikje] *m* shopkeeper

bouton [butɔ̃] *m* button; pimple; doorknob; bud; **bouton de puissance** volume control

bouton-d'argent [butɔ̃darʒɑ̃] *m* (*pl* **boutons-d'argent**) sneezewort

bouton-d'or [butɔ̃dɔr] *m* (*pl* **boutons-d'or**) buttercup

boutonner [butɔne] *tr* to button ‖ *intr* to bud

bouton·neux [butɔnø] **bouton·neuse** [butɔnøz] *adj* pimply

boutonnière [butɔnjɛr] *f* buttonhole

bouton-pression [butɔ̃presjɔ̃] *m* (*pl* **boutons-pression**) snap fastener

bouture [butyr] *f* cutting (*from a plant*)

bouturer [butyre] *tr* to propagate (*plants*) by cuttings ‖ *intr* to shoot suckers

bouverie [buvri] *f* cowshed

bou·vier [buvje] **-vière** [vjɛr] *mf* cowherd

bouvillon [buvijɔ̃] *m* steer, young bullock

bouvreuil [buvrœj] *m* bullfinch; **bouvreuil cramoisi** scarlet grosbeak

box [bɔks] *m* (*pl* **boxes**) stall

boxe [bɔks] *f* boxing

boxer [bɔksœr] *m* boxer (*dog*) ‖ [bɔkse] *tr* & *intr* to box

boxeur [bɔksœr] *m* (sports) boxer

boy [bɔj] *m* houseboy; chorus boy

boyau [bwajo] *m* (*pl* **boyaux**) intestine, gut; inner tube; (mil) communication trench

boycottage [bɔjkɔtaʒ] *m* boycott

boycotter [bɔjkɔte] *tr* to boycott

boy-scout [bɔjskut] *m* (*pl* **-scouts**) boy scout

b. p. f. *abbr* (**bon pour francs**) value in francs

bracelet [brasle] *m* bracelet; wristband; **bracelet de caoutchouc** rubber band; **bracelet de cheville** anklet

bracelet-montre [braslemɔ̃tr] *m* (*pl* **bracelets-montres**) wrist watch

braconnage [brakɔnaʒ] *m* poaching

braconner [brakɔne] *intr* to poach

bracon·nier [brakɔnje] **bracon·nière** [brakɔnjɛr] *mf* poacher

brader [brade] *tr* to sell off

braderie [bradri] *f* clearance sale

braguette [braget] *f* fly (*of trousers*)

brahmane [braman] *m* Brahman

brai [brɛ] *m* resin, pitch

braille [braj] *m* braille

brailler [braje] *tr* & *intr* to bawl

brail·leur [brajœr] **brail·leuse** [brajøz] *adj* loudmouthed ‖ *mf* loudmouth

braiment [brɛmɑ̃] *m* bray

braire [brɛr] §68 (usually used in: *inf*; *ger*; *pp*; 3d *sg* & *pl*) *intr* to bray

braise [brɛz] *f* embers, coals

braiser [brɛze] *tr* to braise

braisière [brɛzjɛr] *f* braising pan

bramer [brame] *intr* to bell

bran [brɑ̃] *m* bran; (slang) dung; **bran de scie** sawdust

brancard [brɑ̃kar] *m* stretcher; shaft (*of carriage*)

brancardier [brɑ̃kardje] *m* stretcherbearer

branche [brɑ̃ʃ] *f* branch

brancher [brɑ̃ʃe] *tr* to branch, fork; to hook up, connect; (elec) to plug in ‖ *intr* to perch

brande [brɑ̃d] *f* heather; heath

brandir [brɑ̃dir] *tr* to brandish

brandon [brɑ̃dɔ̃] *m* torch; firebrand; **brandon de discorde** mischief-maker

bran·lant [brɑ̃lɑ̃] **-lante** [lɑ̃t] *adj* shaky, tottering, unsteady

branle [brɑ̃l] *m* oscillation; impetus; **mener le branle** to lead the dance; **mettre en branle** to set in motion

branle-bas [brɑ̃ləba] *m invar* call to battle stations; bustle, commotion

branler [brɑ̃le] *tr* to shake (*the head*) ‖ *intr* to shake; to oscillate; to be loose (*said of tooth*); **branler dans le manche** to be about to fall

braque [brak] *adj* (coll) featherbrained ‖ *mf* (coll) featherbrain ‖ *m* pointer (*dog*)

braquer [brake] *tr* to aim, point; to fix (*the eyes*); to turn (*a steering wheel*); **braquer contre** to turn (*e.g., an audience*) against ‖ *intr* to steer

bras [brɑ] *m* arm; handle; shaft; **à bras raccourcis** violently; **bras de mer** sound (*passage of water*); **bras de pick-up** pickup arm, tone arm; **bras dessus bras dessous** arm in arm; **en bras de chemise** in shirt sleeves; **manquer de bras** to be short-handed

braser [braze] *tr* to braze

brasero [brazero] *m* brazier

brasier [brazje] *m* glowing coals; blaze

bras-le-corps [bralkɔr] *m*—**à bras-le-corps** around the waist

brassage [brasaʒ] *m* brewing

brasse [bras], [brɑs] *f* fathom; breast stroke

brassée [brase] *f* armful; stroke (*in swimming*)

brasser [brase] *tr* to brew

brasserie [brasri] *f* brewery; restaurant, lunchroom

bras·seur [brasœr] **bras·seuse** [brasøz] *mf* brewer; swimmer doing the breast stroke; **brasseur d'affaires** person with many irons in the fire

brassière [brasjɛr] *f* sleeved shirt (*for an infant*); shoulder strap; **brassière de sauvetage** life preserver

bravache [bravaʃ] *adj* & *m* braggart

bravade [bravad] *f* bravado

brave [brav] *adj* brave ‖ (when standing before noun) *adj* worthy, honest ‖ *m* brave man

braver [brave] *tr* to brave

bravoure [bravur] *f* bravery, gallantry

break [brɛk] *m* station wagon

brebis [brəbi] *f* ewe; sheep, lamb; **brebis galeuse** black sheep

brèche [brɛʃ] *f* breach (*in a wall*); gap (*between mountains*); nick (*e.g., on china*); (fig) dent (*in a fortune*);

battre en brèche to batter; (fig) to disparage; **mourir sur la brèche** to go down fighting

bredouille [brəduj]—**rentrer** or **revenir bredouille** to return empty-handed

bredouiller [brəduje] *tr* to stammer out (*an excuse*) || *intr* to mumble

bref [bref] **brève** [brɛv] *adj* brief, short; curt || *m* papal brief || *f* short syllable; **brèves et longues** dots and dashes || **bref** *adv* briefly, in short

brelan [brəlɑ̃] *m* (cards) three of a kind

breloque [brələk] *f* trinket, charm; **battre la breloque** to sound the all clear; to keep irregular time; (coll) to have a screw loose somewhere

brème [brɛm] *f* (ichth) bream

Brésil [brezil] *m*—**le Brésil** Brazil

brési·lien [breziljɛ̃] **-lienne** [ljɛn] *adj* Brazilian || (*cap*) *mf* Brazilian

Bretagne [brətaɲ] *f* Brittany; **la Bretagne** Brittany

bretelle [brətel] *f* strap, sling; access route; **bretelles** suspenders

bre·ton [brətɔ̃] **-tonne** [tɔn] *adj* Breton || *m* Breton (*language*) || (*cap*) *mf* Breton (*person*)

bretteur [brɛtœr] *m* swashbuckler

bretzel [brɛtzel] *m* pretzel

breuvage [brœvaʒ] *m* beverage, drink

brevet [brəve] *m* diploma; license; (mil) commission; **brevet d'invention** patent

breve·té **-tée** [brəvte] *adj* commissioned; patented; **non breveté** noncommissioned || *m* commissioned officer

breveter [brəvte] §34 *tr* to patent

bréviaire [brevjer] *m* (eccl) breviary

bribe [brib] *f* hunk of bread; **bribes** scraps, leavings, fragments

bric [brik] *m*—**de bric et de broc** with odds and ends; somehow

bric-à-brac [brikabrak] *m invar* secondhand merchandise; junk shop

brick [brik] *m* brig (*kind of ship*)

bricolage [brikɔlaʒ] *m* do-it-yourself

bricoler [brikɔle] *intr* to do odd jobs; to putter around

brico·leur [brikɔlœr] **-leuse** [løz] *mf* jack-of-all-trades || *m* handyman

bride [brid] *f* bridle; strap; clamp; **à toute bride** or **à bride abattue** full speed ahead

bridge [bridʒ] *m* (cards, dentistry) bridge

bridger [bridʒe] *intr* to play bridge

brid·geur [bridʒœr] **-geuse** [ʒøz] *mf* bridge player

briefing [brifiŋ] *m* briefing

brièvement [brijɛvmɑ̃] *adv* briefly

brièveté [brijɛvte] *f* brevity

brigade [brigad] *f* brigade

brigadier [brigadje] *m* corporal; police sergeant; noncom

brigand [brigɑ̃] *m* brigand

brigantin [brigɑ̃tɛ̃] *m* brigantine

brigue [brig] *f* intrigue, lobbying

briguer [brige] *tr* to influence underhandedly; to lobby for (*s.th.*); to court (*favor, votes*)

brigueur [brigœr] *m* schemer

bril·lant [brijɑ̃] **bril·lante** [brijɑ̃t] *adj* brilliant, bright || *m* brilliancy, luster; fingernail polish

briller [brije] *intr* to shine; to sparkle; **faire briller** to show (*s.o.*) off

brimade [brimad] *f* hazing

brimborion [brɛ̃bɔrjɔ̃] *m* mere trifle

brimer [brime] *tr* to haze

brin [brɛ̃] *m* blade; sprig, shoot; staple (*of hemp, linen*); strand (*of rope*); belt (*of pulley*); (coll) (little) bit, e.g., **un brin d'air** a (little) bit of air; **ne . . . brin** §90 (archaic) not a bit, not a single; **un beau brin de fille** (coll) a fine figure of a girl

brinde [brɛ̃d] *f* (archaic) toast

brindille [brɛ̃dij] *f* twig, sprig

brioche [brijɔʃ] *f* brioche, breakfast roll

brique [brik] *f* brick

briquer [brike] *tr* (coll) to polish up, scour

briquet [brike] *m* lighter

briquetage [briktaʒ] *m* brickwork

briqueter [brikte] §34 *tr* to brick (up)

briqueterie [briketri] *f* brickyard

briqueteur [briktœr] *m* bricklayer

brisant [brizɑ̃] *m* breakers; **brisants** surf

brise [briz] *f* breeze

bri·sé **-sée** [brize] *adj* broken; folding (*door*) || *fpl* see **brisées**

brise-bise [brizbiz] *m invar* weather stripping; café curtain

brisées [brize] *fpl* track, footsteps

brise-glace [brizglas] *m invar* (naut) icebreaker

brise-jet [brizʒe] *m invar* (anti)splash attachment (*for water faucet*), spray filter

brise-lames [brizlam] *m invar* breakwater

brisement [brizmɑ̃] *m* breaking

briser [brize] *tr, intr, & ref* to break

brise-tout [briztu] *m invar* (coll) butterfingers, clumsy person

bri·seur [brizœr] **-seuse** [zøz] *mf* breaker (*person*); **briseur de grève** strikebreaker

brise-vent [brizvɑ̃] *m invar* windbreak

brisque [brisk] *f* service stripe

bristol [bristol] *m* Bristol board, pasteboard; visiting card

brisure [brizyr] *f* break; joint

britannique [britanik] *adj* British || (*cap*) *mf* Briton

broc [bro] *m* pitcher, jug

brocanter [brɔkɑ̃te] *tr* to buy, sell, or trade (*secondhand articles*) || *intr* to deal in secondhand articles

brocan·teur [brɔkɑ̃tœr] **-teuse** [tøz] *mf* secondhand dealer

brocard [brɔkar] *m* lampoon, brickbat; (zool) brocket; **lancer des brocards** to make sarcastic remarks, to gibe

brocart [brɔkar] *m* brocade

broche [brɔʃ] *f* brooch; pin; (culin) spit, skewer

bro·ché **-chée** [brɔʃe] *adj* paperback, paperbound

brocher [brɔʃe] *tr* to brocade; to sew (*book bindings*); (coll) to hurry through

brochet [brɔʃe] *m* (ichth) pike

brochette [brɔʃɛt] f skewer; skewerful; string (of decorations)

bro·cheur [brɔʃœr] -cheuse [ʃøz] mf bookbinder || f stapler

brochure [brɔʃyr] f brochure, pamphlet

brocoli [brɔkɔli] m broccoli

brodequin [brɔdkɛ̃] m buskin

broder [brɔde] tr & intr to embroider

broderie [brɔdri] f embroidery

brome [brom] m (chem) bromine

bromure [brɔmyr] m bromide

bronche [brɔ̃ʃ] f bronchial tube

broncher [brɔ̃ʃe] intr to stumble; to flinch; to grumble

bronchique [brɔ̃ʃik] adj bronchial

bronchite [brɔ̃ʃit] f bronchitis

bronze [brɔ̃z] m bronze

bron·zé -zée [brɔ̃ze] adj bronze; suntanned

bronzer [brɔ̃ze] tr & ref to bronze; to sun-tan

brook [bruk] m (turf) water jump

broquette [brɔkɛt] f brad, tack

brossage [brɔsaʒ] m brushing

brosse [brɔs] f brush; brosse à cheveux hairbrush; brosse à dents toothbrush; brosse à habits clothesbrush; brosse de chiendent scrubbing brush; brosses shrubs, bushes

brosser [brɔse] tr to brush; to paint the broad outlines of (a picture); (fig) to sketch; (slang) to beat, conquer || ref to brush one's clothes; (coll) to skimp, to scrimp

brouet [brue] m gruel, broth

brouette [bruɛt] f wheelbarrow

brouetter [bruɛte] tr to carry in a wheelbarrow

brouhaha [bruaa] m (coll) babel, hubbub

brouillage [brujaʒ] m (rad) jamming

brouillamini [brujamini] m (coll) mess

brouillard [brujar] adj masc blotting (paper) || m fog, mist; (com) daybook

brouillasse [brujas] f (coll) drizzle

brouillasser [brujase] intr (coll) to drizzle

brouille [bruj] f discord, misunderstanding

brouiller [bruje] tr to mix up; to jam (a broadcast); to scramble (eggs); brouiller mes (ses, etc.) pistes to cover my (his, etc.) tracks || ref to quarrel; to cloud over

brouil·lon [brujɔ̃] brouil·lonne [brujɔn] adj crackpot; blundering; at loose ends || mf crackpot || m scratch pad; draft; outline

broussailles [brusaj] fpl underbrush, brushwood; en broussailles disheveled

broussail·leux [brusajø] broussail·leuse [brusajøz] adj bushy

broussard [brusar] m (coll) bushman, colonist

brousse [brus] f veldt, bush

broutage [brutaʒ] m grazing (of animal); ratatat (of a machine)

brouter [brute] intr to browze, graze; to jerk, to grab (said of clutch, cutting tool, brake)

broutille [brutij] f twig; trifle, bauble

broyage [brwajaʒ] m grinding, crushing

broyer [brwaje] §47 tr to grind, crush; broyer du noir (coll) to be down in the dumps

broyeur [brwajœr] broyeuse [brwajøz] adj grinding, crushing || mf grinder, crusher || f (mach) grinder

bru [bry] f daughter-in-law

bruant [bryɑ̃] m (orn) bunting; bruant jaune yellowhammer

brucelles [brysɛl] fpl tweezers

brugnon [bryɲɔ̃] m nectarine

bruine [bryin] f drizzle

bruiner [bryine] intr to drizzle

bruire [bryir] (usually used in: inf; 3d sg pres ind bruit; 3d sg & pl imperf ind bruyait or bruissait, bruyaient or bruissaient) intr to rustle; to hum, buzz; to splash

bruissement [bryismɑ̃] m rustling

bruit [bryi] m noise; stir, fuss; le bruit court que it is rumored that

bruitage [bryitaʒ] m sound effects

brû·lant [brylɑ̃] -lante [lɑ̃t] adj burning; ardent; ticklish (question)

brû·lé -lée [bryle] adj burned || m smell of burning; burned taste || f (slang) beating

brûle-gueule [brylgœl] m invar (slang) short pipe (for smoking)

brûle-parfum [brylparfœ̃] m invar incense burner

brûle-pourpoint [brylpurpwɛ̃] —à brûle-pourpoint point-blank

brûler [bryle] tr to burn; to burn out (a fuse); to go through (a red light); to pass (another car); to roast (coffee); to distil (liquor); brûler la cervelle à qn to blow s.o.'s brains out || intr to burn, burn up || ref to burn up, to be burned

brû·leur [brylœr] -leuse [løz] mf arsonist; distiller || m (mach) burner; brûleur à café coffee roaster

brûloir [brylwar] m roaster

brûlure [brylyr] f burn

brume [brym] f fog, mist

brumer [bryme] intr to be foggy

bru·meux [brymø] -meuse [møz] adj foggy, misty

brun [brœ̃] brune [bryn] adj dark-brown; dark || m brunet; dark brown || f see brune

brunâtre [brynatr] adj brownish

brune [bryn] f brunette; twilight

bru·net [bryne] -nette [net] adj black-haired || m dark-haired man, brunet || f brunette

bru·ni -nie [bryni] adj burnished, polished || m burnishing, polish

brunir [brynir] tr to brown; to burnish, polish || intr to turn brown

brunissoir [bryniswar] m (mach) buffer

brusque [brysk] adj brusque; sudden; surprise (attack); quick (movements; decision)

brusquer [bryske] tr to hurry, rush through; to be blunt with

brusquerie [bryskri] f brusqueness; suddenness

brut [bry] brute [bryt] adj crude, unpolished, unrefined, uncivilized; un-cut (*diamond*); raw (*material*); dry (*champagne*); brown (*sugar*); gross (*weight*) || *f* see **brute** || **brut** *adv*— **peser brut** to have a gross weight of

bru·tal -tale [brytal] (*pl* **-taux** [to]) *adj* brutal, rough; outspoken; coarse, beastly || *mf* brute, bully

brutaliser [brytalize] *tr* to bully; to mistreat

brutalité [brytalite] *f* brutality; **bruta-lité policière** police brutality

brute [bryt] *f* brute

Bruxelles [brysel] *f* Brussels

bruxel·lois [bryselwa] **bruxel·loise** [bryselwaz] *adj* of Brussels || (*cap*) *mf* native or inhabitant of Brussels

bruyamment [bryijamã] *adv* noisily

bruyant [bryijã] **bruyante** [bryijãt] *adj* noisy

bruyère [bryijer] *f* heather; heath

buanderie [bɥãderi] *f* laundry room

buan·dier [bɥãdje] **-dière** [djer] *mf* laundry worker || *f* laundress

bubonique [bybɔnik] *adj* bubonic

bûche [byʃ] *f* log; (slang) dunce; **bûche de Noël** yule log; cake deco-rated as a yule log; **ramasser une bûche** (slang) to take a tumble

bûcher [byʃe] *m* woodshed; pyre; stake (*e.g., for burning witches*) || *tr* to rough-hew; (slang) to bone up on || *intr* (slang) to keep on working; to slave away || *ref* (slang) to fight

bûche·ron [byʃrɔ̃] **-ronne** [rɔn] *mf* woodcutter || *m* lumberjack

bûchette [byʃet] *f* stick of wood

bû·cheur [byʃœr] **-cheuse** [ʃøz] *mf* (coll) eager beaver

budget [bydʒe] *m* budget; **boucler son budget** (coll) to make ends meet

budgétaire [bydʒeter] *adj* budgetary

buée [bɥe] *f* steam; mist

buffet [byfe] *m* buffet; snack bar; sta-tion restaurant; **danser devant le buffet** to miss a meal

buf·fle [byfl] **buf·flonne** [byflɔn] *mf* water buffalo; Cape buffalo

bugle [bygl] *m* (mus) saxhorn, bugle || *f* (bot) bugle

building [bildiŋ] *m* large office build-ing, skyscraper

buire [bɥir] *f* ewer

buis [bɥi] *m* boxwood

buisson [bɥisɔ̃] *m* bush

buisson·neux [bɥisɔnø] **buisson·neuse** [bɥisɔnøz] *adj* bushy

buisson·nier [bɥisɔnje] **buisson·nière** [bɥisɔnjer] *adj*—**faire l'école buis-sonnière** (coll) to play hooky

bulbe [bylb] *m* bulb

bul·beux [bylbø] **-beuse** [bøz] *adj* bulbous

bulgare [bylgar] *adj* Bulgarian || *m* Bulgarian (*language*) || (*cap*) *mf* Bul-garian (*person*)

Bulgarie [bylgari] *f* Bulgaria; **la Bul-garie** Bulgaria

bulle [byl] *m* wrapping paper || *f* bubble; blister; (eccl) bull

bulletin [byltɛ̃] *m* bulletin; ballot; **bul-letin de bagages** baggage check; **bulletin de commande** order blank;

bulletin de naissance birth certifi-cate; **bulletin scolaire** report card

bul·leux [bylø] **bul·leuse** [byløz] *adj* blistery

bure [byr] *m* mine shaft || *f* drugget, sackcloth

bu·reau [byro] *m* (*pl* **-reaux**) desk; office; **bureau à cylindre** roll-top desk; **bureau ambulant** post-office car; **bureau d'aide sociale** welfare de-partment; **Bureau de l'état civil** Bureau of Vital Statistics; **bureau de location** box office; **bureau de place-ment** employment agency; **bureau de poste** post office; **bureau des objets trouvés** lost-and-found department; **bureau de tabac** tobacco shop; **bu-reau directoire** cabinet, committee; **deuxième bureau** intelligence division

bureaucrate [byrokrat] *mf* bureaucrat

bureaucratie [byrokrasi] *f* bureaucracy

bureaucratique [byrokratik] *adj* bu-reaucratic

burette [byret] *f* cruet; oilcan

burin [byrɛ̃] *m* engraving; burin (*tool*)

burlesque [byrlesk] *adj* & *m* burlesque

busard [byzar] *m* harrier, marsh hawk

busc [bysk] *m* whalebone

buse [byz] *f* buzzard

business [biznes] *m* (slang) work; (slang) complicated business

bus·qué -quée [byske] *adj* arched

buste [byst] *m* bust

but [by], [byt] *m* mark, goal, target; aim, end, purpose; point (*scored in game*); **aller droit au but** to come straight to the point; **de but en blanc** point-blank

bu·té -tée [byte] *adj* obstinate, head-strong || *f* abutment

buter [byte] *tr* to prop up; (slang) to bump off, kill || *intr*—**buter contre** to bump into, to stumble on || *ref*— **se buter à** to butt up against; (fig) to be dead set on

buteur [bytœr] *m* scorekeeper

butin [bytɛ̃] *m* booty; profits, savings

butiner [bytine] *tr* to pillage; to gather honey from || *intr* to pillage; to gather honey (*said of bees*); **bu-tiner dans** to browse among (*books*)

butoir [bytwar] *m* buffer, stop, catch

bu·tor [bytɔr] **-torde** [tɔrd] *mf* (slang) lout, good-for-nothing

butte [byt] *f* butte, knoll; **butte de tir** butt, mound (*for target practice*); **être en butte à** to be exposed to

butter [byte] *tr* to hill (*plants*)

buttoir [bytwar] *m* (agr) hiller

buty·reux [bytirø] **-reuse** [røz] *adj* buttery

buvable [byvabl] *adj* drinkable; (pharm) to be taken by mouth

buvard [byvar] *adj* blotting (*paper*) || *m* blotter

buvette [byvet] *f* bar, fountain

buvette-buffet [byvetbyfe] *f* (coll) snack bar

bu·veur [byvœr] **-veuse** [vøz] *mf* drinker; **buveur d'eau** abstainer; va-cationist at a spa

byzan·tin [bizɑ̃tɛ̃] **-tine** [tin] *adj* Byzantine

C

C, c [se] *m invar* third letter of the French alphabet

C/ *abbr* (**compte**) account

ça [sa] *pron indef* (coll) that; **ah ça non!** no indeed!; **avec ça!** tell me another!; **ça y est** that's that; that's it, that's right; **comment ça!** how so?; **et avec ça?** what else?; **où ça,** where?

çà [sa] *adv*—**ah çà!** now then! **çà et là** here and there

cabale [kabal] *f* cabal, intrigue

cabaler [kabale] *intr* to cabal, intrigue

caban [kabɑ̃] *m* (naut) peacoat

cabane [kaban] *f* cabin, hut

cabanon [kabanɔ̃] *m* hut; padded cell

cabaret [kabarɛ] *m* tavern; cabaret, night club; liquor closet

cabas [kaba] *m* basket

cabestan [kabɛstɑ̃] *m* capstan

cabillaud [kabijo] *m* haddock; (coll) fresh cod

cabine [kabin] *f* cabin (*of ship or airplane*); bathhouse; car (*of elevator*); cab (*of locomotive or truck*); **cabine téléphonique** telephone booth

cabinet [kabinɛ] *m* (*ministry*) cabinet; study (*of scholar*); office (*of professional man*); clientele; staff (*of a cabinet officer*); toilet; storeroom closet; **cabinet d'aisance** rest room; **cabinet de débarras** storeroom closet; **cabinet de toilette** powder room; **cabinets** rest rooms

câble [kabl] *m* cable

câbler [kable] *tr & intr* to cable

câblier [kablije] *m* cable ship

câblogramme [kablɔgram] *m* cablegram

cabo·chard [kabɔʃar] **-charde** [ʃard] *adj* obstinate, pigheaded

caboche [kabɔʃ] *f* hobnail; (coll) noodle (*head*)

cabochon [kabɔʃɔ̃] *m* uncut gem; stud, upholstery nail

cabot [kabo] *m* (ichth) miller's-thumb, bullhead; (coll) ham (*actor*)

cabotage [kabɔtaʒ] *m* coastal navigation, coasting trade

cabo·tin [kabotɛ̃] **-tine** [tin] *mf* barnstormer; (coll) ham actor; **cabotin de la politique** (coll) corny politician, political orator given to histrionics

cabotinage [kabɔtinaʒ] *m* barnstorming; (coll) ham acting

cabotiner [kabɔtine] *intr* to barnstorm; (coll) to play to the grandstand

cabrer [kabre] *tr* to make (*a horse*) rear; to nose up (*a plane*) ‖ *ref* to rear; to kick over the traces; (aer) to nose up

cabri [kabri] *m* (zool) kid

cabriole [kabrijɔl] *f* caper

cabrioler [kabrijɔle] *intr* to caper

cacahouète [kakawɛt] or **cacahuète** [kakaɥɛt] *f* peanut

cacao [kakao] *m* cocoa; cocoa bean

cacaotier [kakaɔtje] *m* (bot) cacao

cacaoyer [kakaɔje] *m* (bot) cacao

cacarder [kakarde] *intr* to cackle

cacatoès [kakatɔɛs] or **cacatois** [kakatwa] *m* cockatoo

cachalot [kaʃalo] *m* sperm whale

cache [kaʃ] *m* masking tape ‖ *f* hiding place

cache-cache [kaʃkaʃ] *m invar* hide-and-seek

cache-col [kaʃkɔl] *m invar* scarf

cachemire [kaʃmir] *m* cashmere

cache-nez [kaʃne] *m invar* muffler

cache-poussière [kaʃpusjɛr] *m invar* duster (*overgarment*)

cacher [kaʃe] *tr* to hide; **cacher q.ch. à qn** to hide s.th. from s.o. ‖ *ref* to hide; **se cacher à** to hide from; **se cacher de q.ch.** to make a secret of s.th.

cache-radiateur [kaʃradjatœr] *m invar* radiator cover

cache-sexe [kaʃsɛks] *m invar* G-string

cachet [kaʃɛ] *m* seal; postmark; fee; price of a lesson; meal ticket; (pharm, phila) cachet; (fig) seal; stylishness; **payer au cachet** to pay a set fee

cacheter [kaʃte] §34 *tr* to seal, to seal up; to seal with wax

cachette [kaʃɛt] *f* hiding place; **en cachette** secretly

cachot [kaʃo] *m* dungeon; prison

cacophonie [kakɔfɔni] *f* cacophony

cactier [kaktje] or **cactus** [kaktys] *m* cactus

c.-à-d. *abbr* (**c'est-à-dire**) that is

cadastre [kadastr] *m* land-survey register

cadavre [kadavr] *m* corpse, cadaver; (slang) dead soldier (*bottle*)

ca·deau [kado] *m* (*pl* **-deaux**) gift

cadenas [kadna] *m* padlock

cadenasser [kadnase] *tr* to padlock

cadence [kadɑ̃s] *f* cadence, rhythm, time; output (*of worker, of factory, etc.*); **cadence de tir** rate of firing

cadencer [kadɑ̃se] §51 *tr* to cadence ‖ *intr* to call out cadence

ca·det [kadɛ] **-dette** [dɛt] *adj* younger ‖ *mf* youngest; junior; (sports) player fifteen to eighteen years old; **le cadet de mes soucis** (coll) the least of my worries ‖ *m* caddy; (mil) cadet; younger brother; younger son ‖ *f* younger sister; younger daughter

cadmium [kadmjɔm] *m* cadmium

cadrage [kadraʒ] *m* (mov, telv) framing; (phot) centering

cadran [kadrɑ̃] *m* dial; **cadran d'appel** telephone dial; **cadran solaire** sundial; **faire le tour du cadran** to sleep around the clock

cadre [kadr] *m* frame; framework; setting; outline, framework (*of a literary work*); limits, scope (*of activities or duties*); (mil) cadre; (naut) cot; **cadres** officials; (mil) regulars; **cadres sociaux** memorable dates or events

cadrer [kadre] *tr* to frame (*film*) ‖ *intr* to conform, tally

ca·duc **-duque** [kadyk] *adj* decrepit,

frail; outlived (*custom*); deciduous (*leaves*); lapsed (*insurance policy*); (law) null and void

caducée [kadyse] *m* caduceus

C.A.F. *abbr* (**coût, assurance, fret**) C.I.F. (*cost, insurance, and freight*)

ca·fard [kafar] **-farde** [fard] *adj* sanctimonious || *mf* hypocrite; (coll) squealer || *m* (coll) cockroach; (coll) blues

café [kafe] *adj invar* tan || *m* coffee; café; coffeehouse; **café chantant** music hall (*with tables*); **café complet** coffee, hot milk, rolls, butter, and jam; **café nature, café noir** black coffee

café-concert [kafekɔ̃ser] *m* (*pl* **cafés-concerts**) music hall (*with tables*), cabaret

caféier [kafeje] *m* coffee plant

caféière [kafejer] *f* coffee plantation

caféine [kafein] *f* caffeine

cafe·tier [kaftje] **-tière** [tjer] *mf* café owner || *f* coffeepot

cafouiller [kafuje] *intr* (slang) to miss (*said of engine*); (slang) to flounder around

cage [kaʒ] *f* cage; **cage d'un ascenseur** elevator shaft; **cage d'un escalier** stairwell; **cage thoracique** thoracic cavity; **en cage** (coll) in the clink, in the pen

cageot [kaʒo] *m* crate

ca·gnard [kaɲar] **-gnarde** [ɲard] *adj* indolent, lazy || *m* (coll) sunny spot

ca·gneux [kaɲø] **-gneuse** [ɲøz] *adj* knock-kneed; pigeon-toed

cagnotte [kaɲɔt] *f* kitty, pool

ca·got [kago] **-gotte** [gɔt] *adj* hypocritical || *mf* hypocrite

cagoule [kagul] *f* cowl; hood (*with eyeholes*)

cahier [kaje] *m* notebook; **cahier à feuilles mobiles** loose-leaf notebook; **cahier des charges** (com) specifications

cahin-caha [kaɛ̃kaa] *adv* (coll) so-so

cahot [kao] *m* jolt, bump

cahoter [kaɔte] *tr & intr* to jolt

caho·teux [kaɔtø] **-teuse** [tøz] *adj* bumpy (*road*)

cahute [kayt] *f* hut, shack

caille [kɑj] *f* quail

cail·lé -lée [kɑje] *adj* curdled || *m* curd

caillebotis [kɑjbɔti] *m* boardwalk; (mil) duckboard; (naut) grating

caillebotte [kɑjbɔt] *f* curds

caillebotter [kɑjbɔte] *tr & intr* to curdle

cailler [kɑje] *tr & ref* to clot, curdle, curd

caillot [kɑjo] *m* clot; blood clot

cail·lou [kaju] *m* (*pl* **-loux**) pebble; (coll) bald head; **caillou du Rhin** rhinestone

caillou·teux [kajutø] **-teuse** [tøz] *adj* stony (*road*); pebbly (*beach*)

cailloutis [kajuti] *m* crushed stone, gravel

Caïn [kaɛ̃] *m* Cain

Caire [ker] *m*—**Le Caire** Cairo

caisse [kes] *f* chest, box; case (*for packing; of a clock or piano*); chest-ful, boxful; till, cash register, coffer, safe; cashier, cashier's window; desk (*in a hotel*); **caisse à eau** water tank; **caisse claire** snare drum; **caisse d'épargne** savings bank; **caisse des écoles** scholarship fund; **grosse caisse** bass drum; bass drummer; **petite caisse** petty cash

caisson [kesɔ̃] *m* caisson

cajoler [kaʒɔle] *tr* to cajole, wheedle

cajolerie [kaʒɔlri] *f* cajolery

cajou [kaʒu] *m* cashew nut

cake [kek] *m* fruit cake

cal [kal] *m* (*pl* **cals**) callus, callosity; **cal vicieux** badly knitted bone

calage [kalaʒ] *m* wedging, chocking; stalling (*of motor*)

calamité [kalamite] *f* calamity

calami·teux [kalamitø] **-teuse** [tøz] *adj* calamitous

calandre [kalɑ̃dr] *f* mangle (*for clothes*); calender (*for paper*); grill (*for car radiator*); (ent) weevil; (orn) lark

calandrer [kalɑ̃dre] *tr* to calender

calcaire [kalker] *adj* calcareous; chalky; hard (*water*) || *m* limestone

calcifier [kalsifje] *tr & ref* to calcify

calciner [kalsine] *tr & ref* to burn to a cinder

calcium [kalsjɔm] *m* calcium

calcul [kalkyl] *m* calculation; (math, pathol) calculus; **calcul biliaire** gallstone; **calcul mental** mental arithmetic; **calcul rénal** kidney stone

calcula·teur [kalkylatœr] **-trice** [tris] *adj* calculating || *mf* calculator (*person*) || *m* (mach) calculator || *f* (mach) computer

calculer [kalkyle] *tr & intr* to calculate

cale [kal] *f* wedge, chock; hold (*of ship*); **cale de construction** stocks; **cale sèche** dry dock

ca·lé -lée [kale] *adj* stalled; (coll) well-informed; (slang) involved, difficult; **calé en** (coll) strong in, up on

calebasse [kalbas] *f* calabash

calèche [kalɛʃ] *f* open carriage

caleçon [kalsɔ̃] *m* drawers, shorts; **caleçon de bain** swimming trunks

calembour [kalɑ̃bur] *m* pun

calendes [kalɑ̃d] *fpl* calends; **aux calendes grecques** (coll) when pigs fly

calendrier [kalɑ̃drije] *m* calendar

calepin [kalpɛ̃] *m* notebook

caler [kale] *tr* to wedge, to chock; to jam; to stall; to lower (*sail*); (naut) to draw || *intr* to stall (*said of motor*); (coll) to give in || *ref* to stall; to get nicely settled

calfater [kalfate] *tr* to caulk

calfeutrer [kalføtre] *tr* to stop up || *ref* to shut oneself up

calibre [kalibr] *m* caliber

calibrer [kalibre] *tr* to calibrate

calice [kalis] *m* chalice; (bot) calyx

calicot [kaliko] *m* calico; sign, banner; (slang) sales clerk

califat [kalifa] *m* caliphate

calife [kalif] *m* caliph

Californie [kaliforni] *f* California; **la basse Californie** Lower California; **la Californie** California

califourchon [kalifur/ʃ5]—**à califourchon** astride, astraddle; **s'asseoir à califourchon** to straddle

câ·lin [kɑlɛ̃] **-line** [lin] *adj* coaxing; caressing

câliner [kaline] *tr* to coax; to caress

cal·leux [kalø] **cal·leuse** [kaløz] *adj* callous, calloused

callisthénie [kalisteni] *f* calisthenics

cal·mant [kalmɑ̃] **-mante** [mɑ̃t] *adj* calming ‖ *m* sedative

calmar [kalmar] *m* squid

calme [kalm] *adj & m* calm

calmement [kalməmɑ̃] *adv* calmly

calmer [kalme] *tr* to calm ‖ *ref* to become calm, to calm down

calmir [kalmir] *intr* to abate

calomnie [kalɔmni] *f* calumny, slander

calomnier [kalɔmnje] *tr* to calumniate

calorie [kalɔri] *f* calory

calorifère [kalɔrifɛr] *adj* heating, heat-conducting ‖ *m* heater; **calorifère à air chaud** hot-air heater; **calorifère à eau chaude** hot-water heater

calorifuge [kalɔrifyʒ] *adj* insulating ‖ *m* insulator

calorifuger [kalɔrifyʒe] §38 *tr* to insulate

calorique [kalɔrik] *adj* caloric

calot [kalo] *m* policeman's hat, kepi

calotte [kalɔt] *f* skullcap; dome; (coll) box on the ear; (coll) clergy; **calotte des cieux** vault of heaven; **flanquer une calotte à** (coll) to box on the ear

calotter [kalɔte] *tr* (coll) to box on the ear, to cuff; (slang) to snitch

calque [kalk] *m* tracing; decal; word-for-word correspondence (*between two languages*); slavish imitation; spitting image

calquer [kalke] *tr* to trace; to imitate slavishly

calumet [kalyme] *m* calumet; **calumet de paix** peace pipe

calvados [kalvados] *m* applejack

calvaire [kalvɛr] *m* calvary

calvinisme [kalvinist] *adj & mf* Calvinist

calvitie [kalvisi] *f* baldness

camarade [kamarad] *mf* comrade; **camarade de chambre** roommate; **camarade de travail** fellow worker; **camarade d'étude** schoolmate

camaraderie [kamaradri] *f* comradeship; camaraderie, fellowship

ca·mard [kamar] **-marde** [mard] *adj* snub-nosed

cambouis [kɑ̃bwi] *m* axle grease

cambrer [kɑ̃bre] *tr* to curve, arch

cambrioler [kɑ̃brijɔle] *tr* to break into, to burglarize

cambrio·leur [kɑ̃brijɔlœr] **-leuse** [løz] *mf* burglar

cambrure [kɑ̃bryr] *f* curve, arch

cambuse [kɑ̃byz] *f* (naut) storeroom between decks

came [kam] *f* cam

camée [kame] *m* cameo

caméléon [kameleɔ̃] *m* chameleon

camélia [kamelja] *m* camellia

camelot [kamlo] *m* cheap woolen cloth; huckster; newsboy

camelote [kamlɔt] *f* shoddy merchandise, rubbish, junk

caméra [kamera] *f* (mov, telv) camera

camion [kamjɔ̃] *m* truck; paint bucket; **camion à remorque** trailer (truck); **camion à semi-remorque** semitrailer; **camion d'enregistrement** (mov) sound truck

camion-benne [kamjɔ̃bɛn] *m* (*pl* **camions-bennes**) dump truck

camion-citerne [kamjɔ̃sitɛrn] *m* (*pl* **camions-citernes**) tank truck

camion-grue [kamjɔ̃gry] *m* (*pl* **camions-grues**) tow truck

camionnage [kamjɔnaʒ] *m* trucking

camionner [kamjɔne] *tr* to truck

camionnette [kamjɔnet] *f* van; **camionnette de police** police wagon; **camionnette sanitaire** mobile health unit

camionneur [kamjɔnœr] *m* trucker; truckdriver, teamster

camisole [kamizɔl] *f* camisole; **camisole de force** strait jacket

camouflage [kamuflaʒ] *m* camouflage

camoufler [kamufle] *tr* to camouflage

camp [kɑ̃] *m* camp

campa·gnard [kɑ̃paɲar] **-gnarde** [ɲard] *adj & m* rustic

campagne [kɑ̃paɲ] *f* campaign; country

cam·pé -pée [kɑ̃pe] *adj* encamped; **bien campé** well-built (*man*); clearly presented (*story*); firmly fixed

campement [kɑ̃pmɑ̃] *m* encampment; camping

camper [kɑ̃pe] *tr* to camp; (coll) to clap (*e.g., one's hat on one's head*); **camper là qn** (coll) to run out on s.o. ‖ *intr & ref* to camp

cam·peur [kɑ̃pœr] **-peuse** [pøz] *mf* camper

camphre [kɑ̃fr] *m* camphor

camping [kɑ̃piŋ] *m* campground; trailer; camping

campos [kɑ̃po] *m* (coll) vacation, day off

campus [kɑ̃pys] *m* campus

ca·mus [kamy] **-muse** [myz] *adj* snub-nosed, pug-nosed, flat-nosed

Canada [kanada] *m*—**le Canada** Canada

cana·dien [kanadjɛ̃] **-dienne** [djen] *adj* Canadian ‖ *f* sheepskin jacket; station wagon ‖ (*cap*) *mf* Canadian

canaille [kanaj] *adj* vulgar, coarse ‖ *f* rabble, riffraff; scoundrel

ca·nal [kanal] *m* (*pl* **-naux** [no]) canal; tube, pipe; ditch, drain; (rad, telv) channel; **canal de Panama** Panama Canal; **canal de Suez** [syez] Suez Canal; **par le canal de** through the good offices of

canapé [kanape] *m* sofa, davenport; (culin) canapé; **canapé à deux places** settee

canapé-lit [kanapeli] *m* (*pl* **canapés-lits**) sofa bed, day bed

canard [kanar] *m* duck; sugar soaked in coffee, brandy, etc.; (mus) false note; (coll) hoax; (coll) rag, paper; **canard mâle** drake; **canard publicitaire** publicity stunt; **canard sauvage** wild duck

canarder [kanarde] *tr* to snipe at ‖ *intr* to snipe

canari [kanari] *m* canary

cancan [kɑ̃kɑ̃] *m* cancan (*dance*); (coll) gossip

cancaner [kɑ̃kane] *intr* to quack; (coll) to gossip

canca•nier [kɑ̃kanje] **-nière** [njer] *adj* (coll) catty ‖ *mf* (coll) gossip

cancer [kɑ̃ser] *m* cancer

cancé•reux [kɑ̃serø] **-reuse** [røz] *adj* cancerous

cancre [kɑ̃kr] *m* (coll) dunce, lazy student; (coll) tightwad; (zool) crab

candélabre [kɑ̃delɑbr] *m* candelabrum; espaliered fruit tree; cactus; lamppost

candeur [kɑ̃dœr] *f* naïveté

candi [kɑ̃di] *adj* candied (*fruit*) ‖ *m* rock candy

candi•dat [kɑ̃dida] **-date** [dat] *mf* candidate; nominee

candidature [kɑ̃didatyr] *f* candidacy

candide [kɑ̃did] *adj* naïve

candir [kɑ̃dir] *intr*—**faire candir** to candy, to crystallize (*sugar*) ‖ *ref* to candy, to crystallize

cane [kan] *f* duck, female duck

caner [kane] *intr* (slang) to chicken out

caneton [kantɔ̃] *m* duckling

canette [kanet] *f* female duckling; beer bottle; **canette de bière** can of beer

canevas [kanva] *m* canvas (*cloth*); outline (*of novel, story, etc.*); embroidery netting; (*in artillery, in cartography*) triangulation

canezou [kanzu] *m* sleeveless lace blouse

caniche [kaniʃ] *m* poodle

canicule [kanikyl] *f* dog days

canif [kanif] *m* penknife, pocketknife

ca•nin [kanɛ̃] **-nine** [nin] *adj* canine ‖ *f* canine (*tooth*)

canitie [kanisi] *f* grayness (*of hair*)

cani•veau [kanivo] *m* (*pl* **-veaux**) gutter; (elec) conduit

cannaie [kane] *f* sugar plantation

canne [kan] *f* cane; reed; cane, walking stick; **canne à pêche** fishing rod; **canne à sucre** sugar cane

canneberge [kanberʒ] *f* cranberry

canneler [kanle] §34 *tr* to groove; to corrugate; to flute (*a column*)

cannelle [kanel] *f* cinnamon; spout

cannelure [kanlyr] *f* groove, channel, corrugation; fluting (*of column*)

canner [kane] *tr* to cane (*a chair*)

cannibale [kanibal] *adj* & *mf* cannibal

canoë [kanɔe] *m* canoe

canoéiste [kanɔeist] *mf* canoeist

canon [kanɔ̃] *m* canon; cannon; gun barrel; tube; nozzle, spout; **canon à électrons** electron gun

cañon [kaɲɔ̃] *m* canyon

cano•nial -niale [kanɔnjal] *adj* (*pl* **-niaux** [njo]) canonical

canonique [kanɔnik] *adj* canonical

canoniser [kanɔnize] *tr* to canonize

canonnade [kanɔnad] *f* cannonade

canonner [kanɔne] *tr* to cannonade

canonnier [kanɔnje] *m* cannoneer

canonnière [kanɔnjer] *f* gunboat; pop-gun

canot [kano] *m* rowboat, launch; **canot automobile** speedboat, motorboat; **canot de sauvetage** lifeboat

canotage [kanɔtaʒ] *m* boating

canoter [kanɔte] *intr* to go boating

canotier [kanɔtje] *m* rower; skimmer

cant [kɑ̃] *m* cant

cantaloup [kɑ̃talu] *m* cantaloupe

cantate [kɑ̃tat] *f* cantata

cantatrice [kɑ̃tatris] *f* singer

cantilever [kɑ̃tilevœr] *adj* & *m* cantilever

cantine [kɑ̃tin] *f* canteen (*restaurant*); **cantine d'officier** officer's kit

cantique [kɑ̃tik] *m* canticle, ode; **cantique de Noël** (eccl) Christmas carol; **Cantique des Cantiques** (Bib) Song of Songs

canton [kɑ̃tɔ̃] *m* canton, district; **Cantons de l'Est** Eastern Townships (*in Canada*)

cantonade [kɑ̃tɔnad] *f* (theat) wings; **à la cantonade** (theat) offstage; **crier à la cantonade** to yell out (*s.th.*); **parler à la cantonade** to seem to be talking to oneself; (theat) to speak toward the wings

cantonnement [kɑ̃tɔnmɑ̃] *m* billeting

cantonner [kɑ̃tɔne] *tr* to billet

cantonnier [kɑ̃tɔnje] *m* road laborer; (rr) section hand

canular [kanylar] *m* (coll) practical joke, hoax, canard

canule [kanyl] *f* nozzle (*of syringe or injection needle*)

canuler [kanyle] *tr* (slang) to bother

caoutchouc [kautʃu] *m* rubber; **caoutchouc mousse** foam rubber; **caoutchoucs** rubbers, overshoes

caoutchouter [kautʃute] *tr* to rubberize

caoutchou•teux [kautʃutø] **-teuse** [tøz] *adj* rubbery

cap [kap] *m* cape, headland; bow, head (*of ship*); **Cap de Bonne Espérance** Cape of Good Hope; **mettre le cap sur** (coll) to set a course for

capable [kapabl] *adj* capable

capacité [kapasite] *f* capacity; ability

cape [kap] *f* cape; hood; derby; outer leaf, wrapper (*of cigar*); **à la cape** (naut) hove to; **de cape et d'épée** cloak-and-dagger (*novel, movie, etc.*); **rire sous cape** to laugh up one's sleeve; **vendre sous cape** (coll) to sell under the counter

C.A.P.E.S. [kapes] *m* (acronym) (certificat d'aptitude au professorat de l'enseignement du second degré) secondary-school teachers certificate

capillaire [kapiler] *adj* capillary ‖ *m* (bot) maidenhair (*fern*)

capitaine [kapiten] *m* captain

capi•tal -tale [kapital] *adj* (*pl* **-taux** [to] **-tales**) *adj* capital, principal, essential; capital (*city; punishment; crime; letter*); death (*sentence*); deadly (*sins*) ‖ *m* capital, assets; principal (*main sum*); **avec de minces capitaux** capital on a shoestring; **capitaux** capital ‖ *f* capital (*city; letter*)

capitalisation [kapitalizɑsjɔ̃] *f* capitalization; hoarding (*of money*)

capitaliser [kapitalize] *tr* to capitalize (*an income*); to compound (*interest*) ‖ *intr* to hoard

capitalisme [kapitalism] *m* capitalism

capitaliste [kapitalist] *adj* capitalist ‖ *mf* capitalist; investor

capi·teux [kapitø] **-teuse** [tøz] *adj* heady (*wine, champagne, etc.*)

Capitole [kapitɔl] *m* Capitol

capitonner [kapitɔne] *tr* to upholster

capituler [kapityle] *intr* to capitulate; to parley

ca·pon [kapɔ̃] **-ponne** [pɔn] *adj* cowardly ‖ *mf* coward; sneak; tattletale

capo·ral [kapɔral] *m* (*pl* **-raux** [ro]) corporal; shag, caporal (*tobacco*); **Caporal a dit . . . Simon says . . .**

caporalisme [kapɔralism] *m* militarism; dictatorial government

capot [kapo] *adj invar* speechless, confused; (*cards*) trickless ‖ *m* cover; hood (*of automobile*); (naut) hatch

capotage [kapɔtaʒ] *m* overturning

capote [kapɔt] *f* coat with a hood; hood (*of baby carriage*); **capote rebattable** (aut) folding top

capoter [kapɔte] *intr* to capsize; to overturn, upset

câpre [kɑpr] *f* (bot) caper

caprice [kapris] *m* caprice, whim

capri·cieux [kaprisjø] **-cieuse** [sjøz] *adj* capricious, whimsical

capsule [kapsyl] *f* capsule; bottle cap; percussion cap; (bot) capsule, pod; (rok) capsule; **capsules surrénales** adrenal glands

capsuler [kapsyle] *tr* to cap

capter [kapte] *tr* to win over; to harness (*a river*); to tap (*electric current; a water supply*); (rad, telv) to receive, pick up

cap·tieux [kapsjø] **-tieuse** [sjøz] *adj* captious, insidious; specious

cap·tif [kaptif] **-tive** [tiv] *adj & mf* captive

captiver [kaptive] *tr* to captivate

captivité [kaptivite] *f* captivity

capture [kaptyr] *f* capture

capturer [kaptyre] *tr* to capture

capuce [kapys] *m* (eccl) pointed hood

capuchon [kapyʃɔ̃] *m* hood (*of coat*); cap (*of pen*); (aut) valve cap; (eccl) cowl

capucine [kapysin] *f* nasturtium

caque [kak] *f* keg, barrel

caquet [kakɛ] *m* cackle

caqueter [kakte] §34 *intr* to cackle; to gossip

car [kar] *m* bus, sightseeing bus, interurban; **car de police** patrol wagon; **car sonore** loudspeaker truck ‖ *conj* for, because

carabe [karab] *m* ground beetle

carabine [karabin] *f* carbine

carabi·né -née [karabine] *adj* (coll) violent (*wind, cold, criticism*)

caraco [karako] *m* loose blouse

caractère [karaktɛr] *m* character; **caractères gras** (typ) boldface

caractériser [karakterize] *tr* to characterize

caractéristique [karakteristik] *adj & f* characteristic

carafe [karaf] *f* carafe; **rester en carafe** (slang) to be left out in the cold

carafon [karafɔ̃] *m* small carafe

caraïbe [karaib] *adj* Caribbean, Carib ‖ (*cap*) *mf* Carib (*person*)

carambolage [karɑ̃bɔlaʒ] *m* jostling; (coll) bumping (*e.g., of autos*)

caramboler [karɑ̃bɔle] *tr* (coll) to strike, bump into ‖ *intr* (billiards) to carom

caramel [karamɛl] *m* caramel

carapace [karapas] *f* turtle shell, carapace

carapater [karapate] *ref* (slang) to beat it

carat [kara] *m* carat

caravane [karavan] *f* caravan; house trailer; group (*of tourists*)

caravaning [karavaniŋ] *m* trailer camping

caravansérail [karavɑ̃seraj] *m* caravansary; (fig) world crossroads

caravelle [karavɛl] *f* caravel

carbonade [karbɔnad] *f* see **carbonnade**

carbone [karbɔn] *m* carbon

carbonique [karbɔnik] *adj* carbonic

carboniser [karbɔnize] *tr* to carbonize, char

carbonnade [karbɔnad] *f* charcoalgrilled steak (ham, etc.); beef and onion stew (*in northern France*); **à la carbonnade** charcoal-grilled

carburant [karbyrɑ̃] *m* motor fuel

carburateur [karbyratœr] *m* carburetor

carbure [karbyr] *m* carbide

carburéacteur [karbyreaktœr] *m* jet fuel

carcan [karkɑ̃] *m* pillory

carcasse [karkas] *f* skeleton; framework; (coll) carcass

cardan [kardɑ̃] *m* (mach) universal joint

carde [kard] *f* card; leaf rib; teasel head

carder [karde] *tr* to card

cardiaque [kardjak] *adj & mf* cardiac

cardi·nal -nale [kardinal] *adj & m* (*pl* **-aux** [no]) cardinal

cardiogramme [kardjɔgram] *m* cardiogram

carême [karɛm] *m* Lent; **de carême** Lenten

carême-prenant [karɛmprənɑ̃] *m* (*pl* **carêmes-prenants**) Shrovetide

carence [karɑ̃s] *f* lack, deficiency; failure

carène [karɛn] *f* hull

caréner [karene] §10 *tr* to streamline; (naut) to careen

caren·tiel -tielle [karɑ̃sjɛl] *adj* deficiency (*disease*)

cares·sant [karɛsɑ̃] **cares·sante** [karɛsɑ̃t] *adj* caressing; lovable; nice to pet; soothing (*e.g., voice*)

caresse [karɛs] *f* caress; endearment

caresser [karɛse] *tr* to caress; to pet; to nourish (*a hope*)

cargaison [kargɛzɔ̃] *f* cargo

cargo [kargo] *m* freighter; **cargo mixte** freighter carrying passengers

cari [kari] *m* curry

caricature [karikatyr] *f* caricature; cartoon

caricaturer [karikatyre] *tr* to caricature

caricaturiste [karikatyrist] *mf* caricaturist; cartoonist

carie [kari] *f* caries; **carie sèche** dry rot

carillon [karijɔ̃] *m* carillon

carillonner [karijɔne] *tr & intr* to carillon, to chime

carlingue [karlɛ̃g] *f* (aer) cockpit

carmin [karmɛ̃] *adj & m* carmine

carnage [karnaʒ] *m* carnage

carnas·sier [karnasje] **carnas·sière** [karnasjer] *adj* carnivorous ‖ *m* carnivore ‖ *f* game bag

carnation [karnɑsjɔ̃] *f* flesh tint

carna·val [karnaval] *m* (*pl* **-vals**) carnival; parade dummy

car·né -née [karne] *adj* flesh-colored; meat (*diet*)

carnet [karnɛ] *m* notebook, address book; memo pad; book (*of tickets, checks, stamps, etc.*); **carnet à feuilles mobiles** loose-leaf notebook

carnier [karnje] *m* hunting bag

carotte [karɔt] *f* carrot; (min) core sample; **tirer une carotte à** (coll) to cheat

carotter [karɔte] *tr* (coll) to cheat

carpe [karp] *m* (anat) wrist bones ‖ *f* carp; **être muet comme une carpe** to be still as a mouse

carpette [karpɛt] *f* rug, mat

carquois [karkwa] *m* quiver

carre [kar] *f* thickness (*of board*); crown (*of hat*); edge (*of ice skate*); square toe (*of shoe*); **d'une bonne carre** broad-shouldered (*man*)

car·ré -rée [kare] *adj* square; forthright ‖ *m* square; landing (*of staircase*); patch (*in garden*); (cards) four of a kind; (naut) wardroom ‖ *f* (slang) room, pad

car·reau [karo] *m* (*pl* **-reaux**) tile, flagstone; windowpane; stall (*in market*); pithead (*of mine*); goose (*of tailor*); quarrel (*square-headed arrow*); (cards) diamond; (cards) diamonds; **à carreaux** checked (*design*); **rester sur le carreaux** (coll) to be left out of the running; **se garder à carreau** (coll) to be on one's guard

carrefour [karfur] *m* crossroads; square (*in a city*)

carrelage [karlaʒ] *m* tiling

carreler [karle] §34 *tr* to tile

carrément [karemã] *adv* squarely; frankly

carrer [kare] *tr* to square ‖ *ref* (coll) to plunk oneself down; (coll) to strut

carrier [karje] *m* quarryman

carrière [karjer] *f* career; course (*e.g., of the sun*); quarry; **donner carrière à** to give free rein to

carriole [karjɔl] *f* light cart, trap; (coll) jalopy

carrossable [karɔsabl] *adj* passable

carrosse [karɔs] *m* carriage, coach

carrosserie [karɔsri] *f* (aut) body

carrossier [karɔsje] *m* coachmaker

carrousel [karuzɛl] *m* carrousel; parade ground; tiltyard

carrure [karyr] *f* width (*of shoulders, garment, etc.*); **d'une belle carrure** broad-shouldered (*man*)

cartable [kartabl] *m* briefcase

cartayer [karteje] §49 *intr* to avoid the ruts

carte [kart] *f* card; map, chart; bill (*to pay*); bill of fare, menu; **carte d'abonnement** commutation ticket; season ticket; **carte d'entrée** pass, ticket of admission; **carte des vins** wine list; **carte grise** automobile registration; **carte postale** post card; **cartes truquées** marked cards, stacked deck; **tirer les cartes à qn** to tell s.o.'s fortunes with cards

cartel [kartɛl] *m* cartel; wall clock; challenge (*to a duel*)

carte-lettre [kartəletr] *f* (*pl* **cartes-lettres**) gummed letter-envelope

carter [karter] *m* housing; bicycle chain guard; (aut) crankcase

cartilage [kartilaʒ] *m* cartilage, gristle

cartographe [kartɔgraf] *m* cartographer

cartomancie [kartɔmɑ̃si] *f* fortunetelling with cards

carton [kartɔ̃] *m* pasteboard, cardboard; cardboard box, carton; carton (*of cigarettes*); cartoon (*preliminary sketch*); (typ) cancel; **carton à chapeau** hatbox; **carton à dessin** portfolio for drawings and plans

carton-pâte [kartɔ̃pɑt] *m* papier-mâché

cartouche [kartuʃ] *m* (archit) cartouche, tablet ‖ *f* cartridge; carton (*of cigarettes*); canister (*of gas mask*); refill (*of pen*); **cartouche à blanc** blank cartridge

cartouchière [kartuʃjer] *f* cartridge belt, cartridge case

carvi [karvi] *m* caraway

cas [kɑ] *m* case; **cas urgent** emergency; **en cas de** in the event of, in a time of; **en cas d'imprévu** in case of emergency; **en cas que, au cas que, au cas où, dans le cas où** in the event that; **faire cas de** to esteem, to make much of; **le cas échéant** should the occasion arise, if necessary; **selon le cas** as the case may be

casa·nier [kazanje] **-nière** [njer] *adj* home-loving ‖ *mf* homebody

casaque [kazak] *f* jockey coat; blouse; **tourner casaque** to be a turncoat

cascade [kaskad] *f* cascade; jerk; spree; **prendre à la cascade** to ad-lib

cascader [kaskade] *intr* to cascade; (slang) to lead a wild life

casca·deur [kaskadœr] **-deuse** [døz] *mf* (mov) double ‖ *m* stunt man ‖ *f* stunt girl

case [kɑz] *f* compartment; pigeonhole; square (*e.g., of checkerboard or ledger*); box (*to be filled out on a form*); hut, cabin; **case postale** post-office box

caséine [kazein] *f* casein

caser [kaze] *tr* to put away (*e.g., in a drawer*); to arrange (*e.g., a counter display in a store*); (coll) to place, to find a job for ‖ *ref* (coll) to get settled

caserne [kazern] *f* barracks; **de caserne** off-color (*jokes*); regimented

caserner [kazerne] *tr & intr* to barrack

ca·sher -shère [kaʃer] *adj* kosher

casier [kasje] *m* rack (*for papers, magazines, letters, bottles*); cabinet; **casier à homards** lobster pot; **casier à tiroirs** music cabinet; **casier judiciaire** police record

casque [kask] *m* helmet; earphones, headset; comb (*of rooster*); **casque à mèche** nightcap; **casque à pointe** spiked helmet; **casque blindé** crash helmet

casquer [kaske] *intr* to fall into a trap; (slang) to shell out

casquette [kasket] *f* cap

cas·sant [kasɑ̃] **cas·sante** [kasɑ̃t] *adj* brittle; abrupt, curt

casse [kɑs] *m* (slang) burglarizing || *f* breakage || [kas], [kɑs] *f* ladle, scoop; crucible; (bot) cassia; (pharm) senna; (typ) case; (coll) scrap heap, junk

cas·sé -sée [kase] *adj* broken-down; shaky, weak (*voice*)

casse-cou [kasku] *m invar* (coll) daredevil; (coll) stunt man; (coll) danger spot || *interj* look out!

casse-croûte [kaskrut] *m invar* snack

casse-gueule [kasgœl] *adj invar* (slang) risky || *m invar* (coll) risky business

casse-noisettes [kasnwazet] *m invar* nutcracker

casse-noix [kasnwɑ], [kasnwa] *m invar* nutcracker

casse-pieds [kaspje] *m invar* (coll) pain in the neck

casser [kase] *tr* to break; to crack, to shatter; (law) to break (*a will*); (mil) to break, to bust; (coll) to split (*one's eardrums*); **casser sa pipe** (coll) to kick the bucket || *ref* to break; (coll) to rack (*one's brains*); **se casser le nez** (coll) to fail

casserole [kasrɔl] *f* saucepan

casse-tête [kastet] *m invar* truncheon; din; brain teaser, puzzler; **casse-tête chinois** jigsaw puzzle

cassette [kaset], [kaset] *f* strongbox, coffer; casket (*for jewels*)

cassis [kasi], [kasis] *m* black currant; cassis (*liqueur*); gutter

cassolette [kasɔlet] *f* incense burner

cassonade [kasɔnad] *f* brown sugar

cassoulet [kasule] *m* pork and beans

cassure [kasyr] *f* break; crease; rift

castagnettes [kastaɲet] *fpl* castanets

caste [kast] *f* caste; **hors caste** outcaste

castil·lan [kastijɑ̃] **castil·lane** [kastijan] *adj* Castilian || *m* Castilian (*language*) || (*cap*) *mf* Castilian (*person*)

Castille [kastij] *f* Castile; **la Castille** Castile

castor [kastɔr] *m* beaver

castrat [kastra] *m* castrato

castrer [kastre] *tr* to castrate

ca·suel -suelle [kazɥel] *adj* casual; (coll) brittle || *m* perquisites

cataclysme [kataklism] *m* cataclysm

catacombes [katakɔ̃b] *fpl* catacombs

catafalque [katafalk] *m* catafalque

cataire [kater] *f* catnip

Catalogne [katalɔɲ] *f* Catalonia; **la Catalogne** Catalonia

catalogue [katalɔg] *m* catalogue

cataloguer [katalɔge] *tr* to catalogue

catalyseur [katalizœr] *m* catalyst

cataplasme [kataplasm] *m* poultice

catapulte [katapylt] *f* catapult

catapulter [katapylte] *tr* to catapult

cataracte [katarakt] *f* cataract

catarrhe [katar] *m* catarrh; bad cold

catastrophe [katastrɔf] *f* catastrophe

catch [katʃ] *m* wrestling

catcheur [katʃœr] *m* wrestler

catéchiser [kateʃize] *tr* to catechize; to reason with

catéchisme [kateʃism] *m* catechism

catégorie [kategɔri] *f* category

catégorique [kategɔrik] *adj* categorical

catgut [katgyt] *m* (surg) catgut

cathédrale [katedral] *f* cathedral

cathéter [kateter] *m* (med) catheter

cathode [katɔd] *f* cathode

catholicisme [katɔlisism] *m* Catholicism

catholicité [katɔlisite] *f* catholicity; Catholicism; Catholics

catholique [katɔlik] *adj* catholic; Catholic; orthodox; **pas très catholique** (coll) questionable || *mf* Catholic

cati [kati] *m* glaze, gloss

catimini [katimini]—**en catimini** (coll) on the sly

catir [katir] *tr* to glaze

cauca·sien [kokazjɛ̃] **-sienne** [zjɛn] *adj* Caucasian || (*cap*) *mf* Caucasian

caucasique [kokazik] *adj* Caucasian

cauchemar [koʃmar] *m* nightmare

cause [koz] *f* cause; (law) case; **à cause de** because of, on account of, for the sake of; **et pour cause** with good reason; **hors de cause** irrelevant, beside the point; **mettre q.ch. en cause** to question s.th.; **mettre qn en cause** to implicate s.o.

causer [koze] *tr* to cause || *intr* to chat

causerie [kozri] *f* chat; informal lecture

causette [kozet] *f*—**faire la causette** (coll) to chat

cau·seur [kozœr] **-seuse** [zøz] *adj* talkative, chatty || *mf* speaker, conversationalist || *f* love seat

caustique [kostik] *adj* caustic

caute·leux [kotlø] **-leuse** [løz] *adj* crafty, wily; cunning (*mind*)

cautériser [koterize] *tr* to cauterize

caution [kosjɔ̃] *f* security, collateral; guarantor, bondsman; **mettre en liberté sous caution** to let out on bail; **se porter caution pour qn** to put up bail for s.o.; **sujet à caution** unreliable; **verser une caution** to make a deposit

cautionnement [kosjɔnmɑ̃] *m* surety bond, guaranty; bail; deposit

cautionner [kosjɔne] *tr* to bail out; to guarantee

cavalcade [kavalkad] *f* cavalcade

cavalerie [kavalri] *f* cavalry

cava·lier [kavalje] **-lière** [ljer] *adj* cavalier; bridle (*path*) || *mf* horseback rider; dance partner || *m* cavalier, horseman; escort; (chess) knight || *f* horsewoman

cave [kav] *adj* hollow (*cheeks*) || *f* cellar; liquor cabinet; liquor store; night club; bank (*in game of chance*); stake (*in gambling*); **cave à vin** wine cellar

ca·veau [kavo] *m* (*pl* **-veaux**) small cellar; vault, crypt; rathskeller

caver [kave] *tr* to hollow out || *intr* to ante || *ref* to become hollow (*said of eyes*); to wager

caverne [kavɛrn] *f* cave, cavern; (*pathol*) cavity (*e.g., in lung*)

caver·neux [kavɛrnø] **-neuse** [nøz] *adj* cavernous; hollow (*voice*)

caviar [kavjar] *m* caviar

caviarder [kavjarde] *tr* to censor

cavité [kavite] *f* cavity, hollow

caw·cher -chère [kaʃer] *adj* kosher

Cayes [kaj] *fpl*—**Cayes de la Floride** Florida Keys

C.C.P. *abbr* (**Compte chèques postaux**) postal banking account

ce [sə] (or **cet** [sɛt] before vowel or mute h) **cette** [sɛt] *adj dem* (*pl* **ces** [se]) §82A || **ce** *pron* §82B, §85A4

C.E.A. *abbr* (**Commissariat à l'Énergie atomique**) Atomic Energy Commission

céans [seã] *adv* herein

ceci [səsi] *pron dem indef* this, this thing, this matter

cécité [sesite] *f* blindness

céder [sede] §10 *tr* to cede, transfer; to yield, give up; **ne le céder à personne** to be second to none || *intr* to yield, succumb, give way

cédille [sedij] *f* cedilla

cédrat [sedra] *m* citron

cèdre [sɛdr] *m* cedar

cédule [sedyl] *f* rate, schedule; (law) notification

C.E.E. *abbr* (**Communauté économique européenne**) Common Market

cégétiste [seʒetist] *mf* unionist

ceindre [sɛ̃dr] §50 *tr* to buckle on, to gird; to encircle; to wreathe (*one's head*); **ceindre la couronne** to assume the crown || *ref*—**se ceindre de** to gird on

ceinture [sɛ̃tyr] *f* belt; waist, waistline; sash, waistband; girdle; **ceinture de sauvetage** life belt; **ceinture de sécurité** safety belt; **se mettre la ceinture** or **se serrer la ceinture** to tighten one's belt

ceinturer [sɛ̃tyre] *tr* to girdle, to belt; to encircle, to belt; (wrestling) to grip around the waist

cela [səla] *pron dem indef* that, that thing; that matter; **à cela près** with that one exception; **et cela? et cela?** what else?

célébrant [selebrã] *m* (eccl) celebrant

célébration [selebrasjɔ̃] *f* celebration

célèbre [selebr] *adj* famous

célébrer [selebre] §10 *tr* to celebrate

célébrité [selebrite] *f* celebrity

celer [səle] §2 *tr* to hide, conceal

céleri [selri], [selri] *m* celery

céleste [selest] *adj* celestial

célibat [seliba] *m* celibacy

célibataire [selibater] *adj* single || *mf* celibate || *m* bachelor || *f* spinster

celle [sɛl] §83

celle-ci [sɛlsi] §84

celle-là [sɛlla] §84

cellier [selje] *m* wine cellar; fruit cellar

cellophane [selofan] *f* cellophane

cellule [selyl], [selyl] *f* cell

celluloïd [selyloid] *m* celluloid

celte [sɛlt] *adj* Celtic || (*cap*) *mf* Celt

celtique [sɛltik] *adj* & *m* Celtic

celui [səlɥi] **celle** [sɛl] (*pl* **ceux** [sø] **celles**) §83

celui-ci [səlɥisi] **celle-ci** [sɛlsi] (*pl* **ceux-ci** [søsi] **celles-ci**) §84

celui-là [səlɥila] **celle-là** [sɛlla] (*pl* **ceux-là** [søla] **celles-là**) §84

cémentation [semãtasjɔ̃] *f* casehardening

cendre [sãdr] *f* cinder; **cendres** ashes

cendrée [sãdre] *f* shot; buckshot; (sports) cinder track

cendrer [sãdre] *tr* to cinder

cendrier [sãdrije] *m* ashtray

Cendrillon [sãdrijɔ̃] *f* Cinderella

cène [sɛn] *f* (eccl) Holy Communion || (*cap*) *f* (eccl) Last Supper

cens [sãs] *m* census; poll tax

cen·sé -sée [sãse] *adj* supposed to, e.g., **je ne suis pas censé le savoir** I am not supposed to know it; reputed to be, e.g., **il est censé juge infaillible** he is reputed to be an infallible judge

censément [sãsemã] *adv* supposedly, apparently, allegedly

censeur [sãsœr] *m* censor; census taker; critic; auditor; proctor

censure [sãsyr] *f* censure; censorship; (psychoanal) censor

censurer [sãsyre] *tr* to censure; to censor

cent [sã] *adj* & *pron* (*pl* **cents** in multiples when standing before modified noun, e.g., **trois cents œufs** three hundred eggs) one hundred, a hundred; **cent pour cent** one hundred percent; **cent un** [sãœ̃] one hundred and one, a hundred and one; **l'an dix-neuf cent** the year nineteen hundred; **page deux cent** page two hundred || *m* hundred, one hundred || [sãt] *m* cent

centaine [sãten] *f* hundred; **par centaines** by the hundreds; **une centaine de** about a hundred

centaure [sãtor] *m* centaur

centenaire [sãtner] *adj* centenary || *mf* centenarian || *m* centennial

centen·nal -nale [sãtennal] *adj* (*pl* **-naux** [no]) centennial

centième [sãtjem] *adj*, *pron* (*masc, fem*), & *m* hundredth || *f* hundredth performance

centigrade [sãtigrad] *adj* & *m* centigrade

centime [sãtim] *m* centime

centimètre [sãtimetr] *m* centimeter; tape measure

centrage [sãtraʒ] *m* centering

cen·tral -trale [sãtral] *adj* (*pl* **-traux** [tro]) central; main (*office*) || *m* (telp) central || *f* powerhouse; labor union; **centrale atomique** or **nucléaire** atomic generator

centralisation [sãtralizasjɔ̃] *f* centralization

centraliser [sãtralize] *tr & ref* to centralize

centre [sãtr] *m* center; **centre commercial** shopping district; **centre de dépression** storm center; **centre de triage** (rr) switchyard; **centre d'études** college; **centre de villégiature** resort; **centre social des étudiants** student center, student union

centrer [sãtre] *tr* to center

centrifuge [sãtrifyʒ] *adj* centrifugal

centuple [sãtypl] *adj & m* hundredfold; **au centuple** hundredfold

cep [sɛp] *m* vine stock

cépage [sepaʒ] *m* (bot) vine

cèpe [sɛp] *f* cepe mushroom

cependant [səpãdã] *adv* meanwhile; however, but, still; **cependant que** while, whereas; **et cependant** and yet

céramique [seramik] *adj* ceramic || *f* (art of) ceramics; ceramic piece; **céramiques** ceramics (*objects*)

cerbère [sɛrber] *m* (coll) watchdog || (*cap*) *m* Cerberus

cer·ceau [sɛrso] *m* (*pl* **-ceaux**) hoop; **cerceaux** pinfeathers

cercle [sɛrkl] *m* circle, club, society; clubhouse; hoop; **en cercle** in the cask

cercler [sɛrkle] *tr* to ring, encircle; to hoop

cercueil [sɛrkœj] *m* coffin

céréale [sereal] *adj & f* cereal

céré·bral -brale [serebral] *adj* (*pl* **-braux** [bro]) cerebral

cérémo·nial -niale [seremɔnjal] *adj & m* ceremonial

cérémonie [seremɔni] *f* ceremony; **faire des cérémonies** to stand on ceremony

cérémo·niel -nielle [seremɔnjɛl] *adj* ceremonial

cérémo·nieux [seremɔnjø] **-nieuse** [njøz] *adj* ceremonious, formal, stiff

cerf [sɛr] *m* deer, red deer; stag, buck

cerf-volant [sɛrvɔlã] *m* (*pl* **cerfs-volants**) kite

cerisaie [sərize] *f* cherry orchard

cerise [səriz] *f* cherry

cerisier [sərizje] *m* cherry tree

cerne [sɛrn] *m* annual ring (*of tree*); ring (*around moon, black eye, wound*)

cer·neau [sɛrno] *m* (*pl* **-neaux**) unripe nutmeat

cerner [sɛrne] *tr* to ring, encircle; to hem in, besiege; to shell (*nuts*)

cer·tain -taine [tɛn] *adj* certain, sure || (*when standing before noun*) *adj* certain, some; **certain auteur** a certain author; **depuis un certain temps** for some time; **d'un certain âge** middle-aged || **certains** *pron indef pl* certain people

certainement [sɛrtɛnmã] *adv* certainly

certes [sɛrt] *adv* indeed, certainly

certificat [sɛrtifika] *m* certificate

certifier [sɛrtifje] *tr* to certify

certitude [sɛrtityd] *f* certainty

cérumen [serymɛn] *m* earwax

céruse [seryz] *f* white lead

cer·veau [sɛrvo] *m* (*pl* **-veaux**) brain; mind; **cerveau brûlé** (coll) hothead

cervelas [sɛrvəla] *m* salami

cervelet [sɛrvəle] *m* cerebellum

cervelle [sɛrvel] *f* brains; **brûler la cervelle à qn** (coll) to shoot s.o.'s brains out

ces [se] §82A

césa·rien [sezarjɛ̃] **-rienne** [rjen] *adj* Caesarean || *f* Caesarean section

cesse [sɛs] *f* cessation, ceasing; **sans cesse** unceasingly, incessantly

cesser [sese] *tr* to stop, to cease, to leave off (*e.g., work*) || *intr* to cease, stop; **cesser de** + *inf* to stop, cease, quit + *ger*

cessez-le-feu [seselfø] *m invar* ceasefire

cession [sesjɔ̃] *f* ceding, surrender; (law) transfer

c'est-à-dire [setadir] *conj* that is, namely

césure [sezyr] *f* caesura

cet [set] §82A

cette [set] §82A

ceux [sø] §83

ceux-ci [søsi] §84

ceux-là [søla] §84

Ceylan [selã] *m* Ceylon

C.G.T. [seʒete] *f* (letterword) (confédération générale du travail) national labor union || *abbr* (Cie Générale transatlantique) French Line

cha·cal [ʃakal] *m* (*pl* **-cals**) jackal

cha·cun [ʃakœ̃] **-cune** [kyn] *pron indef* each, each one, every one; everybody, everyone; **chacun pour soi** every man for himself; **chacun son goût** every man to his own taste; **tout chacun** (coll) every Tom, Dick, and Harry

chadburn [tʃadbœrn] *m* (naut) public-address system

chadouf [ʃaduf] *m* well sweep

cha·grin [ʃagrɛ̃] **-grine** [grin] *adj* sad, downcast || *m* grief, sorrow

chagriner [ʃagrine] *tr* to grieve, distress; to make into shagreen leather || *intr* to grieve, worry

chah [ʃa] *m* shah

chahut [ʃay] *m* (coll) horseplay, row

chahuter [ʃayte] *tr* (coll) to upset; (coll) to boo, heckle || *intr* (coll) to create a disturbance

chai [ʃe] *m* wine cellar

chaîne [ʃen] *f* chain; warp (*of fabric*); necklace; (archit) band; (archit) tie; (naut) cable; (rad, telv) network; (telv) channel; **chaîne de fabrication** or **chaîne de montage** assembly line; **faire la chaîne** to form a bucket brigade

chaînon [ʃenɔ̃] *m* link

chair [ʃer] *f* flesh; pulp (*of fruits*); meat (*of animals*); **chair de poule** gooseflesh; **chair de sa chair** one's flesh and blood; **chairs** (painting, sculpture) nude parts; **en chair et en os** in the flesh; **ni chair ni poisson** neither fish nor fowl

chaire [ʃer] *f* pulpit; lectern; chair (*held by university professor*)

chaise [ʃɛz] f chair; bowline knot; (mach) bracket; **chaise à bascule** rocking chair; **chaise à porteurs** sedan chair; **chaise berceuse** rocking chair; **chaise brisée** folding chair; **chaise d'enfant** high chair; **chaise électrique** electric chair; **chaise percée** commode, toilet; **chaise pliante** folding chair

cha·land [ʃalɑ̃] **-lande** [lɑ̃d] mf customer ‖ m barge; **chaland de débarquement** (mil) landing craft

châle [ʃɑl] m shawl

chalet [ʃalɛ] m chalet, cottage, summer home; **chalet de nécessité** public rest room

chaleur [ʃalœr] f heat; warmth; **les grandes chaleurs de l'été** the hot weather of summer

chaleu·reux [ʃalœrø] **-reuse** [røz] adj warm, heated

châlit [ʃali] m bedstead

chaloupe [ʃalup] f launch

chalu·meau [ʃalymo] m (pl **-meaux**) reed; blowtorch; (mus) pipe; **chalumeau oxhydrique** or **chalumeau oxyacétylénique** acetylene torch

chalut [ʃaly] m trawl

chalutier [ʃalytje] m trawler

chamade [ʃamad] f—**battre la chamade** to beat wildly (said of the heart)

chamailler [ʃamaje] ref to squabble

chamarrer [ʃamare] tr to decorate, to ornament; to bedizen, to bedeck; (slang) to cover (s.o.) with ridicule

chambarder [ʃɑ̃barde] tr (slang) to upset, to turn upside down

chambellan [ʃɑ̃bɛllɑ̃] m chamberlain

chambouler [ʃɑ̃bule] tr (slang) to upset, to turn topsy-turvy

chambranle [ʃɑ̃brɑ̃l] m frame (of a door or window); mantelpiece

chambre [ʃɑ̃br] f chamber; room; **chambre à air** inner tube; **chambre à coucher** bedroom; **chambre d'ami** guest room; **chambre de compensation** clearing house; **chambre noire** darkroom

chambrée [ʃɑ̃bre] f dormitory, barracks; bunkmates

chambrer [ʃɑ̃bre] tr to keep under lock and key; to keep (wine) at room temperature

cha·meau [ʃamo] **-melle** [mɛl] mf (pl **-meaux**) camel ‖ m (slang) bitch (person)

chamois [ʃamwa] adj & m chamois

champ [ʃɑ̃] m field; **aux champs** salute (played on trumpet or drum); **champ clos** lists, dueling field; **champ de courses** race track; **champ de repos** cemetery; **champ de tir** firing range; **champ libre** clear field; **champs Élysées** Elysian Fields; **Champs-Élysées** Champs Élysées (street)

champagne [ʃɑ̃paɲ] m champagne; **champagne brut** extra dry champagne; **champagne d'origine** vintage champagne ‖ (cap) f Champagne; **la Champagne** Champagne

champe·nois [ʃɑ̃pənwa] **-noise** [nwaz] adj Champagne ‖ m Champagne

dialect ‖ (cap) mf inhabitant of Champagne

champêtre [ʃɑ̃pɛtr] adj rustic, rural

champignon [ʃɑ̃piɲɔ̃] m mushroom; fungus; (slang) accelerator pedal; **champignon de couche** cultivated mushroom; **champignon vénéneux** toadstool

champignonner [ʃɑ̃piɲɔne] intr to mushroom

cham·pion [ʃɑ̃pjɔ̃] **-pionne** [pjɔn] m champion ‖ f championess

championnat [ʃɑ̃pjɔna] m championship

champlever [ʃɑ̃lve] §2 tr to chase out, to gouge out

chan·card [ʃɑ̃sar] **-carde** [sard] adj (slang) in luck ‖ mf (slang) lucky person

chance [ʃɑ̃s] f luck; good luck; **avoir de la chance** to be lucky; **bonne chance** good luck; **chance moyenne** off chance; **chances** chances, risks, probability, possibility

chance·lant [ʃɑ̃slɑ̃] **-lante** [lɑ̃t] adj shaky, unsteady, tottering; delicate (health, constitution)

chanceler [ʃɑ̃sle] §34 intr to stagger, to totter, to teeter; to waver

chancelier [ʃɑ̃səlje] m chancellor

chancellerie [ʃɑ̃sɛlri] f chancellery

chan·ceux [ʃɑ̃sø] **-ceuse** [søz] adj lucky; risky

chanci [ʃɑ̃si] m manure pile for mushroom growing

chancir [ʃɑ̃sir] intr to grow moldy

chancre [ʃɑ̃kr] m chancre; ulcer, canker

chandail [ʃɑ̃daj] m sweater; **chandail à col roulé** turtleneck sweater

chandeleur [ʃɑ̃dlœr] f—**la chandeleur** Candlemas

chandelier [ʃɑ̃dəlje] m candlestick; chandler

chandelle [ʃɑ̃dɛl] f tallow candle; prop, stay (used in construction); **chandelle de glace** icicle; **en chandelle** vertically; **voir trente-six chandelles** to see stars (on account of a blow)

chanfrein [ʃɑ̃frɛ̃] m forehead (of a horse); chamfer, beveled edge

chanfreiner [ʃɑ̃frene] tr to chamfer, to bevel

change [ʃɑ̃ʒ] m exchange; rate of exchange; **de change** in reserve, extra; **donner le change à** to throw off the trail; **prendre le change** to let one self be duped; **rendre le change à qn** to give s.o. a taste of his own medicine

changeable [ʃɑ̃ʒabl] adj changeable

chan·geant [ʃɑ̃ʒɑ̃] **-geante** [ʒɑ̃t] adj changeable, changing, fickle; iridescent

changement [ʃɑ̃ʒmɑ̃] m change; shift, shifting; **changement de propriétaire** under new ownership; **changement de vitesse** gearshift

changer [ʃɑ̃ʒe] §38 tr to change; **changer contre** to exchange for ‖ intr to change; **changer d'avis** to change one's mind; **changer de place** to change one's seat; **changer de ton**

(coll) to change one's tune; **changer de visage** to blush; to change color || *ref* to change, change clothes

chanoine [ʃanwan] *m* (eccl) canon

chanson [ʃɑ̃sɔ̃] *f* song; **chanson bachique** drinking song; **chanson de geste** medieval epic; **chanson de Noël** Christmas carol; **chanson du terroir** folk song; **chanson sentimentale** torch song

chansonner [ʃɑ̃sɔne] *tr* to lampoon in a satirical song

chansonneur [ʃɑ̃sɔnœr] *m* lampooner (*who writes satirical songs*)

chanson-nier [ʃɑ̃sɔnje] **chanson-nière** [ʃɑ̃sɔnjɛr] *mf* songwriter || *m* chansonnier; song book

chant [ʃɑ̃] *m* singing; song, chant; canto; crowing (*of rooster*); side (*e.g., of a brick*); **chant du cygne** swan song; **chant de Noël** Christmas carol; **chant national** national anthem; **chants** poetry; **de chant** on end, edgewise

chantage [ʃɑ̃taʒ] *m* blackmail

chan-tant [ʃɑ̃tɑ̃] **-tante** [tɑ̃t] *adj* singable, melodious; singsong (*accent*); musical (*evening*)

chan-teau [ʃɑ̃to] *m* (*pl* **-teaux**) chunk (*of bread*); remnant

chantepleure [ʃɑ̃tplœr] *f* wine funnel; tap (*of cask*); sprinkler; weep hole

chanter [ʃɑ̃te] *tr* to sing || *intr* to sing; to crow (*as a rooster*); to pay blackmail; **chanter faux** to sing out of tune; **chanter juste** to sing in tune; **faire chanter** to blackmail

chanterelle [ʃɑ̃trɛl] *f* first string (*of violin*); decoy bird; mushroom; **appuyer sur la chanterelle** (coll) to rub it in

chan-teur [ʃɑ̃tœr] **-teuse** [tøz] *adj* singing; song (*bird*) || *mf* singer; **chanteur de charme** crooner; **chanteur de rythme** jazz singer

chantier [ʃɑ̃tje] *m* shipyard; stocks; slip; workshop, yard; gantry, stand (*for barrels*); (public sign) men at work; **chantier de démolition** junkyard, scrap heap; **mettre en** or **sur le chantier** to start work on

chantilly [ʃɑ̃tiji] *m* whipped cream

chantonner [ʃɑ̃tɔne] *tr & intr* to hum

chantoung [ʃɑ̃tuŋ] *m* shantung

chantourner [ʃɑ̃turne] *tr* to jigsaw

chantre [ʃɑ̃tr] *m* cantor, chanter; precentor; songster; bard, poet

chanvre [ʃɑ̃vr] *m* hemp; **en chanvre** hempen; flaxen (*color*)

chan-vrier [ʃɑ̃vrije] **-vrière** [vrijɛr] *adj* hemp (*industry*) || *mf* dealer in hemp; hemp dresser

chaos [kao] *m* chaos

chaotique [kaotik] *adj* chaotic

chaparder [ʃaparde] *tr* (coll) to pilfer, to filch

chape [ʃap] *f* cover, covering; tread (*of tire*); coping (*of bridge*); frame, shell (*of pulley block*); (eccl) cope

cha-peau [ʃapo] *m* (*pl* **-peaux**) hat; head (*of mushroom*); lead (*of magazine or newspaper article*); cap (*of fountain pen; of valve*); cowl (*of*

chimney); **chapeau à cornes** cocked hat; **chapeau bas** hat in hand; **chapeau bas!** hats off!; **chapeau chinois** Chinese bells; **chapeau de roue** hubcap; **chapeau haut de forme** top hat; **chapeau melon** derby; **chapeau mou** fedora

chapeau-cloche [ʃapoklɔʃ] *m* (*pl* **chapeaux-cloches**) cloche (*hat*)

chapeauter [ʃapote] *tr* (coll) to put a hat on (*e.g., a child*)

chapelain [ʃaplɛ̃] *m* chaplain (*of a private chapel*)

chapeler [ʃaple] §34 *tr* to scrape the crust off of (*bread*)

chapelet [ʃaple] *m* chaplet, rosary; string (*of onions; of islands; of insults*); chain (*of events; of mountains*); series (*e.g., of attacks*); (mil) stick (*of bombs*); **chapelet hydraulique** bucket conveyor; **défiler son chapelet** (coll) to speak one's mind; **dire son chapelet** to tell one's beads; **en chapelet** (elec) in series

chape-lier [ʃaplje] **-lière** [ljɛr] *mf* hatter || *f* Saratoga trunk

chapelle [ʃapel] *f* chapel; clique, coterie; **chapelle ardente** mortuary chamber lighted by candles; hearse

chapellerie [ʃapelri] *f* hatmaking; millinery; hat shop; millinery shop

chapelure [ʃaplyr] *f* bread crumbs

chaperon [ʃaprɔ̃] *m* chaperon; hood; cape with a hood; coping (*of wall*); **le Petit Chaperon rouge** Little Red Ridinghood

chaperonner [ʃaprɔne] *tr* to chaperon

chapi-teau [ʃapito] *m* (*pl* **-teaux**) capital (*of column*); circus tent

chapitre [ʃapitr] *m* chapter; **commencer un nouveau chapitre** to turn over a new leaf

chapon [ʃapɔ̃] *m* capon; (culin) crust rubbed with garlic

chaque [ʃak] *adj indef* each, every || *pron indef* (coll) each, each one

char [ʃar] *m* chariot; float (*in parade*); (mil) tank; **char d'assaut** or **char de combat** (mil) tank; **char funèbre** hearse

charabia [ʃarabja] *m* gibberish

charançon [ʃarɑ̃sɔ̃] *m* weevil

charbon [ʃarbɔ̃] *m* coal; soft coal; charcoal; carbon (*of an electric cell or arc*); cinder (*in the eye*); **charbon ardent** live coal; **charbon de bois** charcoal; **charbon de terre** coal; **être sur les charbons ardents** to be on pins and needles

charbonnage [ʃarbɔnaʒ] *m* coal mining; coal mine

charbonner [ʃarbɔne] *tr* to char; to draw (*a picture*) with charcoal || *intr & ref* to char, to carbonize

charbon-neux [ʃarbɔnø] **charbon-neuse** [ʃarbɔnøz] *adj* sooty; anthrax-carrying

charbon-nier [ʃarbɔnje] **charbon-nière** [ʃarbɔnjɛr] *adj* coal (*e.g., industry*) || *mf* coal dealer || *m* charcoal burner; coaler || *f* coal scuttle; charcoal kiln; (orn) coal titmouse

charcuter [ʃarkyte] *tr* to butcher, mangle

charcuterie [ʃarkytri] *f* delicatessen; pork butcher shop

charcu·tier [ʃarkytje] **-tière** [tjɛr] *mf* pork butcher; (coll) sawbones

chardon [ʃardɔ̃] *m* thistle

chardonneret [ʃardɔnrɛ] *m* (orn) goldfinch

charge [ʃarʒ] *f* charge; load, burden; caricature; public office; **à charge de** on condition of, with the proviso of; **à charge de revanche** on condition of getting the same thing in return; **charges de famille** dependents; **être à charge à** to be dependent upon; **être à la charge de** to be supported by; **faire la charge de** to do a takeoff of

char·gé -gée [ʃarʒe] *adj* loaded; full; overcast (*sky*); registered (*letter*) ‖ *m* assistant, deputy, envoy; **chargé de cours** assistant professor

chargement [ʃarʒəmɑ̃] *m* charging; loading; cargo

charger [ʃarʒe] §38 *tr* to charge; to drive, to take (*s.o. in one's car*) ‖ *intr* (mil) to charge; (naut) to load; *ref* to be loaded; **se charger de** to take charge of; to take up (*a question*)

chargeur [ʃarʒœr] *m* loader; stoker; shipper; clip (*of gun*); (elec) charger

chariot [ʃarjo] *m* wagon, cart; typewriter carriage; **chariot d'enfant** walker; **chariot élévateur** fork-lift truck; **Grand Chariot, Chariot de David** Big Dipper; **Petit Chariot** Little Dipper

charitable [ʃaritabl] *adj* charitable

charité [ʃarite] *f* charity; **faire la charité** to give alms; **faites la charité de** or **ayez la charité de** have the goodness to; **par charité** for charity's sake

charlatan [ʃarlatɑ̃] *m* charlatan

charlemagne [ʃarləmaɲ] *m* (cards) king of hearts; **faire charlemagne** to quit while winning

char·mant [ʃarmɑ̃] **-mante** [mɑ̃t] *adj* charming

charme [ʃarm] *m* charm; (*Carpinus betulus*) hornbeam; **se porter comme un charme** to be fit as a fiddle

charmer [ʃarme] *tr* to charm

char·meur [ʃarmœr] **-meuse** [møz] *adj* charming ‖ *mf* charmer

charmille [ʃarmij] *f* bower, arbor

char·nel -nelle [ʃarnɛl] *adj* carnal

charnière [ʃarnjɛr] *f* hinge

char·nu -nue [ʃarny] *adj* fleshy; plump; pulpy

charogne [ʃarɔɲ] *f* carrion

charpentage [ʃarpɑ̃taʒ] *m* carpentry

charpente [ʃarpɑ̃t] *f* framework; scaffolding; frame, build (*of body*)

charpenter [ʃarpɑ̃te] *tr* to square (*timber*); to outline, map out, plan (*a novel, speech, etc.*); **être solidement charpenté** to be well built or well constructed ‖ *intr* to carpenter

charpenterie [ʃarpɑ̃tri] *f* carpentry; structure (*of building*)

charpentier [ʃarpɑ̃tje] *m* carpenter

charpie [ʃarpi] *f* lint; **en charpie in shreds**

charrée [ʃare] *f* lye

charre·tier [ʃartje] **-tière** [tjɛr] *mf* teamster; **jurer comme un charretier** to swear like a trooper

charrette [ʃarɛt] *f* cart

charriage [ʃarjaʒ] *m* cartage; drifting (*of ice*); (slang) exaggeration

charrier [ʃarje] *tr* to cart, to transport; to carry away (*sand, as the river does*); (slang) to poke fun at ‖ *intr* to be full of ice (*said of river*); (slang) to exaggerate

charroi [ʃarwa], [ʃarwa] *m* cartage

charron [ʃarɔ̃], [ʃarɔ̃] *m* wheelwright, cartwright

charroyer [ʃarwaje] §47 *tr* to cart

charrue [ʃary] *f* plow; **mettre la charrue devant les bœufs** to put the cart before the horse

charte [ʃart] *f* charter; title deed; fundamental principle

chas [ʃa] *m* eye (*of needle*)

chasse [ʃas] *f* hunt, hunting; hunting song; chase; bag (*game caught*); **aller à la chasse** to go hunting; **chasse à courre** riding to the hounds; **chasse aux appartements** house hunting; **chasse aux fauves** big-game hunting; **chasse d'eau** flush; **chasse gardée** game preserve; **chasse réservée** (public sign) no shooting; **tirer la chasse** to pull the toilet chain

châsse [ʃas] *f* reliquary; frame (*as for eyeglasses*) ‖ **châsses** *mpl* (slang) blinkers, eyes

chasse-bestiaux [ʃasbestjo] *m invar* cowcatcher

chasse-clou [ʃasklu] *m* (*pl* **-clous**) punch, nail set

chassé-croisé [ʃasekrwaze] *m* (*pl* **chassés-croisés**) futile efforts

chasselas [ʃasla] *m* white table grape

chasse-mouches [ʃasmuʃ] *m invar* fly swatter; fly net

chasse-neige [ʃasnɛʒ] *m invar* snowplow

chasse-pierres [ʃaspjɛr] *m invar* (rr) cowcatcher

chasser [ʃase] *tr* to hunt; to chase; to chase away, to put to flight; to drive (*e.g., a herd of cattle*); (coll) to fire (*e.g., a servant*) ‖ *intr* to hunt; to skid; to come, e.g., **le vent chasse du nord** the wind is coming from the north; **chasser de race** (coll) to be a chip off the old block

chasseresse [ʃasrɛs] *f* huntress

chas·seur [ʃasœr] **chas·seuse** [ʃasøz] *mf* hunter; bellhop ‖ *m* chasseur; fighter pilot; **chasseur à réaction** jet fighter; **chasseur d'assaut** fighter plane; **chasseur de chars** antitank tank; **chasseur de sous-marins** submarine chaser

chasseur-bombardier [ʃasœrbɔ̃bardje] *m* fighter-bomber

chassie [ʃasi] *f* gum (*on eyelids*)

chas·sieux [ʃasjø] **chas·sieuse** [ʃasjøz] *adj* gummy (*eyelids*)

châssis [ʃasi] *m* chassis; window frame; chase (*for printing*); **châssis à**

demeure or dormant sealed window frame; **châssis couche** (hort) hotbed; **châssis mobile** movable sash

châssis-presse [ʃɑsipres] m (pl **-presses**) printing frame

chaste [ʃast] adj chaste

chasteté [ʃastəte] f chastity

chat [ʃa] **chatte** [ʃat] mf cat ‖ m tomcat; **à bon chat bon rat** tit for tat; **acheter chat en poche** (coll) to buy a pig in a poke; **appeler un chat un chat** (coll) to call a spade a spade; **chat à neuf queues** cat-o'-nine-tails; **chat dans la gorge** (coll) frog in the throat; **chat de gouttière** alley cat; **chat sauvage** wildcat; **d'autres chats à fouetter** (coll) other fish to fry; **il ne faut pas réveiller le chat qui dort** let sleeping dogs lie; **le Chat botté** Puss in Boots; **mon petit chat!** darling!; **pas un chat** (coll) not a soul ‖ f see **chatte**

châtaigne [ʃatɛɲ] f chestnut

châtaignier [ʃatɛɲe] m chestnut tree

chataire [ʃater] f catnip

châ·teau [ʃato] m (pl **-teaux**) chateau; palace; estate; manor; **château d'eau** water tower; **château de cartes** house of cards; **château fort** castle, fort, citadel; **châteaux en Espagne** castles in the air; **mener une vie de château** to live like a prince

châteaubriand or **châteaubriant** [ʃatobriɑ̃] m grilled beefsteak

châte·lain [ʃatlɛ̃] **-laine** [len] mf proprietor of a country estate ‖ f wife of the lord of the manor; bracelet

châtelet [ʃatlɛ] m small chateau

chat-huant [ʃaɥɑ̃] m (pl **chats-huants** [ʃaɥɑ̃]) screech owl

châtier [ʃatje] tr to chasten, chastise; to correct; to purify (style)

chatière [ʃatjer] f ventilation hole; cathole

châtiment [ʃatimɑ̃] m punishment

chatoiement [ʃatwamɑ̃] m glisten, sparkle; sheen, shimmer; play of colors

chaton [ʃatɔ̃] m kitten; setting (of ring); (bot) catkin

chatonner [ʃatɔne] tr to set (a gem) ‖ intr to have kittens

chatouillement [ʃatujmɑ̃] m tickle; tickling sensation

chatouiller [ʃatuje] tr to tickle; (fig) to excite, arouse ‖ intr to tickle

chatouil·leux [ʃatujø] **chatouil·leuse** [ʃatujøz] adj ticklish; touchy

chatoyer [ʃatwaje] §47 intr to glisten, to sparkle; to shimmer

chat-pard [ʃapar] m (pl **chats-pards**) ocelot

châtrer [ʃatre] tr to castrate

chatte [ʃat] adj fem kittenish ‖ f cat, female cat

chatterie [ʃatri] f cajoling; sweets

chatterton [ʃatertɔn] m friction tape

chaud [ʃo] **chaude** [ʃod] adj hot, warm; last-minute (news flash); **il fait chaud** it is warm (weather); **pleurer à chaudes larmes** to cry one's eyes out ‖ m heat, warmth; **à chaud** emergency (operation); (med) in the acute stage; **avoir chaud** to be warm, to be hot (said of person); **il a eu chaud** (coll) he had a narrow escape ‖ adv—**coûter chaud** (coll) to cost a pretty penny; **servir chaud** to serve (s.th.) piping hot

chaudière [ʃodjer] f boiler

chaudron [ʃodrɔ̃] m cauldron

chaudron·nier [ʃodrɔnje] **chaudron·nière** [ʃodrɔnjer] mf coppersmith; boilermaker

chauffage [ʃofaʒ] m heating; stoking; (coll) coaching

chauffard [ʃofar] m road hog, Sunday driver

chauffe [ʃof] f stoking; furnace

chauffe-assiettes [ʃofasjet] m invar hot plate

chauffe-bain [ʃofbɛ̃] m (pl **-bains**) bathroom water heater

chauffe-eau [ʃofo] m invar water heater

chauffe-lit [ʃofli] m (pl **-lits**) bed-warmer

chauffe-pieds [ʃofpje] m invar foot warmer

chauffe-plats [ʃofpla] m invar chafing dish

chauffer [ʃofe] tr to heat; to warm up; to limber up; (coll) to coach; (slang) to snitch, filch ‖ intr to heat up; to get up steam; to overheat; **ça va chauffer!** (coll) watch the fur fly! ‖ ref to warm oneself; to heat up

chaufferette [ʃofret] f foot warmer; space heater; car heater

chauffeur [ʃofœr] m driver; chauffeur; (rr) stoker, fireman

chauffeuse [ʃoføz] f fireside chair

chaume [ʃom] m stubble; thatch

chaumière [ʃomjer] f thatched cottage

chaussée [ʃose] f pavement, road; causeway

chausse-pied [ʃospje] m (pl **-pieds**) shoehorn

chausser [ʃose] tr to put on (shoes, skis, glasses, tires, etc.); to shoe; to fit ‖ intr to fit (said of shoe); **chausser de** to wear (a certain size shoe) ‖ ref to put one's shoes on

chausses [ʃos] fpl hose (in medieval dress); **aux chausses de** on the heels of; **c'est elle qui porte les chausses** (coll) she wears the pants

chausse-trape [ʃostrap] f (pl **-trapes**) trap

chaussette [ʃoset] f sock

chausseur [ʃosœr] m shoe salesman

chausson [ʃosɔ̃] m pump, slipper, savate; **chausson aux pommes** apple turnover

chaussure [ʃosyr] f footwear, shoes; shoe; **trouver chaussure à son pied** to find what one needs

chauve [ʃov] adj bald

chauve-souris [ʃovsuri] f (pl **chauves-souris**) (zool) bat

chau·vin [ʃovɛ̃] **-vine** [vin] adj chauvinistic ‖ mf chauvinist

chauvir [ʃovir] intr—**chauvir de l'oreille** or **chauvir des oreilles** to prick up the ears (said of horse, mule, donkey)

chaux [ʃo] f lime

chavirement [ʃavirmɑ̃] *m* capsizing, overturning

chavirer [ʃavire] *tr & intr* to tip over, to capsize

chef [ʃɛf] *m* head, chief, leader; boss; scoutmaster; **chef de bande** ringleader, gang leader; **chef de cuisine** chef; **chef de file** leader, standard-bearer; **chef de gare** stationmaster; **chef de l'exécutif** chief executive; **chef de musique** bandmaster; **chef de rayon** floorwalker; **chef de tribu** chieftain; **chef d'orchestre** conductor; bandleader; **de son propre chef** by one's own authority, on one's own

chef-d'œuvre [ʃedœvr] *m* (*pl* **chefs-d'œuvre**) masterpiece

chef-lieu [ʃefljø] *m* (*pl* **chefs-lieux**) county seat, capital city

cheftaine [ʃeften] *f* Girl Scout unit leader

cheik [ʃɛk] *m* sheik

chelem [ʃlɛm] *m* slam (*at bridge*); **être chelem** (*cards*) to be shut out

chemin [ʃmɛ̃] *m* way; road; **chemin battu** beaten path; **chemin de la Croix** (eccl) Way of the Cross; **chemin de fer** railroad; **chemin des écoliers** (coll) long way around; **chemin de table** table runner; **chemin de traverse** side road; shortcut; **chemin de velours** primrose path; **n'y pas aller par quatre chemins** (coll) to come straight to the point

chemi•neau [ʃmino] *m* (*pl* **-neaux**) hobo, tramp; deadbeat

cheminée [ʃmine] *f* chimney, stack, smokestack; fireplace; (naut) funnel

cheminer [ʃmine] *intr* to trudge, tramp; to make headway

cheminot [ʃmino] *m* railroader

chemise [ʃmiz] *f* shirt; dust jacket (*of book*); folder, file; jacket, shell, metal casing; **chemise de mailles** coat of mail; **chemise de nuit** nightgown

chemiser [ʃmize] *tr* (mach) to case, to jacket

chemiserie [ʃmizri] *f* haberdashery

chemisette [ʃmizet] *f* short-sleeved shirt

chemi•sier [ʃmizje] **-sière** [zjer] *mf* haberdasher ‖ *m* shirtwaist

che•nal [ʃnal] *m* (*pl* **-naux** [no]) channel; millrace

chenapan [ʃnapɑ̃] *m* rogue, scoundrel

chêne [ʃen] *m* oak

ché•neau [ʃeno] *m* (*pl* **-neaux**) rain spout

chêne-liège [ʃenljeʒ] *m* (*pl* **chênes-lièges**) cork oak

chenet [ʃnɛ] *m* andiron

chènevis [ʃɛnvi] *m* hempseed, birdseed

chenil [ʃni] *m* kennel

chenille [ʃnij] *f* caterpillar; chenille; caterpillar tread

chenil•lé -lée [ʃnije] *adj* with a caterpillar tread

che•nu -nue [ʃny] *adj* hoary

cheptel [ʃɛptel], [ʃtel] *m* livestock; **cheptel mort** implements and buildings

chèque [ʃɛk] *m* check; **chèque de voyage** traveler's check; **chèque prescrit** lapsed check; **chèque sans provision** worthless check

chéquier [ʃekje] *m* checkbook

cher chère [ʃer] *adj* expensive, dear ‖ (when standing before noun) *adj* dear, beloved ‖ *f* see **chère** ‖ **cher** *adv* dear(ly); **coûter cher** to cost a great deal

chercher [ʃerʃe] *tr* to look for, search for, seek, hunt; to try to get; **aller chercher** to go and get; **envoyer chercher** to send for ‖ *intr* to search; **chercher à** to try to, to endeavor to ‖ *ref* to look for each other; to feel one's way

cher•cheur [ʃerʃœr] **-cheuse** [ʃøz] *adj* inquiring (*mind*); homing (*device*) ‖ *mf* seeker; researcher, scholar; investigator; prospector (*for gold, uranium, etc.*)

chère [ʃer] *f* fare, food and drink; **faire bonne chère** to live high

ché•ri -rie [ʃeri] *adj & mf* darling

chérir [ʃerir] *tr* to cherish

cherry [ʃeri] *m* cherry cordial

cherté [ʃerte] *f* high price; **cherté de la vie** high cost of living

chérubin [ʃerybɛ̃] *m* cherub

ché•tif [ʃetif] **-tive** [tiv] *adj* puny, sickly; poor, wretched

che•val [ʃəval] *m* (*pl* **-vaux** [vo]) horse; metric or French horsepower (*735 watts*); **à cheval** on horseback; **à cheval sur** astride; insistent upon; **cheval de bois** or **cheval d'arçons** horse (*for vaulting*); **cheval de course** race horse; **cheval de race** thoroughbred; **cheval de retour** (coll) jailbird; **cheval entier** stallion; **monter sur ses grands chevaux** (fig) to get up on one's high horse

chevalement [ʃəvalmɑ̃] *m* support, shoring; (min) headframe

chevaler [ʃəvale] *tr* to shore up

chevaleresque [ʃəvalresk] *adj* knightly, chivalrous

chevalerie [ʃəvalri] *f* chivalry

chevalet [ʃəvale] *m* easel; sawhorse; stand, frame; bridge (*of violin*)

chevalier [ʃəvalje] *m* knight; (orn) sandpiper; **chevalier d'industrie** manipulator, swindler; **chevalier errant** knight-errant; **Chevaliers du taste-vin** wine-tasting club

chevalière [ʃəvaljer] *f* signet ring

cheva•lin -line [ʃəvalɛ̃] **-lin** [lin] *adj* equine

cheval-vapeur [ʃəvalvapœr] *m* (*pl* **chevaux-vapeur**) metric or French horsepower (*735 watts*)

chevauchée [ʃəvoʃe] *f* ride

chevaucher [ʃəvoʃe] *tr* to straddle ‖ *intr* to ride horseback; to overlap

cheve•lu -lue [ʃəvly] *adj* hairy; long-haired

chevelure [ʃəvlyr] *f* hair, head of hair; tail (*of a comet*)

chevet [ʃəve] *m* headboard; bolster; **de chevet** bedside (*lamp, table, book*)

che•veu [ʃəvø] *m* (*pl* **-veux** hair; **avoir mal aux cheveux** (coll) to have a hangover; **cheveux hair** (*of the head*); hairs; **cheveux en brosse** crew cut; **couper les cheveux en quatre** (coll) to split hairs; **en cheveux** hatless; **faire dresser les cheveux** (coll) to make one's hair stand on end; **ne tenir qu'à un cheveu** (coll) to hang by a thread; **saisir l'occasion aux cheveux** (coll) to take time by the forelock; **se faire des cheveux** (coll) to worry oneself gray; **tiré par les cheveux** (coll) far-fetched

chevillard [ʃəvijar] *m* wholesale cattle dealer or jobber

cheville [ʃəvij] *f* peg; pin; bolt; padding (*of verse*); ankle; **cheville ouvrière** (mach) kingbolt; (fig) mainspring (*of an enterprise*); **être en cheville avec** (coll) to be in cahoots with; **ne pas arriver à la cheville de qn** (coll) not to hold a candle to s.o.

chèvre [ʃevr] *f* goat; nanny goat

che-vreau [ʃəvro] *m* (*pl* -**vreaux**) kid

chèvrefeuille [ʃevrəfœj] *m* honeysuckle

chevrette [ʃəvrɛt] *f* kid; doe (*roe deer*); shrimp; tripod

chevreuil [ʃəvrœj] *m* roe deer; roebuck

chevron [ʃəvrɔ̃] *m* rafter; chevron, hash mark; **en chevron** in a herringbone pattern

chevron·né -née [ʃəvrəne] *adj* wearing chevrons; experienced, oldest

chevronner [ʃəvrəne] *tr* to put rafters on; to give chevrons to

chevroter [ʃəvrəte] *intr* to bleat; to sing or speak in a quavering voice

chewing-gum [ʃwiŋɡɔm], [tʃuwiŋɡɔm] *m* chewing gum

chez [ʃe] *prep* at the house, home, office, etc., of, e.g., **chez mes amis** at my friends' house; e.g., **chez le boulanger** at the baker's; in the country of, among, e.g., **chez les Français** among the French; in the time of, e.g., **chez les anciens Grecs** in the time of the ancient Greeks; in the work of, e.g., **chez Homère** in Homer's works; with, e.g., **c'est chez lui une habitude** it's a habit with him

chez-soi [ʃeswa] *m invar* home

chialer [ʃjale] *intr* (slang) to cry

chiasse [ʃjas] *f* flyspecks; (metallurgy) dross; (coll) loose bowels

chic [ʃik] *adj invar* stylish, chic; **un chic type** (coll) a good egg ‖ *m* style; skill, knack; (coll) smartness, elegance; (slang) ovation; **de chic** from memory ‖ *interj* (coll) fine!, grand!

chicane [ʃikan] *f* chicanery; shady lawsuit; baffle, baffle plate; **chercher chicane à** to engage in a petty quarrel with; **en chicane** staggered, zigzag; curved (*tube*)

chicaner [ʃikane] *tr* to pick a fight with; **chicaner q.ch. à qn** to quibble over s.th. with s.o. ‖ *intr* to quibble

chicanerie [ʃikanri] *f* chicanery

chiche [ʃiʃ] *adj* stingy; small, dwarf ‖ *interj* (coll) I dare you!

chicon [ʃikɔ̃] *m* (coll) romaine

chicorée [ʃikɔre] *f* chicory; **chicorée frisée** endive

chicot [ʃiko] *m* stump (*of tree*); (coll) stump, stub (*of tooth*)

chien [ʃjɛ̃] **chienne** [ʃjen] *mf* dog ‖ *m* hammer (*of gun*); glamour; **à la chien**

(coll) with bangs; **chien couchant** setter; (slang) apple polisher; **chien d'arrêt** pointer; **chien d'aveugle** Seeing Eye dog; **chien de** or **chienne de** (coll) dickens of a; **chien de garde** watchdog; **chien du jardinier** (coll) dog in the manger; **chien savant** performing dog; **de chien** (coll) miserable (*weather, life, etc.*); **en chien de fusil** (coll) curled up (*e.g., to sleep*); **entre chien et loup** (coll) at dusk; **les chiens écrasés** (slang) the accident page (*of newspaper*); **petit chien** pup; **se regarder en chiens de faïence** (coll) to glare at one another ‖ *f* see **chienne**

chiendent [ʃjɛ̃dɑ̃] *m* couch grass; (coll) trouble

chienlit [ʃjɑ̃li] *mf* (vulgar) person who soils his bed ‖ *m* carnival mask; masquerade, fantastic costume

chien-loup [ʃjɛ̃lu] *m* (*pl* **chiens-loups**) wolfhound

chienne [ʃjen] *f* bitch

chienner [ʃjene] *intr* to whelp

chiennerie [ʃjenri] *f* stinginess, meanness

chiffe [ʃif] *f* rag; (coll) weakling

chiffon [ʃifɔ̃] *m* rag; scrap of paper; **chiffons** (coll) fashions

chiffonnade [ʃifɔnad] *f* salad greens

chiffonner [ʃifɔne] *tr* to rumple, crumple; to make (*a dress*); (coll) to ruffle (*tempers*), to bother ‖ *intr* to pick rags; to make dresses

chiffon·nier [ʃifɔnje] **chiffon·nière** [ʃifɔnjer] *mf* scavenger, ragpicker ‖ *m* chiffonier

chiffre [ʃifr] *m* figure, number; cipher, code; sum total; combination (*of lock*); monogram; **chiffre d'affaires** turnover; **chiffres romains** roman numerals

chiffrer [ʃifre] *tr* to number; to monogram; to figure the cost of; to cipher, code ‖ *intr* to calculate; to mount up; to cipher, code ‖ *ref*—**se chiffrer par** to amount to

chignole [ʃiɲɔl] *f* breast drill, hand drill; (coll) jalopy

chignon [ʃiɲɔ̃] *m* chignon, bun, knot

Chili [ʃili] *m*—**le Chili** Chile

chimère [ʃimer] *f* chimera; **se forger des chimères** to indulge in wishful thinking

chimie [ʃimi] *f* chemistry

chimique [ʃimik] *adj* chemical

chimiste [ʃimist] *mf* chemist

chimpanzé [ʃɛ̃pɑ̃ze] *m* chimpanzee

Chine [ʃin] *f* China; **la Chine** China

chi·né -née [ʃine] *adj* mottled, figured

chiner [ʃine] *tr* to mottle (*cloth*); (coll) to make fun of

chi·nois [ʃinwa] **-noise** [nwaz] *adj* Chinese ‖ *m* Chinese (*language*) ‖ (*cap*) *mf* Chinese (*person*)

chinoiserie [ʃinwazri] *f* Chinese curio; **chinoiseries administratives** (coll) red tape

chiot [ʃjo] *m* puppy

chiourme [ʃjurm] *f* chain gang

chiper [ʃipe] *tr* (slang) to swipe

chiple [ʃipl] *f* (coll) shrew

chipoter [ʃipɔte] *intr* to haggle
chips [ʃips] *mpl* potato chips
chique [ʃik] *f* chew, quid (*of tobacco*); (ent) chigger
chiqué [ʃike] *m* (slang) sham, bluff
chiquenaude [ʃiknod] *f* fillip, flick
chiquer [ʃike] *tr* to chew (*tobacco*) || *intr* to chew tobacco
chiromancie [kirɔmɑ̃si] *f* palmistry
chiroman·cien [kirɔmɑ̃sjɛ̃] -**cienne** [sjɛn] *mf* palm reader
chiropracteur [kirɔpraktœr] *m* chiropractor
chirurgi·cal -**cale** [ʃiryʒikal] *adj* (*pl* -**caux** [ko]) surgical
chirurgie [ʃiryʒi] *f* surgery
chirur·gien [ʃiryʒjɛ̃] -**gienne** [ʒjɛn] *mf* surgeon
chirurgien-dentiste [ʃiryʒjɛ̃dɑ̃tist] *m* (*pl* **chirurgiens-dentistes**) dental surgeon
chiure [ʃjyr] *f* flyspeck
chlore [klɔr] *m* chlorine
chlo·ré -**rée** [klɔre] *adj* chlorinated
chlorhydrique [klɔridrik] *adj* hydrochloric
chloroforme [klɔrɔfɔrm] *m* chloroform
chloroformer [klɔrɔfɔrme] *tr* to chloroform
chlorophylle [klɔrɔfil] *f* chlorophyll
chlorure [klɔryr] *m* chloride; **chlorure de soude** sodium chloride
choc [ʃɔk] *m* shock; clash; bump; clink (*of glasses*)
chocolat [ʃɔkɔla] *adj invar* & *m* chocolate
chocolaterie [ʃɔkɔlatri] *f* chocolate factory
chœur [kœr] *m* choir, chorus
choir [ʃwar] (usually used only in *inf* and *pp* **chu**; sometimes used in *pres ind* **chois**, etc.; *pret* **chus**, etc.; *fut* **choirai**, etc.) *intr* (*aux*: ÊTRE or AVOIR) to fall; **se laisser choir** to drop, to flop
choi·si -**sie** [ʃwazi] *adj* choice, select; chosen; selected (*works*)
choisir [ʃwazir] *tr* & *intr* to choose
choix [ʃwa] *m* choice; **au choix** at one's discretion; **de choix** choice
choléra [kɔlera] *m* cholera
cholérique [kɔlerik] *mf* cholera victim
cholestérol [kɔlesterɔl] *m* cholesterol
chômage [ʃomaʒ] *m* unemployment; **en chômage** unemployed
chô·mé -**mée** [ʃome] *adj* closed for business, off, e.g., **jour chômé** day off
chômer [ʃome] *tr* to take (*a day*) off; to observe (*a holiday*) || *intr* to take off (*from work*); to be unemployed
chô·meur [ʃomœr] -**meuse** [møz] *mf* unemployed worker
chope [ʃɔp] *f* stein, beer mug
chopine [ʃɔpin] *f* half-liter measure; (slang) bottle
chopper [ʃɔpe] *intr* to stumble; to blunder
choquer [ʃɔke] *tr* to shock; to bump; to clink (*glasses*); (elec) to shock || *ref* to collide; to take offense
cho·ral -**rale** [kɔral] *adj* (*pl* -**raux** [ro]) choral || *m* (*pl* -**rais**) chorale || *f* choral society, glee club

chorégraphie [kɔregrafi] *f* choreography
choriste [kɔrist] *mf* chorister
chorus [kɔrys] *m*—**faire chorus** to repeat in unison; to chime in; to approve unanimously
chose [ʃoz] *adj invar* (coll) odd; **être tout chose** (coll) to feel funny || *m* thingamajig; **Monsieur Chose** (coll) Mr. what's-his-name || *f* thing || *pron indef masc*—**autre chose** something else; **quelque chose** something
chou [ʃu] **choute** [ʃut] *mf*—**ma choute**, **mon chou** (coll) sweetheart || *m* (*pl* **choux**) cabbage; **chou à la crème** cream puff; **choux de Bruxelles** Brussels sprouts; **de chou** (coll) of little value; **faire chou blanc** (coll) to draw a blank; **finir dans le chou** (coll) to come in last
choucas [ʃuka] *m* jackdaw
choucroute [ʃukrut] *f* sauerkraut; **choucroute garnie** sauerkraut with ham or sausage
chouette [ʃwɛt] *adj* (coll) swell; **chouette alors!** (coll) oh boy! || *f* owl; (coll) radio; **chouette épervière** hawk owl
chou-fleur [ʃuflœr] *m* (*pl* **choux-fleurs**) cauliflower
chou-rave [ʃurav] *m* (*pl* **choux-raves**) kohlrabi
chow-chow [ʃuʃu] *m* (*pl* -**chows**) chow (*dog*)
choyer [ʃwaje] §47 *tr* to pamper, coddle; to cherish (*a hope*); to entertain (*an idea*)
chrestomatie [krestɔmati], [krestɔmasi] *f* chrestomathy
chré·tien [kretjɛ̃] -**tienne** [tjɛn] *adj* & *mf* Christian
chrétiennement [kretjɛnmɑ̃] *adv* in the faith
chrétienté [kretjɛ̃te] *f* Christendom
christ [krist] *m* crucifix || (*cap*) *m* Christ; **le Christ** Christ
christianiser [kristjanize] *tr* to Christianize
christianisme [kristjanism] *m* Christianity
chromatique [krɔmatik] *adj* chromatic
chrome [krom] *m* chrome, chromium
chromer [krome] *tr* to chrome
chromosome [krɔmozɔm] *m* chromosome
chronique [krɔnik] *adj* chronic || *f* chronicle; column (*in newspaper*); **chronique financière** financial page; **chronique mondaine** society news; **chronique théâtrale** theater page
chroniqueur [krɔnikœr] *m* chronicler; columnist; **chroniqueur dramatique** drama critic
chrono [krɔno] *m*—**faire du 60 chrono** (coll) to do 60 by the clock
chronologie [krɔnɔlɔʒi] *f* chronology
chronologique [krɔnɔlɔʒik] *adj* chronological
chronomètre [krɔnɔmetr] *m* chronometer; stopwatch
chronométrer [krɔnɔmetre] §10 *tr* to clock, to time

chronométreur [krɔnɔmetrœr] *m* time-keeper

chrysalide [krizalid] *f* chrysalis

chrysanthème [krizɑ̃tɛm] *m* chrysanthemum

chuchotement [ʃyʃɔtmɑ̃] *m* whisper, whispering

chuchoter [ʃyʃɔte] *tr & intr* to whisper

chuinter [ʃɥɛ̃te] *intr* to hoot (*said of owl*); to make a swishing sound, to hiss (*said of escaping gas*); to pronounce [ʃ] instead of [s] and [ʒ] instead of [z]

chut [ʃyt] *interj* sh!

chute [ʃyt] *f* fall; downfall; drop (*in prices, voltage, etc.*); **chute d'eau** waterfall

chuter [ʃyte] *tr* to hush; to hiss (*an actor*) ‖ *intr* (coll) to fall; (cards) to be down

Chypre [ʃipr] *f* Cyprus

ci [si] *pron indef*—**comme ci comme ça** so-so ‖ *adv*—**entre ci et là** between now and then

-ci [si] §82, §84

ci-après [siapre] *adv* hereafter, below, further on

ci-bas [siba] *adv* below

cible [sibl] *f* target

ciboule [sibul] *f* scallion

ciboulette [sibulɛt] *f* chive, chives

cicatrice [sikatris] *f* scar

cicatriser [sikatrize] *tr* to heal; to scar ‖ *ref* to heal

Cicéron [siserɔ̃] *m* Cicero

cicérone [siserɔn] *m* guide

ci-contre [sikɔ̃tr] *adv* opposite, on the opposite page; in the margin

ci-dessous [sidəsu] *adv* further on, below, hereunder

ci-dessus [sidəsy] *adv* above

ci-devant [sidəvɑ̃] *mf invar* (hist) aristocrat; (coll) back number ‖ *adv* previously, formerly

cidre [sidr] *m* cider

Cie *abbr* (**Compagnie**) Co.

ciel [sjɛl] *m* (*pl* **cieux** [sjø]) sky, heavens (*firmament*); heaven (*state of great happiness*) ‖ *m* (*pl* **ciels**) heaven (*abode of the blessed*); sky (*upper atmosphere, especially with reference to meteorological conditions; representation of sky in a painting*); canopy (*of a bed*) ‖ *m* (*pl* **cieux** or **ciels**) clime, sky

cierge [sjɛrʒ] *m* wax candle; cactus; **droit comme un cierge** straight as a ramrod; **en cierge** straight up

cigale [sigal] *f* cicada, grasshopper

cigare [sigar] *m* cigar

cigarette [sigarɛt] *f* cigarette

ci-gît [siʒi] see **gésir**

cigogne [sigɔɲ] *f* stork

ciguë [sigy] *f* hemlock (*herb and poison*)

ci-in·clus [siɛ̃kly] **-cluse** [klyz] *adj* enclosed ‖ **ci-inclus** *adv* enclosed

ci-joint [siʒwɛ̃] **-jointe** [ʒwɛ̃t] *adj* enclosed ‖ **ci-joint** *adv* enclosed

cil [sil] *m* eyelash; **cils** eyelash (*fringe of hair*)

cilice [silis] *m* hair shirt

ciller [sije] *tr & intr* to blink

cime [sim] *f* summit, top

ciment [simɑ̃] *m* cement; **ciment armé** reinforced concrete

cimentation [simɑ̃tasjɔ̃] *f* cementing

cimenter [simɑ̃te] *tr* to cement

cimeterre [simtɛr] *m* scimitar

cimetière [simtjɛr] *m* cemetery

cinéaste [sineast] *mf* film producer; movie director; scenarist; movie technician

cinégraphiste [sinegrafist] *mf* scenarist

cinéma [sinema] *m* movies; moving-picture theater; cinema; **cinéma auto** drive-in movie; **cinéma d'essai** preview theater; **cinéma muet** silent movie

cinémathèque [sinematek] *f* film library

cinématographique [sinematɔgrafik] *adj* motion-picture, film

cinéphile [sinefil] *mf* movie fan

cinéprojecteur [sineprɔʒektœr] *m* motion-picture projector

ciné-roman [sinerɔmɑ̃] *m* (*pl* **-romans**) published story (*of a film*)

cinétique [sinetik] *adj* kinetic ‖ *f* kinetics

cin·glant [sɛ̃glɑ̃] **-glante** [glɑ̃t] *adj* scathing

cin·glé -glée [sɛ̃gle] *adj* (slang) screwy ‖ *mf* (slang) screwball

cingler [sɛ̃gle] *tr* to whip; to cut to the quick ‖ *intr* to go full sail

cinq [sɛ̃(k)] *adj & pron* five; the Fifth, e.g., **Jean cinq** John the Fifth; **cinq heures** five o'clock ‖ *m* five; fifth (*in dates*); **il était moins cinq** (coll) it was a close shave

cinquantaine [sɛ̃kɑ̃tɛn] *f* about fifty; age of fifty, fifty mark, fifties

cinquante [sɛ̃kɑ̃t] *adj, pron, & m* fifty; **cinquante et un** fifty-one; **cinquante et unième** fifty-first

cinquantième [sɛ̃kɑ̃tjɛm] *adj, pron* (*masc, fem*), & *m* fiftieth

cinquième [sɛ̃kjɛm] *adj, pron* (*masc, fem*), & *m* fifth

cintre [sɛ̃tr] *m* arch; coat hanger; bend; **plein cintre** semicircular arch

cin·tré -trée [sɛ̃tre] *adj* (slang) crazy

cintrer [sɛ̃tre] *tr* to arch, to bend

cirage [siraʒ] *m* waxing; shoe polish; **dans le cirage** (coll) in the dark

circoncire [sirkɔ̃sir] §66 (*pp* **circoncis**) *tr* to circumcise

circoncision [sirkɔ̃sizjɔ̃] *f* circumcision

circonférence [sirkɔ̃ferɑ̃s] *f* circumference

circonflexe [sirkɔ̃flɛks] *adj & m* circumflex

circonscription [sirkɔ̃skripsjɔ̃] *f* circumscription; ward, district

circonscrire [sirkɔ̃skrir] §25 *tr* to circumscribe

circons·pect [sirkɔ̃spe], [sirkɔ̃spɛk(t)] **-pecte** [pɛkt] *adj* circumspect

circonstance [sirkɔ̃stɑ̃s] *f* circumstance; **circonstances et dépendances** appurtenances; **de circonstance** proper for the occasion, topical; emergency (*measure*); guest, e.g., **orateur de circonstance** guest speaker circonstan·cié -ciée [sirkɔ̃stɑ̃sje] *adj* circumstantial, in detail

circonstan·ciel -cielle [sirkɔ̃stɑ̃sjɛl] *adj* (gram) adverbial

circonvenir [sirkɔ̃vnir] §72 *tr* to circumvent

circonvoi·sin [sirkɔ̃vwazɛ̃] -sine [zin] *adj* nearby, neighboring

circuit [sirkɥi] *m* circuit; circumference; detour; tour

circulaire [sirkyler] *adj* & *f* circular

circulation [sirkylasjɔ̃] *f* circulation; traffic; circulation interdite (public sign) no thoroughfare

circuler [sirkyle] *intr* to circulate

cire [sir] *f* wax; cire à cacheter sealing wax; cire molle (fig) wax in one's hands

ci·ré -rée [sire] *adj* waxed || *m* waterproof garment; raincoat

cirer [sire] *tr* to wax; to polish

ci·reur [sirœr] -reuse [røz] *mf* waxer, polisher (*person*); shoeblack, bootblack || *f* floor waxer (*machine*)

ci·reux [sirø] -reuse [røz] *adj* waxy

ciron [sirɔ̃] *m* mite

cirque [sirk] *m* circus; amphitheater

cirrhose [siroz] *f* cirrhosis

cisaille [sizaj] *f* metal clippings, scissel; cisailles clippers, shears; wire cutter

cisailler [sizaje] *tr* to shear

ci·seau [sizo] *m* (*pl* -seaux) chisel; ciseau à froid cold chisel; ciseaux scissors; ciseaux à ongles nail scissors; ciseaux à raisin pruning shears; ciseaux à tondre sheep shears

ciseler [sizle] §2 *tr* to chisel; to chase; to cut, shear; to prune

ciseleur [sizlœr] *m* chaser, tooler

citadelle [sitadɛl] *f* citadel

cita·din [sitadɛ̃] -dine [din] *adj* urban || *mf* city dweller

citation [sitasjɔ̃] *f* citation, quotation; citation, summons

cité [site] *f* housing development; (hist) fortified city, citadel; cité ouvrière low-cost housing development; cité sainte Holy City; cité universitaire university dormitory complex; la Cité the City (*district within ancient boundaries*)

citer [site] *tr* to cite, quote; to summon, subpoena

citerne [sitɛrn] *f* cistern; tank; citerne flottante tanker

cithare [sitar] *f* cither, zither

citoyen [sitwajɛ̃] citoyenne [sitwajɛn] *mf* citizen; (coll) individual, person; citoyens citizenry

citoyenneté [sitwajɛnte] *f* citizenship; citizenry

citrique [sitrik] *adj* citric

citron [sitrɔ̃] *adj* & *m* lemon

citronnade [sitrɔnad] *f* lemonade

citron·né -née [sitrɔne] *adj* lemon-flavored

citronnelle [sitrɔnɛl] *f* citronella

citronner [sitrɔne] *tr* to flavor with lemon

citronnier [sitrɔnje] *m* lemon tree

citrouille [sitruj] *f* pumpkin, gourd

cive [siv] *f* scallion

civet [sive] *m* stew

civette [sivet] *f* civet; civet cat; chive, chives

civière [sivjer] *f* stretcher, litter

ci·vil -vile [sivil] *adj* civil; civilian; secular || *m* civilian; layman; en civil plain-clothes (*man*); in civies

civilisation [sivilizasjɔ̃] *f* civilization

civiliser [sivilize] *tr* to civilize || *ref* to become civilized

civilité [sivilite] *f* civility; civilités kind regards; amenities

civique [sivik] *adj* civic; civil (*rights*); national (*guard*)

civisme [sivism] *m* good citizenship

clabauder [klabode] *intr* to clamor

claie [kle] *f* wickerwork; trellis

clair claire [kler] *adj* clear, bright; evident, plain; light, pale || *m* light, brightness; clair de lune moonlight; clairs highlights || *f* oyster bed

clai·ret [klere] -rette [klerɛt] *adj* light-red; thin, high-pitched (*voice*) || *m* light, red wine || *f* light sparkling wine

claire-voie [klervwa] *f* (*pl* claires-voies) latticework, slats; clerestory; à claire-voie with open spaces

clairière [klerjer] *f* clearing, glade

clairon [klerɔ̃] *m* bugle; bugler

claironner [klerɔne] *tr* to announce || *intr* to sound the bugle

clairse·mé -mée [klersəme] *adj* scattered, sparse; thin, thinned out

clairvoyance [klervwajɑ̃s] *f* clear-sightedness, clairvoyance

clairvoyant [klervwajɑ̃] clairvoyante [klervwajɑ̃t] *adj* clear-sighted, clairvoyant

clamer [klame] *tr* & *intr* to cry out

clameur [klamœr] *f* clamor, outcry

clamp [klɑ̃] *m* (med) clamp

clampin [klɑ̃pɛ̃] *m* (mil) straggler

clan [klɑ̃] *m* clan, clique

clandes·tin [klɑ̃destɛ̃] -tine [tin] *adj* clandestine

clapet [klape] *m* valve; ferme ton clapet! (slang) shut your trap!

clapier [klapje] *m* rabbit hutch

clapoter [klapɔte] *intr* to splash; to be choppy

claque [klak] *m* opera hat || *f* slap, smack, slap, claque, paid applauders

claquemurer [klakmyre] *tr* to shut in || *ref* to shut oneself up at home

claquer [klake] *tr* to slap; to clap; to smack (*the lips*); to slam (*the door*); to crack (*the whip*); to click (*the heels*); to snap (*the fingers*); (coll) to tire out; (coll) to waste || *intr* to clap, slap, slam; to crack; (slang) to fail; (slang) to die || *ref* (*with dat of reflex pron*) to sprain; (slang) to work oneself to death

claquettes [klaket] *fpl* tap-dancing

claqueur [klakœr] *m* applauder, member of a claque

clarifier [klarifje] *tr* to clarify || *ref* to become clear

clarine [klarin] *f* cowbell

clarinette [klarinεt] f clarinet

clarté [klarte] f clarity; brightness; clarté du soleil sunshine

classe [klas] f class; classroom; classe de rattrapage refresher course (for backward children); classe de travaux pratiques lab class

clas·sé -sée [klase] adj pigeonholed, tabled; standard (literary work); listed; non classé (sports) also-ran

classer [klase] tr to class; to sort out, to file; to pigeonhole, to table

classeur [klasœr] m file (for letters, documents); filing cabinet

classicisme [klasisism] m classicism

classification [klasifikasjɔ̃] f classification

classifier [klasifje] tr to classify; to sort out

classique [klasik] adj classic, classical; standard (author, work) || mf classicist || m classic; standard work

claudication [klodikasjɔ̃] f limping

clause [kloz] f clause, stipulation, provision; clause additionnelle rider; clause ambiguë joker clause; clause de style unwritten provision

claustration [klostrasjɔ̃] f confinement; cloistering

clavecin [klavsε̃] m harpsichord

claveciniste [klavsinist] mf harpsichordist

clavette [klavεt] f pin, cotter pin; key

clavicule [klavikyl] f collarbone

clavier [klavje] m keyboard; key ring; range (e.g., of the voice); clavier universel standard keyboard

clayère [klεjεr] f oyster bed

clé [kle] f see clef

clef [kle] adj invar key || f key; wrench; (wrestling) lock; clef anglaise monkey wrench; clef à tube socket wrench; clef crocodile alligator wrench; clef des champs vacation; clef de voûte keystone; sous clef under lock and key

clémence [klemɑ̃s] f clemency

clé·ment [klemɑ̃] -mente [mɑ̃t] adj mild, clement

clenche [klɑ̃ʃ] f latch

cleptomane [klεptɔman] mf kleptomaniac

clerc [klεr] m cleric, clergyman; scholar; clerk

clergé [klεrʒe] m clergy

clergie [klεrʒi] f learning, scholarship; clergy

cléri·cal -cale [klerikal] adj & mf (pl -caux [ko]) clerical

cliché [kliʃe] m cliché; (phot) negative; (typ) plate, stereotype; prendre un cliché (phot) to make an exposure

clicher [kliʃe] tr (typ) to stereotype

client [klijɑ̃] cliente [kljɑ̃t] mf client; patient; customer; guest (of a hotel)

clientèle [klijɑ̃tεl] f clientele; adherents

cligner [kliɲe] tr to squint (one's eyes) || intr to squint, to blink; cligner de l'œil à to wink at

cligno·tant [kliɲɔtɑ̃] -tante [tɑ̃t] adj blinking || m (aut) directional signal

clignotement [kliɲɔtmɑ̃] m blinking; twinkling; flickering

clignoter [kliɲɔte] intr to blink; to twinkle; to flicker

clignoteur [kliɲɔtœr] m (aut) directional signal

climat [klima], [klima] m climate

climatisation [klimatizasjɔ̃] f air conditioning

climati·sé -sée [klimatize] adj air-conditioned

climatiseur [klimatizœr] m air conditioner

clin [klε̃] m—à clin (carpentry) overlapping, covering; clin d'œil wink; en un clin d'œil in the twinkling of an eye

clinicien [klinisjε̃] adj masc clinical || m clinician

clinique [klinik] adj clinical || f clinic; private hospital

clinquant [klε̃kɑ̃] m foil, tinsel; flashiness, tawdriness

clip [klip] m clip, brooch

clique [klik] f drum and bugle corps; (coll) gang; cliques wooden shoes

cliquet [klikε] m (mach) pawl, catch

cliqueter [klikte] §34 intr to click, to clink, to clank, to jangle

cliquetis [klikti] m click, clink, clank, jangle

cliquette [klikεt] f castanets; (fishing) sinker

clisse [klis] f draining rack, wicker bottleholder

clivage [klivaʒ] m cleavage

cliver [klive] tr to cleave; to cut

cloaque [klɔak] m cesspool

clo·chard [klɔʃar] -charde [ʃard] mf beggar, tramp

cloche [klɔʃ] adj bell-shape (skirt) || f bell; bell glass; blister (on skin); cloche à plongeurs diving bell; cloche de sauvetage escape hatch (on submarine); déménager à la cloche de bois (coll) to skip out without paying; la cloche (slang) beggars

clochement [klɔʃmɑ̃] m limp, limping

cloche-pied [klɔʃpje]—à cloche-pied on one foot, hopping

clocher [klɔʃe] m steeple; belfry; parish, home town; de clocher local (politics) || intr to limp; quelque chose cloche something jars, is not right

clocheton [klɔʃtɔ̃] m little steeple

clochette [klɔʃεt] f little bell; (bot) bellflower

cloison [klwazɔ̃] f partition; division, barrier (e.g., between classes); (anat, bot) septum, dividing membrane; (naut) bulkhead; cloison étanche (naut) watertight compartment

cloisonner [klwazone] tr to partition

cloître [klwatr] m cloister

cloîtrer [klwatre] tr to cloister; to confine

clopin-clopant [klɔpε̃klɔpɑ̃] adv (coll) so-so; aller clopin-clopant (coll) to go hobbling along

clopiner [klɔpine] intr to hobble

cloque [klɔk] f blister

cloquer [klɔke] tr & intr to blister

clore [klɔr] §24 tr & intr to close

clos [klo] **close** [kloz] *adj* closed ‖ *m* enclosure; **clos de vigne** vineyard

clôture [klotyr] *f* fence; wall; cloistered life; closing of an account

clôturer [klotyre] *tr* to enclose, to wall in; to close out (*an account*); to conclude (*a discussion*)

clou [klu] *m* nail; (coll) boil; (coll) jalopy; (coll) feature attraction; (slang) pawnshop; **clou de girofle** clove; **clous** pedestrian crossing; **des clous!** (slang) nothing at all!

clouer [klue] *tr* to nail; to immobilize, rivet; **clouer le bec à qn** (coll) to shut s.o.'s mouth

clouter [klute] *tr* to stud; to trim or border with studs, e.g., **passage clouté** pedestrian crossing (bordered with studs)

clown [klun] *m* clown; **faire le clown** to clown (around)

clownerie [klunri] *f* high jinks, clowning

club [klyb] *m* (literary) society; (political) association ‖ [klœb] *m* **club** (*for social and athletic purposes, etc.*); clubhouse; (golf) club; armchair

clubiste [klybist] *mf* (coll) club member; (coll) joiner

clubman [klœbman] *m* club member

coaccu·sé -sée [kɔakyze] *mf* codefendant

coaguler [kɔagyle] *tr & ref* to coagulate

coaliser [kɔalize] *tr* to form into a coalition ‖ *ref* to form a coalition

coalition [kɔalisjɔ̃] *f* coalition

coassement [kɔasmɑ̃] *m* croak, croaking

coasser [kɔase] *intr* to croak

coasso·clé -ciée [kɔasɔsje] *mf* copartner

coauteur [kɔotœr] *m* coauthor

cobalt [kɔbalt] *m* cobalt

cobaye [kɔbaj] *m* guinea pig

cocaïne [kɔkain] *f* cocaine

cocarde [kɔkard] *f* cockade; rosette of ribbons; **avoir sa cocarde** (coll) to be tipsy; **prendre la cocarde** (coll) to enlist

cocasse [kɔkas] *adj* (coll) funny, ridiculous

coccinelle [kɔksinel] *f* ladybug

coche [kɔʃ] *m* coach, stagecoach; two-door sedan; barge ‖ *f* notch, score; (zool) sow

cocher [kɔʃe] *m* coachman, driver ‖ *tr* to notch, to score; to check off

cochère [kɔʃer] *adj* carriage (*entrance*)

co·chon -chonne [ʃɔn] *mf* (coll) skunk, slob ‖ *m* pig, hog; **cochon de lait** suckling pig; **cochon de mer** porpoise; **cochon d'Inde** guinea pig

cochonnerie [kɔʃɔnri] *f* (slang) dirty trick; (slang) filthy speech, smut

cocker [kɔker] *m* cocker spaniel

cockpit [kɔkpit] *m* (aer) cockpit

cocktail [kɔktel] *m* cocktail; cocktail party

coco [kɔko] *m* (koko) coconut; licorice water; **mon coco** (coll) my darling; **un joli coco** (coll) a stinker ‖ *f* (slang) cocaine

cocon [kɔkɔ̃] *m* cocoon

cocorico [kɔkɔriko] *m* cockcrow ‖ *interj* cock-a-doodle-doo!

cocotier [kɔkɔtje] *m* coconut tree

cocotte [kɔkɔt] *f* saucepan; cocotte, floozy; **ma cocotte** (coll) my little chick, my baby doll

co·cu -cue [kɔky] *adj & m* cuckold

cocufier [kɔkyfje] *tr* (slang) to cuckold

code [kɔd] *m* code; **code de la route** traffic regulations; **code pénal** criminal code; **codes** (slang) dimmers; **se mettre en code** to dip one's headlights

codex [kɔdeks] *m* pharmacopoeia

codicille [kɔdisil] *m* codicil

codifier [kɔdifje] *tr* to codify

coéducation [kɔedykasjɔ̃] *f* coeducation

coefficient [kɔefisjɑ̃] *m* coefficient

coéqui·pier -pière [kɔekipje] [pjer] *mf* teammate

coercition [kɔersisjɔ̃] *f* coercion

cœur [kœr] *m* heart; core; courage, spirit; bosom, breast; depth (*of winter*); (cards) heart; (cards) hearts; **à cœur joie** to one's heart's content; **avoir du cœur** to be kind-hearted; **avoir du cœur au ventre** (coll) to have guts; **avoir le cœur sur la main** (coll) to be open-handed; **avoir le cœur sur les lèvres** to wear one's heart on one's sleeve; **cœur de bronze** heart of stone; **de bon cœur** willingly, heartily; **de mauvais cœur** reluctantly; **en avoir le cœur net** to get to the bottom of it; **épancher son cœur à** to open one's heart to; **fendre le cœur à** to break the heart of; **le cœur gros** with a heavy heart; **mal au cœur** or **mal de cœur** stomach ache; nausea; **par cœur** by heart; **prendre à cœur** to take to heart; **ronger le cœur** to eat one's heart out; **soulever le cœur** to turn the stomach

coexistence [kɔegzistɑ̃s] *f* coexistence

coexister [kɔegziste] *intr* to coexist

coffre [kɔfr] *m* chest; coffer, bin; safe-deposit box; trunk (*of car*); buoy (*for mooring*); cofferdam

coffre-fort [kɔfrəfɔr] *m* (*pl* **coffres-forts**) safe, strongbox, vault

coffret [kɔfre] *m* gift box

cognac [kɔɲak] *m* cognac

cognat [kɔɲa] *m* blood kin

cognée [kɔɲe] *f* ax, hatchet

cogner [kɔɲe] *tr, intr, & ref* to knock, bump

cohabiter [kɔabite] *intr* to cohabit

cohé·rent -rente [kɔerɑ̃] [rɑ̃t] *adj* coherent

cohériter [kɔerite] *intr* to inherit jointly

cohéri·tier -tière [kɔeritje] [tjer] *mf* coheir

cohésion [kɔezjɔ̃] *f* cohesion

cohorte [kɔɔrt] *f* cohort

cohue [kɔy] *f* crowd, throng, mob

coi [kwa] **coite** [kwat] *adj* quiet; **demeurer** or **se tenir coi** to keep still

coiffe [kwaf] *f* cap; headdress; caul

coif·fé -fée [kwafe] *adj*—**coiffé de** wearing (*a hat*); (fig) crazy about (*a person*); **être coiffé** to be wearing a hairdo; **être né coiffé** (fig) to be lucky

coiffer [kwafe] tr to put a hat or cap on (s.o.); to dress or do the hair of; (mil) to reach (an objective) || intr—**coiffer de** to wear (a certain size hat) || ref to do one's hair; **se coiffer de** (coll) to set one's cap for

coif·feur [kwafœr] **coif·feuse** [kwafØz] mf hairdresser; barber; **coiffeur pour dames** coiffeur || f dresser, dressing table

coiffure [kwafyr] f coiffure; headdress; **coiffure en brosse** crew cut

coin [kwɛ̃] m corner; angle; nook; wedge, coin; stamp, die (for coining money); (typ) quoin; **le petit coin** (coll) the powder room

coinçage [kwɛ̃saʒ] m wedging

coincer [kwɛ̃se] §51 tr to wedge, jam; (coll) to pinch, arrest || ref to jam

coincidence [kɔɛ̃sidɑ̃s] f coincidence

coincider [kɔɛ̃side] intr to coincide

coin-coin [kwɛ̃kwɛ̃] m invar quack (of duck); toot (of horn)

coing [kwɛ̃] m quince

coït [kɔit] m coition

coke [kɔk] m coke

cokéfier [kɔkefje] tr & ref to coke

col [kɔl] m neck (of bottle; of womb); collar (of dress); mountain pass; (coll) head (on beer); **col de fourrure** neckpiece; **col roulé** turtleneck; **faux col** detachable collar

colback [kɔlbak] m busby

colère [kɔler] f anger; **en colère** angry; **se mettre en colère** to become angry

colé·reux [kɔlerØ] **-reuse** [rØz] adj irascible, choleric

colérique [kɔlerik] adj choleric

colibri [kɔlibri] m hummingbird

colimaçon [kɔlimasɔ̃] m snail; **en colimaçon** spiral

colin [kɔlɛ̃] m hake

colin-maillard [kɔlɛ̃majar] m blind-man's buff

colique [kɔlik] f colic

colis [kɔli] m piece of baggage, package, parcel; **colis postal** parcel post

colisée [kɔlize] m coliseum

collabora·teur [kɔlabɔratœr] **-trice** [tris] mf collaborator; contributor

collaborationniste [kɔlabɔrasjɔnist] mf collaborationist

collaborer [kɔlabɔre] intr to collaborate; **collaborer à** to contribute to

collage [kɔlaʒ] m pasting, mounting; collage; sizing; clarifying (of wine); (coll) common-law marriage

col·lant [kɔlɑ̃] **col·lante** [kɔlɑ̃t] adj sticky; tight, close-fitting || m tights

collapsus [kɔlapsys] m (pathol) collapse

collaté·ral -rale [kɔlateral] (pl -raux [ro]) adj collateral; parallel; intermediate (points of the compass) || mf collateral (relative) || m side aisle of a church

collation [kɔlasjɔ̃] f conferring (of titles, degrees, etc.); collation (of texts) || [kɔlasjɔ̃] f snack

collationner [kɔlasjɔne] tr to collate, to compare; **faire collationner un télégramme** to request a copy of a telegram || intr to have a snack

colle [kɔl] f paste, glue; (coll) brain-teaser, stickler; (slang) detention; (slang) oral exam; (slang) flunking; **colle forte** glue; **poser une colle** (slang) to ask a hard one

collecte [kɔlekt] f collection (for charitable cause); (eccl) collect

collecteur [kɔlektœr] adj main, e.g., **égout collecteur** main sewer || m collector; commutator (of motor or dynamo); (aut) manifold; **collecteur d'ondes** aerial

collec·tif [kɔlektif] **-tive** [tiv] adj collective

collection [kɔleksjɔ̃] f collection

collectionner [kɔleksjɔne] tr to collect

collection·neur [kɔleksjɔnœr] **collection·neuse** [kɔleksjɔnØz] mf collector

collège [kɔleʒ] m high school; preparatory school; college (of cardinals, electors, etc.); **collège universitaire** junior college

collé·gial -giale [kɔleʒjal] (pl -giaux [ʒjo]) adj collegiate || f collegiate church

collé·gien [kɔleʒjɛ̃] **-gienne** [ʒjen] adj high-school || m schoolboy || f schoolgirl; coed

collègue [kɔleg] mf colleague

coller [kɔle] tr to paste, stick, glue; to clarify (wine); to mat (e.g., with blood); (coll) to floor, to stump; (coll) to punish (a pupil); (coll) to flunk; (coll) to sock (e.g., on the jaw) || intr to cling, to fit tightly (said of dress); (coll) to stick close; **ça colle!** (slang) O.K.! || ref (slang) to have a common-law marriage; **se coller contre** to stand close to; to cling to

collet [kɔle] m collar; neck (of person; of tooth); neck, scrag (e.g., of mutton); cape; snare; stalk and roots; lasso, noose; **collet monté** (coll) stuffed shirt

colleter [kɔlte] §34 tr to collar || ref to fight, scuffle

collier [kɔlje] m necklace; collar; dog collar; horse collar; **à collier** ring-necked; **reprendre le collier** (coll) to get back into harness

colliger [kɔlliʒe] §38 tr to make a collection of

colline [kɔlin] f hill

collision [kɔllizjɔ̃] f collision

colloï·dal -dale [kɔllɔidal] adj (pl -daux [do]) colloid, colloidal

colloïde [kɔllɔid] m colloid

colloque [kɔllɔk] m colloquy, symposium

colloquer [kɔllɔke] tr to classify (creditors' claims); **colloquer q.ch. à qn** (coll) to palm off s.th. on s.o.

collusion [kɔllyzjɔ̃] f collusion

collyre [kɔllir] m (med) eyewash

Cologne [kɔlɔɲ] f Cologne

Colomb [kɔlɔ̃] m Columbus

colombe [kɔlɔ̃b] f dove

Colombie [kɔlɔ̃bi] f Colombia; **la Colombie** Colombia

colombier [kɔlɔ̃bje] *m* dovecote; large-size paper

colom·bin [kɔlɔ̃bɛ̃] **-bine** [bin] *adj* columbine || *m* stock dove; lead ore || *f* bird droppings; (bot) columbine

colon [kɔlɔ̃] *m* colonist; tenant farmer; summer camper

côlon [kolɔ̃] *m* (anat) colon

colonel [kɔlɔnɛl] *m* colonel

colonelle [kɔlɔnɛl] *f* colonel's wife; (theat) performance for the press

colonie [kɔlɔni] *f* colony; **colonie de déportation** penal settlement; **colonie de vacances** summer camp

coloniser [kɔlɔnize] *tr* to colonize

colonnade [kɔlɔnad] *f* colonnade

colonne [kɔlɔn] *f* column; pillar; **cinquième colonne** fifth column; **colonne vertébrale** spinal column

colophane [kɔlɔfan] *f* rosin

colophon [kɔlɔfɔ̃] *m* colophon

colo·rant [kɔlɔrɑ̃] **-rante** [rɑ̃t] *adj* coloring || *m* dye, stain

colorer [kɔlɔre] *tr & ref* to color

colorier [kɔlɔrje] *tr* to paint, color

coloris [kɔlɔri] *m* hue; brilliance

colos·sal -sale [kɔlɔsal] *adj* (*pl* **colossaux** [kɔlɔso]) colossal

colosse [kɔlɔs] *m* colossus

colporter [kɔlpɔrte] *tr* to peddle

colporteur [kɔlpɔrtœr] *m* peddler

coltiner [kɔltine] *tr* to lug on one's back or on one's head

coma [kɔma] *m* (pathol) coma

coma·teux [kɔmatø] **-teuse** [tøz] *adj* comatose || *mf* person in a coma

combat [kɔ̃ba] *m* combat; **combat tournoyant** (aer) dogfight; **hors de combat** disabled

comba·tif [kɔ̃batif] **-tive** [tiv] *adj* combative

combat·tant [kɔ̃batɑ̃] **combat·tante** [kɔ̃batɑ̃t] *adj & mf* combatant; **anciens combattants** veterans

combattre [kɔ̃batr] §7 *tr & intr* to combat

combien [kɔ̃bjɛ̃] *adv* how much, how many; how far; how long; how, e.g., **combien il était brave!** how brave he was! || *m invar*—**du combien chaussez-vous?** what size shoes do you wear?; **du combien coiffez-vous?** what size hat do you wear?; **le combien?** which one (*in a series*)?; **le combien êtes-vous?** (coll) what rank do you have?; **le combien sommes-nous?** (coll) what day of the month is it?; **tous les combien?** how often?

combinaison [kɔ̃binezɔ̃] *f* combination; coveralls; slip, undergarment

combi·né -née [kɔ̃bine] *adj* combined || *m* French telephone, handset; radio phonograph

combiner [kɔ̃bine] *tr* to combine; to arrange, group; to concoct (*a scheme*) || *ref* (chem) to combine

comble [kɔ̃bl] *adj* full, packed || *m* summit; roof, coping; **au comble de** at the height of; **c'est le comble!**, **c'est un comble!** (coll) that's the limit!, that takes the cake!; **sous les combles** in the attic

combler [kɔ̃ble] *tr* to heap up; to fill to the brim; to overwhelm; **combler d'honneurs** to shower honors upon

combustible [kɔ̃bystibl] *adj & m* combustible, fuel

combustion [kɔ̃bystjɔ̃] *f* combustion

comédie [kɔmedi] *f* comedy; play; sham

comé·dien [kɔmedjɛ̃] **-dienne** [djɛn] *mf* comedian; actor; hypocrite; **comédien ambulant** strolling player || *f* comedienne; actress

comédon [kɔmedɔ̃] *m* blackhead

comestible [kɔmestibl] *adj* edible || **comestibles** *mpl* foodstuffs

comète [kɔmɛt] *f* comet

comique [kɔmik] *adj & m* comic

comité [kɔmite] *m* committee

commandant [kɔmɑ̃dɑ̃] *m* commandant, commander; major

commande [kɔmɑ̃d] *f* order (*for goods or services*); control, command; **à la commande** (paid) down; **commande postale** mail order; **de commande** operating; (fait) **sur commande** (made) to order

commandement [kɔmɑ̃dmɑ̃] *m* command, order; commandment

commander [kɔmɑ̃de] *tr* to order (*goods or services*); to command, order || *intr* (mil) to command; **commander à** to control, to have command over; **commander à qn de +** *inf* to order s.o. to + *inf* || *ref* to control oneself

commanditaire [kɔmɑ̃diter] *adj* sponsoring || *mf* (com) sponsor, backer

commandite [kɔmɑ̃dit] *f* joint-stock company

commanditer [kɔmɑ̃dite] *tr* to back, to finance; (rad, telv) to sponsor

comme [kɔm] *adv* as; how; **comme ci comme ça** so-so || *prep* as, like || *conj* as; since

commémorer [kɔmmemɔre] *tr* to commemorate

commen·çant [kɔmɑ̃sɑ̃] **-çante** [sɑ̃t] *mf* beginner

commencement [kɔmɑ̃smɑ̃] *m* beginning

commencer [kɔmɑ̃se] §51 *tr & intr* to begin; **commencer à** to begin to

comment [kɔmɑ̃] *m invar* how; wherefore || *adv* how; why; **mais comment donc!** by all means!; **n'importe comment** any way || *interj* what!; indeed!

commentaire [kɔmɑ̃ter] *m* commentary; unfriendly comment

commenta·teur [kɔmɑ̃tatœr] **-trice** [tris] *mf* commentator

commenter [kɔmɑ̃te] *tr* to comment on; to make a commentary on; to criticize

commérage [kɔmeraʒ] *m* (coll) gossip

commer·çant [kɔmersɑ̃] **-çante** [sɑ̃t] *adj* commercial, business || *mf* merchant, dealer

commerce [kɔmers] *m* commerce, trade

commercer [kɔmerse] §51 *intr* to trade

commer·cial -ciale [kɔmersjal] *adj* (*pl* **-ciaux** [sjo] **-ciales**) commercial || *f* station wagon

commercialisation [kɔmersjalizasjɔ̃] *f* marketing

commercialiser [kɔmersjalize] *tr* to commercialize

commère [kɔmer] *f* (coll) busybody, gossip

commettre [kɔmetr] §42 *tr* to commit; to compromise || *ref* to compromise oneself

commis [kɔmi] *m* clerk; **commis voyageur** traveling salesman

commisération [kɔmizerasjɔ̃] *f* commiseration

commissaire [kɔmiser] *m* commissioner; commissary

commissaire-priseur [kɔmiserprizœr] *m* (*pl* **commissaires-priseurs**) appraiser; auctioneer

commissariat [kɔmisarja] *m* commissariat; **commissariat de police** police station

commission [kɔmisjɔ̃] *f* commission; errand; committee

commissionnaire [kɔmisjɔner] *m* agent, broker; messenger

commissionner [kɔmisjɔne] *tr* to commission

commissure [kɔmisyr] *f* corner (*of* lips)

commode [kɔmɔd] *adj* convenient; comfortable; easygoing || *f* chest of drawers, bureau

commodité [kɔmɔdite] *f* comfort, accommodation; **à votre commodité** at your convenience; **commodités** comfort station

commotion [kɔmosjɔ̃] *f* commotion; concussion; shock

commotionner [kɔmosjɔne] *tr* to shake up, injure, shock

commuer [kɔmɥe] *tr* (law) to commute

com·mun [kɔmœ̃] **com·mune** [kɔmyn] *adj* common || *m* common run || *f* see **commune**

commu·nal -nale [kɔmynal] (*pl* **-naux** [no]) *adj* communal, common || *mpl* common property, commons

communautaire [kɔmynoter] *adj* communal

communauté [kɔmynote] *f* community; **Communauté économique européenne** Common Market

commune [kɔmyn] *f* commune; **communes** Commons

commu·niant [kɔmynjɑ̃] **-niante** [njɑ̃t] *mf* communicant

communicable [kɔmynikabl] *adj* communicable

communi·cant [kɔmynikɑ̃] **-cante** [kɑ̃t] *adj* communicating

communica·teur [kɔmynikatœr] **-trice** [tris] *adj* connecting (*wire*)

communica·tif [kɔmynikatif] **-tive** [tiv] *adj* communicative; infectious (*laughter*)

communication [kɔmynikasjɔ̃] *f* communication; telephone call; (telp) connection; **communication avec avis d'appel** (telp) messenger call; **communication avec préavis** person-to-person call; **communication payable à l'arrivée, communication P.C.V.** collect call; **en communication** in touch; **fausse communication** (telp)

wrong number; **vous avez la communication!** (telp) go ahead!

communier [kɔmynje] *intr* to take communion; to have a common bond of sympathy, to be in accord

communion [kɔmynjɔ̃] *f* communion

communiqué [kɔmynike] *m* communiqué

communiquer [kɔmynike] *tr & intr* to communicate

communi·sant [kɔmynizɑ̃] **-sante** [zɑ̃t] *adj* fellow-traveling || *mf* fellow traveler

communisme [kɔmynism] *m* communism

communiste [kɔmynist] *adj & mf* communist

commutateur [kɔmytatœr] *m* (elec) changeover switch, two-way switch

commutation [kɔmytasjɔ̃] *f* commutation

commutatrice [kɔmytatris] *f* (elec) rotary converter

com·pact -pacte [kɔ̃pakt] *adj* compact

compagne [kɔ̃paɲ] *f* companion; helpmate

compagnie [kɔ̃paɲi] *f* company; **de compagnie or en compagnie** together; **fausser compagnie à** to give (*s.o.*) the slip; **tenir compagnie à** to keep (*s.o.*) company

compagnon [kɔ̃paɲɔ̃] *m* companion; **compagnon d'armes** comrade in arms; **compagnon de jeu** playmate; **compagnon de route** fellow traveler; **compagnon d'infortune** fellow sufferer; **joyeux compagnon** good fellow

comparaison [kɔ̃parezɔ̃] *f* comparison; **en comparaison de** compared to; **par comparaison** in comparison; **sans comparaison** beyond comparison

comparaître [kɔ̃paretr] §12 *intr* (law) to appear (in court)

compara·tif [kɔ̃paratif] **-tive** [tiv] *adj & m* comparative

compa·ré -rée [kɔ̃pare] *adj* comparative

comparer [kɔ̃pare] *tr* to compare

comparoir [kɔ̃parwar] (used only in: *inf*; *ger* **comparant**) *intr* (law) to appear in court

comparse [kɔ̃pars] *mf* (theat) walk-on; (fig) nobody, unimportant person

compartiment [kɔ̃partimɑ̃] *m* compartment

comparution [kɔ̃parysjɔ̃] *f* appearance in court

compas [kɔ̃pa] *m* compasses (*for drawing circles*); calipers; (naut) compass; **avoir le compas dans l'œil** to have a sharp eye

compas·sé -sée [kɔ̃pase] *adj* stiff, studied

compasser [kɔ̃pase] *tr* to measure out, to lay off; **compasser ses discours** to speak like a book

compassion [kɔ̃pasjɔ̃] *f* compassion

compatibilité [kɔ̃patibilite] *f* compatibility

compatir [kɔ̃patir] *intr*—**compatir à** to take pity on, to feel for; to be indulgent toward; to share in (*s.o's* *bereavement*); **ne pouvoir compatir** to be unable to agree

compatis·sant [kɔ̃patisɑ̃] **compatis·sante** [kɔ̃patisɑ̃t] *adj* compassionate, sympathetic, indulgent

compatriote [kɔ̃patriɔt] *mf* compatriot

compensa·teur [kɔ̃pɑ̃satœr] **-trice** [tris] *adj* compensating, equalizing

compensation [kɔ̃pɑ̃sɑsjɔ̃] *f* compensation

compenser [kɔ̃pɑ̃se] *tr* to compensate; to compensate for || *ref* to balance each other

compérage [kɔ̃peraʒ] *m* complicity

compère [kɔ̃per] *m* accomplice; comrade; stooge (*for a clown*)

compétence [kɔ̃petɑ̃s] *f* competence, proficiency; (law) jurisdiction

compé·tent [kɔ̃petɑ̃] **-tente** [tɑ̃t] *adj* competent, proficient; (law) having jurisdiction, expert

compéter [kɔ̃pete] §10 *intr*—**compéter à** to belong to by right; to be within the competency of (*a court*)

compéti·teur [kɔ̃petitœr] **-trice** [tris] *mf* rival, competitor

compétition [kɔ̃petisjɔ̃] *f* competition

compilation [kɔ̃pilɑsjɔ̃] *f* compilation

compiler [kɔ̃pile] *tr* to compile

complainte [kɔ̃plɛ̃t] *f* sad ballad; (law) complaint

complaire [kɔ̃pler] §52 *intr* (with *dat*) to please, gratify || *ref*—**se complaire à** to take pleasure in

complaisance [kɔ̃plezɑ̃s] *f* compliance; courtesy; complacency; **auriez-vous la complaisance de . . . ?** would you be so kind as to . . . ?; **de complaisance** out of kindness

complai·sant [kɔ̃plezɑ̃] **-sante** [zɑ̃t] *adj* complaisant, obliging; complacent

complément [kɔ̃plemɑ̃] *m* complement; (gram) object; **complément d'attribution** (gram) indirect object

com·plet [kɔ̃ple] **-plète** [plet] *adj* complete, full; **c'est complet!** that's the last straw! || *m* suit (*of clothes*); **au complet** full (*house*); **au grand complet** at full strength

compléter [kɔ̃plete] §10 *tr* to complete || *ref* to be completed; to complement one another

complet-veston [kɔ̃plevestɔ̃] *m* (*pl* complets-veston) man's suit

complexe [kɔ̃pleks] *adj & m* complex; **complexe de culpabilité** guilt complex

complexé complexée [kɔ̃plekse] *adj* (coll) timid, withdrawn || *mf* person with complexes

complexion [kɔ̃pleksjɔ̃] *f* constitution, disposition

complication [kɔ̃plikɑsjɔ̃] *f* complication

complice [kɔ̃plis] *adj* accessory, abetting || *mf* accomplice; **complice d'adultère** corespondent

complicité [kɔ̃plisite] *f* complicity

compliment [kɔ̃plimɑ̃] *m* compliment

complimenter [kɔ̃plimɑ̃te] *tr* to compliment; to congratulate

complimen·teur [kɔ̃plimɑ̃tœr] **-teuse** [tøz] *adj* complimentary || *mf* flatterer, yes man

compli·qué -quée [kɔ̃plike] *adj* complicated

compliquer [kɔ̃plike] *tr* to complicate || *ref* to become complicated; to have complications

complot [kɔ̃plo] *m* plot, conspiracy

comploter [kɔ̃plɔte] *tr & intr* to plot, conspire

comploteur [kɔ̃plɔtœr] *m* conspirator

comportement [kɔ̃pɔrtəmɑ̃] *m* behavior

comporter [kɔ̃pɔrte] *tr* to permit; to include || *ref* to behave

compo·sant [kɔ̃pozɑ̃] **-sante** [zɑ̃t] *adj* constituent || *m* (chem) component || *f* (mech) component

compo·sé -sée [kɔ̃poze] *adj & m* compound

composer [kɔ̃poze] *tr* to compose; to compound; to dial (*a telephone number*) || *intr* to take an exam; to come to terms || *ref*—**se composer de** to be composed of

composi·teur [kɔ̃pozitœr] **-trice** [tris] *mf* composer; compositor; **amiable compositeur** (law) arbitrator

composition [kɔ̃pozisjɔ̃] *f* composition; compound; dialing (*of telephone number*); term paper; **de bonne composition** easygoing, reasonable; **entrer en composition** to reach an agreement

compositeur [kɔ̃pɔstœr] *m* composing stick; dating and numbering machine, dating stamp

compote [kɔ̃pɔt] *f* compote; **compote de pommes** applesauce

compotier [kɔ̃pɔtje] *m* compote (*dish*)

compréhensible [kɔ̃preɑsibl] *adj* comprehensible

compréhen·sif [kɔ̃preɑsif] **-sive** [siv] *adj* understanding; comprehensive

compréhension [kɔ̃preɑsjɔ̃] *f* comprehension, understanding

comprendre [kɔ̃prɑ̃dr] §56 *tr* to understand; to comprehend, to include, to comprise || *intr* to understand || *ref* to be understood; to be included

compresse [kɔ̃pres] *f* (med) compress

compresseur [kɔ̃presœr] *m* compressor

compression [kɔ̃presjɔ̃] *f* compression; repression; reduction

compri·mé -mée [kɔ̃prime] *adj* compressed || *m* (pharm) tablet, lozenge

comprimer [kɔ̃prime] *tr* to compress; to repress

com·pris [kɔ̃pri] **-prise** [priz] *adj* understood; included; including, e.g., **la ferme comprise** or **y compris la ferme** the farm included, including the farm

compromet·tant [kɔ̃prɔmetɑ̃] **compromet·tante** [kɔ̃prɔmetɑ̃t] *adj* compromising, incriminating

compromettre [kɔ̃prɔmetr] §42 *tr* to compromise || *intr* to submit to arbitration || *ref* to compromise oneself

compromis [kɔ̃prɔmi] *m* compromise

comptabiliser [kɔ̃tabilize] *tr* (com) to enter into the books

comptabilité [kɔ̃tabilite] *f* bookkeeping, accounting; accounting department, accounts; **comptabilité à partie double** double-entry bookkeeping; **comptabilité simple** single-entry bookkeeping; **tenir la comptabilité** to keep the books

comptable [kɔ̃tabl] *adj* accountable, responsible; accounting (*machine*) || *mf* bookkeeper; **comptable agréé** or **expert comptable** certified public accountant; **comptable contrôleur** auditor

comp·tant [kɔ̃tɑ̃] -tante [tɑ̃t] *adj* spot (*cash*); down, e.g., **argent comptant** cash down || *m*—**au comptant** cash, for cash || **comptant** *adv* cash (down), e.g., **payer comptant** to pay cash

compte [kɔ̃t] *m* account; accounting; (sports) count; **à bon compte** cheap; **à ce compte** in that case; **à compte** on account; **au bout du compte** or **en fin de compte** when all is said and done; **compte à rebours** countdown; **compte courant** current account; **charge account**; **compte de dépôt** checking account; **compte de profits et pertes** profit and loss statement; **compte en banque** bank account; **compte rendu** report, review; **compte rond** round numbers; **donner son compte à** to give the final paycheck to, to discharge; **être en compte à demi** to go fifty-fifty; **loin de compte** wide of the mark; **rendre compte de** to review; **se rendre compte de** to realize, to be aware of; **tenir compte de** to bear in mind

compte-fils [kɔ̃tfil] *m invar* cloth prover

compte-gouttes [kɔ̃tgut] *m invar* dropper; **au compte-gouttes** in driblets

compter [kɔ̃te] *tr* to count; to number, have; **compter** + *inf* to count on + *ger*; **sans compter** not to mention || *intr* to count; **à compter de** starting from; **compter avec** to reckon with; **compter sur** to count on

compte-tours [kɔ̃tatur] *m invar* tachometer, r.p.m. counter

comp·teur [kɔ̃tœr] -teuse [tøz] *mf* counter, checker (*person*) || *m* meter; counter; speedometer; **compteur de gaz** gas meter; **compteur de Geiger** Geiger counter; **compteur de stationnement** parking meter; **relever le compteur** to read the meter

compteur-indicateur [kɔ̃tœrɛ̃dikatœr] *m* (*pl* **compteurs-indicateurs**) speedometer

comptine [kɔ̃tin] *f* counting-out rhyme

comptoir [kɔ̃twar] *m* counter; branch bank; bank; **comptoir postal** mailorder house

compulser [kɔ̃pylse] *tr* to go through, examine (*books, papers, etc.*)

computer [kɔ̃pyte] *tr* to compute

comte [kɔ̃t] *m* count

comté [kɔ̃te] *m* county

comtesse [kɔ̃tes] *f* countess

concasser [kɔ̃kase] *tr* to crush, pound

concasseur [kɔ̃kasœr] *adj masc* crushing || *m* (mach) crusher

concave [kɔ̃kav] *adj* concave

concéder [kɔ̃sede] §10 *tr & intr* to concede

concen·tré -trée [kɔ̃sɑ̃tre] *adj* concentrated; condensed (*milk*); reserved (*person*)

concentrer [kɔ̃sɑ̃tre] *tr* to concentrate; to repress, hold back

concentrique [kɔ̃sɑ̃trik] *adj* concentric

concept [kɔ̃sɛpt] *m* concept

conception [kɔ̃sɛpsjɔ̃] *f* conception

concerner [kɔ̃sɛrne] *tr* to concern; **en ce qui concerne** concerning

concert [kɔ̃sɛr] *m* concert; **de concert** together, in concert

concer·tant [kɔ̃sɛrtɑ̃] -tante [tɑ̃t] *adj* performing together || *mf* (mus) performer

concerter [kɔ̃sɛrte] *tr & ref* to concert, to plan

concertiste [kɔ̃sɛrtist] *mf* concert performer

concession [kɔ̃sɛsjɔ̃] *f* concession

concessionnaire [kɔ̃sɛsjɔner] *mf* grantee, licensee; dealer (*in automobiles*); agent (*for insurance*)

concetti [kɔ̃tʃeti] *mpl* conceits

concevable [kɔ̃səvabl] *adj* conceivable

concevoir [kɔ̃səvwar] §59 *tr* to conceive; to compose (*a letter, telegram*)

concierge [kɔ̃sjerʒ] *mf* concierge, building superintendent

concile [kɔ̃sil] *m* (eccl) council

concilia·teur [kɔ̃siljatœr] -trice [tris] *adj* conciliating || *mf* conciliator

conciliatoire [kɔ̃siljatwar] *adj* conciliatory

concilier [kɔ̃silje] *tr* to reconcile (*two parties, two ideas, etc.*); to win (*e.g., favor*) || *ref* to win over, gain (*e.g., esteem*); to agree

con·cis [kɔ̃si] -cise [siz] *adj* concise

concitoyen [kɔ̃sitwajɛ̃] concitoyenne [kɔ̃sitwajen] *mf* fellow citizen

conclu·ant [kɔ̃klyɑ̃] concluante [kɔ̃klyɑ̃t] *adj* conclusive

conclure [kɔ̃klyr] §11 *tr* to conclude || *intr* to conclude; **conclure à** to decide on, to decide in favor of

conclusion [kɔ̃klyzjɔ̃] *f* conclusion

concombre [kɔ̃kɔ̃br] *m* cucumber

concomi·tant [kɔ̃kɔmitɑ̃] -tante [tɑ̃t] *adj* concomitant

concordance [kɔ̃kɔrdɑ̃s] *f* agreement; concordance (*of Bible*)

concorde [kɔ̃kɔrd] *f* concord

concorder [kɔ̃kɔrde] *intr* to agree

concourir [kɔ̃kurir] §14 *intr* to compete; to cooperate; to converge, concur

concours [kɔ̃kur] *m* crowd; cooperation; contest, competition; meet; competitive examination; **concours de beauté** beauty contest; **concours de créanciers** meeting of creditors; **concours hippique** horse show; **hors concours** not competing; in a class by itself

con·cret [kɔ̃kre] -crète [kret] *adj & m* concrete

concrétiser [kɔ̃kretize] tr to put in concrete form

concubine [kɔ̃kybin] f concubine

concurrence [kɔ̃kyrãs] f competition; competitors; jusqu'à concurrence de to the amount of; libre concurrence free enterprise

concurrencer [kɔ̃kyrãse] §51 tr to rival, to compete with

concur·rent [kɔ̃kyrã] concur·rente [kɔ̃kyrãt] adj competitive || mf competitor; contestant

concurren·tiel -tielle [kɔ̃kyrãsjel] adj competitive

concussion [kɔ̃kysjɔ̃] f extortion; embezzlement

condamnable [kɔ̃danabl] adj blameworthy

condamnation [kɔ̃danasjɔ̃] f condemnation

condamner [kɔ̃dane] tr to condemn; to give up (an incurable patient); to forbid the use of; to board up (a window); to batten down (the hatches)

condensateur [kɔ̃dãsatœr] m (elec) condenser

condenser [kɔ̃dãse] tr & ref to condense

condenseur [kɔ̃dãsœr] m condenser

condescendance [kɔ̃desãdãs] f condescension

condescen·dant [kɔ̃desãdã] -dante [dãt] adj condescending

condescendre [kɔ̃desãdr] intr to condescend; to yield, comply

condiment [kɔ̃dimã] m condiment

condisciple [kɔ̃disipl] mf classmate

condition [kɔ̃disjɔ̃] f condition; à condition, sous condition conditionally; on approval; à condition que on condition that; dans de bonnes conditions in good condition; sans conditions unconditional

condition·nel -nelle [kɔ̃disjɔnel] adj & m conditional

conditionner [kɔ̃disjɔne] tr to condition; (com) to package

condoléances [kɔ̃dɔleãs] fpl condolence

conduc·teur [kɔ̃dyktœr] -trice [tris] adj conducting; driving; (elec) power (line); (elec) lead (wire) || adj masc (elec, phys) (in predicate after être, it may be translated by a noun) conductor, e.g., les métaux sont bons conducteurs de l'électricité metals are good conductors of electricity || mf guide; leader; driver || m motorman; foreman; pressman; (elec, phys) conductor

conduire [kɔ̃dɥir] §19 tr to conduct; to lead; to drive; to see (s.o. to the door) || intr to drive || ref to conduct oneself

conduit [kɔ̃dɥi] m conduit; conduit auditif auditory canal; conduits lacrymaux tear ducts

conduite [kɔ̃dɥit] f conduct, behavior; management, command; driving (of a car; of cattle); pipe line; duct, flue; avoir de la conduite to be well behaved; conduite d'eau water main; conduite intérieure closed car; faire la conduite à to escort; faire une conduite de Grenoble à qn (coll) to kick s.o. out

cône [kon] m cone

confection [kɔ̃feksjɔ̃] f manufacture; construction (e.g., of a machine); ready-made clothes; de confection ready-made (suit, dress, etc.)

confectionner [kɔ̃feksjɔne] tr to manufacture; to prepare (a dish)

confection·neur [kɔ̃feksjɔnœr] confec·tion·neuse [kɔ̃feksjɔnøz] mf manufacturer (esp. of ready-made clothes)

confédération [kɔ̃federasjɔ̃] f confederation, confederacy

confédérer [kɔ̃federe] §10 tr & ref to confederate

conférence [kɔ̃ferãs] f conference; lecture, speech; conférence au sommet summit conference; conférence de presse press conference

conféren·cier [kɔ̃ferãsje] -cière [sjer] mf lecturer, speaker

conférer [kɔ̃fere] §10 tr to confer, award; to administer (a sacrament); to collate, compare || intr to confer

confesse [kɔ̃fes] f—à confesse to confession; de confesse from confession

confesser [kɔ̃fese] tr to confess; (coll) to pump (s.o.) || ref to confess

confesseur [kɔ̃fesœr] m confessor

confession [kɔ̃fesjɔ̃] f confession; (eccl) denomination

confessionnal [kɔ̃fesjɔnal] m confessional

confession·nel -nelle [kɔ̃fesjɔnel] adj denominational

confiance [kɔ̃fjãs] f confidence; confiance en soi self-confidence; de confiance reliable; confidently; en confiance with confidence

con·fiant [kɔ̃fjã] -fiante [fjãt] adj confident; confiding, trusting

confidence [kɔ̃fidãs] f confidence, secret

confi·dent [kɔ̃fidã] -dente [dãt] mf confident

confiden·tiel -tielle [kɔ̃fidãsjel] adj confidential

confier [kɔ̃fje] tr to entrust; to confide, disclose; to commit (to memory); to consign; confier à to put (seed) in (the ground) || ref—se confier à to confide in, to trust; se confier en to put one's trust in

confinement [kɔ̃finmã] m imprisonment

confiner [kɔ̃fine] tr to confine || intr—confiner à to border on, to verge on || ref to confine oneself; se confiner dans to confine oneself to

confins [kɔ̃fɛ̃] mpl confines

confire [kɔ̃fir] §66 (pp confit) tr to preserve; to pickle; to candy; to can (goose, chicken, etc.); to dip (skins) || ref to become immersed (in work, prayer, etc.)

confirmer [kɔ̃firme] tr to confirm

confiserie [kɔ̃fizri] f confectionery

confi·seur [kɔ̃fizœr] -seuse [zøz] mf confectioner, candymaker

confisquer [kɔ̃fiske] tr to confiscate

con·fit [kɔ̃fi] -fite [fit] adj preserved; pickled; candied; steeped (e.g., in *piety*); incrusted (*in bigotry*) ‖ *m* canned chicken, goose, etc.

confiture [kɔ̃fityr] *f* preserves, jam

confitu·rier [kɔ̃fityrje] **-rière** [rjer] *mf* manufacturer of jams ‖ *m* jelly glass, jam jar

conflagration [kɔ̃flagrɑsjɔ̃] *f* conflagration, turmoil

conflit [kɔ̃fli] *m* conflict

confluer [kɔ̃flye] *intr* to meet, come together (*said of two rivers*)

confondre [kɔ̃fɔ̃dr] *tr* to confuse, mix up, mingle; to confound ‖ *ref* to become bewildered, mixed up; **se confondre en excuses** to fall all over oneself apologizing

conforme [kɔ̃fɔrm] *adj* corresponding; certified, e.g., **pour copie conforme** certified copy; **conforme à** conformable to, consistent with; **conforme à l'échantillon** identical with sample; **conforme aux normes** according to specifications; **conforme aux règles** in order

confor·mé -mée [kɔ̃fɔrme] *adj* shaped, built; **bien conformé** well-built; **mal conformé** misshapen

conformément [kɔ̃fɔrmemɑ̃] *adv*—**conformément à** in compliance with

conformer [kɔ̃fɔrme] *tr & ref* to conform

conformiste [kɔ̃fɔrmist] *mf* conformist

conformité [kɔ̃fɔrmite] *f* conformity, conformance

confort [kɔ̃fɔr] *m* comfort; convenience; **pneu confort** balloon tire

confortable [kɔ̃fɔrtabl] *adj* comfortable ‖ *m* comfort; easy chair

confrère [kɔ̃frɛr] *m* confrere, colleague

confrérie [kɔ̃freri] *f* brotherhood

confronter [kɔ̃frɔ̃te] *tr* to confront; to compare, collate

con·fus [kɔ̃fy] **-fuse** [fyz] *adj* confused, vague, blurred; embarrassed

confusion [kɔ̃fyzjɔ̃] *f* confusion

congé [kɔ̃ʒe] *m* leave; vacation; dismissal; **congé libérable** military discharge; **congé payé** vacation with pay; **donner congé à** to lay off; **donner son congé à** to give notice to; **prendre congé de** to take leave of

congédiement [kɔ̃ʒedimɑ̃] *m* dismissal, discharge; paying off (*of crew*)

congédier [kɔ̃ʒedje] *tr* to dismiss

congélateur [kɔ̃ʒelatœr] *m* freezer (*for frozen foods*)

congélation [kɔ̃ʒelɑsjɔ̃] *f* freezing

congeler [kɔ̃ʒle] §2 *tr & ref* to freeze; to congeal; **congeler à basse température** to deep-freeze

congéni·tal -tale [kɔ̃ʒenital] *adj* (*pl* **-taux** [to]) congenital

congère [kɔ̃ʒer] *f* snowdrift

congestion [kɔ̃ʒɛstjɔ̃] *f* congestion; **congestion cérébrale** stroke; **congestion pulmonaire** pneumonia

congestionner [kɔ̃ʒɛstjɔne] *tr & ref* to congest

conglomération [kɔ̃glɔmerɑsjɔ̃] *f* conglomeration

conglomérer [kɔ̃glɔmere] §10 *tr & ref* to conglomerate

congratulation [kɔ̃gratylɑsjɔ̃] *f* congratulation

congratuler [kɔ̃gratyle] *tr* to congratulate

congre [kɔ̃gr] *m* conger eel

congréer [kɔ̃gree] *tr* to worm (*rope*)

congrégation [kɔ̃gregɑsjɔ̃] *f* (eccl) congregation

congrès [kɔ̃grɛ] *m* congress, convention

congressiste [kɔ̃gresist] *mf* delegate ‖ *m* congressman ‖ *f* congresswoman

con·gru -grue [kɔ̃gry] *adj* precise, suitable; scanty; (math) congruent

conifère [kɔnifer] *adj* coniferous ‖ *m* conifer

conique [kɔnik] *adj* conical ‖ *f* conic section

conjecture [kɔ̃ʒektyr] *f* conjecture

conjecturer [kɔ̃ʒektyre] *tr & intr* to conjecture, to surmise

conjoindre [kɔ̃ʒwɛ̃dr] §35 *tr* to join in marriage

con·joint [kɔ̃ʒwɛ̃] **-jointe** [ʒwɛ̃t] *adj* united, joint ‖ *mf* spouse, consort

conjoncteur [kɔ̃ʒɔ̃ktœr] *m* automatic switch

conjonction [kɔ̃ʒɔ̃ksjɔ̃] *f* conjunction

conjugaison [kɔ̃ʒygɛzɔ̃] *f* conjugation

conju·gal -gale [kɔ̃ʒygal] *adj* (*pl* **-gaux** [go]) conjugal, connubial

conjuguer [kɔ̃ʒyge] *tr* to combine (*e.g., forces*); to conjugate

conjuration [kɔ̃ʒyrɑsjɔ̃] *f* conjuration; conspiracy; **conjurations** entreaties

conju·ré -rée [kɔ̃ʒyre] *mf* conspirator

conjurer [kɔ̃ʒyre] *tr* to conjure; to conjure away; to conjure up; to conspire for, to plot; **conjurer qn de** + *inf* to entreat s.o. to + *inf* ‖ *intr* to hatch a plot ‖ *ref* to plot together, conspire

connaissance [kɔnesɑ̃s] *f* knowledge; acquaintance; consciousness; attention; **connaissance des temps** nautical almanac; **connaissances** knowledge; **en connaissance de** with full knowledge of; **faire connaissance avec** to become acquainted with; **faire la connaissance de** to meet; **parler en connaissance de cause** to know what one is talking about; **perdre connaissance** to lose consciousness; **sans connaissance** unconscious

connaissement [kɔnesmɑ̃] *m* bill of lading

connais·seur [kɔnesœr] **connais·seuse** [kɔnesøz] *mf* connoisseur; expert

connaître [kɔnɛtr] §12 *tr* to know; to be acquainted with ‖ *intr*—**connaître de** (law) to have jurisdiction over ‖ *ref* to be acquainted; to become acquainted; **se connaître à** or **en** to know a lot about; **s'y connaître** to know what one is talking about; **s'y connaître en** to know a lot about

connecter [kɔnekte] *tr* to connect

connétable [kɔnetabl] *m* constable

connexe [kɔnɛks] *adj* connected

connexion [kɔnɛksjɔ̃] *f* connection

connexité [kɔnɛksite] *f* connection

con·nu -nue [kɔny] *adj* well-known ‖ *m*—**le connu** the known

conque [kɔ̃k] *f* conch

conqué·rant [kɔ̃kerɑ̃] **-rante** [rɑ̃t] *adj* (coll) swaggering ‖ *mf* conqueror

conquérir [kɔ̃kerir] §3 *tr* to conquer

conquête [kɔ̃ket] *f* conquest

consa·cré -crée [kɔ̃sakre] *adj* accepted, time-honored, stock

consacrer [kɔ̃sakre] *tr* to consecrate; to devote, dedicate *(time, energy, effort)*; to give, to spare *(e.g., time)*; to sanction, confirm ‖ *ref*—**se consacrer à** to devote or dedicate oneself to

consan·guin [kɔ̃sɑ̃gɛ̃] **-guine** [gin] *adj* consanguineous; on the father's side ‖ *mf* blood relation

consciemment [kɔ̃sjamɑ̃] *adv* consciously

conscience [kɔ̃sjɑ̃s] *f* conscience; conscientiousness; consciousness; **avoir la conscience large** to be broadminded; **en conscience** conscientiously

conscien·cieux [kɔ̃sjɑ̃sjø] **-cieuse** [sjøz] *adj* conscientious

cons·cient [kɔ̃sjɑ̃] **cons·ciente** [kɔ̃sjɑ̃t] *adj* conscious, aware, knowing

conscription [kɔ̃skripsjɔ̃] *f* draft, conscription

conscrit [kɔ̃skri] *m* draftee, conscript

consécration [kɔ̃sekrasjɔ̃] *f* consecration; confirmation

consécu·tif [kɔ̃sekytif] **-tive** [tiv] *adj* consecutive; dependent *(clause)*; **consécutif à** resulting from

conseil [kɔ̃sej] *m* advice, counsel; counselor; council, board, committee; **conseil d'administration** board of directors; **conseil de guerre** courtmartial; staff meeting of top brass; **conseil de prud'hommes** arbitration board; **conseil de révision** draft board; **conseils** advice; **un conseil** a piece of advice

conseil·ler [kɔ̃seje] **conseil·lère** [kɔ̃sejer] *mf* councilor; counselor, adviser ‖ *f* councillor's wife; counselor's wife ‖ **conseiller** *tr* to advise, to counsel *(s.o. or s.th.)*; **conseiller q.ch. à qn** to recommend s.th. to s.o. ‖ *intr* to advise, to counsel; **conseiller à qn de** + *inf* to advise s.o. to + *inf*

conseil·leur [kɔ̃sejer] **conseil·leuse** [kɔ̃sejøz] *mf* adviser; know-it-all

consensus [kɔ̃sɛ̃sys] *m* consensus

consentement [kɔ̃sɑ̃tmɑ̃] *m* consent

consentir [kɔ̃sɑ̃tir] §41 *tr* to grant, allow; to accept, recognize; **consentir que** + *subj* to permit *(s.o.)* to + *inf* ‖ *intr* to consent; **consentir à** to consent to, to agree to, to approve of

conséquemment [kɔ̃sekamɑ̃] *adv* consequently; consistently

conséquence [kɔ̃sekɑ̃s] *f* consequence; consistency; **en conséquence** accordingly

consé·quent [kɔ̃sekɑ̃] **-quente** [kɑ̃t] *adj* consequent; consistent; important ‖ *m* (logic, math) consequent; **par conséquent** consequently

conserva·teur [kɔ̃sɛrvatœr] **-trice** [tris] *adj* conservative ‖ *mf* conservative;

curator, keeper; warden, ranger; registrar

conservation [kɔ̃sɛrvasjɔ̃] *f* conservation, preservation; curatorship; curator's office

conservatisme [kɔ̃sɛrvatism] *m* conservatism

conservatoire [kɔ̃sɛrvatwar] *m* conservatory *(of music)*; museum, academy

conserve [kɔ̃sɛrv] *f* canned food, preserves; escort, convoy; **conserves** dark glasses; **conserves au vinaigre** pickles; **mettre en conserve** to can; **voler de conserve avec** to fly alongside of

conserver [kɔ̃sɛrve] *tr* to conserve; to preserve; to keep *(one's health; one's equanimity; a secret)*; to escort, to convoy *(a ship)* ‖ *ref* to stay in good shape; to take care of oneself

conserverie [kɔ̃sɛrvəri] *f* canning factory; canning

considérable [kɔ̃siderabl] *adj* considerable; important; large, great

considérant [kɔ̃siderɑ̃] *m* motive, grounds; **considérant que** whereas

considération [kɔ̃siderasjɔ̃] *f* consideration

considérer [kɔ̃sidere] §10 *tr* to consider, examine; to esteem, consider

consignataire [kɔ̃siɲater] *m* consignee, trustee

consignation [kɔ̃siɲasjɔ̃] *f* consignment; **en consignation** on consignment

consigne [kɔ̃siɲ] *f* password; baggage room, checkroom; checking fee; confinement to barracks, detention; deposit; (mil) orders, instructions; **en consigne à la douane** held up in customs; **être de consigne** to be on duty; **manquer à la consigne** to disobey orders

consigner [kɔ̃siɲe] *tr* to consign; to check *(baggage)*; to put down in writing, to enter in the record; to confine to barracks, to keep *(a student)* in; to put out of bounds *(e.g., for military personnel)*; to close *(a port)*; **consigner sa** (or **la**) **porte** to be at home to no one

consistance [kɔ̃sistɑ̃s] *f* consistency; stability *(of character)*; credit, reality, standing; **en consistance de** consisting of

consis·tant [kɔ̃sistɑ̃] **-tante** [tɑ̃t] *adj* consistent; stable *(character)*; **consistant en** consisting of

consister [kɔ̃siste] *intr*—**consister à** + *inf* to consist in + *ger*; **consister dans** or **en** to consist in; to consist of

consistoire [kɔ̃sistwar] *m* consistory

consola·teur [kɔ̃sɔlatœr] **-trice** [tris] *adj* consoling ‖ *mf* comforter

consolation [kɔ̃sɔlasjɔ̃] *f* consolation

console [kɔ̃sɔl] *f* console; console table; bracket

consoler [kɔ̃sɔle] *tr* to console

consolider [kɔ̃sɔlide] *tr* to consolidate; to fund *(a debt)*

consomma·teur [kɔ̃sɔmatœr] **-trice**

[tris] *mf* consumer; customer (*in a restaurant or bar*)

consommation [kɔ̃sɔmasjɔ̃] *f* consummation (*e.g., of a marriage*); perpetration (*e.g., of a crime*); consumption, use; drink (*e.g., in a café*)

consom·mé **-mée** [kɔ̃sɔme] *adj* consummate; skilled (*e.g., technician*); consumed, used up ‖ *m* consommé

consommer [kɔ̃sɔme] *tr* to consummate, complete; to perpetrate (*e.g., a crime*); to consume

consomp·tif [kɔ̃sɔ̃ptif] **-tive** [tiv] *adj* wasting away

consomption [kɔ̃sɔ̃psjɔ̃] *f* wasting away, decline

conso·nant [kɔ̃sɔnɑ̃] **-nante** [nɑ̃t] *adj* consonant, harmonious

consonne [kɔ̃sɔn] *f* consonant

consorts [kɔ̃sɔr] *mpl* partners, associates, (pej) confederates

conspira·teur [kɔ̃spiratœr] **-trice** [tris] *mf* conspirator

conspiration [kɔ̃spirasjɔ̃] *f* conspiracy

conspirer [kɔ̃spire] *tr & intr* to conspire

conspuer [kɔ̃spɥe] *tr* to boo, hiss

constamment [kɔ̃stamɑ̃] *adv* constantly

constance [kɔ̃stɑ̃s] *f* constancy

cons·tant [kɔ̃stɑ̃] **-tante** [tɑ̃t] *adj* constant; true; established, evident ‖ *f* constant

constat [kɔ̃sta] *m* affidavit

constatation [kɔ̃statasjɔ̃] *f* authentication; declaration, claim

constater [kɔ̃state] *tr* to certify; to find out; to prove, establish

constellation [kɔ̃stellasjɔ̃] *f* constellation

consteller [kɔ̃stelle] *tr* to spangle

consterner [kɔ̃sterne] *tr* to dismay

constipation [kɔ̃stipasjɔ̃] *f* constipation

constiper [kɔ̃stipe] *tr* to constipate

consti·tuant [kɔ̃stitɥɑ̃] **-tuante** [tɥɑ̃t] *adj & m* constituent

constituer [kɔ̃stitɥe] *tr* to constitute; to settle (*a dowry*); to form (*a cabinet; a corporation*); to empanel (*a jury*); to appoint (*a lawyer*) ‖ *ref* to be formed; **se constituer prisonnier** to give oneself up

constitu·tif [kɔ̃stitytif] **-tive** [tiv] *adj* constituent

constitution [kɔ̃stitysjɔ̃] *f* constitution; settlement (*of a dowry*); **constitution en société** incorporation

construc·teur [kɔ̃stryktœr] **-trice** [tris] *adj* constructive, building ‖ *mf* constructor, builder

construc·tif [kɔ̃stryktif] **-tive** [tiv] *adj* constructive

construction [kɔ̃stryksjɔ̃] *f* construction; **construction mécanique** mechanical engineering

construire [kɔ̃strɥir] §19 *tr* to construct, to build; to draw (*e.g., a triangle*); (gram) to construe

consul [kɔ̃syl] *m* consul

consulaire [kɔ̃syler] *adj* consular

consulat [kɔ̃syla] *m* consulate

consul·tant [kɔ̃syltɑ̃] **-tante** [tɑ̃t] *adj* consulting ‖ *mf* consultant

consulta·tif [kɔ̃syltatif] **-tive** [tiv] *adj* advisory

consultation [kɔ̃syltasjɔ̃] *f* consultation; **consultation externe** outpatient clinic; **consultation populaire** poll, referendum

consulte [kɔ̃sylt] *f* (eccl, law) consultation

consulter [kɔ̃sylte] *tr* to consult ‖ *intr* to give consultations ‖ *ref* to deliberate

consumer [kɔ̃syme] *tr* to consume, use up, destroy ‖ *ref* to burn out; to waste away; to fail

contact [kɔ̃takt] *m* contact; **mettre en contact** to put in touch, to connect; **prendre contact** to make contact

contacter [kɔ̃takte] *tr* (coll) to contact

conta·gieux [kɔ̃taʒjø] **-gieuse** [ʒjøz] *adj* contagious

contagion [kɔ̃taʒjɔ̃] *f* contagion

contamination [kɔ̃taminasjɔ̃] *f* contamination

contaminer [kɔ̃tamine] *tr* to contaminate

conte [kɔ̃t] *m* tale, story; **conte à dormir debout** cock-and-bull story, baloney; **conte de fées** fairy tale

contemplation [kɔ̃tɑ̃plasjɔ̃] *f* contemplation

contempler [kɔ̃tɑ̃ple] *tr* to contemplate

contempo·rain [kɔ̃tɑ̃porɛ̃] **-raine** [ren] *adj & m* contemporary

contemp·teur [kɔ̃tɑ̃ptœr] **-trice** [tris] *mf* scoffer

contenance [kɔ̃tnɑ̃s] *f* capacity; area; countenance; **faire bonne contenance** to put up a bold front

conte·nant [kɔ̃tnɑ̃] **-nante** [nɑ̃t] *adj* containing ‖ *m* container

contenir [kɔ̃tnir] §72 *tr* to contain; to restrain ‖ *ref* to contain oneself, to hold oneself back

con·tent [kɔ̃tɑ̃] **-tente** [tɑ̃t] *adj* content; happy, glad, pleased; **content de** satisfied with ‖ *m* fill, e.g., **avoir son content** to have one's fill

contentement [kɔ̃tɑ̃tmɑ̃] *m* contentment

contenter [kɔ̃tɑ̃te] *tr* to content, satisfy ‖ *ref* to satisfy one's desires; **se contenter de** to be content or satisfied with

conten·tieux [kɔ̃tɑ̃sjø] **-tieuse** [sjøz] *adj* contentious ‖ *m* contention, litigation; claims department

contention [kɔ̃tɑ̃sjɔ̃] *f* application, intentness

conte·nu **-nue** [kɔ̃tny] *adj* contained, restrained, stifled ‖ *m* contents

conter [kɔ̃te] *tr* to relate, tell; **en conter à** (coll) to take (*s.o.*) in; **en conter (de belles)** (coll) to tell tall tales ‖ *intr* to narrate, to tell a story

contestation [kɔ̃testasjɔ̃] *f* argument, dispute; **sans contestation** without opposition

conteste [kɔ̃test] *f*—**sans conteste** incontestably, unquestionably

contester [kɔ̃teste] *tr & intr* to contest

con·teur [kɔ̃tœr] **-teuse** [tøz] *mf* storyteller

contexte [kɔ̃tɛkst] *m* context

conti·gu -guë [kɔ̃tigy] *adj* contiguous; **contigu à** adjoining

continence [kɔ̃tinɑ̃s] *f* continence

conti·nent [kɔ̃tinɑ̃] **-nente** [nɑ̃t] *adj* & *m* continent

continen·tal -tale [kɔ̃tinɑ̃tal] *adj* (*pl* **-taux** [to]) continental

contingence [kɔ̃tɛ̃ʒɑ̃s] *f* contingency

contin·gent [kɔ̃tɛ̃ʒɑ̃] **-gente** [ʒɑ̃t] *adj* contingent ‖ *m* contingent; quota

conti·nu -nue [kɔ̃tiny] *adj* continuous; direct (*current*) ‖ *m* continuum

continuation [kɔ̃tinyɑsjɔ̃] *f* continuation

conti·nuel -nuelle [kɔ̃tinyɛl] *adj* continual

continuité [kɔ̃tinyite] *f* continuity

continûment [kɔ̃tinymɑ̃] *adv* continuously

contorsion [kɔ̃tɔrsjɔ̃] *f* contortion

contour [kɔ̃tur] *m* contour

contourner [kɔ̃turne] *tr* to contour; to go around, to skirt; to get around (*the law*); to twist, distort

contrac·tant [kɔ̃traktɑ̃] **-tante** [tɑ̃t] *adj* contracting (*parties*) ‖ *mf* contracting party

contracter [kɔ̃trakte] *tr* to contract; to float (*a loan*) ‖ *ref* to contract; to be contracted

contraction [kɔ̃traksjɔ̃] *f* contraction

contradiction [kɔ̃tradiksjɔ̃] *f* contradiction

contradictoire [kɔ̃tradiktwar] *adj* contradictory

contraindre [kɔ̃trɛ̃dr] §15 *tr* to compel, force, constrain; to restrain, to curb ‖ *ref* to restrain oneself

con·traint [kɔ̃trɛ̃] **-trainte** [trɛ̃t] *adj* constrained, forced; stiff (*person*) ‖ *f* constraint; restraint; exigencies (*e.g., of the rhyme*)

contraire [kɔ̃trɛr] *adj* contrary; opposite (*e.g., direction*); injurious (*e.g., to health*) ‖ *m* contrary, opposite; antonym; **au contraire** on the contrary

contrairement [kɔ̃trɛrmɑ̃] *adv* contrary

contrarier [kɔ̃trarje] *tr* to thwart; to vex, annoy; to contrast (*e.g., colors*)

contrariété [kɔ̃trarjete] *f* vexation, annoyance; clashing (*e.g., of colors*)

contraste [kɔ̃trast] *m* contrast

contraster [kɔ̃traste] *tr* & *intr* to contrast

contrat [kɔ̃tra] *m* contract

contravention [kɔ̃travɑ̃sjɔ̃] *f* infraction; **dresser une contravention** to write out a (traffic) ticket; **recevoir une contravention** to get a ticket

contre [kɔ̃tr] *m* opposite, con; (cards) double; **par contre** on the contrary ‖ *adv* against; nearby; **contre à contre** alongside ‖ *prep* against; contrary to; to, e.g., **dix contre un** ten to one; for, e.g., **échanger contre** to exchange for; e.g., **remède contre la toux** remedy for a cough; (sports) versus; **contre remboursement** (com) collect on delivery

contre-allée [kɔ̃trale] *f* (*pl* **-allées**) parallel walk

contre-amiral [kɔ̃tramiral] *m* (*pl* **-amiraux** [amiro]) rear admiral

contre-appel [kɔ̃trapel] *m* (*pl* **-appels**) second roll call; double-check

contre-attaque [kɔ̃tratak] *f* (*pl* **-attaques**) counterattack

contre-attaquer [kɔ̃tratake] *tr* to counterattack

contrebalancer [kɔ̃trəbalɑ̃se] §51 *tr* to counterbalance

contrebande [kɔ̃trəbɑ̃d] *f* contraband; smuggling; **faire la contrebande** to smuggle

contreban·dier [kɔ̃trəbɑ̃dje] **-dière** [djɛr] *adj* smuggled, contraband ‖ *mf* smuggler

contrebas [kɔ̃trəba]—**en contrebas** downwards

contrebasse [kɔ̃trəbas] *f* contrabass

contre-biais [kɔ̃trəbjɛ]—**à contre-biais** the wrong way, against the grain

contre-boutant [kɔ̃trəbutɑ̃] *m* (*pl* **-boutants**) shore

contrecarrer [kɔ̃trəkare] *tr* to stymie, to thwart

contre-chant [kɔ̃trəʃɑ̃] *m* (*pl* **-chants**) counter melody

contrecœur [kɔ̃trəkœr] *m* smoke shelf; **à contrecœur** unwillingly

contrecoup [kɔ̃trəku] *m* rebound, recoil, backlash; repercussion

contre-courant [kɔ̃trəkurɑ̃] *m* (*pl* **-courants**) countercurrent; **à contre-courant** upstream; behind the times

contredire [kɔ̃trədir] §40 *tr* to contradict ‖ *ref* to contradict oneself

contrée [kɔ̃tre] *f* region, countryside

contre-écrou [kɔ̃trekru] *m* (*pl* **-écrous**) lock nut

contre-espion [kɔ̃trespjɔ̃] *m* (*pl* **-espions**) counterspy

contre-espionnage [kɔ̃trespjɔnaʒ] *m* (*pl* **-espionnages**) counterespionage

contrefaçon [kɔ̃trəfasɔ̃] *f* infringement (*of patent or copyright*); forgery; counterfeit; plagiarism

contrefacteur [kɔ̃trəfaktœr] *m* forger; counterfeiter; plagiarist

contrefaction [kɔ̃trəfaksjɔ̃] *f* forgery; counterfeiting

contrefaire [kɔ̃trəfɛr] §29 *tr* to forge; to counterfeit; to imitate, to mimic; to disguise

contre-fait [kɔ̃trəfɛ] **-faite** [fɛt] *adj* counterfeit; deformed

contre-fenêtre [kɔ̃trəfnɛtr] *f* (*pl* **-fenêtres**) inner sash; storm window

contre-feu [kɔ̃trəfø] *m* (*pl* **-feux**) backfire (*in fire fighting*)

contreficher [kɔ̃trəfiʃe] *ref* (slang) to not give a rap

contre-fil [kɔ̃trəfil] *m* (*pl* **-fils**) opposite direction, wrong way; **à contre-fil** upstream; against the grain

contre-filet [kɔ̃trəfilɛ] *m* short loin (*club and porterhouse steaks*)

contrefort [kɔ̃trəfɔr] *m* buttress, abutment; foothills

contre-haut [kɔ̃trəo]—**en contre-haut** on a higher level; from top to bottom

contre-interrogatoire [kɔ̃trɛ̃terɔgatwar] *m* cross-examination

contre-interroger [kɔ̃trɛ̃teroʒe] §38 *tr* to cross-examine

contre-jour [kɔ̃traʒur] *m invar* backlighting; **à contre-jour** against the light

contremaî·tre [kɔ̃trəmetr] **-tresse** [tres] *mf* overseer || *m* foreman; (naut) (hist) boatswain's mate; (nav) petty officer || *f* forewoman

contremander [kɔ̃trəmɑ̃de] *tr* to countermand; to call off

contremarche [kɔ̃trəmarʃ] *f* countermarch; riser (*of stair step*)

contremarque [kɔ̃trəmark] *f* countersign; pass-out check

contremarquer [kɔ̃trəmarke] *tr* to countersign

contre-mesure [kɔ̃trəmzyr] *f* (*pl* **-mesures**) countermeasure

contre-offensive [kɔ̃trɔfɑ̃siv] *f* (*pl* **-offensives**) counteroffensive

contrepartie [kɔ̃trəparti] *f* counterpart; (bk) duplicate entry; **en contrepartie** as against this

contre-pas [kɔ̃trəpɑ] *m invar* half step (*taken in order to get in step*)

contre-pente [kɔ̃trəpɑ̃t] *f* (*pl* **-pentes**) reverse slope

contre-performance [kɔ̃trəperformɑ̃s] *f* (*pl* **-performances**) unexpected defeat

contrepèterie [kɔ̃trəpetri] *f* spoonerism

contre-pied [kɔ̃trəpje] *m* (*pl* **-pieds**) backtrack; opposite opinion; **à contre-pied** off balance

contre-plaqué [kɔ̃trəplake] *m* (*pl* **-plaqués**) plywood

contre-plaquer [kɔ̃trəplake] *tr* to laminate

contrepoids [kɔ̃trəpwa] *m invar* counterweight, counterbalance

contre-poil [kɔ̃trəpwal] *m* wrong way (*e.g., of fur*); **à contre-poil** the wrong way; at the wrong end

contrepoint [kɔ̃trəpwɛ̃] *m* counterpoint

contre-pointe [kɔ̃trəpwɛ̃t] *f* (*pl* **-pointes**) false edge (*of sword*); tailstock (*of lathe*)

contre-pointer [kɔ̃trəpwɛ̃te] *tr* to quilt

contrepoison [kɔ̃trəpwazɔ̃] *m* antidote

contrer [kɔ̃tre] *tr & intr* (cards) to double; (coll) to counter

contreseing [kɔ̃trəsɛ̃] *m* countersignature

contresens [kɔ̃trəsɑ̃s] *m invar* misinterpretation; mistranslation; wrong way; **à contresens** in the wrong sense; in the wrong direction

contresigner [kɔ̃trəsiɲe] *tr* to countersign

contretemps [kɔ̃trətɑ̃] *m*—**à contretemps** at the wrong moment; syncopated

contre-torpilleur [kɔ̃trətɔrpijœr] *m* (*pl* **-torpilleurs**) (nav) torpedo-boat destroyer

contreve·nant [kɔ̃trəvnɑ̃] **-nante** [nɑ̃t] *mf* lawbreaker, delinquent

contrevenir [kɔ̃trəvnir] §72 *intr* (with *dat*) to contravene, to break (*a law*)

contrevent [kɔ̃trəvɑ̃] *m* shutter, window shutter

contre-voie [kɔ̃trəvwa] *f* (*pl* **-voies**) parallel route; **à contre-voie** in reverse (*of the usual direction*); on the side opposite the platform

contribuable [kɔ̃tribɥabl] *adj* taxpaying || *mf* taxpayer

contribuer [kɔ̃tribɥe] *intr* to contribute

contribution [kɔ̃tribysjɔ̃] *f* contribution; tax

contrister [kɔ̃triste] *tr* to sadden

con·trit [kɔ̃tri] **-trite** [trit] *adj* contrite

contrôlable [kɔ̃trolabl] *adj* verifiable

contrôle [kɔ̃trol] *m* inspection, verification, check; supervision, observation; auditing; inspection booth, ticket window; (mil) muster roll; **contrôle des naissances** birth control; **contrôle de soi** self-control; **contrôle par sondage** spot check

contrôler [kɔ̃trole] *tr* to inspect, verify, check; to supervise, to put under observation; to audit; to criticize || *ref* to control oneself

contrô·leur [kɔ̃trolœr] **-leuse** [løz] *mf* inspector, checker; supervisor, observer; auditor, comptroller; conductor, ticket collector || *m* gauge; **contrôleur de vitesse** speedometer; **contrôleur de vol** flight indicator

controversable [kɔ̃trɔversabl] *adj* controversial

controverse [kɔ̃trɔvers] *f* controversy

controverser [kɔ̃trɔverse] *tr* to controvert

contumace [kɔ̃tymas] *f* contempt of court

con·tus [kɔ̃ty] **-tuse** [tyz] *adj* bruised

contusion [kɔ̃tyzjɔ̃] *f* contusion, bruise

contusionner [kɔ̃tyzjɔne] *tr* to bruise

convain·cant [kɔ̃vɛ̃kɑ̃] **-cante** [kɑ̃t] *adj* convincing

convaincre [kɔ̃vɛ̃kr] §70 *tr* to convince; to convict || *ref* to be satisfied

convain·cu **-cue** [kɔ̃vɛ̃ky] *adj* convinced, dyed-in-the-wool; convicted

convalescence [kɔ̃valesɑ̃s] *f* convalescence

convales·cent [kɔ̃valesɑ̃] **convales·cente** [kɔ̃valesɑ̃t] *adj & mf* convalescent

convenable [kɔ̃vnabl] *adj* suitable, proper; opportune (*moment*)

convenance [kɔ̃vnɑ̃s] *f* suitability, propriety; conformity; **convenances** conventions

convenir [kɔ̃vnir] §72 *intr* to agree; (with *dat*) to fit, suit; **convenir de** to admit, to admit to, to admit the truth of; to agree on || *ref* to agree with one another || *impers*—**il convient** it is fitting, it is appropriate

convention [kɔ̃vɑ̃sjɔ̃] *f* convention

conven·tion·nel **-nelle** [kɔ̃vɑ̃sjɔnel] *adj* conventional

conve·nu **-nue** [kɔ̃vny] *adj* settled; stipulated (*price*); appointed (*time, place*); trite, stereotyped (*language*)

converger [kɔ̃verʒe] §38 *intr* to converge

conversation [kɔ̃versɑsjɔ̃] *f* conversation

converser [kɔ̃verse] *intr* to converse

conversion [kɔ̃versjɔ̃] *f* conversion; turning

conver·ti -tie [kɔ̃verti] *adj* converted || *mf* convert

convertible [kɔ̃vertibl] *adj* convertible

convertir [kɔ̃vertir] *tr* to convert || *ref* to convert, to be converted; to change one's mind

convertissable [kɔ̃vertisabl] *adj* convertible

convertisseur [kɔ̃vertisœr] *m* converter; (elec) converter

convexe [kɔ̃veks] *adj* convex

conviction [kɔ̃viksjɔ̃] *f* conviction

convier [kɔ̃vje] *tr* to invite

convive [kɔ̃viv] *mf* dinner guest; table companion

convocation [kɔ̃vɔkɑsjɔ̃] *f* convocation, summoning

convoi [kɔ̃vwa] *m* convoy; funeral procession

convoiter [kɔ̃vwate] *tr* to covet

convoi·teur [kɔ̃vwatœr] **-teuse** [tøz] *adj* covetous || *mf* covetous person

convoitise [kɔ̃vwatiz] *f* covetousness, cupidity

convoquer [kɔ̃vɔke] *tr* to convoke; to summon

convoyer [kɔ̃vwaje] §47 *tr* to convoy

convoyeur [kɔ̃vwajœr] *adj* convoying || *m* (mach) conveyor; (nav) escort

convulser [kɔ̃vylse] *tr* to convulse

convulsion [kɔ̃vylsjɔ̃] *f* convulsion

convulsionner [kɔ̃vylsjɔne] *tr* to convulse

coordon·né -née [kɔɔrdɔne] *adj & f* coordinate

coordonner [kɔɔrdɔne] *tr* to coordinate

co·pain [kɔpɛ̃] **-pine** [pin] *mf* (coll) pal, chum

co·peau [kɔpo] *m* (*pl* **-peaux**) chip, shaving

copie [kɔpi] *f* copy; exercise, composition (*at school*); **pour copie conforme** true copy

copier [kɔpje] *tr & intr* to copy

co·pieux [kɔpjø] **-pieuse** [pjøz] *adj* copious

copilote [kɔpilɔt] *m* copilot

copiste [kɔpist] *mf* copyist; copier

coposséder [kɔpɔsede] §10 *tr* to own jointly

copropriété [kɔprɔprijete] *f* joint ownership

copula·tif [kɔpylatif] **-tive** [tiv] *adj* (gram) coordinating

copulation [kɔpylɑsjɔ̃] *f* copulation

copule [kɔpyl] *f* (gram) copula

coq [kɔk] *adj* bantam || *m* cock rooster; (naut) cook

coq-à-l'âne [kɔkɑlɑn] *m invar* cock-and-bull story

coque [kɔk] *f* shell; cocoon; hull; **coque de noix** coconut

coquelicot [kɔkliko] *m* poppy

coqueluche [kɔklyʃ] *f* whooping cough; (coll) rage, vogue

coquemar [kɔkmar] *m* teakettle

coquerie [kɔkri] *f* (naut) galley

coqueriquer [kɔkrike] *intr* to crow

co·quet [kɔkɛ] **-quette** [kɛt] *adj* coquettish; stylish; considerable (*sum*)

coqueter [kɔkte] §34 *intr* to flirt

coquetier [kɔkətje] *m* eggcup; egg man

coquetterie [kɔkɛtri] *f* coquetry

coquillage [kɔkijaʒ] *m* shellfish; shell

coquille [kɔkij] *f* shell; typographical error (*of transposed letters*); pat (*of butter*); **coquille de noix** nutshell; **coquille Saint-Jacques** scallop

co·quin [kɔkɛ̃] **-quine** [kin] *adj* deceitful; roguish || *mf* scoundrel; rogue

cor [kɔr] *m* horn; corn (*on foot*); prong (*of antler*); horn player; **à cor et à cri** with hue and cry; **cor anglais** English horn; **cor de chasse** hunting horn; **cor d'harmonie** French horn

co·rail [kɔraj] *m* (*pl* **-raux** [ro]) coral

cor·beau [kɔrbo] *m* (*pl* **-beaux**) crow, raven

corbeille [kɔrbej] *f* basket; flower bed; (theat) dress circle; **corbeille à papier** wastebasket; **corbeille de mariage** wedding present

corbillard [kɔrbijar] *m* hearse

corbillon [kɔrbijɔ̃] *m* small basket; word game

cordage [kɔrdaʒ] *m* cordage, rope; (naut) rigging

corde [kɔrd] *f* rope, cord; tightrope; inside track; (geom) chord; **corde à or de boyau** catgut (*for, e.g., violin*); **corde à linge** wash line; **corde à nœuds** knotted rope; **cordes vocales** vocal cords; **être sur la corde raide** to be out on a limb; **les cordes** (mus) the strings; **toucher la corde sensible** to touch a sympathetic chord; **usé jusqu'à la corde** threadbare

cor·dé -dée [kɔrde] *adj* heart-shaped || *f* cord (*of wood*); roped party (*of mountain climbers*)

cor·deau [kɔrdo] *m* (*pl* **-deaux**) tracing line; tracing thread; mine fuse; **tiré au cordeau** in a straight line

cordelier [kɔrdəlje] *m* Franciscan friar

corder [kɔrde] *tr* to twist; to string (*a tennis racket*)

cor·dial -diale [kɔrdjal] *adj & m* (*pl* **-diaux** [djo]) cordial

cordialité [kɔrdjalite] *f* cordiality

cordier [kɔrdje] *m* ropemaker; tailpiece (*of violin*)

cordon [kɔrdɔ̃] *m* cordon; cord; latchstring; **cordon de sonnette** bellpull; **cordon de soulier** shoestring

cordon-bleu [kɔrdɔ̃blø] *m* (*pl* **cordons-bleus**) cordon bleu

cordonnerie [kɔrdɔnri] *f* shoemaking; shoe repairing; shoe store; shoemaker's

cordon·nier [kɔrdɔnje] **cordon·nière** [kɔrdɔnjer] *mf* shoemaker

Corée [kɔre] *f* Korea; **la Corée** Korea

coré·en [kɔreɛ̃] **coréenne** [kɔreen] *adj* Korean || *m* Korean (*language*) || (*cap*) *mf* Korean (*person*)

coriace [kɔrjas] *adj* tough, leathery; (coll) stubborn

coricide [kɔrisid] *m* corn remover

cormoran [kɔrmɔrɑ̃] *m* cormorant

cornac [kɔrnak] *m* mahout

cor·nard [kɔrnar] **-narde** [nard] *adj* horned; (slang) cuckold; (*of horse*) wheezing || *m* (slang) cuckold

corne [kɔrn] *f* horn; dog-ear (*of page*); hoof; shoehorn; **corne d'abondance**

horn of plenty; **faire les cornes à** (coll) to make a face at

cor·né -née [kɔrne] *adj* horny ‖ *f* cornea

corneille [kɔrnej] *f* crow, rook; **corneille d'église** jackdaw

cornemuse [kɔrnəmyz] *f* bagpipe

cornemuseur [kɔrnəmyzœr] *m* bagpiper

corner [kɔrne] *tr* to dog-ear; to give (*s.o.*) the horn; (coll) to trumpet (*news*) about ‖ *intr* to blow the horn, to honk; to ring (*said of ears*); (mus) to blow a horn; **cornez!** sound your horn!

cornet [kɔrne] *m* cornet; horn; dice-box; cornetist; mouthpiece (*of microphone*); receiver (*of telephone*); **cornet acoustique** ear trumpet; **cornet à pistons** cornet; **cornet de glace** ice-cream cone

cornette [kɔrnet] *m* (mil) cornet ‖ *f* (*headdress*) cornet

cornettiste [kɔrnetist] *mf* cornetist

corniche [kɔrni/] *f* cornice

cornichon [kɔrni/ɔ̃] *m* pickle, gherkin; (*fool*) (coll) dope, drip

cor·nier -nière [kɔrnje] (**-nière** [njer]) *adj* corner ‖ *f* valley (*joining roofs*); angle iron

corniste [kɔrnist] *mf* horn player

Cornouailles [kɔrnwaj] *f* Cornwall

cornouiller [kɔrnuje] *m* dogwood

cor·nu -nue [kɔrny] *adj* horned; preposterous (*ideas*) ‖ *f* (chem) retort

corollaire [kɔrɔller] *m* corollary

coronaire [kɔrɔner] *adj* coronary

coroner [kɔrɔnœr] *m* coroner

corporation [kɔrpɔrɑsjɔ̃] *f* association, guild

corpo·rel -relle [kɔrpɔrel] *adj* corporal, bodily

corps [kɔr] *m* body; corps; **à corps perdu** without thinking; **à mon (ton, etc.) corps défendant** in self-defense; reluctantly; **corps à corps** hand-to-hand; in a clinch; **corps céleste** heavenly body; **corps composé** (chem) compound; **corps de garde** guardhouse, guardroom; **corps de logis** main part of the building; **corps du délit** corpus delicti; **corps enseignant** faculty; **corps simple** (chem) simple substance; **prendre corps** to take shape; **saisir au corps** (law) to arrest

corps-à-corps [kɔrakɔr] *m* hand-to-hand combat; (boxing) infighting

corpulence [kɔrpylɑ̃s] *f* corpulence

corpuscule [kɔrpyskyl] *m* (phys) corpuscle

corral [kɔral] *m* corral

cor·rect -recte [kɔrrekt] *adj* correct

correc·teur -trice [kɔrrektœr] (**-trice** [tris]) *mf* corrector; proofreader

correc·tif -tive [kɔrrektif] (**-tive** [tiv]) *adj* & *m* corrective

correction [kɔrreksjɔ̃] *f* correction; correctness; proofreading

corrélation [kɔrrelɑsjɔ̃] *f* correlation

correspondance [kɔrespɔ̃dɑ̃s] *f* correspondence; transfer, connection

correspon·dant [kɔrespɔ̃dɑ̃] (**-dante** [dɑ̃t]) *adj* corresponding, correspondent ‖ *mf* correspondent; party (*person who gets a telephone call*)

correspondre [kɔrespɔ̃dr] *intr* to correspond; **correspondre à** to correspond to, to correlate with; **correspondre avec** to correspond with (*a letter writer*); to connect with (*e.g., a train*)

corridor [kɔridɔr] *m* corridor

corriger [kɔriʒe] §38 *tr* to correct; to proofread

corroborer [kɔrrɔbɔre] *tr* to corroborate

corroder [kɔrrɔde] *tr* & *ref* to corrode; to erode

corrompre [kɔrɔ̃pr] (3d *sg pres ind* **corrompt**) *tr* to corrupt; to rot; to bribe; to seduce; to spoil

corro·sif -sive [kɔrrozif] (**-sive** [ziv]) *adj* & *m* corrosive

corrosion [kɔrrozjɔ̃] *f* corrosion; erosion

corroyer [kɔrwaje] §47 *tr* to weld; to plane (*wood*); to prepare (*leather*)

corruption [kɔrrypsjɔ̃] *f* corruption; bribery; seduction

corsage [kɔrsaʒ] *m* blouse, corsage

corsaire [kɔrser] *m* corsair; **corsaire de finance** ruthless businessman, robber baron

corse [kɔrs] *adj* Corsican ‖ *m* Corsican (*language*) ‖ (*cap*) *f* Corsica; **la Corse** Corsica ‖ (*cap*) *mf* Corsican (*person*)

cor·sé -sée [kɔrse] *adj* full-bodied, heavy; spicy, racy

corser [kɔrse] *tr* to spike, to give body to (*wine*); to spice up (*a story*) ‖ *ref* to become serious; **ça se corse** the plot thickens

corset [kɔrse] *m* corset

cortège [kɔrteʒ] *m* cortege; parade; **cortège funèbre** funeral procession

cortisone [kɔrtizɔn] *f* cortisone

corvée [kɔrve] *f* chore; forced labor; work party

coryphée [kɔrife] *m* coryphée; (fig) leader

cosaque [kɔzak] *adj* Cossack ‖ (*cap*) *mf* Cossack

cosmétique [kɔsmetik] *adj* cosmetic ‖ *m* cosmetic; hair set, hair spray ‖ *f* beauty culture

cosmique [kɔsmik] *adj* cosmic

cosmonaute [kɔsmɔnot] *mf* cosmonaut

cosmopolite [kɔsmɔpɔlit] *adj* & *mf* cosmopolitan

cosmos [kɔsmos], [kɔsmɔs] *m* cosmos; outer space

cosse [kɔs] *f* pod; **avoir la cosse** (slang) to be lazy

cos·su -sue [kɔsy] *adj* rich; well-to-do

cos·taud -taude [kɔsto] (**-taude** [tod]) *adj* (slang) husky, strapping ‖ *m* (slang) muscleman

costume [kɔstym] *m* costume; suit; **costume sur mesure** custom-made or tailor-made suit; **costume tailleur** lady's tailor-made suit

costumer [kɔstyme] *tr* & *ref* to dress up (*for a fancy-dress ball*); **se costumer en** to come dressed as a

costu·mier -mière [kɔstymje] (**-mière** [mjer]) *mf* costumer

cote [kɔt] *f* assessment, quota; identification mark, letter, or number; call number (*of book*); altitude (*above sea level*); bench mark; book value (*of, e.g., used cars*); racing odds; (telv) rating; **avoir la cote** (coll) to be highly thought of; **cote d'alerte** danger point; **cote d'amour** moral qualifications; **cote de la Bourse** stock-market quotations; **cote mal taillée** rough compromise

côte [kot] *f* rib; chop; coast; slope; **à côtes** ribbed, corded; **aller** or **se mettre à la côte**, **faire côte** to run aground; **avoir les côtes en long** (coll) to feel lazy; **côte à côte** side by side; **côte d'Azur** French Riviera; **côtes découvertes**, **plates côtes** spareribs; **en côte** uphill; **être à la côte** to be broke; **faire côte** to run aground

co·té -tée [kote] *adj* listed (*on the stock market*); (fig) esteemed

côté [kote] *m* side; **à côté** in the next room; near; **à côté de** beside; **côté cour** (theat) stage right; **côté jardin** (theat) stage left; **d'à côté** next-door; **de côté** sideways; sidelong; aside; **de mon côté** for my part; **donner, passer**, or **toucher à côté** to miss the mark; **du côté de** in the direction of, toward; on the side of; **d'un côté . . . de l'autre côté** or **d'un autre côté** on the one hand . . . on the other hand; **répondre à côté** to miss the point

co·teau [koto] *m* (*pl* **-teaux**) knoll; slope

Côte-de-l'Or [kotdəlɔr] *f* Gold Coast

côte·lé -lée [kotle] *adj* ribbed, corded

côtelette [kotlet] *f* cutlet, chop; **côtelettes découvertes** spareribs

coter [kote] *tr* to assess; to mark; to number; to esteem; (com) to quote, to give a quotation on; (geog) to mark the elevations on

coterie [kotri] *f* coterie, clique

cothurne [kotyrn] *m* buskin

cô·tier -tière [kotje] [tjer] *adj* coastal

cotir [kotir] *tr* to bruise (*fruit*)

cotisation [kotizasjɔ̃] *f* dues; assessment

cotiser [kotize] *tr* to assess (*each member of a group*) || *intr* to pay one's dues || *ref* to club together

coton [kotɔ̃] *m* cotton; **c'est coton** (slang) it's difficult; **coton de verre** glass wool; **coton hydrophile** absorbent cotton; cotton batting; **élever dans le coton** to coddle; **filer un mauvais coton** (coll) to be in a bad way

cotonnade [kotonad] *f* cotton cloth

cotonner [kotone] *tr* to pad or stuff with cotton || *ref* to become fluffy; to become spongy or mealy

cotonnerie [kotonri] *f* cotton field; cotton mill

coton·neux [kotonø] **coton·neuse** [kotonøz] *adj* cottony; spongy, mealy

coton·nier -nière [kotonje] [njer] *adj* cotton || *mf* cotton picker || *m* cotton plant

côtoyer [kotwaje] §47 *tr* to skirt (*the* edge); to hug (*the shore*); to border on (*the truth, the ridiculous, etc.*)

cotre [kotr] *m* (naut) cutter

cotte [kot] *f* petticoat; peasant skirt; overalls; **cotte de mailles** coat of mail

cou [ku] *m* neck; **sauter au cou de** to throw one's arms around

couard [kwar] **couarde** [kward] *adj* *mf* coward

couardise [kwardiz] *f* cowardice

couchage [kuʃaʒ] *m* bedding; bed for the night

cou·chant [kuʃɑ̃] **-chante** [ʃɑ̃t] *adj* setting || *m* west; decline, old age

couche [kuʃ] *f* layer, stratum; coat (*of paint*); diaper; (hort) hotbed; **couche de fond** primer, prime coat; **couches** strata; childbirth, e.g., **une femme en couches** a woman in childbirth; **fausse couche** miscarriage

coucher [kuʃe] *m* setting (*of sun*); going to bed; **coucher du soleil** sunset; **le coucher et la nourriture** room and board || *tr* to put to bed; to put down, lay down; to bend down, flatten; to mention (*in one's will*); **coucher en joue** to aim at; **coucher par écrit** to set down in writing || *intr* to spend the night; (naut) to heel over || *ref* to go to bed, to lie down; to set (*said of sun*); to bend; **allez vous coucher!** (coll) go to blazes!

couchette [kuʃet] *f* berth; crib

couci-couça [kusikusa] or **couci-couci** [kusikusi] *adv* so-so

coucou [kuku] *m* cuckoo; cuckoo clock; (coll) marsh marigold

coude [kud] *m* elbow; angle, bend, turn; **coude à coude** shoulder to shoulder; **jouer des coudes à travers** to elbow one's way through (*a crowd*)

coudée [kude] *f* cubit; **avoir ses coudées franches** to have a free hand; to have elbowroom

cou-de-pied [kudpje] *m* (*pl* **cous-de-pied**) instep

couder [kude] *tr* to bend like an elbow

coudoiement [kudwamɑ̃] *m* elbowing

coudoyer [kudwaje] §47 *tr* to elbow, to jostle; to rub shoulders with

coudraie [kudre] *f* hazel grove

coudre [kudr] §13 *tr* & *intr* to sew

coudrier [kudrije] *m* hazel tree

couenne [kwan] *f* pigskin; rind, crackling; mole, birthmark

couette [kwet] *f* feather bed; (little) tail; (mach) bearing; **couette de lapin** scut; **couettes** (naut) slip

cougouar or **couguar** [kugwar] *m* cougar

couiner [kwine] *intr* to send Morse code; (coll) to squeak (*said of animal*)

coulage [kulaʒ] *m* flow; leakage; casting (*of metal*); pouring (*of concrete*); (naut) scuttling; (coll) wasting

cou·lant [kulɑ̃] **-lante** [lɑ̃t] *adj* flowing, running; accommodating (*person*) || *m* sliding ring; (bot) runner

coule [kul] *f* cowl; **être à la coule** (slang) to know the ropes

cou·lé -lée [kule] *adj* cast; sunken;

(coll) sunk ‖ *m* (mus) slur ‖ *f* casting; run (*of wild beasts*); **coulée volcanique** outflow of lava

couler [kule] *tr* to pour; to cast (*e.g., a statue*); to scuttle; to pass (*e.g., many happy hours*); (mus) to slur ‖ *intr* to flow; to run; to leak; to sink; to slip (*away*) ‖ *ref* to slip, slide; (coll) to be done for, to be sunk; **se la couler douce** (coll) to take it easy

couleur [kulœr] *f* color; policy (*of newspaper*); (cards) suit; **de couleur** colored; **les trois couleurs** the tricolor; **sous couleur de** with the pretext of, with a show of

couleuvre [kulœvr] *f* snake; **avaler des couleuvres** (coll) to swallow insults; (coll) to be gullible; **couleuvre à collier** grass snake

coulis [kuli] *m*—**coulis de tomates** tomato sauce

coulisse [kulis] *f* groove; slide (*of trombone*); (com) curb exchange; (pol) lobby; **à coulisse** sliding; **coulisses** (theat) wings; (theat) backstage; **dans les coulisses** behind the scenes, out of sight; **travailler dans les coulisses** to pull strings

coulis-seau [kuliso] *m* (*pl* -seaux) slide, runner

couloir [kulwar] *m* corridor; hallway; lobby

couloire [kulwar] *f* strainer

coup [ku] *m* blow; stroke; blast (*of whistle*); jolt; **à coup de** with the aid of; **à coup sûr** certainly; **après coup** when it is too late; **à tout coup** each time; **boire à petits coups** to sip; **coup de bélier** water hammer (*in pipe*); **coup de coude** nudge; **coup de dés** throw of the dice; risky business; **coup de fer** pressing, ironing; **coup de feu, coup de fusil** shot, gunshot; **coup de fion** (slang) finishing touch; **coup de foudre** thunderbolt; love at first sight; bolt from the blue; **coup de fouet** whiplash; stimulus; **coup de froid** cold snap; **coup de grâce** last straw; deathblow; **coup de Jarnac** [ʒarnak] stab in the back; **coup de patte** expert stroke (*e.g., of the brush*); (coll) dig, insult; **coup de pied** kick; **coup d'épingle** pinprick; **coup de poing** punch; **coup de sang** (pathol) stroke; **coup de semence** warning shot; **coup de sifflet** whistle, toot; **coup de soleil** sunburn; (coll) sunstroke; **coup de téléphone** telephone call; **coup de tête** butt; sudden impulse; **coup de théâtre** dramatic turn of events; **coup de tonnerre** thunderclap; **coup d'œil** glance, look; **coup manqué, coup raté** miss; **coup monté** put-up job, frame-up; **coups et blessures** assault and battery; **coup sur coup** one right after the other; **donner un coup de main (à)** to lend a helping hand (to); **encore un coup** once again; **en venir aux coups** to come to blows; **être dans le coup** (coll) to be in on it; **faire coup double** to kill two birds with one stone; **faire les quatre coups** (coll) to

live it up, to dissipate; **faire un coup de main** to go on a raid; **manquer son coup** to miss one's chance; **se faire donner un coup de piston** (coll) to pull wires, to use influence; **sous le coup de** under the (immediate) influence of; **sur le coup** on the spot, outright; **tout à coup** suddenly; **tout d'un coup** at one shot, at once

coupable [kupabl] *adj* guilty ‖ *mf* culprit

cou·pant [kupɑ̃] **-pante** [pɑ̃t] *adj* cutting, sharp ‖ *m* (cutting) edge

coup-de-poing [kudpwɛ̃] *m* (*pl* **coups-de-poing**) brass knuckles

coupe [kup] *f* champagne glass; loving cup, trophy; cup competition; cutting; cross section; wood acreage to be cut; cut (*of cloth; of clothes; of playing cards*); division (*of verse*); **coupe claire** cutover forest; **coupe de cheveux** haircut; **coupe sombre** harvested forest; **être sous la coupe de qn** (coll) to be under s.o.'s thumb; **il y a loin de la coupe aux lèvres** there is many a slip between the cup and the lip; **mettre en coupe réglée** (coll) to fleece

cou·pé **-pée** [kupe] *adj* cut, cut off; interrupted (*sleep*); diluted (*wine*) ‖ *m* coupé ‖ *f* gangway

coupe-circuit [kupsirkɥi] *m invar* (elec) fuse

coupe-coupe [kupkup] *m invar* machete

coupe-feu [kupfø] *m invar* firebreak

coupe-fil [kupfil] *m invar* wire cutter

coupe-file [kupfil] *m invar* police pass (*for emergency vehicles*)

coupe-gorge [kupgɔrʒ] *m invar* deathtrap, dangerous territory

coupe-jarret [kupʒarɛ] *m* (*pl* **-jarrets**) cutthroat

coupe-ongles [kupɔ̃gl] *m invar* nail clippers

coupe-papier [kuppapje] *m invar* paper knife, letter opener

couper [kupe] *tr* to cut; to cut off; to cut out; to break off, interrupt; to cut, water down; to turn off; to trump; to castrate, geld; **ça te la coupe!** (coll) top that!; **couper la file** (aut) to leave one's lane; **couper la parole à** to interrupt; **couper menu** to mince ‖ *intr* to cut; **couper court à** to cut (*s.o. or s.th.*) short ‖ *ref* to cut oneself; to intersect; (coll) to contradict oneself; (coll) to give oneself away

couperet [kuprɛ] *m* cleaver; guillotine blade

couperose [kuproz] *f* (pathol) acne

cou·peur [kupœr] **-peuse** [pøz] *mf* cutter; **coupeur de bourses** (coll) purse snatcher; **coupeur d'oreilles** (coll) hatchet man, hired thug

couplage [kuplaʒ] *m* (mach) coupling

couple [kupl] *m* couple (*e.g., of friends, cronies, thieves, etc.; man and wife*); pair (*e.g., of pigeons*); (mech) couple, torque; **couple thermo-électrique** thermoelectric couple;

maître couple (naut) midship frame ‖ *f* yoke (*of oxen*); couple; leash

coupler [kuple] *tr* to couple; to pair

coupleur [kuplœr] *m* (mach) coupler

coupole [kupɔl] *f* cupola

coupon [kupɔ̃] *m* coupon; remnant (*of cloth*); theater ticket

coupon-réponse [kupɔ̃repõs] *m*—**coupon-réponse international** international (postal) reply coupon; **coupon-réponse postal** return-reply post card or letter

coupure [kupyr] *f* cut, incision, slit; cut, deletion; newspaper clipping; small note; interruption, break; drain (*e.g., through a marsh*)

cour [kur] *f* court; courtyard; courtship; **bien en cour** in favor; **cour anglaise** courtyard or court (*of apartment building*); **cour d'appel** appellate court; **cour d'assises** criminal court; **cour de cassation** supreme court of appeals; **cour d'école** school playground; **faire la cour à** to court; **mal en cour** out of favor

courage [kuraʒ] *m* courage; **reprendre courage** to take heart; **travailler avec courage** to work hard ‖ *interj* buck up!, cheer up!

coura·geux [kuraʒø] **-geuse** [ʒøz] *adj* courageous; hard-working

courailler [kurɑje] *intr* to gallivant

couramment [kuramɑ̃] *adv* currently; fluently, easily

cou·rant [kurɑ̃] **-rante** [rɑ̃t] *adj* current; running (*water*); present-day (*language, customs, etc.*) ‖ *m* current; flow; shift (*of opinion, population, etc.*); **courant alternatif** alternating current; **courant continu** direct current; **courant d'air** draft; **Courant du Golfe** Gulf Stream; **dans le courant du mois** (de la semaine, etc.) in the course of the month (of the week, etc.); **être au courant de** to be informed about

courba·tu ·tue [kurbaty] *adj* stiff in the joints, aching all over

courbature [kurbatyr] *f* stiffness, aching

courbaturer [kurbatyre] *tr* to make stiff; to exhaust (*the body*)

courbe [kurb] *adj* curved ‖ *f* curve; **courbe de niveau** contour line

cour·bé ·bée [kurbe] *adj* curved, bent, crooked

courber [kurbe] *tr* to bend, curve ‖ *intr & ref* to bend, curve; to give in

courbure [kurbyr] *f* curve, curvature; **double courbure** S-curve

courette [kuret] *f* small courtyard

cou·reur [kurœr] **-reuse** [røz] *mf* runner; **coureur cycliste** bicycle racer; **coureur de cotillons** (coll) wolf; **coureur de dot** fortune hunter; **coureur de filles** Casanova, Don Juan; **coureur de girls** stage-door Johnny; **coureur de spectacles** playgoer; **coureur de vitesse** sprinter

courge [kurʒ] *f* gourd, squash

courir [kurir] §14 *tr* to run; to run after; to roam; to frequent ‖ *intr* to run; **le bruit court que** rumor has it that; **par le temps qui court** at the present time

courlis [kurli] *m* curlew

couronne [kurɔn] *f* crown; wreath; coronet; rim (*of atomic structures*)

couronnement [kurɔnmɑ̃] *m* crowning; coronation; coping

couronner [kurɔne] *tr* to crown; to top, cap; to reward ‖ *ref* to be crowned; to be covered (*with flowers*)

courrier [kurje] *m* courier; mail; **courrier du cœur** advice to the lovelorn; **courrier mondain** gossip column; **courrier théâtral** theater section

courriériste [kurjerist] *mf* columnist

courroie [kurwa] *f* strap; belt

courroucer [kuruse] §51 *tr* (lit) to anger

courroux [kuru] *m* (lit) wrath, anger

cours [kur] *m* course; current (*of river*); tree-lined walk; rate (*of exchange*); market quotation; style, vogue; **au cours de** in the course of; **avoir cours** to be in circulation; to be legal tender; to have classes; **cours d'eau** stream, river; **cours d'été** or **cours de vacances** summer school; **cours du soir** night school; **de cours** in length (*said of a river*); **de long cours** long-range; **suivre un cours** to take a course (*in school*)

course [kurs] *f* running; race; errand; trip; ride (*e.g., in a taxi*); course, path; privateering; stroke (*of a piston*); **course à pied** foot race; **course attelée** harness race; **course au trot** trotting race; **course aux armements** arms race; **course de chevaux** horse race; **course de côte** hill climb; **course de taureaux** bullfight; **course de vitesse** sprint; **course d'obstacles** steeplechase; **courses sur route** road racing; **de course** at a run; racing (*car; track; crowd*); (mil) on the double; **en pleine course** in full swing; **faire des courses** to go shopping

cour·sier [kursje] **-sière** [sjer] *mf* messenger ‖ *m* errand boy; steed

coursive [kursiv] *f* (naut) alleyway, gangway (*connecting staterooms*)

court [kur] **courte** [kurt] *adj* short; brief; concise; choppy (*sea*); thick (*sauce, gravy*); **à court** short; **de court** by surprise; **prendre le plus court** to take a shortcut; **tenir de court** to hold on a short leash ‖ (*when standing before noun*) *adj* short, brief (*interval, time, life*) ‖ *m* court (*for tennis*) ‖ *adv* short; **demeurer court** to forget what one wanted to say; **tourner court** to turn sharp; to stop short, to change the subject; **tout court** simply, merely; plain

courtage [kurtaʒ] *m* brokerage; broker's commission

cour·taud [kurto] **-taude** [tod] *adj* stocky, short and stocky

court-circuit [kursirkɥi] *m* (*pl* **courts-circuits**) short circuit

court-circuiter [kursirkɥite] *tr* to short-circuit

courtepointe [kurtəpwɛ̃t] *f* counterpane

cour·tier [kurtje] -tière [tjɛr] *mf* broker; agent; **courtier électoral** canvasser

courtisan [kurtizɑ̃] *m* courtier

courtisane [kurtizan] *f* courtesan

courtiser [kurtize] *tr* to court

cour·tois [kurtwa] -toise [twaz] *adj* courteous; courtly

courtoisie [kurtwazi] *f* courtesy

court-vê·tu -tue [kurvety] *adj* short-skirted

cou·ru -rue [kuru] *adj* sought after, popular; **c'est couru** (coll) it's a sure thing

cou·seur [kuzœr] -seuse [zøz] *mf* sewer || *f* seamstress; (mach) stitcher

cou·sin [kuzɛ̃] -sine [zin] *mf* cousin; **cousin germain** first cousin; **cousins issus de germains** first cousins once removed || *m* mosquito

cousinage [kuzinaʒ] *m* cousinship; (coll) relatives

coussin [kusɛ̃] *m* cushion

coussinet [kusinɛ] *m* little cushion; (mach) bearing

coût [ku] *m* cost; **coût de la vie** cost of living

cou·teau [kuto] *m* (*pl* -teaux) knife; **couteau à cran d'arrêt** clasp knife with safety catch; switchblade knife; **couteau à découper** carving knife; **couteau à ressort** switchblade knife; **couteau pliant, couteau de poche** jackknife

coutelas [kutla] *m* cutlass; butcher knife

coutellerie [kutɛlri] *f* cutlery

coûter [kute] *tr* to cost; **coûte que coûte** cost what it may; **il m'en coûte de** + *inf* it's hard for me to + *inf*

coû·teux [kutø] -teuse [tøz] *adj* costly, expensive

coutil [kuti] *m* duck (*cloth*); mattress ticking

coutume [kutym] *f* custom; habit; common law; **de coutume** ordinarily

coutu·mier [kutymje] -mière [mjɛr] *adj* customary; common (*law*); accustomed || *m* book of common law

couture [kutyr] *f* needlework; sewing; seam; suture; scar; **battre qn à plate couture** (coll) to beat s.o. hollow; **examiner sur toutes les coutures** to examine inside and out or from every angle; **haute couture** fashion designing, haute couture; **sans couture** seamless

couturer [kutyre] *tr* to scar

coutu·rier [kutyrje] -rière [rjɛr] *mf* dressmaker || *m* dress designer || *f* seamstress

couvaison [kuvezɔ̃] *f* incubation period

couvée [kuve] *f* brood

couvent [kuvɑ̃] *m* convent; monastery; convent school

couver [kuve] *tr* to brood, hatch || *intr* to brood; to smolder

couvercle [kuvɛrkl] *m* cover, lid

cou·vert [kuvɛr] -verte [vɛrt] *adj* covered; dressed, clothed; cloudy (*weather*); wooded (*countryside*) || *m* cover; setting (*of table*); service (*fork and spoon*); cover charge; room, lodging;

authority (*given by a superior*); **à couvert** sheltered; **mettre le couvert** to set the table; **sous le couvert de** under cover of; **sous les couverts** under cover (*of trees*) || *f* glaze

couverture [kuvɛrtyr] *f* cover; coverage; covering; wrapper; blanket; bedspread

couveuse [kuvøz] *f* brood hen; incubator

couvre-chef [kuvrəʃɛf] *m* (*pl* -chefs) (coll) headgear

couvre-feu [kuvrəfø] *m* (*pl* -feux) curfew

couvre-lit [kuvrəli] *m* (*pl* -lits) bedspread

couvre-livre [kuvrəlivr] *m* (*pl* -livres) dust jacket

couvre-pieds [kuvrəpje] *m invar* bedspread; quilt

couvre-plat [kuvrəpla] *m* (*pl* -plats) dish cover

couvre-théière [kuvrətejer] *m* (*pl* -théières) tea cozy

couvreur [kuvrœr] *m* roofer

couvrir [kuvrir] §65 *tr* to cover || *ref* to cover; to cover oneself; to get cloudy; to put one's hat on

cow-boy [kaubɔj], [kobɔj] *m* (*pl* -boys) cowboy

C.P. *abbr* (**case postale**) post-office box

C.R. [seer] *adv* (letterword) (**contre remboursement**) C.O.D.; **envoyez-le-moi C.R.** send it to me C.O.D.

crabe [krab], [krab] *m* crab; caterpillar (tractor)

crachat [kraʃa] *m* sputum, spit

cra·ché -chée [kraʃe] *adj* (coll) spitting (*image*)

cracher [kraʃe] *tr & intr* to spit

crachin [kraʃɛ̃] *m* light drizzle

crachoir [kraʃwar] *m* spittoon; **tenir le crachoir** (slang) to have the floor, to speak

crachoter [kraʃote] *intr* to keep on spitting; to sputter

crack [krak] *m* favorite (*the horse favored to win*); (coll) champion, ace; (coll) crackerjack

cracking [krakiŋ] *m* cracking (*of oil*)

craie [krɛ] *f* chalk; piece of chalk

crailler [kraje] *intr* to caw

craindre [krɛ̃dr] §15 *tr* to fear, to be afraid of, to dread; to respect || *intr* to be afraid

crainte [krɛ̃t] *f* fear, dread; **dans la crainte que** or **de crainte que** for fear that

crain·tif [krɛ̃tif] -tive [tiv] *adj* fearful; timid

cramoi·si -sie [kramwazi] *adj & m* crimson

crampe [krɑ̃p] *f* cramp (*in a muscle*)

crampon [krɑ̃pɔ̃] *m* clamp; cleat (*on a shoe*); (coll) pest, bore

cramponner [krɑ̃pɔne] *tr* to clamp together; (coll) to pester || *ref* to hold fast, hang on, cling

cran [krɑ̃] *m* notch; cog, catch, tooth; **avoir du cran** (coll) to be game (*for anything*); **baisser un cran** to come down a peg; **être à cran** (coll) to be exasperated, cross

crâne [krɑn] *adj* bold, daring ‖ *m* skull, cranium; **bourrer le crâne à qn** (coll) to hand s.o. a line

crâner [krɑne] *intr* (coll) to swagger

cra·neur [krɑnœr] **-neuse** [nøz] *adj & mf* (coll) braggart

crapaud [krapo] *m* toad; baby grand; flaw (*in diamond*); low armchair; (coll) brat; **avaler un crapaud** (coll) to put up with a lot

crapule [krapyl] *f* underworld; scum; bum, punk; **vivre dans la crapule** to live in debauchery

crapu·leux [krapylø] **-leuse** [løz] *adj* debauched; lewd, filthy

craquage [krakaʒ] *m* cracking (*of petroleum*)

craquement [krakmɑ̃] *m* crack, crackle

craquer [krake] *intr* to crack; to burst; (coll) to crash, fail

craqueter [krakte] §34 *intr* to crackle

crash [kraʃ] *m* crash landing

crasse [kras] *adj* gross; crass (*ignorance*) ‖ *f* filth, squalor; avarice; dross; **faire une crasse à qn** (slang) to play a dirty trick on s.o.

cras·seux [krasø] **cras·seuse** [krasøz] *adj* filthy, squalid; (coll) stingy

crassier [krasje] *m* slag heap

cratère [krater] *m* crater; ewer

cravache [kravaʃ] *f* riding whip, horsewhip

cravacher [kravaʃe] *tr* to horsewhip

cravate [kravat] *f* necktie, cravat; scarf; sling (*for unloading goods*); **cravate de chanvre** (coll) noose; **cravate de drapeau** pennant

cravater [kravate] *tr* to tie a necktie on (*s.o.*) ‖ *intr* (slang) to tell a fish story

crawl [krol] *m* crawl (*in swimming*)

crayeux [krejø] **crayeuse** [krejøz] *adj* chalky

crayon [krejɔ̃] *m* pencil; **crayon de pastel** wax crayon; **crayon de rouge à lèvres** lipstick

crayonner [krejone] *tr* to crayon, to pencil, to sketch

créance [kreɑ̃s] *f* belief, credence; **créances gelées** frozen assets; **créances véreuses** bad debts

créan·cier [kreɑ̃sje] **-cière** [sjer] *mf* creditor; **créancier hypothécaire** mortgage holder

créa·teur [kreatœr] **-trice** [tris] *adj* creative ‖ *mf* creator; originator

création [kreasjɔ̃] *f* creation

créature [kreatyr] *f* creature

crécelle [kresɛl] *f* rattle; chatterbox; **de crécelle** rasping

crèche [krɛʃ] *f* manger; crèche; day nursery

crédence [kredɑ̃s] *f* buffet, sideboard, credenza

crédibilité [kredibilite] *f* credibility

crédit [kredi] *m* credit; (govt) appropriation

créditer [kredite] *tr* (com) to credit

crédi·teur [kreditœr] **-trice** [tris] *adj* credit (*side, account*) ‖ *mf* creditor

credo [kredo] *m invar* credo, creed

crédule [kredyl] *adj* credulous

créer [kree] *tr* to create

crémaillère [kremajer] *f* pothook;

rack; rack rail; **crémaillère et pignon** rack and pinion; **pendre la crémaillère** to have a housewarming

crémation [kremasjɔ̃] *f* cremation

crématoire [krematwar] *adj & m* crematory

crème [krɛm] *f* cream; **crème chantilly** whipped cream; **crème de démaquillage** cleansing cream; **crème fouettée** whipped cream; **crème glacée** ice cream

crémer [kreme] §10 *intr* to cream

crémerie [kremri] *f* dairy; milkhouse (*on a farm*); dairy luncheonette

cré·meux [kremø] **-meuse** [møz] *adj* creamy

crémier [kremje] *m* dairyman

crémière [kremjer] *f* dairymaid; cream pitcher

crémone [kremɔn] *f* casement bolt

cré·neau [kreno] *m* (*pl* **-neaux**) crenel; loophole; **créneaux** battlements

créneler [krenle] §34 *tr* to crenelate; to tooth (*a wheel*); to mill (*a coin*)

créole [kreɔl] *adj* Creole ‖ *m* Creole (*language*) ‖ (*cap*) *mf* Creole (*person*)

crêpe [krɛp] *m* crepe ‖ *f* pancake

crépitation [krepitasjɔ̃] *f* crackle

crépitement [krepitmɑ̃] *m* crackling

crépiter [krepite] *intr* to crackle

cré·pu -pue [krepy] *adj* crimped, frizzly, crinkled

crépuscule [krepyskyl] *m* twilight

cresson [kresɔ̃] *m* cress; **cresson de fontaine** watercress

crête [krɛt] *f* crest; **crête de coq** cockscomb

Crète [krɛt] *f* Crete; **la Crète** Crete

crête-de-coq [krɛtdəkɔk] *f* (*pl* **crêtes-de-coq**) (bot) cockscomb

cré·tin [kretɛ̃] **-tine** [tin] *mf* cretin; (coll) jackass, fathead

cré·tois [kretwa] **-toise** [twaz] *adj* Cretan ‖ (*cap*) *mf* Cretan

creuser [krøze] *tr* to dig, excavate; to hollow out; to furrow; to go into thoroughly ‖ *ref*—**se creuser la tête** (coll) to rack one's brains

creuset [krøze] *m* crucible

creux creuse [krø] [krøz] *adj* hollow; concave; sunken, deep-set; empty (*stomach*); deep (*voice*); off-peak (*hours*); **songer creux** to dream idle dreams; **sonner creux** to sound hollow ‖ *m* hollow (*of hand*); hole (*in ground*); pit (*of stomach*); trough (*of wave*); **creux de l'aisselle** armpit; **creux des reins** small of the back

crevaison [krəvezɔ̃] *f* blowout

crevasse [krəvas] *f* crevice; crack (*in skin*); rift (*in clouds*); flaw (*in metal*)

crevasser [krəvase] *tr* to chap ‖ *intr & ref* to crack, to chap

crève-cœur [krɛvkœr] *m invar* heartbreak, keen disappointment

crever [krəve] §2 *tr* to burst; to work to death (*e.g., a horse*) ‖ *intr* to burst; to split; to burst, go flat (*said of a tire*); (slang) to die, kick the bucket ‖ *ref* to work oneself to death

crevette [krəvet] *f* shrimp; **crevette**

grise shrimp; **crevette rose, crevette bouquet** prawn

C.-R.F. *abbr* (**Croix-Rouge française**) French Red Cross

cri [kri] *m* cry; shout; whine, squeal; **dernier cri** last word, latest thing

criailler [kriɑje] *intr* to honk (*said of goose*); (coll) to whine, complain, grouse; **criailler après, criailler contre** (coll) to nag at

criaillerie [kriɑjri] *f* (coll) shouting; (coll) whining, complaining; (coll) nagging

criant [krijɑ̃] **criante** [krijɑ̃t] *adj* crying (*shame*); obvious (*truth*); flagrant (*injustice*)

criard [krijar] **criarde** [krijard] *adj* complaining; shrill (*voice*); loud (*color*); pressing (*debts*) || *mf* complainer || *f* scold, shrew

crible [kribl] *m* sieve; **crible à gravier** gravel screen; **crible à mineral** jig; **passer au crible** to sift or screen

cri·blé -blée [krible] *adj* riddled (*with, e.g., debts*); pitted (*by, e.g., smallpox*)

cribler [krible] *tr* to sift; screen; to riddle; **cribler de ridicule** to cover with ridicule

cric [krik] *m* (aut) jack || *interj* crack!, snap!

cricket [kriket] *m* (sports) cricket

cricri [krikri] *m* (ent) cricket

crier [krije] *tr* to cry; to cry out; to shout; to cry for (*revenge*); **crier misère** to complain of being poor; **to cry poverty** (*said of clothing, furniture, etc.*) || *intr* to cry; to cry out; to shout; to creak, to squeak; to squeal; **crier à** to cry out against (*scandal, injustice, etc.*); to cry for (*help*); **crier après** to yell at, to bawl out; **crier contre** to cry out against; to rail at

crieur [krijœr] **crieuse** [krijøz] *mf* crier; hawker, peddler; **crieur public** town crier

crime [krim] *m* crime; felony

crimi·nel -nelle [kriminɛl] *adj & mf* criminal

crin [krɛ̃] *m* horsehair (*on mane and tail*); **à tous crins** out-and-out, hardcore (*e.g., revolutionist*)

crinière [krinjer] *f* mane

crique [krik] *f* cove

criquet [krike] *m* locust; weak wine; (coll) shrimp (*person*)

crise [kriz] *f* crisis; **crise d'appendicite** appendicitis attack; **crise de foi** shaken faith; **crise de main-d'œuvre** labor shortage; **crise de nerfs** fit of hysterics; **crise du foie** liver upset; **crise du logement** housing shortage; **crise économique** (com) depression

cris·pant [krispɑ̃] **-pante** [pɑ̃t] *adj* irritating, annoying

crispation [krispɑsjɔ̃] *f* contraction, shriveling up; (coll) fidgeting

crisper [krispe] *tr* to contract, clench; (coll) to make fidgety || *ref* to contract, to curl up

crisser [krise] *tr* to grind or grit (*one's teeth*) || *intr* to grate, crunch

cris·tal [kristal] *m* (*pl* -taux [to]) crystal; **cristal de roche** rock crystal; **cristal taillé** cut glass; **cristaux glassware; cristaux de soude** washing soda

cristal·lin [kristalɛ̃] **cristal·line** [kristalin] *adj* crystalline || *m* crystalline lens (*of the eye*)

cristalliser [kristalize] *tr, intr, & ref* to crystallize

critère [kriter] *m* criterion

critérium [kriterjɔm] *m* championship game

critiquable [kritikabl] *adj* open to criticism, questionable

critique [kritik] *adj* critical || *mf* critic || *f* criticism; critics; **critiques** censure

critiquer [kritike] *tr* to criticize, find fault with || *intr* to find fault

critiqueur [kritikœr] *m* critic, faultfinder

croassement [krɔasmɑ̃] *m* croak, caw, croaking (*of raven*)

croasser [krɔase] *intr* to croak, to caw

croate [krɔat] *adj* Croatian || *m* Croat, Croatian (*language*) || (*cap*) *mf* Croatian (*person*)

croc [kro] *m* hook; fang (*of dog*); tusk (*of walrus*)

croc-en-jambe [krɔkɑ̃jɑ̃b] *m* (*pl* **crocs-en-jambes** [krɔkɑ̃jɑ̃b])—**faire un croc-en-jambe à qn** to trip s.o. up

croche [krɔʃ] *f* (mus) quaver

crochet [krɔʃe] *m* hook; fang (*of snake*); crochet work; crochet needle; picklock; **crochet radiophonique** talent show; **crochets** (typ) brackets; **faire un crochet** to swerve; **vivre aux crochets de** to live on or at the expense of

crocheter [krɔʃte] §2 *tr* to pick (*a lock*)

crocheteur [krɔʃtœr] *m* picklock; porter

cro·chu -chue [krɔʃy] *adj* hooked (*e.g., nose*); crooked; **avoir les mains crochues** to be light-fingered

crocodile [krɔkɔdil] *m* crocodile

crocus [krɔkys] *m* crocus

croire [krwar] §16 *tr* to believe; **croire + inf** to think that + *ind*; **croire qn + adj** to believe s.o. to be + *adj*; **croire que non** to think not; **croire que oui** to think so; **je crois bien** or **je le crois bien** I should say so || *intr* to believe; **croire à** to believe in; **croire en Dieu** to believe in God; **j'y crois** I believe in it || *ref* to believe oneself to be

croisade [krwazad] *f* crusade

croi·sé -sée [krwaze] *adj* crossed; twilled (*cloth*); double-breasted (*suit*); alternate (*rhymes*) || *m* Crusader || *f* crossing, crossroads

croisement [krwazmɑ̃] *m* crossing; intersection; meeting, passing (*of two vehicles*); cross-breeding; **croisement en trèfle** cloverleaf, cloverleaf intersection

croiser [krwaze] *tr* to cross; to fold over; to meet, to pass || *intr* to fold over, to lap; to cruise || *ref* to cross, intersect; to go on a crusade

croiseur [krwazœr] *m* cruiser; **croiseur de bataille** battle cruiser

croisière [krwazjɛr] *f* cruise; **en croisière** cruising

croissance [krwasãs] *f* growth

crois·sant [krwasã] **crois·sante** [krwasãt] *adj* growing, increasing, rising || *m* crescent; crescent roll; billhook

croître [krwatr] §17 *intr* to grow; to increase, to rise

croix [krwa] *f* cross; (typ) dagger; **croix gammée** swastika; **en croix** crossed, crosswise

Croix-Rouge [krwaruʒ] *f* Red Cross

cro·quant [krɔkã] **-quante** [kãt] *adj* crisp, crunchy || *m* wretch

croque-mitaine [krɔkmiten] *m* (*pl* **-mitaines**) bugaboo, bogeyman

croque-monsieur [krɔkməsjø] *m invar* grilled ham-and-cheese sandwich

croque-mort [krɔkmɔr] *m* (*pl* **-morts**) (coll) funeral attendant

croquer [krɔke] *tr* to munch; to sketch; to dissipate (*a fortune*) || *intr* to crunch

croquet [krɔkɛ] *m* croquet; almond cookie

croquis [krɔki] *m* sketch; draft, outline; **croquis coté** diagram, sketch

crosse [krɔs] *f* crosier; butt (*of gun*); hockey stick; lacrosse stick; golf club; **chercher des crosses à** (slang) to pick a fight with; **mettre la crosse en l'air** to show the white flag, to surrender

crotale [krɔtal] *m* rattlesnake

crotte [krɔt] *f* dung; mud; **crotte de chocolat** chocolate cream (candy)

crotter [krɔte] *tr* to dirty || *ref* to get dirty; to commit a nuisance (*said of dog*)

crottin [krɔtɛ̃] *m* horse manure

crouler [krule] *intr* to collapse

croup [kru] *m* (pathol) croup

croupe [krup] *f* croup, rump; ridge, brow; **en croupe** behind the rider

croupetons [kruptɔ̃]—**à croupetons** squatting

crou·pi·pie [krupi] *adj* stagnant

croupier [krupje] *m* croupier; financial partner

croupière [krupjɛr] *f* crupper; **tailler des croupières à** (coll) to make it hard for

croupion [krupjɔ̃] *m* rump

croupir [krupir] *intr* to stagnate; to wallow (*in vice, filth*); to remain (*e.g., in ignorance*)

croustil·lant [krustijã] **croustil·lante** [krustijãt] *adj* crisp, crunchy; spicy (*story*)

croustille [krustij] *f* piece of crust; snack; **croustilles** potato chips

croustiller [krustije] *intr* to munch, to nibble

croustil·leux [krustijø] **croustil·leuse** [krustijøz] *adj* spicy (*story*)

croûte [krut] *f* crust; pastry shell (*of meat pie*); scab (*of wound*); (coll) daub, worthless painting; **casser la croûte** (coll) to have a snack

croû·teux [krutø] **-teuse** [tøz] *adj* scabby

croûton [krutɔ̃] *m* crouton; heel (*of bread*); **vieux croûton** (coll) old dodo

croyable [krwajabl], [krwajabl] *adj* believable

croyance [krwajãs] *f* belief

croy·ant [krwajã] **croyante** [krwajãt] *adj* believing || *mf* believer

C.R.S. [seeres] *fpl* (letterword) (Compagnies républicaines de sécurité) state troopers

cru crue [kry] *adj* raw, uncooked; indigestible; crude (*language*; *art*); glaring, harsh (*light*); hard (*water*); plain (*terms*); **à cru** directly; bareback || *m* region (*in which s.th. is grown*); vineyard; vintage; **de son cru** of his own invention; **du cru** local, at the vineyard || *see* **crue**

cruauté [kryote] *f* cruelty

cruche [kryʃ] *f* pitcher, jug

cruchon [kryʃɔ̃] *m* small pitcher or jug

cru·cial -ciale [krysjal] *adj* (*pl* **-ciaux** [sjo]) crucial; cross-shaped

crucifiement [krysifimã] *m* crucifixion

crucifier [krysifje] *tr* to crucify

crucifix [krysifi] *m* crucifix

crucifixion [krysifiksjɔ̃] *f* crucifixion

crudité [krydite] *f* crudity; indigestibility; rawness (*of food*); harshness (*of light*); hardness (*of water*); **crudités** raw fruits and vegetables; off-color remarks

crue [kry] *f* overflow (*of river*); growth

cruel cruelle [kryɛl] *adj* cruel

cruellement [kryɛlmã] *adv* cruelly; sorely

crû·ment [krymã] *adv* crudely; roughly

crustacé [krystase] *m* crustacean

crypte [kript] *f* crypt

C^teC^t *abbr* (**compte courant**) current account

cubage [kybaʒ] *m* volume

cu·bain [kybɛ̃] **-baine** [ben] *adj* Cuban || (*cap*) *mf* Cuban

cube [kyb] *adj* cubic || *m* cube

cuber [kybe] *tr* to cube

cubique [kybik] *adj* cubic

cueillaison [kœjɛzɔ̃] *f* picking, gathering; harvest time

cueil·leur [kœjœr] **cueil·leuse** [kœjøz] *mf* picker; fruit picker

cueillir [kœjir] §18 *tr* to pick; to pluck; to gather; to win (*laurels*); to steal (*a kiss*); (coll) to nab (*a thief*); (coll) to pick up (*a friend*)

cuiller *or* **cuillère** [kɥijɛr] *f* spoon; ladle (*for molten metal*); scoop (*of a dredger*); **cuiller à bouche** tablespoon; **cuiller à café** teaspoon; **cuiller à pot** ladle; **cuiller à soupe** soupspoon; **cuiller et fourchette** fork and spoon

cuillerée [kɥijre] *f* spoonful

cuilleron [kɥijrɔ̃] *m* bowl (*of spoon*)

cuir [kɥir] *m* leather; hide; **cuir chevelu** scalp; **cuir verni** patent leather; **cuir vert** rawhide; **faire des cuirs** to make mistakes in liaison

cuirasse [kɥiras] *f* cuirass, breastplate; armor

cuiras·sé -sée [kɥirase] *adj* armored || *m* battleship

cuirasser [kɥirase] *tr* to armor || *ref* to steel oneself

cuire [kɥir] §19 *tr* to cook; to ripen || *intr* to cook; to sting, smart; **faire cuire** to cook; **il vous en cuira** you'll suffer for it

cui·sant [kɥizɑ̃] **-sante** [zɑ̃t] *adj* stinging, smarting

cuisine [kɥizin] *f* kitchen; cooking; cuisine; (coll) skulduggery; **cuisine roulante** chuck wagon, field kitchen; **faire la cuisine** to cook

cuisiner [kɥizine] *tr* to cook; (coll) to grill (*a suspect*); (coll) to fix (*an election*) || *intr* to cook

cuisi·nier [kɥizinje] **-nière** [njɛr] *mf* cook || *f* kitchen stove, cookstove

cuisse [kɥis] *f* thigh; (culin) drumstick; **cuisses de grenouille** frogs' legs; **il se croit sorti de la cuisse de Jupiter** (coll) he thinks he is the Lord God Almighty

cuis·seau [kɥiso] *m* (*pl* **-seaux**) leg of veal

cuisson [kɥisɔ̃] *f* baking, cooking; (fig) burning sensation, smarting; **en cuisson** on the stove, on the grill, in the oven

cuissot [kɥiso] *m* leg (*of game*)

cuistre [kɥistr] *m* pedant, prig

cuit [kɥi] **cuite** [kɥit] *adj* cooked; **nous sommes cuits** (coll) our goose is cooked || *f* firing (*in a kiln*); **prendre une cuite** (slang) to get soused

cuivre [kɥivr] *m* copper; **cuivre jaune** brass; **les cuivres** (mus) the brasses

cui·vré **-vrée** [kɥivre] *adj* coppercolored, bronzed; brassy, metallic (*sound or voice*)

cuivrer [kɥivre] *tr* to copper; to bronze, tan; to make (*a sound or one's voice*) brassy or metallic || *ref* to become copper-colored

cui·vreux [kɥivrø] **-vreuse** [vrøz] *adj* (chem) cuprous

cul [ky] *m* bottom (*of bottle, bag*); (slang) ass, hind end, rump; **faire cul sec** (slang) to chug-a-lug

culasse [kylas] *f* breechblock; (mach) cylinder head

cul-blanc [kyblɑ̃] *m* (*pl* **culs-blancs**) wheatear, whitetail

culbute [kylbyt] *f* somersault; tumble, bad fall; (coll) failure; (coll) fall (*of a cabinet*); **faire la culbute** to sell at double the purchase price

culbuter [kylbyte] *tr* to overthrow; to overwhelm (*the enemy*) || *intr* to tumble, to fall backwards; to somersault

culbuteur [kylbytœr] *m* (mach) rocker arm

cul-de-basse-fosse [kydbɑsfos] *m* (*pl* **culs-de-basse-fosse**) dungeon

cul-de-jatte [kydəʒat] *mf* (*pl* **culs-de-jatte**) legless person

cul-de-sac [kydəsak] *m* (*pl* **culs-de-sac**) dead end; (public sign) no outlet

culée [kyle] *f* abutment

culer [kyle] *intr* to back water

culinaire [kyliner] *adj* culinary

culmi·nant [kylminɑ̃] **-nante** [nɑ̃t] *adj* culminating; highest (*point*)

culmination [kylminasjɔ̃] *f* (astr) culmination

culminer [kylmine] *intr* to rise high, to tower; (astr) to culminate

culot [kylo] *m* base, bottom; (coll) baby of the family; **avoir du culot** (slang) to have a lot of nerve

culotte [kylot] *f* breeches, pants; forked pipe; panties (*feminine undergarment*); (culin) rump; **culotte de golf** plus fours; **culotte de peau** (slang) old soldier; **culotte de sport** shorts; **porter la culotte** (coll) to wear the pants; **prendre une culotte** (slang) to lose one's shirt; (slang) to have a jag on

culot·té -tée [kylote] *adj* (coll) nervy, fresh

culotter [kylote] *tr* to cure (*a pipe*) || *ref* to put one's pants on

culte [kylt] *m* worship; cult; divine service, ritual; religion, creed; **avoir un culte pour** to worship (*e.g., one's parents*)

cul-terreux [kyterø] *m* (*pl* **culs-terreux**) (coll) clodhopper, hayseed

cultivable [kyltivabl] *adj* arable, tillable

cultiva·teur [kyltivatœr] **-trice** [tris] *adj* farming || *mf* farmer || *m* (mach) cultivator

cultiver [kyltive] *tr* to cultivate; to culture

cultu·ral -rale [kyltyral] *adj* (*pl* **-raux** [ro]) agricultural

culture [kyltyr] *f* culture; cultivation

cultu·rel -relle [kyltyrel] *adj* cultural

cumula·tif [kymylatif] **-tive** [tiv] *adj* cumulative

cunéiforme [kyneifɔrm] *adj* cuneiform

cupide [kypid] *adj* greedy

cupidité [kypidite] *f* cupidity

Cupidon [kypidɔ̃] *m* Cupid

curage [kyraʒ] *m* cleansing, cleaning out; unstopping (*of a drain*)

curatelle [kyratel] *f* guardianship, trusteeship

cura·teur [kyratœr] **-trice** [tris] *mf* guardian, trustee

cura·tif [kyratif] **-tive** [tiv] *adj* curative

cure [kyr] *f* treatment, cure; vicarage, rectory; parish; sun porch; **n'avoir cure de rien** or **n'en avoir cure** not to care

curé [kyre] *m* parish priest

cure-dent [kyrdɑ̃] *m* (*pl* **-dents**) toothpick

curée [kyre] *f* quarry (*given to the hounds*); scramble, mad race (*for gold, power, recognition, etc.*)

cure-oreille [kyrɔrɛj] *m* (*pl* **-oreilles**) earpick

cure-pipe [kyrpip] *m* (*pl* **-pipes**) pipe cleaner

curer [kyre] *tr* to clean out; to dredge || *ref* (with *dat* of *reflex pron*) to pick (*one's nails, one's teeth, etc.*)

cu·rieux [kyrjø] **-rieuse** [rjøz] *adj* curious

curiosité [kyrjozite] *f* curiosity; curio; connoisseurs, e.g., **le langage de la curiosité** the jargon of connoisseurs;

curiosités sights; **visiter les curiosités** to go sightseeing

curseur [kyrsœr] *m* slide, runner

cur·sif [kyrsif] **-sive** [siv] *adj* cursory; cursive (*handwriting*) ‖ *f* cursive

cuta·né -née [kytane] *adj* cutaneous

cuticule [kytikyl] *f* cuticle

cuve [kyv] *f* vat, tub, tank

cu·veau [kyvo] *m* (*pl* **-veaux**) small vat or tank

cuver [kyve] *tr* to leave to ferment; **cuver son vin** (coll) to sleep it off ‖ *intr* to ferment in a wine vat

cuvette [kyvɛt] *f* basin, pan; bulb (*of a thermometer*); (chem, phot) tray

cuvier [kyvje] *m* washtub

C.V. [seve] *m* (letterword) **(cheval-vapeur)** hp, horsepower

cyanamide [sjanamid] *f* cyanamide

cyanose [sjanoz] *f* cyanosis

cyanure [sjanyr] *m* cyanide

cyclable [siklabl] *adj* reserved for bicycles

cycle [sikl] *m* cycle

cyclique [siklik] *adj* cyclic(al)

cycliste [siklist] *mf* cyclist

cyclomoteur [siklɔmɔtœr] *m* motorbike

cyclone [siklon] *m* cyclone

cyclope [siklɔp] *m* cyclops

cyclotron [siklɔtrɔ̃] *m* cyclotron

cygne [siɲ] *m* swan

cylindrage [silɛ̃draʒ] *m* rolling (*of roads, gardens, etc.*); calendering, mangling

cylindre [silɛ̃dr] *m* cylinder; roller (*e.g., of rolling mill*); steam roller

cylindrée [silɛ̃dre] *f* piston displacement

cylindrer [silɛ̃dre] *tr* to roll (*a road, garden, etc.*); to calender, to mangle

cylindrique [silɛ̃drik] *adj* cylindrical

cymbale [sɛ̃bal] *f* cymbal

cynique [sinik] *adj & m* cynic

cynisme [sinism] *m* cynicism

cyprès [siprɛ] *m* cypress

cyrillique [sirilik] *adj* Cyrillic

cytoplasme [sitɔplasm] *m* cytoplasm

czar [ksar] *m* czar

czarine [ksarin] *f* czarina

D

D, d [de] *m invar* fourth letter of the French alphabet

d' = de before vowel or mute **h**

d'abord [dabɔr] see **abord**

dactylo [daktilo] *mf* (coll) typist

dactylographe [daktilɔgraf] *mf* typist

dactylographier [daktilɔgrafje] *tr* to type

dactyloscopie [daktilɔskɔpi] *f* finger-printing

dada [dada] *m* hobby-horse; hobby, fad, pet subject; **enfourcher son dada** to ride one's hobby

dague [dag] *f* dagger; first antler; tusk

dahlia [dalja] *m* dahlia

daigner [deɲe] *intr*—**daigner + inf** to deign to, to condescend to + *inf*; **daignez** please

d'ailleurs [dajœr] see **ailleurs**

daim [dɛ̃] *m* fallow deer; suede

daine [dɛn] *f* doe

dais [dɛ] *m* canopy

dalle [dal] *f* flagstone, slab, paving block; **se rincer la dalle** (slang) to wet one's whistle

daller [dale] *tr* to pave with flagstones

dalto·nien [daltɔnjɛ̃] **-nienne** [njɛn] *adj* color-blind ‖ *mf* color-blind person

dam [dɑ̃] *m*—**au dam de** to the detriment of

damas [damɑ] *m* damask ‖ (*cap*) [damɑs] *f* Damascus

damasquiner [damaskine] *tr* to dama-scene

damas·sé -sée [damase] *adj & m* damask

dame [dam] *f* dame; lady; tamp, tamper; rowlock; (cards, chess) queen; (checkers) king; **aller à dame** (checkers) to crown a man king; (chess) to queen a pawn; **dames** (public sign) ladies ‖ *interj* for heaven's sake!

damer [dame] *tr* to tamp (*the earth*); (checkers) to crown (*a checker*); (chess) to queen (*a pawn*); **damer le pion à qn** to outwit s.o.

damier [damje] *m* checkerboard

damnation [dɑnasjɔ̃] *f* damnation

dam·né -née [dɑne] *adj & mf* damned

damner [dɑne] *tr* to damn

damoi·seau [damwazo] **-selle** [zɛl] *mf* (*pl* **-seaux**) (archaic) young member of the nobility ‖ *m* lady's man ‖ *f* (archaic) damsel

dancing [dɑ̃siŋ] *m* dance hall

dandiner [dɑ̃dine] *tr* to dandle ‖ *ref* to waddle along

dandy [dɑ̃di] *m* dandy

Danemark [danmark] *m*—**le Danemark** Denmark

danger [dɑ̃ʒe] *m* danger

dange·reux [dɑ̃ʒrø] **-reuse** [røz] *adj* dangerous

da·nois [danwa] **-noise** [nwaz] *adj* Danish ‖ *m* Danish (*language*) ‖ (*cap*) *mf* Dane

dans [dɑ̃] *prep* in; into; **boire dans un verre** to drink out of a glass; **dans la suite** later

danse [dɑ̃s] *f* dance; **danse guerrière** war dance

danser [dɑ̃se] *tr & intr* to dance; **faire danser** to mistreat

dan·seur [dɑ̃sœr] **-seuse** [søz] *mf* dancer; **danseur de corde** tightrope walker; **en danseuse** in a standing position (*taken by cyclist*)

Danube [danyb] *m* Danube

d'après [dapre] see **après**

dard [dar] *m* dart; sting; snake's tongue; harpoon

darder [darde] *tr* to dart, to hurl

dare-dare [dardar] *adv* (coll) on the double

darse [dars] *f* wet dock

date [dat] *f* date; **de fraîche date** recent; **de longue date** of long standing; **en date de** from; **faire date** to mark an epoch; **prendre date** to make an appointment

dater [date] *tr & intr* to date; **à dater de** dating from

datif [datif] *m* dative

datte [dat] *f* date

dattier [datje] *m* date palm

daube [dob] *f* braised meat; **en daube** braised

dauber [dobe] *tr* to braise; to heckle; to slander; (coll) to pummel ‖ *intr*— **dauber sur qn** to heckle s.o., to slander s.o.

dau•beur [dobœr] **-beuse** [bøz] *mf* heckler

dauphin [dofɛ̃] *m* dolphin; dauphin

dauphine [dofin] *f* dauphiness

dauphinelle [dofinɛl] *f* delphinium

davantage [davɑ̃taʒ] §90 *adv* more; any more; any longer; ne . . . davantage no more; **pas davantage** no longer

de [də] §77, §78, §79 *prep* of, from; with, e.g., **frapper d'une épée** to strike with a sword; (to indicate the agent with the passive voice) by, e.g., **ils sont aimés de tous** they are loved by all; (to indicate the point of departure) from, e.g., **de Paris à Madrid** from Paris to Madrid; (to indicate the point of arrival) for, e.g., **le train de Paris** the train for Paris; (with a following infinitive after certain verbs) to, e.g., **il essaie d'écrire la lettre** he is trying to write the letter; (with a following infinitive after an adjective used with the impersonal expression **il est**) to, e.g., **il est facile de chanter cette chanson** it is easy to sing that song; (after **changer, se souvenir, avoir besoin,** etc.), e.g., **changer de vêtements** to change clothes; (after a comparative and before a numeral) than, e.g., **plus de quarante** more than forty; (to express the indefinite plural or partitive idea), e.g., **de l'eau** water, some water; (to form prepositional phrases with some adverbs), e.g., **auprès de vous** near you; (with the historical infinitive), e.g., **et chacun de pleurer** and everyone cried

dé [de] *m* die (*singular of dice*); thimble; domino; golf tee; **dés dice**

déambuler [deɑ̃byle] *intr* to stroll

débâcle [debɑkl] *m* debacle; breakup (*of ice*)

débâcler [debɑkle] *intr* to break up (*said of ice in a river*)

déballage [debalaʒ] *m* unpacking; cutrate merchandise (*sold by street vendor*)

déballer [debale] *tr* to unpack (*merchandise*); to display (*merchandise*)

débandade [debɑ̃dad] *f* rout, stampede; **à la débandade** in confusion, helter-skelter

débander [debɑ̃de] *tr* to rout, to stampede; to slacken (*s.th. under tension*); to unwind; **débander les yeux à qn** to take the blindfold from s.o.'s eyes ‖ *intr* to flee, to stampede

débaptiser [debatize] *tr* to change the name of, to rename

débarbouiller [debarbuje] *tr* to wash the face of

débarcadère [debarkader] *m* wharf, dock, landing platform

débarder [debarde] *tr* to unload

débardeur [debardœr] *m* stevedore, longshoreman

débar•qué -quée [debarke] *adj* disembarking ‖ *mf* new arrival ‖ *m* disembarkment; **au débarqué** on arrival

débarquement [debarkmɑ̃] *m* disembarkation

débarquer [debarke] *m*—**au débarquer de qn** at the moment of s.o.'s arrival ‖ *tr* to unload; to lower (*a lifeboat, seaplane, etc.*); (coll) to sack (*s.o.*) ‖ *intr* to disembark, get off

débarras [debara] *m* catchall

débarrasser [debarase] *tr* to disencumber, to disentangle; to clear (*the table*); to rid ‖ *ref*—**se débarrasser de** to get rid of

débarrer [debare] *tr* to unbar

débat [deba] *m* debate; dispute; **débats** discussion (*in a meeting*); proceedings (*in a court*)

débâter [debate] *tr* to unsaddle

débattre [debatr] §7 *tr* to debate, argue, discuss; to haggle over (*a price*); to question (*items in an account*) ‖ *ref* to struggle; to be debated

débauche [deboʃ] *f* debauch, debauchery; riot (*e.g., of colors*); overeating; striking, quitting work

débaucher [deboʃe] *tr* to debauch; to induce (*a worker*) to strike; to lay off (*workers*); to steal (*a worker*) from another employer ‖ *ref* to become debauched

débile [debil] *adj* weak ‖ *mf* mental defective

débilité [debilite] *f* debility

débiliter [debilite] *tr* to debilitate

débiner [debine] *tr* (slang) to run (*s.o.*) down ‖ *ref* (slang) to fly the coop

débit [debi] *m* debit; retail sale; shop; cutting up (*of wood*); output; way of speaking

débiter [debite] *tr* to debit; to cut up in pieces; to retail; to produce; to speak (*one's part*); to repeat thoughtlessly

débi•teur [debitœr] **-trice** [tris] *adj* debit (*account, balance*); delivery (*spool*) ‖ *mf* debtor ‖ **-teur** [tœr] **-teuse** [tøz] *mf* gossip, talebearer; salesclerk

déblai [deble] *m* excavation; **déblais** rubble, fill

déblaiement [deblemɑ̃] *m* clearing away

déblatérer [deblatere] §10 *tr* to bluster or fling (*threats, abuse*) ‖ *intr*—**déblatérer contre** to rail at

déblayer [debleje] §49 *tr* to clear, to clear away

débloquer [debloke] *tr* to unblock; to unfreeze (*funds, credits, etc.*)

déboire [debwar] *m* unpleasant aftertaste; disappointment

déboisement [debwazmã] *m* deforestation

déboîter [debwate] *tr* to disconnect (*pipe*); to dislocate (*a shoulder*) ‖ *intr* to move into another lane (*said of automobile*); (naut) to haul (*out of a line*)

débonder [debɔ̃de] *tr* to unbung

débonnaire [deboner] *adj* good-natured, easygoing; (Bib) meek

débor·dant [debordã] **-dante** [dãt] *adj* overflowing

débor·dé **-dée** [deborde] *adj* overwhelmed

déborder [deborde] *tr* to extend beyond, to jut out over; to trim the border from; to overwhelm; to untuck (*a bed*); (mil) to outflank ‖ *intr* to overflow; (naut) to shove off

débotté [debote] *m*—au débotté immediately upon arrival, at once

débouché [debuʃe] *m* outlet; opening (*for trade; of an attack*)

déboucher [debuʃe] *tr* to free from obstruction; to uncork ‖ *intr*—**déboucher dans** to empty into (*said of river*); **déboucher sur** to open onto, to emerge into

déboucler [debukle] *tr* to unbuckle; to take the curls out of

débouler [debule] *tr* to fly down (*e.g., a stairway*) ‖ *intr* to run suddenly out of cover (*said of rabbits*); to dash; **débouler dans** to roll down (*a stairway*)

déboulonner [debulone] *tr* to unbolt; (coll) to ruin, have fired; (coll) to debunk

débourber [deburbe] *tr* to clear of mud, to clean

débourrer [debure] *tr* to unhair (*a hide*); to remove the stuffing from (*a chair*); to knock (*a pipe*) clean

débours [debur] *m* disbursement; **rentrer dans ses débours** to recover one's investment

déboursement [debursmã] *m* disbursing

débourser [deburse] *tr* to disburse

debout [dəbu] *adv* upright, on end; standing; up (*out of bed*)

déboutonner [debutone] *tr* to unbutton; **à ventre déboutonné** immoderately ‖ *ref* (coll) to get something off one's chest

débrail·lé **-lée** [debraje] *adj* untidy, mussed up, unkempt; loose (*morals*); vulgar (*speech*) ‖ *m* untidiness

débrancher [debrãʃe] *tr* to switch (*railroad cars*) to a siding; (elec) to disconnect

débrayage [debrejaʒ] *m* (aut) clutch release; (coll) walkout

débrayer [debreje] §49 *tr* to disengage, throw out (*the clutch*) ‖ *intr* to throw out the clutch; (coll) to walk out (*said of strikers*)

débri·dé **-dée** [debride] *adj* unbridled

débris [debri] *mpl* debris; remains

débrouil·lard [debrujar] **débrouil·larde** [debrujard] *adj* (coll) resourceful ‖ *mf* (coll) smart customer

débrouiller [debruje] *tr* to disentangle, to unravel; to clear up (*a mystery*); to make out (*e.g., a signature*); (coll) to teach (*s.o.*) to be resourceful ‖ *ref* to clear (*said of sky*); (coll) to manage to get along, to take care of oneself; (coll) to extricate oneself (*from a difficult situation*)

débucher [debyʃe] *tr* to flush out (*game*) ‖ *intr* to run out of cover (*said of game*)

débusquer [debyske] *tr* to flush out (*game; the enemy*)

début [deby] *m* debut; beginning, commencement; opening play

débu·tant [debytã] **-tante** [tãt] *adj* beginning ‖ *mf* beginner; newcomer (*e.g., to stage or screen*) ‖ *f* debutante

débuter [debyte] *intr* to make one's debut, to begin; to start up a business; to make the opening play

deçà [dəsa] *adv*—**deçà delà** here and there; **en deçà de** on this side of

décacheter [dekaʃte] §34 *tr* to unseal

décade [dekad] *f* period of ten days; (hist, lit) decade

décadence [dekadãs] *f* decadence

déca·dent [dekadã] **-dente** [dãt] *adj* & *mf* decadent

décaféi·né **-née** [dekafeine] *adj* decaffeinated, caffeine-free

décagénaires [dekaʒener] *mfpl* teenagers

décaisser [dekese] *tr* to uncrate; to disburse, pay out

décalage [dekalaʒ] *m* unkeying; shift; slippage; (aer) stagger

décalcomanie [dekalkomani] *f* decal

décaler [dekale] *tr* to unkey; to shift

décalquage [dekalkaʒ] or **décalque** [dekalk] *m* decal

décalquer [dekalke] *tr* to transfer (*a decal*) onto paper, canvas, metal, etc.; **décalquer sur** to transfer (*a decal*) onto (*e.g., paper*)

décamper [dekãpe] *intr* to decamp

décanat [dekana] *m* deanship

décanter [dekãte] *tr* to decant

décapant [dekapã] *m* scouring agent

décaper [dekape] *tr* to scour, scale

décapiter [dekapite] *tr* to behead, to decapitate; to top (*a tree*)

décapotable [dekapotabl] *adj* & *f* (aut) convertible

déca·ti -tie [dekati] *adj* haggard, worn-out, faded

décatir [dekatir] *tr* to steam (*cloth*)

décaver [dekave] *tr* (coll) to fleece

décéder [desede] §10 *intr* (aux: ÊTRE) to die (*said of human being*)

décèlement [deselmã] *m* disclosure

déceler [desle] §2 *tr* to uncover, detect; to betray (*confusion*)

décélération [deselerasjɔ̃] *f* deceleration

décembre [desãbr] *m* December

décennie [deseni] *f* decade

dé·cent [desã] **-cente** [sãt] *adj* decent

décentraliser [desãtralize] *tr* to decentralize

déception [desɛpsjɔ̃] *f* disappointment

décernement [desɛrnəmã] *m* awarding

décerner [desɛrne] *tr* to award (*a prize*); to confer (*an honor*); to issue (*a writ*)

décès [dese] *m* decease, demise

déce·vant [desvã] **-vante** [vãt] *adj* disappointing; deceptive

décevoir [desvwar] §59 *tr* to disappoint; to deceive

déchaînement [deʃɛnmã] *m* unchaining, unleashing; outburst, wave

déchaîner [deʃɛne] *tr* to unchain, let loose ‖ *ref* to fly into a rage; to break out (*said of storm*)

déchanter [deʃãte] *intr* (coll) to sing a different tune

décharge [deʃarʒ] *f* discharge; drain; rubbish heap; storeroom, shed; **à décharge** for the defense

déchargement [deʃarʒəmã] *m* unloading

décharger [deʃarʒe] §38 *tr* to discharge; to unload; to unburden; to exculpate (*a defendant*) ‖ *ref* to vent one's anger; to go off (*said of gun*); to run down (*said of battery*); **se décharger de q.ch. sur qn** to shift the responsibility for s.th. on s.o.

déchargeur [deʃarʒœr] *m* porter (*e.g., in a market*); dock hand

déchar·né [deʃarne] **-née** [deʃarne] *adj* emaciated, skinny; bony

décharner [deʃarne] *tr* to strip the flesh from; to emaciate ‖ *ref* to waste away

déchaus·sé [deʃose] **-sée** *adj* barefoot

déchausser [deʃose] *tr* to take the shoes off of (*s.o.*); to expose the roots of (*a tree, a tooth*) ‖ *ref* to take off one's shoes; to shrink (*said of gums*)

déchéance [deʃeãs] *f* downfall; lapse, forfeiture (*of a right*); expiration, term (*of a note or loan*)

déchet [deʃɛ] *m* loss, decrease; **déchet de route** loss in transit; **déchets** waste products

décheveler [deʃəvle] §34 *tr* to dishevel, to muss (*s.o.'s hair*)

déchiffonner [deʃifɔne] *tr* to iron (*wrinkled material*)

déchiffrable [deʃifrabl] *adj* legible; decipherable

déchiffrement [deʃifrəmã] *m* deciphering, decoding; sight-reading

déchiffrer [deʃifre] *tr* to decipher; to sight-read (*music*)

déchif·freur [deʃifrœr] **déchif·freuse** [deʃifrøz] *mf* decipherer, decoder; sight-reader

déchique·té [deʃikte] **-tée** *adj* jagged, torn

déchiqueter [deʃikte] §34 *tr* to cut into strips; to shred; to slash

déchi·rant [deʃirã] **-rante** [rãt] *adj* heartrending

déchi·ré [deʃire] **-rée** [deʃire] *adj* torn; sorry

déchirer [deʃire] *tr* to tear, to tear up; to split (*a country; one's eardrums*);

to pick (*s.o.'s character*) to pieces ‖ *ref* (with *dat* of *reflex pron*) to skin (*e.g., one's knee*)

déchirure [deʃiryr] *f* tear, rent; sprain

déchoir [deʃwar] (usually used only in: *inf; pp* **déchu;** sometimes used in: *pres ind* **déchois,** etc.; *fut* **déchoirai,** etc.; *cond* **déchoirais,** etc.) *intr* (aux: AVOIR or ÊTRE) to fall (*from high estate*); to decline, to fail

dé·chu [deʃy] **-chue** [deʃy] *adj* fallen; deprived (*of rights*); expired (*insurance policy*)

décider [deside] *tr* to decide, to decide on; **décider qn à + *inf*** to persuade s.o. to + *inf* ‖ *intr* to decide; **décider de** to decide, determine the outcome of, e.g., **le coup a décidé de la partie** the trick decided the (outcome of the) game; **décider de + *inf*** to decide to + *inf* ‖ *ref* to decide, to make up one's mind, to resolve; **se décider à + *inf*** to decide to + *inf*

déci·mal [desimal] **-male** *adj* (*pl* **-maux** [mo]) decimal ‖ *f* decimal

décimer [desime] *tr* to decimate

déci·sif [desizif] **-sive** [ziv] *adj* decisive

décision [desizjɔ̃] *f* decision; decisiveness

déclama·teur [deklamatœr] **-trice** [tris] *adj* bombastic ‖ *mf* declaimer

déclamatoire [deklamatwar] *adj* declamatory

déclamer [deklame] *tr* to declaim ‖ *intr* to rant; **déclamer contre** to inveigh against

déclara·tif [deklaratif] **-tive** [tiv] *adj* declarative

déclaration [deklarasjɔ̃] *f* declaration; **déclaration de revenus** income-tax return

déclarer [deklare] *tr & intr* to declare ‖ *ref* to declare oneself; to arise, break out, occur

déclassement [deklasmã] *m* disarrangement; drop in social status; transfer to another class (*on ship, train, etc.*); dismantling; demoting

déclasser [deklase] *tr* to disarrange; to dismantle; to demote

déclenchement [deklãʃmã] *m* releasing; launching (*of an attack*)

déclencher [deklãʃe] *tr* to unlatch, disengage; to release (*the shutter*); to open (*fire*); to launch (*an attack*)

déclencheur [deklãʃœr] *m* (mach, phot) release

déclic [deklik] *m* pawl, catch; hair trigger

déclin [deklɛ̃] *m* decline

déclinaison [deklinɛzɔ̃] *f* (astr) declination; (gram) declension

décliner [dekline] *tr & intr* to decline

déclive [dekliv] *adj* sloping ‖ *f* slope

déclivité [deklivite] *f* declivity

dé·clos [deklo] **-close** [kloz] *adj* in bloom

décocher [dekɔʃe] *tr* to let fly; to flash (*a smile*)

décoder [dekɔde] *tr* to decode

décoiffer [dekwafe] *tr* to loosen or muss the hair of; to uncap (*a bottle*)

|| *ref* to muss one's hair; to take one's hair down

décoincer [dekwɛ̃se] §51 *tr* to unwedge, to loosen (*a jammed part*)

décolérer [dekɔlere] §10 *intr* to calm down

décollage [dekɔlaʒ] *m* unsticking, ungluing; takeoff (*of airplane*)

décoller [dekɔle] *tr* to unstick, detach || *intr* (aer) to take off

décolletage [dekɔltaʒ] *m* low-cut neck; screw cutting; topping

décolle·té -tée [dekɔlte] *adj* décolleté || *m* low-cut neckline; bare neck and shoulders

décolleter [dekɔlte] §34 *tr* to cut the neck of (*a dress*) low; to bare the neck and shoulders of || *ref* to wear a low-necked dress

décoloration [dekɔlɔrɑsjɔ̃] *f* discoloration

décolorer [dekɔlɔre] *tr & ref* to bleach; to fade

décombres [dekɔ̃br] *mpl* debris, ruins

décommander [dekɔmɑ̃de] *tr* to cancel an order for; to call off (*a dinner*); to cancel the invitation to (*a guest*) || *ref* to cancel a meeting

décompléter [dekɔ̃plete] §10 *tr* to break up (*a set*)

décomposer [dekɔ̃poze] *tr & ref* to decompose

décomposition [dekɔ̃pozisjɔ̃] *f* decomposition

décompression [dekɔ̃presjɔ̃] *f* decompression

décomprimer [dekɔ̃prime] *tr* to decompress

décompte [dekɔ̃t] *m* itemized statement; discount (*to be deducted from total*); disappointment

décompter [dekɔ̃te] *tr* to deduct (*a sum from an account*) || *intr* to strike the wrong hour

déconcerter [dekɔ̃sɛrte] *tr* to disconcert

décon·fit [dekɔ̃fi] **-fite** [fit] *adj* discomfited, baffled, confused

déconfiture [dekɔ̃fityr] *f* discomfiture; downfall, rout; business failure

décongeler [dekɔ̃ʒle] §2 *tr* to thaw; to defrost

décongestionner [dekɔ̃ʒɛstjɔne] *tr* to relieve congestion in

déconseiller [dekɔ̃seje] *tr* to dissuade; **déconseiller q.ch. à qn** to advise s.o. against s.th. || *intr*—**déconseiller à qn de** + *inf* to advise s.o. against + *ger*

déconsidération [dekɔ̃siderɑsjɔ̃] *f* disrepute

déconsidérer [dekɔ̃sidere] §10 *tr* to bring into disrepute, to discredit

déconsigner [dekɔ̃siɲe] *tr* to take (*one's baggage*) out of the checkroom; to free (*soldiers*) from detention

décontenancer [dekɔ̃tnɑ̃se] §51 *tr* to discountenance, abash || *ref* to lose one's self-assurance

décontrac·té -tée [dekɔ̃trakte] *adj* relaxed, at ease; indifferent

décontracter [dekɔ̃trakte] *tr* to loosen

up (*one's muscles*) || *intr* to stretch one's muscles; to relax

déconvenue [dekɔ̃vny] *f* disappointment, mortification

décor [dekɔr] *m* décor, decoration; (theat) setting; **décor découpé** cutout; **décors** (theat) set, stage setting

décora·teur [dekɔratœr] **-trice** [tris] *mf* interior decorator; stage designer

décora·tif [dekɔratif] **-tive** [tiv] *adj* decorative, ornamental

décoration [dekɔrɑsjɔ̃] *f* decoration

décorum [dekɔrɔm] *m invar* decorum

découcher [dekuʃe] *intr* to sleep away from home

découdre [dekudr] §13 *tr* to unstitch, to rip up; to gore || *intr*—**en découdre** to cross swords || *ref* to come unsewn, to rip at the seam

découler [dekule] *intr* to trickle; to proceed, arise, be derived

découpage [dekupaʒ] *m* shooting script

découper [dekupe] *tr* to carve (*e.g., a turkey*); to cut out (*a design*); to indent (*the coast*) || *ref*—**se découper sur** to stand out against (*the horizon*)

décou·plé -plée [dekuple] *adj* wellbuilt, brawny

découpler [dekuple] *tr* to unleash

découpure [dekupyr] *f* cutting out; ornamental cutout; indentation (*in coast*)

découragement [dekuraʒmɑ̃] *m* discouragement

décourager [dekuraʒe] §38 *tr* to discourage || *ref* to become discouraged

décours [dekur] *m* wane

décou·su -sue [dekuzy] *adj* unsewn; disjointed, unsystematic; incoherent (*words*); desultory (*remarks*)

décou·vert -verte [vert] *adj* uncovered, open, exposed || *m* deficit; overdraft || *f* uncovering; discovery

décou·vreur [dekuvrœr] **-vreuse** [vrøz] *mf* discoverer

découvrir [dekuvrir] §65 *tr* to discover; to discern (*in the distance*); to pick out (*with a searchlight*); to uncover || *intr* to become visible (*said of rocks at low tide*) || *ref* to take off one's hat; to lower one's guard; to clear up (*said of the sky*); to say what one is thinking; to come to light, to be revealed

décrasser [dekrase] *tr* to clean; to polish up

décré·pit [dekrepi] **-pite** [pit] *adj* decrepit

décret [dekre] *m* decree

décrier [dekrije] *tr* to decry, disparage, run down

décrire [dekrir] §25 *tr* to describe

décrocher [dekrɔʃe] *tr* to unhook, take down; (coll) to wangle; **décrocher la timbale** (coll) to hit the jackpot || *intr* to withdraw

décrochez-moi-ça [dekrɔʃemwasa] *m invar* (coll) secondhand clothing store

décroît [dekrwa] *m* last quarter (*of moon*)

décroître [dekrwatr] §17 (*pp* **décru**; *pres ind* **décrois**, etc.; *pret* **décrus**, etc.) *intr* to decrease; to shorten (*said of days*); to fall (*said of river*)

décrotter [dekrɔte] *tr* to remove mud from; (coll) to teach how to behave

décrotteur [dekrɔtœr] *m* shoeshine boy

décrottoir [dekrɔtwar] *m* doormat; scraper (*for shoes*)

décrue [dekry] *f* fall, drop, subsiding

décrypter [dekripte] *tr* to decipher

déculotter [dekylɔte] *tr* to take the pants off of ‖ *ref* to take off one's pants

décuple [dekypl] *adj & m* tenfold

décupler [dekyple] *tr & intr* to increase tenfold

dédaigner [dedeɲe] *tr* to disdain; to reject (*e.g., an offer*); **dédaigner de** + *inf* not to condescend to + *inf*

dédai·gneux [dedeɲø] **-gneuse** [ɲøz] *adj* disdainful

dédain [dedɛ̃] *m* disdain

dedans [dədɑ̃] *m* inside; **en dedans** inside ‖ *adv* inside, within; **mettre dedans** (coll) to take in, to fool

dédicace [dedikas] *f* dedication

dédicacer [dedikase] §51 *tr* to dedicate, to autograph

dédicatoire [dedikatwar] *adj* dedicatory

dédier [dedje] *tr* to dedicate; to offer (*e.g., a collection to a museum*)

dédire [dedir] §40 *tr—***dédire qn** to disavow s.o.'s words or actions ‖ *ref* to make a retraction, to back down; **se dédire de** to go back on, to fail to keep

dédit [dedi] *m* penalty (*for breaking a contract*); breach of contract

dédommagement [dedɔmaʒmɑ̃] *m* compensation, damages, indemnity

dédommager [dedɔmaʒe] §38 *tr* to compensate for a loss, to indemnify

dédouaner [dedwane] *tr* to clear through customs; to rehabilitate (*a politician, statesman, etc.*)

dédoublement [dedubləmɑ̃] *m* splitting; subdivision; unfolding

dédoubler [deduble] *tr* to divide or split in two; to remove the lining from; to unfold; to put on another section of (*a train*)

déduction [dedyksjɔ̃] *f* deduction

déduire [deduir] §19 *tr* to deduce; to infer; (com) to deduct

déesse [dees] *f* goddess

défaillance [defajɑ̃s] *f* failure, failing; faint; lapse (*of memory*); nonappearance (*of witness*); **défaillance cardiaque** heart failure; **sans défaillance** unflinching

défail·lant [defajɑ̃] **défail·lante** [defajɑ̃t] *adj* failing, faltering

défaillir [defajir] §69 *intr* to fail; to falter, weaken, flag; to faint

défaire [defer] §29 *tr* to undo; to untie, unwrap, unpack; to rearrange; to let down (*one's hair*); to rid; to defeat, to rout; to wear (*s.o.*) down, to tire (*s.o.*) out ‖ *ref* to come undone; **se défaire de** to get rid of

dé·fait [defe] **-faite** [fet] *adj* undone, untied; loose; disheveled; drawn

(*countenance*) ‖ *f* defeat; disposal, turnover; (fig) loophole

défaitisme [defetism] *m* defeatism

défaitiste [defetist] *mf* defeatist

défalcation [defalkasjɔ̃] *f* deduction

défalquer [defalke] *tr* to deduct

défaufiler [defofile] *tr* to untack

défausser [defose] *tr* to straighten ‖ *ref—***se défausser (de)** to discard

défaut [defo] *m* defect, fault; lack (*of knowledge, memory, etc.*); flaw; chink (*in armor*); **à défaut de** in default of, lacking; **faire défaut à** to abandon, fail (*e.g., one's friends*); (law) to default; **mettre en défaut** to foil

défaveur [defavœr] *f* disfavor

défavorable [defavɔrabl] *adj* unfavorable

défavoriser [defavɔrize] *tr* to handicap, to put at a disadvantage

défécation [defekasjɔ̃] *f* defecation

défec·tif [defektif] **-tive** [tiv] *adj* (gram) defective

défection [defeksjɔ̃] *f* defection; **faire défection** to defect

défec·tueux [defektɥø] **-tueuse** [tɥøz] *adj* defective, faulty

défectuosité [defektɥozite] *f* imperfection

défen·deur [defɑ̃dœr] **-deresse** [dres] *mf* defendant

défendre [defɑ̃dr] *tr* to defend; to protect (*e.g., against the cold*); **à son corps défendant** in self-defense; against one's will; **défendre q.ch. à qn** to forbid s.o. s.th. ‖ *intr—***défendre à qn de** + *inf* to forbid s.o. to + *inf* ‖ *ref* to defend oneself; (coll) to hold one's own; **se défendre de** to deny (*e.g., having said s.th.*); to refrain from, to keep from

défen·du -due [defɑ̃dy] *adj* forbidden

défense [defɑ̃s] *f* defense; tusk; **défense passive** civil defense (*against air raids*); (public signs): **défense d'afficher** post no bills; **défense de dépasser** no passing; **défense de déposer des ordures** no dumping, no littering; **défense de doubler** no passing; **défense de faire des ordures** commit no nuisance; **défense de fumer** no smoking; **défense d'entrer** private, keep out, no admittance

défenseur [defɑ̃sœr] *m* defender; lawyer for the defense; stand-by

défen·sif [defɑ̃sif] **-sive** [siv] *adj & f* defensive

déférence [deferɑ̃s] *f* deference

défé·rent [deferɑ̃] **-rente** [rɑ̃t] *adj* deferential

déférer [defere] §10 *tr* to confer, award; to refer (*a case to a court*); **déférer en justice** to haul into court ‖ *intr* to comply; **déférer à** to defer to, to comply with

déferler [deferle] *tr* to unfurl; to set (*the sails of a ship*) ‖ *intr* to spread out (*said of a crowd*); to break (*said of waves*)

défeuiller [defœje] *tr* to defoliate ‖ *ref* to lose its leaves

défi [defi] *m* challenge, dare; **défi à**

l'autorité defiance of authority; **porter un défi à** to defy; **relever un défi** to take a dare

défiance [defjᾶs] *f* distrust

dé•fiant [defjᾶ] **-fiante** [fjᾶt] *adj* distrustful

déficeler [defisle] §34 *tr* to untie

déficience [defisjᾶs] *f* deficiency

défi•cient [defisjᾶ] **-ciente** [sjᾶt] *adj* deficient

déficit [defisit] *m* deficit

déficitaire [defisiter] *adj* deficit; meager (*crop*); lean (*year*)

défier [defje] *tr* to challenge; to defy (*death, time, etc.*); **défier qn de** to dare s.o. to || *ref*—se **défier de** to mistrust

défiger [defiʒe] §38 *tr* to liquefy

défiguration [defigyrasjɔ̃] *f* disfigurement; defacement

défigurer [defigyre] *tr* to disfigure; to deface; to distort

défilé [defile] *m* defile (*in mountains*); parade, procession, line of march

défilement [defilmᾶ] *m* (mil) defilade, cover

défiler [defile] *tr* to unstring; (mil) to put under cover || *intr* to march by, to parade, to defile || *ref* to come unstrung; to take cover; (coll) to gold-brick

défi•ni -nie [defini] *adj* definite; defined

définir [definir] *tr* to define || *ref* to be defined

définissable [definisabl] *adj* definable

défini•tif [definitif] **-tive** [tiv] *adj* definitive; standard (*edition*); **en définitive** in short, all things considered

définition [definisjɔ̃] *f* definition

définitivement [definitivmᾶ] *adv* definitively, for good, permanently

déflation [deflasjɔ̃] *f* deflation (*of currency*); sudden drop (*in wind*)

défleurir [deflœrir] *tr* to deflower, to strip of flowers || *intr & ref* to lose its flowers

déflexion [defleksjɔ̃] *f* deflection

défloraison [deflorezɔ̃] *f* dropping of petals

déflorer [deflore] *tr* to deflower

défon•cé -cée [defɔ̃se] *adj* battered, smashed, crumpled; bumpy

défoncer [defɔ̃se] §51 *tr* to batter in; to stave in (*a cask*); to remove the seat of (*a chair*); to break up (*ground; a road*) || *ref* to be broken up (*said of road*)

déformation [deformasjɔ̃] *f* deformation, distortion; **déformation professionnelle** narrow professionalism

défor•mé -mée [deforme] *adj* out of shape; rough (*road*)

déformer [deforme] *tr* to deform, distort || *ref* to become deformed

défoulement [defulmᾶ] *m* (psychoanal) insight, recall; (coll) relief

défraî•chi -chie [defreʃi] *adj* dingy, faded

défraîchir [defreʃir] *tr* to make stale, to fade

défrayer [defreje] §49 *tr* to defray the

expenses of (*s.o.*); **défrayer la conversation** to be the subject of the conversation

défricher [defriʃe] *tr* to reclaim; to clear up (*a puzzler*)

défricheur [defriʃœr] *m* pioneer, explorer

défriser [defrize] *tr & ref* to uncurl

défroncer [defrɔ̃se] §51 *tr* to remove the wrinkles from

défroque [defrɔk] *f* piece of discarded clothing

défroquer [defrɔke] *tr* to unfrock || *ref* to give up the frock

dé•funt [defœ̃] **-funte** [fœ̃t] *adj & mf* deceased

déga•gé -gée [degaʒe] *adj* breezy, jaunty, nonchalant; free, detached

dégagement [degaʒmᾶ] *m* disengagement; clearing, relieving of congestion; liberation (*e.g., of heat*); exit; retraction (*of promise*); redemption, taking out of hock

dégager [degaʒe] §38 *tr* to disengage; to free, clear, release; to draw, extract (*the moral or essential points*); to give off, liberate; to take back (*one's word*); to redeem, to take out of hock

dégaine [degɛn] *f* (coll) awkward bearing; ridiculous posture

dégainer [degɛne] *tr* to unsheathe || *intr* to take up a sword

dégar•ni -nie [degarni] *adj* empty, depleted, stripped

dégarnir [degarnir] *tr* to clear (*a table*); to withdraw soldiers from (*a sector*); to prune || *ref* to thin out

dégât [dega] *m* damage, havoc

dégauchir [degoʃir] *tr* to smooth out the rough edges of (*stone, wood; an inexperienced person*)

dégel [deʒel] *m* thaw

dégeler [deʒle] §2 *tr* to thaw, to defrost; to loosen up, relax || *intr* to thaw out; **il dégèle** it is thawing

dégéné•ré -rée [deʒenere] *adj & mf* degenerate

dégénérer [deʒenere] §10 *intr* to degenerate

dégénérescence [deʒeneresᾶs] *f* degeneration

dégingan•dé -dée [deʒɛ̃gᾶde] *adj* gangling, ungainly

dégivrage [deʒivraʒ] *m* defrosting

dégivrer [deʒivre] *tr* to defrost, to deice

dégivreur [deʒivrœr] *m* defroster, deicer

déglacer [deglase] §51 *tr* to deice; to remove the glaze from (*paper*)

dégommer [degome] *tr* to ungum; (coll) to fire (*s.o.*)

dégon•flé -flée [degɔ̃fle] *adj* flat (*tire*)

dégonflement [degɔ̃fləmᾶ] *m* deflation

dégonfler [degɔ̃fle] *tr* to deflate || *ref* to go flat; to go down, to subside (*said of swelling*); (slang) to lose one's nerve

dégorger [degɔrʒe] §38 *tr* to disgorge; to unstop, open (*a pipe*); to scour (*e.g., wool*) || *intr* to discharge, to overflow

dégour·di -die [degurdi] *adj* limbered up, lively, sharp, adroit || *mf* smart aleck

dégourdir [degurdir] *tr* to remove stiffness or numbness from (*e.g., legs*); to stretch (*one's limbs*); to take the chill off; to teach (*s.o.*) the ropes, to polish (*s.o.*) || *ref* to limber up

dégoût [degu] *m* distaste, dislike

dégoû·tant [degutã] **-tante** [tãt] *adj* disgusting, distasteful

dégoû·té -tée [degute] *adj* fastidious, hard to please || *mf* finicky person

dégoûter [degute] *tr* to disgust; **dégoûter qn de** to make s.o. dislike || *ref* to become fed up

dégoutter [degute] *intr* to drip, trickle

dégradation [degradasjɔ̃] *f* degradation; defacement; shading off, graduation; worsening (*of a situation*); (mil) demotion; **dégradation civique** loss of civil rights

dégrader [degrade] *tr* to degrade, to bring down; to deface; to shade off, to graduate; (mil) to demote, to break || *ref* to debase oneself; to become dilapidated

dégrafer [degrafe] *tr* to unhook, to unclasp

dégraissage [degrɛsaʒ] *m* dry cleaning

dégraisser [degrɛse] *tr* to remove grease from; to dry-clean

dégrais·seur [degrɛsœr] **dégrais·seuse** [degrɛsøz] *mf* dry cleaner, cleaner and dyer

degré [dəgre] *m* degree; step (*of stairs*); **monter d'un degré** to take a step up (*on the ladder of success*)

dégringolade [degrɛ̃gɔlad] *f* (coll) tumble; (coll) comedown, collapse, downfall

dégringoler [degrɛ̃gɔle] *tr* to bring down (*a government*) || *intr* (coll) to tumble, to tumble down

dégriser [degrize] *tr & ref* to sober up

dégrossir [degrosir] *tr* to rough-hew; to make the preliminary sketches of; to refine or polish (*a hick*)

déguenil·lé -lée [degənije] *adj* ragged, in tatters || *mf* ragamuffin

déguerpir [degɛrpir] *intr* (coll) to clear out, to beat it; **faire déguerpir** to evict

déguisement [degizmã] *m* disguise

déguiser [degize] *tr* to disguise

dégusta·teur [degystatœr] **-trice** [tris] *mf* winetaster

dégustation [degystasjɔ̃] *f* tasting, art of tasting; consumption (*of beverages*)

déguster [degyste] *tr* to taste discriminatingly; to sip, drink; to consume

déhancher [deɑ̃ʃe] *tr* to dislocate the hip of || *intr* to swing one's hips

déharnacher [dearnaʃe] *tr* to unsaddle, unharness || *ref* (coll) to throw off one's heavy clothing

dehors [dəɔr] *m* outside; **dehors** *mpl* outward appearance; **du dehors** from without, foreign, external; **en dehors** outside; **en dehors de** outside of; beyond || *adv* outside, out; out-of-doors

déification [deifikɑsjɔ̃] *f* deification

déifier [deifje] *tr* to deify

déiste [deist] *adj & mf* deist

déité [deite] *f* deity

déjà [deʒa] *adv* already

déjanter [deʒɑ̃te] *tr* to take (*a tire*) off the rim || *ref* to come off

déjection [deʒɛksjɔ̃] *f* excretion; volcanic debris

déjeter [deʒte] §34 *tr & ref* to warp, to spring

déjeuner [deʒœne] *m* lunch; breakfast; breakfast set; **petit déjeuner** breakfast || *intr* to have lunch; to have breakfast

déjouer [deʒwe] *tr* to foil, thwart

déjucher [deʒyʃe] *tr* to unroost || *intr* to come off the roost (*said of fowl*)

déjuger [deʒyʒe] §38 *ref* to change one's mind

delà [dəla] *adv*—**au delà de** beyond; **par delà** beyond

délabrement [delabrəmã] *m* decay, dilapidation; impairment (*of health*)

délabrer [delabre] *tr* to ruin, wreck || *ref* to become dilapidated

délacer [delase] §51 *tr* to unlace

délai [delɛ] *m* term, duration, period (*of time*); postponement, extension; **à bref délai** at short notice; **dans le plus bref délai** in the shortest possible time; **dans un délai de** within; **dans un délai record** in record time; **dernier délai** deadline; **sans délai** without delay

délais·sé -sée [delɛse] *adj* forsaken, forlorn, neglected

délaissement [delɛsmã] *m* abandonment

délaisser [delɛse] *tr* to abandon, desert; to relinquish (*a right*)

délassement [delasmã] *m* relaxation

délasser [delase] *tr* to rest, refresh, relax || *ref* to rest up

déla·teur [delatœr] **-trice** [tris] *mf* informer

délation [delasjɔ̃] *f* paid informing

déla·vé -vée [delave] *adj* washed-out, weak

délayer [deleje] §49 *tr* to add water to, to dilute; **délayer un discours** to stretch out a speech

deleatur [deleatyr] *m* dele

délébile [delebil] *adj* erasable

délectable [delɛktabl] *adj* delectable

délectation [delɛktasjɔ̃] *f* pleasure

délecter [delɛkte] *ref*—**se délecter à** to find pleasure in

délégation [delegasjɔ̃] *f* delegation

délé·gué -guée [delege] *adj* delegated || *mf* delegate, spokesman

déléguer [delege] §10 *tr* to delegate

délester [delɛste] *tr* to unballast; to unburden, relieve

délétère [deletɛr] *adj* deleterious

délibération [deliberasjɔ̃] *f* deliberation

délibé·ré -rée [delibere] *adj* deliberate, firm, decided

délibérer [delibere] §10 *tr & intr* to deliberate

déli·cat [delika] **-cate** [kat] *adj* delicate; fine, sensitive (*ear, mind, taste*); touchy; tactful; scrupulous, honest

délicatesse [delikates] *f* delicacy; refinement, fineness; fastidiousness; fragility, weakness

délice [delis] *m* great pleasure || **délices** *fpl* delights, pleasures

déli·cieux [delisjø] **-cieuse** [sjøz] *adj* delicious; delightful, charming

dé·lié -liée [delje] *adj* slender (*figure*); nimble (*mind*); fine (*handwriting*); glib (*tongue*) || *m* upstroke, thin stroke

délier [delje] *tr* to untie, to loosen, to release || *ref* to come loose

délinéament [delineamᾶ] *m* delineation

délinéer [delinee] *tr* to delineate

délinquance [delɛ̃kɑ̃s] *f* delinquency; **délinquance juvénile** juvenile delinquency

délin·quant [delɛ̃kɑ̃] **-quante** [kɑ̃t] *adj & mf* delinquent; **délinquant primaire** first offender

déli·rant [delirɑ̃] **-rante** [rɑ̃t] *adj* delirious, raving

délire [delir] *m* delirium; **en délire** delirious, in a frenzy

délirer [delire] *intr* to be delirious, to rave

délit [deli] *m* offense, wrong, crime; **en flagrant délit** in the act

délivrance [delivrɑ̃s] *f* deliverance; delivery

délivre [delivr] *m* afterbirth, placenta

délivrer [delivre] *tr* to deliver

déloger [deloʒe] §38 *tr* to dislodge; (coll) to oust, to evict || *intr* to move out (*of a house*)

déloyal déloyale [delwajal] *adj* (*pl* **déloyaux** [delwajo]) disloyal; unfair, dishonest

déloyauté [delwajote] *f* disloyalty; disloyal act; dishonesty

delta [delta] *m* delta

déluge [delyʒ] *m* deluge, flood

délu·ré -rée [delyre] *adj* smart, clever; smart-alecky, forward

délurer [delyre] *tr & ref* to wise up

délustrer [delystre] *tr* to take the gloss off of

démagnétiser [demaɲetize] *tr* to demagnetize

démagogie [demagɔʒi] *f* demagogy

démagogique [demagɔʒik] *adj* demagogic

démagogue [demagɔg] *adj* demagogic || *mf* demagogue

démaigrir [demegrir] *tr* to thin down

démailler [demaje] *tr* to unshackle (*a chain*); to unravel (*e.g., a knitted sweater*); to make a run in (*a stocking*) || *ref* to run (*said of stocking*)

démailloter [demajote] *tr* to take the diaper off of

demain [dǝmɛ̃] *adv & m* tomorrow; **à demain** until tomorrow; so long; **de demain en huit** a week from tomorrow; **de demain en quinze** two weeks from tomorrow; **demain matin** tomorrow morning

démancher [demᾶʃe] *tr* to remove the handle of; (coll) to dislocate

demande [dǝmᾶd] *f* request; application (*for a position*); inquiry; demand (*by buyers for goods*)

demander [dǝmᾶde] *tr* to ask (*a favor; one's way*); to ask for (*a package; a porter*); to require, to need (*attention*); **demander q.ch. à qn** to ask s.o. for s.th. || *intr*—**demander à** or **de** + *inf* to ask permission to + *inf*; to insist upon + *ger*; **demander après** to ask about, ask for (*s.o.*); **demander à qn de** + *inf* to ask s.o. to + *inf*; **je ne demande pas mieux** I wish I could || *ref* to be needed; to wonder

deman·deur [dǝmᾶdœr] **-deuse** [døz] *mf* asker; buyer || **-deur** [dœr] **-deresse** [drɛs] *mf* plaintiff

démangeaison [demᾶʒɛz] *f* itch

démanger [demᾶʒe] §38 *tr & intr* to itch || *intr* (with *dat*) to itch; **la langue lui démange** he is itching to speak

démanteler [demᾶtle] §2 *tr* to dismantle (*a fort or town*); to uncover (*a spy ring*)

démaquillage [demakijaʒ] *m* removal of paint or make-up

démaquillant [demakijᾶ] *m* cleansing cream, make-up remover

démaquiller [demakije] *tr & ref* to take the paint or make-up off

démarcation [demarkɑsjɔ̃] *f* demarcation

démarche [demarʃ] *f* gait, step, bearing; method; step, move, action

démarier [demarje] *tr* to thin out (*plants*)

démarque [demark] *f* (com) markdown

démarquer [demarke] *tr* to remove the identification marks from; to plagiarize; to mark down

démarrage [demaraʒ] *m* start

démarrer [demare] *tr* to unmoor || *intr* to cast off (*said of ship*); to start (*said of train or car*); to spurt (*said of racing contestant; said of economy*); **démarrer trop tôt** to jump the gun; **faire démarrer** to start (*a car*); **ne démarrez pas!** don't stir!

démarreur [demarœr] *m* starter (*of car*)

démasquer [demaske] *tr & ref* to unmask

démâter [demate] *tr* to dismast || *intr* to lose her masts (*said of ship*)

démêlé [demele] *m* quarrel, dispute; **avoir des démêlés avec** to be at odds with, to run afoul of

démêler [demele] *tr* to disentangle, unravel; to bring to light, uncover (*a plot*); to make out, discern

démembrement [demᾶbrǝmᾶ] *m* dismemberment

déménagement [demenaʒmᾶ] *m* moving

déménager [demenaʒe] §38 *tr* to move (*household effects*) to another residence; to move the furniture from (*a house*) || *intr* to move, to change one's residence; (coll) to become childish; **tu déménages!** (coll) you're out of your mind!

déménageur [demenaʒœr] *m* mover

démence [demɑ̃s] *f* madness, insanity; **en démence** demented

démener [demne] §2 *ref* to struggle, to be agitated; to take great pains

dé-ment [demɑ̃] **-mente** [mɑ̃t] *adj & mf* lunatic

démenti [demɑ̃ti] *m* contradiction, denial; proof to the contrary; (coll) shame (*on account of a failure*)

démentir [demɑ̃tir] §41 *tr* to contradict, to deny; to give the lie to, to belie ‖ *intr* to go back on one's word; to be inconsistent

démériter [demerite] *intr* to lose esteem, to become unworthy

démesure [demɑzyr] *f* lack of moderation, excess

démesu·ré -rée [demɑzyre] *adj* measureless, immense; immoderate, excessive

démettre [demetr] §42 *tr* to dismiss (*from a job or position*); to dislocate (*an arm*) ‖ *ref* to resign, retire

démeubler [demœble] *tr* to remove the furniture from

demeurant [dəmœrɑ̃]—**au demeurant** all things considered, after all

demeure [dəmœr] *f* home, abode, dwelling; **à demeure** permanently; **dernière demeure** final resting place; **en demeure** in arrears; **mettre qn en demeure de** to oblige s.o. to; **sans plus longue demeure** without further delay

demeurer [dəmœre] *intr* to live, dwell ‖ *intr* (*aux:* ÊTRE) to stay, remain; **en demeurer** to leave off; **en demeurer là** to stop, rest there; to leave it at that

demi [dəmi] *m* half; (sports) center; (sports) halfback; **à demi** half; **et demi** and a half, e.g., **un centimètre et demi** a centimeter and a half; (after **midi** or **minuit**) half past, e.g., **midi et demi** half past twelve

demi-bas [dəmiba] *m* half hose

demi-botte [dəmibɔt] *f* (*pl* **-bottes**) half boot

demi-cercle [dəmiserkl] *m* (*pl* **-cercles**) semicircle

demi-clef [dəmikle] *f* (*pl* **-clefs**) half hitch; **demi-clef à capeler** clove hitch; **deux demi-clefs** two half hitches

demi-congé [dəmikɔ̃ʒe] *m* (*pl* **-congés**) half-holiday

demi-deuil [dəmidœj] *m* (*pl* **-deuils**) half mourning

demi-dieu [dəmidjø] *m* (*pl* **-dieux**) demigod

demie [dəmi] *f* half hour; **et demie** half past, e.g., **deux heures et demie** half past two

demi-finale [dəmifinal] *f* (*pl* **-finales**) semifinal

demi-frère [dəmifrer] *m* (*pl* **-frères**) half brother; stepbrother

demi-heure [dəmiœr] *f* (*pl* **-heures**) half-hour; **toutes les demi-heures à la demi-heure juste** every half-hour on the half-hour

demi-jour [dəmiʒur] *m invar* twilight, half-light

demi-journée [dəmiʒurne] *f* (*pl* **-journées**) half-day; **à demi-journée** half-time

démilitariser [demilitarize] *tr* to demilitarize

demi-longueur [dəmilɔ̃gœr] *f* half-length

demi-lune [dəmilyn] *f* (*pl* **-lunes**) half-moon

demi-mondaine [dəmimɔ̃den] *f* (*pl* **-mondaines**) demimondaine

demi-monde [dəmimɔ̃d] *m* demimonde

demi-mot [dəmimo] *m* (*pl* **-mots**) understatement, euphemism; **comprendre à demi-mot** to get the drift of; to take the hint

déminer [demine] *tr* to clear of mines

demi-pause [dəmipoz] *f* (*pl* **-pauses**) (mus) half rest

demi-pension [dəmipɑ̃sjɔ̃] *f* (*pl* **-pensions**) breakfast and one meal

demi-place [dəmiplas] *f* (*pl* **-places**) half fare; half-price seat

demi-reliure [dəmirəljyr] *f* (*pl* **-reliures**) quarter binding; **demi-reliure à petits coins** half binding

demi-saison [dəmisezɔ̃] *f* in-between season; **de demi-saison** spring-and-fall (*coat*)

demi-sang [dəmisɑ̃] *m invar* half-bred horse

demi-sœur [dəmisœr] *f* (*pl* **-sœurs**) half sister; stepsister

demi-solde [dəmisɔld] *m invar* pensioned officer ‖ *f* (*pl* **-soldes**) army pension, half pay

demi-soupir [dəmisupir] *m* (*pl* **-soupirs**) (mus) eighth rest

démission [demisjɔ̃] *f* resignation

démissionnaire [demisjɔner] *adj* outgoing ‖ *mf* former incumbent

démissionner [demisjɔne] *tr* (coll) to fire ‖ *intr* to resign

demi-tasse [dəmitas] *f* (*pl* **-tasses**) half-cup; small cup, demitasse

demi-teinte [dəmitɛ̃t] *f* (*pl* **-teintes**) halftone

demi-ton [dəmitɔ̃] *m* (*pl* **-tons**) (mus) half tone

demi-tour [dəmitur] *m* (*pl* **-tours**) about-face; half turn; **demi-tour, (à) droite!** about face!; to the rear!; **faire demi-tour** to do an about-face; to turn back

démobiliser [demɔbilize] *tr* to demobilize

démocrate [demɔkrat] *mf* democrat

démocratie [demɔkrasi] *f* democracy

démocratique [demɔkratik] *adj* democratic

démo·dé -dée [demɔde] *adj* old-fashioned, out-of-date, outmoded

démoder [demɔde] *ref* to be outmoded

demoiselle [dəmwazel] *f* single girl, young lady, miss; dragonfly; (slang) girl; **demoiselle de magasin** salesgirl; **demoiselle d'honneur** maid of honor, bridesmaid; lady-in-waiting

démolir [demɔlir] *tr* to demolish; to overturn (*a cabinet or government*)

démolition [demɔlisjɔ̃] *f* demolition; **démolitions** scrap, rubble

démon [demɔ̃] *m* demon

démoniaque [demɔnjak] *adj* demonic, demoniac(al) ‖ *mf* demoniac

démonstra·teur [demɔ̃stratœr] **-trice** [tris] *mf* demonstrator

démonstra·tif [demɔ̃stratif] **-tive** [tiv] *adj* & *m* demonstrative

démontable [demɔ̃tabl] *adj* collapsible, detachable; knockdown

démonte-pneu [demɔ̃tpnø] *m* (*pl* **-pneus**) tire iron

démonter [demɔ̃te] *tr* to dismount; to dismantle ‖ *ref* to come apart; to go to pieces (*while taking an exam*)

démontrable [demɔ̃trabl] *adj* demonstrable

démontrer [demɔ̃tre] *tr* to demonstrate

démoraliser [demɔralize] *tr* to demoralize

démouler [demule] *tr* to remove from a mold

dému·ni -nie [demyni] *adj* out of money; **démuni de** out of; devoid of

démunir [demynir] *tr* to strip, deprive; to deplete (*a garrison*) ‖ *ref* to deprive oneself

démystifier [demistifje] *tr* to debunk

dénationaliser [denasjɔnalize] *tr* to denationalize

dénaturaliser [denatyralize] *tr* to denaturalize

dénatu·ré -rée [denatyre] *adj* denatured; unnatural, perverse

dénaturer [denatyre] *tr* to denature; to pervert; to distort

dénégation [denegasjɔ̃] *f* denial

déni [deni] *m* refusal; (law) denial

dénicher [deni/e] *tr* to dislodge; to take out of the nest; to make (*s.o.*) move; to search out ‖ *intr* to leave the nest

déni·cheur [deni/œr] **-cheuse** [/øz] *mf* hunter (*of rare books, antiques, etc.*); **dénicheur de vedettes** talent scout

denier [dənje] *m* (fig) penny, farthing; **denier à Dieu** gratuity; **deniers** money, funds; **de ses deniers** with his own money

dénier [denje] *tr* to deny, refuse

dénigrer [denigre] *tr* to disparage

déniveler [denivle] §34 *tr* to make uneven, to change the level of

dénivellation [denivellasjɔ̃] *f* or **dénivellement** [denivelmã] *m* unevenness; depression, settling

dénombrement [denɔ̃brəmã] *m* census, enumeration

dénombrer [denɔ̃bre] *tr* to take a census of, to enumerate

dénomination [denɔminasjɔ̃] *f* denomination, appellation, designation

dénommer [denɔme] *tr* to denominate, to name

dénoncer [denɔ̃se] §51 *tr* to renounce; to indicate, reveal ‖ *ref* to give oneself up

dénonciation [denɔ̃sjasjɔ̃] *f* denunciation; declaration

dénoter [denɔte] *tr* to denote

dénouement [denumã] *m* outcome, denouement; untying

dénouer [denwe] *tr* to untie; to unravel

dénoyer [denwaje] §47 *tr* to pump out

denrée [dãre] *f* commodity; **denrées** provisions, products

dense [dãs] *adj* dense

densité [dãsite] *f* density

dent [dã] *f* tooth; cog; scallop (*of an edge*); **dent d'éléphant** tusk; **dents de lait** baby teeth; **dents de sagesse** wisdom teeth; **sur les dents** on one's toes

dentaire [dãter] *adj* dental

den·tal -tale [dãtal] *adj* & *f* (*pl* **-taux** [to] **-tales**) dental

dent-de-chien [dãdə/jɛ̃] *f* (*pl* **dents-de-chien**) dogtooth violet

dent-de-lion [dãdəljɔ̃] *f* (*pl* **dents-de-lion**) dandelion

denteler [dãtle] §34 *tr* to notch, to indent

dentelle [dãtel] *f* lace; lacework

dentelure [dãtlyr] *f* notching; serration; scalloping; (phila) perforation

denter [dãte] *tr* to furnish with cogs or teeth

dentier [dãtje] *m* false teeth, denture

dentifrice [dãtifris] *m* dentifrice

dentiste [dãtist] *mf* dentist

denture [dãtyr] *f* denture; **denture artificielle** false teeth

dénuder [denyde] *tr* to strip, denude

dénuement [denymã] *m* destitution

dénuer [denɥe] *tr* to deprive, strip

déontologie [deɔ̃tɔlɔʒi] *f* study of ethics; **déontologie médicale** (med) code of medical ethics

dépannage [depanaʒ] *m* emergency service, repairs

dépanner [depane] *tr* to give emergency service to; (coll) to get (*s.o.*) out of a scrape

dépan·neur [depanœr] **dépan·neuse** [depanøz] *adj* repairing ‖ *m* serviceman, repairman ‖ *f* tow truck, wrecker

dépaqueter [depakte] §34 *tr* to unpack, unwrap

dépareil·lé -lée [depareje] *adj* incomplete, broken (*set*); odd (*sock*)

dépareiller [depareje] *tr* to break (a *set*)

déparer [depare] *tr* to mar, to spoil the beauty of; to strip of ornaments

déparier [deparje] *tr* to break, split up the pair of

départ [depar] *m* departure; beginning; division; sorting out; **départ usine F.O.B.**; **faux départ** false start

département [departəmã] *m* (govt) department

départir [departir] §64 (or sometimes like **finir**) *tr* to divide up, to distribute ‖ *ref*—**se départir de** to give up; to depart from

dépassement [depasmã] *m* passing

dépasser [depase] *tr* to pass, overtake; to go beyond; to overshoot (*the mark*); to exceed; to extend beyond; to be longer than; (coll) to surprise ‖ *intr* to pass; to stick out, to overlap, to show

dépayser [depeize] *tr* to take out of one's familiar surroundings; to bewilder ‖ *ref* to leave one's country

dépecer [depəse] §20 *tr* to carve, to cut up

dépêche [depeʃ] *f* dispatch; telegram

dépêcher [depeʃe] *tr* to dispatch || *ref* to hurry

dépeigner [depeɲe] *tr* to tousle, to muss up (*the hair*)

dépeindre [depɛ̃dr] §50 *tr* to depict

dépendance [depɑ̃dɑ̃s] *f* dependence; **dépendances** outbuildings, annex; dependencies, possessions

dépen•dant [depɑ̃dɑ̃] **-dante** [dɑ̃t] *adj* dependent

dépendre [depɑ̃dr] *tr* to take down || *intr* to depend; **dépendre de** to depend on; to belong to; **il dépend de vous de** it is for you to

dépens [depɑ̃] *mpl* expenses, costs; **aux dépens de** at the expense of

dépense [depɑ̃s] *f* expense; pantry; dispensary (*of hospital*); flow (*of water*); consumption (*of fuel*)

dépenser [depɑ̃se] *tr* to spend, expend || *ref* to exert oneself, to spend one's energy

dépen•sier [depɑ̃sje] **-sière** [sjer] *adj & mf* spendthrift

dépérir [deperir] *intr* to waste away, decline

dépêtrer [depetre] *tr* to get (*s.o.*) out of a jam

dépeupler [depœple] *tr* to depopulate; to unstock (*a pond*)

dépha•sé -sée [defaze] *adj* out of phase

déplauter [depjote] *tr* to skin

dépécer [depjese] §58 *tr* to dismember

dépiler [depile] *tr* to remove the hair from

dépister [depiste] *tr* to track down

dépit [depi] *m* spite, resentment; **en dépit de** in spite of

dépiter [depite] *tr* to spite, to vex || *ref* to take offense

dépla•cé -cée [deplase] *adj* displaced (*person*); misplaced, out of place

déplacement [deplasmɑ̃] *m* displacement; movement; travel; transfer (*of an official*); shift (*in votes*); change (*in schedule*); (*naut*) displacement

déplacer [deplase] §51 *tr* to displace; to move; **déplacer la question** to stray from the subject || *ref* to move

déplaire [depler] §52 *intr* (with *dat*) to displease; (with *dat*) to dislike, e.g., **le lait lui déplaît** he dislikes milk; **ne vous en déplaise** if you have no objection, by your leave || *ref* to be displeased, e.g., **ils se sont déplu** they were displeased; **se déplaire à** not to like it in, e.g., **je me déplais à la campagne** I don't like it in the country

déplai•sant [deplezɑ̃] **-sante** [zɑ̃t] *adj* unpleasant, disagreeable

déplaisir [deplezir] *m* displeasure

déplanter [deplɑ̃te] *tr* to dig up for transplanting

déplantoir [deplɑ̃twar] *m* garden trowel

dépliant [deplijɑ̃] *m* folder, brochure

déplier [deplie] *tr & ref* to unfold

déplisser [deplise] *tr* to unpleat

déploiement [deplwamɑ̃] *m* unfolding,
unfurling; display, array; (mil) deployment

déplorable [deplɔrabl] *adj* deplorable

déplorer [deplɔre] *tr* to deplore; to grieve over

déployer [deplwaje] §47 *tr* to unfold, to unfurl; to display; (mil) to deploy || *ref* (mil) to deploy

déplumer [deplyme] *tr* to pluck (*a chicken*) || *ref* (coll) to lose one's hair

dépolariser [depɔlarize] *tr* to depolarize

dépo•li -lie [depɔli] *adj* ground (*glass*)

dépolir [depɔlir] *tr* to remove the polish from; to frost (*glass*)

déport [depɔr] *m* disqualifying of oneself; (com) commission; **sans déport** without delay

déportation [depɔrtasjɔ̃] *f* deportation; internment in a concentration camp

dépor•té -tée [depɔrte] *mf* deported criminal, convict; prisoner in a concentration camp

déportement [depɔrtəmɑ̃] *m* swerve; **déportements** misconduct, immoral conduct, bad habits

déporter [depɔrte] *tr* to deport; to send to a concentration camp; to make (*an automobile*) swerve; to deflect (*an airplane*) from its course || *intr* to swerve

dépo•sant [depozɑ̃] **-sante** [zɑ̃t] *adj* testifying; depositing || *mf* deponent, witness; depositor

dépose [depoz] *f* removal

déposer [depoze] *tr* to deposit; to depose; to drop, leave off; to register (*a trademark*); to lodge (*a complaint*); to file (*a petition*) || *intr & ref* to depose; to settle, to form a deposit

dépositaire [depoziter] *mf* trustee, holder; dealer

déposséder [deposede] §10 *tr* to dispossess

dépôt [depo] *m* deposit; depository, depot; warehouse; delivery, handing in; **dépôt d'autobus** carbarn; **dépôt de locomotives** roundhouse; **dépôt de mendicité** poorhouse; **dépôt d'épargne** savings account; **dépôt des bagages** baggage room; **dépôt d'essence** filling station; **dépôt de vivres** commissary; **dépôt d'ordures** dump

dépouille [depuj] *f* castoff skin; hide (*taken from animal*); **dépouille mortelle** mortal remains; **dépouilles** spoils (*of war*)

dépouillement [depujmɑ̃] *m* gathering, selection, sifting; despoilment; counting (*of votes*); **dépouillement volontaire** relinquishing

dépouiller [depuje] *tr* to skin; to strip; to gather, select, sift; to count (*votes*) || *ref* to shed one's skin (*said of insects and reptiles*); to strip oneself, to divest oneself

dépour•vu -vue [depurvy] *adj* destitute; **au dépourvu** unaware; **dépourvu de** devoid of, lacking in

dépoussiérer [depusjere] §10 *tr* to vacuum

dépravation [depravɑsjɔ̃] *f* depravity

dépraver [deprave] *tr* to deprave

déprécation [deprekɑsjɔ̃] *f* supplication

dépréciation [depresjɑsjɔ̃] *f* depreciation

déprécier [depresje] *tr & ref* to depreciate

déprédation [depredɑsjɔ̃] *f* depredation; embezzlement, misappropriation

déprendre [deprãdr] §56 *ref* to detach oneself; to come loose; to melt

dépres•sif [depresif] **dépres•sive** [depresiv] *adj* depressive

dépression [depresjɔ̃] *f* depression

déprimer [deprime] *tr* to depress, to lower || *ref* to be depressed

dépriser [deprize] *tr* to undervalue

depuis [dəpɥi] *adv* since; **depuis que** since || *prep* since, for, e.g., **je suis à Paris depuis trois jours** I have been in Paris for three days; **depuis . . . jusqu'à** from . . . to

dépurer [depyre] *tr* to purify

députation [depytɑsjɔ̃] *f* deputation

député [depyte] *m* deputy

députer [depyte] *tr* to deputize

der [der] *f*—**la der des der** (coll) the war to end all wars

déraci•né -née [derasine] *adj* uprooted || uprooted person, wanderer

déraciner [derasine] *tr* to uproot, to root out; to eradicate

déraillement [derɑjmã] *m* derailment

dérailler [derɑje] *intr* to jump the track; (coll) to get off the track

déraison [derezɔ̃] *f* unreasonableness, irrationality

déraisonnable [derezɔnabl] *adj* unreasonable

déraisonner [derezɔne] *intr* to talk nonsense

dérangement [derɑ̃ʒmã] *m* derangement; breakdown; disturbance, bother

déranger [derɑ̃ʒe] §38 *tr* to derange, to put out of order; to disturb, trouble || *ref* to move, to change jobs; to become disordered, upset; **ne vous dérangez pas!** don't get up!; don't bother!

déraper [derape] *intr* to skid, to sideslip; to weigh anchor

dératé [derate] *m*—**courir comme un dératé** to run like a jack rabbit

dératiser [deratize] *tr* to derat

derby [derbi] *m* derby *(race)*

derechef [dərəʃef] *adv* (lit) once again

déré•glé -glée [deregle] *adj* out of order; irregular *(pulse)*; disorderly, excessive

dérégler [deregle] §10 *tr* to put out of order, upset || *ref* to get out of order; to run wild

dérider [deride] *tr* to smooth, unwrinkle; to cheer up || *ref* to cheer up

dérision [derizjɔ̃] *f* derision

dérisoire [derizwar] *adj* derisive

dérivation [derivɑsjɔ̃] *f* derivation; drift; by-pass; diversion *(of river, stream, etc.)*; **en dérivation** shunted *(circuit)*

dérive [deriv] *f* drift; (aer) fin; (naut) centerboard; **à la dérive** adrift

déri•vé -vée [derive] *adj* drifting; shunted *(current)* || *m* derivative

dériver [derive] *tr* to derive; to divert *(e.g., a river)*; to unrivet || *intr* to derive; to be derived; to result; to drift

dermatologie [dermatɔlɔʒi] *f* dermatology

der•nier -nière [njer] *adj* last; latest; latter; final; last *(just elapsed)*, e.g., **la semaine dernière** last week || (when standing before noun) *adj* last *(in a series)*, e.g., **la dernière semaine de la guerre** the last week of the war

dernièrement [dernjermã] *adv* lately

dernier-né [dernjene] **dernière-née** [dernjerne] *mf (pl* **-nés -nées)** lastborn child

déro•bé -bée [derɔbe] *adj* secret; **à la dérobée** stealthily, on the sly

dérober [derɔbe] *tr* to steal; to hide, **dérober à** to steal from; to rescue from *(e.g., death)* || *ref* to steal away, disappear; to hide; to shy away, balk; to shirk; to give way *(said of knees or one's footing)*; se **dérober à** to slip away from, to escape from

dérogation [derɔgɑsjɔ̃] *f*—**dérogation à** departure from *(custom)*; waiving of *(principle)*; deviation from *(instructions)*; **par dérogation à** notwithstanding

déroger [derɔʒe] §38 *intr*—**déroger à** to depart from *(custom)*; to waive *(a principle)*; to derogate from *(dignity, one's rank)*

dérouiller [deruje] *tr* to remove the rust from; to polish *(s.o.)*; (coll) to limber up; (coll) to brush up on || *ref* to lose its rust; to brush up; to limber up

dérouler [derule] *tr & ref* to unroll, unfold

dérou•tant [derutã] **-tante** [tãt] *adj* baffling, misleading

déroute [derut] *f* rout, downfall

dérouter [derute] *tr* to steer off the course; to reroute; to disconcert, baffle || *ref* to go astray; to become confused

derrick [derik] *m* oil derrick

derrière [derjer] *m* rear, backside || *adv & prep* behind

derviche [dervi] *m* dervish

des [de] §77

dès [de] *prep* by *(a certain time)*; from *(a certain place)*; as early as, as far back as; from, beginning with; **dès lors** from that time, ever since; **dès lors que** since, inasmuch as; **dès que** as soon as

désabonner [dezabɔne] *tr* to cancel the subscription of || *ref* to cancel one's subscription

désabu•sé -sée [dezabyze] *adj* disillusioned

désabuser [dezabyze] *tr* to disabuse, disillusion || *ref* to have one's eyes opened

désaccord [dezakɔr] *m* disagreement, discord

désaccorder [dezakɔrde] *tr* to put (*an instrument*) out of tune.‖ *ref* to get out of tune

désaccoupler [dezakuple] *tr* to unpair; to uncouple

désaccoutumer [dezakutyme] *tr* to break (*s.o.*) of a habit ‖ *ref* to break oneself of a habit

désaffecter [dezafekte] *tr* to turn from its intended use

désagréable [dezagreabl] *adj* disagreeable; unpleasant

désagréger [dezagreʒe] §1 *tr* to break up, to dissolve, to disintegrate

désagrément [dezagremã] *m* unpleasantness, annoyance

désaimanter [dezɛmãte] *tr* to demagnetize

désalté·rant [dezaltɛrã] **-rante** [rãt] *adj* thirst-quenching, refreshing

désaltérer [dezaltere] §10 *tr* to quench the thirst of; to refresh with a drink ‖ *ref* to quench one's thirst

désamorcer [dezamɔrse] §51 *tr* to de-activate, to disconnect the fuse of; to unprime

désappointement [dezapwɛtmã] *m* disappointment

désappointer [dezapwɛte] *tr* to disappoint; to break the point of, to blunt

désapprendre [dezaprãdr] §56 *tr* to unlearn, to forget

désapproba·teur [dezaprɔbatœr] **-trice** [tris] *adj* disapproving ‖ *mf* critic

désapprouver [dezapruve] *tr* to disapprove of, to disapprove

désarçonner [dezarsɔne] *tr* to unhorse, buck off; (coll) to dumfound

désarmement [dezarməmã] *m* disarmament; disarming; dismantling (*of ship*)

désarmer [dezarme] *tr* to disarm; to deactivate; to dismantle; to appease ‖ *intr* to disarm; to slacken, let up (*said of hostility*)

désarroi [dezarwa] *m* disorder, disarray, confusion

désarticulation [dezartikylasjɔ̃] *f* dislocation

désassembler [dezasãble] *tr* to disassemble

désastre [dezastr] *m* disaster

désas·treux [dezastrø] **-treuse** [trøz] *adj* disastrous

désavantage [dezavãtaʒ] *m* disadvantage

désavantager [dezavãtaʒe] §38 *tr* to put at a disadvantage, to handicap

désavanta·geux [dezavãtaʒø] **-geuse** [ʒøz] *adj* disadvantageous

désa·veu [dezavø] *m* (*pl* **-veux**) disavowal, denial, repudiation

désavouer [dezavwe] *tr* to disavow, to deny, to repudiate, to disown

désaxé désaxée [dezakse] *adj* unbalanced, out of joint

desceller [desele] *tr* to unseal

descendance [desãdãs] *f* descent

descendeur [desãdœr] *m* ski jumper

descendre [desãdr], [desãdr] *tr* to descend, to go down (*a hill, street,*

stairway); to take down, to lower (*a picture*); (coll) to bring down (*an airplane; luggage*); (coll) to drop off, let off at the door ‖ *intr* (aux: ÊTRE) to descend; to go down, to go downstairs; to stay, to stop (*at a hotel*). **descendre** + *inf* to go down to + *inf*; to stop off to + *inf*; **descendre court** to undershoot (*said of airplane*). **descendre de** to come down from (*a mountain, ladder, tree*); to be descended from

descente [desãt] *f* descent; invasion; raid; stay (*at a hotel*); stop (*en route*); **descente à terre** (nav) shore leave; **descente de lit** bedside rug

descriptible [dɛskriptibl] *adj* describable

descrip·tif [dɛskriptif] **-tive** [tiv] *adj* descriptive

description [dɛskripsjɔ̃] *f* description

déségrégation [desegregasjɔ̃] *f* desegregation

désempa·ré -rée [dezãpare] *adj* disconcerted; disabled (*ship*)

désemparer [dezãpare] *tr* to disable (*a ship*) ‖ *intr* **—sans désemparer** continuously, without intermission

désemplir [dezãplir] *intr*—**ne pas désemplir** to be always full

désenchaîner [dezãʃene] *tr* to unchain

désenchantement [dezãʃãtmã] *m* disenchantment

désenchanter [dezãʃãte] *tr* to disenchant

désencombrer [dezãkɔ̃bre] *tr* to disencumber, to clear, to free

désengager [dezãgaʒe] §38 *tr* to release from a promise

désengorger [dezãgɔrʒe] §38 *tr* to unstop

désengrener [dezãgrəne] §2 *tr* to disengage, to throw out of gear

désenivrer [dezãnivre] *tr & intr* to sober up

désenlacer [dezãlase] §51 *tr* to unbind

désennuyer [dezãnɥije] §27 *tr* to divert; cheer up ‖ *ref* to find relief from boredom

désensabler [dezãsable] *tr* to free (*a ship*) from the sand; to dredge the sand from (*a canal*)

désensibiliser [dezãsibilize] *tr* to desensitize

désensorceler [dezãsɔrsəle] §34 *tr* to remove the spell from

désentortiller [dezãtɔrtije] *tr* to straighten out

désenvelopper [dezãvlɔpe] *tr* to unwrap

déséquilibre [dezekilibr] *m* mental instability

déséquili·bré -brée [dezekilibre] *adj* mentally unbalanced ‖ *mf* unbalanced person

déséquilibrer [dezekilibre] *tr* to unbalance

dé·sert [dezer] **-serte** [zert] *adj & m* desert

déserter [dezerte] *tr & intr* to desert

déserteur [dezertœr] *m* deserter

désertion [dezersjɔ̃] *f* desertion

désespérance [dezesperãs] *f* despair

désespé·ré -rée [dezespere] *adj* desperate, hopeless ‖ *mf* desperate person"

désespérer [dezespere] §10 *tr* to be the despair of ‖ *ref* to lose hope

désespoir [dezespwar] *m* despair; **en désespoir de cause** as a last resort

déshabillage [dezabijaʒ] *m* striptease

déshabillé [dezabije] *m* morning wrap

déshabiller [dezabije] *tr & ref* to undress; **déshabiller saint Pierre pour habiller saint Paul** to rob Peter to pay Paul

déshabituer [dezabitɥe] *tr* to break (*s.o.*) of a habit

déshéri·té -tée [dezerite] *adj* underprivileged; **les déshérités** the underprivileged

déshériter [dezerite] *tr* to disinherit; to disadvantage

déshonnête [dezɔnɛt] *adj* improper, immodest

déshonnêteté [dezɔnɛtəte] *f* impropriety, immodesty, indecency

déshonneur [dezɔnœr] *m* dishonor

déshono·rant -rante [dezɔnɔrɑ̃] **-rante** [rɑ̃t] *adj* dishonorable, discreditable

déshonorer [dezɔnɔre] *tr* to dishonor

déshydratation [dezidratasjɔ̃] *f* dehydration

déshydrater [dezidrate] *tr* to dehydrate

désignation [deziɲasjɔ̃] *f* designation; appointment, nomination

dési·gné -gnée [deziɲe] *mf* nominee

désigner [deziɲe] *tr* to designate; to indicate, point out; to appoint, nominate; to signify, mean; to set (*the hour of an appointment*) ‖ *ref*—**se désigner à l'attention de** to bring oneself to the attention of

désillusion [dezillyzjɔ̃] *f* disillusion; disappointment

désillusionner [dezillyzjone] *tr* to disillusion; to disappoint

désinence [dezinɑ̃s] *f* (gram) ending

désinfecter [dezɛ̃fɛkte] *tr* to disinfect

désintégration [dezɛ̃tegrasjɔ̃] *f* disintegration

désintégrer [dezɛ̃tegre] §10 *tr & ref* to disintegrate

désintéres·sé -sée [dezɛ̃terese] *adj* disinterested, impartial; unselfish

désintéressement [dezɛ̃teresmɑ̃] *m* disinterestedness, impartiality; payment, satisfaction (*of a debt*); paying off (*of a creditor*)

désintéresser [dezɛ̃terese] *tr* to pay off; to buy out ‖ *ref*—**se désintéresser de** to lose interest in

désintoxication [dezɛ̃tɔksikasjɔ̃] *f* treatment for alcoholism, drug addiction, or poisoning; disintoxification

désinvolte [dezɛ̃vɔlt] *adj* free and easy, casual; offhanded, impertinent

désinvolture [dezɛ̃vɔltyr] *f* free and easy manner, offhandedness; impertinence

désir [dezir] *m* desire

désirable [dezirabl] *adj* desirable

désirer [dezire] *tr* to desire, wish

dési·reux -reuse [dezirø] **-reuse** [røz] *adj* desirous

désister [deziste] *ref* to desist; to withdraw from a runoff election; **se dé-**

sister de to waive (*a claim*); to drop (*a lawsuit*)

désobéir [dezɔbeir] *intr* to disobey; (with *dat*) to disobey; **être désobéi** to be disobeyed

désobli·geant [dezɔbliʒɑ̃] **-geante** [ʒɑ̃t] *adj* disagreeable, ungracious

désobliger [dezɔbliʒe] §38 *tr* to offend, displease, disoblige

désodori·sant [dezɔdɔrizɑ̃] **-sante** [zɑ̃t] *adj & m* deodorant

désodoriser [dezɔdɔrize] *tr* to deodorize

désœu·vré -vrée [dezœvre] *adj* idle, unoccupied, out of work; **les désœuvrés** the unemployed

désœuvrement [dezœvrəmɑ̃] *m* idleness, unemployment

déso·lant [dezɔlɑ̃] **-lante** [lɑ̃t] *adj* distressing, sad

désolation [dezɔlasjɔ̃] *f* desolation; grief, distress

déso·lé -lée [dezɔle] *adj* desolate; distressed

désoler [dezɔle] *tr* to desolate, destroy; to distress ‖ *ref* to be distressed

désopi·lant [dezɔpilɑ̃] **-lante** [lɑ̃t] *adj* hilarious, sidesplitting

désordon·né -née [dezɔrdɔne] *adj* disordered; untidy; disorderly

désordonner [dezɔrdɔne] *tr* to upset, confuse

désordre [dezɔrdr] *m* disorder, confusion; moral laxity

désorganisa·teur [dezɔrganizatœr] **-trice** [tris] *adj* disorganizing ‖ *mf* troublemaker

désorganisation [dezɔrganizasjɔ̃] *f* disorganization

désorganiser [dezɔrganize] *tr* to disorganize

désorien·té -tée [dezɔrjɑ̃te] *adj* disoriented, bewildered

désorienter [dezɔrjɑ̃te] *tr* to disorient; to mislead; to disconcert ‖ *ref* to become confused; to lose one's bearings

désormais [dezɔrmɛ] *adv* henceforth

désosser [dezɔse] *tr* to bone

despote [dɛspɔt] *m* despot

despotique [dɛspɔtik] *adj* despotic

despotisme [dɛspɔtism] *m* despotism

des·quels -quelles [dekɛl] §78

dessaisir [desezir] *tr* to dispossess; to let go, to release ‖ *ref*—**se dessaisir de** to relinquish

dessalement [desalmɑ̃] *m* desalinization

dessaler [desale] *tr* to desalt, to desalinate ‖ *ref* (coll) to wise up

dessécher [deseʃe] §10 *tr* to dry up, wither; to drain (*a pond*); to dehydrate (*the body*); to sear (*the heart*) ‖ *ref* to dry up; to waste away

dessein [desɛ̃] *m* design, plan, intent; **à dessein** on purpose

desseller [desele] *tr* to unsaddle

desserrer [desere] *tr* to loosen; **ne pas desserrer les dents** to keep mum

dessert [deser] *m* dessert, last course

desserte [desert] *f* buffet, sideboard; branch (*of railroad or bus line*); ministry (*of a substituting clergyman*)

dessertir [desertir] *tr* to remove (*a gem*) from its setting

desservant [deservã] *m* parish priest

desservir [deservir] §63 *tr* to clear (*the table*); to be of disservice to, to harm; (aer, aut, rr) to stop at (*a town or station*); (aer, aut, eccl, rr) to serve (*a locality*); (elec) to supply (*a region*)

dessiller [desije] *tr*—**dessiller les yeux à qn** or **de qn** to open s.o.'s eyes, to undeceive s.o.

dessin [desẽ] *m* drawing, sketch, design; profile (*of face*); **dessins animés** (mov) animated cartoons

dessina·teur [desinatœr] **-trice** [tris] *mf* designer; cartoonist

dessiner [desine] *tr* to draw, sketch, design; to delineate, outline || *ref* to stand out, to be outlined

dessoûler or **dessouler** [desule] *tr* & *intr* to sober up

dessous [dəsu] *m* underpart; reverse side, wrong side; coaster (*underneath a glass*); seamy side, machinations behind the scenes; **au dessous de** below; **avoir le dessous** to get the short end of the deal; **du dessous** below; **en dessous** underneath; **les dessous** lingerie, undergarments || *adv & prep* under, underneath, below

dessous-de-bouteille [dəsudəbutej] *m invar* coaster

dessous-de-bras [dəsudəbra] *m invar* underarm pad

dessous-de-carafe [dəsudəkaraf] *m invar* coaster

dessous-de-plat [dəsudəpla] *m invar* hot pad

dessous-de-table [dəsudətabl] *m invar* under-the-counter money

dessus [dəsy] *m* upper part; back (*of the hand*); right side (*of material*); (mus) treble part; **au dessus de** beyond; **avoir le dessus** to have the upper hand; **le dessus du panier** the cream of the crop || *adv* above || *prep* on, above, over

dessus-de-cheminée [dəsydəʃmine] *m invar* mantelpiece

dessus-de-lit [dəsydəli] *m invar* bedspread

dessus-de-porte [dəsydəpɔrt] *m invar* overdoor

dessus-de-table [dəsydətabl] *m invar* table cover

destin [destẽ] *m* destiny, fate

destinataire [destinater] *mf* addressee; payee; **destinataire inconnu** or **absent** (formula stamped on envelope) not at this address

destination [destinasjɔ̃] *f* destination; **à destination de** to, bound for

destinée [destine] *f* destiny

destiner [destine] *tr* to destine; to set aside, to reserve; **destiner q.ch. à qn** to mean or intend s.th. for s.o.

destituer [destitɥe] *tr* to remove from office

destitution [destitysjɔ̃] *f* dismissal, removal from office

destrier [destrije] *m* (hist) steed, charger

destroyer [destrɔjœr] *m* (nav) destroyer

destruc·teur [destryktœr] **-trice** [tris] *adj* destroying, destructive || *mf* destroyer

destruc·tif [destryktif] **-tive** [tiv] *adj* destructive

destruction [destryksjɔ̃] *f* destruction

dé·suet [dezɥe] **-suète** [zɥet] *adj* obsolete, antiquated, out-of-date

désuétude [dezɥetyd] *f* desuetude, disuse

désu·ni -nie [dezyni] *adj* at odds, divided against itself; uncoordinated

désunion [dezynjɔ̃] *f* dissension

désunir [dezynir] *tr* to disunite, divide; to estrange

déta·ché -chée [detaʃe] *adj* detached; clean; spare (*parts*); acting, temporary (*official*); staccato (*note*)

détachement [detaʃmã] *m* detachment; (mil) detail

détacher [detaʃe] *tr* to detach; to let loose; to clean; to make (*s.th.*) stand out in relief || *ref* to come loose; to break loose; to stand out in relief

détacheur [detaʃœr] *m* spot remover

détail [detaj] *m* detail; retail; item (*of an account*); **au détail** at retail; **en détail** detailed

détail·lant [detajã] **détail·lante** [detajãt] *adj* retail || *mf* retailer

détailler [detaje] *tr* to detail; to cut up into pieces; to retail; to itemize (*an account*)

détartrer [detartre] *tr* to remove the scale from (*a boiler*); to remove the tartar from (*teeth*)

détaxation [detaksasjɔ̃] *f* lowering or removal of taxes

détaxer [detakse] *tr* to lower or remove the tax from

détecter [detekte] *tr* to detect

détecteur [detektœr] *m* detector; **détecteur de mines** mine detector

détection [deteksjɔ̃] *f* detection

détective [detektiv] *m* detective, private detective; box camera

déteindre [detẽdr] §50 *tr* to fade, bleach || *intr* to fade, run

dételer [detle] §34 *tr* to unharness || *intr* to let up; to settle down

détendre [detãdr] *tr* to relax; to stretch out (*one's legs*); to lower (*the gas*) || *ref* to relax, to enjoy oneself

détenir [detnir] §72 *tr* to detain (*in prison*); to hold, withhold; to own

détente [detãt] *f* trigger; relaxation, easing (*of tension*); relaxation of tension (*in international affairs*)

déten·teur [detãtœr] **-trice** [tris] *mf* holder (*of stock; of a record*); keeper (*of a secret*)

détention [detãsjɔ̃] *f* detention, custody; possession; **détention préventive** pretrial imprisonment, custody

déte·nu -nue [detny] *adj* detained, imprisoned || *mf* prisoner

déterger [deterʒe] §38 *tr* to clean

détérioration [deterjɔrasjɔ̃] *f* deterioration

détériorer [deterjɔre] *tr* to damage || *intr* to deteriorate

détermination [determinɑsjɔ̃] *f* determination

déterminer [determine] *tr* to determine || *ref* to decide

déter·ré -rée [detere] *adj* disinterred || *mf* (fig) corpse, ghost

déterrer [detere] *tr* to dig up; to exhume

déter·sif [detersif] **-sive** [siv] *adj & m* detergent

détester [deteste] *tr* to detest, to hate

déto·nant [detɔnɑ̃] **-nante** [nɑ̃t] *adj & m* explosive

détoner [detɔne] *intr* to detonate, to explode

détonner [detɔne] *intr* to sing or play off key; to clash (*said of colors*)

détordre [detɔrdr] *tr* to untwist

détortiller [detɔrtije] *tr* to untangle

détour [detur] *m* turn, curve, bend; roundabout way, detour; **sans détour** frankly, honestly

détour·né -née [deturne] *adj* off the beaten track, isolated; indirect, roundabout; twisted (*meaning*)

détourner [deturne] *tr* to divert; to deter; to embezzle; to lead astray; to distort, twist

détrac·teur [detraktœr] **-trice** [tris] *adj* disparaging || *mf* detractor

détra·qué -quée [detrake] *adj* out of order; broken (*in health*); unhinged, deranged || *mf* nervous wreck

détraquer [detrake] *tr* to put out of commission; (coll) to upset, unhinge || *ref* to break down

détrempe [detrɑ̃p] *f* distemper (*painting*); annealing (*of steel*)

détremper [detrɑ̃pe] *tr* to soak; to dilute; to anneal (*steel*)

détresse [detres] *f* distress

détriment [detrimɑ̃] *m* detriment

détritus [detritys] *m* debris, rubbish, refuse

détroit [detrwa] *m* strait, sound

détromper [detrɔ̃pe] *tr* to undeceive, to enlighten

détrôner [detrone] *tr* to dethrone

détrousser [detruse] *tr* to let down (*e.g., one's sleeves*); to hold up (*s.o.*) in the street || *ref* to let down a garment

détrousseur [detrusœr] *m* highwayman

détruire [detrɥir] §19 *tr* to destroy; to put an end to || *ref* (coll) to commit suicide

dette [det] *f* debt; **dette active** asset; **dette passive** liability

deuil [dœj] *m* mourning; grief, sorrow; bereavement; funeral procession; **deuil de veuve** widow's weeds; **faire son deuil de** (coll) to say good-by to

deux [dø] *adj & pron* two; the Second, e.g., **Charles deux** Charles the Second; **deux heures** two o'clock || *m* two; second (*in dates*)

deuxième [døzjem] *adj & m* second

deux-pièces [døpjes] *m invar* two-piece suit

deux-points [døpwɛ̃] *m invar* colon

deux-ponts [døpɔ̃] *m invar* (aer, naut) double-decker

dévaler [devale] *tr* to descend (*a slope*) || *intr* to descend quickly

dévaluation [devalɥasjɔ̃] *f* devaluation

dévaluer [devalɥe] *tr* to devaluate

devant [dəvɑ̃] *m* front; **par devant** in front; **prendre les devants** to make the first move; to get ahead; to take precautions || *adv* before, in front || *prep* before, in front of

devanture [dəvɑ̃tyr] *f* show window; display; storefront

dévasta·teur [devastatœr] **-trice** [tris] *adj* devastating

dévastation [devastɑsjɔ̃] *f* devastation

dévaster [devaste] *tr* to devastate

déveine [deven] *f* bad luck

développé [devlɔpe] *m* press (*in weight lifting*)

développement [devlɔpmɑ̃] *m* development; unwrapping (*of package*); expansion

développer [devlɔpe] *tr* to develop; to unwrap (*a package*); to reveal, show (*e.g., a card*); to spread out, open out; to expand (*an algebraic expression*) || *ref* to develop

devenir [dəvnir] §72 *intr* (aux: ÊTRE) to become; **qu'est devenu Robert?** what has become of Robert?

dévergondage [devergɔ̃daʒ] *m* profligacy

dévergon·dé -dée [devergɔ̃de] *adj & mf* profligate

dévergonder [devergɔ̃de] *ref* to become dissolute

dévernir [devernir] *tr* to remove the varnish from

déverrouiller [deveruje] *tr* to unbolt

dé·vers [dever] **-verse** [vers] *adj* warped; out of alignment || *m* inclination, slope; banking

déverser [deverse] *tr* to pour out; to slope, bank || *intr* to pour out; to lean, to become lopsided || *ref* to empty, flow (*said of river*)

dévêtir [devetir] §73 *tr & ref* to undress

déviation [devjɑsjɔ̃] *f* deviation; detour

dévider [devide] *tr* to unwind, to reel off

dévier [devje] *tr* to deflect, to by-pass || *intr* to deviate, to swerve

de·vin [dəvɛ̃] **-vineresse** [vinres] *mf* fortuneteller

deviner [dəvine] *tr* to guess

devinette [dəvinet] *f* riddle

dévirer [devire] *tr* to turn back; to bend back; to feather (*an oar*)

devis [dəvi] *m* estimate

dévisager [devizaʒe] §38 *tr* to stare at, to stare down

devise [dəviz] *f* motto, slogan; heraldic device; name of a ship; currency; **devise forte** strong currency

deviser [dəvize] *intr* to chat

dévisser [devise] *tr* to unscrew

dévitaliser [devitalize] *tr* to kill the nerve of (*a tooth*)

dévoiler [devwale] *tr* to unveil; to straighten (*e.g., a bent wheel*) || *ref* to unveil; to come to light

devoir [dəvwar] *m* duty; exercise,

homework; **devoirs** respects; homework || §21 *tr* to owe || *aux* used to express 1) necessity, e.g., **il doit s'en aller** he must go away; **il devra s'en aller** he will have to go away; **il a dû s'en aller** he had to go away; 2) obligation, e.g., **il devrait s'en aller** he ought to go away, he should go away; **il aurait dû s'en aller** he ought to have gone away, he should have gone away; 3) conjecture, e.g., **il doit être malade** he must be ill; **il a dû être malade** he must have been ill; 4) what is expected or scheduled, e.g., **que dois-je faire maintenant?** what am I to do now?; **le train devait arriver à six heures** the train was to arrive at six o'clock

dévo·lu -lue [devɔly] *adj*—**dévolu à** devolving upon, vested in || *m*—**son dévolu sur** to fix one's choice upon

dévora·teur [dévɔratœr] **-trice** [tris] *adj* devouring

dévorer [devɔre] *tr* to devour, eat up

dévo·reur [devɔrœr] **-reuse** [røz] *mf* devourer; (fig) glutton

dé·vot [devo] **-vote** [vɔt] *adj* devout, pious || *mf* devout, pious person; devotee; **faux dévot** hypocrite

dévotion [devosjɔ̃] *f* devotion, devoutness; **à votre dévotion** at your service, at your disposal; **être à la dévotion de qn** to be at s.o.'s beck and call

dé·voué -vouée [devwe] *adj* devoted; **dévoué à vos ordres** (complimentary close) at your service; **votre dévoué** (complimentary close) yours truly

dévouement [devumɑ̃] *m* devotion

dévouer [devwe] *tr* to dedicate, sacrifice || *ref* to devote oneself

dévoyé dévoyée [devwaje] *adj* delinquent (*young person*) || *mf* delinquent

dévoyer [devwaje] §47 *tr* to lead astray

dextérité [deksterite] *f* dexterity

dextrose [dekstroz] *m* dextrose

diabète [djabet] *m* diabetes

diabétique [djabetik] *adj & mf* diabetic

diable [djɑbl] *m* devil; hand truck, dolly; (coll) fellow; **à la diable** haphazardly; **c'est là le diable** (coll) there's the rub; **diable à ressort** jack-in-the-box; **du diable** extreme; **en diable** extremely; **faire le diable à quatre** (coll) to raise Cain; **tirer le diable par la queue** (coll) to be hard up

diablerie [djɑbləri] *f* deviltry

diabolique [djɑbɔlik] *adj* diabolic(al)

diaconesse [djakɔnes] *f* deaconess

diacre [djakr] *m* deacon

diacritique [djakritik] *adj* diacritical

diadème [djadem] *m* diadem; (*woman's headdress*) tiara, coronet

diagnose [djagnoz] *f* diagnostics, diagnosis

diagnostic [djagnɔstik] *m* diagnosis

diagnostiquer [djagnɔstike] *tr* to diagnose

diago·nal -nale [djagɔnal] *adj & f* (*pl* **-naux** [no] **-nales**) diagonal

diagonalement [djagɔnalmɑ̃] *adv* diagonally, cater-cornered

diagramme [djagram] *m* diagram

dialecte [djalekt] *m* dialect

dialogue [djalɔg] *m* dialogue

diamant [djamɑ̃] *m* diamond

diamantaire [djamɑ̃ter] *adj* diamond-bright || *m* dealer in diamonds

diamé·tral -trale [djametral] *adj* (*pl* **-traux** [tro]) diametric(al)

diamètre [djametr] *m* diameter

diane [djan] *f* reveille

diantre [djɑ̃tr] *interj* the dickens!

diapason [djapazɔ̃] *m* range (*of voice or instrument*); pitch, standard pitch; tuning fork

diaphane [djafan] *adj* diaphanous

diaphragme [djafragm] *m* diaphragm

diapo [djapo] *f* (coll) slide

diapositive [djapozitiv] *f* (phot) transparency, slide

diaprer [djapre] *tr* to variegate

diarrhée [djare] *f* diarrhea

diastole [djastɔl] *f* diastole

diathermie [djatermi] *f* diathermy

diatribe [djatrib] *f* diatribe

dichotomie [dikɔtɔmi] *f* dichotomy; split fee (*between physicians*)

dictaphone [diktafɔn] *m* dictaphone

dictateur [diktatœr] *m* dictator

dictature [diktatyr] *f* dictatorship

dictée [dikte] *f* dictation; **écrire sous la dictée de** to take dictation from

dicter [dikte] *tr & intr* to dictate

diction [diksjɔ̃] *f* diction

dictionnaire [diksjɔner] *m* dictionary; **dictionnaire vivant** (coll) walking encyclopedia

dicton [diktɔ̃] *m* saying, proverb

didactique [didaktik] *adj* didactic(al)

dièdre [djedr] *adj & m* dihedral

diérèse [djerez] *f* diaeresis

dièse [djez] *adj & m* (mus) sharp

diesel [dizel] *m* Diesel motor

diéser [djeze] §10 *tr* to sharp

diète [djet] *f* diet

diététi·cien [djetetisjɛ̃] **-cienne** [sjen] *mf* dietitian

diététique [djetetik] *adj* dietetic || *f* dietetics

dieu [djø] *m* (*pl* **dieux**) god || (*cap*) *m* God; **Dieu merci!** thank heavens!; **mon Dieu!** good gracious!

diffamation [difamasjɔ̃] *f* defamation

diffamer [difame] *tr* to defame

diffé·ré -rée [difere] *adj* deferred; delayed (*action*) || *m* (rad, telv) pre-recording; **en différé** (rad, telv) pre-recorded

différemment [diferamɑ̃] *adv* differently

différence [diferɑ̃s] *f* difference; **à la différence de** unlike, contrary to

différencier [diferɑ̃sje] *tr & ref* to differentiate

différend [diferɑ̃] *m* dispute, disagreement, difference; **partager le différend** to split the difference

diffé·rent [diferɑ̃] **-rente** [rɑ̃t] *adj* different

différen·tiel -tielle [diferɑ̃sjel] *adj* differential ‖ *m* (mach) differential ‖ *f* (math) differential

différer [difere] §10 *tr* to defer, to put off ‖ *intr* to differ; to disagree

difficile [difisil] *adj* difficult, hard; hard to please, crotchety; **faire le difficile** to be hard to please

difficulté [difikylte] *f* difficulty

difforme [diform] *adj* deformed

difformité [diformite] *f* deformity

dif·fus [dify] **dif·fuse** [difyz] *adj* diffuse; verbose, windy

diffuser [difyze] *tr* to broadcast ‖ *ref* to diffuse

diffuseur [difyzœr] *m* spreader (*of news*); loudspeaker; nozzle

digérer [diʒere] §10 *tr & intr* to digest ‖ *ref* to be digested

digeste [diʒest] *adj* (coll) easy to digest ‖ *m* (law) digest

digestible [diʒestibl] *adj* digestible

diges·tif [diʒestif] **-tive** [tiv] *adj* digestive

digestion [diʒestjɔ̃] *f* digestion

digi·tal -tale [diʒital] *adj* (*pl* **-taux** [to]) digital ‖ *f* digitalis, foxglove

digitaline [diʒitalin] *f* (pharm) digitalis

digne [diɲ] *adj* worthy; dignified; haughty, uppish

dignitaire [diɲiter] *mf* dignitary

dignité [diɲite] *f* dignity

digression [digresjɔ̃] *f* digression

digue [dig] *f* dike; breakwater; (fig) barrier

dilacérer [dilasere] §10 *tr* to lacerate

dilapider [dilapide] *tr* to squander; to embezzle

dilater [dilate] *tr & ref* to dilate

dilatoire [dilatwar] *adj* dilatory

dilemme [dilem] *m* dilemma

dilettante [diletɑ̃t] *mf* dilettante

diligemment [diliʒamɑ̃] *adv* diligently

diligence [diliʒɑ̃s] *f* diligence; **à la diligence de** at the request of

dili·gent [diliʒɑ̃] **-gente** [ʒɑ̃t] *adj* diligent

diluer [dilɥe] *tr* to dilute

dilution [dilysjɔ̃] *f* dilution

dimanche [dimɑ̃ʃ] *m* Sunday; **du dimanche** (coll) Sunday (*driver*); (coll) amateur (*painter*); **le dimanche des Rameaux** Palm Sunday

dîme [dim] *f* tithe

dimension [dimɑ̃sjɔ̃] *f* dimension

diminuer [diminɥe] *tr & intr* to diminish

diminu·tif [diminytif] **-tive** [tiv] *adj & m* diminutive

dinde [dɛ̃d] *f* turkey; (culin) turkey; (coll) silly girl

dindon [dɛ̃dɔ̃] *m* turkey

dindonner [dɛ̃dɔne] *tr* to dupe, take in

dîner [dine] *m* dinner; **dîner de garçons** stag dinner; **dîner prié** formal dinner ‖ *intr* to dine

dînette [dinet] *f* family meal; children's playtime meal

dî·neur [dinœr] **-neuse** [nøz] *mf* diner, dinner guest

dinosaure [dinozɔr] *m* dinosaur

diocèse [djɔsez] *m* diocese

diode [djɔd] *f* diode

dionée [djɔne] *f* Venus's-flytrap

diphtérie [difteri] *f* diphtheria

diphtongue [diftɔ̃g] *f* diphthong

diplomate [diplɔmat] *adj* diplomatic ‖ *mf* diplomat

diplomatie [diplɔmasi] *f* diplomacy

diplomatique [diplɔmatik] *adj* diplomatic

diplôme [diplom] *m* diploma

dire [dir] *m* statement; **au dire de** according to ‖ §22 *tr* to say, tell, relate; **à l'heure dite** at the appointed time; **à qui le dites-vous?** (coll) you're telling me!; **autrement dit** in other words; **dire que . . .** to think that; **dites-lui bien des choses de ma part** say hello for me; **tu l'as dit!** (coll) you said it! ‖ *intr* to say; **à vrai dire** to tell the truth; **cela va sans dire** it. goes without saying; **c'est beaucoup dire** (coll) that's going rather far; **c'est pas peu dire** (slang) that's saying a lot; **comme on dit** as the saying goes; **dites donc!** hey!, say!; **il n'y a pas à dire** make no mistake about it ‖ *ref* to be said; to say to oneself or to each other; to claim to be, to call oneself

di·rect -recte [dirɛkt] *adj* direct ‖ *m* (boxing) solid punch; **en direct** (rad, telv) live

direc·teur [dirɛktœr] **-trice** [tris] *adj* directing, guiding; principal; driving (*rod, wheel*) ‖ *mf* director ‖ *f* directress

direction [dirɛksjɔ̃] *f* direction; administration, management, board; head office; (aut) steering

direction·nel -nelle [dirɛksjɔnel] *adj* directional

directorat [dirɛktɔra] *m* directorship

dirigeable [diriʒabl] *adj & m* dirigible

diri·geant [diriʒɑ̃] **-geante** [ʒɑ̃t] *adj* governing, ruling ‖ *mf* ruler, leader, head, executive

diriger [diriʒe] §38 *tr* to direct, control, manage; to steer ‖ *ref* to go; **se diriger vers** to head for

dirigisme [diriʒism] *m* government economic planning and control

discernable [disernabl] *adj* discernible

discernement [disernəmɑ̃] *m* discernment, perception

discerner [diserne] *tr* to discern

disciple [disipl] *m* disciple

disciplinaire [disipliner] *adj* disciplinary ‖ *m* military policeman

discipline [disiplin] *f* discipline; scourge

discipliner [discipline] *tr* to discipline

disconti·nu -nue [diskɔ̃tiny] *adj* discontinuous

discontinuer [diskɔ̃tinɥe] *tr* to discontinue

disconvenir [diskɔ̃vnir] §72 *tr* to deny ‖ *intr* (with *dat*) to not suit, discplease ‖ *intr* (aux: ÊTRE)—**ne pas disconvenir de** to admit, not deny

discophile [diskɔfil] *mf* record collector

discord [diskɔr] *adj masc* out of tune ‖ *m* instrument out of tune

discordance [diskɔrdɑ̃s] *f* discordance

discor·dant [diskɔrdɑ̃] **-dante** [dɑ̃t] *adj* discordant

discorde [diskɔrd] f discord
discorder [diskɔrde] intr to be discordant, to jar
discothèque [diskɔtɛk] f record cabinet; record library; discotheque
discourir [diskurir] §14 intr to discourse
discours [diskur] m discourse; speech
discour·tois [diskurtwa] **-toise** [twaz] adj discourteous
discourtoisie [diskurtwazi] f discourtesy
discrédit [diskredi] m discredit
discréditer [diskredite] tr to discredit
dis·cret [diskrɛ] **-crète** [krɛt] adj discreet; discrete
discrétion [diskresjɔ̃] f discretion; à discrétion as much as one wants
discrimination [diskriminasjɔ̃] f discrimination
discriminatoire [diskriminatwar] adj discriminatory
discriminer [diskrimine] tr to discriminate
disculper [diskylpe] tr to clear, exonerate ‖ ref to clear oneself
discur·sif [diskyrsif] **-sive** [siv] adj discursive
discussion [diskysjɔ̃] f discussion
discuter [diskyte] tr & intr to discuss; to question, debate
di·sert [dizɛr] **-serte** [zɛrt] adj eloquent, fluent
disertement [dizɛrtəmɑ̃] adv eloquently, fluently
disette [dizɛt] f shortage, scarcity; famine
di·seur [dizœr] **-seuse** [zøz] mf talker, speaker; monologuist; **diseuse de bonne aventure** fortuneteller
disgrâce [disgrɑs] f disfavor; misfortune; surliness, gruffness
disgra·cié -ciée [disgrasje] adj out of favor; ill-favored, homely; unfortunate
disgracier [disgrasje] tr to deprive of favor
disgra·cieux [disgrasjø] **-cieuse** [sjøz] adj awkward; homely, ugly; disagreeable
disjoindre [disʒwɛ̃dr] §35 tr to sever, to separate
disjoncteur [disʒɔ̃ktœr] m circuit breaker
dislocation [dislɔkasjɔ̃] f dislocation; separation; dismemberment
disloquer [dislɔke] tr to dislocate; to disperse; to dismember ‖ ref to break up, disperse
disparaître [disparɛtr] §12 intr to disappear
disparate [disparat] adj incongruous ‖ f incongruity; clash (of colors)
disparité [disparite] f disparity
disparition [disparisjɔ̃] f disappearance
dispa·ru -rue [dispary] adj disappeared; missing (in battle) ‖ mf missing person; **le disparu** the deceased
dispen·dieux [dispɑ̃djø] **-dieuse** [djøz] adj expensive
dispensaire [dispɑ̃sɛr] m dispensary, outpatient clinic

dispensa·teur [dispɑ̃satœr] **-trice** [tris] mf dispenser
dispense [dispɑ̃s] f dispensation, exemption
dispenser [dispɑ̃se] tr to dispense; **dispensé du timbrage** (label on envelope) mailing permit
disperser [dispɛrse] tr & ref to disperse
dispersion [dispɛrsjɔ̃] f dispersion, dissipation
disponibilité [dispɔnibilite] f availability; **disponibilités** liquid assets; **en disponibilité** in the reserves
disponible [dispɔnibl] adj available; vacant (seat); (govt, mil) subject to call
dis·pos [dispo] **-pose** [poz] adj alert, fit, in good condition
dispo·sé -sée [dispoze] adj disposed; arranged; **disposé d'avance** predisposed; **peu disposé** reluctant
disposer [dispoze] tr to dispose ‖ intr to dispose; **disposer de** to dispose of, to have at one's disposal; to have at hand; to make use of; **disposer pour** to provide for (e.g., the future); **vous pouvez disposer** you may leave ‖ ref —**se disposer à** to be disposed to; to plan on
dispositif [dispozitif] m apparatus, device; (mil) disposition
disposition [dispozisjɔ̃] f disposition; disposal; **dispositions** arrangements; aptitude; provisions (of a legal document)
dispropor·tion·né -née [disprɔpɔrsjɔne] adj disproportionate, incompatible
dispute [dispyt] f dispute
disputer [dispyte] tr to dispute; (coll) to bawl out ‖ ref to dispute
disquaire [diskɛr] m record dealer
disqualification [diskalifikasjɔ̃] f disqualification
disqualifier [diskalifje] tr & ref to disqualify
disque [disk] m disk; record, disk; (sports) discus; **changer de disque** (coll) to change the subject; **disque de longue durée** long-playing record
dissection [disɛksjɔ̃] f dissection
dissemblable [disɑ̃blabl] adj dissimilar
dissemblance [disɑ̃blɑ̃s] f dissimilarity
disséminer [disemine] tr to disseminate
dissension [disɑ̃sjɔ̃] f dissension
dissentiment [disɑ̃timɑ̃] m dissent
disséquer [diseke] §10 tr to dissect
dissertation [disɛrtasjɔ̃] f dissertation; (in school) essay, term paper
dissidence [disidɑ̃s] f dissent
dissi·dent [disidɑ̃] **-dente** [dɑ̃t] adj dissenting ‖ mf dissenter, dissident
dissimiler [disimile] tr (phonet) to dissimilate
dissimulation [disimylasjɔ̃] f dissemblance
dissimuler [disimyle] tr & intr to dissemble; **dissimuler q.ch. à qn** to conceal s.th. from s.o. ‖ ref to hide, skulk
dissipation [disipasjɔ̃] f dissipation
dissi·pé -pée [disipe] adj dissipated; pleasure-seeking; unruly (schoolboy)
dissiper [disipe] tr & ref to dissipate

dissocier [disɔsje] *tr & ref* to dissociate

disso·lu -lue [disɔly] *adj* dissolute ‖ *mf* profligate

dissolution [disɔlysjɔ̃] *f* dissolution; dissoluteness; rubber cement

dissol·vant [disɔlvã] **-vante** [vãt] *adj & m* solvent

dissonance [disɔnãs] *f* dissonance

dissoudre [disudr] §60 (*pp* **dissous, dissoute**; no *pret* or *imperf subj*) *tr & ref* to dissolve

dissuader [disɥade] *tr* to dissuade

distance [distãs] *f* distance; **à distance** at a distance

distancer [distãse] §51 *tr* to outdistance; to distance (*a race horse*)

dis·tant -tante [distã] [tãt] *adj* distant

distendre [distãdr] *tr & ref* to distend; to strain (*a muscle*)

distillation [distilasjɔ̃] *f* distillation

distiller [distile] *tr* to distill

distillerie [distilri] *f* distillery; distilling industry

dis·tinct [distɛ̃], [distɛ̃kt] **-tincte** [tɛ̃kt] *adj* distinct

distinc·tif [distɛ̃ktif] **-tive** [tiv] *adj* distinctive

distinction [distɛ̃ksjɔ̃] *f* distinction

distin·gué -guée [distɛ̃ge] *adj* distinguished; famous; sincere, e.g., **veuillez accepter nos sentiments distingués** (*complimentary close*) please accept our sincere regards

distinguer [distɛ̃ge] *tr* to distinguish ‖ *ref* to be distinguished; to distinguish oneself

distordre [distɔrdr] *tr* to twist, to sprain

dis·tors [distɔr] **-torse** [tɔrs] *adj* twisted

distorsion [distɔrsjɔ̃] *f* sprain; convulsive twist; (electron, opt) distorsion

distraction [distraksjɔ̃] *f* distraction; heedlessness, lapse; embezzlement; appropriation (*of a sum of money*)

distraire [distrer] §68 *tr* to distract, amuse; to separate, set aside (*e.g., part of one's savings*) ‖ *ref* to amuse oneself

dis·trait [distre] **-traite** [tret] *adj* absent-minded

distribuer [distribɥe] *tr* to distribute; to arrange the furnishings of (*an apartment*)

distribu·teur [distribytœr] **-trice** [tris] *mf* distributor (*person*) ‖ *m* (mach) distributor; **distributeur automatique** vending machine; **distributeur de musique** jukebox

distribution [distribysjɔ̃] *f* distribution; mail delivery; supply system (*of gas, water, or electricity*); valve gear (*of steam engine*); timing gears (*of internal-combustion engine*); (theat) cast

district [distrik], [distrikt] *m* district

dit [di] **dite** [dit] *adj* agreed upon, stated ‖ *m* saying

dito [dito] *adv* ditto

diva [diva] *f* diva

divaguer [divage] *intr* to ramble

divan [divã] *m* divan

diverger [diverʒe] §38 *intr* to diverge

di·vers [diver] **-verse** [vers] *adj* changing, varied ‖ **di·vers -verses** *adj pl* diverse, different, several

diversifier [diversifje] *tr & ref* to diversify

diversion [diversjɔ̃] *f* diversion

diversité [diversite] *f* diversity

divertir [divertir] *tr* to divert, amuse ‖ *ref* to be diverted, amused

dividende [dividãd] *m* dividend

di·vin [divɛ̃] **-vine** [vin] *adj* divine

divination [divinasjɔ̃] *f* divination

divinité [divinite] *f* divinity

diviser [divize] *tr & ref* to divide

diviseur [divizœr] *m* (math) divisor; (fig) troublemaker

divisible [divizibl] *adj* divisible

division [divizjɔ̃] *f* division

divisionnaire [divizjɔner] *adj* divisional ‖ *m* division head

divorce [divɔrs] *m* divorce

divor·cé -cée [divɔrse] *mf* divorced person ‖ *f* divorcee

divorcer [divɔrse] §51 *tr* to divorce (*a married couple*) ‖ *intr* to divorce, to get a divorce; **divorcer avec** to withdraw from (*the world*); **divorcer d'avec** to get a divorce from, to be divorced from, to divorce (*husband or wife*); to withdraw from (*the world*)

divulguer [divylge] *tr* to divulge

dix [di(s)] *adj & pron* ten; the Tenth, e.g., **Jean dix** John the Tenth; **dix heures** ten o'clock ‖ *m* ten; tenth (*in dates*)

dix-huit [dizɥi], [dizɥit] *adj & pron* eighteen; the Eighteenth, e.g., **Jean dix-huit** John the Eighteenth ‖ *m* eighteen; eighteenth (*in dates*)

dix-huitième [dizɥitjem] *adj & m* eighteenth

dixième [dizjem] *adj, pron* (*masc, fem*), & *m* tenth

dix-neuf [diznœf] *adj & pron* nineteen; the Nineteenth, e.g., **Jean dix-neuf** John the Nineteenth ‖ *m* nineteen; nineteenth (*in dates*)

dix-neuvième [diznœvjem] *adj & m* nineteenth

dix-sept [disset] *adj & pron* seventeen; the Seventeenth, e.g., **Jean dix-sept** John the Seventeenth ‖ *m* seventeen; seventeenth (*in dates*)

dix-septième [dissetjem] *adj & m* seventeenth

djinn [dʒin] *m* jinn

do *abbr* (dito) do. (ditto)

docile [dɔsil] *adj* docile

dock [dɔk] *m* dock; warehouse; **dock flottant** floating dry dock

docker [dɔker] *m* dock worker

docte [dɔkt] *adj* learned, scholarly ‖ *mf* scholar ‖ *m* learned man

doc·teur [dɔktœr] **-toresse** [tɔres] *mf* doctor

docto·ral -rale [dɔktɔral] *adj* (*pl* **-raux** [ro]) doctoral

doctorat [dɔktɔra] *m* doctorate

doctrine [dɔktrin] *f* doctrine

document [dɔkymã] *m* document

documentaire [dɔkymåter] adj & m documentary

documentation [dɔkymåtɑsjɔ̃] ƒ documentation; literature (*about a region, business, etc.*)

documenter [dɔkymåte] tr to document ‖ ref to gather documentary evidence

dodeliner [dɔdline] tr & intr to sway, rock

dodo [dodo] m (orn) dodo; (baby talk) to go to bed; **faire dodo** to sleep

do·du -due [dɔdy] adj (coll) plump

dogmatique [dɔgmatik] adj dogmatic ‖ mƒ dogmatic person ‖ ƒ dogmatics

dogmatiser [dɔgmatize] intr to dogmatize

dogme [dɔgm] m dogma

dogue [dɔg] m bulldog

doigt [dwa] m finger; **à deux doigts de** a hairbreadth away from; **doigt annulaire** ring finger; **doigt de Dieu** hand of God; **doigt du pied** toe; **mettre le doigt dessus** to hit the nail on the head; **mon petit doigt m'a dit** (coll) a little bird told me; **montrer du doigt** to single out (*for ridicule*); to point at; **petit doigt** little finger; **se mettre le doigt dans l'œil** (coll) to put one's foot in one's mouth; **se mordre les doigts** to be sorry

doigté [dwate] m touch; adroitness, skillfulness; fingering

doigter [dwate] m fingering ‖ tr & intr to finger

doigtier [dwatje] m fingerstall

doit [dwa] m debit

doléances [dɔleãs] fpl grievances

do·lent -lente [dɔlã] [lãt] adj doleful

dollar [dɔlar] m dollar

domaine [dɔmen] m domain

dôme [dom] m dome; cathedral

domestication [dɔmestikasjɔ̃] ƒ domestication

domesticité [dɔmestisite] ƒ domestication; staff of servants

domestique [dɔmestik] adj & mƒ domestic

domestiquer [dɔmestike] tr to domesticate

domicile [dɔmisil] m residence

domicilier [dɔmisilje] tr to domicile ‖ ref to take up residence

dominance [dɔminãs] ƒ (genetics) dominance

domi·nant [dɔminã] **-nante** [nãt] adj dominant ‖ ƒ dominating trait; (mus) dominant

domina·teur [dɔminatœr] **-trice** [tris] adj domineering, overbearing ‖ mƒ ruler, conqueror

domination [dɔminɑsjɔ̃] ƒ domination

dominer [dɔmine] tr & intr to dominate ‖ ref to control oneself

domini·cal -cale [dɔminikal] adj (pl **-caux** [ko]) Sunday; dominical

domino [dɔmino] m domino

dommage [dɔmaʒ] m loss; injury; **c'est dommage!** that's too bad! **dommages et intérêts** (law) damages; **quel dommage!** what a pity!

dommageable [dɔmaʒabl] adj injurious

dommages-intérêts [dɔmaʒɛ̃tere] mpl (law) damages

dompter [dɔ̃te] tr to tame; to train (*animals*); to subdue

domp·teur [dɔ̃tœr] **-teuse** [tøz] mƒ tamer, trainer; conquerer

don [dɔ̃] m gift; don (*Spanish title*)

donataire [dɔnater] mƒ legatee

dona·teur [dɔnatœr] **-trice** [tris] mƒ (law) donor, legator

donation [dɔnasjɔ̃] ƒ donation, gift, grant

donc [dɔ̃k], [dɔ̃] adv therefore, then; thus; now, of course; (often used for emphasis), e.g., **entrez donc!** do come in!

donjon [dɔ̃ʒɔ̃] m keep, donjon; (nav) turret

don·nant [dɔnã] **don·nante** [dɔnãt] adj generous, open-handed; **donnant** tit for tat; cash down; **peu donnant** closefisted

donne [dɔn] ƒ (cards) deal; doña (*Spanish title*); **fausse donne** misdeal

don·né -née [dɔne] adj given; **étant donné que** whereas, since ‖ ƒ datum; **données** data, facts

donner [dɔne] tr to give; (cards) to deal ‖ intr to give; **donner sur** to open onto, to look out on; **donner sur les doigts** to rap one's knuckles

don·neur [dɔnœr] **don·neuse** [dɔnøz] mƒ donor; **donneur universel** type-O blood donor ‖ m (cards) dealer

dont [dɔ̃] §79

donzelle [dɔ̃zel] ƒ woman of easy virtue

doper [dɔpe] tr to dope

doping [dɔpiŋ] m dope, pep pill

dorade [dɔrad] ƒ gilthead

dorénavant [dɔrenavã] adv henceforth

dorer [dɔre] tr to gild; (fig) to sugarcoat

d'ores [dɔr] see ores

dorlotement [dɔrlɔtmã] m coddling

dorloter [dɔrlɔte] tr to coddle

dor·mant [dɔrmã] **-mante** [mãt] adj stagnant, immovable ‖ m doorframe

dor·meur [dɔrmœr] **-meuse** [møz] adj sleeping ‖ mƒ sleeper ‖ ƒ earring

dormir [dɔrmir] §23 intr to sleep; to lie dormant; **à dormir debout** boring, dull; **dormir debout** to sleep standing up; **dormir sur les deux oreilles** to feel secure

dortoir [dɔrtwar] m dormitory

dorure [dɔryr] ƒ gilding; gilt; icing

dos [do] m back; bridge (*of nose*); **dans le dos de** behind the back of; **en dos d'âne** saddle-backed, hog-backed; **se mettre qn à dos** to make an enemy of s.o.; **voir au dos** see other side

dosage [dozaʒ] m dosage

dose [doz] ƒ dose

doser [doze] tr to dose out, to measure out, to proportion

dossier [dosje] m chair back; dossier

dot [dɔt] ƒ dowry

dotation [dɔtɑsjɔ̃] ƒ endowment

doter [dɔte] tr to endow; to dower; to give a dowry to

douaire [dwer] m dower

douairière [dwerjer] ƒ dowager

douane [dwan] *f* customs, duty; customhouse

doua·nier [dwanje] **-nière** [njer] *adj* customs ‖ *m* customs officer

doublage [dublaʒ] *m* doubling; metal plating of a ship; lining (*act of lining*); dubbing (*on tape or film*)

double [dubl] *adj & adv* double; à double face two-faced ‖ *m* double; duplicate, copy; **au double** twice; **double au carbone** carbon copy; **en double** in duplicate

doublement [dubləmɑ̃] *m* doubling ‖ *adv* doubly

doubler [duble] *tr* to double; to parallel, to run alongside; to pass (*s.o., s.th. going in the same direction*); to line (*a coat*); to dub (*a film*); to copy, dub (*a sound tape*); to replace (*an actor*); to gain one lap on (*another contestant*); (coll) to cheat ‖ *intr* to double; to pass (*on highway*)

doublure [dublyr] *f* lining; (theat) understudy, replacement

douce-amère [dusamɛr] *f* (*pl* **douces-amères**) (bot) bittersweet

douceâtre [dusɑtr] *adj* sweetish; mawkish

doucement [dusmɑ̃] *adv* softly; slowly ‖ *interj* easy now!, just a minute!

douce-reux [dusrø] **-reuse** [røz] *adj* unpleasantly sweet, cloying, mealy-mouthed

douceur [dusœr] *f* sweetness; softness, gentleness; **douceurs** sweets

douche [duʃ] *f* shower bath; douche; (coll) dressing down; (coll) shock, disappointment

doucher [duʃe] *tr* to give a shower bath to; (coll) to reprimand; (coll) to disappoint ‖ *ref* to take a shower bath

doucir [dusir] *tr* to polish, rub

doué douée [dwe] *adj* gifted, endowed

douer [dwe] *tr* to endow; **douer de** to endow or gift (*s.o.*) with

douille [duj] *f* cartridge case; sconce (*of candlestick*); bushing; (elec) socket

douil·let [duje] **douil·lette** [dujet] *adj* soft, delicate; oversensitive ‖ *f* child's padded coat

douleur [dulœr] *f* pain; sorrow; soreness

doulou·reux [dulurø] **-reuse** [røz] *adj* painful; sad; sore

doute [dut] *m* doubt; **sans doute** no doubt

douter [dute] *tr* to doubt, e.g., **je doute qu'il vienne** I doubt that he will come ‖ *intr* to doubt; **à n'en pas douter** beyond a doubt; **douter de** to doubt; to distrust ‖ *ref*—**se douter de** to suspect; **se douter que** to suspect that

dou·teur [dutœr] **-teuse** [tøz] *adj* doubting ‖ *mf* doubter

dou·teux [dutø] **-teuse** [tøz] *adj* doubtful; dubious

Douvres [duvr] Dover

doux [du] **douce** [dus] *adj* sweet; soft; pleasing, suave; quiet; new (*wine*); fresh (*water*); gentle (*slope*); mild

(*weather, climate*); **en douce** on the sly, on the q.t. ‖ **doux** *interj*—**tout doux!** easy there!

douzain [duzɛ̃] *m* twelve-line verse

douzaine [duzen] *f* dozen; **à la douzaine** by the dozen; **une douzaine de** a dozen

douze [duz] *adj & pron* twelve; the Twelfth, e.g., **Jean douze** John the Twelfth ‖ *m* twelve; twelfth (*in dates*)

douzième [duzjem] *adj, pron* (*masc, fem*), *& m* twelfth

doyen [dwajɛ̃] **doyenne** [dwajen] *mf* dean; **doyen d'âge** oldest member

doyenneté [dwajente] *f* seniority

Dʳ *abbr* (**Docteur**) Dr.

drachme [drakm] *m* drachma; dram

dragage [dragaʒ] *m* dredging

dragée [draʒe] *f* sugar-coated almond; (pharm) pill; (coll) bitter pill; **tenir la dragée haute à qn** to make s.o. pay through the nose; to be high-handed with s.o.

drageon [draʒɔ̃] *m* (bot) sucker

dragon [dragɔ̃] *m* dragon; dragoon; shrew; **dragon de vertu** prude

dragonne [dragon] *f* tassel, sword knot

drague [drag] *f* dredge; minesweeping apparatus

draguer [drage] *tr* to dredge, drag; to sweep for mines

dragueur [dragœr] *adj* minesweeping ‖ *m* dredger; **dragueur de mines** mine-sweeper

drain [drɛ̃] *m* drainpipe; (med) drain

drainage [drenaʒ] *m* drainage

drainer [drene], [drene] *tr* to drain

draisine [drezin] *f* (rr) handcar

dramatique [dramatik] *adj* dramatic

dramatiser [dramatize] *tr* to dramatize

dramaturge [dramatyrʒ] *mf* playwright

dramaturgie [dramatyrʒi] *f* dramatics

drame [dram] *m* drama; tragic event

drap [dra] *m* cloth; sheet; **être dans de beaux draps** to be in a pretty pickle

dra·peau [drapo] *m* (*pl* **-peaux**) flag; **au drapeau!** colors (bugle call)!; **drapeau parlementaire** flag of truce; **être sous les drapeaux** to be a serviceman

draper [drape] *tr* to drape ‖ *ref* to drape oneself

draperie [drapri] *f* drapery; drygoods business; textile industry

dra·pier [drapje] **-pière** [pjer] *mf* draper; textile manufacturer

drastique [drastik] *adj* (med) drastic

drèche [drɛʃ] *f* draff, residue of malt

drège [drɛʒ] *f* dragnet

drelin [drəlɛ̃] *m* ting-a-ling

dressage [dresaʒ] *m* training (*of animals*); erection

dresser [drese] *tr* to raise, to hold erect; to train; to put up, to erect; to set (*the table; a trap*); to draw up, to draft; to plane, smooth; **dresser l'oreille** to prick up one's ears ‖ *ref* to stand or sit up straight; **se dresser contre** to be dead set against

dressoir [dreswar] *m* sideboard, buffet, dish closet

dribble [dribl] *m* (sports) dribble

dribbler [drible] *tr & intr* (sports) to dribble

drille [drij] *m*—joyeux drille gay blade || *f* jeweler's drill brace; **drilles** rags *(for papermaking)*

drisse [dris] *f* halyard, rope

drogue [drɔg] *f* drug; chemical; nostrum, concoction; narcotic; (coll) trash, rubbish

droguer [drɔge] *tr* to drug or dope *(with too much medicine)* || *intr* (coll) to cool one's heels || *ref* to drug or dope oneself

droguerie [drɔgri] *f* drysaltery (Brit)

droguiste [drɔgist] *mf* drysalter (Brit)

droit [drwa], [drwa] **droite** [drwat], [drwat] *adj* right; honest, sincere; fair, just || *m* law; right, justice; tax; right angle; **à bon droit** with reason; **de (plein) droit** rightfully, by rights, incontestably; **droit coutumier** common law; **droit de cité** key to the city; acceptability; **droits civils** rights to manage property; **droits civiques**, **droits politiques** civil rights; **droits d'auteur** royalty; **droits de reproduction réservés** copyrighted; **tous droits réservés** all rights reserved, copyrighted || *f* right, right-hand side; right hand; straight line; **à droite** to or on the right || **droit** *adv* —droit au but straight to the point; **tout droit** straight ahead

droi-tier [drwatje], [drwatje] -tière [tjer] *adj* right-handed || *mf* right-handed person; rightist

droiture [drwatyr], [drwatyr] *f* integrity

drolatique [drɔlatik] *adj* droll, comic

drôle [drol] *adj* droll, funny, strange; drôle de funny, e.g., **une drôle d'idée** a funny idea; **drôle de guerre** phony war; **drôle d'homme, de corps, de pistolet, or de pierrot** (coll) queer duck || *mf* (coll) queer duck, strange person

drôlerie [drolri] *f* drollery

drôlesse [droles] *f* wench, hussy

dromadaire [drɔmader] *m* dromedary

dronte [drɔt] *m* (orn) dodo

droppage [drɔpaʒ] *m* airdrop

drosser [drɔse] *tr* to drive, carry *(as the wind drives a ship ashore)*

dru drue [dry] *adj* thick, dense; fine *(rain)* || **dru** *adv* thickly, heavily

druide [druid] *m* druid

du [dy] §77

dû due [dy] *adj & m* due

duc [dyk] *m* duke; horned owl

ducat [dyka] *m* ducat

duché [dyʃe] *m* duchy, dukedom

duchesse [dyʃes] *f* duchess

duègne [dyɛɲ] *f* duenna

duel [dyɛl] *m* duel; dual number; **duel oratoire** verbal battle

duelliste [dyelist] *m* duelist

dulcifier [dylsifje] *tr* to sweeten

dûment [dymɑ̃] *adv* duly

dune [dyn] *f* dune

dunette [dynet] *f* (naut) poop

Dunkerque [dœkerk] *f* Dunkirk

duo [dyo] *m* duet; duo; **duo d'injures** exchange of words, insults

duodénum [dyɔdenɔm] *m* duodenum

dupe [dyp] *f* dupe

duper [dype] *tr* to dupe

duperie [dypri] *f* deception, trickery

duplicata [dyplikata] *m* duplicate

duplicateur [dyplikatœr] *m* duplicating machine

duplication [dyplikasjɔ̃] *f* duplication

duplicité [dyplisite] *f* duplicity

duquel [dykel] §78

dur dure [dyr] *adj* hard; tough; difficult; **coucher sur la dure** to sleep on the bare ground or floor; **dur à la détente** tight-fisted; **dur d'oreille** hard of hearing; **élever un enfant à la dure** to give a child a strict upbringing || *mf* (coll) tough customer || *m* hard material, concrete || **dur** *adv* hard, e.g., **travailler dur** to work hard

durable [dyrabl] *adj* durable

durant [dyrɑ̃] *prep* during; (sometimes stands after noun), e.g., **sa vie durant** during his life

durcir [dyrsir] *tr, intr & ref* to harden

durcissement [dyrsismɑ̃] *m* hardening

durée [dyre] *f* duration; wear

durer [dyre] *intr* to last, endure

dureté [dyrte] *f* hardness; cruelty

durillon [dyrijɔ̃] *m* callus, corn

duvet [dyve] *m* down, fuzz; nap *(of cloth)*

duve-té -tée [dyvte] *adj* downy

duve-teux [dyvtø] -teuse [tøz] *adj* fuzzy

dynamique [dinamik] *adj* dynamic || *f* dynamics

dynamite [dinamit] *f* dynamite

dynamiter [dinamite] *tr* to dynamite

dynamo [dinamo] *f* dynamo

dynaste [dinast] *m* dynast

dynastie [dinasti] *f* dynasty

dysenterie [disɑ̃tri] *f* dysentery

dyspepsie [dispepsi] *f* dyspepsia

E

E, e [ə], *[ə] m invar* fifth letter of the French alphabet

eau [o] *f* (*pl* eaux) water; wake *(of ship)*; **à l'eau de rose** maudlin; **de la plus belle eau** of the first water; **eau calcaire** hard water; **eau de cale** bilge water; **eau de Javel** bleach; **eau dentifrice** mouthwash; **eau douce** soft water; fresh water; **eau dure** hard water; **eau lourde** heavy water;

eau oxygénée hydrogen peroxide; **eau vive** running water; **eaux waters**; waterworks; **eaux juvéniles** mineral waters; **eaux thermales** hot springs; **eaux usées, eaux résiduelles** polluted water; **eaux vives** swift current; **être en eau** to sweat; **faire de l'eau** to take in water; **faire eau** to leak; **grandes eaux** fountains; **nager entre deux eaux** to float under the surface; to play both sides of the street; **pêcher en eau trouble** to fish in troubled waters; **porter de l'eau à la rivière** or **à la mer** to carry coals to Newcastle; **tomber à l'eau** to fizzle out

eau-de-vie [odvi] f (pl **eaux-de-vie**) brandy; spirits

eau-forte [ofort] f (pl **eaux-fortes**) aqua fortis; etching

éba·hi -hie [ebai] adj dumfounded

ébattre [ebatr] §7 ref to frolic, to gambol

ébauche [eboʃ] f rough sketch or draft; suspicion (of a smile)

ébaucher [eboʃe] tr to sketch, to make a rough draft of

ébène [eben] f ebony

ébénier [ebenje] m ebony (tree)

ébéniste [ebenist] m cabinetmaker

ébénisterie [ebenistri] f cabinetmaking

éberluer [eberlɥe] tr to astonish

éblouir [ebluir] tr to dazzle, blind

éblouissement [ebluismɑ̃] m dazzle; glare; (pathol) dizziness

éboueur [ebwœr] m street cleaner, trash man; garbage collector

ébouillanter [ebujɑ̃te] tr to scald

éboulement [ebulmɑ̃] m cave-in, landslide

ébouler [ebule] tr & ref to cave in

ébourif·fant [eburifɑ̃] **ébourif·fante** [eburifɑ̃t] adj (coll) astounding

ébouriffer [eburife] tr to ruffle; (coll) to astound

ébouter [ebute] tr to cut off the end of

ébranchage [ebrɑ̃ʃaʒ] m pruning

ébrancher [ebrɑ̃ʃe] tr to prune

ébranlement [ebrɑ̃lmɑ̃] m shaking; shock

ébranler [ebrɑ̃le] tr to shake, jar || ref to start out; to be shaken

ébrécher [ebreʃe] §10 tr to nick, chip; to make a dent in (e.g., a fortune) || ref to be nicked, chipped; (with dat of reflex pron) to break off (a tooth)

ébriété [ebrijete] f inebriation

ébrouer [ebrue] ref to snort (said of horse); to splash about; to shake the water off oneself

ébruiter [ebrɥite] tr to noise about, to blab || ref to get around (said of news); to leak out (said of secret)

ébullition [ebylisjɔ̃] f boiling; ebullience, ferment

ébur·né -née [ebyrne] adj ivory

écaille [ekɑj] f scale (of fish, snake); shell; tortoise shell

écail·ler [ekɑje] **écail·lère** [ekɑjer] mf oyster opener || m oysterman || f oysterwoman || **écailler** tr & ref to scale

écale [ekal] f shell, husk, hull

écaler [ekale] tr to shell, husk, hull

écarlate [ekarlat] adj & f scarlet

écarquiller [ekarkije] tr (coll) to open wide, to spread apart

écart [ekar] m swerve, side step; digression, flight (of imagination); difference, gap, spread; error (in range); lapse (in good conduct); (cards) discard; **à l'écart** aside; aloof; **à l'écart de** far from; **faire le grand écart** to do the splits; **faire un écart** to shy (said of horse); to swerve (said of car); to step aside (said of person)

écar·té -tée [ekarte] adj lonely, secluded; wide-apart

écartèlement [ekartɛlmɑ̃] m quartering

écarteler [ekartəle] §2 tr to quarter

écartement [ekartəmɑ̃] m removal, separation; spreading; space between; spark gap; gauge (of rails)

écarter [ekarte] tr to put aside; to keep away; to ward off; to draw aside; to spread; (cards) to discard || ref to turn away; to stray

ecchymose [ekimoz] f black-and-blue mark

ecclésiastique [eklezjastik] adj & m ecclesiastic

écerve·lé -lée [eservəle] adj scatterbrained || mf scatterbrain

échafaud [eʃafo] m scaffold

échafaudage [eʃafodaʒ] m scaffolding

échafauder [eʃafode] tr to pile up; to lay the groundwork for || intr to erect a scaffolding

échalasser [eʃalase] tr to stake

échalote [eʃalɔt] f shallot

échancrer [eʃɑ̃kre] tr to make a V-shaped cut in (the neck of a dress); to cut (a dress) low in the neck; to indent; to hollow out

échange [eʃɑʒ] m exchange

échanger [eʃɑʒe] §38 tr to exchange; **échanger pour** or **contre** to exchange (s.th.) for

échangeur [eʃɑʒœr] m interchange

échanson [eʃɑ̃sɔ̃] m cupbearer

échantillon [eʃɑ̃tijɔ̃] m sample; **comparer à l'échantillon** to spot-check

échantillonnage [eʃɑ̃tijɔnaʒ] m sampling; spot check

échantillonner [eʃɑ̃tijɔne] tr to cut samples of; to spot-check; to select (a sampling to be polled)

échappatoire [eʃapatwar] f loophole, way out

échap·pé -pée [eʃape] mf escapee || f escape; short period; glimpse; (sports) spurt; **à l'échappée** stealthily

échappement [eʃapmɑ̃] m escape, leak; exhaust; escapement (of watch); **échappement libre** cutout

échapper [eʃape] tr—**l'échapper belle** to have a narrow escape || intr to escape; **échapper à** to escape from; **échapper de** to slip out of || ref to escape

écharde [eʃard] f splinter

écharpe [eʃarp] f scarf; sash; sling; **en écharpe** diagonally, crosswise; in a sling; across the shoulder

écharper [eʃarpe] tr to slash, cut up

échasse [eʃɑs] *f* stilt

échauder [eʃode] *tr* to scald; to white-wash; to gouge (*a customer*)

échauffement [eʃofmɑ̃] *m* heating; overexcitement

échauffer [eʃofe] *tr* to heat; to warm; **échauffer les oreilles à qn** to get s.o.'s dander up || *ref* to heat up; to become excited

échauffourée [eʃofure] *f* skirmish; rash undertaking

èche [ɛʃ] *f* bait

échéance [eʃeɑ̃s] *f* due date, expiration

échec [eʃɛk] *m* check; chessman; failure; **échec et mat** checkmate; **échecs** [eʃe] chess; chess set; **être échec** to be in check; **jouer aux échecs** to play chess

échelle [eʃɛl] *f* ladder; scale; **échelle de sauvetage** fire escape; **échelle mobile** sliding scale; **échelle pliante** stepladder; **monter à l'échelle** (coll) to bite, be fooled

échelon [eʃlɔ̃] *m* echelon; rung (*of ladder*)

échelonner [eʃlɔne] *tr* to spread out, to space out

écheniller [eʃnije] *tr* to remove cater-pillars from; to exterminate (*pests*); to eradicate (*corruption*)

éche·veau [eʃvo] *m* (*pl* **-veaux**) skein

éche·velé -lée [eʃəvle] *adj* disheveled; wild (*dance, race*)

écheveler [eʃəvle] §34 *tr* to dishevel

échevin [eʃvɛ̃] *m* (hist) alderman

échine [eʃin] *f* spine, backbone; **avoir l'échine souple** (coll) to be a yes man

échiner [eʃine] *tr* to break the back of; to beat, kill || *ref* to tire oneself out

échiquier [eʃikje] *m* chessboard; ex-chequer

écho [eko] *m* echo; piece of gossip; **échos** gossip column; **faire écho to** echo

échoir [eʃwar] (usually used only in: *inf*; *ger* **échéant**; *pp* **échu**; 3d *sg*: *pres ind* **échoit**; *pret* **échut**; *fut* **échoira**; *cond* **échoirait**) *intr* (*aux*: AVOIR or ÊTRE) to fall, devolve; to fall due

échoppe [eʃɔp] *f* burin; (com) stand, booth; workshop

échopper [eʃɔpe] *tr* to scoop out

échotier [ekotje] *m* gossip columnist, society editor

échouer [eʃwe] *tr* to ground, to beach || *intr* to sink; to run aground; to fail || *ref* to run aground

é·chu -chue [eʃy] *adj* due, payable

écimer [esime] *tr* to top

éclaboussement [eklabusmɑ̃] *m* splash

éclabousser [eklabuse] *tr* to splash

éclair [eklɛr] *adj* lightning (*e.g., speed*); flash (*bulb*) || *m* flash (*of light, of lightning, of the eyes, of wit*); (culin) éclair; **éclairs** lightning; **éclairs de chaleur** heat lightning; **éclairs en nappe** sheet lightning; **il fait des éclairs** it is lightening; **passer comme un éclair** to flash by

éclairage [eklɛraʒ] *m* lighting; **sous cet éclairage** (fig) in this light

éclaircie [eklɛrsi] *f* break, clearing; spell of good weather

éclaircissement [eklɛrsismɑ̃] *m* expla-nation, clearing up

éclairement [eklɛrmɑ̃] *m* illumination

éclairer [eklɛre] *tr* to light; to en-lighten; **éclairer sa lanterne** (fig) to ring a bell for s.o. || *intr* to light up, to glitter; **il éclaire** it is lightening || *ref* to be lighted

éclai·reur [eklɛrœr] **-reuse** [røz] *mf* scout || *m* boy scout || *f* girl scout

éclat [ekla] *m* splinter; ray (*of sun-shine*); peal (*of thunder*); burst (*of laughter*); brightness, splendor

éclatement [eklatmɑ̃] *m* explosion; blowout (*of tire*); (fig) split

éclater [eklate] *intr* to splinter; to sparkle, glitter; to burst; to break out; to blow up

éclateur [eklatœr] *m* spark gap (*of induction coil*)

éclectique [eklɛktik] *adj* eclectic

éclipse [eklips] *f* eclipse; **à éclipses** flashing, blinking

éclipser [eklipse] *tr* to eclipse || *ref* to be eclipsed; (coll) to vanish; (coll) to sneak off

éclisse [eklis] *f* splinter; (med) splint; (rr) fishplate

éclisser [eklise] *tr* to splint

éclo·pé -pée [eklope] *adj* lame || *mf* cripple

éclore [eklɔr] §24 *intr* (*aux*: ÊTRE) to hatch; to blossom out

éclosion [eklozjɔ̃] *f* hatching; blooming

écluse [eklyz] *f* lock (*of canal, river, etc.*); floodgate

écluser [eklyze] *tr* to close (*a canal*) by a lock; to pass (*a boat*) through a lock

écœurer [ekœre] *tr* to sicken; to dis-hearten

école [ekɔl] *f* school; **école à tir** artil-lery practice; **école d'application** model school; **école d'arts et métiers** trade school; **école dominicale**, **école du dimanche** Sunday School; **école libre** private school; **école maternel-le** nursery school; **école mixte** co-educational school; **être à bonne école** to be in good hands; **faire école** to set a fashion; to form a school (*to set up a doctrine, gain adherents*); **faire l'école buissonnière** (coll) to play hooky

éco·lier [ekɔlje] **-lière** [ljer] *adj* schoolboy || *mf* pupil, scholar; nov-ice || *m* schoolboy || *f* schoolgirl

écologie [ekɔlɔʒi] *f* ecology

éconduire [ekɔ̃dɥir] §19 *tr* to show out

économat [ekɔnɔma] *m* comptroller's office; commissary, company or co-op store; **économats** chain stores

économe [ekɔnɔm] *adj* economical || *mf* treasurer; housekeeper || *m* bursar

économie [ekɔnɔmi] *f* economy; **éco-nomie de marché** free enterprise; **économies** savings

économique [ekɔnɔmik] *adj* economic; economical || *f* economics

économiser [ekɔnɔmize] *tr & intr* to economize, save

écope [ekɔp] *f* scoop (*for bailing*)

écoper [ekɔpe] *tr* to bail out ‖ *intr* (coll) to get a bawling out

écorce [ekɔrs] *f* bark (*of tree*); peel, rind; crust (*of earth*)

écorcer [ekɔrse] §51 *tr* to peel, to strip off

écorcher [ekɔrʃe] *tr* to peel; to chafe; to fleece, overcharge; to grate on (*the ears*); to burn (*the throat*); to murder (*a language*) ‖ *ref* (with *dat of reflex pron*) to skin (*e.g., one's arm*)

écor·cheur [ekɔrʃœr] **-cheuse** [ʃøz] *mf* skinner; fleecer, swindler

écorchure [ekɔrʃyr] *f* scratch, abrasion

écorner [ekɔrne] *tr* to poll, break the horns of; to dog-ear; to make a hole in (*e.g., a fortune*)

écornifler [ekɔrnifle] *tr* to cadge; **écornifler un dîner à qn** to bum a dinner off s.o.

écorni·fleur [ekɔrniflœr] **-fleuse** [fløz] *mf* sponger, moocher

écos·sais [ekɔse] **écos·saise** [ekɔsez] *adj* Scotch, Scottish ‖ *m* Scotch, Scottish (*language*); Scotch plaid ‖ (*cap*) *mf* Scot; **les Écossais** the Scotch ‖ *m* Scotchman

Écosse [ekɔs] *f* Scotland; **l'Écosse** Scotland

écosser [ekɔse] *tr* to shell, hull, husk

écot [eko] *m* share; tree stump; **payer son écot** to pay one's share

écoulement [ekulmɑ̃] *m* flow; (com) sale, turnover; (pathol) discharge; **écoulement d'eau** drainage

écouler [ekule] *tr* to sell, dispose of ‖ *ref* to run (*said, e.g., of water*); to flow; to drain; to leak; to elapse, to go by

écourter [ekurte] *tr* to shorten (*a dress, coat, etc.*); to crop (*the tail, ears, etc.*); to cut short, curtail

écoute [ekut] *f* listening post; monitoring; (naut) sheet; **écoutes** wild boar's ears; **être aux écoutes** to eavesdrop, to keep one's ears to the ground; **se mettre à l'écoute** to listen to the radio

écouter [ekute] *tr* to listen to; **écouter parler** to listen to (*s.o.*) speaking ‖ *intr* to listen; **écouter aux portes** to eavesdrop ‖ *ref* to coddle oneself; **s'écouter parler** to be pleased with the sound of one's own voice

écou·teur [ekutœr] **-teuse** [tøz] *mf* listener; **écouteur aux portes** eavesdropper ‖ *m* telephone receiver; earphone

écoutille [ekutij] *f* hatchway

écouvillon [ekuvijɔ̃] *m* swab, mop

écrabouiller [ekrabuje] *tr* (coll) to squash

écran [ekrɑ̃] *m* screen; (phot) filter; **écran de cheminée** fire screen; **écran de protection aérienne** air umbrella; **le petit écran** television screen; **porter à l'écran** to put on the screen

écra·sant -sante [ekrazɑ̃] **-sante** [zɑ̃t] *adj* crushing

écraser [ekraze] *tr* to crush; to overwhelm; to run over ‖ *ref* to be crushed; to crash

écrémer [ekreme] §10 *tr* to skim; (fig) to skim the cream off

écrémeuse [ekremøz] *f* cream separator

écrevisse [ekrəvis] *f* crayfish

écrier [ekrije] *ref* to cry out, exclaim

écrin [ekrɛ̃] *m* jewel case

écrire [ekrir] §25 *tr* to write; to spell ‖ *intr* to write ‖ *ref* to write to each other; to be written; to be spelled

é·crit [ekri] **-crite** [krit] *adj* written; **c'était écrit** it was fate ‖ *m* writing, written word; written examination; **écrits** writings, works; **par écrit** in writing

écri·teau [ekrito] *m* (*pl* **-teaux**) sign, placard

écritoire [ekritwar] *f* desk set

écriture [ekrityr] *f* handwriting; writing (*style of writing*); **écriture de chat** scrawl; **écritures** accounts; **Écritures** Scriptures; **écritures publiques** government documents

écrivailleur [ekrivɑjœr] *m* (coll) scribbler, hack writer

écrivain [ekrivɛ̃] *adj*—**femme écrivain** woman writer ‖ *m* writer; **écrivain public** public letter writer

écrivasser [ekrivase] *intr* (coll) to scribble

écrou [ekru] *m* nut (*with internal thread*); register (*on police blotter*); **écrou à oreille** thumb nut

écrouer [ekrue] *tr* to jail, to book

écrouler [ekrule] *ref* to collapse; to crumble; to flop (*in a chair*)

é·cru -crue [ekry] *adj* raw; unbleached

écu [eky] *m* shield; crown (*money*); **écus** money

écubier [ekybje] *m* (naut) hawsehole

écueil [ekœj] *m* reef, sandbank; stumbling block

écuelle [ekɥɛl] *f* bowl

éculer [ekyle] *tr* to wear down at the heel

écu·mant [ekymɑ̃] **-mante** [mɑ̃t] *adj* foaming; fuming (*with rage*)

écume [ekym] *f* foam; froth; lather; dross; scum (*on liquids; on metal; of society*); **écume de mer** meerschaum

écumer [ekyme] *tr* to skim, scum; to pick up (*e.g., gossip*); to scour (*the seas*) ‖ *intr* to foam; to scum; to fume (*with anger*)

écu·meur [ekymœr] **-meuse** [møz] *mf* drifter; **écumeur de marmite** hanger-on; **écumeur de mer** pirate

écu·meux -meuse [ekymø] **-meuse** [møz] *adj* foamy, frothy

écumoire [ekymwar] *f* skimmer

écurage [ekyraʒ] *m* scouring; cleaning out

écurer [ekyre] *tr* to scour; to clean out

écureuil [ekyrœj] *m* squirrel

écurie [ekyri] *f* stable (*for horses, mules, etc.*); string of horses

écusson [ekysɔ̃] *m* escutcheon; bud (*for grafting*); (mil) identification tag

écuyer [ekɥije] *mf* horseback rider ‖ *m* horseman; squire; riding master ‖ *f* horsewoman

eczéma [ekzema], [egzema] *m* eczema

edelweiss [edəlvajs], [edɛlves] *m* edelweiss

éden [edɛn] *m* Eden || (*cap*) *m* Garden of Eden

éden·té -tée [edɑ̃te] *adj* toothless

E.D.F. *abbr* (**Électricité de France**) French national electric company

édicter [edikte] *tr* to decree, to promulgate

édicule [edikyl] *m* kiosk; street urinal

édi·fiant [edifjɑ̃] **-fiante** [fjɑ̃t] *adj* edifying

édification [edifikɑsjɔ̃] *f* edification; construction, building

édifice [edifis] *m* edifice, building

édifier [edifje] *tr* to edify; to inform, enlighten; to construct, to build; to found

édit [edi] *m* edict

éditer [edite] *tr* to publish; to edit (*a manuscript*)

édi·teur [editœr] **-trice** [tris] *mf* publisher; editor (*of a manuscript*)

édition [edisjɔ̃] *f* edition; publishing

édito·rial -riale [editɔrjal] *adj* & *m* (*pl* **-riaux** [rjo]) editorial

édredon [edrədɔ̃] *m* eiderdown

éduca·teur [edykatœr] **-trice** [tris] *adj* educational || *mf* educator

éduca·tif [edykatif] **-tive** [tiv] *adj* educational

éducation [edykɑsjɔ̃] *f* education, bringing-up, nurture

éduquer [edyke] *tr* to bring up (*children*); to educate, train

éfaufiler [efofile] *tr* to unravel

effacement [efasmɑ̃] *m* effacement, erasing; self-effacement

effacer [efase] §51 *tr* to efface; to erase || *ref* to efface oneself; to stand aside

effarement [efarmɑ̃] *m* fright, scare

effaroucher [efaru/e] *tr* to frighten, scare off

effec·tif [efektif] **-tive** [tiv] *adj* actual, real || *m* personnel, manpower; strength (*of military unit*); complement (*of ship*); size (*of class*)

effectivement [efektivmɑ̃] *adv* actually, really, sure enough

effectuer [efektɥe] *tr* to effect

effémi·né -née [efemine] *adj* effeminate

efféminer [efemine] *tr* to make a sissy of; to unman || *ref* to become effeminate

effervescence [efervesɑ̃s] *f* effervescence; excitement, ferment

efferves·cent [efervesɑ̃] **efferves·cente** [efervesɑ̃t] *adj* effervescent

effet [efe] *m* effect; (billiards) english; **à cet effet** for that purpose; **en effet** indeed, actually, sure enough; **effet de commerce** bill of exchange; **effets publics** government bonds; **faire de l'effet** to be striking; **faire l'effet de** to give the impression of

effeuillage [efœjaʒ] *m* thinning of leaves

effeuillaison [efœjezɔ̃] *f* fall of leaves

effeuiller [efœje] *tr* to thin out the leaves of, to pluck off the petals of || *ref* to shed its leaves

effeuilleuse [efœjøz] *f* (coll) stripteaser

efficace [efikas] *adj* effective

efficacement [efikasmɑ̃] *adv* effectively

efficacité [efikasite] *f* efficacy, efficiency

efficience [efisjɑ̃s] *f* efficiency

effi·cient [efisjɑ̃] **-ciente** [sjɑ̃t] *adj* efficient

effigie [efiʒi] *f* effigy

effiler [efile] *tr* to unravel; to taper

effilocher [efilɔ/e] *tr* to unravel

efflan·qué -quée [eflɑ̃ke] *adj* skinny

effleurer [eflœre] *tr* to graze; to touch on

effluve [eflyv] *m* effluvium, emanation

effondrement [efɔ̃drəmɑ̃] *m* collapse

effondrer [efɔ̃dre] *tr* to break open; to break (*ground*) || *ref* to collapse, cave in; to sink

efforcer [efɔrse] §51 *ref*—**s'efforcer à** or **de** to try hard to, to strive to

effort [efɔr] *m* effort; (med) hernia, rupture; **effort de rupture** breaking stress; **effort de tension** torque; **faire effort sur soi-même** to get a hold of oneself

effraction [efraksjɔ̃] *f* housebreaking

effraie [efre] *f* screech owl

effranger [efrɑ̃ʒe] §38 *tr* & *ref* to fray

effrayant [efrejɑ̃] **effrayante** [efrejɑ̃t] *adj* frightful, dreadful

effrayer [efreje] §49 *tr* to frighten || *ref* to be frightened

effré·né -née [efrene] *adj* unbridled

effritement [efritmɑ̃] *m* crumbling

effriter [efrite] *tr* & *ref* to crumble

effroi [efrwɑ], [efrwa] *m* fright

effron·té -tée [efrɔ̃te] *adj* impudent; shameless; (slang) saucy, sassy

effronterie [efrɔ̃tri] *f* effrontery

effroyable [efrwɑjabl] *adj* frightful

effusion [efyzjɔ̃] *f* effusion; shedding (*of blood*); (fig) gushing

égailler [egaje] *ref* to scatter

é·gal -gale [egal] (*pl* **-gaux** [go]) *adj* equal; level; (coll) indifferent; **ça m'est égal** (coll) it's all the same to me, it's all right || *mf* equal; **à l'égal de** as much as, no less than

également [egalmɑ̃] *adv* equally, likewise, also

égaler [egale] *tr* to equal, match

égaliser [egalize] *tr* to equalize; to equate

égalitaire [egaliter] *adj* & *mf* equalitarian

égalité [egalite] *f* equality; evenness; **être à égalité** to be tied

égard [egar] *m* respect; **à l'égard de** with regard to; **à tous (les) égards** in all respects; **eu égard à** in consideration of

éga·ré -rée [egare] *adj* stray, lost

égarement [egarmɑ̃] *m* wandering (*of mind, senses, etc.*); frenzy (*of sorrow, anger, etc.*)

égarer [egare] *tr* to mislead; to misplace; to bewilder || *ref* to get lost, to stray; to be on the wrong track

égayer [egeje] §49 *tr* & *ref* to cheer up; to brighten

égide [eʒid] *f* aegis
églefin [egləfɛ̃] *m* haddock
église [egliz] *f* church
églogue [eglɔg] *f* eclogue
égoïne [egoin] *f* handsaw
égoïsme [egoism] *m* egoism
égoïste [egoist] *adj* selfish ‖ *mf* egoist
égorgement [egɔrʒəmɑ̃] *m* slaughter
égorger [egɔrʒe] §38 *tr* to cut the throat of; (coll) to overcharge
égosiller [egozije] *ref* to shout oneself hoarse
égotisme [egɔtism] *m* egotism
égotiste [egɔtist] *adj* egotistical ‖ *mf* egotist
égout [egu] *m* drainage; sewer; sink, cesspool (*e.g., of iniquity*)
égoutier [egutje] *m* sewer worker
égoutter [egute] *tr* to drain; to let drip ‖ *ref* to drip
égouttoir [egutwar] *m* drainboard
égrapper [egrape] *tr* to pick off from the cluster
égratigner [egratiɲe] *tr* to scratch; to take a dig at, to tease
égratignure [egratiɲyr] *f* scratch; gibe, dig
égrener [egrəne] §2 *tr* to shell (*e.g., peas*); to gin (*cotton*); to pick off (*grapes*); to unstring (*pearls*); to tell (*beads*) ‖ *ref* to drop one by one; to be strung out
égril·lard [egrijar] **égril·larde** [egrijard] *adj* spicy, lewd ‖ *mf* shameless, unblushing person
égrugeoir [egryʒwar] *m* mortar (*for pounding or grinding*)
égruger [egryʒe] §38 *tr* to pound (*in a mortar*)
égueuler [egœle] *tr* to break the neck of (*e.g., a bottle*)
Égypte [eʒipt] *f* Egypt; **l'Égypte** Egypt
égyp·tien [eʒipsjɛ̃] **-tienne** [sjɛn] *adj* Egyptian ‖ (*cap*) *mf* Egyptian
éhon·té -tée [eɔ̃te] *adj* shameless
eider [ɛjder] *m* eider duck
éjaculation [eʒakylɑsjɔ̃] *f* ejaculation; (eccl) short, fervent prayer
éjaculer [eʒakyle] *tr & intr* to ejaculate
éjecter [eʒɛkte] *tr* to eject; (coll) to oust
éjection [eʒɛksjɔ̃] *f* ejection
élabo·ré -rée [elabɔre] *adj* elaborated; prepared, elaborate
élaborer [elabɔre] *tr* to elaborate; to work out, develop
élaguer [elage] *tr* to prune
élan [elɑ̃] *m* dash; impulse, outburst; spirit, glow; (zool) elk, moose; **avec élan** with enthusiasm
élan·cé -cée [elɑ̃se] *adj* slender, slim
élancement [elɑ̃smɑ̃] *m* throbbing, twinge; yearning (*e.g., for God*)
élancer [elɑ̃se] §51 *intr* to throb, to twinge ‖ *ref* to rush, spring, dash; to spurt out
élargir [elarʒir] *tr* to widen; to broaden; to release (*a prisoner*) ‖ *ref* to widen; to become more lax
élasticité [elastisite] *f* elasticity
élastique [elastik] *adj* elastic ‖ *m* elastic; rubber band

élec·teur [elɛktœr] **-trice** [tris] *adj* voting ‖ *mf* voter, constituent; (hist) elector; **électeurs** electorate
élec·tif [elɛktif] **-tive** [tiv] *adj* elective
élection [elɛksjɔ̃] *f* election; choice
électorat [elɛktɔra] *m* right to vote; (hist) electorate
électri·cien [elɛktrisjɛ̃] **-cienne** [sjɛn] *adj* electrical (*worker*) ‖ *mf* electrician
électricité [elɛktrisite] *f* electricity
électrifier [elɛktrifje] *tr* to electrify
électrique [elɛktrik] *adj* electric(al)
électriser [elɛktrize] *tr* to electrify
électro [elɛktro] *m* electromagnet
électro-aimant [elɛktroɛmɑ̃] *m* (*pl* **-aimants**) electromagnet
électrochoc [elɛktrɔʃɔk] *m* (med) electric shock treatment
électro-culinaire [elɛktrɔkyliner] *adj* electric kitchen (*appliances*)
électrocuter [elɛktrɔkyte] *tr* to electrocute
électrode [elɛktrɔd] *f* electrode
électrolyse [elɛktrɔliz] *f* electrolysis
électrolyte [elɛktrɔlit] *m* electrolyte
électromagnétique [elɛktrɔmaɲetik] *adj* electromagnetic
électroména·ger [elɛktrɔmenaʒe] **-gère** [ʒer] *adj* household-electric
électromo·teur [elɛktrɔmɔtœr] **-trice** [tris] *adj* electromotive ‖ *m* electric motor
électron [elɛktrɔ̃] *m* electron
électronique [elɛktrɔnik] *adj* electronic ‖ *f* electronics
électron-volt [elɛktrɔ̃vɔlt] *m* (*pl* **électrons-volts**) electron-volt
électrophone [elɛktrɔfɔn] *m* electric phonograph
électrotype [elɛktrɔtip] *m* electrotype
électrotyper [elɛktrɔtipe] *tr* to electrotype
élégance [elegɑ̃s] *f* elegance
élé·gant [elegɑ̃] **-gante** [gɑ̃t] *adj* elegant
élégiaque [eleʒjak] *adj* elegiac ‖ *mf* elegist
élégie [eleʒi] *f* elegy
élément [elemɑ̃] *m* element; (*of an electric battery*) cell, element; (elec, mach) unit; **élément standard** standard part
élémentaire [elemɑ̃ter] *adj* elementary
éléphant [elefɑ̃] *m* elephant
éléphantesque [elefɑ̃tesk] *adj* (coll) gigantic, elephantine
élevage [elvaʒ], [ɛlvaʒ] *m* rearing, raising, breeding; ranch
éléva·teur [elevatœr] **-trice** [tris] *adj* lifting ‖ *m* elevator; hoist
élévation [elevɑsjɔ̃] *f* elevation; promotion; increase; (rok) lift-off
élève [elev] *mf* pupil, student; **ancien élève** alumnus; **élève externe** day student; **élève interne** boarding student ‖ *f* breeder (*animal*); (hort) seedling
éle·vé -vée [elve] *adj* high, elevated; lofty, noble; **bien élevé** well-bred; **mal élevé** ill-bred
élever [elve] §2 *tr* to raise; to raise,

bring up, nurture; to erect || *ref* to rise; to arise; to be built, to stand

éle·veur [elvœr] **-veuse** [vøz] *mf* breeder, rancher

elfe [elf] *m* elf

élider [elide] *tr* to elide

éligible [eliʒibl] *adj* eligible

élimer [elime] *tr & ref* to wear threadbare

éliminatoire [eliminatwar] *adj* (sports) preliminary || *f* (sports) preliminaries

éliminer [elimine] *tr* to eliminate

élire [elir] §36 *tr* to elect

élision [elizjɔ̃] *f* elision

élite [elit] *f* elite

elle [el] *pron disj* §85 || *pron conj* §87

elle-même [elmem] §86

ellipse [elips] *f* (gram) ellipsis; (math) ellipse

elliptique [eliptik] *adj* elliptic(al)

élocution [elɔkysjɔ̃] *f* elocution; choice and arrangement of words

éloge [elɔʒ] *m* eulogy; praise

élo·gieux [elɔʒjø] **-gieuse** [ʒjøz] *adj* full of praise

éloi·gné -gnée [elwaɲe] *adj* distant

éloignement [elwaɲəmɑ̃] *m* remoteness; aversion; postponement

éloigner [elwaɲe] *tr* to move away; to remove; to drive away; to postpone || *ref* to move away; to digress, deviate; to become estranged

élongation [elɔ̃gasjɔ̃] *f* stretching

élonger [elɔ̃ʒe] §38 *tr* to lay (*e.g., a cable*); **élonger la terre** to skirt the coast

éloquence [elɔkɑ̃s] *f* eloquence

élo·quent [elɔkɑ̃] **-quente** [kɑ̃t] *adj* eloquent

é·lu -lue [ely] *adj* elected || *mf* chosen one; **les élus** the elect

élucider [elyside] *tr* to elucidate

éluder [elyde] *tr* to elude, avoid

éma·cié -ciée [emasje] *adj* emaciated

émacier [emasje] *ref* to become emaciated

é·mail [emaj] *m* (*pl* **-maux** [mo]) enamel || *m* (*pl* **-mails**) nail polish; car or bicycle paint

émaillage [emajaʒ] *m* enameling

émailler [emaje] *tr* to enamel; to sprinkle (*e.g., with quotations, metaphors, etc.*); to dot (*e.g., the fields, as flowers do*)

émanation [emanasjɔ̃] *f* emanation; manifestation (*e.g., of authority*)

émanciper [emɑ̃sipe] *tr* to emancipate || *ref* to be emancipated; (coll) to get out of hand

émaner [emane] *intr* to emanate

émarger [emarʒe] §38 *tr* to trim (*e.g., a book*); to initial (*a document*) || *intr* to get paid; **émarger à** to be paid from

émasculer [emaskyle] *tr* to emasculate

embâcle [ɑ̃bɑkl] *m* pack ice, ice floe

emballage [ɑ̃balaʒ] *m* packing, wrapping

emballer [ɑ̃bale] *tr* to wrap up, to pack; to race (*a motor*); (coll) to thrill; (coll) to bawl out || *ref* to bolt, to run away; (mach) to race; (coll) to get worked up

embal·leur [ɑ̃balœr] **embal·leuse** [ɑ̃baløz] *mf* packer

embarbouiller [ɑ̃barbuje] *tr* to besmear; (coll) to muddle, confuse || *ref* (coll) to get tangled up

embarcadère [ɑ̃barkader] *m* wharf; (rr) platform

embarcation [ɑ̃barkasjɔ̃] *f* small boat

embardée [ɑ̃barde] *f* lurch; (aut) swerve; (aer, naut) yaw

embarder [ɑ̃barde] *intr* (aut) to swerve; (aer, naut) to yaw

embargo [ɑ̃bargo] *m* embargo

embarquement [ɑ̃barkəmɑ̃] *m* embarkation; shipping; loading

embarquer [ɑ̃barke] *tr* to embark; to ship (*a sea*); to load (*in car, plane, etc.*); (coll) to put in the clink || *ref* to embark; to board; to get into a car

embarras [ɑ̃bara] *m* embarrassment; trouble, inconvenience; encumbrance; obstruction; perplexity; financial difficulties; **embarras de voitures** traffic jam; **embarras du choix** too much to choose from; **faire des embarras** (coll) to put on airs

embarrasser [ɑ̃barase] *tr* to embarrass; to hamper, to obstruct; to stump, to perplex || *ref*—**s'embarrasser de** to take an interest in; to bother with

embaucher [ɑ̃boʃe] *tr* to hire, to sign on; (coll) to entice (*soldiers*) to desert || *intr* to hire; **on n'embauche pas** (public sign) no help wanted

embauchoir [ɑ̃boʃwar] *m* shoetree

embaumement [ɑ̃bomɑ̃] *m* embalming; perfuming

embaumer [ɑ̃bome] *tr* to embalm; to perfume || *intr* to smell good

embaumeur [ɑ̃bomœr] *m* embalmer

embellir [ɑ̃belir] *tr* to embellish || *intr* to clear up (said of weather); to improve in looks || *ref* to grow more beautiful

embellissement [ɑ̃belismɑ̃] *m* embellishment

embêtement [ɑ̃bɛtmɑ̃] *m* (coll) annoyance

embêter [ɑ̃bete], [ɑ̃bete] *tr* (coll) to annoy

emblave [ɑ̃blav] *f* grainfield

emblaver [ɑ̃blave] *tr* to sow

emblée [ɑ̃ble]—**d'emblée** then and there, right off; without difficulty

emblématique [ɑ̃blematik] *adj* emblematic(al)

emblème [ɑ̃blɛm] *m* emblem

embobeliner [ɑ̃bɔbline] *tr* (coll) to bamboozle

embobiner [ɑ̃bɔbine] *tr* to wind up (*e.g., on a reel*); (coll) to bamboozle

emboîter [ɑ̃bwate] *tr* to encase; to nest (*boxes, boats, etc.*); (mach) to interlock, joint; **emboîter le pas** to fall into step

embolie [ɑ̃bɔli] *f* (pathol) embolism

embonpoint [ɑ̃bɔ̃pwɛ̃] *m* portliness; **prendre de l'embonpoint** to put on flesh

embouche [ɑ̃buʃ] *f* pasture

embou·ché -chée [ãbuʃe] *adj—***mal embouché** foul-mouthed
emboucher [ãbuʃe] *tr* to blow, sound
embouchoir [ãbuʃwar] *m* mouthpiece
embouchure [ãbuʃyr] *f* mouth (*of a river*); mouthpiece
embourber [ãburbe] *tr* to stick in the mud; to vilify, to implicate
embout [ãbu] *m* tip, ferrule; rubber tip (*for chair*)
embouteillage [ãbutejaʒ] *m* bottling; bottleneck, traffic jam
emboutir [ãbutir] *tr* to stamp, emboss; to smash (*e.g., a fender*) ‖ *ref* to bump
embranchement [ãbrãʃmã] *m* branching (off); branch; branch line; junction (*of roads, track, etc.*)
embrasement [ãbrazmã] *m* conflagration; illumination, glow
embraser [ãbraze] *tr* to set aflame or aglow ‖ *ref* to flame up; to glow
embrassade [ãbrasad] *m* embrace; kissing
embrasse [ãbrɑs] *f* curtain tieback
embrassement [ãbrasmã] *m* embrace
embrasser [ãbrase] *tr* to embrace; to kiss; to join; to undertake; to take in (*at a glance*); to take (*the opportunity*) ‖ *ref* to embrace; to neck
embras·seur [ãbrasœr] **embras·seuse** [ãbrasøz] *mf* smoocher
embrasure [ãbrazyr] *f* embrasure, loophole; opening (*for door or window*)
embrayage [ãbrejaʒ] *m* coupling, engagement; (aut) clutch
embrayer [ãbreje], [ãbreje] §49 *tr* to engage, connect; to throw into gear ‖ *intr* to throw the clutch in
embrocher [ãbrɔʃe] *tr* to put on a spit
embrouiller [ãbruje] *tr* to embroil ‖ *ref* to become embroiled
embroussail·lé -lée [ãbrusaje] *adj* bushy; tangled; complicated, complex
embru·mé -mée [ãbryme] *adj* foggy, misty
embruns [ãbrœ̃] *mpl* spray
embryologie [ãbrijɔlɔʒi] *f* embryology
embryon [ãbrijõ] *m* embryo
embryonnaire [ãbrijɔnɛr] *adj* embryonic
em·bu -bue [ãby] *adj* lifeless, dull ‖ *m* dull tone (*of a painting*)
embûche [ãbyʃ] *f* snare, trap
embuer [ãbɥe] *tr* to cloud with steam; **embué de larmes** dimmed with tears
embuscade [ãbyskad] *f* ambush
embus·qué -quée [ãbyske] *adj* in ambush; **se tenir embusqué** to lie in ambush ‖ *m* (mil) goldbricker, shirker
embusquer [ãbyske] *tr* to ambush, trap ‖ *ref* to lie in ambush; (mil) to get a safe assignment
émé·ché -chée [emeʃe] *adj* (coll) tipsy, high
émender [emãde] *tr* to amend (*a sentence, decree, etc.*)
émeraude [emrod] *f* emerald
émergence [emɛrʒãs] *f* emergence
émerger [emɛrʒe] §38 *intr* to emerge
émeri [emri] *m* emery

émerillon [emrijõ] *m* swivel; (orn) merlin
émerillon·né -née [emrijone] *adj* lively, gay
émérite [emerit] *adj* experienced; distinguished, remarkable; confirmed (*smoker*); (obs) retired, emeritus
émersion [emɛrsjõ] *f* emersion
émerveillement [emɛrvejmã] *m* wonderment
émerveiller [emɛrveje] *tr* to astonish, amaze
émétique [emetik] *adj & m* emetic
émet·teur [emetœr] **émet·trice** [emetris] *adj* issuing; transmitting ‖ *mf* maker (*of check, draft*); issuer ‖ *m* broadcasting station; (rad) transmitter
émetteur-récepteur [emetœrreseptœr] *m* (*pl* **émetteurs-récepteurs**) (rad) walkie-talkie
émettre [emetr] §42 *tr* to emit; to express (*an opinion*); to issue (*stamps, bank notes, etc.*); to transmit (*a radio signal*) ‖ *intr* to transmit, broadcast
é·meu [emø] *m* (*pl* **-meus**) (zool) emu
émeute [emøt] *f* riot
émeutier [emøtje] *m* rioter
émietter [emjete] *tr* to crumble; to break up (*an estate*)
émi·grant [emigrã] **-grante** [grãt] *adj & mf* emigrant; migrant
émi·gré -grée [emigre] *adj* emigrating ‖ *mf* emigrant; émigré
émigrer [emigre] *intr* to emigrate; to migrate
émincer [emɛ̃se] §51 *tr* to cut in thin slices
éminemment [eminamã] *adv* eminently
éminence [eminãs] *f* eminence
émi·nent -nente [eminã] **-nente** [nãt] *adj* eminent
émissaire [emiser] *m* emissary; outlet (*of lake, basin, etc.*)
émission [emisjõ] *f* emission; utterance; issue (*of stamps, bank notes, etc.*); (rad) transmission, broadcast
emmagasiner [ãmagazine] *tr* to put in storage; to store up; to stockpile
emmailloter [ãmajote] *tr* to swathe; to bandage
emmancher [ãmãʃe] *tr* to put a handle on ‖ *ref* (coll) to begin; **s'emmancher bien** (coll) to get off to a good start; **s'emmancher mal** (coll) to get off to a bad start
emmêler [ãmele], [ãmele] *tr* to tangle up; to mix up
emménagement [ãmenaʒmã] *m* moving in; installation
emménager [ãmenaʒe] §38 *tr & intr* to move in
emmener [ãmne] §2 *tr* to take or lead away; to take out (*e.g., to dinner*); to take (*on a visit*)
emmenthal [emɛ̃tal], [emental] *m* Swiss cheese
emmiel·lé -lée [ãmjele], [ãmjele] *adj* honeyed (*e.g., words*)
emmitoufler [ãmitufle] *tr & ref* to bundle up (*in warm clothing*)
emmurer [ãmyre] *tr* to wall in, immure

émol [emwa] *m* agitation, alarm

émolument [emɔlymã] *m* share; **émoluments** emolument, fee, salary

émonder [emɔ̃de] *tr* to prune, trim

émo·tif -tive [emɔtif] [tiv] *adj* emotional || *mf* emotional person

émotion [emosjɔ̃] *f* emotion; commotion

émotionnable [emosjɔnabl] *adj* emotional

émotion·nant [emosjɔnã] **émotionnante** [emosjɔnãt] *adj* stirring, moving

émotionner [emosjɔne] *tr* to move deeply, thrill, affect || *ref* to get excited, flustered

émoucher [emuʃe] *tr* to chase flies away from

émouchet [emuʃɛ] *m* sparrow hawk

émouchoir [emuʃwar] *m* whisk, fly swatter

émoudre [emudr] §43 *tr* to grind, sharpen

émoulage [emulaʒ] *m* grinding, sharpening

émou·lu -lue [emuly] *adj*—**frais émoulu de** (fig) fresh from, just back from

émous·sé -sée [emuse] *adj* blunt

émousser [emuse] *tr* to dull, blunt

émoustiller [emustije] *tr* (coll) to exhilarate, to rouse

émouvoir [emuvwar] §45 (*pp* ému) *tr* to move; to excite || *ref* to be moved; to be excited

empailler [ãpaje] *tr* to stuff (*animals*); to cane (*a chair*)

empail·leur [ãpajœr] **empail·leuse** [ãpajøz] *mf* taxidermist; caner

empaler [ãpale] *tr* to impale

empan [ãpã] *m* span (*of hand*)

empanacher [ãpanaʃe] *tr* to plume

empaquetage [ãpaktaʒ] *m* packaging; package

empaqueter [ãpakte] §34 *tr* to package

emparer [ãpare] *ref*—**s'emparer de** to seize, take hold of

empâter [ãpate] *tr* to make sticky; to fatten up (*chickens, turkeys, etc.*); to coat (*the tongue*); (typ) to overink || *ref* to put on weight; to become coated (*said of tongue*); to become husky (*said of voice*)

empattement [ãpatmã] *m* foundation, footing; (aut) wheelbase

empaumer [ãpome] *tr* to catch in the hand; to hit with a racket; to palm (*a card*); (coll) to hoodwink

empêchement [ãpɛʃmã] *m* impediment, bar; hindrance, obstacle

empêcher [ãpɛʃe] *tr* to hinder; **empêcher qn de** + *inf* to prevent or keep s.o. from + *ger*; **n'empêche que** all the same, e.g., **n'empêche qu'il est très poli** he's very polite all the same || *ref*—**ne pouvoir s'empêcher de** + *inf* not to be able to help + *ger*, e.g., **je n'ai pu m'empêcher de rire** I could not help laughing

empê·cheur [ãpɛʃœr] **-cheuse** [ʃøz] *mf*—**empêcheur de danser en rond** (coll) wet blanket

empeigne [ãpɛɲ] *f* upper (*of shoe*)

empennage [ãpennaʒ] *m* feathers (*of arrow*); fins, vanes; (aer) empennage

empereur [ãprœr] *m* emperor

emperler [ãperle] *tr* to ornament with pearls; to cover with drops; **la sueur emperlait son front** his forehead was covered with beads of perspiration

empe·sé -sée [ãpəze] *adj* starched; stiff, wooden (*style*)

empeser [ãpəze] §2 *tr* to starch

empes·té -tée [ãpeste] *adj* pestilential; stinking, reeking; depraved

empester [ãpeste] *tr* to stink; to corrupt || *intr* to stink

empêtrer [ãpetre] *tr* to hamper; to involve, entangle || *ref* to become involved, entangled

emphase [ãfaz] *f* overemphasis; bombast, pretentiousness

emphatique [ãfatik] *adj* overemphasized; bombastic, pretentious

emphysème [ãfizem] *m* emphysema

empiècement [ãpjesmã] *m* yoke (*of shirt, blouse, etc.*)

empierrer [ãpjere] *tr* to pave with stones; (rr) to ballast

empiétement [ãpjetmã] *m* encroachment, incursion

empiéter [ãpjete] §10 *intr* to encroach

empiffrer [ãpifre] *tr* (coll) to stuff, fatten || *ref* (coll) to stuff oneself, to guzzle

empiler [ãpile] *tr* to pile up, stack; (slang) to dupe || *ref* to pile up; **se faire empiler** (slang) to be had

empire [ãpir] *m* empire; control, supremacy

empirer [ãpire] *tr* to make worse, to aggravate || *intr* (*aux*: AVOIR or ÊTRE) to grow worse

empirique [ãpirik] *adj* empiric(al) || *m* empiricist; charlatan, quack

emplacement [ãplasmã] *m* emplacement; location, site

emplâtre [ãplatr] *m* patch (*on tire*); (med) plaster; (coll) boob

emplette [ãplet] *f* purchase; **aller faire des emplettes** to go shopping

emplir [ãplir] *tr* & *ref* to fill up

emploi [ãplwa] *m* employment, job; employment, use; (theat) type (*of role*); **double emploi** useless duplication; **emploi du temps** schedule

employé employée [ãplwaje] *mf* employee; clerk

employer [ãplwaje] §47 *tr* to employ; to use || *ref* to be employed; **s'employer à** to try to, to do one's best to

employeur [ãplwajœr] **employeuse** [ãplwajøz] *mf* employer

empocher [ãpoʃe] *tr* (coll) to pocket

empoi·gnant [ãpwaɲã] **-gnante** [ɲãt] *adj* exciting, arresting, thrilling

empoigner [ãpwaɲe] *tr* to grasp; to collar (*a crook*); to grip, move (*an audience*)

empois [ãpwa] *m* starch

empoisonnement [ãpwazɔnmã] *m* poisoning; **avoir des empoisonnements** (coll) to be annoyed

empoisonner [ãpwazɔne] *tr* to poison; to infect (*the air*); to corrupt; (coll) to bother || *intr* to reek || *ref* to be poisoned

empoison·neur [ɑ̃pwazɔnœr] **empoison·neuse** [ɑ̃pwazɔnǿz] *adj* poisoning || *mf* poisoner; corrupter

empoissonner [ɑ̃pwasɔne] *tr* to stock with fish

empor·té -tée [ɑ̃pɔrte] *adj* quick-tempered, impetuous

emportement [ɑ̃pɔrtəmɑ̃] *m* anger, temper

emporte-pièce [ɑ̃pɔrtəpjɛs] *m* (*pl* -**pièces**) punch; **à l'emporte-pièce** trenchant, cutting, biting (*style, words, etc.*)

emporter [ɑ̃pɔrte] *tr* to take away; to carry off; to remove; **à emporter** to take out, to go (*e.g., said of food to take out of the restaurant*); **l'emporter sur** to have the upper hand over || *ref* to be carried away; to lose one's temper; to run away

empo·té -tée [ɑ̃pɔte] *adj* (coll) clumsy || *mf* (coll) butterfingers

empoter [ɑ̃pɔte] *tr* to pot (*a plant*)

empourprer [ɑ̃purpre] *tr* to set aglow || *ref* to turn crimson; to flush

empoussiérer [ɑ̃pusjere] §10 *tr* to cover with dust

empreindre [ɑ̃prɛ̃dr] §50 *tr* to imprint, stamp

empreinte [ɑ̃prɛ̃t] *f* imprint, stamp; **empreinte des roues** wheel tracks; **empreinte digitale** fingerprint; **empreinte du pied** or **empreinte de pas** footprint

empres·sé -sée [ɑ̃prese] *adj* eager

empressement [ɑ̃presmɑ̃] *m* haste, alacrity; eagerness, readiness

empresser [ɑ̃prese] *ref* to hasten; **s'empresser à** to be anxious to; **s'empresser auprès de** to be attentive to, make a fuss over; to press around; **s'empresser de** to hasten to

emprise [ɑ̃priz] *f* expropriation; control, ascendancy

emprisonnement [ɑ̃prizɔnmɑ̃] *m* imprisonment

emprisonner [ɑ̃prizɔne] *tr* to imprison

emprunt [ɑ̃prœ̃] *m* loan; loan word; **d'emprunt** feigned, assumed

emprunter [ɑ̃prœ̃te] *tr* to borrow; to take (*a road, a route*); to take on (*false appearances*); **emprunter q.ch. à** to borrow s.th. from; to get s.th. from

empuantir [ɑ̃pɥɑ̃tir] *tr* to stink up

empyème [ɑ̃pjem] *m* empyema

empyrée [ɑ̃pire] *m* empyrean

é·mu -mue [emy] *adj* moved, touched; tender (*memory*); **ému de** alarmed by

émulation [emylɑsjɔ̃] *f* emulation, rivalry

émule [emyl] *mf* emulator, rival

émulsion [emylsjɔ̃] *f* emulsion

émulsionner [emylsjɔne] *tr* to emulsify

en [ɑ̃] *pron indef & adv* §87 || *prep* in; into; to; to, *e.g.*, **aller en France** to go to France; *e.g.*, **de mal en pis** from bad to worse; at, *e.g.*, **en mer** at sea; *e.g.*, **en guerre** at war; on, *e.g.*, **en congé** on leave; by, *e.g.*, **en chemin**

de fer by rail; of, made of, *e.g.*, **en bois** (made) of wood

enamourer [ɑ̃namure] *ref* to become enamored, to fall in love

encabaner [ɑ̃kabane] *ref* (Canad) to hole up, to dig in (*e.g., for the winter*)

encablure [ɑ̃kablyr] *f* cable's length (*unit of measure*)

encadrement [ɑ̃kadrəmɑ̃] *m* framing; frame; framework; window frame; doorframe; border, edge; staffing; officering (*furnishing with officers*)

encadrer [ɑ̃kadre] *tr* to frame; to staff (*an organization*); to officer (*troops*); to incorporate (*recruits*) into a unit

encadreur [ɑ̃kadrœr] *m* framer (*person*)

encager [ɑ̃kaʒe] §38 *tr* to cage

encaisse [ɑ̃kes] *f* cash on hand, cash balance; **encaisse métallique** bullion

encais·sé -sée [ɑ̃kese] *adj* deeply embanked, sunken

encaissement [ɑ̃kesmɑ̃] *m* cashing (*e.g., of check*); boxing, crating; embankment

encaisser [ɑ̃kese], [ɑ̃kese] *tr* to cash; to box, to crate; to receive (*a blow*); to embank (*a river*); (coll) to put up with || *ref* to be steeply embanked

encaisseur [ɑ̃kesœr] *m* collector; payee; cashier

encan [ɑ̃kɑ̃] *m* auction

encanailler [ɑ̃kanaje] *tr* to debase || *ref* to acquire bad habits; to keep low company

encapuchonner [ɑ̃kapyʃɔne] *tr* to hood

encaquer [ɑ̃kake] *tr* to barrel; to pack (*sardines*); (coll) to pack in like sardines

encart [ɑ̃kar] *m* inset, insert

encarter [ɑ̃karte] *tr* to card (*buttons, pins, etc.*); (bb) to tip in

en-cas [ɑ̃kɑ] *m invar* snack; reserve, emergency supply

encasernement [ɑ̃kazernəmɑ̃] *m*—**encasernement de conscience** thought control, regimentation

encaserner [ɑ̃kazerne] *tr* to quarter, to barrack (*troops*)

encastrement [ɑ̃kastrəmɑ̃] *m* groove; fitting

encastrer [ɑ̃kastre] *tr & ref* to fit

encaustique [ɑ̃kostik] *f* furniture polish; floor wax; encaustic painting

encaustiquer [ɑ̃kostike] *tr* to wax

encaver [ɑ̃kave] *tr* to cellar (*wine*)

enceindre [ɑ̃sɛ̃dr] §50 *tr* to enclose, to encircle

enceinte [ɑ̃sɛ̃t] *adj fem* pregnant || *f* enclosure; walls, ramparts; precinct, compass; (boxing) ring

encens [ɑ̃sɑ̃] *m* incense; flattery

encenser [ɑ̃sɑ̃se] *tr* to incense, perfume with incense; to flatter

encensoir [ɑ̃sɑ̃swar] *m* censer

encéphalite [ɑ̃sefalit] *f* encephalitis

encercler [ɑ̃serkle] *tr* to encircle

enchaînement [ɑ̃ʃenmɑ̃] *m* chaining up; chain, sequence

enchaîner [ɑ̃ʃene], [ɑ̃ʃene], *tr* to chain; to connect || *intr* to go on speaking || *ref* to be connected

enchan·té -tée [ãʃãte] *adj* delighted, pleased

enchantement [ãʃãtmã] *m* enchantment

enchanter [ãʃãte] *tr* to enchant

enchan·teur [ãʃãtœr] **-teresse** [tres] *adj* enchanting, bewitching ‖ *m* enchanter, magician ‖ *f* enchantress

enchâsser [ãʃase] *tr* to enshrine; to insert; to set, chase (*a gem*)

enchère [ãʃɛr] *f* bid, bidding; **folle enchère** bid that cannot be made good; folly

enchérir [ãʃerir] *tr* to bid on; to raise the price of ‖ *intr* to bid; to rise in price; **enchérir sur** to improve on; to outbid

enchérisseur [ãʃerisœr] *m* bidder; **dernier enchérisseur** highest bidder

enchevêtrement [ãʃvetrəmã] *m* entanglement; network; jumble

enchevêtrer [ãʃvetre] *tr* to tangle up; to halter (*a horse*) ‖ *ref* to become complicated or confused

enchifre·né -née [ãʃifrəne] *adj* stuffed-up (*with a cold*)

enclave [ãklav] *f* enclave

enclaver [ãklave] *tr* to enclose; to dovetail

enclencher [ãklãʃe] *tr & ref* to interlock

en·clin [ãklɛ̃] **-cline** [klin] *adj* inclined, prone

encliquetage [ãkliktaʒ] *m* ratchet

encliqueter [ãklikte] §34 *tr* to cog, to mesh

enclitique [ãklitik] *adj & m & f* enclitic

enclore [ãklɔr] §24 (has also 1st & 2d pl pres ind **enclosons, enclosez**) *tr* to close in, to wall in

enclos [ãklo] *m* enclosure, close

enclume [ãklym] *f* anvil; **se trouver entre l'enclume et le marteau** (coll) to be between the devil and the deep blue sea

encoche [ãkɔʃ] *f* notch, nick; slot; thumb index

encocher [ãkɔʃe] *tr* to notch, to nick; to slot

encoignure [ãkɔɲyr] *f* corner; corner piece; corner cabinet

encollage [ãkɔlaʒ] *m* gluing; sizing

encoller [ãkɔle] *tr* to glue; to size

encolure [ãkɔlyr] *f* collar size; neck line; neck and withers (*of horse*); **gagner par une encolure** to win by a neck

encombre [ãkɔ̃br] *m*—**sans encombre** without a hitch, without hindrance

encombrement [ãkɔ̃brəmã] *m* encumbrance, congestion

encombrer [ãkɔ̃bre] *tr* to encumber; to crowd, congest; to block up, to jam; to litter; to load down ‖ *ref*—**s'encombrer de** (coll) to be saddled with

encontre [ãkɔ̃tr] [ãkɔ̃tr]—**à l'encontre de** counter to, against; contrary to

encore [ãkɔr] *adv* still, e.g., **il est encore ici** he is still here; yet, e.g., **encore mieux** better yet; e.g., **pas encore** not yet; only, e.g., **si encore vous m'en aviez parlé!** if only you had told me!; **encore que** although;

encore une fois once more, once again; **en voulez-vous encore?** do you want some more? ‖ *interj* again!, oh no, not again! (*expressing impatience or astonishment*)

encorner [ãkɔrne] *tr* to gore, to toss

encouragement [ãkuraʒmã] *m* encouragement

encourager [ãkuraʒe] §38 *tr* to encourage

encourir [ãkurir] §14 *tr* to incur

encrasser [ãkrase] *tr* to soil, to dirty; to soot up (*a chimney*); to foul (*a gun*) ‖ *ref* to get dirty; to stop up, clog; to soot up

encre [ãkr] *f* ink; **encre de Chine** India ink; **encre sympathique** invisible ink

encrer [ãkre] *tr* to ink

encreur [ãkrœr] *adj* inking (*ribbon, roller*) ‖ *m* ink roller

encrier [ãkrije] *m* inkwell

encroûter [ãkrute] *tr* to encrust; to plaster (*walls*) ‖ *ref* to become encrusted; to get rusty; to become hidebound, prejudiced

encyclique [ãsiklik] *adj & f* encyclical

encyclopédie [ãsiklɔpedi] *f* encyclopedia

encyclopédique [ãsiklɔpedik] *adj* encyclopedic

endauber [ãdobe] *tr* to braise

endémie [ãdemi] *f* endemic

endémique [ãdemik] *adj* endemic

endenter [ãdãte] *tr* to tooth, to cog; to mesh (*gears*); **bien endenté** (coll) with plenty of teeth; (coll) with a hearty appetite

endetter [ãdete] *tr & ref* to run into debt

endêver [ãdeve] *intr*—**faire endêver** to bedevil, to drive wild

endia·blé -blée [ãdjable] *adj* devilish, reckless; full of pep

endiguement [ãdigmã] *m* damming up; embankment

endiguer [ãdige] *tr* to dam up

endimancher [ãdimãʃe] *tr & ref* to put on Sunday clothes, to dress up

endive [ãdiv] *f* endive

endocrine [ãdɔkrin] *adj* endocrine

endoctriner [ãdɔktrine] *tr* to indoctrinate; to win over

endolo·ri -rie [ãdɔlɔri] *adj* painful, sore

endommagement [ãdɔmaʒmã] *m* damage

endommager [ãdɔmaʒe] §38 *tr* to damage ‖ *ref* to suffer damage

endor·mi -mie [ãdɔrmi] *adj* asleep, sleeping; sluggish, apathetic; dormant; numb (*arm or leg*)

endormir [ãdɔrmir] §23 *tr* to put to sleep; to lull, to put off guard ‖ *ref* to go to sleep; to slack off; to let down one's guard

endos [ãdo] *m* endorsement

endosse [ãdos] *f* responsibility

endossement [ãdosmã] *m* endorsement

endosser [ãdose] *tr* to endorse; to take on the responsibility of

endosseur [ãdosœr] *m* endorser

endroit [ãdrwa], [ãdrwa] *m* place, spot; right side (*of cloth*); **à l'endroit**

right side out; **à l'endroit de** with regard to; **le petit endroit** (coll) the toilet; **mettre à l'endroit** to put on right side out

enduire [ãdɥir] §19 *tr* to coat, smear

enduit [ãdɥi] *m* coat, coating

endurance [ãdyrãs] *f* endurance

endu·rant [ãdyrã] **-rante** [rãt] *adj* untiring; meek, patient

endur·ci -cie [ãdyrsi] *adj* hardened; tough, calloused; inveterate

endurcir [ãdyrsir] *tr* to harden; to inure, to toughen ‖ *ref* to harden; **s'endurcir à** to become accustomed to, to become inured to

endurcissement [ãdyrsismã] *m* hardening

endurer [ãdyre] *tr* to endure

énergétique [enerʒetik] *adj* energy, power

énergie [enerʒi] *f* energy

énergique [enerʒik] *adj* energetic

énergumène [energymen] *mf* ranter, wild person, nut

éner·vant [enervã] **-vante** [vãt] *adj* annoying, nerve-racking

énerver [enerve] *tr* to enervate; to unnerve ‖ *ref* to get nervous; to be exasperated

enfance [ãfãs] *f* childhood; infancy; dotage, second childhood; **c'est l'enfance de l'art** (coll) it's child's play; **enfance délinquante** juvenile delinquents; **première enfance** infancy

enfant [ãfã] *adj invar* childish, childlike; **bon enfant** good-natured ‖ *mf* child; **enfant de chœur** altar boy; **enfant de la balle** child who follows in his father's footsteps; **enfant en bas âge** infant; **enfant terrible** (fig) stormy petrel; **enfant trouvé** foundling; **mon enfant!** my boy!; **petit enfant** infant

enfantement [ãfãtmã] *m* childbirth

enfanter [ãfãte] *tr* to give birth to

enfantillage [ãfãtijaʒ] *m* childishness

enfan·tin [ãfãtɛ̃] **-tine** [tin] *adj* childish, infantile

enfari·né -née [ãfarine] *adj* smeared with flour

enfer [ãfer] *m* hell

enfermer [ãferme] *tr* to enclose; to shut up, to lock up ‖ *ref* to shut oneself in; to closet oneself

enferrer [ãfere] *tr* to pierce, to run through ‖ *ref* to run oneself through with a sword; to bite (*said of fish*); (fig) to be caught in one's own trap

enfiévrer [ãfjevre] §10 *tr* to inflame, to make feverish

enfilade [ãfilad] *f* row, string, series; (mil) enfilade; **en enfilade** connecting, e.g., **chambres en enfilade** connecting rooms

enfile-aiguille [ãfilegɥij] *m invar* threader, needle threader

enfiler [ãfile] *tr* to pierce; to thread (*a needle*); to string (*beads*); to start down (*a street*); (coll) to put on (*clothes*)

enfin [ãfɛ̃] *adv* finally, at last; in short; after all, anyway

enflam·mé -mée [ãflɑme], [ãflame] *adj* flaming; bright red; inflamed

enflammer [ãflɑme], [ãflame] *tr* to inflame ‖ *ref* to be inflamed; to flare up

enfler [ãfle] *tr* to swell; to puff up or out; to exaggerate ‖ *intr & ref* to swell, to puff up

enflure [ãflyr] *f* swelling; (fig) exaggeration

enfon·cé -cée [ãfɔ̃se] *adj* sunken, deep; deep-set; broken (*ribs*); (coll) taken, had (*bested*)

enfoncement [ãfɔ̃smã] *m* driving in; breaking open; hollow, recess

enfoncer [ãfɔ̃se] §51 *tr* to drive in; to push in, break open; (coll) to get the better of ‖ *intr* to sink to the bottom ‖ *ref* to sink, plunge; to give way; to disappear; to penetrate (*said of root, bullet, etc.*)

enforcir [ãforsir] *tr* to reinforce ‖ *intr & ref* to become stronger; to grow

enfouir [ãfwir] *tr* to bury; to hide ‖ *ref* to burrow; to bury oneself (*e.g., in an out-of-the-way locality*)

enfourcher [ãfurʃe] *tr* to stick a pitchfork into; to mount, straddle

enfourchure [ãfurʃyr] *f* crotch

enfourner [ãfurne] *tr* to put in the oven; (coll) to gobble down

enfreindre [ãfrɛ̃dr] §50 *tr* to violate, break (*e.g., a law*)

enfuir [ãfɥir] §31 *ref* to run away; to escape; to elope

enfu·mé -mée [ãfyme] *adj* blackened; smoky (*color*)

enfumer [ãfyme] *tr* to smoke up, blacken; to smoke out

enfutailler [ãfytaje] *tr* to cask, to barrel

enga·gé -gée [ãgaʒe] *adj* committed; hocked ‖ *m* (mil) enlisted man

engagement [ãgaʒmã] *m* engagement; hocking; obligation; promise; (mil) enlistment; (mil) engagement

engager [ãgaʒe] §38 *tr* to engage; to hock; to enlist, urge, involve; to open, to begin (*negotiations, the conversation, etc.*) ‖ *ref* to commit oneself; to promise, to pledge; to enter a contest; to become engaged to be married; (mil) to enlist; **s'engager dans** to begin (*battle; a conversation*); to plunge into; to fit into

engainer [ãgene], [ãgene] *tr* to sheathe, to envelop

engazonner [ãgazɔne] *tr* to sod

engeance [ãʒɑ̃s] *f* (pej) breed, brood

engelure [ãʒlyr] *f* chilblain

engendrer [ãʒɑ̃dre] *tr* to engender

engin [ãʒɛ̃] *m* device; **engin balistique** ballistic missile; **engin guidé** or **engin spécial** guided missile; **engins de pêche** fishing tackle

englober [ãglɔbe] *tr* to put together, to unite; to embrace, to comprise

engloutir [ãglutir] *tr* to gobble down; to swallow up, to engulf

engluer [ãglye] *tr* to lime (*a trap*); to catch; to take in, hoodwink ‖ *ref* to be caught; to fall into a trap, to be taken in

engommer [ãgɔme] *tr* to gum

engon·cé -cée [ãgɔ̃se] *adj* awkward, stiff (*air*)

engoncer [ãgɔ̃se] §51 *tr* to bundle up; to cramp

engorgement [ãgɔrʒəmã] *m* obstruction, blocking

engorger [ãgɔrʒe] §38 *tr* to obstruct, block

engouement [ãgumã] *m* infatuation; (pathol) obstruction

engouer [ãgwe] *tr* to obstruct ‖ *ref*—**s'engouer de** (coll) to be infatuated with, to be wild about

engouffrer [ãgufre] *tr* to engulf; to gobble up; to eat up (*e.g., a fortune*) ‖ *ref* to be swallowed up; to dash; to surge

engour·di -die [ãgurdi] *adj* numb

engourdir [ãgurdir] *tr* to numb; to dull ‖ *ref* to grow numb

engourdissement [ãgurdismã] *m* numbness; dullness, torpidity

engrais [ãgrɛ] *m* fertilizer; manure; fodder; **mettre à l'engrais** to fatten

engraisser [ãgrese], [ãgrese] *tr* to fatten; to fertilize; to enrich ‖ *intr* (*aux:* AVOIR *or* ÊTRE) to fatten up, to get fat ‖ *ref* to become fat; to become rich

engranger [ãgrãʒe] §38 *tr* to garner; to get in, to put in the barn

engraver [ãgrave] *tr, intr, & ref* to silt up; (naut) to run aground

engrenage [ãgrənaʒ] *m* gear; gearing; (coll) mesh, toils; **engrenage à vis sans fin** worm gear; **engrenages de distribution** timing gears

engrener [ãgrəne] §2 *tr* to feed (*a hopper, a thresher; a fowl*); to put into gear, to mesh ‖ *intr & ref* (mach) to mesh, engage

engrenure [ãgrənyr] *f* engaging (*of toothed wheels*)

engrumeler [ãgrymle] §34 *tr & ref* to clot, to curdle

engueuler [ãgœle] *tr* (slang) to bawl out

enguirlander [ãgirlãde] *tr* to garland; to adorn; (coll) to bawl out

enhardir [ãardir] *tr* to embolden ‖ *ref* —**s'enhardir à** to be so bold as to

énième [enjɛm] *adj* nth

énigmatique [enigmatik] *adj* enigmatic(al), puzzling

énigme [enigm] *f* enigma, riddle, puzzle

enivrement [ãnivrəmã] *m* intoxication

enivrer [ãnivre] *tr* to intoxicate; to elate ‖ *ref* to get drunk

enjambée [ãʒãbe] *f* stride

enjambement [ãʒãbmã] *m* enjambment

enjamber [ãʒãbe] *tr* to stride over, to span ‖ *intr* to stride along; to run on (*said of line of poetry*); **enjamber sur** to project over; to encroach on

en·jeu [ãʒø] *m* (*pl* **-jeux**) stake, bet

enjoindre [ãʒwɛ̃dr] §35 *tr* to enjoin

enjôler [ãʒole] *tr* (coll) to cajole

enjô·leur [ãʒolœr] **-leuse** [løz] *adj* cajoling ‖ *mf* cajoler, wheedler

enjoliver [ãʒolive] *tr* to embellish

enjoli·veur [ãʒolivœr] **-veuse** [vøz] *mf* embellisher ‖ *m* hubcap

en-joué -jouée [ãʒwe] *adj* sprightly

enjouement [ãʒumã] *m* playfulness

enlacement [ãlasmã] *m* embrace, hug; lacing, interweaving

enlacer [ãlase] §51 *tr & ref* to enlace, to entwine; to embrace

enlaidir [ãledir], [ãledir] *tr* to disfigure ‖ *intr* to grow ugly ‖ *ref* to disfigure oneself

enlèvement [ãlɛvmã] *m* removal; kidnaping, abduction

enlever [ãlve] §2 *tr* to take away, take off, remove; to carry off; to lift, lift up; to send up (*a balloon*); (fig) to carry away (*an audience*); **enlever le couvert** to clear the table; **enlever q.ch. à** to take s.th. from, remove s.th. from ‖ *ref* to come off, wear off; to rise; to boil over; (fig) to flare up

enliasser [ãljase] *tr* to tie up in bundles

enliser [ãlize] *ref* to get stuck

enluminer [ãlymine] *tr* to illuminate; to make colorful

enluminure [ãlyminyr] *f* illuminated drawing; (painting) illumination

enneiger [ãneʒe], [ãneʒe] §38 *tr* to cover with snow

enne·mi -mie [enmi] *adj* hostile, inimical; enemy, e.g., **en pays ennemi** in enemy country ‖ *mf* enemy

ennoblir [ãnɔblir] *tr* to ennoble

ennui [ãnɥi] *m* ennui, boredom; nuisance, bother; worry, trouble

ennuyer [ãnɥije] §27 *tr* to bore; to bother ‖ *ref* to be bored

énon·cé -cée [enɔ̃se] *m* statement; wording (*of a document*); terms (*of a theorem*)

énoncer [enɔ̃se] §51 *tr* to state, enunciate; to utter

énorgueillir [ãnɔrgœjir] *tr* to make proud or boastful ‖ *ref*—**s'enorgueillir de** to pride oneself on, to boast of, to glory in

énorme [enɔrm] *adj* enormous; (coll) shocking; (coll) outrageous

énormément [enɔrmemã] *adv* enormously, tremendously; (coll) awfully; **énormément de** lots of

énormité [enɔrmite] *f* enormity; (coll) nonsense; (coll) blunder

enquérir [ãkerir] §3 *ref*—**s'enquérir de** to ask or inquire about

enquête [ãkɛt] *f* investigation, inquiry; inquest; **enquête par sondage** public-opinion poll

enquêter [ãkete] *intr* to conduct an investigation

enraciner [ãrasine] *tr* to root; to instill ‖ *ref* to take root

enra·gé -gée [ãraʒe] *adj* enraged, hotheaded; mad (*dog*); rabid (*communist*); out-and-out (*socialist*); inveterate (*gambler*); enthusiastic (*sportsman*) ‖ *mf* enthusiast, fan; fanatic, fiend

enrager [ãraʒe] §38 *intr* to be mad; **faire enrager** to enrage

enrayer [ãreje], [ãreje] §49 *tr* to put

spokes to; to jam, lock; to stem, halt || *ref* to jam

enrayure [ãrejyr] *f* (mach) skid, shoe

enrégimenter [ãrezimãte] *tr* to regiment

enregistrement [ãrǝzistrǝmã] *m* recording; registration; transcription; checking (*of baggage*); **enregistrement sur bande** or **sur ruban** tape recording

enregistrer [ãrǝzistre] *tr* to record; to register; to transcribe; to check (*baggage*)

enregis·treur [ãrǝzistrœr] **-treuse** [trøz] *adj* recording || *mf* recorder

enrhumer [ãryme] *tr* to give a cold to || *ref* to catch cold

enrichir [ãri/ir] *tr* to enrich || *ref* to become rich

enrichissement [ãri/ismã] *m* enrichment

enrober [ãrobe] *tr* to coat; to wrap

enrôlement [ãrolmã] *m* enrollment; enlistment

enrôler [ãrole] *tr & ref* to enroll, enlist

enrouement [ãrumã] *m* hoarseness, huskiness

enrouer [ãrwe] *tr* to make hoarse || *ref* to become hoarse

enrouiller [ãruje] *tr & ref* to rust

enroulement [ãrulmã] *m* coil; (archit) volute; (elec) winding

enrouler [ãrule] *tr & ref* to wind, coil; to roll up

ensabler [ãsable] *tr & ref* to run aground on the sand

ensacher [ãsa/e] *tr* to bag

ensanglanter [ãsãglãte] *tr* to stain with blood; to steep in blood

ensel·gnant [ãsɛɲã] **-gnante** [ɲãt] *adj* teaching || *mf* teacher

enseigne [ãsɛɲ] *m* (nav) ensign || *f* flag, ensign; sign (*on tavern, store*)

enseignement [ãsɛɲǝmã] *m* teaching, instruction, education; **enseignement confessionnel** parochial school education; **enseignement libre** or **privé** private-school education; **enseignement supérieur** higher education

enseigner [ãsɛɲe] *tr* to teach; to show; **enseigner q.ch. à qn** to teach s.o. s.th. || *intr* to teach; **enseigner à qn à + *inf*** to teach s.o. to **+ *inf***

ensemble [ãsãbl] *m* ensemble; **avec ensemble** in harmony, with one mind; **dans son ensemble** as a whole; **d'ensemble** general, comprehensive, overall; **grand ensemble** housing development || *adv* together

ensemencement [ãsmãsmã] *m* sowing

ensemencer [ãsmãse] §51 *tr* to seed, sow; to culture (*microorganisms*)

enserrer [ãsere] *tr* to enclose; to squeeze, clasp

ensevelir [ãsǝvlir] *tr* to bury; to shroud

ensevelissement [ãsǝvlismã] *m* burial; shrouding

ensilage [ãsilaʒ] *m* storing in a pit or silo

ensiler [ãsile] *tr* to ensilage

ensoleiller [ãsɔleje] *tr* to make sunny, to brighten

ensommeil·lé -lée [ãsɔmeje], [ãsɔmeje] *adj* drowsy

ensorceler [ãsɔrsǝle] §34 *tr* to bewitch, to enchant

ensorce·leur [ãsɔrsǝlœr] **-leuse** [løz] *adj* bewitching, enchanting || *m* sorcerer, wizard; charmer || *f* witch; enchantress

ensorcellement [ãsɔrsɛlmã] *m* sorcery, enchantment; spell, charm

ensuite [ãsɥit] *adv* then, next; afterwards, after; **ensuite?** what then?, what next?; anything else?

ensuivre [ãsɥivr] §67 (used only in 3d *sg & pl*) *ref* to ensue; **il s'ensuit que . . .** it follows that . . .

entacher [ãta/e] *tr* to blemish; **entaché de nullité** null and void

entaille [ãtaj] *f* notch, nick; gash

entailler [ãtaje] *tr* to notch, to nick; to gash

entame [ãtam] *f* top slice, first slice, end slice

entamer [ãtame] *tr* to cut the first slice of; to begin; to engage in, to start (*a conversation*); to make a break in (*the skin; a battle line*); to cast a slur upon; to open (*a bottle; negotiations; a card suit*); (coll) to make a dent in (*e.g., one's savings*)

entartrer [ãtartre] *tr & ref* to scale, fur

entassement [ãtasmã] *m* piling up

entasser [ãtase] *tr & ref* to pile up, to accumulate; to crowd

ente [ãt] *f* paintbrush handle; (hort) graft, scion

entendement [ãtãdmã] *m* understanding; consciousness

entendre [ãtãdr] *tr* to hear; to understand; to mean; **entendre chanter** to hear (*s.o.*) singing, to hear (*s.o.*) sing; to hear (*s.th.*) sung; **entendre dire que** to hear that; **entendre parler de** to hear of or about; **entendre raison** to listen to reason; **il entend que je le fasse** he expects me to do it, he insists that I do it || *intr* to hear || *ref* to understand one another; to get along; **s'entendre à** to be skilled in, to know

enten·du -due [ãtãdy] *adj* agreed; **bien entendu** of course; **c'est entendu!** all right!

enténébrer [ãtenebre] §10 *tr* to plunge into darkness

entente [ãtãt] *f* understanding; agreement, pact; **à double entente** with a double meaning, e.g., **expression à double entente** expression with a double meaning, double entendre; **entente industrielle** (com) combine

enter [ãte] *tr* to graft; to splice (*pieces of wood*)

entérinement [ãterinmã] *m* ratification

entériner [ãterine] *tr* to ratify

enterrement [ãtɛrmã] *m* burial, interment; funeral procession; funeral; funeral expenses; pigeonholing

enterrer [ãtere] *tr* to bury, inter; to pigeonhole, sidetrack; (coll) to attend the funeral services of; **enterrer sa vie de garçon** (coll) to give a farewell stag party ‖ *ref* to bury oneself; (mil) to dig oneself in

en-tête [ãtɛt] *m* (*pl* **-têtes**) headline; chapter heading; letterhead

entê·té -tée [ãtete] *adj* obstinate, stubborn

entêtement [ãtɛtmã] *m* obstinacy, stubbornness

entêter [ãtete] *tr* to give a headache to; to make giddy ‖ *intr* to go to one's head ‖ *ref* to persist

enthousiasme [ãtuzjasm] *m* enthusiasm

enthousiasmer [ãtuzjasme] *tr & ref* to enthuse

enthousiaste [ãtuzjast] *adj* enthusiastic ‖ *mf* enthusiast, fan, buff

entichement [ãti/mã] *m* infatuation

enticher [ãti/e] *tr* to infatuate ‖ *ref* to become infatuated

en·tier [ãtje] **-tière** [tjɛr] *adj* entire, whole, full; obstinate ‖ *m* whole, entirety; **en entier** in full

entièrement [ãtjɛrmã] *adv* entirely

entité [ãtite] *f* entity, being

entoiler [ãtwale] *tr* to put a backing on, to mount

entomologie [ãtɔmɔlɔʒi] *f* entomology

entonner [ãtɔne] *tr* to barrel; to intone, start off (*a song*); to sing (*s.o.'s praises*) ‖ *ref* to rush up and down (*said of wind*)

entonnoir [ãtɔnwar] *m* funnel; shell hole

entorse [ãtɔrs] *f* sprain; infringement (*of a rule*); stretching (*of the truth*)

entortiller [ãtɔrtije] *tr & ref* to twist

entour [ãtur] *m*—**à l'entour** in the vicinity; **à l'entour de** around; **entours** surroundings

entourage [ãturaʒ] *m* setting, surroundings; entourage; (mach) casing

entourer [ãture] *tr* to surround

entourloupette [ãturlupɛt] *f* (coll) double cross; **faire une entourloupette à** (coll) to double-cross

entournure [ãturnyr] *f* armhole; **gêné dans les entournures** ill at ease

entraccuser [ãtrakyze] *ref* to accuse one another

entracte [ãtrakt] *m* intermission

entraide [ãtrɛd] *f* mutual assistance

entrailles [ãtraj] *fpl* entrails; tenderness, pity; bowels (*of the earth*); **sans entrailles** (fig) heartless

entr'aimer [ãtreme], [ãtrɛme] *ref* to love each other

entrain [ãtrɛ̃] *m* spirit, gusto, pep

entraînement [ãtrɛnmã] *m* training; enthusiasm

entraîner [ãtrene] *tr* to carry along or away, to entrain; to involve, entail; to pull (*railroad cars*); to work (*a pump*); to train (*an athlete*) ‖ *ref* (sports) to train

entraîneur [ãtrenœr] *m* trainer, coach

entraîneuse [ãtrenøz] *f* B-girl

entr'apercevoir [ãtrapɛrsəvwar] §59 *tr* to catch a glimpse of

entrave [ãtrav] *f* shackle; hindrance

entra·vé -vée [ãtrave] *adj* impeded, hampered; checked (*vowel*)

entraver [ãtrave] *tr* to shackle; to hinder, impede

entre [ãtr] *prep* between; among; in or into, e.g., **entre les mains de** in or into the hands of; **d'entre** among; from among, out of; of, e.g., **l'un d'entre eux** one of them; **entre deux eaux** under the surface of the water

entrebâillement [ãtrəbajmã] *m* chink, slit, crack

entrebâiller [ãtrəbaje] *tr* to leave ajar

entrechat [ãtrə/a] *m* caper; entrechat

entrechoquer [ãtrə/ɔke] *tr* to bump together ‖ *ref* to clash

entrecôte [ãtrəkot] *f* sirloin steak, loin of beef; top chuck roast

entrecouper [ãtrəkupe] *tr* to interrupt; to intersect ‖ *ref* to intersect

entrecroiser [ãtrəkrwaze] *tr & ref* to interlace; to intersect

entre-deux [ãtrədø] *m invar* space between; interval; partition; (sports) jump ball

entre-deux-guerres [ãtrədøgɛr] *m & f invar* period between the wars (*the First and Second World War*)

entrée [ãtre] *f* entrance, entry; admission, admittance; beginning; customs duty; (culin) entree; **avoir ses entrées à, chez,** or **dans** to have the entree into; **d'entrée** at the start, right off; **entrée de serrure** keyhole; **entrée d'un chapeau** hat size; **entrée interdite** (public sign) keep out, no admittance

entrefaites [ãtrəfɛt] *fpl*—**sur ces entrefaites** meanwhile

entrefer [ãtrəfɛr] *m* (elec) air gap

entrefermer [ãtrəfɛrme] *tr* to close part way

entrefilet [ãtrəfilɛ] *m* short feature, special item

entregent [ãtrəʒã] *m* tact, diplomacy, savoir-faire; **avoir de l'entregent** to be a good mixer

entrejambe [ãtrəʒãb] *m* crotch

entrelacer [ãtrəlase] §51 *tr & ref* to interlace, to entwine, intertwine

entrelarder [ãtrəlarde] *tr* to lard; to interlard

entre-ligne [ãtrəliɲ] *m* (*pl* **-lignes**) space (*between the lines*); insertion (*written between the lines*); **à l'entre-ligne** double-spaced

entremêler [ãtrəmele] *tr* to mix, mingle; to intersperse

entremets [ãtrəmɛ] *m* side dish; dessert

entremet·teur [ãtrəmetœr] **entremet·teuse** [ãtrəmetøz] *mf* go-between ‖ *m* (pej) pimp

entremettre [ãtrəmetr] §42 *ref* to intervene, to intercede

entremise [ãtrəmiz] *f* intervention; **par l'entremise de** through the medium of

entre-nuire [ãtrənɥir] §19 (*pp* **nui**) *ref* (with *dat* of *reflex pron*) to hurt each other

entrepont [ãtrəpɔ̃] *m* (naut) between-decks

entreposer [ãtrəpoze] *tr* to place in a warehouse, to store; to bond

entrepôt [ãtrəpo] *m* warehouse; **en entrepôt** in bond

entrepre·nant [ãtrəprənã] **-nante** [nãt]

adj enterprising; bold, audacious; gallant

entreprendre [ătrəprădr] §56 *tr* to undertake; to contract for; to enter upon; (coll) to try to win over ‖ *intr*—**entreprendre sur** to encroach upon

entre•pre•neur [ătrəprənœr] **-neuse** [nøz] *mf* contractor; **entrepreneur de camionnage** trucker; **entrepreneur de pompes funèbres** undertaker

entreprise [ătrəpriz] *f* undertaking; business, firm; contract

entrer [ătre] *tr* to introduce, bring in ‖ *intr* (*aux:* ÊTRE) to enter; to go in, to come in; **entrer à, dans,** or **en** to enter; to enter into; to begin; **entrer pour** to enter into, to be an ingredient of

entre-rail [ătrəraj] *m* (rr) gauge

entre-regarder [ătrərəgarde] *ref* to exchange glances

entresol [ătrəsɔl] *m* mezzanine

entre-temps [ătrətă] *m invar* interval; **dans l'entre-temps** in the meantime ‖ *adv* meanwhile

entreteneur [ătrətnœr] *m* keeper of a mistress

entretenir [ătrətnir] §72 *tr* to maintain, keep up; to carry on (*a conversation*); to keep (*a mistress*); to entertain, harbor ‖ *ref* to converse, talk

entrete•nu -nue [ătrətny] *adj* kept (*woman*); continuous, undamped (*waves*)

entretien [ătrətjĕ] *m* maintenance, upkeep; support (*of family, army, etc.*); interview

entretoise [ătrətwaz] *f* strut, brace, crosspiece

entre-tuer [ătrətɥe] *ref* to kill each other, to fight to the death

entre-voie [ătrəvwa] *f* (rr) gauge

entrevoir [ătrəvwar] §75 *tr* to glimpse; to foresee

entre-vu -vue [ătrəvy] *adj* half-seen; vaguely foreseen ‖ *f* interview

entrouvrir [ătruvrir] §65 *tr & ref* to open part way

enture [ătyr] *f* splice (*of pieces of wood*)

énumérer [enymere] §10 *tr* to enumerate

envahir [ăvair] *tr* to invade

envahissement [ăvaismă] *m* invasion

envaser [ăvaze] *tr* to fill with mud; to stick in the mud

enveloppe [ăvlɔp] *f* envelope; **enveloppe à fenêtre** window envelope

envelopper [ăvlɔpe] *tr* to envelop; to wrap up

envenimer [ăvnime] *tr* to inflame, make sore; (fig) to envenom, embitter

envergure [ăvergyr] *f* span; wingspread; spread of sail; span, scope

envers [ăver] *m* wrong side, reverse, back; **à l'envers** inside out; upside down; back to front; topsy-turvy; **mettre à l'envers** to put on backwards ‖ *prep* towards; with regard to; **envers et contre tous** in spite of everyone else

envi [ăvi]—**à l'envi** vying with each other; **à l'envi de** vying with

enviable [ăvjabl] *adj* enviable

envie [ăvi] *f* desire, longing; envy; birthmark; hangnail; **avoir envie de** to feel like, to have a notion to

envier [ăvje] *tr* to envy; to desire; **envier q.ch. à qn** to begrudge s.o. s.th.

en•vieux [ăvjø] **-vieuse** [vjøz] *adj* envious ‖ *mf* envious person

environ [ăvirŏ] *m* outlying section; **aux environs de** in the vicinity of; around, about; **environs** surroundings ‖ *adv* about, approximately

environnement [ăvirɔnmă] *m* environment

environner [ăvirɔne] *tr* to surround

envisager [ăvizaʒe] §38 *tr* to envisage ‖ *intr*—**envisager de** + *inf* to plan to + *inf*, to expect to + *inf*

envoi [ăvwa] *m* consignment; remittance; envoy (*of ballad*)

envol [ăvɔl] *m* flight; (aer) takeoff

envolée [ăvɔle] *f* flight; (aer) takeoff

envoler [ăvɔle] *ref* to fly (*said of time*); (aer) to take off

envoûtement [ăvutmă] *m* spell, voodoo

envoûter [ăvute] *tr* to cast a spell on

envoyé envoyée [ăvwaje] *mf* envoy; messenger; **envoyé spécial** special correspondent (*of newspaper*)

envoyer [ăvwaje] §26 *tr* to send; to send out; to throw (*e.g., a stone*); to give (*a kick*); **envoyer promener** or **envoyer qn promener** to send (*s.o.*) about his business; **envoyer qn** + *inf* to send s.o. to + *inf*; **envoyer qn chercher q.ch.** or **qn** to send s.o. for s.th. or s.o. ‖ *intr*—**envoyer chercher** to send for (*s.o. or s.th.*) ‖ *ref* (coll) to gulp down

enzyme [ăzim] *m & f* enzyme

épa•gneul -gneule [epanœl] *mf* spaniel

épais épaisse [epe] [epes] *adj* thick ‖ **épais** *adv* thickly

épaisseur [epesœr] *f* thickness

épaissir [epesir] *tr, intr, & ref* to thicken

épanchement [epăʃmă] *m* outpouring, effusion; (pathol) discharge

épancher [epă/e] *tr* to pour out; to unburden (*e.g., one's feelings*) ‖ *ref* to pour out; **s'épancher auprès de** to unbosom oneself to; **s'épancher de q.ch.** to get s.th. off one's chest

épandre [epădr] *tr & ref* to spread; to scatter

épanouir [epanwir] *tr* to make (*flowers*) bloom; to light up (*the face*) ‖ *ref* to bloom; to beam (*said of face*)

épanouissement [epanwismă] *m* blossoming; brightening up (*of a face*)

épar•gnant -gnante [eparnă] [năt] *adj* thrifty ‖ *m* depositor

épargne [eparn] *f* saving, thrift; **épargnes** savings

épargner [eparne] *tr* to save; to spare; to husband

éparpillement [eparpijmă] *m* scattering

éparpiller [eparpije] *tr* to scatter; to dissipate (*e.g., one's efforts*)

épars [epar] **éparse** [epars] *adj* scattered, sparse; in disorder

épa·tant [epatã] **-tante** [tãt] *adj* (coll) wonderful, terrific

épate [epat] *f*—**faire de l'épate** (slang) to make a big show, to splurge

épa·té -tée [epate] *adj* flattened; (slang) flabbergasted

épater [epate] *tr* (coll) to shock, amaze

épaulard [epolar] *m* killer whale

épaule [epol] *f* shoulder; **donner un coup d'épaule à qn** (coll) to give s.o. a hand; **par-dessus l'épaule** (fig) contemptuously

épaulé-jeté [epoleʒte] *m* clean and jerk (*in weight lifting*)

épaulement [epolmã] *m* breastworks

épauler [epole] *tr* to back, support ‖ *intr* to take aim

épaulette [epolet] *f* epaulet

épave [epav] *f* wreck; derelict, stray; **épaves** wreckage

épée [epe] *f* sword

épéiste [epeist] *m* swordsman

épeler [eple] §34 *tr* to spell, to spell out; to read letter by letter

épellation [epelɑsjɔ̃] *f* spelling

éper·du -due [eperdy] *adj* bewildered; desperate (*resistance*); mad (*with pain*); wild (*with joy*)

éperdument [eperdymã] *adv* desperately, madly, wildly

éperlan [eperlã] *m* smelt

éperon [eprɔ̃] *m* spur

éperonner [eprɔne] *tr* to spur

épervier [epervje] *m* sparrow hawk; fish net

éphémère [efemer] *adj* ephemeral ‖ *m* mayfly

épi [epi] *m* ear, cob, spike; cowlick

épice [epis] *f* spice

épicéa [episea] *m* Norway spruce

épicer [epise] §51 *tr* to spice

épicerie [episri] *f* grocery store; canned goods

épi·cier [episje] **-cière** [sjer] *mf* grocer

épidémie [epidemi] *f* epidemic

épidémiologie [epidemjɔlɔʒi] *f* epidemiology

épidémique [epidemik] *adj* epidemic; contagious (*e.g.*, *laughter*)

épiderme [epiderm] *m* epidermis

épier [epje] *tr* to spy upon; to be on the lookout for ‖ *intr* to ear, to head

épieu [epjø] *m* (*pl* épieux) pike

épiglotte [epiglɔt] *f* epiglottis

épigramme [epigram] *f* epigram

épigraphe [epigraf] *f* epigraph

épilepsie [epilɛpsi] *f* epilepsy

épileptique [epilɛptik] *adj* & *mf* epileptic

épiler [epile] *tr* to pluck (*one's eyebrows*); to remove hair from

épilogue [epilɔg] *m* epilogue

épiloguer [epilɔge] *intr* to split hairs; **épiloguer sur** to carp at

épinard [epinar] *m* spinach; **des épinards** spinach (*leaves used as food*)

épine [epin] *f* thorn; **épine dorsale** backbone; **épine noire** blackthorn; **être sur les épines** to be on pins and needles

épinette [epinɛt] *f* spinet; hencoop

épi·neux [epinø] **-neuse** [nøz] *adj* thorny; ticklish (*question*)

épingle [epɛ̃gl] *f* pin; **épingle à chapeau** hatpin; **épingle à cheveux** hairpin; **épingle à linge** clothespin; **épingle anglaise** safety pin; **épingle dans une meule de foin** needle in a haystack; **épingle de cravate** stickpin; **épingle de sûreté** safety pin; **monter en épingle** (coll) to make much of; **tiré à quatre épingles** (coll) spic-and-span; (coll) all dolled up; **tirer son épingle du jeu** (coll) to get out by the skin of one's teeth

épingler [epɛ̃gle] *tr* to pin; (coll) to pin down (*s.o.*)

épinière [epinjer] *adj fem* spinal (*cord*)

Épiphanie [epifani] *f* Epiphany, Twelfth-night

épique [epik] *adj* epic

épisco·pal -pale [episkɔpal] (*pl* -**paux** [po]) *adj* episcopal; Episcopalian ‖ *mf* Episcopalian

épisode [epizɔd] *m* episode

épisodique [epizɔdik] *adj* episodic

épisser [epise] *tr* to splice

épissure [episyr] *f* splice

épistémologie [epistemɔlɔʒi] *f* epistemology

épitaphe [epitaf] *f* epitaph

épithète [epitɛt] *f* epithet

épitoge [epitɔʒ] *f* shoulder band (*worn by French lawyers and holders of French degrees*)

épitomé [epitome] *m* epitome

épître [epitr] *f* epistle

éplo·ré -rée [eplɔre] *adj* in tears

épluchage [eplyʃaʒ] *m* peeling; examination

éplucher [eplyʃe] *tr* to peel, pare; to clean, pick; (fig) to find fault with, to pick holes in

éplu·cheur [eplyʃœr] **-cheuse** [ʃøz] *mf* (coll) faultfinder ‖ *m* potato peeler, orange peeler, peeling knife ‖ *f*—**éplucheuse électrique** electric peeler

épluchure [eplyʃyr] *f* peelings; **épluchure de maïs** cornhusks

épointer [epwɛ̃te] *tr* to dull the point of

éponge [epɔ̃ʒ] *f* sponge

éponger [epɔ̃ʒe] §38 *tr* to sponge off, to mop up

épopée [epɔpe] *f* epic

époque [epɔk] *f* epoch; time; period; **à l'époque de** at the time of; **d'époque** a real antique; **faire époque** to be epoch-making

épouiller [epuje] *tr* to delouse

époumoner [epumɔne] *ref* to shout oneself out of breath

épousailles [epuzaj] *fpl* wedding

épouser [epuze] *tr* to marry; to espouse; **épouser la forme de** to take the exact shape of

époussetage [epustaʒ] *m* dusting

épousseter [epuste] §34 *tr* to dust

époussette [epuset] *f* duster

épouvantable [epuvãtabl] *adj* frightful, terrible

épouvantail [epuvãtaj] *m* scarecrow

épouvante [epuvãt] *f* fright, terror

épouvanter [epuvɑ̃te] *tr* to frighten, terrify

époux [epu] **épouse** [epuz] *mf* spouse || *m* husband; **les époux** husband and wife || *f* wife

éprendre [eprɑ̃dr] §56 *ref*—**s'éprendre de** to fall in love with; to hold fast to (*liberty, justice, etc.*)

épreuve [eprœv] *f* proof, test, trial; ordeal; examination; (phot, typ) proof

épris [epri] **éprise** [epriz] *adj* infatuated; **épris de** in love with

éprouver [epruve] *tr* to prove, test, try; to experience, to feel; to put to the test

éprouvette [epruvet] *f* test tube; specimen; (med) probe

epsomite [epsɔmit] *f* Epsom salts

épucer [epyse] §51 *tr* to clean of fleas, to delouse

épui·sé -sée [epɥize] *adj* exhausted, tired out; sold out

épuisement [epɥizmɑ̃] *m* exhaustion; diminution, draining off

épuiser [epɥize] *tr* to exhaust, use up; to wear out; to tire out || *ref* to run out; to wear out

épuration [epyrɑsjɔ̃] *f* purification; refining (*e.g., of petroleum*); (pol) purge

épure [epyr] *f* working drawing

épurement [epyrmɑ̃] *m* expurgation

épurer [epyre] *tr* to purify; to expurgate; to weed out, to purge

équanimité [ekwanimite] *f* equanimity

équarrir [ekarir] *tr* to cut up, quarter (*an animal*); to square off

équateur [ekwatœr] *m* equator; **l'Équateur** Ecuador

équation [ekwɑsjɔ̃] *f* equation

équato·rial -riale [ekwatɔrjal] *adj* (*pl* **-riaux** [rjo]) equatorial

équerrage [ekeraʒ] *m* bevel; beveling

équerre [eker] *f* square (*L- or T-shaped instrument*); **d'équerre** square, true; **mettre d'équerre** to square, to true

équerrer [ekere] *tr* to bevel

équestre [ekestr] *adj* equestrian

équilaté·ral -rale [ekɥilateral] *adj* (*pl* **-raux** [ro]) equilateral

équilibre [ekilibr] *m* equilibrium, balance; equipoise

équilibrer [ekilibre] *tr* & *ref* to balance

équilibriste [ekilibrist] *mf* balancer, ropedancer

équinoxe [ekinɔks] *m* equinox

équipage [ekipaʒ] *m* crew; retinue, suite; attire

équipe [ekip] *f* team; crew; gang, work party; (naut) train of boats; **équipe de jour** day shift; **équipe de nuit** night shift; **équipe de secours** rescue squad

équipée [ekipe] *f* escapade, lark; crazy project

équipement [ekipmɑ̃] *m* equipment

équiper [ekipe] *tr* to equip

équi·pier [ekipje] **-pière** [pjer] *mf* teammate; crew member

équitable [ekitabl] *adj* equitable

équitation [ekitɑsjɔ̃] *f* horseback riding

équité [ekite] *f* equity

équiva·lent [ekivalɑ̃] **-lente** [lɑ̃t] *adj* & *m* equivalent

équivaloir [ekivalwar] §71 *intr*—**équivaloir à** to be equivalent to; to be tantamount to

équivoque [ekivɔk] *adj* equivocal; questionable (*e.g., reputation*) || *f* double entendre; uncertainty; **sans équivoque** without equivocation

équivoquer [ekivɔke] *intr* to equivocate, quibble; to pun

érable [erabl] *m* maple; **érable à sucre** sugar maple

érafler [erafle] *tr* to graze, scratch

éraflure [eraflyr] *f* graze, scratch

érail·lé -lée [eraje] *adj* bloodshot (*eyes*); hoarse (*voice*)

érailler [eraje] *tr* to fray

ère [er] *f* era

érection [ereksjɔ̃] *f* erection

érein·té -tée [erɛ̃te] *adj* all in, worn out, tired out

éreinter [erɛ̃te] *tr* to exhaust, tire out; (coll) to criticize unmercifully, to run down (*an author, play, etc.*) || *ref* to wear oneself out; to drudge

erg [erg] *m* erg

ergot [ergo] *m* spur (*of rooster*); **monter or se dresser sur ses ergots** (fig) to get up on a high horse

ergotage [ergotaʒ] *m* (coll) quibbling

ergoter [ergɔte] *tr* (coll) to quibble

ériger [eriʒe] §38 *tr* to erect || *ref*—**s'ériger en** to set oneself up as

ermitage [ermitaʒ] *m* hermitage

ermite [ermit] *m* hermit

éroder [erode] *tr* to erode

érosion [erozjɔ̃] *f* erosion

érotique [erotik] *adj* erotic

érotisme [erotism] *m* eroticism

er·rant [erɑ̃] **er·rante** [erɑ̃t] *adj* wandering, stray; errant

erratique [eratik] *adj* intermittent, irregular, erratic

erre [er] *f* (naut) headway; **erres** track (*e.g., of deer*)

errements [ermɑ̃] *mpl* ways, methods; (pej) erring ways, bad habits

errer [ere] *intr* to wander; to err; to play (*said of smile*)

erreur [erœr] *f* error, mistake; **erreur de frappe** typing error

erro·né -née [erone] *adj* erroneous

éructation [eryktɑsjɔ̃] *f* belch

éructer [erykte] *tr* (fig) to belch forth || *intr* to belch

éru·dit [erydi] **-dite** [dit] *adj* erudite, learned || *mf* scholar, erudite

érudition [erydisjɔ̃] *f* erudition

éruption [erypsjɔ̃] *f* eruption

ès [es] *prep* §77

esc. *abbr* (escompte) discount

esca·beau [eskabo] *m* (*pl* **-beaux**) stool; stepladder

escadre [eskadr] *f* squadron; fleet

escadron [eskadrɔ̃] *m* (mil) squadron

escalade [eskalad] *f* scaling, climbing

escalader [eskalade] *tr* to scale, to climb; to clamber over or up

escalator [eskalatɔr] *m* escalator

escale [eskal] *f* port of call, stop; **faire escale** to make a stop; **sans escale** nonstop

escalier [ɛskalje] *m* stairway; **escalier à vis** circular stairway; **escalier de sauvetage** fire escape; **escalier en colimaçon** spiral staircase; **escalier mécanique** or **roulant** escalator

escalope [ɛskalɔp] *f* scallop

escamotable [ɛskamɔtabl] *adj* retractable (*e.g., landing gear*); concealable (*piece of furniture*)

escamotage [ɛskamɔtaʒ] *m* sleight of hand; side-stepping, avoiding; theft

escamoter [ɛskamɔte] *tr* to palm (*a card*); to pick (*a wallet*); to dodge (*a question*); to slur (*a word*); to hush up (*a scandal*); (aer) to retract (*landing gear*)

escamo·teur [ɛskamɔtœr] **-teuse** [tøz] *mf* prestidigitator; pickpocket

escapade [ɛskapad] *f* escapade, escape

escarbille [ɛskarbij] *f* cinder, clinker

escarbot [ɛskarbo] *m* beetle

escarboucle [ɛskarbukl] *f* (mineral) carbuncle

escargot [ɛskargo] *m* snail

escarmouche [ɛskarmuʃ] *f* skirmish

escarmoucher [ɛskarmuʃe] *intr* to skirmish

escarpe [ɛskarp] *m* ruffian, bandit ‖ *f* escarpment (*of a fort*)

escar·pé -pée [ɛskarpe] *adj* steep

escarpement [ɛskarpəmɑ̃] *m* escarpment

escarpin [ɛskarpɛ̃] *m* pump, dancing shoe

escarpolette [ɛskarpɔlet] *f* swing

escarre [ɛskar] *f* scab

escarrifier [ɛskarifje] *tr* to form a scab on

esche [ɛʃ] *f* bait

Eschyle [ɛsil], [eʃil] *m* Aeschylus

escient [ɛsjɑ̃]—**à bon escient** knowingly, wittingly; **à mon (ton, etc.) escient** to my (your, etc.) certain knowledge

esclaffer [ɛsklafe] *ref* to burst out laughing

esclandre [ɛsklɑ̃dr] *m* scandal

esclavage [ɛsklavaʒ] *m* slavery

esclavagiste [ɛsklavaʒist] *adj* pro-slavery ‖ *mf* advocate of slavery

esclave [ɛsklav] *adj & mf* slave

escompte [ɛskɔ̃t] *m* discount, rebate; **escompte de caisse** cash discount; **escompte en dehors** bank discount; **prendre à l'escompte** to discount

escompter [ɛskɔ̃te] *tr* to discount (*a premature note*); to anticipate

escompteur [ɛskɔ̃tœr] *adj* discounting (*banker*) ‖ *m* discount broker

escopette [ɛskɔpet] *f* blunderbuss

escorte [ɛskɔrt] *f* escort

escorter [ɛskɔrte] *tr* to escort

escouade [ɛskwad] *f* infantry section; gang (*of laborers*)

escrime [ɛskrim] *f* fencing

escrimer [ɛskrime] *intr & ref* to fence; **s'escrimer à** to work with might and main at; **s'escrimer contre** to fence with

escri·meur [ɛskrimœr] **-meuse** [møz] *mf* fencer

escroc [ɛskro] *m* crook, swindler

escroquer [ɛskrɔke] *tr* to swindle

escroquerie [ɛskrɔkri] *f* swindling, cheating; racket, swindle

ésotérique [ɛzɔterik] *adj* esoteric

espace [ɛspas] *m* space; room; **espace cosmique** outer space ‖ *f* (typ) space

espacement [ɛspasmɑ̃] *m* spacing

espacer [ɛspase] §51 *tr* to space

espadon [ɛspadɔ̃] *m* swordfish

espadrille [ɛspadrij] *f* tennis shoe; beach sandal; esparto sandal

Espagne [ɛspaɲ] *f* Spain; **l'Espagne** Spain

espa·gnol -gnole [ɛspaɲɔl] *adj* Spanish ‖ *m* Spanish (*language*) ‖ (*cap*) *mf* Spaniard (*person*); **les Espagnols** the Spanish

espagnolette [ɛspaɲɔlet] *f* espagnolette (*door fastener for French casement window*)

espalier [ɛspalje] *m* espalier

espèce [ɛspes] *f* species; sort, kind; **en espèces** in specie; **en l'espèce** in the matter; **espèces sonnantes** hard cash; **sale espèce** cad, bounder ‖ *mf*— **espèce de** (coll) damn, e.g., **cet espèce d'idiot** that damn fool

espérance [ɛsperɑ̃s] *f* hope; **espérances** expectations; prospects

espérer [ɛspere] §10 *tr* to hope, to hope for; (coll) to wait for; **espérer + inf** to hope to + *inf* ‖ *intr* to trust; (coll) to wait

espiègle [ɛspjegl] *adj* mischievous ‖ *mf* rogue

espièglerie [ɛspjeglri] *f* mischievousness; prank

es·pion [ɛspjɔ̃] **-pionne** [pjɔn] *mf* spy ‖ *m* concealed microphone; busybody (*mirror*)

espionnage [ɛspjɔnaʒ] *m* espionage

espionner [ɛspjɔne] *tr* to spy on

espoir [ɛspwar] *m* hope; promise

esprit [ɛspri] *m* spirit; mind; intelligence; wit; spirits (*of wine*); **à l'esprit clair** clearheaded; **avoir l'esprit de l'escalier** to think of what to say too late; **bel esprit** man of letters; **esprit d'équipe** teamwork; **esprit de système** love of order; (pej) pigheadedness; **esprit fort** freethinker; **rendre l'esprit** to give up the ghost

esquif [ɛskif] *m* skiff

esqui·mau [ɛskimo] **-maude** [mod] (*mod*) (*pl* **-maux**) *adj* Eskimo ‖ *m* husky, Eskimo dog; Eskimo (*language*) ‖ (*cap*) *mf* Eskimo (*person*)

esquinter [ɛskɛ̃te] *tr* (coll) to tire out; (coll) to wear out; (coll) to run down, knock, criticize

esquisse [ɛskis] *f* sketch; outline, draft; beginning (*e.g., of a smile*)

esquisser [ɛskise] *tr* to sketch; to outline, draft; to begin

esquiver [ɛskive] *tr* to dodge, to sidestep; **esquiver de la tête** to duck ‖ *ref* to sneak away

essai [ɛse] *m* essay; trial, test; **à l'essai** on trial; **essais** first attempts (*of artist, writer, etc.*); **faire l'essai de** to try out

essaim [ɛsɛ̃] *m* swarm

essaimer [ɛseme] *intr* to swarm

essarter [ɛsarte] *tr* to clear (*brush*)

essarts [esar] *mpl* clearings

essayage [esejaʒ] *m* fitting, trying on

essayer [eseje], [eseje] §49 *tr* to try on or try out; to assay (*ore*) ‖ *intr* to try; essayer de to try to ‖ *ref*—s'essayer à to try one's skill at

essayeur [esejœr] essayeuse [esejøz] *mf* assayer

essayiste [esejist] *mf* essayist

esse [es] *f* S-hook; sound hole (*of violin*)

essence [esɑ̃s] *f* essence; gasoline; kind, species; par essence by definition

essen•tiel -tielle [esɑ̃sjel] *adj* & *m* essential

esseu•lé -lée [escele] *adj* abandoned

es•sieu [esjø] *m* (*pl* -sieux) axle

essor [esɔr] *m* flight; development; boom (*in business*); donner libre essor à to give vent to; to give full scope to; prendre son essor to take wing

essorer [esɔre] *tr* to spin-dry; to wring; to centrifuge

essoreuse [esɔrøz] *f* spin-drier; wringer; centrifuge

essouf•flé -flée [esufle] *adj* breathless, out of breath

essuie-glace [esɥiglas] *m* (*pl* -glaces) windshield wiper

essuie-mains [esɥimɛ̃] *m invar* towel

essuie-plume [esɥiplym] *m* (*pl* -plumes) penwiper

essuyer [esɥije], [esɥije] §27 *tr* to wipe; to wipe off; to wipe away; to suffer, endure; to undergo; to weather (*a storm*); essuyer les plâtres (coll) to be the first to occupy a house

est [est] *adj invar* & *m* east

estacade [estakad] *f* breakwater; pier; boom (*barrier of floating logs*); railway trestle

estafette [estafet] *f* messenger

estaminet [estamine] *m* bar, café

estampe [estɑ̃p] *f* print, engraving; (*tool*) stamp

estamper [estɑ̃pe] *tr* to stamp (*with a design*); to engrave; to overcharge, to fleece

estampille [estɑ̃pij] *f* identification mark; trademark; hallmark

ester [ester] *m* ester ‖ [este] *intr*— ester en justice to go to law, to sue

esthète [estet] *mf* aesthete

esthéti•cien [estetisjɛ̃] -cienne [sjɛn] *mf* aesthetician ‖ *f* beautician

esthétique [estetik] *adj* aesthetic ‖ *f* aesthetics

estimable [estimabl] *adj* estimable

estimateur [estimatœr] *m* estimator, appraiser

estimation [estimasjɔ̃] *f* estimation, appraisal

estime [estim] *f* esteem; à l'estime by guesswork; (naut) by dead reckoning

estimer [estime] *tr* to esteem; to estimate, to assess; estimer + *inf* to think that + *ind*, e.g., j'estime avoir fait mon devoir I think that I did my duty

esti•val -vale [estival] *adj* (*pl* -vaux [vo]) summer

esti•vant [estivɑ̃] -vante [vɑ̃t] *mf* summer vacationist, summer resident

estiver [estive] *intr* to summer

estocade [estɔkad] *f* thrust (*in fencing*); unexpected attack

estomac [estɔma] *m* stomach

estomaquer [estɔmake] *tr* (coll) to astound ‖ *ref* (coll) to be angered

estomper [estɔ̃pe] *tr* to shade off, to rub away (*a drawing*); to blur ‖ *ref* to be blurred

Estonie [estɔni] *f* Estonia; l'Estonie Estonia

estrade [estrad] *f* platform

estragon [estragɔ̃] *m* tarragon

estro•pié -piée [estrɔpje] *adj* crippled ‖ *mf* cripple

estuaire [estɥer] *m* estuary

estudian•tin [estydjɑ̃tɛ̃] -tine [tin] *adj* student

esturgeon [estyrʒɔ̃] *m* sturgeon

et [e] *conj* and; et . . . et both . . . and

Établ. *abbr* (Établissement) company, establishment

étable [etabl] *f* stable, cowshed

établer [etable] *tr* to stable

établi [etabli] *m* workbench

établir [etablir] *tr* to establish ‖ *ref* to settle down; to set up headquarters

établissement [etablismɑ̃] *m* establishment

étage [etaʒ] *m* floor, story; tier, level; rank, social level; (rok) stage; de bas étage lower-class; dernier étage top floor; premier étage first floor above ground floor

étager [etaʒe] §38 *tr* to arrange in tiers; to stagger; to perform in stages

étagère [etaʒer] *f* rack, shelf

étai [ete] *m* prop, stay

étain [etɛ̃] *m* tin; pewter

étal [etal] *m* (*pl* étals or étaux [eto]) stall, stand; butcher's block

étalage [etalaʒ] *m* display

étalager [etalaʒe] §38 *tr* to display

étalagiste [etalaʒist] *mf* window dresser, display artist; demonstrator

étaler [etale] *tr* to display; to spread out ‖ *ref* (coll) to sprawl

étalon [etalɔ̃] *m* stallion; monetary standard

étalonner [etalɔne] *tr* to verify, control; to standardize; to graduate, calibrate

étalon-or [etalɔ̃ɔr] *m* gold standard

étambot [etɑ̃bo] *m* (naut) sternpost

étamer [etame] *tr* to tin-plate; to silver (*a mirror*)

étamine [etamin] *f* stamen; sieve; cheesecloth

étampe [etɑ̃p] *f* stamp, die, punch

étamper [etɑ̃pe] *tr* to stamp, punch

étanche [etɑ̃ʃ] *adj* watertight, airtight

étancher [etɑ̃ʃe] *tr* to check, stanch the flow of; to quench (*one's thirst*); to make watertight or airtight

étang [etɑ̃] *m* pond

étape [etap] *f* stage; stop, halt; day's march; (sports) lap; brûler les étapes to go straight through

état [eta] *m* state; statement, record; trade, occupation; government; (hist) estate; en tout état de cause at all costs; in any case; **état civil** marital status; **état tampon** buffer state; **être dans tous ses états** to stew; **être en état de** to be in a position to; **faire état de** to take into account; to expect to; **hors d'état** out of order, unfit; **tenir en état** to keep in shape, to repair

étatisation [etatizɑsjɔ̃] *f* nationalization

étatiser [etatize] *tr* to nationalize

étatisme [etatism] *m* statism

état-major [etamaʒɔr] *m* (*pl* **états-majors**) headquarters; staff

état-providence [etaprɔvidɑ̃s] *m* welfare state

États-Unis [etazyni] *mpl* United States

étau [eto] *m* (*pl* **étaux**) vise

étayer [eteje] §49 *tr* to prop, stay

et Cⁱᵉ *abbr* (**et Compagnie**) & Co.

été [ete] *m* summer

éteignoir [etɛɲwar] *m* candle snuffer; (coll) kill-joy, wet blanket

éteindre [etɛ̃dr] §50 *tr* to extinguish, put out; to turn off; to wipe out; to appease (*e.g., one's thirst*); to dull (*a color*) || *intr* to put out the light || *ref* to go out; (fig) to die, pass away

éteint [etɛ̃] **éteinte** [etɛ̃t] *adj* extinguished; extinct; dull, dim

étendard [etɑ̃dar] *m* flag, banner

étendoir [etɑ̃dwar] *m* clothesline; drying rack

étendre [etɑ̃dr] *tr* to extend, spread out || *ref* to stretch out; to spread

éten·du -due [etɑ̃dy] *adj* outspread; extensive; vast; diluted, adulterated || *f* stretch; range, scope

éter·nel -nelle [eternel] *adj* eternal

éterniser [eternize] *tr* to perpetuate (*a name*); to drag out || *ref* (coll) to drag on; **s'éterniser chez qn** (coll) to overstay an invitation

éternité [eternite] *f* eternity

éternuement [eternymɑ̃] *m* sneeze; sneezing

éternuer [eternɥe] *intr* to sneeze

étêter [etete] *tr* to top (*a tree*); to take the head off (*a fish, nail, etc.*)

éteule [etœl] *f* stubble

éther [eter] *m* ether

éthé·ré -rée [etere] *adj* ethereal

Éthiopie [etjɔpi] *f* Ethiopia; **l'Éthiopie** Ethiopia

éthio·pien [etjɔpjɛ̃] **-pienne** [pjɛn] *adj* Ethiopian || *m* Ethiopian (*language*) || (*cap*) *mf* Ethiopian (*person*)

éthique [etik] *adj* ethical || *f* ethics

ethnique [etnik] *adj* ethnic(al)

ethnographie [etnɔgrafi] *f* ethnography

ethnologie [etnɔlɔʒi] *f* ethnology

éthyle [etil] *m* ethyl

éthylène [etilen] *m* ethylene

étiage [etjaʒ] *m* low-water mark

étince·lant [etɛ̃slɑ̃] **-lante** [lɑ̃t] *adj* sparkling, glittering

étinceler [etɛ̃sle] §34 *intr* to sparkle, glitter

étincelle [etɛ̃sɛl] *f* spark; (fig) flash

étiolement [etjɔlmɑ̃] *m* wilting

étioler [etjɔle] *tr* & *ref* to wilt

étique [etik] *adj* lean, emaciated

étiqueter [etikte] §34 *tr* to label

étiquette [etikɛt] *f* etiquette; label; **étiquette gommée** sticker

étirer [etire] *tr* to stretch, lengthen, elongate || *ref* (coll) to stretch one's limbs

étoffe [etɔf] *f* stuff; material, fabric; quality, worth

étoile [etwal] *f* star; traffic circle; **à la belle étoile** out of doors; **étoile de mer** starfish; **étoile filante** shooting or falling star; **étoile polaire** polestar

étoi·lé -lée [etwale] *adj* star-spangled, starry

étole [etɔl] *f* stole

éton·nant [etɔnɑ̃] **éton·nante** [etɔnɑ̃t] *adj* astonishing

étonnement [etɔnmɑ̃] *m* surprise, astonishment; fissure, crack

étonner [etɔne] *tr* to surprise, astonish; to shake or crack (*masonry*) || *ref* to be surprised

étouf·fant [etufɑ̃] **étouf·fante** [etufɑ̃t] *adj* suffocating; sweltering

étouffée [etufe] *f* braising; **cuire à l'étouffée** to braise

étouffer [etufe] *tr*, *intr*, & *ref* to suffocate; to stifle; to choke

étoupe [etup] *f* oakum, tow

étourderie [eturdri] *f* thoughtlessness

étour·di -die [eturdi] *adj* scatter-brained || *mf* scatterbrain

étourdir [eturdir] *tr* to stun, daze; to numb; to deafen (*with loud noise*) || *ref* to try to forget, get in a daze

étourdissement [eturdismɑ̃] *m* dizziness; numbing

étour·neau [eturno] *m* (*pl* **-neaux**) starling

étrange [etrɑ̃ʒ] *adj* strange

étran·ger [etrɑ̃ʒe] **-gère** [ʒer] *adj* foreign; irrelevant; unknown, strange; **être étranger à** to be unacquainted with || *mf* foreigner; stranger; **à l'étranger** abroad, in a foreign country

étrangeté [etrɑ̃ʒte] *f* strangeness

étrangler [etrɑ̃gle] *tr* & *intr* to strangle || *ref* to choke; to narrow (*said of passageway, valley, etc.*)

étran·gleur [etrɑ̃glœr] **-gleuse** [gløz] *mf* strangler

étrave [etrav] *f* (naut) stempost; **de l'étrave à l'étambot** from stem to stern

être [etr] *m* being || §28 *intr* to be; **en être pour sa peine** to have nothing for one's trouble; **être à** + *pron disj* to be + *pron poss*, e.g., **le livre est à moi** the book is mine; **n'est-ce pas** see **ne** || *aux* (used with some intransitive verbs and all reflexive verbs) to have, e.g., **elles sont arrivées** they have arrived; (used to form the passive voice) to be, e.g., **il est aimé de tout le monde** he is loved by everybody

étrécir [etresir] *tr* & *ref* to shrink

étreindre [etrɛ̃dr] §50 *tr* to embrace; to grip, seize

étreinte [etrɛ̃t] *f* embrace; hold, grasp

étrenne [etren] *f* first sale of the day;

avoir l'étrenne de to have the first use of; étrennes New-Year gifts

étrenner [etrene] *tr* to put on for the first time; to be the first to wear || *intr* (coll) to be the first to catch it

étrier [etrije] *m* stirrup

étrille [etrij] *f* currycomb

étriller [etrije] *tr* to curry; (coll) to thrash, to tan the hide of; (coll) to overcharge, to fleece

étriper [etripe] *tr* to gut, disembowel

étri·qué ·quée [etrike] *adj* skimpy, tight; narrow, cramped

étriquer [etrike] *tr* to make too tight; to shorten (*e.g., a speech*)

étroit [etrwa] étroite [etrwat] *adj* narrow; strict; tight; close; à l'étroit confined, cramped

étroitesse [etrwates] *f* narrowness; étroitesse d'esprit narrow-mindedness

étude [etyd] *f* study; law office; law practice; spadework, planning; à l'étude under consideration; mettre à l'étude to study; terminer ses études to finish one's courses

étu·diant [etydjã] -diante [djãt] *mf* student

étu·dié -diée [etydje] *adj* studied; set (*speech*); artificial, affected

étudier [etydje] *tr* to study; to practice, rehearse; to learn by heart; to design || *intr* to study || *ref* to be overly introspective; s'étudier à to take pains to, to make a point of

étui [etɥi] *m* case, box

étuve [etyv] *f* steam bath or room; drying room; steam sterilizer; incubator (*for breeding cultures*)

étuver [etyve] *tr* to stew; to steam; to dry

étymologie [etimɔlɔʒi] *f* etymology

étymon [etimɔ̃] *m* etymon

eucalyptus [økaliptys] *m* eucalyptus

Eucharistie [økaristi] *f* Eucharist

eunuque [ønyk] *m* eunuch

euphé·mique [øfemik] *adj* euphemistic

euphémisme [øfemism] *m* euphemism

euphonie [øfɔni] *f* euphony

euphonique [øfɔnik] *adj* euphonic

euphorie [øfɔri] *f* euphoria

Europe [ørɔp] *f* Europe; l'Europe Europe

euro·péen [ørɔpeɛ̃] euro·péenne [ørɔpeɛn] *adj* European || (*cap*) *mf* European

eux [ø] §85

eux-mêmes [ømɛm] §86

évacuer [evakɥe] *tr & ref* to evacuate

éva·dé -dée [evade] *mf* escapee

évader [evade] *ref* to escape, evade

évaluer [evalɥe] *tr* to evaluate, appraise; to estimate

évanes·cent [evanesɑ̃] évanes·cente [evanesɑ̃t] *adj* evanescent

évangélique [evɑ̃ʒelik] *adj* evangelic(al)

évangéliste [evɑ̃ʒelist] *m* evangelist

évangile [evɑ̃ʒil] *m* gospel

évanouir [evanwir] *ref* to faint; to lose consciousness; to vanish; (rad) to fade

évanouissement [evanwismɑ̃] *m* fainting; disappearance

évapo·ré -rée [evapɔre] *adj* flighty, fickle, giddy

évaporer [evapɔre] *tr & ref* to evaporate

évaser [evɑze] *tr & ref* to widen

éva·sif [evazif] -sive [ziv] *adj* evasive

évasion [evɑzjɔ̃] *f* evasion; escape; d'évasion escapist (*literature*)

Ève [ev] *f* Eve; je ne le connais ni d'Ève ni d'Adam (coll) I don't know him from Adam

évêché [eve/e] *m* bishopric

éveil [evej] *m* awakening; alarm, warning

éveil·lé -lée [eveje] *adj* alert, lively; sharp, intelligent

éveiller [eveje] *tr & ref* to wake up

événement [evenəmɑ̃], [evenmɑ̃] *m* event; outcome, development; faire événement to cause quite a stir

évent [evɑ̃] *m* vent; staleness

éventail [evɑ̃taj] *m* fan; range, spread; screen

éventaire [evɑ̃ter] *m* tray (*carried by flower girl, cigarette girl, etc.*); sidewalk display

éventer [evɑ̃te] *tr* to fan; to ventilate; to get wind of (*a secret*); éventer la mèche (coll) to let the cat out of the bag || *ref* to fan oneself; to fade away (*said of odor*); to go stale or flat

éventrer [evɑ̃tre] *tr* to disembowel; to smash open

éventualité [evɑ̃tɥalite] *f* eventuality; possibility

éven·tuel -tuelle [evɑ̃tɥel] *adj* eventual; possible, contingent; forthcoming || *m* eventuality; possibility; possibilities (*e.g., of a job*)

éventuellement [evɑ̃tɥelmɑ̃] *adv* eventually; possibly; if need be

évêque [evɛk] *m* bishop

évertuer [evertɥe] *ref*—s'évertuer à or pour + *inf* to strive to + *inf*

éviction [eviksjɔ̃] *f* eviction, removal; éviction scolaire quarantine

évidement [evidmɑ̃] *m* hollowing out

évidemment [evidamɑ̃] *adv* evidently

évidence [evidɑ̃s] *f* evidence, obviousness; conspicuousness; de toute évidence by all appearances; se mettre en évidence to come to the fore

évi·dent [evidɑ̃] -dente [dɑ̃t] *adj* evident

évider [evide] *tr* to hollow out

évier [evje] *m* sink

évincer [evɛ̃se] §51 *tr* to evict, to oust; to discriminate against

éviter [evite] *tr* to avoid, escape

évoca·teur [evɔkatœr] -trice [tris] *adj* evocative, suggestive

évocation [evɔkɑsjɔ̃] *f* evocation

évoluer [evɔlɥe] *intr* to evolve; to change one's mind

évolution [evɔlysjɔ̃] *f* evolution

évoquer [evɔke] *tr* to evoke; to recall, to call to mind

exact [egza], [ɛgzakt] exacte [ɛgzakt] *adj* exact

exactitude [ɛgzaktityd] *f* exactness; punctuality

exagérer [egzaʒere] §10 *tr* to exaggerate; to overdo

exal·té -tée [egzalte] *adj* impassioned;

high-strung, wrought-up || *mf* hot-head, fanatic

exalter [egzalte] *tr* to exalt; to excite (*e.g., the imagination*) || *ref* to get excited

examen [egzamɛ̃] *m* examination; à l'examen under consideration; on approval; examen de fin d'études or examen de fin de classe final examination; examen probatoire placement exam; libre examen free inquiry; se présenter à, passer, or subir un examen to take an examination

examina·teur [egzaminatœr] **-trice** [tris] *mf* examiner

examiner [egzamine] *tr* to examine

exaspération [egzasperasjɔ̃] *f* exasperation; crisis, aggravation

exaspérer [egzaspere] §10 *tr* to exasperate; to make worse

exaucer [egzose] §51 *tr* to answer the prayer of; to fulfill (*a wish*)

excava·teur [ekskavatœr] **-trice** [tris] *m & f* excavator, steam shovel

excaver [ekskave] *tr* to excavate

excé·dant [eksedɑ̃] **-dante** [dɑ̃t] *adj* excess; tiresome

excédent [eksedɑ̃] *m* excess, surplus

excédentaire [eksedɑ̃ter] *adj* excess

excéder [eksede] §10 *tr* to exceed; to tire out; to overtax

excellence [ekselɑ̃s] *f* excellence; **Votre Excellence** Your Excellency

exceller [eksele] *intr* to excel

excentricité [eksɑ̃trisite] *f* eccentricity

excentrique [eksɑ̃trik] *adj* eccentric; remote, outlying || *mf* eccentric || *m* (mach) eccentric

excep·té -tée [eksepte] *adj* excepted || excepté *adv*—excepté que except that || excepté *prep* except, except for

exception [eksepsjɔ̃] *f* exception; à l'exception de with the exception of

exception·nel -nelle [eksepsjonel] *adj* exceptional

excès [ekse] *m* excess; excès de pose (phot) overexposure; excès de vitesse speeding

exces·sif [eksesif] **exces·sive** [eksesiv] *adj* excessive

exciper [eksipe] *intr*—**exciper de** (law) to offer a plea of, to allege

excitable [eksitabl] *adj* excitable

exci·tant [eksitɑ̃] **-tante** [tɑ̃t] *adj* stimulating || *m* stimulant

exciter [eksite] *tr* to excite, stimulate; to stir, incite; to provoke (*e.g., laughter*)

exclamation [eksklamasjɔ̃] *f* exclamation

exclamer [eksklame] *ref* to exclaim

exclure [eksklyr] §11 *tr* to exclude

exclu·sif [eksklyzif] **-sive** [ziv] *adj* exclusive

exclusion [eksklyzjɔ̃] *f* exclusion; à l'exclusion de exclusive of, excluding

exclusivité [eksklyzivite] *f* exclusiveness; exclusive rights; newsbeat; en exclusivité (public sign in front of a theater) exclusive showing

excommunication [ekskomynikasjɔ̃] *f* excommunication

excommunier [ekskomynje] *tr* to excommunicate

excorier [ekskorje] *tr* to scratch, skin

excrément [ekskremɑ̃] *m* excrement

excroissance [ekskrwasɑ̃s] *f* growth, tumor

excursion [ekskyrsjɔ̃] *f* excursion; tour, trip; outing

excursionner [ekskyrsjone] *intr* to go on an excursion

excusable [ekskyzabl] *adj* excusable

excuse [ekskyz] *f* excuse; des excuses apologies

excuser [ekskyze] *tr* to excuse || *ref* to excuse oneself, to apologize; je m'excuse! (coll) excuse me!

exécrer [egzekre] §10 *tr* to execrate

exécu·tant [egzekytɑ̃] **-tante** [tɑ̃t] *mf* performer

exécuter [egzekyte] *tr* to execute; to perform; to make (*copies*) || *ref* to comply

exécuteur [egzekytœr] *m*—**exécuteur testamentaire** executor; **exécuteur des hautes œuvres** hangman

exécu·tif [egzekytif] **-tive** [tiv] *adj & m* executive

exécution [egzekysjɔ̃] *f* execution; performance; fulfillment; mettre à exécution to carry out

exécutrice [egzekytris] *f* executrix

exemplaire [egzɑ̃pler] *adj* exemplary || *m* exemplar, model; sample, specimen; copy (*e.g., of book*); en double exemplaire with carbon copy; exemplaire dédicacé autographed copy; exemplaires de passe extra copies

exemple [egzɑ̃pl] *m* example; à l'exemple de after the example of; par exemple for example; par exemple! the idea!, well I never!; prêcher d'exemple to practice what one preaches; sans exemple unprecedented

exempt [egzɑ̃] **exempte** [egzɑ̃t] *adj* exempt || *m* (hist) police officer

exempter [egzɑ̃te] *tr* to exempt

exemption [egzɑ̃psjɔ̃] *f* exemption

exer·cé -cée [egzerse] *adj* practiced, experienced

exercer [egzerse] §51 *tr* to exercise; to exert; to practice (*e.g., medicine*) || *ref* to exercise; to practice, to drill

exercice [egzersis] *m* exercise; drill; practice; **exercice budgétaire** fiscal year

exhalaison [egzalezɔ̃] *f* exhalation (*of gas, vapors, etc.*)

exhalation [egzalasjɔ̃] *f* exhalation (*of air from lungs*)

exhaler [egzale] *tr, intr, & ref* to exhale

exhaure [egzor] *f* pumping out (*of a mine*); drain pumps

exhaussement [egzosmɑ̃] *m* raising; rise

exhausser [egzose] *tr* to raise, to increase the height of || *ref* to rise

exhaus·tif [egzostif] **-tive** [tiv] *adj* exhaustive

exhiber [egzibe] *tr* to exhibit; to show (*a ticket, passport, etc.*) || *ref* to make an exhibition of oneself

exhibition [egzibisjɔ̃] *f* exhibition

exhorter [egzɔrte] *tr* to exhort

exhumer [egzyme] *tr* to exhume

exi·geant [egziʒɑ̃] **-geante** [ʒɑ̃t] *adj* exigent, exacting; unreasonable

exigence [egziʒɑ̃s] *f* demand, claim; requirement; unreasonableness; **exigences** exigencies

exiger [egziʒe] §38 *tr* to demand, require, exact

exigible [egziʒibl] *adj* required; due, on demand

exi·gu -guë [egzigy] *adj* tiny; insufficient

exiguïté [egziguite] *f* smallness; insufficiency

exil [egzil] *m* exile

exi·lé -lée [egzile] *adj & mf* exile

exiler [egzile] *tr* to exile

existence [egzistɑ̃s] *f* existence

exister [egziste] *intr* to exist

exode [egzɔd] *m* exodus; flight (*of capital; of emigrants, refugees, etc.*)

exonération [egzɔnerasjɔ̃] *f* exemption, exoneration

exonérer [egzɔnere] §10 *tr* to exempt, exonerate || *ref* to pay up a debt

exorbi·tant [egzɔrbitɑ̃] **-tante** [tɑ̃t] *adj* exorbitant

exorciser [egzɔrsize] *tr* to exorcise

exotique [egzɔtik] *adj* exotic

expan·sif [ekspɑ̃sif] **-sive** [siv] *adj* expansive

expansion [ekspɑ̃sjɔ̃] *f* expansion; expansiveness; spread (*of a belief*)

expa·trié -triée [ekspatrije] *adj & mf* expatriate

expatrier [ekspatrije] *tr* to expatriate

expectorer [ekspektɔre] *tr & intr* to expectorate

expé·dient [ekspedjɑ̃] **-diente** [djɑ̃t] *adj* expedient || *m* expedient; (coll) makeshift; **expédient provisoire** emergency measure; **vivre d'expédients** to live by one's wits

expédier [ekspedje] *tr* to expedite; to ship; to make a certified copy of; (coll) to dash off, do hurriedly

expédi·teur [ekspeditœr] **-trice** [tris] *adj* forwarding (*station, agency, etc.*) || *mf* sender, shipper

expédi·tif [ekspeditif] **-tive** [tiv] *adj* expeditious

expédition [ekspedisjɔ̃] *f* expedition; shipping; shipment; certified copy

expéditionnaire [ekspedisjɔner] *adj* expeditionary || *mf* sender; clerk

expérience [eksperjɑ̃s] *f* experience; experiment

expérimen·té -tée [eksperimɑ̃te] *adj* experienced

expérimenter [eksperimɑ̃te] *tr* to try out, to test || *intr* to conduct experiments

ex·pert [eksper] **-perte** [pert] *adj* expert || *m* expert; connoisseur; appraiser

expert-comptable [eksperkɔ̃tabl] *m* (pl **experts-comptables**) certified public accountant

expertise [ekspertiz] *f* expert appraisal

expertiser [ekspertize] *tr* to appraise

expier [ekspje] *tr* to expiate, to atone for

expirer [ekspire] *tr & intr* to expire; to exhale

explicable [eksplikabl] *adj* explicable, explainable

explica·tif [eksplikatif] **-tive** [tiv] *adj* explanatory

explication [eksplikasjɔ̃] *f* explanation; interpretation (*of a text*); **avoir une explication avec qn** to have it out with s.o.

explicite [eksplisit] *adj* explicit

expliciter [eksplisite] *tr* to make explicit

expliquer [eksplike] *tr* to explain; to give an interpretation of || *ref* to explain oneself; to understand

exploit [eksplwa] *m* exploit; **exploit d'ajournement** subpoena; **signifier un exploit** to serve a summons

exploi·tant [eksplwatɑ̃] **-tante** [tɑ̃t] *adj* operating, working || *mf* operator (*of enterprise*); developer; cultivator; (mov) exhibitor

exploitation [eksplwatasjɔ̃] *f* exploitation; management, development, cultivation; land under cultivation

exploiter [eksplwate] *tr* to exploit; to manage, develop, cultivate || *intr* to serve summonses

explora·teur [eksplɔratœr] **-trice** [tris] *mf* explorer

exploration [eksplɔrasjɔ̃] *f* exploration

explorer [eksplɔre] *tr* to explore; (telv) to scan

exploser [eksploze] *intr* to explode

explosible [eksplozibl] *adj* explosive

explo·sif [eksplozif] **-sive** [ziv] *adj & m* explosive

explosion [eksplozjɔ̃] *f* explosion; **à explosion** internal-combustion (*engine*)

exporta·teur [ekspɔrtatœr] **-trice** [tris] *adj* exporting || *mf* exporter

exportation [ekspɔrtasjɔ̃] *f* export; exportation

exporter [ekspɔrte] *tr & intr* to export

expo·sant [ekspozɑ̃] **-sante** [zɑ̃t] *mf* exhibitor; petitioner || *m* (math) exponent

exposé [ekspoze] *m* exposition, account, statement; report (*given by a student in class*)

exposer [ekspoze] *tr* to expose; to explain, expound; to exhibit, display

exposition [ekspozisjɔ̃] *f* exposition; exposure (*to one of the points of the compass*); introduction (*of a book*); lying in state; **exposition canine** dog show; **exposition d'horticulture** flower show; **exposition hippique** horse show

ex·près [ekspre] **-presse** [pres] *adj* express || **exprès** *adj invar* special-delivery (*letter, package, etc.*) || *m* express; **par exprès** by special delivery || **exprès** *adv* expressly, on purpose

express [ekspres] *adj & m* express (*train*)

expressément [ɛksprɛsemɑ̃] adv expressly

expres·sif [ɛksprɛsif] expres·sive [ɛksprɛsiv] adj expressive

expression [ɛksprɛsjɔ̃] f expression; d'expression française native French-speaking

exprimer [ɛksprime] tr to express; to squeeze out

exproprier [ɛksprɔprije] tr to expropriate

expul·sé -sée [ɛkspylse] adj deported || mf deportee

expulser [ɛkspylse] tr to expel; to evict; to throw out

expulsion [ɛkspylsjɔ̃] f expulsion

expurger [ɛkspyrʒe] §38 tr to expurgate

ex·quis [ɛkski] -quise [kiz] adj exquisite; sharp (pain)

exsangue [ɛksɑ̃g] adj bloodless, anemic

exsuder [ɛksyde] tr & intr to exude

extase [ɛkstaz] f ecstasy

exta·sié -siée [ɛkstazje] adj enraptured, ecstatic, in ecstasy

extasier [ɛkstazje] ref to be enraptured

extatique [ɛkstatik] adj & mf ecstatic

extempora·né -née [ɛkstɑ̃pɔrane] adj (law) unpremeditated; (pharm) ready for use

exten·sif [ɛkstɑ̃sif] -sive [siv] adj wide (meaning); (mech) tensile

extension [ɛkstɑ̃sjɔ̃] f extension

exténuer [ɛkstenɥe] tr to exhaust, tire out || ref to tire oneself out

exté·rieur -rieure [ɛksterjœr] adj exterior; external; outer, outside; foreign (policy) || m exterior; outside; (mov) location shot; à l'extérieur outside; abroad; en extérieur (mov) on location

extérieurement [ɛksterjœrmɑ̃] adv externally; superficially; on the outside

extérioriser [ɛksterjɔrize] tr to reveal, to show || ref to open one's heart

exterminer [ɛkstɛrmine] tr to exterminate

externat [ɛkstɛrna] m day school

externe [ɛkstɛrn] adj external || m day student; outpatient; (med) nonresident intern

extinc·teur [ɛkstɛ̃ktœr] -trice [tris] adj extinguishing || m fire extinguisher

extinction [ɛkstɛ̃ksjɔ̃] f extinction; extinguishing; loss (of voice); l'extinction des feux (mil) lights out, taps

extirper [ɛkstirpe] tr to extirpate

extorquer [ɛkstɔrke] tr to extort

extor·queur [ɛkstɔrkœr] -queuse [køz] mf extortionist

extorsion [ɛkstɔrsjɔ̃] f extortion

extra [ɛkstra] adj invar (coll) extra-special, extra || m invar extra

extraction [ɛkstraksjɔ̃] f extraction

extrader [ɛkstrade] tr to extradite

extradition [ɛkstradisjɔ̃] f extradition

extra-fin [ɛkstrafɛ̃] -fine [fin] adj high-quality

extraire [ɛkstrɛr] §68 tr to extract; to excerpt; to get out || ref to extricate oneself

extrait [ɛkstrɛ] m extract; excerpt; abstract; certified copy; extrait de baptême baptismal certificate; extrait de naissance birth certificate; extraits selections (e.g., in an anthology)

extra-muros [ɛkstramyros] adj invar extramural; suburban || adv outside the town

extraordinaire [ɛkstraɔrdiner], [ɛkstrɔrdiner] adj extraordinary

extrapoler [ɛkstrapɔle] tr to extrapolate

extra-sensoriel -sensorielle [ɛkstrasɑ̃sɔrjɛl] adj extrasensory

extravagance [ɛkstravagɑ̃s] f extravagance; excess; absurdity, wildness

extrava·gant [ɛkstravagɑ̃] -gante [gɑ̃t] adj excessive, extravagant; absurd, wild, eccentric || mf eccentric, screwball

extraver·ti -tie [ɛkstraverti] adj & mf extrovert

extrême [ɛkstrɛm] adj & m extreme

extrêmement [ɛkstrɛmemɑ̃] adv extremely

extrême-onction [ɛkstrɛmɔ̃ksjɔ̃] f extreme unction

Extrême-Orient [ɛkstrɛmɔrjɑ̃] m Far East

extrémiste [ɛkstremist] adj & mf extremist

extrémité [ɛkstremite] f extremity; en venir à des extrémités to resort to violence; être à toute extrémité to be at death's door

extrinsèque [ɛkstrɛ̃sɛk] adj extrinsic

exubé·rant [ɛgzyberɑ̃] -rante [rɑ̃t] adj exuberant

exulter [ɛgzylte] intr to exult

ex-voto [ɛksvɔto] m invar votive inscription or tablet

F

F, f [ɛf], *[ɛf] m invar sixth letter of the French alphabet

F abbr (franc) franc

fable [fɑbl] f fable; laughingstock

fabri·cant [fabrikɑ̃] -cante [kɑ̃t] mf manufacturer

fabrica·teur [fabrikatœr] -trice [tris] mf fabricator (e.g., of lies); forger; counterfeiter

fabrication [fabrikasjɔ̃] f manufacture; forging; counterfeiting

fabrique [fabrik] f factory; factory

workers; mill hands; (obs) church trustees; (obs) church revenue; **fabrique de papier** paper mill

fabriquer [fabrike] *tr* to manufacture; to fabricate; to forge; to counterfeit

fabu·leux [fabylø] **-leuse** [løz] *adj* fabulous

façade [fasad] *f* façade; frontage; **en façade sur** facing, overlooking

face [fas] *f* face; side (*of a diamond; of a phonograph record*); surface; heads (*of coin*); **de face** full-faced (*portrait*); **en face (de)** opposite, facing; **faire face à** to face; to face up to; to meet (*an obligation*); **perdre la face** to lose face; **sauver la face** to save face

face-à-main [fasamɛ̃] *m* (*pl* **faces-à-main**) lorgnette

facétie [fasesi] *f* off-color joke; practical joke

facé·tieux [fasesjø] **-tieuse** [sjøz] *adj* droll, funny ‖ *mf* wag

facette [faset] *f* facet

fâ·ché -chée [faʃe] *adj* angry; sorry; **fâché avec** at odds with; **fâché contre** angry with (*a person*); **fâché de** angry at (*a thing*); sorry for

fâcher [faʃe] *tr* to anger ‖ *ref* to get angry; to be sorry

fâ·cheux [faʃø] **-cheuse** [ʃøz] *adj* annoying, tiresome; unfortunate ‖ *mf* nuisance, bore

fa·cial -ciale [fasjal] *adj* (*pl* **-ciaux** [sjo]) facial; face (*value*)

facile [fasil] *adj* easy; easygoing; facile, glib

facilité [fasilite] *f* facility; opportunity (*e.g., to meet s.o.*); **facilités de paiement** installments; easy terms

faciliter [fasilite] *tr* to facilitate

façon [fasɔ̃] *f* fashion; fashioning; way, manner; fit (*of clothes*); **à façon** job (*work; workman*); **à la façon de** like; **de façon à** so as to; **de façon que** or **de telle façon que** so that, e.g., **parlez de telle façon qu'on vous comprenne** speak so that you can be understood; **de toute façon** in any event; **façons** manners; **faire des façons** to stand on ceremony; **sans façon** informal

faconde [fakɔ̃d] *f* glibness, gift of gab

façonner [fasɔne] *tr* to fashion, shape; to work (*the land*); to accustom

façon·nier [fasɔnje] **façon·nière** [fasɔnjɛr] *adj* jobbing; fussy ‖ *mf* piece-worker; stuffed shirt

fac-similé [faksimile] *m* (*pl* **-similés**) facsimile

factage [faktaʒ] *m* delivery service; home delivery

facteur [faktœr] *m* factor; mailman; expressman; auctioneer (*at a market*); maker (*of musical instruments*)

factice [faktis] *adj* imitation, artificial

fac·tieux [faksjø] **-tieuse** [sjøz] *adj* factious, seditious ‖ *mf* trouble-maker, agitator

faction [faksjɔ̃] *f* faction; **être de faction** to be on sentry duty

factionnaire [faksjɔnɛr] *m* sentry

factorerie [faktɔrəri] *f* trading post

factotum [faktɔtɔm] *m* factotum; meddler; jack-of-all-trades

factum [faktɔm] *m* political pamphlet; (law) brief

facturation [faktyrasjɔ̃] *f* billing, invoicing

facture [faktyr] *f* invoice; bill; workmanship; **établir une facture** to make out an invoice; **suivant facture** as per invoice

facturer [faktyre] *tr* to bill

factu·rier [faktyrje] **-rière** [rjer] *mf* billing clerk ‖ *m* invoice book

faculta·tif [fakyltatif] **-tive** [tiv] *adj* optional

faculté [fakylte] *f* faculty; school, college (*of law, medicine, etc.*); **la Faculté** medical men

fadaise [fadez] *f* piece of nonsense; **fadaises** drivel

fade [fad] *adj* tasteless, flat; insipid, namby-pamby

fader [fade] *tr* (coll) to beat; (coll) to share the swag with; **il est fadé** (coll) he's done for

fadeur [fadœr] *f* insipidity; pointlessness; **fadeurs** platitudes

fagot [fago] *m* faggot; **fagot d'épines** ill-tempered person; **sentir le fagot** to smell of heresy

fagoter [fagote] *tr* to tie up in bundles, to faggot; (coll) to dress like a scarecrow

faible [febl] *adj* feeble, weak; low (*figure; moan*); poor (*harvest*); slight (*difference*) ‖ *mf* weakling ‖ *m* weakness; foible, weak spot; **faible d'esprit** feeble-minded person

faiblesse [febles] *f* feebleness, weakness, frailty

faiblir [feblir] *intr* to weaken; to diminish

faïence [fajɑ̃s] *f* earthenware, pottery

faille [faj] *f* (geol) fault; (tex) faille; (fig) defect; (fig) rift

fail·li -lie [faji] *adj & mf* bankrupt

faillible [fajibl] *adj* fallible

faillir [fajir] *intr* to fail, to go bankrupt ‖ (used only in: *inf*; *ger* **faillant**; *pp* & compound tenses; *pret*; *fut*; *cond*) *intr* to fail; to give way; (with *dat*) to fail, let (*s.o.*) down; **faillir à** to fail in (*a duty*); to fail to keep (*a promise*); **faillir à** + *inf* to fail to + *inf*; **sans faillir** without fail ‖ (used only in *pret* and *past indef*) *intr*—nearly, almost, e.g., **il a failli être écrasé** he was nearly run over

faillite [fajit] *f* bankruptcy; **faire faillite** to go bankrupt

faim [fɛ̃] *f* hunger; **avoir faim** to be hungry; **avoir une faim de loup** to be hungry as a bear; **manger à sa faim** to eat one's fill

fainéant [feneɑ̃] **fainéante** [feneɑ̃t] *adj* lazy ‖ *mf* loafer, do-nothing

fainéanter [feneɑ̃te] *intr* (coll) to loaf

faire [fer] *m* making, doing ‖ §29 *tr* to make; to do; to give (*an order; a lecture; alms, a gift; thanks*); to take (*a walk; a step*); to pack (*a trunk*); to clean (*the room, the shoes, etc.*); to follow (*a trade*); to keep (*silence*);

to perform (*a play; a miracle*); to play the part of; to charge for, e.g., **combien faites-vous ces souliers?** how much do you charge for these shoes?; to say, e.g., **oui, fit-il** yes, said he; (coll) to estimate the cost of; for expressions like **il fait chaud** it is warm, see the noun; **cela ne fait rien** it doesn't matter; **faire** + *inf* to have + *inf*, e.g., **je le ferai aller** I shall have him go; **faire** + *inf* to make + *inf*, e.g., **je le ferai parler** I will make him talk; **faire** + *inf* to have + *pp*, e.g., **je vais faire faire un complet** I am going to have a suit made; **il n'en fait pas d'autres** that's just like him; **ne faire que** + *inf* to keep on + *ger*, e.g., **il ne fait que crier** he keeps on yelling ‖ *intr* to go, e.g., **la cravate fait bien avec la chemise** the tie goes well with the shirt; to act; **comment faire?** what shall I do?; **faire dans** to make a mess in; **ne faire que de** + *inf* to have just + *pp*, e.g., **il ne fait que d'arriver** he has just arrived ‖ *ref* to become (*a doctor, lawyer, etc.*); to grow (*e.g., old*); to improve; to happen; to pretend to be; **se faire à** to get accustomed to, to adjust to; **s'en faire** to worry, e.g., **ne vous en faites pas!** don't worry!

faire-part [ferpar] *m invar* announcement (*of birth, marriage, death*)

faire-valoir [fervalwar] *m invar* turning to account; **faire-valoir direct** farming by the owner

faisable [fəzabl] *adj* feasible

fai·san [fəzã] **-sane** [zan] or **-sande** [zãd] *mf* pheasant

faisander [fəzãde] *tr* to jerk (*game*) ‖ *intr* to become gamy, to get high

fais·ceau [feso] *m* (*pl* **-ceaux**) bundle, cluster; beam (*of light*); pencil (*of rays*); **faisceaux** fasces; **faisceaux de preuves** cumulative evidence; **former les faisceaux** to stack or pile arms

fai·seur [fəzœr] **-seuse** [zøz] *mf*—**bon faiseur** first-rate workman; **faiseur de mariages** matchmaker; **faiseur de vers** versifier, poetaster ‖ *m* bluffer; schemer

fait [fe] **faite** [fet] *adj* well-built, shapely; full-grown; made-up (*with cosmetics*); **fait à la main** hand-made; **tout fait** ready-made ‖ *m* deed, act; fact; **dire son fait à qn** (coll) to give s.o. a piece of one's mind; **prendre fait et cause pour** to take up the cudgels for; **si fait** yes, indeed; **sur le fait** redhanded, in the act; **tout à fait** entirely ‖ [fet] *m*—**au fait** to the point; after all; **de fait** de facto; **du fait que** owing to the fact that; **en fait** as a matter of fact

faîtage [fetaʒ] *m* ridgepole; roofs; roofing

fait-divers [fediver] *m* (*pl* **faits-divers**) news item

faîte [fet] *m* peak; top (*of tree*); ridge (*of roof*)

faîtière [fetjer] *adj fem* ridge ‖ *f* ridge tile; skylight

fait-tout [fetu] *m invar* stewpan, casserole

faix [fe] *m* load, burden; (archit) settling; (physiol) fetus and placenta

falaise [falez] *f* cliff, bluff

falla·cieux [falasjø] **-cieuse** [sjøz] *adj* fallacious

falloir [falwar] §30 *impers* to be necessary; **c'est plus qu'il n'en faut** that's more than enough; **comme il faut** proper; properly; the right kind of, e.g., **un chapeau comme il faut** the right kind of hat; **il fallait le dire!** why didn't you say so!; **il faut** + *inf* it is necessary to + *inf*, one must + *inf*; **il faut qu'il** + *subj* it is necessary that he + *subj*, it is necessary for him to + *inf*; he must + *inf* (expressing conjecture), e.g., **il n'est pas venu, il faut qu'il soit malade** he did not come, he must be sick; **il faut qu'il ne** + *subj* + **pas** he must not + *inf*, e.g., **il faut qu'il ne vienne pas** he must not come; **il faut une connaissance des affaires à ce travail** the work requires business experience; **il faut une heure** it takes an hour; **il leur a fallu trois jours** it took them three days; **il leur faut** + *inf* they have to + *inf*, they must + *inf*; **il leur faut du repos** they need rest; **il leur faut sept dollars** they need seven dollars; **il ne faut pas** + *inf* one must or should not + *inf*, e.g., **il ne faut pas se fier à ce garçon** one must not trust that boy; **il ne faut pas qu'il** + *subj* he must not + *inf*; **que leur faut-il?** what do they need?, what do they require?; **qu'il ne fallait pas** wrong, e.g., **la police a arrêté l'homme qu'il ne fallait pas** the police arrested the wrong man ‖ *ref*—**il s'en faut de beaucoup** not by a long shot, far from it, not by any means; **il s'en faut de dix dollars** there is a shortage of ten dollars; **peu m'en est fallu que . . .** it very nearly happened that . . . ; **peu s'en faut** very nearly; **tant s'en faut que** far from, e.g., **tant s'en faut qu'il soit artiste** he is far from being an artist

fa·lot [falo] **-lotte** [lɔt] *adj* wan, colorless; quaint, droll ‖ *m* lantern

falsification [falsifikɑsjɔ̃] *f* falsification; adulteration; debasement (*of coin*)

falsifier [falsifje] *tr* to falsify; to adulterate; to debase (*coin*)

fa·mé -mée [fame] *adj*—**mal famé** disreputable

famélique [famelik] *adj* famished

fa·meux [famø] **-meuse** [møz] *adj* famous ‖ (when standing before noun) *adj* (coll) notorious; well-known

fami·lial -liale [familjal] *adj* (*pl* **-liaux** [ljo]) family, domestic ‖ *f* station wagon

familiariser [familjarize] *tr* to familiarize ‖ *ref* to become familiar

familiarité [familjarite] *f* familiarity

fami·lier [familje] **-lière** [ljer] *adj*

familiar, intimate; household (*gods*); pet (*animal*) || *mf* familiar, intimate; pet animal

famille [famij] *f* family; **en famille** in the family circle, at home; (Canad) pregnant

famine [famin] *f* famine

fa·nal [fanal] *m* (*pl* **-naux** [no]) lantern; (naut) running light

fanatique [fanatik] *adj* fanatic(al) || *mf* fanatic; enthusiast, fan

fanatisme [fanatism] *m* fanaticism

faner [fane] *tr & ref* to fade

fanfare [fɑ̃far] *f* fanfare; brass band

fanfa·ron [fɑ̃farɔ̃] **-ronne** [rɔn] *adj* bragging || *mf* braggart

fanfaronner [fɑ̃farɔne] *intr* to brag

fange [fɑ̃ʒ] *f* mire, mud; (fig) mire, gutter

fan·geux [fɑ̃ʒø] **-geuse** [ʒøz] *adj* muddy; (fig) dirty, soiled

fanion [fanjɔ̃] *m* pennant, flag

fanon [fanɔ̃] *m* dewlap (*of cow*); whalebone; fetlock; wattle

fantaisie [fɑ̃tezi] *f* imagination; fantasy, fancy, whim; **de fantaisie** fanciful; fancy, e.g., **pain de fantaisie** fancy bread

fantaisiste [fɑ̃tezist] *adj* fantastic, whimsical || *mf* whimsical person; singing comedian

fantasque [fɑ̃task] *adj* fantastic; whimsical, temperamental

fantassin [fɑ̃tasɛ̃] *m* foot soldier

fantastique [fɑ̃tastik] *adj* fantastic

fantoche [fɑ̃tɔʃ] *m* puppet

fantôme [fɑ̃tom] *adj* shadow (*government*) || *m* phantom, ghost

fanum [fanɔm] *m* hallowed ground

faon [fɑ̃] *m* fawn

faonner [fane] *intr* to bring forth young (*said especially of deer*)

faquin [fakɛ̃] *m* rascal

fa·raud [faro] **-raude** [rod] *adj* (coll) swanky || *mf* (coll) fop, bumpkin; **faire le faraud** (coll) to show off

farce [fars] *f* farce; trick, joke; (culin) stuffing

far·ceur [farsœr] **-ceuse** [søz] *mf* practical joker; phony

farcir [farsir] *tr* to stuff

fard [far] *m* make-up; **parler sans fard** to speak plainly, to tell the unvarnished truth; **piquer un fard** (coll) to blush

far·deau [fardo] *m* (*pl* **-deaux**) load, burden; weight (*of years*)

farder [farde] *tr* to make up (*an actor*); to disguise (*the truth*) || *ref* to weigh heavily; (archit) to sink; (theat) to make up

fardier [fardje] *m* dray, cart

farfe·lu -lue [farfəly] *adj* (coll) harebrained, cockeyed; bizarre

farfouiller [farfuje] *tr* (coll) to rummage about in || *intr* (coll) to rummage about; **farfouiller dans** (coll) to rummage about in

farine [farin] *f* flour, meal; **farine de froment** whole-wheat flour; **farine de riz** ground rice; **farine lactée** malted milk

fariner [farine] *tr* (culin) to flour

fari·neux [farinø] **-neuse** [nøz] *adj* white with flour; mealy; starchy

farouche [faruʃ] *adj* wild, savage; unsociable; shy; stubborn (*resistance*); fierce (*look*)

fascicule [fasikyl] *m* fascicle; **fascicule de mobilisation** marching orders

fascina·teur [fasinatœr] **-trice** [tris] *adj* fascinating || *mf* spellbinder

fasciner [fasine] *tr* to fascinate; to spellbind

fascisme [faʃism] *m* fascism

fasciste [faʃist] *adj & mf* fascist

faste [fast] *adj* auspicious; feast (*day*) || *m* pomp; **fastes** annals

fasti·dieux [fastidjø] **-dieuse** [djøz] *adj* tedious, wearisome

fas·tueux [fastɥø] **-tueuse** [tɥøz] *adj* pompous, ostentatious

fat [fat] *adj masc* conceited, foppish || *m* fop

fa·tal -tale [fatal] *adj* (*pl* **-tals**) fatal; fateful; inevitable

fatalisme [fatalism] *m* fatalism

fataliste [fatalist] *adj* fatalistic || *mf* fatalist

fatalité [fatalite] *f* fatality; fatalism; fate; curse, misfortune

fatidique [fatidik] *adj* fateful; prophetic

fati·gant [fatigɑ̃] **-gante** [gɑ̃t] *adj* fatiguing; tiresome (*person*)

fatigue [fatig] *f* fatigue

fati·gué -guée [fatige] *adj* fatigued; worn-out (*clothing*); well-thumbed (*book*)

fatiguer [fatige] *tr* to fatigue; to wear out; to weary || *intr* to strain, labor; to pull (*said of engine*); to bear a heavy strain (*said of beam*) || *ref* to get tired

fatras [fatra] *m* jumble, hodgepodge

fatuité [fatɥite] *f* conceit; foppishness

faubert [fober] *m* (naut) swab

faubourg [fobur] *m* suburb; outskirts; quarter, district (*especially of Paris*)

faubou·rien [foburjɛ̃] **-rienne** [rjɛn] *adj* working-class, vulgar || *mf* resident of the outskirts of a city; local inhabitant

fau·ché -chée [foʃe] *adj* (coll) broke (*without money*)

faucher [foʃe] *tr* to mow, reap; (coll) to swipe

fau·cheur [foʃœr] **-cheuse** [ʃøz] *mf* reaper || *m* (ent) daddy-longlegs || *f* (mach) reaper, mower

faucheux [foʃø] *m* (ent) daddy-longlegs

faucille [fosij] *f* sickle

faucon [fokɔ̃] *m* falcon

fauconnier [fokɔnje] *m* falconer

faufil [fofil] *m* basting thread

faufiler [fofile] *tr* to baste || *ref* to thread one's way, to worm one's way

faune [fon] *m* faun || *f* fauna

faunesse [fones] *f* female faun

faussaire [foser] *mf* forger

fausser [fose] *tr* to falsify, distort; to bend, twist; to warp (*the judgment*); to force (*a lock*); to strain (*the voice*); **fausser compagnie à qn** (coll) to give s.o. the slip || *intr* to sing or play out of tune ‖ *ref* to bend, buckle; to crack (*said of voice*)

fausset [fosɛ] *m* falsetto; plug (*for wine barrel*)

fausseté [foste] *f* falsity; double-dealing

faute [fot] *f* fault; mistake; blame; lack, need, want; (sports) foul; (sports) error; **faire faute** to be lacking; **faute de** for want of; **faute de copiste** clerical error; **faute de frappe** typing error; **faute d'impression** misprint; **sans faute** without fail

fauter [fote] *intr* (coll) to go wrong (*said of a woman*)

fauteuil [fotœj] *m* armchair, easy chair; seat (*of member of an academy*); chair (*of presiding officer; presiding officer himself*); **fauteuil à bascule** or **à balançoire** rocking chair; **fauteuil à oreilles** wing chair; **fauteuil d'orchestre** orchestra seat; **fauteuil pliant** folding chair; **fauteuil roulant pour malade** wheelchair; **siéger au fauteuil présidentiel** to preside

fau·teur [fotœr] **-trice** [tris] *mf* instigator, agitator

fau·tif [fotif] **-tive** [tiv] *adj* faulty

fauve [fov] *adj* fawn (*color*); musky (*odor*); wild (*beast*) ‖ *m* fawn color; wild beast; **fauves** big game

fauvette [fovɛt] *f* warbler

faux [fo] **fausse** [fos] *adj* false; counterfeit; wrong, e.g., **fausse date** wrong date; e.g., **fausse note** wrong note ‖ *m* imitation; forgery; **à faux** wrongly ‖ *faux f* scythe ‖ *faux adv* out of tune, off key

faux-bourdon [foburdɔ̃] *m* (*pl* **-bourdons**) *m* (ent) drone

faux-col [fokɔl] *m* (*pl* **-cols**) collar, detachable collar

faux-filet [fofilɛ] *m* (*pl* **-filets**) sirloin

faux-fuyant [fofɥijɑ̃] *m* (*pl* **-fuyants**) subterfuge, pretext

faux-jour [foʒur] *m* (*pl* **-jours**) halflight

faux-monnayeur [fomɔnɛjœr] *m* (*pl* **-monnayeurs**) counterfeiter

faux-pas [fopɑ] *m invar* faux pas, slip, blunder

faux-semblant [fosɑ̃blɑ̃] *m* (*pl* **-semblants**) false pretense

faveur [favœr] *f* favor; **à la faveur de** under cover of; **en faveur de** in favor of; on behalf of

favorable [favorabl] *adj* favorable

favo·ri [favori] **-rite** [rit] *adj* & *mf* favorite ‖ **favoris** *mpl* sideburns ‖ *f* mistress

favoriser [favorize] *tr* to favor; to encourage, promote

Fco or **fco** *abbr* (**franco**) postpaid

fébrile [febril] *adj* feverish

fèces [fɛs] *fpl* feces

fé·cond [fekɔ̃] **-conde** [kɔ̃d] *adj* fecund, fertile

féconder [fekɔ̃de] *tr* to impregnate

fécondité [fekɔ̃dite] *f* fecundity, fertility

fécule [fekyl] *f* starch; **fécule de maïs** cornstarch

fécu·lent [fekylɑ̃] **-lente** [lɑ̃t] *adj* starchy ‖ *m* starchy food

fédé·ral -rale [federal] *adj* & *m* (*pl* **-raux** [ro]) federal

fédéra·tif [federatif] **-tive** [tiv] *adj* federated, federative

fédération [federasjɔ̃] *f* federation

fédérer [federe] §10 *tr* & *ref* to federate

fée [fe] *f* fairy; **de fée** fairy; meticulous (*work*); **vieille fée** old hag

féerie [feri] *f* fairyland; fantasy

féerique [ferik] *adj* fairy, magic(al)

feindre [fɛ̃dr] §21 *tr* to feign ‖ *intr* to feign; to limp (*said of horse*)

feinte [fɛ̃t] *f* feint

feinter [fɛ̃te] *tr* (coll) to trick ‖ *intr* to feint

feldspath [fɛldspat], [fɛlspat] *m* feldspar

fê·lé -lée [fele] *adj* (coll) cracked, crazy

fêler [fele] *tr* to crack

félicitations [felisitasjɔ̃] *fpl* congratulations

féliciter [felisite] *tr* to congratulate; **féliciter qn de** + *inf* to congratulate s.o. for + *ger*; **féliciter qn de** or **pour** to congratulate s.o. for ‖ *ref*—**se féliciter de** to congratulate oneself on, to be pleased with oneself because of

fé·lon [felɔ̃] **-lonne** [lɔn] *adj* disloyal, treasonable

félonie [feloni] *f* disloyalty, treason

fêlure [felyr] *f* crack, chink

femelle [fəmɛl] *adj* & *f* female

fémi·nin [feminɛ̃] **-nine** [nin] *adj* & *m* feminine

féminisme [feminism] *m* feminism

femme [fam] *f* woman; wife; bride; **bonne femme** (coll) simple, goodnatured woman; **femme agent** (*pl* **femmes agents**) policewoman; **femme auteur** (*pl* **femmes auteurs**) authoress; **femme de chambre** chambermaid; **femme de charge** housekeeper; **femme de journée** cleaning woman; **femme de ménage** cleaning woman; **femme d'intérieur** homebody; **femme docteur** woman doctor (*e.g., with Ph.D. degree*); **femme juge** woman judge; **femme médecin** woman doctor (*physician*); **femme pasteur** woman preacher

fendiller [fɑ̃dije] *tr* & *ref* to crack

fendoir [fɑ̃dwar] *m* cleaver, chopper

fendre [fɑ̃dr] *tr* to crack; to split (*e.g., wood*); to cleave (*e.g., the air*); to break (*one's heart*); to elbow one's way through (*a crowd*) ‖ *ref* to crack; (escr) to lunge

fenêtre [fənɛtr] *f* window; **fenêtre à battants** casement window, French window; **fenêtre à guillotine** sash window; **fenêtre en saillie** bay window

fenil [fənil], [fəni] *m* hayloft

fenouil [fənuj] *m* fennel; **fenouil bâtard** dill

fente [fɑ̃t] *f* crack, split, fissure; notch; slot (*e.g., in a coin telephone*); (escr) lunge

féo·dal -dale [feɔdal] *adj* (*pl* **-daux** [do]) feudal

féodalisme [feɔdalism] *m* feudalism

fer [fer] *m* iron; head (*of tool*); point (*of weapon*); **croiser le fer avec** to cross swords with; **fer à cheval** horseshoe; **fer à friser** curling iron; **fer à marquer** *or* **flétrir** branding iron; **fer à repasser** iron, flatiron; **fer à souder** soldering iron; **fer de fonte** cast iron; **fer forgé** wrought iron; **fers** irons, chains, fetters; **marquer au fer** to brand; **remuer le fer dans la plaie** (coll) to rub it in

ferblanterie [ferblãtri] *f* tinware; tinwork, sheet-metal work; tinsmith's shop

ferblantier [ferblãtje] *m* tinsmith

fé·rié -riée [ferje] *adj* feast (*day*)

férir [ferir] *tr*—**sans coup férir** without striking a blow

ferler [ferle] *tr* (naut) to furl

fermage [fermaʒ] *m* tenant farming; rent

ferme [ferm] *adj* firm || *f* farm, tenant farm; farmhouse || *adv* firmly, fast

fer·mé -mée [ferme] *adj* exclusive, restricted; inscrutable (*countenance*)

ferment [fermã] *m* ferment

fermenter [fermãte] *intr* to ferment

fermer [ferme] *tr* to close, to shut; to turn off; **fermer à clef** to lock; **fermer au verrou** to bolt; **la ferme!** (slang) shut up!, shut your trap! || *intr & ref* to close, to shut

fermeté [fermte] *f* firmness

fermeture [fermətyr] *f* closing; fastening; **fermeture éclair** zipper

fer·mier [fermje] **-mière** [mjer] *adj* farming || *m* farmer; tenant farmer; lessee || *f* farmer's wife

fermoir [fermwar] *m* snap, clasp

féroce [ferɔs] *adj* ferocious

férocité [ferɔsite] *f* ferocity

ferraille [feraj] *f* scrap iron; (coll) small change; **mettre à la ferraille** to junk

ferrailleur [ferajœr] *m* dealer in scrap iron; sword rattler

fer·ré -rée [fere] *adj* ironclad; hobnailed (*shoe*); paved (*road*); **ferré sur** well versed in

ferrer [fere] *tr* to shoe (*a horse*)

ferret [fere] *m* tag (*of shoelace*); (geol) hard core

ferronnerie [ferɔnri] *f* ironwork; hardware

ferron·nier [ferɔnje] **ferron·nière** [ferɔnjer] *mf* ironworker; hardware dealer

ferrotypie [ferɔtipi] *f* tintype

ferroviaire [ferɔvjer] *adj* railway

ferrure [feryr] *f* horseshoeing; **ferrures** hardware; metal trim

ferry-boat [feribot] *m* (*pl* **-boats**) train ferry

fertile [fertil] *adj* fertile

fertiliser [fertilize] *tr* to fertilize

fertilité [fertilite] *f* fertility

fé·ru -rue [fery] *adj*—**féru de** wrapped up in (*an idea, an interest*)

fer·vent [fervã] **-vente** [vãt] *adj* fervent || *mf* devotee

ferveur [fervœr] *f* fervor

fesse [fes] *f* buttock

fessée [fese] *f* spanking

fesse-mathieu [fesmatjø] *m* (*pl* **-mathieux**) usurer; skinflint

fesser [fese] *tr* to spank

fes·su -sue [fesy] *adj* broad-bottomed

festin [festẽ] *m* feast, banquet

festi·val [festival] *m* (*pl* **-vals**) music festival

festivité [festivite] *f* festivity

feston [festɔ̃] *m* festoon

festonner [festɔne] *tr* to festoon; to scallop

festoyer [festwaye] §47 *tr* to fete, regale || *intr* to feast

fê·tard [fetar] **-tarde** [tard] *mf* merrymaker

fête [fet] *f* festival; feast day, holiday; name day; party, festivity; **être à la fête** (coll) to be very pleased or gratified; **faire fête à** to receive with open arms; **faire la fête** (coll) to carouse; **fête foraine** carnival; **fête légale** *or* **fête nationale** legal holiday; **la fête des Mères** Mother's Day; **la fête des Morts** All Souls' Day; **la fête des Rois** Twelfth-night; **se faire une fête de** to look forward with pleasure to; **souhaiter une bonne fête à qn** to wish s.o. many happy returns

Fête-Dieu [fetdjø] *f* (*pl* **Fêtes-Dieu**)— **la Fête-Dieu** Corpus Christi

fêter [fete] *tr* to fete; to celebrate (*a special event*)

fétiche [fetiʃ] *m* fetish

fétu [fety] *m* straw; trifle

feu feue [fø] *adj* (*pl* **feus**) (standing before noun) late, deceased, e.g., **la feue reine** the late queen || **feu** *adj invar* (standing before article and noun) late, deceased, e.g., **feu la reine** the late queen || *m* (*pl* **feux**) fire; flame; traffic light; burner (*of stove*); **à petit feu** by inches; **du feu à light** (*to ignite a cigar, etc.*); **être sous les feux de la rampe** to be in the limelight; **faire du feu** to light a fire; **faire long feu** to hang fire; to fail; (arti) to miss; **feu d'artifice** fireworks; **feu de joie** bonfire; **feu de paille** (fig) flash in the pan; **feu follet** will-o'-the-wisp; **feux de position**, **feux de stationnement** parking lights; **mettre le feu à** to set on fire; **prendre feu** to catch fire || **feu** *interj* fire! (*command to fire*); **au feu!** fire! (*warning*)

feuillage [fœjaʒ] *m* foliage; **feuillages** fallen branches

feuille [fœj] *f* leaf; sheet; form (*to be filled out*); **feuille de chou** (coll) rag (*newspaper of little value*); **feuille de présence** time sheet; **feuille d'étain** tin foil; **feuille de température** temperature chart; **feuille d'imposition** income-tax blank

feuil·lé feuil·lée [fœje] *adj* leafy, foliaged || *f* bower; **feuillées** (mil) camp latrine

feuiller [fœje] *intr* to leaf

feuille·té -tée [fœjte] *adj* foliated; in flaky layers

feuilleter [fœjte] §34 *tr* to leaf through; to foliate; (culin) to roll into thin layers

feuilleton [fœjtɔ̃] *m* newspaper serial (*printed at bottom of page*); (rad, telv) serial

feuil·lu feuil·lue [fœjy] *adj* leafy ‖ *m* foliage

feuillure [fœjyr] *f* groove

feuler [fœle] *intr* to growl (*said of cat*)

feutre [føtr] *m* felt

feu·tré -trée [føtre] *adj* velvetlike; muffled (*steps*)

feutrer [føtre] *tr* to felt

fève [fεv] *f* bean; **fève des Rois** bean or figurine baked in the Twelfth-night cake; **fèves au lard** pork and beans

février [fevrie] *m* February

fi [fi] *interj* fie!; **faire fi de** to scorn

fiacre [fjakr] *m* horse-drawn cab

fiançailles [fjãsaj] *fpl* engagement, betrothal

fian·cé -cée [fjãse] *mf* betrothed ‖ *m* fiancé ‖ *f* fiancée

fiancer [fjãse] §51 *tr* to betroth ‖ *ref* to become engaged

fiasco [fjasko] *m* (coll) fiasco, failure; **faire fiasco** to flop, fail

fibre [fibr] *f* fiber; (fig) feeling, sensibility; **avoir la fibre sensible** to be easily moved

fi·breux [fibrø] -breuse [brøz] *adj* fibrous

ficeler [fisle] §34 *tr* to tie up

ficelle [fisεl] *adj* (coll) knowing ‖ *f* string; **connaître les ficelles** (fig) to know the ropes; **tenir** or **tirer les ficelles** (fig) to pull strings; **vieille ficelle** (coll) old hand

fiche [fi∫] *f* peg; slip, form, blank; filing card, index card; membership card; (cards) chip, counter; (elec) plug; **fiche de consolation** booby prize; **fiche femelle** (elec) jack; **fiche perforée** punch card; **fiche scolaire** report card

ficher [fi∫e] *tr* to drive in (*a stake*); to take down (*information on a form*); to fasten, fix, stick; **ficher qn à la porte** (coll) to kick s.o. out; **ficher une gifle à qn** (coll) to box s.o. on the ear; **fichez-moi le camp!** (slang) beat it! ‖ *ref*—**se ficher de** (slang) to make fun of

fichier [fi∫je] *m* card catalogue; cabinet, file (*for cards or papers*)

fichtre [fi∫trə] *interj* (coll) gosh!

fi·chu -chue [fi∫y] *adj* (coll) wretched, ugly; **fichu de** capable of ‖ *m* scarf, shawl

fic·tif [fiktif] **-tive** [tiv] *adj* fictitious

fiction [fiksjɔ̃] *f* fiction

fidéicommis [fideikɔmi] *m* (law) trust

fidèle [fidεl] *adj* faithful ‖ *mf* supporter; **les fidèles** (eccl) the congregation, the faithful

fidélité [fidelite] *f* fidelity, faithfulness; **haute fidélité** high fidelity

fief·fé fief·fée [fjεfe] *adj* (coll) downright, real, regular (*liar, coward, etc.*)

fiel [fjεl] *m* bile; gall

fiel·leux [fjεlø] fiel·leuse [fjεløz] *adj* galling

fiente [fjãt] *f* droppings

fier 'fière [fjεr] *adj* proud; haughty ‖ **fier** [fje] *tr* (archaic) to entrust ‖ *ref*—**se fier à** or **en** to trust, to have confidence in, to rely upon; **se fier à qn de** to entrust s.o. with; **s'y fier** to trust in

fier-à-bras [fjεrabra] *m* (*pl* **fier-à-bras** or **fiers-à-bras** [fjεrabra]) braggart

fierté [fjεrte] *f* pride

fièvre [fjεvr] *f* fever; **fièvre aphteuse** foot-and-mouth disease

fifre [fifr] *m* fife; fife player

fi·gé -gée [fiʒe] *adj* curdled; fixed, set; frozen (*smile*); **figé sur place** rooted to the spot

figement [fiʒmã] *m* clotting, coagulation

figer [fiʒe] §38 *tr* to curdle; to stop dead ‖ *ref* to curdle; to set, to freeze (*said, e.g., of smile*)

fignoler [fiɲɔle] *tr* to work carefully at ‖ *intr* to be finicky

figue [fig] *f* fig; **figue de Barbarie** prickly pear

figuier [figje] *m* fig tree

figu·rant [figyrã] **-rante** [rãt] *mf* (theat) supernumerary, extra

figura·tif [figyratif] **-tive** [tiv] *adj* figurative, emblematic

figure [figyr] *f* figure; face (*of a person*); face card; **faire figure** to cut a figure; **figure de proue** (naut) figurehead; **prendre figure** to take shape

figu·ré -rée [figyre] *adj* figurative; figured ‖ *m* figurative sense

figurer '[figyre] *tr* to figure ‖ *intr* to figure, take part; (theat) to walk on ‖ *ref* to imagine, believe

fil [fil] *m* thread; wire; edge (*e.g., of knife*); grain (*of wood*); **au fil de l'eau** with the stream; **droit fil** with the grain; **elle lui a donné du fil à retordre** (fig) she gave him more than he bargained for; **fil à plomb** plumb line; **fil de fer barbelé** barbed wire; **fil de lin** yarn; **fil d'or** spun gold; **fils de la vierge** gossamer; **passer au fil de l'épée** to put to the sword; **plein de fils** stringy; **sans fil** wireless

filament [filamã] *m* filament

filamen·teux [filamãtø] -teuse [tøz] *adj* stringy

filan·dreux [filãdrø] -dreuse [drøz] *adj* stringy (*meat*); long, drawn-out

fi·lant [filã] **-lante** [lãt] *adj* ropy (*liquid*); shooting (*star*)

filasse [filas] *f* tow, oakum

filature [filatyr] *f* manufacture of thread; spinning mill; shadowing (*of a suspect*)

fil-de-fériste [fildəferist] *mf* tightwire walker

file [fil] *f* file, row, lane; **à la file** one after another, in a row; **file d'attente** waiting line; **marcher en file indienne** to walk Indian file

filer [file] *tr* to spin (*rope, cable*); to prolong; to pay out (*rope, cable*); to prolong; to shadow (*a suspect*) ‖ *intr* to ooze; to smoke (*said of lamp*); (coll) to go fast; **filer à**

l'anglaise (coll) to take French leave; **filer doux** (coll) to back down, to give in; **filez!** (coll) get out!

filet [file] *m* net; trickle (*of water*); streak (*of light*); thread (*of screw or nut*); (culin) fillet; (typ) rule; **faux filet** sirloin; **filet à bagage** baggage rack; **filet à cheveux** hair net; **filet à provisions** string bag, mesh bag

fileter [filte] §2 *tr* to thread (*a screw*); to draw (*wire*)

fi·leur [filœr] **-leuse** [løz] *mf* spinner

fi·lial -liale [filjal] *adj* (*pl* **-liaux** [ljo]) filial || *f* (com) branch, subsidiary

filiation [filjɑsjɔ̃] *f* filiation

fillère [filjɛr] *f* (mach) die; (mach) drawplate; **filière administrative** official channels; **passer par la filière** (coll) to go through channels; (coll) to work one's way up

filigrane [filigran] *m* filigree; watermark (*in paper*)

filigraner [filigrane] *tr* to filigree

filin [filɛ̃] *m* (naut) rope

fille [fij] *f* daughter; unmarried girl; servant; (pej) tart; **fille de joie, des rues, or de vie, fille publique** prostitute; **fille de salle** nurse's aid; **fille d'honneur** bridesmaid; **jeune fille** girl; **vieille fille** old maid

fillette [fijet] *f* young girl, little lass

fil·leul fil·leule [fijœl] *mf* godchild || *m* godson || *f* goddaughter

film [film] *m* film; (fig) train (*of events*); **film sonore** sound film

filmage [filmaʒ] *m* filming

filmer [filme] *tr* to film

filmique [filmik] *adj* film

filon [filɔ̃] *m* vein, lode; (coll) soft job; (coll) bonanza, strike; **filon guide** leader vein

filoselle [filozɛl] *f* floss silk

filou [filu] *m* sneak thief; cheat, sharper

filouter [filute] *tr* (coll) to swindle, cheat; **filouter q.ch. à qn** (coll) to do s.o. out of s.th. || *intr* to cheat at cards

fils [fis] *m* son; (when following proper name) junior; **fils à papa** (coll) rich man's son, playboy; **fils de ses œuvres** (fig) self-made man

filtrage [filtraʒ] *m* filtering; surveillance (*by the police*)

fil·trant [filtrɑ̃] **-trante** [trɑ̃t] *adj* filterable; filter, e.g., **papier filtrant** filter paper

filtre [filtrə] *m* filter

filtrer [filtre] *tr & intr* to filter

fin [fɛ̃] **fine** [fin] *adj* fine || (when standing before noun) *adj* clever, sly, smart; secret, hidden || *m* fine linen; smart person; **le fin du fin** the finest of the fine || **fin** *f* end; **à la fin** at last; **à seule fin de** for the sole purpose of; **à toutes fins utiles** for your information; **c'est la fin des haricots** (slang) that takes the cake; **en fin de compte** in the end; to get to the point; **fin d'interdiction de dépasser** (public sign) end of no passing; **mot de la fin** clincher; **sans**

fin endless || **fin** *adv* absolutely; finely (*ground*); small, e.g., **écrire fin** to write small

fi·nal -nale [final] (*pl* **-nals** or **-naux** [no]) *adj* final || *m* finale || *f* last syllable or letter; (mus) keynote; (sports) finals

finalement [finalmɑ̃] *adv* finally

finaliste [finalist] *mf* finalist

financement [finɑ̃smɑ̃] *m* financing

financer [finɑ̃se] §51 *tr* to finance

finan·cier [finɑ̃sje] **-cière** [sjɛr] *adj* financial; spicy (*sauce for vol-au-vent*) || *m* financier

finasser [finase] *intr* (coll) to use finesse, to finagle

finasserie [finasri] *f* shrewdness

fi·naud [fino] **-naude** [nod] *adj* wily, sly || *mf* sly fox; smart aleck

finesse [fines] *f* finesse; fineness; **savoir les finesses** to know the fine points or niceties

fi·ni -nie [fini] *adj* finished; finite; ruined (*in health, financially, etc.*); arrant (*rogue*) || *m* finish; finite

finir [finir] *tr & intr* to finish; **en finir avec** to have done with; **finir de + inf** to finish + *ger*; **finir par + inf** to finish by + *inf*

finissage [finisaʒ] *m* finishing touch, final step

finition [finisjɔ̃] *f* finish; **finitions** finishing touches

finlan·dais [fɛ̃lɑ̃dɛ] **-daise** [dez] *adj* Finnish || *m* Finnish (*language*) || (*cap*) *mf* Finn

Finlande [fɛ̃lɑ̃d] *f* Finland; **la Finlande** Finland

fin·nois [finwa] **fin·noise** [finwaz] *adj* Finnish || *m* Finnish (*language*; Finnic (*branch of Uralic*) || (*cap*) *mf* Finn

fiole [fjɔl] *f* phial

fioriture [fjɔrityr] *f* flourish, curlicue

firmament [firmamɑ̃] *m* firmament

firme [firm] *f* firm, house, company

fisc [fisk] *m* bureau of internal revenue, tax-collection agency

fis·cal -cale [fiskal] *adj* (*pl* **-caux** [ko]) fiscal; revenue, taxation

fiscaliser [fiskalize] *tr* to subject to tax

fiscalité [fiskalite] *f* tax collections; fiscal policy

fissile [fisil] *adj* fissionable

fission [fisjɔ̃] *f* fission

fissure [fisyr] *f* fissure, crack

fissurer [fisyre] *tr & ref* to fissure

fiston [fistɔ̃] *m* (slang) sonny

fixation [fiksɑsjɔ̃] *f* fixation; fixing

fixe [fiks] *adj* fixed; permanent (*ink*); glassy (*stare*); regular (*time*); set (*price*); standing (*rule*) || *m* fixed income || *interj* (mil) eyes front!

fixe-chaussette [fiksəʃosɛt] *m* (*pl* **-chaussettes**) garter (*for men's socks*)

fixement [fiksəmɑ̃] *adv* fixedly

fixer [fikse] *tr* to fix; to appoint; (coll) to stare at; **fixer son choix sur** to fix on; **pour fixer ses idées** for the sake of argument || *ref* to be fastened; to establish residence; to make up one's mind

flacon [flakɔ̃] *m* small bottle; flask

flageller [flaʒelle] *tr* to flagellate

flageoler [flaʒɔle] *intr* to quiver

flageolet [flaʒɔle] *m* flageolet; kidney bean

flagorner [flagɔrne] *tr* to flatter

fla·grant [flagrã] **-grante** [grãt] *adj* flagrant, glaring, obvious

flair [fler] *m* scent, sense of smell; (*discernment*) flair, keen nose

flairer [flere] *tr* to smell, to sniff; to scent, to smell out

fla·mand [flamã] **-mande** [mãd] *adj* Flemish || *m* Flemish (*language*) || (*cap*) *mf* Fleming (*person*)

flamant [flamã] *m* flamingo

flam·bant [flãbã] **-bante** [bãt] *adj* flaming; **flambant neuf** (coll) brand-new

flam·beau [flãbo] *m* (*pl* **-beaux**) torch; candlestick; large wax candle; (fig) light

flambée [flãbe] *f* blaze

flamber [flãbe] *tr* to singe; to sterilize; **être flambé** (coll) to be all washed up, ruined || *intr* to flame

flamberge [flãberʒ] *f* (archaic) sword, blade; **mettre flamberge au vent** to unsheathe the sword

flamboiement [flãbwamã] *m* glow, flare

flamboyant [flãbwajã] **flamboyante** [flãbwajãt] *adj* flaming, blazing; (archit) flamboyant

flamboyer [flãbwaje] §47 *intr* to flame

flamme [flam], [flam] *f* flame; pennant

flammèche [flameʃ] *f* ember, large spark

flan [flã] *m* custard; blank (*coin, medal, record*); **à la flan** (slang) happy-go-lucky; botched (*job*); **c'est du flan** (slang) it's ridiculous

flanc [flã] *m* flank; side (*of ship, mountain, etc.*); **battre du flanc** to pant; **être sur le flanc** (coll) to be laid up; **flancs** (archaic) womb; bosom; **prêter le flanc à** to lay oneself open to; **se battre les flancs** to go to a lot of trouble for nothing; **tirer au flanc** (coll) to gold-brick, to malinger

flancher [flãʃe] *intr* (coll) to give in; (coll) to weaken, give way

flanchet [flãʃe] *m* flank (*of beef*)

Flandre [flãdr] *f* Flanders; **la Flandre** Flanders

flanelle [flanel] *f* flannel

flâner [flɑne] *intr* to stroll, saunter; to loaf

flânerie [flɑnri] *f* strolling; loafing

flâ·neur [flɑnœr] **-neuse** [nøz] *mf* stroller; loafer

flanquer [flɑke] *tr* to flank; (coll) to throw, fling; **flanquer à la porte** (coll) to kick out; **flanquer un coup à** (coll) to take a swing at

fla·pi -pie [flapi] *adj* (coll) tired out, fagged out

flaque [flak] *f* puddle, pool

flash [flaʃ] *m* (*pl* **flashes**) news flash; (phot) flash attachment; (phot) flash bulb

flasque [flask] *adj* flabby || *m* metal trim || *f* flask; powder horn

flatter [flate] *tr* to flatter; to stroke; to delight; to cater to; to delude || *intr* to flatter || *ref*—**se flatter de** to flatter oneself on

flatterie [flatri] *f* flattery

flat·teur [flatœr] **flat·teuse** [flatøz] *adj* flattering || *mf* flatterer

flatulence [flatylãs] *f* (pathol) flatulence

flatuosité [flatɥozite] *f* (pathol) flatulence

fléau [fleo] *m* (*pl* **fléaux**) flail; beam (*of balance*); (fig) scourge, plague

flèche [flɛʃ] *f* arrow; spire (*of church*); boom (*of crane*); flitch (*of bacon*); **en flèche** like an arrow; in tandem; **faire flèche de tout bois** to leave no stone unturned; **flèche d'eau** (bot) arrowhead

fléchette [fleʃet] *f* dart (*used in game*)

fléchir [fleʃir] *tr* to bend; to move (*e.g., to pity*) || *intr* to bend, give way; to weaken, to flag; to go down, to sag (*said of prices*)

flegmatique [flegmatik] *adj* phlegmatic, stolid

flegme [flegm] *m* phlegm

flemme [flem] *f* (slang) sluggishness; **tirer sa flemme** (slang) to not lift a finger

flet [fle] *m* flounder

flétan [fletã] *m* halibut

flétrir [fletrir] *tr & ref* to fade, wither; to weaken

flétrissure [fletrisyr] *f* fading, withering; branding (*of criminals*); blot, stigma

fleur [flœr] *f* flower; blossom; **à fleur de** level with, even with; on the surface of; **à fleur de peau** skin-deep; **à fleur de tête** bulging (*eyes*); **en fleur** in bloom; **en fleurs** in bloom (*said of group of different varieties*); **fleur de farine** fine white flour; **fleur de l'âge** prime of life; **fleur de lis** [flœrdəlis] fleur-de-lis; **fleur des pois** (coll) pick of the lot; **fleurs** mold (*on wine, cider, etc.*)

fleurer [flœre] *intr* to exhale or give off an odor; **fleurer bon** to smell good

fleuret [flœre] *m* fencing foil

fleurette [flœret] *f* little flower; **conter fleurette** to flirt

fleu·ri -rie [flœri] *adj* in bloom; flowery; florid (*complexion; style*)

fleurir [flœrir] *tr* to decorate with flowers || *intr* to flower, bloom || *intr* (ger **florissant**; *imperf* **florissais**, etc.) to flourish

fleuriste [flœrist] *mf* florist; floral gardener; maker or seller of artificial flowers

fleuron [flœrɔ̃] *m* floret; (archit) finial; **fleuron à sa couronne** feather in his cap

fleuve [flœv] *m* river (*flowing directly to the sea*); (fig) river (*of tears, blood, etc.*)

flexible [fleksibl] *adj* flexible; (fig) pliant

flexion [flɛksjɔ̃] *f* bending, flexion; (gram) inflection

flibuster [flibyste] *tr* to rob, to snitch || *intr* to filibuster

flibustier [flibystje] *m* filibuster (*pirate*)

flic [flik] *m* (slang) copper, fuzz

flirt [flœrt] *m* flirt; flirtation

flirter [flœrte] *intr* to flirt

flir·teur [flœrtœr] **-teuse** [tøz] *adj* flirtatious || *mf* flirt

flocon [flɔkɔ̃] *m* flake; snowflake; tuft (*e.g., of wool*); **flocons d'avoine** oatmeal; **flocons de maïs** cornflakes; **flocons de neige** snowflakes

floconner [flɔkɔne] *intr* to form flakes; to become fleecy

flocon·neux [flɔkɔnø] **flocon·neuse** [flɔkɔnøz] *adj* flaky; fleecy

floraison [flɔrɛzɔ̃] *f* flowering, blooming

flo·ral -rale [flɔral] *adj* (*pl* **-raux** [ro]) floral

floralies [flɔrali] *fpl* flower show

flore [flɔr] *f* flora

floren·tin [flɔrɑ̃tɛ̃] **-tine** [tin] *adj* Florentine; **à la florentine** with spinach || (*cap*) *mf* Florentine (*native or inhabitant of Florence*)

Floride [flɔrid] *f* Florida; **la Floride** Florida

florilège [flɔrilɛʒ] *m* anthology

floris·sant [flɔrisɑ̃] **floris·sante** [flɔrisɑ̃t] *adj* flourishing

floss [flɔs] *m* (coll) dental floss

flot [flo] *m* wave; tide; flood, multitude; **à flot** afloat; **à flots** in torrents, abundantly; **flots** waters (*of a lake, the sea, etc.*); **flots de** lots of

flottabilité [flɔtabilite] *f* buoyancy

flottable [flɔtabl] *adj* buoyant; navigable (*for rafts*)

flottage [flɔtaʒ] *m* log driving

flottaison [flɔtɛzɔ̃] *f* water line

flot·tant [flɔtɑ̃] **flot·tante** [flɔtɑ̃t] *adj* floating; vacillating, undecided

flotte [flɔt] *f* fleet; buoy; float (*on fishline*); (slang) water, rain

flottement [flɔtmɑ̃] *m* floating; hesitation, vacillation; undulation

flotter [flɔte] *intr* to float; to waver, hesitate; to fly (*said of flag*); **il flotte** (slang) it is raining

flotteur [flɔtœr] *m* log driver; float (*of fishline, carburetor, etc.*); pontoon, float (*of seaplane*)

flottille [flɔtij] *f* flotilla; **flottille de pêche** fishing fleet

flou floue [flu] *adj* blurred, hazy; fluffy (*hair*); loose-fitting (*dress*); light and soft (*tones, lines in a painting*) || *m* blur, fuzziness; dressmaking

fluctuation [flyktɥasjɔ̃] *f* fluctuation

fluctuer [flyktɥe] *intr* to fluctuate

fluet [flye] **fluette** [flyet] *adj* thin, slender

fluide [flɥid] *adj & m* fluid

fluidifier [flɥidifje] *tr* to liquefy

fluor [flyɔr] *m* fluorine

fluores·cent [flyɔresɑ̃] **fluores·cente** [flyɔresɑ̃t] *adj* fluorescent

fluoridation [flyɔridasjɔ̃] *f* fluoridation

fluorider [flyɔride] *tr & intr* to fluoridate

fluorure [flyɔryr] *m* fluoride

flûte [flyt] *f* flute; long thin loaf of French bread; tall champagne glass; **flûte à bec** recorder; **flûte de Pan** Pan's pipes; **flûtes** (slang) legs; **grande flûte** concert flute; **jouer ou se tirer des flûtes** (slang) to run for it; **petite flûte** piccolo || *interj* shucks!, rats!

flûtiste [flytist] *mf* flutist

flux [fly] *m* flow; flood tide; (cards) flush; (chem, elec, med, metallurgy) flux; **flux de sang** flush, blush; dysentery; **flux de ventre** diarrhea; **flux et reflux** ebb and flow

fluxion [flyksjɔ̃] *f* inflammation

foc [fɔk] *m* (naut) jib

fo·cal -cale [fɔkal] *adj* (*pl* **-caux** [ko]) focal

fœtus [fetys] *m* fetus

foi [fwa] *f* faith; word (*of a gentleman*); **ajouter foi à** to give credence to; **bonne foi** good faith, sincerity; **de bonne foi** sincere; sincerely; **de mauvaise foi** dishonest; dishonestly; **en foi de quoi** in witness whereof; **faire foi de** to be evidence of; **ma foi!** upon my word; **manquer de foi à** to break faith with; **mauvaise foi** bad faith, insincerity; **sur la foi de** on the strength of

foie [fwa] *m* liver; **avoir les foies** (slang) to be scared stiff; **foie gras** goose liver

foin [fwɛ̃] *m* hay; **avoir du foin dans ses bottes** (coll) to be well heeled; **faire du foin** (slang) to kick up a fuss

foire [fwar] *f* fair; market; (coll) chaos, mess; **foire d'empoigne** free-for-all

foirer [fware] *intr* (slang) to flop, fail; (slang) to hang fire; (slang) to be stripped (*said of screw, nut, etc.*)

fois [fwa] *f* time, *e.g.,* **visiter trois fois par semaine** to visit three times a week; times, *e.g.,* **deux fois deux font quatre** two times two is four; **à la fois** at the same time, together; **deux fois** twice; twofold; **encore une fois** once more, again; **il y avait une fois** once upon a time there was; **maintes et maintes fois** time and time again; **une fois** one time, once; **une fois pour toutes** or **une bonne fois** once and for all

foison [fwazɔ̃] *f*—**à foison** in abundance

foison·nant [fwazɔnɑ̃] **foison·nante** [fwazɔnɑ̃t] *adj* abundant, plentiful

foisonner [fwazɔne] *intr* to abound

folâtre [folɑtr] *adj* frisky, playful

folâtrer [folɑtre] *intr* to frolic, romp

folie [fɔli] *f* madness, insanity; folly, piece of folly; country lodge, hideaway (*for romantic trysts*); **à la folie** madly, passionately; **faire une folie** to do something crazy; **folie de la persécution** persecution complex

folio [fɔljo] *m* folio

folioter [fɔljote] *tr* to folio

folle [fɔl] *f* crazy woman

follement [fɔlmɑ̃] *adv* madly

fol·let [fɔlɛ] **fol·lette** [fɔlɛt] *adj* merry, playful; elfish

follicule [fɔlikyl] *m* follicle

fomenta·teur [fɔmɑ̃tatœr] **-trice** [tris] *mf* agitator, troublemaker

fomenter [fɔmɑ̃te] *tr* to foment

fon·cé -cée [fɔ̃se] *adj* dark; deep

foncer [fɔ̃se] §51 *tr* to darken; to dig (*a well*); to fit a bottom to (*a cask*) || *intr* to charge, to rush

fon·cier [fɔ̃sje] **-cière** [sjɛr] *adj* landed (*property*); property (*tax*); funda-mental, natural || *m* real-estate tax

foncièrement [fɔ̃sjɛrmɑ̃] *adv* funda-mentally, naturally

fonction [fɔ̃ksjɔ̃] *f* function; duty; **faire fonction de** to function as

fonctionnaire [fɔ̃ksjɔnɛr] *mf* civil serv-ant; officeholder

fonctionnarisme [fɔ̃ksjɔnarism] *m* bu-reaucracy

fonction·nel -nelle [fɔ̃ksjɔnɛl] *adj* functional

fonctionner [fɔ̃ksjɔne] *intr* to function, to work

fond [fɔ̃] *m* bottom; back, far end; background; foundation; dregs; core, inner meaning, main issue; **à fond** thoroughly; **à fond de train** at full speed; **au fond, dans le fond,** or **par le fond** actually, really, basically; **de fond** fundamental, main; **de fond en comble** from top to bottom; **faire fond sur** to rely on; **fond sonore** background noise; **râcler les fonds du tiroir** to scrape the bottom of the barrel; **sans fond** bottomless; **y aller au fond** to go the whole way || *see* **fonds**

fondamen·tal -tale [fɔ̃damɑ̃tal] *adj* (*pl* **-taux** [to]) fundamental, basic

fon·dant [fɔ̃dɑ̃] **-dante** [dɑ̃t] *adj* melt-ing; juicy, luscious || *m* fondant (*candy*); (metallurgy) flux

fonda·teur [fɔ̃datœr] **-trice** [tris] *mf* founder

fondation [fɔ̃dasjɔ̃] *f* foundation; founding; endowment

fon·dé -dée [fɔ̃de] *adj* founded; justi-fied; authorized; **bien fondé** well-founded || *m*—**fondé de pouvoir** proxy, authorized agent

fondement [fɔ̃dmɑ̃] *m* foundation, basis; (coll) behind; **sans fondement** unfounded

fonder [fɔ̃de] *tr* to found

fonderie [fɔ̃dri] *f* foundry; smelting

fondeur [fɔ̃dœr] *m* founder, smelter

fondre [fɔ̃dr] *tr* to melt, dissolve; to smelt; to cast (*metal*); to blend (*colors*); to merge (*companies*) || *intr* to melt; (coll) to lose weight; **fondre en larmes** to burst into tears; **fondre sur** to pounce on

fondrière [fɔ̃drijɛr] *f* quagmire; mud-hole, rut, pothole

fonds [fɔ̃] *m* land (*of an estate*); busi-ness, good will; fund; **bon fonds** good nature; **fonds** *mpl* business house; **fonds de commerce** business house; **fonds de prévoyance** reserve fund; **fonds d'État** *mpl* government bonds

fon·du -due [fɔ̃dy] *adj* melted; molten

|| *m* blending (*of colors*); (mov, telv) dissolve, fade-out

fontaine [fɔ̃tɛn] *f* fountain; spring; well; cistern; **fontaine de Jouvence** Fountain of Youth

fonte [fɔ̃t] *f* melting; casting; cast iron; holster; (typ) font; **venir de fonte** avec to be cast in one piece with

fonts [fɔ̃] *mpl*—**fonts baptismaux** bap-tismal font

football [futbol] *m* soccer

footing [futiŋ] *m* walking

for [fɔr] *m*—**dans son for intérieur** in his heart of hearts; **for intérieur** con-science

forage [fɔraʒ] *m* drilling

fo·rain [fɔrɛ̃] **-raine** [rɛn] *adj* travel-ing, itinerant || **forains** *mpl* carnival people

forban [fɔrbɑ̃] *m* pirate

forçage [fɔrsaʒ] *m* (agr) forcing

forçat [fɔrsa] *m* convict; (hist) galley slave; (fig) drudge

force [fɔrs] *f* force; strength; **à force de** by dint of, as a result of; **à toute force at all costs**; **de première force** foremost (*musician, artist, scientist, etc.*); **de toutes ses forces** with all one's might; **force de frappe** striking force; **force m'est de . . .** (lit) I am obliged to . . . ; **force majeure** (law) act of God; **forces sheep shears**; **force vive** (phys) kinetic energy; **la force de l'âge** the prime of life || *adj invar* (archaic) many

forcément [fɔrsemɑ̃] *adv* inevitably, necessarily

force·né -née [fɔrsəne] *adj* frenzied, frantic || *m* madman || *f* crazy wom-an

forceps [fɔrsɛps] *m* (obstet) forceps

forcer [fɔrse] §51 *tr* to force; to do violence to; to bring to bay; to in-crease (*the dose*); to strain (*a mus-cle*); to mark up (*a receipt*); **forcer la main à qn** to force s.o.'s hand; **forcer la note** (coll) to overdo it; **forcer le respect de qn** to compel respect from s.o.; **forcer qn à** or **de + inf** to force s.o. to + *inf* || *ref* to overdo; to do violence to one's feel-ings

forclore [fɔrklɔr] (used only in *inf* and *pp* **forclos**) *tr* to foreclose

forclusion [fɔrklyzjɔ̃] *f* foreclosure

forer [fɔre] *tr* to drill, to bore

fores·tier [fɔrɛstje] **-tière** [tjɛr] *adj* forest || *m* forester

foret [fɔre] *m* drill

forêt [fɔre] *f* forest

fo·reur [fɔrœr] **-reuse** [røz] *adj* drill-ing || *mf* driller || *f* drill, machine drill

forfaire [fɔrfɛr] §29 (used only in *inf*; 1st, 2d, & 3d *sg pres ind*; compound tenses) *intr*—**forfaire à** to forfeit (*one's honor*); to fail in (*a duty*)

forfait [fɔrfɛ] *m* heinous crime; con-tract; package deal; (turf) forfeit; **à forfait** for a lump sum

forfaitaire [fɔrfɛtɛr] *adj* contractual

forfaiture [fɔrfɛtyr] *f* malfeasance

forfanterie [fɔrfɑ̃tri] *f* bragging

forge [fɔrʒ] *f* forge; steel mill

forger [fɔrʒe] §38 *tr* to forge

forgeron [fɔrʒərɔ̃] *m* blacksmith

forgeur [fɔrʒœr] *m* forger, smith; coiner (*e.g., of new expressions*); fabricator (*of false stories*)

formaliser [fɔrmalize] *ref* to take offense

formaliste [fɔrmalist] *adj* formalistic, conventional || *mf* formalist

formalité [fɔrmalite] *f* formality, convention

format [fɔrma] *m* size, format

formation [fɔrmasjɔ̃] *f* formation; education, training

forme [fɔrm] *f* form; **en forme** fit, in shape; **en bonne forme,** or **en bonne et due forme,** in order, in due form; **pour la forme** for appearances

for·mel -melle [fɔrmɛl] *adj* explicit; strict; formal, superficial

formellement [fɔrmɛlmɑ̃] *adv* absolutely, strictly

former [fɔrme] *tr & ref* to form

formidable [fɔrmidabl] *adj* formidable; (coll) tremendous, terrific

formulaire [fɔrmyler] *m* formulary; form (*with spaces for answers*)

formule [fɔrmyl] *f* formula; form, blank; format; **formule de politesse** complimentary close

formuler [fɔrmyle] *tr* to formulate; to draw up

fort [fɔr] **forte** [fɔrt] *adj* strong; fortified (*city*); **c'est fort!** it's hard to believe! || (when standing before noun) *adj* high (*fever*); large (*sum*); hard (*task*) || *m* fort; strong man; forte; height (*of summer*) || **fort** *adv* exceedingly; loud; hard

forteresse [fɔrtəres] *f* fortress, fort

forti·fiant [fɔrtifjɑ̃] **-fiante** [fjɑ̃t] *adj & m* tonic

fortification [fɔrtifikasjɔ̃] *f* fortification

fortifier [fɔrtifje] *tr* to fortify; to confirm (*one's opinions*)

fortin [fɔrtɛ̃] *m* small fort

for·tuit [fɔrtɥi] **-tuite** [tɥit] *adj* fortuitous, accidental

fortune [fɔrtyn] *f* fortune; **faire fortune** to make a fortune

fortu·né -née [fɔrtyne] *adj* fortunate; rich

fosse [fos] *f* pit; grave; **fosse aux lions** lions' den; **fosse commune** pauper's grave; **fosse d'aisances** cesspool; **fosse septique** septic tank

fossé [fose] *m* ditch, trench; moat; **sauter le fossé** to take the plunge

fossette [fosɛt] *f* dimple

fossile [fosil] *adj & m* fossil || *mf* fossil (*person*)

fossoyeur [foswajœr] *m* gravedigger

fou [fu] or **fol** [fɔl] **folle** [fɔl] (*pl* **fous folles**) *adj* mad, insane; foolish; extravagant; unsteady; loose (*pulley*); (coll) tremendous (*success*); **être fou à lier** to be raving mad; **être fou de** to be wild about; to be wild with (*joy, pain, etc.*) || **fou** *m* madman; fool; jester; (cards) joker; (chess) bishop || *f* see **folle**

foucade [fukad] *f* whim, impulse

foudre [fudr] *m* thunderbolt (*of Zeus*); large cask; **foudre de guerre** great captain; **foudre d'éloquence** powerful orator || *f* lightning; **foudres** displeasure (*e.g., of a prince*); **foudres de l'Église** excommunication

foudroyant [fudrwajɑ̃] **foudroyante** [fudrwajɑ̃t] *adj* lightning-like; crushing, overwhelming

foudroyer [fudrwaje] §47 *tr* to strike with lightning; to strike suddenly; to dumfound; **foudroyer d'un regard** to cast a withering glance at || *intr* to hurl thunderbolts

fouet [fwe] *m* whip; (culin) beater

fouetter [fwete] *tr & intr* to whip

fougère [fuʒer] *f* fern

fougue [fug] *f* spirit, ardor

fou·gueux [fugø] **-gueuse** [gøz] *adj* spirited, fiery, impetuous

fouille [fuj] *f* excavation; search

fouiller [fuje] *tr* to excavate; to search, comb, inspect

fouillis [fuji] *m* jumble, disorder

fouine [fwin] *f* beech marten; pitchfork; harpoon

fouiner [fwine] *intr* (coll) to pry, meddle

fouir [fwir] *tr* to dig, burrow

foulard [fular] *m* scarf, neckerchief

foule [ful] *f* crowd, mob; **en foule** in great numbers

fouler [fule] *tr* to tread on, to press; to sprain || *ref* (with *dat* of *reflex pron*) to sprain; (slang) to put oneself out, to tire oneself out

foulque [fulk] *f* (zool) coot

foulure [fulyr] *f* sprain

four [fur] *m* oven; kiln, furnace; (coll) flop, turkey; **faire cuire au four** to bake; to roast; **faire four** (coll) to flop; **four à briques** brickkiln; **four à chaux** limekiln; **petit four** teacake

fourbe [furb] *adj* deceiving, cheating || *mf* deceiver, cheat

fourberie [furbəri] *f* deceit, cheating

fourbir [furbir] *tr* to furbish, polish

fourbissage [furbisaʒ] *m* furbishing, polishing

four·bu -bue [furby] *adj* broken-down (*horse*); (coll) dead tired, all in

fourche [furʃ] *f* fork; pitchfork; **fourche avant** front fork (*of bicycle*); **fourches patibulaires** (hist) gallows

fourcher [furʃe] *tr & intr* to fork; **la langue lui a fourché** (coll) he made a slip of the tongue

fourchette [furʃɛt] *f* fork; wishbone

four·chu -chue [furʃy] *adj* forked; cloven

fourgon [furgɔ̃] *m* truck; poker; (rr) baggage car; (rr) boxcar; **fourgon bancaire** armored car; **fourgon de queue** caboose; **fourgon funèbre** hearse

fourmi [furmi] *f* ant; **fourmi blanche** white ant, termite

fourmilier [furmilje] *m* anteater

fourmilière [furmiljer] *f* ant hill

fourmiller [furmije] *intr* to swarm; to tingle (*said, e.g., of foot*); **fourmiller de** to teem with

fournaise [furnɛz] *f* furnace; (fig) oven
four·neau [furno] *m* (*pl* **-neaux**) furnace; cooking stove; **haut fourneau** blast furnace
fournée [furne] *f* batch
four·ni -nie [furni] *adj* bushy, thick; **bien fourni** well-stocked
fourniment [furnimɑ̃] *m* (mil) kit
fournir [furnir] *tr* to furnish, to supply, to provide; to follow (*a suit in cards*) ‖ *intr* (with *dat*) to supply (*s.o.'s needs*); (with *dat*) to defray (*expenses*); (with *dat*) (cards) to follow (*suit*) ‖ *ref* to grow thick; to be a customer
fournissement [furnismɑ̃] *m* contribution, holdings (*of each shareholder*); statement of holdings
fournisseur [furnisœr] *m* supplier, dealer
fourniture [furnityr] *f* furnishing, supplying; (culin) seasoning; **fournitures** supplies
fourrage [furaʒ] *m* fodder
fourrager [furaʒe] §38 *tr* to forage; to rummage, to rummage through ‖ *intr* to rummage (about), to forage
fourragère [furaʒɛr] *f* lanyard; tailboard
four·ré -rée [fure] *adj* lined with fur; furred (*tongue*); stuffed (*dates*); filled (*candies*); sham, hollow (*peace*) ‖ *m* thicket
four·reau [furo] *m* (*pl* **-reaux**) sheath; scabbard; tight skirt; **coucher dans son fourreau** (coll) to sleep in one's clothes
fourrer [fure] *tr* to line with fur; (coll) to cram, stuff; (coll) to shut up (*in prison*); (coll) to stick, poke ‖ *ref* (coll) to turn, go; (coll) to curl up (*in bed*); **se fourrer dans** (coll) to stick one's nose in
fourre-tout [furtu] *m invar* catchall; duffel bag
fourreur [furœr] *m* furrier
fourrier [furje] *m* quartermaster
fourrière [furjɛr] *f* pound (*for automobiles; for stray dogs*)
fourrure [furyr] *f* fur
fourvoyer [furvwaje] §47 *tr* to lead astray
fox [fɔks] *m* fox terrier
fox-terrier [fɔksterje] *m* fox terrier
fox-trot [fɔkstrɔt] *m invar* fox trot
foyer [fwaje] *m* foyer, lobby; hearth, fireside; firebox; focus; home; greenroom; center (*of learning; of infection*); **à double foyer** bifocal; **foyer des étudiants** student center; **foyer du soldat** service club; **foyers** native land
frac [frak] *m* cutaway coat
fracas [fraka] *m* crash; roar (*of waves*); peal (*of thunder*)
fracasser [frakase] *tr & ref* to break; to shatter, break to pieces
fraction [fraksjɔ̃] *f* fraction; breaking (*e.g., of bread*)
fractionnaire [fraksjɔnɛr] *adj* fractional
fractionnement [fraksjɔnmɑ̃] *m* cracking (*of petroleum*)

fractionner [fraksjɔne] *tr* to divide into fractions
fracture [fraktyr] *f* fracture; breaking open
fracturer [fraktyre] *tr* to fracture; to break open
fragile [fraʒil] *adj* fragile
fragment [fragmɑ̃] *m* fragment
fragmenter [fragmɑ̃te] *tr* to fragment
frai [fre] *m* spawning; spawn, roe
fraîche [frɛʃ] *f* cool of the day
fraîchement [freʃmɑ̃] *adv* in the open air; recently; (coll) cordially
fraîcheur [freʃœr] *f* coolness; freshness; newness
fraîchir [freʃir] *intr* to become cooler; to freshen (*said of wind*)
frais [fre] **fraîche** [frɛʃ] *adj* cool; fresh; wet (*paint*); **il fait frais** it is cool out ‖ (when standing before noun) *adj* recent (*date*) ‖ *m* cool place; fresh air; **aux frais de** at the expense of; **de frais** just, freshly; **faire les frais de la conversation** (coll) to take the lead in the conversation; to be the subject of the conversation; **frais** *mpl* expenses; **se mettre en frais** (coll) to go to a great deal of expense or trouble ‖ *f* see **fraîche** ‖ **frais** *adv*—**boire frais** to have a cool drink ‖ **frais fraîche** *adv* (agrees with following *pp*) just, freshly, e.g., **garçon frais arrivé de l'école** boy just arrived from school; e.g., **roses fraîches cueillies** freshly gathered roses
fraise [frez] *f* strawberry; wattle (*of turkey*); (mach) countersink
fraiser [freze] *tr* (mach) to countersink
fraisier [frezje] *m* strawberry plant
framboise [frɑ̃bwaz] *f* raspberry
framboisier [frɑ̃bwazje] *m* raspberry bush
franc [frɑ̃] **franche** [frɑ̃ʃ] *adj* free; frank, sincere; complete ‖ (when standing before noun) *adj* arrant (*knave*); downright (*fool*) ‖ **franc franque** [frɑ̃k] *adj* Frankish ‖ *m* franc (*unit of currency*) ‖ (*cap*) *m* Frank (*medieval German*) ‖ **franc** *adv* frankly
fran·çais [frɑ̃sɛ] **-çaise** [sez] *adj* French ‖ *m* French (*language*); **en bon français** in correct French ‖ (*cap*) *m* Frenchman; **les Français** the French ‖ *f* Frenchwoman
franc-alleu [frɑ̃kalø] *m* (*pl* **francs-alleux** [frɑ̃kalø]) (hist) freehold
France [frɑ̃s] *f* France; **la France** France
franchement [frɑ̃ʃmɑ̃] *adv* frankly, sincerely; without hesitation
franchir [frɑ̃ʃir] *tr* to cross, to go over or through; to jump over; to overcome (*an obstacle*)
franchise [frɑ̃ʃiz] *f* exemption; frankness; freedom; **franchise postale** frank
francique [frɑ̃sik] *m* Frankish
franciser [frɑ̃size] *tr* to make French
franc-maçon [frɑ̃masɔ̃] *m* (*pl* **francs-maçons**) Freemason

franc-maçonnerie [frãmɔsɔnri] *f* Freemasonry

franco [frãko] *adv* free, without shipping costs; **franco de bord** free on board; **franco de port** postpaid

franco-cana·dien [frãkokanadjẽ] **-dienne** [djen] *adj* French-Canadian || **Franco-Cana·dien -dienne** *mf* French Canadian

francophone [frãkofɔn] *adj* French-speaking || *mf* French speaker

franc-parler [frãparle] *m*—**avoir son franc-parler** to be free-spoken

franc-tireur [frãtirœr] *m* (*pl* **francs-tireurs**) free lance; sniper

frange [frãʒ] *f* fringe; **à frange** fringed

franger [frãʒe] §38 *tr* to fringe

franquette [frãket] *f*—**à la bonne franquette** (coll) simply, without fuss

frap·pant [frapã] **frap·pante** [frapãt] *adj* striking, surprising

frappe [frap] *f* minting, striking; stamp (*on coins, medals, etc.*); touch (*in typing*)

frap·pé [frape] **frap·pée** [frape] *adj* struck; iced; (slang) crazy || *m* (mus) downbeat

frapper [frape] *tr* to strike, hit, knock; to mint (*coin*); to stamp (*cloth*); to ice (*e.g., champagne*) || *intr* to strike, hit, knock || *ref* (coll) to become panic-stricken

frasque [frask] *f* escapade

frater·nel -nelle [fraternel] *adj* fraternal, brotherly

fraterniser [fraternize] *intr* to fraternize

fraternité [fraternite] *f* fraternity, brotherhood

fraude [frod] *f* fraud; smuggling; **en fraude** fraudulently; **faire la fraude** to smuggle; **fraude fiscale** tax evasion

fraudu·leux [frodylø] **-leuse** [løz] *adj* fraudulent

frayer [freje], [freje] §49 *tr* to mark out (*a path*) || *intr* to spawn; **frayer avec** to associate with

frayeur [frejœr] *f* fright, scare

fredaine [frɛden] *f* (coll) escapade, prank, spree

fredon [frədɔ̃] *m* (cards) three of a kind

fredonnement [frədɔnmã] *m* hum, humming

fredonner [frədɔne] *tr & intr* to hum

frégate [fregat] *f* frigate

frein [frɛ̃] *m* bit (*of bridle*); brake (*of car*); **frein à main** hand brake; **frein à pied** foot brake; **mettre le frein** to put the brake on; **mettre un frein à** to curb, check; **ronger son frein** to champ at the bit

freiner [frene] *tr & intr* to brake

frelater [frəlate] *tr* to adulterate

frêle [frel] *adj* frail

frelon [frəlɔ̃] *m* hornet

frémir [fremir] *intr* to shudder

frémissement [fremismã] *m* shudder

frêne [fren] *m* ash tree

frénésie [frenezi] *f* frenzy

frénétique [frenetik] *adj* frenzied

fréquemment [frekamã] *adv* frequently

fréquence [frekãs] *f* frequency; **basse fréquence** low frequency; **fréquence du pouls** pulse rate; **haute fréquence** high frequency

fré·quent [frekã] **-quente** [kãt] *adj* frequent; rapid (*pulse*)

fréquenter [frekãte] *tr* to frequent; to associate with; (coll) to go steady with (*a boy or girl*)

frère [frer] *m* brother; **frère consanguin** half brother (*by the father*); **frère convers** (eccl) lay brother; **frère de lait** foster brother; **frère germain** whole brother; **frère jumeau** twin brother; **frères siamois** Siamese twins; **frère utérin** half brother (*by the mother*)

fresque [fresk] *f* fresco

fret [fre] *m* freight; chartering; cargo

fréter [frete] §10 *tr* to charter (*a ship*); to rent (*a car*)

fréteur [fretœr] *m* shipowner

frétiller [fretije] *intr* to wriggle; to quiver; **frétiller de** to wag (*its tail*)

fretin [frətẽ] *m*—**le menu fretin** small fry

frette [fret] *f* hoop, iron ring

freudisme [frødism] *m* Freudianism

freux [frø] *m* rook, crow

friand [frijã] **friande** [frijãd] *adj* tasty; fond (*of food, praise, etc.*) || *m* sausage roll

friandise [frijãdiz] *f* candy, sweet; delicacy, tidbit

fric [frik] *m* (slang) jack, money

fricasser [frikase] *tr* to fricassee; to squander

friche [friʃ] *f* fallow land; **en friche** fallow

friction [friksjɔ̃] *f* friction; massage

frictionner [friksjone] *tr* to rub, massage

frigide [friʒid] *adj* frigid

frigidité [friʒidite] *f* frigidity

frigorifier [frigorifje] *tr* to refrigerate

frigorifique [frigorifik] *adj* refrigerating || *m* cold-storage plant

fri·leux [frilø] **-leuse** [løz] *adj* chilly, shivery

frimas [frima] *m* icy mist, rime

frime [frim] *f* (coll) sham, fake, hoax

frimousse [frimus] *f* (coll) little face, cute face

fringale [frẽgal] *f* (coll) mad hunger

frin·gant [frẽgã] **-gante** [gãt] *adj* dashing, spirited

fringuer [frẽge] *tr* (slang) to dress || *intr* (obs) to frisk about

fringues [frẽg] *fpl* (slang) duds

fri·pé -pée [fripe] *adj* rumpled, mussed; worn, tired (*face*)

friper [fripe] *tr* to wrinkle, rumple

friperie [fripri] *f* secondhand clothes; secondhand furniture

fri·pier [fripje] **-pière** [pjer] *mf* old-clothes dealer; junk dealer

fri·pon [fripɔ̃] **-ponne** [pɔn] *adj* roguish || *mf* rogue, rascal

friponnerie [fripɔnri] *f* rascality, cheating

fripouille [fripuj] *f* (slang) scoundrel

frire [frir] §22 (used in *inf*; *pp*; 1st, 2d, 3d *sg pres ind*; *sg imperv*; rarely used in *fut; cond*) *tr* to fry; to deep-fry; **être frit** (coll) to be done for ‖ *intr* to fry

frise [friz] *f* frieze

friselis [frizli] *m* soft rustling; gentle lapping (*of water*)

friser [frize] *tr* to curl; to border on; to graze ‖ *intr* to curl

frisoir [frizwar] *m* curling iron

fri·son [frizɔ̃] **-sonne** [zɔn] *adj* Frisian ‖ *m* wave, curl; Frisian (*language*) ‖ (*cap*) *mf* Frisian

fris·quet [friske] **-quette** [ket] *adj* (coll) chilly

frisson [frisɔ̃] *m* shiver; shudder, thrill; **frissons** shivering

frissonner [frisɔne] *intr* to shiver

frisure [frizyr] *f* curling; curls

frites [frit] *fpl* French fries

frittage [fritaʒ] *m* (metallurgy) sintering

friture [frityr] *f* frying; deep fat; fried fish; (rad, telv) static

frivole [frivɔl] *adj* frivolous, trifling

froc [frɔk] *m* (eccl) frock

froid [frwa] **froide** [frwad] *adj* cold; chilly (*manner*) ‖ *m* cold; coolness (*between persons*); **avoir froid** to be cold; **il fait froid** it is cold; **jeter un froid sur** (fig) to put a damper on **froideur** [frwadœr] *f* coldness; coolness

froissement [frwasmɑ̃] *m* bruising; rumpling, crumpling; clash (*of interests*); ruffling (*of feelings*)

froisser [frwase] *tr* to bruise; to rumple, crumple ‖ *ref* to take offense

frôlement [frolmɑ̃] *m* grazing; rustle

frôler [frole] *tr* to graze, to brush against; (coll) to have a narrow escape from

fromage [frɔmaʒ] *m* cheese; (coll) soft job; **fromage blanc** cream cheese; **fromage de tête** headcheese

froma·ger [frɔmaʒe] **-gère** [ʒer] *adj* cheese (*industry*) ‖ *m* cheesemaker; (bot) silk-cotton tree

fromagerie [frɔmaʒri] *f* cheese factory; cheese store

froment [frɔmɑ̃] *m* wheat

fronce [frɔ̃s] *f* crease, fold; **à fronces** shirred

froncement [frɔ̃smɑ̃] *m* puckering; **froncement de sourcils** frown

froncer [frɔ̃se] §51 *tr* to pucker; **froncer les sourcils** to frown, to wrinkle one's brow

frondaison [frɔ̃dezɔ̃] *f* foliation; foliage

fronde [frɔ̃d] *f* slingshot

fronder [frɔ̃de] *tr* to scoff at

fron·deur [frɔ̃dœr] **-deuse** [døz] *adj* bantering, irreverent ‖ *mf* scoffer

front [frɔ̃] *m* forehead; impudence; brow (*of hill*); (geog, mil, pol) front; **de front** abreast; frontal; at the same time; **faire front à** to face up to

fronta·lier [frɔ̃talje] **-lière** [ljer] *adj* frontier ‖ *m* frontiersman ‖ *f* frontier woman

frontière [frɔ̃tjer] *adj & f* frontier

frontispice [frɔ̃tispis] *m* frontispiece; title page

frottement [frɔtmɑ̃] *m* rubbing, friction

frotter [frɔte] *tr* to rub; to polish; to strike (*a match*); **frotter les oreilles à qn** (coll) to box s.o.'s ears ‖ *ref*— **se frotter à** (coll) to attack, to challenge; (coll) to rub shoulders with

froufrou [frufru] *m* rustle, swish

frousse [frus] *f* (slang) jitters

fructifier [fryktifje] *intr* to bear fruit

fruc·tueux [fryktɥø] **-tueuse** [tɥøz] *adj* fruitful, profitable

fru·gal -gale [frygal] *adj* (*pl* **-gaux** [go]) temperate; frugal (*meal*)

fruit [frɥi] *m* fruit; **des fruits** fruit; **fruits civils** income (*from rent, interest, etc.*); **fruits de mer** seafood; **fruit sec** (fig) flop, failure

fruiterie [frɥitri] *f* fruit store

frui·tier [frɥitje] **-tière** [tjer] *adj* fruit; fruit-bearing ‖ *mf* fruit vendor

fruste [fryst] *adj* worn; rough, uncouth

frustrer [frystre] *tr* to frustrate, disappoint; to cheat, defraud

fugace [fygas] *adj* fleeting, evanescent

fugi·tif [fyʒitif] **-tive** [tiv] *adj & mf* fugitive

fugue [fyg] *f* sudden disappearance; (mus) fugue

fuir [fɥir] §31 *tr* to flee, to run away from ‖ *intr* to flee; to leak; to recede (*said of forehead*)

fuite [fɥit] *f* flight; leak

fulgu·rant [fylgyrɑ̃] **-rante** [rɑ̃t] *adj* flashing; vivid; stabbing (*pain*)

fulguration [fylgyrasjɔ̃] *f* sheet lightning

fulgurer [fylgyre] *intr* to flash

fuligi·neux [fyliʒinø] **-neuse** [nøz] *adj* sooty

fumage [fymaʒ] *m* smoking (*of meat*); manuring (*of fields*)

fume-cigare [fymsigar] *m invar* cigar holder

fume-cigarette [fymsigaret] *m invar* cigarette holder

fumée [fyme] *f* smoke; steam; **fumées** fumes

fumer [fyme] *tr & intr* to smoke; to fume; to manure

fumerie [fymri] *f* opium den; smoking room

fumet [fyme] *m* aroma; bouquet (*of wine*)

fu·meur [fymœr] **-meuse** [møz] *mf* smoker; **fumeur à la file** chain smoker

fu·meux [fymø] **-meuse** [møz] *adj* smoky; foggy, hazy (*ideas*)

fumier [fymje] *m* manure; dunghill; (slang) skunk, scoundrel

fumiger [fymiʒe] §38 *tr* to fumigate

fumiste [fymist] *m* heater man; (coll) practical joker

fumisterie [fymistri] *f* heater work; heater shop; (coll) hooey

fumoir [fymwar] *m* smoking room; smokehouse

funambule [fynɑ̃byl] *mf* tightrope walker

funèbre [fynebr] *adj* funereal; funeral (*march, procession, service*)

funérailles [fyneraj] *fpl* funeral

funéraire [fynerer] *adj* funeral

funeste [fynest] *adj* baleful, fatal

funiculaire [fynikylɛr] *adj & m* funicular

fur [fyr] *m*—**au fur et à mesure** progressively, gradually; **au fur et à mesure de** in proportion to; **au fur et à mesure que** as, in proportion as

furet [fyrɛ] *m* ferret; snoop; ring-in-the-circle (*parlor game*)

fureter [fyrte] §2 *intr* to ferret

fureur [fyrœr] *f* fury; **à la fureur** passionately; **faire fureur** to be the rage

furi·bond [fyribɔ̃] **-bonde** [bɔ̃d] *adj* furious; withering (*look*) ‖ *mf* irascible individual

furie [fyri] *f* fury; termagant

fu·rieux [fyrjø] **-rieuse** [rjøz] *adj* furious; angry (*wind*)

furoncle [fyrɔ̃kl] *m* boil

fur·tif [fyrtif] **-tive** [tiv] *adj* furtive, stealthy

fusain [fyzɛ̃] *m* charcoal; charcoal drawing; spindle tree

fu·seau [fyzo] *m* (*pl* **-seaux**) spindle; **à fuseau** tapering; **fuseau horaire** time zone (*between two meridians*)

fusée [fyze] *f* rocket; spindleful; spindle (*of axle*); (coll) ripple, burst (*of laughter*); **fusée à retard** delayed-action fuse; **fusée d'artifice** or **fusée volante** skyrocket; **fusée éclairante** flare; **fusée engin** rocket engine; **fusée fusante** time fuse; **fusée percutante** percussion fuse

fuselage [fyzlaʒ] *m* fuselage

fuse·lé -lée [fyzle] *adj* spindle-shaped; tapering, slender (*fingers*); streamlined

fuseler [fyzle] §34 *tr* to taper; to streamline

fuser [fyze] *intr* to melt; to run (*said of colors*); to fizz, to spurt; to stream in or out (*said of light*)

fusible [fyzibl] *adj* fusible ‖ *m* fuse

fusil [fyzi] *m* gun, rifle; whetstone; rifleman; **fusil à deux coups** double-barreled gun; **fusil de chasse** shotgun; **fusil mitrailleur** light machine gun; **un bon fusil** a good shot (*person*)

fusillade [fyzijad] *f* fusillade

fusiller [fyzije] *tr* to shoot, to execute by a firing squad

fusion [fyzjɔ̃] *f* fusion

fusionner [fyzjɔne] *tr & intr* to blend, to fuse; (com) to merge

fustiger [fystiʒe] §38 *tr* to thrash, flog; to castigate

fût [fy] *m* cask, keg; barrel (*of drum*); stock (*of gun*); trunk (*of tree*); shaft (*of column*); stem (*of candelabrum*)

futaie [fytɛ] *f* stand of timber; **de haute futaie** full-grown

futaille [fytaj] *f* cask, barrel

futaine [fytɛn] *f* fustian

fu·té -tée [fyte] *adj* (coll) cunning, shrewd ‖ *f* mastic, filler

futile [fytil] *adj* futile

futilité [fytilite] *f* futility; **futilités** trifles

fu·tur -ture [fytyr] *adj* future ‖ *m* future; husband-to-be ‖ *f* future wife

fuyant [fɥijɑ̃] **fuyante** [fɥijɑ̃t] *adj* fleeting; receding (*forehead*)

fuyard [fɥijar] **fuyarde** [fɥijard] *adj & mf* runaway

G

G, g [ʒe] *m invar* seventh letter of the French alphabet

gabardine [gabardin] *f* gabardine

gabare [gabar] *f* barge

gabarit [gabari] *m* templet; (rr) maximum structure; (coll) size

gabelle [gabɛl] *f* (hist) salt tax

gâche [gɑʃ] *f* catch (*at a door*); trowel; wooden spatula

gâcher [gɑʃe] *tr* to mix (*cement*); to spoil, bungle; to squander

gâchette [gɑʃɛt] *f* trigger; pawl, spring catch

gâ·cheur [gɑʃœr] **-cheuse** [ʃøz] *adj* bungling ‖ *mf* bungler

gâchis [gɑʃi] *m* wet cement; mud, slush; (coll) mess, muddle

gaélique [gaelik] *adj & m* Gaelic

gaffe [gaf] *f* gaff; (coll) social blunder, faux pas

gaffer [gafe] *tr* to hook with a gaff ‖ *intr* (coll) to make a blunder

gaga [gaga] *adj* (coll) doddering ‖ *mf* (coll) dotard

gage [gaʒ] *m* pledge, pawn; forfeit (*in a game*); **gages** wage, wages; **prêter sur gages** to pawn

gager [gaʒe] §38 *tr* to wager, to bet; to pay wages to

ga·geur [gaʒœr] **-geuse** [ʒøz] *mf* bettor

gageure [gaʒyr] *f* wager, bet

gagiste [gaʒist] *mf* pledger; wage earner; (theat) extra

ga·gnant [gaɲɑ̃] **-gnante** [ɲɑ̃t] *adj* winning ‖ *mf* winner

gagne-pain [gaɲpɛ̃] *m invar* breadwinner; livelihood, bread and butter

gagne-petit [gaɲpəti] *m invar* cheapjack, low-salaried worker

gagner [gaɲe] *tr* to gain; to win; to earn; to reach; to save (*time*) ‖ *intr* to improve; to gain; to spread ‖ *ref* to be catching (*said of disease*)

ga·gneur [gaɲœr] **-gneuse** [ɲøz] *mf* winner; earner

gai gaie [ge] *adj* gay; (coll) tipsy

gaiement [gemɑ̃] *adv* gaily

gaieté [gete] *f* gaiety; **de gaieté de cœur** of one's own free will

gail·lard [gajar] **gail·larde** [gajard] *adj*

healthy, hearty; merry; ribald, spicy
‖ *m* sturdy fellow; tricky fellow;
gaillard d'arrière quarter-deck; **gaillard d'avant** forecastle ‖ *f* bold young
lady; husky young woman
gaillardise [gajardiz] *f* cheerfulness;
gaillardises spicy stories
gain [gɛ̃] *m* gain; earnings; winning
(*e.g., of bet*); **avoir gain de cause**
to win one's case
gaine [gɛn] *f* sheath; case, covering;
girdle (*corset*); **gaine d'aération** ventilation shaft
gainer [gene] *tr* to sheath, to encase
gaîté [gete] *f* gaiety
gala [gala] *m* gala; state dinner
galamment [galamɑ̃] *adv* gallantly
ga·lant [galɑ̃] **-lante** [lɑ̃t] *adj* gallant;
amorous; kept (*woman*) ‖ *m* gallant;
vert galant gay old blade
galanterie [galɑ̃tri] *f* gallantry; liber-
tinism
galaxie [galaksi] *f* galaxy
galbe [galb] *m* curve, sweep, graceful
outline
gale [gal] *f* mange; (coll) backbiter,
cad
galée [gale] *f* (typ) galley
galéjade [galeʒad] *f* joke, far-fetched
story
galère [galɛr] *f* galley; drudgery; mason's hand truck
galerie [galri] *f* gallery; cornice, rim;
baggage rack; **galerie marchande**
shopping center
galérien [galerjɛ̃] *m* galley slave
galet [galɛ] *m* pebble; (mach) roller
galetas [galta] *m* hovel
galette [galɛt] *f* cake; buckwheat pancake; hardtack; (slang) dough,
money; **galette des Rois** twelfth-cake
(*eaten at Epiphany*)
ga·leux [galø] **-leuse** [løz] *adj* mangy
galimatias [galimatja] *m* nonsense,
gibberish
galion [galjɔ̃] *m* galleon
Galles [gal]—**le pays de Galles** Wales;
prince de Galles Prince of Wales
gal·lois [galwa] **gal·loise** [galwaz] *adj*
Welsh ‖ *m* Welsh (*language*) ‖ (*cap*)
m Welshman; **les Gallois** the Welsh
‖ (*cap*) *f* Welshwoman
gallon [galɔ̃] *m* gallon (*imperial or
American*)
galoche [galɔʃ] *f* clog (*shoe*); **de** or **en
galoche** pointed (*chin*)
galon [galɔ̃] *m* galloon, braid; (mil)
stripe, chevron; **prendre du galon** to
move up
galonner [galɔne] *tr* to trim with braid
galop [galo] *m* gallop; **petit galop**
canter
galoper [galɔpe] *tr & intr* to gallop
galopin [galɔpɛ̃] *m* (coll) urchin
galvaniser [galvanize] *tr* to galvanize
galvauder [galvode] *tr* (coll) to botch;
(coll) to waste (*e.g., one's talent*);
(coll) to sully (*a name*) ‖ *intr* (slang)
to walk the streets ‖ *ref* (slang) to
go bad
gambade [gɑ̃bad] *f* gambol
gambader [gɑ̃bade] *intr* to gambol
gambit [gɑ̃bi] *m* gambit

gamelle [gamɛl] *f* mess kit
ga·min [gamɛ̃] **-mine** [min] *mf* street
urchin; youngster
gaminerie [gaminri] *f* mischievousness
gamme [gam] *f* gamut, range; set (*of
tools*); (mus) scale, gamut
Gand [gɑ̃] *m* Ghent
ganglion [gɑ̃glijɔ̃] *m* ganglion
gangrène [gɑ̃gren] *f* gangrene
gangrener [gɑ̃grəne] §2 *tr & ref* to
gangrene
ganse [gɑ̃s] *f* braid, piping
gant [gɑ̃] *m* glove; **jeter le gant** to
throw down the gauntlet; **prendre
des gants pour** to put on kid gloves
to; **relever le gant** to take up the
gauntlet; **se donner des gants** to take
all the credit
gantelet [gɑ̃tlɛ] *m* protective glove
ganter [gɑ̃te] *tr* to put gloves on (*s.o.*);
to fit, to become (*s.o.; said of gloves*)
cela me gante (coll) that suits me ‖
intr—**ganter de** to wear, to take (*a
certain size of glove*) ‖ *ref* to put on
one's gloves
garage [garaʒ] *m* garage; turnout
garagiste [garaʒist] *m* garageman,
mechanic
ga·rant [garɑ̃] **-rante** [rɑ̃t] *adj* guaran-
teeing ‖ *mf* guarantor, warrantor;
se porter garant de to guarantee ‖ *m*
guarantee, warranty
garantie [garɑ̃ti] *f* guarantee
garantir [garɑ̃tir] *tr* to guarantee; to
vouch for; to shelter, protect
garce [gars] *f* (coll) wench; (coll) bitch
garçon [garsɔ̃] *m* boy; young man;
bachelor; apprentice; waiter; **garçon
de courses** errand boy; **garçon de
recette** bank messenger; **garçon de
salle** orderly; **garçon d'honneur** best
man; **garçon manqué** tomboy; **vieux
garçon** old bachelor
garçonne [garsɔn] *f* bachelor girl
garçonnet [garsɔnɛ] *m* little boy
garçon·nier [garsɔnje] **garçon·nière**
[garsɔnjer] *adj* bachelor; tomboyish
‖ *f* bachelor apartment; tomboy
garde [gard] *m* guard, guardsman;
keeper, custodian; **garde champêtre**
constable; **garde de nuit** night watchman; **garde forestier** ranger ‖ *f*
guard; custody; nurse; flyleaf; **de
garde** on duty; **garde à vous!** (mil)
attention!; **garde civique** national
guard; **monter la garde** to go on
guard duty; **prendre garde à** to look
out for, to take notice of; **prendre
garde de** to take care not to; to be
careful to; **prendre garde que** to
notice that; **prendre garde que . . .
ne + subj** to be careful lest, to be
careful that . . . not; **sur ses gardes**
on one's guard
garde-à-vous [gardavu] *m invar* (*military position*) attention
garde-à-vue [gardavy] *f* custody, imprisonment
garde-barrière [gardəbarjer] *mf* (*pl
gardes-barrière* or *gardes-barrières*)
crossing guard
garde-bébé [gardəbebe] *mf* (*pl* -**bébés**)
baby-sitter

garde-boue [gardəbu] *m invar* mudguard

garde-chasse [gardəʃas] *m* (*pl* gardeschasse *or* gardes-chasses) gamekeeper

garde-corps [gardəkɔr] *m invar* guardrail; (naut) life line

garde-côte [gardəkot] *m* (*pl* -côtes) coast-guard cutter ‖ *m* (*pl* gardescôtes) (obs) coastguardsman; (obs) coast guard

garde-feu [gardəfø] *m invar* fire screen

garde-fou [gardəfu] *m* (*pl* -fous) guardrail

garde-frein [gardəfrɛ̃] *m* (*pl* gardesfrein *or* gardes-freins) brakeman

garde-magasin [gardəmagazɛ̃] *m* (*pl* gardes-magasin *or* gardes-magasins) warehouseman

garde-malade [gardəmalad] *mf* (*pl* gardes-malades) nurse

garde-manger [gardəmɑ̃ʒe] *m invar* icebox; larder

garde-meuble [gardəmœbl] *m* (*pl* -meuble *or* meubles) furniture warehouse

garde-nappe [gardənap] *m* (*pl* -nappe *or* nappes) table mat, place mat

garde-pêche [gardəpɛʃ] *m* (*pl* gardespêche) fish warden ‖ *m invar* fishery service boat

garder [garde] *tr* to guard; to keep; **garder à vue** to hold in custody; **garder jusqu'à l'arrivée** (formula on envelope) hold for arrival; **garder la chambre** to stay in one's room; **garder la ligne** to keep one's figure ‖ *ref* to keep (*to stay free of deterioration*); **se garder de** to protect oneself from; to watch out for; to take care not to

garde-rats [gardəra] *m invar* rat guard

garderie [gardəri] *f* nursery; forest reserve

garde-robe [gardərɔb] *f* (*pl* -robes) wardrobe

garde-voie [gardəvwa] *m* (*pl* gardesvoie *or* gardes-voies) trackwalker

garde-vue [gardəvy] *m invar* eyeshade, visor

gar·dien [gardjɛ̃] **-dienne** [djen] *adj* guardian (*angel*) ‖ *mf* guard, guardian; keeper; caretaker; attendant (*at a garage*); **gardien de but** goalkeeper; **gardien de la paix** policeman

gare [gar], [gɑr] *f* station; **gare aérienne** airport; **gare de triage** switchyard; **gare maritime** port, dock; **gare routière** *or* **gare d'autobus** bus station ‖ [gar] *interj* look out!

garer [gare] *tr* to park; to put in the garage; (naut) to dock; (rr) to shunt; (coll) to secure (*e.g., a fortune*) ‖ *ref* to get out of the way; to park, park one's car; **se garer de** to look out for

gargariser [gargarize] *ref* to gargle

gargarisme [gargarism] *m* gargle

gargote [gargɔt] *f* (coll) hash house, beanery

gargouille [garguj] *f* gargoyle

gargouillement [gargujmɑ̃] *m* gurgling; rumbling (*in stomach*)

gargouiller [garguje] *intr* to gurgle

garnement [garnəmɑ̃] *m* scamp, bad boy

gar·ni **-nie** [garni] *adj* furnished (*room*) ‖ *m* furnished room; furnished house

garnir [garnir] *tr* to garnish, adorn; to furnish; to strengthen; to line (*a brake*) ‖ *ref* to fill up (*said of crowded room, theater seats, etc.*)

garnison [garnizɔ̃] *f* garrison

garniture [garnityr] *f* garniture, decoration; fittings; accessories; complete set; (culin) garnish; **garniture de feu** fire irons; **garniture de lit** bedding

garrot [garo] *m* garrote (*instrument of torture*); (med) tourniquet; (zool) withers

garrotte [garɔt] *f* garrote (*torture*)

garrotter [garote] *tr* to garrote; to pinion

gars [gɑ] *m* (coll) lad

Gascogne [gaskɔɲ] *f* Gascony; **la Gascogne** Gascony

gasconnade [gaskɔnad] *f* gasconade; insincere invitation

gas-oil [gazwal] *m* diesel oil

Gaspésie [gaspezi] *f* Gaspé Peninsula

gaspiller [gaspije] *tr* to waste, squander

gastrique [gastrik] *adj* gastric

gastronomie [gastrɔnɔmi] *f* gastronomy

gâ·teau [gɑto] *adj invar* (coll) fond (*papa*); (coll) fairy (*godmother*) ‖ *m* (*pl* -teaux) cake; (coll) booty, loot; **gâteau de miel** honeycomb; **gâteau des Rois** twelfth-cake

gâte-métier [gɑtmetje] *m invar* undercutter

gâte-papier [gɑtpapje] *m invar* hack writer

gâter [gate] *tr & ref* to spoil

gâte-sauce [gatsos] *m invar* poor cook; kitchen boy

gâ·teux [gɑtø] **-teuse** [tøz] *adj* (coll) senile ‖ *mf* (coll) dotard

gâtisme [gatism] *m* senility

gauche [goʃ] *adj* left; left-hand; crooked; awkward ‖ *f* left hand; left side; (pol) left wing; **à gauche** to the left; **à gauche, gauche!** (mil) left, face!

gau·cher [goʃe] **-chère** [ʃer] *adj* left-handed ‖ *mf* left-hander

gauchir [goʃir] *tr & ref* to warp

gauchiste [goʃist] *adj & mf* leftist

gaudriole [godrijɔl] *f* broad joke

gaufre [gofr] *f* waffle; **gaufre de miel** honeycomb

gaufrer [gofre] *tr* to emboss, figure; to flute; to corrugate

gaufrette [gofret] *f* wafer

gaufrier [gofrije] *m* waffle iron

gaule [gol] *f* pole; **la Gaule** Gaul

gauler [gole] *tr* to bring down (*e.g., fruit*) with a pole

gau·lois [golwa] **-loise** [lwaz] *adj* Gaulish, Gallic; broad (*humor*) ‖ *m* Gaulish (*language*) ‖ (cap) *mf* Gaul ‖ (cap) *f* gauloise (*cigarette*)

gauloiserie [golwazri] *f* racy joking

gaulthérie [goteri] *f* (bot) wintergreen

gausser [gose] *ref*—**se gausser de** (coll) to poke fun at

gaver [gave] *tr & ref* to cram

gavroche [gavrɔʃ] *mf* street urchin

gaz [gaz] *m* gas; gaslight; gas company; **gaz d'échappement** exhaust; **gaz d'éclairage** illuminating gas; **gaz de combat** poison gas; **gaz en cylindre** bottled gas; **gaz hilarant** laughing gas; **gaz lacrimogène** tear gas; **mettre les gaz** (aut) to step on the gas

gaze [gaz] *f* gauze; cheesecloth

ga·zé -zée [gaze] *adj* gassed || *mf* gas casualty

gazéifier [gazeifje] *tr* to gasify; to carbonate, charge

gazelle [gazɛl] *f* gazelle

gazer [gaze] *tr* to gas; to cover with gauze; to tone down || *intr* (coll) to go full steam ahead; **ça gaze?** (coll) how goes it?

ga·zeux -zeuse [gazø] -[zøz] *adj* gaseous; carbonated

ga·zier [gazje] -**zière** [zjer] *adj* gas || *m* gasman; gas fitter

gazoduc [gazɔdyk] *m* gas pipe line

gazogène [gazɔʒɛn] *m* gas producer

gazoline [gazɔlin] *f* petroleum ether

gazomètre [gazɔmetr] *m* gasholder, gas tank

gazon [gazɔ̃] *m* lawn; turf, sod

gazonner [gazɔne] *tr* to sod

gazouiller [gazuje] *intr* to chirp, twitter; to warble; to babble

gazouillis [gazuji] *m* chirping; warbling; babbling

geai [ʒɛ] *m* jay

géant [ʒeɑ̃] **géante** [ʒeɑ̃t] *adj* gigantic || *m* giant || *f* giantess

Gédéon [ʒedeɔ̃] *m* (Bib) Gideon

gei·gnard [ʒeɲar] -**gnard** [ɲard] *adj* (coll) whining || *mf* (coll) whiner

geignement [ʒeɲmɑ̃] *m* whining, whimper

geindre [ʒɛ̃dr] §50 *intr* to whine, whimper; (coll) to complain

gel [ʒɛl] *m* frost, freezing; (chem) gel

gélatine [ʒelatin] *f* gelatin

gelée [ʒəle] *f* frost; (culin) jelly; **gelée blanche** hoarfrost

geler [ʒəle] §2 *tr, intr & ref* to freeze; to congeal

gelure [ʒəlyr] *f* frostbite

gémi·né -née [ʒemine] *adj* twin; coeducational (*school*)

gémir [ʒemir] *intr* to groan, moan

gémissement [ʒemismɑ̃] *m* groaning, moaning

gemme [ʒem] *f* gem; bud; pine resin

gemmer [ʒeme] *tr* to tap for resin || *intr* to bud

gê·nant [ʒenɑ̃] -**nante** [nɑ̃t] *adj* troublesome, embarrassing

gencive [ʒɑ̃siv] *f* (anat) gum

gendarme [ʒɑ̃darm] *m* policeman; rock pinnacle; flaw (*of gem*); (coll) virago; (slang) red herring

gendarmerie [ʒɑ̃darmri] *f* police headquarters

gendre [ʒɑ̃dr] *m* son-in-law

gêne [ʒen] *f* discomfort, embarrassment; **être dans la gêne** to be hard up; **être sans gêne** (coll) to be rude, casual

gène [ʒen] *m* (biol) gene

généalogie [ʒenealɔʒi] *f* genealogy

gêner [ʒene] *tr* to embarrass; to inconvenience; to hinder; to embarrass financially; to pinch (*the feet*)

géné·ral -rale [ʒeneral] *adj & m* (*pl* -**raux** [ro]) general; **en général** in general; **général de brigade** brigadier general; **général de corps d'armée** lieutenant general; **général de division** major general || *f* general's wife; (theat) opening night; **battre la générale** (mil) to sound the alarm

généralat [ʒenerala] *m* generalship

généraliser [ʒeneralize] *tr & intr* to generalize

généralissime [ʒeneralisim] *m* generalissimo

généralité [ʒeneralite] *f* generality; **la généralité de** the general run of

généra·teur [ʒeneratœr] -**trice** [tris] *adj* generating || *m* boiler || *f* generator

génération [ʒeneɾasjɔ̃] *f* generation

générer [ʒenere] §10 *tr* to generate

géné·reux [ʒenerø] -**reuse** [røz] *adj* generous; full (*bosom*); rich, full (*wine*)

générique [ʒenerik] *adj* generic || *m* (mov) credit line

générosité [ʒenerozite] *f* generosity; **générosités** acts of generosity

Gênes [ʒen] *f* Genoa

genèse [ʒənez] *f* genesis

genet [ʒəne] *m* jennet (*horse*)

genêt [ʒəne] *m* (bot) broom; **genêt épineux** furze

génétique [ʒenetik] *adj* genetic || *f* genetics

gê·neur [ʒenœr] -**neuse** [nøz] *mf* intruder, spoilsport

Genève [ʒənev] *f* Geneva

gene·vois [ʒənvwa], [ʒɛnvwa] -**voise** [vwaz] *adj* Genevan || (*cap*) *mf* Genevan (*person*)

genévrier [ʒənevrije] *m* juniper

gé·nial -niale [ʒenjal] *adj* (*pl* -**niaux** [njo]) brilliant, ingenious; genius-like, of genius

génie [ʒeni] *m* genius; bent, inclination; genie; engineer corps; **génie civil** civil engineering; **génie industriel** industrial engineering; **génie maritime** naval construction

genièvre [ʒənjevr] *m* juniper; juniper berry; gin

génisse [ʒenis] *f* heifer

géni·tal -tale [ʒenital] *adj* (*pl* -**taux** [to]) genital

géni·teur [ʒenitœr] -**trice** [tris] *adj* engendering || *m* sire || *f* genetrix

géni·tif [ʒenitif] -**tive** [tiv] *adj & m* genitive

génocide [ʒenɔsid] *m* genocide

gé·nois [ʒenwa] -**noise** [nwaz] *adj* Genoese || (*cap*) *mf* Genoese

ge·nou [ʒənu] *m* (*pl* -**noux**) knee; (mach) joint

genouillère [ʒənujer] *f* kneecap; kneepad

genre [ʒɑ̃r] *m* genre; genus; kind, sort;

manner, way; fashion, taste; (gram) gender; **de genre** (fa) genre; **faire du genre** (coll) to put on airs; **genre humain** humankind

gens [ʒɑ̃] *mpl* (an immediately preceding adjective that varies in its feminine form is put in that form, and so are **certain, quel, tel,** and **tout** that precede that preceding adjective, but the noun remains masculine for pronouns that stand for it, for past participles that agree with it, and for adjectives in all other positions, e.g., **toutes ces vieilles gens sont intéressants** all these old people are interesting) people; nations, e.g., **droit des gens** law of nations; men, e.g., **gens de lettres** men of letters; **gens d'affaires** businessmen; **gens d'Église** clergy; **gens de la presse** newsmen; **gens de mer** seamen; **gens de robe** bar; **jeunes gens** young people (*men and women*); young men

gent [ʒɑ̃] *f* (obs) nation, race

gentiane [ʒɑ̃sjan] *f* gentian

gen·til [ʒɑ̃ti] **-tille** [tij] *adj* nice, kind || (*cap*) *m* pagan, gentile

gentilhomme [ʒɑ̃tijɔm] *m* (*pl* **gentils-hommes** [ʒɑ̃tizɔm]) nobleman

gentillesse [ʒɑ̃tijɛs] *f* niceness, kindness; **gentillesses** nice things, kind words

gentil·let [ʒɑ̃tijɛ] **gentil·lette** [ʒɑ̃tijɛt] *adj* rather nice

gentiment [ʒɑ̃timɑ̃] *adv* nicely; gracefully

géographie [ʒeɔgrafi] *f* geography

geôle [ʒol] *f* jail

geô·lier [ʒolje] **-lière** [ljɛr] *mf* jailer

géologie [ʒeɔlɔʒi] *f* geology

géologique [ʒeɔlɔʒik] *adj* geologic(al)

géomé·tral -trale [ʒeɔmetral] *adj* (*pl* **-traux** [tro]) flat (*projection*)

géométrie [ʒeɔmetri] *f* geometry

géométrique [ʒeɔmetrik] *adj* geometric(al)

géophysique [ʒeɔfizik] *f* geophysics

géopolitique [ʒeɔpɔlitik] *f* geopolitics

Georges [ʒɔrʒ] *m* George

gérance [ʒerɑ̃s] *f* management; board of directors

géranium [ʒeranjɔm] *m* geranium

gé·rant [ʒerɑ̃] **-rante** [rɑ̃t] *mf* manager; **gérant d'une publication** managing editor

gerbe [ʒɛrb] *f* sheaf; spray (*of flowers; of water; of bullets*); shower (*of sparks*)

gerbée [ʒɛrbe] *f* straw

gerber [ʒɛrbe] *tr* to sheave; to stack

gerce [ʒɛrs] *f* crack, split; clothes moth

gercer [ʒɛrse] §51 *tr, intr, & ref* to crack, to chap

gerçure [ʒɛrsyr] *f* crack, chap

gérer [ʒere] §10 *tr* to manage, to run

gériatrie [ʒerjatri] *f* geriatrics

ger·main [ʒɛrmɛ̃] **-maine** [mɛn] *adj* german, first (*cousin*)

germe [ʒɛrm] *m* germ

germer [ʒɛrme] *intr* to germinate

germicide [ʒɛrmisid] *adj* germicidal || *m* germicide

gérondif [ʒerɔ̃dif] *m* gerund

gérontologie [ʒerɔ̃tɔlɔʒi] *f* gerontology

gésier [ʒesje] *m* gizzard

gésir [ʒezir] (used only in *inf*; **ger gisant**; 3d *sg pres ind* **gît**; 1st, 2d, 3d *pl pres ind* **gisons, gisez, gisent**; *imperf ind* **gisais, gisait, gisions, gisiez, gisaient**) *intr* to lie; **ci-gît** here lies (*buried*)

gesse [ʒɛs] *f* vetch; **gesse odorante** sweet pea

gestation [ʒɛstasjɔ̃] *f* gestation

geste [ʒɛst] *m* gesture || *f* medieval epic poem

gesticuler [ʒɛstikyle] *intr* to gesticulate

gestion [ʒɛstjɔ̃] *f* management, administration

gestionnaire [ʒɛstjɔnɛr] *adj* managing || *mf* manager, administrator

geyser [ʒezɛr], [ʒejzɛr] *m* geyser

ghetto [geto], [gɛto] *m* ghetto

gib·beux [ʒibø] **gib·beuse** [ʒibøz] *adj* humped, hunchbacked

gibecière [ʒibsjɛr] *f* game bag; sack (*for papers, books, etc.*)

gibelotte [ʒiblɔt] *f* rabbit stew

gibet [ʒibɛ] *m* gibbet, gallows

gibier [ʒibje] *m* game; **gibier à plume** feathered game; **gibier de potence** gallows bird

giboulée [ʒibule] *f* shower; hailstorm

giboyeux [ʒibwajø] **giboyeuse** [ʒibwajøz] *adj* full of game

gibus [ʒibys] *m* opera hat

giclée [ʒikle] *f* spurt

gicler [ʒikle] *intr* to spurt

gicleur [ʒiklœr] *m* atomizer; (aut) spray nozzle (*of carburetor*)

gifle [ʒifl] *f* slap in the face

gifler [ʒifle] *tr* to slap in the face

gigantesque [ʒigɑ̃tɛsk] *adj* gigantic

gigogne [ʒigɔɲ] *adj—***table gigogne** nest of tables || (*cap*) *f—***la mère Gigogne** the old woman who lived in a shoe

gigolo [ʒigolo] *m* (coll) gigolo

gigot [ʒigo] *m* leg of lamb, leg of mutton; **à gigot** leg-of-mutton (*sleeve*)

gigue [ʒig] *f* jig; haunch (*of venison*); (coll) leg; (slang) long-legged gawky girl

gilet [ʒile] *m* vest; **gilet de sauvetage** life jacket; **gilet pare-balles** bullet-proof vest; **pleurer dans le gilet de qn** (coll) to cry on s.o.'s shoulder

gingembre [ʒɛ̃ʒɑ̃br] *m* ginger

girafe [ʒiraf] *f* giraffe

giration [ʒirasjɔ̃] *f* gyration

girl [gœrl] *f* chorus girl

girofle [ʒirɔfl] *m* clove

giroflée [ʒirɔfle] *f* gillyflower

giron [ʒirɔ̃] *m* lap; bosom (*of the Church*)

girouette [ʒirwɛt] *f* weather vane

gisement [ʒizmɑ̃] *m* deposit; lode, seam; (naut) bearing; **gisement de pétrole** oil field

gi·tan [ʒitɑ̃] **-tane** [tan] *adj & mf* gypsy

gîte [ʒit] *m* lodging; lair, cover; deposit (*of ore*); **gîte à la noix** round steak || *f* (naut) list; **donner de la gîte** to heel

giter [ʒite] *intr* to lodge; to lie, couch;

to perch; (naut) to list, heel || *ref* to find shelter

givre [ʒivr] *m* rime, hoarfrost

givrer [ʒivre] *tr* to frost

glabre [glabr] *adj* beardless

glaçage [glasaʒ] *m* icing (*on cake*)

glace [glas] *f* ice; ice cream; mirror; plate glass; car window; glaze, icing; flaw (*of gem*); **être de glace** (fig) to be hard as stone; **glace au sirop** sundae; **glace panachée** Neapolitan ice cream; **rompre la glace** (fig) to break the ice

gla·cé -cée [glase] *adj* frozen; iced, chilled; icy, frosty; glazed, glossy

glacer [glase] §51 *tr* to freeze; to chill; to glaze; to ice (*a cake*)

glacerie [glasri] *f* glass factory

glaciaire [glasjɛr] *adj* glacial

gla·cial -ciale [glasjal] *adj* (*pl* -**cials**) glacial

glacier [glasje] *m* glacier; ice-cream man

glacière [glasjɛr] *f* icehouse; icebox; freezer

glacis [glasi] *m* slope; ramp; (mil) glacis; (painting) glaze

glaçon [glasɔ̃] *m* icicle; ice cube; ice floe; (fig) cold fish, iceberg

glaçure [glasyr] *f* (ceramics) glaze

gladiateur [gladjatœr] *m* gladiator

glaïeul [glajœl] *m* gladiola

glaire [glɛr] *f* white of egg; mucus

glaise [glɛz] *f* clay, loam

glaisière [glezjɛr] *f* clay pit

glaive [glɛv] *m* (lit) sword

gland [glɑ̃] *m* acorn; tassel

glande [glɑ̃d] *f* gland

glane [glan] *f* gleaning; cluster

glaner [glane] *tr* to glean

glanure [glanyr] *f* gleaning

glapir [glapir] *intr* to yelp, yap

glas [gla] *m* knell, tolling

glauque [glok] *adj & m* blue-green

glèbe [glɛb] *f* clod (*sod*); soil (*land*)

glène [glɛn] *f* (anat) socket; (naut) coil of rope

glissade [glisad] *f* slip; sliding; (dancing) glide; **glissade de terre** landslide; **glissade sur l'aile** (aer) sideslip; **glissade sur la queue** (aer) tail dive

glis·sant [glisɑ̃] **glis·sante** [glisɑ̃t] *adj* slippery

glissement [glismɑ̃] *m* sliding; gliding

glisser [glise] *tr* to slip; to drop (*a word into s.o.'s ear*); *intr* to slip; to slide; to skid; to glide || *ref* to slip

glissière [glisjɛr] *f* slide, groove; à **glissière** sliding; zippered

glissoire [gliswar] *f* slide (*on ice or snow*)

glo·bal -bale [glɔbal] *adj* (*pl* -**baux** [bo]) global; lump (*sum*)

globe [glɔb] *m* globe; **globe de feu** fireball; **globe de l'œil** eyeball

globule [glɔbyl] *m* globule; (physiol) corpuscle

gloire [glwar] *f* glory; pride; halo; **pour la gloire** for fun, for nothing; **se faire gloire de** to glory in

gloriette [glɔrjɛt] *f* arbor, summerhouse

glo·rieux [glɔrjø] **-rieuse** [rjøz] *adj* glorious; blessed; vain

glorifier [glɔrifje] *tr* to glorify || *ref* **se glorifier de** to glory in

gloriole [glɔrjɔl] *f* vainglory

glose [gloz] *f* gloss; (coll) gossip

gloser [gloze] *intr* (coll) to gossip

glossaire [glɔsɛr] *m* glossary

glotte [glɔt] *f* glottis

glouglou [gluglu] *m* gurgle; glug; gobble-gobble; coo (*of dove*)

glouglouter [gluglute] *intr* to gurgle; to gobble (*said of turkey*)

glousser [gluse] *intr* to cluck; to chuckle

glou·ton [glutɔ̃] **-tonne** [tɔn] *adj* gluttonous || *mf* glutton || *m* (zool) glutton, wolverine

gloutonnerie [glutɔnri] *f* gluttony

glu [gly] *f* birdlime; (coll) trap

gluant [glyɑ̃] **gluante** [glyɑ̃t] *adj* sticky, gummy; (fig) tenacious

glucose [glykoz] *m* glucose

glycérine [gliserin] *f* glycerine

gnognote [nɔɲɔt] *f* (coll) junk

gnome [gnom] *m* gnome

gnomon [gnɔmɔ̃] *m* sundial

gnon [nɔ̃] *m* (slang) blow, punch

go [go]—**tout de go** (coll) straight off, at once

goal [gol] *m* goalkeeper

gobelet [gɔblɛ] *m* cup, tumbler, mug; **gobelets utilisés** (public sign) used paper drinking cups

gobe-mouches [gɔbmuʃ] *m invar* (zool) flycatcher; (fig) sucker, gull

gober [gɔbe] *tr* to gulp down, to gobble; to suck (*an egg*); (coll) to swallow, to be a sucker for

goberger [gɔberʒe] §38 *ref* (coll) to guzzle; (coll) to live in comfort

gobeter [gɔbte] §34 *tr* to plaster, to fill in the cracks of

go·beur [gɔbœr] **-beuse** [bøz] *mf* (coll) sucker, gullible person

godet [gɔdɛ] *m* cup; basin; bucket (*of water wheel*); (bot) calyx; à **godets** flared

godille [gɔdij] *f* scull, oar

godiller [gɔdije] *intr* to scull

godillot [gɔdijo] *m* (slang) clodhopper (*shoe*)

goéland [gɔelɑ̃] *m* sea gull

goélette [gɔelɛt] *f* (naut) schooner

goémon [gɔemɔ̃] *m* seaweed

gogo [gɔgo] *m* (coll) sucker, gull; à **gogo** (coll) galore

gogue·nard [gɔgnar] **-narde** [nard] *adj* jeering, mocking

goguenarder [gɔgnarde] *intr* to jeer

goguette [gɔgɛt] *f*—**en goguette** (coll) tipsy

goinfre [gwɛ̃fr] *m* glutton, guzzler

goitre [gwatr] *m* goiter

golf [gɔlf] *m* golf

golfe [gɔlf] *m* gulf

gomme [gɔm] *f* gum; eraser; **gomme à mâcher** chewing gum; **gomme d'épinette** spruce gum; **gomme de sapin** balsam; **gomme élastique** India rubber; **mettre la gomme** (slang) to speed it up

gomme-laque [gɔmlak] *f* (*pl* **gommes-laques**) shellac

gommelaquer [gɔmlake] *tr* to shellac

gommer [gɔme] *tr* to gum; to erase ‖ *intr* to stick, to gum up

gond [gɔ̃] *m* hinge; **sortir de ses gonds** (coll) to fly off the handle

gondole [gɔ̃dɔl] *f* gondola

gondoler [gɔ̃dɔle] *intr & ref* to buckle up

gondolier [gɔ̃dɔlje] *m* gondolier

gonfalon [gɔ̃falɔ̃] *m* pennant

gonflement [gɔ̃flɔmɑ̃] *m* swelling

gonfler [gɔ̃fle] *tr* to swell, inflate ‖ *intr* to swell up, puff up ‖ *ref* to become inflated; (coll) to swell up with pride

gonfleur [gɔ̃flœr] *m* tire pump

gong [gɔ̃g] *m* gong

goret [gɔre] *m* piglet; (coll) slob

gorge [gɔrʒ] *f* throat; bust, breasts (*of woman*); gorge; **à pleine gorge** or **à gorge déployée** at the top of one's voice; **avoir la gorge serrée** to have a lump in one's throat; **faire des gorges chaudes de** (coll) to scoff at; to gloat over; **rendre gorge** to make restitution

gorger [gɔrʒe] §38 *tr & ref* to gorge, stuff

gorille [gɔrij] *m* gorilla; (slang) strongarm man, bodyguard; (slang) bouncer (*in a night club*)

gosier [gozje] *m* throat, gullet; **à plein gosier** loudly, lustily; **gosier serré** with one's heart in one's mouth; **s'humecter** or **se rincer le gosier** (slang) to wet one's whistle

gosse [gɔs] *mf* (coll) kid, youngster

gothique [gɔtik] *adj* Gothic ‖ *m* Gothic (*language*); Gothic art ‖ *f* black letter, Old English

gouailler [gwaje] *tr* to jeer at ‖ *intr* to jeer

gouape [gwap] *f* (slang) hoodlum, blackguard

gouaper [gwape] *intr* (slang) to lead a disreputable life

goudron [gudrɔ̃] *m* tar

goudronner [gudrone] *tr* to tar

gouffre [gufr] *m* gulf, abyss; whirlpool

gouge [guʒ] *f* gouge; harlot

gouger [guʒe] §38 *tr* to gouge

goujat [guʒa] *m* boor, cad

goujon [guʒɔ̃] *m* gudgeon, pin; pintle (*of hinge*); dowel; (ichth) gudgeon; **taquiner le goujon** to go fishing

goulasch [gula/] *m & f* goulash

goule [gul] *f* ghoul

goulet [gule] *m* narrows, sound; **goulet d'étranglement** bottleneck

goulot [gulo] *m* neck (*of bottle*); **boire au goulot** to drink right out of the bottle

gou·lu **-lue** [guly] *adj* gluttonous

goupil [gupi] *m* (obs) fox

goupille [gupij] *f* pin; **goupille fendue** cotter pin

goupiller [gupije] *tr* to cotter; (slang) to contrive, wangle

goupillon [gupijɔ̃] *m* bottle brush; sprinkler (*for holy water*); **goupillon nettoie-pipes** pipe cleaner

gourd [gur] **gourde** [gurd] *adj* numb (*with cold*) ‖ *adj fem* (coll) dumb ‖

f gourd; canteen, metal flask; (coll) dumbbell

gourdin [gurdɛ̃] *m* cudgel

gourgandine [gurgɑ̃din] *f* (hist) low-necked bodice; (coll) trollop

gour·mand [gurmɑ̃] **-mande** [mɑ̃d] *adj & mf* gourmand, gourmet

gourmander [gurmɑ̃de] *tr* to bawl out

gourmandise [gurmɑ̃diz] *f* gluttony; love of good food; **gourmandises** delicacies

gourme [gurm] *f* impetigo; **jeter sa gourme** (coll) to sow one's wild oats

gour·mé **-mée** [gurme] *adj* stiff, stuck-up

gourmet [gurmɛ] *m* gourmet

gourmette [gurmɛt] *f* curb (*of harness*); curb watch chain

gousse [gus] *f* pod; clove (*of garlic*)

gousset [gusɛ] *m* vest pocket; fob, watch pocket (*in trousers*)

goût [gu] *m* taste; flavor; sense of taste; **au goût du jour** up to date

goûter [gute] *m* afternoon snack ‖ *tr* to taste; to sample; to relish, enjoy ‖ *intr* to have a bite to eat; **goûter à** to sample, try; **goûter de** (coll) to try out (*e.g., a trade*)

goutte [gut] *f* drop, drip; (pathol) gout; **boire la goutte** (coll) to take a nip of brandy; **la goutte d'eau qui a fait déborder le vase** the straw which broke the camel's back; **ne ... goutte** §90 (used only with **comprendre**, **connaître**, **entendre**, and **voir**) (archaic & hum) not at all, e.g., **je n'y vois goutte** I don't see at all; **tomber goutte à goutte** to drip

goutte-à-goutte [gutagut] *m invar* (med) dropping bottle (*for intravenous drip*)

gouttelette [gutlɛt] *f* droplet

goutter [gute] *intr* to drip

gouttière [gutjɛr] *f* eavestrough, gutter; (med) splint

gouvernail [guvɛrnaj] *m* rudder, helm; **gouvernail de profondeur** (aer) elevator

gouver·nant [guvɛrnɑ̃] **-nante** [nɑ̃t] *adj* governing ‖ **gouvernants** *mpl* powers that be, rulers ‖ *f* governess; housekeeper

gouverne [guvɛrn] *f* guidance; **gouvernes** (aer) controls; **pour votre gouverne** for your guidance

gouvernement [guvɛrnɔmɑ̃] *m* government; **gouvernement fantoche** puppet government

gouvernemen·tal **-tale** [guvɛrnɔmɑ̃tal] *adj* (*pl* **-taux** [to]) governmental

gouverner [guvɛrne] *tr* to govern, to control; to steer; to manage with care ‖ *intr* to govern; (naut) to answer to the helm

gouverneur [guvɛrnœr] *m* governor; tutor; director (*e.g., of a bank*)

goyave [gɔjav] *f* guava

goyavier [gɔjavje] *m* guava tree

Graal [gral] *m* Grail

grabat [graba] *m* pallet, straw bed

grâce [grɑs] *f* grace; **de bonne grâce** willingly; **de grâce** for mercy's sake; **de mauvaise grâce** unwillingly; **faire**

grâce à to pardon; to spare; **faites-moi la grâce de** be kind enough to; **grâce!** mercy!; **grâce à** thanks to

gracier [grasje] *tr* to reprieve

gra•cieux [grasjø] **-cieuse** [sjøz] *adj* gracious; graceful

gracile [grasil] *adj* slender, slim

gradation [gradɑsjɔ̃] *f* gradation

grade [grad] *m* grade; rank; degree (*in school*); **en prendre pour son grade** (coll) to get called down

gra•dé -dée [grade] *adj* noncommissioned ‖ *mf* noncommissioned officer

gradient [gradjɑ̃] *m* gradient

gradin [gradɛ̃] *m* tier

graduation [graduɑsjɔ̃] *f* graduation

gra•dué -duée [gradɥe] *adj* graduated (*scale*); graded (*lessons*) ‖ *mf* graduate

gra•duel -duelle [gradɥel] *adj & m* gradual

graduer [gradɥe] *tr* to graduate

grailler [graje] *intr* to speak hoarsely; to sound the horn to recall the dogs

grain [grɛ̃] *m* grain; particle, speck; bean; squall; **grain de beauté** beauty spot, mole; **grain de raisin** grape; **grains** grain, cereals; **veiller au grain** (fig) to be on one's guard

graine [grɛn] *f* seed; **graine d'anis** aniseed; **mauvaise graine** (coll) shady character; **monter en graine** to run to seed; to soon be on the shelf (*said of young girl*); (coll) to grow; **prendre de la graine de** (coll) to follow the example of

graissage [gresaʒ] *m* (aut) lubrication

graisse [gres] *f* grease; fat; mother (*of wine*)

graisser [grese], [grɛse] *tr* to grease; to lubricate; to get grease stains on; **graisser la patte à qn** (coll) to grease s.o.'s palm

grais•seux [gresø] **grais•seuse** [gresøz] *adj* greasy

grammaire [gramer] *f* grammar

grammai•rien [gramerjɛ̃] **-rienne** [rjen] *mf* grammarian

grammati•cal -cale [gramatikal] *adj* (*pl* **-caux** [ko]) grammatical

gramme [gram] *m* gram

grand [grɑ̃] **grande** [grɑ̃d] *adj* tall ‖ (when standing before noun) *adj* large; great; important; high (*priest; mass; society; explosive*); vain, empty (*words*); broad (*daylight*); grand (*dignitary; officer; lady*); main (*road*); (fig) big (*heart*) ‖ *m* adult, grownup; grandee, noble; **en grand** life-size; on a grand scale; enlarged (*copy*); wide (*open*); **grands et petits** young and old ‖ **grand** *adv*—**voir grand** to see big, to envisage great projects

grand-chose [grɑ̃ʃoz] *mf invar*—**pas grand-chose** (coll) nobody, person of no importance ‖ *adv*—**pas grand-chose** not much

grand-duc [grɑ̃dyk] *m* (*pl* **grands-ducs**) grand duke

grand-duché [grɑ̃dyʃe] *m* (*pl* **grands-duchés**) grand duchy

Grande-Bretagne [grɑ̃dbrətaɲ] *f* Great Britain; **la Grande-Bretagne** Great Britain

grande-duchesse [grɑ̃dədyʃes] *f* (*pl* **grandes-duchesses**) grand duchess

grande•let [grɑ̃dle] **-lette** [let] *adj* tall for his or her age

grandement [grɑ̃dmɑ̃] *adv* highly; handsomely; **se tromper grandement** to be very mistaken

grand-erre [grɑ̃ter] *adv* at full speed

gran•det [grɑ̃de] **-dette** [det] *adj* rather big; rather tall

grandeur [grɑ̃dœr] *f* size; height; greatness; (astr) magnitude

grandiose [grɑ̃djoz] *adj* grandiose

grandir [grɑ̃dir] *tr* to enlarge; to increase ‖ *intr* to grow; to grow up

grandissement [grɑ̃dismɑ̃] *m* magnification, enlargement; growth

grand-livre [grɑ̃livr] *m* (*pl* **grands-livres**) ledger

grand-maman [grɑ̃mamɑ̃] *f* (*pl* **-mamans**) grandma

grand-mère [grɑ̃mer] *f* (*pl* **-mères** or **grands-mères**) grandmother; (coll) old lady

grand-messe [grɑ̃mes] *f* (*pl* **-messes**) high mass

grand-oncle [grɑ̃tɔ̃kl] *m* (*pl* **grands-oncles**) granduncle

Grand-Orient [grɑ̃tɔrjɑ̃] *m* grand lodge

grand-papa [grɑ̃papa] *m* (*pl* **grands-papas**) grandpa

grand-peine [grɑ̃pen]—**à grand-peine** with great difficulty

grand-père [grɑ̃per] *m* (*pl* **grands-pères**) grandfather

grand-route [grɑ̃rut] *f* (*pl* **-routes**) highway

grand-rue [grɑ̃ry] *f* (*pl* **-rues**) main street

Grands Lacs [grɑ̃lak] *mpl* Great Lakes

grands-parents [grɑ̃parɑ̃] *mpl* grandparents

grand-tante [grɑ̃tɑ̃t] *f* (*pl* **-tantes**) grandaunt

grange [grɑ̃ʒ] *f* barn

granit [grani], [granit] *m* granite

granite [granit] *m* granite

granulaire [granyler] *adj* granular

granule [granyl] *m* granule

granu•lé -lée [granyle] *adj* granulated ‖ *m* little pill; medicine in granulated form

granuler [granyle] *tr & ref* to granulate

graphie [grafi] *f* spelling

graphique [grafik] *adj* graphic(al) ‖ *m* graph

graphite [grafit] *m* graphite

grappe [grap] *f* bunch, cluster; string (*of onions*); **une grappe humaine** a bunch of people

grappillage [grapijaʒ] *m* gleaning; (coll) graft

grappiller [grapije] *tr & intr* (*in vineyard*) to glean; (coll) to pilfer

grappillon [grapijɔ̃] *m* little bunch

grappin [grapɛ̃] *m* grapnel; **jeter** or **mettre le grappin sur qn** (coll) to get one's hooks into s.o.

gras [grɑ] **grasse** [grɑs] *adj* fat; greasy; rich (*soil*); carnival (*days*); smutty (stories); (typ) bold-faced ‖ *m* fatty part; calf (*of leg*); foggy weather; **au gras** with meat sauce; **faire gras** to eat meat ‖ **gras** *adv*—**parler gras** to speak with uvular r; to tell smutty stories

gras-double [grɑdubl] *m* (*pl* **-doubles**) tripe

grassement [grɑsmɑ̃] *adv* comfortably; generously

grasseyer [grɑseje] §32 *tr* to make (*one's r's*) uvular ‖ *intr* to speak with uvular r

grassouil·let [grɑsuje] **grassouil·lette** [grɑsujɛt] *adj* (coll) plump, chubby

gratification [gratifikɑsjɔ̃] *f* tip, gratuity

gratifier [gratifje] *tr* to favor, reward; **gratifier qn de q.ch.** to bestow s.th. upon s.o.

gratin [gratɛ̃] *m* (culin) crust; (coll) upper crust; **au gratin** breaded

gratiner [gratine] *tr* to cook au gratin ‖ *intr* to brown, to crisp

gratis [gratis] *adv* gratis

gratitude [gratityd] *f* gratitude

gratte [grat] *f* scraper; (coll) graft

gratte-ciel [gratsjɛl] *m invar* skyscraper

gratte-cul [gratky] *m invar* (bot) hip

gratte-dos [gratdo] *m invar* back scratcher

gratte-papier [gratpapje] *m invar* (coll) pencil pusher, office drudge

gratte-pieds [gratpje] *m invar* shoe-scraper

gratter [grate] *tr* to scratch; to scratch out; to scrape up, scrape together; to itch; (coll) to pocket ‖ *intr* to knock gently ‖ *ref* to scratch; (with *dat* of *reflex pron*) to scratch (*e.g., one's arm*)

grattoir [gratwar] *m* scraper; knife eraser

gra·tuit [gratɥi] **-tuite** [tɥit] *adj* free of charge; gratuitous; unfounded

gratuité [gratɥite] *f* gratuity

grave [grav], [grɑv] *adj* grave; low (*frequency*); (mus) bass; (mus) flat

grave·leux [gravlø] **-leuse** [løz] *adj* gravelly, gritty; smutty, licentious

gravelle [gravɛl] *f* (pathol) gravel

graver [grave] *tr* to engrave; to cut (*a phonograph record*)

graveur [gravœr] *m* engraver; etcher

gravier [gravje] *m* gravel

gravir [gravir] *tr* to climb, climb up

gravitation [gravitɑsjɔ̃] *f* gravitation

gravité [gravite] *f* gravity

graviter [gravite] *intr* to gravitate

gravure [gravyr] *f* engraving; etching; cutting (*of phonograph record*)

gré [gre] *m* will; **à son gré** to one's liking; **bon gré mal gré** willy-nilly; **de bon gré** willingly; **de gré à gré** by mutual consent; **de gré ou de force** willy-nilly; **savoir** (**bon**) **gré de** to be grateful for; **savoir mauvais gré de** to be displeased with

grec grecque [grɛk] *adj* Greek; classic (*profile*) ‖ *m* Greek (*language*) ‖ *f* Greek fret ‖ (*cap*) *mf* Greek

Grèce [grɛs] *f* Greece; **la Grèce** Greece

gre·din [grədɛ̃] **-dine** [din] *mf* scoundrel

gréement [gremɑ̃] *m* (naut) rigging

gréer [gree] *tr* (naut) to rig

greffe [grɛf] *m* (jur) office of the court clerk ‖ *f* grafting; (hort, med) graft; **greffe du cœur** heart transplant

greffer [grefe] *tr* to graft; to add ‖ *ref* to be added

greffier [grefje] *m* clerk of court, recorder; court reporter

greffon [grefɔ̃] *m* (hort) graft; (surg) transplant

grégaire [greger] *adj* gregarious

grège [grɛʒ] *adj* raw (*silk*) ‖ *f* raw silk

grégo·rien [gregɔrjɛ̃] **-rienne** [rjɛn] *adj* Gregorian

grêle [grɛl] *adj* slender, slim; thin, high-pitched ‖ *f* hail; (fig) shower

grê·lé -lée [grele] *adj* pockmarked

grêler [grele] *tr* to damage by hail; to pockmark ‖ *intr* (fig) to rain down thick; **il grêle** it is hailing

grêlon [grɛlɔ̃] *m* hailstone

grelot [grəlo] *m* sleigh bell

grelottement [grəlɔtmɑ̃] *m* shivering, trembling; jingle, jingling

grelotter [grəlɔte] *intr* to shiver, tremble; to jingle

grenade [grənad] *f* grenade; (bot) pomegranate; **grenade à main** hand grenade; **grenade éclairante** flare; **grenade lacrymogène** tear bomb; **grenade sous-marine** depth charge

grenadier [grənadje] *m* pomegranate tree; (mil) grenadier

grenadine [grənadin] *f* grenadine

grenaille [grənaj] *f* shot; **grenaille de plomb** buckshot

grenailler [grənaje] *tr* to granulate

grenat [grəna] *adj invar* & *m* garnet

grenier [grənje] *m* attic, loft; granary

grenouille [grənuj] *f* frog; **grenouille mugissante** or **taureau** bullfrog; **manger la grenouille** (coll) to make off with the money, to abscond

grenouillère [grənujer] *f* marsh

gre·nu -nue [grəny] *adj* full of grain; grainy (*leather*); granular (*marble*) ‖ *m* graininess; granularity

grès [grɛ] *m* gritstone, sandstone; stoneware; terra cotta (*for drainpipes*)

grésil [grezil] *m* sleet

grésillement [grezijmɑ̃] *m* sizzling; chirping (*of cricket*)

grésiller [grezije] *tr* to scorch, to shrivel up ‖ *intr* to sizzle, to sputter; **il grésille** it is sleeting

grève [grɛv] *f* beach; strike; (armor) greave; **faire** (**la**) **grève** to strike; **faire la grève de la faim** to go on a hunger strike; **grève de solidarité** sympathy strike; **grève du zèle** slowdown (*caused by rigid application of rules*); **grève improvisée**, **grève inattendue**, **grève surprise** walkout; **grève perlée** slowdown; **grève sauvage**, **grève spontanée** wildcat strike; **grève sur le tas** sitdown strike; **grève tournante** strike in one industry at a time or for several hours at a time; **se met-tre en grève** to go on strike

grever [grəve] §2 *tr* to burden; to assess (*property*); **grever de** to burden with

gréviste [grevist] *mf* striker

gribouillage [gribujaʒ] *m* (coll) scribble, scrawl; (coll) daub (*in painting*)

gribouiller [gribuje] *tr* (coll) to scribble off (*a note*) ‖ *intr* (coll) to scribble, scrawl; (coll) to daub

grief [grijɛf] *m* grievance, complaint; **faire grief de q.ch. à qn** to complain to s.o. about s.th.

grièvement [grijɛvmɑ̃] *adv* seriously, badly

griffe [grif] *f* claw, talon; signature stamp; (bot) tendril; (mach) hook, grip; **faire ses griffes** to sharpen its claws (*said of cat*); **griffe à papiers** paper clip; **porter la griffe de** to carry the stamp of; **tomber sous la griffe de** (coll) to fall into the clutches of

griffer [grife] *tr* to claw, scratch

griffon [grifɔ̃] *m* griffin

griffonner [grifɔne] *tr* to scrawl; (coll) to scribble off (*a letter*)

grignoter [griɲɔte] *tr* to nibble on or at; to wear down (*e.g., the enemy*) ‖ *intr* (coll) to make a little profit, to get a cut

gril [gril] *m* gridiron, grid, grill; (theat) upper flies; **être sur le gril** (coll) to be on tenterhooks

grillade [grijad] *f* grilled meat; broiling

grillage [grijaʒ] *m* grating, latticework, trellis; broiling; roasting; toasting; burning out (*of a light bulb*); (tex) singeing

grille [grij] *f* grille; grate, grating; bars; railing; gate; squares (*of crossword puzzle*); grid (*of storage battery and vacuum tube*); **grille des salaires** salary schedule

grille-pain [grijpɛ̃] *m invar* toaster

griller [grije] *tr* to grill, broil; to put a grill on; to roast (*coffee*); to toast (*bread*); to burn out (*a fuse, lamp, electric iron, etc.*); to singe, scorch; to nip (*a bud, as the frost does*) ‖ *intr* to grill; to toast; to burn out; **griller de** to long to

grilloir [grijwar] *m* roaster; (culin) broiler

grillon [grijɔ̃] *m* cricket

grimace [grimas] *f* grimace; **faire des grimaces** to make faces; to smirk, simper; to be full of wrinkles

grimacer [grimase] §51 *intr* to grimace; to make wrong creases

grime [grim] *m* dotard, old fogey

grimer [grime] *tr* to make up (*an actor*) ‖ *ref* to make up

grimper [grɛ̃pe] *tr* to climb ‖ *intr* to climb; **grimper à or sur** to climb up on

grimpe-reau [grɛ̃pro] *m* (*pl* -reaux) (orn) tree creeper

grim-peur [grɛ̃pœr] -**peuse** [pøz] *adj* climbing ‖ *m* climber

grincement [grɛ̃smɑ̃] *m* grating

grincer [grɛ̃se] §51 *tr* to gnash, grit (*the*

teeth*) ‖ *intr* to grate, grind, creak; to scratch (*said of pen*)

grin-cheux [grɛ̃ʃø] -**cheuse** [ʃøz] *adj* grumpy ‖ *mf* grumbler, sorehead

gringa-let [grɛ̃galɛ] -**lette** [lɛt] *adj* weak, puny ‖ *m* (coll) weakling, shrimp

griot [grijo] **griotte** [grijɔt] *mf* witch doctor ‖ *m* seconds (*in milling grain*) ‖ *f* sour cherry

grippe [grip] *f* grippe; **prendre en grippe** to take a dislike to

grippeminaud [gripmino] *m* (coll) smoothy, hypocrite

gripper [gripe] *tr* to snatch; (slang) to steal ‖ *intr* (mach) to jam ‖ *ref* to get stuck

grippe-sou [gripsu] *m* (*pl* -sou or -sous) (coll) tightwad, skinflint

gris [gri] **grise** [griz] *adj* gray; cloudy; brown (*paper*); (coll) tipsy

grisailler [grizaje] *tr* to paint gray ‖ *intr* to turn gray

grisâtre [grizatr] *adj* grayish

griser [grize] *tr* to paint gray; (coll) to intoxicate; **les succès l'ont grisé** (coll) success has gone to his head ‖ *ref* to get tipsy; **se griser de** (coll) to revel in

griserie [grizri] *f* intoxication

grisette [grizet] *f* gay working girl

gris-gris [grigri] *m* lucky charm

grisonner [grizɔne] *intr* to turn gray

grisotte [grizɔt] *f* clock (*in stocking*)

grisou [grizu] *m* firedamp

grive [griv] *f* thrush; **grive mauvis** song thrush; **grive migratoire** (*Turdus migratorius*) robin

grive-lé -**lée** [grivle] *adj* speckled

grivèlerie [grivelri] *f* sneaking out without paying the check

gri-vois [grivwa] -**voise** [vwaz] *adj* spicy, off-color

grizzly [grizli] *m* grizzly bear

Groënland [grɔɛnlɑ̃d] *m*—**le Groën-land** Greenland

grog [grɔg] *m* grog

gro-gnard [grɔɲar] -**gnarde** [ɲard] *adj* grumbling ‖ *mf* grumbler

grogner [grɔɲe] *intr* to grunt, to growl; to grumble, to grouch

gro-gnon [grɔɲɔ̃] -**gnonne** [ɲɔn] *adj* grouchy, grumbling ‖ *mf* grouch, grumbler

grognonner [grɔɲɔne] *intr* to grunt; to be a complainer, to whine

groin [grwɛ̃] *m* snout; (coll) ugly mug

grommeler [grɔmle] §34 *tr* & *intr* to mutter, grumble; to growl

grondement [grɔ̃dmɑ̃] *m* growl; rumble

gronder [grɔ̃de] *tr* to scold ‖ *intr* to scold; to growl; to grumble

gron-deur [grɔ̃dœr] -**deuse** [døz] *adj* scolding; grumbling ‖ *mf* grumbler

groom [grum] *m* bellhop, pageboy

gros [gro] **grosse** [gros] *adj* big (*with child*); heavy (*heart*) ‖ (when standing before noun) *adj* big, large, bulky; course; plain (*common sense*); main (*walls*); high (*stakes*); rich (*merchant*); booming (*voice*); bad (*weather*); heavy, rough (*sea*); swear (*words*) ‖ *m* bulk, main part; **en gros**

wholesale; roughly, without going into detail; **faire le gros et le détail** to deal in wholesale and retail || *f* see **grosse** || **gros** *adv* much, a great deal; (fig) probably

gros•bec [grobek] *m* (*pl* -**becs**) grosbeak

groseille [grozej] *f* currant; **groseille à maquereau** gooseberry

groseillier [grozeje] *m* currant bush

Gros-Jean [groʒɑ̃] *m*—**être Gros-Jean comme devant** to be in the same fix again

grosse [gros] *f* fat woman; (com) gross; (law) engrossed copy

grosserie [grosri] *f* silver dishes

grossesse [groses] *f* pregnancy

grosseur [grosœr] *f* size; swelling, tumor

gros•sier [grosje] **gros•sière** [grosjer] *adj* coarse; crude, rude; vulgar, ribald; glaring (*error*)

grossièrement [grosjermɑ̃] *adv* grossly

grossièreté [grosjerte] *f* coarseness, grossness, vulgarity

grossir [grosir] *tr* to enlarge; to increase || *intr* to grow larger; to put on weight

grossis•sant [grosisɑ̃] **grossis•sante** [grosisɑ̃t] *adj* swelling; magnifying (*glasses*)

grossiste [grosist] *m* wholesaler, jobber

grotesque [grotesk] *adj* grotesque || *mf* grotesque person || *m* grotesque || *f* grotesque (*ornament*)

grotte [grot] *f* grotto

grouillement [grujmɑ̃] *m* swarming, rumbling

grouiller [gruje] *intr* to swarm; **grouiller de** to teem with || *ref* (slang) to get a move on

groupe [grup] *m* group; (mach & mil) unit; **groupe franc** (mil) commando; **groupe sanguin** blood type

groupement [grupmɑ̃] *m* grouping; organization

grouper [grupe] *tr* & *ref* to group

gruau [gryo] *m* (*pl* **gruaux**) groats; (culin) gruel; (orn) small crane

grue [gry] *f* crane; (orn) crane; (coll) tart

gruger [gryʒe] §38 *tr* to sponge on, exploit; to crunch

grume [grym] *f* bark; **en grume** rough (*timber*)

gru•meau [grymo] *m* (*pl* -**meaux**) gob, curd

grumeler [grymle] §34 *intr* to curdle, clot

gruyère [gryjer] *m* Gruyère cheese

guatémaltèque [gwatemaltek] *adj* Guatemalan || (*cap*) *mf* Guatemalan

gué [ge] *m* ford, crossing; **sonder le gué** (coll) to see how the land lies || *interj* hurrah!

guéable [geabl] *adj* fordable

guéer [gee] *tr* to ford; to water (*a horse*)

guelte [gelt] *f* commission, percentage

guenille [gənij] *f* ragged garment; **en guenilles** in tatters

guenon [gənɔ̃] *f* female monkey; long-tailed monkey; (coll) hag, old bag

guépard [gepar] *m* cheetah

guêpe [gep] *f* wasp

guère [ger] §90 *adv* hardly ever; **ne . . . guère** hardly, scarcely; hardly ever; not very; **ne . . . guère de** hardly any; **ne . . . guère que** hardly any but; hardly anyone but; **ne . . . plus guère** hardly ever any more; not much longer

guères [ger] *adv* (poetic) var of **guère**

guéret [gere] *m* fallow land

guéridon [geridɔ̃] *m* pedestal table

guérilla [gerija] *f* guerrilla warfare

guérillero [gerijero] *m* guerrilla

guérir [gerir] *tr* to cure || *intr* to get well; to get better; to heal || *ref* to cure oneself; to recover

guérison [gerizɔ̃] *f* cure, healing; recovery

guérissable [gerisabl] *adj* curable

guéris•seur [gerisœr] **guéris•seuse** [gerisøz] *mf* healer; quack

guérite [gerit] *f* sentry box; (rr) signal box; **guérite téléphonique** call box

guerre [ger] *f* war; **de guerre lasse** for the sake of peace and quiet; **être de bonne guerre** to be fair, to be cricket; **guerre à outrance** all-out war; **Guerre de Troie** Trojan War; **guerre d'usure** war of attrition; **guerre éclair** blitzkrieg; **guerre froide** cold war; **guerre presse-bouton** push-button war

guer•rier [gerje] **guer•rière** [gerjer] *adj* warlike, martial || *m* warrior || *f* amazon

guerroyant [gerwajɑ̃] **guerroyante** [gerwajɑ̃t] *adj* warlike, bellicose

guerroyer [gerwaje] §47 *intr* to make war

guerroyeur [gerwajœr] **guerroyeuse** [gerwajøz] *adj* fighting (*spirit*) || *mf* fighter

guet [ge] *m* watch, lookout

guet-apens [getapɑ̃] *m* (*pl* **guets-apens** [getapɑ̃]) ambush, trap

guêtre [getr] *f* gaiter, legging

guêtrer [getre] *tr* & *ref* to put gaiters on

guetter [gete] *tr* to watch; to watch for; (coll) to lie in wait for

guetteur [getœr] *m* lookout, sentinel

gueu•lard [gœlar] -**larde** [lard] *adj* (slang) loud-mouthed; (slang) fond of good eating || *mf* gourmet; (slang) loud-mouth || *m* mouth (*of blast furnace; of cannon*); (naut) megaphone

gueule [gœl] *f* mouth (*of animal; of furnace, cannon, etc.*); (slang) mouth, mug (*of person*); **avoir de la gueule** (coll) to have a certain air; **avoir la gueule de bois** (coll) to have a hangover; **fine gueule** (coll) gourmet; **gueule cassée** (coll) disabled veteran; **gueule noire** (coll) miner; **ta gueule!** (slang) shut up!

gueule-de-loup [gœldəlu] *f* (*pl* **gueules-de-loup**) (bot) snapdragon

gueuler [gœle] *tr* & *intr* (slang) to bellow

gueuleton [gœltɔ̃] *m* (slang) big feed

gueux [gø] **gueuse** [gøz] *adj* beggarly, wretched || *mf* beggar; scamp || *f* pig iron; pig (*mold*); woolen jacket; (coll) whore; **courir la gueuse** (coll) to go whoring

gugusse [gygys] *m* clown

gui [gi] *m* mistletoe; (naut) boom

guichet [giʃe] *m* window (*in post office, bank, box office, etc.*); counter (*e.g., in bank*); wicket

guidage [gidaʒ] *m* (rok) guidance

guide [gid] *m* guide; guidebook || *f* rein; **mener la vie à grandes guides** to live extravagantly

guide-âne [gidɑn] *m* (*pl* -âne or -ânes) manual, guide

guider [gide] *tr* to guide

guidon [gidɔ̃] *m* handlebars; sight, bead (*of gun*); (naut) pennant

guigne [giɲ] *f* heart cherry; (coll) jinx

guigner [giɲe] *tr* to steal a glance at; (coll) to covet || *intr* to peep

guignol [giɲɔl] *m* Punch (*puppet*); Punch and Judy show; (aer) king post

guignolet [giɲɔle] *m* cherry brandy

guillaume [gijom] *m* rabbet plane; **Guillaume** William

guilledou [gijdu] *m*—**courir le guilledou** (coll) to make the rounds

guillemet [gijme] *m* quotation mark; **fermer les guillemets** to close quotes; **ouvrir les guillemets** to quote

guillemeter [gijmǝte] §34 *tr* to put in quotes

guiller [gije] *intr* to ferment

guille·ret [gijre] -**rette** [ret] *adj* chipper, lively, gay

guillotine [gijotin] *f* guillotine; **à guillotine** sliding; sash (*window*)

guillotiner [gijotine] *tr* to guillotine

guimauve [gimov] *f* (bot) marshmallow

guimbarde [gɛ̃bard] *f* (mus) jew's-harp; (coll) jalopy

guimpe [gɛ̃p] *f* wimple

guin·dé -dée [gɛ̃de] *adj* affected, stiff

guin·deau [gɛ̃do] *m* (*pl* -deaux) windlass

guinder [gɛ̃de] *tr* to hoist || *ref* to put on airs

guinée [gine] *f* guinea (*coin*); **Guinée** Guinea; **la Guinée** Guinea

guingan [gɛ̃gɑ̃] *m* gingham

guingois [gɛ̃gwa] *m*—**de guingois** askew; lopsidedly

guinguette [gɛ̃get] *f* roadside inn, roadside park

guipage [gipaʒ] *m* wrapping, lapping

guiper [gipe] *tr* to wind; to cover (*a wire*)

guipure [gipyr] *f* pillow lace

guirlande [girlɑ̃d] *f* garland, wreath

guirlander [girlɑ̃de] *tr* to garland

guise [giz] *f* manner; **à sa guise** as one pleases; **en guise de** by way of

guitare [gitar] *f* guitar

guitariste [gitarist] *mf* guitarist

guppy [gypi] *m* guppy

gustation [gystasjɔ̃] *f* tasting; drinking

guttu·ral -rale [gytyral] (*pl* -raux [ro] -rales) *adj & f* guttural

Guyane [gɥijan] *f* Guiana; **la Guyane** Guiana

gymnase [ʒimnɑz] *m* gymnasium

gymnaste [ʒimnast] *mf* gymnast

gymnote [ʒimnɔt] *m* electric eel

gynécologie [ʒinekɔlɔʒi] *f* gynecology

gypse [ʒips] *m* gypsum

gyrocompas [ʒirɔkɔ̃pa] *m* gyrocompass

gyroscope [ʒirɔskɔp] *m* gyroscope

H

H, h [aʃ], *[aʃ] m invar* eighth letter of the French alphabet

habile [abil] *adj* skillful; clever

habileté [abilte] *f* skill; cleverness

habiliter [abilite] *tr* to qualify, entitle

habillement [abijmɑ̃] *m* clothing; clothes

habiller [abije] *tr* to dress; to clothe; to put together || *intr* to be becoming, e.g., **robe qui habille bien** becoming dress || *ref* to dress; to get dressed; **s'habiller chez** to buy one's clothes at or from

habit [abi] *m* dress suit; habit, frock; **habit de cérémonie** or **soirée, habit à queue de pie, habit à queue de morue** tails; **habits** clothes

habitacle [abitakl] *m* (aer) cockpit; (naut) binnacle; (poetic) dwelling

habi·tant [abitɑ̃] -**tante** [tɑ̃t] *mf* inhabitant

habitat [abita] *m* habitat; living conditions, housing

habitation [abitasjɔ̃] *f* habitation; dwelling; residence; **habitation à bon marché** or **à loyer modéré** low-rent apartment

habi·té -tée [abite] *adj* inhabited; (rok) manned

habiter [abite] *tr* to live in, to inhabit || *intr* to live, reside

habitude [abityd] *f* habit, custom; **comme d'habitude** as usual; **d'habitude** usually

habi·tuel -tuelle [abitɥel] *adj* habitual

habituer [abitɥe] *tr* to accustom

hâbler *[able] intr* to brag, to boast

hâblerie *[abləri] f* bragging

hâ·bleur *[ablœr] -bleuse** [bløz] *adj* boastful || *m* braggart, boaster

hache *[aʃ] f* ax, hatchet

ha·ché -chée *[aʃe] adj* ground, chopped; hachured; choppy (*sea*); jerky (*style*); dotted (*line*)

hacher *[aʃe] tr* to hack; to grind, chop up; **hacher menu** to mince

hache·reau *[aʃro] m* (*pl* -reaux) hatchet

hachette * [aʃɛt] f hatchet
hachis * [aʃi] m hash, forcemeat
hachisch * [aʃiʃ] m hashish
hachoir * [aʃwar] m cleaver; chopping board
hachure * [aʃyr] f shading
hachurer * [aʃyre] tr to shade, hatch
haddock * [adɔk] m finnan haddie
ha·gard [agar] -garde [gard] adj haggard
haie * [ɛ] f hedge; hurdle; line, row
haie * [aj] interj giddap!
haillon * [ajɔ̃] m old piece of clothing; en haillons in rags and tatters
haillon·neux * [ajɔnø] haillon·neuse * [ajɔnøz] adj ragged, tattered
haine * [ɛn] f hate
hai·neux * [ɛnø] -neuse [nøz] adj full of hate, spiteful, malevolent
haïr * [air] §33 tr to hate, to detest || intr—haïr de to hate to
haire * [ɛr] f hair shirt
haïssable * [aisabl] adj hateful
Haïti [aiti] f Haiti
haï·tien [aisjɛ̃] -tienne [sjɛn] adj Haitian || (cap) mf Haitian
halcyon [alsjɔ̃] m (orn) kingfisher
hâle * [ɑl] m sun tan
haleine [alɛn] f breath; avoir l'haleine courte to be short-winded; (fig) to have little inspiration; de longue haleine hard, arduous (work); en haleine in good form; hors d'haleine out of breath; perdre haleine to get out of breath; reprendre haleine to catch one's breath; tenir en haleine to hold (e.g., an audience) breathless
halenée [alne] f whiff; strong breath
haler * [ale] tr to haul, to tow
hâler * [ale] tr to tan
hale·tant * [altɑ̃] -tante [tɑ̃t] adj breathless, panting
haleter * [alte] §2 intr to pant, puff
hall * [ol] m lobby; hall, auditorium
halle * [al] f market, marketplace; exchange
hallebarde * [albard] f halberd; il pleut des hallebardes (coll) it's raining cats and dogs
hallier * [alje] m thicket
hallucination [allysinasjɔ̃] f hallucination
halo * [alo] m halo
halogène [alɔʒɛn] m halogen
halte * [alt] f halt; stop; (rr) flag stop, way station; faire faire halte à to halt || interj halt!
halte-là * [altla] interj (mil) halt!
haltère [alter] m dumbbell
haltérophile [alterɔfil] m weight lifter
haltérophilie [alterɔfili] f weight lifting
hamac * [amak] m hammock
ha·meau * [amo] m (pl -meaux) hamlet
hameçon * [amsɔ̃] m hook, fishhook; (fig) bait
hammam * [ammam] m Turkish bath
hampe * [ɑ̃p] f staff, pole; shaft; downstroke; (culin) flank
hamster * [amster] m hamster
han * [ɑ̃], [hɑ̃] m grunt
hanap * [anap] m hanap, goblet
hanche * [ɑ̃ʃ] f hip; haunch

hancher * [ɑ̃ʃe] intr to lean on one leg || ref (mil) to stand at ease
handball * [ɑ̃bol] m handball
handicap * [ɑ̃dikap] m handicap
handicaper * [ɑ̃dikape] tr to handicap
hangar * [ɑ̃gar] m hangar; shed
hanneton * [antɔ̃] m June bug, chafer
hanter * [ɑ̃te] tr to haunt
hantise * [ɑ̃tiz] f obsession
happe * [ap] f crucible tongs; (carp) cramp, staple
happer * [ape] tr to snap up; (coll) to nab || intr to stick
haquenée [akne] f palfrey
haquet * [ake] m dray; haquet à main pushcart
harangue * [arɑ̃g] f harangue
haranguer * [arɑ̃ge] tr & intr to harangue
haras * [arɑ] m stud farm
harasser * [arase] tr to tire out
harceler * [arsəle] §2 or §34 tr to harass, to harry; to pester; to dun
harde * [ard] f herd; leash; set (of dogs); hardes old clothes
har·di -die * [ardi] adj bold || hardi interj up and at them!
hardiesse * [ardjɛs] f boldness
harem * [arem] m harem
hareng * [arɑ̃] m herring; hareng fumé kipper; hareng saur red herring; sec comme un hareng (coll) long and thin; serrés comme des harengs (coll) packed like sardines
harengère * [arɑ̃ʒɛr] f fishwife; (coll) shrew
harenguet * [arɑ̃gɛ] m sprat
hargne * [arɲ] f bad temper
har·gneux * [arɲø] -gneuse [ɲøz] adj bad-tempered, peevish, surly
haricot * [ariko] m bean; haricot beurre lima bean, butter bean; haricot de Lima lima bean; haricot de mouton haricot (stew); haricot de Soissons kidney bean; haricot vert string bean
harmonica [armɔnika] m mouth organ
harmonie [armɔni] f harmony; (mus) band
harmo·nieux [armɔnjø] -nieuse [njøz] adj harmonious
harmonique [armɔnik] adj harmonic
harmoniser [armɔnize] tr & ref to harmonize
harnachement * [arnaʃmɑ̃] m harness; harnessing
harnacher * [arnaʃe] tr to harness; to rig out
harnais * [arne] m harness
haro * [aro] m—crier haro sur (coll) to make a hue and cry against
harpagon [arpagɔ̃] m scrooge
harpe * [arp] f harp
harpie * [arpi] f harpy
harpiste * [arpist] mf harpist
harpon * [arpɔ̃] m harpoon
harponner * [arpɔne] tr to harpoon; (coll) to nab (e.g., a thief)
hart * [ar] f noose
hasard * [azar] m hazard, chance; à tout hasard just in case, come what may; au hasard at random; par hasard by chance

hasar·dé -dée *[azarde] *adj* hazardous

hasar·deux *[azardø] -deuse [døz] *adj* risky, uncertain

hase *[az] *f* doe hare

hâte *[at] *f* haste; à la hâte hastily; avoir hâte de to be eager to; en hâte, en toute hâte posthaste

hâter *[ate] *tr & ref* to hasten

hâ·tif *[atif] -tive [tiv] *adj* premature; (hort) early

hauban *[obɑ̃] *m* (naut) shroud; (naut) guy

haubert *[ober] *m* coat of mail

hausse *[os] *f* rise, increase; block, wedge, prop; (mil) elevation, range; jouer à la hausse to bull the market

haussement *[osmɑ̃] *m* shrug

hausser *[ose] *tr* to raise, to lift; to shrug (one's shoulders) || *intr* to rise

haussier *[osje] *m* bull (on the stock exchange)

haussière *[osjer] *f* (naut) hawser

haut *[o] *haute *[ot] *adj* high; loud; high and mighty || (when standing before noun) *adj* high; loud; upper, higher; extra (pay); early (antiquity, Middle Ages, etc.) || *m* top; height; de haut en bas from top to bottom; en haut up; upstairs; haut de casse (typ) upper case; haut des côtes sparerib; le prendre de haut to get on one's high horse; traiter de haut en bas to high-hat || *f* see haute || *haut adv* high; up high; loudly; haut les bras! start working!; haut les cœurs! lift up your hearts!; haut les mains! hands up!

hau·tain *[otɛ̃] -taine [ten] *adj* haughty

hautbois *[obwa] *m* oboe

haut-de-chausses *[odəʃos] *m* (pl hauts-de-chausses) trunk hose, breeches

haut-de-forme *[odəform] *m* (pl hauts-de-forme) top hat

haute *[ot] *f* high society

hautement *[otmɑ̃] *adv* loudly; openly, clearly; highly (qualified); proudly

hauteur *[otœr] *f* height; hill, upland; altitude; haughtiness; (phys) pitch (of sound); à la hauteur de equal to, up to; (naut) off

haut-fond *[ofɔ̃] *m* (pl hauts-fonds) shoal, shallows

haut-le-cœur *[olækœr] *m invar* nausea

haut-le-corps *[oləkɔr] *m invar* jump, sudden start

haut-parleur *[oparlœr] *m* (pl haut-parleurs) loudspeaker

hautu·rier *[otyrje] -rière [rjer] *adj* deep-sea

havage *[avaʒ] *m* (min) cutting

havane *[avan] *adj invar* tan, brown || *m* Havana cigar || (cap) *f*—La Havane Havana

hâve *[av] *adj* haggard, peaked

havir *[avir] *tr* (culin) to sear

havre *[avr] *m* haven, harbor

havresac *[avrəsak] *m* haversack, knapsack; tool bag

hawaïen or **hawaiien** [awajɛ̃], [avajɛ̃] **hawaïenne** or **hawaiienne** [awajen],

[avajen] *adj* Hawaiian || (cap) *mf* Hawaiian

Haye *[ɛ] *f*—La Haye The Hague

H.B.M. [aʃbeem] *f* (letterword) (habitation à bon marché) low-rent apartment

he *[e], [he] *interj* hey!

heaume *[om] *m* helmet

hebdomadaire [ebdɔmader] *adj & m* weekly

héberger [eberʒe] §38 *tr* to lodge

hébé·té -tée [ebete] *adj* dazed

hébéter [ebete] §10 *tr* to daze, stupefy

hébraïque [ebraik] *adj* Hebrew

hébraï·sant [ebraizɑ̃] -sante [zɑ̃t] *mf* Hebraist

hébraïser [ebraize] *tr & intr* to Hebraize

hé·breu [ebrø] (pl -breux) *adj masc* Hebrew || *m* Hebrew (language); c'est de l'hébreu pour moi it's Greek to me || (cap) *m* Hebrew (man)

hécatombe [ekatɔ̃b] *f* hecatomb

hein *[ɛ̃] *interj* (coll) eh!, what!

hélas [elas] *interj* alas!

Hélène [elen] *f* Helen

héler [ele] §10 *tr* to hail, to call

hélice [elis] *f* (aer) propeller; (math) helix, spiral; (naut) screw

hélicoptère [elikɔpter] *m* helicopter

héliport [elipɔr] *m* heliport

hélium [eljɔm] *m* helium

hélix [eliks] *m* helix

hellène [elen] *adj* Hellenic || (cap) *mf* Hellene

helvétique [elvetik] *adj* Swiss

hématie [emati] *f* red blood corpuscle

hémisphère [emisfer] *m* hemisphere

hémistiche [emisti] *m* hemistich

hémoglobine [emɔglɔbin] *f* hemoglobin

hémophilie [emɔfili] *f* hemophilia

hémorragie [emɔraʒi] *f* hemorrhage

hémorroïdes [emɔrɔid] *fpl* hemorrhoids

hémostatique [emɔstatik] *adj* hemostatic || *m* hemostatic, hemostat

henné *[ene] *m* henna

hennir *[enir] *intr* to neigh, whinny

hennissement *[enismɑ̃] *m* neigh, whinny

Henri *[ɑ̃ri], *[ari] *m* Henry

héraldique [eraldik] *adj* heraldic

héraut *[ero] *m* herald

herbe *[erb] *f* grass; lawn; herb; couper l'herbe sous le pied de qn (coll) to pull the rug from under s.o.'s feet; en herbe unripe; budding; fines herbes herbs for seasoning; herbe à la puce (Canad) poison ivy; herbe aux chats catnip; herbes médicinales or officinales (pharm) herbs; herbes potagères potherbs; mauvaise herbe weed

her·beux *[erbø] -beuse [bøz] *adj* grassy

herboristerie [erbɔristri] *f* herb shop

her·bu -bue *[erby] *adj* grassy

herculéen [erkyleɛ̃] **herculéenne** [erkyleen] *adj* herculean

hère *[er] *m* wretch

héréditaire [erediter] *adj* hereditary

hérédité [eredite] *f* heredity

hérésie [erezi] *f* heresy

hérétique [eretik] *adj & mf* heretic

héris·sé héris·sée *[erise] *adj* bristly; shaggy; prickly; surly
hérisser *[erise] *tr & intr* to bristle
hérisson *[erisɔ̃] *m* hedgehog
héritage [eritaʒ] *m* heritage; inheritance
hériter [erite] *tr* to inherit ‖ *intr* to inherit; **hériter de** to become the heir of; to inherit, to come into
héri·tier [eritje] **·tière** [tjer] *mf* heir ‖ *f* heiress
hermétique [ermetik] *adj* hermetic(al), airtight; (fig) obscure
hermine [ermin] *f* ermine
herminette [erminet] *f* adze
hernie *[erni] *f* hernia
her·nieux *[ernjø] **·nieuse** [njøz] *adj* ruptured
héroïne [erɔin] *f* heroine; (drug) heroin
héroïque [erɔik] *adj* heroic
héroïsme [erɔism] *m* heroism
héron *[erɔ̃] *m* heron
héros *[ero] *m* hero
herse *[ers] *f* harrow; portcullis; **les herses** (theat) stage lights
herser *[erse] *tr* to harrow
hési·tant [ezitɑ̃] **·tante** [tɑ̃t] *adj* hesitant
hésitation [ezitasjɔ̃] *f* hesitation
hésiter [ezite] *intr* to hesitate
hétéroclite [eterɔklit] *adj* unusual, odd
hétérodoxe [eterɔdɔks] *adj* heterodox
hétérodyne [eterɔdin] *adj* heterodyne
hétérogène [eterɔʒɛn] *adj* heterogeneous
hêtre *[etr] *m* beech, beech tree
heur *[œr] *m* pleasure; **heur et malheur** joys and sorrows
heure [œr] *f* hour; time (of day); o'clock; **à la bonne heure!** fine!; **à l'heure on time;** by the hour, per hour; **à l'heure juste, à l'heure sonnante on the hour; à tout à l'heure!** see you later!; **à toute heure** at any time; **de bonne heure** early; **heure d'été** daylight-saving time; **heure H** zero hour; **heure légale** twelve-month daylight time (standard time); **heure militaire** sharp, e.g., **huit heures, heure militaire** eight hours sharp; **heures d'affluence** rush hours; **heures de consultation** office hours; **heures de pointe** rush hours; **heures d'ouverture** business hours; **heures supplémentaires** overtime; **l'heure du déjeuner** lunch hour; **tout à l'heure** in a little while; a little while ago
heu·reux *[œrø], [ørø] **·reuse** [røz] *adj* happy, pleased; lucky, fortunate
heurt *[œr] *m* knock, bump; clash; bruise; **sans heurt** without a hitch
heur·té ·tée *[œrte] *adj* clashing (colors); abrupt (style)
heurter *[œrte] *tr* to knock against, to bump into; to antagonize ‖ *intr*— **heurter contre** to bump into ‖ *ref* to clash, to collide; **se heurter à** to come up against
heurtoir *[œrtwar] *m* door knocker; (rr) buffer
hi *[i] *m invar*—**hi hi hi!** ho ho ho!;

pousser des hi et des ha to sputter in amazement
hiatus [jatys], *[jatys] *m* hiatus
hiberner [iberne] *intr* to hibernate
hibiscus [ibiskys] *m* hibiscus
hi·bou *[ibu] *m* (pl **·boux**) owl
hic *[ik] *m*—**voilà le hic!** (coll) there's the rub!
hi·deux *[idø] **·deuse** [døz] *adj* hideous
hie *[i] *f* pile driver
hièble [jebl] *f* (bot) elder
hié·mal ·male [jemal] *adj* (pl **·maux** [mo]) winter
hier [jer] *adv & m* yesterday; **hier soir** last evening, last night
hiérarchie *[jerarʃi] *f* hierarchy
hiéroglyphe [jerɔglif] *m* hieroglyphic
hiéroglyphique [jerɔglifik] *adj* hieroglyphic
hila·rant [ilarɑ̃] **·rante** [rɑ̃t] *adj* hilarious; laughing (gas)
hilare [ilar] *adj* hilarious
hin·dou ·doue [ɛ̃du] *adj* Hindu ‖ (cap) *mf* Hindu
hippique [ipik] *adj* horse (race, show)
hippisme [ipism] *m* horse racing
hippodrome [ipɔdrom] *m* hippodrome, race track
hippopotame [ipɔpɔtam] *m* hippopotamus
hirondelle [irɔdɛl] *f* (orn) swallow; (coll) bicycle cop
hispanique [ispanik] *adj* Hispanic
hispani·sant [ispanizɑ̃] **·sante** [zɑ̃t] *mf* Hispanist
hisser *[ise] *tr* to hoist, to raise
histoire [istwar] *f* history; story; **faire des histoires à** (coll) to make trouble for; **histoire à dormir debout** (coll) tall tale; **histoire de rire** (coll) just for fun; **histoire de s'informer** (coll) out of curiosity; **pas d'histoires** (coll) no fuss
histologie [istɔlɔʒi] *f* histology
histo·rien [istɔrjɛ̃] **·rienne** [rjɛn] *mf* historian
historier [istɔrje] *tr* to illustrate, adorn
historique [istɔrik] *adj* historic(al) ‖ *m* historical account
histrion [istrijɔ̃] *m* ham actor
hiver [iver] *m* winter
hiver·nal ·nale [ivernal] *adj* (pl **·naux** [no]) winter
hiverner [iverne] *intr* to winter
H.L.M. [aʃɛlɛm] *m* (letterword) (habitation à loyer modéré) low-rent apartment
ho *[o], [ho] *interj* hey there!; what!
hobe·reau *[ɔbro] *m* (pl **·reaux**) (orn) hobby; (coll) squire
hoche *[ɔʃ] *f* nick on a blade
hochement *[ɔʃmɑ̃] *m* shake, toss
hochepot *[ɔʃpo] *m* (culin) hotchpotch
hochequeue *[ɔʃkø] *m* (orn) wagtail
hocher *[ɔʃe] *tr* to shake; to nod
hochet *[ɔʃɛ] *m* rattle (toy); bauble
hockey *[ɔkɛ] *m* hockey; **hockey sur glace** ice hockey
hoirie [wari] *f* legacy
holà *[ɔla], [hɔla] *m invar*—**mettre le**

holà à (coll) to put a stop to || *interj* hey!; stop!

holding * [ɔldiŋ] *m* holding company

hold-up * [ɔldœp] *m invar* holdup

hollan·dais * [ɔlɑ̃de] **-daise** [dez] *adj* Dutch || *m* Dutch (*language*) || (*cap*) *mf* Hollander (*person*)

hollande * [ɔlɑ̃d] *m* Edam cheese || *f* Holland (*linen*) || (*cap*) *f* Holland; **la Hollande** Holland

holocauste [ɔlɔkost] *m* holocaust

homard * [ɔmar] *m* lobster

home * [om] *m* home

homélie [ɔmeli] *f* homily

homéopathie [ɔmeɔpati] *f* homeopathy

homicide [ɔmisid] *adj* homicidal || *mf* homicide (*person*) || *m* homicide (*act*)

hommage [ɔmaʒ] *m* homage; **hommage de l'auteur** (formula in presenting complimentary copies) with the compliments of the author; **hommages** respects, compliments

hommasse [ɔmas] *adj* mannish (*woman*)

homme [ɔm] *m* man; **brave homme** fine man, honest man; **être homme à** to be the man to, to be capable of; **homme à tout faire** jack-of-all-trades; handyman; **homme d'affaires** businessman; **homme d'armes** man-at-arms; **homme de droite** rightist; **homme de gauche** leftist; **homme d'église** churchman; **homme de guerre** or **d'épée** military man; **homme de la rue** man in the street, first comer; **homme de l'espace** spaceman; **homme de lettres** man of letters; **homme de paille** figurehead, stooge; **homme de peine** working-man; **homme des bois** orang-utan; **homme d'État** statesman; **homme de troupe** (*pl* **hommes des troupes**) (mil) enlisted man, private; **homme d'expédition** go-getter; **homme d'intérieur** homebody; **homme du monde** man of the world; **homme galant** ladies' man; **hommes de bien** men of good will; **honnête homme** upright man; **man of culture, gentleman**; **jeune homme** young man; **teen-age boy**; **le vieil homme** (Bib) the old Adam; **un homme à la mer!** man overboard!

homme-grenouille [ɔmgrənuj] *m* (*pl* **hommes-grenouilles**) frogman

homme-sandwich [ɔmsɑ̃dwitʃ], [ɔmsɑ̃dwiʃ] *m* (*pl* **hommes-sandwichs**) sandwich man

homogène [ɔmɔʒɛn] *adj* homogeneous

homogénéiser [ɔmɔʒeneize] *tr* to homogenize

homologation [ɔmɔlɔgɑsjɔ̃] *f* validation

homologue [ɔmɔlɔg] *adj* homologous || *mf* (fig) opposite number

homologuer [ɔmɔlɔge] *tr* to confirm, endorse; to probate (*e.g., a will*)

homonyme [ɔmɔnim] *adj* homonymous || *m* homonym; namesake

homosexuel homosexuelle [ɔmɔseksɥel] *adj* & *mf* homosexual

hongre * [ɔ̃gr] *adj* gelded || *m* gelding

hongrer * [ɔ̃gre] *tr* to geld

Hongrie * [ɔ̃gri] *f* Hungary; **la Hongrie** Hungary

hon·grois * [ɔ̃grwɑ] **-groise** [grwɑz] *adj* Hungarian || *m* Hungarian (*language*) || (*cap*) *mf* Hungarian (*person*)

honnête [ɔnet] *adj* honest, honorable

honnêteté [ɔnetəte] *f* honesty, uprightness

honneur [ɔnœr] *m* honor; **faire honneur à sa parole** to keep one's word

honnir * [ɔnir] *tr* to shame

honorabilité [ɔnɔrabilite] *f* respectability

honorable [ɔnɔrabl] *adj* honorable

honoraire [ɔnɔrer] *adj* honorary, emeritus || **honoraires** *mpl* honorarium, fee

honorer [ɔnɔre] *tr* to honor || *ref*—**s'honorer de** to pride oneself on

honorifique [ɔnɔrifik] *adj* honorific

honte * [ɔ̃t] *f* shame; **avoir honte** to be ashamed; **faire honte à qn** to make s.o. ashamed; **faire honte à ses parents** to be a disgrace to one's parents; **fausse honte** bashfulness; **sans honte** unashamedly

hon·teux * [ɔ̃tø] **-teuse** [tøz] *adj* ashamed; shameful

hop * [ɔp] *interj* go!, off with you!

hôpi·tal [ɔpital] *m* (*pl* **-taux** [to]) hospital; charity hospital

hoquet * [ɔke] *m* hiccough

hoqueter * [ɔkte] §34 *intr* to hiccough

horaire [ɔrer] *adj* hourly, by hour || *m* timetable; schedule

horde * [ɔrd] *f* horde

horion * [ɔrjɔ̃] *m* punch, clout

horizon [ɔrizɔ̃] *m* horizon

horizon·tal -tale [ɔrizɔ̃tal] (*pl* **-taux** [to] **-tales**) *adj* & *f* horizontal

horloge [ɔrlɔʒ] *f* clock

horlo·ger [ɔrlɔʒe] **-gère** [ʒer] *adj* clockmaking, watchmaking || *mf* clockmaker, watchmaker

horlogerie [ɔrlɔʒri] *f* clockmaking, watchmaking; **d'horlogerie** clockwork

hormis * [ɔrmi] *prep* (lit) except for

hormone [ɔrmɔn] *f* hormone

horoscope [ɔrɔskɔp] *m* horoscope; **tirer l'horoscope de qn** to cast s.o.'s horoscope

horreur [ɔrœr] *f* horror; **avoir horreur de** to have a horror of; **commettre des horreurs** to commit atrocities; **dire des horreurs** to say obscene things; **dire des horreurs de qn** to say shocking things about

horrible [ɔribl] *adj* horrible

horrifier [ɔrifje] *tr* to horrify

horripi·lant -lante [ɔrripilɑ̃] **-lante** [lɑ̃t] (coll) *adj* hair-raising

horripilation [ɔrripilɑsjɔ̃] *f* gooseflesh, (coll) exasperation

horripiler [ɔrripile] *tr* to give gooseflesh to; (coll) to exasperate

hors * [ɔr] *prep* out, beyond, outside; except, except for, save; **hors de** out of, outside of; **hors de soi** beside oneself, frantic; **hors d'ici!** get out!; **hors tout** overall

hors-bord *['ɔrbɔr] *m invar* outboard (*motor or motorboat*)

hors-caste *['ɔrkast] *mf invar* outcaste

hors-concours *['ɔrkɔ̃kur] *adj invar* excluded from competition ‖ *m invar* contestant excluded from competition

hors-d'œuvre *['ɔrdœvr] *m invar* hors-d'œuvre

hors-jeu *['ɔrʒø] *m invar* offside position

hors-la-loi *['ɔrlalwa] *m invar* outlaw

hors-ligne *['ɔrliɲ] *adj invar* (coll) exceptional ‖ *m invar* roadside

hors-texte *['ɔrtɛks] *m invar* (bb) insert

hortensia [ɔrtɑ̃sja] *m* hydrangea

horticole [ɔrtikɔl] *adj* horticultural

horticulture [ɔrtikyltyr] *f* horticulture

hospice [ɔspis] *m* hospice; home (*for the old, infirm, orphaned, etc.*)

hospita·lier [ɔspitalje] **-lière** [ljɛr] *adj* hospitable; hospital ‖ *mf* hospital employee

hospitaliser [ɔspitalize] *tr* to hospitalize

hospitalité [ɔspitalite] *f* hospitality

hostie [ɔsti] *f* (eccl) Host

hostile [ɔstil] *adj* hostile

hostilité [ɔstilite] *f* hostility

hôte [ot] *m* host; guest

hôtel [otel], [ɔtel] *m* hotel; mansion; **hôtel des Monnaies** mint; **hôtel des Postes** main post office; **hôtel de ville** city hall; **hôtel meublé** rooming house, residential hotel

hôtel-Dieu [oteldjø], [ɔteldjø] *m* (*pl* **hôtels-Dieu**) city hospital

hôte·lier [otəlje], [ɔtəlje] **-lière** [ljɛr] *adj* hotel (*business*) ‖ *mf* hotel manager

hôtellerie [otelri], [ɔtelri] *f* hotel business; fine restaurant; hostelry, hostel

hôtesse [otes] *f* hostess; **hôtesse de l'air** air hostess, stewardess

hotte *['ɔt] *f* basket (*carried on back*); hod (*of mason*); hood (*of chimney*)

hou *['u] *interj* oh no!

houache *['waʃ] *f* wake (*of ship*)

houblon *['ublɔ̃] *m* hop (*vine*); hops (*dried flowers*)

houe *['u] *f* hoe

houer *['we] *tr* to hoe

houille *['uj] *f* coal; **houille blanche** water power; **houille bleue** tide power; **houille d'or** energy from the sun; **houille grasse** or **collante** soft coal; **houille incolore** wind power; **houille maigre** or **éclatante** hard coal; **houille rouge** energy from the heat of the earth

houil·ler *['uje] **houil·lère** *['ujɛr] *adj* coal-bearing, carboniferous; coal (*industry*) ‖ *f* coal mine

houilleur *['ujœr] *m* coal miner

houle *['ul] *f* swell

houlette *['ulɛt] *f* crook (*of shepherd*); (hort) trowel

hou·leux *['ulø] **-leuse** *['løz] *adj* swelling (*sea*); (fig) stormy, turbulent

houp *['up], *['hup] *interj* go to it!

houppe *['up] *f* tuft; crest; tassel; **houppe à poudre** powder puff

houppelande *['uplɑ̃d] *f* greatcoat

houppette *['upɛt] *f* tuft; powder puff

hourra *['ura], *['hura] *m*—**pousser trois hourras** to give three cheers ‖ *interj* hurrah!

hourvari *['urvari] *m* call to the hounds; (coll) uproar

houspiller *['uspije] *tr* to jostle, knock around; to rake over the coals, to tell off

housse *['us] *f* slipcover; cover (*e.g., for typewriter*); garment bag; housing, horsecloth; (aut) seat cover

housser *['use] *tr* to dust (*with feather duster*)

houssine *['usin] *f* rug beater; switch

houssoir *['uswar] *m* feather duster; whisk broom

houx *['u] *m* holly

hoyau *['wajo] *m* (*pl* **hoyaux**) mattock; pickax

hublot *['yblo] *m* porthole

huche *['yʃ] *f* hutch; bin

hucher *['yʃe] *tr* to call, to shout to

hue *['y] *interj* gee up! **tirer à hue et à dia** (fig) to pull in opposite directions

huée *['ɥe] *f* hoot, boo

huer *['ɥe] *tr* & *intr* to hoot, to boo

hugue·not *['ygno] **-note** *[nɔt] *adj* Huguenot ‖ *f* pipkin ‖ (*cap*) *mf* Huguenot (*person*)

huile [ɥil] *f* oil; big shot; **d'huile** calm, e.g., **mer d'huile** calm sea; **huile de coude** elbow grease; **huile de foie de morue** cod-liver oil; **huile de freins** brake fluid; **huile de ricin** castor oil; **huile lourde** diesel fuel; **huile solaire** suntan oil; **les huiles** (coll) the VIP's; **sentir l'huile** (fig) to smell of midnight oil; **verser de l'huile sur le feu** (fig) to add fuel to the fire

huiler [ɥile] *tr* to oil; to grease

hui·leux [ɥilø] **-leuse** [ɥiløz] *adj* oily; greasy

huis [ɥi] *m* (archaic) door; **à huis clos** behind closed doors; (law) in camera; **à huis ouvert** spectators admitted ‖ *['ɥi] *m*—**demander le huis clos** to request a closed-door session

huisserie [ɥisri] *f* doorframe

huissier [ɥisje] *m* doorman; usher (*before a person of rank*); **huissier audiencier** bailiff; **huissier exploitant** process server

huit *['ɥi(t)] *adj* & *pron* eight; the Eighth, e.g., **Jean huit** John the Eighth; **huit heures** eight o'clock ‖ *m* eight; eighth (*in dates*); **faire des huit** to cut figures of eight (*in figure skating*)

huitain *['ɥitɛ̃] *m* eight-line verse

huitaine *['ɥiten] *f* (grouping of) eight; week; **à huitaine** the same day next week; **une huitaine de** about eight

huitième *['ɥitjem] *adj, pron* (*masc, fem*), & *m* eighth

huître [ɥitr] *f* oyster

huit-reflets *['ɥirəfle] *m invar* top hat

huî·trier [ɥitrije] **-trière** [trijer] *adj* oyster (*industry*) ‖ *m* (orn) oyster-catcher ‖ *f* oyster bed

hulotte * [ylɔt] f hoot owl
hululer * [ylyle] intr to hoot
hum * [œm], [hœm] interj hum!
hu·main [ymɛ̃] **-maine** [men] adj human; humane
humaniste [ymanist] adj & mf humanist
humanitaire [ymaniter] adj & mf humanitarian
humanité [ymanite] f humanity; **humanités classiques** humanities (Greek & Latin classics); **humanités modernes** humanities, belles-lettres; **humanités scientifiques** liberal studies (concerned with the observation and classification of facts)
humble [œ̃bl] adj humble
humecter [ymekte] tr to moisten || ref to become damp; **s'humecter le gosier** (slang) to wet one's whistle
humer * [yme] tr to suck, to suck up; to sip; to inhale, to breathe in
humérus [ymerys] m humerus
humeur [ymœr] f humor, body fluid; humor, mood, spirits; **avec humeur** testily; **avoir de l'humeur** to be in a bad mood; **être de bonne humeur** to be in a good humor
humide [ymid] adj humid, damp; wet
humidifier [ymidifje] tr to humidify
humidité [ymidite] f humidity
humi·liant [ymiljɑ̃] **-liante** [ljɑ̃t] adj humiliating
humiliation [ymiljɑsjɔ̃] f humiliation
humilier [ymilje] tr to humiliate, to humble || ref to humble oneself
humilité [ymilite] f humility
humoriste [ymɔrist] adj humorous (writer) || mf humorist
humoristique [ymɔristik] adj humorous
humour [ymur] m humor; **humour noir** macabre humor, sick humor
humus [ymys] m humus
hune * [yn] f (naut) top; **hune de vigie** (naut) crow's-nest
huppe * [yp] f tuft, crest (of bird); (orn) hoopoe
hup·pé -pée * [ype] adj tufted, crested; (coll) smart, stylish
hure * [yr] f head (of boar, salmon, etc.); (culin) headcheese
hurlement * [yrlmɑ̃] m howl, roar; howling, roaring (e.g., of wind)
hurler * [yrle] tr to cry out, yell || intr to howl, to roar
hur·leur * [yrlœr] **-leuse** [løz] adj howling || mf howler || m (zool) howler
hurluberlu [yrlyberly] m (coll) scatterbrain
hu·ron [yrɔ̃] **-ronne** [rɔn] adj (coll) boorish, uncouth || mf (coll) boor
hurricane * [urikan], * [œriken] m hurricane
hutte * [yt] f hut, cabin
hyacinthe [jasɛ̃t] f hyacinth (stone)
hya·lin [jalɛ̃] **-line** [lin] adj glassy
hybride [ibrid] adj & m hybrid
hydrate [idrat] m hydrate
hydrater [idrate] tr & ref to hydrate

hydraulique [idrolik] adj hydraulic || f hydraulics
hydravion [idravjɔ̃] m hydroplane
hydre [idr] f hydra
hydrocarbure [idrokarbyr] m hydrocarbon
hydro-électrique [idroelektrik] adj hydroelectric
hydrofoil [idrofɔjl] m hydrofoil
hydrofuge [idrofyʒ] adj waterproof
hydrofuger [idrofyʒe] §38 tr to waterproof
hydrogène [idroʒɛn] m hydrogen
hydroglisseur [idroglisœr] m speedboat
hydromètre [idrometr] m hydrometer || f (ent) water spider
hydrophile [idrofil] adj absorbent || m —**hydrophile brun** (ent) water devil
hydrophobie [idrofɔbi] f hydrophobia
hydropisie [idropizi] f dropsy
hydroscope [idroskɔp] m dowser
hydroxyde [idroksid] m hydroxide
hyène [jen] f hyena
hygiène [iʒjen] f hygiene
hygiénique [iʒjenik] adj hygienic
hymnaire [imner] m hymnal
hymne [imnə], [im] m hymn, ode, anthem; **hymne national** national anthem || f (eccl) hymn, canticle
hyperacidité [iperasidite] f hyperacidity
hyperbole [iperbɔl] f (math) hyperbola; (rhet) hyperbole
hypersensible [ipersɑ̃sibl] adj hypersensitive, supersensitive
hypersensi·tif [ipersɑ̃sitif] **-tive** [tiv] adj hypersensitive, supersensitive
hypertension [ipertɑ̃sjɔ̃] f high blood pressure, hypertension
hypnose [ipnoz] f hypnosis
hypnotique [ipnotik] adj & m hypnotic
hypnotiser [ipnotize] tr to hypnotize || ref—**s'hypnotiser sur** (fig) to be hypnotized by
hypnoti·seur [ipnotizœr] **-seuse** [zøz] mf hypnotist
hypnotisme [ipnotism] m hypnotism
hypocondriaque [ipokɔ̃drijak] adj & mf hypochondriac
hypocrisie [ipokrizi] f hypocrisy
hypocrite [ipokrit] adj hypocritical || mf hypocrite
hypodermique [ipodermik] adj hypodermic
hyposulfite [iposylfit] m hyposulfite
hypotension [ipotɑ̃sjɔ̃] f low blood pressure
hypoténuse [ipotenyz] f hypotenuse
hypothèque [ipotek] f mortgage; **prendre une hypothèque sur** to put a mortgage on; **purger une hypothèque** to pay off a mortgage
hypothéquer [ipoteke] §10 tr to mortgage
hypothèse [ipotez] f hypothesis
hypothétique [ipotetik] adj hypothetic(al)
hystérie [isteri] f hysteria
hystérique [isterik] adj hysteric(al)

I

I, i [i], *[i] *m invar* ninth letter of the French alphabet

iambique [jãbik] *adj* iambic

ibé·rien [iberjẽ] **-rienne** [rjen] *adj* Iberian ‖ (*cap*) *mf* Iberian

ibérique [iberik] *adj* Iberian

iceberg [isberg] *m* iceberg

ichtyologie [iktjɔlɔʒi] *f* ichthyology

ici [isi] *adv* here; this is, e.g., **ici Paris** (rad, telv) this is Paris; e.g., **ici Robert** (telp) this is Robert; **d'ici** hereabouts; from today; **d'ici demain** before tomorrow; **d'ici là** between now and then, in the meantime; **d'ici peu** before long; **jusqu'ici** up to now, hitherto; **par ici** this way, through here

ici-bas [isibɑ] *adv* here below, on earth

icône [ikon] *f* icon

iconoclaste [ikɔnɔklast] *adj* iconoclastic ‖ *mf* iconoclast

iconographie [ikɔnɔgrafi] *f* iconography; pictures, pictorial material

iconoscope [ikɔnɔskɔp] *m* iconoscope

ictère [ikter] *m* jaundice

ictérique [ikterik] *adj* jaundiced

idéal idéale [ideal] *adj & m* (*pl* **idéaux** [ideo] or **idéals**) ideal

idéaliser [idealize] *tr* idealize

idéaliste [idealist] *adj & mf* idealist

idée [ide] *f* idea; mind, head; opinion, esteem; (coll) shade, touch; **changer d'idée** to change one's mind

identification [idãtifikasjɔ̃] *f* identification

identifier [idãtifje] *tr* to identify

identique [idãtik] *adj* identic(al)

identité [idãtite] *f* identity

idéologie [ideɔlɔʒi] *f* ideology; (pej) utopianism

idéologique [ideɔlɔʒik] *adj* ideologic(al); conceptual

ides [id] *fpl* ides

idiomatique [idjɔmatik] *adj* idiomatic

idiome [idjom] *m* idiom, language

idiosyncrasie [idjɔsẽkrazi] *f* idiosyncrasy

i·diot [idjo] **-diote** [djɔt] *adj* idiotic ‖ *mf* idiot

idiotie [idjɔsi] *f* idiocy

idiotisme [idjɔtism] *m* idiom, idiomatic expression

idolâtrer [idɔlatre] *tr* to idolize

idolâtrie [idɔlatri] *f* idolatry

idole [idɔl] *f* idol

idylle [idil] *f* idyll; romance, love affair

idyllique [idilik] *adj* idyllic

if [if] *m* yew

IGAME [igam] *m* (acronym) (**Inspecteur Général de l'Administration en Mission Extraordinaire**) head prefect

igname [iɲam], [iɲam] *f* yam

ignare [iɲar] *adj* ignorant

ig·né -née [iɲe] *adj* igneous

ignifuge [iɲifyʒ] *adj* fireproof ‖ *m* fireproofing

ignifuger [iɲifyʒe] §38 *tr* to fireproof

ignition [ignisjɔ̃] *f* ignition; red heat (*of metal*)

ignoble [iɲɔbl] *adj* ignoble; disgusting

ignomi·nieux [iɲɔminjø] **-nieuse** [njøz] *adj* ignominious

ignorance [iɲɔrɑ̃s] *f* ignorance

igno·rant [iɲɔrɑ̃] **-rante** [rɑ̃t] *adj* ignorant ‖ *mf* ignoramus

ignorer [iɲɔre] *tr* not to know, to be ignorant of; to be unacquainted with

il [il] §87

île [il] *f* island, isle; **les îles Normandes** the Channel Islands

illé·gal -gale [illegal] *adj* (*pl* **-gaux** [go]) illegal

illégitime [illeʒitim] *adj* illegitimate; unjustified

illet·tré -trée [illetre] *adj & mf* illiterate

illicite [illisit] *adj* illicit; foul (*blow*)

illimi·té -tée [illimite] *adj* unlimited

illisible [illizibl] *adj* illegible; unreadable (*book*)

illogique [illɔʒik] *adj* illogical

illumination [illyminasjɔ̃] *f* illumination

illumi·né -née [illymine] *adj & mf* fanatic, visionary

illuminer [illymine] *tr* to illuminate

illusion [illyzjɔ̃] *f* illusion; **illusion de la vue** optical illusion; **se faire des illusions** to indulge in wishful thinking

illusionner [illyzjɔne] *tr* to delude ‖ *ref* to delude oneself

illusionniste [illyzjɔnist] *mf* magician

illusoire [illyzwar] *adj* illusory, illusive

illustra·teur [illystratœr] *m* illustrator

illustration [illystrasjɔ̃] *f* illustration; glorification; glory; celebrity

illustre [illystr] *adj* illustrious, renowned

illus·tré -trée [illystre] *adj* illustrated ‖ *m* illustrated magazine

illustrer [illystre] *tr* to illustrate ‖ *ref* to distinguish oneself

îlot [ilo] *m* small island, isle; block (*of houses*)

ils [il] §87

image [imaʒ] *f* image; picture; **images** imagery

imager [imaʒe] §38 *tr* to embellish with metaphors, to color

imagerie [imaʒri] *f*—**imagerie d'Épinal** cardboard cutouts

imaginaire [imaʒiner] *adj* imaginary

imagination [imaʒinasjɔ̃] *f* imagination

imaginer [imaʒine] *tr* to imagine; to invent ‖ *intr* to imagine; **imaginer de** + *inf* to have the idea of + *ger* ‖ *ref* to imagine oneself; (with *dat* of *reflex pron*) to imagine

imbattable [ẽbatabl] *adj* unbeatable

imbat·tu -tue [ẽbaty] *adj* unbeaten

imbécile [ẽbesil] *adj & mf* imbecile

imbécillité [ẽbesilite] *f* imbecility

imberbe [ẽberb] *adj* beardless

imbiber [ẽbibe] *tr & ref* to soak; **s'imbiber de** to soak up; to be imbued with imbri·qué ·quée [ɛbrike] *adj* overlapping

imbrisable [ɛbrizabl] *adj* unbreakable

imbrûlable [ɛbrylabl] *adj* fireproof

im·bu ·bue [ɛby] *adj*—imbu de imbued with, steeped in

imita·teur [imitatœr] ·trice [tris] *mf* imitator

imitation [imitasjɔ̃] *f* imitation

imiter [imite] *tr* to imitate

immacu·lé ·lée [immakyle] *adj* immaculate

immangeable [ɛmɑ̃ʒabl] *adj* inedible

immanquable [ɛmɑ̃kabl] *adj* infallible; inevitable

immaté·riel ·rielle [immaterjel] *adj* immaterial

immatriculation [immatrikylasjɔ̃] *f* registration; enrollment

immatriculer [immatrikyle] *tr* to register

immature [immatyr] *adj* unmatured

immé·diat ·diate [immedja] ·diate [djat] *adj* immediate

immédiatement [immedjatmã] *adv* immediately

immémo·rial ·riale [immemɔrjal] *adj* (*pl* ·riaux [rjo]) immemorial

immense [immɑ̃s] *adj* immense

immensurable [immɑ̃syrabl] *adj* immeasurable, immensurable

immerger [immerʒe] §38 *tr* to immerse, to dip; to throw overboard; to lay (*a cable*)

imméri·té ·tée [immerite] *adj* undeserved

immersion [immersjɔ̃] *f* immersion

immettable [ɛmetabl] *adj* unwearable

immeuble [immœbl] *adj* real, e.g., biens immeubles real estate ‖ *m* building, apartment building

immi·grant [immigrɑ̃] ·grante [grɑ̃t] *adj* & *mf* immigrant

immigration [immigrasjɔ̃] *f* immigration

immi·gré ·grée [immigre] *adj* & *mf* immigrant

immigrer [immigre] *intr* to immigrate

immi·nent [imminɑ̃] ·nente [nɑ̃t] *adj* imminent, impending

immiscer [immise] §51 *ref*—s'immiscer dans to interfere with, to meddle with

immixtion [immiksjɔ̃] *f* interference

immobile [immɔbil] *adj* motionless; immobile (*resolute*); dead (*typewriter key*)

immobi·lier [immɔbilje] ·lière [ljer] *adj* real-estate, property; real, e.g., biens immobiliers real estate

immobiliser [immɔbilize] *tr* to immobilize; to tie up ‖ *ref* to come to a stop

immodé·ré ·rée [immɔdere] *adj* immoderate

immonde [immɔ̃d] *adj* foul, filthy; (eccl) unclean

immondices [immɔ̃dis] *fpl* garbage, refuse

immo·ral ·rale [immɔral] *adj* (*pl* ·raux [ro]) immoral

immortaliser [immɔrtalize] *tr* to immortalize

immor·tel ·telle [immɔrtel] *adj* & *mf* immortal ‖ *f* (bot) everlasting

immoti·vé ·vée [immɔtive] *adj* groundless

immuable [immɥabl] *adj* changeless

immuniser [immynize] *tr* to immunize

immunité [immynite] *f* immunity

im·pair ·paire [ɛper] *adj* odd, uneven ‖ *m* (coll) blunder

impardonnable [ɛpardɔnabl] *adj* unpardonable

impar·fait [ɛparfe] ·faite [fet] *adj* & *m* imperfect

imparité [ɛparite] *f* inequality, disparity

impar·tial ·tiale [ɛparsjal] *adj* (*pl* ·tiaux [sjo]) impartial

impartir [ɛpartir] *tr* to grant

impasse [ɛpɑs] *f* blind alley, dead-end street; impasse, deadlock; (cards) finesse; faire l'impasse à (cards) to finesse

impassible [ɛpasibl] *adj* impassible; impassive (*look, face, etc.*)

impatience [ɛpasjɑ̃s] *f* impatience; impatiences (coll) attack of nerves

impa·tient [ɛpasjɑ̃] ·tiente [sjɑ̃t] *adj* impatient

impatienter [ɛpasjɑ̃te] *tr* to make impatient ‖ *ref* to lose patience

impatroniser [ɛpatrɔnize] *ref* to take charge; to take hold

impavide [ɛpavid] *adj* fearless

impayable [ɛpejabl] *adj* (coll) priceless, very funny

impayé impayée [ɛpeje] *adj* unpaid

impeccable [ɛpekabl] *adj* impeccable

impénétrable [ɛpenetrabl] *adj* impenetrable

impéni·tent [ɛpenitɑ̃] ·tente [tɑ̃t] *adj* impenitent, obdurate, inveterate

impensable [ɛpɑ̃sabl] *adj* unthinkable

imper [ɛper] *m* (coll) raincoat

impéra·tif [ɛperatif] ·tive [tiv] *adj* & *m* imperative

impératrice [ɛperatris] *f* empress

imperceptible [ɛperseptibl] *adj* imperceptible; negligible

imperdable [ɛperdabl] *adj* unlosable

imperfection [ɛperfeksjɔ̃] *f* imperfection, defect

impé·rial ·riale [ɛperjal] *adj* (*pl* ·riaux [rjo]) imperial ‖ *f* goatee; upper deck (*of bus, coach, etc.*)

impérialiste [ɛperjalist] *adj* & *mf* imperialist

impé·rieux [ɛperjø] ·rieuse [rjøz] *adj* imperious, haughty; imperative, urgent

impérissable [ɛperisabl] *adj* imperishable

impéritie [ɛperisi] *f* incompetence

imperméabiliser [ɛpermeabilize] *tr* to waterproof

imperméable [ɛpermeabl] *adj* waterproof; impervious ‖ *m* raincoat

imperson·nel ·nelle [ɛpersɔnel] *adj* impersonal; commonplace; ordinary

imperti·nent [ɛpertinɑ̃] ·nente [nɑ̃t] *adj* impertinent ‖ *mf* impertinent person

impé·trant [ɛpetrɑ̃] ·trante [trɑ̃t] *mf* holder (*of a title or degree*)

impé·tueux [ɛ̃petɥø] **-tueuse** [tɥøz] *adj* impetuous

impie [ɛ̃pi] *adj* impious, ungodly; blasphemous ‖ *mf* unbeliever; blasphemer

impiété [ɛ̃pjete] *f* impiety; disrespect

impitoyable [ɛ̃pitwajabl] *adj* unmerciful

implanter [ɛ̃plɑ̃te] *tr* to implant; to introduce ‖ *ref* to take root; **s'implanter chez** (coll) to thrust oneself upon

implication [ɛ̃plikɑsjɔ̃] *f* implication

implicite [ɛ̃plisit] *adj* implicit

impliquer [ɛ̃plike] *tr* to implicate; to imply

implorer [ɛ̃plɔre] *tr* to implore

imployable [ɛ̃plwajabl] *adj* pitiless; inflexible

impo·li -lie [ɛ̃pɔli] *adj* impolite

impolitique [ɛ̃pɔlitik] *adj* ill-advised

impondérable [ɛ̃pɔ̃derabl] *adj & m* imponderable

impopulaire [ɛ̃pɔpyler] *adj* unpopular

impopularité [ɛ̃pɔpylarite] *f* unpopularity

importance [ɛ̃pɔrtɑ̃s] *f* importance; size; **d'importance** large, of consequence; thoroughly, very hard

impor·tant [ɛ̃pɔrtɑ̃] **-tante** [tɑ̃t] *adj* important; large, considerable ‖ *m* main thing; **faire l'important** (coll) to act big

importa·teur [ɛ̃pɔrtatœr] **-trice** [tris] *mf* importer

importer [ɛ̃pɔrte] *tr* to import ‖ *intr* to matter; to be important; **n'importe** no matter, never mind; **n'importe comment** any way; **n'importe où** anywhere; **n'importe quand** anytime; **n'importe quel . . .** any . . . ; **n'importe qui** anybody; **n'importe quoi** anything; **peu m'importe** it doesn't matter to me; **qu'importe?** what does it matter?

impor·tun [ɛ̃pɔrtœ̃] **-tune** [tyn] *adj* bothersome ‖ *mf* pest, nuisance

importuner [ɛ̃pɔrtyne] *tr* to importune

imposable [ɛ̃pozabl] *adj* taxable

impo·sant -sante [ɛ̃pozɑ̃] [zɑ̃t] *adj* imposing

impo·sé -sée [ɛ̃poze] *adj* taxed; fixed (*price*) ‖ *mf* taxpayer

imposer [ɛ̃poze] *tr* to impose; to levy a tax on ‖ *intr*—**en imposer à** to make an impression on; to impose on ‖ *ref* to assert oneself; to be indispensable; **s'imposer à** to force itself upon; **s'imposer chez** to foist oneself upon

imposition [ɛ̃pozisjɔ̃] *f* imposition; taxation; laying on, levying

impossible [ɛ̃pɔsibl] *adj* impossible

imposte [ɛ̃pɔst] *f* transom; (archit) impost

imposteur [ɛ̃pɔstœr] *m* impostor

imposture [ɛ̃pɔstyr] *f* imposture

impôt [ɛ̃po] *m* tax; **impôt du sang** military duty; **impôt foncier** property tax; **impôt indirecte** sales tax; **impôt retenu à la source** withholding tax; **impôt sur le revenu** income tax

impotence [ɛ̃pɔtɑ̃s] *f* lameness, infirmity

impo·tent [ɛ̃pɔtɑ̃] **-tente** [tɑ̃t] *adj* crippled; bedridden ‖ *mf* cripple

impraticable [ɛ̃pratikabl] *adj* impracticable; impassable (*e.g., road*)

impré·cis [ɛ̃presi] **-cise** [siz] *adj* vague, hazy

imprégner [ɛ̃preɲe] §10 *tr* to impregnate

imprenable [ɛ̃prənabl] *adj* impregnable

impréparation [ɛ̃preparasjɔ̃] *f* unpreparedness

imprésario [ɛ̃presarjo] *m* impresario

impression [ɛ̃presjɔ̃] *f* impression; printing

impression·nant [ɛ̃presjɔnɑ̃] **impression·nante** [ɛ̃presjɔnɑ̃t] *adj* impressive

impressionner [ɛ̃presjɔne] *tr* to impress, to affect; (phot) to expose

imprévisible [ɛ̃previzibl] *adj* unforeseeable

imprévision [ɛ̃previzjɔ̃] *f* lack of foresight

imprévoyant [ɛ̃prevwajɑ̃] **imprévoyante** [ɛ̃prevwajɑ̃t] *adj* improvident, shortsighted

impré·vu -vue [ɛ̃prevy] *adj & m* unforeseen, unexpected; **sauf imprévu** unless something unforeseen happens

impri·mé -mée [ɛ̃prime] *adj* printed ‖ *m* print, calico; printed work, book; printing (*as opposed to script*); **imprimés** printed matter

imprimer [ɛ̃prime] *tr* to print; to imprint; to impress; to impart (*e.g., movement*)

imprimerie [ɛ̃primri] *f* printing; printing office, print shop

imprimeur [ɛ̃primœr] *m* printer

imprimeur-éditeur [ɛ̃primœreditœr] *m* (*pl* **imprimeurs-éditeurs**) printer and publisher

imprimeur-libraire [ɛ̃primœrlibrer] *m* (*pl* **imprimeurs-libraires**) printer and publisher

imprimeuse [ɛ̃primøz] *f* printing press

improbable [ɛ̃prɔbabl] *adj* improbable

improba·tif [ɛ̃prɔbatif] **-tive** [tiv] *adj* disapproving

improbité [ɛ̃prɔbite] *f* dishonesty

improduc·tif [ɛ̃prɔdyktif] **-tive** [tiv] *adj* unproductive

impromp·tu -tue [ɛ̃prɔ̃pty] *adj* impromptu ‖ *m* impromptu play; (mus) impromptu ‖ **impromptu** *adv* impromptu

impropre [ɛ̃prɔpr] *adj* improper (*not right*); **impropre à** unfit for

impropriété [ɛ̃prɔprijete] *f* incorrectness

improviser [ɛ̃prɔvize] *tr & intr* to improvise

improviste [ɛ̃prɔvist]—**à l'improviste** unexpectedly, impromptu; **prendre à l'improviste** to catch napping

impru·dent [ɛ̃prydɑ̃] **-dente** [dɑ̃t] *adj* imprudent

impubère [ɛ̃pyber] *adj* under the age of puberty

impubliable [ɛ̃pybljabl] *adj* unpublishable, not fit to print

impu·dent [ɛ̃pydɑ̃] **-dente** [dɑ̃t] *adj* impudent

impudeur [ɛ̃pydœr] *f* immodesty

impudicité [ɛ̃pydisite] *f* indecency
impudique [ɛ̃pydik] *adj* immodest
impuissance [ɛ̃pɥisɑ̃s] *f* impotence; **être dans l'impuissance de faire q.ch.** to be powerless to do s.th.
impuis·sant [ɛ̃pɥisɑ̃] **impuis·sante** [ɛ̃pɥisɑ̃t] *adj* impotent, powerless, helpless; (pathol) impotent
impul·sif -sive [ɛ̃pylsif] -sive [siv] *adj* impulsive || *mf* impulsive person
impulsion [ɛ̃pylsjɔ̃] *f* impulse; **donner l'impulsion à** to give an impetus to; **sous l'impulsion du moment** on the spur of the moment
impunément [ɛ̃pynemɑ̃] *adv* with impunity
impu·ni -nie [ɛ̃pyni] *adj* unpunished
impunité [ɛ̃pynite] *f* impunity
im·pur -pure [ɛ̃pyr] *adj* impure
impureté [ɛ̃pyrte] *f* impurity
imputation [ɛ̃pytasjɔ̃] *f* imputation; (com) charge; (com) deduction
imputer [ɛ̃pyte] *tr* to impute, ascribe; (com) **imputer q.ch. à** to charge s.th. to
inaccessible [inaksesibl] *adj* inaccessible
inac·tif [inaktif] **-tive** [tiv] *adj* inactive
inaction [inaksjɔ̃] *f* inaction
inactivité [inaktivite] *f* inactivity
inadaptation [inadaptasjɔ̃] *f* maladjustment
inadap·té -tée [inadapte] *adj* maladjusted || *mf* misfit
inadvertance [inadvɛrtɑ̃s] *f*—**par inadvertance** inadvertently
inalté·ré -rée [inaltere] *adj* unspoiled
inani·mé -mée [inanime] *adj* inanimate
inappréciable [inapresjabl] *adj* inappreciable, imperceptible; invaluable
inapprivoisable [inaprivwazabl] *adj* untamable
inapte [inapt] *adj* inept; **inapte à** unfit for, unsuitable for || *mf* dropout, washout; **les inaptes** the unfit; the unemployable
inaptitude [inaptityd] *f* unfitness
inarticu·lé -lée [inartikyle] *adj* inarticulate
inassou·vi -vie [inasuvi] *adj* unsatisfied
inattaquable [inatakabl] *adj* unquestionable; unassailable; **inattaquable par** unaffected by, resistant to
inatten·du -due [inatɑ̃dy] *adj* unexpected
inaten·tif [inatɑ̃tif] **-tive** [tiv] *adj* inattentive; careless
inattention [inatɑ̃sjɔ̃] *f* inattentiveness, carelessness
inaudible [inodibl] *adj* inaudible
inaugu·ral -rale [inogyral] *adj* (pl -raux [ro]) inaugural
inauguration [inogyrasjɔ̃] *f* inauguration
inaugurer [inogyre] *tr* to inaugurate; to unveil (*a statue*)
inauthentique [inotɑ̃tik] *adj* unauthentic
inavouable [inavwabl] *adj* shameful
ina·voué -vouée [inavwe] *adj* unacknowledged
inca [ɛ̃ka] *adj invar* Inca || (cap) *m* Inca

incandes·cent [ɛ̃kɑ̃desɑ̃] **incandes·cente** [ɛ̃kɑ̃desɑ̃t] *adj* incandescent; wild, stirred up (*crowd*)
incapable [ɛ̃kapabl] *adj* incapable; (law) incompetent || *mf* (law) incompetent person
incapacité [ɛ̃kapasite] *f* incapacity; disability
incarcérer [ɛ̃karsere] §10 *tr* to incarcerate
incar·nat -nate [ɛ̃karna] -nate [nat] *adj* flesh-colored; rosy || *m* flesh color
incarnation [ɛ̃karnasjɔ̃] *f* incarnation
incar·né -née [ɛ̃karne] *adj* incarnate; ingrowing (*nail*)
incarner [ɛ̃karne] *tr* to incarnate, to embody || *ref* to become incarnate; (pathol) to become ingrown; **s'incarner dans** to become the embodiment of
incartade [ɛ̃kartad] *f* indiscretion; prank
incassable [ɛ̃kasabl] *adj* unbreakable
incendiaire [ɛ̃sɑ̃djɛr] *adj & mf* incendiary
incendie [ɛ̃sɑ̃di] *m* fire, conflagration; **incendie volontaire** arson
incen·dié -diée [ɛ̃sɑ̃dje] *adj* burnt down || *mf* fire victim
incendier [ɛ̃sɑ̃dje] *tr* to set on fire; to burn down; (fig) to fire, inflame; (slang) to give a tongue-lashing to
incer·tain -taine [ɛ̃sɛrtɛ̃] -taine [ten] *adj* uncertain; indistinct; unsettled (*weather*)
incertitude [ɛ̃sɛrtityd] *f* incertitude, uncertainty; **dans l'incertitude** in doubt
incessamment [ɛ̃sesamɑ̃] *adv* incessantly; without delay, at any moment
inces·sant [ɛ̃sesɑ̃] **inces·sante** [ɛ̃sesɑ̃t] *adj* incessant
inceste [ɛ̃sɛst] *m* incest
inces·tueux [ɛ̃sɛstɥø] **-tueuse** [tɥøz] *adj* incestuous
inchan·gé -gée [ɛ̃ʃɑ̃ʒe] *adj* unchanged
incidemment [ɛ̃sidamɑ̃] *adv* incidentally
incidence [ɛ̃sidɑ̃s] *f* incidence
inci·dent [ɛ̃sidɑ̃] **-dente** [dɑ̃t] *adj & m* incident
incinérer [ɛ̃sinere] §10 *tr* to incinerate; to cremate
incirconcis [ɛ̃sirkɔ̃si] *adj masc* uncircumcised
inciser [ɛ̃size] *tr* to make an incision in; to tap (*a tree*); (med) to lance
inci·sif [ɛ̃sizif] **-sive** [ziv] *adj* incisive || *f* incisor
incision [ɛ̃sizjɔ̃] *f* incision
incitation [ɛ̃sitasjɔ̃] *f* incitement
inciter [ɛ̃site] *tr* to incite
inci·vil -vile [ɛ̃sivil] *adj* uncivil
incivili·sé -sée [ɛ̃sivilize] *adj* uncivilized
inclassable [ɛ̃klasabl] *adj* unclassifiable
inclé·ment -mente [ɛ̃klemɑ̃] -mente [mɑ̃t] *adj* inclement
inclinaison [ɛ̃klinezɔ̃] *f* inclination; slope
inclination [ɛ̃klinasjɔ̃] *f* inclination; bow; love, affection
incliner [ɛ̃kline] *tr & ref* to incline; to bend; to bow

inclure [ɛklyr] §11 (*pp* **inclus**) *tr* to include; to enclose

in·clus [ɛkly] **-cluse** [klyz] *adj* including, e.g., **jusqu'à la page dix incluse** up to and including page ten; inclusive, e.g., **de mercredi à samedi inclus** from Wednesday to Saturday inclusive

inclu·sif [ɛklyzif] **-sive** [ziv] *adj* inclusive

inclusivement [ɛklyzivmɑ̃] *adv* inclusively, inclusive

incognito [ɛkɔɲito] *m & adv* incognito

incohé·rent [ɛkɔerɑ̃] **-rente** [rɑ̃t] *adj* incoherent; inconsistent, illogical

incolore [ɛkɔlɔr] *adj* colorless

incomber [ɛkɔbe] *intr*—**incomber à** to devolve on, to fall upon; **il incombe à qn de** it behooves s.o. to

incombustible [ɛkɔbystibl] *adj* incombustible; fireproof

incommode [ɛkɔmɔd] *adj* inconvenient; unwieldy

incommoder [ɛkɔmɔde] *tr* to inconvenience

incommodité [ɛkɔmɔdite] *f* inconvenience

incomparable [ɛkɔparabl] *adj* incomparable

incompatible [ɛkɔpatibl] *adj* incompatible; conflicting

incompétence [ɛkɔpetɑ̃s] *f* incompetence; lack of jurisdiction

incompé·tent [ɛkɔpetɑ̃] **-tente** [tɑ̃t] *adj* incompetent; lacking jurisdiction

incom·plet [ɛkɔple] **-plète** [plet] *adj* incomplete

incompréhensible [ɛkɔpreɑ̃sibl] *adj* incomprehensible

incom·pris [ɛkɔpri] **-prise** [priz] *adj* misunderstood

inconcevable [ɛkɔsvabl] *adj* inconceivable

inconciliable [ɛkɔsiljabl] *adj* irreconcilable

incondition·nel -nelle [ɛkɔdisjɔnel] *adj* unconditional

inconduite [ɛkɔdɥit] *f* misconduct

inconfort [ɛkɔfɔr] *m* discomfort

incon·gru -grue [ɛkɔgry] *adj* incongruous

incon·nu -nue [ɛkɔny] *adj* unknown; **inconnu à cette adresse** address unknown || *mf* unknown (*person*) || *m* unknown (*what is not known*) || *f* (math) unknown

inconsciemment [ɛkɔsjamɑ̃] *adv* subconsciously; unconsciously

inconscience [ɛkɔsjɑ̃s] *f* unconsciousness; unawareness

incons·cient [ɛkɔsjɑ̃] **incons·ciente** [ɛkɔsjɑ̃t] *adj* unconscious, unaware, oblivious; thoughtless; subconscious || *mf* dazed person || *m* unconscious

inconséquence [ɛkɔsekɑ̃s] *f* inconsistency; thoughtlessness, inconsiderateness

inconsé·quent [ɛkɔsekɑ̃] **-quente** [kɑ̃t] *adj* inconsistent; thoughtless, inconsiderate

inconsidé·ré -rée [ɛkɔsidere] *adj* inconsiderate

inconsistance [ɛkɔsistɑ̃s] *f* inconsistency; flimsiness, instability

inconsis·tant [ɛkɔsistɑ̃] **-tante** [tɑ̃t] *adj* inconsistent; flimsy, unstable

inconsolable [ɛkɔsɔlabl] *adj* inconsolable

incons·tant [ɛkɔstɑ̃] **-tante** [tɑ̃t] *adj* inconstant

inconstitution·nel -nelle [ɛkɔstitysjɔnel] *adj* unconstitutional

inconti·nent [ɛkɔtinɑ̃] **-nente** [nɑ̃t] *adj* incontinent || **incontinent** *adv* at once, forthwith

incontrôlable [ɛkɔtrolabl] *adj* unverifiable

incontrô·lé -lée [ɛkɔtrole] *adj* unverified; unchecked, uncontrollable

inconvenance [ɛkɔvnɑ̃s] *f* impropriety

inconve·nant [ɛkɔvnɑ̃] **-nante** [nɑ̃t] *adj* improper, indecent

inconvénient [ɛkɔvenjɑ̃] *m* inconvenience, disadvantage; **voir un inconvénient à** to have an objection to

incorporation [ɛkɔrpɔrasjɔ̃] *f* incorporation; (mil) induction

incorpo·ré -rée [ɛkɔrpɔre] *adj* built-in

incorpo·rel -relle [ɛkɔrpɔrel] *adj* incorporeal; intangible (*property*)

incorporer [ɛkɔrpɔre] *tr* to incorporate; (mil) to induct || *ref* to incorporate

incor·rect -recte [ɛkɔrekt] *adj* incorrect; unfair

incrédule [ɛkredyl] *adj* incredulous; unbelieving || *mf* unbeliever, freethinker

incrédulité [ɛkredylite] *f* incredulity; disbelief

increvable [ɛkrəvabl] *adj* punctureproof; (slang) untiring

incriminer [ɛkrimine] *tr* to incriminate

incrochetable [ɛkrɔʃtabl] *adj* burglarproof (*lock*)

incroyable [ɛkrwajabl] *adj* unbelievable

incroy·ant [ɛkrwajɑ̃] **incroyante** [ɛkrwajɑ̃t] *adj* unbelieving || *mf* unbeliever

incrustation [ɛkrystasjɔ̃] *f* incrustation; inlay; (sewing) insert

incruster [ɛkryste] *tr* to incrust; to inlay || *ref* to take root, to become ingrained

incubateur [ɛkybatœr] *m* incubator

incuber [ɛkybe] *tr* to incubate

inculpation [ɛkylpasjɔ̃] *f* indictment; **sous l'inculpation de** on a charge of

incul·pé -pée [ɛkylpe] *adj* indicted; **inculpé de** charged with, accused of || *mf* accused, defendant

inculper [ɛkylpe] *tr* to indict, to charge

inculquer [ɛkylke] *tr* to inculcate

inculte [ɛkylt] *adj* uncultivated; uncouth

incunables [ɛkynabl] *mpl* incunabula

incurable [ɛkyrabl] *adj & mf* incurable

incurie [ɛkyri] *f* carelessness

incursion [ɛkyrsjɔ̃] *f* incursion, foray

Inde [ɛd] *f* India; **Indes Occidentales** West Indies; **Indes Orientales Néerlandaises** Dutch East Indies; **l'Inde** India

indébrouillable [ɛdebrujabl] *adj* inextricable, hopelessly involved

indécence [ɛ̃desɑ̃s] *f* indecency
indé·cent [ɛ̃desɑ̃] **-cente** [sɑ̃t] *adj* indecent
indéchiffrable [ɛ̃deʃifrabl] *adj* undecipherable; incomprehensible; illegible
indé·cis [ɛ̃desi] **-cise** [siz] *adj* indecisive; uncertain, undecided; blurred
indéclinable [ɛ̃deklinabl] *adj* indeclinable
indécrottable [ɛ̃dekrɔtabl] *adj* (coll) incorrigible, hopeless
indéfectible [ɛ̃defektibl] *adj* everlasting; unfailing
indéfendable [ɛ̃defɑ̃dabl] *adj* indefensible
indéfi·ni -nie [ɛ̃defini] *adj* indefinite
indéfinissable [ɛ̃definisabl] *adj* indefinable
indéfrisable [ɛ̃defrizabl] *adj* permanent (*wave*) || *f* permanent wave
indélébile [ɛ̃delebil] *adj* indelible
indéli·cat -cate [ɛ̃delika] [kat] *adj* indelicate; dishonest
indémaillable [ɛ̃demajabl] *adj* runproof
indemne [ɛ̃demn] *adj* undamaged, unharmed
indemnisation [ɛ̃demnizasjɔ̃] *f* indemnification, compensation
indemniser [ɛ̃demnize] *tr* to compensate
indemnité [ɛ̃demnite] *f* indemnity; allowance, grant; compensation; **indemnité journalière** workmen's compensation; **indemnité parlementaire** salary of members (*of parliamentary body*)
indéniable [ɛ̃denjabl] *adj* undeniable
indépendance [ɛ̃depɑ̃dɑ̃s] *f* independence
indépen·dant [ɛ̃depɑ̃dɑ̃] **-dante** [dɑ̃t] *adj & mf* independent
indéréglable [ɛ̃dereglabl] *adj* foolproof
indescriptible [ɛ̃deskriptibl] *adj* indescribable
indésirable [ɛ̃dezirabl] *adj* undesirable
indestructible [ɛ̃destryktibl] *adj* indestructible
indétermi·né -née [ɛ̃determine] *adj* indeterminate
indétraquable [ɛ̃detrakabl] *adj* foolproof
index [ɛ̃deks] *m* index; forefinger; index number; **Index** (eccl) Index
indica·teur [ɛ̃dikatœr] **-trice** [tris] *adj* indicating || *mf* informer || *m* gauge; indicator, pointer; timetable; road sign; guidebook; street guide
indica·tif [ɛ̃dikatif] **-tive** [tiv] *adj* indicative, suggestive || *m* (gram) indicative; (rad) station identification; **indicatif d'appel** (rad, telg) call letters or number
indication [ɛ̃dikasjɔ̃] *f* indication; **fausse indication** wrong piece of information; **indications** directions; **sauf indication contraire** unless otherwise directed; **sur l'indication de** at the suggestion of
indice [ɛ̃dis] *m* indication, sign; clue; **indice des prix** price index; **indice d'octane** octane number; **indice du coût de la vie** cost-of-living index

indicible [ɛ̃disibl] *adj* inexpressible
in·dien [ɛ̃djɛ̃] **-dienne** [djɛn] *adj* Indian || *f* calico, chintz || (*cap*) *mf* Indian
indifféremment [ɛ̃diferamɑ̃] *adv* indiscriminately
indiffé·rent [ɛ̃diferɑ̃] **-rente** [rɑ̃t] *adj* indifferent; unimportant; **cela m'est indifférent** it's all the same to me
indigence [ɛ̃diʒɑ̃s] *f* indigence, poverty
indigène [ɛ̃diʒɛn] *adj* indigenous, native || *mf* native
indi·gent [ɛ̃diʒɑ̃] **-gente** [ʒɑ̃t] *adj* indigent || *mf* pauper; **les indigents** the poor
indigeste [ɛ̃diʒɛst] *adj* indigestible; heavy, stodgy; undigested, mixed up
indigestion [ɛ̃diʒɛstjɔ̃] *f* indigestion
indignation [ɛ̃diɲasjɔ̃] *f* indignation
indigne [ɛ̃diɲ] *adj* unworthy; shameful
indi·gné -gnée [ɛ̃diɲe] *adj* indignant
indigner [ɛ̃diɲe] *tr* to outrage || *ref* to be indignant
indignité [ɛ̃diɲite] *f* unworthiness; indignity, outrage
indigo [ɛ̃digo] *adj invar & m* indigo
indi·qué -quée [ɛ̃dike] *adj* advisable, appropriate; **être tout indiqué pour** to be just the thing for; to be just the man for
indiquer [ɛ̃dike] *tr* to indicate; to name; **indiquer du doigt** to point to, to point out
indi·rect -recte [ɛ̃dirɛkt] *adj* indirect
indisciplinable [ɛ̃disiplinabl] *adj* unruly
indiscipline [ɛ̃disiplin] *f* lack of discipline, disobedience
indiscipli·né -née [ɛ̃disipline] *adj* undisciplined
indis·cret -crète [ɛ̃diskre] [kret] *adj* indiscreet
indiscrétion [ɛ̃diskresjɔ̃] *f* indiscretion; **sans indiscrétion...** if I may ask...
indiscutable [ɛ̃diskytabl] *adj* unquestionable
indiscu·té -tée [ɛ̃diskyte] *adj* unquestioned
indispensable [ɛ̃dispɑ̃sabl] *adj & m* indispensable, essential
indisponible [ɛ̃dispɔnibl] *adj* unavailable; out of commission (*said of car, machine, etc.*)
indispo·sé -sée [ɛ̃dispoze] *adj* indisposed (*slightly ill*); ill-disposed
indisposer [ɛ̃dispoze] *tr* to indispose
indissoluble [ɛ̃disɔlybl] *adj* indissoluble
indis·tinct [ɛ̃distɛ̃], [ɛ̃distɛ̃kt] *adj* indistinct
indistinctement [ɛ̃distɛ̃ktəmɑ̃] *adv* indistinctly; indiscriminately
individu [ɛ̃dividy] *m* individual; (coll) fellow, guy
individualiser [ɛ̃dividɥalize] *tr* to individualize
individualité [ɛ̃dividɥalite] *f* individuality
indivi·duel -duelle [ɛ̃dividɥɛl] *adj* individual; separate
indi·vis -vise [ɛ̃divi] **-vise** [viz] *adj* joint; **par indivis** jointly
indivisible [ɛ̃divizibl] *adj* indivisible
Indochine [ɛ̃dɔʃin] *f* Indochina; **l'Indochine** Indochina

indocile [ɛ̃dɔsil] *adj* rebellious, unruly

indo-européen [ɛ̃dɔørɔpeɛ̃] **-européenne** [ørɔpeen] *adj* Indo-European ‖ *m* Indo-European (*language*) ‖ (*cap*) *mf* Indo-European

indo·lent [ɛ̃dɔlɑ̃] **-lente** [lɑ̃t] *adj* indolent; apathetic; painless (*e.g., tumor*) ‖ *mf* idler

indolore [ɛ̃dɔlɔr] *adj* painless

indomptable [ɛ̃dɔ̃tabl] *adj* indomitable

indomp·té -tée [ɛ̃dɔ̃te] *adj* untamed

Indonésie [ɛ̃dɔnezi] *f* Indonesia; **l'Indonésie** Indonesia

indoné·sien [ɛ̃dɔnezjɛ̃] **-sienne** [zjen] *adj* Indonesian ‖ *m* Indonesian (*language*) ‖ (*cap*) *mf* Indonesian (*person*)

in-douze [ɛ̃duz] *adj invar* & *m invar* duodecimo

in·du -due [ɛ̃dy] *adj* unseemly (*e.g., hour*); undue (*haste*); unwarranted (*remark*) ‖ *m* something not due

inducteur [ɛ̃dyktœr] *m* (elec) field

induction [ɛ̃dyksjɔ̃] *f* (elec, logic) induction

induire [ɛ̃dɥir] §19 *tr* to induce; **induire en** to lead into (*temptation, error, etc.*)

in·duit -duite [ɛ̃dɥi] *adj* induced ‖ *m* (elec) armature

indulgence [ɛ̃dylʒɑ̃s] *f* indulgence

indul·gent -gente [ɛ̃dylʒɑ̃] *adj* indulgent

indûment [ɛ̃dymɑ̃] *adv* unduly

indurer [ɛ̃dyre] *tr* & *ref* to harden

industrialiser [ɛ̃dystrijalize] *tr* to industrialize ‖ *ref* to become industrialized

industrie [ɛ̃dystri] *f* industry; trickery; (obs) occupation, trade; **l'industrie du spectacle** show business

industrie-clef [ɛ̃dystrikle] *f* (*pl* industries-clefs*) key industry

indus·triel -trielle [ɛ̃dystrijel] *adj* industrial ‖ *m* industrialist

indus·trieux [ɛ̃dystrijø] **-trieuse** [trijøz] *adj* industrious; skilled

inébranlable [inebrɑ̃labl] *adj* unshakable

inéchangeable [ineʃɑ̃ʒabl] *adj* unexchangeable

iné·dit [inedi] **-dite** [dit] *adj* unpublished; new, novel

inéducable [inedykabl] *adj* unteachable

ineffable [inefabl] *adj* ineffable

ineffaçable [inefasabl] *adj* indelible

inefficace [inefikas] *adj* ineffective, inefficient

iné·gal -gale [inegal] *adj* (*pl* -gaux [go]) unequal; uneven

inégalité [inegalite] *f* inequality; unevenness

inéligible [ineliʒibl] *adj* ineligible

inéluctable [inelyktabl] *adj* unavoidable

inénarrable [inenarabl] *adj* beyond words, too funny for words

inepte [inept] *adj* inept, inane

ineptie [inepsi] *f* ineptitude, inanity; inane remark

inépuisable [inepɥizabl] *adj* inexhaustible

inerme [inerm] *adj* thornless

inertie [inersi] *f* inertia

inescomptable [ineskɔ̃tabl] *adj* not subject to discount

inespé·ré -rée [inespere] *adj* unhoped-for, unexpected

inévitable [inevitabl] *adj* inevitable

inexact inexacte [inegzakt] *adj* inexact, inaccurate; unpunctual

inexactitude [inegzaktityd] *f* inexactness, inaccuracy; unpunctuality

inexau·cé -cée [inegzose] *adj* unfulfilled, unanswered

inexcitable [ineksitabl] *adj* unexcitable

inexcusable [inekskyzabl] *adj* inexcusable

inexécutable [inegzekytabl] *adj* impracticable

inexécution [inegzekysjɔ̃] *f* nonfulfillment

inexer·cé -cée [inegzerse] *adj* untried; untrained

inexhaustible [inegzostibl] *adj* inexhaustible

inexigible [inegziʒibl] *adj* uncollectable

inexis·tant [ineksistɑ̃] **-tante** [tɑ̃t] *adj* nonexistent

inexorable [inegzɔrabl] *adj* inexorable

inexpérience [ineksperjɑ̃s] *f* inexperience

inexpérimen·té -tée [ineksperimɑ̃te] *adj* inexperienced; untried

inex·pié -piée [inekspje] *adj* unexpiated

inexplicable [ineksplikabl] *adj* inexplicable, unexplainable

inexpli·qué -quée [ineksplike] *adj* unexplained

inexploi·té -tée [ineksplwate] *adj* untapped

inexplo·ré -rée [ineksplɔre] *adj* unexplored

inexpres·sif [inekspresif] **inexpres·sive** [inekspresiv] *adj* expressionless

inexprimable [ineksprimabl] *adj* inexpressible

inexpri·mé -mée [ineksprime] *adj* unexpressed

inexpugnable [inekspygnabl] *adj* impregnable

inextinguible [inekstɛ̃gibl], [inekstɛ̃gɥibl] *adj* inextinguishable; uncontrollable; unquenchable

infaillible [ɛ̃fajibl] *adj* infallible

infaisable [ɛ̃fəzabl] *adj* unfeasible

infa·mant [ɛ̃famɑ̃] **-mante** [mɑ̃t] *adj* opprobrious

infâme [ɛ̃fɑm] *adj* infamous; squalid

infamie [ɛ̃fami] *f* infamy; **dire des infamies à** to hurl insults at; **noter d'infamie** to brand as infamous

infant [ɛ̃fɑ̃] *m* infante

infante [ɛ̃fɑ̃t] *f* infanta

infanterie [ɛ̃fɑ̃tri] *f* infantry; **infanterie de l'air, infanterie aéroportée** parachute troops; **infanterie de marine** overseas troops; **infanterie portée, infanterie motorisée** motorized troops

infantile [ɛ̃fɑ̃til] *adj* infantile

infatigable [ɛ̃fatigabl] *adj* indefatigable

infatuation [ɛ̃fatɥasjɔ̃] *f* conceit, false pride

infa·tué -tuée [ɛ̃fatɥe] *adj* infatuated with oneself, conceited

infé·cond [ɛ̃fekɔ̃] **-conde** [kɔ̃d] *adj* sterile, barren

in·fect -fecte [ɛ̃fɛkt] *adj* stinking; foul, vile

infecter [ɛ̃fɛkte] *tr* to infect; to pollute; to stink up

infec·tieux [ɛ̃fɛksjø] **-tieuse** [sjøz] *adj* infectious

infection [ɛ̃fɛksjɔ̃] *f* infection; stench

inférer [ɛ̃fere] §10 *tr* to infer, conclude

infé·rieur -rieure [ɛ̃ferjœr] *adj* lower; inferior; **inférieur à** below; less than ‖ *mf* subordinate, inferior

infériorité [ɛ̃ferjɔrite] *f* inferiority

infer·nal -nale [ɛ̃fɛrnal] *adj* (*pl* **-naux** [no]) infernal

infester [ɛ̃feste] *tr* to infest

infidèle [ɛ̃fidɛl] *adj* infidel; unfaithful ‖ *mf* infidel ‖ *m* unfaithful husband ‖ *f* unfaithful wife

infidélité [ɛ̃fidelite] *f* infidelity; inaccuracy, unfaithfulness

infiltration [ɛ̃filtrasjɔ̃] *f* infiltration

infiltrer [ɛ̃filtre] *ref* to infiltrate; to seep, percolate; **s'infiltrer à travers** or **dans** to infiltrate

infime [ɛ̃fim] *adj* very small, infinitesimal; very low; trifling, negligible

infi·ni -nie [ɛ̃fini] *adj* infinite ‖ *m* infinite; (math) infinity; **à l'infini** infinitely

infiniment [ɛ̃finimɑ̃] *adv* infinitely; (coll) greatly, deeply, terribly

infinité [ɛ̃finite] *f* infinity

infini·tif [ɛ̃finitif] **-tive** [tiv] *adj* & *m* infinitive

infirme [ɛ̃firm] *adj* infirm, crippled, disabled ‖ *mf* invalid, cripple

infirmer [ɛ̃firme] *tr* (law) to invalidate

infirmerie [ɛ̃firməri] *f* infirmary; (nav) sick bay

infir·mier [ɛ̃firmje] **-mière** [mjer] *mf* nurse; **infirmière bénévole** volunteer nurse; **infirmière diplômée** registered nurse ‖ *m* male nurse; orderly, attendant

infirmière-major [ɛ̃firmjɛrmaʒɔr] *f* head nurse

infirmité [ɛ̃firmite] *f* infirmity

infixe [ɛ̃fiks] *m* infix

inflammable [ɛ̃flamabl] *adj* inflammable

inflammation [ɛ̃flamasjɔ̃] *f* inflammation

inflammatoire [ɛ̃flamatwar] *adj* inflammatory

inflation [ɛ̃flasjɔ̃] *f* inflation

inflationniste [ɛ̃flasjɔnist] *adj* inflationary

infléchir [ɛ̃fleʃir] *tr* to inflect, bend ‖ *ref* to bend, curve

inflexible [ɛ̃fleksibl] *adj* inflexible

inflexion [ɛ̃fleksjɔ̃] *f* inflection; change; bend, curve; metaphony

infliger [ɛ̃fliʒe] §38 *tr* to inflict; **infliger q.ch. à** to inflict s.th. on

influence [ɛ̃flyɑ̃s] *f* influence

influencer [ɛ̃flyɑ̃se] §51 *tr* to influence

nfluent [ɛ̃flyɑ̃] **influente** [ɛ̃flyɑ̃t] *adj* influential

nfluenza [ɛ̃flyɑ̃za] *f* influenza

nfluer [ɛ̃flye] *intr*—**influer sur** to influence

in-folio [ɛ̃fɔljo] *adj* & *m* (*pl* **-folio** or **-folios**) folio

informa·teur [ɛ̃fɔrmatœr] **-trice** [tris] *mf* informant

information [ɛ̃fɔrmasjɔ̃] *f* information; piece of information; (law) investigation; **aller aux informations** to make inquiries; **information génétique** genetic characteristics; **informations** news; information; **informations de presse** press reports

informatique [ɛ̃fɔrmatik] *adj* informational ‖ *f* information storage

informe [ɛ̃fɔrm] *adj* formless, shapeless

informer [ɛ̃fɔrme] *tr* to inform, advise ‖ *intr*—**informer contre** to inform on ‖ *ref* to inquire, to keep oneself informed

infortune [ɛ̃fɔrtyn] *f* misfortune

infortu·né -née [ɛ̃fɔrtyne] *adj* unfortunate

infraction [ɛ̃fraksjɔ̃] *f* infraction

infranchissable [ɛ̃frɑ̃ʃisabl] *adj* insuperable; impassable (*e.g., mountain*)

infrarouge [ɛ̃fraruʒ] *adj* & *m* infrared

infrason [ɛ̃frasɔ̃] *m* infrasonic vibration

infrastructure [ɛ̃frastryktyr] *f* infrastructure; (rr) roadbed

infroissable [ɛ̃frwasabl] *adj* creaseless, wrinkleproof

infruc·tueux [ɛ̃fryktɥø] **-tueuse** [tɥøz] *adj* unfruitful, fruitless

in·fus [ɛ̃fy] **-fuse** [fyz] *adj* inborn, innate, intuitive

infuser [ɛ̃fyze] *tr* to infuse; to brew; **infuser un sang nouveau à** to put new blood or life into ‖ *intr* to steep

infusion [ɛ̃fyzjɔ̃] *f* steeping; brew

ingambe [ɛ̃gɑ̃b] *adj* spry, nimble, alert

ingénier [ɛ̃ʒenje] *ref* to strive hard

ingénierie [ɛ̃ʒeniri] or **ingéniérie** [ɛ̃ʒenjeri] *f* engineering

ingénieur [ɛ̃ʒenjœr] *m* engineer; **ingénieur des ponts et chaussées** civil engineer

ingé·nieux [ɛ̃ʒenjø] **-nieuse** [njøz] *adj* ingenious

ingéniosité [ɛ̃ʒenjozite] *f* ingenuity

ingé·nu -nue [ɛ̃ʒeny] *adj* ingenuous, artless ‖ *mf* naïve person ‖ *f* ingénue

ingénuité [ɛ̃ʒenɥite] *f* ingenuousness

ingérer [ɛ̃ʒere] §10 *tr* to ingest ‖ *ref* to meddle

ingouvernable [ɛ̃guvernabl] *adj* unruly, unmanageable

in·grat -grate [ɛ̃gra] *adj* ungrateful; disagreeable; thankless (*task*); unprofitable (*work*); barren (*soil*); awkward (*age*) ‖ *mf* ingrate

ingratitude [ɛ̃gratityd] *f* ingratitude

ingrédient [ɛ̃gredjɑ̃] *m* ingredient

inguérissable [ɛ̃gerisabl] *adj* & *mf* incurable

ingurgiter [ɛ̃gyrʒite] *tr* to swallow; to gulp down

inhabile [inabil] *adj* unskilled; unfitted, unqualified

inhabileté [inabilte] *f* inability; clumsiness; unfitness

inhabitable [inabitabl] *adj* uninhabitable

inhabi·té -tée [inabite] *adj* uninhabited

inhabi·tuel -tuelle [inabitɥɛl] *adj* unusual

inhé·rent [inerã] **-rente** [rãt] *adj* inherent

inhiber [inibe] *tr* to inhibit

inhibition [inibisjɔ̃] *f* inhibition

inhospita·lier [inɔspitalje] **-lière** [ljɛr] *adj* inhospitable

inhu·main [inymɛ̃] **-maine** [mɛn] *adj* inhuman

inhumanité [inymanite] *f* inhumanity

inhumation [inymasjɔ̃] *f* burial

inhumer [inyme] *tr* to bury, to inter

inimitié [inimitje] *f* enmity

inintelli·gent [inɛ̃teliʒɑ̃] **-gente** [ʒɑ̃t] *adj* unintelligent

inintéres·sant [inɛ̃teresɑ̃] **inintéressante** [inɛ̃teresɑ̃t] *adj* uninteresting

ininterrom·pu -pue [inɛ̃terɔ̃py] *adj* uninterrupted

inique [inik] *adj* iniquitous, unjust

iniquité [inikite] *f* iniquity

ini·tial -tiale [inisjal] (*pl* **-tiaux** [sjo] **-tiales**) *adj & f* initial

initia·teur [inisjatœr] **-trice** [tris] *adj* initiating || *mf* initiator

initiation [inisjasjɔ̃] *f* initiation

initiative [inisjativ] *f* initiative

initier [inisje] *tr* to initiate; to introduce || *ref* to become initiated

injecter [ɛ̃ʒekte] *tr* to inject; to impregnate || *ref* to become bloodshot

injec·teur [ɛ̃ʒektœr] **-trice** [tris] *adj* injecting || *m* injector; nozzle (*in motor*)

injection [ɛ̃ʒeksjɔ̃] *f* injection; impregnation; redness (*of eyes*); (geog) intrusion

injonction [ɛ̃ʒɔ̃ksjɔ̃] *f* injunction, order

injouable [ɛ̃ʒwabl] *adj* unplayable

injure [ɛ̃ʒyr] *f* insult; wrong; **l'injure des ans** the ravages of time

injurier [ɛ̃ʒyrje] *tr* to insult, to abuse

inju·rieux [ɛ̃ʒyrjø] **-rieuse** [rjøz] *adj* insulting, abusive; harmful, offensive

injuste [ɛ̃ʒyst] *adj* unjust

injustice [ɛ̃ʒystis] *f* injustice

injusti·fié -fiée [ɛ̃ʒystifje] *adj* unjustified

inlassable [ɛ̃lasabl] *adj* untiring

in·né -née [inne] *adj* innate, inborn

innocence [inɔsɑ̃s] *f* innocence

inno·cent [inɔsɑ̃] **-cente** [sɑ̃t] *adj & mf* innocent

innocenter [inɔsɑ̃te] *tr* to exonerate

innocuité [inɔkɥite] *f* innocuousness

innombrable [inɔ̃brabl] *adj* innumerable

innova·teur [inɔvatœr] **-trice** [tris] *adj* innovating || *mf* innovator

innovation [inɔvasjɔ̃] *f* innovation

innover [inɔve] *tr & intr* to innovate

inoccu·pé -pée [inɔkype] *adj* unoccupied; unemployed, idle || *mf* idler

in-octavo [inɔktavo] *adj & m* (*pl* **-octavo** or **-octavos**) octavo

inoculation [inɔkylasjɔ̃] *f* inoculation

inoculer [inɔkyle] *tr* to inoculate

inodore [inɔdɔr] *adj* odorless

inoffen·sif [inɔfɑ̃sif] **-sive** [siv] *adj* inoffensive

inondation [inɔ̃dasjɔ̃] *f* flood

inonder [inɔ̃de] *tr* to flood

inopi·né -née [inɔpine] *adj* unexpected

inoppor·tun [inɔpɔrtœ̃] **-tune** [tyn] *adj* untimely, inconvenient

inopportunité [inɔpɔrtynite] *f* untimeliness

inorganique [inɔrganik] *adj* inorganic

inorgani·sé -sée [inɔrganize] *adj* unorganized (*workers*), nonunion

inoubliable [inublijabl] *adj* unforgettable

inouï inouïe [inwi] *adj* unheard-of

inoxydable [inɔksidabl] *adj* inoxidizable, stainless, rustproof

inqualifiable [ɛ̃kalifjabl] *adj* unspeakable

in·quiet -quiète [kjɛt] *adj* anxious, worried, uneasy; restless

inquié·tant [ɛ̃kjetɑ̃] **-tante** [tɑ̃t] *adj* disquieting, worrisome

inquiéter [ɛ̃kjete] §10 *tr & intr* to worry

inquiétude [ɛ̃kjetyd] *f* uneasiness, worry

inquisi·teur [ɛ̃kizitœr] **-trice** [tris] *adj* inquisitorial; searching (*e.g.*, *look*) || *m* inquisitor

inquisition [ɛ̃kizisjɔ̃] *f* inquisition; investigation

inracontable [ɛ̃rakɔ̃tabl] *adj* untellable

insaisissable [ɛ̃sezisabl] *adj* hard to catch; elusive

insalubre [ɛ̃salybr] *adj* unhealthy

insane [ɛ̃san] *adj* insane, crazy

insanité [ɛ̃sanite] *f* insanity; piece of folly

insatiable [ɛ̃sasjabl] *adj* insatiable

insatisfaction [ɛ̃satisfaksjɔ̃] *f* dissatisfaction

inscription [ɛ̃skripsjɔ̃] *f* inscription; registration, enrollment; **inscription de or en faux** (law) plea of forgery; **prendre ses inscriptions** to register at a university

inscrire [ɛ̃skrir] §25 *tr* to inscribe; to register; to record || *ref* to register, enroll; **s'inscrire à** to join; **s'inscrire en faux contre** to deny; **s'inscrire pour** to sign up for

ins·crit [ɛ̃skri] **-crite** [krit] *adj* inscribed; registered, enrolled || *mf* registered student; (sports) entry; **inscrit maritime** naval recruit

insecte [ɛ̃sekt] *m* insect, bug

insecticide [ɛ̃sektisid] *adj* insecticidal || *m* insecticide

insen·sé -sée [ɛ̃sɑ̃se] *adj* senseless, insane, crazy || *m* madman || *f* madwoman

insensible [ɛ̃sɑ̃sibl] *adj* insensitive; imperceptible

inséparable [ɛ̃separabl] *adj* inseparable || *m* lovebird

insérer [ɛ̃sere] §10 *tr* to insert

insertion [ɛ̃sersjɔ̃] *f* insertion

insi·dieux [ɛ̃sidjø] **-dieuse** [djøz] *adj* insidious

insigne [ɛ̃siɲ] *adj* signal, noteworthy; notorious || *m* badge, mark; **insignes** insignia

insigni·fiant [ɛ̃siɲifjɑ̃] **-fiante** [fjɑ̃t] *adj* insignificant

insincère [ɛ̃sɛ̃ser] *adj* insincere

insinuation [ɛ̃sinɥasjɔ̃] *f* insinuation

insinuer [ɛ̃sinɥe] *tr* to insinuate; to

hint, hint at; to work **in**, introduce ‖ *ref*—**s'insinuer dans** to worm one's way into

insipide [ɛ̃sipid] *adj* insipid, tasteless; insipid, dull

insister [ɛ̃siste] *intr* to insist; (coll) to continue, persevere; **insister pour** to insist on; **insister sur** to stress

insociable [ɛ̃sɔsjabl] *adj* unsociable

insolation [ɛ̃sɔlɑsjɔ̃] *f* exposure to the sun; sunstroke

insolence [ɛ̃sɔlɑ̃s] *f* insolence

inso·lent [ɛ̃sɔlɑ̃] **-lente** [lɑ̃t] *adj* insolent; extraordinary, unexpected

insolite [ɛ̃sɔlit] *adj* bizarre

insoluble [ɛ̃sɔlybl] *adj* insoluble

insolvabilité [ɛ̃sɔlvabilite] *f* insolvency

insolvable [ɛ̃sɔlvabl] *adj* insolvent

insomnie [ɛ̃sɔmni] *f* insomnia

insondable [ɛ̃sɔ̃dabl] *adj* unfathomable

insonore [ɛ̃sɔnɔr] *adj* soundproof; noiseless

insonoriser [ɛ̃sɔnɔrize] *tr* to soundproof

insouciance [ɛ̃susjɑ̃s] *f* carefreeness; indifference, carelessness

insou·ciant [ɛ̃susjɑ̃] **-ciante** [sjɑ̃t] *adj* carefree, unconcerned

insou·cieux [ɛ̃susjø] **-cieuse** [sjøz] *adj* carefree, unmindful

insou·mis [ɛ̃sumi] **-mise** [miz] *adj* unruly; unsubjugated ‖ *mf* rebel ‖ *m* (mil) A.W.O.L.

insoumission [ɛ̃sumisjɔ̃] *f* insubordination, rebellion; (mil) absence without leave

insoupçonnable [ɛ̃supsɔnabl] *adj* above suspicion

insoupçon·né -née [ɛ̃supsɔne] *adj* unsuspected

insoutenable [ɛ̃sutnabl] *adj* untenable; unbearable

inspecter [ɛ̃spɛkte] *tr* to inspect

inspec·teur [ɛ̃spɛktœr] **-trice** [tris] *mf* inspector

inspection [ɛ̃spɛksjɔ̃] *f* inspection; inspectorship

inspiration [ɛ̃spirɑsjɔ̃] *f* inspiration

inspirer [ɛ̃spire] *tr* to inspire; to breathe in; **inspirer à qn de** to inspire s.o. to; **inspirer q.ch. à qn** to inspire s.o. with s.th. ‖ *ref*—**s'inspirer de** to be inspired by

instable [ɛ̃stabl] *adj* unstable

installateur [ɛ̃stalatœr] *m* heater man; fitter, plumber

installation [ɛ̃stalɑsjɔ̃] *f* installation; equipment, outfit; appointments, fittings

installer [ɛ̃stale] *tr* to install; to equip, furnish; **être bien installé** to be comfortably settled ‖ *ref* to settle down, to set up shop; **s'installer chez** to foist oneself on

instamment [ɛ̃stamɑ̃] *adv* urgently, earnestly

instance [ɛ̃stɑ̃s] *f* insistence; **avec instance** earnestly; **en instance** pending; **en instance de** on the point of; **en seconde instance** on appeal; **instances** entreaties; **introduire une instance** to start proceedings

ins·tant [ɛ̃stɑ̃] **-tante** [tɑ̃t] *adj* urgent, pressing ‖ *m* instant, moment; **à cha-** que **instant, à tout instant** continually; **à l'instant** at once, right away; just now; at the moment; **par instants** from time to time

instanta·né -née [ɛ̃stɑ̃tane] *adj* instantaneous ‖ *m* snapshot

instantanément [ɛ̃stɑ̃tanemɑ̃] *adv* instantaneously; instantly

instar [ɛ̃star]—**à l'instar de** in the manner of

instauration [ɛ̃stɔrɑsjɔ̃] *f* establishment

instaurer [ɛ̃stɔre] *tr* to establish

instigation [ɛ̃stigɑsjɔ̃] *f* instigation

instiller [ɛ̃stile] *tr* to instill

instinct [ɛ̃stɛ̃] *m* instinct; **d'instinct, par instinct** by instinct

instinc·tif [ɛ̃stɛktif] **-tive** [tiv] *adj* instinctive

instituer [ɛ̃stitɥe] *tr* to found; to institute (*e.g., proceedings*)

institut [ɛ̃stity] *m* institute; **institut de beauté** beauty parlor; **institut de coupe** tonsorial parlor; **institut dentaire** dental school

institu·teur [ɛ̃stitytœr] **-trice** [tris] *mf* schoolteacher; founder

institution [ɛ̃stitysjɔ̃] *f* institution

instructeur [ɛ̃stryktœr] *m* instructor

instruc·tif [ɛ̃stryktif] **-tive** [tiv] *adj* instructive

instruction [ɛ̃stryksjɔ̃] *f* instruction; education; **instruction judiciaire** (law) preliminary investigation; **instructions permanentes** standing orders

instruire [ɛ̃strɥir] §19 *tr* to instruct; **instruire qn de** to inform s.o. of ‖ *ref* to improve one's mind

instrument [ɛ̃strymɑ̃] *m* instrument; **instrument à anche** reed instrument; **instrument à cordes** stringed instrument; **instrument à vent** wind instrument; **instrument en bois** woodwind; **instrument en cuivre** brass

instrumen·tal -tale [ɛ̃strymɑ̃tal] *adj* (*pl* **-taux** [to]) instrumental

instrumenter [ɛ̃strymɑ̃te] *tr* to instrument

instrumentiste [ɛ̃strymɑ̃tist] *mf* instrumentalist

insu [ɛ̃sy] *m*—**à l'insu de** unknown to; **à mon insu** unknown to me

insubmersible [ɛ̃sybmɛrsibl] *adj* unsinkable

insubordon·né -née [ɛ̃sybɔrdɔne] *adj* insubordinate

insuccès [ɛ̃syksɛ] *m* failure

insuffi·sant [ɛ̃syfizɑ̃] **-sante** [zɑ̃t] *adj* insufficient

insulaire [ɛ̃syler] *adj* insular ‖ *mf* islander

insuline [ɛ̃sylin] *f* insulin

insulte [ɛ̃sylt] *f* insult

insulter [ɛ̃sylte] *tr* to insult ‖ *intr* (with *dat*) to offend, outrage

insupportable [ɛ̃sypɔrtabl] *adj* unbearable

insur·gé -gée [ɛ̃syrʒe] *adj & mf* insurgent

insurger [ɛ̃syrʒe] §38 *ref* to revolt, rebel

insurmontable [ɛ̃syrmɔ̃tabl] *adj* insurmountable

insurrection [ɛ̃syrɛksjɔ̃] f insurrection

in·tact -tacte [ɛ̃takt] adj intact, untouched

intangible [ɛ̃tɑ̃ʒibl] adj intangible

intarissable [ɛ̃tarisabl] adj inexhaustible

inté·gral -grale [ɛ̃tegral] adj (pl -graux [gro]) integral; complete (e.g., edition); full (e.g., payment) || f complete works; (math) integral

inté·grant [ɛ̃tegrɑ̃] -grante [grɑ̃t] adj integral

intégration [ɛ̃tegrasjɔ̃] f integration

intègre [ɛ̃tegr] adj honest, upright

intégrer [ɛ̃tegre] §10 tr to integrate || ref to form an integral part; (slang) to be accepted (at an exclusive school)

intégrité [ɛ̃tegrite] f integrity

intellect [ɛ̃telɛkt] m intellect

intellec·tuel -tuelle [ɛ̃telɛktɥɛl] adj & mf intellectual

intelligence [ɛ̃teliʒɑ̃s] f intelligence; intellect (person); en bonne intelligence avec on good terms with; être d'intelligence to be in collusion

intelli·gent [ɛ̃teliʒɑ̃] -gente [ʒɑ̃t] adj intelligent

intelligible [ɛ̃teliʒibl] adj intelligible

intempé·rant [ɛ̃tɑ̃perɑ̃] -rante [rɑ̃t] adj intemperate

intempéries [ɛ̃tɑ̃peri] fpl bad weather

intempes·tif [ɛ̃tɑ̃pɛstif] -tive [tiv] adj untimely

intenable [ɛ̃tnabl] adj untenable

intendance [ɛ̃tɑ̃dɑ̃s] f stewardship; controllership, office of bursar; Intendance (mil) Quartermaster Corps

inten·dant [ɛ̃tɑ̃dɑ̃] -dante [dɑ̃t] mf steward, superintendent; controller, bursar; intendant militaire quartermaster

intense [ɛ̃tɑ̃s] adj intense

inten·sif [ɛ̃tɑ̃sif] -sive [siv] adj intensive

intensifier [ɛ̃tɑ̃sifje] tr & ref to intensify

intensité [ɛ̃tɑ̃site] f intensity

intenter [ɛ̃tɑ̃te] tr to start (a suit); to bring (an action)

intention [ɛ̃tɑ̃sjɔ̃] f intention, intent; à l'intention de for (the sake of)

intention·né -née [ɛ̃tɑ̃sjone] adj motivated; bien intentionné well-meaning; mal intentionné ill-disposed

intention·nel -nelle [ɛ̃tɑ̃sjonɛl] adj intentional

inter [ɛ̃ter] m (coll) long distance

interaction [ɛ̃teraksjɔ̃] f interaction, interplay

intercaler [ɛ̃terkale] tr to intercalate; to insert, to sandwich

intercéder [ɛ̃tersede] §10 intr to intercede

intercepter [ɛ̃tersɛpte] tr to intercept

intercepteur [ɛ̃tersɛptœr] m interceptor

interchangeable [ɛ̃terʃɑ̃ʒabl] adj interchangeable

interclasse [ɛ̃terklɑs] m (educ) break between classes

intercourse [ɛ̃terkurs] f (naut) free entry

interdépen·dant [ɛ̃terdepɑ̃dɑ̃] -dante [dɑ̃t] adj interdependent

interdiction [ɛ̃terdiksjɔ̃] f interdiction; suspension; interdiction de séjour forbidden entry

interdire [ɛ̃terdir] §40 tr to prohibit, to forbid; to confound, to abash; to interdict; to suspend; interdire q.ch. à qn to forbid s.o. s.th.

inter·dit [ɛ̃terdi] -dite [dit] adj prohibited, forbidden; dumfounded, abashed; deprived of rights; (mil) off limits || m interdict

intéres·sant [ɛ̃teresɑ̃] intéres·sante [ɛ̃teresɑ̃t] adj interesting; attractive (offer)

intéres·sé -sée [ɛ̃terese] adj interested; self-seeking || mf interested party

intéresser [ɛ̃terese] tr to interest; to involve || ref—s'intéresser à or dans to be interested in

intérêt [ɛ̃tere] m interest; intérêts composés compound interest

interférence [ɛ̃terferɑ̃s] f interference

interférer [ɛ̃terfere] §10 intr (phys) to interfere || ref to interfere with each other

inté·rieur -rieure [ɛ̃terjœr] adj interior; inner, inside || m interior; inside; house, home

intérieurement [ɛ̃terjœrmɑ̃] adv inwardly, internally; to oneself

intérim [ɛ̃terim] m invar interim; dans l'intérim in the meantime; par intérim acting, pro tem, interim

intérimaire [ɛ̃terimer] adj temporary, acting

interjection [ɛ̃terʒɛksjɔ̃] f interjection

interligne [ɛ̃terliɲ] m space between the lines; writing in the space between the lines; à double interligne double-spaced || f lead

interligner [ɛ̃terliɲe] tr to interline; (typ) to lead out

interlocu·teur [ɛ̃terlɔkytœr] -trice [tris] mf interlocutor; intermediary; party (with whom one is conversing)

interlope [ɛ̃terlɔp] adj illegal, shady || m (naut) smuggling vessel

interloquer [ɛ̃terlɔke] tr to disconcert

interlude [ɛ̃terlyd] m interlude

intermède [ɛ̃termed] m (theat & fig) interlude

intermédiaire [ɛ̃termedjer] adj intermediate, intermediary || mf intermediary || m (com) middleman; par l'intermédiaire de by means of, by the medium of

interminable [ɛ̃terminabl] adj interminable

intermit·tent [ɛ̃termitɑ̃] intermit·tente [ɛ̃termitɑ̃t] adj intermittent

internat [ɛ̃terna] m boarding school; boarding-school life; (med) internship

internatio·nal -nale [ɛ̃ternasjonal] adj (pl -naux [no]) international

interne [ɛ̃tern] adj inner; (math) interior || mf boarder (at a school); (med) intern

inter·né -née [ɛ̃terne] mf internee

internement [ɛ̃ternəmɑ̃] m internment; confinement (of a mental patient)

interner [ɛ̃tɛrne] *tr* to intern
interpeller [ɛ̃tɛrpɛle] *tr* to question, to interrogate; to yell at; to heckle
interphone [ɛ̃tɛrfɔn] *m* intercom
interplanétaire [ɛ̃tɛrplanetɛr] *adj* interplanetary
interpoler [ɛ̃tɛrpɔle] *tr* to interpolate
interposer [ɛ̃tɛrpoze] *tr* to interpose
interprétation [ɛ̃tɛrpretasjɔ̃] *f* interpretation
interprète [ɛ̃tɛrprɛt] *mf* interpreter
interpréter [ɛ̃tɛrprete] §10 *tr* to interpret; **mal interpréter** to misinterpret
interrogation [ɛ̃terɔgasjɔ̃] *f* interrogation
interroger [ɛ̃terɔʒe] §38 *tr* to interrogate, to question
interrompre [ɛ̃terɔ̃pr] (3d *sg pres ind* **interrompt** [ɛ̃terɔ̃]) *tr* to interrupt; to heckle || *ref* to break off, to be interrupted
interrup·teur [ɛ̃teryptœr] **-trice** [tris] *adj* interrupting; circuit-breaking || *m* switch; **interrupteur à couteau** knife switch; **interrupteur à culbuteur** or **à bascule** toggle switch; **interrupteur d'escalier** two-way switch; **interrupteur encastré** flush switch; **interrupteur olive** pear switch
interruption [ɛ̃terypsjɔ̃] *f* interruption
intersection [ɛ̃terseksjɔ̃] *f* intersection
intersigne [ɛ̃tersiɲ] *m* omen, portent
interstellaire [ɛ̃tersteler] *adj* interstellar
interstice [ɛ̃terstis] *m* interstice
interur·bain [ɛ̃teryrbɛ̃] **-baine** [bɛn] *adj* interurban; (telp) long-distance || *m* (telp) long distance
intervalle [ɛ̃terval] *m* interval
intervenir [ɛ̃tervnir] §72 (*aux:* ÊTRE) *intr* to intervene; to take place, happen; (med) to operate; **faire intervenir** to call in
intervention [ɛ̃tervɑ̃sjɔ̃] *f* intervention; (med) operation
intervertir [ɛ̃tervertir] *tr* to invert, to transpose
interview [ɛ̃tervju] *f* (journ) interview
interviewer [ɛ̃tervjuvœr] *m* interviewer || [ɛ̃tervjuve] *tr* to interview
intestat [ɛ̃testa] *adj* & *mf invar* intestate
intes·tin [ɛ̃testɛ̃] **-tine** [tin] *adj* intestine, internal || *m* intestine; **gros intestin** large intestine; **intestin grêle** small intestine
intimation [ɛ̃timasjɔ̃] *f* (law) summons
intime [ɛ̃tim] *adj* & *mf* intimate
inti·mé -mée [ɛ̃time] *mf* (law) defendant
intimer [ɛ̃time] *tr* to notify; to give (*an order*)
intimider [ɛ̃timide] *tr* to intimidate
intimité [ɛ̃timite] *f* intimacy; privacy; depths (*of one's being*)
intituler [ɛ̃tityle] *tr* to entitle
intolérable [ɛ̃tɔlerabl] *adj* intolerable
intolé·rant [ɛ̃tɔlerɑ̃] **-rante** [rɑ̃t] *adj* intolerant
intonation [ɛ̃tɔnasjɔ̃] *f* intonation
intouchable [ɛ̃tuʃabl] *adj* & *mf* untouchable
intoxication [ɛ̃tɔksikasjɔ̃] *f* poisoning
intoxiquer [ɛ̃tɔksike] *tr* to poison

intraitable [ɛ̃tretabl] *adj* intractable
intransi·geant [ɛ̃trɑ̃ziʒɑ̃] **-geante** [ʒɑ̃t] *adj* intransigent || *mf* diehard, standpatter
intransi·tif [ɛ̃trɑ̃zitif] **-tive** [tiv] *adj* intransitive
intravei·neux [ɛ̃travɛnø] **-neuse** [nøz] *adj* intravenous
intrépide [ɛ̃trepid] *adj* intrepid; persistent
intri·gant [ɛ̃trigɑ̃] **-gante** [gɑ̃t] *adj* intriguing || *mf* plotter, schemer
intrigue [ɛ̃trig] *f* intrigue, plot; love affair; **intrigues de couloir** lobbying
intriguer [ɛ̃trige] *tr* & *intr* to intrigue
intrinsèque [ɛ̃trɛ̃sɛk] *adj* intrinsic
introduction [ɛ̃trodyksjɔ̃] *f* introduction; admission
introduire [ɛ̃trodɥir] §19 *tr* to introduce, to bring in; to show in; to interject (*e.g., a remark*) || *ref* to be introduced; **s'introduire dans** to slip in
intronisation [ɛ̃trɔnizasjɔ̃] *f* investiture, inauguration
introniser [ɛ̃trɔnize] *tr* to enthrone
introspec·tif [ɛ̃trɔspɛktif] **-tive** [tiv] *adj* introspective
introuvable [ɛ̃truvabl] *adj* unfindable
introver·ti -tie [ɛ̃trɔverti] *adj* & *mf* introvert
intrusion [ɛ̃tryzjɔ̃] *f* intrusion
in·trus [ɛ̃try] **-truse** [tryz] *adj* intruding || *mf* intruder
intuition [ɛ̃tɥisjɔ̃] *f* intuition
inusable [inyzabl] *adj* durable, wearproof
inusi·té -tée [inyzite] *adj* obsolete
inutile [inytil] *adj* useless, unnecessary
inutilement [inytilmɑ̃] *adv* in vain, uselessly; unnecessarily
inutilité [inytilite] *f* uselessness
invain·cu -cue [ɛ̃vɛ̃ky] *adj* unconquered
invalide [ɛ̃valid] *adj* invalid || *mf* invalid, cripple; **invalide de guerre** disabled veteran
invalider [ɛ̃valide] *tr* to invalidate
invalidité [ɛ̃validite] *f* invalidity; disability
invariable [ɛ̃varjabl] *adj* invariable
invasion [ɛ̃vazjɔ̃] *f* invasion
invective [ɛ̃vɛktiv] *f* invective
invectiver [ɛ̃vɛktive] *tr* to rail at || *intr* to inveigh
invendable [ɛ̃vɑ̃dabl] *adj* unsalable
inven·du -due [ɛ̃vɑ̃dy] *adj* unsold || *m* —**les invendus** the unsold copies; the unsold articles
inventaire [ɛ̃vɑ̃tɛr] *m* inventory
inventer [ɛ̃vɑ̃te] *tr* to invent
inven·teur [ɛ̃vɑ̃tœr] **-trice** [tris] *mf* inventor; (law) finder
inven·tif [ɛ̃vɑ̃tif] **-tive** [tiv] *adj* inventive
invention [ɛ̃vɑ̃sjɔ̃] *f* invention
inventorier [ɛ̃vɑ̃tɔrje] *tr* to inventory
inversable [ɛ̃vɛrsabl] *adj* untippable, uncapsizable
inverse [ɛ̃vɛrs] *adj* & *m* inverse; **faire l'inverse de** to do the opposite of
inverser [ɛ̃vɛrse] *tr* to invert, to reverse || *intr* (elec) to reverse

inverseur [ɛ̃versœr] *m* reversing device; **inverseur des phares (aut)** dimmer

inversion [ɛ̃versjɔ̃] *f* inversion

inverté·bré -brée [ɛ̃vertebre] *adj* & *m* invertebrate

inver·ti -tie [ɛ̃verti] *mf* invert

invertir [ɛ̃vertir] *tr* to invert, reverse

investiga·teur [ɛ̃vestigatœr] **-trice** [tris] *adj* investigative; searching || *mf* investigator

investigation [ɛ̃vestigasjɔ̃] *f* investigation

investir [ɛ̃vestir] *tr* to invest; to vest; **investir qn du sa confiance** to place one's confidence in s.o.

investissement [ɛ̃vestismã] *m* investment

investiture [ɛ̃vestityr] *f* investiture; nomination (*as a candidate for election*)

invété·ré -rée [ɛ̃vetere] *adj* inveterate

invétérer [ɛ̃vetere] *ref* to become inveterate

invincible [ɛ̃vɛ̃sibl] *adj* invincible

invisible [ɛ̃vizibl] *adj* invisible; (coll) hiding, keeping out of sight

invitation [ɛ̃vitasjɔ̃] *f* invitation

invite [ɛ̃vit] *f* invitation, inducement; **répondre à l'invite de qn** (cards) to return s.o.'s lead; (fig) to respond to s.o.'s advances

invi·té -tée [ɛ̃vite] *adj* invited || *mf* guest

inviter [ɛ̃vite] *tr* to invite

involontaire [ɛ̃vɔlɔ̃ter] *adj* involuntary

invoquer [ɛ̃vɔke] *tr* to invoke

invraisemblable [ɛ̃vresɑ̃blabl] *adj* improbable, unlikely, hard to believe; (coll) strange, weird

invraisemblance [ɛ̃vresɑ̃blɑ̃s] *f* improbability, unlikelihood; (coll) queerness

invulnérable [ɛ̃vylnerabl] *adj* invulnerable

Iode [jɔd] *m* iodine

Iodure [jɔdyr] *m* iodide

ion [jɔ̃] *m* ion

ioniser [jɔnize] *tr* to ionize

iota [jɔta] *m* iota

Irak [irak] *m*—l'Irak Iraq

ira·kien [irakjɛ̃] **-kienne** [kjen] *adj* Iraqi || (*cap*) *mf* Iraqi

Iran [irɑ̃] *m*—l'Iran Iran

ira·nien [iranjɛ̃] **-nienne** [njen] *adj* Iranian || *m* Iranian (*language*) || (*cap*) *mf* Iranian (*person*)

iris [iris] *m* iris

irlan·dais [irlɑ̃de] **-daise** [dez] *adj* Irish || *m* Irish (*language*) || (*cap*) *m* Irishman; **les Irlandais** the Irish || (*cap*) *f* Irishwoman

Irlande [irlɑ̃d] *f* Ireland; **l'Irlande** Ireland

ironie [irɔni] *f* irony

ironique [irɔnik] *adj* ironic(al)

ironiser [irɔnize] *tr* to say ironically || *intr* to speak ironically, to jeer

irradier [iradje] *tr* & *ref* to irradiate

irraison·né -née [irezɔne] *adj* unreasoning

irration·nel -nelle [irasjɔnel] *adj* irrational

irréalisable [irealizabl] *adj* impractical, unattainable

irréalité [irealite] *f* unreality

irrécouvrable [irekuvrabl] *adj* uncollectible

irrécupérable [irekyperabl] *adj* irretrievable

irrécusable [irekyzabl] *adj* unimpeachable, incontestable, indisputable

irréel irréelle [ireel] *adj* unreal

irréfléchi -chie [ireflefi] *adj* rash, thoughtless

irréfutable [irefytabl] *adj* irrefutable

irrégu·lier [iregylje] **-lière** [ljer] *adj* & *m* irregular

irréli·gieux [irelizjø] **-gieuse** [zjøz] *adj* irreligious

irrémédiable [iremedjabl] *adj* irremediable

irremplaçable [irɑ̃plasabl] *adj* irreplaceable

irréparable [ireparabl] *adj* irreparable; irretrievable (*loss, mistake, etc.*)

irrépressible [irepresibl] *adj* irrepressible

irréprochable [ireprɔfabl] *adj* irreproachable

irrésistible [irezistibl] *adj* irresistible

irréso·lu -lue [irezɔly] *adj* irresolute

irrespect [irespe] *m* disrespect

irrespec·tueux [irespektɥø] **-tueuse** [tɥøz] *adj* disrespectful

irrespirable [irespirabl] *adj* unbreathable

irresponsable [irespɔ̃sabl] *adj* irresponsible

irrétrécissable [iretresisabl] *adj* preshrunk, unshrinkable

irrévéren·cieux [ireverɑ̃sjø] **-cieuse** [sjøz] *adj* irreverent

irréversible [ireversibl] *adj* irreversible

irrévocable [irevɔkabl] *adj* irrevocable

irrigation [irigasjɔ̃] *f* irrigation

irriguer [irige] *tr* to irrigate

irri·tant -tante [iritɑ̃] **-tante** [tɑ̃t] *adj* irritating || *m* irritant

irritation [iritasjɔ̃] *f* irritation

irriter [irite] *tr* to irritate || *ref* to become irritated

irruption [irypsjɔ̃] *f* irruption; invasion; **faire irruption** to burst in

isabelle [izabel] *m* dun or light-bay horse || (*cap*) *f* Isabel

Isaïe [izai] *m* Isaiah

Islam [islam] *m*—l'Islam Islam

islan·dais [islɑ̃de] **-daise** [dez] *adj* Icelandic || *m* Icelandic (*language*) || (*cap*) *mf* Icelander

Islande [islɑ̃d] *f* Iceland; **l'Islande** Iceland

isocèle [izɔsel] *adj* isosceles

iso·lant [izɔlɑ̃] **-lante** [lɑ̃t] *adj* insulating || *m* insulator

isolateur [izɔlatœr] *m* insulator

isolation [izɔlasjɔ̃] *f* insulation; **isolation phonique** soundproofing

isolationniste [izɔlasjɔnist] *adj* & *mf* isolationist

iso·lé -lée [izɔle] *adj* isolated; independent; insulated

isolement [izɔlmɑ̃] *m* isolation; insulation

isolément [izɔlemɑ̃] *adv* separately, independently

isoler [izɔle] *tr* to isolate; to insulate || *ref* to cut oneself off

isoloir [izɔlwar] *m* polling booth

isotope [izɔtɔp] *m* isotope

Israël [israel] *m*—l'Israël Israel

israé·lien [israeljɛ̃] **-lienne** [ljɛn] *adj* Israeli || (*cap*) *mf* Israeli

israélite [israelit] *adj* Israelite || (*cap*) *mf* Israelite

is·su is·sue [isy] *adj*—issu de descended from, born of || *f* exit, way out; outlet; outcome, issue; **à l'issue de** on the way out from; at the end of; **issues** sharps, middlings (*in milling flour*); offal (*in butchering*); **sans issue** without exit; without any way out

isthme [ism] *m* isthmus

Italie [itali] *f* Italy; **l'Italie** Italy

ita·lien [italjɛ̃] **-lienne** [ljɛn] *adj* Ital-ian || *m* Italian (*language*) || (*cap*) *mf* Italian (*person*)

italique [italik] *adj* Italic; (*typ*) italic || *m* (*typ*) italics

item [item] *m* question (*in a test*) || *adv* ditto

itinéraire [itinerer] *adj & m* itinerary

itiné·rant [itinerɑ̃] **-rante** [rɑ̃t] *adj & mf* itinerant

itou [itu] *adv* (*slang*) also, likewise

ivoire [ivwar] *m* ivory

ivraie [ivre] *f* darnel, cockle; (Bib) tares

ivre [ivr] *adj* drunk, intoxicated

ivresse [ivres] *f* drunkenness; ecstasy, rapture

ivrogne [ivrɔɲ] *adj* hard-drinking || *m* drunkard

ivrognerie [ivrɔɲri] *f* drunkenness

ivrognesse [ivrɔɲes] *f* drinking woman

J

J, j [ʒi] *m invar* tenth letter of the French alphabet

jabot [ʒabo] *m* jabot; crop (*of bird*)

jabotage [ʒabɔtaʒ] *m* jabbering

jaboter [ʒabɔte] *tr & intr* to jabber

jacasse [ʒakas] *f* magpie; chatterbox

jacasser [ʒakase] *intr* to chatter, to jabber

jacasserie [ʒakasri] *f* chatter, jabber

jachère [ʒaʃer] *f* fallow ground

jacinthe [ʒasɛ̃t] *f* hyacinth; **jacinthe des bois** bluebell

Jacques [ʒak] *m* James, Jacob; **Jacques Bonhomme** the typical Frenchman

jactance [ʒaktɑ̃s] *f* bragging

jade [ʒad] *m* jade

jadis [ʒadis] *adv* formerly, of yore

jaguar [ʒagwar] *m* jaguar

jaillir [ʒajir] *intr* to gush, to burst forth

jaillissement [ʒajismɑ̃] *m* gush

jais [ʒe] *m* jet

jalon [ʒalɔ̃] *m* stake; landmark; surveying staff

jalonner [ʒalɔne] *tr* to stake out; to mark (*a way, a channel*)

jalousie [ʒaluzi] *f* jealousy; awning; Venetian blind

ja·loux [ʒalu] **-louse** [luz] *adj* jealous

jamais [ʒame] *adv* ever; never; **jamais de la vie!** not on your life!; **jamais plus** never again; **ne . . . jamais** §90 never; **pour jamais** forever

jambe [ʒɑ̃b] *f* leg; **à toutes jambes** as fast as possible; **prendre ses jambes à son cou** to take to one's heels

jambon [ʒɑ̃bɔ̃] *m* ham; **jambon d'York** boiled ham

jambon·neau [ʒɑ̃bɔno] *m* (*pl* **-neaux**) ham knuckle

jamboree [ʒɑ̃bɔre], [dʒɑ̃bɔri] *m* jamboree

jante [ʒɑ̃t] *f* felloe; rim (*of auto wheel*)

janvier [ʒɑ̃vje] *m* January

Japon [ʒapɔ̃] *m*—**le Japon** Japan

japo·nais [ʒapɔne] **-naise** [nez] *adj* Japanese || *m* Japanese (*language*) || (*cap*) *mf* Japanese (*person*)

japper [ʒape] *intr* to yap, to yelp

jaquemart [ʒakmar] *m* jack (*figurine striking the time on a bell*)

jaquette [ʒaket] *f* coat, jacket; cutaway coat, morning coat; book jacket

jardin [ʒardɛ̃] *m* garden; **jardin d'acclimatation** zoo; **jardin d'enfants** kindergarten; **jardin d'hiver** greenhouse

jardiner [ʒardine] *tr* to clear out, to trim || *intr* to garden

jardi·nier [ʒardinje] **-nière** [njer] *adj* garden || *mf* gardener || *m* flower stand; mixed vegetables; spring wagon || *f* kindergartner (*teacher*)

jargon [ʒargɔ̃] *m* jargon

jarre [ʒar] *f* earthenware jar

jarret [ʒare] *m* hock, gambrel; shin (*of beef or veal*); back of the knee

jarretelle [ʒartel] *f* garter

jarretière [ʒartjer] *f* garter

jars [ʒar] *m* gander

jaser [ʒaze] *intr* to babble, prattle; to blab, gossip

jasmin [ʒasmɛ̃] *m* jasmine

jaspe [ʒasp] *m* jasper; (bb) marbling

jasper [ʒaspe] *tr* to marble, speckle

jatte [ʒat] *f* bowl

jauge [ʒoʒ] *f* gauge; dipstick; (agr) trench; (naut) tonnage

jauger [ʒoʒe] §38 *tr* to gauge, measure; (naut) to draw

jaunâtre [ʒonatr] *adj* yellowish; sallow

jaune [ʒon] *adj* yellow || *mf* yellow

person (*Oriental*) ‖ *m* yellow; yolk (*of egg*); scab, strikebreaker

jaunir [ʒonir] *tr* & *intr* to yellow

jaunisse [ʒonis] *f* jaundice

Javel [ʒavɛl] *f*—**eau de Javel** bleach

javelle [ʒavɛl] *f* swath (*of grain*); bunch (*of twigs*)

javelliser [ʒavelize] *tr* to chlorinate (*water*)

javelot [ʒavlo] *m* javelin

jazz [dʒaz] *m* jazz

je [ʒə] §87

Jean [ʒɑ̃] *m* John

Jeanne [ʒɑn] *f* Jane, Jean, Joan

jeannette [ʒanɛt] *f* gold cross (*ornament*); sleeveboard

Jeannot [ʒano] *m* (coll) Johnny, Jack

jeep [dʒip] *f* jeep

Jéhovah [ʒeova] *m* Jehovah

je-m'en-fichisme [ʒmɑ̃fiʃism] *m* (slang) what-the-hell attitude

je-ne-sais-quoi [ʒənsekwa] *m invar* what-you-call-it

Jérôme [ʒerom] *m* Jerome

jerrycan [dʒerikan] *m* gasoline can

jersey [ʒɛrse] *m* jersey, sweater

Jérusalem [ʒeryzalɛm] *f* Jerusalem

Jésuite [ʒezɥit] *m* Jesuit

Jésus [ʒezy] *m* Jesus

Jésus-Christ [ʒezykri] *m* Jesus Christ

jet [ʒɛ] *m* throw, cast; jet; spurt, gush; flash (*of light*); **du premier jet** at the first try; **jet à la mer** jettison; **jet d'eau** fountain; **jet de pierre** stone's throw

jetée [ʒəte] *f* breakwater, jetty

jeter [ʒəte] §34 *tr* to throw; to throw away; to throw down; to hurl, fling; to toss; to cast (*a glance*); to shed (*the skin*); to pour forth; to utter; to drop (*anchor*); to lay (*the foundations*) ‖ *intr* to sprout ‖ *ref* to throw oneself; to rush; to empty (*said of a river*)

jeton [ʒətɔ̃] *m* token, counter; slug

jeu [ʒø] *m* (*pl* **jeux**) play; game, sport; gambling; pack, deck (*of cards*); set (*of chessmen; of tools*); playing; acting; execution, performance; **en jeu** in gear; at stake; **franc jeu** fair play; **gros jeu** high stakes; **jeu d'eau** dancing waters; **jeu de dames** checkers; **jeu de hasard** game of chance; **jeu de massacre** hit-the-baby (*game at fair*); **jeu de mots** pun, play on words; **jeu d'enfant** child's play; **jeu de patience** jigsaw puzzle; **jeu de puce** tiddlywinks; **jeu de société** parlor game; **jeu d'orgue** organ stop; **jouer un jeu d'enfer** to play for high stakes; **vieux jeu** old hat

jeudi [ʒødi] *m* Thursday; **jeudi saint** Maundy Thursday

jeun [ʒœ̃]—**à jeun** fasting; on an empty stomach

jeune [ʒœn] *adj* young; youthful; junior, younger ‖ *m* young man; **jeunes délinquants** juvenile delinquents; **les jeunes** young people; the young (*of an animal*)

jeûne [ʒøn] *m* fast, fasting

jeûner [ʒøne] *intr* to fast; to abstain; to eat sparingly

jeunesse [ʒœnɛs] *f* youth; youthfulness; boyhood, girlhood; **jeunesse dorée** young people of wealth and fashion

jeu-net [ʒœne] **-nette** [nɛt] *adj* youngish

jeû-neur [ʒønœr] **-neuse** [nøz] *mf* faster

joaillerie [ʒoajri] *f* jewelry; jewelry business; jewelry shop

joail-lier [ʒoaje] **joail-lière** [ʒoajer] *mf* jeweler

jobard [ʒobar] *m* (coll) dupe

jobarderie [ʒobardri] *f* gullibility

jockey [ʒoke] *m* jockey

jodler [ʒodle] *tr* & *intr* to yodel

joie [ʒwa] *f* joy; **joies** pleasures

joindre [ʒwɛ̃dr] §35 *tr* to join; to add; to adjoin; to catch up with; **joindre les deux bouts** to make both ends meet ‖ *intr* to join ‖ *ref* to join, unite; to be adjacent, to come together

joint [ʒwɛ̃] **jointe** [ʒwɛ̃t] *adj* joined; joint (*effort*); **joint à** added to ‖ *m* joint; **joint de cardan** (mach) universal joint; **joint de culasse** (aut) gasket (*of cylinder head*); **joint de dilatation thermique** expansion joint; **trouver le joint** (coll) to hit on the solution

jointure [ʒwɛ̃tyr] *f* knuckle; joint

joker [ʒɔker] *m* joker

jo-li -lie [ʒɔli] *adj* pretty; tidy (*income*)

joliment [ʒɔlimɑ̃] *adv* nicely; (coll) extremely, awfully

Jonas [ʒonas], [ʒonɑ] *m* Jonah

jonc [ʒɔ̃] *m* rush; **jonc d'Inde** rattan

jonchée [ʒɔ̃ʃe] *f* litter (*things strewn about*); cottage cheese

joncher [ʒɔ̃ʃe] *tr* to strew; to litter

jonction [ʒɔ̃ksjɔ̃] *f* junction

jongler [ʒɔ̃gle] *intr* to juggle

jonglerie [ʒɔ̃gləri] *f* jugglery

jongleur [ʒɔ̃glœr] *m* juggler; jongleur

jonque [ʒɔ̃k] *f* (naut) junk

jonquille [ʒɔ̃kij] *adj invar* pale-yellow ‖ *m* pale yellow ‖ *f* jonquil

Jordanie [ʒordani] *f* Jordan; **la Jordanie** Jordan

joue [ʒu] *f* cheek; **se caler les joues** (slang) to stuff oneself

jouer [ʒwe] *tr* to play; to gamble away; to feign; to act (*a part*) ‖ *intr* to play; to gamble; to feign; **faire jouer** to spring (*a lock*); **jouer à** to play (*a game*); **jouer à la baisse** to bear the market; **jouer à la hausse** to bull the market; **jouer de** to play (*a musical instrument*) ‖ *ref* to frolic; **se jouer de** to make fun of; to be independent of; to make light of

jouet [ʒwe] *m* toy, plaything

joueur [ʒwœr] **joueuse** [ʒwøz] *mf* player (*of games; of musical instruments*); gambler; **beau joueur** good sport; **joueur à la baisse** bear; **joueur à la hausse** bull; **mauvais joueur** poor sport

jouf-flu -flue [ʒufly] *adj* chubby

joug [ʒu] *m* yoke

jouir [ʒwir] *intr* to enjoy oneself, enjoy life; **jouir de** to enjoy

jouissance [ʒwisãs] *f* enjoyment; use, possession

jouis-seur [ʒwisœr] **jouis-seuse** [ʒwisøz] *adj* pleasure-loving || *mf* pleasure lover

jou·jou [ʒuʒu] *m* (*pl* -joux) toy, plaything

jour [ʒur] *m* day; daylight; light, window, opening; **à jour** openwork; up to date; **de nos jours** nowadays; **grand jour** broad daylight; **huit jours** a week; **il fait jour** it is getting light; **jour chômé** day off; **jour de ma fête** my birthday; **jour férié** legal holiday; **jour ouvrable** workday; **le jour de l'An** New Year's day; **le jour J** D-Day; **quinze jours** two weeks; **sous un faux jour** in a false light; **vivre au jour le jour** to live from hand to mouth

Jourdain [ʒurdẽ] *m* Jordan (*river*)

jour·nal [ʒurnal] *m* (*pl* -naux [no]) newspaper; journal; diary; (*naut*) logbook, journal; **journal parlé** newscast; **journal télévisé** telecast

journa·lier [ʒurnalje] **-lière** [ljer] *adj* daily || *m* day laborer

journalisme [ʒurnalism] *m* journalism

journaliste [ʒurnalist] *mf* journalist

journée [ʒurne] *f* day; day's journey; day's pay; day's work; **journée d'accueil** open house; **toute la journée** all day long

journellement [ʒurnelmã] *adv* daily

joute [ʒut] *f* joust

jouter [ʒute] *intr* to joust

jo·vial -viale [ʒɔvjal] *adj* (*pl* -vials or -viaux [vjo] -viales) jovial, jocose

joyau [ʒwajo] *m* (*pl* joyaux) jewel

joyeux [ʒwajø] **joyeuse** [ʒwajøz] *adj* joyful, cheerful; jocose

jubi·lant -lante [ʒybilã] -lante [lãt] *adj* jubilant

jubilé [ʒybile] *m* jubilee; golden-wedding anniversary

jucher [ʒyʃe] *tr & intr* to perch || *ref* to go to roost

judaïque [ʒydaik] *adj* Jewish

judaïsme [ʒydaism] *m* Judaism

judas [ʒyda] *m* peephole || (*cap*) *m* Judas

judicature [ʒydikatyr] *f* judiciary

judiciaire [ʒydisjer] *adj* legal, judicial

judi·cieux [ʒydisjø] -cieuse [sjøz] *adj* judicious, judicial

juge [ʒyʒ] *m* judge; umpire; **juge assesseur** associate judge

jugement [ʒyʒmã] *m* judgment

juger [ʒyʒe] §38 *tr & intr* to judge

jugulaire [ʒygyler] *adj* jugular || *f* chin strap

juif [ʒyif] **juive** [ʒyiv] *adj* Jewish || (*cap*) *mf* Jew

juillet [ʒyije] *m* July

juin [ʒɥẽ] *m* June

Jules [ʒyl] *m* Julius; (coll) Mack; (slang) pimp; (slang) chamber pot

ju·lien [ʒyljẽ] **-lienne** [ljen] *adj* Julian || *f* (*soup*) julienne; (bot) rocket

ju·meau [ʒymo] **-melle** [mel] (*pl* -meaux -melles) *adj & mf* twin || *f* see jumelles

jumelage [ʒymlaʒ] *m* twinning

jume·lé -lée [ʒymle] *adj* double; twin (*cities*); semidetached (*house*); bilingual (*text*)

jumeler [ʒymle] §34 *tr* to couple, to join; to pair

jumelles [ʒymel] *fpl* opera glasses; field glasses; **jumelles de manchettes** cuff links

jument [ʒymã] *f* mare

jungle [ʒɔ̃gl] *f* jungle

jupe [ʒyp] *f* skirt

jupon [ʒypɔ̃] *m* petticoat

juré [ʒyre] *m* juror; member of an examining board

jurer [ʒyre] *tr* to swear || *intr* to swear; to clash

juridiction [ʒyridiksjɔ̃] *f* jurisdiction

juridique [ʒyridik] *adj* legal, judicial

juriste [ʒyrist] *m* writer on legal matters

juron [ʒyrɔ̃] *m* oath

jury [ʒyri] *m* jury; examining board

jus [ʒy] *m* juice; gravy; (slang) drink (*body of water*)

jusqu'au-boutiste [ʒyskobutist] *mf* (coll) bitterender; diehard

jusque [ʒysk(ə)] *adv* even; **jusqu'à** as far as, down to, up to; until; even; **jusqu'à ce que** until; **jusqu'après** until after; **jusqu'à quand** how long || *prep* as far as; until; **jusques et y compris** [ʒyskəzeikɔ̃pri] up to and including; **jusqu'ici** this far; until now; **jusqu'où** how far

jusque-là [ʒyskəla] *adv* that far; until then

jusquiame [ʒyskjam] *f* henbane

juste [ʒyst] *adj* just, righteous; accurate; just enough; sharp, e.g., **à six heures justes** at six o'clock sharp; (mus) in tune, on key || *adv* justly; correctly, exactly

justement [ʒystəmã] *adv* just; justly; exactly; as it happens

juste-milieu [ʒystəmiljø] *m* happy medium, golden mean

justesse [ʒystes] *f* justness; precision, accuracy; **de justesse** barely

justice [ʒystis] *f* justice; **faire justice de** to mete out just punishment to; to make short work of

justiciable [ʒystisjabl] *adj*—**justiciable de** accountable to; subject to

justifier [ʒystifje] *tr* to justify || *intr*—**justifier de** to account for, to prove || *ref* to clear oneself

jute [ʒyt] *m* jute

ju·teux [ʒytø] **-teuse** [tøz] *adj* juicy

juvénile [ʒyvenil] *adj* juvenile, youthful

juxtaposer [ʒykstapoze] *tr* to juxtapose

K

K, k [ka] *m invar* eleventh letter of the French alphabet
kaki [kaki] *adj invar* & *m* khaki
kaléidoscope [kaleidɔskɔp] *m* kaleidoscope
kangourou [kãguru] *m* kangaroo
keepsake [kipsɛk] *m* giftbook, keepsake
képi [kepi] *m* kepi
kermesse [kermɛs] *f* charity bazaar
kérosène [kerozen] *m* kerosene
ketchup [ketʃœp] *m* ketchup
khan [kã] *m* khan
kidnapper [kidnape] *tr* to kidnap
kidnap·peur [kidnapœr] **kidnap·peuse** [kidnapøz] *mf* kidnaper
kif [kif] *m* (coll) pot, marijuana
kif-kif [kifkif] *adj invar* (coll) all the same; **c'est kif-kif** (coll) it's fifty-fifty
kilo [kilo] *m* kilo, kilogram
kilocycle [kilɔsikl] *m* kilocycle
kilogramme [kilɔgram] *m* kilogram
kilomètre [kilɔmetr] *m* kilometer, kilo
kilowatt [kilɔwat] *m* kilowatt
kilowatt-heure [kilɔwatœr] *m* (*pl* **kilowatts-heures**) kilowatt-hour

kilt [kilt] *m* kilt
kimono [kimɔno] *m* kimono
kinescope [kineskɔp] *m* kinescope
kiosque [kjɔsk] *m* newsstand; bandstand; summerhouse
kipper [kipœr], [kiper] *m* kipper
klaxon [klaksɔn] *m* (aut) horn
klaxonner [klaksɔne] *intr* to sound the horn
kleptomane [klɛptɔman] *adj* & *mf* kleptomaniac
km/h *abbr* (**kilomètres-heure**, **kilomètres à l'heure**) kilometers per hour
knock-out [nɔkaut], [nɔkut] *adj invar* (boxing) knocked out, groggy ‖ *m* (boxing) knockout
k.o. [kao] (letterword) (**knock-out**) *adj* k.o., knocked out; **mettre k.o.** to knock out ‖ *m* k.o., knockout
kraft [kraft] *m* strong wrapping paper
krak [krak] *m* crash (*e.g., on stock market*)
kyrielle [kirjel] *f* rigmarole, string
kyste [kist] *m* cyst

L

L, l [ɛl], *** [ɛl] *m invar* twelfth letter of the French alphabet
la [la] *art* §77 ‖ *m* (mus) la ‖ *pron* §87
là [la] *adv* there; here, e.g., **je suis là** I am here; in, e.g., **est-il là?** is he in?; **il n'était pas là** he was out; là, là! there, there! (*it's not as bad as that!*)
-là [la] §82, §84
là-bas [laba] *adv* yonder, over there
label [label] *m* union label
labeur [labœr] *m* labor, toil
la·bial -biale [labjal] (*pl* **-biaux** [bjo] **-biales**) *adj* & *f* labial
laboran·tin [labɔrãtɛ̃] **-tine** [tin] *mf* laboratory assistant
laboratoire [labɔratwar] *m* laboratory
labo·rieux [labɔrjø] **-rieuse** [rjøz] *adj* laborious; arduous; industrious; working (*classes*); **c'est laborieux!** (coll) it's endless!
labour [labur] *m* tilling, plowing
labourable [laburabl] *adj* arable, tillable
labourer [labure] *tr* to till, to plow; to furrow (*the brow*); to scratch
laboureur [laburœr] *m* farm hand, plowman
Labrador [labradɔr] *m*—**le Labrador** Labrador
labyrinthe [labirɛ̃t] *m* labyrinth, maze
lac [lak] *m* lake; **Grands Lacs** Great Lakes
lacer [lase] §51 *tr* to lace; to tie (*one's shoes*)

lacération [laserasjɔ̃] *f* tearing
lacérer [lasere] §10 *tr* to lacerate; to tear up
lacet [lase] *m* lace; snare, noose; bowstring (*for strangling*); hairpin curve; **en lacet** winding (*road*); **lacet de soulier** shoelace
lâche [laʃ] *adj* slack, loose; lax, careless; cowardly ‖ *mf* coward
lâcher [laʃe] *tr* to loosen; to let go, to release; to turn loose; to blurt out (*a word*); to fire (*a shot*); (coll) to drop (*one's friends*); **lâcher pied** to give ground; **lâcher prise** to let go
lâcheté [laʃte] *f* cowardice
lâ·cheur [laʃœr] **-cheuse** [ʃøz] *mf* fickle friend, turncoat
lacis [lasi] *m* network (*of threads, nerves*)
laconique [lakɔnik] *adj* laconic
lacrymogène [lakrimɔʒen] *adj* tear (*gas*)
lacs [lɑ] *m* noose, snare; **lacs d'amour** love knot
lac·té -tée [lakte] *adj* milky; milk (*diet*)
lacune [lakyn] *f* lacuna, gap, blank
lad [lad] *m* stableboy
là-dedans [ladədã] §85A *adv* in it, within, in that, in there
là-dessous [ladəsu] §85A *adv* under it, under that, under there
là-dessus [ladəsy] §85A *adv* on it, on that; thereupon

ladre [lɑdr] *adj* stingy, niggardly ‖ *mf* miser

ladrerie [lɑdrəri] *f* miserliness

lagon [lagɔ̃] *m* lagoon

lagune [lagyn] *f* lagoon

lai laie [lɛ] *adj* lay ‖ *m* lay (*poem*) ‖ *f* see **laie**

laïc laïque [laik] *adj* lay, secular ‖ *mf* layman ‖ *f* laywoman

laiche [lɛʃ] *f* (bot) sedge, reed grass

laïcisation [laisizasjɔ̃] *f* secularization

laïciser [laisize] *tr* to secularize

laid [lɛ] **laide** [lɛd] *adj* ugly; plain, homely; mean, low-down

laide·ron [lɛdrɔ̃] **-ronne** [rɔn] *adj* homely, ugly ‖ **laideron** *m* or *f* ugly wench

laideur [lɛdœr] *f* ugliness; meanness

laie [lɛ] *f* (zool) wild sow

lainage [lɛnaʒ] *m* woolens

laine [lɛn] *f* wool; **laine d'acier** steel wool; **manger** or **tondre la laine sur le dos à** (fig) to fleece

lainer [lɛne] *tr* to teasel, to nap

lai·neux [lɛnø] **-neuse** [nøz] *adj* wooly; downy

lai·nier [lɛnje] **-nière** [njɛr] *adj* wool (*industry*) ‖ *mf* dealer in wool; worker in wool

laïque [laik] *adj* lay, secular ‖ *mf* layman ‖ *f* laywoman

laisse [lɛs] *f* leash; foreshore; laisse

laissé-pour-compte laissée-pour-compte [lesepurkɔ̃t] *adj* returned (*merchandise*) ‖ *m* (*pl* **laissés-pour-compte**) reject; leftover merchandise

laisser [lese], [lɛse] *tr* to leave, to quit; to let, to allow; to let go (*at a low price*); to let have, e.g., **il me l'a laissé pour trois dollars** he let me have it for three dollars; **laisser +** *inf* = **qn** to let s.o. **+** *inf*, e.g., **il a laissé Marie aller au théâtre** he let Mary go to the theater; e.g., **il me l'a laissé peindre** or **il m'a laissé le peindre** he let me paint it ‖ *intr*—**ne pas laisser de** to not fail to, to not stop ‖ *ref* to let oneself, e.g., **se laisser aller** to let oneself go; **se laisser aller à** to give way to

laisser-aller [leseale] *m* abandon, easy-goingness; slovenliness, negligence

laisser-passer [lesepase] *m invar* permit, pass

lait [lɛ] *m* milk; **lait de chaux** whitewash; **lait de poule** eggnog; **lait écrémé** skim milk; **se mettre au lait** to go on a milk diet

laitage [lɛtaʒ] *m* dairy products

laitance [lɛtɑ̃s] *f* milt

laiterie [lɛtri] *f* dairy, creamery; dairy farming

lai·tier [lɛtje] **-tière** [tjɛr] *adj* dairy; milch (*cow*) ‖ *m* milkman; (metallurgy) slag, dross ‖ *f* dairymaid; milch cow

laiton [lɛtɔ̃] *m* brass

laitonner [lɛtɔne] *tr* to plate with brass

laitue [lɛty] *f* lettuce; **laitue romaine** romaine

laïus [lajys] *m* (coll) speech, impromptu remarks; (coll) hot air

laïus·seur [lajysœr] **laïus·seuse** [lajysøz] *mf* (coll) windbag

laize [lɛz] *f* width (*of cloth*)

lamanage [lamanaʒ] *m* harborage

lamaneur [lamanœr] *m* harbor pilot

lam·beau [lɑ̃bo] *m* (*pl* **-beaux**) scrap, bit; rag; **en lambeaux** in tatters, in shreds

lam·bin [lɑ̃bɛ̃] **-bine** [bin] *adj* (coll) slow ‖ *mf* (coll) slowpoke

lambiner [lɑ̃bine] *intr* (coll) to dawdle

lambris [lɑ̃bri] *m* paneling, wainscoting; plaster (*of ceiling*); **lambris dorés** (fig) palatial home

lambrisser [lɑ̃brise] *tr* to panel, to wainscot; to plaster

lame [lam] *f* blade; slat (*of blinds*); runner (*of skate*); wave; lamina, thin plate; sword; (fig) swordsman; **lame de fond** ground swell

la·mé -mée [lame] *adj* gold-trimmed, silver-trimmed, spangled ‖ *m*—**de lamé**, e.g., **une robe de lamé** a spangled dress

lamelle [lamɛl] *f* lamella, thin strip; slide (*of microscope*)

lamentable [lamɑ̃tabl] *adj* lamentable

lamentation [lamɑ̃tasjɔ̃] *f* lamentation, lament

lamenter [lamɑ̃te] *intr* & *ref* to lament

laminer [lamine] *tr* to laminate; to roll (*a metal*)

laminoir [laminwar] *m* rolling mill; calender

lampadaire [lɑ̃pader] *m* lamppost; floor lamp

lampe [lɑ̃p] *f* lamp; (electron) tube; **lampe à pétrole** kerosene lamp; **lampe à rayons ultraviolets** sun lamp; **lampe à souder** blowtorch; **lampe au néon** neon light; **lampe de chevet** bedlamp; **lampe de poche** flashlight; **lampe survoltée** photoflood bulb; **s'en mettre plein la lampe** (slang) to fill one's belly

lampée [lɑ̃pe] *f* (coll) gulp, swig

lamper [lɑ̃pe] *tr* (coll) to gulp down, to guzzle

lampe-tempête [lɑ̃ptɑ̃pɛt] *f* (*pl* **lampes-tempête**) hurricane lamp

lampion [lɑ̃pjɔ̃] *m* Chinese lantern

lampiste [lɑ̃pist] *m* lightman; (coll) scapegoat; (coll) underling

lamproie [lɑ̃prwa] *f* lamprey

lampyre [lɑ̃pir] *m* glowworm

lance [lɑ̃s] *f* lance; nozzle (*of hose*); **rompre une lance avec** to cross swords with

lan·cé -cée [lɑ̃se] *adj* flying (*start*); in the swim

lance-bombes [lɑ̃sbɔ̃b] *m invar* trench mortar; (aer) bomb release

lancée [lɑ̃se] *f* impetus

lance-flammes [lɑ̃sflam] *m invar* flamethrower

lance-fusées [lɑ̃sfyze] *m invar* rocket launcher

lancement [lɑ̃smɑ̃] *m* launching, throwing; (*of ship; of new product on the market*) launching; (aer) airdrop; (aer) release; (baseball) pitching

lance-mines [lɑ̃smin] *m invar* minelayer

lance-pierres [lãspjɛr] *m invar* sling-shot

lancer [lãse] §51 *tr* to throw, fling, cast; to launch (*e.g., a ship, a new product*); to issue (*e.g., an appeal*); (baseball) to pitch ‖ *ref* to rush, dash; **se lancer dans** to launch out into, to take up

lance-roquettes [lãsrɔket] *m invar* (arti) bazooka

lance-torpilles [lãstɔrpij] *m invar* torpedo tube

lancette [lãset] *f* (surg) lancet

lan·ceur [lãsœr] **-ceuse** [søz] *mf* promoter; (baseball) pitcher; (sports) hurler, thrower ‖ *m* (rok) booster

lanci·nant [lãsinã] **-nante** [nãt] *adj* shooting, throbbing (*pain*); gnawing (*regret*)

lanciner [lãsine] *tr* to torment ‖ *intr* to shoot; to throb

lan·dau [lãdo] *m* (*pl* **-daus**) landau; baby carriage

lande [lãd] *f* moor, heath

landier [lãdje] *m* kitchen firedog with pothangers

langage [lãgaʒ] *m* language, speech

lange [lãʒ] *m* diaper

langer [lãʒe] §38 *tr* to swaddle, diaper

langou·reux [lãgurø] **-reuse** [røz] *adj* languorous

langouste [lãgust] *f* spiny lobster, crayfish

langous·tier [lãgustje] **-tière** [tjer] *m & f* lobster net ‖ *m* lobster boat

langoustine [lãgustin] *f* prawn

langue [lãg] *f* tongue; language, speech; **avoir la langue bien pendue** (coll) to have the gift of gab; **donner sa langue au chat** (coll) to give up; **langue cible** target language; **langue source** source language; **langues vivantes** modern languages; **langue verte** slang; **mauvaise langue** backbiter, gossip; **prendre langue avec** to open up a conversation with; **tirer la langue à** to stick out one's tongue at

langue-de-chat [lãgdəʃa] *f* (*pl* **langues-de-chat**) (culin) ladyfinger

languette [lãget] *f* tongue (*e.g., of shoe*); pointer (*of scale*); flap, strip

langueur [lãgœr] *f* languor

languir [lãgir] *intr* to languish; to pine away

languis·sant [lãgisã] **languis·sante** [lãgisãt] *adj* languid; languishing; long-drawn-out, tiresome

lanière [lanjer] *f* strap, strip, thong

lanoline [lanɔlin] *f* lanolin

lanterne [lãtern] *f* lantern; (aut) parking light; (obs) street lamp; **conter des lanternes** (coll) to talk nonsense; **lanterne d'agrandissement** (phot) enlarger; **lanterne de projection, lanterne à projections** slide projector, filmstrip projector; **lanterne rouge** (slang) tail end, last to arrive; **lanterne sourde** dark lantern; **lanterne vénitienne** Japanese lantern; **oublier d'éclairer** or **d'allumer sa lanterne** (coll) to leave out the most important point

lanterner [lãterne] *tr* (coll) to string along, to put off ‖ *intr* to loaf around, to dawdle; **faire lanterner qn** to keep s.o. waiting

lapider [lapide] *tr* to stone; to vilify

la·pin [lapɛ̃] **-pine** [pin] *mf* rabbit; **lapin de garenne** wild rabbit; **lapin russe** albino rabbit; **poser un lapin à qn** (coll) to stand s.o. up

la·pon [lapɔ̃] **-pone** [pɔn] *adj* Lappish ‖ *m* Lapp, Lappish (*language*) ‖ (*cap*) *mf* Lapp, Laplander (*person*)

Laponie [lapɔni] *f* Lapland; **la Laponie** Lapland

lapsus [lapsys] *m* slip (*of tongue, pen, etc.*)

laquais [lake] *m* lackey, footman

laque [lak] *m & f* lacquer ‖ *m* lacquer ware ‖ *f* lac; shellac; hair spray

laquelle [lakɛl] §78

laquer [lake] *tr* to shellac; to lacquer

larcin [larsɛ̃] *m* petty larceny; plagiarism

lard [lar] *m* bacon, side pork; (coll) fat (*of a person*); (slang) fat slob; **se faire du lard** (coll) to get fat

larder [larde] *tr* to lard; to pierce, riddle

large [larʒ] *adj* wide, broad; generous; ample; large, e.g., **pour une large part** to a large extent ‖ *m* width, breadth; open sea; room, e.g., **donner du large à** qn to give s.o. room; **au large** in the offing; **au large de** off, e.g., **au large du Havre** off Le Havre; **prendre le large** (coll) to shove off ‖ *adv* boldly; **calculer large** to figure roughly; **habiller large** to dress in loose-fitting clothes; **il n'en mène pas large** (fig) he gets rattled in a tight spot; **voir large** (fig) to think big

largement [larʒəmã] *adv* widely; abundantly; fully; plenty, e.g., **vous avez largement le temps** you have plenty of time

largesse [larʒes] *f* largess

largeur [larʒœr] *f* width, breadth; (naut) beam

larguer [large] *tr* to let go, to release

larme [larm] *f* tear; (coll) drop; **fondre en larmes** to burst into tears; **pleurer à chaudes larmes** to shed bitter tears

larmoyant [larmwajã] **larmoyante** [larmwajãt] *adj* tearful; watery (*eyes*)

larmoyer [larmwaje] §47 *intr* to water (*said of eyes*); to snivel, to blubber

lar·ron [larɔ̃] **lar·ronnesse** [larɔnes] *mf* thief; **s'entendre comme larrons en foire** to be as thick as thieves

larve [larv] *f* larva

laryn·gé ·gée [larɛ̃ʒe] *adj* laryngeal

laryn·gien [larɛ̃ʒjɛ̃] **-gienne** [ʒjɛn] *adj* laryngeal

laryngite [larɛ̃ʒit] *f* laryngitis

laryngoscope [larɛ̃gɔskɔp] *m* laryngoscope

larynx [larɛ̃ks] *m* larynx

las [lɑ] **lasse** [lɑs] *adj* weary ‖ **las** [lɑs], [la] *interj* alas!

las·cif [lasif] **las·cive** [lasiv] *adj* lascivious

lasciveté [lasivte] *f* lasciviousness

laser [lazer] *m* laser

las·sant [lɑsɑ̃] las·sante [lɑsɑ̃t] *adj* tiring, tedious

lasser [lɑse] *tr* to tire, to weary; to wear out (*s.o.'s patience*) || *ref*—sans se lasser unceasingly; se lasser de + *inf* to tire of + *ger*; to tire oneself out + *ger*

lassitude [lɑsityd] *f* lassitude, weariness

lasso [lɑso] *m* lasso

latence [lɑtɑ̃s] *f* latency

la·tent [lɑtɑ̃] -tente [tɑ̃t] *adj* latent

laté·ral -rale [lateral] *adj* (*pl* -raux) lateral

la·tin [lɑtɛ̃] -tine [tin] *adj* Latin || *m* Latin (*language*) || (*cap*) *mf* Latin (*person*)

latino-améri·cain [latinɔamerikɛ̃] -caine [ken] (*pl* -américains) *adj* Latin-American || (*cap*) *mf* Latin American

latitude [latityd] *f* latitude

latrines [latrin] *fpl* latrine

latte [lat] *f* lath; broadsword

latter [late] *tr* to lath

lattis [lati] *m* lathing, laths

laudanum [lodanɔm] *m* laudanum

lauda·tif [lodatif] -tive [tiv] *adj* laudatory

lauréat [lɔrea] lauréate [lɔreat] *adj* laureate || *mf* winner, laureate

laurier [lɔrje] *m* laurel, sweet bay; laurier rose rosebay; s'endormir sur ses lauriers to rest on one's laurels

lavable [lavabl] *adj* washable

lavabo [lavabo] *m* washbowl; washroom; lavabos toilet, lavatory

lavage [lavaʒ] *m* washing; lavage de cerveau (coll) brainwashing; lavage des titres wash sale; lavage de tête (coll) dressing down

lavallière [lavaljer] *f* loosely tied bow

lavande [lavɑ̃d] *f* lavender

lavandière [lavɑ̃djer] *f* washerwoman

lave [lav] *f* lava

lave-glace [lavglas] *m* (*pl* -glaces) (aut) windshield washer

lavement [lavmɑ̃] *m* enema

laver [lave] *tr* to wash; laver le cerveau à (coll) to brainwash || *intr* to wash || *ref* to wash oneself, wash; (with *dat* of *reflex pron*) to wash (*e.g., one's hands*)

laverie [lavri] *f* (min) washery; laverie automatique, laverie libre-service self-service laundry

lavette [lavet] *f* dishcloth

la·veur [lavœr] -veuse [vøz] *mf* washer; laveur de vaisselle dishwasher (*person*); laveur de vitres window washer (*person*) || *f* washerwoman; washing machine

lavoir [lavwar] *m* place for washing clothes

lavure [lavyr] *f* dishwater; (coll) swill, hogwash

laxa·tif [laksatif] -tive [tiv] *adj & m* laxative

layer [leje] §49 *tr* to blaze a trail through; to blaze (*trees to mark a trail*)

layette [lejet] *f* layette; packing case

lazzi [lazi] *mpl* jeers

le [lə] *art* §77 || *pron* §87

leader [lidœr] *m* leader

lèche [leʃ] *f* (coll) thin slice (*e.g., of bread*); faire de la lèche à qn (slang) to lick s.o.'s boots

lèche-carreaux [leʃkaro] *m invar* (slang) window-shopping

lèchefrite [leʃfrit] *f* dripping pan

lécher [leʃe] §10 *tr* to lick; to overpolish (*one's style*)

lé·cheur [leʃœr] -cheuse [ʃøz] *mf* (coll) bootlicker, flatterer

lèche-vitrines [leʃvitrin] *m invar* window-shopping; faire du lèche-vitrines to go window-shopping

leçon [ləsɔ̃] *f* lesson; reading (*of manuscript*); faire la leçon à to lecture, sermonize; to prime on what to say

lec·teur [lektœr] -trice [tris] *mf* reader; lecturer (*of university rank*) || *m* playback

lecture [lektyr] *f* reading; playback; lecture sur les lèvres lip reading

ledit [lədi] ladite [ladit] *adj* (*pl* lesdits [ledi] lesdites [ledit]) the aforesaid

lé·gal -gale [legal] *adj* (*pl* -gaux [go]) legal; statutory

légaliser [legalize] *tr* to legalize

légalité [legalite] *f* legality

légat [lega] *m* papal legate

légataire [legater] *mf* legatee; légataire universel residual heir

légation [legɑsjɔ̃] *f* legation

légendaire [leʒɑ̃der] *adj* legendary

légende [leʒɑ̃d] *f* legend; caption

lé·ger [leʒe] -gère [ʒer] *adj* light; slight (*accent, difference, pain, mistake, etc.*); faint (*sound, tint, etc.*); delicate (*odor, perfume, etc.*); mild, weak (*drink*); scanty (*dress*); graceful (*figure*); empty (*stomach*); agile, active; frivolous, carefree; à la légère lightly; without due consideration

légèreté [leʒerte] *f* lightness; gracefulness; frivolity; fickleness

leggings [legins] *mpl & fpl* leggings

leghorn [legɔrn] *f* leghorn (*chicken*)

légiférer [leʒifere] §10 *intr* to legislate

légion [leʒjɔ̃] *f* legion

législa·teur [leʒislatœr] -trice [tris] *mf* legislator

législa·tif [leʒislatif] -tive [tiv] *adj* legislative

législation [leʒislɑsjɔ̃] *f* legislation

législature [leʒislatyr] *f* legislative session; legislature

légiste [leʒist] *m* jurist

légitime [leʒitim] *adj* legitimate || *f* (slang) lawful spouse; ma légitime (slang) my better half

légitimer [leʒitime] *tr* to legitimate; to justify

légitimité [leʒitimite] *f* legitimacy

legs [le], [leg] *m* legacy

léguer [lege] §10 *tr* to bequeath

légume [legym] *m* vegetable; legume (*pod*) || *f*—grosse légume (slang) bigwig, big wheel

légu·mier [legymje] -mière [mjer] *adj* vegetable (*garden, farming, etc.*) || *m* vegetable dish

lendemain [lɑ̃dmɛ̃] *m* next day; results,

outcome, e.g., **avoir d'heureux lende-mains** to have happy results or a happy outcome; **au lendemain de** the day after; **le lendemain matin** the next morning; **sans lendemain** short-lived

lénifier [lenifje] *tr* (med) to soothe

lent [lɑ̃] **lente** [lɑ̃t] *adj* slow || *f* nit

lentement [lɑ̃tmɑ̃] *adv* slowly; deliberately

lenteur [lɑ̃tœr] *f* slowness, sluggishness; **lenteurs** delays, dilatoriness

lentille [lɑ̃tij] *f* lens; (bot) lentil; **lentilles** freckles

léopard [leɔpar] *m* leopard

lèpre [lepr] *f* leprosy

lé-preux [leprø] **-preuse** [prøz] *adj* leprous || *mf* leper

lequel [ləkel] §78

les [le] *art* §77 || *pron* §87 || *prep* near (*in place names*)

les-bien [lesbjɛ̃] **-bienne** [bjen] *adj* Lesbian || *f* lesbian || (*cap*) *mf* Lesbian

lèse-majesté [lezmaʒeste] *f*—**crime de lèse-majesté** lese majesty, high treason

léser [leze] §10 *tr* to injure

lésine [lezin] *f* stinginess

lésiner [lezine] *intr* to haggle, to be stingy

lésion [lezjɔ̃] *f* lesion; wrong, damage

les-quels -quelles [lekel] §78

lessivage [lesivaʒ] *m* washing; **lessivage de crâne** (coll) brainwashing

lessive [lesiv] *f* washing (*of clothes*); wash; washing soda, lye; **faire la lessive** to do the wash

lessiver [lesive] *tr* to wash; to scrub (*with a cleaning agent*); (slang) to clean out (*e.g., another poker player*); **être lessivé** (slang) to be exhausted

lessiveuse [lesivøz] *f* washing machine

lest [lest] *m* ballast

leste [lest] *adj* nimble, quick; suggestive, broad; flippant

lestement [lestəmɑ̃] *adv* nimbly, deftly

lester [leste] *tr* to ballast; (coll) to fill (*one's stomach, pockets, etc.*) || *ref* (coll) to stuff oneself

léthargie [letarʒi] *f* lethargy

léthargique [letarʒik] *adj* lethargic || *mf* lethargic person

Lettonie [letɔni] *f* Latvia; **la Lettonie** Latvia

lettrage [letraʒ] *m* lettering

lettre [letr] *f* letter; **à la lettre, au pied de la lettre** to the letter; **avant la lettre** before complete development; **en toutes lettres** in full; in so many words; **lettre de change** bill of exchange; **lettre de faire-part** announcement; **lettre de voiture** bill of lading; **lettre d'imprimerie** printed letter; **lettre majuscule** capital letter; **lettres numérales** roman numerals; **mettre une lettre à la poste** to mail a letter

let-tré -trée [letre] *adj* lettered, literate || *mf* learned person

lettre-morte [letrəmɔrt] *f* letter returned to sender

lettrine [letrin] *f* catchword; initial letter

leu [lø] *m*—**à la queue leu leu** in single file

leucémie [løsemi] *f* leukemia

leucorrhée [løkɔre] *f* leucorrhea

leur [lœr] *adj poss* §88 || *pron poss* §89 || *pron pers* §87

leurre [lœr] *m* lure; delusion

leurrer [lœre] *tr* to lure; to trick, delude || *ref* to be deceived

levain [ləvɛ̃] *m* leaven

levant [ləvɑ̃] *adj masc* rising (*sun*) || *m* east || (*cap*) *m* Levant

levan-tin [ləvɑ̃tɛ̃] **-tine** [tin] *adj* Levantine || (*cap*) *mf* Levantine

le-vé -vée [ləve] *adj* rising (*sun*); raised (*e.g., hand*); up, e.g., **le soleil est levé** the sun is up || *m* (mus) upbeat; (surv) survey || *f* levee, embankment; collection (*of mail*); levying (*of troops, taxes, etc.*); raising (*of siege*); lifting (*of embargo*); striking (*of camp*); breaking (*of seals*); upstroke (*of piston*); **faire une levée** (cards) to take a trick; **levée de boucliers** public protest, outcry; **levée d'écrou** discharge (*from prison*); **levée de séance** adjournment; **levée du corps** removal of the body; funeral service (*in front of the coffin*); **levées manquantes** (cards) undertricks

lever [ləve] *m* rising; (surv) survey; **lever du rideau** rise of the curtain; curtain raiser; **lever du soleil** sunrise || §2 *tr* to lift; to raise; to collect; to pick up (*the mail*); to levy (*troops, taxes, etc.*); to strike (*camp*); to adjourn (*a meeting*); to weigh (*anchor*); to relieve (*a guard*); to remit (*a punishment*); to flush (*e.g., a partridge*); to effect (*a survey*); to break (*the seals*) || *intr* to come up (*said of plants*); to rise (*said of dough*) || *ref* to get up; to stand up; to rise; to heave (*said of sea*); to clear up (*said of weather*)

léviathan [levjatɑ̃] *m* leviathan

levier [ləvje] *m* lever; crowbar; **être aux leviers de commande** (aer) to be at the controls; (fig) to be in control; **levier de changement de vitesse** gearshift lever

lévitation [levitasjɔ̃] *f* levitation

levraut [ləvro] *m* young hare, leveret

lèvre [levr] *f* lip; rim; **du bout des lèvres** half-heartedly, guardedly; **embrasser sur les lèvres** to kiss; **serrer les lèvres** to purse one's lips

lévrier [levrije] *m* greyhound

levure [ləvyr] *f* yeast; **levure anglaise** or **chimique** baking powder; **levure de bière** brewer's yeast

lexi-cal -cale [leksikal] *adj* (*pl* **-caux** [ko]) lexical

lexicographe [leksikɔgraf] *mf* lexicographer

lexicographie [leksikɔgrafi] *f* lexicography

lexicographique [leksikɔgrafik] *adj* lexicographic(al)

lexicologie [leksikɔlɔʒi] *f* lexicology

lexique [leksik] *m* lexicon, vocabulary; abridged dictionary

lez [le] *prep* near (*in place names*)

lézard [lezar] *m* lizard; **faire le lézard** (coll) to sun oneself, to loaf

lézarde [lezard] *f* crack, split, crevice; gimp (*of furniture*); braid; (mil) gold braid

lézarder [lezarde] *tr & ref* to crack, to split || *intr* (coll) to bask in the sun

liaison [ljezɔ̃] *f* liaison

liant [ljɑ̃] **liante** [ljɑ̃t] *adj* flexible, supple; sociable, affable || *m* flexibility; sociability; binder, binding material; **avoir du liant** to be a good mixer

liard [ljar] *m* (fig) farthing

liasse [ljas] *f* packet, bundle (*e.g., of letters*); wad (*of bank notes*)

Liban [libɑ̃] *m*—**le Liban** Lebanon

liba·nais [libane] **-naise** [nez] *adj* Lebanese || (*cap*) *mf* Lebanese

libation [libasjɔ̃] *f* libation

libelle [libel] *m* lampoon

libellé [libelle] *m* wording

libeller [libele], [libelle] *tr* to word; to draw up (*e.g., a contract*); to make out (*a check*)

libellule [libellyl] *f* dragonfly

libé·ral **-rale** [liberal] *adj & mf* (*pl* **-raux** [ro]) liberal

libéralisme [liberalism] *m* liberalism

libéralité [liberalite] *f* liberality

libéra·teur [liberatœr] **-trice** [tris] *adj* liberating || *mf* liberator

libération [liberasjɔ̃] *f* liberation

libérer [libere] §10 *tr* to liberate || *ref* to free oneself; to pay up

liberté [liberte] *f* liberty, freedom; **liberté d'association** or **liberté de réunion** right of assembly; **liberté de langage** freedom of speech; **liberté de la presse** freedom of the press; **liberté de la propriété** right to own private property; **liberté du commerce et de l'industrie** free enterprise; **liberté du culte** freedom of worship

liber·tin [libertɛ̃] **-tine** [tin] *adj* libertine; (archaic) freethinking || *mf* libertine; (archaic) freethinker

libidi·neux [libidinø] **-neuse** [nøz] *adj* libidinous

libido [libido] *f* libido

libraire [librer] *mf* bookseller; publisher

libraire-éditeur [librereditœr] *m* (*pl* **libraires-éditeurs**) publisher and bookseller

librairie [libreri] *f* bookstore; book trade; publishing house

libre [libr] *adj* free; **je suis libre de mon temps** my time is my own; **libre arbitre** free will; **libre de** free to, at liberty to

libre-échange [libreʃɑʒ] *m* free trade

libre-échangiste [libreʃaʒist] *m* (*pl* **-échangistes**) free trader

libre-pen·seur [librəpɑ̃sœr] **-seuse** [søz] *mf* (*pl* **libres-penseurs**) freethinker

libre-service [librəservis] *m* (*pl* **libres-services**) self-service; self-service store

lice [lis] *f* enclosure or fence (*of race track, fairground, tiltyard, etc.*); (zool) hound bitch; **de basse lice** (tex) low-warp; **de haute lice** (tex) high-warp; **entrer en lice** to enter the lists

licence [lisɑ̃s] *f* license; **licence ès lettres** advanced liberal-arts degree, master of arts; **prendre des licences avec** to take liberties with

licen·cié -ciée [lisɑ̃sje] *mf* holder of a master's degree

licenciement [lisɑ̃simɑ̃] *m* discharge, layoff

licencier [lisɑ̃sje] *tr* to discharge, lay off

licen·cieux [lisɑ̃sjø] **-cieuse** [sjøz] *adj* licentious

lichen [liken] *m* lichen

licher [liʃe] *tr* (slang) to gulp down

licite [lisit] *adj* lawful, licit

licorne [likorn] *f* unicorn

licou [liku] *m* halter

lie [li] *f* dregs, lees; (fig) dregs, scum

lie-de-vin [lidvɛ̃] *adj invar* maroon

liège [ljeʒ] *m* cork

lien [ljɛ̃] *m* tie, bond, link

lier [lje] *tr* to tie, to bind, to link || *ref* to bind together; to make friends; **lier conversation avec** to fall into conversation with; **se lier d'amitié avec** to become friends with

lierre [ljer] *m* ivy

liesse [ljes] *f*—**en liesse** in festive mood, gay

lieu [ljø] *m* (*pl* **lieux**) place; **au lieu de** instead of, in lieu of; **avoir lieu** to take place; **avoir lieu de** to have reason to; **donner lieu à** to give rise to; **en aucun lieu** nowhere; **en dernier lieu** finally; **en haut lieu** high up, in responsible circles; **en premier lieu** first of all; **en quelque lieu que** wherever; **en tous lieux** everywhere; **il y a lieu à** there is room for; **lieu commun** commonplace; platitude; **lieu de villégiature** resort; **lieu géométrique** locus; **lieux** premises; **lieux d'aisances** rest rooms; **lieux payants** comfort station, public lavatory; **sur les lieux** on the spot; on the premises; **tenir lieu** to take place; **tenir lieu de** to take the place of

lieu-dit [ljødi] *m* (*pl* **lieux-dits**)—**le lieu-dit . . .** the place called . . .

lieue [ljø] *f* league

lieur [ljœr] **lieuse** [ljøz] *mf* binder || *f* (mach) binder

lieutenant [ljøtnɑ̃] *m* lieutenant; (merchant marine) mate; **lieutenant de port** harbor master; **lieutenant de vaisseau** (nav) lieutenant commander

lieutenant-colonel [ljøtnɑ̃kɔlɔnel] *m* (*pl* **lieutenants-colonels**) lieutenant colonel

lièvre [ljevr] *m* hare; **c'est là que gît le lièvre** there's the rub; **lever un lièvre** (fig) to raise an embarrassing question; **prendre le lièvre au gîte** (fig) to catch s.o. napping

ligament [ligamɑ̃] *m* ligament

ligature [ligatyr] *f* ligature

ligaturer [ligatyre] *tr* to tie up

ligne [liɲ] *f* line; figure, waistline; (*of an automobile*) lines; **aller à la ligne** to begin a new paragraph; **avoir de la ligne** to have a good figure; **en première ligne** of the first importance; on the firing line; **garder sa ligne** to keep one's figure; **grande ligne** (rr) main line; **grandes lignes** broad outline; **hors ligne** unrivaled, outstanding; **ligne à postes groupés** (telp) party line; **ligne de changement de date** international date line; **ligne de flottaison** water line; **ligne de mire** (arti) line of sight; **ligne de partage des eaux** watershed; **ligne partagée** (telp) party line; **ligne pointillée** or **hachée** dotted line

lignée [liɲe] *f* lineage, offspring

li·gneux -gneuse [liɲø] [ɲøz] *adj* woody

lignifier [liɲifje] *tr & ref* to turn into wood

ligot [ligo] *m* firewood (*in tied bundle*)

ligoter [ligote] *tr* to tie up, to bind

ligue [lig] *f* league

liguer [lige] *tr & ref* to league

lilas [lila] *adj invar & m* lilac

li·lial -liale [liljal] *adj* (*pl* -liaux [ljo]) lily-white, lily-like

lilliputien -tienne [lilipysjɛ̃] [tjɛn] *adj & mf* Lilliputian

limace [limas] *f* (zool) slug; (coll) slowpoke; (slang) shirt

limaçon [limasɔ̃] *m* snail; **en limaçon** spiral

limaille [limaj] *f* filings

limbe [lɛ̃b] *m* (astr, bot) limb; **limbes** limbo

lime [lim] *f* file; (*Citrus limetta*) sweet lime; **dernier coup de lime** finishing touches; **enlever à la lime** to file off; **lime à ongles** nail file; **lime émeri** emery board

limer [lime] *tr* to file; to fray; (fig) to polish

limette [limet] *f* (*Citrus limetta*) sweet lime

limier [limje] *m* bloodhound; (coll) sleuth

liminaire [liminer] *adj* preliminary

limitation [limitasjɔ̃] *f* limitation

limite [limit] *f* limit; maximum, e.g., **vitesse limite** maximum speed; **dernière limite** deadline

limiter [limite] *tr* to limit || *ref* to be limited; to limit oneself

limitrophe [limitrɔf] *adj* frontier; **limitrophe de** adjacent to

limogeage [limɔʒaʒ] *m* (coll) removal from office

limoger [limɔʒe] §38 *tr* (coll) to remove from office, to relieve of a command

limon [limɔ̃] *m* silt; clay; mud; shaft (*of wagon*)

limonade [limɔnad] *f* lemon soda

limona·dier -dière [limɔnadje] [djer] *mf* soft-drink manufacturer; café manager

limo·neux -neuse [limɔnø] [nøz] *adj* silty; muddy

limousine [limuzin] *f* heavy cloak; (aut) limousine

limpide [lɛ̃pid] *adj* limpid

lin [lɛ̃] *m* flax; linen

linceul [lɛ̃sœl] *m* shroud; cover (*of snow*)

linéament [lineamɑ̃] *m* lineament

linge [lɛ̃ʒ] *m* linen (*sheets, tablecloths, underclothes, etc.*); piece of linen; **laver le linge** to do the wash; **linge de corps** underclothes

lingère [lɛ̃ʒer] *f* linen maid; linen closet

lingerie [lɛ̃ʒri] *f* linen (*sheets, tablecloths, underclothes, etc.*); linen closet; **lingerie de dame** lingerie; **lingerie d'homme** men's underwear

lingot [lɛ̃go] *m* ingot

lin·gual -guale [lɛ̃gwal] (*pl* -guaux [gwo] -guales) *adj & f* lingual

linguiste [lɛ̃gɥist] *mf* linguist

linguistique [lɛ̃gɥistik] *adj* linguistic || *f* linguistics

liniment [linimɑ̃] *m* liniment

linoléum [linɔleɔm] *m* linoleum

linon [linɔ̃] *m* lawn (*sheer linen*)

linotte [linɔt] *f* (orn) linnet

linotype [linɔtip] *f* linotype

linotypiste [linɔtipist] *mf* linotype operator

lin·teau [lɛ̃to] *m* (*pl* -teaux) lintel

lion [ljɔ̃] **lionne** [ljɔn] *mf* lion || *f* lioness

lion·ceau [ljɔ̃so] *m* (*pl* -ceaux) lion cub

lippe [lip] *f* thick lower lip, blubber lip

lip·pu ·pue [lipy] *adj* thick-lipped

liquéfier [likefje] *tr* to liquefy

liqueur [likœr] *f* liqueur; liquid; (chem, pharm) liquor

liquidation [likidasjɔ̃] *f* liquidation; settlement; clearance sale

liquide [likid] *adj & m* liquid || *f* liquid (*consonant*)

liquider [likide] *tr* to liquidate; to settle (*a score*); to wind up (*a piece of business*); (coll) to get rid of; to put an end to

liquidité [likidite] *f* liquidity

liquo·reux -reuse [likɔrø] [røz] *adj* sweet

lire [lir] §36 *tr & intr* to read; **lire à haute voix** to read aloud; **lire à vue** to sight-read; **lire sur les lèvres** to lip-read || *ref* to read; to show, e.g., **la surprise se lit sur votre visage** your face shows surprise

lis [lis] *m* lily; **lis blanc** lily; **lis jaune** day lily

Lisbonne [lizbɔn] *f* Lisbon

liséré [lizere] or **liseré** [lizere] *m* braid, border, strip

li·seur -seuse [lizœr] [zøz] *mf* reader || *f* bookmark; reading lamp; book jacket; bed jacket

lisibilité [lizibilite] *f* legibility

lisible [lizibl] *adj* legible; readable

lisière [lizjer] *f* edge, border; list, selvage; **tenir en lisières** to keep in leading strings

lisse [lis] *adj* smooth, polished, sleek || *f* (naut) handrail

lisser [lise] *tr* to smooth, to polish, to

sleek; to glaze (paper) ‖ ref to become smooth; se lisser les plumes to preen its feathers

liste [list] f list

lit [li] m bed; layer; stratum; **dans le lit de la marée** in the tideway; **dans le lit du vent** in the wind's eye; **du premier lit** by or of the first marriage; **lit de mort** deathbed; **lit d'époque** period bed; **lit de sangle, lit de camp** folding cot, camp bed; **lit en portefeuille** apple-pie bed; **lit pliant, lit escamotable, lit à rabattement** foldaway bed; **lits jumeaux** twin beds

litanie [litani] f litany; tale of woe

lit-cage [lika3] m (pl **lits-cages**) foldaway bed

litée [lite] f litter (of animals)

literie [litri] f bedding, bedclothes

lithine [litin] f lithia

lithium [litjɔm] m lithium

lithographe [litɔgraf] mf lithographer

lithographie [litɔgrafi] f lithography; lithograph

lithographier [litɔgrafje] tr to lithograph

litière [litjer] f litter (bedding for animals); **faire litière de** to trample

litige [liti3] m litigation

liti·gieux [liti3jø] **-gieuse** [3jøz] adj litigious

litre [litr] m liter

littéraire [literer] adj literary ‖ mf teacher of literature; belletrist

litté·ral -rale [literal] adj (pl **-raux** [ro]) literal; literary, written

littérature [literatyr] f literature

litto·ral -rale [litɔral] (pl **-raux** [ro]) adj littoral, coastal ‖ m coast, coastline

Lituanie [lituani] f Lithuania; **la Lituanie** Lithuania

litua·nien [lituanjɛ̃] **-nienne** [njɛn] adj Lithuanian ‖ m Lithuanian (language) ‖ (cap) mf Lithuanian (person)

liturgie [lityr3i] f liturgy

liturgique [lityr3ik] adj liturgic(al)

livide [livid] adj livid

Livourne [livurn] f Leghorn

livrable [livrabl] adj ready for delivery

livraison [livrezɔ̃] f delivery; installment; **livraison contre remboursement** cash on delivery

livre [livr] m book; **à livre ouvert** at sight; **faire un livre** to write a book; (racing) to make book; **feuilleter un livre** to glance through a book; **grand livre** (bk) ledger; **livre de bord** (aer, naut) logbook; **livre de classe** textbook; **livre de cuisine, livre de recettes** cookbook; **livre d'or** blue book; testimonial volume; **livre jaune** white book; **petit livre** (bk) journal, day book; **porter au grand livre** (bk) to post ‖ f pound (weight; currency)

livrée [livre] f livery; appearances; coat (of horse, deer, etc.)

livrer [livre] tr to deliver; to surrender; to betray ‖ ref—**se livrer à** to sur-

render oneself to; to give way to; to indulge in

livresque [livresk] adj bookish

livret [livre] m booklet; (mus) libretto; **livret de caisse d'épargne** bankbook; **livret de famille** marriage certificate; **livret militaire** military record; **livret scolaire** transcript (of grades)

li·vreur [livrœr] **-vreuse** [vrøz] mf deliverer (of parcels, packages, etc.) ‖ m deliveryman ‖ f woman who makes deliveries; delivery truck

lobe [lɔb] m lobe

lo·cal -cale [lɔkal] (pl **-caux** [ko]) adj local ‖ m place, premises, quarters; headquarters; **locaux** (sports) home team; **locaux commerciaux** office space

localiser [lɔkalize] tr to locate; to localize

localité [lɔkalite] f locality

locataire [lɔkater] mf tenant, renter

location [lɔkasjɔ̃] f rental; reservation

loch [lɔk] m (naut) log (to determine speed)

locomotive [lɔkɔmɔtiv] f locomotive; (fig) mover

locuste [lɔkyst] f (ent) locust

locu·teur [lɔkytœr] **-trice** [tris] mf speaker

locution [lɔkysjɔ̃] f locution; phrase

lof [lɔf] m windward side; **aller or venir au lof** to sail into the wind

logarithme [lɔgaritm] m logarithm

loge [lɔ3] f lodge; circus cage; concierge's room; chamber, cell; (theat) dressing room; (theat) box

logeabilité [lɔ3abilite] f spaciousness

logeable [lɔ3abl] adj livable, inhabitable

logement [lɔ3mɑ̃] m lodging, lodgings

loger [lɔ3e] §38 tr, intr, & ref to lodge

lo·geur [lɔ3œr] **-geuse** [3øz] mf proprietor of a boardinghouse ‖ m landlord ‖ f landlady

logi·cien [lɔ3isjɛ̃] **-cienne** [sjɛn] mf logician

logique [lɔ3ik] adj logical ‖ f logic

logis [lɔ3i] m abode

logistique [lɔ3istik] adj logistic(al) ‖ f logistics

loi [lwa] f law; **faire des lois** to legislate; **faire la loi** to lay down the law; **loi exceptionnelle** emergency legislation

loin [lwɛ̃] adv far; far away, far off; **au loin** in the distance; **d'aussi loin que, du plus loin que** as soon as; as far back as; **de loin from afar**; far from; far be it from (e.g., me); **de loin en loin** now and then; **il y a loin de** it is a far cry from

loin·tain [lwɛ̃tɛ̃] **-taine** [tɛn] adj faraway, distant, remote; early (e.g., memories) ‖ m distance, background; **le lointain** (theat) upstage

loir [lwar] m dormouse; **dormir comme un loir** to sleep like a log

loisible [lwazibl] adj—**il m'est** (lui est, etc.) **loisible de** I am (he is, etc.) free to or entitled to, it is open for me (him, etc.) to

loisir [lwazir] *m* leisure, spare time; **loisirs** diversions
lolo [lolo] *m* (coll) milk (*in baby talk*)
lombes [lɔ̃b] *mpl* loins
londo·nien [lɔ̃dɔnjɛ̃] **-nienne** [njɛn] *adj* London || (*cap*) *mf* Londoner
Londres [lɔ̃dr] *m* London
londrès [lɔ̃dres] *m* Havana cigar
long [lɔ̃] **longue** [lɔ̃g] *adj* long; lengthy (*speech*); long (*syllable, vowel*); thin, weak (*sauce, gravy*); slow (*to understand, to decide*) || (*when standing before noun*) *adj* long; **de longue main** of long standing || *m* length; extent; **au long** at length; **de long** lengthwise; **de long en large** up and down, back and forth; **le long de** along || *f* see **longue** || **long** *adv* much; **en dire long** to talk a long time; to speak volumes; **en savoir long sur** to know a great deal about; **en savoir plus long** to know more about it
longanimité [lɔ̃ganimite] *f* long-suffering
long-courrier [lɔ̃kurje] (*pl* **-courriers**) *adj* long-range || *m* airliner; liner, ocean liner
longe [lɔ̃ʒ] *f* tether, leash; (culin) loin
longer [lɔ̃ʒe] §38 *tr* to walk along, to go beside; to extend along, to skirt
longeron [lɔ̃ʒrɔ̃] *m* crossbeam, girder
longévité [lɔ̃ʒevite] *f* longevity
longitude [lɔ̃ʒityd] *f* longitude
longtemps [lɔ̃tɑ̃] *m* a long time; **avant longtemps** before long; **depuis longtemps** for a long time; long since; **ne . . . plus longtemps** no . . . longer || *adv* long; for a long time
longue [lɔ̃g] *f* long syllable; long vowel; long suit (*in cards*); **à la longue** in the long run
longuement [lɔ̃gmɑ̃] *adv* at length, a long time
lon·guet [lɔ̃gɛ] **-guette** [gɛt] *adj* (coll) longish, rather long
longueur [lɔ̃gœr] *f* length; lengthiness; **de longueur, dans la longueur** lengthwise; **d'une longueur** by a length, by a head; **longueur d'onde** wavelength
longue-vue [lɔ̃gvy] *f* (*pl* **longues-vues**) telescope, spyglass
looping [lupiŋ] *m* loop-the-loop
lopin [lɔpɛ̃] *m* patch of ground, plot
loquace [lɔkwas], [lɔkas] *adj* loquacious
loque [lɔk] *f* rag; **être comme une loque** to feel like a dishrag; **être en loques** to be in tatters
loquet [lɔkɛ] *m* latch
loque·teux [lɔktø] **-teuse** [tøz] *adj* in tatters || *mf* tatterdemalion
lorgner [lɔrɲe] *tr* to cast a sidelong glance at; to ogle; to have one's eyes on (*a job, an inheritance, etc.*)
lorgnette [lɔrɲɛt] *f* opera glasses
lorgnon [lɔrɲɔ̃] *m* pince-nez; lorgnette
loriot [lɔrjo] *m* golden oriole
lorry [lɔri] *m* lorry, small flatcar
lors [lɔr] *adv*—**lors de** at the time of; **lors même que** even if
lorsque [lɔrsk] *conj* when

losange [lɔzɑ̃ʒ] *m* (geom) lozenge; **en losange** diamond-shaped; oval-shaped
lot [lo] *m* lot; prize (*e.g., in lottery*); **gagner le gros lot** to hit the jackpot
loterie [lɔtri] *f* lottery
lo·ti -tie [lɔti] *adj*—**bien loti** well off; **mal loti** badly off
lotion [losjɔ̃] *f* lotion; **lotion capillaire** hair tonic
lotionner [losjɔne] *tr* to bathe (*a wound*)
lotir [lɔtir] *tr* to parcel out; **lotir qn de q.ch.** to allot s.th. to s.o.
lotissement [lɔtismɑ̃] *m* allotment, apportionment; building lot
louable [lwabl] *adj* praiseworthy; for hire
louage [lwaʒ] *m* hire
louange [lwɑ̃ʒ] *f* praise; **à la louange de** in praise of
louanger [lwɑ̃ʒe] §38 *tr* to praise, extol
louan·geur [lwɑ̃ʒœr] **-geuse** [ʒøz] *adj* laudatory, flattering
louche [luʃ] *adj* ambiguous; suspicious, shady; cross-eyed; cloudy (*e.g., wine*) || *f* ladle; basting spoon
loucher [luʃe] *intr* to be cross-eyed, to squint; **faire loucher qn de jalousie** (coll) to turn s.o. green with envy; **loucher sur** (coll) to cast longing eyes at
louchet [luʃɛ] *m* spade (*for digging*)
louer [lwe] *tr* to rent, hire; to reserve (*a seat*); to praise || *ref* to be rented; to hire oneself out; **se louer de** to be satisfied with
loueur [lwœr] **loueuse** [lwøz] *mf* operator of a rental service; flatterer
loufoque [lufɔk] *adj* (slang) cracked || *m* (slang) crackpot
lougre [lugr] *m* (naut) lugger
Louisiane [lwizjan] *f* Louisiana; **la Louisiane** Louisiana
lou·lou [lulu] **-loute** [lut] *mf* (coll) darling, pet || *m*—**loulou de Poméranie** Pomeranian, spitz
loup [lu] *m* wolf; mask; flaw; **avoir vu le loup** to have lost one's innocence; **crier au loup** to cry wolf; **loup de mer** (ichth) wolf eel; (coll) old salt; **mon petit loup** (coll) my pet
loup-cervier [luservje] *m* (*pl* **loups-cerviers**) lynx
loupe [lup] *f* magnifying glass; gnarl (*on tree*); (pathol) wen
lou·pé -pée [lupe] *adj* bungled; defective || *m* defect
louper [lupe] *tr* (coll) to goof up, to muff; (coll) to miss (*e.g., one's train*) || *intr* (coll) to fail, to goof
loup-garou [lugaru] *m* (*pl* **loups-garous**) werewolf
lou·piot [lupjo] **-piotte** [pjɔt] *mf* (coll) kid, child; **loupiots** (coll) small fry
lourd [lur] **lourde** [lurd] *adj* heavy; hefty; clumsy; sultry (*weather*); off-color (*joke*); dull (*mind*); (agr) hard to cultivate || (*when standing before noun*) *adj* heavy; grave; clumsy (*e.g., compliments*); off-color (*joke*) || **lourd** *adv* heavy, heavily

lour·daud [lurdo] **-daude** [dod] *adj*
clumsy, loutish, dull || *mf* lout, oaf
lourdement [lurdəmã] *adv* heavily;
clumsily; **avancer or rouler lourde-**
ment to lumber along
lourdeur [lurdœr] *f* heaviness; clumsiness; sultriness; dullness
loustic [lustik] *m* wag, clown; (coll)
screwball, character
loutre [lutr] *f* otter
louve [luv] *f* she-wolf
louve·teau [luvto] *m* (*pl* **-teaux**) wolf
cub; cub scout
louvoyer [luvwaje] §47 *intr* to be evasive; (naut) to tack
lovelace [lɔvlas] *m* seducer, Don Juan
lover [lɔve] *tr & ref* to coil
loyal loyale [lwajal] *adj* (*pl* **loyaux**
[lwajo]) loyal; honest; fair, just
loyaliste [lwajalist] *mf* loyalist
loyauté [lwajote] *f* loyalty; honesty;
fairness
loyer [lwaje] *m* rent
lubie [lybi] *f* whim
lubricité [lybrisite] *f* lubricity, lewdness
lubri·fiant [lybrifjã] **-fiante** [fjãt] *adj*
& *m* lubricant
lubrifier [lybrifje] *tr* to lubricate
lucarne [lykarn] *f* dormer window;
skylight
lucide [lysid] *adj* lucid
luciole [lysjɔl] *f* firefly
lucra·tif [lykratif] **-tive** [tiv] *adj* lucrative
lucre [lykr] *m* lucre
luette [lɥet] *f* uvula
lueur [lɥœr] *f* glimmer, gleam; flash,
blink
luge [lyʒ] *f* sled
lugubre [lygybr] *adj* gloomy
lui [lɥi] *pron disj* §85 || *pron conj* §87
lui-même [lɥimem] §86
luire [lɥir] §37 *intr* to shine; to gleam,
glow, glisten; to dawn
lui·sant [lɥizã] **-sante** [zãt] *adj* shining
lulu [lyly] *m* (orn) tree pipit
lumbago [lɔ̃bago] *m* lumbago
lumière [lymjer] *f* light; aperture; (*person*) luminary; **avoir des lumières de**
to have knowledge of
lumignon [lymiɲɔ̃] *m* feeble light
luminaire [lyminer] *m* luminary
lumines·cent [lyminesã] **lumines·cente**
[lyminesãt] *adj* luminescent
lumi·neux [lyminø] **-neuse** [nøz] *adj*
luminous; light (*e.g., spot*); bright
(*idea*)
lunaire [lyner] *adj* lunar || *f* (bot)
honesty
lunatique [lynatik] *adj* whimsical, ec-
centric || *mf* whimsical person, ec-
centric
lunch [lœntʃ], [lœ̃ʃ] *m* buffet lunch
lundi [lœ̃di] *m* Monday
lune [lyn] *f* moon; **être dans la lune**
to be daydreaming; **lune de miel**
honeymoon; **lune des moissons** harvest moon; **vieilles lunes** good old
days, bygone days
lu·né **-née** [lyne] *adj* moon-shaped;

bien luné in a good mood; **mal luné**
in a bad mood
lune·tier [lyntje] **-tière** [tjer] *mf* optician
lunette [lynet] *f* telescope, spyglass;
toilet seat; hole (*in toilet seat*); wishbone (*of turkey, chicken*); (archit)
lunette; (aut) rear window; **lunettes**
eyeglasses, spectacles, goggles; **lunettes de lecture, lunettes pour lire**
reading glasses; **lunettes de soleil**
sunglasses; **lunettes noires** dark
glasses
lurette [lyret] *f*—**il y a belle lurette**
(coll) ages ago
luron [lyrɔ̃] *m* (coll) playboy
luronne [lyron] *f* (coll) hussy
lustre [lystr] *m* luster; five-year period;
chandelier
lus·tré -trée [lystre] *adj* lustrous, glossy
lustrine [lystrin] *f* cotton satin
lut [lyt] *m* (chem) lute
luth [lyt] *m* (mus) lute
lutherie [lytri] *f* violin making
luthé·rien [lyterjẽ] **-rienne** [rjen] *adj*
Lutheran || (*cap*) *mf* Lutheran
luthier [lytje] *m* violin maker
lu·tin [lytẽ] **-tine** [tin] *adj* impish || *m*
imp
lutiner [lytine] *tr* to tease
lutrin [lytrẽ] *m* lectern
lutte [lyt] *f* struggle, fight; wrestling;
de bonne lutte aboveboard; **de haute
lutte** by force; in open competition;
hard-won; **lutte à la corde de traction** tug of war; **lutte libre** catch-as-
catch-can
lutter [lyte] *intr* to fight, to struggle;
to wrestle
lut·teur [lytœr] **lut·teuse** [lytøz] *mf*
wrestler; (fig) fighter
luxation [lyksasjɔ̃] *f* dislocation
luxe [lyks] *m* luxury
Luxembourg [lyksãbur] *m*—**le Luxembourg** Luxembourg
luxer [lykse] *tr* to dislocate
luxueux [lyksɥø] **luxueuse** [lyksɥøz]
adj luxurious
luxure [lyksyr] *f* lechery, lust
luxu·riant [lyksyrjã] **-riante** [rjãt] *adj*
luxuriant
luxu·rieux [lyksyrjø] **-rieuse** [rjøz]
adj lecherous, lustful
luzerne [lyzern] *f* alfalfa
lycée [lise] *m* high school; lyceum
lycéen [liseẽ] **lycéenne** [liseen] *mf*
high-school student
lymphatique [lẽfatik] *adj* lymphatic
lymphe [lẽf] *f* lymph
lynchage [lẽʃaʒ] *m* lynching
lyncher [lẽʃe] *tr* to lynch
lynx [lẽks] *m* lynx
Lyon [ljɔ̃] *m* Lyons
lyon·nais [lione] **lyon·naise** [ljonez]
adj Lyonese; **à la lyonnaise** lyonnaise
lyre [lir] *f* lyre
lyrique [lirik] *adj* lyric(al) || *m* lyric
poet || *f* lyric poetry
lyrisme [lirism] *m* lyricism
lys [lis] *m* lily; **lys blanc** lily; **lys jaune**
day lily
lysimaque [lizimak] *f* loosestrife

M, m [ɛm], *[ɛm] *m invar* thirteenth letter of the French alphabet
M. *abbr* (Monsieur) Mr.
ma [ma] §88
ma·boul -boule [mabul] *adj* (slang) nuts, balmy || *mf* (slang) nut
macabre [makabr] *adj* macabre
macadam [makadam] *m* macadam
macadamiser [makadamize] *tr* to macadamize
macaron [makarɔ̃] *m* macaroon
macchabée [makabe] *m* (slang) stiff (*corpse*)
macédoine [masedwan] *f* macédoine, medley; **macédoine de fruits** fruit salad; **macédoine de légumes** mixed vegetables
macérer [masere] §10 *tr* to macerate; to mortify (*the flesh*); to soak, to steep || *intr* to soak, to steep
mâchefer [maʃfɛr] *m* clinker
mâcher [maʃe] *tr* to chew; **mâcher la besogne à qn** to do all one's work for one; **ne pas mâcher ses mots** to not mince words
machin [maʃɛ̃] *m* (coll) what-do-you-call-it; (coll) what's-his-name, so-and-so
machi·nal -nale [maʃinal] *adj* (*pl* -naux [no]) mechanical
machination [maʃinɑsjɔ̃] *f* machination
machine [maʃin] *f* machine; engine; **faire machine arrière** to go into reverse; **machine à calculer** adding machine; **machine à coudre** sewing machine; **machine à écrire** typewriter; **machine à laver** washing machine; **machine à laver la vaisselle** dishwasher; **machine à vapeur** steam engine; **machines** machinery
machine-outil [maʃinuti] *f* (*pl* machines-outils) machine tool
machinerie [maʃinri] *f* machinery; engine room
machiniste [maʃinist] *m* (theat) stagehand
mâchoire [maʃwar] *f* jaw; jawbone; lower jaw
mâchonner [maʃɔne] *tr* to chew, munch; to mumble (*e.g., the end of a sentence*)
mâchurer [maʃyre] *tr* to crush; to smudge
maçon [masɔ̃] *m* mason
maçonner [masɔne] *tr* to mason, to wall up
maçonnerie [masɔnri] *f* masonry
macule [makyl] *f* spot, blotch; inkblot; birthmark
maculer [makyle] *tr* to soil, spot; (typ) to smear
madame [madam] *f* (*pl* mesdames [medam]) madam; Mrs.; (not translated), e.g., **madame votre femme** your wife
Madeleine [madlɛn] *f* Madeleine, Magdalen; sponge cake; **pleurer comme une Madeleine** to weep bitterly
mademoiselle [madmwazɛl] *f* (*pl* mesdemoiselles [medmwazɛl]) Miss;

eldest daughter; (not translated), e.g., **mademoiselle votre fille** your daughter
Madone [madɔn] *f* Madonna
ma·dré -drée [madre] *adj* sly, cagey || *mf* sly one
madrier [madrije] *m* beam
maf·flu -flue [mafly] *adj* heavy-jowled
magasin [magazɛ̃] *m* store; warehouse; magazine (*of gun or camera; for munitions or powder*); **avoir en magasin** to have in stock; **grands magasins** department store; **magasin à libre service** self-service store; **magasin à succursales multiples** chain store; **magasin d'antiquités** antique shop; **magasin de modes** dress shop
magasinage [magazinaʒ] *m* storage, warehousing; storage charges; (Canad) shopping
magasinier [magazinje] *m* warehouseman
magazine [magazin] *m* magazine; (mov, telv) hour, program, e.g., **magazine féminin** woman's hour
mages [maʒ] *mpl* Magi
magi·cien [maʒisjɛ̃] **-cienne** [sjɛn] *mf* magician
magie [maʒi] *f* magic
magique [maʒik] *adj* magic
magis·tral -trale [maʒistral] *adj* (*pl* -traux [tro]) masterful, masterly; magisterial; (pharm) magistral
magistrat [maʒistra] *m* magistrate
magnanime [maɲanim] *adj* magnanimous
magnat [magna] *m* magnate
magnésium [maɲezjɔm] *m* magnesium
magnétique [maɲetik] *adj* magnetic; hypnotic
magnétiser [maɲetize] *tr* to magnetize; to hypnotize; to spellbind
magnétisme [maɲetism] *m* magnetism
magnéto [maɲeto] *f* magneto
magnétophone [maɲetɔfɔn] *m* tape recorder
magnétoscope [maɲetɔskɔp] *m* video tape recorder; video tape recording
magnifier [maɲifje] *tr* to extol, glorify
magnifique [maɲifik] *adj* magnificent; lavishly generous
magnitude [magnityd] *f* (astr) magnitude
magot [mago] *m* Barbary ape; figurine; (coll) hoard, pile (*of money*)
Mahomet [maɔme] *m* Mahomet
mahomé·tan [maɔmetɑ̃] **-tane** [tan] *adj & m* Mohammedan
mai [me] *m* May; Maypole
maie [me] *f* bread bin; kneading trough
maigre [megr] *adj* lean; thin; meager; meatless (*day*); **faire maigre** to abstain from meat
maigreur [megrœr] *f* leanness; meagerness
maigri·chon [megriʃɔ̃] **-chonne** [ʃɔn] *adj* (coll) skinny

maigrir [megrir] *tr* to slim; to make (*s.o.*) look thinner || *intr* to lose weight

mail [maj] *m* mall

maille [maj] *f* link; stitch; mesh, loop; **avoir maille à partir avec qn** to have a bone to pick with s.o.; **mailles** mail

maillet [maje] *m* mallet

maillon [majɔ̃] *m* link (*of a chain*)

maillot [majo] *m* swimming suit; jersey; **maillot de bain** swimming suit; **maillot de corps** undershirt; **maillot de danseur** tights; **maillot des acrobates** tights

main [mɛ̃] *f* hand; quire; **à la main** by hand; **à main levée** in one stroke; **avoir la haute main sur** to control; **avoir la main, être la main** (*cards*) to be the dealer; **battre des mains** to applaud; **de la main à la main** privately; **de longue main** carefully; for a long time; **de main à main** from one person to another; **de première main** firsthand; **donner les mains à q.ch.** to be in favor of s.th.; **en venir aux mains** to come to blows; **faire main basse sur** to grab, to steal; **haut les mains!** hands up!; **passer la main dans le dos à qn** to soft-soap s.o.; **serrer la main à** to shake hands with; **sous main** secretly; **tout main** handmade

main-d'œuvre [mɛ̃dœvr] *f* (*pl* **mains-d'œuvre**) labor; laborers, manpower

maint [mɛ̃] **mainte** [mɛ̃t] *adj* many a; **à maintes reprises** time and again

maintenant [mɛ̃tənɑ̃] *adv* now

maintenir [mɛ̃tnir] §72 *intr* to maintain; to hold up || *ref* to keep on; to keep up

maintien [mɛ̃tjɛ̃] *m* maintenance; bearing

maire [mer] *m* mayor

mairesse [meres] *f* (coll) mayor's wife

mairie [meri] *f* town hall, city hall

mais [me] *m* but || *adv* why, well; **mais non** certainly not || *conj* but

maïs [mais] *m* corn, maize

maison [mezɔ̃] *f* house; home; household, family; house, firm, business; **à la maison** at home, home; **fait à la maison** homemade; **maison centrale** state or federal prison; **maison close, borgne, publique, mal famée, de débauche, de passe, de rendezvous, de tolérance** house of ill fame; **maison d'accouchement** lying-in hospital; **maison d'antiquités, de meubles d'époque,** or **d'originaux** antique shop; **maison de commerce** firm; **maison de confiance** (com) trustworthy firm; **maison de correction** reform school; **maison de couture** dressmaking establishment; **maison de fous** madhouse; **maison de jeux** gambling house; **maison de plaisance** or **de campagne** cottage, summer home; **maison de rapport** apartment house; **maison de repos** rest home; **maison de retraite** old-people's home; **maison de santé** nursing home; **maison jumelée** semi-detached house; **maison mère** head office; **maison mortuaire** home of the deceased; **maison religieuse** convent

maisonnée [mezɔne] *f* household

maisonnette [mezɔnet] *f* little house, cottage

maître-tresse [metr] **-tresse** [tres] *adj* expert, capable; basic, key; main (*beam, girder*); utter (*fool*); arrant (*knave*); high (*card*) || *m* master; Mr. (*when addressing a lawyer*); (naut) mate; (naut) petty officer; **être passé maître en** to be a past master of or in; **maître chanteur** blackmailer; **maître d'armes** fencing master; **maître de chapelle** choirmaster; **maître d'école** schoolmaster; **maître de conférences** associate professor; **maître de forges** ironmaster; **maître de maison** man of the house, householder; **maître d'équipage** boatswain; **maître d'études** monitor, supervisor; **maître d'hôtel** headwaiter; butler; **maître d'œuvre** foreman; **maître Jacques** jack-of-all-trades; **maître mécanicien** chief engineer; **maître mineur** mine foreman; **maître queue** chef; **passer maître** to know one's trade § *f* see **maîtresse**

maître-autel [metrotel] *m* (*pl* **maîtres-autels**) high altar

maîtresse [metres] *f* mistress; **maîtresse d'école** schoolmistress; **maîtresse de maison** lady of the house

maîtrise [metriz] *f* mastery, command; master's degree; **maîtrise de soi** self-control

maîtriser [metrize] *tr* to master, control; to subdue

maj. *abbr* (**majuscule**) cap.

majesté [maʒeste] *f* majesty

majes-tueux [maʒestɥø] **-tueuse** [tɥøz] *adj* majestic

ma-jeur -jeure [maʒœr] *adj & m* major

major [maʒɔr] *m* regimental quartermaster; army doctor; **être le major de sa promotion** to be at the head of one's class

majordome [maʒɔrdɔm] *m* major-domo

majorer [maʒɔre] *tr* to increase the price of; to overprice; to raise (*the price*)

majoritaire [maʒɔriter] *adj* majority

majorité [maʒɔrite] *f* majority

Majorque [maʒɔrk] *f* Majorca

major-quin [maʒɔrkɛ̃] **-quine** [kin] *adj* Majorcan || (*cap*) *mf* Majorcan

majuscule [maʒyskyl] *adj* capital (*letter*) || *f* capital letter

mal [mal] *adj*—**de mal** bad, e.g., **dire q.ch. de mal** to say s.th. bad; **pas mal** not bad, quite good-looking || *m* (*pl* **maux** [mo]) evil; trouble; hurt; pain; wrong; **avoir du mal à** + *inf* to have a hard time + *ger*, to have difficulty in + *ger*; **avoir mal à la tête** to have a headache; **avoir mal au cœur** to be nauseated; **avoir mal aux dents** to have a toothache; **avoir mal de gorge** to have a sore throat; **dire du mal de qn** to speak ill of s.o.; **faire mal à, faire du mal à** to hurt, to harm; **le Mal** Evil; **mal aux reins**

backache; **mal blanc** whitlow; **mal de l'air** airsickness; **mal de la route** carsickness; **mal de mer** seasickness; **mal des rayons** radiation sickness; **mal du pays** homesickness; **mal du siècle** Weltschmerz, romantic melancholy; **se donner du mal** to take pains || *adv* §91 badly, bad; **de mal en pis** from bad to worse; **être mal avec qn** to be on bad terms with s.o.; **pas mal** not bad; **pas mal de** a lot of, quite a few

malade [malad] *adj* sick, ill || *mf* patient, sick person

maladie [maladi] *f* disease, sickness; distemper; **elle va en faire une maladie** (coll) she'll be terribly upset over it; **maladie de carence** or **par carence** deficiency disease; **maladie de cœur** heart trouble; **maladie des caissons** bends; **maladie diplomatique** malingering; **revenir de maladie** to convalesce

mala·dif [maladif] **-dive** [div] *adj* sickly; morbid

maladresse [maladres] *f* awkwardness; blunder

mala·droit [maladrwa] **-droite** [drwat] *adj* clumsy, awkward

ma·lais [male] **-laise** [lez] *adj* Malay -|| *m* Malay (*language*) || see **malaise** *m* || (*cap*) *mf* Malay (*person*)

malaise [malez] *m* malaise, discomfort

malai·sé **-sée** [maleze] *adj* difficult

malap·pris [malapri] **malap·prise** [malapriz] *adj* uncouth, ill-bred || *mf* ill-bred person

malard [malar] *m* (orn) mallard

malaria [malarja] *f* malaria

malavi·sé **-sée** [malavize] *adj* ill-advised, indiscreet

malaxer [malakse] *tr* to knead; to churn (*butter*); to massage

malaxeur [malaksœr] *m* churn; (mach) mixer

malchance [malʃɑ̃s] *f* bad luck; **par malchance** unluckily; **une malchance** a piece of bad luck

malchan·ceux [malʃɑ̃sø] **-ceuse** [søz] *adj* unlucky

malcommode [malkɔmɔd] *adj* inconvenient; unsuitable, impractical

maldonne [maldɔn] *f* misdeal

mâle [mɑl] *adj* male; energetic, virile || *m* male

malédiction [malediksjɔ̃] *f* curse

maléfice [malefis] *m* evil spell

maléfique [malefik] *adj* baleful

malencon·treux [malɑ̃kɔ̃trø] **-treuse** [trøz] *adj* untimely, unfortunate

malentendu [malɑ̃tɑ̃dy] *m* misunderstanding

malfaçon [malfasɔ̃] *f* defect

malfai·sant [malfəzɑ̃] **-sante** [zɑ̃t] *adj* mischievous, harmful

malfaiteur [malfetœr] *m* malefactor

malfa·mé **-mée** [malfame] *adj* ill-famed

malgra·cieux [malgrasjø] **-cieuse** [sjøz] *adj* ungracious

malgré [malgre] *prep* in spite of; **malgré que** in spite of the fact that, although

malhabile [malabil] *adj* inexperienced, clumsy

malheur [malœr] *m* misfortune; unhappiness; bad luck; **faire un malheur** to commit an act of violence; **jouer de malheur** to be unlucky

malheu·reux [malœrø] **-reuse** [røz] *adj* unfortunate; unhappy; unlucky; paltry || *m* poor man, wretch; **les malheureux** the unfortunate || *f* poor woman, wretch

malhonnête [malɔnet] *adj* dishonest; (slang) rude, uncivil

malhonnêteté [malɔnette] *f* dishonesty

malice [malis] *f* mischievousness

mali·cieux [malisjø] **-cieuse** [sjøz] *adj* malicious, mischievous

malignité [maliɲite] *f* malignancy

ma·lin [malɛ̃] **-ligne** [liɲ] *adj* cunning, sly, smart; mischievous; malignant (*e.g., tumor*); **ce n'est pas malin** (coll) it's easy || *mf* sly one; **Le Malin** the Evil One

malingre [malɛ̃gr] *adj* weakly, puny

malintention·né **-née** [malɛ̃tɑ̃sjɔne] *adj* evil-minded, ill-disposed

mal-jugé [malʒyʒe] *m* miscarriage (*of justice*)

malle [mal] *f* trunk; mailboat; **faire ses malles** to pack

malléable [maleabl] *adj* malleable; compliant, pliable

mallette [malet] *f* suitcase; small trunk

malmener [malməne] §2 *tr* to rough up

malodo·rant [malɔdɔrɑ̃] **-rante** [rɑ̃t] *adj* malodorous; bad (*breath*)

malo·tru **-true** [malɔtry] *adj* coarse, uncouth || *mf* ill-bred person, oaf

malpropre [malprɔpr] *adj* dirty; improper; crude, clumsy (*workmanship*)

mal·sain [malsɛ̃] **-saine** [sen] *adj* unhealthy

malséant [malseɑ̃] **malséante** [malseɑ̃t] *adj* improper

maison·nant [malsɔnɑ̃] **maison·nante** [malsɔnɑ̃t] *adj* offensive, objectionable

malt [malt] *m* malt

maltraiter [maltrete] *tr* to mistreat

malveil·lant [malvejɑ̃] **malveil·lante** [malvejɑ̃t] *adj* malevolent

malve·nu **-nue** [malvəny] *adj* ill-advised, out of place; poorly developed

malversation [malversasjɔ̃] *f* embezzlement

maman [mamɑ̃] *f* mamma

mamelle [mamel] *f* breast; udder

mamelon [mamlɔ̃] *m* nipple, teat; knoll

mamie [mami] *f* (coll) my dear

mammifère [mamifer] *adj* mammalian || *m* mammal

mammouth [mamut] *m* mammoth

mamours [mamur] *mpl* (coll) caresses

mam'selle or **mam'zelle** [mamzel] *f* (coll) Miss

manant [manɑ̃] *m* hick, yokel

manche [mɑ̃ʃ] *m* handle; stick, stock; neck (*of violin*); (culin) knuckle; **branler au manche** or **dans le manche** to be shaky; **manche à balai** broomstick; (aer) joy stick; **manche à gigot** holder (*for carving*) || *f* sleeve; hose; channel; game, heat, round; shaft, chute; (baseball) inning; (bridge) game; (tennis) set; **en manches de chemise** in shirt sleeves; **la Manche** the English Channel; **manche à air** windsock; **manche à manche** neck and neck, even up; **manches à gigot** leg-of-mutton sleeves

manchette [mɑ̃ʃet] *f* cuff; (journ) headline

manchon [mɑ̃ʃɔ̃] *m* muff; (*of gaslight*) mantle; (mach) casing, sleeve

man·chot [mɑ̃ʃo] **-chote** [ʃɔt] *adj* one-armed; one-handed; (coll) clumsy ‖ *mf* one-armed person; one-handed person ‖ *m* (orn) penguin

mandarine [mɑ̃darin] *f* mandarin orange

mandat [mɑ̃da] *m* mandate; term of office; money order; power of attorney; proxy; **mandat d'arrêt** warrant; **mandat de perquisition** search warrant

mandataire [mɑ̃dater] *mf* representative; proxy; defender

mandat-carte [mɑ̃dakart] *m* (*pl* **mandats-carte**) postal-card money order

mandat-poste [mɑ̃dapɔst] *m* (*pl* **mandats-poste**) postal money order

Mandchourie [mɑ̃t∫uri] *f* Manchuria; **la Mandchourie** Manchuria

mander [mɑ̃de] *tr* to summon

mandoline [mɑ̃dɔlin] *f* mandolin

mandragore [mɑ̃dragɔr] *f* mandrake

mandrin [mɑ̃drɛ̃] *m* (mach) punch; (mach) chuck

manécanterie [manekɑ̃tri] *f* choir school

manège [manɛʒ] *m* horsemanship; riding school; trick, little game; **manège de chevaux de bois** merry-go-round

mânes [mɑn] *mpl* shades, spirits (*of ancestors*)

maneton [mantɔ̃] *m* crank handle; pin (*of crankshaft*)

manette [manet] *f* lever, switch

manganèse [mɑ̃ganez] *m* manganese

mangeable [mɑ̃ʒabl] *adj* edible; barely fit to eat

mangeaille [mɑ̃ʒaj] *f* swill; (coll) grub, chow

mangeotter [mɑ̃ʒɔte] *tr* to pick at (*one's food*)

manger [mɑ̃ʒe] *m* food, e.g., **le boire et le manger** food and drink; (slang) meal ‖ §38 *tr* to eat; to eat up; to mumble (*one's words*); **manger du bout des lèvres** to nibble at ‖ *intr* to eat

mangerie [mɑ̃ʒri] *f* (coll) big meal

mange-tout [mɑ̃ʒtu] *m invar* sugar pea

man·geur [mɑ̃ʒœr] **-geuse** [ʒøz] *mf* eater; wastrel, spendthrift; **mangeur d'hommes** man-eater

mangouste [mɑ̃gust] *f* mongoose

maniable [manjabl] *adj* maneuverable, easy to handle, supple

maniaque [manjak] *adj & mf* maniac

manie [mani] *f* mania

maniement [manimɑ̃] *m* handling

manier [manje] *tr* to handle ‖ *ref* (coll) to get a move on

manière [manjer] *f* manner; **à la ma-**

nière de in the manner of; **de manière à** so as to; **de manière que** so that; **de toute manière** in any case; **d'une manière ou d'une autre** one way or another; **en aucune manière** by no means; **faire des manières** to pretend to be indifferent, to want to be coaxed; **manière de voir** point of view; **manières** manners

manié·ré -rée [manjere] *adj* mannered, affected

maniérisme [manjerism] *m* mannerism

ma·nieur [manjœr] **-nieuse** [njøz] *mf* handler; **grand manieur d'argent** tycoon

manifes·tant [manifestɑ̃] **-tante** [tɑ̃t] *mf* demonstrator

manifestation [manifestasjɔ̃] *f* demonstration, manifestation

manifeste [manifest] *adj* manifest ‖ *m* manifesto; (naut) manifest

manifester [manifeste] *tr* to manifest ‖ *intr* to demonstrate ‖ *ref* to reveal oneself

manigance [manigɑ̃s] *f* trick, intrigue

manipuler [manipyle] *tr* to manipulate; to handle (*e.g., packages*); to arrange (*equipment*) for an experiment

manitou [manitu] *m* manitou; (coll) bigwig

manivelle [manivel] *f* crank

manne [man] *f* manna

mannequin [mankɛ̃] *m* mannequin; scarecrow

manœuvre [manœvr] *m* hand, laborer ‖ *f* maneuver; (naut) handling, maneuvering; (rr) shifting; **fausse manœuvre** wrong move; **manœuvres** rigging

manœuvrer [manœvre] *tr & intr* to maneuver; (rr) to shift

manoir [manwar] *m* manor, manor house

man·quant [mɑ̃kɑ̃] **-quante** [kɑ̃t] *adj* missing ‖ *mf* absentee ‖ *m* missing article; **manquants** shortages

manque [mɑ̃k] *m* lack; shortage; insufficiency; **manque à gagner** lost opportunity; **manque de parole** breach of faith; **par manque de** for lack of ‖ *f*—**à la manque** (coll) rotten, poor, dud

man·qué -quée [mɑ̃ke] *adj* missed, unsuccessful; broken (*engagement*); (with abilities which were not professionally developed), e.g., **le docteur est un cuisinier manqué** the doctor could have been a cook by profession

manquement [mɑ̃kmɑ̃] *m* breach, lapse

manquer [mɑ̃ke] *tr* to miss; to flunk ‖ *intr* to misfire; to be missing, e.g., **il en manque trois** three are missing; to be missed, e.g., **vous lui manquez beaucoup** you are very much missed by him, he misses you very much; to be short, e.g., **il lui manque cinq francs** he is five francs short; **manquer à** to break (*one's word*); to disobey (*an order*); to fail to observe (*a rule*); to fail, e.g., **le cœur lui a manqué** his heart failed him; **manquer de** to lack, to be short of, to run out of; **manquer de** + *inf* to nearly + *inf*, e.g., **il a manqué de se noyer** he nearly drowned; **sans manquer** without fail ‖ *ref* to miss each other; to fail

mansarde [mɑ̃sard] *f* mansard roof; mansard

manse [mɑ̃s] *m & f* (hist) small manor

mante [mɑ̃t] *f* mantle; **mante religieuse** (ent) praying mantis

man·teau [mɑ̃to] *m* (*pl* **-teaux**) overcoat; mantle, cloak; mantelpiece; **sous le manteau** sub rosa

mantille [mɑ̃tij] *f* mantilla

manucure [manykyr] *mf* manicurist

ma·nuel -nuelle [manɥɛl] *adj* manual ‖ *mf* laborer, blue-collar worker ‖ *m* manual, handbook

manufacture [manyfaktyr] *f* factory, plant

manufacturer [manyfaktyre] *tr* to manufacture

manus·crit [manyskri] **-crite** [krit] *adj & m* manuscript

manutention [manytɑ̃sjɔ̃] *f* handling (*of merchandise*)

manutentionner [manytɑ̃sjɔne] *tr* to handle (*merchandise*)

mappemonde [mapmɔ̃d] *f* world map; **mappemonde céleste** map of the heavens

maque·reau [makro] **-relle** [rɛl] (*pl* **-reaux -relles**) *mf* (slang) procurer ‖ *m* mackerel; (slang) pimp ‖ *f* (slang) madam (*of a brothel*)

maquette [makɛt] *f* maquette, model; dummy (*of book*); rough sketch

maquignon [makiɲɔ̃] *m* horse trader; wholesale cattle dealer; (coll) go-between

maquignonnage [makiɲɔnaʒ] *m* horse trading

maquignonner [makiɲɔne] *intr* to horse-trade

maquillage [makijaʒ] *m* make-up; fakery

maquiller [makije] *tr* to make up; to fake, to distort ‖ *ref* to make up

maquil·leur [makijœr] **maquil·leuse** [makijøz] *mf* make-up artist ‖ *m* make-up man

maquis [maki] *m* bush; maquis; **prendre le maquis** to go underground

maraî·cher [marɛʃe] **-chère** [ʃɛr] *adj* truck-farming ‖ *mf* truck farmer

marais [marɛ] *m* marsh; truck farm; **marais salant** saltern

marasme [marasm] *m* depression; doldrums, standstill

marathon [maratɔ̃] *m* marathon

marâtre [marɑtr] *f* stepmother; cruel mother

maraude [marod] *f* marauding; **en maraude** cruising (*taxi*)

marauder [marode] *intr* to maraud; to cruise (*said of taxi*)

marau·deur [marodœr] **-deuse** [døz] *adj* marauding ‖ *mf* marauder

marbre [marbr] *m* marble; (typ) stone

marbrer [marbre] *tr* to marble; to mottle, vein; to bruise, blotch

marc [mar] *m* mark (*old coin*); marc, pulp; **marc de café** coffee grounds;

marc de thé tea leaves ‖ [mark] (*cap*) *m* Mark

marcassin [markasɛ̃] *m* young wild boar

mar·chand [marʃɑ̃] **-chande** [ʃɑ̃d] *adj* marketable; sale (*value*); trading (*center*); wholesale (*price*); merchant (*marine*) ‖ *mf* merchant; **marchand ambulant** peddler; **marchand de canons** munitions maker; **marchand de couleurs** paint dealer, dealer in household articles; **marchand de ferraille** junk dealer; **marchand de journaux** newsdealer; **marchand des quatre-saisons** fruit vendor; **marchand en gros** wholesaler; **marchand forain** hawker ‖ *f*—**marchande d'amour** or **de plaisir** prostitute

marchandage [marʃɑ̃daʒ] *m* bargaining; haggling; deal, underhanded arrangement

marchander [marʃɑ̃de] *tr* to bargain over; to haggle over; to be stingy with (e.g., *one's compliments*) ‖ *intr* to haggle

marchan·deur [marʃɑ̃dœr] **-deuse** [døz] *mf* bargainer; haggler

marchandise [marʃɑ̃diz] *f* merchandise; marchandises goods

mar·chant [marʃɑ̃] **-chante** [ʃɑ̃t] *adj* marching; militant (*wing of political party*); (mil) wheeling (*flank*)

marche [marʃ] *f* march; step (*of stairway*); walking; movement; progress, course; (aut) gear; **à dix minutes de marche** ten minutes walk from here; **attention à la marche!** watch your step!; **en marche** in motion, running, operating; **faire marche arrière** to back up, to reverse; **fermer la marche** to bring up the rear; **marche funèbre** funeral march; **ouvrir la marche** to lead off the procession

marché [marʃe] *m* market; marketing, shopping; deal, bargain; **à bon marché** cheap; cheaply; **à meilleur marché** cheaper; more cheaply; **bon marché** cheapness; cheap; cheaply; **faire bon marché de** to set little store by; **faire son marché** to do the marketing; **lancer, mettre,** or **vendre sur le marché** to market; **marché noir** black market; **par-dessus le marché** into the bargain

marchepied [marʃəpje] *m* footstool; little stepladder; running board; (fig) stepping stone

marcher [marʃe] *intr* to walk; to run, operate; to march; **marcher à grands pas** to stride; **marcher au pas** to walk in step; **marcher dans l'espace** to take a space walk; **marcher sur** to tread on, to walk on; **marchez au pas** (public sign) drive slowly

mar·cheur [marʃœr] **-cheuse** [ʃøz] *mf* walker

mardi [mardi] *m* Tuesday; **mardi gras** Shrove Tuesday; Mardi gras

mare [mar] *f* pool, pond

marécage [marekaʒ] *m* marsh, swamp

maréca·geux [marekaʒø] **-geuse** [ʒøz] *adj* marshy, swampy

maré·chal [mareʃal] *m* (*pl* **-chaux**

[ʃo]) marshal; blacksmith; **maréchal des logis** artillery or cavalry sergeant
maréchale [mareʃal] f marshal's wife
maréchal-ferrant [mareʃalferɑ̃] m (pl **maréchaux-ferrants**) blacksmith, farrier
marée [mare] f tide; fresh seafood; **marée descendante** ebb tide; **marée montante** flood tide
marelle [marɛl] f hopscotch
marémo·teur [maremɔtœr] **-trice** [tris] adj tide-driven
margarine [margarin] f margarine
marge [marʒ] f margin; border, edge; leeway, room; **en marge de** on the fringe of; a footnote to; **marge bénéficiaire** margin of profit; **marge de sécurité** margin of safety
margelle [marʒɛl] f curb, edge (of well, fountain, etc.)
margeur [marʒœr] m margin stop
margi·nal -nale [marʒinal] adj (pl **-naux** [no]) marginal
margot [margo] f (coll) magpie; (coll) chatterbox; **Margot** (coll) Maggie
margotin [margotɛ̃] m kindling
margouillis [marguji] m (coll) rotten stinking mess
margou·lin [margulɛ̃] **-line** [lin] mf sharpster, shyster
marguerite [margərit] f daisy; **Marguerite** Margaret
marguillier [margije] m churchwarden
mari [mari] m husband
mariable [marjabl] adj marriageable
mariage [marjaʒ] m marriage; wedding; blend, combination
Marianne [marjan] f Marian; Marianne (symbol of the French Republic)
ma·rié -riée [marje] adj married ‖ m bridegroom; **jeunes mariés** newlyweds; **les mariés** the bride and groom ‖ f bride
marier [marje] tr to marry, join in wedlock; to marry off; to blend, harmonize ‖ ref to get married; **se marier avec** to marry
marie-salope [marisalɔp] f (pl **maries-salopes**) dredger; (slang) slut
ma·rieur [marjœr] **-rieuse** [rjøz] mf (coll) matchmaker
marihuana [mariɥana] or **marijuana** [mariʒɥana] f marijuana
ma·rin [marɛ̃] **-rine** [rin] adj marine; seagoing; sea, e.g., **brise marine** sea breeze ‖ m sailor, seaman; sailor suit ‖ f navy; seascape; **marine marchande** merchant marine
mariner [marine] tr & intr to marinate
mari·nier [marinje] **-nière** [njɛr] adj naval; petty (officer); **à la marinière** cooked in gravy with onions ‖ m waterman ‖ f blouse; (swimming) sidestroke
marionnette [marjɔnɛt] f marionette; (fig) puppet
mari·tal -tale [marital] adj (pl **-taux** [to]) of the husband
maritime [maritim] adj maritime
maritorne [maritɔrn] f slut
marivaudage [marivodaʒ] m playful flirting; sophisticated conversation
marjolaine [marʒɔlɛn] f marjoram

marlou [marlu] m (slang) pimp
marmaille [marmaj] f (coll) brats
marmelade [marməlad] f marmalade; (coll) mess
marmite [marmit] f pot, pan; (geol) pothole; (mil) shell, heavy shell; **marmite autoclave, marmite sous pression** pressure cooker; **marmite norvégienne** double boiler
marmiton [marmitɔ̃] m cook's helper
marmonner [marmɔne] tr & intr to mumble
marmot [marmo] m (coll) lad; (coll) grotesque figurine (on knocker); **croquer le marmot** (coll) to cool one's heels; **marmots** (coll) urchins, kids
marmotte [marmɔt] f woodchuck; **dormir comme une marmotte** to sleep like a log; **marmotte d'Amérique** groundhog; **marmotte de commis voyageur** traveling salesman's sample case
marmouset [marmuze] m grotesque figurine; little man
marner [marne] tr to marl
marner [marne] tr to marl
Maroc [marɔk] m—**le Maroc** Morocco
maro·cain [marɔkɛ̃] **-caine** [ken] adj Moroccan ‖ (cap) mf Moroccan
maronner [marɔne] intr (coll) to grumble
maroquin [marɔkɛ̃] m morocco leather
maroquinerie [marɔkinri] f leather goods
marotte [marɔt] f fad; whim; dummy head (of milliner); jester's staff
mar·quant [markɑ̃] **-quante** [kɑ̃t] adj remarkable, outstanding; purple (passages)
marque [mark] f mark; brand, make; hallmark; token, stamp; de marque distinguished; **marque déposée** trademark
marquer [marke] tr to mark; to brand; to score; to indicate, show ‖ intr to make a mark, to leave an impression
marqueterie [markətri], [marketri] f marquetry, inlay
mar·queur [markœr] **-queuse** [køz] mf marker ‖ m scorekeeper; scorer ‖ f (mach) stenciler
marquis [marki] m marquis
marquise [markiz] f marchioness, marquise; marquee, awning; (rr) roof (over platform)
marraine [marɛn] f godmother, sponsor; christener; **marraine de guerre** war mother
mar·rant [marɑ̃] **mar·rante** [marɑ̃t] adj (slang) sidesplitting; (slang) funny, queer
marre [mar] adv—**en avoir marre** (coll) to be fed up
marrer [mare] ref (slang) to have a good laugh
mar·ron [marɔ̃] **mar·ronne** [marɔn] adj quack (doctor); shyster (lawyer) ‖ **marron** adj invar reddish-brown, chestnut ‖ m chestnut; **marron d'Inde** horse chestnut
marronnier [marɔnje] m chestnut tree; **marronnier d'Inde** horse-chestnut tree

mars [mars] *m* March; Mars Mars

Marseille [marsɛj] *f* Marseilles

marsouin [marswɛ̃] *m* porpoise

marte [mart] *f* (zool) marten

mar·teau [marto] *m* (*pl* **-teaux**) *adj* (coll) cracked; balmy || *m* hammer; (ichth) hammerhead; **marteau de porte** knocker

marteau-pilon [martopilɔ̃] *m* (*pl* **marteaux-pilons**) drop hammer

marteler [martəle] §2 *tr* to hammer; to hammer at; **to hammer out**

Marthe [mart] *f* Martha

mar·tial -tiale [marsjal] *adj* (*pl* **-tiaux** [sjo]) martial

martinet [martinɛ] *m* triphammer; scourge, cat-o'-nine-tails; (orn) martin, swift

martin-pêcheur [martɛ̃peʃœr] *m* (*pl* **martins-pêcheurs**) (orn) kingfisher

martre [martr] *f* (zool) marten

mar·tyr -tyre [martir] *adj & mf* martyr || **martyre** *m* martyrdom

martyriser [martirize] *tr* to martyr

marxiste [marksist] *adj & mf* Marxist

maryland [marilɑ̃] *m* choice tobacco || (*cap*) *m*—**le Maryland** Maryland

mas [mɑ], [mɑs] *m* farmhouse or farm (*in Provence*)

mascarade [maskarad] *f* masquerade

mascaret [maskarɛ] *m* bore

mascaron [maskarɔ̃] *m* mask, mascaron

mascotte [maskɔt] *f* mascot

mascu·lin [maskylɛ̃] **-line** [lin] *adj & m* masculine

masque [mask] *m* mask; **masque à gaz** gas mask; **masque mortuaire** death mask

masquer [maske] *tr & ref* to mask

massacre [masakr] *m* massacre; botched job

massacrer [masakre] *tr* to massacre; to botch

massage [masaʒ] *m* massage

masse [mas] *f* mass; sledge hammer; mace; pool, common fund; (elec) ground (*e.g., of an automobile*); **masse d'air froid** cold front; **mettre à la masse** (elec) to ground; **une masse de** (coll) a lot of

massepain [maspɛ̃] *m* marzipan

masser [mase] *tr* to mass; to massage || *ref* to mass; to massage oneself

massette [masɛt] *f* sledge hammer (*of stonemason*); (bot) bulrush

mas·seur [masœr] **mas·seuse** [masøz] *mf* masseur || *m* masseuse (*instrument*)

mas·sif [masif] **mas·sive** [masiv] *adj* massive; heavyset; solid (*e.g., gold*) || *m* massif, high plateau; clump (*of flowers, trees, etc.*)

massue [masy] *f* club, bludgeon

mastic [mastik] *m* putty

mastiquer [mastike] *tr* to masticate; to putty

mastoc [mastɔk] *adj invar* heavy, massive

masturber [mastyrbe] *tr & ref* to masturbate

m'as-tu-vu -vue [matyvy] (*pl* **-vu -vue**) *adj* (coll) stuck-up || *mf* (coll) show-

off, smart aleck; (coll) bragging actor

masure [mazyr] *f* hovel, shack, shanty

mat mate [mat] *adj* dull, flat || **mat** *adj invar* checkmated || *m* checkmate || **mat** *adv* dull

mât [mɑ] *m* mast; pole

matamore [matamɔr] *m* braggart

match [matʃ] *m* match, contest, game

matelas [matla] *m* mattress; (coll) roll (*of bills*)

matelasser [matlase] *tr* to pad, to cushion

matelot [matlo] *m* sailor, seaman

matelote [matlɔt] *f* fish stew in wine

mater [mate] *tr* to dull; to checkmate; to subdue

matérialiser [materjalize] *ref* to materialize

matérialiste [materjalist] *adj* materialistic || *mf* materialist

maté·riau [materjo] *m* (*pl* **-riaux**) material

maté·riel -rielle [materjɛl] *adj* material; materialistic || *m* material; equipment; (mil) matériel; **matériel roulant** (rr) rolling stock || *f* (slang) living

mater·nel -nelle [matɛrnɛl] *adj* maternal || *f* nursery school

maternité [matɛrnite] *f* maternity; maternity hospital

math or **maths** [mat] *fpl* (coll) math

mathémati·cien [matematisjɛ̃] **-cienne** [sjɛn] *mf* mathematician

mathématique [matematik] *adj* mathematical || **mathématiques** *fpl* mathematics

matière [matjɛr] *f* matter; subject matter; material; **matière première** raw material

matin [matɛ̃] *m* morning; early part of the morning; **au petit matin** in the wee hours of the morning; **de bon matin, de grand matin** very early; **du matin** in the morning, A.M., e.g., **onze heures du matin** eleven o'clock in the morning, eleven A.M. || *adv* early

mâ·tin [matɛ̃] **-tine** [tin] *mf* (coll) sly one || *m* (zool) mastiff || **mâtin** *adv* indeed!, well I'll be!

mati·nal -nale [matinal] *adj* (*pl* **-naux** [no]) morning; early-rising

mâti·né -née [matine] *adj* crossbred; **mâtiné de** mixed with, crossbred with

matinée [matine] *f* morning; matinée; **faire la grasse matinée** to sleep late

mâtiner [matine] *tr* to crossbreed

matines [matin] *fpl* matins

matité [matite] *f* dullness

ma·tois -toise [matwa] [twaz] *adj* sly, cunning || *mf* sly dog

matou [matu] *m* tomcat

matraque [matrak] *f* bludgeon; club, billy

matraquer [matrake] *tr* to club, bludgeon

matriarcat [matrijarka] *m* matriarchy

matrice [matris] *f* matrix

matricide [matrisid] *mf* matricide (*person*) || *m* matricide (*action*)

matricule [matrikyl] *adj* serial (*num-

ber) || *m* serial number || *f* roll, register

matrimo‧nial -niale [matrimɔnjal] *adj* (*pl* **-niaux** [njo]) matrimonial, marital

matrone [matrɔn] *f* matron; matriarch; old hag; midwife; abortionist

mâture [matyr] *f* masts (*of ship*)

maudire [modir] §39 *tr* to curse, to damn

mau‧dit [modi] **-dite** [dit] *adj* cursed

maugréer [mogree] *intr* to grumble, gripe

maure [mɔr] *adj* Moorish || (*cap*) *m* Moor

mauresque [mɔresk] *adj* Moorish || (*cap*) *f* Moorish woman

mausolée [mozɔle] *m* mausoleum

maussade [mosad] *adj* sullen, gloomy

mau‧vais [mɔve], [move] **-vaise** [vez] *adj* §91 bad; evil; wrong; **il fait mauvais** the weather is bad; **sentir mauvais** to smell bad || *mf* wicked person; **le Mauvais** the Evil One || *m* evil

mauve [mov] *adj* mauve || *f* (bot) mallow

mauviette [movjet] *f* (orn) lark; (coll) milquetoast

mauvis [movi] *m* (orn) redwing

maxillaire [maksiller] *m* jawbone

maxime [maksim] *f* maxim

maximum [maksimɔm] *adj* & *m* maximum

mayonnaise [majɔnez] *f* mayonnaise

mazette [mazet] *f* duffer || *interj* gosh!

mazout [mazut] *m* fuel oil

mazouter [mazute] *intr* to fuel up

Me *abbr* (**Maître**) Mr.

me [mə] §87

méandre [meɑ̃dr] *m* meander

mec [mek] *m* (slang) guy; (slang) tough egg

mécanicien [mekanisjɛ̃] *m* mechanic; machinist; engineer (*of locomotive*)

mécanicienne [mekanisjen] *f* sewing-machine operator

mécanique [mekanik] *adj* mechanical || *f* mechanism; mechanics

mécaniser [mekanize] *tr* to mechanize

mécanisme [mekanism] *m* mechanism

mécano [mekano] *m* (coll) mechanic

mécène [mesen] *m* patron, Maecenas

méchanceté [meʃɑ̃ste] *f* malice, wickedness; nastiness

mé‧chant [meʃɑ̃] **-chante** [ʃɑ̃t] *adj* malicious, wicked; nasty; naughty (*child*) || *mf* mean person; **faire le méchant** to threaten; (coll) to strike back; **les méchants** the wicked; **méchant!** naughty boy!

mèche [meʃ] *f* wick; fuse; lock (*of hair*); bit (*of drill*); **être de mèche avec** (coll) to be in cahoots with; **éventer** or **découvrir la mèche** to discover the plot; **il n'y a pas mèche** (coll) it's no go, nothing doing; **vendre la mèche** (coll) to let the cat out of the bag

mécompte [mekɔ̃t] *m* miscalculation; disappointment

méconnaissable [mekɔnesabl] *adj* unrecognizable

méconnaître [mekɔnetr] §12 *tr* to ignore; to underestimate

mécon‧nu -nue [mekɔny] *adj* underestimated, misunderstood

mécon‧tent [mekɔtɑ̃] **-tente** [tɑ̃t] *adj* dissatisfied, displeased || *mf* grumbler

mécontentement [mekɔ̃tɑ̃tmɑ̃] *m* dissatisfaction, displeasure

mécontenter [mekɔ̃tɑ̃te] *tr* to displease

Mecque [mek] *f*—**La Mecque** Mecca

mécréant [mekreɑ̃] **mécréante** [mekreɑ̃t] *adj* unbelieving || *mf* unbeliever

médaille [medaj] *f* medal

médaillon [medajɔ̃] *m* medallion; locket; thin round slice (*e.g., of meat*); pat (*of butter*)

médecin [medsɛ̃], [metsɛ̃] *m* doctor; **femme médecin** woman doctor

médecine [medsin], [metsin] *f* medicine (*science and art*)

mé‧dian [medjɑ̃] **-diane** [djan] *adj* & *f* median

média‧teur [medjatœr] **-trice** [tris] *mf* mediator

médiation [medjɑsjɔ̃] *f* mediation

médi‧cal -cale [medikal] *adj* (*pl* **-caux** [ko]) medical

médicament [medikamɑ̃] *m* (pharm) medicine

médicamenter [medikamɑ̃te] *tr* to dose

médicamen‧teux [medikamɑ̃tø] **-teuse** [tøz] *adj* medicinal

médici‧nal -nale [medisinal] *adj* (*pl* **-naux** [no]) medicinal

médié‧val -vale [medjeval] *adj* (*pl* **-vaux** [vo]) medieval

médiéviste [medjevist] *mf* medievalist

médiocre [medjɔkr] *adj* mediocre, poor; average

médiocrité [medjɔkrite] *f* mediocrity

médire [medir] §40 *intr* to backbite; **médire de** to run down, to disparage

médisance [medizɑ̃s] *f* disparagement, backbiting

médi‧sant [medizɑ̃] **-sante** [zɑ̃t] *adj* disparaging, backbiting || *mf* slanderer

méditation [meditɑsjɔ̃] *f* meditation

méditer [medite] *tr* & *intr* to meditate

méditerra‧né -née [mediterane] *adj* Mediterranean; inland || (*cap*) *f* Mediterranean (Sea)

méditerranéen [mediteraneɛ̃] **méditerranéenne** [mediteraneen] *adj* Mediterranean

médium [medjɔm] *m* medium (*in spiritualism*); range (*of voice*)

médiumnique [medjɔmnik] *adj* psychic

médius [medjys] *m* middle finger

méduse [medyz] *f* jellyfish, medusa || (*cap*) *f* Medusa

méduser [medyze] *tr* to petrify (*with terror*)

meeting [mitiŋ] *m* rally, meet, meeting

méfait [mefe] *m* misdeed; **méfaits** ravages

méfiance [mefjɑ̃s] *f* mistrust

mé‧fiant [mefjɑ̃] **-fiante** [fjɑ̃t] *adj* mistrustful

méfier [mefje] *ref* to beware; **se méfier de** to guard against, to mistrust

mégacycle [megasikl] *m* megacycle

mégaphone [megafɔn] *m* megaphone

mégarde [megard] *f*—**par mégarde** inadvertently

mégère [meʒer] *f* shrew

mégohm [megom] *m* megohm

mégot [mego] *m* butt (*of cigarette or cigar*)

meil·leur -leure [mejœr] §91 *adj comp & super* better; best; **meilleur marché** cheaper

mélancolie [melɑ̃kɔli] *f* melancholy, melancholia

mélancolique [melɑ̃kɔlik] *adj* melancholy

mélange [melɑ̃ʒ] *m* mixing, blending; mixture, blend

mélanger [melɑ̃ʒe] §38 *tr* to mix, to blend

mélan·geur -geuse [melɑ̃ʒœr] [ʒøz] *m & f* mixer

mélasse [melas] *f* molasses; **dans la mélasse** (coll) in the soup

mê·lé -lée [mele] *adj* mixed ‖ *f* melee

mêler [mele] *tr* to mix; to tangle; to shuffle (*the cards*) ‖ *ref* to mix; **se mêler à** to mingle with; to join in; **se mêler de** to meddle with, to interfere with

mélèze [melez] *m* (bot) larch

mélodie [melɔdi] *f* melody

mélo·dieux [melɔdjø] **-dieuse** [djøz] *adj* melodious

mélodique [melɔdik] *adj* melodic

mélodramatique [melɔdramatik] *adj* melodramatic

mélomane [melɔman] *adj* music-loving ‖ *mf* music lover

melon [məlɔ̃] *m* melon; derby; **melon d'eau** watermelon

mélopée [melɔpe] *f* singsong, chant

membrane [mɑ̃bran] *f* membrane; **membrane vibrante** (elec) diaphragm

membre [mɑ̃br] *m* member; limb, member; **membre de phrase** clause

membrure [mɑ̃bryr] *f* frame, limbs

même [mem] *adj indef* very, e.g., **le jour même** on that very day ‖ (when standing before noun) *adj indef* same, e.g., **en même temps** at the same time ‖ *pron indef* same, same one; **à même de** + *inf* up to + *ger*, in a position to + *inf*; **à même le** (la, etc.) straight out of the (*e.g., bottle*); flush with the (*e.g., pavement*); next to one's (*e.g., skin*); on the bare (*ground, sand, etc.*); **cela revient au même** that amounts to the same thing; **de même** likewise; **de même que** in the same way as; **tout de même** nevertheless ‖ *adv* even; **même quand** even when; **même si** even if **-même** [mem] §86

mémento [memɛ̃to] *m* memento; memo book

mémère [memer] *f* (coll) granny; (coll) blowsy dame

mémoire [memwar] *m* memorandum; statement, account; term paper; treatise; petition; **mémoires** memoirs ‖ *f* memory; **de mémoire** from memory; **de mémoire d'homme** within memory; **pour mémoire** for the record

mémorandum [memɔrɑ̃dɔm] *m* memorandum; **mémorandum de combat** battle orders

mémo·rial [memɔrjal] *m* (*pl* **-riaux** [rjo]) memorial; (dipl) memorandum; memoirs

menace [mənas] *f* menace, threat

menacer [mənase] §51 *tr & intr* to menace, to threaten

ménage [menaʒ] *m* household; family; married couple; furniture; **de ménage** homemade; **faire bon ménage** to get along well; **faire des ménages** to do housework (*for hire*); **faire le ménage** to do the housework; **se mettre en ménage** to set up housekeeping; (coll) to live together (*without being married*)

ménagement [menaʒmɑ̃] *m* discretion; consideration

ména·ger [menaʒe] **-gère** [ʒer] *adj* household; **ménager de** thrifty with ‖ *f* housewife, homemaker; silverware; silverware case ‖ **ménager** §38 *tr* to be careful with, to spare; to save (*money; one's strength*); to husband (*one's resources, one's strength*); to be considerate of, to handle with kid gloves; to arrange, to bring about; to install, to provide; to make (*e.g., a hole*) ‖ *intr* to save ‖ *ref* to take good care of oneself

ménagerie [menaʒri] *f* menagerie

men·diant [mɑ̃djɑ̃] **-diante** [djɑ̃t] *adj & mf* beggar; **des mendiants** dessert (*of dried fruits and nuts*)

mendier [mɑ̃dje] *tr & intr* to beg

menées [məne] *fpl* intrigues, schemes

mener [məne] §2 *tr* to lead; to take; to manage; to draw (*e.g., a line*) ‖ *intr* to lead

ménestrel [menestrel] *m* wandering minstrel

ménétrier [menetrije] *m* fiddler

me·neur [mənœr] **-neuse** [nøz] *mf* leader; ringleader; **meneur de jeu** master of ceremonies; narrator; moving spirit

menotte [mənɔt] *f* tiny hand; **menottes** handcuffs; **mettre** or **passer les menottes à** to handcuff

mensonge [mɑ̃sɔ̃ʒ] *m* lie; **pieux mensonge** white lie

menson·ger [mɑ̃sɔ̃ʒe] **-gère** [ʒer] *adj* lying, false; illusory, deceptive

menstrues [mɑ̃stry] *fpl* menses

mensualité [mɑ̃sɥalite] *f* monthly installment; monthly salary

men·suel -suelle [mɑ̃sɥel] *adj* monthly

men·tal -tale [mɑ̃tal] *adj* (*pl* **-taux** [to]) mental

mentalité [mɑ̃talite] *f* mentality

men·teur [mɑ̃tœr] **-teuse** [tøz] *adj* lying ‖ *mf* liar

menthe [mɑ̃t] *f* mint; **menthe poivrée** peppermint; **menthe verte** spearmint

mention [mɑ̃sjɔ̃] *f* mention; **avec mention** with honors; **biffer les mentions inutiles** to cross out the questions which do not apply; **être reçu sans mention** to receive just a passing grade

mentionner [mɑ̃sjɔne] *tr* to mention

mentir [mãtir] §41 *intr* to lie

menton [mãtɔ̃] *m* chin

mentonnière [mãtɔnjɛr] *f* chin rest; chin strap

me•nu -nue [məny] *adj* small, little; tiny, fine ‖ *m* menu; minute detail

menuet [mənɥɛ] *m* minuet

menuiserie [mənɥizri] *f* carpentry; woodwork

menuisier [mənɥizje] *m* carpenter

méprendre [meprãdr] §56 *ref* to be mistaken; **à s'y méprendre** enough to take one for the other; **il n'y a pas à s'y méprendre** there's no mistake about it

mépris [mepri] *m* contempt, scorn

méprisable [meprizabl] *adj* contemptible, despicable

mépri•sant -sante [meprizã] -**sante** [zãt] *adj* contemptuous, scornful

méprise [mepriz] *f* mistake

mépriser [meprize] *tr* to despise, scorn

mer [mɛr] *f* sea; **basse mer** low tide; **de haute mer** seagoing; **haute mer, pleine mer** high seas; high tide; **mer des Indes** Indian Ocean; **sur mer** afloat

mercanti [mɛrkãti] *m* profiteer

mercantile [mɛrkãtil] *adj* profiteering, mercenary

mercenaire [mɛrsənɛr] *adj & mf* mercenary

mercerie [mɛrsəri] *f* notions

merci [mɛrsi] *m* thanks, thank you; **merci de** + *inf* thank you for + *ger*; **merci de** or **pour** thank you for ‖ *f*— **à la merci de** at the mercy of; **Dieu merci!** thank heavens! ‖ *interj* thanks!, thank you!; no thanks!, no thank you!

mercredi [mɛrkrədi] *m* Wednesday; **mercredi des Cendres** Ash Wednesday

mercure [mɛrkyr] *m* mercury

mercuriale [mɛrkyrjal] *f* reprimand; market quotations; mercury (*weed*)

merde [mɛrd] *f* excrement; **merde alors!** (coll) well I'll be!

mère [mɛr] *f* mother; **la mère Gigogne** the old woman who lived in a shoe

méri•dien [meridjɛ̃] -**dienne** [djɛn] *adj & m* meridian ‖ *f* meridian line; couch, sofa; siesta

méridio•nal -nale [meridjɔnal] (*pl* -**naux** [no]) *adj* meridional, southern ‖ (*cap*) *mf* inhabitant of the Midi

meringue [mərɛ̃g] *f* meringue

merise [məriz] *f* wild cherry

merisier [mərizje] *m* wild cherry (tree)

méri•tant -tante [meritã] -**tante** [tãt] *adj* deserving, worthy

mérite [merit] *m* merit

mériter [merite] *tr* to merit, to deserve; to win, earn ‖ *intr*—**mériter bien de** to deserve the gratitude of

méritoire [meritwar] *adj* deserving, meritorious

merlan [mɛrlã] *m* (ichth) whiting

merle [mɛrl] *m* (orn) blackbird; **merle blanc** (fig) rara avis; **vilain merle** (fig) dirty dog

merlin [mɛrlɛ̃] *m* ax; poleax; (naut) marline

merluche [mɛrlyʃ] *f* (ichth) hake, cod

merveille [mɛrvɛj] *f* marvel, wonder; **à merveille** marvelously, wonderfully

merveil•leux [mɛrvɛjø] **merveil•leuse** [mɛrvɛjøz] *adj* marvelous, wonderful

mes [me] §88

mésalliance [mezaljãs] *f* misalliance, mismatch

mésallier [mezalje] *tr* to misally ‖ *ref* to marry beneath one's station

mésange [mezãʒ] *f* (orn) chickadee, titmouse

mésaventure [mezavãtyr] *f* misadventure

mésentente [mezãtãt] *f* misunderstanding

mésestimer [mezestime] *tr* to underestimate

mésintelligence [mezɛ̃teliʒãs] *f* misunderstanding, discord

mes•quin [mɛskɛ̃] -**quine** [kin] *adj* mean; stingy; petty

mess [mes] *m* officer's mess

message [mesaʒ] *m* message

messa•ger [mesaʒe] -**gère** [ʒɛr] *mf* messenger

messagerie [mesaʒri] *f* express; **messageries** express company

messe [mes] *f* (eccl) Mass; **dire** or **faire des messes basses** (coll) to speak in an undertone; **messe basse, petite messe** Low Mass; **première messe, messe du début** early Mass

Messie [mesi] *m* Messiah

messieurs-dames [mesjødam] *interj* ladies and gentlemen!

mesure [məzyr] *f* measure; measurement; (mus, poetic) measure; **à mesure** successively, one by one; **à mesure que** as; according as, proportionately as; **battre la mesure** to keep time; **dans une certaine mesure** to a certain extent; **être en mesure de** to be in a position to; **faire sur mesure** to make (*clothing*) to order; (fig) to tailormake; **mesure de circonstance** emergency measure; **mesure en ruban** tape measure; **prendre des mesures de** to take measures to; **prendre la mesure de** to size up; **prendre les mesures de** to measure

mesurer [məzyre] *tr* to measure; to measure off or out ‖ *ref* to measure; **se mesurer avec** to measure swords with

métairie [meteri] *f* farm (*of a sharecropper*)

mé•tal [metal] *m* (*pl* -**taux** [to]) metal

métallique [metalik] *adj* metallic

métalloïde [metalɔid] *m* nonmetal

métallurgie [metalyrʒi] *f* metallurgy

métamorphose [metamɔrfoz] *f* metamorphosis

métaphore [metafɔr] *f* metaphor

métaphorique [metafɔrik] *adj* metaphorical

métathèse [metatez] *f* metathesis

métayage [metejaʒ] *m* sharecropping, tenant farming

métayer [meteje] **métayère** [metejer] *mf* sharecropper

méteil [metɛj] *m* wheat and rye

météo [meteo] *adj invar* meteorological || *m* weatherman || *f* meteorology; weather bureau; weather report

météore [meteɔr] *m* meteor (*atmospheric phenomenon*)

météorite [meteɔrit] *m & f* meteorite

météorologie [meteɔrɔlɔʒi] *f* meteorology; weather bureau; weather report

métèque [metɛk] *m* (pej) foreigner

méthane [metan] *m* methane

méthode [metɔd] *f* method

méthodique [metɔdik] *adj* methodic(al)

méthodiste [metɔdist] *adj & mf* Methodist

méticu·leux [metikylø] **-leuse** [løz] *adj* meticulous

métier [metje] *m* trade, craft; loom; **faites votre métier!** mind your own business!; **sur le métier** on the stocks

mé·tis -tisse [metis] *adj & mf* half-breed

métisser [metise] *tr* to crossbreed

métrage [metraʒ] *m* length in meters; length (*of remnant, film, etc.*); (mov) length of film in meters (*in English: footage, i.e., length of film in feet*); **court métrage** (mov) short subject, short; **long métrage** (mov) full-length movie, feature

mètre [mɛtr] *m* meter; **mètre à ruban** tape measure; **mètre pliant** folding rule

métrer [metre] §10 *tr* to measure out by the meter

métrique [metrik] *adj* metric(al) || *f* metrics

métro [metro] *m* subway

métronome [metrɔnɔm] *m* metronome

métropole [metrɔpɔl] *f* metropolis; mother country

métropoli·tain [metrɔpɔlitɛ̃] **-taine** [tɛn] *adj* metropolitan || *m* subway; (eccl) metropolitan

mets [mɛ] *m* dish, food

mettable [metabl] *adj* wearable

met·teur [metœr] **met·teuse** [metøz] *mf* **metteur au point** mechanic; **metteur en œuvre** setter; (fig) promoter; **metteur en ondes** (rad) director, producer; **metteur en pages** (typ) make-up man; **metteur en scène** (mov, theat) director, producer

mettre [metr] §42 *tr* to put, lay, place; to put on (*clothes*); to set (*the table*); to take (*time*); **mettre à feu** (rok) to fire; **mettre au point** to carry out, complete; to tune up, adjust; (opt) to focus; (rad) to tune; **mettre au rancart** to pigeonhole; **mettre en accusation** to indict; **mettre en marche** to start; **mettre en œuvre** to put into action; **mettre en valeur** to develop, improve; to set off, enhance; **mettre en vigueur** to enforce; **mettre feu à** to set fire to; **mettre que** (coll) to suppose that || *intr*—**mettre bas** (zool) to litter || *ref* to sit or stand; to go; **se mettre à** to begin to; **se mettre à table** to sit down to eat; (slang) to confess; **se mettre en colère** to get angry; **se mettre en route** to set out; **se mettre mal avec** to quarrel with

meuble [mœbl] *adj* uncemented; loose (*ground*); personal (*property*) || *m* piece of furniture; **meubles furniture; meubles d'occasion** secondhand furniture

meubler [mœble] *tr* to furnish

meuglement [møgləmɑ̃] *m* lowing (*of cow*)

meugler [møgle] *intr* to low

meule [møl] *f* millstone; grindstone; stack (*e.g., of hay*)

meuler [møle] *tr* to grind

meu·nier [mønje] **-nière** [njɛr] *adj* milling (*e.g., industry*) || *m* miller || *f* miller's wife; **à la meunière** sautéed in butter

meurt-de-faim [mœrdəfɛ̃] *mf invar* starveling; **de meurt-de-faim** starvation (*wages*)

meurtre [mœrtr] *m* manslaughter; (fig) shame, crime; **meurtre commis avec préméditation** murder

meur·trier [mœrtrije] **-trière** [trijɛr] *adj* murderous, deadly || *m* murderer || *f* murderess; gun slit, loophole

meurtrir [mœrtrir] *tr* to bruise

meute [møt] *f* pack, band

mévente [mevɑ̃t] *f* slump (*in sales*)

mexi·cain [meksikɛ̃] **-caine** [kɛn] *adj* Mexican || *f* (cap) *mf* Mexican

Mexico [meksiko] Mexico City

Mexique [meksik] *m*—**le Mexique** Mexico

mezzanine [medzanin] *m & f* (theat) mezzanine || *f* mezzanine; mezzanine window

miaou [mjau] *m* meow

miaulement [mjolmɑ̃] *m* meow; caterwauling; catcall

miauler [mjole] *intr* to meow

mi-bas [miba] *m invar* half hose

mica [mika] *m* mica

miche [miʃ] *f* round loaf of bread

mi-chemin [miʃmɛ̃] *m*—**à mi-chemin** halfway

mi-clos [miklo] **-close** [kloz] *adj* (*pl* **-clos -closes**) half-shut

micmac [mikmak] *m* (coll) underhand dealing

mi-corps [mikɔr] *m*—**à mi-corps** to the waist

mi-côte [mikot] *f*—**à mi-côte** halfway up the hill

microbe [mikrɔb] *m* microbe

microbicide [mikrɔbisid] *adj & m* germicide

microbiologie [mikrɔbjɔlɔʒi] *f* microbiology

microfilm [mikrɔfilm] *m* microfilm

microfilmer [mikrɔfilme] *tr* to microfilm

micro-onde [mikrɔɔ̃d] *f* (*pl* **-ondes**) microwave

microphone [mikrɔfɔn] *m* microphone

microscope [mikrɔskɔp] *m* microscope

microscopique [mikrɔskɔpik] *adj* microscopic

microsillon [mikrɔsijɔ̃] *adj & m* microgroove

midi [midi] *m* noon; south; twelve, e.g., **midi dix** ten minutes after twelve; **chercher midi à quatorze heures** (fig) to look for difficulties where there are none; **Midi** south of France

midinette [midinɛt] *f* dressmaker's assistant; working girl

mie [mi] *f* soft part, crumb; female friend; **ne . . . mie** §90 (archaic) not a crumb, not, e.g., **je n'en veux mie** I don't want any

miel [mjɛl] *m* honey

miel·leux [mjɛlø] **miel·leuse** [mjɛløz] *adj* honeyed, unctuous

mien [mjɛ̃] **mienne** [mjɛn] §89

miette [mjɛt] *f* crumb

mieux [mjø] §91 *adv comp & super* better; **aimer mieux** to prefer; **à qui mieux mieux** trying to outdo each other; **de mieux en mieux** better and better; **être mieux, aller mieux** to feel better; **tant mieux** so much the better; **valoir mieux** to be better

mieux-être [mjøzetr] *m* improved well-being

mièvre [mjɛvr] *adj* dainty, affected

mi-figue [mifig] *f*—**mi-figue mi-raisin** half one way half the other; half in jest half in earnest

mi·gnard [miɲar] **-gnarde** [ɲard] *adj* affected, mincing

mi·gnon [miɲɔ̃] **-gnonne** [ɲɔn] *adj* cute, darling || *mf* darling

mignon·net [miɲɔnɛ] **mignon·nette** [miɲɔnɛt] *adj* dainty || *f* fine lace; pepper; (bot) pink

mignoter [miɲɔte] *tr* (coll) to pet (*a child*)

migraine [migrɛn] *f* migraine; headache

migratoire [migratwar] *adj* migratory

mi-jambe [miʒɑ̃b] *f*—**à mi-jambe** up to one's knee

mijoter [miʒɔte] *tr* to simmer; (coll) to cook up, to brew || *intr* to simmer

mil [mil] *adj* one thousand, e.g., **l'an mil neuf cent soixante-six** the year one thousand nine hundred and sixty-six || *m* Indian club; millet

milan [milɑ̃] *m* (orn) kite

milice [milis] *f* militia

mi·lieu [miljø] *m* (*pl* **-lieux**) middle; milieu; **milieu de table** centerpiece

militaire [militɛr] *adj* military || *m* soldier; **le militaire** the military

mili·tant [militɑ̃] **-tante** [tɑ̃t] *adj & mf* militant

militariser [militarize] *tr* to militarize

militarisme [militarism] *m* militarism

militer [milite] *intr* to militate

mille [mil] *adj & pron* thousand || *m* thousand; mile; **mettre dans le mille** to hit the bull's-eye; **mille marin** international nautical mile

millefeuille [milfœj] *m* napoleon (*pastry*)

mille-feuille [milfœj] *f* (*pl* **-feuilles**) (bot) yarrow

millénaire [milener] *adj* millennial || *m* millennium

mille-pattes [milpat] *m invar* centipede

millésime [milezim] *m* date, vintage

millet [mijɛ] *m* millet; birdseed

milliard [miljar] *m* billion

milliardaire [miljardɛr] *mf* billionaire

millième [miljɛm] *adj, pron* (*masc, fem*) thousandth || *m* thousandth; mill (*thousandth part of a dollar*)

millier [milje] *m* thousand; about a thousand; **par milliers** by the thousands; **un millier de** a thousand

milligramme [miligram] *m* milligram

millimètre [milimɛtr] *m* millimeter

million [miljɔ̃] *m* million; **un million de** a million

millionième [miljɔnjɛm] *adj, pron* (*masc, fem*), *m* millionth

millionnaire [miljɔnɛr] *adj & m* millionaire

mime [mim] *mf* mime; mimic

mimer [mime] *tr & intr* to mime; to mimic

mimique [mimik] *adj* sign (*language*) || *f* mimicry

minable [minabl] *adj* wretched, shabby; (coll) pitiful (*performance, existence, etc.*) || *mf* unfortunate

minaret [minarɛ] *m* minaret

minauder [minode] *intr* to simper, smirk

minau·dier [minodje] **-dière** [djɛr] *adj* mincing

mince [mɛ̃s] *adj* thin, slim, slight; **mince!** or **mince alors!** golly!

mine [min] *f* mine; lead (*of pencil*); look, face; looks; (fig) mine (*of information*); **avoir bonne mine** to look well; **avoir la mine d'être** to look to be; **avoir mauvaise mine** to look badly; **faire bonne mine à** to be nice to; **faire des mines** to simper; **faire la mine à** to pout at; **faire mauvaise mine à** to be unpleasant to; **faire mine de** to make as if to

miner [mine] *tr* to mine; to undermine; to wear away

mineral [minre] *m* ore

miné·ral -rale [mineral] (*pl* **-raux** [ro]) *adj & m* mineral

minéralogie [mineralɔʒi] *f* mineralogy

mi·net [minɛ] **-nette** [nɛt] *mf* (coll) kitty, pussy; (coll) darling

mi·neur -neure [minœr] *adj & mf* minor || *m* miner

miniature [minjatyr] *f* miniature

miniaturisation [minjatyrizɑsjɔ̃] *f* miniaturization

miniaturiser [minjatyrize] *tr* to miniaturize

minijupe [miniʒyp] *f* miniskirt

mini·mal -male [minimal] *adj* (*pl* **-maux** [mo]) minimum (*temperature*)

minime [minim] *adj* tiny, derisory (*salary*)

minimiser [minimize] *tr* to minimize

minimum [minimɔm] *adj & m* minimum; **minimum vital** minimum wage

ministère [ministɛr] *m* ministry; **ministère des Affaires étrangères** Department of State

ministé·riel -rielle [ministerjɛl] *adj* ministerial

ministre [ministr] *m* minister; **ministre des Affaires étrangères** secretary of state; **premier ministre** prime minister

minium [minjəm] *m* red lead

minois [minwa] *m* (coll) pretty little face

minoritaire [minɔriter] *adj* minority

minorité [minɔrite] *f* minority

Minorque [minɔrk] *f* Minorca

minoterie [minɔtri] *f* flour mill; flour industry

minotier [minɔtje] *m* miller

minuit [minɥi] *m* midnight; twelve, e.g., **minuit et demi** twelve thirty

minuscule [minyskyl] *adj* tiny; small (*letter*) || *f* small letter

minus habens [minysabɛ̃s] *mf invar* (coll) moron, idiot

minutage [minytaʒ] *m* timing

minute [minyt] *f* minute; moment, instant; **à la minute** that very moment || *interj* (coll) just a minute!

minuter [minyte] *tr* to itemize; to time

minuterie [minytri] *f* delayed-action switch; (mach) timing mechanism

minutie [minysi] *f* minute detail; great care; **minuties** minutiae

minu·tieux [minysjø] **-tieuse** [sjøz] *adj* meticulous, thorough

mioche [mjɔʃ] *mf* (coll) brat

mi-pente [mipɑ̃t]—**à mi-pente** halfway up or halfway down

mirabilis [mirabilis] *m* (bot) marvel-of-Peru

miracle [mirakl] *m* miracle; wonder, marvel; miracle play; **crier au miracle** to go into ecstasies

miracu·leux [mirakylø] **-leuse** [løz] *adj* miraculous; wonderful, marvelous

mirador [miradɔr] *m* watchtower

mirage [miraʒ] *m* mirage

mire [mir] *f* sight (*of gun*); surveyor's pole; (telv) test pattern

mire-œufs [mirø] *m invar* candler

mirer [mire] *tr* to candle (*eggs*) || *ref* to look at oneself; to be reflected

mirifique [mirifik] *adj* (coll) marvelous

mirobo·lant [mirobɔlɑ̃] **-lante** [lɑ̃t] *adj* (coll) astounding

miroir [mirwar] *m* mirror; **miroir à alouettes** decoy

miroiter [mirwate] *intr* to sparkle, gleam; **faire miroiter q.ch. à qn** to lure s.o. with s.th.

miroton [mirotɔ̃] *m* Irish stew

misaine [mizen] *f* foresail

misanthrope [mizɑ̃trɔp] *mf* misanthrope

miscellanées [miselane], [misɛllane] *fpl* miscellany

mise [miz] *f* placing, putting; dress, attire; (cards) stake, ante; **de mise** acceptable, proper; **mise à feu** firing (*e.g., of missile*); **mise à l'eau** launching; **mise à prix** opening bid; **mise au point** carrying out, completion; tuning up, adjustment; (opt) focusing; (rad) tuning; **mise au rancart** pigeonholing; **mise bas** delivery (*of litter*); **mise de fonds** investment; **mise en accusation** indictment; **mise en demeure** (law) injunction; **mise en marche** starting; **mise en œuvre** putting into action; **mise en scène** (theat) direction; (theat & fig) staging; **mise**

en valeur development, improvement; **mise en vigueur** enforcement

miser [mize] *tr & intr* to ante; to stake, bet; to bid (*e.g., at auction*)

misérable [mizerabl] *adj* miserable || *mf* wretch

misère [mizer] *f* misery, wretchedness; poverty; worry; (coll) trifle; **crier misère** to make a poor mouth; to look forsaken; **faire des misères à** to pester

misé·reux [mizerø] **-reuse** [røz] *adj* destitute, wretched || *mf* pauper

miséricorde [mizerikɔrd] *f* mercy

miséricor·dieux [mizerikɔrdjø] **-dieuse** [djøz] *adj* merciful

missel [misel] *m* missal

missile [misil] *m* guided missile

mission [misjɔ̃] *f* mission

missionnaire [misjɔner] *adj & m* missionary

missive [misiv] *adj & f* missive

mitaine [miten] *f* mitt

mite [mit] *f* (ent) mite; (ent) clothes moth

mi·té -tée [mite] *adj* moth-eaten; (coll) shabby

mi-temps [mitɑ̃] *f invar* (sports) half time; **à mi-temps** half time

miter [mite] *ref* to become moth-eaten

mi·teux [mitø] **-teuse** [tøz] *adj* shabby || *mf* (coll) shabby-looking person

mitiger [mitiʒe] §38 *tr* to mitigate

mitonner [mitone] *tr* to simmer; to pamper; (coll) to contrive, devise || *intr* to simmer

mi·toyen [mitwajɛ̃] **mitoyenne** [mitwajen] *adj* midway, intermediate, dividing; jointly owned, common

mitraille [mitraj] *f* scrap iron; grapeshot; artillery fire

mitrailler [mitraje] *tr* to machine-gun; to pepper (*with gunfire, flash bulbs, etc.*)

mitraillette [mitrajet] *f* submachine gun, Tommy gun

mitrail·leur [mitrajœr] **mitrail·leuse** [mitrajøz] *adj* repeating, automatic (*firearm*) || *m* machine gunner || *f* machine gun

mitre [mitr] *f* miter; chimney pot

mitron [mitrɔ̃] *m* baker's boy

mi-voix [mivwa]—**à mi-voix** in a low voice, under one's breath

mixte [mikst] *adj* mixed; coeducational; composite; joint (*e.g., commission*); (rr) freight-and-passenger

mixtion [mikstjɔ̃] *f* mixing; mixture

mixture [mikstyr] *f* mixture

Mlle *abbr* (**Mademoiselle**) Miss

MM. *abbr* (**Messieurs**) Messrs.

Mme *abbr* (**Madame**) Mrs.; Mme.

mobile [mɔbil] *adj* mobile || *m* motive; (fa) mobile

mobi·lier [mɔbilje] **-lière** [ljer] *adj* personal || *m* furniture

mobilisable [mɔbilizabl] *adj* (mil) subject to call

mobilisation [mɔbilizasjɔ̃] *f* mobilization

mobiliser [mɔbilize] *tr & intr* to mobilize

mobilité [mɔbilite] *f* mobility

moche [mɔʃ] *adj* (coll) ugly; (coll) lousy

modalité [mɔdalite] *f* modality, manner, method; **modalités** terms

mode [mɔd] *m* kind, method, mode; (gram) mood; (mus) mode; **mode d'emploi** directions for use || *f* fashion; **à la mode** in style, fashionable; **à la mode de** in the manner of; **modes** fashions; millinery

modèle [mɔdel] *adj & m* model

modeler [mɔdle] §2 *tr* to model; to shape, mold || *ref*—**se modeler sur** to take as a model

modéliste [mɔdelist] *mf* model-airplane designer, etc.; dress designer

modéra·teur [mɔderatœr] **-trice** [tris] *adj* moderating || *mf* moderator; regulator; moderator (*for slowing down neutrons*); **modérateur de son** volume control

modé·ré -rée [mɔdere] *adj* moderate

modérer [mɔdere] §10 *tr & ref* to moderate

moderne [mɔdern] *adj* modern

moderniser [mɔdernize] *tr* to modernize

modeste [mɔdest] *adj* modest

modestie [mɔdesti] *f* modesty

modicité [mɔdisite] *f* paucity (*of resources*); lowness (*of price*)

modifica·teur [mɔdifikatœr] **-trice** [tris] *adj* modifying || *m* modifier

modifier [mɔdifje] *tr* to modify

modique [mɔdik] *adj* moderate, reasonable

modiste [mɔdist] *f* milliner

modulation [mɔdylɑsjɔ̃] *f* modulation; **modulation d'amplitude** amplitude modulation; **modulation de fréquence** frequency modulation

module [mɔdyl] *m* module; **module lunaire** (rok) lunar module

moduler [mɔdyle] *tr & intr* to modulate

moelle [mwal] *f* marrow; (bot) pith; **moelle épinière** spinal cord

moel·leux [mwalø] **moel·leuse** [mwaløz] *adj* soft; mellow; flowing (*brush stroke*)

moellon [mwalɔ̃] *m* building stone

mœurs [mœr], [mœrs] *fpl* customs, habits; morals

mohair [mɔer] *m* mohair

moi [mwa] §85, §87

moignon [mwaɲɔ̃] *m* stump

moi-même [mwamem] §86

moindre [mwɛ̃dr] §91 *adj comp & super* less; lesser; least, slightest

moine [mwan] *m* monk

moi·neau [mwano] *m* (*pl* -neaux) sparrow

moins [mwɛ̃] *m* less; minus; **au moins** or **du moins** at least; **(le) moins** (the) least; **moins de** fewer || *adv comp & super* §91 less; fewer; **à moins de** + *inf* without + *ger*, unless + *ind*; **à moins que** unless; **de moins en moins** less and less; **en moins de rien** in no time at all; **moins de** (followed by numeral) less than; **moins que** less than; **rien moins que** anything but ||

prep minus; to, e.g., **dix heures moins le quart** a quarter to ten

moire [mwar] *f* moire; **moire de soie** watered silk

moi·ré -rée [mware] *adj* watered (*silk*) || *m* wavy sheen

mois [mwa] *m* month

Moïse [mɔiz] *m* Moses

moi·si -sie [mwazi] *adj* moldy || *m* mold; **sentir le moisi** to have a musty smell

moisir [mwazir] *tr* to mold || *intr* to become moldy, to mold; (fig) to vegetate || *ref* to mold

moisissure [mwazisyr] *f* mold

moisson [mwasɔ̃] *f* harvest

moissonner [mwasɔne] *tr* to harvest, reap

moisson·neur [mwasɔnœr] **moisson·neuse** [mwasɔnøz] *mf* reaper || *f* (mach) reaper

moite [mwat] *adj* moist, damp; clammy

moiteur [mwatœr] *f* moistness, dampness; **moiteur froide** clamminess

moitié [mwatje] *f* half; (coll) better half (*wife*); **à moitié, la moitié** half; **à moitié chemin** halfway; **à moitié prix** at half price; **de moitié** by half || *adv* half

moka [mɔka] *m* mocha coffee; mocha cake

molaire [mɔler] *adj & f* molar

môle [mol] *m* mole, breakwater || *f* (ichth) sunfish

molécule [mɔlekyl] *f* molecule

moleskine [mɔleskin] *f* (*fabric*) moleskin; imitation leather

molester [mɔleste] *tr* to molest

moleter [mɔlte] §34 *tr* to knurl, to mill

mollas·son [mɔlasɔ̃] **mollas·sonne** [mɔlasɔn] *mf* (coll) softy

mollement [mɔlmɑ̃] *adv* flabbily; listlessly

mollesse [mɔles] *f* flabbiness, apathy; softness (*of contour*); mildness (*of climate*)

mol·let [mɔle] **mol·lette** [mɔlet] *adj* soft, downy; soft-boiled (*egg*) || *m* (anat) calf

molletière [mɔltjer] *f* puttee, legging

molleton [mɔltɔ̃] *m* flannel

mollir [mɔlir] *intr* to weaken

mollusque [mɔlysk] *m* mollusk

molosse [mɔlɔs] *m* watchdog

molybdène [mɔlibden] *m* molybdenum

môme [mom] *m* (slang) little || *mf* (coll) kid || *f* (slang) babe

moment [mɔmɑ̃] *m* moment; **à aucun moment** at no time; **à ce moment-là** then, at that time; **à tout moment, à tous moments** continually; **au moment où** just when; **c'est le moment** now is the time; **d'un moment à l'autre** at any moment; **en ce moment** now; at this moment; **par moments** now and then; **sur le moment** at the very moment; **un petit moment** a little while

momenta·né -née [mɔmɑ̃tane] *adj* momentary

momerie [mɔmri] *f* mummery

momie [mɔmi] *f* mummy

mon [mɔ̃] §88

Mon abbr (**Maison**) (com) House

mona·cal -cale [mɔnakal] adj (pl -**caux** [ko]) monastic, monkish

monachisme [mɔna/ism], [mɔnakism] m monasticism

monarchique [mɔnar/ik] adj monarchic

monarque [mɔnark] m monarch

monastère [mɔnaster] m monastery

monastique [mɔnastik] adj monastic

mon·ceau [mɔ̃so] m (pl -**ceaux**) heap, pile

mon·dain [mɔ̃dɛ̃] -**daine** [dɛn] adj worldly; social (life, functions, etc.); sophisticated ‖ mf worldly-minded person; socialite

mondanité [mɔ̃danite] f worldliness; **mondanités** social events; (journ) social news

monde [mɔ̃d] m world; people; **avoir du monde chez soi** to have company; **il y a du monde, il y a un monde fou** there is a big crowd; **le beau monde, le grand monde** high society, fashionable society; **mettre au monde** to give birth to; **tout le monde** everybody, everyone

monder [mɔ̃de] tr to hull; to blanch; to stone

mon·dial -diale [mɔ̃djal] adj (pl -**diaux** [djo]) world; world-wide

monétaire [mɔnetɛr] adj monetary

mon·gol -gole [mɔ̃gɔl] adj Mongol ‖ m Mongol (language) ‖ (cap) mf Mongol (person)

moni·teur [mɔnitœr] -**trice** [tris] mf coach, trainer, instructor; monitor (at school)

monnaie [mɔnɛ] f change, small change; money (legal tender of a country); **fausse monnaie** counterfeit money; **la Monnaie** the Mint; **monnaie forte** hard currency; **payer en monnaie de singe** to give lip service to

monnayer [mɔneje] §49 tr to mint, to coin; to convert into cash; to cash in on

monnayeur [mɔnejœr] m—**faux monnayeur** counterfeiter

monocle [mɔnɔkl] m monocle

monogamie [mɔnɔgami] f monogamy

monogramme [mɔnɔgram] m monogram

monographie [mɔnɔgrafi] f monograph

monolithique [mɔnɔlitik] adj monolithic

monologue [mɔnɔlɔg] m monologue

monologuer [mɔnɔlɔge] tr to soliloquize

monomanie [mɔnɔmani] f monomania

monôme [mɔnom] m single file (of students); (math) monomial

monoplan [mɔnɔplɑ̃] m monoplane

monopole [mɔnɔpɔl] m monopoly

monopoliser [mɔnɔpɔlize] tr to monopolize

monorail [mɔnɔraj] m monorail

monosyllabe [mɔnɔsilab] m monosyllable

monothéiste [mɔnɔteist] adj & mf monotheist

monotone [mɔnɔtɔn] adj monotonous

monotonie [mɔnɔtɔni] f monotony

monotype [mɔnɔtip] adj monotypic ‖

m monotype ‖ f Monotype (machine to set type)

monseigneur [mɔ̃seɲœr] m (pl **messeigneurs** [meseɲœr]) monseigneur

monsieur [məsjø] m (pl **messieurs** [mesjø]) gentleman; sir; mister; Mr.

monstre [mɔ̃str] adj huge, monster ‖ m monster; freak; **monstres sacrés** (fig) sacred cows, idols

mons·trueux [mɔ̃stryø] -**trueuse** [tryøz] adj monstrous

mont [mɔ̃] m mount; mountain; **par monts et par vaux** over hill and dale; **passer les monts** to cross the Alps

montage [mɔ̃taʒ] m hoisting; setting up (of a machine); (elec) hookup; (mov) cutting, editing

monta·gnard [mɔ̃taɲar] -**gnarde** [ɲard] adj mountain ‖ mf mountaineer

montagne [mɔ̃taɲ] f mountain; **montagnes russes** roller coaster

monta·gneux [mɔ̃taɲø] -**gneuse** [ɲøz] adj mountainous

mon·tant [mɔ̃tɑ̃] -**tante** [tɑ̃t] adj rising, ascending; uphill; vertical; high-necked (dress) ‖ m upright, riser; gatepost; total (sum); (culin) tang; **montants** goal posts; (slang) pair of trousers

mont-de-piété [mɔ̃dpjete] m (pl **monts-de-piété**) pawnshop

mon·té -tée [mɔ̃te] adj mounted; organized; equipped, well-provided; worked-up, angry ‖ f climb; slope

monte-charge [mɔ̃tarʒ] m invar freight elevator

monte-plats [mɔ̃tpla] m invar dumbwaiter

monter [mɔ̃te] tr to go up, to climb; to mount; to set up; to carry up, take up, bring up ‖ intr (aux: ÊTRE) to go up, to come up; to come upstairs; to rise; to come in (said of tide); **monter + inf** to go up to + inf; **monter à** or **en** to go up, to climb, to ascend; to mount; **monter sur** to mount (the throne); to go on (the stage) ‖ ref—**se monter à** to amount to; **se monter en** to lay in a supply of; **se monter la tête** to get excited

montre [mɔ̃tr] f show, display; watch; **en montre** in the window, on display; **faire montre de** to show off, to parade; **montre à remontoir** stemwinder; **montre à répétition** repeater

montre-bracelet [mɔ̃trabraslɛ] f (pl **montres-bracelets**) wrist watch

montrer [mɔ̃tre] tr to show; **montrer du doigt** to point out or at ‖ ref to appear; to show oneself to be (e.g., patient)

mon·treur [mɔ̃trœr] -**treuse** [trøz] mf showman, exhibitor

mon·tueux [mɔ̃tɥø] -**tueuse** [tɥøz] adj rolling, hilly

monture [mɔ̃tyr] f mounting; assembling; mount (e.g., horse)

monument [mɔnymɑ̃] m monument; **monument aux morts** memorial monument

moquer [mɔke] tr & ref to mock; **se moquer de** to make fun of, to laugh at

moquerie [mɔkri] f mockery
moquette [mɔket] f pile carpet
mo·ral -rale [mɔral] (pl -raux [ro])
adj moral ‖ m morale ‖ f ethics;
moral (of a fable); **faire la morale
à qn** to lecture s.o.
moralité [mɔralite] f morality; moral
(e.g., of a fable)
morasse [mɔras] f final proof (of newspaper)
moratoire [mɔratwar] m moratorium
moratorium [mɔratɔrjɔm] m moratorium
morbide [mɔrbid] adj morbid
morbleu [mɔrblø] interj (obs) zounds!
mor·ceau [mɔrso] m (pl -ceaux) piece,
bit; morsel; **bas morceaux** (culin)
cheap cuts; **en morceaux** in cubes
(of sugar); **morceaux choisis** selected
passages
morceler [mɔrsəle] §34 tr to parcel out
morcellement [mɔrselmɑ̃] m parceling
out, division
mordancer [mɔrdɑ̃se] §51 tr to size
mor·dant -dante [mɔrdɑ̃] [dɑ̃t] adj
mordant, caustic ‖ m mordant; cutting edge; fighting spirit; (mus)
mordent
mordicus [mɔrdikys] adv (coll) stoutly,
tenaciously
mordiller [mɔrdije] tr & intr to nibble;
to nip
mordo·ré -rée [mɔrdɔre] adj golden-
brown, bronze-colored
mordre [mɔrdr] tr to bite ‖ intr to bite;
mordre à to bite on; to take to, to
find easy; **mordre dans** to bite into;
mordre sur to encroach upon ‖ ref
to bite
mor·du -due [mɔrdy] adj bitten;
smitten ‖ mf (coll) fan (person)
morelle [mɔrel] f nightshade
morfondre [mɔrfɔ̃dr] tr to chill to the
bone ‖ ref to be bored waiting
morgue [mɔrg] f morgue; haughtiness
mori·caud [mɔriko] -caude [kod] adj
(coll) dark-skinned, dusky
morigéner [mɔriʒene] §10 tr to scold
morillon [mɔrijɔ̃] m rough emerald;
duck; **morillon à dos blanc** canvas-
back
mor·mon [mɔrmɔ̃] -mone [mɔn] adj
& mf Mormon
morne [mɔrn] adj dismal, gloomy ‖ m
hillock, knoll
mornifle [mɔrnifl] f (coll) slap
morose [mɔroz] adj morose
morphine [mɔrfin] f morphine
morphologie [mɔrfɔlɔʒi] f morphology
morpion [mɔrpjɔ̃] m tick-tack-toe;
(youngster) (slang) squirt; (Phthirius
pubis) (slang) crab louse
mors [mɔr] m bit; jaw (of vise)
morse [mɔrs] m Morse code; walrus
morsure [mɔrsyr] f bite
mort [mɔr] **morte** [mɔrt] adj dead;
spent (bullet); (aut) neutral ‖ mf
dead person, corpse ‖ m (bridge)
dummy; **faire le mort** to play dead
‖ **mort** f death; **attraper la mort** to
catch one's death of cold
mortadelle [mɔrtadel] f bologna

mortaise [mɔrtez] f mortise
mortaiser [mɔrteze] tr to mortise
mortalité [mɔrtalite] f mortality
mort-aux-rats [mɔrtora], [mɔrora] f
invar rat poison
mort-bois [mɔrbwa] m deadwood
morte-eau [mɔrto] f (pl **mortes-eaux**
[mɔrtezo]) low tide
mor·tel -telle [mɔrtel] adj & mf mortal
morte-saison [mɔrtəsezɔ̃] f (pl **mortes-
saisons**) off-season
mortier [mɔrtje] m mortar; round
judicial cap
mortifier [mɔrtifje] tr to mortify; to
tenderize (meat)
mort-né -née [mɔrne] (pl -nés) adj stillborn ‖ mf stillborn child
mortuaire [mɔrtyer] adj mortuary;
funeral (e.g., service); death (notice)
morue [mɔry] f cod
morve [mɔrv] f snot
mor·veux [mɔrvø] -veuse [vøz] adj
snotty ‖ mf (coll) young snot, brat,
whippersnapper
mosaïque [mɔzaik] adj mosaic; Mosaic
‖ f mosaic
Moscou [mɔsku] m Moscow
mosquée [mɔske] f mosque
mot [mo] m word; answer (to riddle);
à mots couverts guardedly; **au bas
mot** at least; **avoir toujours le mot
pour rire** to be always cracking
jokes; **bon mot** witticism; **gros mots**
foul words; **le mot à mot** the word-
for-word translation; **mot à double
sens** double entendre; **mot de passe**
password; **mot d'ordre** slogan; **mot
pour mot** word for word; **mots croisés**
crossword puzzle; **ne . . . mot** §90
(archaic) not a word, nothing; **placer
un mot** to put in a word; **prendre qn
au mot** to take s.o. at his word; **sans
mot dire** without a word
motard [mɔtar] m (coll) motorcyclist;
(coll) motorcycle cop
mot-clé [mɔkle] m (pl **mots-clés**) key
word
motel [mɔtel] m motel
mo·teur [mɔtœr] -trice [tris] adj driving (wheel); drive (shaft); motive
(power); power (brake); motor
(nerve) ‖ m motor, engine; prime
mover; instigator; **moteur à deux
temps** two-cycle engine; **moteur à
explosion** internal-combustion engine; **moteur à quatre temps** four-
cycle engine; **moteur à réaction** jet
engine; **moteur hors bord** outboard
motor
moteur-fusée m (pl **moteurs-fusées**)
rocket engine
motif [mɔtif] m motive; (fa, mus)
motif
motion [mosjɔ̃] f (parl) motion
motiver [mɔtive] tr to motivate
moto [mɔto] f motorcycle
motoriser [mɔtɔrize] tr to motorize
mot-outil [mɔuti] m (pl **mots-outils**)
link word
mot-piège [mɔpjeʒ] m (pl **mots-pièges**)
tricky word

mots-croisés [mɔkrwaze] *mpl* cross-word puzzle

mot-souche [mosuʃ] *m* (*pl* **mots-souches**) entry word; (typ) catch-word

motte [mɔt] *f* clod, lump; slab (*of butter*); **motte de gazon** turf

motus [motys] *interj* mum's the word!

mou [mu] (or **mol** [mɔl] before vowel or mute h) **molle** [mɔl] (*pl* **mous molles**) *adj* soft; limp, flabby, slack; spineless, listless || *m* slack; lights, lungs; (coll) softy

mou·chard [muʃar] **-charde** [ʃard] *mf* (coll) stool pigeon, squealer

moucharder [muʃarde] *tr* (coll) to spy on; (coll) to squeal on || *intr* (coll) to squeal

mouche [muʃ] *f* fly; beauty spot; **faire d'une mouche un éléphant** to make a mountain out of a molehill; **faire la mouche** to fly into a rage; **faire mouche** to hit the bull's-eye; **mouche à miel** honeybee; **mouche d'Espagne** (pharm) Spanish fly; **mouche du coche** busybody

moucher [muʃe] *tr* to blow (*one's nose*); to snuff, to trim; (coll) to scold || *ref* to blow one's nose

moucherolle [muʃrɔl] *f* (orn) fly-catcher

moucheron [muʃrɔ̃] *m* gnat; snuff (*of candle*)

moucheter [muʃte] §34 *tr* to speckle

mouchoir [muʃwar] *m* handkerchief

moudre [mudr] §43 *tr* to grind

moue [mu] *f* wry face; **faire la moue** to pout

mouette [mwet] *f* gull, sea gull; **mouette rieuse** black-headed gull

mouffette [mufet] *f* skunk

moufle [mufl] *m* & *f* pulley block || *f* mitten

mouillage [mujaʒ] *m* anchorage; wetting; watering, diluting

mouil·lé-lée [muje] *adj* wet; at anchor; palatalized; liquid (*l*)

mouiller [muje] *tr* to wet; to water, dilute; to palatalize; to drop (*anchor*) || *intr* to drop anchor || *ref* to get wet; to water; (coll) to become involved

moulage [mulaʒ] *m* molding, casting; mold, cast; grinding, milling

moule [mul] *m* mold, form || *f* mussel; (slang) fleabrain; (slang) jellyfish

mouler [mule] *tr* to mold; to outline, e.g., **corsage qui moule le buste** blouse which outlines the bosom

moulin [mulɛ̃] *m* mill; **moulin à café** coffee grinder; **moulin à paroles** (coll) windbag; **moulin à vent** windmill

moulinet [muline] *m* winch; reel (*of casting rod*); turnstile; pinwheel (*child's toy*); **faire le moulinet avec** to twirl

moult [mult] *adv* (obs) much, many

mou·lu -lue [muly] *adj* ground; (coll) done in

moulure [mulyr] *f* molding

mou·rant [murɑ̃] **-rante** [rɑ̃t] *adj* dying || *mf* dying person

mourir [murir] §44 *intr* (aux: ÊTRE) to die || *ref* to be dying

mouron [murɔ̃] *m* (bot) starwort, stitchwort; (bot) pimpernel

mousquetaire [muskater] *m* musketeer

mousse [mus] *adj* dull || *m* cabin boy || *f* moss; froth, foam; lather, suds; whipped cream

mousseline [muslin] *f* muslin; **mousseline de soie** chiffon

mousser [muse] *intr* to froth, to foam; to lather; **faire mousser** (coll) to crack up, to build up; (slang) to enrage

mous·seux [musø] **mous·seuse** [musøz] *adj* mossy; frothy, foamy, sudsy; sparkling (*wine*)

mousson [musɔ̃] *f* monsoon

moustache [mustaʃ] *f* moustache; **moustaches** whiskers (*of, e.g., cat*); **moustaches en croc** handle-bar mustache

moustiquaire [mustiker] *f* mosquito net

moustique [mustik] *m* mosquito

moût [mu] *m* must; wort

moutard [mutar] *m* (slang) kid

moutarde [mutard] *f* mustard

moutier [mutje] *m* (obs) monastery

mouton [mutɔ̃] *m* sheep; mutton; (slang) stool pigeon; **doux comme un mouton** gentle as a lamb; **moutons** whitecaps; **moutons de Panurge** (fig) chameleons, yes men; **revenons à nos moutons** let's get back to our subject

mouton·né -née [mutone] *adj* fleecy; frothy (*sea*); mackerel (*sky*)

moutonner [mutone] *tr* to curl || *intr* to break into whitecaps

mouton·neux [mutonø] **mouton·neuse** [mutonøz] *adj* frothy; fleecy (*e.g., cloud*)

mouture [mutyr] *f* grinding; mixture of wheat, rye, and barley; (fig) reworking

mouvement [muvmɑ̃] *m* movement; motion; **mouvement d'horlogerie** clockwork; **mouvement d'humeur** fit of bad temper; **mouvement ondulatoire** wave motion

mouvemen·té -tée [muvmɑ̃te] *adj* lively; eventful; hilly, broken (*terrain*)

mouvementer [muvmɑ̃te] *tr* to enliven

mouvoir [muvwar] §45 *tr* to move; to set in motion, to drive || *ref* to move, stir

moyen [mwajɛ̃] **moyenne** [mwajen] *adj* average; ordinary; middle, intermediate; medium || *m* way, manner; **au moyen de** by means of; **moyens** means || *f* average; mean; passing mark; **en moyenne** on an average

moyen-âge [mwajɛnɑʒ] *m* Middle Ages

moyen-courrier [mwajɛ̃kurje] *m* (*pl* **moyens-courriers**) medium-range plane

moyennant [mwajɛnɑ̃] *prep* in exchange for || *conj* provided that

Moyen-Orient [mwajɛnɔrjɑ̃] *m* Middle East

moyeu [mwajø] *m* (*pl* **moyeux**) hub
mû mue [my] *adj* driven, propelled || *f* see **mue**
mucosité [mykozite] *f* mucus
mucus [mykys] *m* mucus
mue [my] *f* molt, shedding
muer [mɥe] *intr* to molt; to shed; (*said of voice*) to break, change
muet [mɥe] **muette** [mɥet] *adj* mute; silent; non-speaking (*rôle*); blank; dead (*key*) || *mf* mute || *m* silent movie
mufle [myfl] *m* muzzle, snout; (coll) cad, skunk
mugir [myʒir] *intr* to bellow
mugissement [myʒismɑ̃] *m* bellow
muguet [myge] *m* lily of the valley
mulâtre [mylɑtr] **-tresse** [tres] *mf* mulatto
mule [myl] *f* mule
mulet [myle] *m* mule; (ichth) mullet
mule-tier [myltje] **-tière** [tjer] *adj* mule (*e.g., trail*) || *m* muleteer
mulette [mylet] *f* fresh-water clam
mulot [mylo] *m* field mouse
multilaté-ral -rale [myltilateral] *adj* (*pl* **-raux** [ro]) multilateral
multiple [myltipl] *adj & m* multiple
multiplicité [myltiplisite] *f* multiplicity
multiplier [myltiplije] *tr & ref* to multiply
multitude [myltityd] *f* multitude
munici-pal -pale [mynisipal] *adj* (*pl* **-paux** [po]) municipal
municipalité [mynisipalite] *f* municipality; city officials; city hall
munifi-cent [mynifisɑ̃] **-cente** [sɑ̃t] *adj* munificent
munir [mynir] *tr* to provide, equip || *ref*—**se munir de** to provide oneself with
munitions [mynisjɔ̃] *fpl* munitions
mu-queux [mykø] **-queuse** [køz] *adj* mucous || *f* mucous membrane
mur [myr] *m* wall; **mettre au pied du mur** to corner; **mur de soutènement** retaining wall; **mur sonique, mur du son** sound barrier
mûr mûre [myr] *adj* ripe, mature || *f* see **mûre**
muraille [myraj] *f* wall, rampart
mu-ral -rale [myral] *adj* (*pl* **-raux** [ro]) mural
mûre [myr] *f* mulberry; blackberry
murer [myre] *tr* to wall up or in || *ref* to shut oneself up
mûrier [myrje] *m* mulberry tree
mûrir [myrir] *tr & intr* to ripen, mature
murmure [myrmyr] *m* murmur
murmurer [myrmyre] *tr & intr* to murmur
musaraigne [myzarɛɲ] *f* (zool) shrew
musarder [myzarde] *intr* to dawdle
musc [mysk] *m* musk
muscade [myskad] *f* nutmeg; **passez muscade!** presto!
muscardin [myskardɛ̃] *m* dormouse
muscat [myska] *m* muscatel
muscle [myskl] *m* muscle

mus-clé -clée [myskle] *adj* muscular; (coll) powerful (*e.g., drama*); (slang) difficult
musculaire [myskyler] *adj* muscular
muscu-leux [myskylø] **-leuse** [løz] *adj* muscular
muse [myz] *f* muse; **les Muses** the Muses
mu-seau [myzo] *m* (*pl* **-seaux**) snout; (coll) mug, face
musée [myze] *m* museum
museler [myzle] §34 *tr* to muzzle
muselière [myzəljer] *f* muzzle
muser [myze] *intr* to dawdle
musette [myzet] *f* feed bag; kit bag; haversack
muséum [myzeɔm] *m* museum of natural history
musi-cal -cale [myzikal] *adj* (*pl* **-caux** [ko]) musical
music-hall [myzikol] *m* (*pl* **-halls**) vaudeville; vaudeville house; music hall (Brit)
musi-cien [myzisjɛ̃] **-cienne** [sjen] *mf* musician
musicologie [myzikɔlɔʒi] *f* musicology
musique [myzik] *f* music; band; **toujours la même musique** (coll) the same old song
mus-qué -quée [myske] *adj* musk-scented
musul-man -mane [myzylmɑ̃] [man] *adj & mf* Mussulman
mutation [mytasjɔ̃] *f* mutation; transfer; (biol) mutation, sport
muter [myte] *tr* to transfer
muti-lé -lée [mytile] *mf* disabled veteran
mutiler [mytile] *tr* to mutilate; to deface; to disable; to garble (*e.g., the truth*)
mu-tin [mytɛ̃] **-tine** [tin] *adj* roguish || *mf* mutineer
muti-né -née [mytine] *adj* mutinous || *mf* mutineer
mutiner [mytine] *ref* to mutiny
mutualité [mytɥalite] *f* mutual insurance
mu-tuel -tuelle [mytɥel] *adj* mutual || *f* mutual benefit association
myope [mjɔp] *adj* near-sighted || *mf* near-sighted person
myriade [mirjad] *f* myriad
myrrhe [mir] *f* myrrh
myrte [mirt] *m* myrtle
myrtille [mirtij] *f* blueberry
mystère [mister] *m* mystery
mysté-rieux [misterjø] **-rieuse** [rjøz] *adj* mysterious
mysticisme [mistisism] *m* mysticism
mystification [mistifikasjɔ̃] *f* mystification; hoax
mystifier [mistifje] *tr* to mystify; to hoax
mystique [mistik] *adj & mf* mystic
mythe [mit] *m* myth
mythique [mitik] *adj* mythical
mythologie [mitɔlɔʒi] *f* mythology
mythologique [mitɔlɔʒik] *adj* mythological

N

N, n [ɛn], *[ɛn] *m invar* fourteenth letter of the French alphabet

na·bot [nabo] **-bote** [bɔt] *adj* dwarfish || *mf* dwarf, midget

nacelle [nasɛl] *f* (aer) nacelle; (naut) wherry, skiff; (fig) boat

nacre [nakr] *f* mother-of-pearl

na·cré -crée [nakre] *adj* pearly

nage [naʒ] *f* swimming; rowing, paddling; **être (tout) en nage** to be wet with sweat; **nage à la pagaie** paddling; **nage de côté** sidestroke; **nage en couple** sculling; **nage en grenouille** breaststroke

nagée [naʒe] *f* swimming stroke

nageoire [naʒwar] *f* fin; flipper (*of seal*); float (*for swimmers*)

nager [naʒe] §38 *intr* to swim; to float; to row; **nager à culer** (naut) to back water; **nager debout** to tread water; to row standing up; **nager entre deux eaux** to swim under water; (fig) to carry water on both shoulders

na·geur [naʒœr] **-geuse** [ʒøz] *adj* swimming; floating || *mf* swimmer; rower

naguère or **naguères** [nager] *adv* lately, just now

naïf [naif] **naïve** [naiv] *adj* naïve || *mf* simple-minded person

nain [nɛ̃] **naine** [nɛn] *adj & mf* dwarf

naissain [nɛsɛ̃] *m* seed oysters

naissance [nɛsɑ̃s] *f* birth; lineage; descent; beginning; (archit) springing line; **de basse naissance** lowborn; **de haute naissance** highborn; **de naissance** by birth; **donner naissance à** to give birth to; to give rise to; **naissance de la gorge** bosom; throat; **naissance des cheveux** hairline; **naissance du jour** daybreak; **prendre naissance** to arise, originate

nais·sant [nɛsɑ̃] **nais·sante** [nɛsɑ̃t] *adj* nascent, rising, budding

naître [nɛtr] §46 *intr* (*aux:* ÊTRE) to be born; to bud; to arise, originate; to dawn; **faire naître** to give birth to; to give rise to

naïveté [naivte] *f* naïveté; artlessness

nanan [nɑnɑ̃], [nɑ̃nɑ̃] *m* (coll) goody; **du nanan** (coll) nice

nantir [nɑ̃tir] *tr* to give security or a pledge to; **nantir de** to provide with || *intr* to stock up; to feather one's nest || *ref*—**se nantir de** to provide oneself with

nantissement [nɑ̃tismɑ̃] *m* security

napée [nape] *f* wood nymph

napel [napɛl] *m* monkshood, wolfsbane

naphte [naft] *m* naphtha

napoléo·nien [napɔleɔnjɛ̃] **-nienne** [njɛn] *adj* Napoleonic

nappage [napaʒ] *m* table linen

nappe [nap] *f* tablecloth; sheet (*of water, flame*); net (*for fishing; for bird catching*); **mettre la nappe** to set the table; **nappe d'autel** altar cloth; **ôter la nappe** to clear the table

napperon [naprɔ̃] *m* tablecloth cover; **petit napperon** doily

narcisse [narsis] *m* narcissus; **narcisse des bois** daffodil; **Narcisse** Narcissus

narcotique [narkɔtik] *adj & m* narcotic

narcotiser [narkɔtize] *tr* to dope

nargue [narg] *f* scorn, contempt; **faire nargue de** to defy; **nargue de . . . !** fie on . . . !

narguer [narge] *tr* to flout, to snap one's fingers at

narguilé [nargile] *m* hookah

narine [narin] *f* nostril

nar·quois [narkwa] **-quoise** [kwaz] *adj* sly, cunning; sneering

narra·teur [naratœr] **-trice** [tris] *mf* narrator, storyteller

narra·tif [naratif] **-tive** [tiv] *adj* narrative

narration [narɑsjɔ̃] *f* narration; narrative

narrer [nare] *tr* to narrate, relate

na·sal -sale [nazal] *adj* (*pl* **-saux** [zo]) nasal || *f* nasal (*vowel*)

nasaliser [nazalize] *tr & intr* to nasalize

nasarde [nazard] *f* fillip on one's nose (*in contempt*); snub, insult

na·seau [nazo] *m* (*pl* **-seaux**) nostril (*of horse, etc.*); **naseaux** (coll) snout

nasil·lard [nazijar] **nasil·larde** [nazijard] *adj* nasal

nasiller [nazije] *intr* to talk through one's nose; to squawk, quack

nasse [nas] *f* fish trap; (sports) basket

na·tal -tale [natal] *adj* (*pl* **-tals**) natal, of birth, native

natalité [natalite] *f* birth rate

natation [natɑsjɔ̃] *f* swimming

na·tif [natif] **-tive** [tiv] *adj & mf* native

nation [nɑsjɔ̃] *f* nation; **Nations Unies** United Nations

natio·nal -nale [nɑsjɔnal] *adj & mf* (*pl* **-naux** [no] **-nales**) national

nationaliser [nɑsjɔnalize] *tr* to nationalize

nationalité [nɑsjɔnalite] *f* nationality

nativité [nativite] *f* nativity; nativity scene; **Nativité** Nativity

natte [nat] *f* mat, matting; braid

natter [nate] *tr* to weave; to braid

naturalisation [natyralizɑsjɔ̃] *f* naturalization

naturaliser [natyralize] *tr* to naturalize

naturalisme [natyralism] *m* naturalism

naturaliste [natyralist] *adj & mf* naturalist

nature [natyr] *adj invar* raw; black (*coffee*) || *f* nature; **nature morte** (painting) still life

natu·rel -relle [natyrɛl] *adj* natural; native || *m* naturalness; native, citizen

naturellement [natyrɛlmɑ̃] *adv* naturally; of course

naufrage [nofraʒ] *m* shipwreck

naufra·gé -gée [nofraʒe] *adj* shipwrecked || *mf* shipwrecked person

nauséa·bond [nozeabɔ̃] **-bonde** [bɔ̃d] *adj* nauseating

nausée [noze] *f* nausea

nauséeux [nozeø] **nauséeuse** [nozeøz] *adj* nauseous

nautique [notik] *adj* nautical

nautisme [notism] *m* yachting

nauto·nier [notɔnje] **-nière** [njer] *mf* pilot

na·val -vale [naval] *adj* (*pl* **-vals**) naval; nautical, maritime

navel [navel] *f* navel orange

navet [nave] *m* turnip

navette [navet] *f* shuttle; shuttle train; **faire la navette** to shuttle, to ply back and forth

navigable [navigabl] *adj* navigable (*river*); seaworthy (*ship*)

naviga·teur [navigatœr] **-trice** [tris] *adj* seafaring || *m* navigator

navigation [navigasjɔ̃] *f* navigation; sailing; **navigation de plaisance** (*sports*) sailing

naviguer [navige] *intr* to navigate, sail; **naviguer sur** to navigate, sail (*the sea*)

navire [navir] *m* ship; **navire de débarquement** landing craft; **navire marchand** merchantman

navire-citerne [navirsitern] *m* (*pl* **navires-citernes**) tanker

navire-école [navirekɔl] *m* (*pl* **navires-écoles**) training ship

navire-jumeau [navirʒymo] *m* (*pl* **navires-jumeaux**) sister ship

na·vrant -vrante [navrɑ̃] **-vrante** [vrɑ̃t] *adj* distressing, heartrending

na·vré -vrée [navre] *adj* sorry, grieved

navrer [navre] *tr* to distress, grieve

nazaréen [nazareɛ̃] **nazaréenne** [nazareen] *adj* Nazarene || (*cap*) *mf* Nazarene

N.-D. *abbr* (**Notre-Dame**) Our Lady

ne [nə] §87, §90; **n'est-ce pas?** isn't that so? La traduction précédente est généralement remplacée par diverses locutions. Si l'énoncé est négatif, la question qui équivaut à **n'est-ce pas?** sera affirmative, par ex., **Vous ne travaillez pas. N'est-ce pas?** You are not working. Are you? Si l'énoncé est affirmatif, la question sera négative, par ex., **Vous travaillez. N'est-ce pas?** You are working. Are you not? ou **Aren't you?** Si l'énoncé contient un auxiliaire, la question contiendra cet auxiliaire moins l'infinitif ou moins le participe passé, par ex., **Il arrivera demain. N'est-ce pas?** He will arrive tomorrow. Won't he?; par ex., **Paul est déjà arrivé. N'est-ce pas?** Paul has already arrived. Hasn't he? Si l'énoncé ne contient ni auxiliaire ni forme de la copule "to be," la question contiendra l'auxiliaire "do" ou "did" moins l'infinitif, par ex., **Marie parle anglais. N'est-ce pas?** Mary speaks English. Doesn't she?

né née [ne] *adj* born; by birth; **bien né** highborn; **né pour** cut out for

néanmoins [neɑ̃mwɛ̃] *adv* nevertheless

néant [neɑ̃] *m* nothing, nothingness; worthlessness; obscurity; none (*as a response on the appropriate blank of an official form*)

nébu·leux [nebylø] **-leuse** [løz] *adj* nebulous; gloomy (*facial expression*); worried (*brow*) || *f* nebula

nécessaire [neseser] *adj* necessary, needful; **nécessaire à** required for || *m* necessities; kit, dressing case

nécessairement [nesesermɑ̃] *adv* necessarily

nécessité [nesesite] *f* necessity; need; **nécessité préalable** prerequisite

nécessiter [nesesite] *tr* to necessitate

nécessi·teux [nesesitø] **-teuse** [tøz] *adj* needy || *mf* needy person; **les nécessiteux** the needy

nécrologie [nekrɔlɔʒi] *f* necrology, obituary

nectar [nektar] *m* nectar

néerlan·dais [neerlɑ̃dɛ] **-daise** [dez] *adj* Dutch || *m* Dutch (*language*) || (*cap*) *mf* Netherlander

nef [nef] *f* nave; (*archaic*) ship; **nef latérale** aisle

néfaste [nefast] *adj* ill-starred, unlucky

nèfle [nefl] *f* medlar

néflier [neflije] *m* medlar tree

néga·teur [negatœr] **-trice** [tris] *adj* negative

néga·tif [negatif] **-tive** [tiv] *adj* negative || *m* (*phot*) negative || *f* negative (*side of a question*)

négation [negasjɔ̃] *f* negation; (*gram*) negative

négli·gé -gée [negliʒe] *adj* careless; unadorned, unstudied || *m* carelessness; negligee, dressing gown

négligeable [negliʒabl] *adj* negligible

négligence [negliʒɑ̃s] *f* negligence; **avec négligence** slovenly

négli·gent [negliʒɑ̃] **-gente** [ʒɑ̃t] *adj* negligent || *mf* careless person

négliger [negliʒe] §38 *tr* to neglect || *ref* to neglect oneself

négoce [negɔs] *m* trade, commerce; (*com*) company

négociable [negɔsjabl] *adj* negotiable

négo·ciant [negɔsjɑ̃] **-ciante** [sjɑ̃t] *mf* wholesaler, dealer

négocia·teur [negɔsjatœr] **-trice** [tris] *mf* negotiator

négociation [negɔsjasjɔ̃] *f* negotiation

négocier [negɔsje] *tr* to negotiate || *intr* to negotiate; to deal

nègre [negr] *adj* Negro; dark brown || *m* Negro; ghost writer; **petit nègre** pidgin, Creole

négrerie [negrəri] *f* slave quarters

négrier [negrije] *adj masc* slave || *m* slave driver; slave ship

neige [neʒ] *f* snow

neiger [neʒe] §38 *intr* to snow

Némésis [nemezis] *f* Nemesis

nenni [nani], [neni], [neni] *adv* (*archaic*) no, not

nénuphar [nenyfar] *m* water lily

néologisme [neɔlɔʒism] *m* neologism

néon [neɔ̃] *m* neon

néophyte [neɔfit] *mf* neophyte, convert

neptunium [neptynjɔm] *m* neptunium

nerf [ner] *m* nerve; tendon, sinew; (archit, bb) rib; (fig) backbone, sinew; **avoir du nerf** to have nerves of steel; **avoir les nerfs à fleur de peau** to be on edge; **nerf de bœuf**

scourge; **porter sur les nerfs à qn** to get on s.o.'s nerves

Néron [nerɔ̃] *m* Nero

ner·veux [nervø] **-veuse** [vøz] *adj* nervous; nerve; jittery; sinewy, muscular; forceful (*style*)

nervure [nervyr] *f* rib

net nette [nɛt] *adj* clean; clear, sharp, distinct; net; **net d'impôt** tax-exempt || *m*—**mettre au net** to make a fair copy of || **net** *adv* flatly, point-blank, outright

netteté [nɛtəte] *f* neatness; clearness, sharpness

nettoiement [netwamɑ̃] *m* cleaning

nettoyage [netwajaʒ] *m* cleaning; **nettoyage à sec** dry cleaning

nettoyer [netwaje] §47 *tr* to clean; to wash up or out; **nettoyer à sec** to dry-clean || *ref* to wash up, to clean oneself

nettoyeur [netwajœr] **nettoyeuse** [netwajøz] *mf* cleaner

neuf [nœf] **neuve** [nœv] *adj* new; flambant neuf, **tout neuf** brand-new || **neuf** *adj* & *pron* nine; the Ninth, e.g., **Jean le Neuf** John the Ninth; **neuf heures** nine o'clock || *m* nine; ninth (*in dates*)

neutraliser [nøtralize] *tr* to neutralize

neutralité [nøtralite] *f* neutrality

neutre [nøtr] *adj* & *m* neuter; neutral

neuvième [nœvjɛm] *adj, pron (masc, fem)*, & *m* ninth

ne·veu [nəvø] *m* (*pl* **-veux**) nephew; **nos neveux** our posterity

névralgie [nevralʒi] *f* neuralgia

névrose [nevroz] *f* neurosis

névro·sé -sée [nevroze] *adj* & *mf* neurotic

New York [nujɔrk], [nœjɔrk] *m* New York

newyor·kais [nœjɔrkɛ] **-kaise** [kez] *adj* New York || (*cap*) *mf* New Yorker

nez [ne] *m* nose; cape, headland; **nez à nez** face to face

ni [ni] §90 *conj*—**ne . . . ni . . . ni** neither . . . nor, e.g., **elle n'a ni papier ni stylo** she has neither paper nor pen; **ni . . . ni** neither . . . nor; **ni . . . non plus** nor . . . either

niable [njabl] *adj* deniable

niais [nje] **niaise** [njez] *adj* foolish, silly, simple-minded || *mf* fool, simpleton

niaiserie [njezəri] *f* foolishness, silliness, simpleness

niche [niʃ] *f* niche; alcove; prank; **niche à chien** doghouse

nichée [niʃe] *f* brood

nicher [niʃe] *tr* to niche, to lodge || *intr* to nestle; to nest; to hide || *ref* to nest

nickeler [nikle] §34 *tr* to nickel-plate

nickelure [niklyr] *f* nickel plate

nicotine [nikɔtin] *f* nicotine

nid [ni] *m* nest; **en nid d'abeilles** honeycombed; **nid de pie** crow's-nest

nièce [njes] *f* niece

nième [njem] *adj* nth

nier [nje] *tr* to deny || *intr* to plead not guilty

ni·gaud [nigo] **-gaude** [god] *adj* silly || *mf* nincompoop

nigauderie [nigodri] *f* silliness

nihilisme [niilism] *m* nihilism

Nil [nil] *m* Nile

nimbe [nɛ̃b] *m* halo, nimbus

nimber [nɛ̃be] *tr* to halo

nimbus [nɛ̃bys] *m* (meteo) nimbus

nipper [nipe] *tr* (coll) to tog || *ref* (coll) to tog oneself out

nippes [nip] *fpl* (coll) worn-out clothes; (slang) duds

nique [nik] *f*—**faire la nique à** to turn up one's nose at

nitrate [nitrat] *m* nitrate

nitre [nitr] *m* niter, nitrate

ni·treux [nitrø] **-treuse** [trøz] *adj* nitrous

nitrière [nitrijer] *f* saltpeter bed

nitrique [nitrik] *adj* nitric

nitrogène [nitrɔʒen] *m* nitrogen

nitroglycérine [nitrɔgliserin] *f* nitroglycerin

ni·veau [nivo] *m* (*pl* **-veaux**) level; **au niveau de** on a par with; **niveau à bulle d'air** spirit level; **niveau à lunettes** surveyor's level; **niveau d'essence** gasoline gauge; **niveau de vie** standard of living; **niveau d'huile** oil gauge; **niveau mental** I.Q.

niveler [nivle] §34 *tr* to level; to survey

nive·leur [nivlœr] **-leuse** [løz] *mf* leveler || *m* harrow || *f* (agr) leveler

nivellement [nivelmɑ̃] *m* leveling; surveying

N°, n° *abbr* (**numéro**) no.

noble [nɔbl] *adj* & *mf* noble

noblesse [nɔbles] *f* nobility; nobleness

noce [nɔs] *f* wedding; wedding party; **faire la noce** to go on a spree; **ne pas être à la noce** to be in trouble; **noces** wedding

no·ceur [nɔsœr] **-ceuse** [søz] *adj* (coll) bacchanalian, reveling || *mf* (coll) reveler, debauchee

no·cif [nɔsif] **-cive** [siv] *adj* noxious

noctambule [nɔktɑ̃byl] *mf* nighthawk; sleepwalker

nocturne [nɔktyrn] *adj* nocturnal; night; nightly || *m* (mus) nocturne || *f* open night (*of store*)

nodosité [nɔdozite] *f* nodule (*of root*); node, wart

Noé [nɔe] *m* Noah

noël [nɔel] *m* Christmas carol; (coll) Christmas present; **Noël** Christmas

nœud [nø] *m* knot; rosette; finger joint; **Adam's apple; tie, alliance; crux** (*of question, plot, crisis*); node; (naut) knot; **nœud de vache** granny knot; **nœud plat** square knot; **nœuds** coils (*of snake*); **nœud vital** nerve center

noir noire [nwar] *adj* black; **noir comme poix** pitch-black || **mf** Negro || *m* black; bruise; **broyer du noir** to be blue, down in the dumps; **noir de fumée** lampblack || *f* (mus) quarter note

noirâtre [nwaratr] *adj* blackish

noi·raud [nwaro] **-raude** [rod] *adj* swarthy

noirceur [nwarsœr] *f* blackness; black spot

noircir [nwarsir] *tr* to blacken || *intr & ref* to burn black; to turn dark

noircissure [nwarsisyr] *f* black spot, smudge

noise [nwaz] *f* squabble; **chercher noise à** to pick a quarrel with

noisetier [nwaztje] *m* hazelnut tree

noisette [nwazet] *adj invar* reddish-brown || *f* hazelnut

noix [nwa], [nwa] *f* walnut; nut; **à la noix** (slang) trifling; **noix d'acajou, noix de cajou** cashew nut; **noix du Brésil** Brazil nut; **noix de coco** coconut; **noix de galle** nutgall; **noix de muscade** nutmeg; **noix de veau** round of veal

nolis [nɔli] *m* freight

noliser [nɔlize] *tr* to charter (*a ship*)

nom [nɔ̃] *m* name; noun; **de nom** by name; **nom à rallonges, nom à tiroirs** (coll) word made up of several parts; **nom commercial** trade name; **nom de baptême** baptismal name, Christian name; **nom de demoiselle** maiden name; **nom de famille** surname; **nom de guerre** fictitious name, assumed name; **nom de jeune fille** maiden name; **nom d'emprunt** assumed name; **nom de théâtre** stage name; **nom marchand** trade name; **petit nom** first name; **petit nom d'amitié** pet name; **sans nom** nameless; **sous le nom de** by the name of

nomade [nɔmad] *adj & mf* nomad

nombre [nɔ̃br] *m* number, quantity

nombrer [nɔ̃bre] *tr* to number

nom·breux [nɔ̃brø] **-breuse** [brøz] *adj* numerous; rhythmic, harmonious (*e.g., prose*)

nombril [nɔ̃bri] *m* navel

nomenclature [nɔmɑ̃klatyr] *f* nomenclature; vocabulary; body (*of dictionary*)

nomi·nal -nale [nɔminal] *adj* (*pl* -naux [no]) nominal; **appel nominal** roll call

nomina·tif [nɔminatif] **-tive** [tiv] *adj* nominative; registered (*stocks, bonds, etc.*) || *m* nominative

nomination [nɔminɑsjɔ̃] *f* appointment

nom·mé -mée [nɔme] *adj* named; appointed; called || *m*—**le nommé . . .** the man called . . .

nommément [nɔmemɑ̃] *adv* namely, particularly

nommer [nɔme] *tr* to name, call; to appoint || *ref* to be named, e.g., **je me nomme . . .** my name is . . .

non [nɔ̃] *m invar* no || *adv* no, not; **non pas** not so; **non plus** neither, not, nor . . . either, e.g., **moi non plus nor I** either; **non point!** by no means!; **que non!** no indeed!

non-belli·ge·rant [nɔ̃bellizerɑ̃] **-rante** [rɑ̃t] *adj & mf* nonbelligerent

nonce [nɔ̃s] *m* nuncio

noncha·lant [nɔ̃ʃalɑ̃] **-lante** [lɑ̃t] *adj* nonchalant

non-com·bat·tant [nɔ̃kɔ̃batɑ̃] **non-combat·tante** [nɔ̃kɔ̃batɑ̃t] *adj & mf* noncombatant

non-conformiste [nɔ̃kɔ̃fɔrmist] *adj & mf* nonconformist

non-enga·gé -gée [nɔ̃ɑ̃gaʒe] *adj* unaligned, uncommitted

nonnain [nɔnɛ̃] *f* (pej) nun

nonne [nɔn] *f* nun

nonobstant [nɔnɔpstɑ̃] *adv* notwithstanding; **nonobstant que** although || *prep* in spite of

non-pesanteur [nɔ̃pəzɑ̃tœr] *f* weightlessness

non-rési·dent [nɔ̃rezidɑ̃] **-dente** [dɑ̃t] *adj & mf* nonresident

non-réussite [nɔ̃reysit] *f* failure

non-sens [nɔ̃sɑ̃s] *m* absurdity, nonsense

non-usage [nɔnyzaʒ] *m* disuse

non-violence [nɔ̃vjɔlɑ̃s] *f* nonviolence

nord [nɔr] *adj invar* north, northern || *m* north; **du nord** northern; **faire le nord** to steer northward; **vers le nord** northward

nord-est [nɔrest] *adj invar & m* northeast

nord-ouest [nɔrwest] *adj invar & m* northwest

nor·mal -male [nɔrmal] *adj* (*pl* -maux [mo]) normal; regular, standard; perpendicular || *f* normal; perpendicular

norma·lien [nɔrmaljɛ̃] **-lienne** [ljen] *mf* student at a teachers college

nor·mand [nɔrmɑ̃] **-mande** [mɑ̃d] *adj* Norman || *m* Norman (*dialect*) || (*cap*) *mf* Norman (*person*)

Normandie [nɔrmɑ̃di] *f* Normandy; **la Normandie** Normandy

norme [nɔrm] *f* norm; specifications

nor·rois [nɔrwa] **nor·roise** [nɔrwaz] *adj* Norse || *m* Norse (*language*) || (*cap*) *m* Norseman

Norvège [nɔrveʒ] *f* Norway; **la Norvège** Norway

norvé·gien [nɔrveʒjɛ̃] **-gienne** [ʒjen] *adj* Norwegian || *m* Norwegian (*language*) || *f* round-stemmed rowboat || (*cap*) *mf* Norwegian (*person*)

nos [no] §88

nostalgie [nɔstalʒi] *f* nostalgia, homesickness

nostalgique [nɔstalʒik] *adj* nostalgic, homesick

notable [nɔtabl] *adj* notable, noteworthy || *m* notable

notaire [nɔter] *m* notary; lawyer

notamment [nɔtamɑ̃] *adv* especially

notation [nɔtɑsjɔ̃] *f* notation

note [nɔt] *f* note; bill (*to be paid*); grade, mark (*in school*); footnote; **être dans la note** to be in the swing of things; **note de rappel** reminder; **prendre note de** to note down

noter [nɔte] *tr* to note; to note down; to notice; to mark (*a student*); to write down (*a tune*)

notice [nɔtis] *f* notice (*review, sketch*)

notification [nɔtifikɑsjɔ̃] *f* notification, notice

notifier [nɔtifje] *tr* to report on; to serve (*a summons*)

notion [nɔsjɔ̃] *f* notion

notoire [nɔtwar] *adj* well-known

notoriété [nɔtɔrjete] *f* fame

notre [nɔtr] §88

nôtre [notr] §89; **serez-vous des nô-tres? will you join us?**

noue [nu] *f* pasture land; roof gutter

noué nouée [nwe] *adj* afflicted with rickets

nouer [nwe] *tr* to knot; to tie; to form; to cook up (*a plot*) ‖ *ref* to form knots; to be tied; (*hort*) to set

noueux [nwø] **noueuse** [nwøz] *adj* knotty, gnarled

nouille [nuj] *f* noodle

nounou [nunu] *f* nanny

nour·ri -rie [nuri] *adj* heavy, sustained; rich (*style*)

nourrice [nuris] *f* wet nurse; can; (*aut*) reserve tank

nourricerie [nurisri] *f* baby farm; stock farm; silkworm farm

nourri·cier [nurisje] **-cière** [sjɛr] *adj* nutritive; nourishing; foster

nourrir [nurir] *tr* to nourish; to suckle; to feed (*a fire*); to nurse (*plants; hopes*) ‖ *intr* to be nourishing ‖ *ref* to feed; to thrive

nourrisseur [nurisœr] *m* stock raiser, dairyman

nourrisson [nurisɔ̃] *m* nursling, suckling; foster child

nourriture [nurityr] *f* nourishment, food; nourishing; nursing; breast-feeding; **nourriture du feu** firewood

nous [nu] §85, §87; **nous autres Amé-ricains** we Americans

nous-mêmes [numem] §86

nou·veau [nuvo] (or **-vel** [vɛl] before vowel or mute *h*) **-velle** [vɛl] (*pl* **-veaux -velles**) *adj* new (*recent*) ‖ (when standing before noun) *adj* new (*other, additional, different*) ‖ *m* freshman; **à nouveau** anew; **de nouveau** again; **du nouveau** something new; **le nouveau** the new ‖ *f* see **nouvelle**

nouveau-né -née [nuvone] *adj & mf* (*pl* **-nés**) newborn

nouveauté [nuvote] *f* newness, novelty

nouvelle [nuvɛl] *f* piece of news; novelette, short story; **donnez-moi de vos nouvelles** let me hear from you; **nouvelles** news

Nouvelle-Angleterre [nuvɛlãɡlətɛr] *f* New England; **la Nouvelle-Angle-terre** New England

Nouvelle-Écosse [nuvɛlekɔs] *f* Nova Scotia; **la Nouvelle-Écosse** Nova Scotia

Nouvelle-Orléans [nuvɛlɔrleã] *f*—**la Nouvelle-Orléans** New Orleans

nouvelliste [nuvelist] *mf* short-story writer

nova·teur [nɔvatœr] **-trice** [tris] *adj* innovating ‖ *mf* innovator

novembre [nɔvãbr] *m* November

novice [nɔvis] *adj* inexperienced, new ‖ *mf* novice, neophyte

noviciat [nɔvisja] *m* novitiate

novocaïne [nɔvokain] *f* novocaine

noyade [nwajad] *f* drowning

noyau [nwajo] *m* (*pl* **noyaux**) nucleus; stone, kernel; pit (*of fruit*); core (*of electromagnet*); newel; hub; (*fig*) cell (*of conspirators*); (*fig*) bunch (*of*

card players); **noyau d'atome** atomic nucleus

noyautage [nwajotaʒ] *m* infiltration (*e.g., of communists*)

noyer [nwaje] *m* walnut tree; **en noyer** in walnut (*wood*) ‖ §47 *tr & ref* to drown

nu nue [ny] *adj* naked, nude; bare; barren; uncarpeted; unharnassed, un-saddled (*horse*); (*aut*) stripped ‖ *m* nude; **à nu** exposed; bareback ‖ *f* see **nue**

nuage [nɥaʒ] *m* cloud

nua·geux [nɥaʒø] **-geuse** [ʒøz] *adj* cloudy

nuance [nɥãs] *f* hue, shade, tone, nuance

nucléaire [nykleer] *adj* nuclear

nucléole [nykleɔl] *m* nucleolus

nucléon [nykleɔ̃] *m* nucleon

nudiste [nydist] *adj & mf* nudist

nudité [nydite] *f* nakedness; nudity; plainness (*of style*); nude

nue [ny] *f* clouds; sky; **mettre** or **porter aux nues** to praise to the skies

nuée [nɥe] *f* cloud, storm cloud; flock

nuire [nɥir] §19 (*pp* **nui**) *intr* (with *dat*) to harm, to injure

nuisible [nɥizibl] *adj* harmful

nuit [nɥi] *f* night; **à la nuit** close after dark; **bonne nuit** good night; **cette nuit** last night; **nuit blanche** sleepless night

nuitamment [nɥitamã] *adv* at night

nu-jambes [nyʒãb] *adj invar* bare-legged

nul nulle [nyl] *adj indef* no; **ne . . . nul** or **nul . . . ne** §90 no; **nul et non avenu, nulle et non avenue** [nylenɔ̃avny] null and void ‖ *f* dummy word or letter ‖ **nul** *pron indef*—**nul ne** §90B no one, nobody

nullement [nylmã] §90 *adv* not at all

nullité [nyllite] *f* nonentity, nobody

nûment [nymã] *adv* candidly, frankly

numé·ral -rale [nymeral] *adj & m* (*pl* **-raux** [ro]) numeral

numération [nymerasjɔ̃] *f* numeration; **numération globulaire** blood count

numérique [nymerik] *adj* numerical

numéro [nymero] *m* numeral; number; issue, number (*of a periodical*), e.g., **dernier numéro** current issue; e.g., **numéro ancien** back number; (*slang*) queer duck; **faire un numéro** to dial; **numéro de vestiaire** check (*of check-room*); **numéro d'ordre** serial number

numéroter [nymerɔte] *tr* to number

numismatique [nymismatik] *adj* nu-mismatic ‖ *f* numismatics

nu-pieds [nypje] *adj invar* barefooted

nup·tial -tiale [nypsjal] *adj* (*pl* **-tiaux** [sjo]) nuptial

nuque [nyk] *f* nape, scruff

nurse [nœrs] *f* children's nurse

nu-tête [nytɛt] *adj invar* bareheaded

nutri·tif [nytritif] **-tive** [tiv] *adj* nu-tritive; nutritious

nutrition [nytrisjɔ̃] *f* nutrition

nylon [nilɔ̃] *m* nylon

nymphe [nɛ̃f] *f* nymph

O

O, o [o], *[o] *m invar* fifteenth letter of the French alphabet

oasis [ɔazis] *f* oasis

obéir [ɔbeir] *intr* to obey; (with *dat*) to obey, yield to; (with *dat*) to be subject to; **être obéi** to be obeyed; **obéir au doigt et à l'œil** to obey blindly

obéissance [ɔbeisɑ̃s] *f* obedience

obéis·sant [ɔbeisɑ̃] **obéis·sante** [ɔbeisɑ̃t] *adj* obedient

obélisque [ɔbelisk] *m* obelisk

obérer [ɔbere] §10 *tr* to burden with debt ‖ *ref* to run into debt

obèse [ɔbez] *adj* obese

obésité [ɔbezite] *f* obesity

objecter [ɔbʒɛkte] *tr* to object, e.g., **objecter que . . .** to object that . . . ; to bring up, e.g., **objecter q.ch. à qn** to bring up s.th. against s.o.; to put forward (*in opposition*), e.g., **objecter de bonnes raisons à or contre un argument** to put forward good reasons against an argument

objecteur [ɔbʒɛktœr] *m*—**objecteur de conscience** conscientious objector

objec·tif [ɔbʒɛktif] **-tive** [tiv] *adj* objective ‖ *m* objective; object lens; (mil) target

objection [ɔbʒɛksjɔ̃] *f* objection; **faire des objections** to object

objectivité [ɔbʒɛktivite] *f* objectivity

objet [ɔbʒɛ] *m* object; **menus objets** notions; **objet d'art** work of art; **objet de risée** laughingstock; **objets de première nécessité** articles of everyday use; **remplir son objet** to attain one's end

obligation [ɔbligasjɔ̃] *f* obligation; (com) bond, debenture; **être dans l'obligation de** to be obliged to

obligatoire [ɔbligatwar] *adj* required, obligatory; (coll) inevitable

obli·gé -gée [ɔbliʒe] *adj* obliged, compelled; necessary, indispensable; **bien obligé** much obliged; **c'est obligé** (coll) it has to be; **être obligé de** to be obliged to

obli·geant [ɔbliʒɑ̃] **-geante** [ʒɑ̃t] *adj* obliging

obliger [ɔbliʒe] §38 *tr* to oblige ‖ *ref*—**s'obliger à** + *inf* to undertake to + *inf*; **s'obliger pour qn** to stand surety for s.o.

oblique [ɔblik] *adj* oblique

oblitération [ɔbliterasjɔ̃] *f* obliteration; cancellation (*of postage stamp*); (pathol) occlusion

oblitérer [ɔblitere] §10 *tr* to obliterate; to cancel (*a postage stamp*); to obstruct (*e.g., a vein*)

o·blong [ɔblɔ̃] **-blongue** [blɔ̃g] *adj* oblong

obnubiler [ɔbnybile] *tr* to cloud, befog

obole [ɔbɔl] *f* widow's mite

obscène [ɔpsɛn] *adj* obscene

obscénité [ɔpsenite] *f* obscenity

obs·cur -cure [ɔpskyr] *adj* obscure

obscurcir [ɔpskyrsir] *tr* to obscure; to dim ‖ *ref* to grow dark; to grow dim

obscurité [ɔpskyrite] *f* obscurity

obséder [ɔpsede] §10 *tr* to obsess; to importune, to harass

obsèques [ɔpsɛk] *fpl* obsequies, funeral rites

obsé·quieux [ɔpsekjø] **-quieuse** [kjøz] *adj* obsequious

observance [ɔpsɛrvɑ̃s] *f* observance

observa·teur [ɔpsɛrvatœr] **-trice** [tris] *adj* observant ‖ *mf* observer

observation [ɔpsɛrvasjɔ̃] *f* observation

observatoire [ɔpsɛrvatwar] *m* observatory

observer [ɔpsɛrve] *tr* to observe ‖ *ref* to watch oneself; to watch each other

obsession [ɔpsesjɔ̃] *f* obsession

obsolète [ɔpsɔlɛt] *adj* obsolete

obstacle [ɔpstakl] *m* obstacle

obstétrique [ɔpstetrik] *adj* obstetrical ‖ *f* obstetrics

obstination [ɔpstinasjɔ̃] *f* obstinacy

obsti·né -née [ɔpstine] *adj* obstinate

obstruction [ɔpstryksjɔ̃] *f* obstruction; (sports) blocking; **faire de l'obstruction** (pol) to filibuster; **obstruction systématique** filibustering

obstruer [ɔpstrye] *tr* to obstruct

obtempérer [ɔptɑ̃pere] §10 *intr* (with *dat*) to comply with, to obey

obtenir [ɔptənir] §72 *tr* to obtain, get

obtention [ɔptɑ̃sjɔ̃] *f* obtaining

obtura·teur [ɔptyratœr] **-trice** [tris] *adj* stopping, closing ‖ *m* (mach) stopcock; (phot) shutter

obturation [ɔptyrasjɔ̃] *f* stopping up; filling (*of tooth*); **obturation des lumières** blackout

obturer [ɔptyre] *tr* to stop up; to fill (*a tooth*)

ob·tus [ɔpty] **-tuse** [tyz] *adj* obtuse

obus [ɔby] *m* (mil) shell; plunger (*of tire valve*); **obus à balles** shrapnel; **obus à mitraille** shrapnel; **obus de rupture** armor-piercing shell

obvier [ɔbvje] *intr* (with *dat*) to obviate, to prevent

oc [ɔk] *adv* (Old Provençal) yes

occasion [ɔkazjɔ̃], [ɔkazjɔ̃] *f* occasion; opportunity; bargain; **à l'occasion** on occasion; **à l'occasion de** for (*e.g., s.o.'s birthday*); **d'occasion** second-hand (*clothing*); used (*car*)

occasion·nel -nelle [ɔkazjɔnɛl] *adj* occasional; chance (*meeting*); determining (*cause*)

occasionnellement [ɔkazjɔnɛlmɑ̃] *adv* occasionally; by chance, accidentally

occasionner [ɔkazjɔne] *tr* to occasion

occident [ɔksidɑ̃] *m* occident, west

occiden·tal -tale [ɔksidɑtal] *adj & mf* (*pl* **-taux** [to]) occidental

occlu·sif [ɔklyzif] **-sive** [ziv] *adj & f* occlusive

occlusion [ɔklyzjɔ̃] *f* occlusion

occulte [ɔkylt] *adj* occult

occu·pant [ɔkypɑ̃] **-pante** [pɑ̃t] *adj* occupying ‖ *mf* occupant

occupation [ɔkypasjɔ̃] *f* occupation

occu·pé -pée [ɔkype] *adj* occupied; **occupé** (public sign) in use

occuper [ɔkype] *tr* to occupy ‖ *ref* to find something to do; **s'occuper de** to be occupied with, to be busy with; to take care of, to handle

occurrence [ɔkyrãs] *f* occurrence; **en l'occurrence** under the circumstances; **être en occurrence** to occur; **selon l'occurrence** as the case may be

océan [ɔseã] *m* ocean; **océan glacial arctique** Arctic Ocean; **océan Indien** Indian Ocean

océanique [ɔseanik] *adj* oceanic

ocre [ɔkr] *f* ochre

octane [ɔktan] *m* octane

octave [ɔktav] *f* octave

octa·von [ɔktavõ] **-vonne** [vɔn] *mf* octoroon

octobre [ɔktɔbr] *m* October

octroi [ɔktrwa] *m* granting (*of a favor*); tax on provisions being brought into town

octroyer [ɔktrwaje] §47 *tr* to grant, concede; to bestow

oculaire [ɔkyler] *adj* ocular, eye ‖ *m* ocular, eyepiece

oculariste [ɔkylarist] *mf* optician (*who specializes in glass eyes*)

oculiste [ɔkylist] *mf* oculist

ode [ɔd] *f* ode

odeur [ɔdœr] *f* odor, scent

o·dieux [ɔdjø] **-dieuse** [djøz] *adj* odious ‖ *m* odium, odiousness

odo·rant [ɔdɔrã] **-rante** [rãt] *adj* fragrant

odorat [ɔdɔra] *m* (sense of) smell

Odyssée [ɔdise] *f* Odyssey

œcuménique [ekymenik] *adj* ecumenical

œdème [edɛm] *m* (pathol) edema

Œdipe [edip] *m* Oedipus

œil [œj] *m* (*pl* **yeux** [jø] **les yeux** [lezjø]) eye; typeface, font; bud; **avoir l'œil (américain)** (coll) to be observant; **coûter les yeux de la tête** (coll) to cost a fortune; **donner de l'œil à** to give a better appearance to; **entre quatre yeux** [ãtrəkatzjø] (coll) between you and me; **faire les gros yeux à** (coll) to glare at; **faire les yeux doux à** to make eyes at; **ne pas avoir les yeux dans la poche** (coll) to keep one's eyes peeled; (coll) to be no shrinking violet; **œil au beurre noir** (coll) black eye; **œil de pie** (naut) eyelet; **œil de verre** glass eye; **œil électrique** electric eye; **pocher un œil à qn** to give s.o. a black eye; **sale œil** disapproving or dirty look; **sauter aux yeux**, **crever les yeux** to be obvious; **se mettre le doigt dans l'œil** (coll) to put one's foot in one's mouth; **se rincer l'œil** (slang) to get an eyeful; **taper dans l'œil à or de qn** (coll) to take s.o.'s fancy; **voir d'un mauvais œil** to take a dim view of

œil-de-bœuf [œjdəbœf] *m* (*pl* **œils-de-bœuf**) bull's-eye, small oval window

œil-de-chat [œjdəʃa] *m* (*pl* **œils-de-chat**) cat's-eye (*gem*)

œil-de-perdrix [œjdəperdri] *m* (*pl* **œils-de-perdrix**) (pathol) soft corn

œillade [œjad] *f* glance, leer, wink; **lancer, jeter,** or **décocher une œillade à** to ogle

œillère [œjɛr] *f* eyecup; blinker; **avoir des œillères** to be biased

œillet [œjɛ] *m* eyelet; eyelet hole; carnation, clove pink; **œillet d'Inde** (*Tagetes*) marigold

œilleton [œjtõ] *m* eye, bud; eyepiece; sight (*of rifle, camera, etc.*)

œillette [œjɛt] *f* opium poppy

œnologie [enɔlɔʒi] *f* science of viniculture, oenology

œsophage [ezɔfaʒ] *m* esophagus

œstres [ɛstr] *mpl* botflies, nose flies

œuf [œf] *m* (*pl* **œufs** [ø]) egg; **marcher sur des œufs** to walk on thin ice; **œuf à la coque** soft-boiled egg; **œuf à repriser** darning egg; **œuf de Colomb** ingenious, though obvious, solution to a problem; **œuf de Pâques** Easter egg; **œuf rouge** Easter egg; **œuf dur** hard-boiled egg; **œuf mollet** soft-boiled egg; **œuf poché** poached egg; **œufs** spawn, roe; **œufs au lait** custard; **œufs au miroir** fried eggs; **œufs brouillés** scrambled eggs; **œuf sur le plat** fried egg; **plein comme un œuf** chock-full; **tondre un œuf** to squeeze blood out of a turnip; **tuer, écraser,** or **étouffer dans l'œuf** to nip in the bud

œuvre [œvr] *m* works (*of a painter*); **dans œuvre** inside (*measurements*); **hors d'œuvre** out of alignment; **le grand œuvre** the philosopher's stone; **le gros œuvre** (archit) the foundation, walls, and roof ‖ *f* work; piece of work; **bonnes œuvres** good works; **mettre en œuvre** to implement, to use; **mettre qn à l'œuvre** to set s.o. to work; **mettre tout en œuvre** to leave no stone unturned; **œuvres complètes** collected works; **œuvres mortes** (naut) topsides; **œuvre pie** good deed, good work; **œuvres vives** (naut) hull below water line; **se mettre à l'œuvre** to get to work

offen·sant [ɔfãsã] **-sante** [sãt] *adj* offensive

offense [ɔfãs] *f* offense; **faire offense à qn** to offend s.o.; **soit dit sans offense** with all due respect

offenser [ɔfãse] *tr* to offend ‖ *ref* to be offended

offen·sif [ɔfãsif] **-sive** [siv] *adj* & *f* offensive

office [ɔfis] *m* office, (eccl) office, service; **d'office** ex officio; **faire l'office de** to act as; **office d'ami** friendly turn; **remplir son office** (fig) to do its job ‖ *f* pantry

offi·ciel -cielle [ɔfisjɛl] *adj* & *mf* official

officier [ɔfisje] *m* officer; (naut) mate; **officier de service** (mil) officer of the day; **officier ministériel** notary public; **officier supérieur** (mil) field officer ‖ *intr* to officiate

offi·cieux [ɔfisjø] **-cieuse** [sjøz] *adj* unofficial, off-the-cuff; zealous; well-meant (*lie*); **faire l'officieux** to be officious

offrant [ɔfrɑ̃] *m*—**le plus offrant** the highest bidder

offre [ɔfr] *f* offer; **l'offre et la demande** supply and demand; **offres d'emploi** (formula in want ads) help wanted

offrir [ɔfrir] §65 *tr* to offer ‖ *ref* to offer oneself; to offer itself, to occur

offset [ɔfsɛt] *m invar* offset

offusquer [ɔfyske] *tr* to obfuscate, obscure; to irritate, displease ‖ *ref*—**s'offusquer de** to take offense at

ogive [ɔʒiv] *f* ogive; (rok) nose cone

ogre [ɔgr] **ogresse** [ɔgres] *mf* ogre; **manger comme un ogre** (coll) to eat like a horse

ohé [ɔe] *interj* hey!; **ohé du navire!** ship ahoy!

ohm [om] *m* ohm

oie [wa] *f* goose; simpleton; **oie blanche** simple little goose (*naïve girl*); **oie sauvage** wild goose

oignon [ɔɲɔ̃] *m* onion; (hort) bulb; (pathol) bunion; (coll) turnip, pocket watch; **aux petits oignons** (coll) perfect; **occupe-toi de tes oignons** (coll) mind your own business

oil [ɔil], [ɔj] *adv* (Old French) yes

oindre [wɛ̃dr] §35 *tr* to anoint

oi·seau [wazo] *m* (*pl* -seaux) bird; hod (*of mason*); (coll) character; **être comme l'oiseau sur la branche** to be here today and gone tomorrow; **oiseau de paradis, oiseau des îles** bird of paradise; **oiseau des tempêtes** stormy petrel; **oiseaux domestiques, oiseaux de basse-cour** poultry

oiseau-mouche [wazomuʃ] *m* (*pl* -mouches) hummingbird

oiseler [wazle] §34 *tr* to train (*hawks*) ‖ *intr* to trap birds

oiselet [wazlɛ] *m* little bird

oiseleur [wazlœr] *m* fowler

oise·lier [wazəlje] **-lière** [ljɛr] *mf* bird fancier

oi·seux [wazø] **-seuse** [zøz] *adj* useless

oi·sif [wazif] **-sive** [ziv] *adj* idle ‖ *mf* idler

oisillon [wazijɔ̃] *m* fledgling

oisiveté [wazivte] *f* idleness

oison [wazɔ̃] *m* gosling; (coll) ninny

O.K. [oke] *interj* (letterword) O.K.!

oléagi·neux [ɔleaʒinø] **-neuse** [nøz] *adj* oily

olfac·tif [ɔlfaktif] **-tive** [tiv] *adj* olfactory

olibrius [ɔlibrijys] *m* pedant; pest; braggart (*in medieval plays*)

oligarchie [ɔligarʃi] *f* oligarchy

olivaie [ɔlivɛ] *f* olive grove

olivâtre [ɔlivɑtr] *adj* olive (*complexion*)

olive [ɔliv] *adj invar* & *f* olive

olivette [ɔlivɛt] *f* olive grove

olivier [ɔlivje] *m* olive tree; olive wood; **Olivier** Oliver

olympiade [ɔlɛ̃pjad] *f* olympiad

olym·pien [ɔlɛ̃pjɛ̃] **-pienne** [pjɛn] *adj* Olympian

olympique [ɔlɛ̃pik] *adj* Olympic

ombilic [ɔ̃bilik] *m* umbilicus

ombili·cal -cale [ɔ̃bilikal] *adj* (*pl* -caux [ko]) umbilical

ombrage [ɔ̃braʒ] *m* shade; **porter ombrage à** to offend; **prendre ombrage (de)** to take offense (at)

ombrager [ɔ̃braʒe] §38 *tr* to shade

ombra·geux [ɔ̃braʒø] **-geuse** [ʒøz] *adj* shy, skittish; touchy; distrustful

ombre [ɔ̃br] *f* shadow; shade; **ombres (chinoises)** shadow play, shadowgraph; **une ombre au tableau** (coll) a fly in the ointment

ombrelle [ɔ̃brɛl] *f* parasol; (aer) umbrella

ombrer [ɔ̃bre] *tr* to shade; to apply eye shadow to

om·breux [ɔ̃brø] **-breuse** [brøz] *adj* shady

omelette [ɔmlɛt] *f* omelet

omettre [ɔmɛtr] §42 *tr* to omit

omission [ɔmisjɔ̃] *f* omission

omnibus [ɔmnibys] *adj* omnibus; local (*train*) ‖ *m* omnibus; local (*train*)

omnipo·tent [ɔmnipɔtɑ̃] **-tente** [tɑ̃t] *adj* omnipotent

omnis·cient [ɔmnisjɑ̃] **omnis·ciente** [ɔmnisjɑ̃t] *adj* omniscient

omnium [ɔmnjɔm] *m* (com) holding company, general trading company; (sports) open race

omnivore [ɔmnivɔr] *adj* omnivorous

omoplate [ɔmɔplat] *f* shoulder blade

on [ɔ̃] §87 *pron indef* one, they, people; (coll) we, e.g., **y va-t-on?** are we going there?; (coll) I, e.g., **on est fatigué** I am tired; (often translated by passive forms), e.g., **on sait que** it is generally known that

once [ɔ̃s] *f* ounce

oncle [ɔ̃kl] *m* uncle

onction [ɔ̃ksjɔ̃] *f* unction; eloquence

onc·tueux [ɔ̃ktɥø] **-tueuse** [tɥøz] *adj* unctuous; greasy; bland

onde [ɔ̃d] *f* wave; watering (*of silk*); (poetic) water; **les petites ondes** (rad) shortwave; **mettre en ondes** to put on the air; **onde de choc** (aer) shock wave; **onde porteuse** (rad) carrier wave; **ondes amorties** (rad) damped waves; **ondes entretenues** (rad) continuous waves; **ondes radiophoniques** airwaves; **onde sonore** sound wave

ondée [ɔ̃de] *f* shower

on-dit [ɔ̃di] *m invar* gossip, scuttlebutt

ondoyant [ɔ̃dwajɑ̃] **ondoyante** [ɔ̃dwajɑ̃t] *adj* undulating, wavy; wavering (*person*)

ondoyer [ɔ̃dwaje] §47 *tr* to baptize in an emergency ‖ *intr* to undulate, wave

ondulation [ɔ̃dylɑsjɔ̃] *f* undulation, waving; flowing (*e.g., of drapery*); wave (*of hair*); **à ondulations** rolling (*ground*); **ondulation permanente** permanent wave

ondu·lé -lée [ɔ̃dyle] *adj* wavy; corrugated

onduler [ɔ̃dyle] *tr* to wave (*hair*) ‖ *intr* to wave, to undulate

oné·reux [ɔnerø] **-reuse** [røz] *adj* onerous

ongle [ɔ̃gl] *m* nail, fingernail; **jusqu'au bout des ongles** to or at one's fingertips; **ongle des pieds** toenail

onglée [ɔ̃gle] *f* numbness in the fingertips

onglet [ɔ̃glɛ] m nail hole, groove (in blade); thimble; **à onglets** thumb-indexed; **monter sur onglet** (bb) to insert (a page)

onguent [ɔ̃gɑ̃] m ointment, salve

O.N.U. [ɔny] (acronym) or [ɔeny] (letterword) (**Organisation des Nations Unies**) f UN

onyx [ɔniks] m onyx

onzain *[ɔ̃zɛ̃] m eleven-line verse

onze *[ɔ̃z] adj & pron eleven; the Eleventh, e.g., **Jean onze** John the Eleventh; **onze heures** eleven o'clock ‖ m eleven; eleventh (in dates), e.g., **le onze mai** the eleventh of May

onzième *[ɔ̃zjɛm] adj, pron (masc, fem), & m eleventh

opale [ɔpal] f opal

opaque [ɔpak] adj opaque

opéra [ɔpera] m opera; opera house; **grand opéra, opéra sérieux** grand opera, **opéra bouffe** comic opera, opéra bouffe

opéra-comique [ɔperakɔmik] m (pl **opéras-comiques**) light opera

opéra·teur [ɔperatœr] **-trice** [tris] mf operator ‖ m cameraman

opération [ɔperasjɔ̃] f operation

opé·ré -rée [ɔpere] mf surgical patient

opérer [ɔpere] §10 tr to operate on; **opérer à chaud** to perform an emergency operation on (s.o.); **opérer qn de q.ch.** (med) to operate on s.o. for s.th. ‖ intr to operate; to work ‖ ref to occur, take place

opérette [ɔperet] f operetta, musical comedy

opia·cé -cée [ɔpjase] adj opiate

opiner [ɔpine] intr to opine; **opiner du bonnet** (coll) to be a yes man

opiniâtre [ɔpinjɑtr] adj stubborn

opiniâtreté [ɔpinjɑtrəte] f stubbornness

opinion [ɔpinjɔ̃] f opinion; public opinion; **avoir bonne opinion de** to think highly of; **avoir une piètre opinion de** to take a dim view of

opium [ɔpjɔm] m opium

oponce [ɔpɔ̃s] m prickly pear

opossum [ɔpɔsɔm] m opossum

oppor·tun [ɔpɔrtœ̃] **-tune** [tyn] adj opportune, timely, expedient

opportunisme [ɔpɔrtynist] adj opportunistic ‖ mf opportunist

opportunité [ɔpɔrtynite] f opportuneness

oppo·sant [ɔpozɑ̃] **-sante** [zɑ̃t] adj opposing ‖ mf opponent

oppo·sé -sée [ɔpoze] adj & m opposite, contrary; **à l'opposé de** contrary to

opposer [ɔpoze] tr to raise (an objection); **opposer q.ch. à** to set up s.th. against; to place s.th. opposite; to contrast s.th. with ‖ ref—**s'opposer à** to oppose, object to

opposite [ɔpozit] m—**à l'opposite (de)** opposite

opposition [ɔpozisjɔ̃] f opposition; contrast

oppresser [ɔprese] tr to oppress; to impede (respiration); to weigh upon (one's heart)

oppresseur [ɔprescœr] m oppressor

oppres·sif [ɔpresif] **oppres·sive** [ɔpresiv] adj oppressive

oppression [ɔpresjɔ̃] f oppression; difficulty in breathing

opprimer [ɔprime] tr to oppress

opprobre [ɔprɔbr] m opprobrium, shame

opter [ɔpte] intr to opt, to choose

opticien [ɔptisjɛ̃] m optician

optimisme [ɔptimism] m optimism

optimiste [ɔptimist] adj optimistic ‖ mf optimist

option [ɔpsjɔ̃] f option

optique [ɔptik] adj optic(al) ‖ f optics; perspective; **sous cette optique** from that point of view

opu·lent [ɔpylɑ̃] **-lente** [lɑ̃t] adj opulent

opuscule [ɔpyskyl] m opuscule, treatise; brochure, pamphlet

or [ɔr] m gold; **rouler sur l'or** to be rolling in money ‖ adv now; therefore

oracle [ɔrakl] m oracle

orage [ɔraʒ] m storm

ora·geux [ɔraʒø] **-geuse** [ʒøz] adj stormy

oraison [ɔrezɔ̃] f prayer; **oraison dominicale** Lord's Prayer; **oraison funèbre** funeral oration; **prononcer l'oraison funèbre de** (coll) to write off (a custom, institution, etc.)

o·ral -rale [ɔral] adj (pl **-raux** [ro]) oral

orange [ɔrɑ̃ʒ] adj invar orange (color) ‖ m orange (color) ‖ f orange (fruit)

oran·gé -gée [ɔrɑ̃ʒe] adj & m orange (color)

orangeade [ɔrɑ̃ʒad] f orangeade

oranger [ɔrɑ̃ʒe] m orange tree

orangeraie [ɔrɑ̃ʒre] f orange grove

orangerie [ɔrɑ̃ʒri] f orangery; orange grove

orang-outan [ɔrɑ̃utɑ̃] m (pl **orangs-outans**) orang-outang

ora·teur [ɔratœr] **-trice** [tris] mf orator; speaker

oratoire [ɔratwar] adj oratorical ‖ m (eccl) oratory

oratorio [ɔratɔrjo] m oratorio

orbite [ɔrbit] f orbit; socket (of eye); **placer sur son orbite, mettre en orbite** to orbit; **sur orbite** in orbit

orchestre [ɔrkɛstr] m orchestra; band; **orchestre de typique** rumba band

orchestrer [ɔrkɛstre] tr to orchestrate

orchidée [ɔrkide] f orchid

ordalie [ɔrdali] f (hist) ordeal

ordinaire [ɔrdiner] adj ordinary ‖ m ordinary; regular bill of fare; (mil) mess; **d'ordinaire, à l'ordinaire** ordinarily

ordi·nal -nale [ɔrdinal] adj & m (pl **-naux** [no]) ordinal

ordinateur [ɔrdinatœr] m (electron) computer

ordination [ɔrdinasjɔ̃] f ordination

ordonnance [ɔrdɔnɑ̃s] f ordinance; order, arrangement; (pharm) prescription

ordonna·teur [ɔrdɔnatœr] **-trice** [tris]

mf organizer; marshal; **ordonnateur des pompes funèbres** funeral director

ordon•né -née [ɔrdɔne] *adj* orderly

ordonner [ɔrdɔne] *tr* to arrange, put in order; to order; to prescribe (*e.g., medicine*); (eccl) to ordain; **ordonner à qn de** + *inf* to order s.o. to + *inf*; **ordonner q.ch. à qn** to order s.o. to do s.th.

ordre [ɔrdr] *m* order; **avoir de l'ordre** to be neat, orderly; **à vos ordres** at your service; **dans l'ordre d'entrée en scène** (theat) in order of appearance; **en ordre in order**; **jusqu'à nouvel ordre** until further notice; as things stand; **les ordres** (eccl) orders; **ordre du jour** (mil) order of the day; (parl) agenda; **ordre public** law and order; **payez à l'ordre de** (com) pay to the order of; **sous les ordres de** under the command of

ordure [ɔrdyr] *f* rubbish, filth; **ordures ménagères** garbage

ordu•rier [ɔrdyrje] **-rière** [rjɛr] *adj* lewd, filthy

orée [ɔre] *f* edge (*of a forest*)

oreille [ɔrɛj] *f* ear; **avoir l'oreille basse** to be humiliated; **dormir sur les deux oreilles** to sleep soundly; **dresser or tendre l'oreille** to prick up one's ears; **échauffer les oreilles à qn** to rile s.o. up; **faire la sourde oreille** to turn a deaf ear; **rompre les oreilles à qn** (coll) to talk s.o.'s head off; **se faire tirer l'oreille** (coll) to play hard to get

oreiller [ɔreje] *m* pillow

oreillette [ɔrejɛt] *f* earflap (*of cap*); (anat) auricle

oreillons [ɔrejɔ̃] *mpl* mumps

ores [ɔr] *adv*—**d'ores et déjà** [dɔrzedeʒa] from now on

Orfée [ɔrfe] *m* Orpheus

orfèvre [ɔrfɛvr] *m* goldsmith; silversmith; **être orfèvre en la matière** (coll) to know one's onions

orfèvrerie [ɔrfɛvrəri] *f* goldsmith's shop; goldsmith's trade; gold plate; gold or silver jewelry

orfraie [ɔrfrɛ] *f* osprey, fish hawk

organdi [ɔrgɑ̃di] *m* organdy

organe [ɔrgan] *m* organ; part (*of a machine*)

organique [ɔrganik] *adj* organic

organisa•teur [ɔrganizatœr] **-trice** [tris] *adj* organizing ‖ *mf* organizer

organisation [ɔrganizasjɔ̃] *f* organization

organiser [ɔrganize] *tr* to organize

organisme [ɔrganism] *m* organism; organization

organiste [ɔrganist] *mf* organist

orgasme [ɔrgasm] *m* orgasm

orge [ɔrʒ] *f* barley

orgelet [ɔrʒəle] *m* (pathol) sty

orgie [ɔrʒi] *f* orgy

orgue [ɔrg] *m* organ; **orgue de Barbarie** hand organ; **orgue de cinéma** theater organ ‖ *f*—**les grandes orgues** the pipe organ

orgueil [ɔrgœj] *m* pride, conceit; **avoir l'orgueil de** to take pride in

orgueil•leux [ɔrgœjø] **orgueil•leuse** [ɔrgœjøz] *adj* proud, haughty

orient [ɔrjɑ̃] *m* orient; east; **Orient** Orient, East

orien•tal -tale [ɔrjɑ̃tal] (*pl* -**taux** [to]) *adj* oriental; eastern, east ‖ (cap) *mf* Oriental (*person*)

orientation [ɔrjɑ̃tasjɔ̃] *f* orientation; **orientation professionnelle** vocational guidance

orienter [ɔrjɑ̃te] *tr* to orient; to guide ‖ *ref* to take one's bearings

orien•teur [ɔrjɑ̃tœr] **-teuse** [tøz] *mf* guidance counselor

orifice [ɔrifis] *m* orifice, hole, opening

origan [ɔrigɑ̃] *m* marjoram

originaire [ɔriʒinɛr] *adj* native; original, first

origi•nal -nale [ɔriʒinal] *adj* (*pl* -**naux** [no]) original; eccentric, peculiar ‖ *m* antique (*piece of furniture*); eccentric, card (*person*); (typ) copy, original

originalité [ɔriʒinalite] *f* originality; eccentricity

origine [ɔriʒin] *f* origin

origi•nel -nelle [ɔriʒinɛl] *adj* original (*sin; meaning*); primitive, early

ori•gnal [ɔriɲal] *m* (*pl* -**gnaux** [ɲo]) moose, elk

orillon [ɔrijɔ̃] *m* ear, handle; (archit) projection

ori•peau [ɔripo] *m* (*pl* -**peaux**) tinsel; **oripeaux** cheap finery

Orléans [ɔrleɑ̃] *f* Orléans; **la Nouvelle Orléans** New Orleans

orme [ɔrm] *m* elm; **attendez-moi sous l'orme** (coll) I won't be there

or•né -née [ɔrne] *adj* ornate

ornement [ɔrnəmɑ̃] *m* ornament

ornemen•tal -tale [ɔrnəmɑ̃tal] *adj* (*pl* -**taux** [to]) ornamental

orner [ɔrne] *tr* to ornament, to adorn

ornière [ɔrnjɛr] *f* rut, groove

ornithologie [ɔrnitɔlɔʒi] *f* ornithology

orphe•lin [ɔrfəlɛ̃] **-line** [lin] *adj* & *mf* orphan

orphelinat [ɔrfəlina] *m* orphanage (*asylum*)

orphéon [ɔrfeɔ̃] *m* male choir, glee club; brass band

orteil [ɔrtɛj] *m* toe; big toe; **gros orteil** big toe

O.R.T.F. [ɔɛrteɛf] *m* (letterword) (office de radio-télévision française) French radio and television system

orthodoxe [ɔrtɔdɔks] *adj* orthodox

orthographe [ɔrtɔgraf] *f* spelling, orthography

orthographier [ɔrtɔgrafje] *tr* to spell

ortie [ɔrti] *f* nettle

orviétan [ɔrvjetɑ̃] *m* nostrum

os [ɔs] *m* (*pl* os [o]) bone; **à gros os** big-boned; **os à moelle** marrowbone; **trempé jusqu'aux os** soaked to the skin

osciller [ɔsile] *intr* to oscillate; to waver, hesitate

o•sé -sée [oze] *adj* daring, bold; risqué, off-color

oseille [ozɛj] *f* sorrel; (slang) dough

oser [oze] *tr* & *intr* to dare

osier [ozje] *m* osier; **d'osier** wicker

osmose [ɔsmoz] f osmosis
ossature [ɔsatyr] f bone structure; framework, skeleton
ossements [ɔsmɑ̃] mpl bones, remains
os·seux [ɔsø] os·seuse [ɔsøz] adj bony
ossifier [ɔsifje] tr & ref to ossify
os·su -sue [ɔsy] adj bony; big-boned
ostensible [ɔstɑ̃sibl] adj conspicuous, ostensible; ostentatious
ostensoir [ɔstɑ̃swar] m monstrance
ostentatoire [ɔstɑ̃tatwar] adj ostentatious
ostracisme [ɔstrasism] m ostracism
otage [ɔtaʒ] m hostage
otalgie [ɔtalʒi] f earache
O.T.A.N. or OTAN [ɔtan], [ɔtɑ̃], [ɔtɑ̃] f (acronym) (Organisation du traité de l'Atlantique Nord)—l'O.T.A.N. NATO
otarie [ɔtari] f sea lion
OTASE [ɔtaz] f (acronym) (Organisation du traité de l'Asie du Sud-Est)—l'OTASE SEATO
ôter [ote] tr to remove, to take away; to take off; to tip (one's hat); ôter q.ch. à qn to remove or take away s.th. from s.o.; ôter q.ch. de q.ch. to take s.th. away from s.th. || ref to withdraw, to get out of the way
otto·man [ɔtɔmɑ̃] -mane [man] adj Ottoman || m ottoman (corded fabric) || f ottoman (divan) || (cap) mf Ottoman (person)
ou [u] conj or; ou . . . ou either . . . or
où [u] adv where; d'où from where, whence; où que wherever; par où which way || conj where; when; d'où from where, whence; par où through which; partout où wherever
ouailles [waj] fpl (eccl) flock
ouais [we] interj (coll) oh yeah!
ouate *[wat] f cotton batting, wadding
ouater *[wate] tr to pad, to wad
oubli [ubli] m forgetfulness; omission, oversight; tomber dans l'oubli to fall into oblivion
oublier [ublije] tr & intr to forget || ref to forget oneself; to be forgotten
oubliettes [ublijet] fpl dungeon of oblivion
ou·blieux [ublijø] -blieuse [blijøz] adj forgetful, oblivious, unmindful
ouche [u/ʃ] f orchard; vegetable garden
ouest [west] adj invar & m west
ouest-alle·mand [westalmɑ̃] -mande [mɑ̃d] adj West German || (cap) mf West German
ouf *[uf] interj whew!
oui [wi] m invar yes; les oui l'emportent the ayes have it || adv yes; je crois que oui I think so; oui madame yes ma'am; oui monsieur yes sir; oui mon capitaine (mon général, etc.) yes sir
ouï-dire [widir] m invar hearsay; simples ouï-dire (law) hearsay evidence
ouïe [wi] f hearing; être tout ouïe (tutwi) to be all ears; ouïes gills; sound holes (of violin) || interj oh my!
ouïr [wir] (used only in: inf, compound tenses with pp ouï, and 2d pl impv

oyez) tr to hear; oyez . . . ! hear ye . . . !
ouragan [uragɑ̃] m hurricane
ourdir [urdir] tr to warp (cloth before weaving); to hatch (e.g., a plot)
ourler [urle] tr to hem; ourler à jour to hemstitch
ourlet [urle] m hem; ourlet de la jupe hemline
ours [urs] m bear; (fig) lone wolf; ours en peluche teddy bear; ours mal léché unmannerly boor; ours marin (zool) seal; vendre la peau de l'ours avant de l'avoir tué to count one's chickens before they are hatched
ourse [urs] f she-bear; la Grande Ourse the Big Dipper, the Great Bear; la Petite Ourse the Little Dipper, the Little Bear
oursin [ursɛ̃] m sea urchin
ourson [urs5] m bear cub
ouste [ust] interj (coll) out!, out you go!
outarde [utard] f (orn) bustard
outil [uti] m tool, implement
outillage [utijaʒ] m tools; equipment
outil·lé -lée [utije] adj equipped with tools; tooled-up (factory)
outiller [utije] tr to equip with tools; to tool up (a factory) || ref to supply oneself with equipment; to tool up
outilleur [utijœr] m toolmaker
outrage [utraʒ] m outrage, affront; ravages (of time); contempt of court; faire outrage à qn to outrage s.o.; outrage aux bonnes mœurs traffic in pornography; outrage public à la pudeur indecent exposure
outrager [utraʒe] §38 tr to outrage, to affront
outra·geux [utraʒø] -geuse [ʒøz] adj outrageous, insulting
outrance [utrɑ̃s] f excess; exaggeration; à outrance to the limit
outran·cier [utrɑ̃sje] -cière [sjer] adj extreme, excessive, out-and-out || mf extremist, out-and-outer
outre [utr] f goatskin canteen || adv further; d'outre en d'outre right through; en outre besides, moreover; passer outre à to ignore (e.g., an order) || prep in addition to, apart from; beyond
ou·tré -trée [utre] adj overdone, exaggerated; exasperated
outrecui·dant [utrəkɥidɑ̃] -dante [dɑ̃t] adj self-satisfied; insolent, presumptuous
outre-Manche [utrəmɑ̃ʃ] adv across the Channel
outremer [utrəmer] m ultramarine, lapis lazuli (color)
outre-mer [utrəmer] adv overseas
outre-monts [utrəm5] adv over the mountains (i.e., the Alps)
outrepasser [utrəpase] tr to go beyond, to exceed
outrer [utre] tr to overdo, to exaggerate; to exasperate
outre-tombe [utrət5b] adv—d'outre-tombe posthumous
ou·vert [uver] -verte [vert] adj open;

exposed; frank, candid; on (*said of meter, gas, etc.*)

ouverture [uvertyr] *f* opening; hole, gap; (mus) overture; (phot) aperture

ouvrable [uvrabl] *adj* working, e.g., **jour ouvrable** working day

ouvrage [uvraʒ] *m* work, handiwork; piece of work; work, treatise

ouvrager [uvraʒe] §38 *tr* to work (*e.g., iron*); to turn (*wood*)

ou·vré -vrée [uvre] *adj* worked, wrought; finished (*product*)

ouvre-boîtes [uvrəbwat] *m invar* can opener

ouvre-bouteilles [uvrəbutej] *m invar* bottle opener

ouvreur [uvrœr] *m* opener (*in poker*)

ouvreuse [uvrøz] *f* usher

ou·vrier [uvrije] **-vrière** [vrijer] *adj* working, worker, worker's, workingman's || *mf* worker || *m* workman, laborer; workingman || *f* workingwoman

ouvrir [uvrir] §65 *tr* to open; to turn on (*the light; the radio or television; the gas*); **ouvrir boutique** to set up shop || *intr* to be open; to open (*said of store, school, etc.; said of card player*) || *ref* to open; to be opened; **s'ouvrir à** to open up to, confide in

ouvroir [uvrwar] *m* workroom

ovaire [ɔver] *m* ovary

ovale [ɔval] *adj* & *m* oval

ovation [ɔvasjɔ̃] *f* ovation

ovationner [ɔvasjɔne] *tr* to give an ovation to

Ovide [ɔvid] *m* Ovid

oxford [ɔksfɔr] *m* oxford cloth

oxyde [ɔksid] *m* oxide

oxyder [ɔkside] *tr* & *ref* to oxidize

oxygène [ɔksiʒen] *m* oxygen

oxygéner [ɔksiʒene] §10 *tr* to oxygenate; to bleach (*hair*) || *ref*—**s'oxygéner les poumons** (coll) to fill one's lungs full of ozone

oxyton [ɔksitɔ̃] *adj* & *m* oxytone

ozone [ozɔn] *m* ozone

P

P, p [pe] *m invar* sixteenth letter of the French alphabet

pacage [pakaʒ] *m* pasture

pacifica·teur [pasifikatœr] **-trice** [tris] *mf* pacifier

pacifier [pasifje] *tr* to pacify

pacifique [pasifik] *adj* pacific || **Pacifique** *adj* & *m* Pacific

pacifisme [pasifism] *m* pacifism

pacifiste [pasifist] *mf* pacifist

pacotille [pakotij] *f* junk; **de pacotille** shoddy; junky

pacte [pakt] *m* pact, covenant

pactiser [paktize] *intr* to compromise; to traffic (*with the enemy*)

paf [paf] *adj* (slang) tipsy, tight || *interj* bang!

pagaie [page] *f* paddle

pagaïe or **pagaille** [pagaj] *f* disorder; **en pagaïe** (coll) in great quantity; (coll) in a mess

paganisme [paganism] *m* paganism

pagayer [pageje] §49 *tr* & *intr* to paddle

page [paʒ] *m* page || *f* page (*of a book*); **être à la page** to be up to date

paginer [paʒine] *tr* to page

pagne [paɲ] *m* loincloth

paie [pe] *f* pay, wages

paiement [pemã] *m* payment

païen [pajɛ̃] **païenne** [pajen] *adj* & *mf* pagan

pail·lard [pajar] **pail·larde** [pajard] *adj* ribald || *mf* debauchee

paillasse [pajas] *m* buffoon || *f* straw mattress; (slang) whore

paillasson [pajasɔ̃] *m* doormat

paille [paj] *f* straw; flaw; (Bib) mote; **paille de fer** iron shavings

pail·lé -lée [paje] *adj* rush-bottomed (*chair*)

pailler [paje] *m* straw stack || *tr* to bottom (*a chair*) with straw; to mulch

pailleter [pajte] §34 *tr* to spangle

paillette [pajet] *f* spangle; flake (*of mica; of soap*); grain (*of gold*); flaw (*in a diamond*)

pain [pɛ̃] *m* bread; loaf (*of bread, of sugar*); cake (*of soap*); pat (*of butter*); **avoir du pain sur la planche** (coll) to have a lot to do; **pain à cacheter** sealing wafer; **pain aux raisins** raisin roll; **pain bis** brown bread; **pain complet** whole-wheat bread; **pain de fantaisie** bread sold by the loaf (*instead of by weight*); **pain de mie** sandwich bread; **pain d'épice** gingerbread; **pain grillé** toast; **pain perdu** French toast; **petit pain** roll; **se vendre comme des petits pains** (coll) to sell like hot cakes

pair paire [per] *adj* even (*number*) || *m* peer; equal; (com) par; **hors de pair, hors pair** unrivaled; **marcher de pair avec** to keep abreast of; **travailler au pair** (coll) to work for one's keep; **au pair** at par || *f* pair; couple; brace (*of dogs, pistols, etc.*); yoke (*of oxen*)

pairesse [peres] *f* peeress

pairie [peri], [peri] *f* peerage

paisible [pezibl] *adj* peaceful

paître [petr] §48 *tr* & *intr* to graze; **envoyer paître** (coll) to send packing

paix [pe] *f* peace

Pakistan [pakistã] *m*—**le Pakistan** Pakistan

pakista·nais [pakistane] **-naise** [nez] *adj* Pakistani || (cap) *mf* Pakistani

pal [pal] *m* (*pl* **paux** [po] or **pals**) pale, stake

palabre [palabr] *m & f* palaver

palace [palas] *m* luxury hotel

palais [palɛ] *m* palace; palate; court-house, law courts

palan [palɑ̃] *m* block and tackle

palanque [palɑ̃k] *f* stockade

pala·tal -tale [palatal] (*pl* **-taux** [to] **-tales**) *adj & f* palatal

pale [pal] *f* blade (*of, e.g., oar*); stake; sluice gate; (eccl) pall

pâle [pɑl] *adj* pale

palefrenier [palfrənje] *m* groom; (coll) hick, oaf

palefroi [palfrwa] *m* palfrey

paleron [palrɔ̃] *m* bottom chuck roast

palet [palɛ] *m* disk, flat stone; puck

paletot [palto] *m* topcoat

palette [palɛt] *f* palette; paddle

pâleur [pɑlœr] *f* pallor; paleness

palier [palje] *m* landing (*of stairs*); plateau (*of curve of a graph*); (mach) bearing; **en palier** on the level; **palier à billes** ball bearing; **par paliers** graduated (*e.g., tax*)

pâlir [pɑlir] *tr & intr* to pale, turn pale

palis [pali] *m* picket fence

palissade [palisad] *f* palisade; fence

palissandre [palisɑ̃dr] *m* rosewood

pallier [palje] *tr* to palliate; to mitigate || *intr* (with *dat*) to mitigate

palmarès [palmares] *m* list of winners

palme [palm] *f* (bot) palm

palmeraie [palmərɛ] *f* palm grove

palmier [palmje] *m* palm tree

palmipède [palmiped] *adj* webfooted || *m* webfoot

palombe [palɔ̃b] *f* ringdove

palourde [palurd] *f* clam

palpable [palpabl] *adj* palpable; plain, obvious

palper [palpe] *tr* to feel; to palpate; (coll) to pocket (*money*)

palpiter [palpite] *intr* to palpitate

palsambleu [palsɑ̃blø] *interj* zounds!

paltoquet [paltɔkɛ] *m* nonentity

palu·déen -déenne [palydeɛ̃] **-déenne** [deɛn] *adj* marsh (*plant*); swamp (*fever*)

paludisme [palydism] *m* malaria

pâmer [pɑme] *ref* to swoon

pâmoison [pɑmwazɔ̃] *f* swoon

pamphlet [pɑ̃flɛ] *m* lampoon

pamplemousse [pɑ̃pləmus] *m & f* grapefruit

pan [pɑ̃] *m* tail (*of shirt or coat*); section; side, face; patch (*of sky*); **Pan** Pan || *interj* bang!

panacée [panase] *f* panacea

panachage [panaʃaʒ] *m* mixing; **faire du panachage** to split one's vote

panache [panaʃ] *m* plume; wreath (*of smoke*); **aimer le panache** to be fond of show; **avoir son panache** (coll) to be tipsy; **faire panache** to somersault, to turn over

pana·ché -chée [panaʃe] *adj* variegated; mixed (*salad*); motley (*crowd*)

panacher [panaʃe] *tr* to variegate; to plume; to split (*one's vote*) || *ref* to become variegated

panais [panɛ] *m* parsnip

panama [panama] *m* panama hat; **le**

Panama Panama; **Panama** Panama City

panaris [panari] *m* (pathol) whitlow, felon

pancarte [pɑ̃kart] *f* placard; poster, sign

panchromatique [pɑ̃krɔmatik] *adj* panchromatic

pancréas [pɑ̃kreas] *m* pancreas

pandémonium [pɑ̃demɔnjɔm] *m* den of iniquity; pandemonium

pa·né -née [pane] *adj* breaded

panetière [pantjɛr] *f* breadbox

panier [panje] *m* basket; hoop (*of skirt*); creel (*trap*); **être dans le même panier** to be in the same boat; **panier à ouvrage** work basket; **panier à papier** wastepaper basket; **panier à provisions** shopping basket; **panier à salade** wire salad washer; (coll) paddy wagon; **panier percé** spendthrift

panier-repas [panjerəpa] *m* (*pl* **paniers-repas**) box lunch

panique [panik] *adj & f* panic

panne [pan] *f* breakdown, trouble; plush; fat (*of pig*); peen (*of hammer*); tip (*of soldering iron*); bank (*of clouds*); purlin (*of roof*); daub; (theat) small part; (en) **panne sèche** (public sign) out of gas; **être dans la panne** (coll) to be hard up; **être en panne** (coll) to be unable to continue; **être en panne de** (coll) to be deprived of; **laisser en panne** to leave in the lurch; **mettre en panne** (naut) to heave to; **panne fendue** claw (*of hammer*); **rester en panne** to come to a standstill; **tomber en panne** to have a breakdown

pan·né -née [pane] *adj* (slang) hard up

pan·neau [pano] *m* (*pl* **-neaux**) panel; snare, net; **condamner les panneaux** (naut) to batten down the hatches; **donner dans le panneau** to walk into the trap; **panneau d'affichage** billboard; **panneau de tête** headboard (*of bed*); **panneaux** paneling; **panneaux de signalisation** traffic signs; **tomber** or **donner dans le panneau** to be taken in, to fall into a trap

panoplie [panɔpli] *f* panoply

panorama [panɔrama] *m* panorama

panoramiquer [panɔramike] *intr* (mov, telv) to pan

panse [pɑ̃s] *f* belly; rumen, first stomach

pansement [pɑ̃smɑ̃] *m* (surg) dressing

panser [pɑ̃se] *tr* to dress, bandage; to groom (*an animal*)

pan·su -sue [pɑ̃sy] *adj* potbellied

pantalon [pɑ̃talɔ̃] *m* trousers, pair of trousers; panties; slacks; **pantalon à pattes d'éléphant** bell-bottomed trousers; **pantalon corsaire** pedal pushers; **pantalon de coutil** ducks; blue jeans; **pantalon de golf** knickers; **pantalon de ski** ski pants

pante [pɑ̃t] *m* (slang) guy

panteler [pɑ̃tle] §34 *intr* to pant

panthéisme [pɑ̃teism] *m* pantheism

panthéon [pɑ̃teɔ̃] *m* pantheon

panthère [pɑ̃tɛr] *f* panther

pantin [pɑ̃tɛ̃] *m* puppet; jumping jack; **pantin articulé** string puppet

pantomime [pɑ̃tɔmim] *f* pantomime

pantou·flard [pɑ̃tuflar] **-flarde** [flard] *mf* (coll) homebody

pantoufle [pɑ̃tufl] *f* slipper

pantoufler [pɑ̃tufle] *intr* to leave government service

paon [pɑ̃] *m* peacock, peafowl; peacock butterfly

paonne [pan] *f* peahen

papa [papa] *m* papa; **à la papa** (coll) cautiously; **de papa** (coll) outmoded; **papa gâteau** (coll) sugar daddy

papas [papɑs] *m* pope (*in Orthodox Church*)

papauté [papote] *f* papacy

pape [pap] *m* pope

pape·lard [paplar] **-larde** [lard] *adj* hypocritical ‖ *mf* hypocrite ‖ *m* scrap of paper

paperasse [papras] *f* old paper

paperasserie [paprasri] *f* red tape

paperas·sier [paprasje] **paperas·sière** [paprasjɛr] *adj* fond of red tape ‖ *mf* bureaucrat

papeterie [paptri] *f* paper mill; stationery store

pape·tier [paptje] **-tière** [tjɛr] *mf* stationer

papier [papje] *m* paper; newspaper article; document; piece of paper; **être dans les petits papiers de** (coll) to be in the good graces of; **gratter du papier** to scribble; **papier à calquer, papier végétal** tracing paper; **papier à en-tête** letterhead; **papier à lettres** writing paper; **papier à machine** typewriter paper; **papier à musique** staff paper; **papier bible, indien,** or **pelure** Bible paper, onionskin; **papier buvard** blotting paper; **papier carbone** carbon paper; **papier collant** Scotch tape; **papier d'emballage** wrapping paper; **papier de soie** tissue paper; **papier d'étain** tin foil; **papier de verre** sandpaper; **papier hygiénique** toilet paper; **papier journal** newsprint; **papier kraft** cardboard (*for packing*); **papier mâché** papier-mâché; **papier ministre** foolscap; **papier paraffiné** wax paper; **papier peint** wallpaper; **papier rayé** lined paper; **papier sensible** photographic paper; **papier tue-mouches** flypaper; **rayez cela de vos papiers!** (coll) don't count on it!

papier-filtre [papjefiltrə] *m* filter paper

papier-monnaie [papjemɔnɛ] *m* paper money

papier-pierre [papjepjɛr] *m* (*pl* **papiers-pierre**) papier-mâché

papille [papij] [papil] *f* papilla; **papille gustative** taste bud

papillon [papijɔ̃] *m* butterfly; flier, handbill; inset; form, application; thumbscrew, wing nut; butterfly valve; rider (*to document*); (coll) parking ticket; **papillon de nuit** moth; **papillons noirs** gloomy thoughts

papillonner [papijɔne] *intr* to flit about

papillote [papijɔt] *f* curlpaper; (culin) paper wrapper

papilloter [papijɔte] *intr* to blink; to flicker

papoter [papɔte] *intr* to chitchat

paprika [paprika] *m* paprika

papyrus [papirys] *m* papyrus

pâque [pɑk] *f* Passover; **la pâque russe** Russian Easter; **Pâque** Passover

paquebot [pakbo] *m* liner

pâquerette [pɑkrɛt] *f* white daisy

Pâques [pɑk] *m* Easter ‖ *fpl* Easter; **faire ses pâques** or **Pâques** to take Easter Communion; **Pâques fleuries** Palm Sunday

paquet [pakɛ] *m* packet, bundle; package; parcel; pack (*of cigarettes*); dressing down; **être un paquet d'os** [dos] to be nothing but skin and bones; **faire son paquet** (coll) to pack up; **mettre le paquet** (coll) to shoot the works; **paquet de mer** heavy sea; **petit paquet** parcel (*under a kilogram*); **petits paquets** parcel post; **un paquet de** a lot of

par [par] *prep* by; through; out of, e.g., **par la fenêtre** out of the window; per, a, e.g., **huit dollars par jour** eight dollars per day, eight dollars a day; on, e.g., **par une belle matinée** on a beautiful morning; in, e.g., **par temps de brume** in foggy weather; **de par la loi** in the name of the law; **par avion** (formula on envelope) air mail; **par delà** beyond; **par derrière** at the back, the back way; **par devant** in front, before; **par exemple** for example; **par ici** this way; **par là** that way; **par où?** which way?

para [para] *m* (coll) paratrooper

parabole [parabɔl] *f* parable; (*curve*) parabola

parachever [paraʃve] §2 *tr* to finish off

parachutage [paraʃytaʒ] *m* airdrop, airdropping

parachute [paraʃyt] *m* parachute

parachuter [paraʃyte] *tr* to airdrop; (coll) to appoint in haste

parachutisme [paraʃytism] *m* parachuting; (sports) skydiving

parachutiste [paraʃytist] *mf* parachutist; (sports) skydiver ‖ *m* paratrooper

parade [parad] *f* show; parry; sudden stop (*of horse*); come-on (*in front of sideshow*); (mil) inspection, parade; **à la parade** on parade; **faire parade de** to show off, to display

parader [parade] *intr* to show off

paradis [paradi] *m* paradise; (theat) peanut gallery

paradoxal paradoxale [paradɔksal] *adj* (*pl* **paradoxaux** [paradɔkso]) paradoxical

paradoxe [paradɔks] *m* paradox

parafe [paraf] *m* flourish; initials

parafer [parafe] *tr* to initial

paraffine [parafin] *f* paraffin

paraffiner [parafine] *tr* to paraffin

parages [paraʒ] *mpl* region, vicinity; **dans ces parages** in these parts

paragraphe [paragraf] *m* paragraph

Paraguay [parage] *m*—le Paraguay Paraguay

paraguayen [paragejɛ̃] **paraguayenne** [paragejen] *adj* Paraguayan || (*cap*) *mf* Paraguayan

paraître [parɛtr] §12 *intr* to appear; to seem; to come out; to show off; **à ce qu'il paraît** from all appearances; **faire paraître** to publish; **vient de paraître** just out

parallèle [paralɛl] *adj* parallel || *m* parallel, comparison; (geog) parallel || *f* (geom) parallel

paralyser [paralize] *tr* to paralyze

paralysie [paralizi] *f* paralysis

paralytique [paralitik] *adj & mf* paralytic

parangon [parɑ̃gɔ̃] *m* paragon

paranoïaque [paranɔjak] *adj & mf* paranoiac

parapet [parapɛ] *m* railing, parapet; (mil) parapet

paraphe [paraf] *m* flourish; initials

parapher [parafe] *tr* to initial

paraphrase [parafraz] *f* circumlocution, paraphrase; commentary

paraphraser [parafraze] *tr* to paraphrase

parapluie [paraplɥi] *m* umbrella

parasite [parazit] *adj* parasitic(al) || *m* parasite; **parasites** (rad) static

parasiter [parazite] *tr* to live as a parasite on or in (*a host*); (fig) to sponge on

parasol [parasɔl] *m* parasol; beach umbrella

paratonnerre [paratoner] *m* lightning rod

parâtre [parɑtr] *m* stepfather; cruel father

paravent [paravɑ̃] *m* folding screen

parbleu [parblø] *interj* rather!, by Jove!, you bet!

parc [park] *m* park; sheepfold; corral, pen; playpen; grounds, property; (mil) supply depot; (rr) rolling stock; **parc à huîtres** oyster bed; **parc automobile** motor pool; **parc de stationnement (payant)** parking lot

parcage [parkaʒ] *m* parking

parcelle [parsɛl] *f* particle; plot

parce que [pars(ə)kə] *conj* because

parchemin [parʃəmɛ̃] *m* parchment; (coll) sheepskin (*diploma*)

parchemi·né **-née** [parʃəmine] *adj* wrinkled

parcheminer [parʃəmine] *tr* to parchmentize || *ref* to shrivel up

par-ci [parsi] *adv*—**par-ci par-là** here and there

parcimo·nieux [parsimɔnjø] **-nieuse** [njøz] *adj* parsimonious

parcomètre [parkɔmetr] *m* parking meter

parcourir [parkurir] §14 *tr* to travel through, to tour; to wander about; to cover (*a distance*); to scour (*the country*); to glance through

parcours [parkur] *m* run, trip; route, distance covered; round (*e.g., of golf*); stroke (*of piston*)

par-delà [pardəla] *adv & prep* beyond

par-derrière [pardɛrjer] *adv & prep* behind

par-dessous [pardəsu] *adv & prep* underneath

pardessus [pardəsy] *m* overcoat

par-dessus [pardəsy] *adv* on top, over || *prep* on top of, over

par-devant [pardəvɑ̃] *adv* in front || *prep* in front of, before

par-devers [pardəver] *prep* in the presence of; **par-devers soi** in one's own possession

pardi [pardi] *interj* (coll) of course!

pardon [pardɔ̃] *m* pardon; Breton pilgrimage || *adv* (to contradict a negative statement or question) yes, e.g., **Vous ne parlez pas français, n'est-ce pas? Pardon, je le parle très bien** You don't speak French, do you? Yes, I speak it very well || *interj* pardon me!; (slang) oh boy!

pardonnable [pardɔnabl] *adj* pardonable

pardonner [pardɔne] *tr* to pardon; **pardonner q.ch. à qn** to pardon s.o. for s.th. || *intr* (with *dat*) to pardon, to forgive; **ne pas pardonner** to be fatal (*said of illness, mistake, etc.*)

pare-balles [parbal] *adj invar* bulletproof

pare-boue [parbu] *m invar* mudguard

pare-brise [parbriz] *m invar* windshield

pare-chocs [parʃɔk] *m invar* (aut) bumper

pare-étincelles [paretɛ̃sel] *m invar* fire screen

pa·reil -reille [parej] *adj* identical, the same; such, such a || *mf* equal, match; **sans pareil, sans pareille** without parallel, unequaled || *m*—**c'est du pareil au même** (coll) it's six of one and half dozen of the other || *f* same (*thing*); **rendre la pareille à qn** to pay s.o. back in his own coin

pareillement [parejmɑ̃] *adv* likewise

parement [parmɑ̃] *m* cuff; facing; trimming; (eccl) parament

pa·rent [parɑ̃] **-rente** [rɑ̃t] *adj* like || *mf* relative; **parents** parents; relatives; ancestors; **plus proche parent** next of kin

parenté [parɑ̃te] *f* relationship; relations

parenthèse [parɑ̃tez] *f* parenthesis; **entre parenthèses** in parentheses

parer [pare] *tr* an adorn; to parry; to prepare || *intr*—**parer à** to provide for || *ref* to show off

pare-soleil [parsɔlej] *m invar* sun visor

paresse [parɛs] *f* laziness

paresser [parese] *intr* (coll) to loaf

pares·seux [paresø] **-seuse** [paresøz] *adj* lazy || *mf* lazy person, lazybones; malingerer || *m* (zool) sloth

par ex. *abbr* (**par exemple**) e.g.

parfaire [parfer] §29 *tr* to perfect; to make up (*e.g., a sum of money*)

par·fait -faite [parfɛ] **-faite** [fɛt] *adj & m* perfect || **parfait** *interj* fine!, excellent!

parfaitement [parfɛtmɑ̃] *adv* perfectly; completely; certainly, of course

parfois [parfwa] *adv* sometimes

parfum [parfœ̃] *m* perfume; aroma; bouquet (*of wines*); flavor (*of ice cream*)

parfumer [parfyme] *tr* to perfume; to flavor || *ref* to use perfume

pari [pari] *m* bet, wager

paria [parja] *m* pariah

parier [parje] *tr & intr* to bet, wager

Paris [pari] *m* Paris

pari·sien [parizjɛ̃] **-sienne** [zjɛn] *adj* Parisian || (*cap*) *mf* Parisian

parité [parite] *f* parity; likeness; evenness (*of numbers*)

parjure [parʒyr] *adj* perjured || *mf* perjurer || *m* perjury

parking [parkiŋ] *m* parking lot

par·lant [parlɑ̃] **-lante** [lɑ̃t] *adj* speaking; talking (*e.g., picture*); eloquent, expressive

parlement [parləmɑ̃] *m* parliament

parlementaire [parləmɑ̃tɛr] *adj* parliamentary || *mf* peace envoy; member of a parliament, legislator

parlementer [parləmɑ̃te] *intr* to parley

parler [parle] *m* speech, way of speaking; dialect || *tr & intr* to speak, to talk

par·leur [parlœr] **-leuse** [løz] *mf*—**beau parleur** good talker; windbag

parloir [parlwar] *m* reception room

parlote [parlɔt] *f* (coll) talk, gossip, rumor

parmi [parmi] *prep* among

Parnasse [parnɑs] *m*—**le Parnasse** Parnassus (*poetry*); Mount Parnassus

parodie [parɔdi] *f* parody, travesty

parodier [parɔdje] *tr* to parody, to travesty

paroi [parwa] *f* partition, wall; inner side; (anat) wall

paroisse [parwas] *f* parish

parois·sial -siale [parwasjal] *adj* (*pl* **parois·siaux** [parwasjo]) parochial, parish

parois·sien [parwasjɛ̃] **parois·sienne** [parwasjɛn] *mf* parishioner || *m* prayer book; (coll) fellow

parole [parɔl] *f* word; speech; word, promise; **avoir la parole** to have the floor; **donner la parole à** to recognize, to give the floor to; **sur parole** on one's word

paro·lier [parɔlje] **-lière** [ljɛr] *mf* lyricist; librettist

parpaing [parpɛ̃] *m* concrete block; building block

parquer [parke] *tr* to park; to pen in || *intr* to be penned in || *ref* to park

Parques [park] *fpl* Fates

parquet [parke] *m* parquet, floor; floor (*of stock exchange*); public prosecutor's office

parqueter [parkəte] §34 *tr* to parquet, to floor

parrain [parɛ̃] *m* godfather; sponsor

parricide [parisid] *mf* parricide, patricide (*person*) || *m* parricide, patricide (*act*)

parsemer [parsəme] §2 *tr* to sprinkle; to spangle

part [par] *m* newborn child; dropping (*of young by animal in labor*) || *f* part, share; **aller quelque part** (coll)

to go to the toilet; **à part** aside; aside from; **à part entière** with full privileges; **autre part** elsewhere; **avoir part au gâteau** (coll) to have a slice in the pie; **d'autre part** besides; **de la part de** on the part of, from; **de part en part** through and through; **de toutes parts** on all sides; **d'une part . . . d'autre part**; on the one hand . . . on the other hand; **faire la part de** to make allowance for; **faire part de** to announce; **faire part de q.ch. à qn** to inform s.o. of s.th.; **nulle part** nowhere; **nulle part ailleurs** nowhere else; **pour ma part** as for me, for my part; **prendre en bonne part** to take good-naturedly; **prendre en mauvaise part** to take offense at; **prendre part à** to take part in; **quelque part** somewhere

partage [partaʒ] *m* division, partition; sharing; share; tie vote; **échoir en partage à qn** to fall to s.o.'s lot

partager [partaʒe] §38 *tr* to share; to divide

partance [partɑ̃s] *f* departure; **en partance** leaving; **en partance pour** bound for

partant [partɑ̃] *m* (sports) starter; **partants** departing guests, departing travelers, etc. || *adv* (lit) consequently

partenaire [partənɛr] *mf* partner; sparring partner

parterre [partɛr] *m* orchestra circle; flower bed

parti [parti] *m* party; side; match, good catch; **faire un mauvais parti à** to rough up, to mistreat; **parti pris** fixed opinion; prejudice; **prendre le parti de** to decide to; **prendre le parti de qn** to take s.o.'s side; **prendre parti** to take sides; **prendre son parti** to make up one's mind; **prendre son parti de** to resign oneself to; **tirer parti de** to take advantage of

par·tial -tiale [parsjal] *adj* (*pl* **-tiaux** [sjo]) partial, biased

partici·pant [partisipɑ̃] **-pante** [pɑ̃t] *adj & mf* participant

participation [partisipɑsjɔ̃] *f* participation

participe [partisip] *m* participle

participer [partisipe] *intr*—**participer à** to participate in; **participer de** to partake of

particulariser [partikylarize] *tr* to specify || *ref* to make oneself conspicuous

particularité [partikylarite] *f* peculiarity; detail

particule [partikyl] *f* particle

particu·lier [partikylje] **-lière** [ljɛr] *adj* particular; special; private || *mf* private citizen; (coll) odd person || *m* particular

partie [parti] *f* part; line, specialty; game, winning score; contest; party (*diversion*); (law) party; **avoir partie liée avec** to be in league with; **faire partie de** to belong to; **faire partie intégrante de** to. be part and parcel of; **partie civile** plaintiff; **partie de chasse** hunting party; **partie de plai-**

sir outing, picnic; **partie nulle** tie game; **prendre à partie** to take to task

par·tiel -tielle [parsjɛl] *adj* partial

partir [partir] (used only in *inf*) *tr*—**avoir maille à partir** to have a bone to pick ‖ §64 *intr* (*aux:* ÊTRE) to leave; to go off (*said of firearm*); to begin; **à partir de** from; from . . . on, e.g., **à partir de maintenant** from now on; **faire partir** to send off; to remove (*a spot*); to set off (*an explosive*); to fire (*a gun*); **partir** + *inf* to leave in order to + *inf*; **partir de** to come from; to start with; **partir pour** or **à** to leave for

parti·san [partizɑ̃] **-sane** [zan] *adj & mf* partisan

partition [partisjɔ̃] *f* (mus) score

partout [partu] *adv* everywhere; **partout ailleurs** anywhere else; everywhere else; **partout où** wherever; everywhere

parure [paryr] *f* ornament; set; finery; necklace

parution [parysjɔ̃] *f* appearance, publication

parvenir [parvənir] §72 *intr* (*aux:* ÊTRE)—**parvenir à** to reach; **parvenir à** + *inf* to succeed in + *ger*

parve·nu -nue [parvəny] *adj & mf* upstart

parvis [parvi] *m* square (*in front of a church*)

pas [pɑ] *m* step; pace; footprint; footfall; pass; straits; pitch (*of screw*); **allonger le pas** to quicken one's pace; to put one's best foot forward; **à pas comptés** with measured tread; **à pas de loup, à pas feutrés** stealthily; **à pas de tortue** at a snail's pace; **à quatre pas** nearby; **au pas at** a walk; **céder le pas (à)** to stand aside (for); to keep clear (*in front of a driveway*); **de ce pas** at once; **être au pas** to be in step; **faire le premier pas** to make the first move; **faire les cent pas** to come and go; **faux pas** misstep; blunder; **marcher sur les pas de** to follow in the footsteps of; **marquer le pas** to mark time; **mauvais pas** tight squeeze; fix; **pas à pas** little by little, cautiously; **pas d'armes** passage at arms; **Pas de Calais** Straits of Dover; **pas de cheval** hoofbeat; **pas de clerc** blunder; **pas de deux** two-step; **pas de la porte** doorstep; **pas de l'oie** goosestep; **pas de porte** (com) price paid for good will; **prendre le pas sur** to get ahead of ‖ *adv*—**ne . . . pas** §90 not, e.g., **je ne sais pas** I do not know; e.g., **ne pas signer** to not sign; (used with **non**), e.g., **non pas** no; (used without **ne**) (slang) not, e.g., **je fais pas de politique** I don't meddle in politics; **n'est-ce pas?** see **ne**; **pas?** (coll) not so?; **pas de** no; **pas du tout** not at all; **pas encore** not yet

pas·cal -cale [paskal] *adj* (*pl* **-caux** [ko]) Passover; Easter

passable [pɑsabl] *adj* passable, fair; mediocre, so-so

passade [pɑsad] *f* passing fancy

passage [pɑsaʒ] *m* passage; crossing; pass; **barrer le passage** to block the way; **livrer passage à** to let through; **passage à niveau** grade crossing; **passage au-dessous de la voie, passage souterrain** underpass; **passage au-dessus de la voie** overpass; **passage clouté, passage zébré** pedestrian crossing; **passage de vitesses** gear shifting; **passage interdit** (public sign) do not enter; (public sign) no thoroughfare; **passage protégé** arterial crossing (*vehicles intersecting highway must stop*)

passa·ger [pɑsaʒe] **-gère** [ʒer] *adj* passing, fleeting, migratory; busy (*road*) ‖ *mf* passenger; **passager clandestin, passager de cale** stowaway; **passager d'entrepont** steerage passenger

pas·sant [pɑsɑ̃] **pas·sante** [pɑsɑ̃t] *adj* busy (*street*) ‖ *mf* passer-by

passation [pɑsasjɔ̃] *f* handing over

passavant [pɑsavɑ̃] *m* permit; (naut) gangway

passe [pɑs] *m* master key ‖ *f* pass; channel; **être en bonne passe de** to be in a fair way to; **être en passe de** to be about to; **mauvaise passe** tight spot

pas·sé -sée [pɑse] *adj* past; faded; overripe; last (*week*) ‖ *m* past; past tense ‖ **passé** *prep* past, beyond, after

passe-bouillon [pɑsbujɔ̃] *m invar* soup strainer

passe-droit [pɑsdrwa] *m* (*pl* **-droits**) illegal favor; injustice

passe-lacet [pɑslase] *m* (*pl* **-lacets**) bodkin

passe-lait [pɑsle] *m invar* milk strainer

passe-lettres [pɑsletr] *m* (*pl* **-lettres**) letter drop

passement [pɑsmɑ̃] *m* braid, trimming

passementer [pɑsmɑ̃te] *tr* to trim

passementerie [pɑsmɑ̃tri] *f* trimmings

passe-montagne [pɑsmɔ̃taɲ] *m* (*pl* **-montagnes**) storm hood, ski mask

passe-partout [pɑspartu] *m invar* master key; slip mount

passe-passe [pɑspɑs] *m invar* legerdemain

passepoil [pɑspwal] *m* piping, braid

passeport [pɑspɔr] *m* passport

passer [pɑse] *tr* to pass; to ferry; to get across (*e.g., a river*); to spend; to pass (*e.g., the evening*); to take (*an exam*); to slip on (*e.g., a dressing gown*); to show (*a film*); to make (*a telephone call*); to go on (*one's way*); **passer q.ch. à qn** to hand or lend s.o. s.th.; to forgive s.o. s.th. ‖ *intr* (*aux:* AVOIR or ÊTRE) to pass; to pass away; to become; **en passer par là** to knuckle under; **faire passer** to get (*e.g., a message*) through; to while away (*the time*); **passer à** to pass over to; **passer chez** or **passer voir** to drop in on; **passer outre à** to override; **passer par** to pass through, to go through; **passer pour** to pass for or as; **passons!** let's skip it! ‖ *ref* to happen, to take place; **se passer de** to do without

passe·reau [pɑsro] *m* (*pl* **-reaux**) sparrow

passerelle [pɑsrel] *f* footbridge; gangplank; (naut) bridge

passe-temps [pɑstɑ̃] *m invar* pastime, hobby

passe-thé [pɑste] *m invar* tea strainer

pas·seur [pɑsœr] **pas·seuse** [pɑsøz] *mf* smuggler || *m* ferryman

passible [pɑsibl] *adj*—**passible de** liable for, subject to

pas·sif [pɑsif] **pas·sive** [pɑsiv] *adj* passive || *m* passive; debts, liabilities

passiflore [pɑsiflɔr] *f* passionflower

passion [pɑsjɔ̃], [pɑsjɔ̃] *f* passion

passion·nant [pɑsjɔnɑ̃] **passion·nante** [pɑsjɔnɑ̃t] *adj* thrilling, fascinating

passion·né -née [pɑsjɔne] *adj* passionate; impassioned; **passionné de** or **pour** passionately fond of || *mf* enthusiast, fan

passion·nel -nelle [pɑsjɔnel] *adj* of passion, of jealousy

passionner [pɑsjɔne] *tr* to excite the interest of, to arouse || *ref*—**se passionner pour** or **à** to be passionately fond of

passoire [pɑswar] *f* colander; strainer; (fig) sieve

pastel [pɑstel] *m* pastel; (bot) woad

pastèque [pɑstek] *f* watermelon

pasteur [pɑstœr] *m* pastor, minister; shepherd

pasteuriser [pɑstœrize] *tr* to pasteurize

pastiche [pɑstiʃ] *m* pastiche; parody

pastille [pɑstij] *f* lozenge, drop; tire patch; polka dot; **pastille pectorale** cough drop

pasto·ral -rale [pɑstɔral] (*pl* **-raux** [ro] **-rales**) *adj* & *f* pastoral

pastorat [pɑstɔra] *m* pastorate

pat [pɑt] *adj invar* (chess) in stalemate; **faire pat** to stalemate || *m* (chess) stalemate

patache [pɑtaʃ] *f* police boat; (coll) rattletrap

patachon [pɑtaʃɔ̃] *m*—**mener une vie de patachon** to lead a wild life

patapouf [pɑtapuf] *m* (coll) roly-poly || *interj* flop!

pataquès [pɑtakes] *m* faulty liaison; blooper, goof

patate [pɑtat] *f* sweet potato; (coll) spud

patati [pɑtati]—**et patati et patata!** (coll) and so on and on!

patatras [pɑtatra] *interj* bang!, crash!

pa·taud -taude [pɑto] [tod] *adj* clumsy, loutish || *mf* lout

patauger [pɑtoʒe] §38 *intr* to splash; (coll) to flounder

pâte [pɑt] *f* paste; dough, batter; **en pâte** (typ) pied; **mettre la main à la pâte** to put one's shoulder to the wheel; **pâte à papier** wood pulp; **pâte brisée**, **pâte feuilletée** puff paste; **pâte dentifrice** toothpaste; **pâte molle** spineless person; **pâtes alimentaires** pastas (*macaroni, noodles, spaghetti, etc.*); **peindre à la pâte** to paint with a full brush; **une bonne pâte d'homme** (coll) a good sort

pâté [pɑte] *m* blot, splotch; (typ) pi;

pâté de foie gras minced goose livers; **pâté de maisons** block of houses; **pâté en croûte** meat or fish pie; **pâté maison** chef's-special pâté

pâtée [pɑte] *f* dog food, cat food; chicken feed

pate·lin [pɑtlɛ̃] **-line** [lin] *adj* fawning, wheedling || *m* wheedler; (coll) native village

patenôtre [pɑtnotr] *f* prayer; (archaic) mumbo jumbo

pa·tent [pɑtɑ̃] **-tente** [tɑ̃t] *adj* patent || *f* license; tax; **patente (de santé)** (naut) bill of health

paten·té -tée [pɑtɑ̃te] *adj* licensed || *mf* licensed dealer

patenter [pɑtɑ̃te] *tr* to license

Pater [pɑter] *m invar* Lord's Prayer

patère [pɑter] *f* clothes hook; curtain hook

paterne [pɑtern] *adj* mawkish, mealy-mouthed

pater·nel -nelle [pɑternel] *adj* paternal; fatherly || *m* (slang) pop, dad

paternité [pɑternite] *f* paternity; fatherhood; authorship

pâ·teux [pɑtø] **-teuse** [tøz] *adj* pasty; thick; coated (*tongue*)

pathétique [pɑtetik] *adj* pathetic || *m* pathos

pathologie [pɑtɔlɔʒi] *f* pathology

pathos [pɑtos] *m* bathos

patibulaire [pɑtibyler] *adj* hangdog (*look*)

patience [pɑsjɑ̃s] *f* patience

pa·tient [pɑsjɑ̃] **-tiente** [sjɑ̃t] *adj* & *mf* patient

patienter [pɑsjɑ̃te] *intr* to be patient

patin [pɑtɛ̃] *m* skate; runner; sill, sleeper; (sole) pieds; (aer) skid; (rr) base, flange (*of rails*); **patin à glace** ice skate; **patin à roulettes** roller skate; **patin de frein** brake shoe

patiner [pɑtine] *intr* to skate; to slide; to skid

patinette [pɑtinet] *f* scooter

pati·neur [pɑtinœr] **-neuse** [nøz] *mf* skater

patinoire [pɑtinwar] *f* skating rink

patio [pɑtjo], [pɑsjo] *m* patio

pâtir [pɑtir] *intr*—**pâtir de** to suffer from

pâtisserie [pɑtisri] *f* pastry; pastry shop; pastry making

pâtis·sier [pɑtisje] **pâtis·sière** [pɑtisjer] *mf* pastry cook; proprietor of a pastry shop

patoche [pɑtɔʃ] *f* (coll) hand, paw

patois [pɑtwa] *m* patois; jargon, lingo

patouiller [pɑtuje] *tr* (coll) to paw, maul || *intr* (coll) to splash

patraque [pɑtrak] *adj* in bad shape || *f* (coll) turnip (*old watch*)

pâtre [pɑtr] *m* herdsman

patriarche [pɑtrijarʃ] *m* patriarch

patrice [pɑtris] *m* patrician; **Patrice** Patrick

patri·cien [pɑtrisjɛ̃] **-cienne** [sjen] *adj* & *mf* patrician

patrie [pɑtri] *f* native land, fatherland

patrimoine [pɑtrimwan] *m* patrimony

patrio·tard [pɑtrijɔtar] **-tarde** [tard] *adj* flag-waving, chauvinistic

patriote [patrijɔt] *adj* patriotic ‖ *mf* patriot

patriotique [patrijɔtik] *adj* patriotic

patriotisme [patrijɔtism] *m* patriotism

pa·tron [patrɔ̃] **-tronne** [trɔn] *mf* patron saint; proprietor; boss; sponsor ‖ *m* pattern, model; captain, skipper; coxswain; master, lord; medium size; **grand patron** large size; **patron à jours** stencil; **patron de thèse** thesis sponsor ‖ *f* mistress of the house; (slang) better half

patronage [patrɔnaʒ] *m* patronage, protection; sponsorship; (eccl) social center

patronat [patrɔna] *m* management

patronner [patrɔne] *tr* to patronize, to protect; to sponsor; to stencil

patrouille [patruj] *f* patrol

patrouiller [patruje] *intr* to patrol

patte [pat] *f* paw; foot (*of bird*); leg (*of insect*); flap, tab; hook; (coll) hand, foot, or leg (*of person*); **à pattes d'éléphant** bell-bottom (*trousers*); **à quatre pattes** on all fours; **faire patte de velours** (coll) to pull in one's claws; **graisser la patte** (coll) to grease the palm of; **patte d'épaule** shoulder strap; **pattes de mouche** (coll) scrawl

patte-d'oie [patdwa] *f* (*pl* **pattes-d'oie**) crow's-foot; crossroads; (bot) goosefoot

pattemouille [patmuj] *f* damp cloth

pâturage [pɑtyraʒ] *m* pasture; pasturage; pasture rights

pâture [pɑtyr] *f* fodder; pasture; (fig) food

paume [pom] *f* palm; (archaic) tennis

pau·mé -mée [pome] *adj* (coll) lost

paupière [popjɛr] *f* eyelid

pause [poz] *f* pause; (mus) full rest; **pause café** coffee break

pauvre [povr] *adj* poor; **pauvre de moi!** woe is me!; **pauvre d'esprit** (coll) dim-witted ‖ (when standing before noun) *adj* poor, wretched; late (*deceased*) ‖ *mf* pauper; **les pauvres** *f* the poor

pauvreté [povrəte] *f* poverty

P.A.V. [peave] *adj* (letterword) (**payable avec préavis**) person-to-person (*telephone call*)

pavaner [pavane] *ref* to strut

pavé [pave] *m* pavement, street; paving stone; paving block; (culin) slab; **sur le pavé** pounding the streets, out of work

pavement [pavmɑ̃] *m* paving (*act*); mosaic or marble flooring

paver [pave] *tr* to pave

pavillon [pavijɔ̃] *m* pavilion; tent, canopy; lodge, one-story house; wing, pavilion; flag; bell (*of trumpet*); **amener son pavillon** to strike one's colors; **baisser pavillon** to knuckle under

pavois [pavwa] *m* shield; **élever sur le pavois** to extol

pavoiser [pavwaze] *tr* to deck out with bunting, to decorate

pavot [pavo] *m* poppy

payable [pejabl] *adj* payable

payant [pejɑ̃] **payante** [pejɑ̃t] *adj* paying

paye [pɛj] *f* pay, wages

payement [pɛjmɑ̃] *m* payment

payer [peje] §49 *tr* to pay; to pay for; **payer comptant** to pay cash for; **payer de retour** to pay back; **payer q.ch. à qn** to pay s.o. for s.th.; to pay for s.th. for s.o.; **payer qn de q.ch.** to pay s.o. for s.th.; **payer rubis sur l'ongle** to pay down on the nail ‖ *intr* to pay ‖ *ref* to treat oneself to; to take what is due; **pouvoir se** (*dat*) **payer** to be able to afford; **se payer de** to be satisfied with

pays [pei] *m* country; region; town; (coll) fellow countryman; **du pays** local; **le pays de** the land of; **pays de cocagne** land of milk and honey

paysage [peizaʒ] *m* landscape, scenery; (painting) landscape

paysagiste [peizaʒist] *m* landscape painter

pay·san [peizɑ̃] **-sane** [zan] *adj* & *mf* peasant

Pays-Bas [peibɑ], [peibɑ] *mpl*—**les Pays-Bas** The Netherlands

paysé [peiz] *f* countrywoman

P.C. [pese] *m* (letterword) (**parti communiste**) Communist party; (**poste de commandement**) command post

P.c.c. *abbr* (**pour copie conforme**) certified copy

p.c.v. or **P.C.V.** [peseve] *m* (letterword) (**payable chez vous**) or (**à percevoir**)—**téléphoner en p.c.v.** to telephone collect

péage [peaʒ] *m* toll

peau [po] *m* (*pl* **peaux**) skin; pelt; hide; film (*on milk*); (slang) bag, whore; **entrer dans la peau d'un personnage** (theat) to get right inside a part; **faire peau neuve** to turn over a new leaf; **la peau!** (slang) nothing doing!; **peau d'âne** (coll) sheepskin; **peau de tambour** drumhead; **vendre la peau de l'ours avant de l'avoir tué** to count one's chickens before they are hatched

peau-rouge [poruʒ] *mf* (*pl* **peaux-rouges**) redskin

pêche [pɛʃ] *f* peach; fishing; **pêche à la mouche noyée** fly casting; **pêche au coup** fishing with hook, line, and pole; **pêche au lancer** casting; **pêche sous-marine** deep-sea fishing; **pêche sportive** fishing with a fly rod or casting rod

péché [peʃe] *m* sin

pécher [peʃe] §10 *intr* to sin

pêcher [peʃe] *m* peach tree ‖ *tr* to fish, fish for; (coll) to get ‖ *intr* to fish; **pêcher à la mouche** to fly-fish

pêcherie [peʃri] *f* fishery

pé·cheur [peʃœr] **-cheresse** [ʃrɛs] *mf* sinner

pê·cheur [peʃœr] **-cheuse** [ʃøz] *mf* fisher; **pêcheur de perles** pearl diver ‖ *m* fisherman

pécore [pekɔr] *f* (coll) silly goose

pecque [pɛk] *f* (coll) silly affected woman

péculat [pekyla] *m* embezzlement

pécule [pekyl] *m* nest egg

pédagogie [pedagɔʒi] *f* pedagogy, education

pédagogue [pedagɔg] *adj* pedagogical || *mf* pedagogue; teacher

pédale [pedal] *f* pedal; treadle; (vulg) pederast; **pédale d'embrayage** (aut) clutch pedal

pédaler [pedale] *intr* to pedal

pédalier [pedalje] *m* pedal keyboard; pedal and sprocket-wheel assembly

pédalo [pedalo] *m* water bicycle

pé·dant [pedɑ̃] **-dante** [dɑ̃t] *adj* pedantic || *mf* pedant

pédanterie [pedɑ̃tri] *f* pedantry

pédantesque [pedɑ̃tɛsk] *adj* pedantic

pédestre [pedɛstr] *adj* on foot

pédiatrie [pedjatri] *f* pediatrics

pédicure [pedikyr] *mf* chiropodist

pedigree [pedigri] *m* pedigree

Pégase [pegɑz] *m* Pegasus

pègre [pɛgr] *f* underworld

peigne [pɛɲ] *m* comb; card (*for wool*); reed (*of loom*); (zool) scallop

peigner [pɛɲe] *tr* to comb; to card || *ref* to comb one's hair

peignoir [pɛɲwar] *m* bathrobe; dressing gown, peignoir

peindre [pɛ̃dr] §50 *tr & intr* to paint

peine [pɛn] *f* pain; trouble; difficulty; penalty; **à peine** hardly, scarcely; **en être pour sa peine** to have nothing to show for one's trouble; **faire (de la) peine à** to grieve; **faire peine à voir** to be pathetic; **peine capitale** capital punishment; **peine de cœur** heartache; **peine de mort** death penalty; **peine pécuniaire** financial distress; **purger sa peine** to serve one's sentence; **valoir la peine** to be worth while; **veuillez vous donner la peine de** please be so kind as to

peiner [pene] *tr* to pain, grieve; to fatigue || *intr* to labor

peintre [pɛ̃tr] *m* painter

peinture [pɛ̃tyr] *f* paint; painting; attention **à la peinture** (public sign) wet paint; **je ne peux pas le voir en peinture** (coll) I can't stand him

peinturer [pɛ̃tyre] *tr* to lay a coat of paint on; to daub

peinturlurer [pɛ̃tyrlyre] *tr* (coll) to paint in all the colors of the rainbow

péjora·tif [peʒɔratif] **-tive** [tiv] *adj & m* pejorative

pékin [pekɛ̃] *m* pekin; **en pékin** (slang) in civies; **Pékin** Peking

péki·nois [pekinwa] **-noise** [nwaz] *adj* Pekingese || *m* Pekingese (*language; dog*) || (cap) *mf* Pekingese (*inhabitant*)

pelage [pəlaʒ] *m* coat (*of animal*)

pe·lé ·lée [pəle] *adj* bald; bare

pêle-mêle [pɛlmɛl] *m invar* jumble || *adv* pell-mell

peler [pəle] §2 *tr, intr, & ref* to peel, to peel off

pèle·rin [pɛlrɛ̃] **-rine** [rin] *mf* pilgrim || *m* peregrine falcon; basking shark || *f see* **pèlerine**

pèlerinage [pɛlrinaʒ] *m* pilgrimage

pèlerine [pɛlrin] *f* pelerine, cape; hooded cape

péllade [pɛljad] *f* adder

pélican [pelikɑ̃] *m* pelican

pellagre [pelagr] *f* pellagra

pelle [pɛl] *f* shovel; scoop; **pelle à poussière** dustpan; **pelle à vapeur** steam shovel; **pelle mécanique** power shovel; **ramasser à la pelle** to shovel, to shovel up

pelletée [pɛlte] *f* shovelful

pelleter [pɛlte] §34 *tr* to shovel

pelleterie [pɛltri] *f* fur trade; skin, pelt

pelleteuse [pɛltøz] *f* power shovel

pellicule [pelikyl] *f* film; pellicle; speck of dandruff; (phot) film; **pellicules** dandruff

pelote [plɔt] *f* ball (*of string, of snow, etc.*); **faire sa pelote** (coll) to make one's pile; **pelote basque** pelota; **pelote d'épingles** pincushion

peloter [plɔte] *tr* to wind into a ball; (fig) to flatter; (slang) to feel up, to paw || *intr* to bat the ball back and forth

pelo·teur [plɔtœr] **-teuse** [tøz] *adj* flattering, ingratiating; (coll) fresh, amorous, spoony || *mf* (coll) masher, spooner

peloton [plɔtɔ̃] *m* little ball (*e.g., of wool*); group (*of racers*); (mil) platoon, troop, detachment; **peloton d'exécution** firing squad

pelotonner [plɔtɔne] *tr* to wind into a ball || *ref* to curl up, to snuggle

pelouse [pluz] *f* lawn; (golf) green

peluche [plyʃ] *f* plush

pelure [plyr] *f* peel, peeling, skin; rind; (coll) coat

pénaliser [penalize] *tr* to penalize

pénalité [penalite] *f* penalty

pe·naud [pəno] **-naude** [nod] *adj* bashful, shy; shamefaced; crestfallen

penchant [pɑ̃ʃɑ̃] *m* penchant, bent

pen·ché ·chée [pɑ̃ʃe] *adj* leaning; stooping, bent over

pencher [pɑ̃ʃe] *tr, intr, & ref* to lean, to bend, to incline; **se pencher sur** to make a close study of

pendable [pɑ̃dabl] *adj* outrageous; (archaic) hangable

pendaison [pɑ̃dɛzɔ̃] *f* hanging

pen·dant [pɑ̃dɑ̃] **-dante** [dɑ̃t] *adj* hanging; pending || *m* pendant; counterpart; **pendant d'oreille** eardrop; **se faire pendant** to make a pair || *pendant adv*—**pendant que** while || *pendant prep* during

pendeloque [pɑ̃dlɔk] *f* pendant; jewel (*of eardrop*)

pendentif [pɑ̃dɑ̃tif] *m* pendant; eardrop; lavaliere

penderie [pɑ̃dri] *f* clothes closet

pendoir [pɑ̃dwar] *m* meat hook

pendre [pɑ̃dr] *tr* to hang; to hang up; **être pendu à** to hang on (*e.g., the telephone*) || *intr* to hang; to hang down; to sag; **ça lui pend au nez** he's got it coming to him || *ref* to hang oneself; **se pendre à** to hang on to

pen·du ·due [pɑ̃dy] *adj* hanging; hanged || *mf* hanged person

pendule [pɑ̃dyl] *m* pendulum || *f* clock; **pendule à pile** battery clock

pêne [pen] *m* bolt; latch

pénétration [penetrasjɔ̃] *f* penetration; permeation

pénétrer [penetre] §10 *tr* to penetrate, to permeate || *intr* to penetrate; to enter || *ref* to mix; **se pénétrer de** to become imbued with

pénible [penibl] *adj* hard, painful

péniche [peniʃ] *f* barge; houseboat; **péniche de débarquement** landing craft

pénicilline [penisilin] *f* penicillin

péninsulaire [penɛ̃syler] *adj* peninsular

péninsule [penɛ̃syl] *f* large peninsula

pénitence [penitɑ̃s] *f* penitence; penalty (*in games*); punishment; **en pénitence** in disgrace; **faire pénitence** to do penance

pénitencier [penitɑ̃sje] *m* penitentiary; penal colony

péni•tent [penitɑ̃] -tente [tɑ̃t] *adj & mf* penitent

penne [pɛn] *f* quill, feather

Pennsylvanie [pɛnsilvani] *f* Pennsylvania; **la Pennsylvanie** Pennsylvania

pénombre [penɔ̃br] *f* penumbra; half-light; **dans la pénombre** out of the limelight

pense-bête [pɑ̃sbɛt] *m* (*pl* -bêtes) (coll) reminder

pensée [pɑ̃se] *f* thought; thinking; (bot) pansy

penser [pɑ̃se] *tr* to think; **penser de** to think of (*to have as an opinion of*); **penser + inf** to intend to + *inf* || *intr* to think; **penser à** to think of (*to direct one's thoughts toward*); **y penser** to think of it, e.g., **pendant que j'y pense** while I think of it

penseur [pɑ̃sœr] *m* thinker

pen•sif [pɑ̃sif] -sive [siv] *adj* pensive; absent-minded

pension [pɑ̃sjɔ̃] *f* pension (*annuity; room and board; boardinghouse*); **avec pension complète** with three meals; **pension de famille** residential hotel; **pension de retraite, pension viagère** annuity; **prendre pension** to board; **sans pension** without meals

pensionnaire [pɑ̃sjɔner] *mf* boarder; guest (*in hotel*); resident student || *f* naïve girl

pensionnat [pɑ̃sjɔna] *m* boarding school

pension•né -née [pɑ̃sjɔne] *adj* pensioned || *mf* pensioner

pensionner [pɑ̃sjɔne] *tr* to pension

pensum [pɛ̃sɔm] *m* thankless task

Pentagone [pɛ̃tagɔn] *m* Pentagon

pente [pɑ̃t] *f* slope; inclination; bent; fall (*of river*); **en pente** sloping

Pentecôte [pɑ̃tkot] *f*—**la Pentecôte** Pentecost, Whitsunday

pénultième [penyltjɛm] *adj* next to the last || *f* penult

pénurie [penyri] *f* lack, shortage

pépé [pepe] *m* (slang) grandpa

pépée [pepe] *f* doll; (slang) doll

pépère [peper] *adj* (coll) easygoing || *m* grandpa; (coll) old duffer; (coll) overgrown boy

pépètes [pepet] *fpl* (slang) dough

pépie [pepi] *f* (vet) pip; **avoir la pépie** (coll) to be thirsty

pépiement [pepimɑ̃] *m* chirp

pépier [pepje] *intr* to chirp

pépin [pepɛ̃] *m* pip, seed; (coll) umbrella; **avoir un pépin** (coll) to strike a snag

pépinière [pepinjer] *f* (hort) nursery; (fig) training school; (fig) hotbed

pépiniériste [pepinjerist] *m* nurseryman

pépite [pepit] *f* nugget

péque•naud [pekno] -naude [nod] *adj & mf* (slang) peasant

péquenot [pekno] *m* (slang) peasant

perçage [persaʒ] *m* drilling, boring

per•çant [persɑ̃] -çante [sɑ̃t] *adj* piercing, penetrating

perce [pers] *f* drill, bore; **en perce** on tap

perce-neige [persəneʒ] *m invar* (bot) snowdrop

percepteur [persɛptœr] *m* tax collector

perception [persɛpsjɔ̃] *f* perception; tax collection; tax; tax department, bureau of internal revenue

percer [perse] §51 *tr* to pierce; to drill; to tap (*a barrel*); to break through || *intr* to come through or out; to burst (*said, e.g., of abscess*); **to make a name for oneself**

perceuse [persøz] *f* drill; machine drill

percevoir [persəvwar] §59 *tr* to perceive; to collect

perche [perʃ] *f* pole; (ichth) perch; (coll) beanpole; **perche à sauter** vaulting pole; **perche à son** microphone stand; **tendre la perche à** to lend a helping hand to

percher [perʃe] *tr* to perch || *intr* to perch, to roost

perchoir [perʃwar] *m* perch

per•clus [pɛrkly] -cluse [klyz] *adj* crippled, paralyzed

percolateur [pɛrkɔlatœr] *m* large coffee maker

percuter [pɛrkyte] *tr* to strike; to crash into; to percuss || *intr* to crash

percuteur [pɛrkytœr] *m* firing pin

per•dant [pɛrdɑ̃] -dante [dɑ̃t] *adj* losing || *mf* loser

perdition [pɛrdisjɔ̃] *f* perdition; **en perdition** (naut) in distress

perdre [pɛrdrə] *tr* to lose; to ruin || *intr* to lose; to leak; to deteriorate || *ref* to get lost; to disappear

per•dreau [pɛrdro] *m* (*pl* -dreaux) young partridge

perdrix [pɛrdri] *f* partridge

per•du -due [pɛrdy] *adj* lost; spare (*time*); stray (*bullet*); remote (*locality*); advance (*sentry*)

père [pɛr] *m* father; senior, e.g., **M. Martin père** Mr. Martin, senior; **père de famille** head of the household; **père spirituel** father confessor

péréquation [perekwasjɔ̃] *f* equalizing

perfection [pɛrfɛksjɔ̃] *f* perfection

perfectionner [pɛrfɛksjɔne] *tr* to perfect || *ref* to improve

perfide [pɛrfid] *adj* perfidious || *mf* treacherous person

perfidie [pɛrfidi] *f* perfidy

perforation [perfɔrasjɔ̃] *f* perforation

perforatrice [perfɔratris] *f* pneumatic drill; perforator; keypunch (machine)

perforer [perfɔre] *tr* to perforate; to drill, bore; to punch (*a card*)

performance [perfɔrmɑ̃s] *f* (sports) performance

péricliter [periklite] *intr* to fail

péril [peril] *m* peril

péril·leux [perijø] **péril·leuse** [perijøz] *adj* perilous

péri·mé -mée [perime] *adj* expired, elapsed; out-of-date

périmer [perime] *intr & ref* to lapse

période [perjɔd] *f* period; (phys) cycle

périodique [perjɔdik] *adj* periodic(al)

péripétie [peripesi] *f* vicissitude

périphérie [periferi] *f* periphery

périphérique [periferik] *adj* peripheral

périple [peripl] *m* journey

périr [perir] *intr* to perish

périscope [periskɔp] *m* periscope

périssable [perisabl] *adj* perishable

perle [perl] *f* pearl; bead

perler [perle] *tr* to pearl; to do to perfection || *intr* to form beads

permanence [permanɑ̃s] *f* permanence; headquarters, station; **en permanence** at all hours

perma·nent [permanɑ̃] **-nente** [nɑ̃t] *adj* permanent; standing; continuous, nonstop || *f* permanent

perme [perm] *f* (coll) furlough

permettre [permetr] §42 *tr* to permit; **permettre q.ch. à qn** to allow s.o. s.th. || *intr*—**permettez!** excuse me!; **permettre à qn de** + *inf* to permit s.o. to or let s.o. + *inf*; **vous permettez?** may I? || *ref*—**se permettre de** to take the liberty of

permis [permi] *m* permit, license; **permis de conduire** driver's license

permission [permisjɔ̃] *f* permission; (mil) furlough, leave

permissionnaire [permisjɔner] *m* soldier on leave

permutation [permytasjɔ̃] *f* permutation; exchange of posts; transposition

permuter [permyte] *tr* to permute; to exchange || *intr* to change places

perni·cieux [pernisjø] **-cieuse** [sjøz] *adj* pernicious

péroné [perɔne] *m* (anat) fibula

pérorer [perɔre] *intr* to hold forth

Pérou [peru] *m*—**le Pérou** Peru

peroxyde [perɔksid] *m* peroxide

perpendiculaire [perpɑ̃dikyler] *adj & f* perpendicular

perpète [perpet]—**à perpète** (slang) forever

perpétrer [perpetre] §10 *tr* to perpetrate

perpé·tuel -tuelle [perpetɥel] *adj* perpetual; life (*imprisonment*); constant, continual

perpétuer [perpetɥe] *tr* to perpetuate || *ref* to be perpetuated

perpétuité [perpetɥite] *f* perpetuity; **à perpétuité** forever; for life

perplexe [perpleks] *adj* perplexed; **rendre perplexe** to perplex

perplexité [perpleksite] *f* perplexity

perquisition [perkizisjɔ̃] *f* search

perquisitionner [perkizisjɔne] *intr* to make a search

perron [perɔ̃] *m* front-entrance stone steps

perroquet [perɔke] *m* parrot

perruche [peryʃ] *f* parakeet; hen parrot

perruque [peryk] *f* wig; **vieille perruque** (coll) old fogey

per·san [persɑ̃] **-sane** [san] *adj* Persian || *m* Persian (*language*) || (*cap*) *mf* Persian (*person*)

perse [pers] *adj* Persian || (*cap*) *mf* Persian || (*cap*) *f* Persia; **la Perse** Persia

persécuter [persekyte] *tr* to persecute

persécution [persekysjɔ̃] *f* persecution

persévérer [persevere] §10 *intr* to persevere

persienne [persjen] *f* Persian blind, slatted shutter

persil [persi] *m* parsley

persis·tant [persistɑ̃] **-tante** [tɑ̃t] *adj* persistent

persister [persiste] *intr* to persist; **persister à** to persist in

personnage [persɔnaʒ] *m* personage; (theat) character

personnalité [persɔnalite] *f* personality

personne [persɔn] *f* person; self; appearance; lady, e.g., **belle personne** beautiful lady; e.g., **jolie personne** pretty lady; **grande personne** grown-up; **par personne** per person; **payer de sa personne** to not spare one's efforts; **s'assurer de la personne de** to arrest; **une tierce personne** a third party || *pron indef* no one, nobody; **personne ne or ne . . . personne** §90B no one, nobody, not anyone

person·nel -nelle [persɔnel] *adj* personal || *m* personnel

personnifier [persɔnifje] *tr* to personify

perspective [perspektiv] *f* perspective; outlook; **en perspective** in view

perspicace [perspikas] *adj* perspicacious

persuader [persɥade] *tr* to persuade; **persuader q.ch. à qn or persuader qn de q.ch.** to persuade s.o. of s.th. || *intr*—**persuader à qn de** to persuade s.o. to || *ref* to be convinced

persuasion [persɥazjɔ̃] *f* persuasion

perte [pert] *f* loss; ruin, downfall; **à perte de vue** as far as the eye can see; **en pure perte** uselessly

perti·nent [pertinɑ̃] **-nente** [nɑ̃t] *adj* pertinent

perturba·teur [pertyrbatœr] **-trice** [tris] *adj* disturbing || *mf* troublemaker

perturber [pertyrbe] *tr* to perturb

péru·vien [peryvjɛ̃] **-vienne** [vjen] *adj* Peruvian || (*cap*) *mf* Peruvian

pervenche [pervɑ̃ʃ] *f* periwinkle

per·vers [perver] **-verse** [vers] *adj* perverted || *mf* pervert

perversion [perversjɔ̃] *f* perversion

perversité [pɛrversite] f perversity, depravity

pervertir [pɛrvertir] tr to pervert

pesage [pəzaʒ] m weigh-in; paddock

pe·sant [pəzɑ̃] **-sante** [zɑ̃t] adj heavy ‖ m—**valoir son pesant d'or** to be worth one's weight in gold

pesanteur [pəzɑ̃tœr] f heaviness; weight; (phys) gravity

pèse-bébé [pɛzbebe] m (pl **-bébés**) baby scale

pesée [pəze] f weighing; leverage

pèse-lettre [pɛzletr] m (pl **-lettres**) letter scale

pèse-personne [pɛzpɛrsɔn] m (pl **-personnes**) bathroom scale

peser [pəze] §2 tr to weigh ‖ intr to weigh; **peser à** to hang heavy on; **peser sur** to bear down on; to lie down on; to lie heavy on; to stress ‖ ref to weigh oneself; to weigh in

peson [pəzɔ̃] m spring scale

pessimisme [pesimism] m pessimism

pessimiste [pesimist] adj pessimistic ‖ mf pessimist

peste [pɛst] f plague; pest, nuisance ‖ interj gosh!

pester [pɛste] intr to grouse; **pester contre** to rail at

pestifé·ré -rée [pɛstifere] adj plague-ridden ‖ mf victim of the plague

pestilence [pɛstilɑ̃s] f pestilence

pet [pɛ] m (slang) scandal; (vulgar) wind; **ça ne vaut pas un pet (de lapin)** (coll) it's not worth a wooden nickel ‖ interj (coll) look out!

pétale [petal] m petal

pétarade [petarad] f series of explosions; backfire

pétard [petar] m firecracker; blast; (slang) gat, revolver; (slang) backside; **faire du pétard** (coll) to kick up a fuss; **lancer un pétard** (coll) to drop a bombshell

pet-de-loup [pedlu] m (pl **pets-de-loup**) absent-minded professor

pet-de-nonne [pednɔn] m (pl **pets-de-nonne**) fritter

pet-en-l'air [petɑ̃ler] m invar short jacket

péter [pete] §10 tr—**péter du feu** (coll) to be a live wire ‖ intr (coll) to go bang; (vulg) to break wind

pètesec [pɛtsek] adj invar (coll) bossy, despotic ‖ m invar (coll) martinet, bossy fellow

pétil·lant [petijɑ̃] **pétil·lante** [petijɑ̃t] adj crackling; sparkling

pétiller [petije] intr to crackle; to sparkle

pe·tiot [pətjo] **-tiote** [tjɔt] adj (coll) tiny, wee ‖ mf (coll) tot

pe·tit [pəti] **-tite** [tit] adj §91 small, little; short; minor, lower; **en petit** shortened; miniature; **petit à petit** little by little, bit by bit ‖ mf youngster; young (of an animal); poor little thing ‖ m little boy ‖ f little girl

petit-beurre [pətibœr] m (pl **petits-beurre**) cookie

petit-cou·sin [pətikuzɛ̃] **-sine** [zin] mf (pl **petits-cousins**) second cousin

petite-fille [pətitfij] f (pl **petites-filles**) granddaughter

petite-nièce [pətitnjes] f (pl **petites-nièces**) great-niece

petitesse [pətites] f smallness

petit-fils [pətifis] m (pl **petits-fils**) grandson; grandchild

petit-gris [pətigri] m (pl **petits-gris**) miniver; snail

pétition [petisjɔ̃] f petition; **faire une pétition de principe** to beg the question

petit-lait [pətile] m (pl **petits-laits**) whey

petit-neveu [pətinvø] m (pl **petits-neveux**) great-nephew

petits-enfants [pətizɑ̃fɑ̃] mpl grandchildren

petit-suisse [pətisɥis] m (pl **petits-suisses**) cream cheese

peton [pətɔ̃] m (coll) tiny foot

pétoncle [petɔ̃kl] m scallop

Pétrarque [petrark] m Petrarch

pétrifier [petrifje] tr & ref to petrify

pétrin [petrɛ̃] m kneading trough; (coll) mess, jam

pétrir [petrir] tr to knead; to mold

pétrole [petrɔl] m petroleum; **à pétrole** kerosene (lamp); **pétrole brut** crude oil; **pétrole lampant** kerosene

pétro·lier [petrɔlje] **-lière** [ljer] adj oil ‖ m tanker; oil baron

P et T [peete] fpl (letterword) (**Postes et télécommunications**) post office, telephone, and telegraph

pétu·lant [petylɑ̃] **-lante** [lɑ̃t] adj lively, frisky

peu [pø] m bit, little; **peu de** few; not much; not many; **peu de chose** not much ‖ adv §91 little; not very; **à peu près** about, practically; **depuis peu** of late; **peu ou prou** more or less; **peu probable** improbable; **peu s'en faut** very nearly; **pour peu que, si peu que** however little; **quelque peu** somewhat; **sous peu** before long; **tant soit peu** ever so little

peuplade [pœplad] f tribe

peuple [pœpl] adj plebeian, common ‖ m people

peuplement [pœpləmɑ̃] m populating; planting; stocking (e.g., with fish)

peupler [pœple] tr to people; to plant; to stock ‖ intr to multiply, to breed

peuplier [pøplje] m poplar

peur [pœr] f fear; **avoir peur (de)** to be afraid (of); **de peur que** lest, for fear that; **une peur bleue** (coll) an awful fright

peu·reux -reuse [pœrø] [røz] adj fearful, timid

peut-être [pøtetr] adv perhaps; **peut-être que non** perhaps not

p. ex. abbr (par exemple) e.g.

phalange [falɑ̃ʒ] f phalanx

phalène [falen] m & f moth

Pharaon [faraɔ̃] m Pharaoh

phare [far] m lighthouse; beacon; (aut) headlight; **phares code** dimmers

phari·sien [farizjɛ̃] **-sienne** [zjen] adj pharisaic ‖ mf pharisee

pharmaceutique [farmasøtik] *adj* pharmaceutical ‖ *f* pharmaceutics

pharmacie [farmasi] *f* drugstore, pharmacy; medicine chest; drugs

pharma·cien [farmasjɛ̃] **-cienne** [sjen] *mf* pharmacist

pharynx [farɛ̃ks] *m* pharynx

phase [faz] *f* phase

Phébé [febe] *f* Phoebe

Phénicie [fenisi] *f* Phoenicia; **la Phénicie** Phoenicia

phéni·cien [fenisjɛ̃] **-cienne** [sjen] *adj* Phoenician ‖ (*cap*) *mf* Phoenician

phénix [feniks] *m* phoenix

phénomé·nal **-nale** [fenɔmenal] *adj* (*pl* **-naux** [no]) phenomenal

phénomène [fenɔmen] *m* phenomenon; (*coll*) monster, freak

philanthrope [filɑ̃trɔp] *mf* philanthropist

philanthropie [filantrɔpi] *f* philanthropy

philatélie [filateli] *f* philately

philatéliste [filatelist] *mf* philatelist

philip·pin [filipɛ̃] **-pine** [pin] *adj* Philippine ‖ (*cap*) *mf* Filipino

Philippines [filipin] *fpl* Philippines

philistin [filistɛ̃] *adj* masc & *m* Philistine

philologie [filɔlɔʒi] *f* philology

philologue [filɔlɔg] *mf* philologist

philosophe [filɔzɔf] *adj* philosophic ‖ *mf* philosopher

philosophie [filɔzɔfi] *f* philosophy

philosophique [filɔzɔfik] *adj* philosophic(al)

philtre [filtr] *m* philter

phlébite [flebit] *f* phlebitis

phobie [fɔbi] *f* phobia

phonétique [fɔnetik] *adj* phonetic ‖ *f* phonetics

phoniatrie [fɔnjatri] *f* speech therapy

phono [fɔno] *m* (*coll*) phonograph

phonographe [fɔnɔgraf] *m* phonograph

phonologie [fɔnɔlɔʒi] *f* phonology

phonothèque [fɔnɔtek] *f* record library

phoque [fɔk] *m* seal

phosphate [fɔsfat] *m* phosphate

phosphore [fɔsfɔr] *m* phosphorus

phosphores·cent [fɔsfɔresã] **phosphores·cente** [fɔsfɔresãt] *adj* phosphorescent

photo [fɔto] *f* photo, snapshot

photocopier [fɔtɔkɔpje] *tr* to photocopy, to photostat

photogénique [fɔtɔʒenik] *adj* photogenic

photographe [fɔtɔgraf] *mf* photographer

photographie [fɔtɔgrafi] *f* photography; photograph

photographier [fɔtɔgrafje] *tr* to photograph

photogravure [fɔtɔgravyr] *f* photoengraving

photostat [fɔtɔsta] *m* photostat

phrase [frɑz] *f* sentence; (mus) phrase; **phrase de choc** punch line

phrénologie [frenɔlɔʒi] *f* phrenology

physi·cien [fizisjɛ̃] **-cienne** [sjen] *mf* physicist

physiologie [fizjɔlɔʒi] *f* physiology

physiologique [fizjɔlɔʒik] *adj* physiological

physionomie [fizjɔnɔmi] *f* physiognomy

physique [fizik] *adj* physical; material ‖ *m* physique; appearance ‖ *f* physics

piaffer [pjafe] *intr* to paw the ground; to fidget, fume

piailler [pjaje] *intr* (coll) to cheep; (coll) to squeal

pianiste [pjanist] *mf* pianist

piano [pjano] *m* piano; **piano à queue** grand piano; **piano droit** upright piano ‖ *adv* (coll) quietly

pianoter [pjanɔte] *intr* to strum; to drum, to thrum; to rattle away

piastre [pjastr] *f* (Canad) dollar

piauler [pjole] *intr* to peep; to screech (*said of pulley*); (coll) to whine

pic [pik] *m* peak; (tool) pick; (orn) woodpecker; **à pic** sheer, steep; (coll) in the nick of time; **couler à pic** to sink like a stone

picaillons [pikajɔ̃] *mpl* (slang) dough

picaresque [pikaresk] *adj* picaresque

piccolo [pikɔlo] *m* piccolo

pichet [piʃɛ] *m* pitcher, jug

pick-up [pikœp] *m invar* pickup; record player; pickup truck

picoler [pikɔle] *intr* (slang) to get pickled

picorer [pikɔre] *tr & intr* to peck

picoter [pikɔte] *tr* to prick; to peck at; to sting

picotin [pikɔtɛ̃] *m* peck (*measure*)

pictu·ral **-rale** [piktyral] *adj* (*pl* **-raux** [ro]) pictorial

pie [pi] *adj invar* piebald ‖ *f* magpie

pièce [pjes] *f* piece; patch; room; play; document; coin; wine barrel; **à la pièce** separately; **donner la pièce à** to tip; **faire pièce à** to play a trick on; to put a check on; **inventé de toutes pièces** made up out of the whole cloth; **la pièce** apiece; **pièce à conviction** (law) exhibit; **pièce comptable** voucher; **pièce d'eau** ornamental pond; **pièce de rechange**, **pièce détachée** spare part; **pièce de résistance** pièce de résistance; (culin) entree; **tout d'une pièce** in one piece; (coll) rigid; (coll) stiffly ‖ *adv* apiece

pied [pje] *m* foot; foothold; **à pied** on foot; **au pied de la lettre** literally; **au pied levé** offhand; **de pied en cap** from head to toe; **faire le pied de grue** (coll) to cool one's heels, to stand around waiting; **faire les pieds à** (coll) to give what's coming to; **faire un pied de nez** (coll) to thumb one's nose; **lever le pied** to abscond; **mettre à pied** to dismiss, fire; **mettre les pieds dans le plat** (coll) to put one's foot in one's mouth; **mettre pied à terre** to dismount; **pied équin** clubfoot; **travailler comme un pied** (coll) to botch one's work

pied-à-terre [pjetater] *m invar* hangout, temporary base

pied-bot [pjebo] *m* (*pl* **pieds-bots**) clubfooted person pied-d'alouette [pjedalwet] m (pl pieds-d'alouette) delphinium

pied-droit [pjedrwa] m (pl pieds-droits) (archit) pier

piédes-tal -tale [pjedestal] m (pl -taux [to]) pedestal

pied-noir [pjenwar] m (pl pieds-noirs) Algerian of European descent

piège [pjɛʒ] m trap, snare

piéger [pjeʒe] §1 tr to trap, to snare; to booby-trap

pie-grièche [pigrijɛʃ] f (pl pies-grièches) shrike; shrew

pierraille [pjeraj] f rubble

pierre [pjer] f stone; faire d'une pierre deux coups to kill two birds with one stone; Pierre Peter; pierre à aiguiser whetstone; pierre à briquet flint; pierre à chaux, pierre à plâtre gypsum; pierre à feu, pierre à fusil gunflint; pierre angulaire cornerstone; pierre à rasoir hone; pierre calcaire limestone; pierre d'achoppement stumbling block; pierre de gué stepping stone; pierre de touche touchstone; pierre tombale tombstone

pierreries [pjerri] fpl precious stones

pier-reux [pjerø] pier-reuse [pjerøz] adj stony || f (coll) streetwalker

pierrot [pjero] m clown; sparrow; (coll) oddball; (coll) greenhorn

piété [pjete] f piety; devotion

piéter [pjete] §10 intr to toe the line || ref to stand firm

piétiner [pjetine] tr to trample on || intr to stamp; to mark time

piéton [pjetɔ̃] m pedestrian

piètre [pjetr] adj poor, wretched

pieu [pjø] m (pl pieux) post, stake; (archit) pile

pieuvre [pjœvr] f octopus; (coll) leech

pieux [pjø] pieuse [pjøz] adj pious; dutiful; white (lie)

pif [pif] m (slang) snout (nose) || interj bang!

pige [piʒ] f (slang) year; à la pige (journ) so much a line; faire la pige à (slang) to outdo

pigeon [piʒɔ̃] m pigeon; pigeon voyageur homing pigeon

pigeonner [piʒɔne] tr (coll) to dupe

pigeonnier [piʒɔnje] m dovecote

piger [piʒe] §38 tr (slang) to look at; (slang) to get || intr—tu piges? (slang) do you get it?

pigment [pigmã] m pigment

pignocher [piɲɔʃe] intr to pick at one's food

pignon [piɲɔ̃] m gable; (mach) pinion; avoir pignon sur rue (coll) to have a home of one's own; (coll) to be well off; pignon de chaîne sprocket wheel

pile [pil] f stack, pile; pier; (elec) battery (primary cell); (coll) thrashing; pile atomique atomic pile; pile ou face heads or tails; pile sèche dry cell || adv (coll) short; (coll) exactly

piler [pile] tr to grind, to crush

pilier [pilje] m pillar; pilier de cabaret barfly

pillage [pijaʒ] m looting

pil-lard [pijar] pil-larde [pijard] adj looting || mf looter

piller [pije] tr & intr to loot; to plagiarize

pil-leur [pijœr] pil-leuse [pijøz] mf pillager

pilon [pilɔ̃] m pestle; (coll) drumstick (of chicken); (coll) wooden leg; pilon à vapeur steam hammer

pilonnage [pilɔnaʒ] m crushing; pilonnage aérien saturation bombing

pilonner [pilɔne] tr to crush; to bomb

pilori [pilɔri] m pillory

pilot [pilo] m pile (in piling); rags (for paper)

pilotage [pilɔtaʒ] m piloting; pilotage sans visibilité blind flying

pilote [pilɔt] m pilot; pilote de ligne airline pilot; pilote d'essai test pilot

piloter [pilɔte] tr to pilot; to guide; to drive piles into || intr to pilot; to be a guide

pilotis [pilɔti] m piles

pilule [pilyl] f pill; (coll) bitter pill; dorer la pilule to gild the lily

piment [pimã] m allspice (berry); (fig) spice; piment doux sweet pepper; piment rouge red or hot pepper

pimenter [pimãte] tr to season with red pepper; (fig) to spice

pim-pant [pɛ̃pã] -pante [pãt] adj smart, spruce

pin [pɛ̃] m pine; pin de Weymouth (Pinus strobus) white pine; pin sylvestre (Pinus sylvestris) Scotch pine

pinacle [pinakl] m pinnacle

pince [pɛ̃s] f tongs; pliers; forceps; crowbar; gripper; grip; pleat; claw (of crab); aller à pinces (slang) to hoof it; petites pinces, pince à épiler tweezers; pince à linge clothespin; pince à sucre sugar tongs; pince hémostatique hemostat; pinces tongs; pincers, pliers; pinces de cycliste bicycle clips; serrer la pince à (slang) to shake hands with

pin-cé -cée [pɛ̃se] adj prim, tight-lipped; thin, pinched || f see pincée

pin-ceau [pɛ̃so] m (pl -ceaux) paintbrush; pencil (of light)

pincée [pɛ̃se] f pinch

pincement [pɛ̃smã] m pinching; plucking

pince-monseigneur [pɛ̃smɔ̃seɲœr] f (pl pinces-monseigneur) jimmy

pince-nez [pɛ̃sne] m invar nose glasses

pincer [pɛ̃se] §51 tr to pinch; to grip; to nip off; to pluck; to top (plants); to purse (the lips); to pleat; (coll) to nab, to catch || intr to bite (said of cold); en pincer pour (slang) to have a crush on; pincer de (mus) to strum on

pince-sans-rire [pɛ̃ssãrir] adj invar deadpan || mf invar deadpan comic

pincette [pɛ̃set] f tweezers; pincettes tweezers; fire tongs

pinçon [pɛ̃sɔ̃] m bruise (from pinch)

pinède [pined] f pine grove

pingouin [pɛ̃gwɛ̃] m (family: Alcidae) auk

pingre [pɛ̃gr] *adj* (coll) stingy ‖ *mf* (coll) tightwad

pinson [pɛ̃sɔ̃] *m* (orn) finch

pintade [pɛ̃tad] *f* guinea fowl

pin up [pinœp] *f invar* (coll) pinup girl

pioche [pjɔʃ] *f* pickax

piocher [pjɔʃe] *tr & intr* to dig, to pick; (coll) to cram

pio·cheur [pjɔʃœr] **-cheuse** [ʃøz] *mf* digger; (coll) grind ‖ *f* (mach) cultivator

piolet [pjɔlɛ] *m* ice ax

pion [pjɔ̃] *m* (checkers) man; (chess & fig) pawn; (slang) proctor; **damer le pion à** (coll) to get the better of

pionnier [pjɔnje] *m* pioneer

pipe [pip] *f* pipe; **casser sa pipe** (slang) to kick the bucket

pi·peau [pipo] *m* (*pl* **-peaux**) bird call; shepherd's pipe; lime twig

piper [pipe] *tr* to snare, to catch; to load (*the dice*); to mark (*the cards*) ‖ *intr*—**ne pipe pas!** (coll) not a peep out of you!

pi·quant [pikã] **-quante** [kãt] *adj* piquant, intriguing; racy, spicy ‖ *m* sting; prickle; quill (*of porcupine*); piquancy, pungency; point (*of story*); (fig) bite

pique [pik] *m* (cards) spade; (cards) spades ‖ *f* pike; pique

pi·qué -quée [pike] *adj* stung; sour; (mus) staccato; (coll) batty; **piqué de** studded with ‖ *m* quilt; **descendre en piqué** to nose-dive

pique-assiette [pikasjɛt] *mf* (*pl* **-assiettes**) (coll) sponger

pique-feu [pikfø] *m invar* poker

pique-nique [piknik] *m* (*pl* **-niques**) picnic

pique-niquer [piknike] *intr* to picnic

piquer [pike] *tr* to sting; to prick; to pique; to stimulate; to quilt; to spur; to give a shot to; (mus) to play staccato; (slang) to filch; (slang) to pinch, to nab ‖ *intr* to turn sour; (aer) to nose-dive ‖ *ref* to be piqued; to spot; to give oneself a shot; **se piquer de** to take pride in; **se piquer pour** to take a fancy to

piquet [pike] *m* peg, stake; picket; **piquet de grève** picket line

piqueter [pikte] §34 *tr* to stake out; to spot, dot

piquette [pikɛt] *f* poor wine; (coll) crushing defeat

pi·queur [pikœr] **-queuse** [køz] *mf* stitcher ‖ *m* huntsman; outrider

piqûre [pikyr] *f* sting, bite; prick; injection, shot; stitching; puncture; **piqûre de ver** moth hole

pirate [pirat] *m* pirate; **pirate de l'air** hijacker

pirater [pirate] *intr* to pirate

piraterie [piratri] *f* piracy; **piraterie aérienne** hijacking

pire [pir] §91 *adj comp & super* worse; worst ‖ *m* (the) worst

pirouette [pirwɛt] *f* pirouette

pirouetter [pirwete] *intr* to pirouette

pis [pi] *adj comp & super* worse;

worst ‖ *m* udder; **au pis aller** at worst; **de pis en pis** worse and worse; **(le) pis** (the) worst; **qui pis est** what's worse; **tant pis** so much the worse ‖ *adv comp & super* §91 worse; worst

pis-aller [pizale] *m invar* makeshift

piscine [pisin] *f* swimming pool

pissenlit [pisãli] *m* dandelion

pisser [pise] *tr* (coll) to spout (*water*); (coll) to leak; (slang) to pass (*e.g., blood*); **pisser de la copie** (slang) to be a hack writer ‖ *intr* (slang) to urinate

pisse-vinaigre [pisvinegr] *m invar* (coll) skinflint

pissoir [piswar] *m* (coll) urinal

pissotière [pisotjɛr] *f* (coll) street urinal

pistache [pistaʃ] *f* pistachio

piste [pist] *f* track; trail; ring (*of, e.g., circus*); rink; lane (*of highway*); **à double piste** four-lane (*highway*); **piste cavalière** bridle path; **piste cyclable** bicycle track; **piste d'atterrissage** landing strip; **piste de danse** dance floor; **piste d'envoi** runway; **piste pour skieurs** ski run; **piste sonore** sound track

pister [piste] *tr* to track, trail

pistolet [pistɔlɛ] *m* pistol; spray gun; (coll) card; **pistolet à bouchon** popgun; **pistolet d'arçon** horse pistol; **pistolet mitrailleur** submachine gun

piston [pistɔ̃] *m* piston; (coll) pull

pistonner [pistɔne] *tr* (coll) to push, to back

pitance [pitãs] *f* ration; food

pi·teux [pitø] **-teuse** [tøz] *adj* pitiful, sorry, sad

pitié [pitje] *f* pity; **à faire pitié** (coll) very badly; **par pitié!** for pity's sake!; **quelle pitié!** how awful!

piton [pitɔ̃] *m* screw eye; peak

pitou [pitu] *m* (Canad) dog; (Canad) tyke

pitoyable [pitwajabl] *adj* pitiful

pitre [pitr] *m* clown

pittoresque [pitɔrɛsk] *adj* picturesque

pivoine [pivwan] *f* peony

pivot [pivo] *m* pivot

pivoter [pivɔte] *intr* to pivot

P.J. [peʒi] *f* (letterword) (**police judiciaire**) (coll) police (*dealing with criminal cases*)

placage [plakaʒ] *m* veneering; plating

placard [plakar] *m* cupboard; closet; placard, poster; (typ) galley

placarder [plakarde] *tr* to placard; (typ) to print in galleys

place [plas] *f* place; city square; room; seat; job, position; fare; **sur place** on the spot

placement [plasmã] *m* placement; investment; **de placement** employment (*agency*)

placer [plase] §51 *tr* to place; to invest; to slip in ‖ *ref* to seat oneself; to rank; to get a job; to take place

pla·ceur [plasœr] **-ceuse** [søz] *mf* employment agent ‖ *m* usher

placide [plasid] *adj* placid

pla·cier [plasje] **-cière** [sjɛr] *mf* agent, representative

plafond [plafɔ̃] *m* ceiling

plafonner [plafɔne] *intr*—**plafonner (à)** to hit the top (at)

plafonnier [plafɔnje] *m* ceiling light; (aut) dome light

plage [plaʒ] *f* beach; band (*of record*); (poetic) clime

plagiaire [plaʒjɛr] *mf* plagiarist

plagiat [plaʒja] *m* plagiarism

plagier [plaʒje] *tr* & *intr* to plagiarize

plagiste [plaʒist] *mf* beach concessionaire

plaider [plede] *tr* to argue (*a case*); to plead (*e.g., ignorance*) || *intr* to plead; to go to law

plai·deur [pledœr] **-deuse** [døz] *mf* litigant

plaidoirie [pledwari] *f* pleading

plaidoyer [pledwaje] *m* appeal (*of lawyer to judge or jury*)

plaie [plɛ] *f* wound, sore; plague; **plaie en séton** flesh wound

plai·gnant [plɛɲɑ̃] **-gnante** [ɲɑ̃t] *mf* plaintiff

plain [plɛ̃] *m* high tide

plaindre [plɛ̃dr] §15 *tr* to pity || *ref* to complain

plaine [plɛn] *f* plain

plain-pied [plɛ̃pje] *m*—**de plain-pied** on the same floor; (fig) on an equal footing

plainte [plɛ̃t] *f* complaint; moan

plain·tif [plɛ̃tif] **-tive** [tiv] *adj* plaintive

plaire [plɛr] §52 *intr* (with *dat*) to please; (with *dat*) to like, e.g., **le lait lui plaît** he likes milk; **s'il vous plaît** please || *ref* to be pleased; to enjoy oneself; to like one another; **se plaire à** to like it in, e.g., **je me plais à la campagne** I like it in the country

plaisance [plezɑ̃s] *f*—**de plaisance** pleasure (*e.g., boat*)

plai·sant [plezɑ̃] **-sante** [zɑ̃t] *adj* pleasant; funny || *m*—**mauvais plaisant** practical joker

plaisanter [plezɑ̃te] *tr* to poke fun at || *intr* to joke

plaisanterie [plezɑ̃tri] *f* joke; joking

plaisantin [plezɑ̃tɛ̃] *adj masc* roguish, waggish || *m* wag

plaisir [plezir] *m* pleasure; **à plaisir** without cause; at one's pleasure; **au plaisir (de vous revoir)** good-by; **faire plaisir à** to please, give pleasure to

plan [plɑ̃] **plane** [plan] *adj* even, flat; plane (*angle*) || *m* plan; design; (geom) plane; **au deuxième plan** in the background; **au premier plan** in the foreground; downstage; **au troisième plan** far in the background; **gros plan** (mov) close-up; **laisser en plan** (coll) to leave stranded; (coll) to put off, delay; **lever un plan** to survey; **plan de travail** work schedule; **rester en plan** (coll) to remain in suspense; **sur le plan de** from the point of view of || *f* see **plane**

planche [plɑ̃ʃ] *f* board; plank; (hort) bed; (typ) plate; (slang) blackboard; **faire la planche** to float on one's back; **planche de bord** instrument panel; **planche de débarquement** gangplank; **planche de salut** sheet anchor

planchéier [plɑ̃ʃeje] *tr* to floor; to board

plancher [plɑ̃ʃe] *m* floor; **le plancher des vaches** (coll) terra firma

plane [plan] *f* drawknife

planer [plane] *tr* to plane || *intr* to hover; to glide; to float; **planer sur** to overlook, to sweep (*e.g., a landscape with one's eyes*); (fig) to hover over

planète [planɛt] *f* planet

planeur [planœr] *m* glider

planeuse [planøz] *f* planing machine

planification [planifikasjɔ̃] *f* planning

planifier [planifje] *tr* to plan

planning [planiŋ] *m* detailed plan; **planning familial** birth control

plan-plan [plɑ̃plɑ̃] *adv* (coll) quietly, without hurrying

planque [plɑ̃k] *f* (coll) soft job; (slang) hideout

planquer [plɑ̃ke] *tr* to hide || *ref* (mil) to take cover; (slang) to hide out

plant [plɑ̃] *m* planting; bed, patch; seedling, sapling

plantation [plɑ̃tasjɔ̃] *f* planting; plantation; **plantation de cheveux** hairline; head of hair

plante [plɑ̃t] *f* plant; sole

plan·té -tée [plɑ̃te] *adj* set, situated

planter [plɑ̃te] *tr* to plant; to set; **planter là** to give the slip to || *ref* to stand

planteur [plɑ̃tœr] *m* planter

plantoir [plɑ̃twar] *m* (hort) dibble

planton [plɑ̃tɔ̃] *m* (mil) orderly

plantu·reux [plɑ̃tyrø] **-reuse** [røz] *adj* abundant; fertile; (coll) buxom

plaque [plak] *f* plate; plaque; splotch; **plaque à crêpes** pancake griddle; **plaque croûteuse** scab; **plaque d'immatriculation** (aut) license plate; **plaque minéralogique** (aut) license plate; **plaque tournante** (rr) turntable; (fig) hub (*of a city*)

plaquer [plake] *tr* to plate; to veneer; to plaster down (*one's hair*); to strike (*a chord*); (football) to tackle; (coll) to jilt; **plaquer à l'électricité** to electroplate || *ref* to lie flat; (aer) to pancake

plaquette [plakɛt] *f* plaque; pamphlet; (histology) platelet

plastic [plastik] *m* plastic bomb

plastique [plastik] *adj* plastic || *m* plastics || *f* plastic art

plastron [plastrɔ̃] *m* shirt front; breastplate; hostile contingent (*in war games*)

plastronner [plastrɔne] *intr* (fig) to throw out one's chest

plat [pla] **plate** [plat] *adj* flat; even; smooth (*sea*); dead (*calm*); corny (*joke*); **à plat** run-down; flat || *m* dish; platter; course (*of meal*); flat (*of hand*); blade (*of oar*); face (*of hammer*); **plat cuisiné** platter, short-order meal; **plat de côtes** sparerib; **plat du jour** today's special, chef's special; **plat principal, plat de résistance** entree; **plats** (bb) boards

platane [platan] *m* plane tree; **faux platane** sycamore

pla·teau [plato] *m* (*pl* -**teaux**) plateau; tray; shelf; platform; plate; pan (*of scale*); (mov, telv) set; (rr) flatcar; (theat) stage; **plateau porte-disque** turntable (*of phonograph*); **plateau tournant** revolving stage

plate-bande [platbɑ̃d] *f* (*pl* **plates-bandes**) flower bed

plate-forme [platform] *f* (*pl* **plates-formes**) platform; (rr) flatcar

platine [platin] *m* platinum ‖ *f* plate; platen; lock (*of gun*); stage (*of microscope*)

plati·né -née [platine] *adj* platinum-plated; platinum

platitude [platityd] *f* platitude; flatness; obsequiousness

Platon [platɔ̃] *m* Plato

plâtre [plɑtr] *m* plaster; plaster cast; **essuyer les plâtres** to be the first occupant of a new house; **plâtre à mouler** plaster of Paris

plâtrer [plɑtre] *tr* to plaster; to put in a cast; to fertilize ‖ *ref* (coll) to pile on the make-up or face powder

plausible [plozibl] *adj* plausible

plébéien [plebejɛ̃] **plébéienne** [plebejen] *adj* & *mf* plebeian

plein [plɛ̃] **pleine** [plen] *adj* full; round, plump; solid (*bar, wheel, wire, etc.*); continuous (*line*); heavy (*heart*); in foal, with calf, etc.; (coll) drunk; **plein aux as** (coll) well-heeled; **plein de** full of; covered with; preoccupied with; **plein de soi** self-centered ‖ (when standing before noun) *adj* full; high (*tide*); **en plein + noun** in the midst of the + *noun*, right in the + *noun*; at the height of the (*season*); in the open (*air*); out at (*sea*), on the high (*seas*); in broad (*daylight*); in the dead of (*winter*); **en** full (*of the moon*); bull's-eye; downstroke; **battre son plein** to be in full swing; **en plein** plumb, plump, squarely; **faire le plein (de)** to fill up the tank (with) ‖ **plein** *adv* full; **tout plein** very much

plein-emploi [plɛ̃ɑ̃plwa] *m* full employment

pleu·rard [plœrar] -**rarde** [rard] *adj* (coll) whimpering ‖ *mf* (coll) whimperer

pleurer [plœre] *tr* to weep over; **pleurer misère** to complain of being poor ‖ *intr* to cry, weep; **pleurer à chaudes larmes** to weep bitterly

pleurésie [plœrezi] *f* pleurisy

pleu·reur [plœrœr] -**reuse** [røz] *adj* weeping ‖ *f* paid mourner

pleurnicher [plœrniʃe] *intr* to whimper, snivel

pleurs [plœr] *mpl* tears

pleutre [pløtr] *adj* (coll) cowardly ‖ *m* (coll) coward

pleuvasser [pløvase] *intr* (coll) to drizzle

pleuvoir [pløvwar] §53 *intr* & *impers* to rain; **pleuvoir à verse, à flots,** or **à seaux** to rain buckets

pli [pli] *m* fold; pleat; bend (*of arm or leg*); hollow (*of knee*); letter; envelope; undulation (*of ground*); (cards) trick; **faux pli** crease, wrinkle; **petit pli** tuck; **sous ce pli** enclosed, herewith; **sous pli cacheté** in a sealed envelope; **sous pli distinct** or **séparé** under separate cover

pliage [plijaʒ] *m* folding

pliant [plijɑ̃] **pliante** [plijɑ̃t] *adj* folding; collapsible; pliant ‖ *m* campstool, folding chair

plier [plije] *tr* to fold; to bend; to force ‖ *intr* to fold; to bend; to yield; **ne pas plier, s.v.p.** (formula on envelope) please do not bend ‖ *ref* to fold; to yield; to fall back (*said of army*)

plisser [plise] *tr* to pleat; to crease; to wrinkle; to squint (*the eyes*) ‖ *intr* to fold ‖ *ref* to wrinkle; to pucker up (*said of mouth*)

plomb [plɔ̃] *m* lead; shot; seal; plumb; sinker (*of fishline*); (elec) fuse; **à plomb** plumb, vertical; straight down, directly; **faire sauter un plomb** to burn or blow out a fuse

plombage [plɔ̃baʒ] *m* filling (*of tooth*); sealing (*e.g., at customs*)

plombagine [plɔ̃baʒin] *f* graphite

plom·bé -bée [plɔ̃be] *adj* leaden; in bond, sealed; filled (*tooth*); livid (*hue*)

plomber [plɔ̃be] *tr* to cover with lead; to seal; to plumb; to fill (*a tooth*); to make livid; to roll (*the ground*)

plomberie [plɔ̃bri] *f* plumbing; plumbing-supply store; leadwork

plombeur [plɔ̃bœr] *m* (mach) roller

plombier [plɔ̃bje] *m* plumber; worker in lead

plonge [plɔ̃ʒ] *f* dishwashing

plon·geant [plɔ̃ʒɑ̃] -**geante** [ʒɑ̃t] *adj* plunging; from above

plongée [plɔ̃ʒe] *f* plunge; dive; dip, slope; **en plongée** submerged

plongeoir [plɔ̃ʒwar] *m* diving board

plongeon [plɔ̃ʒɔ̃] *m* plunge; dive; (football) tackle; **plongeon de haut vol** high dive

plonger [plɔ̃ʒe] §38 *tr* to plunge; to thrust, to stick ‖ *intr* to plunge; to dive; (coll) to have a good view; **plonger raide** to crash-dive ‖ *ref*—se **plonger dans** to immerse oneself in; to give oneself over to

plon·geur [plɔ̃ʒœr] -**geuse** [ʒøz] *adj* diving ‖ *mf* diver; dishwasher (*in restaurant*) ‖ *m* (mach) plunger; (orn) diver

plot [plo] *m* (elec) contact point

ployer [plwaje] §47 *tr* & *intr* to bend

pluches [plyʃ] *fpl* (mil) K.P.

pluie [plɥi] *f* rain; shower; **pluies radioactives** fallout

plumage [plymaʒ] *m* plumage

plumard [plymar] *m*—**aller au plu-mard** (slang) to hit the hay

plume [plym] *f* feather; pen; penpoint

plu·meau [plymo] *m* (*pl* -**meaux**) feather duster

plumer [plyme] *tr* to pluck; (coll) to fleece ‖ *intr* to feather one's oar

plumet [plyme] *m* plume

plu·meux [plymø] -**meuse** [møz] *adj* feathery

plumier [plymje] *m* pencil box

plupart [plypar] *f*—**la plupart** most; the most; for the most part; **la plupart de** most; the most; most of, the majority of; **la plupart d'entre nous** (eux) most of us (them); **pour la plupart** for the most part

plu·riel -rielle [plyrjɛl] *adj* & *m* plural; **au pluriel** in the plural

plus [ply] ([plyz] before vowel; [plys] in final position) *m* plus; **au plus, tout au plus** at the most, at best; at the latest; at the outside; **d'autant plus** all the more so; **de plus** more; moreover, besides; **de plus en plus** more and more; **en plus** extra; **en plus de** in addition to, besides; **le plus, la plus, les plus** (the) most; **le plus de** the most; **le plus que** as much as, as fast as; **ni . . . non plus** nor . . . either, e.g., **ni moi non plus** nor I either; **ni plus ni moins** neither more nor less; **non plus** neither, not . . . either; **plus de** more, e.g., **plus de chaleur** more heat; no more, e.g., **plus de potage** no more soup; **qui plus est** what is more, moreover ‖ *adv comp* & *super* §91 more; **des plus . . .** (le) most; **plus + *adj*** most + *adj*, extremely + *adj*; (le) **plus . . .** (the) most, e.g., **ce que j'aime le plus** what I like (the) most; **le** (or **son**, etc.) **plus + *adj*** the (or his, etc.) most; **ne . . . plus** §90 no more, no longer; **ne . . . plus que** §90 now only, e.g., **il n'y a plus que mon oncle** there is now only my uncle; **on ne peut plus + *adj*** or *adv* extremely + *adj* or *adv*; **plus de** (followed by numeral) more than; **plus jamais** never more; **plus . . . plus** (or **moins**) the more . . . the more (or the less); **plus que** more than; **plus tôt** sooner ‖ *prep* plus

plusieurs [plyzjœr] *adj* & *pron indef* several

plus-que-parfait [plyskəparfɛ] *m* pluperfect

plus-value [plyvaly] *f* (*pl* -**values**) appreciation; increase; surplus; extra cost; surplus value (*in Marxian economics*)

Plutarque [plytark] *m* Plutarch

Pluton [plytɔ̃] *m* Pluto

plutonium [plytɔnjɔm] *m* plutonium

plutôt [plyto] *adv* rather; instead; **plutôt . . . que** rather . . . than

pluvier [plyvje] *m* (orn) plover

plu·vieux [plyvjø] -**vieuse** [vjøz] *adj* rainy

pneu [pnø] *m* (*pl* **pneus**) tire; express letter (*by Parisian tube*); **pneu ballon**

or **confort** balloon tire; **pneu de se-cours** spare tire

pneumatique [pnømatik] *adj* pneumatic ‖ *m* tire; express letter (*by Parisian tube*)

pneumonie [pnømɔni] *f* pneumonia

pochade [pɔʃad] *f* sketch

po·chard [pɔʃar] -**charde** [ʃard] *mf* (coll) boozer, guzzler

poche [pɔʃ] *f* pocket; bag, pouch; crop (*of bird*)

po·ché -chée [pɔʃe] *adj* poached; black (*eye*)

pocher [pɔʃe] *tr* to poach; to dash off (*a sketch*)

pochette [pɔʃet] *f* folder; book (*of matches*); kit; fancy handkerchief; **pochette à disque** record jacket; **pochette surprise** surprise package

pocheuse [pɔʃøz] *f* egg poacher

pochoir [pɔʃwar] *m* stencil

poêle [pwal] *m* stove; pall; canopy ‖ *f* frying pan

poêlon [pwalɔ̃] *m* saucepan

poème [pɔem] *m* poem; **poème symphonique** tone poem

poésie [pɔezi] *f* poetry; poem

poète [pɔet] *mf* poet

poétesse [pɔetes] *f* poetess

poétique [pɔetik] *adj* poetic(al) ‖ *f* poetics

pogrom [pɔgrɔm] *m* pogrom

poids [pwa], [pwɑ] *m* weight; **poids lourd** truck

poi·gnant [pwaɲɑ̃] -**gnante** [ɲɑ̃t] *adj* poignant

poignard [pwaɲar] *m* dagger

poignarder [pwaɲarde] *tr* to stab

poigne [pwaɲ] *f* grip, grasp; **à poigne** strong, energetic

poignée [pwaɲe] *f* handful; handle; grip; hilt; **poignée de main** handshake

poignet [pwaɲe] *m* wrist; cuff; **poignet mousquetaire** French cuff

poil [pwal] *m* hair; bristle; nap, pile; coat (*of animals*); **à long poil** shaggy; **à poil** naked; bareback; **au poil** (slang) peachy; **avoir un poil dans la main** (coll) to be lazy; **de mauvais poil** (coll) in a bad mood; **de tout poil** (coll) of every shade and hue; **poil follet** down; **reprendre du poil de la bête** (coll) to be one's own self again; **se mettre à poil** to strip to the skin

poi·lu -lue [pwaly] *adj* hairy ‖ *m* (mil) doughboy

poinçon [pwɛ̃sɔ̃] *m* punch; stamp; hallmark; **poinçon à glace** ice pick

poinçonner [pwɛ̃sɔne] *tr* to punch; to stamp; to prick; to hallmark

poinçonneuse [pwɛ̃sɔnøz] *f* stamping machine; ticket punch

poindre [pwɛ̃dr] §35 *intr* to dawn; to sprout

poing [pwɛ̃] *m* first; **dormir à poings fermés** to sleep like a log

point [pwɛ̃] *m* point; stitch; period (*used also in French to mark the divisions of whole numbers*); hole (*in a strap*); mark (*on a test*); (aer,

naut) position; (typ) point; **à point**
at the right moment; to a turn, medium; **à point nommé** in the nick of
time; **à tel point que** to such a degree that; **au dernier point** to the
utmost degree; **de point en point** exactly to the letter; **de tout point, en
tout point** entirely; **deux points** colon; **faire le point** to take stock, to
get one's bearings; **mettre au point**
to focus; to adjust, to tune up; to develop, to perfect; **mettre les points
sur les i** to dot one's i's; **point d'appui** fulcrum; base of operations;
point de bâti (sewing) tack; **point de
départ** starting point; **point de repère**
point of reference, guide; (surv)
bench mark; (fig) landmark; **point
d'estime** dead reckoning; **point
d'exclamation** exclamation point;
point d'interrogation question mark;
point d'orgue (mus) pause; **point du
jour** break of day; **point et virgule**
semicolon; **point mort** dead center;
(aut) neutral; **points et traits** dots
and dashes ‖ *adv*—**ne . . . point** §90
not; not at all

pointage [pwɛtaʒ] *m* checking; check
mark; aiming

pointe [pwɛt] *f* point; tip; peak; head
(*of arrow*); nose (*e.g., of bullet*); toe
(*of shoe*); twinge (*of pain*); dash (*of,
e.g., vanilla*); suggestion, touch; witty
phrase, quip; (geog) cape, point;
(mil) spearhead; **à pointes** spiked
(*shoes*); **de pointe** peak (*e.g., hours*);
discuter sur les pointes d'épingle to
split hairs; **en pointe** tapering; **faire
des pointes** to toe-dance; **pointe
d'aiguille** needlepoint; **pointe de
Paris** wire nail; **pointe de vitesse**
spurt; **pointe du jour** daybreak; **sur
la pointe des pieds** on tiptoe

poin·teau [pwɛto] *m* (*pl* **-teaux**) checker; needle

pointer [pwɛtœr] *m* pointer (*dog*) ‖
[pwɛte] *tr* to check off; to check in;
to prick up (*the ears*); to dot ‖ *intr*
to rise, to soar skywards; to stand
out; to sprout ‖ *ref* to check in, to
show up

poin·teur [pwɛtœr] **-teuse** [tøz] *mf*
checker; scorer; timekeeper; gunner;
(*dog*) pointer

pointillé [pwɛtije] *m* perforated line

pointil·leux [pwɛtijø] **pointil·leuse**
[pwɛtijøz] *adj* punctilious; touchy;
captious

poin·tu -tue [pwɛty] *adj* pointed; shrill;
(fig) touchy

pointure [pwɛtyr] *f* size

poire [pwar] *f* pear; bulb (*of camera,
syringe, horn, etc.*); (slang) mug;
(slang) sucker, sap; **couper la poire
en deux** to split the difference; **garder une poire pour la soif** to put
something aside for a rainy day;
poire à poudre powder flask; **poire
électrique** pear-shaped switch

poi·reau [pwaro] *m* (*pl* **-reaux**) (bot)
leek

poirée [pware] *f* (bot) Swiss chard

poirier [pwarje] *m* pear tree
pois [pwa], [pwɑ] *m* pea; polka dot;
petits pois, pois verts peas; **pois
cassés** split peas; **pois chiche** chick-
pea; **pois de senteur** sweet pea
poison [pwazɔ̃] *m* poison
pois·sard [pwasar] **pois·sarde** [pwa-
sard] *adj* vulgar ‖ *f* fishwife
poisser [pwase] *tr* to coat with wax or
pitch ‖ *intr* to be sticky
pois·seux [pwasø] **pois·seuse** [pwasøz]
adj sticky
poisson [pwasɔ̃] *m* fish; **poisson d'avril**
April Fool (*joke, trick*); **poisson
rouge** goldfish
poisson-chat [pwasɔ̃ʃa] *m* (*pl* **poissons-
chats**) catfish
poissonnerie [pwasɔnri] *f* fish market
poisson·nier [pwasɔnje] **poisson·nière**
[pwasɔnjɛr] *mf* dealer in fish ‖ *f*
fishwife; fish kettle
poitrail [pwatraj] *m* breast
poitrinaire [pwatrinɛr] *adj & mf*
(pathol) consumptive
poitrine [pwatrin] *f* chest; breast;
bosom
poivre [pwavr] *m* pepper
poivrer [pwavre] *tr* to pepper
poivrier [pwavrije] *m* pepper plant;
pepper shaker
poivrière [pwavrijɛr] *f* pepper shaker;
pepper plantation
poivron [pwavrɔ̃] *m* pepper; sweet
pepper plant
poix [pwa], [pwɑ] *f* pitch; **poix sèche**
resin
poker [pɔker] *m* poker; four of a kind
polaire [pɔlɛr] *adj* pole, polar
polariser [pɔlarize] *tr* to polarize
pôle [pol] *m* pole
po·li -lie [pɔli] *adj* polished; polite ‖
m polish, gloss
police [pɔlis] *f* police; policy; **police
d'assurance** insurance policy
policer [pɔlise] §51 *tr* to civilize; (obs)
to police
Polichinelle [pɔliʃinɛl] *m* Punch; **de
polichinelle** open (*secret*)
poli·cier [pɔlisje] **-cière** [sjɛr] *adj* police (*investigation, dog, etc.*); detective (*e.g., story*) ‖ *m* plain-clothes
man, detective
polio [pɔljo] *mf* (coll) polio victim ‖ *f*
(coll) polio
polir [pɔlir] *tr* to polish
polissoir [pɔliswar] *m* polisher
polis·son [pɔlisɔ̃] **polis·sonne** [pɔlisɔn]
adj smutty ‖ *mf* scamp, rascal
politesse [pɔlites] *f* politeness; **polites-
ses** civilities, compliments
politicard [pɔlitikar] *m* unscrupulous
politician
politi·cien [pɔlitisjɛ̃] **-cienne** [sjɛn] *adj*
short-sighted; insincere ‖ *mf* poli-
tician
politique [pɔlitik] *adj* political; prudent, wise ‖ *m* politician; statesman
‖ *f* politics; policy; cunning, shrewdness
pollen [pɔlɛn] *m* pollen
polluer [pɔllɥe] *tr* to pollute
polo [pɔlo] *m* polo

Pologne [pɔlɔɲ] *f* Poland; **la Pologne** Poland

polo·nais [pɔlɔnɛ] **-naise** [nɛz] *adj* Polish || *m* Polish (*language*) || (*cap*) *mf* Pole

polonium [pɔlɔnjɔm] *m* polonium

pol·tron [pɔltrɔ̃] **-tronne** [trɔn] *adj* cowardly || *mf* coward

polycopie [pɔlikɔpi] *f* mimeographing; tiré à **la polycopie** mimeographed

polycopié [pɔlikɔpje] *m* mimeographed university lectures

polycopier [pɔlikɔpje] *tr* to mimeograph

polygame [pɔligam] *adj* polygamous || *mf* polygamist

polyglotte [pɔliglɔt] *adj* polyglot || *mf* polyglot, linguist

polygone [pɔligɔn] *m* polygon; shooting range

polynôme [pɔlinom] *m* polynomial

polype [pɔlip] *m* polyp

polythéiste [pɔliteist] *adj* polytheistic || *mf* polytheist

pom [pɔ̃] *interj* bang!

pommade [pɔmad] *f* pomade; **passer de la pommade à** (coll) to soft-soap

pomme [pɔm] *f* apple; ball, knob; head (*of lettuce*); **pomme de discorde** bone of contention; **pomme de pin** pine cone; **pomme de terre** potato; **pommes chips** potato chips; **pommes de terre au four** baked potatoes; scalloped potatoes; **pommes de terre en robe de chambre, en robe des champs,** or **en chemise** potatoes in their jackets; **pommes de terre sautées** fried potatoes; **pommes frites** French fried potatoes; **pommes soufflées** potato puffs; **pommes vapeur** boiled potatoes; steamed potatoes

pom·meau [pɔmo] *m* (*pl* **-meaux**) pommel; butt (*of fishing pole*)

pomme·lé -lée [pɔmle] *adj* dappled; fleecy (*clouds*); mackerel (*sky*)

pommette [pɔmɛt] *f* cheekbone

pommier [pɔmje] *m* apple tree

pompe [pɔ̃p] *f* pomp; pump; **à la pompe** on draught; **pompe à incendie** fire engine; **pompe aspirante** suction pump; **pompes funèbres** funeral

pomper [pɔ̃pe] *tr* to pump; to suck in

pompette [pɔ̃pɛt] *adj* (coll) tipsy

pom·peux [pɔ̃pø] **-peuse** [pøz] *adj* pompous; high-flown

pom·pier [pɔ̃pje] **-pière** [pjɛr] *adj* conventional; pretentious || *mf* fitter || *m* fireman

pompiste [pɔ̃pist] *mf* filling-station attendant

pomponner [pɔ̃pɔne] *tr* & *ref* to dress up

ponçage [pɔ̃saʒ] *m* sandpapering; pumicing

ponce [pɔ̃s] *f* pumice stone

pon·ceau [pɔ̃so] (*pl* **-ceaux**) *adj* poppy-red || *m* rude bridge; culvert

poncer [pɔ̃se] §51 *tr* to sandpaper; to pumice

poncho [pɔ̃tʃo] *m* poncho

poncif [pɔ̃sif] *m* banality

ponctualité [pɔ̃ktɥalite] *f* punctuality

ponctuation [pɔ̃ktɥasjɔ̃] *f* punctuation

ponc·tuel -tuelle [pɔ̃ktɥɛl] *adj* punctual

ponctuer [pɔ̃ktɥe] *tr* to punctuate

pondération [pɔ̃derasjɔ̃] *f* balance; weighting

pondé·ré -rée [pɔ̃dere] *adj* moderate, well-balanced; weighted

pondérer [pɔ̃dere] §10 *tr* to balance; to weight

pondeuse [pɔ̃døz] *f* layer (*hen*); (coll) prolific woman

pondre [pɔ̃dr] *tr* to lay (*an egg*); (coll) to turn out (*a book*); (slang) to bear (*a child*) || *intr* to lay

poney [pɔnɛ] *m* pony

pont [pɔ̃] *m* bridge; (naut) deck; **faire le pont** (coll) to take the intervening day or days off; **pont aérien** airlift; **pont arrière** (aut) rear-axle assembly; **pont cantilever, pont à consoles** cantilever bridge; **ponts et chaussées** [pɔ̃zeʃose] highway department; **pont suspendu** suspension bridge

ponte [pɔ̃t] *f* egg laying; eggs

pontet [pɔ̃tɛ] *m* trigger guard

pontife [pɔ̃tif] *m* pontiff

pont-levis [pɔ̃lvi] *m* (*pl* **ponts-levis**) drawbridge

ponton [pɔ̃tɔ̃] *m* pontoon; landing stage

pont-promenade [pɔ̃prɔmnad] *m* (*pl* **ponts-promenades**) promenade deck

pool [pul] *m* pool (*combine*)

pope [pɔp] *m* Orthodox priest

popeline [pɔplin] *f* poplin

popote [pɔpɔt] *adj invar* (coll) stay-at-home || *f* (mil) mess; (coll) cooking; **faire la popote** (coll) to do the cooking oneself

populace [pɔpylas] *f* populace, rabble

populaire [pɔpylɛr] *adj* popular; vulgar, common

populariser [pɔpylarize] *tr* to popularize

popularité [pɔpylarite] *f* popularity

population [pɔpylasjɔ̃] *f* population

popu·leux -leuse [pɔpylø] [løz] *adj* populous; crowded

populo [pɔpylo] *m* (coll) rabble

porc [pɔr] *m* pig, hog; pork

porcelaine [pɔrsəlɛn] *f* porcelain; china

porcelet [pɔrsəlɛ] *m* piglet

porc-épic [pɔrkepik] *m* (*pl* **porcs-épics** [pɔrkepik]) porcupine

porche [pɔrʃ] *m* porch, portico

porcher [pɔrʃe] *m* swineherd

porcherie [pɔrʃəri] *f* pigpen

pore [pɔr] *m* pore

po·reux -reuse [pɔrø] [røz] *adj* porous

pornographie [pɔrnɔgrafi] *f* pornography

porphyre [pɔrfir] *m* porphyry

port [pɔr] *m* port; carrying; wearing; bearing; shipping charges; **arriver à bon port** to arrive safe; **port d'attache** home port; **port d'escale** port of call; **port franc** duty-free; free port; **port payé** postpaid

portable [pɔrtabl] *adj* portable; wearable

portail [pɔrtaj] *m* portal, gate

por·tant [pɔrtɑ̃] **-tante** [tɑ̃t] *adj* bearing; lifting; **être bien portant** to be in good health || *m* handle

porta·tif [pɔrtatif] **-tive** [tiv] *adj* portable

porte [pɔrt] *f* door; doorway; gate; **fausse porte** blind door; **porte à deux battants** double door; **porte à tambour** revolving door; **porte battante** swinging door; **porte cochère** covered carriage entrance

porte-à-faux [pɔrtafo] *m* invar—**en porte-à-faux** out of line; (fig) in an untenable position

porte-aiguilles [pɔrtegɥi] *m* invar needle case

porte-allumettes [pɔrtalymet] *m* invar matchbox

porte-assiette [pɔrtasjet] *m* (*pl* **-assiette** or **-assiettes**) place mat

porte-avions [pɔrtavjɔ̃] *m* invar aircraft carrier

porte-bagages [pɔrtbagaʒ] *m* invar baggage rack

porte-bannière [pɔrtbanjer] *mf* (*pl* **-bannière** or **-bannières**) colorbearer

porte-bonheur [pɔrtbɔnœr] *m* invar good-luck charm

porte-carte [pɔrtəkart] *m* (*pl* **-carte** or **-cartes**) card case

porte-chapeaux [pɔrtʃapo] *m* invar hatrack

porte-cigarette [pɔrtsigaret] *m* invar cigarette holder

porte-cigarettes [pɔrtsigaret] *m* invar cigarette case

porte-clés or **porte-clefs** [pɔrtəkle] *m* invar key ring

porte-disques [pɔrtdisk] *m* invar record case

porte-documents [pɔrtdɔkymɑ̃] *m* invar letter case, portfolio

porte-drapeau [pɔrtdrapo] *m* (*pl* **-drapeau** or **-drapeaux**) standard-bearer

portée [pɔrte] *f* range, reach; import, significance; litter; (mus) staff; **à la portée de** within reach of; **à portée de la voix** within speaking distance; **à portée de l'oreille** within hearing distance; **hors de la portée de** out of reach of

portefaix [pɔrtəfe] *m* porter; dock hand

porte-fenêtre [pɔrtfənetr], [pɔrtəfnetr] *f* (*pl* **portes-fenêtres**) French window, French door

portefeuille [pɔrtəfœj] *m* portfolio; wallet; billfold

porteman·teau [pɔrtmɑ̃to] *m* (*pl* **-teaux**) clothes tree; **en portemanteau** square (*shoulders*)

porte-mine [pɔrtəmin] *m* (*pl* **-mine** or **mines**) mechanical pencil

porte-monnaie [pɔrtmɔne] *m* invar change purse

porte-parapluies [pɔrtparaplɥi] *m* invar umbrella stand

porte-parole [pɔrtparɔl] *m* invar spokesman, mouthpiece

porte-plume [pɔrtəplym] *m* invar penholder; **porte-plume réservoir** fountain pen

porter [pɔrte] *tr* to carry; to bear; to wear; to propose (*a toast*); **porté à** to be inclined to; **être porté sur** to have a weakness for; **porter à l'écran** (mov) to put on the screen || *intr* to carry; **porter sur** to bear down on, to emphasize; to be aimed at || *ref* to be worn; to proceed, to go; to be, e.g., **comment vous portez-vous?** how are you?; **se porter à** to indulge in; **se porter candidat** to run as a candidate

porte-savon [pɔrtsavɔ̃] *m* (*pl* **-savon** or **-savons**) soap dish

porte-serviettes [pɔrtservjet] *m* invar towel rack

por·teur [pɔrtœr] **-teuse** [tøz] *mf* porter; bearer; holder

porte-vêtement [pɔrtəvetmɑ̃] *m* invar clothes hanger

porte-voix [pɔrtəvwa] *m* invar megaphone; **mettre les mains en porte-voix** to cup one's hands

por·tier [pɔrtje] **-tière** [tjer] *mf* concierge || *m* doorman || *f* door (*of car*); portière

portillon [pɔrtijɔ̃] *m* gate; (rr) side gate (*at crossing*); **refouler du portillon** (slang) to have bad breath

portion [pɔrsjɔ̃] *f* portion; share

portique [pɔrtik] *m* portico

porto [pɔrto] *m* port wine

portori·cain [pɔrtorikɛ̃] **-caine** [ken] *adj* Puerto Rican || (*cap*) *mf* Puerto Rican

Porto Rico [pɔrtoriko] *f* Puerto Rico

portrait [pɔrtre] *m* portrait; **être tout le portrait de** to be the very image of; **portrait à mi-corps** half-length portrait; **portrait de face** full-faced portrait

portraitiste [pɔrtretist] *mf* portrait painter

portu·gais [pɔrtyge] **-gaise** [gez] *adj* Portuguese || *m* Portuguese (*language*) || (*cap*) *mf* Portuguese (*person*)

Portugal [pɔrtygal] *m*—**le Portugal** Portugal

pose [poz] *f* pose; laying, setting in place; (phot) exposure

po·sé **-sée** [poze] *adj* poised, steady; trained (*voice*)

posément [pozemɑ̃] *adv* calmly, steadily, carefully

posemètre [pozmetr] *m* (phot) light meter, exposure meter

poser [poze] *tr* to place; to arrange; to ask (*a question*); to set up (*a principle*) || *intr* to pose || *ref* to pose; to alight; to land; **se poser en** to set oneself up as

po·seur [pozœr] **-seuse** [zøz] *mf* layer; poseur; phony; **poseur d'affiches** billposter

posi·tif [pozitif] **-tive** [tiv] *adj* & *m* positive

position [pozisjɔ̃] *f* position

posséder [pɔsede] §10 *tr* to possess, own; to have a command of, to know perfectly || *ref* to control oneself

possession [pɔsesjɔ̃] *f* possession

possibilité [pɔsibilite] *f* possibility
possible [pɔsibl] *adj & m* possible
postage [pɔstaʒ] *m* mailing
pos·tal -tale [pɔstal] *adj* (*pl* **-taux** [to]) postal
postdate [pɔstdat] *f* postdate
postdater [pɔstdate] *tr* to postdate
poste [pɔst] *m* post; station; set; position, job; **poste de douane** port of entry; **poste d'émetteur** broadcasting station; **poste de radio** radio set; **poste de repérage** tracking station; **poste de secours** first-aid station; **poste des malades** (nav) sick bay; **poste d'essence** gas station; **poste d'incendie** fire station; **poste supplémentaire** (telp) extension || *f* post, mail; **mettre à la poste** to mail; **poste restante** general delivery; **postes** post office department
poster [pɔste] *tr* to post || *ref* to lie in wait
postérité [pɔsterite] *f* posterity
posthume [pɔstym] *adj* posthumous
postiche [pɔstiʃ] *adj* false; detachable || *m* toupee; switch, false hair
pos·tier [pɔstje] **-tière** [tjer] *mf* postal clerk
postscolaire [pɔstskɔler] *adj* adult (*education*); extension (*courses*)
post-scriptum [pɔstskriptɔm] *m invar* postscript
postu·lant [pɔstylã] **-lante** [lãt] *mf* applicant, candidate; postulant
postuler [pɔstyle] *tr* to apply for || *intr* to apply; **postuler pour** to represent (*a client*)
posture [pɔstyr] *f* posture; situation
pot [po] *m* pot; pitcher; jug; jar; can; **découvrir le pot aux roses** (coll) to discover the secret; **payer les pots cassés** (coll) to pay the piper; **pot à bière** beer mug; **pot à fleurs** flowerpot; **pot d'échappement** (aut) muffler; **pot de noir** cloudy weather; **pot d'étain** pewter tankard; **tourner autour du pot** (coll) to beat about the bush
potable [pɔtabl] *adj* drinkable; (coll) acceptable, passable
potache [pɔtaʃ] *m* (coll) schoolboy
potage [pɔtaʒ] *m* soup; **potage de maïs** hominy; **pour tout potage** (lit) all told
pota·ger [pɔtaʒe] **-gère** [ʒer] *adj* vegetable || *m* vegetable garden
potasse [pɔtas] *f* potash
potasser [pɔtase] *tr* (coll) to bone up on || *intr* (coll) to grind away
potas·seur [pɔtasœr] **potas·seuse** [pɔtasøz] *mf* (coll) grind
potassium [pɔtasjɔm] *m* potassium
pot-au-feu [pɔtofø] *adj invar* (coll) home-loving || *m invar* beef stew
pot-de-vin [pɔdvẽ] *m* (*pl* **pots-de-vin**) bribe, money under the table
po·teau [pɔto] *m* (*pl* **-teaux**) post, pole; **poteau de but** goal post; **poteau indicateur** signpost
pote·lé -lée [pɔtle] *adj* chubby
potence [pɔtãs] *f* gallows; bracket
potentat [pɔtãta] *m* potentate

poten·tiel -tielle [pɔtãsjel] *adj & m* potential
poterie [pɔtri] *f* pottery; metalware; **poterie mordorée** lusterware
poterne [pɔtern] *f* postern
potiche [pɔtiʃ] *f* large Oriental vase; (fig) figurehead
potin [pɔtẽ] *m* piece of gossip; racket; **faire du potin** (coll) to raise a row; **potins** gossip
potiner [pɔtine] *intr* to gossip
potion [posjɔ̃] *f* potion
potiron [pɔtirɔ̃] *m* pumpkin; **potiron lumineux** jack-o'-lantern
pou [pu] *m* (*pl* **poux**) louse
poubelle [pubel] *f* garbage can
pouce [pus] *m* thumb; big toe; inch; **manger sur le pouce** (coll) to eat on the run
poudre [pudr] *f* powder; face powder; **en poudre** powdered; granulated (*sugar*); **il n'a pas inventé la poudre** (coll) he's not so smart; **jeter de la poudre aux yeux de** to deceive; **poudre dentifrice** tooth powder; **se mettre de la poudre** to powder one's nose
poudrer [pudre] *tr* to powder
poudrerie [pudrəri] *f* powder mill
pou·dreux [pudrø] **-dreuse** [drøz] *adj* powdery; dusty || *f* sugar shaker
poudrier [pudrije] *m* compact
poudrière [pudrijer] *f* powder magazine; (fig) powder keg
poudroyer [pudrwaje] §47 *intr* to raise the dust; to shine through the dust
pouf [puf] *m* hassock, pouf || *interj* plop!; **faire pouf** (slang) to flop
pouffer [pufe] *intr* to burst out laughing
pouil·leux [pujø] **pouil·leuse** [pujøz] *adj* lousy; sordid || *mf* person covered with lice
pouillot [pujo] *m* (orn) warbler
poulailler [pulaje] *m* henhouse; (theat) peanut gallery
poulain [pulẽ] *m* colt, foal
poule [pul] *f* hen; chicken; (*in games*) pool; jackpot; (turf) sweepstakes; (coll) skirt, dame; (slang) tart, mistress; **ma poule** (coll) my pet; **poule au pot** chicken stew; **poule d'Inde** turkey hen; **poule mouillée** (coll) milksop; **tuer la poule aux œufs d'or** to kill the goose that lays the golden eggs
poulet [pule] *m* chicken, (coll) love letter; **mon petit poulet** (coll) my pet; **poulet d'Inde** turkey cock
poulette [pulet] *f* pullet; (coll) gal; **ma poulette** (coll) darling
pouliche [puliʃ] *f* filly
poulie [puli] *f* pulley; block
poulpe [pulp] *m* octopus
pouls [pu] *m* pulse; **tâter le pouls à** to feel the pulse of
poumon [pumɔ̃] *m* lung
poupe [pup] *f* (naut) stern, poop
poupée [pupe] *f* doll; dummy; sore finger; (mach) headstock
pou·pon [pupɔ̃] **-ponne** [pɔn] *mf* baby; chubby-faced youngster

pouponnière [pupɔnjɛr] *f* nursery
pour [pur] *m*—le **pour** et le **contre** the pros and the cons || *adv*—**pour lors** then; **pour peu que** however little; **pour que** in order that; **pour . . . que** however, e.g., **pour charmante qu'elle soit** however charming she may be || *prep* for; in order to; **pour ainsi dire** so to speak; **pour cent** per cent
pourboire [purbwar] *m* tip
pour·ceau [purso] *m* (pl **-ceaux**) swine, hog, pig
pourcentage [pursɑ̃taʒ] *m* percentage
pourchasser [purʃase] *tr* to hound
pourlécher [purleʃe] §10 *ref* to smack one's lips
pourparlers [purparle] *mpl* talks, parley, conference
pourpoint [purpwɛ̃] *m* doublet
pourpre [purpr] *adj* purple || *m* purple (*violescent*) || *f* purple (*deep red, crimson*)
pourquoi [purkwa] *m* why; **le pourquoi et le comment** the why and the wherefore || *adv & conj* why; **pourquoi pas?** why not?
pour·ri -rie [puri] *adj* rotten; spoiled || *m* rotten part
pourrir [purir] *tr, intr, & ref* to rot; to spoil; to corrupt
pourriture [purityr] *f* rot; decay; corruption
poursuite [pursᵾit] *f* pursuit; (*law*) action, suit; (coll) spotlight
poursui·vant -vante [pursᵾivɑ̃] -[vɑ̃t] *mf* pursuer; (law) plaintiff
poursuivre [pursᵾivr] §67 *tr* to pursue, chase; to proceed with; to persecute; to sue || *intr* to continue || *ref* to be continued
pourtant [purtɑ̃] *adv* however, nevertheless, yet
pourtour [purtur] *m* circumference
pourvoi [purvwa] *m* (law) appeal
pourvoir [purvwar] §54 *tr*—**pourvoir de** to supply with, to provide with; to favor with || *intr*—**pourvoir à** to provide for, to attend to || *ref* (law) to appeal
pourvoyeur [purvwajœr] **pourvoyeuse** [purvwajøz] *mf* provider, supplier, caterer; **pourvoyeurs** gun crew
pourvu que [purvykə] *conj* provided that
pousse [pus] *f* shoot, sprout
pous·sé -sée [puse] *adj* elaborate, searching, exhaustive || *f* push, shove; thrust; rise; pressure; (rok) thrust
pousse-café [puskafe] *m invar* liqueur
pousser [puse] *tr* to push, to shove, to egg on, to urge; to utter (*a cry*); to heave (*a sigh*); **pousser plus loin** to carry further || *intr* to push, shove; to grow; to push on || *ref* to push oneself forward
poussette [pusɛt] *f* baby carriage
poussier [pusje] *m* coal dust
poussière [pusjɛr] *f* dust; powder; **poussière d'eau** spray; **une pous-**

sière a trifle; **une poussière de** a lot of
poussié·reux [pusjerø] **-reuse** [røz] *adj* dusty; powdery
pous·sif [pusif] **pous·sive** [pusiv] *adj* wheezy
poussin [pusɛ̃] *m* chick
poussoir [puswar] *m* push button
poutre [putr] *f* beam; joist; girder
poutrelle [putrɛl] *f* small girder
pouvoir [puvwar] *m* power; **pouvoir d'achat** purchasing power || §55 *tr* to be able to do; **je n'y puis rien** I can't or cannot help it, I can do nothing about it || *intr* to be able; **on ne peut mieux** couldn't be better; **on ne peut plus** I (we, they, etc.) can do no more; **on** I (we're, they're, etc.) all in || *aux* used to express 1) ability, e.g., **elle peut prédire l'avenir** she is able to predict the future, she can predict the future; 2) permission, e.g., **vous pouvez partir** you may go; e.g., **puis-je partir?** may I go?; 3) possibility, e.g., **il peut pleuvoir** it may rain; e.g., **il a pu oublier son parapluie** he may have forgotten his umbrella; 4) optative, e.g., **puisse-t-il venir!** may he come! || *impers ref*—**il se peut que** it is possible that, e.g., **il se peut qu'il vienne ce soir** it is possible that he may come this evening; **il se pourrait bien que** it might well be that, e.g., **il se pourrait bien qu'il vînt ce soir** it might well be that he will come this evening, he might come this evening || *ref* to be possible; **cela ne se peut pas** that is not possible
pragmatique [pragmatik] *adj* pragmatic(al)
prairie [preri], [preri] *f* meadow; **les Prairies** the prairie
praticable [pratikabl] *adj* practicable; passable || *m* practicable stage property; (mov, telv) camera platform
prati·cien [pratisjɛ̃] **-cienne** [sjɛn] *mf* practitioner
prati·quant [pratikɑ̃] **-quante** [kɑ̃t] *adj* practicing (*e.g., Catholic*); churchy || *mf* churchgoer
pratique [pratik] *adj* practical || *f* practice; contact, company; customer; **libre pratique** freedom of worship; (naut) freedom from quarantine
pratiquement [pratikmɑ̃] *adv* practically, in practice
pratiquer [pratike] *tr* to practice; to cut, make (*e.g., a hole*); to frequent; to read a great deal of (*e.g., of doctor*); to practice one's religion || *ref* to be practiced, done; to rule, prevail (*said of prices*)
pré [pre] *m* meadow; **sur le pré** on the field of honor (*dueling ground*)
préalable [prealabl] *adj* previous; preliminary || *m* prerequisite; **au préalable** before, in advance
préambule [preɑ̃byl] *m* preamble
préau [preo] *m* (pl **préaux**) yard
préavis [preavi] *m* advance warning;

avec **préavis** person-to-person (*telephone call*)

précaire [preker] *adj* precarious

précaution [prekosjɔ̃] *f* precaution

précautionner [prekosjone] *tr* to caution || *intr* to be on one's guard

précaution·neux [prekosjɔnø] **précaution·neuse** [prekosjɔnøz] *adj* precautious

précé·dent [presedɑ̃] **-dente** [dɑ̃t] *adj* preceding || *m* precedent

précéder [presede] §10 *tr* & *intr* to precede

précepte [presept] *m* precept

précep·teur [preseptœr] **-trice** [tris] *mf* tutor

prêche [prɛʃ] *m* sermon

prêcher [preʃe] *tr* to preach; to preach to || *intr* to preach; **prêcher d'exemple** to practice what one preaches

prê·cheur [preʃœr] **-cheuse** [ʃøz] *adj* preaching || *mf* sermonizer

pré·cieux [presjø] **-cieuse** [sjøz] *adj* precious; valuable; affected

préciosité [presjozite] *f* preciosity (*French literary style corresponding to English euphuism*)

précipice [presipis] *m* precipice

précipi·té -tée [presipite] *adj* hurried, precipitous || *m* precipitate

précipiter [presipite] *tr* to hurl || *ref* to hurl oneself; to precipitate; to hurry, rush

pré·cis [presi] **-cise** [siz] *adj* precise; sharp, e.g., **trois heures précises** three o'clock sharp || *m* abstract, summary

préciser [presize] *tr* to specify || *intr* to be precise || *ref* to become clear; to take shape, to jell

précision [presizjɔ̃] *f* precision; **précisions** data

préci·té -tée [presite] *adj* aforementioned

précoce [prekɔs] *adj* precocious; (bot) early

précon·çu -çue [prekɔ̃sy] *adj* preconceived

préconiser [prekɔnize] *tr* to advocate, recommend

précurseur [prekyrsœr] *adj masc* precursory || *m* forerunner, harbinger

préda·teur [predatœr] *adj masc* predatory || *m* predatory animal

prédécesseur [predesesœr] *m* predecessor

prédicateur [predikatœr] *m* preacher

prédiction [prediksjɔ̃] *f* prediction

prédire [predir] §40 *tr* to predict

prédisposer [predispoze] *tr* to predispose

prédomi·nant [predɔminɑ̃] **-nante** [nɑ̃t] *adj* predominant

préémi·nent [preeminɑ̃] **-nente** [nɑ̃t] *adj* preeminent

préfabri·qué -quée [prefabrike] *adj* prefabricated

préface [prefas] *f* preface

préfacer [prefase] §51 *tr* to preface

préfecture [prefektyr] *f* prefecture; **préfecture de police** police headquarters

préférable [preferabl] *adj* preferable

préférence [preferɑ̃s] *f* preference

préférer [prefere] §10 *tr* to prefer

préfet [prefe] *m* prefect; **préfet de police** police commissioner

préfixe [prefiks] *m* prefix

préfixer [prefikse] *tr* to prefix

préhistorique [preistɔrik] *adj* prehistoric

préjudice [preʒydis] *m* prejudice, detriment; **porter préjudice à** to injure, to harm; **sans préjudice de** without affecting

préjudiciable [preʒydisjabl] *adj* detrimental

préjudicier [preʒydisje] *intr* (with *dat*) to harm, damage

préjugé [preʒyʒe] *m* prejudice

préjuger [preʒyʒe] §38 *tr* to foresee || *intr*—**préjuger de** to prejudge

prélart [prelar] *m* tarpaulin

prélasser [prelase] *ref* to lounge

prélat [prela] *m* prelate

prélèvement [prelevmɑ̃] *m* deduction; sample; levy

prélever [prelve] §2 *tr* to set aside, deduct; to take (*a sample*); to levy; **prélever à** to take from

préliminaire [preliminer] *adj* & *m* preliminary

prélude [prelyd] *m* prelude

préluder [prelyde] *intr* to warm up (*said of singer, musician, etc.*); **préluder à** to prelude

prématu·ré -rée [prematyre] *adj* premature

préméditer [premedite] *tr* to premeditate

prémices [premis] *fpl* first fruits; beginning

pre·mier [prǝmje] **-mière** [mjer] *adj* first; raw (*materials*); prime (*number*); the First, e.g., **Jean premier John the First** || (*when standing before noun*) *adj* first; prime (*minister*); maiden (*voyage*); early (*infancy*) || *m* first; **jeune premier** leading man; **premier de cordée leader** || *f* first; first class; (theat) première; **jeune première** leading lady || *pron* (*masc & fem*) first

premier-né [prǝmjene] **première-née** [prǝmjerne] (*pl* **premiers-nés**) *adj* & *mf* first-born

prémisse [premis] *f* premise

prémonition [premɔnisjɔ̃] *f* premonition

prémunir [premynir] *tr* to forewarn || *ref*—**se prémunir contre** to protect oneself against

pre·nant [prǝnɑ̃] **-nante** [nɑ̃t] *adj* sticky; winning; pleasing

prendre [prɑ̃dr] §56 *tr* to take; to take on; to take up; to catch; to get (*to obtain and bring*); to steal (*a kiss*); to buy (*a ticket*); to make (*an appointment*); **à tout prendre** all things considered; **prendre de l'âge** to be getting old; **prendre la mer** to take to sea; **prendre l'eau** to leak; **prendre le large** to take to the open sea; **prendre q.ch. à qn** to take s.th. from s.o.; to charge s.o. s.th. (*i.e., a cer-*

tain sum of money); **prendre son temps** to take one's time || *intr* to catch (*said of fire*); to take root; to form (*said of ice*); to set (*said of mortar*); to stick (*to a pan or dish*); to catch on (*said of a style*); to turn (*right or left*); **prendre à droite** to bear to the right; **qu'est-ce qui lui prend?** what's come over him? || *ref* to get caught, to catch (*e.g., on a nail*); to congeal; to clot; to curdle; to jam; to take from each other; **pour qui se prend-il?** who does he think he is?; **s'en prendre à qn de q.ch.** to blame s.o. for s.th.; **se prendre à** to begin to; **se prendre d'amitié** to strike up a friendship; **se prendre de vin** to get drunk; **s'y prendre** to go about it

pre•neur [prənœr] -neuse [nøz] *mf* taker; buyer; payee; lessee

prénom [prenɔ̃] *m* first name

prénommer [prenɔme] *tr* to name || *ref* —il (elle, etc.) se prénomme his (her, etc.) first name is

préoccupation [preɔkypasjɔ̃] *f* preoccupation

préoccuper [preɔkype] *tr* to preoccupy || *ref* —se préoccuper de to pay attention to; to be concerned about

prépara•teur [preparatœr] -trice [tris] *mf* laboratory assistant

préparatifs [preparatif] *mpl* preparations

préparation [preparasjɔ̃] *f* preparation; notice, warning

préparatoire [preparatwar] *adj* preparatory

préparer [prepare] *tr, intr, & ref* to prepare

prépondé•rant [prepɔ̃derã] -rante [rãt] *adj* preponderant

prépo•sé -sée [prepoze] *mf* employee, clerk; **préposé de la douane** customs officer; **préposée au vestiaire** hatcheck girl

préposer [prepoze] *tr*—**préposer qn à q.ch.** to put s.o. in charge of s.th.

préposition [prepozisjɔ̃] *f* preposition

prérogative [prerɔgativ] *f* prerogative

près [pre] *adv* near; à beaucoup près by far; à cela près except for that; à peu d'exceptions près with few exceptions; à peu près about, practically; à . . . près except for; within, e.g., je peux vous dire l'heure à cinq minutes près I can tell you what time it is within five minutes; au plus près to the nearest point; de près close; closely; ici près near here; près de near; nearly, about; alongside, at the side of; près de + *inf* about to + *inf*; tout près nearby, right here || *prep* near; to, at

présage [preza3] *m* presage, foreboding

présager [preza3e] §38 *tr* to presage, forebode; to anticipate

pré•salé [presale] *m* (*pl* prés-salés) salt-meadow sheep; salt-meadow mutton

presbyte [presbit] *adj* far-sighted || *mf* far-sighted person

presbytère [presbiter] *m* presbytery

presbyté•rien [presbiterjɛ̃] -rienne [rjen] *adj* & *mf* Presbyterian

presbytie [presbisi] *f* far-sightedness

prescription [preskripsjɔ̃] *f* prescription

prescrire [preskrir] §25 *tr* to prescribe || *ref* to be prescribed

préséance [preseɑ̃s] *f* precedence

présence [prezɑ̃s] *f* presence; attendance; en présence face to face

pré•sent [prezɑ̃] -sente [zɑ̃t] *adj* present || *m* present, gift; (*gram*) present; les présents those present

présentable [prezɑ̃tabl] *adj* presentable

présenta•teur [prezɑ̃tatœr] -trice [tris] *mf* (*rad*) announcer; présentateur de disques disk jockey

présentation [prezɑ̃tasjɔ̃] *f* presentation; introduction; appearance; look, form (*of a new product*)

présentement [prezɑ̃tmɑ̃] *adv* right now

présenter [prezɑ̃te] *tr* to present; to introduce; to offer; to pay (*one's respects*) || *ref* to present oneself; to present itself; se présenter à to be a candidate for

présérie [preseri] *f* (*com*) trial run, sample run

préservatif [prezervatif] *m* preventive; condom

préserver [prezerve] *tr* to preserve

présidence [prezidɑ̃s] *f* presidency; chairmanship; presidential mansion

prési•dent [prezidɑ̃] -dente [dɑ̃t] *mf* president; chairman; presiding judge || *f* president's wife; chairwoman; madame la présidente madam chairman

présiden•tiel -tielle [prezidɑ̃sjel] *adj* presidential

présider [prezide] *tr* to preside over || *intr* to preside; présider à to preside over

présomp•tif [prezɔ̃ptif] -tive [tiv] *adj* presumptive, presumed

présomption [prezɔ̃psjɔ̃] *f* presumption

présomp•tueux [prezɔ̃ptɥø] -tueuse [tɥøz] *adj* presumptuous

presque [presk(ə)] *adv* almost, nearly; presque jamais hardly ever; presque personne scarcely anybody

presqu'île [preskil] *f* peninsula

pres•sant [presɑ̃] pres•sante [presɑ̃t] *adj* pressing, urgent

presse [pres] *f* press; hurry, rush; crowd; hand screw, clamp; mettre sous presse to go to press

pres•sé -sée [prese] *adj* pressed; pressing, urgent; squeezed

presse-bouton [presbutɔ̃] *adj invar* push-button (*warfare*)

presse-citron [presitrɔ̃] *m invar* lemon squeezer

pressentiment [presɑ̃timɑ̃] *m* presentiment, foreboding

pressentir [presɑ̃tir] §41 *tr* to have a foreboding of; to sound out

presse-papiers [prespapje] *m invar* paperweight

presse-purée [prespyre] *m invar* potato masher

presser [prese], [prese] *tr* to press; to squeeze; to hurry, hasten || *intr* to be urgent || *ref* to hurry; **se presser à** to crowd around

pressing [presiŋ] *m* dry cleaner's, tailor shop

pression [presjɔ̃] *f* pressure; snap fastener; **à la pression** on draught; **pression artérielle** blood pressure

pressoir [preswar] *m* press

pressurer [presyre] *tr* to press, squeeze; to bleed white, to wring money out of

pressuriser [presyrize] *tr* to pressurize

prestance [prestɑ̃s] *f* commanding appearance, dignified bearing

prestation [prestasjɔ̃] *f* taking (*of oath*); tax; allotment, allowance, benefit

preste [prest] *adj* nimble

prestidigita·teur [prestidiʒitatœr] **-trice** [tris] *mf* magician

prestidigitation [prestidiʒitasjɔ̃] *f* sleight of hand, legerdemain

prestige [prestiʒ] *m* prestige; illusion, magic

presti·gieux [prestiʒjø] **-gieuse** [ʒjøz] *adj* prestigious, famous; marvelous

présumer [prezyme] *tr* to presume; to presume to be || *intr* to presume; **présumer de** to presume upon

présupposer [presypoze] *tr* to presuppose

présure [prezyr] *f* rennet

prêt [pre] **prête** [pret] *adj* ready; **prêt à porter** ready-to-wear, ready-made; **prêt à tout** ready for anything || *m* loan

prêt-à-porter [pretaporte] *m* (*pl* **prêts-à-porter** [pretaporte]) ready-to-wear, ready-made clothes

prêt-bail [prebaj] *m invar* lend-lease

préten·dant [pretɑ̃dɑ̃] **-dante** [dɑ̃t] *mf* pretender || *m* suitor

prétendre [pretɑ̃dr] *tr* to claim; to require || *intr*—**prétendre à** to aspire to; to lay claim to

préten·du -due [pretɑ̃dy] *adj* so-called, alleged || *m* fiancé || *f* fiancée

prête-nom [pretnɔ̃] *m* (*pl* **-noms**) dummy, figurehead, straw man

prétentaine [pretɑ̃ten] *f*—**courir la prétentaine** (coll) to be on the loose; (coll) to have many love affairs

préten·tieux [pretɑ̃sjø] **-tieuse** [sjøz] *adj* pretentious

prétention [pretɑ̃sjɔ̃] *f* pretention, pretense; claim, pretensions

prêter [prete], [prete] *tr* to lend; to give (*e.g., help*); to pay (*attention*); to take (*an oath*); to impart (*e.g., luster*); to attribute, ascribe || *intr* to lend; to stretch; **prêter à** to lend itself to || *ref*—**se prêter à** to lend itself to; to be a party to, to countenance; to indulge in

prê·teur [pretœr] **-teuse** [tøz] *mf* lender; **prêteur sur gages** pawnbroker

prétexte [pretekst] *m* pretext

prétexter [pretekste] *tr* to give as a pretext

prétonique [pretɔnik] *adj* pretonic

prêtre [pretr] *m* priest

prêtresse [pretres] *f* priestess

prêtrise [pretriz] *f* priesthood

preuve [prœv] *f* proof, evidence

preux [prø] *adj masc* valiant || *m* doughty knight

prévaloir [prevalwar] §71 (*subj* **prévale**, etc.) *intr* to prevail || *ref*—**se prévaloir de** to avail oneself of; to pride oneself on

prévarication [prevarikasjɔ̃] *f* breach of trust

prévariquer [prevarike] *intr* to betray one's trust

prévenance [prevnɑ̃s] *f* kindness, thoughtfulness

préve·nant [prevnɑ̃] **-nante** [nɑ̃t] *adj* attentive, considerate; prepossessing

prévenir [prevnir] §72 *tr* to anticipate; to avert, forestall; to ward off, to prevent; to notify, inform; to bias, to prejudice

préven·tif [prevɑ̃tif] **-tive** [tiv] *adj* preventive; pretrial (*detention*)

prévention [prevɑ̃sjɔ̃] *f* bias, prejudice; custody, imprisonment; prevention (*of accidents*); **prévention routière** traffic police; road safety

préve·nu -nue [prevny] *adj* biased, prejudiced; forewarned; accused || *mf* prisoner, accused, defendant

prévision [previzjɔ̃] *f* anticipation, estimate; **prévision du temps** weather forecast; **prévisions** expectations

prévoir [prevwar] §57 *tr* to foresee, anticipate; to forecast

prévoyance [prevwajɑ̃s] *f* foresight

prévo·yant [prevwajɑ̃] **prévoyante** [prevwajɑ̃t] *adj* far-sighted, provident

prie-dieu [pridjø] *m invar* prie-dieu || *f* praying mantis

prier [prije] *tr* to ask, to beg; to pray (*God*); **je vous en prie!** I beg your pardon!; by all means!; you are welcome!; please have some!; **je vous prie!** please!; **prier qn de** + *inf* to ask, to beg s.o. + *inf* || *intr* to pray

prière [prijer] *f* prayer; **prière de . . .** please . . . ; **prière d'insérer** publisher's insert for reviewers

primaire [primer] *adj* primary; first (*offender*); (coll) narrow-minded || *m* (elec) primary; (coll) primitive

primat [prima] *m* (eccl) primate

primate [primat] *m* (zool) primate

primauté [primote] *f* supremacy

prime [prim] *adj* early (*youth*); (math) prime || *f* premium; bonus; free gift; (eccl) prime; **prime de transport** traveling expenses

primer [prime] *tr* to excel; to take priority over; to award a prize to

primerose [primroz] *f* hollyhock

primesau·tier [primsotje] **-tière** [tjer] *adj* impulsive, quick

primeur [primœr] *f* freshness; first fruit; early vegetable; (journ) beat, scoop; **primeurs** fruits and vegetables out of season

primevère [primvɛr] f primrose

primi·tif [primitif] **-tive** [tiv] adj primitive; original, early; primary (colors; tense) ‖ mf primitive

primo [primo] adv firstly

primor·dial -diale [primɔrdjal] adj (pl **-diaux** [djo]) primordial; fundamental, prime, primary

prince [prɛ̃s] m prince; **prince de Galles** Prince of Wales

princesse [prɛ̃sɛs] f princess

prin·cier [prɛ̃sje] **-cière** [sjɛr] adj princely

princi·pal -pale [prɛ̃sipal] adj & m (pl **-paux** [po]) principal, chief

principauté [prɛ̃sipote] f principality

principe [prɛ̃sip] m principle; beginning; source

printa·nier [prɛ̃tanje] **-nière** [njer] adj spring; springlike

printemps [prɛ̃tɑ̃] m spring; springtime; **au printemps** in the spring

priorité [priɔrite] f priority; right of way; **de priorité** preferred (stock); main (road); **priorité à droite, priorité à gauche** (public sign) yield

pris [pri] **prise** [priz] adj set, frozen; **être pris** to be busy; **pris de vin** drunk ‖ f capture, seizure; taking; hold; setting; tap, faucet; (med) dose; (naut) prize; **donner prise à** to lay oneself open to; **être aux prises avec** to be struggling with; **hors de prise** out of gear; **lâcher prise** to let go; **prise d'air** ventilator; **prise d'antenne** (rad) lead-in; **prise d'armes** military parade; **prise d'eau** water faucet; hydrant; **prise de bec** (coll) quarrel; **prise de conscience** awakening, awareness; **prise de courant** (elec) plug; (elec) tap, outlet; **prise de position** statement of opinion; **prise de sang** blood specimen; **prise de son** recording; **prise de tabac** pinch of snuff; **prise de terre** (elec) ground connection; **prise de vue(s)** (phot) shot, picture taking; **prise de vue directe** (telv) live broadcast; **prise directe** high gear

prisée [prize] f appraisal

priser [prize] tr to value; to snuff up ‖ intr to take snuff

pri·seur [prizœr] **-seuse** [zøz] mf snuffer ‖ m appraiser

prisme [prism] m prism

prison [prizɔ̃] f prison

prison·nier [prizɔnje] **prison·nière** [prizɔnjer] mf prisoner

privautés [privote] fpl liberties

pri·vé -vée [prive] adj private; tame, pet ‖ m private life

priver [prive] tr to deprive ‖ ref to deprive oneself; **se priver de** to do without, to abstain from

privilège [privilɛʒ] m privilege

privilé·gié -giée [privileʒje] adj privileged; preferred (stock)

prix [pri] m price; prize; value; **à aucun prix** not at any price; by no means; **à tout prix** at all costs; au

prix de at the price of; at the rate of; compared with; **dans mes prix** within my means; **grand prix** championship race; **hors de prix** at a prohibitive cost; **prix courant** list price; **prix de départ** upset price; **prix de détail** retail price; **prix de fabrique** factory price; **prix de gros** wholesale price; **prix de la vie** cost of living; **prix de location** rent; **prix de revient** cost price; **prix de vente** selling price; **prix fixe** table d'hôte

probabilité [prɔbabilite] f probability

probable [prɔbabl] adj probable, likely

pro·bant [prɔbɑ̃] **-bante** [bɑ̃t] adj convincing; conclusive (evidence)

probe [prɔb] adj honest, upright

problème [prɔblɛm] m problem

procédé [prɔsede] m process; procedure; tip (of cue); **procédés** proceedings; behavior

procéder [prɔsede] §10 intr to proceed; (with dat) to perform, carry out; **procéder de** to arise from

procédure [prɔsedyr] f procedure; proceedings

procès [prɔsɛ] m lawsuit, case; trial; **intenter un procès à** to sue; to prosecute; **sans autre forme de procès** then and there, without appeal

proces·sif [prɔsesif] **proces·sive** [prɔsesiv] adj litigious

procession [prɔsesjɔ̃] f procession

processus [prɔsesys] m process

procès-verbal [prɔsevɛrbal] m (pl **-verbaux** [verbo]) report; minutes; ticket (e.g., for speeding)

pro·chain [prɔʃɛ̃] **-chaine** [ʃɛn] adj next; impending; (lit) nearest, immediate; **la prochaine semaine** the next week; **la semaine prochaine** next week ‖ m neighbor, fellow-man ‖ f—**à la prochaine!** (coll) so long!

prochainement [prɔʃɛnmɑ̃] adv shortly

proche [prɔʃ] adj near; nearby; close (relative) ‖ **proches** mpl close relatives ‖ adv—**de proche en proche** little by little

proclamer [prɔklame] tr to proclaim

proclitique [prɔklitik] adj & m proclitic

procuration [prɔkyrasjɔ̃] f power of attorney; **par procuration** by proxy

procurer [prɔkyre] tr & ref to procure, to get

procureur [prɔkyrœr] m attorney; **procureur de la république** district attorney; **procureur général** attorney general

prodige [prɔdiʒ] m prodigy; wonder

prodi·gieux [prɔdiʒjø] **-gieuse** [ʒjøz] adj prodigious, wonderful; terrific

prodigue [prɔdig] adj prodigal, lavish ‖ mf prodigal, spendthrift

prodiguer [prɔdige] tr to squander, waste; to lavish ‖ ref to not spare oneself; to show off

prodrome [prɔdrom] m harbinger; introduction

produc·teur [prɔdyktœr] **-trice** [tris] adj productive ‖ mf producer

produc·tif [prɔdyktif] **-tive** [tiv] *adj* productive; producing

production [prɔdyksjɔ̃] *f* production

produire [prɔdɥir] §19 *tr* to produce; to create; to introduce || *ref* to take place; to be produced; to show up

produit [prɔdɥi] *m* product; proceeds; offspring; **produit de luxe** luxury item; **produit pharmaceutique** patent medicine, drug; **produits agricoles** agricultural produce; **produits de beauté** cosmetics

proémi·nent [prɔeminã] **-nente** [nãt] *adj* prominent, protuberant

profane [prɔfan] *adj* profane; lay, uninformed || *mf* profane; layman

profaner [prɔfane] *tr* to profane; (fig) to prostitute

proférer [prɔfere] §10 *tr* to utter

professer [prɔfese] *tr* to profess; to teach || *intr* to teach

professeur [prɔfesœr] *m* teacher; professor

profession [prɔfesjɔ̃] *f* profession; occupation, trade

profession·nel -nelle [prɔfesjɔnɛl] *adj* & *mf* professional

profil [prɔfil] *m* profile; side face; cross section; skyline (*of city*)

profi·lé -lée [prɔfile] *adj* streamlined, aerodynamic

profiler [prɔfile] *tr* to profile || *ref—* **se profiler sur** to stand out against

profit [prɔfi] *m* profit; **mettre à profit** to take advantage of; **profits et pertes** profit and loss

profitable [prɔfitabl] *adj* profitable

profiter [prɔfite] *intr* to profit; to grow; (with *dat*) to profit; **profiter à, dans,** or **en** to profit from

profi·teur [prɔfitœr] **-teuse** [tøz] *mf* profiteer

pro·fond -fonde [fɔ̃d] *adj* profound; deep; low (*bow; voice*); **peu profond** shallow || *m* depths || *f* (slang) pocket || **profond** *adv* deep

profondément [prɔfɔ̃demã] *adv* profoundly, deeply; soundly; deep

profondeur [prɔfɔ̃dœr] *f* depth

progéniture [prɔʒenityr] *f* progeny; offspring, child

programma·teur [prɔgramatœr] **-trice** [tris] *mf* (mov, rad, telv) programmer

programmation [prɔgramasjɔ̃] *f* programming

programme [prɔgram] *m* program; **programme de prévoyance** retirement program; **programme des études** curriculum

programmer [prɔgrame] *tr* to program

program·meur [prɔgramœr] **programmeuse** [prɔgramøz] *mf* (comp) programmer

progrès [prɔgre] *m* progress; **faire des progrès** to make progress

progresser [prɔgrese] *intr* to progress

progres·sif [prɔgresif] **progres·sive** [prɔgresiv] *adj* progressive

progressiste [prɔgresist] *adj* & *mf* progressive

prohiber [prɔibe] *tr* to prohibit

prohibition [prɔibisjɔ̃] *f* prohibition

proie [prwa], [prwɑ] *f* prey; **de proie** predatory; **en proie à** a prey to

projecteur [prɔʒektœr] *m* projector; searchlight; (mov) projection machine

projectile [prɔʒektil] *m* projectile; **projectile téléguidé** guided missile

projection [prɔʒeksjɔ̃] *f* projection

projet [prɔʒe] *m* project; draft; sketch, plan; **faire des projets** to make plans; **projet de loi** bill

projeter [prɔʒte] §34 *tr* to project; to pour forth (*smoke*); to cast (*a shadow*); to plan || *intr* to plan

prolétaire [prɔleter] *m* proletarian

prolétariat [prɔletarja] *m* proletariat

proléta·rien [prɔletarjɛ̃] **-rienne** [rjɛn] *adj* proletarian

proliférer [prɔlifere] §10 *intr* to proliferate

prolifique [prɔlifik] *adj* prolific

prolixe [prɔliks] *adj* prolix

prologue [prɔlɔg] *m* prologue; preface

prolonger [prɔlɔ̃ʒe] §38 *tr* to prolong; to extend || *ref* to be prolonged; to continue, extend

promenade [prɔmnad] *f* promenade; walk; ride; drive; sail; **faire une promenade** (en auto, à cheval, à motocyclette, en bateau, etc.) to take a ride

promener [prɔmne] §2 *tr* to take for a walk or drive; to walk (*e.g., a dog*); to take along; **envoyer promener qn** (coll) to send s.o. packing; **promener . . . sur** to run (*e.g., one's hand, eyes*) over || *ref* to stroll; to go for a walk, ride, drive, or sail; **allez vous promener!** get out of here!

prome·neur [prɔmnœr] **-neuse** [nøz] *mf* walker, stroller

promenoir [prɔmnwar] *m* ambulatory, cloister; (theat) standing room

promesse [prɔmes] *f* promise

promettre [prɔmetr] §42 *tr* to promise; **promettre q.ch. à qn** to promise s.th. to s.o. || *intr* to look promising; **promettre à qn de** + *inf* to promise s.o. to + *inf* || *ref* to promise oneself; (with *dat of reflex pron*) to promise oneself (*e.g., a vacation*); **se promettre de** to resolve to

pro·mis [prɔmi] **-mise** [miz] *adj* promised; **promis à** headed for

promiscuité [prɔmiskɥite] *f* indiscriminate mixture; lack of privacy

promontoire [prɔmɔ̃twar] *m* promontory

promo·teur [prɔmotœr] **-trice** [tris] *mf* promoter; originator

promotion [prɔmosjɔ̃] *f* promotion; uplift; class (*in school*)

promouvoir [prɔmuvwar] §45 (*pp* **promu**) *tr* to promote

prompt [prɔ̃] **prompte** [prɔ̃t] *adj* prompt, ready, quick

promptitude [prɔ̃tityd] *f* promptness

promulguer [prɔmylge] *tr* to promulgate

prône [pron] *m* homily

prôner [prone] *tr* to extol

pronom [prɔnɔ̃] *m* pronoun

pronomi·nal -nale [prɔnɔminal] *adj* (*pl*

-naux [no]) pronominal; reflexive (*verb*)

pronon·cé -cée [prɔnɔ̃se] *adj* marked; sharp (*curve*); prominent (*nose*)

prononcer [prɔnɔ̃se] §51 *tr* to pronounce; to utter; to deliver (*a speech*); to pass (*judgment*) || *intr* to decide || *ref* to be pronounced; to express an opinion

prononciation [prɔnɔ̃sjɑsjɔ̃] *f* pronunciation

pronostic [prɔnɔstik] *m* prognosis

pronostiquer [prɔnɔstike] *tr* to prognosticate

propagande [prɔpagɑ̃d] *f* propaganda; publicity, advertising

propager [prɔpaʒe] §38 *tr* to propagate; to spread || *ref* to be propagated; to spread

propédeutique [prɔpedøtik] *f* (*educ*) preliminary study

propension [prɔpɑ̃sjɔ̃] *f* propensity

prophète [prɔfɛt] *m* prophet

prophétesse [prɔfetɛs] *f* prophetess

prophétie [prɔfesi] *f* prophecy

prophétiser [prɔfetize] *tr* to prophesy

prophylactique [prɔfilaktik] *adj* prophylactic

propice [prɔpis] *adj* propitious; lucky (*star*)

proportion [prɔpɔrsjɔ̃] *f* proportion; en proportion de in proportion to

proportion·né -née [prɔpɔrsjɔne] *adj* proportionate

proportion·nel -nelle [prɔpɔrsjɔnɛl] *adj* proportional

proportionner [prɔpɔrsjɔne] *tr* to proportion

propos [prɔpo] *m* remark; purpose; à ce propos in this connection; à propos by the way; timely, fitting; at the right moment; à propos de with regard to, concerning; à tout propos at every turn; changer de propos to change the subject; de propos délibéré on purpose; des propos en l'air idle talk; hors de propos out of place; irrelevant

proposer [prɔpoze] *tr* to propose; to nominate; to recommend (*s.o.*) || *ref* to have in mind; to apply (*for a job*); se proposer de to intend to

proposition [prɔpozisjɔ̃] *f* proposition; proposal; clause

propre [prɔpr] *adj* clean, neat; original (*meaning*); proper (*name*); literal (*meaning*); propre à fit for, suited to || (*when standing before noun*) *adj* own || *m* characteristic; au propre in the literal sense; c'est du propre! (*coll*) what a dirty trick!; en propre in one's own right

pro·pret [prɔprɛ] -prette [prɛt] *adj* (*coll*) clean, bright

propreté [prɔprəte] *f* cleanliness, neatness

propriétaire [prɔprijetɛr] *mf* proprietor, owner; landowner || *m* landlord || *f* proprietress; landlady

propriété [prɔprijete] *f* property; propriety, appropriateness

propulseur [prɔpylsœr] *m* engine, motor; outboard motor; (rok) booster

propulsion [prɔpylsjɔ̃] *f* propulsion; propulsion à réaction jet propulsion

prorata [prɔrata] *m invar*—au prorata de in proportion to

proroger [prɔrɔʒe] §38 *tr* to postpone; to extend; to adjourn || *ref* to be adjourned

prosaïque [prozaik] *adj* prosaic

prosateur [prozatœr] *m* prose writer

proscrire [prɔskrir] §25 *tr* to proscribe; to banish, outlaw

pros·crit [prɔskri] -crite [krit] *adj* banished || *mf* outlaw

prose [proz] *f* prose; (coll) style (*of writing*)

prosélyte [prozelit] *mf* proselyte

prosodie [prozɔdi] *f* prosody

prospecter [prɔspekte] *tr* & *intr* to prospect

prospec·teur [prɔspektœr] -trice [tris] *mf* prospector

prospectus [prɔspektys] *m* prospectus; handbill

prospère [prɔspɛr] *adj* prosperous

prospérer [prɔspere] §10 *intr* to prosper, to thrive

prospérité [prɔsperite] *f* prosperity

prosternation [prɔsternɑsjɔ̃] *f* prostration; groveling

prosterner [prɔsterne] *tr* to bend over || *ref* to prostrate oneself; to grovel

prostituée [prɔstitɥe] *f* prostitute

prostituer [prɔstitɥe] *tr* to prostitute

prostration [prɔstrɑsjɔ̃] *f* prostration

pros·tré -trée [prɔstre] *adj* prostrate

protagoniste [prɔtagɔnist] *m* protagonist

prote [prɔt] *m* (typ) foreman

protection [prɔtɛksjɔ̃] *f* protection; protection civile civil defense

proté·gé -gée [prɔteʒe] *adj* guarded; arterial (*crossing*) || *mf* protégé, dependent; pet

protège-cahier [prɔtɛʒkaje] *m* (*pl -cahiers*) notebook cover

protège-livre [prɔtɛʒlivr] *m* (*pl -livres*) dust jacket

protéger [prɔteʒe] §1 *tr* to protect; to be a patron of

protéine [prɔtein] *f* protein

protes·tant [prɔtɛstɑ̃] -tante [tɑ̃t] *adj* & *mf* Protestant; protestant

protestation [prɔtɛstɑsjɔ̃] *f* protest

protester [prɔtɛste] *tr* & *intr* to protest; protester de to protest

protêt [prɔtɛ] *m* (com) protest

protocole [prɔtɔkɔl] *m* protocol

proton [prɔtɔ̃] *m* proton

protoplasme [prɔtɔplasm] *m* protoplasm

prototype [prɔtɔtip] *m* prototype

protozoaire [prɔtɔzɔɛr] *m* protozoan

protubérance [prɔtyberɑ̃s] *f* protuberance

proue [pru] *f* prow, bow

prouesse [prɥɛs] *f* prowess

prouver [prɥve] *tr* to prove

provenance [prɔvnɑ̃s] *f* origin; en provenance de from

proven·çal -çale [prɔvɑ̃sal] (*pl -çaux* [so]) *adj* Provençal || *m* Provençal (*language*) || (*cap*) *mf* Provençal (*person*)

provenir [prɔvnir] §72 *intr* (*aux:* ÊTRE) —**provenir de** to come from

proverbe [prɔvɛrb] *m* proverb

providence [prɔvidɑ̃s] *f* providence

providen‧tiel -tielle [prɔvidɑ̃sjɛl] *adj* providential

province [prɔvɛ̃s] *adj invar* (coll) provincial ‖ *f* province; **la province** the provinces (*all of France outside of Paris*)

proviseur [prɔvizœr] *m* headmaster

provision [prɔvizjɔ̃] *f* stock, store; deposit; **aller aux provisions** to go shopping; **faire provision de** to stock up on; **provisions** provisions, foodstuffs; **sans provision** bad (*check*)

provisoire [prɔvizwar] *adj* provisional, temporary; emergency

provo‧cant [prɔvɔkɑ̃] **-cante** [kɑ̃t] *adj* provocative

provoquer [prɔvɔke] *tr* to provoke; to cause, bring about; to arouse

proxénète [prɔksenɛt] *mf* procurer ‖ *m* pimp

proximité [prɔksimite] *f* proximity; **à proximité de** near

prude [pryd] *adj* prudish ‖ *f* prude

prudence [prydɑ̃s] *f* prudence

pru‧dent [prydɑ̃] **-dente** [dɑ̃t] *adj* prudent

pruderie [prydri] *f* prudery

prud'homme [prydɔm] *m* arbitrator; (obs) solid citizen

prudhommesque [prydɔmɛsk] *adj* pompous

pruine [prɥin] *f* bloom

prune [pryn] *f* plum; **des prunes!** (slang) nuts!; **pour des prunes** (coll) for nothing

pru‧neau [pryno] *m* (*pl* **-neaux**) prune; (slang) bullet

prunelle [prynɛl] *f* pupil (*of eye*); sloe; sloe gin; **jouer de la prunelle** (coll) to ogle; **prunelle de ses yeux** apple of his (one's, etc.) eye

prunellier [prynɛlje] *m* sloe, blackthorn

prunier [prynje] *m* plum tree

prus‧sien [prysjɛ̃] **prus‧sienne** [prysjɛn] *adj* Prussian ‖ (*cap*) *mf* Prussian

P.-S. [pees] *m* (letterword) (**postscriptum**) P.S.

psalmodier [psalmɔdje] *tr* & *intr* to speak in a singsong

psaume [psom] *m* psalm

psautier [psotje] *m* psalter

pseudonyme [psødɔnim] *adj* pseudonymous ‖ *m* pseudonym; nom de plume

psit [psit] *interj* (coll) hist!

P.S.V. [peesve] *m* (letterword) (**pilotage sans visibilité**) blind flying

psychanalyse [psikanaliz] *f* psychoanalysis

psychanalyser [psikanalize] *tr* to psychoanalyze

psyché [psi/e] *f* psyche; cheval glass

psychiatre [psikjatr] *mf* psychiatrist

psychiatrie [psikjatri] *f* psychiatry

psychique [psi/ik] *adj* psychic

psychologie [psikɔlɔʒi] *f* psychology

psychologique [psikɔlɔʒik] *adj* psychologic(al)

psychologue [psikɔlɔg] *mf* psychologist

psychopathe [psikɔpat] *mf* psychopath

psychose [psikoz] *f* psychosis

psychotique [psikɔtik] *adj* & *mf* psychotic

ptomaïne [ptɔmain] *f* ptomaine

P.T.T. [petete] *fpl* (letterword) (**Postes, télégraphes, et téléphones**) post office, telephone, and telegraph

puant [pɥɑ̃] **puante** [pɥɑ̃t] *adj* stinking

puanteur [pɥɑ̃tœr] *f* stench, stink

puberté [pybɛrte] *f* puberty

pu‧blic -blique [pyblik] *adj* public; notorious ‖ *m* public; audience

publication [pyblikasjɔ̃] *f* publication; proclamation

publicitaire [pyblisitɛr] *adj* advertising ‖ *m* advertising man

publicité [pyblisite] *f* publicity; advertising; **publicité aérienne** skywriting

publier [pyblije] *tr* to publish; to publicize, proclaim

puce [pys] *f* flea; **mettre la puce à l'oreille à qn** (fig) to put a bug in s.o.'s ear

pu‧ceau [pyso] **-celle** [sɛl] (*pl* **-ceaux**) *adj* & *mf* (coll) virgin ‖ *f* maid

puceron [pysrɔ̃] *m* plant louse

pudding [pudiŋ] *m* plum pudding

puddler [pydle] *tr* to puddle

pudeur [pydœr] *f* modesty

pudi‧bond [pydibɔ̃] **-bonde** [bɔ̃d] *adj* prudish

pudibonderie [pydibɔ̃dri] *f* false modesty

pudique [pydik] *adj* modest, chaste

puer [pɥe] *tr* to reek of ‖ *intr* to stink

pué‧ril -rile [pɥeril] *adj* puerile

puérilité [pɥerilite] *f* puerility

pugilat [pyʒila] *m* fight, brawl

pugiliste [pyʒilist] *m* pugilist

pugnace [pygnas] *adj* pugnacious

puî‧né -née [pɥine] *adj* younger ‖ *mf* younger child

puis [pɥi] *adv* then; next; **et puis** besides; **et puis après?** (coll) what next?

puisard [pɥizar] *m* drain, cesspool; sump

puisatier [pɥizatje] *m* well digger

puiser [pɥize] *tr* to draw (*water*); **puiser à** or **dans** to draw (*s.th.*) from ‖ *intr*—**puiser à** or **dans** to draw from or on; to dip or reach into

puisque [pɥisk(ə)] *conj* since, as, seeing that

puissamment [pɥisamɑ̃] *adv* powerfully; exceedingly

puissance [pɥisɑ̃s] *f* power

puis‧sant [pɥisɑ̃] **puis‧sante** [pɥisɑ̃t] *adj* powerful

puits [pɥi] *m* well; pit; (min) shaft; (naut) locker; **puits absorbant, puits perdu** cesspool; **puits de pétrole** oil well; **puits de science** fountain of knowledge

pull-over [pulɔvœr], [pylɔver] *m* (*pl* **-overs**) sweater, pullover

pulluler [pylyle] *intr* to swarm, to teem

pulmonaire [pylmɔnɛr] *adj* pulmonary ‖ *f* (bot) lungwort pulpe [pylp] f pulp

pulsation [pylsɑsjɔ̃] f pulsation, beat; pulse

pulsion [pylsjɔ̃] f (psychoanal) impulse

pulvérisateur [pylverizatœr] m spray, atomizer

pulvériser [pylverize] tr to pulverize; to spray

punaise [pynez] f bug; bedbug; thumbtack

punch [pɔ̃ʃ] m punch (drink) || [pœnʃ] m (boxing) punch

punching-ball [pœnʃiŋbol] m punching bag

punir [pynir] tr & intr to punish

punition [pynisjɔ̃] f punishment

pupille [pypil], [pypij] mf ward || f pupil (of eye)

pupitre [pypitr] m desk; stand, rack; lectern; console, controls; pupitre à musique music stand

pur pure [pyr] adj pure || mf diehard; les purs the pure in heart

purée [pyre] f purée; mashed potatoes; (coll) wretch; être dans la purée (coll) to be broke; purée de pois (culin, fig) pea soup || interj (slang) how awful!

pureté [pyrte] f purity

purga·tif [pyrgatif] -tive [tiv] adj & m purgative

purgatoire [pyrgatwar] m purgatory

purge [pyrʒ] f purge

purger [pyrʒe] §38 tr to purge; to pay off (e.g., a mortgage); to serve (a sentence)

purifier [pyrifje] tr to purify

puri·tain [pyritɛ̃] -taine [ten] adj & mf puritan; Puritan

pur-sang [pyrsɑ̃] adj & m invar thoroughbred

pus [py] m pus

pusillanime [pyzilanim] adj pusillanimous

pustule [pystyl] f pimple

putain [pytɛ̃] adj invar (coll) amiable, agreeable || f (vulg) whore

putois [pytwa] m skunk, polecat

putréfier [pytrefje] tr & ref to decompose, to rot

putride [pytrid] adj putrid

puy [pɥi] m volcanic peak

puzzle [pœzl] m jigsaw puzzle

p.-v. [peve] m (letterword) (procès-verbal) (coll) ticket, e.g., attraper un p.-v. to get a ticket

pygargue [pigarg] m osprey, fish hawk

pygmée [pigme] m pygmy

pygméen [pigmeɛ̃] pygméenne [pigmeen] adj pygmy

pyjama [piʒama] m pajamas; un pyjama a pair of pajamas

pylône [pilon] m pylon; tower

pyramide [piramid] f pyramid

Pyrénées [pirene] fpl Pyrenees

pyrite [pirit] f pyrites

pyrotechnie [pirotekni] f pyrotechnics

pyrotechnique [piroteknik] adj pyrotechnical

python [pitɔ̃] m python

pythonisse [pitɔnis] f pythoness

pyxide [piksid] f pyx

Q

Q, q [ky] m invar seventeenth letter of the French alphabet

quadrant [kwadrɑ̃], [kadrɑ̃] m (math) quadrant

quadrilatère [kwadrilater] m quadrilateral

quadrupède [kwadryped] m quadruped

quadruple [kwadrypl] adj & m quadruple

quadrupler [kwadryple] tr & intr to quadruple

quadru·plés -plées [kwadryple] mfpl quadruplets

quai [ke] m quay, wharf; platform (e.g., in a railroad station); embankment, levee; amener à quai to berth; le Quai d'Orsay the French foreign office

qua·ker [kwekœr] -keresse [kwaker] -keresse [kres] mf Quaker

qualifiable [kalifjabl] adj describable

quali·fié -fiée [kalifje] adj qualified; qualifying; aggravated (crime)

qualifier [kalifje] tr & intr to qualify

qualité [kalite] f quality; title, capacity; avoir qualité pour to be authorized to; en qualité de in the capacity of

quand [kɑ̃] adv when; how soon; n'importe quand anytime; quand même though, just the same || conj when; quand même even if

quant [kɑ̃] adv—quant à as for, as to, as far as; quant à cela for that matter

quant-à-soi [kɑ̃taswa] m dignity, reserve; rester or se tenir sur son quant-à-soi to keep one's distance

quantique [kwɑ̃tik] adj quantum

quantité [kɑ̃tite] f quantity

quan·tum [kwɑ̃tɔm] m (pl -ta [ta]) quantum

quarantaine [karɑ̃ten] f age of forty, forty mark, forties; quarantine; une quarantaine de about forty

quarante [karɑ̃t] adj, pron, & m forty; quarante et un forty-one; quarante et unième forty-first

quarante-deux [karɑ̃tdø] adj, pron, & m forty-two

quarante-deuxième [karɑ̃tdøzjem] adj, pron (masc, fem), & m forty-second

quarantième [karɑ̃tjem] adj, pron (masc, fem), & m fortieth

quart [kar] m quarter; fourth (in fractions); quarter of a pound; quarter of a liter; **bon quart!** (naut) all's well!; **passer un mauvais quart d'heure** to have a trying time; **petit quart** (naut) dogwatch; **prendre le quart** (naut) to come on watch; **quart de cercle** quadrant; **quart de soupir** (mus) sixteenth-note rest; **quart d'heure de Rabelais** day of reckoning; **tous les quarts d'heure au quart d'heure juste** every quarter-hour on the quarter-hour; **un petit quart d'heure** a quarter of an hour or so

quarte [kart] *adj* quartan (*fever*) || *f* half-gallon; (escr) quarte; (mus) fourth

quarte·ron [kartərɔ̃] **-ronne** [rɔn] *mf* quadroon || *m* handful (*e.g., of people*)

quartette [kwartet] *m* combo (*foursome*)

quartier [kartje] *m* quarter; neighborhood; section (*of orange*); portion; **à quartier** aloof; apart; **avoir quartier libre** (mil) to have a pass; to be off duty; **les beaux quartiers** the upper-class residential district; **mettre en quartiers** to dismember; **quartier d'affaires** business district; **quartier général** (mil) headquarters; **quartier réservé** red-light district; **quartiers** quarters, barracks

quartier-maître [kartjemetr] *m* (*pl* **quartiers-maîtres**) quartermaster

quartz [kwarts] *m* quartz

quasar [kwazar] *m* quasar

quasi [kazi] *m* butt (*of a loin cut*) || *adv* almost

quasiment [kazimɑ̃] *adv* (coll) almost

quatorze [katɔrz] *adj & pron* fourteen; the Fourteenth, e.g., **Jean quatorze** John the Fourteenth || *m* fourteen; fourteenth (*in dates*)

quatorzième [katɔrzjem] *adj, pron* (*masc, fem*), & *m* fourteenth

quatrain [katrɛ̃] *m* quatrain

quatre [katr] *adj & pron* four; the Fourth, e.g., **Jean quatre** John the Fourth; **quatre à quatre** four at a time; **quatre heures** four o'clock || *m* four; fourth (*in dates*); **se mettre en quatre pour** to fall all over oneself for; **se tenir à quatre** to keep oneself under control

quatre-épices [katrepis] *m & f invar* allspice (*plant*); **des quatre-épices** allspice (*spice*)

quatre-saisons [katrəsezɔ̃], [katsezɔ̃] *f invar* everbearing small strawberry

quatre-temps [katrətɑ̃] *mpl* Ember days

quatre-vingt-dix [katrəvɛ̃di(s)] *adj, pron, & m* ninety

quatre-vingt-dixième [katrəvɛ̃dizjem] *adj, pron* (*masc, fem*), & *m* ninetieth

quatre-vingtième [katrəvɛ̃tjem] *adj, pron* (*masc, fem*), & *m* eightieth

quatre-vingt-onze [katrəvɛ̃ɔ̃z] *adj, pron, & m* ninety-one

quatre-vingt-onzième [katrəvɛ̃ɔ̃zjem] *adj, pron* (*masc, fem*), & *m* ninety-first

quatre-vingts [katrəvɛ̃] *adj & pron*

eighty; **quatre-vingt** eighty, e.g., **page quatre-vingt** page eighty || *m* eighty

quatre-vingt-un [katrəvɛ̃œ̃] *adj, pron, & m* eighty-one

quatre-vingt-unième [katrəvɛ̃ynjem] *adj, pron* (*masc, fem*), & *m* eighty-first

quatrième [katrijem] *adj, pron* (*masc, fem*), & *m* fourth

quatuor [kwatɥɔr] *m* (*mus*) quartet

que [kə] (or qu' [k] before a vowel or mute h) *pron rel* whom; which, that; **ce que** that which, what || *pron interr* what; **qu'est-ce que . . . ?** what (as direct object) . . . ?; **qu'est-ce qui . . . ?** what (as subject) . . . ? || *adv* why, e.g., **qu'avez-vous besoin de tant de livres?** why do you need so many books?; how!, e.g., **que cette femme est belle!** how beautiful that woman is!; **que de** what a lot of, e.g., **que de difficultés!** what a lot of difficulties! || *conj* that; when, e.g., **un jour que je suis allé chez le dentiste** once when I went to the dentist; since, e.g., **il y a trois jours qu'il est arrivé** it is three days since he came; until, e.g., **attendez qu'il vienne** wait until he comes; than, e.g., **plus grand que moi** taller than I; as, e.g., **aussi grand que moi** as tall as I; but, e.g., **personne que vous** no one but you; whether, e.g., **qu'il parte ou qu'il reste** whether he leaves or stays; (in a conditional sentence without **si**, to introduce the conditional in a dependent clause which represents the main clause of the corresponding sentence in English), e.g., **il ferait faillite que cela ne m'étonnerait pas** if he went bankrupt it would not surprise me; (as a repetition of another conjunction), e.g., **si elle chante et que la salle soit comble** if she sings and there is a full house; e.g., **comme il avait soif et que le vin était bon** as he was thirsty and the wine was good; (in a prayer or exhortation), e.g., **que Dieu vous bénisse!** may God bless you!, God bless you!; (in a command), e.g., **qu'il parle** (aille, parte, etc.) let him speak (go, leave, etc.); **ne . . . que** §90 only, but

quel quelle [kel] §80

quelconque [kelkɔ̃k] *adj indef* any; any, whatever; any at all, some kind of || (when standing before noun) *adj indef* some, some sort of || *adj* ordinary, nondescript, mediocre

quelque [kelkə] *adj indef* some, any; **quelque chose** (always *masc*) something; **quelque chose de bon** something good; **quelque part** somewhere; **quelque . . . qui** or **quelque . . . que** whatever . . . ; whichever . . . ; **quelques** a few || *adv* some, about; **quelque peu** somewhat; **quelque + adj or adv . . . que** however + *adj* or *adv*

quelquefois [kelkəfwa] *adv* sometimes

quel·qu'un [kelkœ̃] **-qu'une** [kyn] §81

quémander [kemɑ̃de] *tr* to beg for || *intr* to beg

qu'en-dira-t-on [kɑ̃diratɔ̃] *m invar* what other people will say, gossip

quenotte [kənɔt] *f* (coll) baby tooth

quenouille [kənuj] *f* distaff; distaff side

querelle [kərɛl] *f* quarrel; **chercher querelle à** to pick a quarrel with; **une querelle d'Allemand, une mauvaise querelle** a groundless quarrel

quereller [kərɛle] *tr* to nag, scold ‖ *ref* to quarrel

querel·leur [kərɛlœr] **querel·leuse** [kərɛløz] *adj* quarrelsome ‖ *mf* wrangler ‖ *f* shrew

quérir [kerir] (used only in *inf*) *tr* to go for, to fetch

question [kɛstjɔ̃] *f* question

questionnaire [kɛstjɔner] *m* questionnaire

questionner [kɛstjɔne] *tr* to question

question·neur [kɛstjɔnœr] **question·neuse** [kɛstjɔnøz] *adj* inquisitive ‖ *mf* inquisitive person ‖ *m* (rad, telv) quizmaster

quête [kɛt] *f* quest; **faire la quête** to take up the collection

quêter [kɛte] *tr* to beg or fish for (*votes, praise, etc.*); to hunt for (*game*); to collect (*contributions*) ‖ *intr* to take up a collection

quetsche [kwɛtʃ] *f* quetsch

queue [kø] *f* tail; queue; billiard cue; train (*of dress*); handle (*of pan*); bottom (*of class*); stem, stalk; **à la queue leu leu** in single file; **faire la queue** to line up, to queue up; **fausse queue** miscue; **queue de cheval** (bot) horsetail; **queue de loup** (bot) purple foxglove; **queue de poisson** (aut) fishtail; **queue de vache** cat's-tail (*cirrus*); **sans queue ni tête** without head or tail; **venir en queue** to bring up the rear

queue-d'aronde [kødarɔ̃d] *f* (*pl* **queues-d'aronde**) dovetail; **assembler à queue-d'aronde** to dovetail

queue-de-morue [kødmɔry] *f* (*pl* **queues-de-morue**) tails, swallow-tailed coat; (painting) flat brush

queue-de-rat [kødəra] *f* (*pl* **queues-de-rat**) rat-tail file; taper

qui [ki] *pron rel* who, whom; which, that; **ce qui** that which, what; **n'importe qui** anyone; **qui que** anyone, no one; whoever, e.g., **qui que vous soyez** whoever you are ‖ *pron interr* who, whom; **qui est-ce que . . . ?** whom . . . ?; **qui est-ce qui . . . ?** who . . . ?

quia [kɥija]—**mettre** or **réduire qn à quia** (obs) to stump or floor s.o.

quiconque [kikɔ̃k] *pron indef* whoever, whosoever; whomever; anyone

quidam [kɥidam], [kidam] *m* individual, person

quiétude [kɥijetyd], [kjetyd] *f* peace of mind; quiet, calm

quignon [kiɲɔ̃] *m* hunk (*of bread*)

quille [kij] *f* keel; pin (*for bowling*); **quilles** ninepins

quincaillerie [kɛ̃kajri] *f* hardware; hardware store

quincail·lier [kɛ̃kaje] **quincail·lière** [kɛ̃kajer] *mf* hardware dealer

quinconce [kɛ̃kɔ̃s] *m* quincunx; **en quinconce** quincuncially

quinine [kinin] *f* quinine

quinquen·nal -nale [kɥɛ̃kɥennal] *adj* (*pl* **-naux** [no]) five-year

quinquet [kɛ̃ke] *m*—**allume tes quinquets!** (slang) open your eyes!

quinquina [kɛ̃kina] *m* cinchona

quin·tal [kɛ̃tal] *m* (*pl* **-taux** [to]) hundredweight; one hundred kilograms

quinte [kɛ̃t] *f* whim; (cards) sequence of five; (mus) fifth; **quinte de toux** fit of coughing

quintessence [kɛ̃tesɑ̃s] *f* quintessence

quintette [kɥɛ̃tet], [kɛ̃tet] *m* (mus) quintet; (coll) five-piece combo; **quintette à cordes** string quintet

quin·teux [kɛ̃tø] **-teuse** [tøz] *adj* crotchety, fitful, restive

quintu·plés -plées [kɛ̃typle] *mfpl* quintuplets

quinzaine [kɛ̃zen] *f* (group of) fifteen; two weeks, fortnight; **une quinzaine de** about fifteen

quinze [kɛ̃z] *adj & pron* fifteen; the Fifteenth, e.g., **Jean quinze** John the Fifteenth ‖ *m* fifteen; fifteenth (*in dates*)

quinzième [kɛ̃zjem] *adj, pron* (*masc, fem*), *& m* fifteenth

quiproquo [kiprɔko] *m* mistaken identity, misunderstanding

quiscale [kɥiskal] *m* (orn) purple grackle

quittance [kitɑ̃s] *f* receipt

quitte [kit] *adj* free (*from obligation*); clear (*of debts*); (en) **être quitte pour** to get off with; **être quitte to be quits; **tenir qn quitte de** to release s.o. from ‖ *m*—**jouer (à) quitte ou double** to play double or nothing ‖ *adv*—**quitte à** even if one has to, e.g., **commençons par en rire, quitte à en pleurer plus tard** let us begin by laughing, even if we have to cry later on

quitter [kite] *tr* to leave; to take off (*e.g., a coat*) ‖ *intr* to leave, go away; **ne quittez pas!** (telp) hold the line! ‖ *ref* to part, separate

quitus [kɥitys] *m* discharge, acquittance

qui-vive [kiviv] *m invar*—**sur le qui-vive** on the qui vive ‖ *interj* (mil) who goes there?

quoi [kwa] *pron indef* what, which; **à quoi bon?** what's the use?; **de quoi enough; **moyennant quoi** in exchange for which; **n'importe quoi** anything; **quoi que** whatever; **quoi qu'il en soit** be that as it may; **sans quoi** otherwise

quoique [kwakə] *conj* although, though

quolibet [kɔlibɛ] *m* gibe, quip

quorum [kwɔrɔm], [kɔrɔm] *m* quorum

quota [kwɔta], [kɔta] *m* quota

quote-part [kɔtpar] *f invar* quota, share

quoti·dien [kɔtidjɛ̃] **-dienne** [djɛn] *adj* daily ‖ *m* daily newspaper

quotient [kɔsjɑ̃] *m* quotient

quotité [kɔtite] *f* share, amount

R

R, r [ɛr], *[ɛr] *m invar* eighteenth letter of the French alphabet

rabâcher [rabaʃe] *tr* to harp on ‖ *intr* to harp on the same thing

rabais [rabɛ] *m* reduction, discount

rabaisser [rabese] *tr* to lower; to disparage

rabat [raba] *m* flap (*vestment*)

rabat-joie [rabaʒwa] *m invar* kill-joy

rabattre [rabatr] §7 *tr* to lower; to discount; to turn down; to fold up; to pull down; to cut back; to flush (*game*) ‖ *intr* to turn; **en rabattre** to come down a peg or two; **rabattre de** to reduce (*a price*) ‖ *ref* to fold; to drop down; to turn the other way; **se rabattre sur** to fall back on

rabat·tu -tue [rabaty] *adj* turndown

rabbin [rabɛ̃] *m* rabbi

rabibocher [rabiboʃe] *tr* (coll) to patch up ‖ *ref* (coll) to make up

rabiot [rabjo] *m* overtime; extra bit; (mil) extra service; (coll) graft

rabioter [rabjɔte] *tr* to graft

râ·blé -blée [rɑble] *adj* husky

rabot [rabo] *m* plane

raboter [rabɔte] *tr* to plane

rabo·teux [rabɔtø] **-teuse** [tøz] *adj* rough, uneven ‖ *f* (mach) planer

rabou·gri -grie [rabugri] *adj* scrub, scrawny

rabrouer [rabrue] *tr* to snub

racaille [rakɑj] *f* riffraff

raccommodage [rakɔmɔdaʒ] *m* mending; darning; patching

raccommodement [rakɔmɔdmɑ̃] *m* (coll) reconciliation

raccommoder [rakɔmɔde] *tr* to mend; to darn; to patch; (coll) to patch up

raccompagner [rakɔ̃paɲe] *tr* to see back, to see home

raccord [rakɔr] *m* connection; coupling; joint; adapter; **faire un raccord à** to touch up

raccordement [rakɔrdəmɑ̃] *m* connecting, linking, joining

raccorder [rakɔrde] *tr & ref* to connect

raccour·ci -cie [rakursi] *adj* shortened; abridged; squat, dumpy; bobbed (*hair*) ‖ *m* abridgment; shortcut, cutoff; foreshortening; **en raccourci** in miniature; in a nutshell

raccourcir [rakursir] *tr* to shorten; to abridge; to foreshorten ‖ *intr* to grow shorter

raccourcissement [rakursismɑ̃] *m* shortening; abridgment; shrinking

raccroc [rakro] *m* fluke

raccrocher [rakroʃe] *tr & intr* to hang up ‖ *ref*—**se raccrocher à** to hang on to

race [ras] *f* race; **de race** thoroughbred

ra·cé -cée [rase] *adj* thoroughbred

rachat [raʃa] *m* repurchase; redemption; ransom

racheter [raʃte] §2 *tr* to buy back; to redeem; to ransom

rachitique [raʃitik] *adj* rickety

rachitisme [raʃitism] *m* rickets

ra·cial -ciale [rasjal] *adj* (*pl* **-ciaux** [sjo]) race, racial

racine [rasin] *f* root; **racine carrée** square root; **racine cubique** cube root

racket [raket] *m* (coll) racket

racketter or **racketteur** [raketœr] *m* racketeer

raclée [rakle] *f* beating

racler [rakle] *tr* to scrape

raclette [raklet] *f* scraper; hoe; (phot) squeegee

racloir [raklwar] *m* scraper

raclure [raklyr] *f* scrapings

racolage [rakɔlaʒ] *m* soliciting

racoler [rakɔle] *tr* (coll) to solicit; (archaic) to shanghai

raco·leur [rakɔlœr] **-leuse** [løz] *mf* recruiter ‖ *f* (coll) hustler, streetwalker

racontar [rakɔ̃tar] *m* (coll) gossip

raconter [rakɔ̃te] *tr* to tell, narrate; to describe

racon·teur [rakɔ̃tœr] **-teuse** [tøz] *mf* storyteller

racornir [rakɔrnir] *tr & intr* to harden; to shrivel

radar [radar] *m* radar

rade [rad] *f* roadstead; **en rade** (coll) abandoned

ra·deau [rado] *m* (*pl* **-deaux**) raft

ra·diant [radjɑ̃] **-diante** [djɑ̃t] *adj* (astr, phys) radiant

radiateur [radjatœr] *m* radiator

radiation [radjɑsjɔ̃] *f* radiation; striking off

radi·cal -cale [radikal] *adj & mf* (*pl* **-caux** [ko]) radical ‖ *m* (chem, gram, math) radical

radier [radje] *tr* to cross out, to strike out or off

ra·dieux [radjø] **-dieuse** [djøz] *adj* radiant

radin [radɛ̃] *adj masc & fem* (slang) stingy

radio [radjo] *m* radiogram; radio operator ‖ *f* radio; radio set; X ray

radioac·tif [radjɔaktif] **-tive** [tiv] *adj* radioactive

radio-crochet [radjokroʃɛ] *m* (*pl* **-crochets**) talent show

radiodiffuser [radjɔdifyze] *tr* to broadcast

radiodiffusion [radjɔdifyzjɔ̃] *f* broadcasting

radiofréquence [radjɔfrekɑ̃s] *f* radiofrequency

radiogramme [radjɔgram] *m* radiogram

radiographier [radjɔgrafje] *tr* to X-ray

radio-journal [radjɔʒurnal] *m* (*pl* **-journaux** [ʒurno]) radio newscast

radiologie [radjɔlɔʒi] *f* radiology

radiophare [radjɔfar] *m* radio beacon

radioreportage [radjɔrəpɔrtaʒ] *m* news broadcast; sports broadcast

radioscopie [radjɔskɔpi] *f* radioscopy, fluoroscopy

radiotélévi·sé -sée [radjɔtelevize] *adj* broadcast over radio and television

radis [radi] *m* radish

radium [radjɔm] *m* radium

radius [radjys] *m* (anat) radius
radotage [radɔtaʒ] *m* drivel, twaddle
radoter [radɔte] *intr* to talk nonsense, to ramble
radoub [radu] *m* (naut) graving
radouber [radube] *tr* (naut) to grave
radoucir [radusir] *tr & ref* to calm down
rafale [rafal] *f* squall, gust; burst of gunfire
raffermir [rafermir] *tr & ref* to harden
raffinage [rafinaʒ] *m* refining
raffinement [rafinmɑ̃] *m* refinement
raffiner [rafine] *tr* to refine || *intr* to be subtle; **raffiner sur** to overdo
raffinerie [rafinri] *f* refinery
raffoler [rafɔle] *intr*—**raffoler de** to dote on, to be wild about
raffut [rafy] *m* (coll) uproar
rafistolage [rafistɔlaʒ] *m* (coll) patching up
rafistoler [rafistɔle] *tr* (coll) to patch up
rafle [rafl] *f* raid, mass arrest; stalk; corncob
rafler [rafle] *tr* (coll) to carry away, to make a clean sweep of
rafraîchir [rafreʃir] *tr* to cool; to refresh; to freshen up; to trim (*the hair*) || *intr* to cool || *ref* to cool off; to refresh oneself
rafraîchissement [rafreʃismɑ̃] *m* refreshment; cooling off
ragaillardir [ragajardir] *tr* to cheer up
rage [raʒ] *f* rage; rabies; **à la rage** madly; **faire rage** to rage
rager [raʒe] §38 *intr* (coll) to be enraged
ra‧geur [raʒœr] **-geuse** [ʒøz] *adj* bad-tempered
ragot [rago] *m* (coll) gossip
ragoût [ragu] *m* stew, ragout; (obs) spice, relish
ragoû‧tant [ragutɑ̃] **-tante** [tɑ̃t] *adj* tempting, inviting; pleasing; **peu ragoûtant** not very appetizing
rai [re] *m* ray; spoke
raid [red] *m* raid; air raid; endurance test
raide [red] *adj* stiff; tight, taut; steep; (coll) incredible || *adv* suddenly
raideur [redœr] *f* stiffness
raidillon [redijɔ̃] *m* short steep path
raidir [redir] *tr & ref* to stiffen
raie [re] *f* stripe, streak; stroke; line (*of spectrum*); part (*of hair*); (ichth) ray, skate
raifort [refɔr] *m* horseradish
rail [rɑj] *m* rail; **rail conducteur** third rail; **remettre sur les rails** (fig) to put back on the track; **sortir des rails** to jump the track
railler [rɑje] *tr* to make fun of || *intr* to joke || *ref*—**se railler de** to make fun of
raillerie [rɑjri] *f* raillery, banter
rail‧leur [rɑjœr] **rail‧leuse** [rɑjøz] *adj* teasing, bantering || *mf* teaser
rainette [renet] *f* tree frog
rainure [renyr] *f* groove
raisin [rezɛ̃] *m* grapes; grape; **raisin d'ours** (bot) bearberry; **raisins de Corinthe** currants; **raisins de mer** cuttlefish eggs; **raisins de Smyrne** seedless raisins; **raisins secs** raisins
raisiné [rezine] *m* grape jelly; (slang) blood
raison [rezɔ̃] *f* reason; ratio, rate; **à raison de** at the rate of; **avoir raison** to be right; **avoir raison de** to get the better of; **donner raison à** to back, support; **en raison de** because of; **raison sociale** trade name; **se faire une raison** to resign oneself
raisonnable [rezɔnabl] *adj* reasonable; rational
raison‧né -née [rezɔne] *adj* rational; detailed
raisonnement [rezɔnmɑ̃] *m* reasoning; argument
raisonner [rezɔne] *tr* to reason out; to reason with || *intr* to reason; to argue || *ref* to reason with oneself
raison‧neur [rezɔnœr] **raison‧neuse** [rezɔnøz] *adj* rational; argumentative || *mf* reasoner; arguer
rajeunir [raʒœnir] *tr* to rejuvenate || *intr* to grow young again || *ref* to pretend to be younger than one is
rajeunissement [raʒœnismɑ̃] *m* rejuvenation
rajouter [raʒute] *tr* to add again; (coll) to add more
rajuster [raʒyste] *tr* to readjust; to adjust || *ref* to adjust one's clothes
râle [rɑl] *m* rale; death rattle; (orn) rail
ralen‧ti ‧tie [ralɑ̃ti] *adj* slow || *m* slowdown; **au ralenti** slowdown (*work*); go-slow (*policy*); slow-motion (*moving picture*); idling (*motor*); **tourner au ralenti** (aut) to idle
ralentir [ralɑ̃tir] *tr, intr, & ref* to slow down; **ralentir** (public sign) slow
ralliement [ralimɑ̃] *m* rally
rallier [ralje] *tr & ref* to rally
rallonge [ralɔ̃ʒ] *f* extra piece; leaf (*of table*); (coll) under-the-table payment; **à rallonges** extension (*table*)
rallonger [ralɔ̃ʒe] §38 *tr & intr* to lengthen
rallumer [ralyme] *tr* to relight; (fig) to rekindle || *intr* to put on the lights again || *ref* to be rekindled
rallye [rali] *m* rallye
ramage [ramaʒ] *m* floral design; warbling
ramas [ramɑ] *m* heap; pack (*e.g., of thieves*)
ramassage [ramasaʒ] *m* gathering; ramassage scolaire school-bus service
ramas‧sé -sée [ramase] *adj* stocky, compact (*style*)
ramasser [ramase] *tr* to gather; to gather together; to pick up; (coll) to catch (*a scolding; a cold*) || *ref* to gather; to gather oneself together
rambarde [rɑ̃bard] *f* handrail
rame [ram] *f* prop, stick; oar, pole; ream (*of paper*); string (*e.g., of barges*); (rr) train, section; **rame de métro** subway train
ra‧meau [ramo] *m* (*pl* **-meaux**) branch; sprig
ramée [rame] *f* boughs

ramener [ramne] §2 *tr* to lead back; to bring back; to reduce; to restore

ramer [rame] *tr* to stake (*a plant*) ‖ *intr* to row

ra·meur [ramœr] **-meuse** [møz] *mf* rower

ramier [ramje] *m* wood pigeon

ramifier [ramifje] *tr & ref* to ramify, to branch out

ramol·li -lie [ramɔli] *adj* sodden; (coll) half-witted ‖ *mf* (coll) half-wit

ramollir [ramɔlir] *tr & ref* to soften

ramoner [ramɔne] *tr* to sweep (*a chimney*)

ramoneur [ramɔnœr] *m* chimney sweep

ram·pant -pante [rɑ̃pɑ̃] [pɑ̃t] *adj* crawling, creeping; (hum) ground (*crew*)

rampe [rɑ̃p] *f* ramp; grade, gradient; banister; flight (*of stairs*); (aer) runway lights; (theat) footlights; **rampe de lancement** launching pad

ramper [rɑ̃pe] *intr* to crawl; to grovel; (bot) to creep

ramure [ramyr] *f* branches; antlers

rancart [rɑ̃kar] *m* (slang) rendezvous; **mettre au rancart** (coll) to scrap, to shelve

rance [rɑ̃s] *adj* rancid

ranch [rɑ̃tʃ] *m* ranch

rancir [rɑ̃sir] *intr & ref* to turn rancid

rancœur [rɑ̃kœr] *f* rancor

rançon [rɑ̃sɔ̃] *f* ransom

rançonner [rɑ̃sɔne] *tr* to ransom

rancune [rɑ̃kyn] *f* grudge

rancu·nier [rɑ̃kynje] **-nière** [njer] *adj* vindictive

randonnée [rɑ̃dɔne] *f* long walk; long ride

rang [rɑ̃] *m* rank; **au premier rang** in the first row; ranking; **en rang d'oignons** in a line

ran·gé -gée [rɑ̃ʒe] *adj* orderly; pitched (*battle*); steady (*person*)

ranger [rɑ̃ʒe] §38 *tr* to range; to rank ‖ *ref* to take one's place; to get out of the way; to mend one's ways; **se ranger à** to adopt, take (*e.g., a suggestion*)

ranimer [ranime] *tr & ref* to revive

raout [raut] *m* reception

rapace [rapas] *adj* rapacious ‖ *m* bird of prey

rapatriement [rapatrimɑ̃] *m* repatriation

rapatrier [rapatrije] *tr* to repatriate

râpe [rɑp] *f* rasp; grater

râ·pé -pée [rɑpe] *adj* grated; threadbare ‖ *m* (coll) grated cheese

râper [rɑpe] *tr* to rasp, to grate

rapetasser [raptase] *tr* (coll) to patch up

rapetisser [raptise] *tr, intr, & ref* to shrink, shorten

râ·peux [rɑpø] **-peuse** [pøz] *adj* raspy, grating

ra·piat [rapja] **-piate** [pjat] *adj* (coll) stingy ‖ *mf* (coll) skinflint

rapide [rapid] *adj* rapid; steep ‖ *m* rapids; (rr) express; **rapides** rapids

rapidité [rapidite] *f* rapidity; steepness

rapiéçage [rapjesaʒ] *m* patching

rapiécer [rapjese] §58 *tr* to patch

rapière [rapjer] *f* rapier

rapin [rapɛ̃] *m* dauber; (coll) art student

rapine [rapin] *f* rapine, pillage

rappel [rapel] *m* recall; reminder; call-up; recurrence; booster (*shot*); (theat) curtain call; **battre le rappel** to call to arms; **rappel au règlement** point of order; **rappel de chariot** backspacer

rappeler [raple] §34 *tr* to recall; to remind; to call back; to call up ‖ *ref* to remember

rapport [rapɔr] *m* yield, return; report; connection, bearing; (math) ratio; **en rapport avec** in touch with; in keeping with; **par rapport à** in comparison with; **rapports** relations; sexual relations; **sous tous les rapports** in all respects

rapporter [rapɔrte] *tr* to bring back; to yield; to report; to relate; to repeal, call off; to attach; to retrieve (*game*); (bk) to post ‖ *intr* to yield; (coll) to squeal ‖ *ref*—**s'en rapporter à** to leave it up to; **se rapporter à** to be related to, to refer to

rappor·teur [rapɔrtœr] **-teuse** [tøz] *mf* tattletale ‖ *m* recorder; (geom) protractor

rapprochement [raprɔʃmɑ̃] *m* bringing together; parallel; rapprochement

rapprocher [raprɔʃe] *tr* to bring closer; to reconcile; to compare ‖ *ref* to draw closer, to approach; **se rapprocher de** to approximate, to resemble

rapt [rapt] *m* kidnapping

raquette [raket] *f* racket; snowshoe; tennis player; (bot) prickly pear

rare [rar] *adj* rare; scarce; sparse, thin (*hair*)

rarement [rarmɑ̃] *adv* rarely, seldom

rareté [rarte] *f* rarity; scarcity; rareness

ras [rɑ] **rase** [rɑz] *adj* short (*hair, nap, etc.*); level; close-cropped; close-shaven; open (*country*) ‖ *m*—**à ras de, au ras de** flush with; **ras d'eau** water line; **ras du cou** crew neck; **voler au ras du sol** to skim along the ground

rasade [rɑzad] *f* bumper, glassful

rasage [rɑzaʒ] *m* shearing; shaving

ra·sant [rɑzɑ̃] **-sante** [zɑ̃t] *adj* level; grazing; close to the ground; (coll) boring

rase-mottes [rɑzmɔt] *m invar*—**faire du rase-mottes** or **voler en rase-mottes** to hedgehop

raser [rɑze] *tr* to shave; to raze; to graze ‖ *ref* to shave

ra·seur [rɑzœr] **-seuse** [zøz] *adj* (coll) boring ‖ *mf* (coll) bore

rasoir [rɑzwar] *adj invar* (slang) boring ‖ *m* razor; (slang) bore; **rasoir à manche** straight razor; **rasoir de sûreté** safety razor

rassasiement [rasazimɑ̃] *m* satiation

rassasier [rasazje] *tr* to satisfy; to satiate ‖ *ref* to have one's fill

rassemblement [rasɑ̃bləmɑ̃] *m* assembling; crowd; muster; (*trumpet call*) assembly; **rassemblement!** (mil) fall in!

rassembler [rasɑ̃ble] *tr* & *ref* to gather together

rasseoir [raswar] §5 *tr* to reseat; to set in place again || *ref* to sit down again

rasséréner [raserene] §10 *tr* & *ref* to calm down

rassir [rasir] *intr* & *ref* (coll) to get stale

ras·sis [rasi] **ras·sise** [rasiz] *adj* level-headed; stale (*bread*)

rassortir [rasɔrtir] *tr* to restock || *ref* to lay in a new stock

rassurer [rasyre] *tr* to reassure || *ref* to be reassured

rastaquouère [rastakwer] *m* (coll) flashy stranger

rat [ra] *m* rat; (coll) tightwad; **fait comme un rat** caught like a rat in a trap; **mon rat** (coll) my turtledove; **rat à bourse** gopher; **rat de bibliothè-que** bookworm; **rat de cale** stowaway; **rat de cave** thin candle; tax collector; **rat d'égout** sewer rat; **rat des champs** field mouse; **rat d'hôtel** hotel thief; **rat d'Opéra** ballet girl; **rat musqué** muskrat

ratatiner [ratatine] *ref* to shrivel up

ratatouille [ratatuj] *f* (coll) stew; (coll) bad cooking; (coll) blows

rate [rat] *f* spleen; female rat

ra·té ·tée [rate] *adj* miscarried; bad (*shot, landing, etc.*) || *mf* failure, dropout

râ·teau [rɑto] *m* (pl **-teaux**) rake

râteler [rɑtle] §34 *tr* to rake

râtelier [rɑtəlje] *m* rack; set of false teeth; **manger à deux râteliers** (coll) to play both sides of the street; **râtelier d'armes** gun rack

rater [rate] *tr* to miss || *intr* to miss, to misfire; to fail

ratiboiser [ratibwaze] *tr* (coll) to take to the cleaners; **ratiboiser q.ch. à qn** (coll) to clean s.o. out of s.th.

ratifier [ratifje] *tr* to ratify

ration [rɑsjɔ̃] *f* ration

ration·nel -nelle [rasjɔnɛl] *adj* rational

rationnement [rasjɔnmɑ̃] *m* rationing

rationner [rasjɔne] *tr* to ration

ratisser [ratise] *tr* to rake; to rake in; to search with a fine-tooth comb; (coll) to fleece

ratissoire [ratiswar] *f* hoe

raton [ratɔ̃] *m* little rat; **raton laveur** raccoon

rattacher [rataʃe] *tr* to tie again; to link; to unite || *ref* to be connected

rattrapage [ratrapaʒ] *m* catch-up; (typ) catchword

rattraper [ratrape] *tr* to catch up to; to recover; to recapture || *ref* to catch up; **se rattraper à** to catch hold of; **se rattraper de** to make good, to recoup

rature [ratyr] *f* erasure

raturer [ratyre] *tr* to cross out

rauque [rok] *adj* hoarse, raucous

ravage [ravaʒ] *m* ravage

ravager [ravaʒe] §38 *tr* to ravage

ravalement [ravalmɑ̃] *m* trimming down; resurfacing; disparagement

ravaler [ravale] *tr* to choke down; to disparage; ¡to drag down; to resurface; to eat (*one's words*) || *ref* to lower oneself

ravaudage [ravodaʒ] *m* mending; darning; (fig) patchwork

ravauder [ravode] *tr* to mend; to darn

ravier [ravje] *m* hors-d'oeuvre dish

ravigoter [ravigɔte] *tr* (coll) to revive

ravilir [ravilir] *tr* to debase

ravin [ravɛ̃] *m* ravine

ravine [ravin] *f* mountain torrent

raviner [ravine] *tr* to furrow

ravir [ravir] *tr* to ravish; to kidnap, abduct; to delight, entrance; **ravir q.ch. à qn** to snatch or take s.th. from s.o. || *intr*—**à ravir** marvelously

raviser [ravize] *ref* to change one's mind

ravis·sant [ravisɑ̃] **ravis·sante** [ravisɑ̃t] *adj* ravishing, entrancing

ravis·seur [raviscer] **ravis·seuse** [ravisøz] *mf* kidnaper

ravitaillement [ravitajmɑ̃] *m* supplying; supplies

ravitailler [ravitaje] *tr* to supply; to fill up the gas tank of (*a vehicle*) || *ref* to lay in supplies; to fill up (*to get gas*)

raviver [ravive] *tr* to revive; to brighten up; to reopen (*an old wound*) || *ref* to revive; to break out again

ravoir [ravwar] (used only in inf) *tr* to get back again

rayer [reje] §49 *tr* to cross out, to strike out; to rule, to line; to stripe; to rifle (*a gun*)

rayon [rejɔ̃] *m* ray; radius; spoke; shelf; honeycomb; department (in a store); point (of star); **ce n'est pas mon rayon** (coll) that's not in my line; **rayon de lune** moonbeam; **rayons X** X rays; **rayon visuel** line of sight

rayon·nant [rejɔnɑ̃] **rayon·nante** [rejɔnɑ̃t] *adj* radiant; radiating; radioactive; (rad) transmitting

rayonne [rejɔn] *f* rayon

rayonner [rejɔne] *intr* to radiate

rayure [rejyr] *f* stripe; scratch; rifling

raz [rɑ] *m* race (*channel and current of water*); **raz de marée** tidal wave; landslide (*in an election*)

razzia [razja] *f* raid

razzier [razje] *tr* to raid

réacteur [reaktœr] *m* reactor; **réacteur nucléaire** nuclear reactor

réactif [reaktif] *m* (chem) reagent

réaction [reaksjɔ̃] *f* reaction; kick (of rifle); **à réaction** jet; **réaction en chaîne** chain reaction

réactionnaire [reaksjɔner] *adj* & *mf* reactionary

réadaptation [readaptasjɔ̃] *f* rehabilitation; **réadaptation fonctionnelle** occupational therapy

réadapter [readapte] *tr* to rehabilitate || *ref* to be rehabilitated

réaffirmer [reafirme] *tr* to reaffirm

réagir [reaʒir] *intr* to react

réalisable [realizabl] *adj* feasible; (com) saleable

réalisa·teur [realizatœr] **-trice** [tris]

adj producing ‖ *mf* achiever; producer ‖ *m* (mov, rad, telv) director

réalisation [realizasjɔ̃] *f* accomplishment; work; (mov, rad, telv) production; (com) liquidation

réaliser [realize] *tr* to realize; to accomplish; to sell out; (mov) to produce ‖ *ref* to come to pass, to be realized

réalisme [realism] *m* realism

réaliste [realist] *adj* realistic ‖ *mf* realist

réalité [realite] *f* reality

réanimer [reanime] *tr* to revive

réapparaître [reaparetr] §12 *intr* to reappear

réapparition [reaparisjɔ̃] *f* reappearance

réarmement [rearməmɑ̃] *m* rearmament

réassortir [reasɔrtir] *tr* to restock ‖ *ref* to lay in a new stock

réassurer [reasyre] *tr* to reinsure

rébarba·tif [rebarbatif] -**tive** [tiv] *adj* forbidding, repulsive

rebâtir [rəbatir] *tr* to rebuild

rebattre [rəbatr] §7 *tr* to beat; to reshuffle; to repeat over and over again

rebat·tu -tue [rəbaty] *adj* hackneyed

rebelle [rəbel] *adj* rebellious ‖ *mf* rebel

rebeller [rəbele], [rəbelle] *ref* to rebel

rébellion [rebeljɔ̃] *f* rebellion

rebiffer [rəbife] *ref* to kick over the traces

reboisement [rəbwazmɑ̃] *m* reforestation

rebond [rəbɔ̃] *m* rebound

rebon·di -die [rəbɔ̃di] *adj* plump, buxom; paunchy

rebondir [rəbɔ̃dir] *intr* to bounce; (fig) to come up again

rebord [rəbɔr] *m* edge, border; sill, ledge; hem; brim (*of hat*); rim (*of saucer*); lip (*of cup*)

reboucher [rəbuʃe] *tr* to recork; to stop up ‖ *ref* to be stopped up

rebours [rəbur] *m*—**à rebours** backwards; against the grain; the wrong way; backhanded (*compliment*); **à** or **au rebours de** contrary to

rebouter [rəbute] *tr* to set (*a bone*)

rebrousse-poil [rəbruspwal]—**à rebrousse-poil** against the grain, the wrong way

rebrousser [rəbruse] *tr* to brush up; rebrousser **chemin** to turn back; rebrousser **qn** (coll) to rub s.o. the wrong way ‖ *ref* to turn up, to bend back

rebuffade [rəbyfad] *f* rebuff; **essuyer une rebuffade** to be snubbed

rebut [rəby] *m* castoff; waste; scum (*of society*); rebuff; **de rebut** castoff; waste; unclaimed (*letter*); **mettre au rebut** to discard

rebu·tant [rəbytɑ̃] -**tante** [tɑ̃t] *adj* dull, tedious; repugnant

rebuter [rəbyte] *tr* to rebuff; to bore; to be repulsive to

recaler [rəkale] *tr* (coll) to flunk

récapitulation [rekapitylasjɔ̃] *f* recapitulation

recéder [rəsede] §10 *tr* to give or sell back

recel [rəsel] *m* concealment (*of stolen goods; of criminals*)

receler [rəsle] §2 or **recéler** [rəsele] §10 *tr* to conceal; to receive (*stolen goods*); to harbor (*a criminal*) ‖ *intr* to hide

rece·leur [rəslœr] -**leuse** [løz] *mf* fence, receiver of stolen goods

récemment [resamɑ̃] *adv* recently, lately

recensement [rəsɑ̃smɑ̃] *m* census; **recensement du contingent** draft registration

recenser [rəsɑ̃se] *tr* to take the census of; to take a count of

recenseur [rəsɑ̃sœr] *m* census taker

ré·cent [resɑ̃] -**cente** [sɑ̃t] *adj* recent

récépissé [resepise] *m* receipt

réceptacle [reseptakl] *m* receptacle

récep·teur [reseptœr] -**trice** [tris] *adj* receiving ‖ *m* receiver

récep·tif [reseptif] -**tive** [tiv] *adj* receptive

réception [resepsjɔ̃] *f* reception; receipt; approval; admission (*to a club*); registration desk (*of hotel*); landing (*of, e.g., a parachutist*); (sports) catch; **accuser réception de** to acknowledge receipt of

réceptionnaire [resepsjɔner] *mf* consignee; chief receptionist

récession [resesjɔ̃] *f* recession

recette [rəset] *f* receipt; collection (*of debts, taxes, etc.*); (culin) recipe; **faire recette** to be a box-office attraction; **recettes de métier** tricks of the trade

recevable [rəsvabl] *adj* acceptable; admissible

rece·veur [rəsvœr] -**veuse** [vøz] *mf* collector; conductor (*of bus, streetcar, etc.*); blood recipient; **receveur des postes** postmaster; **receveur universel** recipient of blood from a universal donor

recevoir [rəsvwar] §59 *tr* to receive; to accommodate; to admit (*to a school, club, etc.*); **être reçu** to be admitted; to pass ‖ *intr* to receive

rechange [rəʃɑ̃ʒ] *m* replacement, change; **de rechange** spare (*e.g., parts*)

rechaper [rəʃape] *tr* to recap, to retread

réchapper [reʃape] *intr*—**en réchapper** to get away with it; to get well; **réchapper à** or **de** to escape from

recharge [rəʃarʒ] *f* refill; recharging; reloading

recharger [rəʃarʒe] §38 *tr* to recharge; to refill; to reload; to ballast (*a roadbed*)

réchaud [reʃo] *m* hot plate

réchauffer [reʃofe] *tr* & *ref* to warm up

rêche [reʃ] *adj* rough, harsh

recherche [rəʃerʃ] *f* search; quest; investigation, piece of research; refinement; **recherches** research

recher·ché -chée [rəʃerʃe] *adj* sought-after, in demand; elaborate; studied; affected

rechercher [rəʃerʃe] *tr* to seek, to look for

rechigner [rəʃiɲe] *intr*—**rechigner à** to balk at

rechute [rəʃyt] *f* relapse

rechuter [rəʃyte] *intr* to relapse

récidive [residiv] *f* recurrence; second offense

récidiver [residive] *intr* to recur; to relapse

récif [resif] *m* reef

récipiendaire [resipjɑ̃der] *m* new member, inductee; recipient

récipient [resipjɑ̃] *m* recipient, vessel

réciprocité [resiprɔsite] *f* reciprocity

réciproque [resiprɔk] *adj* reciprocal || *f* converse

récit [resi] *m* recital, account

réci·tal -tale [resital] *m* (*pl* **-tals**) recital

récitation [resitasjɔ̃] *f* recitation

réciter [resite] *tr* to recite

récla·mant [reklamɑ̃] **-mante** [mɑ̃t] *mf* claimant

réclamation [reklamasjɔ̃] *f* complaint; demand

réclame [reklam] *f* advertising; advertisement; (theat) cue; (typ) catchword; **faire de la réclame** to advertise, to ballyhoo; **réclame à éclipse** flashing sign; **réclame lumineuse** illuminated sign

réclamer [reklame] *tr* to claim; to clamor for; to demand || *intr* to lodge a complaint; to intercede || *ref* —**se réclamer de** to appeal to; to claim kinship with; **se réclamer de qn** to use s.o.'s name as a reference

reclassement [rəklasmɑ̃] *m* reclassification

reclasser [rəklase] *tr* to reclassify

re·clus [rəkly] **-cluse** [klyz] *adj & mf* recluse

recoin [rəkwɛ̃] *m* nook, cranny

récollection [rekɔleksjɔ̃] *f* religious meditation

recoller [rəkɔle] *tr* to paste again

récolte [rekɔlt] *f* harvest

récolter [rekɔlte] *tr* to harvest

recommander [rəkɔmɑ̃de] *tr* to recommend; to register (*a letter*) || *ref*—**se recommander à** to seek the protection of; **se recommander de** to ask (*s.o.*) for a reference

recommencer [rəkɔmɑ̃se] §51 *tr & intr* to begin again

récompense [rekɔ̃pɑ̃s] *f* recompense, reward; award

récompenser [rekɔ̃pɑ̃se] *tr* to recompense

réconcilier [rekɔ̃silje] *tr* to reconcile

reconduire [rəkɔ̃dɥir] §19 *tr* to escort; (coll) to kick out, to send packing

réconfort [rekɔ̃fɔr] *m* comfort

réconfor·tant [rekɔ̃fɔrtɑ̃] **-tante** [tɑ̃t] *adj* consoling; stimulating

réconforter [rekɔ̃fɔrte] *tr* to comfort; to revive || *ref* to recuperate; to cheer up

reconnaissance [rəkɔnesɑ̃s] *f* recognition; gratitude; (mil) reconnaissance; **aller en reconnaissance** to reconnoiter; **reconnaissance de** or **pour** gratitude for

reconnais·sant [rəkɔnesɑ̃] **reconnaissante** [rəkɔnesɑ̃t] *adj* grateful; **être reconnaissant de** + *inf* to be grateful for + *ger*; **être reconnaissant de** or **pour** to be grateful for

reconnaître [rəkɔnetr] §12 *tr* to recognize; (mil) to reconnoiter || *ref* to recognize oneself; to know where one is; to acknowledge oneself (*e.g., guilty*); **s'y reconnaître** to know where one is

reconquérir [rəkɔ̃kerir] §3 *tr* to reconquer

reconquête [rəkɔ̃ket] *f* reconquest

reconsidérer [rəkɔ̃sidere] §10 *tr* to reconsider

reconstituant [rəkɔ̃stitɥɑ̃] *m* tonic

reconstituer [rəkɔ̃stitɥe] *tr* to reconstruct; to restore

reconstruire [rəkɔ̃strɥir] §19 *tr* to reconstruct

record [rəkɔr] *adj invar & m* record

recordman [rəkɔrdman] *m* record holder

recoudre [rəkudr] §13 *tr* to sew up

recouper [rəkupe] *tr* to cut again; to blend (*wines*)

recourir [rəkurir] §14 *intr* to run again; **recourir à** to resort to; to appeal to

recours [rəkur] *m* recourse; **recours en grâce** petition for pardon

recouvrement [rəkuvrəmɑ̃] *m* recovery

recouvrer [rəkuvre] *tr* to recover

recouvrir [rəkuvrir] §65 *tr* to cover; to cover up; to mask; to resurface (*e.g., a road*) || *ref* to overlap

récréation [rekreasjɔ̃] *f* recreation; recess (*at school*)

recréer [rəkree] *tr* to re-create

récréer [rekree] *tr & ref* to relax

récrier [rekrje] *ref* to cry out

récrire [rekrir] §25 *tr* to rewrite; to write again

recroquevil·lé -lée [rəkrɔkvije] *adj* shriveled up, curled up; huddled up

recroqueviller [rəkrɔkvije] *tr & ref* to shrivel up, to curl up

re·cru -crue [rəkry] *adj* exhausted

recrue [rəkry] *f* recruit

recruter [rəkryte] *tr* to recruit || *ref* to be recruited

rectangle [rektɑ̃gl] *m* rectangle

rectificateur [rektifikatœr] *m* rectifier

rectifier [rektifje] *tr* to rectify; to true up; to grind (*a cylinder*)

rectum [rektɔm] *m* rectum

reçu [rəsy] *m* receipt

recueil [rəkœj] *m* collection; compilation

recueillement [rəkœjmɑ̃] *m* meditation

recueillir [rəkœjir] §18 *tr* to collect, to gather; to take in (*a needy person*); to receive (*a legacy*) || *ref* to collect oneself, to meditate

recuire [rəkɥir] §19 *tr* to anneal, to temper; to cook over again || *intr* (fig) to stew

recul [rəkyl] *m* backing, backward movement; kick, recoil; **être en recul** to be losing ground; **prendre du recul** to consider in perspective

reculer [rəkyle] *tr* to move back; to put off (*e.g., a decision*) ‖ *intr* to move back; to back out; to recoil; **reculer devant** to shrink from ‖ *ref* to move back

reculons [rəkylɔ̃]—**à reculons** backwards

récupération [rekyperɑsjɔ̃] *f* recovery

récupérer [rekypere] §10 *tr* to salvage, to recover; to recuperate; to make up (*e.g., lost hours*); to find another job for ‖ *intr* to recuperate

récurer [rekyre] *tr* to scour

récur·rent [rekyrɑ̃] **récur·rente** [rekyrɑ̃t] *adj* recurrent

récuser [rekyze] *tr* to take exception to ‖ *ref* to refuse to give one's opinion

rédac·teur [redaktœr] **-trice** [tris] *mf* editor; **rédacteur en chef** editor in chief; **rédacteur gérant** managing editor; **rédacteur publicitaire** copywriter; **rédacteur sportif** sports editor

rédaction [redaksjɔ̃] *f* editorial staff; editorial office; edition; editing

reddition [redisjɔ̃] *f* surrender

redécouvrir [rədekuvrir] §65 *tr* to rediscover

rédemp·teur [redɑ̃ptœr] **-trice** [tris] *adj* redemptive ‖ *mf* redeemer

rédemption [redɑ̃psjɔ̃] *f* redemption

redevable [rədvabl] *adj* indebted

redevance [rədvɑ̃s] *f* dues, fees; rent; tax (*on radio sets*)

rédiger [rediʒe] §38 *tr* to edit; to draft; to write up

redingote [rədɛ̃gɔt] *f* frock coat

redire [rədir] §22 *tr* to repeat; to give away (*a secret*) ‖ *intr*—**trouver à redire à** to find fault with

redon·dant [rədɔ̃dɑ̃] **-dante** [dɑ̃t] *adj* redundant

redoutable [rədutabl] *adj* frightening

redoute [rədut] *f* redoubt

redouter [rədute] *tr* to dread

redressement [rədresmɑ̃] *m* straightening out; redress; (elec) rectifying

redresser [rədrese] *tr* to straighten; to hold up (*e.g., the head*); to redress; (elec) to rectify ‖ *ref* to straighten up

redresseur [rədresœr] *m* (elec) rectifier; **redresseur de torts** knight-errant; (coll) reformer

réduction [redyksjɔ̃] *f* reduction

réduire [reduir] §19 *tr* to reduce; to set (*a bone*)

réduit [redui] *m* retreat, nook; redoubt

rééditer [reedite] *tr* to reedit

réel réelle [reel] *adj & m* real, actual

réélection [reeleksjɔ̃] *f* reelection

réellement [reelmɑ̃] *adv* really

réescompte [reeskɔ̃t] *m* rediscount

réexamen [reegzamɛ̃] *m* reexamination

réexpédier [reekspedje] *tr* to reship; to return to sender

réexpédition [reekspedisjɔ̃] *f* reshipment; return

refaire [rəfɛr] §29 *tr* to redo ‖ *intr*—**à refaire** to be done over; to be dealt over ‖ *ref* to recover; to make good one's losses

référence [referɑ̃s] *f* reference

référendum or **referendum** [referɛ̃dɔm] *m* referendum

référer [refere] §10 *intr*—**en référer à** to appeal to ‖ *ref*—**s'en référer à** to leave it up to; **se référer à** to refer to

refermer [rəfɛrme] *tr & ref* to close again, to close

refiler [rəfile] *tr*—**refiler à qn** (slang) to palm off on s.o.

réfléchir [refleʃir] *tr & intr* to reflect ‖ *ref* to be reflected

reflet [rəflɛ] *m* reflection; glint, gleam

refléter [rəflete] §10 *tr* to reflect ‖ *ref* to be mirrored

réflexe [reflɛks] *adj & m* reflex

réflexion [refleksjɔ̃] *f* reflection

refluer [rəflye] *intr* to ebb

reflux [rəfly] *m* ebb

refonte [rəfɔ̃t] *f* recasting

réforma·teur [reformatœr] **-trice** [tris] *mf* reformer

réformation [reformasjɔ̃] *f* reformation

réforme [reform] *f* reform; **la Réforme** the Reformation

réfor·mé -mée [reforme] *adj* (eccl) Reformed; (mil) disabled

réformer [reforme] *tr & ref* to regroup

réformer [reforme] *tr* to reform; (mil) to discharge ‖ *ref* to reform

refou·lé -lée [rəfule] *adj* (coll) inhibited

refoulement [rəfulmɑ̃] *m* driving back; (psychoanal) repression

refouler [rəfule] *tr* to drive back; to choke back (*a sob*); to sail against (*the current*); to compress, stem; (psychoanal) to repress ‖ *intr* to flow back

réfractaire [refraktɛr] *adj* refractory; rebellious ‖ *mf* insubordinate

réfraction [refraksjɔ̃] *f* refraction

refrain [rəfrɛ̃] *m* refrain; hum; **le même refrain** the same old tune

réfréner [refrene] §10 *tr* to curb

réfrigérateur [refriʒeratœr] *m* refrigerator

réfrigérer [refriʒere] §10 *tr* to refrigerate; (coll) to chill to the bone

refroidir [rəfrwadir] *tr* to cool; (slang) to rub out ‖ *intr* to cool ‖ *ref* to cool; to catch cold

refroidissement [rəfrwadismɑ̃] *m* cooling

refuge [rəfyʒ] *m* refuge; shelter; safety zone

réfu·gié -giée [refyʒje] *mf* refugee

réfugier [refyʒje] *ref* to take refuge

refus [rəfy] *m* refusal; **refus seulement** regrets only (*to invitation*)

refuser [rəfyze] *tr* to refuse; to refuse to recognize; to flunk; to decline ‖ *intr* to refuse; **refuser de** or **à** to refuse to ‖ *ref* to be refused; **se refuser à** to refuse to accept

réfuter [refyte] *tr* to refute

regagner [rəgaɲe] *tr* to regain

regain [rəgɛ̃] *m* second growth; (fig) aftermath; **regain de** new lease on

ré·gal [regal] *m* (*pl* **-gals**) treat

régaler [regale] *tr* to treat; to level ‖ *intr* to treat

regard [rəgar] *m* look, glance; **couver du regard** to gloat over; to look fondly at; to look greedily at; **en regard** facing, opposite

regar·dant [rəgardɑ̃] **-dante** [dɑ̃t] *adj* (coll) penny-pinching

regarder [rəgarde] *tr* to look at; to face; to concern || *intr* to look; **regarder à** to pay attention to; to watch (*one's money*); to mind (*the price*); **y regarder à deux fois** to watch one's step, think twice || *ref* to face each other

régate [regat] *f* regatta

régence [reʒɑ̃s] *f* regency

régénérer [reʒenere] §10 *tr & ref* to regenerate

ré·gent [reʒɑ̃] **-gente** [ʒɑ̃t] *mf* regent

régenter [reʒɑ̃te] *tr & intr* to boss

régicide [reʒisid] *mf* regicide (*person*) || *m* regicide (*act*)

régie [reʒi] *f* commission, administration; excise tax; stage management; **en régie** state owned or operated

regimber [rəʒɛ̃be] *intr & ref* to revolt; to balk

régime [reʒim] *m* government, form of government; administration; system; diet; performance, working conditions; rate (*of speed; of flow; of charge or discharge of a storage battery*); bunch, cluster; stem (*of bananas*); (gram) complement; (gram) government; **en régime permanent** under steady working conditions

régiment [reʒimɑ̃] *m* regiment

régimentaire [reʒimɑ̃ter] *adj* regimental

région [reʒjɔ̃] *f* region

régir [reʒir] *tr* to govern

régisseur [reʒisœr] *m* manager; stage manager

registre [rəʒistr] *m* register; damper; throttle valve

réglable [reglabl] *adj* adjustable

réglage [reglaʒ] *m* setting, adjusting; lines (*on paper*); (mach, rad, telv) tuning

règle [regl] *f* rule; ruler; **en règle in** order; **en règle générale** as a general rule; **règle à calcul** slide rule; **règles** menstrual period

ré·glé -glée [regle] *adj* regulated; adjusted, tuned; well-behaved, orderly; ruled (*paper*); finished, decided

règlement [regləmɑ̃] *m* regulation, rule; settlement; **règlement intérieur** by-laws

réglementaire [regləmɑ̃ter] *adj* regular; regulation

réglementer [regləmɑ̃te] *tr* to regulate, to control

régler [regle] §10 *tr* to regulate, to put in order; to set (*a watch*); to settle (*an account*); to rule (*paper*); (aut, rad, telv) to tune || *intr* to pay

réglisse [reglis] *m & f* licorice

règne [reɲ] *m* reign; (biol) kingdom

régner [reɲe] §10 *intr* to reign

regorger [rəgɔrʒe] §38 *intr* to overflow; **regorger de** to abound in

régratter [rəgrate] *tr* to scrape || *intr* to pinch pennies

regret [rəgre] *m* regret; **à regret** regretfully

regrettable [rəgretabl] *adj* regrettable

regretter [rəgrete] *tr* to regret; to long for, to miss || *intr* to be sorry

régulariser [regylarize] *tr* to regularize; to adjust, regulate

régularité [regylarite] *f* regularity

régula·teur [regylatœr] **-trice** [tris] *adj* regulating || *m* (mach) governor

régulation [regylasjɔ̃] *f* regulation

régu·lier [regylje] **-lière** [ljer] *adj* regular; (coll) aboveboard, fair || *m* regular

réhabiliter [reabilite] *tr* to rehabilitate

rehausser [rəose] *tr* to heighten; to enhance

Reims [rɛ̃s] *m* Rheims

rein [rɛ̃] *m* kidney

réincarnation [reɛ̃karnɑsjɔ̃] *f* reincarnation

reine [ren] *f* queen

reine-claude [renklod] *f* (*pl* **-claudes** or **reines-claudes**) greengage

reine-des-prés [rendepre] *f* (*pl* **reines-des-prés**) meadowsweet

reine-marguerite [renmargərit] *f* (*pl* **reines-marguerites**) aster

réintégrer [reɛ̃tegre] §10 *tr* to reinstate; to return to

réitérer [reitere] §10 *tr* reiterate

rejaillir [rəʒajir] *intr* to spurt out; to bounce; to splash; **rejaillir sur** to reflect on

rejet [rəʒe] *m* casting up; rejection; enjambment; (bot) shoot

rejeter [rəʒte] §34 *tr* to reject; to throw back; to throw up; to shift (*responsibility*) || *ref* to fall back

rejeton [rəʒtɔ̃] *m* shoot; offshoot, offspring; (coll) child

rejoindre [rəʒwɛ̃dr] §35 *tr* to rejoin; to overtake || *ref* to meet

réjouir [reʒwir] *tr* to gladden, cheer || *ref* to rejoice, to be delighted

réjouissance [reʒwisɑ̃s] *f* rejoicing; **réjouissances** festivities

réjouis·sant [reʒwisɑ̃] **réjouis·sante** [reʒwisɑ̃t] *adj* cheery; amusing

relâche [rəlɑʃ] *m & f* respite, letup || *f* (naut) stop; **faire relâche** (naut) to make a call; (theat) to close (*for a day or two*); **relâche** (public sign) no performance today

relâ·ché -chée [rəlɑʃe] *adj* lax; loose

relâchement [rəlɑʃmɑ̃] *m* relaxation; letting up

relâcher [rəlɑʃe] *tr* to loosen; to relax; to release || *intr* (naut) to make a call || *ref* to loosen; to become lax

relais [rəle] *m* relay; shift

relance [rəlɑ̃s] *f* raise (*e.g., in poker*); outbreak

relancer [rəlɑ̃se] §51 *tr* to start up again; to harass, to hound; to return (*the ball*); to raise (*the ante*) || *intr* (cards) to raise

re·laps -lapse [rəlaps] *mf* backslider

relater [rəlate] *tr* to relate

rela·tif [rəlatif] **-tive** [tiv] *adj* relative

relation [rəlɑsjɔ̃] *f* relation; **en relation avec, en relations avec** in touch with; **relations** connections

relativité [rəlativite] *f* relativity

relaxation [rəlaksɑsjɔ̃] *f* relaxation

▸

relaxer [rəlakse] *tr* to relax; to free ‖ *ref* to relax

relayer [rəleje] §49 *tr* to relay; to relieve ‖ *ref* to work in relays or shifts

reléguer [rəlege] §10 *tr* to relegate

relent [rəlɑ̃] *m* musty smell

relève [rəlɛv] *f* relief; change *(of the guard)*; **prendre la relève** to take over

rele·vé -vée [rəlve] *adj* lofty, elevated; turned up; graded *(curve)*; spicy ‖ *m* check list; tuck *(in dress)*; (culin) next course; **faire le relevé de** to survey; to check off; **relevé de compte** bank statement; **relevé de compteur** meter reading; **relevé de notes des écoles** transcript of grades

relèvement [rəlɛvmɑ̃] *m* raising; recovery, improvement; picking up *(e.g., of wounded)*; (naut) bearing

relever [rəlve] §2 *tr* to raise; to turn up; to restore; to relieve, enhance; to pick out; to take a reading of; to season; (mil) to relieve ‖ *intr*—**relever de** to recover from; to depend on ‖ *ref* to rise; to recover; to right itself; to take turns

relief [rəljɛf] *m* relief; **en relief** in relief; **reliefs** leavings

relier [rəlje] *tr* to bind; to link

re·lieur [rəljœr] **-lieuse** [ljøz] *mf* bookbinder

reli·gieux [rəliʒjø] **-gieuse** [ʒjøz] *adj* religious ‖ *m* monk ‖ *f* nun; cream puff

religion [rəliʒjɔ̃] *f* religion

reliquat [rəlika] *m* remainder

relique [rəlik] *f* relic

relire [rəlir] §36 *tr* to read again; to read over again

reliure [rəljyr] *f* binding; bookbinding

reloger [rələʒe] §38 *tr* to find a new home for, to relocate

reluire [rəlɥir] §37 *intr* to shine, gleam, sparkle

relui·sant [rəlɥizɑ̃] **-sante** [zɑ̃t] *adj* shiny, gleaming; **peu reluisant** unpromising, not brilliant

reluquer [rəlyke] *tr* to have an eye on

remâcher [rəmaʃe] *tr* (coll) to stew over

remailler [rəmaje] *tr* to mend the meshes of

remanier [rəmanje] *tr* to revise, revamp; to reshuffle

remarier [rəmarje] *tr & ref* to remarry

remarquable [rəmarkabl] *adj* remarkable

remarquer [rəmarke] *tr & intr* to remark, to notice; **faire remarquer** to point out ‖ *ref*—**se faire remarquer** to make oneself conspicuous

remballer [rɑ̃bale] *tr* to repack

rembarquer [rɑ̃barke] *tr, intr, & ref* to reembark

rembarrer [rɑ̃bare] *tr* to snub, rebuff

remblai [rɑ̃blɛ] *m* fill; embankment

remblayer [rɑ̃bleje] §49 *tr* to fill

rembobiner [rɑ̃bɔbine] *tr* to rewind

remboîter [rɑ̃bwate] *tr* to reset *(a bone)*; to recase *(a book)*

rembourrer [rɑ̃bure] *tr* to upholster; to stuff; to pad

rembourrure [rɑ̃buryr] *f* stuffing

remboursement [rɑ̃bursəmɑ̃] *m* reimbursement

rembourser [rɑ̃burse] *tr* to reimburse

rembrunir [rɑ̃brynir] *tr* to darken; to sadden ‖ *ref* to cloud over

remède [rəmɛd] *m* remedy

remédier [rəmedje] *intr* (with *dat*) to remedy

remembrement [rəmɑ̃brəmɑ̃] *m* regrouping

remémorer [rəmemɔre] *tr*—**remémorer q.ch. à qn** to remind s.o. of s.th. ‖ *ref* to remember

remerciement [rəmɛrsimɑ̃] *m* thanking; **remerciements** thanks; **mille remerciements de** or **pour** a thousand thanks for

remercier [rəmɛrsje] *tr* to thank; to dismiss *(an employee)*; to refuse with thanks; **remercier qn de** + *inf* to thank s.o. for + *ger*; **remercier qn de** or **pour** to thank s.o. for

remettre [rəmɛtr] §42 *tr* to remit, to deliver; to put back; to put back on; to give back; to put off; to reset ‖ *ref* to resume; to recover; to pull oneself together; *(said of weather)* to clear; **s'en remettre à** to leave it up to, to depend on

remise [rəmiz] *f* remittance; discount; delivery; postponement; surrender, return; garage; cover *(for game)*; **de remise** rented *(car)*

remiser [rəmize] *tr* to put away; to park ‖ *ref* to take cover

rémission [remisjɔ̃] *f* remission

remmailler [rɑ̃maje] *tr* to darn

remmener [rɑ̃mne] §2 *tr* to take back

remon·tant [rəmɔ̃tɑ̃] **-tante** [tɑ̃t] *adj* fortifying; remontant *(rose)* ‖ *m* tonic

remonte [rəmɔ̃t] *f* ascent

remontée [rəmɔ̃te] *f* climb; surfacing; comeback

remonte-pente [rəmɔ̃tpɑ̃t] *m* (*pl* **-pentes**) ski lift

remonter [rəmɔ̃te] *tr* to remount; to pull up; to wind *(a clock)*; to pep up; (theat) to put on again ‖ *intr* (*aux*: ÊTRE) to go up again; to date back ‖ *ref* to pep up

remontoir [rəmɔ̃twar] *m* knob *(of stem-winder)*

remontrance [rəmɔ̃trɑ̃s] *f* remonstrance

remontrer [rəmɔ̃tre] *tr* to show again; to point out ‖ *intr*—**en remontrer à** to outdo, to best

remords [rəmɔr] *m* remorse

remorque [rəmɔrk] *f* tow rope; trailer; **à la remorque** in tow

remorquer [rəmɔrke] *tr* to tow; to haul

remorqueur [rəmɔrkœr] *m* tugboat

rémouleur [remulœr] *m* knife grinder, scissors grinder

remous [rəmu] *m* eddy; wash *(of boat)*; agitation

rempailler [rɑ̃paje] *tr* to cane

rempart [rɑ̃par] *m* rampart

remplaçable [rɑ̃plasabl] *adj* replaceable

rempla·çant [rɑ̃plasɑ̃] **-çante** [sɑ̃t] *mf* replacement, substitute

remplacement [rãplasmã] *m* replacement

remplacer [rãplase] §51 *tr* to replace; to take the place of; **remplacer par** to replace with

rem·pli -plie [rãpli] *adj* full ‖ *m* tuck

remplir [rãplir] *tr* to fill; to fill up; to fill out or in; to fulfill ‖ *ref* to fill up

remplissage [rãplisaʒ] *m* filling up

remplumer [rãplyme] *ref* (coll) to put on flesh again; (coll) to make a comeback

remporter [rãpɔrte] *tr* to take back; to carry off; to win

remue-ménage [rəmymenaʒ] *m invar* stir, bustle, to-do

remuer [rəmɥe] *tr* to move; to stir; to remove (*e.g., a piece of furniture*) ‖ *intr* to move ‖ *ref* to move; to hustle

rémunération [remyneʀasjõ] *f* remuneration

renâcler [rənakle] *intr* to snort; **renâcler à** (coll) to shrink from, to bridle at

renaissance [rənɛsãs] *f* renascence, rebirth; renaissance

renais·sant [rənɛsã] **renais·sante** [rənɛsãt] *adj* renascent, reviving; Renaissance

renaître [rənɛtr] §46 *tr* to be reborn; to revive; to grow again

re·nard [rənar] **-narde** [nard] *mf* fox

renché·ri -rie [rãʃeri] *adj* fastidious

renchérir [rãʃerir] *tr* to make more expensive ‖ *intr* to go up in price; **renchérir sur** to improve on

rencontre [rãkõtr] *f* meeting, encounter; clash; collision; **aller à la rencontre de** to go to meet

rencontrer [rãkõtre] *tr* to meet, encounter ‖ *ref* to meet; to collide; to occur

rendement [rãdmã] *m* yield; (mech) output, efficiency

rendez-vous [rãdevu] *m* appointment, date; rendezvous; **sur rendez-vous** by appointment

rendre [rãdr] *tr* to render; to yield; to surrender; to make; to translate; to vomit ‖ *intr* to bring in, yield ‖ *ref* to surrender; **se rendre à** to go to; **se rendre compte de** to realize

ren·du -due [rãdy] *adj* arrived; translated; all in, exhausted ‖ *m* rendering; returned article

rêne [rɛn] *f* rein

réné·gat [rənega] **-gate** [gat] *mf* renegade

renfer·mé -mée [rãferme] *adj* closemouthed, stand-offish ‖ *m* close smell; **sentir le renfermé** to smell stuffy

renfermer [rãferme] *tr* to contain; to include ‖ *ref*—**se renfermer dans** to withdraw into; to confine oneself to

renfler [rãfle] *ref* to swell up

renflouer [rãflue] *tr* to keep afloat; to salvage

renfoncement [rãfõsmã] *m* recess; hollow; dent

renfoncer [rãfõse] §51 *tr* to recess; to dent; to pull down (*e.g., one's hat*) ‖ *ref* to recede; to draw back

renforcement [rãfɔrsəmã] *m* reinforcement

renforcer [rãfɔrse] §51 *tr* to reinforce

renforcir [rãfɔrsir] *tr* (slang) to strengthen ‖ *intr* (slang) to grow stronger

renfort [rãfɔr] *m* reinforcement

renfro·gné -gnée [rãfrɔɲe] *adj* sullen, glum

renfrogner [rãfrɔɲe] *ref* to scowl

rengager [rãgaʒe] §38 *tr* to rehire ‖ *intr & ref* to reenlist

rengaine [rãgen] *f*—**la même rengaine** the same old story; **vieille rengaine** old refrain

rengorger [rãgɔrʒe] §38 *ref* to strut

reniement [rənimã] *m* denial

renier [rənje] *tr* to deny; to repudiate

renifler [rənifle] *tr & intr* to sniff

renne [ren] *m* reindeer

renom [rənõ] *m* renown, fame

renom·mé -mée [rənɔme] *adj* renowned, well-known ‖ *f* fame; reputation

renommer [rənɔme] *tr* to reelect; to reappoint

renoncement [rənõsmã] *m* renunciation

renoncer [rənõse] §51 *tr* to renounce, repudiate ‖ *intr* to give up; (cards) to renege; (with *dat*) to renounce; (with *dat*) to give up, to abandon; **y renoncer** to give it up

renonciation [rənõsjasjõ] *f* renunciation; waiver

renoncule [rənõkyl] *f* buttercup; **renoncule double** bachelor's-button; **renoncule langue** spearwort

renouer [rənwe] *tr* to tie again; to resume (*e.g., a conversation*) ‖ *intr* to renew a friendship

renou·veau [rənuvo] *m* (*pl* **-veaux**) springtime; revival

renouvelable [rənuvlabl] *adj* renewable

renouveler [rənuvle] §34 *tr & ref* to renew

renouvellement [rənuvɛlmã] *m* renewal

rénover [renɔve] *tr* to renew; to renovate

renseignement [rãsɛɲmã] *m* piece of information; **de renseignements** (mil) intelligence; **renseignements** information

renseigner [rãsɛɲe] *tr* to inform ‖ *ref* to find out; **se renseigner auprès de qn** to inquire of s.o.

rentable [rãtabl] *adj* profitable

rente [rãt] *f* revenue, income; annuity; dividend, return; **rente viagère** life annuity

ren·té -tée [rãte] *adj* well-off

renter [rãte] *tr* to endow

ren·tier [rãtje] **-tière** [tjer] *mf* person of independent means

ren·tré -trée [rãtre] *adj* sunken (*eyes*); suppressed (*feelings*) ‖ *f* return; reopening (*of school*); yield

rentrer [rãtre] *tr* to bring in or back; to put in; to hold back (*e.g., one's tears*); to draw in (*claws*) ‖ *intr* (*aux:* ÊTRE) to return, to reenter; to go or come home; to be paid or collected; **rentrer dans** to fit into; to come back to; to get back, recover; **rentrer en soi-même** to take stock of oneself

renverse [rãvers] *f* shift, turn; **à la renverse** backwards

renversement [rãversəmã] *m* reversal, shift; upset, overturn; overthrow

renverser [rãverse] *tr* to reverse; to overthrow ‖ *intr & ref* to capsize

renvoi [rãvwa] *m* dismissal; postponement; reference; return; belch

renvoyer [rãvwaje] §26 *tr* to dismiss; to fire (*an employee*); to postpone; to refer; to send back

réorganiser [reorganize] *tr & ref* to reorganize

réouverture [reuvertyr] *f* reopening

repaire [rəper] *m* den

repaître [rəpetr] §12 *tr* to graze; **repaître de** to feast (*e.g., one's eyes*) on ‖ *ref* to eat one's fill (*said of animals*); **se repaître de** to indulge in, to wallow in

répandre [repãdr] *tr* to spread; to strew, scatter; to spill; to shed ‖ *ref* to spread; **se répandre en** to be profuse in

répan·du ·due [repãdy] *adj* widespread; widely known

reparaître [rəparetr] §12 *intr* to reappear

répara·teur [reparatœr] **-trice** [tris] *adj* restorative ‖ *m* repairman

réparation [reparasjõ] *f* repair; reparation; restoration

réparer [repare] *tr* to repair; to mend, patch; to make up (*a loss*); to redress (*a wrong*); to restore (*one's strength*)

repartie [rəparti], [reparti] *f* repartee

repartir [rəpartir] §64 *tr* to retort ‖ *intr* (*aux:* ÊTRE) to start again; to leave again

répartir [repartir] *tr* to distribute

répartiteur [repartitœr] *m* distributor; assessor

répartition [repartisjõ] *f* distribution; apportionment; range (*of words*)

repas [rəpa] *m* meal, repast; **dernier repas** (rel) last supper; **repas champêtre** picnic; **repas de noce** wedding breakfast; **repas froid** cold snack; **repas sur le pouce** takeout meal

repassage [rəpasaʒ] *m* recrossing; ironing; stropping; whetting

repasser [rəpase] *tr* to pass again; to go over, to review; to iron; to strop; to whet ‖ *intr* to pass by again; to drop in again

repêcher [rəpeʃe] *tr* to fish out; to give another chance to; (coll) to get (*s.o.*) out of a scrape

repentance [rəpãtãs] *f* repentance

repen·tant [rəpãtã] **-tante** [tãt] *adj* repentant

repen·ti ·tie [rəpãti] *adj* repentant

repentir [rəpãtir] *m* repentance ‖ §41 *ref* to repent; **se repentir de** to be sorry for, to repent

repérage [reperaʒ] *m* spotting, locating; tracking; marking with a reference mark; (mov) synchronization

répercussion [reperkysjõ] *f* repercussion

répercuter [reperkyte] *tr* to reflect ‖ *ref* to reverberate; to have repercussions

repère [rəper] *m* mark, reference

repérer [repere] §10 *tr* to locate, spot; to mark with a reference mark; (mov) to synchronize

répertoire [repertwar] *m* repertory; index; **répertoire à onglets** thumb index; **répertoire d'adresses** address book; **répertoire vivant** walking encyclopedia

répéter [repete] §10 *tr & ref* to repeat

répéti·teur [repetitœr] **-trice** [tris] *mf* assistant teacher; coach, tutor

répétition [repetisjõ] *f* repetition; private lesson, tutoring; rehearsal; **répétition des couturières** next to last dress rehearsal; **répétition générale** final dress rehearsal

repeupler [rəpœple] *tr* to repeople; to restock

repiquer [rəpike] *tr* to plant out (*seedlings*); to repave; to restitch; to re-record; (phot) to retouch ‖ *intr*—**repiquer à** (slang) to come back to

répit [repi] *m* respite, letup

replacement [rəplasmã] *m* replacement; reinvestment

replacer [rəplase] §51 *tr* to replace; to find a new job for; to reinvest ‖ *ref* to find a new job

replâtrage [rəplɑtraʒ] *m* replastering; makeshift; (fig) patchwork

re·plet ·plète [rəple] [plet] *adj* fat, plump

repli [rəpli] *m* crease, fold; dip, depression; (mil) falling back

replier [rəplije] *tr* to refold; to turn up; to close (*e.g., an umbrella*) ‖ *ref* to curl up, to coil up; (mil) to fall back

réplique [replik] *f* reply, retort; replica; **donner la réplique à qn** to answer s.o.; (theat) to give s.o. his cue; (theat) to play the straight man or stooge for s.o.

répliquer [replike] *tr & intr* to reply

replonger [rəplõʒe] §38 *tr* to plunge again ‖ *intr* to dive again ‖ *ref*—**se replonger dans** to get back into

répon·dant ·dante [repõdã] *mf* guarantor; (eccl) server; **avoir du répondant** (coll) to have money behind one

répondre [repõdr] *tr* to answer (*e.g., yes or no*); to assure ‖ *intr* to answer, reply; to answer back; to be saucy; to reecho; **répondre à** to answer (*e.g., a question, a letter*); to correspond to; **répondre de** to answer for (*a person*); to guarantee (*a thing*) ‖ *ref* to answer each other; to correspond to each other; to be in harmony

réponse [repõs] *f* answer, response; **réponse normande** evasive answer

report [rəpɔr] *m* carrying forward or over; carry-over

reportage [rəpɔrtaʒ] *m* reporting

reporter [rəpɔrter] *m* reporter ‖ [rəpɔrte] *tr* to carry back; to postpone; (math) to carry forward ‖ *intr* (com) to carry stock; **à reporter** carried forward || *ref*—**se reporter à** to be carried back to (*e.g., childhood days*); to refer to

reporteur [rəpɔrtœr] *m* broker

repos [rəpo] *m* rest, repose; **au repos** not running, still; **de tout repos** reliable; **en repos** at rest; **repos!** (mil) at ease!

repo·sé -sée [rəpoze] *adj* refreshed, relaxed

reposer [rəpoze] *tr* to rest || *intr* to rest; **ici repose . . . here lies . . .** || *ref* to rest; **s'en reposer sur** to rely on

repous·sant [rəpusɑ̃] **repous·sante**, [rəpusɑ̃t] *adj* repulsive

repousser [rəpuse] *tr* to push, shove; to repulse, repel; to reject, refuse; to postpone; to emboss || *intr* to grow again; to be offensive; (arti) to recoil

repoussoir [rəpuswar] *m* foil; contrast; (mach) driving bolt

reprendre [rəprɑ̃dr] §56 *tr* to take back; to resume; to regain (*consciousness*); to find fault with; to take in (*e.g., a dress*); to catch (*one's breath*); (theat) to put on again || *intr* to start again; to pick up, to improve; to criticize || *ref* to pull oneself together; to correct oneself in speaking

représailles [rəprezaj] *fpl* reprisal

représentant [rəprezɑ̃tɑ̃] *m* representative

représenta·tif [rəprezɑ̃tatif] **-tive** [tiv] *adj* representative

représentation [rəprezɑ̃tɑsjɔ̃] *f* representation; performance; remonstrance

représenter [rəprezɑ̃te] *tr* to represent; to put on, to perform || *intr* to make a good showing

répression [rəpresjɔ̃] *f* repression

réprimande [rəprimɑ̃d] *f* reprimand

réprimander [rəprimɑ̃de] *tr* to reprimand

réprimer [rəprime] *tr* to repress

re·pris [rəpri] **-prise** [priz] *adj* recaptured; **être repris de** to suffer from a recurrence of || *m*—**repris de justice** hardened criminal, habitual offender || *f see* **reprise**

reprisage [rəprizaʒ] *m* darning

reprise [rəpriz] *f* recapture; resumption; darning; pickup (*acceleration of motor*); (theat) revival; **à plusieurs reprises** several times; **faire une reprise à** to darn; **par reprises** a little at a time

repriser [rəprize] *tr* to darn; to mend

réproba·teur [rəprɔbatœr] **-trice** [tris] *adj* reproving

reproche [rəprɔʃ] *m* reproach

reprocher [rəprɔʃe] *tr* to reproach; to begrudge; (law) to take exception to (*a witness*); **reprocher q.ch. à qn** to reproach s.o. for s.th.; to begrudge s.o. s.th.; to remind s.o. reproachfully of s.th.

reproduction [rəprɔdyksjɔ̃] *f* reproduction

reproduire [rəprɔdɥir] §19 *tr & ref* to reproduce

réprou·vé -vée [repruve] *adj & mf* outcast; damned

réprouver [repruve] *tr* to disapprove

reptile [reptil] *m* reptile

re·pu -pue [rapy] *adj* satiated

républi·cain [repyblikɛ̃] **-caine** [ken] *adj & mf* republican

république [repyblik] *f* republic

répudier [repydje] *tr* to repudiate

répu·gnant [repyɲɑ̃] **-gnante** [ɲɑ̃t] *adj* repugnant

répugner [repyɲe] *intr* (with *dat*) to disgust; to balk at; **répugner à + inf** to be loath to + *inf*

répul·sif [repylsif] **-sive** [siv] *adj* repulsive

réputation [repytasjɔ̃] *f* reputation

répu·té -tée [repyte] *adj* of high repute; **être réputé** to be reputed to be

requérir [rəkerir] §3 *tr* to demand; to ask; to require; to summon; to requisition

requête [rəkɛt] *f* petition, appeal

requiem [rekɥijem] *m* requiem

requin [rəkɛ̃] *m* shark

réquisition [rekizisjɔ̃] *f* requisition

réquisitionner [rekizisjɔne] *tr* to requisition

réquisitoire [rekizitwar] *m* indictment

res·capé -capée [reskape] *adj* rescued || *mf* survivor

rescinder [resɛ̃de] *tr* to rescind

rescousse [reskus] *f* rescue

ré·seau [rezo] *m* (*pl* **-seaux**) net; network, system; **réseau de barbelés** barbed wire entanglement

réséda [rezeda] *m* mignonette

réservation [rezervɑsjɔ̃] *f* reservation

réserve [rezerv] *f* reserve; reservation; **de réserve** emergency, reserve (*rations, fund, etc.*); **sous réserve que** on condition that; **sous toutes réserves** without committing oneself

réserver [rezerve] *tr* to reserve; to set aside || *ref* to set aside for oneself; to wait and see, to hold off

réserviste [rezervist] *m* reservist

réservoir [rezervwar] *m* reservoir, tank; **réservoir de bombes** bomb bay

résidence [rezidɑ̃s] *f* residence

rési·dent [rezidɑ̃] **-dente** [dɑ̃t] *mf* alien, foreigner; (dipl) resident

résiden·tiel -tielle [rezidɑ̃sjel] *adj* residential

résider [rezide] *intr* to reside

résidu [rezidy] *m* residue; refuse

résignation [reziɲɑsjɔ̃] *f* resignation

résigner [reziɲe] *tr* to resign || *ref* to be or become resigned

résilier [rezilje] *tr* to cancel

résille [rezij] *f* hair net

résine [rezin] *f* resin

résistance [rezistɑ̃s] *f* resistance

résis·tant [rezistɑ̃] **-tante** [tɑ̃t] *adj* resistant; strong; fast (*color*)

résister [reziste] *intr* to be fast, not run (*said of colors or dyes*); (with *dat*) to resist, to withstand, to hold out against; (with *dat*) to weather (*e.g., a storm*); **résister à + inf** to resist + ger

réso·lu -lue [rezɔly] *adj* resolute, resolved

résolution [rezɔlysjɔ̃] *f* resolution; canceling

résonance [rezɔnɑ̃s] *f* resonance

résonner [rezɔne] *intr* to resound; to re-echo

résorber [rezɔrbe] *tr* to absorb || *ref* to become absorbed

résoudre [rezudr] §60 *tr* to resolve; to decide; to solve; to persuade; to cancel; **être résolu à** to be resolved to || *intr*—**résoudre de** to decide to || *ref*—**se résoudre à** to decide to; to reconcile oneself to; **se résoudre en** to turn into

respect [respe] *m* respect; **présenter ses respects (à)** to pay one's respects (to); **respect de soi** or **soi-même** self-respect; **respect humain** [respekymɛ̃] fear of what people might say; **sauf votre (mon,** etc.) **respect** with all due respect; **pardon the language**

respectable [respektabl] *adj* respectable

respecter [respekte] *tr* to respect || *ref* to keep one's self-respect

respec•tif [respektif] **-tive** [tiv] *adj* respective

respec•tueux [respektɥø] **-tueuse** [tɥøz] *adj* respectful

respirer [respire] *tr* to breathe || *intr* to breathe; to catch one's breath

resplendis•sant [resplɑ̃disɑ̃] **resplendis•sante** [resplɑ̃disɑ̃t] *adj* resplendent

responsabilité [respɔ̃sabilite] *f* responsibility

responsable [respɔ̃sabl] *adj* responsible; **responsable de** responsible for; **responsable envers** accountable to || *mf* person responsible, person in charge

resquiller [reskije] *tr* (coll) to obtain by fraud || *intr* (coll) to crash the gate

resquil•leur [reskijœr] **resquil•leuse** [reskijøz] *mf* (coll) gate-crasher

ressac [rəsak] *m* surf; undertow

ressaisir [rəsezir] *tr* to recapture || *ref* to regain one's self-control

ressasser [rəsɑse] *tr* to go over and over again

ressaut [rəso] *m* projection; sharp rise

ressemblance [rəsɑ̃blɑ̃s] *f* resemblance

ressembler [rəsɑ̃ble] *intr* (with *dat*) to resemble, look like || *ref* to resemble one another; to be alike, to look alike

ressemeler [rəsəmle] §34 *tr* to resole

ressentiment [rəsɑ̃timɑ̃] *m* resentment

ressentir [rəsɑ̃tir] *tr* to feel keenly, to be hurt by (*an insult*); to experience (*joy, pain, surprise*) || *ref*—**se ressentir de** to feel the aftereffects of

resserre [rəser] *f* shed, storeroom

resserrer [rəsere] *tr* to tighten; to contract; to close; to lock up (*e.g., valuables*) again || *ref* to tighten; to contract

ressort [rəsɔr] *m* spring; springiness; motive; **du ressort de** within the jurisdiction of; **en dernier ressort** without appeal; **as a last resort; ressort à boudin** coil spring; **sans ressort** slack

ressortir [rəsɔrtir] *intr*—**ressortir à** to come under the jurisdiction of; to

fall under the head of || §64 *intr* (aux: ÊTRE) to go out again; to stand out, to be evident; **faire ressortir** to set off; **il ressort de** it follows from; **il ressort que** it follows that

ressortis•sant [rəsɔrtisɑ̃] **ressortis•sante** [rəsɔrtisɑ̃t] *adj*—**ressortissant à** under the jurisdiction of || *mf* national

ressource [rəsurs] *f* resource

ressouvenir [rəsuvnir] §72 *ref* to reminisce; **se ressouvenir de** to recall

ressusciter [resysite] *tr* to resuscitate; to resurrect || *intr* (aux: ÊTRE) to rise from the dead; to get well

res•tant [restɑ̃] **-tante** [tɑ̃t] *adj* remaining || *m* remainder

restaurant [restɔrɑ̃] *m* restaurant; **restaurant libre-service** self-service restaurant

restauration [restɔrasjɔ̃] *f* restoration; restaurant business

restaurer [restɔre] *tr* to restore || *ref* (coll) to take some nourishment

reste [rest] *m* rest, remainder; remnant; relic; **au reste, du reste** moreover; **de reste** spare; **restes** remains; leftovers

rester [reste] *intr* (aux: ÊTRE) to remain, to stay; to be left over; **en rester** to stop, to leave off; **en rester là** to stop right there; **il me (te, leur,** etc.) **reste q.ch.** I (you, they, etc.) have s.th. left

restituer [restitɥe] *tr* to restore; to give back

restitution [restitysjɔ̃] *f* restitution; restoration

restoroute [restɔrut] *m* drive-in restaurant

restreindre [restrɛ̃dr] §50 *tr* to restrict; to curtail || *ref* to become limited; to cut down expenses

res•treint [restrɛ̃] **-treinte** [trɛ̃t] *adj* limited

restriction [restriksjɔ̃] *f* restriction

résultat [rezylta] *m* result

résulter [rezylte] *intr* to result; **il en résulte que** it follows that

résumé [rezyme] *m* summary, recapitulation; **en résumé** in short, in a word

résumer [rezyme] *tr* to summarize || *ref* to be summed up

résurrection [rezyreksjɔ̃] *f* resurrection

rétablir [retablir] *tr* to restore || *ref* to recover

rétablissement [retablismɑ̃] *m* restoration; recovery

retailler [rətaje] *tr* to resharpen

retape [rətap] *f* (slang) streetwalking

retaper [rətape] *tr* (coll) to straighten up; (coll) to give a lick and a promise to || *ref* (coll) to perk up

retard [rətar] *m* delay; **en retard** late; slow (*clock*); **en retard sur** behind

retardataire [rətardater] *adj* tardy; retarded || *mf* latecomer, straggler

retarder [rətarde] *tr* to delay; to put off; to set back || *intr* to go slow, to be behind

retenir [rətnir] §72 *tr* to hold or keep back; to detain; to remember, note; to reserve; to retain (*a lawyer*); to carry (*a number*) || *ref*—**se retenir à** to cling to; **se retenir de** to refrain from

retentir [rətãtir] *intr* to resound

rete·nu -nue [rətny] *adj* reserved; held back || *f* withholding; reserve; **retenue à la source** withholding tax

réticence [retisãs] *f* evasiveness, concealment; hesitation; reservation, misgiving

réti·cent [retisã] **-cente** [sãt] *adj* evasive; hesitant; reserved, withdrawn

réticule [retikyl] *m* handbag

ré·tif [retif] **-tive** [tiv] *adj* restive

rétine [retin] *f* retina

retirement [rətirmã] *m* contraction

retirer [rətire] *tr* to withdraw; to take off; to fire again || *intr* to fire again || *ref* to withdraw; to retire

retombée [rətõbe] *f* fall; hang (*of cloth*); **retombées radioactives** fallout

retomber [rətõbe] *intr* (*aux:* ÊTRE) to fall again; to fall; to fall back; to hang, hang down; to relapse

retordre [rətɔrdr] *tr* to twist; to wring out

rétorquer [retɔrke] *tr* to retort

re·tors [rətɔr] **-torse** [tɔrs] *adj* twisted; wily; curved (*beak*) || *mf* rascal

retouche [rətuʃ] *f* retouch; (phot) retouching; **retouches** alterations

retoucher [rətuʃe] *tr* to retouch; to make alterations on

retour [rətur] *m* return; turn, bend; reversal (*e.g., of opinion*); **en retour d'équerre** at right angles; **être de retour** to be back; **par retour du courrier** by return mail; **retour à la masse** (elec) ground (*on chassis of auto, radio, etc.*); **retour à la terre** (elec) ground; **retour d'âge** change of life; **retour de flamme** backfire; **retour de manivelle** kick (of the crank); (fig) backlash; **retour en arrière** flashback

retourner [rəturne] *tr* to send back, to return; to upset; to turn over (*e.g., the soil*); to turn inside out || *intr* (*aux:* ÊTRE) to go back, to return || *ref* to turn around, to look back; to turn over; (fig) to veer, to shift; **s'en retourner** to go back; **se retourner contre** to turn against

retracer [rətrase] §51 *tr* to retrace; to bring to mind, to recall || *ref* to come to mind again; to recall

rétracter [retrakte] *tr & ref* to retract

rétraction [retraksjõ] *f* contraction

retrait [rətre] *m* withdrawal; shrinkage; running out (*of tide*); **en retrait** set back, recessed; (typ) indented; **retrait de permis** suspension of driver's license

retraite [rətret] *f* retreat; retirement; pension; **battre en retraite** to retreat; **en retraite** retired; **prendre sa retraite** to retire; **toucher sa retraite** to draw one's pension

retrai·té -tée [rətrete] *adj* pensioned, retired || *mf* pensioner

retranchement [rətrãʃmã] *m* retrenchment; cutting out

retrancher [rətrãʃe] *tr* to cut off or

out, to retrench || *ref* to become entrenched

retransmettre [rətrãsmetr] §42 *tr* to retransmit; to rebroadcast

retransmission [rətrãsmisjõ] *f* retransmission; rebroadcast

rétré·ci -cie [retresi] *adj* narrow; shrunk

rétrécir [retresir] *tr* to shrink; to take in (*a garment*) || *intr & ref* to shrink; to narrow

retremper [rətrãpe] *tr* to soak again; to retemper; to give new strength or life to || *ref* to take another dip; to get new vigor

rétribuer [retribɥe] *tr* to remunerate

rétribution [retribysjõ] *f* retribution; salary, fee

rétroaction [retroaksjõ] *f* feedback; retroaction

rétrofusée [retrɔfyze] *f* retrorocket

rétrograder [retrɔgrade] *intr* to retrogress

rétrospection [retrɔspeksjõ] *f* retrospection

retrousser [rətruse] *tr* to roll up, to turn up; to curl up (*one's lip*) || *ref* to turn up or pull up one's clothes

retrouver [rətruve] *tr* to find again; to recover || *ref* to be back again; to meet again; to get one's bearings

rétroviseur [retrɔvizœr] *m* rear-view mirror

rets [re] *m*—**prendre dans des rets** to snare

réunification [reynifikɑsjõ] *f* reunification

réunion [reynjõ] *f* reunion; meeting

réunir [reynir] *tr* to unite, join; to reunite; to call together, convene || *ref* to meet; to reunite

réus·si -sie [reysi] *adj* successful

réussir [reysir] *tr* to make a success of, to be good at || *intr* to succeed; **réussir à** to succeed in; to pass (*an exam*)

réussite [reysit] *f* success; **faire une réussite** (cards) to play solitaire

revaloir [rəvalwar] §71 *tr*—**revaloir q.ch. à qn** to pay s.o. back for s.th.

revan·chard [rəvãʃar] **-charde** [ʃard] *adj* (coll) vengeful || *mf* (coll) avenger

revanche [rəvãʃ] *f* revenge; return bout or engagement, return match; **en revanche** on the other hand; **prendre sa revanche sur** to get even with

revancher [rəvãʃe] *ref* to get even

rêvasser [revase] *intr* to daydream

rêvasserie [revasri] *f* fitful dreaming; daydreaming

rêve [rev] *m* dream

revêche [rəveʃ] *adj* sullen, crabbed

réveil [revej] *m* awakening; alarm clock; (mil) reveille

réveille-matin [revejmatɛ̃] *m invar* alarm clock

réveiller [reveje] *tr & ref* to wake up

réveillon [revejõ] *m* Christmas Eve supper; New Year's Eve party

réveillonner [revejɔne] *intr* to celebrate Christmas Eve or New Year's Eve

révéla·teur [revelatœr] **-trice** [tris] *adj*

revealing; telltale || *mf* informer || *m* (phot) developer

révélation [revelasjɔ̃] *f* revelation

révéler [revele] §10 *tr* to reveal; (phot) to develop

revenant [rəvnɑ̃] *m* ghost

reven•deur [rəvɑ̃dœr] **-deuse** [døz] *mf* retailer; secondhand dealer

revendication [rəvɑ̃dikasjɔ̃] *f* claim

revendiquer [rəvɑ̃dike] *tr* to claim; to insist upon; to assume (*a responsibility*)

revendre [rəvɑ̃dr] *tr* to resell

revenez-y [rəvnezi] *m invar* (coll) return; **un goût de revenez-y** (coll) a taste like more

revenir [rəvnir] §72 *intr* (*aux:* ÊTRE) to return, come back; (with *dat*) to suit, to please; **en revenir** to have a narrow escape; **faire revenir** (culin) to brown; **n'en pas revenir** to not get over it; **revenir à** to come to, amount to; to come to (*e.g.,* mind); **revenir à soi** to come to; **revenir bredouille** to come back empty-handed; **revenir de** to recover from; to realize (*a mistake*); **revenir de loin** to have been at death's door; **revenir sur** to go back on (*e.g., one's word*) || *ref*—**s'en revenir** to come back

revente [rəvɑ̃t] *f* resale

revenu [rəvny] *m* revenue, income

revenue [rəvny] *f* new growth (*of trees*)

rêver [reve] *tr* to dream || *intr* to dream; **rêver à** to dream of (*think about*); **rêver de** to dream of (*in sleep; to long to*)

réverbère [reverber] *m* streetlight

réverbérer [reverbere] §10 *tr* to reflect (*light, heat, etc.*) || *ref* to be reflected

reverdir [rəverdir] *tr* to make green || *intr* to grow green; to become young again

révérence [reverɑ̃s] *f* reverence; curtsy; **révérence parler** (coll) pardon the language; **tirer sa révérence** to bow out

révéren•cieux [reverɑ̃sjø] **-cieuse** [sjøz] *adj* obsequious

révé•rend [reverɑ̃] **-rende** [rɑ̃d] *adj & m* reverend

révérer [revere] §10 *tr* to revere

rêverie [revri] *f* reverie

revers [rəver] *m* reverse; lapel; (tennis) backhand; **à revers** from behind; **revers de main** slap with the back of the hand

reverser [rəverse] *tr* to pour back; to pour out again

réversible [reversibl] *adj* reversible

revêtement [rəvɛtmɑ̃] *m* surfacing; facing; lining; casing

revêtir [rəvɛtir] §73 *tr* to put on; to clothe, to dress up; to invest; to surface; to line; to face; to assume (*a form; an aspect*)

rê•veur [revœr] **-veuse** [vøz] *adj* dreamy || *mf* dreamer; **cela me laisse rêveur** that leaves me puzzled

revirement [rəvirmɑ̃] *m* sudden reversal; (naut) tack

réviser [revize] *tr* to revise; to review; to overhaul; to recondition

réviseur [revizœr] *m* proofreader

révision [revizjɔ̃] *f* revision; review; overhauling; proofreading

révisionniste [revizjɔnist] *adj & mf* revisionist

revivre [rəvivr] §74 *tr* to live again, relive || *intr* to live again

révocation [revɔkasjɔ̃] *f* dismissal; revocation

revoici [rəvwasi] *prep*—**me (vous, etc.)** **revoici** (coll) here I am (you are, etc.) again

revoilà [rəvwala] *prep*—**le (la, etc.)** **voilà** (coll) there it is (he, she, etc.) is again

revoir [rəvwar] *m*—**au revoir** good-by || §75 *tr* to see again; to review; to revise || *ref* to meet again

révol•tant [revɔltɑ̃] **-tante** [tɑ̃t] *adj* revolting

révolte [revɔlt] *f* revolt, rebellion

révol•té -tée [revɔlte] *adj & mf* rebel

révolter [revɔlte] *tr & ref* to revolt; **se révolter devant** to be revolted by

révo•lu -lue [revɔly] *adj* completed; elapsed; bygone

révolution [revɔlysjɔ̃] *f* revolution

révolutionnaire [revɔlysjɔner] *adj & mf* revolutionary

revolver [revɔlver] *m* revolver

révoquer [revɔke] *tr* to revoke; to countermand; to dismiss; to recall

re•vu -vue [rəvy] *adj* revised || *f* see revue

revue [rəvy] *f* review; magazine, journal; (theat) revue; **passer en revue** to review (*past events; troops*)

rez-de-chaussée [red͡ʒose] *m invar* first floor, ground floor

R.F. *abbr* (**République Française**) French Republic

rhabiller [rabije] *tr* to repair; to dress again; to refurbish || *ref* to change one's clothes; **va te rhabiller!** (pej) get out!

rhapsodie [rapsɔdi] *f* rhapsody

Rhénanie [renani] *f* Rhineland

rhéostat [reɔsta] *m* rheostat

rhétorique [retɔrik] *adj* rhetorical || *f* rhetoric

Rhin [rɛ̃] *m* Rhine

rhinocéros [rinɔseros] *m* rhinoceros

rhubarbe [rybarb] *f* rhubarb

rhum [rɔm] *m* rum

rhumati•sant [rymatizɑ̃] **-sante** [zɑ̃t] *adj & mf* rheumatic

rhumatis•mal -male [rymatismal] *adj* (*pl* **-maux** [mo]) rheumatic

rhumatisme [rymatism] *m* rheumatism

rhume [rym] *m* cold; **rhume des foins** hay fever

riant [rjɑ̃] **riante** [rjɑ̃t] *adj* smiling; cheerful, pleasant

ribambelle [ribɑ̃bel] *f* (coll) long string, swarm, lot

ri•baud [ribo] **-baude** [bod] *adj* licentious || *mf* camp follower; debauchee

ricanement [rikanmɑ̃] *m* snicker

ricaner [rikane] *intr* to snicker

ri•chard [ri/ar] **-charde** [/ard] *mf* (coll) moneybags

riche [ri/] *adj* rich || *m* rich man; **nouveaux riches** newly rich

riche·lieu [riʃəljø] m (pl **-lieu** or **-lieus**) oxford

richesse [riʃɛs] f wealth; richness; **richesses** riches; **richesses naturelles** natural resources

ricin [risɛ̃] m castor-oil plant; castor bean

ricocher [rikɔʃe] intr to ricochet, rebound

ricochet [rikɔʃɛ] m ricochet; **faire des ricochets** to play ducks and drakes; **par ricochet** indirectly

rictus [riktys] m rictus; grin

ride [rid] f wrinkle; ripple

ri·deau [rido] m (pl **-deaux**) curtain; **rideau d'arbres** line of trees; **rideau de fer** iron curtain; safety blind (of a store); (theat) fire curtain; **rideau de feu** (mil) cover of artillery fire; **rideau de fumée** smoke screen

ridelle [ridɛl] f rave, side rails (of wagon)

rider [ride] tr to wrinkle; to ripple

ridicule [ridikyl] adj ridiculous || m ridicule

ridiculiser [ridikylize] tr to ridicule

rien [rjɛ̃] m trifle; **comme un rien** with no trouble at all; **un rien de** just a little (bit) of; **un rien de temps no time at all** || pron indef—**de rien** don't mention it, you're welcome; of no importance; **il n'en est rien** such is not the case; **rien ne or ne . . . rien** §90B nothing, not anything; **rien de moins (que)** nothing less (than); **rien que** nothing but

rieur [rjœr] **rieuse** [rjøz] adj laughing || mf laugher, mocker || f (orn) black-headed gull

riflard [riflar] m coarse file; jack plane; paring chisel

rigide [riʒid] adj rigid; stiff; strict

rigolade [rigɔlad] f (coll) good time, fun; (coll) big joke

rigole [rigɔl] f drain; ditch

rigoler [rigɔle] intr (slang) to laugh, to joke

rigo·lo [rigɔlo] **-lote** [lɔt] adj (coll) comical; (coll) queer, funny || mf (coll) card || m (slang) rod, gat

rigou·reux [rigurø] **-reuse** [røz] adj rigorous; severe

rigueur [rigœr] f rigor, strictness; **à la rigueur** to the letter; as a last resort; **de rigueur** compulsory, de rigueur

rillons [rijɔ̃] mpl cracklings

rimail·leur [rimajœr] **rimail·leuse** [rimajøz] mf (coll) rhymester

rime [rim] f rhyme; **rimes croisées** alternate rhymes; **rimes plates** couplets of alternate masculine and feminine rhymes

rimer [rime] tr & intr to rhyme

rinçage [rɛ̃saʒ] m rinse

rince-bouche [rɛ̃sbuʃ] m invar mouthwash

rince-bouteilles [rɛ̃sbutɛj] m invar (mach) bottle-washing machine

rince-doigts [rɛ̃sdwa] m invar fingerbowl

rincer [rɛ̃se] §51 tr to rinse; (slang) to ruin, to take to the cleaners

rinçure [rɛ̃syr] f rinsing water

ring [riŋ] m ring (for, e.g., boxing)

ringard [rɛ̃gar] m poker (for fire)

ripaille [ripaj] f (coll) blowout; **faire ripaille** (coll) to carouse

ripe [rip] f scraper

riper [ripe] tr to scrape; (naut) to slip || intr to slip; to skid

riposte [ripɔst] f riposte, retort

riposter [ripɔste] tr to riposte, to retort

rire [rir] m laugh; laughter; laughing || §61 intr to laugh; to joke; to smile; **pour rire** for fun, in jest; **rire dans sa barbe, rire sous cape** to laugh up one's sleeve; **rire de** to laugh at or over; **rire du bout des lèvres, rire du bout des dents** to titter; **rire jaune** to force a laugh || ref—**se rire de** to laugh at

ris [ri] m (naut) reef; (obs) laughter; **ris d'agneau** or **de veau** sweetbread

risée [rize] f scorn; laughingstock; light squall

risible [rizibl] adj laughable

risque [risk] m risk

ris·qué -quée [riske] adj risky; risqué

risquer [riske] tr to risk; to hazard (e.g., a remark) || intr—**risquer de** + inf to risk + ger; **to have a good chance of** + ger

risque-tout [riskətu] mf invar daredevil

rissoler [risɔle] tr & intr to brown

ristourne [risturn] f rebate, refund; dividend

ristourner [risturne] tr to refund

ritournelle [riturnɛl] f—**c'est toujours la même ritournelle** it's always the same old story; **ritournelle publicitaire** advertising jingle or slogan

ri·tuel -tuelle [rituɛl] adj & m ritual

rivage [rivaʒ] m shore; bank

ri·val -vale [rival] (pl **-vaux** [vo] **-vales**) adj & mf rival

rivaliser [rivalize] intr to compete; **rivaliser avec** to compete with, to rival

rivalité [rivalite] f rivalry

rive [riv] f shore; bank

river [rive] tr to rivet

rive·rain -raine [rivrɛ̃] **-raine** [rɛn] adj waterfront; bordering || mf riversider; dweller along a street or road

riveraineté [rivrɛnte] f riparian rights

rivet [rivɛ] m rivet

rivière [rivjɛr] f river, stream, tributary; (turf) water jump; **rivière de diamants** diamond necklace

rixe [riks] f brawl

riz [ri] m rice; **riz au lait** rice pudding; **riz glacé** polished rice

rizière [rizjɛr] f rice field

robe [rɔb] f dress; gown; robe; wrapper (of cigar); skin (of onion, sausage, etc.); husk (of, e.g., bean); **robe de chambre** dressing gown; **robe d'intérieur** housecoat

rober [rɔbe] tr to husk, to skin; to wrap (a cigar)

roberts [rɔbɛr] mpl (slang) breasts

robin [rɔbɛ̃] m (coll) judge; (pej) shyster

robinet [rɔbinɛ] m faucet, tap; cock;

robinet d'eau tiède (coll) bore; **robinet mélangeur** mixing faucet

robinier [rɔbinje] *m* (bot) locust tree

robot [rɔbo] *m* robot

robre [rɔbr] *m* rubber (*in bridge*)

robuste [rɔbyst] *adj* robust; firm

roc [rɔk] *m* rock

rocaille [rɔkaj] *adj* rococo || *f* stones; rocky ground; stonework

rocail·leux [rɔkajø] **rocail·leuse** [rɔkajøz] *adj* rocky, stony; harsh

roche [rɔʃ] *f* rock; boulder

rocher [rɔʃe] *m* rock; crag

rochet [rɔʃɛ] *m* ratchet; bobbin

ro·cheux [rɔʃø] **-cheuse** [ʃøz] *adj* rocky

rodage [rɔdaʒ] *m* grinding; breaking in; **en rodage** being broken in, new

roder [rɔde] *tr* to grind (*a valve*); to break in (*a new car*); to polish up (*a new play*)

rôder [rode] *intr* to prowl

rô·deur [rodœr] **-deuse** [døz] *adj* prowling || *mf* prowler

rogatons [rɔgatɔ̃] *mpl* (coll) scraps

rogne [rɔɲ] *f* (coll) anger; **mettre qn en rogne** (coll) to make s.o. see red

rogner [rɔɲe] *tr* to pare, to trim

rognon [rɔɲɔ̃] *m* kidney

rogomme [rɔgɔm] *m*—**de rogomme** (coll) husky, beery (*voice*)

rogue [rɔg] *adj* arrogant

roi [rwa], [rwɑ] *m* king; **tirer les rois** to gather to eat the Twelfth-night cake

roitelet [rwatlɛ] *m* kinglet; (orn) kinglet

rôle [rol] *m* role; roll, muster

ro·main [rɔmɛ̃] **-maine** [men] *adj* Roman; roman (*type*); romaine (*lettuce*) || *m* (typ) roman || *f* romaine (*lettuce*) || (*cap*) *mf* Roman (*person*)

ro·man [rɔmɑ̃] **-mane** [man] *adj* Romance (*language*); (archit) Romanesque || *m* novel; **roman d'anticipation** science-fiction novel; **roman policier** detective story

romance [rɔmɑ̃s] *f* ballad

romanche [rɔmɑ̃ʃ] *m* Romansh

roman·cier [rɔmɑ̃sje] **-cière** [sjer] *mf* novelist; **romancier d'anticipation** science-fiction writer

ro·mand [rɔmɑ̃] **-mande** [mɑ̃d] *adj* French-speaking (*Switzerland*)

romanesque [rɔmanesk] *adj* romanesque, romantic, fabulous

roman-feuilleton [rɔmɑ̃fœjtɔ̃] *m* (pl **romans-feuilletons**) newspaper serial

roman-fleuve [rɔmɑ̃flœv] *m* (pl **romans-fleuves**) saga novel

romani·chel **-chelle** [rɔmaniʃɛl] *mf* gypsy, vagrant

romantique [rɔmɑ̃tik] *adj & mf* romantic

romantisme [rɔmɑ̃tism] *m* romanticism

romarin [rɔmarɛ̃] *m* (bot) rosemary

Rome [rɔm] *f* Rome

rompre [rɔ̃pr] (3d *sg pres ind* **rompt** [rɔ̃]) *tr* to break; to burst; to break in, train; to break off || *intr & ref* to break

romsteck [rɔmstɛk] *m* rump steak

ronce [rɔ̃s] *f* bramble; curly grain (*of wood*); **en ronces artificielles** barbed-wire (*fence*)

ronchonner [rɔ̃ʃɔne] *intr* (coll) to bellyache, grumble

rond [rɔ̃] **ronde** [rɔ̃d] *adj* round; rounded; plump; straightforward; (slang) tight, drunk || *m* ring, circle; round slice; (coll) dough, money; **en rond** in a circle; **rond de fumée** smoke ring; **rond de serviette** napkin ring || *f* round; beat, round; round dance; radius; round hand; (mus) whole note; **à la ronde** around; **s'amuser à la ronde, faire la ronde** to go ring-around-a-rosy || **rond** *adv* —**tourner rond** to work or go smoothly

rond-de-cuir [rɔ̃dkɥir] *m* (pl **ronds-de-cuir**) leather seat; (pej) bureaucrat

ron·deau [rɔ̃do] *m* (pl **-deaux**) rondeau; field roller

ronde·let [rɔ̃dlɛ] **-lette** [lɛt] *adj* plump; tidy (*sum*)

rondelle [rɔ̃dɛl] *f* disk; slice; washer (*of faucet, bolt, etc.*)

rondement [rɔ̃dmɑ̃] *adv* briskly; **mener rondement** to make short work of; **parler rondement** to be blunt

rondeur [rɔ̃dœr] *f* roundness; plumpness; frankness

rond-point [rɔ̃pwɛ̃] *m* (pl **ronds-points**) intersection, crossroads; traffic circle; circus, roundabout (Brit)

ronéo [rɔneo] *f* Mimeograph machine

ronéotyper [rɔneotipe] *tr* to mimeograph

ron·flant [rɔ̃flɑ̃] **-flante** [flɑ̃t] *adj* snoring; roaring; whirring, humming; (pej) high-sounding, pretentious

ronflement [rɔ̃fləmɑ̃] *m* snore; roar; whirr, hum

ronfler [rɔ̃fle] *intr* to snore; to roar; to whirr, to hum

ron·fleur [rɔ̃flœr] **-fleuse** [fløz] *mf* snorer || *m* vibrator (*replacing bell*)

ronger [rɔ̃ʒe] §38 *tr* to gnaw, nibble; to eat away; to bite (*one's nails*); to corrode; to torment || *ref* to be worn away; to be eaten away; to eat one's heart out, to fret

ron·geur [rɔ̃ʒœr] **-geuse** [ʒøz] *adj* gnawing || *m* rodent

ronron [rɔ̃rɔ̃] *m* purr; drone

ronronnement [rɔ̃rɔnmɑ̃] *m* purring

ronronner [rɔ̃rɔne] *intr* to purr

roquer [rɔke] *intr* (chess) to castle

roquet [rɔkɛ] *m* cur, yapper; (*breed of dog*) pug

roquette [rɔkɛt] *f* (plant; missile) rocket

rosace [rɔzas] *f* rose window; (archit) rosette

rosa·cé -cée [rɔzase] *adj* roselike || *f* skin eruption

rosaire [rɔzer] *m* rosary

rosâtre [rozɑtr] *adj* dusty-pink

rosbif [rɔsbif] *m* roast beef

rose [roz] *adj & m* rose, pink (*color*) || *f* rose; rose window; **dire la rose** to box the compass; **rose des vents** compass card; **rose d'Inde** (*Tagetes*) marigold

ro·sé -sée [roze] *adj* rose, rose-colored || *m* rosé wine || *f* see **rosée**

ro·seau [rozo] *m* (*pl* -seaux) reed
rosée [roze] *f* dew
roséole [rozeɔl] *f* rash; rose rash
roseraie [rozre] *f* rose garden
rosette [rozet] *f* bowknot; rosette; red ink; red chalk
rosier [rozje] *m* rosebush; **rosier églantier** sweetbrier
rosse [rɔs] *adj* nasty, mean; strict, stern; cynical || *f* (coll) beast, stinker; (coll) nag; **sale rosse** (coll) dirty bitch
rossée [rɔse] *f* (coll) thrashing
rosser [rɔse] *tr* to beat up, thrash; (coll) to beat, to best
rossignol [rɔsiɲɔl] *m* skeleton key; (orn) nightingale; (coll) piece of junk, drug on the market
rot [ro] *m* (slang) burp, belch
rota·tif [rɔtatif] -**tive** [tiv] *adj* rotary || *f* rotary press
rotation [rɔtasjɔ̃] *f* rotation; turnover (*of merchandise*)
rotatoire [rɔtatwar] *adj* rotary
roter [rɔte] *intr* (slang) to burp
rô·ti -**tie** [roti] *adj* roasted || *m* roast || *f* piece of toast; **rôtie à l'anglaise** Welsh rarebit
rotin [rɔtɛ̃] *m* rattan; de or en rotin cane (*chair*); **pas un rotin** not a penny!
rôtir [rotir] *tr, intr, & ref* to roast; to toast; to scorch
rôtisserie [rotisri] *f* rotisserie shop (*where roasted fowl is sold*); grill-room (*restaurant*)
rôtissoire [rotiswar] *f* rotisserie
rotonde [rɔtɔ̃d] *f* rotunda; (rr) round-house
rotor [rɔtɔr] *m* rotor
rotule [rɔtyl] *f* kneecap
roture [rɔtyr] *f* common people
rotu·rier [rɔtyrje] -**rière** [rjer] *adj* plebeian, of the common people || *mf* commoner
rouage [rwaʒ] *m* cog; **rouages** movement (*of a watch*)
rou·blard [rublar] -**blarde** [blard] *adj* (coll) wily || *mf* (coll) schemer
roublardise [rublardiz] *f* (coll) cunning
roucoulement [rukulmɑ̃] *m* cooing; billing and cooing
roucouler [rukule] *tr & intr* to coo
roue [ru] *f* wheel; **faire la roue** to turn cartwheels; to strut; **roue de secours** spare wheel (*with tire*)
roué rouée [rwe] *adj* slick; knocked out || *mf* slicker || *m* rake
rouelle [rwel] *f* fillet (*of veal*)
rouer [rwe] *tr* to break upon the wheel; **rouer de coups** to thrash, beat up
rouerie [ruri] *f* trickery; trick
rouet [rwe] *m* spinning wheel
rouge [ruʒ] *adj* red || *m* red; rouge; blush; **porter au rouge** to heat red-hot; **rouge à lèvres** lipstick || *adv* red
rou·geaud [ruʒo] -**geaude** [ʒod] *adj* ruddy || *mf* ruddy-faced person
rouge-gorge [ruʒgɔrʒ] *m* (*pl* **rouges-gorges**) robin (*Erithacus rubecula*)
rougeole [ruʒɔl] *f* measles

rougeur [ruʒœr] *f* redness; blush; **rougeurs** red spots
rougir [ruʒir] *tr* to redden || *intr* to turn red; to blush
rouille [ruj] *f* rust
rouil·lé -**lée** [ruje] *adj* rusty; (*out of practice; blighted*) rusty
rouiller [ruje] *tr, intr, & ref* to rust
roulade [rulad] *f* trill; (mus) run
rou·lant [rulɑ̃] -**lante** [lɑ̃t] *adj* rolling; (coll) funny
rou·leau [rulo] *m* (*pl* -leaux) roller; roll; spool; rolling pin; **rouleau compresseur** road roller
roulement [rulmɑ̃] *m* roll; rotation; rattle, clatter; exchange; **par roulement** in rotation; **roulement à billes** ball bearing
rouler [rule] *tr* to roll; (coll) to take in, cheat || *intr* to roll; to roll along; **rouler sur** to roll in (*wealth*); to turn on || *ref* to roll; to roll up; to toss and turn; (with *dat of reflex pron*) to twiddle (*one's thumbs*); **se les rouler** (coll) to not turn a hand
roule-ta-bille [rultabij] *m invar* (coll) rolling stone
roulette [rulet] *f* small wheel; castor; roulette; **aller comme sur des roulettes** to go well, to work smoothly
rou·leur [rulœr] -**leuse** [løz] *mf* drifter (*from one job to another*) || *m* freight handler || *f* streetwalker
roulis [ruli] *m* (naut) roll
roulotte [rulot] *f* trailer; gypsy wagon
rou·main [rumɛ̃] -**maine** [men] *adj* Rumanian || *m* Rumanian (*language*) || (*cap*) *mf* Rumanian (*person*)
roupiller [rupije] *intr* to take a snooze
rou·quin [rukɛ̃] -**quine** [kin] *adj* (coll) red-headed; || *mf* (coll) redhead || *m* (slang) red wine; **Rouquin** Red (*nickname*)
rouspéter [ruspete] §10 *intr* (coll) to bellyache, to kick
rouspé·teur [ruspetœr] -**teuse** [tøz] *mf* (coll) bellyacher, complainer
roussâtre [rusɑtr] *adj* auburn
rousse [rus] *f* redhead, auburn-haired woman; (slang) cops
rousseur [rusœr] *f* reddishness; freckle
roussir [rusir] *tr* to scorch; to singe || *intr* to become brown; **faire roussir** (culin) to brown
route [rut] *f* road; route, itinerary; **bonne route!** happy motoring!; **en route!** let's go!; **faire fausse route** to take the wrong road; (fig) to be on the wrong track; **mettre en route** to start; **route déformée** rough road; **route déviée** detour
rou·tier [rutje] -**tière** [tjer] *adj* road (*e.g., map*) || *m* trucker; bicycle racer; Explorer, Rover (*boy scout*); (naut) track chart; **vieux routier** veteran, old hand
routine [rutin] *f* routine
routi·nier [rutinje] -**nière** [njer] *adj* routine; one-track (*mind*)
rouvieux [ruvjø] *adj masc* mangy || *m* mange
rouvrir [ruvrir] §65 *tr & intr* to reopen
roux [ru] **rousse** [rus] *adj* russet, red-

dish; red, auburn (*hair*); browned (*butter*) ‖ *mf* redhead ‖ *m* russet, reddish brown, auburn (*color*); brown sauce ‖ *f* see **rousse**

royal royale [rwajal] *adj* (*pl* **royaux** [rwajo]) royal ‖ *f* imperial, goatee

royaliste [rwajalist] *adj & mf* royalist

royaume [rwajom] *m* kingdom

royauté [rwajote] *f* royalty

R.S.V.P. [eresvepe] *m* (letterword) (**répondez, s'il vous plaît**) R.S.V.P.

R.T.F. [erteef] *f* (letterword) (**radio-diffusion-télévision française**) French radio and television

ruade [ryad] *f* kick, buck

ruban [rybã] *m* ribbon; tape; **ruban adhésif** adhesive tape; **ruban adhésif transparent** transparent tape; **ruban de chapeau** hatband; **ruban de frein** brake lining; **ruban encreur** typewriter ribbon; **ruban magnétique** recording tape

rubéole [rybeɔl] *f* German measles

rubis [rybi] *m* ruby; jewel (*of watch*); **payer rubis sur l'ongle** to pay down on the nail

rubrique [rybrik] *f* rubric; caption, heading; label (*in a dictionary*)

ruche [ryʃ] *f* beehive

rude [ryd] *adj* rude, rough; rugged; hard; steep; (*coll*) amazing

rudement [rydmã] *adv* roughly; (*coll*) awfully, mighty

rudesse [rydes] *f* rudeness, roughness; harshness

rudiment [rydimã] *m* rudiment

rudoyer [rydwaje] §47 *tr* to bully, browbeat; to abuse, treat roughly

rue [ry] *f* street; **rue barrée** (public sign) no thoroughfare; (public sign) closed for repairs; **rue sans issue** (public sign) no outlet

ruée [rɥe] *f* rush; **ruée vers l'or** gold rush

ruelle [rɥel] *f* alley, lane; space between bed and wall

ruer [rɥe] *intr* to kick, to buck; **ruer dans les brancards** to kick over the traces ‖ *ref*—**se ruer sur** to rush at

rugir [ryʒir] *intr* to roar, bellow

rugissement [ryʒismã] *m* roar

ru·gueux [rygø] **-gueuse** [gøz] *adj* rough, rugged

ruine [rɥin] *f* ruin

ruiner [rɥine] *tr* to ruin

ruis·seau [rɥiso] *m* (*pl* **-seaux**) stream, brook; (fig) gutter

ruisseler [rɥisle] §34 *intr* to stream; to drip, to trickle

ruisselet [rɥisle] *m* little stream

ruissellement [rɥiselmã] *m* streaming; (*e.g., of light*) flood

rumeur [rymœr] *f* rumor; hum (*e.g., of voices*); roar (*of the sea*); **rumeur publique** public opinion

ru·pin [rypɛ̃] **-pine** [pin] *adj* (slang) rich ‖ *mf* (slang) swell

rupiner [rypine] *tr & intr* (coll) to do well

rupteur [ryptœr] *m* (elec) contact breaker

rupture [ryptyr] *f* rupture; breach; break; breaking off

ru·ral -rale [ryral] (*pl* **-raux** [ro]) *adj* rural ‖ *mf* farmer; **ruraux** country people

ruse [ryz] *f* ruse

ru·sé -sée [ryze] *adj* cunning, crafty ‖ *mf* sly one

russe [rys] *adj* Russian ‖ *m* Russian (*language*) ‖ (*cap*) *mf* Russian (*person*)

Russie [rysi] *f* Russia; **la Russie** Russia

rus·taud [rysto] **-taude** [tod] *adj* rustic, clumsy ‖ *mf* bumpkin

rustique [rystik] *adj* rustic; hardy

rustre [rystr] *adj* oafish ‖ *m* bumpkin, oaf; (obs) peasant

rut [ryt] *m* (zool) rut

ruti·lant -lante [lãt] *adj* bright-red; gleaming

rutiler [rytile] *intr* to gleam, to glow

rythme [ritm] *m* rhythm; rate (*of production*)

ryth·mé -mée [ritme] *adj* rhythmic(al); cadenced

rythmer [ritme] *tr* to cadence; to mark with a rhythm

rythmique [ritmik] *adj* rhythmic(al)

S

S, s [es], *[es] *m invar* nineteenth letter of the French alphabet

S. *abbr* (**saint**) St.

sa [sa] §88

S.A. [esa] *f* (letterword) (**Société anonyme**) Inc.

sabbat [saba] *m* Sabbath; witches' Sabbath; racket, uproarious gaiety; **sabbat des chats** caterwauling

sabir [sabir] *m* pidgin

sable [sabl] *m* sand; sable; **sable mouvant** quicksand

sabler [sable] *tr* to sandblast; to drink in one gulp; to toss off (*some champagne*)

sa·bleux [sablø] **-bleuse** [bløz] *adj* sandy ‖ *f* sandblast; sandblaster

sablier [sablije] *m* hourglass; (*for drying ink*) sandbox; dealer in sand

sablière [sablijer] *f* sandpit; wall plate; (rr) sandbox

sablon·neux [sablɔnø] **sablon·neuse** [sablɔnøz] *adj* sandy

sablonnière [sablɔnjer] *f* sandpit

sabord [sabɔr] *m* porthole

saborder [sabɔrde] *tr* to scuttle

sabot [sabɔ] *m* wooden shoe; hoof; whipping top; bungled work; ferrule; caster cup; **dormir comme un sabot** to sleep like a top; **sabot de frein** brake shoe; **sabot d'enrayage** wedge, block, scotch

sabotage [sabɔtaʒ] *m* sabotage

saboter [sabɔte] *tr* to sabotage; to bungle ‖ *intr* (coll) to make one's wooden shoes clatter

sabo·teur [sabɔtœr] **-teuse** [tøz] *mf* saboteur; bungler

sabo·tier [sabɔtje] **-tière** [tjɛr] *mf* maker and seller of wooden shoes ‖ *f* clog dance

sabre [sɑbr] *m* saber

sabrer [sɑbre] *tr* to saber; (coll) to botch; (coll) to cut, condense

sac [sak] *m* sack, bag; **être un sac d'os** [dos] to be nothing but skin and bones; **sac à main** handbag; **sac à malice** bag of tricks; **sac à provisions** shopping bag; **sac de couchage** sleeping bag

saccade [sakad] *f* jerk

sacca·dé -dée [sakade] *adj* jerky

saccager [sakaʒe] §38 *tr* to sack; (coll) to upset, to turn topsy-turvy

saccha·rin [sakarɛ̃] **-rine** [rin] *adj* saccharine ‖ *f* saccharin

saccharose [sakaroz] *m* sucrose

sacerdoce [saserdɔs] *m* priesthood

sacerdo·tal -tale [saserdɔtal] *adj* (*pl* **-taux** [to]) sacerdotal, priestly

sachet [saʃe] *m* sachet; packet (*of needles, medicine, etc.*); powder charge

sacoche [sakɔʃ] *f* satchel

sacramen·tel -telle [sakramɑ̃tɛl] *adj* sacramental

sacre [sakr] *m* crowning, consecration

sa·cré -crée [sakre] *adj* sacred; (anat) sacral ‖ (when standing before noun) *adj* (coll) darned, blasted

sacrement [sakrəmɑ̃] *m* sacrament

sacrer [sakre] *tr* to crown, to consecrate ‖ *intr* to curse

sacrifice [sakrifis] *m* sacrifice

sacrifier [sakrifje] *tr* to sacrifice

sacrilège [sakrilɛʒ] *adj* sacrilegious ‖ *mf* sacrilegious person ‖ *m* sacrilege

sacristain [sakristɛ̃] *m* sexton

sadique [sadik] *adj* sadistic ‖ *mf* sadist

safran [safrɑ̃] *m* saffron

sagace [sagas] *adj* sagacious, shrewd

sage [saʒ] *adj* wise; well-behaved; modest (*woman*); good (*child*); **soyez sage!** be good! ‖ *mf* sage

sage-femme [saʒfam] *f* (*pl* **sages-femmes**) midwife

sagesse [saʒɛs] *f* wisdom; good behavior

sai·gnant [seɲɑ̃] **-gnante** [ɲɑ̃t] *adj* bleeding; (*wound*) fresh; (*meat*) rare

saignée [seɲe] *f* bloodletting; bend of the arm, small of the arm; (fig) drain on the purse

saignement [seɲmɑ̃] *m* bleeding; **saignement de nez** nosebleed

saigner [seɲe], [seɲe] *tr & intr* to bleed; **saigner à blanc, saigner aux quatre veines** to bleed white

sail·lant [sajɑ̃] **sail·lante** [sajɑ̃t] *adj* prominent, salient; projecting; high (*cheekbones*)

saillie [saji] *f* projection; spurt; sally, outburst; **faire saillie** to jut out, project

saillir [sajir] (used only in *inf, ger,* & 3d *sg* & *pl*) *tr* (agr) to cover ‖ §69 *intr* to protrude, to project; to spurt

sain [sɛ̃] **saine** [sɛn] *adj* healthy; **sain d'esprit** sane; **sain et sauf** safe and sound

saindoux [sɛ̃du] *m* lard

sainement [sɛnmɑ̃] *adv* soundly

saint [sɛ̃] **sainte** [sɛ̃t] *adj* saintly; sacred, holy ‖ *mf* saint

sainteté [sɛ̃təte] *f* holiness

saisie [sezi] *f* seizure; foreclosure

saisie-arrêt [seziarɛ] *f* (*pl* **-arrêts**) attachment, garnishment

saisir [sezir] *tr* to seize; to sear (*meat*); to grasp (*to understand*); to strike, startle; to overcome; **saisir un tribunal de** to lay before a court ‖ *ref* **—se saisir de** to take possession of

saisissement [sezismɑ̃] *m* chill; shock

saison [sɛzɔ̃] *f* season

salace [salas] *adj* salacious

salade [salad] *f* salad; (fig) mess; **salade russe** mixed vegetable salad with mayonnaise

saladier [saladje] *m* salad bowl

salaire [salɛr] *m* salary, wage; recompense, punishment

salariat [salarja] *m* salaried workers, employees; salary (*fixed wage*)

sala·rié -riée [salarje] *adj* salaried, hired ‖ *mf* wage earner; employee

sa·laud [salo] **-laude** [lod] *adj* (coll) slovenly ‖ *mf* (slang) skunk, scoundrel

sale [sal] *adj* dirty; dull (*color*) ‖ *mf* dirty person

sa·lé -lée [sale] *adj* salty, salted; dirty (*joke*); padded (*bill*); (slang) exaggerated ‖ *m* salt pork

saler [sale] *tr* to salt

saleté [salte] *f* dirtiness; piece of dirt; (slang) dirty trick; (slang) dirt

salière [saljɛr] *f* saltcellar

salir [salir] *tr & ref* to soil

salive [saliv] *f* saliva

salle [sal] *f* room; hall; auditorium; ward (*in a hospital*); (theat) audience, house; **salle à manger** dining room; **salle d'armes** fencing room; **salle d'attente** waiting room; **salle de bains** bathroom; **salle d'écoute** language laboratory; **salle de police** guardhouse; **salle des accouchées** maternity ward; **salle de séjour** living room; **salle des machines** engine room; **salle des pas perdus** lobby, waiting room; **salle de rédaction** city room; **salle de spectacle** movie house; **salle des ventes** salesroom, showroom; **salle de travail** delivery room; **salle d'exposition** showroom

salon [salɔ̃] *m* living room, parlor; exposition; salon (*ship's lounge*); **salon de beauté** beauty parlor; **salon de l'automobile** automobile show; **salon de thé** tearoom

salon·nard [salɔnar] **salon·narde** [salɔnard] *mf* sycophant
saloperie [salɔpri] *f* (slang) trash
salopette [salɔpɛt] *f* coveralls, overalls; bib; smock
salpêtre [salpetr] *m* saltpeter
salsepareille [salsəparej] *f* sarsaparilla
saltimbanque [saltɛ̃bɑ̃k] *mf* tumbler; mountebank, charlatan
salubre [salybr] *adj* salubrious, healthful
saluer [salɥe] *tr* to salute; to greet, to bow to, to wave to
salut [saly] *m* health; safety; salvation; salute; greeting, bow; nod; **salut!** (coll) hi!, howdy!; **salut les gars!**, **salut les copains!** hi, fellows!
salutation [salytɑsjɔ̃] *f* greeting; **salutations distinguées**, or **sincères salutations** (complimentary close) yours truly
salve [salv] *f* salvo, salute
samari·tain [samaritɛ̃] **-taine** [tɛn] *adj* Samaritan ‖ (*cap*) *mf* Samaritan
samedi [samdi] *m* Saturday
sanatorium [sanatɔrjɔm] *m* sanitarium
sanctifier [sɑ̃ktifje] *tr* to sanctify
sanction [sɑ̃ksjɔ̃] *f* sanction; penalty
sanctionner [sɑ̃ksjɔne] *tr* to sanction; to penalize
sanctuaire [sɑ̃ktɥer] *m* sanctuary
sandale [sɑ̃dal] *f* sandal; gym shoe
sandwich [sɑ̃dwitʃ], [sɑ̃dwiʃ] *m* (*pl* **sandwiches, sandwichs**) sandwich
sang [sɑ̃] *m* blood; **avoir le sang chaud** (coll) to be a go-getter; **bon sang!** (coll) darn it all!; **sang et tripes** blood and guts; **se faire du mauvais sang** to get all stewed up
sang-froid [sɑ̃frwa], [sɑ̃frwɑ] *m* self-control
san·glant [sɑ̃glɑ̃] **-glante** [glɑ̃t] *adj* bloody; cruel
sangle [sɑ̃gl] *f* cinch
sanglier [sɑ̃glije] *m* wild boar
sanglot [sɑ̃glo] *m* sob
sangloter [sɑ̃glɔte] *intr* to sob
sang-mêlé [sɑ̃mele] *m invar* half-breed
sangsue [sɑ̃sy] *f* bloodsucker, leech
san·guin [sɑ̃gɛ̃] **-guine** [gin] *adj* sanguine ‖ *f* (fa) sanguine
sanitaire [saniter] *adj* sanitary; hospital, e.g., **avion sanitaire** hospital plane
sans [sɑ̃] *adv*—**sans que** without; **sans quoi** or else ‖ *prep* without; **sans cesse** ceaselessly; **sans façon** informally; **sans fil** wireless
sans-abri [sɑ̃zabri] *mf invar* homeless person
sans-cœur [sɑ̃kœr] *mf invar* heartless person
sans-filiste [sɑ̃filist] *mf* (*pl* **-filistes**) radio operator; radio amateur
sans-gêne [sɑ̃ʒɛn] *adj invar* offhanded ‖ *mf invar* offhanded person ‖ *m* offhandedness
sansonnet [sɑ̃sɔne] *m* starling; blackbird
sans-travail [sɑ̃travaj] *mf invar* unemployed worker
san·tal [sɑ̃tal] *m* (*pl* **-taux** [to]) (bot) sandalwood

santé [sɑ̃te] *f* health; sanity; **santé publique** public health service
sape [sap] *f* sap (*undermining*)
saper [sape] *tr* to sap, to undermine
sapeur [sapœr] *m* (mil) sapper; **fumer comme un sapeur** (coll) to smoke like a chimney
sapeur-pompier [sapœrpɔ̃pje] *m* (*pl* **sapeurs-pompiers**) fireman; **sapeurs-pompiers** fire department
saphir [safir] *m* sapphire; sapphire needle
sapin [sapɛ̃] *m* fir
sapristi [sapristi] *interj* hang it!
saquer [sake] *tr* (slang) to fire, to sack
sarbacane [sarbakan] *f* blowgun
sarcasme [sarkasm] *m* sarcasm
sarcler [sarkle] *tr* to weed, root out
sarcloir [sarklwar] *m* hoe
Sardaigne [sardɛn] *f* Sardinia; **la Sardaigne** Sardinia
sarde [sard] *adj* Sardinian ‖ *m* Sardinian (*language*) ‖ (*cap*) *mf* Sardinian (*person*)
sardine [sardin] *f* sardine
S.A.R.L. *abbr* (**Société à responsabilité limitée**) corporation
sarment [sarmɑ̃] *m* vine; vine shoot
sarra·sin [sarazɛ̃] **-sine** [zin] *adj* Saracen ‖ *m* buckwheat ‖ *f* portcullis ‖ (*cap*) *mf* Saracen
sar·rau [saro] *m* (*pl* **-raus**) smock
sarriette [sarjet] *f* (bot) savory
sas [sɑ], [sɑs] *m* sieve; lock (*of canal, submarine, etc.*); air lock (*of caisson, spaceship, etc.*); **sas d'évacuation** (aer) escape hatch
sasser [sase] *tr* to sift, screen; to pass through a lock
satelliser [satelize] *tr* to make a satellite of; (rok) to put into orbit
satellite [satelit] *adj & m* satellite
satin [satɛ̃] *m* satin
satinette [satinet] *f* sateen
satire [satir] *f* satire
satirique [satirik] *adj* satiric(al)
satiriser [satirize] *tr* to satirize
satisfaction [satisfaksjɔ̃] *f* satisfaction
satisfaire [satisfer] §29 *tr* to satisfy ‖ *intr* to satisfy; (with *dat*) to fulfill; (with *dat*) to meet (*a need*) ‖ *ref* to be satisfied
satisfai·sant [satisfəzɑ̃] **-sante** [zɑ̃t] *adj* satisfactory; satisfying
saturer [satyre] *tr* to saturate
Saturne [satyrn] *m* Saturn
saturnisme [satyrnism] *m* lead poisoning
sauce [sos] *f* sauce; gravy; drawing pencil; (tech) solution
saucer [sose] §51 *tr* to dip in sauce or gravy; (coll) to soak to the skin; (coll) to reprimand severely
saucière [sosjer] *f* gravy bowl
saucisse [sosis] *f* sausage; frankfurter
saucisson [sosisɔ̃] *m* bologna, sausage
sauf [sof] **sauve** [sov] *adj* safe ‖ **sauf** *prep* save, except; barring; subject to (*e.g., correction*)
sauf-conduit [sofkɔ̃dɥi] *m* (*pl* **-conduits**) safe-conduct
sauge [soʒ] *f* (bot) sage, salvia

saugre·nu -nue [sogrəny] *adj* absurd, silly

saule [sol] *m* willow

saumâtre [somɑtr] *adj* brackish

saumon [som5] *m* salmon; pig (*of crude metal*)

saumure [somyr] *f* brine

sauner [sone] *intr* to make salt

saupoudrer [sopudre] *tr* to sprinkle (*with powder, sugar; citations*)

saurer [sɔre] *tr* to kipper

saut [so] *m* leap, jump; falls, waterfall; **au saut du lit** on getting out of bed; **faire le saut** to take the fatal step; **faire un saut chez** to drop in on; **par sauts et par bonds** by fits and starts; **saut à la perche** pole vault; **saut de carpe** jackknife; **saut de l'ange** swan dive; **saut en chute libre** skydiving; **saut périlleux** somersault

saut-de-lit [sodli] *m invar* wrap

saut-de-mouton [sodmut5] *m* (*pl* **sauts-de-mouton**) cloverleaf (*intersection*)

saute [sot] *f* change in direction, shift

saute-mouton [sotmut5] *m* leapfrog

sauter [sote] *tr* to leap over; to skip || *intr* to leap, jump; to blow up; **faire sauter** to sauté; to flip (*a pancake*); to fire (*an employee*) || *m* **à cloche-pied** to hop on one foot; **sauter à pieds joints** to do a standing jump; **sauter aux nues** to get mad

sauterelle [sotrɛl] *f* grasshopper

sauterie [sotri] *f* (coll) hop (*dancing party*)

sau·teur [sotœr] **-teuse** [tøz] *adj* jumping || *mf* jumper || *m* jumper, jumping horse || *f* frying pan

sautiller [sotije] *intr* to hop

sautoir [sotwar] *m* St. Andrew's cross; **en sautoir** crossways

sauvage [sovaʒ] *adj* savage; wild; shy || *mf* savage

sauvagerie [sovaʒri] *f* savagery; wildness; shyness

sauvegarde [sovgard] *f* safeguard

sauvegarder [sovgarde] *tr* to safeguard

sauve-qui-peut [sovkipø] *m invar* panic, stampede, rout

sauver [sove] *tr* to save; to rescue || *intr*—**sauve qui peut!** every man for himself! || *ref* to run away; to escape; (theat) to exit; **sauve-toi!** (coll) scram!

sauvetage [sovtaʒ] *m* salvage; lifesaving, rescue

sauveteur [sovtœr] *adj masc* lifesaving || *m* lifesaver

sau·veur [sovœr] *adj masc* Saviour || *m* savior; **Le Sauveur** the Saviour

savamment [savamã] *adv* knowingly; skillfully

savane [savan] *f* prairie, savanna

sa·vant [savã] **-vante** [vãt] *adj* scholarly, learned || *mf* scientist, scholar, savant; **savant atomiste** nuclear physicist

savate [savat] *f* old slipper; foot boxing; (coll) butterfingers; **traîner la savate** to be down at the heel

saveur [savœr] *f* savor, taste

savoir [savwar] *m* learning || §62 *tr & intr* to know; to know how to; **à**

savoir namely, to wit; **à savoir que** with the understanding that; **en savoir long** to know all about it; **pas que je sache** not that I know of

savoir-faire [savwarfer] *m invar* knowhow

savon [sav5] *m* soap; (slang) sharp reprimand; **savon en paillettes** soap flakes

savonnage [savonaʒ] *m* soaping

savonner [savone] *tr* to soap

savonnerie [savonri] *f* soap factory

savonnette [savonɛt] *f* toilet soap

savon·neux [savonø] **savon·neuse** [savonøz] *adj* soapy

savourer [savure] *tr* to savor

savou·reux [savurø] **-reuse** [røz] *adj* savory, tasty

saxon [saks5] **saxonne** [saksɔn] *adj* Saxon || *m* Saxon (*language*) || (*cap*) *mf* Saxon (*person*)

saxophone [saksofɔn] *m* saxophone

saynète [senɛt] *f* sketch, playlet

sca·bieux [skabjø] **-bieuse** [bjøz] *adj* scabby || *f* scabious

sca·breux [skɑbrø] **-breuse** [brøz] *adj* rough (*road*); risky (*business*); scabrous (*remark*)

scalpel [skalpɛl] *m* scalpel

scalper [skalpe] *tr* to scalp

scandale [skɑdal] *m* scandal; disturbance

scanda·leux [skɑdalø] **-leuse** [løz] *adj* scandalous

scandaliser [skɑdalize] *tr* to lead astray; to scandalize || *ref* to take offense

scander [skɑde] *tr* to scan (*verses*)

scandinave [skɑdinav] *adj* Scandinavian || *m* Scandinavian (*language*) || (*cap*) *mf* Scandinavian (*person*); **Scandinaves** Scandinavian countries

scaphandre [skafɑdr] *m* diving suit; spacesuit; **scaphandre autonome** aqualung

scaphandrier [skafɑdrije] *m* diver

scarlatine [skarlatin] *f* scarlet fever

scarole [skarɔl] *f* escarole

sceau [so] *m* (*pl* **sceaux**) seal

scélé·rat [selera] **-rate** [rat] *adj* villainous || *mf* villain

scellé [sele] *m* seal

sceller [sele] *tr* to seal

scénario [senarjo] *m* scenario

scène [sen] *f* scene; stage; theater

scénique [senik] *adj* scenic

scepticisme [septisism] *m* skepticism

sceptique [septik] *adj & mf* skeptic

sceptre [septr] *m* scepter

schah [ʃa] *m* shah

schelem [ʃlem] *m* slam (*at bridge*)

schéma [ʃema] *m* diagram

schisme [ʃism] *m* schism

schizophrène [skizofren] *adj & mf* schizophrenic

schlague [ʃlag] *f* flogging

schooner [skunœr], [ʃunœr] *m* schooner

sciatique [sjatik] *adj* sciatic || *f* (pathol) sciatica

scie [si] *f* saw; (coll) bore, nuisance; **scie à découper** jig saw

sciemment [sjamã] *adv* knowingly

science [sjɑ̃s] *f* science; learning, knowledge

science-fiction [sjɑ̃sfiksjɔ̃] *f* science fiction

scientifique [sjɑ̃tifik] *adj* scientific || *mf* scientist

scier [sje] *tr* to saw; (coll) to bore || *intr* (naut) to row backwards

scierie [siri] *f* sawmill

scieur [sjœr] *m* sawyer

scinder [sɛ̃de] *tr* to divide || *ref* to be divided

scintil·lant [sɛ̃tijɑ̃] **scintil·lante** [sɛ̃tijɑ̃t] *adj* scintillating; twinkling

scintillation [sɛ̃tijɑsjɔ̃] *f* twinkling, twinkle; (phys) scintillation

scintillement [sɛ̃tijmɑ̃] *m* twinkling

scintiller [sɛ̃tije] *intr* to scintillate; to twinkle

scion [sjɔ̃] *m* scion; tip (*of fishing rod*)

scission [sisjɔ̃] *f* schism; (biol & phys) fission

sciure [sjyr] *f* sawdust

sclérose [skleroz] *f* sclerosis

scolaire [skɔler] *adj* school

scolastique [skɔlastik] *adj & m* scholastic || *f* scholasticism

sconse [skɔ̃s] *m* skunk fur; skunk

scories [skɔri] *fpl* slag, dross

scorpion [skɔrpjɔ̃] *m* scorpion

scout scoute [skut] *adj & m* scout

scoutisme [skutism] *m* scouting

scribe [skrib] *m* scribe

script [skript] *m* scrip; (typ) script

scripturaire [skriptyrer] *adj* Scriptural || *m* fundamentalist

scrofule [skrɔfyl] *f* scrofula

scrotum [skrɔtɔm] *m* scrotum

scrupule [skrypyl] *m* scruple

scrupu·leux [skrypylø] **-leuse** [løz] *adj* scrupulous

scruter [skryte] *tr* to scrutinize

scrutin [skrytɛ̃] *m* ballot; balloting, voting, poll; **dépouiller le scrutin** to count the votes; **scrutin de ballottage** runoff election

scrutiner [skrytine] *intr* to ballot

sculpter [skylte] *tr* to sculpture; to carve (*wood*)

sculpteur [skyltœr] *m* sculptor

sculpture [skyltyr] *f* sculpture

s.d. *abbr* (**sans date**) n.d.

S.D.N. [esdeen] *f* (letterword) (**Société des Nations**) League of Nations

se [sə] §87

séance [seɑ̃s] *f* session, sitting, seat (*in an assembly*); performance, showing; séance; **séance tenante** on the spot

séant [seɑ̃] **séante** [seɑ̃t] *adj* fitting, decent; sitting (*as a king or a court in session*) || *m* buttocks, bottom; **se mettre sur son séant** to sit up (*in bed*)

seau [so] *m* (*pl* **seaux**) bucket, pail; **il pleut à seaux** it's raining cats and dogs; **seau à charbon** coal scuttle

sébile [sebil] *f* wooden bowl

sec [sek] **sèche** [sɛʃ] *adj* dry; sharp; rude; unguarded (*card*); total (*loss*); **en cinq sec** in a jiffy; **sec comme un hareng** (coll) long and thin; **tout sec** and nothing more || *f* dryness; **à sec** dry; (coll) broke || *f see* **sèche** || **sec** *adv*—**aussi sec** (slang) on the spot;

boire sec to drink one's liquor straight; **frapper sec** to land a hard fast punch; **parler sec** to talk tough

sécession [sesesjɔ̃] *f* secession

sèche [sɛʃ] *f* (slang) fag, cigarette

sèche-cheveux [sɛʃʃəvø] *m invar* hair drier

sécher [seʃe] §10 *tr* to dry; to season; to cut (*a class*) || *intr* to become dry

sécheresse [seʃres] *f* dryness; drought; baldness (*of style*); curtness; (fig) coldness

séchoir [seʃwar] *m* drier; drying room; clotheshorse

se·cond [səgɔ̃] **-conde** [gɔ̃d] *adj & pron* second; **en second** next in rank || *m* second || *f see* **seconde**

secondaire [səgɔ̃der] *adj & m* secondary

seconde [səgɔ̃d] *f* second (*in time*; *musical interval*; *of angle*); second class

seconder [səgɔ̃de] *tr* to help, second

secouer [səkwe] *tr* to shake; to shake off or down || *ref* to pull oneself together

secourable [səkurabl] *adj* helpful

secourir [səkurir] §14 *tr* to help, aid

secourisme [səkurism] *m* first aid

secouriste [səkurist] *mf* first-aider; first-aid worker

secours [səkur] *m* help, aid; **au secours!** help!; **de secours** emergency; spare (*tire*); **des secours** supplies, relief

secousse [səkus] *f* shake, jolt; (elec) shock

se·cret [səkre] **-crète** [kret] *adj* secret; secretive || *m* secret; secrecy; **au secret** in solitary confinement || *f see* **secrète**

secrétaire [səkreter] *mf* secretary || *m* secretary (*desk*)

secrète [səkret] *f* central intelligence

secréter [sekrete] §10 *tr* to secrete

sectaire [sekter] *adj & mf* sectarian

secte [sekt] *f* sect

secteur [sektœr] *m* sector; (elec) house current, local supply circuit; **secteur postal** postal zone; (mil) A.P.O. number

section [seksjɔ̃] *f* section; cross section

sectionner [seksjɔne] *tr* to section; to cut || *ref* to break apart

séculaire [sekyler] *adj* secular

sécu·lier [sekylje] **-lière** [ljer] *adj & m* secular

sécurité [sekyrite] *f* security

séda·tif [sedatif] **-tive** [tiv] *adj & m* sedative

sédation [sedasjɔ̃] *f* sedation

sédentaire [sedɑ̃ter] *adj* sedentary

sédiment [sedimɑ̃] *m* sediment

sédi·tieux [sedisjø] **-tieuse** [sjøz] *adj* seditious

sédition [sedisjɔ̃] *f* sedition

séduc·teur [sedyktœr] **-trice** [tris] *adj* seducing, bewitching || *mf* seducer || *f* vamp

séduction [sedyksjɔ̃] *f* seduction

séduire [sedɥir] §19 *tr* to seduce; to charm, to bewitch; to bribe

sédui·sant [sedɥizɑ̃] **-sante** [zɑ̃t] *adj* seductive, tempting

segment [sɛgmã] *m* segment; **segment de piston** piston ring

ségrégation [segregasjɔ̃] *f* segregation

ségrégationniste [segregasjɔnist] *adj* segregationist

seiche [sɛʃ] *f* cuttlefish

séide [seid] *m* henchman

seigle [sɛgl] *m* rye

seigneur [sɛɲœr] *m* lord

sein [sɛ̃] *m* breast; bosom; womb; **au sein de** in the heart of

seine [sɛn] *f* dragnet

seing [sɛ̃] *m* signature; **sous seing privé** privately witnessed

seize [sɛz] *adj & pron* sixteen; the Sixteenth, e.g., **Jean seize** John the Sixteenth || *m* sixteen; sixteenth (*in dates*)

seizième [sɛzjɛm] *adj, pron* (*masc, fem*), & *m* sixteenth

séjour [seʒur] *m* stay, visit

séjourner [seʒurne] *intr* to reside; to stay, to visit

sel [sɛl] *m* salt; **gros sel** coarse salt; (*fig*) dirty joke; **sel ammoniac** sal ammoniac; **sel gemme** rock salt

sélec•tif -tive [selɛktif] [tiv] *adj* selective

sélection [selɛksjɔ̃] *f* selection

sélectionner [selɛksjɔne] *tr* to select

self [sɛlf] *f* (elec) coil, spark coil

self-service [selfsɛrvis] *m* self-service

selle [sɛl] *f* saddle; seat (*of bicycle, motorcycle, etc.*); sculptor's tripod; stool, movement; (culin) saddle; **aller à la selle** to go to the toilet

seller [sele] *tr* to saddle

sellier [selje] *m* saddler

selon [səlɔ̃] *adv*—**c'est selon** that depends; **selon que** according as || *prep* according to; after (*e.g., my own heart*)

semailles [səmaj] *fpl* sowing, seeding

semaine [səmen] *f* week; week's wages; set of seven; **à la petite semaine** day-to-day, hand-to-mouth; short-sighted; **de semaine** on duty during the week; **la semaine des quatre jeudis** (coll) never; **semaine anglaise** five-day workweek

semai•nier [səmenje] **-nière** [njer] *mf* week worker || *m* highboy; office calendar

sémantique [semãtik] *adj* semantic || *f* semantics

sémaphore [semafɔr] *m* semaphore

semblable [sãblabl] *adj* similar, like || *m* fellow-man, equal

semblant [sãblã] *m* semblance, appearance; **faire semblant** to pretend

sembler [sãble] *intr* to seem; to seem to

semelle [səmel] *f* sole; foot (*of stocking*); tread (*of tire*); bed (*of concrete*)

semence [səmãs] *f* seed; semen; brad; **semence de perles** seed pearls

semer [səme] §2 *tr* to seed, to sow; to scatter, strew; to lay (*mines*); (slang) to outdistance; (slang) to drop (*an acquaintance*)

semestre [səmestr] *m* semester; six-month period

semes•triel -trielle [səmestrijel] *adj* six-month; semester

se•meur [səmœr] **-meuse** [møz] *mf* sower; spreader of gossip || *f* seeder, drill

semi-chenillé [səmi/nije] *m* half-track

semi-conduc•teur [səmikɔ̃dyktœr] **-trice** [tris] *adj* semiconductive || *m* semiconductor

semifi•ni -nie [səmifini] *adj* unfinished

sémil•lant [semijã] **sémil•lante** [semijãt] *adj* sprightly, lively

séminaire [seminer] *m* seminary; seminar; conference

semi-remorque [səmirəmɔrk] *f* (*pl* **-remorques**) semitrailer

semis [səmi] *m* sowing; seedling; seed-bed

sémite [semit] *adj* Semitic || (*cap*) *mf* Semite

sémitique [semitik] *adj* Semitic

semoir [səmwar] *m* seeder, drill

semonce [səmɔ̃s] *f* reprimand; (naut) order to heave to

semoncer [səmɔ̃se] §51 *tr* to reprimand; (naut) to order to heave to

semoule [səmul] *f* (culin) semolina

sénat [sena] *m* senate

sénateur [senatœr] *m* senator

sénile [senil] *adj* senile

sens [sãs] *m* sense, meaning; opinion; direction; **en sens inverse** in the opposite direction; **sens dessus dessous** [sãdəsydəsu] upside down; **sens devant derrière** [sãdəvãderjer] back to front; **sens interdit** (public sign) no entry; **sens obligatoire** (public sign) right way, this way; **sens unique** (public sign) one way

sensation [sãsasjɔ̃] *f* sensation

sensation•nel -nelle [sãsasjɔnel] *adj* sensational

sen•sé -sée [sãse] *adj* sensible

sensibiliser [sãsibilize] *tr* to sensitize

sensibilité [sãsibilite] *f* sensibility; sensitivity

sensible [sãsibl] *adj* sensitive; sensible; appreciable, perceptible

sensi•tif -tive [sãsitif] [tiv] *adj* sensory; sensitive, touchy

senso•riel -rielle [sãsɔrjel] *adj* sensory

sen•suel -suelle [sãsɥel] *adj* sensual

sent-bon [sãbɔ̃] *m invar* odor, perfume

sentence [sãtãs] *f* proverb; (law) sentence

senteur [sãtœr] *f* odor, perfume

sentier [sãtje] *m* path; **hors des sentiers battus** off the beaten track

sentiment [sãtimã] *m* sentiment, feeling

sentimen•tal -tale [sãtimãtal] *adj* (*pl* **-taux** [to]) sentimental

sentine [sãtin] *f* bilge

sentinelle [sãtinel] *f* sentinel

sentir [sãtir] §41 *tr* to feel; to smell; to smell like, smell of; to taste of; to have all the earmarks of; to show the effects of; **ne pas pouvoir sentir qn** to be unable to stand s.o. || *intr* to smell; to smell bad || *ref* to feel; to be felt; **se sentir de** to feel the effects of

seoir [swar] §5A (3d *pl pres ind* **siéent**;

used only in 3d *sg* & *pl* of most simple tenses) *intr* (with *dat*) to be suitable to, to become; to be fitting to, to be proper for ‖ (used only in *inf* and 2d *sg* & *pl* and 1st *pl impv*) *ref* (coll & poetic) to sit down, have a seat

séparation [separasjɔ̃] *f* separation

séparer [separe] *tr* & *ref* to separate, to divide

sept [set] *adj* & *pron* seven; the Seventh, e.g., **Jean sept** John the Seventh; **sept heures** seven o'clock ‖ *m* seven; seventh (*in dates*)

septembre [septãbr] *m* September

septième [setjem] *adj, pron* (*masc, fem*), & *m* seventh

septique [septik] *adj* septic

sépulcre [sepylkr] *m* sepulcher

sépulture [sepyltyr] *f* grave, tomb, burial place; burial

séquelle [sekel] *f* gang; (*pathol*) complications; **séquelles** aftermath

séquence [sekãs] *f* sequence; (*in poker*) straight

séquestrer [sekestre] *tr* to sequester

séraphin [serafɛ̃] *m* seraph; (coll) angel

serbe [serb] *adj* Serb ‖ (*cap*) *mf* Serb

se·rein [sərɛ̃] **-reine** [ren] *adj* serene ‖ *m* night dew

sérénade [serenad] *f* serenade

sérénité [serenite] *f* serenity

serf [ser], [serf] serve [serv] *mf* serf

serge [serʒ] *f* serge

sergent [serʒã] *m* sergeant

série [seri] *f* series, string, set; (elec) series; **de série** standard; stock (*car*); **en série in** (a) series; mass, e.g., **fabrication en série** mass production; **hors série** outsize (*wearing apparel*); discontinued (*as an item of manufacture*); custom-built; almost unheard of; **série noire** run of bad luck

sé·rieux [serjø] **-rieuse** [rjøz] *adj* serious

serin [sərɛ̃] *m* canary; (coll) simpleton

seringa [sərɛ̃ga] *m* mock orange

seringue [sərɛ̃g] *f* syringe; (hort) spray gun; **seringue à graisse** grease gun; **seringue à injections** hypodermic syringe; **seringue à instillations** nasal spray

serment [sermã] *m* oath; **prêter serment** to take oath

sermon [sermɔ̃] *m* sermon

sermonner [sermone] *tr* to sermonize

serpe [serp] *f* billhook

serpent [serpã] *m* snake, serpent; **serpent à sonnettes** rattlesnake; **serpent caché sous les fleurs** snake in the grass

serpenter [serpãte] *intr* to wind

serpen·tin [serpãtɛ̃] **-tine** [tin] *adj* serpentine ‖ *m* coil; worm (*of still*); paper streamer

serpillière [serpijer] *f* floorcloth; sacking, burlap

serpolet [serpole] *m* thyme

serre [ser] *f* greenhouse; **serres** claws, talons

ser·ré -rée [sere] *adj* tight; narrow; compact; close ‖ **serré** *adv*—**jouer serré** to play it close to the vest

serre-fils [serfil] *m invar* (elec) binding post

serre-freins [serfrɛ̃] *m invar* brakeman

serre-livres [serlivr] *m invar* book end

serrement [sermã] *m* squeezing, pressing; (min) partition (*to keep out water*); (pathol) pang; **serrement de cœur** heaviness of heart; **serrement de main** handshake

serrer [sere] *tr* to press; to squeeze; to wring; to tighten; to close up (*ranks*); to clasp, shake, e.g., **serrer la main à** to shake hands with; to grit (*one's teeth*); to put on (*the brakes*) ‖ *intr*—**serrez à droite** (public sign) squeeze to right ‖ *ref* to squeeze together, to be close together

serre-tête [sertet] *m invar* headband; kerchief; crash helmet; (telp) headset

serrure [seryr] *f* lock; **serrure de sûreté** safety lock

serrurier [seryrje] *m* locksmith

sertir [sertir] *tr* to set (*a stone*)

sérum [serom] *m* serum

servage [servaʒ] *m* serfdom

ser·veur [servœr] **-veuse** [vøz] *mf* (tennis) server ‖ *m* waiter; barman ‖ *f* waitress; barmaid; extra maid; (mach) coffee maker

serviable [servjabl] *adj* obliging

service [servis] *m* service; agency; **être de service** to be on duty; **service compris** tip included; **service de garde** twenty-four-hour service; **service des abonnés absents** telephone answering service; **service des renseignements téléphoniques** information; **service sanitaire** ambulance corps

serviette [servjet] *f* napkin; towel; brief case; **serviette de bain** bath towel; **serviette éponge** washcloth; Turkish towel; **serviette hygiénique** sanitary napkin

servile [servil] *adj* servile

servir [servir] §63 *tr* to serve; to deal (*cards*) ‖ *intr* to serve; **servir à** to be useful for, to serve as; **servir à qn de** to serve s.o. as; **servir de** to serve as, to function as ‖ *ref* to help oneself; **se servir chez** to patronize; **se servir de** to use

serviteur [servitœr] *m* servant

servitude [servityd] *f* servitude; (law) easement

servofrein [servofrɛ̃] *m* power brake

ses [se] §8

sésame [sezam] *m* sesame

session [sesjɔ̃] *f* session

seuil [sœj] *m* threshold

seul seule [sœl] *adj* alone; lonely ‖ (when standing before noun) *adj* sole, single, only ‖ *pron indef* single one, only one; single person, only person ‖ **seul** *adv* alone

seulement [sœlmã] *adv* only, even ‖ *conj* but

sève [sev] *f* sap; vim

sévère [sever] *adj* severe; stern; strict

sévices [sevis] *mpl* cruelty, brutality

sévir [sevir] *intr* to rage

sevrage [səvraʒ] *m* weaning

sevrer [səvre] §2 tr to wean

sexe [seks] m sex; le beau sexe the fair sex; le sexe fort the sterner sex

sextant [sekstã] m sextant

sextuor [sekstɥɔr] m (mus) sextet

sexuel sexuelle [seksɥel] adj sexual

seyant [sejã] seyante [sejãt] adj becoming

shampooing [ʃãpwɛ̃] m shampoo

shérif [ʃerif] m sheriff

short [ʃɔrt] m shorts

si [si] m invar if; des si et des car ifs and buts || adv so; as; (to contradict a negative statement or question) yes, e.g., Vous ne le saviez pas. Si! You didn't know. Yes, I did!; si bien que so that, with the result that; si peu que so little that; si peu que ce soit however little it may be; si + adj or adv + que + subj however + adj or adv + ind, e.g., si vite qu'il s'en aille however fast he goes away || conj if; whether; si . . . ne unless, e.g., si je ne me trompe unless I am mistaken; si ce n'est unless; si tant est que if it is true that

sia-mois [sjamwa] -moise [mwaz] adj Siamese || (cap) mf Siamese

sibé-rien [siberjɛ̃] -rienne [rjen] adj Siberian || (cap) mf Siberian

sibylle [sibil] f sibyl

Sicile [sisil] f Sicily; la Sicile Sicily

sici-lien [sisiljɛ̃] -lienne [ljen] adj Sicilian || (cap) mf Sicilian

sidé-ral -rale [sideral] adj (pl -raux [ro]) sidereal

sidérer [sidere] §10 tr (coll) to flabbergast

sidérurgie [sideryrʒi] f iron-and-steel industry

sidérurgique [sideryrʒik] adj iron-and-steel

siècle [sjekl] m century; age; (eccl) world

siège [sjeʒ] m seat; headquarters; (eccl) see; (mil) siege; siège à glissière glider; siège baquet (pl sièges baquets) bucket seat; siège éjectable ejection seat

siéger [sjeʒe] §1 intr to sit, to be in session; (said of malady) to be seated

sien [sjɛ̃] sienne [sjen] §89

sieste [sjest] f siesta; faire la sieste to take a siesta

sifflement [sifləmã] m whistle; hiss; swish, whiz

siffler [sifle] tr to whistle (e.g., a tune); to hiss, boo; to whistle to || intr to whistle; to hiss; to swish, to whiz

sifflet [sifle] m whistle

sif-fleur [siflœr] sif-fleuse [sifløz] mf whistler

sigle [sigl] m abbreviation; word formed by literation; acronym

si-gnal [sinal] m (pl -gnaux [no]) signal; sign; (telp) busy signal

signa-lé -lée [sinale] adj signal, noteworthy

signalement [sinalmã] m description

signaler [sinale] tr to signal; to point out || ref to distinguish oneself

signalisation [sinalizasjɔ̃] f signs

signataire [sinater] adj & mf signatory

signature [sinatyr] f signature; signing

signe [sin] m sign; faire signe à to motion to, to signal; signe de ponctuation punctuation mark; signe de tête nod

signer [sine] tr to sign || ref to cross oneself

signet [sine], [sine] m bookmark

significa-tif [sinifikatif] -tive [tiv] adj significant

signifier [sinifje] tr to signify; to mean

silence [silãs] m silence

silen-cieux [silãsjø] -cieuse [sjøz] adj silent || m (aut) muffler

silex [sileks] m flint

silhouette [silwet] f silhouette

silhouetter [silwete] tr to silhouette

silicium [silisjɔm] m silicon

silicone [silikɔn] f silicone

sillage [sijaʒ] m wake

sillet [sije] m (mus) nut

sillon [sijɔ̃] m furrow; groove; sillon sonore sound track

sillonner [sijɔne] tr to furrow; to groove; to cross, to streak

silo [silo] m silo

silure [silyr] m catfish

simagrée [simagre] f pretense

similaire [similer] adj similar

similigravure [similigravyr] f halftone

similitude [similityd] f similarity

similor [similor] m ormolu

simple [sɛ̃pl] adj simple; passer en simple police to go to police court; simple particulier private citizen; simple soldat private || mf simpleminded person || m simple (herb); (tennis) singles

sim-plet [sɛ̃ple] -plette [plet] adj artless

simplifier [sɛ̃plifje] tr to simplify

simpliste [sɛ̃plist] adj oversimple

simulacre [simylakr] m sham; simulacre de combat sham battle

simuler [simyle] tr to simulate

simulta-né -née [simyltane] adj simultaneous

sinapisme [sinapism] m mustard plaster

sincère [sɛ̃ser] adj sincere

sincérité [sɛ̃serite] f sincerity

sinécure [sinekyr] f sinecure

singe [sɛ̃ʒ] m monkey; (slang) boss; grimacer comme un vieux singe to grin like a Cheshire cat

singer [sɛ̃ʒe] §38 tr to ape

singerie [sɛ̃ʒri] f monkeyshine; grimace; monkey cage

singulariser [sɛ̃gylarize] tr to draw attention to || ref to stand out

singu-lier [sɛ̃gylje] -lière [ljer] adj & m singular

sinistre [sinistr] adj sinister || m disaster

sinis-tré -trée [sinistre] adj damaged, ruined; homeless; shipwrecked || mf victim

sinon [sinɔ̃] adv if not; perhaps even; sinon que except for the fact that || prep except for, except to || conj except, unless; or else, else, otherwise

si-nueux [sinɥø] -nueuse [nɥøz] adj sinuous, winding

sinus [sinys] m sinus; (trig) sine

sionisme [sjonism] *m* Zionism
siphon [sifɔ̃] *m* siphon; siphon bottle; trap (*double-curved pipe*)
siphonner [sifone] *tr* to siphon
sirène [siren] *f* siren; foghorn
sirop [siro] *m* syrup; **sirop pectoral** cough syrup
siroter [sirote] *tr & intr* (coll) to sip
sis [si] **sise** [siz] *adj* located
sismographe [sismɔgraf] *m* seismograph
sismologie [sismɔlɔʒi] *f* seismology
site [sit] *m* site; lay of the land
sitôt [sito] *adv* immediately; **sitôt dit, sitôt fait** no sooner said than done; **sitôt que** as soon as
sittelle [sitɛl] *f* (orn) nuthatch
situation [situɑsjɔ̃] *f* situation; **situation sans issue** deadlock, impasse
situer [sitɥe] *tr* to situate, to locate
six [si(s)] *adj & pron* six; the Sixth, e.g., **Jean six** John the Sixth; **six heures** six o'clock ‖ *m* six; sixth (*in dates*)
sixième [sizjɛm] *adj, pron* (*masc, fem*), *& m* sixth
six-quatre-deux [siskatdø]—**à la six-quatre-deux** (coll) slapdash
sizain [sizɛ̃] *m* six-line verse; pack (*of cub scouts*)
sizerin [sizrɛ̃] *m* (orn) redpoll
ski [ski] *m* ski; skiing; **faire du ski to go skiing; ski nautique** water-skiing
skier [skje] *intr* to ski
skieur [skjœr] **skieuse** [skjøz] *mf* skier
slalom [slalɔm] *m* slalom
slave [slav] *adj* Slav; Slavic ‖ *m* Slavic (*language*) ‖ (*cap*) *mf* Slav (*person*)
slogan [slɔgɑ̃] *m* (com) slogan
slovaque [slɔvak] *adj* Slovak ‖ *m* Slovak (*language*) ‖ (*cap*) *mf* Slovak (*person*)
smoking [smɔkiŋ] *m* tuxedo
snack [snak] *m* snack bar
S.N.C.F. [esenseef] *f* (letterword) (Société nationale des Chemins de fer français) French railroad
snob [snɔb] *adj invar* snobbish ‖ *mf* (*pl* snob or snobs) snob
snober [snɔbe] *tr* to snub
snobisme [snɔbism] *m* snobbery
sobre [sɔbr] *adj* sober, moderate; simple (*ornamentation*)
sobriété [sɔbrijete] *f* sobriety; moderation (*in eating, speaking*)
sobriquet [sɔbrikɛ] *m* nickname
soc [sɔk] *m* plowshare
sociable [sɔsjabl] *adj* sociable, neighborly; social (*creature*)
so·cial -ciale [sɔsjal] *adj* (*pl* **-ciaux** [sjo]) social
sociali·sant [sɔsjalizɑ̃] **-sante** [zɑ̃t] *adj* socialistic ‖ *mf* socialist sympathizer
socialiser [sɔsjalize] *tr* to socialize
socialisme [sɔsjalism] *m* socialism
socialiste [sɔsjalist] *adj & mf* socialist
sociétaire [sɔsjeter] *mf* stockholder; member (*e.g., of an acting company*)
société [sɔsjete] *f* society; company; firm, partnership; **société anonyme** stock company, corporation; **société de prévoyance** benefit society; **Société des Nations** League of Nations

sociologie [sɔsjɔlɔʒi] *f* sociology
socle [sɔkl] *m* pedestal; footing, socle
socque [sɔk] *m* clog, sabot; (theat) comedy
socquette [sɔkɛt] *f* anklet
Socrate [sɔkrat] *m* Socrates
soda [sɔda] *m* soda water
sodium [sɔdjɔm] *m* sodium
sœur [sœr] *f* sister; **et ta sœur!** (slang) knock it off!; **ma sœur** (eccl) sister
sofa [sɔfa] *m* sofa
soi [swa] §85, §85B; **à part soi** to oneself (himself, etc.); **de soi, en soi** in itself
soi-disant [swadizɑ̃] *adj invar* so-called, self-styled ‖ *adv* supposedly
soie [swa] *f* silk; bristle
soierie [swari] *f* silk goods; silk factory
soif [swaf] *f* thirst; **avoir soif** to be thirsty
soi·gné -gnée [swaɲe] *adj* well-groomed, trim; polished (*speech*)
soigner [swaɲe] *tr* to nurse, take care of; to groom; to polish (*one's style*)
soigneur [swaɲœr] *m* (sports) trainer
soi·gneux [swaɲø] **-gneuse** [ɲøz] *adj* careful, meticulous
soi-même [swamɛm] §86
soin [swɛ̃] *m* care, attention; treatment; **aux bons soins de** in care of (*c/o*); **être aux petits soins auprès de** to wait on (*s.o.*) hand and foot; **premiers soins** first aid; **soins d'urgence** first aid
soir [swar] *m* evening, night; **hier soir** last night; **le soir** in the evening, at night
soirée [sware] *f* evening; evening party; **en soirée** evening (*performance*); **soirée dansante** dance
soit [swa], [swat] *conj* take for instance, e.g., **soit quatre multiplié par deux** take for instance four multiplied by two; say, e.g., **bien des hommes étaient perdus, soit un million** many men were lost, say a million; **soit ... soit** either ... or, whether ... or; **soit que ... soit que** whether ... or ‖ [swat] *interj* so be it!, all right!
soixante [swasɑ̃t] *adj, pron, & m* sixty; **soixante et onze** seventy-one; **soixante et onzième** seventy-first; **soixante et un** sixty-one; **soixante et unième** sixty-first
soixante-dix [swasɑ̃di(s)] *adj, pron, & m* seventy
soixante-dixième [swasɑ̃tdizjɛm] *adj, pron* (*masc, fem*), *& m* seventieth
soixantième [swasɑ̃tjɛm] *adj, pron* (*masc, fem*), *& m* sixtieth
soja [sɔʒa] *m* soybean
sol [sɔl] *m* soil; ground; floor
solaire [sɔler] *adj* solar
soldat [sɔlda] *m* soldier
soldatesque [sɔldatesk] *adj* barrack-room (*humor; manners*) ‖ *f* rowdies
solde [sɔld] *m* balance (*of an account*); remnant; clearance sale; **en solde** reduced (*in price*) ‖ *f* (mil) pay
solder [sɔlde] *tr* to settle (*an account*); to sell out; (mil) to pay ‖ *intr* to sell out

sol·deur [sɔldœr] **-deuse** [døz] *mf* dealer in seconds and remnants

sole [sɔl] *f* sole (*fish*); field (*used for crop rotation*)

soleil [sɔlej] *m* sun; sunshine, sunlight; sunflower; pinwheel; **il fait du soleil** or **il fait soleil** it is sunny

solen·nel -nelle [sɔlanel] *adj* solemn

solénoïde [sɔlenɔid] *m* solenoid

solfège [sɔlfɛʒ] *m* sol-fa

solidage [sɔlidaʒ] *f* goldenrod

solidaire [sɔlider] *adj* interdependent; jointly binding; **solidaire de responsible for; answerable to; integral with, in one piece with

solidariser [sɔlidarize] *ref* to join together

solidarité [sɔlidarite] *f* solidarity, interdependence

solide [sɔlid] *adj & m* solid

solidité [sɔlidite] *f* solidity; soundness; strength (*e.g., of a fabric*)

soliloque [sɔlilɔk] *m* soliloquy

soliste [sɔlist] *mf* soloist

solitaire [sɔliter] *adj* solitary; lonely ‖ *m* solitary, anchorite; old wild boar; solitaire

solitude [sɔlityd] *f* solitude

solive [sɔliv] *f* joist

soli·veau [sɔlivo] *m* (*pl* -**veaux**) small joist; (coll) nobody

solliciter [sɔllisite] *tr* to solicit; to apply for; to incite; to attract (*attention; iron*); to induce ‖ *intr* to seek favors

sollici·teur [sɔllisitœr] **-teuse** [tøz] *mf* solicitor, office seeker, petitioner, lobbyist

solo [sɔlo] *adj invar & m* solo

solstice [sɔlstis] *m* solstice

soluble [sɔlybl] *adj* soluble; solvable

solution [sɔlysjɔ̃] *f* solution

solutionner [sɔlysjɔne] *tr* to solve

solvabilité [sɔlvabilite] *f* solvency

solvable [sɔlvabl] *adj* solvent

solvant [sɔlvã] *m* solvent

sombre [sɔ̃br] *adj* somber; sullen

sombrer [sɔ̃bre] *intr* to sink; to vanish (*as a fortune*)

sommaire [sɔmer] *adj & m* summary

sommation [sɔmasjɔ̃] *f* summons; sentry challenge; **faire les trois sommations** to read the riot act

somme [sɔm] *m* nap ‖ *f* sum; **en somme, somme toute** in short, when all is said and done

sommeil [sɔmej] *m* sleep; **avoir sommeil** to be sleepy

sommeiller [sɔmeje] *intr* to doze; to lie dormant

sommelier [sɔməlje] *m* wine steward

sommer [sɔme] *tr* to add up; to summon, to issue a legal writ to

sommet [sɔme] *m* summit, top; apex (*of a triangle*); vertex (*of an angle*); (fig) acme

sommier [sɔmje] *m* bedspring; ledger; crossbeam; (archaic) pack animal; **sommier élastique** spring mattress

sommité [sɔmite] *f* pinnacle, crest; leader, authority

somnambule [sɔmnãbyl] *adj* sleepwalking ‖ *mf* sleepwalker

somnifère [sɔmnifer] *adj & m* soporific

somnolence [sɔmnɔlãs] *f* drowsiness; indolence, laziness

somno·lent [sɔmnɔlã] **-lente** [lãt] *adj* somnolent, drowsy; indolent

somnoler [sɔmnɔle] *intr* to doze

somptuaire [sɔ̃ptɥer] *adj* luxury (*tax*)

somp·tueux [sɔ̃ptɥø] **-tueuse** [tɥøz] *adj* sumptuous

son [sɔ̃] *adj poss* §88 ‖ *m* sound; bran

sonate [sɔnat] *f* sonata

sondage [sɔ̃daʒ] *m* sounding, probing; **sondage de l'opinion** public-opinion poll; **sondage d'exploration** wildcat (*well*)

sonde [sɔ̃d] *f* lead, probe; borer, drill

sonder [sɔ̃de] *tr* to sound, probe, bore, fathom; to explore, reconnoiter; to poll (*e.g., public opinion*); to sound out (*s.o.*)

son·deur [sɔ̃dœr] **-deuse** [døz] *mf* prober, sounder

songe [sɔ̃ʒ] *m* dream

songe-creux [sɔ̃ʒkrø] *m invar* visionary, pipe dreamer

songer [sɔ̃ʒe] §38 *tr* to dream up ‖ *intr* to dream; to think; to intend to; **songer à** to think of; to imagine, to dream of; **songez-y!** think it over!

songerie [sɔ̃ʒri] *f* reverie, daydreaming

son·geur [sɔ̃ʒœr] **-geuse** [ʒøz] *adj* dreamy, preoccupied ‖ *mf* daydreamer

sonique [sɔnik] *adj* sonic, of sound

sonnaille [sɔnaj] *f* cowbell, sheepbell

sonnailler [sɔnaje] *m* bellwether ‖ *intr* to ring often and without cause

son·nant [sɔnã] **son·nante** [sɔnãt] *adj* striking (*clock*); metal (*money*); at the stroke of, e.g., **à huit heures sonnantes** at the stroke of eight

son·né -née [sɔne] *adj* past, e.g., **deux heures sonnées** past two o'clock; over, e.g., **il a soixante ans sonnés** he is over sixty; (slang) cuckoo, nuts; (slang) stunned

sonner [sɔne] *tr* to ring; to ring for; to sound ‖ *intr* to ring; to strike; to sound

sonnerie [sɔnri] *f* chimes, chiming; set of bells, carillon; fanfare; ring (*of a telephone, doorbell, etc.*); alarm or striking mechanism (*of clock*)

sonnet [sɔne] *m* sonnet

sonnette [sɔnet] *f* doorbell; pile driver

sonneur [sɔnœr] *m* bellringer; trumpeter

sonore [sɔnɔr] *adj* sonorous; sound (*wave, track*); echoing (*hall, cathedral, etc.*); (phonet) voiced ‖ *f* voiced consonant

sonoriser [sɔnɔrize] *tr* to record sound effects on (*a film*); to equip (*an auditorium*) with loudspeakers

sonorité [sɔnɔrite] *f* sonority, resonance

sonotone [sɔnɔtɔn] *m* hearing aid

sophistication [sɔfistikɑsjɔ̃] *f* adulteration

sophisti·qué -quée [sɔfistike] *adj* adulterated; artificial, counterfeit

sophistiquer [sɔfistike] *tr* to adulterate; to stubilize

Sophocle [sɔfɔkl] *m* Sophocles

sopraniste [sɔpranist] *m* male soprano

sopra·no [sɔprano] *mf* (*pl* **-ni** [ni] or **-nos**) soprano ‖ *m* soprano (*voice*)

sorbet [sɔrbɛ] *m* sherbet

sorbetière [sɔrbətjɛr] *f* ice-cream freezer

sorbon·nard [sɔrbɔnar] **sorbon·narde** [sɔrbɔnard] *mf* (coll) Sorbonne student; (coll) Sorbonne professor

sorcellerie [sɔrsɛlri] *f* sorcery

sor·cier [sɔrsje] **-cière** [sjɛr] *adj* sorcerer's; **cela n'est pas sorcier** there's no trick to that ‖ *m* sorcerer, wizard ‖ *f* sorceress, witch; **vieille sorcière** old hag

sordide [sɔrdid] *adj* sordid

sornette [sɔrnɛt] *f* nonsense

sort [sɔr] *m* fate, destiny; fortune, lot; spell, charm

sortable [sɔrtabl] *adj* suitable, acceptable; presentable

sor·tant [sɔrtã] **-tante** [tãt] *adj* retiring (*congressman*); winning (*number*) ‖ *mf* person leaving

sorte [sɔrt] *f* sort, kind; state, condition; way, manner; **de la sorte** this way, thus; **de sorte que** so that, thus, with the result that; **en quelque sorte** in a certain way; **en sorte que** in such a way that

sortie [sɔrti] *f* exit, way out; outing, jaunt; quitting time; outburst, tirade; (mil) sortie; **sortie de bain** bathrobe; **sortie de bal** evening wrap; **sortie de secours** emergency exit; **sortie de voiture(s)** driveway

sortilège [sɔrtilɛʒ] *m* spell, charm

sortir [sɔrtir] §64 *tr* to take out, to bring out; to publish ‖ *intr* (*aux:* ÊTRE) to go out, to come out; to come forth; to stand out; **au sortir de** on coming out of; **sortir de** + *inf* (coll) to have just + *pp*

S.O.S. [ɛsoɛs] *m* (letterword) S.O.S.

sosie [sozi] *m* double

sot [so] **sotte** [sɔt] *adj* stupid, silly ‖ *mf* fool, simpleton

sottise [sɔtiz] *f* stupidity, silliness, foolishness

sou [su] *m* sou; (fig) penny, farthing; **sans le sou** penniless; **sou à sou** or **sou par sou** a penny at a time

soubassement [subasmã] *m* subfoundation, infrastructure

soubresaut [subreso] *m* sudden start, jerk; palpitation, jump (*of the heart*)

soubrette [subrɛt] *f* (theat) soubrette; (coll) attractive chambermaid

souche [suʃ] *f* stump; stock; stack (*of fireplace*); strain (*of virus*); (coll) dolt

souci [susi] *m* care; marigold; **sans souci** carefree

soucier [susje] *ref* to care, concern oneself

soucieusement [susjøzmã] *adv* uneasily, anxiously; with concern

sou·cieux [susjø] **-cieuse** [sjøz] *adj* solicitous, concerned; uneasy, anxious

soucoupe [sukup] *f* saucer; **soucoupe volante** flying saucer

soudage [sudaʒ] *m* soldering; welding

sou·dain [sudɛ̃] **-daine** [dɛn] *adj* sudden ‖ **soudain** *adv* suddenly

soudainement [sudɛnmã] *adv* suddenly

soudaineté [sudɛnte] *f* suddenness

souda·nais [sudanɛ] **-naise** [nɛz] *adj* Sudanic ‖ *m* Sudanic (*language*) ‖ (*cap*) *mf* Sudanese (*person*)

soude [sud] *f* (chem) soda

souder [sude] *tr* to solder; to weld ‖ *ref* to knit (*as bones do*)

soudeur [sudœr] *m* welder

soudoyer [sudwaje] §47 *tr* to bribe; to hire (*assassins*)

soudure [sudyr] *f* solder; soldering; soldered joint; knitting (*of bones*); **faire la soudure** to bridge the gap; **soudure autogène** welding

soue [su] *f* pigsty

soufflage [suflaʒ] *m* blowing; glass blowing

souffle [sufl] *m* breath; breathing

souf·flé -flée [sufle] *adj* puffed up ‖ *m* soufflé

souffler [sufle] *tr* to blow; to blow out (*a candle*); to blow up (*a balloon*); to prompt (*an actor*); to huff (*a checker*); to suggest (*an idea*); **ne pas souffler mot** to not breathe a word; **souffler à l'oreille** to whisper; **souffler q.ch. à qn** to take s.th. from s.o. ‖ *intr* to blow; to pant, puff; to take a breather, to catch one's breath

soufflerie [sufləri] *f* bellows; wind tunnel

soufflet [suflɛ] *m* slap in the face; affront, insult; bellows; gore (*of dress*); (rr) flexible cover (*between two cars*)

souffleter [sufləte] §34 *tr* to slap in the face; to affront

souf·fleur [suflœr] **souf·fleuse** [sufløz] *mf* (theat) prompter ‖ *m* glass blower ‖ *f* (mach) blower

soufflure [suflyr] *f* blister, bubble

souffrance [sufrãs] *f* suffering; **en souffrance** unfinished (*business*); outstanding (*bill*); unclaimed (*parcel*); at a standstill, suspended

souf·frant [sufrã] **souf·frante** [sufrãt] *adj* suffering; sick, ailing

souffre-douleur [sufrədulœr] *m invar* butt (*of a joke*), laughingstock

souffre·teux [sufrətø] **-teuse** [tøz] *adj* sickly; destitute, half-starved

souffrir [sufrir] §65 *tr* to suffer; to stand, bear, tolerate; to permit ‖ *intr* to suffer ‖ *ref* to put up with each other

soufre [sufr] *m* sulfur

soufrer [sufre] *tr* to sulfurate

souhait [swɛ] *m* wish; **à souhait** to one's liking, to perfection; **à vos souhaits!** (salutation) gesundheit!; **souhaits** good wishes; **souhaits de bonne année** New Year's greetings

souhaitable [swɛtabl] *adj* desirable

souhaiter [swɛte] *tr* to wish; to wish for; to wish to; **je vous la souhaite bonne et heureuse** I wish you a happy New Year

souille [suj] *f* wallow

souiller [suje] *tr* to dirty, spot, stain, soil, sully

souillon [sujɔ̃] *f* (coll) scullery maid

souillure [sujyr] *f* spot, stain
soûl [su] **soûle** [sul] *adj* drunk; sottish ‖ *m* fill, e.g., **manger son soûl** to eat one's fill
soulagement [sulaʒmã] *m* relief; comfort
soulager [sulaʒe] §38 *tr* to relieve; to comfort
soûler [sule] *tr* (slang) to cram down one's throat; (slang) to get (*s.o.*) drunk ‖ *ref* (fig) to have one's fill; (slang) to get drunk
soulèvement [sulɛvmã] *m* upheaval; uprising; surge; **soulèvement de cœur** nausea
soulever [sulve] §2 *tr* to raise, heave, lift (up); to stir up ‖ *ref* to rise; to raise oneself; to revolt
soulier [sulje] *m* shoe
soulignement [sulinəmã] *m* underlining
souligner [suline] *tr* to underline; to emphasize
soulte [sult] *f* balance due
soumettre [sumɛtr] §42 *tr* to submit; to subject; to overcome, subdue ‖ *ref* to submit, surrender
sou·mis [sumi] **-mise** [miz] *adj* submissive, subservient; subject; amenable (*to a law*)
soumission [sumisjɔ̃] *f* submission, surrender; bid (*to perform a service*); guarantee
soumissionnaire [sumisjɔnɛr] *mf* bidder
soupape [supap] *f* valve; **soupape à réglage** or **à papillon** damper; **soupape de sûreté** safety valve; **soupape électrique** rectifier
soupçon [supsɔ̃] *m* suspicion; misgiving; dash, touch (*small amount*)
soupçonner [supsɔne] *tr & intr* to suspect
soupçon·neux [supsɔnø] **soupçon·neuse** [supsɔnøz] *adj* suspicious
soupe [sup] *f* vegetable soup; sop (*bread*); (mil) mess; **de soupe on K.P.**; **soupe au lait** (coll) mean-tempered person; **soupe populaire** soup kitchen; **trempé comme une soupe** soaking wet
soupente [supɑ̃t] *f* attic
souper [supe] *m* supper ‖ *intr* to have supper
soupeser [supəze] §2 *tr* to heft, to weigh (*e.g., a package*) in one's hand
soupière [supjɛr] *f* soup tureen
soupir [supir] *m* sigh; breath; (mus) quarter rest
soupi·rail [supiraj] *m* (*pl* **-raux** [ro]) cellar window
soupirant [supirã] *m* suitor
soupirer [supire] *intr* to sigh; **soupirer après** or **pour** to long for
souple [supl] *adj* supple; flexible, pliant; versatile, adaptable
souplesse [suples] *f* suppleness, flexibility
souquer [suke] *tr* to haul taut ‖ *intr* to pull hard (*on the oars*)
source [surs] *f* source; spring, fountain; **source de pétrole** oil well; **source jaillissante** gusher
sourcier [sursje] *m* dowser
sourcil [sursi] *m* eyebrow

sourciller [sursije] *intr* to knit one's brows; **sans sourciller** without batting an eye
sourcil·leux [sursijø] **sourcil·leuse** [sursijøz] *adj* supercilious
sourd [sur] **sourde** [surd] *adj* deaf; quiet; dull (*sound, color*); deep (*voice*); undeclared (*war*); (phonet) unvoiced; **sourd comme un pot** (coll) stone-deaf ‖ *mf* deaf person ‖ *f* unvoiced consonant
sourdement [surdəmã] *adv* secretly; heavily; dully
sourdine [surdin] *f* (mus) mute; **à la sourdine** muted; **en sourdine** on the sly
sourd-muet [surmɥe] **sourde-muette** [surdəmɥet] (*pl* **sourds-muets**) *adj* deaf and dumb, deaf-mute ‖ *mf* deaf-mute
sourdre [surdr] (used in: *inf*; 3d *sg* & *pl pres ind* **sourd, sourdent**) *intr* to spring, well up
souricier [surisje] *m* mouser
souricière [surisjer] *f* mousetrap; (fig) trap
sourire [surir] *m* smile ‖ §61 *intr* to smile; **sourire à** to smile at; to smile on; to look good to
souris [suri] *m* (obs) smile ‖ *f* mouse
sour·nois [surnwa] **-noise** [nwaz] *adj* sly, cunning, artful
sous [su] *prep* under; on (*a certain day; certain conditions*); **sous caoutchouc** rubber-covered; **sous clef** under lock and key; **sous la main** at hand; **sous les drapeaux** in the army; **sous main** underhandedly; **sous peu** shortly; **sous un certain angle** from a certain point of view
sous-alimentation [suzalimãtasjɔ̃] *f* undernourishment
sous-bois [subwa] *m* underbrush, undergrowth
sous-chef [suʃef] *m* (*pl* **-chefs**) assistant (*to the head man*), deputy, second-in-command
souscripteur [suskriptœr] *m* subscriber (*to a loan or charity*); signer (*of a commercial paper*)
souscription [suskripsjɔ̃] *f* signature; subscription; **souscription de soutien** sustaining membership
souscrire [suskrir] §25 *tr & intr* to subscribe
sous-cuta·né -née [sukytane] *adj* subcutaneous
sous-dévelop·pé -pée [sudɛvlɔpe] *adj* underdeveloped
sous-diacre [sudjakr] *m* subdeacon
sous-direc·teur [sudirɛktœr] **-trice** [tris] *mf* (*pl* **-directeurs**) second-in-command
sous-entendre [suzãtãdr] *tr* to understand (*what is not expressed*); to imply
sous-entendu [suzãtãdy] *m* inference, implication, innuendo, double meaning, double entendre
sous-entente [suzãtãt] *f* mental reservation; hidden, cryptic meaning

sous-entrepreneur [suzɑ̃trəprɑ̃nœr] *m* (*pl* -entrepreneurs) subcontractor

sous-estimer [suzestime] *tr* to underestimate

sous-fifre [sufifr] *m* (*pl* -fifres) (coll) underling

sous-garde [sugard] *f* trigger guard

sous-lieutenant [suljøtnɑ̃] *m* (*pl* -lieutenants) second lieutenant

sous-location [sulɔkasjɔ̃] *f* sublease

sous-louer [sulwe] *tr* to sublet, sublease

sous-main [sumɛ̃] *m invar* desk blotter; en sous-main underhandedly

sous-marin [sumarɛ̃] -marine [marin] *adj & m* (*pl* -marins) submarine

sous-marinier [sumarinje] *m* (*pl* -mariniers) submarine crewman

sous-mentonnière [sumɑ̃tɔnjər] *f* (*pl* -mentonnières) chin strap

sous-nappe [sunap] *f* (*pl* -nappes) table pad

sous-off [suzɔf] *m* (*pl* -offs) noncom

sous-officier [suzofisje] *m* (*pl* -officiers) noncommissioned officer

sous-ordre [suzɔrdr] *m* (*pl* -ordres) underling, subordinate; (biol) suborder; en sous-ordre subordinate; subordinately

sous-production [suprɔdyksjɔ̃] *f* underproduction

sous-produit [suprɔdɥi] *m* (*pl* -produits) by-product

sous-secrétaire [suskreter] *m* (*pl* -secrétaires) undersecretary

sous-secrétariat [suskretarja] *m* undersecretaryship

sous-seing [susɛ̃] *m invar* privately witnessed document

soussi-gné -gnée [susiɲe] *adj & mf* undersigned

sous-sol [susɔl] *m* (*pl* -sols) subsoil; basement

sous-titre [sutitr] *m* (*pl* -titres) subtitle

sous-titrer [sutitre] *tr* to subtitle

soustraction [sustraksjɔ̃] *f* subtraction; (law) purloining

soustraire [sustrer] §68 *tr* to remove; take away; to subtract; to deduct; soustraire de to subtract from; soustraire q.ch. à qn to take s.th. away from s.o.; to steal s.th. from s.o. ‖ *ref* to withdraw; se soustraire à to escape from

sous-traitant [sutretɑ̃] *m* (*pl* -traitants) subcontractor; sublessee

sous-traité [sutrete] *m* (*pl* -traités) subcontract

sous-traiter [sutrete] *tr & intr* to subcontract

sous-ventrière [suvɑ̃trijer] *f* (*pl* -ventrières) girth

sous-verre [suver] *m invar* passe-partout; coaster

sous-vêtement [suvetmɑ̃] *m* (*pl* -vêtements) undergarment

soutache [sutaʃ] *f* braid

soutacher [sutaʃe] *tr* to trim with braid

soutane [sutan] *f* soutane, cassock

soutanelle [sutanɛl] *f* frock coat; choir robe

soute [sut] *f* (naut) storeroom; soute à charbon coal bunker

soutenable [sutnabl] *adj* supportable, tenable

soutenance [sutnɑ̃s] *f* defense (*of an academic thesis*)

soutènement [sutenmɑ̃] *m* support

souteneur [sutnœr] *m* pimp

soutenir [sutnir] §72 *tr* to support, bear; to sustain; to insist, claim; to defend (*a thesis*) ‖ *ref* to stand up; to keep afloat

soute·nu -nue [sutny] *adj* sustained; elevated (*style*); steady (*market*); true (*colors*)

souter·rain [suterɛ̃] souter·raine [suterɛn] *adj* subterranean, underground; underhanded ‖ *m* tunnel, subway (*for pedestrians*)

soutien [sutjɛ̃] *m* support; stand-by

soutien-gorge [sutjɛ̃gɔrʒ] *m* (*pl* soutiens-gorge) brassiere

soutirage [sutiraʒ] *m* racking

soutirer [sutire] *tr* to rack (*wine*); soutirer q.ch. à qn to get s.th. out of s.o., to sponge on s.o. for s.th.

souvenir [suvnir] *m* memory, remembrance; souvenir ‖ §72 *intr*—faire souvenir qn de q.ch. to remind s.o. of s.th. ‖ *ref* to remember; se souvenir de to remember

souvent [suvɑ̃] *adv* often

souve·rain [suvrɛ̃] -raine [ren] *adj & mf* sovereign ‖ *m* sovereign (*coin*)

souveraineté [suvrente] *f* sovereignty

soviet [sɔvjet] *m* soviet

soviétique [sɔvjetik] *adj* Soviet ‖ (*cap*) *mf* Soviet Russian

soya [sɔja] *m* soybean

soyeux [swajø] soyeuse [swajøz] *adj* silky

S.P. *abbr* (sapeurs-pompiers) fire department

spa·cieux [spasjø] -cieuse [sjøz] *adj* spacious, roomy

spadassin [spadasɛ̃] *m* hatchet man, hired thug

spaghetti [spagetti] *m* spaghetti

sparadrap [sparadra] *m* adhesive tape

spartiate [sparsjat] *adj* Spartan ‖ (*cap*) *mf* Spartan

spasme [spasm] *m* spasm

spasmodique [spasmɔdik] *adj* spasmodic; (pathol) spastic

spath [spat] *m* (mineral) spar

spa·tial -tiale [spasjal] *adj* (*pl* -tiaux [sjo]) spatial

spatule [spatyl] *f* spatula; (orn) spoonbill

spea·ker [spikœr] -kerine [krin] *mf* (rad, telv) announcer ‖ *m* speaker (*presiding officer*)

spé·cial -ciale [spesjal] *adj* (*pl* -ciaux [sjo]) special

spécialiser [spesjalize] *tr & ref* to specialize

spécialiste [spesjalist] *mf* specialist; expert

spécialité [spesjalite] *f* specialty; specialization; patent medicine

spé·cieux [spesjø] -cieuse [sjøz] *adj* specious

spécifier [spesifje] *tr* to specify

spécifique [spesifik] *adj & m* specific
spécimen [spesimɛn] *adj & m* specimen
spectacle [spektakl] *m* spectacle, sight; show; play; **à grand spectacle** spectacular (*production*)
specta·teur [spektatœr] -trice [tris] *mf* spectator
spectre [spektr] *m* ghost; spectrum; (fig) specter
spécula·teur [spekylatœr] -trice [tris] *mf* speculator
spéculer [spekyle] *tr* to speculate
spéléologie [speleɔlɔʒi] *f* speleology
sperme [spɛrm] *m* sperm
sphère [sfɛr] *f* sphere
sphérique [sferik] *adj* spherical
sphinx [sfɛ̃ks] *m* sphinx
spider [spider] *m* (aut) rumble seat
spi·nal -nale [spinal] *adj* (*pl* -naux [no]) spinal
spi·ral -rale [spiral] (*pl* -raux [ro]) *adj* spiral || *m* hairspring (*of watch*) || *f* spiral; **en spirale** spiral
ıire [spir] *f* turn (*in a wire*); whorl (*of a shell*)
spirée [spire] *f* (bot) spirea
spirite [spirit] *adj & mf* spiritualist
spiri·tuel -tuelle [spiritɥel] *adj* spiritual; sacred (*music*); witty || *m* ecclesiastical power
spiri·tueux [spiritɥø] -tueuse [tɥøz] *adj* spirituous || *m* spirituous liquor
spleen [splin] *m* boredom, melancholy
splendeur [splɑ̃dœr] *f* splendor
splendide [splɑ̃did] *adj* splendid; bright, brilliant
spolia·teur [spɔljatœr] -trice [tris] *adj* despoiling || *mf* despoiler
spolier [spɔlje] *tr* to despoil
spon·gieux [spɔ̃ʒjø] -gieuse [ʒjøz] *adj* spongy
sponta·né -née [spɔ̃tane] *adj* spontaneous
sporadique [spɔradik] *adj* sporadic(al)
sport [spɔr] *adj invar* sport, sporting; sportsmanlike || *m* sport
spor·tif [spɔrtif] -tive [tiv] *adj* sport, sporting || *mf* athlete, player || *m* sportsman
spot [spot] *m* spotlight; (radar) blip
spoutnik [sputnik] *m* sputnik
spu·meux [spymø] -meuse [møz] *adj* frothy, foamy
squale [skwal] *m* (ichth) dogfish
squelette [skəlɛt] *m* skeleton
squelettique [skəletik] *adj* skeletal
S.R. *abbr* (**Service de renseignements**) information desk or bureau
stabiliser [stabilize] *tr* to stabilize
stabilité [stabilite] *f* stability
stable [stabl] *adj* stable
stade [stad] *m* stadium; (fig) stage (*of development*)
stage [staʒ] *m* probationary period, apprenticeship
stagiaire [staʒjɛr] *adj & mf* apprentice
stag·nant [stagnɑ̃] -nante [nɑ̃t] *adj* stagnant
stalle [stal] *f* stall
stance [stɑ̃s] *f* stanza
stand [stɑ̃d] *m* stands; shooting gallery; pit (*for motor racing*)

standard [stɑ̃dar] *adj invar* standard || *m* standard; switchboard
standardiser [stɑ̃dardize] *tr* to standardize
standardiste [stɑ̃dardist] *mf* switchboard operator, telephone operator
standing [stɑ̃diŋ] *m* status, standing; standard of living; **de grand standing** luxury (*apartments*)
star [star] *f* (mov, theat) star
starter [starter], [startœr] *m* (aut) choke; (sports) starter
station [stɑsjɔ̃] *f* station; resort; (rr) flag station; **station d'écoute** monitoring station; **station d'émission** broadcasting station; **station de repérage** tracking station; **station de taxis** taxi stand; **station orbitale** space station
stationnaire [stɑsjɔner] *adj* stationary || *m* gunboat
stationnement [stɑsjɔnmɑ̃] *m* parking; **stationnement interdit** (public sign) no parking
stationner [stɑsjɔne] *intr* to stop; to park
station-service [stɑsjɔ̃servis] *f* (*pl* **stations-service**) service station
statique [statik] *adj* static
statisti·cien [statistisjɛ̃] -cienne [sjen] *mf* statistician
statistique [statistik] *adj* statistical || *f* statistics
statuaire [statɥer] *adj* statuary || *mf* sculptor || *f* statuary
statue [staty] *f* statue
statuer [statɥe] *tr* to hand down (*a ruling*) || *intr* to hand down a ruling
statu quo [statykwo], [statuko] *m* status quo
stature [statyr] *f* stature
statut [staty] *m* statute; legal status
statutaire [statyter] *adj* statutory
Ste *abbr* (**Sainte**) St. (*female saint*)
Sté *abbr* (**Société**) Inc.
sténo [steno] *f* stenographer; stenography
sténodactylo [stenɔdaktilo] *f* shorthand typist; shorthand typing
sténogramme [stenɔgram] *m* shorthand notes
sténographe [stenɔgraf] *mf* stenographer
sténographie [stenɔgrafi] *f* stenography
sténographier [stenɔgrafje] *tr* to take down in shorthand
stéréo [stereo] *adj invar* stereo || *f*—**en stéréo** (electron) in stereo
stéréophonie [stereɔfɔni] *f* stereophonic sound system; **en stéréophonie** stereophonic (*e.g., broadcast*)
stéréoscopique [stereɔskɔpik] *adj* stereo, stereoscopic
stéréoty·pé -pée [stereɔtipe] *adj* stereotyped
stérile [steril] *adj* sterile
stériliser [sterilize] *tr* to sterilize
stérilité [sterilite] *f* sterility
sterling [sterliŋ] *adj invar* sterling
stéthoscope [stetɔskɔp] *m* stethoscope
stick [stik] *m* walking stick
stigmate [stigmat] *m* stigma
stigmatiser [stigmatize] *tr* to stigmatize

stimu·lant [stimylɑ̃] **-lante** [lɑ̃t] *adj &* m stimulant
stimuler [stimyle] *tr* to stimulate
stimu·lus [stimylys] *m* (*pl* **-li** [li]) (physiol) stimulus
stipendier [stipɑ̃dje] *tr* to hire (*e.g., an assassin*); to bribe
stipuler [stipyle] *tr* to stipulate
stock [stɔk] *m* goods, stock; hoard
stocker [stɔke] *tr &* intr to stockpile
stockiste [stɔkist] *m* authorized dealer (*carrying parts, motors, etc.*)
stoï·cien [stɔisjɛ̃] **-cienne** [sjen] *adj & mf* Stoic
stoïque [stɔik] *adj* stoical ‖ *mf* stoic
stop [stɔp] *m* stop; stoplight; **du stop** (coll) hitchhiking ‖ *interj* stop!
stoppage [stɔpaʒ] *m* reweaving, invisible mending
stopper [stɔpe] *tr* to reweave; to stop ‖ *intr* to stop
store [stɔr] *m* blind; window awning; outside window shade
strabique [strabik] *adj* squint-eyed
strabisme [strabism] *m* squint
strapontin [strapɔ̃tɛ̃] *m* jump seat; (theat) attached folding seat
strass [stras] *m* paste (*jewelry*)
stratagème [strataʒem] *m* stratagem
strate [strat] *f* (geol) stratum
stratège [strateʒ] *m* strategist
stratégie [strateʒi] *f* strategy
stratégique [strateʒik] *adj* strategic(al)
stratégiste [strateʒist] *m* strategist
stratifier [stratifje] *tr &* ref to stratify
stratosphère [stratɔsfer] *f* stratosphere
strict stricte [strikt] *adj* strict
stri·dent [stridɑ̃] **-dente** [dɑ̃t] *adj* strident
strie [stri] *f* streak; stripe
strier [strije] *tr* to streak; to score, groove
strontium [strɔ̃sjɔm] *m* strontium
strophe [strɔf] *f* verse, stanza; strophe
structu·ral -rale [stryktyral] *adj* (*pl* **-raux** [ro]) structural
structure [stryktyr] *f* structure
strychnine [striknin] *f* strychnine
stuc [styk] *m* stucco; **enduire de stuc** to stucco
stu·dieux [stydjø] **-dieuse** [djøz] *adj* studious
studio [stydjo] *m* studio
stupé·fait [stypefe] **-faite** [fet] *adj* dumfounded, amazed
stupé·fiant [stypefjɑ̃] **-fiante** [fjɑ̃t] *adj* astounding ‖ *m* drug, narcotic
stupéfier [stypefje] *tr* to astound; to stupefy (*as with a drug*)
stupeur [stypœr] *f* stupor; amazement
stupide [stypid] *adj* stupid
stupidité [stypidite] *f* stupidity
stuquer [styke] *tr* to stucco
style [stil] *m* style; stylus
styler [stile] *tr* to train
stylet [stile] *m* stiletto
styliser [stilize] *tr* to stylize
stylo [stilo] *m* pen, fountain pen; **stylo à bille** ball-point pen
styptique [stiptik] *adj & m* styptic
suaire [sɥer] *m* shroud, winding sheet

suave [sɥav] *adj* sweet (*perfume, music, etc.*); bland (*food*); suave
subcons·cient [sypkɔ̃sjɑ̃] **subcons·ciente** [sypkɔ̃sjɑ̃t] *adj & m* subconscious
subdiviser [sybdivize] *tr* to subdivide
subir [sybir] *tr* to submit to; to undergo; to feel, experience; to take (*an exam*); to serve (*a sentence*)
su·bit [sybi] **-bite** [bit] *adj* sudden
subjec·tif [sybʒektif] **-tive** [tiv] *adj* subjective
subjonc·tif [sybʒɔ̃ktif] **-tive** [tiv] *adj & m* subjunctive
subjuguer [sybʒyge] *tr* to dominate; to spellbind
sublime [syblim] *adj* sublime
sublimer [syblime] *tr* to sublimate
submerger [sybmerʒe] **§38** *tr* to submerge
submersible [sybmersibl] *adj & m* submersible
submersion [sybmersjɔ̃] *f* submersion
subodorer [sybɔdɔre] *tr* to scent (*game*); (fig) to scent (*a plot*)
subordon·né -née [sybɔrdɔne] *adj & m* subordinate
subordonner [sybɔrdɔne] *tr* to subordinate
suborner [sybɔrne] *tr* to bribe
subrécargue [sybrekarg] *m* supercargo
subreptice [sybreptis] *adj* surreptitious
subsé·quent [sypsekɑ̃] **-quente** [kɑ̃t] *adj* subsequent
subside [sypsid], [sybzid] *m* subsidy
subsidiaire [sypsidjer] *adj* subsidiary
subsistance [sybzistɑ̃s], [sypsistɑ̃s] *f* subsistence; (mil) rations
subsister [sybziste], [sypsiste] *intr* to subsist
substance [sypstɑ̃s] *f* substance; **en substance** briefly
substan·tiel -tielle [sypstɑ̃sjel] *adj* substantial
substan·tif [sypstɑ̃tif] **-tive** [tiv] *adj & m* substantive
substituer [sypstitɥe] *tr*—**substituer qn** or **q.ch. à** to substitute s.o. or s.th. for, e.g., **une biche fut substituée à Iphigénie** a hind was substituted for Iphigenia ‖ *ref*—**se substituer à** to take the place of
substitut [sypstity] *m* substitute
substitution [sypstitysjɔ̃] *f* substitution
substrat [sypstra] *m* substratum
subterfuge [sypterfyʒ] *m* subterfuge
sub·til -tile [syptil] *adj* subtle; fine (*powder, dust, etc.*); quick (*poison*); delicate (*scent*); clever (*crook*)
subtiliser [syptilize] *tr* to pick (*a purse*) ‖ *intr* to split hairs
subtilité [syptilite] *f* subtlety
subur·bain [sybyrbɛ̃] **-baine** [ben] *adj* suburban
subvenir [sybvənir] **§72** *intr* (with *dat*) to supply, provide, satisfy
subvention [sybvɑ̃sjɔ̃] *f* subsidy, subvention
subventionner [sybvɑ̃sjɔne] *tr* to subsidize
subver·sif [sybversif] **-sive** [siv] *adj* subversive
subvertir [sybvertir] *tr* to subvert

suc [syk] *m* juice; sap; (fig) essence

succéda·né -née [syksedane] *adj* & *m* substitute

succéder [syksede] §10 *intr* to happen; (with *dat*) to succeed, follow; **succéder à** to succeed to (*the throne, a fortune*) || *ref* to follow one after the other, to follow one another

succès [sykse] *m* success; outcome; **avoir du succès** to be a success

succes·sif [syksesif] **succes·sive** [syksesiv] *adj* successive

succession [syksesjɔ̃] *f* succession; inheritance; heirs

suc·cinct [syksɛ̃] **-cincte** [sɛ̃t] *adj* succinct; scanty; meager

succion [syksjɔ̃] *f* suction

succomber [sykɔ̃be] *intr* to succumb

succursale [sykyrsal] *f* branch

sucer [syse] §51 *tr* to suck

sucette [syset] *f* pacifier; lollipop, sucker

su·ceur [sysœr] **-ceuse** [søz] *adj* sucking || *m* nozzle

suçoter [sysɔte] *tr* to suck away at

sucre [sykr] *m* sugar; **sucre brut** brown sugar; **sucre candi** rock candy; **sucre de canne** cane sugar; **sucre glace** confectioners' sugar

su·cré -crée [sykre] *adj* sugary; with sugar, e.g., **du café sucré** coffee with sugar || *f*—**faire la sucrée** to be mealy-mouthed

sucrer [sykre] *tr* to sugar; (slang) to take away, to cut out || *ref* (slang) to grab the lion's share

sucrerie [sykrəri] *f* sugar refinery; **sucreries** candy

su·crier [sykrije] **-crière** [krijer] *adj* sugar || *m* sugar bowl

sud [syd] *adj invar* & *m* south

sud-améri·cain [sydamerikɛ̃] **-caine** [ken] *adj* South American || (*cap*) *mf* (*pl* **Sud-Américains**) South American

sudation [sydasjɔ̃] *f* sweating

sud-est [sydɛst] *adj invar* & *m* southeast

sudiste [sydist] *mf* Southerner (*in U.S.A.*)

sud-ouest [sydwest] *adj invar* & *m* southwest

sud-vietna·mien [sydvjetnamjɛ̃] **-mienne** [mjɛn] *adj* South Vietnamese || (*cap*) *mf* (*pl* **Sud-Vietnamiens**) South Vietnamese

suède [sɥed] *m* suede || (*cap*) *f* Sweden; **la Suède** Sweden

sué·dois [sɥedwa] **-doise** [dwaz] *adj* Swedish || *m* Swedish (*language*) || (*cap*) *mf* Swede

suée [sɥe] *f* sweating

suer [sɥe] *tr* & *intr* to sweat

sueur [sɥœr] *f* sweat

suffire [syfir] §66 *intr* to suffice; (with *dat*) to suffice; **il suffit de** + *inf* it suffices to + *inf*; **suffire à** + *inf* to suffice to + *inf*; **suffit!** enough! || *ref* to be self-sufficient

suffisance [syfizɑ̃s] *f* sufficiency; self-sufficiency, smugness

suffi·sant [syfizɑ̃] **-sante** [zɑ̃t] *adj* sufficient; smug, sophomoric; impudent || *mf* prig

suffixe [syfiks] *m* suffix

suffoquer [syfɔke] *tr* & *intr* to suffocate, choke, stifle, smother

suffrage [syfraʒ] *m* suffrage, vote; public approval; **au suffrage universel** by popular vote; **suffrage capacitaire** suffrage contingent upon literacy tests; **suffrage censitaire** suffrage upon payment of taxes

suggérer [syɡʒere] §10 *tr* to suggest

sugges·tif [syɡʒestif] **-tive** [tiv] *adj* suggestive

suggestion [syɡʒestjɔ̃] *f* suggestion

suggestionner [syɡʒestjɔne] *tr* to influence by means of suggestion

suicide [sɥisid] *adj* suicidal || *m* suicide (*act*)

suici·dé -dée [sɥiside] *adj* dead by suicide || *mf* suicide (*person*)

suicider [sɥiside] *ref* to commit suicide

suie [sɥi] *f* soot

suif [sɥif] *m* tallow

suint [sɥɛ̃] *m* wool fat, wool grease

suinter [sɥɛ̃te] *intr* to seep, to ooze; to sweat (*said of wall*); to run (*said of wound*)

suisse [sɥis] *adj* Swiss; **faire suisse** to eat or drink by oneself; to go Dutch || *m* Swiss guard; uniformed usher; **petit suisse** cream cheese || (*cap*) *f* Switzerland; **la Suisse** Switzerland || **Suisse Suissesse** [sɥises] *mf* Swiss (*person*)

suite [sɥit] *f* suite; consequence; continuation, sequel (*of literary work*); sequence, series; **à la suite de** after; **de suite** in succession; in a row; **par la suite** later on; **par suite** consequently; **par suite de** because of

sui·vant [sɥivɑ̃] **-vante** [vɑ̃t] *adj* next, following, subsequent || *mf* follower; next (person) || *f* servant, confidante || **suivant** *adv*—**suivant que** according as || **suivant** *prep* according to

sui·veur [sɥivœr] **-veuse** [vøz] *adj* follow-up (*e.g., car*) || *mf* follower

sui·vi -vie [sɥivi] *adj* connected, coherent; popular

suivre [sɥivr] §67 *tr* to follow; to take (*a course in school*); **suivre la mode** (fig) to follow suit || *intr* to follow; **à suivre** to be continued || *ref* to follow in succession; to follow one after the other

su·jet [syʒe] **-jette** [ʒet] *adj* subject; apt, liable; inclined || *mf* subject (*of a government*); **mauvais sujet** ne'er-do-well || *m* subject, topic; (gram) subject; **au sujet de** about, concerning

sujétion [syʒesjɔ̃] *f* subjection

sulfamide [sylfamid] *m* sulfa drug

sulfure [sylfyr] *m* sulfide

sulfurique [sylfyrik] *adj* sulfuric

sultan [syltɑ̃] *m* sultan

sumac [symak] *m* sumac; **sumac vénéneux** poison ivy

super [syper] *m* (coll) high-test gas

superbe [sypɛrb] *adj* superb; proud ‖ *m* proud person ‖ *f* pride

supercarburant [syperkarbyrã] *m* high-test gasoline

supercherie [syperʃəri] *f* hoax, swindle

superfétatoire [syperfetatwar] *adj* redundant

superficie [syperfisi] *f* surface, area

superfi·ciel -cielle [syperfisjɛl] *adj* superficial

super·flu -flue [syperfly] *adj* superfluous ‖ *m* superfluity, excess

supé·rieur -rieure [syperjœr] *adj* superior; higher; upper (*e.g.*, *story*); **supérieur à** above; more than ‖ *mf* superior

supérieurement [syperjœrmã] *adv* superlatively, exceptionally

supériorité [syperjɔrite] *f* superiority

superla·tif [syperlatif] **-tive** [tiv] *adj & m* superlative; **au superlatif** superlatively; in the superlative

supermarché [sypermarʃe] *m* supermarket

superposer [syperpoze] *tr* to superimpose ‖ *ref* to intervene

supersonique [sypersɔnik] *adj* supersonic

supersti·tieux [syperstisjø] **-tieuse** [sjøz] *adj* superstitious

superstition [syperstisjɔ̃] *f* superstition

superstrat [syperstra] *m* superstratum

superviser [sypervize] *tr* to inspect; to revise; to correct; to supervise

supplanter [syplãte] *tr* to supplant

suppléance [sypleãs] *f* substituting; temporary post

suppléant [sypleã] **suppléante** [sypleãt] *adj* substituting ‖ *mf* substitute (*e.g.*, *a teacher, judge*)

suppléer [syplee] *tr* to supply; to take the place of; to make up for (*what is lacking*); to fill in (*the gaps*); to substitute for (*s.o.*); to fill (*a vacancy*) ‖ *intr*—**suppléer à** to make up for (*s.th.*)

supplément [syplemã] *m* supplement

supplé·tif [sypletif] **-tive** [tiv] *adj & m* (mil) auxiliary

suppliant [syplijã] **suppliante** [syplijãt] *adj & mf* suppliant, supplicant

supplice [syplis] *m* torture; punishment; **être au supplice** to be in agony

supplicier [syplisje] *tr* to torture to death; to torment

supplier [syplije] *tr* to beseech, implore, supplicate; **je vous en supplie** I beg you; **supplier qn de** to implore s.o. to

supplique [syplik] *f* petition

support [sypɔr] *m* support, prop, pillar, bracket, strut; standard (*e.g.*, *for a lamp*)

support-chaussette [sypɔrʃoset] *m* (pl **supports-chaussette**) garter (*for men*)

supporter [sypɔrtœr], [sypɔrter] *m* fan, devotee, supporter, partisan ‖ [sypɔrte] *tr* to support, to prop up; to bear, to endure; to stand, to tolerate, to put up with ‖ *intr*—**supporter de** + *inf* to tolerate or stand

for + *ger* ‖ *ref* to be tolerated; to put up with each other

suppo·sé -sée [sypoze] *adj* supposed, admitted; spurious, assumed ‖ **supposé** *prep* supposing, admitting, granting

supposer [sypoze] *tr* to suppose; to imply; **à supposer que . . .** suppose that **. . .** ; **supposer un testament** to palm off a forged will

supposition [sypozisjɔ̃] *f* supposition; forgery, fraudulent substitution or alteration; **supposition de part** or **supposition d'enfant** false claim of maternity and maternal rights

suppositoire [sypozitwar] *m* suppository

suppôt [sypo] *m* henchman, tool, agitator, hireling; **suppôt de Bacchus** drunkard; **suppôt du diable** imp

suppression [sypresjɔ̃] *f* suppression; elimination (*of a job*); discontinuance (*of a festival*); killing (*of a person*); **suppression de part** or **suppression d'enfant** concealment of a child's birth or death

supprimer [syprime] *tr* to suppress, to cancel, to abolish; to cut out, to omit; (slang) to eliminate, liquidate ‖ *ref* to kill oneself

suppurer [sypyre] *intr* to suppurate

supputation [sypytasjɔ̃] *f* calculation, evaluation, reckoning

supputer [sypyte] *tr* to calculate (*e.g.*, *forthcoming profits, expenses*)

suprême [syprem] *adj* supreme; last

sur sure [syr] *adj* sour ‖ **sur** *prep* on, over; about, concerning; with (*on the person of*); out of, in, e.g., **un jour sur quatre** one day out of four, one day in four; after, e.g., **page sur page** page after page; **sur ce, sur quoi** whereupon; **sur le fait** in the act

sûr sûre [syr] *adj* sure; trustworthy; safe; certain; **à coup sûr, pour sûr** for sure, without fail

surabon·dant [syrabɔ̃dã] **-dante** [dãt] *adj* superabundant

surabonder [syrabɔ̃de] *intr* to superabound; **surabonder de** or **en** to be glutted with

surajouter [syraʒute] *tr* to add on

suralimentation [syralimãtasjɔ̃] *f* forced feeding; (aut) supercharging

suran·né -née [syrane] *adj* outmoded, out-of-date, superannuated; expired (*driver's license, passport, etc.*)

surboum [syrbum] *f* (slang) dance, hop

surcharge [syrʃarʒ] *f* surcharge; overwriting; (sports) handicap (*of weight on a horse*)

surcharger [syrʃarʒe] §38 *tr* to surcharge; to write a word over (*another word*); to write a word over a crossed-out word on (*a document*)

surchauffe [syrʃof] *f* superheating; overheating (*of the economy*)

surchauffer [syrʃofe] *tr* to superheat (*steam; an oven*); to overheat (*an oven, iron, etc.*)

surchoix [syrʃwa] *m* finest quality

surclasser [syrklɑse] *tr* to outclass

surcompo-sé -sée [syrkɔ̃poze] *adj* (gram) double-compound

surcompression [syrkɔ̃presjɔ̃] *f* pressurization, high compression

surcompri-mé -mée [syrkɔ̃prime] *adj* high-compression (*engine*)

surcomprimer [syrkɔ̃prime] *tr* to supercharge; to pressurize

surcontrer [syrkɔ̃tre] *tr* (cards) to redouble

surcouper [syrkupe] *tr* (cards) to overtrump

surcroît [syrkrwa], [syrkrwa] *m* addition, increase; de surcroît or par surcroît in addition, extra

surdi-mutité [syrdimμtite] *f* deaf-muteness

surdité [syrdite] *f* deafness

su-reau [syro] *m* (*pl* -reaux) elderberry

surélévation [syrelevasjɔ̃] *f* escalation, excessive increase; extra story (*added to a building*)

surélever [syrelve] §2 *tr* to raise, raise up; to drive up; to jack up

surenchère [syrɑ̃ʃer] *f* higher bid; surenchère électorale campaign promise, political outbidding

surenchérir [syrɑ̃ʃerir] *intr* to make a higher bid; surenchérir sur qn to outbid s.o.

surestimer [syrestime] *tr* to overestimate

su-ret [syre] -rette [ret] *adj* tart

sûreté [syrte] *f* safety, security; sureness (*of touch; of taste*); surety; en sûreté out of harm's way; in custody, confined (*e.g., in prison*); sûreté individuelle legal protection (*e.g., against arbitrary arrest*); Sûreté nationale or la Sûreté central intelligence; sûretés precautions; guarantees, security (*for a loan*)

surévaluer [syrevalμe] *tr* to overvalue

surexciter [syreksite] *tr* to overexcite

surexposer [syrekspoze] *tr* (phot) to overexpose

surexposition [syrekspozisjɔ̃] *f* (phot) overexposure

surface [syrfas] *f* surface; financial backing; faire surface to surface (*said of a submarine*)

surfaire [syrfer] §29 *tr & intr* to overprice; to overrate

sur-fin [syrfɛ̃] -fine [fin] *adj* superfine

surge-lé -lée [syrʒəle] *adj* frozen (*foods*)

surgeon [syrʒɔ̃] *m* offshoot, sucker

surgir [syrʒir] *intr* to spring up; arise, appear; to arrive, reach port

surglacer [syrglase] §51 *tr* to glaze; to ice (*cake*)

surhaussement [syrosmɑ̃] *m* heightening, raising; banking (*of road*)

surhausser [syrose] *tr* to heighten, to raise; to force up (*prices*); to force up the price of (*s.th.*); to bank (*a road*)

surhomme [syrɔm] *m* superman

surhu-main [syrymɛ̃] -maine [mɛn] *adj* superhuman

surimpression [syrɛ̃presjɔ̃] *f* superimposition; (mov) montage

surintendant [syrɛ̃tɑ̃dɑ̃] *m* superintendent, administrator

surir [syrir] *intr* to turn sour

sur-le-champ [syrlʃɑ̃] *adv* on the spot, immediately

surlendemain [syrlɑ̃dmɛ̃] *m*—le surlendemain the second day after, two days later

surlier [syrlje] *tr* to whip (*a rope*)

surmenage [syrmənaʒ] *m* overworking, fatigue

surmener [syrməne] §2 *tr & ref* to overwork

sur-moi [syrmwa] *m* superego

surmonter [syrmɔ̃te] *tr* to surmount ‖ *intr* to come to the top (*said of oil in water*)

surmouler [syrmule] *tr* to cast from another mold

surmultiplication [syrmyltiplikasjɔ̃] *f* (aut) overdrive

surnager [syrnaʒe] §38 *intr* to float; to survive

surnatu-rel -relle [syrnatyrel] *adj & m* supernatural

surnom [syrnɔ̃] *m* nickname, sobriquet

surnombre [syrnɔ̃br] *m* excess number; en surnombre supernumerary; spare; rester en surnombre to be odd man; surnombre des habitants overpopulation

surnommer [syrnɔme] *tr* to name, call, nickname

surnuméraire [syrnymerer] *adj* supernumerary, extra ‖ *mf* substitute, supernumerary

suroffre [syrɔfr] *f* better or higher offer

suroît [syrwa] *m* southwest wind

surpasser [syrpase] *tr* to surpass; to astonish ‖ *ref* to outdo oneself

surpaye [syrpej] *f* extra pay

surpayer [syrpeje] §49 *tr* to pay too much to; to pay too much for

surpeu-plé -plée [syrpœple] *adj* overpopulated

surpeuplement [syrpœpləmɑ̃] *m* overpopulation

surplis [syrpli] *m* surplice

surplomber [syrplɔ̃be] *tr & intr* to overhang

surplus [syrply] *m* surplus; au surplus moreover

surpopulation [syrpɔpylasjɔ̃] *f* overpopulation

surprendre [syrprɑ̃dr] §56 *tr* to surprise; to come upon by chance; to detect; to overtake, catch

surprise [syrpriz] *f* surprise

surprise-party or surprise-partie [syrprizparti] *f* (*pl* surprises-parties) private dancing party

surproduction [syrprɔdyksjɔ̃] *f* overproduction

surréalisme [syrealism] *m* surrealism

sursaut [syrso] *m* sudden start; en sursaut with a start

sursauter [syrsote] *intr* to give a jump, to start, to jerk

surseoir [syrswar] §5B (*fut* **surseoirai,** etc.) *tr* to postpone, defer, put off || *intr*—**surseoir** (with *dat*) to stay (*an investigation; an execution*)

sursis [syrsi] *m* suspension (*of penalty*); postponement, deferment, stay; **en sursis, avec sursis** suspended (*sentence*)

surtaxe [syrtaks] *f* surtax, surcharge; **surtaxe postale** postage due

surtaxer [syrtakse] *tr* to surtax

surtension [syrtɑ̃sjɔ̃] *f* (elec) surge

surtout [syrtu] *m* topcoat; centerpiece, epergne || *adv* especially, particularly (*by the police*) surveillance

surveillance [syrvejɑ̃s] *f* supervision; (*by the police*) surveillance

surveil·lant [syrvejɑ̃] **surveil·lante** [syrvejɑ̃t] *mf* supervisor, superintendent, overseer; **surveillant d'études** study-hall proctor

surveiller [syrveje] *tr* to inspect, to put under surveillance; to supervise, watch over, monitor

survenir [syrvənir] §72 *intr* (*aux:* ÊTRE) to arrive unexpectedly, to happen suddenly, to crop up

survenue [syrvəny] *f* unexpected arrival

survêtement [syrvetmɑ̃] *m* track suit, sweat shirt

survie [syrvi] *f* survival; afterlife; (law) survivorship

survivance [syrvivɑ̃s] *f* survival

survi·vant [syrvivɑ̃] **-vante** [vɑ̃t] *adj* surviving || *mf* survivor

survivre [syrvivr] §74 *intr* to survive; (with *dat*) to survive, outlive

survoler [syrvɔle] *tr* to fly over; to skim over (*e.g., a problem*)

survol·té -tée [syrvɔlte] *adj* electrified, charged with emotion

sus [sys], [sy] *adv*—**en sus de** in addition to || *interj* up and at it (them)!

susceptible [syseptibl] *adj* susceptible; **susceptible de** capable of

susciter [sysite] *tr* to stir up, evoke, rouse; (lit) to raise up

sus·dit [sysdi] **-dite** [dit] *adj* aforesaid

susmention·né -née [sysmɑ̃sjone] *adj* aforementioned

sus·pect [syspe], [syspekt] **-pecte** [pekt] *adj* suspect, suspicious || *mf* suspect

suspecter [syspekte] *tr* to suspect

suspendre [syspɑ̃dr] *tr* to suspend; to hang, to hang up; **être suspendu aux lèvres de qn** to hang on s.o.'s every word || *ref* to be hung; to hang on

suspen·du -due [syspɑ̃dy] *adj* suspended; hanging

suspens [syspɑ̃] *m* suspense; **en suspens** suspended; in abeyance; outstanding

suspension [syspɑ̃sjɔ̃] *f* suspension

suspi·cieux [syspisj∅] **-cieuse** [sj∅z] *adj* suspicious

suspicion [syspisjɔ̃] *f* suspicion

sustenter [systɑ̃te] *tr* to sustain || *ref* to sustain oneself

susurrer [sysyre] *tr & intr* to murmur, to whisper

susvi·sé -sée [sysvize] *adj* above-mentioned

suture [sytyr] *f* suture

suturer [sytyre] *tr* to suture

suze·rain [syzrɛ̃] **-raine** [ren] *adj & mf* suzerain

svastika [svastika] *m* swastika

svelte [svelt] *adj* slender, lithe, willowy

S.V.P. [esvepe] *m* (letterword) (**s'il vous plaît**) if you please, please

sweater [switɶr] *m* sweater

sycophante [sikɔfɑ̃t] *m* informer

syllabe [silab] *f* syllable

syllogisme [silɔʒism] *m* syllogism

sylphe [silf] *m* sylph

sylvestre [silvestr] *adj* sylvan

symbole [sɛ̃bɔl] *m* symbol; **Symbole des apôtres** Apostles' Creed

symbolique [sɛ̃bɔlik] *adj* symbolic(al)

symboliser [sɛ̃bɔlize] *tr* to symbolize

symbolisme [sɛ̃bɔlism] *m* symbolism

symétrie [simetri] *f* symmetry

symétrique [simetrik] *adj* symmetric(al)

sympathie [sɛ̃pati] *f* fondness, liking; sympathy

sympathique [sɛ̃patik] *adj* likable, attractive; sympathetic

sympathi·sant [sɛ̃patizɑ̃] **-sante** [zɑ̃t] *adj* sympathetic || *mf* sympathizer

sympathiser [sɛ̃patize] *intr* to get along well; **sympathiser avec** to be drawn toward

symphonie [sɛ̃fɔni] *f* symphony

symptôme [sɛ̃ptom] *m* symptom

synagogue [sinagɔg] *f* synagogue

synchrone [sɛ̃krɔn] *adj* synchronous

synchroniser [sɛ̃krɔnize] *tr* to synchronize

syncope [sɛ̃kɔp] *f* faint, swoon, syncope; syncopation

syndicat [sɛ̃dika] *m* labor union; **syndicat d'initiative** chamber of commerce; **syndicat patronal** employers' association

syndicats-patrons [sɛ̃dikapatrɔ̃] *adj invar* labor-management

syndiquer [sɛ̃dike] *tr & ref* to syndicate

synonyme [sinɔnim] *adj* synonymous || *m* synonym

synopsis [sinɔpsis] *m & f* (mov) synopsis

syntaxe [sɛ̃taks] *f* syntax

synthèse [sɛ̃tez] *f* synthesis

synthétique [sɛ̃tetik] *adj* synthetic

synthétiser [sɛ̃tetize] *tr* to synthesize

syntonisation [sɛ̃tɔnizasjɔ̃] *f* tuning (*of radio*)

syntoniser [sɛ̃tɔnize] *tr* to tune in

syphilis [sifilis] *f* syphilis

Syrie [siri] *f* Syria; **la Syrie** Syria

sy·rien [sirjɛ̃] **-rienne** [rjen] *adj* Syrian || (*cap*) *mf* Syrian (*person*)

systématique [sistematik] *adj* systematic

systématiser [sistematize] *tr* to systematize

système [sistem] *m* system; **courir, porter,** or **taper sur le système à qn** (slang) to get on s.o.'s nerves; **système D** (coll) resourcefulness

systole [sistɔl] *f* systole

T

T, t [te] *m invar* twentieth letter of the French alphabet

t. *abbr* (tome) vol.

ta [ta] §88

tabac [taba] *m* tobacco; tobacco shop; **avoir le gros tabac** (slang) to be a hit; **passer qn à tabac** (coll) to give s.o. the third degree; **tabac à chiquer** chewing tobacco; **tabac à priser** snuff

tabagie [tabaʒi] *f* smoke-filled room

tabasser [tabase] *tr* (slang) to give a licking to, to shellac

tabatière [tabatjɛr] *f* snuffbox; skylight, dormer window

tabernacle [tabɛrnakl] *m* tabernacle

table [tabl] *f* table; **aimer la table** to like good food; **à table!** dinner is served!; **dresser** or **mettre la table** to set the table; **faire table rase** to make a clean sweep; **sainte table** altar rail; **se mettre à table** (slang) to tell all, to confess, to squeal; **table à abattants** gate-leg table; **table à ouvrage** worktable; **table à rallonges** extension table; **table de chevet**, **table de nuit** bedside table; **table d'écoute** wiretap; **table de jeu** card table; **table des matières** table of contents; **table de toilette** dressing table; **table d'hôte** table d'hôte; chef's special; **table d'opération** operating table; **table gigogne** nest of tables; **table interurbaine** long-distance switchboard; **table roulante** serving cart; **tenir table ouverte** to keep open house

ta·bleau [tablo] *m* (*pl* **-bleaux**) painting, picture; scoreboard; board; table, catalogue; panel (*of jurors*); **tableau d'affichage** bulletin board; **tableau d'avancement** seniority list; **tableau de bord** dashboard; instrument panel; **tableau de distribution** switchboard; **tableau d'honneur** honor roll; **tableau noir** blackboard; **tableau vivant** tableau

tabler [table] *intr*—**tabler sur** to count on; to use as a base

tablette [tablɛt] *f* shelf; mantelpiece; bar (*e.g., of chocolate*); **rayez cela de vos tablettes** don't count on it; **tablettes** pocket notebook

table-valise [tabləvaliz] *f* (*pl* **tables-valises**) folding table

tablier [tablije] *m* apron; roadway (*of bridge*); hood (*of chimney*); **tablier de fer** protective shutter (*on store window*)

ta·bou **-bou** or **boue** [tabu] *adj & m* taboo

tabouret [tabure] *m* stool; footstool

tabulaire [tabylɛr] *adj* tabular

tabulateur [tabylatœr] *m* tabulator

tac [tak] *m* click, clack; **du tac au tac** tit for tat; **tac tac tac!** rat-a-tat-tat!

tache [taʃ] *f* spot, stain; blemish, flaw; blot, smear; speck; **faire tache** to be out of place; **faire tache d'huile** to spread; **sans tache** spotless, unblemished; **tache de rousseur**, **tache de son** freckle; **tache de vin** birthmark; **tache originelle** original sin; **tache solaire** sunspot

tâche [taʃ] *f* task, job; **prendre à tâche de** to try to; **travailler à la tâche** to do piecework

tacher [taʃe] *tr & ref* to spot, stain

tâcher [taʃe] *tr*—**tâcher que** to see to it that || *intr*—**tâcher de** to try to; **tâcher** to try

tâcheron [taʃrɔ̃] *m* small jobber; piece-worker; hard worker; wage slave

tacheter [taʃte] §34 *tr* to spot, to speckle

tacite [tasit] *adj* tacit

taciturne [tasityrn] *adj* taciturn

tacot [tako] *m* (coll) jalopy

tact [takt] *m* tact; sense of touch

tacticien [taktisjɛ̃] *m* tactician

tactique [taktik] *adj* tactical || *f* tactics

taffetas [tafta] *m* taffeta; **taffetas gommé** adhesive tape

Tage [taʒ] *m* Tagus

taïaut [tajo] *interj* tallyho!

taie [te] *f* (pathol) leukoma; **avoir une taie sur l'œil** (fig) to be blinded by prejudice; **taie d'oreiller** pillowcase

taillader [tajade] *tr & ref* to slash, cut

taille [taj] *f* cutting (*e.g., of diamond*); trimming (*e.g., of hedge*); height, stature; waist, waistline; size; cut (*of garment*); **à la taille de**, **de la taille de** to the measure of, suitable for; **avoir la taille fine** to have a slim waist; **de taille** big enough, strong enough; (coll) big; **être de taille à** to be up to, to be big enough to; **taille de guêpe** wasp waist; **taille en dessous** next size smaller; **taille en dessus** next size larger

tail·lé **-lée** [taje] *adj* cut; trimmed; **bien taillé** well-built; **taillé pour** cut out for

taille-crayon [tajkrejɔ̃] *m* (*pl* **-crayon** or **-crayons**) pencil sharpener

taille-douce [tajdus] *f* (*pl* **tailles-douces**) copperplate

taille-pain [tajpɛ̃] *m invar* bread knife; bread slicer

tailler [taje] *tr* to cut; to sharpen (*a pencil*); to prune, trim (*a tree*); to carve (*stone*); to clip (*hair*) || *intr* (cards) to deal || *ref* to carve out (*a path; a career*); (coll) to beat it

tailleur [tajœr] *m* tailor; woman's suit; (cards) dealer; **en tailleur** squatting (*while tailoring*); **tailleur de diamants** diamond cutter; **tailleur de pierre** stonecutter; **tailleur sur mesure** lady's tailor-made suit

taillis [taji] *m* thicket, copse

tain [tɛ̃] *m* silvering (*of mirror*)

taire [tɛr] §52 (3d *sg pres ind* **tait**) *tr* to hush up, to hide; **la tairas-tu?** (slang) will you shut your trap?; **taire q.ch. à qn** to keep s.th. from s.o. || *intr*—**faire taire** to silence || *ref* to keep quiet, keep still; **se taire sur** to say nothing about; **tais-toi!** shut up!

talent [talɑ̃] *m* talent

talen·tueux [talɑ̃tyǿ] **-tueuse** [tyǿz] *adj* talented

taloche [talɔʃ] *f* plastering trowel; (coll) clout, smack

talon [talɔ̃] *m* heel; stub

talonner [talɔne] *tr* to tail; to harass; to dig one's spurs into || *intr* to bump

talus [taly] *m* slope; embankment

tambour [tɑ̃bur] *m* drum; drummer; entryway; spool (*of reel*); **tambour battant** (coll) roughly; (coll) quickly; **tambour cylindrique** revolving door; **tambour de basque** tambourine; **tambour de freins** brake drum; **tambour de ville** town crier

tambouriner [tɑ̃burine] *tr* & *intr* to drum; to broadcast far and wide || *intr* to beat a tattoo; to drum

tambour-major [tɑ̃burmaʒɔr] *m* (*pl* **tambours-majors**) drum major

tamis [tami] *m* sieve; **passer au tamis** to sift; **tamis à farine** flour sifter

Tamise [tamiz] *f* Thames

tamiser [tamize] *tr* & *intr* to sift

tampon [tɑ̃pɔ̃] *m* plug; bung; swab; rubber stamp; buffer; cancellation, postmark; (surg) tampon; **tampon buvard** hand blotter; **tampon encreur** stamp pad

tamponner [tɑ̃pɔne] *tr* to swab, to dab; to bump, to bump into; (surg) to tampon

tan [tɑ̃] *adj invar* tan || *m* tanbark

tancer [tɑ̃se] §51 *tr* to scold

tandem [tɑ̃dɛm] *m* tandem; **en tandem** tandem

tandis que [tɑ̃dikə], [tɑ̃diskə] *conj* while; whereas

tangage [tɑ̃gaʒ] *m* (naut) pitching

Tanger [tɑ̃ʒe] *m* Tangier

tangible [tɑ̃ʒibl] *adj* tangible

tanguer [tɑ̃ge] *intr* to pitch (*said of ship*)

tanière [tanjɛr] *f* den, lair

tanker [tɑ̃kɛr] *m* oil tanker

tan·nant [tɑ̃nɑ̃] **tan·nante** [tɑ̃nɑ̃t] *adj* (coll) boring

tanne [tan] *f* spot (*on leather*); blackhead

tanner [tane] *tr* to tan; (coll) to pester

tannerie [tanri] *f* tannery

tanneur [tanœr] *m* tanner

tan·sad [tɑ̃sad] *m* (*pl* **-sads**) rear seat (*of motorcycle*)

tant [tɑ̃] *adv* so, so much; so long; **en tant que** as; in so far as; **si tant est que** if it is true that; **tant bien que mal** somehow or other; **tant de** so many; so much; **tant mieux** so much the better; **tant pis** so much the worse; never mind; **tant qu'à faire** while we're (you've, etc.) at it; **tant que** as well as; as long as; **tant s'en faut** far from it; **tant soit peu** ever so little; **vous m'en direz tant** (coll) you've just said a mouthful

tante [tɑ̃t] *f* aunt; (slang) fairy; **ma tante** (coll) the hockshop

tantième [tɑ̃tjɛm] *m* percentage

tantine [tɑ̃tin] *f* (coll) auntie

tantôt [tɑ̃to] *m* (coll) afternoon || *adv* in a little while; a little while ago; (coll) in the afternoon; **à tantôt** see you soon; **tantôt . . . tantôt** sometimes . . . sometimes

taon [tɑ̃] *m* horsefly

tapage [tapaʒ] *m* uproar

tapa·geur [tapaʒœr] **-geuse** [ʒǿz] *adj* loud

tape [tap] *f* tap, slap

ta·pé -pée [tape] *adj* dried (*fruit*); rotten in spots; (coll) crazy; (slang) worn (*with age or fatigue*); **bien tapé** (coll) well done; (coll) nicely served; (coll) to the point

tape-à-l'œil [tapalœj] *adj* gaudy, showy || *m invar* mere show

taper [tape] *tr* to tap, to slap; to type; (coll) to hit (*s.o. for money*) || *intr* to tap, to slap; to type; (coll) to go to the head (*said of wine*); **ça tape ici** (slang) it hurts here; **taper dans** (coll) to use; **taper dans le mille** (coll) to succeed; **taper dans l'œil de qn** (coll) to make a hit with s.o.; **taper de** to hit (*e.g., 100 m.p.h.*); **taper des pieds** to stamp one's feet; **taper sur** (coll) to get on (*s.o.'s nerves*); **taper sur le ventre de qn** (coll) to give s.o. a poke in the ribs; **taper sur qn** (coll) to run down s.o., to give s.o. a going-over

tapette [tapɛt] *f* carpet beater; fly swatter; handball; (slang) fairy; **avoir une fière tapette** (coll) to be a chatterbox

tapin [tapɛ̃] *m* (coll) drummer boy; (slang) solicitation (*by a prostitute*)

tapinois [tapinwa] **—en tapinois** stealthily

tapir [tapir] *ref* to crouch, to squat; to hide

tapis [tapi] *m* carpet; rug; game of chance; **mettre sur le tapis** to bring up for discussion; **tapis de bain** bath mat; **tapis de sol** ground cloth; **tapis de table** table covering; **tapis roulant** conveyor belt; moving sidewalk

tapis-brosse [tapibrɔs] *m* (*pl* **-brosses**) doormat

tapisser [tapise] *tr* to upholster; to tapestry; to wallpaper

tapisserie [tapisri] *f* upholstery; tapestry; **faire tapisserie** to be a wallflower

tapis·sier [tapisje] **tapis·sière** [tapisjɛr] *mf* upholsterer; tapestry maker; paperhanger

tapoter [tapɔte] *tr* & *intr* to tap

taquet [takɛ] *m* wedge, peg; (mach) tappet; (naut) cleat; **taquet d'arrêt** (rr) scotch, wedge

ta·quin [takɛ̃] **-quine** [kin] *adj* teasing || *mf* tease

taquiner [takine] *tr* to tease

taquinerie [takinri] *f* teasing

taraud [taro] *m* (mach) tap

tarauder [tarode] *tr* (mach) to tap; (coll) to pester

taraudeuse [tarodǿz] *f* tap wrench

tard [tar] *m*—**sur le tard** late in the day; late in life || *adv* late; **pas plus tard que** no later than; **plus tard** later on

tarder [tarde] *intr* to delay; **tarder à to be long in** || *impers*—**il tarde** (with *dat*) **de** long to, e.g., **il lui tarde de vous voir** he longs to see you

tar·dif [tardif] [*dive* [div] *adj* late; backward; tardy

tardivement [tardivmã] *adv* belatedly

tare [tar] *f* defect, blemish; taint; loss in value; tare (*weight*)

tarer [tare] *tr* to damage; to taint; to tare || *ref* to spoil

targette [target] *f* latch

targuer [targe] *ref*—**se targuer de** to pride oneself on

tarière [tarjer] *f* auger, drill

tarif [tarif] *m* price list; rate, tariff; **plein tarif** full fare; **tarifs postaux** postal rates

tarifaire [tarifer] *adj* tariff

tarifer [tarife] *tr* to price; to rate

tarir [tarir] *tr* to drain, exhaust, dry up || *intr* to dry up, to run dry; **ne pas tarir** to never run out || *ref* to dry up; to be exhausted

tarse [tars] *m* tarsus; instep

tartare [tartar] *adj* tartar (*sauce*); Tartar || (*cap*) *mf* Tartar

tarte [tart] *adj* (coll) silly, stupid; (coll) ugly || *f* pie, tart; (slang) slap

tartine [tartin] *f* slice of bread and butter or jam; (coll) long-winded speech; (coll) rambling article

tartiner [tartine] *tr* to spread

tartre [tartr] *m* tartar; scale

tartuferie [tartyfri] *f* hypocrisy

tas [tɑ] *m* heap, pile; **mettre en tas** to pile up; **prendre sur le tas** to catch red-handed; **tas de foin** haystack; **un tas de** (coll) a lot of

tasse [tɑs] *f* cup; **tasse à café** coffee cup; **tasse à thé** teacup; **tasse de café** cup of coffee

tas·seau [tɑso] *m* (*pl* -**seaux**) bracket; cleat; lug (*on casting*)

tasser [tɑse] *tr* to cram; to tamp; **bien tassé** (coll) brimful || *intr* to grow thick || *ref* to settle; to huddle; (coll) to go back to normal

taste-vin [tastəvɛ̃] *m invar* wine taster (*cup*); sampling tube

tata [tata] *f* (slang) auntie

tâter [tate] *tr* to feel, to touch; to test, to feel out; **tâter le pouls à qn** to feel s.o.'s pulse || *intr*—**tâter de** to taste; to experience; to try one's hand at || *ref* to stop to think, to ponder

tâte-vin [tatvɛ̃] *m invar* wine taster (*cup*); sampling tube

tatil·lon [tatijɔ̃] **tatil·lonne** [tatijɔn] *adj* fussy, hairsplitting || *mf* hair-splitter

tâtonner [tatɔne] *intr* to grope

tâtons [tatɔ̃]—**à tâtons** gropingly

tatouage [tatwaʒ] *m* tattoo

tatouer [tatwe] *tr* to tattoo

taudis [todi] *m* hovel; **taudis** *mpl* slums

taule [tol] *f* (slang) fleabag; **faire de la taule** (slang) to do a stretch

taupe [top] *f* mole; moleskin

taupin [topɛ̃] *m* (mil) sapper; (coll) engineering student

taupinière [topinjer] *f* molehill

tau·reau [toro] *m* (*pl* -**reaux**) bull

taux [to] *m* rate; **taux d'escompte** discount rate

taveler [tavle] §34 *tr* to spot || *ref* to become spotted

taverne [tavern] *f* inn, tavern

taxation [taksɑsjɔ̃] *f* fixing (*of prices, wages, etc.*); assessment; taxation

taxe [taks] *f* fixed price; rate; tax; **taxe à la valeur ajoutée** value-added tax; **taxe de luxe** luxury tax; **taxe de séjour** nonresident tax; **taxe directe** sales tax; **taxe perçue** postage paid; **taxe supplémentaire** postage due; **taxe sur les spectacles** entertainment tax

taxer [takse] *tr* to fix the price of; to regulate the rate of; to assess; to tax; **taxer qn de** to tax or charge s.o. with || *ref* to set an offering price; **se taxer de** to accuse oneself of

taxi [taksi] *m* taxi; (coll) cabdriving; **hep taxi!** taxi! || *mf* (coll) cabdriver

taxidermie [taksidɛrmi] *f* taxidermy

taxiphone [taksifɔn] *m* pay phone

Tchécoslovaquie [tʃekɔslɔvaki] *f* Czechoslovakia; **la Tchécoslovaquie** Czechoslovakia

tchèque [tʃɛk] *adj* Czech || *m* Czech (*language*) || (*cap*) *mf* Czech (*person*)

te [tə] §87

techni·cien [teknisjɛ̃] **-cienne** [sjɛn] *mf* technician; engineer

technique [teknik] *adj* technical || *f* technique; engineering

teck [tek] *m* teak

teigne [teɲ] *f* moth; ringworm; (fig) pest, nuisance

teindre [tɛ̃dr] §50 *tr* to dye; to tint || *ref* to be tinted; to dye or tint one's hair; (with *dat* of *reflex pron*) to dye or tint (*one's hair*)

teint [tɛ̃] **teinte** [tɛ̃t] *adj* dyed; with dyed hair || *m* dye; complexion; **bon teint** fast color || *f* tint, shade; (fig) tinge

teinter [tɛ̃te] *tr* to tint; to tinge

teinture [tɛ̃tyr] *f* dye; dyeing; tincture; (fig) smattering; **teinture d'iode** (pharm) iodine

teinturerie [tɛ̃tyrri] *f* dry cleaner's; dyer's; dyeing

teintu·rier [tɛ̃tyrje] **-rière** [rjer] *mf* dry cleaner; dyer

tel telle [tel] *adj* such; like, e.g., **tel père tel fils** like father like son; **de telle sorte que** so that; **tel ou tel** such and such a; **tel que** such as, the same as, as; **tel quel** as is || *mf*—**un tel** or **une telle** so-and-so || *pron* such a one, such

télé [tele] *f* (coll) TV; (coll) TV set

télécommander [telekɔmɑ̃de] *tr* to operate by remote control; (fig) to inspire, influence

téléférique [teleferik] *m* skyride, cableway

télégramme [telegram] *m* telegram

télégraphe [telegraf] *m* telegraph

télégraphier [telegrafje] *tr* & *intr* to telegraph

télégraphiste [telegrafist] *mf* telegrapher

téléguider [telegide] *tr* to guide (*e.g., a missile*); (*coll*) to influence

téléimprimeur [teleẽprimœr] *m* teletype, teleprinter

télémètre [telemetr] *m* telemeter; range finder

téléobjectif [teleɔbʒektif] *m* telephoto lens

télépathie [telepati] *f* telepathy

téléphérique [teleferik] *m* skyride, cableway

téléphone [telefon] *m* telephone

téléphoner [telefone] *tr & intr* to telephone

téléphoniste [telefonist] *mf* telephone operator || *m* lineman || *f* telephone girl

télescope [teleskɔp] *m* telescope

télescoper [teleskɔpe] *tr & ref* to telescope

télescopique [teleskɔpik] *adj* telescopic

téléscripteur [teleskriptœr] *m* teletype, teletypewriter

télésiège [telesjeʒ] *m* chair lift

téléski [teleski] *m* ski lift

téléspecta·teur [telespektatœr] **-trice** [tris] *mf* (television) viewer

télétype [teletip] *m* teletype

téléviser [televize] *tr* to televise

téléviseur [televizœr] *m* television set; **téléviseur à servo-réglage** remote-control television set

télévision [televizjɔ̃] *f* television; (*coll*) television set

télévi·suel -suelle [televizɥɛl] *adj* television

tellement [telmã] *adv* so much, so; **tellement de** so much, so many; **tellement que** to such an extent that

téméraire [temerer] *adj* rash, reckless, foolhardy

témérité [temerite] *f* temerity, rashness

témoignage [temwaɲaʒ] *m* testimony, witness; **en témoignage de quoi** in witness whereof; **rendre témoignage à** or **pour** to testify in favor of

témoigner [temwaɲe] *tr* to show; to testify || *intr* to testify; **témoigner de** to give evidence of; to bear witness to

témoin [temwẽ] *adj invar* type, model; pilot || *m* witness; control (*in scientific experiment*); second (*in duel*); **prendre à témoin** to call to witness; **témoin à charge** witness for the prosecution; **témoin à décharge** witness for the defense; **témoin oculaire** eyewitness

tempe [tãp] *f* (anat) temple

tempérament [tãperamã] *m* temperament; amorous nature; **à tempérament** on the installment plan

tempérance [tãperãs] *f* temperance

tempé·rant -rante [tãperã] **-rãt**] *adj* temperate

température [tãperatyr] *f* temperature

tempé·ré -rée [tãpere] *adj* temperate; tempered; restrained

tempérer [tãpere] §10 *tr* to temper || *ref* to moderate

tempête [tãpet] *f* tempest, storm; **affronter la tempête** (fig) to face the music; **tempête dans un verre d'eau** tempest in a teapot; **tempête de neige** blizzard; **tempête de poussière** dust storm; **tempête de sable** sandstorm

tempêter [tãpete] *intr* to storm

tempé·tueux [tãpetɥø] **-tueuse** [tɥøz] *adj* tempestuous

temple [tãpl] *m* temple; chapel, church

tempo [tempo], [tɛpo] *m* tempo

temporaire [tãporer] *adj* temporary

tempo·ral -rale [tãporal] *adj* (*pl* **-raux** [ro]) (anat) temporal

tempo·rel -relle [tãporel] *adj* temporal

temporiser [tãporize] *intr* to temporize, to stall

temps [tã] *m* time; times; cycle (*of internal-combustion engine*); position, movement (*in gymnastics, fencing, carrying of arms*); weather, *e.g.,* **quel temps fait-il?** what is the weather like?; (gram) tense; (mus) beat, measure; **à temps** in time; **avoir fait son temps** to have seen better days; **dans le temps** formerly; **de temps en temps** from time to time; **en même temps** at the same time; **en temps et lieu** in due course; **en temps utile** in due course; **faire son temps** to do time (*in prison*); **gagner du temps** to save time; **le bon vieux temps** the good old days; **Le Temps** Father Time; **temps atomique** atomic era; **temps d'arrêt** pause, halt

tenable [tənabl] *adj*—**pas tenable** untenable; unbearable

tenace [tənas] *adj* tenacious

ténacité [tenasite] *f* tenacity

tenailler [tənaje] *tr* to torture

tenailles [tənaj] *fpl* pincers

tenan·cier [tənãsje] **-cière** [sjer] *mf* sharecropper; lessee; keeper (*e.g., of a dive*)

te·nant [tənã] **-nante** [nãt] *adj* attached (*collar*) || *mf* (sports) holder (*of a title*) || *m* champion, supporter; **connaître les tenants et les aboutissants** to know the ins and outs; **d'un seul tenant** in one piece

tendance [tãdãs] *f* tendency

tendan·cieux [tãdãsjø] **-cieuse** [sjøz] *adj* tendentious, slanted

ten·deur [tãdœr] **-deuse** [døz] *mf* paperhanger; layer (*of traps*) || *m* stretcher

tendoir [tãdwar] *m* clothesline

tendon [tãdɔ̃] *m* tendon

tendre [tãdr] *adj* tender || *tr* to stretch; to hang; to bend (*a bow*); to lay (*a trap*); to strain (*one's ear*); to hold out, to reach out || *intr*—**tendre à** to aim at; to tend toward || *ref* to become strained

tendresse [tãdres] *f* tenderness, love, affection; (coll) partiality; **mille tendresses** (*closing of letter*) fondly

tendreté [tãdrəte] *f* tenderness

ten·du -due [tãdy] *adj* tense, taut; strained; stretched out; **tendu de** hung with

ténèbres [tenebr] *fpl* darkness

téné·breux [tenebrø] **-breuse** [brøz] *adj* dark; somber (*person*); shady (*deal*); obscure (*style*)

te·neur [tənœr] **-neuse** [nøz] *mf* holder; **teneur de livres** bookkeeper

|| **teneur** *f* tenor, gist; text; grade (*e.g., of ore*)

ténia [tenja] *m* tapeworm

tenir [tənir], §72 *tr* to hold; to keep; to take up (*space*); **être tenu à** to be obliged to; **être tenu de** to be responsible for || *intr* to hold; **il ne tient qu'à vous** it's up to you; **tenez!** here!; **tenir à** to insist upon; to care for, to value; to be caused by; **tenir de** to take after, to resemble; **tenir debout** (fig) to hold water, to ring true; **tenir q.ch. de qn** to have s.th. from s.o., to learn s.th. from s.o.; **tiens!** well!, hey! || *ref* to stay, remain; to sit up; to stand up; to behave; to contain oneself; **à quoi s'en tenir** what to believe; **s'en tenir à** to limit oneself to; to abide by

tennis [tenis] *m* tennis; tennis court

ténor [tenor] *adj masc* tenor || *m* tenor; star performer

tension [tɑ̃sjɔ̃] *f* tension; blood pressure; **avoir de la tension** to have high blood pressure; **haute tension** (elec) high tension; **tension artérielle** blood pressure

tentacule [tɑ̃takyl] *m* tentacle

tenta·teur [tɑ̃tatœr] **-trice** [tris] *mf* tempter

tentation [tɑ̃tasjɔ̃] *f* temptation

tentative [tɑ̃tativ] *f* attempt

tente [tɑ̃t] *f* tent; awning

tente-abri [tɑ̃tabri] *f* (*pl* **tentes-abris** [tɑ̃tabri]) pup tent

tenter [tɑ̃te] *tr* to tempt; to attempt || *intr*—**tenter de** to attempt to

tenture [tɑ̃tyr] *f* drape; hangings; wallpaper

te·nu -nue [təny] *adj* firm (*securities, market, etc.*); **bien tenu** well-kept || *f* see **tenue**

té·nu -nue [teny] *adj* tenuous; thin

tenue [təny] *f* holding; managing; upkeep, maintenance; behavior; bearing; dress, costume; uniform; session; (mus) hold; **avoir de la tenue** to have good manners; **avoir une bonne tenue** (horsemanship) to have a good seat; **en tenue** in uniform; **grande tenue** (mil) full dress; **petite tenue** (mil) undress; **tenue des livres** bookkeeping; **tenue de soirée** evening clothes; **tenue de ville** street clothes

térébenthine [terebɑ̃tin] *f* turpentine

tergiverser [terʒiverse] *intr* to duck, equivocate, vacillate

terme [term] *m* term; end, limit; quarterly payment; **avant terme** prematurely; **terme fatal** last day of grace

terminaison [terminɛzɔ̃] *f* ending, termination

termi·nal -nale [terminal] *adj* (*pl* **-naux** [no]) terminal

terminer [termine] *tr & ref* to terminate

terminus [terminys] *m* terminal || *interj* the end has come!

termite [termit] *m* termite

terne [tern] *adj* dull, drab

ternir [ternir] *tr & ref* to tarnish

terrain [terɛ̃] *m* ground; terrain; playing field; dueling field; **ne pas être**

---

sur son terrain to be out of one's depth; **tâter le terrain** to find out the lay of the land; **terrain à bâtir** or **à lotir** building plot; **terrain brûlant** (fig) unsafe ground; **terrain d'atterrissage** landing field; **terrain d'aviation** airfield; **terrain de courses** race track; **terrain de jeux** playground; **terrain de manœuvres** parade ground; **terrain vague** vacant lot

terrasse [teras] *f* terrace; sidewalk café; **terrasse en plein air** outdoor café

terrasser [terase] *tr* to embank; to floor, to knock down

terre [ter] *f* earth; land; (elec) ground; **descendre à terre** to go ashore; **la Terre Sainte** the Holy Land; **mettre pied à terre** to dismount; **par terre** on the floor; on the ground; **terre cuite** terra cotta; **Terre de Feu** Tierra del Fuego; **terre ferme** terra firma; **terre franche** loam

ter·reau [tero] *m* (*pl* **-reaux**) compost

terre-neuve [ternœv] *m invar* Newfoundland dog ||—**Terre-Neuve** *f* Newfoundland

terre-plein [terplɛ̃] *m* (*pl* **-pleins**) median, divider (*of road*); fill, embankment; earthwork, rampart; terrace; (rr) roadbed

terrer [tere] *tr* to earth up (*e.g., a tree*); to earth over (*seed*) || *ref* to burrow; to entrench oneself

terrestre [terestr] *adj* land; terrestrial

terreur [terœr] *f* terror; **la Terreur** the Reign of Terror

ter·reux [terø] **ter·reuse** [terøz] *adj* earthy; dirty; sallow (*complexion*)

terrible [teribl] *adj* terrible; terrific

ter·rien [terjɛ̃] **ter·rienne** [terjen] *adj* landed (*gentry*) || *mf* landowner; landlubber || *m* earthman

terrier [terje] *m* hole, burrow; (dog) terrier

terrifier [terifje] *tr* to terrify

terrir [terir] *intr* to come close to shore (*said of fish*)

territoire [teritwar] *m* territory

terroir [terwar] *m* soil; homeland

terroriser [terɔrize] *tr* to terrorize

tertiaire [tersjer] *adj* tertiary

tertre [tertr] *m* mound, knoll

tes [te] §888

tesson [tesɔ̃] *m* shard; broken glass

test [test] *m* test; (zool) shell; **test de niveau** placement test

testament [testamɑ̃] *m* testament; will

testa·teur [testatœr] **-trice** [tris] *mf* testator

tester [teste] *tr* to test || *intr* to make one's will

testicule [testikyl] *m* testicle

tétanos [tetanos] *m* tetanus

têtard [tetar] *m* tadpole; (bot) pollard

tête [tet] *f* head; heading (*e.g., of chapter*); **à la tête de** in charge of, at the head of; **à tête reposée** at one's (own) leisure; **avoir la tête près du bonnet** (coll) to be quick-tempered; **avoir une bonne tête** to have a pleasant look or expression; **de tête** in one's mind's eye, mentally; capable, e.g., **une femme de tête** a capable woman;

en avoir par-dessus la tête (coll) to be fed up with it; **en tête foremost,** at the front, leading; **en tête à tête avec** alone with; **faire la tête à** to frown at, to give a dirty look to; **faire une tête** to wear a long face; **forte tête** strong-minded person; **jeter à la tête à qn** (fig) to cast in s.o.'s face; **la tête en bas** head downwards, upside down; **la tête la première** headfirst, headlong; **laver la tête à qn** (coll) to give s.o. a dressing down; **mauvaise tête** troublemaker; **monter à la tête de qn** to go to s.o.'s head; **n'en faire qu'à sa tête** to be a law unto oneself; **par tête** per capita, per head; **piquer une tête** to take a header, to dive; **saluer de la tête** to nod; **se mettre en tête de** to take it into one's head to; **se payer la tête de qn** (coll) to pull s.o.'s leg; **tenir tête à** to face up to, to stand up to; **tête baissée** headlong, heedless; **tête brûlée** daredevil; **tête chercheuse** homing head (*of missile*); **tête d'affiche** (theat) headliner; **tête de bois** blockhead; **tête de cuvée** choice wine; **tête de lecture** (elec) playback head; **tête de ligne** truck terminal; **tête de linotte** scatterbrain; **tête de pont** (mil) bridgehead, beachhead; **tête de Turc** butt, scapegoat, fall guy; **tête montée** excitable person; **tête morte et tibias** skull and crossbones; **tomber sur la tête** (coll) to be off one's rocker

tête-à-queue [tɛtakø] *m invar* about-face, slue

tétée [tete] *f* sucking; feeding time

téter [tete] §10 *tr & intr* to suck

tétine [tetin] *f* nipple; teat

téton [tetɔ̃] *m* (coll) tit

tétras [tetrɑ] *m* grouse

tette [tɛt] *f* (coll) tit

tê·tu -tue [tety] *adj* stubborn

teuf-teuf [tœftœf] *m* (*pl* **teuf-teuf** or **teufs-teufs**) (coll) jalopy ‖ *interj* chug!, chug!

tévé [teve] *f* (acronym) (*télévision*) TV

texte [tɛkst] *m* text; **apprendre son texte** (theat) to learn one's lines

textile [tɛkstil] *adj & m* textile

tex·tuel -tuelle [tɛkstɥɛl] *adj* textual; verbatim

texture [tɛkstyr] *f* texture

thaï [tai] *adj invar & m* Thai

thaïlan·dais [tajlɑ̃dɛ] **-daise** [dɛz] *adj* Thai ‖ (*cap*) *mf* Thai

Thaïlande [tajlɑ̃d] *f* Thailand

thaumaturge [tomatyrʒ] *m* miracle worker, magician

thé [te] *m* tea

théâ·tral -trale [teatral] *adj* (*pl* **-traux** [tro]) theatrical

théâtre [teɑtr] *m* theater; stage, boards; scene (*e.g., of the crime*)

théier [teje] **théière** [tejɛr] *adj* tea ‖ *m* tea (*shrub*) ‖ *f* see **théière**

théière [tejɛr] *f* teapot

thème [tɛm] *m* theme; translation (*into a foreign language*)

théologie [teɔlɔʒi] *f* theology

théorème [teɔrɛm] *m* theorem

théorie [teɔri] *f* theory; procession

théorique [teɔrik] *adj* theoretical

thérapeutique [terapøtik] *adj* therapeutic ‖ *f* therapeutics

thérapie [terapi] *f* therapy

Thérèse [terɛz] *f* Theresa

ther·mal -male [tɛrmal] *adj* (*pl* **-maux** [mo]) thermal

thermique [tɛrmik] *adj* thermal

thermocouple [tɛrmokupl] *m* thermocouple

thermodynamique [tɛrmɔdinamik] *adj* thermodynamic ‖ *f* thermodynamics

thermomètre [tɛrmɔmɛtr] *m* thermometer

thermonucléaire [tɛrmɔnykleɛr] *adj* thermonuclear

Thermopyles [tɛrmɔpil] *fpl*—**les Thermopyles** Thermopylae

thermos [tɛrmos] *f* thermos bottle

thermosiphon [tɛrmɔsifɔ̃] *m* hot-water heater

thermostat [tɛrmɔsta] *m* thermostat

thésauriser [tezorize] *tr & intr* to hoard

thésauri·seur [tezorizœr] **-seuse** [zøz] *mf* hoarder

thèse [tɛz] *f* thesis

thon [tɔ̃] *m* tuna

thorax [tɔraks] *m* thorax

thrène [trɛn] *m* threnody

thuriféraire [tyriferɛr] *m* incense bearer; flatterer

thym [tɛ̃] *m* thyme

thyroïde [tiroid] *adj & f* thyroid

tiare [tjar] *f* tiara (*papal miter*); papacy

tibia [tibja] *m* tibia; shin; **tibias croisés et tête de mort** skull and crossbones

tic [tik] *m* (pathol) tic; **tic tac** ticktock

ticket [tikɛ] *m* ticket (*of bus, subway, etc.*); check (*for article in baggage room*); ration stamp; **sans tickets** unrationed; **ticket de quai** platform ticket

tic-tac [tiktak] *m invar* tick

tiède [tjɛd] *adj* lukewarm; mild

tiédeur [tjedœr] *f* lukewarmness; mildness

tiédir [tjedir] *tr* to take the chill off ‖ *intr* to become lukewarm

tien [tjɛ̃] **tienne** [tjɛn] §89

tiens [tjɛ̃] *interj* welll, hey!

tiers [tjɛr] **tierce** [tjɛrs] *adj* third; tertian (*fever*) ‖ *m* third (*in fractions*); **le tiers** a third; the third party; **le tiers et le quart** (coll) everybody and anybody ‖ *f* (typ) press proof

tige [tiʒ] *f* stem; trunk; shaft; shank; piston rod; leg (*of boot*); stock (*of genealogy*)

tignasse [tiɲas] *f* shock, mop (*of hair*)

tigre [tigr] *m* tiger

ti·gré -grée [tigre] *adj* striped; speckled, spotted

tigresse [tigrɛs] *f* tigress

tillac [tijak] *m* top deck (*of old-time ships*)

tilleul [tijœl] *m* linden

timbale [tɛ̃bal] *f* metal cup, mug; (culin) mold; (mus) kettledrum; **décrocher la timbale** (coll) to carry off the prize

timbalier [tɛ̃balje] *m* kettledrummer

timbrage [tɛ̃braʒ] *m* stamping; cancellation (*of mail*)

timbre [tɛ̃br] *m* bell; doorbell; buzzer; seal, stamp; postage stamp; postmark; snare (*of drum*); (phonet, phys) timbre

tim·bré ·brée [tɛ̃bre] *adj* stamped; ringing (*voice*); (coll) cracked, crazy

timbre-poste [tɛ̃brəpɔst] *m* (*pl* **timbres-poste**) postage stamp

timbrer [tɛ̃bre] *tr* to stamp; to postmark

timbres-prime [tɛ̃brəprim] *mpl* trading stamps

timide [timid] *adj* timid, shy

timon [timɔ̃] *m* pole (*of carriage*); beam (*of plow*); (naut) helm

timonier [timɔnje] *m* helmsman; wheelhorse

timo·ré ·rée [timɔre] *adj* timorous

tin [tɛ̃] *m* chock

tinette [tinɛt] *f* firkin (*tub*); bucket (*for fecal matter*)

tintamarre [tɛ̃tamar] *m* uproar

tintement [tɛ̃tmɑ̃] *m* tolling (*of bell*); tinkle (*of bell*); ringing (*in ears*)

tinter [tɛ̃te] *tr* to toll || *intr* to toll; to tinkle; to jingle, to clink; to ring (*said of ears*)

tintin [tɛ̃tɛ̃] *m*—**faire tintin** (slang) to do without || *interj* (slang) nothing doing!

tintouin [tɛ̃twɛ̃] *m* (coll) trouble

tique [tik] *f* (ent) tick

tiquer [tike] *intr* to twitch; (coll) to wince; **sans tiquer** (coll) without turning a hair

tir [tir] *m* shooting; firing; aim; shooting gallery; **tir à la cible** target practice; **tir à l'arc** archery; **tir au fusil** gunnery; **tir au pigeon** trapshooting

tirade [tirad] *f* (theat) long speech

tirage [tiraʒ] *m* drawing; towing; draft (*of chimney*); printing; circulation (*of newspaper*); (coll) tension, friction; **tirage à part** offprint; **tirage au sort** lottery drawing; **tirage de luxe** deluxe edition

tiraillement [tirɑjmɑ̃] *m* pain, cramp; conflict, tension

tirailler [tirɑje] *tr* to pull about, to tug at; to pester || *intr* to blaze away; **tirailler sur** to snipe at || *ref* to have a misunderstanding

tirailleur [tirɑjœr] *m* sharpshooter; sniper; (fig) free lance

tirant [tirɑ̃] *m* string; strap; **tirant d'eau** draft (*of ship*)

tire [tir] *f* (heral) row (*of vair*); (slang) car, auto; (Canad) taffy pull

ti·ré ·rée [tire] *adj* drawn; printed || *m* shooting preserve; payee; **tiré à part** offprint

tire-au-flanc [tiroflɑ̃] *m invar* malingerer, shirker

tire-botte [tirbɔt] *m* (*pl* **-bottes**) bootjack

tire-bouchon [tirbuʃɔ̃] *m* (*pl* **-bouchons**) corkscrew; corkscrew curl

tire-bouchonner [tirbuʃɔne] *tr* to twist in a spiral

tire-bouton [tirbutɔ̃] *m* (*pl* **-boutons**) buttonhook

tire-clou [tirklu] *m* (*pl* **-clous**) nail puller

tire-d'aile [tirdɛl]—**à tire-d'aile** with wings outspread, swiftly

tire-fond [tirfɔ̃] *m invar* spike; screw eye

tire-larigot [tirlarigo]—**boire à tire-larigot** to drink like a fish

tire-ligne [tirliɲ] *m* (*pl* **-lignes**) ruling pen

tirelire [tirlir] *f* piggy bank; (*face*) (coll) mug; (*head*) (coll) noggin; (slang) belly

tire-l'œil [tirlœj] *m invar* eye catcher

tirer [tire] *tr* to draw; to pull, to tug; to shoot, to fire; to run off, to print; to take out; to take, to get; to stick out (*one's tongue*); **tirer au clair** to bring out into the open; **tirer parti de** to turn to account || *intr* to pull; to shoot; to draw (*e.g., to a close*); to draw (*said of chimney*); **tirer à, vers,** or **sur** to border on || *ref* to extricate oneself; **s'en tirer** to manage; **se tirer d'affaire** to pull through, to get along

tiret [tire] *m* dash; blank (*to be filled in*)

tirette [tiret] *f* slide (*of desk*); damper (*of chimney*)

tireur [tirœr] *m* marksman; drawer; payer (*of check*); printer; **tireur de bois flotté** log driver; **tireur d'élite** sharpshooter; **tireur d'épée** fencer; **tireur isolé** sniper

tireuse [tirøz] *f* markswoman; **tireuse de cartes** fortuneteller

tiroir [tirwar] *m* drawer; (mach) slide valve; **à tiroirs** episodic (*play, novel, etc.*)

tiroir-caisse [tirwarkɛs] *m* (*pl* **tiroirs-caisses**) cash register

tisane [tizan] *f* tea, infusion; (coll) bad champagne; (slang) slap

tison [tizɔ̃] *m* ember; (fig) firebrand

tisonner [tizɔne] *tr* to poke

tisonnier [tizɔnje] *m* poker

tissage [tisaʒ] *m* weaving

tisser [tise] *tr & intr* to weave

tisse·rand [tisrɑ̃] **·rande** [rɑ̃d] *mf* weaver

tis·seur [tisœr] **tis·seuse** [tisøz] *mf* weaver

tissu [tisy] *m* tissue; cloth; fabric, material; pack (*of lies*)

tissu-éponge [tisyepɔ̃ʒ] *m* (*pl* **tissus-éponges**) toweling, terry cloth

tissure [tisyr] *f* texture; (fig) framework

titane [titan] *m* titanium

titi [titi] *m* (slang) street urchin

Titien [tisjɛ̃] *m*—**le Titien** Titian

titre [titr] *m* title; title page; heading; fineness (*of coinage*); claim, right; concentration (*of a solution*); **à juste titre** rightly so; **à titre de** in the capacity of; by virtue of; **à titre d'emprunt** as a loan; **à titre d'essai** on trial; **à titre gratuit** or **gracieux** free of charge; **titres** qualifications; (com) securities

titrer [titre] *tr* to title; to subtitle (*films*)

tituber [titybe] *intr* to stagger
titulaire [tityler] *adj* titular ‖ *mf* incumbent; holder (*of passport, license, degree, post*)
titulariser [titylarize] *tr* to confirm the appointment of
toast [tost] *m* toast; **porter un toast à** to toast
toboggan [tɔbɔgã] *m* toboggan; toboggan run; slide, chute
toc [tɔk] *adj invar* (coll) worthless; (coll) crazy ‖ *m* (mach) chuck; (coll) imitation; **en toc** (coll) worthless; **toc, toc!** knock, knock!
tohu-bohu [tɔybɔy] *m* hubbub
toi [twa] §85, §87
toile [twal] *f* cloth; linen; canvas, painting; (theat) curtain; **toile à coton** calico; **toile à laver** dishrag; **toile à matelas** ticking; **toile à voile** sailcloth; **toile cirée** oilcloth; **toile d'araignée** cobweb; **toile de fond** backdrop
toilette [twalɛt] *f* toilet; dressing table; dress, outfit (*of a woman*); **aimer la toilette** to be fond of clothing; **faire la toilette de** to lay out (*a corpse*)
toi-même [twamɛm] §86
toise [twaz] *f* fathom; **passer à la toise** to measure the height of
toiser [twaze] *tr* to size up
toison [twazɔ̃] *f* fleece; mop (*of hair*); **Toison d'or** Golden Fleece
toit [twa] *m* roof; rooftop; home, house; **crier sur les toits** to shout from the housetops
toiture [twatyr] *f* roofing
tôle [tol] *f* sheet metal; tole (*decorative metalware*); **tôle de blindage** armor plate; **tôle étamée** tin plate; **tôle galvanisée** galvanized iron; **tôle noire** sheet iron; **tôle ondulée** corrugated iron
tolérable [tɔlerabl] *adj* tolerable, bearable
tolérance [tɔlerãs] *f* tolerance
tolérer [tɔlere] §10 *tr* to tolerate
tôlerie [tolri] *f* sheet metal; rolling mill
tolet [tɔle] *m* oarlock
tomaison [tɔmezɔ̃] *f* volume number
tomate [tɔmat] *f* tomato
tombe [tɔ̃b] *f* tomb; grave; tombstone
tom-beau [tɔ̃bo] *m* (*pl* -beaux) tomb; **à tombeau couvert** lickety-split
tombée [tɔ̃be] *f* fall (*of rain, snow, etc.*); **tombée de la nuit** nightfall
tomber [tɔ̃be] *tr* to throw (*a wrestler*); (coll) to remove (*a piece of clothing*); (slang) to seduce (*a woman*) ‖ *intr* (*aux:* ÊTRE) to fall, to drop; **tomber amoureux** to fall in love; **tomber bien** to happen just in time; **tomber en panne** to have a breakdown; **tomber sur** to run into, chance upon; to turn to (*said of conversation*)
tombe-reau [tɔ̃bro] *m* (*pl* -reaux) dump truck; dumpcart; load
tombola [tɔ̃bɔla] *m* raffle
tome [tɔm] *m* tome, volume
ton [tɔ̃] *adj poss* §88 ‖ *m* tone; (mus) key

to-nal -nale [tɔnal] *adj* (*pl* -nals) tonal
ton-deur -deuse [tɔ̃dœr] **-deuse** [døz] *mf* shearer ‖ *f* shears; **tondeuse à cheveux** hair clippers; **tondeuse à gazon** lawn mower; **tondeuse (à gazon) à moteur** power mower; **tondeuse électrique** electric clippers; **tondeuse mécanique** cropper; power mower
tondre [tɔ̃dr] *tr* to clip; to shear; to mow
toni-fiant -fiante [tɔnifjɑ̃] **-fiante** [fjɑ̃t] *adj* & *m* tonic
tonifier [tɔnifje] *tr* to tone up
tonique [tɔnik] *adj* & *m* tonic
toni-truant -truante [tɔnitryɑ̃] **-truante** [tryɑ̃t] *adj* (coll) thunderous
tonne [tɔn] *f* ton; tun
ton-neau [tɔno] *m* (*pl* -neaux) barrel; cart; roll (*of automobile, airplane, etc.*); (naut) ton; **au tonneau** on draught; **tonneau de poudre** powder keg
tonnelet [tɔnle] *m* keg
tonnelier [tɔnəlje] *m* cooper
tonnelle [tɔnɛl] *f* arbor
tonner [tɔne] *intr* to thunder
tonnerre [tɔnɛr] *m* thunder
tonte [tɔ̃t] *f* clipping; shearing; mowing
tonton [tɔ̃tɔ̃] *m* (slang) uncle
top [tɔp] *m* beep
topaze [tɔpaz] *f* topaz
toper [tɔpe] *intr* to shake hands on it; **tope là!** it's a deal!
topinambour [tɔpinãbur] *m* Jerusalem artichoke
topique [tɔpik] *adj* local, regional
topographie [tɔpɔgrafi] *f* topography
toquade [tɔkad] *f* (coll) infatuation
toquante [tɔkãt] *f* (coll) ticker (*watch*)
toque [tɔk] *f* toque; cap (*of chef; of judge*)
to-qué -quée [tɔke] *adj* (coll) crazy, cracked ‖ *mf* (coll) nut
toquer [tɔke] *tr* to infatuate ‖ *intr* (coll) to rap, tap ‖ *ref*—**se toquer de** to be infatuated with
torche [tɔrʃ] *f* torch; **se mettre en torche** to fail to open (*said of parachute*); **torche électrique** flashlight
torcher [tɔrʃe] *tr* to wipe clean; to rush through; to botch; to daub with clay and straw
torchère [tɔrʃɛr] *f* candelabrum; floor lamp
torchis [tɔrʃi] *m* adobe
torchon [tɔrʃɔ̃] *m* dishcloth; rag; (coll) scribble; **le torchon brûle** they're squabbling
torchonner [tɔrʃɔne] *tr* (coll) to botch
tor-dant -dante [tɔrdã] **-dante** [dãt] *adj* (coll) sidesplitting
tord-boyaux [tɔrbwajo] *m invar* (coll) rotgut
tordeuse [tɔrdøz] *f* moth
tordoir [tɔrdwar] *m* wringer; rope-making machine
tordre [tɔrdr] *tr* to twist; to wring ‖ *ref* to twist; to writhe; **se tordre de rire** to split one's sides laughing
tornade [tɔrnad] *f* tornado
toron [tɔrɔ̃] *m* strand (*of rope*)
torpédo [tɔrpedo] *f* (archaic) open touring car

torpeur [tɔrpœr] *f* torpor
torpille [tɔrpij] *f* torpedo; (arti) mine
torpiller [tɔrpije] *tr* to torpedo
torpilleur [tɔrpijœr] *m* torpedo boat; torpedoman
torque [tɔrk] *f* coil of wire; twist (*of tobacco*)
torréfaction [tɔrefaksjɔ̃] *f* roasting
torréfier [tɔrefje] *tr* to roast
torrent [tɔrɑ̃] *m* torrent
torride [tɔrid] *adj* torrid
tors [tɔr] *torse* [tɔrs] *adj* twisted; crooked || *m* twist | see **torse** *m*
torsade [tɔrsad] *f* twisted cord; coil (*of hair*); **à torsades** fringed
torsader [tɔrsade] *tr* to twist
torse [tɔrs] *m* torso, trunk
torsion [tɔrsjɔ̃] *f* twisting, torsion
tort [tɔr] *m* wrong; harm; **à tort** wrongly; **à tort et à travers** at random, wildly; carelessly, inconsiderately; **à tort ou à raison** rightly or wrongly; inconsiderately; **avoir tort** to be wrong; **donner tort à** to lay the blame on; **faire tort à** to wrong
torticolis [tɔrtikɔli] *m* stiff neck
tortillard [tɔrtijar] *adj masc* knotty || *m* (coll) jerkwater train
tortiller [tɔrtije] *tr* to twist, to twirl; (slang) to gulp down || *intr* to wriggle; (coll) to beat about the bush || *ref* to wriggle, squirm; to writhe, twist
tor·tu -tue [tɔrty] *adj* crooked || *f* turtle, tortoise
tor·tueux -tueuse [tɔrtyø] [tyøz] *adj* winding; devious, underhanded
torture [tɔrtyr] *f* torture
torturer [tɔrtyre] *tr* to torture
torve [tɔrv] *adj* menacing
tos·can -cane [tɔskã] [kan] *adj* Tuscan || *m* Tuscan (*dialect*) || (*cap*) *mf* Tuscan (*person*)
tôt [to] *adv* soon; early; **au plus tôt** as soon as possible; at the earliest; **le plus tôt possible** as soon as possible; **pas de si tôt** not soon; **tôt ou tard** sooner or later
to·tal -tale [tɔtal] *adj & m* (*pl* -taux [to]) total
totaliser [tɔtalize] *tr* to total
totalitaire [tɔtaliter] *adj* totalitarian
totem [tɔtɛm] *m* totem
toton [tɔtɔ̃] *m* teetotum
toubib [tubib] *m* (coll) medical officer; (coll) doctor, physician
tou·chant [tu/ɑ̃] **-chante** [ʃɑ̃t] *adj* touching || **touchant** *prep* touching, concerning
touche [tu/] *f* touch; key (*of piano or typewriter*); stop (*of organ*); fret (*of guitar*); fingerboard (*of violin*); hit (*in fencing*); bite (*on fishline*); goad (*for cattle*); tab (*of file index*); thumb index; (elec) contact; (coll) look, appearance; **touche de blocage** shift lock; **touche de manœuvre** shift key
touche-à-tout [tu/atu] *m invar* (coll) busybody
toucher [tu/e] *m* touch, sense of touch || *tr* to touch; to concern; to cash (*a check*); to draw out (*money*); to goad

(*cattle*); (mus) to pluck (*the strings*) || *intr* to touch; **toucher à** to touch (*one's food, capital, etc.*); to touch on; to call at (*a port*); to be about to achieve (*one's aim*); **toucher de** to play (*e.g., the piano*) || *ref* to touch
touer [twe] *tr* to warp; to kedge
touffe [tuf] *f* tuft; clump (*of trees*)
touffeur [tufœr] *f* suffocating heat
touf·fu -fue [tufy] *adj* bushy; (fig) dense
touille [tuj] *m* dogfish, shark
touiller [tuje] *tr* (coll) to stir; (coll) to mix; (coll) to shuffle
toujours [tuʒur] *adv* always; still; anyhow; **M. Toujours** (coll) yes man; **pour toujours** forever
toupet [tupe] *m* tuft (*of hair*); forelock (*of horse*); (coll) nerve, brass
toupie [tupi] *f* top; molding board; silly woman
tour [tur] *m* turn; tour; trick; lathe; **à tour de bras** with all one's might; **à tour de rôle** in turn; **en un tour de main** in a jiffy; **faire le tour de** to tour, to twist; to walk or ride around; **faire un tour de** to take a walk or ride in; **tour à tour** by turns; **tour de bâton** (coll) rake-off, killing; **tour de main, tour d'adresse** sleight of hand; **tour de poitrine** chest size; **tour de taille** waist measurement; **tour de tête** hat size; **tours et retours** twists and turns || *f* tower; (chess) castle, rook; (mil) turret; **tour de contrôle** control tower; **tour de guet** lookout tower
tourbe [turb] *f* peat; mob
tourbillon [turbijɔ̃] *m* whirl; whirlpool; whirlwind
tourbillonner [turbijɔne] *intr* to whirl, to swirl
tourelle [turɛl] *f* turret
tourillon [turijɔ̃] *m* axle; trunnion
touriste [turist] *adj & mf* tourist
tourment [turmã] *m* torment
tourmente [turmɑ̃t] *f* storm
tourmenter [turmɑ̃te] *tr* to torment || *ref* to fret
tour·nant [turnã] **-nante** [nãt] *adj* turning, revolving || *m* turn; turning point; water wheel
tourne-à-gauche [turnagoʃ] *m invar* wrench; saw set; diestock
tournebroche [turnəbrɔʃ] *m* roasting jack, turnspit
tourne-disque [turnədisk] *m* (*pl* -disques) record player
tournedos [turnədo] *m* filet mignon
tournée [turne] *f* round; **en tournée** (theat) on tour; **faire une tournée** to take a trip; **tournée électorale** political campaign
tournemain [turnəmɛ̃]—**en un tournemain** in a split second
tourne-pierre [turnəpjer] *m* (*pl* -pierres) (orn) turnstone
tourner [turne] *tr* to turn; to turn over; to shoot (*a moving picture; a scene*); to outflank; **tourner et retourner** to turn over and over || *intr* to turn; (mov) to shoot a picture; (theat) to tour; **la tête me** (lui, etc.) **tourne** my

(his, etc.) head is turning, I feel (he feels, etc.) dizzy; **silence, on tourne!** quiet on the set!; **tourner à** or **en to** turn into; **tourner autour du pot** (coll) to beat about the bush; **tourner bien** to turn out well; **tourner en rond** to go around in circles, to spin; **tourner mal** to go bad || *ref* to turn

tournesol [turnəsɔl] *m* litmus; sunflower

tournevis [turnəvis] *m* screwdriver

tourniquet [turnikε] *m* turnstile; revolving door; revolving display stand; (surg) tourniquet; **passer au tourniquet** (slang) to be courtmartialed

tournoi [turnwa] *m* tournament

tournoyer [turnwaje] §47 *intr* to turn, to wheel; to twirl; to tourney

tournure [turnyr] *f* turn, course (*of events*); wording, phrasing, turn (*of phrase*); expression; shape, figure

tourte [turt] *adj* (slang) stupid || *f* (coll) dolt; **tourte à la viande** meat pie

tour·teau [turto] *m* (*pl* -**teaux**) oil cake; crab

tourte·reau [turtəro] *m* (*pl* -**reaux**) turtledove, young lover

tourterelle [turtərεl] *f* turtledove

tourtière [turtjεr] *f* pie pan

toussailler [tusaje] *intr* to keep on coughing

Toussaint [tusε̃] *f* All Saints' Day; **la Toussaint** All Saints' Day

tousser [tuse] *intr* to cough; to clear one's throat

tousserie [tusri] *f* constant coughing

toussotement [tusɔtmɑ̃] *m* slight coughing

toussoter [tusɔte] *intr* to cough slightly

tout [tu] **toute** [tut] (*pl* **tous toutes**) *adj* any, every, all; **tous les** all, all of, e.g., **tous les hommes** all men, all of the men; whole, entire, e.g., **toute la journée** the whole day; **à tout coup** every time; **à toute heure** at any time; **tous les deux** both || *m* (*pl* **touts**) whole, all; everything; sum; **du tout** (coll) not at all; **en tout** wholly, in all; **pas du tout** not at all || **tout toute** (*pl* **tous** [tus] **toutes**) *pron* all, everything, anything; **à tout prendre** on the whole; **tout compté** all things considered; **tout** *adv* all, quite, completely; very, e.g., **un des tout premiers** one of the very foremost; **tout à côté de** right next to; **tout à coup** suddenly; **tout à fait** quite; **tout à l'heure** in a little while; a little while ago; **tout au plus** at most; **tout de même** however, all the same; **tout de suite** at once, immediately; **tout en** while, e.g., **tout en parlant** while talking; **tout éveillé** wide awake; **tout fait** ready-made; **tout haut** aloud; **tout neuf** brand-new; **tout nu** stark-naked; **tout près** nearby; **tout . . . que** despite the fact that, e.g., **tout vieux qu'il était** despite the fact that he was old || **toute toutes** *adv* (before a feminine word beginning with a

consonant or an aspirate **h**) all, quite, completely, e.g., **elles sont toutes seules** they are all (or quite or completely) alone .

tout-à-l'égout [tutalegu] *m invar* sewerage

toute-épice [tutepis] *f* (*pl* **toutes-épices** [tutepis]) allspice (*berry*)

toutefois [tutfwa] *adv* however

toute-puissance [tutpɥisɑ̃s] *f* omnipotence

toutou [tutu] *m* (coll) doggie

Tout-Paris [tupari] *m invar* high society, smart set (*in Paris*)

tout-petit [tupəti] *m* (*pl* -**petits**) toddler

tout-puissant [tupɥisɑ̃] **toute-puissante** [tutpɥisɑ̃t] (*pl* **tout-puissants toutes-puissantes**) *adj* almighty || **le Tout-Puissant** the Almighty

tout-venant [tuvnɑ̃] *m invar* all comers; run-of-the-mine coal; run-of-the-mill product; ordinary run of people

toux [tu] *f* cough

toxicomane [tɔksikɔman] *adj* addicted || *mf* drug addict

toxicomanie [tɔksikɔmani] *f* drug addiction

toxique [tɔksik] *adj* toxic || *m* poison

trac [trak] *m* (coll) stage fright; **avoir le trac** (coll) to lose one's nerve; **tout à trac** without thinking

tracas [traka] *m* worry, trouble

tracasser [trakase] *tr* & *ref* to worry

tracasserie [trakasri] *f* bother; **tracasseries** interference

tracassin [trakasε̃] *m* (coll) worry

trace [tras] *f* trace; track, trail; sketch; footprint; **marcher sur les traces de** to follow in the footsteps of

tracé [trase] *m* tracing; **faire le tracé de** to lay out; (math) to plot

tracer [trase] §51 *tr* to trace, draw

tra·ceur [trasœr] -**ceuse** [søz] *mf* tracer || *m* tracer (*radioactive substance*)

trachée [traʃe] *f* trachea, windpipe

trachée-artère [traʃearter] *f* (*pl* **trachées-artères**) windpipe

tract [trakt] *m* tract

tractation [traktasjɔ̃] *f* underhanded deal

tracteur [traktœr] *m* tractor

traction [traksjɔ̃] *f* traction; **faire des tractions** to do chin-ups; **traction avant** front-wheel drive

tradition [tradisjɔ̃] *f* tradition

tradition·nel -**nelle** [tradisjɔnεl] *adj* traditional

traduc·teur [tradyktœr] -**trice** [tris] *mf* translator

traduction [tradyksjɔ̃] *f* translation

traduire [tradɥir] §19 *tr* to translate; **traduire en justice** to haul into court

trafic [trafik] *m* traffic, trade; **trafic d'influence** influence peddling; **trafic routier** highway traffic

trafi·quant [trafikɑ̃] -**quante** [kɑ̃t] *mf* racketeer; **trafiquant en stupéfiants** dope peddler

trafiquer [trafike] *tr* to traffic in || *intr* to traffic; **trafiquer de** to traffic in or on

trafi·queur [trafikœr] -**queuse** [køz] *mf* racketeer

tragédie [traʒedi] *f* tragedy

tragé·dien [traʒedjɛ̃] **-dienne** [djɛn] *mf* tragedian

tragique [traʒik] *adj* tragic

trahir [trair] *tr* to betray

trahison [traizɔ̃] *f* betrayal; treason

train [trɛ̃] *m* pace, speed; manner, way; series; raft (*of logs*); (rr) train; (coll) row, racket; **être en train de** + *inf* to be in the act or process of + *ger*; (translated by a progressive form of the verb), e.g., **je suis en train d'écrire** I am writing; **mettre en train** to start; **train arrière** (aut) rear-axle assembly; (rr) rear car; **train avant** (aut) front-axle assembly; **train d'atterrissage** landing gear; **train de banlieue** suburban train; **train de marchandises** freight train; **train de vie** way of life; standard of living; **train direct** through train; **train omnibus** local train; **train sanitaire** military hospital train

traî·nant [trenɑ̃] **-nante** [nɑ̃t] *adj* trailing; creeping; drawling; languid

traî·nard [trenar] **-narde** [nard] *mf* straggler

traîne [trɛn] *f* train (*of dress*); dragnet; **à la traîne** dragging; straggling; in tow

traî·neau [treno] *m* (*pl* **-neaux**) sleigh; sled; sledge; dragnet

traînée [trene] *f* trail, train; (coll) streetwalker

traîner [trene] *tr* to drag, to lug; to drawl; to shuffle (*the feet*) || *intr* to drag; to straggle; to lie around || *ref* to crawl; to creep; to limp

traî·neur [trenœr] **-neuse** [nøz] *mf* straggler; loiterer

train-train [trɛ̃trɛ̃] *m* routine

traire [trɛr] §68 *tr* to milk

trait [trɛ] *m* arrow, dart; dash; stroke; feature (*of face*); trait, characteristic; trace (*of harness*); **avoir trait à** to refer to; **de trait** draft (*horse*); **d'un trait** in one gulp; **partir comme un trait** to be off like a shot; **tracer à grands traits** to trace in broad outlines; **trait d'esprit** witticism; **trait d'héroïsme** heroic deed; **trait d'union** hyphen; **trait pour trait** exactly

traitable [tretabl] *adj* tractable

traite [trɛt] *f* trade, traffic; milking; (com) draft; **tout d'une traite** at a single stretch

traité [trete] *m* treatise; treaty

traitement [tretmɑ̃] *m* treatment; salary; **mauvais traitements** affront, mistreatment

traiter [trete] *tr* to treat; to receive; **traiter qn de** to call s.o. (*a name*) || *intr* to negotiate; **traiter de** to deal with

traiteur [tretœr] *m* caterer; (obs) restaurateur

traî·tre [tretr] **-tresse** [trɛs] *adj* traitorous; treacherous; (coll) single || *mf* traitor; (theat) villain || *f* traitress

traîtrise [tretriz] *f* treachery

trajectoire [traʒɛktwar] *f* trajectory

trajet [traʒɛ] *m* distance, trip, passage; (aer) flight

tralala [tralala] *m* (coll) fuss

trame [tram] *f* weft; web (*of life*); conspiracy

tramer [trame] *tr* to weave; to hatch (*a plot*) || *ref* to be plotted

traminot [tramino] *m* traction-company employee

tramontane [tramɔ̃tan] *f* north wind; **perdre la tramontane** to lose one's bearings

tramp [trɑp] *m* tramp steamer

tramway [tramwɛ] *m* streetcar

tran·chant [trɑ̃ʃɑ̃] **-chante** [ʃɑ̃t] *adj* cutting; glaring; trenchant || *m* cutting edge; knife; side (*of hand*); **à double tranchant** or **à deux tranchants** two-edged

tranche [trɑ̃ʃ] *f* slice; section; portion, installment; group (*of figures*); cross section; **doré sur tranches** (bb) gilt-edged; (coll) gilded (*e.g., youth*); **une tranche de vie** a slice of life

tranchée [trɑ̃ʃe] *f* trench; **tranchées** colic

trancher [trɑ̃ʃe] *tr* to cut off; to slice; to decide, settle || *intr* to decide once and for all; to stand out; **trancher avec** to contrast with; **trancher dans le vif** to cut to the quick; (fig) to take drastic measures; **trancher de** (lit) to affect the manners of

tranquille [trɑ̃kil] *adj* quiet, tranquil; **laissez-moi tranquille** leave me alone; **soyez tranquille** don't worry

tranquilli·sant [trɑ̃kilizɑ̃] **-sante** [zɑ̃t] *adj* tranquilizing || *m* tranquilizer

tranquilliser [trɑ̃kilize] *tr* to tranquilize; to reassure || *ref* to calm down

tranquillité [trɑ̃kilite] *f* tranquillity

transaction [trɑ̃zaksjɔ̃] *f* transaction; compromise

transat [trɑ̃zat] *m* (coll) transatlantic liner; (coll) deck chair || **la Transat** (coll) the French Line

transatlantique [trɑ̃zatlɑ̃tik] *adj* & *m* transatlantic

transbordement [trɑ̃sbɔrdəmɑ̃] *m* transshipment, transfer

transborder [trɑ̃sbɔrde] *tr* to transship, to transfer

transbordeur [trɑ̃sbɔrdœr] *m* transporter bridge

transcender [trɑ̃sɑ̃de] *tr* & *ref* to transcend

transcription [trɑ̃skripsjɔ̃] *f* transcription

transcrire [trɑ̃skrir] §25 *tr* to transcribe; **transcrire en clair** to decode

transe [trɑ̃s] *f* apprehension, anxiety; trance; **être dans des transes** to be quaking in one's boots

transept [trɑ̃sɛpt] *m* transept

transférer [trɑ̃sfere] §10 *tr* to transfer; to convey

transfert [trɑ̃sfɛr] *m* transfer, transference

transfo [trɑ̃sfo] *m* (coll) transformer

transforma·teur [trɑ̃sfɔrmatœr] **-trice** [tris] *adj* (elec) transforming || *m* (elec) transformer; **transformateur abaisseur (de tension)** step-down transformer; **transformateur de sonnerie** doorbell transformer; **transfor-**

mateur élévateur (de tension) step-up transformer

transformer [trāsfɔrme] *tr & ref* to transform

transfuge [trāsfyʒ] *m* turncoat

transfuser [trāsfyze] *tr* to transfuse; to instill

transfusion [trāsfyzjɔ̃] *f* transfusion

transgresser [trāsgrese] *tr* to transgress

transgression [trāsgresjɔ̃] *f* transgression

transhumer [trāzyme] *tr & intr* to move from winter to summer pasture

tran·si -sie [trāzi], [trāsi] *adj* chilled to the bone; numb, transfixed (*with fright*)

transiger [trāziʒe] §38 *intr* to compromise

transistor [trāzistɔr] *m* transistor

transit [trāzit] *m* transit

transi·tif [trāzitif] -tive [tiv] *adj* transitive

transition [trāzisjɔ̃] *f* transition

transitoire [trāzitwar] *adj* transitory; transitional

translation [trāslɑsjɔ̃] *f* transfer, translation

translitérer [trāslitere] §10 *tr* to transliterate

translucide [trāslysid] *adj* translucent

transmetteur [trāsmetœr] *adj masc* transmitting || *m* (telg, telp) transmitter; **transmetteur d'ordres** (naut) engine-room telegraph

transmettre [trāsmetr] §42 *tr* to transmit; to transfer; (sports) to pass

transmission [trāsmisjɔ̃] *f* transmission; broadcast; **transmission en différé** recorded broadcast; **transmission en direct** live broadcast; **transmissions** (mil) signal corps

transmuer [trāsmɥe] *tr* to transmute

transmuter [trāsmyte] *tr* to transmute

transparaître [trāsparetr] §12 *intr* to show through

transpa·rent [trāsparā] -rente [rāt] *adj* transparent

transpercer [trāsperse] §51 *tr* to transfix

transpiration [trāspirɑsjɔ̃] *f* perspiration

transpirer [trāspire] *tr* to sweat || *intr* to sweat, perspire; to leak out (*said of news*)

transplanter [trāsplāte] *tr* to transplant

transport [trāspɔr] *m* transport; transportation; **transport au cerveau** cerebral hemorrhage

transpor·té -tée [trāspɔrte] *adj* enraptured, carried away

transporter [trāspɔrte] *tr* to transport

transposer [trāspoze] *tr* to transpose

transver·sal -sale [trāsversal] *adj* (*pl* -saux [so]) transversal; cross (*street*)

trapèze [trapɛz] *m* trapeze; trapezoid

trappe [trap] *f* trap door; pitfall, trap; **Trappist** monastery; **Trappe** Trappist order

trappeur [trapœr] *m* trapper

tra·pu -pue [trapy] *adj* stocky, squat

traque [trak] *f* driving of game

traquenard [traknar] *m* trap, booby trap, pitfall

traquer [trake] *tr* to hem in, to bring to bay

traumatique [tromatik] *adj* traumatic

tra·vail [travaj] *m* (*pl* -vaux [vo]) work; workmanship; **en travail** in labor; **Travail** Labor; **travail à la pièce, travail à la tâche** piecework; **travail d'équipe** teamwork; **travail de Romain** herculean task; **travaux forcés** hard labor; **travaux ménagers** housework || *m* (*pl* -vails) stocks (*for horses*)

travail·lé -lée [travaje] *adj* finely wrought, elaborate; labored

travailler [travaje] *tr* to work; to worry || *intr* to work; to warp (*said of wood*)

travail·leur [travajœr] **travail·leuse** [travajøz] *adj* hardworking || *mf* worker, toiler

travailliste [travajist] *adj & mf* Labourite (Brit)

travée [trave] *f* span (*of bridge*); row of seats; (archit) bay

traveling [travliŋ] *m* (mov, telv) dolly (*for camera*)

travers [traver] *m* breadth; fault, failing; **à travers** across, through; **de travers** awry; **en travers de** across; **par le travers de** abreast of

traverse [travers] *f* crossbeam; cross street; setback; rung (*of ladder*); (rr) tie; **de traverse** cross (*e.g., street*); **mettre à la traverse de** to oppose

traversée [traverse] *f* crossing

traverser [traverse] *tr* to cross; to cut across

traver·sier [traversje] -sière [sjer] *adj* cross, crossing

traversin [traversɛ̃] *m* bolster (*of bed*)

traves·ti -tie [travesti] *adj* disguised; costume (*ball*) || *m* fancy costume, disguise; transvestite; female impersonator

travestir [travestir] *tr* to travesty; to disguise

travestissement [travestismā] *m* travesty; disguise

trébucher [trebyʃe] *intr* to stumble

tréfiler [trefile] *tr* to wiredraw

trèfle [trefl] *m* clover; trefoil; cloverleaf (*intersection*); (cards) club; (cards) clubs

tréfonds [trefɔ̃] *m* secret depths

treillage [trejaʒ] *m* trellis

treillager [trejaʒe] §38 *tr* to trellis

treille [trej] *f* grape arbor

treillis [treji] *m* latticework; iron grating; denim; **treillis métallique** wire netting

treillisser [trejise] *tr* to trellis

treize [trez] *adj & pron* thirteen; the Thirteenth, e.g., **Jean treize** John the Thirteenth || *m* thirteen; thirteenth (*in dates*); **treize à la douzaine** baker's dozen

treizième [trezjem] *adj, pron* (*masc, fem*), *& m* thirteenth

tréma [trema] *m* dieresis

tremble [trābl] *m* aspen (*tree*)

tremblement [trābləmā] *m* trembling; **tremblement de terre** earthquake

trembler [trāble] *intr* to tremble

trembleur [trãblœr] *m* vibrator, buzzer; (rel) Shaker; (rel) Quaker

trembloter [trãblɔte] *intr* to quiver; to quaver

trémie [tremi] *f* hopper

trémoussement [tremusmã] *m* fluttering, flutter; jiggling, jiggle

trémousser [tremuse] *ref* to flutter; to jiggle; (coll) to bustle

trempage [trãpaʒ] *m* soaking

trempe [trãp] *f* temper; soaking; (slang) scolding

trempée [trãpe] *f* tempering

tremper [trãpe] *tr* to temper; to dilute; to dunk ‖ *intr* to soak; to become involved (*in, e.g., a crime*)

trempette [trãpɛt] *f*—**faire la trempette** to dunk; **faire trempette** to take a dip

tremplin [trãplɛ̃] *m* springboard, diving board; trampoline; ski jump; (fig) springboard

trentaine [trãtɛn] *f* age of thirty; **une trentaine de** about thirty

trente [trãt] *adj & pron* thirty; **sur son trente et un** (coll) all spruced up; **trente et un** thirty-one; **trente et unième** thirty-first ‖ *m* thirty; thirtieth (*in dates*); **trente et un** thirty-one; thirty-first (*in dates*); **trente et unième** thirty-first

trente-deux [trãtdø] *adj, pron, & m* thirty-two

trente-deuxième [trãtdøzjɛm] *adj, pron* (*masc, fem*), *& m* thirty-second

trente-six [trãtsi(s)] *adj, pron, & m* thirty-six; **tous les trente-six du mois** (coll) once in a blue moon

trentième [trãtjɛm] *adj, pron* (*masc, fem*), *& m* thirtieth

trépas [trepa] *m* (lit) death; **passer de vie à trépas** (lit) to pass away

trépasser [trepase] *intr* (lit) to die

trépied [trepje] *m* tripod

trépigner [trepiɲe] *intr* to stamp one's feet

très [trɛ] *adv* very; **le très honorable** the Right Honorable

trésor [trezɔr] *m* treasure; **Trésor** Treasury

trésorerie [trezɔrri] *f* treasury

tréso·rier [trezɔrje] **-rière** [rjɛr] *mf* treasurer

tressaillement [tresajmã] *m* start, quiver

tressaillir [tresajir] §69 *intr* to give a start, to quiver

tressauter [tresote] *intr* to start

tresse [tres] *f* tress

tresser [trese] *tr* to braid, to plait; to weave (*e.g., a basket*)

tré·teau [treto] *m* (*pl* **-teaux**) trestle; **sur les tréteaux** (theat) on the boards

treuil [trœj] *m* windlass; winch

trève [trɛv] *f* truce; respite; **trève de . . .** that's enough . . .

tri [tri] *m* sorting

triage [trijaʒ] *m* sorting, selection; classification; (rr) shifting

triangle [trijãgl] *m* triangle

tribord [tribɔr] *m* starboard

tribu [triby] *f* tribe

tribu·nal [tribynal] *m* (*pl* **-naux** [no]) tribunal, court; **en plein tribunal** in

open court; **tribunal de police** police court; **tribunaux pour enfants** juvenile courts

tribune [tribyn] *f* rostrum, tribune; gallery; grandstand; **monter à la tribune** to take the floor; **tribune des journalistes** press box; **tribune d'orgue** organ loft; **tribune libre** open forum

tribut [triby] *m* tribute

tributaire [tribytɛr] *adj & m* tributary; **être tributaire de** to be dependent upon

tricher [triʃe] *tr & intr* to cheat

tricherie [triʃri] *f* cheating

tri·cheur [triʃœr] **-cheuse** [ʃøz] *mf* cheater; **tricheur professionnel** cardsharper

tricolore [trikɔlɔr] *adj & m* tricolor

tricot [triko] *m* knitting; knitted garment

tricotage [trikotaʒ] *m* knitting

tricoter [trikote] *tr & intr* to knit

trier [trije] *tr* to pick out, to screen; **trier sur le volet** to hand-pick

trieur [trijœr] **trieuse** [trijøz] *mf* sorter ‖ *m & f* (mach) sorter

trigonométrie [trigonɔmetri] *f* trigonometry

trille [trij] *m* trill

triller [trije] *tr & intr* to trill

trillion [triljɔ̃] *m* quintillion (U.S.A.); trillion (Brit)

trilogie [trilɔʒi] *f* trilogy

trimbaler [trɛ̃bale] *tr* to cart around

trimer [trime] *intr* to slave

trimestre [trimɛstr] *m* quarter (*of a year*); quarter's salary; quarter's rent; (educ) term

tringle [trɛ̃gl] *f* rod; **tringle de rideau** curtain rod

trinité [trinite] *f* trinity

trinquer [trɛ̃ke] *intr* to clink glasses, to toast; (slang) to drink; **trinquer avec** to hobnob with

trio [trijo] *m* trio

triom·phant [trijɔ̃fã] **-phante** [fãt] *adj* triumphant

triomphe [trijɔ̃f] *m* triumph; **faire triomphe à** to welcome in triumph

tripar·ti ·tie [triparti] *adj* tripartite

tripartite [tripartit] *adj* tripartite

tripatouiller [tripatuje] *tr* (coll) to tamper with

tripette [tripɛt] *f*—**ça ne vaut pas tripette** it's not worth a wooden nickel

triple [tripl] *adj & m* triple

tri·plé ·plée [triple] *mf* triplet

tripler [triple] *tr & intr* to triple

triplicata [triplikata] *m invar* triplicate

tripot [tripo] *m* gambling den; house of ill repute

tripoter [tripote] *tr* to finger, toy with ‖ *intr* to dabble, to potter around; to rummage

trique [trik] *f* (coll) cudgel

triste [trist] *adj* sad

tristesse [tristes] *f* sadness, sorrow

triturer [trityre] *tr* to pulverize, to grind ‖ *ref*—**se triturer la cervelle** to rack one's brain

tri·vial ·viale [trivjal] *adj* (*pl* **-viaux** [vjo]) trivial; vulgar, coarse

trivialité [trivjalite] *f* triviality; vulgarity, coarseness

troc [trɔk] *m* barter; swap; **troc pour troc** even up

troglodyte [trɔglɔdit] *m* cave dweller; (orn) wren

trognon [trɔɲɔ̃] *m* core; (slang) darling, pet

Troie [trwa], [trwa] *f* Troy

trois [trwa] *adj & pron* three; the Third, e.g., **Jean trois** John the Third; **trois heures** three o'clock || *m* three; third (*in dates*)

troisième [trwazjɛm] *adj, pron (masc, fem), & m* third

trolley [trɔle] *m* trolley

trolleybus [trɔlebys] *m* trackless trolley

trombe [trɔ̃b] *f* waterspout; **entrer en trombe** to dash in; **trombe d'eau** deluge

trombone [trɔ̃bɔn] *m* trombone; paper clip

trompe [trɔ̃p] *f* horn; trunk (*of elephant*); beak (*of insect*); **trompe d'Eustache** Eustachian tube

trompe-la-mort [trɔ̃plamɔr] *mf invar* daredevil

trompe-l'œil [trɔ̃plœj] *m invar* dummy effect; (coll) bluff, fake; **en trompe-l'œil** in perspective

tromper [trɔ̃pe] *tr* to deceive, to cheat || *ref* to be wrong; **se tromper de** to be mistaken about

tromperie [trɔ̃pri] *f* deceit; fraud; illusion

trompeter [trɔ̃pte] §34 *tr & intr* to trumpet

trompette [trɔ̃pet] *m* trumpeter || *f* trumpet; **en trompette** turned up

trom·peur [trɔ̃pœr] **-peuse** [pøz] *adj* false, lying || *mf* deceiver

tronc [trɔ̃] *m* trunk; (slang) head; **tronc des pauvres** poor box

tronche [trɔ̃ʃ] *f* (slang) noodle

tronçon [trɔ̃sɔ̃] *m* stump; section (*e.g., of track*)

trône [tron] *m* throne

trôner [trone] *intr* to sit in state || *ref* —**se trôner sur** to lord it over

tronquer [trɔ̃ke] *tr* to truncate, to cut off; to mutilate

trop [tro] *m* excess; too much; **de trop** too much; to excess; in the way, e.g., **il est de trop ici** he is in the way here; **par trop** altogether, excessively; **trop de . . .** too much . . . ; too many . . . || *adv* too; too much; **trop lourd** overweight

trophée [trɔfe] *m* trophy

tropi·cal -cale [trɔpikal] *adj (pl -caux* [ko]) tropical

trop-plein [trɔplɛ̃] *m (pl -pleins)* overflow

troquer [trɔke] *tr* to barter; **troquer contre** to swap for

trot [tro] *m* trot; **au trot** at a trot; (coll) on the double, quickly

trotte [trɔt] *f* (coll) quite a distance to walk

trotter [trɔte] *intr* to trot

trot·teur [trɔtœr] **trot·teuse** [trɔtøz] *mf* (turf) trotter || *f* second hand; **trotteuse centrale** sweep-second

trottin [trɔtɛ̃] *m* errand girl

trottinette [trɔtinet] *f* scooter

trottoir [trɔtwar] *m* sidewalk; **faire le trottoir** to walk the streets (*said of prostitute*); **trottoir roulant** escalator

trou [tru] *m* hole; pothole; eye (*of needle*); gap; jerkwater town; **faire son trou** to feather one's nest; **faire un trou à la lune** to fly the coop; **trou d'air** air pocket; **trou de clef** keyhole (*of clock*); **trou de la serrure** keyhole; **trou d'obus** shell hole; **trou du souffleur** prompter's box; **trou individuel** (mil) foxhole

trouble [trubl] *adj* muddy, cloudy, turbid (*liquid*); murky (*sky*); misty (*glass*); blurred (*image; sight*); dim (*light*); vague, disquieting || *m* disquiet; unrest; trouble (*illness*)

trouble-fête [trublafɛt] *mf invar* wet blanket, kill-joy

troubler [truble] *tr* to upset, trouble; to make muddy; to disturb; to make cloudy; to blur || *ref* to become muddy or cloudy; to lose one's composure

trouée [true] *f* gap, breach; (mil) breakthrough

trouille [truj] *f*—**avoir la trouille** (slang) to get cold feet

troupe [trup] *f* troop; band, party; (theat) troupe

trou·peau [trupo] *m (pl -peaux)* flock; herd; **attention aux troupeaux** (public sign) cattle crossing

troupier [trupje] *m* (coll) soldier; **jurer comme un troupier** to swear like a trooper

trousse [trus] *f* case, kit; **avoir qn à ses trousses** to have s.o. at one's heels; **trousse de première urgence** first-aid kit

trous·seau [truso] *m (pl -seaux)* trousseau; outfit; bunch (*of keys*)

troussequin [truskɛ̃] *m* cantle

trousser [truse] *tr* to turn up; to tuck up; to polish off; (culin) to truss || *ref* to lift one's skirts

trouvaille [truvaj] *f* find

trouver [truve] *tr* to find || *ref* to be found; to find oneself; to be, e.g., **où se trouve-t-il?** where is he?; **il se trouve que . . .** it happens that . . . ; **se trouver mal** to feel ill

troyen [trwajɛ̃] **troyenne** [trwajen] *adj* Trojan || (*cap*) *mf* Trojan

truand [tryɑ̃] **truande** [tryɑ̃d] *adj & m* good-for-nothing

truc [tryk] *m* gadget, device; (coll) trick, gimmick; (coll) thing; (coll) what's-his-name

truchement [tryʃmɑ̃] *m* spokesman; interpreter; **par le truchement de** thanks to, through

trucu·lent [trykylɑ̃] **-lente** [lɑ̃t] *adj* truculent

truelle [tryel] *f* trowel

truffe [tryf] *f* truffle

truie [trɥi] *f* sow

truisme [trɥism] *m* truism

truite [trɥit] *f* trout

tru·meau [trymo] *m (pl -meaux)* trumeau (*mirror with painting above in same frame*)

truquage [tryka3] *m* faking

truquer [tryke] *tr* to fake; to cook (*the accounts*); to stack (*the deck*); to load (*the dice*); to fix (*the outcome of a fight*) || *intr* to resort to fakery

trust [trœst] *m* trust, holding company

T.S.F. [teesef] *f* (letterword) (**télégraphie sans fil**) wireless; radio

t. s. v. p. *abbr* (**tournez s'il vous plaît**) over (*please turn the page*)

tu [ty] §87; **être à tu et à toi avec to** hobnob with

T.U. [tey] *m* (letterword) (**temps universel**) universal time, Greenwich Mean Time

tube [tyb] *m* tube; pipe; (anat) duct; (slang) hit

tubercule [tyberkyl] *m* tubercle; tuber

tuberculose [tyberkyloz] *f* tuberculosis

tue-mouches [tymu] *m invar* flypaper

tuer [tɥe] *tr* to kill || *ref* to be killed; to kill oneself

tuerie [tɥri] *f* slaughter

tue-tête [tytet]—**à tue-tête** at the top of one's voice

tuile [tɥil] *f* tile; (coll) nasty blow

tuilerie [tɥilri] *f* tileworks

tulipe [tylip] *f* tulip

tumeur [tymœr] *f* tumor

tumulte [tymylt] *m* tumult, hubbub

tungstène [tœksten] *m* tungsten

tunique [tynik] *f* tunic

tunnel [tynɛl] *m* tunnel; **passer sous un tunnel** to go through a tunnel; **tunnel aérodynamique** wind tunnel

turban [tyrbã] *m* turban

turbine [tyrbin] *f* turbine

turbu·lent [tyrbylã] **-lente** [lãt] *adj* turbulent

turc turque [tyrk] *adj* Turkish || *m* Turkish (*language*) || (*cap*) *mf* Turk (*person*)

turf [tyrf] *m*—**le turf** the turf, the track

turfiste [tyrfist] *m* turfman, racegoer

turlututu [tyrlytyty] *interj* fiddlesticks!, nonsense!

Turquie [tyrki] *f* Turkey; **la Turquie** Turkey

turquoise [tyrkwaz] *m* turquoise (*color*) || *f* turquoise (*stone*)

tutelle [tytel] *f* guardianship, tutelage; trusteeship

tu·teur [tytœr] **-trice** [tris] *mf* guardian || *m* (hort) stake, prop

tutoyer [tytwaje] §47 *tr* to thou, to address familiarly || *ref* to thou each other, to be on a first-name basis

tuyau [tɥijo], [tjjo] *m* (*pl* **tuyaux**) pipe, tube; fluting; (coll) tip; **tuyau d'arrosage** garden hose; **tuyau d'échappement** exhaust; **tuyau d'incendie** fire hose

tuyauter [tɥijote], [tjjote] *tr* to flute; (coll) to tip off || *intr* (coll) to crib

tuyauterie [tɥijotri] *f* pipe mill; piping; (aut) manifold; **tuyauterie d'admission** intake manifold; **tuyauterie d'échappement** exhaust manifold

tympan [tɛ̃pã] *m* eardrum; (archit, mus) tympanum

type [tip] *m* type; (coll) fellow, character

typer [tipe] *tr* to type

typhoïde [tifoid] *adj & f* typhoid

typhon [tifɔ̃] *m* typhoon

typique [tipik] *adj* typical; South American (*music*)

typographie [tipɔgrafi] *f* typography

typographique [tipɔgrafik] *adj* typographic(al)

tyran [tirã] *m* tyrant; (orn) kingbird

tyrannie [tirani] *f* tyranny

tyrannique [tiranik] *adj* tyrannic(al)

U

U, u [y], *[y] *m invar* twenty-first letter of the French alphabet

Ukraine [ykren] *f* Ukraine

ukrai·nien [ykrenjɛ̃] **-nienne** [njen] *adj* Ukrainian || *m* Ukrainian (*language*) || (*cap*) *mf* Ukrainian (*person*)

ulcère [ylser] *m* ulcer, sore

ulcérer [ylsere] §10 *tr* to ulcerate; to embitter || *ref* to ulcerate; to fester

ulté·rieur -rieure [ylterjœr] *adj* ulterior; subsequent

ultimatum [yltimatɔm] *m* ultimatum

ultime [yltim] *adj* ultimate, final

ultra-court [yltrakur] **-courte** [kurt] *adj* (electron) ultrashort

ultravio·let [yltravjɔle] **-lette** [let] *adj & m* ultraviolet

ululer [ylyle] *intr* to hoot

un [œ̃] **une** [yn] *adj & pron* one; **l'un à l'autre** to each other, to one another; **l'un et l'autre** both; **l'un l'autre** each other, one another; **ni**

l'un ni l'autre neither, neither one; **un à un** one by one; **une heure une** o'clock || *art indef* a || *m* one || *f*—**la une** the front page

unanime [ynanim] *adj* unanimous

unanimité [ynanimite] *f* unanimity

Unesco [ynesko] *f* (acronym) (**Organisation des Nations Unies pour l'Éducation, la Science et la Culture**)—**l'Unesco** UNESCO

u·ni -nie [yni] *adj* united; smooth, level; uneventful; plain; solid (*color*); together (*said, e.g., of the hands of a clock*) || *m* plain cloth

unicorne [ynikɔrn] *m* unicorn

unification [ynifikɑsjɔ̃] *f* unification

unifier [ynifje] *tr* to unify || *ref* to consolidate, merge; to become unified

uniforme [ynifɔrm] *adj & m* uniform

uniformiser [ynifɔrmize] *tr* to make uniform

uniformité [ynifɔrmite] *f* uniformity

unijambiste [yniʒābist] *adj* one-legged ‖ *mf* one-legged person

unilaté·ral -rale [ynilateral] *adj* (*pl* -raux [ro]) unilateral

union [ynjɔ̃] *f* union; **union libre** common-law marriage

unique [ynik] *adj* only, single; unique

unir [ynir] *tr & ref* to unite

unisson [ynisɔ̃] *m* unison

unitaire [yniter] *adj* unit

unité [ynite] *f* unity; unit; battleship; (coll) one million old francs

univers [yniver] *m* universe

univer·sel -selle [yniversɛl] *adj & m* universal

universitaire [yniversiter] *adj* university

université [yniversite] *f* university

uranium [yranjɔm] *m* uranium

ur·bain [yrbɛ̃] **-baine** [bɛn] *adj* urban; urbane

urbaniser [yrbanize] *tr* to urbanize

urbanisme [yrbanism] *m* city planning

urbaniste [yrbanist] *adj* zoning (*ordinance*) ‖ *mf* city planner

urbanité [yrbanite] *f* urbanity

urètre [yretr] *m* urethra

urgence [yrʒɑ̃s] *f* urgency; emergency; emergency case; **d'urgence** emergency (*e.g., hospital ward*); right away, without delay

ur·gent [yrʒɑ̃] **-gente** [ʒɑ̃t] *adj* urgent; emergency (*case*); (formula on letter or envelope) rush ‖ *m* urgent matter

urinaire [yriner] *adj* urinary

uri·nal [yrinal] *m* (*pl* -naux [no]) urinal (*for use in bed*)

urine [yrin] *f* urine

uriner [yrine] *tr & intr* to urinate

urinoir [yrinwar] *m* urinal (*place*)

urne [yrn] *f* urn; ballot box; **aller aux urnes** to go to the polls

urologie [yrɔlɔʒi] *f* urology

U.R.S.S. [yreses] *f* (letterword) (**Union des Républiques Socialistes Soviétiques**) U.S.S.R.

Ursse [yrs] *f* (acronym) (**Union des Républiques Socialistes Soviétiques**) U.S.S.R.

urticaire [yrtiker] *f* hives

urubu [yryby] *m* turkey vulture

us [ys] *mpl*—**les us et (les) coutumes** the manners and customs

U.S. [yes] *adj* (letterword) (**United States**) U.S., e.g., **l'aviation U.S.** U.S. aviation

U.S.A. [yesa] *mpl* (letterword) (**United States of America**) U.S.A.

usage [yzaʒ] *m* usage; custom; use; **faire de l'usage** to wear well; **hors d'usage** outmoded; (gram) obsolete; **manquer d'usage** to lack good breeding; **usage du monde** good breeding, savoir-vivre

usa·gé -gée [yzaʒe] *adj* secondhand; worn-out, used

usa·ger [yzaʒe] **-gère** [ʒer] *mf* user

usant [yzɑ̃] **usante** [yzɑ̃t] *adj* exhausting, wearing

u·sé -sée [yze] *adj* worn-out; trite, commonplace

user [yze] *tr* to wear out; to wear away; to ruin (*e.g., health*) ‖ *intr*—**en user bien avec** to treat well; **user de** to use ‖ *ref* to wear out

usine [yzin] *f* factory, mill, plant; **usine à gaz** gasworks

usiner [yzine] *tr* to machine, to tool

usi·nier [yzinje] **-nière** [njer] *adj* manufacturing; factory (*town*) ‖ *m* manufacturer

usi·té -tée [yzite] *adj* used, in use; **peu usité** out of use, rare

ustensile [ystɑ̃sil] *m* utensil, implement

u·suel -suelle [yzɥel] *adj* usual

usure [yzyr] *f* usury; wear; wear and tear

usurper [yzyrpe] *tr* to usurp

utérus [yterys] *m* uterus, womb

utilisable [ytilizabl] *adj* usable

utilisa·teur [ytilizatœr] **-trice** [tris] *mf* user

utilitaire [ytiliter] *adj* utilitarian; utility (*vehicle, goods, etc.*)

utilité [ytilite] *f* utility, usefulness, use; (theat) support; (theat) supporting rôle; **jouer les utilités** (fig) to play second fiddle; **utilités** (theat) small parts

utopique [ytɔpik] *adj* utopian

utopiste [ytɔpist] *mf* utopian

V

V, v [ve] *m invar* twenty-second letter of the French alphabet

v. *abbr* (**voir**) see; (**volume**) vol.

vacance [vakɑ̃s] *f* vacancy, opening; **vacances** vacation

vacancier [vakɑ̃sje] *m* vacationist

va·cant [vakɑ̃] **-cante** [kɑ̃t] *adj* vacant

vacarme [vakarm] *m* din, racket

vacation [vakɑsjɔ̃] *f* investigation; **vacations** fee; recess

vaccin [vaksɛ̃] *m* vaccine

vaccination [vaksinɑsjɔ̃] *f* vaccination

vaccine [vaksin] *f* cowpox

vacciner [vaksine] *tr* to vaccinate

vache [vaʃ] *adj* embarrassing (*question*); cantankerous (*person*) ‖ *f* cow; cowhide; (*woman*) (slang) bitch; (*man*) (slang) swine, rat; (*policeman*) (slang) flatfoot, bull; en **vache** leather (*e.g., suitcase*); **manger de la vache enragée** (coll) not to have a red cent to one's name; **oh, la vache!** damn it!; **parler français comme une vache espagnole** (coll) to murder the French language; **vache à eau** canvas bucket (*for camping*); **vache à lait** milch cow; (coll) gull, sucker

vachement [vaʃmã] *adv* (slang) tremendously

va·cher [vaʃe] **-chère** [ʃer] *mf* cowherd

vacherie [vaʃri] *f* cowshed; dairy farm; (coll) dirty trick

vachette [vaʃet] *f* young calf; calf (*leather*)

vaciller [vasije] *intr* to vacillate, waver; to flicker; to totter

vacuité [vakɥite] *f* vacuity, emptiness

vacuum [vakɥɔm] *m* vacuum

vade-mecum [vademekɔm] *m invar* handbook, vade mecum

vadrouille [vadruj] *f* (naut) mop, swab; (slang) bender, spree

vadrouiller [vadruje] *intr* (slang) to ramble around, to gad about

vadrouil·leur [vadrujœr] **vadrouil·leuse** [vadrujøz] *mf* (slang) rounder

va-et-vient [vaevjẽ] *m invar* backward-and-forward motion; hurrying to and fro; comings and goings; ferryboat; (elec) two-way switch

vaga·bond [vagabɔ̃] **-bonde** [bɔ̃d] *adj* vagabond ǁ *mf* vagabond, tramp

vagabondage [vagabɔ̃daʒ] *m* vagrancy; **vagabondage interdit** (public sign) no loitering, no begging

vagabonder [vagabɔ̃de] *intr* to wander about, to roam, to tramp

vagir [vaʒir] *intr* to cry, wail

vague [vag] *adj* vague (*look; lot*); waste (*land*) ǁ *m* vagueness, (fig) space, thin air ǁ *f* wave; **la nouvelle vague** the wave of the future; **vague de fond** ground swell

vaguemestre [vagmestr] *m* (mil, nav) mail clerk

vaguer [vage] *intr* to wander

vaillance [vajãs] *f* valor

vail·lant [vajã] **vail·lante** [vajãt] *adj* valiant; up to scratch

vain [vẽ] **vaine** [ven] *adj* vain; **en vain** in vain

vaincre [vẽkr] §70 *tr* to defeat, conquer; to overcome (*fear, instinct, etc.*) ǁ *intr* to conquer ǁ *ref* to control oneself

vain·cu -cue [vẽky] *adj* defeated, beaten, conquered ǁ *mf* loser

vainqueur [vẽkœr] *adj masc* victorious ǁ *m* victor, winner

vairon [verɔ̃] *adj masc* whitish (*eye*); **vairons** of different colors (*said of eyes*) ǁ *m* (ichth) minnow

vais·seau [veso] *m* (*pl* **-seaux**) vessel; nave (*of church*); **vaisseau amiral** flagship; **vaisseau sanguin** blood vessel; **vaisseau spatial** spaceship

vaisseau-école [vesoekɔl] *m* (*pl* **vaisseaux-écoles**) (nav) training ship

vaisselier [vesəlje] *m* china closet

vaisselle [vesel] *f* dishes; **faire la vaisselle** to wash the dishes; **vaisselle plate** plate (*of gold or silver*)

val [val] *m* (*pl* **vaux** [vo] or **vals**) (obs) valley; **à val** going down the valley; **à val de** (obs) down from

valable [valabl] *adj* valid; worthwhile (*e.g., experience*)

valence [valãs] *f* (chem) valence

valen·tin [valãtẽ] **-tine** [tin] *mf* valentine (*sweetheart*)

valet [vale] *m* valet; holdfast, clamp; (cards) jack; **valet de chambre** valet; **valet de ferme** hired man; **valet de pied** footman

valeur [valœr] *f* value, worth, merit; valor; (*person, thing, or quality worth having*) asset; (com) security, stock; **de valeur** able; valuable; (Canad) too bad, unfortunate; **envoyer en valeur déclarée** to insure (*a package*); **mettre en valeur** to develop (*e.g., a region*); to set off, enhance

valeu·reux [valœrø] **-reuse** [røz] *adj* valorous, brave

validation [validɑsjɔ̃] *f* validation

valide [valid] *adj* valid; fit, able-bodied

valider [valide] *tr* to validate

validité [validite] *f* validity

valise [valiz] *f* suitcase; **faire ses valises** to pack, to pack one's bags; **valise diplomatique** diplomatic pouch

vallée [vale] *f* valley

vallon [valɔ̃] *m* vale, dell

valoir [valwar] §71 *tr* to equal; **un service en vaut un autre** one good turn deserves another; **valoir q.ch. à qn** to get or bring s.o. s.th., e.g., **cela lui a valu une amélioration** that got him a raise; e.g., **la condamnation lui a valu cinq ans de prison** the verdict brought him five years in prison ǁ *intr* to be worth; **autant vaut y renoncer** might as well give up; **cela ne vaut rien** it's worth nothing; **faire valoir** to set off to advantage; to use to advantage; to develop (*one's land*); to invest (*funds, capital*); to put forward (*one's reasons*); **faire valoir que . . .** to argue that . . . ǁ *impers*—**il vaut mieux** it would be better to, e.g., **il vaut mieux attendre** it would be better to wait; **mieux vaut tard que jamais** better late than never ǁ *ref*—**les deux se valent** one is as good as the other

valse [vals] *f* waltz

valser [valse] *tr & intr* to waltz

valve [valv] *f* (aut, bot, zool) valve; (elec) vacuum tube

valvule [valvyl] *f* valve

vamp [vãp] *f* vamp

vamper [vãpe] *tr* (coll) to vamp

vampire [vãpir] *m* vampire

van [vã] *m* van (*for moving horses*)

vandale [vãdal] *adj* vandal; Vandal ǁ *m* vandal ǁ (*cap*) *mf* Vandal

vandalisme [vãdalism] *m* vandalism

vanille [vanij] *f* vanilla

vani·teux [vanitø] **-teuse** [tøz] *adj* vain, conceited

vanne [van] *f* sluice gate, floodgate; butterfly valve; (slang) gibe

van·neau [vano] *m* (*pl* **-neaux**) (orn) lapwing

vanner [vane] *tr* to winnow; to tire out

vannerie [vanri] *f* basketry

vannier [vanje] *m* basket maker

van·tail [vãtaj] *m* (*pl* **-taux** [to]) leaf (*of door, shutter, sluice gate, etc.*)

van·tard [vãtar] **-tarde** [tard] *adj* bragging, boastful || *mf* braggart

vantardise [vãtardiz] *f* bragging, boasting

vanter [vãte] *tr* to praise; to boost, to push (*a product on the market*) || *ref* to brag, to boast

va-nu-pieds [vanypje] *mf invar* (coll) tramp

vapeur [vapœr] *m* steamship || *f* steam; vapor, mist; **à la vapeur** steamed (*e.g., potatoes*); under steam; (coll) at full speed; **à vapeur** steam (*e.g., engine*); **vapeurs** low spirits

vaporisateur [vaporizatœr] *m* atomizer, spray

vaporiser [vaporize] *tr & ref* to vaporize; to spray

vaquer [vake] *intr* to take a recess; **vaquer à** to attend to || *impers*—**il vaque** there is vacant

varappe [varap] *f* cliff; rock climbing

varech [varek] *m* wrack, seaweed

vareuse [varøz] *f* (mil) blouse; (nav) peacoat

variable [varjabl] *adj & f* variable

va·riant -riante [varjã] [rjãt] *adj & f* variant

variation [varjɑsjɔ̃] *f* variation

varice [varis] *f* varicose veins

varicelle [varisɛl] *f* chicken pox

va·rié -riée [varje] *adj* varied

varier [varje] *tr & intr* to vary

variété [varjete] *f* variety; **variétés** selections (*from literary works*); vaudeville

variole [varjɔl] *f* smallpox

vari·queux -queuse [varikø] [køz] *adj* varicose

Varsovie [varsɔvi] *f* Warsaw

vase [vɑz] *m* vase; vessel; **en vase clos** shut up; in an airtight chamber; **vase de nuit** chamber pot || *f* mud, slime

vaseline [vazlin] *f* vaseline

va·seux -seuse [vazø] [zøz] *adj* muddy, slimy; (coll) all in, tired; (coll) fuzzy, obscure

vasistas [vazistas] *m* transom

vasouiller [vazuje] *tr* (coll) to make a mess of || *intr* (coll) to go badly

vasque [vask] *f* basin (*of fountain*)

vas·sal -sale [vasal] (*pl* **vas·saux** [vaso] **-sales**) *adj & mf* vassal

vaste [vast] *adj* vast

vastement [vastəmɑ̃] *adv* (coll) very

Vatican [vatikã] *m* Vatican

vaticane [vatikan] *adj fem* Vatican

va-tout [vatu] *m*—**jouer son va-tout** to stake one's all

vaudeville [vodvil] *m* vaudeville (*light theatrical piece interspersed with songs*); (obs) satirical song

vaudou [vodu] *adj invar & m* voodoo

vau-l'eau [volo]—**à vau-l'eau** downstream; **s'en aller à vau-l'eau** (fig) to go to pot

vau·rien [vorjɛ̃] **-rienne** [rjen] *mf* good-for-nothing

vautour [votur] *m* vulture

vautrer [votre] *ref* to wallow

veau [vo] *m* (*pl* **veaux**) calf; veal; calfskin; (coll) lazybones, dope; **pleurer**

comme un veau to cry like a baby; **veau marin** seal

vé·cu -cue [veky] *adj* true to life

vedette [vədet] *f* patrol boat; scout; lead, star; **en vedette** in the limelight; **mettre en vedette** to headline, to highlight; **vedette de l'écran** movie star; **vedette du petit écran** television star

végé·tal -tale [veʒetal] (*pl* **-taux** [to]) *adj* vegetable, vegetal || *m* vegetable

végéta·rien [veʒetarjɛ̃] **-rienne** [rjen] *adj & mf* vegetarian

végétation [veʒetɑsjɔ̃] *f* vegetation; **végétations (adénoïdes)** adenoids

végéter [veʒete] §10 *intr* to vegetate

véhémence [veemɑ̃s] *f* vehemence

véhé·ment -mente [veemɑ̃] [mɑ̃t] *adj* vehement

véhicule [veikyl] *m* vehicle

veille [vɛj] *f* watch, vigil; wakefulness; **à la veille de** on the eve of; just before; on the verge or point of; **la veille de the eve of**; the day before; **la Veille de Noël** Christmas Eve; **la Veille du jour de l'An** New Year's Eve; **veilles** sleepless nights, late nights; night work

veillée [veje] *f* evening; social evening; **veillée funèbre, veillée du corps** wake

veiller [veje] *tr* to sit up with, to watch over || *intr* to sit up, to stay up; to keep watch; **veiller à** to look after, to see to

veil·leur [vejœr] **veil·leuse** [vejøz] *mf* watcher || *m* watchman; **veilleur de nuit** night watchman || *f see* **veilleuse**

veilleuse [vejøz] *f* night light; rushlight; pilot light; **mettre en veilleuse** to turn down low; to dim (*the headlights*); to slow down (*production in a factory*)

vei·nard [venar] **-narde** [nard] *adj* (coll) lucky || *mf* (coll) lucky person

veine [ven] *f* vein; luck; **veine alors!** (coll) swell!

veiner [vene] *tr* to vein

vei·neux -neuse [venø] [nøz] *adj* veined; venous

vélaire [veler] *adj & f* velar

vêler [vele] *intr* to calve

vélin [velɛ̃] *m* vellum

velléitaire [veleiter] *adj & mf* erratic

velléité [veleite] *f* stray impulse, fancy; **velléité de sourire** slight smile

vélo [velo] *m* bike; **faire du vélo** to go bicycle riding

vélocité [velɔsite] *f* velocity; speed; agility

vélomoteur [velɔmɔtœr] *m* motorbike

velours [vəlur] *m* velvet; **velours côtelé** corduroy

velou·té -tée [vəlute] *adj* velvety || *m* velvetiness

velouter [vəlute] *tr* to make velvety

ve·lu -lue [vəly] *adj* hairy

velum [velom] *m* awning

velvet [velvet] *m* velveteen

venaison [vənezɔ̃] *f* venison

ve·nant [vənã] **-nante** [nãt] *adj* coming; thriving || *mf* comer; **à tout venant** to all comers

vendange [vãdãʒ] *f* grape harvest; vintage

vendanger [vãdãʒe] §38 *tr* to pick (*the grapes*) ‖ *intr* to harvest grapes

ven·deur [vãdœr] **-deuse** [døz] *mf* seller, vendor; salesclerk; **vendeur ambulant** peddler ‖ *m* salesman ‖ *f* salesgirl, saleslady

vendre [vãdr] *tr* to sell; to sell out, to betray; **à vendre** for sale; **vendre au détail** to retail; **vendre aux enchères** to auction off; **vendre en gros** to wholesale ‖ *ref* to sell; to sell oneself, to sell out

vendredi [vãdrədi] *m* Friday; **vendredi saint** Good Friday

ven·du -due [vãdy] *adj* sold; corrupt ‖ *mf* traitor

véné·neux [venenø] **-neuse** [nøz] *adj* poisonous

vénérable [venerabl] *adj* venerable

vénérer [venere] §10 *tr* to venerate

véné·rien [venerjɛ̃] **-rienne** [rjɛn] *adj* venereal ‖ *mf* person with venereal disease

vengeance [vãʒãs] *f* vengeance, revenge

venger [vãʒe] §38 *tr* to avenge ‖ *ref* to get revenge

ven·geur [vãʒœr] **-geuse** [ʒøz] *adj* avenging ‖ *mf* avenger

veni·meux [vənimø] **-meuse** [møz] *adj* venomous

venin [vənɛ̃] *m* venom

venir [vənir] §72 *intr* to come; **à venir** forthcoming; **faire venir** to send for; **où voulez-vous en venir?** what are you getting at?; **venez avec** (coll) come along; **venir de** to have just, e.g., **il vient de partir** he has just left ‖ *impers*—**il me (nous, etc.) vient à l'esprit que** it occurs to me (to us, etc.) that

Venise [vəniz] *f* Venice

véni·tien [venisjɛ̃] **-tienne** [sjɛn] *adj* Venetian ‖ (*cap*) *mf* Venetian

vent [vã] *m* wind; **avoir le vent en poupe** to be in luck; **avoir vent de** to get wind of; **contre vents et marées** through thick and thin; **en plein vent** in the open air; **être dans le vent** to be up to date; **il fait du vent** it is windy; **les vents** (mus) the woodwinds; **vent arrière** tailwind; **vent coulis** draft; **vent debout** headwind; **vent en poupe** (naut) tailwind

vente [vãt] *f* sale; felling (*of timber*); **en vente** on sale; **en vente libre** (pharm) on sale without a prescription; **jeunes ventes** new overgrowth; **vente amiable** private sale; **vente à tempérament** installment selling; **vente à terme** sale on time; **vente au détail** retailing; **vente en gros** wholesaling

ventilateur [vãtilatœr] *m* ventilator; fan; electric fan

ventiler [vãtile] *tr* to ventilate; to value separately; (bk) to apportion

ventouse [vãtuz] *f* sucker; suction cup; suction grip; nozzle (*of vacuum cleaner*); vent

ventre [vãtr] *m* belly; stomach; womb;

à plat ventre prostrate; **à ventre déboutonné** (coll) excessively; (coll) with all one's might; **avoir q.ch. dans le ventre** (coll) to have s.th. on the ball; **bas ventre** (fig) genitals; **ventre à terre** (coll) lickety-split

ventricule [vãtrikyl] *m* ventricle

ventriloque [vãtrilɔk] *mf* ventriloquist

ventriloquie [vãtrilɔki] *f* ventriloquism

ventripo·tent [vãtripotã] **-tente** [tãt] *adj* (coll) potbellied

ven·tru -true [vãtry] *adj* potbellied

ve·nu -nue [vəny] *adj*—**bien venu** successful; welcome ‖ *mf*—**le premier venu** the first comer; just anyone; **les nouveaux venus** the newcomers ‖ *f* coming, advent

Vénus [venys] *f* Venus

vénusté [venyste] *f* charm, grace

vêpres [vepr] *fpl* vespers

ver [ver] *m* worm; **tirer les vers du nez à** to worm secrets out of, to pump; **ver à soie** silkworm; **ver de terre** earthworm; **ver luisant** glowworm

véracité [verasite] *f* veracity

véranda [verãda] *f* veranda

ver·bal -bale [verbal] *adj* (*pl* **-baux** [bo]) verbal; (gram) verb

verbaliser [verbalize] *intr* to write out a report or summons; **verbaliser contre qn** to give s.o. a ticket (*e.g., for speeding*)

verbe [verb] *m* verb; **avoir le verbe haut** to talk loud; **Verbe** (eccl) Word

ver·beux [verbø] **-beuse** [bøz] *adj* verbose, wordy

verbiage [verbjaʒ] *m* verbiage

verdâtre [verdɑtr] *adj* greenish

verdeur [verdœr] *f* greenness; vigor, spryness; crudeness (*of speech*)

verdict [verdik], [verdikt] *m* verdict

verdir [verdir] *tr & intr* to turn green

verdoyer [verdwaje] §47 *intr* to become green

verdure [verdyr] *f* verdure; greens

vé·reux [verø] **-reuse** [røz] *adj* wormy

verge [verʒ] *f* rod; shank (*of anchor*); penis

verger [verʒe] *m* orchard

verglas [vergla] *m* glare ice; sleet

vergogne [vergɔɲ] *f*—**sans vergogne** immodest, brazen; immodestly, brazenly

véridique [veridik] *adj* veracious

vérifica·teur [verifikatœr] **-trice** [tris] *mf* inspector, examiner; **vérificateur comptable** auditor

vérification [verifikɑsjɔ̃] *f* verification; auditing; ascertainment

vérifier [verifje] *tr* to verify; to audit; to ascertain

véritable [veritabl] *adj* veritable; real, genuine

vérité [verite] *f* truth; **à la vérité** to tell the truth; **dire à qn ses quatre vérités** (coll) to give s.o. a piece of one's mind; **en vérité** truly, in truth

ver·meil -meille [vermej] *adj* rosy

vermillon [vermijɔ̃] *adj invar & m* vermilion

vermine [vermin] *f* vermin

vermou·lu -lue [vermuly] *adj* worm-eaten

vermout or **vermouth** [vermut] *m* vermouth

vernaculaire [vernakyler] *adj* vernacular

vernir [vernir] *tr* to varnish; **être verni** (coll) to be lucky

vernis [verni] *m* varnish; (fig) veneer

vernissage [vernisaʒ] *m* varnishing; private viewing (*of pictures*)

vernisser [vernise] *tr* to glaze

vérole [verɔl] *f* (slang) syphilis; **petite vérole** smallpox

verre [ver] *m* glass; crystal (*of watch*); **verre à vitre** windowpane; **verre consigné** bottle with deposit; **verre de contact** contact lens; **verre de lampe** lamp chimney; **verre dépoli** frosted glass; **verre perdu** disposable bottle (*no deposit*); **verres eyeglasses**; **verres de soleil** sunglasses; **verres grossissants** magnifying glasses; **verre taillé** cut glass

verrière [verjer] *f* stained-glass window

verrou [veru] *m* bolt; **être sous les verrous** to be locked up

verrouiller [veruje] *tr* to bolt; to lock up ‖ *ref* to lock oneself in

verrue [very] *f* wart

vers [ver] *m* verse; **les vers** verse, poetry ‖ *prep* toward; about, e.g., **vers les cinq heures** about five o'clock

Versailles [versaj] *f* Versailles

versant [versã] *m* slope, side

versatile [versatil] *adj* fickle

verse [vers] *f*—**pleuvoir à verse** to pour

ver·sé -sée [verse] *adj*—**versé dans** versed in

versement [versəmã] *m* deposit; installment; **versement anticipé** payment in advance

verser [verse] *tr* to pour; to upset; to tip over; to deposit ‖ *intr* to overturn

verset [verse] *m* (Bib) verse

versification [versifikasjɔ̃] *f* versification

versifier [versifje] *tr & intr* to versify

version [versjɔ̃] *f* version; translation from a foreign language

verso [verso] *m* verso; **au verso** on the back

vert [ver] **verte** [vert] *adj* green; verdant; vigorous (*person*); new (*wine*); raw (*leather*); sharp (*scolding*); spicy (*story*); **ils sont trop verts!** sour grapes! ‖ *m* green; greenery; **mettre au vert** to put out to pasture; **se mettre au vert** to take a rest in the country

vert-de-gris [verdəgri] *m invar* verdigris

vertèbre [vertebr] *f* vertebra

verté·bré -brée [vertebre] *adj & m* vertebrate

verti·cal -cale [vertikal] (*pl* **-caux** [ko] **-cales**) *adj* vertical ‖ *m* (astr) vertical circle ‖ *f* vertical

vertige [vertiʒ] *m* vertigo, dizziness

vertigo [vertigo] *m* staggers (*of horse*); caprice

vertu [verty] *f* virtue

ver·tueux [vertɥø] **-tueuse** [tɥøz] *adj* virtuous

verve [verv] *f* verve

ver·veux [vervø] **-veuse** [vøz] *adj* lively, animated ‖ *m* fishnet

vésanie [vezani] *f* madness

vesce [ves] *f* vetch

vésicule [vezikyl] *f* vesicle; blister; **vésicule biliaire** gall bladder

vespasienne [vespazjen] *f* street urinal

vessie [vesi] *f* bladder; **vessie à glace** ice bag

veste [vest] *f* coat, suit coat; **remporter une veste** (coll) to suffer a setback; **retourner sa veste** (coll) to do an about-face; **veste croisée** double-breasted coat; **veste de pyjama** pajama top; **veste de sport** sport coat; **veste d'intérieur, veste d'appartement** lounging robe; **veste droite** single-breasted coat

vestiaire [vestjer] *m* checkroom, cloakroom

vestibule [vestibyl] *m* vestibule

vestige [vestiʒ] *m* vestige; footprint

veston [vestɔ̃] *m* coat

Vésuve [vezyv] *m*—**le Vésuve** Vesuvius

vêtement [vetmã] *m* garment; **vêtements** clothes

vétéran [veterã] *m* veteran

vétérinaire [veteriner] *adj & mf* veterinary

vétille [vetij] *f* trifle

vétiller [vetije] *intr* to split hairs

vêtir [vetir] §73 *tr & ref* to dress

veto [veto] *m* veto; **mettre** or **opposer son veto à** to veto

vétuste [vetyst] *adj* decrepit, rickety

veuf [vœf] **veuve** [vœv] *adj* widowed ‖ *m* widower ‖ *f* see **veuve**

veule [vøl] *adj* (coll) feeble, weak

veuvage [vœvaʒ] *m* widowhood; widowerhood

veuve [vœv] *f* widow

vexation [veksasjɔ̃] *f* vexation

vexer [vekse] *tr* to vex

via [vja] *prep* via

viaduc [vjadyk] *m* viaduct

via·ger [vjaʒe] **-gère** [ʒer] *adj* life, for life ‖ *m* life annuity

viande [vjãd] *f* meat; **amène ta viande!** (slang) get over here!

vibration [vibrasjɔ̃] *f* vibration

vibrer [vibre] *intr* to vibrate

vicaire [viker] *m* vicar

vice [vis] *m* vice; defect; **vice de conformation** physical defect; **vice de forme** (law) irregularity, flaw; **vice versa** vice versa

vice-amiral [visamiral] *m* (*pl* **-amiraux** [amiro]) vice-admiral

vice-président [visprezidã] **-présidente** [prezidãt] *mf* (*pl* **-présidents**) vice-president

vice-roi [visrwa] *m* (*pl* **-rois**) viceroy

vice-versa [viseversa], [visversa] *adv* vice versa

vi·cié -ciée [visje] *adj* foul, polluted; poor, thin (*blood*)

vicier [visje] *tr* to foul, to pollute; to taint, to spoil

vi·cieux [visjø] **-cieuse** [sjøz] *adj* vicious; wrong (*use*)

vici·nal -nale [visinal] *adj* (*pl* **-naux** [no]) local, side (*road*)

vicissitude [visisityd] *f* vicissitude

vicomte [vikɔ̃t] *m* viscount

victime [viktim] *f* victim

victoire [viktwar] *f* victory

victo·rieux [viktɔrjø] **-rieuse** [rjøz] *adj* victorious

victuailles [viktɥaj] *fpl* victuals, foods

vidange [vidɑ̃ʒ] *f* draining; night soil; drain (*of pipe, sink, etc.*)

vidanger [vidɑ̃ʒe] §38 *tr* to drain

vide [vid] *adj* empty; blank; vacant ‖ *m* emptiness, void; vacuum

vi·dé -dée [vide] *adj* cleaned (*fish, fowl, etc.*); played out, exhausted

vide-bouteille [vidbutej] *m* (*pl* **-bouteilles**) siphon

vide-cave [vidkav] *m invar* sump pump

vide-citron [vidsitrɔ̃] *m* (*pl* **-citrons**) lemon squeezer

vide-gousset [vidguse] *m* (*pl* **-goussets**) (hum) thief

vide-ordures [vidɔrdyr] *m invar* garbage shoot

vide-poches [vidpɔʃ] *m invar* dresser; pin tray; (aut) glove compartment

vider [vide] *tr* to empty; to drain; to clean (*fish, fowl, etc.*); to settle (*a question*); **se faire vider de** (coll) to get thrown out of; to be fired from; to be expelled from

vi·deur [vidœr] **-deuse** [døz] *mf* (coll) bouncer (*in a night club*)

viduité [vidɥite] *f* widowhood

vidure [vidyr] *f* guts (*e.g., of cleaned fish*); **vidures de poubelle** garbage

vie [vi] *f* life; livelihood, living; **à vie** for life; **de ma** (**sa, etc.**) **vie** in my (his, etc.) life, e.g., **je ne l'ai jamais vu de ma vie** I have never seen it in my life; **jamais de la vie!** not on your life!; **vie de bâton de chaise** disorderly life; **vie de château** life of ease

vieillard [vjejar] *m* old man; **les vieillards** old people

vieille [vjej] *f* old woman

vieilleries [vjejri] *fpl* old things; old ideas

vieillesse [vjejes] *f* old age

vieil·li -lie [vjeji] *adj* aged; out-of-date, antiquated

vieillir [vjejir] *tr* to age; to make (*s.o.*) look older ‖ *intr* to age, to grow old ‖ *ref* to make oneself look older

vieil·lot [vjejo] **vieil·lotte** [vjejɔt] *adj* (coll) oldish, quaint

vielle [vjel] *f* (hist) hurdy-gurdy

Vienne [vjen] *f* Vienna; Vienne (*city in France*)

vien·nois [vjenwa] **vien·noise** [vjenwaz] *adj* Viennese ‖ (*cap*) *mf* Viennese

vierge [vjerʒ] *adj* virginal; virgin; blank; unexposed (*film*) ‖ *f* virgin

Vietnam [vjetnam] *m*—**le Vietnam** Vietnam

vietna·mien [vjetnamjɛ̃] **-mienne** [mjen] *adj* Vietnamese ‖ (*cap*) *mf* Vietnamese

vieux [vjø] (or **vieil** [vjej] before vowel or mute h) **vieille** [vjej] *adj* old (*wine*) ‖ (when standing before noun) *adj* old; old-fashioned; obsolete (*word, meaning, etc.*) ‖ *mf* old person ‖ *m* old man; **les vieux** old people; **mon vieux** (coll) my boy ‖ *f* see **vieille**

vif [vif] **vive** [viv] *adj* alive, living; lively, quick; bright, intense; hearty, heartfelt; sharp (*criticism*); keen (*pleasure*); spring (*water*) ‖ *m* quick; **couper dans le vif** to take drastic measures; **entrer dans le vif de** to get to the heart of; **peindre au vif** to paint from life; **piqué au vif** stung to the quick

vif-argent [vifarʒɑ̃] *m* quicksilver; (*person*) live wire

vigie [viʒi] *f* lookout

vigilance [viʒilɑ̃s] *f* vigilance

vigi·lant [viʒilɑ̃] **-lante** [lɑ̃t] *adj* vigilant ‖ *m* night watchman

vigile [viʒil] *m* night watchman ‖ *f* (eccl) vigil

vigne [viɲ] *f* vine; vineyard; **vigne blanche** clematis; **vigne de Judas** bittersweet; **vigne vierge** Virginia creeper

vigne·ron [viɲrɔ̃] **-ronne** [rɔn] *mf* vine-grower; vintner

vignette [viɲet] *f* vignette; tax stamp; gummed tab

vignoble [viɲɔbl] *m* vineyard

vigou·reux [vigurø] **-reuse** [røz] *adj* vigorous

vigueur [vigœr] *f* vigor; **entrer en vigueur** to go into effect

vil vile [vil] *adj* vile; cheap

vi·lain [vilɛ̃] **-laine** [len] *adj* nasty; ugly; naughty ‖ *mf* nasty person

vilebrequin [vilbrəkɛ̃] *m* brace (*of brace and bit*); crankshaft

vilenie [vilni] *f* villainy; abuse

villa [villa] *f* villa; cottage, small one-story home

village [vilaʒ] *m* village

villa·geois [vilaʒwa] **-geoise** [ʒwaz] *mf* villager

ville [vil] *f* city; town; **aller en ville** to go downtown; **la Ville Lumière** the City of Light (*Paris*); **ville champignon** boom town; **ville satellite** suburban town; **villes jumelées** twin cities; **villes réunies** twin cities

villégiature [vileʒjatyr] *f* vacation

vin [vɛ̃] *m* wine; **avoir le vin gai** to be hilariously drunk; **être entre deux vins** to be tipsy; **vin d'honneur** reception (*at which toasts are offered*); **vin d'orange** sangaree; **vin mousseux** sparkling wine; **vin ordinaire** table wine

vinaigre [vinegr] *m* vinegar

vinaigrette [vinegret] *f* French dressing, vinaigrette sauce

vindica·tif [vɛ̃dikatif] **-tive** [tiv] *adj* vindictive

vingt [vɛ̃] *adj & pron* twenty; the Twentieth, e.g., **Jean vingt** John the Twentieth; **vingt et un** [vɛ̃teœ̃] twenty-one; twenty-first, e.g., **Jean vingt et un** John the Twenty-first; **vingt et unième** twenty-first ‖ *m* twenty; twentieth (*in dates*); **vingt et**

un twenty-one; twenty-first (*in dates*); **vingt et unième** twenty-first

vingtaine [vɛ̃tɛn] *f* score; **une vingtaine de** about twenty

vingt-deux [vɛ̃tdø] *adj & pron* twenty-two; the Twenty-second, e.g., **Jean vingt-deux** John the Twenty-second ‖ *m* twenty-two; twenty-second (*in dates*) ‖ *interj* (slang) beware!; cheese it!

vingt-deuxième [vɛ̃tdøzjɛm] *adj, pron* (*masc, fem*), & *m* twenty-second

vingt-et-un [vɛ̃teœ̃] *m* (cards) twenty-one

vingtième [vɛ̃tjɛm] *adj, pron* (*masc, fem*), & *m* twentieth

vinyle [vinil] *m* vinyl

viol [vjɔl] *m* rape

violation [vjɔlɑsjɔ̃] *f* violation

violence [vjɔlɑ̃s] *f* violence

vio·lent [vjɔlɑ] **-lente** [lɑ̃t] *adj* violent

violenter [vjɔlɑ̃te] *tr* to do violence to

violer [vjɔle] *tr* to violate; to break (*the faith*); to rape, ravish

vio·let [vjɔle] **-lette** [let] *adj & m* violet (*color*) ‖ *f* (bot) violet

violon [vjɔlɔ̃] *m* violin; (slang) calaboose, jug; **payer les violons** (coll) to pay the piper; **violon d'Ingres** hobby

violoncelle [vjɔlɔ̃sɛl] *m* violoncello

violoniste [vjɔlɔnist] *mf* violinist

vipère [vipɛr] *f* viper

virage [viraʒ] *m* turning; turn, e.g., **pas de virage à gauche** no left turn; (aer) bank; (phot) toning; **virage en épingle à cheveux** hairpin curve; **virages** (public sign) winding road; **virage sur place** U-turn

virago [virago] *f* mannish woman

virée [vire] *f* (coll) spin (*in a car*); (coll) round (*of bars*)

virement [virmɑ̃] *m* transfer (*of funds*); (naut) tacking

virer [vire] *tr* to transfer (*funds*); (phot) to tone ‖ *intr* to turn; (aer) to bank; **virer à** to turn (*sour, red, etc.*); **virer de bord** (naut) to tack

virevolte [virvɔlt] *f* turn; about-face

virevolter [virvɔlte] *intr* to make an about-face; to go hither and thither

virginité [virʒinite] *f* virginity, maidenhood

virgule [virgyl] *f* (gram) comma; (*used in French to set off the decimal fraction from the integer*) decimal point

virilité [virilite] *f* virility

virole [virɔl] *f* ferrule

virologie [virɔlɔʒi] *f* virology

vir·tuel -tuelle [virtɥel] *adj* potential; (mech, opt, phys) virtual

virtuose [virtɥoz] *mf* virtuoso

virtuosité [virtɥozite] *f* virtuosity

virulence [virylɑ̃s] *f* virulence

viru·lent [virylɑ̃] **-lente** [lɑ̃t] *adj* virulent

virus [virys] *m* virus

vis [vis] *f* screw; thread (*of screw*); spiral staircase; **fermer à vis** to screw shut; **serrer la vis à** (fig) to put the screws on; **vis à métaux** machine screw; **vis de blocage** setscrew

visa [viza] *m* visa; (fig) approval

visage [vizaʒ] *m* face; **à deux visages** two-faced; **faire bon visage à** to pretend to be friendly to; **trouver visage de bois** to find the door closed; **visages pâles** palefaces; **voir qn sous son vrai visage** to see s.o. in his true colors

visagiste [vizaʒist] *mf* beautician

vis-à-vis [vizavi] *adv* vis-à-vis; **vis-à-vis de** vis-à-vis; towards; in the presence of ‖ *m* vis-à-vis; **en vis-à-vis** facing

viscère [visɛr] *m* organ; **viscères** viscera

visée [vize] *f* aim

viser [vize] *tr* to aim; to aim at; to concern; to visa ‖ *intr* to aim; **viser à** to aim at; to aim to

viseur [vizœr] *m* viewfinder; sight (*of gun*); **viseur de lancement** bombsight

visibilité [vizibilite] *f* visibility; **sans visibilité** blind (*flying*)

visible [vizibl] *adj* visible; obvious; (coll) at home, free; (coll) open to the public

visière [vizjɛr] *f* visor; sight (*of gun*); **rompre en visière à** to take a stand against

vision [vizjɔ̃] *f* vision

visionnaire [vizjɔnɛr] *adj & mf* visionary

visionner [vizjɔne] *tr* to view, inspect

visionneuse [vizjɔnøz] *f* viewer

visite [vizit] *f* visit; inspection; **en, de visite** visiting; **faire, rendre visite à** to visit

visiter [vizite] *tr* to visit; to inspect

visi·teur [vizitœr] **-teuse** [tøz] *adj* visiting (*e.g., nurse*) ‖ *mf* visitor; inspector

vison [vizɔ̃] *m* mink

vis·queux [viskø] **-queuse** [køz] *adj* viscous

visser [vise] *tr* to screw; to screw on; (coll) to put the screws on

visualiser [vizɥalize] *tr* to visualize

vi·suel -suelle [vizɥel] *adj* visual

vi·tal -tale [vital] *adj* (*pl* **-taux** [to]) vital

vitaliser [vitalize] *tr* to vitalize

vitalité [vitalite] *f* vitality

vitamine [vitamin] *f* vitamin

vite [vit] *adj* fast, swift ‖ *adv* fast, quickly; **faites vite!** hurry up!

vitesse [vites] *f* speed, velocity; rate; **à toute vitesse** at full speed; **changer de vitesse** (aut) to shift gears; **en grande vitesse** (rr) by express; **en petite vitesse** (rr) by freight; **en première (seconde**, etc.) **vitesse** (aut) in first (second, etc.) gear; **vitesse acquise** momentum

viticole [vitikɔl] *adj* wine

vitrage [vitraʒ] *m* glasswork; small window curtain; sash; glazing

vi·trail [vitraj] *m* (*pl* **-traux** [tro]) stained-glass window

vitre [vitr] *f* windowpane, pane; (aut) window; **casser les vitres** (coll) to kick up a fuss

vi·tré -trée [vitre] *adj* glazed; vitreous (*humor*); glassed-in

vi·treux [vitrø] **-treuse** [trøz] *adj* glassy; vitreous

vitrier [vitrije] *m* glazier

vitrine [vitrin] *f* show window; showcase; glass cabinet; **lécher les vitrines** (coll) to go window-shopping

vitupérer [vitypere] §10 *tr* to vituperate, abuse || *intr*—**vitupérer contre** (coll) to vituperate

vivace [vivas] *adj* hardy, vigorous; long-lived; (bot) perennial

vivacité [vivasite] *f* vivacity

vivan·dier [vivãdje] **-dière** [djer] *mf* sutler || *f* camp follower

vi·vant [vivã] **-vante** [vãt] *adj* living, alive; lively; modern (*language*) || *m*—**bon vivant** high liver, jolly companion; **du vivant de** during the lifetime of; **les vivants et les morts** the quick and the dead

vivat [viva] *m* viva || *interj* viva!

vivement [vivmã] *adv* quickly; warmly; deeply; sharply, briskly

viveur [vivœr] *m* pleasure seeker, rounder

vivier [vivje] *m* fish preserve, fishpond

vivifier [vivifje] *tr* to vivify, vitalize

vivisection [viviseksjõ] *f* vivisection

vivoir [vivwar] *m* (Canad) living room

vivoter [vivote] *intr* (coll) to live from hand to mouth

vivre [vivr] *m*—**le vivre et le couvert** room and board; **le vivre et le vêtement** food and clothing; **vivres** provisions; (mil) rations, supplies || §74 *tr* to live (*one's life, faith, art*); (to) live through, to experience || *intr* to live; **être difficile à vivre** to be difficult to live with; **qui vive?** (mil) who is there?; **qui vivra verra** time will tell; **vive!, vivent! viva!, long live!; vivre au jour le jour** to live from hand to mouth; **vivre de** to live on

vizir [vizir] *m* vizier

vlan [vlã] *interj* whack!

vocable [vɔkabl] *m* word

vocabulaire [vɔkabyler] *m* vocabulary

vo·cal -cale [vɔkal] *adj* (*pl* -caux [ko]) vocal

vocaliser [vɔkalize] *tr, intr,* & *ref* to vocalize

vocatif [vɔkatif] *m* vocative

vocation [vɔkasjõ] *f* vocation, calling; **vocation pédagogique** teaching career

vociférer [vɔsifere] §10 *tr* to shout (*e.g., insults*) || *intr* to vociferate

vœu [vø] *m* (*pl* **vœux**) vow; wish; resolution; **meilleurs vœux!** best wishes!; **tous mes vœux!** my best wishes!

vogue [vɔg] *f* vogue, fashion; **en vogue** in vogue, in fashion

voguer [vɔge] *intr* to sail; **vogue la galère!** let's chance it, here goes!

voici [vwasi] *prep* here is, here are; for, e.g., **voici quatre jours qu'elle est partie** she has been gone for four days; **le voici here he is; nous voici** here we are; **que voici** here, e.g., **mon frère que voici va vous accompagner** my brother here is going to accompany you

voie [vwa] *f* way; road; lane (*of highway*); (anat) tract; (rr) track; **en voie de** on the road to, nearing; **être en bonne voie** to be doing well; **voie d'eau** leak; **voie de garage** driveway; **voie d'évitement** siding; **Voie lactée** Milky Way; **voie maritime** seaway; **voie(s) de fait** (law) assault and battery; **voie surface** surface mail

voilà [vwala] *prep* there is, there are; here is, here are; that's, e.g., **voilà pourquoi** that's why; ago, e.g., **voilà quatre jours qu'elle est partie** she left four days ago; **voilà, monsieur** there you are, sir

voile [vwal] *m* veil; (phot) fog (*on negative*); **voile du palais** soft palate; **voile noir** (pathol) blackout || *f* sail; sailboat; **faire voile sur** to set sail for

voi·lé -lée [vwale] *adj* veiled; overcast; muffled; warped; husky (*voice*); (phot) fogged; **peu voilé** thinly veiled, broad (*e.g., hint*)

voiler [vwale] *tr* to veil; (phot) to fog || *ref* to cloud over; to become warped

voi·lier [vwalje] **-lière** [ljer] *adj* sailing || *m* sailboat; sailmaker; migratory bird

voilure [vwalyr] *f* sails; warping

voir [vwar] §75 *tr* to see; **faire voir** to show; **voie jouer** to see (*s.o.*) playing, to see (*s.th.*) played; **voir qn qui vient** to see s.o. coming, to see s.o. come; **voir venir qn** to see s.o. coming, to see s.o. come; (fig) to see through s.o. || *intr* to see; **faites voir!** let's see it!, let me see it!; **j'en ai vu bien d'autres** I have seen worse than that; **n'avoir rien à voir avec, à,** or **dans** to have nothing to do with; **voir à** + *inf* to see that + *inf*, e.g., **voir à nous loger** to see that we are housed; **voir au dos** see other side, turn the page; **voyons!** see here!, come now! || *ref* to see oneself; to see one another; to be obvious; to be seen, to be found

voire [vwar] *adv* nay, indeed; **voire même** or even, and even

voirie [vwari] *f* highway department; garbage collection; dump

voi·sé -sé [vwaze] *adj* voiced

voi·sin [vwazɛ̃] **-sine** [zin] *adj* neighboring; adjoining; **voisin de** near || *mf* neighbor

voisinage [vwazinaʒ] *m* neighborhood; neighborliness

voisiner [vwazine] *intr* to visit one's neighbors; **voisiner avec** to be placed next to

voiture [vwatyr] *f* vehicle; carriage; (aut, rr) car; **en voiture!** all aboard!; **petite voiture** (coll) wheelchair; **voiture à bras** handcart; **voiture d'enfant** baby carriage; **voiture de pompier** fire engine; **voiture de remise** rented car; **voiture de série** stock car; **voiture de tourisme** pleasure car; **voiture d'infirme** wheelchair; **voiture d'occasion** used car

voiture-bar [vwatyrbar] *f* (*pl* **voitures-bars**) club car

voiture-lit [vwatyrli] *f* (*pl* **voitures-lits**) sleeping car

voiturer [vwatyre] *tr* to transport, to convey

voiture-restaurant [vwatyrrɛstorɑ̃] *f* (*pl* **voitures-restaurants**) dining car

voiture-salon [vwatyrsalɔ̃] *f* (*pl* **voitures-salons**) parlor car

voix [vwa], [vwɑ] *f* voice; vote; **à haute voix** aloud; in a loud voice; **à pleine voix** at the top of one's voice; **à voix basse** in a low voice; **à voix haute** in a loud voice; **de vive voix** by word of mouth; **voix de tête, voix de fausset** falsetto

vol [vɔl] *m* theft, robbery; flight; flock; **au vol** in flight; in passing; **à vol d'oiseau** as the crow flies; **de haut vol** high-flying; big-time (*crook*); **vol avec effraction** burglary; **vol cosmique** space flight; **vol plané** volplane; **vol sans visibilité** blind flying

volage [vɔlaʒ] *adj* fickle, changeable

volaille [vɔlaj] *f* fowl; (slang) hens (*women*); (slang) gal

vo·lant [vɔlɑ̃] **-lante** [lɑ̃t] *adj* flying || *m* steering wheel; flywheel; shuttlecock; sail (*of windmill*); flounce (*of dress*); leaf (*attached to stub*); **volant de sécurité** safety margin, reserve

vola·til -tile [vɔlatil] *adj* volatile || *m* bird; fowl

volatiliser [vɔlatilize] *tr & ref* to volatilize

volcan [vɔlkɑ̃] *m* volcano

volcanique [vɔlkanik] *adj* volcanic

vole [vɔl] *f*—**faire la vole** to take all the tricks

volée [vɔle] *f* volley; flight (*of birds; of stairs*); flock; **à la volée** on the wing; at random; **à toute volée** loud and clear; **de haute volée** upperclass; **de la première volée** first-class, crack; **sonner à toute volée** to peal out

voler [vɔle] *tr* to rob; to steal; to fly at; **ne l'avoir pas volé** to deserve all that is coming; **voler à** to steal from || *intr* to rob; to steal; to fly

volet [vɔle] *m* shutter; inside flap; end paper; (aer) flap; **trier sur le volet** to choose with care

voleter [vɔlte] §34 *intr* to flutter

vo·leur [vɔlœr] **-leuse** [løz] *adj* thievish || *mf* thief; **au voleur!** stop thief!; **voleur à la tire** pickpocket; **voleur à l'étalage** shoplifter; **voleur de grand chemin** highwayman

volition [vɔlisjɔ̃] *f* volition

volley-ball [vɔlebol] *m* volleyball

volontaire [vɔlɔ̃tɛr] *adj* voluntary; headstrong, willful; determined (*chin*) || *mf* volunteer

volonté [vɔlɔ̃te] *f* will; wishes; **à volonté** at will; **bonne volonté** good will; **faire ses quatre volontés** (coll) to do just as one pleases; **mauvaise volonté** ill will

volontiers [vɔlɔ̃tje] *adv* gladly, willingly

volt [vɔlt] *m* volt

voltage [vɔltaʒ] *m* voltage

volte-face [vɔltəfas] *f invar* volte-face

voltige [vɔltiʒ] *f* acrobatics

voltiger [vɔltiʒe] §38 *intr* to flit about; to flutter

voltmètre [vɔltmɛtr] *m* voltmeter

volubile [vɔlybil] *adj* voluble

volume [vɔlym] *m* volume; **faire du volume** (coll) to put on airs

volumi·neux [vɔluminø] **-neuse** [nøz] *adj* voluminous

volupté [vɔlypte] *f* voluptuousness, ecstasy

volup·tueux [vɔlyptɥø] **-tueuse** [tɥøz] *adj* voluptuous || *mf* voluptuary

vomir [vɔmir] *tr & intr* to vomit

vomissure [vɔmisyr] *f* vomit

vorace [vɔras] *adj* voracious

voracité [vɔrasite] *f* voracity

vos [vo] §88

vo·tant [vɔtɑ̃] **-tante** [tɑ̃t] *mf* voter

vote [vɔt] *m* vote; **passer au vote** to vote on; **vote affirmatif** yea; **vote négatif** nay; **vote par correspondance** absentee ballot; **vote par procuration** proxy

voter [vɔte] *tr* to vote; to vote for || *intr* to vote; **voter à mains levées** to vote by show of hands; **voter par assis et levé** to give one's vote by standing or by remaining seated

vo·tif [vɔtif] **-tive** [tiv] *adj* votive

votre [vɔtr] §88

vôtre [votr] §89

vouer [vwe] *tr* to vow, to dedicate; to doom, to condemn; **voué à** headed for; doomed to || *ref*—**se vouer à** to dedicate oneself to

vouloir [vulwar] *m* will || §76 *tr* to want, to wish; to require; **je voudrais** I would like; I would like to; **veuillez** + *inf* please + *inf*; **voulez-vous vous taire?** will you be quiet?; **vouloir bien** to be glad to, to be willing to; **vouloir dire** to mean || *intr*—**en vouloir à** to bear a grudge against; **je veux!** (slang) and how!; **je veux bien** I'm quite willing; **si vous voulez bien** if you don't mind || *ref*—**s'en vouloir** to have it in for each other

vou·lu -lue [vuly] *adj* required; deliberate

vous [vu] §85, §87; **vous autres Américains** you Americans

vous-même [vumɛm] §86

voussoir [vuswar] *m* (archit) arch stone

voussure [vusyr] *f* arch, arching

voûte [vut] *f* vault; **voûte céleste** canopy of heaven

voûter [vute] *tr* to vault; to bend || *ref* to become round-shouldered

vouvoyer [vuvwaje] §47 *tr* to address with the pronoun **vous** (*instead of* **tu**)

voy. *abbr* (**voyez**) see

voyage [vwajaʒ] *m* trip, journey, voyage; ride (*in car, train, plane, etc.*); **voyage à forfait** all-expense tour; **voyage aller et retour** round trip; **voyage de noces** honeymoon

voyager [vwajaʒe] §38 *intr* to travel

voya·geur [vwajaʒœr] **-geuse** [ʒøz] *mf* traveler; passenger

voyance [vwajɑ̃s] *f* clairvoyance

voyant [vwajɑ̃] **voyante** [vwajɑ̃t] *adj* loud, gaudy || *mf* clairvoyant || *m* signal; (aut) gauge || *f* fortuneteller

voyelle [vwajɛl] *f* vowel

voyeur [vwajœr] **voyeuse** [vwajøz] *mf* voyeur ‖ *m* Peeping Tom

voyou [vwaju] **voyoute** [vwajut] *adj* gutter, low ‖ *mf* gutter-snipe; brat; hoodlum

vrac [vrak]—**en vrac** unpacked, loose; in bulk; in disorder

vrai vraie [vrɛ], [vrɛ] *adj* true, real, genuine ‖ *m* truth; **à vrai dire** to tell the truth; **pour vrai** (coll) for good

vraiment [vrɛmã] *adv* truly, really

vraisemblable [vrɛsãblabl] *adj* probable, likely; true to life, realistic (*play, novel*)

vraisemblance [vrɛsãblãs] *f* probability, likelihood; realism

vrille [vrij] *f* drill; (aer) spin; (bot) tendril

vriller [vrije] *tr* to bore ‖ *intr* to go into a tailspin

vrombir [vrɔ̃bir] *intr* to throb; to buzz; to hum, to purr (*said of motor*)

vu vue [vy] *adj* seen, regarded; **bien vu de** in favor with; **mal vu de** out of favor with ‖ *m*—**au vu de** upon presentation of; **au vu et au su de tout le monde** openly ‖ *f* view; sight; eyesight; **avoir à vue** to have in mind; **à vue** in sight; (com) on demand; **à vue de nez** at first sight; **à vue d'œil** visibly; quickly; **de vue** by sight; **en vue** in evidence; in sight; **en vue de** in order to; **garder à vue** to keep under observation, to keep locked up; **perdre qn de vue** to lose sight of s.o.; to get out of touch with s.o.; **vue à vol d'oiseau** bird's-eye view; **vues sur** designs on ‖ **vu** *prep* considering, in view of; **vu que** whereas

vulcaniser [vylkanize] *tr* to vulcanize

vulgaire [vylgɛr] *adj* common, vulgar; ordinary, everyday; vernacular ‖ *m* common herd; vernacular

vulgariser [vylgarize] *tr* to popularize; to make vulgar

vulgarité [vylgarite] *f* vulgarity

vulnérable [vylnerabl] *adj* vulnerable

Vve *abbr* (veuve) widow

W

W, w [dubləvə] *m invar* twenty-third letter of the French alphabet

wagon [vagɔ̃] *m* (rr) car, coach; (coll) big car; **un wagon** (coll) a lot; **wagon à bagages** baggage car; **wagon à bestiaux** cattle car; **wagon couvert** boxcar; **wagon de marchandises** freight car; **wagon frigorifique** or **réfrigérant** refrigerator car; **wagon plat** flat car

wagon-bar [vagɔ̃bar] *m* (*pl* **wagons-bars**) club car

wagon-citerne [vagɔ̃sitern] *m* (*pl* **wagons-citernes**) tank car

wagon-lit [vagɔ̃li] *m* (*pl* **wagons-lits**) sleeping car

wagon-poste [vagɔ̃pɔst] *m* (*pl* **wagons-poste**) mail car

wagon-réservoir [vagɔ̃rezɛrvwar] *m* (*pl* **wagons-réservoirs**) tank car

wagon-restaurant [vagɔ̃rɛstɔrã] *m* (*pl* **wagons-restaurants**) dining car

wagon-salon [vagɔ̃salɔ̃] *m* (*pl* **wagons-salons**) parlor car

wagon-tombereau [vagɔ̃tɔ̃bro] *m* (*pl* **wagons-tombereaux**) dump truck

wallace [valas] *f* drinking fountain

wal·lon [walɔ̃] **wal·lonne** [walɔn] *adj* Walloon ‖ *m* Walloon (*dialect*) ‖ (*cap*) *mf* Walloon

warrant [warã], [varã] *m* receipt

water-polo [waterpolo] *m* water polo

waterproof [waterpruf] *adj invar* waterproof ‖ *m invar* raincoat

waters [water], [vater] *mpl* toilet

watt [wat] *m* watt

watt-heure [watœr] *m* (*pl* **watts-heures**) watt-hour

wattman [watman] *m* motorman

wattmètre [watmetr] *m* wattmeter

week-end [wikɛnd] *m* (*pl* **-ends**) week-end

whisky [wiski] *m* whiskey; **whisky écossais** Scotch

wolfram [vɔlfram] *m* wolfram

X

X, x [iks], *[iks] *m invar* twenty-fourth letter of the French alphabet

Xavier [gzavje] *m* Xavier

xénon [ksenɔ̃] *m* xenon

xénophobe [ksenofɔb] *adj* xenophobic ‖ *mf* xenophobe

Xérès [keres], [gzeres] *m* Jerez; sherry

Xerxès [gzerses] *m* Xerxes

xylophone [ksilofɔn] *m* xylophone

Y

Y, y [igrek], *[igrek] *m invar* twenty-fifth letter of the French alphabet

y [i] *pron pers* §87 to it, to them; at it, at them; in it, in them; by it, by them; of it, of them, e.g., **j'y pense** I am thinking of it or them; (untranslated with certain verbs), e.g., **je n'y vois pas** I don't see; e.g., **il s'y connaît** (coll) he's an expert, he knows what he's talking about; him, her, e.g., **je m'y fie** I trust him; **allez-y!** go ahead!, start!; **ça y est!** that's it!; **je n'y suis pour personne** I am not at home for anybody; **je n'y suis pour rien** I have nothing to do with it; **j'y suis!** I've got it! || *adv* there; here, in, e.g., **Monsieur votre père y est-il?** is your father here?, is your father in?

yacht [jɔt], [jak] *m* yacht; **yacht à glace** iceboat

yacht-club [jɔtklœb] *m* yacht club

yankee [jɑ̃ki] *adj masc* Yankee || (*cap*) *mf* Yankee

yèble [jebl] *f* (bot) elder; **l'yèble** the elder

yeoman [jɔman] *m* yeoman

yeuse [jøz] *f* holm oak; **l'yeuse** the holm oak

yeux [jø] *mpl* see **œil**

yé-yé [jeje] (*pl* -**yés**) *adj & mf* jitterbug

yiddish [jidiʃ] *adj invar & m* Yiddish

yogourt [jɔgur] *m* yogurt

yole [jɔl] *f* yawl

Yonne [jɔn] *f* Yonne; **l'Yonne** the Yonne

yougoslave [jugɔslav] *adj* Yugoslav || (*cap*) *mf* Yugoslav

Yougoslavie [jugɔslavi] *f* Yugoslavia; **la Yougoslavie** Yugoslavia

youyou [juju] *m* dinghy

Z

Z, z [zɛd] *m invar* twenty-sixth letter of the French alphabet

za·zou -**zoue** [zazu] *adj* (coll) jazzy || *m* (coll) zoot suiter

zèbre [zebr] *m* zebra; (slang) guy

zébrer [zebre] §10 *tr* to stripe; **le soleil zèbre** the sun casts streaks of light on

zébrure [zebryr] *f* stripe

zéla·teur [zelatœr] -**trice** [tris] *mf* zealot

zèle [zel] *m* zeal

zénith [zenit] *m* zenith

zéphyr [zefir] *m* zephyr

zeppelin [zeplɛ̃] *m* zeppelin

zéro [zero] *m* zero

zest [zest] *m*—**entre le zist et le zest** (coll) betwixt and between || *interj* tush!

zeste [zest] *m* peel (*of citrus fruit*); dividing membrane (*of nut*); **pas un zeste** (fig) not a particle of difference

Zeus [zøs] *m* Zeus

zézaiement [zezemɑ̃] *m* lisp

zézayer [zezeje] §49 *intr* to lisp

zibeline [ziblin] *f* sable

zieuter [zjøte] *tr* (slang) to get a load of

zigzag [zigzag] *m* zigzag

zigzaguer [zigzage] *intr* to zigzag

zinc [zɛ̃g] *m* zinc; (coll) bar

zizanie [zizani] *f* wild rice; tare; **semer la zizanie** to sow discord

zodiaque [zɔdjak] *m* zodiac

zone [zon] *f* zone; **zone bleu** center city with limited parking

zoo [zoo] *m* zoo

zoologie [zɔɔlɔʒi] *f* zoology

zoologique [zɔɔlɔʒik] *adj* zoologic(al)

zouave [zwav] *m* Zouave; **faire le zouave** (coll) to play the fool

zut [zyt] *interj* heck!, hang it!

PART TWO

Anglais-Français

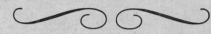

La prononciation de l'anglais

Les signes suivants représentent à peu près tous les sons de la langue anglaise.

VOYELLES

SIGNE	SON	EXEMPLE
[æ]	Plus fermé que a dans **patte**.	**hat** [hæt]
[ɑ]	Comme a dans **pâte**.	**father** ['fɑðər] **proper** ['prɑpər]
[e]	Comme e dans **sec**.	**met** [met]
[e]	Comme e dans **récit**. Surtout en position finale, [e] se prononce comme s'il était suivi de [ɪ].	**fate** [fet] **they** [ðe]
[ə]	C'est e muet, par ex., e dans **gouvernement**.	**heaven** ['hevən] **pardon** ['pɑrdən]
[i]	Comme i dans **mine**.	**she** [ʃi] **machine** [mə'ʃin]
[ɪ]	Moins fermé que i dans **mirage**.	**fit** [fɪt] **beer** [bɪr]
[o]	Comme au dans **haut**. Surtout en position finale, [o] se prononce comme s'il était suivi de [ʊ].	**nose** [noz] **road** [rod] **row** [ro]
[ɔ]	Un peu plus fermé que o dans **donne**.	**bought** [bɔt] **law** [lɔ]
[ʌ]	Plus ou moins comme eu dans **peur**.	**cup** [kʌp] **come** [kʌm] **mother** ['mʌðər]
[ʊ]	Moins fermé que ou dans **doublage**.	**pull** [pʊl] **book** [bʊk] **wolf** [wʊlf]
[u]	Comme ou dans **doublage**.	**move** [muv] **tomb** [tum]

DIPHTONGUES

SIGNE	SON	EXEMPLE
[aɪ]	Comme ai dans **ail**.	**night** [naɪt] **eye** [aɪ]
[aʊ]	Comme aou dans **caoutchouc**.	**found** [faʊnd] **cow** [kaʊ]
[ɔɪ]	Comme oy dans **boy**.	**voice** [vɔɪs] **oil** [ɔɪl]

CONSONNES

SIGNE	SON	EXEMPLE
[b]	Comme b dans **bébé**.	**bed** [bed] **robber** ['rɑbər]
[d]	Comme d dans **don**.	**dead** [ded] **add** [æd]

3

SIGNE	SON	EXEMPLE
[dʒ]	Comme dj dans djinn.	gem [dʒɛm] jail [dʒel]
[ð]	Comme la consonne castillane d intervocalique de moda.	this [ðɪs] father ['faðər]
[f]	Comme f dans fin.	face [fes] phone [fon]
[g]	Comme g dans gallois.	go [go] get [gɛt]
[h]	Comme la consonne allemande h de Haus ou comme la consonne espagnole j de jota mais moins aspiré.	hot [hat] alcohol ['ælkə,hɔl]
[j]	Comme i dans hier ou comme y dans yod.	yes [jɛs] unit ['junɪt]
[k]	Comme k dans kiosque ou comme c dans cote, mais accompagné d'une aspiration.	cat [kæt] chord [kɔrd] kill [kɪl]
[l]	Comme l ou ll dans pulluler.	late [let] allow [ə'lau]
[m]	Comme m dans mère.	more [mor] command [kə'mænd]
[n]	Comme n dans note.	nest [nɛst] manner ['mænər]
[ŋ]	Comme ng dans parking.	king [kɪŋ] conquer ['kaŋkər]
[p]	Comme p dans père, mais accompagné d'une aspiration.	pen [pɛn] cap [kæp]
[r]	Le r le plus commun dans une grande partie de l'Angleterre et dans la plus grande partie des États-Unis et du Canada, c'est le r rétroflexe, une semi-voyelle dont l'articulation se produit par la pointe de la langue élevée vers la voûte du palais. Cette consonne est très faible dans la position intervocalique ou à la fin de la syllabe et, par conséquent, elle y est très peu audible. L'articulation de cette consonne tend à colorier le son des voyelles voisines.	run [rʌn] far [far] art [art] carry ['kæri]
	Le r, précédé des sons [ʌ] ou [ə], donne sa propre couleur à ces sons et disparaît complètement en tant que son consonant.	burn [bʌrn] learn [lʌrn] weather ['wɛðər] send [sɛnd]
[s]	Comme ss dans classe.	cellar ['sɛlər]
[ʃ]	Comme ch dans chose.	shall [ʃæl] machine [mə'ʃin] nation ['neʃən]
[t]	Comme t dans table, mais accompagné d'une aspiration.	ten [tɛn] dropped [drapt]
[tʃ]	Comme tch dans caoutchouc.	child [tʃaɪld] much [mʌtʃ] nature ['netʃər]
[θ]	Comme la consonne castillane c de cinco.	think [θɪŋk] truth [truθ]
[v]	Comme v dans veuve.	vest [vɛst] over ['ovər] of [ɑv]
[w]	Comme w dans watt; comme le [w] produit en prononçant le mot bois.	work [wʌrk] tweed [twid] queen [kwin]
[z]	Comme s dans rose ou comme z dans zèbre.	zeal [zil] busy ['bɪzi] his [hɪz] winds [wɪndz]
[ʒ]	Comme j dans jardin.	azure ['eʒər] measure ['mɛʒər]

4

L'accent tonique principal, indiqué par le signe graphique ¹ , et l'accent secondaire, indiqué par le signe graphique ₍ , précèdent la syllabe à laquelle ils s'appliquent, par ex., **fascinate** [ˈfæsɪ͵net].

La prononciation des mots composés

Dans la partie anglais-français du Dictionnaire la prononciation figurée de tous les mots anglais simples est indiquée selon une nouvelle adaptation de la méthode de l'Association phonétique internationale, et placée entre crochets à la suite du mot-souche.

Il y a trois genres de mots composés en anglais: (1) les mots dont les éléments composants sont soudés en un mot simple, par ex., **steamboat** vapeur, (2) les mots dont les éléments composants sont reliés entre eux par un trait d'union, par ex., **short-circuit** court-circuiter, et (3) les mots dont les éléments composants restent graphiquement indépendants, par ex., **post card** carte postale. La prononciation des mots composés anglais n'est pas indiquée dans ce Dictionnaire lorsque celle des éléments composants a déjà été indiquée à la suite de ces éléments là où ils apparaissent comme mots-souches. Néanmoins, les accents principaux et secondaires sont indiqués dans l'écriture de ces mots composés, ex.: **steamˈboatˈ, shortˈ-cirˈcuit, postˈ cardˈ, eyeˈ of the mornˈing.**

En ce qui concerne les éléments composants qui se terminent par **-ing** [ɪŋ] dans les mots composés, l'accent seul est précisé lorsque ces éléments se présentent également comme mots-souches suivis de la prononciation figurée, par ex., **playˈing cardˈ.**

Dans les noms dans lesquels les éléments composants **-man** et **-men** portent l'accent secondaire, les voyelles de ces éléments se prononcent comme dans les mots simples **man** et **men**, par ex., **mailman** [ˈmel͵mæn] et **mailmen** [ˈmel͵mæn]. Dans les noms dans lesquels ces éléments composants sont inaccentués, les voyelles se prononcent dans les deux formes comme e muet, par ex., **policeman** [pəˈlismən] et **policemen** [pəˈlismən]. Il y a des noms dans lesquels ces éléments composants se prononcent des deux façons, c'est-à-dire, avec l'accent secondaire ou sans accent, par ex., **doorman** [ˈdɔr͵mæn] ou [ˈdɔrmən] et **doormen** [ˈdɔr͵men] ou [ˈdɔrmən]. Dans ce Dictionnaire la transcription phonétique de ces mots est omise si le premier élément composant se présente ailleurs comme mot-souche suivi de la prononciation figurée. Cependant, l'accentuation de ces mots est indiquée dans le mot-souche même:

> **mailˈmanˈ** *s* (*pl* -menˈ)
> **policeˈman** *s* (*pl* -men)
> **doorˈmanˈ** or doorˈman *s* (*pl* -menˈ or -men)

La prononciation des participes passés

Lorsqu'un mot a pour désinence **-ed** (ou **-d** après un e muet), et une prononciation conforme aux principes énoncés plus bas, celle-ci ne figurera pas dans ce Dictionnaire, si elle est indiquée quand la forme du mot sans cette désinence se présente comme mot-souche.

La désinence **-ed** (ou **-d** après un e muet) du prétérit, du participe passé, et de certains adjectifs possède trois prononciations différentes selon le son de la dernière consonne du radical.

1) Si le radical se termine par le son d'une consonne sonore (sauf [d]), que voici: [b], [g], [l], [m], [n], [ŋ], [r], [v], [z], [ð], [ʒ], ou [dʒ] ou par le son d'une voyelle, -ed se prononce [d].

SON DU RADICAL	INFINITIF	PRÉTÉRIT ET PARTICIPE PASSÉ
[b]	ebb [eb] rob [rɑb] robe [rob]	ebbed [ebd] robbed [rɑbd] robed [robd]
[g]	egg [eg] sag [sæg]	egged [egd] sagged [sægd]
[l]	mail [mel] scale [skel]	mailed [meld] scaled [skeld]
[m]	storm [stɔrm] bomb [bɑm] name [nem]	stormed [stɔrmd] bombed [bɑmd] named [nemd]
[n]	tan [tæn] sign [saɪn] mine [maɪn]	tanned [tænd] signed [saɪnd] mined [maɪnd]
[ŋ]	hang [hæŋ]	hanged [hæŋd]
[r]	fear [fɪr] care [ker]	feared [fɪrd] cared [kerd]
[v]	rev [rev] save [sev]	revved [revd] saved [sevd]
[z]	buzz [bʌz] fuse [fjuz]	buzzed [bʌzd] fused [fjuzd]
[ð]	smooth [smuð] bathe [beð]	smoothed [smuðd] bathed [beðd]
[ʒ]	massage [mə'sɑʒ]	massaged [mə'sɑʒd]
[dʒ]	page [pedʒ]	paged [pedʒd]
son de voyelle	key [ki] sigh [saɪ] paw [pɔ]	keyed [kid] sighed [saɪd] pawed [pɔd]

2) Si le radical se termine par le son d'une consonne sourde (sauf [t]), que voici: [f], [k], [p], [s], [θ], [ʃ], ou [tʃ], -ed se prononce [t].

SON DU RADICAL	INFINITIF	PRÉTÉRIT ET PARTICIPE PASSÉ
[f]	loaf [lof] knife [naɪf]	loafed [loft] knifed [naɪft]
[k]	back [bæk] bake [bek]	backed [bækt] baked [bekt]
[p]	cap [kæp] wipe [waɪp]	capped [kæpt] wiped [waɪpt]
[s]	hiss [hɪs] mix [mɪks]	hissed [hɪst] mixed [mɪkst]
[θ]	lath [læθ]	lathed [læθt]
[ʃ]	mash [mæʃ]	mashed [mæʃt]
[tʃ]	match [mætʃ]	matched [mætʃt]

3) Si le radical se termine par le son d'une dentale, que voici: [t] ou [d], -ed se prononce [ɪd] ou [əd].

SON DU RADICAL	INFINITIF	PRÉTÉRIT ET PARTICIPE PASSÉ
[t]	wait [wet] mate [met]	waited ['wetɪd] mated ['metɪd]
[d]	mend [mend] wade [wed]	mended ['mendɪd] waded ['wedɪd]

6

Notez que le redoublement orthographique de la consonne finale après une voyelle simple accentuée n'altère pas la prononciation de la désinence **-ed: batted** [ˈbætɪd], **dropped** [drɒpt], **robbed** [rɒbd].

Ces règles s'appliquent aussi aux adjectifs composés qui se terminent par **-ed.** On n'indique que l'accent de ces adjectifs lorsque les éléments composants (le dernier, bien entendu, sans la désinence **-ed**) se présentent ailleurs comme motssouches suivis de la prononciation figurée, par ex., **flat′-nosed′**.

Cependant, le **-ed** de quelques adjectifs formés sur un radical qui se termine par un son consonantique en plus de ceux qui se terminent par [d] et [t], est prononcé [ɪd] et cette irrégularité s'indique en donnant la prononciation figurée complète, par ex., **blessed** [ˈblesɪd], **crabbed** [ˈkræbɪd].

ANGLAIS—FRANÇAIS

A

A, a [e] *s* Iière lettre de l'alphabet
a *art indef* un
aback [ə'bæk] *adv* avec le vent dessus; **taken aback** déconcerté
abandon [ə'bændən] *s* abandon *m* ‖ *tr* abandonner
abase [ə'bes] *tr* abaisser, humilier
abasement [ə'besmənt] *s* abaissement *m*
abash [ə'bæʃ] *tr* décontenancer
abashed *adj* confus, confondu
abate [ə'bet] *tr* diminuer, réduire; (*part of price*) rabattre ‖ *intr* se calmer; (*said of wind*) tomber
abbess ['æbɪs] *s* abbesse *f*
abbey ['æbi] *s* abbaye *f*
abbot ['æbət] *s* abbé *m*
abbreviate [ə'brivɪˌet] *tr* abréger
abbreviation [əˌbrivɪ'eʃən] *s* abréviation *f*
A B C's [ˌeˌbi'siz] *spl* (letterword) a b c *m*
abdicate ['æbdɪˌket] *tr & intr* abdiquer
abdomen ['æbdəmən], [æb'domən] *s* abdomen *m*
abduct [ə'dʌkt] *tr* enlever, ravir
abeam [ə'bim] *adv* par le travers
abed [ə'bed] *adv* au lit
abet [ə'bet] *v* (*pret & pp* **abetted**; *ger* **abetting**) *tr* encourager
abettor [ə'betər] *s* complice *mf*
abeyance [ə'be-əns] *s* suspension *f*; **in abeyance** en suspens
ab·hor [æb'hɔr] *v* (*pret & pp* **-horred**; *ger* **-horring**) *tr* abhorrer, détester
abhorrent [æb'hɑrənt], [æb'hɔrənt] *adj* détestable, répugnant
abide [ə'baɪd] *v* (*pret & pp* **abode** or **abided**) *tr* attendre ‖ *intr* demeurer, continuer, persister; **to abide by** s'en tenir à; rester fidèle à
abili·ty [ə'bɪlɪti] *s* (*pl* -**ties**) capacité *f*, habileté *f*; talent *m*
abject ['æbdʒɛkt] *adj* abject
ablative ['æblətɪv] *adj & s* ablatif *m*
ablaut ['æblaut] *s* apophonie *f*
ablaze [ə'blez] *adj* enflammé; (*colorful*) resplendissant ‖ *adv* en feu
able ['ebəl] *adj* capable, habile; **to be able to** pouvoir
a'ble-bod'ied *adj* robuste, vigoureux; (*seaman*) breveté
abloom [ə'blum] *adj & adv* en fleur
abnormal [æb'nɔrməl] *adj* anormal
abnormali·ty [ˌæbnɔr'mælɪti] *s* (*pl* -**ties**) anomalie *f*, irrégularité *f*; (*of body*) difformité *f*
aboard [ə'bɔrd] *adv* à bord; **all aboard!** en voiture!; **to go aboard** s'embarquer ‖ *prep* à bord de
abode [ə'bod] *s* demeure *f*, résidence *f*

abolish [ə'bɑlɪʃ] *tr* abolir
A-bomb ['eˌbɑm] *s* bombe *f* atomique
abomination [əˌbɑmɪ'neʃən] *s* abomination *f*
aborigines [ˌæbə'rɪdʒɪˌniz] *spl* aborigènes *mpl*
abort [ə'bɔrt] *intr* avorter
abortion [ə'bɔrʃən] *s* avortement *m*
abound [ə'baund] *intr* abonder
about [ə'baut] *adv* à la ronde, tout autour; (*almost*) presque; (*here and there*) çà et là; **to be about to** sur le point de ‖ *prep* autour de, aux environs de; (*approximately*) environ; au sujet de; vers, e.g., **about six o'clock** vers six heures; **it is about . . .** il s'agit de . . .
about'-face' or **about'-face'** *s* volte-face *f*; (mil) demi-tour *m* ‖ **about'-face'** *intr* faire volte-face
above [ə'bʌv] *adv* en haut; au-dessus, ci-dessus ‖ *prep* au-dessus de; plus que, outre; (*another point on the river*) en amont de; **above all** surtout
above'-men'tioned *adj* susmentionné
abrasive [ə'bresɪv], [ə'brezɪv] *adj & s* abrasif *m*
abreast [ə'brest] *adj & adv* de front; **three abreast** par rangs de trois; **to be abreast of** or **with** être en ligne avec; **to keep abreast of** se tenir au courant de
abridge [ə'brɪdʒ] *tr* abréger
abridgment [ə'brɪdʒmənt] *s* abrégé *m*, résumé *m*; réduction *f*
abroad [ə'brɔd] *adv* au loin; (*in foreign parts*) à l'étranger
abrogate ['æbrəˌget] *tr* abroger
abrupt [ə'brʌpt] *adj* (*steep; impolite*) abrupt; (*hasty*) brusque, précipité
abscess ['æbsɛs] *s* abcès *m*
abscond [æb'skɑnd] *intr* s'enfuir, déguerpir; **to abscond with** lever le pied avec
absence ['æbsəns] *s* absence *f*
absent ['æbsənt] *adj* absent ‖ [æb'sɛnt] *tr*—**to absent oneself** s'absenter
absentee [ˌæbsən'ti] *s* absent *m*
ab'sent-mind'ed *adj* absent, distrait
absolute ['æbsəˌlut] *adj & s* absolu *m*
absolutely ['æbsəˌlutli] *adv* absolument ‖ [ˌæbsə'lutli] *adv* (coll) absolument
absolve [æb'sɑlv] *tr* absoudre
absorb [æb'sɔrb] *tr* absorber; **to be or become absorbed in** s'absorber dans
absorbent [æb'sɔrbənt] *adj & s* absorbant; (*cotton*) hydrophile ‖ *s* absorbant *m*
absorbing [æb'sɔrbɪŋ] *adj* absorbant
abstain [æb'sten] *intr* s'abstenir

abstemious [æb'stimɪ·əs] *adj* abstinent, sobre

abstinent ['æbstɪnənt] *adj* abstinent

abstract ['æbstrækt] *adj* abstrait ‖ *s* abrégé *m*, résumé *m* ‖ *tr* résumer ‖ [æb'strækt] *tr* abstraire; (*to remove*) soustraire

abstractedly [æb'stræktɪdli] *adv* d'un œil distrait

abstruse [æb'strus] *adj* abstrus

absurd [əb'sʌrd], [əb'zʌrd] *adj* absurde

absurdi·ty [əb'sʌrdɪti], [əb'zʌrdɪti] *s* (*pl* -**ties**) absurdité *f*

abundance [ə'bʌndəns] *s* abondance *f*

abundant [ə'bʌndənt] *adj* abondant

abuse [ə'bjus] *s* abus *m*; (*mistreatment*) maltraitement *m*; (*insulting words*) insultes *fpl* ‖ [ə'bjuz] *tr* abuser de; maltraiter; insulter

abusive [ə'bjusɪv] *adj* (*insulting*) injurieux; (*wrong*) abusif

abut [ə'bʌt] *v* (*pret & pp* **abutted**; *ger* **abutting**) *intr*—**to abut on** border, confiner

abutment [ə'bʌtmənt] *s* (*of wall*) contrefort *m*; (*of bridge*) culée *f*; (*of arch*) pied-droit *m*

abyss [ə'bɪs] *s* abîme *m*

A.C. ['e'si] *s* (letterword) (**alternating current**) courant *m* alternatif

academic [ˌækə'dɛmɪk] *adj* académique; théorique ‖ *s* étudiant *m* or professeur *m* de l'université

academical [ˌækə'dɛmɪkəl] *adj* académique; théorique ‖ **academicals** *spl* costume *m* académique

academician [əˌkædə'mɪʃən] *s* académicien *m*

acade·my [ə'kædəmi] *s* (*pl* -**mies**) académie *f*; (*preparatory school*) collège *m*

accede [æk'sid] *intr* acquiescer; **to accede to** accéder à; (*the throne*) monter sur

accelerate [æk'sɛlə ˌret] *tr & intr* accélérer

accelerator [æk'sɛlə ˌretər] *s* accélérateur *m*

accent ['æksɛnt] *s* accent *m* ‖ ['æksɛnt], [æk'sɛnt] *tr* accentuer

accentuate [æk'sɛntʃu ˌet] *tr* accentuer

accept [æk'sɛpt] *tr* accepter

acceptable [æk'sɛptəbəl] *adj* acceptable

acceptance [æk'sɛptəns] *s* acceptation *f*; (*approval*) approbation *f*

acceptation [ˌæksɛp'teʃən] *s* acceptation *f*; (*meaning*) acception *f*

access ['æksɛs] *s* accès *m*

accessible [æk'sɛsɪbəl] *adj* accessible

accession [æk'sɛʃən] *s* accession *f*

accesso·ry [æk'sɛsəri] *adj* accessoire ‖ *s* (*pl* -**ries**) accessoire *m*; (*to a crime*) complice *mf*

ac'cess route' *s* voie *f* de raccordement, bretelle *f*

accident ['æksɪdənt] *s* accident *m*; **by accident** par accident

accidental [ˌæksɪ'dɛntəl] *adj* accidentel ‖ *s* (mus) accident *m*

ac'cident-prone' *adj* prédisposé aux accidents

acclaim [ə'klem] *tr* acclamer

acclimate ['æklɪ ˌmet] *tr* acclimater

accommodate [ə'kɑmə ˌdet] *tr* accommoder; (*to oblige*) rendre service à; (*to lodge*) loger

accommodating [ə'kɑmə ˌdetɪŋ] *adj* accommodant, serviable

accommodation [əˌkɑmə'deʃən] *s* accommodation *f*; **accommodations** commodités *fpl*; (*in a train*) place *f*; (*in a hotel*) chambre *f*; (*room and board*) le vivre et le couvert

accompaniment [ə'kʌmpənimənt] *s* accompagnement *m*

accompanist [ə'kʌmpənɪst] *s* accompagnateur *m*

accompa·ny [ə'kʌmpəni] *v* (*pret & pp* -**nied**) *tr* accompagner

accomplice [ə'kɑmplɪs] *s* complice *mf*

accomplish [ə'kɑmplɪʃ] *tr* accomplir

accomplishment [ə'kɑmplɪʃmənt] *s* accomplissement *m*, réalisation *f*; (*thing itself*) œuvre *f* accomplie; **accomplishments** arts *mpl* d'agrément, talents *mpl*

accord [ə'kɔrd] *s* accord *m*; **in accord** d'accord; **of one's own accord** de son plein gré ‖ *tr* accorder ‖ *intr* se mettre d'accord

accordance [ə'kɔrdəns] *s* accord *m*; **in accordance with** conformément à

according [ə'kɔrdɪŋ] *adj*—**according as** selon que; **according to** selon, d'après, suivant; **according to expert advice** au dire d'experts

accordingly [ə'kɔrdɪŋli] *adv* en conséquence

accordion [ə'kɔrdɪ·ən] *s* accordéon *m*

accost [ə'kɔst], [ə'kɑst] *tr* accoster

account [ə'kaunt] *s* compte *m*; profit *m*, calcul *m*; (*narration*) récit *m*; (*report*) compte rendu; (*explanation*) explication *f*; **of no account** sans importance; **on account of** à cause de; **on no account** en aucune façon; **to call to account** demander des comptes à ‖ *intr*—**to account for** expliquer; (*money*) rendre compte de

accountable [ə'kauntəbəl] *adj* responsable; (*explainable*) explicable

accountant [ə'kauntənt] *s* comptable *mf*

account' book' *s* registre *m* de comptabilité

accounting [ə'kauntɪŋ] *s* règlement *m* de comptes; (*profession*) comptabilité *f*

accouterments [ə'kutərmənts] *spl* équipement *m*

accredit [ə'krɛdɪt] *tr* accréditer

accretion [ə'kriʃən] *s* accroissement *m*

accrue [ə'kru] *intr* s'accroître; **to accrue from** dériver de; **to accrue to** échoir à

accumulate [ə'kjumjə ˌlet] *tr* accumuler ‖ *intr* s'accumuler

accuracy ['ækjərəsi] *s* exactitude *f*

accurate ['ækjərɪt] *adj* exact; (*aim*) juste; (*translation*) fidèle

accursed [ə'kʌrsɪd], [ə'kʌrst] *adj* maudit

accusation [ˌækjə'zeʃən] *s* accusation *f*

accusative [ə'kjuzətɪv] *adj & s* accusatif *m*

accuse [ə'kjuz] *tr* accuser

accused *s* accusé *m*, inculpé *m*

accustom [ə'kʌstəm] *tr* accoutumer; **to become accustomed** s'accoutumer

ace [es] *s* as *m*; **to have an ace up one's sleeve** avoir un atout dans la manche

acetate ['æsɪ,tet] *s* acétate *m*

ace'tic ac'id [ə'sitɪk] *s* acide *m* acétique

acetone ['æsɪ,ton] *s* acétone *f*

acet'ylene torch' [ə'setɪ,lin] *s* chalumeau *m* oxyacétylénique

ache [ek] *s* douleur *f* || *intr* faire mal; **my head aches** j'ai mal à la tête; **to be aching to** (coll) brûler de

achieve [ə't∫iv] *tr* accomplir, atteindre; (*a victory*) remporter

achievement [ə't∫ivmənt] *s* accomplissement *m*, réalisation *f*; (*thing itself*) œuvre *f* remarquable, réussite *f*; (*heroic deed*) exploit *m*

Achil'les' heel' [ə'kɪliz] *s* talon *m* d'Achille

acid ['æsɪd] *adj & s* acide *m*

acidi·ty [ə'sɪdɪti] *s* (*pl* -ties) acidité *f*

ac'id test' *s* (fig) épreuve *f* définitive

acknowledge [æk'nɑlɪdʒ] *tr* reconnaître; **to acknowledge receipt of** accuser réception de

acknowledgment [æk'nɑlɪdʒmənt] *s* reconnaissance *f*; (*of a letter*) accusé *m* de réception; (*receipt*) récépissé *m*

acme ['ækmi] *s* comble *m*, sommet *m*

acolyte ['ækə,lart] *s* enfant *m* de chœur; (*priest*) acolyte *m*; assistant *m*

acorn ['ekɔrn], ['ekərn] *s* gland *m*

acoustic [ə'kustɪk] *adj* acoustique || **acoustics** *s & spl* acoustique *f*

acquaint [ə'kwent] *tr* informer; **to be acquainted** se connaître; **to be acquainted with** connaître

acquaintance [ə'kwentəns] *s* connaissance *f*

acquiesce [,ækwɪ'es] *intr* acquiescer

acquiescence [,ækwɪ'esəns] *s* acquiescement *m*, consentement *m*

acquire [ə'kwaɪr] *tr* acquérir; (*friends; a reputation*) s'acquérir

acquirement [ə'kwaɪrmənt] *s* acquisition *f*

acquisition [,ækwɪ'zɪ∫ən] *s* acquisition *f*

acquisitive [ə'kwɪzɪtɪv] *adj* âpre au gain, avide

acquit [ə'kwɪt] *v* (*pret & pp* **acquitted**; *ger* **acquitting**) *tr* acquitter; **to acquit oneself** se comporter

acquittal [ə'kwɪtəl] *s* acquittement *m*

acre ['ekər] *s* acre *f*

acrid ['ækrɪd] *adj* âcre

acrimonious [,ækrɪ'monɪ-əs] *adj* acrimonieux

acrobat ['ækrə,bæt] *s* acrobate *mf*

acrobatic [,ækrə'bætɪk] *adj* acrobatique || **acrobatics** *s* (*profession*) acrobatie *f*; **acrobatics** *spl* (*stunts*) acrobaties

acronym ['ækrənɪm] *s* sigle *m*

acropolis [ə'krapəlɪs] *s* acropole *f*

across [ə'krɔs], [ə'krɑs] *adv* en travers, à travers; (*sidewise*) en largeur || *prep* en travers de; (*e.g., the street*) de l'autre côté de; **across country** à travers champs; **to come across** rencontrer par hasard; **to go across** traverser

acrostic [ə'krɔstɪk], [ə'krɑstɪk] *s* acrostiche *m*

act [ækt] *s* action *f*, acte *m*; (circus, rad, telv) numéro *m*; (govt) loi *f*; (law, theat) acte; (coll) allure *f* affectée, comédie *f*; **in the act** sur le fait, en flagrant délit || *tr* jouer; **to act the fool** faire le pitre || *intr* agir; se conduire; (theat) jouer; **to act as** servir de; **to act on** influer sur

acting ['æktɪŋ] *adj* intérimaire || (*actor's art*) jeu *m*; (*profession*) théâtre *m*

action ['æk∫ən] *s* action *f*; (law) acte *m*; (mach) jeu *m*; (theat) intrigue *f*; **out of action** hors de service; **to go into action** (mil) aller au feu; **to suit the action to the word** joindre le geste à la parole; **to take action** prendre des mesures

activate ['æktɪ,vet] *tr* activer

active ['æktɪv] *adj* actif

activi·ty [æk'tɪvɪti] *s* (*pl* -ties) activité *f*

actor ['æktər] *s* acteur *m*

actress ['æktrɪs] *s* actrice *f*

actual ['ækt∫u·əl] *adj* véritable, réel, effectif

actually ['ækt∫u·əli] *adv* réellement, en réalité, effectivement

actuar·y ['ækt∫u,eri] *s* (*pl* -ies) actuaire *m*

actuate ['ækt∫u,et] *tr* actionner; (*to motivate*) animer

acuity [ə'kju·ɪti] *s* acuité *f*

acumen [ə'kjumən] *s* finesse *f*

acute [ə'kjut] *adj* aigu; (fig) avisé

acutely [ə'kjutli] *adv* profondément

A.D. ['e'di] *adj* (letterword) (**Anno Domini**) ap. J.-C.

ad [æd] *s* (coll) annonce *f*

adage ['ædɪdʒ] *s* adage *m*

Adam ['ædəm] *s* Adam *m*; **I don't know him from Adam** (coll) je ne le connais ni d'Ève ni d'Adam

adamant ['ædəmənt] *adj* inflexible

Ad'am's ap'ple *s* pomme *f* d'Adam

adapt [ə'dæpt] *tr* adapter

adaptation [,ædæp'te∫ən] *s* adaptation *f*

adapter [ə'dæptər] *s* adaptateur *m*, raccord *m*; (phot) bague *f* porte-objectif

add [æd] *tr* ajouter; **to add up** additionner || *intr* additionner; **to add up to** s'élever à

adder ['ædər] *s* (zool) vipère *f*

addict ['ædɪkt] *s* toxicomane *mf*; (sports) fanatique *mf* || [ə'dɪkt] *tr* atteindre de toxicomanie; **to be addicted to** (*to enjoy*) s'adonner à

addiction [ə'dɪk∫ən] *s* toxicomanie *f*; **addiction to** penchant *m* pour

add'ing machine' *s* machine *f* à calculer, additionneuse *f*

addition [ə'dɪʃən] s addition f; **in addition to** en plus de

additive ['ædɪtɪv] adj & s additif m

addle ['ædəl] tr brouiller

address [ə'dres], ['ædres] s adresse f || [ə'dres] s discours m; **to deliver an address** prononcer un discours || tr adresser; s'adresser à; (an audience) faire un discours à

address' book' s carnet m d'adresses

addressee [,ædre'si] s destinataire mf

adduce [ə'd(j)us] tr alléguer; (proof) fournir

adenoids ['ædə,nɔɪdz] spl végétations fpl adénoïdes

adept [ə'dept] adj habile || s adepte mf

adequate ['ædɪkwɪt] adj suffisant, adéquat; **adequate to** à la hauteur de, proportionné à

adhere [æd'hɪr] intr adhérer

adherence [æd'hɪrəns] s adhérence f

adherent [æd'hɪrənt] adj & s adhérent m

adhesion [æd'hiʒən] s adhésion f; (pathol) adhérence f

adhesive [æd'hisɪv], [æd'hizɪv] adj & s adhésif m

adhe'sive tape' s sparadrap m

adieu [ə'd(j)u] s (pl adieus or adieux) adieu m || interj adieu!

ad infinitum [æd,ɪnfɪ'naɪtəm] adv sans fin

adjacent [ə'dʒesənt] adj adjacent

adjective ['ædʒɪktɪv] adj & s adjectif m

adjoin [ə'dʒɔɪn] tr avoisiner || intr être contigu

adjoining [ə'dʒɔɪnɪŋ] adj contigu

adjourn [ə'dʒʌrn] tr (to postpone) remettre, reporter; (a meeting, a session) lever; (sine die; for resumption at another time or place) ajourner || intr s'ajourner; lever la séance

adjournment [ə'dʒʌrnmənt] s suspension f de séance

adjudge [ə'dʒʌdʒ] tr adjuger; (a criminal) condamner

adjudicate [ə'dʒudɪ,ket] tr & intr juger

adjunct ['ædʒʌŋkt] adj & s adjoint m; **adjuncts** accessoires mpl

adjust [ə'dʒʌst] tr ajuster || intr s'adapter

adjustable [ə'dʒʌstəbəl] adj réglable

adjustment [ə'dʒʌstmənt] s ajustage m, réglage m; (arrangement) ajustement m, règlement m; (telv) mise f au point

adjutant ['ædʒətənt] s adjutant m

ad-lib [,æd'lɪb] adj improvisé || v (pret & pp -libbed; ger -libbing) tr & intr improviser (en cascade)

administer [æd'mɪnɪstər] tr administrer; **to administer an oath** faire prêter serment || intr—**to administer to** pourvoir à, aider, assister

administration [æd,mɪnɪs'treʃən] s administration f; gouvernement m

administrator [æd'mɪnɪs,tretər] s administrateur m

admiral ['ædmɪrəl] s amiral m

admiral·ty ['ædmɪrəlti] s (pl -ties) amirauté f; ministère m de la marine

admiration [,ædmɪ'reʃən] s admiration f

admire [æd'maɪr] tr admirer

admirer [æd'maɪrər] s admirateur m; (suitor) soupirant m

admission [æd'mɪʃən] s admission f; (price) entrée f; (confession) aveu m

ad·mit [æd'mɪt] v (pret & pp -mitted; ger -mitting) tr admettre; (e.g., a mistake) avouer; **admit bearer** laisser passer

admittance [æd'mɪtəns] s entrée f

admittedly [æd'mɪtɪdli] adv manifestement

admonish [æd'mɑnɪʃ] tr admonester

ad nauseam [æd'nɔʃɪ,æm], [æd'nɔsɪəm] adv jusqu'au dégoût

ado [ə'du] s agitation f; **much ado about nothing** beaucoup de bruit pour rien; **without further ado** sans plus de façons

adolescence [,ædə'lesəns] s adolescence f

adolescent [,ædə'lesənt] adj & s adolescent m

adopt [ə'dɑpt] tr adopter

adoption [ə'dɑpʃən] s adoption f

adoptive [ə'dɑptɪv] adj adoptif

adorable [ə'dorəbəl] adj adorable

adoration [,ædə'reʃən] s adoration f

adore [ə'dor] tr adorer

adorn [ə'dɔrn] tr orner, parer

adornment [ə'dɔrnmənt] s parure f

adre'nal glands' [æd'rinəl], [ə'drinəl] spl (capsules) surrénales fpl

adrenalin [æd'drenəlɪn] s adrénaline f

Adriatic [,edrɪ'ætɪk], [,ædrɪ'ætɪk] adj & s Adriatique f

adrift [ə'drɪft] adj & adv à la dérive

adroit [ə'drɔɪt] adj adroit, habile

adulate ['ædʒə,let] tr aduler

adult [ə'dʌlt], ['ædʌlt] adj & s adulte mf

adulterate [ə'dʌltə,ret] tr frelater

adulteration [ə,dʌltə'reʃən] s frelatage m

adulterer [ə'dʌltərər] s adultère m

adulteress [ə'dʌltərɪs] s adultère f

adulterous [ə'dʌltərəs] adj adultère

adulter·y [ə'dʌltəri] s (pl -ies) adultère m

adumbrate [æd'ʌmbret], ['ædəm,bret] tr ébaucher; (to foreshadow) présager

advance [æd'væns], [æd'vɑns] s avance f; **advances** propositions fpl; propositions malhonnêtes; **in advance** d'avance; en avance || tr avancer || intr avancer, s'avancer; (said of prices) augmenter; (said of stocks) monter

advancement [æd'vænsmənt], [æd-'vɑnsmənt] s avancement m

advance' pay'ment s versement m anticipé

advantage [æd'væntɪdʒ], [æd'vɑntɪdʒ] s avantage m; **to take advantage of** profiter de

advent ['ædvent] s venue f; **Advent** (eccl) Avent m

adventitious [,ædven'tɪʃəs] adj adventice

adventure [æd'vɛntʃər] s aventure f
adventurer [æd'vɛntʃərər] s aventurier m
adventuress [æd'vɛntʃərɪs] s aventurière f
adventurous [æd'vɛntʃərəs] adj aventureux
adverb ['ædvʌrb] s adverbe m
adversary ['ædvər‚sɛri] s (pl -ies) adversaire mf
adverse [æd'vʌrs], ['ædvʌrs] adj adverse
adversity [æd'vʌrsɪti] s (pl -ties) adversité f
advertise ['ædvər‚taɪz], [‚ædvər'taɪz] tr & intr annoncer
advertisement [‚ædvər'taɪzmənt], [æd-'vʌrtɪzmənt] s annonce f
advertiser ['ædvər‚taɪzər], [‚ædvər-'taɪzər] s annonceur m
advertising ['ædvər‚taɪzɪŋ] s réclame f
ad'vertising a'gency s agence f de publicité
ad'vertising man' s entrepreneur m de publicité
advice [æd'vaɪs] s conseil m; conseils; **a piece of advice** un conseil
advisable [æd'vaɪzəbəl] adj opportun, recommandable
advise [æd'vaɪz] tr conseiller; (to inform) aviser; **to advise against** déconseiller; **to advise s.o. to** + inf conseiller à qn de + inf
advisedly [æd'vaɪzɪdli] adv en connaissance de cause
advisement [æd'vaɪzmənt] s conseils mpl; **to take under advisement** mettre en délibération
adviser [æd'vaɪzər] s conseiller m
advisory [æd'vaɪzəri] adj consultatif
advocacy ['ædvəkəsi] s plaidoyer m
advocate ['ædvə‚ket] s partisan m; (lawyer) avocat m || tr préconiser
Aegean Sea' [ɪ'dʒi‐ən] s mer f Égée, mer de l'Archipel
aegis ['idʒɪs] s égide f
aerate ['ɛret] tr aérer
aerial ['ɛrɪ‐əl] adj aérien || s antenne f
aerodynamic [‚ɛrodaɪ'næmɪk] adj aérodynamique || **aerodynamics** s aérodynamique f
aeronautic [‚ɛro'nɔtɪk] adj aéronautique || **aeronautics** s aéronautique f
aerosol ['ɛrə‚sɔl] s aérosol m
aerospace ['ɛrə‚spes] adj aérospatial
Aeschylus ['ɛskɪləs] s Eschyle m
aesthete ['ɛsθit] s esthète mf
aesthetic [ɛs'θɛtɪk] adj esthétique || **aesthetics** s esthétique f
afar [ə'fɑr] adv au loin
affable ['æfəbəl] adj affable
affair [ə'fɛr] s affaire f; (of lovers) affaire de cœur
affect [ə'fɛkt] tr affecter
affectation [‚æfɛk'teʃən] s affectation f
affected adj affecté, maniéré
affection [ə'fɛkʃən] s affection f
affectionate [ə'fɛkʃənɪt] adj affectueux
affidavit [‚æfɪ'devɪt] s déclaration f sous serment
affiliate [ə'fɪlɪ‚et] s (com) société f affiliée || tr affilier || intr s'affilier

affinity [ə'fɪnɪti] s (pl -ties) affinité f; (inlawry) alliance f
affirm [ə'fʌrm] tr & intr affirmer
affirmative [ə'fʌrmətɪv] adj affirmatif || s affirmative f
affix ['æfɪks] s affixe m || [ə'fɪks] tr annexer; (a signature) apposer; (guilt) attribuer; (on the wall) afficher
afflict [ə'flɪkt] tr affliger
affliction [ə'flɪkʃən] s (sorrow) affliction f; (disorder) infirmité f
affluence ['æflu‐əns] s affluence f de biens, richesse f
afford [ə'fɔrd] tr fournir; se permettre, avoir de quoi payer
affront [ə'frʌnt] s affront m || tr insulter
Afghanistan [æf'gænɪ‚stæn] s l'Afghanistan m
afire [ə'faɪr] adj & adv en feu
aflame [ə'flem] adj & adv en flammes
afloat [ə'flot] adj & adv à flot; (rumor) en circulation; **to keep afloat on the water** se tenir sur l'eau
afoot [ə'fut] adj & adv à pied; (underway) en œuvre
aforesaid [ə'fɔr‚sɛd] adj susdit; ci-dessus mentionné
afraid [ə'fred] adj effrayé; **to be afraid** avoir peur
afresh [ə'frɛʃ] adv à nouveau
Africa ['æfrɪkə] s Afrique f; l'Afrique
African ['æfrɪkən] adj africain || s Africain m
after ['æftər], ['ɑftər] adj suivant, postérieur || adv après, plus tard || prep après, à la suite de; (in the manner or style of) d'après; (not translated in expressions of time), e.g., **eight minutes after ten** dix heures huit || conj après que
af'ter-din'ner adj d'après dîner
af'ter-ef'fect s contrecoup m; **aftereffects** (pathol) séquelles fpl
af'ter-glow' s lueur f du coucher
af'ter-im'age s image f consécutive
af'ter-life' s survie f
aftermath ['æftər‚mæθ], ['ɑftər‚mæθ] s conséquences fpl sérieuses, suites fpl; (agr) regain m
af'ter-noon' s après-midi m & f; **good afternoon!** bonjour!
af'ter-shav'ing lo'tion s eau f de Cologne pour la barbe
af'ter-taste' s arrière-goût m
af'ter-thought' s réflexion f après coup
afterward ['æftərwərd], ['ɑftərwərd] adv après, ensuite
again [ə'gɛn] adv encore, de plus; de nouveau, encore une fois; **now and again** de temps en temps
against [ə'gɛnst] prep contre; **against the grain** à rebrousse-poil; **over against** en face de; par contraste avec
age [edʒ] s âge m; (about a hundred years) siècle m; **for ages** depuis longtemps; **of age** majeur; **to come of age** atteindre sa majorité; **under age** mineur || tr & intr vieillir
aged [edʒd] adj (wine, cheese, etc.)

vieilli; (of the age of) âgé de ‖ ['edʒɪd] adj âgé, vieux

agen·cy ['edʒənsi] s (pl -cies) agence f; (means) action f

agenda [ə'dʒɛndə] s ordre m du jour

agent ['edʒənt] s agent m; (means) moyen m; (com) commissionnaire m

agglomeration [ə‚glamə'reʃən] s agglomération f

aggrandizement [ə'grændɪzmənt] s agrandissement m

aggravate ['ægrə‚vet] tr aggraver; (coll) exaspérer

aggregate ['ægrɪ‚get] adj global ‖ s agrégat m ‖ tr rassembler; (coll) s'élever à

aggression [ə'grɛʃən] s agression f

aggressive [ə'grɛsɪv] adj agressif; (livewire) entreprenant

aggressor [ə'grɛsər] s agresseur m

aghast [ə'gæst], [ə'gɑst] adj abasourdi

agile ['ædʒɪl] adj agile

agility [ə'dʒɪlɪti] s agilité f

agitate ['ædʒɪ‚tet] tr agiter

agitator ['ædʒɪ‚tetər] s agitateur m

aglow [ə'glo] adj & adv rougeoyant

agnostic [æg'nɑstɪk] adj & s agnostique mf

ago [ə'go] adv il y a, e.g., two days ago il y a deux jours

agog [ə'gag] adj & adv en émoi

agonizing ['ægə‚naɪzɪŋ] adj angoissant

ago·ny ['ægəni] s (pl -nies) angoisse f; (death struggle) agonie f

agrarian [ə'grɛrɪ‚ən] adj agraire; (law) agrarien ‖ s agrairien m

agree [ə'gri] intr être d'accord, s'accorder; **agreed!** d'accord!; **to agree to** consentir à

agreeable [ə'gri‚əbəl] adj agréable, sympathique; (consenting) d'accord

agreement [ə'grimənt] s accord m; contrat m

agriculture ['ægrɪ‚kʌltʃər] s agriculture f

aground [ə'graund] adj (naut) échoué ‖ adv—**to run aground** échouer

ague ['egju] s fièvre f intermittente; accès m de frisson

ahead [ə'hɛd] adj & adv en avant; **ahead of** avant; devant; **straight ahead** tout droit; **to get ahead of** devancer

ahem [ə'hɛm] interj hum!

ahoy [ə'hɔɪ] interj—**ship ahoy!** ohé du navire!

aid [ed] s (assistance) aide f; (assistant) aide mf ‖ tr aider

aide-de-camp ['eddə'kæmp] s (pl aides-de-camp) officier m d'ordonnance, aide m de camp

ail [el] tr affliger; **what ails you?** qu'avez-vous? ‖ intr être souffrant

ailment ['elmənt] s indisposition f, maladie f

aim [em] s but m, objectif m; (of gun) pointage m ‖ tr diriger; (a blow) allonger; (a telescope, cannon, etc.) pointer, viser ‖ intr viser

air [er] s air m; **on the air** à la radio, à la télévision, à l'antenne; **to put on airs** prendre des airs; **to put on the**

air radiodiffuser; **to walk on air** ne pas toucher terre; **up in the air** confondu, sidéré; (angry) très monté ‖ tr aérer; (a question) ventiler; (feelings) donner libre cours à

air-borne ['er‚born] adj aéroporté

air′ brake′ s frein m à air comprimé

air′-condi′tion tr climatiser

air′ condi′tioner s climatiseur m

air′ condi′tioning s climatisation f

air′craft′ s aéronef m, appareil m d'aviation

air′craft car′rier s porte-avions m

air′drop′ s parachutage m ‖ tr parachuter

air′field′ s terrain m d'aviation, aérodrome m

air′ force′ s forces fpl aériennes

air′ gap′ s (elec) entrefer m

air′ let′ter s aérogramme m

air′lift′ s pont m aérien

air′line′ s ligne f aérienne

air′line pi′lot s pilote m de ligne

air′lin′er s avion m de transport

air′mail′ adj aéropostal ‖ s poste f aérienne; **by airmail** par avion

air′plane′ s avion m

air′ pock′et s trou m d'air

air′ pollu′tion s pollution f de l'air

air′port′ s aéroport m

air′ raid′ s attaque f aérienne

air′-raid drill′ s exercice m d'alerte aérienne

air′-raid shel′ter s abri m

air′-raid ward′en s chef m d'îlot

air′-raid warn′ing s alarme f aérienne

air′sick′ adj atteint du mal de l'air

air′sick′ness s mal m de l'air

air′ sleeve′ or **sock′** s manche f à air

air′strip′ s piste f

air′ term′inal s aérogare f

air′tight′ adj hermétique

air′waves′ spl ondes fpl radiophoniques

air′way′ s route f aérienne

air·y ['eri] adj (comp -ier; super -iest) aérien; gracieux; (coll) maniéré

aisle [aɪl] s (through rows of seats) passage m central, allée f; (in a train) couloir m; (long passageway in a church) nef f latérale

ajar [ə'dʒar] adj entrebâillé

akimbo [ə'kɪmbo] adj & adv—**with arms akimbo** les poings sur les hanches

akin [ə'kɪn] adj apparenté

alabaster ['ælə‚bæstər], ['ælə‚bɑstər] s albâtre m

alacrity [ə'lækrɪti] s vivacité f, empressement m

alarm [ə'larm] s alarme f; (of clock) sonnerie f ‖ tr alarmer

alarm′ clock′ s réveille-matin m, réveil m

alarming [ə'larmɪŋ] adj alarmant

alas [ə'læs], [ə'lɑs] interj hélas!

Albanian [æl'benɪ‚ən] adj albanais ‖ s (language) albanais m; (person) Albanais

albatross ['ælbə‚trɔs], ['ælbə‚trɑs] s albatros m

albi·no [æl'baɪno] adj albinos ‖ s (pl -nos) albinos m

album ['ælbəm] *s* album *m*
albumen [æl'bjumən] *s* albumen *m*
alchemy ['ælkɪmi] *s* alchimie *f*
alcohol ['ælkə,hɔl], ['ælkə,hɑl] *s* alcool *m*
alcoholic [,ælkə'hɔlɪk], [,ælkə'hɑlɪk] *adj & s* alcoolique *mf*
alcove ['ælkov] *s* niche *f*; (*for a bed*) alcôve *f*
alder ['ɔldər] *s* aune *m*
alder-man ['ɔldərmən] *s* (*pl* **-men**) conseiller *m* municipal
ale [el] *s* ale *f*
alembic [ə'lɛmbɪk] *s* alambic *m*; (fig) creuset *m*
alert [ə'lʌrt] *adj & s* alerte *f* ‖ *tr* alerter
alfalfa [æl'fælfə] *s* luzerne *f*
algebra ['ældʒɪbrə] *s* algèbre *f*
Algeria [æl'dʒɪrɪə] *s* Algérie *f*
Algerian [æl'dʒɪrɪ·ən] *adj* (*of Algeria*) algérien; (*of Algiers, the Barbary state*) algérois ‖ *s* Algérien *m*; Algérois *m*
Algiers [æl'dʒɪrz] *s* Alger *m*
alias ['elɪ·əs] *s* nom *m* d'emprunt ‖ *adv* alias, autrement dit
ali·bi ['ælɪ,baɪ] *s* (*pl* **-bis**) excuse *f*; (law) alibi *m*
alien ['eljən], ['elɪ·ən] *adj & s* étranger *m*
alienate ['eljə,net], ['elɪ·ə,net] *tr* s'aliéner; (*to transfer*) aliéner
alight [ə'laɪt] *adj* allumé ‖ *v* (*pret & pp* **alighted** or **alit** [ə'lɪt]) *intr* descendre, se poser; (*on land*) atterrir; (*on sea*) amerrir
align [ə'laɪn] *tr* aligner ‖ *intr* s'aligner
alike [ə'laɪk] *adj* pareils, e.g., *these books are alike* ces livres sont pareils; **to look alike** se ressembler ‖ *adv* de la même façon
alimony ['ælɪ,moni] *s* pension *f* alimentaire après divorce
alive [ə'laɪv] *adj* vivant; vif; **alive to** sensible à
alka·li ['ælkə,laɪ] *s* (*pl* **-lis** or **-lies**) alcali *m*
alkaline ['ælkə,laɪn], ['ælkəlɪn] *adj* alcalin
all [ɔl] *adj indef* tout; tout le ‖ *s* tout *m* ‖ *pron indef* tout; tous; **all of** tout le; **first of all** tout d'abord; **is that all?** c'est tout?; (*ironically*) ce n'est que ça?; **not at all** pas du tout ‖ *adv* tout; **all at once** tout à coup; **all but** presque; **all in** (coll) éreinté; **all in all** à tout prendre; **all off** (slang) abandonné; **all right** bon, ça va, très bien; **all's well!** (naut) bon quart!; **all the better** tant mieux; **all told** en tout; **fifteen (thirty, etc.) all** (tennis) égalité à quinze (trente, etc.); **to be all for** ne demander mieux que
allay [ə'le] *tr* apaiser
all'-clear' *s* fin *f* d'alerte
allege [ə'lɛdʒ] *tr* alléguer; déclarer sous serment; affirmer sans preuve
alleged *adj* présumé, prétendu, censé
allegedly [ə'lɛdʒɪdli] *adv* prétendument, censément
allegiance [ə'lidʒəns] *s* allégeance *f*

allegoric(al) [,ælɪ'gɑrɪk(əl)], [,ælɪ'gɔrɪk(əl)] *adj* allégorique
allego·ry ['ælɪ,gori] *s* (*pl* **-ries**) allégorie *f*
aller·gy ['ælərdʒi] *s* (*pl* **-gies**) allergie *f*
alleviate [ə'livɪ,et] *tr* soulager, alléger
alley ['æli] *s* ruelle *f*; **that is up my alley** (slang) cela est dans mes cordes
al'ley cat' *s* chat *m* de gouttière
alliance [ə'laɪ·əns] *s* alliance *f*
alligator ['ælɪ,getər] *s* alligator *m*
al'ligator pear' *s* poire *f* d'avocat
al'ligator wrench' *s* clef *f* à machoires dentées
alliteration [ə,lɪtə're/ən] *s* allitération *f*
all'-know'ing *adj* omniscient
allocate ['ælə,ket] *tr* allouer, assigner
allot [ə'lɑt] *v* (*pret & pp* **allotted**; *ger* **allotting**) *tr* répartir
allotment [ə'lɑtmənt] *s* allocation *f*; (*from social security*) prestation *f*
all'-out' *adj* total
allow [ə'laʊ] *tr* permettre; (*a fact; a privilege*) accorder; (*as an allocation*) allouer ‖ *intr*—**to allow for** tenir compte de
allowance [ə'laʊ·əns] *s* allocation *f*, indemnité *f*; concession *f*; tolérance *f*
alloy ['ælɔɪ], [ə'lɔɪ] *s* alliage *m* ‖ [ə'lɔɪ] *tr* allier
all' right' *interj* bon!, très bien!, ça va! (*agreed!*) c'est entendu!, d'accord!
all'-round' *adj* (*athlete*) complet; (*man*) universel; total, global
All' Saints'' Day' *s* la Toussaint
All' Souls'' Day' *s* la fête des Morts
all'spice' *s* (*plant*) quatre-épices *f*; (*berry*) toute-épice *f*; piment *m*
all'-time' *adj* record
allude [ə'lud] *intr*—**to allude to** faire allusion à
allure [ə'lur] *tr* séduire, tenter
allurement [ə'lurmənt] *s* charme *m*
alluring [ə'lurɪŋ] *adj* séduisant
all' wet' *adj* (coll) fichu, erroné
al·ly ['ælaɪ], [ə'laɪ] *s* (*pl* **-lies**) allié *m* ‖ [ə'laɪ] *v* (*pret & pp* **-lied**) *tr* allier
almanac ['ɔlmə,næk] *s* almanach *m*
almighty [ɔl'maɪti] *adj* omnipotent
almond ['ɑmənd], ['æmənd] *s* amande *f*
al'mond tree' *s* amandier *m*
almost ['ɔlmost], [ɔl'most] *adv* presque; **I almost fell** j'ai failli tomber
alms [ɑmz] *s & spl* aumône *f*
alms'house' *s* hospice *m*
aloe ['ælo] *s* aloès *m*
aloft [ə'lɔft], [ə'lɑft] *adv* en l'air; (aer) en vol; (naut) en haut
alone [ə'lon] *adj* seul, e.g., **my arm alone** suffices mon bras seul suffit; e.g., **the metropolis alone** la seule métropole; **let alone . . .** sans compter . . . ; **to leave alone** laisser tranquille ‖ *adv* seulement
along [ə'lɔŋ], [ə'lɑŋ] *adv* avec; **all along** tout le temps; **come along!** venez donc!; **to get along** s'en aller; se porter, faire des progrès ‖ *prep* le long de; sur
along'side' *adv* à côté ‖ *prep* à côté de

aloof [ə'luf] *adj* isolé, peu abordable ‖ *adv* à l'écart, à distance
aloud [ə'laud] *adv* à haute voix
alpenstock ['ælpən،stɑk] *s* bâton *m* ferré
alphabet ['ælfə،bet] *s* alphabet *m*
alpine ['ælpaɪn] *adj* alpin
Alps [ælps] *spl*—**the Alps** les Alpes *fpl*
already [ɔl'redɪ] *adv* déjà
Alsatian [æl'seʃən] *adj* alsacien ‖ *s* (*dialect*) alsacien *m*; (*person*) Alsacien *m*
also ['ɔlso] *adv* aussi, également
altar ['ɔltər] *s* autel *m*
al'tar boy' *s* enfant *m* de chœur
al'tar cloth' *s* nappe *f* d'autel
al'tar-piece' *s* rétable *m*
al'tar rail' *s* grille *f* du chœur
alter ['ɔltər] *tr* altérer; (*a suit of clothes*) retoucher, faire des retouches à; (*an animal*) châtrer ‖ *intr* se modifier
alteration [،ɔltə'reʃən] *s* altération *f*; (*in a building*) modification *f*; **alterations** (*in clothing*) retouches *fpl*
alternate ['ɔltərnɪt], ['æltərnɪt] *adj* alternatif; (*angle*) alterne; (*rhyme*) croisé ‖ ['ɔltər،net], ['æltər،net] *tr* faire alternance à ‖ *intr* alterner
al'ternating cur'rent *s* courant *m* alternatif
alternative [ɔl'tʌrnɪtɪv], [æl'tʌrnɪtɪv] *adj & s* alternatif *m*
although [ɔl'ðo] *conj* bien que, quoique
altitude ['æltɪ،t(j)ud] *s* altitude *f*
al·to ['ælto] *s* (*pl* -tos) alto *m*
altogether [،ɔltə'gɛðər] *adv* ensemble; entièrement; tout compris
altruist ['æltru،ɪst] *adj & s* altruiste *mf*
alum ['æləm] *s* alun *m*
aluminum [ə'lumɪnəm] *s* aluminium *m*
alum·nus [ə'lʌmnəs] *s* (*pl* -ni [naɪ]) diplômé *m*, ancien étudiant *m*
alveo·lus [æl'vi،ələs] *s* (*pl* -li [،laɪ]) alvéole *m*
always ['ɔlwɪz], ['ɔlwez] *adv* toujours
A.M. ['e'em] *adv* (letterword) (ante meridiem) du matin
amalgam [ə'mælgəm] *s* amalgame *m*
amalgamate [ə'mælgə،met] *tr* amalgamer ‖ *intr* s'amalgamer
amass [ə'mæs] *tr* amasser
amateur ['æmət∫ər] *adj & s* amateur *m*
amaze [ə'mez] *tr* étonner
amazing [ə'mezɪŋ] *adj* étonnant
amazon ['emə،zɑn], ['emə،zən] *s* amazone *f*; **Amazon** Amazone *f*; (*river*) fleuve *m* des Amazones
ambassador [æm'bæsədər] *s* ambassadeur *m*
ambassadress [æm'bæsədrɪs] *s* ambassadrice *f*, ambassadeur *m*
amber ['æmbər] *adj* ambré ‖ *s* ambre *m* jaune, ambre succin
ambidextrous [،æmbɪ'dɛkstrəs] *adj* ambidextre
ambigui·ty [،æmbɪ'gju،ɪti] *s* (*pl* -ties) ambiguïté *f*
ambition [æm'bɪʃən] *s* ambition *f*
ambitious [æm'bɪʃəs] *adj* ambitieux

amble ['æmbəl] *s* amble *m* ‖ *intr* (to stroll) déambuler; (equit) ambler
ambulance ['æmbjələns] *s* ambulance *f*
am'bulance corps' *s* service *m* sanitaire
am'bulance driv'er *s* ambulancier *m*
ambulatory ['æmbjələ،tori] *adj* ambulatoire
ambush ['æmbuʃ] *s* embuscade *f* ‖ *tr* embusquer
ameliorate [ə'miljə،ret] *tr* améliorer ‖ *intr* s'améliorer
amen ['e'men], ['ɑ'men] *s* amen *m* ‖ *interj* ainsi soit-il!
amenable [ə'minəbəl], [ə'mɛnəbəl] *adj* docile; **amenable to** (*a court*) justiciable de; (*a fine*) passible de; (*a law*) soumis à; (*persuasion*) disposé à; (*a superior*) responsable envers
amend [ə'mɛnd] *tr* amender ‖ *intr* s'amender
amendment [ə'mɛndmənt] *s* amendement *m*
amends [ə'mɛndz] *spl* dédommagement *m*; **to make amends** to dédommager
ameni·ty [ə'minɪti], [ə'mɛnɪti] *s* (*pl* -ties) aménité *f*; **amenities** agréments *mpl*; civilités *fpl*
America [ə'mɛrɪkə] *s* Amérique *f*; l'Amérique
American [ə'mɛrɪkən] *adj* américain *f*; *s* Américain *m*
Amer'ican Eng'lish *s* anglais *m* d'Amérique, américain *m*
Amer'ican In'dian *s* amérindien *m*
Americanism [ə'mɛrɪkə،nɪzəm] *s* (*word*) américanisme *m*; patriotisme *m* américain
Amer'ican plan' *s* pension *f* complète
Amer'ican way of life' *s* mode *m* de vie américain
amethyst ['æmɪθɪst] *s* améthyste *f*
amiable ['emɪ،əbəl] *adj* aimable
amicable ['æmɪkəbəl] *adj* amical
amid [ə'mɪd] *prep* au milieu de
amid'ships *adv* au milieu du navire
amidst [ə'mɪdst] *prep* au milieu de
amiss [ə'mɪs] *adv* détraqué; **not amiss** pas mal; **something amiss** quelque chose qui manque, quelque chose qui cloche ‖ *adv* de travers; **to take amiss** prendre en mauvaise part
ami·ty ['æmɪti] *s* (*pl* -ties) amitié *f*
ammeter ['æm،mɪtər] *s* ampèremètre *m*
ammonia [ə'monjə] *s* (*gas*) ammoniac *m*; (*gas dissolved in water*) ammoniaque *f*
ammunition [،æmjə'nɪʃən] *s* munitions *fpl*
amnesia [æm'niʒɪ،ə], [æm'niʒə] *s* amnésie *f*
amnes·ty ['æmnɪsti] *s* (*pl* -ties) amnistie *f* ‖ *v* (*pret & pp* -tied) *tr* amnistier
amoeba [ə'mibə] *s* amibe *f*
among [ə'mʌŋ] *prep* entre, parmi
amorous ['æmərəs] *adj* amoureux
amorphous [ə'mɔrfəs] *adj* amorphe
amortize ['æmər،taɪz] *tr* amortir
amount [ə'maunt] *s* montant *m*, quantité *f* ‖ *intr*—**to amount to** s'élever à
ampere ['æmpɪr] *s* ampère *m*

amphibian [æm'fɪbɪ-ən] *adj & s* amphibie *mf*; amphibien *m*
amphibious [æm'fɪbɪ-əs] *adj* amphibie *m*
amphitheater ['æmfɪ ,θi-ətər] *s* amphithéâtre *m*
ample ['æmpəl] *adj* ample; (*speech*) satisfaisant; (*reward*) suffisant
amplifier ['æmplɪ ,faɪ-ər] *s* amplificateur *m*
ampli·fy ['æmplɪ ,faɪ] *v* (*pret & pp* **-fied**) *tr* amplifier
amplitude ['æmplɪ ,t(j)ud] *s* amplitude *f*
am/plitude modula/tion *s* modulation *f* d'amplitude
amputate ['æmpjə ,tet] *tr* amputer
amputee [,æmpjə'ti] *s* amputé *m*
amuck [ə'mʌk] *adv*—**to run amuck** s'emballer
amulet ['æmjəlɪt] *s* amulette *f*
amuse [ə'mjuz] *tr* amuser
amusement [ə'mjuzmənt] *s* amusement *m*
amusing [ə'mjuzɪŋ] *adj* amusant
an [æn], [ən] *art indef* (devant un son vocalique) un
anachronism [ə'nækrə ,nɪzəm] *s* anachronisme *m*
analogous [ə'næləgəs] *adj* analogue
analo·gy [ə'nælədʒɪ] *s* (*pl* **-gies**) analogie *f*
analy·sis [ə'nælɪsɪs] *s* (*pl* **-ses** [,sɪz]) analyse *f*
analyst ['ænəlɪst] *s* analyste *mf*
analytic(al) [,ænə'lɪtɪk(əl)] *adj* analytique
analyze ['ænə ,laɪz] *tr* analyser
anarchist ['ænərkɪst] *s* anarchiste *mf*
anarchy ['ænərkɪ] *s* anarchie *f*
anathema [ə'næθɪmə] *s* anathème *m*
anatomic(al) [,ænə'tɑmɪk(əl)] *adj* anatomique
anato·my [ə'nætəmɪ] *s* (*pl* **-mies**) anatomie *f*
ancestor ['ænsestər] *s* ancêtre *m*
ances·try ['ænsestrɪ] *s* (*pl* **-tries**) ancêtres *mpl*, aïeux *mpl*; (*line*) ascendance *f*
anchor ['æŋkər] *s* ancre *f*; **anchors aweigh!** ancres levées!; **to cast anchor** jeter l'ancre, mouiller l'ancre; **to weigh anchor** lever l'ancre || *tr & intr* ancrer
ancho·vy ['ænt/ovi] *s* (*pl* **-vies**) anchois *m*
ancient ['en/ənt] *adj* ancien
and [ænd] *conj* et; **and/or** et/ou; **and so forth** et ainsi de suite
andiron ['ænd ,aɪ-ərn] *s* chenet *m*
anecdote ['ænɪk ,dot] *s* anecdote *f*
anemia [ə'nimɪ-ə] *s* anémie *f*
anesthesia [,ænɪs'θiʒə] *s* anesthésie *f*
anesthetic [,ænɪs'θetɪk] *adj & s* anesthésique *m*
anesthetist [æ'nesθɪtɪst] *s* anesthésiste *mf*
anesthetize [æ'nesθɪ ,taɪz] *tr* anesthésier
aneurysm ['ænjə ,rɪzəm] *s* anévrisme *m*
anew [ə'n(j)u] *adv* à (or de) nouveau
angel ['endʒəl] *s* ange *m*; (*financial backer*) (coll) bailleur *m* de fonds

angelic(al) [æn'dʒelɪk(əl)] *adj* angélique
anger ['æŋgər] *s* colère *f* || *tr* mettre en colère, fâcher
angina pectoris [æn'dʒaɪnə'pektərɪs] *s* angine *f* de poitrine
angle ['æŋgəl] *s* angle *m* || *tr* (journ) présenter sous un certain angle || *intr* pêcher à la ligne; **to angle for** essayer d'attraper; (*a compliment*) quêter
angler ['æŋglər] *s* pêcheur *m* à la ligne; (*schemer*) intrigant *m*
an·gry ['æŋgri] *adj* (*comp* **-grier**; *super* **-griest**) fâché; **angry at** fâché de; **angry with** fâché contre; **to become angry** se mettre en colère
anguish ['æŋgwɪ/] *s* angoisse *f*
angular ['æŋgələr] *adj* angulaire; (*features*) anguleux
animal ['ænɪməl] *adj & s* animal *m*
animate ['ænɪmɪt] *adj* animé || ['ænɪ ,met] *tr* animer
an/imated cartoon/ *s* dessins *mpl* animés
animation [,ænɪ'me/ən] *s* animation *f*
animosi·ty [,ænɪ'mɑsɪtɪ] *s* (*pl* **-ties**) animosité *f*
animus ['ænɪməs] *s* animosité *f*; intention *f*
anion ['æn ,aɪ-ən] *s* anion *m*
anise ['ænɪs] *s* anis *m*
aniseed ['ænɪ ,sid] *s* graine *f* d'anis
ankle ['æŋkəl] *s* cheville *f*
anklet ['æŋklɪt] *s* socquette *f*; bracelet *m* de cheville
annals ['ænəlz] *spl* annales *fpl*
anneal [ə'nil] *tr* recuire, détremper
annex ['æneks] *s* annexe *f* || [ə'neks] *tr* annexer, rattacher
annexation [,æneks'e/ən] *s* annexion *f*, rattachement *m*
annihilate [ə'naɪ-ɪ ,let] *tr* annihiler
annihilation [ə,naɪ-ɪ'le/ən] *s* anéantissement *m*
anniversa·ry [,ænɪ'vʌrsəri] *adj* anniversaire || *s* (*pl* **-ries**) anniversaire *m*
annotate ['ænə ,tet] *tr* annoter
announce [ə'nauns] *tr* annoncer
announcement [ə'naunsmənt] *s* annonce *f*, avis *m*
announcer [ə'naunsər] *s* annonceur *m*; (rad) présentateur *m*, speaker *m*
annoy [ə'nɔɪ] *tr* ennuyer, tourmenter
annoyance [ə'nɔɪ-əns] *s* ennui *m*
annoying [ə'nɔɪ-ɪŋ] *adj* ennuyeux
annual ['ænju-əl] *adj* annuel || *s* annuaire *m*; plante *f* annuelle
annui·ty [ə'n(j)u-ɪtɪ] *s* (*pl* **-ties**) (*annual payment*) annuité *f*; (*of a retired person*) pension *f* de retraite, pension viagère
an·nul [ə'nʌl] *v* (*pret & pp* **-nulled**; *ger* **-nulling**) *tr* annuler; abolir
anode ['ænod] *s* anode *f*
anodyne ['ænə ,daɪn] *adj & s* anodin *m*
anoint [ə'nɔɪnt] *tr* oindre
anon [ə'nɑn] *adv* tout à l'heure
anonymity [,ænə'nɪmɪtɪ] *s* anonymat *m*
anonymous [ə'nɑnɪməs] *adj* anonyme
another [ə'nʌðər] *adj & pron indef* un autre; (*an additional*) encore un; **many another** beaucoup d'autres

answer ['ænsər], ['ɑnsər] s réponse f; (math) solution f || tr (e.g., yes or no) répondre; (a question, a letter) répondre à || intr répondre; **to answer for** répondre de

an'swer book' s livre m du maître

an'swering ser'vice s (telp) service m des abonnés absents

ant [ænt] s fourmi f

antagonism [æn'tægə,nɪzəm] s antagonisme m

antagonize [æn'tægə,naɪz] tr contrarier; (a friend) s'aliéner

Antarctic [ænt'ɑrktɪk] adj & s Antarctique f

Antarctica [ænt'ɑrktɪkə] s l'Antarctique f

Antarc'tic O'cean s Océan m glacial antarctique

ante ['æntɪ] s mise f || tr miser || intr miser, caver; **ante up!** misez!

anteater ['ænt,itər] s fourmilier m

antecedent [,æntɪ'sidənt] adj & s antécédent m

antechamber ['æntɪ,tʃembər] s antichambre f

antelope ['æntɪ,lop] s antilope f

anten-na [æn'tɛnə] s (pl -nae [ni]) (ent) antenne f || s (pl -nas) (rad) antenne f

antepenult [,æntɪ'pinʌlt] s antépénultième f

anterior [æn'tɪrɪ-ər] adj antérieur

anthem ['ænθəm] s hymne m; (eccl) antienne f, hymne f

ant' hill' s fourmilière f

antholo-gy [æn'θalədʒɪ] s (pl -gies) anthologie f

anthropoid ['ænθro,pɔɪd] adj & s anthropoïde m

antiaircraft [,æntɪ'er,kræft], [,æntɪ'er,krɑft] adj antiaérien, contre-avions

antibiotic [,æntɪbaɪ'ɑtɪk] adj & s antibiotique m

antibod-y ['æntɪ,bɑdɪ] s (pl -ies) anticorps m

anticipate [æn'tɪsɪ,pet] tr anticiper; (to expect) s'attendre à

anticipation [æn,tɪsɪ'peʃən] s anticipation f

anticlimax [,æntɪ'klaɪmæks] s chute f dans le trivial, désillusion f

antics ['æntɪks] spl bouffonnerie f

antidote ['æntɪ,dot] s antidote m

antifreeze [,æntɪ'friz] s antigel m

antiglare ['æntɪ'gler] adj antiaveuglant

antiknock [,æntɪ'nɑk] adj & s antidétonant m

an'timis'sile mis'sile [,æntɪ'mɪsəl] s missile m antimissile

antimony ['æntɪ,monɪ] s antimoine m

antipa-thy [æn'tɪpəθɪ] s (pl -thies) antipathie f

antiperspirant [,æntɪ'pʌrspərənt] s antitranspirant m

antiphon ['æntɪ,fɑn] s antienne f

antiquated ['æntɪ,kwetɪd] adj vieilli, démodé

antique [æn'tik] adj antique; ancien || s (piece of furniture) original m; **antiques** meubles mpl d'époque

antique' deal'er s antiquaire m

antique' shop' s magasin m d'antiquités, maison f de meubles d'époque

antiqui-ty [æn'tɪkwɪtɪ] s (pl -ties) antiquité f; (oldness) ancienneté f

anti-Semitic [,æntɪsɪ'mɪtɪk] adj antisémite, antisémitique

antiseptic [,æntɪ'septɪk] adj & s antiseptique m

an'titank' gun' [,æntɪ'tæŋk] s canon m antichar

antithe-sis [æn'tɪθɪsɪs] s (pl -ses [,siz]) antithèse f

antitoxin [,æntɪ'tɑksɪn] s antitoxine f

antiwar [,æntɪ'wɔr] adj antimilitariste

antler ['æntlər] s andouiller m

antonym ['æntənɪm] s antonyme m

anvil ['ænvɪl] s enclume f

anxie-ty [æŋ'zaɪ-ətɪ] s (pl -ties) anxiété f, inquiétude f

anxious ['æŋkʃəs] adj inquiet, soucieux; **to be anxious to** avoir envie de, tenir beaucoup à

any ['ɛnɪ] adj indef quelque, du; aucun; **any day** n'importe quel jour; **any place** n'importe où; **any time** n'importe quand, à tout moment; **any way** n'importe comment, de toute façon || pron indef quiconque; quelques-uns §81; **not . . . any** ne . . . aucun §90; ne . . . en . . . pas, e.g., **I will not give him any** je ne lui en donnerai pas || adv un peu

an'y·bod'y pron indef quelqu'un §81; n'importe qui; **not . . . anybody** ne . . . personne

an'y·how' adv en tout cas; cependant

an'y·one' pron indef quelqu'un §81; n'importe qui; quiconque; **not . . . anyone** ne . . . personne, e.g., **I don't see anyone** je ne vois personne

an'y·thing' pron indef quelque chose; n'importe quoi; **anything at all** quoi que ce soit, si peu que ce soit; **anything but** rien moins que; **anything else?** et avec ça?, ensuite?; **not . . . anything** ne . . . rien

an'y·way' adv en tout cas

an'y·where' adv n'importe où; **not . . . anywhere** ne . . . nulle part

aor·ta [e'ɔrtə] s (pl -tas or -tae [ti]) aorte f

apace [ə'pes] adv vite, rapidement

apache [ə'paʃ], [ə'pæʃ] s apache m || **Apache** [ə'pætʃi] s apache m

apart [ə'pɑrt] adj séparé || adv à part, à l'écart; **apart from** en dehors de

apartment [ə'pɑrtmənt] s appartement m

apart'ment house' s maison f de rapport, immeuble m d'habitation

apathetic [,æpə'θetɪk] adj apathique

apa·thy ['æpəθɪ] s (pl -thies) apathie f

ape [ep] s singe m || tr singer

aperture ['æpərtʃər] s ouverture f; (phonet) aperture f

apex ['epeks] s (pl apexes or apices ['æpɪ,siz]) sommet m; (astr) apex m

aphid ['efɪd], ['æfɪd] s puceron m

aphorism ['æfə,rɪzəm] s aphorisme m

aphrodisiac [,æfrə'dɪzɪ,æk] adj & s aphrodisiaque m

apiar·y ['epɪ ˌerɪ] *s* (*pl* **-ies**) rucher *m*
apiece [ə'pis] *adv* la pièce, chacun
apish ['epɪʃ] *adj* simiesque; (fig) imitateur
aplomb [ə'plɑm], [ə'plɔm] *s* aplomb *m*
apocalyptic(al) [ə ˌpɑkə'lɪptɪk(əl)] *adj* apocalyptique
Apocrypha [ə'pɑkrɪfə] *s* apocryphes *mpl*
apogee ['æpə ˌdʒi] *s* apogée *m*
Apollo [ə'pɑlo] *s* Apollon *m*
apologetic [ə ˌpɑlə'dʒɛtɪk] *adj* prêt à s'excuser, humble, penaud
apologize [ə'pɑlə ˌdʒaɪz] *intr* faire des excuses, s'excuser
apolo·gy [ə'pɑlədʒɪ] *s* (*pl* **-gies**) excuse *f*; (*makeshift*) semblant *m*, prétexte *m*; (*apologia*) apologie *f*
A.P.O. **number** ['e'pi'o ˌnʌmbər] *s* (letterword) (*Army Post Office*) secteur *m* postal
apoplectic [ˌæpə'plektɪk] *adj* & *s* apoplectique *mf*
apoplexy ['æpə ˌpleksɪ] *s* apoplexie *f*
apostle [ə'pɑsəl] *s* apôtre *m*
Apos′tles′ Creed′ *s* symbole *m* des apôtres
apos·tle·ship′ [ə'pɑsələt *m*
apostrophe [ə'pɑstrəfɪ] *s* apostrophe *f*
apothecar·y [ə'pɑθɪ ˌkerɪ] *s* (*pl* **-ies**) apothicaire *m*
appall [ə'pɔl] *tr* épouvanter, effrayer, consterner
appalling [ə'pɔlɪŋ] *adj* épouvantable
appara·tus [ˌæpə'retəs], [ˌæpə'rætəs] *s* (*pl* **-tus** or **-tuses**) appareil *m*, dispositif *m*
appar·el [ə'pærəl] *s* (*equipment*; *clothes*) appareil *m*; (*clothes*) habillement *m* ‖ *v* (*pret & pp* **-eled** or **-elled**; *ger* **-eling** or **-elling**) *tr* habiller, vêtir; parer
apparent [ə'pærənt], [ə'perənt] *adj* apparent; (*heir*) présomptif
apparition [ˌæpə'rɪʃən] *s* apparition *f*
appeal [ə'pil] *s* appel *m*, recours *m*; charme *m*, attrait *m*; (law) pourvoi *m* ‖ *tr* (*a case*) faire appeler ‖ *intr* séduire, charmer; s'adresser, recourir; (law) appeler, pourvoir en cassation
appealing [ə'pilɪŋ] *adj* séduisant, attrayant, sympathique
appear [ə'pɪr] *intr* (*to come into view; to be published; to seem*) paraître; (*to come into view*) apparaître
appearance [ə'pɪrəns] *s* (*look*) apparence *f*, aspect *m*; (*act of showing up*) apparition *f*; (*in print*) parution *f*; **to all appearances** selon toute vraisemblance; **to make one's appearance** faire acte de présence
appease [ə'piz] *tr* apaiser
appeasement [ə'pizmənt] *s* apaisement *m*
appeaser [ə'pizər] . *s* conciliateur *m*, pacificateur *m*
appel′late court′ [ə'pelɪt], [ə'pelet] *s* tribunal *m* d'appel; **highest appellate court** cour *f* de cassation
append [ə'pend] *tr* apposer, ajouter

appendage [ə'pendɪdʒ] *s* dépendance *f*, accessoire *m*
appendecto·my [ˌæpən'dektəmɪ] *s* (*pl* **-mies**) appendicectomie *f*
appendicitis [ə ˌpendɪ'saɪtɪs] *s* appendicite *f*
appen·dix [ə'pendɪks] *s* (*pl* **-dixes** or **-dices** [dɪ ˌsiz]) appendice *m*
appertain [ˌæpər'ten] *intr* se rapporter
appetite ['æpɪ ˌtaɪt] *s* appétit *m*
appetizer ['æpɪ ˌtaɪzər] *s* apéritif *m*
appetizing ['æpɪ ˌtaɪzɪŋ] *adj* appétissant
applaud [ə'plɔd] *tr* applaudir; (*to approve*) applaudir à; **to applaud s.o.** for applaudir qn de ‖ *intr* applaudir
applause [ə'plɔz] *s* applaudissements *mpl*
apple ['æpəl] *s* pomme *f*; (*tree*) pommier *m*
ap′ple·jack′ *s* calvados *m*
ap′ple of the eye′ *s* prunelle *f* des yeux
ap′ple or′chard *s* pommeraie *f*, verger *m* à pommes
ap′ple pie′ *s* tarte *f* aux pommes
ap′ple pol′isher *s* (coll) chien *m* couchant, flagorneur *m*
ap′ple·sauce′ *s* compote *f* de pommes; (slang) balivernes *fpl*
ap′ple tree′ *s* pommier *m*
ap′ple turn′over *s* chausson *m* (aux pommes)
appliance [ə'plaɪəns] *s* appareil *m*; application *f*; **appliances** accessoires *mpl*
applicable ['æplɪkəbəl] *adj* applicable
applicant ['æplɪkənt] *s* candidat *m*, postulant *m*
application [ˌæplɪ'keʃən] *s* application *f*; (*for a job*) demande *f*, sollicitation *f*
applica′tion blank′ *s* formule *f*
applied′ arts′ *spl* arts *mpl* industriels
ap·ply [ə'plaɪ] *v* (*pret & pp* **-plied**) *tr* appliquer ‖ *intr* s'appliquer; **to apply for** solliciter, postuler; **to apply to s.o.** s'adresser à qn
appoint [ə'pɔɪnt] *tr* nommer, désigner; (obs) équiper
appointed *adj* désigné; (*time*) convenu, dit
appointment [ə'pɔɪntmənt] *s* (*engagement*) rendez-vous *m*; (*to a position*) désignation *f*, nomination *f*; **appointments** (*of a room*) aménagements *mpl*; **by appointment** sur rendez-vous
apportion [ə'pɔrʃən] *tr* répartir; (com) ventiler
appraisal [ə'prezəl] *s* appréciation *f*, estimation *f*, évaluation *f*; (*by an appraiser*) expertise *f*
appraise [ə'prez] *tr* priser, estimer, évaluer; faire l'expertise de
appraiser [ə'prezər] *s* priseur *m*, estimateur *m*, évaluateur *m*; expert *m*, commissaire-priseur *m*
appreciable [ə'priʃɪ·əbəl] *adj* appréciable, sensible
appreciate [ə'priʃɪ ˌet] *tr* apprécier; (*to be grateful for*) reconnaître; (*to be aware of*) être sensible à, s'apercevoir de ‖ *intr* augmenter, hausser

appreciation [ə͵priʃɪ'eʃən] s appréciation f; reconnaissance f, gratitude f; (*rise in value*) plus-value f

appreciative [ə'priʃɪ͵etɪv] adj reconnaissant

apprehend [͵æprɪ'hɛnd] tr comprendre; (*to seize; to fear*) appréhender

apprehension [͵æprɪ'hɛn/ən] s appréhension f

apprehensive [͵æprɪ'hɛnsɪv] adj craintif

apprentice [ə'prɛntɪs] s apprenti m

appren'tice·ship' s apprentissage m

apprise [ə'praɪz] tr prévenir, informer, mettre au courant

approach [ə'protʃ] s approche f; **to make approaches to** faire des avances à || tr approcher, approcher de, s'approcher de || intr approcher, s'approcher

approachable [ə'protʃəbəl] adj abordable, accessible

approbation [͵æprə'beʃən] s approbation f

appropriate [ə'proprɪ·ɪt] adj approprié || [ə'proprɪ͵et] tr (*to take for oneself*) s'approprier; (*to assign*) affecter

appropriation [ə͵proprɪ'eʃən] s appropriation f; (*assigning*) affectation f; (govt) crédit m budgétaire

approval [ə'pruvəl] s approbation f, consentement m; **on approval** à l'essai, à condition

approve [ə'pruv] tr approuver || intr être d'accord; **to approve of** approuver

approximate [ə'praksɪmɪt] adj approximatif || [ə'praksɪ͵met] tr se rapprocher de

appurtenance [ə'pʌrtɪnəns] s appartenance f; attirail m; **appurtenances** dépendances fpl

apricot ['eprɪ͵kat], ['æprɪ͵kat] s abricot m; (*tree*) abricotier m

April ['eprɪl] s avril m

A'pril fool' s (*joke*) poisson m d'avril; (*victim*) dupe f, dindon m

A'pril Fools'' Day' s le jour du poisson d'avril

apron ['eprən] s tablier m; (aer) aire f de manœuvre

apropos [͵æprə'po] adj opportun || adv opportunément; **apropos of** quant à, à l'égard de

apse [æps] s abside f

apt [æpt] adj apte; bien à propos; **apt to** enclin à, porté à

aptitude ['æptɪ͵t(j)ud] s aptitude f

aquacade ['ækwə͵ked] s féerie f sur l'eau, spectacle m aquatique

aqualung ['ækwə͵lʌŋ] s scaphandre m autonome

aquamarine [͵ækwəmə'rin] s aigue-marine f

aquaplane ['ækwə͵plen] s aquaplane m

aquari·um [ə'kwɛrɪ·əm] s (pl **-ums** or **-a** [ə]) aquarium m

aquatic [ə'kwætɪk], [ə'kwɑtɪk] adj aquatique || **aquatics** spl sports mpl nautiques

aqueduct ['ækwə͵dʌkt] s aqueduc m

aquiline ['ækwɪ͵laɪn] adj aquilin

Arab ['ærəb] adj arabe || s (*horse*) arabe m; (*person*) Arabe mf

Arabian [ə'rebɪ·ən] adj arabe || s Arabe mf

Arabic ['ærəbɪk] adj arabique || s (*language*) arabe m

Ar'abic nu'meral s chiffre m arabe

arbiter ['arbɪtər] s arbitre m

arbitrary ['arbɪ͵trɛri] adj arbitraire

arbitrate ['arbɪ͵tret] tr & intr arbitrer

arbitration [͵arbɪ'treʃən] s arbitrage m

arbitrator ['arbɪ͵tretər] s arbitre m; (law) amiable compositeur m

arbor ['arbər] s berceau m, charmille f; (mach) arbre m

arbore·tum [͵arbə'ritəm] s (pl **-tums** or **-ta** [tə]) jardin m botanique d'arbres

arbutus [ar'bjutəs] s arbousier m

arc [ark] s (elec, geom) arc m

arcade [ar'ked] s arcade f; galerie f

arcane [ar'ken] adj mystérieux

arch [artʃ] adj insigne; espiègle || s (*of a building, cathedral, etc.*) arc m; (*of bridge*) arche f; (*of vault*) voûte f || tr voûter; (*the back*) arquer || intr se voûter; s'arquer

archaic [ar'ke·ɪk] adj archaïque

archaism ['arke͵ɪzəm], ['arki͵ɪzəm] s archaïsme m

archangel ['ark͵endʒəl] s archange m

arch'bish'op s archevêque m

arch'duke' s archiduc m

arched [artʃt] adj voûté, courbé, arqué

archeologist [͵arkɪ'alədʒɪst] s archéologue mf

archeology [͵arkɪ'alɪdʒi] s archéologie f

archer ['artʃər] s archer m

archery ['artʃəri] s tir m à l'arc

archetype ['arkɪ͵taɪp] s archétype m

archipela·go [͵arkɪ'peləgo] s (pl **-gos** or **-goes**) archipel m

architect ['arkɪ͵tɛkt] s architecte m

architecture ['arkɪ͵tɛktʃər] s architecture f

archives ['arkaɪvz] spl archives fpl

arch'priest' s archiprêtre m

arch'way' s voûte f, arcade f

Arctic ['arktɪk] adj & s (*ocean*) Arctique m; (*region*) Arctique f

arc' weld'ing s soudure f à l'arc

ardent ['ardənt] adj ardent

ardor ['ardər] s ardeur f

arduous ['ardʒu·əs], ['ardju·əs] adj ardu, difficile

area ['ɛrɪ·ə] s aire f, surface f; territoire m; (mil) secteur m, zone f

arena [ə'rinə] s arène f

Argentina [͵ardʒən'tinə] s Argentine f; l'Argentine

argue ['argju] tr (*a question*) discuter; (*a case*) plaider; (*a point*) soutenir; (*to imply*) arguer; **to argue s.o. into** + ger persuader à qn de + inf || intr discuter, argumenter; plaider

argument ['argjəmənt] s (*proof; reason; theme*) argument m; discussion f, argumentation f; dispute f

argumentative [͵argjə'mɛntətɪv] adj disposé à argumenter, raisonneur

aria ['arɪ·ə], ['ɛrɪ·ə] s aria f

arid ['ærɪd] *adj* aride

aridity [ə'rɪdɪti] *s* aridité *f*

arise [ə'raɪz] *v* (*pret* **arose** [ə'roz]; *pp* **arisen** [ə'rɪzən]) *intr* (*to rise*) se lever; (*to originate*) provenir, prendre naissance; (*to occur*) se produire; (*to be raised, as objections*) s'élever

aristocra·cy [,ærɪs'takrəsi] *s* (*pl* **-cies**) aristocratie *f*

aristocrat [ə'rɪstə,kræt] *s* aristocrate *mf*

aristocratic [ə,rɪstə'krætɪk] *adj* aristocrate

Aristotle ['ærɪ,statəl] *s* Aristote *m*

arithmetic [ə'rɪθmətɪk] *s* arithmétique *f*

arithmetician [ə,rɪθmə'tɪʃən] *s* arithméticien *m*

ark [ɑrk] *s* arche *f*

arm [ɑrm] *s* bras *m*; (*mil*) arme *f*; **arm in arm** bras dessus bras dessous; **at arm's length** à bout de bras; **under my (your, etc.) arm** sous mon (ton, etc.) aisselle; **up in arms** en rébellion ouverte ‖ *tr* armer ‖ *intr* s'armer

armada [ɑr'madə], [ɑr'medə] *s* armada *f*, grande flotte *f*

armadil·lo [,ɑrmə'dɪlo] *s* (*pl* **-los**) tatou *m*

armament ['ɑrməmənt] *s* armement *m*

armature ['ɑrmə,tʃər] *s* (*elec*) induit *m*

arm'band' *s* brassard *m*

arm'chair' *s* fauteuil *m*

Armenian [ɑr'minɪən] *adj* arménien ‖ *s* (*language*) arménien *m*; (*person*) Arménien

armful ['ɑrm,fʊl] *s* brassée *f*

arm'hole' *s* emmanchure *f*, entournure *f*

armistice ['ɑrmɪstɪs] *s* armistice *m*

armor ['ɑrmər] *s* (*personal*) armure *f*; (*on ships, tanks, etc.*) cuirasse *f*, blindage *m* ‖ *tr* cuirasser, blinder ‖ *intr* se mettre l'armure

ar'mored car' *s* fourgon *m* blindé

ar'mor plate' *s* plaque *f* de blindage

ar'mor-plate' *tr* cuirasser, blinder

armor·y ['ɑrməri] *s* (*pl* **-ies**) ateliers *mpl* d'armes, salle *f* d'armes

arm'pit' *s* aisselle *f*

arm'rest' *s* appui-bras *m*, accoudoir *m*

arms' race' *s* course *f* aux armements

ar·my ['ɑrmi] *adj* militaire ‖ *s* (*pl* **-mies**) armée *f*

aroma [ə'romə] *s* arôme *m*

aromatic [,ærə'mætɪk] *adj* aromatique

around [ə'raʊnd] *adv* autour, alentour; de tous côtés ‖ *prep* autour de; **around 1950** (*coll*) vers 1950

arouse [ə'raʊz] *tr* éveiller; (*from sleep*) réveiller

arpeg·gio [ɑr'pɛdʒo] *s* (*pl* **-gios**) arpège *m*

arraign [ə'ren] *tr* accuser; (*law*) mettre en accusation

arrange [ə'rendʒ] *tr* arranger ‖ *intr* s'arranger

arrangement [ə'rendʒmənt] *s* arrangement *m*

array [ə're] *s* ordre *m*; (*display*) étalage *m*; (*adornment*) parure *f*; (*mil*) rangée *f*, rangs *mpl* ‖ *tr* ranger, disposer; (*to adorn*) parer

arrearage [ə'rɪrɪdʒ] *s* arriéré *m*

arrears [ə'rɪrz] *spl* arriéré *m*; **in arrears** arriéré

arrest [ə'rɛst] *s* (*capture*) arrestation *f*; (*halt*) arrêt *m* ‖ *tr* arrêter; fixer; (*attention*) retenir

arrival [ə'raɪvəl] *s* arrivée *f*; (*of goods or ships*) arrivage *m*

arrive [ə'raɪv] *intr* arriver

arrogance ['ærəgəns] *s* arrogance *f*

arrogant ['ærəgənt] *adj* arrogant

arrogate ['ærə,get] *tr*—**to arrogate to oneself** s'arroger

arrow ['æro] *s* flèche *f*

ar'row·head' *s* tête *f* de flèche; (*bot*) sagittaire *m*

arsenal ['ɑrsənəl] *s* ateliers *mpl* d'armes, manufacture *f* d'armes

arsenic ['ɑrsɪnɪk] *s* arsenic *m*

arson ['ɑrsən] *s* incendie *m* volontaire

arsonist ['ɑrsənɪst] *s* incendiaire *mf*

art [ɑrt] *s* art *m*

arterial [ɑr'tɪrɪ·əl] *adj* artériel

arteriosclerotic [ɑr,tɪrɪ·osklɪ'rɑtɪk] *adj* artérioscléreux

arter·y ['ɑrtəri] *s* (*pl* **-ies**) artère *f*

arte'sian well' [ɑr'tiʒən] *s* puits *m* artésien

artful ['ɑrtfəl] *adj* ingénieux; (*crafty*) artificieux, sournois; artificiel

arthritis [ɑr'θraɪtɪs] *s* arthrite *f*

artichoke ['ɑrtɪ,tʃok] *s* artichaut *m*

article ['ɑrtɪkəl] *s* article; **article of clothing** article *m* d'habillement

articulate [ɑr'tɪkjəlɪt] *adj* articulé; (*expressing oneself clearly*) clair, expressif; (*speech*) intelligible; (*creature*) doué de la parole ‖ [ɑr'tɪkjə,let] *tr* articuler ‖ *intr* s'articuler

artifact ['ɑrtɪ,fækt] *s* artefact *m*

artifice ['ɑrtɪfɪs] *s* artifice *m*

artificial [,ɑrtɪ'fɪʃəl] *adj* artificiel

artificiali·ty [,ɑrtɪ,fɪʃɪ'ælɪti] *s* (*pl* **-ties**) manque *m* de naturel

artillery [ɑr'tɪləri] *s* artillerie *f*

artil'lery·man *s* (*pl* **-men**) artilleur *m*

artisan ['ɑrtɪzən] *s* artisan *m*

artist ['ɑrtɪst] *s* artiste *mf*

artistic [ɑr'tɪstɪk] *adj* artistique, artiste

artistry ['ɑrtɪstri] *s* art *m*, habileté *f*

artless ['ɑrtlɪs] *adj* naturel; ingénu, naïf; sans art

arts' and crafts' *spl* arts et métiers *mpl*

Aryan ['ɛrɪ·ən], ['ɑrjən] *adj* aryen ‖ *s* (*person*) Aryen *m*

as [æz], [əz] *pron rel* que, e.g., **the same as** le même que ‖ *adv* aussi, e.g., **as . . . as** aussi . . . que; **as for** quant à; **as is** tel quel; **as of** (*a certain date*) en date du; **as regards** en ce qui concerne; **as soon as** aussitôt que; **as though** comme si; **as yet** jusqu'ici ‖ *prep* comme ‖ *conj* puisque; comme; que

asbestos [æs'bɛstəs] *s* amiante *m*, asbeste *m*

ascend [ə'sɛnd] *tr* (*a ladder*) monter à; (*a mountain*) gravir; (*a river*) remonter ‖ *intr* monter, s'élever

ascendancy [ə'sɛndənsi] *s* supériorité *f*, domination *f*

ascension [ə'sɛnʃən] *s* ascension *f*

Ascen'sion Day' *s* Ascension *f*

ascent [ə'sent] s ascension f
ascertain [,æsər'ten] tr vérifier
ascertainment [,æsər'tenmənt] s constatation f
ascetic [ə'setɪk] adj ascétique || s ascète mf
asceticism [ə'setɪ ,sɪzəm] s ascétisme m, ascèse f
ascor'bic ac'id [ə'skɔrbɪk] s acide m ascorbique
ascribe [ə'skraɪb] tr attribuer, imputer
aseptic [e'septɪk], [e'septɪk] adj aseptique
ash [æʃ] s cendre f; (tree) frêne m
ashamed [ə'ʃemd] adj honteux; to be ashamed avoir honte
ash'can' s poubelle f
ashen ['æʃən] adj cendré
ashore [ə'ʃor] adv à terre; to go ashore débarquer
ash'tray' s cendrier m
Ash' Wednes'day s le mercredi des Cendres
Asia ['eʒə], ['eʃə] s Asie f; l'Asie
A'sia Mi'nor s Asie f Mineure; l'Asie Mineure
aside [ə'saɪd] s aparté m || adv de côté, à part; (aloof, at a distance) à l'écart; aside from en dehors de, à part; to step aside s'écarter; (fig) quitter la partie
asinine ['æsɪ ,naɪn] adj stupide
ask [æsk], [ɑsk] tr (a favor; one's way) demander; (a question) poser; to ask s.o. about s.th. interroger qn au sujet de q.ch.; to ask s.o. for s.th. demander q.ch. à qn; to ask s.o. to + inf demander à qn de + inf, prier qn de + inf || intr—to ask about s'enquérir de; to ask for (a package; a porter) demander; (to inquire about) demander après; you asked for it (you're in for it) (coll) c'est bien fait pour vous
askance [ə'skæns] adv de côté; to look askance at regarder de travers
askew [ə'skju] adj & adv de travers, en biais, de biais
asleep [ə'slip] adj endormi; to fall asleep s'endormir
asp [æsp] s aspic m
asparagus [ə'spærəgəs] s asperge f; (stalks and tips used as food) des asperges
aspect ['æspekt] s aspect m
aspen ['æspən] s tremble m
aspersion [ə'spʌrʒən], [ə'spʌrʃən] s (sprinkling) aspersion f; (slander) calomnie f
asphalt ['æsfɔlt], ['æsfælt] s asphalte m
asphyxiate [æs'fɪksɪ ,et] tr asphyxier
aspirate ['æspɪrɪt] adj & s (phonet) aspiré m || ['æspɪ ,ret] tr aspirer
aspire [ə'spaɪr] intr—to aspire to aspirer à
aspirin ['æspɪrɪn] s aspirine f
ass [æs] s âne m
assail [ə'sel] tr assaillir
assailant [ə'selənt] s assaillant m
assassin [ə'sæsɪn] s assassin m
assassinate [ə'sæsɪ ,net] tr assassiner

assassination [ə ,sæsɪ'neʃən] s assassinat m
assault [ə'sɔlt] s assaut m; (rape) viol m; (law) voie f de fait || tr assaillir
assault' and bat'tery s (law) voies fpl de fait
assay [ə'se], ['æse] s essai m; métal m titré || [ə'se] tr essayer; titrer
assayer [ə'se·ər] s essayeur m
as'say val'ue s teneur f
assemblage [ə'semblɪdʒ] s assemblage m
assemble [ə'sembəl] tr assembler || intr s'assembler, se réunir
assem·bly [ə'semblɪ] s (pl -blies) (meeting) assemblée f, réunion f; (assembling) assemblage m, montage m
assem'bly hall' s salle f de conférences; (educ) grand amphithéâtre m
assem'bly line' s chaîne f de fabrication, chaîne de montage
assem'bly room' s salle f de réunion; (mach) atelier m de montage
assent [ə'sent] s assentiment m || intr assentir
assert [ə'sʌrt] tr affirmer; (one's rights) revendiquer; to assert oneself imposer le respect, s'imposer
assertion [ə'sʌrʃən] s assertion f
assess [ə'ses] tr (damages, taxes, etc.) évaluer; (value of property) coter; (property for tax purposes) grever
assessment [ə'sesmənt] s évaluation f; cote f; charge f, taxe f
assessor [ə'sesər] s répartiteur m d'impôts
asset ['æset] s avantage m; possession f; assets biens mpl, avoirs mpl, actif m
assiduous [ə'sɪdʒu·əs], [ə'sɪdju·əs] adj assidu
assign [ə'saɪn] tr assigner; (mil) affecter
assignation [,æsɪg'neʃən] s assignation f; rendez-vous m illicite
assignment [ə'saɪnmənt] s attribution f; (schoolwork) devoirs mpl; (law) assignation f, transfer m; (mil) affectation f
assimilate [ə'sɪmɪ ,let] tr assimiler || intr s'assimiler
assimilation [ə ,sɪmɪ'leʃən] s assimilation f
assist [ə'sɪst] tr assister, aider, secourir || intr être assistant
assistance [ə'sɪstəns] s assistance f, aide f, secours m
assistant [ə'sɪstənt] adj & s assistant m, adjoint m
assizes [ə'saɪzɪz] spl assises fpl
associate [ə'soʃɪ·ɪt], [ə'soʃɪ ,et] adj & s associé m || [ə'soʃɪ ,et] tr associer || intr s'associer
association [ə ,soʃɪ'eʃən] s association f
assonance ['æsənəns] s assonance f
assort [ə'sɔrt] tr assortir || intr s'associer
assorted adj assorti
assortment [ə'sɔrtmənt] s assortiment m
assuage [ə'swedʒ] tr assouvir; soulager, apaiser
assume [ə's(j)um] tr supposer; (various

forms) affecter; (a fact) présumer; (a name) emprunter; (duties) assumer, se charger de

assumed adj supposé; (borrowed) d'emprunt, emprunté; (feigned) feint

assumed/ name/ s nom m d'emprunt, nom de guerre

assuming [ə's(j)umɪŋ] adj prétentieux

assumption [ə'sʌmp/ən] s présomption f, hypothèse f; (of virtue) affectation f; (of power) appropriation f; **Assumption** (eccl) Assomption f

assurance [ə'/urəns] s assurance f, confiance f; promesse f

assure [ə'/ur] tr assurer, garantir

astatine ['æstə,tin] s astate m

aster ['æstər] s aster m; (China aster) reine-marguerite f

asterisk ['æstə,rɪsk] s astérisque m

astern [ə'stʌrn] adv à l'arrière

asthma ['æzmə], ['æsmə] s asthme m

astonish [ə'stɑnɪ/] tr étonner

astonishing [ə'stɑnɪ/ɪŋ] adj étonnant

astonishment [ə'stɑnɪ/mənt] s étonnement m

astound [ə'staund] tr stupéfier, ahurir, étonner

astounding [ə'staundɪŋ] adj étonnant, abasourdissant; (success) foudroyant

astraddle [ə'strædəl] adv à califourchon

astray [ə'stre] adv—to go astray s'égarer; to lead astray égarer

astride [ə'straɪd] adv à califourchon || prep à califourchon sur

astrologer [ə'strɑlədʒər] s astrologue m

astrology [ə'strɑlədʒɪ] s astrologie f

astronaut ['æstrə,nɔt] s astronaute mf

astronautics [,æstrə'nɔtɪks] s astronautique f

astronomer [ə'strɑnəmər] s astronome m

astronomic(al) [,æstrə'nɑmɪk(əl)] adj astronomique

as/tronom/ical year/ s année f solaire, année tropique

astronomy [ə'strɑnəmɪ] s astronomie f

astute [ə'st(j)ut] adj astucieux, fin

asunder [ə'sʌndər] adj séparé || adv en deux

asylum [ə'saɪləm] s asile m

at [æt], [ət] prep à, e.g., at Paris à Paris; chez, e.g., at John's chez Jean; en, e.g., at the same time en même temps

atheism ['eθɪ,ɪzəm] s athéisme m

atheist ['eθɪ-ɪst] s athée mf

atheistic [,eθɪ'ɪstɪk] adj athée

Athens ['eθɪnz] s Athènes f

athlete ['æθlit] s athlète m, sportif m

ath/lete's foot/ s pied m d'athlète

athletic [æθ'letɪk] adj athlétique || **athletics** s athlétisme m

athwart [ə'θwɔrt] adv par le travers

Atlantic [ət'læntɪk] adj & s Atlantique m

atlas ['ætləs] s atlas m

atmosphere ['ætməs,fɪr] s atmosphère f

atmospheric [,ætməs'ferɪk] adj atmosphérique || **atmospherics** spl parasites mpl atmosphériques

atom ['ætəm] s atome m

atomic [ə'tɑmɪk] adj atomique

atom/ic bomb/ s bombe f atomique

atom/ic nuc/leus s noyau m d'atome

atom/ic pile/ s pile f atomique

atom/ic struc/ture s édifice m atomique

atomize ['ætə,maɪz] tr atomiser

atomizer ['ætə,maɪzər] s atomiseur m, vaporisateur m

atone [ə'ton] intr—to atone for expier

atonement [ə'tonmənt] s expiation f

atrocious [ə'tro/əs] adj atroce

atroci·ty [ə'trɑsɪtɪ] s (pl -ties) atrocité f

atro·phy ['ætrəfɪ] s atrophie f || v (pret & pp -phied) tr atrophier || intr s'atrophier

attach [ə'tæt/] tr attacher; (property) saisir; (salary) mettre opposition sur; to be attached to s'attacher à

attachment [ə'tæt/mənt] s attache f; (of the sentiments) attachement m; (law) opposition f, saisie-arrêt f

attack [ə'tæk] s attaque f || tr attaquer; s'attaquer à || intr attaquer

attacker [ə'tækər] s assaillant m

attain [ə'ten] tr atteindre

attainment [ə'tenmənt] s acquisition f, réalisation f; **attainments** connaissances fpl

attar ['ætər] s essence f

attempt [ə'tempt] s tentative f, essai m; (assault) attentat m || tr tenter; (s.o.'s life) attenter à

attend [ə'tend] tr (a performance) assister à; (a sick person) soigner; (a person) servir; to attend classes suivre des cours || intr—to attend to vaquer à, s'occuper de

attendance [ə'tendəns] s assistance f; présence f; (med) soins mpl

attendant [ə'tendənt] adj concomitant || s assistant m; (to royalty) serviteur m; **attendants** suite f

attention [ə'ten/ən] s attention f; **attention:** Mr. Doe à l'attention de M. Dupont; **attentions** égards mpl || interj attention!; (mil) garde à vous!

attentive [ə'tentɪv] adj attentif

attenuate [ə'tenju,et] tr amincir; (words; bacteria) atténuer

attest [ə'test] tr attester || intr—to attest to attester

Attic ['ætɪk] adj attique || (l.c.) s mansarde f, grenier m, soupente f

attire [ə'taɪr] s vêtement m, parure f || tr habiller, vêtir; parer

attitude ['ætɪ,t(j)ud] s attitude f

attorney [ə'tʌrnɪ] s avoué m, avocat m

attor/ney gen/eral s procureur m général, ministre m de justice

attract [ə'trækt] tr attirer

attraction [ə'træk/ən] s attraction f; attrait m, attirance f

attractive [ə'træktɪv] adj attirant, attrayant; (said, e.g., of a force) attractif

attribute ['ætrɪ,bjut] s attribut m || [ə'trɪbjut] tr attribuer

attrition [ə'trɪ/ən] s attrition f, usure f

attune [ə't(j)un] tr accorder

auburn ['ɔbərn] adj auburn, brun rougeâtre

auction ['ɔkʃən] s vente f aux enchères || tr vendre aux enchères

auctioneer [,ɔkʃən'ɪr] s adjudicateur m, commissaire-priseur m || tr & intr vendre aux enchères

audacious [ɔ'deʃəs] adj audacieux

audacity [ɔ'dæsɪti] s audace f

audience ['ɔdɪ-əns] s (hearing; formal interview) audience f; (assembly of hearers or spectators) assistance f, salle f, auditoire m; (those who follow what one says or writes) public m

au'dio fre'quency ['ɔdɪ,o] s audio-fréquence f

audiometer [,ɔdɪ'amɪtər] s audiomètre m

audit ['ɔdɪt] s apurement m || tr apurer; to audit a class assister à la classe en auditeur libre

audition [ɔ'dɪʃən] s audition f || tr & intr auditionner

auditor ['ɔdɪtər] s (com) comptable m agréé, expert comptable m; (educ) auditeur m libre

auditorium [,ɔdɪ'tɔrɪ-əm] s auditorium m, salle f, amphithéâtre m

auditory ['ɔdɪ,tɔri] adj auditif

auger ['ɔgər] s tarière f

aught [ɔt] s zéro m || pron indef—for aught I know autant que je sache || adv du tout

augment [ɔg'mɛnt] tr & intr augmenter

augur ['ɔgər] s augure m || tr & intr augurer; to augur well être de bon augure

augu·ry ['ɔgjəri] s (pl -ries) augure m

august [ɔ'gʌst] adj auguste || August ['ɔgəst] s août m

auk [ɔk] s guillemot m

aunt [ænt], [ɑnt] s tante f

aureomycin [,ɔri-o'maɪsɪn] s (pharm) auréomycine f

auricle ['ɔrɪkəl] s auricule f, oreillette f

aurora [ɔ'rɔrə] s aurore f

auscultate ['ɔskəl,tet] tr ausculter

auspices ['ɔspɪsɪz] spl auspices mpl

auspicious [ɔs'pɪʃəs] adj propice, favorable

austere [ɔs'tɪr] adj austère

Australia [ɔs'treljə] s Australie f; l'Australie

Australian [ɔs'treljən] adj australien || s (person) Australien m

Austria ['ɔstrɪ-ə] s Autriche f; l'Autriche

Austrian ['ɔstrɪ-ən] adj autrichien || s (person) Autrichien m

authentic [ɔ'θɛntɪk] adj authentique

authenticate [ɔ'θɛntɪ,ket] tr authentifier, constater l'authenticité de

author ['ɔθər] s auteur m

authoress ['ɔθərɪs] s femme f auteur

authoritarian [ə,θɔrɪ'tɛrɪ-ən], [ɔ,θɔrɪ-'tɛrɪ-ən] adj autoritaire || s homme m autoritaire

authoritative [ɔ'θɔrɪ,tetɪv], [ɔ'θɔrɪ-,tetɪv] adj autorisé; (dictatorial) autoritaire

authori·ty [ɔ'θɑrɪti], [ɔ'θɔrɪti] s (pl -ties) autorité f; on good authority de bonne part

authorize ['ɔθə,raɪz] tr autoriser

au'thor·ship' s paternité f

au·to ['ɔto] s (pl -tos) (coll) auto f, voiture f

autobiogra·phy [,ɔtobaɪ'agrəfi], [,ɔtobi'agrəfi] s (pl -phies) autobiographie f

autocrat ['ɔtə,kræt] s autocrate mf

autocratic(al) [,ɔtə'krætɪk(əl)] adj autocratique

autograph ['ɔtə,græf], ['ɔtə,grɑf] s autographe m || tr écrire l'autographe sur, dédicacer

au'tographed cop'y s exemplaire m dédicacé

au'to·intox'ica'tion s auto-intoxication f

automat ['ɔtə,mæt] s restaurant m libre service

automate ['ɔtə,met] tr automatiser

automatic [,ɔtə'mætɪk] adj automatique || s revolver m

automat'ic transmis'sion s changement m de vitesse automatique

automation [,ɔtə'meʃən] s automatisation f, automation f

automa·ton [ɔ'tamə,tan] s (pl -tons or -ta [tə]) automate m

automobile [,ɔtəmo'bil], [ɔtə'mobil] s automobile f

au'tomobile' show' s salon m de l'automobile

automotive [,ɔtə'motɪv] adj automobile; automoteur

autonomous [ɔ'tanəməs] adj autonome

autonomy [ɔ'tanəmi] s autonomie f

autop·sy [ɔ'tapsi] s (pl -sies) autopsie f

autumn ['ɔtəm] s automne m

autumnal [ɔ'tʌmnəl] adj automnal, d'automne

auxilia·ry [ɔg'zɪljəri] adj auxiliaire || s (pl -ries) auxiliaire mf; auxiliaries (mil) troupes fpl auxiliaires

avail [ə'vel] s utilité f || tr profiter à; to avail oneself of avoir recours à, profiter de || intr être utile, servir

available [ə'veləbəl] adj disponible; (e.g., train) accessible; to make available to mettre à la disposition de

avalanche ['ævə,læntʃ], ['ævə,lantʃ] s avalanche f

avarice ['ævərɪs] s avarice f

avaricious [,ævə'rɪʃəs] adj avaricieux

avenge [ə'vɛndʒ] tr venger

avenger [ə'vɛndʒər] s vengeur m

avenue ['ævə,n(j)u] s avenue f

aver [ə'vʌr] v (pret & pp averred; ger averring) tr avérer, affirmer

average ['ævərɪdʒ] adj moyen || s moyenne f; on the average en moyenne || tr prendre la moyenne de || intr atteindre une moyenne

averse [ə'vʌrs] adj—averse to hostile à, opposé à, ennemi de

aversion [ə'vʌrʒən] s aversion f

avert [ə'vʌrt] tr détourner, écarter; empêcher, éviter

aviar·y ['evi,eri] s (pl -ies) volière f

aviation [,evi'eʃən] s aviation f

aviator ['evi,etər] s aviateur m

avid ['ævɪd] adj avide; avid for avide de

avidity [ə'vɪdɪti] s avidité f
avoca·do [ˌævo'kado] s (pl -dos) avo-cat m
avocation [ˌævə'keʃən] s occupation f, profession f; distraction f
avoid [ə'vɔɪd] tr éviter
avoidable [ə'vɔɪdəbəl] adj évitable
avoidance [ə'vɔɪdəns] s dérobade f
avow [ə'vau] tr avouer
avowal [ə'vau·əl] s aveu m
avowedly [ə'vau·ɪdli] adv ouvertement, franchement
await [ə'wet] tr attendre
awake [ə'wek] adj éveillé || v (pret & pp awoke [ə'wok] or awaked) tr éveiller || intr s'éveiller
awaken [ə'wekən] tr éveiller, réveiller || intr se réveiller
awakening [ə'wekənɪŋ] s réveil m; (disillusionment) désabusement m
award [ə'wɔrd] s prix m; (law) dom-mages et intérêts mpl || tr décerner; accorder
aware [ə'wer] adj conscient; **to be-come aware of** se rendre compte de
awareness [ə'wernɪs] s conscience f
away [ə'we] adj absent || adv au loin, loin; **away from** éloigné de, loin de; **to do away with** abolir; **to get away** s'absenter; (to escape) échapper; **to go away** s'en aller; **to make away with** (to steal) dérober; **to run away** se sauver; **to send away** renvoyer; **to take away** enlever || interj hors d'ici!; **away with!** à bas!
awe [ɔ] s crainte f révérentielle || tr inspirer de la crainte à

awesome ['ɔsəm] adj impressionnant
awful ['ɔfəl] adj terrible; (coll) terri-ble, affreux
awfully ['ɔfəli] adv terriblement; (coll) joliment, rudement
awhile [ə'hwaɪl] adv quelque temps, un peu, un moment
awkward ['ɔkwərd] adj gauche, mala-droit; (moment) embarrassant
awl [ɔl] s alène f
awning ['ɔnɪŋ] s tente f; (in front of store) banne f
A.W.O.L. [ˈeˈdʌbəlˌjuˈoˈɛl] (letter-word ['ewɔl] (acronym) s (absent without leave) absence f illégale; **to be A.W.O.L.** être absent sans per-mission
awry [ə'raɪ] adv de travers
ax [æks] s hache f
axiom ['æksɪ·əm] s axiome m
axiomatic [ˌæksɪ·ə'mætɪk] adj axio-matique
axis ['æksɪs] s (pl axes ['æksiz]) axe m
axle ['æksəl] s essieu m
ax'le grease' s cambouis m
ay or **aye** [aj] s oui m; **aye aye, sir!** oui, commandant!, bien, capitaine!; **the ayes have it** les oui l'emportent || [e] adv toujours
azalea [ə'zeljə] s azalée f
azimuth ['æzɪməθ] s azimut m
Azores [ə'zorz], ['ezorz] spl Açores fpl
Aztecs ['æzteks] spl Aztèques mpl
azure ['æʒər], ['eʒər] adj azuré, d'azur || s azur m || tr azurer

B

B, b [bi] s IIe lettre de l'alphabet
babble ['bæbəl] s babil m || tr (secrets) dire à tort et à travers || intr babiller; (said of birds) jaser; (said of brook) murmurer
babbling ['bæblɪŋ] adj (gossiper) ba-billard; (brook) murmurant || s ba-billage m
babe [beb] s bébé m, bambin m; (naive person) (coll) enfant mf; (pretty girl) (coll) pépée f, môme f
babel ['bebəl] s brouhaha m, vacarme m
baboon [bæ'bun] s babouin m
ba·by ['bebi] s (pl -bies) bébé m; (youngest child) cadet m, benjamin m; **baby!** (honey!) (coll) ma choute! || v (pret & pp -bied) tr traiter en bébé, dorloter; (e.g., a machine) traiter avec soin
ba'by car'riage s voiture f d'enfant, poussette f; (with hood) landau m
ba'by grand' s piano m demi-queue
ba'by-sit'ter s gardienne f d'enfants, garde-bébé mf
ba'by talk' s babil m enfantin

ba'by teeth' spl dents fpl de lait
baccalaureate [ˌbækə'lɔrɪ·ɪt] s bac-calauréat m
bacchanal ['bækənəl] adj bachique || s bacchanale f; (person) noceur m
bachelor ['bætʃələr] s célibataire m; (graduate) bachelier m
bach'elor apart'ment s garçonnière f
bach'elor girl' s garçonne f
bach'elor·hood' s célibat m
bach'elor's-but'ton s (bot) bluet m, barbeau m
bach'elor's degree' s baccalauréat m
bacil·lus [bə'sɪləs] s (pl -li [laɪ]) ba-cille m
back [bæk] adj postérieur || s dos m; (of house; of head or body) derrière m; (of house; of car) arrière m; (of room) fond m; (of fabric) envers m; (of seat) dossier m; (of medal; of hand) revers m; (of page) verso m; (sports) arrière m; **back to back** dos à dos; **with one's back to the wall** poussé au pied du mur, aux abois || adv en arrière, à l'arrière; **as far back as** déjà en, dès; **back and forth**

de long en large; **back of** derrière; **back to front** sens devant derrière; **in back** par derrière; **some weeks back** il y a quelques semaines; **to be back** être de retour; **to come back** revenir; **to go back** retourner; **to go back home** rentrer; **to go back on** (coll) abandonner; **to go back to** (*to hark back to*) remonter à; **to make one's way back** s'en retourner ∥ *tr* faire faire marche arrière à; (*e.g., a car*) faire reculer; (*to support*) appuyer, soutenir; (*to reinforce*) renforcer; (*e.g., a racehorse*) parier pour; **to back s.o. up** soutenir qn; **to back water** nager à culer ∥ *intr* reculer; faire marche arrière; **to back down** (fig) se rétracter, se retirer; **to back out of** (*e.g., an agreement*) se dédire de, se soustraire à; **to back up** reculer

back'ache' *s* mal *m* de dos

back'bite' *v* (*pret* -**bit**; *pp* -**bitten** or **bit**) *tr* médire de ∥ *intr* médire

back'bit'er *s* médisant *m*

back'bone' *s* colonne *f* vertébrale, épine *f* dorsale, échine *f*; (*of a fish*) grande arête *f*; (*of an enterprise*) colonne *f*, appui *m*; (fig) caractère *m*, cran *m*; **to have no backbone** (fig) avoir l'échine souple

back'break'ing *adj* éreintant, dur

back'door' *adj* (fig) secret, clandestin

back' door' *s* porte *f* de derrière; (fig) petite porte

back'down' *s* (coll) palinodie *f*

back'drop' *s* toile *f* de fond

backer ['bækər] *s* (*of team, party, etc.*) supporter *m*; (com) bailleur *m* de fonds, commanditaire *m*

back'fire' *s* retour *m* de flamme, pétarade *f*; (*for firefighting*) contre-feu *m*; (mach) contre-allumage *m* ∥ *intr* donner des retours de flamme; (fig) produire un résultat imprévu

backgammon ['bæk,gæmən], [,bæk-'gæmən] *s* trictrac *m*, jacquet *m*

back'ground' *s* fond *m*; (*of person*) origines *fpl*, éducation *f*; (*music, sound effects, etc.*) fond sonore

back'hand' *s* (tennis) revers *m*

back'hand'ed *adj* de revers; (*compliment*) à rebours, équivoque

backing ['bækɪŋ] *s* (*support*) appui *m*, soutien *m*; (*reinforcement*) renforcement *m*; (*backing up*) recul *m*

back' in'terest *m* arrérage *m*; arrérages *mpl*

back'lash' *s* contrecoup *m*

back'light'ing *s* contre-jour *m*

back'log' *s* arriéré *m*, accumulation *f*

back' num'ber *s* (*of newspaper, magazine*) vieux numéro *m*; (coll) vieux jeu *m*

back' pay' *s* salaire *m* arriéré; (mil) arriéré *m* de solde

back' pay'ment *s* arriéré *m*

back' scratch'er *s* gratte-dos *m*; (slang) lèche-bottes *m*

back' seat' *s* banquette *f* arrière; **to take a back seat** (fig) aller au second plan

back'side' *s* derrière *m*, postérieur *m*

back'slide' *intr* récidiver

back'slid'er *s* récidiviste *mf*, relaps *m*

back'space key' *s* rappel *m* de chariot

back'spac'er *s* rappel *m* de chariot

back'spin' *s* (*of ball*) coup *m* en bas, effet *m*

back'stage' *adv* dans les coulisses

back'stairs' *adj* caché, indirect

back' stairs' *spl* escalier *m* de service

back'stitch' *s* point *m* arrière

back'stop' *s* (baseball) attrapeur *m* ∥ *v* (*pret & pp* -**stopped**; *ger* -**stopping**) *tr* (coll) soutenir

back'stroke' *s* (*of piston*) course *f* de retour; (swimming) brasse *f* sur le dos

back'swept wing' *s* aile *f* en flèche

back' talk' *s* réplique *f* impertinente

back' tax'es *spl* impôts *mpl* arriérés

back'track' *intr* rebrousser chemin

back'up' *s* appui *m*, soutien *m*

back'up light' *s* phare *m* de recul

backward ['bækwərd] *adj* (*in direction*) en arrière, rétrograde; (*in time*) en retard; (*in development*) arriéré, attardé ∥ *adv* en arrière; (*opposite to the normal*) à rebours; (*walking*) à reculons; (*flowing*) à contre-courant; (*stroking of the hair*) à contre-poil; **backward and forward** de long en large; **to go backward and forward** aller et venir

back'ward-and-for'ward mo'tion *s* vaet-vient *m*

backwardness ['bækwərdnɪs] *s* retard *m*, lenteur *f*

backwards ['bækwərdz] *adv* var of **backward**

back'wash' *s* remous *m*

back'wa'ter *s* (*of river*) bras *m* mort; (*e.g., of water wheel*) remous *m*; (fig) endroit *m* isolé, trou *m*

back' wheel' *s* roue *f* arrière

back'woods' *spl* forêts *fpl* de l'intérieur; bled *m*, brousse *f*

back'woods'man *s* (*pl* -**men**) défricheur *m* de forêts, coureur *m* des bois

back'yard' *s* derrière *m* (de la maison)

bacon ['bekən] *s* lard *m*, bacon *m*; (slang) butin *m*; **to bring home the bacon** (coll) remporter la timbale

bacteria [bæk'tɪrɪ-ə] *spl* bactéries *fpl*

bacteriology [bæk,tɪrɪ'alədʒɪ] *s* bactériologie *f*

bacteri-um [bæk'tɪrɪ-əm] *s* (*pl* -**a** [ə]) bactérie *f*

bad [bæd] *adj* mauvais §91; (*wicked*) méchant; (*serious*) grave; **from bad to worse** de mal en pis; **too bad!** c'est dommage!

bad' breath' *s* haleine *f* forte

bad' com'pany *s* mauvaises fréquentations *fpl*

bad' debt' *s* mauvaise créance *f*

bad' egg' *s* (slang) mauvais sujet *m*

bad' exam'ple *s* exemple *m* pernicieux

badge [bædʒ] *s* insigne *m*, plaque *f*

badger ['bædʒər] *s* blaireau *m* ∥ *tr* harceler, ennuyer

bad' lot' *s* voyous *mpl*, racaille *f*

badly ['bædli] *adv* mal §91; (*seriously*) gravement; **to want badly** avoir grande envie de

bad'man' *s* (*pl* **-men'**) bandit *m*

badness ['bædnɪs] *s* mauvaise qualité *f*; (*of character*) méchanceté *f*

bad'-tem'pered *adj* susceptible, méchant; (*e.g., horse*) vicieux, rétif

baffle ['bæfəl] *s* déflecteur *m*, chicane *f* || *tr* déconcerter, confondre

baffling ['bæflɪŋ] *adj* déconcertant

bag [bæg] *s* sac *m*; (*suitcase*) valise *f*; (*of game*) chasse *f* || *v* (*pret & pp* **bagged**; *ger* **bagging**) *tr* ensacher, mettre en sac; (*game*) abattre, tuer || *intr* (*said of clothing*) faire poche

bagful ['bæg,ful] *s* sachée *f*

baggage ['bægɪdʒ] *s* bagage *m*, bagages

bag'gage car' *s* (rr) fourgon *m* à bagages

bag'gage check' *s* bulletin *m* de bagages

bag'gage room' *s* bureau *m* de gare expéditeur; (*checkroom*) consigne *f*

bag'gage truck' *s* chariot *m* à bagages; (*hand truck*) diable *m*

bag·gy ['bægi] *adj* (*comp* **-gier**; *super* **-giest**) bouffant

bag' of tricks' *s* sac *m* à malice

bag'pipe' *s* cornemuse *f*

bail [bel] *s* caution *f*; **to be out on bail** être libre sous caution; **to put up bail** se porter caution || *tr* cautionner; **to bail out** se porter caution pour; (*a boat*) écoper || *intr*—**to bail out** (aer) sauter en parachute

bailiff ['belɪf] *s* (*of a court*) huissier *m*, bailli *m*; (*on a farm*) régisseur *m*

bailiwick ['belɪwɪk] *s* bailliage *m*, rayon *m*; (fig) domaine *m*

bait [bet] *s* appât *m*, amorce *f* || *tr* appâter, amorcer; (*to harass*) harceler

bake [bek] *tr* faire cuire au four; **to bake bread** boulanger, faire le pain || *intr* cuire au four

baked' pota'toes *spl* pommes *fpl* de terre au four

bakelite ['bekə,laɪt] *s* bakélite *f*

baker ['bekər] *s* boulanger *m*

bak'er's doz'en *s* treize *m* à la douzaine

bak·er·y ['bekəri] *s* (*pl* **-ies**) boulangerie *f*

baking ['bekɪŋ] *s* cuisson *f* au four

bak'ing pow'der *s* levure *f* anglaise

bak'ing so'da *s* bicarbonate *m* de soude

balance ['bæləns] *s* balance *f*, équilibre *m*; (*scales*) balance *f*; (*what is left*) reste *m*; (com) solde *m*, report *m* || *tr* balancer; (*an account*) solder || *intr* se balancer; se solder

bal'ance of pay'ments *s* balance *f* des comptes

bal'ance of pow'er *s* équilibre *m* politique

bal'ance of trade' *s* balance du commerce

bal'ance sheet' *s* bilan *m*

bal'ance wheel' *s* balancier *m*

balancing ['bælənsɪŋ] *s* balancement

m; équilibrage *m*; ajustement *m*; (com) règlement *m* des comptes

balco·ny ['bælkəni] *s* (*pl* **-nies**) balcon *m*; (*in a theater*) galerie *f*

bald [bɔld] *adj* chauve; (*fact, statement, etc.*) simple, net, carré

balderdash ['bɔldər,dæʃ] *s* galimatias *m*, fatras *m*

baldness ['bɔldnɪs] *s* calvitie *f*

bale [bel] *s* balle *f* || *tr* emballer

Balear'ic Is'lands [,bælɪ'ærɪk] *spl* Baléares *fpl*

baleful ['belfəl] *adj* funeste, fatal; triste

balk [bɔk] *s* déception *f*, contretemps *m*; (*beam*) poutre *f*; (agr) billon *m* || *tr* frustrer || *intr* regimber

Balkan ['bɔlkən] *adj* balkanique

balk·y ['bɔki] *adj* (*comp* **-ier**; *super* **-iest**) regimbé, rétif

ball [bɔl] *s* balle *f*; (*in billiards; in bearings*) bille *f*; (*spherical body*) boule *f*; (*dance*) bal *m*; (sports) ballon *m*; **to be on the ball** (slang) être toujours là pour le coup; **to have s.th. on the ball** (slang) avoir q.ch. dans le ventre; **to play ball** jouer au ballon; (slang) coopérer; (*to be in cahoots*) (slang) être en tandem || *tr*—**to ball up** (slang) bousiller, embrouiller

ballad ['bæləd] *s* (*song*) romance *f*, complainte *f*; (*poem*) ballade *f*

ball' and chain' *s* boulet *m*; (slang) femme *f*, épouse *f*

ball'-and-sock'et joint' *s* joint *m* à rotule

ballast ['bæləst] *s* (aer, naut) lest *m*; (rr) ballast *m* || *tr* lester; ballaster

ball' bear'ing *s* bille *f*, roulement *m* à billes

ball' cock' *s* robinet *m* à flotteur

ballerina [,bælə'rinə] *s* ballerine *f*

ballet ['bæle] *s* ballet *m*

ballistic [bə'lɪstɪk] *adj* balistique || **ballistics** *s* balistique *f*

ballis'tic mis'sile *s* engin *m* balistique

balloon [bə'lun] *s* ballon *m* || *tr* ballonner || *intr* ballonner, se ballonner

ballot ['bælət] *s* scrutin *m*; (*individual ballot*) bulletin *m* || *intr* scrutiner, voter

bal'lot box' *s* urne *f*; **to stuff the ballot boxes** bourrer les urnes

balloting ['bælətɪŋ] *s* scrutin *m*

ball'-point pen' *s* stylo *m* à bille

ball'room' *s* salon *m* de bal, salle *f* de danse

ballyhoo ['bælɪ,hu] *s* publicité *f* tapageuse || *tr* faire de la réclame pour

balm [bam] *s* baume *m* || *tr* parfumer

balm·y ['bami] *adj* (*comp* **-ier**; *super* **-iest**) embaumé; (slang) toqué

baloney [bə'loni] *s* (culin) mortadelle *f*; (slang) fadaises *fpl*

balsam ['bɔlsəm] *s* baume *m*

bal'sam fir' *s* sapin *m* baumier

bal'sam pop'lar *s* peuplier *m* baumier

Balt [bɔlt] *s* Balte *mf*

Bal'timore o'riole ['bɔltɪ,mor] *s* loriot *m* de Baltimore

baluster ['bæləstər] *s* balustre *m*

balustrade [ˌbæləsˈtred] s balustrade f, rampe f

bamboo [bæmˈbu] s bambou m

bamboozle [bæmˈbuzəl] tr (slang) mystifier

ban [bæn] s ban m, interdiction f; bans bans mpl || v (pret & pp banned; ger banning) tr mettre au ban

banal [ˈbenəl], [bəˈnæl] adj banal

banali·ty [bəˈnælɪti] s (pl -ties) banalité f

banana [bəˈnænə] s banane f

banan'a tree' s bananier m

band [bænd] s bande, lien m; musique f, fanfare f; (dance band) orchestre m; (strip of color) raie f; to beat the band (slang) sans pareille; (hastily) vivement || tr entourer de bandes; (a bird) marquer de bandes || intr—to band together se grouper

bandage [ˈbændɪdʒ] s (dressing) pansement m; (holding the dressing in place) bandage m || tr panser; bander

band'box' s carton m de modiste

bandit [ˈbændɪt] s bandit m

band'mas'ter s chef m de musique

band' saw' s scie f à ruban

band'stand' s kiosque m

band'wag'on s char m de la victoire; to jump on the bandwagon suivre la majorité victorieuse

ban·dy [ˈbændi] adj tortu || v (pret & pp -died) tr renvoyer, échanger; to bandy words se renvoyer des paroles || intr se disputer

ban'dy-leg'ged adj bancal

bane [ben] s poison m; ruine f

baneful [ˈbenfəl] adj funeste, nuisible

bang [bæŋ] s coup m; (of a door) claquement m; (of fireworks; of a gun) détonation f; bangs frange f; to go off with a bang détoner; (slang) réussir || tr frapper; (a door) faire claquer; to bang down (e.g., a lid) abattre violemment; to bang up (slang) rosser, cogner || intr claquer avec fracas; to bang against cogner; to bang on frapper à || interj pan!; pom!

bang'-up' adj (slang) de premier ordre, à la hauteur

banish [ˈbænɪʃ] tr bannir, exiler

banishment [ˈbænɪʃmənt] s bannissement m

banister [ˈbænɪstər] s balustre m; banisters balustrade f, rampe f

bank [bæŋk] s banque f; (of river) rive f, bord m; (shoal) banc m; (slope) talus m, terrasse f; (in a gambling game) cave f; (aer) virage m incliné; to break the bank faire sauter la banque || tr terrasser; (money) déposer; (an airplane) incliner || intr (aer) virer, virer sur l'aile, s'incliner; to bank on compter sur

bank' account' s compte m en banque

bank'book' s carnet m de banque

banked adj incliné

banker [ˈbæŋkər] s banquier m

banking [ˈbæŋkɪŋ] adj bancaire

bank' note' s billet m de banque

bank'roll' s paquet m de billets, liasse f de billets

bankrupt [ˈbæŋkrʌpt] adj & s failli m; (with guilt) banqueroutier m; to go bankrupt faire banqueroute || tr mettre en faillite

bankrupt·cy [ˈbæŋkrʌptsi] s (pl -cies) banqueroute f

bank' vault' s chambre f forte

banner [ˈbænər] s bannière f

ban'ner cry' s cri m de guerre

ban'ner year' s année f record

banquet [ˈbæŋkwɪt] s banquet m || intr banqueter

bantam [ˈbæntəm] adj nain || s poulet m nain, poulet de Bantam

ban'tam·weight' s poids m bantam

banter [ˈbæntər] s badinage m || tr & intr badiner

bantering [ˈbæntərɪŋ] adj railleur, goguenard

baptism [ˈbæptɪzəm] s baptême m

baptismal [bæpˈtɪzməl] adj baptismal

baptis'mal certif'icate s extrait m baptême, bulletin m de naissance

baptis'mal font' s fonts mpl baptismaux

Baptist [ˈbæptɪst] s baptiste mf

baptister·y [ˈbæptɪstəri] s (pl -ies) baptistère m

baptize [bæpˈtaɪz], [ˈbæptaɪz] tr baptiser

bar [bɑr] s barre f, barreau m; (obstacle) barrière f, empêchement m; (barroom; counter) bar m; (profession of law) barreau; (of chocolate) tablette f; (mus) mesure f; (phys) bar; behind bars sous les barreaux || prep —bar none sans exception || v (pret & pp barred; ger barring) tr barrer

barb [bɑrb] s barbillon m; dent f d'une flèche; (in metalwork) barbe f || tr garnir de barbillons

Barbados [bɑrˈbedoz] s la Barbade

barbarian [bɑrˈberi·ən] adj & s barbare mf

barbaric [bɑrˈbærɪk] adj barbare

barbarism [ˈbɑrbəˌrɪzəm] s barbarie f; (in speech or writing) barbarisme m

barbari·ty [bɑrˈbærɪti] s (pl -ties) barbarie f

barbarous [ˈbɑrbərəs] adj barbare

barbecue [ˈbɑrbɪˌkju] s grillade f en plein air || tr griller à la sauce piquante

bar'becue pit' s rôtisserie f en plein air

barbed adj barbelé, pointu

barbed' wire' s fil m de fer barbelé

barbed'-wire entan'glement s réseau m de barbelés

barber [ˈbɑrbər] s coiffeur m; (who shaves) barbier m

bar'ber pole' s enseigne f de barbier

bar'ber-shop' s salon m de coiffeur

bar'ber-shop quartet' s ensemble m harmonique de chanteurs amateurs

barbiturate [bɑrˈbɪtʃə·ret], [ˌbɑrbɪˈtjuret] adj & s barbiturique m

bard [bɑrd] s barde m

bare [ber] adj nu; découvert; simple || tr mettre à nu

bare'back' adv à nu

bare'faced' adj éhonté, effronté, sans déguisement

bare'foot' adj nu-pieds

bare'head'ed adj nu-tête

bare'leg'ged adj nu-jambes

barely ['berli] adv à peine

bareness ['bernɪs] s nudité f, dénuement m; (of style) pauvreté f

bar'fly' s (pl -flies) (slang) pilier m de cabaret

bargain ['bargɪn] s (deal) marché m, affaire f; (cheap purchase) solde m, occasion f; **into the bargain** par-dessus le marché || intr entrer en négociations; **she gave him more than he bargained for** (fig) elle lui a donné du fil à retordre; **to bargain over** marchander; **to bargain with** traiter avec

bar'gain count'er s rayon m des soldes

bar'gain sale' s vente f de soldes

barge [bardʒ] s barge f, chaland m, péniche f || intr—**to barge into** entrer sans façons

baritone ['bærɪ,ton] adj de baryton || s baryton m

barium ['berɪ-əm] s baryum m

bark [bark] s (of tree) écorce f; (of dog) aboiement m; (boat) trois-mâts m; **his bark is worse than his bite** il fait plus de bruit que de mal || tr—**to bark out** dire d'un ton sec || intr aboyer; **to bark up the wrong tree** suivre une mauvaise piste

bar'keep'er s barman m

barker ['barkər] (coll) s bonimenteur m, barnum m

barley ['barli] s orge f

bar'maid' s fille f de comptoir, demoiselle f de comptoir, serveuse f

barn [barn] s (for grain) grange f; (for horses) écurie f; (for livestock) étable f

barnacle ['barnəkəl] s (on a ship) anatife m, patelle f; (goose) bernacle f

barn'owl' s (Tyto alba) effraie f

barn'storm' intr aller en tournée

barn'yard' s basse-cour f

barometer [bə'ramɪtər] s baromètre m

barometric [,bærə'metrɪk] adj barométrique

baron ['bærən] s baron m; (of steel, coal, lumber) (coll) magnat m

baroness ['bærənɪs] s baronne f

baroque [bə'rok] adj & s baroque m

bar'rack-room' adj (humor; manners) soldatesque, de caserne || s chambrée f

barracks ['bærəks] spl caserne f

barrage [bə'raʒ] s barrage m

barred adj barré; (excluded) exclu

barrel ['bærəl] s tonneau m, fût m; large barrel barrique f; small barrel baril m, baricaut m, barillet m

bar'rel or'gan s orgue m de Barbarie

barren ['bærən] adj stérile; (bare) nu; (of style) aride, sec

barricade [,bærɪ'ked] s barricade f || tr barricader

barrier ['bærɪ-ər] s barrière f

bar'rier reef' s récif-barrière m

barring ['barɪŋ] prep sauf

barrister ['bærɪstər] s (Brit) avocat m

bar'room' s cabaret m, bar m, bistrot m

bar'tend'er s barman m

barter ['bartər] s échange m, troc m || tr échanger

ba'sal metab'olism ['besəl] s métabolisme m basal

basalt [bə'sɔlt], ['bæsɔlt] s basalte m

base [bes] adj bas, vil || s base f; fondement m, ligne f d'appui, principe m; (pedestal) socle m || tr baser; fonder

base'ball' s base-ball m

base'board' s moulure f de base

basement ['besmənt] s sous-sol m, cave f

base'ment win'dow s soupirail m

bash [bæʃ] tr cogner, assommer

bashful ['bæʃfəl] adj timide

basic ['besɪk] adj fondamental, de base, essentiel; (alkaline) basique

basil ['bæzəl] s basilic m

basilica [bə'sɪlɪkə] s basilique f

basin ['besɪn] s bassin m; (washbasin) cuvette f; (bowl) bol m

ba•sis ['besɪs] s (pl -ses [siz]) base f, fondement m; **on the basis of** sur la base de

bask [bæsk], [bask] intr se chauffer

basket ['bæskɪt], ['baskɪt] s panier m; (with a handle) corbeille f; (carried on the back) hotte f

bas'ket-ball' s basket-ball m, basket m

bas'ket lunch' s panier-repas m

bas'ket-mak'er s vannier m

bas'ket-work' s vannerie f

Basque [bæsk] adj basque || s (language) basque m; (person) Basque mf

bass [bes] adj grave, bas || s (mus) basse f || [bæs] s (ichth) bar m

bass' drum' [bes] s grosse caisse f

bassinet [,bæsɪ'net], ['bæsɪ,net] s berceaunette f

bassoon [bə'sun] s basson m

bass viol ['bes'vaɪ-əl] s basse f de viole

basswood ['bæs,wud] s tilleul m

bastard ['bæstərd] adj & s bâtard m

baste [best] tr (to thrash) rosser; (to scold) éreinter; (culin) arroser; (sewing) faufiler, baguer, bâtir

bastion ['bæstʃən], ['bæstɪ-ən] s bastion m

bat [bæt] s bâton m; (for cricket) bat m; (sports) batte f; (zool) chauve-souris f; (blow) (coll) coup m; **to be at bat** tenir la batte; **to go to bat for** (coll) intervenir au profit de; **to have bats in the belfry** (coll) avoir une araignée dans le plafond || v (pret & pp batted; ger batting) tr battre

batch [bætʃ] s (of papers) liasse f; (coll) fournée f, lot m

bated ['betɪd] adj—**with bated breath** en baissant la voix, dans un souffle

bath [bæθ], [baθ] s bain m; (bathroom) salle f de bains; **to take a bath** prendre un bain, se baigner

bathe [beð] tr baigner || intr se baigner

bather ['beðər] s baigneur m
bath'house' s établissement m de bains; (at the seashore) cabine f
bath'ing suit' s costume m de bain
bath'ing trunks' s slip m de bain
bath' mat' s tapis m de bain
bath'robe' s peignoir m
bath'room' s salle f de bains
bath'room fix'tures spl appareils mpl sanitaires
bath'room scale' s pèse-personne m
bath' tow'el s serviette f de bain
bath'tub' s baignoire f
baton [bæ'tɒn], ['bætɒn] s baguette f, bâton m de chef d'orchestre
battalion [bə'tæljən] s bataillon m
batten ['bætən] tr—to batten down the hatches condamner les panneaux
batter ['bætər] s (culin) pâte f; (sports) batteur m || tr battre
bat'tering ram' s bélier m
batter·y ['bætəri] s (pl -ies) (elec, mil, mus) batterie f; (primary cell) pile f; (secondary cell or cells) accumulateur m, accu m
battle ['bætəl] s bataille f; to do battle livrer combat || tr & intr combattre
bat'tle-ax' s hache f d'armes; (shrew) (slang) harpie f, mégère f
bat'tle cruis'er s croiseur m de bataille
bat'tle cry' s cri m de guerre
bat'tle-field' s champ m de bataille
bat'tle-front' s front m de bataille
bat'tle line' s ligne f de feu
battlement ['bætəlmənt] s créneau m; battlements parapet m, rempart m
bat'tle roy'al s mêlée f générale
bat'tle-ship' s cuirassé m, navire m de guerre
bat·ty ['bæti] adj (comp -tier; super -tiest) (slang) dingo, maboul, braque
bauble ['bɒbəl] s babiole f, bagatelle f; (of jester) marotte f
Bavaria [bə'vɛri·ə] s la Bavière
Bavarian [bə'vɛri·ən] adj bavarois || s Bavarois m
bawd·y ['bɒdi] adj (comp -ier; super -iest) obscène, impudique
bawl [bɒl] tr—to bawl out (slang) engueuler || intr gueuler; (to cry) sangloter
bawl'ing out' s (slang) engueulade f
bay [be] adj & s baie f; at bay aux abois || intr aboyer, hurler
bay'ber'ry s (pl -ries) baie f
bay'berry tree' s laurier m
bayonet ['be·ɒnɪt] s baïonnette f || tr percer d'un coup de baïonnette
bayou ['baɪ·u], ['baɪ·o] s anse f
bay' rum' s eau f de toilette au laurier
bay' win'dow s fenêtre f en saillie; (slang) bedaine f, gros ventre m
bazaar [bə'zar] s bazar m; (social event) kermesse f
B.C. ['bi'si] adv (letterword) (before Christ) av. J.-C.
be [bi] v (pres am [æm], is [ɪz], are [ɑr]; pret was [wɑz] or [wʌz], were [wʌr]; pp been [bɪn] intr être; avoir, e.g., to be five years old avoir cinq ans; e.g., to be ten feet long

avoir dix pieds de long; e.g., what is the matter with you? qu'avez-vous?; here is or here are voici; how are you? comment allez-vous?, ça va?, comment vous portez-vous?; how much is that? combien coûte cela?, c'est combien ça?; so be it ainsi soit-il; there is or there are il y a; (in directing the attention) voilà; for expressions like it is warm il fait chaud or I am cold j'ai froid, see the noun || aux (to form the passive voice) être, e.g., he is loved by everybody il est aimé de tout le monde; (progressive not expressed in French), e.g., he is eating il mange; to be to + inf devoir + inf, e.g., I am to give a speech je dois prononcer un discours
beach [bitʃ] s plage f, bord m de la mer; grève f, rivage m || tr & intr échouer
beach'comb'er s batteur m de grève
beach'head' s (mil) tête f de pont
beach' umbrel'la s parasol m de plage
beacon ['bikən] s signal m, phare m || tr éclairer || intr briller
bead [bid] s perle f, grain m; (of a gun) guidon m; beads collier m; (of sweat) gouttes fpl; (eccl) chapelet m; to draw a bead on viser; to tell one's beads égrener son chapelet
beadle ['bidəl] s bedeau m, appariteur m
beagle ['bigəl] s beagle m, briquet m
beak [bik] s bec m; (nose) (slang) pif m; (slang) grand nez m crochu
beaker ['bikər] s coupe f, vase m à bec, verre m à expérience
beam [bim] s poutre f; (plank) madrier m; (of roof) solive f; (of ship) bau m, barrot m; (of light; of hope) rayon m; (rad) faisceau m; on the beam (slang) sur la bonne piste; to be off the beam (slang) faire fausse route || tr (light, waves, etc.) émettre; to beam a broadcast faire une émission || intr rayonner
bean [bin] s haricot m; fève f; (slang) caboche f; to spill the beans (coll) vendre la mèche
beaner·y ['binəri] s (pl -ies) (slang) gargote f
bean'pole' s perche f à fèves; (person) (slang) asperge f
bean'stalk' s tige f de fève, tige de haricot
bear [bɛr] s ours m; (in the stock market) baissier m || v (pret bore [bor]; pp borne [born]) tr porter; (a child) enfanter; (interest on money) rapporter; (to put up with) souffrir, supporter; to bear the market jouer à la baisse || intr porter; to bear down appuyer; to bear up against résister à; to bear upon avoir du rapport à; to bring to bear mettre en jeu
bearable ['bɛrəbəl] adj supportable
bear' cub' s ourson m
beard [bɪrd] s barbe f || tr braver, narguer
bearded adj barbu

beardless ['bɪrdlɪs] *adj* imberbe, sans barbe

bearer ['bɛrər] *s* porteur *m*

bearing ['bɛrɪŋ] *s* port *m*, maintien *m*; (mach) roulement *m*, coussinet *m*; (naut) relèvement *m*; to get one's **bearings** se retrouver; to have a bearing on s'appliquer à; to take **bearings** (naut) faire le point

bear' mar'ket *s* marché *m* à la baisse

bear'skin' *s* peau *f* d'ours; colback *m*

beast [bist] *s* bête *f*, animal *m*; (person) brute *f*, animal *m*

beast·ly ['bistli] *adj* (*comp* **-lier**; *super* **-liest**) brutal, bestial; (coll) abominable, détestable

beast' of bur'den *s* bête *f* de somme, bête de charge

beat [bit] *s* battement *m*; (of policeman) ronde *f*; (mus) mesure *f*, temps *m* || *v* (*pret* **beat**; *pp* **beat** or **beaten**) *tr* battre; (*to defeat*) vaincre, battre; that beats me! (slang) ça me dépasse!; to beat back or down rabattre; to beat in enfoncer; to beat it (slang) filer, décamper; to beat s.o. **hollow** (coll) battre qn à plate couture; to beat s.o. out of money (slang) escroquer qn; to beat time battre la mesure; to beat up (slang) rosser || *intr* battre; to beat around the bush (coll) tourner autour du pot

beater ['bitər] *s* batteur *m*; (culin) fouet *m*

beati·fy [bi'æti,faɪ] *v* (*pret* & *pp* **-fied**) *tr* béatifier

beating ['bitɪŋ] *s* battement *m*; (blows) bastonnade *f*, rossée *f*; (defeat) (coll) raclée *f*

beatitude [bi'æti,t(j)ud] *s* béatitude *f*

beau [bo] *s* (*pl* **beaus** or **beaux** [boz]) beau *m*, galant *m*

beautician [bju'tɪʃən] *s* coiffeur *m*, coiffeuse *f*, esthéticienne *f*

beautiful ['bjutɪfəl] *adj* beau

beautifully ['bjutɪfəli] *adv* admirablement

beauti·fy ['bjuti,faɪ] *v* (*pret* & *pp* **-fied**) *tr* embellir

beau·ty ['bjuti] *s* (*pl* **-ties**) beauté *f*

beau'ty con'test *s* concours *m* de beauté

beau'ty par'lor or **beau'ty shop'** *s* salon *m* or institut *m* de beauté

beau'ty queen' *s* reine *f* de beauté

beau'ty sleep' *s* sommeil *m* avant minuit

beau'ty spot' *s* (place) coin *m* délicieux; (on face) grain *m* de beauté

beaver ['bivər] *s* castor *m*

becalm [bi'kɑm] *tr* calmer, apaiser; (naut) abriter

because [bi'kɔz] *conj* parce que; because of à cause de, par suite de

beck [bɛk] *s*—to be at s.o.'s beck and **call** obéir à qn au doigt et à l'œil

beckon ['bɛkən] *tr* faire signe à, appeler || *intr* appeler

be·come [bi'kʌm] *v* (*pret* **-came**; *pp* **-come**) *tr* convenir à, aller à, seoir à || *intr* devenir; se faire, e.g., to become a doctor se faire médecin; e.g., to become known se faire connaître;

to become accustomed s'accoutumer; to become old vieillir; what has become of him? qu'est-ce qu'il est devenu?

becoming [bi'kʌmɪŋ] *adj* convenable, seyant

bed [bed] *s* lit *m*; couche *f*; to go to **bed** se coucher; to put to bed coucher

bed' and board' *s* le vivre et le couvert

bed'bug' *s* punaise *f* (des lits)

bed'clothes' *spl* couvertures *fpl* et draps *mpl*

bedding ['bedɪŋ] *s* literie *f*

bedeck [bi'dek] *tr* parer, orner, chamarrer; to bedeck oneself s'attifer

bed'fast' *adj* cloué au lit

bed'fel'low *s* camarade *m* de lit

bedizen [bi'daɪzən], [bi'dɪzən] *tr* attifer, chamarrer

bed'jack'et *s* liseuse *f*

bedlam ['bedləm] *s* pétaudière *f*, tumulte *m*

bed'lamp' *s* lampe *f* de chevet

bed' lin'en *s* literie *f*, draps *mpl* en toile de fil

bed'pan' *s* bassin *m* (de lit)

bed'post' *s* pied *m* de lit

bedraggled [bi'drægəld] *adj* crotté, échevelé

bedridden ['bed,rɪdən] *adj* alité, cloué au lit

bed'rock' *s* roche *f* de fond; tuf *m*; (fig) fondement *m*

bed'room' *s* chambre *f* à coucher

bed'room lamp' *s* lampe *f* de chevet

bed'side' *s* bord *m* du lit, chevet *m*

bed'side book' *s* livre *m* de chevet

bed'sore' *s* escarre *f*

bed'spread' *s* dessus-de-lit *m*

bed'spring' *s* sommier *m*

bed'stead' *s* bois *m* de lit

bed'tick' *s* coutil *m*

bed'time' *s* l'heure *f* du coucher

bed' warm'er *s* chauffe-lit *m*

bed'wet'ting *s* énurésie *f*

bee [bi] *s* abeille *f*; (get-together) réunion *f*; (contest) concours *m*

beech [bitʃ] *s* hêtre *m*

beech' mar'ten *s* (zool) fouine *f*

beech'nut' *s* faîne *f*

beef [bif] *s* bœuf *m* || *tr*—to beef up (coll) renforcer || *intr* (slang) rouspéter

beef' cat'tle *s* bœufs *mpl* de boucherie

beef'steak' *s* bifteck *m*

beef' stew' *s* ragoût *m* de bœuf

bee'hive' *s* ruche *f*

bee'keep'er *s* apiculteur *m*

bee'keep'ing *s* apiculture *f*

bee'line' *s*—to make a beeline for aller en droite ligne à

beer [bɪr] *s* bière *f*

beer' bot'tle *s* canette *f* (de bière)

bees'wax' *s* cire *f* d'abeille

beet [bit] *s* betterave *f*

beetle ['bitəl] *s* scarabée *m*, escarbot *m*

bee'tle-browed' *adj* à sourcils épais, à sourcils fournis

be·fall [bi'fɔl] *v* (*pret* **-fell**; *pp* **-fallen**) *tr* arriver à || *intr* arriver

befitting [bɪˈfɪtɪŋ] *adj* convenable, seyant

before [bɪˈfor] *adv* avant, auparavant ‖ *prep* avant; (*in front of*) devant; **before** + *ger* avant de + *inf* ‖ *conj* avant que

before'hand' *adv* d'avance, préalablement, auparavant

befriend [bɪˈfrend] *tr* venir en aide à

befuddle [bɪˈfʌdəl] *tr* embrouiller

beg [beg] *v* (*pret & pp* **begged**; *ger* **begging**) *tr* mendier; (*to entreat*) prier ‖ *intr* mendier; (*said of dog*) faire le beau; **I beg of you** je vous en prie; **to beg for** solliciter; **to beg off** s'excuser; **to go begging** (fig) rester pour compte

be·get [bɪˈget] *v* (*pret* **-got**; *pp* **-gotten** or **-got**; *ger* **-getting**) *tr* engendrer

beggar [ˈbegər] *s* mendiant *m*

beggarly [ˈbegərli] *adj* chétif, misérable

be·gin [bɪˈgɪn] *v* (*pret* **-gan** [ˈgæn]; *pp* **-gun** [ˈgʌn]; *ger* **-ginning**) *tr & intr* commencer; **beginning with** à partir de; **to begin to** commencer à

beginner [bɪˈgɪnər] *s* débutant *m*, commençant *m*; (*tyro*) blanc-bec *m*, novice *m*, béjaune *m*; (nil) bleu *m*

beginning [bɪˈgɪnɪŋ] *s* commencement *m*, début *m*

begrudge [bɪˈgrʌdʒ] *tr* donner à contrecœur; **to begrudge s.o. s.th.** envier q.ch. à qn

beguile [bɪˈgaɪl] *tr* charmer, tromper

behalf [bɪˈhæf], [bɪˈhɑf] *s*—**on behalf of** de la part de, au nom de

behave [bɪˈhev] *intr* se comporter, se conduire; se comporter bien

behavior [bɪˈhevjər] *s* comportement *m*, conduite *f*

behead [bɪˈhed] *tr* décapiter

beheading [bɪˈhedɪŋ] *s* décapitation *f*

behest [bɪˈhest] *s* ordre *m*, demande *f*

behind [bɪˈhaɪnd] *s* derrière *m* ‖ *adv* derrière, par derrière; **to be behind** être en retard; **to fall behind** traîner en arrière ‖ *prep* derrière; en arrière de; **behind the back of** dans le dos de; **behind time** en retard

be·hold [bɪˈhold] *v* (*pret & pp* **-held** [ˈheld]) *tr* contempler ‖ *interj* voyez!, voici!

behoove [bɪˈhuv] *impers*—**it behooves him to** il lui appartient de; **it does not behoove him to** mal lui sied de

being [ˈbi·ɪŋ] *adj*—**for the time being** pour le moment ‖ *s* être *m*

belabor [bɪˈlebər] *tr* rosser; (fig) trop insister sur

belated [bɪˈletɪd] *adj* attardé, tardif

belch [beltʃ] *s* éructation *f*; rot *m* (slang) ‖ *tr & intr* éructer

bel·fry [ˈbelfri] *s* (*pl* **-fries**) beffroi *m*, clocher *m*

Belgian [ˈbeldʒən] *adj* belge ‖ *s* Belge *mf*

Belgium [ˈbeldʒəm] *s* Belgique *f*; la Belgique

be·lie [bɪˈlaɪ] *v* (*pret & pp* **-lied** [ˈlaɪd]; *ger* **-lying** [ˈlaɪ·ɪŋ]) *tr* démentir

belief [bɪˈlif] *s* croyance *f*

believable [bɪˈlivəbəl] *adj* croyable

believe [bɪˈliv] *tr & intr* croire; **to believe in** croire à or en; **to make believe** faire semblant, feindre

believer [bɪˈlivər] *s* croyant *m*

belittle [bɪˈlɪtəl] *tr* rabaisser

bell [bel] *s* cloche *f*; (*of a clock or gong*) timbre *m*; (*small bell*) sonnette *f*, clochette *f*; (*big bell*) bourdon *m*; (*on animals*) grelot *m*, clarine *f*, sonnaille *f*; (*of a trumpet*) pavillon *m*; **bells** sonnerie *f* ‖ *tr* attacher un grelot à

belladonna [ˌbeləˈdɑnə] *s* belladone *f*

bell'-bot'tom trou'sers *spl* pantalon *m* à pattes d'éléphant

bell'boy' *s* chasseur *m*, garçon *m* d'hôtel

bell' glass' *s* globe *m*, garde-poussière *m*

bell'hop' *s* chasseur *m*, garçon *m* d'hôtel

bellicose [ˈbelɪˌkos] *adj* belliqueux

belligerent [bəˈlɪdʒərənt] *adj & s* belligérant *m*

bell' jar' *s var of* **bell glass**

bellow [ˈbelo] *s* mugissement *m*; **bellows** (*of camera*; *of fireplace*) soufflet *m*; (*of organ*; *of forge*) soufflerie *f* ‖ *intr* mugir, beugler

bell'pull' *s* cordon *m* de sonnette

bell' ring'er *s* sonneur *m*; carillonneur *m*

bell'-shaped' *adj* en forme de cloche

bell' tow'er *s* clocher *m*, campanile *m*

bellwether [ˈbelˌweðər] *s* sonnailler *m*

bel·ly [ˈbeli] *s* (*pl* **-lies**) ventre *m* ‖ *v* (*pret & pp* **-lied**) *intr*—**to belly out** s'enfler

bel'ly·ache' *s* (coll) mal *m* de ventre ‖ *intr* (slang) rouspéter

bel'ly dance' *s* (coll) danse *f* du ventre

bel'ly flop' *s* plat ventre *m* (acrobatique)

bellyful [ˈbelɪˌful] *s* (slang) ventrée *f*

bel'ly-land' *intr* (aer) aterrir sur le ventre

belong [bɪˈlɔŋ], [bɪˈlɑŋ] *intr* (*to have the proper qualities*) aller bien; **to belong in** devoir être dans, e.g., **this chair belongs in that corner** cette chaise doit être dans ce coin-là; **to belong to** appartenir à; **to belong together** aller ensemble

belongings [bɪˈlɔŋɪŋz], [bɪˈlɑŋɪŋz] *spl* biens *mpl*, effets *mpl*

beloved [bɪˈlʌvɪd], [bɪˈlʌvd] *adj & s* bien-aimé *m*

below [bɪˈlo] *adv* dessous, au-dessous, en bas; (*as follows, following*) ci-dessous, ci-après ‖ *prep* sous, au-dessous de; (*another point on the river*) en aval de

belt [belt] *s* ceinture *f*; zone *f*; (*of a machine*) courroie *f*; **to tighten one's belt** se serrer la ceinture ‖ *tr* ceindre; (slang) cogner

belt' buck'le *s* boucle *f* de ceinturon

belt' convey'or *s* tapis *m* roulant

belted *adj* à ceinture

belt'way' *s* route *f* de ceinture, boulevard *m* périphérique

bemoan [bɪˈmon] *tr* déplorer

bemuse [bɪˈmjuz] *tr* stupéfier, hébéter

bench [bentʃ] *s* banc *m*; (law) siège *m*

bench' mark' *s* repère *m*

bend [bend] *s* courbure *f*; (*of road*) tournant *m*; (*of river*) sinuosité *f*; bends *mpl m* des caissons || *v* (*pret & pp* bent [bent]) *tr* courber; (*the elbow; a person to one's will*) plier; (*the knee*) fléchir || *intr* courber; plier; do not bend (label) ne pas plier; to bend down se courber

bender [ˈbendər] *s*—to go on a bender (slang) faire la bombe

beneath [bɪˈniθ] *adv* dessous, au-dessous, en bas || *prep* sous, au-dessous de

benediction [ˌbenɪˈdɪkʃən] *s* bénédiction *f*

benefactor [ˈbenɪˌfæktər], [ˌbenɪˈfæktər] *s* bienfaiteur *m*

beneficence [bɪˈnefɪsəns] *s* bienfaisance *f*

beneficent [bɪˈnefɪsənt] *adj* bienfaisant

beneficial [ˌbenɪˈfɪʃəl] *adj* profitable, avantageux; (*remedy*) salutaire

beneficiar·y [ˌbenɪˈfɪʃɪˌerɪ] *s* (*pl* -ies) bénéficiaire *mf*, ayant droit *m*

benefit [ˈbenɪfɪt] *s* profit *m*; (theat) bénéfice *m*; benefits bienfaits *mpl*, avantages *mpl*; for the benefit of au profit de || *tr* profiter (with *dat*) || *intr* bénéficier

ben'efit soci'ety *s* société *f* de prévoyance

benevolent [bɪˈnevələnt] *adj* bienveillant, bienfaisant, bénévole

benign [bɪˈnaɪn] *adj* bénin

bent [bent] *adj* courbé, plié; (*person's back*) voûté; (*determined*) résolu; bent over (*shoulders*) voûté; (*figure, person*) courbé; to be bent on être acharné à || *s* penchant *m*; to have a bent for avoir du goût pour

benzene [ˈbenˈzin] *s* (chem) benzène *m*

benzine [ˈbenˈzin] *s* benzine *f*

bequeath [bɪˈkwið], [bɪˈkwiθ] *tr* léguer

bequest [bɪˈkwest] *s* legs *m*

berate [bɪˈret] *tr* gronder

be·reave [bɪˈriv] *v* (*pret & pp* -reaved or -reft [ˈreft]) *tr* priver; (*to cause sorrow to*) affliger

bereavement [bɪˈrivmənt] *s* privation *f*; (*sorrow*) deuil *m*, affliction *f*

Berlin [bərˈlɪn] *adj* berlinois || *s* Berlin *m*

Berliner [bərˈlɪnər] *s* berlinois *m*

Bermuda [bərˈmjudə] *s* les Bermudes *fpl*

ber·ry [ˈberɪ] *s* (*pl* -ries) baie *f*; (*seed*) grain *m*

berserk [bərˈsʌrk], [bərˈzʌrk] *adv* frénétiquement; to go berserk frapper à tort et à travers

berth [bʌrθ] *s* couchette *f*; (*at a dock*) emplacement *m*; (*space to move about*) évitage *m*; (fig) poste *m*, situation *f* || *tr* (*a ship*) accoster

beryllium [bəˈrɪlɪəm] *s* béryllium *m*

be·seech [bɪˈsitʃ] *v* (*pret & pp* -sought [ˈsɔt] or -seeched) *tr* supplier

be·set [bɪˈset] *v* (*pret & pp* -set; *ger* -setting) *tr* assiéger, assaillir

beside [bɪˈsaɪd] *prep* à côté de, auprès de; to be beside oneself être hors de soi; to be beside oneself with (*e.g., joy*) être transporté de

besides [bɪˈsaɪdz] *adv* en outre, de plus; (*otherwise*) d'ailleurs || *prep* en sus de, en plus de, outre

besiege [bɪˈsidʒ] *tr* assiéger

besmear [bɪˈsmɪr] *tr* barbouiller

besmirch [bɪˈsmʌrtʃ] *tr* souiller

best [best] *adj super* (le) meilleur §91 || *s* (le) meilleur *m*; at best au mieux; to do one's best faire de son mieux; to get the best of it avoir le dessus; to make the best of s'accommoder de || *adv super* (le) mieux §91 || *tr* l'emporter sur

bestial [ˈbestjəl], [ˈbestʃəl] *adj* bestial, brutal

best' man' *s* garçon *m* d'honneur

bestow [bɪˈsto] *tr* accorder, conférer

bestowal [bɪˈstoəl] *s* don *m*, dispensation *f*

best' sell'er *s* livre *m* à succès, succès *m* de librairie

bet [bet] *s* pari *m*, gageure *f*; make your bet! faites vos jeux! || *v* (*pret & pp* bet or betted; *ger* betting) *tr & intr* parier; you bet! (slang) je vous crois!, tu parles!

be·take [bɪˈtek] *v* (*pret* -took; *pp* -taken) *tr*—to betake oneself se rendre

betray [bɪˈtre] *tr* trahir

betrayal [bɪˈtreəl] *s* trahison *f*

betrayer [bɪˈtreər] *s* traître *m*

betroth [bɪˈtroð], [bɪˈtroθ] *tr*—to be betrothed se fiancer

betrothal [bɪˈtroðəl], [bɪˈtroθəl] *s* fiançailles *fpl*

better [ˈbetər] *adj comp* meilleur §91; better than meilleur que || *adv comp* mieux §91; better than mieux que; (followed by numeral) plus de; it is better to il vaut mieux de; so much the better tant mieux; to be better (*in better health*) aller mieux; to be better to valoir mieux; to get better s'améliorer; to get the better of l'emporter sur; to think better se raviser || *tr* améliorer || *intr* s'améliorer

bet'ter half' *s* (coll) chère moitié *f*

bet'ting odds' *spl* cote *f* (des paris)

bettor [ˈbetər] *s* parieur *m*, gageur *m*

between [bɪˈtwin] *adv* au milieu; dans l'intervalle || *prep* entre; between friends dans l'intimité

between'-decks' *s* (naut) entrepont *m*

bev·el [ˈbevəl] *adj* biseauté, taillé en biseau || *s* (*instrument*) équerre *f*; (*sloping part*) biseau *m* || *v* (*pret & pp* -eled or -elled; *ger* -eling or -elling) *tr* biseauter, chanfreiner, équerrer

beverage [ˈbevərɪdʒ] *s* boisson *f*

bev·y [ˈbevɪ] *s* (*pl* -ies) bande *f*

bewail [bɪˈwel] *tr* lamenter, pleurer

beware [bɪˈwer] *tr* se bien garder de || *intr* prendre garde; to beware of prendre garde à || *interj* gare!, prenez garde!

bewilder [bɪ'wɪldər] *tr* confondre, ahurir

bewilderment [bɪ'wɪldərmənt] *s* confusion *f*, ahurissement *m*

bewitch [bɪ'wɪtʃ] *tr* ensorceler

bewitching [bɪ'wɪtʃɪŋ] *adj* enchanteur

beyond [bɪ'jɑnd] *s*—**the beyond** l'au-delà *m* || *adv* au-delà || *prep* au-delà de; **beyond a doubt** hors de doute; **it's beyond me** (coll) je n'y comprends rien; **to go beyond** dépasser

biannual [baɪ'ænjuəl] *adj* semi-annuel

bias ['baɪəs] *adj* biais || *s* biais *m*; (fig) prévention *f*, préjugé *m* || *tr* prédisposer, prévenir, rendre partial

bib [bɪb] *s* bavette *f*

Bible ['baɪbəl] *s* Bible *f*

Biblical ['bɪblɪkəl] *adj* biblique

bibliographer [,bɪblɪ'ɑgrəfər] *s* bibliographe *m*

bibliogra·phy [,bɪblɪ'ɑgrəfi] *s* (*pl* -**phies**) bibliographie *f*

biceps ['baɪseps] *s* biceps *m*

bicker ['bɪkər] *intr* se quereller, se chamailler

bickering ['bɪkərɪŋ] *s* bisbille *f*

bicuspid [baɪ'kʌspɪd] *s* prémolaire *f*

bicycle ['baɪsɪkəl] *s* bicyclette *f*, vélo *m* || *intr* faire de la bicyclette, aller à bicyclette

bi'cycle path' *s* piste *f* cyclable

bicyclist ['baɪsɪklɪst] *s* cycliste *mf*

bid [bɪd] *s* enchère *f*, offre *f*, mise *f*; (*e.g.*, *to build a school*) soumission *f*; (cards) demande *f* || *v* (*pret* **bade** [bæd] *or* **bid**; *ger* **bidden** ['bɪdən]) *tr* inviter; (*to order*) commander; (cards) demander; **to bid ten thousand on** mettre une enchère de dix mille *sur* || *intr*—**to bid on** mettre une enchère sur

bidder ['bɪdər] *s* enchérisseur *m*, offrant *m*; (*person who submits an estimate*) soumissionnaire *mf*

bidding ['bɪdɪŋ] *s* enchères *fpl*; **at s.o.'s bidding** aux ordres de qn

bide [baɪd] *tr*—**to bide one's time** attendre l'heure or le bon moment

biennial [baɪ'ɛnɪəl] *adj* biennal

bier [bɪr] *s* (*frame or stand*) catafalque *m*; (*coffin*) cercueil *m*

biff [bɪf] *s* (slang) gnon *m*, beigne *f* || *tr* (slang) gifler, cogner

bifocal [baɪ'fokəl] *adj* bifocal || **bifocals** *spl* lunettes *fpl* bifocales

big [bɪg] *adj* (*comp* **bigger**; *super* **biggest**) gros, grand; (*man*) de grande taille || *adv*—**to grow big** grossir, grandir; **to talk big** (slang) se vanter

bigamist ['bɪgəmɪst] *s* bigame *mf*

bigamous ['bɪgəməs] *adj* bigame

bigamy ['bɪgəmi] *s* bigamie *f*

big'-boned' *adj* ossu, à gros os

big' busi'ness *s* (pej) les grosses affaires *fpl*

Big' Dip'per *s* Grande Ourse *f*

big' game' *s* fauves *mpl*, gros gibier *m*

big'-heart'ed *adj* généreux, cordial

big'mouth' *s* (slang) gueulard *m*

bigot ['bɪgət] *s* bigot *m*

bigoted ['bɪgətɪd] *adj* bigot

bigot·ry ['bɪgətri] *s* (*pl* -**ries**) bigoterie *f*

big' shot' *s* (slang) grand manitou *m*, gros bonnet *m*

big' splash' *s* (slang) sensation *f* à tout casser

big' stiff' *s* (slang) personnage *m* guindé

big'-time op'erator *s* (slang) gros trafiquant *m*

big' toe' *s* orteil *m*, gros orteil

big' top' *s* (*circus tent*) chapiteau *m*

big' wheel' *s* (slang) gros bonnet *m*, grand manitou *m*, grosse légume *f*

big'wig' *s* (coll) gros bonnet *m*, grand manitou *m*, grosse légume *f*

bike [baɪk] *s* (coll) bécane *f*, vélo *m*

bile [baɪl] *s* bile *f*

bilge [bɪldʒ] *s* sentine *f*, cale *f*

bilge' wa'ter *s* eau *f* de cale

bilingual [baɪ'lɪŋgwəl] *adj* bilingue

bilious ['bɪljəs] *adj* bilieux

bilk [bɪlk] *s* tromperie *f*, escroquerie *f* || *tr* tromper, escroquer

bill [bɪl] *s* (*invoice*) facture *f*, mémoire *m*; (*in a hotel*) note *f*; (*in a restaurant*) addition *f*; (*currency*) billet *m*; (*of a bird*) bec *m*; (*posted*) affiche *f*, placard *m*, écriteau *m*; (*in a legislature*) projet *m* de loi; **post no bills** (public sign) défense d'afficher; **to head the bill** (theat) avoir la vedette || *tr* facturer

bill'board' *s* tableau *m* d'affichage, panneau *m* d'affichage

billet ['bɪlɪt] *s* (*order*) billet *m* de logement; (*of metal or wood*) billette *f* || *tr* loger, cantonner

bill'fold' *s* portefeuille *m*

bil'liard ball' *s* bille *f*

billiards ['bɪljərdz] *s* & *spl* billard *m*

bil'liard ta'ble *s* billard *m*

billion ['bɪljən] *s* (U.S.A.) milliard *m*; (Brit) billion *m*

billionaire [,bɪljən'ɛr] *s* milliardaire *mf*

bill' of exchange' *s* lettre *f* de change, traite *f*

bill' of fare' *s* carte *f* du jour

bill' of health' *s* patente *f* de santé

bill' of lad'ing *s* connaissement *m*

bill' of rights' *s* déclaration *f* des droits de l'homme

bill' of sale' *s* acte *m* de vente

billow ['bɪlo] *s* flot *m*, grosse vague *f* || *intr* ondoyer

billowy ['bɪlo·i] *adj* onduleux, ondoyant

bill'post'er *s* colleur *m* d'affiches, afficheur *m*

bil·ly ['bɪli] *s* (*pl* -**lies**) bâton *m*

bil'ly goat' *s* (coll) bouc *m*

bimonthly [baɪ'mʌnθli] *adj* bimestriel

bin [bɪn] *s* huche *f*, coffre *m*

binary ['baɪnəri] *adj* binaire

binaural [baɪ'nɔrəl], [bɪn'ɔrəl] *adj* stéréophonique; à deux oreilles

bind [baɪnd] *v* (*pret* & *pp* **bound** [baund]) *tr* lier, attacher; (*a book*) relier; (*s.o. to an agreement*) obliger

binder ['baɪndər] s (*person*) lieur m; (*of books*) relieur m; (*agreement*) conventions fpl; (*mach*) lieuse f

binder·y ['baɪndəri] s (*pl* -ies) atelier m de reliure

binding ['baɪndɪŋ] adj obligatoire; (*med*) astringent; **binding on all concerned** solidaire || s reliure f

bind'ing post' s (elec) borne f

binge [bɪndʒ] s (coll) noce f, bombe f

bingo ['bɪŋgo] s loto m

binocular [bɪ'nɑkjələr] adj & s binoculaire m; **binoculars** jumelles fpl

binomial [baɪ'nomɪ·əl] adj & s binôme m

biochemistry [,baɪ·o'kemɪstri] s biochimie f

biographer [baɪ'ɑgrəfər] s biographe mf

biographic(al) [,baɪ·ə'græfɪk(əl)] adj biographique

biogra·phy [baɪ'ɑgrəfi] s (*pl* -phies) biographie f

biologist [baɪ'ɑlədʒɪst] s biologiste mf

biology [baɪ'ɑlədʒi] s biologie f

biophysics [,baɪ·ə'fɪzɪks] s biophysique f

biop·sy ['baɪ·ɑpsi] s (*pl* -sies) biopsie f

bipartisan [baɪ'pɑrtɪzən] adj & s bipartite m

bipartite [baɪ'pɑrtaɪt] adj biparti

biped ['baɪped] adj & s bipède m

biplane ['baɪ,plen] s biplan m

birch [bʌrtʃ] s bouleau m; (*for whipping*) verges fpl || tr battre à coups de verges

birch' rod' s verges fpl

bird [bʌrd] s oiseau m; (slang) type m, individu m; **a bird in the hand is worth two in the bush** un "tiens" vaut mieux que deux "tu l'auras"; **to give s.o. the bird** (slang) envoyer qn promener; **to kill two birds with one stone** faire d'une pierre deux coups

bird' bath' s baignoire f pour oiseaux, bain m pour oiseaux

bird'cage' s cage f d'oiseau

bird' call' s appeau m, pipeau m

bird' dog' s chien m pour la plume

bird' fan'cier s oiselier

birdie ['bʌrdi] s oiselet m, oisillon m

bird'lime' s glu f

bird' of pas'sage s oiseau m de passage

bird' of prey' s oiseau m de proie

bird'seed' s alpiste m, chènevis m

bird's'-eye' s (*pattern*) œil-de-perdrix m

bird's'-eye view' s vue f à vol d'oiseau, tour m d'horizon, vue d'ensemble

biretta [bɪ'retə] s barette f

birth [bʌrθ] s naissance f; **by birth** de naissance; **to give birth to** donner naissance à

birth' certif'icate s acte m de naissance, bulletin m de naissance

birth' control' s contrôle m des naissances, procréation f dirigée

birth'day' s anniversaire m; **happy birthday!** heureux anniversaire!

birth'day cake' s gâteau m d'anniversaire

birth'day pres'ent s cadeau m d'anniversaire

birth'mark' s tache f, envie f

birth'place' s lieu m de naissance

birth' rate' s natalité f, taux m de natalité

birth'right' s droit m de naissance; droit d'aînesse

biscuit ['bɪskɪt] s petit pain m, crêpe f au beurre, gâteau m feuilleté

bisect [baɪ'sekt] tr couper en deux, diviser en deux

bisexual [baɪ'sek/ʊ·əl] adj bissexuel

bishop ['bɪʃəp] s évêque m; (chess) fou m

bishopric ['bɪʃəprɪk] s évêché m

bison ['baɪsən], ['baɪzən] s bison m

bisulfate [baɪ'sʌlfet] s bisulfate m

bisulfite [baɪ'sʌlfaɪt] s bisulfite m

bit [bɪt] s morceau m, bout m, brin m; (*of a bridle*) mors m; (*of a drill*) mèche f; **bit by bit** petit à petit

bitch [bɪtʃ] s (dog) chienne f; (*fox*) renarde f; (*wolf*) louve f; (vulgar) vache f

bite [baɪt] s (*of food*) bouchée f; (*by an animal*) morsure f; (*by an insect*) piqûre f; (*by a fish on a hook*) touche f || v (*pret* bit [bɪt]; *pp* bit or bitten ['bɪtən]) tr mordre; (*said of an insect or snake*) piquer

biting ['baɪtɪŋ] adj mordant; (cold) piquant; (wind) coupant

bit' play'er s figurant m

bitter ['bɪtər] adj amer; (cold) âpre, noir; (*fight*) acharné; (style) mordant || **bitters** spl bitter m

bit'ter end' s—**to the bitter end** jusqu'au bout

bit'ter-end'er s (coll) intransigeant m, jusqu'au-boutiste mf

bitterness ['bɪtərnɪs] s amertume f; (*of winter*) âpreté f; (fig) aigreur f

bit'ter-sweet' adj aigre-doux || s douce-amère f

bitumen [bɪ't(j)umən] s bitume m

bivou·ac ['bɪvu·æk], ['bɪvwæk] s bivouac m, cantonnement m || v (*pret* & *pp* -acked; *ger* -acking) intr bivouaquer

biweekly [baɪ'wikli] adj bimensuel || adv bimensuellement

biyearly [baɪ'jɪrli] adj semestriel || adv semestriellement

bizarre [bɪ'zɑr] adj bizarre

blab [blæb] v (*pret* & *pp* blabbed; *ger* blabbing) tr ébruiter || intr jaser

blabber ['blæbər] intr jaser

blab'ber-mouth' s (slang) jaseur m

black [blæk] adj & s noir m || tr noircir; **to black out** faire le black-out dans

black'-and-blue' adj meurtri

black'-and-white' adj en blanc et noir

black'ball' s blackbouler

black'ber'ry s (*pl* -ries) mûre f, mûre de ronce

black'berry bush' s mûrier m sauvage

black'bird' s (*Turdus merula*) merle m

black'board' s tableau m noir

black'board eras'er s éponge f, chiffon m

black' cur'rant s cassis m

black' damp' s mofete f

blacken ['blækən] *tr* noircir

black' eye' *s* œil *m* poché; **to give s.o. a black eye** pocher l'œil à qn; (*fig*) ruiner la réputation de qn

black'-eyed Su'san ['suzən] *s* marguerite *f* américaine

blackguard ['blægɑrd] *s* vaurien *m*, salaud *m*

black'head' *s* comédon *m*, tanne *f*

black'-headed gull' *s* mouette *f* rieuse

blacking ['blækɪŋ] *s* cirage *m* noir

blackish ['blækɪʃ] *adj* noirâtre

black'jack' *s* assommoir *m*; (cards) vingt-et-un *m* || *tr* assommer

black' lead' [led] *s* mine *f* de plomb

black' let'ter *s* caractère *m* gothique

black' list' *s* liste *f* noire

black'-list' *tr* mettre à l'index, mettre en quarantaine

black' lo'cust *s* (bot) faux acacia *m*

black' mag'ic *s* magie *f* noire

black'mail' *s* chantage *m* || *tr* faire chanter || *intr* faire du chantage

blackmailer ['blæk,melər] *s* maître *m* chanteur

black' mark' *s* (of censure) tache *f*

black' mar'ket *s* marché *m* noir

black' marketeer' [,mɑrkɪ'tɪr] *s* trafiquant *m* du marché noir

black'out' *s* black-out *m*; (of aviator) cécité *f* temporaire

black' pep'per *s* poivre *m* noir

black' sheep' *s* (fig) brebis *f* galeuse

black'smith' *s* forgeron *m*, maréchalferrant *m*

bladder ['blædər] *s* vessie *f*

bladderwort ['blædər,wʌrt] *s* utriculaire *f*

blade [bled] *s* lame *f*; (of grass) brin *m*; (of propeller) aile *f*, pale *f*; (of oar) plat *m*; (young man) gaillard *m*; (mach) ailette *f*, palette *f*, aube *f*

blah [blɑ] *s* (slang) sornettes *fpl*, fadaises *fpl*, bêtises *fpl*

blah-blah ['blɑ'blɑ] *s* baratin *m*

blamable ['blemǝbǝl] *adj* blâmable, coupable

blame [blem] *s* blâme *m*; reproches *mpl* || *tr* blâmer; reprocher; **s'en prendre à**

blameless ['blemlɪs] *adj* sans reproche

blame'wor'thy *adj* blâmable

blanch [blænt ʃ], [blɑnt ʃ] *tr* & *intr* blanchir

bland [blænd] *adj* doux, suave; (with dissimulation) narquois

blandish ['blændɪʃ] *tr* flatter, cajoler

blandishment ['blændɪʃmǝnt] *s* flatterie *f*; attrait *m*, charme *m*

blank [blæŋk] *adj* blanc; (check; form) en blanc; (mind) confondu, déconcerté || *s* blanc *m*; trou *m*, vide *m*, lacune *f*; (metal mold) flan *m*; (form to be filled out) fiche *f*, formule *f*, feuille *f*; (space to be filled in) tiret *m* || *tr*—**to blank out** effacer || *intr*—**to blank out** (coll) s'évanouir

blank' check' *s* chèque *m* en blanc; (fig) chèque en blanc

blanket ['blæŋkɪt] *adj* général || *s* couverture *f* || *tr* envelopper; traiter sous une rubrique générale

blank' verse' *s* vers *mpl* blancs

blare [bler] *s* bruit *m*; (of trumpet) sonnerie *f* || *tr* faire retentir; (like a trumpet) sonner || *intr* retentir

blarney ['blɑrni] *s* (coll) flagornerie *f* || *tr* (coll) flagorner

blaspheme [blæs'fim] *tr* & *intr* blasphémer

blasphemous ['blæsfǝmǝs] *adj* blasphématoire, blasphémateur

blasphe·my ['blæsfɪmi] *s* (pl **-mies**) blasphème *m*

blast [blæst], [blɑst] *s* rafale *f*, souffle *m*; explosion *f*; (of dynamite) charge *f*; (of whistle) coup *m*; (of trumpet) sonnerie *f*; **at full blast** à toute allure || *tr* (to blow up) faire sauter; (hopes) ruiner; (a plant) flétrir || *intr* (said of plant) se faner; **to blast off** (said of rocket) se mettre à feu

blast' fur'nace *s* haut fourneau *m*

blasting ['blæstɪŋ], ['blɑstɪŋ] *s* abattage *m* à la poudre; (of hopes) anéantissement *m*; (coll) abattage *m*, verte semonce *f*

blast'ing cap' *s* capsule *f* fulminante

blast'off' *s* mise *f* à feu

blatant ['bletǝnt] *adj* criard; (injustice) criant

blaze [blez] *s* flamme *f*, flambée *f*; (e.g., blazing house) incendie *m*; **to run like blazes** (slang) courir furieusement || *tr*—**to blaze the trail** frayer la piste || *intr* flamboyer, s'embraser

blazing ['blezɪŋ] *adj* embrasé, en feu; (sun) flamboyant

blazon ['blezǝn] *s* (heral) blason *m* || *tr* célébrer; exalter; (heral) blasonner; **to blazon out** proclamer

bleach [blit ʃ] *s* décolorant *m*, eau *f* de Javel; (for hair) eau oxygénée || *tr* blanchir, décolorer

bleachers ['blit ʃərz] *spl* gradins *mpl*, tribune *f*

bleak [blik] *adj* froid, morne, nu

blear-eyed ['blɪr'aɪd] *adj* chassieux, larmoyant; (dull) d'un esprit épais

blear·y ['blɪri] *adj* (comp **-ier**; super **-iest**) (eyes) chassieux; (prospect) voilé, incertain

bleat [blit] *s* bêlement *m* || *intr* bêler, bégueter

bleed [blid] *v* (pret & pp bled [bled]) *tr* & *intr* saigner; **to bleed white** saigner à blanc

bleeding ['blidɪŋ] *adj* saignant || *s* saignement *m*; (bloodletting) saignée *f*

blemish ['blemɪʃ] *s* défaut *m*, tache *f* || *tr* défigurer; (a reputation) tacher

blench [blent ʃ] *intr* pâlir; (to draw back) broncher

blend [blend] *s* mélange *m* || *v* (pret & pp blended or blent [blent]) *tr* mêler, mélanger; fondre, marier || *intr* se fondre, se marier

bless [bles] *tr* bénir

blessed ['blesɪd] *adj* béni, saint; (happy) bienheureux

blessing ['blesɪŋ] *s* bénédiction *f*; (at meals) bénédicité *m*

blight [blaɪt] *s* rouille *f*, nielle *f*; (*of peaches*) cloque *f*; (*of potatoes; of vines*) brunissure *f*; (fig) flétrissure *f* ‖ *tr* rouiller, nieller; (*hopes, aspirations*) flétrir, frustrer

blimp [blɪmp] *s* vedette *f* (aérienne)

blind [blaɪnd] *adj* aveugle; **blind by birth** aveugle-né; **blind in one eye** borgne; **blind person** aveugle *m* ‖ *s* store *m*; (*for hunting*) guet-apens *m*; (fig) feinte *f*; (cards) talon *m* ‖ *tr* aveugler; (*by dazzling*) éblouir

blind/ al/ley *s* cul-de-sac *m*, impasse *f*

blinder ['blaɪndər] *s* œillère *f*

blind/ flight/ *s* vol *m* à l'aveuglette

blind/ fly/ing *s* (aer) pilotage *m* sans visibilité

blind/fold/ *adj* les yeux bandés ‖ *s* bandeau *m* ‖ *tr* bander les yeux

blindly ['blaɪndli] *adv* aveuglément

blind/ man/ *s* aveugle *m*

blind/man's buff/ *s* colin-maillard *m*

blindness ['blaɪndnɪs] *s* cécité *f*; (fig) aveuglement *m*

blind/ spot/ *s* côté *m* faible

blink [blɪŋk] *s* clignotement *m* ‖ *tr* faire clignoter ‖ *intr* clignoter

blinker ['blɪŋkər] *s* feu *m* clignotant; (*for horses*) œillère *f*; (*for signals*) projecteur *m* clignotant

blink/er light/ *s* feu *m* à éclipses

blip [blɪp] *s* spot *m*

bliss [blɪs] *s* félicité *f*, béatitude *f*

blissful ['blɪsfəl] *adj* bienheureux

blister ['blɪstər] *s* ampoule *f*, bulle *f* ‖ *tr* couvrir d'ampoules; (*paint*) boursoufler ‖ *intr* se couvrir d'ampoules; se boursoufler

blithe [blaɪð], [blaɪθ] *adj* gai, joyeux

blitzkrieg ['blɪts‚krig] *s* guerre *f* éclair

blizzard ['blɪzərd] *s* tempête *f* de neige

bloat [blot] *tr* boursoufler, enfler ‖ *intr* se boursoufler, enfler

blob [blab] *s* motte *f*; (*of color*) tache *f*; (*of ink*) pâté *m*

block [blak] *s* bloc *m*; (*toy*) cube *m*; (*of shares*) tranche *f*; (*of houses*) pâté *m*, îlot *m* ‖ *tr* (*a project*) contrecarrer; (*a wall*) condamner, murer; **to block up** boucher, bloquer

blockade [bla'ked] *s* blocus *m*; **to run the blockade** forcer le blocus ‖ *tr* bloquer

block/ and tac/kle *s* palan *m*

block/head/ *s* sot *m*, niais *m*

blond [bland] *adj & s* blond *m*

blonde [bland] *adj & s* blonde *f*

blood [blʌd] *s* sang *m*; parenté *f*, race *f*; **in cold blood** de sang-froid; **to put new blood into** infuser un sang nouveau à

blood/ and guts/ *spl* sang *m* et tripes

blood/ bank/ *s* banque *f* du sang

blood/ count/ *s* numération *f* globulaire

blood/curd/ling *adj* horripilant

blood/hound/ *s* limier *m*

bloodless ['blʌdlɪs] *adj* exsangue; (*revolution*) sans effusion de sang

bloodletting ['blʌd‚lɛtɪŋ] *s* saignée *f*; (fig) effusion *f* de sang

blood/ or/ange *s* sanguine *f*

blood/ plas/ma *s* plasma *m* sanguin

blood/ poi/soning *s* septicémie *f*, empoisonnement *m* du sang

blood/ pres/sure *s* tension *f* artérielle

blood/shed/ *s* effusion *f* de sang

blood/shot/ *adj* injecté, éraillé

blood/ spec/imen *s* prise *f* de sang

blood/stained/ *adj* taché de sang

blood/stream/ *s* circulation *f* du sang

blood/suck/er *s* sangsue *f*

blood/ test/ *s* examen *m* du sang

blood/thirst/y *adj* sanguinaire

blood/ transfu/sion *s* transfusion *f* de sang, transfusion sanguine

blood/ type/ *s* groupe *m* de sang

blood/ ves/sel *s* vaisseau *m* sanguin

blood·y ['blʌdi] *adj* (*comp* -ier; *super* -iest) sanglant

bloom [blum] *s* fleur *f*; fraîcheur *f*; (*of a fruit*) velouté *m*, duvet *m*; **in bloom** en fleur ‖ *intr* fleurir

bloomers ['blumərz] *spl* culotte *f* de femme

blooper ['blupər] *s* (coll) gaffe *f*, bévue *f*; (rad) poste *m* brouilleur

blossom ['blasəm] *s* fleur *f*; **in blossom** en fleur ‖ *intr* fleurir; **to blossom out** s'épanouir

blot [blat] *s* tache *f*; (*of ink*) pâté *m* ‖ *v* (*pret & pp* blotted; *ger* blotting) *tr* tacher, barbouiller; (*ink*) sécher; **to blot out** rayer ‖ *intr* (*said of ink*) boire

blotch [blatʃ] *s* tache *f*; (*on face*) pustule *f* ‖ *tr* couvrir de taches; (*the skin*) marbrer

blotch·y ['blatʃi] *adj* (*comp* -ier; *super* -iest) brouillé, tacheté

blotter ['blatər] *s* buvard *m*

blot/ting pa/per *s* papier *m* buvard

blouse [blaus] *s* corsage *m*; (*children's*) chemise *f*; (mil) vareuse *f*

blow [blo] *s* coup *m*; **to come to blows** en venir aux coups ‖ *v* (*pret* blew [blu]; *pp* blown) *tr* souffler; **to blow one's nose** se moucher; **to blow out** (*a candle*) éteindre; **to blow up** faire sauter; (*a photograph*) agrandir; (*a balloon*) gonfler ‖ *intr* souffler; (slang) décamper en vitesse; **to blow out** (*said of a tire*) éclater; **to blow over** passer; **to blow up** éclater; (slang) se mettre en colère

blower ['blo·ər] *s* soufflerie *f*; (mach) ventilateur *m*

blow/fly/ *s* (*pl* -flies) mouche *f* à viande

blow/gun/ *s* sarbacane *f*

blow/hard/ *s* (slang) hâbleur *m*

blow/hole/ *s* (*of tunnel*) ventilateur *m*; (*of whale*) évent *m*

blowing ['blo·ɪŋ] *s* soufflage *m*; (*of the wind*) soufflement *m*

blow/out/ *s* (*of a tire*) éclatement *m*; (*orgy*) (slang) gueuleton *m*

blow/pipe/ *s* chalumeau *m*

blow/torch/ *s* lampe *f* à souder

blubber ['blʌbər] *s* graisse *f* de baleine ‖ *tr* bredouiller ‖ *intr* pleurer comme un veau

bludgeon ['blʌdʒən] *s* matraque *f* ‖ *tr* assommer

blue [blu] *adj* bleu; **to be blue** (coll) broyer du noir, avoir le cafard ‖ *s* bleu m; from out of the blue du ciel, à l'improviste; the blues le cafard, l'humeur f noire || tr bleuir

blue'bell' s jacinthe f des bois

blue'ber'ry s (pl -ries) myrtille f

blue'bird' s oiseau m bleu

blue'-black' adj noir tirant sur le bleu

blue' blood' s sang m royal; aristocrate mf

blue'bot'tle s bluet m, barbeau m

blue' cheese' s roquefort m américain

blue' chip' s valeur-vedette f, valeur f de tout repos

blue'-gray' adj gris bleuté, gris-bleu

blue'jay' s geai m bleu

blue' jeans' spl blue-jean m

blue' moon' s—once in a blue moon tous les trente-six du mois

blue'nose' s puritain m, collet m monté

blue'-pen'cil v (pret & pp -ciled or -cilled; ger -ciling or -cilling) tr corriger au crayon bleu; couper, censurer

blue'print' s dessin m négatif, photocalque m; (fig) plan m, schéma m || tr planifier

blue'stock'ing s (coll) bas-bleu m

bluff [blʌf] adj abrupt; (cliff) accore, escarpé; (person) brusque || s (cliff) falaise f, cap m à pic; (deception) bluff m; to call s.o.'s bluff relever un défi || tr & intr bluffer

bluffer ['blʌfər] s bluffeur m

bluish ['bluɪʃ] adj bleuté, bleuâtre

blunder ['blʌndər] s bévue f, gaffe f || intr faire une bévue, gaffer; to blunder into se heurter contre; to blunder upon découvrir par hasard; tomber sur

blunt [blʌnt] adj (blade) émoussé, (point) épointé; (person) brusque || tr émousser; épointer

bluntly ['blʌntli] adv brusquement, sans façons; carrément, sans ménagements

blur [blʌr] s barbouillage m || v (pret & pp blurred; ger blurring) tr embrouiller, voiler

blurb [blʌrb] s annonce f; publicité f au protège-livre

blurt [blʌrt] tr—to blurt out laisser échapper, lâcher

blush [blʌʃ] s rougeur f; at first blush au premier abord || intr rougir

bluster ['blʌstər] s rodomontade f, fanfaronnade f || intr (of wind) souffler en rafales; (of person) faire du fracas

blustery ['blʌstəri] adj (wind) orageux; (person) bravache, fanfaron

boar [bor] s (male swine) verrat m; (wild hog) sanglier m

board [bord] s planche f; (e.g., of directors) conseil m, commission f; (meals) le couvert; above board cartes sur table; on board à bord || tr (a ship) monter à bord de; (paying guests) nourrir || intr monter à bord; (said of paying guest) prendre pension

board' and room' s pension f et chambre f

boarder ['bordər] s pensionnaire mf; (student) interne mf

board'ing-house' s pension f (de famille)

board' of direc'tors s conseil m d'administration, gérance f

board' of trade' s association f des industriels et commerçants

board' of trustees' s comité m administrateur (e.g., of a university)

board'walk' s promenade f planchéiée au bord de la mer; (over mud) caillebotis m

boast [bost] s vanterie f || intr se vanter

boastful ['bostfəl] adj vantard

boasting ['bostɪŋ] s jactance f

boat [bot] s bateau m; (small boat) embarcation f; to miss the boat (coll) manquer le coche

boat' hook' s gaffe f

boat'house' s hangar m à bateaux or à canots

boating ['botɪŋ] s canotage m; to go boating faire du canotage

boat'load' s batelée f

boat'man s (pl -men) batelier m

boat' race' s régate f

boatswain ['bosən], ['bot,swen] s maître m d'équipage

bob [bab] s plomb m; (of hair) chignon m || v (pret & pp bobbed; ger bobbing) intr s'agiter, danser

bobbin ['babɪn] s bobine f

bob'by pin' s épingle f à cheveux

bob'by-socks' spl (coll) socquettes fpl, chaussettes fpl basses

bobbysoxer ['babɪ,saksər] s (coll) zazou m, jeune lycéenne f

bob'sled' s bobsleigh m

bob'tail' adj à queue écartée || tr couper court

bode [bod] tr & intr présager

bodily ['badɪli] adj corporel, physique || adv corporellement, en corps

bod-y ['badi] s (pl -ies) corps m; (dead body) cadavre m; (solidity) consistance f; (flavor of wine) sève f, générosité f; (aer) fuselage m; (aut) carrosserie f; to come in a body venir en corps

bod'y-guard' s garde m du corps; (group) garde f du corps

bog [bag] s marécage m, fondrière f || v (pret & pp bogged; ger bogging) intr—to bog down s'enliser

bogey-man ['bogi,mæn] s (pl -men) croque-mitaine m

bogus ['bogəs] adj faux, simulé

Bohemia [bo'himɪ-ə] s (country) Bohême f, la Bohême; (of artistic world) la bohème

Bohemian [bo'himɪ-ən] adj bohémien; (unconventional, arty) bohème, de bohème || s (person living in the country of Bohemia) Bohémien m; (artist) bohème mf

boil [bɔɪl] s ébullition f; (on the skin) furoncle m, clou m || tr faire bouillir || intr bouillir

boiled' din'ner s pot-au-feu m

boiled' ham' s jambon m d'York

boiled' pota'toes spl pommes fpl bouillies, pommes vapeur

boiler ['bɔɪlər] *s* chaudière *f*

boi/ler-mak/er *s* chaudronnier *m*

boiling ['bɔɪlɪŋ] *adj* bouillonnant || *s* ébullition *f*, bouillonnement *m*

boisterous ['bɔɪstərəs] *adj* bruyant, débordant

bold [bold] *adj* hardi, osé, téméraire; (*headland*) à pic; (*look*) assuré

bold/face/ *s* (*typ*) caractères *mpl* gras

bold/-faced/ *adj* (*forward*) effronté

boldness ['boldnɪs] *s* hardiesse *f*; effronterie *f*

boll/ wee/vil [bol] *s* anthonome *m* du coton, charançon *m* du coton

bologna [bə'lonə], [bə'lonjə] *s* mortadelle *f*, gros saucisson *m*

Bolshevik ['bɑl/əvɪk], ['bol/əvɪk] *adj* bolcheviste, bolchevique || *s* Bolcheviste *mf*, Bolchevique *mf*

bolster ['bolstər] *s* traversin *m* || *tr* soutenir

bolt [bolt] *s* verrou *m*; (*with a thread at one end*) boulon *m*; (*of cloth*) rouleau *m* || *tr* verrouiller; (*food*) gober; (*e.g., a political party*) lâcher || *intr* décamper

bomb [bɑm] *s* bombe *f* || *tr* bombarder

bombard [bɑm'bɑrd] *tr* bombarder

bombardier [,bɑmbər'dɪr] *s* bombardier *m*

bombardment [bɑm'bɑrdmənt] *s* bombardement *m*

bombast ['bɑmbæst] *s* boursouflure *f*

bombastic [bɑm'bæstɪk] *adj* boursouflé

bomb/ bay/ *s* (aer) soute *f* à bombes

bomb/ cra/ter *s* entonnoir *m*, trou *m* d'obus

bomber ['bɑmər] *s* avion *m* de bombardement, bombardier *m*

bombing ['bɑmɪŋ] *s* bombardement *m*

bomb/proof/ *adj* à l'épreuve des bombes

bomb/shell/ *s* obus *m*; **to fall like a bombshell** tomber comme une bombe

bomb/ shel/ter *s* abri *m* à l'épreuve des bombes

bomb/sight/ *s* viseur *m* de lancement

bona fide ['bonə,faɪdə] *adj & adv* de bonne foi

bonanza [bo'nænzə] *s* aubaine *f*, filon *m*

bonbon ['bɑn,bɑn] *s* bonbon *m*

bond [bɑnd] *s* lien *m*; (com) obligation *f*; **in bond** en entrepôt || *tr* (com) entreposer, mettre en entrepôt

bondage ['bɑndɪdʒ] *s* esclavage *m*

bond/hold/er *s* obligataire *mf*

bone [bon] *s* os *m*; (*of a fish*) arête *f*; **to have a bone to pick** avoir maille à partir || *tr* (*meat or fish*) désosser || *intr*—**to bone up on** (*a subject*) (slang) potasser, piocher

bone/head/ *s* (slang) ignorant *m*

boneless ['bonlɪs] *adj* sans os; sans arêtes

bone/ of conten/tion *s* pommé *f* de discorde

boner ['bonər] *s* (coll) bourde *f*

bonfire ['bɑn,faɪr] *s* feu *m* de joie; (*for burning trash*) feu de jardin

bonnet ['bɑnɪt] *s* bonnet *m*; chapeau *m* à brides; (fig) chapeau

bonus ['bonəs] *s* boni *m*, prime *f*

bon-y ['boni] *adj* (*comp* -ier; *super* -iest) osseux; (*thin*) décharné

boo [bu] *s* huée *f*, sifflement *m*; **not to say boo** ne pas souffler mot || *tr & intr* huer, siffler

boob [bub] *s* (coll) emplâtre *m*

boo-by ['bubi] *s* (*pl* -bies) (coll) nigaud *m*

boo/by hatch/ *s* (slang) asile *m* d'aliénés (prison) (slang) violon *m*

boo/by prize/ *s* fiche *f* de consolation

boo/by trap/ *s* engin *m* piégé; (fig) attrape-nigaud *m*

boo/by-trap/ *v* (*pret & pp* -trapped; *ger* -trapping) *tr* piéger

book [buk] *s* livre *m*; (*of tickets*) carnet *m*; (*libretto*) livret *m*; **by the book** d'après le texte, selon les règles; **to make book** (sports) inscrire les paris || *tr* (*a seat or room*) retenir, réserver

book/bind/er *s* relieur *m*

book/bind/er-y *s* (*pl* -ies) atelier *m* de reliure

book/bind/ing *s* reliure *f*

book/case/ *s* bibliothèque *f*, étagère *f*

book/ end/ *s* serre-livres *m*, appui-livres *m*

booking ['bukɪŋ] *s* réservation *f*; (theat) location *f*

bookish ['bukɪʃ] *adj* livresque; (*person*) studieux

book/keep/er *s* comptable *mf*, teneur *m* de livres

book/keep/ing *s* comptabilité *f*

book/ learn/ing *s* science *f* livresque

booklet ['buklɪt] *s* livret *m*; (*notebook*) cahier *m*; (*pamphlet*) brochure *f*

book/lov/er *s* bibliophile *mf*

book/mark/ *s* signet *m*

bookmobile ['bukmo,bil] *s* bibliobus *m*

book/plate/ *s* ex-libris *m*

book/rack/ *s* étagère *f*

book/ review/ *s* compte *m* rendu

book/sel/ler *s* libraire *m*

book/shelf/ *s* (*pl* -shelves) rayon *m*, étagère *f*

book/stand/ *s* étalage *m* de livres; (*in a station*) bibliothèque *f*

book/store/ *s* librairie *f*

book/ val/ue *s* (com) valeur *f* comptable

book/worm/ *s* ciron *m*; (fig) rat *m* de bibliothèque

boom [bum] *s* retentissement *m*, grondement *m*; (*rapid rise or growth*) vague *f* de prospérité, boom *m*; (naut) bout-dehors *m* || *intr* retentir; (com) prospérer || *interj* boum!

boomerang ['bumə,ræŋ] *s* boomerang *m*

boom/ town/ *s* ville *f* champignon

boon [bun] *s* bienfait *m*, avantage *m*; (archaic) don *m*, faveur *f*

boon/ compan/ion *s* joyeux compagnon *m*

boor [bur] *s* rustre *m*, goujat *m*

boost [bust] *s* relèvement *m*; (*help*)

aide *f* ‖ *tr* soulever par derrière; (*prices*) hausser; (*to praise*) faire la réclame pour

booster ['bustər] *s* (*enthusiastic backer*) réclamiste *mf*; (*go-getter*) homme *m* d'expédition, lanceur *m* d'affaires; (elec) survolteur *m*; (rok) booster *m*, propulseur *m*

boost′er rock′et *s* fusée *f* de lancement

boost′er shot′ *s* piqûre *f* de rappel

boot [but] *s* botte *f*, bottine *f*; **to boot** en sus; **to lick s.o.'s boots** (coll) lécher les bottes à qn ‖ *tr* botter

boot′black′ *s* cireur *m* de bottes

booth [buθ] *s* (*at fair*) baraque *f*; (*e.g., for telephoning*) cabine *f*

boot′leg′ *adj* (slang) clandestin, de contrebande ‖ *v* (*pret & pp* -legged; *ger* -legging) *tr* (slang) faire la contrebande de ‖ *intr* (slang) faire la contrebande

bootlegger ['but‚legər] *s* (slang) contrebandier *m*; (slang) contrebandier *m* d'alcool, bootlegger *m*

boot′leg′ging *s* contrebande *f*

boot′lick′ *tr* (coll) lécher les bottes à

boo•ty ['buti] *s* (*pl* -ties) butin *m*

booze [buz] *s* (coll) boisson *f* alcoolique ‖ *intr* (coll) s'adonner à la boisson

border ['bordər] *s* bord *m*, bordure *f*; (*of field and forest*; *of a piece of cloth*) lisière *f*; (*of a road*) marge *f*; (*of a country*) frontière *f*; (*edging*) galon *m*, bordé *m* ‖ *tr* border; (*a handkerchief*) lisérer ‖ *intr*—**to border on** confiner à, toucher à; (*a color*) tirer sur

bor′der-line′ *adj* indéterminé ‖ *s* ligne *f* de démarcation

bore [bor] *s* trou *m*, bordure *f*; (*of gun*) calibre *m*; (*of cannon*) âme *f*; (*of cylinder*) alésage *m*; (*nuisance*) ennui *m*; (*person*) raseur *m* ‖ *tr* percer; (*a cylinder*) aléser; (*to annoy*) ennuyer

boreal ['bori•əl] *adj* boréal

boredom ['bordəm] *s* ennui *m*

boring ['boriŋ] *adj* ennuyeux, rasant, rasoir ‖ *s* perçage *m*, percement *m*

born [born] *adj* né; **to be born** naître

borough ['bʌro] *s* (*town*) bourg *m*; circonscription *f* électorale

borrow ['baro], ['bɔro] *tr* emprunter; **to borrow from** emprunter à

borrower ['baro•ər], ['bɔro•ər] *s* emprunteur *m*

bor′rower's card′ *s* bulletin *m* de prêt

borrowing ['baro•iŋ], ['bɔro•iŋ] *s* emprunt *m*

borzoi ['bɔrzɔi] *s* lévrier *m* russe

bosom ['buzəm] *s* sein *m*, poitrine *f*; (*of the Church*) giron *m*

boss [bɔs], [bas] *s* patron *m*, chef *m*; (*foreman*) contremaître *m* ‖ *tr* diriger

boss•y ['bɔsi], ['basi] *adj* (*comp* -ier; *super* -iest) autoritaire; **to be bossy** jordonner

botanical [bə'tænɪkəl] *adj* botanique

botanist ['batənɪst] *s* botaniste *mf*

botany ['batəni] *s* botanique *f*

both [boθ] *adj* deux, e.g., **with both hands** à deux mains; les deux, e.g.,

both books les deux livres ‖ *pron* les deux, tous les deux ‖ *conj* à la fois; **both . . . and** aussi bien . . . que, e.g., **both in England and France** aussi bien en Angleterre qu'en France

bother ['baðər] *s* ennui *m* ‖ *tr* ennuyer, déranger ‖ *intr* se déranger

bothersome ['baðərsəm] *adj* importun

bottle ['batəl] *s* bouteille *f* ‖ *tr* mettre en bouteille, embouteiller

bot′tle cap′ *s* capsule *f*

bot′tled gas′ *s* gaz *m* en cylindre

bot′tle-neck′ *s* goulot *m*; (fig) embouteillage *m*

bot′tle o′pener *s* ouvre-bouteilles *m*

bottler ['batlər] *s* metteur *m* en bouteilles

bottling ['batliŋ] *s* mise *f* en bouteilles

bottom ['batəm] *s* fond *m*; **at the bottom of** au fond de; (*the page*) en bas de; **to reach the bottom of the barrel** (coll) être à fond de cale

bot′tom dol′lar *s* dernier sou *m*

bottomless ['batəmlɪs] *adj* sans fond

bough [bau] *s* rameau *m*

boulder ['boldər] *s* bloc *m*, rocher *m*

boulevard ['bulə‚vard] *s* boulevard *m*

bounce [bauns] *s* (*elasticity*) rebond *m*; (*of a ball*) rebond *m* ‖ *tr* faire rebondir; (slang) flanquer à la porte ‖ *intr* rebondir

bouncer ['baunsər] *s* (*in night club*) (coll) videur *m*, gorille *m*

bound [baund] *adj* (*tied*) lié; (*obliged*) obligé, tenu; **bound for** en partance pour ‖ *s* bond *m*, saut *m*; **bounds** bornes *fpl*, limites *fpl*; **out of bounds** hors jeu; (*prohibited*) défendu ‖ *tr* borner, limiter ‖ *intr* bondir

bound•a•ry ['baundəri] *s* (*pl* -ries) borne *f*, limite *f*

boun′dary stone′ *s* borne *f*

boundless ['baundlɪs] *adj* sans bornes

boun•ty ['baunti] *s* (*pl* -ties) largesse *f*; (*award*) prime *f*

bouquet [bu'ke], [bo'ke] *s* bouquet *m*

bout [baut] *s* rencontre *f*; (*e.g., of fever*) accès *m*; (sports) match *m*

bow [bau] *s* inclination *f*, révérence *f*; (*of ship*) avant *m*, proue *f* ‖ *tr* incliner, courber ‖ *intr* s'incliner, se courber; **to bow down** se prosterner; **to bow out** se retirer; **to bow to** saluer ‖ [bo] *s* (*weapon*) arc *m*; (bowknot) nœud *m*; (*of violin*) archet *m* ‖ *intr* (mus) tirer l'archet

bowdlerize ['baudlə‚raiz] *tr* expurger

bowel ['bau•əl] *s* intestin *m*, boyau *m*; **bowels** entrailles *fpl*

bow′el move′ment *s* selle *f*; **to have a bowel movement** aller à la selle

bower ['bau•ər] *s* berceau *m*, tonnelle *f*

bow′ie knife′ ['bo•i], ['bu•i] *s* couteau-poignard *m*

bowknot ['bo‚nat] *s* nœud *m* en forme de rose, rosette *f*

bowl [bol] *s* bol *m*, jatte *f*; (*of pipe*) fourneau *m*; (*of spoon*) cuilleron *m*; **bowls** (sports) boules *fpl* ‖ *tr* rouler, lancer; **to bowl over** (*to overturn*) (coll) renverser; (slang) déconcerter

|| *intr*—**to bowl along** rouler rapidement

bowlegged ['bo͵lɛgd], ['bo͵lɛgɪd] *adj* aux jambes arquées

bowler ['bolər] *s* (*hat*) chapeau *m* melon; (*in cricket*) lanceur *m*; (*in bowling*) joueur *m* de boules

bowling ['bolɪŋ] *s* jeu *m* de boules, jeu de quilles

bowl′ing al′ley *s* boulodrome *m*

bowl′ing green′ *s* boulingrin *m*

bowl′ing pin′ *s* quille *f*

bowsprit ['bausprɪt], ['bosprɪt] *s* beaupré *m*

bow′ tie′ [bo] *s* nœud *m* papillon

box [baks] *s* boîte *f*; (*law*) barre *f*; (*theat*) loge *f*, baignoire *f*; **box on the ear** claque *f* || *tr* emboîter; (*to hit*) boxer; **to box the compass** réciter la rose des vents || *intr* (*sports*) boxer

box′car′ *s* (rr) wagon *m* couvert

boxer ['baksər] *s* (*person*) boxeur *m*; (*dog*) boxer *m*

boxing ['baksɪŋ] *s* emboîtage *m*; (*sports*) boxe *f*

box′ of′fice *s* bureau *m* de location

box′-office flop′ *s* (slang) four *m*

box′-office hit′ *s* pièce *f* à succès

box′wood′ *s* buis *m*

boy [bɔɪ] *s* garçon *m*; (*little boy*) garçonnet *m*

boycott ['bɔɪkat] *s* boycottage *m* || *tr* boycotter

boy′ friend′ *s* ami *m*, camarade *m*; (*of a girl*) bon ami *m*

boyhood ['bɔɪhud] *s* enfance *f*, jeunesse *f*, adolescence *f*

boyish ['bɔɪ·ɪʃ] *adj* de garçon

boy′ scout′ *s* boy-scout *m*

bra [brɑ] *s* (coll) soutien-gorge *m*

brace [bres] *s* attache *f*, lien *m*; (*of game birds*) couple *f*; (*of pistols*) paire *f*; (*to impart a rotary movement to a bit*) vilebrequin *m*; (aer, aut) entretoise *f*; (mus, typ) accolade *f* || *tr* ancrer, entretoiser; (*to tone up*) fortifier, remonter || *intr*—**to brace up** prendre courage

brace′ and bit′ *s* vilebrequin *m*

bracelet ['breslɪt] *s* bracelet *m*

bracer ['bresər] *s* tonique *m*

bracing ['bresɪŋ] *adj* tonique, fortifiant

bracket ['brækɪt] *s* console *f*; (*grouping*) niveau *m*; (mach) chaise *f*; (typ) crochet *m* || *tr* grouper; (typ) mettre entre crochets

brackish ['brækɪʃ] *adj* saumâtre

brad [bræd] *s* semence *f*, clou *m* (sans tête)

brag [bræg] *s* (*pret & pp* **bragged**; *ger* **bragging**) *intr* se vanter

braggadoci·o [͵brægə'doʃɪ͵o] *s* (*pl* -os) fanfaronnade *f*; (*person*) fanfaron *m*

braggart ['brægərt] *s* vantard *m*

bragging ['brægɪŋ] *s* vanterie *f*

Brah·man ['brɑmən] *s* (*pl* -mans) brahmane *m*

braid [bred] *s* tresse *f*, passement *m*; (mil) galon *m*; **to trim . with braid** soutacher || *tr* passementer; (*the hair*) tresser

braille [brel] *s* braille *m*

brain [bren] *s* cerveau *m*; **brains** cervelle *f*; (fig) intelligence *f*, cerveau; **to rack one's brains** se creuser la cervelle || *tr* casser la tête à

brain′ child′ *s* idée *f* de génie

brainless ['brenlɪs] *adj* sans cervelle

brain′storm′ *s* accès *m* de folie; (coll) confusion *f* mentale; (coll) trouvaille *f*, bonne idée *f*

brain′wash′ *tr* (*by use of torture, drugs, etc.*) faire un lavage de cerveau à; (*by means of commercials, sales talk, etc.*) bourrer le crâne de

brain′wash′ing *s* lavage *m* de cerveau; bourrage *m* de crâne

brain′work′ *s* travail *m* intellectuel

brain·y ['breni] *adj* (*comp* -ier; *super* -iest) (coll) intelligent, à l'esprit vif

braise [brez] *tr* braiser, endauber

brais′ing pan′ *s* braisière *f*

brake [brek] *s* frein *m*; **to put on the brakes** serrer les freins || *tr & intr* freiner

brake′ drum′ *s* tambour *m* de frein

brake′ light′ *s* (aut) feu *m* de freinage

brake′ lin′ing *s* garniture *f* de frein

brake′man *s* (*pl* -men) serre-freins *m*

brake′ ped′al *s* pédale *f* de frein

brake′ shoe′ *s* sabot *m* de frein

bramble ['bræmbəl] *s* ronce *f*

bran [bræn] *s* son *m*, bran *m*

branch [bræntʃ] *s* branche *f*; (*of tree*) rameau *m*, branche; (*of a business*) succursale *f*, filiale *f* || *intr*—**to branch off** s'embrancher, se bifurquer; **to branch out** se ramifier

branch′ line′ *s* embranchement *m*

branch′ of′fice *s* succursale *f*; bureau *m* de quartier

branch′ road′ *s* embranchement *m*

brand [brænd] *s* (*trademark*) marque *f*; (*torch*) brandon *m*; (*coal*) tison *m*; (*on a criminal*) flétrissure *f*; (*on cattle*) marque || *tr* marquer au fer rouge, flétrir

brand′ing i′ron *s* fer *m* à flétrir

brandish ['brændɪʃ] *tr* brandir

brand′-new′ *adj* tout neuf, flambant neuf

bran·dy ['brændi] *s* (*pl* -dies) eau-de-vie *f*

brash [bræʃ] *adj* impertinent

brass [bræs], [brɑs] *s* laiton *m*; (mil) (coll) officiers *mpl* supérieurs, galonnard *m*; (slang) toupet *m*, culot *m*; **big brass** (slang) grosses légumes *fpl*; **the brasses** (mus) les cuivres

brass′ band′ *s* fanfare *f*, musique *f*

brassiere [brə'zɪr] *s* soutien-gorge *m*

brass′ knuck′les *spl* coup-de-poing *m*

brass′ tack′ *s* semence *f* (de tapissier); **to get down to brass tacks** (coll) en venir aux faits

brat [bræt] *s* (coll) gamin *m*, gosse *mf*

brava·do [brə'vado] *s* (*pl* -does or -dos) bravade *f*

brave [brev] *adj* brave || *s* guerrier *m* peau-rouge || *tr* braver

bravery ['brevəri] *s* bravoure *f*

bra·vo ['brɑvo] *s* (*pl* -vos) bravo *m* || *interj* bravo!

brawl [brɔl] s bagarre f, querelle f || intr se bagarrer, se quereller

brawler ['brɔlər] s bagarreur m

brawn [brɔn] s muscle m; muscles bien développés; (culin) fromage m de cochon

brawn·y ['brɔni] adj (comp -ier; super -iest) bien découplé, musclé

bray [bre] s braiment m || intr braire

braze [brez] tr braser

brazen ['brezən] adj effronté || tr—to brazen through mener à bonne fin avec une effronterie audacieuse

Brazil [brə'zɪl] s le Brésil

Brazilian [brə'zɪljən] adj brésilien || s (person) Brésilien m

Brazil' nut' s noix f du Brésil

breach [britʃ] s (in a wall) brèche f; (violation) infraction f || tr ouvrir une brèche dans

breach' of con'tract s rupture f de contrat

breach' of prom'ise s rupture f de fiançailles

breach' of the peace' s attentat m contre l'ordre public

breach' of trust' s abus m de confiance

bread [brɛd] s pain m || tr paner, gratiner

bread' and but'ter s (fig) gagne-pain m

bread'bas'ket s panier m à pain, corbeille f à pain

bread'board' s planche f à pain

bread' crumbs' spl chapelure f

breaded adj (culin) au gratin

bread'ed veal' cut'let s escalope f panée de veau

bread'fruit' s fruit m à pain; (tree) arbre m à pain, jacquier m

bread' knife' s couteau m à pain

breadth [brɛdθ] s largeur f

bread'win'ner s soutien m de famille

break [brek] s rupture f; (of an object) brisure f, cassure f; (in time or space) trou m, pause f; (slang) chance f || v (pret broke [brok]; pp broken) tr rompre, briser, casser; (a law) violer; (the heart) fendre; (one's word) manquer à; (a will; a soldier by reducing his rank) casser; to break bread rompre le pain; to break down (for analysis) analyser; to break in (a door) enfoncer; (a new car) roder || intr rompre, briser, se briser; (said of clouds) se dissiper; (said of waves) déferler; to break down avoir une panne

breakable ['brekəbəl] adj fragile

breakage ['brekɪdʒ] s casse f

break'down' s (stoppage) arrêt m; (disaster) débâcle f; (of health) épuisement m; (of negotiations) rupture f; (for analysis) analyse f, ventilation f; (mach) panne f

breaker ['brekər] s brisant m

breakfast ['brɛkfəst] s petit déjeuner m || intr prendre le petit déjeuner

break'fast food' s céréales fpl (pour le petit déjeuner)

break'neck' adj vertigineux; at breakneck speed à tombeau ouvert

break' of day' s point m du jour

break'through' s (mil) percée f; (fig) découverte f sensationnelle

break'up' s dissolution f; écroulement m; (in health) abattement m

break'wa'ter s digue f, brise-lames m

breast [brɛst] s sein m; (of cooked chicken) blanc m; to make a clean breast of it se déboutonner

breast'bone' s sternum m; (of fowl) bréchet m

breast' feed'ing s allaitement m

breast'plate' s (of high priest) pectoral m; (of armor) plastron m

breast'stroke' s brasse f

breast'work' s (mil) parapet m

breath [brɛθ] s haleine f, souffle m; last breath dernier soupir m; out of breath hors d'haleine

breathe [brɪð] tr & intr respirer, souffler; not to breathe a word ne pas souffler mot

breathing ['brɪðɪŋ] s souffle m

breath'ing space' s répit m

breathless ['brɛθlɪs] adj haletant, hors d'haleine; inanimé

breath'tak'ing adj émouvant, sensationnel

breech [britʃ] s culasse f

breech'es bu'oy s (naut) bouée-culotte f

breed [brid] s race f || v (pret & pp bred [brɛd]) tr engendrer; (e.g., cattle) élever || intr se reproduire

breeder ['bridər] s éleveur m

breeding ['bridɪŋ] s (of animals) élevage m; good breeding savoir-vivre m

breeze [briz] s brise f

breez·y ['brizi] adj (comp -ier; super -iest) aéré; (coll) désinvolte, dégagé

brethren ['brɛðrɪn] spl frères mpl

Breton ['brɛtən] adj breton; s (language) breton m; (person) Breton m

breviary ['brivi‚ɛri], ['brɛvi‚ɛri] s (pl -ies) (eccl) bréviaire m

brevi·ty ['brɛvɪti] s (pl -ties) brièveté f

brew [bru] s breuvage m, infusion f || tr infuser; (beer) brasser || intr s'infuser

brewer ['bru·ər] s brasseur m

brew'er's yeast' s levure f de bière

brewer·y ['bru·əri] s (pl -ies) brasserie f

brewing ['bru·ɪŋ] s brassage m

bribe [braɪb] s pot-de-vin m || tr corrompre, suborner, soudoyer

briber·y ['braɪbəri] s (pl -ies) corruption f, subornation f

brick [brɪk] s brique f || tr briqueter

brick'bat' s brocard m; to hurl brickbats lancer des brocards

brick'lay'er s briqueteur m

brick'work' s briquetage m

brick'yard' s briqueterie f

bridal ['braɪdəl] adj nuptial

bride [braɪd] s (nouvelle) mariée f

bride'groom' s (nouveau) marié m

brides'maid' s demoiselle f d'honneur

bride'-to-be' s future femme f

bridge [brɪdʒ] s pont m; (cards, dentistry) bridge m; (naut) passerelle f; to burn one's bridges couper les ponts || tr construire un pont sur; to bridge a gap combler une lacune

bridge'head' s (mil) tête f de pont

bridle ['braɪdəl] s bride f; (fig) frein m || tr brider; (fig) freiner || intr se raidir

bri'dle path' s piste f cavalière

brief [brif] adj bref || s résumé m; (law) dossier m; **briefs** slip m; **to hold a brief for** plaider pour || tr mettre au courant

brief'case' s serviette f

briefing ['brifɪŋ] s briefing m, renseignements mpl tactiques

briefly ['brifli] adv bref, brièvement, en substance

brier ['braɪ·ər] s ronce f

brig [brɪg] s prison f navale; (ship) brick m

brigade [brɪ'ged] s brigade f

brigadier [,brɪgə'dɪr] s général m de brigade

brigand ['brɪgənd] s brigand m

brigantine ['brɪgən,tin], ['brɪgən,taɪn] s brigantin m

bright [braɪt] adj brillant; (day) clair; (color) vif; (person) (fig) brillant

brighten ['braɪtən] tr faire briller; égayer, réjouir || intr s'éclaircir

bright' ide'a s (coll) idée f lumineuse

brightness ['braɪtnɪs] s éclat m, clarté f; (of mind) vivacité f

brilliance ['brɪljəns] or **brilliancy** ['brɪljənsi] s brillant m, éclat m

brilliant ['brɪljənt] adj & s brillant m

brim [brɪm] s bord m || v (pret & pp brimmed; ger brimming; intr—to brim over (with) déborder (de)

brimful ['brɪm,ful] adj à ras bords

brim'stone' s soufre m

brine [braɪn] s saumure f

bring [brɪŋ] v (pret & pp brought [brɔt]) tr apporter; (a person) amener, conduire; **to bring back** rapporter; (a person) ramener; **to bring down** (baggage) descendre; (with a gun) abattre; **to bring in** entrer, introduire; **to bring out** faire ressortir; (e.g., a book) publier; **to bring together** réunir; **to bring to pass** causer, opérer; **to bring up** éduquer, élever; (baggage) monter

bring'ing-up' s éducation f

brink [brɪŋk] s bord m

brisk [brɪsk] adj vif, actif, animé

brisket ['brɪskɪt] s (culin) poitrine f

bristle ['brɪsəl] s soie f; (of brush) poil m || tr hérisser || intr se hérisser

bristling ['brɪslɪŋ] adj hérissé

Bris'tol board' ['brɪstəl] s bristol m

Britain ['brɪtən] s Grande-Bretagne f; la Grande-Bretagne

British ['brɪtɪʃ] adj britannique || the British les Britanniques

Britisher ['brɪtɪʃər] s Britannique mf

Briton ['brɪtən] s Britannique mf

Brittany ['brɪtəni] s Bretagne f; la Bretagne

brittle ['brɪtəl] adj fragile, cassant

broach [brotʃ] s broche f; (for tapping casks) mèche f à percer || tr (e.g., a keg of beer) mettre en perce; (a subject) entamer

broad [brɔd] adj (wide) large; (immense) vaste; (mind, views) libéral, tolérant; (accent) fort, prononcé; (use, sense) répandu, général; (daylight) plein; (joke, story) grossier, salé

broad'-backed' adj d'une belle carrure

broad'brimmed' adj à larges bords

broad'cast' adj diffusé; (rad) radiodiffusé || s (rad) radiodiffusion f, émission f || v (pret & pp -cast) tr diffuser, répandre || (pret & pp -cast or -casted) tr radiodiffuser || intr (rad) émettre

broad'casting sta'tion s station f d'émission

broad'cloth' s popeline f

broaden ['brodən] tr élargir || intr s'élargir

broad'-gauge' adj à voie large

broad' jump' s saut m en longueur

broad'-mind'ed adj à l'esprit large

broad'side' s bordée f; (typ) placard m

brocade [bro'ked] s brocart m || tr brocher

broccoli ['brokəli] s brocoli m

brochure [bro'ʃur] s brochure f

brogue [brog] s accent m irlandais; (shoe) soulier m grossier

broil [brɔɪl] s grillade f; (quarrel) rixe f || tr & intr griller

broiler ['brɔɪlər] s gril m

broke [brok] adj (slang) fauché

broken ['brokən] adj brisé, cassé; (promise; ranks; beam) rompu

brok'en-down' adj délabré; en panne

bro'ken-heart'ed adj au cœur brisé

broker ['brokər] s courtier m

brokerage ['brokərɪdʒ] s courtage m

bromide ['bromaɪd] s bromure m; (coll) platitude f

bromine ['bromin] s brome m

bronchial ['brɑŋkɪ·əl] adj bronchique

bron'chial tube' s bronche f

bronchitis [brɑŋ'kaɪtɪs] s bronchite f

bron·co ['brɑŋko] s (pl -cos) cheval m sauvage

bronze [brɑnz] adj bronzé || s bronze m || tr bronzer || intr se bronzer

brooch [brotʃ], [brutʃ] s broche f

brood [brud] s couvée f; (of children) nichée f || intr couver; (to sulk) broyer du noir; **to brood over** songer sombrement à

brood' hen' s couveuse f

brood'mare' s poulinière f

brook [bruk] s ruisseau m || tr—to brook no ne pas tolérer

brooklet ['bruklɪt] s ruisseau m

broom [brum], [brum] s balai m; (bot) genêt m

broom'stick' s manche m à balai

broth [brɔθ], [brɑθ] s bouillon m, consommé m

brothel ['brɑθəl], ['brɑðəl] s bordel m

brother ['brɑðər] s frère m

broth'er-hood' s fraternité f

broth'er-in-law' s (pl brothers-in-law) beau-frère m

brotherly ['brɑðərli] adj fraternel || adv fraternellement

brow [brau] s (forehead) front m;

(*eyebrow*) sourcil *m*; **to knit one's brow** froncer le sourcil

brow'beat' *v* (*pret* **-beat**; *pp* **-beaten**) *tr* rabrouer, brusquer

brown [braun] *adj* marron; (*paper*) gris; (*bread*) bis; (*shoes*) jaune; (*butter*) roux, noir; (*hair*) brun, châtain || *tr* brunir; (*culin*) rissoler, dorer

brownish ['braunɪʃ] *adj* brunâtre

brown' stud'y *s*—**in a brown study** absorbé dans des méditations

brown' sug'ar *s* cassonade *f*, sucre *m* brut

browse [brauz] *intr* (*said of animals*) brouter; (*said of booklovers*) butiner; (*said of customers for secondhand books*) bouquiner

bruise [bruz] *s* (*on body or fruit*) meurtrissure *f*; (*on body*) contusion *f* || *tr* meurtrir, contusionner

bruiser ['bruzər] *s* (coll) costaud *m*

bruit [brut] *tr* ébruiter; **to bruit about** répandre

brunette [bru'nɛt] *adj* & *s* brune *f*, brunette *f*

brunt [brʌnt] *s* choc *m*, assaut *m*; **to bear the brunt of** (fig) faire tous les frais de

brush [brʌʃ] *s* brosse *f*; (*countryside*) brousse *f*; (elec) balai *m* || *tr* brosser; **to brush aside** écarter || *intr*—**to brush against** frôler; **to brush up on** repasser, rafraîchir

brush'-off' *s* (slang) affront *m*; **to give a brush-off to** (slang) expédier avec rudesse

brush'wood' *s* broussailles *fpl*, brindilles *fpl*

brusque [brʌsk] *adj* brusque

Brussels ['brʌsəlz] *s* Bruxelles *f*

Brus'sels sprouts' *mpl* chou *m* de Bruxelles

brutal ['brutəl] *adj* brutal

brutal·i·ty [bru'tælɪti] *s* (*pl* **-ties**) brutalité *f*

brute [brut] *adj* brutal || *s* bête *f*, animal *m*; (*person*) brute *f*, animal *m*

brutish ['brutɪʃ] *adj* grossier, brut, brutal

bubble ['bʌbəl] *s* bulle *f* || *intr* bouillonner; (*said of drink*) pétiller; **to bubble over** déborder

bub'ble gum' *s* gomme *f* à claquer

bub·bly ['bʌbli] *adj* (*comp* **-blier**; *super* **-bliest**) bouillonnant, gazeux

bubon'ic plague' [bju'bɑnɪk] *s* peste *f* bubonique

buccaneer [,bʌkə'nɪr] *s* boucanier *m*

buck [bʌk] *s* (*red deer*) cerf *m*; (*fallow deer*) daim *m*; (*roebuck*) chevreuil *m*; (slang) dollar *m*; the male of many animals such as: (*goat*) bouc *m*; (*rabbit*) lapin *m*; (*hare*) lièvre *m*; **to pass the buck** (coll) renvoyer la balle || *tr*—**to buck off** (*a rider*) désarçonner; **to buck up** (coll) remonter le courage de || *intr*—**to buck up** (coll) reprendre courage

bucket ['bʌkɪt] *s* seau *m*; **to kick the bucket** (slang) casser sa pipe

buck'et seat' *s* siège *m* baquet

buckle ['bʌkəl] *s* boucle *f* || *tr* boucler || *intr* arquer, gauchir; **to buckle down** s'appliquer

buck' pri'vate *s* simple soldat *m*

buckram ['bʌkrəm] *s* bougran *m*

buck'saw' *s* scie *f* à bûches

buck'shot' *s* gros plomb *m*

buck'tooth' *s* (*pl* **-teeth**) dent *f* saillante

buck'wheat' *s* sarrasin *m*

buck'wheat cake' *s* crêpe *f* de sarrasin

bud [bʌd] *s* bouton *m*, bourgeon *m* || *v* (*pret* & *pp* **budded**; *ger* **budding**) *intr* boutonner, bourgeonner

Buddhism ['budɪzəm] *s* bouddhisme *m*

Buddhist ['budɪst] *adj* & *s* bouddhiste *mf*

budding ['bʌdɪŋ] *adj* en bouton; (*beginning*) en germe, naissant

bud·dy ['bʌdi] *s* (*pl* **-dies**) (coll) copain *m*

budge [bʌdʒ] *tr* faire bouger || *intr* bouger

budget ['bʌdʒɪt] *s* budget *m* || *tr* comptabiliser, inscrire au budget

budgetary ['bʌdʒɪ,tɛri] *adj* budgétaire

buff [bʌf] *adj* (*color*) chamois || *s* (coll) fanatique *mf*, enthousiaste *mf* || *tr* polir, émeuler

buffa·lo ['bʌfə,lo] *s* (*pl* **-loes** or **-los**) bison *m*; (*water buffalo*; *Cape buffalo*) buffle *m*

buffer ['bʌfər] *s* (mach) brunissoir *m*; (rr) (*on cars*) tampon *m*; (rr) (*at end of track*) butoir *m*

buff'er state' *s* état *m* tampon

buff'er zone' *s* zone *f* tampon

buffet [bu'fe] *s* buffet *m* || ['bʌfɪt] *tr* frapper (violemment)

buffet' lunch' [bu'fe] *s* lunch *m*

buffoon [bə'fun] *s* bouffon *m*

buffooner·y [bə'funəri] *s* (*pl* **-ies**) bouffonnerie *f*

bug [bʌɡ] *s* insecte *m*; (germ) microbe *m*; (*in a mechanical device*) vice *m*, défaut *m*; (coll) idée *f* fixe, lutin *m*; (Brit) punaise *f*; **he's a bug for . . .** (coll) il est fou de . . . || *v* (*pret* & *pp* **bugged**; *ger* **bugging**) *tr* (slang) installer une table d'écoute dans; installer un microphone dans; (*to annoy*) (slang) embêter, emmerder

bug'bear' *s* épouvantail *m*, croquemitaine *m*; (*pet peeve*) bête *f* noire

bug'-eyed' *adj* (slang) aux yeux saillants

bug·gy ['bʌɡi] *adj* (*comp* **-gier**; *super* **-giest**) infesté d'insectes; infesté; (slang) fou || *s* (*pl* **-gies**) buggy *m* à quatre roues; (*two-wheeled*) buggy, boguet *m*

bug'house' *s* (slang) cabanon *m*

bugle ['bjuɡəl] *s* (bot) bugle *f*; (mus) clairon *m* || *tr* & *intr* claironner

bu'gle call' *s* sonnerie *f* de clairon

bugler ['bjuɡlər] *s* clairon *m*

build [bɪld] *s* structure *f*; (*of human body*) taille *f*, charpente *f* || *v* (*pret* & *pp* **built** [bɪlt]) *tr* bâtir, construire

builder ['bɪldər] *s* constructeur *m*; (*of bridges, roads, etc.*) entrepreneur *m*

building ['bɪldɪŋ] *s* immeuble *m*, bâtiment *m*, édifice *m*

build'ing and loan' associa'tion *s* société *f* de prêt à la construction

build'ing lot' *s* terrain *m* à bâtir

built'-in' *adj* incorporé

built'-up' *adj* aggloméré; *(heel)* renforcé; *(land)* bâti

bulb [bʌlb] *s* bulbe *m*; *(of vaporizer)* poire *f*; *(bot)* oignon *m*; *(elec)* ampoule *f*

bulbous ['bʌlbəs] *adj* bulbeux

Bulgaria [bʌl'gɛrɪ·ə] *s* Bulgarie *f*; la Bulgarie

Bulgarian [bʌl'gɛrɪ·ən] *adj* bulgare || *s (language)* bulgare *m*; *(person)* Bulgare *m*

bulge [bʌldʒ] *s* bosse *f*, bombement *m*; *(mil)* saillant *m* || *tr* bourrer, gonfler || *intr* faire une bosse, bomber

bulk [bʌlk] *s* masse *f*, volume *m*: **in bulk** en bloc; *(com)* en vrac || *tr* entasser (en vrac) || *intr* tenir de la place; **to bulk large** devenir important

bulk'head' *s* (naut) cloison *f*

bulk·y ['bʌlki] *adj (comp* -ier*; super* -iest*)* volumineux

bull [bul] *s* taureau *m*; *(on the stock exchange)* haussier *m*, spéculateur *m* à la hausse; *(eccl)* bulle *f*; *(policeman)* (slang) flic *m*, vache *f*; *(exaggeration)* (slang) blague *f*, boniment *m*, chiqué *m*; **like a bull in a china shop** comme un éléphant dans un magasin de porcelaine; **to take the bull by the horns** (fig) prendre le taureau par les cornes || *tr*—**to bull the market** jouer à la hausse

bull'dog' *s* bouledogue *m*

bull'doze' *tr* passer au bulldozer; *(coll)* intimider

bulldozer ['bul,dozər] *s* chasse-terre *m*, bulldozer *m*

bullet ['bulɪt] *s* balle *f*

bulletin ['bulɪtɪn] *s* bulletin *m*; *(e.g., of a university)* annuaire *m*

bul'letin board' *s* tableau *m* d'affichage

bul'let-proof' *adj* à l'épreuve des balles || *tr* blinder

bul'let-proof vest' *s* gilet *m* pare-balles

bull'fight' *s* course *f* de taureaux

bull'fight'er *s* torero *m*

bull'fight'ing *s* tauromachie *f*

bull'finch' *s* bouvreuil *m*

bull'frog' *s* grenouille *f* d'Amérique

bull'head' *s* (ichth) chabot *m*, cabot *m*; *(miller's-thumb)* meunier *m*, cabot *m*

bull'head'ed *adj* entêté

bullion ['buljən] *s (of gold)* or *m*; *(of silver)* argent *m*; encaisse *f* métallique, lingots *mpl* d'or, lingots d'argent; *(on uniform)* cordonnet *m* d'or, cordonnet d'argent

bull' mar'ket *s* marché *m* à la hausse

bullock ['bulək] *s* bœuf *m*

bull' pen' *s* toril *m*; *(jail)* poste *m* de détention préventive

bull'ring' *s* arène *f*, arène pour les courses de taureaux

bull's-eye' *s* mouche *f*; **to hit the bull's-eye** faire mouche

bull's-eye win'dow *s* œil-de-bœuf *m*

bull'ter'rier *s* bull-terrier *m*

bul·ly ['buli] *adj* (coll) épatant || *s (pl* -lies*)* brute *f*, brutal *m*; *(at school)* brimeur *m*, tyranneau *m* || *v (pret & pp* -lied*) tr* brutaliser, malmener; *(at school)* brimer, tyranniser

bulrush ['bul,rʌʃ] *s* jonc *m* des marais

bulwark ['bulwərk] *s* rempart *m*; (naut) pavois *m* || *tr* garnir de remparts; (fig) protéger

bum [bʌm] *adj* (slang) moche, de camelote || *s* (slang) clochard *m* || *v (pret & pp* bummed*; ger* bumming*) tr & intr* (slang) écornifler

bumble ['bʌmbəl] *tr* bâcler || *intr (to stumble)* trébucher; *(in speaking)* bafouiller; *(said of bee)* bourdonner

bum'ble-bee' *s* bourdon *m*

bump [bʌmp] *s* choc *m*; *(protuberance)* bosse *f*; *(of car on rough road)* cahot *m* || *tr* cogner, tamponner, heurter; **to bump off** *(to kill)* (slang) buter || *intr* se cogner; **to bump along** *(said of car)* cahoter; **to bump into** buter contre, choquer

bumper ['bʌmpər] *adj* exceptionnel || *s* (aut) pare-chocs *m*; *(rr)* tampon *m*

bumpkin ['bʌmpkɪn] *s* péquenot *m*, rustre *m*

bumptious ['bʌmp/əs] *adj* outrecuidant

bump·y ['bʌmpi] *adj (comp* -ier*; super* -iest*)* bosselé; *(road)* cahoteux

bun [bʌn] *s* brioche *f*, petit pain *m*; *(hair)* chignon *m*

bunch [bʌntʃ] *s (of bananas)* régime *m*; *(of flowers)* bouquet *m*; *(of grapes)* grappe *f*; *(of keys)* trousseau *m*; *(of people)* groupe *m*, bande *f*; *(of ribbons)* flot *m*; *(of twigs)* paquet *m*; *(on body)* bosse *f* || *tr* grouper || *intr* se serrer

buncombe ['bʌŋkəm] *s* (coll) baliver-nes *fpl*, sornettes *fpl*

bundle ['bʌndəl] *s* paquet *m*; *(of banknotes, papers, etc.)* liasse *f* || *tr* empaqueter, mettre en paquet; **to bundle up** *(in warm clothing)* emmitoufler || *intr*—**to bundle up** s'emmitoufler

bung [bʌŋ] *s* bonde *f* || *tr* mettre une bonde à

bungalow ['bʌŋgə,lo] *s* bungalow *m*

bung'hole' *s* bonde *f*

bungle ['bʌŋgəl] *s* gâchis *m*, bousillage *m* || *tr* saboter, bousiller || *intr* saboter

bungler ['bʌŋglər] *s* gâcheur *m*, bousilleur *m*

bungling ['bʌŋglɪŋ] *adj* gauche, maladroit || *s* maladresse *f*

bunion ['bʌnjən] *s* oignon *m* (au pied)

bunk [bʌŋk] *s* couchette *f*, (slang) ba-livernes *fpl*, sornettes *fpl* || *intr* (coll) se coucher

bunk' bed' *s* (naut) cadre *m*

bunker ['bʌŋkər] *s* (golf) banquette *f*; (naut) soute *f*

bun·ny ['bʌni] *s (pl* -nies*)* petit lapin *m*

bunting ['bʌntɪŋ] *s* drapeaux *mpl*; *(cloth)* étamine *f*; *(orn)* bruant *m*

buoy [bɔɪ], ['bu·i] *s* bouée *f* || *tr*—**to buoy up** faire flotter; (fig) soutenir

buoyancy ['bɔɪ·ənsɪ], ['bujənsɪ] s flottabilité f
buoyant ['bɔɪ·ənt], ['bujənt] adj flottant; (cheerful) plein d'allant, plein de ressort
bur [bʌr] s (of chestnut) bogue f; (ragged metal edge) bavure f, barbe f
burble ['bʌrbəl] s murmure m || intr murmurer
burden ['bʌrdən] s fardeau m, charge f; (mus) refrain m || tr charger
burdensome ['bʌrdənsəm] adj onéreux
burdock ['bʌrdɑk] s bardane f
bureau ['bjuro] s commode f, chiffonier m; (office) bureau m
bureaucra·cy [bju'rɑkrəsɪ] s (pl -cies) bureaucratie f
bureaucrat ['bjurə,kræt] s bureaucrate mf
bureaucratic [,bjurə'krætɪk] adj bureaucratique
bu'reau of vi'tal statis'tics s bureau m de l'état civil
burg [bʌrg] s (coll) hameau m, patelin m; (coll) ville f
burglar ['bʌrglər] s cambrioleur m
bur'glar alarm' s signalisateur m anti-vol, sonnette f d'alarme
burglarize ['bʌrglə,raɪz] tr cambrioler
bur'glar-proof' adj incrochetable
burglar·y ['bʌrgləri] s (pl -ies) cambriolage m
Burgundian [bər'gʌndɪ·ən] adj bourguignon || s (dialect) bourguignon m; (person) Bourguignon m
Burgundy ['bʌrgəndɪ] s Bourgogne f; la Bourgogne || **burgun·dy** s (-dies) (wine) bourgogne m
burial ['berɪ·əl] s enterrement m, inhumation f
bur'ial ground' s cimetière m
burlap ['bʌrlæp] s toile f d'emballage, serpillière f
burlesque [bər'lesk] adj & s burlesque m || tr parodier
burlesque' show' s music-hall m
bur·ly ['bʌrlɪ] adj (comp -lier; super -liest) solide, costaud
Burma ['bʌrmə] s Birmanie f; la Birmanie
Bur·mese [bər'miz] adj birman || s (pl -mese) (language) birman m; (person) Birman m
burn [bʌrn] s brûlure f || v (pret & pp burned or burnt [bʌrnt]) tr & intr brûler; **to burn out** (elec) griller
burner ['bʌrnər] s brûleur m; (using gas) bec m; (of a stove) feu m
burning ['bʌrnɪŋ] adj brûlant; (in flames) en feu || s brûlure f; (fire) incendie m
burnish ['bʌrnɪʃ] tr brunir, polir
burrow ['bʌro] s terrier m || tr creuser || intr se terrer
bursar ['bʌrsər] s économe m
burst [bʌrst] s éclat m, explosion f || v (pret & pp burst) tr faire éclater; (a balloon) crever; (a boiler; one's buttons) faire sauter || intr éclater, exploser; (said of tire) crever; **to burst into tears** fondre en larmes; **to burst out laughing** éclater de rire

bur·y ['berɪ] v (pret & pp -ied) tr enterrer, ensevelir; (e.g., pirate treasure) enfouir
bus [bʌs] s (pl busses or buses) autobus m; (interurban or sightseeing) car m, autocar m || v (pret & pp bused or bussed; ger busing or bussing) tr transporter en autobus
bus'boy' s aide-serveur m
bush [buʃ] s buisson m; (shrub) arbuste m; (in Africa and Australia) brousse f; **to beat around the bush** tourner autour du pot, tortiller
bushed [buʃt] adj (coll) éreinté
bushel ['buʃəl] s boisseau m
bushing ['buʃɪŋ] s manchon m, douille f, bague f, coussinet m
bush·y ['buʃɪ] adj (comp -ier; super -iest) (countryside) buissonneux; (hair) touffu; (eyebrows) broussailleux
business ['bɪznɪs] adj commercial || s affaires fpl; (subject) sujet m; (theat) jeux mpl de scène; **it's none of your business** cela ne vous regarde pas; **mind your own business!** occupez-vous de vos affaires!, faites votre métier!; **to mean business** (coll) ne pas plaisanter; **to send about one's business** envoyer paître
busi'ness dis'trict s quartier m commerçant
busi'ness hours' s heures fpl d'ouverture
busi'ness house' s maison f de commerce
busi'ness·like' adj pratique; (manner, transaction) sérieux
busi'ness·man' s (pl -men') homme m d'affaires; **big businessman** grand industriel m, chef m d'industrie
busi'ness man'ager s directeur m commercial
busi'ness reply' card' s carte f postale avec réponse payée
busi'ness suit' s complet m veston
busi'ness·wom'an s (pl -wom'en) femme f d'affaires
buskin ['bʌskɪn] s brodequin m
bus' sta'tion s gare f routière
bus' stop' s arrêt m d'autobus
bust [bʌst] s buste m; (of woman) gorge f, buste; (slang) faillite f || tr (mil) limoger; (slang) casser || intr (slang) échouer
busting ['bʌstɪŋ] s (mil) cassation f
bustle ['bʌsəl] s remue-ménage m, affairement m, branle-bas m || intr se remuer, s'affairer
bustling ['bʌslɪŋ] adj affairé
bus·y ['bɪzɪ] adj (comp -ier; super -iest) occupé || v (pret & pp -ied) tr —**to busy oneself with** s'occuper de
bus'y·bod'y s (pl -ies) officieux m
bus'y sig'nal s (telp) signal m de ligne occupée
but [bʌt] adv seulement; ne . . . que, e.g., **to have nothing but trouble** n'avoir que des ennuis; **but for** sans; **but for that** à part cela || prep sauf, excepté; **all but** presque || conj mais
butcher ['butʃər] s boucher m || tr (an

animal for meat) abattre, dépecer; (*to massacre; to bungle*) massacrer
butch′er knife′ *s* couperet *m*, coutelas *m* (de boucher)
butch′er shop′ *s* boucherie *f*
butler ['bʌtlər] *s* maître *m* d'hôtel, intendant *m*
butt [bʌt] *s* bout *m*; (*cask*) futaille *f*; (*of a gun*) crosse *f*; (*of a cigarette*) mégot *m*; (*of a joke*) souffre-douleur *m*, plastron *m*; (*blow*) coup *m* de tête, coup de corne; (*slang*) postérieur *m*, derrière *m* ‖ *tr* (*like a goat*) donner un coup de corne à ‖ *intr*— **to butt up against** buter contre; **to butt in** (coll) intervenir sans façon
butte [bjut] *s* butte *f*, tertre *m*, puy *m*
butt′ end′ *s* gros bout *m*
butter ['bʌtər] *s* beurre *m* ‖ *tr* beurrer; **to butter up** (coll) passer de la pommade à, pateliner
but′ter-cup′ *s* renoncule *f*, bouton-d'or *m*
but′ter dish′ *s* beurrier *m*, beurrière *f*
but′ter-fat′ *s* crème *f*
but′ter-fin′gered *adj* maladroit
but′ter-fin′gers *s* brise-tout *mf*
but′ter-fly′ *s* (*pl* **-flies**) papillon *m*
but′ter knife′ *s* couteau *m* à beurre
but′ter-milk′ *s* babeurre *m*
but′ter-scotch′ *s* caramel *m* au beurre
buttocks ['bʌtəks] *spl* fesses *fpl*
button ['bʌtən] *s* bouton *m* ‖ *tr* boutonner
but′ton-hole′ *s* boutonnière *f* ‖ *tr* (coll) retenir (*qqn*) par le pan de sa veste
but′ton-hook′ *s* tire-bouton *m*
buttress ['bʌtrɪs] *s* contrefort *m* ‖ *tr* arc-bouter; (fig) étayer
buxom ['bʌksəm] *adj* plantureuse
buy [baɪ] *s*—**a good buy** (coll) une bonne affaire ‖ *v* (*pret & pp* **bought** [bɔt]) *tr* acheter; (*a ticket*) prendre; **to buy a drink** for payer un verre à; **to buy back** racheter; **to buy from** acheter à or de; **to buy out** (*a part-*

ner) désintéresser; **to buy s.o. off** se débarrasser de qn, racheter qn; **to buy up** accaparer
buyer ['baɪ·ər] *s* acheteur *m*
buzz [bʌz] *s* bourdonnement *m*; **to give s.o. a buzz** (*on the telephone*) (coll) passer un coup de fil à ‖ *tr* (aer) survoler à basse altitude ‖ *intr* bourdonner
buzzard ['bʌzərd] *s* buse *f*
buzz′ bomb′ *s* bombe *f* volante
buzzer ['bʌzər] *s* trembleur *m*
buzz′ saw′ *s* scie *f* circulaire
by [baɪ] *adv* près, auprès; (*aside*) de côté; **by and by** tout à l'heure, sous peu; **by and large** généralement parlant ‖ *prep* par; (*near*) près de; **by a head** (*taller*) d'une tête; **by day** pendant la journée; **by far** de beaucoup; **by Monday** d'ici à lundi; **by profession** de profession; **by the way** à propos; **to be followed** (**loved,** etc.) **by** être suivi (aimé, etc.) de
by-and-by ['baɪ·ən'baɪ] *s* proche avenir *m*; **in the sweet by-and-by** à la Saint-Glinglin
by′gone′ *adj* d'autrefois, passé
by′law′ *s* ordonnance *f*, règlement *m*
by′-line′ *s* signature *f* de journaliste
by′-pass′ *s* déviation *f*; (elec) dérivation *f* ‖ *tr* éviter, contourner; (mach) amener or placer en dérivation
by′-play′ *s* (theat) jeu *m* en aparté
by′-prod′uct *s* sous-produit *m*
by′-road′ *s* chemin *m* détourné
bystander ['baɪ‚stændər] *s* spectateur *m*, assistant *m*
by′way′ *s* chemin *m* écarté, voie *f* indirecte
by′word′ *s* dicton *m*, proverbe *m*; objet *m* de dérision
Byzantine ['bɪzən‚tin], [bɪ'zæntin] *adj & s* byzantin *m*
Byzantium [bɪ'zænʃ ɪ·əm], [bɪ'zæntɪ·əm] *s* Byzance *f*

C

C, c [si] *s* IIIᵉ lettre de l'alphabet
cab [kæb] *s* taxi *m*; (*of locomotive or truck*) cabine *f*; (*hansom*) fiacre *m*, cab *m*
cabaret [‚kæbə're] *s* boîte *f* de nuit, cabaret *m*
cabbage ['kæbɪdʒ] *s* chou *m*
cab′driv′er *s* chauffeur *m* de taxi
cabin ['kæbɪn] *s* case *f*, cabane *f*; (*of ship or airplane*) cabine *f*
cab′in boy′ *s* (naut) mousse *m*
cabinet ['kæbɪnɪt] *s* cabinet *m*; (*cupboard; radio cabinet*) meuble *m*; meuble à tiroirs; (*of professional men*) étude *f*, cabinet; (*of officers*) cabinet, bureau *m* directoire, comité *m*, conseil *m*

cab′inet-mak′er *s* ébéniste *m*, menuisier *m*
cab′inet mem′ber *s* ministre *m*
cable ['kebəl] *s* câble *m* ‖ *tr & intr* câbler
ca′ble car′ *s* funiculaire *m*, téléférique *m*
ca′ble-gram′ *s* câblogramme *m*
ca′ble ship′ *s* câblier *m*
ca′ble's length′ *s* encablure *f*
caboose [kə'bus] *s* (naut) coquerie *f*; (rr) fourgon *m* de queue, wagon *m* du personnel
cab′stand′ *s* station *f* de taxi
cache [kæʃ] *s* cachette *f*, cache *f* ‖ *tr* mettre dans une cachette, cacher
cachet [kæ'ʃe] *s* cachet *m*

cackle ['kækəl] s caquet m || intr caqueter; (said of goose) cacarder

cacopho·ny [kə'kɑfəni] s (pl -nies) cacophonie f

cac·tus ['kæktəs] s (pl -tuses or -ti [taɪ]) cactus m

cad [kæd] s malotru m

cadaver [kə'dævər] s cadavre m

cad·dy ['kædi] s (pl -dies) boîte f à thé; (person) cadet m, caddie m

cadence ['kedəns] s cadence f

cadet [kə'dɛt] s cadet m

cadmium ['kædmɪ·əm] s cadmium m

Caesar'ean opera'tion [sɪ'zɛrɪ·ən] s césarienne f

café [kæ'fe] s cabaret m; café-restaurant m

ca'fé soci'ety s gens mpl chic des cabarets à la mode

cafeteria [,kæfə'tɪrɪ·ə] s cafétéria f, restaurant m de libre-service

caffeine ['kæfin], ['kæfin], ['kæfi·ɪn] s caféine f

cage [kedʒ] s cage f || tr mettre en cage

ca·gey ['kedʒi] adj (comp -gier; super -giest) (coll) rusé, fin

cahoots [kə'huts] s—in cahoots (slang) de mèche

Cain [ken] s Caïn m; to raise Cain (coll) faire le diable à quatre

Cairo ['kaɪro] s Le Caire

caisson ['kesən] s caisson m

cais'son disease' s maladie f des caissons

cajole [kə'dʒol] tr cajoler, enjôler

cajoler·y [kə'dʒoləri] s (pl -ies) cajolerie f, enjôlement m

cake [kek] s gâteau m; (one-layer cake) galette f; (pastry) pâtisserie f; (of soap, wax) pain m; (of ice) bloc m; (crust) croûte f; to sell like hot cakes (coll) se vendre comme des petits pains; to take the cake (coll) être la fin des haricots || tr couvrir d'une croûte || intr s'agglutiner, faire croûte

calabash ['kælə,bæʃ] s calebasse f; (tree) calebassier m

calaboose ['kælə,bus] s (coll) violon m, tôle f

calamitous [kə'læmɪtəs] adj calamiteux

calami·ty [kə'læmɪti] s (pl -ties) calamité f

calci·fy ['kælsɪ,faɪ] v (pret & pp -fied) tr calcifier || intr se calcifier

calcium ['kælsɪ·əm] s calcium m

calculate ['kælkjə,let] tr & intr calculer

calculating ['kælkjə,letɪŋ] adj calculateur

calculation [,kælkjə'leʃən] s calcul m

calcu·lus ['kælkjələs] s (pl -luses or -li [,laɪ]) (math, pathol) calcul m

caldron ['kɔldrən] s (culin) chaudron m; (mach) chaudière f

calendar ['kæləndər] s calendrier m

cal'endar year' s année f civile

calender ['kæləndər] s calandre f || tr calandrer, cylindrer

calf [kæf], [kɑf] s (pl calves [kævz], [kɑvz]) veau m; (of leg) mollet m

calf'skin' s veau m, peau f de veau

calf's' liv'er s foie m de veau

caliber ['kælɪbər] s calibre m

calibrate ['kælɪ,bret] tr calibrer

cali·co ['kælɪ,ko] s (pl -coes or -cos) calicot m, indienne f

California [,kælɪ'fɔrnɪ·ə] s Californie f; la Californie

calipers ['kælɪpərz] spl compas m à calibrer

caliph ['kelɪf], ['kælɪf] s calife m

caliphate ['kælɪ,fet] s califat m

calisthenic [,kælɪs'θɛnɪk] adj callisthénique || calisthenics spl callisthénie f

calk [kɔk] s crampon m à glace || tr calfater

call [kɔl] s appel m; (cry) cri m; (visit) visite f; (at a port) escale f; to have no call to n'avoir aucune raison de || tr appeler; (e.g., the doctor) faire venir; (a meeting) convoquer; to call aside prendre à part; to call back rappeler; to call down (from upstairs) faire descendre; (the wrath of the gods) invoquer; (to scold) (coll) gronder; to call off (a dog) rappeler; (coll) annuler, décommander; to call the roll faire l'appel; to call in rappeler; to call to order rappeler à l'ordre; to call up (coll) passer un coup de fil à; (mil) mobiliser || intr appeler; crier; (to visit) faire une visite; (naut) faire escale; to call upon faire appel à; to call upon s.o. to speak inviter qn à prendre la parole

call' bell' s sonnette f

call' box' s guérite f téléphonique

call' boy' s (in a hotel) chasseur m; (theat) avertisseur m

caller ['kɔlər] s visiteur m

call' girl' s call-girl f

calling ['kɔlɪŋ] s vocation f, profession f; (of a meeting) convocation f

cal'ling card' s carte f de visite

call' let'ter s (telg, rad) indicatif m d'appel

call' mon'ey s prêts mpl au jour le jour

callous ['kæləs] adj (foot, hand, etc.) calleux; (unfeeling) endurci, insensible

callow ['kælo] adj inexpérimenté, novice

cal'low youth' s blanc-bec m

callus ['kæləs] s (on skin) cal m, durillon m, callosité f; (bot) cal m

calm [kɑm] adj & s calme m || tr calmer; to calm down pacifier || intr —to calm down se calmer; (said of wind or sea) calmir

calorie ['kæləri] s calorie f

calum·ny ['kæləmni] s (pl -nies) calomnie f

calva·ry ['kælvəri] s (pl -ries) calvaire m; Calvary le Calvaire

calve [kæv], [kɑv] intr vêler

cam [kæm] s came f

cambric ['kembrɪk] s batiste f

camel ['kæməl] s chameau m

camellia [kə'miljə] s camélia m

came·o ['kæmi,o] s (pl -os) camée m

camera ['kæmərə] *s* appareil *m* (photographique)

cam/era·man/ *s* (*pl* **-men/**) photographe *m*

camouflage ['kæmə,flɑʒ] *s* camouflage *m* ‖ *tr* camoufler

camp [kæmp] *s* camp *m* ‖ *intr* camper; **to go camping** faire du camping

campaign [kæm'pen] *s* campagne *f* ‖ *intr* faire campagne

campaigner [kæm'penər] *s* propagandiste *mf*; vétéran *m*

camp/ bed/ *s* lit *m* de camp, lit de sangle

camp/ chair/ *s* chaise *f* pliante

camper ['kæmpər] *s* campeur *m*

camp/fire/ *s* feu *m* de camp

camp/ground/ *s* camping *m*

camphor ['kæmfər] *s* camphre *m*

camping ['kæmpɪŋ] *s* camping *m*

camp/stool/ *s* pliant *m*

campus ['kæmpəs] *s* campus *m*, terrain *m* universitaire

cam/shaft/ *s* arbre *m* à cames

can [kæn] *s* boîte *f*; (*e.g., for gasoline*) bidon *m* ‖ *v* (*pret & pp* **canned**; *ger* **canning**) *tr* mettre en boîte, conserver; (*to dismiss*) (slang) dégommer ‖ *v* (*pret & cond* **could** [kud]) *aux*—**Albert can't do it** Albert ne peut (pas) le faire; **can he swim?** sait-il nager?

Canada ['kænədə] *s* le Canada

Canadian [kə'nedɪ·ən] *adj* canadien ‖ *s* (*person*) Canadien *m*

canal [kə'næl] *s* canal *m*

canar·y [kə'nerɪ] *s* (*pl* **-ies**) canari *m*, serin *m*

can·cel ['kænsəl] *v* (*pret & pp* **-celed** or **-celled**; *ger* **-celing** or **-celling**) *tr* annuler; (*a word*) biffer, rayer; (*a contract*) résilier; (*a postage stamp*) oblitérer; **to cancel an invitation** décommander les invités; **to cancel each other out** s'annuler, se détruire

cancellation [,kænsə'leʃən] *s* annulation *f*; (*of postage stamp*) oblitération *f*; (*of contract*) résiliation *f*

cancer ['kænsər] *s* cancer *m*

cancerous ['kænsərəs] *adj* cancéreux

candela·brum [,kændə'lebrəm] *s* (*pl* **-bra** [brə] or **-brums**) candélabre *m*

candid ['kændɪd] *adj* franc

candida·cy ['kændɪdəsi] *s* (*pl* **-cies**) candidature *f*

candidate ['kændɪ,det] *s* candidat *m*

candied *adj* candi

candied/ fruit/ *s* fruit *m* candi

candle ['kændəl] *s* bougie *f*; (*of tallow*) chandelle *f*; (eccl) cierge *m*

can/dle·hold/er *s* bougeoir *m*

can/dle·light/ *s* lumière *f* de bougie

can/dle·pow/er *s* (phys) bougie *f*

can/dle·stick/ *s* chandelier *m*, bougeoir *m*

can/dle ta/ble *s* guéridon *m*

candor ['kændər] *s* franchise *f*, loyauté *f*

can·dy ['kændɪ] *s* (*pl* **-dies**) confiserie *f*, bonbons *mpl*; **candies** douceurs *fpl*; **piece of candy** bonbon ‖ *v* (*pret & pp* **-died**) *tr* glacer, faire candir ‖ *intr* se candir

can/dy box/ *s* boîte *f* à bonbons

can/dy corn/ *s* grains *mpl* de maïs soufflés et sucrés

can/dy dish/ *s* bonbonnière *f*

can/dy store/ *s* confiserie *f*

cane [ken] *s* canne *f*; (bot) canne ‖ *tr* canner, rempailler

cane/ chair/ *s* chaise *f* cannée

cane/ sug/ar *s* sucre *m* de canne

canine ['kenaɪn] *adj* canin ‖ *s* (*tooth*) canine *f*

canister ['kænɪstər] *s* boîte *f* métallique; (mil) boîte à mitraille

canker ['kæŋkər] *s* chancre *m*; (*in fruit; in society*) ver *m* rongeur ‖ *tr* ronger; (*society*) corrompre

canned/ goods/ *spl* conserves *fpl*, aliments *mpl* conservés

canned/ mu/sic *s* (coll) musique *f* enregistrée

canner·y ['kænəri] *s* (*pl* **-ies**) conserverie *f*

cannibal ['kænɪbəl] *adj & s* cannibale *mf*

canning ['kænɪŋ] *s* conservation *f*

can/ning fac/tory *s* conserverie *f*

cannon ['kænən] *s* canon *m*

cannonade [,kænə'ned] *s* canonnade *f* ‖ *tr* canonner

can/non·ball/ *s* boulet *m* (de canon)

can/non fod/der *s* chair *f* à canon

can·ny ['kæni] *adj* (*comp* **-nier**; *super* **-niest**) prudent, circonspect; rusé, malin

canoe [kə'nu] *s* canoë *m*

canoeist [kə'nu·ɪst] *s* canoéiste *mf*

canon ['kænən] *s* canon *m*

canonical [kə'nɑnɪkəl] *adj* canonique, canonial ‖ **canonicals** *spl* vêtements *mpl* sacerdotaux

canonize ['kænə,naɪz] *tr* canoniser

can/ o/pener *s* ouvre-boîtes *m*

cano·py ['kænəpi] *s* (*pl* **-pies**) dais *m*; (*over an entrance*) marquise *f*

cant [kænt] *s* cant *m*, cafardise *f*; (*argot*) jargon *m* ‖ *tr* (*to tip*) incliner ‖ *intr* (*to tip*) s'incliner; (*to be hypocritical*) papelarder

cantaloupe ['kæntə,lop] *s* cantaloup *m*

cantankerous [kæn'tæŋkərəs] *adj* revêche, acariâtre

cantata [kən'tɑtə] *s* cantate *f*

canteen [kæn'tin] *s* (*shop*) cantine *f*; (*water flask*) bidon *m*; (*service club*) foyer *m* du soldat, du marin, etc.

canter ['kæntər] *s* petit galop *m* ‖ *intr* aller au petit galop

canticle ['kæntɪkəl] *s* cantique *m*, hymne *f*

cantilever ['kæntɪ,livər] *adj & s* cantilever *m*

can/tilever bridge/ *s* pont *m* cantilever, pont à consoles

canton [kæn'tɑn] *s* canton *m*

canvas ['kænvəs] *s* (*cloth*) canevas *m*; (*picture*) toile *f*

canvass ['kænvəs] *s* enquête *f*, sondage *m*; (pol) tournée *f* électorale ‖ *tr* (*a voter*) solliciter la voix de; (*a district*) faire une tournée électorale dans; (com) prospecter ‖ *intr* (com) faire la place; **to canvass for** (*a can-*

didate) faire une campagne électorale en faveur de

canyon ['kænjən] *s* cañon *m*

cap [kæp] *s* (*with visor*) casquette *f*; (*without brim*) bonnet *m*; (*to wear with academic gown*) toque *f*, mortier *m*; (*of bottle*) capsule *f*; (*of cartridge*) amorce *f*, capsule; (*of fountain pen*) capuchon *m*, chapeau *m*; (*of valve; to cover photographic lens*) chapeau; **to set one's cap for** chercher à captiver || *v* (*pret & pp* **capped**; *ger* **capping**) *tr* coiffer; (*a bottle*) capsuler; (*a cartridge*) amorcer; (*a success*) couronner; (*to outdo*) (coll) surpasser

cap. *abbr* (**capital letter**) maj.

capable ['kepəbəl] *adj* capable

capacious [kə'peʃəs] *adj* spacieux, vaste, ample

capaci·ty [kə'pæsɪtɪ] *s* (*pl* **-ties**) capacité *f*; **filled to capacity** comble; **in the capacity of** en tant que, en qualité de, à titre de

cap' and gown' *s* costume *m* académique, toge *f* et mortier *m*; **in cap and gown** en toque et en toge

cape [kep] *s* (*clothing*) cape *f*, pèlerine *f*; (geog) cap *m*, promontoire *m*

Cape' of Good Hope' *s* Cap *m* de Bonne Espérance

caper ['kepər] *s* cabriole *f*, gambade *f*; (bot) câpre *f* || *tr* cabrioler, gambader

Cape'town' *s* Le Cap

capital ['kæpɪtəl] *adj* capital; excellent || *s* (*city*) capitale *f*; (archit) chapiteau *m*; (com) capital *m*; (typ) majuscule *f*, capitale; **small capital** petite capitale

cap'ital and la'bor *spl* le capital et le travail

capitalism ['kæpɪtə,lɪzəm] *s* capitalisme *m*

capitalist ['kæpɪtəlɪst] *adj & s* capitaliste *mf*

capitalize ['kæpɪtə,laɪz] *tr & intr* capitaliser; (typ) écrire avec une majuscule; **to capitalize on** miser sur, tourner à son profit, tirer parti de

cap'ital let'ter *s* majuscule *f*

cap'ital pun'ishment *s* peine *f* capitale

capitol ['kæpɪtəl] *s* capitole *m*

capitulate [kə'pɪtʃə,let] *intr* capituler

capon ['kepən] *s* chapon *m*

caprice [kə'pris] *s* caprice *m*

capricious [kə'prɪʃəs] *adj* capricieux

capsize ['kæpsaɪz] *tr* faire chavirer || *intr* chavirer, capoter

capstan ['kæpstən] *s* cabestan *m*

capsule ['kæpsəl] *s* capsule *f*; (bot, rok) capsule

captain ['kæptən] *s* capitaine *m*; chef *m*; (sports) chef d'équipe || *tr* commander, diriger

captain·cy ['kæptənsi] *s* (*pl* **-cies**) direction *f*, commandement *m*; grade *m* de capitaine

caption ['kæpʃən] *s* légende *f*; (mov) sous-titre *m* || *tr* intituler, donner un sous-titre à

captious ['kæpʃəs] *adj* pointilleux, chicaneux; (*insidious*) captieux

captivate ['kæptɪ,vet] *tr* captiver

captive ['kæptɪv] *adj & s* captif *m*

captivi·ty [kæp'tɪvɪtɪ] *s* (*pl* **-ties**) captivité *f*

captor ['kæptər] *s* ravisseur *m*; (naut) auteur *m* d'une prise

capture ['kæptʃər] *s* capture *f*, prise *f* || *tr* capturer

car [kɑr] *s* auto *f*, voiture *f*; (*of elevator*) cabine *f*; (rr) wagon *m*, voiture; (*for mail, baggage, etc.*) (rr) fourgon *m*

carafe [kə'ræf] *s* carafe *f*

caramel ['kærəməl], ['kɑrməl] *s* caramel *m*

carat ['kærət] *s* carat *m*

caravan ['kærə,væn] *s* caravane *f*

caravansa·ry [,kærə'vænsəri] *s* (*pl* **-ries**) caravansérail *m*

caraway ['kærə,we] *s* carvi *m*

car'away seed' *s* graine *f* de carvi

car'barn' *s* dépôt *m* de tramways

carbide ['kɑrbaɪd] *s* carbure *m*

carbine ['kɑrbaɪn] *s* carabine *f*

carbol'ic ac'id [kɑr'bɑlɪk] *s* acide *m* phénique

carbon ['kɑrbən] *s* (*chemical element*) carbone *m*; (*part of arc light or battery*) charbon *m*; (*in auto cylinder*) calamine *f*; papier *m* carbone

car'bonated wa'ter ['kɑrbə,netɪd] *s* eau *f* gazeuse, soda *m*

car'bon cop'y *s* double *m* au carbone; (fig) calque *m*; (*person*) (fig) sosie *m*

car'bon diox'ide *s* gaz *m* carbonique

car'bon monox'ide *s* oxyde *m* de carbone

car'bon pa'per *s* papier *m* carbone

carbuncle ['kɑrbʌŋkəl] *s* furoncle *m*

carburetor ['kɑrbə,retər] *s* carburateur *m*

carcass ['kɑrkəs] *s* (*dead body*) cadavre *m*; (*without offal*) carcasse *f*

card [kɑrd] *s* carte *f*; (*for filing*) fiche *f*; (*for carding*) carde *f*; (coll) original *m*, numéro *m*, type *m*; **to put one's cards on the table** jouer cartes sur table || *tr* carder, peigner

card'board' *s* carton *m*

card' case' *s* porte-cartes *m*

card' cat'alogue *s* fichier *m*

cardiac ['kɑrdɪ,æk] *adj* cardiaque || *s* (*patient*) (coll) cardiaque *mf*

cardinal ['kɑrdɪnəl] *adj & s* cardinal *m*

card' in'dex *s* fichier *m*

cardiogram ['kɑrdɪo,græm] *s* cardiogramme *m*

card'sharp' *s* tricheur *m*

card' ta'ble *s* table *f* de jeu

card' trick' *s* tour *m* de cartes

care [ker] *s* (*attention*) soin *m*; (*anxiety*) souci *m*; (*responsibility*) charge *f*; (*upkeep*) entretien *m*; **in care of** aux bons soins de, à l'attention de; **take care!** faites attention!; **to take care not to** se garder de; **to take care of** se charger de; (*a sick person*) soigner; **to take care to** avoir soin de || *intr*—**I don't care** ça m'est égal; **to care about** se soucier de, se préoccuper de; **to care for** (*s.o.*) avoir de la sympathie pour; (*s.th.*) trouver plaisir à; (*a sick person*) soigner; **to care to** désirer, vouloir

careen [kə'rin] *tr* faire coucher sur le côté || *intr* donner de la bande, s'incliner

career [kə'rɪr] *s* carrière *f*

care/free/ *adj* sans souci, insouciant

careful ['kɛrfəl] *adj* soigneux, attentif; **be careful!** soyez prudent!

careless ['kɛrlɪs] *adj* (*neglectful*) négligent; (*nonchalant*) insouciant

carelessness ['kɛrlɪsnɪs] *s* négligence *f*

caress [kə'rɛs] *s* caresse *f* || *tr* caresser

caret ['kærət] *s* guidon *m* de renvoi

care/tak'er *s* concierge *mf*, gardien *m*

care/tak'er gov/ernment *s* gouvernement *m* intérimaire

care/worn/ *adj* rongé par les soucis

car/fare/ *s* prix *m* du trajet, place *f*; **to pay carfare** payer le parcours

car-go ['kɑrgo] *s* (*pl* -goes or -gos) cargaison *f*

car/ heat/er *s* chauffage *m* de voiture

Car-ibbe/an Sea/ [,kærɪ'biən], [kə-'rɪbɪ-ən] *s* Mer *f* des Caraïbes, Mer des Antilles

caricature ['kærɪkət/ər] *s* caricature *f* || *tr* caricaturer

caricaturist ['kærɪkət/ərɪst] *s* caricaturiste *mf*

caries ['kɛriz], ['kɛrɪ,iz] *s* carie *f*

carillon ['kærɪ,lɑn], [kə'rɪljən] *s* carillon *m* || *tr & intr* carillonner

car/load/ *s* voiturée *f*

carnage ['kɑrnɪdʒ] *s* carnage *m*

carnal ['kɑrnəl] *adj* charnel; sexuel

car/nal sin/ *s* péché *m* de la chair

carnation [kɑr'neʃən] *s* œillet *m*

carnival ['kɑrnɪvəl] *s* carnaval *m*; fête *f*

car-ol ['kærəl] *s* chanson *f*, cantique *m*; (*Christmas carol*) noël *m* || *v* (*pret & pp* -oled or -olled) *ger* -oling or -olling) *tr & intr* chanter

carom ['kærəm] *s* carambolage *m* || *intr* caramboler

carouse [kə'rauz] *intr* faire la bombe

carp [kɑrp] *s* carpe *f* || *intr* se plaindre

carpenter ['kɑrpəntər] *s* charpentier *m*; (*joiner*) menuisier *m*

carpentry ['kɑrpəntri] *s* charpenterie *f*

carpet ['kɑrpɪt] *s* tapis *m* || *tr* recouvrir d'un tapis

car/pet sweep/er *s* balai *m* mécanique

car/port/ *s* abri *m* pour auto

car/-rent/al serv/ice *s* entreprise *f* de location de voitures

carriage ['kærɪdʒ] *s* voiture *f*; (*used to transport royalty*) carrosse *m*; (*bearing*) port *m*, maintien *m*; (*cost of transport*) frais *mpl* de port; (*of typewriter; of rocket*) chariot *m*; (*of gun*) affût *m*

carrier ['kærɪər] *s* (*person*) porteur *m*; (*e.g., a teamster*) camionneur *m*, voiturier *m*; (*vehicle*) transporteur *m*

car/rier pig/eon *s* pigeon *m* voyageur

car/rier wave/ *s* onde *f* porteuse

carrion ['kærɪ-ən] *s* charogne *f*

carrot ['kærət] *s* carotte *f*

carrousel [,kærə'zɛl] *s* (*merry-go-round*) manège *m* de chevaux de bois; (*hist*) carrousel *m*

car-ry ['kæri] *v* (*pret & pp* -ried) *tr* porter; (*in adding numbers*) retenir; **to be carried** (parl) être voté, être adopté; **to be carried away** (*e.g., with enthusiasm*) être entraîné, s'importer; **to carry away** or **off** emporter, enlever; **to carry back** rapporter; **to carry down** descendre; **to carry forward** avancer; (bk) reporter; **to carry on** continuer; (*e.g., a conversation*) soutenir; **to carry oneself straight** se tenir droit; **to carry out** (*a plan*) exécuter; **to carry over** (bk) reporter; **to carry through** mener à bonne fin; **to carry up** monter; **to carry with one** (*e.g., an audience*) entraîner || *intr* (*said of voice or sound*) porter; **to carry on** continuer; (*in a ridiculous manner*) (coll) faire des espiègleries; (*angrily*) (coll) s'emporter

car/ sick/ness *s* mal *m* de la route

cart [kɑrt] *s* charrette *f*; **to put the cart before the horse** mettre la charrue devant les bœufs || *tr* charrier; (*to truck*) camionner

cartel [kɑr'tɛl] *s* cartel *m*

cartilage ['kɑrtɪlɪdʒ] *s* cartilage *m*

cartographer [kɑr'tɑgrəfər] *s* cartographe *m*

carton ['kɑrtən] *s* carton *m*, boîte *f*

cartoon [kɑr'tun] *s* dessin *m* humoristique; caricature *f*; (*comic strip*) bande *f* dessinée; (mov) dessin animé || *tr* caricaturer

cartoonist [kɑr'tunɪst] *s* caricaturiste *mf*

cartridge ['kɑrtrɪdʒ] *s* cartouche *f*; capsule *f* enregistreuse de pick-up

car/tridge belt/ *s* cartouchière *f*

car/tridge case/ *s* cartouchière *f*

cart/wheel/ *s* roue *f*; **to turn cartwheels** faire la roue

carve [kɑrv] *tr & intr* sculpter; (culin) découper

carver ['kɑrvər] *s* sculpteur *m*; (culin) découpeur *m*

carv/ing knife/ *s* couteau *m* à découper

cascade [kæs'ked] *s* cascade *f* || *intr* cascader

case [kes] *s* (*instance, example*) cas *m*; (*for packing; of clock or piano*) caisse *f*; (*for cigarettes, eyeglasses, cartridges*) étui *m*; (*for jewels, silver, etc.*) écrin *m*; (*for watch*) boîtier *m*; (*for pillow*) taie *f*; (*for surgical instruments*) trousse *f*; (*for sausage*) peau *f*; (*showcase*) vitrine *f*; (*covering*) enveloppe *f*, couverture *f*; (law) cause *f*; (typ) casse *f*; **as the case may be** selon le cas; **in any case** en tout cas; **in case** au cas où; **in case of emergency** en cas d'imprévu; **in no case** en aucun cas; **just in case** à tout hasard; **to win one's case** avoir gain de cause || *tr* (*to put into a case*) encaisser; (*to package*) envelopper; (*to observe*) (slang) observer, épier

case'hard'en tr aciérer, cémenter; (fig) endurcir

casein ['kesi·ɪn] s caséine f

casement ['kesmənt] s croisée f

cash [kæʃ] s espèces fpl; **cash down** argent comptant; **cash offer** offre f réelle; **cash on delivery** livraison contre remboursement; **cash on hand** fonds mpl en caisse; **in cash** en numéraire || tr toucher, encaisser || intr —**to cash in on** (coll) tirer parti de

cash' and car'ry s achat m au comptant et à emporter

cash' bal'ance s solde m de caisse

cash' dis'count s escompte m au comptant

cashew ['kæʃu] s noix f d'acajou, anacarde m; (tree) anacardier m

cash'ew nut' s noix f d'acajou

cashier [kæ'ʃɪr] s caissier m

cashmere ['kæʃmɪr] s cachemire m

cash' reg'ister s caisse f enregistreuse

casing ['kesɪŋ] s enveloppe f, chemise f, coffrage m; (of door or window) chambranle m

cask [kæsk], [kɑsk] s tonneau m, fût m

casket ['kæskɪt], ['kɑskɪt] s (for jewels) écrin m, cassette f; (for interment) cercueil m

casserole ['kæsə·rol] s terrine f

cassock ['kæsək] s soutane f

cast [kæst], [kɑst] s (mold) moule m; (of metal) fonte f; (of fish line) lancer m; (throw) jet m; (for broken limb) plâtre m; (squint) léger strabisme m; (theat) distribution f || v (pret & pp cast) tr fondre, jeter en moule; (to throw) lancer; (a glance) jeter; (a play) distribuer les rôles de; **to be cast in one piece with** venir de fonte avec; **to cast aside** mettre de côté; **to cast lots** tirer au sort; **to cast off** rejeter; **to cast out** mettre à la porte; (a spell) exorciser || intr (fishing) lancer la canne; **to cast about for** chercher; **to cast off** (naut) larguer les amarres

castanets [‚kæstə'nets] spl castagnettes fpl

cast'away' adj & s naufragé m

caste [kæst], [kɑst] s caste f

caster ['kæstər], ['kɑstər] s (wheel) roulette f; (cruet stand) huilier m; (shaker) saupoudreuse f

castigate ['kæstɪ‚get] tr châtier, corriger

Castile [kæs'til] s Castille f; la Castille

Castilian [kæs'tɪljən] adj castillan || s (language) castillan m; (person) Castillan m

casting ['kæstɪŋ] s fonte f; (thing cast) pièce f fondue; (act) lancement m; (fishing) pêche f au lancer; (theat) distribution f

cast'ing rod' s canne f à lancer

cast' i'ron s fonte f

cast'-i'ron adj en fonte

cast'-iron stom'ach s estomac m d'autruche

castle ['kæsəl], ['kɑsəl] s château m; (fortified castle) château fort; (chess) tour f || tr & intr (chess) roquer

cast'off' adj & s rejeté m

cas'tor oil' ['kæstər], ['kɑstər] s huile f de ricin

castrate ['kæstret] tr castrer

casual ['kæʒu·əl] adj casuel; (indifferent) insouciant, désinvolte

casually ['kæʒu·əli] adv nonchalamment, avec désinvolture; (by chance) fortuitement

casual·ty ['kæʒu·əlti] s (pl -ties) accident m; (person) accidenté m; **casualties** (mil) pertes fpl

cas'ualty list' s état m des pertes

cat [kæt] s (tomcat) chat m; (female cat) chatte f; (naut) capon m; (shrew) (coll) cancanière f, chipie f; **a cat may look at a queen** un chien regarde bien un évêque; **to let the cat out of the bag** (coll) vendre ou éventer la mèche; **to rain cats and dogs** (coll) pleuvoir à seaux

cataclysm ['kætə‚klɪzəm] s cataclysme m

catacombs ['kætə‚komz] spl catacombes fpl

catalogue ['kætə‚lɔg], ['kætə‚lag] s catalogue m; (of university) annuaire m || tr cataloguer, classer

Catalonia [‚kætə'loni·ə] s Catalogne f; la Catalogne

catalyst ['kætəlɪst] s catalyseur m

catapult ['kætə‚pʌlt] s catapulte f || tr catapulter

cataract ['kætə‚rækt] s cataracte f

catarrh [kə'tɑr] s catarrhe m

catastrophe [kə'tæstrəfi] s catastrophe f

cat'call' s huée f; (theat) coup m de sifflet || tr & intr (theat) siffler

catch [kætʃ] s prise f; (on door) loquet m; (on buckle) ardillon m; (caught by fisherman) pêche f; (mach) cliquet m, chien m; **there's a catch to it** (coll) c'est une attrape || v (pret & pp caught [kɔt]) tr attraper; (a train; a fish; fire) prendre; (a word or sound) saisir; (e.g., one's coat) accrocher; **caught like a rat in a trap** fait comme un rat; **to catch hold of** saisir, s'accrocher à; **to catch s.o. in the act** prendre qn sur le fait; **to catch up** (in a mistake) surprendre || intr prendre; (said of fire) s'allumer, s'enflammer, se prendre; **to catch on** (a nail, thorn, etc.) s'accrocher à; (to understand) (coll) comprendre; (to become popular) (coll) devenir célèbre, devenir populaire; **to catch up** se rattraper; **to catch up with** rattraper

catch'all' s débarras m, fourre-tout m

catching ['kætʃɪŋ] adj contagieux; (e.g., smile) communicatif

catch' ques'tion s (coll) colle f

catch'word' s mot m de ralliement, slogan m; (cliché) rengaine f, scie f; (at the bottom of page) réclame f; (theat) réplique f; (typ) mot-souche m

catch·y ['kætʃi] adj (comp -ier; super -iest) (tune) facile à retenir, entraînant; (question) insidieux, à traquenard

catechism ['kætɪ‚kɪzəm] s catéchisme m

categorical [ˌkætɪˈgɑrɪkəl], [ˌkætɪˈgɔrɪkəl] *adj* catégorique

cate·go·ry [ˈkætɪˌgori] *s* (*pl* -ries) catégorie *f*

cater [ˈketər] *tr* (*e.g., a wedding*) fournir le buffet de ‖ *intr* être fournisseur; **to cater to** pourvoir à; (*to favor*) entourer de prévenances

cat'er-cor'nered [ˈkætərˌkɔrnərd] *adj* diagonal ‖ *adv* diagonalement

caterer [ˈketərər] *s* fournisseur *m*, traiteur *m*

caterpillar [ˈkætərˌpɪlər] *s* chenille *f*

cat'erpillar trac'tor *s* autochenille *f*

cat'fish' *s* poisson-chat *m*

cat'gut' *s* boyau *m* de chat; (*string*) corde *f* de boyau, boyau; (*surg*) catgut *m*

cathedral [kəˈθidrəl] *s* cathédrale *f*

catheter [ˈkæθɪtər] *s* (med) cathéter *m*

catheterization [ˌkæθɪtərɪˈzeʃən] *s* (surg) cathétérisme *m*

cathode [ˈkæθod] *s* cathode *m*

catholic [ˈkæθəlɪk] *adj* (*universal*) catholique; tolérant, large, e.g., **he has a catholic mind** il a l'esprit large, il est fort tolérant ‖ (*cap*) *adj* & *s* catholique *mf*

Catholicism [kəˈθɑlɪˌsɪzəm] *s* catholicisme *m*

catholicity [ˌkæθəˈlɪsiti] *s* catholicité *f*, universalité *f*; (*tolerance*) largeur *f* d'esprit, tolérance *f*

catkin [ˈkætkɪn] *s* (bot) chaton *m*

cat'nap' *s* petit somme *m*

cat'nip' *s* herbe-aux-chats *f*, cataire *f*

cat-o'-nine-tails [ˌkætəˈnaɪnˌtelz] *s* chat *m* à neuf queues

cat's-paw' *s* (naut) risée *f*; (coll) dupe *f*

catsup [ˈkætsəp], [ˈkætʃəp] *s* sauce *f* tomate

cattle [ˈkætəl] *s* bœufs *mpl*; (*including horses*) gros bétail *m*, bestiaux *mpl*

cat'tle car' *s* fourgon *m* à bestiaux

cat'tle cross'ing *s* passage *m* de troupeaux

cat'tle-man *s* (*pl* -men) éleveur *m* de bétail

cat'tle thief' *s* voleur *m* de bétail

cat·ty [ˈkæti] *adj* (*comp* -tier; *super* -tiest) (coll) cancanier, méchant

cat'ty-cor'ner *adj* (coll) diagonal ‖ *adv* (coll) diagonalement

cat'walk' *s* passerelle *f*

Caucasian [kɔˈkeʒən], [kɔˈkeʃən] *adj* caucasien ‖ *s* Caucasien *m*

caucus [ˈkɔkəs] *s* comité *m* électoral ‖ *intr* se grouper en comité électoral

cauliflower [ˈkɔlɪˌflauˌər] *s* chou-fleur *m*

caulk [kɔk] *tr* calfater

cause [kɔz] *s* cause *f*; **to have cause to** avoir lieu de ‖ *tr* causer; **to cause to** + *inf* faire + *inf*, e.g., **he caused him to stumble** il l'a fait trébucher

cause'way' *s* chaussée *f*

caustic [ˈkɔstɪk] *adj* caustique

cauterize [ˈkɔtəˌraɪz] *tr* cautériser

caution [ˈkɔʃən] *s* prudence *f*, précaution *f*; (*warning*) avertissement *m* ‖ *tr* mettre en garde, avertir

cautious [ˈkɔʃəs] *adj* prudent, circonspect

cavalcade [ˌkævəlˈked], [ˈkævəlˌked] *s* cavalcade *f*

cavalier [ˌkævəˈlɪr] *adj* & *s* cavalier *m*

caval·ry [ˈkævəlri] *s* (*pl* -ries) cavalerie *f*

cav'alry·man' or **cav'alry·man** *s* (*pl* -men' or -men) cavalier *m*

cave [kev] *s* caverne *f* ‖ *intr*—**to cave in** s'effondrer

cave'-in' *s* effondrement *m*

cavern [ˈkævərn] *s* caverne *f*

caviar [ˈkævɪˌɑr], [ˈkɑvɪˌɑr] *s* caviar *m*

cav·il [ˈkævɪl] *v* (*pret* & *pp* -iled or -illed; *ger* -iling or -illing) *intr* ergoter, chicaner

cavi·ty [ˈkævɪti] *s* (*pl* -ties) cavité *f*

cavort [kəˈvɔrt] *intr* gambader, caracoler

caw [kɔ] *s* croassement *m* ‖ *intr* croasser, crialler

cease [sis] *s* cessation *f*; **without cease** sans cesse ‖ *tr* & *intr* cesser; **to cease fire** cesser le feu

cease'-fire' *s* cessez-le-feu *m*

ceaseless [ˈsislɪs] *adj* incessant, continuel

cedar [ˈsidər] *s* cèdre *m*

cede [sid] *tr* & *intr* céder

cedilla [sɪˈdɪlə] *s* cédille *f*

ceiling [ˈsilɪŋ] *s* plafond *m*; **to hit the ceiling** (coll) sortir de ses gonds

ceil'ing lamp' *s* plafonnier *m*

ceil'ing price' *s* prix *m* maximum

celebrant [ˈsɛlɪbrənt] *s* (eccl) célébrant *m*

celebrate [ˈsɛlɪˌbret] *tr* célébrer

celebrated *adj* célèbre

celebration [ˌsɛlɪˈbreʃən] *s* célébration *f*, fête *f*

celebri·ty [sɪˈlɛbrɪti] *s* (*pl* -ties) célébrité *f*; (*e.g., movie star*) vedette *f*

celery [ˈsɛləri] *s* céleri *m*

celestial [sɪˈlɛstʃəl] *adj* céleste

celiba·cy [ˈsɛlɪbəsi] *s* (*pl* -cies) célibat *m*

celibate [ˈsɛlɪˌbet], [ˈsɛlɪbɪt] *adj* & *s* célibataire *mf*

cell [sɛl] *s* cellule *f*; (*of electric battery*) élément *m*

cellar [ˈsɛlər] *s* (*basement; wine cellar*) cave *f*; (*often partly above ground*) sous-sol *m*

cellist or **'cellist** [ˈtʃɛlɪst] *s* violoncelliste *mf*

cel·lo or **'cel·lo** [ˈtʃɛlo] *s* (*pl* -los) violoncelle *m*

cellophane [ˈsɛləˌfen] *s* cellophane *f*

celluloid [ˈsɛljəˌlɔɪd] *s* celluloïd *m*

Celt [sɛlt], [kɛlt] *s* Celte *m*

Celtic [ˈsɛltɪk], [ˈkɛltɪk] *adj* celte, celtique ‖ *s* celtique *m*

cement [sɪˈmɛnt] *s* ciment *m* ‖ *tr* cimenter

cement' mix'er *s* bétonnière *f*

cemeter·y [ˈsɛmɪˌtɛri] *s* (*pl* -ies) cimetière *m*

censer [ˈsɛnsər] *s* encensoir *m*

censor [ˈsɛnsər] *s* censeur *m* ‖ *tr* censurer

cen'sor·ship' s censure f

censure ['sɛnʃər] s blâme m ǁ tr blâmer

census ['sɛnsəs] s recensement m, dénombrement m; (in Roman Empire) cens m

cen'sus tak'er s recenseur m; (in ancient Rome) censeur m

cent [sɛnt] s cent m; not to have a red cent to one's name n'avoir pas un sou vaillant

centaur ['sɛntɔr] s centaure m

centenarian [,sɛntɪ'nɛrɪ·ən] s centenaire mf

centennial [sɛn'tɛnɪ·əl] adj centennal ǁ s centenaire m

center ['sɛntər] adj central ǁ s centre m; (middle) milieu m ǁ tr centrer ǁ intr—to center on concentrer sur

centering ['sɛntərɪŋ] s centrage m; (phot) cadrage m

cen'ter-piece' s surtout m; milieu m de table

centigrade ['sɛntɪ,gred] adj & s centigrade m

centimeter ['sɛntɪ,mitər] s centimètre m

centipede ['sɛntɪ,pid] s mille-pattes m, myriapodes mpl

central ['sɛntrəl] adj & s central m

Cen'tral Amer'ica s l'Amérique f centrale

Cen'tral Intel'ligence s la Sûreté, la Sûreté nationale

centralize ['sɛntrə,laɪz] tr centraliser ǁ intr se centraliser

centrifugal [sɛn'trɪfjʊgəl] adj centrifuge

centrifuge ['sɛntrɪ,fjudʒ] s essoreuse f ǁ tr essorer

centu·ry ['sɛntʃərɪ] s (pl -ries) siècle m

cen'tury-old' adj séculaire

ceramic [sɪ'ræmɪk] adj céramique ǁ ceramics (art) céramique f; spl (objects) céramiques

cereal ['sɪrɪ·əl] adj céréalier ǁ s (grain) céréale f; (oatmeal) flocons mpl d'avoine; (cornflakes) flocons de maïs; (cooked cereal) bouillie f, gruau m

cerebral ['sɛrɪbrəl] adj cérébral

ceremonial [,sɛrɪ'monɪ·əl] adj cérémonial; (e.g., tribal rites) cérémoniel ǁ s cérémonial m

ceremonious [,sɛrɪ'monɪ·əs] adj cérémonieux

ceremo·ny ['sɛrɪ,monɪ] s (pl -nies) cérémonie f; to stand on ceremony faire des cérémonies

certain ['sʌrtən] adj certain; a certain certain; certain people certains; for certain pour sûr, à coup sûr; to make certain of s'assurer de

certainly ['sʌrtənlɪ] adv certainement

certain·ty ['sʌrtəntɪ] s (pl -ties) certitude f

certificate [sər'tɪfɪkɪt] s certificat m; (of birth, of marriage, etc.) bulletin m, acte m, extrait m; (proof) attestation f

cer'tified cop'y s extrait m; (formula used on documents) pour copie conforme

cer'tified pub'lic account'ant s expert-comptable m, comptable m agréé

certi·fy ['sʌrtɪ,faɪ] v (pret & pp -fied) tr certifier

cervix ['sʌrvɪks] s (pl cervices [sər'vaɪsɪz]) nuque f

cessation [sɛ'seʃən] s cessation f, cesse f

cesspool ['sɛs,pul] s fosse f d'aisance, cloaque m

Ceylon [sɪ'lɑn] s Ceylan m

Ceylo·nese [,silə'niz] adj cingalais ǁ s (pl -nese) Cingalais m

chafe [tʃef] tr écorcher, irriter ǁ intr s'écorcher, s'irriter

chaff [tʃæf] s balle f; (banter) raillerie f ǁ tr railler, persifler

chaf'ing dish' s réchaud m de table, chauffe-plats m

chagrin [ʃə'grɪn] s mortification f, humiliation f ǁ tr mortifier, humilier

chain [tʃen] s chaîne f ǁ tr enchaîner

chain' gang' s forçats mpl à la chaîne

chain' reac'tion s (phys) réaction f en chaîne

chain' smok'er s fumeur m à la file

chain'stitch' s point m de chaînette

chain' store' s magasin m à succursales multiples, économat m

chair [tʃer] s chaise f; (held by university professor) chaire f; (of presiding officer; presiding officer himself) fauteuil m; to take a chair prendre un siège, s'asseoir; to take the chair occuper le fauteuil, présider une assemblée ǁ tr présider

chair' lift' s télé-siège m

chair'man s (pl -men) président m

chair'man·ship' s présidence f

chair'wom'an s (pl -wom'en) présidente f

chalice ['tʃælɪs] s calice m

chalk [tʃɔk] s craie f; a piece of chalk une craie, un morceau de craie ǁ tr marquer avec de la craie, écrire à la craie

chalk·y ['tʃɔkɪ] adj (comp -ier; super -iest) crayeux

challenge ['tʃælɪndʒ] s défi m; (objection) contestation f; (mil) qui-vive m; (sports) challenge m ǁ tr défier; (to question) mettre en question, contester; (mil) crier qui-vive à

chamber ['tʃembər] s chambre f

chamberlain ['tʃembərlɪn] s chambellan m

cham'ber·maid' s femme f de chambre

cham'ber mu'sic s musique f de chambre

Cham'ber of Com'merce s syndicat m d'initiative

chameleon [kə'milɪ·ən] s caméléon m

chamfer ['tʃæmfər] s chanfrein m ǁ tr chanfreiner

cham·ois ['tʃæmɪ] s (pl -ois) chamois m

champ [tʃæmp] s mâchonnement m ǁ tr mâcher bruyamment; to champ the bit ronger le frein

champagne [ʃæm'pen] s champagne m ǁ (cap) adj champenois ǁ (cap) s Champagne f; la Champagne

champion ['tʃæmpɪ·ən] s champion m ǁ tr se faire le champion de, défendre

cham·pion·ship s championnat m

chance [tʃæns], [tʃɑns] adj fortuit, de rencontre ‖ s hasard m; risque m; (opportunity) occasion f; **by chance** par hasard, fortuitement; **chances** chances fpl, sort m; **to take a chance** encourir un risque; acheter un billet de loterie; **to take chances** jouer gros jeu ‖ tr hasarder, risquer ‖ intr—**to chance to** venir à, avoir l'occasion de; **to chance upon** rencontrer par hasard

chancel ['tʃænsəl], ['tʃɑnsəl] s chœur m, sanctuaire m

chanceller·y ['tʃænsələri], ['tʃɑnsələri] s (pl -ies) chancellerie f

chancellor ['tʃænsələr], ['tʃɑnsələr] s chancelier m, ministre m

chancre ['ʃæŋkər] s chancre m

chandelier [ˌʃændə'lɪr] s lustre m

change [tʃendʒ] s changement m; (coins) monnaie f; **change in the wind** saute f de vent; **change of address** changement de domicile; **change of clothes** vêtements mpl de rechange; **for a change** comme distraction; pour changer ‖ tr changer; changer de, e.g., **to change religions** changer de culte; **to change sides** tourner casaque ‖ intr changer; (said of voice at puberty) muer; **to change over** (e.g., from one system to another) passer

changeable ['tʃendʒəbəl] adj changeable; (weather) variable; (character) changeant, mobile

changeless ['tʃendʒlɪs] adj immuable

change' of life' s retour m d'âge

change' of voice' s mue f

change'o'ver s changement m, renversement m, relève f

change' purse' s porte-monnaie m

chan·nel ['tʃænəl] s (body of water joining two others) canal m; (bed of river) chenal m; (means of communication) voie f, canal; (passage) conduit m; (groove) cannelure f; (strait) bras m de mer; (for trade) débouché m; (rad) canal m; (rad, telv) chaîne f; (telv) canal (Canad); **through channels** par la voie hiérarchique ‖ v (pret & pp -neled or -nelled; ger -neling or -nelling) tr creuser, canneler

Chan·nel Is·lands spl îles fpl Anglo-Normandes

chant [tʃænt], [tʃɑnt] s chant m; (song sung in a monotone) plain-chant m, psalmodie f ‖ tr & intr psalmodier

chanter ['tʃæntər], ['tʃɑntər] s chantre m

chantey ['ʃænti], ['tʃænti] s chanson f de bord

chaos ['ke·ɑs] s chaos m

chaotic [ke'ɑtɪk] adj chaotique

chap [tʃæp] s crevasse f, gerçure f; (coll) type m, individu m ‖ v (pret & pp chapped; ger chapping) tr crevasser, gercer ‖ intr se crevasser, se gercer

chapel ['tʃæpəl] s chapelle f; (in a

house) oratoire m; (Protestant chapel) temple m

chaperon ['ʃæpəˌron] s chaperon m, duègne f ‖ tr chaperonner

chaplain ['tʃæplɪn] s aumônier m

chaplet ['tʃæplɪt] s chapelet m

chapter ['tʃæptər] s chapitre m; (of an association) bureau m régional

char [tʃɑr] v (pret & pp charred; ger charring) tr & intr charbonner; **to become charred** se charbonner, se carboniser

character ['kærɪktər] s caractère m; (theat) personnage m; (coll) type m, sujet m

characteristic [ˌkærɪktə'rɪstɪk] adj & s caractéristique f

characterize ['kærɪktəˌraɪz] tr caractériser

char'acter ref'erence s certificat m de moralité

char'coal' s charbon m de bois

char'coal burn'er s charbonnier m

char'coal pen'cil s charbon m, crayon m de fusain

charge [tʃɑrdʒ] s charge f; prix m; (against a defendant) chef m d'accusation; (made to a jury) résumé m; **on a charge of** sous l'inculpation de; **to reverse the charges** téléphoner en p.c.v.; **to take charge of** se charger de; **without charge** gratis ‖ tr charger; **to charge s.o. s.th. for s.th.** prendre or demander q.ch. à qn pour q.ch.; **to charge to s.o.'s account** mettre sur le compte de qn ‖ intr (mil) charger; **to charge down on** foncer sur

charge' account' s compte m courant

charger ['tʃɑrdʒər] s cheval m de bataille; (elec) chargeur m

chariot ['tʃæri·ət] s char m

charitable ['tʃærɪtəbəl] adj charitable

charity ['tʃærɪti] s (pl -ties) charité f; (alms) bienfaisance f, aumônes fpl; (institution) société f or œuvre f de bienfaisance; **for charity's sake** par charité

charlatan ['ʃɑrlətən] s charlatan m

charm [tʃɑrm] s charme m; (e.g., on a bracelet) breloque f, porte-bonheur m ‖ tr charmer

charming ['tʃɑrmɪŋ] adj charmeur, charmant

charnel ['tʃɑrnəl] adj de charnier ‖ s charnier m, ossuaire m

chart [tʃɑrt] s (map) carte f; (graph) dessin m graphique; (diagram) diagramme m; (table) tableau m ‖ tr inscrire sur un dessin graphique; (naut) porter sur une carte, dresser la carte de

charter ['tʃɑrtər] s charte f; (of bank) privilège m; (naut) affrètement m ‖ tr accorder une charte à; (a ship) affréter, noliser; (a bus) louer

char'ter mem'ber s membre m fondateur

char'wom'an s (pl -wom'en) nettoyeuse f

chase [t∫es] *s* chasse *f*, poursuite *f*; (*for printing*) châssis *m* ‖ *tr* chasser; (*a gem*) enchâsser; (*gold*) ciseler; (*metal*) repousser; **to chase away** chasser ‖ *intr*—**to chase after** pourchasser, poursuivre

chaser ['t∫esər] *s* chasseur *m*; (*of women*) (coll) coureur *m*; (*taken after an alcoholic drink*) (coll) rince-gueule *m*

chasm ['kæzəm] *s* abîme *m*

chas·sis ['t∫æsi] *s* (*pl* **-sis** [siz]) châssis *m*

chaste [t∫est] *adj* chaste

chasten ['t∫esən] *tr* châtier

chastise [t∫æs'taɪz] *tr* châtier, corriger

chastisement ['t∫æstɪzmənt], [t∫æs-'taɪzmənt] *s* châtiment *m*

chastity ['t∫æstɪti] *s* chasteté *f*

chat [t∫æt] *s* causerie *f*, causette *f* ‖ *v* (*pret & pp* **chatted**; *ger* **chatting**) *intr* causer, bavarder

chattel ['t∫ætəl] *s* bien *m* meuble, objet *m* mobiliaire

chatter ['t∫ætər] *s* bavardage *m*, caquetage *m* ‖ *intr* bavarder, caqueter; (*said of teeth*) claquer

chat'ter·box' *s* bavard *m*, babillard *m*

chauffeur ['∫ofər], [∫o'fʌr] *s* chauffeur *m*

chauvinistic [,∫ovɪ'nɪstɪk] *adj* chauvin

cheap [t∫ip] *adj* bon marché; (coll) honteux; **to get off cheap** (coll) en être quitte à bon compte

cheapen ['t∫ipən] *tr* baisser le prix de; diminuer la valeur de

cheap'skate' *s* (slang) rat *m*

cheat [t∫it] *s* tricheur *m*, fraudeur *m* ‖ *tr* tricher, frauder ‖ *intr* (e.g., *at cards*) tricher; (e.g., *in an examination*) frauder

cheating ['t∫itɪŋ] *s* tricherie *f*, fraude *f*

check [t∫ɛk] *s* (*stopping*) arrêt *m*; (*brake*) frein *m*; (*supervision*) contrôle *m*, vérification *f*; (*in a restaurant*) addition *f*; (*drawn on a bank*) chèque *m*; (e.g., *of a chessboard*) carreau *m*; (*of the king in chess*) échec *m*; (*for baggage*) bulletin *m*; (*pass-out check*) contremarque *f*; (*chip, counter*) jeton *m*; **in check** en échec ‖ *tr* arrêter, freiner; contrôler, vérifier; (*baggage*) faire enregistrer; (e.g., *one's coat*) mettre au vestiaire; (*the king in chess*) faire échec à; **to check off** pointer, cocher ‖ *intr* s'arrêter; **to check in** (*at a hotel*) s'inscrire sur le registre; **to check out** (*of a hotel*) régler sa note; **to check up on** contrôler, examiner

check'book' *s* carnet *m* de chèques, chéquier *m*

checked *adj* (*checkered*) à carreaux; (*syllable*) entravé

checker ['t∫ɛkər] *s* (*inspector*) contrôleur *m*; (*piece used in game*) pion *m*; (*square of checkerboard*) carreau *m*; **checkers** jeu *m* de dames ‖ *tr* quadriller; (*to divide in squares*) quadriller; (*to scatter here and there*) diaprer

check'er·board' *s* damier *m*

checkered *adj* (*divided into squares*) quadrillé, à carreaux; (*varied*) varié, accidenté; (*career, life*) plein de vicissitudes, mouvementé

check' girl' *s* préposée *f* au vestiaire

check'ing account' *s* compte *m* en banque

check' list' *s* liste *f* de contrôle

check' mark' *s* trait *m* de repère, repère *m*, coche *f*

check'mate' *s* échec et mat *m*; (fig) échec *m* ‖ *tr* faire échec et mat à, mater ‖ *intr* faire échec et mat, mater ‖ *interj* échec et mat!

check'-out count'er *s* caisse *f* de supermarché

check'point' *s* contrôle *m* de police

check'room' *s* (*cloakroom*) vestiaire *m*; (*baggage room*) consigne *f*

check'up' *s* vérification *f*, examen *m*

cheek [t∫ik] *s* joue *f*; (coll) aplomb *m*, toupet *m*

cheek'bone' *s* pommette *f*

cheep [t∫ip] *intr* piauler

cheer [t∫ɪr] *s* bonne humeur *f*, gaieté *f*; encouragement *m*, e.g., **word of cheer** parole *f* d'encouragement; **cheers** acclamations *fpl*, bravos *mpl*, vivats *mpl*; **three cheers for...!** vive...!; **to give three cheers** pousser trois hourras ‖ *tr* (*to cheer up*) encourager, égayer; (*to applaud*) acclamer, applaudir ‖ *intr* pousser des vivats, applaudir; **cheer up!** courage!

cheerful ['t∫ɪrfəl] *adj* de bonne humeur, gai; (*place*) d'aspect agréable

cheerfully ['t∫ɪrfəli] *adv* gaiement; (*willingly*) de bon cœur

cheer'lead'er *s* chef *m* de claque

cheerless ['t∫ɪrlɪs] *adj* morne, triste

cheese [t∫iz] *s* fromage *m* ‖ *tr*—**cheese it, the cops!** (slang) vingt-deux, les flics!

cheese'cake' *s* (slang) les pin up *fpl*

cheese' cake' *s* soufflé *m* au fromage, tarte *f* au fromage

cheese'cloth' *s* gaze *f*

chees·y ['t∫izi] *adj* (*comp* **-ier**; *super* **-iest**) caséeux; (slang) miteux

cheetah ['t∫itə] *s* guépard *m*

chef [∫ɛf] *s* chef *m* de cuisine, maître queux *m*

chemical ['kɛmɪkəl] *adj* chimique ‖ *s* produit *m* chimique

chemist ['kɛmɪst] *s* chimiste *mf*

chemistry ['kɛmɪstri] *s* chimie *f*

cherish ['t∫ɛrɪ/] *tr* chérir; (*an idea*) nourrir; (*a hope*) caresser

cher·ry ['t∫ɛri] *s* (*pl* **-ries**) cerise *f*; (*tree*) cerisier *m*

cher'ry or'chard *s* cerisaie *f*

cher'ry tree' *s* cerisier *m*

cher·ub ['t∫ɛrəb] *s* (*pl* **-ubim** [əbɪm]) chérubin *m* ‖ *s* (*pl* **-ubs**) (fig) chérubin *m*

chess [t∫ɛs] *s* échecs *mpl*; **to play chess** jouer aux échecs

chess'board' *s* échiquier *m*

chess'man' *s* (*pl* **-men'**) pièce *f* du jeu d'échecs

chess' set' *s* échecs *mpl*

chest [t∫ɛst] *s* caisse *f*; (*of drawers*)

commode *f*; (anat) poitrine *f*; **to get s.th. off one's chest** (coll) se débou-tonner, dire ce qu'on a sur le cœur

chestnut ['tʃɛsnət] *adj* (color) châtain ‖ *s* (color) châtain *m*; (nut) châ-taigne *f*; (tree) châtaignier *m*

chest/ of drawers/ *s* commode *f*, chif-fonnier *m*

cheval/ glass/ [ʃə'væl] *s* psyché *f*

chevron ['ʃɛvrən] *s* chevron *m*

chew [tʃu] *tr* mâcher; (tobacco) chiquer

chewing ['tʃu·ɪŋ] *s* mastication *f*

chew/ing gum/ *s* gomme *f* à mâcher, chewing-gum *m*

chicaner•y ['tʃɪkɛnəri] *s* (pl -ies) truc *m*, ruse *f*, artifice *m*

chick [tʃɪk] *s* poussin *m*; (girl) (slang) tendron *m*

chickadee ['tʃɪkə‚di] *s* (Parus atrica-pillus) mésange *f* boréale

chicken ['tʃɪkən] *s* poulet *m*; **to be chicken** (slang) avoir la frousse ‖ *intr*—**to chicken out** (slang) caner

chick/en coop/ *s* poulailler *m*

chick/en-heart/ed *adj* froussard, poltron

chick/en pox/ *s* varicelle *f*

chick/en stew/ *s* poule-au-pot *m*

chick/en wire/ *s* treillis *m* métallique

chick/pea/ *s* pois *m* chiche

chico•ry ['tʃɪkəri] *s* (pl -ries) chicorée *f*

chide [tʃaɪd] *v* (pret chided or chid [tʃɪd]; pp chided, chid, or chidden ['tʃɪdən]) *tr & intr* gronder

chief [tʃif] *adj* principal, en chef ‖ *s* chef *m*; (boss) (coll) patron *m*

chief/ exec/utive *s* chef *m* de l'exécutif

chief/ jus/tice *s* président *m* de la Cour suprême

chiefly ['tʃifli] *adv* principalement

chief/ of police/ *s* préfet *m* de police

chief/ of staff/ *s* chef *m* d'état-major

chief/ of state/ *s* chef *m* d'État

chieftain ['tʃiftən] *s* chef *m*

chiffon [ʃɪ'fɑn] *s* mousseline *f* de soie

chiffonier [‚ʃɪfə'nɪr] *s* chiffonnier *m*

chilblain ['tʃɪl‚blen] *s* engelure *f*

child [tʃaɪld] *s* (pl children ['tʃɪldrən]) enfant *mf*; **with child** enceinte

child/birth/ *s* accouchement *m*

child/hood *s* enfance *f*

childish ['tʃaɪldɪʃ] *adj* enfantin, puéril

child/ la/bor *s* travail *m* des enfants

child/like/ *adj* enfantin, d'enfant

child/'s play/ *s* jeu *m* d'enfant; **it's child's play** c'est l'enfance de l'art

child/ wel/fare *s* protection *f* de l'en-fance

Chile ['tʃɪli] *s* le Chili

chil/i pep/per ['tʃɪli] *s* piment *m*

chill [tʃɪl] *adj & s* froid *m*; **sudden chill** saisissement *m*, coup *m* de froid; **to take the chill off** faire tiédir ‖ *tr* refroidir; (a person) transir, faire frissonner; (wine) frapper

chill•y ['tʃɪli] *adj* (comp -ier; super -iest) froid; (sensitive to cold) frileux; **it is chilly** il fait frisquet

chime [tʃaɪm] *s* coup *m* de son; **chimes** (at doorway) sonnerie *f*; (in bell tower) carillon *m* ‖ *tr & intr* caril-lonner

chimera [kaɪ'mɪrə], [kɪ'mɪrə] *s* chi-mère *f*

chiming ['tʃaɪmɪŋ] *s* carillonnement *m*, sonnerie *f*

chimney ['tʃɪmni] *s* cheminée *f*; (of lamp) verre *m*

chim/ney pot/ *s* abat-vent *m*, mitre *f*

chim/ney sweep/ *s* ramoneur *m*

chimpanzee [‚tʃɪm'pænzi], [‚tʃɪmpæn-'zi] *s* chimpanzé *m*

chin [tʃɪn] *s* menton *m*

china ['tʃaɪnə] *s* porcelaine *f* de Chine; **China** Chine *f*; la Chine

chi/na clos/et *s* vitrine *f*

chi/na-ware/ *s* porcelaine *f*

Chi•nese [tʃaɪ'niz] *adj* chinois ‖ *s* (language) chinois *m* ‖ *s* (pl -nese) Chinois *m* (person)

Chi/nese lan/tern *s* lanterne *f* véni-tienne, lampion *m*

chink [tʃɪŋk] *s* fente *f*, crevasse *f*; **chink in one's armor** (coll) défaut *m* de la cuirasse

chin/ strap/ *s* sous-mentonnière *f*, jugu-laire *f*

chip [tʃɪp] *s* copeau *m*, éclat *m*; (in gambling) jeton *m*; **to be a chip off the old block** (coll) chasser de race, être un rejeton de la vieille souche ‖ *v* (pret & pp chipped; ger chipping) *tr* enlever un copeau à ‖ *intr* s'écail-ler; **to chip in** contribuer

chipmunk ['tʃɪp‚mʌŋk] *s* tamias *m* rayé

chipper ['tʃɪpər] *adj* (coll) en forme, guilleret

chiropodist [kaɪ'rapədɪst], [kɪ'rapə-dɪst] *s* pédicure *mf*

chiropractor ['kaɪrə‚præktər] *s* chiro-practeur *m*

chirp [tʃʌrp] *s* gazouillis *m*, pépiement *m* ‖ *intr* gazouiller, pépier

chis•el ['tʃɪzəl] *s* ciseau *m* ‖ *v* (pret & pp -eled or -elled; ger -eling or -el-ling) *tr* ciseler; (a person) (slang) escroquer; **to chisel s.o. out of s.th.** (slang) escroquer q.ch. à qn

chiseler ['tʃɪzələr] *s* ciseleur *m*; (slang) escroc *m*

chit [tʃɪt] *s* note *f*, ticket *m*; (coll) gamin *m*

chit/-chat/ *s* bavardage *m*

chivalrous ['ʃɪvəlrəs] *adj* honorable, courtois; (lit) chevaleresque

chivalry ['ʃɪvəlri] *s* (of Middle Ages) chevalerie *f*; (politeness) courtoisie *f*, galanterie *f*

chive [tʃaɪv] *s* ciboulette *f*, civette *f*

chloride ['kloraɪd] *s* chlorure *m*

chlorinate ['klorɪ‚net] *tr* (water) ver-duniser

chlorination [‚klorɪ'neʃən] *s* verduni-sation *f*

chlorine ['klorɪn] *s* chlore *m*

chloroform ['klorə‚fɔrm] *s* chloro-forme *m* ‖ *tr* chloroformer

chlorophyll ['klorəfɪl] *s* chlorophylle *f*

chock [tʃak] *s* cale *f*; (naut) poulie *f* ‖ *tr* caler

chock/-full/ *adj* bondé, comble, bourré

chocolate ['tʃakəlɪt], ['tʃakəlɪt] *adj & s* chocolat *m*

choc′olate bar′ s tablette f de chocolat

choice [tʃɔɪs] adj de choix, choisi ‖ m choix m; **by choice** par goût, volontairement

choir [kwaɪr] s chœur m

choir′boy′ s enfant m de chœur

choir′mas′ter s chef m de chœur; (eccl) maître m de chapelle

choir′ robe′ s soutanelle f

choke [tʃok] s (aut) starter m ‖ tr étouffer; (to obstruct) obstruer, boucher; **to choke back, down,** or **off** étouffer; **to choke up** obstruer, engorger ‖ intr étouffer; **to choke up** (e.g., with tears) étouffer

choke′ coil′ s (elec) bobine f de réactance

choker [ˈtʃokər] s (scarf) foulard m; (necklace) collier m court

choking [ˈtʃokɪŋ] s étouffement m

cholera [ˈkɑlərə] s choléra m

choleric [ˈkɑlərɪk] adj coléreux

cholesterol [kəˈlɛstəˌrol], [kəˈlɛstəˌral] s cholestérol m

choose [tʃuz] v (pret **chose** [tʃoz]; pp **chosen** [ˈtʃozən]) tr & intr choisir

choos·y [ˈtʃuzi] adj (comp **-ier;** super **-iest**) (coll) difficile à plaire, chipoteur

chop [tʃɑp] s coup m de hache; (culin) côtelette f; **to lick one's chops** (coll) se lécher or s'essuyer les babines ‖ v (pret & pp **chopped;** ger **chopping**) tr hacher, couper; **to chop down** abattre; **to chop off** trancher, couper; **to chop up** couper en morceaux, hacher ‖ intr (said of waves) clapoter

chopper [ˈtʃɑpər] s (of butcher) couperet m; (coll) hélicoptère m; **choppers** (slang) les dents fpl

chop′ping block′ s billot m, hachoir m

chop·py [ˈtʃɑpi] adj (comp **-pier;** ger **-piest**) agité; (waves) clapoteux

chop′stick′ s baguette f, bâtonnet m

choral [ˈkorəl] adj choral

chorale [koˈral] s choral m

cho′ral soci′ety s chorale f

chord [kord] s accord m; (geom) corde f

chore [tʃor] s devoir m; (burdensome chore) corvée f, besogne f

choreography [ˌkoriˈɑgrəfi] s chorégraphie f

chorister [ˈkɑrɪstər], [ˈkɔrɪstər] s choriste mf

chortle [ˈtʃortəl] intr glousser

chorus [ˈkorəs] s chœur m, chorale f; (of song) refrain m; (of protest) concert m ‖ tr répéter en chœur, faire chorus

cho′rus boy′ s boy m

cho′rus girl′ s girl f

cho′sen few′ [ˈtʃozən] s élite f

chow [tʃau] s (dog) chow-chow m; (mil) boustifaille f, mangeaille f

chow′-chow′ s (culin) macédoine f assaisonnée

chowder [ˈtʃaudər] s soupe f au poisson

Christ [kraɪst] s Christ m; le Christ

christen [ˈkrɪsən] tr baptiser

Christendom [ˈkrɪsəndəm] s chrétienté f

christening [ˈkrɪsənɪŋ] s baptême m

Christian [ˈkrɪstʃən] adj & s chrétien m

Christianity [ˌkrɪstʃɪˈæniti] s christianisme m

Christianize [ˈkrɪstʃəˌnaɪz] tr christianiser

Christ′ian name′ s nom m de baptême

Christmas [ˈkrɪsməs] adj de Noël ‖ s Noël m; **Merry Christmas!** Joyeux Noël!

Christ′mas card′ s carte f de Noël

Christ′mas car′ol s chanson f de Noël, chant m de Noël; (eccl) cantique m de Noël

Christ′mas Day′ s le jour de Noël

Christ′mas Eve′ s la veille de Noël

Christ′mas gift′ s cadeau m de Noël

Christ′mas tree′ s arbre m de Noël

Christ′mas tree lights′ s pl guirlandes fpl

chromatic [kroˈmætɪk] adj chromatique

chrome [krom] adj chromé ‖ s acier m chromé; (color) jaune m; (chem) chrome m ‖ tr chromer

chromium [ˈkromɪəm] s chrome m

chromosome [ˈkroməˌsom] s chromosome m

chronic [ˈkrɑnɪk] adj chronique

chronicle [ˈkrɑnɪkəl] s chronique f ‖ tr faire la chronique de

chronicler [ˈkrɑnɪklər] s chroniqueur m

chronologic(al) [ˌkrɑnəˈlɑdʒɪk(əl)] adj chronologique

chronolo·gy [krəˈnɑlədʒi] s (pl **-gies**) chronologie f

chronometer [krəˈnɑmɪtər] s chronomètre m

chrysanthemum [krɪˈsænθɪməm] s chrysanthème m

chub·by [ˈtʃʌbi] adj (comp **-bier;** super **-biest**) joufflu, potelé, dodu

chuck [tʃʌk] s (tap, blow, etc.) petite tape f; (under the chin) caresse f sous le menton; (of lathe) mandrin m; (bottom chuck and chuck rib) paleron m; (top chuck roast and chuck rib) entrecôte f ‖ tr tapoter; **to chuck away** jeter

chuckle [ˈtʃʌkəl] s gloussement m, petit rire m ‖ intr glousser, rire tout bas

chum [tʃʌm] s (coll) copain m ‖ v (pret & pp **chummed;** ger **chumming**) intr—**to chum around with** (coll) fraterniser avec

chum·my [ˈtʃʌmi] adj (comp **-mier;** super **-miest**) intime, familier

chump [tʃʌmp] s (slang) ballot m, lourdaud m

chunk [tʃʌŋk] s gros morceau m; (e.g., of wood) bloc m

church [tʃʌrtʃ] s église f

church′go′er s pratiquant m

church′man s (pl **-men**) (clergyman) ecclésiastique m; (layman) membre m d'une église, fidèle mf, paroissien m

church′ mem′ber s fidèle mf

church′ ser′vice s office m, culte m

church′yard′ s cimetière m

churlish [ˈtʃʌrlɪʃ] adj rustre, grossier; (out of sorts) grincheux

churn [tʃʌrn] s baratte f ‖ tr (cream)

baratter; (*e.g., water*) agiter; **to churn butter** battre le beurre || *intr* bouillonner

chute [ʃut] *s* glissière *f*; parachute *m*; (*of river*) rapide *m*, chute *f* d'eau
Cicero ['sɪsə,ro] *s* Cicéron *m*
cider ['saɪdər] *s* cidre *m*
cigar [sɪ'gɑr] *s* cigare *m*
cigarette [,sɪgə'rɛt] *s* cigarette *f*
cigarette' butt' *s* mégot *m*
cigarette' case' *s* étui *m* à cigarettes
cigarette' fiend' *s* fumeur *m* enragé
cigarette' hold'er *s* fume-cigarette *m*
cigarette' light'er *s* briquet *m*
cigar' hold'er *s* fume-cigare *m*
cigar' store' *s* bureau *m* de tabac
cinch [sɪntʃ] *s* (*of saddle*) sangle *f*; **it's a cinch** (coll) c'est couru d'avance || *tr* sangler; (**to make sure of**) (slang) assurer
cinder ['sɪndər] *s* cendre *f* || *tr* cendrer
Cinderella [,sɪndə'rɛlə] *s* la Cendrillon *f*
cin'der track' *s* piste *f* cendrée
cinema ['sɪnəmə] *s* cinéma *m*
cinnamon ['sɪnəmən] *s* cannelle *f*
cipher ['saɪfər] *s* zéro *m*; (*code*) chiffre *m*; **in cipher** en chiffres || *tr* & *intr* chiffrer
circle ['sʌrkəl] *s* cercle *m*; (*coterie*) milieu *m*, monde *m*; **to have circles around the eyes** avoir les yeux cernés || *tr* ceindre, entourer; (**to travel** *around*) faire le tour de
circuit ['sʌrkɪt] *s* circuit *m*; (*of judge*) tournée *f*
cir'cuit break'er *s* (elec) disjoncteur *m*
cir'cuit court' *s* cour *f* d'assises
circuitous [sər'kju·ɪtəs] *adj* détourné, indirect
circular ['sʌrkjələr] *adj* & *s* circulaire *f*
circulate ['sʌrkjə,let] *tr* faire circuler || *intr* circuler
circulation [,sʌrkjə'leʃən] *s* circulation *f*; (*of newspaper*) tirage *m*
circumcise ['sʌrkəm,saɪz] *tr* circoncire
circumcision [,sʌrkəm'sɪʒən] *s* circoncision *f*
circumference [sər'kʌmfərəns] *s* circonférence *f*
circumflex ['sʌrkəm,flɛks] *adj* & *s* circonflexe *m*
circumlocution [,sʌrkəmlo'kjuʃən] *s* circonlocution *f*
circumscribe [,sʌrkəm'skraɪb] *tr* circonscrire
circumspect ['sʌrkəm,spɛkt] *adv* circonspect
circumstance ['sʌrkəm,stæns] *s* circonstance *f*; (*pomp*) cérémonie *f*; **in easy circumstances** aisé; **under no circumstance** sous aucun prétexte; **under the circumstances** dans ces conditions
circumstantial [,sʌrkəm'stænʃəl] *adj* (*derived from circumstances*) circonstanciel; (*detailed*) circonstancié
cir'cumstan'tial ev'idence *s* preuves *fpl* indirectes
circumvent [,sʌrkəm'vɛnt] *tr* circonvenir
circus ['sʌrkəs] *s* cirque *m*; (Brit) rond-point *m*

cirrhosis [sɪ'rosɪs] *s* cirrhose *f*
cistern ['sɪstərn] *s* citerne *f*
citadel ['sɪtədəl] *s* citadelle *f*
citation [saɪ'teʃən] *s* citation *f*; (*award*) présentation *f*, mention *f*
cite [saɪt] *tr* citer
cither ['sɪθər] *s* cithare *f*
citified ['sɪtɪ,faɪd] *adj* urbain
citizen ['sɪtɪzən] *s* citoyen *m*
citizen-ry ['sɪtɪzənri] *s* (*pl* -ries) citoyens *mpl*
cit'izen-ship' *s* citoyenneté *f*
citric ['sɪtrɪk] *adj* citrique
citron ['sɪtrən] *s* cédrat *m*; (*tree*) cédratier *m*
citronella [,sɪtrə'nɛlə] *s* citronnelle *f*
cit'rus fruit' ['sɪtrəs] *s* agrumes *mpl*
cit-y ['sɪti] *s* (*pl* -ies) ville *f*; **the City** (*district within ancient boundaries*) la Cité
cit'y coun'cil *s* conseil *m* municipal
cit'y hall' *s* hôtel *m* de ville
cit'y plan'ner *s* urbaniste *mf*
cit'y plan'ning *s* urbanisme *m*
civ'et cat' ['sɪvɪt] *s* civette *f*
civic ['sɪvɪk] *adj* civique; **civics** instruction *f* civique
civies ['sɪviz] *spl* (coll) vêtements *mpl* civils; **in civies** en civil, en bourgeois
civil ['sɪvɪl] *adj* civil; (*courteous*) poli
civ'il defense' *s* protection *f* civile
civ'il engineer'ing *s* génie *m* civil
civilian [sɪ'vɪljən] *adj* & *s* civil *m*
civil'ian life' *s* vie *f* civile
civili-ty [sɪ'vɪlɪti] *s* (*pl* -ties) civilité *f*
civilization [,sɪvɪlɪ'zeʃən] *s* civilisation *f*
civilize ['sɪvɪ,laɪz] *tr* civiliser
civ'il rights' *spl* droits *mpl* civiques, droits politiques
civ'il serv'ant *s* fonctionnaire *mf*
civ'il serv'ice *s* fonction *f* publique
civ'il war' *s* guerre *f* civile; **Civil War** (*of the United States*) Guerre de Sécession
clack [klæk] *s* claquement *m* || *intr* claquer
clad [klæd] *adj* vêtu, habillé
claim [klem] *s* demande *f*; (*to a right*) revendication *f*; (*in prospecting*) concession *f* || *tr* (*a right*) réclamer, revendiquer; (*to require*) exiger, demander; **to claim that . . .** prétendre que . . . ; **to claim to** prétendre
claimant ['klemənt] *s* prétendant *m*, ayant droit *m*
clairvoyance [klɛr'vɔɪ·əns] *s* voyance *f*, seconde vue *f*; (*keen insight*) clairvoyance *f*
clairvoyant [klɛr'vɔɪ·ənt] *adj* clairvoyant || *s* voyante *f*; voyant *m*
clam [klæm] *s* palourde *f* || *v* (*pret* & *pp* clammed; *ger* clamming) *intr*—**to clam up** (slang) se taire
clam'bake' *s* pique-nique *m* aux palourdes
clamber ['klæmbər] *intr* grimper; **to clamber over** or **up** escalader
clam-my ['klæmi] *adj* (*comp* -mier; *super* -miest*) moite; (*clinging*) collant
clamor ['klæmər] *s* clameur *f* || *intr* vociférer; **to clamor for** réclamer

clamorous ['klæmərəs] *adj* bruyant

clamp [klæmp] *s* crampon *m*, agrafe *f*; (med) clamp *m* ‖ *tr* fixer, attacher; **to clamp together** cramponner ‖ *intr* —**to clamp down on** (coll) visser

clan [klæn] *s* clan *m*

clandestine [klæn'dɛstɪn] *adj* clandestin

clang [klæŋ] *s* bruit *m* métallique, choc *m* retentissant, cliquetis *m* ‖ *tr* faire résonner ‖ *intr* résonner

clank [klæŋk] *s* bruit *m* sec, bruit métallique, cliquetis *m* ‖ *tr* faire résonner ‖ *intr* résonner

clannish ['klænɪʃ] *adj* partisan

clap [klæp] *s* coup *m*; (*with hand*) tape *f*; (*with the hands*) battement *m* ‖ *v* (*pret & pp* **clapped**; *ger* **clapping**) *tr* battre; (*into jail*) (coll) fourrer; **to clap the hands** claquer ou battre les mains ‖ *intr* applaudir, claquer

clapper ['klæpər] *s* applaudisseur *m*; (*of bell*) battant *m*

claque [klæk] *s* (*paid clappers*) claque *f*; (*crush hat*) claque *m*

claret ['klærɪt] *s* bordeaux *m*

clari·fy ['klærɪ,faɪ] *v* (*pret & pp* -**fied**) *tr* clarifier

clarinet [,klærɪ'nɛt] *s* clarinette *f*

clarity ['klærɪti] *s* clarté *f*

clash [klæʃ] *s* choc *m*; (*conflict*) dispute *f*; (*of colors*) disparate *f* ‖ *intr* se heurter, s'entre-choquer; (*said of colors*) former une disparate

clasp [klæsp], [klɑsp] *s* agrafe *f*, fermoir *m*; (*embrace*) étreinte *f* ‖ *tr* agrafer; (*to embrace*) étreindre

clasp' knife' *s* couteau *m* pliant

class [klæs], [klɑs] *s* classe *f* ‖ *tr* classer

classic ['klæsɪk] *adj & s* classique *m*

classical ['klæsɪkəl] *adj* classique

classicism ['klæsɪ,sɪzəm] *s* classicisme *m*

classicist ['klæsɪsɪst] *s* classique *mf*

classification [,klæsɪfɪ'keʃən] *s* classification *f*, classement *m*

classified *adj* classifié, classé; (*documents*) secret, confidentiel

clas'sified adver'tise'ments *spl* petites annonces *fpl*

classi·fy ['klæsɪ,faɪ] *v* (*pret & pp* -**fied**) *tr* classifier

class'mate' *s* camarade *mf* de classe

class'room' *s* salle *f* de classe, classe *f*

class·y ['klæsi] *adj* (*comp* -**ier**; *super* -**iest**) (slang) chic

clatter ['klætər] *s* fracas *m* ‖ *intr* faire un fracas

clause [klɔz] *s* clause *f*, article *m*; (gram) proposition *f*

clavicle ['klævɪkəl] *s* clavicule *f*

claw [klɔ] *s* (*of animal*) griffe *f*; (*of crab*) pince *f*; (*of hammer*) panne *f* fendue ‖ *tr* griffer, déchirer

clay [kle] *s* argile *f*, glaise *f*

clay' pig'eon *s* pigeon *m* d'argile

clay' pipe' *s* pipe *f* en terre

clay' pit' *s* argilière *f*, glaisière *f*

clean [klin] *adj* propre; (*precise*) net ‖ *adv* net; tout à fait ‖ *tr* nettoyer; (*fish*) vider; (*streets*) balayer; **to clean out** curer; (*a person*) (slang)

mettre à sec, décaver; **to clean up** nettoyer ‖ *intr* faire le nettoyage

clean'-cut' *adj* bien délimité, net; (*e.g., athlete*) bien découplé

cleaner ['klinər] *s* nettoyeur *m*, dégraisseur *m*; **to be taken to the cleaners** (slang) se faire rincer

cleaning ['klinɪŋ] *s* nettoyage *m*

clean'ing wom'an *s* femme *f* de ménage

cleanliness ['klɛnlɪnɪs] *s* propreté *f*, netteté *f*

cleanse [klɛnz] *tr* nettoyer, écurer; (*e.g., a wound*) assainir; (*e.g., one's thoughts*) purifier

cleanser ['klɛnzər] *s* produit *m* de nettoyage; (*soap*) détersif *m*

clean'-shav'en *adj* rasé de frais

cleans'ing cream' *s* crème *f* de démaquillage

clean'up' *s* nettoiement *m*

clear [klɪr] *adj* clair; (*sharp*) net; (*free*) dégagé, libre; (*unmortgaged*) franc d'hypothèque; **to become clear** s'éclaircir; **to keep clear of** éviter ‖ *tr* (*to brighten*) éclaircir; (*e.g., a fence*) franchir; (*obstacles*) dégager; (*land*) défricher; (*goods in customs*) dédouaner; (*an account*) solder; **to clear away** écarter, enlever; **to clear oneself** se disculper; **to clear out** (*e.g., a garden*) jardiner; **to clear the table** desservir, enlever le couvert, ôter la nappe; **to clear up** éclaircir ‖ *intr* (*said of weather*) s'éclaircir; **to clear out** (coll) filer, se sauver

clearance ['klɪrəns] *s* permis *m*, laissez-passer *m*, autorisation *f*; (*between two objects*) espace *m* libre; (com) compensation *f*; (mach) espace *m* mort, jeu *m*

clear'ance sale' *s* vente *f* de soldes

clear'-cut' *adj* net, tranché; (*case*) absolu

clear'-head'ed *adj* lucide, perspicace

clearing ['klɪrɪŋ] *s* (*in clouds*) éclaircie *f*; (*in forest*) clairière *f*, trouée *f*

clear'ing house' *s* (com) comptoir *m* de règlement, chambre *f* de compensation

clearness ['klɪrnɪs] *s* clarté *f*, netteté *f*

clear'-sight'ed *adj* perspicace, clairvoyant

cleat [klit] *s* taquet *m*

cleavage ['klivɪdʒ] *s* clivage *m*

cleave [kliv] *v* (*pret & pp* **cleft** [klɛft] or **cleaved**) *tr* fendre ‖ *intr* se fendre; **to cleave to** s'attacher à, adhérer à

cleaver ['klivər] *s* couperet *m*, hachoir *m*

clef [klɛf] *s* (mus) clef *f*

cleft [klɛft] *adj* fendu ‖ *s* fente *f*, crevasse *f*

cleft' pal'ate *s* palais *m* fendu, fissure *f* palatine

clemen·cy ['klɛmənsi] *s* (*pl* -**cies**) clémence *f*

clement ['klɛmənt] *adj* clément

clench [klɛntʃ] *tr* serrer, crisper

cler·gy ['klʌrdʒi] *s* (*pl* -**gies**) (*members*) clergé *m*; (*profession*) clergie *f*

cler'gy·man *s* (*pl* -**men**) ecclésiastique *m*, clerc *m*

cleric ['klɛrɪk] s clerc m, ecclésiastique m

clerical ['klɛrɪkəl] adj clerical; de bureau || s clerical m; **clericals** habit m ecclésiastique

cler'ical er'ror s faute f de copiste, faute de sténographe

cler'ical work' s travail m de bureau

clerk [klɑrk] s (clerical worker) employé m de bureau, commis m; (in lawyer's office) clerc m; (in store) vendeur m; (in bank) comptable mf; (of court) greffier m; (eccl) clerc

clever ['klɛvər] adj habile, adroit

cliché [kli'ʃe] s cliché m, expression f consacrée

click [klɪk] s cliquetis m, clic m; (of heels) bruit m sec; (of tongue) claquement m; (of a machine) déclic m || intr cliqueter, faire un déclic; (to succeed) (coll) réussir; (to get along well) (coll) s'entendre à merveille

client ['klɑɪənt] s client m

clientele [,klɑɪən'tɛl] s clientèle f

cliff [klɪf] s falaise f, talus m raide

climate ['klɑɪmɪt] s climat m

climax ['klɑɪmæks] s point m culminant, comble m

climb [klɑɪm] s montée f, ascension f || tr & intr monter, gravir; grimper; **to climb down** descendre

climber ['klɑɪmər] s grimpeur m; (bot) plante f grimpante; (social climber) parvenu m, arriviste mf

climbing ['klɑɪmɪŋ] s montée f, escalade f

clinch [klɪntʃ] s crampon m, rivet m; (boxing) corps-à-corps m || tr river; (a bargain) boucler || intr se prendre corps à corps

clincher ['klɪntʃər] s (coll) argument m sans réplique

cling [klɪŋ] v (pret & pp clung [klʌŋ]) intr s'accrocher, se cramponner; **to cling to** (a person) se serrer contre; (a belief) adhérer à

cling'stone peach' s alberge f

clinic ['klɪnɪk] s clinique f

clinical ['klɪnɪkəl] adj clinique

clinician [klɪ'nɪʃən] s clinicien m

clink [klɪŋk] s cliquetis m; (e.g., of glasses) tintement m, choc m || tr (glasses, in a toast) choquer; **to clink glasses with** trinquer avec || intr tinter, cliqueter

clip [klɪp] s attache f; (brooch) agrafe f, clip m; (of gun) chargeur m; (blow) (coll) taloche f; (fast pace) (coll) pas m rapide || v (pret & pp clipped; ger clipping) tr (to fasten) attacher; (hair) rafraîchir; (sheep) tondre; (one's words) avaler

clipper ['klɪpər] s (aer) clipper m; (naut) voilier m de course; **clippers** tondeuse f

clipping ['klɪpɪŋ] s tondage m; (of sheep) tonte f; (of one's hair) taille f; (of newspaper) coupure f (de presse); **clippings** (cuttings, shavings, etc.) rognures fpl, chutes fpl

clip'ping ser'vice s argus m

clique [klik] s coterie f, clan m, chapelle f

cloak [klok] s manteau m || tr masquer

cloak'-and-dag'ger adj (e.g., story) de cape et d'épée

cloak'room' s vestiaire m; (rr) consigne f

clock [klɑk] s pendule f; (e.g., in a tower) horloge f; **to turn back the clock** retarder l'horloge; (fig) revenir en arrière || tr chronométrer

clock'mak'er s horloger m

clock' tow'er s tour f de l'horloge

clock'wise' adj & adv dans le sens des aiguilles d'une montre

clock'work' s mouvement m d'horlogerie; **like clockwork** (coll) comme une horloge

clod [klɑd] s motte f; (person) rustre mf

clod'hop'per s cul-terreux m; (shoe) godillot m

clog [klɑg] s (shoe) galoche f, socque m; (hindrance) entrave f || v (pret & pp clogged; ger clogging) tr (e.g., a pipe) boucher; (e.g., traffic) entraver || intr se boucher

cloister ['klɔɪstər] s cloître m || tr cloîtrer

close [klos] adj proche, tout près; (game; weave; formation; order) serré; (friend) intime; (friendship) étroit; (room) renfermé, étouffant; (translation) fidèle; **close to** près de || adv près, de près || [kloz] s (enclosure) clos m; (end) fin f; (closing) fermeture f || tr fermer; (to end) conclure, terminer; (an account) régler, clôturer; (ranks) serrer, resserrer; (a meeting) lever; **close quotes** fermez les guillemets; **to close in** enfermer; **to close out** (com) liquider, solder || intr se fermer; finir, se terminer; (on certain days) (theat) faire relâche; **to close in on** (the enemy) aborder

close' call' [klos] s—**to have a close call** (coll) l'échapper belle

close-cropped ['klos'krɑpt] adj coupé ras

closed [klozd] adj fermé; (road) barré; (e.g., pipe) obturé, bouché; (ranks) serré; (public sign in front of theater) relâche; **with closed eyes** les yeux clos

closed' car' s conduite f intérieure

closed'-cir'cuit tel'evision s télévision f en circuit fermé

closed' sea'son s fermeture f de la chasse, fermeture de la pêche

closefisted ['klos'fɪstəd] adj ladre, avare

close-fitting ['klos'fɪtɪŋ] adj collant, ajusté, qui moule le corps

close-grained ['klos'grend] adj serré

closely ['klosli] adv (near) de près, étroitement; (exactly) exactement

close-mouthed ['klos'mauðd] adj peu communicatif, économe de mots

closeness ['klosnɪs] s (nearness) proximité f; (accuracy) exactitude f; (stinginess) avarice f; (of weather) lourdeur f; (of air) manque m d'air

close′ shave′ [klos] *s*—**to have a close shave** se faire raser de près; (coll) échapper à un cheveu près

closet [ˈklɑzɪt] *s* placard *m*

clos′et dra′ma *s* spectacle *m* dans un fauteuil

close-up [ˈklos͵ʌp] *s* premier plan *m*, gros plan

closing [ˈklozɪŋ] *adj* dernier, final ‖ *s* fermeture *f*; (*of account; of meeting*) clôture *f*

clos′ing-out′ sale′ *s* soldes *mpl* des fins de séries

clos′ing price′ *s* dernier cours *m*

clot [klɑt] *s* caillot *m* ‖ *v* (*pret & pp* clotted; *ger* clotting) *tr* cailler ‖ *intr* se cailler

cloth [klɔθ], [klɑθ] *s* étoffe *f*; (*fabric*) tissu *m*; (*of wool*) drap *m*; (*of cotton or linen*) toile *f*; cloths (*for cleaning*) chiffons *mpl*, torchons *mpl*, linge *m*; **the cloth** le clergé

clothe [kloð] *v* (*pret & pp* clothed or clad [klæd]) *tr* habiller, vêtir; (*e.g., with authority*) revêtir, investir

clothes [kloz], [kloðz] *spl* vêtements *mpl*, habits *mpl*; (*underclothes, shirts, etc.; wash*) linge *m*; **in plain clothes** en civil; **to put on one's clothes** s'habiller; **to take off one's clothes** se déshabiller

clothes′ bas′ket *s* panier *m* à linge

clothes′ brush′ *s* brosse *f* à habits

clothes′ clos′et *s* garde-robe *f*, penderie *f*, placard *m*

clothes′ dry′er *s* séchoir *m* à linge

clothes′ hang′er *s* cintre *m*

clothes′ horse′ *s* séchoir-chevalet *m*

clothes′ line′ *s* corde *f* à linge, étendoir *m*

clothes′ moth′ *s* gerce *f*

clothes′ pin′ *s* pince *f* à linge

clothes′ rack′ *s* patère *f*

clothier [ˈkloðjər] *s* confectionneur *m*, marchand *m* de confections

clothing [ˈkloðɪŋ] *s* vêtements *mpl*

cloud [klaud] *s* nuage *m*; (*heavy cloud; multitude*) nuée *f*; **in the clouds** dans les nues ‖ *tr* couvrir de nuages; (phot) voiler ‖ *intr* (phot) se voiler; **to cloud over** or **up** se couvrir de nuages

cloud′ burst′ *s* averse *f*, rafale *f* de pluie

cloud′ cham′ber *s* (phys) chambre *f* d'ionisation

cloudless [ˈklaudlɪs] *adj* sans nuages

cloud-y [ˈklaudi] *adj* (*comp* -ier; *super* -iest) nuageux; (phot) voilé

clout [klaut] *s* (coll) gifle *f* ‖ *tr* (coll) gifler

clove [klov] *s* clou *m* de girofle, girofle *m*; (*of garlic*) gousse *f*; (bot) giroflier *m*

clove′ hitch′ *s* demi-clef *f* à capeler

clo′ven hoof′ [ˈklovən] *s* pied *m* fourchu; **to show the cloven hoof** (coll) montrer le bout de l'oreille

clover [ˈklovər] *s* trèfle *m*; **to be in clover** (coll) être sur le velours

clo′ver-leaf′ *s* (*pl* -leaves) feuille *f* de trèfle; (*intersection*) croisement *m* en trèfle, saut-de-mouton *m*

clown [klaun] *s* clown *m*, pitre *m*, bouffon *m* ‖ *intr* faire le pitre

clownish [ˈklaunɪʃ] *adj* bouffon; (*clumsy*) empoté, rustre

cloy [klɔɪ] *tr* rassasier

club [klʌb] *s* massue *f*, gourdin *m*, assommoir *m*; cercle *m*, amicale *f*, club *m*; (cards) trèfle *m*; (golf) crosse *f*, club *m* ‖ *v* (*pret & pp* clubbed; *ger* clubbing) *tr* (*to strike*) assommer; (*to pool*) mettre en commun ‖ *intr*—**to club together** s'associer; se cotiser

club′ car′ *s* voiture-salon *f*

club′ foot′ *s* (*pl* -feet) pied *m* équin, pied bot

club′ foot′ed *adj*—**to be clubfooted** avoir le pied bot, être pied-bot

club′ house′ *s* club *m*, cercle *m*

club′ man *s* (*pl* -men) clubman *m*

club′ room′ *s* salle *f* de réunion

club′ steak′ *s* aloyau *m* de bœuf

club′ wom′an *s* (*pl* -wom′en) cercleuse *f*

cluck [klʌk] *s* gloussement *m* ‖ *intr* glousser

clue [klu] *s* indice *m*, indication *f*; **to find the clue** trouver la clef; **to give s.o. a clue** mettre qn sur la piste; **to have the clue** tenir le bout du fil

clump [klʌmp] *s* (*of earth*) bloc *m*, masse *f*; (*of trees*) bouquet *m*; (*of shrubs or flowers*) massif *m*; (*gait*) pas *m* lourd ‖ *intr*—**to clump along** marcher lourdement

clum-sy [ˈklʌmzi] *adj* (*comp* -sier; *super* -siest) (*worker*) maladroit, gauche; (*work*) bâclé, grossier

cluster [ˈklʌstər] *s* bouquet *m*, massif *m*; (*of grapes*) grappe *f*; (*of pears*) glane *f*; (*of bananas*) régime *m*; (*of diamonds*) épi *m*, nœud *m*; (*of stars*) amas *m* ‖ *tr* grouper ‖ *intr*—**to cluster around** se rassembler; **to cluster together** se conglomérer

clutch [klʌtʃ] *s* (*grasp, grip*) griffe *f*, serre *f*; (aut) embrayage *m*; (aut) pédale *f* d'embrayage; **to fall into the clutches of** tomber sous la patte de; **to let in the clutch** embrayer; **to throw out the clutch** débrayer ‖ *tr* saisir, empoigner ‖ *intr*—**to clutch at** se raccrocher à

clutter [ˈklʌtər] *s* encombrement *m* ‖ *tr*—**to clutter up** encombrer

Co. *abbr* (**Company**) Cⁱᵉ

c/o *abbr* (**in care of**) a/s (aux soins de)

coach [kotʃ] *s* coche *m*, carrosse *f*; (*bus*) autocar *m*, car *m*; (*two-door sedan*) coche *m*; (rr) voiture *f*; (sports) entraîneur *m*, trainer *m* ‖ *tr* donner des leçons particulières à; entraîner; (*for an exam*) préparer à un examen, chauffer; (*an actor*) faire répéter

coach′-and-four′ *s* carrosse *f* à quatre chevaux

coach′ box′ *s* siège *m* du cocher

coach′ house′ *s* remise *f*

coaching [ˈkotʃɪŋ] *s* leçons *fpl* particulières, chauffage *m*, répétitions *fpl*; (sport) entraînement *m*

coach′ man *s* (*pl* -men) cocher *m*

coagulate [ko'ægjə,let] *tr* coaguler ‖ *intr* se coaguler

coal [kol] *adj* charbonnier, houiller ‖ *s* houille *f*, charbon *m*; coals (*embers*) tisons *mpl*, charbons ardents; to carry coals to Newcastle porter de l'eau à la rivière

coal/bin/ *s* coffre *m* à charbon

coal/ bunk/er *s* soute *f* à charbon

coal/ car/ *s* wagon-tombereau *m*

coal/deal/er *s* charbonnier *m*

coalesce [,ko-ə'les] *intr* s'unir, se combiner, fusionner

coal/ field/ *s* bassin *m* houiller

coalition [,ko-ə'lɪʃən] *s* coalition *f*; to form a coalition se coaliser

coal/ mine/ *s* houillère *f*

coal/ oil/ *s* pétrole *m* lampant

coal/ scut/tle *s* seau *m* à charbon

coal/ tar/ *s* goudron *m* de houille

coal/yard/ *s* charbonnerie *f*

coarse [kors] *adj* (*in manners*) grossier; (*composed of large particles*) gros; (*hair, skin*) rude

coarse/-grained/ *adj* à gros grain; (*wood*) à gros fil

coarseness ['korsnɪs] *s* grossièreté *f*; (*of hair, skin*) rudesse *f*

coast [kost] *s* côte *f*; the coast is clear la route est libre ‖ *intr* caboter; (*said of automobile*) aller au débrayé; (*said of bicycle*) aller en roue libre; to coast along continuer sur sa lancée

coastal ['kostəl] *adj* côtier

coaster ['kostər] *s* dessous-de-verre *m*, sous-verre *m*; (*naut*) caboteur *m*

coast/er brake/ *s* frein *m* à contre-pédalage

coast/ guard/ *s* service *m* de guet le long des côtes

coast/-guard cut/ter *s* garde-côte *m*

coast/guards/man *s* (*pl* -men) soldat *m* chargé de la garde des côtes

coasting ['kostɪŋ] *s* (*e.g., on a cycle*) descente *f* en roue libre

coast/ing trade/ *s* cabotage *m*

coast/line/ *s* littoral *m*

coast/wise/ *adj* côtier ‖ *adv* le long de la côte

coat [kot] *s* (*jacket*) veste *f*; (*suitcoat*) veston *m*; (*topcoat*) manteau *m*; (*of an animal*) robe *f*, pelage *m*, livrée *f*; (*of paint*) couche *f* ‖ *tr* enduire; (*with chocolate*) enrober; (*a pill*) dragéifier

coat/ hang/er *s* cintre *m*, portemanteau *m*

coating ['kotɪŋ] *s* enduit *m*, couche *f*

coat/ of arms/ *s* écu *m* armorial; (*bearings*) blason *m*, armoiries *fpl*

coat/ of mail/ *s* cotte *f* de mailles

coat/rack/ *s* portemanteau *m*

coat/room/ *s* vestiaire *m*

coat/tail/ *s* basque *f*

coauthor [ko'ɔθər] *s* coauteur *m*

coax [koks] *tr* cajoler, amadouer

cob [kab] *s* (*of corn*) épi *m* de maïs; (*horse*) cob *m*; (*swan*) cygne *m* mâle

cobalt ['kobɔlt] *s* cobalt *m*

cobbler ['kablər] *s* cordonnier *m*; (*cake*) tourte *f* aux fruits; (*drink*) boisson *f* glacée

cobble•stone ['kabəl,ston] *s* pavé *m*

cob/web/ *s* toile *f* d'araignée

cocaine [ko'ken] *s* cocaïne *f*

cock [kak] *s* coq *m*; (*faucet*) robinet *m*; (*of gun*) chien *m* ‖ *tr* (*one's ears*) dresser, redresser; (*one's hat*) mettre sur l'oreille, retrousser; (*a rifle*) armer

cockade [ka'ked] *s* cocarde *f*

cock-a-doodle-doo ['kakə,dudəl'du] *interj* cocorico!

cock/-and-bull/ sto/ry *s* coq-à-l'âne *m*

cock/crow/ *s* cocorico *m*

cocked/ hat/ *s* chapeau *m* à cornes; to knock into a cocked hat (slang) démolir, aplatir

cock/er span/iel ['kakər] *s* cocker *m*

cock/eyed/ *adj* (coll) de travers, de biais; (slang) insensé

cock/fight/ *s* combat *m* de coqs

cockle ['kakəl] *s* (bot) nielle *f*; (zool) bucarde *f*, clovisse *f*

cock/pit/ *s* (aer) cockpit *m*, carlingue *f*

cock/roach/ *s* blatte *f*, cafard *m*

cockscomb ['kaks,kom] *s* crête *f* de coq; (bot) crête-de-coq *f*

cock/sure/ *adj* (coll) sûr et certain

cock/tail/ *s* cocktail *m*

cock/tail dress/ *s* robe *f* de cocktail

cock/tail par/ty *s* cocktail *m*

cock/tail shak/er *s* shaker *m*

cock•y ['kaki] *adj* (*comp* -ier; *super* -iest) (coll) effronté, suffisant

cocoa ['koko] *s* cacao *m*; (*drink*) chocolat *m*

co/coa bean/ *s* cacao *m*

coconut ['koke,nʌt] *s* noix *f* de coco, coco *m*

co/conut palm/ *s* cocotier *m*

cocoon [ke'kun] *s* cocon *m*

cod [kad] *s* (ichth) morue *f*

C.O.D. ['si'o'di] *s* (letterword) (Collect on Delivery) C.R., contre remboursement, e.g., send it to me C.O.D. envoyez-le-moi C.R.

coddle ['kadəl] *tr* dorloter, gâter

code [kod] *s* code *m*; (*secret code*) chiffre *m* ‖ *tr* chiffrer

code/ word/ *s* mot *m* convenu

codex ['kodeks] *s* (*pl* codices ['kodɪ,siz], ['kadɪ,siz]) manuscrit *m* ancien

cod/fish/ *s* morue *f*

codger ['kadʒər] *s*—old codger (coll) vieux bonhomme *m*

codicil ['kadɪsɪl] *s* (*of will*) codicille *m*; (*of contract, treaty, etc.*) avenant *m*

codi•fy ['kadɪ,faɪ], ['kodɪ,faɪ] *v* (*pret & pp* -fied) *tr* codifier

cod/-liver oil/ *s* huile *f* de foie de morue

coed ['ko,ed] *s* collégienne *f*, étudiante *f* universitaire

coeducation [,ko·edʒə'keʃən] *s* co-éducation *f*

co/educa/tional school/ [,ko·edʒə'keʃənəl] *s* école *f* mixte

coefficient [,ko·ɪ'fɪʃənt] *s* coefficient *m*

coerce [ko'ʌrs] *tr* contraindre, forcer

coercion [ko'ʌrʃən] *s* coercition *f*

coexist [,ko·ɪg'zɪst] intr coexister

, coexistence [,ko·ɪg'zɪstəns] s coexistence f

coffee ['kɔfi], ['kafi] s café m; black coffee café noir, café nature; ground coffee café moulu; roasted coffee café brûlé, café torréfié

cof'fee and rolls' s café m complet

cof'fee bean' s grain m de café

cof'fee break' s pause-café f

cof'fee-cake' s gimblette f (qui se prend avec le café)

cof'fee cup' s tasse f à café

cof'fee grind'er s moulin m à café

cof'fee grounds' spl marc m de café

cof'fee mak'er s percolateur m

cof'fee mill' s moulin m à café

cof'fee planta'tion s caféière f

cof'fee-pot' s cafetière f; (for pouring) verseuse f

cof'fee roast'er s brûloir m

cof'fee shop' s (of hotel) hôtel-restaurant m; (in station) buffet m

cof'fee tree' s caféier m

coffer ['kɔfər], ['kafər] s coffre m, caisse f; (archit) caisson m; coffers trésor m, fonds mpl

cof'fer-dam' s coffre m, bâtardeau m

coffin ['kɔfɪn], ['kafɪn] s cercueil m, bière f

cog [kag] s dent f; (cogwheel) roue f dentée; to slip a cog (coll) avoir des absences

cogency ['kodʒənsi] s force f (de persuasion)

cogent ['kodʒənt] adj puissant, convaincant

cogitate ['kadʒɪ,tet] tr & intr méditer

cognac ['konjæk], ['kanjæk] s cognac m

cognate ['kagnet] adj congénère, apparenté || s congénère mf; (word) mot m apparenté

cognizance ['kagnɪzəns], ['kanɪzəns] s connaissance f

cognizant ['kagnɪzənt], ['kanɪzənt] adj informé

cog'wheel' s roue f dentée

cohabit [ko'hæbɪt] intr cohabiter

coheir [ko'er] s cohéritier

cohere [ko'hɪr] intr s'agglomérer, adhérer; (said of reasoning or style) se suivre logiquement, correspondre

coherent [ko'hɪrənt] adj cohérent

cohesion [ko'hiʒən] s cohésion f

coiffeur [kwa'fʌr] s coiffeur m pour dames

coiffure [kwa'fjur] s coiffure f || tr coiffer

coil [kɔɪl] s (something wound in a spiral) rouleau m; (single turn of spiral) tour m; (of a still) serpentin m; (of hair) boucle f; (elec) bobine f; coils (of snake) nœuds mpl || tr enrouler; (naut) lover, gléner || intr s'enrouler; (said of snake or stream) serpenter

coil' spring' s ressort m en spirale, ressort à boudin

coin [kɔɪn] s monnaie f; (single coin) pièce f de monnaie; (wedge) coin m; in coin en espèces, en numéraire; to pay back s.o. in his own coin rendre à qn la monnaie de sa pièce; to toss a coin jouer à pile ou face || tr (a new word; a story or lie) forger, inventer; to coin money frapper de la monnaie; (coll) faire des affaires d'or, s'enrichir à vue d'œil

coinage ['kɔɪnɪdʒ] s monnayage m; (fig) invention f

coincide [,ko·ɪn'saɪd] intr coïncider

coincidence [ko'ɪnsɪdəns] s coïncidence f

coition [ko'ɪʃən] or coitus ['ko·ɪtəs] s coït m

coke [kok] s coke m || tr cokéfier || intr se cokéfier

colander ['kʌləndər], ['kaləndər] s passoire f

cold [kold] adj froid; it is cold (said of weather) il fait froid; to be cold (said of person) avoir froid || s froid m; (indisposition) rhume m; to be left out in the cold (slang) rester en carafe; to catch a cold attraper un rhume, s'enrhumer

cold' blood' s—in cold blood de sang-froid

cold'-blood'ed adj insensible; (sensitive to cold) frileux; (zool) à sang froid

cold' chis'el s ciseau m à froid

cold' com'fort s maigre consolation f

cold' cream' s cold-cream m

cold' cuts' spl viandes fpl froides, assiette f anglaise

cold' feet' [fit] spl—to have cold feet (coll) avoir froid aux yeux

cold' front' s front m froid

cold'-heart'ed adj au cœur dur, insensible

coldness ['koldnɪs] s froideur f; (in the air) froidure f

cold' should'er s—to give s.o. the cold shoulder (coll) battre froid à qn

cold' snap' s coup m de froid

cold' stor'age s entrepôt m frigorifique; in cold storage en glacière

cold'-stor'age adj frigorifique

cold' war' s guerre f froide

cold' wave' s vague f de froid

coleslaw ['kol,slɔ] s salade f de chou

colic ['kalɪk] s colique f

coliseum [,kalɪ'si·əm] s colisée m

collaborate [kə'læbə,ret] intr collaborer

collaborationist [kə,læbə're/ənɪst] s collaborationniste mf

collaborator [kə'læbə,retər] s collaborateur m

collapse [kə'læps] s écroulement m, effondrement m; (of prices; of government) chute f; (of prices; of a beam) fléchissement m; (pathol) collapsus m || intr s'écrouler, s'effondrer; (said of government) tomber; (said of structure or prices) s'effondrer; (said of balloon) se dégonfler

collapsible [kə'læpsɪbəl] adj démontable, rabattable, pliant

collar ['kalər] s (of dress, shirt) collet m, col m; (worn by dog; on pigeon) collier m; (mach) collier || tr colleter; (coll) empoigner

col/lar·band/ *s* pied *m* de col (d'une chemise)

col/lar·bone/ *s* clavicule *f*

collate [kə'let], ['kalet] *tr* collationner, conférer

collateral [kə'lætərəl] *adj* accessoire; correspondant; *(kin)* collatéral || *s (kin)* collatéral *m;* (com) nantissement *m*

collation [kə'leʃən] *s* collation *f*

colleague ['kalig] *s* collègue *mf*

collect ['kalekt] *s* (eccl) collecte *f* || [kə'lekt] *tr* rassembler; *(taxes)* percevoir, lever; *(stamps, antiques)* collectionner; *(eggs; classroom papers; tickets)* ramasser; *(mail)* faire la levée de; *(debts)* recouvrer; *(gifts, money)* collecter; *(one's thoughts; anecdotes)* recueillir; **to collect oneself** se reprendre, se remettre || *intr (for the poor)* quêter; *(to gather together)* se rassembler, se réunir; *(to pile up)* s'amasser || *adv* en p.c.v., e.g., **to telephone collect** téléphoner en p.c.v.

collect/ call/ *s* (telp) communication *f* P.C.V.

collected *adj* recueilli, maître de soi

collection [kə'lekʃən] *s* collection *f;* (of taxes) perception *f,* levée *f,* recouvrement *m;* (of mail) levée *f;* (of verses) recueil *m*

collec/tion plate/ *s* plateau *m* de quête

collective [kə'lektɪv] *adj* collectif

collector [kə'lektər] *s (of stamps, antiques)* collectionneur *m;* (of taxes) percepteur *m,* receveur *m,* collecteur *m;* (of tickets) contrôleur *m*

college ['kalɪdʒ] *s (of cardinals, electors, etc.)* collège *m;* (school in a university) faculté *f;* (U.S.A.) école *f* des arts et sciences

collegian [kə'lidʒɪ·ən] *s* étudiant *m*

collegiate [kə'lidʒɪ·ɪt] *adj* collégial, de l'université, universitaire

collide [kə'laɪd] *intr* se heurter, se tamponner; **to collide with** se heurter à or contre, heurter contre

collier ['kaljər] *s* houilleur *m;* (ship) charbonnier *m*

collier·y ['kaljərɪ] *s (pl* -ies) houillère *f*

collision [kə'lɪʒən] *s* collision *f*

collocate ['kalo,ket] *tr* disposer en rapport; *(creditors)* colloquer

colloid ['kalɔɪd] *adj* colloïdal || *s* colloïde *m*

colloquial [kə'lokwɪ·əl] *adj* familier

colloquialism [kə'lokwɪ·ə,lɪzəm] *s* expression *f* familière

collo·quy ['kaləkwɪ] *s (pl* -quies) colloque *m*

collusion [kə'luʒən] *s* collusion *f;* **to be in collusion with** être d'intelligence avec

cologne [kə'lon] *s* eau *f* de Cologne

Colombia [kə'lʌmbɪ·ə] *s* Colombie *f;* la Colombie

colon ['kolən] *s* (anat) côlon *m;* (gram) deux points *mpl*

colonel ['kʌrnəl] *s* colonel *m*

colonial [kə'lonɪ·əl] *adj & s* colonial *m*

colonist ['kalənɪst] *s* colon *m*

colonize ['kalə,naɪz] *tr & intr* coloniser

colonnade [,kalə'ned] *s* colonnade *f*

colo·ny ['kalənɪ] *s (pl* -nies) colonie *f*

colophon ['kalə,fan] *s* colophon *m*

color ['kalər] *s* couleur *f;* **the colors** les couleurs, le drapeau; **to call to the colors** appeler sous les drapeaux; **to give or lend color** to colorer; (fig) rendre vraisemblable; **to show one's true colors** se révéler sous son vrai jour; **under color of** sous couleur de; **with flying colors** enseignes déployées || *tr* colorer; *(e.g., a drawing)* colorier; *(to exaggerate)* donner de l'éclat à, imager; *(to dye)* teindre || *intr* se colorer; *(to blush)* rougir

col/or·bear/er *s* porte-drapeau *m*

col/or·blind/ *adj* daltonien, aveugle des couleurs

colored *adj* coloré; *(person)* de couleur; *(drawing)* colorié

colorful ['kalərfəl] *adj* (striking) coloré; *(unusual)* pittoresque

col/or guard/ *s* garde *f* d'honneur du drapeau

coloring ['kalərɪŋ] *s* colorant || *s* colorant *m;* (of painting, complexion, style) coloris *m*

colorless ['kalərlɪs] *adj* incolore

col/or photog/raphy *s* photographie *f* en couleurs

col/or salute/ *s* (mil) salut *m* au drapeau, salut aux couleurs

col/or ser/geant *s* sergent-chef *m,* sergent-major *m*

col/or tel/evision *s* télévision *f* en couleurs

colossal [kə'lasəl] *adj* colossal

colossus [kə'lasəs] *s* colosse *m*

colt [kolt] *s* poulain *m*

Columbus [kə'lʌmbəs] *s* Colomb *m*

column ['kaləm] *s* colonne *f;* (journ) rubrique *f,* chronique *f,* courrier *m;* (mil) colonne *f*

columnar [kə'lʌmnər] *adj* en colonne

columnist ['kaləmɪst] *s* chroniqueur *m,* courriériste *mf*

coma ['komə] *s* (pathol) coma *m*

comb [kom] *s* peigne *m;* (currycomb) étrille *f;* (of rooster; of wave) crête *f;* (filled with honey) rayon *m* || *tr* peigner; explorer minutieusement, fouiller; **to comb out** démêler || *intr (said of waves)* déferler

com·bat ['kambæt] *s* combat *m* || ['kambæt], [kəm'bæt] *v (pret & pp* -bated *or* -batted; *ger* -bating *or* -batting) *tr & intr* combattre

combatant ['kambətənt] *adj & s* combattant *m*

com/bat du/ty *s* service *m* de combat, service au front

combination [,kambɪ'neʃən] *s* combinaison *f*

combine ['kambaɪn] *s* trust *m,* combinaison *f* financière, entente *f* industrielle; (agr) moissonneuse-batteuse *f* || [kəm'baɪn] *tr* combiner || *intr* se liguer, fusionner; (chem) se combiner

combin/ing form/ *s* élément *m* de composition

combo ['kambo] *s* (*of four musicians*) quartette *f*

combustible [kəm'bʌstɪbəl] *adj & s* combustible *m*

combustion [kəm'bʌstʃən] *s* combustion *f*

come [kʌm] *v* (*pret* came [kem]; *pp* come) *intr* venir; **come in!** entrez!; **to come after** succéder à, suivre; (*to come to get*) venir chercher; **to come apart** se séparer, se défaire; **to come around** (*to snap back*) se rétablir; (*to give in*) céder; **to come at** (*to attack*) se jeter sur; **to come back** revenir; (*coll*) revenir en vogue; **to come before** précéder; (*e.g., a legislature*) se mettre devant; **to come between** s'interposer entre; **to come by** (*to get*) obtenir; (*to pass*) passer; **to come down** descendre; **to come downstairs** descendre (en bas); **to come down with** tomber malade avec; **to come for** venir chercher; **to come from** provenir de, dériver de; (*said of wind*) chasser de; **to come in** entrer; entrer dans; (*said of tide*) monter; (*said of style*) entrer en vogue; **to come in for** avoir part à; (*e.g., an inheritance*) succéder à; (*e.g., sympathy*) s'attirer; **to come off** se détacher; (*to take place*) avoir lieu; en sortir, e.g., **to come off victorious** en sortir vainqueur; **to come out** sortir; (*said of sun, stars; said of book*) paraître; (*said of buds*) éclore; (*said of news*) se divulguer; (*said of debutante*) débuter; **to come out for** se prononcer pour; **to come over** se laisser persuader; arriver, e.g., **what's come over him?** qu'est-ce qui lui est arrivé?; **to come through** (*e.g., fields*) passer par, passer à travers; (*e.g., a wall*) pénétrer; (*an illness*) surmonter; se tirer indemne; **to come to** revenir à soi; **to come together** s'assembler, se réunir; **to come true** se réaliser; **to come up** monter; (*to occur*) se présenter; **to come upstairs** monter (en haut); **to come up to** monter jusqu'à, venir à; **to come up with** proposer

come'-and-go' *s* va-et-vient *m*

come'back' *s* (*of style*) (coll) retour *m* en vogue; (*of statesman*) (coll) retour *m* au pouvoir; (slang) réplique *f*, riposte *f*; **to stage a comeback** (coll) se réhabiliter, faire une belle remontée

comedian [kə'midɪ·ən] *s* comique *m*; (*on the legitimate stage*) comédien *m*; auteur *m* comique

comedienne [kə'midɪ'ɛn] *s* comédienne *f*

come'down' *s* humiliation *f*, déchéance *f*

come·dy ['kamədɪ] *s* (*pl* -dies) comédie *f*

come·ly ['kʌmlɪ] *adj* (*comp* -lier; *super* -liest) (*attractive*) avenant, gracieux; (*decorous*) convenable, bienséant

come'-on' *s* (slang) leurre *m*, attrape *f*

comet ['kamɪt] *s* comète *f*

comfort ['kʌmfərt] *s* confort *m*; consolation *f*; (*person*) consolateur *m*; **comforts** commodités *fpl*, agréments *mpl* ‖ *tr* consoler, réconforter

comfortable ['kʌmfərtəbəl] *adj* confortable; (*in a state of comfort*) bien; (*well-off*) à l'aise

comforter ['kʌmfərtər] *s* consolateur *m*; (*bedcover*) couvre-pieds *m* piqué; (*of wool*) cache-nez *m*; (*for baby*) tétine *f*, sucette *f*

comforting ['kʌmfərtɪŋ] *adj* consolateur, réconfortant

com'fort sta'tion *s* châlet *m* de nécessité, lieux *mpl* d'aisances, toilette *f*

comic ['kamɪk] *adj & s* comique *m*; **comics** (*cartoons*) dessins *mpl* humoristiques

com'ic op'era *s* opéra *m* bouffe

com'ic strip' *s* bande *f* humoristique

coming ['kamɪŋ] *adj* qui vient; (*future*) d'avenir, de demain ‖ *s* arrivée *f*, venue *f*; **comings and goings** allées et venues

com'ing out' *s* (*of stocks, bonds, etc.*) émission *f*; (*of a book*) parution *f*; (*of a young lady*) début *m*

comma ['kamə] *s* virgule *f*; (*in French a period or sometimes a small space is used to mark the divisions of whole numbers*) point *m*

command [kə'mænd], [kə'mand] *s* (*leadership*) gouvernement *m*; (*order, direction*) commandement *m*, ordre *m*; (*e.g., of a foreign language*) maîtrise *f*; **to be at s.o.'s command** être aux ordres de qn; **to have a command of** (*a language*) posséder; **to have at one's command** avoir à sa disposition ‖ *tr* commander, ordonner; (*respect*) inspirer; (*to look out over*) dominer; (*a language*) connaître ‖ *intr* (mil) commander, donner les ordres

commandant [,kamən'dænt], [,kamən'dant] *s* commandant *m*

commandeer [,kamən'dɪr] *tr* réquisitionner

commander [kə'mændər], [kə'mandər] *s* commandant *m*

comman'der in chief' *s* commandant *m* en chef

commanding [kə'mændɪŋ], [kə'mandɪŋ] *adj* imposant; (*in charge*) d'autorité

commemorate [kə'mɛməret] *tr* commémorer, célébrer

commence [kə'mɛns] *tr & intr* commencer

commencement [kə'mɛnsmənt] *s* commencement *m*; (educ) jour *m* de la distribution des prix, jour de la collation des grades

commence'ment ex'ercise *s* cérémonie *f* de remise des diplômes

commend [kə'mɛnd] *tr* (*to praise*) louer; (*to entrust*) confier, recommander

commendable [kə'mɛndəbəl] *adj* louable

commendation [,kamən'deʃən] *s* louange *f*, éloge *m*; (mil) citation *f*

comment ['kamənt] *s* remarque *f*, observation *f*, commentaire *m* ‖ *intr* faire des observations; **to comment on** commenter

commentar·y ['kɑmən,teri] s (pl **-ies**) commentaire m

commentator ['kɑmən,tetər] s commentateur m

commerce ['kɑmərs] s commerce m, négoce m

commercial [kə'mʌrʃəl] adj commercial, commerçant ‖ s annonce f publicitaire

commercialize [kə'mʌrʃə,laɪz] tr commercialiser

commiserate [kə'mɪzə,ret] intr—**to commiserate with** compatir aux malheurs de

commiseration [kə,mɪzə'reʃən] s commisération f

commissar [,kɑmɪ'sɑr] s commissaire m

commissar·y ['kɑmɪ,seri] s (pl **-ies**) (person) commissaire m; (canteen) cantine f

commission [kə'mɪʃən] s commission f; (board, council) conseil m; (com) guelte f; (mil) brevet m; **out of commission** hors de service; (naut) désarmé ‖ tr commissionner; (mil) promouvoir

commis'sioned of'ficer s breveté m

commissioner [kə'mɪʃənər] s commissaire m

com·mit [kə'mɪt] v (pret & pp **-mitted**; ger **-mitting**) tr (an error, crime, etc.) commettre; (one's soul, one's money, etc.) confier; (one's word) engager; (to a mental hospital) interner; **to commit to memory** apprendre par cœur; **to commit to prison** envoyer en prison; **to commit to writing** coucher par écrit

commitment [kə'mɪtmənt] s (act of committing) perpétration f; (to a mental institution) internement m; (to prison) emprisonnement m; (to a cause) engagement m

committal [kə'mɪtəl] s (of a crime) perpétration f; (of a task) délégation f; **committal to prison** mise en prison f

commit'tal ser'vice s (eccl) prières fpl au bord de la tombe

committee [kə'mɪti] s comité m, commission f

commode [kə'mod] s (toilet) chaise f percée; (dressing table) grande table f de nuit

commodious [kə'modi-əs] adj spacieux, confortable

commodi·ty [kə'mɑditi] s (pl **-ties**) denrée f, marchandise f

common ['kɑmən] adj commun ‖ s terrain m communal; **commons** communaux mpl; (of school) réfectoire m; **the Commons** (Brit) les communes fpl

com'mon car'rier s entreprise f de transports

commoner ['kɑmənər] s homme m du peuple, roturier m; (Brit) membre m de la Chambre des communes

com'mon law' s droit m coutumier, coutume f

com'mon-law mar'riage s union f libre, collage m

Com'mon Mar'ket s Marché m Commun

com'mon noun' s nom m commun

com'mon-place' adj banal ‖ s banalité f

com'mon sense' s sens m commun

com'mon-sense' adj sensé

com'mon stock' s action f ordinaire, actions ordinaires

commonweal ['kɑmən,wil] s bien m public

com'mon-wealth' s état m, république f

commotion [kə'moʃən] s commotion f

commune [kə'mjun] intr s'entretenir; (eccl) communier

communicant [kə'mjunɪkənt] s informateur m; (eccl) communiant m

communicate [kə'mjunɪ,ket] tr & intr communiquer

communicating [kə'mjunɪ,ketɪŋ] adj communicant

communication [kə,mjunɪ'keʃən] s communication f

communicative [kə'mjunɪ,ketɪv] adj communicatif

communion [kə'mjunjən] s communion f; **to take communion** communier

communism ['kɑmjə,nɪzm] s communisme m

communist ['kɑmjənɪst] adj & s communiste mf

communi·ty [kə'mjunɪti] s (pl **-ties**) (locality) voisinage m; (group of people living together) communauté f

commu'nity chest' s caisse f de secours

commutation [,kɑmjə'teʃən] s commutation f

commuta'tion tick'et s carte f d'abonnement

commutator ['kɑmjə,tetər] s (elec) collecteur m

commute [kə'mjut] tr échanger; (e.g., a prison term) commuer ‖ intr s'abonner au chemin de fer; voyager avec carte d'abonnement

commuter [kə'mjutər] s abonné m au chemin de fer

compact [kəm'pækt] adj compact ‖ ['kɑmpækt] s (agreement) pacte m; (for cosmetics) poudrier m, boîte f à poudre

companion [kəm'pænjən] s compagnon m; (female companion) compagne f

companionable [kəm'pænjənəbəl] adj sociable

compan'ion-ship' s camaraderie f

compan'ion-way' s escalier m des cabines

compa·ny ['kʌmpəni] s (pl **-nies**) compagnie f; (com) société f, compagnie; (naut) équipage m; (theat) troupe f; **to have company** avoir du monde; **to keep bad company** fréquenter la mauvaise compagnie; **to keep company** sortir ensemble; **to keep s.o. company** tenir compagnie à qn; **to part company** se séparer

comparative [kəm'pærətɪv] adj comparatif; (anatomy, literature, etc.) comparé ‖ s comparatif m

compare [kəm'per] s—beyond compare incomparablement, sans égal || tr comparer; compared to en comparaison de; to be compared to se comparer à

comparison [kəm'pærisən] s comparaison f

compartment [kəm'partmənt] s compartiment m

compass ['kʌmpəs] s (for showing direction) boussole f; (range, reach) portée f; (for drawing circles) compas m; to box the compass réciter la rose des vents || tr—to compass about entourer

com'pass card' s rose f des vents

compassion [kəm'pæʃən] s compassion f

compassionate [kəm'pæʃənɪt] adj compatissant

compatibility [kəm,pætɪ'brlɪti] s compatibilité f, convenance f

com·pel [kəm'pel] v (pret & pp -pelled; ger -pelling) tr contraindre, obliger; (respect, silence) imposer

compelling [kəm'pelɪŋ] adj irrésistible; (motive) impérieux

compendious [kəm'pendɪ·əs] adj abrégé, succinct

compensate ['kampən,set] tr compenser; to compensate s.o. for dédommager qn de || intr—to compensate for compenser

compensation [,kampən'seʃən] s compensation f

compete [kəm'pit] intr concourir

competence ['kampɪtəns] or competency ['kampɪtənsi] s compétence f

competent ['kampɪtənt] adj compétent

competition [,kampɪ'tɪʃən] s concurrence f, compétition f; (contest) concours m; (sports) compétition, épreuve f

competitive [kəm'petɪtɪv] adj compétitif

compet'itive exam'ination s concours m

competitor [kəm'petɪtər] s concurrent m

compilation [,kampɪ'leʃən] s compilation f

compile [kəm'paɪl] tr compiler

complacency [kəm'plesənsi] s complaisance f; (self-satisfaction) suffisance f

complacent [kəm'plesənt] adj complaisant; content de soi, suffisant

complain [kəm'plen] intr se plaindre

complainant [kəm'plenənt] s plaignant m

complaint [kəm'plent] s plainte f; (grievance) grief m; (illness) maladie f, mal m

complaisant [kəm'plezənt], ['kamplı,zænt] adj complaisant

complement ['kamplɪmənt] s complément m; (mil) effectif m || ['kamplɪ,ment] tr compléter

complete [kəm'plit] adj complet || tr compléter

complex [kəm'pleks], ['kampleks] adj complexe || ['kampleks] s complexe m

complexion [kəm'plekʃən] s (texture of skin, especially of face) teint m; (general aspect) caractère m; (constitution) complexion f

compliance [kə'plaɪ·əns] s complaisance f; soumission f, conformité f; in compliance with conformément à

complicate ['kamplɪ,ket] tr compliquer

complicated adj compliqué

complication [,kamplɪ'keʃən] s complication f

complici·ty [kəm'plɪsɪti] s (pl -ties) complicité f

compliment ['kamplɪmənt] s compliment m; compliments (kind regards) civilités fpl; to pay a compliment to faire un compliment à; with the compliments of the author hommage de l'auteur || tr complimenter

com'plimen'tary cop'y [,kamplɪ'mentərɪ] s exemplaire m en hommage; to give a complimentary copy of a book faire hommage d'un livre

com'plimen'tary tick'et s billet m de faveur

com·ply [kəm'plaɪ] v (pret & pp -plied) intr—to comply with se conformer à, acquiescer à

component [kəm'ponənt] adj composant || s (chem) composant m; (mech, math) composante f

comportment [kəm'portmənt] s comportement m

compose [kəm'poz] tr composer; to be composed of se composer de; to compose oneself se calmer

composed adj paisible, tranquille

composer [kəm'pozər] s compositeur m

compos'ing stick' s composteur m

composite [kəm'pazɪt] adj & s composé m

composition [,kampə'zɪʃən] s composition f

compositor [kəm'pazɪtər] s compositeur m

compost ['kampost] s compost m

composure [kəm'pozər] s calme m, sang-froid m

compote ['kampot] s (stewed fruits) compote f; (dish) compotier m

compound ['kampaund] adj composé || s composé m; (gram) mot m composé; (math) complexe m; (mil) enceinte f || [kəm'paund] tr composer, combiner; (interest) capitaliser

comprehend [,kamprɪ'hend] tr comprendre

comprehensible [,kamprɪ'hensɪbəl] adj compréhensible

comprehension [,kamprɪ'henʃən] s compréhension f

comprehensive [,kamprɪ'hensɪv] adj compréhensif, étendu; (study, view, measure) d'ensemble

compress ['kampres] s (med) compresse f || [kəm'pres] tr comprimer

compression [kam'preʃən] s compression f

comprise [kəm'praɪz] tr comprendre, renfermer

compromise ['kamprə,maɪz] s compromis m; (with one's conscience) transaction f; rough compromise cote f mal taillée ‖ tr (e.g., one's honor) compromettre ‖ intr (to make concessions) transiger

comptroller [kən'trolər] s vérificateur m, contrôleur m

compulsive [kəm'pʌlsɪv] adj obligatoire; (psychol) compulsif

compulsory [kəm'pʌlsəri] adj obligatoire, forcé

compute [kəm'pjut] tr computer, calculer, supputer ‖ intr calculer

computer [kəm'pjutər] s ordinateur m

comrade ['kɑmræd], ['kɑmrɪd] s camarade mf

com'rade in arms' s compagnon m d'armes

com'rade-ship' s camaraderie f

con [kɑn] s contre m ‖ v (pret & pp **conned**; ger **conning**) tr étudier; (naut) gouverner; (slang) escroquer

concave ['kɑnkev], [kɑn'kev] adj concave

conceal [kən'sil] tr dissimuler

concealment [kən'silmənt] s dissimulation f; (place) cachette f

concede [kən'sid] tr & intr concéder

conceit [kən'sit] s (vanity) vanité f; (witty expression) saillie f, mot m; conceits concetti mpl

conceited adj vaniteux, vain

conceivable [kən'sivəbəl] adj concevable

conceive [kən'siv] tr & intr concevoir

concentrate ['kɑnsən,tret] tr concentrer ‖ intr se concentrer

concentra'tion camp' [,kɑnsən'treʃən] s camp m de concentration

concentric [kən'sentrɪk] adj concentrique

concept ['kɑnsept] s concept m

conception [kən'sepʃən] s conception f

concern [kən'sʌrn] s (business establishment) maison f, compagnie f; (worry) inquiétude f; (relation, reference) intérêt m; (matter) affaire f ‖ tr concerner; as concerns quant à; persons concerned intéressés mpl; to be concerned être inquiet; to be concerned about se préoccuper de; to concern oneself with s'intéresser à; to whom it may concern à qui de droit

concerning [kən'sʌrnɪŋ] prep concernant, en ce qui concerne, touchant

concert ['kɑnsərt] s concert m; in concert de concert ‖ [kən'sʌrt] tr concerter ‖ intr se concerter

con'cert-mas'ter s premier violon m soliste

concerto [kən'tʃerto] s (pl -tos or -ti [ti]) concerto m

concession [kən'seʃən] s concession f

conciliate [kən'sɪlɪ,et] tr concilier

conciliatory [kən'sɪlɪ-ə,tori] adj conciliatoire

concise [kən'saɪs] adj concis

conclude [kən'klud] tr & intr conclure

conclusion [kən'kluʒən] s conclusion f

conclusive [kən'klusɪv] adj concluant

concoct [kən'kɑkt] tr confectionner; (a story) inventer; (a plan) machiner

concoction [kən'kɑkʃən] s confection f; (mixture) mélange m; (pej) drogue f

concomitant [kən'kɑmɪtənt] adj concomitant ‖ s accompagnement m

concord ['kɑnkord] s concorde f; (gram) concordance f; (mus) accord m

concordance [kən'kordəns] s concordance f

concourse ['kɑnkors] s (of people) concours m, foule f; (road) boulevard m; (of railroad station) hall m, salle f des pas perdus

concrete ['kɑnkrit], [kɑn'krit] adj concret; de béton ‖ s concret m; (for construction) béton m ‖ tr (a sidewalk) bétonner

con'crete block' s parpaing m

con'crete mix'er s bétonnière f

concubine ['kɑŋkjə,baɪn] s concubine f

concur [kən'kʌr] v (pret & pp -curred; ger -curring) intr (said of events) concourir; (said of persons) s'accorder

concurrence [kən'kʌrəns] s concours m

concurrent [kən'kʌrənt] adj concourant

concussion [kən'kʌʃən] s secousse f, ébranlement m; (pathol) commotion f

condemn [kən'dem] tr condamner

condemnation [,kɑndem'neʃən] s condamnation f

condense [kən'dens] tr condenser ‖ intr se condenser

condenser [kən'densər] s condenseur m; (elec) condensateur m

condescend [,kɑndɪ'send] intr condescendre

condescending [,kɑndɪ'sendɪŋ] adj condescendant

condescension [,kɑndɪ'senʃən] s condescendance f

condiment ['kɑndɪmənt] s condiment m

condition [kən'dɪʃən] s condition f; on condition that à condition que ‖ tr conditionner

conditional [kən'dɪʃənəl] adj & s conditionnel m

condole [kən'dol] intr—to condole with offrir ses condoléances à

condolence [kən'doləns] s condoléances fpl

condone [kən'don] tr pardonner, tolérer

conducive [kən'd(j)usɪv] adj favorable

conduct ['kɑndʌkt] s conduite f, comportement m ‖ [kən'dʌkt] tr conduire

conductor [kən'dʌktər] s (on bus or streetcar) receveur m; (mus) chef m d'orchestre; (rr) chef de train; (elec, phys) conducteur m; (elec, phys) (in predicate after to be, it may be translated by an adjective) conducteur, e.g., metals are good conductors of electricity les métaux sont bons conducteurs de l'électricité

conduit ['kɑndɪt], ['kɑndʊ·ɪt] s conduit m; (elec) caniveau m

cone [kon] *s* cône *m*; *(for popcorn, ice cream)* cornet *m*, plaisir *m*
confection [kən'fek/ən] *s* confiserie *f*
confectioner [kən'fek/ənər] *s* confiseur *m*
confec'tioners' sug'ar *s* sucre *m* glace
confectioner•y [kən'fek/ə,neri] *s* (*pl* -ies) confiserie *f*
confedera•cy [kən'fədərəsi] *s* (*pl* -cies) confédération *f*; *(for unlawful purposes)* conspiration *f*, entente *f*
confederate [kən'fedərɪt] *adj* confédéré || *s* complice *mf*; **Confederate** (hist) Confédéré *m* || [kən'fedə,ret] *tr* confédérer || *intr* se confédérer
con•fer [kən'fʌr] *v* (*pret & pp* -ferred; *ger* -ferring) *tr & intr* conférer
conference [ˈkɑnfərəns] *s* conférence *f*; *(interview)* entretien *m*; (sports) groupement *m* (d'équipes)
conferment [kən'fʌrmənt] *s* (*of degrees*) collation *f*
confess [kən'fes] *tr* confesser || *intr* se confesser
confession [kən'fe/ən] *s* confession *f*
confessional [kən'fe/ənəl] *s* confessional *m*
confessor [kən'fesər] *s* confesseur *m*
confidant [ˌkɑnfɪ'dænt] [ˈkɑnfɪ,dænt] *s* confident *m*
confide [kən'faɪd] *tr* confier || *intr*—**to confide in** se confier à
confidence [ˈkɑnfɪdəns] *s* confiance *f*; *(secret)* confidence *f*; **in strict confidence** sous toute réserve; **to have confidence in** se confier à
confident [ˈkɑnfɪdənt] *adj* confiant || *s* confident *m*
confidential [ˌkɑnfɪ'den/əl] *adj* confidentiel
confiden'tial sec'retary *s* secrétaire *m* particulier, secrétaire *f* particulière
confine [ˈkɑnfaɪn] *s* (obs) confinement *m*; **the confines** les confins *mpl* || [kən'faɪn] *tr* confiner, enfermer; *(to keep within limits)* limiter; **to be confined** (*said of woman*) accoucher; **to be confined to bed** être alité
confinement [kən'faɪnmənt] *s* limitation *f*; *(in prison)* emprisonnement *m*; *(in childbirth)* accouchement *m*
confirm [kən'fʌrm] *tr* confirmer
confirmed *adj* (*reassured*) confirmé; *(bachelor)* endurci; *(drunkard)* fieffé; *(drinker)* invétéré; *(smoker)* émérite
confiscate [ˈkɑnfɪs,ket] *tr* confisquer
conflagration [ˌkɑnflə'gre/ən] *s* conflagration *f*, incendie *m*
conflict [ˈkɑnflɪkt] *s* conflit *m* || [kən'flɪkt] *intr* être en contradiction, se heurter
conflicting [kən'flɪktɪŋ] *adj* contradictoire; *(events, class hours, etc.)* incompatible
con'flict of in'terest *s* conflit *m* d'intérêts, conflit des intérêts
conform [kən'form] *tr* conformer || *intr* se conformer, s'accommoder
conformist [kən'formɪst] *s* conformiste *mf*
conformi•ty [kən'formɪti] *s* (*pl* -ties)

conformité *f*; **in conformity with** conformément à
confound [kən'faʊnd] *tr* confondre || [ˈkɑn'faʊnd] *tr* maudire; **confound it!** diable!
confounded *adj* confus; *(damned)* sacré
confrere [ˈkɑnfrer] *s* confrère *m*
confront [kən'frʌnt] *tr* (*to face boldly*) affronter, faire face à; *(witnesses; documents)* confronter; **to be confronted by** se trouver en face de
confuse [kən'fjuz] *tr* confondre; **to get confused** devenir confus, s'embrouiller
confusing [kən'fjuzɪŋ] *adj* déroutant, embrouillant
confusion [kən'fjuʒən] *s* confusion *f*
confute [kən'fjut] *tr* réfuter
congeal [kən'dʒil] *tr* congeler || *intr* se congeler
congenial [kən'dʒinjəl] *adj* sympathique, agréable; compatible; **congenial to** *or* **with** apparenté à, conforme au tempérament de
congenital [kən'dʒenɪtəl] *adj* congénital
con'ger eel' [ˈkɑŋgər] *s* congre *m*, anguille *f* de mer
congest [kən'dʒest] *tr* congestionner || *intr* se congestionner
congestion [kən'dʒest/ən] *s* congestion *f*
conglomeration [kən,glɑmə're/ən] *s* conglomération *f*
congratulate [kən'græt/ə,let] *tr* féliciter, congratuler; **to congratulate s.o. for** féliciter qn de *or* pour; **to congratulate s.o. for** + *ger* féliciter qn de + *inf*
congratulations [kən,græt/ə'le/ənz] *spl* félicitations *fpl*
congregate [ˈkɑŋgrɪ,get] *tr* rassembler || *intr* se rassembler
congregation [ˌkɑŋgrɪ'ge/ən] *s* rassemblement *m*; *(parishioners)* fidèles *mfpl*; *(Protestant parishioners; committee of Roman Catholic prelates)* congrégation *f*
congress [ˈkɑŋgrɪs] *s* congrès *m*
congressional [kən'gre/ənəl] *adj* parlementaire
con'gress•man *s* (*pl* -men) congressiste *m*, parlementaire *m*
con'gress•wom'an *s* (*pl* -wom'en) congressiste *f*, parlementaire *f*
congruent [ˈkɑŋgru•ənt] *adj* (math) congru
conical [ˈkɑnɪkəl] *adj* conique
conjecture [kən'dʒekt/ər] *s* conjecture *f* || *tr & intr* conjecturer
conjugal [ˈkɑndʒəgəl] *adj* conjugal
conjugate [ˈkɑndʒə,get] *tr* conjuguer
conjugation [ˌkɑndʒə'ge/ən] *s* conjugaison *f*
conjunction [kən'dʒʌŋk/ən] *s* conjonction *f*
conjuration [ˌkɑndʒə're/ən] *s* conjuration *f*
conjure [kən'dʒur] *tr* (*to appeal to solemnly*) conjurer || [ˈkɑndʒər], [ˈkʌndʒər] *tr* (*to exorcise, drive away*) conjurer; **to conjure up** évoquer || *intr* faire de la sorcellerie

connect [kə'nɛkt] *tr* relier, joindre; (*e.g., two parties on the telephone*) mettre en communication; (*a pipe, an electrical device*) brancher, connecter || *intr* se lier, se joindre; **to connect with** (*said of train*) correspondre avec

connected *adj* (*related*) connexe; (*logical*) suivi

connecting [kə'nɛktɪŋ] *adj* de liaison; (*wire*) de connexion; (*pipe*) de raccord; (*street*) communiquant

connect'ing rod' *s* bielle *f*

connection [kə'nɛkʃən] *s* connexion *f*, liaison *f*; (*between two causes*) connexité *f*; (*in families*) parenté *f*, parent *m*; (*by telephone*) communication *f*; (*of trains*) correspondance *f*; (elec) connexion *f*; **connections** (*in the business world*) clientèle *f*, relations *fpl*; (*in families*) alliés *mpl*, consanguins *mpl*; **in connection with** à propos de

con'ning tow'er ['kɑnɪŋ] *s* (*e.g., on battleship*) poste *m* or tourelle *f* de commandement; (*on sub*) kiosque *m*

conniption [kə'nɪpʃən] *s* (coll) rogne *f*

connive [kə'naɪv] *intr* être de connivence, être complice

connote [kə'not] *tr* (*ta signify*) signifier, vouloir dire; (*to imply*) suggérer, sous-entendre

connubial [kə'n(j)ubɪ·əl] *adj* conjugal

conquer ['kɑŋkər] *tr* conquérir

conqueror ['kɑŋkərər] *s* conquérant

conquest ['kɑŋkwɛst] *s* conquête *f*

conscience ['kɑnʃəns] *s* conscience *f*; **in all conscience** en conscience; **to have on one's conscience** avoir sur la conscience

conscientious [,kɑnʃɪ'ɛnʃəs] *adj* consciencieux

conscien'tious objec'tor [əb'dʒɛktər] *s* objecteur *m* de conscience

conscious ['kɑnʃəs] *adj* conscient; **to be conscious** (*not unconscious*) avoir connaissance; **to be conscious of** avoir conscience de

consciousness ['kɑnʃəsnɪs] *s* (*not sleep or coma*) connaissance *f*; (*awareness*) conscience *f*

conscript ['kɑnskrɪpt] *s* (mil) conscrit *m*; (nav) inscrit *m* maritime || [kən'skrɪpt] *tr* (mil) enrôler; (nav) inscrire

conscription [kən'skrɪpʃən] *s* conscription *f*

consecrate ['kɑnsɪ͵kret] *tr* consacrer; (*e.g., bread*) bénir; (*a king or bishop*) sacrer

consecration [,kɑnsɪ'kreʃən] *s* consécration *f*; (*to a task*) dévouement *m*; (*of a king or bishop*) sacre *m*

consecutive [kən'sɛkjətɪv] *adj* de suite, consécutif

consensus [kən'sɛnsəs] *s* consensus *m*

consent [kən'sɛnt] *s* consentement *m*; **by common consent** d'un commun accord || *intr* consentir

consequence ['kɑnsɪ͵kwɛns] *s* conséquence *f*

consequential [,kɑnsɪ'kwɛnʃəl] *adj* conséquent, logique

consequently ['kɑnsɪ͵kwɛntli] *adv* conséquemment, par conséquent

conservation [,kɑnsər'veʃən] *s* conservation *f*

conservatism [kən'sʌrvə͵tɪzəm] *s* conservatisme *m*

conservative [kən'sʌrvətɪv] *adj & s* conservateur *m*; **at a conservative estimate** au bas mot, au moins

conservato·ry [kən'sʌrvə͵tori] *s* (*pl* -ries) (*of music*) conservatoire *m*; (*greenhouse*) serre *f*

conserve [kən'sʌrv] *tr* conserver

consider [kən'sɪdər] *tr* considérer

considerable [kən'sɪdərəbəl] *adj* considérable

considerate [kən'sɪdərɪt] *adj* prévenant, plein d'égards

consideration [kən͵sɪdə'reʃən] *s* considération *f*; (*remuneration*) rétribution *f*; (*favor*) indulgence *f*; **to take into consideration** tenir compte de; **under consideration** à l'étude

considering [kən'sɪdərɪŋ] *prep* eu égard à; **considering that** vu que

consign [kən'saɪn] *tr* consigner

consignee [,kɑnsaɪ'ni] *s* consignataire *m*

consignment [kən'saɪnmənt] *s* consignation *f*, livraison *f*

consist [kən'sɪst] *intr*—**to consist in** consister dans or en; **to consist in** + *ger* consister à + *inf*; **to consist of** consister dans or en

consisten·cy [kən'sɪstənsi] *s* (*pl* -cies) (*logical connection*) conséquence *f*; (*firmness, amount of firmness*) consistance *f*

consistent [kən'sɪstənt] *adj* (*agreeing with itself or oneself*) conséquent; (*holding firmly together*) consistant; **consistent with** compatible avec

consisto·ry [kən'sɪstəri] *s* (*pl* -ries) consistoire *m*

consolation [,kɑnsə'leʃən] *s* consolation *f*

console ['kɑnsol] *s* console *f* || [kən-'sol] *tr* consoler

con'sole ta'ble *s* console *f*

consolidate [kən'sɑlɪ͵det] *tr* consolider

consonant ['kɑnsənənt] *adj* (*in sound*) consonant; **consonant with** d'accord avec || *s* consonne *f*

consort ['kɑnsɔrt] *s* compagnon *m*; (*husband*) conjoint *m*; (*wife*) conjointe *f*; **prince** *m* **consort**; (*convoy*) conserve *f* || [kən'sɔrt] *tr* unir || *intr* s'associer; (*to harmonize*) s'accorder; **to consort with** s'associer à or avec

conspicuous [kən'spɪkju·əs] *adj* apparent, frappant; (*attracting special attention*) voyant; **to make oneself conspicuous** se faire remarquer

conspira·cy [kən'spɪrəsi] *s* (*pl* -cies) conspiration *f*, conjuration *f*

conspirator [kən'spɪrətər] *s* conspirateur *m*, conjuré *m*

conspire [kən'spaɪr] *intr* conspirer

constable ['kʌnstəbəl], ['kɑnstəbəl] *s* garde *m* champêtre; juge *m* de paix

constancy ['kɑnstænsɪ] s constance f
constant ['kɑnstənt] adj constant ‖ s constante f
constantly ['kɑnstəntlɪ] adv constamment
constellation [,kɑnstə'leʃən] s constellation f
constipate ['kɑnstɪ,pet] tr constiper
constipation [,kɑnstɪ'peʃən] s constipation f
constituen·cy [kən'stɪtʃʊ·ənsɪ] s (pl -cies) électeurs mpl, commettants mpl; circonscription f électorale
constituent [kən'stɪtʃʊ·ənt] adj constituant, constitutif ‖ s élément m, constituant m; (voter, client) électeur m, commettant m
constitute ['kɑnstɪ,t(j)ut] tr constituer
constitution [,kɑnstɪ't(j)uʃən] s constitution f
constrain [kən'stren] tr contraindre
constraint [kən'strent] s contrainte f; (restraint) retenue f; (uneasiness) gêne f
constrict [kən'strɪkt] tr resserrer
construct [kən'strʌkt] tr construire
construction [kən'strʌkʃən] s construction f; interprétation f
constructive [kən'strʌktɪv] adj constructif, constructeur
construe [kən'stru] tr expliquer, interpréter; (gram) construire
consul ['kɑnsəl] s consul m
consular ['kɑns(j)ələr] adj consulaire
consulate ['kɑns(j)əlɪt] s consulat m
consult [kən'sʌlt] tr consulter ‖ intr consulter; se consulter
consultant [kən'sʌltənt] s conseiller m, consultant m
consultation [,kɑnsəl'teʃən] s consultation f; (eccl, law) consulte f
consume [kən's(j)um] tr (to make use of, use up) consommer; (to use up entirely; to destroy) consumer, épuiser
consumer [kən's(j)umər] s consommateur m; (of gas, electricity, etc.) abonné m
consum'er goods' spl denrées fpl de consommation
consummate [kən'sʌmɪt] adj consommé ‖ ['kɑnsə,met] tr consommer
consumption [kən'sʌmpʃən] s consommation f; (pathol) tuberculose f pulmonaire
consumptive [kən'sʌmptɪv] adj destructeur; (pathol) poitrinaire ‖ s (pathol) poitrinaire mf
contact ['kɑntækt] s contact m; to put in contact mettre en contact ‖ tr (coll) prendre contact avec, contacter ‖ intr prendre contact
con'tact lens' s verre m de contact, lentille f de contact
contagion [kən'tedʒən] s contagion f
contagious [kən'tedʒəs] adj contagieux
contain [kən'ten] tr contenir; (one's sorrow) apprivoiser
container [kən'tenər] s boîte f, contenant m, récipient m
containment [kən'tenmənt] s refoulement m, retenue f

contaminate [kən'tæmɪ,net] tr contaminer
contamination [kən,tæmɪ'neʃən] s contamination f
contemplate ['kɑntəm,plet] tr & intr contempler; (e.g., a trip) projeter; to contemplate + ger penser + inf
contemplation [,kɑntəm'pleʃən] s contemplation f
contemporaneous [kən,tempə'renɪ·əs] adj contemporain
contemporar·y [kən'tempə,rerɪ] adj contemporain ‖ s (pl -ies) contemporain m
contempt [kən'tempt] s mépris m, nargue f; (law) contumace f; to hold in contempt mépriser
contemptible [kən'temptɪbəl] adj méprisable
contempt' of court' s outrage m à la justice
contemptuous [kən'temptʃu·əs] adj méprisant
contend [kən'tend] tr prétendre ‖ intr combattre; to contend with lutter contre
contender [kən'tendər] s concurrent m, compétiteur m
content [kən'tent] adj & s content m ‖ ['kɑntent] s contenu m; contents contenu m; (of table of contents) matières fpl ‖ [kən'tent] tr contenter
contented [kən'tentɪd] adj content, satisfait
contention [kən'tenʃən] s (strife) dispute f, différend m; (point argued for) point m discuté, argument m; (law) contentieux m
contentious [kən'tenʃəs] adj contentieux
contentment [kən'tentmənt] s contentement m
contest ['kɑntest] s (struggle, fight) lutte f, dispute f; (competition) concours m, compétition f ‖ [kən'test] tr & intr contester
contestant [kən'testənt] s concurrent m
context ['kɑntekst] s contexte m
contiguous [kən'tɪgju·əs] adj contigu
continence ['kɑntɪnəns] s continence f
continent ['kɑntɪnənt] adj & s continent m
continental [,kɑntɪ'nentəl] adj continental
contingen·cy [kən'tɪndʒənsɪ] s (pl -cies) contingence f
contingent [kən'tɪndʒənt] adj & s contingent m
continual [kən'tɪnju·əl] adj continuel
continuation [kən,tɪnju'eʃən] s continuation f; (e.g., of a story) suite f
continue [kən'tɪnju] tr & intr continuer; continued on page two (three, etc.) suite page deux (trois, etc.); to be continued à suivre
continui·ty [,kɑntɪ'n(j)u·ɪtɪ] s (pl -ties) continuité f; (mov, rad, telv) découpage m, scénario m
continuous [kən'tɪnju·əs] adj continu
contin'uous show'ing s (mov) spectacle m permanent

contin'uous waves' spl ondes fpl entretenues

contortion [kən'tɔrʃən] s contorsion f

contour ['kɑntur] s contour m ‖ tr contourner

con'tour line' s courbe f de niveau

contraband ['kɑntrə,bænd] adj contrebandier ‖ s contrebande f

contrabass ['kɑntrə,bes] s contrebasse f

contraceptive [,kɑntrə'septɪv] adj & s contraceptif m

contract ['kɑntrækt] s contrat m ‖ ['kɑntrækt], [kən'trækt] tr contracter ‖ intr se contracter

contraction [kən'trækʃən] s contraction f

contractor [kən'træktər] s entrepreneur m

contradict [,kɑntrə'dɪkt] tr contredire

contradiction [,kɑntrə'dɪkʃən] s contradiction f

contradictory [,kɑntrə'dɪktəri] adj contradictoire

contral·to [kən'trælto] s (pl -tos) contralto m

contraption [kən'træpʃən] s (coll) machin m, truc m

contra·ry ['kɑntreri] adj contraire ‖ adv contrairement ‖ [kən'treri] adj (coll) obstiné, têtu ‖ ['kɑntreri] s (pl -ries) contraire m; **on the contrary** au contraire, par contre

contrast ['kɑntræst] s contraste m ‖ [kən'træst] tr & intr contraster

contravene [,kɑntrə'vin] tr contredire; (a law) contrevenir (with dat)

contribute [kən'trɪbjut] tr (e.g., a sum of money) contribuer pour ‖ intr (to a newspaper, conference, etc.) collaborer

contribution [,kɑntrɪ'bjuʃən] s contribution f, apport m; (e.g., for charity) souscription f; (to a newspaper, conference, etc.) collaboration f

contributor [kən'trɪbjutər] s (donor) donneur m; (e.g., to a charitable cause) souscripteur m; (to a newspaper, conference, etc.) collaborateur m

contrite [kən'traɪt] adj contrit

contrition [kən'trɪʃən] s contrition f

contrivance [kən'traɪvəns] s invention f, expédient m; (gadget) dispositif m

contrive [kən'traɪv] tr inventer ‖ intr s'arranger; **to contrive to** trouver moyen de

con·trol [kən'trol] s direction f, autorité f; (mastery) maîtrise f; (surveillance) contrôle m; **controls** commandes fpl ‖ v (pret & pp -trolled; ger -trolling) tr diriger; maîtriser; (to give surveillance to) contrôler; (to handle the controls of) commander; **to control oneself** se contrôler

controller [kən'trolər] s contrôleur m, appareil m de contrôle; (elec) controller m

control' pan'el s (aer) planche f de bord, tableau m de bord

control' stick' s (aer) manche m à balai

control' tow'er s poste-vigie m, tourelle f de commandement

controversial [,kɑntrə'vʌrʃəl] adj controversable

controver·sy ['kɑntrə,vʌrsi] s (pl -sies) controverse f; dispute f, querelle f

controvert ['kɑntrə,vʌrt], [,kɑntrə'vʌrt] tr controverser; contredire

contumacious [,kɑnt(j)ʊ'meʃəs] adj rebelle, récalcitrant

contume·ly ['kɑnt(j)ʊmɪli] s (pl -lies) injure f, outrage m, mépris m

contusion [kən't(j)uʒən] s contusion f

conundrum [kə'nʌndrəm] s devinette f, énigme f

convalesce [,kɑnvə'les] intr guérir, se remettre, se rétablir

convalescence [,kɑnvə'lesəns] s convalescence f

convalescent [,kɑnvə'lesənt] adj & s convalescent m

convales'cent home' s maison f de repos

convene [kən'vin] tr assembler, convoquer ‖ intr s'assembler

convenience [kən'vinjəns] s commodité f; (e.g., in the home) confort m; **at your earliest convenience** aussitôt que possible

convent ['kɑnvent] s couvent m (de religieuses)

convention [kən'venʃən] s assemblée f, congrès m; (agreement) convention f; (accepted usage) convention sociale; **conventions** convenances fpl, bienséances fpl

conventional [kən'venʃənəl] adj conventionnel; (in conduct) respectueux des convenances; (everyday) usuel; (model, type) traditionnel

converge [kən'vʌrdʒ] intr converger

conversant [kən'vʌrsənt] adj familier, versé

conversation [,kɑnvər'seʃən] s conversation f

conversational [,kɑnvər'seʃənəl] adj de conversation

converse ['kɑnvʌrs] adj & s contraire m, inverse m, réciproque f ‖ [kən'vʌrs] intr converser

conversion [kən'vʌrʒən] s conversion f

convert ['kɑnvʌrt] s converti m ‖ [kən'vʌrt] tr convertir ‖ intr se convertir

converter [kən'vʌrtər] s convertisseur m

convertible [kən'vʌrtɪbəl] adj (person) convertissable; (thing; security) convertible; (aut) décapotable ‖ s (aut) décapotable f

convex ['kɑnveks], [kɑn'veks] adj convexe, bombé

convey [kən've] tr transporter; (e.g., a message) communiquer; (e.g., property) transmettre; (law) céder

conveyance [kən've·əns] s transport m; (vehicle) moyen m de transport, voiture f; (of message) communication f; (transfer) transmission f; (law) transfert m, cession f

conveyor [kən've·ər] s transporteur m, convoyeur m

convey'or belt' s tapis m roulant

convict ['kɑnvɪkt] s condamné m, forçat *m* || [kən'vɪkt] *tr* condamner, convaincre

conviction [kən'vɪkʃən] *s* condamnation *f*; (*certainty*) conviction *f*

convince [kən'vɪns] *tr* convaincre

convincing [kən'vɪnsɪŋ] *adj* convaincant

convivial [kən'vɪvɪ·əl] *adj* jovial, plein d'entrain

convocation [,kɑnvə'keʃən] *s* (*calling together*) convocation *f*; (*meeting*) assemblée *f*

convoke [kən'vok] *tr* convoquer

convolution [,kɑnvə'luʃən] *s* (*of brain*) circonvolution *f*

convoy ['kɑnvɔɪ] *s* convoi *m*, conserve *f*, e.g., **to sail in convoy** naviguer de conserve || *tr* convoyer

convulse [kən'vʌls] *tr* convulsionner, convulser; **to be convulsed with laughter** se tordre de rire

coo [ku] *intr* roucouler

cooing ['ku·ɪŋ] *s* roucoulement *m*

cook [kʊk] *s* cuisinier *m*, chef *m*; (*female cook*) cuisinière *f* || *tr* cuisiner, faire cuire; **to cook up** (*a plot*) machiner, tramer || *intr* faire la cuisine, cuisiner; (*said of food*) cuire

cook′book′ *s* livre *m* de cuisine

cooker ['kʊkər] *s* réchaud *m*, cuisinière *f*

cookery ['kʊkəri] *s* cuisine *f*

cookie ['kʊki] *s* var of **cooky**

cooking ['kʊkɪŋ] *s* cuisine *f*; (*e.g., of meat*) cuisson *f*

cook′ing uten′sils *spl* batterie *f* de cuisine

cook′stove′ *s* cuisinière *f*

cook·y ['kʊki] *s* (*pl* **-ies**) biscuit *m*, gâteau *m* sec

cool [kul] *adj* frais; (*e.g., to an idea*) indifférent; **it is cool out** il fait frais; **to keep cool** tenir au frais; se tenir tranquille || *s* fraîcheur *f* || *tr* rafraîchir, refroidir; **to cool one's heels** (coll) se morfondre || *intr* se refroidir, se rafraîchir; **to cool down** se calmer; **to cool off** se refroidir

cooler ['kulər] *s* frigorifique *m*; (*prison*) (slang) violon *m*, tôle *f*

cool′-head′ed *adj* imperturbable, de sang-froid

coolness ['kulnɪs] *s* fraîcheur *f*; (*of disposition*) sang-froid *m*, calme *m*; (*stand-offishness*) froideur *f*

coon [kun] *s* raton *m* laveur

coop [kup] *s* poulailler *m*; **to fly the coop** (slang) débiner, décamper || *tr* enfermer dans un poulailler; **to coop up** claquemurer

co-op ['ko·ɑp], [ko'ɑp] *s* entreprise *f* coopérative

cooper ['kupər] *s* tonnelier *m*

cooperate [ko'ɑpə,ret] *intr* coopérer; (*to be helpful*) faire preuve de bonne volonté

cooperation [ko,ɑpə'reʃən] *s* coopération *f*

cooperative [ko'ɑpə,retɪv] *adj* coopératif

coordinate [ko'ɔrdɪnɪt] *adj* coordonné || *s* coordonnée *f* || [ko'ɔrdɪ,net] *tr* coordonner

coot [kut] *s* foulque *f*; **old coot** (coll) vieille baderne *f*

cootie ['kuti] *s* (slang) pou *m*

cop [kɑp] *s* (slang) flic *m* || *v* (*pret & pp* **copped**; *ger* **copping**) *tr* (slang) dérober

copartner [ko'pɑrtnər] *s* coassocié *m*, coparticipant *m*; (*in crime*) complice *mf*

cope [kop] *intr*—**to cope with** faire face à, tenir tête à

cope′stone′ *s* couronnement *m*

copier ['kɑpɪ·ər] *s* (*person who copies*) copiste *m*, imitateur *m*; (*apparatus*) appareil *m* à copier

copilot ['ko,paɪlət] *s* copilote *m*

coping ['kopɪŋ] *s* faîte *m*, comble *m*; (*of bridge*) chape *f*

copious ['kopɪ·əs] *adj* copieux

copper ['kɑpər] *adj* de cuivre, en cuivre; (*color*) cuivré || *s* cuivre *m*; (*coin*) petite monnaie *f*; (slang) flic *m*

cop′per·smith′ *s* chaudronnier *m*

coppery ['kɑpəri] *adj* cuivreux

coppice ['kɑpɪs] *s* taillis *m*

copulate ['kɑpjə,let] *intr* s'accoupler

copulation [,kɑpjə'leʃən] *s* copulation *f*, accouplement *m*

cop·y ['kɑpi] *s* (*pl* **-ies**) copie *f*; (*of a book*) exemplaire *m*; (*of a magazine*) numéro *m*; (*for printer*) original *m*; **to make copies** exécuter des doubles || *v* (*pret & pp* **-ied**) *tr & intr* copier

cop′y·book′ *s* cahier *m*

cop′y·cat′ *s* (coll) imitateur *m*, singe *m*

cop′y·right′ *s* propriété *f* artistique or littéraire, droit *m* de l'artiste or de l'auteur, copyright *m*; (*deposit on printed matter*) dépôt *m* légal || *tr* réserver les droits de publication de

cop′y·right′ed *adj* (formula used on printed material) droits de reproduction réservés

cop′y·writ′er *s* rédacteur *m* d'annonces publicitaires

co·quet [ko'ket] *v* (*pret & pp* **-quetted**; *ger* **-quetting**) *intr* coqueter

coquet·ry ['kokətri], [ko'ketri] *s* (*pl* **-ries**) coquetterie *f*

coquette [ko'ket] *s* coquette *f* || *intr* coqueter

coquettish [ko'ketɪʃ] *adj* coquet

coral ['kɑrəl], ['kɔrəl] *adj* de corail, en corail || *s* corail *m*

cor′al reef′ *s* récif *m* de corail

cord [kɔrd] *s* corde *f*; (*string*) ficelle *f*; (*attached to a bell*) cordon *m*; (elec) fil *m* || *tr* corder

cordage ['kɔrdɪdʒ] *s* cordage *m*

cordial ['kɔrdʒəl] *adj & s* cordial *m*

cordiali·ty [kɔr'dʒælɪti] *s* (*pl* **-ties**) cordialité *f*

corduroy ['kɔrdə,rɔɪ] *s* velours *m* côtelé; **corduroys** pantalon en velours côtelé

core [kor] *s* cœur *m*; (elec) noyau *m*; **rotten to the core** pourri à la base || *tr* vider

corespondent [,korɪs'pɑndənt] *s* complice *mf* d'adultère

cork [kɔrk] *s* liège *m*; *(of bottle)* bouchon *m*; **to take the cork out of** déboucher || *tr* boucher

corking ['kɔrkɪŋ] *adj* (coll) épatant

cork' oak' *s* chêne-liège *m*

cork'screw' *s* tire-bouchon *m*

cork'-tipped' *adj* à bout de liège

cormorant ['kɔrmərənt] *s* cormoran *m*

corn [kɔrn] *s* *(in U.S.A.)* maïs *m*; *(in England)* blé *m*; *(in Scotland)* avoine *f*; *(single seed)* grain *m*; *(on foot)* cor *m*, durillon *m*; *(whiskey)* (coll) eau-de-vie *f* de grain; (slang) platitude *f*, banalité *f*

corn' bread' *s* pain *m* de maïs

corn'cob' *s* épi *m* de maïs; *(without the grain)* rafle *f*

corn'cob pipe' *s* pipe *f* en rafle de maïs

corn'crib' *s* dépôt *m* de maïs

cornea ['kɔrnɪ·ə] *s* cornée *f*

corned' beef' *s* bœuf *m* salé

corner ['kɔrnər] *adj* cornier || *s* coin *m*, angle *m*; *(of room)* encoignure *f*; *(of lips)* commissure *f*; **around the corner** au tournant; **in a corner** (fig) au pied du mur, à l'accul; **to cut a corner close** prendre un virage à la corde; **to cut corners** *(in spending)* rogner les dépenses; *(in work)* bâcler un travail || *tr* coincer, acculer; *(the market)* accaparer

cor'ner cup'board *s* encoignure *f*

cor'ner room' *s* pièce *f* d'angle

cor'ner-stone' *s* pierre *f* angulaire

cornet [kɔr'nɛt] *s* cornet *m*; *(headdress)* cornette *f*; (mil) cornette *m*; (mus) cornet à pistons

corn' exchange' *s* bourse *f* des céréales

corn'field' *s* *(in U.S.A.)* champ *m* de maïs; *(in England)* champ de blé; *(in Scotland)* champ d'avoine

corn'flakes' *spl* paillettes *fpl* de maïs

corn' flour' *s* farine *f* de maïs

corn'flow'er *s* bluet *m*, barbeau *m*

corn' frit'ter *s* crêpes *fpl* de maïs

corn'husk' *s* enveloppe *f* de l'épi de maïs

cornice ['kɔrnɪs] *s* corniche *f*

corn' meal' *s* farine *f* de maïs

corn' on the cob' *s* maïs *m* en épi

corn' pad' *s* bourrelet *m* coricide

corn' pone' *s* pain *m* de maïs

corn' pop'per *s* appareil *m* pour faire éclater le maïs

corn' remov'er *s* coricide *m*

corn' silk' *s* barbe *f* de maïs

corn'stalk' *s* tige *f* de maïs

corn'starch' *s* fécule *f* de maïs

cornucopia [ˌkɔrnə'kopɪ·ə] *s* corne *f* d'abondance

Cornwall ['kɔrn,wɔl], ['kɔrnwəl] *s* la Cornouailles

corn·y ['kɔrnɪ] *adj* (comp **-ier**; super **-iest**) (slang) banal, trivial, fade

corollar·y ['kɑrəˌlɛrɪ], ['kɔrəˌlɛrɪ] *s* (pl **-ies**) corollaire *m*

coronary ['kɑrəˌnɛrɪ], ['kɔrəˌnɛrɪ] *adj* coronaire

coronation [ˌkɑrə'neʃən], [ˌkɔrə'neʃən] *s* couronnement *m*, sacre *m*

cor'oner's in'quest ['kɑrənərz], ['kɔrənərz] *s* enquête *f* judiciaire par-devant jury (en cas de mort violente ou suspecte)

coronet ['kɑrəˌnɛt], ['kɔrəˌnɛt] *s* diadème *m*; *(worn by members of nobility)* couronne *f*; *(worn by earl or baron)* tortil *m*

corporal ['kɔrpərəl] *adj* corporel || *s* (mil) caporal *m*

corporate ['kɔrpərɪt] *adj* incorporé

corporation [ˌkɔrpə'reʃən] *s* société *f* anonyme, compagnie *f* anonyme

corporeal [kɔr'porɪ·əl] *adj* corporel, matériel

corps [kor] *s* (pl **corps** [korz]) corps *m*; (mil) corps d'armée

corpse [kɔrps] *s* cadavre *m*

corps'man *s* (pl **-men**) (mil) infirmier *m*

corpulent ['kɔrpjələnt] *adj* corpulent

corpuscle ['kɔrpəsəl] *s* (phys) corpuscule *m*; (physiol) globule *m*

corpus delicti ['kɔrpəsdɪ'lɪktaɪ] *s* (law) corps *m* du délit

cor·ral [kə'ræl] *s* corral *m*, enclos *m* || *v* (pret & pp **-ralled**; ger **-ralling**) *tr* enfermer dans un corral; (fig) saisir

correct [kə'rɛkt] *adj* correct || *tr* corriger

correction [kə'rɛkʃən] *s* correction *f*

corrective [kə'rɛktɪv] *adj* & *s* correctif *m*

correc'tive lens'es *spl* verres *mpl* correcteurs

correctness [kə'rɛktnɪs] *s* correction *f*

correlate [kɑrəˌlɛt], [kɔrəˌlɛt] *tr* mettre en corrélation || *intr* correspondre; **to correlate with** correspondre à

correlation [ˌkɑrə'leʃən], [ˌkɔrɪ'leʃən] *s* corrélation *f*

correspond [ˌkɑrɪ'spɑnd], [ˌkɔrɪ'spɑnd] *intr* correspondre

correspondence [ˌkɑrɪ'spɑndəns], [ˌkɔrɪ'spɑndəns] *s* correspondance *f*

correspondent [ˌkɑrɪ'spɑndənt], [ˌkɔrɪ'spɑndənt] *adj* & *s* correspondant *m*

corresponding [ˌkɑrɪ'spɑndɪŋ], [ˌkɔrɪ'spɑndɪŋ] *adj* correspondant

corridor ['kɑrɪdər], ['kɔrɪdər] *s* corridor *m*, couloir *m*

corroborate [kə'rɑbəˌret] *tr* corroborer

corrode [kə'rod] *tr* corroder || *intr* se corroder

corrosion [kə'roʒən] *s* corrosion *f*

corrosive [kə'rosɪv] *adj* & *s* corrosif *m*

corrugated ['kɑrəˌgetɪd], ['kɔrəˌgetɪd] *adj* ondulé

corrupt [kə'rʌpt] *adj* corrompu || *tr* corrompre

corruption [kə'rʌpʃən] *s* corruption *f*

corsage [kɔr'sɑʒ] *s* bouquet *m*

corsair ['kɔrˌsɛr] *s* corsaire *m*

corset ['kɔrsɪt] *s* corset *m*

Corsica ['kɔrsɪkə] *s* Corse *f*; la Corse

Corsican ['kɔrsɪkən] *adj* corse || *s* *(dialect)* corse *m*; *(person)* Corse *mf*

cortege [kɔr'teʒ] *s* cortège *m*

cor·tex ['kɔrˌtɛks] *s* (pl **-tices** [tɪˌsiz]) cortex *m*

cortisone ['kɔrtɪˌson] *s* cortisone *f*

coruscate ['kɑrəsˌkɛt], ['kɔrəsˌkɛt] *intr* scintiller

cosmetic [kaz'metɪk] *adj & s* cosmétique *m*

cosmic ['kazmɪk] *adj* cosmique

cosmonaut ['kazmə,nɔt] *s* cosmonaute *mf*

cosmopolitan [,kazmə'palɪtən] *adj & s* cosmopolite *mf*

cosmos ['kazməs] *s* cosmos *m*

Cossack ['ka,sæk] *adj* cosaque ‖ *s* Cosaque *mf*

cost [kɔst], [kast] *s* coût *m*; (*price*) prix *m*; **at all costs** à tout prix, coûte que coûte; **at cost** au prix coûtant; **costs** frais *mpl*; (*law*) dépens *mpl* ‖ *v* (*pret & pp* cost) *intr* coûter

cost' account'ing *s* comptabilité *f* industrielle

costliness ['kɔstlɪnɪs], ['kastlɪnɪs] *s* cherté *f*, haut prix *m*

cost·ly ['kɔstli], ['kastli] *adj* (*comp* -lier; *super* -liest) coûteux, cher

cost' of liv'ing *s* coût *m* de la vie

cost' price' *s* prix *m* coûtant; (*net price*) prix de revient

costume ['kast(j)um] *s* costume *m*

cos'tume ball' *s* bal *m* costumé

cos'tume jew'elry *s* bijoux *mpl* en toc

costumer [kas't(j)umər] *s* costumier *m*

cot [kat] *s* lit *m* de sangle

coterie ['kotəri] *s* coterie *f*

cottage ['katɪdʒ] *s* chalet *m*, cabanon *m*, villa *f*; (*with a thatched roof*) chaumière *f*

cot'tage cheese' *s* lait *m* caillé, caillé *m*, jonchée *f*

cot'ter pin' ['katər] *s* goupille *f* fendue, clavette *f*

cotton ['katən] *adj* cotonnier, de coton ‖ *s* coton *m* ‖ *intr*—to **cotton up to** (coll) éprouver de la sympathie pour

cot'ton bat'ting *s* coton *m* or ouate *f* hydrophile

cot'ton field' *s* cotonnerie *f*

cot'ton gin' *s* égreneuse *f*

cot'ton mill' *s* filature *f* de coton, cotonnerie *f*

cot'ton pick'er *s* cotonnier *m*

cot'ton pick'ing *s* récolte *f* du coton

cot'ton-seed' *s* graine *f* de coton

cot'tonseed oil' *s* huile *f* de coton

cot'ton waste' *s* déchets *mpl* or bourre *f* de coton

cot'ton-wood' *s* peuplier *m* de Virginie

cottony ['katəni] *adj* cotonneux

couch [kautʃ] *s* (*without back*) divan *m*; (*with back*) sofa *m*, canapé *m* ‖ *tr* (*a demand, a letter*) rédiger ‖ *intr* (*to lie in wait*) se tapir

cougar ['kugər] *s* couguar *m*, cougouar *m*

cough [kɔf], [kaf] *s* toux *f* ‖ *tr*—to **cough up** cracher en toussant; (slang) (*money*) cracher ‖ *intr* tousser

cough' drop' *s* pastille *f* pectorale, pastille pour la toux

cough' syr'up *s* sirop *m* pectoral, sirop contre la toux

could [kʊd] *aux*—**he could not come** il ne pouvait pas venir; **he couldn't do it** il n'a (pas) pu le faire; **he couldn't do it if he wanted to** il ne pourrait

(pas) le faire s'il le voulait, il ne saurait (pas) le faire s'il le voulait

council ['kaunsəl] *s* conseil *m*; (eccl) concile *m*

coun'cil-man *s* (*pl* -men) conseiller *m* municipal

councilor ['kaunsələr] *s* conseiller *m*

coun-sel ['kaunsəl] *s* conseil *m*, avis *m*; (*lawyer*) avocat *m* ‖ *v* (*pret & pp* -seled or -selled; *ger* -seling or -selling) *tr & intr* conseiller; to **counsel s.o. to** + *inf* conseiller à qn de + *inf*

counselor ['kaunsələr] *s* conseiller *m*, conseil *m*; (*lawyer*) avocat *m*

count [kaunt] *s* compte *m*; (*nobleman*) comte *m* ‖ *tr* compter; to **count the votes** dépouiller le scrutin ‖ *intr* compter; **count off!** (mil) comptez-vous!; to **count for valoir**; to **count on** (*to have confidence in*) compter sur (*s.o. or s.th.*); to **count on** + *ger* compter + *inf*

countable ['kauntəbəl] *adj* comptable

count'down' *s* compte *m* à rebours

countenance ['kauntɪnəns] *s* mine *f*, contenance *f*; to **give countenance to** appuyer; to **keep one's countenance** garder son sérieux; to **lose countenance** perdre contenance ‖ *tr* soutenir, approver

counter ['kauntər] *adj* contraire ‖ *s* compteur *m*; (*piece of wood or metal for keeping score*) jeton *m*; (*board in shop over which business is transacted*) comptoir *m*; (*in a bar or café*) zinc *m*; **under the counter** en dessous de table, sous le comptoir, sous cape ‖ *adv* contrairement; en sens inverse; to **run counter to** aller à l'encontre de ‖ *tr* contrarier, contrecarrer; (*a move, e.g., in chess*) contrer; (*an opinion*) prendre le contre-pied de ‖ *intr* parer le coup, parer un coup; to **counter with** riposter par

coun'ter-act' *tr* contrebalancer

coun'ter-attack' *s* contre-attaque *f* ‖

coun'ter-attack' *tr* contre-attaquer

coun'ter-bal'ance *s* contrepoids *m* ‖

coun'ter-bal'ance *tr* contrebalancer

coun'ter-clock'wise *adj & adv* en sens inverse des aiguilles d'une montre

coun'ter-cur'rent *s* contre-courant *m*

coun'ter-es'pionage *s* contre-espionnage *m*

counterfeit ['kauntərfɪt] *adj* contrefait; (*beauty*) sophistiqué ‖ *s* contrefaction *f*, contrefaçon *f*; (*money*) fausse monnaie *f* ‖ *tr* contrefaire; (*e.g., an illness*) feindre

counterfeiter ['kauntər,fɪtər] *s* contrefacteur *m*; (*of money*) faux-monnayeur *m*

coun'terfeit mon'ey *s* fausse monnaie *f*, faux billets *mpl*

countermand ['kauntər,mænd], ['kauntər,mand] *s* contre-ordre *m* ‖ *tr* contremander

coun'ter-march' *s* contremarche *f* ‖ *intr* faire une contremarche

coun'ter-meas'ure *s* contre-mesure *f*

coun'ter-offen'sive *s* contre-offensive *f*

coun'ter-pane' *s* courtepointe *f*

coun'ter-part' *s* contrepartie *f*, homologue *m*

coun'ter-point' *s* contrepoint *m*

coun'ter-poise' *s* contrepoids *m* ‖ *tr* faire équilibre à

coun'ter-rev'olu'tionar·y *adj* contrerévolutionnaire ‖ *s* (*pl* -ies) contrerévolutionnaire *mf*

coun'ter-sign' *s* contremarque *f*; (*signature*) contreseing *m*; (*mil*) mot *m* d'ordre ‖ *tr* contresigner

coun'ter-sig'nature *s* contreseing *m*

coun'ter-sink' *s* fraise *f* ‖ *v* (*pret* & *pp* -sunk) *tr* fraiser

coun'ter-spy' *s* (*pl* -spies) contre-espion *m*

coun'ter-stroke' *s* contrecoup *m*

coun'ter-weight' *s* contrepoids *m*

countess ['kauntɪs] *s* comtesse *f*

countless ['kauntlɪs] *adj* innombrable

countrified ['kʌntrɪˌfaɪd] *adj* provincial, compagnard

coun·try ['kʌntrɪ] *s* (*pl* -tries) (*territory of a nation*) pays *m*; (*land of one's birth*) patrie *f*; (*region*) contrée *f*; (*not the city*) campagne *f*

coun'try club' *s* club *m* privé situé hors des agglomérations

coun'try estate' *s* domaine *m*

coun'try·folk' *s* campagnards *mpl*

coun'try·gen'tleman *s* châtelain *m*, propriétaire *m* d'un château

coun'try house' *s* maison *f* de campagne

coun'try·man *s* (*pl* -men) (*of the same country*) compatriote *mf*; (*rural*) compagnard *m*

coun'try·side' *s* paysage *m*, campagne *f*

coun'try town' *s* petite ville *f* de province

coun'try·wide' *adj* national

coun'try·wom'an *s* (*pl* -wom'en) (*of the same country*) compatriote *f*; (*rural*) campagnarde *f*

coun·ty ['kauntɪ] *s* (*pl* -ties) comté *m*

coun'ty seat' *s* chef-lieu *m* de comté

coupé [kupe] *s* coupé *m*

couple ['kʌpəl] *s* (*man and wife; male and female; friends*) couple *m*, paire *f*; (*of eggs, cakes, etc.*) couple *f*; (*elec, mech*) couple *m* ‖ *tr* coupler, accoupler; (*mach*) embrayer ‖ *intr* s'accoupler

coupler ['kʌplər] *s* (*mach*) coupleur *m*

coupling ['kʌplɪŋ] *s* accouplement *m*; (*mach*) couplage *m*

coupon ['k(j)upɑn] *s* coupon *m*, bon *m*

courage ['kʌrɪdʒ] *s* courage *m*

courageous [kə'redʒəs] *adj* courageux

courier ['kʌrɪ·ər], ['kurɪ·ər] *s* courrier *m*; (*on horseback*) estafette *f*

course [kors] *s* cours *m*; carrière *f*, voie *f*, course *f*; (*of a meal*) service *m*, plat *m*; (*of a stream*) parcours *m*, cours *m*; (*direction*) route *f*, chemin *m*; **in due course** en temps voulu; **in the course of** au cours de; **in the course of time** avec le temps; **of course!** naturellement!, bien entendu!; **to give a course** faire un cours; **to set a course for** (naut) mettre le

cap sur; **to take a course** suivre un cours ‖ *tr* & *intr* courir

court [kort] *s* cour *f*; (*of law*) tribunal *m*, cour; (*sports*) terrain *m*, court *m*; **out of court** à l'amiable ‖ *tr* courtiser, faire la cour à; (*favor, votes*) briguer, solliciter; (*danger*) aller au-devant de

courteous ['kʌrtɪ·əs] *adj* poli, courtois

courtesan ['kʌrtɪzən], ['kortɪzən] *s* courtisane *f*

courte·sy ['kʌrtɪsɪ] *s* (*pl* -sies) politesse *f*, courtoisie *f*; **through the courtesy of** avec la gracieuse permission de

court'house' *s* palais *m* de justice

courtier ['kortɪ·ər] *s* courtisan *m*

court' jest'er *s* bouffon *m* du roi

court·ly ['kortlɪ] *adj* (*comp* -lier; *super* -liest) courtois, élégant

court'-mar'tial *s* (*pl* **courts-martial**) conseil *m* de guerre ‖ *v* (*pret* & *pp* -tialed or -tialled; *ger* -tialing or -tialling) *tr* traduire en conseil de guerre; **to be court-martialed** passer en conseil de guerre

court' plas'ter *s* taffetas *m* gommé, sparadrap *m*

court'room' *s* salle *f* du tribunal

court'ship *s* cour *f*

court'yard' *s* cour *f*

cousin ['kʌzɪn] *s* cousin *m*

cove [kov] *s* anse *f*, crique *f*

covenant ['kʌvənənt] *s* contrat *m*, accord *m*, pacte *m*; (Bib) alliance *f*

cover ['kʌvər] *s* couverture *f*; (*lid*) couvercle *m*; (*for furniture*) housse *f*; (*of wild game*) remise *f*, gîte *m*; (com) couverture *f*, provision *f*, marge *f*; (mach) chape *f*; (phila) enveloppe *f*; **from cover to cover de la première page à la dernière; to take cover** se mettre à l'abri; **under cover** (*e.g., of trees*) sous les couverts; (*safe from harm*) à couvert; **under cover of** sous le couvert de, dissimulé dans; **under separate cover** sous pli distinct ‖ *tr* couvrir; (*a certain distance*) parcourir; (*a newspaper story*) faire le reportage de; (*one's tracks*) brouiller; (*with, e.g., chocolate*) enrober; **to cover up** recouvrir ‖ *intr* se couvrir; (*to brood*) couver

coverage ['kʌvərɪdʒ] *s* (*amount or space covered*) portée *f*; (*of news*) reportage *m*; (*insurance*) assurance *f*, couverture *f* d'assurance

cov'er·alls' *spl* salopette *f*, bleus *mpl*

cov'er charge' *s* couvert *m*

cov'ered wag'on *s* chariot *m* couvert

cov'er girl' *s* cover-girl *f*, pin up *f*

covering ['kʌvərɪŋ] *s* couverture *f*, recouvrement *m*

covert ['kʌvərt] *adj* couvert, caché

cov'er-up' *s* subterfuge *m*; (*reply*) réponse *f* évasive

covet ['kʌvɪt] *tr* convoiter

covetous ['kʌvɪtəs] *adj* cupide, avide

covetousness ['kʌvɪtəsnɪs] *s* convoitise *f*, cupidité *f*

covey ['kʌvi] s couvée f; (in flight) volée f

cow [kau] s vache f; (of seal, elephant) femelle f || tr (coll) intimider

coward ['kau.ərd] s lâche mf

cowardice ['kau.ərdɪs] s lâcheté f

cowardly ['kau.ərdli] adj lâche || adv lâchement, peureusement

cow'bell' s grelot m, clarine f

cow'boy' s cow-boy m

cow'catch'er s (rr) chasse-bestiaux m

cower ['kau.ər] intr se tapir

cow'herd' s vacher m, bouvier m

cow'hide' s vache f, peau f de vache; fouet m || tr fouetter

cowl [kaul] s capuchon m, cagoule f; (of chimney) chapeau m; (aer, aut) capot m

cow'lick' s mèche f rebelle

cow'pox' s (pathol) vaccine f

coxcomb ['kaks,kom] s (conceited person) petit-maître m, fat m; (bot) crête-de-coq f

coxswain ['kaksən], ['kak,swen] s patron m de chaloupe; (rowing) barreur m

coy [koɪ] adj réservé, modeste

co·zy ['kozi] adj (comp -zier; super -ziest) douillet, intime || s (pl -zies) couvre-théière m

C.P.A. ['si'pi'e] s (letterword) (certified public accountant) expert-comptable m, comptable m agréé

crab [kræb] s crabe m; (grouch) grincheux m || v (pret & pp crabbed; ger crabbing) intr (coll) se plaindre

crab' ap'ple s pomme f sauvage

crabbed ['kræbɪd] adj acariâtre; (handwriting) de chat; (author) hermétique; (style) entortillé

crab·by ['kræbi] adj (comp -bier; super -biest) (coll) revêche, grognon

crack [kræk] adj (troops) d'élite; (coll) expert, de premier ordre || s (noise) bruit m sec, craquement m; (of whip) claquement m; (fissure) fente f; (e.g., in a dish) fêlure f; (e.g., in a wall) lézarde f; (e.g., in skin) gerçure f; (joke) bon mot m; **crack of dawn** pointe f du jour || tr (one's fingers; petroleum) faire craquer; (a whip) claquer; (to split) fendre; (e.g., a dish) fêler; (e.g., a wall) lézarder; (the skin) gercer; (nuts) casser; **to crack a joke** (slang) faire ou lâcher une plaisanterie; **to crack up** (to praise) (coll) vanter, prôner; (to crash) (coll) écraser || intr (to make a noise) craquer; (said of whip) claquer; (to be split) se fendre; (said of dish) se fêler; (said of wall) se lézarder; (said of skin) se gercer; **to crack up** (to crash) (coll) s'écraser; (to break down) (coll) craquer, s'effondrer

crack'-brained' adj timbré; **to be crack-brained** avoir le cerveau fêlé

crack'down' s (coll) répression f

cracked adj (split) fendu, fêlé; (foolish) (coll) timbré, toqué, cinglé

cracker ['krækər] s biscuit m sec

crack'er-bar'rel adj (coll) en chambre, au petit pied

crack'er-jack' adj (slang) expérimenté, remarquable || s (slang) crack m

cracking ['krækɪŋ] s (of petroleum) cracking m

crackle ['krækəl] s crépitation f || intr crépiter, pétiller

crack'le·ware' s porcelaine f craquelée

crackling ['kræklɪŋ] s crépitement m, pétillement m; (culin) couenne f rissolée; cracklings cretons mpl

crack'pot' adj & s (slang) original m, excentrique m

crack' shot' s (coll) fin tireur m

crack'-up' s (collision) (coll) écrasement m; (breakdown) (coll) effondrement m

cradle ['kredəl] s berceau m || tr bercer

cra'dle-song' s berceuse f

craft [kræft], [kraft] s métier m; (trickery) artifice m; (naut) embarcation f, barque f

craftiness ['kræftɪnɪs], ['kraftɪnɪs] s ruse f, astuce f

crafts'man s (pl -men) artisan m

crafts'man-ship' s habileté f technique; exécution f

craft·y ['kræfti], ['krafti] adj (comp -ier; super -iest) rusé

crag [kræg] s rocher m escarpé

cram [kræm] v (pret & pp crammed; ger cramming) tr (with food) bourrer, gaver; (with people) bonder; (for an exam) (coll) chauffer || intr se bourrer, se gaver; (for an exam) (coll) potasser

cramp [kræmp] s (metal bar; clamp) crampon m; (in a muscle) crampe f; (carpentry) serre-joint m || tr cramponner, agrafer, presser, serrer; (one's movements, style, or manner of living) gêner

cranber·ry ['kræn,beri] s (pl -ries) (Vaccinium oxycoccus or V. uliginosum) canneberge f, airelle f canneberge

crane [kren] s (mach, orn) grue f || tr (one's neck) allonger, tendre || intr allonger le cou

crani·um ['kreni.əm] s (pl -a [ə]) crâne m

crank [kræŋk] s manivelle f; (person) (coll) excentrique mf || tr (a motor) faire partir à la manivelle

crank'case' s carter m

crank'shaft' s vilebrequin m

crank·y ['kræŋki] adj (comp -ier; super -iest) revêche, grincheux; (not working well) détraqué; (queer) excentrique

cran·ny ['kræni] s (pl -nies) fente f, crevasse f; (corner) coin m

crape [krep] s crêpe m

crape'hang'er s (slang) rabat-joie m

craps [kræps] s (slang) jeu m de dés; **to shoot craps** (slang) jouer aux dés

crash [kræʃ] s fracas m, écroulement m; (of thunder) coup m; (e.g., of airplane) écrasement m; (e.g., on stock market) krach m || tr briser, fracasser; (e.g., an airplane) écraser || intr retentir; (said of airplane) s'écraser; (to fail) craquer; **to crash into** em-

boutir, tamponner; **to crash through**
enfoncer
crash′ dive′ *s* brusque plongée *f*
crash′ hel′met *s* casque *m*
crash′-land′ing *s* crash *m*, atterrissage
m violent
crass [kræs] *adj* grossier; (*ignorance*)
crasse
crate [kret] *s* caisse *f* à claire-voie, cageot *m* ‖ *tr* emballer dans une caisse
à claire-voie
crater [′kretər] *s* cratère *m*
cravat [krə′væt] *s* cravate *f*
crave [krev] *tr* désirer ardemment; implorer; requérir, e.g., **the problem
craves serious consideration** le problème requiert une considération sé-
rieuse; **to crave s.o.'s pardon** demander pardon à qn ‖ *intr*—**to crave for**
désirer ardemment; implorer
craven [′krevən] *adj & s* poltron *m*
craving [′krevɪŋ] *s* désir *m* ardent, désir obsédant
craw [krɔ] *s* jabot *m*
crawl [krɔl] *s* rampement *m*; (swimming) crawl *m* ‖ *intr* ramper; **to be
crawling with** fourmiller de, grouiller
de; **to crawl along** se traîner; **to
crawl on one's hands and knees** aller
à quatre pattes; **to crawl over** escala-
lader; **to crawl up** grimper
crayon [′kre·ən] *s* crayon *m* de pastel,
pastel *m* ‖ *tr* crayonner
craze [krez] *s* manie *f*, toquade *f* ‖ *tr*
rendre fou
cra·zy [′krezi] *adj* (*comp* **-zier**; *super*
-ziest) fou; (*rickety*) délabré; **to be
crazy about** (coll) être fou de, être
toqué de; **to drive crazy** rendre fou,
affoler
cra′zy bone′ *s* nerf *m* du coude
cra′zy quilt′ *s* courtepointe *f* multico-
lore
creak [krik] *s* cri *m*, grincement *m* ‖
intr crier, grincer
creak·y [′kriki] *adj* (*comp* **-ier**; *super*
-iest) criard
cream [krim] *s* crème *f*; **creams** (*with
chocolate coating*) chocolats *mpl*
fourrés ‖ *tr* écrémer; (*butter and
sugar together*) mélanger ‖ *intr* crémer
cream′ cheese′ *s* fromage *m* à la
crème, fromage blanc, petit suisse *m*
creamer·y [′kriməri] *s* (*pl* **-ies**) laiterie
f; compagnie *f* laitière
cream′ of tar′tar *s* crème *f* de tartre
cream′ pitch′er *s* crémière *f*
cream′ puff′ *s* chou *m* à la crème
cream′ sep′arator [′sepə‚retər] *s* écrémeuse *f*
cream·y [′krimi] *adj* (*comp* **-ier**; *super*
-iest) crémeux
crease [kris] *s* pli *m*, faux pli *m* ‖ *tr &
intr* plisser
create [kri′et] *tr* créer
creation [kri′eʃən] *s* création *f*
creative [kri′etɪv] *adj* créateur, inventif
creator [kri′etər] *s* créateur *m*
creature [′kritʃər] *s* créature *f*
credence [′kridəns] *s* créance *f*,
croyance *f*, foi *f*

credentials [krɪ′denʃəlz] *spl* papiers
mpl, pièces *fpl* justificatives, lettres
fpl de créance
credibility [‚kredɪ′bɪlɪti] *s* crédibilité *f*
credible [′kredɪbəl] *adj* croyable, digne
de foi
credit [′kredɪt] *s* crédit *m*; (*belief;
claim*) créance *f*; **on credit** à crédit;
to be a credit to faire honneur à; **to
take credit for** s'attribuer le mérite
de ‖ *tr* croire, ajouter foi à; (com)
créditer, porter au crédit
creditable [′kredɪtəbəl] *adj* estimable,
honorable
cred′it card′ *s* carte *f* de crédit
creditor [′kredɪtər] *s* créditeur *m*,
créancier *m*
cre·do [′krido], [′kredo] *s* (*pl* **-dos**)
credo *m*
credulous [′kredʒələs] *adj* crédule
creed [krid] *s* credo *m*; (*denomination*)
foi *f*
creek [krik] *s* ruisseau *m*
creep [krip] *v* (*pret & pp* **crept** [krept])
intr ramper; (*stealthily*) se glisser;
(*slowly*) se traîner, se couler; (*to
climb*) grimper; (*with a sensation of
insects*) fourmiller; **to creep up on
s.o.** s'approcher de qn à pas lents
creeper [′kripər] *s* plante *f* rampante
creeping [′kripɪŋ] *adj* lent, traînant;
(*plant*) rampant ‖ *s* rampement *m*
creep·y [′kripi] *adj* (*comp* **-ier**; *super*
-iest) (coll) mystérieux· **to feel creepy**
fourmiller
cremate [′krimet] *tr* incinérer
cremation [krɪ′meʃən] *s* crémation *f*,
incinération *f*
cremato·ry [′krimə‚tori] *adj* crématoire ‖ *s* (*pl* **-ries**) crématoire *m*, four
m crématoire
Creole [′kri·ol] *adj* créole ‖ *s* (*language*) créole *m*; (*person*) Créole *mf*
crepe [krep] *s* crêpe *m*; (*pancake*)
crêpe *f*
crepe′ pa′per *s* papier *m* crêpe
crescent [′kresənt] *s* croissant *m*
cress [kres] *s* cresson *m*
crest [krest] *s* crête *f*
crested [′krestɪd] *adj* à crête; (*with
feathers*) huppé
crest′fall′en *adj* abattu, découragé
Cretan [′kritən] *adj* crétois ‖ *s* Crétois
m
Crete [krit] *s* Crète *f*; la Crète
cretin [′kritən] *s* crétin *m*
crevice [′krevɪs] *s* crevasse *f*, fente *f*
crew [kru] *s* équipe *f*; (*of a ship*) équipage *m*; (*group, especially of armed
men*) bande *f*, troupe *f*
crew′ cut′ *s* cheveux *mpl* en brosse
crew′ mem′ber *s* équipier *m*
crib [krɪb] *s* lit *m* d'enfant; crèche *f*,
mangeoire *f*; (*for grain*) coffre *m*;
(*student's pony*) corrigé ·*m* employé
subrepticement ‖ *v* (*pret & pp*
cribbed; *ger* **cribbing**) *tr & intr* (coll)
copier à la dérobée
cricket [′krɪkɪt] *s* (ent) grillon *m*;
(sports) cricket *m*; (coll) franc jeu *m*,
jeu loyal; **to be cricket** être de bonne
guerre

crier ['kraɪ-ər] s crieur m
crime [kraɪm] s crime m; (misdemeanor) délit m
criminal ['krɪmɪnəl] adj & s criminel m
crim'inal code' s code m pénal
crim'inal court' s cour f d'assises
crim'inal law' s loi f pénale
crimp [krɪmp] s (in cloth) pli m; (in hair) frisure f; (recruiter) racoleur m; to put a crimp in (coll) mettre obstacle à || tr (cloth) plisser; (hair) friser, crêper; (metal) onduler
crimson ['krɪmzən] adj & s cramoisi m
cringe [krɪndʒ] intr s'humilier, s'abaisser
cringing ['krɪndʒɪŋ] adj craintif, servile || s crainte f, servilité f
crinkle ['krɪŋkəl] s pli m, ride f || tr froisser, plisser || intr se froisser
cripple ['krɪpəl] s estropié m; (lame person) boiteux m || tr estropier; (a machine) disloquer; (business or industry) paralyser; (a ship) désemparer
cri·sis ['kraɪsɪs] s (pl -ses [siz]) crise f
crisp [krɪsp] adj croustillant; (tone) tranchant, brusque; (air) vif, frais
crisscross ['krɪs,krɔs], ['krɪs,krɑs] adj entrecroisé, treillissé || s entrecroisement m; (e.g., of wires) enchevêtrement m || adv en forme de croix || tr entrecroiser || intr s'entrecroiser
criteri·on [kraɪ'tɪrɪ-ən] s (pl -a [ə] or -ons) critère m
critic ['krɪtɪk] s critique mf; (faultfinder) critiqueur m, désapprobateur m
critical ['krɪtɪkəl] adj critique
critically ['krɪtɪkəli] adv en critique; critically ill gravement malade
criticism ['krɪtɪ,sɪzəm] s critique f
criticize ['krɪtɪ,saɪz] tr & intr critiquer
croak [krok] s (of raven) croassement m; (of frog) coassement m || intr (said of raven) croasser; (said of frog) coasser; (to die) (slang) mourir
Croat ['kro-æt] s (language) croate m; (person) Croate mf
Croatian [kro'eʃən] s (language) croate m; (person) Croate mf
cro·chet [kro'ʃe] s crochet m || v (pret & pp -cheted ['ʃed]; ger -cheting ['ʃe-ɪŋ]) tr & intr tricoter au crochet
crochet' nee'dle s crochet m
crock [krɑk] s pot m de terre
crockery ['krɑkəri] s faïence f, poterie f
crocodile ['krɑkə,daɪl] s crocodile m
croc'odile tears' spl larmes fpl de crocodile
crocus ['krokəs] s crocus m
crone [kron] s vieille femme f au visage parcheminé
cro·ny ['kroni] s (pl -nies) copain m
crook [kruk] s (hook) croc m; (of shepherd) houlette f; (of bishop) crosse f; (in road) courbure f; (person) (coll) escroc m || tr courber || intr se courber
crooked ['krukɪd] adj courbé, crochu; (path; conduct) tortueux; (tree; nose; legs) tortu; (person) (coll) malhonnête, fourbe

croon [krun] intr chanter des chansons sentimentales
crooner ['krunər] s chanteur m de charme
crop [krɑp] s récolte f; (head of hair) cheveux mpl ras; (of bird) jabot m; (whip) fouet m; (of whip) manche m; (of appointments, promotions, heroes, discoveries) moisson f || v (pret & pp cropped; ger cropping) tr tondre; (head of hair) couper, tailler; (ears of animal) essoriller || intr—to crop up (coll) surgir, s'élever brusquement
croquet [kro'ke] s croquet m
crosier ['kroʒər] s crosse f
cross [krɔs], [krɑs] adj transversal, oblique; (breed) croisé; (ill-humored) maussade || s croix f; (of races or breeds; of roads) croisement m || tr croiser; (the sea; a street) traverser; (breeds) croiser, métisser; (the threshold) franchir; (said of one road with respect to another) couper; (the letter) barrer; (e.g., s.o.'s plans) (coll) contrecarrer; to cross oneself (eccl) se signer; to cross out biffer, rayer || intr se croiser, passer; to cross over passer de l'autre côté
cross'bones' spl tibias mpl croisés
cross'bow' s arbalète f
cross'breed' v (pret & pp -bred) tr croiser, métisser
cross'-coun'try adj à travers champs
cross'cur'rent s contre-courant m; tendance f contraire
cross'-examina'tion s contre-interrogatoire m
cross'-exam'ine tr contre-interroger, contre-examiner
cross'-eyed' adj louche
crossing ['krɔsɪŋ], ['krɑsɪŋ] s croisement m; (of ocean) traversée f; (of river, mountain, etc.) passage m; (rr) passage m à niveau
cross'ing gate' s barrière f d'un passage à niveau
cross'patch' s (coll) grincheux m, grognon m
cross'piece' s entretoise f
cross'ref'erence s renvoi m
cross'road' s voie f transversale, chemin m de traverse; crossroads carrefour m, croisement m
cross' sec'tion s coupe f transversale; (e.g., of building) section f; (of opinion) sondage m, groupe m représentatif; tranche f de vie
cross'-sec'tion tr couper transversalement
cross' street' s rue f de traverse, rue transversale
cross'wise' adv en croix, en sautoir
cross'word puz'zle s mots mpl croisés
crotch [krɑtʃ] s (forked piece) fourche f; (between legs) entrejambe f, enfourchure f
crotchet ['krɑtʃɪt] s (mus) noire f; (coll) lubie f
crotchety ['krɑtʃɪti] adj capricieux, fantasque

crouch [krautʃ] *s* accroupissement *m* || *intr* s'accroupir, se blottir

croup [krup] *s* (*of horse*) croupe *f*; (pathol) croup *m*

croupier ['krupɪ·ər] *s* croupier *m*

crouton ['krutɑn] *s* croûton *m*

crow [kro] *s* corbeau *m*; (rook) corneille *f*, freux *m*; **as the crow flies** à vol d'oiseau; **to eat crow** (coll) avaler des couleuvres || *intr* (*said of cock*) chanter; (*said of babies*) gazouiller; **to crow over** chanter victoire sur, triompher bruyamment de

crow'bar' *s* levier *m*; (*for forcing doors*) pince-monseigneur *f*

crowd [kraud] *s* foule *f*; (*large flock of people*) affluence *f*, presse *f*; (mob, common people) populace *f*, vulgaire *m*; (clique, set) bande *f*, monde *m*; **a crowd** (*of people*) du monde, beaucoup de monde || *tr* serrer, entasser; (*to push*) pousser; (*a debtor*) presser; **to crowd out** ne pas laisser de place à || *intr* affluer, s'amasser; **to crowd around** se presser autour de; **to crowd in** s'attrouper

crowded *adj* encombré, bondé

crow'foot' *s* renoncule *f*, bouton *m* d'or

crowing ['kro·ɪŋ] *s* chant *m* de coq, cocorico *m*; (*of babies*) gazouillement *m*

crown [kraun] *s* couronne *f*; (*of hat*) calotte *f* || *tr* couronner, sacrer; (checkers) damer; **to crown s.o.** (slang) flanquer un coup sur la tête à qn

crowning ['kraunɪŋ] *s* couronnement *m*

crown' prince' *s* prince *m* héritier

crown' prin'cess *s* princesse *f* héritière

crow's'-foot' *s* (*pl* -feet) patte-d'oie *f*

crow's'-nest' *s* (naut) nid *m* de pie, tonneau *m* de vigie

crucial ['kruʃəl] *adj* crucial

crucible ['krusɪbəl] *s* creuset *m*

crucifix ['krusɪfɪks] *s* crucifix *m*, christ *m*

crucifixion [ˌkrusɪ'fɪkʃən] *s* crucifixion *f*

cruci-fy ['krusɪ·faɪ] *v* (*pret & pp* -fied) *tr* crucifier

crude [krud] *adj* (raw, unrefined) cru, brut; (*lacking culture*) fruste, grossier; (*unfinished*) informe, grossier, mal développé; (*oil*) brut

crudi-ty ['krudɪti] *s* (*pl* -ties) crudité *f*; (*of person*) grossièreté *f*

cruel ['kru·əl] *adj* cruel

cruel-ty ['kru·əlti] *s* (*pl* -ties) cruauté *f*

cruet ['kru·ɪt] *s* burette *f*

cru'et stand' *s* huilier *m*

cruise [kruz] *s* croisière *f* || *intr* croiser

cruiser ['kruzər] *s* croiseur *m*

cruising ['kruzɪŋ] *adj* en croisière; (*taxi*) en maraude

cruis'ing range' *s* autonomie *f*

cruis'ing speed' *s* vitesse *f* de route

cruller ['krʌlər] *s* beignet *m*

crumb [krʌm] *s* miette *f*; (*soft part of bread*) mie *f* || *tr* (cutlets, etc.) paner

crumble ['krʌmbəl] *tr* émietter, ré-

duire en miettes; (*e.g., stone*) effriter || *intr* s'émietter; s'effriter; (*to fall to pieces*) s'écrouler

crum·my ['krʌmi] *adj* (*comp* -mier; *super* -miest) (slang) sale, minable

crumple ['krʌmpəl] *tr* friper, froisser; (*a fender*) mettre en accordéon || *intr* se friper, se froisser

crunch [krʌntʃ] *tr* croquer, broyer || *intr* (*said of snow*) craquer

crupper ['krʌpər] *s* croupière *f*

crusade [kru'sed] *s* croisade *f* || *intr* se croiser, prendre part à une croisade

crush [krʌʃ] *s* écrasement *m*; (*of people*) presse *f*, foule *f*; **to have a crush on** (slang) avoir un béguin pour || *tr* écraser; (*e.g., stone*) broyer, concasser; (*to oppress, grieve*) accabler, aplatir

crush' hat' *s* claque *m*, gibus *m*

crust [krʌst] *s* croûte *f*

crustacean [krʌs'teʃən] *s* crustacé *m*

crust·y ['krʌsti] *adj* (*comp* -ier; *super* -iest) croustillant; (*said of person*) bourru, hargneux

crutch [krʌtʃ] *s* béquille *f*

crux [krʌks] *s* nœud *m*

cry [kraɪ] *s* (*pl* cries) cri *m*; (*of wolf*) hurlement *m*; (*of bull*) mugissement *m*; **to cry one's eyes out** pleurer à chaudes larmes; **to have a good cry** donner libre cours aux larmes || *v* (*pret & pp* cried) *tr* crier; **to cry out** crier || *intr* crier; (*to weep*) pleurer; **to cry for** crier à; **to cry for joy** pleurer de joie; **to cry out** pousser des cris, s'écrier; **to cry out against** crier à

cry'ba·by' *s* (*pl* -bies) pleurard *m*

crypt [krɪpt] *s* crypte *f*

cryptic(al) ['krɪptɪk(əl)] *adj* secret, occulte; (*silence*) énigmatique

crystal ['krɪstəl] *s* cristal *m*

crys'tal ball' *s* boule *f* de cristal

crystalline ['krɪstəlɪn], ['krɪstə·laɪn] *adj* cristallin

crystallize ['krɪstə·laɪz] *tr* cristalliser; (*sugar*) candir || *intr* cristalliser; (*said of sugar*) se candir; (*said of one's thoughts*) (fig) se cristalliser

cub [kʌb] *s* petit *m*; (*of bear*) ourson *m*; (*of fox*) renardeau *m*; (*of lion*) lionceau *m*; (*of wolf*) louveteau *m*

Cuban ['kjubən] *adj* cubain || *s* Cubain *m*

cubbyhole ['kʌbɪˌhol] *s* retraite *f*; (*in wall*) placard *m*; (*in furniture*) case *f*

cube [kjub] *s & s* cube *m*; **in cubes** (*said of sugar*) en morceaux || *tr* cuber

cube' root' *s* racine *f* cubique

cubic ['kjubɪk] *adj* cubique, cube

cu'bic me'ter *s* mètre *m* cube

cub' report'er *s* reporter *m* débutant

cub' scout' *s* louveteau *m*

cuckold ['kʌkəld] *adj & s* cocu *m*, cornard *m* || *tr* cocufier

cuckoo ['kuku] *adj* (slang) niais, benêt || *s* coucou *m*

cuck'oo clock' *s* coucou *m*

cucumber ['kjukʌmbər] *s* concombre *m*

cud [kʌd] *s* bol *m* alimentaire; **to chew the cud** ruminer

cuddle ['kʌdəl] *tr* serrer doucement dans les bras ‖ *intr* (*said of lovers*) s'étreindre; **to cuddle up** se pelotonner

cudg·el ['kʌdʒəl] *s* gourdin *m*, trique *f*; **to take up the cudgels for** prendre fait et cause pour ‖ *v* (*pret & pp* -eled *or* -elled; *ger* -eling *or* -elling) *tr* bâtonner, rosser

cue [kju] *s* avis *m*; (*hint*) mot *m*; (*rod used in billiards; persons in line*) queue *f*; (*mus*) indication *f* de rentrée; (*theat*) réclame *f*; **to give s.o. the cue** faire la leçon à qn, donner le mot à qn; **to take one's cue from** se conformer à

cuff [kʌf] *s* (*of shirt*) poignet *m*, manchette *f*; (*of coat or trousers*) parement *m*; (*blow*) taloche *f*, manchette *f* ‖ *tr* talocher, flanquer une taloche à

cuff' link' *s* bouton *m* de manchette

cuirass [kwɪ'ræs] *s* cuirasse *f*

cuisine [kwɪ'zin] *s* cuisine *f*

culinary ['kjulɪ ˌnɛri] *adj* culinaire

cull [kʌl] *tr* choisir; (*to gather, pluck*) cueillir; **to cull from** recueillir dans

culm [kʌlm] *s* chaume *m*; (*coal dust*) charbonnaille *f*

culminate ['kʌlmɪ ˌnet] *intr* (astr) culminer; **to culminate in** finir par, se terminer en

culmination [ˌkʌlmɪ'neʃən] *s* point *m* culminant; (astr) culmination *f*

culottes [k(j)u'lɑts] *spl* pantalon *m* de plage

culpable ['kʌlpəbəl] *adj* coupable

culprit ['kʌlprɪt] *s* coupable *mf*; (*accused*) accusé *m*, prévenu *m*

cult [kʌlt] *s* culte *m*

cultivate ['kʌltɪ ˌvet] *tr* cultiver

cultivation [ˌkʌltɪ'veʃən] *s* culture *f*

cultivator ['kʌltɪ ˌvetər] *s* (*person*) cultivateur *m*, exploitant *m* agricole; (*mach*) cultivateur *m*, scarificateur *m*

cultural ['kʌltʃərəl] *adj* culturel

culture ['kʌltʃər] *s* culture *f* ‖ *tr* cultiver

cultured *adj* (*learned*) cultivé, lettré

cul'tured pearl' *s* perle *f* de culture

culvert ['kʌlvərt] *s* ponceau *m*, cassis *m*

cumbersome ['kʌmbərsəm] *adj* incommode, encombrant; (*clumsy*) lourd, difficile à manier

cummerbund ['kʌmər ˌbʌnd] *s* ceinture *f* d'étoffe

cumulative ['kjumjə ˌletɪv] *adj* croissant, cumulatif

cunning ['kʌnɪŋ] *adj* (*sly*) astucieux, rusé; (*clever*) habile, fin; (*attractive*) gentil ‖ *s* (*slyness*) astuce *f*, ruse *f*; (*cleverness*) habileté *f*, finesse *f*

cup [kʌp] *s* tasse *f*; (*of metal*) gobelet *m*, timbale *f*; (*bot, eccl*) calice *m*; (*mach*) godet *m* graisseur; (*sports*) coupe *f* ‖ *v* (*pret & pp* **cupped**; *ger* **cupping**) *tr* (surg) ventouser

cupboard ['kʌbərd] *s* armoire *f*; (*in wall*) placard *m*

Cupid ['kjupɪd] *s* Cupidon *m*

cupidity [kju'pɪdɪti] *s* cupidité *f*

cupola ['kjupələ] *s* coupole *f*

cur [kʌr] *s* chien *m* métis, roquet *m*; (*despicable person*) mufle *m*

curate ['kjurɪt] *s* vicaire *m*

curative ['kjurətɪv] *adj* curatif

curator [kju'retər] *s* conservateur *m*

curb [kʌrb] *s* bordure *f* de pavés, bord *m* de trottoir; (*of well*) margelle *f*; (*of bit*) gourmette *f*; (*market*) coulisse *f*; (*check, restraint*) frein *m* ‖ *tr* (*a horse*) gourmer; (*passions, anger, desires*) réprimer, refréner; **curb your dog** (public sign) faites faire votre chien dans le ruisseau

curb' serv'ice *s* restoroute *m*

curb'stone' *s* garde-pavé *m*; **curbstones** bordure *f* de pavés

curd [kʌrd] *s* caillé *m*; **curds** caillebotte *f* ‖ *tr* cailler, caillebotter ‖ *intr* se cailler, se caillebotter

curdle ['kʌrdəl] *tr* cailler; (*the blood*) figer ‖ *intr* se cailler; se figer

curds' and whey' *spl* lait *m* caillé sucré

cure [kjur] *s* guérison *f*; (*treatment*) cure *f*; (*remedy*) remède *m* ‖ *tr* guérir; (*meat; leather*) saler; (*a pipe*) culotter

cure'-all' *s* panacée *f*

curfew ['kʌrfju] *s* couvre-feu *m*

curl·o ['kjurɪ ˌo] *s* (*pl* -os) bibelot *m*

curiosi·ty [ˌkjurɪ'ɑsɪti] *s* (*pl* -ties) curiosité *f*

curious ['kjurɪ·əs] *adj* curieux

curl [kʌrl] *s* boucle *f*, frisure *f*; (*spiral-shaped*) volute *f*; (*of smoke*) spirale *f* ‖ *tr* boucler, friser; (*to coil, to roll up*) enrouler, tire-bouchonner; **to curl one's lip** faire la moue ‖ *intr* boucler, friser; (*said of smoke*) s'élever en spirales; (*said of waves*) onduler, déferler; **to curl up** (*said of leaves, paper, etc.*) se recroqueviller; (*in bed*) se rouler en boule

curlew ['kʌrl(j)u] *s* courlis *m*

curlicue ['kʌrlɪ ˌkju] *s* paraphe *m*

curl'ing i'ron *s* fer *m* à friser

curl'pa'per *s* papillote *f*

curl·y ['kʌrli] *adj* (*comp* -ier; *super* -lest) bouclé, frisé

curmudgeon [kər'mʌdʒən] *s* (*crosspatch*) bourru *m*, sale bougre *m*; (*miser*) ladre *mf*

currant ['kʌrənt] *s* groseille *f*

curren·cy ['kʌrənsi] *s* (*pl* -cies) circulation *f*; (*legal tender*) monnaie *f*, devises *fpl*; **to give currency to** donner cours à

current ['kʌrənt] *adj* courant; (*month*) en cours; (*accepted*) admis, reçu; (*present-day*) actuel ‖ *s* courant *m*; (*stream*) courant, cours *m*

cur'rent account' *s* compte *m* courant

cur'rent events' *spl* actualités *fpl*

cur'rent fail'ure *s* panne *f* de secteur

cur'rent is'sue *s* dernier numéro *m*

curricu·lum [kə'rɪkjələm] *s* (*pl* -lums *or* -la [lə]) programme *m* scolaire, plan *m* d'études

cur·ry ['kʌri] *s* (*pl* -ries) cari *m* ‖ *v* (*pret & pp* -ried) *tr* (*a horse*) étriller; (culin) apprêter au cari; **to curry favor with** faire la cour à

cur'ry·comb' *s* étrille *f* ‖ *tr* étriller

cur'ry pow'der s cari m

curse [kʌrs] s malédiction f; (oath) juron m ǁ tr maudire ǁ intr jurer, sacrer

cursed ['kʌrsɪd], [kʌrst] adj maudit, exécrable, sacré

cursive ['kʌrsɪv] adj cursif ǁ s cursive f

cursory ['kʌrsərɪ] adj superficiel, précipité

curt [kʌrt] adj brusque, court

curtail [kər'tel] tr amoindrir, diminuer; (expenses) restreindre; (rights) enlever

curtailment [kʌr'telmənt] s diminution f; (of expenses) restriction f; (of rights) privation f

curtain ['kʌrtən] s rideau m ǁ tr garnir de rideaux; (to hide) cacher sous des rideaux; **to curtain off** séparer par un rideau

cur'tain call' s rappel m

cur'tain rais'er s (play) lever m de rideau

cur'tain ring' s anneau m de rideau

cur'tain rod' s tringle f de rideau

curt'sy ['kʌrtsɪ] s (pl -sies) révérence f ǁ v (pret & pp -sied) intr faire la révérence

curvature ['kʌrvətʃər] s courbure f; (of spine) déviation f

curve [kʌrv] s courbe f; (of road) virage m; (curvature) courbure f ǁ tr courber ǁ intr se courber

curved adj courbe, courbé

cushion ['kuʃən] s coussin m ǁ tr (a chair) rembourrer; (a shock) amortir

cuspidor ['kʌspɪˌdɔr] s crachoir m

cuss [kʌs] s (person) (coll) vaurien m, chenapan m ǁ tr (coll) maudire ǁ intr (coll) jurer, sacrer

cuss'word' s (coll) juron m

custard ['kʌstərd] s flan m, œufs mpl au lait, crème f caramel

custodian [kʌs'todɪən] s gardien m; concierge mf

custo·dy ['kʌstədɪ] s (pl -dies) garde f; emprisonnement m; **in custody** en sûreté; **to take into custody** mettre en état d'arrestation

custom ['kʌstəm] s coutume f; (customers) clientèle f; **customs** douane f; (duties) droits mpl de douane

customary ['kʌstəˌmerɪ] adj coutumier, ordinaire, habituel

custom-built ['kʌstəm'bɪlt] adj hors série, fait sur commande

customer ['kʌstəmər] s client m, chaland m; (coll) individu m, type m; **customers** clientèle f, achalandage m

cus'tom-house' adj douanier ǁ s douane f

custom-made ['kʌstəm'med] adj fait sur commande; (clothes) sur mesure

cus'toms clear'ance s expédition f douanière

cus'toms of'ficer s douanier m

cus'toms un'ion s union f douanière

cus'tom tai'lor s tailleur m à façon

cut [kʌt] adj coupé; **cut out** taillé, e.g., **he is not cut out for that** il n'est pas taillé pour cela; e.g., **your work is cut out for you** voilà votre besogne taillée ǁ s coupe f; (piece cut off) tranche f, morceau m; (slash) coupure f; (with knife, whip, etc.) coup m; (in prices, wages, etc.) réduction f, baisse f; (of a garment) coupe; (typ) gravure f, planche f; (absence from school) (coll) séchage m; (in winnings, earnings, etc.) (slang) part f; **the cheap cuts** les bas morceaux mpl ǁ v (pret & pp cut; ger cutting) tr couper; (meat, bread) trancher; (prices) réduire, baisser; (e.g., a hole) pratiquer; (glass, diamonds) tailler; (fingernails) rogner; (an article, play, speech) abréger; faire des coupures à; (a phonograph record) enregistrer; (a class) (coll) sécher; **to cut down** faucher, abattre; (expenses) réduire; **to cut off**, cut, or up découper, couper; **to cut short** couper court à ǁ intr couper; trancher; **to cut in** (a conversation) s'immiscer dans; (coll) enlever la danseuse d'un autre; **to cut off** (debate) clore; **to cut up** (slang) faire le pitre

cut'-and-dried' adj décidé d'avance, tout fait; monotone, rasoir

cutaneous [kju'tenɪ·əs] adj cutané

cut'away' s frac m

cut'back' s réduction f; (mov) retour m en arrière

cute [kjut] adj (coll) mignon; (shrewd) (coll) rusé

cut' glass' s cristal m taillé

cuticle ['kjutɪkəl] s cuticule f

cutlass ['kʌtləs] s coutelas m

cutlery ['kʌtlərɪ] s coutellerie f

cutlet ['kʌtlɪt] s côtelette f; (without bone) escalope f

cut'off' s point m de coupure; (road) raccourci m; (of river) bras m mort; (of cylinder) obturateur m

cut'out' s (aut) échappement m libre; (elec) coupe-circuit m; (mov) décor m découpé

cut'-rate' adj à prix réduit

cutter ['kʌtər] s (naut) cotre m

cut'throat' s coup-jarret m

cutting ['kʌtɪŋ] adj tranchant; (tone, remark) mordant, cinglant ǁ s coupe f; (from a newspaper) coupure f; (e.g., of prices) réduction f; (hort) bouture f; (mov) découpage m

cuttlefish ['kʌtəlˌfɪʃ] s seiche f

cut'wa'ter s (naut) étrave f; (of bridge) bec m

cyanamide [saɪ'ænəˌmaɪd] s cyanamide f

cyanide ['saɪəˌnaɪd] s cyanure m

cyanosis [ˌsaɪ·ə'nosɪs] s cyanose f

cycle ['saɪkəl] s cycle m; (of internal-combustion engine) temps m; (phys) période f ǁ intr faire de la bicyclette

cyclic(al) ['saɪklɪk(əl)], ['sɪklɪk(əl)] adj cyclique

cyclist ['saɪklɪst] s cycliste mf

cyclone ['saɪklon] s cyclone m

cyclops ['saɪklɑps] s cyclope m

cyclotron ['saɪkloˌtrɑn], ['sɪkloˌtrɑn] s cyclotron m

cylinder ['sɪlɪndər] s cylindre m; (of revolver) barillet m

cyl'inder block' s cylindre m
cyl'inder bore' s alésage m
cyl'inder head' s culasse f
cylindric(al) [sɪ'lɪndrɪk(əl)] adj cylindrique
cymbal ['sɪmbəl] s cymbale f
cynic ['sɪnɪk] adj & s cynique m
cynical ['sɪnɪkəl] adj cynique
cynicism ['sɪnɪ,sɪzəm] s cynisme m
cynosure ['saɪnə,ʃur], ['sɪnə,ʃur] s guide m, exemple m, norme f; (center of attention) clou m; (astr) cynosure f
cypress ['saɪprəs] s cyprès m

Cyprus ['saɪprəs] s Chypre f
Cyrillic [sɪ'rɪlɪk] adj cyrillique
cyst [sɪst] s kyste m; (on the skin) vésicule f
czar [zar] s tsar m, czar m
czarina [za'rinə] s tsarine f, czarine f
Czech [tʃɛk] adj tchèque ‖ s (language) tchèque m; (person) Tchèque mf
Czecho-Slovak ['tʃɛko'slovæk] adj tchécoslovaque ‖ s Tchécoslovaque mf
Czecho-Slovakia [,tʃɛkoslo'vækɪ-ə] s Tchécoslovaquie f; la Tchécoslovaquie

D

D, d [di] s IVᵉ lettre de l'alphabet
dab [dæb] s touche f; (of ink) tache f; (of butter) petit morceau m ‖ v (pret & pp dabbed; ger dabbing) tr essuyer légèrement; (to pat) tapoter
dabble ['dæbəl] tr humecter ‖ intr barboter; **to dabble in** se mêler de; **to dabble in the stock market** boursicoter
dad [dæd] s (coll) papa m
dad-dy ['dædi] s (pl -dies) papa m
dad'dy-long'legs' s (pl -legs) faucheux m
daffodil ['dæfədɪl] s jonquille f des prés, narcisse m des bois
daff-y ['dæfi] adj (comp -ier; super -iest) (coll) timbré, toqué
dagger ['dægər] s poignard m, dague f; (typ) croix f, obel m; **to look daggers at** foudroyer du regard
dahlia ['dæljə] s dahlia m
dai-ly ['deli] adj quotidien, journalier ‖ s (pl -lies) quotidien m ‖ adv journellement
dain-ty ['denti] adj (comp -tier; super -tiest) délicat ‖ s (pl -ties) friandise f
dair-y ['deri] s (pl -ies) laiterie f; (shop) crémerie f; (farm) vacherie f
dair'y farm' s vacherie f
dair'y-man s (pl -men) laitier m
dais ['de-ɪs] s estrade f
dai-sy ['dezi] s (pl -sies) marguerite f
dal-ly ['dæli] v (pret & pp -lied) intr badiner; (to delay) s'attarder
dam [dæm] s barrage m; (female quadruped) mère f ‖ v (pret & pp dammed; ger damming) tr contenir, endiguer
damage ['dæmɪdʒ] s dommage m, dégâts mpl; (to engine, ship, etc.) avaries fpl; (to one's reputation) tort m; damages (law) dommages-intérêts mpl ‖ tr endommager; (merchandise; a machine) avarier; (a reputation) faire du tort à
damaging ['dæmɪdʒɪŋ] adj dommageable, préjudiciable
damascene ['dæmə,sin], [,dæmə'sin]

adj damasquiné ‖ s damasquinage m ‖ tr damasquiner
Damascus [də'mæskəs] s Damas f
dame [dem] s dame f; (coll) jupon m
damn [dæm] s juron m, gros mot m; **I don't give a damn** (slang) je m'en fiche; **that's not worth a damn** (slang) ça ne vaut pas un pet de lapin, ça ne vaut pas chipette ‖ tr condamner; (to criticize harshly) éreinter; (to curse) maudire; **damn it!** oh, la vache!; **to damn with faint praise** assommer avec des fleurs ‖ intr maudire
damnation [dæm'neʃən] s damnation f
damned [dæmd] adj damné m ‖ s—**the damned** les damnés ‖ adv (slang) diablement, bigrement
damp [dæmp] adj humide, moite ‖ s humidité f; (firedamp) grisou m ‖ (to dampen) humecter, mouiller; (a furnace) étouffer; (sound; electromagnetic waves) amortir
dampen ['dæmpən] tr humecter; (enthusiasm) refroidir; (to muffle) amortir
damper ['dæmpər] s (of chimney) registre m; (of stovepipe) soupape f de réglage; (of piano) étouffoir m; **to put a damper on** (fig) jeter un froid sur
damsel ['dæmzəl] s demoiselle f
dance [dæns], [dɑns] s danse f; bal m, soirée f dansante ‖ tr & intr danser
dance' band' s orchestre m de danse
dance' floor' s piste f de danse
dance' hall' s dancing m, salle f de danse
dance' pro'gram s carnet m de bal
dancer ['dænsər], ['dɑnsər] s danseur m
danc'ing part'ner s danseur m
dandelion ['dændɪ,laɪ-ən] s pissenlit m
dandruff ['dændrəf] s pellicules fpl
dan-dy ['dændi] adj (comp -dier; super -diest) (coll) chic, chouette ‖ s (pl -dies) dandy m, élégant m
Dane [den] s Danois m
danger ['dendʒər] s danger m

dangerous ['dendʒərəs] *adj* dangereux

dangle ['dæŋgəl] *tr* faire pendiller || *intr* pendiller

Danish ['denɪʃ] *adj & s* danois *m*

dank [dæŋk] *adj* humide, moite

Danube ['dænjub] *s* Danube *m*

dapper ['dæpər] *adj* fringant, élégant

dappled ['dæpəld] *adj* tacheté; (*sky*) pommelé; (*horse*) moucheté, miroité

dare [der] *s* défi *m*; **to take a dare** relever un défi || *tr* défier; oser; **to dare s.o. to** + *inf* défier qn de + *inf* || *intr* oser; **to dare** + *inf* oser + *inf*

dare'dev'il *s* risque-tout *mf*

daring ['derɪŋ] *adj* audacieux, hardi || *s* audace *f*, hardiesse *f*

dark [dɑrk] *adj* sombre, obscur; (*color*) foncé; (*complexion*) basané, brun; **it is dark** il fait noir, il fait nuit || *s* obscurité *f*, ténèbres *fpl*

Dark' Ag'es ['ɑrk] âge *m* des ténèbres

darken ['dɑrkən] *tr* assombrir; (*the complexion*) brunir; (*a color*) foncer || *intr* s'assombrir; (*said of forehead*) se rembrunir

dark' horse' *s* (pol) candidat *m* obscur; (sports) outsider *m*

darkly ['dɑrkli] *adv* obscurément; (*mysteriously*) ténébreusement; (*threateningly*) d'un air menaçant

dark' meat' *s* viande *f* brune; (*of game*) viande noire

darkness ['dɑrknɪs] *s* obscurité *f*

dark'room' *s* (phot) chambre *f* noire

darling ['dɑrlɪŋ] *adj & s* chéri *m*, bien-aimé *m*; **my darling** mon chou

darn [dɑrn] *s* reprise *f*, raccommodage *m* || *tr* repriser, raccommoder || *interj* zut!

darn'ing egg' *s* œuf *m* à repriser

darn'ing nee'dle *s* aiguille *f* à repriser

dart [dɑrt] *s* dard *m*; (*small missile used in a game*) fléchette *f* || *intr* se précipiter, aller comme une flèche

dash [dæʃ] *s* trait *m*; (*small amount*) soupçon *m*, petit brin *m*; (*of color*) pointe *f*, touche *f*; (*splash*) choc *m*, floc *m*; (*spirit*) élan *m*, fougue *f*; (*in printing, writing*) tiret *m*; (*in telegraphy*) trait *m*, longue *f* || *tr* (*quickly*) précipiter; (*violently*) heurter; (*hopes*) abattre; **to dash off** écrire d'un trait, esquisser; **to dash to pieces** fracasser || *intr* se précipiter; **to dash against** se heurter contre; **to dash by** filer à grand train; **to dash in** entrer en trombe; **to dash off** or **out** s'élancer, s'élancer dehors

dash'board' *s* tableau *m* de bord

dashing ['dæʃɪŋ] *adj* impétueux, fougueux; (*elegant*) fringant

dastard ['dæstərd] *adj & s* lâche *mf*

data ['detə], ['dætə] *spl* données *fpl*

da'ta proc'essing *s* analyse *f* des renseignements, étude *f* des données

date [det] *s* (*time*) date *f*; (*on books, on coins*) millésime *m*; (*palm*) dattier *m*; (*fruit*) datte *f*; (*of note, of loan*) terme *m*, échéance *f*; (*appointment*) rendez-vous *m*; **out of date** suranné, périmé; **to date** à ce jour; **up to date** à la page, au courant || *tr* dater;

(*e.g., a work of art*) assigner une date à; (coll) fixer un rendez-vous avec || *intr* (*to be outmoded*) dater; **to date from** dater de, remonter à

date' line' *s* ligne *f* de changement de date

date' palm' *s* dattier *m*

dative ['detɪv] *s* datif *m*

daub [dɔb] *s* barbouillage *m* || *tr* barbouiller

daughter ['dɔtər] *s* fille *f*

daugh'ter-in-law' *s* (*pl* **daughters-in-law**) belle-fille *f*, bru *f*

daunt [dɔnt] *tr* intimider, abattre

dauntless ['dɔntlɪs] *adj* intrépide

dauphin ['dɔfɪn] *s* dauphin *m*

davenport ['dævən‚pɔrt] *s* canapé-lit *m*

daw [dɔ] *s* choucas *m*

dawdle ['dɔdəl] *intr* flâner, muser

dawn [dɔn] *s* aube *f*, aurore *f* || *intr* poindre; **to dawn on** venir à l'esprit à

day [de] *adj* (*work*) diurne; (*worker*) de journée || *s* jour *m*; (*of travel, work, worry*) journée *f*; (*of the month*) quantième *m*; **a day** (*per day*) par jour; **by the day** à la journée; **day by day** au jour le jour, jour par jour; **every day** tous les jours, chaque jour; **every other day** tous les deux jours; **from day to day** de jour en jour; **good old days** bon vieux temps; **in less than a day** du jour au lendemain; **in these days** de nos jours; **in those days** à ce moment-là, à cette époque; **one fine day** un beau jour; **the day after** le lendemain; **le lendemain de**; **the day after tomorrow** après-demain; **l'après-demain *m*; **the day before** la veille; **la veille de**; **the day before yesterday** avant-hier; **l'avant-hier *m*

day' bed' *s* canapé-lit *m*

day'break' *s* pointe *f* du jour, lever *m* du jour; **at daybreak** au jour levant

day' coach' *s* (rr) voiture *f*

day'dream' *s* rêvasserie *f*, rêverie *f* || *intr* rêvasser, rêver creux

day'dream'er *s* songe-creux *m*, songeur *m*

day'dream'ing *s* rêvasserie *f*

day' la'borer *s* journalier *m*

day'light' *s* jour *m*; **in broad daylight** en plein jour; **to see daylight** (coll) comprendre; (coll) voir la fin d'une tâche difficile

day'light-sav'ing time' *s* heure *f* d'été

day' lil'y *s* lis *m* jaune, belle-d'un-jour *m*

day' nurs'ery *s* garderie *f* d'enfants, crèche *f*

day' off' *s* jour *m* de congé, jour *m* chômé

day' of reck'oning *s* jour *m* de règlement; (*last judgment*) jour d'expiation

day' shift' *s* équipe *f* de jour

day' stu'dent *s* externe *mf*

day'time' *s* jour *m*, journée *f*

daze [dez] *s* étourdissement *m*; **in a daze** hébété || *tr* étourdir

dazzle ['dæzəl] *s* éblouissement *m* || *tr* éblouir

dazzling ['dæzlɪŋ] *adj* éblouissant

D.C. ['di'si] *s* (letterword) (**District of**

Columbia) le district de Columbia; (direct current) le courant continu

D'day' *s* le jour J

deacon ['dikən] *s* diacre *m*

deaconess ['dikənɪs] *s* diaconesse *f*

dead [dɛd] *adj* mort; (*tired*) épuisé; (*color*) terne; (*business*) stagnant; (*sleep*) profond; (*calm*) plat; (*loss*) sec; (*typewriter key*) immobile; **on a dead level** à franc niveau ‖ *s*—**in the dead of night** au milieu de la nuit; **the dead** les morts; **the dead of winter** le cœur de l'hiver ‖ *adv* absolument; **to stop dead** s'arrêter net

dead'beat' *s* (slang) écornifleur *m*

dead' bolt' *s* pêne *m* dormant

dead' calm' *s* calme *m* plat

dead' cen'ter *s* point *m* mort

dead'-drunk' *adj* ivre mort

deaden ['dɛdən] *tr* amortir; (*sound*) assourdir

dead' end' *s* cul-de-sac *m*, impasse *f*

dead'latch' *s* pêne *m* dormant

dead'-let'ter of'fice *s* bureau *m* des rebuts

dead'line' *s* dernier délai *m*, date *f* limite

dead'lock' *s* serrure *f* à pêne dormant; (fig) impasse *f* ‖ *tr* faire aboutir à une impasse

dead·ly ['dɛdli] *adj* (*comp* **-lier;** *super* **-liest**) mortel; (*sin*) capital

dead' pan' *s* (slang) visage *m* sans expression

dead' reck'oning *s* estime *f*; (*position*) point *m* d'estime

dead' ring'er *s* (coll) portrait *m* vivant

dead' sol'dier *s* (*bottle*) (slang) cadavre *m*

dead' weight' *s* poids *m* lourd

dead'wood' *s* bois *m* mort; (fig) objet *m* or individu *m* inutile

deaf [dɛf] *adj* sourd; **to turn a deaf ear** faire la sourde oreille

deaf'-and-dumb' *adj* sourd-muet

deafen ['dɛfən] *tr* assourdir

deafening ['dɛfənɪŋ] *adj* assourdissant

deaf'-mute' *adj* & *s* sourd-muet *m*

deafness ['dɛfnɪs] *s* surdité *f*

deal [dil] *s* affaire *f*; (*cards*) main *f*, donne *f*; **a good deal (of)** or **a great deal (of)** beaucoup (de); **to think a great deal of s.o.** estimer qn ‖ *v* (*pret* & *pp* **dealt** [dɛlt]) *tr* (*a blow*) donner, porter; (*cards*) donner, distribuer; **to deal out** (*e.g., gifts*) distribuer, répartir; (*alms*) dispenser; (*justice*) rendre ‖ *intr* négocier; (*cards*) faire la donne; **to deal in** faire le commerce de; **to deal with** (*a person*) traiter avec; (*a subject*) traiter de

dealer ['dilər] *s* marchand *m*, négociant *m*; (*of cards*) donneur *m*; (*middleman, e.g., in selling automobiles*) concessionnaire *m*, stockiste *m*

dean [din] *s* doyen *m*

dean'ship *s* doyenné *m*, décanat *m*

dear [dɪr] *adj* cher; **dear me!** mon Dieu!; **Dear Sir** (*salutation in a letter*) Monsieur ‖ *s* chéri *m*

dearie ['dɪri] *s* (coll) petite, chérie *f*

dearth [dʌrθ] *s* disette *f*, pénurie *f*

death [dɛθ] *s* mort *f*; **at death's door** à deux doigts de la mort; **to bore to death** raser; **to put to death** mettre à mort; **to starve to death** mourir de faim; **faire mourir de faim**

death'bed' *s* lit *m* de mort

death'blow' *s* coup *m* mortel

death' certif'icate *s* constatation *f* de décès, extrait *m* mortuaire

death' house' *s* quartier *m* de la mort

death' knell' *s* glas *m* funèbre

deathless ['dɛθlɪs] *adj* immortel

deathly ['dɛθli] *adj* mortel ‖ *adv* mortellement, comme la mort

death' mask' *s* masque *m* mortuaire

death' pen'alty *s* peine *f* capitale

death' rate' *s* mortalité *f*, taux *m* de mortalité

death' rat'tle *s* râle *m* de la mort

death' war'rant *s* ordre *m* d'exécution

death'watch' *s* veillée *f* funèbre

deb [dɛb] *s* (slang) débutante *f*

debacle [de'bakəl] *s* débâcle *m*

de·bar [dɪ'bar] *v* (*pret* & *pp* **-barred;** *ger* **-barring**) *tr* exclure; empêcher

debark [dɪ'bark] *tr* & *intr* débarquer

debarkation [,dibar'keʃən] *s* débarquement *m*

debase [dɪ'bes] *tr* avilir, abaisser; (*e.g., money*) altérer

debatable [dɪ'betəbəl] *adj* discutable

debate [dɪ'bet] *s* débat *m*; **under debate** en discussion ‖ *tr* & *intr* discuter

debauch [dɪ'bɔtʃ] *s* débauche *f* ‖ *tr* débaucher, corrompre

debauchee [,dɛbɔ'ʃi], [,dɛbɔ'tʃi] *s* débauché *m*

debaucher·y [dɪ'bɔtʃəri] *s* (*pl* **-ies**) débauche *f*

debenture [dɪ'bɛntʃər] *s* (*bond*) obligation *f*; (*voucher*) reçu *m*

debilitate [dɪ'bɪlɪ,tet] *tr* débiliter

debili·ty [dɪ'bɪlɪti] *s* (*pl* **-ties**) débilité *f*

debit ['dɛbɪt] *s* débit *m*; (*entry on debit side*) article *m* au débit ‖ *tr* débiter, porter au débit

deb'it bal'ance *s* solde *m* débiteur

debonair [,dɛbə'nɛr] *adj* gai, jovial; élégant, charmant

debris [də'bri], ['dɛbri] *s* débris *mpl*, détritus *m*; (*from ruined buildings*) décombres *mpl*

debt [dɛt] *s* dette *f*; **to run into debt** s'endetter

debtor ['dɛtər] *s* débiteur *m*

debut [de'bju], ['dɛbju] *s* début *m* ‖ *intr* débuter

debutante [,dɛbju'tant], ['dɛbjə,tænt] *s* débutante *f*

decade ['dɛked] *s* décennie *f*, décade *f*

decadence [dɪ'kedəns] *s* décadence *f*

decadent [dɪ'kedənt] *adj* & *s* décadent *m*

decal ['dikæl], [dɪ'kæl], ['dɛkəl] *s* décalcomanie *f*

decamp [dɪ'kæmp] *intr* décamper

decanter [dɪ'kæntər] *s* carafe *f*

decapitate [dɪ'kæpɪ,tet] *tr* décapiter

decay [dɪ'ke] *s* (*rotting*) pourriture *f*; (*decline*) décadence *f*; (*falling to pieces*) délabrement *m*; (*of teeth*)

carie *f* ‖ *tr* pourrir; *(teeth)* carier ‖
intr pourrir, se gâter; *(said of teeth)*
se carier; tomber en décadence or
ruine; délabrer

decease [dɪ'sis] *s* décès *m* ‖ *intr* décéder

deceit [dɪ'sit] *s* tromperie *f*

deceitful [dɪ'sitfəl] *adj* trompeur

deceive [dɪ'siv] *tr & intr* tromper

decelerate [di'sɛlə,ret] *tr & intr* ralentir

December [dɪ'sɛmbər] *s* décembre *m*

decen-cy ['disənsi] *s (pl -cies)* décence
f; decencies convenances *fpl*

decent ['disənt] *adj* décent

decentralize [di'sɛntrə,laɪz] *tr* décentraliser

deception [dɪ'sɛpʃən] *s* tromperie *f*

deceptive [dɪ'sɛptɪv] *adj* trompeur

decide [dɪ'saɪd] *tr* décider; *(the outcome)* décider de ‖ *intr* décider, se
décider; **to decide to** + *inf* décider
de + *inf,* se décider à + *inf;* **to decide upon a day** fixer un jour

deciduous [dɪ'sɪdʒu-əs], [dɪ'sɪdju-əs]
adj caduc

decimal ['dɛsɪməl] *adj* décimal ‖ *s*
décimale *f*

dec'imal point' *s (in French the comma
is used to separate the decimal fraction from the integer)* virgule *f*

decimate ['dɛsɪ,met] *tr* décimer

decipher [dɪ'saɪfər] *tr* déchiffrer

decision [dɪ'sɪʒən] *s* décision *f*

decisive [dɪ'saɪsɪv] *adj* décisif

deck [dɛk] *s (of cards)* jeu *m,* paquet
m; (of ship) pont *m;* **between decks**
(naut) dans l'entrepont ‖ *tr*—**to deck
out** parer, orner

deck' chair' *s* transatlantique *m,* tran-
sat *m,* chaise *f* longue de bord

deck' hand' *s* matelot *m* de pont

deck'-land' *tr* apponter

deck'-land'ing *s* appontage *m*

deck'le edge' ['dɛkəl] *s* barbes *fpl,*
bords *mpl* baveux

declaim [dɪ'klem] *tr & intr* déclamer

declaration [,dɛklə'reʃən] *s* déclaration *f*

declarative [dɪ'klærətɪv] *adj* déclaratif

declare [dɪ'klɛr] *tr & intr* déclarer

declension [dɪ'klɛnʃən] *s* (gram) déclinaison *f*

declination [,dɛklɪ'neʃən] *s* (astr, geog)
déclinaison *f*

decline [dɪ'klaɪn] *s* déclin *m,* décadence *f; (in prices)* baisse *f* ‖ *tr &
intr* décliner

declivi-ty [dɪ'klɪvɪti] *s (pl -ties)* déclivité *f,* pente *f*

decode [dɪ'kod] *tr* décoder, déchiffrer

decompose [,dikəm'poz] *tr* décomposer ‖ *intr* se décomposer

decomposition [,dikɑmpə'zɪʃən] *s* décomposition *f*

decompression [,dikəm'prɛʃən] *s* décompression *f*

decontamination [,dikɑn,tæmɪ'neʃən]
s décontamination *f*

decorate ['dɛkə,ret] *tr* décorer

decoration [,dɛkə'reʃən] *s* décoration *f*

decorator ['dɛkə,retər] *s* décorateur *m*

decorous ['dɛkərəs], [dɪ'korəs] *adj*
convenable, correct, bienséant

decorum [dɪ'korəm] *s* décorum *m*

decoy [dɪ'kɔɪ], ['dikɔɪ] *s* leurre *m,* appât *m; (bird)* appeau *m* ‖ *tr* [dɪ'kɔɪ]
tr leurrer

decrease ['dikris], [dɪ'kris] *s* diminution *f* ‖ [dɪ'kris] *tr & intr* diminuer

decree [dɪ'kri] *s* décret *m,* arrêté *m;
(of divorce)* ordonnance *f* ‖ *tr* décréter, arrêter, ordonner

decrepit [dɪ'krɛpɪt] *adj* décrépit

de-cry [dɪ'kraɪ] *v (pret & pp -cried)*
tr décrier, dénigrer

dedicate ['dɛdɪ,ket] *tr* dédier

dedication [,dɛdɪ'keʃən] *s* consécration
f; (e.g., in a book) dédicace *f*

dedicatory ['dɛdɪkə,tori] *adj* dédicatoire

deduce [dɪ'djus] *tr* déduire, inférer

deduct [dɪ'dʌkt] *tr* déduire

deduction [dɪ'dʌkʃən] *s* déduction *f*

deed [did] *s* action *f,* acte *m;* (law)
acte, titre *m,* contrat *m;* **deed of val-
or** haut fait *m;* **good deed** bonne
action; **in deed** dans le fait ‖ *tr* transférer par un acte

deem [dim] *tr* estimer, juger, croire ‖
intr penser

deep [dip] *adj* profond; *(sound)* grave;
(color) foncé; de profondeur, e.g.,
to be twenty feet deep avoir vingt
pieds de profondeur; **deep in debt**
criblé de dettes; **deep in thought**
plongé dans la méditation ‖ *adv* profondément; **deep into the night** très
avant dans la nuit

deepen ['dipən] *tr* approfondir ‖ *intr*
s'approfondir

deep'-freeze' *v (pret -froze,* pp -frozen)
tr congeler à basse température

deep'-laid' *adj* habilement ourdi

deep' mourn'ing *s* grand deuil *m*

deep'-root'ed *adj* profondément enraciné

deep'-sea fish'ing *s* grande pêche *f* au
large, pêche maritime

deer [dɪr] *s (red deer)* cerf *m; (fallow
deer)* daim *m; (roe deer)* chevreuil *m*

deer'skin' *s* peau *f* de daim

deface [dɪ'fes] *tr* défigurer

de facto [di'fækto] *adv* de fait, de facto

defamation [,dɛfə'meʃən], [,dɪfə'me-
ʃən] *s* diffamation *f,* injures *fpl*

defame [dɪ'fem] *tr* diffamer

default [dɪ'fɔlt] *s* manque *m,* défaut
m; (on an obligation) carence *f;* **by
default** par défaut; (sports) par forfait; **in default of** à défaut de ‖ *tr (a
debt)* manquer de s'acquitter de ‖
intr ne pas tenir ses engagements;
(sports) perdre par forfait

defeat [dɪ'fit] *s* défaite *f;* **unexpected
defeat** contre-performance *f* ‖ *tr*
vaincre, battre, défaire

defeatism [dɪ'fitɪzəm] *s* défaitisme *m*

defeatist [dɪ'fitɪst] *adj & s* défaitiste
mf

defecate ['dɛfɪ,ket] *tr* déféquer

defect [dɪ'fɛkt], ['difɛkt] *s* défaut *m,*
imperfection *f,* vice *m* ‖ [dɪ'fɛkt]
intr faire défection, déserter

defection [dɪ'fɛk/ən] *s* défection *f*
defective [dɪ'fɛktɪv] *adj* défectueux, vicieux; (gram) défectif
defend [dɪ'fɛnd] *tr* défendre
defendant [dɪ'fɛndənt] *s* (law) défendeur *m*, intimé *m*
defense [dɪ'fɛns] *s* défense *f*
defenseless [dɪ'fɛnslɪs] *adj* sans défense
defensive [dɪ'fɛnsɪv] *adj* défensif ‖ *s* défensive *f*
de-fer [dɪ'fʌr] *v* (pret & pp -ferred; ger -ferring) *tr* différer; (mil) mettre en sursis ‖ *intr*—**to defer to** déférer à
deference ['dɛfərəns] *s* déférence *f*
deferential [ˌdɛfə'rɛn/əl] *adj* déférent
deferment [dɪ'fʌrmənt] *s* ajournement *m*, remise *f*; (extension of time) délai *m*; (mil) sursis *m* d'appel
defiance [dɪ'faɪ-əns] *s* défi *m*, provocation *f*, nargue *f*; **in defiance of** au mépris de, en dépit de
defiant [dɪ'faɪ-ənt] *adj* provocant, hostile, de défi
deficien-cy [dɪ'fɪ/ənsi] *s* (pl -cies) déficience *f*, insuffisance *f*; (of vitamins or minerals) carence *f*; (com) déficit *m*
deficient [dɪ'fɪ/ənt] *adj* déficient, insuffisant
deficit ['dɛfɪsɪt] *adj* déficitaire ‖ *s* déficit *m*
defile [dɪ'faɪl], ['dɪfaɪl] *s* défilé *m* ‖ [dɪ'faɪl] *tr* souiller ‖ *intr* défiler
defilement [dɪ'faɪlmənt] *s* souillure *f*
define [dɪ'faɪn] *tr* définir
definite ['dɛfɪnɪt] *adj* défini; (opinions, viewpoints) décidé
definitely ['dɛfɪnɪtli] *adv* décidément, nettement
definition [ˌdɛfɪ'nɪ/ən] *s* définition *f*
definitive [dɪ'fɪnɪtɪv] *adj* définitif
deflate [dɪ'flet] *tr* dégonfler; (currency) amener la déflation de ‖ *intr* se dégonfler
deflation [dɪ'fle/ən] *s* dégonflement *m*; (of prices) déflation *f*
deflect [dɪ'flɛkt] *tr & intr* dévier
deflower [di'flau-ər] *tr* déflorer; (to strip of flowers) défleurir
deforest [di'fɑrɪst], [di'fɔrɪst] *tr* déboiser
deform [dɪ'fɔrm] *tr* déformer
deformed *adj* contrefait, difforme
deformi-ty [dɪ'fɔrmɪti] *s* (pl -ties) difformité *f*
defraud [dɪ'frɔd] *tr* frauder
defray [dɪ'fre] *tr* payer, supporter
defrost [di'frɔst], [di'frast] *tr* décongeler, dégivrer
defroster [di'frɔstər], [di'frastər] *s* déglaceur *m*, dégivreur *m*
defrosting [di'frɔstɪŋ], [di'frastɪŋ] *s* dégélement *m*, dégivrage *m*
deft [dɛft] *adj* adroit, habile; (hand) exercé, preste
defunct [dɪ'fʌŋkt] *adj* défunt; (practice, style, etc.) tombé en désuétude
de-fy [dɪ'faɪ] *v* (pret & pp -fied) *tr* défier, braver, porter un défi à
degeneracy [dɪ'dʒɛnərəsi] *s* dégénérescence *f*

degenerate [dɪ'dʒɛnərɪt] *adj & s* dégénéré *m* ‖ [dɪ'dʒɛnə,ret] *intr* dégénérer
degrade [dɪ'gred] *tr* dégrader
degrading [dɪ'gredɪŋ] *adj* dégradant
degree [dɪ'gri] *s* degré *m*; (from a university) grade *m*; (of humidity) titre *m*; **to take a degree** obtenir ses diplômes, obtenir ses titres universitaires
dehumidi-fy [ˌdihju'mɪdɪˌfaɪ] *v* (pret & pp -fied) *tr* déshumidifier
dehydrate [di'haɪdret] *tr* déshydrater; (the body) dessécher
deice [di'aɪs] *tr* déglacer, dégivrer
deicer [di'aɪsər] *s* dégivreur *m*, antigivrant *m*
dei-fy ['di-ɪ,faɪ] *v* (pret & pp -fied) *tr* déifier
deign [den] *intr*—**to deign to** daigner
dei-ty ['di-ɪti] *s* (pl -ties) divinité *f*; (mythol) déité *f*; **the Deity** Dieu *m*
dejected [dɪ'dʒɛktɪd] *adj* abattu, découragé
dejection [dɪ'dʒɛk/ən] *s* abattement *m*
delay [dɪ'le] *s* retard *m*; (postponement) sursis *m*, remise *f*; **without delay** sans délai; **without further delay** sans plus tarder ‖ *tr* retarder; (to put off) remettre, différer ‖ *intr* tarder, s'attarder
delayed'-ac'tion *adj* à action différée
delayed'-ac'tion switch' *s* minuterie *f* d'escalier
delayed'-time' switch' *s* coupe-circuit *m* à action différée
dele ['dili] *s* (typ) deleatur *m*
delectable [dɪ'lɛktəbəl] *adj* délectable
delegate ['dɛlɪ,get], ['dɛlɪgɪt] *s* délégué *m*; (at a convention) congressiste *mf*, délégué *s* ['dɛlɪ,get] *tr* déléguer
delegation [ˌdɛlɪ'ge/ən] *s* délégation *f*
delete [dɪ'lit] *tr* supprimer
deletion [dɪ'li/ən] *s* suppression *f*; (the deleted part) passage *m* supprimé
deliberate [dɪ'lɪbərɪt] *adj* (premeditated) délibéré, réfléchi; (cautious) circonspect; (slow) lent ‖ [dɪ'lɪbə,ret] *tr & intr* délibérer
deliberately [dɪ'lɪbərɪtli] *adv* (on purpose) exprès, de propos délibéré; (without hurrying) posément, sans hâte
deliberation [dɪ,lɪbə're/ən] *s* délibération *f*; (slowness) lenteur *f*
delica-cy ['dɛlɪkəsi] *s* (pl -cies) délicatesse *f*; (choice food) friandise *f*, gourmandise *f*
delicate ['dɛlɪkɪt] *adj* délicat
delicatessen [ˌdɛlɪkə'tɛsən] *s* charcuterie *f*
delicious [dɪ'lɪ/əs] *adj* délicieux
delight [dɪ'laɪt] *s* délice *m*, délices *fpl*, plaisir *m* ‖ *tr* enchanter, ravir ‖ *intr* —**to delight in** se délecter à
delighted *adj* enchanté, ravi, content
delightful [dɪ'laɪtfəl] *adj* délicieux, ravissant, enchanteur
delineate [dɪ'lɪnɪ,et] *tr* esquisser
delinquen-cy [dɪ'lɪŋkwənsi] *s* (pl -cies) délit *m*, faute *f*; (e.g., of juveniles) délinquance *f*

delinquent [dɪ'lɪŋkwənt] *adj* négligent, coupable; (*in payment*) arriéré; (*in guilt*) délinquant || *s* délinquant *m*; créancier *m* en retard

delirious [dɪ'lɪrɪ·əs] *adj* délirant

deliri·um [dɪ'lɪrɪ·əm] *s* (*pl* -ums or -a [ə]) délire *m*

deliver [dɪ'lɪvər] *tr* délivrer; (*e.g., laundry*) livrer; (*mail*) distribuer; (*a blow*) asséner; (*an opinion*) exprimer; (*a speech*) prononcer; (*energy*) débiter, fournir; **to be delivered of a child** accoucher d'un enfant

deliver·y [dɪ'lɪvəri] *s* (*pl* -ies) *s* remise *f*; (*e.g., of a package*) livraison *f*; (*of mail*) distribution *f*; (*of a speech; of electricity*) débit *m*; (*of a woman in childbirth*) accouchement *m*, délivrance *f*; **free delivery** livraison franco

deliv′ery-man *s* (*pl* -men) livreur *m*

deliv′ery room′ *s* salle *f* d'accouchement, salle de travail

deliv′ery truck′ *s* fourgon *m* à livraison

dell [dɛl] *s* vallon *m*

delouse [di'laus], [di'lauz] *tr* épouiller

delphinium [dɛl'fɪnɪ·əm] *s* dauphinelle *f*, pied-d'alouette *m*

delta ['dɛltə] *s* delta *m*

delude [dɪ'lud] *tr* duper, tromper

deluge ['dɛljudʒ] *s* déluge *m* || *tr* inonder

delusion [dɪ'luʒən] *s* illusion *f*, tromperie *f*; **delusions** (*psychopathol*) hallucinations *fpl*; **delusions of grandeur** folie *f* des grandeurs

delusive [dɪ'lusɪv] or **delusory** [dɪ'lusəri] *adj* trompeur

de luxe [dɪ'luks], [dɪ'lʌks] *adj & adv* de luxe

delve [dɛlv] *intr*—**to delve into** fouiller dans, approfondir

demagnetize [di'mægnɪ,taɪz] *tr* démagnétiser, désaimanter

demagogue ['dɛmə,gag] *s* démagogue *mf*

demand [dɪ'mænd], [dɪ'mɑnd] *s* exigence *f*; (*of the buying public*) demande *f*; **demands** exigences; **in great demand** très recherché; **on demand** sur demande || *tr* exiger

demanding [dɪ'mændɪŋ], [dɪ'mɑndɪŋ] *adj* exigeant

demarcate [dɪ'market], ['dimar,ket] *tr* délimiter

demean [dɪ'min] *tr* dégrader; **to demean oneself** se conduire

demeanor [dɪ'minər] *s* conduite *f*, tenue *f*

demented [dɪ'mɛntɪd] *adj* aliéné, fou

demerit [di'mɛrɪt] *s* démérite *m*

demigod ['dɛmɪ,gad] *s* demi-dieu *m*

demijohn ['dɛmɪ,dʒɑn] *s* dame-jeanne *f*

demilitarize [di'mɪlɪtə,raɪz] *tr* démilitariser

demise [dɪ'maɪz] *s* décès *m*

demitasse ['dɛmɪ,tæs], ['dɛmɪ,tɑs] *s* petite tasse *f* à café; (*contents*) café *m* noir

demobilize [di'mobɪ,laɪz] *tr* démobiliser

democra·cy [dɪ'mɑkrəsi] *s* (*pl* -cies) démocratie *f*

democrat ['dɛmə,kræt] *s* démocrate *mf*

democratic [,dɛmə'krætɪk] *adj* démocratique

demolish [dɪ'mɑlɪʃ] *tr* démolir

demolition [,dɛmə'lɪʃən], [,dimə'lɪʃən] *s* démolition *f*

demon ['dimən] *s* démon *m*

demoniac [dɪ'monɪ,æk] *adj & s* démoniaque *mf*

demonic [dɪ'mɑnɪk] *adj* démoniaque

demonstrate ['dɛmən,stret] *tr* démontrer || *intr* (*to show feelings in public gatherings*) manifester

demonstration [,dɛmən'streʃən] *s* démonstration *f*; (*public show of feeling*) manifestation *f*

demonstrative [dɪ'mɑnstrətɪv] *adj* démonstratif

demonstrator ['dɛmən,stretər] *s* (*salesman*) démonstrateur *m*; (*agitator*) manifestant *m*

demoralize [dɪ'mɑrə,laɪz], [dɪ'mɔrə,laɪz] *tr* démoraliser

demote [dɪ'mot] *tr* rétrograder

demotion [dɪ'moʃən] *s* rétrogradation *f*

de·mur [dɪ'mʌr] *v* (*pret & pp* -murred; *ger* -murring) *intr* faire des objections

demure [dɪ'mjur] *adj* modeste, posé

demurrage [dɪ'mʌrɪdʒ] *s* (naut) surestarie *f*

den [dɛn] *s* (*of animals; of thieves*) repaire *m*, retraite *f*; (*of wild beasts*) antre *m*; (*of lions*) tanière *f*; (*room in a house*) cabinet *m* de travail, fumoir *m*; (Cub Scouts) sizaine *f*

denaturalize [di'nætʃərə,laɪz] *tr* dénaturaliser

denial [dɪ'naɪ·əl] *s* (*contradiction*) dénégation *f*, démenti *m*; (*refusal*) refus *m*, déni *m*

denim ['dɛnɪm] *s* coutil *m*

denizen ['dɛnɪzən] *s* habitant *m*

Denmark ['dɛnmɑrk] *s* le Danemark

denomination [dɪ,nɑmɪ'neʃən] *s* dénomination *f*; (*of coin or stamp*) valeur *f*; (eccl) secte *f*, confession *f*, communion *f*

denote [dɪ'not] *tr* dénoter

denounce [dɪ'nauns] *tr* dénoncer

dense [dɛns] *adj* dense; (*stupid*) bête

densi·ty ['dɛnsɪti] *s* (*pl* -ties) densité *f*

dent [dɛnt] *s* marque *f* de coup, creux *m*; (*in a knife; in a fortune*) brèche *f*; **to make a dent in** faire une brèche à || *tr* ébrécher

dental ['dɛntəl] *adj* dentaire; (phonet) dental || *s* dentale *f*

den′tal floss′ *s* fil *m* dentaire

den′tal sur′geon *s* chirurgien-dentiste *m*

dentifrice ['dɛntɪfrɪs] *s* dentifrice *m*

dentist ['dɛntɪst] *s* dentiste *mf*

dentistry ['dɛntɪstri] *s* odontologie *f*

denture ['dɛntʃər] *s* (*set of teeth*) denture *f*; (*set of artificial teeth*) dentier *m*, râtelier *m*

denunciation [dɪ,nʌnsɪ'eʃən], [dɪ,nʌnʃɪ'eʃən] *s* dénonciation *f*

de·ny [dɪ'naɪ] *v* (*pret & pp* -nied) *tr* nier, démentir; **to deny oneself** se refuser, se priver

deodorant [di'odərənt] *adj* & *s* désodorisant *m*

deodorize [di'odə,raɪz] *tr* désodoriser

depart [dɪ'pɑrt] *intr* partir; **to depart from** se départir de

departed *adj* (*dead*) mort, défunt

department [dɪ'pɑrtmənt] *s* département *m*; (*of hospital*) service *m*; (*of agency*) bureau *m*; (*of store*) rayon *m*, comptoir *m*; (*of university*) section *f*

Depart'ment of State' *s* ministère *m* des affaires étrangères

depart'ment store' *s* grands magasins *mpl*, galerie *f*

departure [dɪ'pɑrtʃər] *s* départ *m*

depend [dɪ'pɛnd] *intr* dépendre; **to depend on** or **upon** dépendre de

dependable [dɪ'pɛndəbəl] *adj* sûr; (*person*) digne de confiance

dependence [dɪ'pɛndəns] *s* dépendance *f*; **dependence on** dépendance de; (*trust in*) confiance en

dependen·cy [dɪ'pɛndənsi] *s* (*pl* -**cies**) dépendance *f*; (*country, territory*) possession *f*, colonie *f*

dependent [dɪ'pɛndənt] *adj* dépendant; **dependent on** dépendant de; (*s.o. for family support*) à la charge de || *s* charge *f* de famille

depend'ent clause' *s* proposition *f* subordonnée

depict [dɪ'pɪkt] *tr* dépeindre, décrire

depiction [dɪ'pɪkʃən] *s* peinture *f*

deplete [dɪ'plit] *tr* épuiser

depletion [dɪ'pliʃən] *s* épuisement *m*

deplorable [dɪ'plorəbəl] *adj* déplorable

deplore [dɪ'plor] *tr* déplorer

deploy [dɪ'plɔɪ] *tr* (mil) déployer || *intr* (mil) se déployer

deployment [dɪ'plɔɪmənt] *s* (mil) déploiement *m*

depolarize [di'polə,raɪz] *tr* dépolariser

depopulate [di'pɑpjə,let] *tr* & *intr* dépeupler

deport [dɪ'port] *tr* déporter; **to deport oneself** se comporter

deportation [,dipor'teʃən] *s* déportation *f*

deportee [,dipor'ti] *s* déporté *m*

deportment [dɪ'portmənt] *s* comportement *m*, tenue *f*, manières *fpl*

depose [dɪ'poz] *tr* & *intr* déposer

deposit [dɪ'pɑzɪt] *s* dépôt *m*; (*as pledge*) cautionnement *m*, arrhes *fpl*, gage *m*; **no deposit** (*bottle*) perdu; **to pay a deposit** verser une provision, un acompte, une caution; **with deposit** (*on a bottle*) consigné || *tr* déposer; laisser comme provision

depos'it account' *s* compte *m* courant

depositor [dɪ'pɑzɪtər] *s* déposant *m*

deposito·ry [dɪ'pɑzɪ,tori] *s* (*pl* -**ries**) dépôt *m*; (*person*) dépositaire *mf*

depot [dipo], ['dɛpo] *s* dépôt *m*; (rr) gare *f*

depraved [dɪ'prevd] *adj* dépravé

depravi·ty [dɪ'prævɪti] *s* (*pl* -**ties**) dépravation *f*

deprecate ['dɛprɪ,ket] *tr* désapprouver

depreciate [dɪ'priʃɪ,et] *tr* déprécier || *intr* se déprécier

depreciation [dɪ,priʃɪ'eʃən] *s* dépréciation *f*

depredation [,dɛprɪ'deʃən] *s* déprédation *f*

depress [dɪ'prɛs] *tr* déprimer; (*prices*) abaisser

depressing [dɪ'prɛsɪŋ] *adj* attristant

depression [dɪ'prɛʃən] *s* dépression *f*

deprive [dɪ'praɪv] *tr* priver

depth [dɛpθ] *s* profondeur *f*; (*in sound*) gravité *f*; **depths** abîme *m*; **in the depth of winter** en plein hiver; **to go beyond one's depth** perdre pied; sortir de sa compétence

depth' bomb' *s* bombe *f* sous-marine

depth' charge' *s* grenade *f* sous-marine

deputation [,dɛpjə'teʃən] *s* députation *f*

deputize ['dɛpjə,taɪz] *tr* députer

depu·ty ['dɛpjəti] *s* (*pl* -**ties**) député *m*

derail [dɪ'rel] *tr* faire dérailler || *intr* dérailler

derailment [dɪ'relmənt] *s* déraillement *m*

derange [dɪ'rendʒ] *tr* déranger

derangement [dɪ'rendʒmənt] *s* dérangement *m*; (*of mind*) aliénation *f*

der·by ['dɑrbi] *s* (*pl* -**bies**) (*race*) derby *m*; (*hat*) chapeau *m* melon

derelict ['dɛrɪlɪkt] *adj* abandonné, délaissé; (*in one's duty*) négligent || *s* épave *f*

dereliction [,dɛrɪ'lɪkʃən] *s* abandon *m*, renoncement *m*

deride [dɪ'raɪd] *tr* tourner en dérision, ridiculiser

derision [dɪ'rɪʒən] *s* dérision *f*

derisive [dɪ'raɪsɪv] *adj* dérisoire

derivation [,dɛrɪ've ʃən] *s* dérivation *f*

derivative [dɪ'rɪvətɪv] *adj* & *s* dérivé *m*

derive [dɪ'raɪv] *tr* & *intr* dériver

dermatology [,dʌrmə'tɑlədʒi] *s* dermatologie *f*

derogatory [dɪ'rɑgə,tori] *adj* péjoratif

derrick ['dɛrɪk] *s* grue *f*; (*for extracting oil*) derrick *m*

dervish ['dʌrvɪʃ] *s* derviche *m*

desalinization [di,sɛlɪnɪ'zeʃən] *s* dessalement *m*

desalt [di'sɔlt] *tr* dessaler

descend [dɪ'sɛnd] *tr* descendre || *intr* descendre; (*said of rain*) tomber; **to be descended from** descendre de; **to descend on** s'abattre sur

descendant [dɪ'sɛndənt] *adj* & *s* descendant *m*

descendent [dɪ'sɛndənt] *adj* descendant

descent [dɪ'sɛnt] *s* descente *f*; (*drop in temperature*) chute *f*; (*lineage*) descendance *f*, naissance *f*

describe [dɪ'skraɪb] *tr* décrire

description [dɪ'skrɪpʃən] *s* description *f*

descriptive [dɪ'skrɪptɪv] *adj* descriptif

de·scry [dɪ'skraɪ] *v* (*pret* & *pp* -**scried**) *tr* découvrir, apercevoir

desecrate ['dɛsɪ,kret] *tr* profaner

desegregate [di'sɛgrɪ,get] *intr* supprimer la ségrégation raciale

desegregation [di,sɛgrɪ'geʃən] *s* déségrégation *f*

desensitize [di'sɛnsɪ,taɪz] *tr* désensibiliser

desert ['dɛzərt] *adj & s* désert *m* ‖ [dɪ'zʌrt] *s* mérite *m*; **to get one's just deserts** recevoir son salaire, recevoir sa juste punition ‖ *tr & intr* déserter

deserted *adj* (*person*) abandonné; (*place*) désert, nu

deserter [dɪ'zʌrtər] *s* déserteur *m*

desertion [dɪ'zʌr/ən] *s* désertion *f*

deserve [dɪ'zʌrv] *tr & intr* mériter

deservedly [dɪ'zʌrvɪdli] *adv* à juste titre, dignement

deserving [dɪ'zʌrvɪŋ] *adj* méritoire, digne

design [dɪ'zaɪn] *s* (*combination of details; art of designing; work of art*) dessin *m*; (*plan, scheme*) dessein *m*, projet *m*, plan *m*; (*model, outline*) modèle *m*, type *m*, grandes lignes *fpl*; **to have designs on** avoir des desseins sur ‖ *tr* inventer, projeter; (*e.g., a dress*) dessiner; (*a secret plan*) combiner; **designed for** destiné à

designate ['dɛzɪg‚net] *tr* désigner

designer [dɪ'zaɪnər] *s* dessinateur *m*

designing [dɪ'zaɪnɪŋ] *adj* artificieux, intrigant ‖ *s* dessin *m*

desirable [dɪ'zaɪrəbəl] *adj* désirable

desire [dɪ'zaɪr] *s* désir *m* ‖ *tr* désirer

desirous [dɪ'zaɪrəs] *adj* désireux

desist [dɪ'zɪst] *intr* cesser

desk [dɛsk] *s* bureau *m*; (*in schoolroom*) pupitre *m*; (*of cashier*) caisse *f*

desk' blot'ter *s* sous-main *m*

desk' clerk' *s* réceptionnaire *mf*

desk' set' *s* écritoire *f*

desolate ['dɛsəlɪt] *adj* désert; (*sad*) désolé; (*alone*) abandonné ‖ ['dɛsə‚let] *tr* désoler

desolation [‚dɛsə'le/ən] *s* désolation *f*

despair [dɪ'spɛr] *s* désespoir *m*, désespérance *f* ‖ *intr* désespérer

despairing [dɪ'spɛrɪŋ] *adj* désespéré

despera·do [‚dɛspə'redo], [‚dɛspə'rado] *s* (*pl* -**does** or -**dos**) hors-la-loi *m*

desperate ['dɛspərɪt] *adj* capable de tout, poussé à bout; (*bitter, excessive*) acharné, à outrance; (*hopeless*) désespéré; (*remedy*) héroïque

desperation [‚dɛspə're/ən] *s* désespoir *m*; (*recklessness*) témérité *f*

despicable ['dɛspɪkəbəl] *adj* méprisable, mesquin

despise [dɪ'spaɪz] *tr* mépriser, dédaigner

despite [dɪ'spaɪt] *prep* en dépit de, malgré

despoil [dɪ'spɔɪl] *tr* dépouiller

desponden·cy [dɪ'spɑndənsi] *s* (*pl* -**cies**) abattement *m*, accablement *m*

despondent [dɪ'spɑndənt] *adj* abattu, accablé, déprimé

despot ['dɛspɑt] *s* despote *m*, tyran *m*

despotic [dɛs'pɑtɪk] *adj* despotique

despotism ['dɛspə‚tɪzəm] *s* despotisme *m*

dessert [dɪ'zʌrt] *s* dessert *m*

dessert' spoon' *s* cuiller *f* à dessert

destination [‚dɛstɪ'ne/ən] *s* destination *f*

destine ['dɛstɪn] *tr* destiner

desti·ny ['dɛstɪni] *s* (*pl* -**nies**) destin *m*, destinée *f*

destitute ['dɛstɪ‚t(j)ut] *adj* indigent; dépourvu

destitution [‚dɛstɪ't(j)u/ən] *s* dénuement *m*, indigence *f*

destroy [dɪ'strɔɪ] *tr* détruire

destroyer [dɪ'strɔɪ·ər] *s* destructeur *m*; (nav) destroyer *m*

destruction [dɪ'strʌk/ən] *s* destruction *f*

destructive [dɪ'strʌktɪv] *adj* destructeur, destructif

desultory ['dɛsəl‚tori] *adj* décousu, sans suite; (*conversation*) à bâtons rompus

detach [dɪ'tæt/] *tr* détacher

detachable [dɪ'tæt/əbəl] *adj* détachable, démontable; (*collar*) faux

detached [dɪ'tæt/] *adj* détaché

detachment [dɪ'tæt/mənt] *s* détachement *m*

detail [dɪ'tel], ['ditel] *s* détail *m*; (mil) extrait *m* de l'ordre du jour; (mil) détachement *m* ‖ [dɪ'tel] *tr* détailler

detailed' state'ment *s* bordereau *m*

detain [dɪ'ten] *tr* retenir, retarder; (*in prison*) détenir

detect [dɪ'tɛkt] *tr* déceler, détecter

detection [dɪ'tɛk/ən] *s* détection *f*

detective [dɪ'tɛktɪv] *adj* (*device*) détecteur; (*film, novel*) policier ‖ *s* détective *m*, agent *m* de la sûreté

detec'tive sto'ry *s* roman *m* policier

detector [dɪ'tɛktər] *s* détecteur *m*

detention [dɪ'tɛn/ən] *s* détention *f*

de·ter [dɪ'tʌr] *v* (*pret* & *pp* -**terred**; *ger* -**terring**) *tr* détourner

detergent [dɪ'tʌrdʒənt] *adj & s* détersif *m*

deteriorate [dɪ'tɪrɪ·ə‚ret] *tr* détériorer ‖ *intr* se détériorer

determination [dɪ‚tʌrmɪ'ne/ən] *s* détermination *f*

determine [dɪ'tʌrmɪn] *tr* déterminer

determined *adj* déterminé, résolu

deterrent [dɪ'tʌrənt] *adj & s* préventif *m*

detest [dɪ'tɛst] *tr* détester

dethrone [dɪ'θron] *tr* détrôner

detonate ['dɛtə‚net], ['ditə‚net] *tr* faire détoner, faire éclater ‖ *intr* détoner

detour ['ditur], [dɪ'tur] *s* déviation *f*; (*indirect manner*) détour *m* ‖ *tr & intr* dévier

detract [dɪ'trækt] *tr* diminuer ‖ *intr*— **to detract from** amoindrir

detractor [dɪ'træktər] *s* détracteur *m*

detriment ['dɛtrɪmənt] *s* détriment *m*

detrimental [‚dɛtrɪ'mɛntəl] *adj* préjudiciable, nuisible

deuce [d(j)us] *s* deux *m*; **what the deuce!** (coll) diantre!, que diable!

devaluate [di'vælju‚et] *tr* dévaluer

devaluation [di‚vælju'e/ən] *s* dévaluation *f*

devastate ['dɛvəs‚tet] *tr* dévaster

devastating ['dɛvəs‚tetɪŋ] *adj* dévastateur; (coll) écrasant, accablant

devastation [‚dɛvəs'te/ən] *s* dévastation *f*

develop [dɪ'vɛləp] *tr* développer; (*a mine*) exploiter; (*e.g., a fever*) contracter; (phot) révéler, développer ‖ *intr* se développer; (*to become evident*) se produire, se manifester

developer [dɪ'veləpər] *s* entrepreneur *m*; (*builder*) maître *m* d'œuvre; (phot) révélateur *m*

development [dɪ'veləpmənt] *s* développement *m*; (*event*) événement *m* récent; (*of housing*) cité *f*, grand ensemble *m*

deviate ['divɪˌet] *s* perverti *m* ‖ *tr* faire dévier ‖ *intr* dévier

deviation [ˌdivɪ'eʃən] *s* déviation *f*

device [dɪ'vaɪs] *s* appareil *m*, dispositif *m*; (*trick*) stratagème *m*, ruse *f*; (*motto*) emblème *m*, devise *f*; **to leave s.o. to his own devices** abandonner qn à ses propres moyens

dev·il ['devəl] *s* diable *m*; **speak of the devil!** (coll) je vois un loup!; **to be between the devil and the deep blue sea** (coll) se trouver entre l'enclume et le marteau; **to raise the devil** (slang) faire le diable à quatre ‖ *v* (*pret & pp* -iled *or* -illed; *ger* -iling *or* -illing) *tr* épicer fortement; (coll) tourmenter

devilish ['devəlɪʃ] *adj* diabolique; (*roguish*) coquin

dev·il-may-care' *adj* insouciant, étourdi

devilment ['devəlmənt] *s* (*mischief*) diablerie *f*; (*evil*) méchanceté *f*

devil·try ['devəltri] *s* (*pl* -tries) méchanceté *f*, cruauté *f*; (*mischief*) espièglerie *f*

devious ['divɪ·əs] *adj* (*straying*) détourné, dévié; (*roundabout; shifty*) tortueux

devise [dɪ'vaɪz] *tr* combiner, inventer; (law) léguer

devoid [dɪ'vɔɪd] *adj* dépourvu, vide, dénué

devolve [dɪ'vɑlv] *intr*—**to devolve on, to,** *or* **upon** échoir à

devote [dɪ'vot] *tr* consacrer

devoted *adj* dévoué; **devoted to** voué à, dévoué à, attaché à

devotee [ˌdevə'ti] *s* dévot *m*, adepte *mf*; (sports) fervent *m*, fanatique *mf*

devotion [dɪ'voʃən] *s* dévotion *f*; (*to study, work, etc.*) dévouement *m*; **devotions** dévotions, prières *fpl*

devour [dɪ'vaur] *tr* dévorer

devout [dɪ'vaut] *adj* dévot, pieux

dew [d(j)u] *s* rosée *f*

dew'drop' *s* goutte *f* de rosée

dew'lap' *s* fanon *m*, double menton *m*

dew·y ['d(j)u·i] *adj* (*comp* -ier; *super* -iest) couvert de rosée

dexterity [deks'terɪti] *s* dextérité *f*, adresse *f*

diabetes [ˌdaɪ·ə'bitis], [ˌdaɪ·ə'bitiz] *s* diabète *m*

diabetic [ˌdaɪ·ə'betɪk], [ˌdaɪ·ə'bitɪk] *adj & s* diabétique *mf*

diabolic(al) [ˌdaɪ·ə'bɑlɪk(əl)] *adj* diabolique

diacritical [ˌdaɪ·ə'krɪtɪkəl] *adj* diacritique

diadem ['daɪ·əˌdem] *s* diadème *m*

diaeresis [daɪ'erɪsɪs] *s* (*pl* -ses [ˌsiz]) diérèse *f*; (*mark*) tréma *m*

diagnose [ˌdaɪ·əg'nos], [ˌdaɪ·əg'noz] *tr* diagnostiquer

diagno·sis [ˌdaɪ·əg'nosɪs] *s* (*pl* -ses [siz]) diagnostic *m*

diagonal [daɪ'ægənəl] *adj* diagonal ‖ *s* diagonale *f*

dia·gram ['daɪ·əˌgræm] *s* diagramme *m*, croquis *m* coté *m* ‖ *v* (*pret & pp* -gramed *or* -grammed; *ger* -graming *or* -gramming) *tr* représenter schématiquement

di·al ['daɪ·əl], [daɪl] *s* cadran *m* ‖ *v* (*pret & pp* -aled *or* -alled; *ger* -aling *or* -alling) *tr* (*a telephone number*) composer ‖ *intr* faire un numéro

dialect ['daɪ·əˌlekt] *s* dialecte *m*

dialing ['daɪ·əlɪŋ] *s* (telp) composition *f* du numéro

dialogue ['daɪ·əˌlog], ['daɪ·əˌlɑg] *s* dialogue *m*

di'al tel'ephone *s* téléphone *m* automatique, automatique *m*

di'al tone' *s* (telp) tonalité *f*

diameter [daɪ'æmɪtər] *s* diamètre *m*

diametric(al) [ˌdaɪ·ə'metrɪk(əl)] *adj* diamétral

diamond ['daɪmənd] *s* diamant *m*; (*figure of a rhombus*) losange *m*; (baseball) petit champ *m*; (cards) carreau *m*

diaper ['daɪ·əpər] *s* lange *m*, couche *f* ‖ *tr* (*to variegate*) diaprer

diaphanous [daɪ'æfənəs] *adj* diaphane

diaphragm ['daɪ·əˌfræm] *s* diaphragme *m*

diarrhea [ˌdaɪ·ə'ri·ə] *s* diarrhée *f*

dia·ry ['daɪ·əri] *s* (*pl* -ries) journal *m*

diastole [daɪ'æstəli] *s* diastole *f*

diathermy ['daɪ·əˌθɜrmi] *s* diathermie *f*

diatribe ['daɪ·əˌtraɪb] *s* diatribe *f*

dice [daɪs] *spl* dés *mpl*; **no dice!** (slang) pas moyen!; **to load the dice** piper les dés ‖ *tr* couper en cubes

dice'box' *s* cornet *m* à dés

dichoto·my [daɪ'kɑtəmi] *s* (*pl* -mies) dichotomie *f*

dictaphone ['dɪktəˌfon] *s* (trademark) dictaphone *m*

dictate ['dɪktet] *s* précepte *m*, règle *f* ‖ *tr & intr* dicter

dictation [dɪk'teʃən] *s* dictée *f*; **to take dictation from** écrire sous la dictée de

dictator ['dɪktetər], [dɪk'tetər] *s* dictateur *m*

dic'tator·ship' *s* dictature *f*

diction ['dɪkʃən] *s* diction *f*

dictionar·y ['dɪkʃənˌeri] *s* (*pl* -ies) dictionnaire *m*

dic·tum ['dɪktəm] *s* (*pl* -ta [tə]) dicton *m*; (law) opinion *f*, arrêt *m*

didactic(al) [daɪ'dæktɪk(əl)], [dɪ'dæktɪk(əl)] *adj* didactique

die [daɪ] *s* (*pl* dice [daɪs]) dé *m*; **the die is cast** le dé en est jeté ‖ *s* (*pl* dies) (*for stamping coins, medals, etc.*) coin *m*; (*for cutting threads*) filière *f*; (*key pattern*) jeu *m* ‖ *v* (*pret & pp* died; *ger* dying) *intr* mourir; **to be dying** se mourir; **to be dying to** (coll) mourir d'envie de; **to die away**

s'éteindre; **to die laughing** (coll) mourir de rire

die'hard' adj intransigeant ‖ s intransigeant m, jusqu'au-boutiste mf

die'sel en'gine ['dizəl] s diesel m, moteur m diesel

die'sel oil' s gas-oil m

die'stock' s porte-filière m

diet ['daɪ·ət] s nourriture f; (congress; abstention from food) diète f; (special menu) régime m ‖ intr être or se mettre au régime, suivre un régime

dietetic [,daɪ·ə'tɛtɪk] adj diététique ‖ **dietetics** s diététique f

dietician [,daɪ·ə'tɪʃən] s diététicien m

differ ['dɪfər] intr différer; **to differ with** être en désaccord avec

difference ['dɪfərəns] s différence f; (controversy) différend m; **to make no difference** ne rien faire; **to split the difference** partager le différend

different ['dɪfərənt] adj différent

differential [,dɪfə'rɛnʃəl] adj différentiel ‖ s (mach) différentiel m; (math) différentielle f

differentiate [,dɪfə'rɛnʃɪ,et] tr différencier ‖ intr se différencier

difficult ['dɪfɪ,kʌlt] adj difficile

difficul·ty ['dɪfɪ,kʌltɪ] s (pl -ties) difficulté f

diffident ['dɪfɪdənt] adj défiant, timide

diffuse [dɪ'fjus] adj diffus ‖ [dɪ'fjuz] tr diffuser ‖ intr se diffuser

dig [dɪg] s—**to give s.o. a dig** (coll) lancer un trait à qn ‖ v (pret & pp **dug** [dʌg]; ger **digging**) tr bêcher, creuser; **to dig up** déterrer ‖ intr bêcher

digest ['daɪdʒɛst] s abrégé m, résumé m; (publication) digest m, sélection f; (law) digeste m ‖ [dɪ'dʒɛst], [daɪ'dʒɛst] tr & intr digérer

digestible [dɪ'dʒɛstɪbəl], [daɪ'dʒɛstɪbəl] adj digestible

digestion [dɪ'dʒɛstʃən], [daɪ'dʒɛstʃən] s digestion f

digestive [dɪ'dʒɛstɪv], [daɪ'dʒɛstɪv] adj digestif

diges'tive tract' s appareil m digestif

digit ['dɪdʒɪt] s chiffre m; (finger) doigt m; (toe) doigt du pied

digitalis [,dɪdʒɪ'telɪs], [,dɪdʒɪ'tɛlɪs] s (bot) digitale f; (pharm) digitaline f

dignified adj distingué; (air) digne

digni·fy ['dɪgnɪ,faɪ] v (pret & pp -fied) tr glorifier, honorer

dignitar·y ['dɪgnɪ,tɛri] s (pl -ies) dignitaire m

digni·ty ['dɪgnɪtɪ] s (pl -ties) dignité f; **to stand on one's dignity** rester sur son quant-à-soi, le prendre de haut

digress [dɪ'grɛs], [daɪ'grɛs] intr faire une digression

digression [dɪ'grɛʃən], [daɪ'grɛʃən] s digression f

dihedral [daɪ'hidrəl] adj & s dièdre m

dike [daɪk] s digue f

dilapidated [dɪ'læpɪ,detɪd] adj délabré, déglingué

dilate [daɪ'let] tr dilater ‖ intr se dilater

dilatory ['dɪlə,tori] adj lent, tardif; (strategy, answer) dilatoire

dilemma [dɪ'lɛmə] s dilemme m

dilettan·te [,dɪlə'tænti] adj dilettante ‖ s (pl -tes or -ti [ti]) dilettante mf

diligence ['dɪlɪdʒəns] s diligence f

diligent ['dɪlɪdʒənt] adj diligent

dill [dɪl] s fenouil m bâtard, aneth m

dillydal·ly ['dɪlɪ,dælɪ] v (pret & pp -lied) intr traînasser

dilute [dɪ'lut], [daɪ'lut] adj dilué ‖ [dɪ'lut] tr diluer, délayer

dilution [dɪ'luʃən] s dilution f

dim [dɪm] adj faible, indistinct; (forebodings) obscur; (memory) effacé; (color) terne; (idea of what is going on) obtus, confus; **to take a dim view of** envisager sans enthousiasme ‖ v (pret & pp **dimmed**; ger **dimming**) tr affaiblir, obscurcir; (beauty) ternir; (the headlights) baisser, mettre en code ‖ intr s'affaiblir, s'obscurcir; (said of color, beauty, etc.) se ternir

dime [daɪm] s monnaie f de dix cents américains

dimension [dɪ'mɛnʃən] s dimension f

diminish [dɪ'mɪnɪʃ] tr & intr diminuer

diminutive [dɪ'mɪnjətɪv] adj & s diminutif m

dimi·ty ['dɪmɪtɪ] s (pl -ties) basin m, brillanté m

dimly ['dɪmlɪ] adv indistinctement

dimmers ['dɪmərz] spl (aut) feux mpl code, feux de croisement; **to put on the dimmers** se mettre en code

dimple ['dɪmpəl] s fossette f

dim'wit' s (slang) sot m, niais m

din [dɪn] s tapage m, fracas m ‖ v (pret & pp **dinned**; ger **dinning**) tr assourdir; répéter sans cesse ‖ intr sonner bruyamment

dine [daɪn] s fêter par un dîner ‖ intr dîner; **to dine out** dîner en ville

diner ['daɪnər] s dîneur m; (short-order restaurant) plats-cuisinés m; (rr) wagon-restaurant m

dinette [daɪ'nɛt] s coin-repas m

ding-dong ['dɪŋ,dɔŋ], ['dɪŋ,dɑŋ] s tintement m, digue-din-don m

din·ghy ['dɪŋgi] s (pl -ghies) canot m, youyou m

din·gy ['dɪndʒi] adj (comp -gier; super -giest) défraîchi, terne

din'ing car' s wagon-restaurant m

din'ing hall' s salle f à manger; (of university) réfectoire m

din'ing room' s salle f à manger

din'ing-room suite' s salle f à manger

dinner ['dɪnər] s dîner m

din'ner coat' s smoking m

din'ner dance' s dîner m suivi de bal

din'ner guest' s convive mf, invité m

din'ner jack'et s smoking m

din'ner pail' s potager m

din'ner set' s service m de table

din'ner time' s heure f du dîner

dinosaur ['daɪnə,sɔr] s dinosaure m

dint [dɪnt] s—**by dint of** à force de

diocese ['daɪ·ə,sis], ['daɪ·əsɪs] s diocèse m

diode ['daɪ·od] s diode f

dioxide [daɪ'ɑksaɪd] s bioxyde m

dip [dɪp] *s* (*immersion*) plongeon *m*; (*swim*) baignade *f*; (*slope*) pente *f*; (*of magnetic needle*) inclinaison *f* ‖ *v* (*pret* & *pp* **dipped**; *ger* **dipping**) *tr* plonger; (*a flag*) marquer ‖ *intr* plonger; (*said of magnetic needle*) incliner; (*said of scale*) pencher; **to dip into** (*a book*) feuilleter; (*one's capital*) prendre dans

diphtheria [dɪf'θɪrɪ·ə] *s* diphtérie *f*

diphthong ['dɪfθɔŋ], ['dɪfθaŋ] *s* diphtongue *f*

diphthongize ['dɪfθɔŋ ,gaɪz], ['dɪfθaŋ ,gaɪz] *tr* diphtonguer ‖ *intr* se diphtonguer

diploma [dɪ'plomə] *s* diplôme *m*

diploma·cy [dɪ'ploməsi] *s* (*pl* -**cies**) diplomatie *f*

diplomat ['dɪplə ,mæt] *s* diplomate *mf*

diplomatic [,dɪplə'mætɪk] *adj* diplomatique, diplomate

dip'lomat'ic pouch' *s* valise *f* diplomatique

dipper ['dɪpər] *s* louche *f*, cuiller *f* à pot

dip'stick' *s* jauge *f*

dire [daɪr] *adj* affreux, terrible

direct [dɪ'rɛkt], [daɪ'rɛkt] *adj* direct; franc, sincère ‖ *tr* diriger; (*to order*) ordonner; (*a letter, question, etc.*) adresser; (*to point out*) indiquer; (*theat*) mettre en scène

direct' cur'rent *s* courant *m* continu

direct' di'aling (*telp*) automatique *m* interurbain

direct' hit' *s* coup *m* or tir *m* direct

direction [dɪ'rɛkʃən], [daɪ'rɛkʃən] *s* direction *f*; (*e.g., of a street*) sens *m*; (*theat*) mise *f* en scène; **directions** instructions *fpl*; (*for use*) mode *m* d'emploi

directional [dɪ'rɛkʃənəl], [daɪ'rɛkʃənəl] *adj* directionnel

direc'tional sig'nal *s* clignotant *m*

directive [dɪ'rɛktɪv], [daɪ'rɛktɪv] *s* ordre *m*, avis *m*

direct' ob'ject *s* (*gram*) complément *m* direct

director [dɪ'rɛktər], [daɪ'rɛktər] *s* directeur *m*, administrateur *m*, chef *m*; (*of a board*) membre *m* du conseil, votant *m*; (*theat*) metteur en scène

direc'tor·ship' *s* direction *f*, directorat *m*

directo·ry [dɪ'rɛktəri], [daɪ'rɛktəri] *s* (*pl* -**ries**) (*board of directors*) conseil *m* d'administration; (*e.g., of telephone*) annuaire *m*; (*e.g., of genealogy*) almanach *m*; (*eccl*) directoire *m*

dirge [dʌrdʒ] *s* hymne *f* or chant *m* funèbre

dirigible ['dɪrɪdʒɪbəl] *adj* & *s* dirigeable *m*

dirt [dʌrt] *s* saleté *f*, ordure *f*; (*on clothes, skin, etc.*) crasse *f*; (*mire*) crotte *f*, boue *f*; (*earth*) terre *f*

dirt'-cheap' *adj* vendu à vil prix

dirt' road' *s* chemin *m* de terre

dirt·y ['dʌrti] *adj* (*comp* -**ier**; *super* -**lest**) sale, malpropre; (*clothes, skin, etc.*) crasseux; (*muddy*) crotté, boueux; (*mean*) méchant, vilain

dir'ty lin'en *s* linge *m* sale; **don't wash your dirty linen in public** il faut laver son linge sale en famille

dir'ty trick' *s* (*slang*) sale tour *m*

disabili·ty [,dɪsə'bɪlɪti] *s* (*pl* -**ties**) incapacité *f*, invalidité *f*

disabil'ity pen'sion *s* pension *f* d'invalidité

disable [dɪs'ebəl] *tr* rendre incapable, mettre hors de combat; (*to hurt the limbs of*) estropier, mutiler

disabled *adj* (*serviceman*) invalide; (*ship*) désemparé

disa'bled vet'eran *s* invalide *m*, réformé *m*

disabuse [,dɪsə'bjuz] *tr* désabuser

disadvantage [,dɪsəd'væntɪdʒ], [,dɪsəd'vantɪdʒ] *s* désavantage *m* ‖ *tr* désavantager

disadvantageous [dɪs ,ædvən'tedʒəs] *adj* désavantageux

disagree [,dɪsə'gri] *intr* différer; **to disagree with** (*to cause discomfort to*) ne pas convenir à; (*to dissent from*) donner tort à

disagreeable [,dɪsə'gri·əbəl] *adj* désagréable; (*mood, weather, etc.*) maussade

disagreement [,dɪsə'grimənt] *s* désaccord *m*, différend *m*

disallow [,dɪsə'lau] *tr* désapprouver, rejeter

disappear [,dɪsə'pɪr] *intr* disparaître; (*phonet*) s'amuïr

disappearance [,dɪsə'pɪrəns] *s* disparition *f*; (*phonet*) amuïssement *m*

disappoint [,dɪsə'pɔɪnt] *tr* décevoir, désappointer

disappointed *adj* déçu

disappointment [,dɪsə'pɔɪntmənt] *s* déception *f*, désappointement *m*

disapproval [,dɪsə'pruvəl] *s* désapprobation *f*

disapprove [,dɪsə'pruv] *tr* & *intr* désapprouver

disarm [dɪs'arm] *tr* & *intr* désarmer

disarmament [dɪs'arməmənt] *s* désarmement *m*

disarming [dɪs'armɪŋ] *adj* désarmant

disarray [,dɪsə're] *s* désarroi *m*, désordre *m*; **in disarray** (*said of apparel*) à demi vêtu ‖ *tr* mettre en désarroi

disassemble [,dɪsə'sɛmbəl] *tr* démonter, désassembler

disassociate [,dɪsə'soʃɪ ,et] *tr* dissocier

disaster [dɪ'zæstər], [dɪ'zastər] *s* désastre *m*

disastrous [dɪ'zæstrəs], [dɪ'zastrəs] *adj* désastreux

disavow [,dɪsə'vau] *tr* désavouer

disavowal [,dɪsə'vau·əl] *s* désaveu *m*

disband [dɪs'bænd] *tr* licencier, congédier ‖ *intr* se débander, se disperser

dis·bar [dɪs'bar] *v* (*pret* & *pp* -**barred**; *ger* -**barring**) *tr* (*law*) rayer du barreau

disbelief [,dɪsbɪ'lif] *s* incroyance *f*

disbelieve [,dɪsbɪ'liv] *tr* & *intr* ne pas croire

disburse [dɪs'bʌrs] *tr* débourser

disbursement [dɪs'bʌrsmənt] *s* déboursement *m*; **disbursements** débours *mpl*

disc [dɪsk] *s* disque *m*

discard [dɪs'kɑrd] *s* rebut *m*; (cards) écart *m*; **discards** marchandises *fpl* de rebut ‖ *tr* mettre de côté, jeter; (cards) écarter ‖ *intr* (cards) se défausser

discern [dɪ'zʌrn], [dɪ'sʌrn] *tr* discerner, percevoir

discernible [dɪ'zʌrnɪbəl], [dɪ'sʌrnɪbəl] *adj* discernable

discerning [dɪ'zʌrnɪŋ], [dɪ'sʌrnɪŋ] *adj* judicieux, pénétrant, éclairé

discernment [dɪ'zʌrnmənt], [dɪ'sʌrnmənt] *s* discernement *m*

discharge [dɪs'tʃɑrdʒ] *s* décharge *f*; (of a prisoner) élargissement *m*; (from a job) congé *m*, renvoi *m*; (from the armed forces) libération *f*; (from the armed forces for unfitness) réforme *f*; (from a wound) suppuration *f* ‖ *tr* décharger; (a prisoner) élargir; (an employee) congédier, renvoyer, licencier; (a soldier) libérer, réformer ‖ *intr* se décharger; (pathol) suppurer

disciple [dɪ'saɪpəl] *s* disciple *m*

disciplinarian [,dɪsɪplɪ'nɛrɪ·ən] *s* partisan *m* d'une forte discipline; personne *f* qui impose une forte discipline

disciplinary ['dɪsɪplɪ,nɛri] *adj* disciplinaire

discipline ['dɪsɪplɪn] *s* discipline *f* ‖ *tr* discipliner

disclaim [dɪs'klem] *tr* désavouer, renier

disclaimer [dɪs'klemər] *s* désaveu *m*

disclose [dɪs'kloz] *tr* découvrir, révéler

disclosure [dɪs'kloʒər] *s* découverte *f*, révélation *f*

discolor [dɪs'kʌlər] *tr* décolorer ‖ *intr* se décolorer

discoloration [dɪs,kʌlə'reʃən] *s* décoloration *f*

discomfit [dɪs'kʌmfɪt] *tr* décontenancer, bafouer

discomfiture [dɪs'kʌmfɪtʃər] *s* déconfiture *f*, déconvenue *f*

discomfort [dɪs'kʌmfərt] *s* malaise *f*; (inconvenience) gêne *f* ‖ *tr* gêner

disconcert [,dɪskən'sʌrt] *tr* déconcerter

disconnect [,dɪskə'nɛkt] *tr* désunir, séparer; (a mechanism) débrayer; (a plug) débrancher; (current) couper

disconsolate [dɪs'kɑnsəlɪt] *adj* désolé, inconsolable

discontent [,dɪskən'tɛnt] *adj* mécontent ‖ *s* mécontentement *m* ‖ *tr* mécontenter

discontented *adj* mécontent

discontinue [,dɪskən'tɪnju] *tr* discontinuer

discontinuous [,dɪskən'tɪnju·əs] *adj* discontinu

discord ['dɪskɔrd] *s* discorde *f*, désaccord *m*; (mus) discordance *f*

discordance [dɪs'kɔrdəns] *s* discordance *f*

discotheque ['dɪskə,tɛk] *s* discothéque *m*

discount ['dɪskaunt] *s* escompte *m*, remise *f*, rabais *m* ‖ ['dɪskaunt], [dɪs'kaunt] *tr* escompter, rabattre

dis'count rate' *s* taux *m* d'escompte

discourage [dɪs'kʌrɪdʒ] *tr* décourager

discouragement [dɪs'kʌrɪdʒmənt] *s* découragement *m*

discourse ['dɪskɔrs], [dɪs'kɔrs] *s* discours *m* ‖ [dɪs'kɔrs] *intr* discourir

discourteous [dɪs'kʌrtɪ·əs] *adj* impoli, discourtois

discourte·sy [dɪs'kʌrtəsi] *s* (*pl* -sies) impolitesse *f*, discourtoisie *f*

discover [dɪs'kʌvər] *tr* découvrir

discoverer [dɪs'kʌvərər] *s* découvreur *m*

discover·y [dɪs'kʌvəri] *s* (*pl* -ies) découverte *f*

discredit [dɪs'krɛdɪt] *s* discrédit *m* ‖ *tr* discréditer

discreditable [dɪs'krɛdɪtəbəl] *adj* déshonorant, peu honorable

discreet [dɪs'krit] *adj* discret

discrepan·cy [dɪs'krepənsi] *s* (*pl* -cies) désaccord *m*, différence *f*

discretion [dɪs'kreʃən] *s* discrétion *f*

discriminate [dɪs'krɪmɪ,net] *tr & intr* discriminer; **to discriminate against** défavoriser

discrimination [dɪs,krɪmɪ'neʃən] *s* discrimination *f*

discriminatory [dɪs'krɪmɪnə,tori] *adj* discriminatoire

discus ['dɪskəs] *s* (sports) disque *m*, palet *m*

discuss [dɪs'kʌs] *tr & intr* discuter

discussion [dɪs'kʌʃən] *s* discussion *f*

disdain [dɪs'den] *s* dédain *m* ‖ *tr* dédaigner

disdainful [dɪs'denfəl] *adj* dédaigneux

disease [dɪ'ziz] *s* maladie *f*

diseased *adj* malade

disembark [,dɪsɛm'bɑrk] *tr & intr* débarquer

disembarkation [dɪs,ɛmbɑr'keʃən] *s* débarquement *m*

disembow·el [,dɪsɛm'bau·əl] *v* (*pret & pp* -eled or -elled; *ger* -eling or -elling) *tr* éventrer

disenchant [,dɪsɛn'tʃænt], [,dɪsɛn'tʃɑnt] *tr* désenchanter

disenchantment [,dɪsɛn'tʃæntmənt], [,dɪsɛn'tʃɑntmənt] *s* désenchantement *m*

disengage [,dɪsɛn'gedʒ] *tr* dégager; (toothed wheels) désengrener; (a motor) débrayer ‖ *intr* se dégager

disengagement [,dɪsɛn'gedʒmənt] *s* dégagement *m*, détachement *m*

disentangle [,dɪsɛn'tæŋgəl] *tr* démêler, débrouiller

disentanglement [,dɪsɛn'tæŋgəlmənt] *s* démêlage *m*, débrouillement *m*

disestablish [,dɪsɛs'tæblɪʃ] *tr* (the Church) séparer de l'État

disfavor [dɪs'fevər] *s* défaveur *f* ‖ *tr* défavoriser

disfigure [dɪs'fɪgjər] *tr* défigurer, enlaidir

disfigurement [dɪs'fɪgjərmənt] *s* défiguration *f*

disfranchise [dɪs'fræntʃaɪz] *tr* priver de ses droits civiques

disgorge [dɪs'gɔrdʒ] *tr & intr* dégorger

disgrace [dɪs'gres] *s* déshonneur *m* || *tr* déshonorer; (*to deprive of favor*) disgracier; **to disgrace oneself** se déshonorer

disgraceful [dɪs'gresfəl] *adj* déshonorant, honteux

disgruntled [dɪs'grʌntəld] *adj* contrarié, de mauvaise humeur

disguise [dɪs'gaɪz] *s* déguisement *m* || *tr* déguiser

disgust [dɪs'gʌst] *s* dégoût *m* || *tr* dégoûter

disgusting [dɪs'gʌstɪŋ] *adj* dégoûtant

dish [dɪʃ] *s* plat *m*; (*food*) mets *m*, plat; **to wash the dishes** faire la vaisselle || *tr*—**to dish up** servir

dish' clos'et *s* étagère *f* à vaisselle

dish'cloth' *s* lavette *f*

dishearten [dɪs'hartən] *tr* décourager

dishev-el [dɪ'ʃɛvəl] *v* (*pret & pp* **-eled** or **-elled**; *ger* **-eling** or **-elling**) *tr* écheveler

dishonest [dɪs'anɪst] *adj* malhonnête, déloyal

dishones-ty [dɪs'anɪsti] *s* (*pl* **-ties**) malhonnêteté *f*, déloyauté *f*, improbité *f*

dishonor [dɪs'anər] *s* déshonneur *m* || *tr* déshonorer

dishonorable [dɪs'anərəbəl] *adj* déshonorant

dish'pan' *s* bassine *f*

dish' rack' *s* égouttoir *m*

dish'rag' *s* lavette *f*

dish'tow'el *s* torchon *m*

dish'wash'er *s* machine *f* à laver la vaisselle, lave-vaisselles *f*; (*person*) plongeur *m*

dish'wa'ter *s* eau *f* de vaisselle

disillusion [,dɪsɪ'luʒən] *s* désillusion *f* || *tr* désillusionner

disillusionment [,dɪsɪ'luʒənmənt] *s* désillusionnement *m*

disinclination [dɪs,ɪnklɪ'neʃən] *s* répugnance *f*, aversion *f*

disinclined [,dɪsɪn'klaɪnd] *adj* indisposé

disinfect [,dɪsɪn'fɛkt] *tr* désinfecter

disinfectant [,dɪsɪn'fɛktənt] *adj & s* désinfectant *m*

disingenuous [,dɪsɪn'dʒɛnju·əs] *adj* insincère, sans franchise

disinherit [,dɪsɪn'hɛrɪt] *tr* déshériter

disintegrate [dɪs'ɪntɪ,gret] *tr* désagréger; (*nucl*) désintégrer || *intr* se désagréger; (*nucl*) se désintégrer

disintegration [dɪs,ɪntɪ'greʃən] *s* désagrégation *f*; (*nucl*) désintégration *f*

disin-ter [,dɪsɪn'tʌr] *v* (*pret & pp* **-terred**; *ger* **-terring**) *tr* déterrer

disinterested [dɪs'ɪntə,rɛstɪd], [dɪs'ɪntrɪstɪd] *adj* désintéressé

disjointed [dɪs'dʒɔɪntɪd] *adj* désarticulé; (*e.g., style*) décousu

disjunctive [dɪs'dʒʌŋktɪv] *adj* disjonctif; (*pronoun*) tonique

disk [dɪsk] *s* disque *m*

disk' jock'ey *s* présentateur *m* de disques

dislike [dɪs'laɪk] *s* aversion *f*; **to take a dislike for** prendre en aversion || *tr* ne pas aimer

dislocate ['dɪslo,ket] *tr* disloquer; (*a joint*) luxer

dislodge [dɪs'ladʒ] *tr* déplacer; (*e.g., the enemy*) déloger

disloyal [dɪs'lɔɪ·əl] *adj* déloyal

disloyal-ty [dɪs'lɔɪ·əlti] *s* (*pl* **-ties**) déloyauté *f*

dismal ['dɪzməl] *adj* sombre, triste

dismantle [dɪs'mæntəl] *tr* démanteler; (*a machine*) démonter; (*a ship*) désarmer

dismay [dɪs'me] *s* consternation *f* || *tr* consterner

dismember [dɪs'mɛmbər] *tr* démembrer

dismiss [dɪs'mɪs] *tr* congédier; (*a servant*) renvoyer; (*an employee*) licencier; (*a government official*) destituer; (*a class in school*) terminer

dismissal [dɪs'mɪsəl] *s* congédiement *m*; (*from a job*) congé *m*, renvoi *m*; (*of an appeal*) (*law*) rejet *m*

dismount [dɪs'maunt] *tr* démonter || *intr* descendre

disobedience [,dɪsə'bidɪ·əns] *s* désobéissance *f*

disobedient [,dɪsə'bidɪ·ənt] *adj* désobéissant

disobey [,dɪsə'be] *tr* désobéir (*with dat*); **to be disobeyed** être désobéi || *intr* désobéir

disorder [dɪs'ɔrdər] *s* désordre *m* || *tr* désordonner

disorderly [dɪs'ɔrdərli] *adj* désordonné, déréglé; (*crowd*) turbulent, effervescent

disor'derly con'duct *s* conduite *f* désordonnée

disor'derly house' *s* maison *f* de prostitution; maison de jeu

disorganize [dɪs'ɔrgə,naɪz] *tr* désorganiser

disoriented [dɪs'ɔrɪ,ɛntɪd] *adj* désorienté

disown [dɪs'on] *tr* désavouer, renier

disparage [dɪ'spærɪdʒ] *tr* dénigrer, déprécier

disparagement [dɪ'spærɪdʒmənt] *s* dénigrement *m*, dépréciation *f*

disparate ['dɪspærɪt] *adj* disparate

dispari-ty [dɪ'spærɪti] *s* (*pl* **-ties**) disparité *f*

dispassionate [dɪs'pæʃənɪt] *adj* calme; impartial

dispatch [dɪ'spætʃ] *s* dépêche *f*; (*shipment*) envoi *m*, expédition *f*; (*promptness*) promptitude *f* || *tr* dépêcher; (*coll*) expédier

dis-pel [dɪ'spɛl] *v* (*pret & pp* **-pelled**; *ger* **-pelling**) *tr* dissiper, disperser

dispensa-ry [dɪ'spɛnsəri] *s* (*pl* **-ries**) dispensaire *m*

dispensation *s* [,dɪspɛn'seʃən] (*dispensing*) dispensation *f*; (*exemption*) dispense *f*

dispense [dɪ'spɛns] *tr* dispenser, distribuer || *intr*—**to dispense with** se passer de; se défaire de

dispenser [dɪ'spɛnsər] *s* dispensateur *m*; (*automatic*) distributeur *m*

disperse [dɪ'spʌrs] tr disperser || intr se disperser

dispersion [dɪ'spʌrʒən], [dɪ'spʌrʃən] s dispersion f

dispirit [dɪ'spɪrɪt] tr décourager

displace [dɪs'ples] tr déplacer; (to take the place of) remplacer

displaced′ per′son s personne f déplacée

displacement [dɪs'plesmənt] s déplacement m; (substitution) remplacement m

display [dɪ'sple] s exposition f, étalage m; (of emotion) manifestation f || tr exposer, étaler; (anger, courage, etc.) manifester; (ignorance) révéler

display′ cab′inet s vitrine f

display′ win′dow s vitrine f, devanture f

displease [dɪs'pliz] tr déplaire (with dat)

displeasing [dɪs'plizɪŋ] adj déplaisant

displeasure [dɪs'plɛʒər] s déplaisir m, mécontentement m

disposable [dɪ'spozəbəl] adj (available) disponible; (made to be disposed of) à jeter; (container) perdu, e.g., **disposable bottle** verre perdu

disposal [dɪ'spozəl] s disposition f; (of a question) résolution f; (of trash, garbage, etc.) destruction f

dispose [dɪ'spoz] tr disposer || intr disposer; **to dispose of** disposer de; (to get rid of) se défaire de; (a question) résoudre, trancher

disposed adj—**to be disposed to** se disposer à, être porté à

disposition [,dɪspə'zɪʃən] s disposition f; (mental outlook) naturel m; (mil) dispositif m

dispossess [,dɪspə'zɛs] tr déposséder; expulser

disproof [dɪs'pruf] s réfutation f

disproportionate [,dɪsprə'porʃənɪt] adj disproportionné

disprove [dɪs'pruv] tr réfuter

dispute [dɪs'pjut] s dispute f; **beyond dispute** incontestable || tr disputer || intr se disputer

disqualify [dɪs'kwɑlɪ,faɪ] v (pret & pp -fied) tr disqualifier

disquiet [dɪs'kwaɪ·ət] s inquiétude f || tr inquiéter

disquisition [,dɪskwɪ'zɪʃən] s essai m, traité m considérable

disregard [,dɪsrɪ'gɑrd] s indifférence f; **disregard for** manque m d'égards envers || tr ne pas faire cas de, passer sous silence

disrepair [,dɪsrɪ'pɛr] s délabrement m

disreputable [dɪs'rɛpjətəbəl] adj déshonorant, suspect; (shabby) débraillé, râpé

disrepute [,dɪsrɪ'pjut] s discrédit m

disrespect [,dɪsrɪ'spɛkt] s irrévérence f; manque m de respect, irrespect m

disrespectful [,dɪsrɪ'spɛktfəl] adj irrévérencieux, irrespectueux; **to be disrespectful to** manquer de respect à

disrobe [dɪs'rob] tr déshabiller || intr se déshabiller

disrupt [dɪs'rʌpt] tr rompre; (to throw into disorder) bouleverser

disruption [dɪs'rʌpʃən] s rupture f; (disorganization) bouleversement m

dissatisfaction [,dɪssætɪs'fækʃən] s mécontentement m

dissatisfied adj mécontent

dissatisfy [dɪs'sætɪs,faɪ] v (pret & pp -fied) tr mécontenter

dissect [dɪ'sɛkt] tr disséquer

dissection [dɪ'sɛkʃən] s dissection f

dissemble [dɪ'sɛmbəl] tr & intr dissimuler

disseminate [dɪ'sɛmɪ,net] tr disséminer

dissension [dɪ'sɛnʃən] s dissension f

dissent [dɪ'sɛnt] s dissentiment m; (nonconformity) dissidence f || intr différer

dissenter [dɪ'sɛntər] s dissident m

dissertation [,dɪsər'teʃən] s dissertation f; (for a degree) thèse f; (speech) discours m

disservice [dɪs'sʌrvɪs] s mauvais service m, tort m

dissidence ['dɪsɪdəns] s dissidence f

dissident ['dɪsɪdənt] adj & s dissident m

dissimilar [dɪ'sɪmɪlər] adj dissemblable

dissimilate [dɪ'sɪmɪ,let] tr (phonet) dissimiler

dissimulate [dɪ'sɪmjə,let] tr & intr dissimuler

dissipate ['dɪsɪ,pet] tr dissiper; (energy, heat, etc.) disperser || intr se dissiper

dissipated adj dissipé; débauché

dissipation [,dɪsɪ'peʃən] s dissipation f; (of energy, heat, etc.) dispersion f

dissociate [dɪ'soʃɪ,et] tr dissocier || intr se dissocier

dissolute ['dɪsə,lut] adj dissolu

dissolution [,dɪsə'luʃən] s dissolution f

dissolve [dɪ'zɑlv] tr dissoudre || intr se dissoudre

dissonance ['dɪsənəns] s dissonance f

dissuade [dɪ'swed] tr dissuader

distaff ['dɪstæf] s quenouille f

dis′taff side′ s côté m maternel

distance ['dɪstəns] s distance f; **at a distance** à distance; **in the distance** au loin, dans le lointain || tr distancer

distant ['dɪstənt] adj distant; (uncle, cousin, etc.) éloigné

distaste [dɪs'test] s dégoût m, aversion f

distasteful [dɪs'testfəl] adj dégoûtant, répugnant

distemper [dɪs'tɛmpər] s (of dog) roupie f; (painting) détrempe f || tr peindre en détrempe

distend [dɪ'stɛnd] tr distendre || intr se distendre

distension [dɪ'stɛnʃən] s distension f

distill [dɪ'stɪl] tr distiller

distillation [,dɪstɪ'leʃən] s distillation f

distillery [dɪs'tɪləri] s (pl -ies) distillerie f

distinct [dɪs'tɪŋkt] adj distinct; (unusual) insigne

distinction [dɪs'tɪŋkʃən] s distinction f

distinctive [dɪs'tɪŋktɪv] adj distinctif

distinguish [dɪs'tɪŋgwɪʃ] tr distinguer; **to distinguish oneself** se distinguer, se faire remarquer

distinguished adj distingué

distort [dɪs'tɔrt] tr déformer
distortion [dɪs'tɔrʃən] s déformation f; (of meaning) sens m forcé; (phot, rad) distorsion f
distract [dɪs'strækt] tr (to amuse) distraire; (to bewilder) bouleverser
distracted adj bouleversé, éperdu
distraction [dɪs'strækʃən] s (amusement) distraction f; (madness) folie f
distraught [dɪs'strɔt] adj bouleversé
distress [dɪs'strɛs] s détresse f || tr affliger
distress' call' s signal m de détresse
distressing [dɪs'strɛsɪŋ] adj affligeant, pénible
distribute [dɪs'strɪbjut] tr distribuer
distribution [ˌdɪstrə'bjuʃən] s distribution f
distributor [dɪs'strɪbjətər] s distributeur m; (for a product) concessionnaire mf
district ['dɪstrɪkt] s contrée f, région f; (of a city) quartier m; (administrative division) district m, circonscription f || tr diviser en districts
dis'trict attor'ney s procureur m de la République, procureur général
distrust [dɪs'trʌst] s défiance f, méfiance f || tr se défier de, se méfier de
distrustful [dɪs'trʌstfəl] adj défiant
disturb [dɪs'stʌrb] tr déranger, troubler; (the peace) perturber
disturbance [dɪs'stʌrbəns] s dérangement m, trouble m; (riot) bagarre f, émeute f; (in the atmosphere or magnetic field) perturbation f
disuse [dɪs'jus] s désuétude f
ditch [dɪtʃ] s fossé m; to the last ditch jusqu'à la dernière extrémité || tr fossoyer; (slang) se défaire de || intr (aer) faire un amerrissage forcé
ditch' reed' s (bot) laîche f
dither ['dɪðər] s agitation f; to be in a dither (coll) s'agiter sans but
dit-to ['dɪto] s (pl -tos) le même; (on a duplicating machine) copie f, duplicata m || adv dito, de même, idem || tr copier, reproduire
dit-ty ['dɪti] s (pl -ties) chansonnette f; old ditty (coll) vieux refrain m
diva ['diva] s diva f
divan ['daɪvæn], [dɪ'væn] s divan m
dive [daɪv] s plongeon m; (of a submarine) plongée f; (aer) piqué m; (coll) gargote f, cabaret m borgne || v (pret & pp dived or dove [dov]) intr plonger; (said of submarine) plonger, effectuer une plongée; (aer) piquer; to dive for (e.g., pearls) pêcher; to dive into (coll) piquer une tête dans
dive'-bomb' tr & intr bombarder en piqué
dive' bomb' s bombardier m à piqué
dive' bomb'ing s bombardement m en piqué, piqué m
diver ['daɪvər] s plongeur m; (person who works under water) scaphandrier m; (orn) plongeon m
diverge [dɪ'vʌrdʒ], [daɪ'vʌrdʒ] intr diverger

divers ['daɪvərz] adj divers
diverse [dɪ'vʌrs], [daɪ'vʌrs], ['daɪvʌrs] adj divers
diversi-fy [dɪ'vʌrsɪˌfaɪ], [daɪ'vʌrsɪˌfaɪ] v (pret & pp -fied) tr diversifier || intr se diversifier
diversion [dɪ'vʌrʒən], [daɪ'vʌrʒən] s diversion f
diversi-ty [dɪ'vʌrsɪti], [daɪ'vʌrsɪti] s (pl -ties) diversité f
divert [dɪ'vʌrt], [daɪ'vʌrt] tr détourner; (to entertain) distraire, divertir
diverting [dɪ'vʌrtɪŋ], [daɪ'vʌrtɪŋ] adj divertissant
divest [dɪ'vɛst], [daɪ'vɛst] tr dépouiller; to divest oneself of se défaire de; (property, holdings) se déposséder de
divide [dɪ'vaɪd] s (geog) ligne f de partage || tr diviser || intr se diviser
dividend ['dɪvɪˌdɛnd] s dividende m
dividers [dɪ'vaɪdərz] spl compas m de mesure
dividing [dɪ'vaɪdɪŋ] s division f; dividing up répartition f, partage m
divination [ˌdɪvɪ'neʃən] s divination f
divine [dɪ'vaɪn] adj divin || s ecclésiastique mf || tr deviner
diviner [dɪ'vaɪnər] s devin m
diving ['daɪvɪŋ] s plongeon m
div'ing bell' s cloche f à plongeur
div'ing board' s plongeoir m, tremplin m
div'ing suit' s scaphandre m
divin'ing rod' [dɪ'vaɪnɪŋ] s baguette f divinatoire
divini-ty [dɪ'vɪnɪti] s (pl -ties) divinité f; (subject of study) théologie f; the Divinity Dieu m
divisible [dɪ'vɪzɪbəl] adj divisible
division [dɪ'vɪʒən] s division f
divisor [dɪ'vaɪzər] s diviseur m
divorce [dɪ'vors] s divorce m; to get a divorce divorcer; to get a divorce from (husband or wife) divorcer d'avec || tr (the married couple) divorcer; (husband or wife) divorcer d'avec || intr divorcer
divorcee [dɪvor'si] s divorcée f
divulge [dɪ'vʌldʒ] tr divulguer
dizziness ['dɪzɪnɪs] s vertige m
diz-zy ['dɪzi] adj (comp -zier; super -ziest) vertigineux; (coll) étourdi, farfelu; to feel dizzy avoir le vertige; to make dizzy étourdir
do [du] v (3d pers does [dʌz]; pret did [dɪd]; pp done [dʌn]; ger doing ['du·ɪŋ]) tr faire; (homage; justice; a good turn) rendre; to do over refaire; to do up emballer, envelopper || intr faire; how do you do? enchanté de faire votre connaissance; comment allez-vous?; that will do c'est bien; en voilà assez; that will never do cela n'ira jamais; to do away with supprimer; to do without se passer de; will I do? suis-je bien comme ça?; will it do? ça va-t-il comme ça? || aux used in English but not specifically expressed in French: 1) in questions, e.g., do you speak French? parlez-vous français?; 2) in negative sentences, e.g., I do not speak French

je ne parle pas français; 3) as a substitute for another verb in an elliptical question, e.g., **I saw him. Did you?** je l'ai vu. L'avez-vous vu?; 4) for emphasis, e.g., **I do believe what you told me** je crois bien ce que vous m'avez dit; 5) in inversions after certain adverbs, e.g., **hardly did we finish when . . .** à peine avions-nous fini que . . . ; 6) in an imperative entreaty, e.g., **do come in!** entrez donc!

do. *abbr* (ditto) d°

docile ['dɑsɪl] *adj* docile

dock [dɑk] *s* embarcadère *m*, quai *m*; *(area including piers and waterways)* bassin *m*, dock *m*; *(bot)* oseille *f*, patience *f*; *(law)* banc *m* des prévenus || *tr* faire entrer au bassin; *(an animal)* couper la queue à; *(s.o.'s salary)* retrancher || *intr (naut)* s'amarrer au quai

docket ['dɑkɪt] *s (law)* rôle *m*; **on the docket** pendant, non jugé; **to put on the docket** (coll) prendre en main

dock' hand' *s* docker *m*

docking ['dɑkɪŋ] *s* (rok) arrimage *m*

dock' work'er *s* docker *m*

dock' yard' *s* chantier *m*

doctor ['dɑktər] *s* docteur *m*; *(woman)* femme *f* docteur; (med) médecin *m*; (med) doctoresse *f*; Doctor Curie *(professor, Ph.D., etc.)* Monsieur Curie; Madame Curie || *tr* soigner; *(e.g., a chipped vase)* réparer; *(e.g., the facts)* falsifier || *intr* pratiquer la médecine; (coll) être en traitement; (coll) prendre des médicaments

doctorate ['dɑktərɪt] *s* doctorat *m*

Doc'tor of Laws' *s* docteur *m* en droit

doctrine ['dɑktrɪn] *s* doctrine *f*

document ['dɑkjəmənt] *s* document *m* || ['dɑkjə‚mɛnt] *tr* documenter

documenta·ry [‚dɑkjə'mɛntəri] *adj* documentaire || *s (pl -ries)* documentaire *m*

documentation [‚dɑkjəmən'teʃən] *s* documentation *f*

doddering ['dɑdərɪŋ] *adj* tremblotant, gâteux

dodge [dɑdʒ] *s* écart *m*, esquive *f*; (coll) ruse *f*, truc *m* || *tr* esquiver; *(a question)* éluder || *intr* s'esquiver

do·do ['dodo] *s (pl -dos or -does)* (orn) dronte *m*, dodo *m*; (coll) vieux fossile *m*, innocent *m*

doe [do] *s (of fallow deer)* daine *f*; *(hind)* biche *f*; *(roe doe)* chevrette *f*; *(of hare)* hase *f*; *(of rabbit)* lapine *f*

doe'skin' *s* peau *f* de daim

doff [dɑf], [dɔf] *tr* ôter

dog [dɔg], [dɑg] *s* chien *m*; **let sleeping dogs lie** il ne faut pas réveiller le chat qui dort; **to go to the dogs** (coll) se débaucher; *(said of business)* (coll) aller à vau-l'eau; **to put on the dog** (coll) faire de l'épate || *v (pret & pp* **dogged;** *ger* **dogging)** *tr* poursuivre

dog'catch'er *s* employé *m* de la fourrière

dog' days' *spl* canicule *f*

doge [dodʒ] *s* doge *m*

dog'face' *s* (slang) troufion *m*

dog'fight' *s* (aer) combat *m* aérien tournoyant et violent; (coll) bagarre *f*

dogged ['dɔgɪd], ['dɑgɪd] *adj* tenace, obstiné

doggerel ['dɔgərəl], ['dɑgərəl] *s* vers *mpl* de mirliton

dog·gy ['dɔgi], ['dɑgi] *adj (comp* **-gier;** *super* **-giest)** canin, de chien || *s (pl* **-gies)** toutou *m*

dog'house' *s* niche *f* à chien; **in the doghouse** (slang) en disgrâce

dog' in the man'ger *s* chien *m* du jardinier

dog' Lat'in *s* latin *m* de cuisine

dogma ['dɔgmə], ['dɑgmə] *s* dogme *m*

dogmatic [dɔg'mætɪk], [dɑg'mætɪk] *adj* dogmatique || **dogmatics** *s* dogmatique *f*

dog' pound' *s* fourrière *f*

dog' rac'ing *s* courses *fpl* de lévriers

dog' rose' *s* rose *f* des haies

dog's'-ear' *s* corne *f* || *tr* corner

dog' show' *s* exposition *f* canine

dog' sled' or **dog' sledge'** *s* traîneau *m* à chiens

dog's' life' *s* vie *f* de chien

Dog' Star' *s* Canicule *f*

dog' tag' *s* (mil) plaque *f* d'identité

dog'-tired' *adj* éreinté, fourbu

dog'tooth' *s (pl* **-teeth)** dent *f* de chien, canine *f*; *(archit, bot, mach)* dent-de-chien *f*

dog'tooth vi'olet *s* dent-de-chien *f*

dog'trot' *s* petit-trot *m*

dog'watch' *s* (naut) petit quart *m*

dog'wood' *s* cornouiller *m*

doi·ly ['dɔɪli] *s (pl* **-lies)** napperon *m*; *(underplate)* garde-nappe *m*

doings ['du·ɪŋz] *spl* actions *fpl*, œuvres *fpl*, faits et gestes *mpl*

do-it-yourself [‚du·ɪt/ər'sɛlf] *adj* de bricolage || *s* bricolage *m*

doldrums ['doldrəmz], ['dɑldrəmz] *spl* marasme *m*; (naut) zone *f* des calmes

dole [dol] *s* aumône *f*; indemnité *f* de chômage || *tr* **—to dole out** distribuer parcimonieusement

doleful ['dolfəl] *adj* dolent

doll [dɑl] *s* poupée *f* || *tr* **—to be dolled up** (coll) être tiré à quatre épingles || *intr* **—to doll up** (coll) se parer, s'endimancher

dollar ['dɑlər] *s* dollar *m*

dol·ly ['dɑli] *s (pl* **-lies)** *(low movable frame)* chariot *m*; *(hand truck)* diable *m*; *(child's doll)* poupée *f*; *(mov, telv)* travelling *m*

dolphin ['dɑlfɪn] *s* dauphin *m*

dolt [dolt] *s* nigaud *m*, lourdaud *m*

doltish ['doltɪʃ] *adj* nigaud, lourdaud

domain [do'men] *s* domaine *m*; *(private estate)* terres *fpl*, propriété *f*

dome [dom] *s* dôme *m*, coupole *f*

dome' light' *s* (aut) plafonnier *m*

domestic [də'mɛstɪk] *adj & s* domestique *mf*

domesticate [də'mɛstɪ‚ket] *tr* domestiquer

domesticity [ˌdɑmɛsˈtɪsɪti] s caractère m casanier; vie f familiale

domicile [ˈdɑmɪsɪl], [ˈdɑmɪˌsaɪl] s domicile m ‖ tr domicilier

dominance [ˈdɑmɪnəns] s prédominance f; (genetics) dominance f

dominant [ˈdɑmɪnənt] adj prédominant, dominant ‖ s (mus) dominante f

dominate [ˈdɑmɪˌnet] tr & intr dominer

dominating [ˈdɑmɪˌnetɪŋ] adj dominateur

domination [ˌdɑmɪˈneʃən] s domination f

domineer [ˌdɑmɪˈnɪr] intr se montrer tyrannique

domineering [ˌdɑmɪˈnɪrɪŋ] adj tyrannique, autoritaire

dominion [dəˈmɪnjən] s domination f; (of British Commonwealth) dominion m

domi‧no [ˈdɑmɪˌno] s (pl -noes or -nos) domino m; **dominoes** sg (game) les dominos

don [dɑn] s (tutor) précepteur m ‖ v (pret & pp **donned**; ger **donning**) tr mettre, enfiler

donate [ˈdonet] tr faire un don de

donation [doˈneʃən] s don m, cadeau m

done [dʌn] adj fait; **are you done?** en avez-vous fini?; **it is done** (it is finished) c'en est fait; **to be done** (e.g., beefsteak) être cuit; **to have done with** en finir avec; **well done!** très bien!, bravo!, à la bonne heure!

done′ for′ adj (tired out) (coll) fourbu; (ruined) (coll) abattu; (out of the running) (coll) hors de combat; (dead) (coll) estourbi

donkey [ˈdɑŋki], [ˈdʌŋki] s âne m, baudet m

donor [ˈdonər] s donneur m; (law) donateur m

doodle [ˈdudəl] tr & intr griffonner

doom [dum] s condamnation f; destin m funeste ‖ tr condamner

dooms′day′ s jugement m dernier

door [dor] s porte f; (of a carriage or automobile) portière f; (one part of a double door) battant m; **behind closed doors** à huis clos; **to see to the door** conduire à la porte; **to show s.o. the door** éconduire qn, mettre qn à la porte

door′bell′ s timbre m, sonnette f

door′bell transform′er s transformateur m de sonnerie

door′bell wire′ s fil m sonnerie

door′ check′ s arrêt m de porte

door′frame′ s chambranle m, huisserie f, dormant m

door′head′ s linteau m

door′jamb′ s jambage m

door′knob′ s bouton m de porte

door′knock′er s heurtoir m, marteau m de porte

door′ latch′ s loquet m

door′man s (pl -men) portier m

door′mat′ s essuie-pieds m, paillasson m

door′nail′ s clou m de porte; **dead as a doornail** (coll) bien mort

door′post′ s montant m de porte

door′ scrap′er [ˈskrepər] s décrottoir m, grattepieds m

door′sill′ s seuil m, traverse f

door′step′ s seuil m, pas m

door′stop′ s entrebâilleur m, butoir m

door′-to-door′ adj porte-à-porte

door′way′ s porte f, portail m

dope [dop] s enduit m; (slang) narcotique m, stupéfiant m; (information) (slang) renseignements mpl; (fool) (slang) cornichon m ‖ tr enduire; (slang) doper, stupéfier; **to dope out** (slang) deviner, déchiffrer

dope′ fiend′ s (slang) toxicomane mf

dope′ ped′dler s trafiquant m de stupéfiants

dormant [ˈdɔrmənt] adj endormi, assoupi; latent; **to lie dormant** dormir

dor′mer win′dow [ˈdɔrmər] s lucarne f

dormito‧ry [ˈdɔrmɪˌtori] s (pl -ries) (room) dortoir m; (building) pavillon m des étudiants, maison f de résidence

dor′mitory com′plex s cité f universitaire

dor‧mouse [ˈdɔrˌmaʊs] s (pl -mice) loir m

dosage [ˈdosɪdʒ] s dosage m

dose [dos] s dose f ‖ tr donner en doses; donner un médicament à

dossier [ˈdɑsɪˌe] s dossier m

dot [dɑt] s point m; **on the dot** (coll) à l'heure tapante; pile, e.g., **at noon on the dot** à midi pile ‖ v (pret & pp **dotted**; ger **dotting**) tr (to make with dots) pointiller; **to dot one's i's** mettre les points sur les i

dotage [ˈdotɪdʒ] s radotage m

dotard [ˈdotərd] s gâteux m, gaga m

dote [dot] intr radoter; **to dote on** raffoler de

doting [ˈdotɪŋ] adj radoteur; (loving to excess) qui aime follement

dots′ and dash′es spl (telg) points et traits mpl

dot′ted line′ s ligne f pointillée, ligne hachée; **to sign on the dotted line** signer aveuglément

double [ˈdʌbəl] adj & adv double, en deux, deux fois ‖ s double m; (cards) contre m; (stunt man) (mov) cascadeur m; **doubles** (tennis) double; **on the double!** (coll) dare-dare!, au trot! ‖ tr doubler; (cards) contrer; **to double up** plier en deux ‖ intr doubler; (cards) contrer; **to double back** faire un crochet; **to double up** se plier, se tordre

dou′ble-act′ing adj à double effet

dou′ble-bar′reled adj (gun) à deux coups

dou′ble bass′ [bes] s contrebasse f

dou′ble bed′ s grand lit m, lit à deux places

dou′ble boil′er s bain-marie m

dou′ble-breast′ed adj croisé

dou′ble chin′ s double menton m

dou′ble cross′ s (slang) entourloupette f, double jeu m

dou′ble-cross′ tr (coll) doubler, rouler, faire une entourloupette à

dou'ble-cross'er s (slang) personne f double, faux jeton m

dou'ble date' s partie f carrée, sortie f à quatre

dou'ble-deal'er s personne f double, homme m à deux visages

dou'ble-deal'ing adj hypocrite ‖ s duplicité f

dou'ble-deck'er s (bed) lits mpl superposés, lits gigognes, lit à deux étages; (bus) autobus m à deux étages; (sandwich) double sandwich m; (aer, naut) deux-ponts m

dou'ble-edged' adj à deux tranchants, à double tranchant

double entendre ['dubəlαn'tαndrə] s expression f à double entente, mot m à double sens

dou'ble-en'try s en partie double

dou'ble-faced' adj à double face

dou'ble fea'ture s (mov) deux grands films mpl, double programme m

dou'ble-joint'ed adj désarticulé

dou'ble-lock' tr fermer à double tour

dou'ble-park' tr faire stationner en double file ‖ intr stationner en double file

dou'ble room' s chambre f à deux lits

dou'ble-spaced' adj à l'interligne

dou'ble stand'ard s code m de morale à deux aspects; **to have a double standard** avoir deux poids et deux mesures

doublet ['dʌblɪt] s (close-fitting jacket) pourpoint m; (counterfeit gem; each of two words having the same origin) doublet m

dou'ble-talk' s (coll) non-sens m; (coll) paroles fpl creuses or ambiguës, mots mpl couverts

dou'ble time' s (for work) salaire m double; (mil) pas m redoublé

doubleton ['dʌbəltən] s deux cartes fpl d'une couleur

dou'ble track' s double piste f

doubling ['dʌblɪŋ] s doublement m

doubly ['dʌbli] adv doublement

doubt [daut] s doute m; **beyond a doubt** à n'en pas douter; **no doubt** sans doute ‖ tr douter de; **to doubt that** douter que; **to doubt whether** douter si ‖ intr douter

doubter ['dautər] s douteur m

doubtful ['dautfəl] adj douteux, indécis, hésitant

doubtless ['dautlɪs] adv sans doute

douche [duʃ] s douche f; (instrument) seringue f à lavement ‖ tr doucher ‖ intr se doucher

dough [do] s pâte f; (slang) fric m; **big dough** (slang) grosse galette f

dough'boy' s (coll) troufion m, biffin m; (in the first World War) poilu m

dough'nut' s beignet m

dough-ty ['dauti] adj (comp -tier; super -tiest) vaillant, preux

dough-y ['do-i] adj (comp -ier; super -iest) pâteux

dour [daur], [dur] adj (severe) austère; (obstinate) buté; (gloomy) mélancolique

douse [daus] tr tremper, arroser; (slang) éteindre

dove [dʌv] s colombe f

dovecote ['dʌv,kot] s pigeonnier m, colombier m

Dover ['dovər] s Douvres

dove'tail' s queue-d'aronde f, adent m ‖ tr assembler à queue-d'aronde, adenter; (fig) raccorder, opérer le raccord entre ‖ intr se raccorder

dove'tailed' adj à queue-d'aronde

dowager ['dau·ədʒər] s douairière f

dow-dy ['daudi] adj (comp -dier; super -diest) gauche, fagoté, mal habillé

dow-el ['dau·əl] s goujon m ‖ v (pret & pp -eled or -elled; ger -eling or -elling) tr goujonner

dower ['dau·ər] s (widow's portion) douaire m; (marriage portion) dot f; (natural gift) don m ‖ tr assigner un douaire à; doter

down [daun] adj bas; (train) descendant; (storage battery) épuisé; (tire) à plat; (sun) couché; (wind, sea, etc.) calmé; (blinds; prices) baissé; (stocks) en moins-value; (sad) abattu, triste ‖ s duvet m; (sand hill) dune f ‖ adv en bas, au bas, vers les bas; à terre; (south) au sud; **down!** (in elevator) on descend!, pour la descente!; **down from** du haut de; **down there** là-bas; **down to** jusqu'à; **down under** aux antipodes; **down with . . .!** à bas . . .!; for expressions like **to go down** descendre or **to pay down** payer comptant, see the verb ‖ prep en bas de; (along) le long de; (a stream) en descendant ‖ tr descendre, abattre; (to swallow) (coll) avaler

down'-and-out' adj décavé

down'beat' s (mus) temps m fort, frappé m, premier accent m

down'cast' adj abattu, baissé

down'fall' s chute f, ruine f

down'grade' adj (coll) descendant ‖ s descente f; **to be on the downgrade** déchoir ‖ adv en déclin ‖ tr déclasser

down'heart'ed adj abattu, découragé

down'hill' adj descendant ‖ adv—**to go downhill** aller en descendant, (fig) décliner

down' pay'ment s acompte m

down'pour' s déluge m, averse f

down'right' adj absolu, véritable ‖ adv tout à fait, absolument

down'stairs' s rez-de-chaussée m ‖ adv en bas; **to go downstairs** descendre

down'stream' adv en aval

down'stroke' s (of piston) course f descendante; (in writing) jambage m

down'town' adj du centre ‖ s centre m ‖ adv en ville

down'trend' s tendance f à la baisse

downtrodden ['daun,trɒdən] adj opprimé

downward ['daunwərd] adj descendant ‖ adv en bas, en descendant

downwards ['daunwərdz] adv en bas, en descendant

down'wash' s (aer) air m déplacé

down·y ['dauni] adj (comp -ier; super

-iest) duveteux; *(velvety)* velouté; *(soft)* mou, moelleux

dow·ry ['dauri] *s (pl* **-ries)** dot *f*

dowser ['dauzər] *s* sourcier *m*, hydroscope *m*

doze [doz] *s* petit somme *m* ‖ *intr* sommeiller; **to doze off** s'assoupir

dozen ['dʌzən] *s* douzaine *f*; **a dozen . . .** une douzaine de . . . ; **by the dozen** à la douzaine

D.P. *abbr* **(displaced person)** personne *f* déplacée

Dr. *abbr* **(Doctor)** Dr

drab [dræb] *adj (comp* **drabber;** *super* **drabbest)** gris ‖ *s* gris *m*

drach·ma ['drækmə] *s (pl* **-mas** *or* **-mae** [mi])** drachme *f*

draft [dræft], [drɑft] *s* courant *m* d'air; *(pulling; current of air in chimney)* tirage *m*; *(sketch, outline)* ébauche *f*; *(of a letter, novel, etc.)* brouillon *m*, premier jet *m*; *(of a bill in Congress)* projet *m*; *(of a law)* avant-projet *m*; *(drink)* trait *m*, gorgée *f*; *(com)* mandat *m*, traite *f*; *(mil)* conscription *f*; *(naut)* tirant *m* d'eau; **drafts** *(game)* dames *fpl*; **on draft** à la pression; **to be exempted from the draft** être exempté du service militaire ‖ *tr (a document)* rédiger, faire le brouillon de; *(a bill in Congress)* dresser; *(a recruit)* appeler sous les drapeaux; **to be drafted** être appelé sous les drapeaux

draft′ beer′ *s* bière *f* pression

draft′ board′ *s* conseil *m* de révision; commission *f* locale des conscriptions

draft′ call′ *s* appel *m* sous les drapeaux

draft′ dodg′er ['dɑdʒər] *s* embusqué *m*

draftee [,dræf′ti], [,drɑf′ti] *s* appelé *m* (sous les drapeaux), conscrit *m*

draft′ horse′ *s* cheval *m* de trait

drafting ['dræftɪŋ], ['drɑftɪŋ] *s* dessin *m* industriel

draft′ing room′ *s* bureau *m* d'études

drafts·man *s (pl* **-men)** dessinateur *m*; *(man who draws up documents)* rédacteur *m*

draft·y ['dræfti], ['drɑfti] *adj (comp* **-ier;** *super* **-iest)** plein de courants d'air

drag [dræg] *s (net)* drège *f*; *(sledge or sled)* traîneau *m*; *(stone drag)* fardier *m*; *(brake)* enrayure *f*; *(impediment)* entrave *f*; *(aer)* résistance *f* à l'avancement ‖ *v (pret & pp* **dragged)**; *ger* **dragging)** *tr* traîner; *(one's feet)* traînasser; *(a net)* draguer; *(a field)* herser; **to drag down** entraîner; **to drag in** introduire de force; **to drag out** faire sortir de force ‖ *intr* traîner à terre; se traîner

drag′net′ *s* traîneau *m*, chalut *m*

dragon ['drægən] *s* dragon *m*

drag′on-fly′ *s (pl* **-flies)** demoiselle *f*, libellule *f*

dragoon [drə′gun] *s* dragon *m* ‖ *tr* tyranniser; forcer, contraindre

drain [dren] *s (sewer)* égout *m*; *(pipe)* tuyau *m* d'égout; *(ditch)* tranchée *f* d'écoulement; *(source of continual expense)* saignée *f*; *(med)* drain *m* ‖

tr (wet ground) drainer; *(a glass or cup)* vider entièrement; *(a crankcase)* vidanger; *(s.o. of strength)* épuiser; *(med)* drainer ‖ *intr* s'égoutter, s'écouler

drainage ['drenɪdʒ] *s* drainage *m*

drain′ board′ *s* égouttoir *m*

drain′ cock′ *s* purgeur *m*

drain′ pipe′ *s* tuyau *m* d'écoulement, drain *m*

drain′ plug′ *s* bouchon *m* de vidange

drake [drek] *s* canard *m* mâle

dram [dræm] *s (weight)* drachme *m*; *(drink)* petit verre *f*, goutte *f*

drama ['drɑmə], ['dræmə] *s* drame *m*

dra′ma crit′ic *s* chroniqueur *m* dramatique

dra′ma review′ *s* avant-première *f*

dramatic [drə′mætɪk] *adj* dramatique ‖ **dramatics** *s* dramaturgie *f*, art *m* dramatique

dramatist ['dræmətɪst] *s* auteur *m* dramatique, dramaturge *mf*

dramatize ['dræmə,taɪz] *tr* dramatiser

drape [drep] *s* rideau *m*; *(hang of a curtain, skirt, etc.)* drapement *m* ‖ *tr* draper, tendre; se draper dans

draper·y ['drepəri] *s (pl* **-ies)** draperie *f*; **draperies** rideaux *mpl*, tentures *fpl*

drastic ['dræstɪk] *adj* énergique, radical; *(laxative)* drastique

draught [dræft], [drɑft] *s (of fish)* coup *m* de filet; *(drink)* trait *m*, gorgée *f*; *(naut)* tirant *m* d'eau; **draughts** *(game)* dames *fpl*; **on draught** à la pression

draught′ beer′ *s* bière *f* pression

draught′ board′ *s* damier *m*

draw [drɔ] *s* tirage *m*; *(in a game or other contest)* partie *f* nulle, match *m* nul ‖ *v (pret* **drew** [dru]; *pp* **drawn** [drɔn]) *tr* tirer; *(a crowd)* attirer; *(a design)* dessiner; *(a card)* tirer; *(trumps)* faire tomber; *(a bow)* bander, tendre; *(water)* puiser; **to draw a conclusion** tirer une conséquence; **to draw aside** prendre à l'écart; **to draw blood** faire saigner; **to draw interest** porter intérêt; **to draw lots** tirer au sort; **to draw off** *(e.g., a liquid)* soutirer; **to draw out** *(a person)* faire parler; *(an activity)* prolonger, traîner; **to draw up** *(a list)* dresser; *(a plan)* rédiger; *(naut)* jauger ‖ *intr* tirer; dessiner; faire partie nulle, faire match nul; **to draw away** s'éloigner; **to draw back** reculer, se retirer; **to draw near** approcher; s'approcher de

draw′back′ *s* désavantage *m*, inconvénient *m*

draw′bridge′ *s* pont-levis *m*

drawee [,drɔ′i] *s* tiré *m*, accepteur *m*

drawer ['drɔ·ər] *s* dessinateur *m*; *(com)* tireur *m* ‖ [drɔr] *s* tiroir *m*; **drawers** caleçon *m*

drawing ['drɔ·ɪŋ] *s* dessin *m*; *(in a lottery)* tirage *m*

draw′ing board′ *s* planche *f* à dessin

draw′ing card′ *s* attrait *m*, attraction *f*

draw′ing room′ *s* salon *m*

draw′knife′ *s (pl* **-knives)** plane *f*

drawl [drɔl] s voix f traînante || tr dire d'une voix traînante || intr traîner la voix en parlant

drawn' but'ter [drɔn] s beurre m fondu; sauce f blanche

drawn' work' s broderie f à fils tirés

dray [dre] s haquet m, charrette f; (sledge) fardier m, schlitte f

drayage ['dre·ɪdʒ] s charriage m, charroi m; frais mpl de transport

dray' horse' s cheval m de trait

dray'man s (pl -men) haquetier m

dread [drɛd] adj redoutable, terrible || s terreur f, crainte f || tr & intr redouter, craindre

dreadful ['drɛdfəl] adj épouvantable

dream [drim] s rêve m, songe m; (fancy, illusion) rêverie f, songerie f || v (pret & pp dreamed or dreamt [drɛmt]) tr—**to dream up** rêver || intr rêver, songer; **to dream of** (future plans) rêver à; (s.o.) rêver de

dreamer ['drimər] s rêveur m

dream'land' s pays m des songes

dream' world' s monde m des rêves

dream·y ['drimi] adj (comp -ier; super -iest) rêveur; (slang) épatant

drear·y ['drɪri] adj (comp -ier; super -iest) triste, morne; monotone

dredge [drɛdʒ] s drague f || tr draguer

dredger ['drɛdʒər] s dragueur m; (mach) drague f

dredging ['drɛdʒɪŋ] s dragage m

dregs [drɛgz] spl lie f

drench [drɛntʃ] tr tremper, inonder

dress [drɛs] s habillement m, costume m; (woman's attire) toilette f, mise f; (woman's dress) robe f || tr habiller, vêtir; (to apply a dressing to) panser; (culin) garnir; **to dress down** (coll) passer au savon à, chapitrer; **to dress up** parer; (ranks) (mil) aligner; **to get dressed** s'habiller || intr s'habiller, se vêtir; (mil) s'aligner; **to dress up** se parer

dress' ball' s bal m paré

dress' cir'cle s corbeille f, premier balcon m

dress' coat' s frac m

dresser ['drɛsər] s coiffeuse f; commode f à miroir; (sideboard) dressoir m; **to be a good dresser** être recherché dans sa mise

dress' form' s mannequin m

dress' goods' spl étoffes fpl pour costumes

dressing ['drɛsɪŋ] s toilette f; (for food) assaisonnement m, sauce f; (stuffing for fowl) farce f; (fertilizer) engrais m; (for a wound) pansement m

dress'ing down' s (coll) savon m, verte réprimande f, algarade f

dress'ing gown' s peignoir m, robe f de chambre

dress'ing room' s cabinet m de toilette; (theat) loge f

dress'ing sta'tion s poste m de secours

dress'ing ta'ble s coiffeuse f, toilette f

dress'mak'er s couturière f

dress'mak'ing s couture f

dress'making estab'lishment s maison f de couture

dress' rehear'sal s répétition f en costume; **final dress rehearsal** répétition générale

dress' shield' s dessous-de-bras m

dress' shirt' s chemise f à plastron

dress' shop' s magasin m de modes

dress' suit' s habit m de cérémonie, tenue f de soirée

dress' tie' s cravate f de smoking, cravate-plastron f

dress' u'niform s (mil) grande tenue f

dress·y ['drɛsi] adj (comp -ier; super -iest) (coll) élégant, chic

dribble ['drɪbəl] s dégouttement m; (of child) bave f; (sports) dribble m || tr (sports) dribbler || intr dégoutter; (said of child) baver; (sports) dribbler

driblet ['drɪblɪt] s chiquet m; **in driblets** au compte-gouttes

dried' ap'ple [draɪd] s pomme f tapée

dried' beef' s viande f boucanée

dried' fig' s figue f sèche

dried' fruit' s fruit m sec

dried' pear' s poire f tapée

drier ['draɪ·ər] s (for clothes) séchoir m, sécheuse f; (for paint) siccatif m; (mach) sécheur m

drift [drɪft] s dérive f; (of sand, snow) amoncellement m; (of meaning) sens m, direction f || intr aller à la dérive; (said of snow) s'amonceler; (aer, naut) dériver; (fig) se laisser aller, flotter

drift' ice' s glaces fpl flottantes

drift'wood' s bois m flotté

drill [drɪl] s foret m; (machine) perforatrice f; (fabric) coutil m, treillis m; (furrow) sillon m; (agricultural implement) semoir m; (in school; on the drill ground) exercice m || tr instruire; (e.g., students) former, entraîner; (mach) forer; (mil) faire faire l'exercice à; **to drill s.th. into s.o.** seriner q.ch. à qn || intr faire l'exercice; forer

driller ['drɪlər] s foreur m

drill' field' or **drill' ground'** s terrain m d'exercice

drill'mas'ter s moniteur m; (mil) instructeur m

drill' press' s foreuse f à colonnes

drink [drɪŋk] s boisson f, breuvage m; boire m, e.g., **food and drink** le boire et le manger || v (pret **drank** [dræŋk]; pp **drunk** [drʌŋk]) tr boire; (e.g., with a meal) prendre; **to drink down** boire d'un trait || intr boire; **to drink out of** (a glass) boire dans; (a bottle) boire à; **to drink to the health of** boire à la santé de

drinkable ['drɪŋkəbəl] adj buvable, potable

drinker ['drɪŋkər] s buveur m

drink'ing cup' s tasse f à boire, gobelet m

drink'ing foun'tain s fontaine f à boire, borne-fontaine f

drink'ing song' s chanson f à boire

drink'ing trough' s abreuvoir m

drink/ing wa/ter s eau f potable

drip [drɪp] s (*drop*) goutte f; (*dripping*) égout m, dégouttement m; (*person*) (slang) cornichon m ‖ v (*pret & pp* **dripped**; *ger* **dripping**) *intr* dégoutter, goutter

drip/ cof/fee s café-filtre m

drip/ cof/fee mak/er s cafetière f à filtre

drip/-dry/ adj à séchage rapide; (*label on shirt*) repassage inutile

dripolator ['drɪpə,letər] s filtre m à café

drip/ pan/ s égouttoir m

dripping ['drɪpɪŋ] s ruissellement m; **drippings** graisse f de rôti

drive [draɪv] s (*in an automobile*) promenade f; (*road*) chaussée f; (*vigor*) énergie f, initiative f; (*fund-raising*) campagne f; (*push forward*) propulsion f; (*aut*) (*point of power application to roadway*) traction f; (*golf*) crossée f; (*mach*) transmission f; **to go for a drive** faire une promenade en auto ‖ v (*pret* **drove** [drov]; *pp* **driven** ['drɪvən] *tr* (*an automobile, locomotive, etc.; an animal; a person in an automobile*) conduire; (*a nail*) enfoncer; (*a bargain*) conclure; (*the ball in a game*) renvoyer, chasser; (*to push, force*) pousser, forcer; (*to overwork*) surmener; **to drive away** chasser; **to drive back** repousser; (*e.g., in a car*) reconduire; **to drive crazy** rendre fou; **to drive in** enfoncer; **to drive out** chasser; **to drive to despair** conduire au désespoir ‖ *intr* conduire; **drive slowly** (*public sign*) marcher au pas; **to drive away** partir, démarrer; **to drive back** rentrer en auto; **to drive on** continuer sa route; **to drive out** sortir

drive/-in/ s (*motion-picture theater*) cinéma m auto; (*restaurant*) restoroute m

driv•el ['drɪvəl] s (*slobber*) bave f; (*nonsense*) bêtises fpl ‖ v (*pret* **-eled** or **-elled**; *ger* **-eling** or **-elling**) *intr* baver; (*to talk nonsense*) radoter

driver ['draɪvər] s chauffeur m, conducteur m; (*of a carriage*) cocher m; (*of a locomotive*) mécanicien m; (*of pack animals*) toucheur m

driv/er's li/cense s permis m de conduire

drive/ shaft/ s arbre m d'entraînement

drive/way/ s voie f de garage, sortie f de voiture

drive/ wheel/ s roue f motrice, roue de transmission

driv/ing school/ s auto-école f

drizzle ['drɪzəl] s pluie f fine, bruine f ‖ *intr* bruiner, brouillasser

droll [drol] adj drôle, drolatique

dromedar•y ['drɑmə,deri] s (*pl* **-ies**) dromadaire m

drone [dron] s bourdonnement m; (*of plane or engine*) vrombissement m, ronron m; fainéant m; (*aer*) avion m téléguidé, avion sans pilote; (*ent*) faux bourdon m ‖ *intr* bourdonner, ronronner

drool [drul] *intr* baver

droop [drup] s inclinaison f ‖ *intr* se baisser; (*to lose one's pep*) s'alanguir; (*bot*) languir

drooping ['drupɪŋ] adj languissant

drop [drɑp] s goutte f; (*fall*) chute f; (*slope*) précipice m; (*depth of drop*) hauteur f de chute; (*in price; in temperature*) baisse f; (*lozenge*) pastille f; (*of supplies from an airplane*) droppage m; **a drop in the bucket** une goutte d'eau dans la mer ‖ v (*pret & pp* **dropped**; *ger* **dropping**) *tr* laisser tomber; (*a curtain; the eyes, voice*) baisser; (*from an airplane*) lâcher; (*e.g., a name from a list*) omettre, supprimer; (*a remark*) glisser; (*a conversation; relations; negotiations*) cesser; (*anchor*) jeter, mouiller; (*an idea, a habit, etc.*) renoncer à; **to drop off** déposer ‖ *intr* tomber; se laisser tomber; baisser; cesser; **to drop in** entrer en passant; **to drop in on** faire un saut chez; **to drop off** se détacher; s'endormir; **to drop out of** (*to quit*) renoncer à, abandonner

drop/ cur/tain s rideau m d'entracte

drop/ ham/mer s marteau-pilon m

drop/ kick/ s coup m tombé

drop/ leaf/ s abattant m

drop/light/ s lampe f suspendue

drop/out/ s raté m; **to become a dropout** abandonner les études

dropper ['drɑpər] s compte-gouttes m

dropsy ['drɑpsi] s hydropisie f

drop/ ta/ble s table f à abattants

dross [drɔs], [drɑs] s scories mpl, écume f

drought [draʊt] s sécheresse f

drove [drov] s troupeau m; (*multitude*) foule f, flots mpl; **in droves** par bandes

drover ['drovər] s bouvier m

drown [draʊn] *tr* noyer; **to drown out** couvrir ‖ *intr* se noyer

drowse [draʊz] *intr* somnoler, s'assoupir

drow•sy ['draʊzi] adj (*comp* **-sier**; *super* **-siest**) somnolent

drub [drʌb] v (*pret & pp* **drubbed**; *ger* **drubbing**) *tr* flanquer une raclée à, rosser

drudge [drʌdʒ] s homme m de peine, piocheur m; **harmless drudge** (*e.g., who compiles dictionaries*) grattepapier m inoffensif

drudger•y ['drʌdʒəri] s (*pl* **-ies**) corvée f, travail m pénible

drug [drʌg] s drogue f, stupéfiant m, produit m pharmaceutique; **drug on the market** rossignol m ‖ v (*pret & pp* **drugged**; *ger* **drugging**) *tr* (*a person*) donner un stupéfiant à, stupéfier; (*food or drink*) ajouter un stupéfiant à

drug/ ad/dict s toxicomane mf

drug/ addic/tion s toxicomanie f

druggist ['drʌgɪst] s pharmacien m

drug/ hab/it s toxicomanie f, vice m des stupéfiants

drug/store/ s pharmacie-bazar f, pharmacie f
drug/ traf/fic s trafic m des stupéfiants
druid ['dru·ɪd] s druide m
drum [drʌm] s (cylinder; instrument of percussion) tambour m; (container for oil, gasoline, etc.) bidon m; to play the drum battre du tambour || v (pret & pp drummed; ger drumming) tr (e.g., a march) tambouriner; rassembler au son du tambour; to drum into fourrer dans; to drum up customers racoler des clients || intr jouer du tambour; (with the fingers) tambouriner; (on the piano) pianoter
drum/ and bu/gle corps/ s clairons et tambours mpl, clique f
drum/ beat/ s coup m de tambour
drum/fire/ s (mil) tir m nourri, feu m roulant
drum/head/ s peau f de tambour; (naut) noix f
drum/ ma/jor s tambour-major m
drummer ['drʌmər] s tambour m; (salesman) (coll) commis m voyageur
drum/stick/ s baguette f de tambour; (of chicken) (coll) cuisse f, pilon m
drunk [drʌŋk] adj ivre, soûl; to get drunk s'enivrer; to get s.o. drunk enivrer qn || s (person) (coll) ivrogne m; (state) ivresse f; to go on a drunk (coll) se soûler
drunkard ['drʌŋkərd] s ivrogne m
drunken ['drʌŋkən] adj enivré
drunk/en driv/ing s conduite f en état d'ivresse
drunkenness ['drʌŋkənnɪs] s ivresse f
dry [draɪ] adj (comp drier; super driest) sec; (thirsty) assoiffé; (boring) aride || s (pl drys) (prohibitionist) antialcoolique mf || v (pret & pp dried) tr sécher; (the dishes) essuyer || intr sécher; to dry up se dessécher; (slang) se taire
dry/ bat/tery s pile f sèche; (number of dry cells) batterie f de piles
dry/ cell/ s pile f sèche
dry/-clean/ tr nettoyer à sec
dry/ clean/er s nettoyeur m à sec, teinturier m
dry/ clean/er's s teinturerie f
dry/ clean/ing s nettoyage m à sec
dry/ dock/ s cale f sèche, bassin m de radoub
dry/-eyed/ adj d'un œil sec
dry/ goods/ spl tissus mpl, étoffes fpl
dry/ ice/ s glace f sèche
dry/ land/ s terre f ferme
dry/ meas/ure s mesure f à grains
dryness ['draɪnɪs] s sécheresse f; (e.g., of a speaker) aridité f
dry/ nurse/ s nourrice f sèche
dry/ rot/ s carie f sèche
dry/ run/ s exercice m simulé, répétition f, examen m blanc
dry/ sea/son s saison f sèche
dry/ wash/ s blanchissage m sans repassage
dual ['d(j)u·əl] adj double || s duel m
dub [dʌb] s (slang) balourd m || v (pret & pp dubbed; ger dubbing) tr (to nickname) donner un sobriquet à; (to

knight) donner l'accolade à, adouber; (a tape recording or movie film) doubler
dubbing ['dʌbɪŋ] s (mov) doublage m
dubious ['d(j)ubɪ·əs] adj (undecided) hésitant; (questionable) douteux
ducat ['dʌkət] s ducat m
duchess ['dʌtʃɪs] s duchesse f
duch·y ['dʌtʃi] s (pl -ies) duché m
duck [dʌk] s canard m; (female) cane f; (motion) esquive f; ducks (trousers) pantalon m de coutil || tr (the head) baisser || intr se baisser; to duck out (coll) s'esquiver
ducking ['dʌkɪŋ] s plongeon m, bain m forcé
duckling ['dʌklɪŋ] s caneton m; (female) canette f
ducks/ and drakes/ s—to play at ducks and drakes faire des ricochets sur l'eau; (fig) jeter son argent par les fenêtres
duck/-toed/ adj qui marche en canard
duct [dʌkt] s conduit m, canal m
duct/less glands/ ['dʌktlɪs] spl glandes fpl closes
duct/work/ s tuyauterie f, canalisation f
dud [dʌd] s (slang) obus m qui a raté; (slang) raté m, navet m; duds (clothes) (coll) frusques fpl, nippes fpl
dude [d(j)ud] s poseur m, gommeux m
dude/ ranch/ s ranch m d'opérette
due [d(j)u] adj dû; (note) échéant; (bill) exigible; (train, bus, person) attendu; due to par suite de; in due form en bonne forme, en règle; to fall due venir à l'échéance; when is the train due? à quelle heure doit arriver le train? || s dû m; dues cotisation f; to pay one's dues cotiser || adv droit vers, e.g., due north droit vers le nord
due/ date/ s échéance f
duel ['d(j)u·əl] s duel m; to fight a duel se battre en duel || v (pret & pp dueled or duelled; ger dueling or duelling) intr se battre en duel
duelist or duellist ['d(j)u·əlɪst] s duelliste m
duenna [d(j)u'ɛnə] s duègne f
dues/-pay/ing adj cotisant
duet [d(j)u'ɛt] s duo m
duke [d(j)uk] s duc m
dukedom ['d(j)ukdəm] s duché m
dull [dʌl] adj (not sharp) émoussé; (color) terne; (sound; pain) sourd; (stupid) lourd; (business) lent; (boring) ennuyeux; (flat) fade, insipide; to become dull s'émousser; (said of senses) s'engourdir || tr (a knife) émousser; (color) ternir; (sound; pain) amortir; (spirits) hébéter, engourdir || intr s'émousser; se ternir; s'amortir; s'engourdir
dullard ['dʌlərd] s lourdaud m, hébété m
dullness ['dʌlnɪs] s (of knife) émoussement m; (e.g., of wits) lenteur f
duly ['d(j)uli] adv dûment, justement
dumb [dʌm] adj (lacking the power to speak) muet; (coll) gourde, imbécile;

completely dumb (coll) bouché à l'émeri; **to play dumb** (coll) feindre l'innocence

dumb′bell′ s (sports) haltère m; (slang) gourde f, imbécile mf

dumb′ crea′ture s animal m, brute f

dumb′wait′er s monte-plats m; (serving table) table f roulante

dumfound [′dʌm′faund] tr abasourdir, ébahir

dum·my [′dʌmi] adj faux, factice || s (pl -mies) (dress form) mannequin; (in card games) mort m; (figurehead, straw man) prête-nom m, homme m de paille; (skeleton copy of a book or magazine) maquette f; (object put in place of the real thing) simulacre m; (slang) bêta m, ballot m

dump [dʌmp] s (pile of rubbish) amas m, tas m; (place) dépotoir m; (mil) dépôt m; (slang) taudis m; **to be down in the dumps** (coll) avoir le cafard || tr décharger, déverser; (on rubbish pile) jeter au rebut; (com) vendre en faisant du dumping

dumping [′dʌmpɪŋ] s (com) dumping m

dumpling [′dʌmplɪŋ] s dumpling m, boulette f

dump′ cart′ s tombereau m

dump·y [′dʌmpi] adj (comp -ier; super -iest) (short and fat) courtaud, trapu; (shabby) râpé, minable

dun [dʌn] adj isabelle || s créancier m importun; (demand for payment) demande f pressante || v (pret & pp dunned; ger dunning) tr (for payment) importuner, poursuivre

dunce [dʌns] s âne m, cancre m

dunce′ cap′ s bonnet m d'âne

dune [d(j)un] s dune f

dung [dʌŋ] s fumier m

dungarees [‚dʌŋgə′riz] spl pantalon m de treillis, treillis m, bleu m

dungeon [′dʌndʒən] s cachot m, cul-de-basse-fosse m; (keep of castle) donjon m

dung′hill′ s tas m de fumier

dunk [dʌŋk] tr & intr tremper

du·o [′d(j)uo] s (pl -os) duo m

duode·num [‚d(j)u·ə′dinəm] s (pl -na [nə]) duodénum m

dupe [d(j)up] s dupe f, dindon m de la farce || tr duper

duplex [′d(j)upleks] adj double, duplex || s maison f double

du′plex house′ s maison f double

duplicate [′d(j)uplɪkɪt] adj double || s duplicata m, polycopie f; **en double, en duplicata** || [′d(j)uplɪ‚ket] tr faire le double de, reproduire; (on a machine) polycopier, ronéocopier

du′plicating machine′ s duplicateur m

duplici·ty [d(j)u′plɪsɪti] s (pl -ties) duplicité f

durable [′d(j)urəbəl] adj durable

duration [d(j)u′reʃən] s durée f

duress [′d(j)uˌres], [d(j)u′res] s contrainte f; emprisonnement m

during [′d(j)urɪŋ] prep pendant

dusk [dʌsk] s crépuscule m; **at dusk** entre chien et loup

dust [dʌst] s poussière f || tr (to free of dust) épousseter; (to sprinkle with dust) saupoudrer; **to dust off** épousseter

dust′ bowl′ s région f dénudée

dust′cloth′ s chiffon m à épousseter

dust′ cloud′ s nuage m de poussière

duster [′dʌstər] s (made of feathers) plumeau m; (made of cloth) chiffon m; (overgarment) cache-poussière m

dust′ jack′et s protège-livre m, couvre-livre m, liseuse f

dust′pan′ s pelle f à ordures

dust′ rag′ s chiffon m à épousseter

dust·y [′dʌsti] adj (comp -ier; super -iest) poussiéreux; (color) cendré

Dutch [dʌtʃ] adj hollandais, néerlandais; (slang) allemand || s (language) hollandais m, néerlandais m; (slang) allemand m; **in Dutch** (slang) en disgrâce; **the Dutch** les Hollandais mpl, les Néerlandais mpl; (slang) les Allemands mpl; **we will go Dutch** (coll) chacun paiera son écot

Dutch′man s (pl -men) Hollandais m, Néerlandais m; (slang) Allemand m

Dutch′ treat′ s—**to have a Dutch treat** (coll) faire suisse, payer son écot

dutiable [′d(j)utɪ·əbəl] adj soumis aux droits de douane

dutiful [′d(j)utɪfəl] adj respectueux, soumis, plein d'égards

du·ty [′d(j)uti] s (pl -ties) devoir m; **duties** fonctions fpl; (taxes, customs) droits mpl; **to be off duty** ne pas être de service, avoir quartier libre; **to be on duty** être de service, être de garde

du′ty-free′ adj exempt de droits

dwarf [dwɔrf] adj & s nain m || tr & intr rapetisser

dwell [dwel] v (pret & pp dwelled or dwelt [dwelt]) intr demeurer; **to dwell on** appuyer sur

dwelling [′dwelɪŋ] s demeure f, habitation f

dwell′ing house′ s maison f d'habitation

dwindle [′dwɪndəl] intr diminuer; **to dwindle away** s'affaiblir

dye [daɪ] s teinture f || v (pret & pp dyed; ger dyeing) tr teindre

dyed′-in-the-wool′ adj intransigeant

dyeing [′daɪ·ɪŋ] s teinture f

dyer [′daɪ·ər] s teinturier m

dying [′daɪ·ɪŋ] adj mourant, moribond

dynamic [daɪ′næmɪk], [dɪ′næmɪk] adj dynamique || **dynamics** s dynamique f

dynamite [′daɪnə‚maɪt] s dynamite f || tr dynamiter

dyna·mo [′daɪnə‚mo] s (pl -mos) dynamo f

dynast [′daɪnæst] s dynaste m

dynas·ty [′daɪnəsti] s (pl -ties) dynastie f

dysentery [′dɪsən‚teri] s dysenterie f

dyspepsia [dɪs′pɛpsɪ·ə], [dɪs′pɛp/ə] s dyspepsie f

E

E, e [i] *s* Vᵉ lettre de l'alphabet

each [it∫] *adj indef* chaque || *pron indef* chacun; **each other** nous, se; l'un l'autre; **to each other** l'un à l'autre || *adv* chacun; *(apiece)* pièce, la pièce

eager ['igər] *adj* ardent, empressé; **eager for** avide de; **to be eager to** brûler de, désirer ardemment

ea'ger bea'ver *s* bûcheur *m*, mouche *f* du coche

eagerness ['igərnɪs] *s* ardeur *f*, empressement *m*

eagle ['igəl] *s* aigle *m*

ea'gle-eyed' *adj* à l'œil d'aigle

ea'gle ray' *s* (ichth) aigle *m* de mer

eaglet ['iglɪt] *s* aiglon *m*

ear [ɪr] *s* oreille *f*; *(of corn or wheat)* épi *m*; **to box s.o.'s ears** frotter les oreilles à qn; **to prick up one's ears** dresser l'oreille; **to turn a deaf ear** faire la sourde oreille || *intr (said of grain)* épier

ear'ache' *s* douleur *m* d'oreille

ear'drop' *s* pendant *m* d'oreille

ear'drum' *s* tympan *m*

ear'flap' *s* lobe *m* de l'oreille; *(on a cap)* protège-oreilles *m*

earl [ʌrl] *s* comte *m*

earldom ['ʌrldəm] *s* comté *m*

ear-ly ['ʌrli] *(comp* -lier; *super* -liest) *adj* primitif; *(first in a series)* premier; *(occurring in the near future)* prochain; *(in the morning)* matinal; *(ahead of time)* en avance; **at an early age** dès l'enfance || *adv* de bonne heure, tôt; anciennement; **as early as** dès

ear'ly bird' *s* matinal *m*

ear'ly mass' *s* première messe *f*

ear'ly-morn'ing *adj* matinal

ear'ly ris'er *s* matinal *m*

ear'ly-ris'ing *adj* matineux, matinal

ear'mark' *s* marque *f*, cachet *m* || *tr (animals)* marquer à l'oreille; *(e.g., money)* spécialiser; **to earmark for** affecter à, assigner à

ear'muff' *s* couvre-oreille *m*

earn [ʌrn] *tr* gagner; *(to get as one's due)* mériter; *(interest)* rapporter

earnest ['ʌrnɪst] *adj* sérieux; **in earnest** sérieusement || *s* gage *m*; (com) arrhes *fpl*

earnings ['ʌrnɪŋz] *spl (wages)* gages *mpl*; *(profits)* profit *m*, bénéfices *mpl*

ear'phone' *s* écouteur *m*; **earphones** casque *m*, écouteurs

ear'ring' *s* boucle *f* d'oreille

ear'split'ting *adj* assourdissant

earth [ʌrθ] *s* terre *f*; **to come down to earth** retomber des nues; **where on earth . . . ?** où diable . . . ?

earthen ['ʌrθən] *adj* de terre, en terre

ear'then-ware' *s* faïence *f*

earthly ['ʌrθli] *adj* terrestre

earth'man' or **earth'man** *s (pl* **men'** or **men)** terrien *m*

earth'quake' *s* tremblement *m* de terre

earth'work' *s* terrassement *m*

earth'worm' *s* lombric *m*, ver *m* de terre

earth-y ['ʌrθi] *adj (comp* -ier; *super* -iest) terreux; *(worldly)* mondain; *(unrefined)* grossier, terre à terre

ear' trum'pet *s* cornet *m* acoustique

ease [iz] *s* aise *f*; *(readiness, naturalness)* désinvolture *f*; *(comfort, wellbeing)* bien-être *m*, tranquillité *f*; **at ease** tranquille; (mil) au repos; **to take one's ease** prendre ses aises; **with ease** facilement || *tr* faciliter; *(a burden)* alléger; *(e.g., one's mind)* calmer, apaiser; *(to let up on)* ralentir || *intr* se calmer, s'apaiser

easel ['izəl] *s* chevalet *m*

easement ['izmənt] *s* (law) servitude *f*

easily ['izli] *adv* facilement, aisément; *(certainly)* sans doute

easiness ['izɪnɪs] *s* facilité *f*; *(of manner)* désinvolture *f*, insouciance *f*

east [ist] *adj & s* est *m* || *adv* à l'est, vers l'est

Easter ['istər] *s* Pâques *m*; **Happy Easter!** Joyeuses Pâques!

East'er egg' *s* œuf *m* de Pâques

East'er Mon'day *s* lundi *m* de Pâques

eastern ['istərn] *adj* oriental, de l'est

East'ern Stand'ard Time' *s* l'heure *f* de l'Est

East'ern Town'ships *spl (in Canada)* Cantons *mpl* de l'Est

eastward ['istwərd] *adv* vers l'est

eas-y ['izi] *adj (comp* -ier; *super* -iest) facile; *(easygoing)* aisé, désinvolte || *adv* (coll) facilement; (coll) lentement; **to take it easy** (coll) en prendre à son aise

eas'y chair' *s* fauteuil *m*, bergère *f*

eas'y-go'ing *adj* insouciant, nonchalant, commode à vivre

eas'y mark' *s* jobard *m*

eas'y pay'ments *spl* facilités *fpl* de paiement

eat [it] *v (pret* **ate** [et]; *pp* **eaten** ['itən]) *tr* manger; **to eat away** ronger || *intr* manger

eatable ['itəbəl] *adj* comestible

eaves [ivz] *spl* avant-toits *mpl*

eaves'drop' *v (pret & pp* **-dropped;** *ger* **-dropping)** *intr* écouter à la porte

ebb [ɛb] *s* reflux *m*, baisse *f* || *intr* refluer, baisser; **to ebb and flow** monter et baisser, fluer et refluer

ebb' and flow' *s* flux et reflux *m*

ebb' tide' *s* marée *f* descendante, jusant *m*

ebon-y ['ɛbəni] *s (pl* -ies) ébène *f*; *(tree)* ébénier *m*

ebullient [ɪ'bʌljənt] *adj* bouillonnant; (fig) enthousiaste, exubérant

eccentric [ɛk'sɛntrɪk] *adj* excentrique || *s (odd person)* excentrique *mf*; *(device)* excentrique *m*

eccentrici·ty [ˌeksɛnˈtrɪsɪti] s (pl -ties) excentricité f

ecclesiastic [ɪˌklizɪˈæstɪk] adj & s ecclésiastique m

echelon [ˈeʃəˌlɑn] s échelon m || tr (mil) échelonner

ech·o [ˈeko] s (pl -oes) écho m || tr répéter || intr faire écho

eclectic [ɛkˈlɛktɪk] adj & s éclectique mf

eclipse [ɪˈklɪps] s éclipse f || tr éclipser

eclogue [ˈɛklɔg], [ˈɛklɑg] s églogue f

ecology [ɪˈkɑlədʒi] s écologie f

economic [ˌikəˈnɑmɪk], [ˌɛkəˈnɑmɪk] adj économique || economics s économique f

economical [ˌikəˈnɑmɪkəl], [ˌɛkə-ˈnɑmɪkəl] adj économe

economize [ɪˈkɑnəˌmaɪz] tr & intr économiser

econo·my [ɪˈkɑnəmi] s (pl -mies) économie f

ecsta·sy [ˈɛkstəsi] s (pl -sies) extase f

ecstatic [ɛkˈstætɪk] adj & s extatique mf

Ecuador [ˈɛkwəˌdɔr] s l'Équateur m

ecumenic(al) [ˌɛkjəˈmɛnɪk(əl)] adj œcuménique

eczema [ˈɛksɪmə], [ɛgˈzimə] s eczéma m

ed·dy [ˈɛdi] s (pl -dies) tourbillon m || v (pret & pp -died) intr tourbillonner

edelweiss [ˈedəlˌvaɪs] s edelweiss m, fleur f de neige

Eden [ˈidən] s (fig) éden m

edge [ɛdʒ] s bord m; (of a knife, sword, etc.) fil m, tranchant m; (of a field, forest, etc.) fil m, tranchant m; (of a strip of cloth) lisière f; (slang) avantage m; **on edge** de chant; (nervous) énervé, crispé; **to be on edge** avoir les nerfs à fleur de peau; **to have the edge on** (coll) enfoncer; **to set the teeth on edge** agacer les dents || tr border; (to sharpen) affiler, aiguiser || intr s'avancer de biais; **to edge away** s'écarter peu à peu; **to edge in** se glisser parmi or dans

edge'ways' adv de côté, de biais

edging [ˈɛdʒɪŋ] s bordure f

edg·y [ˈɛdʒi] adj (comp -ier; super -iest) nerveux crispé, irritable

edible [ˈɛdɪbəl] adj comestible

edict [ˈidɪkt] s édit m

edification [ˌɛdɪfɪˈkeʃən] s édification f

edifice [ˈɛdɪfɪs] s édifice m

edi·fy [ˈɛdɪˌfaɪ] v (pret & pp -fied) tr édifier

edifying [ˈɛdɪˌfaɪ·ɪŋ] adj édifiant

edit [ˈɛdɪt] tr préparer la publication de; (e.g., a newspaper) diriger, rédiger; (a text) éditer

edition [ɪˈdɪʃən] s édition f

editor [ˈɛdɪtər] s (of newspaper or magazine) rédacteur m; (of manuscript) éditeur m; (of feature or column) chroniqueur m, courriériste m

editorial [ˌɛdɪˈtɔrɪ·əl] adj & s éditorial m

edito'rial of'fice s rédaction f

edito'rial pol'icy s ligne f politique

edito'rial staff' s rédaction f

ed'itor in chief' s rédacteur m en chef

educate [ˈɛdʒuˌket] tr instruire, éduquer

educated adj cultivé, instruit

education [ˌɛdʒuˈkeʃən] s éducation f, instruction f

educational [ˌɛdʒuˈkeʃənəl] adj éducatif, éducateur

educator [ˈɛdʒuˌketər] s éducateur m

eel [il] s anguille f

ee·rie or **ee·ry** [ˈɪri] adj (comp -rier; super -riest) mystérieux, spectral

efface [ɪˈfes] tr effacer

effect [ɪˈfɛkt] s effet m; **in effect** en fait, effectivement; **to be in effect** être en vigueur; **to feel the effects of** se ressentir de; **to go into effect, to take effect** prendre effet; (said of law) entrer en vigueur || tr effectuer, mettre à exécution

effective [ɪˈfɛktɪv] adj efficace; (actually in effect) en vigueur; (striking) impressionnant; **to become effective** produire son effet; (to go into effect) entrer en vigueur

effectual [ɪˈfɛktʃʊ·əl] adj efficace

effectuate [ɪˈfɛktʃʊ·ˌet] tr effectuer

effeminacy [ɪˈfɛmɪnəsi] s efféminage f

effeminate [ɪˈfɛmɪnɪt] adj efféminé; **to become effeminate** s'efféminer

effervesce [ˌɛfərˈvɛs] intr être en effervescence

effervescent [ˌɛfərˈvɛsənt] adj effervescent

effete [ɪˈfit] adj stérile, épuisé

efficacious [ˌɛfɪˈkeʃəs] adj efficace

efficacy [ˈɛfɪkəsi] s efficacité f

efficien·cy [ɪˈfɪʃənsi] s (pl -cies) efficacité f; (of business) efficience f; (of machine) rendement m; (of person) compétence f

effi'ciency ex'pert s ingénieur m en organisation

efficient [ɪˈfɪʃənt] adj efficace; (machine) efficient, de bon rendement; (of person) efficient, compétent

effi·gy [ˈɛfɪdʒi] s (pl -gies) effigie f

effort [ˈɛfərt] s effort m

effronter·y [ɪˈfrʌntəri] s (pl -ies) effronterie f

effusion [ɪˈfjuʒən] s effusion f

effusive [ɪˈfjusɪv] adj démonstratif; **to be effusive in** se répandre en

e.g. abbr (Lat: exempli gratia for example) par ex., ex.

egg [ɛg] s œuf m || tr—**to egg on** pousser, inciter

egg'beat'er s fouet m, batteur m à œufs

egg'cup' s coquetier m

egg'head' s (slang) intellectuel m

eggnog [ˈɛgˌnɑg] s lait m de poule

egg'plant' s aubergine f

egg' poach'er s pocheuse f

egg'shell' s coquille f d'œuf

egg' white' s blanc m d'œuf

egoism [ˈɛgoˌɪzəm], [ˈigoˌɪzəm] s égoïsme m

egoist ['ego·ɪst], ['ɪgo·ɪst] s égoïste *mf*

egotism ['ego·ˌtɪzəm], ['ɪgo·ˌtɪzəm] s égotisme *m*

egotist ['egotɪst], ['ɪgotɪst] s égotiste *mf*

egregious [ɪ'gridʒəs] *adj* insigne, notoire

egress ['igres] s sortie *f*, issue *f*

egret ['igret] s aigrette *f*

Egypt ['idʒɪpt] s Égypte *f*; l'Égypte

Egyptian [ɪ'dʒɪpʃən] *adj* égyptien || s Égyptien *m*

ei'der·down/ ['aɪdər] s édredon *m*

ei'der duck/ s eider *m*

eight [et] *adj & pron* huit *m*; || s huit *m*; (*group of eight*) huitaine *f*; **about eight** une huitaine de; **eight o'clock** huit heures

eight'ball/ s—**behind the eightball** (coll) dans le pétrin

eighteen ['et'tin] *adj, pron, & s* dix-huit *m*

eighteenth ['et'tinθ] *adj & pron* dix-huitième (*masc, fem*); **the Eighteenth** dix-huit, e.g., **John the Eighteenth** Jean dix-huit || s dix-huitième *m*; **the eighteenth** (*in dates*) le dix-huit

eighth [etθ] *adj & pron* huitième (*masc, fem*); **the Eighth** huit, e.g., **John the Eighth** Jean huit || s huitième *m*; **the eighth** (*in dates*) le huit

eightieth ['eti·ɪθ] *adj & pron* quatre-vingtième (*masc, fem*) || s quatre-vingtième *m*

eigh'ty ['eti] *adj & pron* quatre-vingts || s (*pl* -ties) quatre-vingts *m*

eight'y-first/ *adj & pron* quatre-vingt-unième (*masc, fem*) || s quatre-vingt-unième *m*

eight'y-one/ *adj, pron, & s* quatre-vingt-un *m*

either ['iðər], ['aɪðər] *adj & pron indef* l'un ou l'autre; l'un et l'autre; **on either side** de chaque côté || *adv*—**not either** non plus || *conj*—**either . . . or** ou . . . ou, soit . . . soit, ou bien . . . ou bien

ejaculate [ɪ'dʒækjəˌlet] *tr & intr* crier; (physiol) éjaculer

eject [ɪ'dʒekt] *tr* éjecter; (*to evict*) expulser, chasser

ejection [ɪ'dʒekʃən] s éjection *f*; (*eviction*) expulsion *f*

ejec'tion seat/ s (aer) siège *m* éjectable

eke [ik] *tr*—**to eke out** gagner avec difficulté

elaborate [ɪ'læbərɪt] *adj* élaboré, soigné; (*ornate*) orné, travaillé; (*involved*) compliqué, recherché || [ɪ'læbəˌret] *tr* élaborer || *intr*—**to elaborate on** or **upon** donner des détails sur

elapse [ɪ'læps] *intr* s'écouler

elastic [ɪ'læstɪk] *adj & s* élastique *m*

elasticity [ɪ,læs'tɪsɪti], [ˌilæs'tɪsɪti] s élasticité *f*

elated [ɪ'letɪd] *adj* transporté, exalté

elation [ɪ'leʃən] s transport *m*, exultation *f*

elbow ['elbo] s coude *m*; **at one's elbow** à portée de la main; **to rub elbows with** coudoyer || *tr* coudoyer; **to elbow one's way** se frayer un chemin à coups de coude || *intr* jouer des coudes

el'bow grease/ s (coll) huile *f* de coude

el'bow·room/ s espace *m*; **to have elbowroom** avoir ses coudées franches

elder ['eldər] *adj* aîné, plus âgé || s aîné *m*; (*senior*) doyen *m*; (*bot*) sureau *m*; (eccl) ancien *m*

el'der·ber'ry s (*pl* -ries) sureau *m*; (*berry*) baie *f* de sureau

elderly ['eldərlɪ] *adj* vieux, âgé

eld'er states'man s vétéran *m* de la politique

eldest ['eldɪst] *adj* (l')aîné, (le) plus âgé

elect [ɪ'lekt] *adj* élu || s—**the elect** les élus *mpl* || *tr* élire

election [ɪ'lekʃən] s élection *f*

electioneer [ɪ,lekʃə'nɪr] *intr* faire la campagne électorale, solliciter des voix

elective [ɪ'lektɪv] *adj* électif; (*optional*) facultatif || s matière *f* à option

elec'toral col'lege [ɪ'lektərəl] s collège *m* électoral

electorate [ɪ'lektərɪt] s corps *m* électoral, électeurs *mpl*, votants *mpl*

electric(al) [ɪ'lektrɪk(əl)] *adj* électrique

elec'trical engineer/ s ingénieur *m* électricien

elec'trical engineer'ing s technique *f* électrique

elec'tric blan'ket s couverture *f* chauffante

elec'tric chair/ s chaise *f* électrique

elec'tric clothes/ ·dri'er s séchoir *m* électrique

elec'tric eel/ s gymnote *m*

elec'tric eye/ s cellule *f* photo-électrique

elec'tric fan/ s ventilateur *m* électrique

elec'tric heat'er s radiateur *m* électrique

electrician [ɪ,lek'trɪʃən], [ˌelek'trɪʃən] s électricien *m*

electricity [ɪ,lek'trɪsɪti], [ˌelek'trɪsɪti] s électricité *f*

elec'tric light/ s lampe *f* électrique

elec'tric me'ter s compteur *m* de courant

elec'tric mix'er s batteur *m* électrique

elec'tric per'colator s cafetière *f* électrique

elec'tric range/ s cuisinière *f* électrique

elec'tric shav'er s rasoir *m* électrique

elec'tric shock/ treat'ment s (med) électrochoc *m*

electri·fy [ɪ'lektrɪˌfaɪ] *v* (*pret & pp* -fied) *tr* (*to provide with electric power*) électrifier; (*to communicate electricity to; to thrill*) électriser

elec·tro [ɪ'lektro] s (*pl* -tros) électrotype *m*

electrocute [ɪ'lektrəˌkjut] *tr* électrocuter

electrode [ɪ'lektrod] s électrode *f*

electrolysis [ɪ,lek'trɑlɪsɪs], [ˌelek'trɑlɪsɪs] s électrolyse *f*

electrolyte [ɪ'lektrəˌlaɪt] s électrolyte *m*

electromagnet [ɪ,lektrə'mægnɪt] s électro-aimant *m*

electromagnetic [ɪ‚lektrəmægˈnetɪk] *adj* électromagnétique

electron [ɪˈlektrɑn] *s* électron *m*

elec′tron gun′ *s* canon *m* à électrons

electronic [ɪ‚lekˈtrɑnɪk], [‚elekˈtrɑn-ɪk] *adj* électronique || **electronics** *s* électronique *f*

elec′tron mi′croscope *s* microscope *m* électronique

electroplate [ɪˈlektrə‚plet] *tr* galvaniser

electrotype [ɪˈlektrə‚taɪp] *s* électrotype *m* || *tr* électrotyper

elegance [ˈelɪgəns] *s* élégance *f*

elegant [ˈelɪgənt] *adj* élégant

elegiac [‚elɪˈdʒaɪ‚æk] [ɪˈlidʒɪ‚æk] *adj* élégiaque

ele‧gy [ˈelɪdʒɪ] *s* (*pl* **-gies**) élégie *f*

element [ˈelɪmənt] *s* élément *m*

elementary [‚elɪˈmentəri] *adj* élémentaire

elephant [ˈelɪfənt] *s* éléphant *m*

elevate [ˈelɪ‚vet] *tr* élever

elevated *adj* élevé; (*style*) soutenu; (*train, railway, etc*) aérien

el′evated rail′way *s* métro *m* aérien

elevation [‚elɪˈveʃən] *s* élévation *f*

elevator [ˈelɪ‚vetər] *s* ascenseur *m*; (*for freight*) monte-charge *m*; (*for hoisting grain*) élévateur *m*; (*warehouse for storing grain*) silo *m* à céréales; (aer) gouvernail *m* d'altitude, gouvernail de profondeur

eleven [ɪˈlevən] *adj* & *pron* onze *m* || onze *m*; **eleven o'clock** onze heures

eleventh [ɪˈlevənθ] *adj* & *pron* onzième (*masc, fem*); **the Eleventh** (onze, *e.g.*, **John the Eleventh** Jean onze || onzième *m*; **the eleventh** (*in dates*) le onze

elev′enth hour′ *s* dernier moment *m*

elf [elf] *s* (*pl* **elves** [elvz]) elfe *m*

elicit [ɪˈlɪsɪt] *tr* (*e.g., a smile*) provoquer, faire sortir; (*e.g., help*) obtenir

elide [ɪˈlaɪd] *tr* élider

eligible [ˈelɪdʒɪbəl] *adj* éligible; (*e.g., bachelor*) sortable

eliminate [ɪˈlɪmɪ‚net] *tr* éliminer

elision [ɪˈlɪʒən] *s* élision *f*

elite [eˈlit] *s* élite *f*

elk [elk] *s* élan *m*

ellipse [ɪˈlɪps] *s* (geom) ellipse *f*

ellip‧sis [ɪˈlɪpsɪs] *s* (*pl* **-ses** [siz]) ellipse *f*; (*punctuation*) points *mpl* de suspension

elliptic(al) [ɪˈlɪptɪk(əl)] *adj* elliptique

elm [elm] *s* orme *m*

elongate [ɪˈlɔŋget], [ɪˈlɑŋget] *tr* allonger, prolonger

elope [ɪˈlop] *intr* s'enfuir avec un amant

elopement [ɪˈlopmənt] *s* enlèvement *m* consenti

eloquence [ˈeləkwəns] *s* éloquence *f*

eloquent [ˈeləkwənt] *adj* éloquent

else [els] *adj*—**nobody else** personne d'autre; **nothing else** rien d'autre; **somebody else** quelqu'un d'autre, un autre; **something else** autre chose; **what else** quoi encore; **who else** qui encore; **who's else** de qui d'autre || *adv* d'une autre façon, autrement; **how(ever) else** de toute autre façon;

nowhere else nulle part ailleurs; **or else** sinon, ou bien, sans quoi; **somewhere else** ailleurs, autre part; **when else** quand encore; **where else** où encore

else′where′ *adv* ailleurs, autre part

elucidate [ɪˈlusɪ‚det] *tr* élucider

elude [ɪˈlud] *tr* éluder, se soustraire à; (*a pursuer*) échapper à

elusive [ɪˈlusɪv] *adj* évasif, fuyant; (*baffling*) insaisissable, déconcertant

emaciated [ɪˈmeʃɪ‚etɪd] *adj* émacié; **to become emaciated** s'émacier

emanate [ˈemə‚net] *intr* émaner

emancipate [ɪˈmænsɪ‚pet] *tr* émanciper

embalm [emˈbɑm] *tr* embaumer

embalming [emˈbɑmɪŋ] *s* embaumement *m*

embankment [emˈbæŋkmənt] *s* (*of river*) digue *f*; (*of road*) remblai *m*

embargo [emˈbɑrgo] *s* (*pl* **-goes**) embargo *m* || *tr* mettre un embargo sur

embark [emˈbɑrk] *intr* s'embarquer

embarkation [‚embɑrˈkeʃən] *s* embarquement *m*

embarrass [emˈbærəs] *tr* faire honte à; (*to make difficult*) embarrasser

embarrassment [emˈbærəsmənt] *s* honte *f*; (*difficulty*) embarras *m*

embas‧sy [ˈembəsi] *s* (*pl* **-sies**) ambassade *f*

em‧bed [emˈbed] *v* (*pret* & *pp* **-bedded**; *ger* **-bedding**) *tr* encastrer

embellish [emˈbelɪʃ] *tr* embellir

embellishment [emˈbelɪʃmənt] *s* embellissement *m*

ember [ˈembər] *s* tison *m*; **embers** braise *f*

Em′ber days′ *spl* quatre-temps *mpl*

embezzle [emˈbezəl] *tr* détourner, s'approprier || *intr* commettre des détournements

embezzler [emˈbezlər] *s* détourneur *m* de fonds

embitter [emˈbɪtər] *tr* aigrir

emblazon [emˈblezən] *tr* embellir; exalter, célébrer

emblem [ˈembləm] *s* emblème *m*

emblematic(al) [‚embləˈmætɪk(əl)] *adj* emblématique

embodiment [emˈbɑdɪmənt] *s* personnification *f*, incarnation *f*

embod‧y [emˈbɑdi] *v* (*pret* & *pp* **-ied**) *tr* personnifier, incarner; (*to include*) incorporer

embolden [emˈboldən] *tr* enhardir

embolism [ˈembə‚lɪzəm] *s* embolie *f*

emboss [emˈbɔs], [emˈbɑs] *tr* (*to raise in relief*) graver en relief; (*metal*) bosseler; (*e.g., leather*) gaufrer, repousser

embouchure [‚ɑmbuˈʃʊr] *s* embouchure *f*; (mus) position *f* des lèvres

embrace [emˈbres] *s* étreinte *f*, embrassement *m* || *tr* étreindre, embrasser || *intr* s'étreindre, s'embrasser

embroider [emˈbrɔɪdər] *tr* broder

embroider‧y [emˈbrɔɪdəri] *s* (*pl* **-ies**) broderie *f*

embroil [emˈbrɔɪl] *tr* (*to throw into confusion*) embrouiller; (*to involve in contention*) brouiller

embroilment [em'brɔɪlmənt] *s* embrouillage *m*, brouillamini *m*, imbroglio *m*

embry·o ['embrɪ‚o] *s* (*pl* -os) embryon *m*

embryology [‚embrɪ'ɑlədʒɪ] *s* embryologie *f*

embryonic [‚embrɪ'ɑnɪk] *adj* embryonnaire

emend [ɪ'mend] *tr* corriger

emendation [‚imen'deʃən] *s* correction *f*

emerald ['emərəld] *s* émeraude *f*

emerge [ɪ'mʌrdʒ] *intr* émerger

emergence [ɪ'mʌrdʒəns] *s* émergence *f*

emergen·cy [ɪ'mʌrdʒənsɪ] *adj* urgent, d'urgence; (*exit*) de secours ‖ *s* (*pl* -cies) cas *m* urgent

emer'gency brake' *s* frein *m* de secours

emer'gency ex'it *s* sortie *f* de secours

emer'gency land'ing *s* atterrissage *m* forcé

emer'gency opera'tion *s* (med) opération *f* à chaud

emer'gency ra'tions *spl* vivres *mpl* de réserve

emer'gency ward' *s* salle *f* d'urgence

emeritus [ɪ'merɪtəs] *adj* honoraire, d'honneur

emersion [ɪ'mʌrʒən], [ɪ'mʌrʃən] *s* émersion *f*

emery ['emərɪ] *s* émeri *m*

em'ery cloth' *s* toile *f* d'émeri

em'ery wheel' *s* meule *f* en émeri

emetic [ɪ'metɪk] *adj* & *s* émétique *m*

emigrant ['emɪgrənt] *adj* & *s* émigrant *m*

emigrate ['emɪ‚gret] *intr* émigrer

eminence ['emɪnəns] *s* éminence *f*

eminent ['emɪnənt] *adj* éminent; **most eminent** (eccl) éminentissime

emissar·y ['emɪ‚serɪ] *s* (*pl* -ies) émissaire *m*

emit [ɪ'mɪt] *v* (*pret & pp* emitted; *ger* emitting) *tr* émettre; (*a gas, an odor, etc.*) exhaler

emolument [ɪ'mɑljəmənt] *s* émoluments *mpl*

emotion [ɪ'moʃən] *s* émotion *f*

emotional [ɪ'moʃənəl] *adj* émotif, émotionnable

emperor ['empərər] *s* empereur *m*

empha·sis ['emfə‚sɪs] *s* (*pl* -ses [‚siz]) accentuation *f*, mise *f* en relief; énergie *f*, force *f*; (*on word or phrase*) accent *m* d'insistance; **to place emphasis on** insister vivement sur; **with emphasis on** en insistant particulièrement sur

emphasize ['emfə‚saɪz] *tr* accentuer, mettre en relief; appuyer sur, souligner

emphatic [em'fætɪk] *adj* accentué, énergique

emphysema [‚emfɪ'simə] *s* emphysème *m*

empire ['empaɪr] *s* empire *m*

empiric(al) [em'pɪrɪk(əl)] *adj* empirique

empiricist [em'pɪrɪsɪst] *s* empirique *m*

emplacement [em'plesmənt] *s* emplacement *m*

employ [em'plɔɪ] *s* service *m* ‖ *tr* employer

employee [em'plɔɪ·i], [‚emplɔɪ'i] *s* employé *m*

employer [em'plɔɪ·ər] *s* employeur *m*, patron *m*, chef *m*

employment [em'plɔɪmənt] *s* emploi *m*

employ'ment a'gency *s* bureau *m* de placement

empower [em'pau·ər] *tr* autoriser

empress ['emprɪs] *s* impératrice *f*

emptiness ['emptɪnɪs] *s* vide *m*

emp·ty ['emptɪ] *adj* (*comp* -tier; *super* -tiest) vide; (*hollow*) creux, vain; (coll) affamé ‖ *v* (*pret & pp* -tied) *tr* vider ‖ *intr* se vider; (*said of river*) se jeter; (*said of auditorium*) se dégarnir

emp'ty-hand'ed *adj* & *adv* les mains vides

emp'ty-head'ed *adj* écervelé

empye·ma [‚empɪ'imə] *s* (*pl* -mata [mətə]) empyème *m*

empyrean [‚empɪ'ri·ən] *s* empyrée *m*

emu ['imju] *s* (zool) émeu *m*

emulate ['emjə‚let] *tr* chercher à égaler, imiter ‖ *intr* rivaliser

emulator ['emjə‚letər] *s* émule *mf*

emulsi·fy [ɪ'mʌlsɪ‚faɪ] *v* (*pret & pp* -fied) *tr* émulsionner

emulsion [ɪ'mʌlʃən] *s* émulsion *f*

enable [en'ebəl] *tr*—**to enable to** rendre capable de, mettre à même de

enact [en'ækt] *tr* (*to decree*) décréter, arrêter; (theat) représenter

enactment [en'æktmənt] *s* loi *f*; (*establishing*) établissement *m*; (govt) promulgation *f*; (law) décret *m*; (theat) représentation *f*

enam·el [ɪ'næməl] *s* émail *m* ‖ *v* (*pret & pp* -eled *or* -elled; *ger* -eling *or* -elling) *tr* émailler

enameling [ɪ'næməlɪŋ] *s* émaillage *m*

enam'el·ware' *s* ustensiles *mpl* en fer émaillé

enamor [en'æmər] *tr* rendre amoureux; **to become enamored with** s'énamourer de

encamp [en'kæmp] *tr* & *intr* camper

encampment [en'kæmpmənt] *s* campement *m*

encase [en'kes] *tr* mettre en caisse; enfermer, envelopper

encephalitis [en‚sefə'laɪtɪs] *s* encéphalite *f*

enchain [en'tʃen] *tr* enchaîner

enchant [en'tʃænt], [en'tʃɑnt] *tr* enchanter

enchanting [en'tʃæntɪŋ], [en'tʃɑntɪŋ] *adj* charmant, ravissant; (*casting a spell*) enchanteur

enchantment [en'tʃæntmənt], [en'tʃɑntmənt] *s* enchantement *m*

enchantress [en'tʃæntrɪs], [en'tʃɑntrɪs] *s* enchanteresse *f*

encircle [en'sʌrkəl] *tr* encercler, cerner; (*a word*) entourer d'un cercle

enclitic [en'klɪtɪk] *adj* & *s* enclitique *m*

enclose [en'kloz] *tr* enclore, entourer; (*in a letter*) inclure, joindre

enclosed *adj* (*in a letter*) ci-joint, ci-inclus

enclosure [enˈkloʒər] *s* clôture *f*, enceinte *f*, enclos *m*; (*e.g., in a letter*) pièce *f* jointe, pièce annexée

encomi·um [enˈkomɪ·əm] *s* (*pl* -ums or -a* [ə]) panégyrique *m*, éloge *m*

encompass [enˈkʌmpəs] *tr* entourer, renfermer

encore [ˈɑnkor] *s* rappel *m*, bis *m* ‖ *tr* bisser ‖ *interj* bis!

encounter [enˈkaʊntər] *s* rencontre *f* ‖ *tr* rencontrer ‖ *intr* se rencontrer, combattre

encourage [enˈkʌrɪdʒ] *tr* encourager

encouragement [enˈkʌrɪdʒmənt] *s* encouragement *m*

encroach [enˈkrotʃ] *intr*—**to encroach on** or **upon** empiéter sur; abuser de

encumber [enˈkʌmbər] *tr* encombrer, embarrasser; (*with debts*) grever

encumbrance [enˈkʌmbrəns] *s* encombrement *m*, embarras *m*; (*law*) charge *f*

encyclical [enˈsɪklɪkəl], [enˈsaɪklɪkəl] *adj & s* encyclique *f*

encyclopedia [en‚saɪkləˈpidɪ·ə] *s* encyclopédie *f*

encyclopedic [en‚saɪkləˈpidɪk] *adj* encyclopédique

end [end] *s* (*in time*) fin *f*; (*in space; small piece*) bout *m*; (*purpose*) but *m*; (*end of set period of time*) terme *m*; **at loose ends** en pagaille; **at the end, in the end** à la fin; **to be at the end of one's rope** être au bout de son rouleau; **to bring to an end** mettre fin à; **to come to an end** prendre fin; **to make both ends meet** joindre les deux bouts; **to stand on end** (*said of hair*) se dresser; **to this end** à cet effet ‖ *tr* achever, terminer ‖ *intr* s'achever, se terminer; **to end up by** finir par

endanger [enˈdendʒər] *tr* mettre en danger

endear [enˈdɪr] *tr* faire aimer; **to endear oneself to** se faire aimer de

endeavor [enˈdevər] *s* effort *m*, tentative *f* ‖ *intr*—**to endeavor to** s'efforcer de, tâcher de

endemic [enˈdemɪk] *adj* endémique

ending [ˈendɪŋ] *s* fin *f*, terminaison *f*; (*gram*) désinence *f*

endive [ˈendaɪv] *s* (*blanched type*) endive *f*; (*Cichorium endivia*) chicorée *f* frisée

endless [ˈendlɪs] *adj* sans fin

end′most′ *adj* extrême

endocrine [ˈendo‚kraɪn], [ˈendokrɪn] *adj* endocrine

endorse [enˈdors] *tr* endosser; (*a candidate*) appuyer; (*a plan*) souscrire à

endorsement [enˈdorsmənt] *s* endos *m*, endossement *m*; (*approval*) appui *m*, approbation *f*

endorser [enˈdorsər] *s* endosseur *m*

endow [enˈdaʊ] *tr* doter, fonder

endowment [enˈdaʊmənt] *s* dotation *f*, fondation *f*; (*talent*) don *m*

endow′ment fund′ *s* caisse *f* de dotation

end′ pa′per *s* pages *fpl* de garde

endurance [enˈd(j)ʊrəns] *s* endurance *f*

endur′ance test′ *s* épreuve *f*. d'endurance

endure [enˈd(j)ʊr] *tr* endurer ‖ *intr* durer

enduring [enˈd(j)ʊrɪŋ] *adj* durable

enema [ˈenəmə] *s* lavement *m*

ene·my [ˈenəmi] *adj* ennemi ‖ *s* (*pl* -mies) ennemi *m*

en′emy al′ien *s* étranger *m* ennemi

energetic [‚enərˈdʒetɪk] *adj* énergique

ener·gy [ˈenərdʒi] *s* (*pl* -gies) énergie *f*

en′ergy bal′ance *s* (nucl) bilan *m* énergétique

enervate [ˈenər‚vet] *tr* énerver

enfeeble [enˈfibəl] *tr* affaiblir

enfold [enˈfold] *tr* envelopper, enrouler; (*to embrace*) embrasser

enforce [enˈfors] *tr* (*a law*) faire exécuter, mettre en vigueur; (*one's rights, one's point of view*) faire valoir, appuyer; (*e.g., obedience*) imposer

enforcement [enˈforsmənt] *s* contrainte *f*; (*of a law*) exécution *f*, mise *f* en vigueur

enfranchise [enˈfræntʃaɪz] *tr* affranchir; donner le droit de vote à

engage [enˈgedʒ] *tr* engager; (*to hire*) engager, embaucher; (*to reserve*) retenir, réserver, louer; (*s.o.'s attention*) fixer, attirer; (*the clutch*) embrayer; (*toothed wheels*) engrener; **to be engaged in** s'occuper de; **to be engaged to be married** être fiancé; **to engage s.o. in conversation** entamer une conversation avec qn ‖ *intr* s'engager; (*mach*) engrener; **to engage in** s'embarquer dans, entrer en or dans

engaged *adj* (*to be married*) fiancé; (*busy*) occupé, pris; (*mach*) en prise; (*mil*) aux prises, aux mains

engagement [enˈgedʒmənt] *s* engagement *m*; (*betrothal*) fiançailles *fpl*; (*appointment*) rendez-vous *m*; (*mach*) embrayage *m*, engrenage *m*; (*mil*) engagement, combat *m*

engage′ment ring′ *s* bague *f* or anneau *m* de fiançailles

engaging [enˈgedʒɪŋ] *adj* engageant, attirant

engender [enˈdʒendər] *tr* engendrer

engine [ˈendʒɪn] *s* machine *f*; (*of automobile*) moteur *m*

engineer [‚endʒəˈnɪr] *s* ingénieur *m*; (*engine driver*) mécanicien *m* ‖ *tr* diriger or construire en qualité d'ingénieur; (coll) manigancer, machiner

engineering [‚endʒəˈnɪrɪŋ] *s* génie *m*

en′gine house′ *s* dépôt *m* de pompes à incendie

en′gine·man′ or **en′gine·man** *s* (*pl* -men′ or -men) mécanicien *m*

en′gine room′ *s* chambre *f* des machines

en′gine-room tel′egraph *s* (naut) transmetteur *m* d'ordres

en′gine trou′ble *s* panne *f* de moteur

England [ˈɪŋglənd] *s* Angleterre *f*; l'Angleterre

English [ˈɪŋglɪʃ] *adj* anglais ‖ *s* (*language*) anglais *m*; (*billiards*) effet *m*; **the English** les Anglais

Eng′lish Chan′nel *s* Manche *f*

Eng′lish dai′sy s marguerite f des champs
Eng′lish horn′ s cor m anglais
Eng′lish-man s (pl -men) Anglais m
Eng′lish-speak′ing adj anglophone, d'expression anglaise; (country) de langue anglaise
Eng′lish-wom′an s (pl -wom′en) Anglaise f
engraft [ɛnˈɡræft], [ɛnˈɡrɑft] tr greffer; (fig) implanter
engrave [ɛnˈɡrev] tr graver
engraver [ɛnˈɡrevər] s graveur m
engraving [ɛnˈɡrevɪŋ] s gravure f
engross [ɛnˈɡros] tr absorber, occuper; (a document) grossoyer
engrossing [ɛnˈɡrosɪŋ] adj absorbant
engulf [ɛnˈɡʌlf] tr engouffrer, engloutir
enhance [ɛnˈhæns], [ɛnˈhɑns] tr rehausser, relever
enhancement [ɛnˈhænsmənt], [ɛnˈhɑnsmənt] s rehaussement m
enigma [ɪˈnɪɡmə] s énigme f
enigmatic(al) [ˌɪnɪɡˈmætɪk(əl)] adj énigmatique
enjoin [ɛnˈdʒɔɪn] tr enjoindre; (to forbid) interdire
enjoy [ɛnˈdʒɔɪ] tr jouir de; **to enjoy +** ger prendre plaisir à + inf; **to enjoy oneself** s'amuser, se divertir
enjoyable [ɛnˈdʒɔɪ-əbəl] adj agréable, plaisant; (show, party, etc.) divertissant
enjoyment [ɛnˈdʒɔɪmənt] s (pleasure) plaisir m; (pleasurable use) jouissance f
enkindle [ɛnˈkɪndəl] tr allumer
enlarge [ɛnˈlɑrdʒ] tr agrandir, élargir; (phot) agrandir ‖ intr s'agrandir, s'élargir; **to enlarge on** or **upon** discourir longuement sur, amplifier
enlargement [ɛnˈlɑrdʒmənt] s agrandissement m
enlighten [ɛnˈlaɪtən] tr éclairer
enlightenment [ɛnˈlaɪtənmənt] s éclaircissements mpl; **the Enlightenment** le siècle des lumières
enlist [ɛnˈlɪst] tr enrôler ‖ intr s'enrôler, s'engager
enlist′ed man′ s homme m de troupe
enlistment [ɛnˈlɪstmənt] s enrôlement m, engagement m
enliven [ɛnˈlaɪvən] tr animer, égayer
enmesh [ɛnˈmɛʃ] tr prendre dans les rets; (e.g., in an evil design) empêtrer; (mach) engrener
enmi·ty [ˈɛnmɪti] s (pl -ties) inimitié f
ennoble [ɛnˈnobəl] tr ennoblir; (to confer a title of nobility upon) anoblir
ennui [ˈɑnwi] s ennui m
enormous [ɪˈnɔrməs] adj énorme
enormously [ɪˈnɔrməsli] adv énormément
enough [ɪˈnʌf] adj, s, & adv assez; **more than enough** plus qu'il n'en faut; **that's enough!** en voilà assez!; **to be intelligent enough** être assez intelligent; **to have enough to live on** avoir de quoi vivre ‖ interj assez!, ça suffit!
enounce [ɪˈnaʊns] tr énoncer

enrage [ɛnˈredʒ] tr faire enrager, rendre furieux; **to be enraged** enrager
enrapture [ɛnˈræptʃər] tr ravir, transporter
enrich [ɛnˈrɪtʃ] tr enrichir
enrichment [ɛnˈrɪtʃmənt] s enrichissement m
enroll [ɛnˈrol] tr enrôler; (a student) inscrire; (to wrap up) enrouler ‖ intr s'enrôler; (said of student) prendre ses inscriptions, se faire inscrire
enrollment [ɛnˈrolmənt] s enrôlement m; (of a student) inscription f; (wrapping up) enroulement m
ensconce [ɛnˈskɑns] tr cacher; **to ensconce oneself** s'installer
ensemble [ɑnˈsɑmbəl] s ensemble m
ensign [ˈɛnsaɪn] s enseigne f ‖ [ˈɛnsən], [ˈɛnsaɪn] s (nav) enseigne m de deuxième classe
ensilage [ˈɛnsɪlɪdʒ] s fourrage m d'un silo américain ‖ tr ensiler
enslave [ɛnˈslev] tr asservir, réduire en esclavage
enslavement [ɛnˈslevmənt] s asservissement m
ensnare [ɛnˈsnɛr] tr prendre au piège, attraper
ensue [ɛnˈs(j)u] intr s'ensuivre, résulter
ensuing [ɛnˈs(j)u-ɪŋ] adj suivant
ensure [ɛnˈʃʊr] tr assurer, garantir
entail [ɛnˈtel] tr occasionner, entraîner
entangle [ɛnˈtæŋɡəl] tr embrouiller
entanglement [ɛnˈtæŋɡəlmənt] s embrouillement m, embarras m
enter [ˈɛntər] tr (a room, a house, etc.) entrer dans; (a school, the army, etc.) entrer à; (e.g., a period of convalescence) entrer en; (a highway, a public square, etc.) déboucher sur; (e.g., a club) devenir membre de; (a request) enregistrer, consigner par écrit; (a student, a contestant, etc.) admettre, faire inscrire; (in the customhouse) déclarer; (to make a record of) inscrire, porter; **to enter one's name for** se faire inscrire à or pour ‖ intr entrer; (theat) entrer en scène; **to enter into** entrer à, dans, or en; (to be an ingredient of) entrer pour; **to enter on** or **upon** entreprendre, débuter dans
enterprise [ˈɛntərˌpraɪz] s (undertaking) entreprise f; (spirit, push) esprit m d'entreprise, allant m, entrain m
enterprising [ˈɛntərˌpraɪzɪŋ] adj entreprenant
entertain [ˌɛntərˈten] tr (to distract) amuser, divertir; (to show hospitality to) recevoir; (at a meal) régaler; (a hope) entretenir, nourrir; (an idea) concevoir ‖ intr recevoir
entertainer [ˌɛntərˈtenər] s (host) hôte m, amphitryon m; amuseur m; (comedian) comique mf
entertaining [ˌɛntərˈtenɪŋ] adj amusant, divertissant
entertainment [ˌɛntərˈtenmənt] s (distraction) amusement m, divertissement m; (show) spectacle m; (as a guest) accueil m, hospitalité f

en'tertain'ment tax' s taxe f sur les spectacles

enthrall [enˈθrɔl] tr (to charm) captiver, charmer; (to enslave) asservir, rendre esclave

enthrone [enˈθron] tr introniser

enthuse [enˈθ(j)uz] tr (coll) enthousiasmer ǁ intr (coll) s'enthousiasmer

enthusiasm [enˈθ(j)uzɪ‚æzəm] s enthousiasme m

enthusiast [enˈθ(j)uzɪ‚æst] s enthousiaste mf; (camera fiend, sports fan, etc.) fanatique mf, enragé m

enthusiastic [en‚θ(j)uzɪˈæstɪk] adj enthousiaste; (for sports, music, a hobby) fanatique, enragé

entice [enˈtaɪs] tr attirer, séduire; (to evil) tenter, chercher à séduire

enticement [enˈtaɪsmənt] s attrait m, appât m; tentation f, séduction f

entire [enˈtaɪr] adj entier

entirely [enˈtaɪrli] adv entièrement, en entier; (absolutely) tout à fait, absolument

entire·ty [enˈtaɪrti] s (pl -ties) totalité f, entier m; **in its entirety** dans sa totalité

entitle [enˈtaɪtəl] tr (to name) intituler; (to qualify) donner le droit à; **to be entitled to** avoir droit à

enti·ty [ˈentɪti] s (pl -ties) entité f

entomb [enˈtum] tr ensevelir

entombment [enˈtummənt] s ensevelissement m

entomology [‚entəˈmɑlədʒi] s entomologie f

entourage [‚ɑntuˈrɑʒ] s entourage m

entrails [ˈentrelz], [ˈentrəlz] spl entrailles fpl

entrain [enˈtren] tr faire prendre le train, embarquer; (to carry along) entraîner ǁ intr embarquer, s'embarquer

entrance [ˈentrəns] s entrée f; (theat) entrée en scène; **entrance to . . .** (public sign) accès à . . . ǁ [enˈtræns], [enˈtrɑns] tr enchanter, ensorceler; **to be entranced** s'extasier

en'trance examina'tion s examen m d'entrée

en'trance fee' s droits mpl d'entrée

entrancing [enˈtrænsɪŋ], [enˈtrɑnsɪŋ] adj enchanteur, ensorceleur

entrant [ˈentrənt] s inscrit m; (in a competition) concurrent m, participant m

en·trap [enˈtræp] v (pret & pp -trapped; ger -trapping) tr attraper

entreat [enˈtrit] tr supplier, prier, conjurer

entreat·y [enˈtriti] s (pl -ies) supplication f, prière f

entree [ˈɑntre] s (entrance; course preceding the roast) entrée f; (main dish) plat m de résistance

entrench [enˈtrentʃ] tr retrancher; **to be entrenched** se retrancher ǁ intr— **to entrench on** or **upon** empiéter sur

entrust [enˈtrʌst] tr—**to entrust s.o. with s.th.,** or **to entrust s.th. to s.o.** confier q.ch. à qn

en·try [ˈentri] s (pl -tries) entrée f; (in a dictionary) article m, entrée; (on a register) inscription f; (in a competition) concurrent m, participant m; (thing entered for judging in a competition) objet m exposé

en'try blank' s feuille f d'inscription

entwine [enˈtwaɪn] tr entrelacer, enlacer ǁ intr s'entrelacer, s'enlacer

enumerate [ɪˈn(j)umə‚ret] tr énumérer

enunciate [ɪˈnʌnsɪ‚et], [ɪˈnʌn/ɪ‚et] tr énoncer, déclarer; (to articulate) articuler, prononcer

envelop [enˈveləp] tr envelopper

envelope [ˈenvə‚lop], [ˈɑnvə‚lop] s enveloppe f; **in an envelope** sous enveloppe, sous pli

envenom [enˈvenəm] tr envenimer, empoisonner

enviable [ˈenvɪ·əbəl] adj enviable, digne d'envie

envious [ˈenvɪ·əs] adj envieux

environment [enˈvaɪrənmənt] s environnement m, milieu m

environs [enˈvaɪrənz] spl environs mpl

envisage [enˈvɪzɪdʒ] tr envisager

envoi [ˈenvɔɪ] s envoi m

envoy [ˈenvɔɪ] s envoyé m, émissaire m; (of poem) envoi m

en·vy [ˈenvi] s (pl -vies) envie f ǁ v (pret & pp -vied) tr envier

enzyme [ˈenzaɪm], [ˈenzɪm] s enzyme m & f

epaulet [ˈepə‚let] s épaulette f

epergne [ɪˈpʌrn], [eˈpern] s surtout m

ephemeral [ɪˈfemərəl] adj éphémère

epic [ˈepɪk] adj épique ǁ s épopée f

epicure [ˈepɪ‚kjur] s gourmet m, gastronome m

epidemic [‚epɪˈdemɪk] adj épidémique ǁ s épidémie f

epidemiology [‚epɪ‚dimɪˈɑlədʒi] s épidémiologie f

epidermis [‚epɪˈdʌrmɪs] s épiderme m

epiglottis [‚epɪˈglɑtɪs] s épiglotte f

epigram [ˈepɪ‚græm] s épigramme f

epilepsy [ˈepɪ‚lepsi] s épilepsie f

epileptic [‚epɪˈleptɪk] adj & s épileptique mf

epilogue [ˈepɪ‚lɔg], [ˈepɪ‚lɑg] s épilogue m

episcopal [ɪˈpɪskəpəl] adj épiscopal

Episcopalian [ɪ‚pɪskəˈpeli·ən] adj épiscopal ǁ s épiscopal m

episode [ˈepɪ‚sod] s épisode m

episodic [‚epɪˈsɑdɪk] adj épisodique

epistle [ɪˈpɪsəl] s épître f

epitaph [ˈepɪ‚tæf] s épitaphe f

epithet [ˈepɪ‚θet] s épithète f

epitome [ɪˈpɪtəmi] s (abridgment) épitomé m; (representative of a class) modèle m, personnification f

epitomize [ɪˈpɪtə‚maɪz] tr abréger; personnifier

epoch [ˈepək], [ˈipɑk] s époque f

epochal [ˈepəkəl] adj mémorable

ep'och-mak'ing adj qui fait époque

Ep'som salts' [ˈepsəm] spl epsomite f, sels mpl d'Epsom

equable [ˈekwəbəl], [ˈikwəbəl] adj uniforme, égal; tranquille

equal [ˈikwəl] adj égal; **to be equal to** égaler, valoir; (e.g., the occasion)

être à la hauteur de; **to be equal to** +
ger être de force à + *inf*, être à même
de + *inf*; **to get equal with** (coll) se
venger de || *s* égal *m*, pareil *m* || *v*
(*pret & pp* equaled *or* equalled; *ger*
equaling *or* equalling) *tr* égaler

equali·ty [ɪˈkwɑlɪti] *s* (*pl* **-ties**) égalité *f*

equalize [ˈikwəˌlaɪz] *tr* égaliser

equally [ˈikwəli] *adv* également

equanimity [ˌikwəˈnɪmɪti] *s* équanimité *f*, égalité *f* d'âme

equate [ɪˈkwet] *tr* égaliser, mettre en
équation

equation [ɪˈkweʒən], [ɪˈkweʃən] *s*
équation *f*

equator [ɪˈkwetər] *s* équateur *m*

equatorial [ˌikwəˈtori·əl] *adj* équato-
rial

equestrian [ɪˈkwɛstri·ən] *adj* équestre
|| *s* cavalier *m*, écuyer *m*

equilateral [ˌikwɪˈlætərəl] *adj* équi-
latéral

equilibrium [ˌikwɪˈlɪbri·əm] *s* équilibre *m*

equinoctial [ˌikwɪˈnɑk/əl] *adj* équi-
noxial

equinox [ˈikwɪˌnɑks] *s* équinoxe *m*

equip [ɪˈkwɪp] *v* (*pret & pp* equipped;
ger equipping) *tr* équiper, outiller; **to
equip with** munir de

equipment [ɪˈkwɪpmənt] *s* équipement
m, matériel *m*

equipoise [ˈikwɪˌpɔɪz], [ˈɛkwɪˌpɔɪz] *s*
équilibre *m* || *tr* équilibrer

equitable [ˈɛkwɪtəbəl] *adj* équitable

equi·ty [ˈɛkwɪti] *s* (*pl* **-ties**) équité *f*;
(com) part *f* résiduaire

equivalent [ɪˈkwɪvələnt] *adj & s* équivalent *m*

equivocal [ɪˈkwɪvəkəl] *adj* équivoque

equivocate [ɪˈkwɪvəˌket] *intr* équivoquer

equivocation [ɪˌkwɪvəˈke/ən] *s* ter-
giversation *f*, équivoque *f*

era [ˈirə], [ˈɪrə] *s* ère *f*, époque *f*

eradicate [ɪˈrædɪˌket] *tr* déraciner,
extirper

erase [ɪˈres] *tr* effacer, biffer

eraser [ɪˈresər] *s* gomme *f* à effacer;
brosse *f*

erasure [ɪˈreʃər] *s* effacement *m*, rature *f*

ere [ɛr] *prép* (poetic) avant || *conj*
(poetic) avant que

erect [ɪˈrɛkt] *adj* droit, debout || *tr* (*to
set in an upright position*) dresser,
élever; (*a building*) ériger, édifier;
(*a machine*) monter

erection [ɪˈrɛk/ən] *s* érection *f*

erg [ʌrg] *s* erg *m*

ermine [ˈʌrmɪn] *s* hermine *f*

erode [ɪˈrod] *tr* éroder

erosion [ɪˈroʒən] *s* érosion *f*

erotic [ɪˈrɑtɪk] *adj* érotique

err [ʌr] *intr* se tromper, faire erreur,
errer; (*to do wrong*) s'égarer, pécher

errand [ˈɛrənd] *s* commission *f*, course
f; **to go on** *or* **to run an errand** faire
une course

er'rand boy' *s* coursier *m*, garçon de
courses

erratic [ɪˈrætɪk] *adj* variable; capricieux, excentrique

erroneous [ɪˈroni·əs] *adj* erroné

error [ˈɛrər] *s* erreur *f*

erudite [ˈɛr(j)uˌdaɪt] *adj* érudit

erudition [ˌɛr(j)uˈdɪ/ən] *s* érudition *f*

erupt [ɪˈrʌpt] *intr* faire éruption

eruption [ɪˈrʌp/ən] *s* éruption *f*

escalate [ˈɛskəˌlet] *tr* escalader

escalation [ˌɛskəˈle/ən] *s* escalade *f*

escalator [ˈɛskəˌletər] *s* escalator *m*,
escalier *m* mécanique *or* roulant

escallop [ɛsˈkæləp] *s* coquille *f* Saint-
Jacques, peigne *m*, pétoncle *m*;
(culin) coquille au gratin || *tr* (*the
edges*) denteler, découper; (culin)
gratiner et cuire au four et à la crème

escapade [ˌɛskəˈped] *s* fredaine *f*,
frasque *f*; (*getting away*) escapade *f*

escape [ɛsˈkep] *s* (*getaway*) évasion *f*,
fuite *f*; (*from responsibilities, duties,
etc.*) évasion, escapade *f*; (*of gas,
liquid, etc.*) échappement *m*, fuite;
(*of a clock*) échappement; **to have a
narrow escape** l'échapper belle; **to
make one's escape** se sauver, s'échap-
per || *tr* échapper à, éviter || *intr*
échapper, s'échapper, s'évader; **to
escape from** échapper à

escape' clause' *s* échappatoire *f*

escapee [ˌɛskəˈpi] *s* évadé *m*, échappé
m

escape' hatch' *s* (aer) sas *m* d'évacuation

escape' lit'erature *s* littérature *f* d'évasion

escapement [ɛsˈkepmənt] *s* issue *f*, débouché *m*; (mach) échappement *m*

escape' wheel' *s* roue *f* de rencontre

escarole [ˈɛskəˌrol] *s* scarole *f*

escarpment [ɛsˈkɑrpmənt] *s* escarpement *m*

eschew [ɛsˈt/u] *tr* éviter, s'abstenir de

escort [ˈɛskɔrt] *s* escorte *f*; (*gentleman
escort*) cavalier *m* || [ɛsˈkɔrt] *tr*
escorter

escutcheon [ɛsˈkʌt/ən] *s* écusson *m*

Es·ki·mo [ˈɛskɪˌmo] *adj* eskimo, esqui-
mau || *s* (*pl* **-mos** *or* **-mo**) (*language;
dog*) esquimau *m*; (*person*) Eskimo
m, Esquimau *m*

Es'kimo wom'an *s* Esquimaude *f*,
femme *f* esquimau

esophagus [iˈsɑfəgəs] *s* (*pl* **-gi** [ˌdʒaɪ])
œsophage *m*

esoteric [ˌɛsoˈtɛrɪk] *adj* ésotérique

especial [ɛsˈpe/əl] *adj* spécial

especially [ɛsˈpe/əli] *adv* surtout, particulièrement

espionage [ˈɛspɪ·əˌnɪdʒ], [ˌɛspɪ·əˈnɑʒ]
s espionnage *m*

espousal [ɛsˈpauzəl] *s* épousailles *f*;
espousal of (*a cause*) adoption de,
adhésion à

espouse [ɛsˈpauz] *tr* épouser; (*to advocate, adopt*) adopter, embrasser

Esq. *abbr* (Esquire)—**John Smith, Esq.**
Monsieur Jean Smith

esquire [ɛsˈkwaɪr], [ˈɛskwaɪr] *s* (hist)
écuyer *m*

essay [ˈɛse] *s* essai *m* || *tr* essayer

essayist [ˈɛseˌɪst] *s* essayiste *mf*

essence ['esəns] s essence f

essential [e'sen/əl] adj & s essentiel m

establish [es'tæblɪʃ] tr établir

establishment [es'tæblɪʃmənt] s établissement m

estate [es'tet] s (landed property) domaine m, propriété f, terres fpl; (a person's possessions) biens mpl, possessions fpl; (left by a decedent) héritage m, succession f; (social status) rang m, condition f; (hist) état m

esteem [es'tim] s estime f || tr estimer

esthete ['esθit] s esthète mf

esthetic [es'θetɪk] adj esthétique || esthetics s esthétique f

estimable ['estɪməbəl] adj estimable

estimate ['estɪˌmet], ['estɪmɪt] s évaluation f, appréciation f; (appraisal) estimation f || ['estɪˌmet] tr (to judge, deem) apprécier, estimer; (the cost) estimer, évaluer

estimation [ˌestɪ'me/ən] s (opinion) jugement m; (esteem) estime f; (appraisal) estimation f; in my estimation à mon avis

Estonia [es'tonɪ-ə] s Estonie f; l'Estonie

estrangement [es'trendʒmənt] s éloignement m; (a becoming unfriendly) désaffection f

estuary ['est/ʊˌeri] s (pl -ies) estuaire m

etch [et/] tr & intr graver à l'eau-forte

etcher ['et/ər] s aquafortiste m

etching ['et/ɪŋ] s eau-forte f

eternal [ɪ'tʌrnəl] adj éternel

eternity [ɪ'tʌrnɪti] s (pl -ties) éternité f

ether ['iθər] s éther m

ethereal [ɪ'θɪrɪ-əl] adj éthéré

ethical ['eθɪkəl] adj éthique

ethics ['eθɪks] s (branch of philosophy) éthique f, morale f; spl (one's conduct, one's moral principles) morale

Ethiopia [ˌiθɪ'opɪ-ə] s Éthiopie f; l'Éthiopie

Ethiopian [ˌiθɪ'opɪ-ən] adj éthiopien || s (language) éthiopien m; (person) Éthiopien m

ethnic(al) ['eθnɪk(əl)] adj ethnique

ethnography [eθ'nɑgrəfi] s ethnographie f

ethnology [eθ'nɑlədʒi] s ethnologie f

ethyl ['eθɪl] s éthyle m

ethylene ['eθɪˌlin] s éthylène m

etiquette ['etɪˌket] s étiquette f

etymology [ˌetɪ'mɑlədʒi] s (pl -gies) étymologie f

etymon ['etɪˌmɑn] s (pl -mons or -ma [mə]) étymon m

eucalyptus [ˌjukə'lɪptəs] s (pl -tuses or -ti [taɪ]) eucalyptus m

Eucharist ['jukərɪst] s Eucharistie f

euchre ['jukər] s euchre m || tr (coll) l'emporter sur

eulogize ['julə,dʒaɪz] tr faire l'éloge de

eulogy ['juलədʒi] s (pl -gies) éloge m

eunuch ['junək] s eunuque m

euphemism ['jufɪˌmɪzəm] s euphémisme m

euphemistic [ˌjufɪ'mɪstɪk] adj euphémique

euphonic [ju'fɑnɪk] adj euphonique

euphony ['jufəni] s (pl -nies) euphonie f

euphoria [ju'forɪ-ə] s euphorie f

euphuism ['jufju,ɪzəm] s euphuisme m; préciosité f

Europe ['jurəp] s Europe f; l'Europe

European [ˌjurə'pi-ən] adj européen || s Européen m

euthanasia [ˌjuθə'neʒə] s euthanasie f

evacuate [ɪ'vækjuˌet] tr évacuer || intr s'évacuer

evade [ɪ'ved] tr échapper à, éviter, esquiver || intr s'évader

evaluate [ɪ'væljuˌet] tr évaluer

Evangel [ɪ'vændʒəl] s évangile m

evangelic(al) [ˌivæn'dʒelɪk(əl)], [ˌɛvæn'dʒelɪk(əl)] adj évangélique

evangelist [ɪ'vændʒəlɪst] s évangéliste m

evaporate [ɪ'væpəˌret] tr évaporer || intr s'évaporer

evasion [ɪ'veʒən] s évasion f; subterfuge m, détour m

evasive [ɪ'vesɪv] adj évasif

eve [iv] s veille f; (poetic) soir m; on the eve of à la veille de; Eve Ève f

even ['ivən] adj (smooth) uni; (number) pair; (equal, uniform) égal; (temperament) calme, rassis, égal; even with à fleur de; to be even être quitte; (cards, sports) être manche à manche or point à point; to get even with (coll) rendre la pareille à || adv même; even + comp encore + comp, e.g., even better encore mieux; even so quand même || tr aplanir, égaliser

evening ['ivnɪŋ] adj du soir || s soir m; all evening toute la soirée; every evening tous les soirs; in the evening le soir; the evening before la veille au soir

evening clothes' s tenue f de soirée; (for women) toilette f de soirée; (for men) habit m de soirée

evening damp' s serein m

evening prim'rose s onagraire f

evening star' s étoile f du soir, étoile du berger

evening wrap' s sortie f de bal

evensong ['ivən,sɔŋ] s (eccl) vêpres fpl

event [ɪ'vent] s événement m; at all events or in any event en tout cas; in the event that dans le cas où

eventful [ɪ'ventfəl] adj mouvementé; mémorable

eventual [ɪ'vent/ʊ-əl] adj final

eventuality [ɪˌvent/ʊ'ælɪti] s (pl -ties) éventualité f

eventually [ɪ'vent/ʊ-əli] adv finalement, à la longue

eventuate [ɪ'vent/ʊˌet] intr—to eventuate in se terminer par, aboutir à

ever ['evər] adv (at all times) toujours; (at any time) jamais; ever since dès lors, depuis; for ever and ever à tout jamais; hardly ever presque jamais

everglade ['evər,gled] s région f marécageuse

evergreen ['evər,grin] adj toujours vert || s arbre m vert; evergreens plantes fpl vertes, verdure f décorative ev·er·last·ing [adj] éternel; *(continual)* sempiternel, perpétuel

ev·er·more' [adv] toujours; for evermore à jamais

every ['evri] *adj* tous les; *(each)* chaque, tout; (coll) tout, e.g., every bit as good as tout aussi bon que; every man for himself sauve qui peut; every now and then de temps en temps; every once in a while de temps à autre; every other day tous les deux jours; every other one un sur deux; every which way (coll) de tous côtés; (coll) en désordre

ev·ery·bod·y [pron indef] tout le monde

ev·ery·day' [adj] de tous les jours

ev·ery·man' [s] Monsieur Tout-le-monde

ev·ery·one' or ev·ery one' [pron indef] chacun, tous, tout le monde

ev·ery·thing [pron indef] tout

ev·ery·where' [adv] partout, de toutes parts; partout où; everywhere else partout ailleurs

evict [ɪ'vɪkt] *tr* évincer, expulser

eviction [ɪ'vɪkʃən] *s* éviction *f*

evidence ['evɪdəns] *s* évidence *f*; *(proof)* preuve *f*, témoignage *m* || *tr* manifester, démontrer

evident ['evɪdənt] *adj* évident

evidently ['evɪdəntli], [ˌevɪ'dentli] *adv* évidemment

evil ['ivəl] *adj* mauvais, méchant || *s* mal *m*, méchanceté *f*

evildoer ['ivəlˌduɐr] *s* malfaisant *m*, méchant *m*

e·vil·do·ing [s] malfaisance *f*

e·vil eye' [s] mauvais œil *m*

e·vil-mind·ed [adj] malintentionné, malin

E·vil One' [s] Esprit *m* malin

evince [ɪ'vɪns] *tr* montrer, manifester

evocative [ɪ'vɑkətɪv] *adj* évocateur

evoke [ɪ'vok] *tr* évoquer

evolution [ˌevə'luʃən] *s* évolution *f*

evolve [ɪ'vɑlv] *tr* développer, élaborer || *intr* évoluer

ewe [ju] *s* brebis *f*

ewer ['juɐr] *s* aiguière *f*

exact [eg'zækt] *adj* exact || *tr* exiger

exacting [eg'zæktɪŋ] *adj* exigeant

exactly [eg'zæktli] *adv* exactement; *(sharp, on the dot)* précisément, justement

exactness [eg'zæktnɪs] *s* exactitude *f*

exaggerate [eg'zædʒəˌret] *tr* exagérer

exalt [eg'zɔlt] *tr* exalter

exam [eg'zæm] *s* (coll) examen *m*

examination [egˌzæmɪ'neʃən] *s* examen *m*; to take an examination se présenter à, passer, or subir un examen

examine [eg'zæmɪn] *tr* examiner

examiner [eg'zæmɪnər] *s* inspecteur *m*, vérificateur *m*; *(in a school)* examinateur *m*

example [eg'zæmpl], [eg'zɑmpl] *s* exemple *m*; for example par exemple

exasperate [eg'zæspəˌret] *tr* exaspérer

exasperation [egˌzæspə'reʃən] *s* exaspération *f*

excavate ['ekskəˌvet] *tr* excaver

exceed [ek'sid] *tr* excéder

exceedingly [ek'sidɪŋli] *adv* extrêmement

excel [ek'sel] *v* *(pret & pp* -celled; *ger* -celling) *tr* surpasser || *intr* exceller; to excel in exceller dans; to excel in + *ger* exceller à + *inf*

excellence ['eksələns] *s* excellence *f*

excellen·cy ['eksələnsi] *s (pl* -cies) excellence *f*; Your Excellency Votre Excellence

excelsior [ek'selsɪ·ər] *s* copeaux *mpl* d'emballage

except [ek'sept] *adv*—except for excepté; except that excepté que || *prep* excepté || *tr* excepter

exception [ek'sepʃən] *s* exception *f*; to take exception to trouver à redire à; with the exception of à l'exception de

exceptional [ek'sepʃənəl] *adj* exceptionnel

excerpt ['eksʌrpt], [ek'sʌrpt] *s* extrait *m*, citation *f* || [ek'sʌrpt] *tr* extraire

excess ['ekses], [ek'ses] *adj* excédentaire || [ek'ses] *s (amount or degree)* excédent *m*, excès *m*; *(excessive amount; immoderate indulgence)* excès *m*; in excess of en plus de

ex·cess bag'gage [s] excédent *m* de bagages

ex·cess fare' [s] supplément *m*

excessive [ek'sesɪv] *adj* excessif

ex·cess-prof·its tax' [s] contribution *f* sur les bénéfices extraordinaires

ex·cess weight' [s] excédent *m* de poids

exchange [eks'tʃendʒ] *s* échange *m*; *(barter)* troc *m*; (com) bourse *f*; (telp) central *m* || *tr* échanger; *(to barter)* troquer; to exchange compliments échanger des politesses; to exchange for échanger contre, échanger pour

exchequer [eks'tʃekər], ['ekstʃekər] *s* trésor *m* public; ministère *m* des finances; (hist) échiquier *m*

excise [ek'saɪz], ['eksaɪz] *s* contributions *fpl* indirectes || *tr* effacer, rayer; (surg) exciser

excitable [ek'saɪtəbəl] *adj* excitable

excite [ek'saɪt] *tr* exciter

excitement [ek'saɪtmənt] *m* agitation *f*, excitation *f*

exciting [ek'saɪtɪŋ] *adj* émotionnant, entraînant, passionnant

exclaim [eks'klem] *tr* s'écrier, e.g., "All is lost!" he exclaimed "Tout est perdu!" s'écria-t-il || *intr* s'exclamer, se récrier

exclamation [ˌeksklə'meʃən] *s* exclamation *f*

exclama'tion mark' [s] point *m* d'exclamation

exclude [eks'klud] *tr* exclure

excluding [eks'kludɪŋ] *prep* à l'exclusion de, sans compter

exclusion [eks'kluʒən] *s* exclusion *f*

exclusive [eks'klusɪv] *adj* exclusif; *(expensive; fashionable)* (coll) choisi, select; exclusive of à l'exclusion de

exclu'sive rights' [spl] exclusivité *f*

exclu'sive show'ing [s] (public sign in front of a theater) en exclusivité

excommunicate [ˌekskə'mjunɪˌket] *tr* excommunier

excommunication [ˌɛkskəˌmjunɪˈkeʃən] s excommunication f

excoriate [ɛksˈkorɪˌet] tr (fig) vitupérer

excrement [ˈɛkskrəmənt] s excrément m

excruciating [ɛksˈkruʃɪˌetɪŋ] adj affreux, atroce

exculpate [ˈɛkskʌlˌpet], [ɛksˈkʌlpet] tr disculper

excursion [ɛksˈkʌrʒən], [ɛksˈkʌrʃən] s excursion f

excusable [ɛksˈkjuzəbəl] adj excusable

excuse [ɛksˈkjus] s excuse f || [ɛksˈkjuz] tr excuser; **excuse me!** pardon!, je m'excuse!, **to excuse oneself** s'excuser

execrate [ˈɛksɪˌkret] tr exécrer; (to curse) maudire

execute [ˈɛksɪˌkjut] tr exécuter

execution [ˌɛksɪˈkjuʃən] s exécution f

executioner [ˌɛksɪˈkjuʃənər] s bourreau m

executive [ɛgˈzɛkjətɪv] adj (powers) exécutif; (position) administratif || s exécutif m; (of school, business, etc.) directeur m, administrateur m

Exec'utive Man'sion s (U.S.A.) demeure f du Président

executor [ɛgˈzɛkjətər] s exécuteur m testamentaire

executrix [ɛgˈzɛkjətrɪks] s exécutrice f testamentaire

exemplary [ɛgˈzɛmpləri], [ˈɛgzəmˌplɛri] adj exemplaire

exempli·fy [ɛgˈzɛmplɪˌfai] v (pret & pp -fied) tr démontrer par des exemples; (to be a model of) servir d'exemple à

exempt [ɛgˈzɛmpt] adj exempt || tr exempter

exemption [ɛgˈzɛmpʃən] s exemption f; **exemptions** (from taxes) déductions fpl

exercise [ˈɛksərˌsaiz] s exercice m; **exercises** cérémonies fpl || tr exercer || intr s'exercer, s'entraîner

exert [ɛgˈzʌrt] tr exercer; **to exert oneself** faire des efforts

exertion [ɛgˈzʌrʃən] s effort m; (e.g., of power) exercice m

exhalation [ˌɛks-həˈleʃən] s (of air) expiration f; (of gas, vapors, etc.) exhalaison f

exhale [ɛksˈhel], [ɛgˈzel]· tr (air from lungs) expirer; (gas, vapor) exhaler || intr expirer; s'exhaler

exhaust [ɛgˈzost] s échappement m; gaz mpl d'échappement || tr épuiser; faire le vide dans

exhaust' fan' s ventilateur m aspirant

exhaustion [ɛgˈzostʃən] s épuisement m

exhaustive [ɛgˈzostɪv] adj exhaustif

exhaust' man'ifold s ·tuyauterie f or collecteur m d'échappement

exhaust' pipe' s tuyau m d'échappement

exhaust' valve' s soupape f d'échappement

exhibit [ɛgˈzɪbɪt] s exhibition f; (of art) exposition f; (law) document m à l'appui, pièce f à conviction || tr

exhiber; (e.g., pictures) exposer || intr faire une exposition

exhibition [ˌɛksɪˈbɪʃən] s exhibition f

exhibitor [ɛgˈzɪbɪtər] s exposant m

exhilarate [ɛgˈzɪləˌret] tr égayer, animer

exhort [ɛgˈzort] tr exhorter

exhume [ɛksˈhjum], [ɛgˈzjum] tr exhumer

exigen·cy [ˈɛksɪdʒənsi] s (pl -cies) exigence f

exigent [ˈɛksɪdʒənt] adj exigeant

exile [ˈɛgzail], [ˈɛksail] s exil m; (person) exilé m || tr exiler

exist [ɛgˈzɪst] intr exister

existence [ɛgˈzɪstəns] s existence f

exit [ˈɛgzɪt], [ˈɛksɪt] s sortie f || intr sortir

exodus [ˈɛksədəs] s exode m

exonerate [ɛgˈzanəˌret] tr (to free from blame) disculper; (to free from an obligation) exonérer, dispenser

exorbitant [ɛgˈzorbɪtənt] adj exorbitant

exorcize [ˈɛksor ˌsaiz] tr exorciser

exotic [ɛgˈzatɪk] adj exotique

expand [ɛksˈpænd] tr (a gas, metal, etc.) dilater; (to enlarge, develop) élargir, développer; (to unfold, stretch out) étendre, déployer; (the chest) gonfler; (math) développer || intr se dilater; s'élargir, se développer; s'étendre, se déployer; se gonfler

expanse [ɛksˈpæns] s étendue f

expansion [ɛksˈpænʃən] s expansion f

expan'sion joint' s joint m de dilatation thermique

expansive [ɛksˈpænsɪv] adj expansif; (broad) large, étendu

expatiate [ɛksˈpeʃɪˌet] intr discourir, s'étendre

expatriate [ɛksˈpetrɪ·ɪt] adj & s expatrié m || [ɛksˈpetrɪˌet] tr expatrier

expect [ɛksˈpɛkt] tr (to await the coming of) attendre; (to look for as likely) s'attendre à; **to expect it** s'y attendre; **to expect s.o. to** + inf s'attendre à ce que qn + subj; **to expect to** + inf s'attendre à + inf

expectan·cy [ɛksˈpɛktənsi] s (pl -cies) attente f, expectative f

expect'ant moth'er [ɛksˈpɛktənt] s future mère f

expectation [ˌɛkspɛkˈteʃən] s expectative f, espérance f

expectorate [ɛksˈpɛktəˌret] tr & intr expectorer

expedien·cy [ɛksˈpidɪ·ənsi] s (pl -cies) convenance f, opportunité f; opportunisme m, débrouillage m

expedient [ɛksˈpidɪ·ənt] adj expédient; (looking out for oneself) débrouillard || s expédient m

expedite [ˈɛkspɪˌdait] tr expédier

expedition [ˌɛkspɪˈdɪʃən] s expédition f; célérité f, promptitude f

expeditionary [ˌɛkspɪˈdɪʃənˌɛri] adj expéditionnaire

expeditious [ˌɛkspɪˈdɪʃəs] adj expéditif

ex·pel [ɛksˈpɛl] v (pret & pp -pelled; ger -pelling) tr expulser; (from school) renvoyer

expend [eks'pend] tr (to pay out) dépenser; (to use up) consommer
expendable [eks'pendəbəl] adj non récupérable; (soldier) sacrifiable
expenditure [eks'pendɪtʃər] s dépense f; consommation f
expense [eks'pens] s dépense f; **at the expense of** aux dépens de; **expenses** frais mpl; (for which a person will be reimbursed) indemnité f; **to meet expenses** faire face aux dépenses
expense' account' s état m de frais, note f de frais
expensive [eks'pensɪv] adj cher, couteux; (tastes) dispendieux
experience [eks'pɪrɪ-əns] s expérience f || tr éprouver
experienced adj expérimenté
experiment [eks'pɛrɪmənt] s expérience f || [eks'pɛrɪ,mɛnt] intr faire des expériences, expérimenter
expert ['ekspərt] adj & s expert m
expertise [,ekspər'tiz] s maîtrise f
expiate ['ekspɪ,et] tr expier
expire [eks'paɪr] tr & intr expirer
expired adj (lease; passport) expiré; (note; permit) périmé; (e.g., driver's license) suranné; (insurance policy) déchu
explain [eks'plen] tr expliquer; **to explain oneself** s'expliquer || intr expliquer
explainable [eks'plenəbəl] adj explicable
explanation [,eksplə'neʃən] s explication f
explanatory [eks'plænə,tori] adj explicatif
explicit [eks'plɪsɪt] adj explicite
explode [eks'plod] tr faire sauter; (a theory, opinion, etc.) discréditer || intr exploser, éclater, sauter
exploit [eks'plɔɪt], ['eksplɔɪt] s exploit m || [eks'plɔɪt] tr exploiter
exploitation [,eksplɔɪ'teʃən] s exploitation f
exploration [,eksplə'reʃən] s exploration f
explore [eks'plor] tr explorer
explorer [eks'plorər] s explorateur m; (boy scout) routier m
explosion [eks'ploʒən] s explosion f
explosive [eks'plosɪv] adj explosif; (mixture) explosible || s explosif m
exponent [eks'ponənt] s interprète mf; (math) exposant m
export ['eksport] s exportation f || [eks'port], ['eksport] tr & intr exporter
exportation [,ekspor'teʃən] s exportation f
exporter ['eksportər], [eks'portər] s exportateur m
expose [eks'poz] tr exposer; (to unmask) démasquer, dévoiler; (phot) impressionner
exposé [,ekspo'ze] s dévoilement m, révélation f, mise f en lumière
exposition [,ekspo'zɪʃən] s exposition f
expostulate [eks'pɑstʃə,let] intr faire des remontrances; **to expostulate with** faire des remontrances à

exposure [eks'poʒər] s exposition f; (unmasking) dévoilement m; (phot) exposition f; (phot) durée f d'exposition
expound [eks'paund] tr exposer
express [eks'pres] adj exprès, formel; (train; gun) express || s (merchandise) messagerie f; (train) express m, rapide m; **by express** (rr) en grande vitesse || adv (rr) en grande vitesse || tr exprimer; (merchandise) envoyer en grande vitesse; (through the express company) expédier par les messageries; **to express oneself** s'exprimer
express' com'pany s messageries fpl
express' high'way s autoroute f
expression [eks'preʃən] s expression f
expressive [eks'presɪv] adj expressif
expressly [eks'presli] adv exprès
express'man s (pl -men) entrepreneur m de messageries; facteur m, agent m d'un service de messageries
express' train' s train m express
express'way' s autoroute f
expropriate [eks'propri,et] tr exproprier
expulsion [eks'pʌlʃən] s expulsion f; (from schools) renvoi m
expunge [eks'pʌndʒ] tr effacer, supprimer, rayer
expurgate ['ekspər,get] tr expurger
exquisite ['ekskwɪzɪt], [eks'kwɪzɪt] adj exquis
ex-service-man [,eks'sʌrvɪs,mæn] s (pl -men) ancien combattant m
extant ['ekstənt], [eks'tænt] adj existant, subsistant
extemporaneous [eks,tɛmpə'renɪ-əs] adj improvisé, impromptu
extemporaneously [eks,tɛmpə'renɪ-əsli] adv à l'impromptu, d'abondance
extempore [eks'tɛmpəri] adj improvisé || adv d'abondance, à l'impromptu
extemporize [eks'tɛmpə,raɪz] tr & intr improviser
extend [eks'tɛnd] tr étendre; (a period of time; a street; a line) prolonger; (a treaty; a session; a right; a due date) proroger; (a helping hand) tendre || intr s'étendre
extended adj étendu, prolongé
extension [eks'tɛnʃən] s extension f; prolongation f; (board for a table) rallonge f; (to building) annexe f; (telp) poste m
exten'sion cord' s cordon m prolongateur, prolongateur m
exten'sion lad'der s échelle f à coulisse
exten'sion ta'ble s table f à rallonges
extensive [eks'tɛnsɪv] adj vaste, étendu
extent [eks'tɛnt] s étendue f; **to a certain extent** dans une certaine mesure; **to a great extent** en grande partie, considérablement; **to the full extent** dans toute la mesure
extenuate [eks'tɛnju,et] tr atténuer; minimiser
exterior [eks'tɪrɪ-ər] adj & s extérieur m
exterminate [eks'tʌrmɪ,net] tr exterminer

external [ɛks'tʌrnəl] *adj* extérieur; (pharm, med) externe || **externals** *spl* dehors *mpl*, apparences *fpl*; (*superficialities*) choses *fpl* secondaires

extinct [ɛks'tɪŋkt] *adj* (*volcano*) éteint; disparu; tombé en désuétude

extinction [ɛks'tɪŋkʃən] *s* extinction *f*

extinguish [ɛks'tɪŋgwɪʃ] *tr* éteindre

extinguisher [ɛks'tɪŋgwɪʃər] *s* (*for candles*) éteignoir *m*; (*for fires*) extincteur *m*

extirpate [ˈɛkstər‚pet], [ɛks'tʌrpet] *tr* extirper

ex-tol [ɛks'tol], [ɛks'tɑl] *v* (*pret & pp* -**tolled**; *ger* -**tolling**) *tr* exalter, vanter

extort [ɛks'tɔrt] *tr* extorquer

extortion [ɛks'tɔrʃən] *s* extorsion *f*

extortionist [ɛks'tɔrʃənɪst] *s* extorqueur *m*

extra [ˈɛkstrə] *adj* supplémentaire; (*of high quality*) extra, extra-fin; (*spare*) de rechange || *s* extra *m*; (*of a newspaper*) édition *f* spéciale; (mov, theat) figurant *m* || *adv* en plus, en sus; (*not on the bill*) non compris

ex'tra board' *s* (*for extension table*) rallonge *f*

ex'tra charge' *s* supplément *m*

extract [ˈɛkstrækt] *s* extrait *m* || [ɛks'trækt] *tr* extraire

extraction [ɛks'trækʃən] *s* extraction *f*

extracurricular [‚ɛkstrəkə'rɪkjələr] *adj* extra-scolaire

extradite [ˈɛkstrə‚daɪt] *tr* extrader

extradition [‚ɛkstrə'dɪʃən] *s* extradition *f*

ex'tra-dry' *adj* (*champagne*) très sec

ex'tra fare' *s* supplément *m* de billet

extramural [‚ɛkstrə'mjurəl] *adj* à l'extérieur de la ville; à l'exterieur de l'université

extraneous [ɛks'trenɪ‚əs] *adj* étranger

extraordinary [ɛks'trɔrdɪ‚nɛri], [‚ɛkstrə'ɔrdɪ‚nɛri] *adj* extraordinaire

extrapolate [ɛks'træpə‚let] *tr & intr* extrapoler

extrasensory [‚ɛkstrə'sɛnsəri] *adj* extrasensoriel

ex'tra-spe'cial *adj* extra

extravagance [ɛks'trævəgəns] *s* (*lavishness*) prodigalité *f*, gaspillage *m*; (*folly*) extravagance *f*

extravagant [ɛks'trævəgənt] *adj* (*person*) dépensier, prodigue; (*price*) exorbitant; (*e.g., praise*) outré; (*e.g., claims*) exagéré, extravagant

extreme [ɛks'trim] *adj & s* extrême *m*; **in the extreme, to extremes** à l'extrême

extremely [ɛks'trimli] *adv* extrêmement

extreme' unc'tion *s* extrême-onction *f*

extremist [ɛks'trimɪst] *adj & s* extrémiste *mf*

extremi·ty [ɛks'trɛmɪti] *s* (*pl* -**ties**) extrémité *f*; **extremities** extrémités

extricate [ˈɛkstrɪ‚ket] *tr* dégager; (*a*

gas) libérer; **to extricate oneself from** se tirer de, se dépêtrer de

extrinsic [ɛks'trɪnsɪk] *adj* extrinsèque

extrovert [ˈɛkstrə‚vʌrt] *adj & s* extraverti *m*

extrude [ɛks'trud] *intr* faire saillie, dépasser

exuberant [ɛg'z(j)ubərənt] *adj* exubérant

exude [ɛg'zud], [ɛk'sud] *tr & intr* exsuder

exult [ɛg'zʌlt] *intr* exulter

exultant [ɛg'zʌltənt] *adj* triomphant

eye [aɪ] *s* œil *m*; (*of needle*) chas *m*, trou *m*; (*of hook and eye*) porte *f*; **to catch s.o.'s eye** tirer l'œil à qn; **to lay eyes on** jeter les yeux sur; **to make eyes at** (coll) faire les yeux doux à; **to see eye to eye with s.o.** voir les choses du même œil que qn; **with an eye to** en vue de; **without batting an eye** (coll) sans sourciller || *v* (*pret & pp* eyed; *ger* eying *or* eyeing) *tr* toiser, reluquer

eye'ball' *s* globe *m* oculaire

eye' bank' *s* banque *f* des yeux

eye'bolt' *s* boulon *m* à œil

eye'brow' *s* sourcil *m*

eye'cup' *s* œillère *f*

eye' drops' *spl* collyre *m*

eyeful [ˈaɪful] *s* vue *f*, coup *m* d'œil; **to get an eyeful** (coll) s'en mettre plein la vue, se rincer l'œil

eye'glass' *s* (*of optical instrument*) oculaire *m*; (*eyecup*) œillère *f*; **eyeglasses** lunettes *fpl*

eye'lash' *s* cil *m*; (*fringe of hair*) cils

eyelet [ˈaɪlɪt] *s* œillet *m*; (*of sail*) œil *m* de pie

eye'lid' *s* paupière *f*

eye' of the morn'ing *s* astre *m* du jour

eye' o'pener [ˈopənər] *s* révélation *f*; (coll) goutte *f* de bonne heure

eye'piece' *s* oculaire *m*

eye'shade' *s* visière *f*, abat-jour *m*

eye' shad'ow *s* fard *m* à paupière

eye'shot' *s* portée *f* de la vue

eye'sight' *s* vue *f*; (*eyeshot*) portée *f* de la vue

eye' sock'et *s* orbite *f* de l'œil

eye'sore' *s* objet *m* déplaisant

eye'strain' *s* fatigue *f* des yeux; **to suffer from eyestrain** avoir les yeux fatigués

eye'-test chart' *s* tableau *m* de lecture pour la vision

eye'tooth' *s* (*pl* -**teeth**) dent *f* œillère *or* canine; **to cut one's eyeteeth** (coll) ne pas être un blanc-bec; **to give one's eyeteeth for** (coll) donner la prunelle de ses yeux pour

eye'wash' *s* collyre *m*; (slang) de l'eau bénite de cour, de la poudre aux yeux

eye'wit'ness *s* témoin *m* oculaire

ey·rie *or* **ey·ry** [ˈɛri] *s* (*pl* -**ries**) aire *f* (de l'aigle); (fig) nid *m* d'aigle

F

F, f [ɛf] s VIᵉ lettre de l'alphabet
fable ['febəl] s fable f
fabric ['fæbrɪk] s tissu m, étoffe f
fabricate ['fæbrɪˌket] tr fabriquer
fabrication [ˌfæbrɪ'keʃən] s fabrication f; (lie) mensonge m
fabulous ['fæbjələs] adj fabuleux
façade [fə'sɑd] s façade f
face [fes] s visage m, figure f; (side) face f; (of the earth) surface f; (appearance, expression) mine f, physionomie f; **about face!** (mil) demitour! **to keep a straight face** montrer un front sérieux; **to lose face** perdre la face; **to make a face** faire une grimace; **to set one's face against** faire front à || tr faire face à; (a wall) revêtir; (a garment) mettre un revers à || intr—**to face about** faire demi-tour; **to face up to** faire face à, affronter
face' card' s figure f
face' lift'ing s ridectomie f
face' pow'der s poudre f de riz
facet ['fæsɪt] s facette f
facetious [fə'siʃəs] adj plaisant
face' tow'el s serviette f de toilette
face' val'ue s valeur f faciale, valeur nominale
facial ['feʃəl] adj facial || s massage m esthétique
fa'cial tis'sue s serviette f à démaquiller
facilitate [fə'sɪlɪˌtet] tr faciliter
facili•ty [fə'sɪlɪti] s (pl -ties) facilité f; **facilities** installations fpl
facing ['fesɪŋ] s revêtement m; (of garment) revers m
facsimile [fæk'sɪmɪli] s fac-similé m
fact [fækt] s fait m; **in fact** en fait, de fait; **the fact is that** c'est que
faction ['fækʃən] s faction f
factor ['fæktər] s facteur m || tr résoudre or décomposer en facteurs
facto•ry ['fæktəri] s (pl -ries) usine f, fabrique f
fac'tory price' s prix m de facture
factual ['fæktʃʊˌəl] adj vrai, réel
facul•ty ['fækəlti] s (pl -ties) faculté f; (teaching staff) corps m enseignant
fad [fæd] s mode f, marotte f; **latest fad** dernier cri m
fade [fed] tr déteindre, décolorer || intr déteindre, se décolorer; (to lose vigor, freshness) se faner; **to fade in** apparaître graduellement; **to fade out** disparaître graduellement
fade'-in' s (mov) apparition f en fondu
fade'-out' s (mov) fondu m
fag [fæg] s (slang) cibiche f || v (pret & ger fagged; ger fagging) tr—**to fag out** éreinter
fagot ['fægət] s fagot m; (for filling up trenches) fascine f || tr fagoter
fail [fel] s—**without fail** sans faute || tr manquer à; (a student) refuser; (an examination) échouer à or dans || intr manquer, faire défaut; (to not succeed) échouer, rater; (said of motor) tomber en panne; (to weaken) baisser, faiblir; **to fail in** faillir à; **to fail to** manquer de, faillir à; **to fail to** do or to keep faillir à
failing ['felɪŋ] adj défaillant || s défaut m || prep à défaut de
failure ['feljər] s insuccès m, échec m; (lack) manque m, défaut m; (person) raté m; (com) faillite f
faint [fent] adj faible; **to feel faint** se sentir mal || s évanouissement m || intr s'évanouir
faint'-heart'ed adj timide, peureux
fair [fer] adj juste, équitable; (honest) loyal, honnête; (average) moyen, passable; (clear) clair; (beautiful) beau; (pleasing) agréable, plaisant; (of hair) blond; (complexion) blanc; **to be fair** (to be just) être de bonne guerre || s foire f, fête f; (bazaar) kermesse f || adv impartialement; **to bid fair to** avoir des chances de; **to play fair** jouer franc jeu
fair' cop'y s copie f au net
fair' ground' s champ m de foire
fairly ['ferli] adv impartialement, loyalement; assez
fair'-mind'ed adj impartial
fairness ['fernɪs] s impartialité f, justice f; (of complexion) clarté f
fair' play' s franc jeu m
fair' sex' s beau sexe m
fair'way' s (golf) parcours m normal; (naut) chenal m
fair'-weath'er adj (e.g., friend) des beaux jours
fair•y ['feri] adj féerique || s (pl -ies) fée f; (homosexual) (coll) tante f
fair'y god'moth'er s marraine f fée; (coll) marraine gâteau
fair'y•land' s royaume m des fées
fair'y tale' s conte m de fées
faith [feθ] s foi f; **to break faith with** manquer de foi à; **to keep faith with** tenir ses engagements envers; **to pin one's faith on** mettre tout son espoir en
faithful ['feθfəl] adj fidèle || s—**the faithful** les fidèles mpl
faithless ['feθlɪs] adj infidèle
fake [fek] adj (coll) faux || s faux m, article m truqué || tr truquer
faker ['fekər] s truqueur m
falcon ['fɔkən], ['fɔlkən] s faucon m
falconer ['fɔkənər], ['fɔlkənər] s fauconnier m
fall [fɔl] adj automnal || s chute f; (of prices) baisse f; (season) automne m & f; **falls** chute d'eau || v (pret fell [fel]; pp fallen ['fɔlən]) intr tomber; (said of prices) baisser; **fall in!** (mil) rassemblement! **fall out!** (mil) rompez les rangs!; **to fall down** (said of person) tomber par terre; (said of building) s'écrouler; **to fall for** (coll)

se laisser prendre à; (*to fall in love with*) (coll) tomber amoureux de; **to fall in** s'effondrer; (mil) former des rangs; **to fall into the trap** donner dans le piège; **to fall off** tomber de; (*to decline*) baisser, diminuer; **to fall out** (*to disagree*) se brouiller; **to fall over oneself to** (coll) se mettre en quatre pour

fallacious [fə'leʃəs] *adj* fallacieux

falla·cy ['fæləsi] *s* (*pl* **-cies**) erreur *f*, fausseté *f*

fall′ guy′ *s* (slang) tête *f* de Turc

fallible ['fælɪbəl] *adj* faillible

fall′ing star′ *s* étoile *f* filante

fall′out′ *s* pluies *fpl* radioactives, retombées *fpl* radioactives

fall′out shel′ter *s* abri *m* antiatomique

fallow ['fælo] *adj* en friche, en jachère || *s* friche *f*, jachère *f* || *tr* laisser en friche or en jachère

false [fɔls] *adj* faux; artificiel, simulé; (*hair*) postiche || *adv* faussement; **to play false** tromper

false′ alarm′ *s* fausse alerte *f*

false′ bot′tom *s* double fond *m*

false′ cog′nate *s* faux ami *m*

false′ eye′lashes *spl* cils *mpl* postiches

false′ face′ *s* masque *m*

false′-heart′ed *adj* perfide, traître

false′hood *s* mensonge *m*

false′ pretens′es *spl* faux-semblants *mpl*

false′ return′ *s* fausse déclaration *f* d'impôts

false′ step′ *s* faux-pas *m*

false′ teeth′ ['tiθ] *spl* fausses dents *fpl*

falset·to [fɔl'seto] *s* (*pl* **-tos**) fausset *m*, voix *f* de tête; (*person*) fausset *m*

falsi·fy ['fɔlsɪˌfaɪ] *v* (*pret & pp* **-fied**) *tr* falsifier, fausser

falsi·ty ['fɔlsɪti] *s* (*pl* **-ties**) fausseté *f*

falter ['fɔltər] *s* vacillation *f*, hésitation *f*; (*of speech*) balbutiement *m* || *intr* vaciller, hésiter; balbutier

fame [fem] *s* renom *m*, renommée *f*

famed *adj* renommé, célèbre

familiar [fə'mɪljər] *adj* & *s* familier *m*; **to become familiar with** se familiariser avec

familiari·ty [fə,mɪlɪ'ærɪti] *s* (*pl* **-ties**) familiarité *f*

familiarize [fə'mɪljəˌraɪz] *tr* familiariser

fami·ly ['fæmɪli] *adj* familial; **in a** or **the family way** (coll) dans une position intéressante; (coll) en famille (Canad) || *s* (*pl* **-lies**) famille *f*

fam′ily man′ *s* (*pl* **men′**) père *m* de famille; (*stay-at-home*) homme *m* casanier, pantouflard *m*

fam′ily name′ *s* nom *m* de famille

fam′ily physi′cian *s* médecin *m* de famille

fam′ily tree′ *s* arbre *m* généalogique

famine ['fæmɪn] *s* famine *f*

famish ['fæmɪʃ] *tr* affamer, priver de vivres || *intr* souffrir de la faim

famished *adj* affamé, famélique; **to be famished** (coll) mourir de faim

famous ['feməs] *adj* renommé, célèbre

fan [fæn] *s* éventail *m*; (mach) ventilateur *m*; (coll) fanatique *mf*, enragé

m || *v* (*pret & pp* **fanned**; *ger* **fanning**) *tr* éventer; (*to winnow*) vanner; (*e.g., passions*) exciter || *intr*—**to fan out** se déployer en éventail

fanatic [fə'nætɪk] *adj* & *s* fanatique *mf*

fanatical [fə'nætɪkəl] *adj* fanatique

fanaticism [fə'nætɪˌsɪzəm] *s* fanatisme *m*

fan′ belt′ *s* (aut) courroie *f* de ventilateur

fancied *adj* imaginaire, supposé

fanciful ['fænsɪfəl] *adj* fantaisiste, capricieux

fan·cy ['fænsi] *adj* (*comp* **-cier**; *super* **-ciest**) ornemental; (*goods, clothes, bread*) de fantaisie; (*high-quaity*) fin, extra, de luxe || *s* (*pl* **-cies**) fantaisie *f*, caprice *m*; **to take a fancy to** prendre du goût pour; (*a loved one*) prendre en affection || *v* (*pret & pp* **-cied**) *tr* s'imaginer, se figurer; **to fancy oneself** s'imaginer; **to fancy that** imaginer que

fan′cy dress′ *s* costume *m* de fantaisie, travesti *m*

fan′cy dress′ ball′ *s* bal *m* costumé, bal travesti

fan′cy foods′ *spl* comestibles *mpl* de fantaisie

fan′cy-free′ *adj* libre, gai, sans amour

fan′cy jew′elry *s* bijouterie *f* de fantaisie

fan′cy skat′ing *s* patinage *m* de fantaisie

fan′cy-work′ *s* broderie *f*, ouvrage *m* d'agrément

fanfare ['fænfer] *s* fanfare *f*

fang [fæŋ] *s* croc *m*; (*of snake*) crochet *m*

fantastic(al) [fæn'tæstɪk(əl)] *adj* fantastique

fanta·sy ['fæntəzi], ['fæntəsi] *s* (*pl* **-sies**) fantaisie *f*

far [fɑr] *adj* lointain; **on the far side of** à l'autre côté de || *adv* loin; **as far as** autant que; (*up to*) jusqu'à; **as far as I am concerned** quant à moi; **as far as I know** pour autant que je sache; **by far** de beaucoup; **far and wide** partout; **far away** au loin; **far from** loin de; **far from it** tant s'en faut; **far into the night** fort avant dans la nuit; **far into the woods** avant dans le bois; **far off** au loin; **how far?** jusqu'où?; **how far is it from . . . ?** combien y a-t-il de . . . ?; **in so far as** dans la mesure où; **so far** or **thus far** jusqu'ici; **to go far** to contribuer pour beaucoup à

far′away′ *adj* éloigné, distant

farce [fɑrs] *s* farce *f*

farcical ['fɑrsɪkəl] *adj* grotesque, ridicule

fare [fer] *s* prix *m*, tarif *m*; (*cost of taxi*) course *f*; (*passenger in taxi*) client *m*; (*passenger in bus*) voyageur *m*; (culin) chère *f*, ordinaire *m*; **fares, please!** vos places, s'il vous plaît! || *intr* se porter; **how did you fare?** comment ça s'est-il passé?

Far′ East′ *s* Extrême-Orient *m*

fare'well' s adieu m; **to bid s.o. fare-well** dire adieu à qn

far'-fetched' adj tiré par les cheveux

far-flung ['far'flʌŋ] adj étendu, vaste, d'une grande envergure

farm [farm] s ferme f; (sharecropper's farm) métairie f || tr cultiver, exploiter; **to farm out** donner à ferme; (work) donner en exploitation à l'extérieur || intr faire de la culture

farmer ['farmər] s fermier m

farm' hand' s valet m de ferme

farm'house' s ferme f, maison f de ferme

farming ['farmɪŋ] s agriculture f, exploitation f agricole

farm'yard' s cour f de ferme

Far' North' s Grand Nord m

far'-off' adj lointain, éloigné

far'-reach'ing adj à longue portée

far'sight'ed adj prévoyant; (physiol) presbyte

farther ['farðər] adj plus éloigné || adv plus loin

farthest ['farðɪst] adj (le) plus éloigné || adv le plus loin; au plus

farthing ['farðɪŋ] s liard m

fascinate ['fæsɪ,net] tr fasciner

fascinating ['fæsɪ,netɪŋ] adj fascinateur, fascinant

fascism ['fæʃɪzəm] s fascisme m

fascist ['fæʃɪst] adj & s fasciste mf

fashion ['fæʃən] s mode f, vogue f; (manner) façon f, manière f; **after a fashion** tant bien que mal; **in fashion** à la mode, en vogue; **out of fashion** démodé || tr façonner

fashionable ['fæʃənəbəl] adj à la mode, élégant, chic

fash'ion design'ing s haute couture f

fash'ion plate' s gravure f de mode; (person) (coll) élégant m

fash'ion show' s présentation f de collection

fast [fæst], [fast] adj rapide; (fixed) solide, fixe; (clock) en avance; (friend) fidèle; (color) grand, bon, e.g., **fast color** grand teint, bon teint; (person) (slang) dévergondé; **to make fast** fixer, fermer || s jeûne m; **to break one's fast** rompre le jeûne || adv vite, rapidement; (firmly) solidement, fermé; (asleep) profondément; **to hold fast** tenir bon; **to live fast** (coll) faire la noce, mener la vie à grandes guides; **to stand fast against** tenir tête à || intr jeûner

fast' day' s jour m de jeûne, jour maigre

fasten ['fæsən], ['fasən] tr attacher, fixer; (e.g., a belt) ajuster || intr s'attacher, se fixer

fastener ['fæsənər], ['fasənər] s attache f, agrafe f

fastidious [fæs'tɪdɪ·əs] adj délicat, dégoûté, difficile

fasting ['fæstɪŋ], ['fastɪŋ] s jeûne m

fat [fæt] adj (comp fatter; super fattest) (plump; greasy) gras; (large) gros; (soil) riche; (spark) nourri; **to get fat** engraisser || s graisse f; (of meat) gras m

fatal ['fetəl] adj fatal

fatalism ['fetə,lɪzəm] s fatalisme m

fatalist ['fetəlɪst] s fataliste mf

fatali·ty [fə'tælɪti] s (pl -ties) fatalité f; (in accidents, war, etc.) mort f, accident m mortel

fate [fet] s sort m, destin m; **the Fates** les Parques fpl

fated adj destiné, voué

fateful ['fetfəl] adj fatal; (prophetic) fatidique

fat'head' s (coll) crétin m, sot m

father ['faðər] s père m; **Father** (salutation given a priest) Monsieur l'abbé || tr servir de père à; (to beget) engendrer; (an idea, project) inventer

fa'ther·hood' s paternité f

fa'ther-in-law' s (pl **fathers-in-law**) beau-père m

fa'ther·land' s patrie f

fatherless ['faðərlɪs] adj sans père, orphelin de père

fatherly ['faðərli] adj paternel

Fa'ther Time' s le Temps

fathom ['fæðəm] s brasse f || tr sonder

fathomless ['fæðəmlɪs] adj insondable

fatigue [fə'tig] s fatigue f; **fatigues** (mil) bleus mpl

fatigue' clothes' spl tenue f de corvée

fatigue' du'ty s (mil) corvée f

fatten ['fætən] tr & intr engraisser

fat·ty ['fæti] adj (comp -tier; super -tiest) gras, grassieux; (tissue) adipeux; (chubby) (coll) potelé, dodu || s (pl -ties) (coll) bon gros m

fatuous ['fætʃʊ·əs] adj sot, idiot

faucet ['fɔsɪt] s robinet m

fault [fɔlt] s faute f; (geol) faille f; **to a fault** à l'excès; **to find fault with** trouver à redire à

fault'find'er s critiqueur m, éplucheur m

fault'find'ing adj chicaneur || s chicanerie f, critique f

faultless ['fɔltlɪs] adj sans défaut

fault·y ['fɔlti] adj (comp -ier; super -iest) fautif, défectueux

faun [fɔn] s faune m

fauna ['fɔnə] s faune f

favor ['fevər] s faveur f; **do me the favor to** faites-moi le plaisir de; **to be in favor of** être partisan de; **to be in favor with** jouir de la faveur de; **to decide in s.o.'s favor** donner gain de cause à qn || tr favoriser; (to look like) (coll) tenir de; (e.g., a sore leg) (coll) ménager

favorable ['fevərəbəl] adj favorable

favorite ['fevərɪt] adj & s favori m

fawn [fɔn] adj (color) fauve || s faon m || intr—**to fawn upon** (said of dog) faire des caresses à; (said of person) faire le chien couchant auprès de

faze [fez] tr (coll) affecter, troubler

FBI [,ef,bi'aɪ] s (letterword) (Federal Bureau of Investigation) Sûreté f nationale, Sûreté (the French equivalent)

fear [fɪr] s crainte f, peur f || tr craindre, avoir peur de || intr craindre, avoir peur

fearful ['fɪrfəl] adj (frightened) peu-

reux, effrayé; (*frightful*) effrayant;
(coll) énorme, effrayant
fearless ['fɪrlɪs] adj sans peur
feasible ['fizɪbəl] adj faisable
feast [fist] s festin m, régal m || tr
régaler || intr faire bonne chère; **to
feast on** se régaler de
feast' day' s fête f, jour m de fête
feat [fit] s exploit m, haut fait m
feather ['fɛðər] s plume f; **feather in
one's cap** (coll) fleuron m à sa couronne; **in fine feather** (coll) plein
d'entrain || tr emplumer; (*an oar*)
ramener à plat; **to feather one's nest**
(coll) faire son beurre
feath'er bed' s lit m de plumes, couette f
feath'er-bed'ding s emploi m de plus
d'ouvriers qu'il n'en faut
feath'er-brained' adj braque, étourdi
feath'er dust'er s plumeau m
feath'er-edge' s (*of board*) biseau m;
(*of tool*) morfil m
feath'er-weight' s poids-plume m
feathery ['fɛðəri] adj plumeux
feature ['fitʃər] s trait m, caractéristique f; (mov) long métrage m, grand
film m || tr caractériser; offrir
comme attraction principale
fea'ture writ'er s rédacteur m
February ['fɛbrʊ ˌɛri] s février m
feces ['fisiz] spl fèces fpl
feckless ['fɛklɪs] adj veule, faible
federal ['fɛdərəl] adj & s fédéral m
federate ['fɛdə ˌret] adj fédéré || tr fé-
dérer || intr se fédérer
federation [ˌfɛdə'reʃən] s fédération f
fedora [fɪ'dorə] s chapeau m mou
fed' up' [fɛd] adj—**to be fed up** (coll)
en avoir marre; **to be fed up with**
(coll) avoir plein le dos de
fee [fi] s honoraires mpl, cachet m; **for
a nominal fee** pour une somme symbolique
feeble ['fibəl] adj faible
fee'ble-mind'ed adj imbécile; obtus,
à l'esprit lourd
feed [fid] s nourriture f, pâture f;
(mach) alimentation f; (slang) grand
repas m || v (pret & pp fed [fed])
tr nourrir, donner à manger à; (*a ma-
chine*) alimenter || intr manger; **to
feed upon** se nourrir de
feed'back' s réalimentation f, régé-
nération f, contre-réaction f
feed' bag' s musette-mangeoire f; **to
put on the feed bag** (slang) casser la
croûte
feeder ['fidər] s alimenteur m; (elec)
canal m d'amenée
feed' pump' s pompe f d'alimentation
feed' trough' s mangeoire f, auge f
feed' wire' s (elec) fil m d'amenée
feel [fil] s sensation f || v (pret & pp
felt [fɛlt]) tr sentir, éprouver; (*the
pulse*) tâter; (*to examine*) palper; **to
feel one's way** avancer à tâtons ||
intr (sick, tired, etc.) se sentir; **to
feel for** tâtonner, chercher à tâtons;
(*to sympathize with*) (coll) être plein
de pitié pour; **to feel like** avoir envie
de

feeler ['filər] s (ent) antenne f; **to put
out a feeler** (coll) tâter le terrain
feeling ['filɪŋ] s (*with senses*) toucher
m, tact m; (*with hands*) tâtage m;
(*impression, emotion*) sentiment m;
feelings sensibilité f
feign [fen] tr & intr feindre
feint [fent] s feinte f || intr feinter
feldspar ['fɛld ˌspar] s feldspath m
felicitate [fə'lɪsɪ ˌtet] tr féliciter
felicitous [fə'lɪsɪtəs] adj heureux, à
propos
fell [fɛl] adj cruel, féroce || tr abattre
felloe ['fɛlo] s jante f
fellow ['fɛlo] s (*of a society*) membre
m; (*holder of a fellowship*) boursier
m; (*friend, neighbor, etc.*) homme m,
compagnon m; (coll) type m, bonhomme m, gars m; **poor fellow!** (coll)
pauvre garçon!
fel'low cit'izen s concitoyen m
fel'low coun'tryman s compatriote m
fel'low crea'ture s semblable mf
fel'low-man' s (pl -men') semblable m,
prochain m
fel'low mem'ber s confrère m
fel'low-ship' s camaraderie f; (*scholarship*) bourse f; (*organization*) association f
fel'low stu'dent s condisciple m
fel'low trav'eler s compagnon m de
voyage; (pol) compagnon de route
felon ['fɛlən] s criminel m; (pathol)
panaris m
felo·ny ['fɛləni] s (pl -nies) crime m
felt [fɛlt] s feutre m || tr feutrer
female ['fimel] adj (sex) féminin; (*animal, plant, piece of a device*) femelle
|| s (*person*) femme f; (*plant, animal*)
femelle f
feminine ['fɛmɪnɪn] adj & s féminin m
feminism ['fɛmɪ ˌnɪzəm] s féminisme m
fen [fɛn] s marécage m
fence [fɛns] s barrière f, clôture f;
palissade f; (*for stolen goods*) rece-
leur m; **on the fence** (coll) indécis,
en balance || tr clôturer || intr faire
de l'escrime
fencing ['fɛnsɪŋ] s (*enclosure*) clôture
f; (sports) escrime f
fenc'ing acad'emy s salle f d'armes
fenc'ing mas'ter s maître m d'armes
fenc'ing match' s assaut m d'armes
fend [fɛnd] tr—**to fend off** parer || intr
—**to fend for oneself** (coll) se débrouiller, se tirer d'affaire
fender ['fɛndər] s (*mudguard*) aile f,
garde-boue m; (*of locomotive*)
chasse-pierres m; (*of fireplace*) garde-
feu m
fennel ['fɛnəl] s fenouil m
ferment ['fɜrmɛnt] s ferment m || [fər-
'mɛnt] tr faire fermenter; (*wine*)
cuver || intr fermenter
fern [fɜrn] s fougère f
ferocious [fə'roʃəs] adj féroce
feroci·ty [fə'rɑsɪti] s (pl -ties) férocité f
ferret ['fɛrɪt] s furet m || tr—**to ferret
out** dénicher || intr fureter
Fer'ris wheel' ['fɛrɪs] s grande roue f
fer·ry ['fɛri] s (pl -ries) bac m; (*to
transport trains*) ferry-boat m || v

(*pret & pp* -ried) *tr & intr* passer en bac

fer'ry-boat' *s* bac *m*; (*to transport trains*) ferry-boat *m*

fer'ry-man *s* (*pl* -men) passeur *m*

fertile [ˈfʌrtɪl] *adj* fertile, fécond

fertilize [ˈfʌrtɪ ˌlaɪz] *tr* fertiliser; (*to impregnate*) féconder

fertilizer [ˈfʌrtɪ ˌlaɪzər] *s* engrais *m*, amendement *m*; (*bot*) fécondateur *m*

fervent [ˈfʌrvənt] *adj* fervent

fervid [ˈfʌrvɪd] *adj* fervent

fervor [ˈfʌrvər] *s* ferveur *f*

fester [ˈfestər] *s* ulcère *m* || *tr* ulcérer || *intr* s'ulcérer

festival [ˈfestɪvəl] *adj* de fête || *s* fête *f*; (*mov, mus*) festival *m*

festive [ˈfestɪv] *adj* de fête, gai

festivi-ty [fesˈtɪvɪti] *s* (*pl* -ties) festivité *f*

festoon [fesˈtun] *s* feston *m* || *tr* festonner

fetch [fetʃ] *tr* aller chercher; (*a certain price*) se vendre à

fetching [ˈfetʃɪŋ] *adj* (coll) séduisant

fete [fet] *s* fête *f* || *tr* fêter

fetish [ˈfetɪʃ], [ˈfitɪʃ] *s* fétiche *m*

fetlock [ˈfetlɑk] *s* boulet *m*; (*tuft of hair*) fanon *m*

fetter [ˈfetər] *s* lien *m*; **fetters** fers *mpl*, chaînes *fpl* || *tr* enchaîner, entraver

fettle [ˈfetəl] *s* condition *f*, état *m*; **in fine fettle** en pleine forme

fetus [ˈfitəs] *s* fœtus *m*

feud [fjud] *s* querelle *f*, vendetta *f* || *intr* quereller, être à couteaux tirés

feudal [ˈfjudəl] *adj* féodal

feudalism [ˈfjudə ˌlɪzəm] *s* féodalisme *m*

fever [ˈfivər] *s* fièvre *f*

fe'ver blis'ter *s* bouton *m* de fièvre

feverish [ˈfivərɪʃ] *adj* fiévreux

few [fju] *adj* peu de; **a few . . .** quelques . . . ; **quite a few** pas mal de; **the few . . .** les rares . . . || *pron indef* peu; **a few** quelques-uns §81; **quite a few** beaucoup

fiancé [ˌfi·ɑnˈse] *s* fiancé *m*

fiancée [ˌfi·ɑnˈse] *s* fiancée *f*

fias-co [fiˈæsko] *s* (*pl* -cos or -coes) fiasco *m*, échec *m*

fiat [ˈfai·ət], [ˈfai·æt] *s* ordonnance *f*, autorisation *f*

fib [fɪb] *s* (coll) petit mensonge *m*, blague *f* || *v* (*pret & pp* fibbed; *ger* fibbing) *intr* (coll) blaguer

fiber [ˈfaɪbər] *s* fibre *f*

fibrous [ˈfaɪbrəs] *adj* fibreux

fickle [ˈfɪkəl] *adj* inconstant, volage

fiction [ˈfɪkʃən] *s* fiction *f*; (*branch of literature*) ouvrages *mpl* d'imagination, romans *mpl*

fictional [ˈfɪkʃənəl] *adj* romanesque, d'imagination

fictionalize [ˈfɪkʃənə ˌlaɪz] *tr* romancer

fictitious [fɪkˈtɪʃəs] *adj* fictif

fiddle [ˈfɪdəl] *s* violon *m* || *tr*—**to fiddle away** (coll) gaspiller || *intr* jouer du violon; **to fiddle around** or **with** (coll) tripoter

fiddler [ˈfɪdlər] *s* (coll) violoneux *m*

fid'dle-stick' *s* (coll) archet *m*; **fiddlesticks!** (coll) quelle blague!

fiddling [ˈfɪdlɪŋ] *adj* (coll) musard

fideli-ty [faɪˈdelɪti], [fɪˈdelɪti] *s* (*pl* -ties) fidélité *f*

fidget [ˈfɪdʒɪt] *intr* se trémousser; **to fidget with** tripoter

fidgety [ˈfɪdʒɪti] *adj* nerveux

fiduciar-y [fɪˈd(j)uʃɪ ˌeri] *adj* fiduciaire || *s* (*pl* -ies) fiduciaire

fie [faɪ] *interj* fi!; **fie on . . . !** nargue de . . . !

field [fild] *s* champ *m*; (*area, activity*) domaine *m*, aire *f*; (*aer, sports*) terrain *m*; (*elec*) champ; (*of motor or dynamo*) (elec) inducteur *m*; (*mil*) aire *f*, théâtre *m*

field' day' *s* (*cleanup*) (mil) manœuvres *fpl* de garnison; (*sports*) manifestation *f* sportive

fielder [ˈfildər] *s* (baseball) chasseur *m*, homme *m* de champ

field' glass'es *spl* jumelles *fpl*

field' hock'ey *s* hockey *m* sur gazon

field' hos'pital *s* ambulance *f*, formation *f* sanitaire

field' mag'net *s* aimant *m* inducteur

field' mar'shal *s* maréchal *m*

field' mouse' *s* mulot *m*

field'piece' *s* pièce *f* de campagne

fiend [find] *s* démon *m*; (*mischief-maker*) (coll) espiègle *mf*; (*enthusiast*) (coll) mordu *m*; (*addict*) (coll) toxicomane *mf*

fiendish [ˈfindɪʃ] *adj* diabolique

fierce [fɪrs] *adj* féroce, farouche; (*wind*) furieux; (coll) très mauvais

fierceness [ˈfɪrsnɪs] *s* férocité *f*

fier-y [ˈfaɪri], [ˈfaɪ·əri] *adj* (*comp* -ier; *super* -iest) ardent; (*speech*) enflammé; (*horse, person, etc.*) fougueux

fife [faɪf] *s* fifre *m*

fifteen [ˈfɪfˈtin] *adj, pron, & s* quinze *m*; **about fifteen** une quinzaine de

fifteenth [ˈfɪfˈtinθ] *adj & pron* quinzième (*masc, fem*); **the Fifteenth** quinze, e.g., **John the Fifteenth** Jean quinze || *s* quinzième *m*; **the fifteenth** (*in dates*) le quinze

fifth [fɪfθ] *adj & pron* cinquième (*masc, fem*); **the Fifth** cinq, e.g., **John the Fifth** Jean cinq || *s* cinquième *m*; (mus) quinte *f*; **the fifth** (*in dates*) le cinq

fifth' col'umn *s* cinquième colonne *f*

fiftieth [ˈfɪftɪ·ɪθ] *adj & pron* cinquantième (*masc, fem*) || *s* cinquantième *m*

fif-ty [ˈfɪfti] *adj & pron* cinquante || *s* (*pl* -ties) cinquante *m*; **about fifty** une cinquantaine *f*; **fifties** (*years of the decade*) années *fpl* cinquante

fif'ty-fif'ty *adv*—**to go fifty-fifty** (coll) être de moitié, être en compte à demi

fig [fɪg] *s* figue *f*; (*tree*) figuier *m*; **a fig for . . . !** (coll) nargue de . . . !

fight [faɪt] *s* combat *m*, bataille *f*; (*spirit*) cœur *m*; **to pick a fight with** chercher querelle à || *v* (*pret & pp* fought [fɔt]) *tr* combattre, se battre contre; **to fight off** repousser || *intr* combattre, se battre; **to fight shy of** se défier de

fighter ['faɪtər] s combattant m; (*game person*) batailleur m; (aer) chasseur m, avion m de chasse

fight′er pi′lot s chasseur m

fig′ leaf′ s feuille f de figuier; (*on statues*) feuille de vigne

figment ['fɪgmənt] s fiction f, invention f

figurative ['fɪgjərətɪv] adj figuratif; (*meaning*) figuré

figure ['fɪgjər] s figure f; (*bodily form*) taille f; (math) chiffre m; **to be good at figures** être bon en calcul; **to have a good figure** avoir de la ligne; **to keep one's figure** garder sa ligne || tr figurer; (*to embellish*) orner de motifs; (*to imagine*) se figurer, s'imaginer; **to figure out** calculer; (coll) déchiffrer || intr figurer; **to figure on** compter sur

fig′ured bass′ [bes] s (mus) basse f chiffrée

fig′ured silk′ s soie f à dessin

fig′ure-head′ s prête-nom m, homme m de paille; (naut) figure f de proue

fig′ure of speech′ s figure f de rhétorique

fig′ure skat′ing s patinage m de fantaisie

filament ['fɪləmənt] s filament m

filbert ['fɪlbərt] s noisette f, aveline f; (*tree*) noisetier m, avelinier m

filch [fɪltʃ] tr chaparder, chiper

file [faɪl] s (*tool*) lime f; (*for papers*) classeur m; (*for cards*) fichier m; (*personal record*) dossier m; (*line*) file f; **in single file** en file indienne, à la queue le leu leu; **to form single file** dédoubler les rangs || tr limer; classer, ranger; (*a petition*) déposer; **to file down** enlever à la lime || intr—**to file off** défiler; **to file out** sortir un à un

file′ case′ s fichier m

file′ clerk′ s employé m, commis m

file′ num′ber s (*e.g., used in answering a letter*) référence f

filial ['fɪlɪəl], ['fɪljəl] adj filial

filiation [,fɪlɪ'eʃən] s filiation f

filibuster ['fɪlɪ,bʌstər] s (*use of delaying tactics*) obstruction f; (*legislator*) obstructionniste mf; (*pirate*) flibustier m || tr (*legislation*) obstruer || intr faire de l'obstruction

filigree ['fɪlɪ,gri] adj filigrané || s filigrane m || tr filigraner

filing ['faɪlɪŋ] s (*of documents*) classement m; (*with a tool*) limage m; **filings** limaille f, grains mpl de limaille

fil′ing cab′inet s classeur m

fil′ing card′ s fiche f

Filipi-no [,fɪlɪ'pino] adj philippin || s (pl -nos) Philippin m

fill [fɪl] s suffisance f; (*earth, stones, etc.*) remblai m; **to have one's fill of** avoir tout son soûl de || tr remplir; (*a prescription*) exécuter; (*a tooth*) plomber; (*a cylinder with gas*) charger; (*a hollow or gap*) combler; (*a job*) occuper; **to fill in** remblayer,

combler; **to fill out** (*a questionnaire*) remplir || intr se remplir; **to fill out** se gonfler; (*said of sail*) s'enfler; **to fill up** se combler; (*to fill the tank full*) faire le plein

filler ['fɪlər] s remplissage m; (*of cigar*) tripe f; (*sizing*) apprêt m, mastic m; (*in notebook*) papier m; (journ) pesée f

fillet ['fɪlɪt] s bande f; (*for hair*) bandeau m; (archit) moulure f || ['fɪle], ['fɪlɪt] s (culin) filet m || tr couper en filets

filling ['fɪlɪŋ] adj (*food*) rassasiant || s (*of job*) occupation f; (*of tooth*) plombage m; (*e.g., of turkey*) farce f; (*of cigar*) tripe f

fill′ing sta′tion s poste m d'essence

fill′ing-station attend′ant s pompiste mf

fillip ['fɪlɪp] s tonique m, stimulant m; (*with finger*) chiquenaude f || tr donner une chiquenaude à

fil-ly ['fɪli] s (pl -lies) pouliche f; (coll) fillette f

film [fɪlm] s film m; (*in a roll*) pellicule f, film || tr filmer

filming ['fɪlmɪŋ] s filmage m

film′ li′brary s cinémathèque f

film′ mak′er s cinéaste m

film′ star′ s vedette f du cinéma

film′strip′ s film m fixe

film-y ['fɪlmi] adj (comp -ier; super -iest) diaphane, voilé

filter ['fɪltər] s filtre m || tr & intr filtrer

filtering ['fɪltərɪŋ] s filtrage m; (*of water*) filtration f

fil′ter pa′per s papier-filtre m

fil′ter tip′ adj à bout-filtre || s bout-filtre m, bout-filtrant m

filth [fɪlθ] s saleté f, ordure f; (fig) obscénité f

filth-y ['fɪlθi] adj (comp -ier; super -iest) sale, immonde

filth′y lu′cre ['lukər] s (coll) lucre m

fin [fɪn] s nageoire f

final ['faɪnəl] adj final; (*last in a series*) ultime, définitif || s examen m final; (sports) finale f

finale [fɪ'nɑli] s (mus) final m

finalist ['faɪnəlɪst] s finaliste mf

finally ['faɪnəli] adv finalement, enfin

finance [fɪ'næns], ['faɪnæns] s finance f || tr financer

financial [fɪ'nænʃəl], [faɪ'nænʃəl] adj financier; (*interest; distress*) pécuniaire

financier [,fɪnən'sɪr], [,faɪnən'sɪr] s financier m

financing [fɪ'nænsɪŋ], ['faɪnænsɪŋ] s financement m

finch [fɪntʃ] s pinson m

find [faɪnd] s trouvaille f || v (pret & pp found [faʊnd]) tr trouver; **to find out** apprendre || intr (law) déclarer; **to find out** (*about*) se renseigner (sur), se mettre au courant (de); **find out!** à vous de trouver!

finder ['faɪndər] s (*of camera*) viseur m; (*of optical instrument*) chercheur m

finding ['faɪndɪŋ] *s* découverte *f*; (*law*) décision *f*; **findings** conclusions *fpl*

fine [faɪn] *adj* fin; (*weather*) beau; (*person, manners, etc.*) distingué, excellent; **that's fine!** bien!, parfait! || *s* amende *f* || *tr* mettre à l'amende

fine' arts' *spl* beaux-arts *mpl*

fineness ['faɪnnɪs] *s* finesse *f*; (*of metal*) titre *m*

fine' print' *s* petits caractères *mpl*

finer·y ['faɪnəri] *s* (*pl* **-ies**) parure *f*

finespun ['faɪn,spʌn] *adj* ténu; (*fig*) subtil

finesse [fɪ'nɛs] *s* finesse *f*; (*in bridge*) impasse *f*; **to use finesse** finasser || *tr* faire l'impasse à

fine'-toothed comb' *s* peigne *m* aux dents fines, peigne fin

finger ['fɪŋɡər] *s* doigt *m*; (slang) mouchard *m*, indicateur *m*; **not to lift a finger** (fig) ne pas remuer le petit doigt; **to burn one's fingers** (fig) se faire échauder; **to put one's finger on the spot** (fig) mettre le doigt dessus; **to slip between the fingers** glisser entre les doigts; **to snap one's fingers at** (fig) faire la figue à, narguer; **to twist around one's little finger** (coll) mener par le bout du nez, faire tourner comme un toton || *tr* toucher du doigt, manier; (mus) doigter; (slang) espionner; (slang) identifier

fin'ger board' *s* (*of guitar*) touche *f*; (*of piano*) clavier *m*

fin'ger bowl' *s* rince-doigts *m*

fin'ger dexter'ity *s* (mus) doigté *m*

fingering ['fɪŋɡərɪŋ] *s* maniement *m*; (mus) doigté *m*

fin'ger·nail' *s* ongle *m*

fin'gernail pol'ish *s* brillant *m*

fin'ger·print' *s* empreinte *f* digitale || *tr* prendre les empreintes digitales de

fin'ger·tip' *s* bout *m* du doigt; **to have at one's fingertips** tenir sur le bout du doigt

finicky ['fɪnɪki] *adj* méticuleux

finish ['fɪnɪʃ] *s* (*perfection*) achevé *m*, fini *m*; (*elegance*) finesse *f*; (*conclusion*) fin *f*; (*gloss, coating, etc.*) fini *m* || *tr* & *intr* finir; **to finish** + *ger* finir de + *inf*; **to finish by** + *ger* finir par + *inf*

fin'ishing touch' *s* dernière main *f*

finite ['faɪnaɪt] *adj* & *s* fini *m*

Finland ['fɪnlənd] *s* Finlande *f*; la Finlande

Finlander ['fɪnləndər] *s* Finlandais *m*

Finn [fɪn] *s* (*member of a Finnish-speaking group of people*) Finnois *m*; (*native or inhabitant of Finland*) Finlandais *m*

Finnish ['fɪnɪʃ] *adj* & *s* finnois *m*

fir [fʌr] *s* sapin *m*

fire [faɪr] *s* feu *m*; (*destructive burning*) incendie *m*; **to catch fire** prendre feu; **to set on fire** mettre le feu à || *tr* mettre le feu à; (*e.g., passions*) enflammer; (*a weapon*) tirer; (*a rocket*) lancer; (*an employee*) (coll) renvoyer || *interj* (*warning*) au feu!; (*command to fire*) feu!

fire' alarm' *s* avertisseur *m* d'incendie; (*box*) poste *m* avertisseur d'incendie

fire'arm' *s* arme *f* à feu

fire'ball' *s* globe *m* de feu; (mil) grenade *f* incendiaire

fire'bird' *s* loriot *m* d'Amérique

fire'boat' *s* bateau-pompe *m*

fire'box' *s* boîte *f* à feu; (rr) foyer *m*

fire'brand' *s* tison *m*; (coll) brandon *m* de discorde

fire'break' *s* tranchée *f* garde-feu, pare-feu *m*

fire'brick' *s* brique *f* réfractaire

fire' brigade' *s* corps *m* de sapeurs-pompiers

fire'bug' *s* (coll) incendiaire *mf*

fire' chief' *s* capitaine *m* des pompiers

fire' com'pany *s* corps *m* de sapeurs-pompiers; (*insurance company*) compagnie *f* d'assurance contre l'incendie

fire'crack'er *s* pétard *m*

fire'damp' *s* grisou *m*

fire' depart'ment *s* service *m* des incendies, sapeurs-pompiers *mpl*

fire'dog' *s* chenet *m*, landier *m*

fire' drill' *s* exercices *mpl* de sauvetage en cas d'incendie

fire' en'gine *s* pompe *f* à incendie

fire' escape' *s* échelle *f* de sauvetage, escalier *m* de secours

fire' extin'guisher *s* extincteur *m*

fire'fly' *s* (*pl* **-flies**) luciole *f*

fire'guard' *s* (*before hearth*) pare-étincelles *m*; (*in forest*) pare-feu *m*

fire' hose' *s* manche *f* d'incendie

fire'house' *s* caserne *f* de pompiers, poste *m* de pompiers

fire' hy'drant *s* bouche *f* d'incendie

fire' insur'ance *s* assurance *f* contre l'incendie

fire' i'rons *spl* garniture *f* de foyer

fire'less cook'er ['faɪrlɪs] *s* marmite *f* norvégienne

fire'man *s* (*pl* **-men**) (*man who stokes fires*) chauffeur *m*; (*man who extinguishes fires*) sapeur-pompier *m*, pompier *m*

fire'place' *s* cheminée *f*, foyer *m*

fire'plug' *s* bouche *f* d'incendie

fire' pow'er *s* puissance *f* de feu

fire'proof' *adj* ignifuge; (*dish*) apyre || *tr* ignifuger

fire' sale' *s* vente *f* après incendie

fire' screen' *s* écran *m* de cheminée, garde-feu *m*

fire' ship' *s* brûlot *m*

fire' shov'el *s* pelle *f* à feu

fire'side' *s* coin *m* du feu

fire'trap' *s* édifice *m* qui invite l'incendie

fire' wall' *s* coupe-feu *m*

fire'ward'en *s* garde *m* forestier, vigie *f*

fire'wa'ter *s* (slang) gnole *f*, whisky *m*

fire'wood' *s* bois *m* de chauffage

fire'works' *spl* feu *m* d'artifice

firing ['faɪrɪŋ] *s* (*of furnace*) chauffe *f*; (*of bricks, ceramics, etc.*) cuite *f*; (*of gun*) tir *m*, feu *m*; (*by a group of soldiers*) fusillade *f*; (*of an internal-combustion engine*) allumage *m*; (*of an employee*) (coll) renvoi *m*

fir′ing line′ s ligne f de feu, chaîne f de combat

fir′ing or′der s rythme m d'allumage

fir′ing pin′ s percuteur m, aiguille f

fir′ing squad′ s peloton m d'exécution; *(for ceremonies)* piquet m d'honneurs funèbres

firm [fʌrm] adj & adv ferme; **to stand firm** tenir bon ‖ s maison f de commerce, firme f

firmament ['fʌrməmənt] s firmament m

firm′ name′ s nom m commercial

firmness ['fʌrmnɪs] s fermeté f

first [fʌrst] adj, pron, & s premier m; **at first** au commencement, au début; **first come first served** les premiers vont devant; **from the first** depuis le premier jour; **John the First** Jean premier ‖ adv premièrement, d'abord; **first and last** en tout et pour tout; **first of all, first off** tout d'abord, de prime abord

first′ aid′ s premiers soins mpl, premiers secours mpl

first′-aid′ kit′ s boîte f à pansements, trousse f de première urgence

first′-aid′ sta′tion s poste m de secours

first′-born′ adj & s premier-né m

first′-class′ adj de première classe, de premier ordre ‖ adv en première classe

first′ cous′in s cousin m germain

first′ draft′ s brouillon m, premier jet m

first′ fin′ger s index m

first′ floor′ s rez-de-chaussée m

first′ fruits′ spl prémices fpl

first′hand′ adj & adv de première main

first′ lieuten′ant s lieutenant m en premier

firstly ['fʌrstli] adv en premier lieu, d'abord

first′ mate′ s (naut) second m

first′ name′ s prénom m, petit nom m

first′ night′ s (theat) première f

first-nighter [,fʌrst'naɪtər] s (theat) habitué m des premières

first′ offend′er s délinquant m primaire

first′ of′ficer s (naut) officier m en second

first′ prize′ s *(in a lottery)* gros lot m; **to win first prize** remporter le prix

first′ quar′ter s *(of the moon)* premier quartier m

first′-rate′ adj de premier ordre, de première qualité; (coll) excellent ‖ adv (coll) très bien, à merveille

first′-run′ mov′ie s film m en exclusivité

fiscal ['fɪskəl] adj fiscal

fis′cal year′ s exercice m budgétaire

fish [fɪʃ] s poisson m; **to be like a fish out of water** être comme un poisson sur la paille; **to be neither fish nor fowl** être ni chair ni poisson; **to drink like a fish** boire comme un trou; **to have other fish to fry** avoir d'autres chiens à fouetter ‖ tr pêcher; (rr) éclisser; **to fish out or up** repêcher ‖ intr pêcher; **to fish for compliments** quêter des compliments; **to go fishing** aller à la pêche; **to take fishing** emmener à la pêche

fish′bone′ s arête f

fish′bowl′ s bocal m

fisher ['fɪʃər] s pêcheur m; (zool) martre f

fish′er·man s (pl -men) pêcheur m

fisher·y ['fɪʃəri] s (pl -ies) *(activity; business)* pêche f; *(grounds)* pêcherie f

fish′ hawk′ s aigle m pêcheur

fish′hook′ s hameçon m

fishing ['fɪʃɪŋ] adj pêcheur, de pêche ‖ s pêche f

fish′ing ground′ s pêcherie f

fish′ing reel′ s moulinet m

fish′ing rod′ s canne f à pêche

fish′ing tack′le s attirail m de pêche

fish′line′ s ligne f de pêche

fish′mar′ket s poissonnerie f

fish′plate′ s (rr) éclisse f

fish′pool′ s vivier m

fish′ spear′ s foène f, fouëne f

fish′ sto′ry s hâblerie f, blague f

fish′tail′ s queue f de poisson; (aer) embardée f ‖ intr (aer) embarder

fish′wife′ s (pl -wives′) poissonnière f; *(foul-mouthed woman)* poissarde f

fish′worm′ s asticot m

fish·y ['fɪʃi] adj (comp -ier; super -iest) *(eyes)* (coll) vitreux; (coll) véreux, louche

fission ['fɪʃən] s (biol) scission f; (nucl) fission f

fissionable ['fɪʃənəbəl] adj fissible, fissile

fissure ['fɪʃər] s fissure f, fente f ‖ tr fissurer ‖ intr se fissurer

fist [fɪst] s poing m; (typ) petite main f; **to shake one's fist at** menacer du poing

fist′fight′ s combat m à coup de poings

fistful ['fɪstful] s poignée f

fisticuffs ['fɪstɪ,kʌfs] spl empoignade f or rixe f à coups de poing; (sports) boxe f

fit [fɪt] adj (comp fitter; super fittest) bon, convenable; capable, digne; *(in good health)* en forme, sain; **fit to be tied** (coll) en colère; **fit to drink** buvable; **fit to eat** mangeable; **to feel fit** être frais et dispos ‖ s ajustement m; *(of clothes)* coupe f, façon f; *(of fever, rage, coughing)* accès m; **by fits and starts** par accès; **fit of coughing** quinte f de toux ‖ v (pret & pp fitted; ger fitting) tr ajuster; *(s.th. in s.th)* emboîter; **to fit for** (e.g., a task) préparer à; **to fit out or up** aménager; **to fit out with** garnir de ‖ intr s'emboîter; **to fit in with** s'accorder avec, convenir à

fitful ['fɪtfəl] adj intermittent

fitness ['fɪtnɪs] s convenance f; *(for a task)* aptitude f; *(good shape)* bonne forme f

fitter ['fɪtər] s ajusteur m; *(of machinery)* monteur m; *(of clothing)* essayeur m

fitting ['fɪtɪŋ] adj convenable, approprié, à propos ‖ s ajustage m; *(of a garment)* essayage m; **fittings** aménagements mpl; *(of metal)* ferrures fpl

five [faɪv] adj & pron cinq || s cinq m;
  five o'clock cinq heures

five'-year plan' s plan m quinquennal

fix [fɪks] s (coll) mauvais pas m; **to be
in a fix** (coll) être dans le pétrin || tr
réparer; (e.g., a date; a photographic
image; prices; one's eyes) fixer;
(slang) donner son compte à

fixedly ['fɪksɪdli] adv fixement

fixing ['fɪksɪŋ] s fixation f; (phot)
fixage m; **fixings** (slang) collation f,
des mets mpl

fix'ing bath' s bain m de fixage, fixa-
teur m

fixture ['fɪkstʃər] s accessoire m, garniture f; **fixtures** meubles mpl à demeure

fizz [fɪz] s pétillement m || intr pétiller

fizzle ['fɪzəl] s (coll) avortement m ||
intr (coll) avorter; **to fizzle out** (coll)
tomber à l'eau, échouer

flabbergasted ['flæbər‚gæstɪd] adj
(coll) éberlué, épaté

flab·by ['flæbi] adj (comp -bier; super
-biest) mou, flasque

flag [flæg] s drapeau m || v (pret & pp
flagged; ger flagging) tr—**to flag s.o.**
transmettre des signaux à qn en agi-
tant un fanion || intr faiblir, se re-
lâcher

flag' cap'tain s (nav) capitaine m de
pavillon

flag'man s (pl -men) signaleur m; (rr)
garde-voie m

flag' of truce' s drapeau m parlementaire

flag'pole' s hampe f de drapeau;
(naut) mât m de pavillon; (surv)
jalon m

flagrant ['flegrənt] adj scandaleux;
(e.g., injustice) flagrant

flag'ship' s (nav) vaisseau m amiral

flag'staff' s hampe f de drapeau

flag'stone' s dalle f

flag' stop' s (rr) halte f, arrêt m facultatif

flag'-wav'ing adj cocardier || s pa-
triotisme m de façade

flail [flel] s fléau m || tr (agr) battre au
fléau; (fig) éreinter

flair [fler] s flair m; aptitude f

flak [flæk] s tir m contre-avions

flake [flek] s (of snow; of cereal) floc-
con m; (of soap; of mica) paillette f;
(of paint) écaille f || intr tomber en
flocons; **to flake off** s'écailler

flak·y ['fleki] adj (comp -ier; super
-iest) floconneux, lamelleux

flamboyant [flæm'bɔɪ‚ənt] adj fleuri,
orné, coloré; (archit) flamboyant

flame [flem] s flamme f; (coll) amant
m, amante f || tr flamber || intr
flamber, flamboyer

flamethrower ['flem‚θro‚ər] s lance-
flammes m

flaming ['flemɪŋ] adj flambant

flamin·go [flə'mɪŋgo] s (pl -gos or
-goes) flamant m

flammable ['flæməbəl] adj inflammable

Flanders ['flændərz] s Flandre f; la
Flandre

flange [flændʒ] s rebord m, saillie f;
(of wheel) jante f; (of rail) patin m

flank [flæŋk] s flanc m || tr flanquer

flannel ['flænəl] s flanelle f

flap [flæp] s (part that can be folded
under) rabat m; (fold in clothing)
pan m; (of a cap) couvre-nuque m;
(of a pocket; of an envelope) patte
f; (of wings) coup m, battement m;
(of a table) battant m; (of a sail,
flag, etc.) claquement m; (slap) tape
f; (aer) volet m || v (pret & pp
flapped; ger flapping) tr (wings,
arms, etc.) battre; (to slap) taper ||
intr battre; (said of sail, flag, etc.)
claquer; (said of curtain) voltiger;
(to hang down) pendre

flap'jack' s (coll) crêpe f

flare [fler] s éclat m vif; (e.g., of skirt;
of pipe or funnel) évasement m; (for
signaling) fusée f éclairante || tr éva-
ser || intr flamboyer; (to spread out-
ward) s'évaser; **to flare up** s'enflammer; (to reappear) se produire
de nouveau; (to become angry) s'emporter

flare'-up' s flambée f soudaine; (of illness) recrudescence f; (of anger)
accès m de colère

flash [flæʃ] s éclair m; (of hope) lueur
f, rayon m; (of wit) trait m; (of
genius) éclair; (brief moment) instant
m; (ostentation) (coll) tape-à-l'œil m;
(last-minute news) (coll) nouvelle f
éclair; **flash in the pan** (coll) feu m
de paille; **in a flash** en un clin d'œil ||
tr projeter; (a gem) faire étinceler;
(to show off) faire parade de; (a mes-
sage) répandre, transmettre || intr
jeter des éclairs; (said of gem, eyes,
etc.) étinceler; **to flash by** passer
comme un éclair

flash'back' s (mov) retour m en arrière,
rappel m

flash' bulb' s ampoule f flash, flash m

flash' flood' s crue f subite

flashing ['flæʃɪŋ] adj éclatant; (light)
à éclats; (signal) clignotant || s bande
f de solin

flash'light' s lampe f torche, lampe de
poche; (phot) lampe éclair

flash'light bat'tery s pile f de torche

flash·y ['flæʃi] adj (comp -ier; super
-iest) (coll) tapageur, criard

flask [flæsk], [flɑsk] s flacon m,
gourde f; (in lab) ballon m, flacon

flat [flæt] adj (comp flatter; super
flattest) plat, uni; (nose) aplati; (refusal) net; (beer) éventé; (tire) dégonflé; (dull, tasteless) fade, terne;
(mus) bémol; s appartement m;
(flat tire) crevaison f; (of sword)
plat m; (mus) bémol m; (theat) châs-
sis m || adv (outright) (coll) nette-
ment, carrément; **to fall flat** tomber à
plat; (fig) manquer son effet; **to sing
flat** chanter faux

flat'boat' s plate f

flat-broke ['flæt'brok] adj (coll) complètement fauché, à la côte

flat'car' s plate-forme f

flat'foot' s (slang) flic m
flat'-foot'ed adj aux pieds plats; (coll) franc, brutal
flat'i'ron s fer m à repasser
flatly ['flætli] adv net, platement
flat'-nosed' adj camard, camus
flatten ['flætən] tr aplatir, aplanir; (metallurgy) laminer || intr s'aplatir, s'aplanir; **to flatten out** (aer) se redresser
flatter ['flætər] tr & intr flatter
flatterer ['flætərər] s flatteur m
flattering ['flætərɪŋ] adj flatteur
flatter·y ['flætəri] s (pl -ies) flatterie f
flat' tire' s pneu m dégonflé, à plat, or crevé, crevaison f
flat'top' s (nav) porte-avions m
flatulence ['flætʃələns] s boursouflure f; (pathol) flatulence f
flat'ware' s couverts mpl; (plates) assiettes fpl
flaunt [flɔnt], [flɑnt] tr faire étalage de
flautist ['flɔtɪst] s flûtiste mf
flavor ['flevər] s saveur f, goût m; (of ice cream) parfum m || tr assaisonner, parfumer
flavoring ['flevərɪŋ] s assaisonnement m; (lemon, rum, etc.) parfum m
flaw [flɔ] s défaut m, tache f; (crack) fêlure f; (in metal) paille f; (in diamond) crapaud m
flawless ['flɔlɪs] adj sans défaut, sans tache
flax [flæks] s lin m
flaxen ['flæksən] adj de lin, blond
flax'seed' s graine f de lin
flay [fle] tr écorcher; (to criticize) rosser, fustiger
flea [fli] s puce f
flea'bite' s piqûre f de puce; (trifle) vétille f
fleck [flek] s tache f; (particle) particule f || tr tacheter
fledgling ['fledʒlɪŋ] adj (lawyer, teacher) en herbe, débutant || s oisillon m; (novice) débutant m, béjaune m
flee [fli] v (pret & pp **fled** [fled]) tr & intr fuir
fleece [flis] s toison f || tr tondre; (to strip of money) (coll) écorcher, plumer
fleec·y ['flisi] adj (comp **-ier;** super **-iest**) laineux; (snow, wool) floconneux; (hair) moutonneux; (clouds) moutonné
fleet [flit] adj rapide || s flotte f
fleet'-foot'ed adj au pied léger
fleeting ['flitɪŋ] adj passager, fugitif
Fleming ['flemɪŋ] s Flamand m
Flemish ['flemɪʃ] adj & s flamand m
flesh [fleʃ] s chair f; **in the flesh** en chair et en os; **to lose flesh** perdre de l'embonpoint; **to put on flesh** prendre de l'embonpoint, s'empâter
flesh' and blood' s nature f humaine; (relatives) famille f, parenté f
flesh'-col'ored adj couleur f de chair, carné
flesh'pot' s (pot for cooking meat) pot-au-feu m; **fleshpots** (high living) luxe m, grande chère f; (evil places) maisons fpl de débauche, mauvais lieux mpl
flesh' wound' [wund] s blessure f en séton, blessure superficielle
flesh·y ['fleʃi] adj (comp **-ier;** super **-iest**) charnu
flex [fleks] tr & intr fléchir
flexible ['fleksɪbəl] adj flexible
flick [flɪk] s (with finger) chiquenaude f; (with whip) petit coup m; **flicks** (coll) ciné m || tr faire une chiquenaude à; (a whip) faire claquer
flicker ['flɪkər] s petite lueur f vacillante; (of eyelids) battement m; (of emotion) frisson m || intr trembloter, vaciller; (said of eyelids) ciller
flier ['flai·ər] s aviateur m; (coll) spéculation f au hasard; (rr) rapide m; (handbill) (coll) prospectus m
flight [flait] s fuite f; (of airplane) vol m; (of birds) volée f; (of stairs) volée f; (of fancy) élan m; **to put to flight** mettre en fuite; **to take flight** prendre la fuite
flight' deck' s (nav) pont m d'envol
flight' rec'ord'er s enregistreur m en vol
flight·y ['flaiti] adj (comp **-ier;** super **-iest**) volage, braque, écervelé
flim-flam ['flɪm,flæm] s (coll) baliverne f; (fraud) (coll) escroquerie f || v (pret & pp **-flammed;** ger **-flamming**) tr (coll) escroquer
flim·sy ['flɪmzi] adj (comp **-sier;** super **-siest**) léger; (e.g., cloth) fragile; (e.g., excuse) frivole
flinch [flɪntʃ] intr reculer, fléchir; **without flinching** sans broncher, sans hésiter
fling [flɪŋ] s jet m; **to go on a fling** faire la noce; **to have a fling at** tenter; **to have one's fling** jeter sa gourme || v (pret & pp **flung** [flʌŋ]) tr lancer; (on the floor, out the window; in jail) jeter; **to fling open** ouvrir brusquement
flint [flɪnt] s silex m; (of lighter) pierre f
flint'lock' s fusil m à pierre
flint·y ['flɪnti] adj (comp **-ier;** super **-iest**) siliceux; (heart) de pierre, insensible
flip [flɪp] adj (comp **flipper;** super **flippest**) (coll) mutin, moqueur || s chiquenaude f; (somersault) culbute f; (aer) petit tour m de vol || v (pret & pp **flipped;** ger **flipping**) tr donner une chiquenaude à; (a page) tourner rapidement; **to flip a coin** jouer à pile ou face; **to flip over** (a phonograph record) retourner
flippancy ['flɪpənsi] s désinvolture f
flippant ['flɪpənt] adj désinvolte
flipper ['flɪpər] s nageoire f
flirt [flʌrt] s flirteur m, flirt m || intr flirter; (said only of a man) conter fleurette
flit [flɪt] v (pret & pp **flitted;** ger **flitting**) intr voleter; **to flit away** passer rapidement; **to flit here and there** voltiger
float [flot] s (raft) radeau m; (on fish line; in carburetor; on seaplane) flot-

teur *m*; (*on fish line or net*) flotte *f*; (*of mason*) aplanissoire *f*; (*in parade*) char *m* de cavalcade, char de Carnaval || *tr* faire flotter; (*a loan*) émettre, contracter || *intr* flotter, nager; (*on one's back*) faire la planche

floater ['flotər] *s* vagabond *m*; (*illegal voter*) faux électeur *m*

floating ['flotɪŋ] *adj* flottant; (*free*) libre || *s* flottement *m*; (*of loan*) émission *f*

float'ing is'land *s* (culin) œufs *mpl* à la neige

flock [flɑk] *s* (*of birds*) volée *f*; (*of sheep*) troupeau *m*; (*of people*) foule *f*, bande *f*; (*of nonsense*) tas *m*; (*of faithful*) ouailles *fpl* || *intr* s'assembler; **to flock in** entrer en foule; **to flock together** s'attrouper

floe [flo] *s* banquise *f*; (*floating piece of ice*) glaçon *m* flottant

flog [flɑg] *v* (*pret & pp* **flogged**; *ger* **flogging**) *tr* fouetter, flageller

flogging ['flɑgɪŋ] *s* fouet *m*

flood [flʌd] *s* inondation *f*; (*caused by heavy rain*) déluge *m*; (*sudden rise of river*) crue *f*; (*of tide*) flot *m*; (*of words, tears, light*) flots *mpl*, déluge || *tr* inonder; (*to overwhelm*) submerger, inonder; (*a carburetor*) noyer || *intr* (*said of river*) déborder, (aut) se noyer

flood'gate' *s* (*of a dam*) vanne *f*; (*of a canal*) porte *f* d'écluse

flood'light' *s* phare *m* d'éclairage, projecteur *m* de lumière || *tr* illuminer par projecteurs

flood' tide' *s* marée *f* montante, flux *m*

floor [flor] *s* (*inside bottom surface of room*) plancher *m*, parquet *m*; (*story of building*) étage *m*; (*of swimming pool, the sea, etc.*) fond *m*; (*of assembly hall*) enceinte *f*, parquet; (*of the court*) prétoire *m*, parquet; (naut) varangue *f*; **to ask for the floor** réclamer la parole; **to give s.o. the floor** donner la parole à qn; **to have the floor** avoir la parole; **to take the floor** prendre la parole || *tr* parqueter; (*an opponent*) terrasser; (*to disconcert*) (coll) désarçonner

flooring ['florɪŋ] *s* planchéiage *m*, parquetage *m*

floor' lamp' *s* lampe *f* à pied, lampadaire *m*

floor' mop' *s* brosse *f* à parquet

floor' show' *s* spectacle *m* de cabaret

floor' tim'ber *s* (naut) varangue *f*

floor'walk'er *s* chef *m* de rayon

floor' wax' *s* cire *f* à parquet, encaustique *f*

flop [flɑp] *s* (coll) insuccès *m*, échec *m*; (*literary work or painting*) (coll) navet *m*; (*play*) (coll) four *m*; **to take a flop** (coll) faire patapouf || *v* (*pret & pp* **flopped**; *ger* **flopping**) *intr* tomber lourdement; (*to fail*) (coll) échouer, rater

flora ['florə] *s* flore *f*

floral ['florəl] *adj* floral

florescence [flo'resəns] *s* floraison *f*

florid ['flɑrɪd], ['flɔrɪd] *adj* fleuri, flamboyant; (*complexion*) rubicond

Florida ['flɑrɪdə], ['flɔrɪdə] *s* Floride *f*; la Floride

Flor'ida Keys' *spl* Cayes *fpl* de la Floride

floss [flɑs], [flɔs] *s* bourre *f*; (*of corn*) barbe *f*

floss' silk' *s* bourre *f* de soie, filoselle *f*

floss·y ['flɔsi], ['flɑsi] *adj* (*comp* **-ier**; *super* **-iest**) soyeux; (slang) pimpant, tapageur

flotsam ['flɑtsəm] *s* épave *f*

flot'sam and jet'sam *s* choses *fpl* de flot et de mer, épaves *fpl*

flounce [flɑuns] *s* volant *m* || *tr* garnir de volants || *intr* s'élancer avec emportement

flounder ['flɑundər] *s* flet *m*; (*plaice*) carrelet *m*, plie *f* || *intr* patauger

flour [flɑur] *s* farine *f* || *tr* fariner

flourish ['flʌrɪʃ] *s* fioriture *f*; (*on a signature*) paraphe *m*; (*of trumpets*) fanfare *m*; (*brandishing*) brandissement *m* || *tr* brandir; (*to wave*) agiter || *intr* fleurir, prospérer

flourishing ['flʌrɪʃɪŋ] *adj* florissant

flour' mill' *s* moulin *m*, minoterie *f*

floury ['flɑuri] *adj* farineux

flout [flɑut] *tr* se moquer de, narguer || *intr* se moquer

flow [flo] *s* écoulement *m*; (*of tide, blood, words*) flot *m*, flux *m*; (*of blood to the head*) afflux *m*; (*rate of flow*) débit *m*; (*current*) courant *m* || *intr* écouler; (*said of tide*) monter; (*said of blood in the body*) circuler; (fig) couler; **to flow into** déboucher dans, se verser dans; **to flow over** déborder

flower ['flɑuər] *s* fleur *f* || *tr & intr* fleurir

flow'er bed' *s* plate-bande *f*, parterre *m*; (*round flower bed*) corbeille *f*

flow'er gar'den *s* jardin *m* de fleurs, jardin d'agrément

flow'er girl' *s* bouquetière *f*; (*at a wedding*) fille *f* d'honneur

flow'er·pot' *s* pot *m* à fleurs

flow'er shop' *s* boutique *f* de fleuriste

flow'er show' *s* exposition *f* horticole, floralies *fpl*

flow'er stand' *s* jardinière *f*

flowery ['flɑuəri] *adj* fleuri

flu [flu] *s* (coll) grippe *f*

fluctuate ['flʌktʃʊ͵et] *intr* fluctuer

flue [flu] *s* tuyau *m*

fluency ['fluənsi] *s* facilité *f*

fluent ['fluənt] *adj* disert, facile; (*flowing*) coulant

fluently ['fluəntli] *adv* couramment

fluff [flʌf] *s* (*velvety cloth*) peluche *f*; (*tuft of fur, dust, etc.*) duvet *m*; (*boner made by actor*) (coll) loup *m* || *tr* lainer, rendre pelucheux; (*one's entrance*) (coll) louper; (*one's lines*) (coll) bouler || *intr* pelucher

fluff·y ['flʌfi] *adj* (*comp* **-ier**; *super* **-iest**) duveteux; (*hair*) flou

fluid ['fluɪd] *adj & s* fluide *m*

fluke [fluk] *s* (*of anchor*) patte *f*; (billiards) raccroc *m*, coup *m* de veine

flume [flum] *s* canalisation *f*, ravin *m*

flunk [flʌŋk] *tr* (*a student*) (coll) recaler, coller; (*an exam*) rater ‖ *intr* être recalé, se faire coller

flunk·y [ˈflʌŋki] *s* (*pl* -ies) laquais *m*

fluorescent [ˌflu·əˈrɛsənt] *adj* fluorescent

fluoridate [ˈflɔrɪˌdet], [ˈflurɪˌdet] *tr & intr* fluorider

fluoridation [ˌflɔrɪˈdeʃən], [ˌflurɪˈde-ʃən] *s* fluoridation *f*

fluoride [ˈflu·əˌraɪd] *s* fluorure *m*

fluorine [ˈflu·əˌrin] *s* fluor *m*

fluoroscopy [ˌflu·əˈrɑskəpi] *s* radioscopie *f*

fluorspar [ˈflu·ərˌspɑr] *s* spath *m* fluor

flur·ry [ˈflʌri] *s* (*pl* -ries) agitation *f*; (*of wind, snow, etc.*) rafale *f* ‖ *v* (*pret & pp* -ried) *tr* agiter

flush [flʌʃ] *adj* (*level*) à ras; (*well-provided*) bien pourvu; (*healthy*) vigoureux; **flush with** au ras de, au niveau de ‖ *s* (*of light*) éclat *m*; (*in the cheeks*) rougeur *f*; (*of joy*) transport *m*; (*of toilet*) chasse *f* d'eau; (*in poker*) flush *m*; **in the first flush of** dans l'ivresse ou le premier éclat de ‖ *adv* à ras, de niveau; (*directly*) droit ‖ *tr* (*a bird*) lever; **to flush a toilet** tirer la chasse d'eau; **to flush out** (*e.g., a drain*) laver à grande eau ‖ *intr* (*to blush*) rougir

flush′ switch′ *s* interrupteur *m* encastré

flush′ tank′ *s* réservoir *m* de chasse

flush′ toi′let *s* water-closet *m* à chasse d'eau

fluster [ˈflʌstər] *s* agitation *f*; **in a fluster** en émoi ‖ *tr* agiter

flute [flut] *s* flûte *f* ‖ *tr* (*a column*) canneler; (*a dress*) tuyauter

flutist [ˈflutɪst] *s* flûtiste *mf*

flutter [ˈflʌtər] *s* battement *m*; **all of a flutter** (coll) tout agité ‖ *intr* voleter; (*said of pulse*) battre fébrilement; (*said of heart*) palpiter

flux [flʌks] *s* flux *m*; (*for fusing metals*) acide *m* à souder; **to be in flux** être dans un état indécis

fly [flaɪ] *s* (*pl* flies) mouche *f*; (*for fishing*) mouche artificielle; (*of trousers*) braguette *f*; (*of tent*) auvent *m*; **flies** (theat) cintres *mpl*; **fly in the ointment** ombre *f* au tableau; **on the fly** au vol ‖ *v* (*pret* flew [flu]; *pp* flown [flon]) *tr* (*a kite*) faire voler; (*an airplane*) piloter; (*freight or passengers*) transporter en avion; (*e.g. the Atlantic*) survoler; (*to flee from*) fuir ‖ *intr* voler; (*to flee*) fuir; (*said of flag*) flotter; **to fly blind** voler à l'aveuglette; **to fly by** voler; **to fly in the face of** porter un défi à; **to fly off** s'envoler; **to fly off the handle** (coll) sortir de ses gonds; **to fly open** s'ouvrir brusquement; **to fly over** survoler

fly′blow′ *s* œufs *mpl* de mouche

fly′-by-night′ *adj* mal financé, indigne de confiance ‖ *s* financier *m* qui lève le pied

fly′ cast′ing *s* pêche *f* à la mouche noyée

fly′catch′er *s* attrape-mouches *m*; (bot) dionée *f*, attrape-mouches; (orn) gobe-mouches *m*

fly′-fish′ *intr* pêcher à la mouche

flying [ˈflaɪ·ɪŋ] *adj* volant; rapide; court, passager ‖ *s* aviation *f*; vol *m*

fly′ing but′tress *s* arc-boutant *m*

fly′ing col′ors—with flying colors drapeau *m* déployé; brillamment

fly′ing field′ *s* champ *m* d'aviation

fly′ing-fish′ *s* poisson *m* volant

fly′ing sau′cer *s* soucoupe *f* volante

fly′ing start′ *s* départ *m* lancé

fly′ing time′ *s* heures *fpl* de vol

fly′leaf′ *s* (*pl* -leaves) feuille *f* de garde, garde *f*

fly′ net′ *s* (*for a bed*) moustiquaire *f*; (*for a horse*) chasse-mouches *m*

fly′ pa′per *s* papier *m* tue-mouches

fly′ rod′ *s* canne *f* à mouche

fly′speck′ *s* chiure *f*, chiasse *f*

fly′ swat′ter [ˌswɑtər] *s* chasse-mouches *m*, émouchoir *m*

fly′trap′ *s* attrape-mouches *m*

fly′wheel′ *s* volant *m*

foal [fol] *s* poulain *m* ‖ *intr* mettre bas

foam [fom] *s* écume *f*; (*on beer*) mousse *f* ‖ *intr* écumer, mousser

foam′ rub′ber *s* caoutchouc *m* mousse

foam·y [ˈfomi] *adj* (*comp* -ier; *super* -iest) écumeux, mousseux

fob [fɑb] *s* (*pocket*) gousset *m*; (*ornament*) breloque *f* ‖ *v* (*pret & pp* fobbed; *ger* fobbing) *tr*—**to fob off s.th. on s.o.** refiler q.ch. à qn

f.o.b. or **F.O.B.** [ˌɛf.oˈbi] *adv* (letter-word) (free on board) franco de bord, départ usine

focal [ˈfokəl] *adj* focal

fo·cus [ˈfokəs] *s* (*pl* -cuses or -ci [saɪ]) foyer *m*; **in focus** au point; **out of focus** non réglé, hors du point focal ‖ *v* (*pret & pp* -cused or -cussed; *ger* -cusing or -cussing) *tr* mettre au point, faire converger; (*a beam of electrons*) focaliser; (*e.g., attention*) concentrer ‖ *intr* converger; **to focus on** se concentrer sur

fodder [ˈfɑdər] *s* fourrage *m*

foe [fo] *s* ennemi *m*, adversaire *mf*

fog [fɑg], [fɔg] *s* brouillard *m*; (naut) brume *f*; (phot) voile *m* ‖ *v* (*pret & pp* fogged; *ger* fogging) *tr* embrumer; (phot) voiler ‖ *intr* s'embrumer; (phot) se voiler

fog′ bank′ *s* banc *m* de brume

fog′ bell′ *s* cloche *f* de brume

fog′bound′ *adj* arrêté par le brouillard, pris dans le brouillard

fog·gy [ˈfɑgi], [ˈfɔgi] *adj* (*comp* -gier; *super* -giest) brumeux; (phot) voilé; (fig) confus, flou; **it is foggy** il fait du brouillard

fog′horn′ *s* sirène *f*, corne *f*, or trompe *f* de brume

foible [ˈfɔɪbəl] *s* faible *m*, marotte *f*

foil [fɔɪl] *s* (*thin sheet of metal*) feuille *f*, lame *f*; (*of mirror*) tain *m*; (*sword*) fleuret *m*; (*person whose personality sets off another's*) repoussoir *m* ‖ *tr* déjouer, frustrer

foil/-wrapped/ adj ceint de papier d'argent

foist [fɔɪst] tr—to foist oneself upon s'imposer chez; to foist s.th. on s.o. imposer q.ch. à qn

fold [fold] s pli m, repli m; (for sheep) parc m, bergerie f; (of fat) bourrelet m; (of the faithful) bercail m || tr plier, replier; (one's arms) se croiser; to fold in (culin) incorporer; to fold up replier || intr se replier; to fold up (theat) faire four; (coll) s'effondrer

folder ['foldər] s (covers for holding papers) chemise f; (pamphlet) dépliant m; (person folding newspapers) plieur m

folderol ['faldə,ral] s sottise f; (piece of foolishness) bagatelle f

folding ['foldɪŋ] adj pliant, repliant, rabattable

fold/ing cam/era s appareil m pliant

fold/ing chair/ s chaise f pliante, chaise brisée

fold/ing cot/ s lit m pliant or escamotable

fold/ing door/ s porte f à deux battants

fold/ing rule/ s mètre m pliant

fold/ing screen/ s paravent m

fold/ing seat/ s strapontin m

foliage ['foli·ɪdʒ] s feuillage m, feuillu m

foli·o ['foli·ˌo] adj in-folio || s (pl -os) (sheet) folio m; (book) in-folio m || tr folioter, paginer

folk [fok] adj populaire, traditionnel, du peuple || s (pl folk or folks) peuple m, race f; folks (coll) gens mpl, personnes fpl; my folks (coll) les miens mpl, ma famille

folk/ dance/ s danse f folklorique

folk/lore/ s folklore m

folk/ mu/sic s musique f populaire

folk/ song/ s chanson f du terroir

folk·sy ['foksi] adj (comp -sier; super -siest) (coll) sociable, liant; (like common people) (coll) du terroir

folk/ways/ spl coutumes fpl traditionnelles

follicle ['falɪkəl] s follicule m

follow ['falo] tr suivre; (to come after) succéder (with dat); (to understand) comprendre; (a profession) embrasser; to follow up poursuivre; (e.g., a success) exploiter || intr suivre; (one after the other) se suivre; as follows comme suit; it follows that il s'ensuit que

follower ['falo·ər] s suivant m; partisan m, disciple m

following ['falo·ɪŋ] adj suivant || s (of a prince) suite f; (followers) partisans mpl, disciples mpl

fol/low the lead/er s jeu m de la queue leu leu

fol/low-up/ adj de continuation, complémentaire; (car) suiveur || s soins mpl post-hospitaliers

fol·ly ['fali] s (pl -lies) sottise f; (madness) folie f; **follies** spectacle m de music-hall, folies fpl

foment [fo'ment] tr fomenter

fond [fand] adj affectueux, tendre; to become fond of s'attacher à

fondle ['fandəl] tr caresser

fondness ['fandnɪs] s affection f, tendresse f; (appetite) goût m, penchant m

font [fant] s source f; (for holy water) bénitier m; (for baptism) fonts mpl; (typ) fonte f

food [fud] adj alimentaire || s nourriture f, aliments mpl; food for thought matière f à réflexion; good food bonne cuisine f

food/ and cloth/ing s le vivre et le vêtement

food/ and drink/ s le boire et le manger

food/stuffs/ spl denrées fpl alimentaires, vivres mpl

fool [ful] s sot m; (jester) fou m; (person imposed on) innocent m, niais m; to make a fool of se moquer de; to play the fool faire le pitre || tr mystifier, abuser; to fool away gaspiller sottement || intr faire la bête; to fool around (coll) gâcher son temps; to fool with (coll) tripoter

fooler·y ['fuləri] s (pl -ies) sottise f, ânerie f

fool/har/dy adj (comp -dier; super -diest) téméraire

fooling ['fulɪŋ] s tromperie f; no fooling! sans blague!

foolish ['fulɪʃ] adj sot, niais; ridicule, absurde

fool/proof/ adj à toute épreuve; infaillible

fools/cap/ s papier m ministre

fool's/ er/rand s—to go on a fool's errand y aller pour des prunes

foot [fut] s (pl feet [fit]) pied m; (of cat, dog, bird) patte f; on foot à pied; to drag one's feet aller à pas de tortue; to have one foot in the grave avoir un pied dans la tombe; to put one's best foot forward (coll) partir du bon pied; to put one's foot down faire acte d'autorité; to put one's foot in it (coll) mettre les pieds dans le plat; to stand on one's own feet voler de ses propres ailes; to tread under foot fouler aux pieds || tr (the bill) payer; to foot it aller à pied

footage ['futɪdʒ] s (mov, telv) (in French métrage m, i.e., length of film in meters) longueur f d'un film en pieds

foot/-and-mouth/ disease/ s (vet) fièvre f aphteuse

foot/ball/ s football m américain; (ball) ballon m

foot/ brake/ s frein m à pédale

foot/bridge/ s passerelle f

foot/fall/ s pas m léger, bruit m de pas

foot/hills/ spl contreforts mpl, collines fpl basses

foot/hold/ s—to gain a foothold prendre pied

footing ['futɪŋ] s équilibre m; (archit) empattement m, base f, socle m; to be on a friendly footing être en bons termes; to be on an equal footing être sur un pied d'égalité; **to lose one's footing** perdre pied

foot'lights' *spl* (theat) rampe *f*

foot'lock'er *s* (mil) cantine *f*

foot'loose' *adj* libre, sans entraves

foot'man *s* (*pl* **-men**) valet *m* de pied

foot'mark' *s* empreinte *f* de pied

foot'note' *s* note *f* au bas de la page

foot'pad' *s* voleur *m* de grand chemin

foot'path' *s* sentier *m* pour piétons

foot'print' *s* empreinte *f* de pas, trace *f*

foot'race' *s* course *f* à pied

foot'rest' *s* cale-pied *m*, repose-pied *m*

foot' sol'dier *s* fantassin *m*

foot'sore' *adj* aux pieds endoloris, éclopé

foot'step' *s* pas *m*; **to follow in s.o.'s footsteps** suivre les traces de qn

foot'stone' *s* pierre *f* tumulaire (au pied d'une tombe); (archit) première pierre

foot'stool' *s* tabouret *m*

foot' warm'er *s* chauffe-pieds *m*

foot'wear' *s* chaussures *fpl*

foot'work' *s* jeu *m* de jambes

foot'worn' *adj* usé; (*person*) aux pieds endoloris

fop [fɑp] *s* petit-maître *m*, bellâtre *m*

for [fɔr], [fər] *prep* pour; de, e.g., **to thank s.o. for** remercier qn de; e.g., **time for dinner** l'heure du dîner; e.g., **to cry for joy** pleurer de joie; e.g., **request for money** demande d'argent; à, e.g., **for sale à** vendre; e.g., **to sell for a high price** vendre à un prix élevé; e.g., **it is for you to decide** c'est à vous de décider; par, e.g., **famous for** célèbre par; e.g., **for example** par exemple; e.g., **for pity's sake** par pitié; contre, e.g., **a remedy for** un remède contre; as for quant à; **for** + *ger* pour + *perf inf*, e.g., **he was punished for stealing** il fut puni pour avoir volé; **for all that** malgré tout cela; **for short** en abrégé; **he has been in Paris for a week** il est à Paris depuis une semaine, il y a une semaine qu'il est à Paris; **he was in Paris for a week** il était à Paris pendant une semaine; **to be for** (*to be in favor of*) être en faveur de, être partisan de or pour; **to use s.th. for s.th.** employer q.ch. comme q.ch.; e.g., **to use coal for fuel** employer le charbon comme combustible ‖ *conj* car, parce que

forage ['fɑrɪdʒ], ['fɔrɪdʒ] *s* fourrage *m* ‖ *tr & intr* fourrager

foray ['fɑre], ['fɔre] *s* incursion *f* ‖ *tr* saccager, fourrager ‖ *intr* faire une incursion

for·bear [fɔr'bɛr] *v* (*pret* **-bore**; *pp* **-borne**) *tr* s'abstenir de ‖ *intr* se montrer patient

forbearance [fɔr'bɛrəns] *s* abstention *f*; patience *f*

for·bid [fɔr'bɪd] *v* (*pret* **-bade** or **-bad** ['bæd]; *pp* **-bidden**; *ger* **-bidding**) *tr* défendre, interdire; **God forbid!** qu'à Dieu ne plaise!; **to forbid s.o. s.th.** défendre q.ch. à qn; **to forbid s.o. to** défendre à qn de

forbidden [fɔr'bɪdən] *adj* défendu

forbidding [fɔr'bɪdɪŋ] *adj* rebutant, rébarbatif, sinistre

force [fɔrs] *s* force *f*; (*of a word*) signification *f*, valeur *f*; **in force** en vigueur; **in full force** en force; **the allied forces** les puissances alliées ‖ *tr* forcer; **to force back** repousser; (*air; water*) refouler; **to force in** (e.g., **a door**) enfoncer; **to force one's way into** (e.g., **a house**) pénétrer de force dans; **to force s.o.'s hand** forcer la main à qn; **to force s.o. to** + *inf* forcer qn à or de + *inf*; **to force s.th. into s.th.** faire entrer q.ch. dans q.ch.; **to force up** (e.g., **prices**) faire monter

forced *adj* tirage *m* forcé

forced' land'ing *s* atterrissage *m* forcé

forced' march' *s* marche *f* forcée

force'-feed' *tr* (*pret & pp* **-fed**) gaver, suralimenter

force'-feed'ing *s* suralimentation *f*

forceful ['fɔrsfəl] *adj* énergique

for·ceps ['fɔrsɛps] *s* (*pl* **-ceps** or **-cipes** [sɪ‚piz]) (dent, surg) pince *f*; (obstet) forceps *m*

force' pump' *s* pompe *f* foulante

forcible ['fɔrsɪbəl] *adj* énergique, vigoureux; (*convincing*) convaincant; (*imposed*) forcé

ford [fɔrd] *s* gué *m* ‖ *tr* franchir à gué

fore [fɔr] *adj* antérieur; (naut) de l'avant ‖ *s* (naut) avant *m*; **to the fore** en vue, en vedette ‖ *adv* à l'avant ‖ *interj* (golf) gare devant!

fore' and aft' *adv* de l'avant à l'arrière

fore'arm' *s* avant-bras *m* ‖ **fore·arm'** *tr* prémunir; (*to warn*) avertir

fore'bear' *s* ancêtre *m*

foreboding [fɔr'bodɪŋ] *s* (*sign*) présage *m*; (*feeling*) pressentiment *m*

fore'cast' *s* prévision *f* ‖ *v* (*pret & pp* **-cast** or **-casted**) *tr* pronostiquer

forecastle ['foksəl], ['fɔr‚kæsəl], ['fɔr‚kasəl] *s* gaillard *m* d'avant

fore·close' *tr* exclure; (law) forclore; **to foreclose the mortgage** saisir l'immeuble hypothéqué

foreclosure [fɔr'kloʒər] *s* saisie *f*, forclusion *f*

fore·doom' *tr* condamner par avance

fore' edge' *s* (bb) tranche *f*

fore'fa'ther *s* aïeul *m*, ancêtre *m*

fore'fin'ger *s* index *m*

fore'foot' *s* (*pl* **-feet**) patte *f* de devant

fore'front' *s* premier rang *m*; **in the forefront** en première ligne

fore·go' *v* (*pret* **-went**; *pp* **-gone**) *tr* (*to give up*) renoncer à

foregoing ['fɔr‚go·ɪŋ], [fɔr'go·ɪŋ] *adj* précédent, antérieur; (*facts, text, etc. already cited*) déjà cité, ci-dessus

fore'gone' *adj* inévitable; (*anticipated*) décidé d'avance, prévu

fore'ground' *s* premier plan *m*

fore'hand'ed *adj* prévoyant; (*thrifty*) ménager

forehead ['fɑrɪd], ['fɔrɪd] *s* front *m*

foreign ['fɑrɪn], ['fɔrɪn] *adj* étranger

for'eign affairs' *spl* affaires *fpl* étrangères

foreigner ['farınər], ['fɔrınər] s étranger m

for'eign exchange' s change m étranger; (currency) devises fpl

for'eign min'ister s ministre m des affaires étrangères

for'eign of'fice s ministère m des affaires étrangères

for'eign serv'ice s (dipl) service m diplomatique; (mil) service m à l'étranger

for'eign trade' s commerce m extérieur

fore'leg' s jambe f de devant

fore'lock' s mèche f sur le front; (of horse) toupet m; to take time by the forelock saisir l'occasion par les cheveux

fore'man s (pl -men) chef m d'équipe; (in machine shop, factory) contremaître m; (of jury) premier juré m

fore'mast' ['fɔrmæst], ['fɔr,mæst], ['fɔr,mɑst] s mât m de misaine

fore'most' adj premier, principal || adv au premier rang

fore'noon' s matinée f

fore'part' s avant m, devant m, partie f avant

fore'paw' s patte f de devant

fore'quar'ter s quartier m de devant

fore'run'ner s précurseur m, avant-coureur m; (sign) signe m avant-coureur

foresail ['fɔrsəl], ['fɔr,sel], s misaine f, voile f de misaine

fore·see' v (pret -saw; pp -seen) tr prévoir

foreseeable [fɔr'si·əbəl] adj prévisible

fore·shad'ow tr présager, préfigurer

fore·short'en tr dessiner en raccourci

fore·short'ening s raccourci m

fore'sight' s prévision f, prévoyance f

fore'sight'ed adj prévoyant

fore'skin' s prépuce m

forest ['farɪst], ['fɔrɪst] adj forestier || s forêt f

fore'stage' s (theat) avant-scène f

fore·stall' tr anticiper, devancer

for'est rang'er s garde m forestier

forestry ['farɪstri], ['fɔrɪstri] s sylviculture f

fore'taste' s avant-goût m

fore·tell' v (pret & pp -told) tr prédire

fore'thought' s prévoyance f; (law) préméditation f

for·ev'er adv pour toujours, à jamais

fore·warn' tr avertir, prévenir

fore'word' s avant-propos m, avis m au lecteur

forfeit ['fɔrfɪt] adj perdu || s (pledge) dédit m, gage m; (fine) amende f; to play at forfeits jouer aux gages || tr être déchu de, être privé de

forfeiture ['fɔrfɪtʃər] s perte f; (fine) amende f, confiscation f

forge [fɔrdʒ] s forge f || tr forger; (e.g., documents) contrefaire, falsifier

forger ['fɔrdʒər] s forgeur m; (e.g., of documents) faussaire mf

forger·y ['fɔrdʒəri] s (pl -ies) contrefaçon f; (of a document, a painting, etc.) faux m

for·get' [fɔr'gɛt] v (pret -got; pp -got or

-gotten; ger -getting) tr & intr oublier; **forget it!** n'y pensez plus!; **to forget to** + inf oublier de + inf

forgetful [fɔr'gɛtfəl] adj oublieux

forget'-me-not' s myosotis m, ne-m'oubliez-pas m

forgivable [fɔr'gɪvəbəl] adj pardonnable

for·give' [fɔr'gɪv] v (pret -gave; pp -given) tr & intr pardonner

forgiveness [fɔr'gɪvnɪs] s pardon m

forgiving [fɔr'gɪvɪŋ] adj indulgent, miséricordieux

for·go' [fɔr'go] v (pret -went; pp -gone) tr renoncer à, s'abstenir de

fork [fɔrk] s fourche f; (of road, tree, stem) fourche f, bifurcation f; (at table) fourchette f || tr & intr fourcher, bifurquer

forked adj fourchu

forked' light'ning s éclairs mpl en zig-zag

fork'lift truck' s chariot m élévateur

forlorn [fɔr'lɔrn] adj (destitute) abandonné; (hopeless) désespéré; (wretched) misérable

forlorn' hope' s tentative f désespérée

form [fɔrm] s forme f; (paper to be filled out) formule f, fiche f, feuille f; (construction to give shape to cement) coffrage m || tr former || intr se former

formal ['fɔrməl] adj cérémonieux, officiel; (formalistic) formaliste; (superficial) formel, de pure forme

for'mal attire' s tenue f de cérémonie

for'mal call' s visite f de politesse

for'mal din'ner s dîner m de cérémonie, dîner prié

formali·ty [fɔr'mælɪti] s (pl -ties) formalité f; (stiffness) cérémonie f; (polite conventions) cérémonie f, étiquette f

for'mal par'ty s soirée f de gala

for'mal speech' s discours m d'apparat

format ['fɔrmæt] s format m

formation [fɔr'meʃən] s formation f

former ['fɔrmər] adj antérieur, précédent; (long past) ancien; (first of two things mentioned) premier || pron—the former celui-là §84; le premier

formerly ['fɔrmərli] adv autrefois, anciennement, jadis

form'fit'ting adj ajusté, moulant

formidable ['fɔrmɪdəbəl] adj formidable

formless ['fɔrmlɪs] adj informe

form' let'ter s lettre f circulaire

formu·la ['fɔrmjələ] s (pl -las or -lae [,li]) formule f

formulate ['fɔrmjə,let] tr formuler

for·sake' [fɔr'sek] v (pret -sook [-suk]; pp -saken [-sekən]) tr abandonner, délaisser

fort [fɔrt] s fort m, forteresse f; **hold the fort!** (coll) je vous confie la maison!

forte [fɔrt] s fort m

forth [fɔrθ] adv en avant; **and so forth** et ainsi de suite; **from this day forth** à partir de ce jour; **to go forth** sortir, se mettre en route

forth'com'ing adj à venir, à paraître

forth'right' adj net, direct || adv droit, carrément; (immediately) tout de suite

forth'with' adv sur-le-champ

fortieth ['fɔrtɪ·ɪθ] adj & pron quarantième (masc, fem) || s quarantième m

fortification [,fɔrtɪfɪ'keʃən] s fortification f

forti·fy ['fɔrtɪ,faɪ] v (pret & pp -fied) tr fortifier; (wine) viner

fortitude ['fɔrtɪ,t(j)ud] s force f d'âme

fortnight ['fɔrt,naɪt], ['fɔrtnɪt] s quinze jours mpl, quinzaine f

fortress ['fɔrtrɪs] s forteresse f

fortuitous [fɔr't(j)u·ɪtəs] adj (accidental) fortuit; (lucky) fortuné

fortunate ['fɔrtʃənɪt] adj heureux

fortune ['fɔrtʃən] s fortune f; **to make a fortune** faire fortune; **to tell s.o. his fortune** dire la bonne aventure à qn

for'tune hunt'er s coureur m de dots

for'tune-tel'ler s diseuse f de bonne aventure

for·ty ['fɔrti] adj & pron quarante || s (pl -ties) quarante m; **about forty** une quarantaine

fo·rum ['fɔrəm] s (pl -rums or -ra [rə]) forum m; (e.g., of public opinion) tribunal m; **open forum** tribune f libre

forward ['fɔrwərd] adj de devant; (precocious) avancé, précoce; (bold) audacieux, effronté || s (sports) avant m || adv en avant; **to bring forward** (bk) reporter; **to come forward** s'avancer; **to look forward to** compter sur, se faire une fête de || tr envoyer, expédier; (a letter) faire suivre; (a project) avancer, favoriser

for'warding address' s adresse f d'expédition, adresse d'envoi

fossil ['fɑsɪl] adj & s fossile m

foster ['fɑstər], ['fɔstər] adj de lait, nourricier || tr encourager, entretenir

fos'ter broth'er s frère m de lait

fos'ter fa'ther s père m nourricier

foul [faʊl] adj immonde; (air) vicié; (wind) contraire; (weather) gros, sale; (breath) fétide; (language) ordurier; (water) bourbeux; (ball) hors jeu || s (baseball) faute f; (boxing) coup m bas || adv déloyalement || tr (sports) commettre une faute contre || intr (said of anchor, propeller, rope, etc.) s'engager

foul-mouthed ['faʊl'maʊðd], ['faʊl'maʊθt] adj mal embouché

foul' play' s malveillance f; (sports) jeu m déloyal

found [faʊnd] tr fonder, établir; (metal) fondre

foundation [faʊn'deʃən] s (basis; masonry support) fondement m; (act of endowing) dotation f; (endowment) fondation f

founder ['faʊndər] s fondateur m; (in foundry) fondeur m || intr (said of horse) boiter bas; (said of building) s'effondrer; (naut) sombrer

foundling ['faʊndlɪŋ] s enfant m trouvé

found'ling hos'pital s hospice m des enfants trouvés

found·ry ['faʊndri] s (pl -ries) fonderie f

found'ry·man s (pl -men) fondeur m

fount [faʊnt] s source f

fountain ['faʊntən] s fontaine f

foun'tain-head' s source f, origine f

Foun'tain of Youth' s fontaine f de Jouvence

foun'tain pen' s stylo m

four [fɔr] adj & pron quatre || s quatre m; **four o'clock** quatre heures; **on all fours** à quatre pattes

four'-cy'cle adj (mach) à quatre temps

four'-cyl'inder adj (mach) à quatre cylindres

four'-flush' intr (coll) bluffer, faire le fanfaron

fourflusher ['fɔr,flʌʃər] s (coll) bluffeur m

four'-foot'ed adj quadrupède

four' hun'dred adj & pron quatre cents || s quatre cents m; **the Four Hundred** la haute société; le Tout Paris

four'-in-hand' s (tie) cravate-plastron f; (team) attelage m à quatre

four'-lane' adj à quatre voies

four'-leaf clo'ver s trèfle m à quatre feuilles

four'-motor plane' s quadrimoteur m

four'-o'clock' s (Mirabilis jalapa) belle-de-nuit f

four' of a kind' s (cards) un carré

four'-post'er s lit m à colonnes

four'score' adj quatre-vingts

foursome ['fɔrsəm] s partie f double

fourteen ['fɔr'tin] adj, pron, & s quatorze m

fourteenth ['fɔr'tinθ] adj & pron quatorzième (masc, fem); **the Fourteenth** quatorze, e.g., **John the Fourteenth** Jean quatorze || s quatorze m; **the fourteenth** (in dates) le quatorze

fourth [fɔrθ] adj & pron quatrième (masc, fem); **the Fourth** quatre, e.g., **John the Fourth** Jean quatre || s quatrième m; (in fractions) quart m; **the fourth** (in dates) le quatre

fourth' estate' s quatrième pouvoir m

fowl [faʊl] s volaille f

fox [fɑks] s renard m || tr (coll) mystifier

fox'glove' s digitale f

fox'hole' s renardière f; (mil) gourbi m, abri m de tranchée

fox'hound' s fox-hound m

fox' hunt' s chasse f au renard

fox' ter'rier s fox-terrier m

fox' trot' s (of animal) petit trot m; (dance) fox-trot m

fox·y ['fɑksi] adj (comp -ier; super -iest) rusé, madré

foyer ['fɔɪ·ər] s (lobby) foyer m; (entrance hall) vestibule m

fracas ['frekəs] s bagarre f, rixe f

fraction ['frækʃən] s fraction f

fractional ['frækʃənəl] adj fractionnaire

frac'tional cur'rency s monnaie f divisionnaire

fracture ['fræktʃər] s fracture f; **to set**

a **fracture** réduire une fracture ‖ *tr* fracturer

fragile ['frædʒɪl] *adj* fragile

fragment ['frægmənt] *s* fragment *m* ‖ *tr* fragmenter

fragrance ['fregrəns] *s* parfum *m*

fragrant ['fregrənt] *adj* parfumé

frail [frel] *adj* frêle; (*e.g., virtue*) fragile, faible ‖ *s* (*basket*) couffe *f*

frail·ty ['frelti] *s* (*pl* -ties) fragilité *f*; (*weakness*) faiblesse *f*

frame [frem] *s* (*of picture, mirror*) cadre *m*; (*of glasses*) monture *f*; (*of window, car*) châssis *m*; (*of window, motor*) bâti *m*; (*support, stand*) armature *f*; (*structure*) charpente *f*; (*for embroidering*) métier *m*; (*of comic strip*) cadre, dessin *m*; (*mov, telv*) image *f* ‖ *tr* former, charpenter; (*a picture*) encadrer; (*film*) cadrer; (*an answer*) formuler; (*slang*) monter une accusation contre

frame' house' *s* maison *f* en bois

frame' of mind' *s* disposition *f* d'esprit

frame'-up' *s* (*slang*) coup *m* monté

frame'work' *s* charpente *f*, squelette *m*

framing ['fremɪŋ] *s* (*mov, phot*) cadrage *m*

France [fræns], [frɑns] *s* France *f*; la France

franchise ['fræntʃaɪz] *s* concession *f*, privilège *m*; droit *m* de vote

frank [fræŋk] *adj* franc ‖ *s* franchise *f* postale; **Frank** (*medieval German person*) Franc *m*; (*masculine name*) François *m* ‖ *tr* affranchir

frankfurter ['fræŋkfərtər] *s* saucisse *f* de Francfort

frankincense ['fræŋkɪn,sɛns] *s* oliban *m*

Frankish ['fræŋkɪʃ] *adj* franc ‖ *s* francique *m*

frankness ['fræŋknɪs] *s* franchise *f*

frantic ['fræntɪk] *adj* frénétique

fraternal [frə'tʌrnəl] *adj* fraternel

fraterni·ty [frə'tʌrnɪti] *s* (*pl* -ties) fraternité *f*; (*association*) confrérie *f*; (*at a university*) club *m* d'étudiants, amicale *f* estudiantine

fraternize ['frætər,naɪz] *intr* fraterniser

fraud [frɔd] *s* fraude *f*; (*person*) imposteur *m*, fourbe *mf*

fraudulent ['frɔdjələnt] *adj* frauduleux, en fraude

fraught [frɔt] *adj*—**fraught with** chargé de

fray [fre] *s* bagarre *f* ‖ *tr* érailler ‖ *intr* s'érailler

freak [frik] *s* (*sudden fancy*) caprice *m*; (*anomaly*) curiosité *f*; (*person, animal*) monstre *m*

freakish ['frikɪʃ] *adj* capricieux, bizarre; (*grotesque*) monstrueux

freckle ['frɛkəl] *s* tache *f* de rousseur, éphélide *f*

freckly ['frɛkli] *adj* couvert de taches de rousseur

free [fri] *adj* (*comp* **freer** ['fri·ər]; *super* **freest** ['fri·ɪst]) libre; (*without charge*) gratuit; (*without extra charge*) franc, exempt; (*e.g., end of a*

rope) dégagé; (*with money, advice, etc.*) libéral, généreux; (*manner, speech, etc.*) franc, ouvert; **to set free** libérer, affranchir ‖ *adv* franco, gratis, gratuitement; (*naut*) largue, e.g., **running free** courant largue ‖ *v* (*pret & pp* **freed** [frid]; *ger* **freeing** ['fri·ɪŋ]) *tr* libérer; (*a prisoner*) affranchir, élargir; (*to disengage*) dégager; (*from an obligation*) exempter

free' and eas'y *adj* désinvolte, dégagé

freebooter ['fri,butər] *s* flibustier *m*, maraudeur *m*

free' compe'tition *s* libre concurrence *f*

freedom ['fridəm] *s* liberté *f*

free'dom of speech' *s* liberté *f* de la parole

free'dom of the press' *s* liberté *f* de la presse

free'dom of the seas' *s* liberté *f* des mers

free'dom of thought' *s* liberté *f* de la pensée

free'dom of wor'ship *s* liberté *f* du culte, libre pratique *f*

free'-for-all' *s* foire *f* d'empoigne, mêlée *f*

free' hand' *s* carte *f* blanche

free'-hand draw'ing *s* dessin *m* à main levée

free'hand'ed *adj* libéral, généreux

free'hold' *s* (*law*) propriété *f* foncière perpétuelle; (*hist*) franc-alleu *m*

free' lance' *s* franc-tireur *m*

free'man *s* (*pl* -men) homme *m* libre; (*citizen*) citoyen *m*

Free'ma'son *s* franc-maçon *m*

Free'ma'sonry *s* franc-maçonnerie *f*

free' of charge' *adj & adv* gratis, exempt de frais

free' on board' *adv* franco de bord, départ usine

free' port' *s* port *m* franc

free' speech' *s* liberté *f* de la parole

free'-spo'ken *adj* franc; **to be free-spoken** avoir son franc-parler

free'think'er *s* libre penseur *m*

free' thought' *s* libre pensée *f*

free' tick'et *s* billet *m* de faveur

free' trade' *s* libre-échange *m*

free' trad'er *s* libre-échangiste *mf*

free'way' *s* autoroute *f*

free' will' *adj* volontaire, de plein gré ‖ *s* libre arbitre *m*; **of one's own free will** de son propre gré

freeze [friz] *s* congélation *f* ‖ *v* (*pret* **froze** [froz]; *pp* **frozen**) *tr* geler, congeler; (*assets, credits, etc.*) geler, bloquer; (*meat*) congeler ‖ *intr* geler; **it is freezing** il gèle

freezer ['frizər] *s* (*for making ice cream*) sorbetière *f*; (*for foods*) congélateur *m*

freight [fret] *s* fret *m*, chargement *m*; (*cost*) fret, prix *m* du transport; **by freight** (rr) en petite vitesse ‖ *tr* transporter; (*a ship, truck, etc.*) charger

freight' car' *s* wagon *m* de marchandises, wagon à caisse

freighter ['fretər] *s* cargo *m*

freight′ plat′form s quai m de déchargement

freight′ sta′tion s gare f de marchandises

freight′ train′ s train m de marchandises

freight′ yard′ s (rr) cour f de marchandises

French [frɛntʃ] adj français || s (language) français m; **the French** les Français

French′ Cana′dian s Franco-Canadien m

French′-Cana′dian adj franco-canadien

French′ chalk′ s craie f de tailleur, stéatite f

French′ cuff′ s poignet m mousquetaire

French′ door′ s porte-fenêtre f

French′ dress′ing s vinaigrette f

French′ fries′ spl frites fpl

French′ horn′ s (mus) cor m d'harmonie

French′ horse′power s (735 watts) cheval-vapeur m, cheval m

French′ leave′ s—**to take French leave** filer à l'anglaise

French′man s (pl -men) Français m

French′ roll′ s petit pain m

French′-speak′ing adj francophone; (country) de langue française

French′ tel′ephone s combiné m

French′ toast′ s pain m perdu

French′ win′dow s porte-fenêtre f

French′wom′an s (pl -wom′en) Française f

frenzied [ˈfrɛnzid] adj frénétique

fren·zy [ˈfrɛnzi] s (pl -zies) frénésie f

frequen·cy [ˈfrikwənsi] s (pl -cies) fréquence f

fre′quency modula′tion s modulation f de fréquence

frequent [ˈfrikwənt] adj fréquent || [friˈkwɛnt], [ˈfrikwənt] tr fréquenter

frequently [ˈfrikwəntli] adv fréquemment

fres·co [ˈfrɛsko] s (pl -coes or -cos) fresque f || tr peindre à fresque

fresh [frɛʃ] adj frais; (water) doux; (e.g., idea) nouveau; (wound) saignant; (cheeky) (coll) osé, impertinent; **fresh paint!** (public sign) attention, peinture fraîche! || adv nouvellement; **fresh in** (coll) récemment arrivé; **fresh out** (coll) récemment épuisé

freshen [ˈfrɛʃən] tr rafraîchir || intr se rafraîchir; (said of wind) fraîchir

freshet [ˈfrɛʃɪt] s crue f

fresh′man s (pl -men) étudiant m de première année, bizut m

freshness [ˈfrɛʃnɪs] s fraîcheur f; (sauciness) impudence f, impertinence f

fresh′-wa′ter adj d'eau douce

fret [frɛt] s (interlaced design) frette f; (uneasiness) inquiétude f; (mus) touchette f || v (pret & pp fretted; ger fretting) tr ajourer || intr s'inquiéter, geindre

fretful [ˈfrɛtfəl] adj irritable, boudeur

fret′work′ s ajour m, ornementation f ajourée

Freudianism [ˈfrɔɪdɪ·ə‚nɪzəm] s freudisme m

friar [ˈfraɪ·ər] s moine m

fricassee [‚frɪkəˈsi] s fricassée f

friction [ˈfrɪkʃən] s friction f

fric′tion tape′ s chatterton m, ruban m isolant

Friday [ˈfraɪdi] s vendredi m

fried [fraɪd] adj frit

fried′ egg′ s œuf m sur le plat

friend [frɛnd] s ami m; **to make friends with** se lier d'amitié avec

friend·ly [ˈfrɛndli] adj (comp -lier; super -liest) amical, sympathique

friendship [ˈfrɛndʃɪp] s amitié f

frieze [friz] s (archit) frise f

frigate [ˈfrɪgɪt] s frégate f

fright [fraɪt] s frayeur f, effroi m; (grotesque or ridiculous person) (coll) épouvantail m; **to take fright at** s'effrayer de

frighten [ˈfraɪtən] tr effrayer; **to frighten away** effaroucher, faire fuir

frightful [ˈfraɪtfəl] adj effroyable; (coll) affreux; (huge) (coll) énorme

frigid [ˈfrɪdʒɪd] adj rigide; (zone) glacial

frigidity [frɪˈdʒɪdɪti] s frigidité f

frill [frɪl] s (on shirt front) jabot m; (frippery) falbala m

fringe [frɪndʒ] s frange f; (border) bordure f; (opt) frange; **on the fringe of** en marge de || tr franger

fringe′ ben′efits spl supplément m de solde, bénéfices mpl marginaux

fripper·y [ˈfrɪpəri] s (pl -ies) (flashiness) clinquant m; (inferior goods) camelote f

frisk [frɪsk] tr (slang) fouiller, palper || intr—**to frisk about** gambader, folâtrer

frisk·y [ˈfrɪski] adj (comp -ier; super -iest) vif, folâtre; (horse) fringant

fritter [ˈfrɪtər] s beignet m || tr—**to fritter away** gaspiller

frivolous [ˈfrɪvələs] adj frivole

frizzle [ˈfrɪzəl] s frisure f || tr frisotter; (culin) faire frire || intr frisotter; (culin) grésiller

friz·zly [ˈfrɪzli] adj (comp -zlier; super -zliest) crépu, crépelu

fro [fro] adv—**to and fro** de long en large; **to go to and fro** aller et venir

frock [frɑk] s robe f; (overalls, smock) blouse f; (eccl) froc m

frock′ coat′ s redingote f

frog [frɑg], [frɔg] s grenouille f; (in throat) chat m

frog′man′ s (pl -men′) homme-grenouille m

frogs′′ legs′ spl cuisses fpl de grenouille

frol·ic [ˈfrɑlɪk] s gaieté f, ébats mpl || v (pret & pp -icked; ger -icking) intr s'ébattre, folâtrer

frolicsome [ˈfrɑlɪksəm] adj folâtre

from [frʌm], [frɑm], [frʌm] prep de; de la part de, e.g., **greetings from your friend** compliments de la part de votre ami; contre, e.g., **a shelter from the rain** un abri contre la pluie; **from a certain angle** sous un certain angle; **from . . . to** depuis . . .

jusqu'à; **from what I hear** d'après ce que j'apprends; **the flight from** le vol en provenance de; **to drink from** (*a glass*) boire dans; (*a bottle*) boire à; **to learn from a book** apprendre dans un livre; **to steal from** voler à

front [frʌnt] *adj* antérieur, de devant || *s* devant *m*; (*first place*) premier rang *m*; (*aut*) avant *m*; (*geog, mil, pol*) front *m*; (*figurehead*) (coll) prête-nom *m*; **in front** par devant; **in front of** en face de, devant; **to put up a bold front** (coll) faire bonne contenance || *tr* (*to face*) donner sur; (*to confront*) affronter || *intr*—**to front on** donner sur

frontage [ˈfrʌntɪdʒ] *s* façade *f*; (*along a street, lake, etc.*) largeur *f*

front/ door/ *s* porte *f* d'entrée

front/ drive/ *s* (aut) traction *f* avant

frontier [frʌnˈtɪr] *adj* frontalier || *s* frontière *f*; (*hist*) front *m* de colonisation, front pionnier

frontiers/man [ˈfrʌntɪrzˌpis] *s* (*pl* -**men**) frontalier *m*, broussard *m*

frontispiece [ˈfrʌntɪsˌpis] *s* frontispice *m*; (*archit*) façade *f* principale

front/ lines/ *spl* avant-postes *mpl*

front/ mat/ter *s* (*of book*) feuilles *fpl* liminaires

front/ of/fice *s* direction *f*

front/ porch/ *s* porche *m*

front/ room/ *s* chambre *f* sur la rue

front/ row/ *s* premier rang *m*

front/ seat/ *s* siège *m* avant; (aut) banquette *f* avant

front/ steps/ *s* perron *m*

front/ view/ *s* vue *f* de face

front/ yard/ *s* devant *m* de la maison

frost [frɔst], [frast] *s* (*freezing*) gelée *f*; (*frozen dew*) givre *m* || *tr* (*to freeze*) geler; (*to cover with frost*) givrer; (culin) glacer

frost/bite/ *s* engelure *f*

frost/ed glass/ *s* verre *m* dépoli

frosting [ˈfrɔstɪŋ], [ˈfrastɪŋ] *s* (*on glass*) dépolissage *m*; (culin) fondant *m*

frost•y [ˈfrɔsti], [ˈfrasti] *adj* (*comp* -**ier**; *super* -**iest**) couvert de givre; (*reception, welcome*) glacé, glacial

froth [frɔθ], [fraθ] *s* écume *f*; (*on soap, beer, chocolate*) mousse *f*; (*frivolity*) futilité *f* || *intr* mousser; (*at the mouth*) écumer

froth•y [ˈfrɔθi], [ˈfraθi] *adj* (*comp* -**ier**; *super* -**iest**) écumeux; (*soap, beer, chocolate*) mousseux; (*frivolous*) creux, futile

froward [ˈfrowərd] *adj* obstiné, revêche

frown [fraun] *s* froncement *m* de sourcils || *intr* froncer les sourcils; **to frown at** *or* **on** être contraire à, désapprouver

frows•y *or* **frowz•y** [ˈfrauzi] *adj* (*comp* -**ier**; *super* -**iest**) malpropre, négligé, peu soigné; (*smelling bad*) malodorant

fro/zen as/sets [ˈfrozən] *spl* fonds *mpl* gelés

fro/zen foods/ *spl* aliments *mpl* surgelés

frugal [ˈfrugəl] *adj* sobre, modéré; (*meal*) frugal

fruit [frut] *adj* fruitier || *s* fruit *m*; les fruits, e.g., **I like fruit** j'aime les fruits

fruit/ cake/ *s* cake *m*

fruit/ cup/ *s* coupe *f* de fruits

fruit/ fly/ *s* mouche *f* du vinaigre

fruitful [ˈfrutfəl] *adj* fructueux, fécond

fruition [fruˈɪʃən] *s* réalisation *f*; **to come to fruition** fructifier

fruit/ juice/ *s* jus *m* de fruits

fruitless [ˈfrutlɪs] *adj* stérile, vain

fruit/ sal/ad *s* macédoine *f* de fruits, salade *f* de fruits

fruit/ stand/ *s* étalage *m* de fruits

fruit/ store/ *s* fruiterie *f*

frumpish [ˈfrʌmpɪʃ] *adj* fagoté, négligé

frustrate [ˈfrʌstret] *tr* frustrer

fry [fraɪ] *s* (*pl* **fries**) (culin) friture *f*; (ichth) fretin *m* || *v* (*pret* & *pp* **fried**) *tr* faire frire; (*to sauté*) faire sauter || *intr* frire

fry/ing pan/ *s* poêle *f* à frire; **to jump from the frying pan into the fire** sauter de la poêle dans le feu

fudge [fʌdʒ] *s* fondant *m* de chocolat; (*humbug*) blague *f*

fuel [ˈfju·əl] *s* combustible *m*; (aut) carburant *m*; (fig) aliment *m* || *v* (*pret* & *pp* **fueled** *or* **fuelled**; *ger* **fueling** *or* **fuelling**) *tr* pourvoir en combustible

fu/el gauge/ *s* jauge *f* de combustible

fu/el line/ *s* conduite *f* de combustible

fu/el oil/ *s* mazout *m*, fuel-oil *m*, fuel *m*

fu/el tank/ *s* réservoir *m* de carburant; (aut) réservoir à essence

fugitive [ˈfjudʒɪtɪv] *adj* & *s* fugitif *m*

ful•crum [ˈfʌlkrəm] *s* (*pl* -**crums** *or* -**cra** [krə]) point *m* d'appui

fulfill [fulˈfɪl] *tr* accomplir; (*an obligation*) s'acquitter de, remplir

fulfillment [fulˈfɪlmənt] *s* accomplissement *m*

full [ful] *adj* plein; (*dress, garment*) ample, bouffant; (*schedule*) chargé; (*lips*) gros, fort; (*brother, sister*) germain; (*having no more room*) complet; **full to overflowing** plein à déborder || *s* plein *m*; **in full** intégralement, entièrement; (*to spell in full*) en toutes lettres; **to the full** complètement || *adv* complètement; **full in the face** en pleine figure; **full many a** bien des; **full well** parfaitement || *tr* (*cloth*) fouler

full/ blast/ *adv* (coll) en pleine activité

full/-blood/ed *adj* robuste; (*thoroughbred*) pur sang

full-blown [ˈfulˈblon] *adj* achevé, développé; en pleine fleur

full/-bod/ied *adj* (e.g., *wine*) corsé

full/ dress/ *s* grande tenue *f*

full/-dress coat/ *s* frac *m*

full/-faced/ *adj* (*portrait*) de face

full-fledged [ˈfulˈfledʒd] *adj* véritable, rien moins que

full-grown [ˈfulˈgron] *adj* (*plant*) mûr; (*tree*) de haute futaie; (*person*) adulte

full′ house′ s (poker) main f pleine; (theat) salle f comble
full′-length′ adj (portrait) en pied
full′-length mir′ror s psyché f
full′-length mov′ie s long métrage m
full′ load′ s plein chargement m
full′ meas′ure s mesure f comble
full′ moon′ s pleine lune f
full′ name′ s nom m et prénoms mpl
full′ pow′ers spl pleins pouvoirs mpl
full′ rest′ s (mus) pause f
full′ sail′ adv toutes voiles dehors
full′ ses′sion s assemblée f plénière
full′-sized′ adj de grandeur nature
full′ speed′ s toute vitesse f
full′ stop′ s (gram) point m final; **to come to a full stop** s'arrêter net
full′ swing′ s—**in full swing** en pleine activité, en train
full′ tilt′ adv à toute vitesse
full′ time′ adv à pleines journées
full′-time′ adj à temps plein
full′ view′ s—**in full view** à la vue de tous
full′ weight′ s poids m juste
fully ['fʊli], ['fʊlɪ] adv entièrement, pleinement
fulsome ['fʊlsəm], ['fʌlsəm] adj écœurant, bas, servile
fumble ['fʌmbəl] tr manier maladroitement; (the ball) ne pas attraper, laisser tomber ‖ intr tâtonner
fume [fjum] s (bad humor) rage f; **fumes** fumées fpl, vapeurs fpl ‖ tr & intr fumer
fumigate ['fjumɪ,get] tr fumiger
fun [fʌn] s amusement m, gaieté f; (badinage) plaisanterie f; **in fun** pour rire; **to have fun** s'amuser; **to make fun of** se moquer de
function ['fʌŋkʃən] s fonction f; (meeting) cérémonie f ‖ intr fonctionner; **to function as** faire fonction de
functional ['fʌŋkʃənəl] adj fonctionnel
functionar·y ['fʌŋkʃə,nɛri] s (pl -ies) fonctionnaire mf
fund [fʌnd] s fonds m; **funds** fonds mpl ‖ tr (a debt) consolider
fundamental [,fʌndə'mɛntəl] adj fondamental ‖ s principe m, base f
fundamentalist [,fʌndə'mɛntəlɪst] s (rel) scripturaire m
funeral ['fjunərəl] adj (march, procession, ceremony) funèbre; (expenses) funéraire ‖ s funérailles fpl
fu′neral direc′tor s entrepreneur m de pompes funèbres
fu′neral home′ or **par′lor** s chapelle f mortuaire; salon m mortuaire (Canad); (business) entreprise f de pompes funèbres
fu′neral proces′sion s convoi m funèbre, enterrement m, deuil m
fu′neral serv′ice s office m des morts
funereal [fju'nɪrɪ·əl] adj funèbre
fungus ['fʌŋgəs] s (pl **funguses** or **fungi** ['fʌndʒaɪ]) (bot) champignon m; (pathol) fongus m
funicular [fju'nɪkjələr] adj & s funiculaire m
funk [fʌŋk] s (coll) frousse f

fun·nel ['fʌnəl] s entonnoir m; (smokestack) cheminée f; (tube for ventilation) tuyau m ‖ v (pret & pp **-neled** or **-nelled**; ger **-neling** or **-nelling**) tr verser avec un entonnoir; (to channel) concentrer
funnies ['fʌniz] spl pages fpl comiques
fun·ny ['fʌni] adj (comp **-nier**; super **-niest**) comique; amusant, drôle; (coll) bizarre, curieux; **to strike s.o. as funny** paraître drôle à qn
fun′ny pa′per s pages fpl comiques
fur [fʌr] s fourrure f; (on tongue) empâtement m; **furs** pelleteries fpl
furbish ['fʌrbɪʃ] tr fourbir; **to furbish up** remettre à neuf
furious ['fjʊrɪ·əs] adj furieux
furl [fʌrl] tr (naut) ferler
fur′-lined′ adj doublé de fourrure
furlough ['fʌrlo] s permission f; **on furlough** en permission ‖ tr donner une permission à
furnace ['fʌrnɪs] s (to heat a house) calorifère m; (to produce steam) chaudière f; (e.g., to smelt ores) fourneau m; (rr) foyer m; (fig) fournaise f
furnish ['fʌrnɪʃ] tr fournir; (a house) meubler
fur′nished apart′ment s garni m, appartement m meublé
furnishings ['fʌrnɪʃɪŋz] spl ameublement m; (things to wear) articles mpl d'habillement
furniture ['fʌrnɪtʃər] s meubles mpl; **a piece of furniture** un meuble; **a suite of furniture** un mobilier
fur′niture deal′er s marchand m de meubles
fur′niture pol′ish s encaustique f
fur′niture store′ s maison f d'ameublement
fur′niture ware′house s garde-meuble m
furor ['fjʊrɔr] s fureur f
furrier ['fʌrɪ·ər] s fourreur m, pelletier m
furrow ['fʌro] s sillon m ‖ tr sillonner
fur·ry ['fʌri] adj (comp **-rier**; super **-riest**) fourré, à fourrure
further ['fʌrðər] adj additionnel, supplémentaire ‖ adv plus loin; (besides) en outre, de plus ‖ tr avancer, favoriser
furtherance ['fʌrðərəns] s avancement m
fur′ther·more′ adv de plus, d'ailleurs
furthest ['fʌrðɪst] adj (le) plus éloigné ‖ adv le plus loin
furtive ['fʌrtɪv] adj furtif
fu·ry ['fjʊri] s (pl -ries) furie f
furze [fʌrz] s genêt m épineux, ajonc m d'Europe
fuse [fjuz] s (tube or wick filled with explosive material) étoupille f, mèche f; (device for exploding a bomb or projectile) fusée f; (elec) fusible m, plomb m de sûreté, plomb fusible; **to burn** or **blow out a fuse** faire sauter un plomb ‖ tr fondre; étoupiller ‖ intr se fondre
fuse′ box′ s boîte f à fusibles

fuselage ['fjuzəlɪdʒ], [,fjuzə'laʒ] s
  fuselage m
fusible ['fjuzɪbəl] adj fusible
fusillade [,fjuzɪ'led] s fusillade f
fusion ['fjuʒən] s fusion f
fuss [fʌs] s fracas m; (dispute) bagarre
  f; to kick up a fuss (coll) faire un tas
  d'histoires; to make a fuss over faire
  grand cas de || intr faire des embar-
  ras, simagrées, or chichis; to fuss
  over être aux petits soins auprès de
fuss•y ['fʌsi] adj (comp -ier; super
  -iest) tracassier, tatillon; (in dress)
  pomponné

fustian ['fʌstʃən] s (cloth) futaine f;
  (bombast) grandiloquence f
futile ['fjutɪl] adj futile
future ['fjutʃər] adj futur, d'avenir || s
  avenir m; (gram) futur m; futures
  (com) valeurs fpl négociées à terme;
  in the future à l'avenir; in the near
  future à brève échéance
fuzz [fʌz] s (on a peach) duvet m; (on
  a blanket) peluche f; (in pockets and
  corners) bourre f
fuzz•y ['fʌzi] adj (comp -ier; super
  -iest) pelucheux; (hair) crêpelu; (indistinct) flou

G

G, g [dʒi] s VIIᵉ lettre de l'alphabet
gab [gæb] s (coll) bavardage m, langue
  f || v (pret & pp gabbed; ger gabbing)
  intr (coll) bavarder
gabardine ['gæbər ,din] s gabardine f
gabble ['gæbəl] s jacasserie f || intr
  jacasser
gable ['gebəl] s (of roof) pignon m;
  (over a door or window) gable m
ga'ble end' s pignon m
ga'ble roof' s comble m sur pignon, toit
  m à deux pentes
gad [gæd] v (pret & pp gadded; ger
  gadding) intr—to gad about courir
  la prétantaine, vadrouiller
gad'about' s vadrouilleur m
gad'fly' s (pl -flies) taon m
gadget ['gædʒɪt] s dispositif m; (un-
  named article) machin m, truc m
Gaelic ['gelɪk] adj & s gaélique m
gaff [gæf] s gaffe f; to stand the gaff
  (slang) ne pas broncher
gaffer ['gæfər] s (coll) vieux bonhomme m
gag [gæg] s bâillon m; (interpolation
  by an actor) gag m; (joke) blague f
  || v (pret & pp gagged; ger gagging)
  tr bâillonner || intr avoir des haut-le-
  cœur
gage [gedʒ] s (pledge) gage m; (challenge) défi m
gaie•ty ['ge·ɪti] s (pl -ties) gaieté f
gaily ['geli] adv gaiement
gain [gen] s gain m; (increase) accrois-
  sement m || tr gagner; (to reach) at-
  teindre, gagner || intr gagner du ter-
  rain; (said of invalid) s'améliorer;
  (said of watch) avancer; to gain on
  prendre de l'avance sur
gainful ['genfəl] adj profitable
gain'say' v (pret & pp -said [,sed],
  [,sed]) tr (to deny) nier; (to contradict) contredire; not to gainsay ne
  pas disconvenir de
gait [get] s démarche f, allure f
gaiter ['getər] s guêtre f
gala ['gælə], ['gelə] adj de gala || s
  gala m
galax•y ['gæləksi] s (pl -ies) galaxie f

gale [gel] s gros vent m; gales of
  laughter éclats ·mpl de rire; to
  weather a gale étaler un coup de vent
gall [gɔl] s bile f, fiel m; (something
  bitter) (fig) fiel m, amertume f; (au-
  dacity) (coll) toupet m || tr écorcher
  par le frottement; (fig) irriter
gallant ['gælənt] adj (spirited, daring)
  vaillant, brave; (stately, grand) fier,
  noble; (showy, gay) élégant, superbe,
  de fête || ['gælənt], [gə'lænt] adj
  galant || s galant m; vaillant m ||
  [gə'lænt] intr faire le galant
gallant•ry ['gæləntri] s (pl -ries) galanterie f; (bravery) vaillance f
gall' blad'der s vésicule f biliaire
gall' duct' s conduit m biliaire
galleon ['gæliən] s (naut) galion m
galler•y ['gæləri] s (pl -ies) galerie f;
  (cheapest seats in theater) poulailler
  m; to play to the gallery poser pour
  la galerie
galley ['gæli] s (ship) galère f; (ship's
  kitchen) coquerie f; (typ) galée f
gal'ley proof' s placard m; épreuve f
  en placard
gal'ley slave' s galérien m
Gallic ['gælɪk] adj gaulois
Gal'lic wit' s esprit m gaulois
galling ['gɔlɪŋ] adj irritant, blessant
gallivant ['gælɪ ,vænt] intr courailler
gall'nut' s noix f de galle
gallon ['gælən] s gallon m américain
galloon [gə'lun] s galon m
gallop ['gæləp] s galop m || tr faire
  galoper || intr galoper
gal·lows ['gæloz] s (pl -lows or -lowses)
  gibet m, potence f
gal'lows bird' s (coll) gibier m de potence
gall'stone' s calcul m biliaire
galore [gə'lor] adv à foison, à gogo
galoshes [gə'laʃɪz] spl caoutchoucs
  mpl
galvanize ['gælvə ,naɪz] tr galvaniser
gal'vanized i'ron s tôle f galvanisée
gambit ['gæmbɪt] s gambit m
gamble ['gæmbl] s risque m, affaire f
  de chance || tr jouer; to gamble away

perdre au jeu || *intr* jouer; jouer à la Bourse; (*fig*) prendre des risques

gambler ['gæmblər] *s* joueur *m*

gambling ['gæmblɪŋ] *s* jeu *m*

gam'bling den' *s* tripot *m*

gam'bling house' *s* maison *f* de jeu

gam'bling ta'ble *s* table *f* de jeu

gam·bol ['gæmbəl] *s* gambade *f* || *v* (*pret & pp* -boled *or* -bolled; *ger* -boling *or* -bolling) *intr* gambader

gambrel ['gæmbrəl] *s* (*hock*) jarret *m*; (*in butcher shop*) jambier *m*

gam'brel roof' *s* toit *m* en croupe

game [gem] *adj* crâne, résolu; (*leg*) boiteux || *s* jeu *m*; (*contest*) match *m*; (*score necessary to win*) partie *f*; (*animal or bird*) gibier *m*; **to make game of** tourner en dérision

game'bag' *s* carnassière *f*, gibecière *f*

game' bird' *s* oiseau *m* que l'on chasse

game'cock' *s* coq *m* de combat

game'keep'er *s* garde-chasse *m*

game' of chance' *s* jeu *m* de hasard

game' preserve' *s* chasse *f* gardée

game' war'den *s* garde-chasse *m*

gamut ['gæmət] *s* gamme *f*

gam·y ['gemi] *adj* (*comp* -ier; *super* -iest) (*having flavor of uncooked game*) faisandé; (*plucky*) crâne

gander ['gændər] *s* jars *m*

gang [gæŋ] *adj* multiple || *s* (*of workmen*) équipe *f*, brigade *f*; (*of thugs*) bande *f*; (*of wrongdoers*) séquelle *f*, clique *f* || *intr*—**to gang up** se concerter; **to gang up on** se liguer contre

gangling ['gæŋglɪŋ] *adj* dégingandé

gangli·on ['gæŋglɪ·ən] *s* (*pl* -ons *or* -a [ə]) ganglion *m*

gang'plank' *s* passerelle *f*, planche *f* de débarquement

gangrene ['gæŋgrin] *s* gangrène *f* || *tr* gangrener || *intr* se gangrener

gangster ['gæŋstər] *s* bandit *m*, gangster *m*

gang'way' *s* (*passageway*) passage *m*, coursive *f*; (*gangplank*) planche *f* de débarquement; (*in ship's side*) coupée *f* || *interj* rangez-vous!, dégagez!

gan·try ['gæntri] *s* (*pl* -tries) (*for barrels*) chantier *m*; (*for crane*) portique *m*; (*rr*) pont *m* à signaux

gan'try crane' *s* grue *f* à portique

gap [gæp] *s* lacune *f*; (*in wall*) brèche *f*; (*between mountains*) col *m*, gorge *f*; (*between two points of view*) abîme *m*, gouffre *m*

gape [gep], [gæp] *s* ouverture *f*, brèche *f*; (*yawn*) bâillement *m*; (*look of astonishment*) badauderie *f* || *intr* (*to yawn*) bâiller; (*to look with astonishment*) badauder; **to gape at** regarder bouche bée

garage [gə'rɑʒ] *s* garage *m*

garb [gɑrb] *s* costume *m* || *tr* vêtir

garbage ['gɑrbɪdʒ] *s* ordures *fpl*

gar'bage can' *s* poubelle *f*

gar'bage collec'tor *s* boueur *m*

gar'bage dispos'al *s* destruction *f* des ordures ménagères

gar'bage truck' *s* benne *f* à ordures

garble ['gɑrbəl] *tr* mutiler, tronquer

garden ['gɑrdən] *s* jardin *m*; (*of vege-*

tables) potager *m*; (*of flowers*) parterre *m* || *intr* jardiner

gar'den cit'y *s* cité-jardin *f*

gardener ['gɑrdnər] *s* jardinier *m*

gardening ['gɑrdnɪŋ] *s* jardinage *m*

gar'den par'ty *s* garden-party *f*

gargle ['gɑrgəl] *s* gargarisme *m* || *v* se gargariser

gargoyle ['gɑrgɔɪl] *s* gargouille *f*

garish ['gɛrɪʃ], ['gærɪʃ] *adj* cru, rutilant, criard

garland ['gɑrlənd] *s* guirlande *f* || *tr* guirlander

garlic ['gɑrlɪk] *s* ail *m*

garment ['gɑrmənt] *s* vêtement *m*

gar'ment bag' *s* housse *f* à vêtements

garner ['gɑrnər] *tr* (*to gather, collect*) amasser; (*cereals*) engranger

garnet ['gɑrnɪt] *adj & s* grenat *m*

garnish ['gɑrnɪʃ] *s* garniture *f* || *tr* garnir; (*law*) effectuer une saisie-arrêt sur

garret ['gærɪt] *s* grenier *m*; (*dormer room*) mansarde *f*

garrison ['gærɪsən] *s* garnison *f* || *tr* (*troops*) mettre en garnison; (*a city*) mettre des troupes en garnison dans

garrote [gə'rɑt], [gə'rot] *s* (*method of execution*) garrotte *f*; (*iron collar used for such an execution*) garrot *m* || *tr* garrotter

garrulous ['gær(j)ələs] *adj* bavard

garter ['gɑrtər] *s* jarretelle *f*, jarretière *f*; (*for men's socks*) support-chaussette *m*, fixe-chaussette *m*

garth [gɑrθ] *s* cour *f* intérieure d'un cloître

gas [gæs] *s* gaz *m*; (*coll*) essence *f*; (*empty talk*) (*coll*) bavardage *m*; **out of gas** en panne sèche || *v* (*pret & pp* gassed; *ger* gassing) *tr* gazer, asphyxier || *intr* dégager des gaz; (*to talk nonsense*) (*coll*) bavarder

gas'bag' *s* enveloppe *f* à gaz; (*coll*) blagueur *m*, baratineur *m*

gas' burn'er *s* bec *m* de gaz

gas' cham'ber *s* chambre *f* à gaz

Gascony ['gæskəni] *s* Gascogne *f*; la Gascogne

gas' en'gine *s* moteur *m* à gaz

gaseous ['gæsɪ·əs] *adj* gazeux

gas' gen'erator *s* gazogène *m*

gash [gæʃ] *s* entaille *f*; (*on face*) balafre *f* || *tr* entailler; balafrer

gas' heat' *s* chauffage *m* au gaz

gas' heat'er *s* (*for hot water*) chauffe-eau *m* à gaz; (*for house heat*) calorifère *m* à gaz

gas'hold'er *s* gazomètre *m*

gasi·fy ['gæsɪ̩faɪ] *v* (*pret & pp* -fied) *tr* gazéifier || *intr* se gazéifier

gas' jet' *s* bec *m* de gaz

gasket ['gæskɪt] *s* joint *m*

gas'light' *s* éclairage *m* au gaz

gas' main' *s* conduite *f* de gaz

gas' mask' *s* masque *m* à gaz

gas' me'ter *s* compteur *m* à gaz

gasoline ['gæsə̩lin], [̩gæsə'lin] *s* essence *f*

gas'oline can' *s* bidon *m* d'essence

gas'oline gauge' *s* voyant *m* d'essence

gas'oline pump' *s* pompe *f* à essence

gasp [gæsp], [gɑsp] *s* halètement *m*; *(of surprise; of death)* hoquet *m* ‖ *tr* —**to gasp out** *(a word)* dire dans un souffle ‖ *intr* haleter

gas' pipe' *s* conduite *f* de gaz

gas' produc'er *s* gazogène *m*

gas' range' *s* fourneau *m* à gaz, cuisinière *f* à gaz

gas' sta'tion *s* poste *m* d'essence

gas' stove' *s* cuisinière *f* à gaz, réchaud *m* à gaz

gas' tank' *s* gazomètre *m*; (aut) réservoir *m* d'essence

gastric ['gæstrɪk] *adj* gastrique

gastronomy [gæs'trɑnəmi] *s* gastronomie *f*

gas'works' *spl* usine *f* à gaz

gate [get] *s* porte *f*; *(in fence or wall)* grille *f*; *(main gate)* portail *f*; *(of sluice)* vanne *f*; *(number paying admission; amount paid)* entrée *f*; barrière *f*; **to crash the gate** resquiller

gate-crasher ['get͵kræʃər] *s* (coll) resquilleur *m*

gate'keep'er *s* portier *m*; (rr) garde-barrière *mf*

gate'-leg ta'ble *s* table *f* à abattants

gate'post' *s* montant *m*

gate'way' *s* passage *m*, entrée *f*; *(main entrance)* portail *m*

gather ['gæðər] *tr* amasser, rassembler; *(the harvest)* rentrer; *(fruits, flowers, etc.)* cueillir, ramasser; *(one's thoughts)* recueillir; (bb) rassembler; (sewing) froncer; *(to deduce)* (fig) conclure; **to gather dust** s'encrasser; **to gather oneself together** se ramasser ‖ *intr* se réunir, s'assembler; *(said of clouds)* s'amonceler

gathering ['gæðərɪŋ] *s* réunion *f*, rassemblement *m*; *(of harvest)* récolte *f*; *(of fruits, flowers, etc.)* cueillette *f*; (bb) assemblage *m*; (sewing) froncis *m*

gaud•y ['gɔdi] *adj* (comp **-ier**; super **-iest**) criard, voyant

gauge [gedʒ] *s* jauge *f*, calibre *m*; *(of liquid in a container)* niveau *m*; *(of gasoline, oil, etc.)* indicateur *m*; *(of carpenter)* trusquin *m*; (rr) écartement *m* ‖ *tr* jauger, calibrer; *(a person; s.o.'s capacities; a distance)* juger, jauger

gauge' glass' *s* indicateur *m* de niveau

Gaul [gɔl] *s* Gaule *f*; la Gaule

Gaulish ['gɔlɪʃ] *adj & s* gaulois *m*

gaunt [gɔnt], [gɑnt] *adj* décharné, étique, efflanqué

gauntlet ['gɔntlɪt], ['gɑntlɪt] *s* gantelet *m*; **to run the gauntlet** passer par les baguettes; **to take up the gauntlet** relever le gant; **to throw down the gauntlet** jeter le gant

gauze [gɔz] *s* gaze *f*

gavel ['gævəl] *s* marteau *m*

gawk [gɔk] *s* (coll) godiche *mf* ‖ *intr* (coll) bayer aux corneilles; **to gawk at** (coll) regarder bouche bée

gawk•y ['gɔki] *adj* (comp **-ier**; super **-iest**) godiche

gay [ge] *adj* gai

gay' blade' *s* (coll) joyeux drille *m*

gaze [gez] *s* regard *m* fixe ‖ *intr* regarder fixement

gazelle [gə'zɛl] *s* gazelle *f*

gazette [gə'zɛt] *s* gazette *f*; journal *m* officiel

gazetteer [͵gæzə'tɪr] *s* dictionnaire *m* géographique

gear [gɪr] *s* attirail *m*, appareil *m*; *(of transmission, steering, etc.)* mécanisme *m*; *(adjustment of automobile transmission)* marche *f*, vitesse *f*; *(two or more toothed wheels meshed together)* engrenage *m*; **out of gear** débrayé; **to throw into gear** embrayer; **to throw out of gear** débrayer; (fig) disloquer ‖ *tr & intr* engrener

gear'box' *s* (aut) boîte *f* de vitesses

gear'shift' *s* changement *m* de vitesse

gear'shift lev'er *s* levier *m* de changement de vitesse

gear'wheel' *s* roue *f* d'engrenage

gee [dʒi] *interj* sapristi!; *(to the right)* hue!; **gee up!** hue!

Gei'ger coun'ter ['gaɪgər] *s* compteur *m* de Geiger

gel [dʒɛl] *s* (chem) gel *m*

gelatine ['dʒɛlətɪn] *s* gélatine *f*

geld [gɛld] *v* (pret & pp **gelded** or **gelt** [gɛlt]) *tr* châtrer

gelding ['gɛldɪŋ] *s* hongre *m*

gem [dʒɛm] *s* gemme *f*; (fig) bijou *m*

gender ['dʒɛndər] *s* (gram) genre *m*; (coll) sexe *m*

gene [dʒin] *s* (biol) gène *m*

genealo•gy [͵dʒɛnɪ'ælədʒɪ], [͵dʒini-'ælədʒɪ] *s* (pl **-gies**) généalogie *f*

general ['dʒɛnərəl] *adj & s* général *m*; **in general** en général

generalissi•mo [͵dʒɛnərə'lɪsimo] *s* (pl **-mos**) généralissime *m*

generali•ty [͵dʒɛnə'rælɪti] *s* (pl **-ties**) généralité *f*

generalize ['dʒɛnərə͵laɪz] *tr & intr* généraliser

generally ['dʒɛnərəli] *adj* généralement

gen'eral practi'tioner *s* médecin *m* de médecine générale

gen'eral-ship' *s* tactique *f*; *(office)* généralat *m*

gen'eral staff' *s* état-major *m*

generate ['dʒɛnə͵ret] *tr* générer; *(to beget)* engendrer; (geom) engendrer

gen'erating sta'tion *s* usine *f* génératrice, centrale *f*

generation [͵dʒɛnə'reʃən] *s* génération *f*

generator ['dʒɛnə͵retər] *s* (chem) gazogène *m*; (elec) générateur *m*

generic [dʒɪ'nɛrɪk] *adj* générique

generosi•ty [͵dʒɛnə'rɑsɪti] *s* (pl **-ties**) générosité *f*

generous ['dʒɛnərəs] *adj* généreux; abondant

gene•sis ['dʒɛnɪsɪs] *s* (pl **-ses** [͵siz]) genèse *f*; **Genesis** (Bib) La Genèse

genetic [dʒɪ'nɛtɪk] *adj* génétique ‖ **genetics** *s* génétique *f*

Geneva [dʒɪ'nivə] *s* Genève *f*

genial ['dʒinɪəl] *adj* affable

genie ['dʒini] *s* génie *m*

genital ['dʒenɪtəl] *adj* génital || **genitals** *spl* organes *mpl* génitaux

genitive ['dʒenɪtɪv] *s* génitif *m*

genius ['dʒinjəs], ['dʒɪnɪ-əs] *s* (*pl* **geniuses**) génie *m* || *s* (*pl* **genii** ['dʒinɪ,aɪ]) génie *m*

Genoa ['dʒeno-ə] *s* Gênes *f*

genocide ['dʒenə,saɪd] *s* génocide *m*

genteel [dʒen'til] *adj* distingué, de bon ton; élégant, chic

gentian ['dʒen/ən] *s* gentiane *f*

gentile ['dʒentaɪl] *s* non-juif *m*, chrétien *m*

gentil·i·ty [dʒen'tɪlɪti] *s* (*pl* **-ties**) (*birth*) naissance *f* distinguée; (*breeding*) politesse *f*

gentle ['dʒentəl] *adj* doux; (*in birth*) noble, bien né; (*e.g., tap on the shoulder*) léger

gen·tle·folk' *s* gens *mpl* de bonne naissance

gen·tle·man *s* (*pl* **-men**) monsieur *m*; (*man of independent means*) rentier *m*; (*hist*) gentilhomme *m*

gentlemanly ['dʒentəlmənli] *adj* bien élevé, de bon ton

gen'tleman's agree'ment *m* sur parole, contrat *m* verbal

gen'tle sex' *s* sexe *m* faible

gentry ['dʒentri] *s* gens *mpl* de bonne naissance; (*Brit*) petite noblesse *f*

genuine ['dʒenjʊ-ɪn] *adj* véritable, authentique; (*person*) sincère, franc

genus ['dʒinəs] *s* (*pl* **genera** ['dʒenərə] or **genuses**) genre *m*

geogra·phy [dʒɪ'agrəfi] *s* (*pl* **-phies**) géographie *f*

geologic(al) [,dʒi-ə'ladʒɪk(əl)] *adj* géologique

geolo·gy [dʒɪ'alədʒi] *s* (*pl* **-gies**) géologie *f*

geometric(al) [,dʒi-ə'metrɪk(əl)] *adj* géométrique

geome·try [dʒɪ'amɪtri] *s* (*pl* **-tries**) géométrie *f*

geophysics [,dʒi-ə'fɪzɪks] *s* géophysique *f*

geopolitics [,dʒi-ə'palɪtɪks] *s* géopolitique *f*

George [dʒɔrdʒ] *s* Georges *m*

geranium [dʒɪ'renɪ-əm] *s* géranium *m*

geriatrics [,dʒerɪ'ætrɪks] *s* gériatrie *f*

germ [dʒʌrm] *s* germe *m*

German ['dʒʌrmən] *adj* allemand || *s* (*language*) allemand *m*; (*person*) Allemand *m*

germane [dʒer'men] *adj* à propos, pertinent; **germane to** se rapportant à

Ger'man mea'sles *s* rubéole *f*

Ger'man sil'ver *s* maillechort *m*, argentan *m*

Germa·ny ['dʒʌrməni] *s* (*pl* **-nies**) Allemagne *f*; l'Allemagne

germicidal [,dʒʌrmɪ'saɪdəl] *adj* germicide

germicide ['dʒʌrmɪ,saɪd] *s* germicide *m*

germinate ['dʒʌrmɪ,net] *intr* germer

germ' war'fare *s* guerre *f* bactériologique

gerontology [,dʒerɑn'talədʒi] *s* gérontologie *f*

gerund ['dʒerənd] *s* gérondif *m*

gestation [dʒes'te/ən] *s* gestation *f*

gesticulate [dʒes'tɪkjə,let] *intr* gesticuler

gesture ['dʒest/ər] *s* geste *m* || *intr* faire des gestes; **to gesture to** faire signe à

get [get] *v* (*pret got* [gɑt]; *pp got* or **gotten** ['gɑtən]; *ger* **getting**) *tr* obtenir, procurer; (*to receive*) avoir, recevoir; (*to catch*) attraper; (*to seek*) chercher, aller chercher; (*to reach*) atteindre; (*to find*) trouver, rencontrer; (*to obtain and bring*) prendre; (*e.g., dinner*) faire; (*rad*) avoir, prendre, accrocher; (*to understand*) (coll) comprendre; **to get across** faire accepter; faire comprendre; **to get a kick out of** (coll) prendre plaisir à; **to get back** ravoir, se faire rendre; **to get down** descendre; (*to swallow*) avaler; **to get in** rentrer; **to get s.o. to** + *inf* persuader à qn de + *inf*; **to get s.th. done** faire faire q.ch. || *intr* (*to become*) devenir, se faire; (*to arrive*) arriver, parvenir; **get up!** (*said to an animal*) huel; **to get about** (*said of news*) se répandre; (*said of convalescent*) être de nouveau sur pied; **to get accustomed to** se faire à; **to get across** traverser; **to get along** circuler; (*to succeed*) se tirer d'affaire; **to get along without** se passer de; **to get angry** se fâcher; **to get away s'évader**; **to get away with** (coll) s'en tirer avec; **to get back** reculer; (*to return*) rentrer; **to get back at** (coll) rendre la pareille à, se venger sur; **to get by** passer; (*to manage, to shift*) (coll) s'en tirer sans peine; **to get dark** faire nuit; **to get down** descendre; **to get going** se mettre en marche; **to get in** or **into** entrer dans; **to get off with** en être quitte pour; **to get on** monter sur; (*a car*) monter dans; continuer; (*to succeed*) faire des progrès; **to get out** sortir; **to get rid of** se défaire de; **to get to** arriver à; (*to have an opportunity to*) avoir l'occasion de; **to get up** se lever; **to not get over it** (coll) ne pas en revenir

get'away' *s* démarrage *m*; (*flight*) fuite *f*

get'-togeth'er *s* réunion *f*

get'up' *s* (*style*) (coll) présentation *f*; (*outfit*) (coll) affublement *m*

geyser ['gaɪzər] *s* geyser *m* || ['gizər] *s* (Brit) chauffe-eau *m* à gaz

ghast·ly ['gæstli], ['gɑstli] *adj* (*comp* **-lier**; *super* **-liest**) livide, blême; horrible, affreux

Ghent [gent] *s* Gand *m*

gherkin ['gʌrkɪn] *s* cornichon *m*

ghet·to ['geto] *s* (*pl* **-tos**) ghetto *m*

ghost [gost] *s* revenant *m*; (*shade, semblance*) ombre *f*; **not the ghost of a chance** pas la moindre chance; **to give up the ghost** rendre l'âme, rendre l'esprit

ghost·ly ['gostli] *adj* (*comp* **-lier**; *super* **-liest**) spectral, fantomatique

ghost' sto'ry *s* histoire *f* de revenants

ghost' town' s ville f morte

ghost' writ'er s nègre m

ghoul [gul] s goule f; (body snatcher) déterreur m de cadavres

ghoulish ['gulɪʃ] adj vampirique

GI ['dʒi'aɪ] (letterword) (General Issue) adj fourni par l'armée || s (pl GI's) soldat m américain, simple soldat

giant ['dʒaɪ·ənt] adj & s géant m

giantess ['dʒaɪ·əntɪs] s géante f

gibberish ['dʒɪbərɪ/], ['ɡɪbərɪ/] s baragouin m

gibbet ['dʒɪbɪt] s gibet m, potence f

gibe [dʒaɪb] s raillerie f, moquerie f || tr & intr railler; **to gibe at** se moquer de, railler

giblets ['dʒɪblɪts] spl abattis m, abats mpl

gid·dy ['ɡɪdɪ] adj (comp -dier; super -diest) étourdi; (height) vertigineux; (foolish) léger, frivole

Gideon ['ɡɪdɪ·ən] s (Bib) Gédéon m

gift [ɡɪft] s cadeau m; (natural ability) don m, talent m || tr douer

gifted adj doué

gift' horse'—**never look a gift horse in the mouth** à cheval donné on ne regarde pas à la bride

gift' of gab' s (coll) bagou m, faconde f

gift' shop' s boutique f de souvenirs, magasin m de nouveautés

gift'-wrap' v (pret & pp -wrapped; ger -wrapping) tr faire un paquet cadeau de

gigantic [dʒaɪ'ɡæntɪk] adj gigantesque

giggle ['ɡɪɡəl] s petit rire m || intr pousser des petits rires, glousser

gigo·lo ['dʒɪɡə‚lo] s (pl -los) gigolo m

GI Joe [‚dʒi‚aɪ'dʒo] s le troufion

gild [ɡɪld] v (pret & pp **gilded** or **gilt** [ɡɪlt]) tr dorer

gilding ['ɡɪldɪŋ] s dorure f

gill [ɡɪl] s (of cock) fanon m; **gills** (of fish) ouïes fpl, branchies fpl

gilt [ɡɪlt] adj & s doré m

gilt'-edged' adj (e.g., book) doré sur tranche; (securities) de premier ordre, de tout repos

gimcrack ['dʒɪm‚kræk] adj de pacotille, de camelote || s babiole f

gimlet ['ɡɪmlɪt] s vrille f, perçoir m

gimmick ['ɡɪmɪk] s (coll) truc m, machin m; (trick) tour m

gin [dʒɪn] s (alcoholic liquor) gin m, genièvre m; (for cotton, corn, etc.) égreneuse f; (snare) trébuchet m || v (pret & pp **ginned**; ger **ginning**) tr égrener

ginger ['dʒɪndʒər] s gingembre m; (fig) entrain m, allant m

gin'ger ale' s boisson f gazeuse au gingembre

gin'ger·bread' s pain m d'épice; ornement m de mauvais goût

gingerly ['dʒɪndʒərlɪ] adj précautionneux || adv tout doux, avec précaution

gin'ger·snap' s gâteau m sec au gingembre

gingham ['ɡɪŋəm] s guingan m

giraffe [dʒɪ'ræf], [dʒɪ'raf] s girafe f

gird [ɡʌrd] v (pret & pp **girt** [ɡʌrt] or **girded**) tr ceindre; **to gird on** se ceindre de; **to gird oneself for** se préparer à

girder ['ɡʌrdər] s poutre f

girdle ['ɡʌrdəl] s ceinture f || tr ceindre, entourer

girl [ɡʌrl] s jeune fille f; (little girl) petite fille; (servant) bonne f

girl' friend' s (sweetheart) petite amie f, bonne amie f; (female friend) amie f, camarade f

girl'hood s enfance f, jeunesse f d'une femme

girlish ['ɡʌrlɪʃ] adj de jeune fille, de petite fille

girl' scout' s éclaireuse f, guide f

girls'' school' s école f de filles

girth [ɡʌrθ] s (band) sangle f; (measure around) circonférence f; (of person) tour m de taille

gist [dʒɪst] s fond m, essence f

give [ɡɪv] s élasticité f || v (pret **gave** [ɡev]; pp **given** ['ɡɪvən]) tr donner; (a speech, a lecture, a class; a smile) faire; **to give away** donner, distribuer; révéler; **to give back** rendre, remettre; **to give forth** or **off** émettre; **to give oneself up** se rendre; **to give up** renoncer à, abandonner || intr donner; **to give in** se rendre; **to give out** manquer; (to become exhausted) s'épuiser; **to give way** faire place, reculer

give'-and-take' s compromis m; échange m de propos plaisants

give'away' s (coll) révélation f involontaire; (coll) trahison f; **to play giveaway** jouer à qui perd gagne

given ['ɡɪvən] adj donné; **given that** vu que, étant donné que

giver ['ɡɪvər] s donneur m, donateur m

giv'en name' s prénom m

gizzard ['ɡɪzərd] s gésier m

glacial ['ɡleʃəl] adj glacial; (chem) en cristaux; (geol) glaciaire

glacier ['ɡleʃər] s glacier m

glad [ɡlæd] adj (comp **gladder**; super **gladdest**) content, heureux; **to be glad to** être content or heureux de

gladden ['ɡlædən] tr réjouir

glade [ɡled] s clairière f, éclaircie f

glad' hand' s (coll) accueil m chaleureux

gladiator ['ɡlædɪ‚etər] s gladiateur m

gladiola [‚ɡlædɪ'olə], [ɡlə'daɪ·ələ] s glaïeul m

gladly ['ɡlædlɪ] adv volontiers, avec plaisir

gladness ['ɡlædnɪs] s joie f, plaisir m

glad' rags' spl (slang) frusques fpl des grands jours

glamorous ['ɡlæmərəs] adj ravissant, éclatant

glamour ['ɡlæmər] s charme m, éclat m

glam'our·girl' s ensorceleuse f

glance [ɡlæns], [ɡlɑns] s coup m d'œil; **at a glance** d'un seul coup d'œil; **at first glance** à première vue || intr jeter un regard; **to glance at** jeter un coup d'œil sur; **to glance off** ricocher, dévier; **to glance through a book**

feuilleter un livre; **to glance up** lever les yeux

gland [glænd] s glande f

glanders ['glændərz] spl (vet) morve f

glare [gler] s lumière f éblouissante; (look) regard m irrité || intr éblouir, briller; **to glare at** lancer un regard méchant à, foudroyer du regard

glare′ ice′ s verglas m

glaring ['glerɪŋ] adj éblouissant; (mistake, fact) évident, qui saute aux yeux; (blunder, abuse) grossier, scandaleux

glass [glæs], [glɑs] s verre m; (mirror) glace f; **glasses** lunettes fpl

glass′ blow′er ['blo·ər] s verrier-souffleur m

glass′ case′ s vitrine f

glass′ cut′ter s (tool) diamant m; (workman) vitrier m

glass′ door′ s porte f vitrée

glassful ['glæsful], ['glɑsful] s̄ verre m

glass′ house′ s serre f; (fig) maison f de verre

glass′ware′ s verrerie f

glass′works′ s verrerie f, glacerie f

glass′ wool′ s laine f de verre

glass·y ['glæsi], ['glɑsi] adj (comp -ier; super -iest) vitreux; (smooth) lisse

glaze [glez] s (ceramics) vernis m; (culin) glace f; (tex) lustre m || tr (to cover with a glossy coating) glacer; (to fit with glass) vitrer

glazier ['glezɪər] s vitrier m

gleam [glim] s rayon m; (of hope) lueur f || intr rayonner, reluire

glean [glin] tr glaner

glee [gli] s allégresse f, joie f

glee′ club′ s orphéon m, société f chorale

glen [glen] s vallon m, ravin m

glib [glɪb] adj (comp glibber; super glibbest) facile; (tongue) délié

glide [glaɪd] s glissement m; (aer) vol m plané; (mus) port m de voix; (phonet) son m transitoire || intr glisser, se glisser; (aer) planer

glider ['glaɪdər] s (porch seat) siège m à glissière; (aer) planeur m

glimmer ['glɪmər] s faible lueur f || intr jeter une faible lueur

glimmering ['glɪmərɪŋ] adj faible, vacillant || s faible lueur f, miroitement m; soupçon m, indice m

glimpse [glɪmps] s aperçu m; **to catch a glimpse of** entrevoir, aviser || tr entrevoir

glint [glɪnt] s reflet m, éclair m || intr jeter un reflet, étinceler

glisten ['glɪsən] s scintillement m || intr scintiller

glitter ['glɪtər] s éclat m, étincellement m || intr étinceler

gloaming ['glomɪŋ] s crépuscule m, jour m crépusculaire

gloat [glot] intr éprouver un malin plaisir; **to gloat over** faire des gorges chaudes de; (e.g., one's victim) couver du regard

global ['globəl] adj sphérique; mondial

globe [glob] s globe m

globe′-trot′ter s globe-trotter m

globule ['glɑbjul] s globule m

gloom [glum] s obscurité f, ténèbres fpl; tristesse f

gloom·y ['glumi] adj (comp -ier; super -iest) sombre, lugubre; (ideas) noir

glori·fy ['glorɪ ˌfaɪ] v (pret & pp -fied) tr glorifier

glorious ['glorɪ·əs] adj glorieux

glo·ry ['glori] s (pl -ries) gloire f; **to be in one's glory** être aux anges; **to go to glory** (slang) aller à la ruine || v (pret & pp -ried) intr—**to glory in** se glorifier de

gloss [glɔs], [glɑs] s lustre m; (on cloth) cati m; (on floor) brillant m; (note, commentary) glose f; **to take off the gloss from** décatir || tr lustrer; **to gloss over** maquiller, farder

glossa·ry ['glɑsəri] s (pl -ries) glossaire m

gloss·y ['glɔsi], ['glɑsi] adj (comp -ier; super -iest) lustré, brillant

glot′tal stop′ ['glɑtəl] s coup m de glotte

glottis ['glɑtɪs] s glotte f

glove [glʌv] s gant m || tr ganter

glove′ compart′ment s boîte f à gants

glow [glo] s rougeoiement m || intr rougeoyer

glower ['glau·ər] s grise mine f || intr avoir l'air renfrogné

glowing ['glo·ɪŋ] adj rougeoyant, incandescent; (healthy) rayonnant; (cheeks) vermeil; (reports) enthousiaste, élogieux

glow′worm′ s ver m luisant

glucose ['glukos] s glucose m

glue [glu] s colle f || tr coller

glue′pot′ s pot m à colle

gluey ['glu·i] adj (comp gluier; super gluiest) gluant

glum [glʌm] adj (comp glummer; super glummest) maussade, renfrogné

glut [glʌt] s surabondance f; (on the market) engorgement m || v (pret & pp glutted; ger glutting) tr (with food) rassasier; (the market) inonder, engorger

glutton ['glʌtən] s glouton m

gluttonous ['glʌtənəs] adj glouton

glutton·y ['glʌtəni] s (pl -ies) gloutonnerie f

glycerine ['glɪsərɪn] s glycérine f

G.M.T. abbr (Greenwich mean time) temps moyen (de Greenwich) T.U., temps m universel

gnarl [nɑrl] s (bot) nœud m || tr tordre || intr grogner

gnarled adj noueux

gnash [næʃ] tr—**to gnash the teeth** grincer des dents or les dents

gnat [næt] s moucheron m, moustique m

gnaw [nɔ] tr ronger

gnome [nom] s gnome m

go [go] s (pl goes) aller m; **a lot of go** (slang) beaucoup d'allant; **it's no go** (coll) ça ne marche pas, pas mèche; **to have a go at** (coll) essayer; **to make a go of** (coll) réussir à || v (*pret* went [went]; *pp* gone [gɔn], [gan]) *tr*—to go it alone le faire tout seul || *intr* aller; (*to work, operate*) marcher; y aller, e.g., **did you go?** y êtes-vous allé?; devenir, e.g., **to go crazy** devenir fou; faire, e.g., **to go quack-quack** faire couin-couin; **going, going, gone!** une fois, deux fois, adjugé!; **go to it!** allez-y!; **to be going to** or **to go to** + *inf* aller + *inf*, e.g., **I am going to the store to buy some shoes** je vais au magasin acheter des souliers; (*to express futurity from the point of view of the present or past*) aller + *inf*, e.g., **he is going to get married** il va se marier; e.g., **he was going to get married** il allait se marier; **to go** (*to take out*) (coll) à emporter; **to go against** contrarier; **to go ahead of** dépasser; **to go away** s'en aller; **to go back** retourner; (*to return home*) rentrer; (*to back up*) reculer; (*to date back*) remonter; **to go by** passer; (*a rule, model, etc.*) agir selon; **to go down** descendre; (*said of sun*) se coucher; (*said of ship*) sombrer; **to go fishing** aller à la pêche; **to go for** or **to go get** aller chercher; **to go in** entrer; entrer dans; (*to fit into*) tenir dans; **to go in for** se consacrer à; **to go in with** s'associer à or avec, se joindre à; **to go off** (*said of bomb, gun, etc.*) partir; **to go on** + *ger* continuer à + *inf*; **to go out** sortir; (*said of light, fire, etc.*) s'éteindre; **to go over** (*to examine*) parcourir, repasser; **to go through** (*e.g., a door*) passer par; (*e.g., a city*) traverser; (*a fortune*) dissiper, dilapider; **to go together** (*said, e.g., of colors*) s'assortir; (*said of lovers*) être très liés; **to go under** succomber; (*said, e.g., of submarine*) plonger; (*a false name*) être connu sous; **to go up** monter; **to go with** accompagner; (*a color, dress, etc.*) s'assortir avec; **to go without** se passer de; **to let go of** lâcher

goad [god] *s* aiguillon *m* || *tr* aiguillonner

go'-ahead' *adj* (coll) entreprenant || *s* (coll) signal *m* d'aller en avant

goal [gol] *s* but *m*

goal'keep'er *s* goal *m*, gardien *m* de but

goal' line' *s* ligne *f* de but

goal' post' *s* montant *m*, poteau *m* de but

goat [got] *s* chèvre *f*; (*male goat*) bouc *m*; (coll) dindon *m*; **to get the goat of** (slang) exaspérer, irriter

goatee [go'ti] *s* barbiche *f*

goat'herd' *s* chevrier *m*

goat'skin' *s* peau *f* de chèvre

goat'suck'er *s* (orn) engoulevent *m*

gob [gab] *s* (coll) grumeau *m*; (coll) marin *m*

gobble ['gabəl] *s* glouglou *m* || *tr* engloutir, bâfrer || *intr* bâfrer; (*said of turkey*) glouglouter

gobbledegook ['gabəldɪˌguk] *s* (coll) palabre *m & f*, charabia *m*

go'-between' *s* intermédiaire *mf*; (*in shady love affairs*) entremetteur *m*

goblet ['gablɪt] *s* verre *m* à pied

goblin ['gablɪn] *s* lutin *m*

go'-by' *s* (coll) affront *m*; **to give s.o. the go-by** (coll) brûler la politesse à qn

go'cart' *s* chariot *m*; (*baby carriage*) poussette *f*; (*handcart*) charrette *f* à bras

god [gad] *s* dieu *m*; **God forbid** qu'à Dieu ne plaise; **God grant** plût à Dieu; **God willing** s'il plaît à Dieu

god'child' *s* (*pl* -children) filleul *m*

god'daugh'ter *s* filleule *f*

goddess ['gadɪs] *s* déesse *f*

god'fa'ther *s* parrain *m*

God'-fear'ing *adj* dévot, pieux

God'forsak'en *adj* abandonné de Dieu; (coll) perdu, misérable

god'head' *s* divinité *f*; **Godhead** Dieu *m*

godless ['gadlɪs] *adj* athée, impie

god-ly ['gadli] *adj* (*comp* -lier; *super* -liest) dévot, pieux

god'moth'er *s* marraine *f*

God's' a'cre *s* le champ de repos

god'send' *s* aubaine *f*

god'son' *s* filleul *m*

God'speed' *s* bonne chance *f*, bon voyage *m*

go-getter ['go͵getər] *s* (coll) homme *m* d'expédition, lanceur *m* d'affaires

goggle ['gagəl] *intr* rouler de gros yeux; (*to open the eyes wide*) écarquiller les yeux

gog'gle-eyed' *adj* aux yeux saillants

goggles ['gagəlz] *spl* lunettes *fpl* protectrices

going ['go·ɪŋ] *adj* en marche; **going on two o'clock** presque deux heures || *s* départ *m*; **good going!** bien joué!

go'ing concern' *s* maison *f* en pleine activité

go'ings on' *spl* (coll) chahut *m*, tapage *m*; (coll) événements *mpl*

goiter ['gɔɪtər] *s* goitre *m*

gold [gold] *s* or *m*, en or || *s* or *m*

gold'beat'er *s* batteur *m* d'or

gold'beater's skin' *s* baudruche *f*

gold'crest' *s* roitelet *m* à tête dorée

golden ['goldən] *adj* d'or; (*gilt*) doré; (*hair*) d'or, d'un blond doré; (*opportunity*) favorable, magnifique

gold'en age' *s* âge *m* d'or

gold'en calf' *s* veau *m* d'or

Gold'en Fleece' *s* Toison *f* d'or

gold'en mean' *s* juste-milieu *m*

gold'en plov'er *s* pluvier *m* doré

gold'en-rod' *s* solidage *f*, gerbe *f* d'or

gold'en rule' *s* règle *f* de la charité chrétienne

gold'en wed'ding *s* noces *fpl* d'or, jubilé *m*

gold'-filled' *adj* (*tooth*) aurifié

gold'finch' *s* chardonneret *m*

gold'fish' *s* poisson *m* rouge

goldilocks ['goldɪˌlaks] *s* jeune fille *f* aux cheveux d'or

gold' leaf' *s* feuille *f* d'or

gold' mine' *s* mine *f* d'or; **to strike a gold mine** (fig) dénicher le bon filon, faire des affaires d'or

gold′ plate′ s vaisselle f d'or
gold′-plate′ tr plaquer d'or
gold′ rush′ s ruée f vers l'or
gold′smith′ s orfèvre m
gold′ stan′dard s étalon-or m
golf [galf] s golf m || intr jouer au golf
golf′ club′ s crosse f de golf, club m; (association) club m de golf
golfer ['galfər] s joueur m de golf
golf′ links′ spl terrain m de golf
gondola ['gandələ] s gondole f
gondolier [,gandə'lɪr] s gondolier m
gone [gɔn], [gan] adj parti, disparu; (used up) épuisé; (ruined) ruiné, fichu; (dead) mort; far gone avancé, épris de, **gone on** (in love with) (coll) entiché de, épris de
gong [gɔn], [gaŋ] s gong m
gonorrhea [,ganə'ri·ə] s blennorragie f
goo [gu] s (slang) matière f collante
good [gud] adj (comp **better**; super **best**) bon §91; (child) sage; (meals) soigné; **good for you!** bien joué!; **to be good at** être fort en, être expert à; **to make good** prospérer; (a loss) compenser; (a promise) tenir; **will you be good enough to** voulez-vous être assez aimable de || s bien m; **for good** pour de bon, définitivement; **goods** biens mpl; (com) marchandises fpl; **to catch with the goods** (slang) prendre la main dans le sac; **to the good** de gagné, e.g., **all or so much to the good** autant de gagné || interj bon!, bien!, à la bonne heure!; **very good!** parfait!
good′ afternoon′ s bonjour m
good′-by′ or **good′-bye′** s adieu m || interj au revoir!; (before a long journey) adieu!
good′ cit′izenship s civisme m
good′ day′ s bonjour m
good′ deed′ s bonne action f
good′ egg′ s (slang) chic type m
good′ eve′ning s bonsoir m
good′ fel′low s brave garçon m, brave type m
good′ fel′lowship s camaraderie f
good′-for-noth′ing adj inutile m || s bon m à rien
Good′ Fri′day s le Vendredi saint
good′ grac′es spl bonnes grâces fpl
good′-heart′ed adj au cœur généreux
good′-hu′mored adj de bonne humeur
good′-look′ing adj beau, joli
good′ looks′ spl belle mine f
good′ luck′ s bonne chance f
good′·ly ['gudli] adj (comp **-lier**; super **-liest**) considérable, important; (quality) bon; (appearance) beau
good′ morn′ing s bonjour m
good′-na′tured adj aimable, accommodant
goodness ['gudnɪs] s bonté f; **for goodness' sake!** pour l'amour de Dieu!; **goodness knows** Dieu seul sait || interj mon Dieu!
good′ night′ s bonne nuit f
good′ sense′ s bon sens m
good′-sized′ adj de grandeur moyenne, assez grand

good′ speed′ s succès m, bonne chance f
good′-tem′pered adj de caractère facile, d'humeur égale
good′ time′ s bon temps m; **to have a good time** prendre du bon temps, bien s'amuser; **to make good time** arriver en peu de temps
good′ turn′ s bienfait m, service m
good′ will′ s bonne volonté f; (com) achalandage m
good′ works′ spl bonnes œuvres fpl
good·y ['gudi] adj (coll) d'une piété affectée || s (pl **-ies**) (coll) petit saint m; **goodies** friandises fpl || interj chouette!; chic!
gooey ['gu·i] adj (comp **gooier**; super **gooiest**) (slang) gluant; (sentimental) (slang) à l'eau de rose
goof [guf] s (slang) toqué m || intr— **to goof off** (slang) tirer au flanc
goof·y ['gufi] adj (comp **-ier**; super **-iest**) (slang) toqué, maboul
goon [gun] s (roughneck) (coll) dur m; (coll) terroriste m professionnel; (slang) niais m
goose [gus] s (pl **geese** [gis]) oie f; **to kill the goose that lays the golden eggs** tuer la poule aux œufs d'or || s (pl **gooses**) (of tailor) carreau m
goose′ber′ry s (pl **-ries**) groseille f verte
goose′ egg′ s œuf m d'oie; (slang) zéro m
goose′ flesh′ s chair f de poule
goose′ neck′ s col m de cygne
goose′ pim′ples spl chair f de poule
goose′ step′ s (mil) pas m de l'oie
goose′-step′ v (pret & pp **-stepped**; ger **-stepping**) intr marcher au pas de l'oie
gopher ['gofər] s citelle m
gore [gor] s (blood) sang m caillé; (sewing) soufflet m || tr percer d'un coup de corne; (sewing) tailler en pointe
gorge [gɔrdʒ] s gorge f || tr gorger || intr se gorger
gorgeous ['gɔrdʒəs] adj magnifique
gorilla [gə'rɪlə] s gorille m
gorse [gɔrs] s (bot) genêt m épineux
gor·y ['gori] adj (comp **-ier**; super **-iest**) ensanglanté, sanglant
gosh [gaʃ] interj (coll) sapristi!, mon Dieu!
goshawk ['gas,hɔk] s autour m
gospel ['gaspəl] s évangile m; **Gospel** Évangile
gos′pel truth′ s parole f d'Évangile
gossamer ['gasəmər] adj ténu || s toile f d'araignée, fils mpl de la Vierge; (gauze) gaze f
gossip ['gasɪp] s commérage m, cancan m; (person) commère f; **piece of gossip** potin m, racontar m || intr cancaner
gos′sip col′umnist s échotier m
Gothic ['gaθɪk] adj & s gothique m
gouge [gaudʒ] s gouge f || tr gouger; (to swindle) empiler
goulash ['gulaʃ] s goulasch m & f
gourd [gord], [gurd] s gourde f

gourmand ['gurmənd] s gourmand m; (glutton) glouton m

gourmet ['gurme] s gourmet m

gout [gaut] s goutte f

govern ['gʌvərn] tr gouverner; (gram) régir ‖ intr gouverner

governess ['gʌvərnɪs] s institutrice f, gouvernante f

government ['gʌvərnmənt] s gouvernement m

governmental [,gʌvərn'mentəl] adj gouvernemental

governor ['gʌvərnər] s gouverneur m; (mach) régulateur m

gown [gaun] s robe f

grab [græb] s prise f; (coll) vol m, coup m ‖ v (pret & pp grabbed; ger grabbing) tr empoigner, saisir ‖ intr —to grab at s'agripper à

grab' bag' s sac m à surprises

grace [gres] s grâce f; (prayer at table before meals) bénédicité m; (prayer at table after meals) grâces; (extension of time) délai m de grâce ‖ tr orner; honorer

graceful ['gresfəl] adj gracieux

grace' note' s note f d'agrément, appoggiature f

gracious ['greʃəs] adj gracieux; (compassionate) miséricordieux

grackle ['grækəl] s (myna) mainate m; (purple grackle) quiscale m

gradation [gre'deʃən] s gradation f

grade [gred] s (rank) grade m; (of oil) grade; qualité f; (school class) classe f, année f; (mark in school) note f; (slope) pente f; **to make the grade** réussir ‖ tr classer; (a school paper) noter; (land) niveler

grade' cross'ing s (rr) passage m à niveau

grade' school' s école f primaire

gradient ['gredɪ·ənt] adj montant ‖ s pente f; (phys) gradient m

gradual ['grædʒʊ·əl] adj & s graduel m

gradually ['grædʒʊ·əli] adv graduellement, peu à peu

graduate ['grædʒʊ·ɪt] s diplômé m ‖ ['grædʒʊ,et] tr conférer un diplôme à, décerner des diplômes à; (to mark with degrees) graduer ‖ intr recevoir son diplôme

grad'uate school' s faculté f des hautes études

grad'uate stu'dent s étudiant m avancé, étudiant de maîtrise, de doctorat

grad'uate work' s études fpl avancées

grad'uat'ing class' s classe f sortante

graduation [,grædʒʊ'eʃən] s collation f des grades; (e.g., marking on beaker) graduation f

graft [græft], [grɑft] s (hort, surg) greffe f; (coll) gratte f, grattage m ‖ tr & intr (hort, surg) greffer; (coll) gratter

grafter ['græftər], ['grɑftər] s (hort) greffeur m; (coll) homme m véreux, concussionnaire m

gra'ham bread' ['gre·əm] s pain m entier

gra'ham flour' s farine f entière

grain [gren] s (small seed; tiny particle of sand, etc.; small unit of weight; small amount) grain m; (cereal seeds) grains mpl, céréales fpl; (in stone) fil m; (in wood) fibres fpl; **against the grain** à contre-fil, à rebrousse-poil ‖ tr grener; (wood, etc.) veiner

grain' el'evator s dépôt m et élévateur m à grains

grain'field' s champ m de blé

graining ['grenɪŋ] s grenage m; (of painting) veinage m

gram [græm] s gramme m

grammar ['græmər] s grammaire f

grammarian [grə'merɪ·ən] s grammairien m

gram'mar school' s école f primaire

grammatical [grə'mætɪkəl] adj grammatical

granary ['grænəri] s (pl -ries) grenier m

grand [grænd] adj magnifique; (person) grand; (coll) formidable

grand'aunt' s grand-tante f

grand'child' s (pl -chil'dren) petit-fils m; petite-fille f; **grandchildren** petits-enfants mpl

grand'daugh'ter s petite-fille f

grand' duch'ess s grande-duchesse f

grand' duch'y s grand-duché m

grand' duke' s grand-duc m

grandee [græn'di] s grand m d'Espagne

grand'fa'ther s grand-père m

grand'father's clock' s pendule f à gaine, horloge f comtoise

grandiose ['grændɪ,os] adj grandiose; pompeux

grand' ju'ry s jury m d'accusation

grand' lar'ceny s grand larcin m

grand' lodge' s grand orient m

grandma ['grænd,mɑ], ['græm,mɑ], ['græmə] s (coll) grand-maman f

grand'moth'er s grand-mère f

grand'neph'ew s petit-neveu m

grand'niece' s petite-nièce f

grand' op'era s grand opéra m

grandpa ['grænd,pɑ], ['græn,pɑ], ['græmpə] s (coll) grand-papa m

grand'par'ent s grand-père m; grand-mère f; **grandparents** grands-parents mpl

grand' pian'o s piano m à queue

grand' slam' s grand chelem m

grand'son' s petit-fils m

grand'stand' s tribune f, gradins mpl

grand' to'tal s total m global

grand'un'cle s grand-oncle m

grand' vizier' s grand vizir m

grange [grendʒ] s ferme f; syndicat m d'agriculteurs

granite ['grænɪt] s granite m, granit m

granny ['græni] s (pl -nies) (coll) grand-mère f

gran'ny knot' s nœud m de vache

grant [grænt], [grɑnt] s concession f; (subsidy) subvention f; (scholarship) bourse f ‖ tr concéder, accorder; (a wish) exaucer; (e.g., a charter) octroyer; (a degree) décerner; **to take for granted** escompter, tenir pour évident; traiter avec indifférence

grantee [græn'ti], [grɑn'ti] s donataire mf

grantor [græn'tɔr], [grɑn'tɔr] s donateur m
granular ['grænjələr] adj granulaire
granulate ['grænjə‚let] tr granuler || intr se granuler
gran'ulated sug'ar s sucre m cristallisé
granule ['grænjul] s granule m, granulé m
grape [grep] s (fruit) raisin m; (vine) vigne f; (single grape) grain m de raisin
grape' ar'bor s treille f
grape'fruit' s (fruit) pamplemousse m & f; (tree) pamplemoussier m
grape' juice' s jus m de raisin
grape'shot' s mitraille f
grape'vine' s vigne f; (chain of gossip) source f de canards
graph [græf], [grɑf] s graphique m; (gram) graphie f
graphic(al) ['græfɪk(əl)] adj graphique; (fig) vivant, net
graphite ['græfaɪt] s graphite m
graph' pa'per s papier m quadrillé
grapnel ['græpnəl] s grappin m
grapple ['græpəl] s grappin m; (fight) corps à corps m || tr saisir au grappin; (a person) empoigner à bras le corps || intr (to fight) lutter corps à corps; **to grapple with** en venir aux prises avec, s'attaquer à
grap'pling i'ron s grappin m
grasp [græsp], [grɑsp] s prise f; **to have a good grasp of** avoir une profonde connaissance de; **within one's grasp** à sa portée || tr saisir || intr—**to grasp** or **to** tâcher de saisir; saisir avidement
grasping ['græspɪŋ], ['grɑspɪŋ] adj avide, rapace
grass [græs], [grɑs] s herbe f; (pasture) herbage m; (lawn) gazon m; **keep off the grass** (public sign) ne marchez pas sur le gazon; **to go to grass** (fig) s'étaler par terre
grass'hop'per s sauterelle f
grass'-roots' adj populaire, du peuple
grass' seed' s graine f fourragère; (for lawns) graine f pour gazon
grass' snake' s (Tropidonotus natrix) couleuvre f à collier
grass' wid'ow s demi-veuve f
grass·y ['græsi], ['grɑsi] adj (comp -ier; super -iest) herbeux
grate [gret] s grille f, grillage m || tr (to put a grate on) griller; (e.g., cheese) râper; **to grate the teeth** grincer des dents || intr grincer; **to grate on** écorcher
grateful ['gretfəl] adj reconnaissant; agréable; **to be grateful for** être reconnaissant de or pour
grater ['gretər] s râpe f
grati·fy ['grætɪ‚faɪ] v (pret & pp -fied) tr faire plaisir à, satisfaire
gratifying ['grætɪ‚faɪ·ɪŋ] adj agréable, satisfaisant
grating ['gretɪŋ] adj grinçant || s grillage m, grille f
gratis ['gretɪs], ['grætɪs] adj gratuit, gracieux || adv gratis, gratuitement
gratitude ['grætɪ‚t(j)ud] s gratitude f,

reconnaissance f; **gratitude for** reconnaissance de or pour
gratuitous [grə't(j)u·ɪtəs] adj gratuit
gratui·ty [grə't(j)u·ɪti] s (pl -ties) gratification f, pourboire m
grave [grev] adj grave || s fosse f, tombe f
gravedigger ['grev‚dɪgər] s fossoyeur m
gravel ['grævəl] s gravier m; (pathol) gravelle f
grav'en im'age ['grevən] s image f taillée
grave'stone' s pierre f tombale
grave'yard' s cimetière m
gravitate ['grævɪ‚tet] intr graviter
gravitation [‚grævɪ'teʃən] s gravitation f
gravi·ty ['grævɪti] s (pl -ties) gravité f; (phys) pesanteur f, gravité
gra·vy ['grevi] s (pl -vies) (juice from cooking meat) jus m; (sauce made with this juice) sauce f; (slang) profit m facile, profit supplémentaire
gra'vy boat' s saucière f
gra'vy train' s (slang) assiette f au beurre
gray [gre] adj gris; (gray-haired) gris, chenu; **to turn gray** grisonner || s gris m || tr grisonner
gray'beard' s barbon m, ancien m
gray'-haired' adj gris, chenu
gray'hound' s lévrier m; (female) levrette f
grayish ['gre·ɪʃ] adj grisâtre
gray' mat'ter s substance f grise
graze [grez] tr (to touch lightly) frôler, effleurer; (to scratch lightly in passing) érafler; (to pasture) faire paître || intr paître
grease [gris] s graisse f || [gris], [griz] tr graisser
grease' cup' [gris] s godet m graisseur
grease' gun' [gris] s graisseur m, seringue f à graisse
grease' paint' [gris] s fard m, grimage m
greas·y ['grisi], ['grizi] adj (comp -ier; super -iest) graisseux, gras
great [gret] adj grand; (coll) excellent, formidable; **a great deal, a great many** beaucoup
great'-aunt' s grand-tante f
Great' Bear' s Grande Ourse f
Great' Brit'ain s Grande Bretagne f; la Grande Bretagne
great'coat' s capote f
Great' Dane' s danois m
Great'er Lon'don s le Grand Londres
Great'er New' York' s le Grand New York
great'-grand'child' s (pl -chil'dren) arrière-petit-fils m; arrière-petite-fille f; **great-grandchildren** arrière-petits-enfants mpl
great'-grand'daugh'ter s arrière-petite-fille f
great'-grand'fa'ther s arrière-grand-père m, bisaïeul m
great'-grand'moth'er s arrière-grand-mère f, bisaïeule f

great′-grand′par′ents *spl* arrière-grands-parents *mpl*

great′-grand′son *s* arrière-petit-fils *m*

greatly ['gretli] *adv* grandement, fort, beaucoup

great′-neph′ew *s* petit-neveu *m*

greatness ['gretnɪs] *s* grandeur *f*

great′-niece′ *s* petite-nièce *f*

great′-un′cle *s* grand-oncle *m*

Great′ War′ *s* Grande Guerre *f*

Grecian ['griʃən] *adj* grec || *s* (*person*) Grec *m*

Greece [gris] *s* Grèce *f*; la Grèce

greed [grid] *s* avidité *f*

greed·y ['gridi] *adj* (*comp* -ier; *super* -iest) avide

Greek [grik] *adj* grec || *s* (*language*) grec *m*; (*unintelligible language*) (*coll*) hébreu *m*, e.g., **it's Greek to me** (*coll*) c'est de l'hébreu pour moi; (*person*) Grec *m*

Greek′ fire′ *s* feu *m* grégeois

green [grin] *adj* vert; inexpérimenté, novice || *s* vert *m*; (*lawn*) gazon *m*; (*golf*) pelouse *f* d'arrivée; **greens** légumes *mpl* verts

green′back′ *s* (U.S.A.) billet *m* de banque

greener·y ['grinəri] *s* (*pl* -ies) verdure *f*

green′-eyed′ *adj* aux yeux verts; (*envious*) jaloux

green′gage′ *s* (bot) reine-claude *f*

green′gro′cer·y *s* (*pl* -ies) fruiterie *f*

green′horn′ *s* blanc-bec *m*, bleu *m*

green′house′ *s* serre *f*

greenish ['grinɪʃ] *adj* verdâtre

Greenland ['grinlənd] *s* le Groënland

green′ light′ *s* feu *m* vert, voie *f* libre

greenness ['grinnɪs] *s* verdure *f*; (*unripeness*) verdeur *f*; inexpérience *f*, naïveté *f*

green′ pep′per *s* poivron *m* vert

green′room′ *s* (theat) foyer *m*

greensward ['grin,sword] *s* pelouse *f*

green′ thumb′ *s*—**to have a green thumb** avoir la main verte

greet [grit] *tr* saluer; (*to welcome*) accueillir

greeting ['gritɪŋ] *s* salutation *f*; (*welcome*) accueil *m*; **greetings** (*on greeting card*) vœux *mpl* || **greetings** *interj* salut!

greet′ing card′ *s* carte *f* de vœux

gregarious [grɪ'gerɪ·əs] *adj* grégaire

Gregorian [grɪ'gorɪ·ən] *adj* grégorien

grenade [grɪ'ned] *s* grenade *f*

grey [gre] *adj, s,* & *intr* var of **gray**

grey′hound′ *s* var of **grayhound**

grid [grid] *s* (*of storage battery and vacuum tube*) grille *f*; (*on map*) quadrillage *m*; (culin) gril *m*

griddle ['grɪdəl] *s* plaque *f* chauffante

grid′dle·cake′ *s* crêpe *f*

grid′i′ron *s* gril *m*; (sports) terrain *m* de football

grid′ leak′ *s* résistance *f* de fuite de la grille

grid′ line′ *s* ligne *f* de quadrillage

grief [grif] *s* chagrin *m*, affliction *f*; **to come to grief** finir mal

grief′-strick′en *adj* affligé, navré

grievance ['grivəns] *s* grief *m*

grieve [griv] *tr* chagriner, affliger || *intr* se chagriner, s'affliger

grievous ['grivəs] *adj* grave, douloureux

griffin ['grɪfɪn] *s* griffon *m*

grill [grɪl] *s* gril *m*; (*grating*) grille *f* || *tr* griller; (*an accused person*) (coll) cuisiner

grille [grɪl] *s* grille *f*; (aut) calandre *f*

grilled′ beef′steak′ *s* châteaubriand *m*

grill′room′ *s* grill-room *m*

grim [grɪm] *adj* (*comp* **grimmer**; *super* **grimmest**) (*fierce*) menaçant; (*repellent*) macabre; (*unyielding*) implacable; (*stern-looking*) lugubre

grimace ['grɪməs], [grɪ'mes] *s* grimace *f* || *intr* grimacer

grime [graɪm] *s* crasse *f*, saleté *f*

grim·y ['graɪmi] *adj* (*comp* -ier; *super* -iest) crasseux, sale

grin [grɪn] *s* grimace *f*; (*smile*) large sourire *m* || *v* (*pret* & *pp* **grinned**; *ger* **grinning**) *intr* avoir un large sourire, rire à belles dents

grind [graɪnd] *s* (*of coffee*) moulure *f*; (*job*) (coll) boulot *m*, collier *m*; (*student*) (coll) bûcheur *m*; **daily grind** (coll) train-train *m* quotidien || *v* (*pret* & *pp* **ground** [graund]) *tr* (*coffee, flour*) moudre; (*food*) broyer; (*meat*) hacher; (*a knife*) aiguiser; (*the teeth*) grincer; (*valves*) roder || *intr* grincer; **to grind away at** (coll) bûcher

grinder ['graɪndər] *s* (*for coffee, pepper, etc.*) moulin *m*, broyeur *m*; (*for meat*) hachoir *m*; (*for tools*) repasseur *m*; (*back tooth*) molaire *f*

grind′stone′ *s* meule *f*, pierre *f* à aiguiser

grip [grɪp] *s* prise *f*; (*with hand*) poigne *f*; (*handle*) poignée *f*; (*handbag*) sac *m* de voyage; (*understanding*) compréhension *f*; **to come to grips** en venir aux prises; **to lose one's grip** lâcher prise || *v* (*pret* & *pp* **gripped**; *ger* **gripping**) *tr* serrer, saisir fortement; (*e.g., a theater audience*) empoigner

gripe [graɪp] *s* (coll) rouspétance *f* || *intr* (coll) rouspéter, ronchonner

grippe [grɪp] *s* grippe *f*

gripping ['grɪpɪŋ] *adj* passionnant

gris·ly ['grɪzli] *adj* (*comp* -lier; *super* -liest) horrible, macabre

grist [grɪst] *s* blé *m* à moudre

gristle ['grɪsəl] *s* cartilage *m*

gris·tly ['grɪsli] *adj* (*comp* -tlier; *super* -tliest) cartilagineux

grist′mill′ *s* moulin *m* à blé

grit [grɪt] *s* grès *m*, sable *m*; (*courage*) cran *m*; **grits** gruau *m* || *v* (*pret* & *pp* **gritted**; *ger* **gritting**) *tr* (*one's teeth*) grincer

grit·ty ['grɪti] *adj* (*comp* -tier; *super* -tiest) sablonneux; (*fig*) plein de cran

griz·zly ['grɪzli] *adj* (*comp* -zlier; *super* -zliest) grisonnant || *s* (*pl* -zlies) ours *m* gris

griz′zly bear′ *s* ours *m* gris

groan [gron] *s* gémissement *m* || *intr* gémir

grocer ['grosər] s épicier m
grocer·y ['grosəri] s (pl -ies) épicerie f; groceries denrées fpl
gro'cery store' s épicerie f
grog [grɑg] s grog m
grog·gy ['grɑgi] adj (comp -gier; super -giest) (coll) vacillant; (shaky, e.g., from a blow) (coll) étourdi; (drunk) (coll) gris, ivre
groin [grɔin] s (anat) aine f; (archit) arête f
groom [grum] s (bridegroom) marié m; (stableboy) palefrenier m || tr soigner, astiquer; (horses) panser; (a politician, a starlet, etc.) dresser, préparer
grooms'man s (pl -men) garçon m d'honneur
groove [gruv] s rainure f; (of pulley) gorge f; (of phonograph record) sillon m; (mark left by wheel) ornière f; (of window, door, etc.) feuillure f; in the groove (coll) comme sur des roulettes; to get into a groove (coll) devenir routinier || tr rainer, canneler
grope [grop] intr tâtonner; to grope for chercher à tâtons
gropingly ['gropiŋli] adv à tâtons
grosbeak ['gros,bik] s gros-bec m
gross [gros] adj gros; (fat, burly) gras, épais; (crass, vulgar) grossier; (weight; receipts) brut; (displacement) global || s invar recette f brute; (twelve dozen) grosse f || tr produire en recette brute, produire brut, e.g., the business grossed a million dollars l'entreprise a produit un million de dollars, brut
gross' na'tional prod'uct s produit m national brut
grotesque [gro'tesk] adj grotesque || s grotesque m; (ornament) grotesque f
grot·to ['grɑto] s (pl -toes or -tos) grotte f
grouch [grautʃ] s (coll) humeur f grognon; (person) (coll) grognon m || intr (coll) grogner
grouch·y ['grautʃi] adj (comp -ier; super -iest) (coll) grognon, maussade
ground [graund] s terre f; (piece of land) terrain m; (basis, foundation) fondement m, base f; (reason) motif m, cause f; (elec) terre f; (body of automobile corresponding to ground) (elec) masse f; ground for complaint grief m; grounds parc m, terrain; fondement, cause; (of coffee) marc m; on the ground of pour raison de, sous prétexte de; to be losing ground être en recul; to break ground donner le premier coup de pioche; to have grounds for avoir matière à; to stand one's ground tenir bon or ferme; to yield ground lâcher pied || tr fonder, baser; (elec) mettre à terre; grounded (aer) interdit de vol, gardé au sol; to ground s.o. in s.th. enseigner à fond q.ch. à qn
ground' connec'tion s prise f de terre
ground' crew' s équipe f au sol, personnel m rampant
ground' floor' s rez-de-chaussée m

ground' glass' s verre m dépoli
ground' hog' s marmotte f d'Amérique
grounding ['graundiŋ] s (aer) interdiction f de vol; (elec) mise f à la masse
ground' installa'tions spl (aer) infrastructure f
ground' lead' [lid] s (elec) conduite f à terre
groundless ['graundlis] adj sans fondement
ground' meat' s viande f hachée
ground' plan' s plan m de base; (archit) plan horizontal
ground' speed' s (aer) vitesse f par rapport au sol
ground' swell' s lame f de fond
ground' troops' spl (mil) effectifs mpl terrestres
ground' wire' s (elec) fil m de terre, fil de masse
ground'work' s fondement m, fond m
group [grup] s groupe m || tr grouper || intr se grouper
grouse [graus] s coq m de bruyère || intr (slang) grogner
grove [grov] s bocage m, bosquet m
grov·el ['grʌvəl], ['grɑvəl] v (pret & pp -eled or -elled; ger -eling or -elling) intr se vautrer; (before s.o.) ramper
grow [gro] v (pret grew [gru]; pp grown [gron]) tr cultiver, faire pousser; (a beard) laisser pousser || intr croître; (said of plants) pousser; (said of seeds) germer; (to become) devenir; to grow angry se mettre en colère; to grow old vieillir; to grow out of se développer de; (e.g., a suit of clothes) devenir trop grand pour; to grow up grandir, profiter
growl [graul] s grondement m, grognement m || tr & intr gronder, grogner
grown'-up' adj adulte || s (pl grown-ups) adulte mf; grown-ups grandes personnes fpl
growth [groθ] s croissance f, développement m; (increase) accroissement m; (of trees, grass, etc.) pousse f; (pathol) excroissance f, grosseur f
grub [grʌb] s asticot m; (person) homme m de peine; (food) (coll) boustifaille f || v (pret & pp grubbed; ger grubbing) tr défricher || intr fouiller
grub·by ['grʌbi] adj (comp -bier; super -biest) sale, malpropre
grudge [grʌdʒ] s rancune f; to have a grudge against garder rancune à || tr donner à contre-cœur
grudgingly ['grʌdʒiŋli] adv à contre-cœur
gruel ['gru·əl] s gruau m, bouillie f
grueling ['gru·əliŋ] adj éreintant
gruesome ['grusəm] adj macabre
gruff [grʌf] adj bourru, brusque; (voice) rauque, gros
grumble ['grʌmbəl] s grognement m || intr grogner, grommeler
grump·y ['grʌmpi] adj (comp -ier; super -iest) maussade, grognon
grunt [grʌnt] s grognement m || intr grogner

G'-string' s (*loincloth*) pagne m; (*worn by women entertainers*) cache-sexe m; (*mus*) corde f de sol

guarantee [ˌgærənˈti] s garantie f; (*guarantor*) garant m, répondant m; (*security*) caution f ‖ tr garantir

guarantor [ˈgærənˌtɔr] s garant m

guaran·ty [ˈgærəntɪ] s (*pl* -ties) garantie f ‖ v (*pret & pp* -tied) tr garantir

guard [gɑrd] s garde f; (*person*) garde m; **on guard** en garde; (*on duty*) de garde; (*mil*) en faction, de faction; **on one's guard** sur ses gardes; **to mount guard** monter la garde; **under guard** gardé à vue ‖ tr garder ‖ intr être de faction; **to guard against** se garder de

guard'du'ty s service m de garde

guarded adj (*remark*) prudent

guard'house' s guérite f, corps-de-garde m; prison f militaire

guardian [ˈgɑrdɪ·ən] adj gardien ‖ s gardien m; (*of a ward*) tuteur m

guard'ian an'gel s ange m gardien, ange tutélaire

guard'ian·ship' s garde f; (*law*) tutelle f

guard'rail' s garde-fou m, parapet m

guard'room' s corps-de-garde m, salle f de police; (*prison*) bloc m, tôle f

guards'man s (*pl* -men) garde m

Guatemalan [ˌgwɑtɪˈmɑlən] adj guatémaltèque ‖ s Guatémaltèque mf

guava [ˈgwɑvə] s goyave f; (*tree*) goyavier m

guerrilla [gəˈrɪlə] s guérillero m; **guerrillas** (*band*) guérilla f

guerril'la war'fare s guérilla f

guess [gɛs] s conjecture f ‖ tr & intr conjecturer; (*a secret, riddle, etc.*) deviner; (*coll*) supposer, penser; **I guess so** je crois que oui; **to guess right** bien deviner

guess'work' s supposition f; **by guesswork** au jugé

guest [gɛst] s invité m, hôte mf; (*in a hotel*) client m, hôte

guest' room' s chambre f d'ami

guest' speak'er s orateur m de circonstance

guffaw [gəˈfɔ] s gros rire m ‖ tr dire avec un gros rire ‖ intr rire bruyamment

Guiana [gɪˈɑnə], [gɪˈænə] s Guyane f; **la Guyane**

guidance [ˈgaɪdəns] s gouverne f; (*guiding*) conduite f; (*in choosing a career*) orientation f; (*of rocket*) guidage m; **for your guidance** pour votre gouverne

guid'ance coun'selor s orienteur m

guide [gaɪd] s guide m ‖ tr guider

guide'book' s guide m

guid'ed mis'sile s engin m téléguidé

guide' dog' s chien m d'aveugle

guide' line' s (fig) norme f, règle f; **guide lines** (*for writing straight lines*) transparent m, guide-âne m

guide'post' s poteau m indicateur

guide' word' s lettrine f

guild [gɪld] s association f, corporation f; (eccl) confrérie f; (hist) guilde f

guild'hall' s hôtel m de ville

guile [gaɪl] s astuce f, artifice m

guileful [ˈgaɪlfəl] adj astucieux, artificieux

guileless [ˈgaɪllɪs] adj candide, innocent

guillotine [ˈgɪlə·ˌtin] s guillotine f ‖ tr guillotiner

guilt [gɪlt] s culpabilité f

guiltless [ˈgɪltlɪs] adj innocent

guilt·y [ˈgɪltɪ] adj (comp -ier; super -iest) coupable; **found guilty** reconnu coupable

guimpe [gɪmp], [gæmp] s empiècement m

guinea [ˈgɪnɪ] s guinée f; **Guinea** Guinée; **la Guinée**

guin'ea fowl' or **hen'** s poule f de Guinée, pintade f

guin'ea pig' s cobaye m

guise [gaɪz] s apparences fpl, déguisement m; **under the guise of** sous un semblant de, sous le masque du

guitar [gɪˈtɑr] s guitare f

guitarist [gɪˈtɑrɪst] s guitariste mf

gulch [gʌltʃ] s ravin m

gulf [gʌlf] s golfe m; (fig) gouffre m

Gulf' of Mex'ico s Golfe m du Mexique

Gulf' Stream' s Courant m du Golfe

gull [gʌl] s mouette f, goéland m; (coll) gogo m, jobard m ‖ tr escroquer, duper

gullet [ˈgʌlɪt] s gosier m

gullible [ˈgʌlɪbəl] adj crédule, naïf

gul·ly [ˈgʌlɪ] s (pl -lies) ravin m; (channel) rigole f

gulp [gʌlp] s gorgée f, lampée f; **at one gulp** d'un trait ‖ tr—**to gulp down** avaler à grandes bouchées, lamper; (e.g., tears) ravaler, refouler ‖ intr avoir la gorge serrée

gum [gʌm] s gomme f; (on eyelids) chassie f; (anat) gencive f ‖ v (pret & pp gummed; ger gumming) tr gommer; **to gum up** encrasser; (coll) bousiller

gum' ar'abic s gomme f arabique

gum'boil' s phlegmon m, fluxion f

gum' boot' s botte f de caoutchouc

gum'drop' s boule f de gomme, pâte f de fruits

gum·my [ˈgʌmɪ] adj (comp -mier; super -miest) gommeux; (eyelids) chassieux

gumption [ˈgʌmpʃən] s (coll) initiative f, cran m

gum'shoe' s caoutchouc m; (coll) détective m ‖ intr rôder en tapinois, marcher furtivement

gun [gʌn] s fusil m; (for spraying) pistolet m; **to stick to one's guns** (coll) ne pas en démordre ‖ v (pret & pp gunned; ger gunning) tr—**to gun down** tuer d'un coup de fusil; **to gun the engine** (slang) appuyer sur le champignon ‖ intr—**to gun for** (game) chasser; (an enemy) pourchasser

gun' bar'rel s canon m

gun'boat' s canonnière f

gun' car'riage s affût m de canon

gun'cot'ton s fulmicoton m

gun′ crew′ *s* peloton *m* de pièce, servants *mpl* de canon

gun′fire′ *s* canonnade *f*, coups *mpl* de feu

gun′man *s* (*pl* -men) *s* bandit *m*

gun′ met′al *s* métal *m* bleui

gunner ['gʌnər] *s* canonnier *m*, artilleur *m*; (aer) mitrailleur *m*

gunnery ['gʌnəri] *s* tir *m*, canonnage *m*

gunnysack ['gʌni‚sæk] *s* sac *m* de serpillière

gun′pow′der *s* poudre *f* à canon

gun′run′ning *s* contrebande *f* d'armes

gun′shot′ *s* coup *m* de feu, coup *m* de fusil

gun′smith′ *s* armurier *m*

gun′stock′ *s* fût *m*

gunwale ['gʌnəl] *s* (naut) plat-bord *m*

gup·py ['gʌpi] *s* (*pl* -pies) guppy *m*

gurgle ['gʌrgəl] *s* glouglou *m*, gargouillement *m* ‖ *intr* glouglouter, gargouiller

gush [gʌʃ] *s* jaillissement *m* ‖ *intr* jaillir; **to gush over** (coll) s'attendrir sur

gusher ['gʌʃər] *s* puits *m* jaillissant

gush·y ['gʌʃi] *adj* (*comp* -ier; *super* -iest) (coll) démonstratif, expansif

gusset ['gʌsɪt] *s* (in garment) soufflet *m*; (mach) gousset *m*

gust [gʌst] *s* bouffée *f*, coup *m*

gusto ['gʌsto] *s* goût *m*, entrain *m*

gust·y ['gʌsti] *adj* (*comp* -ier; *super* -iest) venteux; (wind) à rafales

gut [gʌt] *s* boyau *m*; **guts** (coll) cran *m* ‖ *v* (*pret* & *pp* gutted; *ger* gutting) *tr* raser à l'intérieur; (to take out the guts of) vider

gutter ['gʌtər] *s* (on side of road) caniveau *m*; (in street) ruisseau *m*; (of roof) gouttière *f*; (ditch formed by rain water) rigole *f*

gut′ter·snipe′ *s* (coll) voyou *m*

guttural ['gʌtərəl] *adj* guttural ‖ *s* gutturale *f*

guy [gaɪ] *s* câble *m* tenseur; (naut) hauban *m*; (coll) type *m*, gars *m* ‖ *tr* haubaner; (coll) se moquer de

guy′ wire′ *s* câble *m* tenseur; (naut) hauban *m*

guzzle ['gʌzəl] *tr* & *intr* boire avidement

guzzler ['gʌzlər] *s* soiffard *m*

gym [dʒɪm] *s* (coll) gymnase *m*

gymnasi·um [dʒɪm'nezɪ·əm] *s* (*pl* -ums or -a [ə]) gymnase *m*

gymnast ['dʒɪmnæst] *s* gymnaste *mf*

gynecology [‚gaɪnə'kɑlədʒi], [‚dʒaɪnə'kɑlədʒi] *s* gynécologie *f*

gyp [dʒɪp] *s* (slang) escroquerie *f*; (person) (slang) aigrefin *m* ‖ *v* (*pret* & *pp* gypped; *ger* gypping) *tr* (slang) tirer une carotte à, refaire, gruger

gypsum ['dʒɪpsəm] *s* gypse *m*

gyp·sy ['dʒɪpsi] *adj* bohémien ‖ *s* (*pl* -sies) bohémien *m*; **Gypsy** (language) tsigane, romanichel *m*; (person) gitan *m*, tsigane *mf*, romanichel *m*

gyp′sy moth′ *s* zigzag *m*

gyrate ['dʒaɪret] *intr* tournoyer

gyrocompass ['dʒaɪro‚kʌmpəs] *s* gyrocompas *m*

gyroscope ['dʒaɪrə‚skop] *s* gyroscope *m*

H

H, h [etʃ] *s* VIIIᵉ lettre de l'alphabet

haberdasher ['hæbər‚dæʃər] *s* chemisier *m*

haberdasher·y ['hæbər‚dæʃəri] *s* (*pl* -ies) chemiserie *f*, confection *f* pour hommes

habit ['hæbɪt] *s* habitude *f*; (dress) habit *m*, costume *m*; **to get into the habit of** s'habituer à

habitual [hə'bɪtʃu·əl] *adj* habituel

habituate [hə'bɪtʃu‚et] *tr* habituer

hack [hæk] *s* (notch) entaille *f*; (cough) toux *f* sèche; (hackney) voiture *f* de louage; (old nag) rosse *f*; (writer) écrivassier *m* ‖ *tr* hacher

hackney ['hækni] *s* voiture *f* de louage

hackneyed ['hæknid] *adj* banal, battu

hack′saw′ *s* scie *f* à métaux

haddock ['hædək] *s* églefin *m*

hag [hæg] *s* (ugly woman) guenon *f*; (witch) sorcière *f*; **old hag** vieille fée *f*

haggard ['hægərd] *adj* décharné, hâve; (wild-looking) hagard, farouche

haggle ['hægəl] *intr* marchander; **to haggle over** marchander

Hague [heg] *s*—**The Hague** La Haye

hail [hel] *s* (frozen rain) grêle *f*; **within hail** à portée de la voix ‖ *tr* saluer; (a ship, taxi, etc.) héler ‖ *intr* grêler; **to hail from** venir de ‖ *interj* salut!

Hail′ Mar′y *s* Ave Maria *m*

hail′stone′ *s* grêlon *m*

hail′storm′ *s* tempête *f* de grêle

hair [her] *s* poil *m*; (of person) cheveu *m*; (head of human hair) cheveux *mpl*; **against the hair** à rebrousse-poil, à contre-poil; **hairs** cheveux; **to a hair** à un cheveu près; **to get in s.o.'s hair** (slang) porter sur les nerfs à qn; **to let one's hair down** (slang) en prendre à son aise; **to make s.o.'s hair stand on end** faire dresser les cheveux à qn; **to not turn a hair** ne pas tiquer; **to split hairs** fendre or couper les cheveux en quatre

hair′breadth′ *s* épaisseur *f* d'un cheveu; **to escape by a hairbreadth** l'échapper belle

hair′brush′ *s* brosse *f* à cheveux

hair′cloth′ *s* thibaude *f*; (for furniture) tissu-crin *m*

hair' curl'er [ˌkʌrlər] s frisoir m; (pin) bigoudi m

hair'cut' s coupe f de cheveux; **to get a haircut** se faire couper les cheveux

hair'do' s (pl -dos) coiffure f

hair'dress'er s coiffeur m pour dames; coiffeuse f

hair'dress'ing s cosmétique m

hair' dri'er s sèche-cheveux m, séchoir m à cheveux

hair' dye' s teinture f des cheveux

hair'line' s (on face of type) délié m; (along the upper forehead) naissance f des cheveux, plantation f des cheveux

hair' net' s résille f

hair'pin' s épingle f à cheveux

hair'pin turn' s lacet m

hair'-rais'ing adj (coll) horripilant

hair' rib'bon s ruban m à cheveux

hair' set' s mise f en plis

hair' shirt' s haire f, cilice m

hair'split'ting adj vétilleux, trop subtil ‖ s ergotage m

hair' spray' s (for setting hair) laque f, fixatif m

hair'spring' s spiral m

hair' style' s coiffure f

hair' ton'ic s lotion f capillaire

hair' trig'ger s détente f douce

hair·y ['heri] adj (comp -ier; super -lest) poilu, velu; (on head) chevelu

Haiti ['heti] s Haïti f

Haitian ['hetɪ·ən], ['heʃən] adj haïtien ‖ s Haïtien m

halberd ['hælbərd] s hallebarde f

hal'cyon days' ['hælsɪ·ən] spl jours mpl alcyoniens, jours sereins

hale [hel] adj vigoureux, sain; **hale and hearty** frais et gaillard ‖ tr haler

half [hæf], [hɑf] adj demi ‖ s (pl halves [hævz], [hɑvz]) moitié f, la moitié; (of the hour) demi f; **by half** de moitié, à demi; **half an hour** une demi-heure; **in half** en deux; **to go halves** être de moitié ‖ adv moitié, à moitié; **half . . . half** moitié . . . moitié; **half past** et demie, e.g., **half past three** trois heures et demie

half'-and-half' adj & adv moitié l'un moitié l'autre, en parties égales ‖ s (for coffee) mélange m de lait et de crème; (beer) mélange de bière et eau

half'back' s (football) demi-arrière m, demi m

half'-baked' adj à moitié cuit; (person) inexpérimenté; (plan) prématuré, incomplet

half' bind'ing s (bb) demi-reliure f à petit coins

half'-blood' s métis m; demi-frère m

half' boot' s demi-botte f

half'-bound' adj (bb) en demi-reliure à coins

half'-breed' s métis m, sang-mêlé m; (e.g., horse) demi-sang m

half' broth'er s demi-frère m

half'-cocked' adv (coll) avec trop de hâte

half'-day' s demi-journée f

half'-doz'en s demi-douzaine f

half' fare' s demi-tarif m, demi-place f

half'-full' adj à moitié plein

half'-heart'ed adj sans entrain, hésitant

half'-hol'iday s demi-congé m

half' hose' s chaussettes fpl

half'-hour' s demi-heure f; **every half-hour on the half-hour** toutes les demi-heures à la demi-heure juste; **on the half-hour** à la demie

half' leath'er s (bb) demi-reliure f à petit coins

half'-length' s demi-longueur f

half'-length por'trait s portrait m en buste

half'-light' s demi-jour m

half'-mast' s—**at half-mast** en berne, à mi-mât

half'-moon' s demi-lune f

half' mourn'ing s demi-deuil m

half' note' s (mus) blanche f

half' pay' s demi-solde f

halfpen·ny ['hepənɪ], ['hepnɪ] s (pl -nies) demi-penny m; (fig) sou m

half' pint' s demi-pinte f; (little runt) (slang) petit culot m

half'-seas o'ver adj—**to be half-seas over** avoir du vent dans les voiles

half' shell' s (either half of a bivalve) écaille f; **on the half shell** dans sa coquille

half' sis'ter s demi-sœur f

half' sole' s demi-semelle f

half'-staff' s—**at half-staff** à mi-mât

half'-tim'bered adj à demi-boisage

half' time' s (sports) mi-temps m

half'-time' adj à demi-journée

half' ti'tle s faux titre m, avant-titre m

half'tone' s (painting, phot) demi-teinte f; (typ) similigravure f

half' tone' s (mus) demi-ton m

half'-track' s semi-chenillé m

half'-truth' s demi-vérité f

half'turn' s demi-tour m; (of wheel) demi-révolution f

half'way' adj & adv à mi-chemin; **halfway through** à moitié de; **halfway up** à mi-côte; **to meet s.o. halfway** couper la poire en deux avec qn

half'-wit'ted adj à moitié idiot

halibut ['hælɪbət] s flétan m

halitosis [ˌhælɪˈtosɪs] s mauvaise haleine f

hall [hɔl] s (passageway) corridor m, couloir m; (entranceway) entrée f, vestibule m; (large meeting room) salle f, hall m; (assembly room of a university) amphithéâtre m; (building of a university) bâtiment m

halleluiah or **hallelujah** [ˌhælɪˈlujə] s alléluia m ‖ interj alléluia!

hall'mark' s estampille f, poinçon m; (fig) cachet m, marque f

hal·lo [həˈlo] s (pl -los) holà m ‖ intr huer ‖ interj holà!, ohé!; (hunting) taïaut!

hallow ['hælo] tr sanctifier

hallowed adj sanctifié, saint

Halloween or **Hallowe'en** [ˌhæloˈin] s la veille de la Toussaint

hallucination [həˌlusɪˈneʃən] s hallucination f

hall'way' s corridor m; couloir m

ha·lo ['helo] s (pl -los or -loes) (meteo) auréole f, halo m; (around a head) auréole f

halogen ['hælədʒən] s halogène m

halt [hɔlt] adj boiteux, estropié ‖ s halte f, arrêt m; **to come to a halt** faire halte ‖ tr faire faire halte à ‖ intr faire halte ‖ interj halte!; (mil) halte-là!

halter ['hɔltər] s licou m; (noose) corde f

halting ['hɔltɪŋ] adj boiteux; hésitant

halve [hæv], [hɑv] tr diviser or partager en deux; réduire de moitié

halyard ['hæljərd] s (naut) drisse f

ham [hæm] s (part of leg behind knee) jarret m; (thigh and buttock) fesse f; (culin) cuisse f; (cured) (culin) jambon m; (rad) radio amateur m; (theat) cabotin m; **hams** fesses

hamburger ['hæm,bʌrgər] s sandwich m à la hambourgeoise, hamburger m; (Hamburg steak) biftek m haché

hamlet ['hæmlɪt] s hameau m

hammer ['hæmər] s marteau m; (of gun) chien m, percuteur m ‖ tr marteler; **to hammer out** étendre au marteau; (to resolve) résoudre ‖ intr—**to hammer away at** (e.g., a job) travailler d'arrache-pied à

hammock ['hæmək] s hamac m

hamper ['hæmpər] s manne f ‖ tr embarrasser, gêner, empêcher

hamster ['hæmstər] s hamster m

ham'string' v (pret & pp -strung) tr couper le jarret à; (fig) couper les moyens à

hand [hænd] adj à main, à la main, manuel ‖ s main f; (workman) manœuvre m, ouvrier m; (way of writing) écriture f; (clapping of hands) applaudissements mpl; (of clock or watch) aiguille f; (a round of play) coup m, partie f, main; (of God) doigt m; (measure) palme m; (cards) jeu m; **at hand** sous la main; (said of approaching event) proche, prochain; **by hand** à la main; **hands off!** n'y touchez pas!; **hands up!** haut les mains!; **hand to hand** corps à corps; **on every hand** de toutes parts, de tous côtés; **on the one hand . . . on the other hand** d'une part . . . d'autre part; **to live from hand to mouth** vivre au jour le jour; **to shake hands with** serrer la main à; **to wait on hand and foot** être aux petits soins pour; **to win hands down** gagner dans un fauteuil; **under the hand and seal of** signé et scellé de ‖ tr donner, présenter; (e.g., food at table) passer; **hand down** (e.g., property) léguer; (a verdict) prononcer; **to hand in** remettre; **to hand on** transmettre; **to hand out** distribuer; **to hand over** céder, livrer

hand'bag' s sac m à main

hand' bag'gage s menus bagages mpl

hand'ball' s pelote f; (game) handball m

hand'bill' s prospectus m

hand'book' s manuel m

hand' brake' s frein m à main

hand'car' s (rr) draisine f

hand'cart' s voiture f à bras

hand'clasp' s poignée f de main

hand' control' s commande f à la main

hand'cuff' s menotte f ‖ tr mettre les menottes à

handful ['hænd,ful] s poignée f

hand' glass' s miroir m à main; (magnifying glass) loupe f à main

hand' grenade' s grenade f à main

handi·cap ['hændɪ,kæp] s handicap m ‖ v (pret & pp -capped; ger -capping) tr handicaper

handicraft ['hændɪ,kræft], ['hændɪ,krɑft] s habileté f manuelle; métier m; **handicrafts** produits mpl d'artisanat

handiwork ['hændɪ,wʌrk] s ouvrage m, travail m manuel; (fig) œuvre f

handkerchief ['hæŋkərtʃɪf], ['hæŋkərtʃif] s mouchoir m

handle ['hændəl] s (of basket, crock, pitcher) anse f; (of shovel, broom, knife) manche m; (of umbrella, sword, door) poignée f; (of frying pan) queue f; (of pump) brimbale f; (of handcart) brancard m; (of wheelbarrow) bras m; (opportunity, pretext) prétexte m; (mach) manivelle f, manette f; **to fly off the handle** (coll) sortir de ses gonds ‖ tr manier; (with one's hands) palper, tâter; **handle with care** (shipping label) fragile; **to handle roughly** malmener ‖ intr—**to handle well** (mach) avoir de bonnes réactions

han'dle·bars' spl guidon m

handler ['hændlər] s (sports) entraîneur m

handling ['hændlɪŋ] s (e.g., of tool) maniement m; (e.g., of person) traitement m; (of merchandise) manutention f

hand'made' adj fait à la main

hand'maid' or **hand'maid'en** s servante f; (fig) auxiliaire mf

hand'-me-down' s (coll) vêtement m de seconde main

hand' or'gan s orgue m de Barbarie

hand'out' s (notes) (coll) documentation f; (slang) aumône f

hand'-picked' adj trié sur le volet

hand'rail' s main f courante, rampe f

hand'saw' s égoïne f, scie f à main

hand'set' s combiné m

hand'shake' s poignée f de main

handsome ['hænsəm] adj beau; (e.g., fortune) considérable

hand'spring' s—**to do a handspring** prendre appui sur les mains pour faire la culbute

hand'-to-hand' adj corps-à-corps

hand'-to-mouth' adj—**to lead a hand-to-mouth existence** vivre au jour le jour

hand' truck' s bard m, diable m

hand'work' s travail m à la main

hand'writ'ing s écriture f

handwritten ['hænd,rɪtən] adj manuscrit, autographe

hand·y ['hændɪ] adj (comp **-ier**; super **-iest**) (easy to handle) maniable; (within easy reach) accessible, sous la main; (skillful) adroit, habile; **to come in handy** être très à propos

hand/y-man/ s (pl **-men/**) homme m à tout faire, bricoleur m

hang [hæŋ] s (of dress, curtain, etc.) retombée f, drapé m; (skill; insight) adresse f, sens m; **I don't give a hang!** (coll) je m'en moque pas mal!; **to get the hang** (coll) saisir le truc, attraper le clic || v (pret & pp hung [hʌŋ]) tr pendre; (laundry) étendre; (wallpaper) coller; (one's head) baisser; **hang it all!** zut alors!; **to hang up** suspendre, accrocher; (telp) raccrocher || intr pendre, être accroché; **to hang around** flâner, rôder; **to hang on** se cramponner à, s'accrocher à; (to depend on) dépendre de; (to stay put) tenir bon; **to hang out** pendre dehors; (slang) percher, loger; **to hang over** (to threaten) peser sur, menacer; **to hang together** rester unis; **to hang up** (telp) raccrocher || v (pret & pp hung or hanged) (to execute by hanging) pendre || intr se pendre

hangar ['hæŋər], ['hæŋgɑr] s hangar m

hang/dog/ adj (look) patibulaire

hanger ['hæŋər] s crochet m; (coathanger) cintre m, portemanteau m

hang/er-on/ s (pl **hangers-on**) parasite m, pique-assiette m

hanging ['hæŋɪŋ] adj pendant, suspendu || s pendaison f; **hangings** tentures fpl

hang/man s (pl **-men**) bourreau m

hang/nail/ s envie f

hang/out/ s (coll) repaire m

hang/o/ver s (coll) gueule f de bois

hank [hæŋk] s écheveau m

hanker ['hæŋkər] intr—**to hanker after** or **for** désirer vivement, être affamé de

Hannibal ['hænɪbəl] s Annibal m

haphazard [,hæp'hæzərd] adj fortuit, imprévu; au petit bonheur || adv à l'aventure, au hasard

hapless ['hæplɪs] adj malheureux, malchanceux

happen ['hæpən] intr arriver, se passer; (to be the case by chance) survenir; **happen what may** advienne que pourra; **how does it happen that . . . ?** comment se fait-il que . . . ?, d'où vient-il que . . . ?; **to happen on** tomber sur; **to happen to** + inf se trouver + inf, venir à + inf

happening ['hæpənɪŋ] s événement m

happily ['hæpɪlɪ] adv heureusement

happiness ['hæpɪnɪs] s bonheur m

hap·py ['hæpɪ] adj (comp **-pier**; super **-piest**) heureux; (pleased) content; (hour) propice; **to be happy to** être heureux or content de

hap/py-go-luck/y adj sans souci, insouciant || adv (archaic) à l'aventure

hap/py me/dium s juste-milieu m

Hap/py New/ Year/ interj bonne année!

harangue [hə'ræŋ] s harangue f || tr & intr haranguer

harass ['hærəs], [hə'ræs] tr harceler; tourmenter

harbinger ['hɑrbɪndʒər] s avant-coureur m, précurseur m

harbor ['hɑrbər] s port m; || tr héberger, donner asile à; (a criminal, stolen goods, etc.) receler; (suspicions; a hope) entretenir, nourrir; (a grudge) garder

har/bor mas/ter s capitaine m de port

hard [hɑrd] adj dur; (difficult) difficile; (water) cru, calcaire; (work) assidu, dur; **to be hard on** (to treat severely) être dur or sévère envers; (to wear out fast) user || adv dur, fort; (firmly) ferme; **hard upon** de près, tout contre; **to rain hard** pleuvoir fort; **to try hard** bien essayer

hard/-and-fast/ adj strict, inflexible, établi

hard-bitten ['hɑrd'bɪtən] adj tenace, dur à cuire

hard/-boiled/ adj (egg) dur; (coll) dur, inflexible

hard/ can/dy s bonbons mpl; **piece of hard candy** bonbon m

hard/ cash/ s espèces fpl sonnantes

hard/ ci/der s cidre m

hard/ coal/ s houille f éclatante, anthracite m

hard/ drink/ s boissons fpl alcooliques, liqueurs fpl fortes

hard/ drink/er s grand buveur m

hard/-earned/ adj péniblement gagné

harden ['hɑrdən] tr durcir, endurcir || intr se durcir, s'endurcir

hardening ['hɑrdənɪŋ] s durcissement m; (fig) endurcissement m

hard/ fact/ s fait m brutal; **hard facts** réalités fpl

hard-fought ['hɑrd'fɔt] adj acharné, chaudement disputé

hard/-head/ed adj positif, à la tête froide

hard/-heart/ed adj dur, sans compassion

hardihood ['hɑrdɪ,hʊd] s endurance f; courage m; audace f

hardiness ['hɑrdɪnɪs] s vigueur f

hard/ la/bor s travaux mpl forcés

hard/ luck/ s guigne f, malchance f

hardly ['hɑrdlɪ] adv guère; à peine, ne . . . guère, e.g., **he hardly thinks of anything else** à peine pense-t-il à autre chose, il ne pense guère à autre chose; **hardly ever** presque jamais

hardness ['hɑrdnɪs] s dureté f

hard/ of hear/ing adj dur d'oreille

hard/-pressed/ adj aux abois, gêné

hard/ rub/ber s caoutchouc m durci, ébonite f

hard/-shell/ adj (clam) à carapace dure; (coll) opiniâtre

hard/ship/ s peine f; **hardships** privations fpl; fatigues fpl

hard/tack/ s biscuit m, biscotin m

hard/ times/ spl difficultés fpl, temps mpl difficiles

hard/ to please/ adj difficile à contenter, exigeant

hard′ up′ *adj* (coll) à court d'argent; **to be hard up for** (coll) être à court de

hard′ware′ *s* quincaillerie *f*; (*trimmings*) ferrure *f*

hard′ware′man *s* (*pl* **-men**) quincaillier *m*

hard′ware store′ *s* quincaillerie *f*

hard-won [ˈhɑrdˌwʌn] *adj* chèrement disputé, conquis de haute lutte

hard′wood′ *s* bois *m* dur; arbre *m* de bois dur

hard′wood floor′ *s* parquet *m*

har·dy [ˈhɑrdi] *adj* (*comp* **-dier**; *super* **-diest**) vigoureux, robuste; (*rash*) hardi; (*hort*) résistant

hare [hɛr] *s* lièvre *m*

hare′brained′ *adj* écervelé, farfelu

hare′lip′ *s* bec-de-lièvre *m*

harem [ˈhɛrəm] *s* harem *m*

hark [hɑrk] *intr* écouter; **to hark back to** en revenir à || *interj* écoutez!

harken [ˈhɑrkən] *intr*—**to harken to** écouter

harlequin [ˈhɑrləkwɪn] *s* arlequin *m*

harlot [ˈhɑrlət] *s* prostituée *f*, fille *f* publique

harm [hɑrm] *s* mal *m*, dommage *m* || *tr* nuire (with *dat*), faire du mal (with *dat*)

harmful [ˈhɑrmfəl] *adj* nuisible

harmless [ˈhɑrmlɪs] *adj* inoffensif

harmonic [hɑrˈmɑnɪk] *adj* harmonique

harmonica [hɑrˈmɑnɪkə] *s* harmonica *m*

harmonious [hɑrˈmoni·əs] *adj* harmonieux

harmonize [ˈhɑrməˌnaɪz] *tr* harmoniser || *intr* s'harmoniser

harmo·ny [ˈhɑrməni] *s* (*pl* **-nies**) harmonie *f*

harness [ˈhɑrnɪs] *s* harnais *m*, harnachement *m*; **to die in the harness** (coll) mourir sous le harnais, mourir debout; **to get back in the harness** (coll) reprendre le collier || *tr* harnacher; (*e.g., a river*) aménager, capter

har′ness ma′ker *s* bourrelier *m*, harnacheur *m*

har′ness race′ *s* course *f* attelée

harp [hɑrp] *s* harpe *f* || *intr*—**to harp on** rabâcher

harpist [ˈhɑrpɪst] *s* harpiste *mf*

harpoon [hɑrˈpun] *s* harpon *m* || *tr* harponner

harpsichord [ˈhɑrpsɪˌkɔrd] *s* clavecin *m*

har·py [ˈhɑrpi] *s* (*pl* **-pies**) harpie *f*

harrow [ˈhæro] *s* (agr) herse *f* || *tr* tourmenter; (agr) herser

harrowing [ˈhæro·ɪŋ] *adj* horripilant

har·ry [ˈhæri] *v* (*pret & pp* **-ried**) *tr* harceler; (*to devastate*) ravager

harsh [hɑrʃ] *adj* (life, treatment, etc.) sévère, dur; (*to the touch*) rude; (*to the taste*) âpre; (*to the ear*) discordant

harshness [ˈhɑrʃnɪs] *s* dureté *f*, rudesse *f*; âpreté *f*

hart [hɑrt] *s* cerf *m*

harum-scarum [ˈhɛrəmˈskɛrəm] *adj & s* écervelé || *adv* en casse-cou

harvest [ˈhɑrvɪst] *s* récolte *f*; (*of grain*) moisson *f* || *tr* récolter, moissonner || *intr* faire la récolte ou moisson

harvester [ˈhɑrvɪstər] *s* moissonneur *m*; (mach) moissonneuse *f*

har′vest home′ *s* fin *f* de la moisson; fête *f* de la moisson

har′vest moon′ *s* lune *f* des moissons

has-been [ˈhæzˌbɪn] *s* (coll) vieille croûte *f*

hash [hæʃ] *s* hachis *m* || *tr* hacher

hash′ house′ *s* (slang) gargote *f*

hashish [ˈhæʃiʃ] *s* hachisch *m*

hasp [hæsp], [hɑsp] *s* moraillon *m*

hassle [ˈhæsəl] *s* (coll) querelle *f*, accrochage *m*

hassock [ˈhæsək] *s* pouf *m*

haste [hest] *s* hâte *f*; in haste à la hâte; **to make haste** se hâter

hasten [ˈhesən] *tr* hâter || *intr* se hâter

hast·y [ˈhesti] *adj* (*comp* **-ier**; *super* **-iest**) hâtif, précipité; (*rash*) inconsidéré, emporté

hat [hæt] *s* chapeau *m*; **hat in hand** chapeau bas; **hats off to . . . !** chapeau bas devant . . . !; **to keep under one's hat** (coll) garder strictement pour soi; **to talk through one's hat** (coll) parler à tort et à travers; **to throw one's hat in the ring** (coll) descendre dans l'arène

hat′band′ *s* ruban *m* de chapeau

hat′ block′ *s* forme *f* à chapeaux

hat′box′ *s* carton *m* à chapeaux

hatch [hætʃ] *s* (*brood*) éclosion *f*; (*trap door*) trappe *f*; (*lower half of door*) demi-porte *f*; (*opening in ship's deck*) écoutille *f*; (*hood over hatchway*) capot *m*; (*lid for opening in ship's deck*) panneau *m* de descente || *tr* (*eggs*) couver, faire éclore; (*a plot*) ourdir, manigancer; (*to hachure*) hachurer || *intr* éclore; (*said of chicks*) sortir de la coquille

hat′check girl′ *s* préposée *f* au vestiaire

hatchet [ˈhætʃɪt] *s* hachette *f*; **to bury the hatchet** faire la paix

hatch′way′ *s* écoutille *f*

hate [het] *s* haine *f* || *tr* haïr, détester; **to hate to** haïr de

hateful [ˈhetfəl] *adj* haïssable

hat′pin′ *s* épingle *f* à chapeau

hat′rack′ *s* porte-chapeaux *m*

hatred [ˈhetrɪd] *s* haine *f*

hat′ shop′ *s* chapellerie *f*

hatter [ˈhætər] *s* chapelier *m*

haughtiness [ˈhɔtinɪs] *s* hauteur *f*

haugh·ty [ˈhɔti] *adj* (*comp* **-tier**; *super* **-tiest**) hautain, altier

haul [hɔl] *s* (*pull, tug*) effort *m*; (*amount caught*) coup *m* de filet, prise *f*; (*distance covered*) parcours *m*, distance *f* de transport || *tr* (*to tug*) tirer; (com) transporter

haulage [ˈhɔlɪdʒ] *s* transport *m*; (*cost*) frais *m* de transport

haunch [hɔntʃ], [hɑntʃ] *s* (*hip*) hanche *f*; (*hind quarter of an animal*) quartier *m*; (*leg of animal used for food*) cuissot *m*

haunt [hɔnt], [hɑnt] *s* lieu *m* fréquenté, rendez-vous *m*; (*e.g., of criminals*) repaire *m* || *tr* (*to obsess*) hanter; (*to frequent*) fréquenter

haunt′ed house′ *s* maison *f* hantée par les fantômes

Havana [hə'vænə] *s* La Havane

have [hæv] *s*—the haves and the have-nots les riches et les pauvres || *v* (3d *pers* has [hæz]; *pret & pp* had [hæd]) *tr* avoir; to have + *inf* faire + *inf*, e.g., I shall have him go je le ferai aller; to have + *pp* faire + *inf*, e.g., I am going to have a suit made je vais faire faire un complet; to have nothing to do with n'avoir rien à voir avec; to have on (*clothing*) porter; to have s.th. to + *inf* avoir q.ch. à + *inf*, e.g., I have a lot of work to do j'ai beaucoup de travail à faire || *intr*—to have to avoir à; devoir; falloir, e.g., I have to go il me faut aller; falloir que, e.g., I have to read him the letter il faut que je lui lise la lettre || *aux* (to form compound past tenses) avoir, e.g., I have run too fast j'ai couru trop vite; (to form compound past tenses with some intransitive verbs and all reflexive verbs) être, e.g., they have arrived elles sont arrivées; to have just + *pp* venir de + *inf*, e.g., they have just returned ils viennent de rentrer; e.g., they had just returned ils venaient de rentrer

have′lock′ *s* couvre-nuque *m*

haven [′hevən] *s* havre *m*, asile *m*

haversack [′hævər‚sæk] *s* havresac *m*

havoc [′hævək] *s* ravage *m*; to play havoc with causer des dégâts à

haw [hɔ] *s* (bot) cenelle *f* || *tr & intr* tourner à gauche || *interj* dia!, à gauche!

Hawaiian [hə′wɑɪjən] *adj* hawaïen || *s* Hawaïen *m*

Hawai′ian Is′lands *spl* îles *fpl* Hawaii

haw′-haw′ *s* rire *m* bête || *intr* rire bêtement || *interj* heu!

hawk [hɔk] *s* faucon *m*; (*mortarboard*) taloche *f*; (*sharper*) (coll) vautour *m* || *tr* colporter; to hawk up expectorer || *intr* chasser au faucon; (*to hawk up phlegm*) graillonner

hawker [′hɔkər] *s* colporteur *m*

hawk′ owl′ *s* chouette *f* épervière

hawks′bill tur′tle *s* caret *m*, caouane *f*

hawse [hɔz] *s* (*hole*) écubier *m*; (*prow*) nez *m*; (*distance*) évitage *m*

hawse′hole′ *s* écubier *m*

hawser [′hɔzər] *s* haussière *f*

haw′thorn′ *s* aubépine *f*

hay [he] *s* foin *m*; to hit the hay (slang) aller au plumard; to make hay faire les foins

hay′ fe′ver *s* rhume *m* des foins

hay′field′ *s* pré *m* à foin

hay′fork′ *s* fourche *f* à foin

hay′loft′ *s* fenil *m*, grenier *m* à foin

hay′mak′er *s* (boxing) coup *m* de poing en assommoir

haymow [′he‚mau] *s* fenil *m*; approvisionnement *m* de foin

hay′rack′ *s* râtelier *m*

hay′ride′ *s* promenade *f* en charrette de foin

hay′seed′ *s* graine *f* de foin; (coll) culterreux *m*

hay′stack′ *s* meule *f* de foin

hay′wire′ *adj* (slang) en pagaille; to go haywire (slang) perdre la boussole || *s* fil *m* de fer à lier le foin

hazard [′hæzərd] *s* risque *m*, danger *m*; (golf) obstacle *m*; at all hazards à tout hasard || *tr* hasarder, risquer

hazardous [′hæzərdəs] *adj* hasardé

haze [hez] *s* brume *f*; (fig) obscurité *f* || *tr* brimer

hazel [′hezəl] *adj* couleur de noisette, brun clair || *s* (*tree*) noisetier *m*, avelinier *m*

ha′zel-nut′ *s* noisette *f*, aveline *f*

hazing [′hezɪŋ] *s* brimade *f*; (*at university*) bizutage *m*

ha-zy [′hezi] *adj* (*comp* -zier; *super* -ziest) brumeux; (*notion*) nébuleux, vague

H′-bomb′ *s* bombe *f* H

he [hi] *pron pers* il §87; lui §85; ce §82B; he who celui qui §83

head [hed] *s* tête *f*; (*of bed*) chevet *m*; (*of boil*) tête; (*on glass of beer*) mousse *f*; (*of drum*) peau *f*; (*of cane*) pomme *f*; (*of coin*) face *f*; (*of barrel, cylinder, etc.*) fond *m*; (*of cylinder of automobile engine*) culasse *f*; (*of celery*) pied *m*; (*of ship*) avant *m*; (*of spear, ax, etc.*) fer *m*; (*of arrow*) pointe *f*; (*of business, department, etc.*) chef *m*, directeur *m*; (*of school*) directeur, principal *m*; (*of stream*) source *f*; (*of lake; of the table*) bout *m*, haut bout; (*caption*) titre *m*; (*decisive point*) point *m* culminant, crise *f*; at the head of à la tête de; from head to foot des pieds à la tête; head downwards la tête en bas; head of cattle bœuf *m*; head over heels in love (with) éperdument amoureux (de); heads or tails pile ou face; over one's head (*beyond reach*) hors de la portée de qn; (*going to a higher authority*) sans tenir compte de qn; to be out of one's head (coll) être timbré ou fou; to go to one's head monter à la tête de qn; to keep one's head garder son sang-froid; to keep one's head above water se tenir à flot; to not make head or tail of it n'y comprendre rien; to put heads together prendre conseil; to take it into one's head to avoir l'idée de, se mettre en tête de to win by a head gagner d'une tête || *tr* (*to direct*) diriger; (*a procession*) conduire, mener; (*an organization; a class in school*) être en tête de; (*a list*) venir en tête de; to head off détourner || *intr* (*said of grain*) épier; to head for or towards se diriger vers

head′ache′ *s* mal *m* de tête

head′band′ *s* bandeau *m*

head′board′ *s* panneau *m* de tête

head′cheese′ *s* fromage *m* de tête

head′ cold′ *s* rhume *m* de cerveau

head′dress′ *s* coiffure *f*

head'first' adv la tête la première;
(*impetuously*) précipitamment

head'frame' s (min) chevalement m

head'gear' s garniture f de tête, couvre-
chef m; (*for protection*) casque m

head'hunt'er s chasseur m de têtes

heading ['hɛdɪŋ] s titre m; (*of letter*)
en-tête m; (*of chapter*) tête f

headland ['hɛdlənd] s promontoire m

headless ['hɛdlɪs] adj sans tête; (*leader-
less*) sans chef

head'light' s (aut) phare m; (naut)
fanal m; (rr) feu m d'avant

head'line' s (*of newspaper*) manchette
f; (*of article*) titre m; **to make the
headlines** apparaître aux premières
pages des journaux ‖ tr mettre en
vedette

head'lin'er s (slang) tête f d'affiche

head'long' adj précipité ‖ adv précipitamment

head'man' s (pl -men') chef m

head'mas'ter s principal m, directeur m

head'most' adj de tête, premier

head' of'fice s bureau m central; (*director's office*) direction f; (*of a
corporation*) siège m social

head' of hair' s chevelure f

head'-on' adj & adv de front, face à
face

head'phones' spl écouteurs mpl, casque
m

head'piece' s (*any covering for head*)
casque m; (*headset*) écouteur m;
(*brains, judgment*) tête f, caboche f;
(typ) vignette f, en-tête m

head'quar'ters s bureau m central;
commissariat m de police; (mil) quartier m général; (*staff headquarters*)
(mil) état-major m

head'rest' s appui-tête m

head'set' s casque m, écouteurs mpl

heads'man s (pl -men) bourreau m

head'stone' s pierre f tumulaire (à la
tête d'une tombe); (*cornerstone*)
pierre angulaire

head'strong' adj têtu, entêté

head'wait'er s maître m d'hôtel, steward m

head'wa'ters spl cours m supérieur
d'une rivière

head'way' s progrès m, marche f avant;
(*between buses*) intervalle m; (naut)
erre f; **to make headway** progresser,
aller de l'avant

head'wear' s garniture f de tête

headwind ['hɛd,wɪnd] s vent m contraire, vent debout

head'work' s travail m mental, travail
de tête

head·y ['hɛdi] adj (comp -ier; super
-iest) (*wine*) capiteux; (*conduct*) emporté; (*news*) excitant; (*perfume*)
entêtant

heal [hil] tr guérir; (*a wound*) cicatriser ‖ intr guérir

healer ['hilər] s guérisseur m

healing ['hilɪŋ] s guérison f

health [hɛlθ] s santé f; **to be in good
health** se porter bien, être en bonne
santé; **to be in poor health** se porter mal, être en mauvaise santé; **to**

drink to the health of boire à la santé
de; **to enjoy radiant health** avoir une
santé florissante; **to your health!** à
votre santé!

healthful ['hɛlθfəl] adj sain; (*air, climate, etc.*) salubre; (*recreation, work,
etc.*) salutaire

health·y ['hɛlθi] adj (comp -ier; super
-iest) sain; (*air, climate, etc.*) salubre;
(*person*) bien portant; (*appetite*) robuste

heap [hip] s tas m, amas m ‖ tr entasser, amasser; **to heap** (*honors, praise,
etc.*) **on s.o.** combler qn de; **to heap**
(*insults*) **on s.o.** accabler qn de

hear [hɪr] v (*pret & pp* heard [hʌrd])
tr entendre, ouïr; **to hear it said**
l'entendre dire; **to hear s.o. sing, to
hear s.o. singing** entendre chanter
qn, entendre qn qui chante; **to hear
s.th. sung** entendre chanter q.ch. ‖
intr entendre; **hear! hear!** très bien!,
bravo!; **hear ye! oyez!**; **to hear about**
entendre parler de; **to hear from**
avoir des nouvelles de; **to hear of**
entendre parler de; **to hear tell of**
(coll) entendre parler de; **to hear that**
entendre dire que

hearer ['hɪrər] s auditeur m; **hearers**
auditoire m

hearing ['hɪrɪŋ] s (*sense*) l'ouïe f; (*act,
opportunity to be heard*) audition f;
(law) audience f; **in the hearing of**
en la présence de, devant; **within
hearing** à portée de la voix

hear'ing aid' s sonotone m, micro-
vibrateur m, appareil m de correction
auditive

hear'say' s ouï-dire m

hear'say ev'idence s simples ouï-dire
mpl

hearse [hʌrs] s corbillard m, char m
funèbre

heart [hɑrt] s cœur m; (cards) cœur;
after one's heart selon son cœur; **at
heart** au fond; **by heart** par cœur;
heart and soul corps et âme; **lift up
your hearts!** haut les cœurs!; **to
break the heart of** fendre le cœur à;
to die of a broken heart mourir de
chagrin; **to eat one's heart out** se
ronger le cœur; **to eat to one's heart's
content** manger tout son soûl; **to get
to the heart of the matter** entrer dans
le vif de la question; **to have one's
heart in one's work** avoir le cœur à
l'ouvrage; **to have one's heart in the
right place** avoir le cœur bien placé;
to lose heart perdre courage; **to open
one's heart to** épancher son cœur à;
to take heart prendre courage; **to
take to heart** prendre à cœur; **to wear
one's heart on one's sleeve** avoir le
cœur sur les lèvres; **with a heavy
heart** le cœur gros; **with all one's
heart** de tout son cœur; **with one's
heart in one's mouth** le gosier serré

heart'ache' s peine f de cœur

heart' attack' s crise f cardiaque

heart'beat' s battement m du cœur

heart'break' s crève-cœur m

heartbroken ['hart,brokən] *adj* navré, chagriné
heart'burn' *s* pyrosis *m*
heart' cher'ry *s* guigne *f*
heart' disease' *s* maladie *f* de cœur
hearten ['hartən] *tr* encourager
heart' fail'ure *s* arrêt *m* du cœur
heartfelt ['hart,felt] *adj* sincère, cordial, bien senti
hearth [harθ] *s* foyer *m*, âtre *m*
hearth'stone' *s* pierre *f* de cheminée
heartily ['hartılı] *adv* de bon cœur, sincèrement
heartless ['hartlıs] *adj* sans cœur
heart' of stone' *s* (fig) cœur *m* de bronze
heart'-rend'ing *adj* désolant, navrant
heart'sick' *adj* désolé, chagrin
heart'strings' *spl* fibres *fpl*, replis *mpl* du cœur
heart'-to-heart' *adj* franc, ouvert; sérieux ‖ *adv* à cœur ouvert
heart' trans'plant *s* greffe *f* du cœur, transplantation *f* cardiaque
heart' trou'ble *s* maladie *f* de cœur
heart'wood' *s* bois *m* de cœur
heart•y ['hartɪ] *adj* (comp -ier; super -iest) cordial, sincère; (meal) copieux; (laugh) sonore; (eater) gros
heat [hit] *s* chaleur *f*; (heating) chauffage *m*; (rut of animals) rut *m*; (in horse racing) éliminatoire *f*; in heat en rut ‖ *tr* échauffer; (e.g., a house) chauffer ‖ *intr* s'échauffer; to heat up chauffer
heated *adj* chauffé; (fig) chaud, échauffé
heater ['hitər] *s* (for food) réchaud *m*; (for heating house) calorifère *m*
heath [hiθ] *s* bruyère *f*
hea•then ['hiðən] *adj* païen ‖ *s* (pl -then or -thens) païen *m*
heathendom ['hiðəndəm] *s* paganisme *m*
heather ['heðər] *s* bruyère *f*
heating ['hitɪŋ] *adj* échauffant ‖ *s* chauffage *m*
heat' light'ning *s* éclairs *mpl* de chaleur
heat' shield' *s* (rok) bouclier *m* contre la chaleur, bouclier antithermique
heat'stroke' *s* insolation *f*, coup *m* de chaleur
heat' wave' *s* vague *f* de chaleur; (phys) onde *f* calorifique
heave [hiv] *s* soulèvement *m*; **heaves** (vet) pousse *f* ‖ *v* (pret & pp **heaved** or **hove** [hov]) *tr* soulever; (to throw) lancer; (a sigh) pousser; (the anchor) lever ‖ *intr* se soulever; faire des efforts pour vomir; (said of bosom) palpiter
heaven ['hevən] *s* ciel *m*; **for heaven's sake** pour l'amour de Dieu; **Heaven** le ciel; **heavens** cieux *mpl*, ciel
heavenly ['hevənlɪ] *adj* céleste
heav'enly bod'y *s* corps *m* céleste
heav•y ['hevɪ] *adj* (comp -ier; super -iest) lourd, pesant; (heart; crop; eater; baggage; rain, sea, weather) gros; (meal) copieux; (sleep) profond; (work) pénible; (book, reading, etc.) indigeste; (parts) (theat) tra-

gique, sombre ‖ *adv* lourd, lourdement; **to hang heavy on** peser sur
heav'y drink'er *s* fort buveur *m*
heav'y-du'ty *adj* extra-fort
heav'y-heart'ed *adj* au cœur lourd
heav'y-set' *adj* de forte carrure, costaud
heav'y-weight' *s* (boxing) poids *m* lourd
Hebraist ['hibre·ıst] *s* hébraïsant *m*
Hebrew ['hibru] *adj* hébreu, hébraïque ‖ *s* (language) hébreu *m*, langue *f* hébraïque; (man) Hébreu *m*; (woman) Juive *f*
hecatomb ['hekə,tom] *s* hécatombe *f*
heckle ['hekəl] *tr* interrompre bruyamment, chahuter; (on account of trifles) asticoter, harceler
heckler ['heklər] *s* interrupteur *m* impertinent, interpellateur *m*
hectic ['hektɪk] *adj* fou, bouleversant
hedge [hedʒ] *s* haie *f* ‖ *tr* entourer d'une haie; **to hedge in** entourer de tous côtés ‖ *intr* chercher des échappatoires, hésiter; (com) faire la contrepartie
hedge'hog' *s* hérisson *m*; (porcupine) porc-épic *m*
hedge'hop' *v* (pret & pp **-hopped**; ger **-hopping**) *intr* (aer) voler en rasemottes
hedgerow ['hedʒ,ro] *s* bordure *f* de haies, haie *f* vive
heed [hid] *s* attention *f*, soin *m*; **to take heed** prendre garde ‖ *tr* faire attention à, prendre garde à ‖ *intr* faire attention, prendre garde
heedful ['hidfəl] *adj* attentif
heedless ['hidlıs] *adj* inattentif
heehaw ['hi,ho] *s* hi-han *m* ‖ *intr* pousser des hi-hans
heel [hil] *s* talon *m*; (slang) goujat *m*; **to be down at the heel** traîner la savate; **to cool one's heels** (coll) croquer le marmot, faire le pied de grue
heft•y ['heftɪ] *adj* (comp -ier; super -iest) costaud; (heavy) pesant
heifer ['hefər] *s* génisse *f*
height [haɪt] *s* hauteur *f*; (e.g., of folly) comble *m*
heighten ['haɪtən] *tr* rehausser; (to increase the amount of) augmenter; (to set off, bring out) relever ‖ *intr* se rehausser; augmenter
heinous ['henəs] *adj* odieux, atroce
heir [er] *s* héritier *m*; **to become the heir of** hériter de
heir' appar'ent *s* (pl **heirs apparent**) héritier *m* présomptif
heiress ['erıs] *s* héritière *f*
heir'loom' *s* meuble *m*, bijou *m*, or souvenir *m* de famille
Helen ['helən] *s* Hélène *f*
helicopter ['helɪ,kaptər] *s* hélicoptère *m*
heliport ['helɪ,port] *s* héliport *m*
helium ['hilɪ·əm] *s* hélium *m*
helix ['hilɪks] *s* (pl **helixes** or **helices** ['helɪ,siz]) hélice *f*; (anat) hélix *m*
hell [hel] *s* enfer *m*
hell'bent' *adj* (slang) hardi; **hellbent on** (slang) acharné en diable à

hell'cat' s (*bad-tempered woman*) harpie f; (*witch*) sorcière f
Hellene ['helin] s Hellène mf
Hellenic [he'lɛnɪk], [he'linɪk] adj hellène
hell'fire' s feu m de l'enfer
hellish ['hɛlɪʃ] adj infernal
hel·lo [he'lo] s (pl **-los**) bonjour m || interj bonjour!; (*on telephone*) allô!
helm [hɛlm] s gouvernail m
helmet ['hɛlmɪt] s casque m
helms'man s (pl **-men**) homme m de barre
help [hɛlp] s aide f, secours m; (*workers*) main-d'œuvre f; (*office workers*) employés mpl; (*domestic servants*) domestiques mfpl; **help wanted** (*public sign*) offres d'emploi, on embauche; **there's no help for it** il n'y a pas de remède || tr aider, secourir; **so help me God!** que Dieu me juge!; **to help down** aider à descendre; **to help oneself** se défendre; (*to food*) se servir; **to not be able to help** ne pouvoir s'empêcher de || intr aider || interj au secours!
helper ['hɛlpər] s aide mf, assistant m
helpful ['hɛlpfəl] adj utile; (*person*) serviable, secourable
helping ['hɛlpɪŋ] s (*of food*) portion f
helpless ['hɛlplɪs] adj (*weak*) faible; (*powerless*) impuissant; (*penniless*) sans ressource; (*confused*) désemparé; (*situation*) sans recours
helter-skelter ['hɛltər'skɛltər] adj désordonné s débandade f || adv pêle-mêle
hem [hɛm] s ourlet m, bord m || v (pret & pp **hemmed**; ger **hemming**) tr ourler, border; **to hem in** entourer, cerner || intr faire un ourlet; **to hem and haw** ânonner; (fig) tourner autour du pot || interj hum!
hemisphere ['hɛmɪ,sfɪr] s hémisphère m
hemistich ['hɛmɪ,stɪk] s hémistiche m
hem'line' s ourlet m de la jupe
hem'lock' s (*Tsuga canadensis*) sapin m du Canada, pruche f; (*herb and poison*) ciguë f
hemoglobin [,hɛmə'globɪn], [,himə'globɪn] s hémoglobine f
hemophilia [,hɛmə'fɪlɪ·ə], [,himə'fɪlɪ·ə] s hémophilie f
hemorrhage ['hɛmərɪdʒ] s hémorragie f
hemorrhoids ['hɛmə,rɔɪdz] spl hémorroïdes fpl
hemostat ['hɛmə,stæt], ['himə,stæt] s hémostatique m
hemp [hɛmp] s chanvre m
hem'stitch' s ourlet m à jour || tr ourler à jour || intr faire un ourlet à jour
hen [hɛn] s poule f
hence [hɛns] adv d'ici; (*therefore*) d'où, donc
hence'forth' adv désormais, dorénavant
hench·man ['hɛntʃmən] s (pl **-men**) partisan m, acolyte m, complice mf
hen'coop' s cage f à poules, épinette f
hen'house' s poulailler m

henna ['hɛnə] s henné m || tr teindre au henné
hen'peck' tr mener par le bout du nez
Henry ['hɛnri] s Henri m
hep [hɛp] adj (slang) à la page, dans le train; **to be hep to** (slang) être au courant de
her [hʌr] adj poss son §88 || pron pers elle §85; la §87; lui §87
herald ['hɛrəld] s héraut m; (fig) avant-coureur m || tr annoncer; **to herald in** introduire
herald·ry ['hɛrəldri] s (pl **-ries**) héraldique f, blason m
herb [ʌrb], [hʌrb] s herbe f; (pharm) herbe médicinale or officinale; **herbs for seasoning** fines herbes
herculean [hʌr'kjulɪ·ən], [,hʌrkju'li·ən] adj herculéen
herd [hʌrd] s troupeau m || tr rassembler en troupeau || intr—**to herd together** s'attrouper
herds'man s (pl **-men**) pâtre m; (*of sheep*) berger m; (*of cattle*) bouvier m
here [hɪr] adv ici; **from here to there** d'ici là; **here and there** çà et là, par-ci par-là; **here below** ici-bas; **here is** or **here are** voici; **here lies** ci-gît; **that's neither here nor there** ça n'a rien à y voir || interj tenez!; (*answering roll call*) présent!
hereabouts ['hɪrə,bauts] adv près d'ici
here·af'ter s—**the hereafter** l'autre monde || adv désormais, à l'avenir; (*farther along*) ci-après
here·by' adv par ce moyen, par ceci; (*in legal language*) par les présentes
hereditary [hɪ'rɛdɪ,tɛri] adj héréditaire
heredi·ty [hɪ'rɛdɪti] s (pl **-ties**) hérédité f
here·in' adv ici; (*on this point*) en ceci; (*in this writing*) ci-inclus
here·of' adv de ceci, à ce sujet
here·on' adv là-dessus
here·sy ['hɛrəsi] s (pl **-sies**) hérésie f
heretic ['hɛrətɪk] adj & s hérétique mf
heretical [hɪ'rɛtɪkəl] adj hérétique
heretofore [,hɪrtu'for] adv jusqu'ici
here·upon' adv là-dessus
here·with' adv ci-joint, avec ceci
heritage ['hɛrɪtɪdʒ] s héritage m
hermetic(al) [hʌr'mɛtɪk(əl)] adj hermétique
hermit ['hʌrmɪt] s ermite m
hermitage ['hʌrmɪtɪdʒ] s ermitage m
herni·a ['hʌrnɪ·ə] s (pl **-as** or **-ae** [,i]) hernie f
he·ro ['hɪro] s (pl **-roes**) héros m
heroic [hɪ'ro·ɪk] adj héroïque || **heroics** spl (*verse*) vers m héroïque; (*language*) grandiloquence f
heroin ['hɛro·ɪn] s héroïne f
heroine ['hɛro·ɪn] s héroïne f
heroism ['hɛro,ɪzəm] s héroïsme m
heron ['hɛrən] s héron m
herring ['hɛrɪŋ] s hareng m
her'ring-bone' s (*in fabrics*) point m de chausson; (*in hardwood floors*) parquet m à batons rompus; (*in design*) arête f de hareng
hers [hʌrz] pron poss le sien §89

her·self' *pron pers* elle §85; soi §85; elle-même §86; se §87

hesitan·cy ['hɛzɪtənsɪ] *s* (*pl* **-cies**) hésitation *f*

hesitant ['hɛzɪtənt] *adj* hésitant

hesitate ['hɛzɪ‚tet] *intr* hésiter

hesitation [‚hɛzɪ'teʃən] *s* hésitation *f*

heterodox ['hɛtərə‚dɑks] *adj* hétérodoxe

heterodyne ['hɛtərə‚daɪn] *adj* hétérodyne

heterogeneous [‚hɛtərə'dʒɪnɪ·əs] *adj* hétérogène

hew [hju] *v* (*pret* hewed; *pp* hewed or hewn) *tr* tailler, couper; **to hew down** abattre || *intr*—**to hew close to the line** (coll) agir dans les règles, être très méticuleux

hex [hɛks] *s* porte-guigne *m* || *tr* porter la guigne à

hey [he] *interj* hé!; attention!

hey'day' *s* meilleure période *f*, fleur *f*

hi [haɪ] *interj* salut!

hia·tus [haɪ'etəs] *s* (*pl* **-tuses** or **-tus**) (*gap*) lacune *f*; (*in a text; in verse*) hiatus *m*

hibernate ['haɪbər‚net] *intr* hiberner

hibiscus [hɪ'bɪskəs], [haɪ'bɪskəs] *s* hibiscus *m*, ketmie *f*

hiccough or **hiccup** ['hɪkəp] *s* hoquet *m* || *intr* hoqueter

hick [hɪk] (coll) *adj & s* rustaud *m*

hicko·ry ['hɪkərɪ] *s* (*pl* **-ries**) hickory *m*

hidden ['hɪdən] *adj* caché, dérobée; (*mysterious*) occulte

hide [haɪd] *s* peau *f*, cuir *m* || *v* (*pret* hid [hɪd]; *pp* hid or hidden ['hɪdən]) *tr* cacher; **to hide s.th. from** cacher q.ch. à || *intr* se cacher; **to hide from** se cacher à

hide'-and-seek' *s* cache-cache *m*

hide'bound' *adj* à l'esprit étroit

hideous ['hɪdɪ·əs] *adj* hideux

hide'-out' *s* (coll) repaire *m*, planque *f*

hiding ['haɪdɪŋ] *s* dissimulation *f*; (*punishment*) (coll) raclée *f*, rossée *f*; **in hiding** caché

hid'ing place' *s* cachette *f*

hierar·chy ['haɪ·ə‚rɑrkɪ] *s* (*pl* **-chies**) hiérarchie *f*

hieroglyphic [‚haɪ·ərə'glɪfɪk] *adj* hiéroglyphique || *s* hiéroglyphe *m*

hi-fi ['haɪ'faɪ] *adj* (coll) de haute fidélité || *s* (coll) haute fidélité *f*

hi'-fi' fan' *s* (coll) fanatique *mf* de la haute fidélité

high [haɪ] *adj* haut; (*river, price, rate, temperature, opinion*) élevé; (*fever, wind*) fort; (*sea, wind*) gros; (*cheekbones*) saillant; (*sound*) aigu; (coll) gris; (culin) avancé; **high and dry** à sec; **high and mighty** prétentieux; **to be high** (coll) avoir son pompon || *s* (aut) prise *f* directe; **on high** en haut, dans le ciel || *adv* haut; à un prix élevé; **high and low** partout; **to aim high** viser haut; **to come high** se vendre cher

high' al'tar *s* maître-autel *m*

high'ball' *s* whisky *m* à l'eau

high' blood' pres'sure *s* hypertension *f*

high'born' *adj* de haute naissance

high'boy' *s* chiffonnier *m* semainier *m*

high'brow' *adj & s* (slang) intellectuel *m*

high' chair' *s* chaise *f* d'enfant

high' command' *s* haut commandement *m*

high' cost of liv'ing *s* cherté *f* de la vie

high'er educa'tion ['haɪ·ər] *s* enseignement *m* supérieur

high'er-up' *s* (coll) supérieur *m* hiérarchique

high'est bid'der ['haɪ·ɪst] *s* dernier enchérisseur *m*

high' explo'sive *s* haut explosif *m*, explosif puissant

highfalutin [‚haɪfə'lutən] *adj* (coll) pompeux, ampoulé

high' fidel'ity *s* haute fidélité *f*

high' fre'quency *s* haute fréquence *f*

high' gear' *s* (aut) prise *f* directe

high'-grade' *adj* de qualité supérieure

high'-hand'ed *adj* autoritaire, arbitraire

high' hat' *s* chapeau *m* haut de forme

high'-hat' *adj* (coll) snob, poseur || **high'-hat**' *v* (*pret & pp* **-hatted**; *ger* **-hatting**) *tr* (coll) traiter de haut en bas

high'-heeled' *adj* à talons hauts

high' horse' *s* raideur *f* hautaine; **to get up on one's high horse** monter sur ses grands chevaux

high' jinks' [‚dʒɪŋks] *s* (slang) clownerie *f*, drôlerie *f*

high' jump' *s* saut *m* en hauteur

high'-key' *adj* (phot) lumineux

highland ['haɪlənd] *s* pays *m* de montagne; **highlands** hautes terres *fpl*

high' life' *s* grand monde *m*

high'light' *s* (*big moment*) clou *m*; **highlights** (*in a picture*) clairs *mpl* || *tr* mettre en vedette

highly ['haɪlɪ] *adv* hautement; (*very*) extrêmement, fort; haut, e.g., **highly colored** haut en couleur; **to think highly of** avoir une bonne opinion de

High' Mass' *s* grand-messe *f*

high'-mind'ed *adj* magnanime, noble

highness ['haɪnɪs] *s* hauteur *f*; **Highness** Altesse *f*

high' noon' *s* plein midi *m*

high'-oc'tane *adj* à indice d'octane élevé

high'-pitched' *adj* aigu; (*roof*) à forte pente

high'-powered' *adj* de haute puissance

high'-pres'sure *adj* à haute pression; (fig) dynamique, persuasif || *tr* (coll) gonfler à bloc

high'-priced' *adj* de prix élevé

high' priest' *s* grand prêtre *m*; (fig) pontife *m*

high'road' *s* grand-route *f*; (fig) bonne voie *f*

high' school' *s* école *f* secondaire publique; (*in France*) lycée *m*

high'-school stu'dent *s* lycéen *m*; collégien *m*

high' sea' *s* houle *f*, grosse mer *f*; **high seas** haute mer

high' soci'ety *s* la haute société, le beau monde

high'-sound'ing adj pompeux, prétentieux
high'-speed' adj à grande vitesse
high'-spir'ited adj fougueux, plein
d'entrain
high' spir'its spl gaieté f, entrain m
high' stakes' spl—to play for high
stakes jouer gros jeu
high-strung ['haɪ'strʌŋ] adj tendu,
nerveux
high'-test' gas'oline s supercarburant m
high' tide' s marée f; haute, haute
marée
high' time' s heure f, e.g., it is high
time for you to go c'est certainement
l'heure de votre départ; (slang) bombance f, bombe f
high' trea'son s haute trahison f
high' volt'age s haute tension f
high wa'ter s marée f haute, hautes
eaux fpl
high'way' s grand-route f
high'way commis'sion s administration
f des ponts et chaussées
high'way'man s (pl -men) voleur m de
grand chemin
high'way map' s carte f routière
hijack ['haɪˌdʒæk] tr (coll) arrêter et
voler sur la route; (coll) saisir de
force; (an airplane) (coll) détourner
hijacker ['haɪˌdʒækər] s (coll) bandit
m, bandit de grand chemin; (coll)
pirate m de l'air, pirate aérien
hijacking ['haɪˌdʒækɪŋ] s (coll) piraterie f aérienne, détournement m
hike [haɪk] s excursion f à pied,
voyage m pédestre; (e.g., in rent)
hausse f ‖ tr hausser, faire monter ‖
intr faire de longues promenades à
pied
hiker ['haɪkər] s excursionniste mf à
pied, touriste mf pédestre
hilarious [hɪ'lerɪ·əs], [haɪ'lerɪ·əs] adj
hilare, gai; (joke) hilarant
hill [hɪl] s colline f, coteau m; (incline)
côte f; (mil) cote f; over hill and
dale par monts et par vaux ‖ tr (a
plant) butter, chausser
hill'bil'ly s (pl -lies) montagnard m
rustique
hillock ['hɪlək] s tertre m, butte f
hill'side' s versant m, coteau m
hill·y ['hɪli] adj (comp -ier; super -lest)
montueux, accidenté; (steep) en
pente, à fortes pentes
hilt [hɪlt] s poignée f; up to the hilt
jusqu'à la garde
him [hɪm] pron pers lui §85, §87; le
§87
him·self' pron lui §85; soi §85; lui-
même §86; se §87
hind [haɪnd] adj postérieur, de derrière
‖ s biche f
hinder ['hɪndər] tr empêcher
hind'most' adj dernier, ultime
hind'quar'ter s arrière-train m, train m
de derrière; (of horse) arrière-main m
hindrance ['hɪndrəns] s empêchement
m
hind'sight' s (of firearm) hausse f;
compréhension f tardive

Hindu ['hɪndu] adj hindou ‖ s Hindou
m
hinge [hɪndʒ] s charnière f, gond m;
(of mollusk) charnière f; (bb) onglet m
‖ intr—to hinge on axer sur, dépendre de
hin·ny ['hɪni] s (pl -nies) bardot m
hint [hɪnt] s insinuation f; (small quantity) soupçon m; to take the hint
comprendre à demi-mot, accepter le
conseil ‖ tr insinuer ‖ intr procéder
par insinuation; to hint at laisser entendre
hinterland ['hɪntərˌlænd] s arrière-pays
m
hip [hɪp] adj (slang) à la page, dans le
train; to be hip to (slang) être au
courant de ‖ s hanche f; (of roof)
arête f
hip'bone' s os m coxal, os de la hanche
hipped adj—to be hipped on (coll)
avoir la manie de
hippety-hop ['hɪpɪtɪ'hɑp] adv (coll)
en sautillant
hip·po ['hɪpo] s (pl -pos) (coll) hippopotame m
hippopota·mus [ˌhɪpə'pɑtəməs] s (pl
-muses or -mi [ˌmaɪ]) hippopotame
m
hip'roof' s toit m en croupe
hire [haɪr] s (salary) gages mpl; (rent-
ing) louage m; for hire à louer; in
the hire of aux gages de ‖ tr (a person) engager, embaucher; (to rent)
louer, prendre en location ‖ intr—to
hire out (said of person) se louer,
entrer en service
hired' girl' s servante f, servante de
ferme
hired' man' s (pl men') (coll) valet m
de ferme, garçon m de ferme
hireling ['haɪrlɪŋ] adj & s mercenaire m
hiring ['haɪrɪŋ] s embauchage m
his [hɪz] adj poss son §88 ‖ pron poss
le sien §89
Hispanic [hɪs'pænɪk] adj hispanique
Hispanist ['hɪspənɪst], [hɪs'pænɪst] s
hispanisant m
hiss [hɪs] s sifflement m ‖ tr & intr
siffler
hist [hɪst] interj psitt!, pst!
histology [hɪs'tɑlədʒi] s histologie f
historian [hɪs'tori·ən] s historien m
historic(al) [hɪs'tɑrɪk(əl)], [hɪs'tɔrɪk-
(əl)] adj historique
histo·ry ['hɪstəri] s (pl -ries) histoire f
histrionic [ˌhɪstrɪ'ɑnɪk] adj théâtral ‖
histrionics s art m du théâtre; (fig)
attitude f spectaculaire
hit [hɪt] s coup m; (blow that hits its
mark) coup au but, coup heureux;
(sarcastic remark) coup de patte,
trait m satirique; (on the hit parade)
tube m; (baseball) coup de batte;
(theat) succès m, spectacle m très
couru; (coll) réussite f; to make a hit
(coll) faire sensation ‖ v (pret & pp
hit; ger hitting) tr frapper; (the
mark) atteindre; (e.g., a car) heurter,
heurter contre; (to move the emotions of) toucher; to hit it off (coll)

s'entendre, se trouver d'accord || *intr* frapper; **to hit on** tomber sur, trouver

hit'-and-run' *driv'er s* chauffard *m* qui abandonne la scène d'un accident, qui prend la fuite

hitch [hɪtʃ] *s* saccade *f*, secousse *f*; obstacle *m*, difficulté *f*; *(knot)* nœud *m*, e.g., **timber hitch** nœud de bois; **without a hitch** sans accroc || *tr* accrocher; *(naut)* nouer; **to hitch up** *(e.g., a horse)* atteler

hitch'hike' *intr* (coll) faire de l'auto-stop

hitch'hik'er *s* auto-stoppeur *m*

hitch'hik'ing *s* auto-stop *m*

hitch'ing post' *s* poteau *m* d'attache

hither ['hɪðər] *adv* ici; **hither and thither** çà et là

hith'er•to' *adv* jusqu'ici, jusqu'à présent

hit'-or-miss' *adj* capricieux, éventuel

hit' parade' *s* (coll) chansons *fpl* populaires du moment

hit' rec'ord *s* (coll) disque *m* à succès

hive [haɪv] *s* ruche *f*; **hives** (pathol) urticaire *f*

hoard [hɔrd] *s* entassement *m*, trésor *m* || *tr* accumuler secrètement, thésauriser || *intr* accumuler, entasser, thésauriser

hoarding ['hɔrdɪŋ] *s* accumulation *f* secrète, thésaurisation *f*

hoarfrost ['hɔr,frɔst] *s* givre *m*, gelée *f* blanche

hoarse [hɔrs] *adj* enroué, rauque

hoarseness ['hɔrsnɪs] *s* enrouement *m*

hoar•y ['hɔri] *adj* *(comp* **-ier**; *super* **-iest)** chenu, blanchi

hoax [hoks] *s* mystification *f*, canard *m* || *tr* mystifier

hob [hɑb] *s* *(of fireplace)* plaque *f*; **to play hob** (coll) causer des ennuis; **to play hob with** (coll) bouleverser

hobble ['hɑbəl] *s (limp)* boitillement *m*; *(rope used to tie legs of animal)* entrave *f* || *tr* faire boiter; *(e.g., a horse)* entraver || *intr* boiter, clocher

hob•by ['hɑbi] *s (pl* **-bies)** distraction *f*, violon *m* d'Ingres; *(orn)* hobereau *m*; **to ride one's hobby** enfourcher son dada

hob'by•horse' *s* cheval *m* de bois

hob'gob'lin *s* lutin *m*; *(bogy)* épouvantail *m*

hob'nail' *s* caboche *f*

hob•nob ['hɑb,nɑb] *v (pret & pp* **-nobbed;** *ger* **-nobbing)** *intr* trinquer ensemble; **to hobnob with** être à tu et à toi avec

ho•bo ['hobo] *s (pl* **-bos** or **-boes)** chemineau *m*, vagabond *m*

hock [hɑk] *s (of horse)* jarret *m*; *(wine)* vin *m* du Rhin; *(pawn)* (coll) gage *m*; **in hock** (coll) au clou; *(in prison)* (coll) au bloc || *tr* couper le jarret à; *(to pawn)* (coll) mettre en gage, mettre au clou

hockey ['hɑki] *s* hockey *m*

hock'shop' *s* (slang) mont-de-piété *m*, clou *m*

hocus-pocus ['hokəs'pokəs] *s* tour *m* de passe-passe; *(meaningless formula)* abracadabra *m*

hod [hɑd] *s* oiseau *m*, auge *f*

hod' car'rier *s* aide-maçon *m*

hodgepodge ['hɑdʒ,pɑdʒ] *s* salmigondis *m*, méli-mélo *m*

hoe [ho] *s* houe *f*, binette *f* || *tr* houer, biner

hog [hɑg], [hɔg] *s* pourceau *m*, porc *m*; *(pig)* cochon || *v (pret & pp* **hogged;** *ger* **hogging)** *tr* (slang) s'emparer de, saisir avidement

hog'back' *s* dos *m* d'âne

hoggish ['hɑgɪʃ], ['hɔgɪʃ] *adj* glouton

hogs'head' *s* barrique *f*

hog'wash' *s* eaux *fpl* grasses; vinasse *f*; *(fig)* boniments *mpl* à la noix de coco

hoist [hɔɪst] *s* monte-charge *m*, grue *f*; *(shove)* poussée *f* vers le haut || *tr* lever, guinder; *(a flag, sail, boat, etc.)* hisser

hoity-toity ['hɔɪtɪ'tɔɪtɪ] *adj* hautain; **to be hoity-toity** le prendre de haut

hokum ['hokəm] *s* (coll) boniments *mpl*, fumisterie *f*

hold [hold] *s* prise *f*; *(handle)* poignée *f*, manche *m*; *(domination)* pouvoir *m*, autorité *f*; *(mus)* point *m* d'orgue; *(naut)* cale *f*; **hold for arrival** *(formula on envelope)* garder jusqu'à l'arrivée; **to take hold of** empoigner, saisir || *v (pret & pp* **held** [held]) *tr* tenir; *(one's breath; s.o.'s attention)* retenir; *(to contain)* contenir; *(a job; a title)* avoir, posséder; *(e.g., a university chair)* occuper; *(a fort)* défendre; *(a note)* (mus) tenir, prolonger; **to be held to be . . .** passer pour . . .; **to hold back** or **in** retenir; **to hold one's own** rivaliser, se défendre; **to hold out** tendre, offrir; **to hold over** continuer, remettre; **to hold s.o. . . .** tenir qn pour . . .; **to hold s.o. to his word** obliger qn à tenir sa promesse; **to hold up** *(to delay)* retarder; *(to keep from falling)* retenir, soutenir; *(to rob)* (coll) voler à main armée || *intr (to hold good)* rester valable, rester en vigueur; **hold on!** (telp) restez en ligne!; **to hold back** se retenir, hésiter; **to hold forth** disserter; **to hold off** se tenir à distance; **to hold on** or **out** tenir bon; **to hold on to** s'accrocher à, se cramponner à; **to hold out for** insister pour

holder ['holdər] *s* possesseur *m*; *(of stock)* porteur *m*; *(of stock; of a record)* détenteur *m*; *(of degree, fellowship, etc.)* impétrant *m*; *(for a cigarette)* porte-cigarettes *m*; *(of a post, a right, etc.)* titulaire *mf*; *(for holding, e.g., a hot dish)* poignée *f*

holding ['holdɪŋ] *s* possession *f*; **holdings** valeurs *fpl*; *(of an investor)* portefeuille *m*; *(of a landlord)* propriétés *fpl*

hold'ing com'pany *s* holding trust *m*, holding *m*

hold'up' *s (stop, delay)* arrêt *m*; (coll) attaque *f* à main armée, hold-up *m*; **what's the holdup?** (coll) qu'est-ce qu'on attend?

hole [hol] *s* trou *m*; **in the hole** (coll)

dans l'embarras; **to burn a hole in s.o.'s pocket** (coll) brûler la poche à qn; **to get s.o. out of a hole** (coll) tirer qn d'un mauvais pas; **to pick holes in** (coll) trouver à redire à, démolir; **to wear holes in** (e.g., a garment) trouer || *intr*—**to hole up** se terrer

holiday ['halɪ,de] *s* jour *m* de fête, jour férié; (vacation) vacances *fpl*

holiness ['holɪnɪs] *s* sainteté *f*; **His Holiness** Sa Sainteté

holla ['hala], [hə'la] *interj* holà!

Holland ['haland] *s* Hollande *f*; **la Hollande**

Hollander ['haləndər] *s* Hollandais *m*

hollow ['halo] *adj & s* creux *m* || *adv*—**to beat all hollow** (coll) battre à plate couture || *tr* creuser

hol•ly ['halɪ] *s* (*pl* -**lies**) houx *m*

hol'ly-hock' *s* primerose *f*, rose *f* trémière

holm' oak' [hom] *s* yeuse *f*

holocaust ['hala,kɔst] *s* (*sacrifice*) holocauste *m*; (disaster) sinistre *m*

holster ['holstər] *s* étui *m*; (on saddle) fonte *f*

ho•ly ['holi] *adj* (*comp* -**lier**; *super* -**liest**) saint; (e.g., water) bénit

Ho'ly Ghost' *s* Saint-Esprit *m*

ho'ly or'ders *spl* ordres *mpl* sacrés

Ho'ly Scrip'ture *s* l'Écriture *f* Sainte

Ho'ly See' *s* Saint-Siège *m*

Ho'ly Sep'ulcher *s* Saint Sépulcre *m*

ho'ly wa'ter *s* eau *f* bénite

Ho'ly Writ' *s* l'Écriture *f* Sainte

homage ['hamɪdʒ], ['amɪdʒ] *s* hommage *m*

home [hom] *adj* domestique; national, natal || *s* foyer *m*, chez-soi *m*, domicile *m*; (house) maison *f*; (of the arts; native land) patrie *f*; (for the sick, poor, etc.) asile *m*, foyer, hospice *m*; **at home** à la maison; (at ease) à l'aise; **make yourself at home** faites comme chez vous || *adv* à la maison; **to see s.o. home** raccompagner qn jusqu'à chez lui; **to strike home** frapper juste, toucher au vif

home' ad'dress *s* adresse *f* personnelle

home'bod'y *s* (*pl* -**ies**) casanier *m*, pantouflard *m*

homebred ['hom,bred] *adj* élevé à la maison; du pays, indigène

home'-brew' *s* boisson *f* faite à la maison

home'com'ing *s* retour *m* au foyer; (at university, church, etc.) journée *f* or semaine *f* des anciens

home' coun'try *s* pays *m* natal

home' deliv'ery *s* livraison *f* à domicile

home' econom'ics *s* économie *f* domestique; (instruction) enseignement *m* ménager

home' front' *s* théâtre *m* d'opérations à l'intérieur du pays

home'land' *s* patrie *f*, pays *m* natal

homeless ['homlɪs] *adj* sans foyer

home' life' *s* vie *f* familiale

home'like' *adj* familial, comme chez soi

home'-lov'ing *adj* casanier

home•ly ['homli] *adj* (*comp* -**lier**; *super* -**liest**) (not good-looking) laid, vilain; (not elegant) sans façons

home'made' *adj* fait à la maison, de ménage

home'mak'er *s* maîtresse *f* de maison, ménagère *f*

home' of'fice *s* siège *m* social

homeopathy [,homɪ'apəθɪ], [,hamɪ'apəθɪ] *s* homéopathie *f*

home'own'er *s* propriétaire *mf*

home' plate' *s* (baseball) marbre *m* (Canad)

home' port' *s* port *m* d'attache

home' rule' *s* autonomie *f*, gouvernement *m* autonome

home'sick' *adj* nostalgique; **to be homesick** avoir le mal du pays

home'sick'ness *s* mal *m* du pays, nostalgie *f*

homespun [hom,spʌn] *adj* filé à la maison; (fig) simple, sans apprêt

home'stead *s* bien *m* de famille, ferme *f*

home'stretch' *s* fin *f* de course, dernière étape *f*

home' team' *s* locaux *mpl*, équipe *f* qui reçoit

home'town' *s* ville *f* natale

homeward ['homwərd] *adj* de retour || *adv* vers la maison; vers son pays

home'work' *s* travail *m* à la maison; devoirs *mpl*

homey ['homi] *adj* (*comp* **homier**; *super* **homiest**) (coll) familial, intime

homicidal [,hamɪ'saɪdəl] *adj* homicide

homicide ['hamɪ,saɪd] *s* (act) homicide *m*; (person) homicide *mf*

homi•ly ['hamɪlɪ] *s* (*pl* -**lies**) homélie *f*

hom'ing head' *s* (of missile) tête *f* chercheuse

hom'ing pi'geon *s* pigeon *m* voyageur

hominy ['hamɪnɪ] *s* semoule *f* de maïs

homogeneous [,homə'dʒɪnɪ-əs], [,hamə'dʒɪnɪ-əs] *adj* homogène

homogenize [hə'madʒə,naɪz] *tr* homogénéiser

homonym ['hamənɪm] *s* homonyme *m*

homonymous [hə'manɪməs] *adj* homonyme

homosexual [,homə'sɛkʃʊ-əl] *adj & s* homosexuel *m*

hone [hon] *s* pierre *f* à aiguiser || *tr* aiguiser, affiler

honest ['anɪst] *adj* honnête; (money) honnêtement acquis

honesty ['anɪstɪ] *s* honnêteté *f*; (bot) monnaie *f* du pape

hon•ey ['hʌnɪ] *s* miel *m* || *v* (*pret & pp* -**eyed** or -**ied**) *tr* emmieller

hon'ey-bee' *s* abeille *f* à miel

hon'ey-comb' *s* rayon *m*, gâteau *m* de cire; (anything like a honeycomb) nid *m* d'abeilles || *tr* cribler

honeyed *adj* emmiellé

hon'ey-moon' *s* lune *f* de miel; voyage *m* de noces || *intr* passer la lune de miel

hon'ey-suck'le *s* chèvrefeuille *m*

honk [hʌŋk], [hɔŋk] *s* (aut) klaxon *m* || *tr* (the horn) sonner || *intr* klaxonner

honkytonk ['haŋki,taŋk], ['haŋki-,taŋk] s (slang) boui-boui m
honor ['anər] s honneur m; (award) distinction f; **honors** honneurs ‖ tr honorer
honorable ['anərəbəl] adj honorable
hon'orable dis'charge s (mil) démobilisation f honorable
honorari-um [,anə'rɛri-əm] s (pl **-ums** or **-a** [ə]) s honoraires mpl
honorary ['anə,rɛri] adj honoraire
honorific [,anə'rɪfɪk] adj honorifique ‖ s formule f de politesse
hood [hʊd] s capuchon m, chaperon m; (of chimney) hotte f; (academic hood) capuce m; (aut) capot m; (slang) gangster m ‖ tr capoter
hoodlum ['hʊdləm] s (coll) chenapan m
hoodoo ['hudu] s (bad luck) guigne f; (rites) vaudou m ‖ tr porter la guigne à
hood'wink' s tromper, abuser
hooey ['hu·i] s (slang) blague f
hoof [huf], [hʊf] s sabot m; **on the hoof** sur pied ‖ tr—**to hoof it** (coll) aller à pied
hoof'beat' s pas m de cheval
hook [hʊk] s crochet m; (for fishing) hameçon m; (to join two things) croc m; (boxing) crochet m; **by hook or by crook** (coll) de bric ou de broc, coûte que coûte; **hook line and sinker** (coll) tout à fait, avec tout le bataclan; **to get one's hooks on to** (coll) mettre le grappin sur ‖ tr accrocher; (e.g., a dress) agrafer; (e.g., a boat) crocher, gaffer; (slang) amorcer, attraper; **to hook up** agrafer; (e.g., a loudspeaking system) monter ‖ intr s'accrocher
hookah ['hʊkə] s narguilé m
hook' and eye' s agrafe f et porte f
hook' and lad'der s camion m équipé d'une échelle d'incendie
hooked' rug' s tapis m à points noués
hook'up' s (diagram) (rad, telv) montage m; (network) (rad, telv) chaîne f
hook'worm' s ankylostome m
hooky ['hʊki] s—**to play hooky** (coll) faire l'école buissonnière
hooligan ['hʊlɪgən] s voyou m
hooliganism ['hʊlɪgən,ɪzəm] s voyouterie f
hoop [hup], [hʊp] s cerceau m; (of cask) cercle m ‖ tr cercler, entourer
hoop' skirt' s crinoline f
hoot [hut] s huée f; (of owl) ululement m ‖ tr huer ‖ intr huer; (said of owl) ululer; **to hoot at** huer
hoot' owl' s chat-huant m, hulotte f
hop [hap] s saut m; (dance) (coll) sauterie f, surboum m; (coll) vol m en avion, étape f; **hops** (bot) houblon m ‖ v (pret & pp hopped; ger hopping) tr sauter, franchir; (e.g., a taxi) (coll) prendre ‖ intr sauter, sautiller; **to hop on one foot** sauter a clochepied; **to hop over** sauter
hope [hop] s (feeling of hope) espérance f; (instance of hope) espoir m; (person or thing one puts one's hope in) espérance, espoir ‖ tr & intr espérer; **to hope for** espérer; **to hope to** + inf espérer + inf
hope' chest' s trousseau m
hopeful ['hopfəl] adj (feeling hope) plein d'espoir; (giving hope) prometteur
hopeless ['hoplɪs] adj sans espoir
hopper ['hapər] s (funnel-shaped container) trémie f; (of blast furnace) gueulard m
hop'per car' s wagon-trémie m
hop'scotch' s marelle f
horde [hord] s horde f
horehound ['hor,haʊnd] s (bot) marrube m
horizon [hə'raɪzən] s horizon m
horizontal [,harɪ'zantəl], [,horɪ'zantəl] adj horizontal ‖ s horizontale f
hor'izon'tal hold' s (telv) commande f de stabilité horizontale
hormone ['hormon] s hormone f
horn [horn] s (bony projection on head of certain animals) corne f; (of anvil) bigorne f; (of auto) klaxon m; (of snail; of insect) antenne f; (mus) cor m; (French horn) (mus) cor d'harmonie; **horns** (of deer) bois m; **to blow one's own horn** (coll) se vanter, exalter son propre mérite; **to draw in one's horns** (fig) rentrer les cornes; **to toot the horn corner** ‖ intr—**to horn in** (slang) intervenir sans façon
horn'beam' s (bot) charme m
horned' adj s duc m
hornet ['hornɪt] s frelon m
hor'net's nest' s guêpier m
horn' of plen'ty s corne f d'abondance
horn'pipe' s chalumeau m; (dance) matelote f
horn'rimmed glas'ses spl lunettes fpl à monture en corne
horn·y ['horni] adj (comp **-ier;** super **-iest**) corné, en corne; (callous) calleux; (horned) cornu
horoscope ['harə,skop], ['horə,skop] s horoscope m; **to cast s.o.'s horoscope** tirer l'horoscope de qn
horrible ['harɪbəl], ['horɪbəl] adj horrible; (coll) horrible, détestable
horrid ['harɪd], ['horɪd] adj affreux; (coll) affreux, très désagréable
horri-fy ['harɪ,faɪ], ['horɪ,faɪ] v (pret & pp **-fied**) tr horrifier
horror ['harər], ['horər] s horreur m; **to have a horror of** avoir horreur de
hors d'oeuvre [or'dʌrv] s (pl **hors d'oeuvres** [or'dʌrvz]) hors-d'œuvre m
horse [hors] s cheval m; (of carpenter) chevalet m; **hold your horses!** (coll) arrêtez un moment!; **to back the wrong horse** (coll) miser sur le mauvais cheval; **to be a horse of another color** (coll) être une autre paire de manches; **to eat like a horse** (coll) manger comme un ogre; **to ride a horse** monter à cheval ‖ intr—**to horse around** (slang) muser, se baguenauder
horse'back' s—**on horseback** à cheval ‖ adv—**to ride horseback** monter à cheval

horse'back rid'ing s équitation f, exercice m à cheval
horse' blan'ket s couverture f de cheval
horse' break'er s dompteur m de chevaux
horse'car' s tramway m à chevaux
horse' chest'nut s (tree) marronnier m d'Inde; (nut) marron m d'Inde
horse'cloth' s housse f
horse' col'lar s collier m de cheval
horse' deal'er s marchand m de chevaux
horse' doc'tor s (coll) vétérinaire m
horse' fly' s (pl flies) taon m
horse'hair' s crin m
horse'hide' s peau f or cuir m de cheval
horse'laugh' s gros rire m bruyant
horse'less car'riage ['hɔrslɪs] s voiture f sans chevaux
horse'man s (pl -men) cavalier m; (at race track) turfiste m
horsemanship ['hɔrsmən,ʃɪp] s équitation f
horse' meat' s viande f de cheval
horse' op'era s (coll) western m
horse' pis'tol s pistolet m d'arçon
horse'play' s jeu m de mains, clownerie f
horse'pow'er s (746 watts) cheval-vapeur anglais
horse' race' s course f de chevaux
horse'rad'ish s raifort m
horse' sense' s (coll) gros bon sens m
horse'shoe' s fer m à cheval
horse'shoe'ing s ferrure f, ferrage m
horse'shoe mag'net s aimant m en fer à cheval
horse' show' s exposition f de chevaux, concours m hippique
horse'tail' s queue f de cheval; (bot) prèle f
horse' thief' s voleur m de chevaux
horse' trad'er s maquignon m
horse' trad'ing s maquignonnage m
horse'whip' s cravache f ‖ v (pret & pp -whipped; ger -whipping) tr cravacher
horse'wom'an s (pl -wom'en) s cavalière f, amazone f
hors·y ['hɔrsi] adj (comp -ier; super -iest) chevalin; (coll) hippomane; (awkward in appearance) (coll) maladroit
horticultural [,hɔrtɪ'kʌltʃərəl] adj horticole
horticulture ['hɔrtɪ,kʌltʃər] s horticulture f
hose [hoz] s (flexible tube) tuyau m ‖ s (pl hose) (stocking) bas m; (sock) chaussette f
hosier ['hoʒər] s bonnetier m
hosiery ['hoʒəri] s la bonneterie; (stockings) les bas mpl
hospice ['hɑspɪs] s hospice m
hospitable ['hɑspɪtəbəl], [hɑs'pɪtəbəl] adj hospitalier
hospital ['hɑspɪtəl] s hôpital m, clinique f, maison f de santé
hospitali·ty [,hɑspɪ'tælɪti] s (pl -ties) hospitalité f

hospitalize ['hɑspɪtə,laɪz] tr hospitaliser
hos'pital plane' s avion m sanitaire
hos'pital ship' s navire-hôpital m
hos'pital train' s train m sanitaire
host [host] s hôte m; (who entertains dinner guests) amphitryon m; (multitude) foule f, légion f; (army) armée f; Host (eccl) hostie f
hostage ['hɑstɪdʒ] s otage m
hostel ['hɑstəl] s hôtellerie f; (youth hostel) auberge f de la jeunesse
hostel·ry ['hɑstəlri] s (pl -ries) hôtellerie f
hostess ['hostɪs] s hôtesse f; (taxi dancer) entraîneuse f
hostile ['hɑstɪl] adj hostile
hostili·ty [hɑs'tɪlɪti] s (pl -ties) hostilité f
hostler ['hɑslər], ['ɑslər] s palefrenier m, valet m d'écurie
hot [hɑt] adj (comp hotter; super hottest) chaud; (spicy) piquant; (fight, pursuit, etc.) acharné; (in rut) en chaleur; (radioactive) (coll) fortement radioactif; **hot off** (e.g., the press) (coll) sortant tout droit de; **to be hot** (said of person) avoir chaud; (said of weather) faire chaud; **to get hot under the collar** (coll) s'emporter; **to make it hot for** (coll) rendre la vie intenable à, harceler
hot' air' s (slang) hâblerie f, discours mpl vides
hot'-air' fur'nace s calorifère m à air chaud
hot' and cold' run'ning wa'ter s eau f courante chaude et froide
hot'bed' s (hort) couche f, couche de fumier; (e.g., of vice) foyer m; (e.g., of intrigue) officine f
hot'-blood'ed adj au sang fougueux
hot'box' s (rr) coussinet m échauffé
hot' cake' s crêpe f; **to sell like hot cakes** (coll) se vendre comme des petits pains
hot' dog' s saucisse f de Francfort, saucisse chaude
hotel [ho'tel] adj hôtelier ‖ s hôtel m
hotel'keep'er s hôtelier m
hot'foot' adv (coll) à toute vitesse ‖ tr —**to hotfoot it after** (coll) s'élancer à la poursuite de
hot'head'ed adj exalté, fougueux
hot'house' s serre f chaude
hot' pad' s (for plates at table) garde-nappe m, dessous-de-plat m
hot' pep'per s piment m rouge
hot' plate' s réchaud m
hot' rod' s (slang) bolide m
hot' rod'der [,rɑdər] s (slang) bolide m, casse-cou m
hot' springs' spl sources fpl thermales
hot'-temp'ered adj coléreux, irascible
hot' wa'ter s (coll) mauvaise passe f; **to be in hot water** (coll) être dans le pétrin
hot'-wa'ter boil'er s chaudière f à eau chaude
hot'-wa'ter bot'tle s bouillotte f
hot'-wa'ter heat'er s calorifère m à eau

chaude; (with instantaneous delivery of hot water) chauffe-eau m

hot'-wa'ter heat'ing s chauffage m par eau chaude

hot'-wa'ter tank' s réservoir m d'eau chaude, bâche f

hound [haund] s chien m de chasse, chien courant; to follow the hounds or to ride to hounds chasser à courre || tr poursuivre avec ardeur, pourchasser

hour [aur] s heure f; by the hour à l'heure; on the hour à l'heure sonnante; to keep late hours se coucher tard

hour'glass' s sablier m

hour'-glass fig'ure s taille f de guêpe

hour' hand' s petite aiguille f, aiguille des heures

hourly ['aurli] adj à l'heure, horaire f || adv toutes les heures; (hour by hour) d'heure en heure

house [haus] s (pl houses ['hauzız]) maison f; (legislative body) chambre f; (theat) salle f, e.g., full house salle comble; to be on the house (coll) être au frais du patron; to bring down the house (theat) faire crouler la salle sous les applaudissements; to keep house for tenir la maison de; to put one's house in order (fig) mettre de l'ordre dans ses affaires || [hauz] tr loger, abriter

house' arrest' s—under house arrest en résidence surveillée

house'boat' s bateau-maison m

house'boy' s boy m

house'break'er s cambrioleur m

house'break'ing s effraction f, cambriolage m

housebroken ['haus,broken] adj (dog or cat) dressé à la propreté

house' clean'ing s grand nettoyage m de la maison

house'coat' s peignoir m

house' cur'rent s courant m de secteur, secteur m

house'fly' s (pl -flies) mouche f domestique

houseful ['haus,ful] s pleine maison f

house' fur'nishings spl ménage m

house'hold' adj domestique, du ménage || s ménage m, maisonnée f

house'hold'er s chef m de famille, maître m de maison

house' hunt'ing s chasse f aux appartements

house'keep'er s ménagère f; (employee) femme f de charge; (for a bachelor) gouvernante f

house'keep'ing s le ménage, l'économie f domestique; to set up housekeeping se mettre en ménage

house'maid' s bonne f

house'moth'er s maîtresse f d'internat

house' of cards' s château m de cartes

House' of Com'mons s Chambre f des communes

house' of ill' repute' s maison f mal famée, maison borgne

House' of Represen'tatives s Chambre f des Représentants

house' paint'er s peintre m en bâtiments

house' physi'cian s (in hospital) interne m; (e.g., in hotel) médecin m

house'top' s toit m; to shout from the housetops (coll) crier sur les toits

house' trail'er s caravane f

house'warm'ing s—to have a housewarming pendre la crémaillère

house'wife' s (pl -wives') maîtresse f de maison, ménagère f

house'work' s travaux mpl ménagers; to do the housework faire le ménage

housing ['hauzıŋ] s logement m, habitation f; (horsecloth) housse f; (mach) enchâssure f, carter m

hous'ing devel'opment s (houses) grand ensemble m, habitations fpl neuves; (apartments) cité f

hous'ing short'age s crise f du logement

hovel ['hʌvəl], ['hɑvəl] s bicoque f, masure f; (shed for cattle, tools, etc.) appentis m, cabane f

hover ['hʌvər], ['hʌvər] intr planer, voltiger; (to move to and fro near a person) papillonner; (to hang around threateningly) rôder; (said of smile on lips) errer; hésiter

how [hau] s comment m; the how, the when, and the wherefore (coll) tous les détails || adv comment; how + adj quel + adj, e.g., how beautiful a morning! quelle belle matinée!; comme + c'est + adj, e.g., how beautiful it is! comme c'est beau!; que + c'est + adj, e.g., how beautiful it is! que c'est beau!; how are you? comment allez-vous?, ça va?; how early quand, à quelle heure; how else de quelle autre manière; how far jusqu'où; à quelle distance, e.g., how far is it? à quelle distance est-ce?; how long (in time) jusqu'à quand, combien de temps; how long is the stick? quelle est la longueur du bâton?; how many combien; how much combien; (at what price) à combien; how often combien de fois; how old are you? quel âge avez-vous?; how soon quand, à quelle heure; to know how to savoir

how-do-you-do ['haudəjə'du] s—that's a fine how-do-you-do! (coll) en voilà une affaire!

how-ev'er adv cependant, pourtant, toutefois; however little it may be si peu que ce soit; however much or many it may be autant que ce soit; however pretty she may be quelque jolie qu'elle soit; however that may be quoi qu'il en soit || conj comme, e.g., do it however you want faites-le comme vous voudrez

howitzer ['hau-itsər] s obusier m

howl [haul] s hurlement m || tr hurler; to howl down faire taire en poussant des huées || intr hurler; (said of wind) mugir

howler ['haulər] s hurleur m; (coll) grosse gaffe f, bourde f, bévue f

hoyden ['hɔidən] s petite coquine f

H.P. or **hp** *abbr* (horsepower) CV
hub [hʌb] *s* moyeu *m*; (fig) centre *m*
hubbub [ˈhʌbəb] *s* vacarme *m*, tumulte *m*
hub/cap/ *s* enjoliveur *m*, chapeau *m* de roue
huckster [ˈhʌkstər] *s* (*peddler*) camelot *m*; (*adman*) publicitaire *mf*
huddle [ˈhʌdəl] *s* (coll) conférence *f* secrète; **to go into a huddle** (coll) entrer en conclave ‖ *intr* s'entasser, se presser
hue [hju] *s* teinte *f*, nuance *f*
hue/ and cry/ *s* clameur *f* de haro; **with hue and cry** à cor et à cri
huff [hʌf] *s* accès *m* de colère; **in a huff** vexé, offensé
hug [hʌg] *s* étreinte *f* ‖ *v* (*pret & pp* **hugged;** *ger* **hugging**) *tr* étreindre; (*e.g., the coast*) serrer; (*e.g., the wall*) raser ‖ *intr* s'étreindre
huge [hjudʒ] *adj* énorme, immense
huh [hʌ] *interj* hein!, hé!
hulk [hʌlk] *s* (*body of an old ship*) carcasse *f*; (*old ship used as warehouse, prison, etc.*) ponton *m*; (*heavy, unwieldy person*) mastodonte *m*
hull [hʌl] *s* (*of certain vegetables*) cosse *f*; (*of nuts*) écale *f*; (*of ship or hydroplane*) coque *f* ‖ *tr* (*e.g., peas*) écosser; (*e.g., almonds*) écaler
hullabaloo [ˌhʌləbəˌlu], [ˌhʌləbəˈlu] *s* (coll) boucan *m*, brouhaha *m*
hum [hʌm] *s* (*e.g., of bee*) bourdonnement *m*; (*e.g., of motor*) vrombissement *m*; (*of singer*) fredonnement *m* ‖ *v* (*pret & pp* **hummed**) *ger* **humming**) *tr* (*a melody*) fredonner, chantonner ‖ *intr* (*said of bee*) bourdonner; (*said of machine*) vrombir; (*said of singer*) fredonner, chantonner; (*to be active*) (coll) aller rondement ‖ *interj* hum!
human [ˈhjumən] *adj* humain
hu/man be/ing *s* être *m* humain
humane [hjuˈmen] *adj* humain, compatissant
humanist [ˈhjumənɪst] *adj & s* humaniste *m*
humanitarian [hjuˌmænɪˈterɪən] *adj & s* humanitaire *mf*
humani-ty [hjuˈmænɪti] *s* (*pl* **-ties**) humanité *f*; **humanities** (*Greek and Latin classics*) humanités classiques; (*belles-lettres*) humanités modernes
hu/man-kind/ *s* genre *m* humain
humble [ˈhʌmbəl], [ˈʌmbəl] *adj* humble ‖ *tr* humilier; **to humble oneself** s'humilier
hum/ble pie/ *s*—**to eat humble pie** faire amende honorable, s'humilier
hum/bug/ *s* blague *f*; (*person*) imposteur *m* ‖ *v* (*pret & pp* **-bugged;** *ger* **-bugging**) *tr* mystifier
hum/drum/ *adj* monotone, banal
humer-us [ˈhjumərəs] *s* (*pl* **-i** [ˌaɪ]) humérus *m*
humid [ˈhjumɪd] *adj* humide, moite
humidifier [hjuˈmɪdɪˌfaɪ·ər] *s* humidificateur *m*
humidi-fy [hjuˈmɪdɪˌfaɪ] *v* (*pret & pp* **-fied**) *tr* humidifier

humidity [hjuˈmɪdɪti] *s* humidité *f*
humiliate [hjuˈmɪlɪˌet] *tr* humilier
humiliating [hjuˈmɪlɪˌetɪŋ] *adj* humiliant
humili-ty [hjuˈmɪlɪti] *s* (*pl* **-ties**) humilité *f*
hum/ming-bird/ *s* oiseau-mouche *m*, colibri *m*
humor [ˈhjumər], [ˈjumər] *s* (*comic quality*) humour *m*; (*frame of mind; fluid*) humeur *f*; **out of humor** maussade, grognon; **to be in the humor to** être d'humeur à ‖ *tr* ménager, satisfaire; (*s.o.'s fancies*) se plier à, accéder à
humorist [ˈhjumərɪst], [ˈjumərɪst] *s* humoriste *mf*, comique *mf*
humorous [ˈhjumərəs], [ˈjumərəs] *adj* humoristique; (*writer*) humoriste
hump [hʌmp] *s* bosse *f*
hump/back/ *s* bossu *m*; (*whale*) mégaptère *m*
humus [ˈhjuməs] *s* humus *m*
hunch [hʌntʃ] *s* bosse *f*; (*premonition*) (coll) pressentiment *m* ‖ *tr* arrondir, voûter ‖ *intr* s'accroupir
hunch/back/ *s* bossu *m*
hundred [ˈhʌndrəd] *adj* cent ‖ *s* cent *m*, centaine *f*; **about a hundred** une centaine; **a hundred or one hundred** cent; une centaine; **by the hundreds** par centaines
hun/dred-fold/ *adj & s* centuple *m*; **to increase a hundredfold** centupler ‖ *adv* au centuple
hundredth [ˈhʌndrədθ] *adj, pron, & s* centième *m*
hun/dred-weight/ *s* quintal *m*
Hungarian [hʌŋˈgerɪ·ən] *adj* hongrois ‖ *s* (*language*) hongrois *m*; (*person*) Hongrois *m*
Hungary [ˈhʌŋgəri] *s* Hongrie *f*; la Hongrie
hunger [ˈhʌŋgər] *s* faim *f* ‖ *intr* avoir faim; **to hunger for** être affamé de
hun/ger march/ *s* marche *f* de la faim
hun/ger strike/ *s* grève *f* de la faim
hun-gry [ˈhʌŋgri] *adj* (*comp* **-grier;** *super* **-griest**) affamé; **to be hungry** avoir faim
hunk [hʌŋk] *s* gros morceau *m*
hunt [hʌnt] *s* (*act of hunting*) chasse *f*; (*hunting party*) équipage *m* de chasse; **on the hunt for** à la recherche de ‖ *tr* chasser; (*to seek, look for*) chercher; **to hunt down** donner la chasse à, traquer; **to hunt out** faire la chasse à ‖ *intr* chasser; (*with dogs*) chasser à courre; **to go hunting** aller à la chasse; **to hunt for** chercher; **to take hunting** emmener à la chasse
hunter [ˈhʌntər] *s* chasseur *m*
hunting [ˈhʌntɪŋ] *adj* de chasse ‖ *s* chasse *f*
hunt/ing dog/ *s* chien *m* de chasse
hunt/ing ground/ *s* terrain *m* de chasse, chasse *f*
hunt/ing horn/ *s* cor *m* de chasse
hunt/ing jack/et *s* paletot *m* de chasse
hunt/ing knife/ *s* couteau *m* de chasse

hunt'ing li'cense *s* permis *m* de chasse
hunt'ing lodge' *s* pavillon *m* de chasse
hunt'ing sea'son *s* saison *f* de la chasse
huntress ['hʌntrɪs] *s* chasseuse *f*
hunts'man *s* (*pl* **-men**) chasseur *m*
hurdle ['hʌrdəl] *s* (*hedge over which horses jump*) haie *f*; (*wooden frame over which runners jump*) barrière *f*; (fig) obstacle *m*; **hurdles** course *f* d'obstacles || *tr* sauter
hur'dle race' *s* course *f* d'obstacles; (turf) course de haies
hurdy-gur·dy ['hʌrdɪ‚gʌrdi] *s* (*pl* -dies) orgue *m* de Barbarie
hurl [hʌrl] *s* lancée *f* || *tr* lancer; **to hurl back** repousser, refouler
hurrah [hʌ'rɑ] *or* **hurray** [hu're] *s* hourra *m* || *intr* hourra!; **hurrah for . . . !** vive . . . !
hurricane ['hʌrɪ‚ken] *s* ouragan *m*, hurricane *m*
hurried ['hʌrɪd] *adj* pressé, précipité; (hasty) hâtif, fait à la hâte
hur·ry ['hʌri] *s* (*pl* -ries) hâte *f*; **to be in a hurry** être pressé || *v* (*pret & pp* -ried) *tr* hâter, presser || *intr* se hâter, se presser; **to hurry after** courir après; **to hurry away** s'en aller bien vite; **to hurry back** revenir vite; **to hurry over** venir vite; **to hurry up** se dépêcher
hurt [hʌrt] *adj* blessé || *s* blessure *f*; (pain) douleur *f* || *v* (*pret & pp* **hurt**) *tr* faire mal à || *intr* faire mal, e.g., **does that hurt?** ça fait mal?; avoir mal, e.g., **my head hurts** j'ai mal à la tête
hurtful ['hʌrtfəl] *adj* nuisible
hurtle ['hʌrtəl] *intr* se précipiter
husband ['hʌzbənd] *s* mari *m*, époux *m* || *tr* ménager, économiser
hus'band·man *s* (*pl* -men) cultivateur *m*
husbandry ['hʌzbəndri] *s* agriculture *f*; (raising of livestock) élevage *m*
hush [hʌʃ] *s* silence *m*, calme *m* || *tr* faire taire; **to hush up** (e.g., *a scandal*) étouffer || *intr* se taire || *interj* chut!
hushaby ['hʌʃə‚baɪ] *interj* fais dodo!
hush'-hush' *adj* très secret
hush' mon'ey *s* prix *m* du silence
husk [hʌsk] *s* peau *f*; (*of certain vegetables*) cosse *f*, gousse *f*; (*of nuts*) écale *f*; (*of corn*) enveloppe *f*; (*of oats*) balle *f*; (*of onion*) pelure *f* || *tr* (grain) vanner; (vegetables) éplucher; (peas) écosser; (nuts) écaler
husk'ing bee' *s* réunion *f* pour l'épluchage du maïs
husk·y ['hʌski] *adj* (*comp* **-ier**; *super* **-iest**) costaud; (*voice*) enroué || *s* (*pl* -ies) (dog) chien *m* esquimau
hus·sy ['hʌzi], ['hʌsi] *s* (*pl* -sies) (coll) garce *f*; (coll) coquine *f*
hustle ['hʌsəl] *s* (coll) bousculade *f*, énergie *f*, allant *m* || *tr* pousser, bousculer || *intr* se dépêcher, se presser; (*to work hard*) (coll) se démener, s'activer
hustler ['hʌslər] *s* (*go-getter*) homme *m* d'action; (*swindler*) (slang) filou

hut [hʌt] *s* hutte *f*, cabane *f*; (mil) baraque *f*
hutch [hʌtʃ] *s* (*for rabbits*) clapier *m*; (*used by baker*) huche *f*, pétrin *m*
hyacinth ['haɪ·əsɪnθ] *s* (*stone*) hyacinthe *f*; (*flower*) jacinthe *f*
hybrid ['haɪbrɪd] *adj & s* hybride *m*
hy·dra ['haɪdrə] *s* (*pl* -dras or -drae [dri]) hydre *f*
hydrant ['haɪdrənt] *s* prise *f* d'eau; (faucet) robinet *m*; (fire hydrant) bouche *f* d'incendie
hydrate ['haɪdret] *s* hydrate *m* || *tr* hydrater || *intr* s'hydrater
hydraulic [haɪ'drɔlɪk] *adj* hydraulique || **hydraulics** *s* hydraulique *f*
hydrau'lic ram' *s* bélier *m* hydraulique
hydrocarbon [‚haɪdrə'kɑrbən] *s* hydrocarbure *m*
hy'drochlo'ric ac'id [‚haɪdrə'klorɪk] *s* acide *m* chlorhydrique
hydroelectric [‚haɪdro·ɪ'lektrɪk] *adj* hydro-électrique
hydrofoil ['haɪdrə‚fɔɪl] *s* hydrofoil *m*
hydrogen ['haɪdrədʒən] *s* hydrogène *m*
hy'drogen bomb' *s* bombe *f* à hydrogène
hy'drogen perox'ide *s* eau *f* oxygénée
hy'drogen sul'fide *s* hydrogène *m* sulfuré
hydrometer [haɪ'drɑmɪtər] *s* aréomètre *m*, hydromètre *m*
hydrophobia [‚haɪdrə'fobɪ·ə] *s* hydrophobie *f*
hydroplane ['haɪdrə‚plen] *s* hydravion *m*
hydroxide [haɪ'drɑksaɪd] *s* hydroxyde *m*
hyena [haɪ'inə] *s* hyène *f*
hygiene ['haɪdʒin], ['haɪdʒɪ‚in] *s* hygiène *f*
hygienic [‚haɪdʒɪ'enɪk], [haɪ'dʒinɪk] *adj* hygiénique
hymn [hɪm] *s* hymne *m*; (eccl) hymne *f*, cantique *m*
hymnal ['hɪmnəl] *s* livre *m* d'hymnes
hyperacidity [‚haɪpər·ə'sɪdɪti] *s* hyperacidité *f*
hyperbola [haɪ'pʌrbələ] *s* hyperbole *f*
hyperbole [haɪ'pʌrbəli] *s* hyperbole *f*
hypersensitive [‚haɪpər'sensɪtɪv] *adj* hypersensible, hypersensitif
hypertension [‚haɪpər'tenʃən] *s* hypertension *f*
hyphen ['haɪfən] *s* trait *m* d'union
hyphenate ['haɪfə‚net] *tr* joindre avec un trait d'union
hypno·sis [hɪp'nosɪs] *s* (*pl* -ses [siz]) hypnose *f*
hypnotic [hɪp'nɑtɪk] *adj & s* hypnotique *m*
hypnotism ['hɪpnə‚tɪzəm] *s* hypnotisme *m*
hypnotist ['hɪpnətɪst] *s* hypnotiseur *m*
hypnotize ['hɪpnə‚taɪz] *tr* hypnotiser
hypochondriac [‚haɪpə'kɑndrɪ‚æk], [‚haɪpə'kʌndrɪ‚æk] *adj & s* hypocondriaque *mf*

hypocri·sy [hɪˈpɑkrəsi] s (pl **-sies**) hypocrisie f

hypocrite [ˈhɪpəkrɪt] s hypocrite mf

hypocritical [ˌhɪpəˈkrɪtɪkəl] adj hypocrite

hypodermic [ˌhaɪpəˈdʌrmɪk] adj hypodermique

hyposulfite [ˌhaɪpəˈsʌlfaɪt] s hyposulfite m

hypotenuse [haɪˈpɑtɪˌn(j)us] s hypoténuse f

hypothe·sis [haɪˈpɑθɪsɪs] s (pl **-ses** [ˌsiz]) hypothèse f

hypothetic(al) [ˌhaɪpəˈθɛtɪk(əl)] adj hypothétique

hysteria [hɪsˈtɪrɪ·ə] s agitation f, frénésie f; (pathol) hystérie f

hysteric [hɪsˈtɛrɪk] adj hystérique ‖ **hysterics** spl crise f de nerfs, crise de larmes, fou rire m

hysterical [hɪsˈtɛrɪkəl] adj hystérique

I

I, i [aɪ] s IXᵉ lettre de l'alphabet

I pron je §87; moi §85

iambic [aɪˈæmbɪk] adj ïambique

Iberian [aɪˈbɪrɪ·ən] adj ibérien, ibérique ‖ s Ibérien m

ibex [ˈaɪbɛks] s (pl **ibexes** or **ibices** [ˈɪbɪˌsiz]) bouquetin m

ice [aɪs] s glace f; **to break the ice** (fig) rompre la glace; **to cut no ice** (coll) ne rien casser, ne pas prendre; **to skate on thin ice** (coll) s'engager sur un terrain dangereux ‖ tr glacer; (e.g., champagne) frapper; (e.g., melon) rafraîchir ‖ intr geler; **to ice up** (said of windshield, airplane wings, etc.) se givrer

ice′ age′ s époque f glaciaire

ice′ bag′ s sac m à glace

ice′ bank′ s banquise f

iceberg [ˈaɪsˌbʌrg] s banquise f, iceberg m; (person) (coll) glaçon m

ice′boat′ s (icebreaker) brise-glace m; (for sport) bateau m à patins

icebound [ˈaɪsˌbaʊnd] adj pris dans les glaces

ice′box′ s glacière f

ice′break′er s brise-glace m

ice′cap′ s calotte f glaciaire

ice′ cream′ s glace f

ice′-cream′ cone′ s cornet m de glace, glace f en cornet

ice′-cream′ freez′er s sorbetière f

ice′ cube′ s glaçon m

ice′-cube′ tray′ s bac m à glaçons

iced′ tea′ s thé m glacé

ice′ floe′ s banquise f

ice′ hock′ey s hockey m sur glace

ice′ jam′ s embâcle m

Iceland [ˈaɪslənd] s Islande f; l'Islande

Icelander [ˈaɪsˌlændər], [ˈaɪsləndər] s Islandais m

Icelandic [aɪsˈlændɪk] adj & s islandais m

ice′man′ s (pl **-men′**) glacier m

ice′ pack′ s (pack ice) embâcle m; (med) vessie f de glace

ice′ pail′ s seau m à glace

ice′ pick′ s poinçon m à glace; (of mountain climber) piolet m

ice′ skate′ s patin m à glace

ice′ wa′ter s eau f glacée f

ichthyology [ˌɪkθɪˈɑlədʒi] s ichtyologie f

icicle [ˈaɪsɪkəl] s glaçon m, chandelle f de glace

icing [ˈaɪsɪŋ] s (on cake) glaçage m; (aer) givrage m

icon [ˈaɪkɑn] s icône f

iconoclast [aɪˈkɑnəˌklæst] s iconoclaste m

iconoclastic [aɪˌkɑnəˈklæstɪk] adj iconoclaste

iconoscope [aɪˈkɑnəˌskop] s (trademark) iconoscope m

icy [ˈaɪsi] adj (comp **icier**; super **iciest**) glacé; (slippery) glissant; (fig) froid, glacial

idea [aɪˈdi·ə] s idée f; **the very idea!** par exemple!

ideal [aɪˈdi·əl] adj & s idéal m

idealist [aɪˈdi·əlɪst] adj & s idéaliste mf

idealistic [aɪˌdi·əlˈɪstɪk] adj idéaliste

idealize [aɪˈdi·əˌlaɪz] tr idéaliser

identic(al) [aɪˈdɛntɪk(əl)] adj identique

identification [aɪˌdɛntɪfɪˈkeʃən] s identification f

identifica′tion card′ s carte f d'identité

identifica′tion tag′ s plaque f d'identité

identi·fy [aɪˈdɛntɪˌfaɪ] v (pret & pp **-fied**) tr identifier

identi·ty [aɪˈdɛntiti] s (pl **-ties**) identité f

ideolo·gy [ˌaɪdɪˈɑlədʒi], [ˌɪdɪˈɑlədʒi] s (pl **-gies**) idéologie f

ides [aɪdz] spl ides fpl

idio·cy [ˈɪdɪ·əsi] s (pl **-cies**) idiotie f

idiom [ˈɪdɪ·əm] s (phrase, expression) idiotisme m; (language, style) idiome m

idiomatic [ˌɪdɪ·əˈmætɪk] adj idiomatique

idiosyncra·sy [ˌɪdɪ·əˈsɪŋkrəsi] s (pl **-sies**) idiosyncrasie f

idiot [ˈɪdɪ·ət] s idiot m

idiotic [ˌɪdɪˈɑtɪk] adj idiot

idle [ˈaɪdəl] adj oisif, désœuvré; (futile) oiseux; **to run idle** marcher au ralenti ‖ tr—**to idle away** (time) passer à ne rien faire ‖ intr fainéanter; (mach) tourner au ralenti

idleness [ˈaɪdəlnɪs] s oisiveté f

idler [ˈaɪdlər] s oisif m

idling [ˈaɪdlɪŋ] s (of motor) ralenti m

idol ['aɪdəl] *s* idole *f*
idola·try [aɪ'dɑlətri] *s* (*pl* -tries) idolâtrie *f*
idolize ['aɪdə,laɪz] *tr* idolâtrer
idyll ['aɪdəl] *s* idylle *f*
idyllic [aɪ'dɪlɪk] *adj* idyllique
if [ɪf] *s*—**ifs and buts** des si et des mais || *conj* si; **even if** quand même; **if it is true that** si tant est que; **if not** sinon; **if so** dans ce cas, s'il en est ainsi
ignis fatuus ['ɪgnɪs'fæt/ʊ·əs] *s* (*pl* **ignes fatui** ['ɪgniz'fæt/ʊ,aɪ]) feu *m* follet
ignite [ɪg'naɪt] *tr* allumer || *intr* prendre feu
ignition [ɪg'nɪʃən] *s* ignition *f*; (aut) allumage *m*
igni'tion coil' *s* (aut) bobine *f* d'allumage
igni'tion switch' *s* (key) (aut) clé *f* de contact; (button) (aut) bouton *m* de contact
ignoble [ɪg'nobəl] *adj* ignoble
ignominious [,ɪgnə'mɪnɪ·əs] *adj* ignominieux
ignoramus [,ɪgnə'reməs] *s* ignorant *m*
ignorance ['ɪgnərəns] *s* ignorance *f*
ignorant ['ɪgnərənt] *adj* ignorant; **to be ignorant of** ignorer
ignore [ɪg'nor] *tr* ne pas tenir compte de, ne pas faire attention à; (a suggestion) passer outre à; (to snub) faire semblant de ne pas voir, ignorer à dessein
ilk [ɪlk] *s* espèce *f*; **of that ilk** de cet acabit
ill [ɪl] *adj* (comp **worse** [wʌrs]; super **worst** [wʌrst]) malade, souffrant || *adv* mal; **to take ill** prendre en mauvaise part; (to get sick) tomber malade
ill'-advised' *adj* (person) malavisé; (action) peu judicieux
ill' at ease' *adj* mal à l'aise
ill-bred ['ɪl'bred] *adj* mal élevé
ill'-consid'ered *adj* peu réfléchi, hâtif
ill'-disposed' *adj* mal disposé, malintentionné
illegal [ɪ'ligəl] *adj* illégal
illegible [ɪ'ledʒɪbəl] *adj* illisible
illegitimate [,ɪlɪ'dʒɪtɪmɪt] *adj* illégitime
ill'-famed' *adj* mal famé
ill'-fat'ed *adj* malheureux, infortuné
ill-gotten ['ɪl'gɑtən] *adj* mal acquis
ill' health' *s* mauvaise santé *f*
ill'-hu'mored *adj* de mauvaise humeur, maussade
illicit [ɪ'lɪsɪt] *adj* illicite
illitera·cy [ɪ'lɪtərəsi] *s* (*pl* -cies) ignorance *f*; analphabétisme *m*
illiterate [ɪ'lɪtərɪt] *adj* (uneducated) ignorant, illettré; (unable to read or write) analphabète || *s* analphabète *mf*
ill'-man'nered *adj* malappris, mal élevé
ill'-na'tured *adj* désagréable, méchant
illness ['ɪlnɪs] *s* maladie *f*
illogical [ɪ'lɑdʒɪkəl] *adj* illogique
ill-spent ['ɪl'spent] *adj* gaspillé
ill'-starred' *adj* néfaste, de mauvais augure

ill'-tem'pered *adj* désagréable, de mauvais caractère
ill'-timed' *adj* intempestif, mal à propos
ill'-treat' *tr* maltraiter, rudoyer
illuminate [ɪ'lumɪ,net] *tr* illuminer; (a manuscript) enluminer
illu'minating gas' *s* gaz *m* d'éclairage
illumination [ɪ'lumɪ'neʃən] *s* illumination *f*; (in manuscript) enluminure *f*
illusion [ɪ'luʒən] *s* illusion *f*
illusive [ɪ'lusɪv] *adj* illusoire, trompeur
illusory [ɪ'lusəri] *adj* illusoire
illustrate ['ɪləs,tret], [ɪ'lʌstret] *tr* illustrer
illustration *s* [,ɪləs'treʃən] *s* illustration *f*; (explanation) explication *f*, éclaircissement *m*
illustrative [ɪ'lʌstrətɪv] *adj* explicatif, éclairant
illustrator ['ɪləs,tretər] *s* illustrateur *m*, dessinateur *m*
illustrious [ɪ'lʌstrɪ·əs] *adj* illustre
ill' will' *s* rancune *f*
image ['ɪmɪdʒ] *s* image *f*
image·ry ['ɪmɪdʒri], ['ɪmɪdʒəri] *s* (*pl* -ries) images *fpl*
imaginary [ɪ'mædʒɪ,neri] *adj* imaginaire
imagination [ɪ,mædʒɪ'neʃən] *s* imagination *f*
imagine [ɪ'mædʒɪn] *tr* imaginer, s'imaginer || *intr* imaginer; **imagine!** figurez-vous!
imbecile ['ɪmbɪsɪl] *adj & s* imbécile *mf*
imbecil·ity [,ɪmbɪ'sɪlɪti] *s* (*pl* -ties) imbécillité *f*
imbibe [ɪm'baɪb] *tr* absorber || *intr* boire, lever le coude
imbue [ɪm'bju] *tr* imprégner, pénétrer; **imbued with** imbu de
imitate ['ɪmɪ,tet] *tr* imiter
imitation [,ɪmɪ'teʃən] *adj* d'imitation || *s* imitation *f*
imitator ['ɪmɪ,tetər] *s* imitateur *m*
immaculate [ɪ'mækjəlɪt] *adj* immaculé
immaterial [,ɪmə'tɪrɪ·əl] *adj* immatériel; (pointless) sans conséquence; **it's immaterial to me** cela m'est égal
immature [,ɪmə'tjur] *adj* pas mûr, peu mûr; pas adulte
immeasurable [ɪ'meʒərəbəl] *adj* immensurable
immediacy [ɪ'midɪ·əsi] *s* caractère *m* immédiat, imminence *f*
immediate [ɪ'midɪ·ɪt] *adj* immédiat
immediately [ɪ'midɪ·ɪtli] *adv* immédiatement
immemorial [,ɪmɪ'morɪ·əl] *adj* immémorial
immense [ɪ'mens] *adj* immense
immerse [ɪ'mʌrs] *tr* immerger, plonger
immersion [ɪ'mʌrʃən], [ɪ'mʌrʒən] *s* immersion *f*
immigrant ['ɪmɪgrənt] *adj & s* immigrant *m*
immigrate ['ɪmɪ,gret] *intr* immigrer
immigration [,ɪmɪ'greʃən] *s* immigration *f*
imminent ['ɪmɪnənt] *adj* imminent, très prochain

immobile [ɪˈmobɪl], [ɪˈmobɪl] *adj* immobile

immobilize [ɪˈmobɪˌlaɪz] *tr* immobiliser

immoderate [ɪˈmadərɪt] *adj* immodéré

immodest [ɪˈmadɪst] *adj* impudique

immoral [ɪˈmarəl], [ɪˈmorəl] *adj* immoral

immortal [ɪˈmortəl] *adj & s* immortel *m*

immortalize [ɪˈmortəˌlaɪz] *tr* immortaliser

immune [ɪˈmjun] *adj* dispensé, exempt; (med) immunisé

immunize [ˈɪmjəˌnaɪz], [ɪˈmjunaɪz] *tr* immuniser

imp [ɪmp] *s* suppôt *m* du diable; (child) diablotin *m*, polisson *m*

impact [ˈɪmpækt] *s* impact *m*

impair [ɪmˈper] *tr* endommager, affaiblir; (health, digestion) délabrer

impan•el [ɪmˈpænəl] *v* (pret & pp -eled or -elled; ger -eling or -elling) *tr* appeler à faire partie de; (a jury) dresser la liste de

impart [ɪmˈpart] *tr* imprimer, communiquer; (to make known) communiquer

impartial [ɪmˈparʃəl] *adj* impartial

impassable [ɪmˈpæsəbəl], [ɪmˈpasəbəl] *adj* (road) impraticable; (mountain) infranchissable

impassible [ɪmˈpæsɪbəl] *adj* impassible

impassioned [ɪmˈpæʃənd] *adj* passionné

impassive [ɪmˈpæsɪv] *adj* insensible; (look, face) impassible, composé

impatience [ɪmˈpeʃəns] *s* impatience *f*

impatient [ɪmˈpeʃənt] *adj* impatient

impeach [ɪmˈpitʃ] *tr* accuser; (s.o.'s honor, veracity) attaquer

impeachment [ɪmˈpitʃmənt] *s* accusation *f*; (of honor, veracity) attaque *f*

impeccable [ɪmˈpekəbəl] *adj* impeccable

impecunious [ˌɪmpɪˈkjunɪəs] *adj* besogneux, impécunieux

impede [ɪmˈpid] *tr* entraver, empêcher

impediment [ɪmˈpedɪmənt] *s* obstacle *m*, empêchement *m*

im•pel [ɪmˈpel] *v* (pret & pp -pelled; ger -pelling) *tr* pousser, forcer

impending [ɪmˈpendɪŋ] *adj* imminent

impenetrable [ɪmˈpenətrəbəl] *adj* impénétrable

impenitent [ɪmˈpenɪtənt] *adj* impénitent *m*

imperative [ɪmˈperɪtɪv] *adj & s* impératif *m*

imperceptible [ˌɪmpərˈseptɪbəl] *adj* imperceptible

imperfect [ɪmˈpʌrfɪkt] *adj & s* imparfait *m*

imperfection [ˌɪmpərˈfekʃən] *s* imperfection *f*

imperial [ɪmˈpɪrɪəl] *adj* impérial

imperialist [ɪmˈpɪrɪəlɪst] *adj & s* impérialiste *mf*

imper•il [ɪmˈperɪl] *v* (pret & pp -iled or -illed; ger -iling or -illing) *tr* mettre en péril, exposer au danger

imperious [ɪmˈpɪrɪəs] *adj* impérieux

imperishable [ɪmˈperɪʃəbəl] *adj* impérissable

impersonal [ɪmˈpʌrsənəl] *adj* impersonnel

impersonate [ɪmˈpʌrsəˌnet] *tr* contrefaire, singer; jouer le rôle de

impertinent [ɪmˈpʌrtɪnənt] *adj* impertinent

impetuous [ɪmˈpetʃuˈəs] *adj* impétueux

impetus [ˈɪmpɪtəs] *s* impulsion *f*; (mech) force *f* impulsive; (fig) élan *m*

impie•ty [ɪmˈpaɪˈəti] *s* (pl -ties) impiété *f*

impinge [ɪmˈpɪndʒ] *intr*—to impinge on or upon empiéter sur; (to violate) enfreindre

impious [ˈɪmpɪˈəs] *adj* impie

impish [ˈɪmpɪʃ] *adj* espiègle

implant [ɪmˈplænt] *tr* implanter

implement [ˈɪmplɪmənt] *s* outil *m*, ustensile *m* ‖ *tr* mettre en œuvre, réaliser; (to provide with implements) outiller

implicate [ˈɪmplɪˌket] *tr* impliquer

implicit [ɪmˈplɪsɪt] *adj* implicite

implied [ɪmˈplaɪd] *adj* implicite, sous-entendu

implore [ɪmˈplor] *tr* implorer, supplier, solliciter

im•ply [ɪmˈplaɪ] *v* (pret & pp -plied) *tr* impliquer

impolite [ˌɪmpəˈlaɪt] *adj* impoli

import [ˈɪmport] *s* importance *f*; (meaning) sens *m*, signification *f*; (extent) portée *f*; (com) article *m* d'importation; imports importations *fpl* ‖ [ɪmˈport], [ˈɪmport] *tr* importer; (to mean) signifier, vouloir dire

importance [ɪmˈportəns] *s* importance *f*

important [ɪmˈportənt] *adj* important

importer [ɪmˈportər] *s* importateur *m*

importune [ˌɪmˈportˈt(j)un] *tr* importuner, harceler

impose [ɪmˈpoz] *tr* imposer ‖ *intr*—to impose on or upon en imposer à, abuser de

imposing [ɪmˈpozɪŋ] *adj* imposant

imposition [ˌɪmpəˈzɪʃən] *s* (laying on of a burden or obligation) imposition *f*; (rudeness, taking unfair advantage) abus *m*

impossible [ɪmˈpasɪbəl] *adj* impossible

impostor [ɪmˈpastər] *s* imposteur *m*

imposture [ɪmˈpastjər] *s* imposture *f*

impotence [ˈɪmpətəns] *s* impuissance *f*

impotent [ˈɪmpətənt] *adj* impuissant

impound [ɪmˈpaund] *tr* confisquer, saisir; (a dog, an auto, etc.) mettre en fourrière

impoverish [ɪmˈpavərɪʃ] *tr* appauvrir

impracticable [ɪmˈpræktɪkəbəl] *adj* impraticable, inexécutable

impractical [ɪmˈpræktɪkəl] *adj* peu pratique; (plan) impraticable

impregnable [ɪmˈpregnəbəl] *adj* imprenable, inexpugnable

impregnate [ɪmˈpregnet] *tr* imprégner; (to make pregnant) féconder

impresari•o [ˌɪmprɪˈsarɪˌo] *s* (pl -os) imprésario *m*

impress [ɪmˈpres] *tr* (to have an effect

on the mind or emotions of) impressionner; (to mark by using pressure) imprimer; (on the memory) graver; (mil) enrôler de force; **to impress s.o. with** pénétrer qn de

impression [ɪmˈprɛʃən] s impression f

impressive [ɪmˈprɛsɪv] adj impressionnant

imprint [ˈɪmprɪnt] s empreinte f; (typ) rubrique f, griffe f ‖ [ɪmˈprɪnt] tr imprimer

imprison [ɪmˈprɪzən] tr emprisonner

imprisonment [ɪmˈprɪzənmənt] s emprisonnement m

improbable [ɪmˈprɑbəbəl] adj improbable

impromptu [ɪmˈprɑmpt(j)u] adj & adv impromptu ‖ s (mus) impromptu m

impromp'tu speech' s improvisation f, discours m improvisé

improper [ɪmˈprɑpər] adj (not the right) impropre; (contrary to good taste or decency) inconvenant

improve [ɪmˈpruv] tr améliorer, perfectionner ‖ intr s'améliorer, se perfectionner

improvement [ɪmˈpruvmənt] s amélioration f, perfectionnement m

improvident [ɪmˈprɑvɪdənt] adj imprévoyant

improvise [ˈɪmprəˌvaɪz] tr & intr improviser

imprudent [ɪmˈprudənt] adj imprudent

impudent [ˈɪmpjədənt] adj impudent, effronté

impugn [ɪmˈpjun] tr contester, mettre en doute

impulse [ˈɪmpʌls] s impulsion f

impulsive [ɪmˈpʌlsɪv] adj impulsif

impunity [ɪmˈpjunɪti] s impunité f

impure [ɪmˈpjʊr] adj impur

impuri·ty [ɪmˈpjʊrɪti] s (pl -ties) impureté f

impute [ɪmˈpjut] tr imputer

in [ɪn] adv en dedans, à l'intérieur; (at home) à la maison, chez soi; (pol) au pouvoir; **all in** (tired) (coll) éreinté; **in here** ici, par ici; **in there** là-dedans, là ‖ prep dans; en; (inside) en dedans de, à l'intérieur de; (in ratios) sur, e.g., **one in a hundred** un sur cent; **in that** du fait que ‖ s (coll) entrée f, e.g., **to have an in with** avoir ses entrées chez

inability [ˌɪnəˈbɪlɪti] s incapacité f, impuissance f

inaccessible [ˌɪnækˈsɛsɪbəl] adj inaccessible

inaccura·cy [ɪnˈækjərəsi] s (pl -cies) inexactitude f, infidélité f

inaccurate [ɪnˈækjərɪt] adj inexact, infidèle

inaction [ɪnˈækʃən] s inaction f

inactive [ɪnˈæktɪv] adj inactif

inactivity [ˌɪnækˈtɪvɪti] s inactivité f

inadequate [ɪnˈædɪkwɪt] adj insuffisant

inadvertent [ˌɪnədˈvɑrtənt] adj distrait, étourdi; commis par inadvertance

inadvisable [ˌɪnədˈvaɪzəbəl] adj imprudent, peu sage

inane [ɪnˈen] adj inepte, absurde

inanimate [ɪnˈænɪmɪt] adj inanimé

inappropriate [ˌɪnəˈproprɪˌɪt] adj inapproprié; (word) impropre

inarticulate [ˌɪnɑrˈtɪkjəlɪt] adj inarticulé; (person) muet, incapable de s'exprimer

inartistic [ˌɪnɑrˈtɪstɪk] adj peu artistique; (person) peu artiste

inasmuch as [ˌɪnəzˈmʌtʃ ˌæz] conj attendu que, vu que

inattentive [ˌɪnəˈtɛntɪv] adj inattentif

inaudible [ɪnˈɔdɪbəl] adj inaudible

inaugural [ɪnˈɔgjərəl] adj inaugural ‖ s discours m d'inauguration

inaugurate [ɪnˈɔgjəˌret] tr inaugurer

inauguration [ɪnˌɔgjəˈreʃən] s inauguration f; (investiture) installation f

inborn [ˈɪnˌbɔrn] adj inné, infus

in/breed'ing s croisement m consanguin

Inc. abbr (Incorporated) S.A.

incandescent [ˌɪnkənˈdɛsənt] adj incandescent

incapable [ɪnˈkepəbəl] adj incapable

incapacitate [ˌɪnkəˈpæsɪˌtet] tr rendre incapable

incarcerate [ɪnˈkɑrsəˌret] tr incarcérer

incarnate [ɪnˈkɑrnɪt], [ɪnˈkɑrnet] adj incarné ‖ [ɪnˈkɑrnet] tr incarner

incarnation [ˌɪnkɑrˈneʃən] s incarnation f

incendiar·y [ɪnˈsɛndɪˌɛri] adj incendiaire ‖ s (pl -ies) incendiaire mf

incense [ˈɪnsɛns] s encens m ‖ tr (to burn incense before) encenser ‖ [ɪnˈsɛns] tr exaspérer, irriter

in/cense burn'er s brûle-parfum m

incentive [ɪnˈsɛntɪv] adj & s stimulant m

inception [ɪnˈsɛpʃən] s début m

incessant [ɪnˈsɛsənt] adj incessant

incest [ˈɪnsɛst] s inceste m

incestuous [ɪnˈsɛstʃʊˌəs] adj incestueux

inch [ɪntʃ] s pouce m; **by inches** peu à peu, petit à petit; **not to give way an inch** ne pas reculer d'une semelle; **within an inch of** à deux doigts de ‖ intr—**to inch along** se déplacer imperceptiblement; **to inch forward** avancer peu à peu

incidence [ˈɪnsɪdəns] s incidence f; (range of occurrence) portée f

incident [ˈɪnsɪdənt] adj & s incident m

incidental [ˌɪnsɪˈdɛntəl] adj accidental, fortuit; (expenses) accessoire ‖ **incidentals** spl faux frais mpl

incidentally [ˌɪnsɪˈdɛntəli] adv incidemment, à propos

incinerate [ɪnˈsɪnəˌret] tr incinérer

incipient [ɪnˈsɪpɪənt] adj naissant

incision [ɪnˈsɪʒən] s incision f

incisive [ɪnˈsaɪsɪv] adj incisif

incisor [ɪnˈsaɪzər] s incisive f

incite [ɪnˈsaɪt] tr inciter

inclement [ɪnˈklɛmənt] adj inclément

inclination [ˌɪnklɪˈneʃən] s inclination f; (slope) inclinaison f

incline [ˈɪnklaɪn], [ɪnˈklaɪn] s inclinaison f, pente f ‖ [ɪnˈklaɪn] tr incliner ‖ intr s'incliner

include [ɪnˈklud] tr comprendre, comporter; (to contain) renfermer; (e.g., in a letter) inclure

including [ɪnˈkludɪŋ] prep y compris;

up to and including page ten jusqu'à la page dix incluse

inclusive [ɪnˈklusɪv] *adj* global; (*including everything*) tout compris; **from Wednesday to Saturday inclusive** de mercredi à samedi inclus; **inclusive of . . .** qui comprend . . . ‖ *adv* inclusivement

incogni·to [ɪnˈkɑgnɪˌto] *adj* & *adv* incognito ‖ *s* (*pl -tos*) incognito *m*

incoherent [ˌɪnkoˈhɪrənt] *adj* incohérent

incombustible [ˌɪnkəmˈbʌstɪbəl] *adj* incombustible

income [ˈɪnkʌm] *s* revenu *m*, revenus; (*annual income*) rentes *fpl*

in′come tax′ *s* impôt *m* sur le revenu

in′come-tax return′ *s* déclaration *f* de revenus

in′com′ing *adj* entrant, rentrant; (*tide*) montant ‖ *s* arrivée *f*

incomparable [ɪnˈkɑmpərəbəl] *adj* incomparable

incompatible [ˌɪnkəmˈpætɪbəl] *adj* incompatible

incompetent [ɪnˈkɑmpɪtənt] *adj* & *s* incompétent *m*, incapable *mf*

incomplete [ˌɪnkəmˈplɪt] *adj* incomplet

incomprehensible [ˌɪnkɑmprɪˈhensɪbəl] *adj* incompréhensible

inconceivable [ˌɪnkənˈsivəbəl] *adj* inconcevable

inconclusive [ˌɪnkənˈklusɪv] *adj* peu concluant, non concluant

incongruous [ɪnˈkɑngruˌəs] *adj* incongru, impropre; disparate

inconsequential [ɪnˌkɑnsɪˈkwenʃəl] *adj* sans importance

inconsiderate [ˌɪnkənˈsɪdərɪt] *adj* inconsidéré

inconsisten·cy [ˌɪnkənˈsɪstənsi] *s* (*pl -cies*) (*lack of coherence; instability*) inconsistance *f*; (*lack of logical connection or uniformity*) inconséquence *f*

inconsistent [ˌɪnkənˈsɪstənt] *adj* (*lacking coherence of parts; unstable*) inconsistant; (*not agreeing with itself or oneself*) inconséquent

inconspicuous [ˌɪnkənˈspɪkjuˌəs] *adj* peu apparent; peu impressionnant

inconstant [ɪnˈkɑnstənt] *adj* inconstant

incontinent [ɪnˈkɑntɪnənt] *adj* incontinent

incontrovertible [ˌɪnkɑntrəˈvʌrtɪbəl] *adj* incontestable

inconvenience [ˌɪnkənˈvinɪˌəns] *s* incommodité ‖ *tr* incommoder, gêner

inconvenient [ˌɪnkənˈvinɪˌənt] *adj* incommode, gênant; (*time*) inopportun

incorporate [ɪnˈkɔrpəˌret] *tr* incorporer; (com) constituer en société anonyme ‖ *intr* s'incorporer; (com) se constituer en société anonyme

incorporation [ɪnˌkɔrpəˈreʃən] *s* incorporation *f*; (*of company*) constitution *f* en société anonyme; (*of town*) érection *f* en municipalité

incorrect [ˌɪnkəˈrekt] *adj* incorrect

increase [ˈɪnkris] *s* augmentation *f*; **on the increase** en voie d'accroissement ‖ [ɪnˈkris] *tr* & *intr* augmenter

increasingly [ɪnˈkrisɪŋli] *adv* de plus en plus

incredible [ɪnˈkredɪbəl] *adj* incroyable

incredulous [ɪnˈkredʒələs] *adj* incrédule

increment [ˈɪnkrɪmənt] *s* augmentation *f*

incriminate [ɪnˈkrɪmɪˌnet] *tr* incriminer

incrust [ɪnˈkrʌst] *tr* incruster

incubate [ˈɪnkjəˌbet] *tr* incuber, couver ‖ *intr* couver

incubator [ˈɪnkjəˌbetər] *s* incubateur *m*

inculcate [ɪnˈkʌlket], [ˈɪnkʌlˌket] *tr* inculquer

incumben·cy [ɪnˈkʌmbənsi] *s* (*pl -cies*) charge *f*; période *f* d'exercice

incumbent [ɪnˈkʌmbənt] *adj*—**to be incumbent on** incomber (with *dat*) ‖ *m* titulaire *mf*

incunabula [ˌɪnkjuˈnæbjələ] *spl* origines *fpl*; (*books*) incunables *mpl*

in·cur [ɪnˈkʌr] *v* (*pret* & *pp* **-curred**; *ger* **-curring**) *tr* encourir, s'attirer; (*debt*) contracter

incurable [ɪnˈkjurəbəl] *adj* & *s* incurable *mf*, inguérissable *mf*

incursion [ɪnˈkʌrʒən], [ɪnˈkʌrʃən] *s* incursion *f*

indebted [ɪnˈdetɪd] *adj* endetté; **indebted to s.o. for** redevable à qn de

indecen·cy [ɪnˈdisənsi] *s* (*pl -cies*) indécence *f*, impudeur *f*

indecent [ɪnˈdisənt] *adj* indécent, impudique

inde′cent expo′sure *s* attentat *m* à la pudeur

indecisive [ˌɪndɪˈsaɪsɪv] *adj* indécis

indeclinable [ˌɪndɪˈklaɪnəbəl] *adj* (grám) indéclinable

indeed [ɪnˈdid] *adv* en effet; (*truly*) en vérité ‖ *interj* vraiment!

indefatigable [ˌɪndɪˈfætɪgəbəl] *adj* infatigable

indefensible [ˌɪndɪˈfensɪbəl] *adj* indéfendable

indefinable [ˌɪndɪˈfaɪnəbəl] *adj* indéfinissable

indefinite [ɪnˈdefɪnɪt] *adj* indéfini

indelible [ɪnˈdelɪbəl] *adj* indélébile

indelicate [ɪnˈdelɪkɪt] *adj* indélicat

indemnification [ɪnˌdemnɪfɪˈkeʃən] *s* indemnisation *f*

indemni·fy [ɪnˈdemnɪˌfaɪ] *v* (*pret* & *pp* **-fied**) *tr* indemniser

indemni·ty [ɪnˈdemnɪti] *s* (*pl -ties*) indemnité *f*

indent [ɪnˈdent] *tr* denteler; (*to recess*) renfoncer; (typ) mettre en alinéa, rentrer ‖ *intr* (typ) faire un alinéa

indentation [ˌɪndenˈteʃən] *s* dentelure *f*; (*notch*) entaille *f*; (*recess*) renfoncement *m*; (typ) alinéa *m*

indented *adj* (typ) en alinéa

indenture [ɪnˈdentʃər] *s* contrat *m* d'apprentissage ‖ *tr* mettre en apprentissage

independence [ˌɪndɪˈpendəns] *s* indépendance *f*

independen·cy [ˌɪndɪˈpendənsi] *s* (*pl -cies*) indépendance *f*; nation *f* indépendante

independent [ˌɪndɪˈpendənt] *adj & s* indépendant *m*

indescribable [ˌɪndɪˈskraɪbəbəl] *adj* indescriptible, indicible

indestructible [ˌɪndɪˈstrʌktɪbəl] *adj* indestructible

index [ˈɪndeks] *s* (*pl* indexes *or* indices [ˈɪndɪˌsiz]) index *m*; (*of prices*) indice *m*; (typ) main *f*; **Index** Index ‖ *tr* répertorier; (*a book*) faire un index à

in'dex card' *s* fiche *f*

in'dex fin'ger *s* index *m*

in'dex tab' *s* onglet *m*

India [ˈɪndɪə] *s* Inde *f*; l'Inde

In'dia ink' *s* encre *f* de Chine

Indian [ˈɪndɪən] *adj* indien ‖ *s* Indien *m*

In'dian club' *s* mil *m*, massue *f*

In'dian corn' *s* maïs *m*

In'dian file' *s* file *f* indienne ‖ *adv* en file indienne, à la queue leu leu

In'dian O'cean *s* mer *f* des Indes, océan *m* Indien

In'dian sum'mer *s* été *m* de la Saint-Martin

In'dia rub'ber *s* caoutchouc *m*, gomme *f*

indicate [ˈɪndɪˌket] *tr* indiquer

indication [ˌɪndɪˈkeʃən] *s* indication *f*

indicative [ɪnˈdɪkətɪv] *adj & s* indicatif *m*

indicator [ˈɪndɪˌketər] *s* indicateur *m*

indict [ɪnˈdaɪt] *tr* (law) inculper

indictment [ɪnˈdaɪtmənt] *s* inculpation *f*, mise *f* en accusation

indifferent [ɪnˈdɪfərənt] *adj* indifférent; (*poor*) médiocre

indigenous [ɪnˈdɪdʒɪnəs] *adj* indigène

indigent [ˈɪndɪdʒənt] *adj* indigent

indigestible [ˌɪndɪˈdʒestɪbəl] *adj* indigeste

indigestion [ˌɪndɪˈdʒestʃən] *s* indigestion *f*

indignant [ɪnˈdɪgnənt] *adj* indigné

indignation [ˌɪndɪgˈneʃən] *s* indignation *f*

indigni-ty [ɪnˈdɪgnɪti] *s* (*pl* -ties) indignité *f*

indi-go [ˈɪndɪˌgo] *adj* indigo ‖ *s* (*pl* -gos *or* -goes) indigo *m*

indirect [ˌɪndɪˈrekt], [ˌɪndaɪˈrekt] *adj* indirect

in'direct dis'course *s* discours *m* indirect, style *m* indirect

indiscreet [ˌɪndɪsˈkrit] *adj* indiscret

indispensable [ˌɪndɪsˈpensəbəl] *adj* indispensable

indispose [ˌɪndɪsˈpoz] *tr* indisposer

indisposed *adj* indisposé; (*disinclined*) peu enclin, peu disposé

indissoluble [ˌɪndɪˈsɑljəbəl] *adj* indissoluble

indistinct [ˌɪndɪˈstɪŋkt] *adj* indistinct

individual [ˌɪndɪˈvɪdʒuˌəl] *adj* individuel ‖ *s* individu *m*

individuali-ty [ˌɪndɪˌvɪdʒuˈælɪti] *s* (*pl* -ties) individualité *f*

indivisible [ˌɪndɪˈvɪzɪbəl] *adj* indivisible

Indochina [ˈɪndoˈtʃaɪnə] *s* Indochine *f*; l'Indochine

indoctrinate [ɪnˈdɑktrɪˌnet] *tr* endoctriner, catéchiser

Indo-European [ˈɪndoˌjurəˈpiːən] *adj* indo-européen ‖ *s* (*language*) indo-européen *m*; (*person*) Indo-Européen *m*

indolent [ˈɪndələnt] *adj* indolent

Indonesia [ˌɪndoˈniʒə], [ˌɪndoˈniʒə] *s* Indonésie *f*; l'Indonésie

Indonesian [ˌɪndoˈniʃən], [ˌɪndoˈniʒən] *adj* indonésien ‖ *s* (*language*) indonésien *m*; (*person*) Indonésien *m*

indoor [ˈɪnˌdor] *adj* d'intérieur; (*homeloving*) casanier; (*tennis*) couvert; (*swimming pool*) fermé

indoors [ˈɪnˈdorz] *adv* à l'intérieur

induce [ɪnˈd(j)us] *tr* induire; (*to bring about*) provoquer; **to induce s.o. to** porter qn à

induced *adj* provoqué; (elec) induit

inducement [ɪnˈd(j)usmənt] *s* encouragement *m*, mobile *m*, invite *f*

induct [ɪnˈdʌkt] *tr* installer; (mil) incorporer

inductee [ˈɪnˈdʌkti] *s* appelé *m*

induction [ɪnˈdʌkʃən] *s* installation *f*; (elec, logic) induction *f*; (mil) incorporation *f*

induc'tion coil' *s* bobine *f* d'induction

indulge [ɪnˈdʌldʒ] *tr* favoriser; (*s.o.'s desires*) donner libre cours à; (*a child*) tout passer à ‖ *intr* (coll) boire; (coll) fumer; **to indulge in** se livrer à

indulgence [ɪnˈdʌldʒəns] *s* indulgence *f*; **indulgence in** jouissance de

indulgent [ɪnˈdʌldʒənt] *adj* indulgent

industrial [ɪnˈdʌstrɪəl] *adj* industriel

industrialist [ɪnˈdʌstrɪˌəlɪst] *s* industriel *m*

industrialize [ɪnˈdʌstrɪˌəˌlaɪz] *tr* industrialiser

industrious [ɪnˈdʌstrɪˌəs] *adj* industrieux, appliqué, assidu

indus-try [ˈɪndəstri] *s* (*pl* -tries) industrie *f*; (*zeal*) assiduité *f*

inebriation [ɪnˌibriˈeʃən] *s* ébriété *f*

inedible [ɪnˈedɪbəl] *adj* incomestible

ineffable [ɪnˈefəbəl] *adj* ineffable

ineffective [ˌɪnɪˈfektɪv] *adj* inefficace; (*person*) incapable

ineffectual [ˌɪnɪˈfektʃuˌəl] *adj* inefficace

inefficient [ˌɪnɪˈfɪʃənt] *adj* inefficace; (*person*) incapable

ineligible [ɪnˈelɪdʒɪbəl] *adj* inéligible

inept [ɪnˈept] *adj* inepte

inequali-ty [ˌɪnɪˈkwɑlɪti] *s* (*pl* -ties) inégalité *f*

inequi-ty [ɪnˈekwɪti] *s* (*pl* -ties) injustice *f*

inertia [ɪnˈʌrɪə] *s* inertie *f*

inescapable [ˌɪnesˈkepəbəl] *adj* inéluctable

inevitable [ɪnˈevɪtəbəl] *adj* inévitable

inexact [ˌɪnegˈzækt] *adj* inexact

inexcusable [ˌɪneksˈkjuzəbəl] *adj* inexcusable

inexhaustible [ˌɪnegˈzɔstɪbəl] *adj* inexhaustible, inépuisable

inexorable [ɪnˈeksərəbəl] *adj* inexorable

inexpedient [ˌɪnɛk'spidɪ·ənt] *adj* inopportun, peu expédient

inexpensive [ˌɪnɛk'spɛnsɪv] *adj* pas cher, bon marché

inexperience [ˌɪnɛk'spɪrɪ·əns] *s* inexpérience *f*

inexperienced *adj* inexpérimenté

inexplicable [ɪn'ɛksplɪkəbəl] *adj* inexplicable

inexpressible [ˌɪnɛk'sprɛsɪbəl] *adj* inexprimable, indicible

infallible [ɪn'fælɪbəl] *adj* infaillible

infamous ['ɪnfəməs] *adj* infâme

infa·my ['ɪnfəmi] *s* (*pl* -mies) infamie *f*

infan·cy ['ɪnfənsi] *s* (*pl* -cies) première enfance *f*; (fig) enfance

infant ['ɪnfənt] *adj* infantile; (*in the earliest stage*) (fig) débutant || *s* nourrisson *m*, bébé *m*; enfant *mf* en bas âge

infantile ['ɪnfən‚taɪl], ['ɪnfəntɪl] *adj* infantile; (*childish*) enfantin

in'fantile paral'ysis *s* paralysie *f* infantile

infan·try ['ɪnfəntri] *s* (*pl* -tries) infanterie *f*

in'fantry·man *s* (*pl* -men) militaire *m* de l'infanterie, fantassin *m*

infatuated [ɪn'fætʃu‚etɪd] *adj* entiché, épris; **infatuated with oneself** infatué; **to be infatuated** s'engouer

infect [ɪn'fɛkt] *tr* infecter

infection [ɪn'fɛkʃən] *s* infection *f*

infectious [ɪn'fɛkʃəs] *adj* infectieux; (*laughter*) communicatif, contagieux

in·fer [ɪn'fʌr] *v* (*pret & pp* -ferred; *ger* -ferring) *tr* inférer

inferior [ɪn'fɪrɪ·ər] *adj & s* inférieur *m*

inferiority [ɪn‚fɪrɪ'ɑrɪti] *s* infériorité *f*

inferior'ity com'plex *s* complexe *m* d'infériorité

infernal [ɪn'fʌrnəl] *adj* infernal

infest [ɪn'fɛst] *tr* infester

infidel ['ɪnfɪdəl] *adj & s* infidèle *mf*

infideli·ty [ˌɪnfɪ'dɛlɪti] *s* (*pl* -ties) infidélité *f*

in'field' *s* (baseball) petit champ *m*

infiltrate [ɪn'fɪltret], ['ɪnfɪl‚tret] *tr* s'infiltrer dans, pénétrer; (*with conspirators*) noyauter || *intr* s'infiltrer

infinite ['ɪnfɪnɪt] *adj & s* infini *m*

infinitely ['ɪnfɪnɪtli] *adv* infiniment

infinitive [ɪn'fɪnɪtɪv] *adj & s* infinitif *m*

infini·ty [ɪn'fɪnɪti] *s* (*pl* -ties) infinité *f*; (math) infini *m*

infirm [ɪn'fʌrm] *adj* infirme, maladif

infirma·ry [ɪn'fʌrməri] *s* (*pl* -ries) infirmerie *f*

infirmi·ty [ɪn'fʌrmɪti] *s* (*pl* -ties) infirmité *f*

in'fix' *s* infixe *m*

inflame [ɪn'flem] *tr* enflammer || *intr* s'enflammer

inflammable [ɪn'flæməbəl] *adj* inflammable

inflammation [ˌɪnflə'meʃən] *s* inflammation *f*

inflammatory [ɪn'flæmə‚tori] *adj* incendiaire, provocateur; (pathol) inflammatoire

inflate [ɪn'flet] *tr* gonfler || *intr* se gonfler

inflation [ɪn'fleʃən] *s* gonflement *m*; (com) inflation *f*

inflationary [ɪn'fleʃən‚ɛri] *adj* inflationniste

inflect [ɪn'flɛkt] *tr* infléchir; (*e.g., a noun*) décliner; (*a verb*) conjuguer; (*the voice*) moduler

inflection [ɪn'flɛkʃən] *s* inflexion *f*

inflexible [ɪn'flɛksɪbəl] *adj* inflexible

inflict [ɪn'flɪkt] *tr* infliger

influence ['ɪnflu·əns] *s* influence *f* || *tr* influencer, influer sur

in'fluence ped'dling *s* trafic *m* d'influence

influential [ˌɪnflu'ɛnʃəl] *adj* influent

influenza [ˌɪnflu'ɛnzə] *s* influenza *f*

in'flux' *s* afflux *m*

inform [ɪn'form] *tr* informer, renseigner; **keep me informed** tenez-moi au courant || *intr*—**to inform on** informer contre, dénoncer

informal [ɪn'forməl] *adj* sans cérémonie; (*person; manners*) familier; (*unofficial*) officieux

infor'mal dance' *s* sauterie *f*

informant [ɪn'formənt] *s* informateur *m*; (*in, e.g., language study*) source *f* d'informations

information [ˌɪnfər'meʃən] *s* information *f*, renseignements *mpl*; (telp) service *m* des renseignements téléphoniques; **piece of information** information, renseignement

informational [ˌɪnfər'meʃənəl] *adj* instructif, documentaire; (comp) informatique

informa'tion bu'reau *s* bureau *m* de renseignements

informative [ɪn'formətɪv] *adj* instructif, édifiant

informed' sour'ces *spl* sources *fpl* bien informées

informer [ɪn'formər] *s* délateur *m*, dénonciateur *m*; (*police spy*) indicateur *m*, mouchard *m*

infraction [ɪn'frækʃən] *s* infraction *f*

infrared [ˌɪnfrə'rɛd] *adj & s* infrarouge *m*

infrequent [ɪn'frikwənt] *adj* peu fréquent, rare

infringe [ɪn'frɪndʒ] *tr* enfreindre; (*a patent*) contrefaire || *intr*—**to infringe on** empiéter sur, enfreindre

infringement [ɪn'frɪndʒmənt] *s* infraction *f*; (*on patent rights*) contrefaçon *f*

infuriate [ɪn'fjurɪ‚et] *tr* rendre furieux

infuse [ɪn'fjuz] *tr* infuser

infusion [ɪn'fjuʒən] *s* infusion *f*

ingenious [ɪn'dʒinjəs] *adj* ingénieux

ingenui·ty [ˌɪndʒɪ'n(j)u·ɪti] *s* (*pl* -ties) ingéniosité *f*

ingenuous [ɪn'dʒɛnju·əs] *adj* ingénu, naïf

ingenuousness [ɪn'dʒɛnju·əsnɪs] *s* ingénuité *f*, naïveté *f*

ingest [ɪn'dʒɛst] *tr* ingérer

ingot ['ɪŋgət] *s* lingot *m*

in·grained' *adj* imprégné; (*habit*) invétéré; (*prejudice*) enraciné

ingrate ['ɪngret] *adj & s* ingrat *m*

ingratiate [ɪn'greʃɪ‚et] *tr*—to ingratiate oneself (with) se faire bien voir (de)

ingratiating [ɪn'greʃɪ‚etɪŋ] *adj* insinuant, persuasif

ingratitude [ɪn'grætɪ‚t(j)ud] *s* ingratitude *f*

ingredient [ɪn'gridɪ‚ənt] *s* ingrédient *m*

in'growing nail' *s* ongle *m* incarné

ingulf [ɪn'gʌlf] *tr* engouffrer

inhabit [ɪn'hæbɪt] *tr* habiter

inhabitant [ɪn'hæbɪtənt] *s* habitant *m*

inhale [ɪn'hel] *tr* inhaler, aspirer; (*smoke*) avaler ‖ *intr* (*while smoking*) avaler

inherent [ɪn'hɪrənt] *adj* inhérent

inherit [ɪn'herɪt] *tr* (e.g., *money*) hériter; (e.g., *money to become the heir or successor of*) hériter de; **to inherit s.th. from s.o.** hériter q.ch. de qn

inheritance [ɪn'herɪtəns] *s* héritage *m*

inher'itance tax' *s* droits *mpl* de succession

inheritor [ɪn'herɪtər] *s* héritier *m*

inhibit [ɪn'hɪbɪt] *tr* inhiber

inhibition [‚ɪnɪ'bɪʃən] *s* inhibition *f*

inhospitable [ɪn'hɑspɪtəbəl], [‚ɪnhɑs-'pɪtəbəl] *adj* inhospitalier

inhuman [ɪn'hjumən] *adj* inhumain

inhumane [‚ɪnhju'men] *adj* inhumain, insensible

inhuman·i·ty [‚ɪnhju'mænɪti] *s* (*pl* -ties) inhumanité *f*

inimical [ɪ'nɪmɪkəl] *adj* inamical

iniqui·ty [ɪ'nɪkwɪti] *s* (*pl* -ties) iniquité *f*

ini·tial [ɪ'nɪʃəl] *adj* initial ‖ *s* initiale *f*; **initials** parafe *m*, initiales ‖ *v* (*pret* -tialed *or* -tialled; *ger* -tialing *or* -tialling) *tr* signer de ses initiales, parafer

initiate [ɪ'nɪʃɪ‚et] *s* initié *m* ‖ *tr* initier; (*a project*) commencer

initiation [ɪ‚nɪʃɪ'eʃən] *s* initiation *f*

initiative [ɪ'nɪʃɪ‚etɪv], [ɪ'nɪʃɪetɪv] *s* initiative *f*

inject [ɪn'dʒɛkt] *tr* injecter; (*a remark or suggestion*) introduire

injection [ɪn'dʒɛkʃən] *s* injection *f*

injudicious [‚ɪndʒu'dɪʃəs] *adj* peu judicieux

injunction [ɪn'dʒʌŋkʃən] *s* injonction *f*; (law) mise *f* en demeure

injure ['ɪndʒər] *tr* (*to harm*) nuire (with *dat*); (*to wound*) blesser; (*to offend*) faire tort à, léser

injurious [ɪn'dʒurɪ‚əs] *adj* nuisible, préjudiciable; (*offensive*) blessant, injurieux

inju·ry ['ɪndʒəri] *s* (*pl* -ries) blessure *f*, lésion *f*; (*harm*) tort *m*; injure *f*, offense *f*

injustice [ɪn'dʒʌstɪs] *s* injustice *f*

ink [ɪŋk] *s* encre *f* ‖ *tr* encrer

ink' blot' *s* pâté *m*, macule *f*

inkling ['ɪŋklɪŋ] *s* soupçon *m*, pressentiment *m*

ink' pad' *s* tampon *m* encreur

ink'stand' *s* encrier *m*

ink'well' *s* encrier *m* de bureau

ink·y ['ɪŋki] *adj* (*comp* -ier; *super* -iest) noir foncé; taché d'encre

inlaid ['ɪn‚led], [‚ɪn'led] *adj* incrusté

inland ['ɪnlənd] *adj* & *s* intérieur *m* ‖ *adv* à l'intérieur, vers l'intérieur

in'-law' *s* (coll) parent *m* par alliance; **the in-laws** (coll) la belle-famille, les beaux-parents *mpl*

in·lay ['ɪn‚le] *s* incrustation *f* ‖ [ɪn-'le], ['ɪn‚le] *v* (*pret* & *pp* -laid) *tr* incruster

in'let *s* bras *m* de mer, crique *f*; (e.g., *of air*) arrivée *f*

in'mate *s* habitant *m*; (*of an institution*) pensionnaire *mf*

inn [ɪn] *s* auberge *f*

innate [ɪ'net], ['ɪnet] *adj* inné, infus

inner ['ɪnər] *adj* intérieur *m*; (e.g., *ear*) interne; intime, secret

in'ner-spring mat'tress *s* sommier *m* à ressorts internes

in'ner tube' *s* chambre *f* à air

inning ['ɪnɪŋ] *s* manche *f*, tour *m*

inn'keep'er *s* aubergiste *mf*

innocence ['ɪnəsəns] *s* innocence *f*

innocent ['ɪnəsənt] *adj* & *s* innocent *m*

innocuous [ɪ'nɑkju‚əs] *adj* inoffensif

innovate ['ɪnə‚vet] *tr* & *intr* innover

innovation [‚ɪnə've‚ən] *s* innovation *f*

innuen·do [‚ɪnju'ɛndo] *s* (*pl* -does) allusion *f*, sous-entendu *m*

innumerable [ɪ'n(j)umərəbəl] *adj* innombrable

inoculate [ɪn'ɑkjə‚let] *tr* inoculer

inoculation [ɪn‚ɑkjə'leʃən] *s* inoculation *f*

inoffensive [‚ɪnə'fɛnsɪv] *adj* inoffensif

inopportune [ɪn‚ɑpər't(j)un] *adj* inopportun, mal choisi

inordinate [ɪn'ɔrdɪnɪt] *adj* désordonné, déréglé; (*unrestrained*) démesuré

inorganic [‚ɪnɔr'gænɪk] *adj* inorganique

in'put' *s* consommation *f*; (elec) prise *f*, entrée *f*

inquest ['ɪnkwɛst] *s* enquête *f*

inquire [ɪn'kwaɪr] *tr* s'informer de, e.g., **to inquire the price of** s'informer du prix de ‖ *intr* s'enquérir; **to inquire about** s'enquérir de, se renseigner sur; **to inquire into** faire des recherches sur

inquir·y [ɪn'kwaɪri], ['ɪnkwɪri] *s* (*pl* -ies) investigation *f*, enquête *f*; (*question*) demande *f*; **to make inquiries** s'informer

inquisition [‚ɪnkwɪ'zɪʃən] *s* inquisition *f*

inquisitive [ɪn'kwɪzɪtɪv] *adj* curieux, questionneur

in'road' *s* incursion *f*, empiètement *m*

ins' and outs' *spl* tours et détours *mpl*

insane [ɪn'sen] *adj* dément, fou; (*unreasonable*) insensé, insane

insane' asy'lum *s* asile *m* d'aliénés

insani·ty [ɪn'sænɪti] *s* (*pl* -ties) démence *f*, aliénation *f*

insatiable [ɪn'seʃəbəl] *adj* insatiable

inscribe [ɪn'skraɪb] *tr* inscrire; (*a book*) dédier

inscription [ɪn'skrɪpʃən] *s* inscription *f*; (*of a book*) dédicace *f* inscrutable [ɪn'skrutəbəl] *adj* impénétrable, fermé

insect ['ɪnsɛkt] *s* insecte *m*

insecticide [ɪn'sɛktɪ,saɪd] *adj & s* insecticide *m*

insecure [,ɪnsɪ'kjʊr] *adj* peu sûr; (*nervous*) inquiet

insensitive [ɪn'sɛnsɪtɪv] *adj* insensible

inseparable [ɪn'sɛpərəbəl] *adj* inséparable

insert ['ɪnsʌrt] *s* (sewing) incrustation *f*; (typ) hors-texte *m*, encart *m* ‖ [ɪn-'sʌrt] *tr* insérer, introduire; (typ) encarter

insertion [ɪn'sʌrʃən] *s* insertion *f*; (sewing) incrustation *f*

in·set ['ɪn,sɛt] *s* (*map, picture, etc.*) médaillon *m*; (sewing) incrustation *f*; (typ) hors-texte *m*, encart *m* ‖ [ɪn'sɛt], ['ɪn,sɛt] *v* (*pret & pp* -set; *ger* -setting) *tr* insérer; (*a page or pages*) encarter

in'shore' *adj* côtier ‖ *adv* près de la côte

in'side' *adj* d'intérieur, interne; secret ‖ *s* intérieur *m*, dedans *m*; insides (coll) entrailles *fpl* ‖ *adv* à l'intérieur; inside and out au-dedans et audehors; inside of à l'intérieur de; inside out à l'envers; to turn inside out (*e.g., a coat*) retourner ‖ *prep* à l'intérieur de, dans

in'side informa'tion *s* tuyau *m*, tuyaux *mpl*

insider [,ɪn'saɪdər] *s* initié *m*

in'side track' *s*—to have the inside track prendre à la corde; (fig) avoir un avantage

insidious [ɪn'sɪdɪ·əs] *adj* insidieux

in'sight' *s* pénétration *f*; (psychol) défoulement *m*

insigni·a [ɪn'sɪgnɪ·ə] *s* (*pl* -a or -as) insigne *m*

insignificant [,ɪnsɪg'nɪfɪkənt] *adj* insignifiant

insincere [,ɪnsɪn'sɪr] *adj* insincère, peu sincère

insinuate [ɪn'sɪnju,et] *tr* insinuer

insipid [ɪn'sɪpɪd] *adj* insipide

insist [ɪn'sɪst] *intr* insister; to insist on insister sur; to insist on + *ger* insister pour + *inf*

insofar as [,ɪnso'fɑrəz] *conj* pour autant que, dans la mesure où

insolence ['ɪnsələns] *s* insolence *f*

insolent ['ɪnsələnt] *adj* insolent

insoluble [ɪn'sɑljəbəl] *adj* insoluble

insolven·cy [ɪn'sɑlvənsɪ] *s* (*pl* -cies) insolvabilité *f*

insolvent [ɪn'sɑlvənt] *adj* insolvable

insomnia [ɪn'sɑmnɪ·ə] *s* insomnie *f*

insomuch [,ɪnso'mʌtʃ] *adv*—insomuch as vu que; insomuch that à tel point que

inspect [ɪn'spɛkt] *tr* inspecter

inspection [ɪn'spɛkʃən] *s* inspection *f*

inspector [ɪn'spɛktər] *s* inspecteur *m*

inspiration [,ɪnspɪ'reʃən] *s* inspiration *f*

inspire [ɪn'spaɪr] *tr* inspirer

inspiring [ɪn'spaɪrɪŋ] *adj* inspirant

install [ɪn'stɔl] *tr* installer

installment [ɪn'stɔlmənt] *s* installation *f*; (*delivery*) livraison *f*; (*serial story*)

feuilleton *m*; (*partial payment*) acompte *m*, versement *m*; in installments par acomptes, par tranches

install'ment plan' *s* vente *f* à tempérament ou à crédit; on the installment plan avec facilités de paiement

instance ['ɪnstəns] *s* cas *m*, exemple *m*; for instance par exemple

instant ['ɪnstənt] *adj* imminent, immédiat; on the fifth instant le cinq courant ‖ *s* instant *m*, moment *m*

instantaneous [,ɪnstən'tenɪ·əs] *adj* instantané

instantly ['ɪnstəntlɪ] *adv* à l'instant

instead [ɪn'stɛd] *adv* plutôt, au contraire; à ma (votre, sa, etc.) place; instead of au lieu de

in'step' *s* cou-de-pied *m*

instigate ['ɪnstɪ,get] *tr* inciter

instigation [,ɪnstɪ'geʃən] *s* instigation *f*

instill [ɪn'stɪl] *tr* instiller

instinct ['ɪnstɪŋkt] *s* instinct *m*

instinctive [ɪn'stɪŋktɪv] *adj* instinctif

institute ['ɪnstɪ,t(j)ut] *s* institut *m* ‖ *tr* instituer

institution [,ɪnstɪ't(j)uʃən] *s* institution *f*

instruct [ɪn'strʌkt] *tr* instruire

instruction [ɪn'strʌkʃən] *s* instruction *f*

instructive [ɪn'strʌktɪv] *adj* instructif

instructor [ɪn'strʌktər] *s* instructeur *m*

instrument ['ɪnstrəmənt] *s* instrument *m* ‖ ['ɪnstrə,mɛnt] *tr* instrumenter

instrumental [,ɪnstrə'mɛntəl] *adj* instrumental; to be instrumental in contribuer à

instrumentalist [,ɪnstrə'mɛntəlɪst] *s* instrumentiste *mf*

instrumentali·ty [,ɪnstrəmən'tælɪtɪ] *s* (*pl* -ties) intermédiaire *m*, intervention *f*

in'strument board' *s* tableau *m* de bord

in'strument fly'ing *s* radio-navigation *f*, vol *m* aux instruments

in'strument land'ing *s* atterrissage *m* aux instruments

in'strument pan'el *s* tableau *m* de bord

insubordinate [,ɪnsə'bɔrdɪnɪt] *adj* insubordonné

insufferable [ɪn'sʌfərəbəl] *adj* insupportable, intolérable

insufficient [,ɪnsə'fɪʃənt] *adj* insuffisant

insular ['ɪnsələr], ['ɪnsjʊlər] *adj* insulaire

insulate ['ɪnsə,let] *tr* insoler

in'sulating tape' *s* ruban *m* isolant, chatterton *m*

insulation [,ɪnsə'leʃən] *s* isolation *f*

insulator ['ɪnsə,letər] *s* isolant *m*

insulin ['ɪnsəlɪn] *s* insuline *f*

insult ['ɪnsʌlt] *s* insulte *f* ‖ [ɪn'sʌlt] *tr* insulter

insulting [ɪn'sʌltɪŋ] *adj* insultant, injurieux

insurance [ɪn'ʃʊrəns] *s* assurance *f*

insure [ɪn'ʃʊr] *tr* assurer

insurer [ɪn'ʃʊrər] *s* assureur *m*

insurgent [ɪn'sʌrdʒənt] *adj & s* insurgé *m*

insurmountable [ˌɪnsərˈmaʊntəbəl] *adj* insurmontable

insurrection [ˌɪnsəˈrekʃən] *s* insurrection *f*

intact [ɪnˈtækt] *adj* intact

in'take' *s* (*place*) entrée *f*; (*act or amount*) prise *f*; (*mach*) admission *f*

in'take man'ifold *s* tubulure *f* d'admission, collecteur *m* d'admission

in'take valve' *s* soupape *f* d'admission

intangible [ɪnˈtændʒɪbəl] *adj* intangible

integer [ˈɪntɪdʒər] *s* nombre *m* entier

integral [ˈɪntɪɡrəl] *adj* intégral; (*part*) intégrant; **integral with** solidaire de ‖ *s* intégrale *f*

integrate [ˈɪntɪˌɡret] *tr* intégrer

integration [ˌɪntɪˈɡreʃən] *s* intégration *f*

integrity [ɪnˈteɡrɪti] *s* intégrité *f*

intellect [ˈɪntəˌlekt] *s* intellect *m*; (*person*) intelligence *f*

intellectual [ˌɪntəˈlektʃʊ·əl] *adj & s* intellectuel *m*

intelligence [ɪnˈtelɪdʒəns] *s* intelligence *f*

intel'ligence bu'reau *s* deuxième bureau *m*, service *m* de renseignements

intel'ligence quo'tient *s* quotient *m* intellectuel

intel'ligence test' *s* test *m* d'habileté mentale

intelligent [ɪnˈtelɪdʒənt] *adj* intelligent

intelligible [ɪnˈtelɪdʒɪbəl] *adj* intelligible

intemperate [ɪnˈtempərɪt] *adj* intempérant

intend [ɪnˈtend] *tr* destiner; signifier, vouloir dire; **to intend to** avoir l'intention de, penser; **to intend to become** se destiner à

intended *adj & s* (coll) futur *m*

intense [ɪnˈtens] *adj* intense

intensi·fy [ɪnˈtensɪˌfaɪ] *v* (*pret & pp* **-fied**) *tr* intensifier.‖ *intr* s'intensifier

intensi·ty [ɪnˈtensɪti] *s* (*pl* **-ties**) intensité *f*

intensive [ɪnˈtensɪv] *adj* intensif

intent [ɪnˈtent] *adj* attentif; (*look, gaze*) fixe, intense; **intent on** résolu à ‖ *s* intention *f*; **to all intents and purposes** en fait, pratiquement

intention [ɪnˈtenʃən] *s* intention *f*

intentional [ɪnˈtenʃənəl] *adj* intentionnel, délibéré

intentionally [ɪnˈtenʃənəli] *adv* exprès, à dessein

in·ter [ɪnˈtʌr] *v* (*pret & pp* **-terred**; *ger* **-terring**) *tr* enterrer

interact [ˌɪntərˈækt] *intr* agir réciproquement

interaction [ˌɪntərˈækʃən] *s* interaction *f*

inter·breed [ˌɪntərˈbrid] *v* (*pret & pp* **-bred**) *tr* croiser ‖ *intr* se croiser

intercalate [ɪnˈtʌrkəˌlet] *tr* intercaler

intercede [ˌɪntərˈsid] *intr* intercéder

intercept [ˌɪntərˈsept] *tr* intercepter

interceptor [ˌɪntərˈseptər] *s* intercepteur *m*

interchange [ˈɪntərˌtʃendʒ] *s* échange *m*, permutation *f*; (*transfer point*) correspondance *f*; (*on highway*)

échangeur *m* ‖ [ˌɪntərˈtʃendʒ] *tr* échanger, permuter ‖ *intr* permuter

intercollegiate [ˌɪntərkəˈlidʒɪ·ɪt] *adj* interuniversitaire, entre universités

intercom [ˈɪntərˌkɑm] *s* (coll) interphone *m*

intercourse [ˈɪntərˌkors] *s* relations *fpl*, rapports *mpl*; (*copulation*) copulation *f*, coït *m*

intercross [ˌɪntərˈkrɔs], [ˌɪntərˈkrɑs] *tr* entrecroiser ‖ *intr* s'entrecroiser

interdict [ˈɪntərˌdɪkt] *s* interdit *m* ‖ [ˌɪntərˈdɪkt] *tr* interdire; **to interdict s.o. from** + *ger* interdire à qn de + *inf*

interest [ˈɪntərɪst], [ˈɪntrɪst] *s* intérêt *m*; **the interests** les gens influents; **to pay back with interest** rendre avec usure ‖ [ˈɪntərɪst], [ˈɪntrɪst], [ˈɪntəˌrest] *tr* intéresser

interested *adj* intéressé; **to be interested in** s'intéresser à or dans

interesting [ˈɪntrɪstɪŋ], [ˈɪntəˌrestɪŋ] *adj* intéressant

interfere [ˌɪntərˈfɪr] *intr* (*to meddle*) s'ingérer; (*phys*) interférer; **to interfere with** intervenir dans, se mêler de; (*to come into opposition with*) gêner, entraver; **to interfere with each other** interférer (entre eux)

interference [ˌɪntərˈfɪrəns] *s* interférence *f*, intervention *f*; (*phys*) interférence; (*jamming*) (rad) brouillage *m*

interim [ˈɪntərɪm] *adj* provisoire, par intérim ‖ *s* intérim *m*

interior [ɪnˈtɪrɪ·ər] *adj & s* intérieur *m*

inte'rior dec'orator *s* décorateur *m* d'intérieurs

interject [ˌɪntərˈdʒekt] *tr* interposer; (*questions*) lancer

interjection [ˌɪntərˈdʒekʃən] *s* interjection *f*; (gram) interjection *f*

interlard [ˌɪntərˈlard] *tr* entrelarder

interline [ˌɪntərˈlaɪn] *tr* interligner

interlining [ˈɪntərˌlaɪnɪŋ] *s* doublure *f* intermédiaire

interlock [ˌɪntərˈlɑk] *tr* emboîter, engager ‖ *intr* s'emboîter, s'engager

interloper [ˌɪntərˈlopər] *s* intrus *m*

interlude [ˈɪntərˌlud] *s* (mov, mus, telv) interlude *m*; (theat, fig) intermède *m*

intermediar·y [ˌɪntərˈmidɪˌeri] *adj* intermédiaire ‖ *s* (*pl* **-ies**) intermédiaire *mf*

intermediate [ˌɪntərˈmidɪ·ɪt] *adj* intermédiaire

interment [ɪnˈtʌrmənt] *s* enterrement *m*, sépulture *f*

interminable [ɪnˈtʌrmɪnəbəl] *adj* interminable

intermingle [ˌɪntərˈmɪŋɡəl] *tr* entremêler ‖ *intr* s'entremêler

intermission [ˌɪntərˈmɪʃən] *s* relâche *m*, pause *f*; (theat) entracte *m*

intermittent [ˌɪntərˈmɪtənt] *adj* intermittent

intermix [ˌɪntərˈmɪks] *tr* entremêler ‖ *intr* s'entremêler

intern [ˈɪntʌrn] *s* interne *mf* ‖ [ɪnˈtʌrn] *tr* interner

internal [ɪn'tʌrnəl] *adj* interne

inter'nal-combus'tion en'gine *s* moteur *m* à explosion

inter'nal rev'enue *s* recettes *fpl* fiscales

international [,ɪntər'næʃənəl] *adj* international; (*exposition*) universel

in'terna'tional date' line' *s* ligne *f* de changement de date

in'terna'tional time' zone' *s* fuseau *m* horaire international

internecine [,ɪntər'nisɪn] *adj* domestique, intestin; (*war*) sanguinaire, d'extermination

internee [,ɪntʌr'ni] *s* interné *m*

internment [ɪn'tʌrnmənt] *s* internement *m*

in'tern-ship' *s* internat *m*

interpellate [,ɪntər'pelet], [ɪn'tʌrpɪ-,let] *tr* interpeller

interplanetary [,ɪntər'plænə,teri] *adj* interplanétaire

interplan'etary trav'el *s* voyages *mpl* interplanétaires

interplay ['ɪntər,ple] *s* interaction *f*

interpolate [ɪn'tʌrpə,let] *tr* interpoler

interpose [,ɪntər'poz] *tr* interposer

interpret [ɪn'tʌrprɪt] *tr* interpréter

interpretation [ɪn,tʌrprɪ'teʃən] *s* interprétation *f*

interpreter [ɪn'tʌrprɪtər] *s* interprète *mf*

interrogate [ɪn'terə,get] *tr* interroger

interrogation [ɪn,terə'geʃən] *s* interrogation *f*

interroga'tion mark' *s* point *m* d'interrogation

interrupt [,ɪntə'rʌpt] *tr* interrompre

interruption [,ɪntə'rʌpʃən] *s* interruption *f*

intersect [,ɪntər'sekt] *tr* entrecouper || *intr* s'entrecouper

intersection [,ɪntər'sekʃən] *s* intersection *f*

intersperse [,ɪntər'spʌrs] *tr* entremêler

interstellar [,ɪntər'stelər] *adj* interstellaire

interstice [ɪn'tʌrstɪs] *s* interstice *m*

intertwine [,ɪntər'twaɪn] *tr* entrelacer || *intr* s'entrelacer

interval [ɪn'tʌrvəl] *s* intervalle *m*

intervene [,ɪntər'vin] *intr* intervenir

intervening [,ɪntər'vinɪŋ] *adj* (*period*) intermédiaire; (*party*) intervenant

intervention [,ɪntər'venʃən] *s* intervention *f*

interview ['ɪntər,vju] *s* entrevue *f*; (*journ*) interview *f* || *tr* avoir une entrevue avec; (*journ*) interviewer

inter-weave [,ɪntər'wiv] *v* (*pret* -wove or -weaved; *pp* -wove, woven or weaved) *tr* entrelacer; (*to intermingle*) entremêler

intestate [ɪn'testet], [ɪn'testɪt] *adj & s* intestat *m*

intestine [ɪn'testɪn] *adj & s* intestin *m*

intima·cy ['ɪntɪməsi] *s* (*pl* -cies) intimité *f*; rapports *mpl* sexuels

intimate ['ɪntɪmɪt] *adj & s* intime *mf* || ['ɪntɪ,met] *tr* donner à entendre

intimation [,ɪntɪ'meʃən] *s* suggestion *f*, insinuation *f*

intimidate [ɪn'tɪmɪ,det] *tr* intimider

into ['ɪntu], ['ɪntu] *prep* dans, en

intolerant [ɪn'talərənt] *adj* intolérant

intonation [,ɪnto'neʃən] *s* intonation *f*

intone [ɪn'ton] *tr* (*to begin to sing*) entonner; (*to sing or recite in a monotone*) psalmodier || *intr* psalmodier

intoxicant [ɪn'taksɪkənt] *s* boisson *f* alcoolique

intoxicate [ɪn'taksɪ,ket] *tr* enivrer; (*to poison*) intoxiquer

intoxication [ɪn,taksɪ'keʃən] *s* ivresse *f*; (*poisoning*) intoxication *f*; (fig) enivrement *m*

intractable [ɪn'træktəbəl] *adj* intraitable

intransigent [ɪn'trænsɪdʒənt] *adj* intransigeant

intransitive [ɪn'trænsɪtɪv] *adj* intransitif

intravenous [,ɪntrə'vinəs] *adj* intraveineux

intrepid [ɪn'trepɪd] *adj* intrépide

intricate ['ɪntrɪkɪt] *adj* compliqué

intrigue [ɪn'trig], ['ɪntrig] *s* intrigue *f* || [ɪn'trig] *tr & intr* intriguer

intrinsic(al) [ɪn'trɪnsɪk(əl)] *adj* intrinsèque

introduce [,ɪntrə'd(j)us] *tr* introduire; (*to make acquainted*) présenter

introduction [,ɪntrə'dʌkʃən] *s* introduction *f*; (*of one person to another or others*) présentation *f*

introductory [,ɪntrə'dʌktəri] *adj* préliminaire; (*text*) liminaire; (*speech, letter, etc.*) de présentation

introduc'tory of'fer *s* offre *f* de présentation

introspective [,ɪntrə'spektɪv] *adj* introspectif; (*person*) méditatif

introvert ['ɪntrə,vʌrt] *adj & s* introverti *m*

intrude [ɪn'trud] *intr* s'ingérer, s'immiscer; **to intrude on s.o.** déranger qn

intruder [ɪn'trudər] *s* intrus *m*

intrusion [ɪn'truʒən] *s* intrusion *f*

intrusive [ɪn'trusɪv] *adj* importun

intuition [,ɪnt(j)u'ɪʃən] *s* intuition *f*

inundate ['ɪnən,det] *tr* inonder

inundation [,ɪnən'deʃən] *s* inondation *f*

inure [ɪn'jur] *tr* aguerrir, endurcir || *intr* entrer en vigueur; **to inure to** rejaillir sur

invade [ɪn'ved] *tr* envahir

invader [ɪn'vedər] *s* envahisseur *m*

invalid [ɪn'vælɪd] *adj* invalide, nul || ['ɪnvəlɪd] *adj & s* malade *mf*, invalide *mf*

invalidate [ɪn'vælɪ,det] *tr* invalider

invalidity [,ɪnvə'lɪdɪti] *s* invalidité *f*

invaluable [ɪn'vælju-əbəl] *adj* inappréciable, inestimable

invariable [ɪn'veri-əbəl] *adj* invariable

invasion [ɪn'veʒən] *s* invasion *f*

invective [ɪn'vektɪv] *s* invective *f*

inveigh [ɪn'vе] *intr*—**to inveigh against** invectiver contre

inveigle [ɪn'vegəl], [ɪn'vigəl] *tr* séduire, enjôler; **to inveigle s.o. into** + *ger* entraîner qn à + *inf*

invent [ɪn'vent] *tr* inventer

invention [ɪn'venʃən] *s* invention *f*

inventive [ɪnˈventɪv] *adj* inventif
inventiveness [ɪnˈventɪvnɪs] *s* esprit *m* inventif
inventor [ɪnˈventər] *s* inventeur *m*
invento·ry [ˈɪnvənˌtori] *s* (*pl* -ries) inventaire *m* ‖ *v* (*pret* & *pp* -ried) *tr* inventorier
inverse [ɪnˈvʌrs] *adj* & *s* inverse *m*
inversion [ɪnˈvʌrʒən], [ɪnˈvʌrʃən] *s* interversion *f*, inversion *f*
invert [ɪnˈvʌrt] *adj* & *s* inverti *m* ‖ [ɪnˈvʌrt] *tr* inverser; (*an image*) invertir
invertebrate [ɪnˈvʌrtɪˌbret], [ɪnˈvʌrtɪbrɪt] *adj* & *s* invertébré *m*
invest [ɪnˈvest] *tr* investir; (*money*) investir, placer; **to invest with** investir de ‖ *intr* investir or placer de l'argent
investigate [ɪnˈvestɪˌget] *tr* examiner, rechercher
investigation [ɪnˌvestɪˈgeʃən] *s* investigation *f*
investigator [ɪnˈvestɪˌgetər] *s* investigateur *m*, chercheur *m*
investment [ɪnˈvestmənt] *s* investissement *m*, placement *m*; (*with an office or dignity*) investiture *f*; (*siege*) investissement
investor [ɪnˈvestər] *s* capitaliste *mf*
inveterate [ɪnˈvetərɪt] *adj* invétéré
invidious [ɪnˈvɪdɪ·əs] *adj* odieux
invigorate [ɪnˈvɪgəˌret] *tr* vivifier, fortifier
invigorating [ɪnˈvɪgəˌretɪŋ] *adj* vivifiant, fortifiant
invincible [ɪnˈvɪnsɪbəl] *adj* invincible
invisible [ɪnˈvɪzɪbəl] *adj* invisible
invis'ible ink' *s* encre *f* sympathique
invitation [ˌɪnvɪˈteʃən] *s* invitation *f*
invite [ɪnˈvaɪt] *tr* inviter
inviting [ɪnˈvaɪtɪŋ] *adj* invitant
invoice [ˈɪnvɔɪs] *s* facture *f*; **as per invoice** suivant facture ‖ *tr* facturer
invoke [ɪnˈvok] *tr* invoquer
involuntary [ɪnˈvɑlənˌteri] *adj* involontaire
involve [ɪnˈvɑlv] *tr* impliquer, entraîner, engager
invulnerable [ɪnˈvʌlnərəbəl] *adj* invulnérable
inward [ˈɪnwərd] *adj* intérieur ‖ *adv* intérieurement, en dedans
iodide [ˈaɪ·əˌdaɪd] *s* iodure *m*
iodine [ˈaɪ·əˌdin] *s* (chem) iode *m* ‖ [ˈaɪ·əˌdaɪn] *s* (pharm) teinture *f* d'iode
ion [ˈaɪ·ən], [ˈaɪ·ɑn] *s* ion *m*
ionize [ˈaɪ·əˌnaɪz] *tr* ioniser
I.O.U. [ˈaɪˌoˈju] *s* (letterword) **(I owe you)** reconnaissance *f* de dette
I.Q. [ˈaɪˈkju] *s* (letterword) **(intelligence quotient)** quotient *m* intellectuel
Iran [ɪˈrɑn], [aɪˈræn] *s* l'Iran *m*
Iranian [aɪˈrenɪ·ən] *adj* iranien ‖ *s* (*language*) iranien *m*; (*person*) Iranien *m*
Iraq [ɪˈrɑk] *s* l'Irak *m*
Ira·qi [ɪˈrɑki] *adj* irakien ‖ *s* (*pl* -qis) Irakien *m*
irate [ˈaɪret], [aɪˈret] *adj* irrité
ire [aɪr] *s* courroux *m*, colère *f*

Ireland [ˈaɪrlənd] *s* Irlande *f*; l'Irlande
iris [ˈaɪrɪs] *s* iris *m*
Irish [ˈaɪrɪʃ] *adj* irlandais ‖ *s* (*language*) irlandais *m*; **the Irish** les Irlandais
I'rish·man *s* (*pl* -men) Irlandais *m*
I'rish stew' *s* ragoût *m* irlandais
I'rish·wom'an *s* (*pl* -wom'en) Irlandaise *f*
irk [ʌrk] *tr* ennuyer, fâcher
irksome [ˈʌrksəm] *adj* ennuyeux
iron [ˈaɪ·ərn] *s* fer *m*; (*for pressing clothes*) fer à repasser; **irons** (*fetters*) fers; **to have too many irons in the fire** courir deux lièvres à la fois; **to strike while the iron is hot** battre le fer tant qu'il est chaud ‖ *tr* (*clothes*) repasser; **to iron out** (*a difficulty*) aplanir
i'ron and steel' in'dustry *s* sidérurgie *f*
i'ron-bound' *adj* cerclé; (*unyielding*) inflexible; (*rock-bound*) plein de récifs
ironclad [ˈaɪ·ərnˌklæd] *adj* blindé, cuirassé; (*e.g., contract*) infrangible
i'ron cur'tain *s* rideau *m* de fer
i'ron diges'tion *s* estomac *m* d'autruche
i'ron horse' *s* coursier *m* de fer
ironic(al) [aɪˈrɑnɪk(əl)] *adj* ironique
ironing [ˈaɪ·ərnɪŋ] *s* repassage *m*
i'roning board' *s* planche *f* à repasser
i'ron lung' *s* poumon *m* d'acier
i'ron ore' *s* minerai *m* de fer
i'ron·ware' *s* quincaillerie *f*, ferblanterie *f*
i'ron will' *s* volonté *f* inflexible
i'ron·work' *s* ferrure *f*, ferronnerie *f*
i'ron·work'er *s* ferronnier *m*
iro·ny [ˈaɪrəni] *s* (*pl* -nies) ironie *f*
irradiate [ɪˈredɪˌet] *tr* & *intr* irradier
irrational [ɪˈræʃənəl] *adj* irrationnel
irredeemable [ˌɪrɪˈdiməbəl] *adj* irrémédiable; (*bonds*) non remboursable
irrefutable [ˌɪrɪˈfjutəbəl], [ɪˈrefjutəbəl] *adj* irréfutable
irregular [ɪˈregjələr] *adj* & *s* irrégulier *m*
irrelevant [ɪˈreləvənt] *adj* non pertinent, hors de propos
irreligious [ˌɪrɪˈlɪdʒəs] *adj* irréligieux
irremediable [ˌɪrɪˈmidɪ·əbəl] *adj* irrémédiable
irreparable [ɪˈrepərəbəl] *adj* irréparable
irreplaceable [ˌɪrɪˈplesəbəl] *adj* irremplaçable
irrepressible [ˌɪrɪˈpresɪbəl] *adj* irrépressible, irrésistible
irreproachable [ˌɪrɪˈprotʃəbəl] *adj* irréprochable
irresistible [ˌɪrɪˈzɪstɪbəl] *adj* irrésistible
irrespective [ˌɪrɪˈspektɪv] *adj*—**irrespective of** indépendant de
irresponsible [ˌɪrɪˈspɑnsɪbəl] *adj* irresponsable
irretrievable [ˌɪrɪˈtrivəbəl] *adj* irréparable; (*lost*) irrécupérable
irreverent [ɪˈrevərənt] *adj* irrévérencieux
irrevocable [ɪˈrevəkəbəl] *adj* irrévocable
irrigate [ˈɪrɪˌget] *tr* irriguer

irrigation [ˌɪrɪˈgeʃən] s irrigation f
irritant [ˈɪrɪtənt] adj & s irritant m
irritate [ˈɪrɪˌtet] tr irriter
irritation [ˌɪrɪˈteʃən] s irritation f
irruption [ɪˈrʌpʃən] s irruption f
Isaiah [aɪˈzeɪə] s Isaïe m
isinglass [ˈaɪzɪŋˌglæs], [ˈaɪzɪŋˌglɑs] s gélatine f, colle f de poisson; (mineral) mica m
Islam [ˈɪsləm], [ɪsˈlɑm] s l'Islam m
island [ˈaɪlənd] adj insulaire || s île f
islander [ˈaɪləndər] s insulaire mf
isle [aɪl] s îlot m; (poetic) île f
isolate [ˈaɪsəˌlet], [ˈɪsəˌlet] tr isoler
isolation [ˌaɪsəˈleʃən], [ˌɪsəˈleʃən] s isolement m
isolationist [ˌaɪsəˈleʃənɪst], [ˌɪsəˈleʃənɪst] adj & s isolationniste mf
isosceles [aɪˈsɑsəˌliz] adj isocèle
isotope [ˈaɪsəˌtop] s isotope m
Israel [ˈɪzriəl] s l'Israël m
Israe·li [ɪzˈreli] adj israélien || s (pl -lis [liz]) Israélien m
Israelite [ˈɪzriəˌlaɪt] adj israélite || s Israélite mf
issuance [ˈɪʃuəns] s émission f
issue [ˈɪʃu] s (way out) sortie f, issue f; (outcome) issue; (of a magazine) numéro m; (offspring) descendance f; (of banknotes, stamps, etc.) émission f; (under discussion) point m à discuter; (pathol) écoulement m; at issue en jeu, en litige; to take issue with être en désaccord avec; without issue sans enfants || tr (a book, a magazine) publier; (banknotes, stamps, etc.) émettre; (a summons) lancer; (an order) donner; (a procla-

mation) faire; (a verdict) rendre || intr sortir, déboucher
isthmus [ˈɪsməs] s isthme m
it [ɪt] pron pers ce §82B, §85; lui §85; il §87; le §87; y §87; en §87
Italian [ɪˈtæljən] adj italien || s (language) italien m; (person) Italien m
italic [ɪˈtælɪk] adj (typ) italique; **Italic** italique || **italics** spl italique m
italicize [ɪˈtælɪˌsaɪz] tr mettre en italique
Italy [ˈɪtəli] s Italie f; l'Italie
itch [ɪtʃ] s démangeaison f; (pathol) gale f || tr démanger (with dat) || intr (said of part of body) démanger; (said of person) avoir une démangeaison; to itch to (fig) avoir une démangeaison de
itch·y [ˈɪtʃi] adj (comp -ier; super -iest) piquant; (pathol) galeux
item [ˈaɪtəm] s article m; (in a list) point m; (piece of news) nouvelle f
itemize [ˈaɪtəˌmaɪz] tr spécifier, énumérer
itinerant [aɪˈtɪnərənt], [ɪˈtɪnərənt] adj & s itinérant m
itinerar·y [aɪˈtɪnəˌreri], [ɪˈtɪnəˌreri] adj itinéraire || s (pl -ies) itinéraire m
its [ɪts] adj poss son §88 || pron poss le sien §89
it·self [ɪtˈsɛlf] pron pers soi §85; lui-même §86; se §87
ivied [ˈaɪvid] adj couvert de lierre
ivo·ry [ˈaɪvəri] adj d'ivoire, en ivoire || s (pl -ries) ivoire m; to tickle the ivories (slang) taquiner l'ivoire
i'vory tow'er s (fig) tour f d'ivoire
ivy [ˈaɪvi] s (pl ivies) lierre m

J

J, j [dʒe] s Xᵉ lettre de l'alphabet
jab [dʒæb] s (with a sharp point; with a penknife; with the elbow) coup m; (with a needle) piqûre f; (with the fist) coup sec || v (pret & pp jabbed; ger jabbing) tr donner un coup de coude à; piquer; donner un coup sec à; (a knife) enfoncer
jabber [ˈdʒæbər] tr & intr jaboter
jack [dʒæk] s (aut) cric m; (cards) valet m; (elec) jack m, prise f; (coll) fric m; **Jack** Jeannot m || tr—to **jack up** soulever au cric; (prices) faire monter
jackal [ˈdʒækɔl] s chacal m
jack'ass' s baudet m
jack'daw' s choucas m
jacket [ˈdʒækɪt] s (of a woman; of a book) jaquette f; (of a man's suit) veston m; (metal casing) chemise f
Jack' Frost' s le Bonhomme Hiver
jack'-in-the-box' s diable m à ressort, boîte f à surprise
jack'knife' s (pl -knives) couteau m de poche, couteau pliant; (fancy dive) saut m de carpe
jack'-of-all'-trades' s bricoleur m

jack-o'-lantern [ˈdʒækəˌlæntərn] s potiron m lumineux
jack'pot' s gros lot m, poule f; to hit the jackpot décrocher la timbale
jack' rab'bit s lièvre m des prairies
Jacob [ˈdʒekəb] s Jacques m
jade [dʒed] s (stone; color) jade m; (horse) haridelle f; (woman) coquine f, friponne f
jaded adj éreinté, excédé; blasé
jag [dʒæg] s dentelure f; to have a jag on (slang) être paf
jagged [ˈdʒægɪd] adj dentelé
jaguar [ˈdʒægwɑr] s jaguar m
jail [dʒel] s prison f || tr emprisonner
jail'bird' s cheval m de retour
jailer [ˈdʒelər] s geôlier m
jalop·y [dʒəˈlɑpi] s (pl -ies) bagnole f, tacot m, guimbarde f, clou m
jam [dʒæm] s confiture f; to be in a jam (coll) être dans le pétrin || v (pret & pp jammed; ger jamming) tr coincer || intr se coincer
jamboree [ˌdʒæmbəˈri] s (of boy scouts) jamboree m; (slang) bombance f
James [dʒemz] s Jacques m

jamming ['dʒæmɪŋ] s (rad) brouillage m

Jane [dʒen] s Jeanne f

jangle ['dʒæŋgəl] s cliquetis m || tr faire cliqueter; (nerves) mettre en boule || intr cliqueter

janitor ['dʒænɪtər] s concierge m

janitress ['dʒænɪtrɪs] s concierge f

January ['dʒænju‚erɪ] s janvier m

ja·pan [dʒə'pæn] s laque m du Japon; **Japan** le Japon || v (pret & pp -panned; ger -panning) tr laquer

Japa·nese [‚dʒæpə'niz] adj japonais || s (language) japonais m || s (pl -nese) (person) Japonais m

Jap'anese bee'tle s cétoine f

Jap'anese lan'tern s lanterne f vénitienne

jar [dʒar] s pot m, bocal m; secousse f || v (pret & pp jarred; ger jarring) tr ébranler, secouer § intr trembler, vibrer; (said of sounds, colors, opinions) discorder; **to jar on the nerves** taper sur les nerfs

jargon ['dʒargən] s jargon m

jasmine ['dʒæsmɪn], ['dʒæzmɪn] s jasmin m

jasper ['dʒæspər] s jaspe m

jaundice ['dʒɔndɪs], ['dʒɑndɪs] s jaunisse f, ictère m

jaundiced adj ictérique; (fig) amer

jaunt [dʒɔnt], [dʒɑnt] s excursion f

jaun·ty ['dʒɔntɪ], ['dʒɑntɪ] adj (comp -tier; super -tiest) vif, dégagé; (smart) chic

javelin ['dʒævlɪn], ['dʒævəlɪn] s javelot m

jaw [dʒɔ] s mâchoire f; (of animal) gueule f; **jaws** (e.g., of death) griffes fpl || tr (slang) engueuler || intr (to gossip) (slang) bavarder

jaw'bone' s mâchoire f, maxillaire m

jay [dʒe] s geai m

jay'walk' intr traverser la rue en dehors des clous

jay'walk'er s piéton m distrait

jazz [dʒæz] s jazz m || tr—**to jazz up** (coll) animer, égayer

jazz' band' s orchestre m de jazz

jazz' sing'er s chanteur m de rythme

jealous ['dʒeləs] adj jaloux

jealous·y ['dʒeləsɪ] s (pl -ies) jalousie f

jean [dʒin] s treillis m; **Jean** Jeanne f; **jeans** pantalon m de treillis

jeep [dʒip] s jeep f

jeer [dʒɪr] s raillerie f || intr railler; **to jeer at** se moquer de

Jehovah [dʒɪ'hovə] s Jéhovah m

jell [dʒel] s gelée f || intr se convertir en gelée; (to take hold) prendre forme, se préciser

jel·ly ['dʒelɪ] s (pl -lies) gelée f || v (pret & pp -lied) tr convertir en gelée || intr se convertir en gelée

jel'ly-fish' s méduse f; (person) chiffe f

jeopardize ['dʒepər‚daɪz] tr mettre en danger, compromettre

jeopardy ['dʒepərdɪ] s danger m

jerk [dʒʌrk] s saccade f, secousse f;

(slang) mufle m || tr tirer brusquement, secouer || intr se mouvoir brusquement

jerk'water town' s trou m, petite ville f de province

jerk'water train' s tortillard m

jerk·y ['dʒʌrkɪ] adj (comp -ier; super -iest) saccadé

Jerome [dʒə'rom] s Jérôme m

jersey ['dʒʌrzɪ] s jersey m

Jerusalem [dʒɪ'rusələm] s Jérusalem f

jest [dʒest] s plaisanterie f; **in jest** en plaisantant || intr plaisanter

jester ['dʒestər] s plaisantin m; (medieval clown) bouffon m

Jesuit ['dʒeʒu‚ɪt], ['dʒezju‚ɪt] adj jésuite, jésuitique || s Jésuite m

Jesus ['dʒizəs] s Jésus m

Je'sus Christ' s Jésus-Christ m

jet [dʒet] s (color; mineral) jais m; (of water, gas, etc.) jet m; avion m à réaction || v (pret & pp jetted; ger jetting) intr gicler, jaillir; voyager en jet

jet'-black' adj noir de jais

jet' en'gine s moteur m à réaction

jet' fight'er s chasseur m à réaction

jet' fu'el s carburéacteur m

jet'lin'er s avion m de ligne à réaction

jet' plane' s avion m à réaction

jet' propul'sion s propulsion f par réaction

jetsam ['dʒetsəm] s marchandise f jetée à la mer

jettison ['dʒetɪsən] s jet m à la mer || tr jeter à la mer; (fig) mettre au rebut, rejeter

jet·ty ['dʒetɪ] s (pl -ties) (wharf) pontement m; (breakwater) jetée f

Jew [dʒu] s Juif m; (rel) juif m

jewel ['dʒu‚əl] s joyau m, bijou m; (of a watch) rubis m; (person) bijou

jew'el case' s écrin m

jeweler or **jeweller** ['dʒu‚ələr] s horloger-bijoutier m, bijoutier m

jewelry ['dʒu‚əlrɪ] s joaillerie f

jew'elry store' s bijouterie f; (for watches) horlogerie f

Jewess ['dʒu‚ɪs] s Juive f; (rel) juive f

Jewish ['dʒu‚ɪʃ] adj juif, judaïque

Jews'-harp or **Jew's-harp** ['dʒu‚harp] s guimbarde f

jib [dʒɪb] s (mach) flèche f; (naut) foc m

jibe [dʒaɪb] s moquerie f || intr (coll) concorder; (naut) empanner

jif·fy ['dʒɪfɪ] s (pl -fies)—**in a jiffy** (coll) en un clin d'œil

jig [dʒɪg] s (dance) gigue f; **the jig is up** (slang) il n'y a pas mèche, tout est dans le lac

jigger ['dʒɪgər] s mesure f qui contient une once et demie; (for fishing) leurre m; (tackle) palan m; (flea) puce f; (for separating ore) crible m; (naut) tapecul m; (gadget) (coll) machin m

jiggle ['dʒɪgəl] s petite secousse f || tr agiter, secouer || intr se trémousser

jig'saw' tr chantourner

jig' saw' s scie f à chantourner

jig′saw puz′zle s casse-tête m chinois, puzzle m

jilt [dʒɪlt] tr lâcher, repousser

jim·my ['dʒɪmi] s (pl -mies) pince-monseigneur f || v (pret & pp -mied) tr forcer à l'aide d'une pince-monseigneur

jingle ['dʒɪŋgəl] s (small bell) grelot m; (sound) grelottement m; (poem) rimes fpl enfantines; slogan m à rimes; (rad) réclame f chantée || tr faire grelotter || intr grelotter

jin·go ['dʒɪŋgo] adj & s Jeanne f chauvin m; by jingo! (coll) sapristi!

jingoism ['dʒɪŋgo‚ɪzəm] s chauvinisme m

jinx [dʒɪŋks] s guigne f || tr (coll) porter la guigne à

jitters ['dʒɪtərz] spl (coll) frousse f, trouille f; to give the jitters to (coll) flanquer la trouille à

jittery ['dʒɪtəri] adj froussard

Joan [dʒon] s Jeanne f

job [dʒab] s (piece of work) travail m; (chore) besogne f, tâche f; (employment) emploi m; (work done by contract) travail à forfait; (slang) vol m; bad job (fig) mauvaise affaire f; by the job à la pièce; on the job faisant un stage; (slang) attentif; soft job (coll) filon m, fromage m; to be out of a job être en chômage; to lie down on the job (slang) tirer au flanc

jobber ['dʒabər] s grossiste m; (pieceworker) ouvrier m à la tâche; (dishonest official) agioteur m

job′hold′er s employé m; (in the government) fonctionnaire m

job′ lot′ s solde m de marchandises

job′ print′ing s bilboquet m

jockey ['dʒaki] s jockey m || tr (coll) manœuvrer

jockstrap ['dʒak‚stræp] s suspensoir m

jocose [dʒo'kos] adj jovial, joyeux

jocular ['dʒakjələr] adj facétieux

jog [dʒag] s saccade f || v (pret & pp jogged; ger jogging) tr secouer; (the memory) rafraîchir || intr—to jog along aller au petit trot

John [dʒan] s Jean m; john (slang) toilettes fpl

John′ Bull′ s l'Anglais m typique

John′ Doe′ s M. Dupont, M. Durand

Johnny ['dʒani] s (coll) Jeannot m

john′ny-cake′ s galette f de farine de maïs

John′ny-come′-late′ly s (coll) nouveau venu m

join [dʒɔɪn] tr joindre; (to meet) rejoindre; (a club, a church) se joindre à, entrer dans; (a political party) s'affilier à; (the army) s'engager dans; to join s.o. in + ger se joindre à qn pour + inf || intr se joindre

joiner ['dʒɔɪnər] s menuisier m; (coll) clubiste mf

joint [dʒɔɪnt] adj joint, combiné || s joint m; (culin) rôti m; (slang) boîte f; out of joint disloqué; (fig) de travers

joint′ account′ s compte m indivis

joint′ commit′tee s commission f mixte

joint′ own′er s copropriétaire mf

joint′-stock′ com′pany s société f par actions

joist [dʒɔɪst] s solive f, poutre f

joke [dʒok] s plaisanterie f; to play a joke on faire une attrape à || intr plaisanter

joker ['dʒokər] s farceur m, blagueur m; (cards) joker m, fou m; (coll) clause f ambiguë

jol·ly ['dʒali] adj (comp -lier; super -liest) joyeux, enjoué || adv (coll) rudement

jolt [dʒolt] s cahot m, secousse f || tr cahoter, secouer || intr cahoter

Jonah ['dʒonə] s Jonas m

jonquil ['dʒaŋkwɪl] s jonquille f

Jordan ['dʒɔrdən] s (country) Jordanie f; la Jordanie; (river) Jourdain m

josh [dʒaʃ] tr & intr (coll) blaguer

jostle ['dʒasəl] tr bousculer || intr se bousculer

jot [dʒat] s—not a jot pas un iota || v (pret & pp jotted; ger jotting) tr—to jot down prendre note de

journal ['dʒʌrnəl] s journal m; (magazine) revue f; (mach) tourillon m; (naut) journal de bord

jour′nal box′ s boîte f d'essieu

journalism ['dʒʌrnə‚lɪzəm] s journalisme m

journalist ['dʒʌrnəlɪst] s journaliste mf

journey ['dʒʌrni] s voyage m; trajet m, parcours m || intr voyager

jour′ney·man s (pl -men) compagnon m

joust [dʒʌst], [dʒust], [dʒaust] s joute f || intr jouter

Jove [dʒov] s Jupiter m; by Jove! parbleu!

jovial ['dʒovɪ·əl] adj jovial

jowl [dʒaul] s bajoue f

joy [dʒɔɪ] s joie f

joyful ['dʒɔɪfəl] adj joyeux

joyless ['dʒɔɪlɪs] adj sans joie

joyous ['dʒɔɪ·əs] adj joyeux

joy′ ride′ s (coll) balade f en auto

joy′ stick′ s manche m à balai

Jr. abbr (junior) fils, e.g., Mr. Martin, Jr. M. Martin fils

jubilant ['dʒublənt] adj jubilant

jubilee ['dʒubɪ‚li] s jubilé m

Judaism ['dʒude‚ɪzəm] s judaïsme m

judge [dʒʌdʒ] s juge m || tr & intr juger; judging by à en juger par

judge′ ad′vocate s commissaire m du gouvernement

judgment ['dʒʌdʒmənt] s jugement m

judg′ment day′ s jour m du jugement dernier

judicial [dʒu'dɪʃəl] adj judiciaire; (legal) juridique

judiciar·y [dʒu'dɪʃɪ‚ɛri] adj judiciaire || s (pl -ies) pouvoir m judiciaire; (judges) judicature f

judicious [dʒu'dɪʃəs] adj judicieux

jug [dʒʌg] s (of earthenware) cruche f; (of metal) broc m; (jail) (slang) bloc m

juggle ['dʒʌgəl] *tr* jongler avec; **to juggle away** escamoter || *intr* jongler

juggler ['dʒʌglər] *s* jongleur *m*; imposteur *m*, mystificateur *m*

jugglery ['dʒʌgləri] *or* **juggling** ['dʒʌglɪŋ] *s* jonglerie *f*; (*trickery*) passe-passe *m*

Jugoslavia ['jugo'slɑvɪ-ə] *s* Yougoslavie *f*; la Yougoslavie

jugular ['dʒʌgjələr], ['dʒugjələr] *adj* & *s* jugulaire *f*

juice [dʒus] *s* jus *m*; (coll) courant *m* électrique

juic·y ['dʒusi] *adj* (*comp* -ier; *super* -iest) juteux; (fig) savoureux

jukebox ['dʒuk‚bɑks] *s* pick-up *m* électrique à sous, distributeur *m* de musique

July [dʒu'laɪ] *s* juillet *m*

jumble ['dʒʌmbəl] *s* fouillis *m*, enchevêtrement *m* || *tr* brouiller

jumbo ['dʒʌmbo] *adj* (coll) géant

jump [dʒʌmp] *s* saut *m*, bond *m*; (*nervous start*) sursaut *m*; (sports) saut *m*; (sports) obstacle *m* || *tr* sauter; **to jump ship** tirer une bordée; **to jump the gun** démarrer trop tôt; **to jump the track** dérailler || *intr* sauter, bondir; **to jump at the chance** sauter sur l'occasion

jump' ball' *s* (sports) entre-deux *m*

jump'ing jack' *s* pantin *m*

jump' rope' *s* corde *f* à sauter

jump' seat' *s* strapontin *m*

jump·y ['dʒʌmpi] *adj* (*comp* -ier; *super* -iest) nerveux

junction ['dʒʌŋkʃən] *s* jonction *f*; (*of railroads, roads*) embranchement *m*

juncture ['dʒʌŋktʃər] *s* jointure *f*; (*occasion*) conjoncture *f*; **at this juncture** en cette occasion

June [dʒun] *s* juin *m*

jungle ['dʒʌŋgəl] *s* jungle *f*

jun'gle war'fare *s* guerre *f* de la brousse

junior ['dʒunjər] *adj* cadet; **Bobby Watson, Junior** le jeune Bobby Watson; **Martin, Junior** Martin fils || *s*

cadet *m*; (educ) étudiant *m* de troisième année

jun'ior of'ficer *s* officier *m* subalterne

juniper ['dʒunɪpər] *s* genévrier *m*

ju'niper ber'ry *s* genièvre *m*

junk [dʒʌŋk] *s* (*old metal*) ferraille *f*; (*worthless objects*) bric-à-brac *m*; (*cheap merchandise*) camelote *f*, pacotille *f*; (coll) gnognote *f*; (naut) jonque *f* || *tr* mettre au rebut

junk' deal'er *s* fripier *m*; marchand *m* de ferraille

junket ['dʒʌŋkɪt] *s* excursion *f*; voyage *m* officiel aux frais de la princesse

junk'man' *s* (*pl* -men') ferrailleur *m*; chiffonnier *m*

junk' shop' *s* boutique *f* de bric-à-brac et friperie; bric-à-brac *m*

junk'yard' *s* cimetière *m* de ferraille

jurisdiction [‚dʒurɪs'dɪkʃən] *s* juridiction *f*; **within the jurisdiction of** du ressort de

jurist ['dʒurɪst] *s* légiste *m*

juror ['dʒurər] *s* juré *m*

ju·ry ['dʒuri] *s* (*pl* -ries) jury *m*

just [dʒʌst] *adj* juste || *adv* seulement; justement; **just as** à l'instant où; (*in the same way that*) de même que; **just as it is** tel quel; **just out** vient de paraître; **to have just** venir de

justice ['dʒʌstɪs] *s* justice *f*; (*judge*) juge *m*

jus'tice of the peace' *s* juge *m* de paix

justi·fy ['dʒʌstɪ‚faɪ] *v* (*pret* & *pp* -fied) *tr* justifier

justly ['dʒʌstli] *adv* justement

jut [dʒʌt] *v* (*pret* & *pp* **jutted**; *ger* **jutting**) *intr*—**to jut out** faire saillie

jute [dʒut] *s* jute *m*

juvenile ['dʒuvənɪl], ['dʒuve‚naɪl] *adj* juvénile, adolescent; (*e.g., books*) pour la jeunesse || *s* adolescent *m*

ju'venile delin'quency *s* délinquance *f* juvénile

ju'venile delin'quent *s* délinquant *m* juvénile; **juvenile delinquents** jeunes délinquants *mpl*

juxtapose [‚dʒʌkstə'poz] *tr* juxtaposer

K

K, k [ke] *s* XIᵉ lettre de l'alphabet

kale [kel] *s* chou *m* frisé

kaleidoscope [kə'laɪdə‚skop] *s* kaléidoscope *m*

kangaroo [‚kæŋgə'ru] *s* kangourou *m*

kan'garoo court' *s* tribunal *m* bidon

Kashmir ['kæʃmɪr] *s* le Cachemire

kash'mir shawl' *s* châle *m* de cachemire

keel [kil] *s* quille *f* || *intr*—**to keel over** (naut) chavirer; (coll) tomber dans les pommes

keen [kin] *adj* (*having a sharp edge*) aiguisé, affilé; (*sharp, cutting*) mordant, pénétrant; (*sharp-witted*) perçant, perspicace; (*eager, much inter-*

ested) enthousiaste, vif; (slang) formidable; **keen on** engoué de, passionné de

keep [kip] *s* entretien *m*; (*of medieval castle*) donjon *m*; **for keeps** (*for good*) (coll) pour de bon; (*forever*) (coll) à tout jamais; **to earn one's keep** (coll) gagner sa nourriture, gagner sa vie; **to play for keeps** (coll) jouer le tout pour le tout || *v* (*pret* & *pp* **kept** [kept]) *tr* garder, conserver; (*one's word or promise; accounts, a diary*) tenir; (*animals*) élever; (*a garden*) cultiver; (*a hotel, a school, etc.*) diriger; (*an appointment*) ne pas manquer à; (a holiday) observer; (a person) avoir à sa charge, entretenir; **keep it up!** ne flanchez pas!, continuez!; **to keep away** éloigner; **to keep back** retenir; **to keep down** baisser; (prices) maintenir bas; (a revolt) réprimer; **to keep in** retenir; (a student after school) garder en retenue; (dust, fire, etc.) entretenir; **to keep off** éloigner; **to keep out** tenir éloigné, empêcher d'entrer; **to keep quiet** faire taire; **to keep running** laisser marcher; **to keep score** marquer les points; **to keep servants** avoir des domestiques; **to keep s.o. busy** occuper qn; **to keep s.o. clean (cool, warm,** etc.**)** tenir qn propre (au frais, au chaud, etc.); **to keep s.o. or s.th. from** + ger empêcher qn or q.ch. de + inf; **to keep s.o. informed about** mettre or tenir qn au courant de; **to keep s.o. waiting** faire attendre qn; **to keep up** maintenir; (e.g., all night) faire veiller || intr rester, se tenir; (in good shape) demeurer, se conserver; (e.g., from rotting) se garder; **keep out** (public sign) entrée interdite; **that can keep** (coll) ça peut attendre; **to keep** + ger continuer à + inf; **to keep away** s'éloigner, se tenir à l'écart; **to keep from** + ger s'abstenir de + inf; **to keep in with** rester en bons termes avec; **to keep on** + ger continuer à + inf; **to keep out** rester dehors; **to keep out of** ne pas se mêler de; **to keep quiet** rester tranquille, se taire; **to keep to** (e.g., the right) garder (e.g., la droite); **to keep up** tenir bon, tenir ferme; **to keep up with** aller de pair avec

keeper ['kipər] s gardien m, garde m; (of a game preserve) garde forestier; (of a horseshoe magnet) armature f

keeping ['kipɪŋ] s garde f, surveillance f; (of a holiday) observance f; **in keeping with** en accord avec; **in safe keeping** sous bonne garde; **out of keeping with** en désaccord avec

keep'sake' s souvenir m, gage m d'amitié

keg [kɛg] s tonnelet m; (of herring) caque f

ken [kɛn] s—**beyond the ken of** hors de la portée de

kennel ['kɛnəl] s chenil m

kep·i ['kepi], ['kɛpi] s (pl -is) képi m

kept' wom'an [kɛpt] s (pl wom'en) femme f entretenue

kerchief ['kʌrtʃɪf] s fichu m

kernel ['kʌrnəl] s (inner part of a nut or fruit stone) amande f; (of wheat or corn) grain m; (fig) noyau m, cœur m

kerosene ['kɛrə,sin], [,kɛrə'sin] s kérosène m, pétrole m lampant

ker'osene lamp' s lampe f à pétrole

kerplunk [,kʌr'plʌŋk] interj patatras!

ketchup ['kɛtʃəp] s sauce f tomate, ketchup m

kettle ['kɛtəl] s chaudron m, marmite f; (teakettle) bouilloire f

ket'tle·drum' s timbale f

key [ki] adj clef, clé || s clef f, clé f; (of piano, typewriter, etc.) touche f; (wedge or cotter used to lock parts together) cheville f, clavette f; (reef or low island) caye f; (answer book) livre m du maître; (tone of voice) ton m; (to a map) légende f; (bot) samare f; (mus) tonalité f; (telg) manipulateur m; **key to the city** droit m de cité; **off key** faux; **on key** juste || tr claveter, coincer; **to be keyed up** être surexcité, être tendu

key'board' s clavier m

key'hole' s trou m de la serrure; (of clock) trou de clef

key'man' s (pl -men') pivot m, homme m indispensable

key'note' s (mus) tonique f; (fig) dominante f

key'note speech' s discours m d'ouverture

key'punch' s (mach) perforatrice f

key' ring' s porte-clefs m

key' sig'nature s (mus) armature f de la clé

key'stone' s clef f de voûte

key' word' s mot-clé m

kha·ki ['kɑki], ['kæki] adj kaki || s (pl -kis) kaki m

khan [kɑn] s khan m

kibitz ['kɪbɪts] intr (coll) faire la mouche du coche

kibitzer ['kɪbɪtsər] s (coll) casse-pieds mf, curieux m

kick [kɪk] s coup m de pied; (e.g., of a horse) ruade f; (of a gun) recul m; (complaint) (slang) plainte f; (thrill) (slang) effet m, frisson m; **to get a kick out of** (slang) s'en payer une tranche de || tr donner un coup de pied à; (a ball) botter; **to kick out** (coll) chasser à coups de pied; **to kick s.o. in the pants** (coll) botter le derrière à qn; **to kick the bucket** (coll) casser sa pipe, passer l'arme à gauche; **to kick up a row** (slang) déclencher un chahut || intr donner un coup de pied; (said of gun) reculer; (said of horse) ruer; (sports) botter; **to kick against** regimber contre; **to kick off** (football) donner le coup d'envoi

kick'back' s contrecoup m; (slang) ristourne f

kick'off' s (sports) coup m d'envoi

kid [kɪd] s chevreau m; (coll) gosse mf, mioche mf || v (pret & pp kidded; ger kidding) tr & intr (slang) blaguer; **to kid oneself** (slang) se faire des illusions

kidder ['kɪdər] s (slang) blagueur m

kidding ['kɪdɪŋ] s (slang) blague f; **no kidding!** (slang) sans blague!

kid' gloves' spl gants mpl de chevreau; **to handle with kid gloves** traiter avec douceur, ménager

kid'nap' v (pret & pp -naped or -napped; ger -naping or -napping) tr kidnapper

kidnaper or **kidnapper** ['kɪdnæpər] s kidnappeur m

kidnaping or **kidnapping** [ˈkɪdnæpɪŋ] s kidnappage m

kidney [ˈkɪdni] s rein m; (culin) rognon m

kid'ney bean' s haricot m de Soissons

kid'ney-shaped' adj réniforme

kid'ney stone' s calcul m rénal

kill [kɪl] s mise f à mort; (bag of game) gibier m tué || tr tuer; (an animal) abattre; (a bill, amendment, etc.) mettre son veto à, faire échouer

killer [ˈkɪlər] s assassin m

kill'er whale' s épaulard m, orque f

killing [ˈkɪlɪŋ] adj meurtrier; (exhausting; ridiculous) crevant || s tuerie f; **to make a killing** (coll) réussir un beau coup

kill'-joy' s rabat-joie m, trouble-fête mf

kiln [kɪl], [kɪln] s four m

kil·o [ˈkɪlo], [ˈkilo] s (pl -os) kilo m, kilogramme m; kilomètre m

kilocycle [ˈkɪlə ˌsaɪkəl] s kilocycle m

kilogram [ˈkɪlə ˌgræm] s kilogramme m

kilometer [ˈkɪlə ˌmitər], [kɪˈlɑmɪtər] s kilomètre m

kilowatt [ˈkɪlə ˌwɑt] s kilowatt m

kilowatt-hour [ˈkɪlə ˌwɑtˈaʊr] s (pl -hours) kilowatt-heure m

kilt [kɪlt] s kilt m

kilter [ˈkɪltər] s—**to be out of kilter** (coll) être détraqué

kimo·no [kɪˈmonə], [kɪˈmono] s (pl -nos) kimono m

kin [kɪn] s (family relationship) parenté f; (relatives) les parents mpl; **of kin** apparenté; **the next of kin** le plus proche parent, les plus proches parents

kind [kaɪnd] adj bon, bienveillant; **kind to** bon pour; **to be so kind as to** être assez aimable pour || s espèce f, genre m, sorte f, classe f; **all kinds of** (coll) quantité de; **kind of** (coll) tout à fait; **kind of** (coll) quantité de; **kind of** (coll) plutôt, en quelque sorte; **of a kind** semblable, de même nature; **to pay in kind** payer en nature

kindergarten [ˈkɪndər ˌgɑrtən] s jardin m d'enfants

kindergartner [ˈkɪndər ˌgɑrtnər] s élève mf de jardin d'enfants; (teacher) jardinière f

kind'-heart'ed adj bon, bienveillant

kindle [ˈkɪndəl] tr allumer || intr s'allumer

kindling [ˈkɪndlɪŋ] s allumage m; (wood) bois m d'allumage

kin'dling wood' s bois m d'allumage

kind·ly [ˈkaɪndli] adj (comp -lier; super -liest) (kind-hearted) bon, bienveillant; (e.g., climate) doux; (e.g., terrain) favorable || adv avec bonté, avec bienveillance; **to take kindly** prendre en bonne part; **to take kindly to** prendre en amitié

kindness [ˈkaɪndnɪs] s bonté f, obligeance f

kindred [ˈkɪndrɪd] adj apparenté, de même nature || s parenté f, famille f; parenté, ressemblance f

kinescope [ˈkɪnɪ ˌskop] s (trademark) kinescope m

kinetic [kɪˈnetɪk], [kaɪˈnetɪk] adj cinétique || **kinetics** s cinétique f

kinet'ic en'ergy s énergie f cinétique

king [kɪŋ] s roi m; (cards, chess, & fig) roi; (checkers) pion m doublé, dame f || tr (checkers) damer

king'bolt' s cheville f maîtresse

kingdom [ˈkɪŋdəm] s royaume m; (one of three divisions of nature) règne m

king'fish'er s martin-pêcheur m

king·ly [ˈkɪŋli] adj royal, de roi, digne d'un roi || adv en roi, de roi, comme un roi

king'pin' s cheville f ouvrière; (bowling) quille f du milieu; (coll) ponte m, pontife m

king'post' s poinçon m

kingship [ˈkɪŋ ʃɪp] s royauté f

king'-size' adj grand format, géant

king's' ran'som s rançon f de roi

kink [kɪŋk] s (twist, e.g., in a rope) nœud m; (in a wire) faux pli m; (in hair) frisette f, bouclette f; (soreness in neck) torticolis m; (flaw, difficulty) point m faible; (mental twist) lubie f; (naut) coque f || tr nouer, entortiller || intr se nouer, s'entortiller

kink·y [ˈkɪŋki] adj (comp -ier; super -iest) crépu, bouclé

kinsfolk [ˈkɪnz ˌfok] spl parents mpl

kin'ship s parenté f

kins·man [ˈkɪnzmən] s (pl -men) parent m

kins·woman [ˈkɪnz ˌwʊmən] s (pl -wom'en) parente f

kipper [ˈkɪpər] s kipper m || tr saurer

kiss [kɪs] s baiser m || tr embrasser, donner un baiser à || intr s'embrasser

kit [kɪt] s nécessaire m; (tub) tonnelet m; (of traveler) trousse f de voyage; (mil) équipement m, sac m; **the whole kit and caboodle** (coll) tout le saint-frusquin

kitchen [ˈkɪtʃən] s cuisine f

kitch'en cup'board s vaisselier m

kitchenette [ˌkɪtʃəˈnet] s petite cuisine f

kitch'en gar'den s jardin m potager

kitch'en-maid' s fille f de cuisine

kitch'en police' s (mil) corvée f de cuisine

kitch'en range' s cuisinière f

kitch'en sink' s évier m

kitch'en-ware' s ustensiles mpl de cuisine

kite [kaɪt] s cerf-volant m; (orn) milan m; **to fly a kite** lancer or enlever un cerf-volant

kith' and kin' [kɪθ] spl amis et parents mpl, cousinage m

kitten [ˈkɪtən] s chaton m, petit chat m

kittenish [ˈkɪtənɪʃ] adj enjoué, folâtre; (woman) coquette, chatte

kit·ty [ˈkɪti] s (pl -ties) minet m, minou m; (in card games) cagnotte f, poule f; **kitty, kitty, kitty!** minet, minet, minet!

kleptomaniac [ˌkleptəˈmeni ˌæk] adj & s kleptomane mf

knack [næk] s adresse f, chic m

knapsack ['næp,sæk] s sac m à dos, havresac m

knave [nev] s fripon m; (cards) valet m

knav•er•y ['nevəri] s (pl -ies) friponnerie f

knead [nid] tr pétrir; (to massage) masser

knee [ni] s genou m; **to bring s.o. to his knees** mettre qn à genoux; **to go down on one's knees** se mettre à genoux

knee' breech'es spl culotte f courte

knee'cap' s rotule f; (protective covering) genouillère f

knee'-deep' adj jusqu'aux genoux

knee'-high' adj à la hauteur du genou

knee'hole' s trou m, évidement m pour l'entrée des genoux

knee' jerk' s réflexe m rotulien

kneel [nil] v (pret & pp knelt [nɛlt] or kneeled) intr s'agenouiller, se mettre à genoux

knee'pad' s genouillère f

knee'pan' s rotule f

knee' swell' s (of organ) genouillère f

knell [nɛl] s glas m; **to toll the knell of** sonner le glas de ‖ intr sonner le glas

knickers ['nɪkərz] spl pantalons mpl de golf, knickerbockers mpl

knickknack ['nɪk,næk] s colifichet m

knife [naɪf] s (pl knives [naɪvz]) couteau m; (of paper cutter or other instrument) couperet m, lame f; **to go under the knife** (coll) monter ou passer sur le billard ‖ tr poignarder

knife' sharp'ener s fusil m, affiloir m

knife' switch' s (elec) interrupteur m à couteau

knight [naɪt] s chevalier m; (chess) cavalier m ‖ tr créer ou faire chevalier

knight-errant ['naɪt'ɛrənt] s (pl knights-errant) chevalier m errant —

knighthood ['naɪthud] s chevalerie f

knightly ['naɪtli] adj chevaleresque

knit [nɪt] v (pret & pp knitted or knit; ger knitting) tr tricoter; (one's brows) froncer; **to knit together** lier, unir ‖ intr tricoter; (said of bones) se souder

knit' goods' spl tricot m, bonneterie f

knitting ['nɪtɪŋ] s (action) tricotage m; (product) tricot m

knit'ting nee'dle s aiguille f à tricoter

knit'wear' s tricot m

knob [nɑb] s (lump) bosse f; (of a door, drawer, etc.) bouton m, poignée f; (of a radio) bouton m

knock [nɑk] s coup m, heurt m; (of an internal-combustion engine) cognement m ‖ tr frapper; (repeatedly) cogner à, contre, or sur; (slang) éreinter, dénigrer; **to knock about** bousculer; **to knock against** heurter contre; **to knock down** (with a blow, punch, etc.) renverser; (to the highest bidder) adjuger; **to knock in** enfoncer; **to knock off** faire tomber; **to knock out** faire sortir en cognant; (boxing) mettre knock-out; (to fatigue) (coll) claquer, fatiguer ‖ intr

frapper; (said of internal-combustion engine) cogner; **to knock about** vagabonder, se balader; **to knock against** se heurter contre; **to knock at** or **on** (e.g., a door) heurter à, frapper à; **to knock off** (to stop working) (coll) débrayer

knock'down' adj (dismountable) démontable ‖ s (blow) coup m d'assommoir; (discount) escompte m

knocked'-out' adj éreinté; (boxing) knock-out

knocker ['nɑkər] s (on a door) heurtoir m, marteau m; (critic) (coll) éreinteur m

knock-kneed ['nɑk,nid] adj cagneux

knock'out' s (boxing) knock-out m; (person) (coll) type m renversant; (thing) (coll) chose f sensationnelle

knock'out drops' spl (slang) narcotique m

knoll [nol] s mamelon m, tertre m

knot [nɑt] s nœud m; (e.g., of people) groupe m; (naut) nœud m, mille m marin à l'heure; (loosely) (naut) mille marin; **to tie a knot** faire un nœud; **to tie the knot** (coll) prononcer le conjungo ‖ v (pret & pp knotted; ger knotting) tr nouer; **to knot one's brow** froncer le sourcil ‖ intr se nouer

knot'hole' s trou m de nœud

knot•ty ['nɑti] adj (comp -tier; super -tiest) noueux; (e.g., question) épineux

know [no] s—**to be in the know** (coll) être au courant, être à la page ‖ v (pret knew [n(j)u]; pp known) tr & intr (by reasoning or learning) savoir; (by the senses or by perception; through acquaintance or recognition) connaître; **as far as I know** autant que je sache; **to know about** être informé de, savoir; **to know best** être le meilleur juge; **to know how to** + inf savoir + inf; **to let s.o. know about** faire part à qn de; **you ought to know better** vous devriez avoir honte; **you ought to know better than to . . .** vous devriez vous bien garder de . . . ; **you wouldn't know s.o. from . . .** on prendrait qn pour . . .

knowable ['no-əbəl] adj connaissable

know'-how' s technique f, savoir-faire m

knowing ['no-ɪŋ] adj avisé; (look, smile) entendu

knowingly ['no-ɪŋli] adv sciemment, en connaissance de cause; (on purpose) exprès

know'-it-all' adj (coll) omniscient ‖ s (coll) Monsieur Je-sais-tout m

knowledge ['nɑlɪdʒ] s (faculty) science f, connaissances fpl, savoir m; (awareness, familiarity) connaissance f; **not to my knowledge** pas que je sache; **to have a thorough knowledge of** posséder une connaissance approfondie de; **to my knowledge, to the best of my knowledge** à ma connaissance, autant que je sache; **without my knowledge** à mon insu

knowledgeable ['nɑlɪdʒəbəl] *adj* (coll) intelligent, bien informé

know'-noth'ing *s* ignorant *m*

knuckle ['nʌkəl] *s* jointure *f* or articulation *f* du doigt; (*of a quadruped*) jarret *m*; (mach) joint *m* en charnière; **knuckle of ham** jambonneau *m*; **to rap s.o. over the knuckles** donner sur les doigts or ongles à qn ‖ *intr*—**to knuckle down** se soumettre; (*to work hard*) s'y mettre sérieusement

knurl [nɑrl] *s* molette *f* ‖ *tr* moleter

k.o. ['ke'o] (letterword) (**knockout**) *s* k.o. *m* ‖ *tr* mettre k.o.

Koran [ko'rɑn], [ko'ræn] *s* Coran *m*

Korea [ko'ri·ə] *s* Corée *f*; **la Corée**

Korean [ko'ri·ən] *adj* coréen ‖ *s* (*language*) coréen; (*person*) Coréen *m*

kosher ['koʃər] *adj* casher, cawcher; (coll) convenable

kowtow ['kau'tau], ['ko'tau] *intr* se prosterner à la chinoise; **to kowtow to** faire des courbettes à or devant

K.P. ['ke'pi] *s* (letterword) (**kitchen police**) (mil) corvée *f* de cuisine; **to be on K.P. duty** (mil) être de soupe

kudos ['k(j)udɑs] *s* (coll) gloire *f*, éloges *mpl*, flatteries *fpl*

L

L, l [el] *s* XIIᵉ lettre de l'alphabet

la·bel ['lebəl] *s* étiquette *f*; (*brand*) marque *f*; (*in a dictionary*) rubrique *f*, référence *f* ‖ *v* (*pret & pp* **-beled** or **-belled**) *ger* **-beling** or **-belling**) *tr* étiqueter

labial ['lebɪ·əl] *adj* labial ‖ *s* labiale *f*

labor ['lebər] *s* ouvrier *m*; (*toil*) labeur *m*, peine *f*; (*job, task*) tâche *f*, besogne *f*; (*manual work involved in an undertaking; the wages for such work*) main-d'œuvre *f*; (*wage-earning worker as contrasted with capital and management*) le salariat, le travail; (*childbirth*) couches *fpl*, travail; **to be in labor** être en couches ‖ *tr* (*a point, subject, etc.*) insister sur; (*one's style*) travailler, élaborer ‖ *intr* travailler; (*to toil*) travailler dur, peiner; (*to exert oneself*) s'efforcer; (*said of ship*) fatiguer, bourlinguer; **to labor under** être victime de; **to labor up** (*a hill, slope, etc.*) gravir; **to labor uphill** peiner en côte; **to labor with child** être en travail d'enfant

la'bor and man'agement *spl* la classe ouvrière et le patronat

laborato·ry ['læbərə,tori] *s* (*pl* **-ries**) laboratoire *m*

lab'oratory class' *s* classe *f* de travaux pratiques

labored ['lebərd] *adj* travaillé, trop élaboré; (*e.g., breathing*) pénible

laborer ['lebərər] *s* travailleur *m*, ouvrier *m*; (*unskilled worker*) journalier *m*, manœuvre *m*

laborious [lə'borɪ·əs] *adj* laborieux

la'bor move'ment *s* mouvement *m* syndicaliste

la'bor un'ion *s* syndicat *m*, syndicat ouvrier

Labourite ['lebə,raɪt] *adj & s* (Brit) travailliste *mf*

La'bour Par'ty ['lebər] *s* (Brit) travailliste ‖ *s* parti *m* travailliste

Labrador ['læbrə,dɔr] *s* le Labrador

laburnum [lə'bʌrnəm] *s* cytise *m*

labyrinth ['læbɪrɪnθ] *s* labyrinthe *m*

lace [les] *s* dentelle *f*; (*string to tie shoe, corset, etc.*) lacet *m*, cordon *m*; (*braid*) broderies *fpl* ‖ *tr* garnir or border de dentelles; (*shoes, corset, etc.*) lacer; (*to braid*) entrelacer; (coll) flanquer une rossée à, rosser

lace' trim'ming *s* passementerie *f*

lace'work' *s* dentelles *fpl*, passementerie *f*

lachrymose ['lækrɪ,mos] *adj* larmoyant

lacing ['lesɪŋ] *s* lacet *m*, cordon *m*; (*trimming*) galon *m*, passement *m*; (coll) rossée *f*

lack [læk] *s* manque *m*, défaut *m*; (*lack of necessities*) pénurie *f*; **for lack of** faute de ‖ *tr* manquer de, être dépourvu de ‖ *intr* (*to be lacking*) manquer

lackadaisical [,lækə'dezɪkəl] *adj* languissant, apathique

lackey ['lækɪ] *s* laquais *m*

lacking ['lækɪŋ] *prep* dépourvu de, dénué de

lack'lus'ter *adj* terne, fade

laconic [lə'kɑnɪk] *adj* laconique

lacquer ['lækər] *s* laque *m & f* ‖ *tr* laquer

lac'quer ware' *s* laques *mpl*, objets *mpl* d'art en laque

lacrosse [lə'krɔs], [lə'krɑs] *s* crosse *f*, jeu *m* de crosse; **to play lacrosse** jouer à la crosse

lacu·na [lə'kjunə] *s* (*pl* **-nas** or **-nae** [ni]) lacune *f*

lac·y ['lesɪ] *adj* (*comp* **-ier**; *super* **-iest**) de dentelle; (fig) fin, léger

lad [læd] *s* garçon *m*, gars *m*

ladder ['lædər] *s* échelle *f*; (*stepping stone*) (fig) marchepied *m*, échelon *m*; (*stepladder*) marchepied, escabeau *m*; (*run in stocking*) (Brit) démaillage *m*; (*stairway*) (naut) escalier *m*

lad'der truck' *s* fourgon-pompe *m* à échelle

la'dies' room' *s* toilettes *fpl* pour dames, lavabos *mpl* pour dames

ladle ['ledəl] s louche f || tr servir à la louche

la·dy ['ledɪ] s (pl -dies) dame f; **ladies** (public sign) dames; **ladies and gentlemen!** (formula used in addressing an audience) mesdames, mesdemoiselles, messieurs!; messieurs dames! (coll)

la'dy·bird' or **la'dy·bug'** s coccinelle f, bête f à bon Dieu

la'dy·fin'ger s biscuit m à la cuiller

la'dy-in-wait'ing s (pl ladies-in-waiting) demoiselle f d'honneur

la'dy-kil'ler s bourreau m des cœurs, tombeur m de femmes

la'dy·like' adj de bon ton, de dame

la'dy·love' s bien-aimée f, dulcinée f

la'dy of the house' s maîtresse f de maison

la'dy's maid' s camériste f

la'dy's man' s homme m à succès

lag [læg] s retard m || v (pret & pp lagged; ger lagging) intr traîner; **to lag behind** rester en arrière

la'ger beer' ['lɑgər] s bière f de fermentation basse, lager m

laggard ['lægərd] adj tardif || s traînard m

lagoon [lə'gun] s lagune f

laid' pa'per [led] s papier m vergé

laid' up' adj mis en réserve; (naut) mis en rade; (coll) alité, au lit

lair [ler] s tanière f; (fig) repaire m

laity ['le·ɪti] s profanes mfpl; (eccl) laïques mfpl

lake [lek] adj lacustre || s lac m

lamb [læm] s agneau m

lambaste [læm'best] tr (to thrash) (coll) flanquer une rossée à; (to reprimand harshly) (coll) passer un savon à

lamb' chop' s côtelette f d'agneau

lambkin ['læmkɪn] s agnelet m

lamb'skin' s peau f d'agneau; (dressed with its wool) mouton m, agnelin m

lame [lem] adj boiteux; (sore) endolori; (e.g., excuse) faible, piètre || tr estropier, rendre boiteux

lament [lə'ment] s lamentation f; (dirge) complainte f || tr déplorer || intr lamenter, se lamenter

lamentable ['læməntəbəl] adj lamentable

lamentation [ˌlæmən'teʃən] s lamentation f

laminate ['læmɪˌnet] tr laminer

lamp [læmp] s lampe f

lamp'black' s noir m de fumée

lamp' chim'ney s verre m de lampe

lamp'light' s lumière f de lampe

lamp'light'er s allumeur m de réverbères

lampoon [læm'pun] s libelle m, pasquinade f || tr faire des libelles contre

lamp'post' s réverbère m, poteau m de réverbère

lamprey ['læmprɪ] s lamproie f

lamp'shade' s abat-jour m

lamp'wick' s mèche f de lampe

lance [læns], [lɑns] s lance f; (surg) lancette f, bistouri m || tr percer d'un coup de lance; (surg) donner un coup de lancette or bistouri à

lancet ['lænsɪt], ['lɑnsɪt] s (surg) lancette f, bistouri m

land [lænd] adj terrestre, de terre || s terre f; **land of milk and honey** pays de cocagne; **to make land** toucher terre; **to see how the land lies** sonder or tâter le terrain || tr débarquer, mettre à terre; (an airplane) atterrir; (a fish) amener à terre; (e.g., a job) (coll) décrocher; (a blow) (coll) flanquer || intr débarquer, descendre à terre; (said of airplane) atterrir; **to land on one's feet** retomber sur ses pieds; **to land on the moon** alunir; **to land on the water** amerrir

land' breeze' s brise f de terre

landed adj (owning land) terrien; (realestate) immobilier

land'ed prop'erty s propriété f foncière

land'fall' s (sighting land) abordage m; (landing of ship or plane) atterrissage m; (landslide) glissement m de terrain

landing ['lændɪŋ] s (of plane) atterrissage m; (of ship) mise f à terre, débarquement m; (place where passengers and goods are landed) débarcadère m; (of stairway) palier m; (on the moon) alunissage m

land'ing bea'con s (aer) radiophare m d'atterissage

land'ing craft' s (nav) péniche f de débarquement

land'ing field' s (aer) terrain m d'atterrissage

land'ing force' s (nav) détachement m de débarquement

land'ing gear' s (aer) train m d'atterrissage

land'ing par'ty s (nav) détachement m de débarquement

land'ing stage' s débarcadère m

land'ing strip' s (aer) piste f d'atterrissage

land'la'dy s (pl -dies) (e.g., of an apartment) logeuse f, propriétaire f; (of a lodging house) patronne f; (of an inn) aubergiste f

land'locked' adj entouré de terre

land'lord' s (e.g., of an apartment) logeur m, propriétaire m; (of a lodging house) patron m; (of an inn) aubergiste m

land'lub'ber ['lænd,lʌbər] s marin m d'eau douce

land'mark' s point m de repère, borne f; (important event) étape f importante; (naut) amer m

land' of'fice s bureau m du cadastre

land'own'er s propriétaire m foncier

landscape ['lænd,skep] s paysage m || tr aménager en jardins

land'scape ar'chitect s architecte m paysagiste

land'scape gar'dener s jardinier m paysagiste

land'scape paint'er s paysagiste mf

landscapist ['lænd,skepɪst] s paysagiste mf

land'slide' s glissement m de terrain, éboulement m; (in an election) raz m de marée

landward ['lændwərd] adv du côté de la terre, vers la terre

land' wind' [wɪnd] s vent m de terre

lane [len] s (narrow street or passage) ruelle f; (in the country) sentier m; (of an automobile highway) voie f; (line of cars) file f; (of an air or ocean route) route f de navigation

langsyne ['læŋ'saɪn] s (Scotch) le temps jadis || adv (Scotch) au temps jadis

language ['læŋgwɪdʒ] s langage m; (e.g., of a nation) langue f

languid ['læŋgwɪd] adj languissant

languish ['læŋgwɪʃ] intr languir

languor ['læŋgər] s langueur f

languorous ['læŋgərəs] adj langoureux

lank [læŋk] adj efflanqué, maigre; (hair) plat, e.g., **lank hair** cheveux plats

lank·y ['læŋki] adj (comp **-ier**; super **-iest**) grand et maigre

lanolin ['lænəlɪn] s lanoline f

lantern ['læntərn] s lanterne f

lan'tern slide' s diapositive f

lanyard ['lænjərd] s (around the neck) cordon m; (arti) tire-feu m; (naut) ride f

lap [læp] s (of human body or clothing) genoux mpl, giron m; (of garment) genoux m, pan m; (with the tongue) coup m de langue; (of the waves) clapotis m; (in a race) (sports) tour m; **last lap** dernière étape f || v (pret & pp **lapped**; ger **lapping**) tr (with the tongue) laper; **to lap up** laper; (coll) gober || intr laper; (said of waves) clapoter; **to lap over** déborder

lap' dog' s bichon m, chien m de manchon

lapel [lə'pel] s revers m

Lap'land' s Laponie f; la Laponie

Laplander ['læp,lændər] s Lapon m

Lapp [læp] s (language) lapon m; (person) Lapon m

lap' robe' s couverture f de voyage

lapse [læps] s (passing of time) laps m; (slipping into guilt or error) faute f, écart m; (fall, decline) chute f; (e.g., of an insurance policy) expiration f, échéance f; (of memory) absence f, défaillance f || intr (to elapse) s'écouler, passer; (to err) manquer à ses devoirs; (to decline) déchoir; (said, e.g., of a right) périmer, tomber en désuétude; (said, e.g., of a legacy) devenir caduc; (said, e.g., of an insurance policy) cesser d'être en vigueur

lap'wing' s (orn) vanneau m huppé

larce·ny ['lɑrsəni] s (pl **-nies**) larcin m, vol m

larch [lɑrtʃ] s (bot) mélèze m

lard [lɑrd] s saindoux m || tr larder

larder ['lɑrdər] s garde-manger m

large [lɑrdʒ] adj grand; **at large** en liberté

large' intes'tine s gros intestin m

largely ['lɑrdʒli] adv principalement

largeness ['lɑrdʒnɪs] s grandeur f

large'-scale' adj sur une large échelle, de grande envergure

lariat ['læri·ət] s (for catching animals) lasso m; (for tying grazing animals) longe f

lark [lɑrk] s alouette f; (prank) espièglerie f; **to go on a lark** (coll) faire la bombe

lark'spur' s (rocket larkspur) pied-d'alouette m; (field larkspur) consoude f royale

lar·va ['lɑrvə] s (pl **-vae** [vi]) larve f

laryngeal [lə'rɪndʒɪ·əl], [,lærɪn'dʒi·əl] adj laryngé, laryngien

laryngitis [,lærɪn'dʒaɪtɪs] s laryngite f

laryngoscope [lə'rɪŋgə,skop] s laryngoscope m

larynx ['lærɪŋks] s (pl **larynxes** or **larynges** [lə'rɪndʒiz]) larynx m

lascivious [lə'sɪvɪ·əs] adj lascif

lasciviousness [lə'sɪvɪ·əsnɪs] s lasciveté f

laser ['lezər] s (acronym) (**light amplification by stimulated emission of radiation**) laser m

lash [læʃ] s (cord on end of whip) mèche f; coup m; (splatter of rain on window) fouettement m; (eyelash) cil m || tr fouetter, cingler; (to bind, tie) (naut) amarrer || intr fouetter; **to lash out at** cingler

lashing ['læʃɪŋ] s fouettée f; (rope) amarre f; (naut) amarrage m

lass [læs] s jeune fille f, jeunesse f; bonne amie f

lassitude ['læsɪ,t(j)ud] s lassitude f

las·so ['læso], [læ'su] s (pl **-sos** or **-soes**) lasso m

last [læst], [lɑst] adj (in a series) dernier (before noun), e.g., **the last week of the war** la dernière semaine de la guerre; (just elapsed) dernier (after noun), e.g., **last week** la semaine dernière; **before last** avant-dernier, e.g., **the time before last** l'avant-dernière fois; **the last two** les deux derniers || s dernier m; (the end) fin f, bout m; (for holding shoe) forme f; **at last** enfin, à la fin; **at long last** à la fin des fins; **the last of the month** la fin du mois; **to the last** jusqu'à la fin, jusqu'au bout || intr durer; (to hold out) tenir

last' eve'ning adv hier soir

lasting ['læstɪŋ], ['lɑstɪŋ] adj durable

lastly ['læstli], ['lɑstli] adv pour finir, en dernier lieu, enfin

last'-minute news' s nouvelles fpl de dernière heure

last' name' s nom m, nom de famille

last' night' adv hier soir; cette nuit

last' quar'ter s dernier quartier m

last' sleep' s sommeil m de la mort

last' straw' s—**that's the last straw!** c'est le comble!

Last' Sup'per s (eccl) Cène f

last will' and test'ament s testament m, acte m de dernière volonté

last' word' s dernier mot m; (latest style) (coll) dernier cri m

latch [lætʃ] *s* loquet *m* ‖ *tr* fermer au loquet

latch′key′ *s* clef *f* de porte d'entrée

latch′string′ *s* cordon *m* de loquet

late [let] *adj* (*happening after the usual time*) tardif; (*person; train, bus, etc.*) en retard; (*e.g., art*) de la dernière époque; (*events*) dernier, récent; (*news*) de la dernière heure; (*incumbent of an office*) ancien; (*deceased*) défunt, feu; **at a late hour in** (*the night, the day*) bien avant dans, à une heure avancée de; **in the late seventeenth century (eighteenth century, etc.**) vers la fin du dix-septième siècle (dix-huitième siècle, etc.); **it is late** il est tard; **of late** dernièrement, récemment, depuis peu; **to be late** être en retard; **to be late in** + *ger* tarder à + *inf* ‖ *adv* tard, tardivement; (*after the appointed time*) en retard; **late in** (*the afternoon, the season, the week, the month*) vers la fin de; **late in life** sur le tard; **very late in** (*the night, the day*) bien avant dans, à une heure avancée de

late-comer [′let′kʌmər] *s* (*newcomer*) nouveau venu *m*; (*one who arrives late*) retardataire *mf*

lateen′ sail′ [læ′tin] *s* voile *f* latine

lateen′ yard′ *s* antenne *f*

lately [′letli] *adv* dernièrement, récemment, depuis peu

latency [′letənsi] *s* latence *f*

latent [′letənt] *adj* latent

later [′letər] *adj comp* plus tard, plus tardif; (*event*) subséquent, plus récent; (*kings, luminaries, etc.*) derniers en date; **later than** postérieur à ‖ *adv comp* plus tard; **later on** plus tard, par la suite; **see you later** (coll) à tout à l'heure

lateral [′lætərəl] *adj* latéral

lath [læθ], [lɑθ] *s* latte *f* ‖ *tr* latter

lathe [leð] *s* (mach) tour *m*; **to turn on a lathe** façonner au tour

lather [′læðər] *s* (*of soap*) mousse *f*; (*of horse*) écume *f* ‖ *tr* savonner ‖ *intr* (*said of soap*) mousser; (*said of horse*) être couvert d'écume

lathing [′læθɪŋ], [′lɑθɪŋ] *s* lattage *m*

Latin [′lætɪn], [′lætən] *adj* latin ‖ *s* (*language*) latin *m*; (*person*) Latin *m*

Lat′in Amer′ica *s* l'Amérique *f* latine

Lat′in-Amer′ican *adj* latino-américain ‖ *s* Latino-américain *m*

latitude [′lætɪ ˌt(j)ud] *s* latitude *f*

latrine [lə′trin] *s* latrines *fpl*

latter [′lætər] *adj* dernier; **the latter part of** (*e.g., a century*) la fin de ‖ *pron*—**the latter** celui-ci §84; le dernier

lattice [′lætɪs] *adj* treillissé ‖ *s* treillis *m* ‖ *tr* treillisser

lat′tice gird′er *s* poutre *f* à croisillons

lat′tice-work′ *s* treillis *m*, grillage *m*

laud [lɔd] *tr* louer

laudable [′lɔdəbəl] *adj* louable

laudanum [′lɔdənəm], [′lɔdnəm] *s* laudanum *m*

laudatory [′lɔdə ˌtori] *adj* laudatif, élogieux

laugh [læf], [lɑf] *s* rire *m* ‖ *tr*—**to laugh away** chasser en riant; **to laugh off** tourner en plaisanterie ‖ *intr* rire; **to laugh at** rire de

laughable [′læfəbəl], [′lɑfəbəl] *adj* risible

laughing [′læfɪŋ], [′lɑfɪŋ] *adj* riant, rieur; **it's no laughing matter** il n'y a pas de quoi rire ‖ *s* rire *m*

laugh′ing gas′ *s* gaz *m* hilarant

laugh′ing-stock′ *s* risée *f*, fable *f*

laughter [′læftər], [′lɑftər] *s* rire *m*

launch [lɔntʃ], [lɑntʃ] *s* (*open motorboat*) canot *m* automobile, vedette *f*; (naut) chaloupe *f* ‖ *tr* lancer; (*an attack*) déclencher ‖ *intr*—**to launch into, to launch out on** se lancer dans

launching [′lɔntʃɪŋ], [′lɑntʃɪŋ] *s* lancement *m*

launch′ing pad′ *s* rampe *f* de lancement, aire *f* de lancement

launder [′lɔndər], [′lɑndər] *tr* blanchir

launderer [′lɔndərər], [′lɑndərər] *s* blanchisseur *m*, buandier *m*

laundering [′lɔndərɪŋ], [′lɑndərɪŋ] *s* blanchissage *m*

laundress [′lɔndrɪs], [′lɑndrɪs] *s* blanchisseuse *f*, buandière *f*

laun-dry [′lɔndri], [′lɑndri] *s* (*pl* -dries) linge *m* à blanchir, lessive *f*; (*room*) buanderie *f*; (*business*) blanchisserie *f*

laun′dry-man′ *s* (*pl* -men) blanchisseur *m*, buandier *m*

laun′dry room′ *s* buanderie *f*

laun′dry-wom′an *s* (*pl* -wom′en) blanchisseuse *f*, buandière *f*

laureate [′lɔri ɪt] *adj* & *s* lauréat *m*

lau-rel [′lɔrəl], [′lɑrəl] *s* laurier *m*; **to rest on one's laurels** s'endormir sur ses lauriers ‖ *v* (*pret* & *pp* -reled *or* -relled) *ger* -reling *or* -relling) *tr* couronner de lauriers

lava [′lɑvə], [′lævə] *s* lave *f*

lavaliere [ˌlævə′lɪr] *s* pendentif *m*

lavato-ry [′lævə ˌtori] *s* (*pl* -ries) (*room equipped for washing hands and face; bowl with running water*) lavabo *m*; (*toilet*) lavabos

lavender [′lævəndər] *s* lavande *f*

lav′ender wa′ter *s* eau *f* de lavande

lavish [′lævɪʃ] *adj* prodigue; (*reception, dinner, etc.*) somptueux, magnifique ‖ *tr* prodiguer

law [lɔ] *s* (*of man, of nature, of science*) loi *f*; (*branch of knowledge concerned with law; body of laws; study of law, profession of law*) droit *m*; **to go to law** recourir à la justice; **to go to law with s.o.** citer qn en justice; **to lay down the law** faire la loi; **to practice law** exercer le droit; **to read law** étudier le droit, faire son droit

law′-abid′ing *adj* soumis aux lois, respectueux des lois

law′ and or′der *s* ordre *m* public; **to maintain law and order** maintenir ou faire régner l'ordre

law′break′er *s* transgresseur *m* de la loi

law′ court′ *s* cour *f* de justice, tribunal *m*

lawful ['lɔfəl] adj légal, légitime

lawless ['lɔlɪs] adj sans loi; (*unbridled*) sans frein, déréglé

law'mak'er s législateur m

lawn [lɔn] s pelouse f, gazon m; (*fabric*) batiste f, linon m

lawn' mow'er s tondeuse f de gazon

law' of'fice s étude f (d'avocat)

law' of na'tions s loi f des nations

law' of the jun'gle s loi f de la jungle

law' stu'dent s étudiant m en droit

law'suit' s procès m

lawyer ['lɔjər] s avocat m

lax [læks] adj (*in morals, discipline, etc.*) relâché, négligent; (*loose, not tense*) lâche; (*vague*) vague, flou

laxative ['læksətɪv] adj & s laxatif m

lay [le] adj (*not belonging to clergy*) laïc ou laïque; (*not having special training*) profane ‖ s situation f; (*poem*) lai m ‖ v (*pret & pp* laid [led]). tr poser, mettre; (*a trap*) tendre; (*eggs*) pondre; (*e.g., bricks*) ranger; (*a foundation*) jeter, établir; (*a cable*) poser; (*a mine*) (naut) mouiller; **to be laid in Rome (in France, etc.)** (*said, e.g., of scene*) se passer à Rome (en France, etc.); **to lay aside, away,** or **by** mettre de côté; **to lay down** (*one's life*) sacrifier; (*one's weapons*) déposer; (*conditions*) imposer; **to lay down the law to s.o.** (coll) rappeler qn à l'ordre; **to lay in** (*supplies*) faire provision de; **to lay into s.o.** (coll) sauter dessus qn; **to lay it on thick** (coll) y aller fort; **to lay low** (*to overwhelm*) abattre, terrasser; **to lay off** (*an employee*) congédier; (*to mark the boundaries of*) tracer; (*to stop bothering*) (coll) laisser tranquille; **to lay on** (*paint*) appliquer; (*hands; taxes*) imposer; **to lay open** mettre à nu; **to lay out** arranger; (*to display*) étaler; (*to outline*) tracer; (*money*) débourser; (*a corpse*) faire la toilette de; (*a garden*) aménager; **to lay up** (*to stock up on*) amasser; (*to injure*) aliter; (*a boat*) mettre en rade ‖ intr (*said of hen*) pondre; **to lay about** frapper de tous côtés; **to lay for** être à l'affût de, guetter; **to lay into** (slang) rosser, battre; **to lay off** (coll) cesser; **to lay off smoking** (coll) renoncer au tabac; **to lay over** faire escale; **to lay to** (naut) se mettre à la cape

lay' broth'er s frère m lai, frère convers

layer ['le·ər] s couche f; (*hen*) pondeuse f ‖ tr (hort) marcotter

lay'er cake' s gâteau m sandwich

layette [le'et] s layette f

lay' fig'ure s mannequin m

laying ['le·ɪŋ] s pose f; (*of foundation*) assise f; (*of eggs*) ponte f

lay'man s (*pl* -men) (*person who is not a clergyman*) laïc m ou laïque mf; (*person who has no special training*) profane m

lay'off' s (*discharge*) renvoi m; (*unemployment*) chômage m

lay' of the land' s configuration f du terrain; (fig) aspect m de l'affaire

lay'out' s plan m, dessin m, tracé m; (*of tools*) montage m; (*organization*) disposition f; (*banquet*) (coll) festin m

lay'o'ver s arrêt m en cours de route

lay' sis'ter s sœur f laie, sœur converse

laziness ['lezɪnɪs] s paresse f

la-zy ['lezi] adj (*comp* -zier; *super* -ziest) paresseux

la'zy-bones' s (coll) flemmard m, fainéant m

lb. abbr (**pound**) livre f

lea [li] s (*meadow*) pâturage m, prairie f

lead [led] adj en plomb, de plomb ‖ [led] s plomb m; (*of lead pencil*) mine f (de plombagine); (*for sounding depth*) (naut) sonde f; (typ) interligne f ‖ [led] v (*pret & pp* leaded; *ger* leading) tr plomber; (typ) interligner ‖ [lid] s (*foremost place*) avance f; (*guidance*) direction f, conduite f; (*leash*) laisse f; (*of a newspaper article*) article m de fond; (*leading role*) premier rôle m; (*leading man*) jeune premier m; (elec) câble m de canalisation, conducteur m; (elec, mach) avance; (min) filon m; **to follow s.o.'s lead** suivre l'exemple de qn; **to have the lead** (cards) avoir la main; **to return the lead** (cards) rejouer la couleur; **to take the lead** prendre le pas ‖ [lid] v (*pret & pp* led [led]) tr conduire, mener; (*to command*) commander, diriger; (*to be foremost in*) être à la tête de; (*e.g., an orchestra*) diriger; (*a good or bad life*) mener; (*a certain card*) attaquer de; (*a certain card suit*) attaquer; (elec, mach) canaliser; **to lead away** or **off** emmener; **to lead off** (*to start*) commencer; **to lead on** encourager; **to lead s.o. to believe** mener qn à croire ‖ intr aller devant, tenir la tête; (cards) avoir la main; **to lead to** conduire à, mener à; (*another street, a certain result, etc.*) aboutir à; **to lead up to** (*a great work*) préluder à (*un grand ouvrage*); (*a subject*) amener (*un sujet*)

leaden ['ledən] adj (*of lead; like lead*) de plomb, en plomb; (*heavy as lead*) pesant; (*sluggish*) alangui; (*complexion*) plombé

leader ['lidər] s chef m, guide mf; (*ringleader*) tête f; chef d'orchestre; (*in a dance; among animals*) meneur m; (*in a newspaper*) article m de fond; (*of a reel of tape or film*) amorce f; (*bargain*) article réclame; (*vein of ore*) filon m

leadership ['lidər,ʃɪp] s direction f; don m de commandement

leading ['lidɪŋ] adj principal, premier

lead'ing edge' s (aer) bord m d'attaque

lead'ing la'dy s vedette f, étoile f, jeune première f

lead'ing man' s (*pl* men') jeune premier m

lead'ing ques'tion s question f tendancieuse

lead'-in wire' ['lid,ɪn] s (rad, telv) fil m d'amenée

lead′ pen′cil [lɛd] *s* crayon *m* (à mine de graphite)

lead′ poi′soning [lɛd] *s* saturnisme *m*

leaf [lif] *s* (*pl* **leaves** [livz]) feuille *f*; (*inserted leaf of table*) rallonge *f*; (*hinged leaf of door or table top*) battant *m*; **to shake like a leaf** trembler comme une feuille; **to turn over a new leaf** tourner la page, faire peau neuve ‖ *intr*—**to leaf through** feuilleter

leafless [′liflɪs] *adj* sans feuilles, dénudé

leaflet [′liflɪt] *s* dépliant *m*, papillon *m*, feuillet *m*; (*bot*) foliole *f*

leaf′stalk′ *s* (bot) pétiole *m*

leaf•y [′lifi] *adj* (*comp* -ier; *super* -iest) feuillu, touffu

league [lig] *s* (*unit of distance*) lieue *f*; (*association, alliance*) ligue *f* ‖ *tr* liguer ‖ *intr* se liguer

League′ of Na′tions *s* Société *f* des Nations

leak [lik] *s* fuite *f*; (*in a ship*) voie *f* d'eau; (*of electricity, heat, etc.*) perte *f*, fuite; (*of news, secrets, money, etc.*) fuite; **to spring a leak** avoir une fuite; (naut) faire une voie d'eau ‖ *tr* faire couler; (*gas, steam; secrets, news*) laisser échapper ‖ *intr* fuire, s'écouler; (naut) faire eau; **to leak away** se perdre; **to leak out** (*said of news, secrets, etc.*) transpirer, s'ébruiter

leakage [′likɪdʒ] *s* fuite *f*; (elec) perte *f*

leak•y [′liki] *adj* (*comp* -ier; *super* -iest) percé, troué; qui a des fuites; (*shoes*) qui prennent l'eau; (coll) indiscret

lean [lin] *adj* maigre; (*gasoline mixture*) pauvre ‖ *s* inclinaison *f*; (*of meat*) maigre *m* ‖ *v* (*pret & pp* **leaned** or **leant** [lɛnt]) *tr* incliner; **to lean s.th. against s.th.** appuyer q.ch. contre q.ch. ‖ *intr* s'incliner, pencher; **to lean against** s'appuyer contre; **to lean forward** s'incliner or se pencher en avant; **to lean out of** (*e.g., a window*) se pencher par; **to lean over** se pencher; (*e.g., s.o.'s shoulder*) se pencher sur; **to lean toward** (fig) incliner à or vers, pencher pour or vers

leaning [′linɪŋ] *adj* penché ‖ *s* inclinaison *f*; (fig) inclination *f*, penchant *m*

lean′-to′ *s* (*pl* -tos) appentis *m*

lean′ years′ *spl* années *fpl* maigres

leap [lip] *s* saut *m*, bond *m*; **by leaps and bounds** par sauts et par bonds; **leap in the dark** saut *m* à l'aveuglette ‖ *v* (*pret & pp* **leaped** or **leapt** [lɛpt]) *tr* sauter, franchir ‖ *intr* sauter, bondir; **to leap across** or **over** sauter; **to leap up** sursauter; (*said, e.g., of flame*) jaillir

leap′ day′ *s* jour *m* intercalaire

leap′frog′ *s* saute-mouton *m*

leap′ year′ *s* année *f* bissextile

learn [lʌrn] *v* (*pret & pp* **learned** or **learnt** [lʌrnt]) *tr* apprendre ‖ *intr* apprendre; **to learn to** apprendre à

learned [′lʌrnɪd] *adj* savant, érudit

learn′ed jour′nal *s* revue *f* d'une société savante

learn′ed profes′sion *s* profession *f* libérale

learn′ed soci′ety *s* société *f* savante

learn′ed word′ *s* mot *m* savant

learner [′lʌrnər] *s* élève *mf*; (*beginner*) débutant *m*, apprenti *m*

learn′er's per′mit *s* (aut) permis *m* de conduire (*d'un élève chauffeur*)

learning [′lʌrnɪŋ] *s* (*act and time devoted*) étude *f*; (*scholarship*) savoir *m*, érudition *f*, science *f*

lease [lis] *s* bail *m*; **to give a new lease on life** donner un regain de vie ‖ *tr* (*in the role of landlord*) donner or louer à bail; (*in the role of tenant*) prendre à bail

lease′hold′ *adj* tenu à bail ‖ *s* tenure *f* à bail

leash [liʃ] *s* laisse *f*; **on the leash** en laisse, à l'attache; **to strain at the leash** (fig) ruer dans les brancards ‖ *tr* tenir en laisse

least [list] *adj super* (le) moindre §91 ‖ *s* (le) moins *m*; **at least** du moins; **at the very least** tout au moins; **not in the least** pas le moins du monde, nullement ‖ *adv super* (le) moins §91

leather [′lɛðər] *s* cuir *m*

leath′er·back tur′tle *s* luth *m*

leath′er·neck′ *s* (slang) fusilier *m* marin

leathery [′lɛðəri] *adj* (*e.g., steak*) (coll) coriace

leave [liv] *s* permission *f*; **by your leave** ne vous en déplaise; **on leave** en congé; (mil) en permission; **to give leave to s.o. to** permettre or accorder à qn de; **to take leave of** prendre congé (de), faire ses adieux (à) ‖ *v* (*pret & pp* **left** [lɛft]) *tr* (*to let stay; to stop, give up; to disregard*) laisser; (*to go away from*) partir de, quitter; (*to bequeath*) léguer, laisser; (*a wife*) quitter, abandonner; **to be left** rester, e.g., **the letter was left** unanswered la lettre est restée sans réponse; e.g., **there are three dollars left** il reste trois dollars; **to be left for s.o.** être à qn de; **to be left over** rester; **to leave about** (*without putting away*) laisser traîner; **to leave alone** laisser tranquille; **to leave it up to** s'en remettre à, s'en rapporter à; **to leave no stone unturned** faire flèche de tout bois, mettre tout en œuvre; **to leave off** (*a piece of clothing*) ne pas mettre; (*a passenger*) déposer; **to leave off** + *ger* cesser de + *inf*, renoncer à + *inf*; **to leave out** omettre ‖ *intr* partir, s'en aller; **where did we leave off?** où en sommes-nous restés?

leaven [′lɛvən] *s* levain *m* ‖ *tr* faire lever; (fig) transformer, modifier

leavening [′lɛvənɪŋ] *adj* transformateur ‖ *s* levain *m*

leave′ of ab′sence *s* congé *m*

leave′-tak′ing *s* congé *m*, adieux *mpl*

leavings [′livɪŋz] *spl* restes *mpl*, reliefs *mpl*

Leba•nese [ˌlɛbə′niz] *adj* libanais ‖ *s* (*pl* -nese) Libanais *m*

Lebanon [ˈlɛbənən] *s* le Liban
lecher [ˈlɛtʃər] *s* débauché *m*, libertin *m* ‖ *intr* vivre dans la débauche
lecherous [ˈlɛtʃərəs] *adj* lubrique, lascif
lechery [ˈlɛtʃəri] *s* lubricité *f*, lasciveté *f*
lectern [ˈlɛktərn] *s* lutrin *m*
lecture [ˈlɛktʃər] *s* conférence *f*; (*tedious reprimand*) sermon *m* ‖ *tr* faire une conférence à; (*to rebuke*) sermonner ‖ *intr* faire une conférence or des conférences
lecturer [ˈlɛktʃərər] *s* conférencier *m*
ledge [lɛdʒ] *s* saillie *f*, corniche *f*; (*projection in a wall*) corniche *f*
ledger [ˈlɛdʒər] *s* (*slab*) pierre *f* tombale; (com) grand livre *m*
ledg'er line' *s* (mus) ligne *f* supplémentaire
lee [li] *s* (*shelter*) (naut) abri *m*; (*quarter toward which wind blows*) côté *m* sous le vent; **lees** lie *f*
leech [litʃ] *s* sangsue *f*; **to stick like a leech to s.o.** s'accrocher à qn
leek [lik] *s* poireau *m*
leer [lɪr] *s* regard *m* lubrique, œillade *f* ‖ *intr* lancer or jeter une œillade; **to leer at** lorgner
leer·y [ˈlɪri] *adj* (*comp* -ier; *super* -iest) (coll) soupçonneux, méfiant
leeward [ˈliwərd], [ˈluərd] *adj* & *adv* sous le vent ‖ *s* côté *m* sous le vent; **to pass to leeward of** passer sous le vent de
Lee'ward Is'lands [ˈliwərd] *spl* îles *fpl* Sous-le-Vent
lee'way' *s* (aer, naut) dérive *f*; (*of time, money*) (coll) marge *f*; (*for action*) (coll) champ *m*, liberté *f*
left [lɛft] *adj* gauche; (*left over*) de surplus ‖ *s* (*left hand*) gauche *f*; (boxing) gauche *m*; **on the left, to the left** à gauche; **the Left** (pol) la gauche; **to make a left** tourner à gauche ‖ *adv* à gauche
left' field' *s* (baseball) gauche *f* du grand champ
left'-hand' drive' *s* conduite *f* à gauche
left'-hand'ed *adj* gaucher; (*clumsy*) gauche; (*counterclockwise*) à gauche, en sens inverse des aiguilles d'une montre; (*e.g., compliment*) douteux, ambigu
leftish [ˈlɛftɪʃ] *adj* gauchisant
leftism [ˈlɛftɪzəm] *s* gauchisme *m*
leftist [ˈlɛftɪst] *adj* & *s* gauchiste *mf*
left'o'ver *adj* de surplus, restant ‖ **leftovers** *spl* restes *mpl*
left'-wing' *adj* gauchiste, gauchisant
left'-winger [ˈlɛftˈwɪŋər] *s* (coll) gauchiste *mf*
left·y [ˈlɛfti] *adj* (coll) gaucher ‖ *s* (*pl* -ies) (coll) gaucher *m*
leg [lɛg] *s* jambe *f*; (*of boot or stocking*) tige *f*; (*of fowl, of frogs*) cuisse *f*; (*of journey*) étape *f*; **to be on one's last legs** n'avoir plus de jambes; **to pull the leg of** (coll) se payer la tête de, faire marcher
lega·cy [ˈlɛgəsi] *s* (*pl* -cies) legs *m*
legal [ˈligəl] *adj* légal; (*practice*) juridique
le'gal hol'iday *s* jour *m* férié

legali·ty [lɪˈgælɪti] *s* (*pl* -ties) légalité *f*
legalize [ˈligəˌlaɪz] *tr* légaliser
le'gal ten'der *s* cours *m* légal, monnaie *f* libératoire
legate [ˈlɛgɪt] *s* ambassadeur *m*, envoyé *m*; (eccl) légat *m*
legatee [ˌlɛgəˈti] *s* légataire *mf*
legation [lɪˈgeʃən] *s* légation *f*
legend [ˈlɛdʒənd] *s* légende *f*
legendary [ˈlɛdʒənˌdɛri] *adj* légendaire
legerdemain [ˌlɛdʒərdɪˈmen] *s* escamotage *m*, passe-passe *m*
leggings [ˈlɛgɪŋz] *spl* jambières *fpl*, guêtres *fpl*, leggings *fpl*
leg·gy [ˈlɛgi] *adj* (*comp* -gier; *super* -giest) (*awkward*) dégingandé; (*attractive*) aux longues jambes élégantes
leg'horn' *s* (*hat*) chapeau *m* de paille d'Italie; (*chicken*) leghorn *f*; **Leghorn** Livourne *f*
legibility [ˌlɛdʒɪˈbrlɪti] *s* lisibilité *f*
legible [ˈlɛdʒɪbəl] *adj* lisible
legion [ˈlidʒən] *s* légion *f*
legislate [ˈlɛdʒɪsˌlet] *tr* imposer à force de loi ‖ *intr* faire des lois, légiférer
legislation [ˌlɛdʒɪsˈleʃən] *s* législation *f*
legislative [ˈlɛdʒɪsˌletɪv] *adj* législatif
legislator [ˈlɛdʒɪsˌletər] *s* législateur *m*
legislature [ˈlɛdʒɪsˌletʃər] *s* assemblée *f* législative, législature *f*
legitimacy [lɪˈdʒɪtɪməsi] *s* légitimité *f*
legitimate [lɪˈdʒɪtɪmɪt] *adj* légitime ‖ [lɪˈdʒɪtɪˌmet] *tr* légitimer
legit'imate dra'ma *s* théâtre *m* régulier
legitimize [lɪˈdʒɪtɪˌmaɪz] *tr* légitimer
leg' of lamb' *s* gigot *m* d'agneau
leg' of mut'ton *s* gigot *m*
leg'-of-mut'ton sleeve' *s* manche *f* gigot
legume [ˈlɛgjum], [lɪˈgjum] *s* (*pod*) légume *m*; (bot) légumineuse *f*
leisure [ˈliʒər], [ˈlɛʒər] *s* loisir *m*; **at leisure** à loisir; **in leisure moments** à temps perdu
lei'sure class' *s* désœuvrés *mpl*, rentiers *mpl*
lei'sure hours' *spl* heures *fpl* de loisir
leisurely [ˈliʒərli], [ˈlɛʒərli] *adj* tranquille, posé ‖ *adv* posément, sans hâte
lemon [ˈlɛmən] *s* citron *m*; (*e.g., worthless car*) (coll) clou *m*
lemonade [ˌlɛməˈned] *s* citronnade *f*
lem'on squeez'er *s* presse-citron *m*
lem'on tree' *s* citronnier *m*
lem'on verbe'na [vərˈbinə] *s* verveine *f* citronnelle
lend [lɛnd] *v* (*pret* & *pp* **lent** [lɛnt]) *tr* prêter
lender [ˈlɛndər] *s* prêteur *m*
lend'ing li'brary *s* bibliothèque *f* de prêt
length [lɛŋθ] *s* longueur *f*; (*e.g., of string*) bout *m*, morceau *m*; (*of time*) durée *f*; **at length** longuement, en détail; (*finally*) enfin, à la fin; **in length** de longueur; **to go to any length** to ne reculer devant rien pour; **to keep at arm's length** tenir à distance

lengthen ['lɛŋθən] *tr* allonger, rallonger ‖ *intr* s'allonger

length′wise *adj* longitudinal ‖ *adv* en longueur, dans le sens de la longueur

length·y ['lɛŋθi] *adj* (*comp* -ier; *super* -iest) prolongé, assez long

leniency ['lini·ənsi] *s* douceur *f*, clémence *f*

lenient ['lini·ənt] *adj* doux, clément

lens [lɛnz] *s* lentille *f*; (anat) cristallin *m*

Lent [lɛnt] *s* le Carême

Lenten ['lɛntən] *adj* de carême

lentil ['lɛntəl] *s* lentille *f*

leopard ['lɛpərd] *s* léopard *m*

leper ['lɛpər] *s* lépreux *m*

lep′er house′ *s* léproserie *f*

leprosy ['lɛprəsi] *s* lèpre *f*

leprous ['lɛprəs] *adj* lépreux

lesbian ['lɛzbi·ən] *adj* érotique; **Lesbian** lesbien ‖ *s* (*female homosexual*) lesbienne *f*; **Lesbian** Lesbien *m*

lesbianism ['lɛzbi·ə‚nɪzəm] *s* saphisme *m*

lese majesty ['liz'mædʒɪsti] *s* crime *m* de lèse-majesté

lesion ['liʒən] *s* lésion *f*

less [lɛs] *adj comp* moindre §91 ‖ *s* moins *m* ‖ *adv comp* moins §91; **less and less** de moins en moins; **less than** moins que; (*followed by numeral*) moins de; **the less . . . the less** (or **the more**) moins . . . moins (or plus)

lessee [lɛs'i] *s* preneur *m*; (*e.g., of house*) locataire *mf*; (*e.g., of gasoline station*) concessionnaire *mf*

lessen ['lɛsən] *tr* diminuer, amoindrir ‖ *intr* se diminuer, s'amoindrir

lesser ['lɛsər] *adj comp* moindre §91

lesson ['lɛsən] *s* leçon *f*

lessor ['lɛsər] *s* bailleur *m*

lest [lɛst] *conj* de peur que, de crainte que

let [lɛt] *v* (*pret & pp* let; *ger* letting) *tr* laisser; (*to rent*) louer; **let** + *inf* que + *subj*, e.g., **let him come in** qu'il entre; **let alone** sans parler de, sans compter; **let well enough alone** le mieux est souvent l'ennemi du bien; **let us eat, work, etc.** mangeons, travaillons, etc.; **to be let off with** en être quitte pour; **to let** à louer, e.g., **house to let** maison à louer; **to let alone, to let be** laisser tranquille; **to let by** laisser passer; **to let down** baisser, descendre; (*one's hair*) dénouer, défaire; (*e.g., a garment*) allonger; (*to leave in the lurch*) laisser en panne, faire faux bond à; **to let fly** décocher; **to let go** laisser partir; **to let have** laisser, e.g., **he let Robert have it for three dollars** il l'a laissé à Robert pour trois dollars; **to let in** laisser entrer; **to let in the clutch** (aut) embrayer; **to let into** admettre dans; **to let loose** lâcher; **to let off** laisser partir; (*e.g., steam from a boiler*) laisser échapper, lâcher; (*e.g., a culprit*) pardonner à; **to let oneself go** se laisser aller; **to let on** that (coll) faire croire que; **to let out** faire or laisser sortir; (*e.g., a* *dress*) élargir; (*a cry; a secret; a prisoner*) laisser échapper; (*to reveal*) révéler, divulguer; **to let out on bail** relâcher sous caution; **to let out the clutch** débrayer; **to let slip** laisser tomber; **to let s.o.** + *inf* permettre à qn de + *inf*; laisser qn + *inf*, e.g., **he let Mary go to the theater** il a laissé Marie aller au théâtre; **to let s.o. in on** (*a secret*) (coll) confier à qn; (*e.g., a racing tip*) (coll) tuyauter sur; **to let s.o. know s.th.** faire savoir q.ch. à qn, mettre qn au courant de q.ch.; **to let s.o. off with** faire grâce à qn de; **to let stand** laisser, e.g., **he let the errors stand** il a laissé les fautes; **to let s.th. go** for (*a low price*) laisser q.ch. pour; **to let through** laisser passer; **to let up** laisser monter ‖ *intr* (*said of house, apartment, etc.*) se louer; **to let down** (coll) ralentir; **to let go of** lâcher prise de; **to let out** (*said of class, school, etc.*) finir, se terminer; **to let up** (coll) ralentir, diminuer; (*on discipline; on a person*) devenir moins sévère

let′down′ *s* diminution *f*; (*disappointment*) déception *f*

lethal ['liθəl] *adj* mortel; (*weapon*) meurtrier

lethargic [lɪ'θɑrdʒɪk] *adj* léthargique

lethar·gy ['lɛθərdʒi] *s* (*pl* -gies) léthargie *f*

Lett [lɛt] *s* Letton *m*

letter ['lɛtər] *s* lettre *f*; **to the letter** à la lettre, au pied de la lettre ‖ *tr* marquer avec des lettres

let′ter box′ *s* boîte *f* aux lettres

let′ter car′rier *s* facteur *m*

let′ter drop′ *s* passe-lettres *m*, fente *f* (dans la porte pour le courrier)

lettered *adj* (*person*) lettré

let′ter file′ *s* classeur *m* de lettres

let′ter·head′ *s* en-tête *m*

lettering ['lɛtərɪŋ] *s* (*action*) lettrage *m*; (*title*) inscription *f*

let′ter of cred′it *s* lettre *f* de crédit

let′ter o′pener *s* coupe-papier *m*

let′ter pa′per *s* papier *m* à lettres

let′ter·per′fect *adj* correct; sûr

let′ter press′ *s* presse *f* à copier

let′ter·press′ *s* impression *f* typographique; (*in distinction to illustrations*) texte *m*

let′ter scales′ *spl* pèse-lettre *m*

let′ter·word′ *s* sigle *m*

Lettish ['lɛtɪʃ] *adj & s* letton *m*

lettuce ['lɛtɪs] *s* laitue *f*

let′up′ *s* accalmie *f*, pause *f*; **without letup** sans relâche

leucorrhea [‚lukə'ri·ə] *s* leucorrhée *f*

leukemia [lu'kimi·ə] *s* leucémie *f*

Levant [lɪ'vænt] *s* Levant *m*

Levantine ['lɛvən‚tin], [lɪ'væntin] *adj* levantin ‖ *s* Levantin *m*

levee ['lɛvi] *s* (*embankment*) levée *f*, digue *f*; réception *f* royale

lev·el ['lɛvəl] *adj* de niveau; (*flat*) égal, uni; (*spoonful*) arasé; **level with** de niveau avec, à fleur de ‖ *s* niveau *m*; **on a level with** au niveau de; **to be**

on the level (coll) être de bonne foi;
to find one's level trouver son niveau
|| v (pret & pp -eled or -elled; ger
-eling or -elling) tr niveler; (to
smooth, flatten out) aplanir, araser;
(to bring down) raser; (a gun) braquer; (accusations, sarcasm) lancer,
diriger; to level out égaliser; to level
up (aer) redresser || intr (aer) redres-
ser; to level with (coll) parler franchement à

lev·el·head'ed adj équilibré, pondéré

lev'eling rod' s (surv) jalon-mire m,
jalon m d'arpentage

lever ['lɪvər], ['lɛvər] s levier m || tr
soulever or ouvrir au moyen d'un
levier

leverage ['lɪvərɪdʒ], ['lɛvərɪdʒ] s puissance f or force f de levier; (fig) influence f, avantage m

leviathan [lɪ'vaɪ·əθən] s léviathan m

levitation [,lɛvɪ'teʃən] s lévitation f

levi·ty ['lɛvɪti] s (pl -ties) légèreté f

lev·y ['lɛvi] s (pl -ies) levée f || v (pret
& pp -ied) tr lever; (a fine) imposer

lewd [lud] adj luxurieux, lubrique

lewdness ['ludnɪs] s luxure f, lubricité f

lexical ['lɛksɪkəl] adj lexical

lexicographer [,lɛksɪ'kagrəfər] s lexicographe mf

lexicographic(al) [,lɛksɪkə'græfɪk(əl)]
adj lexicographique

lexicography [,lɛksɪ'kagrəfi] s lexicographie f

lexicology [,lɛksɪ'kalədʒi] s lexicologie f

lexicon ['lɛksɪkən] s lexique m

liabili·ty [,laɪ·ə'brlɪti] s (pl -ties) responsabilité f; (e.g., to disease) prédisposition f; liabilities obligations fpl,
dettes fpl

liabil'ity insur'ance s assurance f tous
risques

liable ['laɪ·əbəl] adj sujet; liable for (a
debt, fine, etc.) passible de, responsable de; we (you, etc.) are liable to
+ inf (coll) il se peut que nous (vous,
etc.) + pres subj; (coll) il est probable que nous (vous, etc.) + pres
ind

liaison ['liɪ·ə,zɑn], ['li·ɛzən] s liaison f

liar ['laɪ·ər] s menteur m

libation [laɪ'beʃən] s libation f

li·bel ['laɪbəl] s diffamation f, calomnie f; (in writing) écrit m diffama-
toire || v (pret & pp -beled or -belled;
ger -beling or -belling) tr diffamer,
calomnier

libelous ['laɪbələs] adj diffamatoire,
calomnieux

liberal ['lɪbərəl] adj libéral; (share,
supply, etc.) libéral, généreux, co-
pieux; (ideas) large || s libéral m

liberali·ty [,lɪbə'rælɪti] s (pl -ties) libéralité f; (breadth of mind) largeur
f de vues

lib'eral-mind'ed adj tolérant

liberate ['lɪbə,ret] tr libérer

liberation [,lɪbə'reʃən] s libération f

liberator ['lɪbə,retər] s libérateur m

libertine ['lɪbər,tin] adj & s libertin m

liber·ty ['lɪbərti] s (pl -ties) liberté f;
at liberty en liberté; at liberty to
libre de; to take the liberty to se permettre de, prendre la liberté de

libidinous [lɪ'bɪdɪnəs] adj libidineux

libido [lɪ'bido], [lɪ'baɪdo] s libido f

librarian [laɪ'brɛrɪ·ən] s bibliothécaire
mf

librar·y ['laɪ,brɛri], ['laɪbrəri] s (pl
-ies) bibliothèque f

li'brary num'ber s cote f

libret·to [lɪ'brɛto] s (pl -tos) livret m,
libretto m

license ['laɪsəns] s permis m, licence f;
(to drive) permis de conduire f || tr
accorder un permis à, autoriser

li'cense num'ber s numéro m d'immatriculation; (aut) numéro minéralogique

li'cense plate' or tag' s plaque f d'immatriculation, plaque minéralogique

licentious [laɪ'sɛnʃəs] adj licencieux

lichen ['laɪkən] s lichen m

lick [lɪk] s coup m de langue; (salt
lick) terrain m salifère; (blow) (coll)
coup m; at full lick (coll) à plein gaz;
to give a lick and a promise to (coll)
nettoyer à la six-quatre-deux; (coll)
faire un brin de toilette à || tr lécher;
(e.g., the fingers) se lécher; (to beat,
thrash) (coll) enfoncer les côtes à,
rosser; (to beat, surpass, e.g., in a
sporting event) (coll) battre, enfoncer; (e.g., a problem) (coll) venir à
bout de; to lick into shape (coll) dégrossir; to lick up lécher

licking ['lɪkɪŋ] s léchage m; (drubbing) (coll) raclée f

licorice ['lɪkərɪs] s réglisse f

lid [lɪd] s couvercle m; (eyelid) paupière f; (hat) (slang) couvre-chef m

lie [laɪ] s mensonge m; to give the lie
to donner le démenti à || v (pret & pp
lied; ger lying) tr—to lie one's way
out se tirer d'affaire par des menson-
ges || intr mentir || v (pret lay; pp
lain [len]; ger lying) intr être
couché; (to be located) se trouver;
(e.g., in the grave) gésir, e.g., here
lies ci-gît; to lie down se coucher

lie' detec'tor s détecteur m de men-
songes

lien [lin], ['li·ən] s privilège m, droit
m de rétention

lieu [lu] s—in lieu of au lieu de

lieutenant [lu'tɛnənt] s lieutenant m;
(nav) lieutenant m de vaisseau

lieuten'ant colo'nel s lieutenant-colonel
m

lieuten'ant comman'der s (nav) capitaine m de corvette

lieuten'ant gov'ernor s (U.S.A.) vice-
gouverneur m; (Brit) lieutenant-gou-
verneur m

lieuten'ant jun'ior grade' s (nav) enseigne m de première classe

life [laɪf] s (pl lives [laɪvz]) vie f; (of
light bulb, lease, insurance policy)
durée f; bigger than life plus grand
que nature; for dear life de toutes
ses forces; for life à vie, pour la vie,

à perpétuité; **for the life of me!** (coll) de ma vie!; **lives lost morts** mpl; **long life** longévité f; **never in my life!, not on your life!** jamais de la vie!; **run for your life!** sauve qui peut!; **such is life!** c'est la vie!; **taken from life** pris sur le vif; **to come to life** revenir à la vie; **to depart this life** quitter ce monde; **to risk life and limb** risquer sa peau

life′ annu′ity s rente f viagère
life′ belt′ s ceinture f de sauvetage
life′blood′ s sang m; (fig) vie f
life′boat′ s chaloupe f de sauvetage; (for shore-based rescue services) canot m de sauvetage
life′ buoy′ s bouée f de sauvetage
life′ float′ s radeau m de sauvetage
life′ guard′ s (mil) garde f du corps
life′ guard′ s sauveteur m, maître nageur m
life′ impris′onment s emprisonnement m à vie
life′ insur′ance s assurance f sur la vie, assurance-vie f
life′ jack′et s gilet m de sauvetage
lifeless ['laɪflɪs] adj sans vie, inanimé; (colors) embu, terne
life′like′ adj vivant, ressemblant
life′ line′ s ligne f or corde f de sauvetage
life′long′ adj de toute la vie, perpétuel
life′ mem′ber s membre m à vie
life′ of lei′sure s vie f de château
life′ of Ri′ley ['raɪlɪ] s (slang) joyeuse vie f, vie oisive
life′ of the par′ty s (coll) boute-entrain m
life′ preserv′er [prɪ'zɜrvər] s appareil m de sauvetage
lifer ['laɪfər] s (slang) condamné m à perpétuité
life′ raft′ s radeau m de sauvetage
lifesaver ['laɪf‚sevər] s sauveteur m; (fig) planche f de salut
life′sav′ing s sauvetage m
life′ sen′tence s condamnation f à perpétuité
life′-size′ adj de grandeur nature
life′time′ adj à vie ‖ s vie f, toute une vie; **in his lifetime** de son vivant
life′work′ s travail m de toute une vie

lift [lɪft] s haussement m, levée f; aide f; (aer) poussée f; (Brit) ascenseur m; (of dumbbell or weight) (sports) arraché m; **to give a lift to** (by offering a ride) conduire d'un coup de voiture, faire monter dans la voiture; (to aid) donner un coup de main à; ranimer ‖ tr lever, soulever; (heart, mind, etc.) élever, ranimer; (a sail) soulager; (an embargo) lever; (e.g., passages from a book) démarquer, plagier; (to rob) (slang) dérober; **to lift up** (the hands) lever; (the head) relever; (the voice) élever ‖ intr se lever, se soulever; (said of clouds, fog, etc.) se lever, se dissiper
lift′ bridge′ s pont m levant, pont-levis m
lift′off′ s (rok) montée verticale, chandelle f

lift′ truck′ s chariot m élévateur
ligament ['lɪgəmənt] s ligament m
ligature ['lɪgət/ər] s ligature f
light [laɪt] adj léger; (having illumination) éclairé; (color, complexion, hair) clair; (beer) blond; (wine) léger; **to make light of** faire peu de cas de ‖ s lumière f; (to control traffic) feu m; (window or other opening in a wall) jour m; (example, shining figure) lumière; (headlight of automobile) phare m; du feu, e.g., **do you have a light?** (e.g., to light a cigarette) avez-vous du feu?; **according to one's lights** selon ses lumières, dans la mesure de son intelligence; **against the light** à contre-jour; **in a false light** sous un faux jour; **in a new light** sous un jour nouveau; **in the same light** sous le même aspect; **it is light** (out) il fait jour; **lights** (navigation lights; parking lights) feux mpl; (of sheep, calf, etc.) mou m; **lights out** (mil) l'extinction f des feux; **to bring to light** mettre au jour; **to come to light** se révéler; **to shed or throw light on** éclairer; **to strike a light** allumer ‖ adv à vide; **to run light** (said of engine) aller haut le pied ‖ v (pret & pp lighted or lit [lɪt]) tr (to furnish with illumination) éclairer, illuminer; (to set afire, ignite) allumer; **to light the way for** éclairer; **to light up** illuminer ‖ intr s'éclairer, s'illuminer; allumer; (to perch) se poser; **to light from or off** (an auto, carriage, etc.) descendre de; **to light into** (to attack; to berate) (slang) tomber sur; **to light out** (to skedaddle) (slang) décamper; **to light up** s'éclairer, s'illuminer; **to light upon** (by happenstance) tomber sur, trouver par hasard
light′ bulb′ s ampoule f électrique, lampe f électrique
light′ complex′ion s teint m clair
lighten ['laɪtən] tr (to make lighter in weight) alléger, soulager; (to provide more light) éclairer, illuminer; (to give a lighter or brighter hue to) éclaircir; (grief, punishment, etc.) adoucir ‖ intr (to become less dark or sorrowful) s'éclairer; (to give off flashes of lightning) faire des éclairs; (to becomes less weighty) s'alléger
lighter ['laɪtər] s (to light cigarette) briquet m; (flat-bottomed barge) chaland m, péniche f
light′-fin′gered adj à doigts agiles
light′-foot′ed adj au pied léger
light′-head′ed adj étourdi
light′-heart′ed adj joyeux, allègre, au cœur léger
light′house′ s phare m
lighting ['laɪtɪŋ] s allumage m, éclairage m
light′ing fix′tures spl appareils mpl d'éclairage
light′ me′ter s posemètre m
lightness ['laɪtnɪs] s (in weight) légèreté f; (in illumination; of complexion) clarté f

light·ning ['laɪtnɪŋ] s (electric discharge) foudre f; (light produced by this discharge) éclairs mpl || v (ger -ning) intr faire des éclairs
light'ning arrest'er [ə ˌrestər] s para-foudre m
light'ning bug' s luciole f
light'ning rod' s paratonnerre m
light' op'era s opérette f
light' read'ing s livres mpl d'agrément; lecture f légère ou amusante
light'ship' s bateau-feu m
light-struck ['laɪt ˌstrʌk] adj (phot) voilé
light' wave' s onde f lumineuse
light'weight' adj léger || s (sports) poids m léger
light'weight coat' s surtout m de demi-saison
light'-year' s année-lumière f
likable ['laɪkəbəl] adj sympathique
like [laɪk] adj (alike) pareils, semblables; pareil à, semblable à; (typical of) caractéristique de; (poles of a magnet) (elec) de même nom; like father like son tel père tel fils; that is like him il n'en fait pas d'autres || s pareil m, semblable m; likes (desires) goût m, inclinations fpl; the likes of him son pareil || adv—like enough probablement; like mad comme un fou || prep comme; like that de la sorte || conj (coll) de la même manière que, comme || tr aimer, aimer bien, trouver bon; plaire (with dat), e.g., I like milk le lait me plaît; se plaire, e.g., I like it in the country je me plais à la campagne || intr vouloir; as you like comme vous voudrez; if you like si vous voulez
likelihood ['laɪklɪ ˌhud] s probabilité f, vraisemblance f
like·ly ['laɪkli] adj (comp -lier; super -liest) probable, vraisemblable; to be likely to + inf être probable que + ind, e.g., Mary is likely to come to see us tomorrow il est probable que Marie viendra nous voir demain || adv probablement, vraisemblablement
like'-mind'ed adj du même avis
liken ['laɪkən] tr comparer, assimiler
likeness ['laɪknɪs] s (picture or image) portrait m; (similarity) ressemblance f
like'wise' adv également, de même; to do likewise en faire autant
liking ['laɪkɪŋ] s sympathie f, penchant m; to one's liking à souhait; to take a liking to (a thing) accueillir avec sympathie; (a person) montrer de la sympathie à, se prendre d'amitié pour
lilac ['laɪlək] adj & s lilas m
Lilliputian [ˌlɪlɪ'pjuʃən] adj & s lilliputien m
lilt [lɪlt] s cadence f
lil·y ['lɪli] s (pl -ies) lis m, lis blanc; (royal arms of France) fleur f de lis; to gild the lily orner la beauté même
lil'y of the val'ley s muguet m
lil'y pad' s feuille f de nénuphar

lil'y-white' adj blanc comme le lis, lilial
Li'ma bean' ['laɪmə] s (Phaseolus limensis) haricot m de Lima
limb [lɪm] s (arm or leg) membre m; (of a tree) branche f; (of a cross; of the sea) bras m; (astr, bot) limbe m; to be out on a limb (coll) être sur la corde raide
limber ['lɪmbər] adj souple, flexible || intr—to limber up se dégourdir
lim·bo ['lɪmbo] s (pl -bos) limbes mpl
lime [laɪm] s (calcium oxide) chaux f; (linden tree) tilleul m; (Citrus aurantifolia) citron m; sweet lime (Citrus limetta) lime f
lime'kiln' s four m à chaux
lime'light' s—to be in the limelight être sous les feux de la rampe
limerick ['lɪmərɪk] s poème m humoristique en cinq vers
lime'stone' adj calcaire || s calcaire m, pierre f à chaux
limit ['lɪmɪt] s limite f, borne f; to be the limit (to be exasperating) (coll) être le comble; (to be bizarre) (coll) être impayable; to go the limit aller jusqu'au bout || tr limiter, borner
limitation [ˌlɪmɪ'teʃən] s limitation f
lim'ited-ac'cess high'way s autoroute f
lim'ited mon'archy s monarchie f constitutionnelle
limitless ['lɪmɪtlɪs] adj sans bornes, illimité
limousine ['lɪmə ˌzin], [ˌlɪmə'zin] s (aut) limousine f
limp [lɪmp] adj mou, flasque, souple || s boiterie f || intr boiter
limpid ['lɪmpɪd] adj limpide
linchpin ['lɪnt ˌpɪn] s cheville f d'essieu, esse f
linden ['lɪndən] s tilleul m
line [laɪn] s ligne f; (of poetry) vers m; (rope, string) cordage m, corde f; (wrinkle) ride f; (dash) trait m; (bar) barre f; (lineage) lignée f; (trade) métier m; (of merchandise) article m; (of traffic) file f; (mil) rang m; (of the spectrum) (phys) raie f; hold the line! (telp) ne quittez pas!; in line aligné, en rang; in line with conforme à, d'accord avec; on the line (telp) au bout du fil; out of line désaligné; en désaccord; to bring into line with mettre d'accord avec; to drop s.o. a line envoyer un mot à qn; to fall into line se mettre en ligne, s'aligner; to hand s.o. a line (slang) faire du baratin à qn, bourrer le crâne de qn; to have a line on (coll) se tuyauter sur; to learn one's lines apprendre son texte ou rôle; to read between the lines lire entre les lignes; to stand or wait in line faire la queue; to toe the line se mettre au pas || tr aligner; (a face) rider; (a suit, coat, etc.) doubler; (brakes) fourrer; to be lined with (e.g., trees) être bordé de || intr—to line up s'aligner, se mettre en ligne; faire la queue

lineage ['lɪnɪ ˌɪdʒ] s lignée f, race f

lineal ['lɪnɪ·əl] *adj* linéal; *(succession)* en ligne directe

lineaments ['lɪnɪ·əmənts] *spl* linéaments *mpl*

linear ['lɪnɪ·ər] *adj* linéaire

lined⁄ pa⁄per *s* papier *m* rayé

line⁄man *s* *(pl* **-men**) *(elec)* poseur *m* de lignes; *(rr)* garde-ligne *m*

linen ['lɪnən] *adj* de lin ‖ *s (fabric)* toile *f* de lin; *(yarn)* fil *m* de lin; *(sheets, tablecloths, underclothes, etc.)* linge *m*, lingerie *f*; **pure linen** pur fil

lin⁄en clos⁄et *s* lingerie *f*

line⁄ of fire⁄ *s* (mil) ligne *f* de tir

line⁄ of sight⁄ *s* ligne *f* de mire

liner ['laɪnər] *s* (naut) paquebot *m*

line⁄-up⁄ *s* mise *f* en rang; personnel *m*; *(arrangement)* disposition *f*; *(of prisoners)* défilé *m* de détenus, alignement *m* de suspects; *(sports)* composition *f*

linger ['lɪŋgər] *intr* s'attarder; *(said of hope, doubt, etc.)* persister; **to linger on** traîner; **to linger over** s'attarder sur

lingerie [ˌlænʒə'ri] *s* lingerie *f* fine pour dames, lingerie de dame

lingering ['lɪŋgərɪŋ] *adj* prolongé, lent

lingual ['lɪŋgwəl] *adj* lingual ‖ *s (consonant)* linguale *f*

linguist ['lɪŋgwɪst] *s (person skilled in several languages)* polyglotte *mf*; *(specialist in linguistics)* linguiste *mf*

linguistic [lɪŋ'gwɪstɪk] *adj* linguistique ‖ **linguistics** *s* linguistique *f*

liniment ['lɪnɪmənt] *s* liniment *m*

lining ['laɪnɪŋ] *s (of a coat)* doublure *f*; *(of a hat)* coiffe *f*; *(of auto brake)* garniture *f*; *(of furnace, wall, etc.)* revêtement *m*

link [lɪŋk] *s* maillon *m*, chaînon *m*; *(fig)* lien *m*; **links** terrain *m* de golf ‖ *tr* enchaîner; **to link** ‖ *intr*—**to link in, on,** or **up** se lier

linnet ['lɪnɪt] *s* (orn) linotte *f*

linoleum [lɪ'nolɪ·əm] *s* linoléum *m*

linotype ['laɪnə,taɪp] (trademark) *s* linotype *f* ‖ *tr & intr* composer à la lino

lin⁄otype op⁄erator *s* linotypiste *mf*

linseed ['lɪn,sid] *s* linette *f*, graine *f* de lin

lin⁄seed oil⁄ *s* huile *f* de lin

lint [lɪnt] *s* bourre *f*, filasse *f*; *(used to dress wounds)* charpie *f*

lintel ['lɪntəl] *s* linteau *m*

lion ['laɪ·ən] *s* lion *m*; *(fig)* lion *m*; **to put one's head in the lion's mouth** se fourrer dans la gueule du loup ou du lion

lioness ['laɪ·ənɪs] *s* lionne *f*

li⁄on-heart⁄ed *adj* au cœur de lion

lionize ['laɪ·ə,naɪz] *tr* faire une célébrité de, traiter en vedette

li⁄ons' den⁄ *s* (Bib) fosse *f* aux lions

li⁄on's share⁄ *s* part *f* du lion

lip [lɪp] *s* lèvre *f*; *(edge)* bord *m*; *(slang)* impertinence *f*; **to hang on the lips of** être suspendu aux lèvres de; **to smack one's lips** se lécher les babines

lip⁄read⁄ *v* *(pret & pp* **-read** [ˌred]) *tr & intr* lire sur les lèvres

lip⁄ read⁄ing *s* lecture *f* sur les lèvres

lip⁄ serv⁄ice *s* dévotion *f* des lèvres

lip⁄stick⁄ *s* bâton *m* de rouge à lèvres

lique-fy ['lɪkwɪ,faɪ] *v* *(pret & pp* **-fied**) *tr* liquéfier

liqueur [lɪ'kʌr] *s* liqueur *f*

liquid ['lɪkwɪd] *adj* liquide ‖ *s* liquide *m*; *(consonant)* liquide *f*

liq⁄uid as⁄sets *spl* valeurs *fpl* disponibles

liquidate ['lɪkwɪ,det] *tr & intr* liquider

liquidity [lɪ'kwɪdɪti] *s* liquidité *f*

liquor ['lɪkər] *s* boisson *f* alcoolique, spiritueux *m*; *(culin)* jus *m*, bouillon *m*

Lisbon ['lɪzbən] *s* Lisbonne *f*

lisle [laɪl] *s* fil *m* d'Écosse, fil retors de coton

lisp [lɪsp] *s* zézayement *m*, blésement *m* ‖ *intr* zézayer, bléser

lissome ['lɪsəm] *adj* souple, flexible; *(nimble)* agile, leste

list [lɪst] *s* liste *f*; *(selvage)* lisière *f*; *(naut)* bande *f*; **to enter the lists** entrer en lice; **to have a list** (naut) donner de la bande ‖ *tr* cataloguer, enregistrer ‖ *intr* (naut) donner de la bande

listen ['lɪsən] *intr* écouter; **to listen in** rester à l'écoute; **to listen to** écouter; **to listen to reason** entendre raison

listener ['lɪsənər] *s* auditeur *m*; *(educ)* auditeur libre

listening ['lɪsənɪŋ] *s* écoute *f*

lis⁄tening post⁄ *s* poste *m* d'écoute

listless ['lɪstlɪs] *adj* apathique, inattentif

list⁄ price⁄ *s* prix *m* courant, cote *f*

lita-ny ['lɪtəni] *s* *(pl* **-nies**) litanie *f*

liter ['litər] *s* litre *m*

literal ['lɪtərəl] *adj* littéral; *(person)* prosaïque

literary ['lɪtəˌreri] *adj* littéraire

literate ['lɪtərɪt] *adj* qui sait lire et écrire; *(well-read)* lettré ‖ *s* personne *f* qui sait lire et écrire; lettré *m*, érudit *m*

literati [ˌlɪtə'rati] *spl* littérateurs *mpl*

literature ['lɪtərətʃər] *s* littérature *f*; *(com)* documentation *f*

lithe [laɪð] *adj* souple, flexible

lithia ['lɪθɪ·ə] *s* (chem) lithine *f*

lithium ['lɪθɪ·əm] *s* (chem) lithium *m*

lithograph ['lɪθə,græf], ['lɪθə,graf] *s* lithographie *f* ‖ *tr* lithographier

lithographer [lɪ'θagrəfər] *s* lithographe *mf*

lithography [lɪ'θagrəfi] *s* lithographie *f*

Lithuania [ˌlɪθu'enɪ·ə] *s* Lituanie *f*; la Lituanie

Lithuanian [ˌlɪθu'enɪ·ən] *adj* lituanien ‖ *s (language)* lituanien *m*; *(person)* Lituanien *m*

litigant ['lɪtɪgənt] *adj* plaidant ‖ *s* plaideur *m*

litigate ['lɪtɪ,get] *tr* mettre en litige ‖ *intr* plaider

litigation [ˌlɪtɪ'geʃən] *s* litige *m*

lit′mus pa′per [′lɪtməs] s papier m de tournesol

litter [′lɪtər] s fouillis m; (things strewn about) jonchée f; (scattered rubbish) ordures fpl; (young brought forth at one birth) portée f; (bedding for animals) litière f; (vehicle carried by men or animals) palanquin m; (stretcher) civière f ‖ tr joncher ‖ intr (to bring forth young) mettre bas

lit′ter-bug′ s souillon m, malpropre m, personne f qui dépose des ordures et des papiers dans la rue

littering [′lɪtərɪŋ] s—no littering (public sign) défense de déposer des ordures

little [′lɪtəl] adj petit; (in amount) peu de, e.g., little money peu d′argent; a little un peu de, e.g., a little money un peu d′argent ‖ s peu m; a little un peu; to make little of, to think little of faire peu de cas de; wait a little attendez un petit moment, attendez quelques instants ‖ adv peu §91; not . . . guère §90, e.g., she little thinks that elle ne se doute guère que; little by little peu à peu, petit à petit

Lit′tle Bear′ s Petite Ourse f

Lit′tle Dip′per s Petit Chariot m

lit′tle fin′ger s petit doigt m, auriculaire m; to twist around one′s little finger mener par le bout du nez

lit′tle-neck′ s coque f de Vénus

littleness [′lɪtəlnɪs] s petitesse f

lit′tle owl′ s (Athene noctua) chouette f chevêche, chevêche f

lit′tle peo′ple spl (fairies) fées fpl; (common people) menu peuple m

Lit′tle Red Rid′ing-hood′ s le Petit Chaperon rouge

lit′tle slam′ s (bridge) petit chelem m

liturgic(al) [lɪ′tʌrdʒɪk(əl)] adj liturgique

litur·gy [′lɪtərdʒi] s (pl -gies) liturgie f

livable [′lɪvəbəl] adj (house) habitable; (life, person) supportable

live [laɪv] adj vivant, vif; (coals, flame) ardent; (elec) sous tension; (telv) en direct ‖ [lɪv] tr vivre; to live down faire oublier ‖ intr vivre; (in a certain locality) demeurer, habiter; live and learn qui vivra verra; to live high mener grand train; to live in (e.g., a city) habiter; to live on continuer à vivre; (e.g., meat) vivre de; (a benefactor) vivre aux crochets de; (one′s capital) manger; to live up to (e.g., one′s reputation) faire honneur à

live′ coal′ [laɪv] s charbon m ardent

livelihood [′laɪvlɪ,hʊd] s vie f; to earn one′s livelihood gagner sa vie

livelong [′lɪv,lɔŋ], [′lɪv,lɑŋ] adj—all the livelong day toute la sainte journée

live·ly [′laɪvli] adj (comp -lier; super -liest) animé, vivant, plein d′entrain; (merry) enjoué, gai; (active, keen) vif; (resilient) élastique

liven [′laɪvən] tr animer ‖ intr s′animer

liver [′lɪvər] s vivant m; (e.g., in cities) habitant m; (anat) foie m

liver·y [′lɪvəri] s (pl -ies) livrée f

liv′ery-man s (pl -men) loueur m de chevaux

liv′ery sta′ble s écurie f de louage

live′ show′ [laɪv] s (telv) prise f de vues en direct

live′stock′ [laɪv] s bétail m, bestiaux mpl, cheptel m

live′ tel′evision broad′cast [laɪv] s prise f de vues en direct

live′ wire′ [laɪv] s fil m sous tension; (slang) type m dynamique

livid [′lɪvɪd] adj livide

living [′lɪvɪŋ] adj vivant, en vie ‖ s vie f; to earn or to make a living gagner sa vie

liv′ing quar′ters spl appartements mpl, habitations fpl

liv′ing room′ s salle f de séjour, salon m

liv′ing space′ s espace m vital

liv′ing wage′ s salaire m suffisant pour vivre, salaire de base

lizard [′lɪzərd] s lézard m

load [lod] s charge f; loads (of) (coll) énormément (de); to get a load of (slang) observer, écouter; to have a load on (slang) avoir son compte ‖ tr charger ‖ intr charger; se charger

loaded adj chargé; (very drunk) (slang) soûl; (very rich) (slang) huppé

load′ed dice′ spl dés mpl pipés

load′stone′ s pierre f d′aimant; (fig) aimant m

loaf [lof] s (pl loaves [lovz]) pain m ‖ intr flâner

loafer [′lofər] s flâneur m

loam [lom] s terre f franche, glaise f; (mixture used in making molds) potée f

loamy [′lomi] adj franc, glaiseux

loan [lon] s prêt m, emprunt m ‖ tr prêter

loan′ shark′ s usurier m

loan′ word′ s mot m d′emprunt

loath [loθ] adj—loath to peu enclin à

loathe [loð] tr détester

loathing [′loðɪŋ] s dégoût m

loathsome [′loðsəm] adj dégoûtant

lob [lab] s (tennis) lob m ‖ v (pret & pp lobbed; ger lobbing) tr frapper en hauteur, lober

lob·by [′labi] s (pl -bies) vestibule m; (e.g., in a theater) foyer m; (pressure group) groupe m de pression, lobby m ‖ v (pret & pp -bied) intr faire les couloirs

lobbying [′labɪ·ɪŋ] s intrigues fpl de couloir

lobbyist [′labɪ·ɪst] s intrigant m de couloir

lobe [lob] s lobe m

lobster [′labstər] s (spiny lobster) langouste f; (Homarus) homard m

lob′ster pot′ s casier m à homards

local [′lokəl] adj local ‖ s (of labor union) succursale f; (journ) informations fpl régionales; (rr) train m omnibus

locale [lo′kæl] s lieu m, milieu m; scène f

locali·ty [loˈkælɪti] s (pl **-ties**) localité f

localize [ˈlokəˌlaɪz] tr localiser

lo′cal supply′ cir′cuit s secteur m

locate [loˈket], [ˈloket] tr (to discover the location of) localiser; (to place, to settle) placer, installer; (to ascribe a particular location to) situer; **to be located** se trouver ‖ intr se fixer, s'établir

location [loˈkeʃən] s (place, position) situation f, emplacement m; (act of placing) établissement m; (act of finding) localisation f, détermination f; (of a railroad line) tracé m; **on location** (mov) en extérieur

loca′tion shot′ s (mov) extérieur m

lock [lɑk] s serrure f; (of a canal) écluse f; (of hair) mèche f, boucle f; (of a firearm) platine f; (wrestling) clef f; **lock, stock, and barrel** tout le bataclan, tout le fourbi; **under lock and key** sous clé ‖ tr fermer à clef; (to key) caler, bloquer; (a boat) écluser, sasser; (a switch) (rr) verrouiller; **to be locked in each other's arms** être enlacés; **to lock in** enfermer à clef; **to lock out** fermer la porte à ou sur; (workers) fermer les ateliers contre; **to lock up** fermer à clef, mettre sous clé; (e.g., a prisoner) boucler, enfermer; (a form) (typ) serrer ‖ intr (said of door) fermer à clef; (said of brake, wheel, etc.) se bloquer; **to lock into** s'engrener dans

locker [ˈlɑkər] s armoire f, coffre m de sûreté (in a station) compartiment m individuel

lock′er room′ s vestiaire m à cases individuelles

locket [ˈlɑkɪt] s médaillon m

lock′jaw′ s trisme m

lock′ nut′ s contre-écrou m

lock′out′ s lock-out m

lock′smith′ s serrurier m

lock′ step′ s—**to march in lock step** emboîter le pas

lock′ stitch′ s point m indécousable

lock′ten′der s éclusier m

lock′up′ s (prison) (coll) bloc m, violon m

lock′ wash′er s rondelle f Grower, rondelle à ressort

locomotive [ˌlokəˈmotɪv] s locomotive f

lo·cus [ˈlokəs] s (pl **-ci** [saɪ]) lieu m; (math) lieu géométrique

locust [ˈlokəst] s (Pachytylus) (ent) criquet m migrateur, locuste f; (Cicada) (ent) cigale f; (bot) faux acacia m

lode [lod] s filon m, veine f

lode′star′ s (astr) étoile f polaire; (fig) pôle m d'attraction

lodge [lɑdʒ] s (of gatekeeper; of animal; of Mason) loge f; (residence, e.g., for hunting) pavillon m; (hotel) relais m, hostellerie f ‖ tr loger; **to lodge a complaint with** porter plainte auprès de ‖ intr loger; (said of arrow, bullet) se loger

lodger [ˈlɑdʒər] s locataire mf, pensionnaire mf

lodging [ˈlɑdʒɪŋ] s logement m; (of a complaint) déposition f

loft [lɔft], [lɑft] s (attic) grenier m, soupente f; (hayloft) fenil m; (in theater or church) tribune f; (in store or office building) atelier m

loft·y [ˈlɔfti], [ˈlɑfti] adj (comp **-ier;** super **-iest**) (towering; sublime) élevé, exalté; (haughty) hautain

log [lɔg], [lɑg] s bûche f, rondin m; (record book) registre m de travail; (aer) livre m de vol; (record book) (naut) journal m de bord; (chip log) (naut) loch m; (pad) carnet m d'écoute; **to sleep like a log** dormir comme une souche ‖ v (pret & pp **logged**; ger **logging**) tr (wood) tronçonner; (an event) porter au journal; (a certain distance) (naut) filer ‖ intr (to cut wood) couper des rondins

logarithm [ˈlɔgəˌrɪðəm], [ˈlɑgəˌrɪðəm] s logarithme m

log′book′ s (aer) livre m de vol; (naut) journal m de bord, livre de loch

log′ cab′in s cabane f en rondins

log′ chip′ s (naut) flotteur m de loch

log′ driv′er s flotteur m

log′ driv′ing s flottage m

logger [ˈlɔgər], [ˈlɑgər] s bûcheron m; (loader) (mach) grue f de chargement; (mach) tracteur m

log′ger·head′ s tête f de bois; **at loggerheads** en bisbille, aux prises

logic [ˈlɑdʒɪk] s logique f

logical [ˈlɑdʒɪkəl] adj logique

logician [loˈdʒɪʃən] s logicien m

logistic(al) [loˈdʒɪstɪk(əl)] adj logistique

logistics [loˈdʒɪstɪks] s logistique f

log′jam′ s embâcle m de bûches; (fig) bouchon m, embouteillage m

log′ line′ s (naut) ligne f de loch

log′roll′ intr faire trafic de faveurs politiques

log′wood′ s bois m de campêche; (tree) campêche m

loin [lɔɪn] s (of beef) aloyau m; (of veal) longe f; (of pork) échine f; **to gird up one's loins** se ceindre les reins

loin′cloth′ s pagne m

loiter [ˈlɔɪtər] tr—**to loiter away** perdre en flânant ‖ intr flâner

loiterer [ˈlɔɪtərər] s flâneur m

loll [lɑl] intr se prélasser, s'allonger, s'affaler

lollipop [ˈlɑliˌpɑp] s sucette f

Lom′bardy pop′lar [ˈlɑmbərdi] s peuplier m noir

London [ˈlʌndən] adj londonien ‖ s Londres m

Londoner [ˈlʌndənər] s Londonien m

lone [lon] adj solitaire, seul; (sole, single) unique

loneliness [ˈlonlɪnɪs] s solitude f

lone·ly [ˈlonli] adj (comp **-lier;** super **-liest**) solitaire, isolé

lonesome [ˈlonsəm] adj solitaire, seul

lone′ wolf′ s (fig) solitaire mf, ours m

long [lɔŋ], [lɑŋ] (comp **longer** [ˈlɔŋ-**

gər], ['laŋgər]; *super* **longest** ['lɔŋ-
gɪst], ['laŋgɪst]) *adj* long; de long, de
longueur, e.g., **two meters long** deux
mètres de long or de longueur || *adv*
longtemps; **as long as** aussi longtemps que; *(provided that)* tant que;
before long sous peu; **how long?**
combien de temps?, depuis combien
de temps?, depuis quand?; **long ago**
il y a longtemps; **long before** longtemps avant; **longer** plus long; **long
since** depuis longtemps; **no longer ne
. . .** plus longtemps; ne . . . plus,
e.g., **I could no longer see him** je ne
pouvais plus le voir; **so long!** (coll)
à bientôt!; **so long as** tant que; **to be
long in** tarder à || *intr*—**to long for**
soupirer pour or après

long'boat' s chaloupe *f*

long' dis'tance *s* (telp) l'interurbain
m; **to call s.o. long distance** appeler
qn par l'interurbain

long'-dis'tance call' *s* (telp) appel *m*
interurbain

long'-dis'tance flight' *s* (aer) vol *m* au
long cours, raid *m* aérien

long'-drawn'-out' *adj* prolongé; *(story)*
délayé

longevity [lɑn'dʒɛvɪti] *s* longévité *f*

long' face' *s* (coll) triste figure *f*

long'hair' *adj* & *s* intellectuel *m*; fanatique *mf* de la musique classique

long'hand' *s* écriture *f* ordinaire; **in
longhand** à la main

longing ['lɔŋɪŋ], ['laŋɪŋ] *adj* ardent ||
s désir *m* ardent

longitude ['landʒɪ,t(j)ud] *s* longitude *f*

long' jump' *s* saut *m* en longueur

long-lived ['lɔŋ'laɪvd], ['laŋ'laɪvd],
['lɔŋ'lɪvd], ['laŋ'lɪvd] *adj* à longue
vie; persistant

long'-play'ing rec'ord *s* disque *m* de
longue durée

long' prim'er ['prɪmər] *s* (typ) philosophie *f*

long'-range' *adj* à longue portée; *(e.g.,
plan)* à long terme

long'shore'man *s* (pl **-men**) arrimeur *m*,
débardeur *m*

long'-stand'ing *adj* de longue date

long'-suf'fering *adj* patient, endurant

long' suit' *s* (cards) couleur *f* longue,
longue *f*; (fig) fort *m*

long'-term' *adj* à longue échéance

long'-wind'ed ['wɪndɪd] *adj* interminable; *(person)* intarissable

look [lʊk] *s* *(appearance)* aspect *m*;
(glance) regard *m*; **looks** apparence
f, mine *f*; **to take a look at** jeter un
coup d'œil sur or à || *tr* regarder;
(e.g., one's age) paraître; **to look
daggers at** lancer un regard furieux
à; **to look the part** avoir le physique
de l'emploi; **to look up** *(e.g., in a
dictionary)* chercher, rechercher; *(to
visit)* aller voir, venir voir || *intr* re-
garder; *(to ꜱeek)* chercher; **it looks
like rain** le temps est à la pluie; **look
here!** dites donc!; **look out!** gare!,
attention!; **to look after** s'occuper
de; *(e.g., an invalid)* soigner; **to look
at** regarder; **to look away** détourner

les yeux; **to look back** regarder en
arrière; **to look down on** mépriser;
to look for chercher; *(to expect)*
s'attendre à; **to look forward to** s'attendre à, attendre avec impatience;
to look ill avoir mauvaise mine; **to
look in on** passer voir; **to look into**
examiner, vérifier; **to look like** *(s.o.
or s.th.)* ressembler à; *(to give promise of)* avoir l'air de; **to look out** faire
attention; *(e.g., the window)* regarder
par; **to look out on** donner sur; **to
look through** *(a window)* regarder
par; *(a telescope)* regarder dans; *(a
book)* feuilleter; **to look toward** regarder du côté de; **to look up** lever
les yeux; **to look up to** respecter; **to
look well** avoir bonne mine

looker-on [,lʊkər'ɑn], [,lʊkər'ɔn] *s*
(pl **lookers-on**) spectateur *m*, assistant *m*

look'ing glass' *s* miroir *m*

look'out' *s* guet *m*; *(person)* guetteur
m; *(place)* poste *m* d'observation;
(person or place) (naut) vigie *f*;
that's his lookout (coll) ça, c'est son
affaire; **to be on the lookout for** être
à l'affût de

loom [lum] *s* métier *m* || *intr* apparaî-
tre indistinctement; s'élever; mena-
cer, paraître imminent

loon [lun] *s* lourdaud *m*, sot *m*; (orn)
plongeon *m*

loon·y ['luni] *adj* (comp **-ier**; super
-iest) (slang) toqué || *s* (pl **-ies**)
(slang) toqué *m*

loop [lup] *s* boucle *f*; *(for fastening a
button)* bride *f*; *(circular route)* boulevard *m* périphérique; *(in skating)*
croisé *m*; **to loop the loop** (aer)
boucler la boucle || *tr* & *intr* boucler

loop'hole' *s* meurtrière *f*, (fig) échappatoire *f*

loop'-the-loop' *s* looping *m*

loose [lus] *adj* lâche; *(stone, tooth)*
branlant; *(screw)* desserré; *(pulley,
wheel)* fou; *(rope)* mou, détendu;
(coat, dress) vague, ample; *(earth,
soil)* meuble, friable; *(bowels)* relâché; *(style)* décousu; *(translation)*
libre, peu exact; *(life, morals)* relâché, dissolu; *(woman)* facile; *(un-
packaged)* en vrac; *(unbound, e.g.,
pages)* détaché; **to become loose** se
détacher; **to break loose** *(from captivity)* s'évader; (fig) se déchaîner;
to let loose lâcher, lâcher la bride à
|| *s*—**to be on the loose** *(to debauch)*
(coll) courir la prétentaine; *(to be
out of work)* (coll) être sans occupa-
tion || *tr* lâcher; *(to untie)* détacher

loose' end' *s* (fig) affaire *f* pendante;
at loose ends désœuvré, indécis

loose'-leaf note'book *s* cahier *m* à
feuilles mobiles

loosen ['lusən] *tr* lâcher, relâcher; *(a
screw)* desserrer || *intr* se relâcher

looseness ['lusnɪs] *s* relâchement *m*;
(of garment) ampleur *f*; *(play of
screw)* jeu *m*, desserrage *m*

loose'strife' *s* *(common yellow type)*

chasse-bosse *f*, grande lysimaque *f*; (*spiked-purple type*) salicaire *f*

loose'-tongued' *adj*—**to be loose-tongued** avoir la langue déliée

loot [lut] *s* butin *m*, pillage *m* ‖ *tr* piller, saccager

lop [lɑp] *v* (*pret & pp* **lopped**; *ger* **lopping**) *tr*—**to lop off** abattre, trancher; (*a tree, a branch*) élaguer ‖ *intr* pendre

lope [lop] *s* galop *m* lent ‖ *intr*—**to lope along** aller doucement

lop'sid'ed *adj* déjeté, bancal

loquacious [loˈkweʃəs] *adj* loquace

lord [lɔrd] *s* seigneur *m*; (*hum & poetic*) époux *m*; (Brit) lord *m* ‖ *tr*—**to lord it over** dominer despotiquement

lord·ly [ˈlɔrdli] *adj* (*comp* **-lier**; *super* **-liest**) de grand seigneur, majestueux; (*arrogant*) hautain, altier

Lord's' Day' *s* jour *m* du Seigneur

lordship [ˈlɔrd/ɪp] *s* seigneurie *f*

Lord's' Prayer' *s* oraison *f* dominicale

Lord's' Sup'per *s* communion *f*, cène *f*; Cène

lore [lor] *s* savoir *m*, science *f*; tradition *f* populaire

lorgnette [lɔrnˈjɛt] *s* (*eyeglasses*) face-à-main *m*; (*opera glasses*) lorgnette *f*

lor·ry [ˈlɑri], [ˈlɔri] *s* (*pl* **-ries**) lorry *m*, wagonnet *m*; (*truck*) (Brit) camion *m*; (*wagon*) (Brit) fardier *m*

lose [luz] *v* (*pret & pp* **lost** [lɔst], [lɑst]) *tr* perdre; (*a patient who dies*) ne pas réussir à sauver; (*several minutes, as a timepiece does*) retarder de; **to lose oneself in** s'absorber dans; **to lose one's way** s'égarer ‖ *intr* perdre; (*said of timepiece*) retarder

loser [ˈluzər] *s* perdant *m*

losing [ˈluzɪŋ] *adj* perdant ‖ **losings** *spl* pertes *fpl*

loss [lɔs], [lɑs] *s* perte *f*; **to be at a loss** ne savoir que faire; **to be at a loss** to avoir de la peine à, être bien embarrassé pour; **to sell at a loss** vendre à perte

loss' of face' *s* perte *f* de prestige

lost [lɔst], [lɑst] *adj* perdu; **lost in thought** perdu or absorbé dans ses pensées; **lost to** perdu pour

lost'-and-found' depart'ment *s* bureau *m* des objets trouvés

lost' sheep' *s* brebis *f* perdue, brebis égarée

lot [lɑt] *s* lot *m*; (*for building*) lotissement *m*, lot; (*fate*) sort *m*, lot; **a bad lot** (coll) un mauvais sujet, dè la mauvaise graine; **a lot of or lots of** (coll) un tas de; **a queer lot** (coll) un drôle de numéro; **in a lot en bloc**; **to cast or to throw in one's lot with** tenter la fortune avec; **to draw or to cast lots** tirer au sort; **such a lot of** tellement de; **what a lot of . . . !** que de . . . !

lotion [ˈloʃən] *s* lotion *f*

lotter·y [ˈlɑtəri] *s* (*pl* **-ies**) loterie *f*

lotto [ˈlɑto] *s* loto *m*

lotus [ˈlotəs] *s* lotus *m*

loud [laʊd] *adj* haut, fort; (*noisy*) bruyant; (*voice*) fort; (*showy*) voyant ‖ *adv* fort; (*noisily*) bruyamment; **out loud** à haute voix

loud·mouthed [ˈlaʊdˌmaʊθt], [ˈlaʊdˌmaʊðd] *adj* au verbe haut

loud'speak'er *s* haut-parleur *m*

Louisiana [luˌiziˈænə] *s* Louisiane *f*; la Louisiane

lounge [laʊndʒ] *s* divan *m*, sofa *m*; (*room*) petit salon *m*, salle *f* de repos; (*in a hotel*) hall *m* ‖ *intr* flâner; (*e.g., in a chair*) se vautrer

lounge' liz'ard *s* (slang) gigolo *m*

louse [laʊs] *s* (*pl* **lice** [laɪs]) pou *m*; (slang) salaud *m* ‖ *tr*—**to louse up** (slang) bâcler

lous·y [ˈlaʊzi] *adj* (*comp* **-ier**; *super* **-iest**) pouilleux; (*mean; ugly*) (coll) moche; (*bungling*) (coll) maladroit, gauche; **lousy with** (slang) chargé de

lout [laʊt] *s* lourdaud *m*, balourd *m*

louver [ˈluvər] *s* abat-vent *m*; (aut) auvent *m*

lovable [ˈlʌvəbəl] *adj* aimable, sympathique

love [lʌv] *s* amour *m*; affection *f*; (tennis) zéro *m*; **in love with** amoureux de; **love at first sight** le coup de foudre; **love to all!** vives amitiés à tous!; **not for love or money** pour rien au monde; **to make love to** faire la cour à; **with much love!** avec mes affectueuses pensées! ‖ *tr & intr* aimer

love' affair' *s* affaire *f* de cœur

love'birds' *spl* inséparables *mpl*; nouveaux mariés *mpl*

love' child' *s* enfant *mf* de l'amour

love' feast' *s* (eccl) agape *f*

love' game' *s* (tennis) jeu *m* blanc

love' knot' *s* lacs *m* d'amour

loveless [ˈlʌvlɪs] *adj* sans amour; (*feeling no love*) insensible à l'amour

love' let'ter *s* billet *m* doux

lovelorn [ˈlʌvˌlɔrn] *adj* délaissé d'amour; éperdu d'amour

love·ly [ˈlʌvli] *adj* (*comp* **-lier**; *super* **-liest**) beau; (*adorable*) charmant, gracieux; (*enjoyable*) (coll) agréable, aimable

love' match' *s* mariage *m* d'amour

love' po'tion *s* philtre *m* d'amour

lover [ˈlʌvər] *s* amoureux *m*, amant *m*; (*of hunting, sports, music, etc.*) amateur *m*, fanatique *mf*

love' seat' *s* causeuse *f*

love'sick' *adj* féru d'amour

love'sick'ness *s* mal *m* d'amour

love' song' *s* romance *f*, chanson *f* d'amour

loving [ˈlʌvɪŋ] *adj* aimant, affectueux; affectionné, e.g., **your loving daughter** votre fille affectionnée

lov'ing cup' *s* coupe *f* de l'amitié; trophée *m*

lov'ing-kind'ness *s* bonté *f* d'âme

low [lo] *adj* bas; (*speed; price*) bas; (*speed; price; number; light*) faible; (*opinion*) défavorable; (*dress*) décolleté; (*sound, note*) bas, grave; (*fever*) lent; (*bow*) profond; **to lay low** étendre, terrasser; **to lie low** se tenir coi || *s* bas *m*; (*moo of cow*) meuglement *m*; (aut) première vitesse *f*; (meteo) dépression *f* || *adv* bas; **to speak low** parler à voix basse || *intr* (*said of cow*) meugler

low/born/ *adj* de basse naissance

low/boy/ *s* commode *f* basse

low/brow/ *adj* (coll) peu intellectuel || *s* (coll) ignorant *m*

low/-cost/ hous/ing *s* habitations *fpl* à loyer modéré ou à bon marché

Low/ Coun/tries *spl* Pays-Bas *mpl*

low/-down/ *adj* (coll) bas, vil || **low/-down/** *s* (slang) faits *mpl* véritables; **to give s.o. the low-down on** (slang) tuyauter qn sur

lower [ˈlo‐ər] *adj* inférieur, bas || *tr* & *intr* baisser || [ˈlau‐ər] *intr* se renfrogner, regarder de travers

low/er berth/ [ˈlo‐ər] *s* couchette *f* inférieure

low/er case/ [ˈlo‐ər] *s* (typ) bas *m* de casse

low/er mid/dle class/ [ˈlo‐ər] *s* petite bourgeoisie *f*

lowermost [ˈlo‐ər,most] *adj* (le) plus bas

low/-fre/quency *adj* à basse fréquence

low/ gear/ *s* première vitesse *f*

lowland [ˈloland] *s* plaine *f* basse; **Lowlands** (*in Scotland*) Basse-Écosse *f*

low‐ly [ˈloli] *adj* (*comp* **-lier**; *super* **-liest**) humble, modeste; (*in growth or position*) bas, infime

Low/ Mass/ *s* messe basse *f*, petite messe

low/-mind/ed *adj* d'esprit vulgaire

low/ neck/ *s* décolleté *m*

low/-necked/ *adj* décolleté

low/-pitched/ *adj* (*sound*) grave; (*roof*) à faible inclinaison

low/-pres/sure *adj* à basse pression

low/-priced/ *adj* à bas prix

low/ shoe/ *s* soulier *m* bas

low/-speed/ *adj* à petite vitesse

low/-spir/ited *adj* abattu

low/ spir/its *spl* abattement *m*, accablement *m*

low/ tide/ *s* marée *f* basse

low/ vis/ibil/ity *s* (aer) mauvaise visibilité *f*

low/-warp/ *adj* (tex) de basse lice

low/ wa/ter *s* (*of river*) étiage *m*; (*of sea*) niveau *m* des basses eaux; marée *f* basse

loyal [ˈlɔɪ‐əl] *adj* loyal

loyalist [ˈlɔɪ‐əlɪst] *s* loyaliste *mf*

loyal‐ty [ˈlɔɪ‐əlti] *s* (*pl* **-ties**) loyauté *f*

lozenge [ˈlazɪndʒ] *s* (*candy cough drop*) pastille *f*; (geom) losange *m*

LP [ˈɛlˈpi] *s* (letterword) (trademark) (**long-playing**) disque *m* de longue durée

lubricant [ˈlubrɪkənt] *adj* & *s* lubrifiant *m*

lubricate [ˈlubrɪ,ket] *tr* lubrifier

lubricous [ˈlubrɪkəs] *adj* (*slippery*) glissant; (*lewd*) lubrique; inconstant

lucerne [luˈsʌrn] *s* luzerne *f*

lucid [ˈlusɪd] *adj* lucide

luck [lʌk] *s* (*good or bad*) chance *f*;

(*good*) chance, bonne chance; **to be down on one's luck, to be out of luck** avoir de la malchance, être dans la déveine; **to be in luck** avoir de la chance, avoir de la veine; **to bring luck** porter bonheur; **to try one's luck** tenter la fortune, tenter l'aventure; **worse luck!** tant pis!, pas de chance!

luckily [ˈlʌkɪli] *adv* heureusement, par bonheur

luckless [ˈlʌklɪs] *adj* malheureux, malchanceux

luck‐y [ˈlʌki] *adj* (*comp* **-ier**; *super* **-iest**) heureux, fortuné; (*supposed to bring luck*) porte-bonheur; **how lucky!** quelle chance!; **to be lucky** avoir de la chance

luck/y charm/ *s* porte-bonheur *m*

luck/y find/ *s* (coll) trouvaille *f*

luck/y hit/ *s* (coll) coup *m* de bonheur

lucrative [ˈlukrətɪv] *adj* lucratif

ludicrous [ˈludɪkrəs] *adj* ridicule, risible

lug [lʌg] *s* oreille *f*; (*pull, tug*) saccade *f* || *v* (*pret* & *pp* **lugged**; *ger* **lugging**) *tr* traîner, tirer; (*to bring up irrelevantly*) (coll) ressortir, amener de force

luggage [ˈlʌgɪdʒ] *s* bagages *mpl*

lug/gage car/rier *s* porte-bagages *m*

lugubrious [luˈg(j)ubrɪ‐əs] *adj* lugubre

lukewarm [ˈluk,wɔrm] *adj* tiède

lull [lʌl] *s* accalmie *f* || *tr* bercer, endormir, calmer

lulla‐by [ˈlʌlə,baɪ] *s* (*pl* **-bies**) berceuse *f*

lumbago [lʌmˈbego] *s* lumbago *m*

lumber [ˈlʌmbər] *s* bois *m* de charpente, bois de construction || *intr* se traîner lourdement

lum/ber‐jack/ *s* bûcheron *m*

lum/ber jack/et *s* canadienne *f*

lum/ber‐man *s* (*pl* **-men**) (*dealer*) exploitant *m* forestier, propriétaire *m* forestier; (*man who cuts down lumber*) bûcheron *m*

lum/ber raft/ *s* train *m* de flottage

lum/ber room/ *s* fourre-tout *m*, débarras *m*

lum/ber‐yard/ *s* chantier *m* de bois, dépôt *m* de bois de charpente

luminar‐y [ˈlumɪ,nɛri] *s* (*pl* **-ies**) corps *m* lumineux; (astr) luminaire *m*; (*person*) (fig) lumière *f*

luminescent [,lumɪˈnɛsənt] *adj* luminescent

luminous [ˈlumɪnəs] *adj* lumineux

lummox [ˈlʌməks] *s* (coll) lourdaud *m*

lump [lʌmp] *s* masse *f*; (*of earth*) motte *f*; (*of sugar*) morceau *m*; (*of salt, flour, porridge, etc.*) grumeau *m*; (*swelling*) bosse *f*; (*of ice, stone, etc.*) bloc *m*; **in the lump** en bloc; **to get a lump in one's throat** avoir un serrement de gorge *f*; **to réunir**; **to lump together** prendre en bloc, englober || *intr*—**to lump along** marcher d'un pas lourd

lumpish [ˈlʌmpɪʃ] *adj* balourd

lump/ sug/ar *s* sucre *m* en morceaux

lump/ sum/ *s* somme *f* globale

lump·y ['lʌmpi] *adj* (*comp* -ier; *super*
-iest) grumeleux; (*covered with*
lumps) couvert de bosses; (*sea*) clapoteux
lu·na·cy ['lunəsi] *s* (*pl* -cies) folie *f*
lu′nar land′ing *s* alunissage *m*
lu′nar mod′ule *s* (*rok*) module *m* lunaire
lunatic ['lunətɪk] *adj & s* fou *m*
lu′natic asy′lum *s* maison *f* de fous
lu′natic fringe′ *s* minorité *f* fanatique
lunch [lʌntʃ] *s* (*midday meal*) déjeuner
m; (*light meal*) collation *f*, petit re-
pas *m* || *intr* déjeuner; (*to snack*)
casser la croûte, manger sur le pouce
lunch′ bas′ket *s* panier *m* à provisions
lunch′ cloth′ *s* nappe *f* à thé
lunch′ coun′ter *s* snack *m*, buffet *m*
luncheon ['lʌntʃən] *s* déjeuner *m*
luncheonette [ˌlʌntʃəˈnet] *s* brasserie
f, café-restaurant *m*
lunch′room′ *s* brasserie *f*, café-restaurant *m*
lunch′time′ *s* heure *f* du déjeuner
lung [lʌŋ] *s* poumon *m*
lunge [lʌndʒ] *s* mouvement *m* en avant;
(*with a sword*) botte *f* || *intr* se pré-
cipiter en avant; (*with a sword*) se
fendre; **to lunge at** porter une botte à
lurch [lʌrtʃ] *s* embardée *f*; (*of person*)
secousse *f*; **to leave in the lurch**
laisser en plan || *intr* faire une em-
bardée; (*said of person*) vaciller
lure [lʊr] *s* (*decoy*) leurre *m*, amorce
f; (fig) attrait *m* || *tr* leurrer; **to lure**
away détourner
lurid ['lʊrɪd] *adj* sensationnel; (*grue-*
some) terrible, macabre; (*fiery*) rougeoyant; (*livid*) blafard
lurk [lʌrk] *intr* se cacher; (*to prowl*)
rôder
luscious ['lʌʃəs] *adj* délicieux, succu-
lent; luxueux, somptueux
lush [lʌʃ] *adj* plein de sève; (*abundant*)
luxuriant; opulent, luxueux
lust [lʌst] *s* désir *m* ardent; (*greed*)

convoitise *f*, soif *f*; (*strong sexual*
appetite) luxure *f*
luster ['lʌstər] *s* lustre *m*
lus′ter·ware′ *s* poterie *f* lustrée, poterie
à reflets métalliques
lustful ['lʌstfəl] *adj* luxurieux, lascif
lustrous ['lʌstrəs] *adj* lustré, chatoyant
lust·y ['lʌsti] *adj* (*comp* -ier; *super*
-iest) robuste, vigoureux
lute [lut] *s* (mus) luth *m*; (*substance*
used to close or seal a joint) (chem)
lut *m*
Lutheran ['luθərən] *adj* luthérien || *s*
Luthérien *m*
Luxemburg ['lʌksəmˌbʌrg] *s* le Luxembourg
luxuriant [lʌgˈʒʊri·ənt], [lʌkˈʃʊri·ənt]
adj luxuriant; (*overornamented*) sur-
chargé
luxurious [lʌgˈʒʊri·əs], [lʌkˈʃʊri·əs]
adj luxueux, somptueux
luxu·ry ['lʌkʃəri], ['lʌgʒəri] *s* (*pl* -ries)
luxe *m*
lux′ury i′tem *s* produit *m* de luxe
lux′ury tax′ *s* impôt *m* somptuaire
lyceum [laɪˈsi·əm] *s* lycée *m*
lye [laɪ] *s* lessive *f*
lying ['laɪ·ɪŋ] *adj* menteur || *s* le men-
songe
ly′ing-in′ hos′pital *s* maternité *f*, clinique *f* d'accouchement
lymph [lɪmf] *s* lymphe *f*
lymphatic [lɪmˈfætɪk] *adj* lymphatique
lynch [lɪntʃ] *tr* lyncher
lynching ['lɪntʃɪŋ] *s* lynchage *m*
lynx [lɪŋks] *s* lynx *m*
Lyons ['laɪ·ənz] *s* Lyon *m*
lyre [laɪr] *s* (mus) lyre *f*
lyric ['lɪrɪk] *adj* lyrique || *s* poème *m*
lyrique; **lyrics** (*of song*) paroles *fpl*;
(theat) chansons *fpl* du livret
lyrical ['lɪrɪkəl] *adj* lyrique
lyricism ['lɪrɪˌsɪzəm] *s* lyrisme *m*
lyricist ['lɪrɪsɪst] *s* poète *m* lyrique;
(*writer of words for songs*) parolier *m*

M

M, m [em] **XIIIᵉ** lettre *f* de l'alphabet
ma′am [mæm], [mɑm] *s* (coll) madame *f*
macadam [məˈkædəm] *s* macadam *m*
macadamize [məˈkædəˌmaɪz] *tr* macadamiser
macaroon [ˌmækəˈrun] *s* macaron *m*
macaw [məˈkɔ] *s* (orn) ara *m*
mace [mes] *s* masse *f*
mace′bear′er *s* massier *m*
machination [ˌmækɪˈneɪʃən] *s* machination *f*
machine [məˈʃin] *s* machine *f*; (*of a*
political party) noyau *m* directeur,
leviers *mpl* de commande || *tr* usiner,
façonner
machine′ gun′ *s* mitrailleuse *f*

ma·chine′-gun′ *v* (*pret & pp* -**gunned**;
ger -**gunning**) *tr* mitrailler
ma·chine′-made′ *adj* fait à la machine
machiner·y [məˈʃinəri] *s* (*pl* -ies) machinerie *f*, machines *fpl*; (*of a watch*;
of government) mécanisme *m*; (*in*
literature) merveilleux *m*
machine′ screw′ *s* vis *f* à métaux
machine′ shop′ *s* atelier *m* d'usinage
machine′ tool′ *s* machine-outil *f*
machine′ transla′tion *s* traduction *f*
automatique
machinist [məˈʃinɪst] *s* mécanicien *m*
mackerel ['mækərəl] *s* maquereau *m*
mack′erel sky′ *s* ciel *m* pommelé *or*
moutonné
mad [mæd] *adj* (*comp* **madder**; *super*

maddest) fou; (*dog*) enragé; (coll) fâché, irrité; **as mad as a hatter** fou à lier; **like mad** (coll) comme un fou, éperdument; **to be mad about** (coll) être fou or passionné de; **to drive mad** rendre fou

madam ['mædəm] s madame f; (*of a brothel*) (slang) tenancière f

mad'cap' adj & s écervelé m, étourdi m

madden ['mædən] tr rendre fou || intr devenir fou

made-to-order ['medtə'ɔrdər] adj fait sur demande; (*clothing*) fait sur mesure

made'-up' adj inventé; (*artificial*) postiche; (*face*) maquillé

mad'house' s maison f de fous

mad'man' s (pl -men') fou m

madness ['mædnɪs] s folie f; (*of dog*) rage f

Madonna [mə'dɑnə] s madone f; (eccl) Madone

maelstrom ['melstrəm] s maelstrom m, tourbillon m

magazine ['mægə,zin], [,mægə'zin] s (*periodical*) revue f, magazine m; (*warehouse; for cartridges of gun or camera; for munitions or powder*) magasin m; (naut) soute f

mag'azine' rack' s casier m à revues

Magdalen ['mægdələn] s Madeleine f

Maggie ['mægi] s (coll) Margot f

maggot ['mægət] s asticot m

Magi ['medʒai] spl mages mpl

magic ['mædʒɪk] adj magique || s magie f; **as if by magic** comme par enchantement

magician [mə'dʒɪʃən] s magicien m

magisterial [,mædʒɪs'tɪrɪ-əl] adj magistral

magistrate ['mædʒɪs,tret] s magistrat m

Magna Charta ['mægnə'kɑrtə] s la Grande Charte f

magnanimous [mæg'nænɪməs] adj magnanime

magnate ['mægnet] s magnat m

magnesium [mæg'ni/ɪ-əm], [mæg'niʒɪ-əm] s magnésium m

magnet ['mægnɪt] s aimant m

magnetic [mæg'netɪk] adj magnétique; (fig) attrayant, séduisant

magnetism ['mægnɪ,tɪzəm] s magnétisme m

magnetize ['mægnɪ,taɪz] tr aimanter

magne-to [mæg'nito] s (pl -tos) magnéto f

magnificent [mæg'nɪfɪsənt] adj magnifique

magni-fy ['mægnɪ,faɪ] v (pret & pp -fied) tr grossir; (opt) grossir

mag'nifying glass' s loupe f

magnitude ['mægnɪ,t(j)ud] s grandeur f; (astr) magnitude f

magpie ['mæg,paɪ] s (orn, fig) pie f

mahlstick ['mɑl,stɪk], ['mɔl,stɪk] s appui-main m

mahoga·ny [mə'hɑgəni] s (pl -nies) acajou m

Mahomet [mə'hɑmɪt] s Mahomet m

mahout [mə'haut] s cornac m

maid [med] s (*servant*) bonne f; (*young girl*) jeune fille f, demoiselle f

maiden ['medən] s jeune fille f, demoiselle f

maid'en·hair' s (bot) capillaire m

maid'en·head' s hymen m

maid'en·hood' s virginité f

maid'en la'dy s demoiselle f, célibataire f

maidenly ['medənli] adj virginal, de jeune fille

maid'en name' s nom m de jeune fille

maid'en voy'age s premier voyage m

maid'-in-wait'ing s (pl maids-in-waiting) fille f d'honneur, dame f d'honneur

maid' of hon'or s demoiselle f d'honneur

maid'serv'ant s fille f de service, servante f

mail [mel] adj postal || s courrier m; (*system*) poste f; (*armor*) mailles fpl, cotte f de mailles; **by return mail** par retour du courrier; **mails** poste || tr mettre à la poste, envoyer par la poste

mail'bag' s sac m postal

mail'boat' s paquebot m, bateau-poste m

mail'box' s boîte f aux lettres

mail' car' s fourgon m postal, bureau m ambulant, wagon-poste m

mail' car'rier s facteur m

mail' clerk' s postier m; (mil, nav) vaguemestre m; (rr) convoyeur m des postes

mailing ['melɪŋ] s envoi m

mail'ing list' s liste f d'adresses; (*of subscribers*) liste d'abonnés

mail'ing per'mit s (label on envelopes) dispensé du timbrage

mail'man' s (pl -men') facteur m

mail' or'der s commande f par la poste

mail'-order house' s établissement m de vente par correspondance or de vente sur catalogue; comptoir m postal (Canad)

mail'-order sell'ing s vente f par correspondance

mail'plane' s avion m postal

mail' train' s train-poste m

maim [mem] tr mutiler, estropier

main [men] adj principal || s égout m collecteur, canalisation f or conduite f principale; **in the main** en général, pour la plupart

main' clause' s proposition f principale

main' course' s (culin) plat m principal, pièce f de résistance

main' deck' s pont m principal

main' floor' s rez-de-chaussée m

mainland ['men,lænd], ['menlənd] s terre f ferme, continent m

main' line' s (rr) grande ligne f

mainly ['menli] adv principalement

mainmast ['menmæst], ['men,mæst], ['men,mɑst] s grand mât m

mainsail ['mensəl], ['men,sel] s grand-voile f

main'spring' s (*of watch*) ressort m moteur, grand ressort m; (fig) mobile m essentiel, principe m

main'stay' s (naut) étai m de grand mât; (fig) point m d'appui

main′ street′ *s* rue *f* principale

maintain [men′ten] *tr* maintenir; (*e.g., a family*) entretenir, faire subsister

maintenance [′mentɪnəns] *s* entretien *m*, maintien *m*; (*department entrusted with upkeep*) services *mpl* d′entretien, maintenance *f*

maître d′hôtel [ˌmetərdo′tel] *s* maître *m* d′hôtel

maize [mez] *s* maïs *m*

majestic [mə′dʒestɪk] *adj* majestueux

majes·ty [′mædʒɪstɪ] *s* (*pl* -ties) majesté *f*

major [′medʒər] *adj* majeur ‖ *s* (*person of full legal age*) majeur *m*; (*educ*) spécialisation *f*; (*mil*) commandant *m* ‖ *intr* (*educ*) se spécialiser

Majorca [mə′dʒɔrkə] *s* Majorque *f*; île *f* de Majorque

Majorcan [mə′dʒɔrkən] *adj* majorquin ‖ *s* Majorquin *m*

ma′jor gen′eral *s* général *m* de division

majori·ty [mə′dʒɑrɪtɪ], [mə′dʒɔrɪtɪ] *adj* majoritaire ‖ *s* (*pl* -ties) majorité *f*; (*mil*) grade *m* de commandant; **the majority of** la plupart de

major′ity vote′ *s* scrutin *m* majoritaire

make [mek] *s* fabrication *f*; (*brand name*) marque *f*; modèle *m* ‖ *v* (*pret & pp* **made** [med]) *tr* faire; rendre, e.g., **to make sick** rendre malade; (*money*) gagner; (*the cards*) battre; (*a train*) attraper; **to make into** transformer en; **to make known** faire savoir; **to make out** déchiffrer, distinguer; (*a bill, receipt, check*) écrire; (*a list*) dresser; **to make s.o.** + *inf* faire + *inf* + qn, e.g., **I will make my uncle talk** je le ferai parler mon oncle ‖ *intr* être, e.g., **to make sure** être sûr; **to make believe** feindre; **to make good** réussir; **to make off** filer, décamper

make′-believe′ *adj* simulé ‖ *s* faux-semblant *m*, feinte *f*

maker [′mekər] *s* fabricant *m*

make′shift′ *s* de fortune, de circonstance ‖ *s* expédient *m*; (*person*) bouche-trou *m*

make′-up′ *s* arrangement *m*, composition *f*; (*cosmetic*) maquillage *m*; (*typ*) mise *f* en pages, imposition *f*

make′-up man′ *s* (*theat*) maquilleur *m*; (*typ*) metteur *m* en pages, imposeur *m*

make′weight′ *s* complément *m* de poids

making [′mekɪŋ] *s* fabrication *f*; (*of a dress; of a cooked dish*) confection *f*; **makings** éléments *mpl* constitutifs; (*money*) recettes *fpl*; **to have the makings of** avoir l′étoffe de

maladjusted [ˌmælə′dʒʌstɪd] *adj* inadapté

maladjustment [ˌmælə′dʒʌstmənt] *s* inadaptation *f*

mala·dy [′mælədɪ] *s* (*pl* -dies) maladie *f*

malaise [mæ′lez] *s* malaise *m*

malaria [mə′lerɪ·ə] *s* malaria *f*, paludisme *m*

Malay [′mele], [mə′le] *adj* malais ‖ *s* (*language*) malais *m*; (*person*) Malais *m*

Malaya [mə′le·ə] *s* Malaisie *f*; **la Malaisie**

malcontent [′mælkən,tent] *adj & s* mécontent *m*

male [mel] *adj & s* mâle *m*

malediction [,mælɪ′dɪk/ən] *s* malédiction *f*

malefactor [′mælɪ,fæktər] *s* malfaiteur *m*

male′ nurse′ *s* infirmier *m*

malevolent [mə′levələnt] *adj* malveillant

malfeasance [,mæl′fizəns] *s* prévarication *f*, trafic *m*

malice [′mælɪs] *s* méchanceté *f*

malicious [mə′lɪ/əs] *adj* méchant

malign [mə′laɪn] *adj* pernicieux; malveillant ‖ *tr* calomnier

malignan·cy [mə′lɪgnənsɪ] *s* (*pl* -cies) malignité *f*

malignant [mə′lɪgnənt] *adj* méchant, malin

malinger [mə′lɪŋgər] *intr* faire le malade

malingerer [mə′lɪŋgərər] *s* simulateur *m*

mall [mɔl], [mæl] *s* mail *m*

mallard [′mælərd] *s* (*orn*) col-vert *m*

malleable [′mælɪ·əbəl] *adj* malléable

mallet [′mælɪt] *s* maillet *m*

mallow [′mælo] *s* (*bot*) mauve *f*

malnutrition [,mæln(ju′trɪ/ən] *s* sous-alimentation *f*, malnutrition *f*

malodorous [mæl′odərəs] *adj* malodorant

malpractice [mæl′præktɪs] *s* incurie *f*; méfait *m*

malt [mɔlt] *s* malt *m*

maltreat [mæl′trit] *tr* maltraiter

mamma [′mɑmə], [mə′mɑ] *s* maman *f*

mammal [′mæməl] *s* mammifère *m*

mammalian [mæ′melɪ·ən] *adj & s* mammifère *m*

mammoth [′mæməθ] *adj* énorme, colossal ‖ *s* mammouth *m*

man [mæn] *s* (*pl* **men** [men]) *s* homme *m*; (*servant*) domestique *m*; (*worker*) ouvrier *m*, employé *m*; (*checkers*) pion *m*; (*chess*) pièce *f*; **a man on**, e.g., **what can a man do?** qu′est-ce qu′on peut faire?; **every man for himself!** sauve qui peut!; **man alive!** (*coll*) tiens!; fichtre!; **man and wife** mari et femme; **men at work** (*public sign*) travaux en cours ‖ *v* (*pret & pp* **manned**) *ger* **manning** *tr* (*a ship*) équiper; (*a fort*) garnir; (*a cannon, the pumps, etc.*) armer; (*a battery*) servir

man′ about town′ *s* boulevardier *m*, coureur *m* de cabarets

manacle [′mænəkəl] *s* manilla *f*; **manacles** menottes *fpl* ‖ *tr* mettre les menottes à

manage [′mænɪdʒ] *tr* gérer, diriger; (*to handle*) manier ‖ *intr* se débrouiller; **how did you manage to . . . ?** comment avez-vous fait pour . . . ?; **to manage to** s′arranger pour

manageable [′mænɪdʒəbəl] *adj* maniable

management ['mænɪdʒmənt] s direction f, gérance f; (group who manage) direction, administration f; (in contrast to labor) patronat m; **under new management** (public sign) changement de propriétaire

manager ['mænədʒər] s directeur m, gérant m; (e.g., of a department) chef m; (impresario) manager m

managerial [,mænə'dʒɪrɪ-əl] adj patronal

man'aging ed'itor s rédacteur m gérant

Manchuria [mæn't∫ʊrɪ-ə] s Mandchourie f; la Mandchourie

man'darin or'ange ['mændərɪn] s mandarine f

mandate ['mændet] s mandat m || tr placer sous le mandat de

mandatory ['mændə,torɪ] adj obligatoire

mandolin ['mændəlɪn] s mandoline f

mandrake ['mændrek] s mandragore f

mane [men] s crinière f

maneuver [mə'nuvər] s manœuvre m || tr & intr manœuvrer

manful ['mænfəl] adj viril, hardi

manganese ['mæŋgə,nis], ['mæŋgə,niz] s manganèse m

mange [mendʒ] s gale f

manger ['mendʒər] s mangeoire f, crèche f

mangle ['mæŋgəl] s calandre f || tr lacérer, mutiler; (to press) calandrer

man-gy ['mendʒɪ] adj (comp -gier; super -giest) galeux; (dirty, squalid) miteux

man'han'dle tr malmener

man'hole' s trou m d'homme, regard m

manhood ['mænhʊd] s virilité f; humanité f

man'hunt' s chasse f à l'homme; chasse au mari

mania ['menɪ-ə] s manie f

maniac ['menɪ,æk] adj & s maniaque mf

maniacal [mə'naɪ-ə-kəl] adj maniaque

manicure ['mænɪ,kjʊr] s soins mpl esthétiques des mains et des ongles; (person) manucure mf || tr manucurer

manicurist ['mænɪ,kjʊrɪst] s manucure mf

manifest ['mænɪ,fest] adj manifeste || s (naut) manifeste m || tr & intr manifester

manifestation [,mænɪfes'te∫ən] s manifestation f

manifes-to [,mænɪ'festo] s (pl -toes) manifeste m

manifold ['mænɪ,fold] adj multiple, nombreux || s (aut) tuyauterie f, collecteur m

manikin ['mænɪkɪn] s mannequin m; (dwarf) nabot m

man' in the moon' s homme m dans la lune

man' in the street' s homme m de la rue

manipulate [mə'nɪpjə,let] tr manipuler

man'kind' s le genre humain, l'humanité f || ['mæn'kaɪnd'] s le sexe fort, les hommes mpl

manliness ['mænlɪnɪs] s virilité f

man•ly ['mænlɪ] adj (comp -lier; super -liest) viril, masculin

manna ['mænə] s manne f

manned' space'craft s vaisseau m spatial habité

mannequin ['mænɪkɪn] s mannequin m

manner ['mænər] s manière f; **by all manner of means** certainement; **by no manner of means** en aucune manière; **in a manner of speaking** pour ainsi dire; **in the manner of** à la, e.g., **in the manner of the French, in the French manner** à la manière française, à la française; **manners** manières; **manners of the time** mœurs fpl de l'époque; **to the manner born** créé et mis au monde pour ça

mannerism ['mænə,rɪzm] s maniérisme m

mannish ['mænɪ∫] adj hommasse

man' of let'ters s homme m de lettres, bel esprit m

man' of parts' s homme m de talent

man' of straw' s homme m de paille

man' of the world' s homme m du monde

man-of-war [,mænəv'wɔr] s (pl men-of-war) navire m de guerre

manor ['mænər] s seigneurie f

man'or house' s château m, manoir m

man' o'verboard' interj un homme à la mer!

man'pow'er s main-d'œuvre f; (mil) effectifs mpl

manse [mæns] s maison f du pasteur

man'serv'ant s (pl men'serv'ants) valet m

mansion ['mæn∫ən] s hôtel m particulier; château m, manoir m

man'slaugh'ter s (law) homicide m involontaire

mantel ['mæntəl] s manteau m de cheminée

man'tel-piece' s manteau m de cheminée; dessus m de cheminée

mantilla [mæn'tɪlə] s mantille f

mantle ['mæntəl] s manteau m, mante f; (of gaslight) manchon m || tr envelopper d'une mante; couvrir, revêtir; (to hide) voiler || intr (said of face) rougir

manual ['mænju-əl] adj manuel || s (book) manuel m; (of arms) (mil) maniement m; (mus) clavier m d'orgue

man'ual dexter'ity s habileté f manuelle

man'ual train'ing s apprentissage m manuel

manufacture [,mænjə'fækt∫ər] s fabrication f; (thing manufactured) produit m fabriqué || tr fabriquer

manufacturer [,mænjə'fækt∫ərər] s fabricant m

manure [mə'n(j)ʊr] s fumier m || tr fumer

manuscript ['mænjə,skrɪpt] adj & s manuscrit m

many ['menɪ] adj beaucoup de; **a good many** bien des, maintes; **how many** combien de; **many another** bien d'autres; **many more** beaucoup d'autres;

so many tant de; **too many** trop de; **twice as many** deux fois autant de || *pron* beaucoup; **as many** as autant de; jusqu'à, e.g., **as many as twenty** jusqu'à vingt; **how many** combien; **many another** bien d'autres; **many more** beaucoup d'autres; **so many** tant; **too many** trop; **twice as many** deux fois autant

man′y-sid′ed *adj* polygonal; (*having many interests or capabilities*) complexe

map [mæp] *s* carte *f*; (*of a city*) plan *m* || *v* (*pret & pp* **mapped**; *ger* **mapping**) *tr* faire la carte de; **to map out** tracer le plan de; **to put on the map** (coll) faire connaître, mettre en vedette

maple [′mepəl] *s* érable *m*

ma′ple sug′ar *s* sucre *m* d'érable

mar [mɑr] *v* (*pret & pp* **marred**; *ger* **marring**) *tr* défigurer, gâcher

marathon [′mærə‚θɑn] *s* marathon *m*

maraud [mə′rɔd] *tr* piller || *intr* marauder

marauder [mə′rɔdər] *s* maraudeur *m*

marauding [mə′rɔdɪŋ] *adj* maraudeur || *s* maraude *f*

marble [′mɑrbəl] *s* marbre *m*; (*little ball of glass*) bille *f*; **marbles** (game) jeu *m* de billes || *tr* marbrer; (*the edge of a book*) jasper

march [mɑrtʃ] *s* marche *f*; **March** mars *m*; **to steal a march on** prendre de l'avance sur || *tr* faire marcher || *intr* marcher

marchioness [′mɑrʃənɪs] *s* marquise *f*

mare [mer] *s* (*female horse*) jument *m*; (*female donkey*) ânesse *f*

Margaret [′mɑrgərɪt] *s* Marguerite *f*

margarine [′mɑrdʒərɪn] *s* margarine *f*

margin [′mɑrdʒɪn] *s* marge *f*; (*border*) bord *m*; (com) acompte *m*

marginal [′mɑrdʒɪnəl] *adj* marginal

mar′gin release′ *s* déclenche-marge *f*

mar′gin stop′ *s* margeur *m*

marigold [′mærɪ‚gold] *s* (*Calendula*) souci *m*; (*Tagetes*) œillet *m* d'Inde

marihuana or **marijuana** [‚mɑrɪ-′hwɑnə] *s* marihuana *f* or marijuana *f*

marinate [′mærɪ‚net] *tr* mariner

marine [mə′rin] *adj* marin, maritime || *s* flotte *f*; (nav) fusilier *m* marin; **tell it to the marines!** (coll) à d'autres!

Marine′ Corps′ *s* infanterie *f* de marine

mariner [′mærɪnər] *s* marin *m*

marionette [‚mærɪ-ə′nɛt] *s* marionnette *f*

marital [′mærɪtəl] *adj* matrimonial

mar′ital sta′tus *s* état *m* civil

maritime [′mærɪ‚taɪm] *adj* maritime

marjoram [′mɑrdʒərəm] *s* marjolaine *f*; origan *m*

mark [mɑrk] *s* marque *f*, signe *m*; (*of punctuation*) point *m*; (*in an examination*) note *f*; (*spot, stain*) tache *f*, marque; (*monetary unit*) mark *m*; (*starting point in a race*) ligne *f* de départ; **as a mark of** en témoignage de; **Mark** Marc *m*; **on your mark!** à vos marques!; **to hit the mark** mettre dans le mille, atteindre le but; **to**

leave one's mark laisser son empreinte; **to make one's mark** se faire un nom, marquer; **to miss the mark** manquer le but; **to toe the mark** se conformer au mot d'ordre || *tr* marquer; (*a student; an exam*) donner une note à; (*e.g., one's approval*) témoigner; **to mark down** noter; (com) démarquer; **to mark off** distinguer; **to mark up** (com) majorer

mark′down′ *s* rabais *m*

marker [′mɑrkər] *s* marqueur *m*; (*of boundary*) borne *f*; (landmark) repère *m*

market [′mɑrkɪt] *s* marché *m*; **to bear the market** jouer à la baisse; **to bull the market** jouer à la hausse; **to play the market** jouer à la bourse; **to put on the market** lancer, vendre, or mettre sur le marché || *tr* commercialiser

marketable [′mɑrkɪtəbəl] *adj* vendable

mar′ket bas′ket *s* panier *m* à provisions

marketing [′mɑrkɪtɪŋ] *s* marché *m*; (*of a product*) commercialisation *f*, exploitation *f*

mar′ket-place′ *s* place *f* du marché

mar′ket price′ *s* cours *m* du marché, prix *m* courant

mark′ing gauge′ *s* trusquin *m*

marks-man [′mɑrksmən] *s* (*pl* **-men**) tireur *m*

marks′man-ship′ *s* habileté *f* au tir, adresse *f* au tir

mark′up′ *s* (*profit*) marge *f* bénéficiaire; (*price increase*) majoration *f* de prix

marl [mɑrl] *s* marne *f* || *tr* marner

marmalade [′mɑrmə‚led] *s* marmelade *f*

maroon [mə′run] *adj & s* (*color*) lie *f* de vin, rouge *m* violacé || *tr* abandonner, isoler

marquee [mɑr′ki] *s* marquise *f*

marquis [′mɑrkwɪs] *s* marquis *m*

marquise [mɑr′kiz] *s* marquise *f*

marriage [′mærɪdʒ] *s* mariage *m*

marriageable [′mærɪdʒəbəl] *adj* mariable

mar′riage certif′icate *s* acte *m* de mariage

mar′riage por′tion *s* dot *f*

mar′riage rate′ *s* taux *m* de nuptialité

mar′ried life′ [′mærɪd] *s* vie *f* conjugale

marrow [′mæro] *s* moelle *f*

mar-ry [′mærɪ] *v* (*pret & pp* **-ried**) *tr* (*to join in wedlock*) marier; (*to take in marriage*) se marier avec; **to get married to** se marier avec; **to marry off** marier || *intr* se marier

Mars [mɑrz] *s* Mars *m*

Marseilles [mɑr′selz] *s* Marseille *f*

marsh [mɑrʃ] *s* marais *m*, marécage *m*

mar-shal [′mɑrʃəl] *s* maître *m* des cérémonies; (*policeman*) shérif *m*; (mil) maréchal *m* || *v* (*pret & pp* **-shaled** or **-shalled**; *ger* **-shaling** or **-shalling**) *tr* conduire; (*one's reasons, arguments, etc.*) ranger, rassembler

marsh′ mal′low *s* (bot) guimauve *f*

marsh′mal′low *s* (*candy*) pâte *f* de guimauve; bonbon *m* à la guimauve

marsh·y ['mɑrʃi] *adj* (*comp* -**ier**; *super* -**iest**) marécageux

mart [mɑrt] *s* marché *m*, foire *f*

marten ['mɑrtən] *s* (*pine marten*) martre *f*; (*beech marten*) fouine *f*

Martha ['mɑrθə] *s* Marthe *f*

martial ['mɑrʃəl] *adj* martial

mar'tial law' *s* loi *f* martiale

martin ['mɑrtɪn] *s* (*orn*) martinet *m*

martinet [,mɑrtɪ'nɛt], ['mɑrtɪ,nɛt] *s* pètesec *m*

martyr ['mɑrtər] *s* martyr *m* || *tr* martyriser

martyrdom ['mɑrtərdəm] *s* martyre *m*

mar·vel ['mɑrvəl] *s* merveille *f* || *v* (*pret* & *pp* -**veled** or -**velled**; *ger* -**veling** or -**velling**) *intr* s'émerveiller; **to marvel at** s'émerveiller de

marvelous ['mɑrvələs] *adj* merveilleux

Marxist ['mɑrksɪst] *adj* & *s* marxiste *mf*

Maryland ['mɛrələnd] *s* le Maryland

marzipan ['mɑrzɪ,pæn] *s* massepain *m*

mascara [mæs'kærə] *s* rimmel *m*

mascot ['mæskɑt] *s* mascotte *f*

masculine ['mæskjəlɪn] *adj* & *s* masculin *m*

mash [mæʃ] *s* (*crushed mass*) bouillie *f*; (*to form wort*) fardeau *m* || *tr* écraser; (*malt, in brewing*) brasser

mashed' pota'toes *spl* purée *f* de pommes de terre

masher ['mæʃər] *s* (*device*) broyeur *m*; (*slang*) tombeur *m*

mask [mæsk], [mɑsk] *s* masque *m*; (*phot*) cache *m* || *tr* masquer; (*phot*) poser un cache à || *intr* se masquer

masked' ball' *s* bal *m* masqué

mason ['mesən] *s* maçon *m*; **Mason** Maçon

mason·ry ['mesənri] *s* (*pl* -**ries**) maçonnerie *f*; **Masonry** Maçonnerie

masquerade [,mæskə'red], [,mɑskə'red] *s* mascarade *f* || *intr* se déguiser; **to masquerade as** se faire passer pour

mass [mæs] *s* masse *f*; (*eccl*) messe *f* || *tr* masser || *intr* se masser

massacre ['mæsəkər] *s* massacre *m* || *tr* massacrer

massage [mə'sɑʒ] *s* massage *m* || *tr* masser

mass' arrest' *s* rafle *f*

masseur [mə'sʌr] *s* masseur *m*

masseuse [mə'suz] *s* masseuse *f*

massive ['mæsɪv] *adj* massif

mass' me'dia ['midɪ·ə] *spl* communication *f* de masse

mass' meet'ing *s* meeting *m* monstre, rassemblement *m*

mass' produc'tion *s* fabrication *f* en série

mast [mæst], [mɑst] *s* mât *m*; (*food for swine*) gland *m*, faîne *f*; **before the mast** comme simple matelot

master ['mæstər], ['mɑstər] *s* maître *m*; (*employer*) chef *m*, patron *m*; (*male head of household*) maître de maison; (*title of respect*) Monsieur *m*; (*naut*) commandant *m* || *tr* maîtriser; (*a subject*) connaître à fond, posséder

mas'ter bed'room *s* chambre *f* du maître

mas'ter build'er *s* entrepreneur *m* de bâtiments

masterful ['mæstərfəl], ['mɑstərfəl] *adj* magistral, expert; impérieux, en maître

mas'ter key' *s* passe-partout *m*

masterly ['mæstərli], ['mɑstərli] *adj* magistral, de maître || *adv* magistralement

mas'ter mechan'ic *s* maître *m* mécanicien

mas'ter·mind' *s* organisateur *m*, cerveau *m* || *tr* organiser, diriger

mas'ter of cer'emonies *s* maître *m* des cérémonies; (*in a night club, on television, etc.*) animateur *m*

mas'ter·piece' *s* chef-d'œuvre *m*

mas'ter stroke' *s* coup *m* de maître

mas'ter·work' *s* chef-d'œuvre *m*

master·y ['mæstəri], ['mɑstəri] *s* (*pl* -**ies**) maîtrise *f*

mast'head' *s* (*of a newspaper*) en-tête *m*; (*naut*) tête *f* de mât

masticate ['mæstɪ,ket] *tr* mastiquer

mastiff ['mæstɪf], ['mɑstɪf] *s* mâtin *m*

masturbate ['mæstər,bet] *tr* masturber || *intr* se masturber

mat [mæt] *s* (*for floor*) natte *f*; (*for a cup, vase, etc.*) dessous *m* de plat; (*before a door*) paillasson *m* || *v* (*pret* & *pp* **matted**; *ger* **matting**) *tr* (*to cover with matting*) couvrir de nattes; (*hair*) emmêler; (*with blood*) coller || *intr* s'emmêler

match [mætʃ] *s* allumette *f*; (*wick*) mèche *f*; (*counterpart*) égal *m*, pair *m*; (*suitable partner in marriage*) parti *m*; (*suitably associated pair*) assortiment *m*; (*game, contest*) match *m*, partie *f*; **to be a match for** être de la force de, être à la hauteur de; **to meet one's match** trouver son pareil || *tr* égaler; (*objects*) faire pendant à, assortir || *intr* s'assortir

match'box' *s* boîte *f* d'allumettes, porte-allumettes *m*

matchless ['mætʃlɪs] *adj* incomparable, sans pareil

match'mak'er *s* marieur *m*

mate [met] *s* compagnon *m*; (*husband*) conjoint *m*; (*wife*) conjointe *f*; (*to a female*) mâle *m*; (*to a male*) femelle *f*; (*checkmate*) mat *m*; (*naut*) officier *m* en second, second maître *m* || *tr* marier; (*zool*) accoupler || *intr* se marier; s'accoupler

material [mə'tɪrɪ·əl] *adj* matériel; important || *s* matériel *m*; (*what a thing is made of*) matière *f*; (*cloth, fabric*) étoffe *f*; (*archit*) matériau *m*; **materials** matériaux *mpl*

materialist [mə'tɪrɪ·əlɪst] *s* matérialiste *mf*

materialistic [mə,tɪrɪ·ə'lɪstɪk] *adj* matérialiste, matériel

materialize [mə'tɪrɪ·ə,laɪz] *intr* se matérialiser; (*to be realized*) se réaliser

matériel [mə,tɪrɪ'ɛl] *s* matériel *m*

maternal [mə'tʌrnəl] *adj* maternel

maternity [mə'tʌrnɪti] s maternité f
mater'nity hos'pital s maternité f
mater'nity room' s salle f d'accouchement
mater'nity ward' s salle f des accouchées
math [mæθ] s (coll) math fpl
mathematical [,mæθɪ'mætɪkəl] adj mathématique
mathematician [,mæθɪmə'tɪʃən] s mathématicien m
mathematics [,mæθɪ'mætɪks] s mathématiques fpl
matinée [,mætɪ'ne] s matinée f
mat'ing sea'son s saison f des amours
matins ['mætɪnz] spl matines fpl
matriarch ['metrɪ,ɑrk] s matriarche f
matriar·chy ['metrɪ,ɑrki] s (pl -chies) matriarcat m
matricide ['metrɪ,saɪd], ['mætrɪ,saɪd] s (person) matricide mf; (action) matricide m
matriculate [mə'trɪkjə,let] tr immatriculer || intr s'inscrire à l'université, prendre ses inscriptions
matriculation [mə,trɪkjə'leʃən] s inscription f, immatriculation f
matrimonial [,mætrɪ'monɪ·əl] adj matrimonial
matrimo·ny ['mætrɪ,moni] s (pl -nies) mariage m, vie f conjugale
ma·trix ['metrɪks], ['mætrɪks] s (pl -trices [trɪ,siz] or -trixes) matrice f
matron ['metrən] s (woman no longer young, and of good standing) matrone f; intendante f, surveillante f
matronly ['metrənli] adj de matrone, digne, respectable
matter ['mætər] s matière f; (pathol) pus m; a matter of affaire de, une question de; for that matter à vrai dire; it doesn't matter cela ne fait rien; no matter n'importe, pas d'importance; no matter when n'importe quand; no matter where n'importe où; no matter who n'importe qui; what is the matter? qu'y a-t-il?; what is the matter with you? qu'avez-vous? || intr importer
mat'ter of course' s chose f qui va de soi
mat'ter of fact' s—as a matter of fact en réalité, effectivement, de fait
matter-of-fact ['mætərəv,fækt] adj prosaïque, terre à terre
mattock ['mætək] s pioche f
mattress ['mætrɪs] s matelas m
mature [mə't/ur], [mə'tur] adj mûr; (due) échu || tr faire mûrir || intr mûrir; (to become due) échoir
maturity [mə't/urɪti], [mə'turiti] s maturité f; (com) échéance f
maudlin ['mɔdlɪn] adj larmoyant
maul [mɔl] tr malmener; (to split) fendre au coin
maulstick ['mɔl,stɪk] s appui-main m
Maun'dy Thurs'day ['mɔndi] s jeudi m saint
mausole·um [,mɔsə'li·əm] s (pl -ums or -a [ə]) mausolée m
maw [mɔ] s (of birds) jabot m; (of fish) poche f d'air

mawkish ['mɔkɪʃ] adj à l'eau de rose; (sickening) écœurant
maxim ['mæksɪm] s maxime f
maximum ['mæksɪməm] adj & s maximum m
May [me] s mai m || (l.c.) v (pret & cond might [maɪt]) aux—it may be il ne peut; may I? vous permettez?; may I + inf puis-je + inf, est-ce que je peux + inf; may I (may we, etc.) + inf peut-on + inf; may you be happy! puissiez-vous être heureux!
maybe ['mebi] adv peut-être
May' Day' s le premier mai m
mayhem ['mehem], ['me·em] s mutilation f
mayonnaise [,me·ə'nez] s mayonnaise f
mayor ['me·ər], [mer] s maire m
May'pole' s mai m
May' queen' s reine f du premier mai
maze [mez] s labyrinthe m, dédale m
me [mi] pron moi §85, §87; me §87
meadow ['medo] s prairie f, pré m
mead'ow·land' s herbage m, prairie f
meager ['migər] adj maigre
meal [mil] s repas m; (grain) farine f; to miss a meal serrer la ceinture d'un cran
meal' tick'et s ticket-repas m; (job) gagne-pain m
meal'time' s heure f du repas
meal·y ['mili] adj (comp -ier; super -iest) farineux
mean [min] adj (intermediate) moyen; (low in station or rank) bas, humble; (shabby) vil, misérable; (stingy) mesquin; (small-minded) bas, vilain, méprisable; (vicious) sauvage, mal intentionné; no mean fameux, excellent || s milieu m, moyen terme m; (math) moyenne f; by all means de toute façon, je vous en prie; by means of au moyen de; by no means en aucune façon; means ressources fpl, fortune f; (agency) moyen m; means to an end moyens d'arriver à ses fins; not by any means! jamais de la vie! || v (pret & pp meant [ment]) tr vouloir dire, signifier; (to intend) entendre; (to entail) entraîner; to mean s.th. for s.o. destiner q.ch. à qn; to mean to avoir l'intention de, compter || intr —to mean well avoir de bonnes intentions
meander [mɪ'ændər] s méandre m || intr faire des méandres
meaning ['minɪŋ] s signification f, sens m; intention f
meaningful ['minɪŋfəl] adj significatif
meaningless ['minɪŋlɪs] adj sans signification, dénué de sens
meanness ['minnɪs] s bassesse f, vilenie f; (stinginess) mesquinerie f
mean'time' s—in the meantime dans l'intervalle, sur ces entrefaites || adv entre-temps, en attendant
mean'while' s & adv var of meantime
measles ['mizəlz] s rougeole f; (German measles) rubéole f
mea·sly ['mizli] adj (comp -slier; super -sliest) rougeoleux; (slang) piètre, insignifiant

measurable ['mɛʒərəbəl] *adj* mesurable

measure ['mɛʒər] *s* mesure *f*; (*step, procedure*) mesure, démarche *f*; (*legislative bill*) projet *m* de loi; (*mus, poetic*) mesure; **in a large measure** en grande partie; **in a measure** dans une certaine mesure; **to take measures** to prendre des mesures pour; **to take s.o.'s measure** (fig) prendre la mesure de qn ‖ *tr* mesurer; **to measure out** mesurer, distribuer ‖ *intr* mesurer

measurement ['mɛʒərmənt] *s* mesure *f*; **to take s.o.'s measurements** prendre les mesures de qn

meas'uring cup' *s* verre *m* gradué

meat [mit] *s* viande *f*; (*food in general*) nourriture *f*; (*gist*) moelle *f*, substance *f*

meat'ball' *s* boulette *f* de viande

meat'hook' *s* croc *m*, allonge *f*

meat' mar'ket *s* boucherie *f*

meat' pie' *s* tourte *f* à la viande, pâté *m* en croûte

meat-y ['miti] *adj* (*comp* -ier; *super* -iest) charnu; (fig) plein de substance, étoffé

Mecca ['mɛkə] *s* La Mecque

mechanic [mə'kænɪk] *s* mécanicien *m*; **mechanics** mécanique *f*

mechanical [mə'kænɪkəl] *adj* mécanique; (fig) mécanique, machinal

mechan'ical draw'ing *s* dessin *m* industriel

mechan'ical engineer' *s* ingénieur *m* mécanicien

mechan'ical toy' *s* jouet *m* mécanique

mechanics [mɪ'kænɪks] *s* mécanique *f*

mechanism ['mɛkə,nɪzəm] *s* mécanisme *m*

mechanize ['mɛkə,naɪz] *tr* mécaniser

medal ['mɛdəl] *s* médaille *f*

medallion [mɪ'dæljən] *s* médaillon *m*

meddle ['mɛdəl] *intr* s'ingérer; **to meddle in** or **with** se mêler de, s'immiscer dans

meddler ['mɛdlər] *s* intrigant *m*, touche-à-tout *m*

meddlesome ['mɛdəlsəm] *adj* intrigant

median ['midɪ·ən] *adj* médian ‖ *s* médiane *f*

me'dian strip' *s* bande *f* médiane

mediate ['midɪ,et] *tr* procurer par médiation, négocier ‖ *intr* s'entremettre, s'interposer

mediation [,midɪ'eʃən] *s* médiation *f*

mediator ['midɪ,etər] *s* médiateur *m*

medical ['mɛdɪkəl] *adj* médical

med'ical stu'dent *s* étudiant *m* en médecine

medicinal [mə'dɪsɪnəl] *adj* médicinal

medicine ['mɛdɪsɪn] *s* (*science and art*) médecine *f*; (pharm) médicament *m*

med'icine cab'inet *s* armoire *f* à pharmacie

med'icine kit' *s* pharmacie *f* portative

med'icine man' *s* (*pl* men') sorcier *m* indien; (*mountebank*) charlatan *m*

medi-co ['mɛdɪ,ko] *s* (*pl* -cos) (slang) carabin *m*, morticole *m*

medieval [,midɪ'ivəl], [,mɛdɪ'ivəl] *adj* médiéval

medievalist [,midɪ'ivəlɪst], [,mɛdɪ'ivəlɪst] *s* médiéviste *mf*

mediocre ['midɪ,okər], [,midɪ'okər] *adj* médiocre

mediocri-ty [,midɪ'ɑkriti] *s* (*pl* -ties) médiocrité *f*

meditate ['mɛdɪ,tet] *tr & intr* méditer

meditation [,mɛdɪ'teʃən] *s* méditation *f*

Mediterranean [,mɛdɪtə'reni·ən] *adj* méditerranéen ‖ *s* Méditerranée *f*

medi-um ['midɪ·əm] *adj* moyen; (culin) à point ‖ *s* (*pl* -ums or -a [ə]) milieu *m*; (*means*) moyen *m*; (*in spiritualism*) médium *m*; (journ) organe *m*; **through the medium of** par l'intermédiaire de

me'dium of exchange' *s* agent *m* monétaire

me'dium-range' *adj* à portée moyenne

me'dium-sized' *adj* de grandeur moyenne

medlar ['mɛdlər] *s* (*fruit*) nèfle *f*; (*tree*) néflier *m*

medley ['mɛdli] *s* mélange *m*; (mus) pot-pourri *m*

medul·la [mɪ'dʌlə] *s* (*pl* -lae [li]) moelle *f*

Medusa [mə'duzə] *s* Méduse *f*

meek [mik] *adj* doux, humble

meekness ['miknɪs] *s* douceur *f*, humilité *f*

meerschaum ['mɪrʃəm], ['mɪrʃəm] *s* écume *f* de mer; pipe *f* d'écume de mer

meet [mit] *adj*—**it is meet that** il convient que ‖ *s* (sports) meeting *m* ‖ *v* (*pret & pp* met [mɛt]) *tr* rencontrer; (*to make the acquaintance of*) faire la connaissance de; (*to go to meet*) aller au-devant de; (*a car in the street; a person on the sidewalk*) croiser; (*by appointment*) retrouver, rejoindre; (*difficulties; expenses*) faire face à; (*one's debts*) honorer; (*one's death*) trouver; (*a need*) satisfaire à; (*an objection*) réfuter; (*the ear*) frapper; **meet my wife (my friend, etc.)** je vous présente ma femme (mon ami, etc.) ‖ *intr* se rencontrer; se retrouver, se rejoindre; (*to assemble*) se réunir; (*to join, touch*) se joindre, se toucher; (*said of rivers*) confluer; (*said of roads; said of cars, persons, etc.*) se croiser; **till we meet again** au revoir; **to meet with** se rencontrer avec, rencontrer; (*difficulties, an affront, etc.*) subir

meeting ['mitɪŋ] *s* rencontre *f*; (*session*) séance *f*; (*assemblage*) réunion *f*, assemblée *f*; (*of two rivers*) confluent *m*; (*of two cars; of two roads*) croisement *m*

meet'ing of the minds' *s* bonne entente *f*

meet'ing place' *s* rendez-vous *m*

megacycle ['mɛgə,saɪkəl] *s* mégacycle *m*

megaphone ['mɛgə,fon] *s* mégaphone *m*, porte-voix *m*

megohm ['mɛg,om] *s* mégohm *m*

melancholia [ˌmelənˈkolɪ·ə] s mélancolie f

melanchol·y [ˈmelənˌkɑli] adj mélancolique || s (pl -ies) mélancolie f

melee [ˈmele], [ˈmele] s mêlée f

mellow [ˈmelo] adj moelleux; enjoué, débonnaire; (ripe) mûr || tr rendre moelleux, mûrir

melodic [mɪˈlɑdɪk] adj mélodique

melodious [mɪˈlodɪ·əs] adj mélodieux

melodramatic [ˌmelədrəˈmætɪk] adj mélodramatique

melo·dy [ˈmelədi] s (pl -dies) mélodie f

melon [ˈmelən] s melon m

melt [melt] tr & intr fondre; **to melt into** (e.g., tears) fondre en

melt'ing pot' s creuset m

member [ˈmembər] s membre m

mem'ber·ship' s membres mpl; (in a club, etc.) association f

membrane [ˈmembren] s membrane f

memen·to [mɪˈmento] s (pl -tos or -toes) mémento m

mem·o [ˈmemo] s (pl -os) (coll) note f, rappel m

mem'o book' s calepin m, mémento m

memoir [ˈmemwɑr] s biographie f; **memoirs** mémoires mpl

mem'o pad' s bloc-notes m, bloc m

memoran·dum [ˌmeməˈrændəm] s (pl -dums or -da [də]) memorandum m; note f, rappel m

memorial [mɪˈmorɪ·əl] adj commémoratif || s mémorial m; pétition f, mémoire m

memo'rial arch' s arc m de triomphe

Memo'rial Day' s la journée du Souvenir

memorialize [mɪˈmorɪ·əˌlaɪz] tr commémorer

memorize [ˈmeməˌraɪz] tr apprendre par cœur

memo·ry [ˈmeməri] s (pl -ries) mémoire f; **from memory** de mémoire; **in memory of** en souvenir de, à la mémoire de

menace [ˈmenɪs] s menace f || tr & intr menacer

menagerie [məˈnæʒəri], [məˈnædʒəri] s ménagerie f

mend [mend] s raccommodage m, reprise f || tr réparer; (to patch) raccommoder; (stockings) repriser; (to reform) améliorer || intr s'améliorer, s'amender

mendacious [menˈdeʃəs] adj mensonger

mendicant [ˈmendɪkənt] adj & s mendiant m

mending [ˈmendɪŋ] s raccommodage m; (of stockings) reprisage m

menfolk [ˈmenˌfok] spl hommes mpl

menial [ˈminɪ·əl] adj servile || s domestique mf

menses [ˈmensiz] spl menstrues fpl

men's fur'nishings s confection f pour hommes

men's' room' s toilettes fpl pour hommes, lavabos mpl pour messieurs

menstruate [ˈmenstru·ˌet] intr avoir ses règles

mental [ˈmentəl] adj mental

men'tal arith'metic s calcul m mental

men'tal defec'tive s débile mf

men'tal ill'ness s maladie f mentale

mentali·ty [menˈtælɪti] s (pl -ties) mentalité f

men'tal reserva'tion s arrière-pensée f

men'tal test' s test m psychologique

mention [ˈmenʃən] s mention f || tr mentionner; **don't mention it** il n'y a pas de quoi, je vous en prie

menu [ˈmenju], [ˈmenju] s menu m, carte f

meow [mɪˈau] s miaou m || intr miauler

Mephistophelian [ˌmefɪstəˈfilɪ·ən] adj méphistophélique

mercantile [ˈmɑrkənˌtil], [ˈmɑrkənˌtaɪl] adj commercial, commerçant

mercenar·y [ˈmɑrsəˌneri] adj mercenaire || s (pl -ies) mercenaire mf

merchandise [ˈmɑrtʃənˌdaɪz] s marchandise f

merchant [ˈmɑrtʃənt] adj & s marchand m

mer'chant·man s (pl -men) navire m marchand

mer'chant marine' s marine f marchande

mer'chant ves'sel s navire m marchand

merciful [ˈmɑrsɪfəl] adj miséricordieux

merciless [ˈmɑrsɪlɪs] adj impitoyable

mercurial [merˈkjurɪ·əl] adj inconstant, versatile; (lively) vif

mercu·ry [ˈmɑrkjəri] s (pl -ries) mercure m

mer·cy [ˈmɑrsi] s (pl -cies) miséricorde f, pitié f; **at the mercy of** à la merci de

mere [mɪr] adj simple, pur; seul, e.g., **at the mere thought of it** à la seule pensée de cela; rien que, e.g., **to shudder at the mere thought of it** frissonner rien que d'y penser

meretricious [ˌmerɪˈtrɪʃəs] adj factice, postiche; de courtisane

merge [mɑrdʒ] tr fusionner || intr fusionner; (said of two roads) converger; **to merge into** se fondre dans

merger [ˈmɑrdʒər] s fusion f

meridian [məˈrɪdɪ·ən] adj & s méridien m

meringue [məˈræŋ] s meringue f

merit [ˈmerɪt] s mérite m || tr mériter

meritorious [ˌmerəˈtorɪ·əs] adj méritoire; (person) méritant

merlin [ˈmɑrlɪn] s (orn) émerillon m

mermaid [ˈmɑrˌmed] s sirène f

merriment [ˈmerɪmənt] s gaieté f, réjouissance f

mer·ry [ˈmeri] adj (comp -rier; super -riest) gai, joyeux; **to make merry** se divertir

Mer'ry Christ'mas s Joyeux Noël m

mer'ry-go-round' s chevaux mpl de bois, manège m forain

mer'ry-mak'er s noceur m, fêtard m

mesh [meʃ] s (network) réseau m; (each open space of net) maille f; (net) filet m; (engagement of gears) engrenage m; **meshes** rets m, filets *mpl* || *tr* (mach) engrener || *intr* s'engrener

mesmerize ['mɛsmə‚raɪz] *tr* magnétiser

mess [mɛs] *s* gâchis *m*; (*refuse*) saleté *f*; (*meal*) (mil) ordinaire *m*; (*for officers*) (mil) mess *m*; **to get into a mess** se mettre dans le pétrin; **to make a mess of** gâcher || *tr*—**to mess up** (*to botch*) gâcher; (*to dirty*) salir || *intr*—**to mess around** (*to putter*) (coll) bricoler; (*to waste time*) (coll) lambiner

message ['mɛsɪdʒ] *s* message *m*

messenger ['mɛsəndʒər] *s* messager *m*; (*one who goes on errands*) commissionnaire *m*

mess′ hall′ *s* cantine *f*; (*for officers*) mess *m*

Messiah [mə'saɪ‚ə] *s* Messie *m*

mess′ kit′ *s* gamelle *f*

mess′mate′ *s* camarade *mf* de table; (nav) camarade *m* de plat

mess′ of pot′tage ['pɑtɪdʒ] *s* (Bib) plat *m* de lentilles

Messrs. ['mɛsərz] *pl* of **Mr.**

mess•y ['mɛsi] *adj* (*comp* **-ier**; *super -iest*) en désordre; (*dirty*) sale, poisseux

metal ['mɛtəl] *s* métal *m*

metallic [mɪ'tælɪk] *adj* métallique

metallurgy ['mɛtə‚lʌrdʒi] *s* métallurgie *f*

met′al pol′ish *s* brillant *m* à métaux

met′al-work′ *s* serrurerie *f*, travail *m* des métaux

metamorpho•sis [‚mɛtə'mɔrfəsɪs] *s* (*pl* **-ses** [‚siz]) métamorphose *f*

metaphony [mə'tæfəni] *s* métaphonie *f*, inflexion *f*

metaphor ['mɛtəfər], ['mɛtə‚fɔr] *s* métaphore *f*

metaphorical [‚mɛtə'farɪkəl], [‚mɛtə'fɔrɪkəl] *adj* métaphorique

metathe•sis [mɪ'tæθɪsɪs] *s* (*pl* **-ses** [‚siz]) métathèse *f*

mete [mit] *tr*—**to mete out** distribuer

meteor ['mitɪ‚ər] *s* étoile *f* filante; (*atmospheric phenomenon*) météore *m*

meteoric [‚mitɪ'arɪk], [‚mitɪ'ɔrɪk] *adj* météorique; (fig) fulgurant

meteorite ['mitɪ‚ə‚raɪt] *s* météorite *m & f*

meteorology [‚mitɪ‚ə'ralədʒi] *s* météorologie *f*

meter ['mitər] *s* (*unit of measurement; verse*) mètre *m*; (*instrument for measuring gas, electricity, water*) compteur *m*; (mus) mesure *f*

me′ter read′er *s* releveur *m* de compteurs

methane ['mɛθen] *s* méthane *m*

method ['mɛθəd] *s* méthode *f*

methodic(al) [mɪ'θɑdɪk(əl)] *adj* méthodique

Methodist ['mɛθədɪst] *adj & s* méthodiste *mf*

Methuselah [mɪ'θuzələ] *s* Mathusalem *m*

meticulous [mɪ'tɪkjələs] *adj* méticuleux

metric(al) ['mɛtrɪk(əl)] *adj* métrique

metrics ['mɛtrɪks] *s* métrique *f*

metronome ['mɛtrə‚nom] *s* métronome *m*

metropolis [mɪ'trapəlɪs] *s* métropole *f*

metropolitan [‚mɛtrə'palɪtən] *adj & s* métropolitain *m*

mettle ['mɛtəl] *s* ardeur *f*, fougue *f*; **to be on one's mettle** se piquer au jeu

mettlesome ['mɛtəlsəm] *adj* ardent, vif, fougueux

mew [mju] *s* miaulement *m* || *intr* miauler

Mexican ['mɛksɪkən] *adj* mexicain || *s* Mexicain *m*

Mexico ['mɛksɪ‚ko] *s* le Mexique

Mex′ico Cit′y *s* Mexico

mezzanine ['mɛzə‚nin] *s* entresol *m*; (theat) mezzanine *m & f*, corbeille *f*

mica ['maɪkə] *s* mica *m*

microbe ['maɪkrob] *s* microbe *m*

microbiology [‚maɪkrəbaɪ'alədʒi] *s* microbiologie *f*

microfilm ['maɪkrə‚fɪlm] *s* microfilm *m* || *tr* microfilmer

microgroove ['maɪkrə‚gruv] *adj & s* microsillon *m*

mi′crogroove rec′ord *s* disque *m* à microsillons

microphone ['maɪkrə‚fon] *s* microphone *m*

microscope ['maɪkrə‚skop] *s* microscope *m*

microscopic [‚maɪkrə'skapɪk] *adj* microscopique

microwave ['maɪkrə‚wev] *s* micro-onde *f*

mid [mɪd] *adj*—**in mid course** à michemin

mid′day′ *s* midi *m*

middle ['mɪdəl] *adj* moyen, du milieu || *s* milieu *m*; **in the middle of** au milieu de

mid′dle age′ *s* âge *m* moyen; **Middle Ages** moyen-âge *m*

middle-aged ['mɪdəl‚edʒd] *adj* d'un âge moyen

mid′dle class′ *s* classe *f* moyenne, bourgeoisie *f*

mid′dle-class′ *adj* bourgeois

Mid′dle East′ *s* Moyen-Orient *m*

Mid′dle Eng′lish *s* moyen anglais *m*

mid′dle fin′ger *s* majeur *m*, doigt *m* du milieu

mid′dle-man′ *s* (*pl* **-men′**) intermédiaire *mf*

middling ['mɪdlɪŋ] *adj* moyen, assez bien, passable || *adv* (coll) assez bien, passablement

mid′dy ['mɪdi] *s* (*pl* **-dies**) (coll) aspirant *m*

mid′dy blouse′ *s* marinière *f*

midget ['mɪdʒɪt] *s* nain *m*, nabot *m*

midland ['mɪdlənd] *adj* de l'intérieur || *s* centre *m* du pays

mid′night′ *adj* de minuit; **to burn the midnight oil** pâlir sur les livres, se crever les livres || *s* minuit *m*

midriff ['mɪdrɪf] *s* diaphragme *m*

mid′ship′man *s* (*pl* **-men**) aspirant *m*

midst [mɪdst] *s* centre *m*; **in our (your, etc.) midst** parmi nous (vous, etc.); **in the midst of** au milieu de

mid'stream' s—**in midstream** au milieu du courant

mid'sum'mer s milieu m de l'été

mid'way' adj & adv à mi-chemin ‖ **mid'way'** s fête f foraine

mid'week' s milieu m de la semaine

mid'wife' s (pl **-wives'**) sage-femme f

mid'win'ter s milieu m de l'hiver

mid'year' s mi-année f

mien [min] s mine f, aspect m

miff [mɪf] s (coll) fâcherie f ‖ tr (coll) fâcher

might [maɪt] s puissance f, force f; **with might and main, with all one's might** de toute sa force ‖ aux used to form the potential mood, e.g., **she might not be able to come** il se pourrait qu'elle ne puisse pas venir

mightily [ˈmaɪtɪli] adv puissamment; (coll) énormément

might·y [ˈmaɪti] adj (comp **-ier;** super **-iest**) puissant; (of great size) grand, vaste ‖ adv (coll) rudement, diablement

mignonette [ˌmɪnjəˈnet] s réséda m

migraine [ˈmaɪgren] s migraine f

migrate [ˈmaɪgret] intr émigrer

migratory [ˈmaɪgrəˌtori] adj migratoire

milch [mɪltʃ] adj laitier

mild [maɪld] adj doux

mildew [ˈmɪlˌd(j)u] s moisissure f; (on vine) mildiou m, blanc m

mildness [ˈmaɪldnɪs] s douceur f

mile [maɪl] s mille m

mileage [ˈmaɪlɪdʒ] s distance f en milles; (charge) tarif m au mille

mile'post' s borne f milliaire

mile'stone' s borne f milliaire; (fig) jalon m

militancy [ˈmɪlɪtənsi] s esprit m militant

militant [ˈmɪlɪtənt] adj & s militant m

militarism [ˈmɪlɪtəˌrɪzəm] s militarisme m

militarize [ˈmɪlɪtəˌraɪz] tr militariser

military [ˈmɪlɪˌteri] adj & s militaire m

mil'itary police'man s (pl **-men**) agent m de la police militaire

militate [ˈmɪlɪˌtet] intr militer

militia [mɪˈlɪʃə] s milice f

mili'tia·man s (pl **-men**) milicien m

milk [mɪlk] adj laitier ‖ s lait m ‖ tr traire; abuser, exploiter; **to milk s.th. from s.o.** soutirer q.ch. à qn

milk' can' s pot m à lait, berthe f

milk' car'ton s boîte f de lait, berlingot m

milk' di'et s régime m lacté

milk'maid' s laitière f

milk'man' s (pl **-men'**) laitier m, crémier m

milk' pail' s seau m à lait

milk'sop' s poule f mouillée

milk' tooth' s dent f de lait

milk'weed' s laiteron m

milk·y [ˈmɪlki] adj (comp **-ier;** super **-iest**) laiteux

Milk'y Way' s Voie f Lactée

mill [mɪl] s moulin m; (factory) fabrique f, usine f; millième m de dollar; **to put through the mill** (coll)

faire passer au laminoir ‖ tr moudre, broyer; (a coin) créneler; (gears) fraiser; (steel) laminer; (ore) bocarder; (chocolate) faire mousser ‖ intr —**to mill around** circuler

millennial [mɪˈleniəl] adj millénaire

millenni·um [mɪˈleniəm] s (pl **-ums** or **-a** [ə]) millénaire m

miller [ˈmɪlər] s meunier m

millet [ˈmɪlɪt] s millet m

milligram [ˈmɪlɪˌgræm] s milligramme m

millimeter [ˈmɪlɪˌmitər] s millimètre m

milliner [ˈmɪlɪnər] s modiste f

mil'linery shop' [ˈmɪlɪˌneri], [ˈmɪlɪnəri] s boutique f de modiste

milling [ˈmɪlɪŋ] s (of grain) mouture f

mill'ing machine' s fraiseuse f

million [ˈmɪljən] adj million de ‖ s million m

millionaire [ˌmɪljənˈer] s millionnaire mf

millionth [ˈmɪljənθ] adj & pron millionième (masc, fem) ‖ s millionième m

mill'pond' s retenue f, réservoir m

mill'race' s bief m

mill'stone' s meule f; (fig) boulet m

mill' wheel' s roue f de moulin

mill'work' s ouvrage m de menuiserie

mime [maɪm] s mime mf ‖ tr & intr mimer

mimeograph [ˈmɪmɪəˌgræf], [ˈmɪmɪəˌgraf] s ronéo f ‖ tr ronéocopier, ronéotyper

mim·ic [ˈmɪmɪk] s mime mf, imitateur m ‖ v (pret & pp **-icked;** ger **-icking**) tr mimer, imiter

mimic·ry [ˈmɪmɪkri] s (pl **-ries**) mimique f, imitation f

minaret [ˌmɪnəˈret], [ˈmɪnəˌret] s minaret m

mince [mɪns] tr (meat) hacher menu ‖ intr minauder

mince'meat' s hachis m de viande et de fruits aromatisés; **to make mincemeat of** (coll) mettre en marmelade

mind [maɪnd] s esprit m; **to be of one mind** être d'accord; **to change one's mind** changer d'avis; **to have a mind to** avoir envie de; **to have in mind** avoir en vue; **to lose one's mind** perdre la raison; **to make up one's mind** to prendre le parti de; **to slip one's mind** échapper à qn; **to speak one's mind** donner son avis ‖ tr (to take care of) garder; (to obey) obéir (with dat); (to be troubled by) s'inquiéter de; (e.g., one's manners) faire attention à; (e.g., a dangerous step) prendre garde à; **mind your own business!** occupez-vous de vos affaires! ‖ intr —**do you mind?** cela ne vous ennuie pas?, cela ne vous gêne pas?; **if you don't mind** si cela ne vous fait rien, si cela vous est égal; **never mind!** n'importe!

mindful [ˈmaɪndfəl] adj attentif; **mindful of** attentif à, soigneux de

mind' read'er s liseur m de la pensée

mind' read'ing s lecture f de la pensée

mine [maɪn] s mine f ‖ pron poss le mien §89; à moi §85 A, 10 ‖ tr (coal, minerals, *etc.*) extraire; (*to under-mine; to lay mines in*) miner

mine'field' *s* champ *m* de mines

mine'lay'er *s* poseur *m* de mines

miner ['maɪnər] *s* mineur *m*

mineral ['mɪnərəl] *adj* & *s* minéral *m*

mineralogy [,mɪnə'rɑlədʒi] *s* minéralogie *f*

min'eral wool' *s* laine *f* minérale, laine de scories

mine'sweep'er *s* dragueur *m* de mines

mingle ['mɪŋɡəl] *tr* mêler, mélanger || *intr* se mêler, se mélanger

miniature ['mɪnɪ·ətʃər], ['mɪnɪt/ər] *s* miniature *f*

miniaturization [,mɪnɪ·ətʃərɪ'zeʃən], [,mɪnɪt/ərɪ'zeʃən] *s* miniaturisation *f*

miniaturize ['mɪnɪ·ətʃə,raɪz], ['mɪnɪt/ə,raɪz] *tr* miniaturiser

minimal ['mɪnɪməl] *adj* minimum

minimize ['mɪnə,maɪz] *tr* minimiser

minimum ['mɪnɪməm] *adj* minimum; (*temperature*) minimal || *s* minimum *m*

min'imum wage' *s* salaire *m* minimum, minimum *m* vital

mining ['maɪnɪŋ] *adj* minier || *s* exploitation *f* des mines; (nav) pose *f* de mines

minion ['mɪnjən] *s* favori *m*; (*henchman*) séide *m*

miniskirt ['mɪnɪ,skʌrt] *s* minijupe *f*

minister ['mɪnɪstər] *s* ministre *m*; (eccl) pasteur *m* || *intr*—**to minister to** (*the needs of*) subvenir à; (*a person*) soigner; (*a parish*) desservir

ministerial [,mɪnɪs'tɪri·əl] *adj* ministériel

minis•try ['mɪnɪstri] *s* (*pl* **-tries**) ministère *m*; (eccl) clergé *m*; (eccl) pastorat *m*

mink [mɪŋk] *s* vison *m*

minnow ['mɪno] *s* vairon *m*

minor ['maɪnər] *adj* & *s* mineur *m*

Minorca [mɪ'nɔrkə] *s* Minorque *f*; île *f* de Minorque

minor•ity [mɪ'nɑrɪti], [mɪ'nɔrɪti] *adj* minoritaire || *s* (*pl* **-ties**) minorité *f*

minstrel ['mɪnstrəl] *s* (*in a minstrel show*) interprète *m* de chants nègres; (hist) ménestrel *m*

mint [mɪnt] *s* hôtel *m* des Monnaies, Monnaie *f*; (bot) menthe *f*; (fig) mine *f* || *tr* frapper, monnayer; (fig) forger

minuet ['mɪnju'ɛt] *s* menuet *m*

minus ['maɪnəs] *adj* négatif || *s* moins *m* || *prep* moins; (coll) sans, dépourvu de

minute [maɪ'n(j)ut] *adj* (*tiny*) minime; (*meticulous*) minutieux || ['mɪnɪt] *s* minute *f*; **minutes** compte *m* rendu, procès-verbal *m* de séance; (*often omitted in expressions of time*), e.g., **ten after two, ten minutes after two** deux heures dix; **up to the minute** de la dernière heure; à la dernière mode; au courant

min'ute hand' ['mɪnɪt] *s* grande aiguille *f*

min'ute steak' ['mɪnɪt] *s* entrecôte *f* minute

minutiae [mɪ'n(j)uʃɪ,i] *spl* minuties *fpl*

minx [mɪŋks] *s* effrontée *f*

miracle ['mɪrəkəl] *s* miracle *m*

mir'acle play' *s* miracle *m*

miraculous [mɪ'rækjələs] *adj* miraculeux

mirage [mɪ'rɑʒ] *s* mirage *m*

mire [maɪr] *s* fange *f*

mirror ['mɪrər] *s* miroir *m*, glace *f* || *tr* refléter

mirth [mʌrθ] *s* joie *f*, gaieté *f*

mir•y ['maɪri] *adj* (*comp* **-ier;** *super* **-iest**) fangeux

misadventure [,mɪsəd'ventʃər] *s* mésaventure *f*

misanthrope ['mɪsən,θrop] *s* misanthrope *mf*

misapprehension [,mɪsæprɪ'henʃən] *s* fausse idée *f*, malentendu *m*

misappropriation [,mɪsə,proprɪ'eʃən] *s* détournement *m* de fonds

misbehave [,mɪsbɪ'hev] *intr* se conduire mal

misbehavior [,mɪsbɪ'hevɪ·ər] *s* mauvaise conduite *f*

miscalculation [,mɪskælkjə'leʃən] *s* mécompte *m*

miscarriage [mɪs'kærɪdʒ] *s* fausse couche *f*; (*e.g., of letter*) perte *f*; (*of justice*) déni *m*, mal-jugé *m*; (fig) avortement *m*, insuccès *m*

miscar•ry [mɪs'kæri] *v* (*pret* & *pp* **-ried**) *intr* faire une fausse couche; (*said, e.g., of letter*) s'égarer; (fig) avorter, échouer

miscellaneous [,mɪsə'lenɪ·əs] *adj* divers, mélangé

miscella•ny ['mɪsə,leni] *s* (*pl* **-nies**) miscellanées *fpl*

mischief ['mɪstʃɪf] *s* (*harm*) tort *m*; (*disposition to annoy*) méchanceté *f*; (*prankishness*) espièglerie *f*

mis'chief-mak'er *s* brandon *m* de discorde

mischievous ['mɪstʃɪvəs] *adj* (*harmful*) nuisible; (*mean*) méchant; (*prankish*) espiègle

misconception [,mɪskən'sepʃən] *s* conception *f* erronée

misconduct [mɪs'kandʌkt] *s* inconduite *f*; (*e.g., of a business*) mauvaise administration *f* || [,mɪskən'dʌkt] *tr* mal administrer; **to misconduct oneself** se conduire mal

misconstrue [,mɪskən'stru], [mɪs'kanstru] *tr* mal interpréter

miscount [mɪs'kaunt] *s* erreur *f* de calcul *f* || *tr* & *intr* mal compter

miscue [mɪs'kju] *s* fausse queue *f*; (*blunder*) bévue *f* || *intr* faire fausse queue; (theat) se tromper de réplique

mis-deal ['mɪs,dil] *s* maldonne *f*, mauvaise donne *f* || [,mɪs'dil] *v* (*pret* & *pp* **-dealt**) *tr* mal distribuer || *intr* faire maldonne

misdeed ['mɪs'did], [,mɪs,did] *s* méfait *m*

misdemeanor [,mɪsdɪ'minər] *s* mauvaise conduite *f*; (law) délit *m* correctionnel

misdirect [ˌmɪsdɪ'rɛkt], [ˌmɪsdaɪ-'rɛkt] *tr* mal diriger

misdoing [mɪs'duːɪŋ] *s* méfait *m*

miser ['maɪzər] *s* avare *mf*

miserable ['mɪzərəbəl] *adj* misérable

miserly ['maɪzərli] *adj* avare

miser·y ['maɪzəri] *s* (*pl* **-ies**) misère *f*, détresse *f*

misfeasance [mɪs'fizəns] *s* (law) abus *m* de pouvoir

misfire [mɪs'faɪr] *s* raté *m* ‖ *intr* rater

mis·fit ['mɪsˌfɪt] *s* (*clothing*) vêtement *m* manqué; (*thing*) laissé-pour-compte *m*; (fig) inadapté *m* ‖ [mɪs-'fɪt] *v* (*pret & pp* **-fitted**; *ger* **-fitting**) *tr* mal aller (with *dat*) ‖ *intr* mal aller

misfortune [mɪs'fortʃən] *s* infortune *f*, malheur *m*

misgiving [mɪs'gɪvɪŋ] *s* pressentiment *m*, appréhension *f*, soupçon *m*

misgovern [mɪs'gʌvərn] *tr* mal gouverner

misguidance [mɪs'gaɪdəns] *s* mauvais conseils *mpl*

misguided [mɪs'gaɪdɪd] *adj* mal placé, hors de propos; (*e.g., youth*) dévoyé

mishap ['mɪshæp], [mɪs'hæp] *s* contretemps *m*, mésaventure *f*

misinform [ˌmɪsɪn'form] *tr* mal renseigner

misinterpret [ˌmɪsɪn'tʌrprɪt] *tr* mal interpréter

misjudge [mɪs'dʒʌdʒ] *tr & intr* mal juger

mis·lay [mɪs'le] *v* (*pret & pp* **-laid**) *tr* égarer, perdre

mis·lead [mɪs'lid] *v* (*pret & pp* **-led**) *tr* égarer; corrompre

misleading [mɪs'lidɪŋ] *adj* trompeur

mismanagement [mɪs'mænɪdʒmənt] *s* mauvaise administration *f*

misnomer [mɪs'nomər] *s* faux nom *m*

misplace [mɪs'ples] *tr* mal placer; (*to mislay*) (coll) égarer, perdre

misprint ['mɪsˌprɪnt] *s* erreur *f* typographique, coquille *f* ‖ [mɪs'prɪnt] *tr* imprimer incorrectement

mispronounce [ˌmɪsprə'naʊns] *tr* mal prononcer

misquote [mɪs'kwot] *tr* citer à faux, citer inexactement

misrepresent [ˌmɪsrɛprɪ'zɛnt] *tr* représenter sous un faux jour; (*e.g., facts*) dénaturer, travestir

miss [mɪs] *s* coup *m* manqué; **Miss** Mademoiselle *f*, Mlle; (*winner of beauty contest*) Miss *f* ‖ *tr* manquer; (*to feel the absence of*) regretter; (*not to run into*) ne pas voir, ne pas rencontrer; (*e.g., one's way*) se tromper de; **he misses you very much** vous lui manquez beaucoup ‖ *intr* manquer

missal ['mɪsəl] *s* missel *m*

misshapen [mɪs'ʃepən] *adj* difforme, contrefait

missile ['mɪsɪl] *s* projectile *m*; (*guided missile*) missile *m*

mis'sile launch'er *s* lance-fusées *m*

missing [mɪsɪŋ] *adj* manquant, absent; perdu; **missing in action** (mil) porté disparu; **to be missing** manquer, e.g., **three are missing** il en manque trois

miss'ing per'sons *spl* disparus *mpl*

mission ['mɪʃən] *s* mission *f*

mission·ar·y ['mɪʃənˌɛri] *adj* missionnaire ‖ *s* (*pl* **-ies**) missionnaire *m*

missis ['mɪsɪz] *s*—**the missis** (coll) votre femme *f*

missive ['mɪsɪv] *adj & s* missive *f*

mis·spell [mɪs'spɛl] *v* (*pret & pp* **-spelled** or **-spelt**) *tr & intr* écrire incorrectement

misspelling [mɪs'spɛlɪŋ] *s* faute *f* d'orthographe

misspent [mɪs'spɛnt] *adj* gaspillé; dissipé

misstatement [mɪs'stetmənt] *s* rapport *m* inexact, erreur *f* de fait

misstep [mɪs'stɛp] *s* faux pas *m*

miss·y ['mɪsi] *s* (*pl* **-ies**) (coll) mademoiselle *f*

mist [mɪst] *s* brume *f*, buée *f*; (*fine spray*) vapeur *f*; (*of tears*) voile *m*

mis·take [mɪs'tek] *s* faute *f*; **by mistake** par erreur, par méprise; **to make a mistake** se tromper ‖ *v* (*pret* **-took**; *pp* **-taken**) *tr* (*to misunderstand*) mal comprendre; (*to be wrong about*) se tromper de; **to mistake s.o. for s.o. else** prendre qn pour qn d'autre

mistaken [mɪs'tekən] *adj* erroné, faux; (*person*) dans l'erreur

mistak'en iden'tity *s* erreur *f* d'identité, erreur sur la personne

mistakenly [mɪs'tekənli] *adv* par erreur

mister ['mɪstər] *s*—**the mister** (coll) votre mari *m* ‖ *interj* (slang & pej) Jules!, mon petit bonhomme!

mistletoe ['mɪsəlˌto] *s* gui *m*

mistreat [mɪs'trit] *tr* maltraiter

mistreatment [mɪs'tritmənt] *s* mauvais traitement *m*

mistress ['mɪstrɪs] *s* maîtresse *f*

mistrial [mɪs'traɪəl] *s* (law) procès *m* entaché de nullité

mistrust [mɪs'trʌst] *s* méfiance *f* ‖ *tr* se méfier de ‖ *intr* se méfier

mistrustful [mɪs'trʌstfəl] *adj* méfiant

mist·y ['mɪsti] *adj* (*comp* **-ier**; *super* **-iest**) brumeux; vague, indistinct

misunderstand [ˌmɪsʌndər'stænd] *v* (*pret & pp* **-stood**) *tr* mal comprendre

misunderstanding [ˌmɪsʌndər'stændɪŋ] *s* malentendu *m*

misuse [mɪs'jus] *s* mauvais usage *m*, abus *m*; (*of words*) emploi *m* abusif ‖ [mɪs'juz] *tr* faire mauvais usage de, abuser de; (*a person*) maltraiter

misword [mɪs'wʌrd] *tr* mal rédiger, mal exprimer

mite [maɪt] *s* (*small contribution*) obole *f*; (*small amount*) brin *m*, bagatelle *f*; (ent) mite *f*

miter ['maɪtər] *s* (*carpentry*) onglet *m*; (eccl) mitre *f* ‖ *tr* tailler à onglet

mi'ter box' *s* boîte *f* à onglets

mitigate ['mɪtɪˌget] *tr* adoucir, atténuer

mitt [mɪt] *s* (*fingerless glove*) mitaine *f*; (*mitten*) moufle *f*; (*baseball*) gant *m* de prise; (*hand*) (slang) main *f*

mitten ['mɪtən] s moufle f

mix [mɪks] tr mélanger, mêler; (cement; a cake) malaxer; (the cards; the salad) touiller; **to mix up** (to confuse) confondre ‖ intr se mélanger, se mêler; **to mix with** s'associer à or avec

mixed adj mélangé; (races; style; colors) mêlé; (feelings; marriage; school; doubles) mixte; (candy) assorti; (salad, vegetables, etc.) panaché; (number) fractionnaire

mixed' drink' s boisson f mélangée

mixer ['mɪksər] s (device) mélangeur m; (for, e.g., concrete) malaxeur m; **to be a good mixer** (coll) avoir le don de plaire

mix'ing fau'cet s robinet m mélangeur

mixture ['mɪkstʃər] s mélange m

mix'-up' s embrouillage m

mizzen ['mɪzən] s artimon m

moan [mon] s gémissement m ‖ intr gémir

moat [mot] s fossé m

mob [mɑb] s populace f; (crush of people) cohue f grouillante; (crowd bent on violence) foule f en colère, ameutement m ‖ v (pret & pp **mobbed**; ger **mobbing**) tr s'attrouper autour de; fondre sur, assaillir

mobile ['mobɪl], ['mobɪl] adj & s mobile m

mobility [mo'bɪlɪti] s mobilité f

mobilization [ˌmobɪlɪ'zeʃən] s mobilisation f

mobilize ['mobɪˌlaɪz] tr & intr mobiliser

mob' rule' s loi f de la populace

mobster ['mɑbstər] s (slang) gangster m

moccasin ['mɑkəsɪn] s mocassin m

Mo'cha cof'fee ['mokə] s moka m

mock [mɑk] adj simulé, contrefait ‖ s moquerie f ‖ tr se moquer de, moquer; (to imitate) contrefaire, singer; (to deceive) tromper ‖ intr se moquer; **to mock at** se moquer de; **to mock up** construire une maquette de

mock' elec'tion s élection f blanche

mocker·y ['mɑkəri] s (pl -ies) moquerie f; (subject of derision) objet m de risée; (poor imitation) parodie f; (e.g., of justice) simulacre m

mockingbird ['mɑkɪŋˌbʌrd] s moqueur m, oiseau m moqueur

mock' or'ange s seringa m

mock' tur'tle soup' s potage m à la tête de veau

mock'-up' s maquette f

mode [mod] s (kind) mode m; (fashion) mode f; (gram, mus) mode m

mod·el ['mɑdəl] adj modèle ‖ s modèle m; (for dressmaker or artist; in a fashion show) mannequin m; (of a statue) maquette f ‖ v (pret & pp **-eled** or **-elled**; ger **-eling** or **-elling**) tr modeler ‖ intr dessiner des modèles; servir de modèle, poser

mod'el-air'plane s aéromodèle m

mod'el-air'plane build'er s aéromodéliste mf

mod'el-air'plane build'ing s aéromodélisme m

moderate ['mɑdərɪt] adj modéré ‖ ['mɑdəˌret] tr modérer; (a meeting) présider ‖ intr se modérer; présider

moderator ['mɑdəˌretər] s (over an assembly) président m; (mediator; substance used for slowing down neutrons) modérateur m

modern ['mɑdərn] adj moderne

modernize ['mɑdərˌnaɪz] tr moderniser

mod'ern lan'guages spl langues fpl vivantes

modest ['mɑdɪst] adj modeste

modes·ty ['mɑdɪsti] s (pl -ties) modestie f

modicum ['mɑdɪkəm] s petite quantité f

modifier ['mɑdɪˌfaɪ·ər] s (gram) modificateur m

modi·fy ['mɑdɪˌfaɪ] v (pret & pp **-fied**) tr modifier

modish ['modɪʃ] adj à la mode, élégant

modulate ['mɑdʒəˌlet] tr & intr moduler

modulation [ˌmɑdʒə'leʃən] s modulation f

mohair ['moˌhɛr] s mohair m

Mohammedan [mo'hæmɪdən] adj mahométan ‖ s mahométan m

Mohammedanism [mo'hæmɪdəˌnɪzəm] s mahométisme m

moist [mɔɪst] adj humide; (e.g., skin) moite

moisten ['mɔɪsən] tr humecter ‖ intr s'humecter

moisture ['mɔɪstʃər] s humidité f

molar ['molər] adj & s molaire f

molasses [mə'læsɪz] s mélasse f

mold [mold] s moule m; (fungus) moisi m, moisissure f; (agr) humus m, terreau m; (fig) trempe f ‖ tr mouler; (to make moldy) moisir ‖ intr moisir, se moisir

molder ['moldər] s mouleur m ‖ intr tomber en poussière

molding ['moldɪŋ] s moulage m; (cornice, shaped strip of wood, etc.) moulure f

mold·y ['moldi] adj (comp **-ier**; super **-iest**) moisi

mole [mol] s (breakwater) môle m; (inner harbor) bassin m; (spot on skin) grain m de beauté; (small mammal) taupe f

molecule ['mɑlɪˌkjul] s molécule f

mole'hill' s taupinière f

mole'skin' s (fur) taupe f; (fabric) moleskine f

molest [mə'lɛst] tr déranger, inquiéter; molester, rudoyer

moll [mɑl] s (slang) femme f du Milieu

molli·fy ['mɑlɪˌfaɪ] v (pret & pp **-fied**) tr apaiser, adoucir

mollusk ['mɑləsk] s mollusque m

mollycoddle ['mɑlɪˌkɑdəl] s poule f mouillée ‖ tr dorloter

molt [molt] s mue f ‖ intr muer

molten ['moltən] adj fondu

molybdenum [mə'lɪbdɪnəm], [ˌmɑlɪb'dinəm] s molybdène m

moment ['momənt] s moment m; **at**

any moment d'un moment à l'autre; at that moment à ce moment-là; at this moment en ce moment; in a moment dans un instant; of great moment d'une grande importance; one moment please! (telp) ne quittez pas!

momentary ['momən,teri] *adj* momentané

momentous [mo'mentəs] *adj* important, d'importance

momen·tum [mo'mentəm] *s* (*pl* -tums or -ta* [tə]) élan *m*; (mech) force *f* d'impulsion, quantité *f* de mouvement

monarch ['monərk] *s* monarque *m*

monarchic(al) [mə'nɑrkɪk(əl)] *adj* monarchique

monar·chy ['monərki] *s* (*pl* -chies) monarchie *f*

monaster·y ['monəs,teri] *s* (*pl* -ies) monastère *m*

monastic [mə'næstɪk] *adj* monastique

monasticism [mə'næstɪ,sɪzəm] *s* monachisme *m*

Monday ['mʌndi] *s* lundi *m*

monetary ['monɪ,teri] *adj* (*pertaining to coinage*) monétaire; (*pertaining to money*) pécuniaire

money ['mʌni] *s* argent *m*; (*legal tender of a country*) monnaie *f*; to get one's money's worth en avoir pour son argent; to make money gagner de l'argent

mon·ey·bag *s* sacoche *f*; moneybags (*wealth*) (coll) sac *m*; (*wealthy person*) (coll) richard *m*

mon·ey belt *s* ceinture *f* porte-monnaie

moneychanger ['mʌni,tʃendʒər] *s* changeur *m*, cambiste *m*

moneyed ['mʌnid] *adj* possédant

mon·ey·lend·er *s* bailleur *m* de fonds

mon·ey·mak·er *s* amasseur *m* d'argent; (fig) source *f* de gain

mon·ey or·der *s* mandat *m* postal

Mongol ['mɑŋgəl], ['mɑŋgal] *adj* mongol || *s* (*language*) mongol *m*; (*person*) Mongol *m*

mon·goose ['mɑŋgus] *s* (*pl* -gooses) mangouste *f*

mongrel ['mʌŋgrəl], ['mɑŋgrəl] *adj* & *s* métis *m*

monitor ['mɑnɪtər] *s* contrôleur *m*; (at school) pion *m*, moniteur *m* || *tr* contrôler; (rad) écouter

monk [mʌŋk] *s* moine *m*

monkey ['mʌŋki] *s* singe *m*; (*female*) guenon *f*; to make a monkey of tourner en ridicule || *intr*—to monkey around tripoter; to monkey around with tripoter; to monkey with (*to tamper with*) tripatouiller

mon·key·shine *s* (slang) singerie *f*

mon·key wrench *s* clé *f* anglaise

monks·hood *s* (bot) napel *m*

monocle ['mɑnəkəl] *s* monocle *m*

monogamy [mə'nɑgəmi] *s* monogamie *f*

monogram ['mɑnə,græm] *s* monogramme *m*

monograph ['mɑnə,græf], ['mɑnə,grɑf] *s* monographie *f*

monolithic [,mɑnə'lɪθɪk] *adj* monolithique

monologue ['mɑnə,lɔg], ['mɑnə,lɑg] *s* monologue *m*

monomania [,mɑnə'meni·ə] *s* monomanie *f*

monomial [mə'nomɪ·əl] *s* monôme *m*

monoplane ['mɑnə,plen] *s* monoplan *m*

monopolize [mə'nɑpə,laɪz] *tr* monopoliser

monopo·ly [mə'nɑpəli] *s* (*pl* -lies) monopole *m*

monorail ['mɑnə,rel] *s* monorail *m*

monosyllable ['mɑnə,sɪləbəl] *s* monosyllabe *m*

monotheist ['mɑnə,θi·ɪst] *adj* & *s* monothéiste *mf*

monotonous [mə'nɑtənəs] *adj* monotone

monotony [mə'nɑtəni] *s* monotonie *f*

monotype ['mɑnə,taɪp] *s* monotype *m*; (*machine to set type*) monotype *f*

monoxide [mə'nɑksaɪd] *s* oxyde *m*, e.g., **carbon monoxide** oxyde *m* de carbone

monsignor [mɑn'sinjər] *s* (*pl* monsignors or monsignori [,mɑnsi'njori]) (eccl) monseigneur *m*

monsoon [mɑn'sun] *s* mousson *f*

monster ['mɑnstər] *adj* & *s* monstre *m*

monstrance ['mɑnstrəns] *s* ostensoir *m*

monstrous ['mɑnstrəs] *adj* monstrueux

month [mʌnθ] *s* mois *m*

month·ly ['mʌnθli] *adj* mensuel || *s* (*pl* -lies) revue *f* mensuelle; **monthlies** (coll) règles *fpl* || *adv* mensuellement

monument ['mɑnjəmənt] *s* monument *m*

moo [mu] *s* meuglement *m* || *intr* meugler

mood [mud] *s* humeur *f*, disposition *f*; (gram) mode *m*; **moods** accès *mpl* de mauvaise humeur

mood·y ['mudi] *adj* (*comp* -ier; *super* -iest) d'humeur changeante; (*melancholy*) maussade

moon [mun] *s* lune *f* || *intr*—to moon about musarder; (*to daydream about*) rêver à

moon·beam *s* rayon *m* de lune

moon·light *s* clair *m* de lune

moon·light·ing *s* deuxième emploi *m*

moon·shine *s* clair *m* de lune; (*idle talk*) baliverne *f*; (coll) alcool *m* de contrebande

moon· shot *s* tir *m* à la lune

moor [mur] *s* lande *f*, bruyère *f*; **Moor** Maure *m* || *tr* amarrer || *intr* s'amarrer

Moorish ['murɪʃ] *adj* mauresque

moose [mus] *s* (*pl* moose) élan *m* du Canada, orignal *m*; (*European elk*) élan *m*

moot [mut] *adj* discutable

mop [mɑp] *s* balai *m* à franges; (*of hair*) tignasse *f* || *v* (*pret* & *pp* mopped; *ger* mopping) *tr* nettoyer avec un balai à franges; (*e.g., one's brow*) s'essuyer; to mop up (mil) nettoyer

mope [mop] *intr* avoir le cafard

moral ['mɑrəl], ['mɔrəl] *adj* moral || *s* (*of a fable*) morale *f*; **morals** mœurs *fpl*

morale [mə'ræl], [mə'rɑl] s moral m
morali•ty [mə'rælɪtɪ] s (pl -ties) morali-té f
morass [mə'ræs] s marais m
moratori•um [,mɑrə'torɪ•əm], [,mærə'torɪ•əm] s (pl -ums or -a [ə]) mora-toire m, moratorium m
morbid ['mɔrbɪd] adj morbide
mordacious [mɔr'deʃəs] adj mordant
mordant ['mɔrdənt] adj & s mordant m
more [mor] adj comp plus de §91; plus nombreux; de plus, e.g., **one minute more** une minute de plus; **more than** plus que; (followed by numeral) plus de || s plus m; **all the more so** d'autant plus; **what is more** qui plus est; **what more do you need?** que vous faut-il de plus? || pron indef plus, da-vantage || adv comp plus §91; davan-tage; **more and more** de plus en plus; **more or less** plus ou moins; **more than** plus que, davantage que; (fol-lowed by numeral) plus de; **neither more nor less** ni plus ni moins; **never more** jamais plus, plus jamais; **no more ne . . .** plus §90; **once more** une fois de plus; **the more . . . the more** (or the less) plus . . . plus (or moins)
more•o'ver adv de plus, du reste
Moresque [mo'resk] adj mauresque
morgue [mɔrg] s institut m médico-légal, morgue f; (journ) archives fpl
Mormon ['mɔrmən] adj & s mormon m
morning ['mɔrnɪŋ] adj matinal, du matin || s matin m; (time between sunrise and noon) matinée f, matin; **in the morning** le matin; **the morning after** le lendemain matin; (coll) le lendemain de bombe
morn'ing coat' s jaquette f
morn'ing-glo'ry s (pl -ries) belle-de-jour f
morn'ing sick'ness s des nausées fpl
morn'ing star' s étoile f du matin
Moroccan [mə'rɑkən] adj marocain || s Marocain m
morocco [mə'rɑko] s (leather) maro-quin m; **Morocco** le Maroc
moron ['mɔrɑn] s arriéré m; (coll) minus mf, minus habens mf
morose [mə'ros] adj morose
morphine ['mɔrfin] s morphine f
morphology [mɔr'fɑlədʒɪ] s morpholo-gie f
morrow ['mɑro], ['mɔro] s—**on the morrow** (of) le lendemain (de)
Morse' code' [mɔrs] s alphabet m morse
morsel ['mɔrsəl] s morceau m
mortal ['mɔrtəl] adj & s mortel m
mortality [mɔr'tælɪtɪ] s mortalité f
mortar ['mɔrtər] s mortier m
mor'tar-board' s bonnet m carré; (of mason) taloche f
mortgage ['mɔrgɪdʒ] s hypothèque f || tr hypothéquer
mortgagee [,mɔrgɪ'dʒi] s créancier m hypothécaire
mortgagor ['mɔrgɪdʒər] s débiteur m hypothécaire
mortician [mɔr'tɪʃən] s entrepreneur m de pompes funèbres

morti•fy ['mɔrtɪ,faɪ] v (pret & pp -fied) tr mortifier
mortise ['mɔrtɪs] s mortaise f || tr mor-taiser
mortuar•y ['mɔrtʃu,ɛri] adj mortuaire || s (pl -ies) morgue f; chapelle f mor-tuaire
mosaic [mo'ze•ɪk] adj & s mosaïque f
Moscow ['mɑskaʊ], ['mɑsko] s Mos-cou m
Moses ['mozɪz], ['mozɪs] s Moïse m
Mos•lem ['mɑzləm], ['mɑsləm] adj musulman || s (pl -lems or -lem) mu-sulman m
mosque [mɑsk] s mosquée f
mosqui•to [məs'kito] s (pl -toes or -tos) moustique m
mosqui'to net' s moustiquaire f
moss [mɔs], [mɑs] s mousse f
moss•y ['mɔsi], ['mɑsi] adj (comp -ier; super -iest) moussu
most [most] adj super (le) plus de §91, (la) plupart de; **for the most part** pour la plupart || s (le) plus, (la) plupart; **at the most** au plus, tout au plus; **most of** la plupart de; **to make the most of** tirer le meilleur parti possible de || pron indef la plupart || adv super (le) plus §91, e.g., **what I like** (the) **most** ce que j'aime le plus; **the** (or **his, etc.**) **most** + adj le (or son, etc.) plus + adj || adv très, bien, fort, des plus
mostly ['mostli] adv pour la plupart, principalement
motel [mo'tel] s motel m
moth [mɔθ], [mɑθ] s teigne f, papillon m nocturne; (clothes moth) mite f
moth'ball' s boule f antimite, boule de naphtaline
moth-eaten ['mɔθ,itən], ['mɑθ,itən] adj mité
mother ['mʌðər] s mère f || tr servir de mère à; (to coddle) dorloter
moth'er coun'try s mère patrie f
Moth'er Goos'e's Nurs'ery Rhymes' spl les Contes de ma mère l'oie
moth'er-hood' s maternité f
moth'er-in-law' s (pl mothers-in-law) belle-mère f
motherless ['mʌðərlɪs] adj orphelin de mère
motherly ['mʌðərli] adj maternel
mother-of-pearl ['mʌðərəv'pʌrl] adj de nacre, en nacre || s nacre f
Moth'er's Day' s fête f des mères
moth'er supe'rior s mère f supérieure
moth'er tongue' s langue f maternelle
moth'er wit' s bon sens m, esprit m
moth' hole' s trou m de mite
moth'proof' adj antimite || tr rendre antimite
moth•y ['mɔθi], ['mɑθi] adj (comp -ier; super -iest) mité, plein de mites
motif [mo'tif] s motif m
motion ['moʃən] s mouvement m; (ges-ture) geste m; (in a deliberating as-sembly) motion f, proposition f || intr —**to motion to** faire signe à
motionless ['moʃənlɪs] adj immobile
mo'tion pic'ture s film m; motion pic-tures cinéma m

mo'tion-pic'ture *adj* cinématographique

mo'tion-pic'ture the'ater *s* cinéma *m*

motivate ['motɪ,vet] *tr* motiver

motive ['motɪv] *adj* moteur || *s* mobile *m*, motif *m*

mo'tive pow'er *s* force *f* motrice

motley ['matlɪ] *adj* bigarré; (*mixed*) mélangé

motor ['motər] *adj* & *s* moteur *m* || *intr* aller en voiture

mo'tor-bike' *s* vélomoteur *m*

mo'tor-boat' *s* canot *m* automobile

mo'tor-bus' *s* autocar *m*

motorcade ['motər,ked] *s* défilé *m* de voitures

mo'tor-car' *s* automobile *f*

mo'tor-cy'cle *s* moto *f*

motorist ['motərɪst] *s* automobiliste *mf*

motorize ['motə,raɪz] *tr* motoriser

mo'tor launch' *s* chaloupe *f* à moteur

mo'tor-man' *s* (*pl* -men) conducteur *m*, wattman *m*

mo'tor pool' *s* parc *m* automobile

mo'tor scoot'er *s* scooter *m*

mo'tor ship' *s* navire *m* à moteurs

mo'tor truck' *s* camion *m* automobile

mo'tor ve'hicle *s* véhicule *m* automobile

mottle ['matəl] *tr* marbrer, tacheter

mot-to ['mato] *s* (*pl* -toes *or* -tos) devise *f*

mound [maund] *s* monticule *m*

mount [maunt] *s* montage *m*; (*hill, mountain*) mont *m*; (*horse for riding*) monture *f* || *tr* & *intr* monter

mountain ['mauntən] *s* montagne *f*

moun'tain climb'ing *s* alpinisme *m*

mountaineer [,mauntə'nɪr] *s* montagnard *m*; (*climber*) alpiniste *mf*

mountainous ['mauntənəs] *adj* montagneux

moun'tain range' *s* chaîne *f* de montagnes

mountebank ['mauntɪ,bæŋk] *s* saltimbanque *mf*

mounting ['mauntɪŋ] *s* montage *m*

mourn [morn] *tr* & *intr* pleurer

mourner ['mornər] *s* affligé *m*; (*woman hired as mourner*) pleureuse *f*; pénitent *m*; mourners deuil *m*

mourn'er's bench' *s* banc *m* des pénitents

mournful ['mornfəl] *adj* lugubre

mourning ['mornɪŋ] *s* deuil *m*

mouse [maus] *s* (*pl* mice [maɪs]) souris *f*

mouse'hole' *s* trou *m* de souris

mouser ['mauzər] *s* souricier *m*

mouse'trap' *s* souricière *f*

moustache [məs'tæʃ], [məs'taʃ] *s* moustache *f*

mouth [mauθ] *s* (*pl* mouths [mauðz]) bouche *f*; (*of gun; of, e.g., wolf*) gueule *f*; (*of river*) embouchure *f*; by mouth par voie buccale; to make s.o.'s mouth water faire venir l'eau à la bouche à qn

mouthful ['mauθ,ful] *s* bouchée *f*

mouth' or'gan *s* harmonica *m*

mouth'piece' *s* embouchure *f*; (*person*) porte-parole *m*

mouth'wash' *s* rince-bouche *m*, eau *f* dentifrice

movable ['muvəbəl] *adj* mobile

move [muv] *s* mouvement *m*; démarche *f*; (*from one house to another*) déménagement *m*; on the move en mouvement || *tr* remuer; (*to excite the feelings of*) émouvoir; to move that (parl) proposer que; to move up (*a date*) avancer || *intr* remuer; (*to stir*) se remuer; (*said of traffic, crowd, etc.*) circuler; (*e.g., to another city*) déménager; don't move! ne bougez pas!; to move away *or* off s'éloigner; to move back reculer; to move in emménager

movement ['muvmənt] *s* mouvement *m*

movie ['muvi] *s* (coll) film *m*; movies (coll) cinéma *m*

mov'ie cam'era *s* caméra *f*

movie-goer ['muvi,go·ər] *s* (coll) amateur *m* de cinéma

mov'ie house' *s* (coll) cinéma *m*, salle *f* de spectacles

moving ['muvɪŋ] *adj* mouvant, en marche; (*touching*) émouvant; (*force*) moteur || *s* mouvement *m*; (*from one house to another*) déménagement *m*

mov'ing pic'ture *s* film *m*; moving pictures cinéma *m*

mov'ing-pic'ture the'ater *s* cinéma *m*

mov'ing spir'it *s* âme *f*

mov'ing stair'way *s* escalier *m* mécanique, escalier roulant

mov'ing van' *s* voiture *f* de déménagement

mow [mo] *v* (*pret* mowed; *pp* mowed *or* mown) *tr* faucher; (*a lawn*) tondre; to mow down faucher

mower ['mo·ər] *s* faucheur *m*; (mach) faucheuse *f*; (*for lawns*) (mach) tondeuse *f*

m.p.h. ['em'pi'etʃ] *spl* (letterword) (miles per hour—six tenths of a mile equaling approximately one kilometer) km/h

Mr. ['mɪstər] *s* Monsieur *m*, M.

Mrs. ['mɪsɪz] *s* Madame *f*, Mme

much [mʌtʃ] *adj* beaucoup de, e.g., much time beaucoup de temps; bien de + *art*, e.g., much trouble bien du mal || *pron indef* beaucoup; too much trop || *adv* beaucoup, bien §91; however much pour autant que; much combien; much less encore moins; too much trop; very much beaucoup

mucilage ['mjusɪlɪdʒ] *s* colle *f* de bureau; (*gummy secretion in plants*) mucilage *m*

muck [mʌk] *s* fange *f*

muck'rake' *intr* (coll) dévoiler des scandales

mucous ['mjukəs] *adj* muqueux

mu'cous lin'ing *s* (anat) muqueuse *f*

mucus ['mjukəs] *s* mucus *m*, mucosité *f*

mud [mʌd] *s* boue *f*; to sling mud at couvrir de boue

muddle ['mʌdəl] *s* confusion *f*, fouillis *m* || *tr* embrouiller || *intr*—to muddle through se débrouiller

mud′dle·head′ s brouillon m
mud·dy ['mʌdi] adj (comp -dier; super -diest) boueux; (clothes) crotté ‖ v (pret & pp -died) tr salir; (clothes) crotter; (a liquid) troubler; (fig) embrouiller
mud′guard′ s garde-boue m
mud′hole′ s bourbier m
mudslinger ['mʌd,slɪŋər] s (fig) calomniateur m
muff [mʌf] s manchon m; (failure) coup m raté ‖ tr rater, louper
muffin ['mʌfɪn] s petit pain m rond, muffin m
muffle ['mʌfəl] tr (a sound) assourdir; (the face) emmitoufler
muffler ['mʌflər] s (scarf) cache-nez m; (aut) pot m d'échappement, silencieux m
mufti ['mʌfti] s vêtement m civil; in mufti en civil, en pékin, en bourgeois
mug [mʌg] s timbale f, gobelet m; (tankard) chope f; (slang) gueule f, museau m ‖ v (pret & pp mugged; ger mugging) tr (e.g., a suspect) (slang) photographier; (a victim) (slang) saisir à la gorge ‖ intr (slang) faire des grimaces
mug·gy ['mʌgi] adj (comp -gier; super -giest) lourd, étouffant
mulat·to [mju'læto], [mə'læto] s (pl -toes) mulâtre m
mulber·ry ['mʌl,beri] s (pl -ries) mûre f; (tree) mûrier m
mulct [mʌlkt] tr (a person) priver, dépouiller; (money) carotter, extorquer
mule [mjul] s (female mule; slipper) mule f; (male mule) mulet m
muleteer [,mjulə'tɪr] s muletier m
mulish ['mjulɪʃ] adj têtu, entêté
mull [mʌl] tr chauffer avec des épices; (to muddle) embrouiller ‖ intr—to mull over réfléchir sur, remâcher
mullion ['mʌljən] s meneau m
multigraph ['mʌltɪ,græf], ['mʌltɪ,grɑf] s (trademark) ronéo f ‖ tr ronéotyper, polycopier
multilateral [,mʌltɪ'lætərəl] adj multilatéral
multiple ['mʌltɪpəl] adj & s multiple m
multiplici·ty [,mʌltɪ'plɪsɪti] s (pl -ties) multiplicité f
multi·ply ['mʌltɪ,plaɪ] v (pret & pp -plied) tr multiplier ‖ intr se multiplier
multitude ['mʌltɪ,t(j)ud] s multitude f
mum [mʌm] adj silencieux; mum's the word! motus!, bouche cousue!; to keep mum ne souffler mot ‖
mumble ['mʌmbəl] tr & intr marmotter
mummer·y ['mʌməri] s (pl -ies) momerie f
mum·my ['mʌmi] s (pl -mies) momie f; (slang) maman f
mumps [mʌmps] s oreillons mpl
munch [mʌntʃ] tr mâchonner
mundane ['mʌnden] adj mondain
municipal [mju'nɪsɪpəl] adj municipal
municipali·ty [mju,nɪsɪ'pælɪti] s (pl -ties) municipalité f
munificent [mju'nɪfɪsənt] adj munificent

munition [mju'nɪʃən] s munition f ‖ tr approvisionner de munitions
muni′tion dump′ s dépôt m de munitions
mural ['mjʊrəl] adj mural ‖ s peinture f murale
murder ['mʌrdər] s assassinat m, meurtre m ‖ tr assassiner; (a language, proper names, etc.) (coll) estropier, écorcher
murderer ['mʌrdərər] s meurtrier m, assassin m
murderess ['mʌrdərɪs] s meurtrière f
murderous ['mʌrdərəs] adj meurtrier
murk·y ['mʌrki] adj (comp -ier; super -iest) ténébreux, nébuleux
murmur ['mʌrmər] s murmure m ‖ tr & intr murmurer
muscle ['mʌsəl] s muscle m
muscular ['mʌskjələr] adj musclé, musculeux; (system, tissue, etc.) musculaire
muse [mjuz] s muse f; the Muses les Muses ‖ tr méditer; to muse on méditer
museum [mju'ziəm] s musée m
muse′um piece′ s pièce f de musée
mush [mʌʃ] s bouillie f; (coll) sentimentalité f de guimauve
mush′room′ s champignon m ‖ intr pousser comme un champignon
mush′room cloud′ s champignon m atomique
mush·y ['mʌʃi] adj (comp -ier; super -iest) mou; (ground) détrempé; (coll) à la guimauve, sentimental
music ['mjuzɪk] s musique f; to face the music (coll) affronter les opposants; to set to music mettre en musique
musical ['mjuzɪkəl] adj musical
mu′sical com′edy s comédie f musicale
musicale [,mjuzɪ'kæl] s soirée f musicale; matinée f musicale
mu′sic box′ s boîte f à musique
mu′sic cab′inet s casier m à musique
mu′sic hall′ s salle f de musique; (Brit) music-hall m
musician [mju'zɪʃən] s musicien m
mu′sic lov′er s mélomane mf
musicology [,mjuzɪ'kalədʒi] s musicologie f
mu′sic rack′ or **mu′sic stand′** s pupitre m à musique
musk [mʌsk] s musc m
musk′ deer′ s porte-musc m
musketeer [,mʌskɪ'tɪr] s mousquetaire m
musk′mel′on s melon m; cantaloup m
musk′rat′ s rat m musqué, ondatra m
Mus·lim ['mʌzlɪm] adj musulman ‖ s (pl -lims or -lim) musulman m
muslin ['mʌzlɪn] s mousseline f
muss [mʌs] tr (the hair) ébouriffer; (the clothing) froisser
Mussulman ['mʌsəlmən] adj & s musulman m
muss·y ['mʌsi] adj (comp -ier; super -iest) en désordre, froissé
must [mʌst] s moût m; nécessité f absolue ‖ aux used to express 1)

necessity, e.g., **he must go away** il doit s'en aller; 2) conjecture, e.g., **he must be ill** il doit être malade; **he must have been ill** il a dû être malade

mustache [məs'tæ/], [məs'tɑ/], ['mʌs-tæ/] s moustache f

mustard ['mʌstərd] s moutarde f

mus'tard plas'ter s sinapisme m

muster ['mʌstər] s rassemblement m; (mil) revue f; **to pass muster** être porté à l'appel; (fig) être acceptable || tr rassembler; **to muster in** enrôler; **to muster out** démobiliser; **to muster up courage** prendre son courage à deux mains

mus'ter roll' s feuille f d'appel

mus-ty ['mʌsti] adj (comp -tier; super -tiest) (moldy) moisi; (stale) renfermé; (antiquated) désuet

mutation [mju'te/ən] s mutation f

mute [mjut] adj muet || s muet m; (mus) sourdine f || tr amortir; (mus) mettre une sourdine à

mutilate ['mjutɪ,let] tr mutiler

mutineer [,mjutɪ'nɪr] s mutin m

mutinous ['mjutɪnəs] adj mutiné

muti-ny ['mjutɪni] s (pl -nies) mutinerie f || v (pret & pp -nied) intr se mutiner

mutt [mʌt] s (dog) (slang) cabot m; (person) (slang) nigaud m

mutter ['mʌtər] tr & intr marmonner

mutton ['mʌtən] s mouton m

mut'ton-chop' s côtelette f de mouton; **muttonchops** favoris mpl en côtelette

mutual ['mjut/u-əl] adj mutuel

mu'tual aid' s entraide f

mu'tual fund' s mutuelle f

muzzle ['mʌzəl] s (projecting part of head of animal) museau m; (device to keep animal from biting) muselière f; (of firearm) gueule f || tr museler

my [maɪ] adj poss mon §88

myriad ['mɪrɪ-əd] adj innombrable || s myriade f

myrrh [mɪr] s myrrhe f

myrtle ['mʌrtəl] s myrte m; (periwinkle) pervenche f

my-self' pron pers moi §85; moi-même §86; me §87

mysterious [mɪs'tɪrɪ-əs] adj mystérieux

myster-y ['mɪstəri] s (pl -ies) mystère m

mystic ['mɪstɪk] adj & s mystique mf

mystical ['mɪstɪkəl] adj mystique

mysticism ['mɪstɪ,sɪzəm] s mysticisme m

mystification [,mɪstɪfɪ'ke/ən] s mystification f

mysti-fy ['mɪstɪ,faɪ] v (pret & pp -fied) tr mystifier

myth [mɪθ] s mythe m

mythical ['mɪθɪkəl] adj mythique

mythological [,mɪθə'lɑdʒɪkəl] adj mythologique

mytholo-gy [mɪ'θɑlədʒi] s (pl -gies) mythologie f

N

N, n [ɛn] s XIVe lettre de l'alphabet

nab [næb] v (pret & pp nabbed; ger nabbing) tr (slang) happer; (to arrest) (slang) pincer, harponner

nag [næg] s bidet m || v (pret & pp nagged; ger nagging) tr & intr gronder constamment; **to nag at** gronder constamment

nail [nel] s (of finger) ongle m; (to be hammered) clou m; **to bite one's nails** se ronger les ongles; **to hit the nail on the head** mettre le doigt dessus, frapper juste || tr clouer; (a lie) mettre à découvert; (coll) saisir, attraper

nail'brush' s brosse f à ongles

nail' clip'pers spl coupe-ongles m

nail' file' s lime f à ongles

nail' pol'ish s vernis m à ongles

nail' scis'sors s & spl ciseaux mpl à ongles

nail' set' s chasse-clou m

naïve [nɑ'iv] adj naïf

naked ['nekɪd] adj nu; **to strip naked** se mettre tout nu; mettre tout nu; **with the naked eye** à l'œil nu

namby-pamby ['næmbi'pæmbi] adj minauder

name [nem] s nom m; (reputation) renom m; **by name** de nom; **by the**

name of sous le nom de; **to call names** traiter de tous les noms; **what is your name?** comment vous appelez-vous? || tr nommer; (a price) fixer, indiquer

name' day' s fête f

nameless ['nemlɪs] adj sans nom, anonyme; (horrid) odieux

namely ['nemli] adv à savoir, nommément

name'sake' s homonyme m

nan-ny ['næni] s (pl -nies) nounou f

nan'ny goat' s (coll) chèvre f, bique f

nap [næp] s (short sleep) somme m, sieste f; (of cloth) poil m, duvet m; **to take a nap** faire un petit somme || v (pret & pp napped; ger napping) intr faire un somme; **to catch napping** prendre au dépourvu

napalm ['nepam] s (mil) napalm m

nape [nep] s nuque f

naphtha ['næfθə] s naphte m

napkin ['næpkɪn] s serviette f

nap'kin ring' s rond m de serviette

Napoleonic [nə,poli'ɑnɪk] adj napoléonien

narcissus [nɑr'sɪsəs] s narcisse m; **Narcissus** Narcisse

narcotic [nar'katık] *adj* & *s* narcotique *m*

narrate [næ'ret] *tr* narrer, raconter

narration [næ're/ən] *s* narration *f*

narrative ['næretiv] *adj* narratif ‖ *s* narration *f*, récit *m*

narrator [næ'retər] *s* narrateur *m*

narrow ['næro] *adj* étroit; (*e.g., margin of votes*) faible ‖ **narrows** *spl* détroit *m*, goulet *m* ‖ *tr* rétrécir ‖ *intr* se rétrécir

nar'row escape' *s*—**to have a narrow escape** l'échapper belle

nar'row gauge' *s* voie *f* étroite

nar'row-mind'ed *adj* à l'esprit étroit, intolérant

nasal ['nezəl] *adj* nasal; (*sound, voice*) nasillard ‖ *s* (phonet) nasale *f*

nasalize ['nezə,laız] *tr* & *intr* nasaliser

nasturtium [nə'stʌr/əm] *s* capucine *f*

nas·ty ['næstı], ['nɑstı] *adj* (*comp* -tier; *super* -tiest) mauvais, sale, dégoûtant; féroce, farouche; désagréable

nation ['ne/ən] *s* nation *f*

national ['næ/ənəl] *adj* & *s* national *m*

na'tional an'them *s* hymne *m* national

nationalism ['næ/ənə,lızəm] *s* nationalisme *m*

nationali·ty [,næ/ən'ælıti] *s* (*pl* -ties) nationalité *f*

nationalize ['næ/ənə,laız] *tr* nationaliser, étatiser

na'tion-wide' *adj* de toute la nation

native ['netıv] *adj* natif; (*land, language*) natal; **native of** originaire de ‖ *s* natif *m*; (*original inhabitant*) naturel *m*, indigène *mf*, autochtone *mf*

na'tive land' *s* pays *m* natal

nativi·ty [nə'tıvıti] *s* (*pl* -ties) naissance *f*; (astrol) nativité *f*; **Nativity** Nativité *f*

NATO ['neto] *s* (acronym) (**North Atlantic Treaty Organization**) l'O.T.A.N. *f*, l'OTAN *f*

nat·ty ['nætı] *adj* (*comp* -tier; *super* -tiest) coquet, élégant, soigné

natural ['næt/ərəl] *adj* naturel ‖ *s* (mus) bécarre *m*; (mus) touche *f* blanche; **a natural** (coll) juste ce qu'il faut

naturalism ['næt/ərə,lızəm] *s* naturalisme *m*

naturalist ['næt/ərəlıst] *s* naturaliste *mf*

naturalization [,næt/ərəlı'ze/ən] *s* naturalisation *f*

naturaliza'tion pa'pers *spl* déclaration *f* de naturalisation

naturalize ['næt/ərə,laız] *tr* naturaliser

nature ['net/ər] *s* nature *f*

naught [nɔt] *s* zéro *m*; rien *m*; **to come to naught** n'aboutir à rien

naugh·ty ['nɔtı] *adj* (*comp* -tier; *super* -tiest) méchant, vilain; (*story*) risqué

nausea ['nɔ/ı·ə], ['nɔsı·ə] *s* nausée *f*

nauseate ['nɔ/ı,et], ['nɔsı,et] *tr* donner la nausée à ‖ *intr* avoir des nausées

nauseating ['nɔ/ı,etıŋ], ['nɔsı,etıŋ] *adj* nauséabond

nauseous ['nɔ/ı·əs], ['nɔsı·əs] *adj* nauséeux

nautical ['nɔtıkəl] *adj* nautique; naval, marin

naval ['nevəl] *adj* naval

na'val acad'emy *s* école *f* navale

na'val of'ficer *s* officier *m* de marine

na'val sta'tion *s* station *f* navale

nave [nev] *s* (*of a church*) nef *f*, vaisseau *m*; (*of a wheel*) moyeu *m*

navel ['nevəl] *s* nombril *m*

na'vel or'ange *s* orange *f* navel

navigable ['nævıgəbəl] *adj* (*river*) navigable; (*aircraft*) dirigeable; (*ship*) bon marcheur

navigate ['nævı,get] *tr* gouverner, conduire; (*the sea*) naviguer sur ‖ *intr* naviguer

navigation [,nævı'ge/ən] *s* navigation *f*

navigator ['nævı,getər] *s* navigateur *m*

na·vy ['nevı] *adj* bleu marine ‖ *s* (*pl* -vies) marine *f* militaire, marine de guerre; (*color*) bleu *m* marine

na'vy bean' *s* haricot *m* blanc

na'vy blue' *s* bleu *m* marine

na'vy yard' *s* chantier *m* naval

nay [ne] *adv* non; voire, même ‖ *s* non *m*; (parl) vote *m* négatif

Nazarene [,næzə'rin] *adj* nazaréen ‖ *s* (*person*) Nazaréen *m*

Nazi ['nɑtsı], ['nætsı] *adj* & *s* nazi *m*

n.d. *abbr* (**no date**) s.d.

Ne'apol'itan ice' cream' [,ni·ə'pɑlıtən] *s* glace *f* panachée

neap' tide' [nip] *s* morte-eau *f*

near [nır] *adj* proche, prochain; d'imitation; **near at hand** tout près; **near side** (*of horse*) côté *m* de montoir ‖ *adv* près, de près; presque; **to come near** s'approcher ‖ *prep* près de; auprès de ‖ *tr* s'approcher de

near'by' *adj* proche ‖ *adv* tout près

Near' East' *s*—**the Near East** le Proche Orient

nearly ['nırlı] *adv* presque, de près; faillir, manquer de, e.g., **I nearly fell** j'ai failli tomber

near'sight'ed *adj* myope

near'sight'edness *s* myopie *f*

neat [nit] *adj* soigné, rangé; concis; (*clever*) adroit; (*liquor*) nature; (slang) chouette

neat's'-foot oil' *s* huile *f* de pied de bœuf

nebu·la ['nebjələ] *s* (*pl* -lae [,li] or -las) nébuleuse *f*

nebulous ['nebjələs] *adj* nébuleux

necessarily [,nesı'serılı] *adv* nécessairement, forcément

necessary ['nesı,serı] *adj* nécessaire

necessitate [nı'sesı,tet] *tr* nécessiter, exiger

necessi·ty [nı'sesıtı] *s* (*pl* -ties) nécessité *f*

neck [nek] *s* cou *m*; (*of bottle*) col *m*, goulot *m*; (*of land*) cap *m*; (*of tooth*) collet *m*; (*of violin*) manche *m*, collet; (*strait*) étroit *m*; **neck and neck** manche à manche; **to break one's neck** (coll) se rompre le cou; **to stick one's neck out** prêter le flanc; **to win**

by a neck gagner par une encolure ‖ *intr* (slang) se peloter
neck/band/ *s* tour *m* de cou
neckerchief ['nɛkərt/ɪf] *s* foulard *m*
necking ['nɛkɪŋ] *s* (slang) pelotage *m*
necklace ['nɛklɪs] *s* collier *m*
neck/piece/ *s* col *m* de fourrure
neck/tie/ *s* cravate *f*
neck/tie pin/ *s* épingle *f* de cravate
necrolo·gy [nɛ'krɑlədʒi] *s* (*pl* -gies) nécrologie *f*
nectar ['nɛktər] *s* nectar *m*
nectarine [‚nɛktə'rin] *s* brugnon *m*
nee [ne] *adj* née
need [nid] *s* besoin *m*; (*want, poverty*) besoin, indigence, *f*, nécessité *f*; if need be au besoin, s'il le faut ‖ *tr* avoir besoin de, falloir, e.g., he needs money il a besoin d'argent, il lui faut de l'argent; demander, e.g., the motor needs oil le moteur demande de l'huile ‖ *aux devoir*
needful ['nidfəl] *adj* nécessaire
needle ['nidəl] *s* aiguille *f* ‖ *tr* (*to prod*) aiguillonner; (coll) taquiner; (*a drink*) (coll) corser
nee/dle-point/ *s* broderie *f* sur canevas; (*lace*) dentelle *f* à l'aiguille
needless ['nidlɪs] *adj* inutile
nee/dle-work/ *s* ouvrage *m* à l'aiguille
need·y ['nidi] *adj* (*comp* -ier; *super* -iest) nécessiteux ‖ *s*—the needy les nécessiteux
ne'er-do-well ['nɛrdu‚wɛl] *adj* propre à rien ‖ *s* vaurien *m*
nefarious [nɪ'fɛrɪ·əs] *adj* scélérat
negate ['nɛget], [nɪ'get] *tr* invalider; nier
negation [nɪ'ge/ən] *s* négation *f*
negative ['nɛgətɪv] *adj* négatif ‖ *s* (*opinion*) négative *f*; (gram) négation *f*; (phot) négatif *m*
neglect [nɪ'glɛkt] *s* négligence *f* ‖ *tr* négliger; to neglect to négliger de
négligée or **negligee** [‚nɛglɪ'ʒe] *s* négligé *m*, robe *f* de chambre
negligence ['nɛglɪdʒəns] *s* négligence *f*
negligent ['nɛglɪdʒənt] *adj* négligent
negligible ['nɛglɪdʒɪbəl] *adj* négligeable
negotiable [nɪ'goʃɪ·əbəl] *adj* négociable
negotiate [nɪ'goʃɪ·et] *tr & intr* négocier
negotiation [nɪ‚goʃɪ'eʃən] *s* négociation *f*
negotiator [nɪ'goʃɪ‚etər] *s* négociateur *m*
Ne·gro ['nigro] *adj* noir, nègre ‖ *s* (*pl* -groes) noir *m*, nègre *m*
neigh [ne] *s* hennissement *m* ‖ *intr* hennir
neighbor ['nebər] *adj* voisin ‖ *s* voisin *m*; (fig) prochain *m* ‖ *tr* avoisiner ‖ *intr* être voisin
neigh/bor·hood/ *s* voisinage *m*; in the neighborhood of aux environs de; (*approximately, about*) (coll) environ
neighborliness ['nebərlɪnɪs] *s* bon voisinage *m*
neighborly ['nebərli] *adj* bon voisin
neither ['niðər], ['naɪðər] *adj indef* ni, e.g., neither one of us ni l'un ni l'autre ‖ *pron indef* ni, e.g., neither ni l'un ni l'autre ‖ *conj* ni; ni . . . non plus, e.g., neither do I ni moi non plus; neither . . . nor ni . . . ni
neme·sis ['nɛmɪsɪs] *s* (*pl* -ses [‚siz]) juste châtiment *m*; Nemesis Némésis *f*
neologism [ni'ɑlə‚dʒɪzəm] *s* néologisme *m*
neon ['ni·ɑn] *s* néon *m*
ne/on lamp/ *s* lampe *f* au néon
ne/on sign/ *s* réclame *f* lumineuse
neophyte ['ni·ə‚faɪt] *s* néophyte *mf*
nephew ['nɛfju], ['nɛvju] *s* neveu *m*
neptunium [nɛp't(j)unɪ·əm] *s* neptunium *m*
Nero ['nɪro] *s* Néron *m*
nerve [nʌrv] *s* nerf *m*; audace *f*; to get on s.o.'s nerves porter sur les nerfs à qn; to have a lot of nerve avoir du toupet; to have nerves of steel avoir du nerf; to lose one's nerve avoir le trac
nerve/ cen/ter *s* nœud *m* vital; (anat) centre *m* nerveux
nerve/-rack/ing *adj* énervant, agaçant
nervous ['nʌrvəs] *adj* nerveux
ner/vous break/down *s* épuisement *m* nerveux, dépression *f* nerveuse
nerv·y ['nʌrvi] *adj* (*comp* -ier; *super* -iest) nerveux, musclé; (coll) audacieux, culotté; (slang) dévergondé
nest [nɛst] *s* nid *m*; (*set of things fitting together*) jeu *m* ‖ *intr* se nicher
nest/ egg/ *s* nichet *m*; (fig) boursicot *m*, bas *m* de laine
nestle ['nɛsəl] *intr* se blottir, se nicher
nest/ of ta/bles *s* table *f* gigogne
net [nɛt] *adj* net ‖ *s* filet *m*; (*for fishing; for catching birds*) nappe *f*; (tex) tulle *m* ‖ *v* (*pret & pp* netted; *ger* netting) *tr* (*a profit*) réaliser
Netherlander ['nɛðər‚lændər], ['nɛðər‚ləndər] *s* Néerlandais *m*
Netherlands ['nɛðərləndz] *s*—The Netherlands les Pays-Bas *mpl*
nettle ['nɛtəl] *s* ortie *f* ‖ *tr* piquer au vif
net/work/ *s* réseau *m*; (rad, telv) chaîne *f*, réseau
neuralgia [n(j)u'rældʒə] *s* névralgie *f*
neuro·sis [n(j)u'rosɪs] *s* (*pl* -ses [siz]) névrose *f*
neurotic [n(j)u'rɑtɪk] *adj & s* névrosé *m*
neuter ['n(j)utər] *adj & s* neutre *m*
neutral ['n(j)utrəl] *adj* neutre ‖ *s* neutre *m*; (gear) point *m* mort
neutrality [n(j)u'trælɪti] *s* neutralité *f*
neutralize ['n(j)utrə‚laɪz] *tr* neutraliser
neutron ['n(j)utrɑn] *s* neutron *m*
neu/tron bomb/ *s* bombe *f* à neutrons
never ['nɛvər] *adv* jamais §90B; ne . . . jamais §90, e.g., he never talks il ne parle jamais
nev/er-more/ *adv* ne . . . plus jamais ‖ *interj* jamais plus!, plus jamais!
nev/er-the-less/ *adv* néanmoins
new [n(j)u] *adj* (*unused*) neuf; (*other, additional, different*) nouveau (before noun); (*recent*) nouveau (after noun); (*inexperienced*) novice; (*wine*)

jeune; **what's new?** quoi de nouveau?, quoi de neuf?

new'born' *adj* nouveau-né

new'born child' *s* nouveau-né *m*

New'cas'tle *s*—**to carry coals to Newcastle** porter de l'eau à la rivière

newcomer ['n(j)u‚kʌmər] *s* nouveau venu *m*

New' Cov'enant *s* (Bib) nouvelle alliance *f*

newel ['n(j)u-əl] *s* (of winding stairs) noyau *m*; (post at end of stair rail) pilastre *m*

New' Eng'land *s* Nouvelle-Angleterre *f*; la Nouvelle-Angleterre

newfangled ['n(j)u‚fæŋgəld] *adj* à la dernière mode, du dernier cri

Newfoundland ['n(j)ufənd‚lænd] *s* Terre-Neuve *f*; **in or to Newfoundland** à Terre-Neuve || [n(j)u'faund-lənd] *s* (dog) terre-neuve *m*

newly ['n(j)uli] *adv* nouvellement

new'ly-wed' *s* nouveau marié *m*

new' moon' *s* nouvelle lune *f*

newness ['n(j)unɪs] *s* nouveauté *f*

New' Or'leans ['ɔrlɪ-ənz] *s* la Nouvelle-Orléans

news [n(j)uz] *s* nouvelles *fpl*; **a news item** un fait-divers; **a piece of news** une nouvelle

news' a'gency *s* agence *f* d'information, agence de presse; agence à journaux

news'beat' *s* exclusivité *f*

news'boy' *s* vendeur *m* de journaux

news'cast' *s* journal *m* parlé; journal télévisé

news'cast'er *s* reporter *m* de la radio

news' con'ference *s* conférence *f* de presse

news' cov'erage *s* reportage *m*

news'deal'er *s* marchand *m* de journaux

news' ed'itor *s* rédacteur *m* publicitaire

news'let'ter *s* circulaire *f* publicitaire

news'man' *s* (pl -men') journaliste *m*; (dealer) marchand *m* de journaux

New' South' Wales' *s* la Nouvelle-Galles du Sud

news'pa'per *adj* journalistique || *s* journal *m*

news'paper clip'ping *s* coupure *f* de presse

news'paper-man' *s* (pl -men') journaliste *m*; (dealer) marchand *m* de journaux

news'paper rack' *s* casier *m* à journaux

news'paper se'rial *s* feuilleton *m*

news'print' *s* papier *m* journal

news'reel' *s* actualités *fpl*

news'room' *s* salle *f* de rédaction

news'stand' *s* kiosque *m*

news'week'ly *s* (pl -lies) hebdomadaire *m*

news'wor'thy *adj* d'actualité

New' Tes'tament *s* Nouveau Testament *m*

New' Year's' Day' *s* le jour de l'an

New' Year's' Eve' *s* la Saint-Sylvestre

New' Year's' greet'ings *spl* souhaits *mpl* de nouvel An

New' Year's' resolu'tion *s* résolution *f* de nouvel An

New' York' [jɔrk] *adj* newyorkais || *s* New York *m*

New' York'er ['jɔrkər] *s* newyorkais *m*

next [nɛkst] *adj* (in time) prochain, suivant; (in place) voisin; (first in the period which follows) prochain (before noun), e.g., **the next time** la prochaine fois; (following the present time) prochain (after noun), e.g., **next week** la semaine prochaine; **next to** à côté de || *adv* après, ensuite; **la prochaine fois; who comes next?** à qui le tour? || *interj* au premier de ces messieurs!, au suivant!

next'-door' *adj* d'à côté, voisin || **next'-door'** *adv* à côté; **next-door to** à côté de; à côté de chez

next' of kin' *s* (pl next of kin) proche parent *m*

Niag'ara Falls' [naɪ'ægərə] *s* la Cataracte du Niagara

nib [nɪb] *s* pointe *f*; (of pen) bec *m*

nibble ['nɪbəl] *s* grignotement *m*; (on fish line) touche *f*; (fig) morceau *m* || *tr & intr* grignoter

nice [naɪs] *adj* agréable, gentil, aimable; (distinction) subtil, fin; (weather) beau; **nice and . . .** (coll) très; **not nice** (coll) vilain

nicely ['naɪsli] *adv* bien; avec délicatesse

nice·ty ['naɪsəti] *s* (pl -ties) précision *f*; (subtlety) finesse *f*

niche [nɪtʃ] *s* niche *f*; (job, position) place *f*, poste *m*

nick [nɪk] *s* (e.g., on china) brèche *f*; **in the nick of time** à point nommé, à pic || *tr* ébrécher; (for money, favors) (slang) cramponner

nickel ['nɪkəl] *s* (metal) nickel *m*; (coin) pièce *f* de cinq sous || *tr* nickeler

nick'el plate' *s* nickelure *f*

nick'el-plate' *tr* nickeler

nicknack ['nɪk‚næk] *s* colifichet *m*

nick'name' *s* sobriquet *m*, surnom *m* || *tr* donner un sobriquet à, surnommer

nicotine ['nɪkə‚tin] *s* nicotine *f*

niece [nis] *s* nièce *f*

nif·ty ['nɪfti] *adj* (comp -tier; super -tiest) (slang) coquet, pimpant

niggard ['nɪgərd] *adj* & *s* avare *mf*

night [naɪt] *s* nuit *f*; (evening) soir *m*; **last night** (night that has just passed) cette nuit; (last evening) hier soir; **night before last** avant-hier soir

night'cap' *s* bonnet *m* de nuit, casque *m* à mèche; (drink) posset *m*

night' club' *s* boîte *f* de nuit

night'fall' *s* tombée *f* de la nuit

night'gown' *s* chemise *f* de nuit

night'hawk' *s* noctambule *mf*; (orn) engoulevent *m*

nightingale ['naɪtən‚gel] *s* rossignol *m*

night'latch' *s* serrure *f* à ressort

night' light' *s* veilleuse *f*

night'long' *adj* de toute la nuit || *adv* pendant toute la nuit

nightly ['naɪtli] *adj* nocturne; de chaque nuit || *adv* nocturnement; chaque nuit

night/mare/ *s* cauchemar *m*

nightmarish ['naɪt,merɪʃ] *adj* (coll) cauchemardeux

night/ owl/ *s* (coll) noctambule *mf*

night/ school/ *s* cours *mpl* du soir

night/shade/ *s* morelle *f*

night/ shift/ *s* équipe *f* de nuit

night/ watch/man *s* (*pl* **-men**) veilleur *m* de nuit

nihilism ['naɪ·ɪ,lɪzəm] *s* nihilisme *m*

nil [nɪl] *s* rien *m*

Nile [naɪl] *s* Nil *m*

nimble ['nɪmbəl] *adj* agile, leste; (*mind*) délié

nim·bus ['nɪmbəs] *s* (*pl* **-buses** or **-bi** [baɪ]) nimbe *m*, auréole *f*; (meteo) nimbus *m*

nincompoop ['nɪnkəm,pup] *s* nigaud *m*

nine [naɪn] *adj & pron* neuf || *s* neuf *m*; **nine o'clock** neuf heures

nine/pins/ *s* quilles *fpl*

nineteen ['naɪn'tin] *adj, pron, & s* dix-neuf *m*

nineteenth ['naɪn'tinθ] *adj & pron* dix-neuvième (*masc, fem*); **the Nineteenth** dix-neuf, e.g., **John the Nineteenth** Jean dix-neuf || *s* dix-neuvième *m*; **the nineteenth** (*in dates*) le dix-neuf

ninetieth ['naɪntɪ·ɪθ] *adj & pron* quatre-vingt-dixième (*masc, fem*) || *s* quatre-vingt-dixième *m*

nine·ty ['naɪntɪ] *adj & pron* quatre-vingt-dix || *s* (*pl* **-ties**) quatre-vingt-dix *m*

nine/ty-first/ *adj & pron* quatre-vingt-onzième (*masc, fem*) || *s* quatre-vingt-onzième *m*

nine/ty-one/ *adj, pron, & s* quatre-vingt-onze *m*

ninth [naɪnθ] *adj & pron* neuvième (*masc, fem*); **the Ninth** neuf, e.g., **John the Ninth** Jean neuf || *s* neuvième *m*; **the ninth** (*in dates*) le neuf

nip [nɪp] *s* pincement *m*, petite morsure *f*; (*of cold weather*) morsure; (*of liquor*) goutte *f* || *v* (*pret & pp* **nipped**; *ger* **nipping**) *tr* pincer, donner une petite morsure à; **to nip in the bud** tuer dans l'œuf || *intr* (coll) biberonner, picoler

nipple ['nɪpəl] *s* mamelon *m*; (*of nursing bottle*) tétine *f*; (mach) raccord *m*

nip·py ['nɪpɪ] *adj* (*comp* **-pier**; *super* **-piest**) piquant; (*cold*) vif; (Brit) leste, rapide

nirvana [nɪr'vanə] *s* le nirvâna

nit [nɪt] *s* pou *m*; (*egg*) lente *f*

niter ['naɪtər] *s* nitrate *m* de potasse; nitrate de soude

nitrate ['naɪtret] *s* azotate *m*, nitrate *m*; (*fertilizer*) engrais *m* nitraté *f* || *tr* nitrater

nitric ['naɪtrɪk] *adj* azotique, nitrique

nitrogen ['naɪtrədʒən] *s* azote *m*

nitroglycerin [,naɪtrə'glɪsərɪn] *s* nitroglycérine *f*

nitrous ['naɪtrəs] *adj* azoteux

ni/trous ox/ide *s* oxyde *m* azoteux, protoxyde *m* d'azote

nit/wit/ *s* (coll) imbécile *mf*

no [no] *adj indef* aucun, nul, pas de §90B; **no admittance** entrée *f* interdite; **no answer** pas de réponse; **no comment!** rien à dire!; **no go** or **no soap** (coll) pas mèche *f*; **no kidding** (coll) blague *f* à part; **no littering** défense *f* de déposer des ordures; **no loitering** vagabondage *m* interdit; **no parking** stationnement *m* interdit; **no place** nulle part; **no place else** nulle part ailleurs; **no shooting** chasse *f* réservée; **no smoking** défense de fumer; **no thoroughfare** circulation *f* interdite, passage *m* interdit; **no use** inutile; **with no** sans || *s* non *m* || *adv* non; **no good** vil; **no longer** ne . . . plus §90, e.g., **he no longer works here** il ne travaille plus ici; **no more** ne . . . plus §90, e.g., **he has no more** il n'en a plus; **no more** . . . (or *comp* in **-er**) **than** ne . . . pas plus . . . que, e.g., **she is no happier than he** elle n'est pas plus heureuse que lui

No/ah's Ark/ ['no·əz] *s* l'arche *f* de Noé

nobili·ty [no'bɪlɪti] *s* (*pl* **-ties**) noblesse *f*

noble ['nobəl] *adj & s* noble *mf*

no/ble·man *s* (*pl* **-men**) noble *m*

nobleness ['nobəlnɪs] *s* noblesse *f*

nobod·y ['no,badɪ], ['nobədɪ] *s* (*pl* **-ies**) nullité *f* || *pron indef* personne; ne . . . personne §90, e.g., **I see nobody there** je n'y vois personne; personne, ne, nul ne §90, e.g., **nobody knows it** personne ne le sait, nul ne le sait

nocturnal [nɑk'tʌrnəl] *adj* nocturne

nocturne ['nɑktʌrn] *s* nocturne *m*

nod [nɑd] *s* signe *m* de tête; (*greeting*) inclination *f* de tête || *v* (*pret & pp* **nodded**; *ger* **nodding**) *tr* (*the head*) incliner; **to nod assent** faire un signe d'assentiment || *intr* (*with sleep*) dodeliner de la tête; (*to greet*) incliner la tête

node [nod] *s* nœud *m*

noise [nɔɪz] *s* bruit *m* || *tr* (*a rumor*) ébruiter

noiseless ['nɔɪzlɪs] *adj* silencieux

nois·y ['nɔɪzɪ] *adj* (*comp* **-ier**; *super* **-iest**) bruyant

nomad ['nomæd] *adj & s* nomade *mf*

no/ man's/ land/ *s* région *f* désolée; (mil) zone *f* neutre

nominal ['nɑmɪnəl] *adj* nominal

nominate ['nɑmɪ,net] *tr* désigner; (*to appoint*) nommer

nomination [,nɑmɪ'neʃən] *s* désignation *f*, investiture *f*

nominative ['nɑmɪnətɪv] *adj & s* nominatif *m*

nominee [,nɑmɪ'ni] *s* désigné *m*, candidat *m*

nonbelligerent [,nɑnbə'lɪdʒərənt] *adj & s* non-belligérant *m*

nonbreakable [nɑn'brekəbəl] *adj* incassable

nonchalant ['nɑnʃələnt], (,nɑnʃə'lɑnt) *adj* nonchalant

noncom ['nɑn,kɑm] *s* (coll) sous-off *m*

noncombatant [nɑn'kɑmbətənt] *adj* & *s* non-combattant *m*

noncommissioned [,nɑnkə'mɪʃənd] *adj* non breveté

non'commis'sioned of'ficer *s* sous-officier *m*

noncommittal [,nɑnkə'mɪtəl] *adj* évasif, réticent

nonconductor [,nɑnkən'dʌktər] *s* non-conducteur *m*, mauvais conducteur *m*

nonconformist [,nɑnkən'fɔrmɪst] *adj* & *s* non-conformiste *mf*

nondenominational [,nɑndɪ,nɑmɪ'neʃənəl] *adj* indépendant, qui ne fait partie d'aucune secte religieuse; (*school*) laïque

nondescript ['nɑndɪ,skrɪpt] *adj* indéfinissable, inclassable

none [nʌn] *pron indef* aucun §90B; (*nobody*) personne, nul §90B; ne . . . aucun, ne . . . nul §90; n'en . . . pas, e.g., **I have none** je n'en ai pas; (*as a response on the blank of an official form*) néant || *adv*—**to be none the wiser** ne pas en être plus sage

nonenti·ty [nɑn'entɪti] *s* (*pl* -ties) nullité *f*

none'such' *s* nonpareil *m*; (*apple*) nonpareille *f*; (*bot*) lupuline *f*, minette *f*

nonfiction [nɑn'frkʃən] *s* littérature *f* autre que le roman

nonfulfillment [,nɑnful'fɪlmənt] *s* inaccomplissement *m*

nonintervention [,nɑnɪntər'venʃən] *s* non-intervention *f*

nonmetal ['nɑn,metəl] *s* métalloïde *m*

nonpartisan [nɑn'partɪzən] *adj* neutre, indépendant

nonpayment [nɑn'pemənt] *s* non-paiement *m*

non-plus ['nɑnplʌs], [nɑn'plʌs] *s* perplexité *f* || *v* (*pret* & *pp* -plused or -plussed; *ger* -plusing or -plussing) *tr* déconcerter, dérouter

nonresident [nɑn'rezɪdənt] *adj* & *s* non-résident *m*

nonresidential [nɑn,rezɪ'denʃəl] *adj* commercial

nonreturnable [,nɑnrɪ'tʌrnəbəl] *adj* (*bottle*) perdu

nonscientific [nɑn,saɪ·ən'tɪfɪk] *adj* anti-scientifique

nonsectarian [,nɑnsek'terɪ·ən] *adj* non-sectaire; qui ne fait partie d'aucune secte religieuse; (*education*) laïque

nonsense ['nɑnsens] *s* bêtise *f*, non-sens *m*

nonskid ['nɑn'skɪd] *adj* antidérapant

nonstop ['nɑn'stɑp] *adj* & *adv* sans arrêt; sans escale

nonviolence [nɑn'vaɪ·ələns] *s* non-violence *f*

noodle ['nudəl] *s* nouille *f*; (*fool*) (slang) niais *m*; (*head*) (slang) tronche *f*

nook [nuk] *s* coin *m*, recoin *m*

noon [nun] *s* midi *m*

no' one' or **no'-one'** *pron indef* personne §90B; ne . . personne §90, e.g., **I see no one there** je n'y vois personne; personne ne, nul ne §90B, e.g., **no one knows it** personne ne le sait, nul ne le sait; **no one else** personne d'autre

noon'time' *s* midi *m*

noose [nus] *s* nœud *m* coulant; (*for hanging*) corde *f*, hart *f*

nor [nɔr] *conj* ni

norm [nɔrm] *s* norme *f*

normal ['nɔrməl] *adj* normal

Norman ['nɔrmən] *adj* normand || *s* (*dialect*) normand *m*; (*person*) Normand *m*

Normandy ['nɔrməndɪ] *s* Normandie *f*; la Normandie

Norse [nɔrs] *adj* & *s* norrois *m*

Norse'man *s* (*pl* -men) Norrois *m*

north [nɔrθ] *adj* & *s* nord *m* || *adv* au nord, vers le nord

North' Af'rican *adj* nord-africain || *s* Nord-Africain *m*

north'east' *adj* & *s* nord-est *m*

north'east'er *s* vent *m* du nord-est

northern ['nɔrðərn] *adj* septentrional, du nord

North' Kore'a *s* Corée *f* du Nord; la Corée du Nord

North' Kore'an *adj* nord-coréen || *s* (*person*) Nord-Coréen *m*

North' Pole' *s* pôle *m* Nord

northward ['nɔrθwərd] *adv* vers le nord

north'west' *adj* & *s* nord-ouest *m*

north' wind' *s* bise *f*

Norway ['nɔrwe] *s* Norvège *f*; la Norvège

Norwegian [nɔr'widʒən] *adj* norvégien || *s* (*language*) norvégien *m*; (*person*) Norvégien *m*

nose [noz] *s* nez *m*; (*of certain animals*) museau *m*; **to blow one's nose** se moucher; **to have a nose for** avoir le flair de; **to keep one's nose to the grindstone** travailler sans relâche, buriner; **to lead by the nose** mener par le bout du nez; **to look down one's nose at** faire un nez à; **to thumb one's nose at** faire un pied de nez à; **to turn up one's nose at** faire la nique à; **under the nose of** à la barbe de || *tr* flairer, sentir; **to nose out** flairer, dépister || *intr*—**to nose about** fouiner; **to nose over** capoter

nose' bag' *s* musette *f*

nose'bleed' *s* saignement *m* de nez

nose' cone' *s* ogive *f*

nose' dive' *s* piqué *m*

nose'-dive' *intr* descendre en piqué

nose' drops' *spl* instillations *fpl* nasales

nose'gay' *s* bouquet *m*

nose' glass'es *spl* pince-nez *m*

nostalgia [nɑ'stældʒə] *s* nostalgie *f*

nostalgic [nɑ'stældʒɪk] *adj* nostalgique

nostril ['nɑstrɪl] *s* narine *f*; (*of horse, cow, etc.*) naseau *m*

nostrum ['nɑstrəm] *s* (*quack and his medicine*) orviétan *m*; panacée *f*

nos·y ['nozi] *adj* (*comp* -ier; *super* -iest) fureteur, indiscret

not [nɑt] *adv* ne §87, §90C; ne ... pas §90, e.g., **he is not here** il n'est pas ici; non, non pas; **not at all** pas du tout; **not much** peu de chose; **not one** pas un; **not that** non pas que; **not yet** pas encore; **to think not** croire que non

notable ['notəbəl] *adj & s* notable *m*

notarize ['notə,raɪz] *tr* authentiquer

notarized *adj* authentique

nota·ry ['notəri] *s* (*pl* **-ries**) notaire *m*

notation [no'teʃən] *s* notation *f*

notch [nɑtʃ] *s* coche *f*, entaille *f*; (*of a belt*) cran *m*; (*of a wheel*) dent *f*; (*gap in a mountain*) brèche *f* || *tr* encocher, entailler

note [not] *s* note *f*; (*short letter*) billet *m*; **notes** commentaires *mpl*; (*of a speech*) feuillets *mpl*; **note to the reader** avis *m* au lecteur || *tr* noter; **to note down** prendre note de

note'book' *s* cahier *m*; (*bill book, memo pad, etc.*) carnet *m*, calepin *m*

note'book cov'er *s* protège-cahier *m*

noted ['notɪd] *adj* éminent, distingué, connu

note' pad' *s* bloc-notes *m*

note'wor'thy *adj* notable, remarquable

nothing ['nʌθɪŋ] *s* rien *m* || *pron indef* rien §90B; ne ... rien §90, e.g., **I have nothing** je n'ai rien; **nothing at all** rien du tout; **nothing doing!** (*slang*) pas mèche! || *adv*—**nothing less than** rien moins que

nothingness ['nʌθɪŋnɪs] *s* néant *m*

notice ['notɪs] *s* (*warning; advertisement*) avis *m*; (*in a newspaper*) annonce *f*; (*observation*) attention *f*; (*of dismissal*) congé *m*; **at short notice** à bref délai; **to take notice of** faire attention à; **until further notice** jusqu'à nouvel ordre || *tr* s'apercevoir de, remarquer

noticeable ['notɪsəbəl] *adj* apparent, perceptible

notification [,notɪfɪ'keʃən] *s* notification *f*, avertissement *m*

noti·fy ['notɪ,faɪ] *v* (*pret & pp* **-fied**) *tr* aviser, avertir

notion ['noʃən] *s* notion *f*; intention *f*; **notions** mercerie *f*; **to have a notion to** avoir dans l'idée, avoir envie de

notorie·ty [,notə'raɪ·ɪti] *s* (*pl* **-ties**) renom *m* déshonorant, triste notoriété *f*

notorious [no'torɪ·əs] *adj* insigne, mal famé; (*person*) d'une triste notoriété

no'-trump' *adj & s* sans-atout *m*

notwithstanding [,nɑtwɪð'stændɪŋ], [,nɑtwɪθ'stændɪŋ] *adv* nonobstant, néanmoins || *prep* malgré || *conj* quoique

nought [nɔt] *s* var of **naught**

noun [naʊn] *s* nom *m*

nourish ['nʌrɪʃ] *tr* nourrir

nourishment ['nʌrɪʃmənt] *s* nourriture *f*, alimentation *f*

Nova Scotia ['novə'skoʃə] *s* Nouvelle-Écosse *f*; la Nouvelle-Écosse

novel ['nɑvəl] *adj* nouveau; original, bizarre || *s* roman *m*

novelette [,nɑvəl'et] *s* nouvelle *f*, bluette *f*

novelist ['nɑvəlɪst] *s* romancier *m*

novel·ty ['nɑvəlti] *s* (*pl* **-ties**) nouveauté *f*; **novelties** bibelots *mpl*, souvenirs *mpl*

November [no'vembər] *s* novembre *m*

novice ['nɑvɪs] *s* novice *mf*

novitiate [no'vɪʃɪ·ɪt] *s* noviciat *m*

novocaine ['novə,ken] *s* novocaïne *f*

now [naʊ] *adv* maintenant; **just now** tout à l'heure, naguère; **now and again** de temps en temps || *interj* allez-y!

nowadays ['naʊ·ə,dez] *adv* de nos jours

no'way' or **no'ways'** *adv* en aucune façon

no'where' *adv* nulle part; ne ... nulle part; **nowhere else** nulle autre part, nulle part ailleurs

noxious ['nɑkʃəs] *adj* nocif

nozzle ['nɑzəl] *s* (*of hose*) ajutage *m*; (*of fire hose*) lance *f*; (*of sprinkling can*) pomme *f*; (*of candlestick*) douille *f*; (*of pitcher; of gas burner*) bec *m*; (*of carburetor*) buse *f*; (*of vacuum cleaner*) suceur *m*; (*nose*) (slang) museau *m*

nth [enθ] *adj* énième, nième; **for the nth time** pour la énième fois; **the nth power** la énième puissance

nuance [nju'ɑns], ['nju·ɑns] *s* nuance *f*

nub [nʌb] *s* protubérance *f*; (*piece*) petit morceau *m*; (slang) nœud *m*

nuclear ['n(j)uklɪ·ər] *adj* nucléaire

nu'clear pow'er plant' *s* centrale *f* nucléaire

nu'clear test' ban' *s* interdiction *f* des essais nucléaires

nucleolus [n(j)u'kli·ələs] *s* nucléole *m*

nucleon ['n(j)ukli·ən] *s* nucléon *m*

nucle·us ['n(j)ukli·əs] *s* (*pl* **-i** [,aɪ] or **-uses**) noyau *m*

nude [n(j)ud] *adj* nu || *s* nu *m*; **in the nude** nu, sans vêtements

nudge [nʌdʒ] *s* coup *m* de coude || *tr* pousser du coude

nudist ['n(j)udɪst] *adj & s* nudiste *mf*

nudity ['n(j)udɪti] *s* nudité *f*

nugget ['nʌgɪt] *s* pépite *f*

nuisance ['n(j)usəns] *s* ennui *m*; (*person*) peste *f*

null [nʌl] *adj indef* nul

null' and void' *adj* nul et non avenu

nulli·fy ['nʌlɪ,faɪ] *v* (*pret & pp* **-fied**) *tr* annuler

numb [nʌm] *adj* engourdi; **to grow numb** s'engourdir || *tr* engourdir

number ['nʌmbər] *s* numéro *m*, chiffre *m*; (*quantity*) nombre *m*; **wrong number** faux numéro || *tr* numéroter; nombrer; (*to amount to*) s'élever à, compter; **to number among** compter parmi

numberless ['nʌmbərlɪs] *adj* innombrable

numbness ['nʌmnɪs] *s* engourdissement *m*

numeral ['n(j)umərəl] *adj* numéral *s* numéro *m*, chiffre *m*

numeration [ˌn(j)uməˈreʃən] s numération f

numerical [n(j)uˈmerɪkəl] adj numérique

numerous [ˈn(j)umərəs] adj nombreux

numismatic [ˌn(j)umɪzˈmætɪk] adj numismatique || **numismatics** s numismatique f

numskull [ˈnʌmˌskʌl] s (coll) sot m

nun [nʌn] s religieuse f, nonne f

nuncio [ˈnʌnʃɪˌo] s (pl -os) nonce m

nuptial [ˈnʌpʃəl] adj nuptial || **nuptials** spl noces fpl

nurse [nʌrs] s infirmière f; (male nurse) infirmier m; (wet nurse) nourrice f; (practical nurse) garde-malade mf; (children's nurse) bonne f d'enfant, nurse f || tr soigner; (hopes; plants; a baby) nourrir

nurse'maid' s bonne f d'enfant

nurser·y [ˈnʌrsəri] s (pl -ies) chambre f des enfants; (for day care) crèche f, pouponnière f; (hort) pépinière f

nurs'ery·man s (pl -men) pépiniériste m

nurs'ery school' s maternelle f

nursing [ˈnʌrsɪŋ] s soins mpl; (profession) métier m d'infirmière; (by mother) allaitement m

nurs'ing bot'tle s biberon m

nurs'ing home' s maison f de repos, maison de santé

nursling [ˈnʌrslɪŋ] s nourrisson m

nurture [ˈnʌrtʃər] s éducation f; nourriture f || tr élever; (to nurse) nourrir

nut [nʌt] s noix f, e.g., **Brazil nut** noix du Brésil; (of walnut tree) noix; (of filbert) noisette f; (to screw on a bolt) écrou m; (slang) extravagant m; **to be nuts about** (slang) être follement épris de

nut'crack'er s casse-noisettes m, casse-noix m; (orn) casse-noix

nut'hatch' s sittelle f

nut'meat' s graine f de fruit sec, graine de noix

nutmeg [ˈnʌtˌmeg] s (seed or spice) noix f muscade, muscade f; (tree) muscadier m

nutriment [ˈn(j)utrɪmənt] s nourriture f

nutrition [n(j)uˈtrɪʃən] s nutrition f

nutritious [n(j)uˈtrɪʃəs] adj nutritif

nut'shell' s coquille f de noix; **in a nutshell** en un mot

nut·ty [ˈnʌti] adj (comp -tier; super -tiest) à goût de noisette, à goût de noix; (slang) cinglé

nuzzle [ˈnʌzəl] tr fouiller du groin || intr fouiller du groin; s'envelopper chaudement; **to nuzzle up to** se pelotonner contre

nylon [ˈnaɪlɑn] s nylon m; **nylons** bas mpl de nylon, bas nylon

nymph [nɪmf] s nymphe f

O

O, o [o] s XVᵉ lettre de l'alphabet

oaf [of] s lourdaud m, rustre m

oak [ok] s chêne m

oaken [ˈokən] adj de chêne, en chêne

oakum [ˈokəm] s étoupe f

oar [or], [ɔr] s rame f, aviron m

oar'lock' s tolet m

oars'man' s (pl -men') rameur m

oa·sis [oˈesɪs] s (pl -ses [siz]) oasis f

oat [ot] s avoine f; **oats** (edible grain) avoine; **to feel one's oats** être imbu de sa personne; **to sow one's wild oats** (coll) jeter sa gourme

oath [oθ] s (pl oaths [oðz]) serment m; (swearword) juron m; **to administer an oath** to (law) faire prêter serment à; **to take an oath** prêter serment

oat'meal' s farine f d'avoine; (breakfast food) flocons mpl d'avoine

obbligato [ˌɑblɪˈgɑto] s accompagnement m à volonté

obdurate [ˈɑbdjərɪt] adj obstiné, endurci

obedience [oˈbidɪəns] s obéissance f

obedient [oˈbidɪənt] adj obéissant

obeisance [oˈbesəns], [oˈbisəns] s hommage m; (greeting) révérence f

obelisk [ˈɑbəlɪsk] s obélisque m

obese [oˈbis] adj obèse

obesity [oˈbisɪti] s obésité f

obey [əˈbe] tr obéir (with dat); **to be obeyed** être obéi || intr obéir

obfuscate [ɑbˈfʌsket], [ˈɑbfəsˌket] tr offusquer

obituar·y [oˈbɪtʃuˌeri] adj nécrologique || s (pl -ies) nécrologie f

object [ˈɑbdʒɪkt] s objet m || [əbˈdʒekt] tr objecter, rétorquer || intr faire des objections; **to object to** s'opposer à, avoir des objections contre

objection [əbˈdʒekʃən] s objection f

objectionable [əbˈdʒekʃənəbəl] adj répréhensible; répugnant, désagréable

objective [əbˈdʒektɪv] adj & s objectif m

obligate [ˈɑblɪˌget] tr obliger

obligation [ˌɑblɪˈgeʃən] s obligation f

obligatory [ˈɑblɪgəˌtori], [əˈblɪgəˌtori] adj obligatoire

oblige [əˈblaɪdʒ] tr obliger; **much obliged** bien obligé, très reconnaissant; **to be obliged to** être obligé de

obliging [əˈblaɪdʒɪŋ] adj accommodant, obligeant

oblique [əˈblik], [əˈblaɪk] adj oblique

obliterate [əˈblɪtəˌret] tr effacer, oblitérer

oblivion [əˈblɪvɪən] s oubli m

oblivious [əˈblɪvɪəs] adj oublieux

oblong [ˈɑblɔŋ], [ˈɑblɑŋ] adj oblong

obnoxious [əb'nɑk/əs] *adj* odieux, désagréable

oboe ['obo] *s* hautbois *m*

oboist ['obo·ɪst] *s* hautboïste *mf*

obscene [ab'sin] *adj* obscène

obsceni·ty [ab'sɛnɪti], [ab'sinɪti] *s* (*pl* -ties) obscénité *f*

obscure [əb'skjʊr] *adj* obscur; (*vowel*) relâché, neutre

obscuri·ty [əb'skjʊrɪti] *s* (*pl* -ties) obscurité *f*

obsequies ['absɪkwiz] *spl* obsèques *fpl*

obsequious [əb'sikwi·əs] *adj* obséquieux

observance [əb'zʌrvəns] *s* observance *f*

observant [əb'zʌrvənt] *adj* observateur

observation [ˌabzər've/ən] *s* observation *f*

observato·ry [əb'zʌrvə,tori] *s* (*pl* -ries) observatoire *m*

observe [əb'zʌrv] *tr* observer; (*silence*) garder; (*a holiday*) célébrer; dire, remarquer

observer [əb'zʌrvər] *s* observateur *m*

obsess [ab'sɛs] *tr* obséder

obsession [ab'sɛ/ən] *s* obsession *f*

obsolescent [ˌabsə'lɛsənt] *adj* vieillissant

obsolete ['absəlit] *adj* désuet, vieilli; (*gram*) obsolète

obstacle ['abstəkəl] *s* obstacle *m*

ob'stacle course' *s* champ *m* d'obstacles, piste *f* d'obstacles

obstetrical [ab'stɛtrɪkəl] *adj* obstétrique

obstetrics [ab'stɛtrɪks] *spl* obstétrique *f*

obstina·cy ['abstɪnəsi] *s* (*pl* -cies) obstination *f*, entêtement *m*

obstinate ['abstɪnɪt] *adj* obstiné

obstreperous [əb'strɛpərəs] *adj* turbulent

obstruct [əb'strʌkt] *tr* obstruer; (*movements*) empêcher, entraver

obstruction [əb'strʌk/ən] *s* obstruction *f*; (*on railroad tracks*) obstacle *m*; (*to movement*) empêchement *m*, entrave *f*

obtain [əb'ten] *tr* obtenir, se procurer || *intr* prévaloir

obtrusive [əb'trusɪv] *adj* importun, intrus

obtuse [əb't(j)us] *adj* obtus

obviate ['abvɪ,et] *tr* obvier (with *dat*)

obvious ['abvɪ·əs] *adj* évident

occasion [ə'keʒən] *s* occasion *f*; **on occasion** en de différentes occasions || *tr* occasionner

occasional [ə'keʒənəl] *adj* fortuit, occasionnel; (*verses*) de circonstance; (*showers*) épars; (*chair*) volant

occasionally [ə'keʒənəli] *adv* de temps en temps, occasionnellement

occident ['aksɪdənt] *s* occident *m*

occidental [ˌaksə'dɛntəl] *adj & s* occidental *m*

occlusion [ə'kluʒən] *s* occlusion *f*

occlusive [ə'klusɪv] *adj* occlusif || *s* occlusive *f*

occult [ə'kʌlt], ['akʌlt] *adj* occulte

occupancy ['akjəpənsi] *s* occupation *f*, habitation *f*

occupant ['akjəpənt] *s* occupant *m*

occupation [ˌakjə'pe/ən] *s* occupation *f*

occupational [ˌakjə'pe/ənəl] *adj* professionnel; de métier

oc'cupa'tional ther'apy *s* thérapie *f* rééducative, réadaptation *f* fonctionnelle

occu·py ['akjə,paɪ] *v* (*pret & pp* -**pied**) *tr* occuper; **to be occupied with** s'occuper de

oc·cur [ə'kʌr] *v* (*pret & pp* -**curred**; *ger* -**curring**) *intr* arriver, avoir lieu; (*to be found; to come to mind*) se présenter; **it occurs to me that** il me vient à l'esprit que

occurrence [ə'kʌrəns] *s* événement *m*; cas *m*, exemple *m*; **everyday occurrence** fait *m* journalier

ocean ['o/ən] *s* océan *m*

oceanic [ˌo/ɪ'ænɪk] *adj* océanique

o'cean lin'er *s* paquebot *m* transocéanique

ocher ['okər] *s* ocre *f*

o'clock [ə'klak] *adv*—**it is one o'clock** il est une heure; **it is two o'clock** il est deux heures

octane ['akten] *s* octane *m*

oc'tane num'ber *s* indice *m* d'octane

octave ['aktɪv], ['aktev] *s* octave *f*

October [ak'tobər] *s* octobre *m*

octo·pus [ˌakto'run] *s* (*pl* -**puses** or -**pi** [ˌpaɪ]) pieuvre *f*, poulpe *m*

octoroon [ˌakto'run] *s* octavon *m*

ocular ['akjələr] *adj & s* oculaire *m*

oculist ['akjəlɪst] *s* oculiste *mf*

odd [ad] *adj* (*number*) impair; (*that doesn't match*) dépareillé, déparié; (*queer*) bizarre, étrange; (*occasional*) divers; quelque, e.g., **three hundred odd horses** quelque trois cents chevaux; et quelques || **odds** *spl* chances *fpl*; (*disparity*) inégalité *f*; (*on a horse*) cote *f*; **at odds** en désaccord, en bisbille; **by all odds** sans aucun doute; **to be at odds with** être mal avec; **to give odds to** donner de l'avance à; **to set at odds** brouiller

oddi·ty ['adɪti] *s* (*pl* -ties) bizarrerie *f*

odd' jobs' *spl* bricolage *m*, petits travaux *mpl*

odd' man' out' *s*—**to be the odd man out** être en trop

odds' and ends' *spl* petits bouts *mpl*, bribes *fpl*; (*trinkets*) bibelots *mpl*; (*food*) restes *mpl*

ode [od] *s* ode *f*

odious ['odɪ·əs] *adj* odieux

odor ['odər] *s* odeur *f*; **to be in bad odor** être mal vu

odorless ['odərlɪs] *adj* inodore

Odyssey ['adɪsi] *s* Odyssée *f*

Oedipus ['ɛdɪpəs], ['idəpəs] *s* Œdipe *m*

of [av], [ʌv], [ʌ] *prep* de; à, e.g., **to think of** penser à; e.g., **to ask s.th. of s.o.** demander q.ch. à qn; en, e.g., **a doctor of medicine** un docteur en médecine; moins, e.g., **a quarter of two** deux heures moins le quart; entre, e.g., **he of all people** lui entre tous; d'entre, e.g., **five of them** cinq d'entre eux; par, e.g., **of necessity** par nécessité; en or de, e.g., **made of**

wood en bois, de bois; (not translated), e.g., **the fifth of March** le cinq mars; e.g., **we often see her of a morning** nous la voyons souvent le matin

off [ɔf], [ɑf] *adj* mauvais, e.g., **off day** (*bad day*) mauvaise journée; libre, e.g., **off day** journée libre; de congé, e.g., **off day** jour de congé; (*account*, *sum*) inexact; (*meat*) avancé; (*electric current*) coupé; (*light*) éteint; (*radio*; *faucet*) fermé; (*street*) secondaire, transversal; (*distant*) éloigné, écarté ‖ *adv* loin; à . . . de distance, e.g., **three kilometers off** à trois kilomètres de distance; parti, e.g., **they're off!** les voilà partis!; bas, e.g., **hats off!** chapeaux bas!; (naut) au large; (theat) à la cantonade ‖ *prep* de; (*at a distance from*) éloigné de, écarté de; (naut) au large de, à la hauteur de; **from off** de dessous de

offal [ˈɑfəl], [ˈɔfəl] *s* (*of butchered meat*) abats *mpl*; (*refuse*) ordures *fpl*

off' and on' *adv* de temps en temps, par intervalles

off'beat' *adj* (slang) insolite, rare

off' chance' *s* chance *f* improbable

off'-col'or *adj* décoloré; (*e.g.*, *story*) grivois, vert

offend [əˈfɛnd] *tr* offenser; **to be offended** s'offenser ‖ *intr*—**to offend against** enfreindre

offender [əˈfɛndər] *s* offenseur *m*; (*criminal*) délinquant *m*, coupable *mf*

offense [əˈfɛns] *s* offense *f*; (law) délit *m*; **to take offense** (**at**) s'offenser (de)

offensive [əˈfɛnsɪv] *adj* offensant, blessant; (mil) offensif ‖ *s* offensive *f*

offer [ˈɔfər], [ˈɑfər] *s* offre *f* ‖ *tr* offrir; (*excuses*; *best wishes*) présenter; (*prayers*) adresser ‖ *intr*—**to offer to** faire l'offre de; faire mine de, e.g., **he offered to fight** il a fait mine de se battre

offering [ˈɔfərɪŋ], [ˈɑfərɪŋ] *s* offre *f*; (eccl) offrande *f*

off'hand' *adj* improvisé; brusque ‖ *adv* au pied levé; brusquement

office [ˈɔfɪs], [ˈɑfɪs] *s* fonction *f*, office *m*; (in business, school, government) bureau *m*; (national agency) office *m*; (of lawyer) étude *f*; (of doctor) cabinet *m*; **elective office** poste *m* électif; **good offices** bons offices; **to run for office** se présenter aux élections

of'fice boy' *s* coursier *m*, commissionnaire *m* de bureau

of'fice desk' *s* bureau *m* ministre

of'fice-hold'er *s* fonctionnaire *mf*

of'fice hours' *spl* heures *fpl* de bureau; (of doctor, counselor, etc.) heures de consultation

officer [ˈɔfɪsər], [ˈɑfɪsər] *s* (of a company) administrateur *m*, dirigeant *m*; (of army, an order, a society, etc.) officier *m*; (police officer) agent *m* de police, officier de police; **officer of the day** (mil) officier de service

of'ficer can'didate *s* élève-officier *m*

of'fice seek'er *s* solliciteur *m*

of'fice supplies' *spl* fournitures *fpl* de bureau, articles *mpl* de bureau

of'fice-supply' store' *s* papeterie *f*

of'fice work' *s* travail *m* de bureau

official [əˈfɪʃəl] *adj* officiel; (*e.g.*, *stationery*) réglementaire ‖ *s* fonctionnaire *mf*, officiel *m*; **officials** cadres *mpl*; (executives) dirigeants *mpl*

offi'cial board' *s* comité *m* directeur

officialese [ə‚fɪʃəˈliz] *s* jargon *m* administratif

officiate [əˈfɪʃɪˌet] *intr* (eccl) officier; **to officiate as** exercer les fonctions de

officious [əˈfɪʃəs] *adj* trop empressé; **to be officious** faire l'officieux

offing [ˈɔfɪŋ], [ˈɑfɪŋ] *s*—**in the offing** au large; (fig) en perspective

off'-lim'its *adj* défendu; (public sign) défense d'entrer, entrée interdite; (mil) interdit aux troupes

off'-peak heat'er *s* thermosiphon *m* à accumulation

off'print' *s* tiré *m* à part

off'-sea'son *s* morte-saison *f*

off'set' *s* compensation *f*; (typ) offset *m* ‖ **off'set'** *tr* (pret & pp -set; ger -setting) compenser

off'shoot' *s* rejeton *m*

off'shore' *adj* éloigné de la côte, du côté de la terre; (wind) de terre ‖ *adv* au large, vers la haute mer

off'side' *adv* (sports) hors jeu

off'spring' *s* descendance *f*; (descendant) rejeton *m*, enfant *mf*; (result) conséquence *f*

off'stage' *adj* dans les coulisses ‖ *adv* à la cantonade

off'-the-cuff' *adj* (coll) impromptu

off'-the-rec'ord *adj* confidentiel

often [ˈɔfən], [ˈɑfən] *adv* souvent; **how often?** combien de fois?; tous les combien?; **not often** rarement; **once too often** une fois de trop

ogive [ˈodʒaɪv], [oˈdʒaɪv] *s* ogive *f*

ogle [ˈogəl] *tr* lancer une œillade à; (to stare at) dévisager

ogre [ˈogər] *s* ogre *m*

ohm [om] *s* ohm *m*

oil [ɔɪl] *s* huile *f*; (painting) huile, peinture *f* à l'huile; **holy oil** huile sainte, saintes huiles; **to pour oil on troubled waters** calmer la tempête, verser de l'huile sur les plaies de qn; **to smell of midnight oil** sentir l'huile; **to strike oil** atteindre une nappe pétrolifère; (fig) trouver le filon ‖ *tr* huiler; (to bribe) graisser la patte à ‖ *intr* (naut) faire le plein de mazout

oil' burn'er *s* réchaud *m* à pétrole

oil'can' *s* bidon *m* d'huile, burette *f* d'huile

oil'cloth' *s* toile *f* cirée

oil' com'pany *s* société *f* pétrolière

oil'cup' *s* (mach) godet *m* graisseur

oil' drum' *s* bidon *m* d'huile

oil' field' *s* gisement *m* pétrolifère

oil' gauge' *s* jauge *f* de niveau d'huile

oil′ lamp′ s lampe f à huile, lampe à pétrole

oil′man′ s (pl **-men′**) (retailer) huilier m; (operator) pétrolier m

oil′ pump′ s pompe f à huile

oil′ stove′ s poêle m à mazout, fourneau m à pétrole

oil′ tank′er s pétrolier m, tanker m

oil′ well′ s puits m à pétrole

oil·y [′ɔɪli] adj (comp **-ier;** super **-iest**) huileux, oléagineux; (fig) onctueux

ointment [′ɔɪntmənt] s onguent m, pommade f

O.K. [′o′ke] (letterword) adj (coll) très bien, parfait || s (coll) approbation f || adv (coll) très bien || v (pret & pp **O.K.′d;** ger **O.K.′ing**) v (coll) approuver || interj O.K.!, ça colle!

okra [′okrə] s gombo m, ketmie f comestible

old [old] adj vieux; (of former times) ancien; (wine) vieux; **any old** n'importe, e.g., **any old time** n'importe quand; quelconque, e.g., **any old book** un livre quelconque; **at . . . years old** à l'âge de . . . ans; **how old is . . .?** quel âge a . . . ?; **of old** d'autrefois, de jadis; **to be . . . years old** avoir . . . ans

old′ age′ s vieillesse f, âge m avancé

old′-clothes′man′ s (pl **-men′**) fripier m

old′ coun′try s mère patrie f

Old′ Cov′enant s (Bib) ancienne alliance f

old′-fash′ioned adj démodé, suranné; (literary style) vieillot

old′ fo′gey or **old′ fo′gy** [′fogi] s (pl **-gies**) vieux bonhomme m, grime f

Old′ French′ s ancien français m

Old′ Glo′ry s le drapeau des États-Unis

old′ hag′ s vieille fée f

old′ hand′ s vieux routier m

old′ lad′y s vieille dame f; (coll) grand-mère f

old′ maid′ s vieille fille f

old′ mas′ter s grand maître m; œuvre f d'un grand maître

old′ moon′ s Lune f à son décours

old′ peo′ple′s home′ s hospice m de vieillards

old′ salt′ s loup m de mer

old′ school′ s vieille école f, vieille roche f

oldster [′oldstər] s vieillard m, vieux m

Old′ Tes′tament s Ancien Testament m

old′-time′ adj du temps jadis, d'autrefois

old′-tim′er s (coll) vieux m de la vieille, vieux routier m

old′ wives′′ tale′ s conte m de bonne femme

Old Wom′an who lived′ in a shoe′ s mère l'Oie f Gigogne

Old′ World′ s vieux monde m

old′-world′ adj de l'ancien monde; du vieux monde

oleander [,oli′ændər] s laurier-rose m

olfactory [ɑl′fæktəri] adj olfactif

oligar·chy [′ɑlɪ,gɑrki] s (pl **-chies**) oligarchie f

olive [′ɑlɪv] adj olive; (complexion) olivâtre || s olive f; (tree) olivier m

ol′ive branch′ s rameau m d'olivier

ol′ive grove′ s olivaie f

ol′ive oil′ s huile f d'olive

Oliver [′ɑlɪvər] s Olivier m

ol′ive tree′ s olivier m

olympiad [o′lɪmpɪ,æd] s olympiade f

Olympian [o′lɪmpɪ·ən] adj olympien

Olympic [o′lɪmpɪk] adj olympique || **Olympics** spl jeux mpl olympiques

omelet [′ɑmə,let], [′ɑmlɪt] s omelette f

omen [′omən] s augure m, présage m

ominous [′ɑmɪnəs] adj de mauvais augure

omission [o′mɪʃən] s omission f

omit [o′mɪt] v (pret & pp **omitted;** ger **omitting**) tr omettre

omnibus [′ɑmnɪ,bʌs], [′ɑmnɪbəs] adj & s omnibus m

omnipotent [ɑm′nɪpətənt] adj omnipotent

omniscient [ɑm′nɪʃənt] adj omniscient

omnivorous [ɑm′nɪvərəs] adj omnivore

on [ɑn], [ɔn] adj (light, radio) allumé; (faucet) ouvert; (machine, motor) en marche; (electrical appliance) branché; (brake) serré; (steak, chops, etc.) dans la poêle; (game, program, etc.) commencé || adv—**and so on** et ainsi de suite; **come on!** (coll) allons donc!; **farther on** plus loin; **from this day on** à dater de ce jour; **later on** plus tard; **move on!** circulez!; **to be on** (theat) être en scène; **to be on to s.o.** (coll) voir clair dans le jeu de qn; **to have on** être vêtu de, porter; **to . . . on** continuer à + inf, e.g., **to sing on** continuer à chanter; **well on** avancé, e.g., **well on in years** d'un âge avancé, e.g., **well on in years** d'un âge avancé || prep sur; (at the time of) lors de; à, e.g., **on foot** à pied; e.g., **on my arrival** à mon arrivée; e.g., **on page three** à la page trois; e.g., **on the first floor** au rez-de-chaussée; e.g., **on the right** à droite; en, e.g., **on a journey** en voyage; e.g., **on arriving** en arrivant; e.g., **on fire** en feu; e.g., **on sale** en vente; e.g., **on the** or **an average** en moyenne; e.g., **on the top of** en dessus de; dans, e.g., **on a farm** dans une ferme; e.g., **on the jury** dans le jury; e.g., **on the street** dans la rue; e.g., **on the train** dans le train; par, e.g., **he came on the train** il est venu par le train; de, e.g., **on a fine day** par un beau jour; de, e.g., **on good authority** de source certaine, de bonne part; e.g., **on the north** du côté du nord; e.g., **on the one hand . . . on the other hand** d'une part . . . d'autre part; e.g., **on this side of** de ce côté-ci; e.g., **to have pity on** avoir pitié de; e.g., **to live on bread and water** vivre de pain et d'eau; sous, e.g., **on a charge of** sous l'inculpation de; e.g., **on pain of death** sous peine de mort; (not translated), e.g., **on Tuesday** mardi; e.g., **on Tuesdays** le mardi, tous les mardis; e.g., **on July fourteenth** le quatorze juillet; contre, e.g., **an attack on** une attaque contre; **it's on me** (*it's my turn to pay*) (coll) c'est ma tournée; **it's on the house** (coll) c'est la tournée du patron; **on examination** après examen; **on it** y, e.g., **there is the shelf; put the book on it** voilà l'étagère; mettez-y le livre; **on or about** (*a certain date*) aux environs de; **on or after** (*a certain date*) à partir de; **on tap** en perce, à la pression; **on the spot** (*immediately*) sur-le-champ; (*there*) sur place; (slang) en danger imminent; **to be on the committee** faire partie du comité; **to march on a city** marcher sur une ville

on′ and on′ *adv* continuellement, sans fin

once [wʌns] *s*—**this once** pour cette fois-ci ‖ *adv* une fois; (*formerly*) autrefois; **all at once** (*all together*) tous à la fois; (*suddenly*) tout à coup; **at once** tout de suite, sur-le-champ; (*at the same time*) à la fois, en même temps; **for once** pour une fois; **once and for all** une bonne fois, une fois pour toutes; **once in a while** de temps en temps; **once more** encore une fois; **once or twice** une ou deux fois; **once upon a time there was** il était une fois ‖ *conj* une fois que, dès que

once′-o′ver *s* (slang) examen *m* rapide; travail *m* hâtif; **to give the once-over to** (slang) jeter un coup d'œil à

one [wʌn] *adj & pron* un; un certain, e.g., **one Dupont** un certain Dupont; un seul, e.g., **with one voice** d'une seule voix; unique, e.g., **one price** prix unique; (not translated when preceded by an adjective), e.g., **the red pencil and the blue one** le crayon rouge et le bleu; **not one** pas un; **one and all** tous; **one and only** unique, e.g., **the one and only closet in the house** l'armoire unique de la maison; seul et unique, e.g., **my one and only umbrella** mon seul et unique parapluie; **one another** l'un l'autre; les uns les autres; **one by one** un à un; **that one** celui-là; **the one that** celui que, celui qui; **this one** celui-ci; **to become one** s'unir, se marier ‖ *s* un *m*; **one o'clock** une heure ‖ *pron indef* on §87, e.g., **one cannot go there alone** on ne peut pas y aller seul; **one's** son, e.g., **one's son** son fils

one′-horse′ *adj* à un cheval; (coll) provincial, insignifiant

one′-horse town′ *s* (coll) trou *m*

onerous [′ɑnərəs] *adj* onéreux

one·self′ *pron* soi §85; soi-même §86; se §87, e.g., **to cut oneself se** couper; **to be oneself** se conduire sans affectation

one′-sid′ed *adj* à un côté, à une face; (*e.g., decision*) unilatéral; (*unfair*) partial, injuste

one′-track′ *adj* à une voie; (coll) routinier

one′-way′ *adj* à sens unique

one′-way tick′et *s* billet *m* d'aller, billet simple

onion [′ʌnjən] *s* oignon *m*; **to know one's onions** (coll) connaître son affaire

on′ion-skin′ *s* papier *m* pelure

on′look′er *s* assistant *m*, spectateur *m*

only [′onli] *adj* seul, unique; (*child*) unique ‖ *adv* seulement; ne . . . que, e.g., **I have only two** je n'en ai que deux; réservé, e.g., **staff only** (public sign) réservé au personnel ‖ *conj* mais, si ce n'était que

on′rush′ *s* ruée *f*

on′set′ *s* attaque *f*; **at the onset of** prime abord, au premier abord

onslaught [′ɑn‚slɔt], [′ɔn‚slɔt] *s* assaut *m*

on′-the-job′ *adj* (*training*) en stage; (coll) alerte

onus [′onəs] *s* charge *f*, fardeau *m*

onward [′ɑnwərd] or **onwards** [′ɑn‚wərdz] *adv* en avant

onyx [′ɑnɪks] *s* onyx *m*

ooze [uz] *s* suintement *m*; (*mud*) vase *f*, limon *m* ‖ *tr* filtrer ‖ *intr* suinter, filtrer; **to ooze out** s'écouler

opal [′opəl] *s* opale *f*

opaque [o′pek] *adj* opaque; (*style*) obscur

open [′opən] *adj* ouvert; (*personality*) franc, sincère; (*job, position*) vacant; (*hour*) libre; (*automobile*) découvert; (*market; trial*) public; (*question*) pendant, indécis; (*wound*) béant; (*to attack, to criticism, etc.*) exposé; (sports) international; **to break or crack open** éventrer; **to throw open the door** ouvrir la porte toute grande ‖ *s* ouverture *f*; (*in the woods*) clairière *f*; **in the open** au grand air, à ciel ouvert; (*in the open country*) en rase campagne; (*in the open sea*) en pleine mer; (*without being hidden*) découvert; (*openly*) ouvertement ‖ *tr* ouvrir; (*a canal lock*) lâcher; **to open fire** déclencher le feu ‖ *intr* ouvrir, s'ouvrir; (*said, e.g., of a play*) commencer, débuter; **to open into** aboutir à, déboucher sur; **to open on** donner sur; **to open up** s'épanouir, s'ouvrir

o′pen-air′ *adj* en plein air, au grand air

o′pen-eyed′ *adj* les yeux écarquillés

o′pen-hand′ed *adj* libéral, la main ouverte

o′pen-heart′ed *adj* ouvert, franc

o′pen-heart′ sur′gery *s* chirurgie *f* à cœur ouvert

o′pen house′ *s* journée *f* d'accueil; **to keep open house** tenir table ouverte

opening [′opənɪŋ] *s* ouverture *f*; (*in the woods*) clairière *f*; (*vacancy*) vacance *f*, poste *m* vacant; (*chance to say something*) occasion *f* favorable

o′pening night′ *s* première *f*

o′pening num′ber *s* ouverture *f*

o′pening price′ *s* cours *m* de début

o′pen-mind′ed *adj* à l'esprit ouvert, sans parti pris

o′pen se′cret *s* secret *m* de Polichinelle

o′pen shop′ *s* atelier *m* ouvert aux non-syndiqués

o'pen·work' s ouvrage m à jour, ajours mpl

opera ['ɑpərə] s opéra m

op'era glass'es spl jumelles fpl de spectacle

op'era hat' s claque m, gibus m

op'era house' s opéra m

operate ['ɑpə‚ret] tr actionner, faire marcher; exploiter || intr fonctionner; s'opérer; (surg) opérer; to operate on (surg) opérer

operatic [‚ɑpə'rætɪk] adj d'opéra

opera'ting expen'ses spl (overhead) frais mpl généraux, frais d'exploitation

op'erating room' s salle f d'opération

op'erating ta'ble s table f d'opération, billard m

operation [‚ɑpə'reʃən] s opération f; (of a business, of a machine, etc.) fonctionnement m; (med) intervention f chirurgicale, opération

operative ['ɑpə‚retɪv], ['ɑpərətɪv] adj opératif; (surg) opératoire || s (workman) ouvrier m; (spy) agent m, espion m

operator ['ɑpə‚retər] s opérateur m; (e.g., of a mine) propriétaire m exploitant; (of an automobile) conducteur m; téléphoniste mf, standardiste mf; (slang) chevalier m d'industrie, aigrefin m

operetta [‚ɑpə'retə] s opérette f

opiate ['opɪ‚ɪt], ['opɪ‚et] adj opiacé || s médicament m opiacé; (coll) narcotique m

opinion [ə'pɪnjən] s opinion f; in my opinion à mon avis

opinionated [ə'pɪnjə‚netɪd] adj fier de ses opinions, dogmatique

opium ['opɪ‚əm] s opium m

o'pium den' s fumerie f

o'pium pop'py s œillette f

opossum [ə'pɑsəm] s opossum m, sarigue f

opponent [ə'ponənt] s adversaire mf, opposant m

opportune [‚ɑpər't(j)un] adj opportun, convenable

opportunist [‚ɑpər't(j)unɪst] s opportuniste mf

opportuni·ty [‚ɑpər't(j)unɪti] s (pl -ties) occasion f; chance f

oppose [ə'poz] tr s'opposer à

opposite ['ɑpəsɪt] adj opposé, contraire; d'en face, e.g., the house opposite la maison d'en face || s opposé m, contraire m || adv en face, vis-à-vis || prep en face de, à l'opposite de

op'posite num'ber s (fig) homologue mf

opposition [‚ɑpə'zɪʃən] s opposition f

oppress [ə'pres] tr opprimer; (to weigh heavily upon) oppresser

oppression [ə'preʃən] s oppression f

oppressive [ə'presɪv] adj oppressif; (stifling) étouffant, accablant

oppressor [ə'presər] s oppresseur m

opprobrious [ə'probrɪ‚əs] adj infamant, injurieux, honteux

opprobrium [ə'probrɪ‚əm] s opprobre m

optic ['ɑptɪk] adj optique || optics s optique f

optical ['ɑptɪkəl] adj optique

op'tical illu'sion s illusion f d'optique

optician [ɑp'tɪʃən] s opticien m

optimism ['ɑptɪ‚mɪzəm] s optimisme m

optimist ['ɑptɪmɪst] s optimiste mf

optimistic [‚ɑptɪ'mɪstɪk] adj optimiste

option ['ɑpʃən] s option f

optional ['ɑpʃənəl] adj facultatif

optometrist [ɑp'tɑmɪtrɪst] s opticien m; optométriste mf (Canad)

opulent ['ɑpjələnt] adj opulent

or [ɔr] conj ou

oracle ['ɔrəkəl], ['ɑrəkəl] s oracle m

oracular [o'rækjələr] adj d'oracle; dogmatique, sentencieux; (ambiguous) équivoque

oral ['ɔrəl] adj oral

orange ['ɑrɪndʒ], ['ɔrɪndʒ] adj orangé, orange || s (color) orangé m, orange m; (fruit) orange f

orangeade [‚ɑrɪndʒ'ed], [‚ɔrɪndʒ'ed] s orangeade f

or'ange blos'som s fleur f d'oranger

or'ange grove' s orangeraie f

or'ange juice' s jus m d'orange

or'ange squeez'er s presse-fruits m

or'ange tree' s oranger m

orang-outang [o'ræŋu‚tæŋ] s orang-outan m

oration [o'reʃən] s discours m

orator ['ɔrətər], ['ɑrətər] s orateur m

oratorical [‚ɔrə'tɑrɪkəl], [‚ɑrə'tɔrɪkəl] adj oratoire

oratori·o [‚ɔrə'torɪ‚o], [‚ɑrə'torɪ‚o] s (pl -os) oratorio m

orato·ry ['ɔrə‚tori], ['ɑrə‚tori] s (pl -ries) art m oratoire; (eccl) oratoire m

orb [ɔrb] s orbe m

orbit ['ɔrbɪt] s orbite f; in orbit sur orbite || tr (e.g., the sun) tourner autour de; (e.g., a rocket) mettre en orbite, satelliser || intr se mettre en orbite

orchard ['ɔrtʃərd] s verger m

orchestra ['ɔrkɪstrə] s orchestre m

orchestrate ['ɔrkɪ‚stret] tr orchestrer

orchid ['ɔrkɪd] s orchidée f

ordain [ɔr'den] tr destiner; (eccl) ordonner; to be ordained (eccl) recevoir les ordres

ordeal [ɔr'dil], [ɔr'di‚əl] s épreuve f; (hist) ordalie f

order ['ɔrdər] s ordre m; (of words) ordonnance f; (for merchandise, a meal, etc.) commande f; (military formation) ordre; (law) arrêt m, arrêté m; in order en ordre; in order of appearance (theat) dans l'ordre d'entrée en scène; in order that pour que, afin que; in order to + inf pour + inf, afin de + inf; on order en commande, commandé; order! à l'ordre!; orders (eccl) les ordres; (mil) la consigne; pay to the order of (com) payez à l'ordre de; to get s.th. out of order détraquer q.ch.; to put in order mettre en règle || tr ordonner; (com) commander; to order around faire aller et venir; **to order s.o. to +** *inf* ordonner à qn de + *inf*

or′der blank′ *s* bon *m* de commande, bulletin *m* de commande

order·ly [′ɔrdərli] *adj* ordonné; (*life*) réglé; **to be orderly avoir de l'ordre** ‖ *s* (*pl* **-lies**) (*med*) ambulancier *m*, infirmier *m*; (*mil*) planton *m*

ordinal [′ɔrdɪnəl] *adj & s* ordinal *m*

ordinance [′ɔrdɪnəns] *s* ordonnance *f*

ordinary [′ɔrdɪˌɛri] *adj* ordinaire; **out of the ordinary** exceptionnel

ordination [ˌɔrdɪ′neʃən] *s* ordination *f*

ordnance [′ɔrdnəns] *s* artillerie *f*; (*branch of an army*) service *m* du matériel

ore [or] *s* minerai *m*

oregano [ə′regəˌno] *s* origan *m*

organ [′ɔrgən] *s* (anat, journ) organe *m*; (mus) orgue *m*

organdy [′ɔrgəndi] *s* organdi *m*

or′gan grind′er *s* joueur *m* d'orgue

organic [ɔr′gænɪk] *adj* organique

organism [′ɔrgəˌnɪzəm] *s* organisme *m*

organist [′ɔrgənɪst] *s* organiste *mf*

organization [ˌɔrgənɪ′zeʃən] *s* organisation *f*

organize [′ɔrgəˌnaɪz] *tr* organiser

organizer [′ɔrgəˌnaɪzər] *s* organisateur *m*

or′gan loft′ *s* tribune *f* d'orgue

orgasm [′ɔrgæzəm] *s* orgasme *m*

or·gy [′ɔrdʒi] *s* (*pl* **-gies**) orgie *f*

orient [′ɔrɪ·ənt] *s* orient *m*; **Orient** Orient ‖ [′ɔrɪˌɛnt] *tr* orienter

oriental [ˌɔrɪ′ɛntəl] *adj* oriental *f*; (*cap*) Oriental *m*

orientate [′ɔrɪ·ɛnˌtet] *tr* orienter

orientation [ˌɔrɪ·ɛn′teʃən] *s* orientation *f*

orifice [′ɑrɪfɪs], [′ɔrɪfɪs] *s* orifice *m*

origin [′ɑrədʒɪn], [′ɔrədʒɪn] *s* origine *f*

original [ə′rɪdʒɪnəl] *adj* (*new, not copied; inventive*) original; (*earliest*) originel, primitif; (*first*) originaire, premier ‖ *s* original *m*

originality [əˌrɪdʒɪ′nælɪti] *s* originalité *f*

originate [ə′rɪdʒəˌnet] *tr* faire naître, créer ‖ *intr* prendre naissance; **to originate from** provenir de

oriole [′ɔrɪˌol], [′ɔrɪˌol] *s* loriot *m*

ormolu [′ɔrməˌlu] *s* bronze *m* doré; (*powdered gold for gilding*) or *m* moulu; (*alloy of zinc and copper*) similor *m*

ornament [′ɔrnəmənt] *s* ornement *m* ‖ [′ɔrnəˌmɛnt] *tr* ornementer, orner

ornamental [ˌɔrnə′mɛntəl] *adj* ornemental

ornate [ɔr′net], [′ɔrnet] *adj* orné, fleuri

ornery [′ɔrnəri] *adj* (coll) acariâtre, intraitable

ornithology [ˌɔrnɪ′θɑlədʒi] *f* ornithologie *f*

orphan [′ɔrfən] *adj & s* orphelin *m*

orphanage [′ɔrfənɪdʒ] *s* (*asylum*) orphelinat *m*; (*orphanhood*) orphelinage *m*

Orpheus [′ɔrfjus], [′ɔrfɪ·əs] *s* Orphée *m*

orthodox [′ɔrθəˌdɑks] *adj* orthodoxe

orthogra·phy [ɔr′θɑgrəfi] *s* (*pl* **-phies**) orthographe *f*

oscillate [′ɑsɪˌlet] *intr* osciller

osier [′oʒər] *s* osier *m*

osmosis [ɑz′mosɪs], [ɑs′mosɪs] *s* osmose *f*

osprey [′ɑspri] *s* aigle *m* pêcheur

ossi·fy [′ɑsɪˌfaɪ] *v* (*pret & pp* **-fied**) *tr* ossifier ‖ *intr* s'ossifier

ostensible [ɑs′tɛnsɪbəl] *adj* prétendu, apparent, soi-disant

ostentatious [ˌɑstɛn′teʃəs] *adj* ostentatoire, fastueux

osteopathy [ˌɑstɪ′ɑpəθi] *s* ostéopathie *f*

ostracism [′ɑstrəˌsɪzəm] *s* ostracisme *m*

ostracize [′ɑstrəˌsaɪz] *tr* frapper d'ostracisme

ostrich [′ɑstrɪtʃ] *s* autruche *f*

other [′ʌðər] *adj* autre; **every other day** tous les deux jours; **every other one** un sur deux ‖ *pron indef* autre ‖ *adv*—**other than** autrement que

otherwise [′ʌðərˌwaɪz] *adv* autrement, à part cela ‖ *conj* sinon, e.g., **come at once, otherwise it will be too late** venez tout de suite, sinon il sera trop tard; sans cela, e.g., **thanks, otherwise I'd have been merci**, sans cela j'aurais oublié

otter [′ɑtər] *s* loutre *f*

Ottoman [′ɑtəmən] *adj* ottoman *f*; (*l.c.*) *s* (*corded fabric*) ottoman *m*; (*divan*) ottomane *f*; (*footstool*) pouf *m*; **Ottoman** (*person*) Ottoman *m*

ouch [autʃ] *interj* aïe!

ought [ɔt] *s* zéro *m*; **for ought I know** pour autant que je sache ‖ *aux* used to express obligation, e.g., **he ought to go away** il devrait s'en aller; e.g., **he ought to have gone away** il aurait dû s'en aller

ounce [auns] *s* once *f*

our [aur] *adj poss* notre §88

ours [aurz] *pron poss* le nôtre §89

our·selves′ [aur′sɛlvz] *pron pers* nous-mêmes §86; nous §85, §87

oust [aust] *tr* évincer, chasser

out [aut] *adj* extérieur; absent; (*fire*) éteint; (*secret*) divulgué; (*tide*) bas; (*flower*) épanoui; (*rope*) filé; (*lease*) expiré; (*gear*) débrayé; (*unconscious person*) évanoui; (*boxer*) knockouté; (*book, magazine, etc.*) paru, publié; (*out of print, out of stock*) épuisé; (*a ball*) (sports) hors jeu; (*a player*) (sports) éliminé ‖ *s* (*pretext*) échappatoire *f*; **to be on the outs with** être brouillé avec ‖ *adv* dehors, au dehors; (*outdoors*) en plein air; **out and out** completement; **out for** en quête de; **out for lunch** parti déjeuner; **out of** (*cash*) démuni de; (*a glass, cup, etc.*) dans; (*a bottle*) à; (*the window; curiosity, friendship, respect, etc.*) par; (*range, sight*) hors de; de, e.g., **to cry out for joy** pleurer de joie; **made out of** fait de; sur, e.g., **nine times out of ten** neuf fois sur dix; **out with it!** allez, dites-le!; **to be out** (*to be absent*) être sorti; faire, e.g., **the sun is out** il fait du soleil; **to be out**

of bounds (sports) être hors jeu ‖ *prep* par ‖ *interj* hors d'ici!, ouste!
out' and away' *adv* de beaucoup, de loin
out'-and-out' *adj* vrai; (*fanatic*) intransigeant; (*liar*) achevé
out'-and-out'er *s* (coll) intransigeant *m*
out'bid' *v* (*pret* -**bid**; *pp* -**bid** or -**bidden**; *ger* -**bidding**) *tr* enchérir sur; (fig) renchérir sur ‖ *intr* surenchérir
out'board mo'tor *s* moteur *m* hors-bord
out'break' *s* déchaînement *m*; (*of hives; of anger;* etc.) éruption *f*; (*of epidemic*) manifestation *f*; (*insurrection*) révolte *f*
out'build'ing *s* annexe *f*, dépendance *f*
out'burst' *s* explosion *f*; (*of anger*) accès *m*; (*of laughter*) éclat *m*; (e.g., *of generosity*) élan *m*
out'cast' *adj* & *s* banni *m*, proscrit *m*
out'caste' *adj* hors caste ‖ *s* hors-caste *mf*
out'come' *s* résultat *m*, dénouement *m*
out'cry' *s* (*pl* -**cries**) clameur *f*; (*of indignation*) levée *f* de boucliers
out-dat'ed *adj* démodé, suranné
out'dis'tance *tr* dépasser; (sports) distancer
out'do' *v* (*pret* -**did**; *pp* -**done**) *tr* surpasser, l'emporter sur; **to outdo oneself** se surpasser
out'door' *adj* au grand air; (sports) de plein air
out'door grill' *s* rôtisserie *f* en plein air
out'doors' *s* rase campagne *f*, plein air *m* ‖ *adv* au grand air, en plein air; en plein air; (*outside of the house*) hors de la maison; (*at night*) à la belle étoile
out'door swim'ming pool' *s* piscine *f* à ciel ouvert
outer ['autər] *adj* extérieur, externe
out'er space' *s* cosmos *m*, espace *m* cosmique
out'field' *s* (baseball) grand champ *m*
out'fit' *s* équipement *m*, attirail *m*; (*caseful of implements*) trousse *f*, nécessaire *m*; (*ensemble*) costume et accessoires *mpl*; (*of a bride*) trousseau *m*; (team) équipe *f*; (*group of soldiers*) unité *f*; (com) compagnie *f* ‖ *v* (*pret* & *pp* -**fitted**; *ger* -**fitting**) *tr* équiper
out'go'ing *adj* en partance, partant; (*officeholder*) sortant; (*friendly*) communicatif, sympathique
out'grow' *v* (*pret* -**grew**; *pp* -**grown**) *tr* devenir plus grand que; (e.g., *childhood clothes, activities,* etc.) devenir trop grand pour; abandonner, se défaire de
out'growth' *s* excroissance *f*; (fig) résultat *m*, conséquence *f*
outing ['autɪŋ] *s* excursion *f*, sortie *f*
outlandish [aut'lændɪʃ] *adj* bizarre, baroque
out'last' *tr* durer plus longtemps que; survivre (with *dat*)
out'law' *s* hors-la-loi *m*, proscrit *m* ‖ *tr* mettre hors la loi, proscrire

out'lay' *s* débours *mpl*, dépenses *fpl* ‖ **out'lay'** *v* (*pret* & *pp* -**laid**) *tr* débourser, dépenser
out'let' *s* sortie *f*, issue *f*; (*escape valve*) déversoir *m*; (for, e.g., *pent-up emotions*) exutoire *m*; (com) débouché *m*; (elec) prise *f* de courant; **no outlet** (public sign) rue sans issue
out'line' *s* (*profile*) contour *m*; (*sketch*) esquisse *f*; (*summary*) aperçu *m*; (*of a work in preparation*) plan *m*; (*main points*) grandes lignes *fpl* ‖ *tr* esquisser; (*a work in preparation*) ébaucher
out'live' *tr* survivre (with *dat*)
out'lived' *adj* caduc, désuet
out'look' *s* perspective *f*, point *m* de vue
out'ly'ing *adj* éloigné, écarté, isolé
outmoded [,aut'modɪd] *adj* démodé
out'num'ber *tr* surpasser en nombre
out'-of-date' *adj* démodé, suranné
out'-of-door' *adj* au grand air
out'-of-doors' *adj* au grand air ‖ *s* rase campagne *f*, plein air *m* ‖ *adv* au grand air, hors de la maison
out' of or'der *adj* en panne; **to be out of order** (*to be out of sequence*) ne pas être dans l'ordre
out' of print' *adj* épuisé
out' of tune' *adj* désaccordé ‖ *adv* faux, e.g., **to sing out of tune** chanter faux
out' of work' *adj* en chômage
out'pa'tient *s* malade *mf* de consultation externe
out'patient clin'ic *s* consultation *f* externe
out'post' *s* avant-poste *m*, antenne *f*
out'put' *s* rendement *m*, débit *m*; (*of a mine;* *of a worker*) production *f*
out'rage *s* outrage *m*; (*wanton violence*) atrocité *f*, attentat *m* honteux ‖ *tr* faire outrage à, outrager; (*a woman*) violer
outrageous [aut'redʒəs] *adj* outrageux; (*intolerable*) insupportable
out'rank' *tr* dépasser en grade, dépasser en rang
out'rid'er *s* explorateur *m*; cow-boy *m*; (*mounted attendant*) piqueur *m*
outrigger ['aut,rɪgər] *s* (*outboard framework*) balancier *m*; (*oar support*) porte-en-dehors *m*
out'right' *adj* pur, absolu; (e.g., *manner*) franc, direct ‖ **out'right'** *adv* complètement; (*frankly*) franchement; (*at once*) sur le coup
out'set' *s* début *m*, commencement *m*
out'side' *adj* du dehors, d'extérieur ‖ **out'side'** *s* dehors *m*, extérieur *m*; surface *f*; **at the outside** tout au plus, au maximum ‖ **out'side'** *adv* dehors, à l'extérieur; (*outdoors*) en plein air; **outside of** en dehors de, à l'extérieur de; (*except for*) sauf ‖ **out'side'** or **out'side'** *prep* en dehors de, à l'extérieur de
outsider [,aut'saɪdər] *s* étranger *m*; (*intruder*) intrus *m*; (*uninitiated*) profane *mf*; (*dark horse*) outsider *m*
out'size' *adj* hors série

out′skirts′ spl approches fpl, périphérie f

out′spo′ken adj franc; **to be outspoken** avoir son franc-parler

out′stand′ing adj saillant; (eminent) hors pair, hors ligne; (debts) à recouvrer, impayé

outward ['autwərd] adj extérieur; (apparent) superficiel; (direction) en dehors || adv au dehors, vers le dehors

out′weigh′ tr peser plus que; (in value) l'emporter en valeur sur

out′wit′ v (pret & pp -witted; ger -witting) tr duper, déjouer; (a pursuer) dépister

oval ['ovəl] adj & s ovale m

ova·ry ['ovəri] s (pl -ries) ovaire m

ovation [o've/ən] s ovation f

oven ['ʌvən] s four m; (fig) fournaise f

over ['ovər] adj fini, passé; (additional) en plus; (excessive) en excès; plus, e.g., **eight and over** huit et plus || adv au-dessus, dessus; (on the other side) de l'autre côté; (again) de nouveau; (on the reverse side of sheet of paper) au verso; (finished) passé, achevé; **all over** (everywhere) partout; (finished) fini; (completely) jusqu'au bout des ongles; **I'll be right over** (coll) j'arrive tout de suite; **over!** (turn the page!) voir au verso!, tournez!; (rad) à vous!; **over again** de nouveau, encore une fois; **over against** en face de; (compared to) auprès de; **over and above** en plus de; **over and out!** (rad) terminé!; **over and over** à coups répétés, à plusieurs reprises; **over here** ici, de ce côté; **over there** là-bas; **to be over** (an illness) s'être remis de; **to hand over** remettre || prep au-dessus de; (on top of) sur, par-dessus; (with motion) par-dessus, e.g., **to jump over a fence** sauter par-dessus une barrière; (a period of time) pendant, au cours de; (near) près de; (a certain number or amount) plus de, au-dessus de; (concerning) à propos de, au sujet de; (on the other side of) au delà de, de l'autre côté de; à, e.g., **over the telephone** au téléphone; (while doing s.th.) tout en prenant, e.g., **over a cup of coffee** tout en prenant une tasse de café; **all over** répandu sur; **over and above** en sus de, en plus de; **to fall over** (e.g., a cliff) tomber du haut de; **to reign over** régner sur

o′ver·all′ adj hors tout, complet; général, total || **overalls** spl combinaison f d'homme, cotte f, salopette f

o′ver·awe′ tr impressionner, intimider

o′ver·bear′ing adj impérieux, tranchant, autoritaire

o′ver·board′ adv par-dessus bord; **man overboard!** un homme à la mer!; **to throw overboard** jeter par-dessus le bord; (fig) abandonner

o′ver·cast′ adj obscurci, nuageux || s ciel m couvert || v (pret & pp -cast) tr obscurcir, couvrir

o′ver·charge′ s prix m excessif, majoration f excessive; (elec) surcharge f || **o′ver·charge′** tr (e.g., an account) majorer; (elec) surcharger; **to overcharge s.o. for s.th.** faire payer trop cher q.ch. à qn

o′ver·coat′ s pardessus m

o′ver·come′ v (pret -came; pp -come) tr vaincre; (difficulties) surmonter

o′ver·con′fidence s témérité f, confiance f exagérée

o′ver·con′fident adj téméraire, excessivement confiant

o′ver·cooked′ adj trop cuit

o′ver·crowd′ tr bonder; (a town, region, etc.) surpeupler

o′ver·do′ v (pret -did; pp -done) tr exagérer; **overdone** (culin) trop cuit || intr se surmener

o′ver·dose′ s dose f excessive

o′ver·draft′ s découvert m, solde m débiteur

o′ver·draw′ v (pret -drew; pp -drawn) tr tirer à découvert || intr excéder son crédit

o′ver·drive′ s (aut) surmultiplication f

o′ver·due′ adj en retard; (com) échu, arriéré

o′ver·eat′ v (pret -ate; pp -eaten) tr & intr trop manger

o′ver·exer′tion s surmenage m

o′ver·expose′ tr surexposer

o′ver·expo′sure s surexposition f

o′ver·flow′ s débordement m; (pipe) trop-plein m || **o′ver·flow′** tr & intr déborder

o′ver·fly′ v (pret -flew; pp -flown) tr survoler

o′ver·grown′ adj démesuré; (e.g., child) trop grand pour son âge; **overgrown with** (e.g., weeds) envahi par, recouvert de

o′ver·hang′ v (pret & pp -hung) tr surplomber, faire saillie au-dessus de; (to threaten) menacer || intr (to jut out) faire saillie

o′ver·haul′ s remise f en état || **o′ver·haul′** tr remettre en état; (to catch up to) rattraper

o′ver·head′ adj élevé; aérien, surélevé || s (overpass) pont-route m; (com) frais mpl généraux || **o′ver·head′** adv au-dessus de la tête, en haut

o′ver·head valve′ s soupape f en tête

o′ver·hear′ v (pret & pp -heard) tr tendre par hasard; (a conversation) surprendre

o′ver·heat′ tr surchauffer

overjoyed [,ovər'dʒɔɪd] adj ravi, transporté de joie

overland ['ovər,lænd], ['ovərlənd] adj & adv par terre, par voie de terre

o′ver·lap′ v (pret & pp -lapped; ger -lapping) tr enchevaucher || intr chevaucher

o′ver·lap′ping s recouvrement m, chevauchement m; (of functions, offices, etc.) double emploi m

o′ver·load′ s surcharge f; **sudden overload** (elec) coup m de collier || **o′ver·load′** tr surcharger o'ver·look' tr donner sur, avoir vue sur; (to ignore) fermer les yeux sur, passer sous silence; (to neglect) oublier, négliger

o'ver·lord' s suzerain m || o'ver·lord' tr dominer, tyranniser

overly ['overli] adv (coll) trop, à l'excès

o'ver·night' adv toute la nuit; du jour au lendemain; to stay overnight passer la nuit

o'ver·night' bag' s sac m de nuit

o'ver·pass' s passage m supérieur, pont-route m

o'ver·pay'ment s surpaye f, rétribution f excessive

o'ver·pop'u·la'tion s surpeuplement m, surpopulation f

o'ver·pow'er tr maîtriser; overpowered with grief accablé de douleur

o'ver·pow'er·ing adj accablant, irrésistible

o'ver·pro·duc'tion s surproduction f

o'ver·rate' tr surestimer

o'ver·reach' tr dépasser

o'ver·ripe' adj blet, trop mûr

o'ver·rule' tr décider contre; (to set aside) annuler, casser

o'ver·run' v (pret -ran; pp -run; ger -running) tr envahir; (to flood) inonder; (limits, boundaries, etc.) dépasser || intr déborder

o'ver·sea' or o'ver·seas' adj d'outre-mer || o'ver·sea' or o'ver·seas' adv outre-mer

o'ver·see' v (pret -saw; pp -seen) tr surveiller

o'ver·se'er s surveillant m, inspecteur m

o'ver·shad'ow tr ombrager; (fig) éclipser

o'ver·shoes' spl caoutchoucs mpl

o'ver·sight' s inadvertance f, étourderie f

o'ver·sleep' v (pret & pp -slept) intr dormir trop longtemps

o'ver·step' v (pret & pp -stepped; ger -stepping) tr dépasser, outrepasser

o'ver·stock' tr surapprovisionner

o'ver·stuffed' adj rembourré

o'ver·sup·ply' s (pl -plies) excédent m, abondance f || o'ver·sup·ply' v (pret & pp -plied) tr approvisionner avec excès

overt [o'vərt], [o'vʌrt] adj ouvert, manifeste; (intentional) prémédité

o'ver·take' v (pret -took; pp -taken) tr rattraper; (a runner) dépasser; (an automobile) doubler; (to surprise) surprendre

o'ver·tax' tr surtaxer; (to tire) surmener, excéder

o'ver-the-coun'ter adj vendu directement à l'acheteur

o'ver·throw' s renversement m || o'ver·throw' v (pret -threw; pp -thrown) tr renverser

o'ver·time' adj & adv en heures supplémentaires || s heures fpl supplémentaires

o'ver·tone' s (mus) harmonique m; (fig) signification f, sous-entendu m

o'ver·trump' tr surcouper

overture ['ovərtʃər] s ouverture f

o'ver·turn' tr renverser, chavirer || intr chavirer; (aer, aut) capoter

overweening [,ovər'winɪŋ] adj arrogant, outrecuidant

o'ver·weight' adj au-dessus du poids normal; (fat) obèse || s excédent m de poids

overwhelm [,ovər'hwɛlm] tr accabler, écraser; (with favors, gifts, etc.) combler

o'ver·work' s surmenage m, excès m de travail || o'ver·work' tr surmener, surcharger; abuser de, trop employer || intr se surmener

Ovid ['avɪd] s Ovide m

ow [au] interj aïe!

owe [o] tr devoir || intr avoir des dettes; to owe for avoir à payer, devoir

owing ['o·ɪŋ] adj dû, redû; owing to à cause de, en raison de

owl [aul] s (Asio) hibou m; (Strix) chouette f, hulotte f; (Tyto alba) effraie f

own [on] adj propre, e.g., my own brother mon propre frère || s—all its own spécial, authentique, e.g., an aroma all its own un parfum spécial, un parfum authentique; my own (your own, etc.) le mien (le vôtre, etc.) §89; of my own (of their own, etc.) bien à moi (bien à eux, etc.); on one's own à son propre compte, de son propre chef; to come into one's own entrer en possession de son bien; (to win out) obtenir des succès; (to receive due praise) recevoir les honneurs qu'on mérite; to hold one's own se maintenir, se défendre || tr posséder; être propriétaire de; (to acknowledge) reconnaître || intr—to own to convenir de, reconnaître; to own up (coll) faire des aveux; to own up to (coll) faire l'aveu de, avouer

owner ['onər] s propriétaire mf, possesseur m

ownership ['onər‚ʃɪp] s propriété f, possession f

own'er's li'cense s carte f grise

ox [aks] s (pl oxen [aksən]) bœuf m

ox'cart' s char m à bœufs

oxfords ['aksfərdz] spl richelieus mpl

oxide ['aksaɪd] s oxyde m

oxidize ['aksɪ‚daɪz] tr oxyder || intr s'oxyder

oxygen ['aksɪdʒən] s oxygène m

oxygenate ['aksɪdʒe‚net] tr oxygéner

ox'ygen tent' s tente f à oxygène

oxytone ['aksɪ‚ton] adj & s oxyton m

oyster ['ɔɪstər] adj huîtrier || s huître f

oys'ter bed' s huîtrière f, banc m d'huîtres

oys'ter cock'tail s huîtres fpl écaillées aux condiments

oys'ter farm' s parc m à huîtres, clayère f

oys'ter fork' s fourchette f à huîtres

oys'ter knife' s couteau m à huîtres

oys'ter·man s (pl -men) écailler m
oys'ter op'ener s (person) écailler m; (implement) ouvre-huîtres m
oys'ter plant' s salsifis m

oys'ter shell' s coquille f d'huître
oys'ter stew' s soupe f à huîtres
ozone ['ozon] s ozone m; (coll) air m frais

P

P, p [pi] s XVIᵉ lettre de l'alphabet
pace [pes] s pas m; **to keep pace with** marcher de pair avec; **to put through one's paces** mettre à l'épreuve; **to set the pace** mener le train ‖ tr arpenter; **to pace off** mesurer au pas ‖ intr aller au pas
pace'mak'er s meneur m de train
pacific [pə'sɪfɪk] adj pacifique ‖ **Pacific** adj & s Pacifique m
pacifier ['pæsɪ,faɪ·ər] s pacificateur m; (teething ring) sucette f
pacifism ['pæsɪ,fɪzəm] s pacifisme m
pacifist ['pæsɪfɪst] adj & s pacifiste mf
paci·fy ['pæsɪ,faɪ] v (pret & pp -fied) tr pacifier
pack [pæk] s paquet m; (of peddler) ballot m; (of soldier) paquetage m, sac m; (of beast of burden) bât m; (of hounds) meute f; (of evildoers; of wolves) bande f; (of lies) tissu m; (of playing cards) jeu m; (of cigarettes) paquet m; (of floating ice) banquise f; (of troubles) foule f; (of fools) tas m; (med) enveloppement m ‖ tr emballer, empaqueter; mettre en boîte; (e.g., earth) tasser; (to stuff) bourrer; **to send packing** (coll) envoyer promener ‖ intr faire ses bagages
package ['pækɪdʒ] s paquet m ‖ tr empaqueter
pack'age plan' s voyage m à forfait
pack' an'imal s bête f de somme
packet ['pækɪt] s paquet m; (naut) paquebot m; (pharm) sachet m
pack'ing box' or **case'** s caisse f d'emballage
pack'ing house' s conserverie f
pack'sad'dle s bât m
pack'thread' s ficelle f
pack'train' s convoi m de bêtes de somme
pact [pækt] s pacte m
pad [pæd] s bourrelet m; (of writing paper) bloc m; (for inking) tampon m; (of an aquatic plant) feuille f; (for launching a rocket) rampe f; (sound of footsteps) pas m ‖ v (pret & pp padded; ger padding) tr rembourrer; (to expand unnecessarily) délayer ‖ intr aller à pied
pad'ded cell' s cellule f matelassée, cabanon m
paddle ['pædəl] s (of a canoe) pagaie f; (for table tennis) raquette f; (of a wheel) aube f; (for beating) palette f ‖ tr pagayer; (to spank) fesser ‖ intr pagayer; (to splash) barboter
pad'dle wheel' s roue f à aubes

paddock ['pædək] s enclos m; (at race track) paddock m
pad'dy wag'on ['pædi] s (slang) panier m à salade
pad'lock' s cadenas m ‖ tr cadenasser
pagan ['pegən] adj & s païen m
paganism ['pegə,nɪzəm] s paganisme m
page [pedʒ] s (of a book) page f; (boy attendant) page m; (in a hotel or club) chasseur m ‖ tr (a book) paginer; appeler, demander, e.g., **you are being paged** on vous demande
pageant ['pædʒənt] s parade f à grand spectacle
pageant·ry ['pædʒəntri] s (pl -ries) grand apparat m; vaines pompes fpl
page' proof' s seconde épreuve f; (journ) morasse f
paginate ['pædʒɪ,net] tr paginer
paging ['pedʒɪŋ] s mise f en pages
paid' in full' [ped] adj (formula stamped on bill) pour acquit
paid' vaca'tion s congé m payé
pail [pel] s seau m
pain [pen] s douleur f; **on pain of** sous peine de; **to take pains** se donner de la peine ‖ tr faire mal (with dat); **it pains me to** il me coûte de ‖ intr faire mal
painful ['penfəl] adj douloureux
pain'kil'er s (coll) calmant m
painless ['penlɪs] adj sans douleur
pains'tak'ing adj soigneux; (work) soigné
paint [pent] s peinture f; **wet paint** peinture fraîche; (public sign) attention à la peinture! ‖ tr & intr peindre
paint'box' s boîte f de couleurs
paint'brush' s pinceau m
paint' buck'et s camion m
painter ['pentər] s peintre mf
painting ['pentɪŋ] s peinture f
paint' remov'er s décapant m
pair [per] s paire f; (of people) couple m ‖ tr accoupler ‖ intr s'accoupler
pair' of scis'sors s ciseaux mpl
pair' of trou'sers s pantalon m
pajamas [pə'dʒɑməz], [pə'dʒæməz] spl pyjama m, pyjamas
Pakistan [,pɑkɪ'stɑn] s le Pakistan
Pakista·ni [,pɑkɪ'stɑni] adj pakistanais ‖ s (pl -nis) Pakistanais m
pal [pæl] s copain m ‖ v (pret & pp palled; ger palling) intr (coll) être de bons copains; **to pal with** être copain de
palace ['pælɪs] s palais m
palatable ['pælətəbəl] adj savoureux; (acceptable) agréable

palatal ['pælətəl] *adj* palatal ‖ *s* palatale *f*

palate ['pælɪt] *s* palais *m*

pale [pel] *adj* pâle ‖ *s* pieux *m*; limites *fpl* ‖ *intr* pâlir

pale'face' *s* visage *m* pâle

palette ['pælɪt] *s* palette *f*

palfrey ['polfrɪ] *s* palefroi *m*

palisade [,pælɪ'sed] *s* palissade *f*; *(line of cliffs)* falaise *f*

pall [pol] *s* poêle *m*, drap *m* mortuaire; *(to cover chalice)* pale *f*; *(vestment)* pallium *m* ‖ *intr* devenir fade; **to pall on** rassasier

pall'bear'er *s* porteur *m* d'un cordon du poêle

pallet ['pælɪt] *s* grabat *m*

palliate ['pælɪ,et] *tr* pallier

pallid ['pælɪd] *adj* pâle, blême

pallor ['pælər] *s* pâleur *f*

palm [pam] *s* *(of the hand)* paume *f*; *(measure)* palme *m*; *(leaf)* palme *f*; *(tree)* palmier *m*; **to carry off the palm** remporter la palme; **to grease the palm of** (slang) graisser la patte à ‖ *tr (a card)* escamoter; **to palm off s.th. on s.o.** refiler q.ch. à qn

palmet•to [pæl'meto] *s* *(pl* **-tos** or **-toes)** palmier *m* nain

palmist ['pamɪst] *s* chiromancien *m*

palmistry ['pamɪstrɪ] *s* chiromancie *f*

palm' leaf' *s* palme *f* de palme

palm' oil' *s* huile *f* de palme

Palm' Sun'day *s* le dimanche des Rameaux

palm' tree' *s* palmier *m*

palpable ['pælpəbəl] *adj* palpable

palpitate ['pælpɪ,tet] *intr* palpiter

pal•sy ['polzɪ] *s* *(pl* **-sies)** paralysie *f* ‖ *v (pret & pp* **-sied)** *tr* paralyser

pal•try ['poltrɪ] *adj* *(comp* **-trier;** *super* **-triest)** misérable

pamper ['pæmpər] *tr* choyer, gâter

pamphlet ['pæmflɪt] *s* brochure *f*

pan [pæn] *s* casserole *f*; *(basin; scale of a balance)* bassin *m*; (slang) binette *f*; **Pan** Pan *m* ‖ *v (pret & pp* **panned)** *ger* **panning)** *tr (gold)* laver à la batée; (coll) débiner, éreinter ‖ *intr* laver à la batée; (mov) panoramiquer; **to pan out well** (coll) réussir

panacea [,pænə'si•ə] *s* panacée *f*

Panama ['pænə,ma], [,pænə'ma] *s* le Panama

Pan'ama Canal' *s* canal *m* de Panama

Pan'ama Canal' Zone' *s* zone *f* canal du Panama

Pan'ama hat' *s* panama *m*

Pan-American [,pænə'merɪkən] *adj* panaméricain

pan'cake' *s* crêpe *f* ‖ *intr* (aer) descendre à plat, se plaquer

pan'cake land'ing *s* atterrissage *m* plaque, sur le ventre, or à plat

panchromatic [,pænkro'mætɪk] *adj* panchromatique

pancreas ['pænkrɪ•əs] *s* pancréas *m*

pander ['pændər] *s* entremetteur *m* ‖ *intr* servir d'entremetteur; **to pander to** se prêter à; encourager

pane [pen] *s* carreau *m*, vitre *f*

pan•el ['pænəl] *s* panneau *m*; *(on wall)* lambris *m*; liste *f*, tableau *m*; groupe *m* de discussion ‖ *v (pret & pp* **-eled** or **-elled)** *ger* **-eling** or **-elling)** *tr (a room)* garnir de boiseries; *(a wall)* lambrisser

pan'el discus'sion *s* colloque *m*

panelist ['pænəlɪst] *s* membre *m* d'un groupe de discussion

pang [pæŋ] *s* élancement *m*, angoisse *f*

pan'han'dle *s* queue *f* de la poêle; (geog) projection *f* d'un territoire dans un autre ‖ *intr* (slang) mendigoter

pan'han'dler *s* (slang) mendigot *m*

pan•ic ['pænɪk] *adj & s* panique *f* ‖ *v (pret & pp* **-icked;** *ger* **-icking)** *tr* semer la panique dans ‖ *intr* être pris de panique

pan'ic-strick'en *adj* pris de panique

pano•ply ['pænəplɪ] *s* *(pl* **-plies)** panoplie *f*

panorama [,pænə'ræmə], [,pænə'ramə] *s* panorama *m*

pan•sy ['pænzɪ] *s* *(pl* **-sies)** pensée *f*; (slang) tapette *f*

pant [pænt] *s* halètement *m*; **pants** pantalon *m*; **to wear the pants** (coll) porter la culotte ‖ *intr* haleter, panteler

pantheism ['pænθɪ,ɪzəm] *s* panthéisme *m*

pantheon ['pænθɪ,an], ['pænθɪ-ən] *s* panthéon *m*

panther ['pænθər] *s* panthère *f*

panties ['pæntɪz] *spl* culotte *f*

pantomime ['pæntə,maɪm] *s* pantomime *f*

pan•try ['pæntrɪ] *s* *(pl* **-tries)** office *m & f*, dépense *f*

pap [pæp] *s* bouillie *f*

papa ['papə], [pə'pa] *s* papa *m*

papa•cy ['pepəsɪ] *s* *(pl* **-cies)** papauté *f*

paper ['pepər] *s* papier *m*; *(newspaper)* journal *m*; *(of needles)* carte *f* ‖ *tr* tapisser

pa'per•back' *s* livre *m* broché; *(pocketbook)* livre de poche

pa'per•boy' *s* vendeur *m* de journaux

pa'per clip' *s* attache *f*, trombone *m*

pa'per cone' *s* cornet *m* de papier

pa'per cup' *s* verre *m* en carton, gobelet *m* de papier

pa'per cut'ter *s* coupe-papier *m*

pa'per hand'kerchief *s* mouchoir *m* à jeter, mouchoir en papier

pa'per•hang'er *s* tapissier *m*

pa'per knife' *s* coupe-papier *m*

pa'per mill' *s* papeterie *f*

pa'per mon'ey *s* papier-monnaie *m*

pa'per nap'kin *s* serviette *f* en papier

pa'per plate' *s* assiette *f* en carton, assiette de papier

pa'per tape' *s* bande *f* de papier

pa'per tow'el *s* serviette *f* de toilette en papier

pa'per•weight' *s* presse-papiers *m*

pa'per work' *s* travail *m* de bureau

papier-mâché [,pepərmə'ʃe] *s* papier-pierre *m*, papier *m* mâché

paprika [pæ'prikə], ['pæprɪkə] *s* paprika *m*

papy·rus [pə'paɪrəs] s (pl -ri [raɪ])
papyrus m

par [par] s pair m; (golf) normale f du
parcours; **at par** au pair; **to be on a
par with** aller de pair avec

parable ['pærəbəl] s parabole f

parabola [pə'ræbələ] s parabole f

parachute ['pærə‚ʃut] s parachute m
‖ tr & intr parachuter

par'achute jump' s saut m en parachute

parachutist ['pærə‚ʃutɪst] s parachutiste mf

parade [pə'red] s défilé m; (ostentation) parade f; (mil) parade ‖ tr
faire parade de ‖ intr défiler; parader

paradise ['pærə‚daɪs] s paradis m

paradox ['pærə‚daks] s paradoxe m

paradoxical [‚pærə'daksɪkəl] adj paradoxal

paraffin ['pærəfɪn] s paraffine f ‖ tr
paraffiner

paragon ['pærə‚gan] s parangon m

paragraph ['pærə‚græf], ['pærə‚graf]
s paragraphe m

Paraguay ['pærə‚gwe], ['pærə‚gwaɪ] s
le Paraguay

Paraguayan [‚pærə'gwe·ən], [‚pærə-
'gwaɪ·ən] adj paraguayen ‖ s Paraguayen m

parakeet ['pærə‚kit] s perruche f

paral·lel ['pærə‚lel] adj parallèle ‖ s
(line) parallèle f; (latitude; declination; comparison) parallèle m; parallels (typ) barres fpl; **without parallel**
sans pareil ‖ v (pret & pp -leled or
-lelled; ger -leling or -lelling) tr mettre en parallèle; entrer en parallèle
avec, égaler

par'allel bars' spl barres fpl parallèles

paraly·sis [pə'rælɪsɪs] s (pl -ses [‚siz])
paralysie f

paralytic [‚pærə'lɪtɪk] adj & s paralytique mf

paralyze ['pærə‚laɪz] tr paralyser

paramount ['pærə‚maunt] adj suprême, capital

paranoiac ['pærə‚nɔɪ·æk] adj & s
paranoïaque mf

parapet ['pærə‚pet] s parapet m

paraphernalia [‚pærəfər'nelɪ·ə] spl effets mpl personnels; attirail m

paraphrase ['pærə‚frez] s remaniement
m ‖ tr remanier

parasite ['pærə‚saɪt] s parasite m

parasitic(al) [‚pærə'sɪtɪk(əl)] adj parasite

parasol ['pærə‚sɔl], ['pærə‚sal] s parasol m, ombrelle f

paratrooper ['pærə‚trupər] s parachutiste m

parboil ['par‚bɔɪl] tr faire cuire légèrement; (vegetables) blanchir

par·cel ['parsəl] s colis m, paquet m ‖
v (pret & pp -celed or -celled; ger
-celing or -celling) tr morceler; **to
parcel out** répartir

par'cel post' s colis mpl postaux

parch [partʃ] tr dessécher; (beans,
grain, etc.) griller

parchment ['partʃmənt] s parchemin m

pardon ['pardən] s pardon m; (remis-

sion of penalty by the state) grâce f;
I beg your pardon je vous demande
pardon ‖ tr pardonner; pardonner
(with dat); (a criminal) grâcier; **to
pardon s.o. for s.th.** pardonner q.ch.
à qn

pardonable ['pardənəbəl] adj pardonnable

pare [per] tr (potatoes, fruit, etc.)
éplucher; (the nails) rogner; (costs)
réduire

parent ['perənt] s père m or mère f;
origine f, base f; parents parents mpl,
père et mère

parentage ['perəntɪdʒ] s paternité f or
maternité f; naissance f, origine f

parenthe·sis [pə'renθɪsɪs] s (pl -ses
[‚siz]) parenthèse f; **in parentheses**
entre parenthèses

parenthood ['perənt‚hud] s paternité f
or maternité f

pariah [pə'raɪ·ə], ['parɪ·ə] s paria m

par'ing knife' s couteau m à éplucher

Paris ['pærɪs] s Paris m

parish ['pærɪʃ] adj paroissien ‖ s paroisse f

parishioner [pə'rɪʃənər] s paroissien m

Parisian [pə'rɪʒən], [pə'rɪʒən] adj & s
parisien m

parity ['pærɪti] s parité f

park [park] s parc m ‖ tr garer, parquer ‖ intr stationner

parked adj en stationnement

parking ['parkɪŋ] s parcage m; (e.g.,
in a city street) stationnement m; **no
parking** (public sign) stationnement
interdit

park'ing lights' spl (aut) feux mpl de
stationnement, feux de position

park'ing lot' s parking m, parc m à
autos

park'ing me'ter s parcomètre m

park'ing tick'et s contravention f, papillon m

park'way' s route f panoramique;
(turnpike) autoroute f

parley ['parli] s pourparlers mpl ‖ intr
parlementer

parliament ['parlɪmənt] s parlement m

parliamentarian [‚parlɪmen'terɪ·ən] s
expert m en usages parlementaires

parlor ['parlər] s salon m; (in an institution) parloir m

par'lor car' s (rr) wagon-salon m

par'lor game' s jeu m de société

Parnassus [par'næsəs] s le Parnasse

parochial [pə'rokɪ·əl] adj paroissial;
(attitude) provincial

paro'chial school' s école f confession-
nelle, école libre

paro·dy ['pærədi] s (pl -dies) parodie f
‖ v (pret & pp -died) tr parodier

parole [pə'rol] s parole f d'honneur;
liberté f sur parole ‖ tr libérer sur
parole

par·quet [par'ke], [par'ket] s parquet
m; (theat) premiers rangs mpl du
parterre ‖ v (pret & pp -queted
['ked], [ketɪd]; ger -queting ['ke·
ɪŋ], ['ketɪŋ]) tr parqueter

parricide ['pærɪ‚saɪd] s (act) parricide
m; (person) parricide mf

parrot [ˈpærət] *s* perroquet *m* ‖ *tr* répéter or imiter comme un perroquet

par·ry [ˈpæri] *s* (*pl* -ries) parade *f* ‖ *v* (*pret & pp* -ried) *tr* parer; (*a question*) éluder

parse [pɑrs] *tr* faire l'analyse grammaticale de

parsimonious [ˌpɑrsɪˈmonɪ·əs] *adj* parcimonieux, regardant

parsley [ˈpɑrsli] *s* persil *m*

parsnip [ˈpɑrsnɪp] *s* panais *m*

parson [ˈpɑrsən] *s* curé *m*; pasteur *m* protestant

parsonage [ˈpɑrsənɪdʒ] *s* presbytère *m*

part [pɑrt] *s* partie *f*; (*share*) part *f*; (*of a machine*) organe *m*, pièce *f*; (*of the hair*) raie *f*; (*theat*) rôle *m*; **for my part** pour ma part; **for the most part** pour la plupart; **in part** en partie; **in these parts** dans ces parages; **on the part of** de la part de; **parts** qualités *fpl*, parties (*génitales*); **to be or form part of** faire partie de; **to be part and parcel of** faire partie intégrante de; **to do one's part** faire son devoir; **to live a part** (theat) entrer dans la peau d'un personnage; **to look the part** avoir le physique de l'emploi; **to take part in** prendre part à; **to take the part of** prendre parti pour; jouer le rôle de ‖ *adv* partiellement, en partie; **part . . . part** moitié . . . moitié ‖ *tr* séparer; **to part the hair** se faire une raie ‖ *intr* se séparer; (*said, e.g., of road*) diverger; (*to break*) rompre; **to part with** se défaire de, se dessaisir de

par·take [pɑrˈtek] *v* (*pret* -took; *pp* -taken) *intr*—**to partake in** participer à; **to partake of** (*e.g., a meal*) prendre; (*e.g., joy*) participer de

partial [ˈpɑrʃəl] *adj* partiel; (*prejudiced*) partial

participant [pɑrˈtɪsɪpənt] *adj & s* participant *m*

participate [pɑrˈtɪsɪˌpet] *intr* participer

participation [pɑrˌtɪsɪˈpeʃən] *s* participation *f*

participle [ˈpɑrtɪˌsɪpəl] *s* participe *m*

particle [ˈpɑrtɪkəl] *s* particule *f*

particular [pərˈtɪkjələr] *adj* particulier; difficile, exigeant; méticuleux; **a particular . . .** un certain . . . ‖ *s* détail *m*

particularize [pərˈtɪkjələˌraɪz] *tr & intr* individualiser, particulariser

parting [ˈpɑrtɪŋ] *s* séparation *f*

partisan [ˈpɑrtɪzən] *adj & s* partisan *m*

partition [pɑrˈtɪʃən] *s* partage *m*; (*wall*) paroi *f*, cloison *f* ‖ *tr* partager; **to partition off** séparer par des cloisons

partner [ˈpɑrtnər] *s* partenaire *mf*; (*husband*) conjoint *m*; (*wife*) conjointe *f*; (*in a dance*) cavalier *m*; (*in business*) associé *m*

part'ner·ship' *s* association *f*; (com) société *f*

part' of speech' *s* partie *f* du discours

part' own'er *s* copropriétaire *mf*

partridge [ˈpɑrtrɪdʒ] *s* perdrix *m*

part'-time' *adj & adv* à mi-temps

par·ty [ˈpɑrti] *adj* de gala ‖ *s* (*pl* -ties) fête *f*, soirée *f*; (*diversion of a group of persons; individual named in contract or lawsuit*) partie *f*; (*with whom one is conversing*) interlocuteur *m*; (mil) détachement *m*, peloton *m*; (pol) parti *m*; (telp) correspondant *m*; (coll) individu *m*; **to be a party to** être complice de

party-goer [ˈpɑrtiˌgo·ər] *s* invité *m*; (*nightlifer*) noceur *m*

par'ty line' *s* (*between two properties*) limite *f*; (telp) ligne *f* à postes groupés ‖ **par'ty line'** *s* ligne du parti; (*of communist party*) directives *fpl* du parti

par'ty pol'itics *s* politique *f* de parti

par'ty wall' *s* mur *m* mitoyen

pass [pæs], [pɑs] *s* (*navigable channel; movement of hands of magician; in sports*) passe *f*; (*straits*) pas *m*; (*in mountains*) col *m*, passage *m*; (*document*) laissez-passer *m*; difficulté *f*; (mil) permission *f*; (theat) billet *m* de faveur ‖ *tr* passer; (*an exam*) réussir à; (*e.g., a student*) recevoir; (*a law*) adopter, voter; (*a red light*) brûler; (*to get ahead of*) dépasser; (*a car going in the same direction*) doubler; (*s.o. or s.th. coming toward one*) croiser; (*a certain place*) passer devant; **to pass around** faire circuler; **to pass oneself off as** se faire passer pour; **to pass out** distribuer; **to pass over** passer sous silence; (*to hand over*) transmettre; **to pass s.th. off on s.o.** repasser or refiler q.ch. à qn ‖ *intr* passer; (educ) être reçu; **to bring to pass** réaliser; **to come to pass** se passer; **to pass as or for** passer pour; **to pass away** disparaître; (*to die out*) s'éteindre; (*to die*) mourir; **to pass by** passer devant; **to pass out** sortir; (slang) s'évanouir; **to pass over** passer sur; (*an obstacle*) franchir; (*said of storm*) s'éloigner; (*to pass through*) traverser; **to pass over to** (*e.g., the enemy*) passer à

passable [ˈpæsəbəl], [ˈpɑsəbəl] *adj* passable; (*road, river, etc.*) franchissable

passage [ˈpæsɪdʒ] *s* passage *m*; (*of time*) cours *m*; (*of a law*) adoption *f*

pass'book' *s* carnet *m* de banque

passenger [ˈpæsəndʒər] *adj* (*e.g., train*) de voyageurs; (*e.g., pigeon*) de passage ‖ *s* voyageur *m*, passager *m*

passer-by [ˈpæsərˈbaɪ], [ˈpɑsərˈbaɪ] *s* (*pl* passers-by) passant *m*

passing [ˈpæsɪŋ], [ˈpɑsɪŋ] *adj* passager *m*; (*act of passing*) dépassement *m*; (*death*) trépas *m*; (*of time*) écoulement *m*; (*of a law*) adoption *f*; (*in an examination*) la moyenne; une mention passable

passion [ˈpæʃən] *s* passion *f*

passionate [ˈpæʃənɪt] *adj* passionné

passive [ˈpæsɪv] *adj & s* passif *m*

pass'key' *s* passe-partout *m*

pass'-out' check' *s* contremarque *f*

Pass/o/ver s Pâque f
pass/port/ s passeport m
pass/word/ s mot m de passe
past [pæst], [past] adj passé, dernier; (e.g., president) ancien || s passé m || prep au-delà de, passé; plus de; hors de, e.g., past all understanding hors de toute compréhension; it's twenty past five il est cinq heures vingt; it's past three o'clock il est trois heures passées
paste [pest] s (glue) colle f de pâte; (jewelry) strass m; (culin) pâte f || tr coller
paste/board/ s carton m
pastel [pæs'tɛl] adj & s pastel m
pasteurize [pæstə,raɪz] tr pasteuriser
pastime [pæs,taɪm], [pas,taɪm] s passe-temps m
past/ mas/ter s expert m en la matière, passé maître
pastor [pæstər], [pastər] s pasteur m
pastoral [pæstərəl], [pastərəl] adj pastoral || s pastorale f
pastorate [pæstərɪt], [pastərɪt] s pastorat m
pastry [pestri] s (pl -tries) pâtisserie f
pas/try cook/ s pâtissier m
pas/try shop/ s pâtisserie f
pasture [pæstʃər], [pastʃər] s pâturage m, pâture f || tr faire paître || intr paître
pasty [pesti] adj (comp -ier; super -iest) pâteux; (face) terreux
pat [pæt] adj à propos; (e.g., excuse) tout prêt || s petite tape f; caresse f; (of butter) coquille f || v (pret & pp patted; ger patting) tr tapoter; caresser; to pat on the back encourager, complimenter
patch [pætʃ] s (e.g., of cloth) pièce f, raccommodage m; (of land) parcelle f; (of ice) plaque f; (of inner tube) rustine f; (e.g., of color) tache f; (beauty spot) mouche f || tr rapiécer; to patch up rapetasser; (e.g., a quarrel) arranger, raccommoder
patent [pætənt] adj patent || [pætənt] adj breveté || s brevet m d'invention; patent applied for une demande de brevet a été déposée || tr breveter
pat/ent leath/er [pætənt] s cuir m verni
pat/ent med/icine [pætənt] s specialité f pharmaceutique
pat/ent rights/ [pætənt] spl propriété f industrielle
paternal [pə'tʌrnəl] adj paternel
paternity [pə'tʌrnɪti] s paternité f
path [pæθ], [paθ] s sentier m; (in garden) allée f; (of bullet, heavenly body, etc.) trajectoire f; (for, e.g., riding horses) piste f; to beat a path frayer un chemin
pathetic [pə'θɛtɪk] adj pathétique
path/find/er s pionnier m
pathology [pə'θalədʒi] s pathologie f
pathos [peθas] s pathétique m
path/way/ s sentier m; (fig) voie f
patience [pe'ʃəns] s patience f
patient [pe'ʃənt] adj patient || s malade mf; (undergoing surgery) patient m

pati·o [pati,o] s (pl -os) patio m
patriarch [petri,ark] s patriarche m
patrician [pə'trɪʃən] adj & s patricien m
patricide [pætrɪ,saɪd] s (act) parricide m; (person) parricide mf
Patrick [pætrɪk] s Patrice m
patrimo·ny [pætrɪ,moni] s (pl -nies) patrimoine m
patriot [petri,ət], [pætrɪ,ət] s patriote mf
patriotic [,petri'atɪk], [,pætrɪ'atɪk] adj patriotique, patriote
patriotism [petri,ə,tɪzəm], [pætrɪ,ə,tɪzəm] s patriotisme m
pa·trol [pə'trol] s patrouille f || v (pret & pp -trolled; ger -trolling) tr faire la patrouille dans || intr patrouiller
patrol/man s (pl -men) agent m de police
patrol/ wag/on s voiture f cellulaire
patron [petrən], [pætrən] adj patron || s protecteur m; (com) client m
patronage [petrənɪdʒ], [pætrənɪdʒ] s patronage m, clientèle f
patronize [petrə,naɪz], [pætrə,naɪz] tr patronner, protéger; traiter avec condescendance; (com) acheter chez
pa/tron saint/ s patron m
patter [pætər] s bruit m; (of rain) fouettement m; (of magician, peddler, etc.) boniment m || intr (said of rain) fouetter; (said of little feet) trottiner
pattern [pætərn] s patron m; modèle m
pat·ty [pæti] s (pl -ties) petit pâté m
paucity [posɪti] s rareté f; manque m, disette f
paunch [pontʃ] s panse f
paunch·y [pontʃi] adj (comp -ier; super -iest) ventru
pauper [popər] s indigent m
pause [poz] s pause f; (mus) point m d'orgue; to give pause to faire hésiter || intr faire une pause; hésiter
pave [pev] tr paver
pavement [pevmənt] s pavé m; (surface) chaussée f
pavilion [pə'vɪljən] s pavillon m
paw [po] s patte f; (coll) main f || tr donner un coup de patte à || intr (said of horse) piaffer
pawl [pol] s cliquet m d'arrêt
pawn [pon] s (in chess) pion m; (security, pledge) gage m; (tool of another person) jouet m || tr mettre en gage; to pawn s.th. off on s.o. (coll) refiler q.ch. à qn
pawn/bro/ker s prêteur m sur gages
pawn/shop/ s mont-de-piété m, crédit m municipal
pawn/ tick/et s reconnaissance f du mont-de-piété
pay [pe] s paye f; (mil) solde f || v (pret & pp paid [ped]) tr payer; (mil) solder; (a compliment; a visit; attention) faire; to pay back payer de retour; to pay down payer comptant; to pay off (a debt) acquitter; (a mortgage) purger; (a creditor) rembourser; to pay s.o. for s.th.

payer qn de q.ch., payer q.ch. à qn ||
intr payer, rapporter; **to pay for**
payer; **to pay off** (coll) avoir du succès; **to pay up** se libérer par un
paiement
payable ['pe.əbəl] *adj* payable
pay′ boost′ *s* augmentation *f*
pay′check′ *s* paye *f*
pay′day′ *s* jour *m* de paye
pay′dirt′ *s* alluvion *f* exploitable; (coll)
source *f* d'argent
payee [pe'i] *s* bénéficiaire *mf*
pay′ en′velope *s* sachet *m* de paye;
paye *f*
payer ['pe.ər] *s* payeur *m*
pay′load′ *s* charge *f* payante; (aer)
poids *m* utile
pay′mas′ter *s* payeur *m*
payment ['pemənt] *m* paiement *m*; (installment, deposit, etc.) versement *m*
pay′ phone′ *s* taxiphone *m*
pay′roll′ *s* bulletin *m* de paye; (for officers) état *m* de solde; (for enlisted
men) feuille *f* de prêt
pay′ sta′tion *s* téléphone *m* public
pea [pi] *s* pois *m*; **green peas** petits
pois
peace [pis] *s* paix *f*
peaceable ['pisəbəl] *adj* pacifique
peaceful ['pisfəl] *adj* paisible, pacifique
peace′mak′er *s* pacificateur *m*
peace′ of mind′ *s* tranquillité *f* d'esprit
peace′ pipe′ *s* calumet *m* de paix
peach [pitʃ] *s* pêche *f*; (slang) bijou *m*
peach′ tree′ *s* pêcher *m*
peach·y ['pitʃi] *adj* (comp **-ier**; super
-iest) (slang) chouette
pea′coat′ *s* (naut) caban *m*
pea′cock′ *s* paon *m*
pea′hen′ *s* paonne *f*
peak [pik] *s* cime *f*, sommet *m*; (mountain; mountain top) pic *m*; (of beard)
pointe *f*; (of a cap) visière *f*; (elec)
pointe
peak′ hour′ *s* heure *f* de pointe
peak′ load′ *s* (elec) charge *f* maximum
peak′ vol′tage *s* tension *f* de crête
peal [pil] *s* retentissement *m*; (of bells)
carillon *m* || *intr* carillonner
peal′ of laugh′ter *s* éclat *m* de rire
peal′ of thun′der *s* coup *m* de tonnerre
pea′nut′ *s* cacahuète *f*; (bot) arachide *f*
pea′nut but′ter *s* beurre *m* de caca-
huètes ou d'arachide
pear [per] *s* poire *f*
pearl [pʌrl] *s* perle *f*
pearl′ oys′ter *s* huître *f* perlière
pear′ tree′ *s* poirier *m*
peasant ['pezənt] *adj & s* paysan *m*
pea′shoot′er *s* sarbacane *f*
pea′ soup′ *s* (culin, fig) purée *f* de pois
peat [pit] *s* tourbe *f*
pebble ['pebəl] *s* caillou *m*; (on seashore) galet *m*
pebbled *adj* (leather) grenu
peck [pek] *s* coup *m* de bec; (eight
quarts) picotin *m*; (kiss) (coll) baiser
m d'oiseau, bécot *m*; (coll) tas *m*
|| *tr* becqueter || *intr* picorer; **to peck
at** picorer; (food) pignocher
peculation [ˌpekjə'leʃən] *s* péculat *m*,
détournement *m* de fonds

peculiar [pɪ'kjuljər] *adj* particulier;
(strange) bizarre
pedagogue ['pedəˌgɑg] *s* pédagogue *mf*
pedagogy ['pedəˌgodʒi], ['pedəˌgodʒi]
s pédagogie *f*
ped·al ['pedəl] *s* pédale *f* || *v* (pret &
pp **-aled** or **-alled**; ger **-aling** or
-alling) *tr* actionner les pédales de ||
intr pédaler
pedant ['pedənt] *s* pédant *m*
pedantic [pɪ'dæntɪk] *adj* pédant
pedant·ry ['pedəntri] *s* (pl **-ries**) pédanterie *f*
peddle ['pedəl] *tr & intr* colporter
peddler ['pedlər] *s* colporteur *m*
pedestal ['pedɪstəl] *s* piédestal *m*
pedestrian [pɪ'destri.ən] *adj* (style)
prosaïque || *s* piéton *m*
pediatrics [ˌpidi'ætrɪks], [ˌpedi'æ-
trɪks] *s* pédiatrie *f*
pedigree ['pedɪˌgri] *s* généalogie *f*;
(table) arbre *m* généalogique; (of
animal) pedigree *m*
pediment ['pedɪmənt] *s* fronton *m*
peek [pik] *s* coup *m* d'œil furtif || *intr*
—**to peek at** regarder furtivement
peel [pil] *s* pelure *f*; (of lemon) zeste
m || *tr* peler; **to peel off** enlever ||
intr se peler; (said of paint) s'écailler
peep [pip] *s* regard *m* furtif; (e.g.,
chickens) piaulement *m* || *intr* piau-
ler; **to peep at** regarder furtivement
peep′hole′ *s* judas *m*
peer [pɪr] *s* pair *m* || *intr* regarder avec
attention; **to peer at** ou **into** scruter
peerless ['pɪrlɪs] *adj* sans pareil
peeve [piv] *s* (coll) embêtement *m* || *tr*
(coll) irriter, embêter, fâcher
peevish ['pivɪʃ] *adj* maussade
peg [peg] *s* cheville *f*; (for tent) piquet
m; **to take down a peg** (coll) rabattre
le caquet de || *v* (pret & pp **pegged**;
ger **pegging**) *tr* cheviller; (e.g., prices)
indexer, fixer; (points) marquer ||
intr piocher; **to peg away at** travailler
ferme à
Pegasus ['pegəsəs] *s* Pégase *m*
peg′ leg′ *s* jambe *f* de bois
peg′ top′ *s* toupie *f*; **peg tops** pantalon
m fuseau
Pekin·ese [ˌpikɪ'niz] *adj* pékinois || *s*
(pl **-ese**) Pékinois *m*
Peking ['pi'kɪŋ] *s* Pékin *m*
pelf [pelf] *s* (pej) lucre *m*
pelican ['pelɪkən] *s* pélican *m*
pellet ['pelɪt] *s* boulette *f*; (bullet)
grain *m* de plomb; (pharm) pilule *f*
pell-mell ['pel'mel] *adj* confus || *adv*
pêle-mêle
pelt [pelt] *s* peau *m*; coup *m* violent;
(of stones, insults, etc.) grêle *f* || *tr*
cribler; (e.g., stones) lancer || *intr*
tomber à verse
pen [pen] *s* plume *f*; (fountain pen)
stylo *m*; (corral) enclos *m*; (fig)
plume; (prison) (slang) bloc *m* || *v*
(pret & pp **penned**; ger **penning**) *tr*
écrire || *v* (pret & pp **penned** or **pent**
[pent]; ger **penning**) *tr* parquer
penalize ['pinəˌlaɪz] *tr* (an action)
sanctionner; (a person) punir;
(sports) pénaliser

penal·ty ['penəlti] s (pl **-ties**) peine f; (for late payment; in a game) pénalité f; **under penalty of** sous peine de

penance ['penəns] s pénitence f

penchant ['penʃənt] s penchant m

pen·cil ['pensəl] s crayon m; (of light) faisceau m ‖ v (pret & pp **-ciled** or **-cilled;** ger **-ciling** or **-cilling**) tr crayonner

pen'cil sharp'ener s taille-crayon m

pendent ['pendent] adj pendant ‖ s pendant m, pendentif m; (of chandelier) pendeloque f

pending ['pendɪŋ] adj pendant ‖ prep en attendant

pendulum ['pendʒələm] s pendule m

pen'dulum bob' s lentille f

penetrate ['penɪ,tret] tr & intr pénétrer

penguin ['peŋgwɪn] s manchot m

pen'hold'er s porte-plume m; (rack) pose-plumes m

penicillin [,penɪ'sɪlɪn] s pénicilline f

peninsula [pə'nɪnsələ] s presqu'île f; (large peninsula like Spain or Italy) péninsule f

peninsular [pə'nɪnsələr] adj péninsulaire

penitence ['penɪtəns] s pénitence f

penitent ['penɪtənt] adj & s pénitent m

pen'knife' s (pl **-knives**) canif m

penmanship ['penmən,ʃɪp] s calligraphie f; (person's handwriting) écriture f

pen' name' s pseudonyme m

pennant ['penənt] s flamme f; (sports) banderole f du championnat

penniless ['penɪlɪs] adj sans le sou

pen·ny ['peni] s (pl **-nies**) (U.S.A.) centime m; **not a penny** pas un sou ‖ s (pl **pence** [pens]) (Brit) penny m

pen'ny-pinch'ing adj regardant

pen'ny-weight' s poids m de 24 grains

pen' pal' s (coll) correspondant m

pen'point' s bec m de plume

pension ['penʃən] s pension f ‖ tr pensionner

pensioner ['penʃənər] s pensionné m

pensive ['pensɪv] adj pensif

Pentagon ['pentə,gɑn] s Pentagone m

Pentecost ['pentɪ,kɑst], ['pentɪ,kɔst] s la Pentecôte

penthouse ['pent,haus] s toit m en auvent, appentis m; appartement m sur toit, maison f à terrasse

pent-up ['pent,ʌp] adj renfermé, refoulé

penult ['pinʌlt] s pénultième f

penum·bra [pɪ'nʌmbrə] s (pl **-brae** [bri] or **-bras**) pénombre f

penurious [pɪ'nurɪ·əs] adj (stingy) mesquin, parcimonieux; (poor) pauvre

penury ['penjəri] s indigence f, misère f

pen'wip'er s essuie-plume m

peo·ny ['pi·əni] s (pl **-nies**) pivoine f

people ['pipəl] spl gens mpl, personnes fpl; **many people** beaucoup de monde; **my people** ma famille, mes parents; **people say** on dit ‖ s (pl **peoples**) peuple m, nation f ‖ tr peupler

pep [pep] s (coll) allant m ‖ v (pret & pp **pepped;** ger **pepping**) tr—**to pep up** (coll) animer

pepper ['pepər] s (spice) poivre m; (fruit) grain m de poivre; (plant) poivrier m; (plant or fruit of the hot or red pepper) piment m rouge; (plant or fruit of the sweet or green pepper) piment doux, poivron m vert ‖ tr poivrer; (e.g., with bullets) cribler

pep'per·box' s poivrière f

pep'per mill' s moulin m à poivre

pep'per·mint' s menthe f poivrée; (lozenge) pastille f de menthe

per [pʌr] prep par; **as per** suivant

perambulator [pər'æmbjə,letər] s voiture f d'enfant

per capita [pər'kæpɪtə] par tête, par personne

perceive [pər'siv] tr (by the senses) apercevoir; (by understanding) percevoir

per cent or **percent** [pər'sent] pour cent

percentage [pər'sentɪdʒ] s pourcentage m; **to get a percentage** (slang) avoir part au gâteau

perceptible [pər'septəbəl] adj perceptible, sensible, appréciable

perception [pər'sepʃən] s perception f; compréhension f, pénétration f

perch [pʌrtʃ] s perchoir m; (ichth) perche f ‖ tr percher ‖ intr percher, se percher

percolate ['pʌrkə,let] tr & intr filtrer

percolator ['pʌrkə,letər] s cafetière f à filtre

percussion [pər'kʌʃən] s percussion f

percus'sion cap' s capsule f fulminante

per diem [pər'daɪ·əm] par jour

perdition [pər'dɪʃən] s perdition f

perennial [pə'renɪ·əl] adj perpétuel; (bot) vivace ‖ s plante f vivace

perfect ['pʌrfɪkt] adj & s parfait m ‖ [pər'fekt] tr perfectionner

perfidious [pər'fɪdɪ·əs] adj perfide

perfi·dy ['pʌrfɪdi] s (pl **-dies**) perfidie f

perforate ['pʌrfə,ret] tr perforer

per'forated line' s pointillé m

perforation [,pʌrfə're'ʃən] s perforation f; (of postage stamp) dentelure f

perforce [pər'fors] adv forcément

perform [pər'fɔrm] tr exécuter; (surg) faire; (theat) représenter ‖ intr jouer; (said of machine) fonctionner

performance [pər'fɔrməns] s exécution f; (production) rendement m; (of a machine) fonctionnement m; (sports) performance f; (theat) représentation f

performer [pər'fɔrmər] s artiste mf

perform'ing arts' spl arts mpl du spectacle

perfume ['pʌrfjum] s parfum m ‖ [pər'fjum] tr parfumer

perfunctory [pər'fʌŋktəri] adj superficiel; négligent

perhaps [pər'hæps] adv peut-être; **perhaps not** peut-être que non

per hour' à l'heure

peril ['perəl] *s* péril *m*
perilous ['perıləs] *adj* périlleux
period ['pırı·əd] *s* période *f*; (*in school*) heure *f* de cours; (gram) point *m*; (sports) division *f*
pe'riod cos'tume *s* costume *m* d'époque
pe'riod fur'niture *s* meubles *m* d'époque
periodic [,pırı'adık] *adj* périodique
periodical [,pırı'adıkəl] *adj* périodique || *s* publication *f* périodique
peripheral [pə'rıfərəl] *adj* périphérique
peripher·y [pə'rıfəri] *s* (*pl* -ies) périphérie *f*
periscope ['perı,skop] *s* périscope *m*
perish ['perıʃ] *intr* périr
perishable ['perıʃəbəl] *adj* périssable
perjure ['pʌrdʒər] *tr*—to perjure oneself se parjurer
perju·ry ['pʌrdʒəri] *s* (*pl* -ries) parjure *m*
perk [pʌrk] *tr*—to perk up (*the head*) redresser; (*the ears*) dresser; (*the appetite*) ravigoter || *intr*—to perk up se ranimer
permanence ['pʌrmənəns] *s* permanence *f*
permanent ['pʌrmənənt] *adj* permanent || *s* permanente *f*
per'manent address' *s* domicile *m* fixe
per'manent ten'ure *s* inamovibilité *f*
per'manent wave' *s* ondulation *f* permanente
per'manent way' *s* (rr) matériel *m* fixe
permeate ['pʌrmı,et] *tr & intr* pénétrer
permissible [pər'mısıbəl] *adj* permis
permission [pər'mıʃən] *s* permission *f*
per·mit ['pʌrmıt] *s* permis *m*; (com) passavant *m* || [pər'mıt] *v* (*pret & pp* -mitted; *ger* -mitting) *tr* permettre; to permit s.o. to permettre à qn de
permute [pər'mjut] *tr* permuter
pernicious [pər'nıʃəs] *adj* pernicieux
pernickety [pər'nıkıti] *adj* (coll) pointilleux
perox·ide' blonde' [pər'aksaıd] *s* blonde *f* décolorée
perpendicular [,pʌrpən'dıkjələr] *adj & s* perpendiculaire *f*
perpetrate ['pʌrpı,tret] *tr* perpétrer
perpetual [pər'pet/u·əl] *adj* perpétuel
perpetuate [pər'pet/u,et] *tr* perpétuer
perplex [pər'pleks] *tr* rendre perplexe
perplexed [pər'plekst] *adj* perplexe
perplexi·ty [pər'pleksıti] *s* (*pl* -ties) perplexité *f*
persecute ['pʌrsı,kjut] *tr* persécuter
persecution [,pʌrsı'kjuʃən] *s* persécution *f*
persevere [,pʌrsı'vır] *intr* persévérer
Persian ['pʌrʒən] *adj* persan || *s* (*language*) persan *m*; (*person*) Persan *m*
Per'sian blind' *s* persienne *f*
Per'sian Gulf' *s* Golfe *m* Persique
Per'sian rug' *s* tapis *m* de Perse
persimmon [pər'sımən] *s* plaquemine *f*; (*tree*) plaqueminier *m*
persist [pər'sıst], [pər'zıst] *intr* persister; to persist in persister dans; + *ger* persister à + *inf*
persistent [pər'sıstənt], [pər'zıstənt] *adj* persistant

person ['pʌrsən] *s* personne *f*; no person personne; per person par personne, chacun
personage ['pʌrsənıdʒ] *s* personnage *m*
personal ['pʌrsənəl] *adj* personnel || *s* (journ) note *f* dans la chronique mondaine
personali·ty [,pʌrsə'nælıti] *s* (*pl* -ties) personnalité *f*
per'sonal prop'erty *s* biens *mpl* mobiliers
personi·fy [pər'sanı,faı] *v* (*pret & pp* -fied) *tr* personnifier
personnel [,pʌrsə'nel] *s* personnel *m*
per'son-to-per'son tel'ephone call' *s* communication *f* avec préavis
perspective [pər'spektıv] *s* perspective *f*
perspicacious [,pʌrspı'keʃəs] *adj* perspicace
perspiration [,pʌrspı'reʃən] *s* transpiration *f*
perspire [pər'spaır] *intr* transpirer
persuade [pər'swed] *tr* persuader; to persuade s.o. of s.th. persuader q.ch. à qn, persuader qn de q.ch.; to persuade s.o. to persuader à qn de
persuasion [pər'sweʒən] *s* persuasion *f*; (faith) (coll) croyance *f*
pert [pʌrt] *adj* effronté; (sprightly) animé
pertain [pər'ten] *intr*—to pertain to avoir rapport à
pertinacious [,pʌrtı'neʃəs] *adj* obstiné, persévérant
pertinent ['pʌrtınənt] *adj* pertinent
perturb [pər'tʌrb] *tr* perturber
Peru [pə'ru] *s* le Pérou
peruse [pə'ruz] *tr* lire; lire attentivement
Peruvian [pə'ruvı·ən] *adj* péruvien || *s* Péruvien *m*
pervade [pər'ved] *tr* pénétrer, s'infiltrer dans
perverse [pər'vʌrs] *adj* pervers; obstiné; capricieux
perversion [pər'vʌrʒən] *s* perversion *f*
perversi·ty [pər'vʌrsıti] *s* (*pl* -ties) perversité *f*; obstination *f*
pervert ['pʌrvərt] *s* pervers *m*, perverti *m* || [pər'vʌrt] *tr* pervertir
pes·ky ['peski] *adj* (*comp* -kier; *super* -kiest) (coll) importun
pessimism ['pesı,mızəm] *s* pessimisme *m*
pessimist ['pesımıst] *s* pessimiste *mf*
pessimistic [,pesı'mıstık] *adj* pessimiste
pest [pest] *s* insecte *m* nuisible; (pestilence) peste *f*; (annoying person) raseur *m*
pester ['pestər] *tr* casser la tête à, importuner
pest'house' *s* lazaret *m*
pesticide ['pestı,saıd] *s* pesticide *m*
pestiferous [pes'tıfərəs] *adj* pestiféré; (coll) ennuyeux
pestilence ['pestıləns] *s* pestilence *f*
pestle ['pesəl] *s* pilon *m*
pet [pet] *s* animal *m* favori; familial *m*; (child) enfant *m* gâté; (anger) accès *m* de mauvaise humeur || *v* (*pret &*

pp petted; *ger* petting) *tr* choyer; (*e.g., an animal's fur*) caresser ‖ *intr* (slang) se bécoter

petal ['petəl] *s* pétale *m*

pet/cock/ *s* robinet *m* de purge

Peter ['pitər] *s* Pierre *m*; **to rob Peter to pay Paul** découvrir saint Pierre pour habiller saint Paul ‖ (*l.c.*) *intr* —**to peter out** (coll) s'épuiser, s'en aller en fumée

petition [pɪ'tɪʃən] *s* pétition *f* ‖ *tr* adresser or présenter une pétition à

pet/ name/ *s* mot *m* doux, nom *m* d'amitié

Petrarch ['pitrark] *s* Pétrarque *m*

petri·fy ['petrɪ,faɪ] *v* (*pret & pp* -fied) *tr* pétrifier ‖ *intr* se pétrifier

petrol ['petrəl] *s* (Brit) essence *f*

petroleum [pɪ'trolɪ·əm] *s* pétrole *m*

pet/ shop/ *s* boutique *f* aux petites bêtes; (*for birds*) oisellerie *f*

petticoat ['petɪ,kot] *s* jupon *m*

pet·ty ['petɪ] *adj* (*comp* -tier; *super* -tiest) insignifiant, petit; (*narrow*) mesquin; intolérant

pet/ty cash/ *s* petite caisse *f*

pet/ty expen/ses *s* menus frais *mpl*

pet/ty lar/ceny *s* vol *m* simple

pet/ty of/ficer *s* (naut) officier *m* marinier

petulant ['petjələnt] *adj* irritable, boudeur

pew [pju] *s* banc *m* d'église

pewter ['pjutər] *s* étain *m*

Pfc. ['pi'ef'si] *s* (letterword) (private first class) soldat *m* de première classe

phalanx ['felæŋks], ['fælæŋks] *s* phalange *f*

phantasm ['fæntæzəm] *s* fantasme *m*

phantom ['fæntəm] *s* fantôme *m*

Pharaoh ['fero] *s* Pharaon *m*

pharisee ['færɪ,si] *s* pharisien *m*; **Pharisee** Pharisien *m*

pharmaceutical [,farmə'sutɪkəl] *adj* pharmaceutique

pharmacist ['farməsɪst] *s* pharmacien *m*

pharma·cy ['farməsɪ] *s* (*pl* -cies) pharmacie *f*

pharynx ['færɪŋks] *s* pharynx *m*

phase [fez] *s* phase *f*; **out of phase** (*said of motor*) décalé ‖ *tr* mettre en phase; développer en phases successives; (coll) inquiéter; **to phase out** faire disparaître peu à peu

pheasant ['fezənt] *s* faisan *m*

phenobarbital [,fino'barbɪ,tæl] *s* phénobarbital *m*

phenomenal [fɪ'namɪ,nəl] *adj* phénoménal

phenome·non [fɪ'namɪ,nan] *s* (*pl* -na [nə]) phénomène *m*

phial ['faɪ·əl] *s* fiole *f*

philanderer [fɪ'lændərər] *s* coureur *m*, galant *m*

philanthropist [fɪ'lænθrəpɪst] *s* philanthrope *m*

philanthro·py [fɪ'lænθrəpɪ] *s* (*pl* -pies) philanthropie *f*

philatelist [fɪ'lætəlɪst] *s* philatéliste *mf*

philately [fɪ'lætəlɪ] *s* philatélie *f*

Philippine ['fɪlɪ,pin] *adj* philippin ‖ **Philippines** *spl* Philippines *fpl*

Philistine [fɪ'lɪstin], ['fɪlɪ,stin], ['fɪlɪ,staɪn] *adj & s* philistin *m*

philologist [fɪ'lalədʒɪst] *s* philologue *mf*

philology [fɪ'lalədʒɪ] *s* philologie *f*

philosopher [fɪ'lasəfər] *s* philosophe *mf*

philosophic(al) [,fɪlə'safɪk(əl)] *adj* philosophique

philoso·phy [fɪ'lasəfɪ] *s* (*pl* -phies) philosophie *f*

philter ['fɪltər] *s* philtre *m*

phlebitis [flɪ'baɪtɪs] *s* phlébite *f*

phlegm [flem] *s* flegme *m*; **to cough up phlegm** cracher des glaires, tousser gras

phlegmatic(al) [fleg'mætɪk(əl)] *adj* flegmatique

phobia ['fobɪ·ə] *s* phobie *f*

Phoebe ['fibi] *s* Phébé *f*

Phoenicia [fɪ'nɪʃə], [fɪ'niʃə] *s* Phénicie *f*; la Phénicie

Phoenician [fɪ'nɪʃən], [fɪ'niʃən] *adj* phénicien ‖ *s* Phénicien *m*

phoenix ['finɪks] *s* phénix *m*

phone [fon] *s* (coll) téléphone *m* ‖ *tr & intr* (coll) téléphoner

phone/ call/ *s* coup *m* de téléphone, coup de fil

phonetic [fo'netɪk] *adj* phonétique ‖ **phonetics** *s* phonétique *f*

phonograph ['fonə,græf], ['fonə,graf] *s* phonographe *m*

phonology [fə'nalədʒɪ] *s* phonologie *f*

pho·ny ['fonɪ] *adj* (*comp* -nier; *super* -niest) faux, truqué ‖ *s* (*pl* -nies) charlatan *m*

pho/ny war/ *s* drôle *f* de guerre

phosphate ['fasfet] *s* phosphate *m*

phosphorescent [,fasfə'resənt] *adj* phosphorescent

phospho·rus ['fasfərəs] *s* (*pl* -ri [,raɪ]) phosphore *m*

pho·to ['foto] *s* (*pl* -tos) (coll) photo *f*

photoengraving [,foto·en'grevɪŋ] *s* photogravure *f*

pho/to fin/ish *s* photo-finish *f*

photogenic [,foto'dʒenɪk] *adj* photogénique

photograph ['fotə,græf], ['fotə,graf] *s* photographie *f* ‖ *tr* photographier ‖ *intr* —**to photograph well** être photogénique

photographer [fə'tagrəfər] *s* photographe *mf*

photography [fə'tagrəfɪ] *s* photographie *f*

photostat ['fotə,stæt] *s* (trademark) photostat *m* ‖ *tr & intr* photocopier

phrase [frez] *s* locution *f*, expression *f*; (mus) phrase *f* ‖ *tr* exprimer, rédiger; (mus) phraser

phrenology [frɪ'nalədʒɪ] *s* phrénologie *f*

phys·ic ['fɪzɪk] *s* médicament *m*; (*laxative*) purgatif *m* ‖ *v* (*pret & pp* -icked; *ger* -icking) *tr* purger

physical ['fɪzɪkəl] *adj* physique

phys/ical de/fect *s* vice *m* de conformation

physician [fɪ'zɪʃən] *s* médecin *m*

physicist ['fɪzɪsɪst] *s* physicien *m*

physics ['fɪzɪks] s physique f

physiogno·my [,fɪzɪ'ɑgnəmɪ], [,fɪzɪ-'ɑnəmɪ] s (pl -mies) physionomie f

physiological [,fɪzɪ·ə'lɑdʒɪkəl] adj physiologique

physiology [,fɪzɪ'ɑlədʒɪ] s physiologie f

physique [fɪ'zik] s physique m

pi [paɪ] s (math) pi m; (typ) pâté m || v (pret & pp pied; ger piing) tr (typ) mettre en pâte

pianist [pɪ'ænɪst], ['pi·ənɪst] s pianiste mf

pian·o [pɪ'æno] s (pl -os) piano m

pian'o stool' s tabouret m de piano

picayune [,pɪkə'jun] adj mesquin

picco·lo ['pɪkəlo] s (pl -los) piccolo m

pick [pɪk] s (tool) pic m, pioche f; (choice) choix m; (choicest) élite f, fleur f || tr choisir; (flowers) cueillir; (fibers) effiler; (one's teeth, nose, etc.) se curer; (a scab) gratter; (a fowl) plumer; (a bone) ronger; (a lock) crocheter; (the ground) piocher; (e.g., guitar strings) toucher; (a quarrel; flaws) chercher; to pick off enlever; (to shoot) descendre; to pick out trier; to pick pockets voler à la tire; to pick to pieces (coll) éplucher; to pick up ramasser; (one's strength) reprendre; (speed) accroître; (a passenger) prendre; (a man overboard) recueillir; (an anchor; a stitch; a fallen child) relever; (information; a language) apprendre; (the scent) retrouver; (rad) capter || intr (said of birds) picorer; to pick at (to scold) (coll) gronder; to pick at one's food manger du bout des dents; to pick on choisir; (coll) gronder; to pick up (coll) se rétablir

pick'ax' s pioche f

picket ['pɪkɪt] s (stake, pale) pieu m; (of strikers; of soldiers) piquet m || tr entourer de piquets de grève || intr faire le piquet

pick'et fence' s palis m

pick'et line' s piquet m de grève

pickle ['pɪkəl] s cornichon m; (brine) marinade f, saumure f; (coll) gâchis m || tr conserver dans du vinaigre

pick'lock' s crochet m; (person) crocheteur m

pick'-me-up' s (coll) remontant m

pick'pock'et s voleur m à la tire

pick'up' s chargement m; passager m; (of a motor) reprise f; (truck; phonograph cartridge) pick-up m; (woman) (coll) racoleuse f

pick'up arm' s bras m de pick-up

pick'up truck' s camionnette f

pic·nic ['pɪknɪk] s pique-nique m || v (pret & pp -nicked; ger -nicking) intr pique-niquer

pictorial [pɪk'torɪ·əl] adj & s illustré m

picture ['pɪktʃər] s tableau m; image f; photographie f; (painting) peinture f; (engraving) gravure f; (mov) film m; (screen) (mov, telv) écran m; the very picture of le portrait de, l'image de; to receive the picture (telv) capter l'image || tr dépeindre, représenter; to picture to oneself s'imaginer

pic'ture gal'lery s musée m de peinture

pic'ture post'card' s carte f postale illustrée

pic'ture show' s exhibition f de peinture; (mov) cinéma m

pic'ture sig'nal s signal m vidéo

picturesque [,pɪktʃə'resk] adj pittoresque

pic'ture tube' s tube m de l'image

pic'ture win'dow' s fenêtre f panoramique

piddling ['pɪdlɪŋ] adj insignifiant

pie [paɪ] s pâté m; (dessert) tarte f; (bird) pie f

piece [pis] s (of music; of bread) morceau m; (cannon, coin, chessman, pastry, clothing) pièce f; (of land) parcelle f; (e.g., of glass) éclat m; a piece of advice un conseil; a piece of furniture un meuble; to break into pieces mettre en pièces, mettre en morceaux; to give s.o. a piece of one's mind (coll) dire son fait à qn; to go to pieces se désagréger; (to be hysterical) avoir ses nerfs; to pick to pieces (coll) éplucher || tr rapiécer; to piece together rassembler, coordonner

piece'meal' adv pièce à pièce

piece'work' s travail m à la tâche

piece'work'er s ouvrier m à la tâche

pied [paɪd] adj bigarré, panaché; (typ) tombé en pâté

pier [pɪr] s quai m; (of a bridge) pile f; (of a harbor) jetée f; (wall between two openings) (archit) trumeau m

pierce [pɪrs] tr & intr percer

piercing ['pɪrsɪŋ] adj perçant; (sharp) aigu

pier' glass' s grand miroir m

pie·ty ['paɪ·ətɪ] s (pl -ties) piété f

piffle ['pɪfəl] s (coll) futilités fpl, sottises fpl

pig [pɪg] s cochon m, porc m

pigeon ['pɪdʒən] s pigeon m

pi'geon·hole' s boulin m; (in desk) case f || tr caser; mettre au rancart

pi'geon house' s pigeonnier m

piggish ['pɪgɪʃ] adj goinfre

piggyback ['pɪgɪ,bæk] adv sur le dos, sur les épaules; en auto-couchette

pig'gy bank' ['pɪgɪ] s tirelire f, grenouille f

pig'head'ed adj cabochard, têtu

pig' i'ron s gueuse f

piglet ['pɪglɪt] s cochonnet m

pigment ['pɪgmənt] s pigment m

pig'pen' s porcherie f

pig'skin' s peau f de porc; (coll) ballon m du football

pig'sty' s (pl -sties) porcherie f

pig'tail' s queue f, natte f; (of tobacco) carotte f

pike [paɪk] s pique f; autoroute f à péage; (fish) brochet m

piker ['paɪkər] s (slang) rat m

pile [paɪl] s tas m; (stake) pieu m; (of rug) poil m; (of building) masse f; (elec, phys) pile f; (coll) fortune f; piles (pathol) hémorroïdes fpl || tr empiler || intr s'empiler

pile' dri'ver s sonnette f

pilfer ['pɪlfər] tr & intr chaparder
pilgrim ['pɪlgrɪm] s pèlerin m
pilgrimage ['pɪlgrɪmɪdʒ] s pèlerinage m
pill [pɪl] s pilule f; (something unpleasant) pilule; (coll) casse-pieds m
pillage ['pɪlɪdʒ] s pillage ‖ tr & intr piller
pillar ['pɪlər] s pilier m
pillo•ry ['pɪləri] s (pl -ries) pilori m ‖ v (pret & pp -ried) tr clouer au pilori
pillow ['pɪlo] s oreiller m
pil'low-case' or **pil'low-slip'** s taie f d'oreiller
pilot ['paɪlət] s pilote m; (of gas range) veilleuse f ‖ tr piloter
pi'lot en'gine s locomotive-pilote f
pi'lot light' s veilleuse f
pimp [pɪmp] s entremetteur m
pimple ['pɪmpəl] s bouton m
pim•ply ['pɪmpli] adj (comp **-plier**; super **-pliest**) boutonneux
pin [pɪn] s épingle f; (of wearing apparel) agrafe f; (bowling) quille f; (mach) clavette f, cheville f, goupille f; **to be on pins and needles** être sur les chardons ardents ‖ v (pret & pp **pinned**; ger **pinning**) tr épingler; (mach) cheviller, goupiller; **to pin down** fixer, clouer
pinafore ['pɪnə‚for] s tablier m d'enfant
pin'ball' s billard m américain
pincers ['pɪnsərz] s & spl pinces fpl
pinch [pɪntʃ] s pinçade f; (of salt) pincée f; (of tobacco) prise f; (of hunger) morsure f; (trying time) moment m critique; (slang) arrestation f; **in a pinch** au besoin ‖ tr pincer; (to press tightly on) serrer; (e.g., one's finger in a door) se prendre; (to arrest) (slang) pincer; (to steal) (slang) chiper ‖ intr (said, e.g., of shoe) gêner; (to save) lésiner
pinchers ['pɪntʃərz] s & spl pinces fpl
pin'cush'ion s pelote f d'épingles
pine [paɪn] s pin m ‖ intr languir; **to pine for** soupirer après
pine'ap'ple s ananas m
pine' cone' s pomme f de pin
pine' nee'dle s aiguille f de pin
ping [pɪŋ] s sifflement m; (in a motor) cognement m ‖ intr siffler; cogner
pin'head' s tête f d'épingle; (coll) crétin m
pink [pɪŋk] adj rose ‖ s rose m; (bot) œillet m; **to be in the pink** se porter à merveille
pin' mon'ey s argent m de poche
pinnacle ['pɪnəkəl] s pinacle m
pin'point' adj exact f ‖ s (fig) point m critique ‖ tr situer avec précision
pin'prick' s piqûre f d'épingle
pint [paɪnt] s chopine f
pin'up girl' s pin up f
pin'wheel' s (fireworks) soleil m; (child's toy) moulinet m
pioneer [‚paɪə'nɪr] s pionnier m ‖ tr défricher ‖ intr faire œuvre de pionnier
pious ['paɪ•əs] adj pieux, dévot
pip [pɪp] s (in fruit) pépin m; (on cards, dice, etc.) point m; (rad) top m; (vet) pépie f
pipe [paɪp] s tuyau m, tube m, conduit m; (to smoke tobacco) pipe f; (of an organ) tuyau m; (mus) chalumeau m ‖ tr canaliser ‖ intr jouer du chalumeau; **pipe down!** (slang) boucle-la!
pipe'clean'er s cure-pipe m
pipe' dream' s rêve m, projet m illusoire
pipe' line' s pipe-line m; (of information) tuyau m
pipe' or'gan s grandes orgues fpl
piper ['paɪpər] s joueur m de chalumeau; (bagpiper) cornemuseur m; **to pay the piper** payer les violons
pipe' wrench' s clef f à tubes
piping ['paɪpɪŋ] s tuyauterie f; (sewing) passepoil m
pippin ['pɪpɪn] s (apple) reinette f; (highly admired person or thing) bijou m
piquancy ['pikənsi] s piquant m
piquant ['pikənt] adj piquant
pique [pik] s pique f ‖ tr piquer; **to pique oneself on** se piquer de
pira•cy ['paɪrəsi] s (pl -cies) piraterie f
Piraeus [paɪ'ri•əs] s Le Pirée
pirate ['paɪrɪt] s pirate m ‖ tr piller ‖ intr pirater
pirouette [‚pɪru'et] s pirouette f ‖ intr pirouetter
pistol ['pɪstəl] s pistolet m
piston ['pɪstən] s piston m
pis'ton ring' s segment m de piston
pis'ton rod' s tige f de piston
pis'ton stroke' s course f de piston
pit [pɪt] s fosse f, trou m; (in the skin) marque f; (of certain fruit) noyau m; (for cockfights, etc.) arène f; (of the stomach) creux m; (min) puits m; (theat) fauteuils mpl d'orchestre derrière les musiciens ‖ v (pret & pp **pitted**; ger **pitting**) tr trouer; (the face) grêler; (fruit) dénoyauter; **to pit oneself against** se mesurer contre
pitch [pɪtʃ] s (black sticky substance) poix f; (throw) lancement m, jet m; (of a boat) tangage m; (of a roof) degré m de pente; (of, e.g., a screw) pas m; (of a tone, of the voice, etc.) hauteur f; (coll) boniment m, tamtam m; **to such a pitch that** à tel point que ‖ tr lancer, jeter; (hay) fourcher; (a tent) dresser; (enduire de poix; (mus) donner le ton de ‖ intr (said of boat) tanguer; **to pitch in** (coll) se mettre à la besogne; (coll) commencer à manger; **to pitch into** (coll) s'attaquer à
pitch' ac'cent s accent m de hauteur
pitcher ['pɪtʃər] s broc m, cruche f; (baseball) lanceur m
pitch'fork' s fourche f; **to rain pitchforks** pleuvoir à torrents
pitch' pipe' s diapason m de bouche
pit'fall' s trappe f; (fig) écueil m, pierre f
pith [pɪθ] s moelle f; (fig) suc m
pith•y ['pɪθi] adj (comp **-ier**; super **-iest**) moelleux; (fig) plein de suc
pitiful ['pɪtɪfəl] adj pitoyable

pitiless ['pɪtɪlɪs] *adj* impitoyable

pit•y ['pɪti] *s* (*pl* -ies) pitié *f*; **for pity's sake!** par pitié!; **what a pity!** quel dommage! ‖ *v* (*pret & pp* -ied) *tr* avoir pitié de, plaindre

pivot ['pɪvət] *s* pivot *m* ‖ *tr* faire pivoter ‖ *intr* pivoter

placard ['plækʊrd] *s* placard *m*, affiche *f* ‖ *tr* placarder

placate ['pleket] *tr* apaiser

place [ples] *s* endroit *m*; (*job*) poste *m*, emploi *m*; (*seat*) place *f*; (*rank*) rang *m*; **everything in its place** chaque chose à sa place; **in no place** nulle part; **in place of** au lieu de; **in your place** à votre place; **out of place** déplacé; **to change places** changer de place; **to keep one's place** (fig) tenir ses distances; **to take place** avoir lieu ‖ *tr* mettre, placer; (*to find a job for; to invest*) placer; (*to recall*) remettre, se rappeler; (*to set down*) poser ‖ *intr* (turf) finir placé

place•bo [plə'sibo] *s* (*pl* -bos *or* -boes) remède *m* factice

place′ card′ *s* marque-place *f*, carton *m* marque-place

place′ mat′ *s* garde-nappe *m*

placement ['plesmənt] *s* placement *m*; (*location*) emplacement *m*

place′ment exam′ *s* examen *m* probatoire

place′-name′ *s* nom *m* de lieu, toponyme *m*

placid ['plæsɪd] *adj* placide

plagiarism ['pledʒə,rɪzəm] *s* plagiat *m*

plagiarize ['pledʒə,raɪz] *tr* plagier

plague [pleg] *s* peste *f*; (*great public calamity*) fléau *m* ‖ *tr* tourmenter

plaid [plæd] *s* plaid *m*

plain [plen] *adj* clair; simple; (*e.g., answer*) franc; (*color*) uni; (*ugly*) sans attraits ‖ *s* plaine *f*

plain′ clothes′ *spl*—**in plain clothes** en civil, en bourgeois

plain′clothes′man *s* (*pl* -men′) agent *m* en civil

plain′ cook′ing *s* cuisine *f* bourgeoise

plain′ om′elet *s* omelette *f* nature

plain′ speech′ *s* franc-parler *m*

plaintiff ['plentɪf] *s* (law) demandeur *m*, plaignant *m*

plaintive ['plentɪv] *adj* plaintif

plan [plæn] *s* plan *m*, projet *m*; (*drawing, diagram*) plan, dessein *m* ‖ *v* (*pret & pp* **planned**) *ger* **planning**) *tr* projeter; **to plan to** se proposer de ‖ *intr* faire des projets

plane [plen] *adj* plan, plat ‖ *s* (aer) avion *m*; (bot) platane *m*; (carpentry) rabot *m*; (geom) plan *m* ‖ *tr* raboter

plane′ sick′ness *s* mal *m* de l'air

planet ['plænɪt] *s* planète *f*

plane′ tree′ *s* platane *m*

plan′ing mill′ *s* atelier *m* de rabotage

plank [plæŋk] *s* planche *f*; (pol) article *m* d'une plate-forme électorale

plant [plænt], [plɑnt] *s* (*factory*) usine *f*; (*building and equipment*) installation *f*; (bot) plante *f* ‖ *tr* planter

plantation [plæn'teʃən] *s* plantation *f*

planter ['plæntər] *s* planteur *m*

plant′ louse′ *s* puceron *m*

plasma ['plæzmə] *s* plasma *m*

plaster ['plæstər], ['plɑstər] *s* plâtre *m*; (*poultice*) emplâtre *m* ‖ *tr* plâtrer; (*a bill, poster*) coller; (slang) griser

plas′ter cast′ *s* plâtre *m*

plas′ter of Par′is *s* plâtre *m* à mouler

plastic ['plæstɪk] *adj* plastique ‖ *s* (*substance*) plastique *m*; (*art*) plastique *f*

plas′tic bomb′ *s* plastic *m*

plas′tic sur′gery *s* chirurgie *f* esthétique, chirurgie plastique

plate [plet] *s* (*dish*) assiette *f*; (*platter*) plateau *m*; (*sheet of metal*) tôle *f*, plaque *f*; vaisselle *f* d'or ou d'argent; (anat, elec, phot, rad, zool) plaque; (typ) planche *f* ‖ *tr* plaquer; (elec) galvaniser; (typ) clicher

plateau [plæ'to] *s* plateau *m*, massif *m*

plate′ glass′ *s* verre *m* cylindré

platen ['plætən] *s* rouleau *m*

platform ['plæt,fɔrm] *s* plate-forme *f*; (*for arrivals and departures*) quai *m*; (*of a speaker*) estrade *f*; (*political program*) plate-forme

plat′form car′ *s* (rr) plate-forme *f*

platinum ['plætɪnəm] *s* platine *m*

plat′inum blonde′ *s* blonde *f* platinée

platitude ['plætɪ,t(j)ud] *s* platitude *f*

Plato ['pleto] *s* Platon *m*

platoon [plə'tun] *s* section *f*

platter ['plætər] *s* plat *m*; (slang) disque *m*

plausible ['plɔzɪbəl] *adj* plausible

play [ple] *s* jeu *m*; (*drama*) pièce *f*; (mach) jeu; **to give full play to** donner libre cours à ‖ *tr* jouer; (*e.g., the fool*) faire; (*cards; e.g., football*) jouer à; (*an instrument*) jouer de; **to play back** (*a tape*) faire repasser; **to play down** diminuer; **to play hooky** faire l'école buissonnière; **to play off** (sports) rejouer; **to play up** accentuer ‖ *intr* jouer; **to play out** s'épuiser; **to play safe** prendre des précautions; **to play sick** faire semblant d'être malade; **to play up to** passer de la pommade à

play′back′ *s* (*device*) lecteur *m*; (*reproduction*) lecture *f*

play′back head′ *s* tête *f* de lecture

play′bill′ *s* programme *m*; (*poster*) affiche *f*

play′er pian′o ['ple-ər] *s* piano *m* mécanique

playful ['plefəl] *adj* enjoué, badin

playgoer ['ple,go-ər] *s* amateur *m* de théâtre

play′ground′ *s* terrain *m* de jeu

play′house′ *s* théâtre *m*; (*dollhouse*) maison *f* de poupée

play′ing card′ *s* carte *f* à jouer

play′ing field′ *s* terrain *m* de sports

play′mate′ *s* compagnon *m* de jeu

play′-off′ *s* finale *f*, match *m* d'appui

play′ on words′ *s* jeu *m* de mots

play′pen′ *s* parc *m* d'enfants

play′room′ *s* salle *f* de jeux

play′thing′ *s* jouet *m*

play'time' s recréation f
playwright ['ple‚raɪt] s auteur m dramatique, dramaturge mf
play'writ'ing s dramaturgie f
plea [pli] s requête f, appel m; prétexte m; (law) défense f
plead [plid] v (pret & pp **pleaded** or **pled** [plɛd]) tr & intr plaider; to **plead not guilty** plaider non coupable
pleasant ['plɛzənt] adj agréable
pleasant-ry ['plɛzəntri] s (pl **-ries**) plaisanterie f
please [pliz] tr plaire (with dat); it **pleases him to** il lui plaît de; **please** + inf veuillez + inf; **to be pleased with** être content or satisfait de ‖ intr plaire; **as you please** comme vous voulez; **if you please** s'il vous plaît
pleasing ['plizɪŋ] adj agréable
pleasure ['plɛʒər] s plaisir m; **at the pleasure of** au gré de; **what is your pleasure?** que puis-je faire pour vous service?, que puis-je faire pour vous?
pleas'ure car' s voiture f de tourisme
pleas'ure trip' s voyage m d'agrément
pleat [plit] s pli m ‖ tr plisser
plebe [plib] s élève m de première année
plebeian [plɪ'bi·ən] adj & s plébéien m
plebiscite ['plɛbɪ‚saɪt] s plébiscite m
pledge [plɛdʒ] s gage m; engagement m d'honneur, promesse f ‖ tr mettre en gage; (one's word) engager
plentiful ['plɛntɪfəl] adj abondant
plenty ['plɛnti] s abondance f; **plenty of** beaucoup de ‖ adv (coll) largement
pleurisy ['plʊrɪsi] s pleurésie f
pliable ['plaɪ·əbəl] adj pliable; docile, maniable
pliers ['plaɪ·ərz] s & spl pinces fpl, tenailles fpl
plight [plaɪt] s embarras m; (promise) engagement m ‖ tr engager; **to plight one's troth** promettre fidélité
plod [plɑd] v (pret & pp **plodded**; ger **plodding**) tr parcourir lourdement et péniblement ‖ intr cheminer; travailler laborieusement
plot [plɑt] s complot m; (of a play or novel) intrigue f; (of ground) lopin m, parcelle f; (map) tracé m, plan m; (of vegetables) carré m ‖ v (pret & pp **plotted**; ger **plotting**) tr comploter, tramer; (a tract of land) faire le plan de; (a point) relever; (lines) tracer ‖ intr comploter; **to plot to** + inf comploter de + inf
plough [plaʊ] s, tr & intr var of **plow**
plover ['plʌvər] s pluvier m
plow [plaʊ] s charrue f; (for snow) chasse-neige m ‖ tr labourer; (the sea; the forehead) sillonner; (snow) déblayer; **to plow back** (com) affecter aux investissements ‖ intr labourer; **to plow through** avancer péniblement dans
plow'man s (pl **-men**) laboureur m
plow'share' s soc m de charrue
pluck [plʌk] s cran m; (tug) saccade f ‖ tr arracher; (flowers) cueillir; (a fowl) plumer; (one's eyebrows)

épiler; (e.g., the strings of a guitar) pincer ‖ intr—**to pluck at** arracher d'un coup sec; **to pluck up** reprendre courage
pluck-y ['plʌki] adj (comp **-ier**; super **-iest**) courageux, crâne
plug [plʌg] s tampon m, bouchon m; (of sink, bathtub, etc.) bonde f; (of tobacco) chique f; (aut) bougie f; (on wall) (elec) prise f; (prongs) (elec) fiche f, prise; (old horse) (coll) rosse f; (hat) (slang) haut-de-forme f; (slang) annonce f publicitaire ‖ v (pret & pp **plugged**; ger **plugging**) tr boucher; (a melon) entamer; **to plug in** (elec) brancher ‖ intr—**to plug away** (coll) persévérer
plum [plʌm] s prune f; (tree) prunier m; (slang) fromage m
plumage ['plumɪdʒ] s plumage m
plumb [plʌm] adj d'aplomb; (coll) pur ‖ s plomb m; **out of plumb** hors d'aplomb ‖ adv d'aplomb; (coll) en plein; (coll) complètement ‖ tr sonder
plumb' bob' s plomb m
plumber ['plʌmər] s plombier m
plumbing ['plʌmɪŋ] s plomberie f
plumb' line' s fil m à plomb
plume [plum] s aigrette f; (of a hat, of smoke, etc.) panache m ‖ tr orner de plumes; (feathers) lisser; **to plume oneself on** se piquer de
plummet ['plʌmɪt] s plomb m ‖ intr tomber d'aplomb, se précipiter
plump [plʌmp] adj grassouillet, potelé, dodu; brusque ‖ s (coll) chute f lourde; (coll) bruit m sourd ‖ adv en plein; brusquement ‖ tr jeter brusquement; **to plump oneself down** s'affaler ‖ intr tomber lourdement
plunder ['plʌndər] s pillage m; (booty) butin m ‖ tr piller
plunge [plʌndʒ] s plongeon m; (pitching movement) tangage m ‖ tr plonger ‖ intr plonger; se précipiter; (fig) se plonger; (naut) tanguer; (slang) risquer de grosses sommes
plunger ['plʌndʒər] s plongeur m; (slang) risque-tout m
plunk [plʌŋk] adv d'un coup sec; (squarely) carrément ‖ tr jeter bruyamment ‖ intr tomber raide
plural ['plʊrəl] adj & s pluriel m
plus [plʌs] adj positif ‖ s (sign) plus m; quantité f positive ‖ prep plus
plush [plʌʃ] adj en peluche; (coll) rupin ‖ s peluche f
plush-y ['plʌʃi] adj (comp **-ier**; super **-iest**) pelucheux; (coll) rupin
plus' sign' s signe m plus
Plutarch ['plutark] s Plutarque m
Pluto ['pluto] s Pluton m
plutonium [plu'toni·əm] s plutonium m
ply [plaɪ] s (pl **plies**) (e.g., of a cloth) pli m; (of rope, wool, etc.) brin m ‖ v (pret & pp **plied**) tr manier; (a trade) exercer; **to ply s.o. with** presser qn de ‖ intr faire la navette
ply'wood' s bois m de placage, contreplaqué m

P.M. ['pi'em] *adv* (letterword) (**post meridiem**) de l'après-midi, du soir
pneumatic [n(j)u'mætɪk] *adj* pneumatique
pneumat'ic drill' *s* foreuse *f* à air comprimé
pneumonia [n(j)u'monɪ'ə] *s* pneumonie *f*
P.O. ['pi'o] *s* (letterword) (**post office**) poste *f*
poach [potʃ] *tr* (*eggs*) pocher || *intr* (*hunting*) braconner
poached' egg' *s* œuf *m* poché
poacher ['potʃər] *s* braconnier *m*
pock [pak] *s* pustule *f*
pocket ['pakɪt] *s* poche *f*; (*billiards*) blouse *f*; (*aer*) trou *m* d'air.|| *tr* empocher; (*a billiard ball*) blouser; (*insults*) avaler
pock'et·book' *s* portefeuille *m*; (*small book*) livre *m* de poche
pock'et hand'kerchief *s* mouchoir *m* de poche
pock'et·knife' *s* (*pl* **-knives**) couteau *m* de poche, canif *m*
pock'et mon'ey *s* argent *m* de poche
pock'mark' *s* marque *f* de la petite vérole
pock'marked' *adj* grêlé
pod [pad] *s* cosse *f*, gousse *f*
poem ['po·ɪm] *s* poème *m*
poet ['po·ɪt] *s* poète *m*
poetess ['po·ɪtɪs] *s* poétesse *f*
poetic [po'etɪk] *adj* poétique || **poetics** *s* poétique *f*
poetry ['po·ɪtri] *s* poésie *f*
pogrom ['pogrəm] *s* pogrom *m*
poignancy ['pɔɪnənsi] *s* piquant *m*
poignant ['pɔɪnənt] *adj* poignant
point [pɔɪnt] *s* (*spot, dot, score, etc.*) point *m*; (*tip*) pointe *f*; (*of pen*) bec *m*; (*of conscience*) cas *m*; (*of a star*) rayon *m*; (*of a joke*) piquant *m*; (*of, e.g., grammar*) question *f*; (*geog, naut*) pointe; (*typ*) point; **beside the point, off the point** hors de propos; **on the point of** sur le point de; (*death*) à l'article de; **on this point** à cet égard, à ce propos; **point of a compass** aire *f* de vent; **point of order** rappel *m* au règlement; **points** (aut) vis *f* platinées; **to carry one's point** avoir gain de cause; **to come to the point** venir au fait; **to have one's good points** avoir ses qualités; **to make a point of** se faire un devoir de || *tr* (*a gun, telescope, etc.*) braquer, pointer; (*a finger*) tendre; (*the way*) indiquer; (*a wall*) jointoyer; (*to sharpen*) tailler en point; **to point out** signaler, faire remarquer || *intr* pointer; (*said of hunting dog*) tomber en arrêt; **to point at** montrer du doigt
point'-blank' *adj* & *adv* (*fired straight at the mark*) à bout portant; (*straightforward*) à brûle-pourpoint
pointed *adj* pointu; (*remark*) mordant
pointer ['pɔɪntər] *s* (*stick*) baguette *f*; (*of a dial*) aiguille *f*; (*dog*) chien *m* d'arrêt, pointeur *m*
poise [pɔɪz] *s* équilibre *m*; (*assurance*)

aplomb *m* || *tr* tenir en équilibre || *intr* être en équilibre; (*in the air*) planer
poison ['pɔɪzən] *s* poison *m* || *tr* empoisonner
poi'son gas' *s* gaz *m* asphyxiant
poi'son i'vy *s* sumac *m* vénéneux
poisonous ['pɔɪzənəs] *adj* toxique; (*plant*) vénéneux; (*snake*) venimeux
poke [pok] *s* poussée *f*; (*with elbow*) coup *m* de coude; (*coll*) traînard *m* || *tr* pousser; (*the fire*) tisonner; **to poke fun at** se moquer de; **to poke one's nose into** (coll) fourrer son nez dans; **to poke s.th. into** fourrer q.ch. dans || *intr* aller sans se presser; **to poke about** fureter
poker ['pokər] *s* tisonnier *m*; (*cards*) poker *m*
pok'er face' *s* visage *m* impassible
pok·y ['poki] *adj* (*comp* **-ier**; *super* **-iest**) (coll) lambin, lent
Poland ['polənd] *s* Pologne *f*; la Pologne
polar ['polər] *adj* polaire
po'lar bear' *s* ours *m* blanc
polarize ['polə͵raɪz] *tr* polariser
pole [pol] *s* (*long rod or staff*) perche *f*; (*of flag*) hampe *f*; (*upright support*) poteau *m*; (astr, biol, elec, geog, math) pôle *m*; **Pole** (*person*) Polonais *m* || *tr* pousser à la perche
pole'cat' *s* putois *m*
pole'star' *s* étoile *f* polaire
pole' vault' *s* saut *m* à la perche
police [pə'lis] *s* police *f* || *tr* maintenir l'ordre dans
police' brutal'ity *s* brutalité *f* policière
police' commis'sioner *s* préfet *m* de police
police'man *s* (*pl* **-men**) agent *m* de police
police' pre'cinct *s* commissariat *m* de police
police' state' *s* régime *m* policier
police' sta'tion *s* poste *m* de police, commissariat *m*
police'wom'an *s* (*pl* **-wom'en**) femme *f* agent
poli·cy ['palɪsi] *s* (*pl* **-cies**) politique *f*; (ins) police *f*
polio ['polɪ͵o] *s* (coll) polio *f*
polish ['palɪʃ] *s* poli *m*; (*for household uses*) cire *f*; (*for shoes*) cirage *m*; (fig) politesse *f*, vernis *m* || *tr* polir; (*shoes, floor, etc.*) cirer; (*one's nails*) vernir; **to polish off** (coll) expédier; (*e.g., a meal*) (slang) engloutir || **Polish** ['polɪʃ] *adj* & *s* polonais *m*
polite [pə'laɪt] *adj* poli
politeness [pə'laɪtnɪs] *s* politesse *f*
politic ['palɪtɪk] *adj* (*prudent*) diplomatique, politique; (*shrewd*) rusé
political [pə'lɪtɪkəl] *adj* politique
politician [͵palɪ'tɪʃən] *s* politicien *m*
politics ['palɪtɪks] *s* & *spl* politique *f*
poll [pol] *s* liste *f* électorale; (*vote*) scrutin *m*; (*head*) tête *f*; **sondage** *m* d'opinion; **to go to the polls** aller aux urnes; **to take a poll** faire une enquête par sondage || *tr* (*e.g., a dele-*)

gation) dépouiller le scrutin de; (*a certain number of votes*) recevoir

pollen ['palən] *s* pollen *m*

poll'ing booth' ['polɪŋ] *s* isoloir *m*

polliwog ['palɪ ,wag] *s* têtard *m*

pol'liwog initia'tion *s* baptême *m* de la ligne

poll' tax' *s* taxe *f* par tête

pollute [pə'lut] *tr* polluer

pollution [pə'luʃən] *s* pollution *f*

polo ['polo] *s* polo *m*

polonium [pə'lonɪ·əm] *s* polonium *m*

polygamist [pə'lɪgəmɪst] *s* polygame *mf*

polygamous [pə'lɪgəməs] *adj* polygame

polyglot ['palɪ ,glat] *adj & s* polyglotte *mf*

polygon ['palɪ ,gan] *s* polygone *m*

polynomial [,palɪ'nomɪ·əl] *s* polynôme *m*

polyp ['palɪp] *s* polype *m*

polytheist ['palɪ ,θi·ɪst] *s* polythéiste *mf*

polytheistic [,palɪθi'ɪstɪk] *adj* polythéiste

pomade [pə'med], [pə'mad] *s* pommade *f*

pomegranate ['pam ,grænɪt] *s* (*shrub*) grenadier *m*; (*fruit*) grenade *f*

pommel ['pʌməl], ['paməl] *s* pommeau *m* ‖ *v* (*pret & pp* -meled or -melled; *ger* -meling or -melling) *tr* rosser

pomp [pamp] *s* pompe *f*

pompous ['pampəs] *adj* pompeux

pon·cho ['pant/o] *s* (*pl* -chos) poncho *m*

pond [pand] *s* étang *m*, mare *f*

ponder ['pandər] *tr* peser ‖ *intr* méditer; **to ponder over** réfléchir sur

ponderous ['pandərəs] *adj* pesant

poniard ['panjərd] *s* poignard *m* ‖ *tr* poignarder

pontiff ['pantɪf] *s* pontife *m*

pontifical [pan'tɪfɪkəl] *adj* (*e.g., air*) de pontife

pontoon [pan'tun] *s* ponton *m*

po·ny ['poni] *s* (*pl* -nies) poney *m*; (*for drinking liquor*) petit verre *m*; (*coll*) aide-mémoire *m* illicite

poodle ['pudəl] *s* caniche *m*

pool [pul] *s* (*small puddle*) mare *f*; (*for swimming*) piscine *f*; (*game*) billard *m*; (*in certain games*) poule *f*; (*of workers*) équipe *f*; (*combine*) pool *m*; (*com*) fonds *m* commun ‖ *tr* mettre en commun

pool'room' *s* salle *f* de billard

pool' ta'ble *s* table *f* de billard

poop [pup] *s* poupe *f*; (*deck*) dunette *f* ‖ *tr* (*slang*) casser la tête à

poor [pur] *adj* pauvre; (*mediocre*) piètre; (*unfortunate*) pauvre (*before noun*); (*without money*) pauvre (*after noun*)

poor' box' *s* tronc *m* des pauvres

poor'house' *s* asile *m* des indigents

poorly ['purli] *adj* souffrant ‖ *adv* mal

pop [pap] *s* bruit *m* sec; (*soda*) boisson *f* gazeuse ‖ *v* (*pret & pp* popped; *ger* popping) *tr* (*corn*) faire éclater ‖ *intr*

(*said, e.g., of balloon*) crever; (*said of cork*) sauter

pop'corn' *s* maïs *m* éclaté, grains *mpl* de maïs soufflés, pop-corn *m*

pope [pop] *s* pape *m*

pop'eyed' *adj* aux yeux saillants

pop'gun' *s* canonnière *f*

poplar ['paplər] *s* peuplier *m*

pop·py ['papi] *s* (*pl* -pies) pavot *m*; (*corn poppy*) coquelicot *m*

pop'py·cock' *s* (coll) fadaises *fpl*

populace ['papjəlɪs] *s* peuple *m*, populace *f*

popular ['papjələr] *adj* populaire

popularize ['papjələ ,raɪz] *tr* populariser, vulgariser

populate ['papjə ,let] *tr* peupler

population [,papjə'leʃən] *s* population *f*

populous ['papjələs] *adj* populeux

porcelain ['pɔrsəlɪn], ['pɔrslɪn] *s* porcelaine *f*

porch [pɔrt/] *s* (*portico*) porche *m*; (*enclosed*) véranda *f*

porcupine ['pɔrkjə ,paɪn] *s* porc-épic *m*

pore [por] *s* pore *m* ‖ *intr*—**to pore over** examiner avec attention, s'absorber dans

pork [pork] *s* porc *m*

pork' and beans' *spl* fèves *fpl* au lard

pork'chop' *s* côtelette *f* de porc

pornography [pɔr'nagrəfi] *s* pornographie *f*

porous ['porəs] *adj* poreux

porphy·ry ['pɔrfɪri] *s* (*pl* -ries) porphyre *m*

porpoise ['pɔrpəs] *s* marsouin *m*

porridge ['parɪdʒ], ['pɔrɪdʒ] *s* bouillie *f*, porridge *m*

port [port] *s* port *m*; (*opening in ship's side*) hublot *m*, sabord *m*; (*left side of ship or airplane*) bâbord *m*; (*wine*) porto *m*; (*mach*) orifice *m*

portable ['pɔrtəbəl] *adj* portatif

portage ['portɪdʒ] *s* transport *m*; portage *m*

portal ['portəl] *s* portail *m*

portcullis [port'kʌlɪs] *s* herse *f*

portend [por'tend] *tr* présager

portent ['portent] *s* présage *m*

portentous [por'tentəs] *adj* extraordinaire; de mauvais augure

porter ['portər] *s* (*doorkeeper*) portier *m*, concierge *m*; (*in hotels and trains*) porteur *m*

portfoli·o [port'folɪ ,o] *s* (*pl* -os) portefeuille *m*

port'hole' *s* hublot *m*

porti·co ['portɪ ,ko] *s* (*pl* -coes or -cos) portique *m*

portion ['porʃən] *s* portion *f*; (*dowry*) dot *f* ‖ *tr*—**to portion out** partager, répartir

port·ly ['portli] *adj* (*comp* -lier; *super* -liest) corpulent

port' of call' *s* port *m* d'escale

portrait ['portret], ['portrɪt] *s* portrait *m*; **to sit for one's portrait** se faire faire son portrait

portray [por'tre] *tr* faire le portrait de; dépeindre, décrire; (*theat*) jouer le rôle de

portrayal [por'tre·əl] s représentation f; description f

Portugal ['port/əgəl] s le Portugal

Por·tu·guese ['port/ə,giz] adj portugais || s (language) portugais m || s (pl -guese) (person) Portugais m

port' wine' s porto m

pose [poz] s pose f || tr & intr poser; **to pose as** se poser comme

posh [paʃ] adj (slang) chic, élégant

position [pə'zɪʃən] s position f; (job) poste m; **in position** en place; **in your position** à votre place

positive ['pazɪtɪv] adj & s positif m

possess [pə'zɛs] tr posséder

possession [pə'zɛʃən] s possession f; **to take possession of** s'emparer de

possible ['pasɪbəl] adj possible

possum ['pasəm] s opossum m; **to play possum** (coll) faire le mort

post [post] s (upright) poteau m; (job, position) poste m; (post office) poste f; (mil) poste m || tr (a notice, placard, etc.) afficher, placarder; (a letter) poster, mettre à la poste; (a sentinel) poster; (with news) tenir au courant; **post no bills** (public sign) défense d'afficher

postage ['postɪdʒ] s port m, affranchissement m

post'age due' s port m dû, affranchissement m insuffisant

post'age me'ter s affranchisseuse f à compteur

post'age stamp' s timbre-poste m

postal [postəl] adj postal

post'al card' s carte f postale

post'al clerk' s postier m

post'al mon'ey or'der s mandat-poste m

post'al per'mit s franchise f postale, dispensé m du timbrage

post'al sav'ings bank' s caisse f d'épargne postale

post' card' s carte f postale

post'date' s postdate f || tr postdater

poster ['postər] s affiche f

posterity [pas'tɛrɪtɪ] s postérité f

postern [postərn] s poterne f

post'haste' adv en toute hâte

posthumous ['pastʃʊməs] adj posthume

post'man s (pl -men) facteur m

post'mark' s cachet m d'oblitération, timbre m || tr timbrer

post'mas'ter s receveur m des postes, administrateur m du bureau de postes

post'master gen'eral s ministre m des Postes et Télécommunications

post-mortem [,post'mortəm] adj après décès; (fig) après le fait || s autopsie f; discussion f après le fait

post' of'fice s bureau m de poste

post'-office box' s case f postale, boîte f postale

post'paid' adv port payé, franc de port, franco de port

postpone [post'pon] tr remettre, différer; (a meeting) ajourner

postponement [post'ponmənt] s remise f, ajournement m

postscript ['post,skrɪpt] s post-scriptum m

posture ['pastʃər] s posture f || intr prendre une posture

post'war' adj d'après-guerre

po·sy ['pozi] s (pl -sies) fleur f; bouquet m

pot [pat] s pot m; (in gambling) mise f; **to go to pot** (slang) s'en aller à vau-l'eau

potash ['pat,æʃ] s potasse f

potassium [pə'tæsɪəm] s potassium m

pota·to [pə'teto] s (pl -toes) pomme f de terre; (sweet potato) patate f

pota'to chips' spl pommes fpl chips, croustille f (Canad)

potbellied ['pat,bɛlid] adj ventru

poten·cy ['potənsi] s (pl -cies) puissance f; virilité f

potent ['potənt] adj puissant, fort; (effective) efficace

potentate ['potən,tet] s potentat m

potential [pə'tɛnʃəl] adj & s potentiel (ielle)

pot'hang'er s crémaillère f

pot'herb' s herbe f potagère

pot'hold'er s poignée f

pot'hole' s nid m de poule

pot'hook' s croc m

potion ['poʃən] s potion f

pot'luck' s—**to take potluck** manger à la fortune du pot

pot' shot' s coup m tiré à courte distance

potter ['patər] s potier m || intr—**to potter around** s'occuper de bagatelles, bricoler

pot'ter's clay' s terre f à potier

pot'ter's field' s fosse f commune

pot'ter's wheel' s roue f or tour m de potier

potter·y ['patəri] s (pl -ies) poterie f

pouch [pautʃ] s poche f, petit sac m; (of kangaroo) poche f ventrale; (for tobacco) blague f

poultice ['poltɪs] s cataplasme m

poultry ['poltri] s volaille f

poul'try·man s (pl -men) éleveur m de volailles; (dealer) volailleur m

pounce [pauns] intr—**to pounce on** fondre sur, s'abattre sur

pound [paund] s (weight) livre f; (for automobiles, stray animals, etc.) fourrière f || tr battre; (to pulverize) piler, broyer; (to bombard) pilonner; (e.g., an animal) mettre en fourrière; (e.g., the sidewalk) (fig) battre || intr battre

pound' ster'ling s livre f sterling

pour [por] tr verser; (tea) servir; **to pour off** décanter || intr écouler; (said of rain) tomber à verse; **to pour out** of sortir à flots

pout [paut] s moue f || intr faire la moue

poverty ['pavərti] s pauvreté f

POW ['pi'o'dʌb,ju] s (letterword) (prisoner of war) P.G.

powder ['paudər] s poudre f || tr réduire en poudre; (to sprinkle with powder) poudrer || intr se poudrer

pow'dered sug'ar s sucre m de confiseur

pow'der puff' s houppe f

pow'der room' *s* toilettes *fpl* pour dames

powdery ['paudəri] *adj (like powder)* poudreux; *(sprinkled with powder)* poussiéreux; *(crumbly)* friable

power ['pau.ər] *s* pouvoir *m*; *(influential nation; energy, force, strength; of a machine, microscope, number)* puissance *f*; *(talent, capacity, etc.)* faculté *f*; **the powers that be** les autorités *fpl*; **to seize power** saisir le pouvoir || *tr* actionner

pow'er brake' *s* (aut) servo-frein *m*

pow'er dive' *s* piqué *m* à plein gaz

pow'er-dive' *intr* piquer à plein gaz

powerful ['pau.ərfəl] *adj* puissant

pow'er-house' *s* usine *f* centrale; (coll) foyer *m* d'énergie

pow'er lawn'mow'er *s* tondeuse *f* à gazon à moteur

powerless ['pau.ərlɪs] *adj* impuissant

pow'er line' *s* secteur *m* de distribution

pow'er mow'er *s* tondeuse *f* à gazon à moteur; motofaucheuse *f*

pow'er of attorn'ey *s* procuration *f*, mandat *m*

pow'er pack' *s* (rad) unité *f* d'alimentation

pow'er plant' *s (powerhouse)* centrale *f* électrique; (aer, aut) groupe *m* motopropulseur

pow'er steer'ing *s* (aut) servo-direction *f*

practicable ['præktɪkəbəl] *adj* praticable

practical ['præktɪkəl] *adj* pratique

prac'tical joke' *s* farce *f*, attrape *f*

prac'tical jok'er *s* fumiste *m*

practically ['præktɪkəli] *adv* pratiquement; *(more or less)* à peu près

prac'tical nurse' *s* garde-malade *mf*

practice ['præktɪs] *s* pratique *f*; *(of a profession)* exercice *m*; *(of a doctor)* clientèle *f*; **in practice** en pratique, pratiquement; *(well-trained)* en forme; **out of practice** rouillé || *tr* pratiquer; *(a profession)* exercer, pratiquer; *(e.g., the violin)* s'exercer à; **to practice what one preaches** prêcher d'exemple || *intr* faire des exercices, s'exercer; *(said of doctor, lawyer, etc.)* exercer

practiced *adj* expert

practitioner [præk'tɪʃənər] *s* praticien *m*

prairie ['preri] *s* steppes *fpl*; **the prairie** les Prairies *fpl*

praise [prez] *s* louange *f* || *tr* louer

praise'wor'thy *adj* louable

pram [præm] *s* voiture *f* d'enfant

prance [præns], [prɑns] *intr* caracoler, cabrioler

prank [præŋk] *s* espièglerie *f*

prate [pret] *intr* bavarder, papoter

prattle ['prætəl] *s* bavardage *m*, papotage *m* || *intr* bavarder, papoter; *(said of children)* babiller

prawn [prɔn] *s* crevette *f* rose, bouquet *m*

pray [pre] *tr & intr* prier

prayer [prer] *s* prière *f*

prayer' book' *s* livre *m* de prières

pray'ing man'tis ['mæntɪs] *s* mante *f* religieuse

preach [pritʃ] *tr & intr* prêcher

preacher ['pritʃər] *s* prédicateur *m*

preamble ['pri,æmbəl] *s* préambule *m*

precarious [prɪ'keri.əs] *adj* précaire

precaution [prɪ'kɔʃən] *s* précaution *f*

precede [prɪ'sid] *tr & intr* précéder

precedent ['presɪdənt] *s* précédent *m*

precept ['prisept] *s* précepte *m*

precinct ['prisɪŋkt] *s* enceinte *f*; circonscription *f* électorale

precious ['preʃəs] *adj* précieux || *adv—* **precious little** (coll) très peu

precipice ['presɪpɪs] *s* précipice *m*

precipitate [prɪ'sɪpɪ,tet] *adj & s* précipité *m* || *tr* précipiter || *intr* se précipiter

precipitous [prɪ'sɪpɪtəs] *adj* escarpé; *(hurried)* précipité

precise [prɪ'saɪs] *adj* précis

precision [prɪ'sɪʒən] *s* précision *f*

preclude [prɪ'klud] *tr* empêcher

precocious [prɪ'koʃəs] *adj* précoce

preconceived [,prikən'sivd] *adj* préconçu

predatory ['predə,tori] *adj* rapace; (zool) prédateur

predicament [prɪ'dɪkəmənt] *s* situation *f* difficile

predict [prɪ'dɪkt] *tr* prédire

prediction [prɪ'dɪkʃən] *s* prédiction *f*

predispose [,pridɪs'poz] *tr* prédisposer

predominant [prɪ'daminənt] *adj* prédominant

preeminent [prɪ'emɪnənt] *adj* prééminent

preempt [prɪ'empt] *tr* s'approprier

preen [prin] *tr* lisser; **to preen oneself** se bichonner; être fier, se piquer

prefabricated [pri'fæbrɪ,ketɪd] *adj* préfabriqué

preface ['prefɪs] *s* préface *f* || *tr* préfacer

pre-fer [prɪ'fʌr] *v (pret & pp* **-ferred;** *ger* **-ferring)** *tr* préférer

preferable ['prefərəbəl] *adj* préférable

preference ['prefərəns] *s* préférence *f*

preferred' stock' *s* actions *f* privilégiées

prefix ['prifɪks] *s* préfixe *m* || *tr* préfixer

pregnan-cy ['pregnənsi] *s (pl* **-cies)** grossesse *f*

pregnant ['pregnənt] *adj* enceinte, grosse; (fig) gros

prehistoric [,prihɪs'tarɪk], [,prihɪs'tɔrɪk] *adj* préhistorique

prejudice ['predʒədɪs] *s* préjugé *m*; *(detriment)* préjudice *m* || *tr* prévenir, prédisposer; *(to harm)* porter préjudice à

prejudicial [,predʒə'dɪʃəl] *adj* préjudiciable

prelate ['prelɪt] *s* prélat *m*

preliminar-y [prɪ'lɪmɪ,neri] *adj* préliminaire || *s (pl* **-ies)** préliminaire *m*

prelude ['preljud], ['prilud] *s* prélude *m* || *tr* introduire; préluder à; *(a piece of music)* préluder par

premature [,primə't(j)ur] *adj* prématuré; *(plant)* hâtif

premeditate [pri'medɪ,tet] *tr* préméditer

premier [prɪ'mɪr], ['primɪ-ər] s premier ministre m
première [prə'mjer], [prɪ'mɪr] s première f; (actress) vedette f
premise ['premɪs] s prémisse f; **on the premises** sur les lieux; **premises** local m, locaux mpl
premium ['primɪ-əm] s prime f
premonition [,primə'nɪʃən] s prémonition f
preoccupation [pri,ɑkjə'peʃən] s préoccupation f
preoccu·py [pri'ɑkjə,paɪ] v (pret & pp -pied) tr préoccuper
prepaid [pri'ped] adj payé d'avance; (letter) affranchi
preparation [,prepə'reʃən] s préparation f; **preparations** (for a trip; for war) préparatifs mpl
preparatory [prɪ'pærə,tori] adj préparatoire
prepare [prɪ'per] tr préparer || intr se préparer
preparedness [prɪ'perɪdnɪs], [prɪ'perdnɪs] s préparation f; armement m préventif
pre·pay [pri'pe] v (pret & pp -paid) tr payer d'avance
preponderant [prɪ'pɑndərənt] adj prépondérant
preposition [,prepə'zɪʃən] s préposition f
prepossessing [,pripə'zesɪŋ] adj avenant, agréable
preposterous [prɪ'pɑstərəs] adj absurde, extravagant
prep' school' [prep] s école f préparatoire
prerecorded [,priri'kərdɪd] adj (rad, telv) différé
prerequisite [pri'rekwɪzɪt] s préalable m; (educ) cours m préalable
prerogative [prɪ'rɑgətɪv] s prérogative f
presage ['presɪdʒ] s présage m; (foreboding) pressentiment m || [prɪ'sedʒ] tr présager; pressentir
Presbyterian [,prezbɪ'tɪrɪ-ən] adj & s presbytérien m
prescribe [prɪ'skraɪb] tr prescrire || intr faire une ordonnance
prescription [prɪ'skrɪpʃən] s prescription f; (pharm) ordonnance f
presence ['prezəns] s présence f
present ['prezənt] adj (at this time) actuel; (at this place or time) présent; **to be present at** assister à || s cadeau m, présent m; (present time or tense) présent; **at present** à présent || [prɪ'zent] tr présenter
presentable [prɪ'zentəbəl] adj présentable, sortable
presentation [,prezən'teʃən], [,prizən-'teʃən] s présentation f
presenta'tion cop'y s exemplaire m offert à titre d'hommage
presentiment [prɪ'zentɪmənt] s pressentiment m
presently ['prezəntli] adv tout à l'heure; (now) à présent
preserve [prɪ'zʌrv] s confiture f; (for game) chasse f gardée || tr préserver, conserver; (to can) conserver

pre-shrunk [pri'ʃrʌŋk] adj irrétrécissable
preside [prɪ'zaɪd] intr présider; **to preside over** présider
presiden·cy ['prezɪdənsi] s (pl -cies) présidence f
president ['prezɪdənt] s président m; (of a university) recteur m
presidential [,prezɪ'denʃəl] adj présidentiel
press [pres] s presse f; (e.g., for wine) pressoir m; (pressure) pression f; (for clothes) armoire f; (in weight lifting) développé m; **in press** (said of clothes) lisse et net; (said of book being published) sous presse; **to go to press** être mis sous presse || tr presser; (e.g., a button) appuyer sur, presser; (clothes) donner un coup de fer à, repasser || intr presser; **to press against** se serrer contre; **to press forward, to press on** presser le pas
press' a'gent s agent m de publicité
press' box' s tribune f des journalistes
press' card' s coupe-file m d'un journaliste
press' con'ference s conférence f de presse
press' gal'lery s tribune f de la presse
pressing ['presɪŋ] adj pressé, pressant
press' release' s communiqué m de presse
pressure ['preʃər] s pression f
pres'sure cook'er s autocuiseur m, cocotte f minute
pressurize ['preʃə,raɪz] tr pressuriser
prestige [pres'tiʒ], ['prestɪdʒ] s prestige m
presumably [prɪ'z(j)uməbli] adv probablement
presume [prɪ'z(j)um] tr présumer; **to presume to** présumer de || intr présumer; **to presume on** or **upon** abuser de
presumption [prɪ'zʌmpʃən] s présomption f
presumptuous [prɪ'zʌmptʃʊ-əs] adj présomptueux
presuppose [,prisə'poz] tr présupposer
pretend [prɪ'tend] tr feindre; **to pretend to** + inf feindre de + inf || intr feindre; **to pretend to** (e.g., the throne) prétendre à
pretender [prɪ'tendər] s prétendant m; (imposter) simulateur m
pretense [prɪ'tens], ['pritens] s prétention f; feinte f; **under false pretenses** par des moyens frauduleux; **under pretense of** sous prétexte de
pretension [prɪ'tenʃən] s prétention f
pretentious [prɪ'tenʃəs] adj prétentieux
pretext ['pritekst] s prétexte m
pretonic [prɪ'tɑnɪk] adj prétonique
pret·ty ['prɪti] adj (comp -tier; super -tiest) joli; (coll) considérable || adv assez; très
prevail [prɪ'vel] intr prévaloir, régner; **to prevail on** or **upon** persuader
prevailing [prɪ'velɪŋ] adj prédominant; (wind) dominant; (fashion) en vogue
prevalent ['prevələnt] adj commun, courant

prevaricate [prɪ'værɪˌket] *intr* mentir

prevent [prɪ'vent] *tr* empêcher

prevention [prɪ'venʃən] *s* empêchement *m*; (*e.g., of accidents*) prévention *f*

preventive [prɪ'ventɪv] *adj & s* préventif *m*

preview ['pri,vju] *s* (*of something to come*) amorce *f*; (*private showing*) (mov) avant-première *f*; (*show of brief scenes for advertising*) film *m* annonce

previous ['privɪ·əs] *adj* précédent, antérieur; (*notice*) préalable; (coll) pressé || *adv*—**previous to** antérieurement à

prewar ['pri,wɔr] *adj* d'avant-guerre

prey [pre] *s* proie *f*; **to be a prey to** être en proie à || *intr*—**to prey on** or **upon** faire sa proie de; (*e.g., a seacoast*) piller; (*e.g., the mind*) ronger, miner

price [praɪs] *s* prix *m* || *tr* mettre un prix à, tarifer; s'informer du prix de

price′ control′ *s* contrôle *m* des prix

price′ cut′ting *s* rabais *m*, remise *f*

price′ fix′ing *s* stabilisation *f* des prix

price′ freez′ing *s* blocage *m* des prix

priceless ['praɪslɪs] *adj* sans prix; (coll) impayable, absurde

price′ list′ *s* liste *f* de prix, tarif *m*

price′ war′ *s* guerre *f* des prix

prick [prɪk] *s* piqûre *f*; (*spur; sting of conscience*) aiguillon *m* || *tr* piquer; **to prick up** (*the ears*) dresser

prick·ly ['prɪkli] *adj* (*comp* -**lier**; *super* -**liest**) épineux

prick′ly heat′ *s* lichen *m* vésiculaire, miliaire *f*

prick′ly pear′ *s* figue *f* de Barbarie; (*plant*) figuier *m* de Barbarie

pride [praɪd] *s* orgueil *m*; (*satisfaction*) fierté *f*; **to take pride in** être fier de || *tr*—**to pride oneself on** or **upon** s'enorgueillir de

priest [prist] *s* prêtre *m*

priestess ['pristɪs] *s* prêtresse *f*

priesthood ['prist·hʊd] *s* sacerdoce *m*

priest·ly ['pristli] *adj* (*comp* -**lier**; *super* -**liest**) sacerdotal

prig [prɪg] *s* poseur *m*, pédant *m*

prim [prɪm] *adj* (*comp* **primmer**; *super* **primmest**) compassé, guindé

prima·ry ['praɪ,meri] *adj* primaire || *s* (*pl* -**ries**) élection *f* primaire; (elec) primaire *m*

primate ['praɪmet] *s* (eccl) primat *m*; (zool) primate *m*

prime [praɪm] *adj* premier, principal; (*of the best quality*) de première qualité, (le) meilleur; (math) prime || *s* fleur *f*, perfection *f*; commencement *m*, premiers jours *mpl*; **prime of life** fleur or force de l'âge || *tr* amorcer; (*a surface to be painted*) appliquer une couche de fond à; (*to supply with information*) mettre au courant

prime′ min′ister *s* premier ministre *m*

primer ['praɪmər] *s* premier livre *m* de lecture; manuel *m* élémentaire || ['praɪmər] *s* (*for paint*) couche *f* de fond, impression *f*; (mach) amorce *f*

primeval [praɪ'mivəl] *adj* primitif

primitive ['prɪmɪtɪv] *adj & s* primitif *m*

primordial [praɪ'mɔrdɪ·əl] *adj* primordial

primp [prɪmp] *tr* bichonner, pomponner || *intr* se bichonner, se pomponner

prim′rose′ *s* primevère *f*

prim′rose path′ *s* chemin *m* de velours

prince [prɪns] *s* prince *m*

prince·ly ['prɪnsli] *adj* (*comp* -**lier**; *super* -**liest**) princier

Prince′ of Wales′ *s* prince *m* de Galles

princess ['prɪnsɪs] *s* princesse *f*

principal ['prɪnsɪpəl] *adj & s* principal *m*

principali·ty [ˌprɪnsɪ'pælɪti] *s* (*pl* -**ties**) principauté *f*

principle ['prɪnsɪpəl] *s* principe *m*

print [prɪnt] *s* empreinte *f*; (*printed cloth*) imprimé *m*; (*design in printed cloth*) estampe *f*; (*lettering*) lettres *fpl* moulées; (*act of printing*) impression *f*; (phot) épreuve *f*; **out of print** épuisé; **small print** petits caractères *mpl* || *tr* imprimer; écrire en lettres moulées; publier; (*an edition; a photographic negative*) tirer

print′ed mat′ter *s* imprimés *mpl*

printer ['prɪntər] *s* imprimeur *m*

prin′ter's dev′il *s* apprenti *m* imprimeur

prin′ter's er′ror *s* faute *f* d'impression, coquille *f*

prin′ter's ink′ *s* encre *f* d'imprimerie

prin′ter's mark′ *s* nom *m* de l'imprimeur

printing ['prɪntɪŋ] *s* imprimerie *f*; (*act*) impression *f*; (*by hand*) écriture *f* en caractères d'imprimerie; édition *f*; tirage *m*; (phot) tirage

print′ing frame′ *s* (phot) châssis-presse *m*

print′ing of′fice *s* imprimerie *f*

prior ['praɪ·ər] *adj* antérieur || *s* prieur *m* || *adv* antérieurement; **prior to** avant; avant de

priori·ty [praɪ'ɑriti], [praɪ'ɔriti] *s* (*pl* -**ties**) priorité *f*

prism ['prɪzəm] *s* prisme *m*

prison ['prɪzən] *s* prison *f* || *tr* emprisonner

prisoner ['prɪzənər], ['prɪznər] *s* prisonnier *m*

pris′on van′ *s* voiture *f* cellulaire

pris·sy ['prɪsi] *adj* (*comp* -**sier**; *super* -**siest**) (coll) bégueule

priva·cy ['praɪvəsi] *s* (*pl* -**cies**) intimité *f*; secret *m*

private ['praɪvɪt] *adj* privé, particulier; confidentiel, secret; (*public sign*) défense d'entrer || *s* simple soldat *m*; **in private** dans l'intimité, en particulier; **privates** parties *fpl*

pri′vate cit′izen *s* simple particulier *m*, simple citoyen *m*

pri′vate first′ class′ *s* soldat *m* de première

pri′vate hos′pital *s* clinique *f*

pri′vate sec′retary *s* secrétaire *m* particulier

privet ['prɪvɪt] *s* troène *m*

privilege ['prɪvɪlɪdʒ] *s* privilège *m*
priv·y ['prɪvɪ] *adj* privé; **privy to** averti de || *s* (*pl* **-ies**) cabinets *mpl* au fond du jardin
prize [praɪz] *s* prix *m*; (*something captured*) prise *f* || *tr* faire cas de, estimer
prize' fight' *s* match *m* de boxe
prize' fight'er *s* boxeur *m* professionnel
prize' ring' *s* ring *m*
prize'win'ner *s* lauréat *m*; **prizewinners** (*list*) palmarès *m*
pro [pro] *s* (*pl* **pros**) vote *m* affirmatif; (*professional*) (coll) pro *m*; **the pros and the cons** le pour et le contre || *prep* en faveur de
probabili·ty [ˌprɑbə'bɪlɪti] *s* (*pl* **-ties**) probabilité *f*
probable ['prɑbəbəl] *adj* probable
probably ['prɑbəbli] *adv* probablement
probate ['probet] *s* homologation *f* || *tr* homologuer
probation [pro'beʃən] *s* liberté *f* surveillée; (*on a job*) stage *m*
probe [prob] *s* sondage *m*; (*instrument*) sonde *f*; (rok) échos *mpl*; (rok) engin *m* exploratoire || *tr* sonder
problem ['prɑbləm] *s* problème *m*
prob'lem child' *s* enfant *mf* terrible
procedure [pro'sidʒər] *s* procédé *m*
proceed [pro'sid] *s*—**proceeds** produit *m*, bénéfices *mpl* || [pro'sid] *intr* avancer, continuer; continuer à parler; **to proceed from** procéder de; **to proceed to** se mettre à; (*to go to*) se diriger à
proceeding [pro'sidɪŋ] *s* procédé *m*; **proceedings** actes *mpl*
process ['prɑsɛs] *s* (*technique*) procédé *m*; (*development*) processus *m*; **in the process of** en train de || *tr* soumettre à un procédé, traiter
procession [pro'sɛʃən] *s* cortège *m*, défilé *m*, procession *f*
pro'cess serv'er *s* huissier *m* exploitant
proclaim [pro'klem] *tr* proclamer
proclitic [pro'klɪtɪk] *adj* & *s* proclitique *m*
procommunist [pro'kɑmjənɪst] *adj* & *s* procommuniste *mf*
procrastinate [pro'kræstɪˌnet] *tr* différer || *intr* remettre les affaires à plus tard
proctor ['prɑktər] *s* surveillant *m*
procure [pro'kjur] *tr* obtenir, se procurer; (*a woman*) entraîner à la prostitution || *intr* faire du proxénétisme
procurement [pro'kjurmənt] *s* obtention *f*, acquisition *f*
procurer [pro'kjurər] *s* proxénète *mf*
prod [prɑd] *s* poussée *f*; (*stick*) aiguillon *m* || *v* (*pret* & *pp* **prodded**) *ger* **prodding**) *tr* aiguillonner
prodigal ['prɑdɪgəl] *adj* & *s* prodigue *mf*
prodigious [pro'dɪdʒəs] *adj* prodigieux
prodi·gy ['prɑdɪdʒi] *s* (*pl* **-gies**) prodige *m*
produce ['prɑd(j)us] *s* produit *m*; (*eatables*) denrées *fpl* || [pro'd(j)us] *tr* produire; (*a play*) mettre en scène; (geom) prolonger

producer [pro'd(j)usər] *s* producteur *m*
product ['prɑdəkt] *s* produit *m*
production [pro'dʌkʃən] *s* production *f*
profane [pro'fen] *adj* profane; (*language*) impie, blasphématoire || *s* profane *mf*; impie *mf* || *tr* profaner
profani·ty [pro'fænɪti] *s* (*pl* **-ties**) blasphème *m*
profess [pro'fɛs] *tr* professer
profession [pro'fɛʃən] *s* profession *f*
professor [pro'fɛsər] *s* professeur *m*
proffer ['prɑfər] *s* offre *f* || *tr* offrir, tendre
proficient [pro'fɪʃənt] *adj* compétent, expert
profile ['profaɪl] *s* profil *m*; courte biographie *f* || *tr* profiler; **to be profiled against** se profiler sur
profit ['prɑfɪt] *s* bénéfice *m*, profit *m* || *tr* profiter (with *dat*) || *intr* profiter; **to profit from** profiter à, de, or en
profitable ['prɑfɪtəbəl] *adj* profitable
prof'it-and-loss' account' *s* compte *m* de profits et pertes
profiteer [ˌprɑfɪ'tɪr] *s* profiteur *m* || *intr* faire des bénéfices excessifs
prof'it tak'ing *s* prise *f* de bénéfices
profligate ['prɑflɪgɪt] *adj* & *s* débauché *m*
pro' for'ma in'voice [ˌpro'fɔrmə] *s* facture *f* simulée
profound [pro'faund] *adj* profond
pro-French' *adj* francophile
profuse [prə'fjuz] *adj* abondant; (*extravagant*) prodigue
proge·ny ['prɑdʒəni] *s* (*pl* **-nies**) progéniture *f*
progno·sis [prɑg'nosɪs] *s* (*pl* **-ses** [siz]) pronostic *m*
prognosticate [prɑg'nɑstɪˌket] *tr* pronostiquer
pro·gram ['progræm] *s* programme *m* || *v* (*pret* & *pp* **-gramed** or **-grammed**) *ger* **-graming** or **-gramming**) *tr* programmer
programmer ['progræmər] *s* (comp) programmeur *m*; (mov, rad, telv) programmateur *m*
programming ['progræmɪŋ] *s* programmation *f*
progress ['prɑgrɛs] *s* progrès *m*; cours *m*, e.g., **work in progress** travaux en cours; **to make progress** faire des progrès || [prə'grɛs] *intr* progresser
progressive [prə'grɛsɪv] *adj* progressif; (pol) progressiste || *s* (pol) progressiste *mf*
prohibit [pro'hɪbɪt] *tr* prohiber, interdire
prohibition [ˌpro·ə'bɪʃən] *s* prohibition *f*
project ['prɑdʒɛkt] *s* projet *m* || [prə'dʒɛkt] *tr* projeter || *intr* (*to jut out*) saillir; (theat) passer la rampe
projectile [prə'dʒɛktɪl] *s* projectile *m*
projection [prə'dʒɛkʃən] *s* projection *f*; (*something jutting out*) saillie *f*
projec'tion booth' *s* (mov) cabine *f* de projection
projector [prə'dʒɛktər] *s* projecteur *m*

proletarian [ˌprolɪˈterɪ·ən] *adj* prolétarien ‖ *s* prolétaire *m*

proletariat [ˌprolɪˈterɪ·ət] *s* prolétariat *m*

proliferate [prəˈlɪfəˌret] *intr* proliférer

prolific [prəˈlɪfɪk] *adj* prolifique

prolix [ˈproliks], [proˈlɪks] *adj* prolixe

prologue [ˈprolɔg], [ˈprolɑg] *s* prologue *m*

prolong [proˈlɔŋ], [proˈlɑŋ] *tr* prolonger

promenade [ˌprɑmɪˈned], [ˌprɑmɪˈnɑd] *s* promenade *f*; bal *m* d'apparat; (theat) promenoir *m* ‖ *intr* se promener

prom′enade′ deck′ *s* (naut) pont-promenade *m*

prominent [ˈprɑmɪnənt] *adj* proéminent; (well-known) éminent

promiscuity [ˌprɑmɪsˈkju·əti] *s* promiscuité *f*

promise [ˈprɑmɪs] *s* promesse *f* ‖ *tr & intr* promettre; **to promise s.o. to** promettre à qn de; **to promise s.th. to s.o.** promettre q.ch. à qn

prom′issory note′ [ˈprɑmɪˌsori] *m* billet *m* à ordre

promontory [ˈprɑmənˌtori] *s* (*pl* **-ries**) promontoire *m*

promote [prəˈmot] *tr* promouvoir

promoter [prəˈmotər] *s* promoteur *m*

promotion [prəˈmoʃən] *s* promotion *f*

prompt [prɑmpt] *adj* prompt; ponctuel ‖ *tr* inciter; (theat) souffler son rôle à

prompter [ˈprɑmptər] *s* (theat) souffleur *m*

promp′ter′s box′ *s* (theat) trou *m* du souffleur

promptness [ˈprɑmptnɪs] *s* promptitude *f*

promulgate [ˈprɑməlˌget], [proˈmʌlget] *tr* promulguer

prone [pron] *adj* à plat ventre, prostré; **prone to** enclin à

prong [prɔŋ], [prɑŋ] *s* dent *f*

pronoun [ˈpronaun] *s* pronom *m*

pronounce [prəˈnauns] *tr* prononcer

pronouncement [prəˈnaunsmənt] *s* déclaration *f*

pronunciation [prəˌnʌnsɪˈeʃən], [prəˌnʌnɪˈeʃən] *s* prononciation *f*

proof [pruf] *adj*—**proof against** à l'épreuve de, résistant à ‖ *s* preuve *f*; (phot, typ) épreuve *f*; **to read proof** corriger les épreuves

proof′read′er *s* correcteur *m*

prop [prɑp] *s* appui *m*; (to hold up a plant) tuteur *m*; **props** (theat) accessoires *mpl* ‖ *v* (*pret & pp* **propped**; *ger* **propping**) *tr* appuyer; (hort) tuteurer

propaganda [ˌprɑpəˈgændə] *s* propagande *f*

propagate [ˈprɑpəˌget] *tr* propager

pro·pel [prəˈpɛl] *v* (*pret & pp* **-pelled**; *ger* **-pelling**) *tr* propulser

propeller [prəˈpɛlər] *s* hélice *f*

propensi·ty [prəˈpɛnsɪti] *s* (*pl* **-ties**) propension *f*

proper [ˈprɑpər] *adj* propre; (fitting, correct) convenable, comme il faut

proper·ty [ˈprɑpərti] *s* (*pl* **-ties**) propriété *f*; **properties** (theat) accessoires *mpl*

prop′erty own′er *s* propriétaire *mf*

prop′erty tax′ *s* impôt *m* foncier

prophe·cy [ˈprɑfɪsi] *s* (*pl* **-cies**) prophétie *f*

prophe·sy [ˈprɑfɪˌsaɪ] *v* (*pret & pp* **-sied**) *tr* prophétiser

prophet [ˈprɑfɪt] *s* prophète *m*

prophetess [ˈprɑfɪtɪs] *s* prophétesse *f*

prophylactic [ˌprofɪˈlæktɪk] *adj* prophylactique ‖ *s* médicament *m* prophylactique

propitiate [prəˈpɪʃɪˌet] *tr* apaiser

propitious [prəˈpɪʃəs] *adj* propice

prop′jet′ *s* turbopropulseur *m*

proportion [prəˈporʃən] *s* proportion *f*; **in proportion as** à mesure que; **in proportion to** en proportion de, en raison de; **out of proportion** hors de proportion ‖ *tr* proportionner

proportionate [prəˈporʃənɪt] *adj* proportionné

proposal [prəˈpozəl] *s* proposition *f*; demande *f* en mariage

propose [prəˈpoz] *tr* proposer ‖ *intr* faire sa déclaration; **to propose to** demander sa main à; (to decide to) se proposer de

proposition [ˌprɑpəˈzɪʃən] *s* proposition *f* ‖ *tr* faire des propositions malhonnêtes à

propound [prəˈpaund] *tr* proposer

proprietor [prəˈpraɪ·ətər] *s* propriétaire *mf*

proprietress [prəˈpraɪ·ətrɪs] *s* propriétaire *f*

proprie·ty [prəˈpraɪ·əti] *s* (*pl* **-ties**) propriété *f*; (of conduct) bienséance *f*; **proprieties** convenances *fpl*

propulsion [prəˈpʌlʃən] *s* propulsion *f*

prorate [proˈret] *tr* partager au prorata

prosaic [proˈze·ɪk] *adj* prosaïque

proscenium [proˈsinɪ·əm] *s* avant-scène *f*

proscribe [proˈskraɪb] *tr* proscrire

prose [proz] *adj* en prose ‖ *s* prose *f*

prosecute [ˈprɑsɪˌkjut] *tr* poursuivre

prosecutor [ˈprɑsɪˌkjutər] *s* (lawyer) procureur *m*; (plaintiff) plaignant *m*

proselyte [ˈprɑsɪˌlaɪt] *s* prosélyte *mf*

prose′ writ′er *s* prosateur *m*

prosody [ˈprɑsədi] *s* prosodie *f*

prospect [ˈprɑspekt] *s* perspective *f*; (future) avenir *m*; (com) client *m* éventuel ‖ *tr & intr* prospecter; **to prospect for** (e.g., gold) chercher

prospector [ˈprɑspektər] *s* prospecteur *m*

prospectus [prəˈspektəs] *s* prospectus *m*

prosper [ˈprɑspər] *intr* prospérer

prosperity [prɑsˈperɪti] *s* prospérité *f*

prosperous [ˈprɑspərəs] *adj* prospère

prostitute [ˈprɑstɪˌt(j)ut] *s* prostituée *f* ‖ *tr* prostituer

prostrate [ˈprɑstret] *adj* prosterné; (exhausted) prostré ‖ *tr* abattre; **to prostrate oneself** se prosterner

prostration [prɑsˈtreʃən] *s* prostration *f*; (abasement) prosternation *f*

protagonist [proˈtægənɪst] *s* protagoniste *m*
protect [prəˈtɛkt] *tr* protéger
protection [prəˈtɛkʃən] *s* protection *f*
protein [ˈprotiɪn], [ˈprotin] *s* protéine *f*
pro-tempore [proˈtɛmpəˌri] *adj* intérimaire, par intérim
protest [ˈprotɛst] *s* protestation *f*
[proˈtɛst] *tr* protester de; protester ‖
intr protester
Protestant [ˈpratɪstənt] *adj & s* protestant *m*
protocol [ˈprotəˌkal] *s* protocole *m*
proton [ˈpratan] *s* proton *m*
protoplasm [ˈprotəˌplæzəm] *s* protoplasme *m*
prototype [ˈprotəˌtaɪp] *s* prototype *m*
protozoan [ˌprotəˈzoən] *s* protozoaire
m
protract [proˈtrækt] *tr* prolonger
protrude [proˈtrud] *intr* saillir
protuberance [proˈt(j)ubərəns] *s* protubérance *f*
proud [praud] *adj* fier; (*vain*) orgueil-
leux
proud' flesh' *s* chair *f* fongueuse
prove [pruv] *v* (*pret* **proved**; *pp*
proved or **proven** [ˈpruvən]) *tr* prouver; (*to put to the test*) éprouver ‖
intr se montrer, se trouver; **to prove
to be** se révéler, s'avérer
proverb [ˈpravərb] *s* proverbe *m*
provide [prəˈvaɪd] *tr* pourvoir, fournir;
to provide s.th. for s.o. fournir q.ch.
à qn ‖ *intr*—**to provide for** pourvoir
à; (*e.g., future needs*) prévoir
provided *conj* pourvu que, à condition
que
providence [ˈpravɪdəns] *s* providence *f*;
(*prudence*) prévoyance *f*
providential [ˌpravɪˈdɛnʃəl] *adj* provi-
dentiel
providing [prəˈvaɪdɪŋ] *conj* pourvu
que, à condition que
province [ˈpravɪns] *s* province *f*;
(*sphere*) compétence *f*
prov'ing ground' *s* terrain *m* d'essai
provision [prəˈvɪʒən] *s* (*supplying*)
fourniture *f*; clause *f*; **provisions** provisions *fpl*
proviso [prəˈvaɪzo] *s* (*pl* -**sos** or -**soes**)
condition *f*, stipulation *f*
provocative [prəˈvakətɪv] *adj* provocant
provoke [prəˈvok] *tr* provoquer; fâcher, contrarier
provoking [prəˈvokɪŋ] *adj* contrariant
prow [prau] *s* proue *f*
prowess [ˈprau·ɪs] *s* prouesse *f*
prowl [praul] *intr* rôder
prowler [ˈpraulər] *s* rôdeur *m*
proximity [prakˈsɪmɪti] *s* proximité *f*
prox·y [ˈpraksi] *s* (*pl* -**ies**) mandat *m*;
(*agent*) mandataire *mf*; **by proxy** par
procuration
prude [prud] *s* prude *mf*
prudence [ˈprudəns] *s* prudence *f*
prudent [ˈprudənt] *adj* prudent
pruder·y [ˈprudəri] *s* (*pl* -**ies**) pruderie *f*
prudish [ˈprudɪʃ] *adj* prude
prune [prun] *s* pruneau *m* ‖ *tr* élaguer

Prussian [ˈprʌʃən] *adj* prussien ‖ *s*
Prussien *m*
pry [praɪ] *v* (*pret & pp* **pried**) *tr*—**to
pry open** forcer avec un levier; **to pry
s.th. out of s.o.** extorquer, soutirer
q.ch. à qn ‖ *intr* fureter; **to pry into**
fourrer son nez dans
P.S. [ˈpiˈɛs] *s* (letterword) (**postscript**)
P.-S.
psalm [sam] *s* psaume *m*
Psalter [ˈsɔltər] *s* psautier *m*
pseudo [ˈs(j)udo] *adj* faux, supposé,
feint, factice
pseudonym [ˈs(j)udənɪm] *s* pseudonyme *m*
psyche [ˈsaɪki] *s* psyché *f*
psychiatrist [saɪˈkaɪ·ətrɪst] *s* psychiatre *mf*
psychiatry [saɪˈkaɪ·ətri] *s* psychiatrie *f*
psychic [ˈsaɪkɪk] *adj* psychique; médiumnique ‖ *s* médium *m*
psychoanalysis [ˌsaɪko·əˈnælɪsɪs] *s*
psychanalyse *f*
psychoanalyze [ˌsaɪkoˈænəˌlaɪz] *tr*
psychanalyser
psychologic(al) [ˌsaɪkoˈladʒɪk(əl)] *adj*
psychologique
psychologist [saɪˈkalədʒɪst] *s* psychologue *mf*
psychology [saɪˈkalədʒi] *s* psychologie *f*
psychopath [ˈsaɪkəˌpæθ] *s* psychopathe *m*
psycho·sis [saɪˈkosɪs] *s* (*pl* -**ses** [siz])
psychose *f*
psychotic [saɪˈkatɪk] *adj & s* psychotique *mf*
ptomaine [ˈtomen] *s* ptomaïne *f*
pub [pʌb] *s* (Brit) bistrot *m*, café *m*
puberty [ˈpjubərti] *s* puberté *f*
public [ˈpʌblɪk] *adj & s* public *m*
publication [ˌpʌbliˈkeʃən] *s* publication *f*
publicity [pʌbˈlɪsɪti] *s* publicité *f*
public'ity stunt' *s* canard *m* publicitaire
publicize [ˈpʌblɪˌsaɪz] *tr* publier
pub'lic li'brary *s* bibliothèque *f* mu-
nicipale
pub'lic-opin'ion poll' *s* sondage *m* de
l'opinion, enquête *f* par sondage
pub'lic school' *s* (U.S.A.) école *f* primaire; (Brit) école privée
pub'lic serv'ant *s* fonctionnaire *mf*
pub'lic speak'ing *s* art *m* oratoire, éloquence *f*
pub'lic toi'let *s* chalet *m* de nécessité
pub'lic util'ity *s* entreprise *f* de service
public; **public utilities** actions *fpl*
émises par les entreprises de service
public
publish [ˈpʌblɪʃ] *tr* publier
publisher [ˈpʌblɪʃər] *s* éditeur *m*
pub'lishing house' *s* maison *f* d'édition
puck [pʌk] *s* palet *m*
pucker [ˈpʌkər] *s* fronce *m*, faux pli *m*
‖ *tr* froncer ‖ *intr* se froncer
pudding [ˈpudɪŋ] *s* entremets *m* sucré
au lait, crème *f*
puddle [ˈpʌdəl] *s* flaque *f* ‖ *tr* puddler
pudg·y [ˈpʌdʒi] *adj* (*comp* -**ier**; *super*
-**iest**) bouffi, rondouillard
puerile [ˈpju·əril] *adj* puéril

puerili·ty [ˌpjuˈrɪlɪti] *s* (*pl* -ties) puérilité *f*

Puerto Rican [ˈpwertoˈrikən] *adj* portoricain ‖ *s* Portoricain *m*

puff [pʌf] *s* souffle *m*; (*of smoke*) bouffée *f*; (*in clothing*) bouillon *m*; (*in sleeve*) bouffant *m*; (*for powder*) houppette *f*; (*swelling*) bouffissure *f*; (*praise*) battage *m*; (culin) moule *m* de pâte feuilletée fourré à la crème, à la confiture, etc. ‖ *tr* lancer des bouffées de; **to puff oneself up** se rengorger; **to puff out** souffler; **to puff up** gonfler ‖ *intr* souffler; (*to swell*) gonfler, se gonfler; **to puff at** or **on** (*a pipe*) tirer sur

puff′ paste′ *s* pâte *f* feuilletée

pugilism [ˈpjudʒɪˌlɪzəm] *s* science *f* pugilistique, boxe *f*

pugilist [ˈpjudʒɪlɪst] *s* pugiliste *m*

pugnacious [pʌgˈneʃəs] *adj* pugnace

pug′-nosed′ *adj* camus

puke [pjuk] *s* (slang) dégobillage *m* ‖ *tr & intr* (slang) dégobiller

pull [pʊl] *s* secousse *f*, coup *m*; (*handle of door*) poignée *f*; (slang) piston *m*, appuis *mpl* ‖ *tr* tirer (*a muscle*) tordre; (*the trigger*) appuyer sur; (*a proof*) (typ) tirer; **to pull about** tirailler; **to pull away** arracher; **to pull down** baisser; (*e.g., a house*) abattre; (*to degrade*) abaisser; **to pull in** rentrer; **to pull off** enlever; (fig) réussir; **to pull on** (*a garment*) mettre; **to pull oneself together** se ressaisir; **to pull out** sortir; (*a tooth*) arracher ‖ *intr* tirer; bouger lentement, bouger avec effort; **to pull at** tirer sur; **to pull for** (slang) plaider en faveur de; **to pull in** rentrer; (*said of train*) entrer en gare; **to pull out** partir; (*said of train*) sortir de la gare; **to pull through** se tirer d'affaire; (*to get well*) se remettre

pull′ chain′ *s* chasse *f* d'eau

pullet [ˈpʊlɪt] *s* poulette *f*

pulley [ˈpʊli] *s* poulie *f*

pulmonary [ˈpʌlməˌneri] *adj* pulmonaire

pulp [pʌlp] *s* pulpe *f*; (*to make paper*) pâte *f*; (*of tooth*) bulbe *m*; **to beat to a pulp** (coll) mettre en bouillie

pulp′ fic′tion *s* romans *mpl* à sensation; le roman de la concierge

pulpit [ˈpʊlpɪt] *s* chaire *f*

pulsate [ˈpʌlset] *intr* palpiter; vibrer

pulsation [pʌlˈseʃən] *s* pulsation *f*

pulse [pʌls] *s* pouls *m*; **to feel** or **take the pulse of** tâter le pouls à

pulverize [ˈpʌlvəˌraɪz] *tr* pulvériser

pu′mice stone′ [ˈpʌmɪs] *s* pierre *f* ponce

pum·mel [ˈpʌməl] *v* (*pret & pp* -meled or -melled; *ger* -meling or -melling) *tr* bourrer de coups

pump [pʌmp] *s* pompe *f*; (*slipperlike shoe*) escarpin *m* ‖ *tr* pomper; (coll) tirer les vers du nez à; **to pump up** pomper; (*a tire*) gonfler ‖ *intr* pomper

pump′han′dle *s* bras *m* de pompe

pumpkin [ˈpʌmpkɪn], [ˈpʌŋkɪn] *s* citrouille *f*, potiron *m*

pun [pʌn] *s* calembour *m*, jeu *m* de mots ‖ *v* (*pret & pp* punned; *ger* punning) *intr* faire des jeux de mots

punch [pʌntʃ] *s* coup *m* de poing; (*to pierce metal*) mandrin *m*; (*to drive a nail or bolt*) poinçon *m*; (*for tickets*) pince *f*, emporte-pièce *m*; (*drink; blow*) punch *m*; (mach) poinçonneuse *f*; (*energy*) (coll) allant *m*, punch; **to pull no punches** parler carrément ‖ *tr* donner un coup de poing à; poinçonner

punch′ bowl′ *s* bol *m* à punch

punch′ card′ *s* carte *f* perforée

punch′ clock′ *s* horloge *f* de pointage

punch′-drunk′ *adj* abruti de coups; (coll) abruti, étourdi

punched′ tape′ *s* bande *f* enregistreuse perforée

punch′ing bag′ *s* punching-ball *m*; (fig) tête *f* de Turc

punch′ line′ *s* point *m* final, phrase *f* clé

punctilious [pʌŋkˈtɪlɪəs] *adj* pointilleux, minutieux

punctual [ˈpʌŋktʃʊəl] *adj* ponctuel

punctuate [ˈpʌŋktʃʊˌet] *tr & intr* ponctuer

punctuation [ˌpʌŋktʃʊˈeʃən] *s* ponctuation *f*

punctua′tion mark′ *s* signe *m* de ponctuation

puncture [ˈpʌŋktʃər] *s* perforation *f*; (*of a tire*) crevaison *f*; (med) ponction *f* ‖ *tr* perforer; (*a tire*) crever; (med) ponctionner

punc′ture-proof′ *adj* increvable

pundit [ˈpʌndɪt] *s* pandit *m*; (*savant*) mandarin *m*; (pej) pontife *m*

pungent [ˈpʌndʒənt] *adj* piquant

punish [ˈpʌnɪʃ] *tr & intr* punir

punishment [ˈpʌnɪʃmənt] *s* punition *f*; (*for a crime*) peine *f*; (*severe handling*) mauvais traitements *mpl*

punk [pʌŋk] *adj* (slang) moche, fichu; **to feel punk** (slang) être mal fichu ‖ *s* amadou *m*; mèche *f* d'amadou; (*decayed wood*) bois *m* pourri; (slang) voyou *m*, mauvais sujet *m*

punster [ˈpʌnstər] *s* faiseur *m* de calembours

pupil [ˈpjupəl] *s* élève *mf*; (*of the eye*) pupille *f*, prunelle *f*

puppet [ˈpʌpɪt] *s* marionnette *f*; (*person controlled by another*) fantoche *m*, pantin *m*

pup′pet gov′ernment *s* gouvernement *m* fantoche

pup′pet show′ *s* spectacle *m* de marionnettes, marionnettes *fpl*

pup·py [ˈpʌpi] *s* (*pl* -pies) petit chien *m*

pup′py love′ *s* premières amours *fpl*

pup′ tent′ *s* tente-abri *f*

purchase [ˈpʌrtʃəs] *s* achat *m*; (*leverage*) point *m* d'appui, prise *f* ‖ *tr* acheter

pur′chasing pow′er *s* pouvoir *m* d'achat

pure [pjur] *adj* pur

purgative ['pʌrgətɪv] *adj & s* purgatif *m*

purgato‧ry ['pʌrgə,tori] *s* (*pl* -ries) purgatoire *m*

purge [pʌrdʒ] *s* purge *f* ‖ *tr* purger

puri‧fy ['pjurɪ,faɪ] *v* (*pret & pp* -fied) *tr* purifier

puritan ['pjurɪtən] *adj & s* puritain *m*; **Puritan** puritain

purity ['pjurɪti] *s* pureté *f*

purloin [pər'lɔɪn] *tr & intr* voler

purple ['pʌrpəl] *adj* pourpre ‖ *s* (*violescent*) pourpre *m*; (*deep red, crimson*) pourpre *f*; **born to the purple** né dans la pourpre

purport ['pʌrport] *s* sens *m*, teneur *f*; (*intention*) but *m*, objet *m* ‖ [pər'port] *tr* signifier, vouloir dire

purpose ['pʌrpəs] *s* intention *f*, dessein *m*; (*goal*) but *m*, objet *m*, fin *f*; **for all purposes** à tous usages; pratiquement; **for the purpose of, with the purpose of** dans le dessein de, dans le but de; **for this purpose** à cet effet; **for what purpose?** à quoi bon?, à quelle fin?; **on purpose** exprès, à dessein; **to good purpose, to some purpose** utilement; **to no purpose** vainement; **to serve the purpose** faire l'affaire

purposely ['pʌrpəsli] *adv* exprès, à dessein, de propos délibéré

purr [pʌr] *s* ronron *m* ‖ *intr* ronronner

purse [pʌrs] *s* bourse *f*, porte-monnaie *m*; (*handbag*) sac *m* à main ‖ *tr* (*one's lips*) pincer

purser ['pʌrsər] *s* commissaire *m*

purse‧ snatch‧er ['snætʃər] *s* voleur *m* à la tire

purse‧ strings‧ *spl* cordons *mpl* de bourse

pursue [pər's(j)u] *tr* poursuivre; (*a profession*) suivre

pursuit [pər's(j)ut] *s* poursuite *f*; profession *f*

pursuit‧ plane‧ *s* chasseur *m*, avion *m* de chasse

purvey [pər've] *tr* fournir

pus [pʌs] *s* pus *m*

push [puʃ] *s* poussée *f* ‖ *tr* pousser; (*a button*) appuyer sur, presser; **to push around** (coll) rudoyer; **to push aside** écarter; **to push away or back** repousser; **to push in** enfoncer; **to push over** faire tomber; **to push through** amener à bonne fin; (*a resolution, bill, etc.*) faire adopter ‖ *intr* pousser; **to push forward or on** avancer; **to push off** se mettre en route; (naut) pousser au large

push‧ but‧ton *s* bouton *m* électrique, poussoir *m*

push‧-but‧ton war‧fare *s* guerre *f* presse-bouton

push‧cart‧ *s* voiture *f* à bras

pushing ['puʃɪŋ] *adj* entreprenant; indiscret; agressif

pusillanimous [,pjusɪ'lænɪməs] *adj* pusillanime

puss [pus] *s* minet *m*; (slang) gueule *f*; **sly puss** (*girl*) (coll) futée *f* ‖ *interj* minet!

Puss‧ in Boots‧ *s* Chat *m* botté

puss‧ in the cor‧ner *s* les quatre coins *mpl*

puss‧y ['pusi] *s* (*pl* -ies) *s* minet *m* ‖ *interj* minet!

puss‧y wil‧low *s* saule *m* nord-américain aux chatons très soyeux

put [put] *v* (*pret & pp* put; *ger* putting) *tr* mettre, placer; (*to throw*) lancer; (*a question*) poser; **to put across** passer; faire accepter; **to put aside** mettre de côté; **to put away** ranger; (*to jail*) mettre en prison; **to put back** remettre; retarder; **to put down** poser; (*e.g., a name*) noter; (*a revolution*) réprimer; (*to lower*) baisser; **to put off** renvoyer; (*to mislead*) dérouter; **to put on** (*clothes*) mettre; (*a play*) mettre en scène, monter; (*a brake*) serrer; (*a light, radio, etc.*) allumer; (*to feign*) feindre, simuler; **to put oneself out** se déranger; **to put on sale** mettre en vente; mettre en solde; **to put out** (*the hand*) étendre; (*the fire, light, etc.*) éteindre; (*s.o.'s eyes*) crever; (*e.g., a book*) publier; (*to show to the door*) mettre dehors; (*to vex*) contrarier; **to put over** (coll) faire accepter; **to put s.o. through s.th.** faire subir q.ch. à qn; **to put through** passer; (*a resolution, bill, etc.*) faire adopter; **to put up** lever; (*a house*) construire, faire construire; (*one's collar, hair, etc.*) relever; (*a picture*) accrocher; (*a notice*) afficher; (*a tent*) dresser; (*an umbrella*) ouvrir; (*the price*) augmenter; (*money as an investment*) fournir; (*resistance*) offrir; (*an overnight guest*) loger; (*fruit, vegetables, etc.*) conserver; (coll) pousser, inciter ‖ *intr* se diriger; **to put on** feindre; **to put up** loger; **to put up with** tolérer

put‧-out‧ *adj* ennuyeux, fâcheux

putrid ['pjutrɪd] *adj* putride

putter ['pʌtər] *intr*—**to putter around** s'occuper de bagatelles

put‧ty ['pʌti] *s* (*pl* -ties) mastic *m* ‖ *v* (*pret & pp* -tied) *tr* mastiquer

put‧ty knife‧ *s* (*pl* knives) couteau *m* à mastiquer

put‧-up‧ *adj* (coll) machiné à l'avance, monté

puzzle ['pʌzəl] *s* énigme *f* ‖ *tr* intriguer; **to puzzle out** déchiffrer ‖ *intr* —**to puzzle over** se creuser la tête pour comprendre

puzzler ['pʌzlər] *s* énigme *f*, colle *f*

puzzling ['pʌzlɪŋ] *adj* énigmatique

PW ['pi'dʌbəl,ju] *s* (letterword) (**prisoner of war**) P.G.

pyg‧my ['pɪgmi] *adj* pygméen ‖ *s* (*pl* -mies) pygmée *m*

pylon ['paɪlɑn] *s* pylône *m*

pyramid ['pɪrəmɪd] *s* pyramide *f* ‖ *tr* augmenter graduellement ‖ *intr* pyramider
pyre [paɪr] *s* bûcher *m* funéraire
Pyrenees ['pɪrɪ,niz] *spl* Pyrénées *fpl*
pyrites [paɪ'raɪtiz], ['paɪraɪts] *s* pyrite *f*
pyrotechnical [,paɪrə'teknɪkəl] *adj* pyrotechnique

pyrotechnics [,paɪrə'teknɪks] *spl* pyrotechnie *f*
python ['paɪθɑn], ['paɪθən] *s* python *m*
pythoness ['paɪθənɪs] *s* pythonisse *f*
pyx [pɪks] *s* (eccl) ciboire *m*; (for carrying Eucharist to sick) (eccl) pyxide *f*; (at a mint) boîte *f* des monnaies

Q

Q, q [kju] *s* XVIIᵉ lettre de l'alphabet
quack [kwæk] *adj* frauduleux, de charlatan ‖ *s* charlatan *m* ‖ *intr* cancaner, faire couin-couin
quacker·y ['kwækəri] *s* (*pl* -ies) charlatanisme *m*
quadrangle ['kwad,ræŋgəl] *s* plan *m* quadrangulaire; cour *f* carrée
quadrant ['kwadrənt] *s* (instrument) quart *m* de cercle, secteur *m*; (math) quadrant *m*
quadroon [kwad'run] *s* quarteron *m*
quadruped ['kwadrə,ped] *adj & s* quadrupède *m*
quadruple ['kwadrupəl] or [kwad'rupəl] *adj & s* quadruple *m* ‖ *tr & intr* quadrupler
quadruplets ['kwadru,plets], [kwad'ruplets] *spl* quadruplés *mpl*
quaff [kwaf], [kwæf] *s* lampée *f* ‖ *tr & intr* boire à longs traits
quagmire ['kwæg,maɪr] *s* bourbier *m*, fondrière *f*
quail [kwel] *s* caille *f* ‖ *intr* fléchir
quaint [kwent] *adj* pittoresque, bizarre
quake [kwek] *s* tremblement *m*; (earthquake) tremblement de terre ‖ *intr* trembler
Quaker ['kwekər] *adj & s* quaker *m*
Quak'er meet'ing *s* réunion *f* de quakers; (coll) réunion où il y a très peu de conversation
quali·fy ['kwalɪ,faɪ] *v* (*pret & pp* -fied) *tr* qualifier; (*e.g.*, *a recommendation*) apporter des réserves à, modifier; **to qualify oneself** se préparer à, se rendre apte à ‖ *intr* se qualifier
quali·ty ['kwalɪti] *s* (*pl* -ties) qualité *f*; (of a sound) timbre *m*
qualm [kwam] *s* scrupule *m*; (remorse) remords *m*; (nausea) soulèvement *m* de cœur
quanda·ry ['kwandəri] *s* (*pl* -ries) incertitude *f*, impasse *f*
quanti·ty ['kwantɪti] *s* (*pl* -ties) quantité *f*
quan·tum ['kwantəm] *adj* quantique ‖ *s* (*pl* -ta [tə]) quantum *m*
quan'tum the'ory *s* théorie *f* des quanta
quarantine ['kwarən,tin], ['kwɔrən,tin] *s* quarantaine *f* ‖ *tr* mettre en quarantaine
quar·rel ['kwarəl], ['kwɔrəl] *s* querelle

f, dispute *f*; **to have no quarrel with** n'avoir rien à redire à; **to pick a quarrel with** chercher querelle à ‖ *v* (*pret & pp* -reled or -relled) *ger* -reling or -relling) *intr* se quereller, se disputer; **to quarrel over** contester sur, se disputer
quarrelsome ['kwarəlsəm], ['kwɔrəlsəm] *adj* querelleur
quar·ry ['kwari], ['kwɔri] *s* (*pl* -ries) carrière *f*; (hunted animal) proie *f* ‖ *v* (*pret & pp* -ried) *tr* extraire ‖ *intr* exploiter une carrière
quart [kwɔrt] *s* quart *m* de gallon, pinte *f*
quarter ['kwɔrtər] *s* quart *m*; (American coin) vingt-cinq cents *mpl*; (of a year) trimestre *m*; (of town; of beef; of moon; of shield) quartier *m*; **a quarter after one** une heure et quart; **a quarter of an hour** un quart d'heure; **a quarter to one** une heure moins le quart; **at close quarters** corps à corps; **quarters** (mil) quartiers *mpl*, cantonnement *m* ‖ *tr & intr* (mil) loger, cantonner
quar'ter·deck' *s* gaillard *m* d'arrière
quar'ter·hour' *s* quart *m* d'heure; **every quarter-hour on the quarter-hour** tous les quarts d'heure au quart d'heure juste
quarter·ly ['kwɔrtərli] *adj* trimestriel ‖ *s* (*pl* -lies) publication *f* or revue *f* trimestrielle ‖ *adv* trimestriellement, par trimestre
quar'ter·mas'ter *s* (mil) quartier-maître *m*, intendant *m* militaire
Quar'ter·master Corps' *s* Intendance *f*, service *m* de l'Intendance
quar'ter note' *s* (mus) noire *f*
quar'ter rest' *s* (mus) soupir *m*
quar'ter tone' *s* (mus) quart *m* de ton
quartet [kwɔr'tet] *s* quatuor *m*
quartz [kwɔrts] *s* quartz *m*
quasar ['kwesar] *s* (astr) quasar *m*
quash [kwɑʃ] *tr* étouffer; (to set aside) annuler, invalider
quatrain ['kwatren] *s* quatrain *m*
quaver ['kwevər] *s* tremblement *m*; (in the singing voice) trémolo *m*; (mus) croche *f* ‖ *intr* trembloter
quay [ki] *s* quai *m*, débarcadère *m*
queen [kwin] *s* reine *f*; (cards, chess) reine

queen/ bee/ s reine f des abeilles
queen/ dow/ager s reine f douairière
queen-ly ['kwinli] adj (comp -lier; super -liest) de reine, digne d'une reine
queen/ moth/er s reine f mère
queen/ post/ s faux poinçon m
queer [kwɪr] adj bizarre, drôle; (suspicious) (coll) suspect; (homosexual) (coll) pervers, inverti; **to feel queer** (coll) se sentir indisposé ‖ s excentrique mf; (homosexual) (coll) tapette f, inverti m ‖ tr (slang) faire échouer, déranger
quell [kwel] tr étouffer, réprimer; (pain, sorrow, etc.) calmer
quench [kwentʃ] tr (the thirst) étancher; (a rebellion) étouffer; (a fire) éteindre
que·ry ['kwɪri] s (pl -ries) question f; doute m; (question mark) point m d'interrogation ‖ v (pret & pp -ried) tr questionner; mettre en doute; (to affix a question mark) marquer d'un point d'interrogation
quest [kwest] s quête f; **in quest of** en quête de
question ['kwestʃən] s question f; doute m; **beyond question** indiscutable, incontestable; **it is a question of** il s'agit de; **out of the question** impossible, impensable; **to ask s.o. a question** poser une question à qn; **to beg the question** faire une pétition de principe; **to call into question** mettre en question; **to move the previous question** (parl) demander la question préalable; **without question** sans aucun doute ‖ tr interroger, questionner; (to cast doubt upon) douter de, contester
questionable ['kwestʃənəbəl] adj discutable, douteux
ques/tion mark/ s point m d'interrogation
questionnaire [,kwestʃən'er] s questionnaire m
queue [kju] s queue f ‖ intr—**to queue up** faire la queue
quibble ['kwɪbəl] intr chicaner, ergoter
quibbling ['kwɪblɪŋ] s chicane f
quick [kwɪk] adj rapide, vif ‖ s—**the quick and the dead** les vivants et les morts; **to cut to the quick** piquer au vif
quicken ['kwɪkən] tr accélérer; (e.g., the imagination) animer ‖ intr s'accélérer; s'animer
quick/lime/ s chaux f vive
quick/ lunch/ s casse-croûte m, repas m léger
quickly ['kwɪkli] adv vite, rapidement
quick/sand/ s sable m mouvant
quick/sil/ver s vif-argent m, mercure m
quick/-tem/pered adj coléreux
quiet ['kwaɪ·ət] adj (still) tranquille, silencieux; (person) modeste, discret; (market) (com) calme; **be quiet!** taisez-vous!; **to keep quiet** rester tranquille; (to not speak) se taire ‖ s tranquillité f; (rest) repos m; **on the quiet** en douce, à la dérobée ‖

tr calmer, tranquilliser; (a child) faire taire ‖ intr—**to quiet down** se calmer
quill [kwɪl] s plume f d'oie; (hollow part) tuyau m (de plume); (of hedgehog, porcupine) piquant m
quilt [kwɪlt] s courtepointe f ‖ tr piquer
quince [kwɪns] s coing m; (tree) cognassier m
quinine ['kwaɪnaɪn] s quinine f
quinsy ['kwɪnzi] s angine f
quintessence [kwɪn'tesəns] s quintessence f
quintet [kwɪn'tet] s quintette m
quintuplets ['kwɪntʊ,plets], [kwɪn'tʌplets], [kwɪn't(j)uplets] spl quintuplés mpl
quip [kwɪp] s raillerie f, quolibet m ‖ v (pret & pp **quipped**; ger **quipping**) tr dire sur un ton railleur ‖ intr railler
quire [kwaɪr] s main f
quirk [kwʌrk] s excentricité f; (subterfuge) faux-fuyant m; **quirk of fate** caprice m du sort
quit [kwɪt] adj quitte; **to be quits** être quitte; **to call it quits** cesser, s'y renoncer; **we are quits** nous voilà quittes ‖ v (pret & pp **quit** or **quitted**; ger **quitting**) tr (e.g., a city) quitter; (one's work, a pursuit, etc.) cesser; **to quit** + ger s'arrêter de + inf ‖ intr partir; (coll) lâcher la partie
quite [kwaɪt] adv tout à fait; **quite a story** (coll) toute une histoire
quitter ['kwɪtər] s défaitiste m, lâcheur m
quiver ['kwɪvər] s tremblement m; (to hold arrows) carquois m ‖ intr trembler
quixotic [kwɪks'ɑtɪk] adj de don Quichotte; visionnaire, exalté
quiz [kwɪz] s (pl **quizzes**) interrogation f, colle f ‖ v (pret & pp **quizzed**; ger **quizzing**) tr examiner, interroger
quiz/ sec/tion s classe f d'exercices
quiz/ show/ s émission-questionnaire f
quizzical ['kwɪzɪkəl] adj curieux; (laughable) risible; (mocking) railleur
quoin [kɔɪn], [kwɔɪn] s angle m; (cornerstone) pierre f d'angle; (wedge) coin m, cale f ‖ tr coincer, caler
quoit [kwɔɪt], [kɔɪt] s palet m; **to play quoits** jouer au palet
quondam ['kwɑndæm] adj ci-devant, d'autrefois
quorum ['kwɔrəm] s quorum m
quota ['kwotə] s quote-part f; (e.g., of immigration) quota m, contingent m
quotation [kwo'teʃən] s (from a book) citation f; (of prices) cours m, cote f
quota/tion marks/ spl guillemets mpl
quote [kwot] s (from a book) citation f; (of prices) cours m, cote f; **in quotes** (coll) entre guillemets ‖ tr (from a book) citer; (values) coter ‖ intr tirer des citations; **to quote out of context** citer hors contexte ‖ interj je cite
quotient ['kwoʃənt] s quotient m

R

R, r [ɑr] *s* XVIIIᵉ lettre de l'alphabet

rabbet ['ræbɪt] *s* feuillure *f* ‖ *tr* feuiller

rab·bi ['ræbaɪ] *s* (*pl* **-bis** or **-bies**) rabbin *m*

rabbit ['ræbɪt] *s* lapin *m*

rab′bit stew′ *s* lapin *m* en civet

rabble ['ræbəl] *s* canaille *f*

rab′ble-rous′er *s* fomentateur *m*, agitateur *m*

rabies ['rebiz], ['rebɪ͵iz] *s* rage *f*

raccoon [ræ'kun] *s* raton *m* laveur

race [res] *s* race *f*; (*contest*) course *f*; (*channel to lead water*) bief *m*; (*rapid current*) raz *m* ‖ *tr* lutter de vitesse avec; (*e.g., a horse*) faire courir; (*a motor*) emballer ‖ *intr* faire une course, courir; (*said of motor*) s'emballer

race′ horse′ *s* cheval *m* de course

race′ ri′ot *s* émeute *f* raciale

race′ track′ *s* champ *m* de courses, hippodrome *m*

racial ['reʃəl] *adj* racial

rac′ing car′ *s* automobile *f* de course

rac′ing odds′ *spl* cote *f*

rack [ræk] *s* (*shelf*) étagère *f*; (*to hang clothes*) portemanteau *m*; (*for baggage*) porte-bagages *m*; (*for guns; for fodder*) râtelier *m*; (*for torture*) chevalet *m*; (*bar made to gear with a pinion*) crémaillère *f*; **to go to rack and ruin** aller à vau-l'eau ‖ *tr* (*with hunger, remorse, etc.*) tenailler; (*one's brains*) se creuser

racket ['rækɪt] *s* raquette *f*; (*noise*) vacarme *m*; (*slang*) racket *m*; **to make a racket** faire du tapage

racketeer [͵rækɪ'tɪr] *s* racketter *m* ‖ *intr* pratiquer l'escroquerie

rack′ rail′way *s* chemin *m* de fer à crémaillère

rac·y ['resi] *adj* (*comp* **-ier**; *super* **-iest**) plein de verve, vigoureux; parfumé; (*off-color*) sale, grivois

radar ['redɑr] *s* (*acronym*) (**radio detecting and ranging**) radar *m*

ra′dar sta′tion *s* poste *m* radar

radiant ['redɪ͵ənt] *adj* radieux, rayonnant; (*astr & phys*) radiant

radiate ['redɪ͵et] *tr* rayonner; (*e.g., happiness*) répandre ‖ *intr* rayonner

radiation [͵redɪ'e/ən] *s* rayonnement *m*, radiation *f*

radia′tion sick′ness *s* mal *m* des rayons

radiator ['redɪ͵etər] *s* radiateur *m*

ra′diator cap′ *s* bouchon *m* de radiateur

radical ['rædɪkəl] *adj* & *s* radical *m*

radi·o ['redɪ͵o] *s* (*pl* **-os**) radio *f* ‖ *tr* radiodiffuser

radioactive [͵redɪ·o'æktɪv] *adj* radioactif

ra′dioac′tive fall′out *s* retombées *fpl* radioactives

ra′dio am′ateur *s* sans-filiste *mf*

ra′dio announ′cer *s* speaker *m*

ra′dio·broad′cast′ing *s* radiodiffusion *f*

ra′dio·fre′quency *s* radiofréquence *f*

radiogram ['redɪ·o͵græm] *s* radiogramme *m*

ra′dio lis′tener *s* auditeur *m* de la radio

radiology [͵redɪ'ɑlədʒɪ] *s* radiologie *f*

ra′dio net′work *s* chaîne *f* de radio-diffusion

ra′dio news′cast *s* journal *m* parlé, radio-journal *m*

ra′dio receiv′er *s* récepteur *m* de radio

radioscopy [͵redɪ'askəpɪ] *s* radioscopie *f*

ra′dio set′ *s* poste *m* de radio

ra′dio sta′tion *s* poste *m* émetteur

ra′dio tube′ *s* lampe *f* de radio

radish ['rædɪʃ] *s* radis *m*

radium ['redɪ·əm] *s* radium *m*

radi·us ['redɪ·əs] *s* (*pl* **-i** [͵aɪ] or **-uses**) rayon *m*; (*anat*) radius *m*; **within a radius of** dans un rayon de, à . . . à la ronde

raffish ['ræfɪʃ] *adj* bravache; (*flashy*) criard

raffle ['ræfəl] *s* tombola *f* ‖ *tr* mettre en tombola

raft [ræft], [rɑft] *s* radeau *m*; **a raft of** (*coll*) un tas de

rafter ['ræftər], ['rɑftər] *s* chevron *m*

rag [ræg] *s* chiffon *m*; **in rags** en haillons; **to chew the rag** (*slang*) tailler une bavette

ragamuffin ['ræɡə͵mʌfɪn] *s* gueux *m*, va-nu-pieds *m*; (*urchin*) gamin *m*

rag′ doll′ *s* poupée *f* de chiffon

rage [redʒ] *s* rage *f*; **to be all the rage** faire fureur; **to fly into a rage** entrer en fureur ‖ *intr* faire rage

rag′ fair′ *s* marché *m* aux puces

ragged ['ræɡɪd] *adj* en haillons; (*edge*) hérissé

ragpicker ['ræɡ͵pɪkər] *s* chiffonnier *m*

rag′time′ *s* rythme *m* syncopé du jazz; musique *f* syncopée du jazz

rag′weed′ *s* ambroisie *f*

ragwort ['ræɡ͵wʌrt] *s* (*Senecio vulgaris*) séneçon *m*; (*S. jacobaea*) jacobée *f*

raid [red] *s* incursion *f*, razzia *f*; (*by police*) descente *f*; (*mil*) raid *m* ‖ *tr* razzier; faire une descente dans

rail [rel] *s* rail *m*; (*railing*) balustrade *f*; (*of stairway*) rampe *f*; (*of, e.g., a bridge*) garde-fou *m*; (*orn*) râle *m*; **by rail** par chemin de fer ‖ *intr* invectiver; **to rail at** invectiver

rail′ fence′ *s* palissade *f* à claire-voie

rail′head′ *s* tête *f* de ligne

railing ['relɪŋ] *s* balustrade *f*

rail′road′ *adj* ferroviaire ‖ *s* chemin *m* de fer ‖ *tr* (*a bill*) faire voter en vitesse; (*coll*) emprisonner à tort

rail′road cros′sing *s* passage *m* à niveau

railroader ['rel͵rodər] *s* cheminot *m*

rail′road sta′tion *s* gare *f*

rail′way′ *adj* ferroviaire ‖ *s* chemin *m* de fer

raiment ['remənt] *s* habillement *m*

rain [ren] *s* pluie *f*; **in the rain** sous la pluie ‖ *tr* faire pleuvoir ‖ *intr* pleuvoir; **it is raining cats and dogs** il pleut à seaux

rainbow ['ren‚bo] s arc-en-ciel m

rain′coat′ s imperméable m

rain′fall′ s chute f de pluie

rain′proof′ adj imperméable

rain′ wa′ter s eau f de pluie

rain•y ['reni] adj (comp -ier; super -iest) pluvieux

raise [rez] s augmentation f; (in poker) relance f || tr augmenter; (plants, animals, children; one's voice; a number to a certain power) élever; (an army, a camp, a siege; anchor; game) lever; (an objection, questions, etc.) soulever; (doubts; a hope; a storm) faire naître; (a window) relever; (one's head, one's voice; prices; the land) hausser; (a flag) arborer; (the dead) ressusciter; (money) se procurer; (the ante) relancer; **to raise up** soulever, dresser

raisin ['rezɪn] s raisin m sec, grain m de raisin sec

rake [rek] s râteau m; (person) débauché m || tr ratisser; **to rake together** râteler

rake′-off′ s (coll) gratte f

rakish ['rekɪʃ] adj gaillard; dissolu

ral•ly ['ræli] s (pl -lies) ralliement m; réunion f politique; (in a game) reprise f; (auto race) rallye m || v (pret & pp -lied) tr rallier || intr se rallier; (from illness) se remettre; (sports) se reprendre; **to rally to the side of** se rallier à

ram [ræm] s bélier m || v (pret & pp rammed; ger ramming) tr tamponner; **to ram down or in** enfoncer || intr se tamponner; **to ram into** tamponner

ramble ['ræmbəl] s flânerie f || intr flâner, errer à l'aventure; (to talk aimlessly) divaguer

rami•fy ['ræmɪ‚faɪ] v (pret & pp -fied) tr ramifier || intr se ramifier

ramp [ræmp] s rampe f

rampage ['ræmpedʒ] s tempête f; **to go on a rampage** se déchaîner

rampart ['ræmpɑrt] s rempart m

ram′rod′ s écouvillon m

ram′shack′le adj délabré

ranch [rænʧ] s ranch m, rancho m

rancid ['rænsɪd] adj rance

rancor ['ræŋkər] s rancœur f

random ['rændəm] adj fortuit; **at random** au hasard

range [rendʒ] s (row) rangée f; (scope) portée f; (mountains) chaîne f; (stove) cuisinière f; (for rifle practice) champ m de tir; (of colors, musical notes, prices, speeds, etc.) gamme f; (of words) répartition f; (of voice) tessiture f; (of vision, of activity, etc.) champ m; (for pasture) grand pâturage m; **within range of** à portée de || tr ranger || intr se ranger; **to range from** s'échelonner entre, varier entre; **to range over** parcourir

range′ find′er s télémètre m

rank [ræŋk] adj fétide, rance; (injustice) criant; (vegetation) luxuriant ||

s rang m || tr ranger || intr occuper le premier rang; **to rank above** être supérieur à; **to rank with** aller de pair avec

rank′ and file′ s hommes mpl de troupe; commun m des mortels; (of the party, union, etc.) commun m

rankle ['ræŋkəl] tr ulcérer; irriter || intr s'ulcérer

ransack ['rænsæk] tr fouiller, fouiller dans; mettre à sac

ransom ['rænsəm] s rançon f || tr rançonner

rant [rænt] intr tempêter

rap [ræp] s tape f; (noise) petit coup m sec; (slang) éreintement m; **to not care a rap** (slang) s'en ficher; **to take the rap** (slang) se laisser châtier || v (pret & pp rapped; ger rapping) tr & intr frapper d'un coup sec

rapacious [rə'peʃəs] adj rapace

rape [rep] s viol m || tr violer

rapid ['ræpɪd] adj rapide || **rapids** spl rapides mpl

rap′id-fire′ adj à tir rapide

rapidity [rə'pɪdəti] s rapidité f

rapier ['repɪ‚ər] s rapière f

rapt [ræpt] adj ravi; absorbé

rapture ['ræptʃər] s ravissement m

rare [rer] adj rare; (meat) saignant; (amusing) (coll) impayable

rare′ bird′ s merle m blanc

rarely ['rerli] adv rarement

rascal ['ræskəl] s coquin m

rash [ræʃ] adj téméraire || s éruption f

rasp [ræsp], [rɑsp] s crissement m; (tool) râpe f || tr râper || intr crisser

raspber•ry ['ræz‚beri], ['rɑz‚beri] s (pl -ries) framboise f

rasp′berry bush′ s framboisier m

rat [ræt] s rat m; (false hair) (coll) postiche m; (deserter) (slang) lâcheur m; (informer) (slang) mouchard m; (scoundrel) (slang) cochon m; **rats!** zut!; **to smell a rat** (coll) soupçonner anguille sous roche

ratchet ['ræʧɪt] s encliquetage m

rate [ret] s taux m; (for freight, mail, a subscription) tarif m; **at any rate** en tout cas; **at the rate of** à raison de || tr évaluer; mériter || intr (coll) être favori

rate′ of exchange′ s cours m

rather ['ræðər], ['rɑðər] adv plutôt; (fairly) assez; **rather than** plutôt que || interj je vous crois!

rathskeller ['ræts‚kelər] s caveau m

rati•fy ['rætɪ‚faɪ] v (pret & pp -fied) tr ratifier

rating ['retɪŋ] s classement m, cote f

ra•tio ['reʃo], ['reʃɪ‚o] s (pl -tios) raison f, rapport m

ration ['reʃən], ['ræʃən] s ration f || tr rationner

rational ['ræʃənəl] adj rationnel

ra′tion book′ s tickets mpl de rationnement

ra′tion card′ s carte f de ravitaillement

rat′ poi′son s mort m aux rats

rat′-tail file′ s queue-de-rat m

rattan [ræ'tæn] s rotin m

rattle ['rætəl] s (*number of short, sharp sounds*) bruit m de ferraille, cliquetis m; (*noisemaking device*) crécelle f; (*child's toy*) hochet m; (*in the throat*) râle m || tr agiter; (*to confuse*) (coll) affoler; **to rattle off** débiter comme un moulin || intr cliqueter; (*said of windows*) trembler

rat'tle-snake' s serpent m à sonnettes

rat'trap' s ratière f

raucous ['rɔkəs] adj rauque

ravage ['rævɪdʒ] s ravage m; **ravages** (*of time*) injure f || tr ravager

rave [rev] s (coll) éloge m enthousiaste || intr délirer; **to rave about** or **over** s'extasier devant or sur

raven ['revən] s corbeau m

ravenous ['rævənəs] adj vorace

rave' review' s article m dithyrambique

ravine [rə'vin] s ravin m

ravish ['rævɪʃ] tr ravir

ravishing ['rævɪʃɪŋ] adj ravissant

raw {rɔ} adj cru; (*sugar, metal*) brut; (*silk*) grège; (*wound*) vif; (*wind*) aigre; (*weather*) humide et froid; novice, inexpérimenté

raw'boned' adj décharné

raw' deal' s (slang) mauvais tour m

raw'hide' s cuir m vert

raw' mate'rial s matière f première, matières premières, matière brute

ray [re] s (*of light*) rayon m; (*fish*) raie f

rayon ['re·ɑn] s rayonne f

raze [rez] tr raser

razor ['rezər] s rasoir m

ra'zor blade' s lame f de rasoir

ra'zor strop' s cuir m à rasoir

razz [ræz] tr (slang) mettre en boîte

reach [ritʃ] s portée f; **out of reach (of)** hors d'atteinte (de), hors de portée (de); **within reach of** à portée de || tr atteindre; arriver à; **to reach out** (*a hand*) tendre; (*an arm*) allonger || intr s'étendre

react [rɪ'ækt] intr réagir

reaction [rɪ'ækʃən] s réaction f

reactionar•y [rɪ'ækʃən‚erɪ] adj réactionnaire || s (pl -ies) réactionnaire mf

reactor [rɪ'æktər] s réacteur m

read [rid] v (pret & pp read [rɛd]) tr lire; **to read over** parcourir || intr lire; (*said of passage, description, etc.*) se lire; (*said, e.g., of thermometer*) marquer; **to read on** continuer à lire; **to read up on** étudier

reader ['ridər] s lecteur m; livre m de lecture

readily ['redɪlɪ] adv (*willingly*) volontiers; (*easily*) facilement

reading ['ridɪŋ] s lecture f

read'ing desk' s pupitre m

read'ing glass' es loupe f; **reading glasses** lunettes fpl pour lire

read'ing lamp' s lampe f de bureau

read'ing room' s salle f de lecture

read•y ['redɪ] adj (comp -ier; super -iest) prêt; (*quick*) vif; (*money*) comptant || v (pret & pp -ied) tr préparer || intr se préparer

read'y cash' s argent m comptant

read'y-made' suit' s (*for men*) complet m de confection; (*for women*) costume m de confection

ready-to-eat ['redɪə'it] adj prêt à servir

ready-to-wear ['redɪə'wer] adj prêt à porter || s prêt-à-porter m

reaffirm [‚ri·ə'fʌrm] tr réaffirmer

reagent [rɪ'edʒənt] s (chem) réactif m

real ['ri·əl] adj vrai, réel

re'al estate' s biens mpl immobiliers

re'al-estate' adj immobilier

realism ['ri·ə‚lɪzəm] s réalisme m

realist ['ri·əlɪst] s réaliste mf

realistic [‚ri·ə'lɪstɪk] adj réaliste

reali•ty [rɪ'ælɪtɪ] s (pl -ties) réalité f

realize ['ri·ə‚laɪz] tr se rendre compte de, s'apercevoir de; (*hopes, profits, etc.*) réaliser

really ['ri·əlɪ] adv vraiment

realm [rɛlm] s royaume m; (*field*) domaine m

realtor ['ri·əl‚tɔr], ['ri·əltər] s agent m immobilier

ream [rim] s rame f; **reams** (coll) masses fpl || tr aléser

reap [rip] tr moissonner; (*to gather*) recueillir

reaper ['ripər] s moissonneur m; (mach) moissonneuse f

reappear [‚ri·ə'pɪr] intr réapparaître

reappearance [‚ri·ə'pɪrəns] s réapparition f

reapportionment [‚ri·ə'pɔrʃənmənt] s nouvelle répartition f

rear [rɪr] adj arrière, d'arrière, de derrière || s derrière m; (*of a car, ship, etc.; of an army*) arrière m; (*of a row*) queue f; **to the rear!** (mil) demitour à droite! || tr élever || intr (*said of animal*) se cabrer

rear' ad'miral s contre-amiral m

rear'-axle assem'bly s (pl -blies) pont m arrière

rear' drive' s traction f arrière

rearmament [rɪ'ɑrməmənt] s réarmement m

rearrange [‚ri·ə'rendʒ] tr arranger de nouveau

rear'-view mir'ror s rétroviseur m

rear' win'dow s (aut) lunette f arrière

reason ['rizən] s raison f; **by reason of** à cause de; **for good reason** pour cause; **to listen to reason** entendre raison; **to stand to reason** être de toute évidence || tr & intr raisonner

reasonable ['rizənəbəl] adj raisonnable

reassessment [‚ri·ə'sɛsmənt] s réévaluation f

reassure [‚ri·ə'ʃʊr] tr rassurer

reawaken [‚ri·ə'wekən] tr réveiller || intr se réveiller

rebate ['ribet], [rɪ'bet] s rabais m, escompte m; ristourne f, bonification f || tr faire un rabais sur

rebel ['rɛbəl] adj & s rebelle mf || **rebel** [rɪ'bɛl] v (pret & pp -belled; ger -belling) intr se rebeller

rebellion [rɪ'bɛljən] s rébellion f

rebellious [rɪ'bɛljəs] adj rebelle

re•bind [rɪ'baɪnd] v (pret & pp -bound) tr (bb) relier à neuf

rebirth ['ribʌrθ] s renaissance f

rebore [ri'bor] tr rectifier

rebound ['ri,baund], [ri'baund] s rebondissement m || [ri'baund] intr rebondir

rebroad-cast [ri'brɑd,kæst], [ri'brɑd,kɑst] s retransmission f || v (pret & pp -cast or -casted) tr retransmettre

rebuff [ri'bʌf] s rebuffade f || tr mal accueillir

re-build [ri'bild] v (pret & pp -built) tr reconstruire

rebuke [ri'bjuk] s réprimande f || tr réprimander

re-but [ri'bʌt] v (pret & pp -butted; ger -butting) tr réfuter, repousser

rebuttal [ri'bʌtəl] s réfutation f

recall [ri'kɔl], ['rikɔl] s rappel m || [ri'kɔl] tr rappeler; se rappeler de

recant [ri'kænt] tr rétracter || intr se rétracter

re-cap ['ri,kæp], [ri'kæp] v (pret & pp -capped; ger -capping) tr rechaper

recapitulate [,rikə,pit/ə'le/ən] s récapitulation f

re-cast ['ri,kæst], ['ri,kɑst], [ri'kæst], [ri'kɑst] s refonte f || ['ri'kæst], [ri'kɑst] v (pret & pp -cast) tr (metal, a play, novel, etc.) refondre; (the actors of a play) redistribuer

recede [ri'sid] intr reculer; (said of forehead, chin, etc.) fuir; (said of sea) se retirer

receipt [ri'sit] s (for goods) récépissé m; (for money) récépissé, reçu m; (recipe) recette f; **receipts** recettes; **to acknowledge receipt of** accuser réception de || tr acquitter

receive [ri'siv] tr recevoir; (stolen goods) recéler; (a station) (rad) capter; **received payment** pour acquit || intr recevoir

receiver [ri'sivər] s (of letter) destinataire mf; (in bankruptcy) syndic m, liquidateur m; (telp) récepteur m

receiv'ing set' s poste m récepteur

recent ['risənt] adj récent

recently ['risəntli] adv récemment

receptacle [ri'septəkəl] s récipient m; (elec) prise f femelle

reception [ri'sep/ən] s réception f; (welcome) accueil m

recep'tion desk' s réception f

receptionist [ri'sep/ənist] s préposé m à la réception

receptive [ri'septiv] adj réceptif

recess [ri'ses], ['rises], ['rises] s (of court, legislature, etc.) ajournement m; (at school) récréation f; (in a wall) niche f || [ri'ses] tr ajourner; (s.th., e.g., in a wall) encastrer || intr s'ajourner

recession [ri'se/ən] s récession f

recipe ['resi,pi] s recette f

recipient [ri'sipi-ənt] s (person) bénéficiaire mf; (of a degree, honor, etc.) récipiendaire m; (of blood) receveur m

reciprocal [ri'siprəkəl] adj réciproque

reciprocity [,resi'prositi] s réciprocité f

recital [ri'saitəl] s récit m; (of music or poetry) récital m

recite [ri'sait] tr réciter; narrer

reckless ['reklis] adj téméraire, imprudent, insouciant

reckon ['rekən] tr calculer; considérer; (coll) supposer, imaginer || intr calculer; **to reckon on** compter sur; **to reckon with** tenir compte de

reclaim [ri'klem] tr récupérer; (e.g., waste land) mettre en valeur; (a person) réformer

reclamation [,reklə'me/ən] s récupération f; (e.g., of waste land) mise f en valeur; (of a person) réforme f

recline [ri'klain] tr appuyer, reposer || intr s'appuyer, se reposer

recluse [ri'klus], ['reklus] adj & s reclus m

recognition [,rekəg'ni/ən] s reconnaissance f

recognize ['rekəg,naiz] tr reconnaître; (parl) donner la parole à

recoil [ri'kɔil] s répugnance f; (of, e.g., firearm) recul m || intr reculer

recollect [,rekə'lekt] tr se rappeler

recollection [,rekə'lek/ən] s souvenir m

recommend [,rekə'mend] tr recommander

recompense ['rekəm,pens] s récompense f || tr récompenser

reconcile ['rekən,sail] tr réconcilier; **to reconcile oneself to** se résigner à

reconnaissance [ri'kɑnisəns] s reconnaissance f

reconnoiter [,rekə'nɔitər], [,rikə'nɔitər] tr & intr reconnaître

reconquer [ri'kɑŋkər] tr reconquérir

reconquest [ri'kɑŋkwest] s reconquête f

reconsider [,rikən'sidər] tr reconsidérer

reconstruct [,rikən'strʌkt] tr reconstruire; (a crime) reconstituer

reconversion [,rikən'vʌrʒən], [,rikən'vʌr/ən] s reconversion f

record ['rekərd] s enregistrement m, registre m; (to play on the phonograph) disque m; (mil) état m de service; (sports) record m; **off the record** en confidence; **records** archives fpl; **to break the record** battre le record; **to have a good record** être bien noté; (at school) avoir de bonnes notes || [ri'kɔrd] tr enregistrer

rec'ord chang'er s tourne-disque m automatique

recorder [ri'kɔrdər] s appareil m enregistreur; (law) greffier m; (mus) flûte f à bec

rec'ord hold'er s recordman m

recording [ri'kɔrdiŋ] adj enregistreur || s enregistrement m

record'ing tape' s ruban m magnétique

rec'ord li'brary s discothèque m

rec'ord play'er s électrophone m

recount [ri'kaunt] s nouveau dépouillement m du scrutin || [ri'kaunt] tr (to count again) recompter || [ri'kaunt] tr (to tell) raconter

recoup [ri'kup] tr recouvrer; **to recoup s.o. for** dédommager qn de

recourse [ri'kors], ['rikors] s recours m; **to have recourse to** recourir à

recover [ri'kʌvər] tr (to get back) recouvrer; (*to cover again*) recouvrir || *intr* (*to get well*) se rétablir

recover·y [rɪˈkʌvəri] *s* (*pl* -ies) récupération *f*, recouvrement *m*; (*e.g., of health*) rétablissement *m*

recreant [ˈrekrɪ·ənt] *adj* & *s* lâche *mf*; traître *m*; apostat *m*

recreation [ˌrekrɪˈeʃən] *s* récréation *f*

recruit [rɪˈkrut] *s* recrue *f* || *tr* recruter; **to be recruited** se recruter

rectangle [ˈrek͵tæŋgəl] *s* rectangle *m*

rectifier [ˈrektəˌfaɪ·ər] *s* rectificateur *m*; (elec) redresseur *m*

recti·fy [ˈrektɪˌfaɪ] *v* (*pret* & *pp* -fied) *tr* rectifier; (elec) redresser

rec·tum [ˈrektəm] *s* (*pl* -ta [tə]) rectum *m*

recumbent [rɪˈkʌmbənt] *adj* couché

recuperate [rɪˈkjupəˌret] *tr* & *intr* récupérer

re·cur [rɪˈkʌr] *v* (*pret* & *pp* -curred; *ger* -curring) *intr* revenir, se reproduire; revenir à la mémoire de

recurrent [rɪˈkʌrənt] *adj* récurrent

red [red] *adj* (*comp* redder; *super* reddest) rouge || *s* (*color*) rouge *m*; **in the red** en déficit; **Red** (*communist*) rouge *mf*; (*nickname*) Rouquin *m*

red′bait′ *tr* taxer de communiste

red′bird′ *s* cardinal *m* d'Amérique, tangara *m*

red′-blood′ed *adj* vigoureux

red′breast′ *s* rouge-gorge *m*

red′cap′ *s* porteur *m*; (Brit) soldat *m* de la police militaire

red′ cell′ *s* globule *m* rouge

Red′ Cross′ *s* Croix-Rouge *f*

redden [ˈredən] *tr* & *intr* rougir

redeem [rɪˈdim] *tr* racheter; (*a pawned article*) dégager; (*a promise*) remplir; (*a debt*) s'acquitter de, acquitter

redeemer [rɪˈdimər] *s* rédempteur *m*

redemption [rɪˈdempʃən] *s* rachat *m*; (rel) rédemption *f*

red′-haired′ *adj* roux

red′hand′ed *adj* & *adv* sur le fait, en flagrant délit

red′head′ *s* (*woman*) rousse *f*

red′ her′ring *s* hareng *m* saur; (fig) faux-fuyant *m*

red′-hot′ *adj* chauffé au rouge; ardent; (*news*) tout frais

rediscount [riˈdɪskaunt] *s* réescompte *m* || *tr* réescompter

rediscover [ˌrɪdɪsˈkʌvər] *tr* redécouvrir

red′-let′ter day′ *s* jour *m* mémorable

red′ light′ *s* feu *m* rouge; **to go through a red light** brûler un feu rouge

red′-light′ dis′trict *s* quartier *m* réservé

red′ man′ *s* (*pl* men′) Peau-Rouge *m*

re·do [ˈriˈdu] *v* (*pret* -did; *pp* -done) *tr* refaire

redolent [ˈredələnt] *adj* parfumé; redolent of exhalant une senteur de; qui fait penser à

redoubt [rɪˈdaut] *s* redoute *f*

redound [rɪˈdaund] *intr* contribuer; **to redound to** tourner à

red′ pep′per *s* piment *m* rouge

redress [rɪˈdres] *s* (rɪˈredrəs) *s* redressement *m* || [rɪˈdres] *tr* redresser

Red′ Rid′ing·hood′ *s* Chaperon rouge *m*

red′skin′ *s* Peau-Rouge *mf*

red′ tape′ *s* paperasserie *f*, chinoiseries *fpl* administratives

reduce [rɪˈd(j)us] *tr* réduire || *intr* maigrir

reduc′ing ex′ercises *spl* exercices *mpl* amaigrissants

reduction [rɪˈdʌkʃən] *s* réduction *f*

redundant [rɪˈdʌndənt] *adj* redondant

red′ wine′ *s* vin *m* rouge

red′wing′ *s* (orn) mauvis *m*

red′wood′ *s* séquoia *m*

reed [rid] *s* (*of instrument*) anche *f*; (bot) roseau *m*; **reeds** (mus) instruments *mpl* à anche

reedit [riˈedɪt] *tr* rééditer

reef [rif] *s* récif *m*; (*of sail*) ris *m* || *tr* (naut) prendre un ris dans

reefer [ˈrifər] *s* caban *m*; (slang) cigarette *f* à marijuana

reek [rik] *intr* fumer; **to reek of** or **with** empester, puer

reel [ril] *s* bobine *f*; (*of film*) rouleau *m*, bobine; (*of fishing rod*) moulinet *m*; (*sway*) balancement *m*; **off the reel** (coll) d'affilée || *tr* bobiner; **to reel off** dévider; (coll) réciter d'un trait || *intr* chanceler

reelection [ˌri·ɪˈlekʃən] *s* réélection *f*

reenlist [ˌri·enˈlɪst] *tr* rengager || *intr* rengager, se rengager

reenlistment [ˌri·enˈlɪstmənt] *s* rengagement *m*; (*person*) engagé *m*

reen·try [rɪˈentri] *s* (*pl* -tries) rentrée *f*; (rok) retour *m* à la Terre

reexamination [ˌri·eg͵zæmɪˈneʃən] *s* réexamen *m*

re·fer [rɪˈfʌr] *v* (*pret* & *pp* -ferred; *ger* -ferring) *tr* renvoyer || *intr*—**to refer to** se référer à

referee [ˌrefəˈri] *s* arbitre *m* || *tr* & *intr* arbitrer

reference [ˈrefərəns] *s* référence *f*

ref′erence room′ *s* bibliothèque *f* de consultation

referen·dum [ˌrefəˈrendəm] *s* (*pl* -da [də]) référendum *m*

refill [ˈrifɪl] *s* recharge *f* || [riˈfɪl] *tr* remplir à nouveau

refine [rɪˈfaɪn] *tr* raffiner

refinement [rɪˈfaɪnmənt] *s* raffinage *m*; (*e.g., of manners*) raffinement *m*

refiner·y [rɪˈfaɪnəri] *s* (*pl* -ies) raffinerie *f*

reflect [rɪˈflekt] *tr* réfléchir || *intr* (*to meditate*) réfléchir; **to reflect on** or **upon** réfléchir à or sur; nuire à la réputation de

reflection [rɪˈflekʃən] *s* (*e.g., of light; thought*) réflexion *f*; (*reflected light; image*) reflet *m*; **to cast reflections on** faire des réflexions à

reflex [ˈrifleks] *adj* & *s* réflexe *m*

reforestation [ˌrifɔrɪsˈteʃən], [ˌrifɔrɪsˈteʃən] *s* reboisement *m*

reform [rɪˈfɔrm] *s* reforme *f* || *tr* réformer || *intr* se réformer

reformation [ˌrefərˈmeʃən] *s* réformation *f*; **the Reformation** la Réforme

reformato·ry [rɪ'fɔrmə,tori] s (pl -ries) maison f de correction

reformer [rɪ'fɔrmər] s réformateur m

reform′ school′ s maison f de correction

refraction [rɪ'fræk/ən] s réfraction f

refrain [rɪ'fren] s refrain m ‖ intr s'abstenir

refresh [rɪ'frɛʃ] tr rafraîchir ‖ intr se rafraîchir

refreshing [rɪ'frɛʃɪŋ] adj rafraîchissant

refreshment [rɪ'frɛʃmənt] s rafraîchissement m

refresh′ment bar′ s buvette f

refrigerate [rɪ'frɪdʒə,ret] tr réfrigérer

refrigerator [rɪ'frɪdʒə,retər] s (icebox) glacière; réfrigérateur m; (condenser) congélateur m

refrig′erator car′ s (rr) wagon m frigorifique

re·fuel [ri'fjul] v (pret & pp -fueled or -fuelled; ger -fueling or -fuelling) tr ravitailler en carburant ‖ intr se ravitailler en carburant

refuge ['rɛfjudʒ] s refuge m; **to take refuge (in)** se réfugier (dans)

refugee [,rɛfju'dʒi] s réfugié m

refund [rɪ'fʌnd] s remboursement m ‖ [rɪ'fʌnd] tr (to pay back) rembourser ‖ [ri'fʌnd] tr (to fund again) consolider

refurnish [ri'fʌrnɪʃ] tr remeubler

refusal [rɪ'fjuzəl] s refus m

refuse ['rɛfjus] s ordures fpl, détritus mpl ‖ [rɪ'fjuz] tr & intr refuser

refute [rɪ'fjut] tr réfuter

regain [rɪ'gen] tr regagner; (consciousness) reprendre

regal ['rigəl] adj royal

regale [rɪ'gel] tr régaler

regalia [rɪ'gelɪ·ə] spl atours mpl, ornements mpl; (of an office) insignes mpl

regard [rɪ'gɑrd] s considération f; (esteem) respect m; (look) regard m; **in** or **with regard to** à l'égard de; **regards sincères amitiés** fpl ‖ tr considérer, estimer; **as regards** quant à

regarding [rɪ'gɑrdɪŋ] prep au sujet de, touchant

regardless [rɪ'gɑrdlɪs] adj inattentif ‖ adv (coll) coûte que coûte; **regardless of** sans tenir compte de

regatta [rɪ'gætə] s régates fpl

regen·cy ['ridʒənsi] s (pl -cies) régence f

regenerate [rɪ'dʒɛnə,ret] tr régénérer ‖ intr se régénérer

regent ['ridʒənt] s régent m

regicide ['rɛdʒɪ,saɪd] s (act) régicide m; (person) régicide mf

regime [re'ʒim] s régime m

regiment ['rɛdʒɪmənt] s régiment m ‖ ['rɛdʒɪ,mɛnt] tr enrégimenter, régenter

regimental [,rɛdʒɪ'mɛntəl] adj régimentaire ‖ **regimentals** spl tenue f militaire

region ['ridʒən] s région f

register ['rɛdʒɪstər] s registre m ‖ tr enregistrer; (a student; an automobile) immatriculer; (a letter) recommander ‖ intr s'inscrire

reg′istered let′ter s lettre f recommandée

reg′istered mail′ s envoi m en recommandé

reg′istered nurse′ s infirmière f diplômée

registrar ['rɛdʒɪs,trɑr] s archiviste mf, secrétaire mf

registration [,rɛdʒɪs'treʃən] s enregistrement m; immatriculation f, inscription f; (of mail) recommandation f

registra′tion blank′ s fiche f d'inscription

registra′tion fee′ s frais mpl d'inscription

registra′tion num′ber s (of soldier or student) numéro m matricule

regret [rɪ'grɛt] s regret m; **regrets excuses** fpl ‖ v (pret & pp -gretted; ger -gretting) tr regretter

regrettable [rɪ'grɛtəbəl] adj regrettable

regular ['rɛgjələr] adj & s régulier m

reg′ular fel′low s (coll) chic type m

regularity [,rɛgjə'lærɪti] s régularité f

regularize ['rɛgjələ,raɪz] tr régulariser

regulate ['rɛgjə,let] tr régler; (to control) réglementer

regulation [,rɛgjə'leʃən] s régulation f; (rule) règlement m

rehabilitate [,rihə'bɪlɪ,tet] tr réadapter; (in reputation, standing, etc.) réhabiliter

rehearsal [rɪ'hʌrsəl] s répétition f

rehearse [rɪ'hʌrs] tr & intr répéter

reign [ren] s règne m ‖ intr régner

reimburse [,ri·ɪm'bʌrs] tr rembourser

rein [ren] s rêne f; **to give free rein to** donner libre cours à ‖ tr contenir, freiner

reincarnation [,ri·ɪnkɑr'neʃən] s réincarnation f

rein′deer′ s renne m

reinforce [,ri·ɪn'fors] tr renforcer; (concrete) armer

reinforcement [,ri·ɪn'forsmənt] s renforcement m

reinstate [,ri·ɪn'stet] tr rétablir

reiterate [ri'ɪtə,ret] tr réitérer

reject ['ridʒɛkt] s pièce f or article m de rebut; **rejects rebuts** mpl ‖ [rɪ'dʒɛkt] tr rejeter

rejection [rɪ'dʒɛk/ən] s rejet m, refus m

rejoice [rɪ'dʒɔɪs] intr se réjouir

rejoin [rɪ'dʒɔɪn] tr rejoindre

rejoinder [rɪ'dʒɔɪndər] s réplique f; (law) réponse f à une réplique

rejuvenation [rɪ,dʒuvɪ'neʃən] s rajeunissement m

rekindle [ri'kɪndəl] tr rallumer

relapse [rɪ'læps] s rechute f ‖ intr rechuter

relate [rɪ'let] tr (to narrate) relater; (e.g., two events) établir un rapport entre; **to be related** être apparenté

relation [rɪ'leʃən] s relation f; récit m, relation; (relative) parent m; (relationship) parenté f; **in relation to** or **with** par rapport à; **relations** (of a sexual nature) rapports mpl

relationship [rɪ'leʃən,ʃɪp] s (connection) rapport m; (kinship) parenté f

relative ['relətɪv] *adj* relatif || *s* parent *m*

relativity [,relə'tɪvəti] *s* relativité *f*

relax [rɪ'læks] *tr* détendre; **to be relaxed** être décontracté or détendu || *intr* se détendre

relaxation [,rɪlæks'eʃən] *s* détente *f*, délassement *m*

relaxing [rɪ'læksɪŋ] *adj* tranquillisant, apaisant; (*diverting*) délassant

relay ['rile], [rɪ'le] *s* relais *m* || *v* (*pret & pp* **-layed**) *tr* relayer; (rad, telg, telp, telv) retransmettre || [rɪ'le] *v* (*pret & pp* **-laid**) *tr* tendre de nouveau

re'lay race' *s* course *f* de relais

release [rɪ'lis] *s* délivrance *f*; (*from jail*) mise *f* en liberté; (*permission*) autorisation *f*; (aer) lâchage *m*; (mach) déclenchement *m* || *tr* délivrer; (*from jail*) mettre en liberté; autoriser; (*a bomb*) lâcher

relegate ['relɪ,get] *tr* reléguer

relent [rɪ'lent] *intr* se laisser attendrir, s'adoucir

relentless [rɪ'lentlɪs] *adj* implacable

relevant ['relɪvənt] *adj* pertinent

reliable [rɪ'laɪəbəl] *adj* digne de confiance, digne de foi

reliance [rɪ'laɪəns] *s* confiance *f*

relic ['relɪk] *s* (rel) relique *f*; (fig) vestige *m*

relief [rɪ'lif] *s* soulagement *m*; (*projection of figures; elevation*) relief *m*; (*aid*) secours *m*; (*welfare program*) aide *f* sociale; (mil) relève *f*; **in relief** en relief

relieve [rɪ'liv] *tr* soulager; (*to aid*) secourir; (*to release from a post*) relever; (*to give variety to*) relever; (mil) relever

religion [rɪ'lɪdʒən] *s* religion *f*

religious [rɪ'lɪdʒəs] *adj* religieux

relinquish [rɪ'lɪŋkwɪʃ] *tr* abandonner

relish ['relɪʃ] *s* goût *m*; (*condiment*) assaisonnement *m*; **relish for** penchant pour || *tr* goûter, apprécier

reluctance [rɪ'lʌktəns] *s* répugnance *f*; **with reluctance** à contrecœur

reluctant [rɪ'lʌktənt] *adj* hésitant, peu disposé

re·ly [rɪ'laɪ] *v* (*pret & pp* **-lied**) *intr*—**to rely on** compter sur, se fier à

remain [rɪ'men] *s*—**remains** restes *mpl*; œuvres *fpl* posthumes || *intr* rester

remainder [rɪ'mendər] *s* reste *m*; **remainders** bouillons *mpl* || *tr* solder

re·make [rɪ'mek] *v* (*pret & pp* **-made**) *tr* refaire

remark [rɪ'mɑrk] *s* remarque *f*, observation *f* || *tr & intr* remarquer, observer; **to remark on** faire des remarques sur

remarkable [rɪ'mɑrkəbəl] *adj* remarquable

remar·ry [rɪ'mæri] *v* (*pret & pp* **-ried**) *tr* remarier; se remarier avec || *intr* se remarier

reme·dy ['remɪdi] *s* (*pl* **-dies**) remède *m* || *v* (*pret & pp* **-died**) *tr* remédier (*with dat*)

remember [rɪ'membər] *tr* se souvenir de, se rappeler; **remember me to** rappelez-moi au bon souvenir de || *intr* se souvenir, se rappeler

remembrance [rɪ'membrəns] *s* souvenir *m*

remind [rɪ'maɪnd] *tr* rappeler

reminder [rɪ'maɪndər] *s* note *f* de rappel, mémento *m*

reminisce [,remɪ'nɪs] *intr* se livrer au souvenirs, raconter ses souvenirs

remiss [rɪ'mɪs] *adj* négligent

remission [rɪ'mɪʃən] *s* rémission *f*

re·mit [rɪ'mɪt] *v* (*pret & pp* **-mitted**; *ger* **-mitting**) *tr* remettre || *intr* se calmer

remittance [rɪ'mɪtəns] *s* remise *f*, envoi *m*

remnant ['remnənt] *s* reste *m*; (*of cloth*) coupon *m*; (*at reduced price*) solde *m*

remod·el [rɪ'mɑdəl] *v* (*pret & pp* **-eled** or **-elled**; *ger* **-eling** or **-elling**) *tr* modeler de nouveau, remanier; (*a house*) transformer

remonstrance [rɪ'mɑnstrəns] *s* remontrance *f*

remonstrate [rɪ'mɑnstret] *intr* protester; **to remonstrate with** faire des remontrances à

remorse [rɪ'mɔrs] *s* remords *m*

remorseful [rɪ'mɔrsfəl] *adj* contrit, repentant, plein de remords

remote [rɪ'mot] *adj* éloigné

remote' control' *s* commande *f* à distance, télécommande *f*

removable [rɪ'muvəbəl] *adj* amovible

removal [rɪ'muvəl] *s* enlèvement *m*; (*from house*) déménagement *m*; (*dismissal*) révocation *f*

remove [rɪ'muv] *tr* enlever, ôter, éloigner; (*furniture*) déménager; (*to dismiss*) révoquer || *intr* se déplacer; déménager

remuneration [rɪ,mjunə'reʃən] *s* rémunération *f*

renaissance [,renə'sɑns], [rɪ'nesəns] *s* renaissance *f*

rend [rend] *v* (*pret & pp* **rent** [rent]) *tr* déchirer; (*to split*) fendre; (*the air; the heart*) fendre

render ['rendər] *tr* rendre; (*a piece of music*) interpréter; (*lard*) fondre

rendez·vous ['rɑndə,vu] *s* (*pl* **-vous** [,vuz]) rendez-vous *m* || *v* (*pret & pp* **-voused** [,vud]; *ger* **-vousing** [,vuɪŋ]) *intr* se rencontrer

rendition [ren'dɪʃən] *s* (*translation*) traduction *f*; (mus) interprétation *f*

renegade ['renɪ,ged] *s* renégat *m*

renege [rɪ'nɪg] *s* renonce *f* || *intr* renoncer; (coll) se dédire, ne pas tenir sa parole

renew [rɪ'n(j)u] *tr* renouveler || *intr* se renouveler

renewable [rɪ'n(j)u-əbəl] *adj* renouvelable

renewal [rɪ'n(j)u-əl] *s* renouvellement *m*

renounce [rɪ'nauns] *s* renonce *f* || *tr* renoncer (*with dat*) || *intr* renoncer

renovate ['renə,vet] *tr* renouveler; (*a room, a house, etc.*) mettre à neuf, rénover, transformer

renown [rɪˈnaun] s renom m
renowned [rɪˈnaund] adj renommé
rent [rent] adj déchiré ‖ s loyer m, location f; (tear, slit) déchirure f; **for rent** à louer ‖ tr louer ‖ intr se louer
rental [ˈrentəl] s loyer m, location f
rent'al a'gen•cy s (pl **-cies**) agence f de location
rent'ed car' s voiture f de louage, voiture de location; (chauffeur-driven limousine) voiture de grande remise
renter [ˈrentər] s locataire mf
renunciation [rɪˌnʌnsɪˈeʃən] s renonciation f
reopen [riˈopən] tr & intr rouvrir
reopening [riˈopənɪŋ] s réouverture f; (of school) rentrée f
reorganize [riˈɔrɡəˌnaɪz] tr réorganiser ‖ intr se réorganiser
repair [rɪˈper] s réparation f; **in good repair** en bon état ‖ tr réparer ‖ intr se rendre
repaper [riˈpepər] tr retapisser
reparation [ˌrepəˈreʃən] s réparation f
repartee [ˌrepərˈti] s repartie f
repast [rɪˈpæst], [rɪˈpast] s repas m
repatriate [riˈpetrɪˌet] tr rapatrier
re•pay [rɪˈpe] v (pret & pp **-paid**) tr rembourser; récompenser
repayment [rɪˈpemənt] s remboursement m; récompense f
repeal [rɪˈpil] s révocation f, abrogation f ‖ tr révoquer, abroger
repeat [rɪˈpit] s répétition f ‖ tr & intr répéter
re•pel [rɪˈpel] v (pret & pp **-pelled**; ger **-pelling**) tr repousser; dégoûter
repent [rɪˈpent] tr se repentir de ‖ intr se repentir
repentance [rɪˈpentəns] s repentir m
repentant [rɪˈpentənt] adj repentant
repercussion [ˌripərˈkʌʃən] s répercussion f, contrecoup m
reperto•ry [ˈrepərˌtori] s (pl **-ries**) répertoire m
repetition [ˌrepɪˈtɪʃən] s répétition f
replace [rɪˈples] tr (to put back) remettre en place; (to take the place of) remplacer
replaceable [rɪˈplesəbəl] adj remplaçable, amovible
replacement [rɪˈplesmənt] s replacement m; (substitution) remplacement m; (substitute part) pièce f de rechange; (person) remplaçant m
replenish [rɪˈplenɪʃ] tr réapprovisionner; remplir
replete [rɪˈplit] adj rempli, plein
replica [ˈreplɪkə] s reproduction f, réplique f
re•ply [rɪˈplaɪ] s (pl **-plies**) réponse f, réplique f ‖ v (pret & pp **-plied**) tr & intr répondre, répliquer
reply' cou'pon s coupon-réponse m
report [rɪˈport] s rapport m; (rumor) bruit m; (e.g., of firearm) détonation f ‖ tr rapporter; dénoncer; **it is reported that** le bruit court que; **reported missing** porté manquant ‖ intr faire un rapport; (to show up) se présenter

report' card' s bulletin m scolaire
reportedly [rɪˈportɪdli] adv au dire de tout le monde
reporter [rɪˈportər] s reporter m
reporting [rɪˈportɪŋ] s reportage m
repose [rɪˈpoz] s repos m ‖ tr reposer; (confidence) placer ‖ intr reposer
reprehend [ˌreprɪˈhend] tr reprendre
represent [ˌreprɪˈzent] tr représenter
representation [ˌreprɪzenˈteʃən] s représentation f
representative [ˌreprɪˈzentətɪv] adj représentatif ‖ s représentant m
repress [rɪˈpres] tr réprimer; (psychoanal) refouler
repression [rɪˈpreʃən] s répression f; (psychoanal) refoulement m
reprieve [rɪˈpriv] s sursis m ‖ tr surseoir à l'exécution de
reprimand [ˈreprɪˌmænd], [ˈreprɪˌmand] s réprimande f ‖ tr réprimander
reprint [ˈriˌprɪnt] s (book) réimpression f; (offprint) tiré m à part ‖ [riˈprɪnt] tr réimprimer
reprisal [rɪˈpraɪzəl] s représailles fpl
reproach [rɪˈprotʃ] s reproche m; opprobre m ‖ tr reprocher; couvrir d'opprobre; **to reproach s.o. for s.th.** reprocher q.ch. à qn
reproduce [ˌriprəˈd(j)us] tr reproduire ‖ intr se reproduire
reproduction [ˌriprəˈdʌkʃən] s reproduction f
reproof [rɪˈpruf] s reproche m
reprove [rɪˈpruv] tr réprimander
reptile [ˈreptɪl] s reptile m
republic [rɪˈpʌblɪk] s république f
republican [rɪˈpʌblɪkən] adj & s républicain m
repudiate [rɪˈpjudɪˌet] tr répudier
repugnant [rɪˈpʌɡnənt] adj répugnant
repulse [rɪˈpʌls] s refus m; (setback) échec m ‖ tr repousser
repulsive [rɪˈpʌlsɪv] adj répulsif
reputation [ˌrepjəˈteʃən] s réputation f
repute [rɪˈpjut] s réputation f; **of ill repute** mal famé ‖ tr—**to be reputed to be** être réputé
reputedly [rɪˈpjutɪdli] adv suivant l'opinion commune
request [rɪˈkwest] s demande f; **on request** sur demande ‖ tr demander
Requiem [ˈrikwɪˌem], [ˈrekwɪˌem] s Requiem m
require [rɪˈkwaɪr] tr exiger
requirement [rɪˈkwaɪrmənt] s exigence f; besoin m
requisite [ˈrekwɪzɪt] adj requis ‖ s chose f nécessaire; condition f nécessaire
requisition [ˌrekwɪˈzɪʃən] s réquisition f ‖ tr réquisitionner
requital [rɪˈkwaɪtəl] s récompense f; (retaliation) revanche f
requite [rɪˈkwaɪt] tr récompenser; (to avenge) venger
re•read [riˈrid] v (pret & pp **-read** [ˈred]) tr relire
resale [ˈriˌsel], [riˈsel] s revente f
rescind [rɪˈsɪnd] tr abroger
rescue [ˈreskju] s sauvetage m; **to the**

rescue au secours, à la rescousse ‖ *tr* sauver, secourir

res′cue par′ty *s* équipe *f* de secours

research [rɪˈsʌrtʃ], [ˈrisʌrtʃ] *s* recherche *f* ‖ *intr* faire des recherches

re-sell [riˈsɛl] *v* (*pret & pp* -**sold**) *tr* revendre

resemblance [rɪˈzɛmbləns] *s* ressemblance *f*

resemble [rɪˈzɛmbəl] *tr* ressembler (with *dat*); **to resemble one another** se ressembler

resent [rɪˈzɛnt] *tr* s'offenser de

resentful [rɪˈzɛntfəl] *adj* offensé

resentment [rɪˈzɛntmənt] *s* ressentiment *m*

reservation [ˌrɛzərˈveʃən] *s* location *f*, réservation *f*; (*Indian land*) réserve *f*; **without reservation** sans réserve

reserve [rɪˈzʌrv] *s* réserve *f* ‖ *tr* réserver

reservist [rɪˈzʌrvɪst] *s* réserviste *m*

reservoir [ˈrɛzərˌvwɑr] *s* réservoir *m*

re-set [riˈsɛt] *v* (*pret & pp* -**set**; *ger* -**setting**) *tr* remettre; (*a gem*) remonter

re-ship [riˈʃɪp] *v* (*pret & pp* -**shipped**; *ger* -**shipping**) *tr* réexpédier; (*on a ship*) rembarquer ‖ *intr* se rembarquer

reshipment [riˈʃɪpmənt] *s* réexpédition *f*; (*on a ship*) rembarquement *m*

reside [rɪˈzaɪd] *intr* résider, demeurer

residence [ˈrɛzɪdəns] *s* résidence *f*, domicile *m*

resident [ˈrɛzɪdənt] *adj & s* habitant *m*

residential [ˌrɛzɪˈdɛnʃəl] *adj* résidentiel

residue [ˈrɛzɪˌd(j)u] *s* résidu *m*

resign [rɪˈzaɪn] *tr* démissionner de, résigner; **to resign oneself to** se résigner à ‖ *intr* démissionner; se résigner; **to resign from** démissionner de

resignation [ˌrɛzɪgˈneʃən] *s* (*from a job, etc.*) démission *f*; (*submissive state*) résignation *f*

resin [ˈrɛzɪn] *s* résine *f*

resist [rɪˈzɪst] *tr* résister (with *dat*); **to resist** + *ger* s'empêcher de + *inf* ‖ *intr* résister

resistance [rɪˈzɪstəns] *s* résistance *f*

resole [riˈsol] *tr* ressemeler

resolute [ˈrɛzəˌlut] *adj* résolu

resolution [ˌrɛzəˈluʃən] *s* résolution *f*

resolve [rɪˈzɑlv] *s* résolution *f* ‖ *tr* résoudre ‖ *intr* résoudre, se résoudre

resonance [ˈrɛzənəns] *s* résonance *f*

resort [rɪˈzɔrt] *s* station *f*, e.g., **health resort** station climatique; (*for help or support*) recours *m*; **as a last resort** en dernier ressort ‖ *intr*—**to resort to** recourir à

resound [rɪˈzaund] *intr* résonner

resource [rɪˈsors], [ˈrisors] *s* ressource *f*

resourceful [rɪˈsorsfəl] *adj* débrouillard

respect [rɪˈspɛkt] *s* respect *m*; **in many respects** à bien des égards; **in this respect** sous ce rapport; **to pay one's respects** (to) présenter ses respects (à); **with respect to** par rapport à ‖ *tr* respecter

respectable [rɪˈspɛktəbəl] *adj* respectable; considérable

respectful [rɪˈspɛktfəl] *adj* respectueux

respectfully [rɪˈspɛktfəli] *adj* respectueusement; **respectfully yours** (complimentary close) veuillez agréer l'assurance de mes sentiments très respectueux

respective [rɪˈspɛktɪv] *adj* respectif

res′piratory tract′ [ˈrɛspɪrəˌtori], [rɪˈspaɪrəˌtori] *s* appareil *m* respiratoire

respite [ˈrɛspɪt] *s* répit *m*; **without respite** sans relâche

resplendent [rɪˈsplɛndənt] *adj* resplendissant

respond [rɪˈspɑnd] *intr* répondre

response [rɪˈspɑns] *s* réponse *f*

responsibil-ity [rɪˌspɑnsɪˈbɪlɪti] *s* (*pl* -**ties**) responsabilité *f*

responsible [rɪˈspɑnsɪbəl] *adj* responsable; (*person*) digne de confiance; (*job, position*) de confiance; **responsible for** responsable de; **responsible to** responsable envers

responsive [rɪˈspɑnsɪv] *adj* sensible, réceptif; prompt à sympathiser

rest [rɛst] *s* repos *m*; (*lack of motion*) pause *f*; (*what remains*) reste *m*; (*mus*) silence *m*; **at rest** en repos; (*dead*) mort; **the rest** les autres; (*the remainder*) le restant; **the rest of us** nous autres; **to come to rest** s'immobiliser; **to lay to rest** enterrer ‖ *tr* reposer ‖ *intr* reposer, se reposer; **to rest on** reposer sur, s'appuyer sur

restaurant [ˈrɛstərənt], [ˈrɛstəˌrɑnt] *s* restaurant *m*

rest′ cure′ *s* cure *f* de repos

restful [ˈrɛstfəl] *adj* reposant; (*calm*) tranquille, paisible

rest′ing place′ *s* lieu *m* de repos, gîte *m*; (*of the dead*) dernière demeure *f*

restitution [ˌrɛstɪˈt(j)uʃən] *s* restitution *f*

restive [ˈrɛstɪv] *adj* rétif

restless [ˈrɛstlɪs] *adj* agité, inquiet; sans repos

restock [riˈstɑk] *tr* réapprovisionner; (*with fish or game*) repeupler

restoration [ˌrɛstəˈreʃən] *s* restauration *f*

restore [rɪˈstor] *tr* restaurer; (*health*) rétablir; (*to give back*) restituer

restrain [rɪˈstren] *tr* retenir, contenir

restraint [rɪˈstrent] *s* restriction *f*, contrainte *f*

restrict [rɪˈstrɪkt] *tr* restreindre

restriction [rɪˈstrɪkʃən] *s* restriction *f*

rest′ room′ *s* cabinet *m* d'aisance

result [rɪˈzʌlt] *s* résultat *m*; **as a result of** par suite de ‖ *intr* résulter; **to result in** aboutir à

resume [rɪˈz(j)um] *tr & intr* reprendre

résumé [ˌrez(j)uˈme] *s* résumé *m*

resumption [rɪˈzʌmpʃən] *s* reprise *f*

resurface [riˈsʌrfɪs] *tr* refaire le revêtement de ‖ *intr* (*said of submarine*) faire surface

resurrect [ˌrɛzəˈrɛkt] *tr & intr* ressusciter

resurrection [,rezə'rekʃən] s résurrection f
resuscitate [rɪ'sʌsɪ,tet] tr & intr ressusciter
retail ['ritel] adj & adv au détail ‖ s vente f au détail ‖ tr vendre au détail, détailler ‖ intr se vendre au détail
retailer ['ritelər] s détaillant m
retain [rɪ'ten] tr retenir; engager
retaliate [rɪ'tælɪ,et] intr prendre sa revanche, user de représailles
retaliation [rɪ,tælɪ'eʃən] s représailles fpl
retard [rɪ'tɑrd] s retard m ‖ tr retarder
retch [retʃ] tr vomir ‖ intr avoir un haut-le-cœur
retching ['retʃɪŋ] s haut-le-cœur m
reticence ['retɪsəns] s réserve f
reticent ['retɪsənt] adj réservé
retina ['retɪnə] s rétine f
retinue ['retɪ,n(j)u] s suite f, cortège m
retire [rɪ'taɪr] tr mettre à la retraite ‖ intr se retirer
retired adj en retraite
retirement [rɪ'taɪrmənt] s retraite f
retire′ment pro′gram s programme m de prévoyance
retiring [rɪ'taɪrɪŋ] adj (shy) effacé; (e.g., congressman) sortant
retort [rɪ'tɔrt] s riposte f, réplique f; (chem) cornue f ‖ tr & intr riposter
retouch [rɪ'tʌtʃ] tr retoucher
retrace [rɪ'tres] tr retracer; (one's steps) revenir sur
retract [rɪ'trækt] tr rétracter ‖ intr se rétracter
retractable [rɪ'træktəbəl] adj (aer) escamotable
re·tread [rɪ,tred] s pneu m rechapé ‖ [rɪ'tred] v (pret & pp -treaded) tr rechaper ‖ v (pret -trod; pp -trod or -trodden) tr & intr repasser
retreat [rɪ'trit] s retraite f; **to beat a retreat** battre en retraite ‖ intr se retirer
retrench [rɪ'trentʃ] tr restreindre ‖ intr faire des économies
retribution [,retrɪ'bjuʃən] s rétribution f
retrieve [rɪ'triv] tr retrouver, recouvrer; (a fortune, a reputation, etc.) rétablir; (game) rapporter ‖ intr (said of hunting dog) rapporter
retriever [rɪ'trivər] s retriever m
retroactive [,retro'æktɪv] adj rétroactif
retrogress ['retrə,gres] intr rétrograder
retrorocket ['retro,rɑkɪt] s rétrofusée f
retrospect ['retrə,spekt] s—**to consider in retrospect** jeter un coup d'œil rétrospectif à
retrospective [,retrə'spektɪv] adj rétrospectif
re·try [rɪ'traɪ] v (pret & pp -tried) tr essayer de nouveau; (law) juger à nouveau
return [rɪ'tʌrn] adj de retour; **by return mail** par retour du courrier ‖ s retour m; (profit) bénéfice m; (yield) rendement m; (unwanted merchandise) rendu m; (of ball) renvoi m; (of income tax) déclaration f; **in return**

(for) en retour (de); **returns** (profits) recettes fpl; (of an election) résultats mpl ‖ tr rendre; (to put back) remettre; (to bring back) rapporter; (e.g., a letter) retourner ‖ intr (to go back) retourner; (to come back) revenir; (to get back home) rentrer; **to return empty-handed** revenir bredouille
return′ address′ s adresse f de l'expéditeur
return′ bout′ s revanche f
return′ game′ or **match′** s match m retour
return′ tick′et s aller et retour m
return′ trip′ s voyage m de retour
reunification [ri,junɪfɪ'keʃən] s réunification f
reunion [ri'junjən] s réunion f
reunite [,riju'naɪt] tr réunir ‖ intr se réunir
rev [rev] s (coll) tour m ‖ v (pret & pp revved; ger revving) tr (coll) accélérer; (to race) (coll) emballer ‖ intr (coll) s'accélérer
revamp [ri'væmp] tr refaire
reveal [rɪ'vil] tr révéler
reveille ['revəli] s réveil m
rev·el ['revəl] s fête f; **revels** ébats mpl, orgie f ‖ v (pret & pp -eled or -elled; ger -eling or -elling) intr faire la fête, faire la bombe; **to revel in** se délecter à
revelation [,revə'leʃən] s révélation f; **Revelation** (Bib) Apocalypse f
revel·ry ['revəlri] s (pl -ries) réjouissances fpl, orgie f
revenge [rɪ'vendʒ] s vengeance f; **to take revenge on s.o. for s.th.** se venger de q.ch. sur qn ‖ tr venger
revengeful [rɪ'vendʒfəl] adj vindicatif
revenue ['revə,n(j)u] s revenu m
rev′enue cut′ter s garde-côte m, vedette f
rev′enue stamp′ s timbre m fiscal
reverberate [rɪ'vʌrbə,ret] intr résonner
revere [rɪ'vɪr] tr révérer
reverence ['revərəns] s révérence f ‖ tr révérer
reverend ['revərənd] adj & s révérend m
reverent ['revərənt] adj révérenciel
reverie ['revəri] s rêverie f
reversal [rɪ'vʌrsəl] s renversement m
reverse [rɪ'vʌrs] adj contraire ‖ s contraire m; (of medal, of fortune) revers m; (of page) verso m; (aut) marche f arrière ‖ tr renverser; (a sentence) (law) révoquer ‖ intr renverser; (said of motor) faire machine arrière; (aut) faire marche arrière
reverse′ lev′er s levier m de renvoi
reverse′ side′ s revers m, dos m
reversible [rɪ'vʌrsɪbəl] adj réversible
revert [rɪ'vʌrt] intr revenir, faire retour
review [rɪ'vju] s revue f; (of a book) compte m rendu; (of a lesson) révision f ‖ tr revoir; (a book) faire la critique de; (a lesson) réviser, revoir; (past events; troops) passer en revue ‖ intr faire des révisions
revile [rɪ'vaɪl] tr injurier, outrager
revise [rɪ'vaɪz] s révision f; (typ)

épreuve *f* de révision ‖ *tr* réviser; (*a book*) revoir

revised′ edi′tion *s* édition *f* revue et corrigée

revision [rɪ'vɪʒən] *s* révision *f*

revisionist [rɪ'vɪʒənɪst] *adj* & *s* révisionniste *mf*

revival [rɪ'vaɪvəl] *s* retour *m* à la vie; (*of learning*) renaissance *f*; (rel) réveil *m*; (theat) reprise *f*

reviv′al meet′ings *spl* (rel) réveils *mpl*

revive [rɪ'vaɪv] *tr* ranimer; (*a victim*) ressusciter; (*a memory*) réveiller; (*a play*) reprendre ‖ *intr* reprendre; se ranimer

revoke [rɪ'vok] *tr* révoquer

revolt [rɪ'volt] *s* révolte *f* ‖ *tr* révolter ‖ *intr* se révolter

revolting [rɪ'voltɪŋ] *adj* dégoûtant, repoussant; rebelle, révolté

revolution [‚revə'luʃən] *s* révolution *f*

revolutionar·y [‚revə'luʃə‚neri] *adj* révolutionnaire ‖ *s* (*pl* -ies) révolutionnaire *mf*

revolve [rɪ'valv] *tr* faire tourner; (*in one's mind*) retourner ‖ *intr* tourner

revolver [rɪ'valvər] *s* revolver *m*

revolv′ing book′case *s* bibliothèque *f* tournante

revolv′ing door′ *s* porte *f* à tambour, tambour *m* cylindrique

revolv′ing fund′ *s* fonds *m* de roulement

revolv′ing stage′ *s* scène *f* tournante

revue [rɪ'vju] *s* (theat) revue *f*

revulsion [rɪ'vʌlʃən] *s* aversion *f*, répugnance *f*; (*change of feeling*) revirement *m*

reward [rɪ'word] *s* récompense *f* ‖ *tr* récompenser

rewarding [rɪ'wordɪŋ] *adj* rémunérateur; (*experience*) enrichissant

re·wind [ri'waɪnd] *v* (*pret & pp* -wound*) *tr* (*film, tape, etc.*) renverser la marche de; (*a typewriter ribbon*) embobiner de nouveau; (*a clock*) remonter

rewire [ri'waɪr] *tr* (*a building*) refaire l'installation électrique dans

re·write [ri'raɪt] *v* (*pret* -wrote; *pp* -written*) *tr* récrire

rhapso·dy ['ræpsədi] *s* (*pl* -dies) *s* rhapsodie *f*

rheostat ['ri·ə‚stæt] *s* rhéostat *m*

rhetoric ['retərɪk] *s* rhétorique *f*

rhetorical [rɪ'tarɪkəl], [rɪ'tɔrɪkəl] *adj* rhétorique

rheumatic [ru'mætɪk] *adj* rhumatismal; (*person*) rhumatisant ‖ *s* rhumatisant *m*

rheumatism ['rumə‚tɪzəm] *s* rhumatisme *m*

Rhine [raɪn] *s* Rhin *m*

Rhineland ['raɪn‚lænd] *s* Rhénanie *f*

rhine′stone′ *s* faux diamant *m*

rhinoceros [raɪ'nasərəs] *s* rhinocéros *m*

rhubarb ['rubarb] *s* rhubarbe *f*

rhyme [raɪm] *s* rime *f*; **in rhyme** en vers ‖ *tr* & *intr* rimer

rhythm ['rɪðəm] *s* rythme *m*

rhythmic(al) ['rɪðmɪk(əl)] *adj* rythmique

rib [rɪb] *s* côte *f*; (*of umbrella*) baleine *f*; (*archit, biol, mach*) nervure *f* ‖ *v* (*pret & pp* ribbed; *ger* ribbing) *tr* garnir de nervures; (slang) taquiner

ribald ['rɪbəld] *adj* grivois

ribbon ['rɪbən] *s* ruban *m*

rice [raɪs] *s* riz *m*

rice′ field′ *s* rizière *f*

rice′ pud′ding *s* riz *m* au lait

rich [rɪtʃ] *adj* riche; (*voice*) sonore; (*wine*) généreux; (*funny*) (coll) impayable; (coll) ridicule; **to get rich** s'enrichir; **to strike it rich** trouver le bon filon ‖ **riches** *spl* richesses *fpl*

rickets ['rɪkɪts] *s* rachitisme *m*

rickety ['rɪkɪti] *adj* (*object*) boiteux, délabré; (*person*) chancelant; (*suffering from rickets*) rachitique

rickshaw ['rɪk‚ʃɔ] *s* pousse-pousse *m*

rid [rɪd] *v* (*pret & pp* rid; *ger* ridding) *tr* débarrasser; **to get rid of** se débarrasser de

riddance ['rɪdəns] *s* débarras *m*; **good riddance!** bon débarras!

riddle ['rɪdəl] *s* devinette *f*, énigme *f* ‖ *tr*—**to riddle with** cribler de

ride [raɪd] *s* promenade *f*; **to take a ride** faire une promenade (en auto, à cheval, à motocyclette, etc.); **to take s.o. for a ride** (to dupe *s.o.*) (slang) faire marcher qn; (to murder *s.o.*) (slang) descendre qn ‖ *v* (*pret* rode [rod]; *pp* ridden ['rɪdən]) *tr* monter à; (coll) se moquer de; **ridden** dominé; **to ride out** (e.g., *a storm*) étaler ‖ *intr* monter à cheval (à bicyclette, etc.); **to let ride** (coll) laisser courir

rider ['raɪdər] *s* (*on horseback*) cavalier *m*; (*on a bicycle*) cycliste *mf*; (*in a vehicle*) voyageur *m*; (*to a document*) annexe *f*

ridge [rɪdʒ] *s* arête *f*, crête *f*; (*of a fabric*) grain *m*

ridge′pole′ *s* faîtage *m*

ridicule ['rɪdɪ‚kjul] *s* ridicule *m* ‖ *tr* ridiculiser

ridiculous [rɪ'dɪkjələs] *adj* ridicule

rid′ing acad′emy *s* école *f* d'équitation

rid′ing boot′ *s* botte *f* de cheval, botte à l'écuyère

rid′ing hab′it *s* habit *m* d'amazone

rife [raɪf] *adj* répandu; **rife with** abondant en

riffraff ['rɪf‚ræf] *s* racaille *f*

rifle ['raɪfəl] *s* fusil *m*; (*spiral groove*) rayure *f* ‖ *tr* piller; (*a gun barrel*) rayer

rift [rɪft] *s* fente *f*, crevasse *f*; (*disagreement*) désaccord *m*

rig [rɪg] *s* équipement *m*; (*carriage*) équipage *m*; (naut) gréement *m*; (*getup*) (coll) accoutrement *m* ‖ *v* (*pret & pp* rigged; *ger* rigging) *tr* équiper; (to *falsify*) truquer; (naut) gréer; **to rig out with** (coll) accoutrer de

rigging ['rɪgɪŋ] *s* gréement *m*; (*fraud*) truquage *m*

right [raɪt] *adj* droit; (*change, time, etc.*) exact; (*statement, answer, etc.*) correct; (*conclusion, word, etc.*)

juste; (*name*) vrai; (*moment, house, road, etc.*) bon, e.g., **it's not the right road** ce n'est pas la bonne route; qu'il faut, e.g., **it's not the right village** (*spot, boy, etc.*) ce n'est pas le village (endroit, garçon, etc.) qu'il faut; **to be all right** aller très bien; **to be right** avoir raison ‖ *s* (*justice*) droit *m*; (*reason*) raison *f*; (*right hand*) droite *f*; (*fist or blow in boxing*) droit; **all rights reserved** tous droits réservés; **by right of** à titre de; **by rights** de plein droit; **by the right!** (*mil*) guide à droite!; **on the right** à droite; **right and wrong** le bien et le mal; **rights** droits; **to be in the right** avoir raison ‖ *adv* directement; correctement; complètement; bien, en bon état; (*to the right*) à droite; (*coll*) même, e.g., **right here** ici même; **all right!** d'accord!; **right and left** à droite et à gauche; **right away** tout de suite; **to put right** mettre bon ordre à, mettre en état *f*; (*right hand*) droite *f*; (*to correct*) corriger; (*to set upright*) redresser ‖ *intr* se redresser ‖ *interj* parfait!

right′ about′ face′ *s* volte-face *f* ‖ *interj* (mil) demi-tour à droite!

righteous [′raɪʧəs] *adj* juste; vertueux

right′ field′ *s* (baseball) champ *m* droit

rightful [′raɪtfəl] *adj* légitime

right′-hand drive′ *s* conduite *f* à droite

right-hander [′raɪt′hændər] *s* droitier *m*

right′-hand man′ *s* bras *m* droit

rightist [′raɪtɪst] *adj & s* droitier *m*

rightly [′raɪtli] *adv* à bon droit, à juste titre; correctement, avec sagesse; **rightly or wrongly** à tort ou à raison

right′ of assem′bly *s* liberté *f* de réunion

right′ of way′ *s* droit *m* de passage; **to yield the right of way** céder le pas

rights′ of man′ *spl* droits *mpl* de l'homme

right to work [′raɪttə′wʌrk] *s* liberté *f* du travail des ouvriers non syndiqués

right′-wing′ *adj* de droite

right-winger [′raɪt′wɪŋər] *s* (coll) droitier *m*

rigid [′rɪʤɪd] *adj* rigide

rigmarole [′rɪgmə‚rol] *s* galimatias *m*

rigor [′rɪgər] *s* rigueur *f*; (pathol) rigidité *f*

rigorous [′rɪgərəs] *adj* rigoureux

rile [raɪl] *tr* (coll) exaspérer

rill [rɪl] *s* ruisselet *m*

rim [rɪm] *s* bord *m*, rebord *m*; (of spectacles) monture *f*; (of wheel) jante *f*

rind [raɪnd] *s* écorce *f*; (of cheese) croûte *f*; (of bacon) couenne *f*

ring [rɪŋ] *s* anneau *m*; (for the finger) bague *f*, anneau; (for some sport or exhibition) piste *f*; (for boxing) ring *m*; (for bullfight) arène *f*; (of a group of people) cercle *m*; (of evildoers) gang *m*; (under the eyes) cerne *m*; (sound) son *m*; (of bell, clock, telephone, etc.) sonnerie *f*; (of a small bell; in the ears; of the glass of glassware) tintement *m*; (to summon a person) coup *m* de sonnette; (quality) timbre *m*; (telp) coup de téléphone ‖ *v* (pret & pp ringed) *tr* cerner ‖ *intr* décrire des cercles ‖ *v* (pret **rang** [ræŋ]; pp **rung** [rʌŋ]) *tr* sonner; **to ring up** (telp) donner un coup de téléphone à ‖ *intr* sonner; (said, e.g., of ears) tinter; **to ring out** résonner

ring′bolt′ *s* piton *m*

ring′dove′ *s* (orn) ramier *m*

ring′ fin′ger *s* annulaire *m*

ringing [′rɪŋɪŋ] *adj* résonnant, retentissant ‖ *s* sonnerie *f*; (in the ears) tintement *m*

ring′lead′er *s* meneur *m*

ringlet [′rɪŋlɪt] *s* bouclette *f*

ring′mas′ter *s* maître *m* de manège, chef *m* de piste

ring′side′ *s* premier rang *m*

ring′snake′ *s* (Tropidonotus natrix) couleuvre *f* à collier

ring′worm′ *s* teigne *f*

rink [rɪŋk] *s* patinoire *f*

rinse [rɪns] *s* rinçage *m* ‖ *tr* rincer

riot [′raɪ‧ət] *s* émeute *f*; (of colors) orgie *f*; **to run riot** se déchaîner; (said of plants or vines) pulluler ‖ *intr* émeuter

rioter [′raɪ‧ətər] *s* émeutier *m*

rip [rɪp] *s* déchirure *f* ‖ *v* (pret & pp **ripped**; ger **ripping**) *tr* déchirer; **to rip away or off** arracher; **to rip open or up** découdre; (a letter, package, etc.) ouvrir en le déchirant ‖ *intr* se déchirer

rip′ cord′ *s* (of parachute) cordelette *f* de déclenchement

ripe [raɪp] *adj* mûr; (cheese) fait; (olive) noir

ripen [′raɪpən] *tr & intr* mûrir

ripple [′rɪpəl] *s* ride *f*; (sound) murmure *m* ‖ *tr* rider ‖ *intr* se rider; murmurer

rise [raɪz] *s* hausse *f*, augmentation *f*; (of ground; of the voice) élévation *f*; (of a heavenly body; of the curtain) lever *m*; (in one's employment, in one's fortunes) ascension *f*; (of water) montée *f*; (of a source of water) naissance *f*; **to get a rise out of** (slang) se payer la tête de; **to give rise to** donner naissance à ‖ *v* (pret **rose** [roz]; pp **risen** [′rɪzən]) *intr* s'élever, monter; (to get out of bed; to ascend up; to ascend in the heavens) se lever; (to revolt) se soulever; (said, e.g., of a danger) se montrer; (said of a fluid) jaillir; (in someone's esteem) grandir; (said of river) prendre sa source; **to rise above** dépasser; (unfortunate events, insults, etc.) se montrer supérieur à; **to rise to** (e.g., the occasion) se montrer à la hauteur de

riser [′raɪzər] *s* (of staircase) contremarche *f*; (of gas or water) colonne *f* montante; **to be a late riser** faire la grasse matinée; **to be an early riser** être matinal

risk [rɪsk] *s* risque *m* ‖ *tr* risquer

risk‧y [′rɪski] *adj* (comp **-ier**; super **-iest**) dangereux, hasardeux, risqué

risqué [rɪs'ke] *adj* risqué, osé
rite [raɪt] *s* rite *m*; **last rites** derniers sacrements *mpl*
ritual ['rɪt/ʊ-əl] *adj* & *s* rituel *m*
ri·val ['raɪvəl] *adj* & *s* rival *m* ‖ *v* (*pret* & *pp* -valed or -valled; *ger* -valing or -valling) *tr* rivaliser avec
rival·ry ['raɪvəlrɪ] *s* (*pl* -ries) rivalité *f*
river ['rɪvər] *adj* fluvial ‖ *s* fleuve *m*; (*tributary*) rivière *f*; (*stream*) cours *m* d'eau; **down the river** en aval; **up the river** en amont
riv'er bas'in *s* bassin *m* fluvial
riv'er·bed' *s* lit *m* de rivière
riv'er·front' *s* rive *f* d'un fleuve
riv'er·side' *adj* riverain ‖ *s* rive *f*
rivet ['rɪvɪt] *s* rivet *m* ‖ *tr* river
riv'et gun' *s* riveuse *f* pneumatique
rivulet ['rɪvjəlɪt] *s* ruisselet *m*
R.N. ['ɑr'ɛn] *s* (letterword) (**registered nurse**) infirmière *f* diplômée
roach [rotʃ] *s* (ent) blatte *f*, cafard *m*; (ichth) gardon *m*
road [rod] *s* route *f*, chemin *m*; (naut) rade *f*; **road under construction** (public sign) travaux
road'bed' *s* assiette *f*; (rr) infrastructure *f*
road'block' *s* barrage *m*
road' hog' *s* écraseur *m*, chauffard *m*
road'house' *s* guinguette *f* au bord de la route
road' map' *s* carte *f* routière
road' serv'ice *s* secours *m* routier
road'side' *s* bord *m* de la route
road' sign' *s* poteau *m* indicateur
road'stead' *s* rade *f*
road'way' *s* chaussée *f*
roam [rom] *tr* parcourir; (*the seas*) sillonner ‖ *intr* errer, rôder
roar [ror] *s* rugissement *m*; (*of cannon, engine, etc.*) grondement *m*; (*of crowd*) hurlement *m*; (*of laughter*) éclat *m* ‖ *intr* rugir; gronder; hurler
roast [rost] *s* rôti *m*; (*of coffee*) torréfaction *f* ‖ *tr* rôtir; (*coffee*) torréfier; (*chestnuts*) griller ‖ *intr* se rôtir; se torréfier
roast' beef' *s* rosbif *m*, rôti *m* de bœuf
roaster ['rostər] *s* (appliance) rôtissoire *f*; (for coffee) brûloir *m*; (fowl) volaille *f* à rôtir
roast' pork' *s* porc *m* rôti
rob [rɑb] *v* (*pret* & *pp* robbed; *ger* robbing) *tr* & *intr* voler; **to rob s.o. of s.th.** voler q.ch. à qn
robber ['rɑbər] *s* voleur *m*
robber·y ['rɑbərɪ] *s* (*pl* -ies) vol *m*
robe [rob] *s* robe *f*; (*of a professor, judge, etc.*) toge *f*; (*dressing gown*) robe *f* de chambre; (*for lap in a carriage*) couverture *f* ‖ *tr* revêtir d'une robe ‖ *intr* revêtir sa robe
robin ['rɑbɪn] *s* (Erithacus rubecula) rouge-gorge *m*; (Turdus migratorius) grive *f* migratoire
robot ['robɑt] *s* robot *m*
robust [ro'bʌst] *adj* robuste
rock [rɑk] *s* roche *f*; (*eminence*) roc *m*, rocher *m*; (*sticking out of water*) rocher; (*one that is thrown*) pierre *f*; (slang) diamant *m*; **on the rocks**

(coll) fauché, à sec; (*said of liquor*) (coll) sur glace ‖ *tr* balancer; (*to rock to sleep*) bercer ‖ *intr* se balancer; se bercer
rock'-bot'tom *adj* (le) plus bas ‖ *s* (le) fin fond *m*
rock' can'dy *s* candi *m*
rock' crys'tal *s* cristal *m* de roche
rocker ['rɑkər] *s* bascule *f*; (*chair*) chaise *f* à bascule; **to go off one's rocker** (slang) perdre la boussole
rock'er arm' *s* culbuteur *m*
rocket ['rɑkɪt] *s* fusée *f*; (arti, bot) roquette *f* ‖ *intr* monter en chandelle; (*said of prices*) monter en flèche
rock'et bomb' *s* bombe *f* volante, fusée *f*
rock'et launch'er *s* lance-fusées *m*; (arti) lance-roquettes *m*
rock'et ship' *s* fusée *f* interplanétaire, fusée interstellaire
rock' gar'den *s* jardin *m* de rocaille
rock'ing chair' *s* fauteuil *m* à bascule
rock'ing horse' *s* cheval *m* à bascule
Rock' of Gibral'tar [dʒɪ'brɔltər] *s* rocher *m* de Gibraltar
rock' salt' *s* sel *m* gemme
rock' wool' *s* laine *f* minérale, laine de verre
rock·y ['rɑkɪ] *adj* (*comp* -ier; *super* -iest) rocheux, rocailleux
Rock'y Moun'tains *spl* Montagnes *fpl* Rocheuses
rod [rɑd] *s* baguette *f*; (*for punishment*) verge *f*; (*of the retina; elongated microorganism*) bâtonnet *m*; (*of authority*) main *f*; (*of curtain*) tringle *f*; (*for fishing*) canne *f*; (Bib) lignée *f*, race *f*; (mach) bielle *f*; (surv) jalon *m*; (*revolver*) (slang) pétard *m*; **rod and gun** la chasse et la pêche
rodent ['rodənt] *adj* & *s* rongeur *m*
roe [ro] *s* (*deer*) chevreuil *m*; (*of fish*) œufs *mpl*
roger ['rɑdʒər] *interj* O.K.!; (rad) message reçu!
rogue [rog] *s* coquin *m*
rogues'/ gal'lery *s* fichier *m* de la police de portraits de criminels
roguish ['rogɪʃ] *adj* espiègle, coquin
roister ['rɔɪstər] *intr* faire du tapage
role or rôle [rol] *s* rôle *m*
roll [rol] *s* rouleau *m*; (*of thunder, drums, etc.*) roulement *m*; (*roll call*) appel *m*; (*list*) rôle *m*; (*of film*) rouleau; (*of paper money*) liasse *f*; (*of dice*) coup *m*; (*of a boat*) roulis *m*; (*of fat*) bourrelet *m*; (culin) petit pain *m*; **to call the roll** faire l'appel ‖ *tr* rouler; **to roll over** retourner; **to roll up** enrouler ‖ *intr* rouler; (*said of thunder*) gronder; (*to sway*) se balancer; (*to overturn*) faire panache; (*said of ship*) rouler; **to roll over** se retourner; **to roll up** se rouler
roll'back' *s* repoussement *m*; (com) baisse *f* de prix
roll' call' *s* appel *m*; (*vote*) appel nominal
roller ['rolər] *s* rouleau *m*; (*of a skate*) roulette *f*; (*wave*) lame *f* de houle

roll′er bear′ing s coussinet m à rouleaux

roll′er coast′er s montagnes fpl russes

roll′er skate′ s patin m à roulettes

roll′er-skate′ intr patiner sur des roulettes

roll′er-skating rink′ s skating m

roll′er tow′el s essuie-mains m à rouleau, serviette f sans fin

roll′ing mill′ s usine f de laminage; (set of rollers) laminoir m

roll′ing pin′ s rouleau m

roll′ing stock′ s (rr) matériel m roulant

roll′-top desk′ s bureau m à cylindre

roly-poly [′roli′poli] adj rondelet

romaine [ro′men] s romaine f

roman [′romən] adj & s (typ) romain m; **Roman** Romain m

Ro′man can′dle s chandelle f romaine

Ro′man Cath′olic adj & s catholique mf

Romance [′romæns], [ro′mæns] adj roman ‖ (l.c.) [ro′mæns], [′romæns] s roman m de chevalerie; (made-up story) conte m bleu; (love affair) idylle f; (mus) romance f ‖ (l.c.) [ro′mæns] intr exagérer, broder

Romanesque [‚romən′ɛsk] adj & s roman m

Ro′man nose′ s nez m aquilin

Ro′man nu′meral s chiffre m romain

romantic [ro′mæntɪk] adj (genre; literature; scenery) romantique; (imagination) romanesque

romanticism [ro′mæntɪ‚sɪzəm] s romantisme m

romanticist [ro′mæntɪsɪst] s romantique mf

romp [rɑmp] intr s'ébattre

rompers [′rɑmpərz] spl barboteuse f

roof [ruf], [rʊf] s toit m; (of the mouth) palais m; **to raise the roof** (slang) faire un boucan de tous les diables

roofer [′rufər], [′rʊfər] s couvreur m

roof′ gar′den s terrasse f avec jardin, pergola f

rook [rʊk] s (chess) tour f; (orn) freux m, corneille f ‖ tr (coll) rouler; **to rook s.o. out of s.th.** (coll) filouter q.ch. à qn

rookie [′rʊki] s (slang) bleu m

room [rum], [rʊm] s pièce f; (especially bedroom) chambre f; (where people congregate) salle f; (space) place f; **to make room for** faire place à ‖ intr vivre en garni; **to room with** partager une chambre avec

room′ and board′ s le vivre et le couvert

room′ clerk′ s employé m à la réception

roomer [′rumər], [′rʊmər] s locataire mf

roomette [ru′mɛt] s chambrette f de sleeping

room′ing house′ s maison f meublée, maison garnie

room′mate′ s camarade mf de chambre

room·y [′rumi], [′rʊmi] adj (comp -ier; super -iest) spacieux, ample

roost [rust] s perchoir m; (coll) logis m, demeure f; **to rule the roost** (coll) faire la loi ‖ intr se percher, percher

rooster [′rustər] s coq m

root [rut], [rʊt] s racine f; **to get to the root of** approfondir; **to take root** prendre racine ‖ tr fouiller; **to root out** déraciner ‖ intr s'enraciner; **to root around in** fouiller dans; **to root for** (coll) applaudir, encourager

rooter [′rutər], [′rʊtər] s (coll) fanatique mf, fana mf

rope [rop] s corde f; (lasso) corde à nœud coulant; **to jump rope** sauter à la corde; **to know the ropes** (slang) connaître les ficelles ‖ tr corder; (cattle) prendre au lasso; **to rope in** (slang) entraîner

rope′ lad′der s échelle f de corde

rope′ walk′er s funambule mf, danseur m de corde

rosa·ry [′rozəri] s (pl -ries) rosaire m

rose [roz] adj rosé ‖ s (color) rose m; (bot) rose f

rose′ bee′tle s cétoine f dorée

rose′bud′ s bouton m de rose

rose′bush′ s rosier m

rose′-col′ored adj rosé, couleur de rose; **to see everything through rose-colored glasses** voir tout en rose

rose′ gar′den s roseraie f

rosemar·y [′roz‚mɛri] s (pl -ies) romarin m

rose′ of Shar′on [′ʃɛrən] s rose f de Saron

rosette [ro′zɛt] s rosette f; (archit, elec) rosace f

rose′ win′dow s rosace f, rose f

rose′wood′ s bois m de rose, palissandre m

rosin [′rɑzɪn] s colophane f

roster [′rɑstər] s liste f, appel m; (educ) heures fpl de classe; (mil) tableau m de service; (naut) rôle m

rostrum [′rɑstrəm] s tribune f

ros·y [′rozi] adj (comp -ier; super -iest) rosé; (complexion) vermeil; (fig) riant

rot [rɑt] s pourriture f; (slang) sottise f ‖ v (pret & pp rotted; ger rotting) tr & intr pourrir

ro′tary press′ [′rotəri] s rotative f

rotate [′rotet], [ro′tet] tr & intr tourner; (agr) alterner

rotation [ro′teʃən] s rotation f; **in rotation** à tour de rôle

rote [rot] s routine f; **by rote** par cœur, machinalement

rot′gut′ s (slang) tord-boyaux m

rotisserie [ro′tɪsəri] s rôtissoire f

rotogravure [‚rotəgrə′vjur], [‚rotə-′grevjur] s rotogravure f

rotten [′rɑtən] adj pourri

rotund [ro′tʌnd] adj rond, arrondi; (e.g., language) ampoulé

rotunda [ro′tʌndə] s rotonde f

rouge [ruʒ] s fard m, rouge m ‖ tr farder ‖ intr se farder, se mettre du rouge

rough [rʌf] adj rude; (uneven) inégal; (coarse) grossier; (unfinished) brut; (road) raboteux; (game) brutal; (sea) agité; (guess) approximatif ‖ tr—to

rough it faire du camping, coucher sur la dure; **to rough up** malmener

rough' draft' s ébauche f, avant-projet m, brouillon f

rough'house' s boucan m, chahut m || intr faire du boucan, chahuter

rough' ide'a s aperçu m

roughly ['rʌfli] adv grossièrement; brutalement; approximativement

rough'neck' s (coll) canaille f

roulette [ru'lɛt] s roulette f

round [raund] adj rond; (rounded) arrondi, rond; (e.g., shoulders) voûté; **three (four, etc.) feet round** trois (quatre, etc.) pieds de tour || s rond m; (inspection) ronde f; (of golf; of drinks; of postman, doctor, etc.) tournée f; (of applause) salve f; (of ammunition) cartouche f; (of veal) noix f; (boxing) round m; **to go the rounds** faire le tour || adv à la ronde; **round about** aux alentours; **the year round** pendant toute l'année; **to pass round** faire circuler, passer à la ronde || prep autour de || tr (to make round) arrondir; (e.g., a corner) tourner, prendre; (a cape) doubler; **to round off or out** arrondir; (to finish) achever; **to round up** rassembler; (suspects) cueillir || intr s'arrondir

roundabout ['raundə,baut] adj indirect || s détour m; (carrousel) (Brit) manège m; (traffic circle) (Brit) rond-point m

rounder ['raundər] s (coll) fêtard m

round'house' s (rr) rotonde f

round'-shoul'dered adj voûté

round' steak' s gîte m à la noix

round' ta'ble s table f ronde; **Round Table** Table ronde

round'-trip' tick'et s billet m d'aller et retour

round'up' s (of cattle) rassemblement m; (of suspects) rafle f

rouse [rauz] tr réveiller || intr se réveiller

rout [raut] s déroute f || tr mettre en déroute

route [rut], [raut] s route f; (of, e.g., bus) ligne f, parcours m || tr acheminer

routine [ru'tin] adj routinier || s routine f

rove [rov] intr errer, vagabonder

rover ['rovər] s vagabond m

row [rau] s (coll) altercation f, prise f de bec; **to raise a row** (coll) faire du boucan || [ro] s rang m; (of, e.g., houses) rangée f; (boat ride) promenade f en barque; **in a row** à la file; (without interruption) de suite; **in rows** par rangs || intr ramer

rowboat ['ro,bot] s bateau m à rames, canot m

row•dy ['raudi] adj (comp -dier; super -diest) tapageur || s (pl -dies) tapageur m

rower ['ro•ər] s rameur m

rowing ['ro•ɪŋ] s nage f, canotage m, sport m de l'aviron

royal ['rɔɪ•əl] adj royal

royalist ['rɔɪ•əlɪst] adj & s royaliste mf

royal•ty ['rɔɪ•əlti] s (pl -ties) royauté f; droit m d'auteur; redevance f, droit d'inventeur

r.p.m. ['ɑr'pi'ɛm] spl (letterword) (revolutions per minute) tours mpl à la minute

rub [rʌb] s frottement m; **there's the rub** (coll) voilà le hic || v (pret & pp rubbed; ger rubbing) tr frotter; **to rub elbows with coudoyer; to rub out** effacer; (slang) descendre, liquider || intr se frotter; (said, e.g., of moving parts) frotter; **to rub off** s'enlever, disparaître

rubber ['rʌbər] s caoutchouc m; (eraser) gomme f à effacer; (in bridge) robre m; **rubbers** (overshoes) caoutchoucs

rub'ber band' s élastique m

rubberize ['rʌbə,raiz] tr caoutchouter

rub'ber-neck' s (coll) badaud m || intr (coll) badauder

rub'ber plant' s figuier m élastique, caoutchoutier m; (tree) arbre m à caoutchouc, hévéa m

rub'ber stamp' s tampon m; (coll) béni-oui-oui m

rub'ber-stamp' tr apposer le tampon sur; (with a person's signature) estampiller; (coll) approuver à tort et à travers

rub'bing al'cohol s alcool m pour les frictions

rubbish ['rʌbɪʃ] s détritus m, rebut m; (coll) imbécillités fpl

rubble ['rʌbəl] s (broken stone) décombres mpl; (used in masonry) moellons mpl

rub'down' s friction f

rubric ['rubrɪk] s rubrique f

ru•by ['rubi] adj (lips) vermeil || s (pl -bies) rubis m

rucksack ['rʌk,sæk] s sac-à-dos m

rudder ['rʌdər] s gouvernail m

rud•dy ['rʌdi] adj (comp -dier; super -diest) rougeaud, coloré

rude [rud] adj (rough, rugged) rude; (discourteous) impoli, grossier

rudeness ['rudnɪs] s rudesse f; impolitesse f

rudiment ['rudɪmənt] s rudiment m

rue [ru] tr regretter amèrement

rueful ['rufəl] adj lamentable; triste

ruffian ['rʌfɪ•ən] s brute f

ruffle ['rʌfəl] s (in water) rides fpl; (sewing) jabot m plissé || tr (to crease; to vex) froisser; (the water) rider; (its feathers) hérisser; (one's hair) ébouriffer

rug [rʌg] s tapis m, carpette f

rugged ['rʌgɪd] adj rude, sévère; (road, country, etc.) raboteux; (person) robuste; (e.g., machine) résistant à toute épreuve

ruin ['ru•ɪn] s ruine f || tr ruiner

rule [rul] s règle f; autorité f; (reign) règne m; (law) décision f; **as a rule** en général; **by rule of thumb** empiriquement, à vue de nez || tr gouverner; (to lead) diriger, guider; (one's passions) contenir; (with lines) régler; (law) décider; **to rule out** écarter, éliminer ‖ intr gouverner; (to be the rule) prévaloir; **to rule over** régner sur

ruler ['rulər] s dirigeant m; souverain m; (for ruling lines) règle f

ruling ['rulɪŋ] adj actuel; (e.g., classes) dirigeant; (quality, trait, etc.) dominant ‖ s (of paper) réglage m; (law) décision f

rum [rʌm] s rhum m

Rumanian [ru'menɪ-ən] adj roumain ‖ s (language) roumain m; (person) Roumain m

rumble ['rʌmbəl] s (of thunder) grondement m; (of a cart) roulement m; (of intestines) gargouillement m; (slang) rixe f entre gangs ‖ intr gronder, rouler

ruminate ['rumɪ‚net] tr & intr ruminer

rummage ['rʌmɪdʒ] intr fouiller

rum′mage sale′ s vente f d'objets usagés

rumor ['rumər] s rumeur f ‖ tr—it is rumored that le bruit court que

rump [rʌmp] s (of animal) croupe f; (of bird) croupion m; (cut of meat) culotte f; (buttocks) postérieur m

rumple ['rʌmpəl] s faux pli m ‖ tr (paper, cloth, etc.) froisser, chiffonner; (one's hair) ébouriffer

rump′ steak′ s romsteck m

rumpus ['rʌmpəs] s (coll) chahut m; (argument) (coll) prise f de bec; **to raise a rumpus** (coll) déclencher un chahut; faire une scène violente

rum′pus room′ s salle f de jeux

run [rʌn] s course f; (e.g., of good or bad luck) suite f; (on a bank by depositors) descente f; (of salmon) remonte f; (of, e.g., a bus) parcours m; (in a stocking) échelle f, maille m; (cards) séquence f; (mus) roulade f; **in the long run** à la longue; **on the run** à la débandade, en fuite; **run of bad luck** série f noire; **the general run** la généralité; **to give free run to** donner libre carrière à; **to give s.o. a run for his money** en donner à qn pour son argent; **to have a long run** (theat) tenir longtemps l'affiche; **to have the run of** avoir libre accès à or dans; **to keep s.o. on the run** ne laisser aucun répit à qn; **to make a run in** (a stocking) démailler ‖ v (pret pan [ræn]; pp run; ger running) tr (the streets; a race; a risk) courir; (a motor, machine, etc.) faire marcher; (an organization, project, etc.) diriger; (a business, factory, etc.) exploiter; (a blockade) forcer; (a line) tracer; (turf) faire courir; **to run aground** échouer; **to run down** (to knock down) renverser; (to find) dépister; (game) mettre aux abois; (to disparage) (coll) dénigrer; **to run in** (a motor) roder; **to run off** (a liquid) faire écouler; (copies, pages, etc.) tirer; **to run through** (e.g., with a sword) transpercer; **to run up** (a flag) hisser; (a debt) (coll) laisser accumuler ‖ intr courir; (said, e.g., of water;

said of fountain pen, nose, etc.) couler; (said of stockings) se démailler; (said of salmon) faire la montaison; (said of colors) s'étaler, se déteindre; (said of sore) suppurer; (said of rumor, news, etc.) circuler, courir; (for office) se présenter; (mach) fonctionner, marcher; (theat) rester à l'affiche, se jouer; **run along!** filez!; **to run across** (to meet by chance) rencontrer par hasard; **to run along** (border, longer; (to go) s'en aller; **to run at** se jeter sur; **to run away** se sauver, s'enfuir; (said of horse) s'emballer, s'emporter; **to run away with** enlever; **to run down** (e.g., a hill) descendre en courant; (said of spring) se détendre; (said of watch) s'arrêter (faute d'être remonté); (said of storage battery) se décharger, s'épuiser; **to run for** (an office) poser sa candidature pour; **to run in the family** tenir de famille; **to run into** heurter; (to meet) (coll) rencontrer; **to run off** se sauver, s'enfuir; (said of liquid) s'écouler; **to run out** (said of passport, lease, etc.) expirer; **to run out of** être à court de; **to run over** (said of a liquid) déborder; (an article, a text, etc.) parcourir; (s.th. in the road) passer sur; (e.g., a pedestrian) écraser; **to run through** (an article, text, etc.) parcourir; (a fortune) gaspiller

run′away′ adj fugitif; (horse) emballé ‖ s fugitif m; cheval m emballé

run′down′ s compte rendu m, récit m

run′-down′ adj délabré; (person; battery) épuisé, à plat; (clock spring) détendu

rung [rʌŋ] s (of ladder or chair) barreau m; (of wheel) rayon m

runner ['rʌnər] s (person) coureur m; (messenger) courrier m; (of ice skate or sleigh) patin m; (narrow rug) rampe f d'escalier; (strip of cloth for table top) chemin m de table; (in stockings) démaillage m; (bot) coulant m

run′ner-up′ s (pl runners-up) bon second m, premier accessit m

running ['rʌnɪŋ] adj (person; water; expenses) courant; (stream; knot; style) coulant; (sore) suppurant; (e.g., motor) en marche ‖ s (of man or animal) course f; (of water) écoulement m; (of machine) fonctionnement m, marche f; (of business) direction f

run′ning board′ s marchepied m

run′ning com/men/tar/y s (pl -ies) (rad, telv) reportage m en direct

run′ning head′ s titre m courant

run′ning start′ s départ m lancé

run′off′ elec′tion s scrutin m de ballottage

run′proof′ adj indémaillable

runt [rʌnt] s avorton m

run′way′ s piste f, rampe f

rupture ['rʌptʃər] s rupture f; (pathol) hernie f ‖ tr rompre; (a ligament, blood vessel, etc.) se rompre ‖ *intr* se rompre

rural ['rʊrəl] *adj* rural

ru'ral free' deliv'ery *s* distribution *f* gratuite par le facteur rural

ru'ral police'man *s* garde *m* champêtre

ruse [ruz] *s* ruse *f*

rush [rʌʃ] *adj* urgent ‖ *s* course *f* précipitée, ruée *f*; précipitation *f*; (bot) jonc *m*; (formula on envelope or letterhead) urgent; **to be in a rush to** être pressé de ‖ *tr* pousser vivement; (e.g., *to the hospital*) transporter d'urgence; (e.g., *a girl*) (slang) insister auprès de; **to rush through** (e.g., *a law*) faire passer à la hâte ‖ *intr* se précipiter, se ruer; **to rush about** courir çà et là; **to rush headlong** foncer tête baissée; **to rush into** (e.g., *a room*) faire irruption dans; (*an affair*) se jeter dans; **to rush out** sortir précipitamment; **to rush through** (one's *lessons, prayers, etc.*) expédier; (e.g., *a town*) traverser à toute vitesse; (*a tourist attraction*) visiter au pas de course; (*a book*) lire à la hâte; **to rush to** s'empresser de; **to rush to**

one's face (*said of blood*) monter au visage à qn

rush'-bot'tomed chair' *s* chaise *f* à fond de paille

rush' hours' *spl* heures *fpl* d'affluence ou de pointe

rush' or'der *s* commande *f* urgente

russet ['rʌsɪt] *adj* roussâtre, roux

Russia ['rʌʃə] *s* Russie *f*; la Russie

Russian ['rʌʃən] *adj* russe ‖ *s* (*language*) russe *m*; (*person*) Russe *mf*

rust [rʌst] *s* rouille *f* ‖ *tr* rouiller ‖ *intr* se rouiller

rustic ['rʌstɪk] *adj* rustique; simple, net; (pej) rustaud ‖ *s* paysan *m*, villageois *m*

rustle ['rʌsəl] *s* bruissement *m*; (of, e.g., *a dress*) froufrou *m* ‖ *tr* faire bruire; (*cattle*) (coll) voler ‖ *intr* bruire; (*said, e.g., of a dress*) froufrouter; **to rustle around** (coll) se démener

rust'proof' *adj* inoxydable

rust•y ['rʌsti] *adj* (*comp* -ier; *super* -iest) rouillé

rut [rʌt] *s* ornière *f*; (zool) rut *m*

ruthless ['ruθlɪs] *adj* impitoyable

rye [raɪ] *s* seigle *m*; whisky *m* de seigle

S

S, s [es] *s* XIXe lettre de l'alphabet

Sabbath ['sæbəθ] *s* sabbat *m*; dimanche *m*

sabbat'ical year' [sə'bætɪkəl] *s* année *f* de congé

saber ['sebər] *s* sabre *m* ‖ *tr* sabrer

sable ['sebəl] *adj* noir ‖ *s* (*animal, fur*) zibeline *f*; noir *m*; **sables** vêtements *mpl* de deuil

sabotage ['sæbə‚taʒ] *s* sabotage *m* ‖ *tr & intr* saboter

saccharin ['sækərɪn] *s* saccharine *f*

sachet [sæ'ʃe] *s* sachet *m* (à parfums)

sack [sæk] *s* sac *m*; (*wine*) xérès *m* ‖ *tr* mettre en sac; (mil) saccager; (coll) saquer, congédier

sack'cloth' *s* grosse toile *f* d'emballage, serpillière *f*; (*worn for penitence*) cilice *m*; **in sackcloth and ashes** sous le sac et la cendre

sacrament ['sækrəmənt] *s* sacrement *m*

sacramental [‚sækrə'mentəl] *adj* sacramentel

sacred ['sekrəd] *adj* sacré

sa'cred cow' *s* (fig) monstre *m* sacré

sacrifice ['sækrɪ‚faɪs] *s* sacrifice *m*; **at a sacrifice** à perte ‖ *tr & intr* sacrifier

sacrilege ['sækrəlɪdʒ] *s* sacrilège *m*

sacrilegious [‚sækrɪ'lɪdʒəs], [‚sækrɪ'lidʒəs] *adj* sacrilège

sacristan ['sækrɪstən] *s* sacristain *m*

sad [sæd] *adj* (*comp* sadder; *super* saddest) triste

sadden ['sædən] *tr* attrister ‖ *intr* s'attrister

saddle ['sædəl] *s* selle *f* ‖ *tr* seller; **to saddle with** charger de, encombrer de

sad'dle•bag' ['sædəl‚bæg] *s* sacoche *f* (de selle)

saddlebow ['sædəl‚bo] *s* arçon *m* de devant

saddler ['sædlər] *s* sellier *m*

sad'dle•tree' *s* arçon *m*

sadist ['sædɪst], ['sedɪst] *s* sadique *mf*

sadistic [sæ'dɪstɪk], [sə'dɪstɪk] *adj* sadique

sadness ['sædnɪs] *s* tristesse *f*

sad' sack' *s* (slang) bidasse *mf*

safe [sef] *adj* (*from danger*) sûr; (*unhurt*) sauf; (*margin*) certain; **safe and sound** sain et sauf; **safe from** à l'abri de ‖ *s* coffre-fort *m*, caisse *f*

safe'-con'duct *s* sauf-conduit *m*

safe'-depos'it box' *s* coffre *m* à la banque; coffret de sûreté (Canad)

safe'guard' *s* sauvegarde *f* ‖ *tr* sauvegarder

safe'keep'ing *s* bonne garde *f*

safe•ty ['sefti] *adj* de sûreté ‖ *s* (*pl* -ties) (*state of being safe*) sécurité *f*, sûreté *f*; (*avoidance of danger*) salut *m*

safe'ty belt' *s* ceinture *f* de sécurité

safe'ty match' *s* allumette *f* de sûreté

safe'ty pin' *s* épingle *f* de sûreté

safe'ty ra'zor *s* rasoir *m* de sûreté

safe'ty valve' *s* soupape *f* de sûreté

saffron ['sæfrən] *adj* safrané ‖ *s* safran *m*

sag [sæg] *s* affaissement *m* ‖ *v* (*pret &*

pp **sagged;** *ger* **sagging)** *intr* s'affaisser

sagacious [səˈgeʃəs] *adj* sagace

sage [sedʒ] *adj* sage ‖ *s* sage *mf*; (*plant*) sauge *f*

sage/brush/ *s* armoise *f*

sail [sel] *s* voile *f*; (*sails*) voilure *f*; (*of windmill*) aile *f*; **full sail** toutes voiles dehors; **to set sail** mettre les voiles; **to take a sail** faire une promenade à la voile; **to take in sail** baisser pavillon ‖ *tr* (*a ship*) gouverner, commander; (*to travel over*) naviguer sur ‖ *intr* naviguer; **to sail along the coast** côtoyer; **to sail into** (coll) assaillir

sail/boat/ *s* bateau *m* à voiles

sail/cloth/ *s* toile *f* à voile

sailing [ˈselɪŋ] *s* navigation *f*; (*working of ship*) manœuvre *f*; (*of pleasure craft*) voile *f*

sail/ing ves/sel *s* voilier *m*

sail/mak/er *s* voilier *m*

sailor [ˈselər] *s* marin *m*; (*simple crewman*) matelot *m*

saint [sent] *adj* & *s* saint *m*

saint/hood *s* sainteté *f*

saintliness [ˈsentlɪnɪs] *s* sainteté *f*

Saint/ Vi/tus's dance/ [ˈvaɪtəsəz] *s* (pathol) danse *f* de Saint-Guy

sake [sek] *s*—**for the sake of** pour l'amour de, dans l'intérêt de; **for your sake** pour vous

salable [ˈseləbəl] *adj* vendable

salacious [səˈleʃəs] *adj* lubrique

salad [ˈsæləd] *s* salade *f*

sal/ad bowl/ *s* saladier *m*

salary [ˈsæləri] *s* (*pl* **-ries**) salaire *m*

sale [sel] *s* vente *f*; **for sale** en vente; **on sale** en solde, en réclame

sales/ clerk/ *s* vendeur *m*

sales/ girl/ *s* vendeuse *f*, demoiselle *f* de magasin

sales/la/dy *s* (*pl* **-dies**) vendeuse *f*

sales/man *s* (*pl* **-men**) vendeur *m*, commis *m*

sales/man-ship/ *s* l'art *m* de vendre

sales/ promo/tion *s* stimulation *f* de la vente

sales/room/ *s* salle *f* de vente

sales/ talk/ *s* raisonnements *mpl* destinés à convaincre le client

sales/ tax/ *s* taxe *f* sur les ventes, impôt *m* indirect

saliva [səˈlaɪvə] *s* salive *f*

sallow [ˈsælo] *adj* olivâtre

sal·ly [ˈsæli] *s* (*pl* **-lies**) saillie *f*; (mil) sortie *f* ‖ *v* (*pret* & *pp* **-lied**) *intr* faire une sortie

salmon [ˈsæmən] *adj* & *s* saumon *m*

saloon [səˈlun] *s* cabaret *m*, estaminet *m*, bistrot *m*; (naut) salon *m*

salt [sɔlt] *s* sel *m* ‖ *tr* saler; **to salt away** (coll) économiser, mettre de côté

salt/cel/lar *s* salière *f*

salt/ lick/ *s* terrain *m* salifère

salt/pe/ter *s* (*potassium nitrate*) salpêtre *m*; (*sodium nitrate*) nitrate *m* du Chili

salt/ pork/ *s* salé *m*

salt/sha/ker *s* salière *f*

salty [ˈsɔlti] *adj* (*comp* **-ier;** *super* **-iest**) salé

salute [səˈlut] *s* salut *m* ‖ *tr* saluer

salvage [ˈsælvɪdʒ] *s* sauvetage *m*; biens *mpl* sauvés ‖ *tr* sauver; récupérer

salvation [sælˈveʃən] *s* salut *m*

Salva/tion Ar/my *s* Armée *f* du Salut

salve [sæv], [sav] *s* onguent *m*, pommade *f*; baume *m* ‖ *tr* appliquer un onguent sur; (fig) apaiser

sal·vo [ˈsælvo] *s* (*pl* **-vos** or **-voes**) salve *f*

Samaritan [səˈmærɪtən] *adj* samaritain ‖ *s* Samaritain *m*

same [sem] *adj* & *pron indef* même (before noun); **at the same time** en même temps, au même moment, à la fois; **it's all the same to me** ça m'est égal; **just the same, all the same** malgré tout, quand même; **the same . . . as** le même . . . que

sameness [ˈsemnɪs] *s* monotonie *f*

sample [ˈsæmpəl] *s* échantillon *m* ‖ *tr* échantillonner; essayer

sam/ple cop/y *s* (*pl* **-ies**) numéro *m* spécimen

sancti·fy [ˈsæŋktɪˌfaɪ] *v* (*pret* & *pp* **-fied**) *tr* sanctifier

sanctimonious [ˌsæŋktɪˈmonɪ·əs] *adj* papelard, bigot

sanction [ˈsæŋkʃən] *s* sanction *f* ‖ *tr* sanctionner

sanctuar·y [ˈsæŋktʃuˌeri] *s* (*pl* **-ies**) sanctuaire *m*; refuge *m*, asile *m*

sand [sænd] *s* sable *m* ‖ *tr* sablonner

sandal [ˈsændəl] *s* sandale *f*

san/dal-wood/ *s* santal *m*

sand/bag/ *s* sac *m* de sable

sand/ bar/ *s* banc *m* de sable

sand/blast/ *s* jet *m* de sable; (*apparatus*) sableuse *f* ‖ *tr* sabler

sand/box/ *s* (rr) sablière *f*

sand/glass/ *s* sablier *m*

sand/pa/per *s* papier *m* de verre ‖ *tr* polir au papier de verre

sand/pi/per *s* bécasseau *m*

sand/stone/ *s* grès *m*

sand/storm/ *s* tempête *f* de sable

sandwich [ˈsændwɪtʃ] *s* sandwich *m* ‖ *tr* intercaler

sand/wich man/ *s* homme-affiche *m*

sand·y [ˈsændi] *adj* (*comp* **-ier;** *super* **-iest**) sablonneux; (*hair*) blond roux

sane [sen] *adj* sain, équilibré; (*principles*) raisonnable

sanguine [ˈsæŋgwɪn] *adj* confiant, optimiste; (*countenance*) sanguin

sanitary [ˈsænɪˌteri] *adj* sanitaire

san/itary nap/kin *s* serviette *f* hygiénique

sanitation [ˌsænɪˈteʃən] *s* hygiène *f*, salubrité *f*; (*drainage*) assainissement *m*

sanity [ˈsænɪti] *s* santé *f* mentale; bon sens *m*

Santa Claus [ˈsæntəˌklɔz] *s* le père Noël

sap [sæp] *s* sève *f*; (mil) sape *f*; (coll) poire *f*, nigaud *m* ‖ *v* (*pret* & *pp* **sapped;** *ger* **sapping)** *tr* tirer la sève de; (*to weaken*) affaiblir; (mil) saper

sapling ['sæplɪŋ] *s* jeune arbre *m*; jeune homme *m*
sapphire ['sæfaɪr] *s* saphir *m*
Saracen ['særəsən] *adj* sarrasin ‖ *s* Sarrasin *m*
sarcasm ['sɑrkæzəm] *s* sarcasme *m*
sardine [sɑr'din] *s* sardine *f*; **packed in like sardines** serrés comme des harengs
Sardinia [sɑr'dɪnɪ-ə] *s* Sardaigne; la Sardaigne
Sardinian [sɑr'dɪnɪ-ən] *adj* sarde ‖ *s* (*language*) sarde *m*; (*person*) Sarde *mf*
sarsaparilla [,sɑrsəpə'rɪlə] *s* salsepareille *f*
sash [sæʃ] *s* ceinture *f*; (*of window*) châssis *m*
sash/ win/dow *s* fenêtre *f* à guillotine
sas·sy ['sæsi] *adj* (*comp* **-ier**; *super* **-siest**) (coll) impudent, effronté
satchel ['sætʃəl] *s* sacoche *f*; (*of schoolboy*) carton *m*
sate [set] *tr* soûler
sateen [sæ'tin] *s* satinette *f*
satellite ['sætə,laɪt] *adj & s* satellite *m*
sat/ellite coun/try *s* pays *m* satellite
satiate ['seʃɪ,et] *adj* rassasié ‖ *tr* rassasier
satin ['sætɪn] *s* satin *m*
satire ['sætaɪr] *s* satire *f*
satiric(al) [sə'tɪrɪk(əl)] *adj* satirique
satirize ['sætɪ,raɪz] *tr* satiriser
satisfaction [,sætɪs'fækʃən] *s* satisfaction *f*
satisfactory [,sætɪs'fæktəri] *adj* satisfaisant
satis·fy ['sætɪs,faɪ] *v* (*pret & pp* **-fied**) *tr* satisfaire; (*a requirement, need, etc.*) satisfaire (with *dat*) ‖ *intr* satisfaire
saturate ['sætʃə,ret] *tr* saturer
Saturday ['sætərdɪ] *s* samedi *m*
Saturn ['sætərn] *s* Saturne *m*
sauce [sɔs] *s* sauce *f*; (coll) insolence *f*, toupet *m* ‖ *tr* assaisonner ‖ [sɔs], [sæs] *tr* (coll) parler avec impudence à
sauce/pan/ *s* casserole *f*
saucer ['sɔsər] *s* soucoupe *f*
sau·cy ['sɔsi] *adj* (*comp* **-cier**; *super* **-ciest**) impudent, effronté
sauerkraut ['saur,kraut] *s* choucroute *f*
saunter ['sɔntər] *s* flânerie *f* ‖ *intr* flâner
sausage ['sɔsɪdʒ] *s* saucisse *f*, saucisson *m*
sauté [so'te] *tr* sauter, faire sauter
savage ['sævɪdʒ] *adj & s* sauvage *mf*
savant ['sævənt] *s* savant *m*, érudit *m*
save [sev] *prep* sauf, excepté ‖ *tr* sauver; (*money*) épargner; (*time*) gagner ‖ *intr* économiser
saving ['sevɪŋ] *adj* économe ‖ **savings** *spl* épargne *f*, économies *fpl*
sav/ings account/ *s* dépôt *m* d'épargne
sav/ings and loan/ associa/tion *s* caisse *f* d'épargne et de prêt
sav/ings bank/ *s* caisse *f* d'épargne
sav/ings book/ *s* livret *m* de caisse d'épargne
savior ['sevjər] *s* sauveur *m*

Saviour ['sevjər] *s* Sauveur *m*
savor ['sevər] *s* saveur *f* ‖ *tr* savourer ‖ *intr*—**to savor of** avoir un goût de
savor·y ['sevəri] *adj* (*comp* **-ier**; *super* **-iest**) (*taste*) savoureux; (*smell*) odorant ‖ *s* (*pl* **-ies**) (bot) sariette *f*
saw [sɔ] *s* scie *f*; (*proverb*) dicton *m* ‖ *tr* scier
saw/dust/ *s* sciure *f* de bois
saw/horse/ *s* chevalet *m*
saw/mill/ *s* scierie *f*
Saxon ['sæksən] *adj* saxon ‖ *s* (*language*) saxon *m*; (*person*) Saxon *m*
saxophone ['sæksə,fon] *s* saxophone *m*
say [se] *s* mot *m*; **to have one's say** avoir son mot à dire ‖ *v* (*pret & pp* **said** [sɛd]) *tr* dire; **I should say not!** absolument pas!; **I should say so!** je crois bien!; **it is said on dit**; **no sooner said than done** sitôt dit, sitôt fait; **that is to say** c'est-à-dire; **to go without saying** aller sans dire; **you said it!** (coll) et comment!, tu parles!
saying ['se·ɪŋ] *s* proverbe *m*
scab [skæb] *s* croûte *f*; (*strikebreaker*) jaune *m*; canaille *f*
scabbard ['skæbərd] *s* fourreau *m*
scab·by ['skæbi] *adj* (*comp* **-bier**; *super* **-biest**) croûteux; (coll) vil
scabrous ['skæbrəs] *adj* scabreux; (*uneven*) rugueux
scads [skædz] *spl* (slang) des tas *mpl*
scaffold ['skæfəld] *s* échafaud *m*; (*used in construction*) échafaudage *m*
scaffolding ['skæfəldɪŋ] *s* échafaudage *m*
scald [skɔld] *tr* échauder
scale [skel] *s* (*of thermometer, map, salaries, etc.*) échelle *f*; (*for weighing*) plateau *m*; (*incrustation*) tartre *m*; (bot, zool) écaille *f*; (mus) échelle; **on a large scale** sur une grande échelle; **scales** balance *f*; **to tip the scales** faire pencher la balance ‖ *tr* escalader; **to scale down** réduire l'échelle de
scallop ['skaləp], ['skæləp] *s* coquille *f* Saint-Jacques, peigne *m*, pétoncle *m*; (*thin slice of meat*) escalope *f*; (*on edge of cloth*) feston *m* ‖ *tr* (*the edges*) denteler, découper; (culin) gratiner et cuire au four et à la crème
scalp [skælp] *s* cuir *m* chevelu; (*Indian trophy*) scalp *m* ‖ *tr* scalper; (*tickets*) (coll) faire le trafic de; (*to hoodwink*) (slang) abuser de
scalpel ['skælpəl] *s* scalpel *m*
scal·y ['skeli] *adj* (*comp* **-ier**; *super* **-iest**) écailleux
scamp [skæmp] *s* garnement *m*
scamper ['skæmpər] *intr* courir allégrement; **to scamper away or off** détaler
scan [skæn] *v* (*pret & pp* **scanned**; *ger* **scanning**) *tr* scruter; (*e.g., a page*) jeter un coup d'œil sur; (*verses*) scander; (telv) balayer
scandal ['skændəl] *s* scandale *m*
scandalize ['skændə,laɪz] *tr* scandaliser
scandalous ['skændələs] *adj* scandaleux
Scandinavian [,skændɪ'nevɪ-ən] *adj*

scandinave ‖ s (*language*) scandinave m; (*person*) Scandinave mf

scanning ['skænɪŋ] s (telv) balayage m

scant [skænt] adj maigre; (*attire*) léger, sommaire ‖ tr réduire; lésiner sur

scant•y ['skæntɪ] adj (comp **-ier;** super **-iest**) rare, maigre; léger

scapegoat ['skep‚got] s bouc m émissaire

scar [skɑr] s cicatrice f; (*on face*) balafre f ‖ v (*pret & pp* **scarred;** ger **scarring**) tr balafrer

scarce [skɛrs] adj rare, peu abondant

scarcely ['skɛrslɪ] adv à peine, presque pas; ne . . . guère §90; **scarcely ever** rarement

scarci•ty ['skɛrsɪtɪ] s (pl **-ties**) manque m, pénurie f

scare [skɛr] s panique f, effroi m ‖ tr épouvanter, effrayer; **to scare away** or **off** effaroucher; **to scare up** (coll) procurer ‖ intr s'effaroucher

scare′crow′ s épouvantail m

scarf [skɑrf] s (pl **scarfs** or **scarves** [skɑrvz]) foulard m, écharpe f

scarlet ['skɑrlɪt] adj & s écarlate f

scar′let fe′ver s scarlatine f

scar•y ['skɛrɪ] adj (comp **-ier;** super **-iest**) (*easily frightened*) (coll) peureux, ombrageux; (*causing fright*) (coll) effrayant

scathing ['skeðɪŋ] adj cinglant

scatter ['skætər] tr éparpiller; (*a mob*) disperser ‖ intr se disperser

scat′ter-brained′ adj (coll) étourdi

scenari•o [sɪ'nɛrɪ‚o], [sɪ'nɑrɪ‚o] s (pl **-os**) scénario m

scene [sin] s scène f; (*landscape*) paysage m; **behind the scenes** dans les coulisses; **to make a scene** faire une scène

scener•y ['sinərɪ] s (pl **-ies**) paysage m; (theat) décor m, décors

sceneshifter ['sin‚ʃɪftər] s (theat) machiniste m

scenic ['sinɪk], ['sɛnɪk] adj pittoresque; spectaculaire; (theat) scénique

sce′nic rail′way s chemin m de fer en miniature des parcs d'attraction

scent [sɛnt] s odeur f; parfum m; (*trail*) piste f ‖ tr parfumer; (*an odor*) renifler; (*game as a dog does; a trap*) flairer

scepter ['sɛptər] s sceptre m

sceptic ['skɛptɪk] adj & s sceptique mf

sceptical ['skɛptɪkəl] adj sceptique

scepticism ['skɛptɪ‚sɪzəm] s scepticisme m

schedule ['skɛdʒul] s (*of work*) plan m; (*of things to do*) emploi m du temps; (*of prices*) barème m; (rr) horaire m; **on schedule** selon l'horaire; selon les prévisions ‖ tr classer; inscrire au programme, à l'horaire, etc.; **scheduled to speak** prévu comme orateur

scheme [skim] s projet m; machination f, truc m ‖ tr projeter ‖ intr ruser

schemer ['skimər] s faiseur m de projets; intrigant m

schism ['sɪzəm] s schisme m, scission f

scholar ['skɑlər] s (*pupil*) écolier m;

(*learned person*) érudit m, savant m; (*holder of scholarship*) boursier m

scholarly ['skɑlərlɪ] adj érudit, savant ‖ adv savamment

schol′ar·ship′ s érudition f; (*award*) bourse f

scholasticism [skə'læstɪ‚sɪzəm] s scolastique f

school [skul] adj scolaire; **school zone** (public sign) ralentir école ‖ s école f; (*of a university*) faculté f; (*of fish*) banc m ‖ tr instruire, discipliner

school′ board′ s conseil m de l'instruction publique

school′book′ s livre m de classe, livre scolaire

school′boy′ s écolier m

school′girl′ s écolière f

school′house′ s maison f d'école

schooling ['skulɪŋ] s instruction f, enseignement m; discipline f; frais mpl de l'éducation

schoolmarm ['skul‚mɑrm] s maîtresse f d'école, institutrice f

school′mas′ter s maître m d'école, instituteur m

school′mate′ s camarade mf d'école, condisciple m

school′room′ s classe f, salle f de classe

school′teach′er s enseignant m, instituteur m

school′yard′ s cour f de récréation

school′ year′ s année f scolaire

schooner ['skunər] s schooner m, goélette f

sciatica [sɑɪ'ætɪkə] s (pathol) sciatique f

science ['sɑɪəns] s science f

sci′ence fic′tion s science-fiction f

scientific [‚sɑɪən'tɪfɪk] adj scientifique

scientist ['sɑɪəntɪst] s homme m de science, savant m

scimitar ['sɪmɪtər] s cimeterre m

scintillate ['sɪntɪ‚let] intr scintiller, étinceler

scion ['sɑɪ·ən] s héritier m; (hort) scion m

scissors ['sɪzərz] s & spl ciseaux mpl

scis′sors-grind′er s rémouleur m; (orn) engoulevent m

scoff [skɔf], [skɑf] s raillerie f ‖ intr —**to scoff at** se moquer de

scold [skold] s harpie f ‖ tr & intr gronder

scolding ['skoldɪŋ] s gronderie f

scoop [skup] s pelle f à main; (*for coal*) seau m; (*kitchen utensil*) louche f; (*of dredge*) godet m; (journ) nouvelle f sensationnelle; (naut) écope f ‖ tr creuser; **to scoop out** excaver à la pelle; (*water*) écoper

scoot [skut] intr (coll) détaler

scooter ['skutər] s trottinette f, patinette f

scope [skop] s (*field*) domaine m, étendue f; (*reach*) portée f, envergure f; **to give free scope to** donner libre carrière à

scorch [skɔrtʃ] tr roussir; flétrir, dessécher

scorched'-earth' pol'icy s politique f de la terre brûlée

scorching ['skɔrtʃɪŋ] adj brûlant; caustique, mordant

score [skor] s compte m, total m; (twenty) vingtaine f; (notch) entaille f; (on metal) rayure f, éraflure f; (mus) partition f; (sports) score m, marque f; **on that score** à cet égard; **to keep score** compter les points || tr (to notch) entailler; (to criticize) blâmer; (metal) rayer, érafler; (a success) remporter; (e.g., a goal) marquer; (mus) orchestrer

score'board' s tableau m

score'keep'er s marqueur m

scorn [skɔrn] s mépris m, dédain m || tr mépriser, dédaigner || intr—**to scorn to** dédaigner de

scorpion ['skɔrpɪ·ən] s scorpion m

Scot [skɑt] s Écossais m

Scotch [skɑtʃ] adj écossais; (slang) avare, chiche || s (dialect) écossais m; whisky m écossais; **the Scotch** les Écossais || (l.c.) s (wedge) cale f; (notch) entaille f || tr caler; entailler; (a rumor) étouffer

Scotch'man s (pl -men) Écossais m

Scotch' pine' s pin m sylvestre

Scotch' tape' s (trademark) ruban m cellulosique, adhésif m scotch

Scotland ['skɑtlənd] s Écosse f; l'Écosse

Scottish ['skɑtɪʃ] adj écossais || s (dialect) écossais m; **the Scottish** les Écossais

scoundrel ['skaundrəl] s coquin m, fripon m, canaille f

scour [skaur] tr récurer; (e.g., the countryside) parcourir

scourge [skʌrdʒ] s nerf m de bœuf, discipline f; (fig) fléau m || tr fouetter, flageller

scout [skaut] adj scout || s éclaireur m; (boy scout) scout m, éclaireur; **a good scout** (coll) un brave gars || tr reconnaître; (to scoff at) repousser avec dédain || intr aller en reconnaissance

scouting ['skautɪŋ] s scoutisme m

scout'ing par'ty s (pl -ties) (mil) détachement m de reconnaissance

scout'mas'ter s chef m de troupe

scowl [skaul] s renfrognement m || intr se renfrogner

scram [skræm] v (pret & pp scrammed; ger scramming) intr (coll) ficher le camp; **scram!** (coll) fiche-moi le camp!

scramble ['skræmbəl] s bousculade f || tr brouiller || intr se disputer; grimper à quatre pattes

scram'bled eggs' spl œufs mpl brouillés

scrap [skræp] s ferraille f; (little bit) petit morceau m; (fight) (coll) chamaillerie f || v (pret & pp scrapped; ger scrapping) tr mettre au rebut || intr (coll) se chamailler

scrap'book' s album m de découpures

scrape [skrep] s grincement m; (coll) mauvaise affaire f || tr gratter, râcler

scrap' heap' s tas m de rebut

scrap' i'ron s ferraille f

scrap' pa'per s bloc-notes m; (refuse) papier m de rebut

scratch [skrætʃ] s égratignure f; **to start from scratch** partir de rien || tr gratter, égratigner

scratch' pad' s bloc-notes m, brouillon m

scratch' pa'per s bloc-notes m

scrawl [skrɔl] s griffonnage m || tr & intr griffonner

scraw·ny ['skrɔni] adj (comp -nier; super -niest) décharné, mince

scream [skrim] s cri m perçant; (slang) personne f ridicule; (slang) chose f ridicule || tr & intr pousser des cris, crier

screech [skritʃ] s cri m perçant || intr jeter des cris perçants

screech' owl' s chat-huant m; (barn owl) effraie f

screen [skrin] s écran m; grillage m en fil de fer, treillis m métallique; (for sifting) crible m || tr abriter; (candidates) trier; (mov) porter à l'écran

screen' grid' s (electron) grille f blindée

screen'play' s scénario m; drame m filmé

screen' test' s bout m d'essai

screw [skru] s vis f; (naut) hélice f; **to have a screw loose** (coll) être toqué || tr visser; **to screw off** dévisser; **to screw tight** visser à bloc; **to screw up** (one's courage) rassembler || intr se visser

screw'ball' adj & s (slang) extravagant m, loufoque m

screw'driv'er s tournevis m

screw' eye' s vis f à œil

screw' press' s cric m à vis

screw' propel'ler s hélice f

screw·y ['skru·i] adj (comp -ier; super -iest) (slang) loufoque m

scrib'al er'ror ['skraɪbəl] s faute f de copiste

scribble ['skrɪbəl] s griffonnage m || tr & intr griffonner

scribe [skraɪb] s scribe m

scrimmage ['skrɪmɪdʒ] s mêlée f

scrimp [skrɪmp] tr lésiner sur || intr lésiner

scrip [skrɪp] s monnaie f scriptural, script m

script [skrɪpt] s manuscrit m, original m; (handwriting) écriture f; (mov) scénario m; (typ) script m

scriptural ['skrɪptʃərəl] adj biblique

scripture ['skrɪptʃər] s citation f tirée de l'Écriture; **Scripture** l'Écriture f; **the Scriptures** les Écritures

script'writ'er s scénariste mf

scrofula ['skrɑfjələ] s scrofule f

scroll [skrol] s rouleau m; (archit) volute f

scroll'work' s ornementation f en volute

scro·tum ['skrotəm] s (pl -ta [tə] or -tums) scrotum m, bourses fpl

scrub [skrʌb] adj rabougri || s arbuste m rabougri; personne f malingre; (sports) joueur m novice || v (pret &

pp **scrubbed;** *ger* **scrubbing)** *tr* frotter, nettoyer, récurer

scrub′bing brush′ *s* brosse *f* de chiendent

scrub′wom′an *s* (*pl* **-wom′en**) nettoyeuse *f*

scruff [skrʌf] *s* nuque *f*

scruple [ˈskrupəl] *s* scrupule *f*

scrupulous [ˈskrupjələs] *adj* scrupuleux

scrutinize [ˈskrutɪˌnaɪz] *tr* scruter

scruti·ny [ˈskrutɪni] *s* (*pl* **-nies**) examen *m* minutieux

scuff [skʌf] *s* usure *f* || *tr* érafler

scuffle [ˈskʌfəl] *s* bagarre *f* || *intr* se bagarrer

scull [skʌl] *s* (*stern oar*) godille *f*; aviron *m* de couple || *tr* godiller || *intr* ramer en couple

sculler·y [ˈskʌləri] *s* (*pl* **-ies**) arrière-cuisine *f*

scul′lery maid′ *s* laveuse *f* de vaisselle

scullion [ˈskʌljən] *s* marmiton *m*

sculptor [ˈskʌlptər] *s* sculpteur *m*

sculptress [ˈskʌlptrɪs] *s* femme *f* sculpteur

sculpture [ˈskʌlptʃər] *s* sculpture *f* || *tr & intr* sculpter

scum [skʌm] *s* écume *f*; (*of society*) canaille *f* || *v* (*pret & pp* **scummed;** *ger* **scumming**) *tr & intr* écumer

scum·my [ˈskʌmi] *adj* (*comp* **-mier;** *super* **-miest**) écumeux; (fig) vil

scurrilous [ˈskʌrɪləs] *adj* injurieux, grossier, outrageant

scur·ry [ˈskʌri] *v* (*pret & pp* **-ried**) *intr* —**to scurry around** galoper; **to scurry away or off** déguerpir

scur·vy [ˈskʌrvi] *adj* (*comp* **-vier;** *super* **-viest**) méprisable, vil || *s* scorbut *m*

scuttle [ˈskʌtəl] *s* (*bucket for coal*) seau *m* à charbon; (*trap door*) trappe *f*; (*run*) course *f* précipitée; (naut) écoutillon *m* || *tr* saborder || *intr* filer, déguerpir

scut′tle-butt′ *s* (coll) on-dit *m*

scythe [saɪð] *s* faux *f*

sea [si] *s* mer *f*; **at sea** en mer; (fig) désorienté; **by the sea** au bord de la mer; **to put to sea** prendre le large

sea′board′ *s* littoral *m*

sea′ breeze′ *s* brise *f* de mer

sea′coast′ *s* côte *f*, littoral *m*

seafarer [ˈsiˌfɛrər] *s* marin *m*; voyageur *m* par mer

sea′food′ *s* fruits *mpl* de mer, marée *f*

seagoing [ˈsiˌgo·ɪŋ] *adj* de haute mer, au long cours

sea′ gull′ *s* mouette *f*, goéland *m*

seal [sil] *s* sceau *m*; (zool) phoque *m* || *tr* sceller

sea′ legs′ *spl* pied *m* marin

sea′ lev′el *s* niveau *m* de la mer

seal′ing wax′ *s* cire *f* à cacheter

seal′skin′ *s* peau *f* de phoque

seam [sim] *s* couture *f*; (*of metal*) joint *m*; (geol) fissure *f*; (min) couche *f*

sea′man *s* (*pl* **-men**) marin *m*

sea′ mile′ *s* mille *m* marin

seamless [ˈsimlɪs] *adj* sans couture; (mach) sans soudure

seamstress [ˈsimstrɪs] *s* couturière *f*

seam·y [ˈsimi] *adj* (*comp* **-ier;** *super* **-iest**) plein de coutures; vil, vilain

séance [ˈse-ɑns] *s* séance *f* de spiritisme

sea′plane′ *s* hydravion *m*

sea′port′ *s* port *m* de mer

sea′ pow′er *s* puissance *f* maritime

sear [sɪr] *adj* desséché || *s* cicatrice *f* de brûlure || *tr* dessécher; marquer au fer rouge

search [sʌrtʃ] *s* recherche *f*; **in search of** à la recherche de || *tr & intr* fouiller; **to search for** chercher

searching [ˈsʌrtʃɪŋ] *adj* pénétrant, scrutateur

search′light′ *s* projecteur *m*

search′ war′rant *s* mandat *m* de perquisition

seascape [ˈsiˌskep] *s* panorama *m* marin; (*painting*) marine *f*

sea′ shell′ *s* coquille *f* de mer

sea′shore′ *s* bord *m* de la mer

sea′sick′ *adj*—**to be seasick** avoir le mal de mer

sea′sick′ness *s* mal *m* de mer

season [ˈsizən] *s* saison *f* || *tr* assaisonner; (*troops*) aguerrir; (*wood*) sécher

seasonal [ˈsizənəl] *adj* saisonnier

seasoning [ˈsizənɪŋ] *s* assaisonnement *m*

sea′son's greet′ings *spl* meilleurs souhaits *mpl*, tous mes vœux *mpl*

sea′son tick′et *s* carte *f* d'abonnement

seat [sit] *s* place *f*, siège *m*; (*of trousers*) fond *m*; **have a seat** asseyez-vous donc; **keep your seat** restez assis || *tr* asseoir; (*a number of persons*) contenir; **to be seated** (*to sit down*) s'asseoir; (*to be in sitting posture*) être assis

seat′ belt′ *s* ceinture *f* de sécurité

seat′ cov′er *s* (aut) housse *f*

SEATO [ˈsito] *s* (acronym) (**Southeast Asia Treaty Organization**) OTASE *f*

sea′ wall′ *s* digue *f*

sea′way′ *s* voie *f* maritime; (*of ship*) sillage *m*; (*rough sea*) mer *f* dure

sea′weed′ *s* algue *f* marine; plante *f* marine

sea′wor′thy *adj* en état de naviguer

secede [sɪˈsid] *intr* se séparer, faire sécession

secession [sɪˈsɛʃən] *s* sécession *f*

seclude [sɪˈklud] *tr* tenir éloigné; (*to shut up*) enfermer

secluded *adj* retiré, écarté

seclusion [sɪˈkluʒən] *s* retraite *f*

second [ˈsɛkənd] *adj & pron* deuxième (*masc, fem*), second; **the Second** deux, e.g., **John the Second** Jean deux; **to be second in command** commander en second; **to be second to none** ne le céder à personne || *s* deuxième *m*, second *m*; (*in time; musical interval; of angle*) seconde *f*; (*in a duel*) témoin *m*, second *m*; (com) article *m* de deuxième qualité; **the second** (*in dates*) le deux || *adv* en second lieu || *tr* affirmer; (*to back up*) seconder

secondar·y [ˈsɛkənˌdɛri] *adj* secondaire || *s* (*pl* **-ies**) (elec) secondaire *m*

sec'ond best' s pis-aller m
sec'ond-best' adj (everyday) de tous les jours; **to come off second-best** être battu
sec'ond-class' adj de second ordre; (rr) de seconde classe
sec'ond hand' s trotteuse f
sec'ond-hand' adj d'occasion, de seconde main
sec'ond-hand book'dealer s bouquiniste mf
sec'ond lieuten'ant s sous-lieutenant m
sec'ond mate' s (naut) second maître m
sec'ond-rate' adj de second ordre
sec'ond sight' s seconde vue f
sec'ond wind' s—**to get one's second wind** reprendre haleine
secre·cy ['sikrəsi] s (pl -cies) secret m; **in secrecy** en secret
secret ['sikrɪt] adj & s secret m; **in secret** en secret
secretar·y ['sekrɪ,teri] s (pl -ies) secrétaire mf; (desk) secrétaire m
se'cret bal'lot s scrutin m secret
secrete [sɪ'krit] tr cacher; (physiol) sécréter
secretive [sɪ'kritɪv] adj cachottier
se'cret serv'ice s deuxième bureau m
sect [sekt] s secte f
sectarian [sek'teri·ən] adj sectaire; (school) confessionnel || s sectaire mf
section ['sekʃən] s section f
sectionalism ['sekʃənə,lɪzəm] s régionalisme m
sec'tion hand' s cantonnier m
sector ['sektər] s secteur m; (instrument) compas m de proportion
secular ['sekjələr] adj (worldly, of this world) séculier; (century-old) séculaire || s séculier m
secularism ['sekjələ,rɪzəm] s laïcisme m, mondanité f
secure [sɪ'kjur] adj sûr || tr obtenir; (to make fast) fixer
securi·ty [sɪ'kjurɪti] s (pl -ties) sécurité f; (pledge) garantie f; (person) garant m; **securities** valeurs fpl
sedan [sɪ'dæn] s (aut) conduite f intérieure
sedan' chair' s chaise f à porteurs
sedate [sɪ'det] adj calme, discret
sedation [sɪ'deʃən] s sédation f
sedative ['sedatɪv] adj & s sédatif m
sedentary ['sedən,teri] adj sédentaire
sedge [sedʒ] s (Carex) laîche f
sediment ['sedɪmənt] s sédiment m
sedition [sɪ'dɪʃən] s sédition f
seditious [sɪ'dɪʃəs] adj séditieux
seduce [sɪ'd(j)us] tr séduire
seducer [sɪ'd(j)usər] s séducteur m
seduction [sɪ'dʌkʃən] s séduction f
seductive [sɪ'dʌktɪv] adj séduisant
sedulous ['sedʒələs] adj assidu
see [si] s (eccl) siège m || v (pret saw [sɔ]; pp seen [sin]) tr voir; **see other side** (turn the page) voir au dos; **to see s.o. play, to see s.o. playing** voir jouer qn, voir qn qui joue; **to see s.th. played** voir jouer q.ch. || intr voir; **to see through s.o.** (fig) voir venir qn
seed [sid] s graine f, semence f; sperme

m; (in fruit) pépin m; (fig) germe m; **to go to seed** monter en graine || tr semer, ensemencer
seed'bed' s semis m
seeder ['sidər] s (mach) semeuse f
seedling ['sidlɪŋ] s semis m
seed·y ['sidi] adj (comp -ier; super -iest) (coll) râpé, miteux
seeing ['si·ɪŋ] adj voyant || s vue f || conj vu que
See'ing Eye' dog' s chien m d'aveugle
seek [sik] v (pret & pp sought [sɔt]) tr chercher || intr chercher; **to seek after** rechercher; **to seek to** chercher à
seem [sim] intr sembler
seemingly ['simɪŋli] adv en apparence
seem·ly ['simli] adj (comp -lier; super -liest) gracieux; (correct) bienséant
seep [sip] intr suinter
seer [sɪr] s prophète m, voyant m
see'saw' s balançoire f, bascule f; (motion) va-et-vient m || intr basculer, balancer
seethe [sið] intr bouillonner
segment ['segmənt] s segment m
segregate ['segrɪ,get] tr mettre à part, isoler
segregation [,segrɪ'geʃən] s ségrégation f
segregationist [,segrɪ'geʃənɪst] s ségrégationniste m
seismograph ['saɪzmə,græf], ['saɪzmə,graf] s sismographe m
seismology [saɪz'malədʒi] s sismologie f
seize [siz] tr saisir
seizure ['siʒər] s prise f; (law) saisie f; (pathol) attaque f
seldom ['seldəm] adv rarement
select [sɪ'lekt] adj choisi || tr choisir, sélectionner
selection [sɪ'lekʃən] s sélection f
selective [sɪ'lektɪv] adj sélectif
self [self] adj de même || s (pl selves [selvz]) moi m, être m; **all by one's self** tout seul; **one's better self** notre meilleur côté || pron—**payable to self** payable à moi-même
self'-addressed en'velope s enveloppe f adressée à l'envoyeur
self'-cen'tered adj égocentrique
self'-con'fidence s confiance f en soi
self'-con'fident adj sûr de soi
self'-con'scious adj gêné, embarrassé
self'-control' s sang-froid m, maîtrise f de soi
self'-defense' s autodéfense f; **in self-defense** en légitime défense
self'-deni'al s abnégation f
self'-deter'mina'tion s autodétermination f
self'-dis'cipline s discipline f personnelle
self'-ed'ucated adj autodidacte
self'-employed' adj indépendant
self'-esteem' s amour-propre m
self'-ev'ident adj évident aux yeux de tout le monde
self'-explan'ator'y adj qui s'explique de soi-même
self'-gov'ernment s autonomie f; maîtrise f de soi

self'-impor'tant adj suffisant, présomptueux

self'-indul'gence s faiblesse f envers soi-même, intempérance f

self'-in'terest s intérêt m personnel

selfish ['sɛlfɪʃ] adj égoïste

selfishness ['sɛlfɪʃnɪs] s égoïsme m

selfless ['sɛlflɪs] adj désintéressé

self'-love' s égoïsme m

self'-made man' s (pl men') fils m de ses œuvres

self'-por'trait s autoportrait m

self'-possessed' adj maître de soi

self'-pres'erva'tion s conservation f de soi-même

self'-reli'ant adj sûr de soi, assuré

self'-respect'ing adj correct, honorable

self'-right'eous adj pharisaïque

self'-sac'rifice' s abnégation f

self'-same' adj identique

self'-sat'isfied' adj content de soi

self'-seek'ing adj égoïste, intéressé

self'-serv'ice s libre-service m

self'-serv'ice laun'dry s (pl -dries) laverie f libre-service, laverie automatique

self'-start'er s démarreur m automatique

self'-styled' adj soi-disant

self'-taught' adj autodidacte

self'-tim'er s (phot) retardateur m

self'-willed' adj obstiné, entêté

self'-wind'ing adj à remontage automatique

sell [sɛl] v (pret & pp **sold** [sold]) tr vendre; **to sell out** solder; (to betray) vendre || intr vendre; **to sell for** (e.g., ten dollars) se vendre à

seller ['sɛlər] s vendeur m

Selt'zer wa'ter ['sɛltsər] s eau f de Seltz

selvage ['sɛlvɪdʒ] s (of fabric) lisière f; (of lock) gâche f

semantic [sɪ'mæntɪk] adj sémantique || **semantics** s sémantique f

semaphore ['sɛmə,for] s sémaphore m

semblance ['sɛmbləns] s semblant m

semen ['simɛn] s sperme m, semence f

semester [sɪ'mɛstər] adj semestriel || s semestre m

semicircle ['sɛmɪ,sʌrkəl] s demi-cercle m

semicolon ['sɛmɪ,kolən] s point-virgule m

semiconductor [,sɛmɪkən'dʌktər] s semi-conducteur m

semiconscious [,sɛmɪ'kɑnʃəs] adj à demi conscient

semifinal [,sɛmɪ'faɪnəl] adj avant-dernière || s demi-finale f

semilearned [,sɛmɪ'lʌrnɪd] adj à moitié savant

seminar ['sɛmɪ,nɑr] s séminaire m

seminar·y ['sɛmɪ,nɛri] s (pl -ies) séminaire m

semiprecious [,sɛmɪ'prɛʃəs] adj fin, semi-précieux

Semite ['sɛmaɪt], ['simaɪt] s Sémite mf

Semitic [sɪ'mɪtɪk] adj (e.g., language) sémitique; (person) sémite

semitrailer ['sɛmɪ,trɛlər] s semi-remorque f

senate ['sɛnɪt] s sénat m

senator ['sɛnətər] s sénateur m

send [sɛnd] v (pret & pp **sent** [sɛnt]) tr envoyer; (rad, telv) émettre; **to send back** renvoyer; **to send out** envoyer; **to send s.o. for s.th.** or **s.o.** envoyer qn chercher q.ch. or qn; **to send s.o. to** + inf envoyer qn + inf || intr (rad, telv) émettre; **to send for** envoyer chercher

sender ['sɛndər] s expéditeur m; (telg) transmetteur m

send'-off' s manifestation f d'adieu

senile ['sinaɪl], ['sɪnɪl] adj sénile

senility [sɪ'nɪlɪti] s sénilité f

senior ['sinjər] adj (clerk, partner, etc.) principal; (rank) supérieur; père, e.g., **Maurice Laporte, Senior** Maurice Laporte père || s aîné m, doyen m; (U.S. upperclassman) étudiant m de dernière année

sen'ior cit'izens spl les vieilles gens fpl

seniority [sin'jɑrɪti], [sin'jɔrɪti] s ancienneté f, doyenneté f

sen'ior staff' s personnel m hors classe

sensation [sɛn'seʃən] s sensation f

sensational [sɛn'seʃənəl] adj sensationnel

sense [sɛns] s sens m; (wisdom) bon sens; (e.g., of pain) sensation f; **to make sense out of** arriver à comprendre || tr percevoir, sentir

senseless ['sɛnslɪs] adj (lacking perception) insensible; (unconscious) sans connaissance; (unreasonable) insensé

sense' of guilt' s remords m

sense' or'gans spl organes mpl des sens

sensibili·ty [,sɛnsɪ'bɪlɪti] s (pl -ties) sensibilité f; susceptibilité f

sensible ['sɛnsɪbəl] adj sensible; (endowed with good sense) sensé, raisonnable

sensitive ['sɛnsɪtɪv] adj sensible; (touchy) susceptible, sensible

sensitize ['sɛnsɪ,taɪz] tr sensibiliser

sensory ['sɛnsəri] adj sensoriel

sensual ['sɛnʃʊ·əl] adj sensuel

sensuous ['sɛnʃʊ·əs] adj sensuel

sentence ['sɛntəns] s (gram) phrase f; (law) sentence f || tr condamner

sentiment ['sɛntɪmənt] s sentiment m

sentimental [,sɛntɪ'mɛntəl] adj sentimental

sentinel ['sɛntɪnəl] s sentinelle f; **to stand sentinel** être en sentinelle

sen·try ['sɛntri] s (pl -tries) sentinelle f

sen'try box' s guérite f

separate ['sɛpərɪt] adj séparé || ['sɛpə,ret] tr séparer || intr se séparer

separation [,sɛpə'reʃən] s séparation f

September [sɛp'tɛmbər] s septembre m

septic ['sɛptɪk] adj septique

sepulcher ['sɛpəlkər] s sépulcre m

sequel ['sikwəl] s conséquence f; (something following) suite f

sequence ['sikwəns] s succession f, ordre m; (cards, mov) séquence f; (of tenses) (gram) concordance f

sequester [sɪ'kwɛstər] tr séquestrer

sequin ['sikwɪn] s paillette f

ser·aph ['sɛrəf] s (pl **-aphs** or **-aphim** [əfɪm]) séraphin m

Serb [sʌrb] adj serbe || s Serbe mf

sere [sɪr] adj sec, desséché

serenade ['ˌsɛrə'ned] s sérénade f || tr donner une sérénade à || intr donner des sérénades

serene [sɪ'rin] adj serein

serenity [sɪ'rɛntɪ] s sérénité f

serf [sʌrf] s serf m

serfdom ['sʌrfdəm] s servage m

serge [sʌrdʒ] s serge f

sergeant ['sʌrdʒənt] s sergent m

ser'geant-at-arms' s (pl **sergeants-at-arms**) huissier m, sergent m d'armes

ser'geant ma'jor s (pl **sergeant majors**) sergent-major m

serial ['sɪrɪ·əl] adj de série || s roman-feuilleton m

serially ['sɪrɪ·əli] adv en série; (in installments) en feuilleton

se'rial num'ber s numéro m d'ordre; (mil) numéro m matricule

se·ries ['sɪriz] s (pl **-ries**) série f; **in series** en série

serious ['sɪrɪ·əs] adj sérieux

seriousness ['sɪrɪ·əsnɪs] s sérieux m, gravité f

sermon ['sʌrmən] s sermon m

sermonize ['sʌrməˌnaɪz] tr & intr sermonner

serpent ['sʌrpənt] s serpent m

se·rum ['sɪrəm] s (pl **-rums** or **-ra** [rə]) sérum m

servant ['sʌrvənt] s domestique mf; (civil servant) fonctionnaire mf; (housemaid) bonne f; (humble servant) (fig) serviteur m

serv'ant girl' s servante f

serv'ant prob'lem s crise f domestique

serve [sʌrv] tr servir; **to serve s.o. as** servir à qn de; **to serve time** purger une peine || intr servir; **to serve as** (to function as) servir de; (to be useful for) servir à

service ['sʌrvɪs] s service m; (eccl) office m; **the services** (mil) les forces fpl armées || tr entretenir, réparer

serviceable ['sʌrvɪsəbəl] adj utile, pratique; résistant

serv'ice club' s foyer m du soldat

serv'ice·man' s (pl **-men'**) réparateur m; (mil) militaire m

serv'ice rec'ord s état m de service

serv'ice sta'tion s station-service f

serv'ice stripe' s chevron m, galon m

servile ['sʌrvɪl] adj servile

servitude ['sʌrvɪˌt(j)ud] s servitude f

sesame ['sɛsəmi] s sésame m; **open sesame!** sésame, ouvre-toi!

session ['sɛʃən] s session f; **to be in session** siéger

set [sɛt] adj (rule) établi; (price) fixe; (time) fixé; (smile; locution) figé || s ensemble m; (of dishes, linen, etc.) assortiment m; (of dishes) service m; (of kitchen utensils) batterie f; (of pans; of weights; of tickets) série f; (of tools, chessmen, oars, etc.) jeu m; (of books) collection f; (of diamonds) parure f; (of tennis)

set m; (of cement) prise f; (of a garment) tournure f; (group of persons) coterie f; (mov) plateau m; (rad) poste m; (theat) mise f en scène; **set of false teeth** dentier m; **set of teeth** denture f || v (pret & pp set; ger setting) tr mettre, placer, poser; (a date, price, etc.) fixer; (a gem) monter; (a trap) tendre; (a timepiece) mettre à l'heure, régler; (the hair) mettre en plis; (a bone) remettre; **to set aside** mettre de côté; annuler; **to set going** mettre en marche; **to set off** mettre en valeur; (e.g., a rocket) lancer, tirer || intr se figer; (said of sun, moon, etc.) se coucher; (said of hen) couver; (said of garment) tomber; **to set about, to set out to** se mettre à; **to set upon** attaquer

set'back' s revers m, échec m

set'screw' s vis f de pression

settee [sɛ'ti] s canapé m; (for two) canapé à deux places, causeuse f

setting ['sɛtɪŋ] s cadre m; (of a gem) monture f; (of cement) prise f; (of sun) coucher m; (of a bone) recollement m; (of a watch) réglage m; (adjustment) ajustage m; (theat) mise f en scène

set'ting-up' ex'ercises spl gymnastique f rythmique, gymnastique suédoise

settle ['sɛtəl] tr établir; (a region) coloniser; (a dispute, account, debt, etc.) régler; (a problem) résoudre; (doubts, fears, etc.) calmer || intr se coloniser; se calmer; (said of weather) se mettre au beau; (said of building) se tasser; (said of sediment, dust, etc.) se déposer; (said of liquid) se clarifier; **to settle down** s'établir; (to be less wild) se ranger; **to settle down to** (a task) s'appliquer à; **to settle on** se décider pour

settlement ['sɛtəlmənt] s établissement m, colonie f; (of an account, dispute, etc.) règlement m; (of a debt) liquidation f; (settlement house) œuvre f sociale

settler ['sɛtlər] s colon m

set'up' s port m, maintien m; (of the parts of a machine) installation f; (coll) organisation f

seven ['sɛvən] adj & pron sept || s sept m; **seven o'clock** sept heures

seventeen ['sɛvən'tin] adj, pron, & s dix-sept

seventeenth ['sɛvən'tinθ] adj & pron dix-septième (masc, fem); **the Seventeenth** dix-sept, e.g., **John the Seventeenth** Jean dix-sept || s dix-septième m; **the seventeenth** (in dates) le dix-sept

seventh ['sɛvənθ] adj & pron septième (masc, fem); **the Seventh** sept, e.g., **John the Seventh** Jean sept || s septième m; **the seventh** (in dates) le sept

seventieth ['sɛvəntɪ·ɪθ] adj & pron soixante-dixième (masc, fem) || s soixante-dixième m

seven·ty ['sɛvənti] adj & pron soixante-dix || s (pl **-ties**) soixante-dix m

sev'enty-first' adj & pron soixante et onzième (masc, fem) ‖ s soixante et onzième m

sev'enty-one' adj, pron, & s soixante et onze m

sever ['sevər] tr séparer; (relations) rompre ‖ intr se séparer

several ['sevərəl] adj & pron indef plusieurs

severance ['sevərəns] s séparation f; (of relations) rupture f; (of communications) interruption f

sev'erance pay' s indemnité f pour cause de renvoi

severe [sɪ'vɪr] adj sévère; (weather) rigoureux; (pain) aigu; (illness) grave

sew [so] v (pret sewed; pp sewed or sewn) tr & intr coudre

sewage ['s(j)uːdʒ] s eaux fpl d'égouts

sewer ['s(j)uːər] s égout m ‖ ['soːər] s (one who sews) couseur m

sewerage ['s(j)uːərɪdʒ] s (removal) vidange f; (system) système m d'égouts; (sewage) eaux fpl d'égouts

sew'ing bas'ket s nécessaire m de couture

sew'ing machine' s machine f à coudre

sex [seks] s sexe m; **the fair sex** le beau sexe; **the sterner sex** le sexe fort; **to have sex with** (coll) avoir des rapports avec

sex' appeal' s sex-appeal m

sextant ['sekstənt] s sextant m

sextet [seks'tet] s sextuor m

sexton ['sekstən] s sacristain m

sexual ['sek/uːəl] adj sexuel

sex·y ['seksi] adj (comp -ier; super -iest) (slang) aguichant, grivois; (story) érotique

sh [ʃ] interj chut!

shab·by ['ʃæbi] adj (comp -bier; super -biest) râpé, usé; (mean) mesquin; (house) délabré

shack [ʃæk] s cabane f, case f

shackle ['ʃækəl] s boucle f; **shackles** entraves fpl ‖ tr entraver

shad [ʃæd] s alose f

shade [ʃed] s ombre f; (of lamp) abatjour m; (of window) store m; (hue; slight difference) nuance f; (little bit) soupçon m ‖ tr ombrager; (to make gradual changes in) nuancer

shadow ['ʃædo] s ombre f ‖ tr ombrager; (to spy on) filer, pister

shad'ow gov'ernment s gouvernement m fantôme

shadowy ['ʃædo·i] adj ombreux, sombre; (fig) vague, obscur

shad·y ['ʃedi] adj (comp -ier; super -iest) ombreux, ombragé; (coll) louche

shaft [ʃæft], [ʃɑft] s (of mine; of elevator) puits m; (of feather) tige f; (of arrow) bois m; (of column) fût m, tige f; (of flag) mât m; (of wagon) brancard m, limon m; (of motor) arbre m; (of light) rayon m; (to make fun of s.o.) trait m

shag·gy ['ʃægi] adj (comp -gier; super -giest) poilu, à longs poils

shag'gy dog' sto'ry s (pl -ries) histoire f sans queue ni tête

shake [ʃek] s secousse f ‖ v (pret shook [ʃʊk]; pp shaken) tr secouer; (the head) hocher, secouer; (one's hand) serrer; **to shake down** faire tomber; (a thermometer) secouer; (slang) escroquer; **to shake off** secouer; (to get rid of) se débarrasser de; **to shake up** (a liquid) agiter, (fig) ébranler ‖ intr trembler

shake'down' s (slang) exaction f, concussion f

shaker ['ʃekər] s (for salt) salière f; (for cocktails) shaker m

shake'up' s bouleversement m; (reorganization) remaniement m

shak·y ['ʃeki] adj (comp -ier; super -iest) tremblant, chancelant; (hand; writing) tremblé; (voice) tremblotant

shall [ʃæl] v (cond should [ʃʊd]) aux used to express 1) the future indicative, e.g., **I shall arrive** j'arriverai; 2) the future perfect indicative, e.g., **I shall have arrived** je serai arrivé; 3) the potential mood, e.g., **what shall he do?** que doit-il faire?

shallow ['ʃælo] adj peu profond; (dish) plat; (fig) creux, superficiel ‖ **shallows** spl haut-fond m

sham [ʃæm] adj feint, simulé ‖ s feinte f, simulacre m; (person) imposteur m ‖ v (pret & pp shammed; ger shamming) tr & intr feindre, simuler

sham' bat'tle s combat m simulé

shambles ['ʃæmbəlz] spl boucherie f; ravage m, ruine f; (disorder) pagaille f

shame [ʃem] s honte f; **shame on you!**, **for shame!** quelle honte! **what a shame!** quel dommage! ‖ tr faire honte à

shame'faced' adj penaud

shameful ['ʃemfəl] adj honteux

shameless ['ʃemlɪs] adj éhonté

shampoo [ʃæm'pu] s shampooing m ‖ tr (the hair) laver; (a person) faire un shampooing à

shamrock ['ʃæmrɑk] s trèfle m d'Irlande

Shanghai ['ʃæŋhaɪ], [ʃæŋ'haɪ] s Changhaï ‖ (l.c.) tr (coll) racoler

Shangri-la [,ʃæŋgrɪ'lɑ] s le pays de Cocagne

shank [ʃæŋk] s jambe f, tibia m; (of horse) canon m; (of anchor) verge f; (culin) manche m; (of a column) fût m

shan·ty ['ʃænti] s (pl -ties) masure f, bicoque f

shan'ty·town' s bidonville m

shape [ʃep] s forme f; **in bad shape** (coll) mal en point; **out of shape** déformé ‖ tr former ‖ intr se former; **to shape up** prendre forme; avancer

shapeless ['ʃeplɪs] adj informe

shape·ly ['ʃepli] adj (comp -lier; super -liest) bien proportionné, bien fait, svelte

share [ʃer] s part f; (of stock in a company) action f ‖ tr partager ‖ intr— **to share in** prendre part à, participer à

sharecropper ['ʃer,krɑpər] s métayer m

share'hold'er s actionnaire mf

shark [ʃɑrk] s requin m; (swindler) escroc m; (slang) as m, expert m

sharp [ʃɑrp] adj aigu; (wind, cold, pain, fight, criticism, edge, trot, mind) vif; (knife) tranchant; (point, tongue) acéré; (slope) raide; (curve) prononcé; (turn) brusque; (photograph) net; (hearing) fin; (step, gait) rapide; (taste) piquant; (reprimand) vert; (keen) éveillé; (cunning) rusé, fin; (mus) dièse; (stylish) coll chic; **sharp features** traits mpl accentués || adv vivement; brusquement; précis, sonnant, tapant, tapant, **at four o'clock sharp** à quatre heures précises, sonnantes, or tapantes; **to stop short** s'arrêter net or pile || s (mus) dièse m || tr (mus) diéser

sharpen [ˈʃɑrpən] tr aiguiser; (a pencil) tailler || intr s'aiguiser

sharpener [ˈʃɑrpənər] s aiguisoir m

sharper [ˈʃɑrpər] s filou m, tricheur m

sharp'shoot'er s tireur m d'élite

shatter [ˈʃætər] tr fracasser, briser || intr se fracasser, se briser

shat'ter-proof' adj de sécurité

shave [ʃev] s—**to get a shave** se faire raser, se faire faire la barbe; **to have a close shave** (coll) l'échapper belle || tr (hair, beard, etc.) raser; (a person) faire la barbe à, raser; (e.g., wood) doler; (e.g., expenses) rogner || intr se raser, se faire la barbe

shaving [ˈʃevɪŋ] s rasage m; **shavings** rognures fpl, copeaux mpl

shav'ing brush' s blaireau m

shav'ing soap' s savon m à barbe

shawl [ʃɔl] s châle m, fichu m

she [ʃi] s femelle f || pron pers elle §85, §87; ce §82B; **she who** celle qui §83

sheaf [ʃif] s (pl **sheaves** [ʃivz]) gerbe f; (of papers) liasse f

shear [ʃɪr] s lame f de ciseau; **shears** ciseaux mpl; (to cut metal) cisaille f || v (pret **sheared**; pp **sheared** or **shorn** [ʃɔrn]) tr (sheep) tondre; (velvet) ciseler; (metal) cisailler; **to shear off** couper

sheath [ʃiθ] s (pl **sheaths** [ʃiðz]) gaine f, fourreau m

sheathe [ʃið] tr envelopper; (a sword) rengainer

shed [ʃed] s hangar m; (for, e.g., tools) remise f; (line from which water flows in two directions) ligne f de faîte || v (pret & pp **shed**; ger **shedding**) tr répandre, verser; (e.g., leaves) perdre; (e.g., light, skin) jeter

sheen [ʃin] s lustre m, brillant m

sheep [ʃip] s (pl **sheep**) mouton m; (ewe) brebis f

sheep'dog' s chien m de berger

sheep'fold' s bergerie f

sheepish [ˈʃipɪʃ] adj penaud; timide

sheep'skin' s (undressed) peau f de mouton; (dressed) basane f; (diploma) (coll) peau d'âne

sheep'skin jack'et s canadienne f

sheer [ʃɪr] adj transparent; léger; (stocking) extra-fin; (steep) à pic; (fig) pur; (fig) vif, e.g., **by sheer force** de vive force || intr faire une embardée

sheet [ʃit] s (e.g., for the bed) drap m; (of paper) feuille f; (of metal) tôle f, lame f; (of water) nappe f; (of ice) couche f; (naut) écoute f; **white as a sheet** blanc comme un linge

sheet' light'ning s fulguration f, éclairs mpl en nappe

sheet' met'al s tôle f

sheet' mu'sic s morceaux mpl de musique

sheik [ʃik] s cheik m; (coll) tombeur m de femmes

shelf [ʃelf] s (pl **shelves** [ʃelvz]) tablette f, planche f; (of cupboard; of library) rayon m; (geog) plateau m; **on the shelf** au rancart, laissé à l'écart

shell [ʃel] s coque f, coquille f; (of nut) écale f, coque; (of pea) cosse f; (of oyster, clam, etc.) écaille f; (of building, ship, etc.) carcasse f; (cartridge) cartouche f; (projectile) obus m; (long, narrow racing boat) yole f || tr écaler, écosser; (mil) bombarder, pilonner; **to shell out** (coll) débourser || intr—**to shell out** (coll) casquer

shel•lac [ʃəˈlæk] s laque f, gomme f laque || v (pret & pp -**lacked**; ger -**lacking**) tr laquer; (slang) tabasser

shell'fish' s fruits mpl de mer, coquillages mpl

shell' hole' s entonnoir m, trou m d'obus

shell' shock' s commotion f cérébrale

shelter [ˈʃeltər] s abri m || tr abriter

shelve [ʃelv] tr (a book) ranger; (merchandise) entreposer; (a project, a question, etc., by putting it aside) enterrer, classer; (to provide with shelves) garnir de tablettes, rayons, or planches

shepherd [ˈʃepərd] s berger m; (fig) pasteur m || tr veiller sur, guider

shep'herd dog' s berger m, chien m de berger

shepherdess [ˈʃepərdɪs] s bergère f

sherbet [ˈʃɑrbət] s sorbet m

sheriff [ˈʃerɪf] s shérif m

sher•ry [ˈʃeri] s (pl -ries) xérès m

shield [ʃild] s bouclier m; (elec) blindage m; (heral, hist) écu m, écusson m || tr protéger; (elec) blinder

shift [ʃɪft] s changement m; (in wind, temperature, etc.) saute f; (group of workmen) équipe f de relais; (fig) expédient m || tr changer; (the blame, the guilt, etc.) rejeter; **to shift gears** changer de vitesse || intr changer; changer de place; changer de direction; **to shift for oneself** se débrouiller tout seul

shift' key' s touche f majuscules

shiftless [ˈʃɪftlɪs] adj mollasse, peu débrouillard

shift•y [ˈʃɪfti] adj (comp -ier; super -iest) roublard; (look) chafouin; (eye) fuyant

shimmer [ˈʃɪmər] s chatoiement m, miroitement m || intr chatoyer, miroiter

shin [ʃɪn] s tibia m; (culin) jarret m ‖ v (pret & pp **shinned**; ger **shinning**) intr—**to shin up** grimper

shin′bone′ s tibia m

shine [ʃaɪn] s brillant m; (of cloth, clothing, etc.) luisant m; (on shoes) coup m de cirage; **to take a shine to** (slang) s'enticher de ‖ v (pret & pp **shined**) tr faire briller, faire reluire; (shoes) cirer ‖ v (pret & pp **shone** [ʃon]) intr briller, reluire

shiner [′ʃaɪnər] s (slang) œil m poché

shingle [′ʃɪŋgəl] s bardeau m; (of doctor, lawyer, etc.) (coll) enseigne f; **shingles** (pathol) zona m

shining [′ʃaɪnɪŋ] adj brillant, luisant

shin-y [′ʃaɪni] adj (comp -ier; super -iest) brillant, reluisant; (from much wear) lustré

ship [ʃɪp] s navire m; (steamer, liner) paquebot m; (aer) appareil m; (nav) bâtiment m ‖ v (pret & pp **shipped**; ger **shipping**) tr expédier; (a cargo; water) embarquer; (oars) armer, rentrer ‖ intr s'embarquer

ship′board′ s bord m; **on shipboard** à bord

ship′build′er s constructeur m de navires

ship′build′ing s construction f navale

ship′mate′ s compagnon m de bord

shipment [′ʃɪpmənt] s expédition f; (goods shipped) chargement m

ship′own′er s armateur m

shipper [′ʃɪpər] s expéditeur m

shipping [′ʃɪpɪŋ] s embarquement m, expédition f; (naut) transport m maritime

ship′ping clerk′ s expéditionnaire mf

ship′ping mem′o s connaissement m

ship′ping room′ s salle f d'expédition

ship′shape′ adj & adv en bon ordre

ship′s′ pa′pers spl papiers mpl de bord

ship′s′ time′ s heure f locale du navire

ship′-to-shore′ ra′di·o [′ʃɪptə′ʃor] s (pl -os) liaison f radio maritime

ship′wreck′ s naufrage m ‖ tr faire naufrager ‖ intr faire naufrage

ship′yard′ s chantier m de construction navale or maritime

shirk [ʃʌrk] tr manquer à, esquiver ‖ intr négliger son devoir

shirred′ eggs′ [ʃʌrd] spl œufs mpl pochés à la crème

shirt [ʃʌrt] s chemise f; **keep your shirt on!** (slang) ne vous emballez pas!; **to lose one's shirt** perdre jusqu'à son dernier sou

shirt′band′ s encolure f

shirt′ front′ s plastron m de chemise

shirt′ sleeve′ s manche f de chemise; **in shirt sleeves** en bras de chemise

shirt′tails′ spl pans mpl de chemise

shirt′waist′ s chemisier m

shiver [′ʃɪvər] s frisson m ‖ intr frissonner

shoal [ʃol] s banc m, bas-fond m

shock [ʃɑk] s (bump, clash) choc m, heurt m; (upset, misfortune; earthquake tremor) secousse f; (of grain) gerbe f, moyette f; (of hair) tignasse f; (elec) commotion f, choc; **to die of**

shock mourir de saisissement ‖ tr choquer; (elec) commotionner, choquer

shock′ absorb′er [æb′sɔrbər] s amortisseur m

shocking [′ʃɑkɪŋ] adj choquant, scandaleux

shock′ troops′ spl troupes fpl de choc

shod-dy [′ʃɑdi] adj (comp -dier; super -diest) inférieur, de pacotille

shoe [ʃu] s soulier m; **to be in the shoes of** être dans la peau de; **to put one's shoes on** se chausser; **to take one's shoes off** se déchausser ‖ v (pret & pp **shod** [ʃɑd]) tr chausser; (a horse) ferrer

shoe′black′ s cireur m de bottes

shoe′horn′ s chausse-pied m

shoe′lace′ s lacet m, cordon m de soulier

shoe′mak′er s cordonnier m

shoe′ pol′ish s cirage m de chaussures

shoe′shine′ s cirage m

shoe′ store′ s magasin m de chaussures

shoe′string′ s lacet m, cordon m de soulier; **on a shoestring** avec de minces capitaux

shoe′tree′ s embauchoir m, forme f

shoo [ʃu] tr chasser ‖ interj ch!, filez!

shoot [ʃut] s (sprout, twig) rejeton m, pousse f; (for grain, sand, etc.) goulotte f; (contest) concours m de tir; (hunting party) partie f de chasse ‖ v (pret & pp **shot** [ʃɑt]) tr tirer; (a person) tuer d'un coup de fusil; (to execute with a discharge of rifles) fusiller; (with a camera) photographier; (a scene; a motion picture) tourner, roder; (the sun) prendre la hauteur de; (dice) jeter; **to shoot down** abattre; **to shoot up** (slang) cribler de balles ‖ intr tirer; s'élancer, se précipiter; (said of pain) lanciner; (said of star) filer; **to shoot at** faire feu sur; (to strive for) viser; **to shoot up** (said of plant) pousser; (said of plant) pousser; (said of flame) jaillir; (said of prices) augmenter

shooting [′ʃutɪŋ] s tir m; (phot) prise f de vues

shoot′ing gal′ler·y s (pl -ies) stand m de tir, tir m

shoot′ing match′ s concours m de tir

shoot′ing script′ s découpage m

shoot′ing star′ s étoile f filante

shop [ʃɑp] s (store) boutique f; (workshop) atelier m; **to talk shop** parler boutique, parler affaires ‖ v (pret & pp **shopped**; ger **shopping**) intr faire des emplettes, faire des courses; magasiner (Canad); **to go shopping** faire des emplettes, faire des courses; **to shop around** être à l'affût de bonnes occasions; **to shop for** chercher à acheter

shop′girl′ s vendeuse f

shop′keep′er s boutiquier m

shoplifter [′ʃɑp,lɪftər] s voleur m à l'étalage

shopper [′ʃɑpər] s acheteur m

shopping [′ʃɑpɪŋ] s achat m; (purchases) achats mpl, emplettes fpl

shop'ping bag' s sac m à provisions

shop'ping cen'ter s centre m commercial

shop'ping dis'trict s quartier m commerçant

shop' stew'ard s délégué m d'atelier

shop'win'dow s vitrine f, devanture f

shop'worn' adj défraîchi

shore [ʃor] s rivage m, rive f, bord m; (sandy beach) plage f; **shores** (poetic) pays m ‖ tr—**to shore up** étayer

shore'bird' s oiseau m de marée

shore' leave' s (nav) descente f à terre

shore'line' s ligne f de côte

shore' patrol' s patrouille f de garde-côte; (police) (nav) police f militaire de la marine

short [ʃort] adj court; (person) petit; (temper) brusque; (phonet) bref; **in short** en somme; **short of breath** poussif; **to be short for** (coll) être le diminutif de; **to be short of** être à court de ‖ s (elec) court-circuit m; (mov) court-métrage m; **shorts** culotte f courte, culotte de sport ‖ adv court, de court; **to run short of** être à court de, manquer de; **to sell short** (com) vendre à découvert; **to stop short** s'arrêter net ‖ tr (elec) court-circuiter ‖ intr (elec) se mettre en court-circuit

shortage [ˈʃortɪdʒ] s manque m, pénurie f; crise f, e.g., **housing shortage** crise du logement; (com) déficit m; **shortages** manquants mpl

short'cake' s gâteau m recouvert de fruits frais m

short'-change' tr ne pas rendre assez de monnaie à; (to cheat) (coll) rouler

short' cir'cuit s court-circuit m

short'-cir'cuit tr court-circuiter

short'com'ing s défaut m

short'cut' s raccourci m

shorten [ˈʃortən] tr raccourcir ‖ intr se raccourcir

shortening [ˈʃortənɪŋ] s raccourcissement m; (culin) saindoux m

short'hand' adj sténographique ‖ s sténographie f; **to take down in shorthand** sténographier

short'hand notes' spl sténogramme m

short'hand typ'ist s sténodactylo mf

short-lived [ˈʃortˈlaɪvd], [ˈʃortˈlɪvd] adj de courte durée, bref

shortly [ˈʃortli] adv tantôt, sous peu; brièvement; (curtly) sèchement; **shortly after** peu après

short'-range' adj à courte portée

short' sale' s vente f à découvert

short'-sight'ed adj myope; **to be short-sighted** (fig) avoir la vue courte

short' sto'ry s nouvelle f, conte m

short'-tem'pered adj vif, emporté

short'-term' adj à court terme

short'wave' adj aux petites ondes, aux ondes courtes ‖ s petite onde f, onde courte

short' weight' s poids m insuffisant

shot [ʃat] adj (silk) changeant; (e.g., chances) (coll) réduit à zéro; (drunk) (slang) paf ‖ s coup m de feu, décharge f; (marksman) tireur m; (pel-

lets) petits plombs mpl; (of a rocket into space) lancement m, tir m; (in certain games) shoot m; (snapshot) instantané m; (mov) plan m; (hypodermic injection) (coll) piqûre f; (drink of liquor) (slang) verre m d'alcool; **a long shot** un gros risque, une chance sur mille; **to fire a shot at** tirer sur; **to start like a shot** partir comme un trait

shot'gun' s fusil m de chasse

shot'-put' s (sports) lancement m du poids

should [ʃʊd] aux used to express 1) the present conditional, e.g., **if I waited for him, I should miss the train** si je l'attendais, je manquerais le train; 2) the past conditional, e.g., **if I had waited for him, I should have missed the train** si je l'avais attendu, j'aurais manqué le train; 3) the potential mood, e.g., **he should go at once** il devrait aller aussitôt; e.g., **he should have gone at once** il aurait dû aller aussitôt; 4) a softened affirmation, e.g., **I should like a drink** je prendrais bien quelque chose à boire; e.g., **I should have thought that you would have known better** j'aurais cru que vous auriez été plus avisé

shoulder [ˈʃoldər] s épaule f; (of a road) accotement m; **across the shoulder** en bandoulière, en écharpe; **shoulders** (of a garment) carrure f ‖ tr (a gun) mettre sur l'épaule; **to shoulder aside** pousser de l'épaule

shoul'der blade' s omoplate f

shoul'der strap' s (of underwear) épaulette f; (mil) bandoulière f

shout [ʃaʊt] s cri m ‖ tr crier; **to shout down** huer ‖ intr crier

shove [ʃʌv] s poussée f, bourrade f ‖ tr pousser, bousculer ‖ intr pousser; **to shove off** pousser au large; (slang) filer, décamper

shov·el [ˈʃʌvəl] s pelle f ‖ v (pret & pp -eled or -elled; ger -eling or -elling) tr pelleter; (e.g., snow) balayer

show [ʃo] s exposition f; apparence f; (display) étalage m; (of hands) levée f; (each performance) séance f; (mov) film m; (theat) spectacle m; **to make a show of** faire parade de ‖ v (pret showed; pp shown [ʃon] or showed) tr montrer; (one's passport) présenter; (a film) projeter; (e.g., to the door) conduire; **to show off** faire étalage de; **to show up** (coll) démasquer ‖ intr se montrer; **to show through** transparaître; **to show up** (against a background) ressortir; (coll) faire son apparition

show' bill' s affiche f

show'boat' s bateau-théâtre m

show' busi'ness s l'industrie f du spectacle

show'case' s vitrine f

show'down' s cartes fpl sur table, moment m critique; **to come to a showdown** en venir au fait

shower [ˈʃaʊ·ər] s averse f, ondée f; (of blows, bullets, kisses, etc.) pluie *f*; (*bath*) douche *f* || *tr* faire pleuvoir; **to shower with** combler de || *intr* pleuvoir *à* verse

show′er bath′ *s* douche *f*

show′ girl′ *s* girl *f*

show′man *s* (*pl* **-men**) impresario *m*; **he′s a great showman** c'est un as pour la mise en scène

show′-off′ *s* (coll) m'as-tu-vu *m*

show′piece′ *s* pièce *f* maîtresse

show′place′ *s* lieu *m* célèbre

show′room′ *s* salon *m* d'exposition

show′ win′dow *s* vitrine *f*

show·y [′ʃo·i] *adj* (*comp* **-ier**; *super* **-iest**) fastueux; (*gaudy*) voyant

shrapnel [′ʃræpnəl] *s* shrapnel *m*, obus *m* à mitraille; éclat *m* d'obus

shred [ʃred] *s* morceau *m*, lambeau *m*; **not a shred of** pas l'ombre de; **to tear to shreds** mettre en lambeaux || *v* (*pret & pp* **shredded** or **shred**; *ger* **shredding**) *tr* mettre en lambeaux, déchiqueter

shrew [ʃru] *s* (*nagging woman*) mégère *f*; (zool) musaraigne *f*

shrewd [ʃrud] *adj* sagace, fin

shriek [ʃrik] *s* cri *m* perçant || *intr* pousser un cri perçant

shrike [ʃraik] *s* pie-grièche *f*

shrill [ʃril] *adj* aigu, perçant

shrimp [ʃrimp] *s* crevette *f*; (*insignificant person*) gringalet *m*

shrine [ʃrain] *s* tombeau *m* de saint; (*reliquary*) châsse *f*; (*holy place*) lieu *m* saint, sanctuaire *m*

shrink [ʃriŋk] *v* (*pret* **shrank** [ʃræŋk] or **shrunk** [ʃrʌŋk]; *pp* **shrunk** or **shrunken**) *tr* rétrécir || *intr* se rétrécir; **to shrink away** or **back from** reculer devant

shrinkage [′ʃriŋkidʒ] *s* rétrécissement *m*

shriv·el [′ʃrivəl] *v* (*pret & pp* **-eled** or **-elled**; *ger* **-eling** or **-elling**) *tr* ratatiner, recroqueviller || *intr* se ratatiner, se recroqueviller

shroud [ʃraud] *s* linceul *m*; (*veil*) voile *m*; **shrouds** (naut) haubans *mpl* || *tr* ensevelir; voiler

Shrove′ Tues′day [ʃrov] *s* mardi *m* gras

shrub [ʃrʌb] *s* arbuste *m*

shrubber·y [′ʃrʌbəri] *s* (*pl* **-ies**) bosquet *m*

shrug [ʃrʌg] *s* haussement *m* d'épaules || *v* (*pret & pp* **shrugged**; *ger* **shrugging**) *tr* (*one′s shoulders*) hausser; **to shrug off** minimiser; ne tenir aucun compte de || *intr* hausser les épaules

shudder [′ʃʌdər] *s* frisson *m*, frémissement *m* || *intr* frissonner, frémir

shuffle [′ʃʌfəl] *s* (*of cards*) battement *m*, mélange *m*; (*of feet*) frottement *m*; (*change of place*) déplacement *m* || *tr* (*cards*) battre; (*the feet*) traîner; (*to mix up*) mêler, brouiller || *intr* battre les cartes; traîner les pieds

shuf′fle-board′ *s* jeu *m* de palets

shun [ʃʌn] *v* (*pret & pp* **shunned**; *ger* **shunning**) *tr* éviter, fuir

shunt [ʃʌnt] *tr* garer, manœuvrer; (elec) shunter, dériver

shut [ʃʌt] *adj* fermé || *v* (*pret & pp* **shut**; *ger* **shutting**) *tr* fermer; **to shut in** enfermer; **to shut off** couper; **to shut up** enfermer; (coll) faire taire || *intr* se fermer; **shut up!** (slang) taistoi!, ferme-la!

shut′down′ *s* fermeture *f*

shutter [′ʃʌtər] *s* volet *m*, contrevent *m*; (*over store window*) rideau *m*; (phot) obturateur *m*

shuttle [′ʃʌtəl] *s* navette *f* || *intr* faire la navette

shut′tle train′ *s* navette *f*

shy [ʃai] *adj* (*comp* **shyer** or **shier**; *super* **shyest** or **shiest**) timide, sauvage; (*said of horse*) ombrageux; **I am shy a dollar** il me faut un dollar; **to be shy of** se méfier de || *v* (*pret & pp* **shied**) *intr* (*said of horse*) faire un écart; **to shy away** éviter

shyster [′ʃaistər] *s* (coll) avocat *m* marron

Sia·mese [ˌsai·ə′miz] *adj* siamois || *s* (*pl* **-mese**) Siamois *m*

Si′amese twins′ *spl* frères *mpl* siamois

Siberian [sai′biri·ən] *adj* sibérien || *s* Sibérien *m*

sibyl [′sibil] *s* sibylle *f*

sic [sik], [sik] *adv* sic || [sik] *v* (*pret & pp* **sicked**; *ger* **sicking**) *tr*—**sic ′em!** (coll) pille!; **to sic on** lancer après

Sicilian [si′siljən] *adj* sicilien || *s* Sicilien *m*

Sicily [′sisili] *s* Sicile *f*; **la Sicile**

sick [sik] *adj* malade; **to be sick and tired of** (coll) en avoir plein le dos de, en avoir marre de; **to be sick at** or **to one′s stomach** avoir mal au cœur, avoir des nausées; **to take sick** tomber malade

sick′bed′ *s* lit *m* de malade

sicken [′sikən] *tr* rendre malade || *intr* tomber malade; (*to be disgusted*) être écœuré

sickening [′sikəniŋ] *adj* écœurant, dégoûtant

sick′ head′ache *s* migraine *f* avec nausées

sickle [′sikəl] *s* faucille *f*

sick′ leave′ *s* congé *m* de maladie

sick·ly [′sikli] *adj* (*comp* **-lier**; *super* **-liest**) maladif, débile

sickness [′siknis] *s* maladie *f*; nausée *f*

side [said] *adj* latéral, de côté || *s* côté *m*; (*of phonograph*) face *f*; (*of team, government, etc.*) camp *m*, parti *m*, côté; **this side up** (*on package*) haut || *intr*—**to side with** prendre le parti de

side′ arms′ *spl* armes *fpl* de ceinturon

side′board′ *s* buffet *m*, desserte *f*

side′burns′ *spl* favoris *mpl*

side′ dish′ *s* plat *m* d'accompagnement

side′ door′ *s* porte *f* latérale, porte *f* de service

side′ effect′ *s* effet *m* secondaire

side′ en′trance *s* entrée *f* latérale

side′ glance′ *s* regard *m* de côté

side′ is′sue *s* question *f* d'intérêt secondaire

side′line′ *s* occupation *f* secondaire; **on the sidelines** sans y prendre part

sidereal [saɪ'dɪrɪ-əl] *adj* sidéral
side' road' *s* chemin *m* de traverse
side' sad'dle *adv* en amazone
side' show' *s* spectacle *m* forain; (fig) événement *m* secondaire
side'slip' *s* glissade *f* sur l'aile
side'split'ting *adj* désopilant
side' step' *s* écart *m*
side'step' *v* (*pret* & *pp* **-stepped**; *ger* **-stepping**) *tr* éviter || *intr* faire un pas de côté
side'stroke' *s* nage *f* sur le côté
side'track' *s* voie *f* de garage || *tr* écarter, dévier; (rr) aiguiller sur une voie de garage
side' view' *s* vue *f* de profil
side'walk' *s* trottoir *m*
side'walk café' *s* terrasse *f* de café
sideward ['saɪdwərd] *adj* latéral || *adv* latéralement, de côté
side'ways' *adj* latéral || *adv* latéralement, de côté
side' whisk'ers *spl* favoris *mpl*
side'wise' *adj* latéral || *adv* latéralement, de côté
siding ['saɪdɪŋ] *s* (rr) voie *f* d'évitement, voie de garage
sidle ['saɪdəl] *intr* avancer de biais; **to sidle up to** se couler auprès de
siege [sidʒ] *s* siège *m*; **to lay siege to** mettre le siège devant
siesta [si'estə] *s* sieste *f*; **to take a siesta** faire la sieste
sieve [sɪv] *s* crible *m*, tamis *m* || *tr* passer au crible, au tamis
sift [sɪft] *tr* passer au crible, passer au tamis; (*flour*) tamiser; (fig) examiner soigneusement
sigh [saɪ] *s* soupir *m* || *intr* soupirer
sight [saɪt] *s* vue *f*; (*of firearm*) mire *f*; (*of telescope, camera, etc.*) viseur *m*; chose *f* digne d'être vue; **a sight of** (coll) énormément de; **at sight** à vue; à livre ouvert; **by sight** de vue; **in sight of** à la vue de; **sad sight** spectacle *m* navrant; **sights** curiosités *fpl*; **to catch sight of** apercevoir; **what a sight you are!** comme vous voilà fait! || *tr* & *intr* viser
sight' draft' *s* (com) effet *m* à vue
sight'-read' *v* (*pret* & *pp* **-read** [ˌred]) *tr* & *intr* lire à livre ouvert; (mus) déchiffrer
sight' read'er *s* déchiffreur *m*
sight'see'ing *s* tourisme *m*; **to go sightseeing** visiter les curiosités
sightseer ['saɪtˌsi·ər] *s* touriste *mf*, excursionniste *mf*
sign [saɪn] *s* signe *m*; (*on a store*) enseigne *f* || *tr* signer; **to sign up** engager, embaucher || *intr* signer; **to sign off** (rad) terminer l'émission; **to sign up for** (coll) s'inscrire à
sig·nal ['sɪgnəl] *adj* signalé, insigne || *s* signal *m* || *v* (*pret* & *pp* **-naled** or **-nalled**; *ger* **-naling** or **-nalling**) *tr* faire signe à, signaler || *intr* faire des signaux
sig'nal tow'er *s* tour *f* de signalisation
signature ['sɪgnətʃər] *s* signature *f*; (mus) armature *f*; (rad) indicatif *m*
sign'board' *s* panneau *m* d'affichage

signer ['saɪnər] *s* signataire *mf*
sig'net ring' ['sɪgnɪt] *s* chevalière *f*
significance [sɪg'nɪfɪkəns] *s* importance *f*; (*meaning*) signification *f*
significant [sɪg'nɪfɪkənt] *adj* important; significatif
signi·fy ['sɪgnɪˌfaɪ] *v* (*pret* & *pp* **-fied**) *tr* signifier
sign'post' *s* poteau *m* indicateur
silence ['saɪləns] *s* silence *m* || *tr* faire taire, réduire au silence
silent ['saɪlənt] *adj* silencieux
si'lent mov'ie *s* film *m* muet
silhouette [ˌsɪlu'et] *s* silhouette *f* || *tr* silhouetter
silicon ['sɪlɪkən] *s* silicium *m*
silicone ['sɪlɪˌkon] *s* silicone *f*
silk [sɪlk] *s* soie *f*
silk'-cotton tree' *s* fromager *m*
silken ['sɪlkən] *adj* soyeux
silk' hat' *s* haut-de-forme *m*
silk'-stock'ing *adj* aristocratique || *s* aristocrate *mf*
silk'worm' *s* ver *m* à soie
silk·y ['sɪlki] *adj* (*comp* **-ier**; *super* **-iest**) soyeux
sill [sɪl] *s* (*of window*) rebord *m*; (*of door*) seuil *m*; (*of walls*) sablière *f*
sil·ly ['sɪli] *adj* (*comp* **-lier**; *super* **-liest**) sot, niais
si·lo ['saɪlo] *s* (*pl* **-los**) silo *m* || *tr* ensiler
silt [sɪlt] *s* vase *f*
silver ['sɪlvər] *s* argent *m* || *tr* argenter; (*a mirror*) étamer
sil'ver·fish' *s* (ent) poisson *m* d'argent
sil'ver foil' *s* feuille *f* d'argent
sil'ver lin'ing *s* beau côté *m*, côté brillant
sil'ver plate' *s* argenterie *f*
sil'ver screen' *s* écran *m*
sil'ver·smith' *s* orfèvre *m*
sil'ver spoon' *s*—**born with a silver spoon in one's mouth** né coiffé
sil'ver-tongued' *adj* à la langue dorée, éloquent
sil'ver·ware' *s* argenterie *f*
similar ['sɪmɪlər] *adj* semblable
similari·ty [ˌsɪmɪ'lærɪti] *s* (*pl* **-ties**) ressemblance *f*, similitude *f*
simile ['sɪmɪli] *s* comparaison *f*
simmer ['sɪmər] *tr* mijoter || *intr* mijoter; **to simmer down** s'apaiser
Simon ['saɪmən] *s* Simon *m*; **Simon says . . .** (game) Caporal a dit . . .
simper ['sɪmpər] *s* sourire *m* niais || *intr* sourire bêtement
simple ['sɪmpəl] *adj* & *s* simple *m*
sim'ple-mind'ed *adj* simple, naïf; niais
simpleton ['sɪmpəltən] *s* niais *m*
simpli·fy ['sɪmplɪˌfaɪ] *v* (*pret* & *pp* **-fied**) *tr* simplifier
simulate ['sɪmjəˌlet] *tr* simuler
simultaneous [ˌsaɪməl'teni·əs], [ˌsɪməl'teni·əs] *adj* simultané
sin [sɪn] *s* péché *m* || *v* (*pret* & *pp* **sinned**; *ger* **sinning**) *intr* pécher
since [sɪns] *adv* & *prep* depuis || *conj* depuis que; (*inasmuch as*) puisque
sincere [sɪn'sɪr] *adj* sincère
sincerity [sɪn'serɪti] *s* sincérité *f*
sine [saɪn] *s* (trig) sinus *m*

sinecure ['saɪnɪˌkjur], ['sɪnɪˌkjur] *s* sinécure *f*

sinew ['sɪnju] *s* tendon *m*; (fig) nerf *m*, force *f*

sinful ['sɪnfəl] *adj* (*person*) pécheur; (*act, intention*) coupable

sing [sɪŋ] *v* (*pret* **sang** [sæŋ] *or* **sung** [sʌŋ]; *pp* **sung**) *tr* & *intr* chanter

singe [sɪndʒ] *v* (*ger* **singeing**) *tr* roussir; (*poultry*) flamber

singer ['sɪŋər] *s* chanteur *m*

single ['sɪŋgəl] *adj* seul, unique; (*unmarried*) célibataire; (*e.g., room in a hotel*) à un lit; (*bed*) à une place; (*e.g., devotion*) simple, honnête ‖ *tr* —**to single out** distinguer, choisir

sin'gle bless'edness ['blɛsɪdnɪs] *s* le bonheur *m* du célibat

sin'gle-breast'ed *adj* droit

sin'gle-en'try *adj* (bk) en partie simple

sin'gle-en'try book'keeping *s* comptabilité *f* simple

sin'gle file' *s*—**in single file** en file indienne, à la file

sin'gle-hand'ed *adj* sans aide, tout seul

sin'gle life' *s* vie *f* de célibataire

sin'gle room' *s* chambre *f* à un lit

sin'gle-track' *adj* (rr) à voie unique; (coll) d'une portée limitée

sing'song' *adj* monotone ‖ *s* mélopée *f*

singular ['sɪŋgjələr] *adj* & *s* singulier *m*

sinister ['sɪnɪstər] *adj* sinistre

sink [sɪŋk] *s* évier *m*; (*drain*) égout *m* ‖ *v* (*pret* **sank** [sæŋk] *or* **sunk** [sʌŋk]; *pp* **sunk**) *tr* enfoncer; (*a ship*) couler, faire sombrer; (*a well*) creuser; (*money*) immobiliser ‖ *intr* s'enfoncer; s'affaisser; (*under the water*) couler, sombrer; (*said of heart*) se serrer; (*said of health, prices, sun, etc.*) baisser; **to sink into** plonger dans; (*an armchair*) s'effondrer dans

sink'ing fund' *s* caisse *f* d'amortissement

sinless ['sɪnlɪs] *adj* sans péché

sinner ['sɪnər] *s* pécheur *m*

sintering ['sɪntərɪŋ] *s* (metallurgy) frittage *m*

sinuous ['sɪnjuˌəs] *adj* sinueux

sinus ['saɪnəs] *s* sinus *m*

sip [sɪp] *s* petite gorgée *f*, petit coup *m* ‖ *v* (*pret* & *pp* **sipped**; *ger* **sipping**) *tr* boire à petit coups, siroter

siphon ['saɪfən] *s* siphon *m* ‖ *tr* siphonner

si'phon bot'tle *s* siphon *m*

sir [sʌr] *s* monsieur *m*; (*British title*) Sir *m*; **Dear Sir** Monsieur

sire [saɪr] *s* sire *m*; (*of a quadruped*) père *m* ‖ *tr* engendrer

siren ['saɪrən] *s* sirène *f*

sirloin ['sʌrlɔɪn] *s* aloyau *m*

sirup ['sɪrəp], ['sʌrəp] *s* sirop *m*

sis·sy ['sɪsi] *s* (*pl* **-sies**) efféminé *m*; fillette *f*; (*cowardly fellow*) poule *f* mouillée

sister ['sɪstər] *adj* (fig) jumeau ‖ *s* sœur *f*

sis'ter-in-law' *s* (*pl* **sisters-in-law**) belle-sœur *f*

sit [sɪt] *v* (*pret* & *pp* **sat** [sæt]; *ger* **sitting**) *intr* s'asseoir; être assis; (*said*

of hen on eggs) couver; (*for a portrait*) poser; (*said of legislature, court, etc.*) siéger; **to sit down** s'asseoir; **to sit still** ne pas bouger; **to sit up** se redresser; se tenir droit; **to sit up and beg** (*said of dog*) faire le beau

sit'-down strike' *s* grève *f* sur le tas

site [saɪt] *s* site *m*

sitting ['sɪtɪŋ] *s* séance *f*

sit'ting duck' *s* (coll) cible *f* facile

sit'ting room' *s* salon *m*

situate ['sɪtʃuˌet] *tr* situer

situation [ˌsɪtʃuˈeʃən] *s* situation *f*; poste *m*, emploi *m*

sitz' bath' [sɪts] *s* bain *m* de siège

six [sɪks] *adj* & *pron* six ‖ *s* six *m*; **at sixes and sevens** de travers, en désaccord; **six o'clock** six heures

sixteen ['sɪks'tin] *adj, pron,* & *s* seize *m*

sixteenth ['sɪks'tinθ] *adj* & *pron* seizième (*masc, fem*); **the Sixteenth** seize, e.g., **John the Sixteenth** Jean seize ‖ *s* seizième *m*; **the sixteenth** (*in dates*) le seize

sixth [sɪksθ] *adj* & *pron* sixième (*masc, fem*); **the Sixth** six, e.g., **John the Sixth** Jean six ‖ *s* sixième *m*; **the sixth** (*in dates*) le six

sixtieth ['sɪkstɪˌtθ] *adj* & *pron* soixantième (*masc, fem*) ‖ *s* soixantième *m*

six·ty ['sɪksti] *adj* & *pron* soixante; **about sixty** une soixantaine de ‖ *s* (*pl* **-ties**) soixante *m*; (*age of*) soixantaine *f*

sizable ['saɪzəbəl] *adj* assez grand, considérable

size [saɪz] *s* grandeur *f*; dimensions *fpl*; (*of a person or garment*) taille *f*; (*of a shoe, glove, or hat*) pointure *f*; (*of a shirt collar*) encolure *f*; (*of a book or box*) format *m*; (*to fill a porous surface*) apprêt *m*; **what size hat do you wear?** de combien coiffez-vous?; **what size shoes do you wear?** du combien chaussez-vous? ‖ *tr* classer; (*wood to be painted*) coller; **to size up** juger

sizzle ['sɪzəl] *s* grésillement *m* ‖ *intr* grésiller

skate [sket] *s* patin *m*; (ichth) raie *f*; **good skate** (slang) brave homme *m* ‖ *intr* patiner; **to go skating** faire du patin

skat'ing rink' *s* patinoire *f*

skein [sken] *s* écheveau *m*

skeleton ['skɛlɪtən] *s* squelette *m*

skel'eton key' *s* crochet *m*

skeptic ['skɛptɪk] *adj* & *s* sceptique *mf*

skeptical ['skɛptɪkəl] *adj* sceptique

skepticism ['skɛptɪˌsɪzəm] *s* scepticisme *m*

sketch [skɛtʃ] *s* esquisse *f*; (*pen or pencil drawing*) croquis *m*, esquisse; (lit) aperçu *m*; (theat) sketch *m* ‖ *tr* esquisser ‖ *intr* croquer

sketch'book' *s* album *m* de croquis

skew [skju] *adj* & *s* biais *m* ‖ *intr* biaiser

skewer ['skjuˌər] *s* brochette *f* ‖ *tr* embrocher

ski [ski] *s* ski *m* ‖ *intr* skier; **to go skiing** faire du ski

ski′ boots′ *spl* chaussures *fpl* de ski

skid [skɪd] *s* (*sidewise*) dérapage *m*; (*forward*) patinage *m*; (*of wheel*) sabot *m*, patin *m* ‖ *v* (*pret & pp* skidded; *ger* skidding) *tr* enrayer, bloquer ‖ *intr* (*sidewise*) déraper; (*forward*) patiner

skid′ row′ [ro] *s* quartier *m* mal famé

skier [′skɪ·ər] *s* skieur *m*

skiff [skɪf] *s* skiff *m*, esquif *m*

skiing [′skɪ·ɪŋ] *s* ski *m*

ski′ jack′et *s* anorak *m*

ski′ jump′ *s* (*place to jump*) tremplin *m*; (*act of jumping*) saut *m* en skis

ski′ lift′ *s* remonte-pente *m*, téléski *m*

skill [skɪl] *s* habileté *f*, adresse *f*; (*job*) métier *m*

skilled *adj* habile, adroit

skillet [′skɪlɪt] *s* casserole *f*; (*frying pan*) poêle *f*

skillful [′skɪlfəl] *adj* habile, expert

skim [skɪm] *v* (*pret & pp* skimmed; *ger* skimming) *tr* (*milk*) écrémer; (*molten metal*) écumer; (*to graze*) raser ‖ *intr* —to skim over passer légèrement sur

ski′ mask′ *s* passe-montagne *m*

skimmer [′skɪmər] *s* écumoire *f*; (*straw hat*) canotier *m*

skim′ milk′ *s* lait *m* écrémé

skimp [skɪmp] *tr* bâcler ‖ *intr* lésiner; to skimp on lésiner sur

skimp·y [′skɪmpi] *adj* (*comp* -ier; *super* -iest) maigre; (*garment*) étriqué; avare, mesquin

skin [skɪn] *s* peau *f*; by the skin of one's teeth de justesse, par un cheveu; soaked to the skin trempé jusqu'aux os; to strip to the skin se mettre à poil ‖ *v* (*pret & pp* skinned; *ger* skinning) *tr* écorcher, dépouiller; (*e.g., an elbow*) s'écorcher; to skin alive (coll) écorcher vif

skin′-deep′ *adj* superficiel; (*beauty*) à fleur de peau

skin′ div′er *s* plongeur *m* autonome

skin′flint′ *s* grippe-sou *m*

skin′ game′ *s* (slang) escroquerie *f*

skin′ graft′ing *s* greffe *f* cutanée, autoplastie *f*

skin·ny [′skɪni] *adj* (*comp* -nier; *super* -niest) maigre, décharné

skip [skɪp] *s* saut *m* ‖ *v* (*pret & pp* skipped; *ger* skipping) *tr* sauter; skip it! ça suffit!, laisse tomber!; to skip rope sauter à la corde ‖ *intr* sauter; to skip out or off filer

ski′ pole′ *s* bâton *m* de skis

skipper [′skɪpər] *s* patron *m* ‖ *tr* commander, conduire

skirmish [′skʌrmɪʃ] *s* escarmouche *f* ‖ *intr* escarmoucher

skirt [skʌrt] *s* jupe *f*; (*woman*) (slang) jupe ‖ *tr* côtoyer, longer; éviter

ski′ run′ *s* descente *f* en skis

ski′ stick′ *s* bâton *m* de skis

skit [skɪt] *s* sketch *m*

skittish [′skɪtɪʃ] *adj* capricieux; timide; (*e.g., horse*) ombrageux

skulduggery [skʌl′dʌgəri] *s* (coll) fourberie *f*, ruse *f*, cuisine *f*

skull [skʌl] *s* crâne *m*

skull′ and cross′bones *s* tibias *mpl* croisés et tête *f* de mort

skull′cap′ *s* calotte *f*

skunk [skʌŋk] *s* mouffette *f*; (*person*) (coll) salaud *m*

sky [skaɪ] *s* (*pl* skies) ciel *m*; to praise to the skies porter aux nues

sky′div′er *s* parachutiste *mf*

sky′div′ing *s* parachutisme *m*, saut *m* en chute libre

sky′lark′ *s* (*Alauda arvensis*) alouette *f*, alouette des champs ‖ *intr* (coll) batifoler

sky′light′ *s* lucarne *f*

sky′line′ *s* ligne *m* d'horizon; (*of city*) profil *m*

sky′rock′et *s* fusée *f* volante ‖ *intr* monter en flèche

sky′scrap′er *s* gratte-ciel *m*

slab [slæb] *s* (*of stone*) dalle *f*; (*slice*) tranche *f*

slack [slæk] *adj* lâche, mou; négligent ‖ *s* mou *m*; (*slowdown*) ralentissement *m*; slacks pantalon *m* ‖ *tr* relâcher; (*lime*) éteindre; to slack off larguer ‖ *intr*—to slack off or up se relâcher

slacken [′slækən] *tr* relâcher; (*to slow down*) ralentir ‖ *intr* se relâcher; ralentir

slacker [′slækər] *s* flemmard *m*; (mil) tire-au-flanc *m*, embusqué *m*

slack′ hours′ *spl* heures *fpl* creuses

slag [slæg] *s* scorie *f*

slake [slek] *tr* apaiser, étancher; (*lime*) éteindre

slalom [′slaləm] *s* slalom *m*

slam [slæm] *s* claquement *m*; (cards) chelem *m*; (coll) critique *f* sévère ‖ *v* (*pret & pp* slammed; *ger* slamming) *tr* claquer; (coll) éreinter; to slam down on flanquer sur ‖ *intr* claquer

slander [′slændər] *s* calomnie *f* ‖ *tr* calomnier

slanderous [′slændərəs] *adj* calomnieux

slang [slæŋ] *s* argot *m*

slant [slænt] *s* pente *f*; (*bias*) point *m* de vue ‖ *tr* mettre en pente, incliner; donner un biais spécial à ‖ *intr* être en pente, s'incliner

slap [slæp] *s* tape *f*, claque *f*; (*in the face*) soufflet *m*, gifle *f* ‖ *v* (*pret & pp* slapped; *ger* slapping) *tr* taper, gifler

slap′dash′ *adj*—in a slapdash manner à la va-comme-je-te-pousse ‖ *adv* à la six-quatre-deux

slap′stick′ *adj* bouffon ‖ *s* bouffonnerie *f*

slash [slæʃ] *s* entaille *f* ‖ *tr* taillader; (*e.g., prices*) réduire beaucoup

slat [slæt] *s* latte *f*

slate [slet] *s* ardoise *f*; (*of candidates*) liste *f* ‖ *tr* couvrir d'ardoises; inscrire sur la liste, désigner

slate′ pen′cil *s* crayon *m* d'ardoise

slate′ roof′ *s* toit *m* d'ardoises

slattern [′slætərn] *s* (*slovenly woman*) marie-salope *f*; (*slut*) voyoute *f*, gueuse *f*

slaughter [′slɔtər] *s* boucherie *f* ‖ *tr* abattre; massacrer

slaught′er·house′ s abattoir m
Slav [slav], [slæv] adj slave ∥ s (language) slave m; (person) Slave mf
slave [slev] adj & s esclave mf ∥ intr besogner, trimer
slave′ driv′er s (hist, fig) négrier m
slavery ['slevəri] s esclavage m; (institution of keeping slaves) esclavagisme m
slave′ ship′ s négrier m
slave′ trade′ s traite f des noirs
Slavic ['slɑvɪk], ['slævɪk] adj & s slave m
slavish ['slevɪʃ] adj servile
slay [sle] v (pret slew [slu]; pp slain [slen]) tr tuer, massacrer
slayer ['sle·ər] s meurtrier m
sled [slɛd] s luge f ∥ v (pret & pp sledded; ger sledding) intr faire de la luge, luger
sledge′ ham′mer [slɛdʒ] s massette f, masse f
sleek [slik] adj lisse, luisant ∥ tr lisser
sleep [slip] s sommeil m; to go to sleep s'endormir; to put to sleep endormir ∥ v (pret & pp slept [slɛpt]) tr—to sleep it over, to sleep on it prendre conseil de son oreiller; to sleep off (a hangover, headache, etc.) faire passer en dormant ∥ intr dormir; (e.g., with a woman) coucher; to sleep late faire la grasse matinée; to sleep like a log dormir comme un loir
sleeper ['slipər] s dormeur m; (girder) poutre f horizontale; (tie) (rr) traverse f
sleep′ing bag′ s sac m de couchage
sleep′ing car′ s wagon-lit m
sleep′ing pill′ s somnifère m
sleepless ['slɪplɪs] adj sans sommeil
sleep′less night′ s nuit f blanche
sleep′walk′er s somnambule mf
sleep·y ['slipi] adj (comp -ier; super -iest) endormi, somnolent; to be sleepy avoir sommeil
sleep′y·head′ s endormi m, grand dormeur m
sleet [slit] s grésil m ∥ intr grésiller
sleeve [sliv] s manche f; (mach) manchon m, douille f; to laugh in or up one's sleeve rire sous cape
sleigh [sle] s traîneau m ∥ intr aller en traîneau
sleigh′ bell′ s grelot m
sleigh′ ride′ s promenade f en traîneau
sleight′ of hand′ [slaɪt] s prestidigitation f, tours mpl de passe-passe
slender ['slɛndər] adj svelte, mince, élancé; (resources) maigre
sleuth [sluθ] s limier m, détective m
slew [slu] s (coll) tas m, floppée f
slice [slaɪs] s tranche f ∥ tr trancher
slick [slɪk] adj lisse; (appearance) élégant; (coll) rusé ∥ s tache f, e.g., **oil slick** tache d'huile ∥ tr lisser; to **slick up** (coll) mettre en ordre
slicker ['slɪkər] s ciré m, imper m; (coll) enjôleur m
slide [slaɪd] s (sliding) glissade f, glissement m; (sliding place) glissoire m; (of microscope) plaque f; (of trombone) coulisse f; (on a slide rule)

curseur m; (piece that slides) glissière f; (phot) diapositive f ∥ v (pret & pp slid [slɪd]) tr glisser ∥ intr glisser; **to let slide** ne faire aucun cas de, laisser aller
slide′ fas′tener s fermeture f éclair
slide′ rule′ s règle f à calcul
slide′ valve′ s soupape f à tiroir
slid′ing con′tact s curseur m
slid′ing door′ s porte f à coulisse
slid′ing scale′ s échelle f mobile
slight [slaɪt] adj léger; (slender; insignificant) mince; (e.g., effort) faible ∥ s affront m ∥ tr faire peu de cas de, dédaigner; (a person) méconnaître
slim [slɪm] adj (comp slimmer; super slimmest) mince, svelte; (chance, excuse) mauvais; (resources) maigre
slime [slaɪm] s limon m, vase f; (of snakes, fish, etc.) bave f
slim·y ['slaɪmi] adj (comp -ier; super -iest) limoneux, vaseux
sling [slɪŋ] s (to shoot stones) fronde f; (to hold up a broken arm) écharpe f; (shoulder strap) bretelle f, bandoulière f ∥ v (pret & pp slung [slʌŋ]) tr—**to sling** lancer; passer en bandoulière
sling′shot′ s fronde f
slink [slɪŋk] v (pret & pp slunk [slʌŋk]) intr—**to slink away** s'esquiver
slip [slɪp] s glissade f, glissement m; bout m de papier; (for indexing, etc.) fiche f; (cutting from plant) bouture f; (piece of underclothing) combinaison f; (blunder) faux pas m, bévue f; (naut) cale f; **to give the slip to** échapper à ∥ v (pret & pp slipped; ger slipping) tr glisser; **to slip off** (a garment) enlever, ôter; **to slip on** (a garment, shoes, etc.) enfiler; **to slip one's mind** sortir de l'esprit, échapper à qn ∥ intr glisser; (blunder) faire un faux pas; **to let slip** laisser échapper; **to slip away** or **off** s'échapper, se dérober; **to slip by** s'échapper; (said of time) s'écouler; **to slip up** se tromper
slip′cov′er s housse f
slipper ['slɪpər] s pantoufle f
slippery ['slɪpəri] adj glissant; (deceitful) rusé
slip′-up′ s (coll) erreur f, bévue f
slit [slɪt] s fente f, fissure f ∥ v (pret & pp slit; ger slitting) tr fendre; (e.g., pages) couper; **to slit the throat of** égorger
slob [slɑb] s (slang) rustaud m
slobber ['slɑbər] s bave f; (fig) sentimentalité f ∥ intr baver
sloe [slo] s (shrub) prunellier m; (fruit) prunelle f
slogan ['slogən] s mot m d'ordre, devise f; (com) slogan m
sloop [slup] s sloop m
slop [slɑp] s lavure f, rinçure f ∥ v (pret & pp slopped; ger slopping) tr répandre ∥ intr se répandre; **to slop over** déborder
slope [slop] s pente f; (of a roof) inclinaison f; (of a region, mountain,

etc.) versant *m* ‖ *tr* pencher, incliner ‖ *intr* se pencher, s'incliner

slop·py ['slɑpi] *adj* (*comp* **-pier;** *super* **-piest**) mouillé; (*dress*) négligé, mal ajusté; (*work*) bâclé

slot [slɑt] *s* entaille *f*, rainure *f*; (*e.g.*, *in a coin telephone*) fente *f*

sloth [sloθ], [slɔθ] *s* paresse *f*; (*zool*) paresseux *m*

slot′ machine′ *s* (*for gambling*) appareil *m* à sous; (*for vending*) distributeur *m* automatique

slouch [slaʊtʃ] *s* démarche *f* lourde; (*person*) lourdaud *m* ‖ *intr* ne pas se tenir droit; (*e.g.*, *in a chair*) se vautrer; **to slouch along** traîner le pas

slouch′ hat′ *s* chapeau *m* mou

slough [slaʊ] *s* bourbier *m* ‖ [slʌf] (*of snake*) dépouille *f*; (*pathol*) escarre *f* ‖ *tr*—**to slough off** se débarrasser de ‖ *intr* muer, se dépouiller

Slovak ['slovæk], [slo'væk] *adj* slovaque *s* (*language*) slovaque *m*; (*person*) Slovaque *mf*

sloven·ly ['slʌvənli] *adj* (*comp* **-lier;** *super* **-liest**) négligé, malpropre

slow [slo] *adj* lent; (*sluggish*) traînard; (*clock, watch*) en retard; (*in understanding*) lourdaud ‖ *adv* lentement ‖ *tr & intr* ralentir; **SLOW** (*public sign*) ralentir; **to slow down** ralentir

slow′ down′ *s* grève *f* perlée

slow′ mo′tion *s* ralenti *m*; **in slow motion** au ralenti, en ralenti

slow′poke′ *s* (*coll*) lambin *m*, traînard *m*

slug [slʌg] *s* (*used as coin*) jeton *m*; (*of linotype*) ligne-bloc *f*; (*zool*) limace *f*; (*blow*) (*coll*) bon coup *m*; (*drink*) (*coll*) gorgée *f* ‖ *v* (*pret & pp* **slugged;** *ger* **slugging**) *tr* (*coll*) flanquer un coup à

sluggard ['slʌgərd] *s* paresseux *m*

sluggish ['slʌgɪʃ] *adj* lent

sluice [slus] *s* canal *m*; (*floodgate*) écluse *f*; (*dam; flume*) bief *m*

sluice′ gate′ *s* vanne *f*

slum [slʌm] *s* bas quartiers *mpl* ‖ *v* (*pret & pp* **slummed;** *ger* **slumming**) *intr*—**to go slumming** aller visiter les taudis

slumber ['slʌmbər] *s* sommeil *m*, assoupissement *m* ‖ *intr* sommeiller

slum′ dwell′ing *s* taudis *m*

slump [slʌmp] *s* affaissement *m*; (*com*) crise *f*, baisse *f* ‖ *intr* s'affaisser; (*said of prices, stocks, etc.*) dégringoler, s'effondrer

slur [slʌr] *s* (*in pronunciation*) mauvaise articulation *f*; (*insult*) affront *m*; (*mus*) liaison *f*; **to cast a slur on** porter atteinte à ‖ *v* (*pret & pp* **slurred;** *ger* **slurring**) *tr* (*a sound, a syllable*) mal articuler; (*a person*) déprécier; (*mus*) lier; **to slur over** glisser sur

slush [slʌʃ] *s* fange *f*, boue *f* liquide; (*gush*) sensiblerie *f*

slut [slʌt] *s* chienne *f*; (*slovenly woman*) marie-salope *f*

sly [slaɪ] *adj* (*comp* **slyer or slier;** *super* **slyest or sliest**) rusé, sournois; (*mischievous*) espiègle, futé; **on the sly** furtivement, en cachette

smack [smæk] *s* claquement *m*; (*with the hand*) gifle *f*, claque *f*; (*trace, touch*) soupçon *m*; (*kiss*) (*coll*) gros baiser *m* ‖ *adv* en plein ‖ *tr* claquer ‖ *intr*—**to smack of** sentir; avoir un goût de

small [smɔl] *adj* petit §91; (*income*) modique; (*short in stature*) court; (*petty*) mesquin; (*typ*) minuscule

small′ arms′ *spl* armes *fpl* portatives

small′ beer′ *s* petite bière *f*; (*slang*) petite bière

small′ busi′ness *s* petite industrie *f*

small′ cap′ital *s* (*typ*) petite capitale *f*

small′ change′ *s* petite monnaie *f*, menue monnaie

small′ fry′ *s* menu fretin *m*

small′ intes′tine *s* intestin *m* grêle

small′-mind′ed *adj* mesquin, étriqué, étroit

small′ of the back′ *s* chute *f* des reins, bas *m* du dos

smallpox ['smɔl,pɑks] *s* variole *f*

small′ print′ *s* petits caractères *mpl*

small′ talk′ *s* ragots *mpl*, papotage *m*

small′-time′ *adj* de troisième ordre, insignifiant, petit

small′-town′ *adj* provincial

smart [smart] *adj* intelligent, éveillé; (*pace*) vif; (*person, clothes*) élégant, chic; (*pain*) cuisant; (*saucy*) impertinent *s* douleur *f* cuisante ‖ *intr* brûler, cuire; (*said of person with hurt feelings*) être cinglé

smart′ al′eck [,ælɪk] *s* (*coll*) fat *m*, présomptueux *m*

smart′ set′ *s* monde *m* élégant, gens *mpl* chic

smash [smæʃ] *s* fracassement *m*, fracas *m*; (*coll*) succès *m* ‖ *tr* fracasser ‖ *intr* se fracasser; **to smash into** emboutir, écraser

smash′ hit′ *s* (*coll*) succès *m*, (*coll*) pièce *f* à succès

smash′-up′ *s* collision *f*; débâcle *f*, culbute *f*

smattering ['smætərɪŋ] *s* légère connaissance *f*, teinture *f*

smear [smɪr] *s* tache *f*; (*vilification*) calomnie *f*; (*med*) frottis *m* ‖ *tr* tacher; calomnier; (*to coat*) enduire

smear′ campaign′ *s* campagne *f* de calomnies

smell [smɛl] *s* odeur *f*; (*aroma*) parfum *m*, senteur *f*; (*sense*) odorat *m* ‖ *v* (*pret & pp* **smelled** or **smelt** [smɛlt]) *tr & intr* sentir; **to smell of** sentir

smell′ing salts′ *spl* sels *m* volatils

smell·y ['smɛli] *adj* (*comp* **-ier;** *super* **-iest**) malodorant, puant

smelt [smɛlt] *s* (*fish*) éperlan *m* ‖ *tr & intr* fondre

smile [smaɪl] *s* sourire *m* ‖ *intr* sourire; **to smile at** sourire à

smirk [smʌrk] *s* minauderie *f* ‖ *intr* minauder

smite [smaɪt] *v* (*pret* **smote** [smot]; *pp* **smitten** ['smɪtən] or **smit** [smɪt]) *tr* frapper; **to smite down** abattre

smith [smɪθ] *s* forgeron *m*

smith·y ['smɪθi] *s* (*pl* -ies) forge *f*

smitten ['smɪtən] *adj* frappé, affligé; (coll) épris, amoureux

smock [smɑk] *s* blouse *f*; (*of artists*) sarrau *m*; (*buttoned in back*) tablier *m*

smock' frock' *s* sarrau *m*

smog [smɑg] *s* (coll) brouillard *m* fumeux

smoke [smok] *s* fumée *f*; (coll) cigarette *f*; **to go up in smoke** s'en aller en fumée ‖ *tr & intr* fumer

smoked' glass'es *spl* verres *mpl* fumés

smoke'-filled room' *s* tabagie *f*

smoke'-less pow'der ['smoklɪs] *s* poudre *f* sans fumée

smoker ['smokər] *s* fumeur *m*; (*room*) fumoir *m*; (*meeting*) réunion *f* de fumeurs; (rr) compartiment *m* pour fumeurs

smoke' rings' *spl* ronds *mpl* de fumée

smoke' screen' *s* rideau *m* de fumée

smoke'stack' *s* cheminée *f*

smoking ['smokɪŋ] *s* le fumer *m*; **no smoking** (*public sign*) défense de fumer

smok'ing car' *s* voiture *f* de fumeurs

smok'ing jack'et *s* veston *m* d'intérieur

smok'ing room' *s* fumoir *m*

smok·y ['smoki] *adj* (*comp* -ier; *super* -iest) fumeux, enfumé

smolder ['smoldər] *s* fumée *f* épaisse; feu *m* qui couve ‖ *intr* brûler sans flamme; (*said of fire, anger, rebellion, etc.*) couver

smooch [smutʃ] *intr* (coll) se bécoter

smooth [smuð] *adj* uni, lisse; (*gentle, mellow*) doux, moelleux; (*operation*) doux, régulier; (*style*) facile ‖ *tr* unir, lisser; **to smooth away** (e.g., *obstacles*) aplanir, enlever; **to smooth down** (*to calm*) apaiser, calmer; **to smooth out** défroisser

smooth'-faced' *adj* imberbe

smooth-shaven ['smuð'ʃevən] *adj* rasé de près

smooth·y ['smuði] *s* (*pl* -ies) (coll) chatteuse *f*, flagorneur *m*

smother ['smʌðər] *tr* suffoquer, étouffer; (culin) recouvrir

smudge [smʌdʒ] *s* tache *f*; (*smoke*) fumée *f* épaisse ‖ *tr* tacher; (agr) fumiger

smudge' pot' *s* fumigène *m*

smug [smʌg] *adj* (*comp* **smugger**; *super* **smuggest**) fat, suffisant

smuggle ['smʌgəl] *tr* introduire en contrebande, faire la contrebande de ‖ *intr* faire la contrebande

smuggler ['smʌglər] *s* contrebandier *m*

smuggling ['smʌglɪŋ] *s* contrebande *f*

smut [smʌt] *s* tache *f* de suie; (*obscenity*) ordure *f*; (agr) nielle *f*

smut·ty ['smʌti] *adj* (*comp* -tier; *super* -tiest) taché de suie, noirci; (*obscene*) ordurier; (agr) niellé

snack [snæk] *s* casse-croûte *m*; **to have a snack** casser la croûte

snack' bar' *s* snack-bar *m*, snack *m*

snag [snæg] *s* (*of tree; of tooth*) chicot *m*; **to hit a snag** se heurter à un obstacle ‖ *v* (*pret & pp* **snagged**; *ger* **snagging**) *tr* (*a stocking*) faire un accroc à

snail [snel] *s* escargot *m*; **at a snail's pace** à pas de tortue, comme un escargot

snake [snek] *s* serpent *m* ‖ *intr* serpenter

snake' in the grass' *s* serpent *m* caché sous les fleurs; ami *m* perfide, traître *m*, individu *m* louche

snap [snæp] *s* (*breaking*) cassure *f*; (*crackling sound*) bruit *m* sec; (*of the fingers*) chiquenaude *f*; (*bite*) coup *m* de dents; (*cookie*) biscuit *m* croquant; (*catch or fastener*) bouton-pression *m*, fermoir *m*; (phot) instantané *m*; (slang) jeu *m* d'enfant, coup facile; **cold snap** coup *m* de froid; **it's a snap!** (slang) c'est du tout cuit! ‖ *v* (*pret & pp* **snapped**; *ger* **snapping**) *tr* casser net; (*one's fingers, a whip, etc.*) faire claquer; (*a picture, a scene*) prendre un instantané de; **to snap up** happer, saisir ‖ *intr* casser net; faire un bruit sec; (*from fatigue*) s'effondrer; **to snap at** donner un coup de dents à; (*speak sharply to*) rembarrer; (*an opportunity*) saisir; **to snap out of it** (slang) se secouer; **to snap shut** se fermer avec un bruit sec

snap' course' *s* (slang) cours *m* tout mâché

snap'drag'on *s* (bot) gueule-de-loup *f*

snap' fas'tener *s* bouton-pression *m*

snap' judg'ment *s* décision *f* prise sans réflexion

snap·py ['snæpi] *adj* (*comp* -pier; *super* -piest) mordant, acariâtre; (*quick, sudden*) vif; **make it snappy!** (slang) grouillez-vous!

snap'shot' *s* instantané *m*

snare [sner] *s* collet *m*; (*trap*) piège *m*; (*of a drum*) timbre *m*, corde *f* de timbre ‖ *tr* prendre au collet, prendre au piège

snare' drum' *s* caisse *f* claire

snarl [snɑrl] *s* (*sound*) grognement *m*; (*intertwining*) enchevêtrement *m* ‖ *tr* dire en grognant; enchevêtrer ‖ *intr* grogner; s'enchevêtrer

snatch [snætʃ] *s* arrachement *m*; petit moment *m*; (*bit, scrap*) bribe *f*, fragment *m*; (*in weight lifting*) arraché *m* ‖ *tr* saisir brusquement, arracher; **to snatch from** arracher à; **to snatch up** ramasser vivement ‖ *intr*—**to snatch at** saisir au vol

sneak [snik] *adj* furtif ‖ *s* chipeur *m*, mauvais type *m* ‖ *tr* (e.g., *a drink*) prendre à la dérobée; glisser furtivement; (coll) chiper ‖ *intr* se glisser furtivement; **to sneak into** se faufiler dans; **to sneak out** s'esquiver

sneaker ['snikər] *s* espadrille *f*

sneak' thief' *s* chipeur *m*, voleur *m* à la tire

sneak·y ['sniki] *adj* (*comp* -ier; *super* -iest) furtif, sournois

sneer [snɪr] *s* ricanement *m* ‖ *intr* ricaner; **to sneer at** se moquer de

sneeze [sniz] *s* éternuement *m* || *intr* éternuer; **it's not to be sneezed at** (coll) il ne faut pas cracher dessus

snicker ['snɪkər] *s* rire *m* bête; (*sneer*) rire narquois; (*in response to smut*) petit rire grivois || *intr* rire bêtement; **to snicker at** se moquer de

sniff [snɪf] *s* reniflement *m*; (*odor*) parfum *m*; (*e.g., of air*) bouffée *f* || *tr* renifler; (*e.g., fresh air*) humer; (*e.g., a scandal*) flairer; (*e.g., a scandal*) flairer || *intr* renifler; **to sniff up** renifler || *intr* renifler; **to sniff at** flairer; (*to disdain*) cracher sur

sniffle ['snɪfəl] *s* reniflement *m*; **to have the sniffles** être enchifrené || *intr* renifler

snip [snɪp] *s* (*e.g., of cloth*) petit bout *m*; (*cut*) coup *m* de ciseaux; (coll) personne *f* insignifiante || *v* (*pret & pp* **snipped**; *ger* **snipping**) *tr* couper; **to snip off** enlever, détacher

snipe [snaɪp] *s* (orn) bécassine *f* || *intr* —**to snipe at** canarder

sniper ['snaɪpər] *s* tireur *m* embusqué

snippet ['snɪpɪt] *s* petit bout *m*, bribe *f*; personne *f* insignifiante

snip·py ['snɪpi] *adj* (*comp* **-pier**; *super* **-piest**) hautain, brusque

snitch [snɪtʃ] *tr* (coll) chaparder || *intr* (coll) moucharder; **to snitch on** (coll) moucharder

sniv·el ['snɪvəl] *s* pleurnicherie *f*; (*mucus*) morve *f* || *v* (*pret & pp* **-eled** or **-elled**; *ger* **-eling** or **-elling**) *intr* pleurnicher; (*to have a runny nose*) être morveux

snob [snɑb] *s* snob *m*

snobbery ['snɑbəri] *s* snobisme *m*

snobbish ['snɑbɪʃ] *adj* snob

snoop [snup] *s* (coll) curieux *m* || *intr* (coll) fouiner, fureter

snoop·y ['snupi] *adj* (*comp* **-ier**; *super* **-iest**) (coll) curieux

snoot [snut] *s* (slang) nez *m*

snoot·y ['snuti] *adj* (*comp* **-ier**; *super* **-iest**) (slang) snob, hautain

snooze [snuz] *s* (coll) petit somme *m* || *intr* (coll) sommeiller

snore [snor] *s* ronflement *m* || *intr* ronfler

snort [snɔrt] *s* ébrouement *m*; (*of person, horse, etc.*) reniflement *m* || *tr* dire en reniflant, grogner || *intr* s'ébrouer, renifler bruyamment

snot [snɑt] *s* (slang) morve *f*

snot·ty ['snɑti] *adj* (*comp* **-tier**; *super* **-tiest**) (coll) morveux; (slang) snob, hautain

snout [snaʊt] *s* museau *m*; (*of pig*) groin *m*; (*of bull*) mufle *m*; (*something shaped like the snout of an animal*) bec *m*, tuyère *f*

snow [sno] *s* neige *f* || *intr* neiger; **it is snowing** il neige; **to shovel snow** balayer la neige

snow'ball' *s* boule *f* de neige || *tr* lancer des boules de neige à || *intr* faire boule de neige

snow'blind'ness *s* cécité *f* des neiges

snow'-capped' *adj* couronné de neige

snow'-clad' *adj* enneigé

snow'drift' *s* congère *f*

snow'fall' *s* chute *f* de neige; (*amount*) enneigement *m*

snow'flake' *s* flocon *m* de neige

snow' flur'ry *s* (*pl* **-ries**) bouffée *f* de neige

snow' line' *s* limite *f* des neiges éternelles

snow'man' *s* (*pl* **-men'**) bonhomme *m* de neige

snow'plow' *s* chasse-neige *m*

snow'shoe' *s* raquette *f*

snow'slide' *s* avalanche *f*

snow'storm' *s* tempête *f* de neige

snow' tire' *s* pneu *m* à neige

snow'white' *adj* blanc comme la neige || **Snowwhite** *s* Blanche-Neige *f*

snow·y ['sno-i] *adj* (*comp* **-ier**; *super* **-iest**) neigeux

snow'y owl' *s* chouette *f* blanche

snub [snʌb] *s* affront *m*, rebuffade *f* || *v* (*pret & pp* **snubbed**; *ger* **snubbing**) *tr* traiter avec froideur, rabrouer

snub·by ['snʌbi] *adj* (*comp* **-bier**; *super* **-biest**) trapu; (*nose*) camus

snub'-nosed' *adj* camard

snuff [snʌf] *s* tabac *m* à priser; (*of a candlewick*) mouchure *f*; **to be up to snuff** (to be shrewd) (slang) être dessalé; (to be up to par) (slang) être dégourdi || *tr* priser; (*a candle*) moucher; **to snuff out** éteindre

snuff'box' *s* tabatière *f*

snuffers ['snʌfərz] *spl* mouchettes *fpl*

snug [snʌg] *adj* (*comp* **snugger**; *super* **snuggest**) confortable; (*garment*) bien ajusté; (*bed*) douillet; (*sheltered*) abrité; (*hidden*) caché; **snug and warm** bien au chaud; **snug as a bug in a rug** comme un poisson dans l'eau

snuggle ['snʌgəl] *tr* serrer dans ses bras || *intr* se pelotonner; **to snuggle up to** se serrer tout près de

so [so] *adv* si, tellement; ainsi; donc, par conséquent, aussi; **or so** plus ou moins; **so as to** afin de, pour; **so far** jusqu'ici; **so long!** (coll) à bientôt!; **so many** tant; tant de; **so much** tant; tant de; **so that** pour que, afin que; de sorte que; **so to speak** pour ainsi dire; **so what?** (slang) et alors?; **to hope so** espérer bien; **to think so** croire que oui || *conj* (coll) de sorte que

soak [sok] *s* trempage *m*; (slang) sac *m* à vin, soûlard *m* || *tr* tremper; (slang) estamper; **to soak to the skin** tremper jusqu'aux os || *intr* tremper

so'-and-so' *s* (*pl* **-sos**) (pej) triste individu *m*, mauvais sujet *m*; **Mr. So-and-so** Monsieur un tel

soap [sop] *s* savon *m* || *tr* savonner

soap'box' *s* caisse *f* à savon; (fig) plateforme *f*

soap'box or'ator *s* orateur *m* de carrefour

soap' bub'ble *s* bulle *f* de savon

soap' dish' *s* plateau *m* à savon

soap' fac'to·ry *s* (*pl* **-ries**) savonnerie *f*

soap' flakes' *spl* savon *m* en paillettes

soap' op'era *s* mélo *m*

soap' pow'der *s* savon *m* en poudre

soap′stone′ *s* pierre *f* de savon; craie *f* de tailleur

soap′suds′ *spl* mousse *f* de savon, eau *f* de savon

soap-y ['sopi] *adj* (*comp* **-ier**; *super* **-iest**) savonneux

soar [sor] *intr* planer dans les airs; prendre l'essor, monter subitement

sob [sab] *s* sanglot *m* ∥ *v* (*pret & pp* **sobbed**; *ger* **sobbing**) *intr* sangloter

sober ['sobər] *adj* sobre; (*expression*) grave; (*truth*) simple; (*not drunk*) pas ivre; (*no longer drunk*) dégrisé ∥ *tr* calmer; **to sober up** dégriser ∥ *intr*— **to sober up** se dégriser

sobriety [so'braɪ-əti] *s* sobriété *f*

sob′ sis′ter *s* (slang) journaliste *f* larmoyante

sob′ sto′ry *s* (*pl* **-ries**) (slang) lamentation *f*, jérémiade *f*

so′-called′ *adj* dit; soi-disant, prétendu; ainsi nommé

soccer ['sakər] *s* football *m*

sociable ['soʃəbəl] *adj* sociable

social ['soʃəl] *adj* social ∥ *s* réunion *f* sans cérémonie

so′cial climb′er *s* parvenu *m*, arriviste *mf*

so′cial events′ *spl* mondanités *fpl*

socialism ['soʃə,lɪzəm] *s* socialisme *m*

socialist ['soʃəlɪst] *s* socialiste *mf*

socialite ['soʃə,laɪt] *s* (coll) membre *m* de la haute société

so′cial reg′ister *s* annuaire *m* de la haute société

so′cial secu′rity *s* sécurité *f* sociale, assistance *f* familiale

so′cial serv′ice *s* assistance *f* sociale, aide *f* sociale, aide familiale

so′cial stra′ta [,streɪtə], [,strætə] *s* couches *fpl* sociales

so′cial work′er *s* assistant *m* social, travailleuse *f* familiale

socie-ty [sə'saɪ-əti] *s* (*pl* **-ties**) société *f*

soci′ety col′umn *s* carnet *m* mondain

soci′ety ed′itor *s* chroniqueur *m* mondain

sociology [,sosɪ'aledʒi], [,soʃɪ'aledʒi] *s* sociologie *f*

sock [sak] *s* chaussette *f*; (slang) coup *m* de poing ∥ *tr* (slang) donner un coup de poing à

socket ['sakɪt] *s* (*of bone*) cavité *f*, glène *f*; (*of candlestick*) tube *m*; (*of caster*) sabot *m*; (*of eye*) orbite *f*; (*of tooth*) alvéole *m*; (elec) douille *f*

sock′et joint′ *s* joint *m* à rotule

sock′et wrench′ *s* clé *f* à tube

sod [sad] *s* gazon *m*; motte *f* de gazon ∥ *v* (*pret & pp* **sodded**; *ger* **sodding**) *tr* gazonner

soda ['sodə] *s* (*soda water*) soda *m*; (chem) soude *f*

so′da crack′er *s* biscuit *m* soda

so′da wa′ter *s* soda *m*

sodium ['sodɪ-əm] *s* sodium *m*

sofa ['sofə] *s* canapé *m*, sofa *m*

soft [sɔft], [saft] *adj* (*yielding*) mou; (*mild*) doux; (*weak in character*) faible; **to go soft** (coll) perdre la boule

soft′-boiled egg′ *s* œuf *m* à la coque

soft′ coal′ *s* houille *f* grasse

soft′ drink′ *s* boisson *f* non-alcoolisée

soften ['sɔfən], ['safən] *tr* amollir; (*e.g., noise*) atténuer; (*one's voice*) adoucir; (*one's moral fiber*) affaiblir; **to soften up** amollir ∥ *intr* s'amollir; s'adoucir; s'affaiblir

soft′ land′ing *s* (rok) arrivée *f* en douceur

soft′ ped′al *s* (mus) pédale *f* sourde

soft′-ped′al *v* (*pret & pp* **-aled** or **-alled**; *ger* **-aling** or **-alling**) *tr* (coll) atténuer, modérer

soft′ soap′ *s* savon *m* mou, savon noir; (coll) pommade *f*

soft′-soap′ *tr* (coll) passer de la pommade à

sog-gy ['sagi] *adj* (*comp* **-gier**; *super* **-giest**) saturé, détrempé

soil [sɔɪl] *s* sol *m*, terroir *m* ∥ *tr* salir, souiller ∥ *intr* se salir

soil′ pipe′ *s* tuyau *m* de descente

sojourn ['sodʒʌrn] *s* séjour *m* ∥ ['sodʒʌrn], [so'dʒʌrn] *intr* séjourner

solace ['salɪs] *s* consolation *f* ∥ *tr* consoler

solar ['solər] *adj* solaire

so′lar bat′tery *s* photopile *f*

sold [sold] *adj*—**sold out** (*no more room*) complet; (*no more merchandise*) épuisé; **to be sold on** (coll) raffoler de ∥ *interj* (*to the highest bidder*) adjugé!

solder ['sadər] *s* soudure *f* ∥ *tr* souder

sol′dering i′ron *s* fer *m* à souder

soldier ['soldʒər] *s* soldat *m*

sole [sol] *adj* seul, unique ∥ *s* (*of shoe*) semelle *f*; (*of foot*) plante *f*; (*fish*) sole *f* ∥ *tr* ressemeler

solemn ['saləm] *adj* sérieux, grave; (*ceremony*) solennel

solicit [sə'lɪsɪt] *tr* solliciter ∥ *intr* quêter; (*with immoral intentions*) racoler

solicitor [sə'lɪsɪtər] *s* solliciteur *m*; agent *m*, représentant *m*; (com) démarcheur *m*; (law) procureur *m*; (Brit) avoué *m*

solicitous [sə'lɪsɪtəs] *adj* soucieux

solid ['salɪd] *adj* solide; (*clouds*) dense; (*gold*) massif; (*opinion*) unanime; (*color*) uni; (*hour, day, week*) entier; (*e.g., three days*) d'affilée ∥ *s* solide *m*

sol′id geom′etry *s* géométrie *f* dans l'espace

solidity [sə'lɪdɪti] *s* solidité *f*, consistance *f*

sollio-quy [sə'lɪləkwi] *s* (*pl* **-quies**) soliloque *m*

solitaire ['salɪ,ter] *s* solitaire *m*; (cards) patience *f*, réussite *f*; **to play solitaire** faire une réussite

solitar-y ['salɪ,teri] *adj* solitaire ∥ *s* (*pl* **-ies**) solitaire *m*

solitude ['salɪ,t(j)ud] *s* solitude *f*

so-lo ['solo] *adj* solo ∥ *s* (*pl* **-los**) solo *m*

soloist ['solo-ɪst] *s* soliste *mf*

solstice ['salstɪs] *s* solstice *m*

soluble ['saljəbəl] *adj* soluble

solution [sə'luʃən] s solution f
solvable ['salvəbəl] adj soluble
solve [salv] tr résoudre
solvency ['salvənsi] s solvabilité f
solvent ['salvənt] adj (substance) solubilisant; (person or business) solvable || s (of a substance) solvant m
somber ['sambər] adj sombre
some [sʌm] adj indef quelque, du; **some way or other** d'une manière ou d'une autre || pron indef certains, quelques-uns §81; **en** §87 || adv un peu, passablement, assez; environ; quelque, e.g., **some two hundred soldiers** quelque deux cents soldats
some'bod'y pron indef quelqu'un §81; **somebody else** quelqu'un d'autre || s (pl -ies) quelqu'un m
some'day' adv un jour
some'how' adv dans un sens, je ne sais comment; **somehow or other** d'une manière ou d'une autre
some'one pron indef quelqu'un §81
somersault ['sʌmər,sɔlt] s saut m périlleux
some'thing s (coll) quelque chose m || pron indef quelque chose (masc) || adv quelque peu, un peu
some'time' adj ancien, ci-devant || adv un jour; un de ces jours
some'times' adv quelquefois, de temps en temps; **sometimes . . . sometimes** tantôt . . . tantôt
some'way' adv d'une manière ou d'une autre
some'what' adv un peu, assez
some'where' adv quelque part; **somewhere else** ailleurs, autre part
somnambulist [sam'næmbjəlist] s somnambule mf
somnolent ['samnələnt] adj somnolent
son [sʌn] s fils m
sonata [sə'natə] s sonate f
song [sɔŋ], [saŋ] s chanson f; (of praise) hymne m; **to buy for a song** (coll) acheter pour une bouchée de pain
song'bird' s oiseau m chanteur
song' book' s recueil m de chansons
Song' of Songs' s (Bib) Cantique m des Cantiques
song' thrush' s grive f musicienne
song'writ'er s chansonnier m
sonic ['sanɪk] adj sonique
son'ic boom' s double bang m
son'-in-law' s (pl **sons-in-law**) gendre m, beau fils m
sonnet ['sanɪt] s sonnet m
son-ny ['sʌni] s (pl -nies) fiston m
soon [sun] adv bientôt; (early) tôt; **as soon as** aussitôt que, dès que, sitôt que; **as soon as possible** le plus tôt possible; **how soon** quand; **no sooner said than done** sitôt dit sitôt fait; **soon after** tôt après; **sooner** plus tôt; (rather) (coll) plutôt; **sooner or later** tôt ou tard; **so soon** si tôt; **too soon** trop tôt
soot [sut], [sut] s suie f || tr—**to soot up** encrasser de suie || intr s'encrasser
soothe [suð] tr calmer, apaiser; flatter

soothsayer ['suθ,se·ər] s devin m
soot·y ['suti], ['suti] adj (comp -ier; super -iest) (color; flame) fuligineux; couvert de suie
sop [sap] s morceau x trempé; (fig) os m à ronger, cadeau m || v (pret & pp **sopped**; ger **sopping**) tr tremper, faire tremper; **to sop up** absorber
sophisticated [sə'fɪstɪ,ketɪd] adj mondain, sceptique; complexe
sophistication [sə,fɪstɪ'keʃən] s mondanité f
sophomore ['safə,mor] s étudiant m de deuxième année
sophomoric [,safə'mɔrɪk] adj naïf, suffisant, présomptueux
sopping ['sapɪŋ] adj détrempé, trempé || s—**sopping wet** trempé comme une soupe
soprano [sə'præno], [sə'prano] adj de soprano || s (pl -os) soprano f; (boy) soprano m
sorcerer ['sɔrsərər] s sorcier m
sorceress ['sɔrsərɪs] s sorcière f
sorcer·y ['sɔrsəri] s (pl -ies) sorcellerie f
sordid ['sɔrdɪd] adj sordide
sore [sor] adj douloureux, enflammé; (coll) fâché || s plaie f, ulcère m
sore'head' s (coll) rouspéteur m, grincheux m
sorely ['sorli] adv gravement, grièvement; cruellement
soreness ['sornɪs] s douleur f, sensibilité f
sore' throat' s—**to have a sore throat** avoir mal à la gorge
sorori·ty [sə'rarɪti], [sə'rɔrɪti] s (pl -ties) club m d'étudiantes universitaires
sorrow ['saro], ['sɔro] s chagrin m, peine f, affliction f, tristesse f || intr s'affliger, avoir du chagrin; être en deuil; **to sorrow for** s'affliger de
sorrowful ['sarəfəl], ['sɔrəfəl] adj (person) affligé, attristé; (news) affligeant
sor·ry ['sari], ['sɔri] adj (comp -rier; super -riest) désolé, navré, fâché; (appearance) piteux, misérable; (situation) triste; **to be or feel sorry** regretter; **to be or feel sorry for** regretter (q.ch.); plaindre (qn); **to be sorry to** + inf regretter de + inf || interj pardon!
sort [sɔrt] s sorte f, espèce f, genre m; **a sort of** une espèce de; **out of sorts** de mauvaise humeur || tr classer; **to sort out** trier
so'-so' adj (coll) assez bon, passable, supportable || adv assez bien, comme ci comme ça
sot [sat] s ivrogne mf
soul [sol] s âme f; **not a soul** (coll) pas un chat; **upon my soul!** par ma foi!
sound [saund] adj sain; solide, en bon état; (sleep) profond || s son m; (probe) sonde f; (geog) goulet m, détroit m, bras m de mer || adj (asleep) profondément || tr sonner; (to take a sounding of) sonder; **to sound out** sonder; **to sound the horn** klaxonner, corner || intr sonner; son-

der; **to sound off** parler haut; **to sound strange** sembler bizarre

sound' bar'rier *s* mur *m* du son

sound' film' *s* film *m* sonore

sound' hole' *s* (*of a violin*) ouïe *f*

soundly ['saundlɪ] *adj* sainement; profondément; (*hard*) bien

sound' post' *s* (*of a violin*) âme *f*

sound'proof' *adj* insonorisé, insonore ‖ *tr* insonoriser

sound' track' *s* piste *f* sonore

sound' wave' *s* onde *f* sonore

soup [sup] *s* potage *m*, bouillon *m*; (*with vegetables*) soupe *f*; **in the soup** (coll) dans le pétrin or la mélasse

soup' kitch'en *s* soupe *f* populaire

soup' spoon' *s* cuiller *f* à soupe

soup' tureen' *s* soupière *f*

sour [saur] *adj* aigre; (*grapes*) vert; (*apples*) sur; (*milk*) tourné ‖ *tr* rendre aigre ‖ *intr* tourner, s'aigrir

source [sors] *s* source *f*

source' lan'guage *s* langue *f* source

source' mate'rial *s* sources *fpl* originales

sour' cher'ry *s* (*pl* **-ries**) griotte *f*; (*tree*) griottier *m*

sour' grapes' *interj* ils sont trop verts!

sour'puss' *s* (slang) grincheux *m*

south [sauθ] *adj* & *s* sud *m*; **the South** (*of France, Italy, etc.*) le Midi; (*of U.S.A.*) le Sud ‖ *adv* au sud, vers le sud

South' Af'rica *s* la République sud-africaine

South' Amer'ica *s* Amérique *f* du Sud; l'Amérique du Sud

South' Amer'ican *adj* sud-américain ‖ *s* (*person*) Sud-Américain *m*

south'east' *adj* & *s* sud-est *m*

southern ['sʌðərn] *adj* du sud, méridional

southerner ['sʌðərnər] *s* Méridional *m*; (U.S.A.) sudiste *mf*

South' Kore'a *s* Corée *f* du Sud; la Corée du Sud

South' Kore'an *adj* sud-coréen ‖ *s* (*person*) Sud-Coréen *m*

south'paw' *adj* & *s* (coll) gaucher *m*

South' Pole' *s* pôle *m* Sud

South' Vietnam-ese' [vɪ͵ɛtnɑ'miz] *adj* sud-vietnamien ‖ *s* (*pl* **-ese**) Sud-Vietnamien *m*

southward ['sauθwərd] *adv* vers le sud

south'west' *adj* & *s* sud-ouest *m*

souvenir [͵suvə'nɪr] *s* souvenir *m*

sovereign ['savrɪn], ['savrɪn] *adj* souverain ‖ *s* (*king; coin*) souverain *m*; (*queen*) souveraine *f*

sovereign-ty ['savrɪntɪ], ['savrɪntɪ] *s* (*pl* **-ties**) souveraineté *f*

soviet ['sovɪ͵ɛt], [͵sovɪ'ɛt] *adj* soviétique ‖ *s* soviet *m*; **Soviet** (*person*) Soviétique *mf*

So'viet Rus'sia *s* la Russie *f* soviétique

So'viet Un'ion *s* Union *f* soviétique

sow [sau] *s* truie *f* ‖ [so] *v* (*pret* **sowed**; *pp* **sown** or **sowed**) *tr* (*seed; a field*) semer; (*a field*) ensemencer

soybean ['sɔɪ͵bin] *s* soya *m*, soja *m*

spa [spɑ] *s* ville *f* d'eau, station *f* thermale, bains *mpl*

space [spes] *s* espace *m*; (typ) espace *f* ‖ *tr* espacer

space' age' *s* âge *m* de l'exploration spatiale

space' bar' *s* barre *f* d'espacement

space'craft' *s* astronef *f*

space' flight' *s* voyage *m* spatial, vol *m* spatial

space' heat'er *s* chaufferette *f*

space' hel'met *s* casque *m* de cosmonaute

space'man or **space'man** *s* (*pl* **-men'** or **-men**) homme *m* de l'espace, astronaute *m*, cosmonaute *m*

space' probe' *s* coup *m* de sonde dans l'espace; (rocket) fusée *f* sonde

spacer ['spesər] *s* (*of typewriter*) barre *f* d'espacement

space'ship' *s* vaisseau *m* spatial, astronef *f*

space' sta'tion *s* station *f* orbitale

space' suit' *s* (rok) scaphandre *m* des cosmonautes

space' walk' *s* promenade *f* dans l'espace

spacious ['speʃəs] *adj* spacieux

spade [sped] *s* bêche *f*; (cards) pique *m*; **to call a spade a spade** (coll) appeler un chat un chat

spade'work' *s* gros travail *m*, défrichage *m*

spaghetti [spə'gɛtɪ] *s* spaghetti *m*

Spain [spen] *s* Espagne *f*; l'Espagne

span [spæn] *s* portée *f*; (*of time*) durée *f*; (*of hand*) empan *m*; (*of wing*) envergure *f*; (*of bridge*) travée *f* ‖ *v* (*pret* & *pp* **spanned**; *ger* **spanning**) *tr* couvrir, traverser

spangle ['spæŋɡəl] *s* paillette *f* ‖ *tr* orner de paillettes

Spaniard ['spænjərd] *s* Espagnol *m*

spaniel ['spænjəl] *s* épagneul *m*

Spanish ['spænɪʃ] *adj* espagnol ‖ *s* (*language*) espagnol *m*; **the Spanish** (*persons*) les Espagnols *mpl*

Span'ish-Amer'ican *adj* hispano-américain ‖ *s* Hispano-Américain *m*

Span'ish broom' *s* genêt *m* d'Espagne

Span'ish fly' *s* cantharide *f*

Span'ish Main' *s* Terre *f* ferme; mer *f* des Antilles

Span'ish moss' *s* tillandsie *f*

spank [spæŋk] *tr* fesser

spanking ['spæŋkɪŋ] *adj* (Brit) de premier ordre; **at a spanking pace** à toute vitesse ‖ *s* fessée *f*

spar [spɑr] *s* (mineral) spath *m*; (naut) espar *m* ‖ *v* (*pret* & *pp* **sparred**; *ger* **sparring**) *intr* s'entraîner à la boxe; se battre

spare [sper] *adj* (*thin*) maigre; (*available*) disponible; (*interchangeable*) de rechange; (*left over*) en surnombre ‖ *tr* (*to save*) épargner, économiser; (*one's efforts*) ménager; (*a person*) faire grâce à, traiter avec indulgence; (*time, money, etc.*) disposer de; (*something*) se passer de

spare' parts' *spl* pièces *fpl* détachées, pièces de rechange

spare'rib' *s* côte *f* découverte de porc, plat *m* de côtes

spare′ room′ s chambre f d'ami
spare′ tire′ s pneu m de rechange
spare′ wheel′ s roue f de secours
sparing ['sperɪŋ] adj économe, frugal
spark [spɑrk] s étincelle f
spark′ coil′ s bobine f d'allumage
spark′ gap′ s (of induction coil) éclateur m; (of spark plug) entrefer m
sparkle ['spɑrkəl] s étincellement m, éclat m || intr étinceler
sparkling ['spɑrklɪŋ] adj étincelant; (wine) mousseux; (soft drink) gazeux
spark′ plug′ s bougie f
sparrow ['spæro] s moineau m
spar′row hawk′ s épervier m
sparse [spɑrs] adj clairsemé, rare; peu nombreux
Spartan ['spɑrtən] adj spartiate || s Spartiate mf
spasm ['spæzəm] s spasme m
spasmodic [spæz'mɑdɪk] adj intermittent, irrégulier; (pathol) spasmodique
spastic ['spæstɪk] adj spasmodique
spat [spæt] s (coll) dispute f, prise f de bec; spats demi-guêtres fpl || v (pret & pp spatted; ger spatting) intr se disputer
spatial ['speʃəl] adj spatial, de l'espace
spatter ['spætər] s éclaboussure f || tr éclabousser
spatula ['spætʃələ] s spatule f
spawn [spɔn] s frai m || tr engendrer || intr frayer
spay [spe] tr châtrer
speak [spik] v (pret spoke [spok]; pp spoken) tr (a word, one's mind, the truth) dire; (a language) parler || intr parler; so to speak pour ainsi dire; speaking! à l'appareil!; to speak out or up parler plus haut, élever la voix; (fig) parler franc
speak′-eas′y s (pl -ies) bar m clandestin
speaker ['spikər] s parleur m; (person addressing a group) conférencier m; (presiding officer) speaker m, président m; (rad) haut-parleur m
spear [spɪr] s lance f || tr percer d'un coup de lance
spear′head′ s fer m de lance; (mil) pointe f, avancée f || tr (e.g., a campaign) diriger
spear′mint′ s menthe f verte
special ['speʃəl] adj spécial, particulier || s train m spécial
spe′cial-deliv′ery let′ter s lettre f exprès
specialist ['speʃəlɪst] s spécialiste mf
specialize ['speʃə,laɪz] tr spécialiser || intr se spécialiser
special·ty ['speʃəlti] s (pl -ties) spécialité f
specie ['spisi] s—in specie en espèces
spe·cies ['spisiz] s (pl -cies) espèce f
specific [spɪ'sɪfɪk] adj & s spécifique m
specif′ic grav′ity s poids m spécifique
specify ['spesɪ,faɪ] v (pret & pp -fied) tr spécifier
specimen ['spesɪmən] s spécimen m; (coll) drôle m de type
specious ['spiʃəs] adj spécieux
speck [spek] s (on fruit, face, etc.) tache f; (in the distance) point m;

(small quantity) brin m, grain m, atome m || tr tacheter
speckle ['spekəl] s petite tache f || tr tacheter, moucheter
spectacle ['spektəkəl] s spectacle m; spectacles lunettes fpl
spec′tacle case′ s étui m à lunettes
spectator ['spektetər], [spek'tetər] s spectateur m
specter ['spektər] s spectre m
spec·trum ['spektrəm] s (pl -tra [trə] or -trums) spectre m
speculate ['spekjə,let] intr spéculer
speculator ['spekjə,letər] s spéculateur m, boursicotier m
speech [spitʃ] s discours m; (language) langage m; (of a people or region) parler m; (power of speech) parole f; (theat) tirade f; to make a speech prononcer un discours
speech′ clin′ic s centre m de rééducation de la parole
speech′ correc′tion s rééducation f de la parole
speechless ['spitʃlɪs] adj sans parole, muet; (fig) sidéré, stupéfié
speed [spid] s vitesse f; at full speed à toute vitesse || v (pret & pp speeded or sped [sped]) tr dépêcher, hâter || intr accélérer; to speed up aller plus vite
speeding ['spidɪŋ] s excès m de vitesse
speed′ king′ s as m du volant
speed′ lim′it s vitesse f maximum
speedometer [spi'dɑmɪtər] s indicateur m de vitesse
speed′ rec′ord s record m de vitesse
speed′-up′ s accélération f
speed′way′ s (racetrack) piste f d'autos; (highway) autoroute f
speed·y ['spidi] adj (comp -ier; super -iest) rapide, vite, prompt
speed′ zone′ s zone f de vitesse surveillée
spell [spel] s sortilège m; intervalle m; (attack) accès m || v (pret & pp spelled or spelt [spelt]) tr (orally) épeler; (in writing) orthographier, écrire; to spell out (coll) expliquer en détail || v (pret & pp spelled) tr (to relieve) remplacer, relever, relayer
spell′bind′er s orateur m fascinant, orateur entraînant
spell′bound′ adj fasciné
spelling ['spelɪŋ] s orthographe f
spell′ing bee′ s concours m d'orthographe
spelunker [spɪ'lʌŋkər] s spéléo m
spend [spend] v (pret & pp spent [spent]) tr dépenser; (a period of time) passer
spender ['spendər] s dépensier m
spend′ing mon′ey s argent m de poche pour les menues dépenses
spend′thrift′ s prodigue mf, grand dépensier m
sperm [spʌrm] s sperme m
sperm′ whale′ s cachalot m
spew [spju] tr & intr vomir
sphere [sfɪr] s sphère f; corps m céleste
spherical ['sferɪkəl] adj sphérique

sphinx [sfɪŋks] s (pl **sphinxes** or **sphinges** ['sfɪndʒiz]) sphinx m

spice [spaɪs] s épice f; (fig) sel m, piquant m || tr épicer

spick-and-span ['spɪkənd'spæn] adj brillant comme un sou neuf; tiré à quatre épingles

spic·y ['spaɪsi] adj (comp -**ier**; super -**iest**) épicé, aromatique; (e.g., gravy) relevé; (conversation, story, etc.) épicé, salé, piquant, grivois

spider ['spaɪdər] s araignée f

spi'der-web' s toile f d'araignée

spiff·y ['spɪfi] adj (comp -**ier**; super -**iest**) (slang) épatant, élégant

spigot ['spɪgət] s robinet m

spike [spaɪk] s pointe f; (nail) clou m à large tête; (bot) épi m; (rr) crampon m || tr clouer; ruiner, supprimer; (a drink) (coll) corser à l'alcool || intr (bot) former des épis

spill [spɪl] s chute f, culbute f || v (pret & pp **spilled** or **spilt** [spɪlt]) tr renverser; (a liquid) répandre; (a rider) désarçonner; (passengers) verser || intr se répandre, s'écouler

spill'way' s déversoir m

spin [spɪn] s tournoiement m, rotation f; (on a ball) effet m; (aer) vrille f; **to go for a spin** (coll) se balader en voiture; **to go into a spin** (aer) descendre en vrille || v (pret & pp **spun** [spʌn]; ger **spinning**) tr filer; faire tournoyer || intr filer; tournoyer

spinach ['spɪnɪtʃ], ['spɪnɪdʒ] s épinard m; (leaves used as food) des épinards

spinal ['spaɪnəl] adj spinal

spi'nal col'umn s colonne f vertébrale

spi'nal cord' s moelle f épinière

spindle ['spɪndəl] s fuseau m

spin'-dri'er s essoreuse f

spin'-dry' v (pret & pp -**dried**) tr essorer

spine [spaɪn] s épine f dorsale, échine f; (quill, fin) épine; (ridge) arête f; (of book) dos m; (fig) courage m

spineless ['spaɪnlɪs] adj sans épines; (weak) mou; **to be spineless** (fig) avoir l'échine souple

spinet ['spɪnɪt] s épinette f

spinner ['spɪnər] s fileur m; machine f à filer

spinning ['spɪnɪŋ] adj tournoyant || s (act) filage m; (art) filature f

spin'ning wheel' s rouet m

spinster ['spɪnstər] s célibataire f, vieille fille f

spiraea [spaɪˈriə] s spirée f

spi·ral ['spaɪrəl] adj spiral, en spirale || s spirale f || v (pret & pp -**raled** or -**ralled**; ger -**raling** or -**ralling**) intr tourner en spirale; (aer) vriller

spi'ral stair'case s escalier m en colimaçon

spire [spaɪr] s aiguille f; (of clock tower) flèche f

spirit ['spɪrɪt] s esprit m; (enthusiasm) feu m; (temper, genius) génie m; (ghost) esprit, revenant m; **high spirits** joie f, abandon m; **spirits** (alcoholic liquor) esprit m, spiritueux m; **to raise the spirits of** remonter le courage de || tr—**to spirit away** enlever, faire disparaître mystérieusement

spirited adj animé, vigoureux

spiritless ['spɪrɪtlɪs] adj sans force, abattu, déprimé

spir'it lev'el s niveau m à bulle

spiritual ['spɪrɪtʃuəl] adj spirituel || s chant m religieux populaire

spiritualism ['spɪrɪtʃuəˌlɪzəm] s spiritisme m

spiritualist ['spɪrɪtʃuəlɪst] s spirite mf; (philos) spiritualiste mf

spir'ituous bev'erages ['spɪrɪtʃuəs] spl boissons fpl spiritueuses

spit [spɪt] s salive f; (culin) broche f || v (pret & pp **spat** [spæt] or **spit**; ger **spitting**) tr & intr cracher

spite [spaɪt] s dépit m, rancune f; **in spite of** en dépit de, malgré || tr dépiter, contrarier

spiteful ['spaɪtfəl] adj rancunier

spit'fire' s mégère f

spit'ting im'age s (coll) portrait m craché

spittoon [spɪˈtun] s crachoir m

splash [splæʃ] s éclaboussure f; (of waves) clapotis m; **to make a splash** (coll) faire sensation || tr & intr éclabousser

splash'down' s (rok) amerrissage m

spleen [splin] s rate f; (fig) maussaderie f, mauvaise humeur f; **to vent one's spleen on** décharger sa bile sur

splendid ['splendɪd] adj splendide; (coll) admirable, superbe

splendor ['splendər] s splendeur f

splice [splaɪs] s (in rope) épissure f; (in wood) enture f || tr (rope) épisser; (wood) enter; (film) réparer, coller; (slang) marier

splint [splɪnt] s éclisse f || tr éclisser

splinter ['splɪntər] s éclat m, éclisse f; (lodged under the skin) écharde f || tr briser en éclats || intr voler en éclats

splin'ter group' s minorité f dissidente, groupe m fragmentaire

split [splɪt] adj fendu; (pea) cassé; (skirt) déchiré || s fente f, fissure f; (quarrel) rupture f; (one's share) part f; (bottle) quart m, demi m; (gymnastics) grand écart m || v (pret & pp **split**; ger **splitting**) tr fendre; (money; work; ticket) partager; (in two) couper; (a hide) dédoubler; **to split hairs** couper les cheveux en quatre; **to split one's sides laughing** se tenir les côtes de rire; **to split the difference** couper la poire en deux || intr se fendre; **to split away (from)** se séparer (de)

split' fee' s (between doctors) dichotomie f

split' personal'ity s personnalité f dédoublée

split' tick'et s (pol) panachage m

splitting ['splɪtɪŋ] adj violent; (headache) atroce || s fendage m; (of the atom) désintégration f; (of the personality) dédoublement m

splotch [splatʃ] s tache f || tr tacher, barbouiller

splurge [splʌrdʒ] *s* (coll) épate *f* ‖ *intr* (coll) se payer une fête; (*to show off*) (coll) faire de l'épate

splutter [ˈsplʌtər] *s* crachement *m* ‖ *tr* —**to splutter out** bredouiller ‖ *intr* crachoter; (*said of candle, grease, etc.*) grésiller

spoil [spɔɪl] *s* (*object of plunder*) prise *f*, proie *f*; **spoils** (*booty*) butin *m*, dépouilles *fpl*; (*emoluments, especially of public office*) assiette *f* au beurre, part *f* du gâteau ‖ *v* (*pret & pp* **spoiled** or **spoilt** [spɔɪlt]) *tr* gâter, abîmer ‖ *intr* se gâter, s'abîmer; **to be spoiling for** (coll) brûler du désir de

spoilage [ˈspɔɪlɪdʒ] *s* déchet *m*

spoiled *adj* gâté

spoil'sport' *s* rabat-joie *m*

spoils' sys'tem *s* système *m* des postes aux petits copains

spoke [spok] *s* rai *m*, rayon *m*; (*of a ladder*) échelon *m*

spokes'man *s* (*pl* -**men**) porte-parole *m*

sponge [spʌndʒ] *s* éponge *f* ‖ *tr* éponger; (*a meal*) (coll) écornifler ‖ *intr* (coll) écornifler; **to sponge on** (coll) vivre aux crochets de

sponge' cake' *s* gâteau *m* de Savoie, gâteau mousseline

sponger [ˈspʌndʒər] *s* écornifleur *m*, pique-assiette *mf*

sponge' rub'ber *s* caoutchouc *m* mousse

spon-gy [ˈspʌndʒi] *adj* (*comp* -**gier**; *super* -**giest**) spongieux

sponsor [ˈspɑnsər] *s* patron *m*; (*godfather*) parrain *m*; (*godmother*) marraine *f*; (law) garant *m*; (rad, telv) commanditaire *m* ‖ *tr* patronner; (law) se porter garant de; (rad, telv) commanditer

spon'sor-ship' *s* patronnage *m*

spontaneous [spɑnˈteni·əs] *adj* spontané

spoof [spuf] *s* (slang) mystification *f*; (slang) parodie *f* ‖ *tr* (slang) mystifier; (slang) blaguer ‖ *intr* (slang) blaguer

spook [spuk] *s* (coll) revenant *m*, spectre *m*

spool [spul] *s* bobine *f*

spoon [spun] *s* cuiller *f*; **to be born with a silver spoon in one's mouth** (coll) être né coiffé ‖ *tr* prendre dans une cuiller; **to spoon off** enlever avec la cuiller ‖ *intr* (coll) se faire des mamours

spooner [ˈspunər] *s* (coll) peloteur *m*

spoonerism [ˈspunə‚rɪzəm] *s* contrepèterie *f*

spoon'-feed' *v* (*pret & pp* -**fed**) *tr* nourrir à la cuiller; (*an industry*) subventionner; (coll) mâcher la besogne à

spoonful [ˈspun‚fʊl] *s* cuillerée *f*

spoon-y [ˈspuni] *adj* (*comp* -**ier**; *super* -**iest**) (coll) peloteur

sporadic(al) [spəˈrædɪk(əl)] *adj* sporadique

spore [spor] *s* spore *f*

sport [sport] *adj* sportif, de sport ‖ *s* sport *m*; amusement *m*, jeu *m*; (biol) mutation *f*; (coll) chic type *m*; **a good**

sport un bon copain; (*a good loser*) un beau joueur; **in sport** par plaisanterie; **to make sport of** tourner en ridicule ‖ *tr* faire parade de, arborer ‖ *intr* s'amuser, jouer

sport' clothes' *spl* vêtements *mpl* de sport

sport'ing goods' *spl* articles *mpl* de sport

sports'cast'er *s* radioreporter *m* sportif

sports' ed'itor *s* rédacteur *m* sportif

sports' fan' *s* fanatique *mf*, enragé *m* des sports

sports'man *s* (*pl* -**men**) sportif *m*

sports'man-like' *adj* sportif

sports'man-ship' *s* sportivité *f*

sports'wear' *s* vêtements *mpl* sport

sports'writ'er *s* reporter *m* sportif

sport·y [ˈsporti] *adj* (*comp* -**ier**; *super* -**iest**) (coll) sportif; (*smart in dress*) (coll) chic; (*flashy*) (coll) criard, voyant; (coll) dissolu, libertin

spot [spɑt] *s* tache *f*; (*place*) endroit *m*, lieu *m*; **on the spot** sur place; (slang) dans le pétrin; **spots** (*before eyes*) mouches *fpl* ‖ *v* (*pret & pp* **spotted**; *ger* **spotting**) *tr* tacher; (coll) repérer, détecter ‖ *intr* se tacher

spot' cash' *s* argent *m* comptant

spot' check' *s* échantillonnage *m*

spot'-check' *tr* échantillonner

spotless [ˈspɑtlɪs] *adj* sans tache

spot'light' *s* spot *m*; (aut) projecteur *m* auxiliaire orientable; **to hold the spotlight** (fig) être en vedette ‖ *tr* diriger les projecteurs sur; (fig) mettre en vedette

spot' remov'er [rɪˌmuvər] *s* détachant *m*

spot' weld'ing *s* soudage *m* par points

spouse [spauz], [spaus] *s* (*man*) époux *m*, conjoint *m*; (*woman*) épouse *f*, conjointe *f*

spout [spaut] *s* tuyau *m* de décharge; (*e.g., of teapot*) bec *m*; (*of sprinkling can*) col *m*, queue *f*; (*of water*) jet *m* ‖ *tr* faire jaillir; (*e.g., insults*) (coll) déclamer ‖ *intr* jaillir; **to spout off** (coll) déclamer

sprain [spren] *s* foulure *f*, entorse *f* ‖ *tr* fouler, se fouler

sprawl [sprɔl] *intr* s'étaler, se carrer

spray [spre] *s* (*of ocean*) embruns *mpl*; (*branch*) rameau *m*; (*for insects*) liquide *m* insecticide; (*for weeds*) produit *m* herbicide; (*for spraying insects or weeds*) pulvérisateur *m*; (*for spraying perfume*) vaporisateur *m* ‖ *tr* pulvériser; (*with a vaporizer*) vaporiser; (hort) désinfecter par pulvérisation d'insecticide; **to spray paint on** peindre au pistolet ‖ *intr*— **to spray out** gicler

sprayer [ˈspre·ər] *s* vaporisateur *m*, pulvérisateur *m*

spray' gun' *s* pulvérisateur *m*; (*for paint*) pistolet *m*; (hort) seringue *f*

spread [spred] *adj* étendu, écarté, ouvert ‖ *s* étendue *f*, rayonnement *m*; (*on bed*) dessus-de-lit *m*, couvre-lit *m*; (*on sandwich*) pâte *f*; (*buffet lunch*) collation *f* ‖ *v* (*pret & pp*

spread) *tr* étendre, étaler; *(news)* répandre; *(disease)* propager; *(the wings)* déployer; *(a piece of bread)* tartiner ‖ *intr* s'étendre, s'étaler; se répandre, rayonner

spree [sprī] *s* bombance *f*, orgie *f*; **to go on a spree** (coll) faire la bombe

sprig [sprīg] *s* brin *m*, brindille *f*

spright•ly ['spraītlī] *adj* (*comp* **-lier**; *super* **-liest**) vif, enjoué

spring [sprīŋ] *adj* printanier ‖ *s* (*of water*) source *f*; *(season)* printemps *m*; *(jump)* saut *m*, bond *m*; *(elastic device)* ressort *m*; *(quality)* élasticité *f* ‖ *v* (*pret* **sprang** [spræŋ] *or* **sprung** [sprʌŋ]; *pp* **sprung**) *tr* (*the frame of a car*) faire déjeter; *(a lock)* faire jouer; *(a leak)* contracter; *(a question)* proposer à l'improviste; *(a prisoner)* (coll) faire sortir de prison ‖ *intr* sauter, bondir; (*said of oil, water, etc.*) jaillir; **to spring up** se lever; naître

spring'-and-fall' *adj* (*coat*) de demi-saison

spring'board' *s* tremplin *m*

spring' fe'ver *s* (hum) malaise *m* des premières chaleurs, flemme *f*

spring'like' *adj* printanier

spring'time' *s* printemps *m*

sprinkle ['sprīŋkəl] *s* pluie *f* fine; (culin) pincée *f* ‖ *tr* (*with water*) asperger, arroser; (*with powder*) saupoudrer; (*to strew*) parsemer ‖ *intr* tomber en pluie fine

sprinkler ['sprīŋklər] *s* arrosoir *m*

sprinkling ['sprīŋklīŋ] *s* aspersion *f*, arrosage *m*; (*with holy water*) aspersion; (*with powder*) saupoudrage *m*; (*of knowledge*) bribes *fpl*, notions *fpl*; (*of persons*) petit nombre *m*

sprin'kling can' *s* arrosoir *m*

sprint [sprīnt] *s* course *f* de vitesse, sprint *m* ‖ *intr* faire une course de vitesse, courir à toute vitesse

sprite [spraīt] *s* lutin *m*

sprocket ['sprakīt] *s* dent *f* de pignon; (*wheel*) pignon *m* de chaîne

sprock'et wheel' *s* pignon *m* de chaîne

sprout [spraūt] *s* pousse *f*, rejeton *m*; (*of seed*) germe *m* ‖ *intr* (*said of plant*) pousser, pointer; (*said of seed*) germer

spruce [sprūs] *adj* pimpant, tiré à quatre épingles ‖ *s* sapin *m*; (*Norway spruce*) épicéa *m* commun ‖ *intr* —**to spruce up** se faire beau, se pomponner

spry [spraī] *adj* (*comp* **spryer** *or* **sprier**; *super* **spryest** *or* **spriest**) vif, alerte

spud [spʌd] *s* (*chisel*) bédane *f*; (agr) arrache-racines *m*; (coll) pomme *f* de terre, patate *f*

spun' glass' [spʌn] *s* coton *m* de verre

spunk [spʌŋk] *s* (coll) cran *m*, courage *m*

spur [spʌr] *s* éperon *m*; (*of rooster*) ergot *m*; (*stimulant*) aiguillon *m*, stimulant *m*; (rr) embranchement *m*; **on the spur of the moment** sous l'impulsion du moment ‖ *v* (*pret & pp*

spurred; *ger* **spurring**) *tr* éperonner; **to spur on** aiguillonner, stimuler

spurious ['spjurī•əs] *adj* faux; (*sentiments*) simulé, feint; (*document*) apocryphe

spurn [spʌrn] *tr* repousser avec mépris, faire fi de

spurt [spʌrt] *s* jaillissement *m*, giclée *f*, jet *m*; (*of enthusiasm*) élan *m*; effort *m* soudain ‖ *intr* jaillir; **to spurt out** gicler

sputnik ['sputnīk], ['spʌtnīk] *s* spoutnik *m*

sputter ['spʌtər] *s* (*manner of speaking*) bredouillement *m*; (*of candle*) grésillement *m*; (*of fire*) crachement *m* ‖ *tr* (*words*) débiter en lançant des postillons ‖ *intr* postillonner; (*said of candle*) grésiller; (*said of fire*) cracher, pétiller

spu•tum ['spjutəm] *s* (*pl* **-ta** [tə]) crachat *m*

spy [spaī] *s* (*pl* **spies**) espion *m* ‖ *v* (*pret & pp* **spied**) *tr* (*to catch sight of*) entrevoir; **to spy out** découvrir par ruse ‖ *intr* espionner; **to spy on** épier, guetter

spy'glass' *s* longue-vue *f*

spying ['spaī•īŋ] *s* espionnage *m*

spy' ring' *s* réseau *m* d'espionnage

squabble ['skwabəl] *s* chamaillerie *f* ‖ *intr* se chamailler

squad [skwad] *s* escouade *f*, peloton *m*; (*of detectives*) brigade *f*

squadron ['skwadrən] *s* (aer) escadrille *f*; (mil) escadron *m*; (nav) escadre *f*

squalid ['skwalīd] *adj* sordide

squall [skwɔl] *s* bourrasque *f*, rafale *f*; (*cry*) braillement *m*; (coll) grabuge *m* ‖ *intr* souffler en bourrasque; brailler

squalor ['skwalər] *s* saleté *f*; misère *f*

squander ['skwandər] *tr* gaspiller

square [skwer] *adj* carré; (*honest*) loyal, franc; (*real*) véritable; (*conventional*) (slang) formaliste; **nine** (**ten, etc.**) **inches square** de neuf (dix, etc.) pouces en carré; **nine** (**ten, etc.**) **square inches** neuf (dix, etc.) pouces carrés; **to get square with** (coll) régler ses comptes avec; **we'll call it square** (coll) nous sommes quittes ‖ *s* carré *m*; (*of checkerboard or chessboard*) case *f*; (*city block*) pâté *m* de maisons; (*open area in town or city*) place *f*; (*of carpenter*) équerre *f*; **to be on the square** (coll) jouer franc jeu ‖ *adv* carrément ‖ *tr* carrer; (*a number*) élever au carré; (*wood, marble, etc.*) équarrir; (*a debt*) régler; (bk) balancer ‖ *intr* —**to square off** (coll) se mettre en posture de combat; **to square with** (*to tally with*) s'accorder avec; régler ses comptes avec

square' dance' *s* quadrille *m* américain

square' deal' *s* (coll) procédé *m* loyal

square' meal' *s* repas *m* copieux

square' root' *s* racine *f* carrée

squash [skwaʃ] *s* écrasement *m*; (bot) courge *f*; (sports) squash *m* ‖ *tr* écraser ‖ *intr* s'écraser

squash·y ['skwɑ/i] *adj* (*comp* **-ier**; *super* **-iest**) mou et humide; (*fruit*) à pulpe molle

squat [skwɑt] *adj* accroupi; (*heavyset*) trapu, ramassé ‖ *s* position *f* accroupie ‖ *v* (*pret & pp* **squatted**; *ger* **squatting**) *intr* s'accroupir; (*to settle*) s'installer sans titre légal

squatter ['skwɑtər] *s* squatter *m*

squaw [skwɔ] *s* femme *f* peau-rouge

squawk [skwɔk] *s* cri *m* rauque; (slang) protestation *f*, piaillerie *f* ‖ *intr* pousser un cri rauque; (slang) protester, piailler

squeak [skwik] *s* grincement *m*; (*of living being*) couic *m*, petit cri *m* ‖ *intr* grincer; pousser des petits cris, couiner

squeal [skwil] *s* cri *m* aigu ‖ *intr* piailler; (slang) manger le morceau; **to squeal on** (slang) moucharder

squealer ['skwilər] *s* (coll) cafard *m*

squeamish ['skwimɪ/] *adj* trop scrupuleux; prude; sujet aux nausées

squeeze [skwiz] *s* pression *f*; (coll) extorsion *f*; **it's a tight squeeze** (coll) ça tient tout juste ‖ *tr* serrer; (*fruit*) presser; **to squeeze from** (coll) extorquer à; **to squeeze into** faire entrer de force dans ‖ *intr* se blottir; **to squeeze through** se frayer un passage à travers

squeezer ['skwizər] *s* presse *f*, presse-fruits *m*

squelch [skwɛlt/] *s* (coll) remarque *f* écrasante ‖ *tr* écraser, réprimer

squid [skwɪd] *s* calmar *m*

squill [skwɪl] *s* (bot) scille *f*; (zool) squille *f*

squint [skwɪnt] *s* coup *m* d'œil furtif; (pathol) strabisme *m* ‖ *tr* fermer à moitié ‖ *intr* loucher; **to squint at** regarder furtivement

squint'-eyed' *adj* bigle, strabique; malveillant

squire [skwaɪr] *s* écuyer *m*; (*lady's escort*) cavalier *m* servant; (*property owner*) propriétaire *m* terrien; juge *m* de paix ‖ *tr* escorter

squirm [skwʌrm] *s* tortillement *m* ‖ *intr* se tortiller; **to squirm out of** se tirer de

squirrel ['skwʌrəl] *s* écureuil *m*

squirt [skwʌrt] *s* giclée *f*, jet *m*; (*syringe*) seringue *f*; (coll) morveux *m* ‖ *tr* faire gicler ‖ *intr* gicler, jaillir

stab [stæb] *s* coup *m* de poignard, de couteau; (*wound*) estafilade *f*; (coll) coup d'essai; **to make a stab at** (coll) s'essayer à ‖ *v* (*pret & pp* **stabbed**; *ger* **stabbing**) *tr* poignarder

stabilize ['stebəl͵aɪz] *tr* stabiliser

stab' in the back' *s* coup *m* de Jarnac, coup de traître

stable ['stebəl] *adj* stable ‖ *s* (*for cows*) étable *f*; (*for horses*) écurie *f*

stack [stæk] *s* tas *m*, pile *f*; (*of hay, straw, etc.*) meule *f*; (*of sheaves*) gerbier *m*; (*e.g., of rifles*) faisceau *m*; (*of ship or locomotive*) cheminée *f*; (*of fireplace*) souche *f*; **stacks** (*in library*) rayons *mpl* ‖ *tr* entasser, empiler; mettre en meule, en gerbier, or en faisceau; (*a deck of cards*) truquer, donner un coup de pouce à; **to stack arms** former les faisceaux

stadi·um ['stedɪ·əm] *s* (*pl* **-ums** or **-a** [ə]) stade *m*

staff [stæf], [stɑf] *s* bâton *m*; (*of pilgrim*) bourdon *m*; (*of flag*) hampe *f*; (*of newspaper*) rédaction *f*; (*employees*) personnel *m*; (*servants*) domestiques *mfpl*; (*support*) soutien *m*; (mil) état-major *m*; (mus) portée *f* ‖ *tr* fournir, pourvoir de personnel; nommer le personnel pour

staff' head'quarters *spl* (mil) état-major *m*

staff' of'ficer *s* officier *m* d'état-major

stag [stæg] *adj* exclusivement masculin; **to go stag** aller sans compagne ‖ *s* homme *m*; (*male deer*) cerf *m*

stage [stedʒ] *s* stade *m*, étape *f*, phase *f*; (*of rocket*) étage *m*; (*stagecoach*) diligence *f*; (*scene*) champ *m* d'action, scène *f*; (*staging*) échafaudage *m*; (*platform*) estrade *f*; (*of microscope*) platine *f*; (theat) scène; **by easy stages** par petites étapes; **by successive stages** par échelons; **to go on the stage** monter sur les planches ‖ *tr* (*a play, demonstration, riot, etc.*) monter; (*a play*) mettre en scène

stage'coach' *s* diligence *f*, coche *m*

stage'craft' *s* technique *f* de la scène

stage' door' *s* entrée *f* des artistes

stage'-door' John'ny *s* (*pl* **-nies**) coureur *m* de girls

stage' effect' *s* effet *m* scénique

stage' fright' *s* trac *m*

stage'hand' *s* machiniste *m*

stage' left' *s* côté *m* jardin

stage' man'ager *s* régisseur *m*

stage' name' *s* nom *m* de théâtre

stage' prop'erties *spl* accessoires *mpl*

stage' right' *s* côté *m* cour

stage'-struck' [strʌk] *adj* entiché de théâtre

stage' whis'per *s* aparté *m*

stagger ['stægər] *tr* ébranler; (*to surprise*) étonner; (*to arrange*) disposer en chicane, en zigzag; (*hours of work, train schedules, etc.*) échelonner ‖ *intr* chanceler, tituber

staggering ['stægərɪŋ] *adj* chancelant; (*amazing*) étonnant

staging ['stedʒɪŋ] *s* échafaudage *m*; (theat) mise *f* en scène

stagnant ['stægnənt] *adj* stagnant

stag' par'ty *s* (*pl* **-ties**) (coll) réunion *f* entre hommes, réunion d'hommes seuls

staid [sted] *adj* posé, sérieux

stain [sten] *s* tache *f*, souillure *f* ‖ *tr* tacher, souiller; (*to tint*) teindre ‖ *intr* se tacher

stained' glass' *s* vitre *f* de couleur

stained'-glass win'dow *s* vitrail *m*

stain'less steel' ['stenlɪs] *s* acier *m* inoxydable

stair [ster] *s* escalier *m*; (*step of a series*) marche *f*, degré *m*; **stairs** escalier *m*

stair'case' *s* escalier *m*

stair′way′ s escalier m

stair′well′ s cage f d'escalier

stake [stek] s pieu m, poteau m; (of tent) piquet m; (marker) jalon m; (for burning condemned persons) bûcher m; (in a game of chance) mise f, enjeu m; **at stake** en jeu; **to pull up stakes** (coll) déménager ‖ tr (a road) bornoyer; (plants) échalasser, ramer; (money) risquer; (to back financially) (slang) fournir aux besoins de; **to stake all** mettre tout en jeu; **to stake off** or **out** jalonner, piqueter

stale [stel] adj (bread) rassis; (wine or beer) éventé; (air) confiné; (joke) vieux; (check) proscrit; (subject) rabattu; (news) défloré, défraîchi; **to smell stale** (said of room) sentir le renfermé

stale′mate′ s (chess) pat m; (fig) impasse f; **in stalemate** pat ‖ tr (chess) faire pat; (fig) paralyser

stalk [stɔk] s tige f; (of flower or leaf) queue f ‖ tr traquer, suivre à la piste ‖ intr marcher fièrement, marcher à grandes enjambées

stall [stɔl] s stalle f; (at a market) étal m, échoppe f; (slang) prétexte m ‖ tr mettre dans une stalle; (a car) caler; (an airplane) mettre en perte de vitesse; **to stall off** (coll) différer sous prétexte ‖ intr (said of motor) se bloquer; **to stall for time** (slang) temporiser

stallion ['stæljən] s étalon m

stalwart ['stɔlwərt] adj robuste; vaillant ‖ s partisan m loyal

stamen ['stemən] s étamine f

stamina ['stæmɪnə] s vigueur f, résistance f

stammer ['stæmər] s bégaiement m, balbutiement m ‖ tr & intr bégayer, balbutier

stammerer ['stæmərər] s bègue mf

stamp [stæmp] s empreinte f; (for postage) timbre m; (for stamping) poinçon m ‖ tr (mail) affranchir; (money; leather; a medal) frapper, estamper; (a document) timbrer; (a passport) viser; **to stamp one's feet** trépigner; **to stamp one's foot** frapper du pied; **to stamp out** (e.g., a rebellion) écraser, étouffer

stampede [stæm'pid] s débandade f; (rush) ruée f; (of people) sauve-quipeut m ‖ tr provoquer la ruée de ‖ intr se débander

stamped′ self′-addressed′ en′velope s enveloppe f timbrée par l'expéditeur

stamp′ing grounds′ spl—**to be on one's stamping grounds** (slang) être sur son terrain, être dans son domaine

stamp′ pad′ s tampon m encreur

stamp′-vend′ing machine′ s distributeur m automatique de timbres-poste

stance [stæns] s attitude f, posture f

stanch [stɑntʃ] adj ferme, solide; vrai, loyal; (watertight) étanche ‖ tr étancher

stand [stænd] s résistance f; position f; (of a merchant) étal m, éventaire m; (of a speaker) tribune f, estrade f; (of a horse) aplombs mpl; (piece of furniture) guéridon m, console f; (to hold music, papers) pupitre m; **stands** tribune f, stand m ‖ v (pret & pp **stood** [stud]) tr mettre, placer, poser; (the cold) supporter; (a shock; an attack) soutenir; (a round of drinks) (coll) payer; **to stand off** repousser; **to stand up** (to keep waiting) (coll) poser un lapin à ‖ intr se lever, se mettre debout; se tenir debout, être debout; en être, e.g., **how does it stand?** où en est-il?; **to stand aloof** or **aside** se tenir à l'écart; **to stand by** se tenir prêt; (e.g., a friend) rester fidèle à; **to stand fast** tenir bon; **to stand for** (to mean) signifier; (to affirm) soutenir; (to allow) tolérer; **to stand in for** doubler, remplacer; **to stand in line** faire la queue; **to stand out** sortir, saillir; **to stand up** se lever, se mettre debout, être debout; **to stand up against** or **to** tenir tête à; **to stand up for** prendre fait et cause pour

standard ['stændərd] adj (product, part, unit) standard, de série, normal; (current) courant; (author, book, work) classique; (edition) définitif; (keyboard of typewriter) universel; (coinage) au titre ‖ s norme f, mesure f, règle f, pratique f; (of quantity, weight, value) standard m; (banner) étendard m; (of lamp) support m; (of wires) pylône m; (of coinage) titre m; (for a monetary system) étalon m; (fig) degré m, niveau m; **standards** critères mpl; **up to standard** suivant la norme

stand′ard-bear′er s porte-drapeau m

stand′ard gauge′ s voie f normale

standardize ['stændər‚daɪz] tr standardiser

stand′ard of liv′ing s niveau m de vie

stand′ard time′ s heure f légale

standee [stæn'di] s voyageur m debout; (theat) spectateur m debout

stand′-in′ s (mov, theat) doublure f, remplaçant m; (coll) appuis mpl, piston m

standing ['stændɪŋ] adj (upright) debout; (statue) en pied; (water) stagnant; (army; committee) permanent; (price; rule; rope) fixe; (custom) établi, courant; (jump) à pieds joints ‖ s standing m, position f, importance f; **in good standing** estimé, accrédité; **of long standing** de longue date

stand′ing ar′my s armée f permanente

stand′ing room′ s places fpl debout

stand′ing vote′ s vote m par assis et levé

stand′pat′ adj & s (coll) immobiliste mf

stand′pat′ter s (coll) immobiliste mf

stand′point′ s point m de vue

stand′still′ s arrêt m, immobilisation f; **to come to a standstill** s'arrêter court

stanza ['stænzə] s strophe f

staple ['stepəl] adj principal ‖ s (product) produit m principal; (for hold-

ing papers together) agrafe *f*; (bb) broche *f*; **staples** denrées *fpl* principales ‖ *tr* agrafer; (*books*) brocher

stapler ['steplər] *s* agrafeuse *f*; (bb) brocheuse *f*

star [star] *s* astre *m*; (*heavenly body except sun and moon; figure that represents a star*) étoile *f*; (*of stage or screen*) vedette *f* ‖ *v* (*pret & pp* **starred**; *ger* **starring**) *tr* étoiler, consteller; (mov, rad, telv, theat) mettre en vedette; (typ) marquer d'un astérisque ‖ *intr* apparaître comme vedette

starboard ['starbərd], ['star,bord] *adj* de tribord ‖ *s* tribord *m* ‖ *adv* à tribord

star′ board′er *s* (coll) pensionnaire *mf* de prédilection

starch [start∫] *s* amidon *m*; (*for fabrics*) empois *m*; (*formality*) raideur *f*; (bot, culin) fécule *f*; (coll) force *f*, vigueur *f* ‖ *tr* empeser

starch•y ['start∫i] *adj* (*comp* **-ier**; *super* **-iest**) empesé; (*foods*) féculent; (*manner*) raide, guindé

stare [ster] *s* regard *m* fixe ‖ *tr*—**to stare s.o. in the face** dévisager qn; (*to be obvious to s.o.*) sauter aux yeux de qn ‖ *intr* regarder fixement; **to stare at** regarder fixement, dévisager

star′fish′ *s* étoile *f* de mer

star′gaze′ *intr* regarder les étoiles; rêvasser, être dans la lune

stark [stark] *adj* pur; rigide; désert, solitaire ‖ *adv* entièrement

stark′-na′ked *adj* tout nu

star′light′ *s* lumière *f* des étoiles

starling ['starlɪŋ] *s* étourneau *m*

star•ry ['stari] *adj* (*comp* **-rier**; *super* **-riest**) étoilé

Stars′ and Stripes′ *spl* bannière *f* étoilée

Star′-Spangled Ban′ner *s* bannière *f* étoilée

start [start] *s* commencement *m*, début *m*; (*sudden start*) sursaut *m*, haut-le-corps *m* ‖ *tr* commencer; (*a car, a motor, etc.*) mettre en marche, démarrer; (*a conversation*) entamer; (*a hare*) lever; (*a deer*) lancer; **to start + ger** se mettre à + *inf* ‖ *intr* commencer, débuter; démarrer; (*to be startled*) sursauter; **starting from or with** à partir de; **to start after** sortir à la recherche de; **to start out** se mettre en route

starter ['startər] *s* initiateur *m*; (aut) démarreur *m*; (sports) starter *m*

start′ing point′ *s* point *m* de départ

startle ['startəl] *tr* faire tressaillir ‖ *intr* tressaillir

startling ['startlɪŋ] *adj* effrayant; (*event*) sensationnel; (*resemblance*) saisissant

starvation [star′ve∫ən] *s* inanition *f*, famine *f*

starva′tion di′et *s* diète *f* absolue

starva′tion wag′es *spl* salaire *m* de famine

starve [starv] *tr* affamer; faire mourir

de faim; **to starve out** réduire par la faim ‖ *intr* être affamé; être dans la misère; mourir de faim; (coll) mourir de faim

state [stet] *s* état *m*; (*pomp*) apparat *m*; **to lie in state** être exposé solennellement ‖ *tr* affirmer, déclarer; (*an hour or date*) régler, fixer; (*a problem*) poser

stateless ['stetlɪs] *adj* apatride

state•ly ['stetli] *adj* (*comp* **-lier**; *super* **-liest**) majestueux, imposant

statement ['stetmənt] *s* énoncé *m*, exposé *m*; (*account, report*) compte rendu *m*, rapport *m*; (*of an account*) (com) relevé *m*

state′ of mind′ *s* état *m* d'esprit, état d'âme

state′room′ *s* (naut) cabine *f*; (rr) compartiment *m*

states′man *s* (*pl* **-men**) homme *m* d'État

static ['stætɪk] *adj* statique; (rad) parasite ‖ *s* (rad) parasites *mpl*

station ['ste∫ən] *s* station *f*; (*for police; for selling gasoline; for broadcasting*) poste *m*; (*of bus, subway, rail line, taxi; for observation*) station; (rr) gare *f* ‖ *tr* poster, placer

sta′tion a′gent *s* chef *m* de gare

stationary ['ste∫ən,eri] *adj* stationnaire

sta′tion break′ *s* (rad) pause *f*

stationer ['ste∫ənər] *s* papetier *m*

stationery ['ste∫ən,eri] *s* papeterie *f*, fournitures *fpl* de bureau

sta′tionery store′ *s* papeterie *f*

sta′tion house′ *s* commissariat *m* de police

sta′tion identifica′tion *s* (rad) indicatif *m*

sta′tion•mas′ter *s* chef *m* de gare

sta′tion wag′on *s* familiale *f*, break *m*

statistical [stə′tɪstɪkəl] *adj* statistique

statistician [,stætɪs′tɪ∫ən] *s* statisticien *m*

statistics [stə′tɪstɪks] *s* (*science*) statistique *f* ‖ *spl* (*data*) statistique, statistiques

statue ['stæt∫u] *s* statue *f*

Stat′ue of Lib′erty *s* Liberté *f* éclairant le monde

statuesque [,stæt∫u′esk] *adj* sculptural

stature ['stæt∫ər] *s* stature *f*, taille *f*; caractère *m*, stature

status ['stetəs] *s* condition *f*; rang *m*, standing *m*

sta′tus quo′ ['kwo] *s* statu quo *m*

sta′tus seek′er *s* obsédé *m* du standing

sta′tus sym′bol *s* symbole *m* du rang social

statute ['stæt∫ut] *s* statut *m*

statutory ['stæt∫u,tori] *adj* statutaire

staunch [stɔnt∫], [stant∫] *adj & tr* var of **stanch**

stave [stev] *s* bâton *m*; (*of barrel*) douve *f*; (*of ladder*) échelon *m*; (mus) portée *f* ‖ *v* (*pret & pp* **staved** or **stove** [stov]) *tr*—**to stave in** défoncer, crever; **to stave off** détourner, éloigner

stay [ste] *s* (*visit*) séjour *m*; (*prop*) étai *m*; (*of a corset*) baleine *f*; (*of execution*) sursis *m*; (fig) soutien *m* ‖

tr arrêter ‖ *intr* rester; séjourner; (*at a hotel*) descendre; **to stay put** ne pas bouger; **to stay up** veiller

stay'-at-home' *adj* & *s* casanier *m*

stead [sted] *s*—in s.o.'s stead à la place de qn; **to stand s.o. in good stead** être fort utile à qn

stead'fast' *adj* ferme; constant

stead•y ['stedi] *adj* (*comp* **-ier;** *super* **-iest**) ferme, solide; régulier; (*market*) soutenu ‖ *v* (*pret* & *pp* **-ied**) *tr* raffermir ‖ *intr* se raffermir

steak [stek] *s* (*slice*) tranche *f*; bifteck *m*

steal [stil] *s* (coll) vol *m*; (*bargain*) (coll) occasion *f* ‖ *v* (*pret* **stole** [stol]; *pp* **stolen**) *tr* voler; **to steal s.th. from s.o.** voler q.ch. à qn ‖ *intr* voler; **to steal away** se dérober; **to steal into** se glisser dans; **to steal upon** s'approcher en tapinois de

stealth [stelθ] *s*—**by stealth** en tapinois, à la dérobée

steam [stim] *s* vapeur *f*; (*e.g., on a window*) buée *f*; **full steam ahead!** en avant à toute vapeur!; **to get up steam** faire monter la pression; **to let off steam** lâcher la vapeur; (fig) s'épancher ‖ *tr* passer à la vapeur; (culin) cuire à la vapeur; **to steam up** (*e.g., a window*) embuer ‖ *intr* dégager de la vapeur, fumer; s'évaporer; **to steam ahead** avancer à la vapeur; (fig) faire des progrès rapides; **to steam up** s'embuer

steam'boat' *s* vapeur *m*

steam' chest' *s* boîte *f* à vapeur

steam' en'gine *s* machine *f* à vapeur

steamer ['stimər] *s* vapeur *m*

steam' heat' *s* chauffage *m* à la vapeur

steam' roll'er *s* rouleau *m* compresseur; (fig) force *f* irrésistible

steam'ship' *s* vapeur *m*

steam' shov'el *s* pelle *f* à vapeur

steam' ta'ble *s* table *f* à compartiments chauffés à la vapeur

steed [stid] *s* coursier *m*

steel [stil] *adj* (industry) sidérurgique ‖ *s* acier *m*; (*for striking fire from flint*) briquet *m*; (*for sharpening knives*) fusil *m* ‖ *tr* aciérer; **to steel oneself against** se cuirasser contre

steel' wool' *s* laine *f* d'acier, paille *f* de fer

steel'works' *spl* aciérie *f*

steelyard ['stil,jard], ['stiljərd] *s* romaine *f*

steep [stip] *adj* raide, abrupt; (*cliff*) escarpé; (*price*) (coll) exorbitant ‖ *tr* tremper; (*e.g., tea*) infuser; **steeped in** saturé de; (*ignorance*) pétri de; (*the classics*) nourri de

steeple ['stipəl] *s* clocher *m*; (*spire*) flèche *f*

stee'ple-chase' *s* course *f* d'obstacles

steer [stɪr] *s* bouvillon *m* ‖ *tr* diriger, conduire; (naut) gouverner ‖ *intr* se diriger; (naut) se gouverner; **to steer clear of** (coll) éviter

steerage ['stɪrɪdʒ] *s* entrepont *m*

steer'age pas'senger *s* passager *m* d'entrepont

steer'ing wheel' *s* volant *m*; (naut) roue *f* de gouvernail

stellar ['stelər] *adj* stellaire; (*rôle*) de vedette

stem [stem] *s* (*of plant; of key*) tige *f*; (*of column; of tree*) fût *m*, tige; (*of fruit*) queue *f*; (*of pipe; of feather*) tuyau *m*; (*of goblet*) pied *m*; (*of watch*) remontoir *m*; (*of word*) radical *m*, thème *m*; (naut) étrave *f*; **from stem to stern** de l'étrave à l'étambot, d'un bout à l'autre ‖ *v* (*pret* & *pp* **stemmed;** *ger* **stemming**) *tr* (*e.g., grapes*) égrapper; (*e.g., the flow of blood*) étancher; (*the tide*) lutter contre, refouler; (*to check*) arrêter, endiguer ‖ *intr*—**to stem from** provenir de

stem'-wind'er *s* montre *f* à remontoir

stench [stentʃ] *s* puanteur *f*

sten-cil ['stensəl] *s* pochoir *m*; (*work produced by it*) travail *m* au pochoir; (*for reproducing typewriting*) stencil *m* ‖ *v* (*pret* & *pp* **-ciled** or **-cilled;** *ger* **-ciling** or **-cilling**) *tr* passer au pochoir; tirer au stencil

stenographer [stə'nɑgrəfər] *s* sténo *f*, sténographe *mf*

stenography [stə'nɑgrəfi] *s* sténographie *f*

step [step] *s* pas *m*; (*of staircase*) marche *f*, degré *m*; (*footprint*) trace *f*; (*of carriage*) marchepied *m*; (*of ladder*) échelon *m*; (*procedure*) démarche *f*; **in step with** au pas avec; **step by step** pas à pas; **watch your step!** prenez garde de tomber!; (fig) évitez tout faux pas! ‖ *v* (*pret* & *pp* **stepped;** *ger* **stepping**) *tr* échelonner; **to step off** mesurer au pas ‖ *intr* faire un pas; marcher; (coll) aller en toute hâte; **to step aside** s'écarter; **to step back** reculer; **to step in** entrer; **to step on it** (coll) mettre tous les gaz; **to step on the starter** appuyer sur le démarreur

step'broth'er *s* demi-frère *m*

step'child' *s* (*pl* **-child'ren**) beau-fils *m*; belle-fille *f*

step'daugh'ter *s* belle-fille *f*

step'fa'ther *s* beau-père *m*

step'lad'der *s* échelle *f* double, marchepied *m*, escabeau *m*

step'moth'er *s* belle-mère *f*

steppe [step] *s* steppe *f*

step'ping stone' *s* pierre *f* de passage; (fig) marchepied *m*

step'sis'ter *s* demi-sœur *f*

step'son' *s* beau-fils *m*

stere•o ['stɛrɪ,o], ['stɪrɪ,o] *adj* (coll) stéréo, stéréophonique; (coll) stéréoscopique ‖ *s* (*pl* **-os**) (coll) disque *m* stéréo; (coll) émission *f* en stéréophonique; (coll) photographie *f* stéréoscopique

stereotyped ['stɛrɪ-ə,taɪpt], ['stɪrɪ-ə,taɪpt] *adj* stéréotypé

sterile ['stɛrɪl] *adj* stérile

sterilize ['stɛrɪ,laɪz] *tr* stériliser

sterling ['stʌrlɪŋ] *adj* de bon aloi ‖ *s* livres *fpl* sterling; argent *m* au titre; vaisselle *f* d'argent

stern [stʌrn] *adj* sévère, austère; (*look*) rébarbatif ‖ *s* poupe *f*

stethoscope ['stɛθə,skop] *s* stéthoscope *m*

stevedore ['stivə,dor] *s* arrimeur *m*

stew [st(j)u] *s* ragoût *m* ‖ *tr* mettre en ragoût ‖ *intr* (coll) être dans tous ses états

steward ['st(j)u-ərd] *s* régisseur *m*, intendant *m*; maître *m* d'hôtel; (aer, naut) steward *m*

stewardess ['st(j)u-ərdɪs] *s* (aer) hôtesse *f* de l'air; (naut) stewardesse *f*

stewed' fruit' *s* compote *f*

stewed' toma'toes *spl* purée *f* de tomates

stick [stɪk] *s* bâtonnet *m*, bâton *m*; (*rod*) verge *f*; (*wand; drumstick*) baguette *f*; (*of chewing gum; of dynamite*) bâton; (*firewood*) bois *m* sec; (*walking stick*) canne *f*; (naut) mât *m*; (typ) composteur *m* ‖ *v* (*pret & pp* **stuck** [stʌk]) *tr* piquer, enfoncer, (*to fasten in position*) clouer, ficher, planter; (*to glue*) coller; (*a pig*) saigner; (coll) confondre; **stick 'em up!** (slang) haut les mains!; **to be stuck** être pris; (*e.g., in the mud*) s'enliser; (*to be unable to continue*) (coll) être en panne; **to stick it out** (coll) tenir jusqu'au bout; **to stick out** (*one's tongue*) tirer; (*one's head*) passer; (*one's chest*) bomber; **to stick up** (*in order to rob*) (slang) voler à main armée ‖ *intr* se piquer, s'enfoncer; se ficher, se planter; (*to be jammed*) être pris, se coincer; (*to adhere*) coller; (*to remain*) continuer, rester; **to stick out** saillir, dépasser; (*to be evident*) sauter aux yeux; **to stick up for** (coll) prendre la défense de

sticker ['stɪkər] *s* étiquette *f* gommée; (*difficult question*) (coll) colle *f*

stick'pin' *s* épingle *f* de cravate

stick'-up' *s* (slang) attaque *f* à main armée, hold-up *m*

stick-y ['stɪki] *adj* (*comp* **-ier**; *super* **-iest**) gluant, collant; (*hands*) poisseux; (*weather*) étouffant; (*question*) épineux; (*unaccommodating*) tatillon

stiff [stɪf] *adj* raide; difficile, ardu; (*joint*) ankylosé; (*brush; batter*) dur; (*style, manner*) guindé, empesé; (*drink*) fort; (*price*) (coll) salé, exagéré ‖ *s* (*corpse*) (slang) macchabée *m*

stiff' col'lar *s* col *m* empesé

stiffen ['stɪfən] *tr* raidir, tendre; (culin) épaissir ‖ *intr* se raidir

stiff' neck' *s* torticolis *m*

stiff'-necked' *adj* obstiné, entêté

stiff' shirt' *s* chemise *f* empesée, chemise à plastron

stifle ['staɪfəl] *tr & intr* étouffer

stig-ma ['stɪgmə] *s* (*pl* **-mas** or **-mata** [mətə]) stigmate *m*

stigmatize ['stɪgmə,taɪz] *tr* stigmatiser

stilet-to [stɪ'lɛto] *s* (*pl* **-tos**) stylet *m*

still [stɪl] *adj* tranquille, calme; immobile; silencieux; (*wine*) non mousseux ‖ *s* alambic *m*; (phot) image *f*; (mov)

photogramme *m*; (poetic) silence *m* ‖ *adv* (*yet*) encore, toujours ‖ *conj* cependant, pourtant ‖ *tr* calmer, apaiser; (*to silence*) faire taire ‖ *intr* se calmer, s'apaiser; se taire

still'born' *adj* mort-né

still' life' *s* (*pl* **still lifes** or **still lives**) nature *f* morte

stilt [stɪlt] *s* échasse *f*; (*in the water*) pilotis *m*

stilted *adj* guindé; (archit) surhaussé

stimulant ['stɪmjələnt] *adj & s* stimulant *m*

stimulate ['stɪmjə,let] *tr* stimuler

stimu-lus ['stɪmjələs] *s* (*pl* **-li** [,laɪ]) stimulant *m*, aiguillon *m*; (physiol) stimulus *m*

sting [stɪŋ] *s* piqûre *f*; (*stinging organ*) aiguillon *m*, dard *m* ‖ *v* (*pret & pp* **stung** [stʌŋ]) *tr & intr* piquer

stin-gy ['stɪndʒi] *adj* (*comp* **-gier**; *super* **-giest**) avare, pingre

stink [stɪŋk] *s* puanteur *f* ‖ *v* (*pret* **stank** [stæŋk]; *pp* **stunk** [stʌŋk]) *tr* —**to stink up** empester, empuantir ‖ *intr* puer, empester; **to stink of** puer, empester

stinker ['stɪŋkər] *s* (slang) peau *f* de vache, chameau *m*

stint [stɪnt] *s* tâche *f*, besogne *f*; **without stint** sans réserve, sans limite ‖ *tr* limiter, réduire; **to stint oneself** se priver ‖ *intr* lésiner, être chiche

stipend ['staɪpɛnd] *s* traitement *m*, honoraires *mpl*

stipulate ['stɪpjə,let] *tr* stipuler

stir [stʌr] *s* remuement *m*, agitation *f*; (*prison*) (slang) bloc *m*; **to create a stir** faire sensation ‖ *v* (*pret & pp* **stirred**) *ger* **stirring**) *tr* remuer, agiter; **to stir up** (*trouble*) fomenter ‖ *intr* remuer, s'agiter, bouger

stirring ['stʌrɪŋ] *adj* entraînant

stirrup ['stʌrəp], ['stɪrəp] *s* étrier *m*

stitch [stɪtʃ] *s* point *m*; (*in knitting*) maille *f*; (surg) point de suture; **not a stitch of** (coll) pas un brin de; **stitch in the side** (coll) point de côté; **to be in stitches** (coll) se tenir les côtes ‖ *tr* coudre; (bb) brocher; (surg) suturer ‖ *intr* coudre

stock [stɑk] *s* approvisionnement *m*, stock *m*; (*assortment*) assortiment *m*; capital *m*, fonds *m*; (*shares*) valeurs *fpl*, actions *fpl*; (*of meat*) bouillon *m*; (*of a tree*) tronc *m*; (*of an anvil*) billot *m*; (*of a rifle*) crosse *f*; (*of a tree; of a family*) souche *f*; (*livestock*) bétail *m*, bestiaux *mpl*; (*handle*) poignée *f*; (*for dies*) tourne-à-gauche *m*; (hort) ente *f*; **in stock** en magasin; **on the stocks** (fig) sur le métier; **out of stock** épuisé; **stocks** (*for punishment*) pilori *m*; (naut) chantier *m*; **to take stock** faire le point; **to take stock in** (coll) faire grand cas de; **to take stock of** faire l'inventaire de ‖ *tr* approvisionner; garder en magasin; (*a forest or lake*) peupler; (*a farm*) monter en bétail; (*a pool*) empoissonner

stockade [stɑ'ked] *s* palanque *f*, palissade *f* ‖ *tr* palissader

stock'breed'er *s* éleveur *m* de bestiaux

stock'breed'ing *s* élevage *m*

stock'bro'ker *s* agent *m* de change, courtier *m* de bourse

stock' car' *s* (aut) voiture *f* de série; (rr) wagon *m* à bestiaux

stock' com'pany *s* (com) société *f* anonyme; (theat) troupe *f* à demeure

stock' div'idend *s* action *f* gratuite

stock' exchange' *s* bourse *f*

stock'hold'er *s* actionnaire *mf*

stocking ['stɑkɪŋ] *s* bas *m*

stock' mar'ket *s* bourse *f*, marché *m* des valeurs; **to play the stock market** jouer à la bourse

stock'pile' *s* stocks *mpl* de réserve ‖ *tr & intr* stocker

stock' rais'ing *s* élevage *m*

stock'room' *s* magasin *m*

stock-y ['stɑki] *adj* (*comp* -**ier**; *super* -**iest**) trapu, costaud

stock'yard' *s* parc *m* à bétail

stoic ['sto·ɪk] *adj & s* stoïque; **Stoic** stoïcien *m*

stoke [stok] *tr* (*a fire*) attiser; (*a furnace*) alimenter, charger

stoker ['stokər] *s* chauffeur *m*; (mach) stoker *m*

stolid ['stɑlɪd] *adj* flegmatique, impassible, lourd

stomach ['stʌmək] *s* estomac *m* ‖ *tr* digérer; (coll) digérer, avaler

stom'ach ache' *s* mal *m* d'estomac

stone [ston] *s* pierre *f*; (*of fruit*) noyau *m*; (pathol) calcul *m*; (typ) marbre *m* ‖ *tr* lapider; (*fruit*) dénoyauter

stone'-broke' *adj* (coll) complètement fauché, raide

stone'-deaf' *adj* sourd comme un pot

stone'ma'son *s* maçon *m*

stone' quar'ry *s* (*pl* -**ries**) carrière *f*

stone's' throw' *s*—**within a stone's throw** à un jet de pierre

ston-y ['stoni] *adj* (*comp* -**ier**; *super* -**iest**) pierreux; (fig) dur, endurci

stooge [studʒ] *s* (theat) compère *m*; (slang) homme *m* de paille, acolyte *m*

stool [stul] *s* tabouret *m*, escabeau *m*; (*bowel movement*) selles *fpl*

stool' pi'geon *s* appeau *m*; (slang) mouchard *m*, mouton *m*

stoop [stup] *s* courbure *f*, inclinaison *f*; (*porch*) véranda *f* ‖ *intr* se pencher; se tenir voûté; (*to debase oneself*) s'abaisser

stoop'-shoul'dered *adj* voûté

stop [stɑp] *s* arrêt *m*; (*in telegrams*) stop *m*; (*full stop*) point *m*; (*of a guitar*) touche *f*; (mus) jeu *m* d'orgue; (public sign) stop; **to put a stop to** mettre fin à ‖ *v* (*pret & pp* **stopped**; *ger* **stopping**) *tr* arrêter; (*a check*) faire opposition à; **to stop up** boucher ‖ *intr* s'arrêter, arrêter; **to stop** + *ger* cesser de + *inf*, s'arrêter de + *inf*; **to stop off** descendre en passant; **to stop off at** s'arrêter un moment à; **to stop over** (aer, naut) faire escale

stop'cock' *s* robinet *m* d'arrêt

stop'gap' *adj* provisoire ‖ *s* bouche-trou *m*

stop'light' *s* signal *m* lumineux; (aut) feu *m* stop, stop *m*

stop'o'ver *s* arrêt *m* en cours de route, étape *f*

stoppage ['stɑpɪdʒ] *s* arrêt *m*; (*of payments*) suspension *f*; (*of wages*) retenue *f*; (obstruction *f*; (pathol) occlusion *f*

stopper ['stɑpər] *s* bouchon *m*, tampon *m*

stop' sign' *s* signal *m* d'arrêt

stop' thief' *interj* au voleur!

stop'watch' *s* chronomètre *m* à déclic, compte-secondes *m*

storage ['storɪdʒ] *s* emmagasinage *m*, entreposage *m*; **to put in storage** entreposer

stor'age bat'ter-y *s* (*pl* -**les**) (elec) accumulateur *m*, accu *m*

store [stor] *s* magasin *m*, boutique *f*; approvisionnement *m*; (*warehouse*) (Brit) entrepôt *m*; **stores** matériel *m*; vivres *mpl*; **to set great store by** faire grand cas de ‖ *tr* emmagasiner; (*warehouse*) entreposer; (*to supply or stock*) approvisionner; **to store away** or **up** accumuler

store'house' *s* magasin *m*, entrepôt *m*; (*of information*) mine *f*

store'keep'er *s* boutiquier *m*

store'room' *s* dépense *f*, office *f*; (*for furniture*) garde-meuble *m*; (naut) soute *f*

stork [stɔrk] *s* cigogne *f*

storm [stɔrm] *s* orage *m*; (mil) assaut *m*; (fig) tempête *f*; **to take by storm** prendre d'assaut ‖ *tr* livrer l'assaut à ‖ *intr* faire de l'orage; (fig) tempêter

storm' cloud' *s* nuage *m* orageux; (fig) nuage noir

storm' door' *s* contre-porte *f*

storm' pet'rel ['petrəl] *s* oiseau *m* des tempêtes

storm' sash' *s* contre-fenêtre *f*

storm' troops' *spl* troupes *fpl* d'assaut

storm' win'dow *s* contre-fenêtre *f*

storm-y ['stɔrmi] *adj* (*comp* -**ier**; *super* -**iest**) orageux

sto-ry ['stori] *s* (*pl* -**ries**) histoire *f*; (*tale*) conte *m*; (*plot*) intrigue *f*; (*floor*) étage *m*; (coll) mensonge *m*, histoire

sto'ry·tel'ler *s* conteur *m*; (*fibber*) menteur *m*

stout [staut] *adj* corpulent, gros; vaillant; ferme, résolu; (*strong*) fort ‖ *s* stout *m*

stout'-heart'ed *adj* au cœur vaillant

stove [stov] *s* (*for heating a house or room*) poêle *m*; (*for cooking*) fourneau *m* de cuisine, cuisinière *f*

stove'pipe' *s* tuyau *m* de poêle; (*hat*) (coll) huit-reflets *m*, tuyau de poêle

stow [sto] *tr* mettre en place, ranger; (naut) arrimer; **to stow with** remplir de ‖ *intr*—**to stow away** s'embarquer clandestinement

stowage ['sto·ɪdʒ] *s* arrimage *m*; (*costs*) frais *mpl* d'arrimage

stow'away' *s* passager *m* clandestin

straddle ['strædəl] *tr* enfourcher, chevaucher ‖ *intr* se mettre à califourchon; (coll) répondre en normand

strafe [straf], [stref] *s* (slang) bombardement *m*, marmitage *m* ‖ *tr* (slang) bombarder, marmiter

straggle ['strægəl] *intr* traîner; (*to be scattered*) s'éparpiller; **to straggle along** marcher sans ordre

straggler ['stræglər] *s* traînard *m*

straight [stret] *adj* droit; direct; loyal, honnête; correct, en ordre; (*hair*) raide; (*whiskey*) sec; (*candid*) franc; (*hanging straight*) d'aplomb; **to set s.o. straight** faire la leçon à qn ‖ *s* (poker) séquence *f* ‖ *adv* droit; directement; loyalement, honnêtement; (*without interruption*) de suite; **straight ahead** tout droit; **straight out** franchement, sans detours; **straight through** de part en part; d'un bout à l'autre; **to go straight** (coll) vivre honnêtement

straighten ['stretən] *tr* redresser; mettre en ordre ‖ *intr* se redresser

straight' face' *s*—**to keep a straight face** montrer un front sérieux

straight'for'ward *adj* franc, direct; loyal

straight' off' *adv* sur-le-champ, d'emblée

straight' ra'zor *s* rasoir *m* à main

straight'way' *adv* sur-le-champ, d'emblée

strain [stren] *s* tension *f*; (*of a muscle*) foulure *f*; (*descendants*) lignée *f*; (*ancestry; type of virus*) souche *f*; (*trait*) héritage *m*, tendance *f*; (*vein*) ton *m*, sens *m*; (*bit*) trace *f*; (coll) grand effort *m*; **mental strain** surmenage *m* intellectuel; **strains** (*of, e.g., the Marseillaise*) accents *mpl*; **sweet strains** doux accords *mpl* ‖ *tr* forcer; (*e.g., a wrist*) se fouler; (*e.g., one's eyes*) se fatiguer; (*e.g., part of a machine*) déformer; (*e.g., a liquid*) filtrer, tamiser; **to strain oneself** se surmener ‖ s'efforcer; filtrer, tamiser; (*to trickle*) suinter; (*said of beam, ship, motor, etc.*) fatiguer; **to strain at** (*a leash, rope, etc.*) tirer sur; (*to balk at*) reculer devant

strained *adj* (*smile*) forcé; (*friendship*) tendu

strainer ['strenər] *s* passoire *f*, filtre *m*

strait [stret] *s* détroit *m*; **straits** détroit; **to be in dire straits** être dans la plus grande gêne

strait' jack'et *s* camisole *f* de force

strait'-laced' *adj* prude, collet monté, puritain

Straits' of Do'ver *spl* Pas *m* de Calais

strand [strænd] *s* (*beach*) plage *f*, grève *f*; (*of rope or cable*) toron *m*; (*of thread*) brin *m*; (*of pearls*) collier *m*; (*of hair*) cheveu *m* ‖ *tr* toronner; (*to undo strands of*) décorder; (*a ship*) échouer

stranded *adj* abandonné; (*lost*) égaré; (*ship*) échoué; (*rope or cable*) à torons; **to leave s.o. stranded** laisser qn en plan

strange [strend3] *adj* étrange; (*unfa-*

miliar) inconnu, étranger; (*unaccustomed*) inhabituel

stranger ['strend3ər] *s* étranger *m*; visiteur *m*

strangle ['stræŋgəl] *tr* étrangler, étouffer ‖ *intr* s'étrangler

strap [stræp] *s* (*of leather, rubber, etc.*) courroie *f*; (*of cloth, metal, leather, etc.*) bande *f*; (*to sharpen a razor*) cuir *m* à rasoir; (*of a harness*) sangle *f* ‖ *v* (*pret & pp* **strapped**) *ger* **strapping**) *tr* attacher avec une courroie, sangler; (*a razor*) repasser sur le cuir

strap'hang'er *s* (coll) voyageur *m* debout

strapping ['stræpɪŋ] *adj* bien découplé, robuste; (coll) énorme, gros

stratagem ['strætədʒəm] *s* stratagème *m*

strategic(al) [strə'tidʒɪk(əl)] *adj* stratégique

strategist ['strætɪdʒɪst] *s* stratège *m*

strate·gy ['strætɪdʒɪ] *s* (*pl* **-gies**) stratégie *f*

strati·fy ['stræti,faɪ] *v* (*pret & pp* **-fied**) *tr* stratifier ‖ *intr* se stratifier

stratosphere ['strætə,sfir], ['stretə,sfir] *s* stratosphère *f*

stra·tum ['stretəm], ['strætəm] *s* (*pl* **-ta** [tə] *or* **-tums**) couche *f*; (*e.g., of society*) classe *f*, couche

straw [strɔ] *s* paille *f*; (*for drinking*) chalumeau *m*, paille; **it's the last straw!** c'est le bouquet!

straw'ber'ry *s* (*pl* **-ries**) fraise *f*; (*plant*) fraisier *m*

straw'hat' *s* chapeau *m* de paille; (*skimmer*) canotier *m*

straw' man' *s* (*pl* **men'**) (*figurehead*) homme *m* de paille; (*scarecrow*) épouvantail *m*; (*red herring*) canard *m*, diversion *f*

straw' mat'tress *s* paillasse *f*

straw' vote' *s* vote *m* d'essai

stray [stre] *adj* égaré; (*bullet*) perdu; (*scattered*) épars ‖ *s* animal *m* égaré ‖ *intr* s'égarer

streak [strik] *s* raie *f*, rayure *f*, bande *f*; (*of light*) trait *m*, filet *m*; (*of lightning*) éclair *m*; (*layer*) veine *f*; (*bit*) trace *f*; **like a streak** comme un éclair; **streak of luck** filon *m* ‖ *tr* rayer, strier, zébrer ‖ *intr* faire des raies; passer comme un éclair

stream [strim] *s* ruisseau *m*; (*steady flow of current*) courant *m*; (*of people, abuse, light, etc.*) flot *m*; (*of, e.g., automobiles*) défilé *m* ‖ *intr* couler; (*said of blood*) ruisseler; (*said of light*) jaillir; (*said of flag*) flotter; **to stream out** sortir à flots

streamer ['strimər] *s* banderole *f*

stream'lined' *adj* aérodynamique, caréné; (fig) abrégé, concis

stream'lin'er *s* train *m* caréné de luxe

street [strit] *s* rue *f*; (*surface of the street*) chaussée *f*

street' Ar'ab *s* gamin *m* des rues

street'car' *s* tramway *m*

street' clean'er *s* balayeur *m*; (mach) balayeuse *f*

street′ clothes′ *spl* vêtements *mpl* de ville

street′ floor′ *s* rez-de-chaussée *m*

street′light′ *s* réverbère *m*

street′ sprink′ler *s* arroseuse *f*

street′ u′rinal *s* vespasienne *f*, édicule *m*, urinoir *m*

street′walk′er *s* racoleuse *f*, fille *f* des rues

strength [strɛŋθ] *s* force *f*; intensité *f*; (*of a fabric*) solidité *f*; (*of spirituous liquors*) degré *m*, titre *m*; (com) tendance *f* à la hausse; (mil) effectif *m*; **on the strength of** sur la foi de

strengthen ['strɛŋθən] *tr* fortifier, renforcer; consolider || *intr* se fortifier, se renforcer

strenuous ['strɛnju·əs] *adj* actif, énergique; (*work*) ardu; (*effort*) acharné; (*objection*) vigoureux

stress [strɛs] *s* tension *f*, force *f*; (mach) stress *m*, tension; (phonet) accent *m* d'intensité; **to lay stress on** insister sur || *tr* (*e.g., a beam*) charger; (*a syllable*) accentuer; insister sur, appuyer sur

stress′ ac′cent *s* accent *m* d'intensité

stretch [strɛtʃ] *s* allongement *m*; (*of the arm; of the meaning*) extension *f*; (*of the imagination*) effort *m*; (*distance in time or space*) intervalle *m*; (*section of road*) section *f*; (*section of country, water, etc.*) étendue *f*; **at a stretch** d'un trait; **in one stretch** d'une seule traite; **to do a stretch** (slang) faire de la taule || *tr* tendre; (*the sense of a word*) forcer; (*a sauce*) allonger; **to stretch oneself** s'étirer; **to stretch out** allonger, étendre; (*the hand*) tendre || *intr* s'étirer; (*said of shoes, gloves, etc.*) s'élargir; **to stretch out** s'allonger, s'étendre

stretcher ['strɛtʃər] *s* (*for gloves, trousers, etc.*) tendeur *m*; (*for a painting*) châssis *m*; (*to carry sick or wounded*) civière *f*, brancard *m*

stretch′er-bear′er *s* brancardier *m*

strew [stru] *v* (*pret* **strewed** or **strewn**) *tr* semer, éparpiller; (*e.g., with flowers*) joncher, parsemer

stricken ['strɪkən] *adj* frappé; (*e.g., with grief*) affligé; (*crossed out*) rayé; **stricken with** atteint de

strict [strɪkt] *adj* strict; (*exacting*) sévère

stricture ['strɪktʃər] *s* critique *f* sévère; (pathol) rétrécissement *m*

stride [straɪd] *s* enjambée *f*; **to hit one's stride** attraper la cadence; **to make great** (or **rapid**) **strides** avancer à grands pas; **to take in one's stride** faire sans le moindre effort || *v* (*pret* **strode** [strod]; *pp* **stridden** ['strɪdən]) *tr* parcourir à grandes enjambées; (*to straddle*) enfourcher || *intr* —**to stride across** or **over** enjamber; **to stride along** marcher à grandes enjambées

strident ['straɪdənt] *adj* strident

strife [straɪf] *s* lutte *f*

strike [straɪk] *s* (*blow*) coup *m*; (*stopping of work*) grève *f*; (*discovery of*

ore, oil, etc.) rencontre *f*; (baseball) coup du batteur; **to go on strike** se mettre en grève || *v* (*pret & pp* **struck** [strʌk]) *tr* frapper; (*coins*) frapper; (*a match*) frotter; (*a bargain*) conclure; (*camp*) lever; (*the sails; the colors*) amener; (*the hour*) sonner; (*root; a pose*) prendre; **how does he strike you?** quelle impression vous fait-il?; **to strike it rich** trouver le filon; **to strike out** rayer; **to strike up** (*a song, piece of music, etc.*) attaquer, entonner; (*an acquaintance, conversation, etc.*) lier || *intr* frapper; (*said of clock*) sonner; (*said of workers*) faire la grève; (mil) donner l'assaut; **to strike out** se mettre en route

strike′break′er *s* briseur *m* de grève, jaune *m*

striker ['straɪkər] *s* frappeur *m*; (*on door*) marteau *m*; (*worker on strike*) gréviste *mf*

striking ['straɪkɪŋ] *adj* frappant, saisissant; (*workers*) en grève

strik′ing pow′er *s* force *f* de frappe

string [strɪŋ] *s* ficelle *f*; (*of onions or garlic; of islands; of pearls; of abuse*) chapelet *m*; (*of words, insults*) enfilade *f*, kyrielle *f*; (*e.g., of cars*) file *f*; (*of beans*) fil *m*; (*for shoes*) lacet *m*; (mus) corde *f*; **strings** instruments *mpl* à cordes; **to pull strings** (fig) tirer les ficelles; **with no strings attached** (coll) sans restriction || *v* (*pret & pp* **strung** [strʌŋ]) *tr* mettre une ficelle à, garnir de cordes; (*e.g., a violin*) mettre les cordes à; (*a bow*) bander; (*a tennis racket*) corder; (*beads, sentences, etc.*) enfiler; (*a cord, a thread, a wire, etc.*) tendre; (*to tune*) monter; **to string along** (slang) lanterner, faire marcher; **to string up** (coll) pendre || *intr*—**to string along with** (slang) collaborer avec, suivre

string′ bean′ *s* haricot *m* vert

stringed′ in′strument *s* instrument *m* à cordes

stringent ['strɪndʒənt] *adj* rigoureux; (*tight*) tendu; (*convincing*) convaincant

string′ quartet′ *s* quatuor *m* à cordes

string-y ['strɪŋi] *adj* (*comp* **-ier**; *super* **-iest**) fibreux, filandreux

strip [strɪp] *s* (*of paper, cloth, land*) bande *f*; (*of metal*) lame *f*, ruban *m* || *v* (*pret & pp* **stripped**; *ger* **stripping**) *tr* dépouiller; (*to strip bare*) mettre à nu; (*the bed*) défaire; (*a screw*) arracher le filet de, faire foirer; (*tobacco*) écoter; **to strip down** (*e.g., a motor*) démonter; **to strip off** enlever; (*e.g., bark*) écorcer || *intr* se déshabiller

stripe [straɪp] *s* raie *f*, bande *f*; (*on cloth*) rayure *f*; (*flesh wound*) marque *f*; (mil, nav) chevron *m*, galon *m*; **to win one's stripes** gagner ses galons || *tr* rayer

strip′ min′ing *s* exploitation *f* minière à ciel ouvert

strip′tease′ s strip-tease m, déshabillage m suggestif

stripteaser ['strɪp,tizər] s effeuilleuse f, strip-teaseuse f

strive [straɪv] v (pret **strove** [strov]; pp **striven** ['strɪvən]) intr s'efforcer; **to strive after** rechercher; **to strive against** lutter contre; **to strive to** s'efforcer à, s'évertuer à

stroke [strok] s coup m; (of pen; of wit) trait m; (of arms in swimming) brassée f; (caress with hand) caresse f de la main; (of a piston) course f; (of lightning) foudre f; (pathol) attaque f d'apoplexie; **at the stroke of** sonnant, e.g., **at the stroke of five** à cinq heures sonnantes; **to not do a stroke of work** ne pas en ficher une ramée || tr caresser de la main

stroll [strol] s promenade f; **to take a stroll** aller faire un tour || intr se promener

stroller ['strolər] s promeneur m; (for babies) poussette f

strong [strɔŋ], [strɑŋ] adj (comp **stronger** ['strɔŋgər], ['strɑŋgər]; super **strongest** ['strɔŋgɪst], ['strɑŋgɪst]) fort; (stock market) ferme; (musical beat) marqué; (spicy) piquant; (rancid) rance

strong′box′ s coffre-fort m

strong′ drink′ s boissons fpl spiritueuses

strong′hold′ s place f forte

strong′ man′ s (pl **men′**) (e.g., in a circus) hercule m forain; (leader, good planner) animateur m; (dictator) chef m autoritaire

strong′-mind′ed adj résolu, décidé; (woman) hommasse

strontium ['strɑnʃɪ‑əm] s strontium m

strop [strɑp] s cuir m à rasoir || v (pret & pp **stropped**; ger **stropping**) tr repasser sur le cuir

strophe ['strofɪ] s strophe f

structure ['strʌkt/ər] s structure f; (building) édifice m

struggle ['strʌgəl] s lutte f || intr lutter; **to struggle along** avancer péniblement

strug′gle for exist′ence s lutte f pour la vie

strum [strʌm] v (pret & pp **strummed**; ger **strumming**) tr (an instrument) gratter de; (a tune) tapoter || intr jouailler; **to strum on** plaquer des arpèges sur

strumpet ['strʌmpɪt] s putain f

strut [strʌt] s (brace, prop) étai m, support m, entretoise f; démarche f orgueilleuse || v (pret & pp **strutted**; ger **strutting**) intr se pavaner

strychnine ['strɪknaɪn], ['strɪknɪn] s strychnine f

stub [stʌb] s (fragment) tronçon m; (of a tree) souche f; (of a pencil; of a cigar, cigarette) bout m; (of a check) talon m, souche || v (pret & pp **stubbed**; ger **stubbing**) tr—**to stub one's toe** se cogner le bout du pied

stubble ['stʌbəl] s éteule f, chaume m; (of beard) poil m court et raide

stubborn ['stʌbərn] adj obstiné; (head‑

strong) têtu; (resolute) acharné; (fever) rebelle; (soil) ingrat

stuc·co ['stʌko] s (pl **-coes** or **-cos**) stuc m || tr stuquer

stuck [stʌk] adj coincé, pris; (glued) collé; (unable to continue) en panne; **stuck on** (coll) entiché de

stuck′-up′ adj (coll) hautain, prétentieux

stud [stʌd] s clou m à grosse tête; (ornament) clou doré; (on shirt) bouton m; (studhorse) étalon m; (horse farm) haras m; (bolt) goujon m; (archit) montant m || v (pret & pp **studded**; ger **studding**) tr clouter; **studded with** jonché de, parsemé de

stud′ bolt′ s goujon m

student ['st(j)udənt] adj estudiantin || s étudiant m; (researcher) chercheur m

stu′dent bod′y s étudiants mpl

stu′dent cen′ter s foyer m d'étudiants, centre m social des étudiants

stu′dent nurse′ s élève f infirmière

stud′ farm′ s haras m

stud′horse′ s étalon m

studied ['stʌdɪd] adj prémédité; recherché

studi·o ['st(j)udɪ,o] s (pl **-os**) studio m, atelier m

studious ['st(j)udɪ‑əs] adj studieux, appliqué

stud·y ['stʌdɪ] s (pl **-ies**) étude f; rêverie f; cabinet m || v (pret & pp **-ied**) tr & intr étudier

stuff [stʌf] s matière f; chose f; **to know one's stuff** (coll) s'y connaître || tr bourrer; (with food) gaver; (furniture) rembourrer; (an animal) empailler; (culin) farcir; **to stuff up** boucher || intr se gaver

stuffed′ shirt′ s collet m monté

stuffing ['stʌfɪŋ] s rembourrage m; (culin) farce f

stuff·y ['stʌfɪ] adj (comp **-ier**; super **-iest**) mal ventilé; (tedious) ennuyeux; (pompous) collet monté; **to smell stuffy** sentir le renfermé

stumble ['stʌmbəl] intr trébucher; (in speaking) hésiter

stum′bling block′ s pierre f d'achoppement

stump [stʌmp] s (of tree) souche f; (e.g., of arm) moignon m; (of tooth) chicot m || tr (a design) estomper; (coll) embarrasser, coller; (a state, district, region) (coll) faire une tournée électorale en, dans, or à || intr clopiner

stump′ speak′er s orateur m de carrefour

stump′ speech′ s harangue f électorale improvisée

stun [stʌn] v (pret & pp **stunned**; ger **stunning**) tr étourdir

stunning ['stʌnɪŋ] adj (coll) étourdissant, épatant

stunt [stʌnt] s atrophie f; (underdeveloped creature) avorton m; (coll) tour m de force, acrobatie f || tr atrophier || intr (coll) faire des acrobaties

stunted *adj* rabougri

stunt/ fly'ing *s* vol *m* de virtuosité, acrobatie *f* aérienne

stunt/ man' *s* (*pl* **men'**) cascadeur *m*, doublure *f*

stupe·fy ['st(j)upɪˌfaɪ] *v* (*pret & pp* **-fied**) *tr* stupéfier

stupendous [st(j)u'pendəs] *adj* prodigieux, formidable

stupid ['st(j)upɪd] *adj* stupide

stupor ['st(j)upər] *s* stupeur *f*

stur·dy ['stʌrdi] *adj* (*comp* **-dier**; *super* **-diest**) robuste, vigoureux; (*resolute*) ferme, hardi

sturgeon ['stʌrdʒən] *s* esturgeon *m*

stutter ['stʌtər] *s* bégaiement *m* || *tr & intr* bégayer

sty [staɪ] *s* (*pl* **sties**) porcherie *f*; (*pathol*) orgelet *m*

style [staɪl] *s* style *m*; (*fashion*) mode *f*; (*elegance*) ton *m*, chic *m*; **to live in great style** mener grand train || *tr* appeler, dénommer; **to style oneself** s'intituler

stylish ['staɪlɪʃ] *adj* à la mode, élégant, chic

sty·mie ['staɪmi] *v* (*pret & pp* **-mied**; *ger* **-mieing**) *tr* contrecarrer

styp/tic pen'cil ['stɪptɪk] *s* crayon *m* styptique

suave [swɑv], [swev] *adj* suave; (*person*) affable; (*manners*) doucereux

sub [sʌb] *s* (coll) sous-marin *m*

subconscious [sʌb'kɑn/əs] *adj & s* subconscient *m*

sub/divide/ or **sub/divide/** *tr* subdiviser || *intr* se subdiviser

subdue [səb'd(j)u] *tr* subjuguer, vaincre, asservir; (*color, light, sound*) adoucir, amortir; (*passions, feelings*) dompter

sub/head/ *s* sous-titre *m*

subject ['sʌbdʒɪkt] *adj* sujet, assujetti, soumis || *s* sujet *m*; (*e.g., in school*) matière *f* || [səb'dʒekt] *tr* assujettir, soumettre

subjection [səb'dʒek/ən] *s* sujétion *f*, soumission *f*

subjective [səb'dʒektɪv] *adj* subjectif

sub/ject mat/ter *s* matière *f*

subjugate ['sʌbdʒəˌget] *tr* subjuguer

subjunctive [səb'dʒʌŋktɪv] *adj & s* subjonctif *m*

sub/lease/ *s* sous-location *f* || **sub/lease/** *tr* sous-louer

sub·let ['sʌb,let], ['sʌb,let] *v* (*pret & pp* **-let**; *ger* **-letting**) *tr* sous-louer

sub/machine/ gun/ *s* mitraillette *f*

sub/marine/ *adj & s* sous-marin *m*

sub/marine chas/er *s* chasseur *m* de sous-marins

submerge [səb'mʌrdʒ] *tr* submerger || *intr* (*said of submarine*) plonger

submersion [səb'mʌrʒən], [səb'mʌr/ən] *s* submersion *f*

submission [səb'mɪ/ən] *s* soumission *f*; (*delivery*) présentation *f*

submissive [səb'mɪsɪv] *adj* soumis

sub·mit [səb'mɪt] *v* (*pret & pp* **-mitted**; *ger* **-mitting**) *tr* soumettre || *intr* se soumettre

subordinate [səb'ɔrdɪnɪt] *adj & s*

subordonné *m* || [sə'bɔrdɪ,net] *tr* subordonner

subpoena [sʌb'pinə], [sə'pinə] *s* assignation *f*, citation *f* || *tr* citer

subscribe [səb'skraɪb] *tr* souscrire || *intr*—**to subscribe to** (*an opinion; a charity; a loan; a newspaper*) souscrire à; (*a newspaper*) s'abonner à

subscriber [səb'skraɪbər] *s* abonné *m*

subscription [səb'skrɪp/ən] *s* souscription *f*; (*to newspaper or magazine*) abonnement *m*; (*to club*) cotisation *f*; **to take out a subscription for s.o.** abonner qn; **to take out a subscription to** s'abonner à

subsequent ['sʌbsɪkwənt] *adj* subséquent, suivant

subservient [səb'sʌrvɪ-ənt] *adj* asservi, subordonné

subside [səb'saɪd] *intr* (*said of water, ground, etc.*) s'abaisser; (*said of storm, excitement, etc.*) s'apaiser

subsidiar·y [səb'sɪdɪ ˌɛri] *adj* subsidiaire || *s* (*pl* **-ies**) filiale *f*

subsidize ['sʌbsɪ ˌdaɪz] *tr* subventionner; suborner

subsi·dy ['sʌbsɪdi] *s* (*pl* **-dies**) subside *m*, subvention *f*

subsist [səb'sɪst] *intr* subsister

subsistence [səb'sɪstəns] *s* (*supplies*) subsistance *f*; existence *f*

sub/soil/ *s* sous-sol *m*

substance ['sʌbstəns] *s* substance *f*

sub·stand/ard *adj* inférieur au niveau normal

substantial [səb'stæn/əl] *adj* substantiel; (*wealthy*) aisé, cossu

substantiate [səb'stæn/ɪ ˌet] *tr* établir, vérifier

substantive ['sʌbstəntɪv] *adj & s* substantif *m*

sub/sta/tion *s* (*of post office*) bureau *m* auxiliaire; (elec) sous-station *f*

substitute ['sʌbstɪ ˌt(j)ut] *s* (*person*) remplaçant *m*, suppléant *m*, substitut *m*; (*e.g., for coffee*) succédané *m* || *tr* remplacer, e.g., **they substituted copper for silver** ils ont remplacé l'argent par le cuivre; substituer, e.g., **a hind was substituted for Iphigenia** une biche fut substituée à Iphigénie || *intr* servir de remplaçant; **to substitute for** remplacer, suppléer

substitution [ˌsʌbstɪ't(j)u/ən] *s* substitution *f*

sub/stra/tum *s* (*pl* **-ta** [tə] or **-tums**) substrat *m*

subterfuge ['sʌbtər ˌfjudʒ] *s* subterfuge *m*, faux-fuyant *m*

subterranean [ˌsʌbtə'renɪ-ən] *adj* souterrain

sub/ti/tle *s* sous-titre *m*

subtle ['sʌtəl] *adj* subtil

subtle·ty ['sʌtəlti] *s* (*pl* **-ties**) subtilité *f*

subtract [səb'trækt] *tr* soustraire

subtraction [səb'træk/ən] *s* soustraction *f*

suburb ['sʌbʌrb] *s* ville *f* de la banlieue; **the suburbs** la banlieue

suburban [sə'bʌrbən] *adj* suburbain

suburbanite [sə'bʌrbə ˌnaɪt] *s* banlieusard *m*

subvention [səb'venʃən] s subvention f
‖ tr subventionner

subversive [səb'vʌrsɪv] adj subversif ‖
s factieux m

subvert [səb'vʌrt] tr corrompre; renverser

sub'way' s métro m; (tunnel for pedestrians) souterrain m

sub'way car' s voiture f de métro

sub'way sta'tion s station f de métro

succeed [sək'sid] tr succéder (with
dat); to succeed one another se succéder ‖ intr réussir; to succeed in +
ger réussir à + inf; to succeed to (the
throne; a fortune) succéder à

success [sək'ses] s succès m, réussite f;
to be a success avoir du succès

successful [sək'sesfəl] adj réussi; heureux, prospère

succession [sək'seʃən] s succession f;
in succession de suite

successive [sək'sesɪv] adj successif

succor ['sʌkər] s secours m ‖ tr secourir

succotash ['sʌkə‚tæʃ] s plat m de fèves
et de maïs

succumb [sə'kʌm] intr succomber

such [sʌtʃ] adj & pron indef tel, pareil,
semblable; such a un tel; such and
such tel et tel; such as tel que

suck [sʌk] s—to give suck to allaiter ‖
tr sucer; (a nipple) téter; to suck in
aspirer; (to absorb) sucer ‖ intr sucer; téter

sucker ['sʌkər] s suceur m; (sucking
organ) suçoir m, ventouse f; (bot)
drageon m; (ichth) rémora m; (gullible person) (coll) gogo m; (lollipop)
(coll) sucette f

suckle ['sʌkəl] tr allaiter

suck'ling pig' s cochon m de lait

suction ['sʌkʃən] s succion f

suc'tion cup' s ventouse f

suc'tion pump' s pompe f aspirante

sudden ['sʌdən] adj brusque, soudain;
all of a sudden tout à coup

suddenly ['sʌdənli] adv tout à coup

suds [sʌdz] spl eau f savonneuse; mousse f de savon

sue [s(j)u] tr poursuivre en justice ‖
intr intenter un procès

suede [swed] s suède m; (for shoes)
daim m

suet ['s(j)u‚ɪt] s graisse f de rognon

suffer ['sʌfər] tr souffrir; (to allow)
permettre; (a defeat) essuyer, subir ‖
intr souffrir

sufferance ['sʌfərəns] s tolérance f

suffering ['sʌfərɪŋ] adj souffrant ‖ s
souffrance f

suffice [sə'faɪs] tr suffire (with dat) ‖
intr suffire; it suffices to + inf il suffit de + inf

sufficient [sə'frʃənt] adj suffisant

suffix ['sʌfɪks] s suffixe m

suffocate ['sʌfə‚ket] tr & intr suffoquer, étouffer

suffrage ['sʌfrɪdʒ] s suffrage m

suffragist ['sʌfrədʒɪst] s partisan m du
droit de vote des femmes

suffuse [sə'fjuz] tr baigner, saturer

sugar ['ʃugər] s sucre m ‖ tr sucrer;

(a cake) saupoudrer de sucre; (a pill)
recouvrir de sucre ‖ intr former du
sucre

sug'ar beet' s betterave f sucrière, betterave à sucre

sug'ar bowl' s sucrier m

sug'ar cane' s canne f à sucre

sug'ar-coat' tr dragéifier; (fig) dorer

sug'ar dad'dy s (pl -dies) papa m gâteau

sug'ar ma'ple s érable m à sucre

sug'ar pea' s mange-tout m

sug'ar tongs' spl pince f à sucre

sugary ['ʃugəri] adj sucré; (fig) doucereux

suggest [səg'dʒest] tr suggérer

suggestion [səg'dʒestʃən] s suggestion
f; nuance f, pointe f, soupçon m

suggestive [səg'dʒestɪv] adj suggestif

suicidal [‚s(j)u‚ɪ'saɪdəl] adj suicidaire

suicide ['s(j)u‚ɪ‚saɪd] s (act) suicide
m; (person) suicidé m; to commit
suicide se suicider

suit [s(j)ut] s costume m; (men's)
complet m, costume; (women's) costume tailleur, tailleur m; (lawsuit)
procès m; (plea) requête f; (cards)
couleur f; to follow suit jouer la couleur; (fig) en faire autant ‖ tr adapter; convenir (with dat), e.g., does
that suit him? cela lui convient?; aller
(with dat), seoir (with dat), e.g., the
dress suits her well la robe lui va
bien, la robe lui sied bien ‖ intr convenir, aller

suitable ['s(j)utəbəl] adj convenable, à
propos; compétent

suit'case' s valise f

suite [swit] s suite f ‖ [s(j)ut] s (of
furniture) ameublement m, mobilier
m

suiting ['s(j)utɪŋ] s étoffe f pour
complets

suit' of clothes' s complet-veston m

suitor ['s(j)utər] s prétendant m, soupirant m

sul'fa drugs' ['sʌlfə] spl sulfamides mpl

sulfide ['sʌlfaɪd] s sulfure m

sulfur ['sʌlfər] adj soufré ‖ s soufre
m ‖ tr soufrer

sulfuric [sʌl'fjurɪk] adj sulfurique

sul'fur mine' s soufrière f

sulk [sʌlk] s bouderie f ‖ intr bouder

sulk·y ['sʌlki] adj (comp -ier; super
-iest) boudeur, maussade

sullen ['sʌlən] adj maussade, rébarbatif

sul·ly ['sʌli] v (pret & pp -lied) tr souiller

sulphur ['sʌlfər] adj, s & tr var of
sulfur

sultan ['sʌltən] s sultan m

sul·try ['sʌltri] adj (comp -trier; super
-triest) étouffant, suffocant

sum [sʌm] s somme f; tout m, total m;
in sum somme toute ‖ v (pret & pp
summed; ger summing) tr—to sum
up résumer

sumac or **sumach** ['ʃumæk], ['sumæk]
s sumac m

summarize ['sʌmə‚raɪz] tr résumer

summa·ry ['sʌməri] adj sommaire ‖ s
(pl -ries) sommaire m

summer ['sʌmər] *adj* estival ‖ *s* été *m* ‖ *intr* passer l'été
sum'mer resort' *s* station *f* estivale
sum'mer school' *s* cours *m* d'été, cours de vacances
summery ['sʌməri] *adj* estival, d'été
summit ['sʌmɪt] *s* sommet *m*
sum'mit con'ference *s* conférence *f* au sommet
summon ['sʌmən] *tr* appeler, convoquer; (law) sommer, citer, assigner
summons ['sʌmənz] *s* appel *m*; (law) citation *f*, assignation *f*, exploit *m*
sumptuous ['sʌmptʃʊ·əs] *adj* somptueux
sun [sʌn] *s* soleil *m* ‖ *v* (pret & pp **sunned**; ger **sunning**) *tr* exposer au soleil ‖ *intr* prendre le soleil
sun' bath' *s* bain *m* de soleil
sun'beam' *s* rayon *m* de soleil
sun'bon'net *s* capeline *f*
sun'burn' *s* coup *m* de soleil ‖ *v* (pret & pp **-burned** or **-burnt**) *tr* hâler, basaner ‖ *intr* se basaner
sun'burned' *adj* brûlé par le soleil
sundae ['sʌndi] *s* coupe *f* de glace garnie de fruits
Sunday ['sʌndi] *adj* dominical ‖ *s* dimanche *m*
Sun'day best' *s* (coll) habits *mpl* du dimanche
Sun'day driv'er *s* chauffeur *m* du dimanche
Sun'day school' *s* école *f* du dimanche
sunder ['sʌndər] *tr* séparer, rompre
sun'di'al *s* cadran *m* solaire, gnomon *m*
sun'down' *s* coucher *m* du soleil
sundries ['sʌndriz] *spl* articles *mpl* divers
sundry ['sʌndri] *adj* divers
sun'fish' *s* poisson-lune *m*
sun'flow'er *s* soleil *m*, tournesol *m*
sun'glass'es *spl* lunettes *fpl* de soleil, verres *mpl* fumés
sunken ['sʌŋkən] *adj* creux, enfoncé; (rock) noyé; (ship) sous-marin
sun' lamp' *s* lampe *f* à rayons ultra-violets
sun'light' *s* lumière *f* du soleil
sun·ny ['sʌni] *adj* (comp **-nier**; super **-niest**) ensoleillé; (happy) enjoué; **it is sunny** il fait du soleil
sun'ny side' *s* côté *m* exposé au soleil; (fig) bon côté
sun' par'lor *s* véranda *f*
sun'rise' *s* lever *m* du soleil
sun'set' *s* coucher *m* du soleil
sun'shade' *s* (over door) banne *f*; parasol *m*; abat-jour *m*, visière *f*
sun'shine' *s* clarté *f* du soleil, soleil *m*; (fig) gaieté *f* rayonnante; **in the sunshine** en plein soleil
sun'spot' *s* tache *f* solaire
sun'stroke' *s* insolation *f*
sun' tan' *s* hâle *m*
sun'-tan oil' *s* huile *f* solaire
sun'up' *s* lever *m* du soleil
sun' vi'sor *s* abat-jour *m*
sup [sʌp] *v* (pret & pp **supped**; ger **supping**) *intr* souper
super ['supər] *adj* (slang) superbe, for-

midable ‖ *s* (theat) figurant *m*; (slang) concierge *mf*
su'per·abun'dant *adj* surabondant
superannuated [,supər'ænju ,etɪd] *adj* (person) retraité; (thing) suranné
superb [su'pʌrb], [sə'pʌrb] *adj* superbe
su'per·car'go *s* (pl **-goes** or **-gos**) subrécargue *m*
su'per·charge' *s* surcompression *f* ‖ *tr* surcomprimer
supercilious [,supər'sɪlɪ·əs] *adj* sourcilleux, hautain, arrogant
superficial [,supər'fɪʃəl] *adj* superficiel
superfluous [su'pʌrflu·əs] *adj* superflu
su'per·high'way' *s* autoroute *f*
su'per·hu'man *adj* surhumain
su'per·impose' *tr* superposer
su'per·intend' *tr* surveiller; diriger
superintendent [,supərɪn'tɛndənt] *s* directeur *m*, directeur en chef; (of a building) concierge *mf*
superior [sə'pɪrɪ·ər], [su'pɪrɪ·ər] *adj* & *s* supérieur *m*
superiority [sə,pɪrɪ'ɑrɪti], [su,pɪrɪ 'ɑrɪti] *s* supériorité *f*
superlative [sə'pʌrlətɪv], [su'pʌrlətɪv] *adj* & *s* superlatif *m*
su'per·man' *s* (pl **-men'**) surhomme *m*
su'per·mar'ket *s* supermarché *m*
su'per·nat'ural *adj* & *s* surnaturel *m*
supersede [,supər'sid] *tr* remplacer
su'per·sen'sitive *adj* hypersensible
su'per·son'ic *adj* supersonique
superstition [,supər'stɪʃən] *s* superstition *f*
superstitious [,supər'stɪʃəs] *adj* superstitieux
supervene [,supər'vin] *intr* survenir
supervise ['supər,vaɪz] *tr* surveiller; diriger
supervision [,supər'vɪʒən] *s* surveillance *f*; direction *f*
supervisor ['supər,vaɪzər] *s* surveillant *m*, inspecteur *m*; directeur *m*
supper ['sʌpər] *s* souper *m*
sup'per·time' *s* heure *f* du souper
supplant [sə'plænt] *tr* supplanter
supple ['sʌpəl] *adj* souple, flexible
supplement ['sʌplɪmənt] *s* supplément *m* ‖ ['sʌplɪ ,ment] *tr* ajouter à
suppliant ['sʌplɪ·ənt] *adj* & *s* suppliant *m*
supplicant ['sʌplɪkənt] *s* suppliant *m*
supplicate ['sʌplɪ ,ket] *tr* supplier
supplier [sə'plaɪ·ər] *s* fournisseur *m*, pourvoyeur *m*
sup·ply [sə'plaɪ] *s* (pl **-plies**) fourniture *f*, provision *f*; (mil) approvisionnement *m*; **supplies** fournitures; (of food) vivres *mpl* ‖ *v* (pret & pp **-plied**) *tr* fournir; (a person, a city, a fort) pourvoir, munir; (a need) répondre à; (what is lacking) suppléer; (mil) approvisionner
supply' and demand' *spl* l'offre *f* et la demande
support [sə'port] *s* soutien *m*, appui *m*; ressources *fpl*, de quoi vivre *m*; (pillar) support *m* ‖ *tr* soutenir, appuyer; (e.g., a wife) entretenir, soutenir; (to

hold up; to corroborate; to tolerate)
supporter; **to support oneself** gagner
sa vie

supporter [sə'portər] *s* partisan *m*, supporter *m*; *(for part of body)* suspensoir *m*

suppose [sə'poz] *tr* supposer; s'imaginer; **I suppose so** probablement; **suppose that . . .** à supposer que . . . ;
suppose we take a walk? si nous faisions une promenade?; **to be supposed to** + *inf* devoir + *inf*; *(to be
considered to)* être censé + *inf*

supposedly [sə'pozidli] *adv* censément

supposition [,sʌpə'zɪʃən] *s* supposition *f*

supposi•to•ry [sə'pɑzɪ,tori] *s (pl* **-ries)**
suppositoire *m*

suppress [sə'pres] *tr* supprimer; *(rebellion; anger)* réprimer, contenir; *(a
yawn)* étouffer, empêcher

suppression [sə'preʃən] *s* suppression *f*;
(of a rebellion) subjugation *f*, répression *f*; *(of a yawn)* empêchement *m*

suppurate ['sʌpjə,ret] *intr* suppurer

supreme [sə'prim], [su'prim] *adj* suprême

supreme′ court′ *s* cour *f* de cassation

surcharge ['sʌr,tʃɑrdʒ] *s* surcharge *f* ‖
[,sʌr'tʃɑrdʒ], ['sʌr,tʃɑrdʒ] *tr* surcharger

sure [ʃur] *adj* sûr, certain; *(e.g., hand)*
ferme; **for sure** à coup sûr, pour sûr;
to be sure to + *inf* ne pas manquer
de + *inf*; **to make sure** s'assurer ‖
adv (coll) certainement; **sure enough**
(coll) effectivement, assurément ‖
interj (slang) mais oui!, bien sûr!,
entendu!

sure′-foot′ed *adj* au pied sûr

sure•ty ['ʃurti], ['ʃurɪti] *s (pl* **-ties)**
sûreté *f*

surf [sʌrf] *s* barre *f*, ressac *m*, brisants
mpl

surface ['sʌrfɪs] *adj* superficiel ‖ *s*
surface *f*; *(area)* superficie *f*; **on the
surface** à la surface, en apparence;
to float under the surface nager entre
deux eaux ‖ *tr* polir la surface de;
(a road) recouvrir, revêtir ‖ *intr (said
of submarine)* faire surface

sur′face mail′ *s* courrier *m* par voie
ordinaire

surf′board′ *s* planche *f* pour le surf,
surfboard *m*

surfeit ['sʌrfɪt] *s* satiété *f* ‖ *tr* rassasier
‖ *intr* se rassasier

surf′rid′ing *s* surfing *m*, planking *m*

surge [sʌrdʒ] *s* houle *f*; (elec) surtension *f* ‖ *intr* être houleux; se répandre; **to surge up** s'enfler, s'élever

surgeon ['sʌrdʒən] *s* chirurgien *m*

surger•y ['sʌrdʒəri] *s (pl* **-ies)** chirurgie *f*; salle *f* d'opération

surgical ['sʌrdʒɪkəl] *adj* chirurgical

sur•ly ['sʌrli] *adj (comp* **-lier;** *super*
-liest) hargneux, maussade, bourru

surmise [sər'maɪz], ['sʌrmaɪz] *s* conjecture *f* ‖ [sər'maɪz] *tr & intr* conjecturer

surmount [sər'maunt] *tr* surmonter

surname ['sʌr,nem] *s* nom *m* de famil-

le; surnom *m* ‖ *tr* donner un nom de
famille à; surnommer

surpass [sər'pæs], [sər'pɑs] *tr* surpasser

surplice ['sʌrplɪs] *s* surplis *m*

surplus ['sʌrplʌs] *adj* excédent, excédentaire, en excédent ‖ *s* surplus *m*,
excédent *m*

sur′plus bag′gage *s* excédent *m* de bagages

surprise [sər'praɪz] *adj* à l'improviste,
brusqué, inopiné ‖ *s* surprise *f*, étonnement *m*; **to take by surprise** prendre à l'improviste, prendre au dépourvu ‖ *tr* surprendre; **to be sur-
prised at** être surpris de

surprise′ attack′ *s* attaque *f* brusquée

surprise′ pack′age *s* surprise *f*, pochette
f surprise

surprise′ par′ty *s (pl* **-ties)** réunion *f* à
l'improviste

surprising [sər'praɪzɪŋ] *adj* surprenant

surrealism [sə'ri•ə,lɪzəm] *s* surréalisme
m

surrender [sə'rendər] *s* reddition *f*, soumission *f*; *(e.g., of prisoners, goods)*
remise *f*; *(e.g., of rights, property)*
cession *f* ‖ *tr* rendre, céder ‖ *intr* se
rendre

surren′der val′ue *s* valeur *f* de rachat

surreptitious [,sʌrep'tɪʃəs] *adj* subreptice

surround [sə'raund] *tr* entourer

surrounding [sə'raundɪŋ] *adj* entou-
rant, environnant ‖ **surroundings** *spl*
environs *mpl*, alentours *mpl*; entourage *m*, milieu *m*

surtax ['sʌr,tæks] *s* surtaxe *f* ‖ *tr* surtaxer

surveillance [sər'vel(j)əns] *s* surveillance *f*

survey ['sʌrve] *s (for verification)* contrôle *m*; *(for evaluation)* appréciation
f, évaluation *f*; *(report)* expertise *f*,
aperçu *m*; *(of a whole)* vue *f* d'ensemble, tour *m* d'horizon; *(measured
plan or drawing)* levé *m*, plan *m*;
(surv) lever *m* or levé *m* des plans; **to
make a survey** *(to map out)* lever un
plan; *(to poll)* effectuer un contrôle
par sondage ‖ [sʌr've], ['sʌrve] *tr*
contrôler; apprécier, évaluer, faire
l'expertise de; *(as a whole)* jeter un
coup d'œil sur; *(to poll)* sonder; *(e.g.,
a farm)* arpenter, faire l'arpentage
de; *(e.g., a city)* faire le levé de

sur′vey course′ *s* cours *m* général

surveying [sʌr've•ɪŋ] *s* arpentage *m*,
géodésie *f*, levé *m* des plans

surveyor [sər've•ər] *s* arpenteur *m*

survival [sər'vaɪvəl] *s* survivance *f*;
(after death) survie *f*

survive [sər'vaɪv] *tr* survivre (with *dat*)
‖ *intr* survivre

surviving [sər'vaɪvɪŋ] *adj* survivant

survivor [sər'vaɪvər] *s* survivant *m*

survivorship [sər'vaɪvər,ʃɪp] *s* (law)
survie *f*

susceptible [sə'septɪbəl] *adj (capable)*
susceptible; *(liable, subject)* sensible;
(to love) facilement amoureux

suspect ['sʌspɛkt], [səs'pɛkt] *adj & s*

suspect *m* ‖ [səs'pɛkt] *tr* soupçonner ‖ *intr* s'en douter

suspend [səs'pɛnd] *tr* suspendre

suspenders [səs'pɛndərz] *spl* bretelles *fpl*

suspense [səs'pɛns] *s* suspens *m*

suspension [səs'pɛnʃən] *s* suspension *f*; **suspension of driver's license** retrait *m* de permis

suspen'sion bridge' *s* pont *m* suspendu

suspicion [səs'pɪʃən] *s* soupçon *m*

suspicious [səs'pɪʃəs] *adj* (*inclined to suspect*) soupçonneux; (*subject to suspicion*) suspect

sustain [səs'ten] *tr* soutenir; (*a loss, injury, etc.*) éprouver

sustenance ['sʌstɪnəns] *s* subsistance *f*; (*food*) nourriture *f*

swab [swɑb] *s* écouvillon *m*; (naut) faubert *m*; (surg) tampon *m* ‖ *v* (*pret & pp* swabbed; *ger* swabbing) *tr* écouvillonner

swaddle ['swɑdəl] *tr* emmailloter

swad'dling clothes' *spl* maillot *m*

swagger ['swægər] *s* fanfaronnade *f* ‖ *intr* faire des fanfaronnades

swain [swen] *s* garçon *m*; jeune berger *m*; soupirant *m*

swallow ['swɑlo] *s* gorgée *f*; (orn) hirondelle *f* ‖ *tr & intr* avaler

swal'low-tailed coat' *s* frac *m*

swamp [swɑmp] *s* marécage *m* ‖ *tr* submerger, inonder

swamp·y ['swɑmpi] *adj* (*comp* -ier; *super* -iest) marécageux

swan [swɑn] *s* cygne *m*

swan' dive' *s* saut *m* de l'ange

swank [swæŋk] *adj* (slang) élégant, chic

swan' knight' *s* chevalier *m* au cygne

swan's'-down' *s* cygne *m*, duvet *m* de cygne

swan' song' *s* chant *m* du cygne

swap [swɑp] *s* (coll) troc *m* ‖ *v* (*pret & pp* swapped; *ger* swapping) *tr & intr* troquer

swarm [swɔrm] *s* essaim *m* ‖ *intr* essaimer; (fig) fourmiller

swarth·y ['swɔrðɪ], ['swɔrθɪ] *adj* (*comp* -ier; *super* -iest) basané, brun, noiraud

swashbuckler ['swɑʃ‚bʌklər] *s* rodomont *m*, bretteur *m*

swat [swɑt] *s* (coll) coup *m* violent ‖ *v* (*pret & pp* swatted; *ger* swatting) *tr* (coll) frapper; (*a fly*) (coll) écraser

sway [swe] *s* balancement *m*; (*domination*) empire *m* ‖ *tr* balancer ‖ *intr* se balancer; (*to hesitate*) balancer

swear [swɛr] *v* (*pret* swore [swor]; *pp* sworn [sworn]) *tr* jurer; **to swear in** faire prêter serment à; **to swear off** jurer de renoncer à ‖ *intr* jurer; **to swear at** injurier; **to swear by** (*e.g., a remedy*) préconiser; **to swear to** déclarer sous serment; jurer de + *inf*

swear' words' *spl* gros mots *mpl*

sweat [swɛt] *s* sueur *f* ‖ *v* (*pret & pp* sweat *or* sweated) *tr* (*e.g., blood*) suer; (slang) faire suer; **to sweat it out** (slang) en baver jusqu'à la fin ‖ *intr* suer

sweater ['swɛtər] *s* chandail *m*

sweat' shirt' *s* maillot *m* de sport

sweat·y ['swɛti] *adj* (*comp* -ier; *super* -iest) suant

Swede [swid] *s* Suédois *m*

Sweden ['swidən] *s* Suède *f*; la Suède

Swedish ['swidɪʃ] *adj & s* suédois *m*

sweep [swip] *s* balayage *m*; étendue *f*; (*curve*) courbe *f*; (*of wind*) souffle *m*; (*of well*) chadouf *m*; **at one sweep** d'un seul coup; **to make a clean sweep of** faire table rase de; (*to win all of*) rafler ‖ *v* (*pret & pp* swept [swɛpt]) *tr* balayer; (*the chimney*) ramoner; (*for mines*) draguer ‖ *intr* balayer; s'étendre

sweeper ['swipər] *s* balayeur *m*; (mach) balai *m* mécanique

sweeping ['swipɪŋ] *adj* (*movement*) vigoureux; (*statement*) catégorique ‖ *s* balayage *m*; **sweepings** balayures *fpl*

sweep'-sec'ond *s* trotteuse *f* centrale

sweep'stakes' *s* *or* *spl* loterie *f*; (turf) sweepstake *m*

sweet [swit] *adj* doux; sucré; (*perfume, music, etc.*) suave; (*sound*) mélodieux; (*milk*) frais; (*person*) charmant, gentil; (*dear*) cher; **to be sweet on** (coll) avoir un béguin pour; **to smell sweet** sentir bon ‖ **sweets** *spl* sucreries *fpl*

sweet'bread' *s* ris *m* de veau

sweet'bri'er *s* églantier *m*

sweeten ['switən] *tr* sucrer; purifier; (fig) adoucir ‖ *intr* s'adoucir

sweet'heart' *s* petite amie *f*, chérie *f*; **sweethearts** amoureux *mpl*

sweet' mar'joram *s* marjolaine *f*

sweet'meats' *spl* sucreries *fpl*

sweet' pea' *s* gesse *f* odorante, pois *m* de senteur

sweet' pep'per *s* piment *m* doux, poivron *m*

sweet' pota'to *s* patate *f* douce

sweet'-scent'ed *adj* parfumé

sweet'-toothed' *adj* friand de sucreries

sweet' wil'liam *s* œillet *m* de poète

swell [swɛl] *adj* (coll) élégant; (slang) épatant *s* gonflement *m*; (*of sea*) houle *f*; (mus) crescendo *m*; (pathol) enflure *f*; (coll) rupin *m* ‖ *v* (*pret* swelled; *pp* swelled *or* swollen ['swolən]) *tr* gonfler, enfler ‖ *intr* se gonfler, s'enfler; (*said of sea*) se soulever; (fig) augmenter

swell'head'ed *adj* suffisant, vaniteux

swelter ['swɛltər] *intr* étouffer de chaleur

swept'back' wing' *s* aile *f* en flèche

swerve [swʌrv] *s* écart *m*, déviation *f*; (aut) embardée *f* ‖ *tr* faire dévier ‖ *intr* écarter, dévier; (aut) faire une embardée

swift [swɪft] *adj* rapide ‖ *adv* vite ‖ *s* (orn) martinet *m*

swig [swɪg] *s* (coll) lampée *f*, trait *m* ‖ *v* (*pret & pp* swigged; *ger* swigging) *tr & intr* lamper

swill [swɪl] *s* eaux *fpl* grasses, ordures *fpl*; (*drink*) lampée *f* ‖ *tr & intr* lamper

swim [swɪm] s nage f; **to be in the swim** (coll) être dans le train ‖ v (pret **swam** [swæm]; pp **swum** [swʌm]; ger **swimming**) tr nager ‖ intr nager; (said of head) tourner; **to swim across** traverser à la nage; **to swim under water** nager entre deux eaux

swimmer ['swɪmər] s nageur m

swimming ['swɪmɪŋ] s natation f, nage f

swim'ming pool' s piscine f

swim'ming suit' s maillot m de bain

swim'ming trunks' spl slip m de bain

swindle ['swɪndəl] s escroquerie f ‖ tr escroquer

swine [swaɪn] s (pl **swine**) cochon m, pourceau m, porc m

swing [swɪŋ] s balancement m, oscillation f; (device used for recreation) escarpolette f; (trip) tournée f; (boxing, mus) swing m; **in full swing** en pleine marche ‖ v (pret & pp **swung** [swʌŋ]) tr balancer, faire osciller; (the arms) agiter; (a sword) brandir; (e.g., an election) mener à bien ‖ intr se balancer; (said of pendulum) osciller; (said of door) pivoter; (said of bell) branler; **to swing open** s'ouvrir tout d'un coup

swing'ing door' s porte f va-et-vient

swinish ['swaɪnɪʃ] adj cochon

swipe [swaɪp] s (coll) coup m à toute volée ‖ tr (coll) frapper à toute volée; (to steal) (slang) chiper

swirl [swʌrl] s remous m, tourbillon m ‖ tr faire tourbillonner ‖ intr tourbillonner

swish [swɪʃ] s (e.g., of a whip) sifflement m; (of a dress) froufrou m; (e.g., of water) susurrement m ‖ tr (a whip) faire siffler; (its tail) battre ‖ intr siffler; froufrouter; susurrer

Swiss [swɪs] adj suisse ‖ s Suisse m; **the Swiss** les Suisses mpl

Swiss' chard' [tʃɑrd] s bette f, poirée f

Swiss' cheese' s emmenthal m, gruyère m

Swiss' Guard' s suisse m

switch [swɪtʃ] s (stick) badine f; (exchange) échange m; (hairpiece) postiche m; (elec) interrupteur m; (rr) aiguille f ‖ tr cingler; (places) échanger; (rr) aiguiller; **to switch off** couper; (a light) éteindre; **to switch on** mettre en circuit; (a light) allumer ‖ intr changer de place

switch'back' s chemin m en lacet

switch'board' s tableau m de distribution; standard m téléphonique

switch'board op'erator s standardiste mf

switch'ing en'gine s locomotive f de manœuvre

switch'man s (pl -men) aiguilleur m

switch' tow'er s poste m d'aiguillage

switch'yard' s gare f de triage

Switzerland ['swɪtsərlənd] s Suisse f; la Suisse

swivel ['swɪvəl] s pivot m; (link) émerillon m ‖ v (pret & pp -eled or -elled; ger -eling or -elling) tr faire pivoter ‖ intr pivoter

swiv'el chair' s fauteuil m tournant

swoon [swun] s évanouissement m ‖ intr s'évanouir

swoop [swup] s attaque f brusque; **at one fell swoop** d'un seul coup ‖ intr foncer, fondre; **to swoop down on** s'abattre sur

sword [sord] s épée f; **to cross swords with** croiser le fer avec; **to put to the sword** passer au fil de l'épée

sword' belt' s ceinturon m

sword'fish' s espadon m

swords'man s (pl -men) épéiste m

sword' swal'lower ['swɑloʊər] s avaleur m de sabres

sword' thrust' s coup m de pointe, coup d'épée

sworn [sworn] adj (enemy) juré; **sworn in** assermenté

sycophant ['sɪkəfənt] s flagorneur m

syllable ['sɪləbəl] s syllabe f

sylla·bus ['sɪləbəs] s (pl -bi [ˌbaɪ] or -buses) programme m

syllogism ['sɪləˌdʒɪzəm] s syllogisme m

sylph [sɪlf] s sylphe m

sylvan ['sɪlvən] adj sylvestre

symbol ['sɪmbəl] s symbole m

symbolic(al) [sɪm'bɑlɪk(əl)] adj symbolique

symbolism ['sɪmbəˌlɪzm] s symbolisme m

symbolize ['sɪmbəˌlaɪz] tr symboliser

symmetric(al) [sɪ'metrɪk(əl)] adj symétrique

symme·try ['sɪmɪtri] s (pl -tries) symétrie f

sympathetic [ˌsɪmpə'θetɪk] adj compatissant; bien disposé; (anat, physiol) sympathique

sympathize ['sɪmpəˌθaɪz] intr—**to sympathize with** compatir à; comprendre

sympa·thy ['sɪmpəθi] s (pl -thies) sympathie f; (shared sorrow) compassion f; **to be in sympathy with** être en sympathie avec; **to extend one's sympathy to** offrir ses condoléances à

sym'pathy strike' s grève f de solidarité

sympho·ny ['sɪmfəni] s (pl -nies) symphonie f

symposi·um [sɪm'pozɪəm] s (pl -a [ə]) colloque m, symposium m

symptom ['sɪmptəm] s symptôme m

synagogue ['sɪnəˌgɔg], ['sɪnəˌgɑg] s synagogue f

synchronize ['sɪŋkrəˌnaɪz] tr synchroniser

synchronous ['sɪŋkrənəs] adj synchrone

syncopation [ˌsɪŋkə'peʃən] s syncope f

syncope ['sɪŋkəˌpi] s syncope f

syndicate ['sɪndɪkɪt] s syndicat m ‖ ['sɪndɪˌket] tr syndiquer ‖ intr se syndiquer

synonym ['sɪnənɪm] s synonyme m

synonymous [sɪ'nɑnɪməs] adj synonyme

synop·sis [sɪ'nɑpsɪs] s (pl -ses [siz]) abrégé m, résumé m; (mov) synopsis m & f

syntax ['sɪntæks] s syntaxe f

synthe·sis ['sɪnθɪsɪs] s (pl -ses [ˌsiz]) synthèse f

synthesize ['sɪnθɪˌsaɪz] tr synthétiser

synthetic(al) [sɪn'θetɪk(əl)] *adj* synthétique

syphilis ['sɪfɪlɪs] *s* syphilis *f*

Syria ['sɪrɪ-ə] *s* Syrie *f*; la Syrie

Syrian ['sɪrɪ-ən] *adj* syrien || *s* (*language*) syrien *m*; (*person*) Syrien *m*

syringe [sɪ'rɪndʒ], ['sɪrɪndʒ] *s* seringue *f* || *tr* seringuer

syrup ['sɪrəp], ['sʌrəp] *s* sirop *m*

system ['sɪstəm] *s* système *m*; (*of lines, wires, pipes, roads*) réseau *m*

systematic(al) [ˌsɪstə'mætɪk(əl)] *adj* systématique

systematize ['sɪstəmə,taɪz] *tr* systématiser

systole ['sɪstəli] *s* systole *f*

T

T, t [ti] *s* XXᵉ lettre de l'alphabet

tab [tæb] *s* patte *f*; (*label*) étiquette *f*; **to keep tab on** (coll) garder à l'œil; **to pick up the tab** (coll) payer l'addition

tab-by ['tæbi] *s* (*pl* **-bies**) chat *m* moucheté; (*female cat*) chatte *f*; (*old maid*) vieille fille *f*; (*spiteful female*) vieille chipie *f*

tabernacle ['tæbər,nækəl] *s* tabernacle *m*

table ['tebəl] *s* table *f*; (*tableland*) plateau *m*; (*list, chart*) tableau *m*, table; **to clear the table** ôter le couvert; **to set the table** mettre le couvert || *tr* ajourner la discussion de

tab·leau ['tæblo] *s* (*pl* **-leaus** or **-leaux** [loz]) tableau *m* vivant

ta'ble-cloth' *s* nappe *f*

table d'hôte ['tabəl'dot] *s* repas *m* à prix fixe

ta'ble-land' *s* plateau *m*

ta'ble lin'en *s* nappage *m*, linge *m* de table

ta'ble man'ners *spl*—**to have good table manners** bien se tenir à table

tab'le-mate' *s* commensal *m*

ta'ble of con'tents *s* table *f* des matières

ta'ble-spoon' *s* cuiller *f* à soupe

tablespoonful ['tebəl,spun,ful] *s* cuillerée *f* à soupe or à bouche

tablet ['tæblɪt] *s* (*writing pad*) bloc-notes *m*, bloc *m*; (*lozenge*) pastille *f*, comprimé *m*; plaque *f* commémorative

ta'ble talk' *s* propos *mpl* de table

ta'ble ten'nis *s* tennis *m* de table

ta'ble-top' *s* dessus *m* de table

ta'ble-ware' *s* ustensiles *mpl* de table

ta'ble wine' *s* vin *m* ordinaire

tabloid ['tæblɔɪd] *adj* (*press, article, etc.*) à sensation || *s* journal *m* de petit format à l'affût du sensationnel

taboo [tæ'bu] *adj* & *s* tabou *m* || *tr* déclarer tabou

tabular ['tæbjələr] *adj* tabulaire

tabulate ['tæbjə,let] *tr* disposer en forme de table or en tableaux, dresser un tableau de, aligner en colonnes

tabulator ['tæbjə,letər] *s* tabulateur *m*

tacit ['tæsɪt] *adj* tacite

taciturn ['tæsɪtərn] *adj* taciturne

tack [tæk] *s* (*nail*) semence *f*; (*plan*) voie *f*, tactique *f*; (*of sail*) amure *f*; (*naut*) bordée *f*; (*sewing*) point *m* de bâti || *tr* clouer; (*sewing*) bâtir || *intr* louvoyer

tackle ['tækəl] *s* attirail *m*; (*for lifting*) treuil *m*; (*football*) plaquage *m*; (*naut*) palan *m* || *tr* empoigner, saisir; (*a problem, job, etc.*) chercher à résoudre, attaquer; (*football*) plaquer

tack-y ['tæki] *adj* (*comp* **-ier**; *super* **-iest**) collant; (coll) râpé, minable

tact [tækt] *s* tact *m*

tactful ['tæktfəl] *adj* plein de tact; **to be tactful** avoir du tact

tactical ['tæktɪkəl] *adj* tactique

tactician [tæk'tɪʃən] *s* tacticien *m*

tactics ['tæktɪks] *spl* tactique *f*

tactless ['tæktlɪs] *adj* sans tact

tadpole ['tæd,pol] *s* têtard *m*

taffeta ['tæfɪtə] *s* taffetas *m*

taffy ['tæfi] *s* pâte *f* à berlingots; (coll) flagornerie *f*

tag [tæg] *s* (*label*) étiquette *f*; (*of shoelace*) ferret *m*; (*game*) chat *m* perché || *v* (*pret* & *pp* **tagged**; *ger* **tagging**) *tr* étiqueter; (*in the game of tag*) attraper || *intr* (coll) suivre de près; **to tag along behind s.o.** (coll) traîner derrière qn

tag' day' *s* jour *m* de collecte publique

tag' end' *s* queue *f*; (*remnant*) coupon *m*

Tagus ['tegəs] *s* Tage *m*

tail [tel] *s* queue *f*; (*of shirt*) pan *m*; **tails** (*of a coin*) pile *f*; (coll) frac *m*; **to turn tail** tourner les talons || *tr* (coll) suivre de tout près || *intr*—**to tail after** marcher sur les talons de; **to tail off** s'éteindre, disparaître

tail' assem'bly *s* (*pl* **-blies**) (aer) empennage *m*

tail' end' *s* queue *f*, fin *f*

tail'light' *s* feu *m* arrière

tailor ['telər] *s* tailleur *m* || *tr* (*a suit*) faire || *intr* être tailleur

tailoring ['telərɪŋ] *s* métier *m* de tailleur

tai'lor-made suit' *s* (*men's*) costume *m* sur mesure, complet *m* sur mesure; (*women's*) costume tailleur, tailleur *m*

tai'lor shop' *s* boutique *f* de tailleur

tail'piece' *s* queue *f*; (*of stringed instrument*) cordier *m*

tail'race' *s* canal *m* de fuite

tail'spin' *s* chute *f* en vrille

tail'wind' *s* (aer) vent *m* arrière; (naut) vent en poupe

taint [tent] *s* tache *f* || *tr* tacher; (*food*) gâter

take [tek] *s* prise *f*; (*mov*) prise de vues; (slang) recette *f* || *v* (*pret* took [tʊk]; *pp* taken) *tr* prendre; (*a walk; a trip*) faire; (*a course; advice*) suivre; (*an examination*) passer; (*a person on a trip*) emmener; (*the occasion*) profiter de; (*a photograph*) prendre; (*a newspaper*) être abonné à; (*a purchase*) garder; (*a certain amount of time*) falloir, e.g., **it takes an hour to walk there** il faut une heure pour y aller à pied; (*to lead*) conduire, mener; (*to tolerate, stand*) supporter; (*a seat*) prendre, occuper, e.g., **this seat is taken** cette place est prise ou occupée; **do you take that to be important?** tenez-vous cela pour important?; **I take it that** je suppose que; **take it easy!** (coll) allez-y doucement!; **to be taken ill** tomber malade; **to take amiss** prendre mal; **to take away** enlever; emmener; (*to subtract*) soustraire, retrancher; **to take down** descendre; (*a building*) démolir; (*in writing*) noter; **to take in** (*a roomer*) recevoir; (*laundry*) prendre à faire à la maison; (*the harvest*) rentrer; (*a seam*) reprendre; (*to include*) embrasser; (*to deceive*) (coll) duper; **to take off** ôter, enlever; (*from the price*) rabattre; (*to imitate*) (coll) singer; **to take on** (*passengers*) prendre; (*a responsibility*) prendre sur soi; (*workers*) embaucher, prendre; **to take out** sortir; (*a bullet from a wound; a passage from a text; an element from a compound*) extraire; (*public sign*) à emporter; **to take place** avoir lieu; **to take s.th. from s.o.** enlever, ôter, ou prendre q.ch. à qn; **to take up** (*to carry up*) monter; (*to remove*) enlever; (*a dress*) raccourcir; (*an idea, method, etc.*) adopter; (*a profession*) embrasser, prendre; (*a question, a study, etc.*) aborder || *intr* prendre; **to not take to** (*a person*) prendre en grippe; **to take after** ressembler à; (*to chase*) poursuivre; **to take off** s'en aller; (aer) décoller; **to take to** (*flight; the woods*) prendre; (*a bad habit*) se livrer à; (*a person*) se prendre d'amitié avec; (*to like*) s'adonner à; **to take to + ger** se mettre à + *inf*; **to take up with s.o.** (coll) se lier avec qn

take/-off/ *s* (aer) décollage *m*; (coll) caricature *f*

tal/cum pow/der [ˈtælkəm] *s* poudre *f* de talc

tale [tel] *s* conte *m*; mensonge *m*; (*gossip*) raconter *m*, histoire *f*

tale/bear/er *s* rapporteur *m*

talent [ˈtælənt] *s* talent *m*; gens *mpl* de talent

talented [ˈtæləntɪd] *adj* doué, talentueux

tal/ent scout/ *s* dénicheur *m* de vedettes

tal/ent show/ *s* crochet *m* radiophonique, radio-crochet *m*

talk [tɔk] *s* paroles *fpl*; (*gossip*) racontars *mpl*, dires *mpl*; (*lecture*) conférence *f*, causerie *f*; **to cause talk** défrayer la chronique; **to have a talk with** s'entretenir avec || *tr* parler; **to talk over** discuter; **to talk up** vanter || *intr* parler; (*to chatter, gossip, etc.*) bavarder, jaser; **to talk back** répliquer; **to talk on** continuer à parler

talkative [ˈtɔkətɪv] *adj* bavard

talker [ˈtɔkər] *s* parleur *m*; **a great talker** (coll) un causeur, un hâbleur

talkie [ˈtɔki] *s* (coll) film *m* parlant

talk/ing doll/ [ˈtɔkɪŋ] *s* poupée *f* parlante

talk/ing pic/ture *s* film *m* parlant

tall [tɔl] *adj* haut, élevé; (*person*) grand; (coll) exagéré

tallow [ˈtælo] *s* suif *m*

tal-ly [ˈtæli] *s* (*pl* -lies) compte *m*, pointage *m* || *v* (*pret & pp* -lied) *tr* pointer, contrôler || *intr* s'accorder

tallyho [ˈtælɪ ˌho] *interj* taïaut!

tal/ly sheet/ *s* feuille *f* de pointage, bordereau *m*

talon [ˈtælən] *s* serre *f*

tamarack [ˈtæmə ˌræk] *s* mélèze *m* d'Amérique

tambourine [ˌtæmbəˈrin] *s* tambour *m* de basque

tame [tem] *adj* apprivoisé; (*e.g., lion*) dompté; (*e.g., style*) fade, terne || *tr* apprivoiser; (*e.g., a lion*) dompter

tamp [tæmp] *tr* bourrer; (*e.g., a hole in the ground*) damer

tamper [ˈtæmpər] *intr*—**to tamper with** se mêler de; (*a lock*) fausser; (*a document*) falsifier; (*a witness*) suborner

tampon [ˈtæmpɑn] *s* (surg) tampon *m* || *tr* (surg) tamponner

tan [tæn] *adj* jaune; (*e.g., skin*) bronzé, hâlé || *v* (*pret & pp* tanned; *ger* tanning) *tr* tanner; (*e.g., the skin*) bronzer, hâler || *intr* se hâler

tandem [ˈtændəm] *adj & adv* en tandem, en flèche || *s* tandem *m*

tang [tæŋ] *s* goût *m* vif, saveur *f*; (*ringing sound*) tintement *m*

tangent [ˈtændʒənt] *adj* tangent || *s* tangente *f*; **to fly off at** or **on a tangent** changer brusquement de sujet

tangerine [ˌtændʒəˈrin] *s* mandarine *f*

tangible [ˈtændʒɪbəl] *adj* tangible

Tangier [tænˈdʒɪr] *s* Tanger *m*

tangle [ˈtæŋgəl] *s* enchevêtrement *m* || *tr* enchevêtrer || *intr* s'enchevêtrer

tank [tæŋk] *s* réservoir *m*; (mil) char *m*

tank/ car/ *s* (rr) wagon-citerne *m*

tanker [ˈtæŋkər] *s* (ship) bateau-citerne *m*; (*truck*) camion-citerne *m*; (*plane*) ravitailleur *m*

tank/ truck/ *s* camion-citerne *m*

tanner [ˈtænər] *s* tanneur *m*

tanner-y [ˈtænəri] *s* (*pl* -ies) tannerie *f*

tantalize [ˈtæntə ˌlaɪz] *tr* tenter, allécher

tantamount [ˈtæntə ˌmaunt] *adj* équivalent

tantrum [ˈtæntrəm] *s* accès *m* de colère; **in a tantrum** en rogne

tap [tæp] *s* petit coup *m*; (*faucet*) robinet *m*; (elec) prise *f*; (mach) taraud *m*; **on tap** au tonneau, en perce;

(*available*) (coll) disponible; **taps** (mil) l'extinction *f* des feux ‖ *v* (*pret & pp* **tapped**; *ger* **tapping**) *tr* taper; (*a cask*) mettre en perce; (*a tree*) entailler; (*a telephone*) passer à la table d'écoute; (*a nut*) tarauder; (*resources, talent, etc.*) drainer; (elec) brancher sur ‖ *intr* taper

tap' dance' *s* danse *f* à claquettes

tap'-dance' *intr* danser les claquettes, faire les claquettes

tap' dan'cer *s* danseur *m* à claquettes

tape [tep] *s* ruban *m* ‖ *tr* (*an electric wire*) guiper; (*land*) mesurer au cordeau; (*to tape-record*) enregistrer sur ruban

tape' meas'ure *s* mètre-ruban *m*, centimètre *m*

taper ['tepər] *s* (*for lighting candles*) allumette-bougie *f*; (eccl) cierge *m* ‖ *tr* effiler ‖ *intr* s'effiler

tape'-record' *tr* enregistrer sur ruban magnétique ou au magnétophone

tape' record'er *s* magnétophone *m*

tapes•try ['tæpɪstri] *s* (*pl* **-tries**) tapisserie *f* ‖ *v* (*pret & pp* **-tried**) *tr* tapisser

tape'worm' *s* ver *m* solitaire

tappet ['tæpɪt] *s* (mach) taquet *m*

tap'room' *s* débit *m* de boissons, buvette *f*

tap' wa'ter *s* eau *f* du robinet

tap' wrench' *s* taraudeuse *f*

tar [tɑr] *s* goudron *m*; (coll) marin *m* ‖ *v* (*pret & pp* **tarred**; *ger* **tarring**) *tr* goudronner; **to tar and feather** enduire de goudron et de plumes

tar•dy ['tɑrdi] *adj* (*comp* **-dier**; *super* **-diest**) lent; retardataire, en retard

tare [tɛr] *s* (*weight*) tare *f*; (Bib) ivraie *f* ‖ *tr* tarer

target ['tɑrgɪt] *s* cible *f*; (*goal*) but *m*; (mil) objectif *m*; (*butt*) (fig) cible

tar'get ar'ea *s* zone *f* de tir

tar'get lan'guage *s* langue *f* cible

tar'get prac'tice *s* tir *m* à la cible

tariff ['tærɪf] *s* (*duties*) droits *mpl* de douane; (*rates in general*) tarif *m*

tarnish ['tɑrnɪʃ] *s* ternissure *f* ‖ *tr* ternir ‖ *intr* se ternir

tar' pa'per *s* papier *m* goudronné

tarpaulin [tɑr'pɔlɪn] *s* bâche *f*, prélart *m*

tarragon ['tærəgən] *s* estragon *m*

tar•ry ['tɑri] *adj* (*comp* **-rier**; *super* **-riest**) goudronneux ‖ ['tæri] *v* (*pret & pp* **-ried**) *intr* tarder; (*to stay*) rester, demeurer

tart [tɑrt] *adj* aigrelet; (*reply*) mordant ‖ *s* tarte *f*; (slang) grue *f*, poule *f*

tartar ['tɑrtər] *adj* (*sauce*) tartare; **Tartar** tartare ‖ *s* (*on teeth*) tartre *m*; **Tartar** Tartare *mf*

task [tæsk], [tɑsk] *s* tâche *f*; **to bring or take to task** prendre à partie

task' force' *s* (mil) groupement *m* stratégique mixte

task'mas'ter *s* chef *m* de corvée; (fig) tyran *m*

tassel ['tæsəl] *s* gland *m*; (*on corn*) barbe *f*; (*on nightcap*) mèche *f*; (bot) aigrette *f*

taste [test] *s* goût *m*, saveur *f*; (*sense of what is fitting*) goût, bon goût ‖ *tr* goûter; (*to sample*) goûter à; (*to try out*) goûter de ‖ *intr* goûter; **to taste like** avoir le goût de; **to taste of** avoir un goût de

taste' bud' *s* papille *f* gustative

tasteless ['testlɪs] *adj* sans saveur, fade; (*in bad taste*) de mauvais goût

tast•y ['testi] *adj* (*comp* **-ier**; *super* **-iest**) (coll) savoureux; (coll) de bon goût

tatter ['tætər] *s* lambeau *m* ‖ *tr* mettre en lambeaux

tatterdemalion [,tætərdɪ'meljən], [,tætərdɪ'mæljən] *s* loqueteux *m*

tattered *adj* en lambeaux, en loques

tattle ['tætəl] *s* bavardage *m*; (*gossip*) cancan *m* ‖ *intr* bavarder; cancaner

tat'tle-tale' *adj* révélateur ‖ *s* rapporteur *m*, cancanier *m*

tattoo [tæ'tu] *s* tatouage *m*; (mil) retraite *f* ‖ *tr* tatouer

taunt [tɔnt], [tɑnt] *s* sarcasme *m* ‖ *tr* bafouer

taut [tɔt] *adj* tendu

tavern ['tævərn], *s* café *m*, bar *m*, bistrot *m*; (*inn*) taverne *f*

taw•dry ['tɔdri] *adj* (*comp* **-drier**; *super* **-driest**) criard, voyant

taw•ny ['tɔni] *adj* (*comp* **-nier**; *super* **-niest**) fauve; (*skin*) basané

tax [tæks] *s* impôt *m*; **to reduce the tax on** dégrever ‖ *tr* imposer; (*e.g., one's patience*) mettre à l'épreuve; **to tax s.o. with** (*e.g., laziness*) taxer qn de

taxable ['tæksəbəl] *adj* imposable

taxation [tæk'seʃən] *s* imposition *f*; charges *fpl* fiscales, impôts *mpl*

tax' collec'tor *s* percepteur *m*

tax' cut' *s* dégrèvement *m* d'impôt

tax' eva'sion *s* fraude *f* fiscale

tax'-exempt' *adj* net d'impôt, exempt d'impôts

tax•i ['tæksi] *s* (*pl* **-is**) taxi *m* ‖ *v* (*pret & pp* **-ied**; *ger* **-iing** *or* **-ying**) *tr* (aer) rouler au sol ‖ *intr* aller en taxi; (aer) rouler au sol ‖ *interj* hep taxi!

tax'i-cab' *s* taxi *m*

tax'i danc'er *s* taxi-girl *f*

taxidermy ['tæksɪ,dɑrmi] *s* taxidermie *f*

tax'i driv'er *s* chauffeur *m* de taxi

tax'i-plane' *s* avion-taxi *m*

tax'i stand' *s* station *f* de taxis

tax'pay'er *s* contribuable *mf*

tax' rate' *s* taux *m* de l'impôt

tea [ti] *s* thé *m*; (*medicinal infusion*) tisane *f*

tea' bag' *s* sachet *m* de thé

tea' ball' *s* boule *f* à thé

tea'cart' *s* table *f* roulante

teach [titʃ] *v* (*pret & pp* **taught** [tɔt]) *tr* enseigner; **to teach s.o. s.th.** enseigner q.ch. à qn; **to teach s.o. to** + *inf* enseigner à qn à + *inf* ‖ *intr* enseigner

teacher ['titʃər] *s* instituteur *m*, enseignant *m*; (*such as adversity*) (fig) maître *m*

teach'er's pet' *s* élève *m* gâté

teaching ['titʃɪŋ] *s* enseignement *m*

teach'ing aids' spl matériel m auxiliaire d'enseignement

teach'ing staff' s corps m enseignant

tea'cup' s tasse f à thé

tea' dance' s thé m dansant

teak [tik] s teck m

tea'ket'tle s bouilloire f

team [tim] s (of horses, oxen, etc.) attelage m; (sports) équipe f || tr atteler || intr—to team up with faire équipe avec

team'mate' s équipier m

teamster ['timstər] s (of horses) charretier m; (of a truck) camionneur m

team'work' s travail m en équipe; (spirit) esprit m d'équipe

tea'pot' s théière f

tear [tɪr] s larme f; to burst into tears fondre en larmes || [ter] s déchirure f || [ter] v (pret tore [tor]; pp torn [torn]) tr déchirer; to tear away, down, off, or out arracher; to tear up (e.g., a letter) déchirer || intr se déchirer; to tear along filer précipitamment, aller à fond de train

tear' bomb' [tɪr] s bombe f lacrymogène

tear' duct' [tɪr] s conduit m lacrymal

tearful ['tɪrfəl] adj larmoyant, éploré

tear' gas' [tɪr] s gaz m lacrymogène

tear-jerker ['tɪr,dʒʌrkər] s (slang) comédie f larmoyante

tea'room' s salon m de thé

tease [tiz] tr taquiner

tea'spoon' s cuiller f à café

teaspoonful ['ti,spun,ful] s cuillerée f à café

teat [tit] s tétine f

tea'time' s l'heure f du thé

technical ['tɛknɪkəl] adj technique

technicali·ty [,tɛknɪ'kælɪti] s (pl -ties) technicité f; (fine point) subtilité f

technician [tɛk'nɪʃən] s technicien m

technique [tɛk'nik] s technique f

ted'dy bear' ['tɛdi] s ours m en peluche

tedious ['tidɪ·əs], ['tidʒəs] adj ennuyeux, fatigant

teem [tim] intr fourmiller; to teem with abonder en, fourmiller de

teeming ['timɪŋ] adj fourmillant; (rain) torrentiel

teen-ager ['tin,edʒər] s adolescent m de 13 à 19 ans

teens [tinz] spl numéros anglais qui se terminent en -teen (de 13 à 19); adolescence f de 13 à 19 ans; to be in one's teens être adolescent

tee·ny ['tini] adj (comp -nier; super -niest) (coll) minuscule, tout petit

teeter ['titər] s branlement m; balançoire f || intr se balancer, chanceler

teethe [tið] intr faire ses dents

teething ['tiðɪŋ] s dentition f

teeth'ing ring' s sucette f

teetotaler [ti'totələr] s antialcoolique mf (qui s'abstient totalement de boissons alcooliques)

tele-cast ['tɛlɪ,kæst], ['tɛlɪ,kɑst] s émission f télévisée || v (pret & pp -cast or -casted) tr & intr téléviser

telegram ['tɛlɪ,græm] s télégramme m

telegraph ['tɛlɪ,græf], ['tɛlɪ,grɑf] s télégraphe m || tr & intr télégraphier

telegrapher [tɪ'lɛgrəfər] s télégraphiste mf

tel'egraph pole' s poteau m télégraphique

telemeter [tɪ'lɛmɪtər] s télémètre m

telepathy [tɪ'lɛpəθi] s télépathie f

telephone ['tɛlɪ,fon] s téléphone m || tr & intr téléphoner

tel'ephone booth' s cabine f téléphonique

tel'ephone call' s appel m téléphonique

tel'ephone direc'tory s annuaire m du téléphone

tel'ephone exchange' s central m téléphonique

tel'ephone op'erator s standardiste mf, téléphoniste mf

tel'ephone receiv'er s récepteur m de téléphone

tel'ephoto lens' ['tɛlɪ,foto] s téléobjectif m

teleprinter ['tɛlɪ,prɪntər] s téléimprimeur m

telescope ['tɛlɪ,skop] s télescope m || tr télescoper || intr se télescoper

telescopic [,tɛlɪ'skɑpɪk] adj télescopique

teletype ['tɛlɪ,taɪp] s (trademark) télétype m

tel'etype'writ'er s téléscripteur m

teleview ['tɛlɪ,vju] tr & intr voir à la télévision

televiewer ['tɛlɪ,vju·ər] s téléspectateur m

televise ['tɛlɪ,vaɪz] tr téléviser

television ['tɛlɪ,vɪʒən] adj télévisuel || s télévision f

tel'evision screen' s écran m de télévision, petit écran

tel'evision set' s téléviseur m

tell [tɛl] v (pret & pp told [told]) tr dire; (a story) raconter; (to count) compter; (to recognize as distinct) distinguer; tell me another! (coll) à d'autres!; to tell off compter; (coll) dire son fait à; to tell s.o. to + inf dire à qn de + inf || intr produire un effet; do tell! (coll) vraiment!; to tell on influer sur; (coll) dénoncer; who can tell? qui sait?

teller ['tɛlər] s narrateur m; (of a bank) caissier m; (of votes) scrutateur m

temper ['tɛmpər] s humeur f, caractère m; (of steel, glass, etc.) trempe f; to keep one's temper retenir sa colère; to lose one's temper se mettre en colère || tr tremper || intr se tremper

temperament ['tɛmpərəmənt] s tempérament m

temperamental [,tɛmpərə'mɛntəl] adj constitutionnel; capricieux, instable

temperance ['tɛmpərəns] s tempérance f

temperate ['tɛmpərɪt] adj tempéré; (in food or drink) tempérant

temperature ['tɛmpərət/ər] s température f

tempest ['tɛmpɪst] s tempête f; tempest in a teapot tempête dans un verre d'eau tempestuous [tem'pestʃʊ-əs] adj tempétueux

temple ['tempəl] s temple m; (side of forehead) tempe f; (of spectacles) branche f

templet ['templɪt] s gabarit m

tem·po ['tempo] s (pl -pos or -pi [pi]) tempo m

temporal ['tempərəl] adj temporel; (anat) temporal

temporary ['tempə,reri] adj temporaire

temporize ['tempə,raɪz] intr temporiser

tempt [tempt] tr tenter

temptation [temp'teʃən] s tentation f

tempter ['temptər] s tentateur m

tempting ['temptɪŋ] adj tentant

ten [ten] adj & pron dix; about ten une dizaine de || s dix m; ten o'clock dix heures

tenable ['tenəbəl] adj soutenable

tenacious [tɪ'neʃəs] adj tenace

tenacity [tɪ'næsɪti] s ténacité f

tenant ['tenənt] s locataire mf

ten'ant farm'er s métayer m

tend [tend] tr soigner; (sheep) garder; (a machine) surveiller || intr—to tend to (to be disposed to) tendre à; (to attend to) vaquer à; to tend towards tendre vers or à

tenden·cy ['tendənsi] s (pl -cies) tendance f

tender ['tendər] adj tendre || s offre f; (aer, naut) ravitailleur m; (rr) tender m || tr offrir

ten'der-heart'ed adj au cœur tendre

ten'der-loin' s filet m

tenderness ['tendərnɪs] s tendresse f; (of, e.g., the skin) sensibilité f; (of, e.g., meat) tendreté f

tendon ['tendən] s tendon m

tendril ['tendrɪl] s vrille f

tenement ['tenɪmənt] s maison f d'habitation

ten'ement house' s maison f de rapport; (in the slums) taudis m

tenet ['tenɪt] s doctrine f, principe m

tennis ['tenɪs] s tennis m

ten'nis court' s court m de tennis

tenor ['tenər] s teneur f, cours m; (mus) ténor m

tense [tens] adj tendu || s (gram) temps m

tension ['tenʃən] s tension f

tent [tent] s tente f

tentacle ['tentəkəl] s tentacule m

tentative ['tentətɪv] adj provisoire; (hesitant) timide

tenth [tenθ] adj & pron dixième (masc, fem); the Tenth dix, e.g., John the Tenth Jean dix || s dixième m; the tenth (in dates) le dix

tent' pole' s montant m de tente

tenuous ['tenjʊ-əs] adj ténu

tenure ['tenjər] s (possession) tenure f; (of an office) occupation f; (protection from dismissal) inamovibilité f

tepid ['tepɪd] adj tiède

term [tʌrm] s terme m; (of imprisonment) temps m; (of office) mandat m; (of the school year) semestre m; terms conditions fpl || tr appeler, qualifier

termagant ['tʌrməgənt] s mégère f

terminal ['tʌrmɪnəl] adj terminal || s (elec) borne f; (rr) terminus m

terminate ['tʌrmɪ,net] tr terminer || intr se terminer

termination [,tʌrmɪ'neʃən] s conclusion f; (extremity) bout m; (of word) désinence f

terminus ['tʌrmɪnəs] s bout m, extrémité f; (boundary) borne f; (rr) terminus m

termite ['tʌrmaɪt] s termite m

term' pa'per s dissertation f

terrace ['terəs] s terrasse f || tr disposer en terrasse

terra firma ['terə'fʌrmə] s terre f ferme

terrain [te'ren] s terrain m

terrestrial [tə'restrɪ-əl] adj terrestre

terrible ['terɪbəl] adj terrible; (extremely bad) atroce

terrific [tə'rɪfɪk] adj terrible, terrifiant; (coll) formidable

terri·fy ['terɪ,faɪ] v (pret & pp -fied) tr terrifier

territo·ry ['terɪ,tori] s (pl -ries) territoire m

terror ['terər] s terreur f

terrorize ['terə,raɪz] tr terroriser

ter'ry cloth' ['teri] s tissu-éponge m

terse [tʌrs] adj concis, succinct

tertiary ['tʌrʃɪ,eri], ['tʌrʃəri] adj tertiaire

test [test] s épreuve f; (exam) examen m; (trial) essai m; (e.g., of intelligence) test m || tr éprouver, mettre à l'épreuve; examiner, tester

testament ['testəmənt] s testament m

test' ban' s interdiction f des essais nucléaires

test' flight' s vol m d'essai

testicle ['testɪkəl] s testicule m

testi·fy ['testɪ,faɪ] v (pret & pp -fied) tr déclarer || intr déposer; to testify to témoigner de

testimonial [,testɪ'moni-əl] s attestation m

testimo·ny ['testɪ,moni] s (pl -nies) témoignage m

test' pat'tern s (telv) mire f

test' pi'lot s pilote m d'essai

test' tube' s éprouvette f

tes·ty ['testi] adj (comp -tier; super -tiest) susceptible

tetanus ['tetənəs] s tétanos m

tether ['teðər] s attache f; at the end of one's tether à bout de ressources || tr mettre à l'attache

tetter ['tetər] s (pathol) dartre f

text [tekst] s texte m

text'book' s manuel m scolaire, livre m de classe

textile ['tekstɪl], ['tekstaɪl] adj & s textile m

textual ['tekstʃʊ-əl] adj textuel

texture ['tekstʃər] s texture f; (woven fabric) tissu m

Thai ['tɑ-i], [taɪ] adj thaï, thaïlandais || s (language) thaï m; (person)

Thaïlandais *m*; **the Thai** les Thaïlandais

Thailand ['taɪlənd] *s* Thaïlande *f*; la Thaïlande

Thames [temz] *s* Tamise *f*

than [ðæn] *conj* que; (*before a numeral*) de, e.g., **more than three** plus de trois

thank [θæŋk] *adj* (*e.g., offering*) de reconnaissance ‖ **thanks** *spl* remerciements *mpl*; **thanks to** grâce à ‖ **thanks** *interj* merci!; **no thanks!** merci! ‖ **thank** *tr* remercier; **thank you** je vous remercie; **thank you for** merci de or pour; **thank you for** + *ger* merci de + *inf*; **to thank s.o.** **for** remercier qn de or pour; **to thank s.o. for** + *ger* remercier qn de + *inf*

thankful ['θæŋkfəl] *adj* reconnaissant

thankless ['θæŋklɪs] *adj* ingrat

Thanksgiv'ing Day' *s* le jour d'action de grâces

that [ðæt] *adj dem* (*pl* **those**) ce §82; **that one** celui-là §84 ‖ *pron dem* (*pl* **those**) celui §83; celui-là §84 ‖ *pron rel* qui; que ‖ *pron neut* cela, ça; **that is** c'est-à-dire; **that's all** voilà tout; **that will do** cela suffit ‖ *adv* tellement, si, aussi; **that far** si loin, aussi loin; **that much, that many** tant ‖ *conj* que; (*in order that*) pour que, afin que; **in that** en ce que

thatch [θæt∫] *s* chaume *m* ‖ *tr* couvrir de chaume

thatched' cot'tage *s* chaumière *f*

thaw [θɔ] *s* dégel *m* ‖ *tr & intr* dégeler

the [ðə], [ðɪ], [ðɪ] *art def* le §77 ‖ *adv* d'autant plus, e.g., **she will be the happier for it** elle en sera d'autant plus heureuse; **the more . . . the more** plus . . . plus

theater ['θiətər] *s* théâtre *m*

the'ater club' *s* association *f* des spectateurs

the'ater-go'er *s* habitué *m* du théâtre

the'ater page' *s* chronique *f* théâtrale

theatrical [θi'ætrɪkəl] *adj* théâtral

thee [ði] *pron pers* (archaic, poetic, Bib) toi §85; te §87

theft [θɛft] *s* vol *m*

their [ðɛr] *adj poss* leur §88

theirs [ðɛrz] *pron poss* le leur §89

them [ðɛm] *pron pers* eux §85; les §87; leur §87; **of them** en §87; **to them** leur §87; y §87

theme [θim] *s* thème *m*; (*essay*) composition *f*; (mus) thème

theme' song' *s* leitmotiv *m*; (rad) indicatif *m*

them·selves' *pron pers* soi §85; eux-mêmes §86; se §87; eux §85

then [ðɛn] *adv* alors; (*next*) ensuite, puis; (*therefore*) donc; **by then** d'ici là; **from then on, since then** depuis lors, dès lors; **then and there** séance tenante; **till then** jusque-là; **what then?** et après?

thence [ðɛns] *adv* de là; (*from that fact*) pour cette raison

thence'forth' *adv* dès lors

theolo·gy [θi'ɑlədʒi] *s* (*pl* **-gies**) théologie *f*

theorem ['θiərəm] *s* théorème *m*

theoretical [ˌθiə'rɛtɪkəl] *adj* théorique

theo·ry ['θiəri] *s* (*pl* **-ries**) théorie *f*

therapeutic [ˌθɛrə'pjutɪk] *adj* thérapeutique ‖ **therapeutics** *spl* thérapeutique *f*

thera·py ['θɛrəpi] *s* (*pl* **-pies**) thérapie *f*

there [ðɛr] *adv* là; y §87; **down there, over there** là-bas; **from there** de là; en §87; **in there** là-dedans; on dit **là-dessus**; **there is** or **there are** il y a; (*pointing out*) voilà; **under there** là-dessous; **up there** là-haut

there'abouts' *adv* aux environs, près de là; (*approximately*) à peu près

there'af'ter *adv* par la suite

there'by' *adv* par là; de cette manière

therefore ['ðɛrˌfor] *adv* par conséquent, donc

there'in' *adv* dedans, là-dedans

there'of' *adv* de cela; en §87

there'upon' *adv* là-dessus §85A; sur ce

there'with' *adv* avec cela

thermal ['θʌrməl] *adj* (*waters*) thermal; (*capacity*) thermique

thermocouple ['θʌrmoˌkʌpəl] *s* thermocouple *m*

thermodynamic [ˌθʌrmodaɪ'næmɪk] *adj* thermodynamique ‖ **thermodynamics** *spl* thermodynamique *f*

thermometer [θər'mɑmɪtər] *s* thermomètre *m*

thermonuclear [ˌθʌrmo'n(j)uklɪər] *adj* thermonucléaire

Thermopylae [θər'mɑpɪˌli] *s* les Thermopyles *fpl*

ther'mos bot'tle ['θʌrməs] *s* thermos *m & f*, bouteille *f* thermos

thermostat ['θʌrməˌstæt] *s* thermostat *m*

thesau·rus [θɪ'sɔrəs] *s* (*pl* **-ri** [raɪ]) trésor *m*; dictionnaire *m* analogique

these [ðiz] *adj dem pl* ces §82 ‖ *pron dem pl* ceux §83; ceux-ci §84

the·sis ['θisɪs] *s* (*pl* **-ses** [siz]) thèse *f*

they [ðe] *pron pers* ils §85; eux §85; on §87, e.g., **they say** on dit; ce §82B

thick [θɪk] *adj* épais; (*pipe, rod, etc.*) gros; (*forest, eyebrows, etc.*) touffu; (*grass, grain, etc.*) dru; (*voice*) pâteux; (*gravy*) court; (coll) stupide, obtus; (coll) intime ‖ *s* (*of thumb, leg, etc.*) gras *m*; **the thick of** (*e.g., a crowd*) le milieu de; (*e.g., a battle*) le fort de; **through thick and thin** contre vents et marées

thicken ['θɪkən] *tr* épaissir ‖ *intr* s'épaissir; (*said, e.g., of plot*) se corser

thicket ['θɪkɪt] *s* fourré *m*, maquis *m*

thick'-head'ed *adj* à la tête dure

thick'-lipped' *adj* lippu

thick'-set' *adj* trapu

thief [θif] *s* (*pl* **thieves** [θivz]) voleur *m*

thieve [θiv] *intr* voler

thiev·er·y ['θivəri] *s* (*pl* **-ies**) volerie *f*

thigh [θaɪ] *s* cuisse *f*

thigh'bone' *s* fémur *m*

thimble ['θɪmbəl] *s* dé *m*

thin [θɪn] *adj* (*comp* **thinner**; *super* **thinnest**) mince; (*person*) élancé, maigre; (*hair*) rare; (*soup*) clair;

(*gravy*) long; (*voice*) grêle; (*excuse*) faible || *v* (*pret* & *pp* **thinned**; *ger* **thinning**) *tr* amincir; (*colors*) délayer; **to thin out** éclaircir || *intr* s'amincir; **to thin out** s'éclaircir

thine [ðaɪn] *adj poss* (archaic, poetic, Bib) ton §88 || *pron poss* (archaic, poetic, Bib) le tien §89

thing [θɪŋ] *s* chose *f*; **for another thing** d'autre part; **for one thing** en premier lieu; **of all things!** par exemple!; **to be the thing** être le dernier cri; **to see things** avoir des hallucinations

thingumbob [ˈθɪŋəmˌbɑb] *s* (coll) truc *m*, machin *m*

think [θɪŋk] *v* (*pret* & *pp* **thought** [θɔt]) *tr* penser; (*to deem, consider*) estimer; **to think of** (*to have an opinion of*) penser de || *intr* penser, songer; **to think fast** avoir l'esprit alerte; **to think of** (*to direct one's thoughts toward*) penser à, songer à; **to think of it or them** y penser, y songer; **to think so** croire que oui

thinker [ˈθɪŋkər] *s* penseur *m*

third [θʌrd] *adj* & *pron* troisième (*masc, fem*); **the Third** trois, e.g., **John the Third** Jean trois || *s* troisième *m*; (*in fractions*) tiers *m*; **the third** (*in dates*) le trois

third′ degree′ *s* (coll) passage *m* à tabac, cuisinage *m*

third′ fin′ger *s* annulaire *m*

third′ rail′ *s* (rr) rail *m* de contact; rail conducteur

third′-rate′ *adj* de troisième ordre

thirst [θʌrst] *s* soif *f* || *intr* avoir soif; **to thirst for** avoir soif de

thirst′-quench′ing *adj* désaltérant

thirst·y [ˈθʌrsti] *adj* (*comp* -ier; *super* -iest) altéré, assoiffé; **to be thirsty** avoir soif

thirteen [ˈθʌrˈtin] *adj, pron,* & *s* treize *m*

thirteenth [ˈθʌrˈtinθ] *adj* & *pron* treizième (*masc, fem*); **the Thirteenth** treize, e.g., **John the Thirteenth** Jean treize || *s* treizième *m*; **the thirteenth** (*in dates*) le treize

thirtieth [ˈθʌrti·ɪθ] *adj* & *pron* trentième (*masc, fem*) || *s* trentième *m*; **the thirtieth** (*in dates*) trente

thir·ty [ˈθʌrti] *adj* & *pron* trente; **about thirty** une trentaine de || *s* (*pl* -ties) trente *m*; **the thirties** les années *fpl* trente

this [ðɪs] *adj dem* (*pl* **these**) ce §82; **this one** celui-ci §84 || *pron dem* (*pl* **these**) celui §83; celui-ci §84 || *pron neut* ceci || *adv* tellement, si, aussi; **this far** si loin, aussi loin; **this much,** this many tant

thistle [ˈθɪsəl] *s* chardon *m*

thither [ˈθɪðər], [ˈðɪðər] *adv* là, de ce côté là

thong [θɔŋ], [θɑŋ] *s* courroie *f*

tho·rax [ˈθoræks] *s* (*pl* -raxes or -races [rəˌsiz]) thorax *m*

thorn [θɔrn] *s* épine *f*

thorn·y [ˈθɔrni] *adj* (*comp* -ier; *super* -iest) épineux

thorough [ˈθʌro] *adj* approfondi, complet; consciencieux, minutieux

thor′ough·bred′ *adj* de race, racé; (*horse*) pur sang || *s* personne *f* racée; (*horse*) pur-sang *m*

thor′ough·fare′ *s* voie *f* de communication; **no thoroughfare** (public sign) rue barrée

thor′ough·go′ing *adj* parfait; consciencieux

thoroughly [ˈθʌroli] *adv* à fond

those [ðoz] *adj dem pl* ces §82 || *pron dem pl* ceux §83; ceux-là §84

thou [ðaʊ] *pron pers* (archaic, poetic, Bib) tu §87 || *tr* & *intr* tutoyer

though [ðo] *adv* cependant || *conj* (*although*) bien que, quoique; (*even if*) même si; **as though** comme si

thought [θɔt] *s* pensée *f*

thought′ control′ *s* asservissement *m* des consciences

thoughtful [ˈθɔtfəl] *adj* pensif; (*considerate*) prévenant, attentif; (*serious*) profond

thoughtless [ˈθɔtlɪs] *adj* étourdi, négligent; inconsidéré

thousand [ˈθaʊzənd] *adj* & *pron* mille; mil, e.g., **the year one thousand nineteen hundred and eighty-one** l'an mil neuf cent quatre-vingt-un || *s* mille *m*; **a thousand** un millier de, mille

thousandth [ˈθaʊzəndθ] *adj* & *pron* millième (*masc, fem*) || *s* millième *m*

thrash [θræʃ] *tr* rosser; (agr) battre; **to thrash out** débattre || *intr* s'agiter; (agr) battre le blé

thread [θrɛd] *s* fil *m*; (bot) filament *m*; (mach) filet *m*; **to hang by a thread** ne tenir qu'à un fil; **to lose the thread of** perdre le fil de || *tr* enfiler; (mach) fileter

thread′bare′ *adj* élimé, râpé; (*tire*) usé jusqu'à la corde

threat [θrɛt] *s* menace *f*

threaten [ˈθrɛtən] *tr* & *intr* menacer

threatening [ˈθrɛtənɪŋ] *adj* menaçant

three [θri] *adj* & *pron* trois || *s* trois *m*; **three o'clock** trois heures; **three of a kind** (cards) un fredon

three′-cor′nered *adj* triangulaire; (*hat*) tricorne

three′-ply′ *adj* à trois épaisseurs; (*e.g., wool*) à trois fils

three′ R's′ [arz] *spl* la lecture, l'écriture et l'arithmétique, premières notions *fpl*

three′score′ *adj* soixante

threno·dy [ˈθrɛnədi] *s* (*pl* -dies) thrène *m*

thresh [θrɛʃ] *tr* (agr) battre; **to thresh out** (*a problem*) débattre || *intr* s'agiter; (agr) battre le blé

thresh′ing floor′ *s* aire *f*

thresh′ing machine′ *s* batteuse *f*

threshold [ˈθrɛʃold] *s* seuil *m*; **to cross the threshold** franchir le seuil

thrice [θraɪs] *adv* trois fois

thrift [θrɪft] *s* économie *f*, épargne *f*

thrift·y [ˈθrɪfti] *adj* (*comp* -ier; *super* -iest) économe, ménager, frugal; prospère

thrill [θrɪl] *s* frisson *m* || *tr* faire frémir || *intr* frémir

thriller ['θrɪlər] *s* roman *m*, film *m*, or pièce *f* à sensation

thrilling ['θrɪlɪŋ] *adj* émouvant, passionnant

thrive [θraɪv] *v* (*pret* thrived or throve [θrov]; *pp* thrived or thriven ['θrɪvən]) *intr* prospérer; (*said of child, plant, etc.*) croître, se développer

throat [θrot] *s* gorge *f*; to clear one's throat s'éclaircir le gosier; to have a sore throat avoir mal à la gorge

throb [θrab] *s* palpitation *f*, battement *m*; (*of motor*) vrombissement *m* || *v* (*pret & pp* throbbed; *ger* throbbing) *intr* palpiter, battre fort; (*said of motor*) vrombir

throes [θroz] *spl* (*of childbirth*) douleurs *fpl*; (*of death*) affres *fpl*; in the throes of luttant avec

throne [θron] *s* trône *m*

throng [θrɔŋ], [θraŋ] *s* foule *f*, affluence *f* || *intr* affluer

throttle ['θratəl] *s* (*of steam engine*) régulateur *m*; (*aut*) étrangleur *m* || *tr* régler; étrangler

through [θru] *adj* direct; (*finished*) fini; (*traffic*) prioritaire || *adv* à travers; complètement || *prep* au travers de, par; grâce à, par le canal de

through-out' *adv* d'un bout à l'autre || *prep* d'un bout à l'autre de; (*during*) pendant tout

through' street' *s* rue *f* à circulation prioritaire

through'way' *s* autoroute *f*

throw [θro] *s* jet *m*, lancement *m*; (*scarf*) châle *m* || *v* (*pret* threw [θru]; *pp* thrown) *tr* jeter, lancer; (*a glance; the dice*) jeter; (*e.g., a baseball*) lancer; (*e.g., a shadow*) projeter; (*blame; responsibility*) rejeter; (*a rider*) désarçonner; (*a game, career, etc.*) perdre à dessein; to throw away jeter; to throw back renvoyer; to throw in ajouter; to throw out expulser, chasser; (*e.g., an odor*) répandre; (*one's chest*) bomber; to throw over abandonner; to throw up jeter en l'air; vomir; (*one's hands*) lever; (*e.g., one's claims*) renoncer à || *intr* jeter, lancer; jeter des dés; to throw up vomir

throw'back' *s* recul *m*; (*setback*) échec *m*; (*reversion*) retour *m* atavique

thrum [θrʌm] *v* (*pret & pp* thrummed; *ger* thrumming) *intr* pianoter

thrush [θrʌʃ] *s* grive *f*

thrust [θrʌst] *s* poussée *f*; (*with a weapon*) coup *m* de pointe; (*with a sword*) coup d'estoc; (*jibe*) trait *m*; (*rok*) poussée *f*; thrust and parry la botte et la parade || *v* (*pret & pp* thrust) *tr* pousser; (*e.g., a dagger*) enfoncer; to thrust oneself on s'imposer à

thud [θʌd] *s* bruit *m* sourd || *v* (*pret & pp* thudded; *ger* thudding) *tr & intr* frapper avec un son mat

thug [θʌg] *s* bandit *m*, assassin *m*

thumb [θʌm] *s* pouce *m*; all thumbs (coll) maladroit; to twiddle one's thumbs se tourner les pouces; under the thumb of sous la coupe de || *tr* tripoter; (*a book*) feuilleter; to thumb a ride faire de l'auto-stop; to thumb one's nose at (coll) faire un pied de nez à

thumb' in'dex *s* onglet *m*, encoche *f*

thumb'print' *s* marque *f* de pouce

thumb'screw' *s* papillon *m*, vis *f* à ailettes

thumb'tack' *s* punaise *f*

thump [θʌmp] *s* coup *m* violent || *tr* cogner || *intr* tomber avec un bruit sourd; (*said, e.g., of marching feet*) sonner lourdement; (*said of heart*) battre fort

thumping ['θʌmpɪŋ] *adj* (coll) énorme

thunder ['θʌndər] *s* tonnerre *m* || *tr* fulminer || *intr* tonner; to thunder at tonner contre, tempêter contre

thun'der-bolt' *s* foudre *f*; (*disaster*) coup *m* de foudre

thun'der-clap' *s* coup *m* de tonnerre

thunderous ['θʌndərəs] *adj* orageux; (*voice; applause*) tonnant

thun'der-show'er *s* pluie *f* d'orage

thun'der-storm' *s* orage *m*

thunderstruck ['θʌndər,strʌk] *adj* foudroyé

Thursday ['θʌrzdi] *s* jeudi *m*

thus [ðʌs] *adv* ainsi; (*therefore*) donc; thus far jusqu'ici

thwack [θwæk] *s* coup *m* || *tr* flanquer un coup à

thwart [θwɔrt] *adj* transversal || *adv* en travers || *tr* déjouer, frustrer

thy [ðaɪ] *adj poss* (archaic, poetic, Bib) ton §88

thyme [taɪm] *s* thym *m*

thyroid ['θaɪrɔɪd] *s* thyroïde *f*; (pharm) extrait *m* thyroïde

thyself [ðaɪ'self] *pron* (archaic, poetic, Bib) toi-même §86; te §87

tiara [taɪ'ɑrə], [taɪ'erə] *s* tiare *f*; (*woman's headdress*) diadème *m*

tic [tɪk] *s* (pathol) tic *m*

tick [tɪk] *s* tic-tac *m*; (*e.g., of pillow*) taie *f*; (*e.g., of mattress*) housse *f* de coutil; (ent) tique *f*; on tick à crédit || *tr*—to tick off (*to check off*) pointer || *intr* tictaquer; (*said of heart*) battre

ticker ['tɪkər] *s* téléimprimeur *m*; (*watch*) (slang) toquante *f*; (*heart*) (slang) cœur *m*

tick'er tape' *s* bande *f* de téléimprimeur

ticket ['tɪkɪt] *s* billet *m*; (*of bus, subway, etc.*) ticket *m*; (*of baggage checkroom*) bulletin *m*; (*of cloakroom*) numéro *m*; (*for boat trip*) passage *m*; (*of a political party*) liste *f* électorale; (*for violation*) (coll) papillon *m* de procès-verbal, contravention *f*; that's the ticket (coll) c'est bien ça, là bonne heure; tickets, please! vos places, s'il vous plaît!

tick'et a'gent *s* guichetier *m*

tick'et collec'tor *s* contrôleur *m*

tick'et of'fice *s* guichet *m*; (theat) bureau *m* de location

tick′et scalp′er [ˌskælpər] s trafiquant m de billets de théâtre

tick′et win′dow s guichet m

ticking [ˈtɪkɪŋ] s coutil m

tickle [ˈtɪkəl] s chatouillement m ‖ tr chatouiller; amuser; plaire (with dat) ‖ intr chatouiller

ticklish [ˈtɪklɪʃ] adj chatouilleux; (touchy) susceptible; (subject, question) épineux, délicat

tick′-tack-toe′ s morpion m

ticktock [ˈtɪkˌtɑk] s tic-tac m ‖ intr faire tic-tac

tid′al wave′ [ˈtaɪdəl] s raz m de marée; (e.g., of popular indignation) vague f

tidbit [ˈtɪdˌbɪt] s bon morceau m

tiddlywinks [ˈtɪdliˌwɪŋks] s jeu m de puce

tide [taɪd] s marée f; **against the tide** à contre-marée; **to go with the tide** suivre le courant ‖ tr—**to tide over** dépanner, remettre à flot; (a difficulty) venir à bout de

tide′land′ s terres fpl inondées aux grandes marées

tide′wa′ter s eaux fpl de marée; bord m de la mer

tide′water pow′er plant′ s usine f marémotrice

tidings [ˈtaɪdɪŋz] spl nouvelles fpl

ti·dy [ˈtaɪdi] adj (comp -dier; super -diest) propre, net, bien tenu; (considerable) (coll) joli, fameux ‖ s (pl -dies) voile m de fauteuil ‖ v (pret & pp -died) tr mettre en ordre, nettoyer ‖ intr—**to tidy up** faire un brin de toilette

tie [taɪ] s lien m, attache f; (knot) nœud m; (necktie) cravate f; (in games) match m nul; (mus) liaison f; (rr) traverse f ‖ v (pret & pp tied; ger tying) tr lier; (a knot, a necktie, etc.) nouer; (shoelaces; a knot; one's apron) attacher; (an artery) ligaturer; (a competitor) être à égalité avec; (mus) lier; **tied up** (busy) occupé; **to tie down** assujettir; **to tie up** attacher; (a package) ficeler; (a person) ligoter; (a wound) bander; (funds) immobiliser; (traffic, a telephone line) emboutiller ‖ intr (sports) faire match nul, égaliser

tie′back′ s embrasse f

tie′pin′ s épingle f de cravate

tier [tɪr] s étage m; (of stadium) gradin m

tiger [ˈtaɪɡər] s tigre m

ti′ger lil′y s lis m tigré

tight [taɪt] adj serré, juste; (e.g., rope) tendu; (clothes) ajusté; (container) étanche; (game) serré; (money) serré; (miserly) (coll) chiche; (drunk) (coll) rond, noir ‖ **tights** spl collant m, maillot m ‖ adv fermement, bien; **to hold tight** tenir serré; se tenir, se cramponner; **to sit tight** (coll) tenir bon

tighten [ˈtaɪtən] tr (a knot, a bolt) serrer, resserrer; (e.g., a rope) tendre ‖ intr se serrer; se tendre

tight-fisted [ˈtaɪtˈfɪstɪd] adj dur à la détente, serré

tight′-fit′ting adj collant, ajusté

tight′rope′ s corde f raide

tight′rope walk′er s funambule mf

tight′ squeeze′ s (coll) situation f difficile, embarras m

tight′wad′ s (coll) grippe-sou m

tigress [ˈtaɪɡrɪs] s tigresse f

tile [taɪl] s (for roof) tuile f; (for floor) carreau m ‖ tr (e.g., a house) couvrir de tuiles; (a floor) carreler

tile′ roof′ s toit m de tuiles

till [tɪl] s tiroir-caisse m ‖ prep jusqu'à ‖ conj jusqu'à ce que ‖ tr labourer

tilt [tɪlt] s pente f, inclinaison f; (contest) joute f; **full tilt** à fond de train ‖ tr pencher, incliner; **to tilt back** renverser en arrière; **to tilt up** redresser ‖ intr se pencher, s'incliner; (with lance) jouter; (naut) donner de la bande; **to tilt at** attaquer, critiquer; **to tilt back** se renverser en arrière

timber [ˈtɪmbər] s bois m de construction; (trees) bois de haute futaie; (rafter) poutre f

tim′ber·land′ s bois m pour exploitation forestière

tim′ber line′ s limite f de la végétation forestière

timbre [ˈtɪmbər] s (phonet, phys) timbre m

time [taɪm] s temps m; heure f, e.g., **what time is it?** quelle heure est-il?; fois, e.g., **five times** cinq fois; e.g., **five times two** is ten cinq fois deux font dix; (phot) temps d'exposition; **at that time** à ce moment-là; à cette époque; **at the present time** à l'heure actuelle; **at the same time** en même temps; **at times** parfois; **behind the times** en retard sur son époque; **between times** entre-temps; **full time** plein temps; **in due time** en temps et lieu; **in no time** en moins de rien; **on time** à l'heure, à temps; **several times** à plusieurs reprises; **time and time again** maintes fois; **to beat time** (mus) battre la mesure; **to do time** (coll) faire son temps; **to have a good time** s'amuser bien, se divertir; **to lose time** (said of timepiece) retarder; **to mark time** marquer le pas; **to play for time** (coll) chercher à gagner du temps ‖ tr mesurer la durée de; (sports) chronométrer

time′ bomb′ s bombe f à retardement

time′ card′ s registre m de présence

time′ clock′ s horloge f enregistreuse

time′ expo′sure s (phot) pose f

time′ fuse′ s fusée f fusante

time′-hon′ored adj consacré par l'usage

time′keep′er s pointeur m, chronométreur m; pendule f; montre f

timeless [ˈtaɪmlɪs] adj sans fin, éternel

time·ly [ˈtaɪmli] adj (comp -lier; super -liest) opportun, à propos

time′piece′ s pendule f; montre f

timer [ˈtaɪmər] s (person) chronométreur m; (of an electrical appliance) minuterie f

time′ sheet′ s feuille f de présence

time′ sig′nal s signal m horaire

time′ta′ble s horaire m; (rr) indicateur m

time′work′ s travail m à l'heure

time′worn′ adj usé par le temps; (venerable) séculaire

time′ zone′ s fuseau m horaire

timid ['tɪmɪd] adj timide

timing ['taɪmɪŋ] s chronométrage m; choix m du moment propice; (of an electrical appliance) minuterie f; (aut, mach) réglage m; (sports) chronométrage; (theat) tempo m

tim′ing gears′ spl engrenage m de distribution

timorous ['tɪmərəs] adj timoré, peureux

tin [tɪn] s (element) étain m; (tin plate) fer-blanc m; (cup, box, etc.) boîte f || v (pret & pp **tinned**; ger **tinning**) tr étamer; (to can) (Brit) mettre en boîte

tin′ can′ s boîte f en fer-blanc, boîte de conserve

tincture ['tɪŋktʃər] s teinture f

tin′ cup′ s timbale f

tinder ['tɪndər] s amadou m

tin′der-box′ s briquet m à amadou; (fig) foyer m de l'effervescence

tin′ foil′ s feuille f d'étain, papier m d'argent

ting-a-ling ['tɪŋə‚lɪŋ] s drelin m

tinge [tɪndʒ] s teinte f, nuance f || v (ger **tingeing** or **tinging**) tr teinter, nuancer

tingle ['tɪŋɡəl] s picotement m, fourmillement m || intr picoter, fourmiller; (e.g., with enthusiasm) tressaillir

tin′ hat′ s (coll) casque m en acier

tinker ['tɪŋkər] s chaudronnier m ambulant; (bungler) bousilleur m || intr bricoler; to tinker with tripatouiller

tinkle ['tɪŋkəl] s tintement m || tr faire tinter || intr tinter

tin′ plate′ s fer-blanc m

tin′-plate′ tr étamer

tin′ roof′ s toit m de fer-blanc

tinsel ['tɪnsəl] s clinquant m; (for a Christmas tree) paillettes fpl, guirlandes fpl clinquantes

tin′smith′ s ferblantier m

tin′ sol′dier s soldat m de plomb

tint [tɪnt] s teinte f || tr teinter

tin′type′ s ferrotypie f

tin′ware′ s ferblanterie f

ti-ny ['taɪni] adj (comp **-nier**; super **-niest**) minuscule

tip [tɪp] s bout m, pointe f; (slant) inclinaison f; (fee to a waiter) pourboire m; (secret information) (slang) tuyau m || v (pret & pp **tipped**; ger **tipping**) tr incliner; (a waiter) donner un pourboire à; (the scales) faire pencher; (a waiter) donner un pourboire à, donner la pièce à; **to tip off** (slang) tuyauter; **to tip over** renverser || intr se renverser; donner un pourboire

tip′cart′ s tombereau m

tip′-in′ s (bb) hors-texte m

tip′-off′ s (coll) tuyau m

tipped′-in′ adj (bb) hors texte

tipple ['tɪpəl] intr biberonner

tip′staff′ s verge f d'huissier; huissier m à verge

tip-sy ['tɪpsi] adj (comp **-sier**; super **-siest**) gris, grisé

tip′toe′ s pointe f des pieds || v (pret & pp **-toed**; ger **-toeing**) intr marcher sur la pointe des pieds

tirade ['taɪred] s diatribe f

tire [taɪr] s pneu m || tr fatiguer || intr se fatiguer

tire′ chain′ s chaîne f antidérapante

tired [taɪrd] adj fatigué, las

tire′ gauge′ s manomètre m

tire′ i′ron s démonte-pneu m

tireless ['taɪrlɪs] adj infatigable

tire′ pres′sure s pression f des pneus

tire′ pump′ s gonfleur m pour pneus

tiresome ['taɪrsəm] adj fatigant, ennuyeux

tissue ['tɪʃu] s tissu m; (thin paper) papier m de soie; (toilet tissue) papier hygiénique; (paper handkerchief) mouchoir m à jeter

tis′sue pa′per s papier m de soie

tit [tɪt] s téton m; (orn) mésange f; **tit for tat** à bon chat bon rat

titanium [taɪ'teni‚əm], [tɪ'teni‚əm] s titane m

tithe [taɪð] s dixième m; (rel) dîme f || tr soumettre à la dîme; payer la dîme sur

Titian ['tɪʃən] s le Titien m

Ti′tian red′ s blond m vénitien

title ['taɪtəl] s titre m || tr intituler

ti′tle deed′ s titre m de propriété

ti′tle-hold′er s tenant m du titre

ti′tle page′ s page f de titre

ti′tle role′ s rôle m principal

tit′mouse′ s (pl **-mice**) (orn) mésange f

titter ['tɪtər] s rire m étouffé || intr rire en catimini

titular ['tɪtʃələr] adj titulaire

to [tu], [tʊ], [tə] adv—**to and fro** de long en large || prep à; (towards) vers; (in order to) afin de, pour; envers, pour, e.g., **good to her** bon envers elle, bon pour elle; jusqu'à, e.g., **to this day** jusqu'à ce jour; e.g., **to count to a hundred** compter jusqu'à cent; moins, e.g., **a quarter to eight** huit heures moins le quart; contre, e.g., **seven to one** sept contre un; dans, e.g., **to a certain extent** dans une certaine mesure; en, e.g., **from door to door** de porte en porte; e.g., **I am going to France** je vais en France; de, e.g., **to try to** + inf essayer de + inf; **to him** lui §87

toad [tod] s crapaud m

toad′stool′ s agaric m; champignon m vénéneux

to-and-fro ['tu-ənd'fro] adj de va-et-vient

toast [tost] s pain m grillé; (with a drink) toast m || tr griller; porter un toast à, boire à la santé de

toaster ['tostər] s grille-pain m

toast′mas′ter s préposé m aux toasts

tobac-co [tə'bæko] s (pl **-cos**) tabac m

tobac′co pouch′ s blague f

toboggan [tə'bɑɡən] s toboggan m

tocsin ['tɑksɪn] *s* tocsin *m*; (*bell*) cloche *f* qui sonne le tocsin

today [tʊ'de] *s & adv* aujourd'hui *m*

toddle ['tɑdəl] *s* allure *f* chancelante ‖ *intr* marcher à petits pas chancelants

toddler ['tɑdlər] *s* tout-petit *m*

tod·dy ['tɑdi] *s* (*pl* **-dies**) grog *m*

to-do [tə'du] *s* (*pl* **-dos**) embarras *mpl*, chichis *mpl*, façons *fpl*

toe [to] *s* doigt *m* du pied, orteil *m*; (*of shoe, of stocking*) bout *m* ‖ *v* (*pret & pp* **toed**; *ger* **toeing**) *tr*—**to toe the line** or **the mark** s'aligner, se mettre au pas

toe'nail' *s* ongle *m* du pied

tog [tɑg] *v* (*pret & pp* **togged**; *ger* **togging**) *tr*—**to tog out** or **up** attifer, fringuer ‖ **togs** *spl* fringues *fpl*

together [tʊ'gɛðər] *adv* ensemble; (*at the same time*) en même temps, à la fois

tog'gle switch' ['tɑgəl] *s* (elec) interrupteur *m* à culbuteur ou à bascule

toil [tɔɪl] *s* travail *m* dur; **toils** filet *m*, piège *m* ‖ *intr* travailler dur

toilet ['tɔɪlɪt] *s* toilette *f*; (*rest room*) cabinet *m* de toilette

toi'let ar'ticles *spl* objets *mpl* de toilette

toi'let bowl' *s* cuvette *f*

toi'let pa'per *s* papier *m* hygiénique

toi'let seat' *s* siège *m* des toilettes

toi'let set' *s* nécessaire *m* de toilette

toi'let soap' *s* savonnette *f*

toi'let wa'ter *s* eaux *fpl* de toilette

token ['tokən] *adj* symbolique ‖ *s* signe *m*, marque *f*; (*keepsake*) souvenir *m*; (*used as money*) jeton *m*; **by the same token** de plus; **in token of** en témoignage de

tolerance ['tɑlərəns] *s* tolérance *f*

tolerate ['tɑlə‚ret] *tr* tolérer

toll [tol] *s* (*of bells*) glas *m*; (*payment*) droit *m* de passage, péage *m*; (*number of victims*) mortalité *f*; (telp) tarif *m* ‖ *tr* sonner; (*to ring the knell for*) sonner le glas de ‖ *intr* sonner le glas

toll' bridge' *s* pont *m* à péage

toll' call' *s* appel *m* interurbain

toll' gate' *s* barrière *f* à péage

toll' road' *s* autoroute *f* à péage

toma·to [tə'meto], [tə'mɑto] *s* (*pl* **-toes**) tomate *f*

tomb [tum] *s* tombeau *m*

tomboy ['tɑm‚bɔɪ] *s* garçon *m* manqué

tomb'stone' *s* pierre *f* tombale

tomcat ['tɑm‚kæt] *s* matou *m*

tome [tom] *s* tome *m*

tomorrow [tʊ'mɑro], [tʊ'mɔro] *adj*, *s*, *& adv* demain *m*; **tomorrow morning** demain matin; **until tomorrow** à demain

tom-tom ['tɑm‚tɑm] *s* tam-tam *m*

ton [tʌn] *s* tonne *f*

tone [ton] *s* ton *m* ‖ *tr* accorder; **to tone down** atténuer; **to tone up** renforcer; (*e.g., the muscles*) tonifier ‖ *intr*—**to tone down** se modérer

tone' po'em *s* poème *m* symphonique

tongs [tɔŋz], [tɑŋz] *spl* pincettes *fpl*; (*e.g., for sugar*) pince *f*; (*of blacksmith*) tenailles *fpl*

tongue [tʌŋ] *s* (*language; part of body*) langue *f*; (*of wagon*) timon *m*; (*of buckle*) ardillon *m*; (*of shoe*) languette *f*; **to hold one's tongue** se mordre la langue

tongue-tied ['tʌŋ‚taɪd] *adj* bouche cousue

tongue' twist'er *s* phrase *f* à décrocher la mâchoire

tonic ['tɑnɪk] *adj & s* tonique *m*

tonight [tʊ'naɪt] *adj & s* ce soir

tonsil ['tɑnsəl] *s* amygdale *f*

tonsillitis [‚tɑnsɪ'laɪtɪs] *s* amygdalite *f*

ton·y ['toni] *adj* (*comp* **-ier**; *super* **-iest**) (slang) élégant, chic

too [tu] *adv* (*also*) aussi; (*more than enough*) trop; (*moreover*) d'ailleurs; **I did too!** mais si!; **too bad!** c'est dommage!; **too many, too much** trop, trop de

tool [tul] *s* outil *m* ‖ *tr* (*a piece of metal*) usiner; (*leather*) repousser; (bb) dorer ‖ *intr*—**to tool along** rouler; **to tool up** s'outiller

tool' box' *s* trousse *f* à outils

tool'mak'er *s* taillandier *m*

toot [tut] *s* son *m* du cor; (*of auto*) coup *m* de klaxon; (*of locomotive*) coup *m* de sifflet ‖ *tr* sonner ‖ *intr* corner; (aut) klaxonner

tooth [tuθ] *s* (*pl* **teeth** [tiθ]) dent *f*; **to grit, grind,** or **gnash the teeth** grincer des dents, crisser des dents

tooth'ache' *s* mal *m* de dents

tooth'brush' *s* brosse *f* à dents

toothless ['tuθlɪs] *adj* édenté

tooth'paste' *s* pâte *f* dentifrice

tooth'pick' *s* cure-dent *m*

tooth' pow'der *s* poudre *f* dentifrice

top [tɑp] *adj* premier, de tête ‖ *s* sommet *m*, cime *f*, faîte *m*; (*of a barrel, table, etc.*) dessus *m*; (*of a page*) haut *m*; (*of a box*) couvercle *m*; (*of a carriage or auto*) capote *f*; (*toy*) toupie *f*; (naut) hune *f*; **at the top of** en haut de; (*e.g., one's class*) à la tête de; **at the top of one's voice** à tue-tête; **from top to bottom** de haut en bas, de fond en comble; **on top of** sur; (*in addition to*) en plus de; **tops** (*e.g., of carrots*) fanes *fpl*; **to sleep like a top** dormir comme un sabot ‖ *v* (*pret & pp* **topped**; *ger* **topping**) *tr* couronner, surmonter; (*to surpass*) dépasser; (*a tree, plant, etc.*) écimer

topaz ['topæz] *s* topaze *f*

top' bill'ing *s* tête *f* d'affiche

top'coat' *s* surtout *m* de demi-saison

toper ['topər] *s* soiffard *m*

top' hat' *s* haut-de-forme *m*

top'-heav'y *adj* trop lourd du haut

topic ['tɑpɪk] *s* sujet *m*

top'knot' *s* chignon *m*

top'mast' *s* mât *m* de hune

top'most' *adj* (le) plus haut

top'notch' *adj* (coll) d'élite

topogra·phy [tə'pɑgrəfi] *s* (*pl* **-phies**) topographie *f*

topple ['tɑpəl] *tr & intr* culbuter

topsail ['tɑpsəl], ['tɑp‚sel] *s* (naut) hunier *m*

top'soil' *s* couche *f* arable

topsy-turvy ['tʌpsɪ'tʌrvi] *adj & adv* sens dessus dessous

torch [tɔrtʃ] *s* torche *f*, flambeau *m*; (Brit) lampe *f* torche; **to carry the torch for** (slang) avoir un amour sans retour pour

torch'bear'er *s* porte-flambeau *m*; (fig) défenseur *m*

torch'light *s* lueur *f* des flambeaux

torch'light proces'sion *s* défilé *m* aux flambeaux

torch' song' *s* chanson *f* de l'amour non partagé

torment ['tɔrment] *s* tourment *m* || [tɔr'ment] *tr* tourmenter

torna·do [tɔr'nedo] *s* (*pl* -does *or* -dos) tornade *f*

torpe·do [tɔr'pido] *s* (*pl* -does) torpille *f* || *tr* torpiller

torpe'do-boat destroy'er *s* contre-torpilleur *m*

torpid ['tɔrpɪd] *adj* engourdi

torque [tɔrk] *s* effort *m* de torsion, couple *m* de torsion

torrent ['tʌrənt], ['tɔrənt] *s* torrent *m*

torrid ['tʌrɪd], ['tɔrɪd] *adj* torride

tor·so ['tɔrso] *s* (*pl* -sos) torse *m*

tort [tɔrt] *s* (law) acte *m* dommageable sauf rupture de contrat ou abus de confiance

tortoise ['tɔrtəs] *s* tortue *f*

tor'toise shell' *s* écaille *f*

torture ['tɔrtʃər] *s* torture *f* || *tr* torturer

toss [tɔs], [tɑs] *s* lancement *m*; (*of the head*) mouvement *m* dédaigneux || *tr* lancer; (*one's head*) relever dédaigneusement; (*a rider*) démonter; (*a coin*) jouer à pile et face avec; **to toss about** agiter, ballotter; **to toss off** (*e.g., work*) expédier; (*in one gulp*) lamper; **to toss up** jeter en l'air || *intr* s'agiter; **to toss and turn** se tourner et retourner

toss'up' *s* (coll) coup *m* de pile ou face; chances *fpl* égales

tot [tɑt] *s* bambin *m*, tout petit *m* || *v* (*pret & pp* totted; *ger* totting) *tr*—**to tot up** additionner

to·tal ['totəl] *adj & s* total *m*; **as a total** au total || *v* (*pret & pp* -taled *or* -talled; *ger* -taling *or* -talling) *tr* additionner, totaliser; (*to amount to*) s'élever à

totalitarian [,to,tælɪ'tɛrɪ·ən] *adj & mf* totalitaire

totem ['totəm] *s* totem *m*

totter ['tɑtər] *intr* chanceler

touch [tʌtʃ] *s* (*act*) attouchement *m*; (*e.g., of color; with a brush*) touche *f*; (*sense; of pianist*) toucher *m*; (*of typist*) frappe *f*; (*little bit*) pointe *f*, brin *m*; **in touch** en communication; **to get in touch with** prendre contact avec || *tr* toucher; (*for a loan*) (slang) taper; **to touch off** déclencher; **to touch up** retoucher || *intr* se toucher; **to touch on** toucher à

touched *adj* touché; (*crazy*) timbré

touching ['tʌtʃɪŋ] *adj* touchant, émouvant || *prep* touchant, concernant

touch·y ['tʌtʃi] *adj* (*comp* -ier; *super* -iest) susceptible, irritable

tough [tʌf] *adj* dur, coriace; (*tenacious*) résistant; (*task*) difficile || *s* voyou *m*

toughen ['tʌfən] *tr* endurcir || *intr* s'endurcir

tough' luck' *s* déveine *f*

tour [tur] *s* tour *m*; (*e.g., of inspection*) tournée *f*; **on tour** en tournée || *tr* faire le tour de; (*e.g., a country*) voyager en; (theat) faire une tournée de, en, ou dans || *intr* voyager

tour'ing car' *s* voiture *f* de tourisme

tourist ['turɪst] *adj & s* touriste *mf*

tournament ['turnəmənt], ['tʌrnəmənt] *s* tournoi *m*

tourney ['turni], ['tʌrni] *s* tournoi *m* || *intr* tournoyer

tourniquet ['turnɪ,ket], ['tʌrnɪ,ke] *s* (surg) garrot *m*, tourniquet *m*

tousle ['tauzəl] *tr* ébouriffer; tirailler, maltraiter

tow [to] *s* remorque *f*; (*e.g., of hemp*) filasse *f*; **to take in tow** prendre en remorque; (fig) se charger de || *tr* remorquer

towage ['to·ɪdʒ] *s* remorquage *m*; droits *mpl* de remorquage

toward(s) [tord(z)], [tə'word(z)] *prep* vers; (*in regard to*) envers

tow'boat' *s* remorqueur *m*

tow·el ['tau·əl] *s* serviette *f*, essuie-main *m* || *v* (*pret & pp* -eled *or* -elled; *ger* -eling *or* -elling) *tr* essuyer avec une serviette

tow'el rack' *s* porte-serviettes *m*

tower ['tau·ər] *s* tour *f* || *intr* s'élever

towering ['tau·ərɪŋ] *adj* élevé, géant; (*e.g., ambition*) sans bornes

tow'er-man *s* (*pl* -men) (aer, rr) aiguilleur *m*

tow'ing serv'ice ['to·ɪŋ] *s* service *m* de dépannage

tow'line' *s* câble *m* de remorque

town [taun] *s* ville *f*; **in town** en ville

town' clerk' *s* secrétaire *m* de mairie

town' coun'cil *s* conseil *m* municipal

town' cri'er *s* crieur *m* public

town' hall' *s* hôtel *m* de ville

town' plan'ning *s* urbanisme *m*

towns'folk' *spl* citadins *mpl*

town'ship *s* commune *f*; (U.S.A.) circonscription *f* administrative de six milles carrés

towns'man ['taunzmən] *s* (*pl* -men) citadin *m*

towns'peo'ple *spl* citadins *mpl*

town' talk' *s* sujet *m* du jour

tow'path' *s* chemin *m* de halage

tow'rope' *s* corde *f* de remorque

tow' truck' *s* dépanneuse *f*, voiture *f* de dépannage

toxic ['tɑksɪk] *adj & s* toxique *m*

toy [tɔɪ] *adj* petit; d'enfant || *s* jouet *m*, joujou *m*; (*trifle*) bagatelle *f* || *intr* jouer, s'amuser; **to toy with** (*a person*) badiner avec; (*an idea*) caresser

toy' dog' *s* chien *m* de manchon

toy' sol'dier *s* soldat *m* de plomb

trace [tres] *s* trace *f*; (*of harness*) trait *m* || *tr* tracer; (*the whereabouts of* s.o. or s.th.) pister; (e.g., an influence) retrouver les traces de; (a design seen through thin paper) calquer; **to trace back** remonter jusqu'à l'origine de

tracer ['tresər] s traceur m

trac′er bul′let s balle f traçante

trache•a ['treki•ə] s (pl **-ae** [ˌi]) trachée f

tracing ['tresɪŋ] s tracé m

trac′ing tape′ s cordeau m

track [træk] s (of foot or vehicle) trace f; (of an animal; in a stadium) piste f; (of a boat) sillage m; (of a railroad) voie f; (of an airplane, of a hurricane) trajet m; (of a tractor) chenille f; (course followed) chemin m tracé; (sports) la course et le saut de barrières; (sports) athlétisme m; **off the beaten track** hors des sentiers battus; **on the right track** sur la bonne voie; **to be on the wrong track** faire fausse route; **to have an inside track** tenir la corde; **to keep track of** ne pas perdre de vue; **to make tracks** (coll) filer ‖ tr traquer; laisser des traces de pas dans; **to track down** dépister

tracking ['trækɪŋ] s (of spaceship) repérage m

track′ing sta′tion s poste m de repérage

track′less trol′ley s trolleybus m

track′ meet′ s concours m de courses et de sauts, épreuve f d'athlétisme

track′walk′er s garde-voie m

tract [trækt] s (of land) étendue f; (leaflet) tract m; (anat) voie f

traction ['trækʃən] s traction f

trac′tion com′pany s entreprise f de transports urbains

tractor ['træktər] s tracteur m

trade [tred] s commerce m, négoce m; clientèle f; (calling, job) métier m; (exchange) échange m; (in slaves) traite f; **to take in trade** reprendre en compte ‖ tr échanger; **to trade in** (e.g., a used car) donner en reprise ‖ intr commercer; **to trade in** faire le commerce de; **to trade on** exploiter

trade′-in′ s reprise f

trade′mark′ s marque f déposée

trade′ name′ s raison f sociale

trader ['tredər] s commerçant m

trade′ school′ s école f des arts et métiers

trades′man s (pl **-men**) commerçant m; (shopkeeper) boutiquier m; (Brit) artisan m

trades′ un′ion or **trade′ un′ion** s syndicat m ouvrier

trade′ winds′ spl vents mpl alizés

trad′ing post′ ['tredɪŋ] s factorerie f

trad′ing stamp′ s timbre-prime m

tradition [trə'dɪʃən] s tradition f

traditional [trə'dɪʃənəl] adj traditionnel

traf•fic ['træfɪk] s (commerce) négoce m; (in the street) circulation f; (illegal) trafic m; (in, e.g., slaves) traite f; (naut, rr) trafic ‖ v (pret & pp **-ficked;** ger **-ficking**) intr trafiquer

traf′fic cir′cle s rond-point m

traf′fic cop′ s agent m de la circulation

traf′fic court′ s tribunal m de simple police (pour les contraventions au code de la route)

traf′fic jam′ s embouteillage m

traf′fic light′ s feu m de circulation

traf′fic sign′ s panneau m de signalisation, poteau m indicateur

traf′fic sig′nal s signal m routier

traf′fic tick′et s contravention f

traf′fic vi′olator s contrevenant m

tragedian [trə'dʒidɪ•ən] s tragédien m

trage•dy ['trædʒɪdi] s (pl **-dies**) tragédie f

tragic ['trædʒɪk] adj tragique

trail [trel] s trace f, piste f; (e.g., of smoke) traînée f ‖ tr traîner; (to look for) pister ‖ intr traîner; (said of a plant) grimper; **to trail off** se perdre

trailer ['trelər] s remorque f; (for vacationing) remorque de plaisance, caravane f; (mov) film-annonce m

trail′er camp′ s camp m pour caravanes

trail′er home′ s caravane f

train [tren] s (of railway cars) train m; (of dress) traîne f; (of thought) enchaînement m; (streak) traînée f ‖ tr entraîner, former; (plants) palisser; (a gun; a telescope) pointer ‖ intr s'entraîner

trained′ an′imals spl animaux mpl savants

trained′ nurse′ s infirmière f diplômée

trainer ['trenər] s (of animals) dresseur m; (sports) entraîneur m

training ['trenɪŋ] s entraînement m; instruction f; (of animals) dressage m

train′ing school′ s école f technique; (reformatory) maison f de correction

train′ing ship′ s navire-école m

trait |tret| s trait m

traitor ['tretər] s traître m

traitress |'tretrɪs| s traîtresse f

trajecto•ry [trə'dʒɛktəri] s (pl **-ries**) trajectoire f

tramp [træmp] s vagabond m; bruit m de pas lourds ‖ tr parcourir à pied; (the street) battre ‖ intr vagabonder; marcher lourdement; **to tramp on** marcher sur

trample ['træmpəl] tr fouler, piétiner ‖ intr—**to trample on** or **upon** fouler, piétiner

trampoline ['træmpəˌlin] s tremplin m de gymnase

tramp′ steam′er s tramp m

trance [træns], [trɑns] s transe f; **in a trance** en transe

tranquil ['træŋkwɪl] adj tranquille

tranquilize ['træŋkwɪˌlaɪz] tr tranquilliser

tranquilizer ['træŋkwɪˌlaɪzər] s tranquillisant m

tranquillity [træn'kwɪlɪti] s tranquillité f

transact [træn'zækt], [træns'ækt] tr traiter, négocier ‖ intr faire des affaires

transaction [træn'zækʃən], [træns'ækʃən] s transaction f; (of business) conduite *f*; **transactions** (*of a society*) actes *mpl*

transatlantic [ˌtrænsət'læntɪk] *adj & s* transatlantique *m*

transcend [træn'sɛnd] *tr* transcender || *intr* se transcender

transcribe [træn'skraɪb] *tr* transcrire

transcript ['trænskrɪpt] *s* copie *f*; (*of a meeting*) procès-verbal *m*; (*educ*) livret *m* scolaire

transcription [træn'skrɪpʃən] *s* transcription *f*

transept ['trænsept] *s* transept *m*

trans·fer ['trænsfər] *s* (*e.g., of stock, property, etc.*) transfert *m*; (*from one place to the other*) translation *f*; (*from one job to the other*) mutation *f*; (*of a design*) décalque *m*; (*for bus or subway*) billet *m* de correspondance; (*public sign*) correspondance || [træns'fʌr], ['trænsfər] *v* (*pret & pp* -ferred; *ger* -ferring) *tr* transférer; transporter; (*e.g., a civil servant*) déplacer; (*a design*) décalquer || *intr* se déplacer; changer de train (de l'autobus, etc.)

transfix [træns'fɪks] *tr* transpercer

transform [træns'fɔrm] *tr* transformer || *intr* se transformer

transformer [træns'fɔrmər] *s* transformateur *m*

transfusion [træns'fjuʒən] *s* transfusion *f*

transgress [træns'grɛs] *tr & intr* transgresser

transgression [træns'grɛʃən] *s* transgression *f*

transient ['trænʃənt] *adj* transitoire, passager; (*e.g., guest*) de passage || *s* hôte *mf* de passage

transistor [træn'sɪstər] *s* transistor *m*

transit ['trænsɪt], ['trænzɪt] *s* transit *m*

transition [træn'zɪʃən] *s* transition *f*

transitional [træn'zɪʃənəl] *adj* transitoire, de transition

transitive ['trænsɪtɪv] *adj* transitif || *s* verbe *m* transitif

transitory ['trænsɪˌtorɪ] *adj* transitoire

translate [træns'let], ['trænslet] *tr* traduire

translation [træns'leʃən] *s* traduction *f*; (*transfer*) translation *f*

translator [træns'letər] *s* traducteur *m*

transliterate [træns'lɪtəˌret] *tr* translitérer

translucent [træns'lusənt] *adj* translucide, diaphane

transmission [træns'mɪʃən] *s* transmission *f*; (*gear change*) changement *m* de vitesse; (*housing for gears*) boîte *f* de vitesses

transmis'sion-gear' box' *s* boîte *f* de vitesses

trans·mit [træns'mɪt] *v* (*pret & pp* -mitted; *ger* -mitting) *tr & intr* transmettre; (*rad*) émettre

transmitter [træns'mɪtər] *s* (telg, telp) transmetteur *m*; (rad) émetteur *m*

transmit'ting sta'tion *s* poste *m* émetteur

transmute [træns'mjut] *tr* transmuer

transom ['trænsəm] *s* (*crosspiece*) lin-

teau *m*; (*window over door*) imposte *f*, vasistas *m*; (*of ship*) barre *f* d'arcasse

transparen·cy [træns'pɛrənsi] *s* (*pl* -cies) transparence *f*; (phot) diapositive *f*

transparent [træns'pɛrənt] *adj* transparent

transpire [træns'paɪr] *intr* se passer; (*to leak out*) transpirer

transplant ['træns‚plænt], ['træns‚plɑnt] *s* (*organ or tissue*) greffon *m*; (*operation*) greffe *f* || [træns-'plænt], [træns'plɑnt] *tr* transplanter; (*e.g., a heart*) greffer

transport ['trænsport] *s* transport *m* || [træns'port] *tr* transporter

transportation [‚trænspor'teʃən] *s* transport *m*; billet *m* de train, de bateau, or d'avion; (*deportation*) transportation *f*

transport'er bridge' [træns'portər] *s* transbordeur *m*

trans'port work'er *s* employé *m* des entreprises de transport

transpose [træns'poz] *tr* transposer

trans·ship [træns'ʃɪp] *v* (*pret & pp* -shipped; *ger* -shipping) *tr* transborder

transshipment [træns'ʃɪpmənt] *s* transbordement *m*

trap [træp] *s* piège *m*; (*pitfall*) trappe *f*; (*double-curved pipe*) siphon *m*; **traps** (mus) batterie *f* de jazz || *v* (*pret & pp* trapped; *ger* trapping) *tr* prendre au piège, attraper

trap' door' *s* trappe *f*

trapeze [trə'piz] *s* trapèze *m*

trapezoid ['træpɪˌzɔɪd] *s* trapèze *m*

trapper ['træpər] *s* trappeur *m*

trappings ['træpɪŋz] *spl* (*adornments*) atours *mpl*; (*of horse's harness*) harnachement *m*

trap'shoot'ing *s* tir *m* au pigeon

trash [træʃ] *s* déchets *mpl*, rebuts *mpl*; (*junk*) camelote *f*; (*nonsense*) ineptie *f*; (*worthless people*) racaille *f*

trash' can' *s* poubelle *f*

travail [trə'vel] *s* labeur *m*; douleur *f* de l'enfantement

trav·el ['trævəl] *s* voyages *mpl*; (mach) course *f* || *v* (*pret & pp* -eled or -elled; *ger* -eling or -elling) *tr* parcourir || *intr* voyager; (mach) se déplacer

trav'el bu'reau *s* agence *f* de voyages

traveler ['trævələr] *s* voyageur *m*

trav'eler's check' *s* chèque *m* de voyage

trav'eling expen'ses *spl* frais *mpl* de voyage

trav'eling sales'man *s* (*pl* -men) commis *m* voyageur

traverse [trə'vʌrs] *tr* parcourir, traverser

traves·ty ['trævɪsti] *s* (*pl* -ties) *s* travestissement *m* || *v* (*pret & pp* -tied) *tr* travestir

trawl [trɔl] *s* chalut *m* || *tr* traîner || *intr* pêcher au chalut

trawler ['trɔlər] *s* chalutier *m*

tray [tre] *s* plateau *m*; (*of refrigerator*) bac *f*; (chem, phot) cuvette *f*

treacherous ['tretʃərəs] *adj* traître

treacher·y ['tretʃəri] *s* (*pl* **-ies**) trahison *f*

tread [tred] *s* (*step; sound of steps*) pas *m*; (*gait*) allure *f*; (*of stairs*) giron *m*; (*of tire*) chape *f*; (*of shoe*) semelle *f*; (*of egg*) cicatricule *f* ‖ *v* (*pret* **trod** [trad]; *pp* **trodden** ['tradən] or **trod**) *tr* marcher sur, piétiner ‖ *intr* marcher

treadle ['tredəl] *s* pédale *f*

tread/mill/ *s* trépigneuse *f*; (*futile drudgery*) besogne *f* ingrate

treason ['trizən] *s* trahison *f*

treasonable ['trizənəbəl] *adj* traître

treasure ['trɛʒər] *s* trésor *m* ‖ *tr* garder soigneusement; (*to prize*) tenir beaucoup à

treasurer ['trɛʒərər] *s* trésorier *m*

treasur·y ['trɛʒəri] *s* (*pl* **-ies**) trésorerie *f*; trésor *m*

treat [trit] *s* régal *m*, plaisir *m* ‖ *tr* traiter; régaler; (*to a drink*) payer à boire à ‖ *intr* traiter

treatise ['tritis] *s* traité *m*

treatment ['tritmənt] *s* traitement *m*

trea·ty ['triti] *s* (*pl* **-ties**) traité *m*

treble ['trebəl] *adj* (*threefold*) triple; (*mus*) de soprano ‖ *s* soprano *mf*; (*voice*) soprano *m* ‖ *tr & intr* tripler

tre/ble clef/ [klef] *s* clef *f* de sol

tree [tri] *s* arbre *m*

tree/ farm/ *s* taillis *m*

treeless ['trilis] *adj* sans arbres

tree/top/ *s* cime *f* d'un arbre

trellis ['trelis] *s* treillis *m*, treillage *m*; (*summerhouse*) tonnelle *f* ‖ *tr* treillager

tremble ['trembəl] *s* tremblement *m* ‖ *intr* trembler

tremendous [trɪ'mendəs] *adj* terrible; (coll) formidable

tremor ['tremər], ['trimər] *s* tremblement *m*

trench [trentʃ] *s* tranchée *f*

trenchant ['trentʃənt] *adj* tranchant

trench/ mor/tar *s* lance-bombes *m*

trend [trend] *s* tendance *f*, cours *m*

trespass ['trespəs] *s* entrée *f* sans permission; délit *m*, offense *f* ‖ *intr* entrer sans permission; **no trespassing** (public sign) défense d'entrer; **to trespass against** offenser; **to trespass on** empiéter sur; (*s.o.'s patience*) abuser de

trespasser ['trespəsər] *s* intrus *m*

tress [tres] *s* tresse *f*; **tresses** chevelure *f*

trestle ['tresəl] *s* tréteau *m*; (*bridge*) pont *m* en treillis

trial ['traɪ·əl] *s* essai *m*; (*difficulty*) épreuve *f*; (law) procès *m*; **on trial** à titre d'essai; (law) en jugement; **to bring to trial** faire passer en jugement

tri/al and er/ror *s*—**by trial and error** par tâtonnements

tri/al balloon/ *s* ballon *m* d'essai

tri/al by ju/ry *s* jugement *m* par jury

tri/al ju/ry *s* jury *m* de jugement

tri/al or/der *s* commande *f* d'essai

tri/al run/ *s* course *f* d'essai

triangle ['traɪˌæŋgəl] *s* triangle *m*

tribe [traɪb] *s* tribu *f*

tribunal [trɪ'bjunəl], [traɪ'bjunəl] *s* tribunal *m*

tribune ['trɪbjun] *s* tribune *f*

tributar·y ['trɪbjəˌteri] *adj* tributaire ‖ *s* (*pl* **-ies**) tributaire *m*

tribute ['trɪbjut] *s* tribut *m*; éloge *m*, compliment *m*; **to pay tribute to** (*e.g., merit*) rendre hommage à

trice [traɪs] *s*—**in a trice** en un clin d'œil

trick [trɪk] *s* tour *m*; (*prank*) farce *f*; (*artifice*) ruse *f*; (cards in one round) levée *f*; (*habit*) manie *f*; (*girl*) (coll) belle *f*; **to be up to one's old tricks again** faire encore des siennes; **to play a dirty trick on** faire un vilain tour à; **tricks of the trade** trucs *mpl* du métier ‖ *tr* duper

tricker·y ['trɪkəri] *s* (*pl* **-ies**) tromperie *f*

trickle ['trɪkəl] *s* filet *m* ‖ *intr* dégoutter

trickster ['trɪkstər] *s* fourbe *mf*

trick·y ['trɪki] *adj* (*comp* **-ier**; *super* **-iest**) rusé; (*difficult*) compliqué, délicat

tricolor ['traɪˌkʌlər] *adj & s* tricolore *f*

tried [traɪd] *adj* loyal, éprouvé

trifle ['traɪfəl] *s* bagatelle *f* ‖ *tr*—**to trifle away** gaspiller ‖ *intr* badiner

trifling ['traɪflɪŋ] *adj* frivole; insignifiant

trifocals [traɪ'fokəlz] *spl* lunettes *fpl* à trois foyers

trigger ['trɪgər] *s* (*of gun*) détente *f*; (*of any device*) déclencheur *m*; **to pull the trigger** appuyer sur la détente ‖ *tr* déclencher

trig/ger-hap/py *adj*—**to be trigger-happy** (coll) avoir la gâchette facile

trigonometry [ˌtrɪgə'nɑmɪtri] *s* trigonométrie *f*

trill [trɪl] *s* trille *m* ‖ *tr & intr* triller

trillion ['trɪljən] *s* (U.S.A.) billion *m*; (Brit) trillion *m*

trilo·gy ['trɪlədʒi] *s* (*pl* **-gies**) trilogie *f*

trim [trɪm] *adj* (*comp* **trimmer**; *super* **trimmest**) ordonné, coquet ‖ *s* état *m*; ornement *m*; (*of sails*) orientation *f* ‖ *v* (*pret & pp* **trimmed**; *ger* **trimming**) *tr* enguirlander; (a Christmas tree) orner; (*hat, dress, etc.*) garnir; (*the hair*) rafraîchir; (*a candle or lamp*) moucher; (*trees, plants*) tailler; (*the edges of a book*) rogner; (*the sails*) orienter; (coll) battre

trimming ['trɪmɪŋ] *s* (*of clothes, hat, etc.*) garniture *f*; (*of hedges*) taille *f*; (*of sails*) orientation *f*; **to get a trimming** (coll) essuyer une défaite

trini·ty ['trɪnɪti] *s* (*pl* **-ties**) trinité *f*; **Trinity** Trinité

trinket ['trɪŋkɪt] *s* colifichet *m*; (*trifle*) babiole *f*

tri·o ['tri·o] *s* (*pl* **-os**) trio *m*

trip [trɪp] *s* voyage *m*; trajet *m*, parcours *m*; (*stumble; blunder*) faux pas *m*; (*act of causing a person to stumble*) croc-en-jambe *m* ‖ *v* (*pret & pp* **tripped**; *ger* **tripping**) *tr* faire trébucher; **to trip up** donner un croc-en-jambe à; prendre en défaut || *intr* trébucher

tripartite [traɪ'pɑrtaɪt] *adj* tripartite

tripe [traɪp] *s* tripe *f*; (slang) fatras *m*

trip/ham/mer *s* marteau *m* à bascule

triple ['trɪpəl] *adj* & *s* triple *m* || *tr* & *intr* tripler

triplet ['trɪplɪt] *s* (*offspring*) triplet *m*; (*stanza*) tercet *m*; (*mus*) triolet *m*; **triplets** (*offspring*) triplés *mpl*

triplicate ['trɪplɪkɪt] *adj* triple || *s* triplicata *m*; **in triplicate** en trois exemplaires

tripod ['traɪpɒd] *s* trépied *m*

triptych ['trɪptɪk] *s* triptyque *m*

trite [traɪt] *adj* banal, rebattu

triumph ['traɪ-əmf] *s* triomphe *m* || *intr* triompher; **to triumph over** triompher de

trium/phal arch/ -[traɪ'ʌmfəl] *s* arc *m* de triomphe

triumphant [traɪ'ʌmfənt] *adj* triomphant

trivia ['trɪvɪ-ə] *spl* vétilles *fpl*

trivial ['trɪvɪ-əl] *adj* trivial, insignifiant

triviali•ty [ˌtrɪvɪ'ælɪti] *s* (*pl* -**ties**) trivialité *f*, insignifiance *f*

Trojan ['trodʒən] *adj* troyen || *s* Troyen *m*

Tro/jan Horse/ *s* cheval *m* de Troie

Tro/jan war/ *s* guerre *f* de Troie

troll [trol] *tr* & *intr* pêcher à la cuiller

trolley ['trɑli] *s* trolley *m*; (*streetcar*) tramway *m*

trol/ley car/ *s* tramway *m*

trol/ley pole/ *s* perche *f*

trolling ['trɒlɪŋ] *s* pêche *f* à la cuiller

trollop ['trɑləp] *s* souillon *f*; (*prostitute*) traînée *f*

trombone ['trɑmbon] *s* trombone *m*

troop [trup] *s* troupe *f*; **troops** (mil) troupes *fpl* || *tr* (*the colors*) présenter || *intr* s'attrouper

trooper ['trupər] *s* cavalier *m*; membre *m* de la police montée; **to swear like a trooper** jurer comme un charretier

tro•phy ['trofi] *s* (*pl* -**phies**) trophée *m*; (sports) coupe *f*

tropic ['trɑpɪk] *adj* & *s* tropique *m*; **tropics** tropiques, zone *f* tropicale

tropical ['trɑpɪkəl] *adj* tropical

trot [trɑt] *s* trot *m* || *v* (*pret* & *pp* **trotted**; *ger* **trotting**) *tr* faire trotter; **to trot out** (slang) exhiber || *intr* trotter

troth [troθ], [troθ] *s* foi *f*; **in troth** en vérité; **to plight one's troth** promettre fidélité; donner sa promesse de mariage

trouble ['trʌbəl] *s* dérangement *m*; (*illness*) trouble *m*; **that's not worth the trouble** cela ne vaut pas la peine; **that's the trouble** voilà le hic; **the trouble is that . . .** la difficulté c'est que . . . ; **to be in trouble** avoir des ennuis; (*said of a woman*) (coll) faire Pâques avant les Rameaux; **to be looking for trouble** chercher querelle; **to get into trouble** se créer des ennuis, s'attirer une mauvaise affaire;

to take the trouble to se donner la peine de; **with very little trouble** à peu de frais || *tr* déranger; affliger; **to be troubled about** se tourmenter au sujet de; **to trouble oneself** s'inquiéter || *intr* se déranger; **to trouble to** se donner la peine de

trou/ble light/ *s* lampe *f* de secours

trou/ble-mak/er *s* fomentateur *m*, perturbateur *m*

troubleshooter ['trʌbəlˌʃutər] *s* dépanneur *m*; (*in disputes*) arbitre *m*

trou/ble-shoot/ing *s* dépannage *m*; (*of disputes*) composition *f*, arbitrage *m*

troublesome ['trʌbəlsəm] *adj* ennuyeux

trou/ble spot/ *s* foyer *m* de conflit

trough [trɔf], [trɑf] *s* (*e.g., to knead bread*) pétrin *m*; (*for water for animals*) abreuvoir *m*; (*for feeding animals*) auge *f*; (*under the eaves*) chéneau *m*; (*between two waves*) creux *m*

troupe [trup] *s* troupe *f*

trouper ['trupər] *s* membre *m* de la troupe; vieil acteur *m*; vieux routier *m*

trousers ['trauzərz] *spl* pantalon *m*

trous•seau [tru'so], ['truso] *s* (*pl* -**seaux** or -**seaus**) trousseau *m*

trout [traut] *s* truite *f*

trowel ['trau-əl] *s* truelle *f*; (*for gardening*) déplantoir *m*

Troy [trɔɪ] *s* Troie *f*

truant ['tru-ənt] *s*—**to play truant** faire l'école buissonnière

truce [trus] *s* trêve *f*

truck [trʌk] *s* camion *m*, poids *m* lourd; (*for baggage*) diable *m*; légumes *mpl*; (coll) rapports *mpl* || *tr* camionner

truck/driv/er *s* camionneur *m*

truck/ farm/ing *s* culture *f* maraîchère

truck/ gar/den *s* jardin *m* maraîcher

trucking ['trʌkɪŋ] *s* camionnage *m*

truculent ['trʌkjələnt], ['trukjələnt] *adj* truculent

trudge [trʌdʒ] *intr* cheminer

true [tru] *adj* vrai; loyal; (*exact*) juste; (*copy*) conforme; **to come true** se réaliser || *tr* rectifier, dégauchir

true/ cop/y *s* (*pl* -**ies**) copie *f* conforme

true/-heart/ed *adj* au cœur sincère

true/love/ *s* bien-aimé *m*

truffle ['trʌfəl], ['trufəl] *s* truffe *f*

truism ['tru-ɪzm] *s* truisme *m*

truly ['truli] *adv* vraiment; sincèrement; **yours truly** (*complimentary close*) veuillez agréer, Monsieur (Madame, etc.), l'assurance de mes sentiments distingués

trump [trʌmp] *s* atout *m*; brave garçon *m*, brave fille *f*; **no trump** sans atout || *tr* couper; **to trump up** inventer || *intr* couper

trumpet ['trʌmpɪt] *s* trompette *f* || *tr* & *intr* trompeter

trumpeter ['trʌmpətər] *s* trompette *m*

truncheon ['trʌntʃən] *s* matraque *f*; (*of policeman*) bâton *m*

trunk [trʌŋk] *s* tronc *m*; (*chest for clothes*) malle *f*; (*of elephant*) trompe *f*; (aut) coffre *m*; **trunks** slip *m*

truss [trʌs] *s* (*framework*) armature *f*; (med) bandage *m* herniaire || *tr* armer; (culin) trousser

trust [trʌst] *s* confiance *f*; *(hope)* espoir *m*; *(duty)* charge *f*; *(safekeeping)* dépôt *m*; (com) trust *m*, cartel *m* ‖ *tr* se fier à; *(to entrust)* confier; (com) faire crédit à ‖ *intr* espérer; **to trust in** avoir confiance en

trust′ com′pany *s* crédit *m*, société *f* de banque

trustee [trʌs′ti] *s* administrateur *m*; *(of a university)* régent *m*; *(of an estate)* fidéicommissaire *mf*

trusteeship [trʌs′ti‚ʃɪp] *s* tutelle *f*

trustful [′trʌstfəl] *adj* confiant

trust′wor′thy *adj* digne de confiance

trust·y [′trʌsti] *adj* *(comp* -ier; *super* -iest)* sûr, loyal ‖ *s* *(pl* -ies) forçat *m* bien noté

truth [truθ] *s* vérité *f*; **in truth** en vérité

truthful [′truθfəl] *adj* véridique

try [traɪ] *s* *(pl* tries) essai *m* ‖ *v* *(pret & pp* tried) *tr* mettre à l'épreuve; (law) juger; **to try on** or **out** essayer ‖ *intr* essayer; **to try to** essayer de

trying [′traɪ‚ɪŋ] *adj* pénible

tryst [trɪst], [traɪst] *s* rendez-vous *m*

T′-shirt′ *s* gilet *m* de peau avec manches

tub [tʌb] *s* cuvier *m*, baquet *m*; *(clumsy boat)* (coll) rafiot *m*

tube [t(j)ub] *s* tube *m*; tunnel *m*; (aut) chambre *f* à air; *(subway)* (Brit) métro *m*

tuber [′t(j)ubər] *s* tubercule *m*

tubercle [t(j)ubərkəl] *s* tubercule *m*

tuberculosis [t(j)u‚bɑrkjə′losɪs] *s* tuberculose *f*

tuck [tʌk] *s* pli *m*, rempli *m* ‖ *tr* plisser, remplier; **to tuck away** reléguer; **to tuck in** rentrer; **to tuck in bed** border; **to tuck up** retrousser

tucker [′tʌkər] *tr*—**to tucker out** (coll) fatiguer

Tuesday [′t(j)uzdi] *s* mardi *m*

tuft [tʌft] *s* touffe *f* ‖ *tr* garnir de touffes ‖ *intr* former une touffe

tug [tʌg] *s* tiraillement *m*, effort *m*; *(boat)* remorqueur *m* ‖ *v* *(pret & pp* tugged; *ger* tugging) *tr* tirer fort; *(a boat)* remorquer ‖ *intr* tirer fort

tug′boat′ *s* remorqueur *m*

tug′ of war′ *s* lutte *f* à la corde (de traction)

tuition [t(j)u′ɪʃən] *s* enseignement *m*; *(fees)* frais *mpl* de scolarité

tulip [′t(j)ulɪp] *s* tulipe *f*

tumble [′tʌmbəl] *s* chute *f*; *(sports)* culbute *f* ‖ *tr* culbuter ‖ *intr* tomber, culbuter; *(sports)* faire des culbutes; *(to catch on)* (slang) comprendre; **to tumble down** dégringoler

tum′ble-down′ *adj* croulant, délabré

tumbler [′tʌmblər] *s* gobelet *m*, verre *m*; acrobate *m*; *(self-righting toy)* poussah *m*, ramponneau *m*

tumor [′t(j)umər] *s* tumeur *f*

tumult [′t(j)umʌlt] *s* tumulte *m*

tun [tʌn] *s* tonne *f*

tuna [′tunə] *s* thon *m*

tune [t(j)un] *s* air *m*; *(manner of acting or speaking)* ton *m*; **in tune** (mus) accordé; (rad) en syntonie; **out of tune** (mus) désaccordé; **to change**

one's tune (coll) changer de disque ‖ *tr* accorder; *(a radio or television set)* régler; **to tune in** (rad) syntoniser; **to tune up** régler

tungsten [′tʌŋstən] *s* tungstène *m*

tunic [′t(j)unɪk] *s* tunique *f*

tuning [′t(j)unɪŋ] *s* réglage *m*; (rad) syntonisation *f*

tun′ing coil′ *s* bobine *f* de syntonisation

tun′ing fork′ *s* diapason *m*

tun·nel [′tʌnəl] *s* tunnel *m*; (min) galerie *f* ‖ *v* *(pret & pp* -neled or -nelled; *ger* -neling or -nelling) *tr* percer un tunnel dans or sous

turban [′tʌrbən] *s* turban *m*

turbid [′tʌrbɪd] *adj* trouble

turbine [′tʌrbɪn], [′tʌrbaɪn] *s* turbine *f*

turbojet [′tʌrbo‚dʒɛt] *s* turboréacteur *m*; avion *m* à turboréacteur

turboprop [′tʌrbo‚prɑp] *s* turbopropulseur *m*; avion *m* à turbopropulseur

turbulent [′tʌrbjələnt] *adj* turbulent

tureen [t(j)u′rin] *s* soupière *f*

turf [tʌrf] *s* gazon *m*; *(sod)* motte *f* de gazon; *(peat)* tourbe *f*; **the turf** le turf

turf′man *s* *(pl* -men) turfiste *mf*

Turk [tʌrk] *s* Turc *m*

turkey [′tʌrki] *s* dindon *m*; (culin) dinde *f*; *(flop)* (slang) four *m*; **Turkey** Turquie *f*; **la Turquie**

Tur′key vul′ture *s* urubu *m*

Turkish [′tʌrkɪʃ] *adj & s* turc *m*

Turk′ish delight′ *s* loukoum *m*

Turk′ish tow′el *s* serviette *f* éponge

turmoil [′tʌrmɔɪl] *s* agitation *f*

turn [tʌrn] *s* tour *m*; *(change of direction)* virage *m*; *(bend)* tournant *m*; *(of events; of an expression)* tournure *f*; *(in a wire)* spire *f*; (coll) coup *m*, choc *m*; **at every turn** à tout propos; **by turns** tour à tour; **in turn** à tour de rôle; **to a turn** (culin) à point; **to do a good turn** rendre un service; **to take turns** alterner; **to wait one's turn** prendre son tour; **whose turn is it?** à qui le tour? ‖ *tr* tourner; **to turn about** or **around** retourner; **to turn aside** or **away** détourner; **to turn back** renvoyer; *(an attack)* repousser; *(a clock)* retarder; **to turn down** *(a collar)* rabattre; *(e.g., the gas)* baisser; *(an offer)* refuser; **to turn from** détourner de; **to turn in** replier; *(a wrongdoer)* dénoncer; **to turn into** changer en; **to turn off** *(the water, the gas, etc.)* fermer; *(the light, the radio, etc.)* éteindre; *(a road)* quitter; **to turn on** *(the water, the gas, etc.)* ouvrir; *(the light, the radio, the gas, etc.)* allumer; **to turn out** mettre dehors; *(to manufacture)* produire; *(e.g., the light)* éteindre; **to turn over and over** tourner et retourner; **to turn up** *(a collar)* relever; *(one's sleeves)* retrousser; *(to unearth)* déterrer ‖ *intr* tourner; se tourner; *(said of milk)* tourner; **to toss and turn** se retourner; *(to be dizzy)* tourner, e.g., **his head is turning** la tête lui tourne; **to turn about** or **around** se retourner, se tourner; **to turn aside** or **away** se détourner; **to turn back** rebrousser chemin; **to turn down** se rabattre; **to turn in** (coll) aller se coucher; **to turn into** tourner à or en; **to turn on** se jeter sur; (*to depend on*) dépendre de; **to turn out to be** se trouver être; **to turn out well** tourner bien; **to turn over** se retourner; (*said of auto*) capoter; **to turn up** se relever; se présenter, arriver

turn′coat′ s transfuge m

turn′down′ adj rabattu ‖ s refus m

turn′ing point′ s moment m décisif

turnip [′tʌrnɪp] s navet m; (*big watch*) (slang) bassinoire f; (slang) tête f de bois

turn′key′ s geôlier m

turn′ of life′ s retour m d'âge

turn′ of mind′ s inclination f naturelle

turn′out′ s (*gathering*) assistance f; (*output*) rendement m; (*equipment*) attelage m

turn′o′ver s renversement m; (com) chiffre m d'affaires

turn′pike′ s autoroute f à péage

turn′spit′ s tournebroche m

turnstile [′tʌrn‚staɪl] s tourniquet m

turn′stone′ s (orn) tourne-pierre m

turn′ta′ble s (*of phonograph*) plateau m porte-disque; (rr) plaque f tournante

turpentine [′tʌrpən‚taɪn] s térébenthine f

turpitude [′tʌrpɪ‚t(j)ud] s turpitude f

turquoise [′tʌrkɔɪz], [′tʌrkwɔɪz] s turquoise f

turret [′tʌrɪt] s tourelle f

turtle [′tʌrtəl] s tortue f

tur′tle-dove′ s tourterelle f

tur′tle-neck′ s col m roulé; chandail m à col roulé

Tuscan [′tʌskən] adj & s toscan m

Tuscany [′tʌskəni] s Toscane f; la Toscane

tusk [tʌsk] s défense f

tussle [′tʌsəl] s bagarre f ‖ intr se bagarrer

tutor [′t(j)utər] s précepteur m, répétiteur m ‖ tr donner des leçons particulières à ‖ intr donner des leçons particulières

tuxe·do [tʌk′sido] s (pl **-dos**) smoking m

TV [′ti′vi] s (letterword) (television) tévé f, télé f

twaddle [′twɑdəl] s fadaises fpl ‖ intr dire des fadaises

twang [twæŋ] s (*of musical instrument*) son m vibrant; (*of voice*) ton m nasillard ‖ tr faire résonner; dire en nasillant ‖ intr nasiller

twang·y [′twæŋi] adj (comp **-ier**; super **-iest**) (*nasal*) nasillard; (*resonant*) vibrant

tweed [twid] s tweed m

tweet [twit] s pépiement m ‖ intr pépier

tweeter [′twitər] s (rad) tweeter m

tweezers [′twizərz] spl brucelles fpl; pince f à épiler

twelfth [twelfθ] adj & pron douzième (*masc, fem*); **the Twelfth** douze, e.g., **John the Twelfth** Jean douze ‖ s

douzième m; **the twelfth** (*in dates*) le douze

twelve [twelv] adj & pron douze; **about twelve** une douzaine de ‖ s douze m; **twelve o'clock** (*noon*) midi m; (*midnight*) minuit m

twentieth [′twentɪ·ɪθ] adj & pron vingtième (*masc, fem*); **the Twentieth** vingt, e.g., **John the Twentieth** Jean vingt ‖ s vingt m; **the twentieth** (*in dates*) le vingt

twen·ty [′twenti] adj & pron vingt; **about twenty** une vingtaine de ‖ s (pl **-ties**) vingt m; **the twenties** les années fpl vingt

twen′ty-first′ adj & pron vingt et unième (*masc, fem*); **the Twenty-first** vingt et un, e.g., **John the Twenty-first** Jean vingt et un ‖ s vingt et unième m; **the twenty-first** (*in dates*) le vingt et un

twen′ty-one′ adj & pron vingt et un ‖ s vingt et un m; (cards) vingt-et-un

twen′ty-sec′ond adj & pron vingt-deuxième (*masc, fem*); **the Twenty-second** vingt-deux, e.g., **John the Twenty-second** Jean vingt-deux ‖ s vingt-deuxième m; **the twenty-second** (*in dates*) le vingt-deux

twen′ty-two′ adj, pron, & s vingt-deux m

twice [twaɪs] adv deux fois; **twice over** à deux reprises

twiddle [′twɪdəl] tr tourner, jouer avec; (*e.g., one's moustache*) tortiller

twig [twɪg] s brindille f

twilight [′twaɪ‚laɪt] adj crépusculaire ‖ s crépuscule m

twill [twɪl] s croisé m ‖ tr croiser

twin [twɪn] adj & s jumeau m ‖ v (pret & pp **twinned**; ger **twinning**) tr jumeler

twin′ beds′ spl lits mpl jumeaux

twine [twaɪn] s ficelle f ‖ tr enrouler ‖ intr s'enrouler

twinge [twɪndʒ] s élancement m ‖ intr élancer

twin′-jet′ plane′ s biréacteur m

twinkle [′twɪŋkəl] s scintillement m; (*of the eye*) clignotement m ‖ intr scintiller; clignoter

twin′-screw′ adj à hélices jumelles

twirl [twʌrl] s tournoiement m ‖ tr faire tournoyer; (*e.g., a cane*) faire des moulinets avec ‖ intr tournoyer

twist [twɪst] s torsion f; (*strand*) cordon m; (*of the wrist, of rope, etc.*) tour m; (*of the road, river, etc.*) coude m; (*of tobacco*) rouleau m; (*of the ankle*) entorse f; (*of mind or disposition*) prédisposition f ‖ tr tordre, tortiller ‖ intr se tordre, se tortiller; **to twist and turn** (*said, e.g., of road*) serpenter; (*said of sleeper*) se tourner et se retourner

twister [′twɪstər] s (coll) tornade f

twit [twɪt] v (pret & pp **twitted**; ger **twitting**) tr taquiner

twitch [twɪtʃ] s crispation f ‖ intr se crisper

twitter [′twɪtər] s gazouillement m ‖ intr gazouiller

two [tu] *adj & pron* deux ǁ *s* deux *m*; **to put two and two together** raisonner juste; **two o'clock** deux heures

two'-cy'cle *adj* (mach) à deux temps

two'-cyl'inder *adj* (mach) à deux cylindres

two'-edged' *adj* à deux tranchants

two' hun'dred *adj, pron, & s* deux cents *m*

twosome ['tusəm] *s* paire *f*; jeu *m* à deux joueurs

two'-time' *tr* (slang) tromper

tycoon [taɪ'kun] *s* (coll) magnat *m*

type [taɪp] *s* type *m* ǁ *tr* typer; (*to typewrite*) taper; (*a sample of blood*) chercher le groupe sanguin sur ǁ *intr* taper

type'face' *s* œil *m*

type'script' *s* manuscrit *m* dactylographié

typesetter ['taɪp,setər] *s* compositeur *m*, typographe *mf*; machine *f* à composer

type'write' *v* (*pret* **-wrote**; *pp* **-written**) *tr & intr* taper à la machine

type'writ'er *s* machine *f* à écrire

type'writ'er rib'bon *s* ruban *m* encreur

type'writ'ing *s* dactylographie *f*

ty'phoid fe'ver ['taɪfɔɪd] *s* fièvre *f* typhoïde

typhoon [taɪ'fun] *s* typhon *m*

typical ['tɪpɪkəl] *adj* typique

typi·fy ['tɪpɪ,faɪ] *v* (*pret & pp* **-fied**) *tr* symboliser; être le type de

typ'ing er'ror *s* faute *f* de frappe

typist ['taɪpɪst] *s* dactylo *f*

typographic(al) [,taɪpə'græfɪk(əl)] *adj* typographique

typograph'ical er'ror *s* erreur *f* typographique

typography [taɪ'pɑgrəfɪ] *s* typographie *f*

tyrannic(al) [tɪ'rænɪk(əl)], [taɪ'rænɪk(əl)] *adj* tyrannique

tyran·ny ['tɪrənɪ] *s* (*pl* **-nies**) tyrannie *f*

tyrant ['taɪrənt] *s* tyran *m*

ty·ro ['taɪro] *s* (*pl* **-ros**) novice *mf*

U

U, u [ju] *s* XXIe lettre de l'alphabet

ubiquitous [ju'bɪkwɪtəs] *adj* ubiquiste, omniprésent

udder ['ʌdər] *s* pis *m*

ugliness ['ʌglɪnɪs] *s* laideur *f*

ug·ly ['ʌglɪ] *adj* (*comp* **-lier**; *super* **-liest**) laid; (*disagreeable; mean*) vilain

Ukraine ['jukren], [ju'kren] *s* Ukraine *f*; l'Ukraine

Ukrainian [ju'krenɪ·ən] *adj* ukrainien ǁ *s* (*language*) ukrainien *m*; (*person*) Ukrainien *m*

ulcer ['ʌlsər] *s* ulcère *m*

ulcerate ['ʌlsə,ret] *tr* ulcérer ǁ *intr* s'ulcérer

ulterior [ʌl'tɪrɪ·ər] *adj* ultérieur; secret, inavoué

ultimate ['ʌltɪmɪt] *adj* ultime, final, définitif

ultima·tum [,ʌltɪ'metəm] *s* (*pl* **-tums** or **-ta** [tə]) ultimatum *m*

ultrashort [,ʌltrə'ʃɔrt] *adj* (electron) ultra-court

ultraviolet [,ʌltrə'vaɪ·əlɪt] *adj & s* ultraviolet *m*

umbil'ical cord' [ʌm'bɪlɪkəl] *s* cordon *m* ombilical

umbrage ['ʌmbrɪdʒ] *s*—**to take umbrage at** prendre ombrage de

umbrella [ʌm'brelə] *s* parapluie *m*; (mil) ombrelle *f* de protection

umbrel'la stand' *s* porte-parapluies *m*

umlaut ['umlaut] *s* métaphonie *f*, inflexion *f* vocalique; (*mark*) tréma *m* ǁ *tr* changer le timbre de; écrire avec un tréma

umpire ['ʌmpaɪr] *s* arbitre *m* ǁ *tr & intr* arbitrer

UN ['ju'en] *s* (letterword) (**United Nations**) ONU *f*

unable [ʌn'ebəl] *adj* incapable; **to be unable to** être incapable de

unabridged [,ʌnə'brɪdʒd] *adj* intégral

unaccented [,ʌn'æksentɪd], [,ʌnæk-'sentɪd] *adj* inaccentué

unacceptable [,ʌnək'septəbəl] *adj* inacceptable

unaccountable [,ʌnə'kauntəbəl] *adj* inexplicable; irresponsable

unaccounted-for [,ʌnə'kauntɪd,fɔr] *adj* inexpliqué, pas retrouvé

unaccustomed [,ʌnə'kʌstəmd] *adj* inaccoutumé

unafraid [,ʌnə'fred] *adj* sans peur

unaligned [,ʌnə'laɪnd] *adj* non-engagé

unanimity [,junə'nɪmɪtɪ] *s* unanimité *f*

unanimous [ju'nænɪməs] *adj* unanime

unanswerable [ʌn'ænsərəbəl] *adj* incontestable, sans réplique; (*argument*) irréfutable

unappreciative [,ʌnə'priʃɪ,etɪv] *adj* ingrat, peu reconnaissant

unapproachable [,ʌnə'protʃəbəl] *adj* inabordable; (fig) incomparable

unarmed [ʌn'ɑrmd] *adj* sans armes

unascertainable [,ʌn,æsər'tenəbəl] *adj* non vérifiable

unasked [ʌn'æskt], [ʌn'ɑskt] *adj* non invité; **to do s.th. unasked** faire q.ch. spontanément

unassembled [,ʌnə'sembəld] *adj* démonté

unassuming [,ʌnə's(j)umɪŋ] *adj* modeste, sans prétentions

unattached [,ʌnə'tæt/t] *adj* indépendant; (*loose*) détaché; (*not engaged to be married*) seul; (mil, nav) en disponibilité

unattainable [ˌʌnəˈtenəbəl] *adj* inaccessible

unattractive [ˌʌnəˈtræktɪv] *adj* peu attrayant, peu séduisant

unavailable [ˌʌnəˈveləbəl] *adj* non disponible

unavailing [ˌʌnəˈvelɪŋ] *adj* inutile

unavoidable [ˌʌnəˈvɔɪdəbəl] *adj* inévitable

unaware [ˌʌnəˈwer] *adj* ignorant; **to be unaware of** ignorer ‖ *adv* à l'improviste; à mon (son, etc.) insu

unawares [ˌʌnəˈwerz] *adv* (*unexpectedly*) à l'improviste; (*unknowingly*) à mon (son, etc.) insu

unbalanced [ʌnˈbælənst] *adj* non équilibré; (*mind*) déséquilibré; (*bank account*) non soldé

unbandage [ʌnˈbændɪdʒ] *tr* débander

un-bar [ʌnˈbɑr] *v* (*pret & pp* **-barred**; *ger* **-barring**) *tr* débarrer

unbearable [ʌnˈberəbəl] *adj* insupportable

unbeatable [ʌnˈbitəbəl] *adj* imbattable

unbecoming [ˌʌnbɪˈkʌmɪŋ] *adj* déplacé, inconvenant; (*dress*) peu seyant

unbelievable [ˌʌnbɪˈlivəbəl] *adj* incroyable

unbeliever [ˌʌnbɪˈlivər] *s* incroyant *m*

unbending [ʌnˈbendɪŋ] *adj* inflexible

unbiased [ʌnˈbaɪəst] *adj* impartial

un-bind [ʌnˈbaɪnd] *v* (*pret & pp* **-bound**) *tr* délier

unbleached [ʌnˈblitʃt] *adj* écru

unbolt [ʌnˈbolt] *tr* (*a gun; a door*) déverrouiller; (*a machine*) déboulonner

unborn [ʌnˈbɔrn] *adj* à naître, futur

unbosom [ʌnˈbuzəm] *tr* découvrir; **to unbosom oneself** ouvrir son cœur

unbound [ʌnˈbaʊnd] *adj* non relié

unbreakable [ʌnˈbrekəbəl] *adj* incassable

unbroken [ʌnˈbrokən] *adj* intact; (*spirit*) indompté; (*horse*) non rompu

unbuckle [ʌnˈbʌkəl] *tr* déboucler

unburden [ʌnˈbʌrdən] *tr* alléger; **to unburden oneself of** se soulager de

unburied [ʌnˈberɪd] *adj* non enseveli

unbutton [ʌnˈbʌtən] *tr* déboutonner

uncalled-for [ʌnˈkɔldˌfɔr] *adj* déplacé; (*e.g., insult*) gratuit

uncanny [ʌnˈkæni] *adj* inquiétant, mystérieux; rare, remarquable

uncared-for [ʌnˈkerdˌfɔr] *adj* négligé; peu soignée

unceasing [ʌnˈsisɪŋ] *adj* incessant

unceremonious [ˌʌnserɪˈmoni-əs] *adj* sans façon

uncertain [ʌnˈsʌrtən] *adj* incertain

uncertain-ty [ʌnˈsʌrtənti] *s* (*pl* **-ties**) incertitude *f*

unchain [ʌnˈtʃen] *tr* désenchaîner

unchangeable [ʌnˈtʃendʒəbəl] *adj* immuable

uncharted [ʌnˈtʃɑrtɪd] *adj* inexploré

unchecked [ʌnˈtʃɛkt] *adj* sans frein, non contenu; non vérifié

uncivilized [ʌnˈsɪvɪˌlaɪzd] *adj* incivilisé

unclad [ʌnˈklæd] *adj* déshabillé

unclaimed [ʌnˈklemd] *adj* non réclamé; (*mail*) au rebut

unclasp [ʌnˈklæsp], [ʌnˈklɑsp] *tr* dégrafer; (*one's hands*) desserrer

unclassified [ʌnˈklæsɪˌfaɪd] *adj* non classé; (*documents, information, etc.*) pas secret

uncle [ˈʌŋkəl] *s* oncle *m*

unclean [ʌnˈklin] *adj* sale, immonde

un-clog [ʌnˈklɑg] *v* (*pret & pp* **-clogged**; *ger* **-clogging**) *tr* dégager, désobstruer

unclouded [ʌnˈklaʊdɪd] *adj* clair, dégagé

uncollectible [ˌʌnkəˈlɛktɪbəl] *adj* irrécouvrable

uncomfortable [ʌnˈkʌmfərtəbəl] *adj* (*causing discomfort*) inconfortable; (*feeling discomfort*) mal à l'aise

uncommitted [ˌʌnkəˈmɪtɪd] *adj* nonengagé

uncommon [ʌnˈkɑmən] *adj* peu commun

uncompromising [ʌnˈkɑmprəˌmaɪzɪŋ] *adj* intransigeant

unconcerned [ˌʌnkənˈsʌrnd] *adj* indifférent

unconditional [ˌʌnkənˈdɪʃənəl] *adj* inconditionnel

uncongenial [ˌʌnkənˈdʒini-əl] *adj* peu sympathique; incompatible; désagréable

unconquerable [ʌnˈkɑŋkərəbəl] *adj* invincible

unconquered [ʌnˈkɑŋkərd] *adj* invaincu, indompté

unconscious [ʌnˈkɑnʃəs] *adj* inconscient; (*temporarily deprived of consciousness*) sans connaissance ‖ *s*— **the unconscious** l'inconscient *m*

unconsciousness [ʌnˈkɑnʃəsnɪs] *s* inconscience *f*; perte *f* de connaissance, évanouissement *m*

unconstitutional [ˌʌnkɑnstɪˈt(j)uʃənəl] *adj* inconstitutionnel

uncontrollable [ˌʌnkənˈtroləbəl] *adj* ingouvernable; (*e.g., desires*) irrésistible; (*laughter*) inextinguible

unconventional [ˌʌnkənˈvɛnʃənəl] *adj* original, peu conventionnel; (*person*) non-conformiste

uncork [ʌnˈkɔrk] *tr* déboucher

uncouple [ʌnˈkʌpəl] *tr* désaccoupler

uncouth [ʌnˈkuθ] *adj* gauche, sauvage; (*language*) grossier

uncover [ʌnˈkʌvər] *tr* découvrir

unction [ˈʌŋkʃən] *s* onction *f*

unctuous [ˈʌŋktʃu-əs] *adj* onctueux

uncultivated [ʌnˈkʌltɪˌvetɪd] *adj* inculte

uncultured [ʌnˈkʌltʃərd] *adj* inculte, sans culture

uncut [ʌnˈkʌt] *adj* non coupé; (*stone, diamond*) brut; (*crops*) sur pied; (*book*) non rogné

undamaged [ʌnˈdæmɪdʒd] *adj* indemne

undaunted [ʌnˈdɔntɪd] *adj* pas découragé; sans peur

undecide 1 [ˌʌndɪˈsaɪdɪd] *adj* indécis

undefeated [ˌʌndɪˈfitɪd] *adj* invaincu

undefended [ˌʌndɪˈfɛndɪd] *adj* sans défense

undefiled [ˌʌndɪˈfaɪld] *adj* sans tache

undeniable [ˌʌndɪˈnaɪ·əbəl] *adj* indéniable

under [ˈʌndər] *adj* (*lower*) inférieur; (*underneath*) de dessous || *adv* dessous; **to go under** sombrer; **to keep under** tenir dans la soumission || *prep* sous, au-dessous de, dessous; moins de, e.g., **under forty** moins de quarante ans; dans, e.g., **under the circumstances** dans les circonstances; en, e.g., **under treatment** en traitement; e.g., **under repair** en voie de réparation; à, e.g., **under the microscope** au microscope; e.g., **under examination** à l'examen; e.g., **under the terms of** aux termes de; e.g., **under the word** (*in dictionary*) au mot; **to serve under** servir sous les ordres de

un'der·age' *adj* mineur

un'der·arm' pad *s* dessous-de-bras *m*

un'der·bid' *v* (*pret & pp* -bid; *ger* -bidding) *tr* offrir moins que

un'der·brush' *s* broussailles *fpl*

un'der·car'riage *s* (aer) train *m* d'atterrissage; (aut) dessous *m*

un'der·clothes' *spl* sous-vêtements *mpl*

un'der·con·sump'tion *s* sous-consommation *f*

un'der·cov'er *adj* secret

un'der·cur'rent *s* courant *m* de fond; (fig) vague *f* de fond

un'der·devel'oped *adj* sous-développé

un'der·dog' *s* opprimé *m*; (sports) parti *m* non favori, outsider *m*

underdone [ˈʌndərˌdʌn] *adj* pas assez cuit

un'der·es'timate *tr* sous-estimer

un'der·gar'ment *s* sous-vêtement *m*

un'der·go' *v* (*pret* -went; *pp* -gone) *tr* subir, éprouver, souffrir

un'der·grad'uate *adj & s* non diplômé *m*

un'der·ground' *adj* souterrain; (fig) clandestin || *s* (*subway*) métro *m*; résistance *f*, maquis *m* || *adv* sous terre; **to go underground** (fig) entrer dans la clandestinité, prendre le maquis

un'der·growth' *s* sous-bois *m*; (*underbrush*) broussailles *fpl*

un'der·hand'ed *adj* sournois, dissimulé

un'der·line' or **un'der·line'** *tr* souligner

underling [ˈʌndərlɪŋ] *s* sous-ordre *m*, sous-fifre *m*

un'der·mine' *tr* miner, saper

underneath [ˌʌndərˈniθ] *adj* de dessous; (*lower*) inférieur || *s* dessous *m* || *adv* dessous, en dessous || *prep* sous, au-dessous de

un'der·nour'ished *adj* sous-alimenté

un'der·nour'ishment *s* sous-alimentation *f*

underpaid [ˌʌndərˈped] *adj* mal rétribué

un'der·pass' *s* passage *m* souterrain

un'der·pin' *v* (*pret & pp* -pinned; *ger* -pinning) *tr* étayer

un'der·priv'ileged *adj* déshérité

un'der·rate' *tr* sous-estimer

un'der·score' *tr* souligner

un'der·sea' *adj* sous-marin || **un'der·sea'** *adv* sous la surface de la mer

un'der·sec'retar'y *s* (*pl* -ies) sous-secrétaire *m*

un'der·sell' *v* (*pret & pp* -sold) *tr* vendre à meilleur marché que; (*for less than the actual value*) solder

un'der·shirt' *s* gilet *m*, maillot *m* de corps

un'der·signed' *adj* soussigné

un'der·skirt' *s* jupon *m*

un'der·stand' *v* (*pret & pp* -stood) *tr & intr* comprendre, entendre

understandable [ˌʌndərˈstændəbəl] *adj* compréhensible; **that's understandable** cela se comprend

un'der·stand'ing *adj* compréhensif || *s* compréhension *f*; (*intellectual faculty, mind*) entendement *m*; (*agreement*) accord *m*, entente *f*; **on the understanding that** à condition que; **to come to an understanding** arriver à un accord

un'der·stud'y *s* (*pl* -ies) doublure *f* || *v* (*pret & pp* -ied) *tr* (*an actor*) doubler

un'der·take' *v* (*pret* -took; *pp* -taken) *tr* entreprendre; (*to agree to perform*) s'engager à faire; **to undertake to** s'engager à

undertaker [ˈʌndərˌtekər] *s* (*mortician*) entrepreneur *m* de pompes funèbres

undertaking [ˌʌndərˈtekɪŋ] *s* entreprise *f*; (*commitment*) engagement *m* || [ˈʌndərˌtekɪŋ] *s* service *m* des pompes funèbres

un'der·tone' *s* ton *m* atténué; (*background sound*) fond *m* obscur; **in an undertone** à voix basse

un'der·tow' *s* (*countercurrent below surface*) courant *m* de fond; (*on beach*) ressac *m*

un'der·wear' *s* sous-vêtements *mpl*

un'der·world' *s* (*criminal world*) bas-fonds *mpl*, pègre *f*; (*pagan world of the dead*) enfers *mpl*

un'der·write' or **un'der·write'** *v* (*pret* -wrote; *pp* -written) *tr* souscrire; (ins) assurer

un'der·writ'er *s* souscripteur *m*; (ins) assureur *m*

undeserved [ˌʌndɪˈzɜrvd] *adj* immérité

undesirable [ˌʌndɪˈzaɪrəbəl] *adj* peu désirable; (*e.g., alien*) indésirable || *s* indésirable *mf*

undetachable [ˌʌndɪˈtætʃəbəl] *adj* inséparable

undeveloped [ˌʌndɪˈvɛləpt] *adj* (*land*) inexploité; (*country*) sous-développé

undigested [ˌʌndɪˈdʒɛstɪd] *adj* indigeste

undignified [ʌnˈdɪgnɪˌfaɪd] *adj* sans dignité, peu digne

undiscernible [ˌʌndɪˈzɜrnɪbəl], [ˌʌndɪˈsɜrnəbəl] *adj* imperceptible

undisputed [ˌʌndɪsˈpjutɪd] *adj* incontesté

undo [ʌnˈdu] *v* (*pret* -did; *pp* -done) *tr* défaire; (fig) ruiner

undoing [ʌnˈdu·ɪŋ] *s* perte *f*, ruine *f*

undone [ʌnˈdʌn] *adj* défait; (*omitted*) inaccompli; **to come undone** se défaire; **to leave nothing undone** ne rien négliger

undoubtedly [ʌn'daʊtɪdlɪ] *adv* sans aucun doute, incontestablement

undramatic [ˌʌndrə'mætɪk] *adj* peu dramatique

undress ['ʌn͵dres], [ʌn'dres] *s* déshabillé *m*; (*scanty dress*) petite tenue *f* || [ʌn'dres] *tr* déshabiller || *intr* se déshabiller

undrinkable [ʌn'drɪŋkəbəl] *adj* imbuvable

undue [ʌn'd(j)u] *adj* indu

undulate ['ʌndjə͵let] *intr* onduler

unduly [ʌn'd(j)ulɪ] *adv* indûment

undying [ʌn'daɪ-ɪŋ] *adj* impérissable

un'earned in'come ['ʌnʌrnd] *s* rente *f*, revenu *m* d'un bien

un'earned in'crement *s* plus-value *f*

unearth [ʌn'ʌrθ] *tr* déterrer

unearthly [ʌn'ʌrθlɪ] *adj* surnaturel, spectral; bizarre; (*hour*) indu

uneasy [ʌn'izɪ] *adj* inquiet; contraint, gêné

uneatable [ʌn'itəbəl] *adj* immangeable

uneconomic(al) [ˌʌnikə'nɑmɪk(əl)], [ˌʌnɛkə'nɑmɪk(əl)] *adj* peu économique; (*person*) peu économe

uneducated [ʌn'edjə͵ketɪd] *adj* ignorant, sans instruction

unemployed [ˌʌnem'plɔɪd] *adj* en chômage, sans travail || *spl* chômeurs *mpl*, sans-travail *mfpl*

unemployment [ˌʌnem'plɔɪmənt] *s* chômage *m*

un'employ'ment insur'ance *s* assurance-chômage *f*

unending [ʌn'endɪŋ] *adj* interminable

unequal [ʌn'ikwəl] *adj* inégal; **to be unequal to** (*a task*) ne pas être à la hauteur de

unequaled or **unequalled** [ʌn'ikwəld] *adj* sans égal, sans pareil

unerring [ʌn'ʌrɪŋ], [ʌn'erɪŋ] *adj* infaillible

UNESCO [ju'nesko] *s* (acronym) (**United Nations Educational, Scientific, and Cultural Organization**) l'Unesco *f*

unessential [ˌʌne'senʃəl] *adj* non essentiel

uneven [ʌn'ivən] *adj* inégal; (*number*) impair

uneventful [ˌʌnɪ'ventfəl] *adj* sans incident, peu mouvementé

unexceptionable [ˌʌnek'sepʃənəbəl] *adj* irréprochable

unexpected [ˌʌnek'spektɪd] *adj* inattendu, imprévu

unexplained [ˌʌnek'splend] *adj* inexpliqué

unexplored [ˌʌnek'splord] *adj* inexploré

unexposed [ˌʌnek'spozd] *adj* (phot) vierge

unfading [ʌn'fedɪŋ] *adj* immarcescible

unfailing [ʌn'felɪŋ] *adj* infaillible; (*inexhaustible*) intarissable

unfair [ʌn'fer] *adj* injuste, déloyal

unfaithful [ʌn'feθfəl] *adj* infidèle

unfamiliar [ˌʌnfə'mɪljər] *adj* étranger, peu familier

unfasten [ʌn'fæsən], [ʌn'fɑsən] *tr* défaire, détacher

unfathomable [ʌn'fæðəməbəl] *adj* insondable

unfavorable [ʌn'fevərəbəl] *adj* défavorable

unfeeling [ʌn'filɪŋ] *adj* insensible

unfilled [ʌn'fɪld] *adj* vide; (*post*) vacant

unfinished [ʌn'fɪnɪʃt] *adj* inachevé

unfit [ʌn'fɪt] *adj* impropre, inapte

unfold [ʌn'fold] *tr* déplier || *intr* se déplier

unforeseeable [ˌʌnfor'si-əbəl] *adj* imprévisible

unforeseen [ˌʌnfor'sin] *adj* imprévu

unforgettable [ˌʌnfər'getəbəl] *adj* inoubliable

unforgivable [ˌʌnfər'gɪvəbəl] *adj* impardonnable

unfortunate [ʌn'fortjənɪt] *adj & s* malheureux *m*

un-freeze [ʌn'friz] *v* (*pret* **-froze**; *pp* **-frozen** *tr* dégeler

unfriend·ly [ʌn'frendlɪ] *adj* (*comp* **-lier**; *super* **-liest**) inamical

unfruitful [ʌn'frutfəl] *adj* infructueux

unfulfilled [ˌʌnfəl'fɪld] *adj* inaccompli

unfurl [ʌn'fʌrl] *tr* déployer

unfurnished [ʌn'fʌrnɪʃt] *adj* non meublé

ungain·ly [ʌn'genlɪ] *adj* gauche, disgracieux

ungentlemanly [ʌn'dʒentəlmənlɪ] *adj* mal élevé, impoli

ungird [ʌn'gʌrd] *tr* déceindre

ungodly [ʌn'gɑdlɪ] *adj* impie; (*dreadful*) (coll) atroce

ungracious [ʌn'greʃəs] *adj* malgracieux

ungrammatical [ˌʌngrə'mætɪkəl] *adj* peu grammatical

ungrateful [ʌn'gretfəl] *adj* ingrat

ungrudgingly [ʌn'grʌdʒɪŋlɪ] *adj* de bon cœur, libéralement

unguarded [ʌn'gɑrdɪd] *adj* sans défense; (*moment*) d'inattention; (*card*) sec

unguent ['ʌŋgwənt] *s* onguent *m*

unhandy [ʌn'hændɪ] *adj* maladroit; (*e.g., tool*) incommode, pas maniable

unhap·py [ʌn'hæpɪ] *adj* (*comp* **-pier**; *super* **-piest**) malheureux, triste; (*unlucky*) malheureux, malencontreux; (*fateful*) funeste

unharmed [ʌn'hɑrmd] *adj* indemne

unharness [ʌn'hɑrnɪs] *tr* dételer

unheal·thy [ʌn'helθɪ] *adj* (*comp* **-thier**; *super* **-thiest**) malsain; (*person*) maladif

unheard-of [ʌn'hʌrd͵ɑv] *adj* inouï

unhinge [ʌn'hɪndʒ] *tr* (fig) détraquer

unhitch [ʌn'hɪtʃ] *tr* décrocher; (*e.g., a horse*) dételer

unho·ly [ʌn'holɪ] *adj* (*comp* **-lier**; *super* **-liest**) profane; (coll) affreux

unhook [ʌn'huk] *tr* décrocher; (*e.g., a dress*) dégrafer

unhoped-for [ʌn'hopt͵for] *adj* inespéré

unhorse [ʌn'hors] *tr* désarçonner

unhurt [ʌn'hʌrt] *adj* indemne

unicorn ['junɪ͵korn] *s* unicorne *m*

unification [ˌjunɪfɪ'keʃən] *s* unification *f*

uniform ['junɪ͵form] *adj & s* uniforme

m ‖ *tr* uniformiser; vêtir d'un uniforme

uniformi·ty [ˌjunɪˈfɔrmɪti] *s* (*pl* -ties) uniformité *f*

uni·fy [ˈjunɪˌfaɪ] *v* (*pret & pp* -fied) unifier

unilateral [ˌjunɪˈlætərəl] *adj* unilatéral

unimpeachable [ˌʌnɪmˈpitʃəbəl] *adj* irrécusable

unimportant [ˌʌnɪmˈpɔrtənt] *adj* peu important, sans importance

uninhabited [ˌʌnɪnˈhæbɪtɪd] *adj* inhabité

uninspired [ˌʌnɪnˈspaɪrd] *adj* sans inspiration, sans vigueur

unintelligent [ˌʌnɪnˈtɛlɪdʒənt] *adj* inintelligent

unintelligible [ˌʌnɪnˈtɛlɪdʒɪbəl] *adj* inintelligible

uninterested [ʌnˈɪntrɪstɪd], [ʌnˈɪntəˌrɛstɪd] *adj* indifférent

uninteresting [ʌnˈɪntrɪstɪŋ], [ʌnˈɪntəˌrɛstɪŋ] *adj* peu intéressant

uninterrupted [ˌʌnɪntəˈrʌptɪd] *adj* ininterrompu

union [ˈjunjən] *adj* (*leader, scale, card, etc.*) syndical ‖ *s* union *f*; (*of workmen*) syndicat *m*

unionize [ˈjunjəˌnaɪz] *tr* syndiquer ‖ *intr* se syndiquer

un'ion shop' *s* atelier *m* syndical

un'ion suit' *s* sous-vêtement *m* d'une seule pièce

unique [juˈnik] *adj* unique

unison [ˈjunɪsən], [ˈjunɪzən] *s* unisson *m*; **in unison (with)** à l'unisson (de)

unit [ˈjunɪt] *adj* unitaire ‖ *s* unité *f*; (elec, mach) groupe *m*

unite [juˈnaɪt] *tr* unir ‖ *intr* s'unir

united [juˈnaɪtɪd] *adj* uni

Unit'ed King'dom *s* Royaume-Uni *m*

Unit'ed Na'tions *fpl* Nations *fpl* Unies

Unit'ed States' *adj* des États-Unis, américain ‖ *s*—**the United States** les États-Unis *mpl*

uni·ty [ˈjunɪti] *s* (*pl* -ties) unité *f*

universal [ˌjunɪˈvʌrsəl] *adj & s* universel *m*

u'niversal joint' *s* joint *m* articulé, cardan *m*

universe [ˈjunɪˌvʌrs] *s* univers *m*

universi·ty [ˌjunɪˈvʌrsɪti] *adj* universitaire ‖ *s* (*pl* -ties) université *f*

unjust [ʌnˈdʒʌst] *adj* injuste

unjustified [ʌnˈdʒʌstɪˌfaɪd] *adj* injustifié

unkempt [ʌnˈkɛmpt] *adj* dépeigné; mal tenu, négligé

unkind [ʌnˈkaɪnd] *adj* désobligeant; (*pitiless*) impitoyable, dur

unknowable [ʌnˈnoˈəbəl] *adj* inconnaissable

unknowingly [ʌnˈnoˈɪŋli] *adv* inconsciemment

unknown [ʌnˈnon] *adj* inconnu; (*not yet revealed*) inédit; **unknown to à** l'insu de ‖ *s* inconnu *m*; (*math*) inconnue *f*

Un'known Sol'dier *s* Soldat *m* inconnu

unlace [ʌnˈles] *tr* délacer

unlatch [ʌnˈlætʃ] *tr* lever le loquet de

unlawful [ʌnˈlɔfəl] *adj* illégal, illicite

unleash [ʌnˈliʃ] *tr* lâcher

unleavened [ʌnˈlɛvənd] *adj* azyme

unless [ʌnˈlɛs] *prep* sauf ‖ *conj* à moins que

unlettered [ʌnˈlɛtərd] *adj* illettré

unlike [ʌnˈlaɪk] *adj* (*not alike*) dissemblables; différent de; (*not typical of*) pas caractéristique de; (*poles of a magnet*) de noms contraires ‖ *prep* (*contrary to*) à la différence de

unlikely [ʌnˈlaɪkli] *adj* peu probable

unlimited [ʌnˈlɪmɪtɪd] *adj* illimité

unlined [ʌnˈlaɪnd] *adj* (*coat*) non fourré; (*paper*) non rayé; (*face*) sans rides

unload [ʌnˈlod] *tr* décharger; (*a gun*) désarmer; (coll) se décharger de ‖ *intr* décharger

unloading [ʌnˈlodɪŋ] *s* déchargement *m*

unlock [ʌnˈlak] *tr* ouvrir; (*a bolted door*) déverrouiller; (*the jaws*) desserrer

unloose [ʌnˈlus] *tr* lâcher; (*to undo*) délier; (*a mighty force*) déchaîner

unloved [ʌnˈlʌvd] *adj* peu aimé, haï

unlovely [ʌnˈlʌvli] *adj* disgracieux

unluck·y [ʌnˈlʌki] *adj* (*comp* -ier; *super* -iest) malchanceux, malheureux

un·make [ʌnˈmek] *v* (*pret & pp* -made) *tr* défaire

unmanageable [ʌnˈmænɪdʒəbəl] *adj* difficile à manier, ingouvernable

unmanly [ʌnˈmænli] *adj* indigne d'un homme, poltron; efféminé

unmannerly [ʌnˈmænərli] *adj* impoli, mal élevé

unmarketable [ʌnˈmɑrkɪtəbəl] *adj* invendable

unmarriageable [ʌnˈmærɪdʒəbəl] *adj* non mariable

unmarried [ʌnˈmærɪd] *adj* célibataire

unmask [ʌnˈmæsk], [ʌnˈmɑsk] *tr* démasquer ‖ *intr* se démasquer

unmatched [ʌnˈmætʃt] *adj* sans égal, incomparable; (*unpaired*) désassorti, dépareillé

unmerciful [ʌnˈmʌrsɪfəl] *adj* impitoyable

unmesh [ʌnˈmɛʃ] *tr* (mach) désengrener ‖ *intr* (mach) se désengrener

unmindful [ʌnˈmaɪndfəl] *adj* oublieux

unmistakable [ˌʌnmɪsˈtekəbəl] *adj* évident, facilement reconnaissable

unmitigated [ʌnˈmɪtɪˌgetɪd] *adj* parfait, fieffé

unmixed [ʌnˈmɪkst] *adj* sans mélange

unmoor [ʌnˈmur] *tr* désamarrer

unmoved [ʌnˈmuvd] *adj* impassible

unmuzzle [ʌnˈmʌzəl] *tr* démuseler

unnatural [ʌnˈnætʃərəl] *adj* anormal, dénaturé; maniéré; artificiel

unnecessary [ʌnˈnɛsəˌsɛri] *adj* inutile

unnerve [ʌnˈnʌrv] *tr* démonter, décontenancer, bouleverser

unnoticeable [ʌnˈnotɪsəbəl] *adj* imperceptible

unnoticed [ʌnˈnotɪst] *adj* inaperçu

unobserved [ˌʌnəbˈzʌrvd] *adj* inobservé, inaperçu

unobtainable [ˌʌnəb'tenəbəl] *adj* introuvable

unobtrusive [ˌʌnəb'trusɪv] *adj* discret, effacé

unoccupied [ʌn'ɑkjə‚paɪd] *adj* libre, inoccupé

unofficial [ˌʌnə'fɪʃəl] *adj* officieux, non officiel

unopened [ʌn'opənd] *adj* fermé; (*letter*) non décacheté

unopposed [ˌʌnə'pozd] *adj* sans opposition; (*candidate*) unique

unorthodox [ʌn'ɔrθə‚dɑks] *adj* peu orthodox

unpack [ʌn'pæk] *tr* déballer

unpalatable [ʌn'pælətəbəl] *adj* fade, insipide

unparalleled [ʌn'pærə‚leld] *adj* sans précédent, sans pareil

unpardonable [ʌn'pɑrdənəbəl] *adj* impardonnable

unpatriotic [ˌʌnpetri'ɑtɪk], [ˌʌnpætri'ɑtɪk] *adj* antipatriotique

unperceived [ˌʌnpər'sivd] *adj* inaperçu

unperturbable [ˌʌnpər'tʌrbəbəl] *adj* imperturbable

unpleasant [ʌn'plezənt] *adj* désagréable, déplaisant

unpopular [ʌn'pɑpjələr] *adj* impopulaire

unpopularity [ʌn‚pɑpjə'læriti] *s* impopularité *f*

unprecedented [ʌn'presɪ‚dentɪd] *adj* sans précédent, inédit

unprejudiced [ʌn'predʒədɪst] *adj* sans préjugés, impartial

unpremeditated [ˌʌnpri'medɪ‚tetɪd] *adj* non prémédité

unprepared [ˌʌnpri'perd] *adj* sans préparation; (*e.g.*, *speech*) improvisé

unprepossessing [ˌʌnpripə'zesɪŋ] *adj* peu engageant

unpresentable [ˌʌnpri'zentəbəl] *adj* peu présentable

unpretentious [ˌʌnpri'tenʃəs] *adj* sans prétentions, modeste

unprincipled [ʌn'prɪnsɪpəld] *adj* sans principes, sans scrupules

unproductive [ˌʌnprə'dʌktɪv] *adj* improductif

unprofitable [ʌn'prɑfɪtəbəl] *adj* peu profitable, inutile

unpronounceable [ˌʌnprə'naunsəbəl] *adj* imprononçable

unpropitious [ˌʌnprə'pɪʃəs] *adj* défavorable

unpublished [ʌn'pʌblɪʃt] *adj* inédit

unpunished [ʌn'pʌnɪʃt] *adj* impuni

unqualified [ʌn'kwɑlə‚faɪd] *adj* incompétent; parfait, fieffé

unquenchable [ʌn'kwentʃəbəl] *adj* inextinguible

unquestionable [ʌn'kwestʃənəbəl] *adj* indiscutable

unravel [ʌn'rævəl] *v* (*pret & pp* -eled or -elled; *ger* -eling or -elling) *tr* effiler; (fig) débrouiller || *intr* s'effiler; (fig) se débrouiller

unreachable [ʌn'ritʃəbəl] *adj* inaccessible

unreal [ʌn'ri·əl] *adj* irréel

unreali·ty [ˌʌnri'æliti] *s* (*pl* -ties) irréalité *f*

unreasonable [ʌn'rizənəbəl] *adj* déraisonnable

unrecognizable [ʌn'rekəg‚naɪzəbəl] *adj* méconnaissable

unreel [ʌn'ril] *tr* dérouler || *intr* se dérouler

unrelenting [ˌʌnri'lentɪŋ] *adj* implacable

unreliable [ˌʌnri'laɪ-əbəl] *adj* peu fidèle, instable, sujet à caution

unremitting [ˌʌnri'mɪtɪŋ] *adj* incessant, infatigable

unrented [ʌn'rentɪd] *adj* libre, sans locataires

unrepentant [ˌʌnri'pentənt] *adj* impénitent

un'requit'ed love' [ˌʌnri'kwaɪtɪd] *s* amour *m* non partagé

unresponsive [ˌʌnri'spɑnsɪv] *adj* peu sensible, froid, détaché

unrest [ʌn'rest] *s* agitation *f*, trouble *m*; inquiétude *f*

un-rig [ʌn'rɪg] *v* (*pret & pp* -rigged; *ger* -rigging) *tr* (naut) dégréer

unrighteous [ʌn'raɪtʃəs] *adj* inique, injuste

unripe [ʌn'raɪp] *adj* vert, pas mûr; précoce

unrivaled or **unrivalled** [ʌn'raɪvəld] *adj* sans rival

unroll [ʌn'rol] *tr* dérouler || *intr* se dérouler

unromantic [ˌʌnro'mæntɪk] *adj* peu romanesque, terre à terre

unruffled [ʌn'rʌfəld] *adj* calme, serein

unruly [ʌn'ruli] *adj* indiscipliné, ingouvernable

unsaddle [ʌn'sædəl] *tr* (*a horse*) desseller; (*a horseman*) désarçonner

unsafe [ʌn'sef] *adj* dangereux

unsaid [ʌn'sed] *adj*—**to leave unsaid** passer sous silence

unsalable [ʌn'seləbəl] *adj* invendable

unsanitary [ʌn'sænɪ‚teri] *adj* peu hygiénique

unsatisfactory [ʌn‚sætɪs'fæktəri] *adj* peu satisfaisant

unsatisfied [ʌn'sætɪs‚faɪd] *adj* insatisfait, inassouvi

unsavory [ʌn'severi] *adj* désagréable; (fig) équivoque, louche

unscathed [ʌn'skeðd] *adj* indemne

unscientific [ˌʌnsaɪ-ən'tɪfɪk] *adj* antiscientifique

unscrew [ʌn'skru] *tr* dévisser

unscrupulous [ʌn'skrupjələs] *adj* sans scrupules

unseal [ʌn'sil] *tr* desceller

unsealed *adj* (*mail*) non clos

unseasonable [ʌn'sizənəbəl] *adj* hors de saison; (*untimely*) inopportun

unseemly [ʌn'simli] *adj* inconvenant

unseen [ʌn'sin] *adj* invisible

unselfish [ʌn'selfɪ] *adj* désintéressé

unsettled [ʌn'setəld] *adj* instable; (*region*) non colonisé; (*question*) en suspens; (*weather*) variable; (*bills*) non réglé

unshackle [ʌn'ʃækəl] *tr* désentraver

unshaken [ʌn'ʃekən] *adj* inébranlé

unshapely [ʌnˈʃepli] *adj* difforme, informe

unshaven [ʌnˈʃevən] *adj* non rasé

unsheathe [ʌnˈʃið] *tr* dégainer

unshod [ʌnˈʃad] *adj* déchaussé; (*horse*) déferré

unshrinkable [ʌnˈʃrɪŋkəbəl] *adj* irrétrécissable

unsightly [ʌnˈsaɪtli] *adj* laid, hideux

unsinkable [ʌnˈsɪŋkəbəl] *adj* insubmersible

unskilled [ʌnˈskɪld] *adj* inexpérimenté; de manœuvre

un'skilled la'borer *s* manœuvre *m*

unskillful [ʌnˈskɪlfəl] *adj* maladroit

unsnarl [ʌnˈsnɑrl] *tr* débrouiller

unsociable [ʌnˈsoʃəbəl] *adj* insociable

unsold [ʌnˈsold] *adj* invendu

unsolder [ʌnˈsadər] *tr* dessouder

unsophisticated [ˌʌnsəˈfɪstɪˌketɪd] *adj* ingénu, naïf, simple

unsound [ʌnˈsaund] *adj* peu solide; (*false*) faux; (*decayed*) gâté; (*mind*) dérangé; (*sleep*) léger

unspeakable [ʌnˈspikəbəl] *adj* indicible; (*disgusting*) sans nom

unsportsmanlike [ʌnˈsportsmən ˌlaɪk] *adj* antisportif

unstable [ʌnˈstebəl] *adj* instable

unsteady [ʌnˈstedi] *adj* chancelant, tremblant, vacillant

unstinted [ʌnˈstɪntɪd] *adj* abondant, sans bornes

unstitch [ʌnˈstɪtʃ] *tr* découdre

un-stop [ʌnˈstap] *v* (*pret & pp* -stopped; *ger* -stopping) *tr* déboucher

unstressed [ʌnˈstrest] *adj* inaccentué

unstrung [ʌnˈstrʌŋ] *adj* détraqué; (*necklace*) défilé; (*mus*) sans cordes

unsuccessful [ˌʌnsəkˈsesfəl] *adj* non réussi; **to be unsuccessful** ne pas réussir

unsuitable [ʌnˈs(j)utəbəl] *adj* impropre; (*time*) inopportun; **unsuitable for** peu fait pour, inapte à

unsuspected [ˌʌnsəsˈpektɪd] *adj* insoupçonné

unswerving [ʌnˈswɜrvɪŋ] *adj* ferme, inébranlable

unsympathetic [ˌʌnsɪmpəˈθetɪk] *adj* peu compatissant

unsystematic(al) [ˌʌnsɪstəˈmætɪk(əl)] *adj* non systématique, sans méthode

untactful [ʌnˈtæktfəl] *adj* indiscret, indélicat

untamed [ʌnˈtemd] *adj* indompté

untangle [ʌnˈtæŋgəl] *tr* démêler, débrouiller

untenable [ʌnˈtenəbəl] *adj* insoutenable

unthankful [ʌnˈθæŋkfəl] *adj* ingrat

unthinkable [ʌnˈθɪŋkəbəl] *adj* impensable

unthinking [ʌnˈθɪŋkɪŋ] *adj* irréfléchi

untidy [ʌnˈtaɪdi] *adj* désordonné, débraillé

un-tie [ʌnˈtaɪ] *v* (*pret & pp* -tied; *ger* -tying) *tr* délier, dénouer

until [ʌnˈtɪl] *prep* jusqu'à || *conj* jusqu'à ce que, en attendant que

untimely [ʌnˈtaɪmli] *adj* inopportun; (*premature*) prématuré

untiring [ʌnˈtaɪrɪŋ] *adj* infatigable

untold [ʌnˈtold] *adj* incalculable; (*suffering*) inouï; (*joy*) indicible; (*tale*) non raconté

untouchable [ʌnˈtʌtʃəbəl] *adj & s* intouchable *mf*

untouched [ʌnˈtʌtʃt] *adj* intact; indifférent; non mentionné

untoward [ʌnˈtord] *adj* malencontreux

untrained [ʌnˈtrend] *adj* inexpérimenté; (*animal*) non dressé

untrammeled *or* **untrammelled** [ʌnˈtræməld] *adj* sans entraves

untried [ʌnˈtraɪd] *adj* inéprouvé

untroubled [ʌnˈtrʌbəld] *adj* calme, insoucieux

untrue [ʌnˈtru] *adj* faux; infidèle

untrustworthy [ʌnˈtrʌst ˌwɜrði] *adj* indigne de confiance

untruth [ʌnˈtruθ] *s* mensonge *m*

untruthful [ʌnˈtruθfəl] *adj* mensonger

untwist [ʌnˈtwɪst] *tr* détordre || *intr* se détordre

unused [ʌnˈjuzd] *adj* inutilisé, inemployé; **unused to** [ʌnˈjuzdtu], [ʌnˈjustu] peu accoutumé à

unusual [ʌnˈjuʒʊ-əl] *adj* insolite, inusité, inhabituel

unutterable [ʌnˈʌtərəbəl] *adj* indicible, inexprimable

unvanquished [ʌnˈvæŋkwɪʃt] *adj* invaincu

unvarnished [ʌnˈvɑrnɪʃt] *adj* non verni; (fig) sans fard, simple

unveil [ʌnˈvel] *tr* dévoiler; (*e.g., a statue*) inaugurer || *intr* se dévoiler

unveiling [ʌnˈvelɪŋ] *s* dévoilement *m*

unventilated [ʌnˈventɪˌletɪd] *adj* sans aération

unvoice [ʌnˈvɔɪs] *tr* dévoiser, assourdir

unwanted [ʌnˈwɑntɪd] *adj* non voulu

unwarranted [ʌnˈwɑrəntɪd] *adj* injustifié; sans garantie

unwary [ʌnˈweri] *adj* imprudent

unwavering [ʌnˈwevərɪŋ] *adj* constant, ferme, résolu

unwelcome [ʌnˈwelkəm] *adj* (*e.g., visitor*) importun; (*e.g., news*) fâcheux

unwell [ʌnˈwel] *adj* indisposé, souffrant; (*menstruating*) indisposée

unwholesome [ʌnˈholsəm] *adj* malsain, insalubre

unwieldy [ʌnˈwildi] *adj* peu maniable

unwilling [ʌnˈwɪlɪŋ] *adj* peu disposé

unwillingly [ʌnˈwɪlɪŋli] *adv* à contre-cœur

un-wind [ʌnˈwaɪnd] *v* (*pret & pp* -wound) *tr* dérouler || *intr* se dérouler

unwise [ʌnˈwaɪz] *adj* peu judicieux, malavisé

unwished-for [ʌnˈwɪʃt ˌfɔr] *adj* non souhaité

unwittingly [ʌnˈwɪtɪŋli] *adv* inconsciemment, sans le savoir

unwonted [ʌnˈwʌntɪd] *adj* inaccoutumé, peu commun

unworldly [ʌnˈwɜrldli] *adj* peu mondain; simple, naïf

unworthy [ʌnˈwɜrði] *adj* indigne

un-wrap [ʌnˈræp] *v* (*pret & pp* -wrapped; *ger* -wrapping) *tr* dépaqueter, désenvelopper

unwrinkled [ʌn'rɪŋkəld] *adj* uni, lisse, sans rides

unwritten [ʌn'rɪtən] *adj* non écrit; oral; *(blank)* vierge, blanc

unwrit'ten law' *s* droit *m* coutumier

unyielding [ʌn'jildɪŋ] *adj* ferme, solide; inébranlable

unyoke [ʌn'jok] *tr* dételer

up [ʌp] *adj* montant, ascendant; *(raised)* levé; *(standing)* debout; *(time)* expiré; *(blinds)* relevé; **up in arms** soulevé, indigné ‖ *adv* haut, en haut; **to be up against** se heurter à; **to be up against it** avoir la déveine; **to be up to** être capable de, être à la hauteur de; être à, e.g., **to be up to you (me, etc.)** être à vous (moi, etc.); **up and down** de haut en bas; *(back and forth)* de long en large; **up there** là-haut; **up to** jusqu'à; *(at the level of)* au niveau de, à la hauteur de; **up to and including** jusques et y compris; **what's up?** qu'est-ce qui se passe?; for expressions like **to go up** monter and **to get up** se lever, see the verb ‖ *prep* en haut de, vers le haut de; *(a stream)* en montant ‖ *v (pret & pp* **upped**; *ger* **upping**) *tr* (coll) faire monter; *(prices, wages)* (coll) élever ‖ *interj* debout!

up-and-coming ['ʌpən'kʌmɪŋ] *adj* (coll) entreprenant

up-and-doing ['ʌpən'du·ɪŋ] *adj* (coll) entreprenant, alerte, énergique

up-and-up ['ʌpən'ʌp] *s*—**to be on the up-and-up** (coll) être en bonne voie; (coll) être honnête

up'braid' *tr* réprimander, reprendre

upbringing ['ʌp,brɪŋɪŋ] *s* éducation *f*

up'coun'try *adv* (coll) à l'intérieur du pays ‖ *s* (coll) intérieur *m* du pays

up'date' *tr* mettre à jour

upheaval [ʌp'hivəl] *s* soulèvement *m*

up'hill' *adj* montant; difficile, pénible ‖ *adv* en montant

up'hold' *v (pret & pp* **-held**) *tr* soutenir, maintenir

upholster [ʌp'holstər] *tr* tapisser

upholsterer [ʌp'holstərər] *s* tapissier *m*

upholster·y [ʌp'holstəri] *s (pl* **-ies**) tapisserie *f*

up'keep' *s* entretien *m*; *(expenses)* frais *mpl* d'entretien

upland ['ʌplənd], ['ʌp,lænd] *adj* élevé ‖ *s* région *f* montagneuse; **uplands** hautes terres *fpl*

up'lift' *s* élévation *f*; *(moral improvement)* édification *f* ‖ **up-lift'** *tr* soulever, élever

upon [ə'pɑn] *prep* sur; à, e.g., **upon my arrival** à mon arrivée; **upon** + *ger* en + *ger*, e.g., **upon arriving** en arrivant

upper ['ʌpər] *adj* supérieur; haut; *(first)* premier ‖ *s (of shoe)* empeigne *f*

up'per berth' *s* couchette *f* du haut, couchette supérieure

up'per-case' *adj* (typ) du haut de casse

up'per clas'ses *spl* hautes classes *fpl*

up'per hand' *s* dessus *m*, haute main *f*

up'per mid'dle class' *s* haute bourgeoisie *f*

up'per·most' *adj* (le) plus haut, (le) plus élevé; (le) premier ‖ *adv* en dessus

uppish ['ʌpɪʃ] *adj* (coll) suffisant, arrogant

up'raise' *tr* lever

up'right' *adj & adv* droit ‖ *s* montant *m*

uprising [ʌp'raɪzɪŋ], ['ʌp,raɪzɪŋ] *s* soulèvement *m*, insurrection *f*

up'roar' *s* tumulte *m*, vacarme *m*

uproarious [ʌp'rori·əs] *adj* tumultueux; *(funny)* comique, impayable

up'root' *tr* déraciner

ups' and downs' *spl* vicissitudes *fpl*

up·set' or **up'set'** *adj (overturned)* renversé; *(disturbed)* bouleversé; *(stomach)* dérangé ‖ **up'set'** *s (overturn)* renversement *m*; *(of emotions)* bouleversement *m* ‖ **up·set'** *v (pret & pp* **-set**; *ger* **-setting**) *tr* renverser; bouleverser ‖ *intr* se renverser

up'set price' *s* prix *m* de départ

upsetting [ʌp'sɛtɪŋ] *adj* bouleversant, inquiétant

up'shot' *s* résultat *m*; point *m* essentiel

up'side down' *adv* sens dessus dessous; **to turn upside down** renverser; se renverser; *(said of carriage)* verser

up'stage' *adj & adv* au second plan, à l'arrière-plan; **to go upstage** remonter ‖ *s* arrière-plan *m* ‖ **up'stage'** *tr* (coll) prendre un air dédaigneux envers

up'stairs' *adj* d'en haut ‖ *s* l'étage *m* supérieur ‖ *adv* en haut; **to go upstairs** monter, monter en haut

up'stand'ing *adj* droit; *(vigorous)* gaillard; *(sincere)* honnête, probe

up'start' *adj & s* parvenu *m*

up'stream' *adj* d'amont ‖ *adv* en amont

up'stroke' *s (in writing)* délié *m*; *(mach)* course *f* ascendante

up'surge' *s* poussée *f*

up'swing' *s* mouvement *m* de montée; *(com)* amélioration *f*

up-to-date ['ʌptə'det] *adj* à la page; *(e.g., account books)* mis à jour

up-to-the-minute ['ʌptəðə'mɪnɪt] *adj* de la dernière heure

up'trend' *s* tendance *f* à la hausse

up'turn' *s* hausse *f*, amélioration *f*

up·turned' *adj (e.g., eyes)* levé; *(part of clothing)* relevé; *(nose)* retroussé

upward ['ʌpwərd] *adj* ascendant ‖ *adv* vers le haut; **upward of** plus de

Ural ['jʊrəl] *adj* Ouralien ‖ *s* Oural *m*; **Urals** Oural

uranium [jʊ'reni·əm] *s* uranium *m*

urban ['ʌrbən] *adj* urbain

urbane [ʌr'ben] *adj* urbain, courtois

urbanite ['ʌrbə,naɪt] *s* citadin *m*, habitant *m* d'une ville

urbanity [ʌr'bænɪti] *s* urbanité *f*

urbanize ['ʌrbə,naɪz] *tr* urbaniser

ur'ban renew'al *s* renouveau *m* urbain

urchin ['ʌrtʃɪn] *s* gamin *m*, galopin *m*

ure·thra [jʊ'riθrə] *s (pl* **-thras** or **-thrae** [θri]) urètre *m*

urge [ʌrdʒ] *s* impulsion *f* ‖ *tr & intr* presser

urgen·cy ['ʌrdʒənsi] *s (pl* **-cies**) urgence *f*; insistance *f*, sollicitation *f*

urgent ['ʌrdʒənt] *adj* urgent, pressant; (*insistent*) pressant, importun
urinal ['jurɪnəl] *s* (*small building or convenience for men*) urinoir *m*, vespasienne *f*; (*for bed*) urinal *m*
urinary ['jurɪ‚nerɪ] *adj* urinaire
urinate ['jurɪ‚net] *tr & intr* uriner; pisser (coll)
urine ['jurɪn] *s* urine *f*
urn [ʌrn] *s* urne *f*; (*for tea, coffee, etc.*) fontaine *f*
urology [jʊ'rɑlədʒɪ] *s* urologie *f*
us [ʌs] *pron pers* nous §85, §87
U.S.A. [‚ju'es'e] *s* (letterword) (**United States of America**) E.-U.A. *mpl* or U.S.A. *mpl*
usable ['juzəbəl] *adj* utilisable
usage ['jusɪdʒ], [‚juzɪdʒ] *s* usage *m*
use [jus] *s* emploi *m*, usage *m*; (*usefulness*) utilité *f*; **in use** occupé; **of what use is it?** à quoi cela sert-il?; **out of use** hors de service; **to be of no use** ne servir à rien; **to have no use for s.o.** tenir qn en mauvaise estime; **to make use of** se servir de; **what's the use?** à quoi bon? ‖ [juz] *tr* employer, se servir de, user de; **to use up** épuiser, user ‖ *intr*—**I used to visit my friend every evening** je visitais mon ami tous les soirs
used [juzd] *adj* usagé, usé; d'occasion, e.g., **used car** voiture *f* d'occasion; **to be used** (*to be put into use*) être usité, être employé; **to be used as** servir de; **to be used to** (*to be useful for*) servir à; **used to** ['justu] accoutumé à; **used up** épuisé
useful ['jusfəl] *adj* utile
usefulness ['jusfəlnɪs] *s* utilité *f*

useless ['juslɪs] *adj* inutile
user ['juzər] *s* usager *m*; (*of a machine, of gas, etc.*) utilisateur *m*
usher ['ʌʃər] *s* placeur *m*; ouvreuse *f*; (*doorkeeper*) huissier *m* ‖ *tr*—**to usher in** inaugurer; (*a person*) introduire
U.S.S.R. [‚ju'es'es'ɑr] *s* (letterword) (**Union of Soviet Socialist Republics**) U.R.S.S. *f*
usual ['juʒʊ-əl] *adj* usuel; **as usual** comme d'habitude
usually ['juʒʊ-əlɪ] *adv* usuellement, d'habitude, d'ordinaire
usurp [ju'zʌrp] *tr* usurper
usu-ry ['juʒərɪ] *s* (*pl* -ries) usure *f*
utensil [ju'tensɪl] *s* ustensile *m*
uter-us ['jutərəs] *s* (*pl* -i [‚aɪ]) utérus *m*
utilitarian [‚jutɪlɪ'terɪ-ən] *adj* utilitaire
utili-ty [ju'tɪlɪtɪ] *s* (*pl* -ties) utilité *f*; service *m* public; **utilities** services en commun (*gaz, transports, etc.*)
utilize ['jutɪ‚laɪz] *tr* utiliser
utmost ['ʌt‚most] *adj* extrême; plus grand; plus éloigné ‖ *s*—**the utmost** l'extrême *m*, le comble *m*; **to do one's utmost** faire tout son possible; **to the utmost** jusqu'au dernier point
utopia [ju'topɪ-ə] *s* utopie *f*
utopian [ju'topɪ-ən] *adj* utopique ‖ *s* utopiste *mf*
utter ['ʌtər] *adj* complet, total, absolu ‖ *tr* proférer, émettre; (*a cry*) pousser
utterance ['ʌtərəns] *s* expression *f*, émission *f*; (gram) énoncé *m*; **to give utterance to** exprimer
utterly ['ʌtərlɪ] *adj* complètement, tout à fait, totalement

V

V, v [vi] *s* XXIIe lettre de l'alphabet
vacan-cy ['vekənsɪ] *s* (*pl* -cies) (*emptiness; gap, opening*) vide *m*; (*unfilled position or job*) vacance *f*; (*in a building*) appartement *m* disponible; (*in a hotel*) chambre *f* de libre; **no vacancy** (public sign) complet
vacant ['vekənt] *adj* (*empty*) vide; (*having no occupant; untenanted*) vacant, libre, disponible; (*expression, look*) distrait, vague
va'cant lot' *s* terrain *m* vague
vacate ['veket] *tr* quitter, évacuer ‖ *intr* (*to move out*) déménager
vacation [ve'keʃən] *s* vacances *fpl*; **on vacation** en vacances ‖ *intr* prendre ses vacances, passer les vacances
vacationist [ve'keʃənɪst] *s* vacancier *m*
vaca'tion with pay' *s* congé *m* payé
vaccinate ['væksɪ‚net] *tr* vacciner
vaccination [‚væksɪ'neʃən] *s* vaccination *f*
vaccine [væk'sin] *s* vaccin *m*
vacillate ['væsɪ‚let] *intr* vaciller

vacui-ty [væ'kju-ɪtɪ] *s* (*pl* -ties) vacuité *f*
vacu-um ['vækju-əm] *s* (*pl* -ums or -a [ə]) vacuum *m*, vide *m* ‖ *tr* passer à l'aspirateur, dépoussiérer
vac'uum clean'er *s* aspirateur *m*
vac'uum pump' *s* pompe *f* à vide
vac'uum tube' *s* tube *m* à vide
vagabond ['vægə‚band] *adj & s* vagabond *m*
vagar-y [və'gerɪ] *s* (*pl* -ies) caprice *m*
vagran-cy ['vegrənsɪ] *s* (*pl* -cies) vagabondage *m*
vague [veg] *adj* vague
vain [ven] *adj* vain; **in vain** en vain
vainglorious [ven'glorɪ-əs] *adj* vaniteux
valance ['væləns] *s* cantonnière *f*, lambrequin *m*
vale [vel] *s* vallon *m*
valedicto-ry [‚vælɪ'dɪktərɪ] *s* (*pl* -ries) ‹ discours *m* d'adieu
valence ['veləns] *s* (chem) valence *f*
valentine ['vælən‚taɪn] *s* (*sweetheart*)

valentin *m*; (*card*) carte *f* de la Saint-Valentin

Val′entine Day′ *s* la Saint-Valentin

vale′ of tears′ *s* vallée *f* de larmes

valet ['vælɪt], ['vælə] *s* valet *m*

valiant ['væljənt] *adj* vaillant

valid ['vælɪd] *adj* valable, valide

validate ['vælɪ‚det] *tr* valider; (*sports*) homologuer

validation [‚vælɪ'deʃən] *s* validation *f*; (*sports*) homologation *f*

validi·ty [və'lɪdɪti] *s* (*pl* -ties) validité *f*

valise [və'lis] *s* mallette *f*

valley ['væli] *s* vallée *f*, vallon *m*; (*of roof*) cornière *f*

valor ['vælər] *s* valeur *f*, vaillance *f*

valorous ['vælərəs] *adj* valeureux

valuable ['vælju‚əbəl], ['væljəbəl] *adj* précieux, de valeur ‖ **valuables** *spl* objets *mpl* de valeur

value ['vælju] *s* valeur *f*; (*bargain*) affaire *f*, occasion *f*; **to set a value on** estimer, évaluer ‖ *tr* (*to think highly of*) priser, estimer; (*to set a price for*) estimer, évaluer; **if you value your life** si vous tenez à la vie

val′ue-added tax′ *s* taxe *f* à la valeur ajoutée, T.V.A.

valueless ['væljulɪs] *adj* sans valeur

valve [vælv] *s* soupape *f*; (*of mollusk; of fruit; of tire*) valve *f*; (*of heart*) valvule *f*; (*mus*) clé *f*

valve′ cap′ *s* chapeau *m*, bouchon *m*

valve′ gear′ *spl* (*of gas engine*) engrenages *mpl* de distribution; (*of steam engine*) mécanisme *m* de distribution

valve′-in-head′ en′gine *s* moteur *m* à soupapes en tête, moteur à culbuteurs

valve′ seat′ *s* siège *m* de soupape

valve′ spring′ *s* ressort *m* de soupape

valve′ stem′ *s* tige *f* de soupape

vamp [væmp] *s* (*of shoe*) empeigne *f*; (*patchwork*) rapiéçage *m*; (*woman who preys on man*) (coll) femme *f* fatale, vamp *f* ‖ *tr* (*a shoe*) mettre une empeigne à; (*to piece together*) rapiécer; (*a susceptible man*) (coll) vamper; (*an accompaniment*) (coll) improviser

vampire ['væmpaɪr] *s* vampire *m*; femme *f* fatale, vamp *f*

van [væn] *s* camion *m*, voiture *f* de déménagement; (mil, fig) avant-garde *f*; (*railway car*) (Brit) fourgon *m*

vandal ['vændəl] *adj* & *s* vandale *m* ‖ (*cap*) *adj* vandale ‖ (*cap*) *s* Vandale *m*

vandalism ['vændə‚lɪzəm] *s* vandalisme *m*

vane [ven] *s* (*weathervane*) girouette *f*; (*of windmill*) aile *f*; (*of propeller or turbine*) ailette *f*; (*of feather*) lame *f*

vanguard ['væn‚ɡɑrd] *s* (mil, fig) avant-garde *f*; **in the vanguard** à l'avant-garde

vanilla [və'nɪlə] *s* vanille *f*

vanish ['vænɪʃ] *intr* s'évanouir, disparaître

van′ishing cream′ *s* crème *f* de jour

vani·ty ['vænɪti] *s* (*pl* -ties) vanité *f*; (*dressing table*) table *f* de toilette, coiffeuse *f*; (*vanity case*) poudrier *m*

van′ity case′ *s* poudrier *m*, nécessaire *m* de toilette

vanquish ['væŋkwɪʃ] *tr* vaincre

van′tage point′ ['væntɪdʒ] *s* position *f* avantageuse

vapid ['væpɪd] *adj* insipide

vapor ['vepər] *s* vapeur *f*

vaporize ['vepə‚raɪz] *tr* vaporiser ‖ *intr* se vaporiser

va′por trail′ *s* (aer) sillage *m* de fumée

variable ['vɛrɪ‚əbl] *adj* & *s* variable *f*

variance ['vɛrɪ‚əns] *s* différence *f*, variation *f*; **at variance with** en désaccord avec

variant ['vɛrɪ‚ənt] *adj* variant ‖ *s* variante *f*

variation [‚vɛrɪ'eʃən] *s* variation *f*

varicose ['værɪ‚kos] *adj* variqueux

var′icose veins′ *spl* (pathol) varice *f*

varied ['vɛrɪd] *adj* varié

variegated ['vɛrɪ‚ɡetɪd], ['vɛrɪ‚ɡetɪd] *adj* varié; (*spotted*) bigarré, bariolé

varie·ty [və'raɪ‚ɪti] *s* (*pl* -ties) variété *f*

vari′ety show′ *s* spectacle *m* de variétés

various ['vɛrɪ‚əs] *adj* divers, différent; (*several*) plusieurs; (*variegated*) bigarré

varnish ['vɑrnɪʃ] *s* vernis *m* ‖ *tr* vernir; (*e.g., the truth*) farder, embellir

varsi·ty ['vɑrsɪti] *adj* universitaire ‖ *s* (*pl* -ties) (sports) équipe *f* universitaire principale

var·y ['vɛri] *v* (*pret* & *pp* -led) *tr* & *intr* varier

vase [ves], [vez] *s* vase *m*

vaseline ['væsə‚lin] *s* (trademark) vaseline *f*

vassal ['væsəl] *adj* & *s* vassal *m*

vast [væst], [vɑst] *adj* vaste

vastness ['væstnɪs], ['vɑstnɪs] *s* vaste étendue *f*, immensité *f*

vat [væt] *s* cuve *f*, bac *m*

Vatican ['vætɪkən] *adj* vaticane ‖ *s* Vatican *m*

vaudeville ['vodvɪl], ['vodəvɪl] *s* spectacle *m* de variétés, music-hall *m*; (*light theatrical piece interspersed with songs*) vaudeville *m*

vault [vɔlt] *s* (*underground chamber*) souterrain *m*; (*of a bank*) chambre *f* forte; (*burial chamber*) caveau *m*; (*leap*) saut *m*; (anat, archit) voûte *f* ‖ *tr* & *intr* sauter

vaunt [vɔnt], [vɑnt] *s* vantardise *f* ‖ *tr* vanter ‖ *intr* se vanter

veal [vil] *s* veau *m*

veal′ chop′ *s* côtelette *f* de veau

veal′ cut′let *s* escalope *f* de veau

veer [vɪr] *s* virage *m* ‖ *tr* faire virer ‖ *intr* virer

vegetable ['vedʒɪtəbəl] *adj* végétal ‖ *s* (*plant*) végétal *m*; (*edible part of plant*) légume *m*

veg′etable gar′den *s* potager *m*

veg′etable soup′ *s* potage *m* aux légumes

vegetarian [‚vedʒɪ'tɛrɪ‚ən] *adj* & *s* végétarien *m*

vegetate ['vedʒɪ‚tet] *intr* végéter

vehemence ['vi·ɪməns] *s* véhémence *f*

vehement ['vi·ɪmənt] *adj* véhément

vehicle ['vi·ɪkəl] s véhicule m

veil [vel] s voile m; to take the veil prendre le voile || tr voiler || intr se voiler

vein [ven] s veine f || tr veiner

velar ['vilər] adj & s vélaire f

vellum ['vɛləm] s vélin m; papier m vélin

veloci·ty [vɪ'lɑsɪti] s (pl -ties) vitesse f

velvet ['vɛlvɪt] s velours m

velveteen [,vɛlvɪ'tin] s velvet m

velvety ['vɛlvɪti] adj velouté

vend [vend] tr vendre, colporter

vend'ing machine' s distributeur m automatique

vendor ['vendər] s vendeur m

veneer [və'nɪr] s placage m; (fig) vernis m || tr plaquer

venerable ['vɛnərəbəl] adj vénérable

venerate ['vɛnə,ret] tr vénérer

venereal [vɪ'nɪrɪ·əl] adj vénérien

Venetian [vɪ'niʃən] adj vénitien || s Vénitien m

Vene'tian blind' s jalousie f, store m vénitien

vengeance ['vendʒəns] s vengeance f; with a vengeance furieusement, à outrance; (to the utmost limit) tant que ça peut

vengeful ['vendʒfəl] adj vengeur

Venice ['vɛnɪs] s Venise f

venison ['vɛnɪsən], ['vɛnɪzən] s venaison f

venom ['vɛnəm] s venin m

venomous ['vɛnəməs] adj venimeux

vent [vent] s orifice m; (for air) ventouse f; to give vent to donner libre cours à || tr décharger

ventilate ['vɛntɪ,let] tr ventiler

ventilator ['vɛntɪ,letər] s ventilateur m

ventricle ['vɛntrɪkəl] s ventricule m

ventriloquism [ven'trɪlə,kwɪzəm] s ventriloquie f

ventriloquist [ven'trɪləkwɪst] s ventriloque mf

venture ['ventʃər] s entreprise f risquée; at a venture à l'aventure || tr aventurer || intr s'aventurer; to venture on hasarder

venturesome ['ventʃərsəm] adj aventureux

venturous ['ventʃərəs] adj aventureux

venue ['vɛnju] s (law) lieu m du jugement; change of venue (law) renvoi m

Venus ['vinəs] s Vénus f

veracious [vɪ're·ʃəs] adj véridique

veraci·ty [vɪ'ræsɪti] s (pl -ties) véracité f

veranda or verandah [və'rændə] s véranda f

verb [vʌrb] adj verbal || s verbe m

verbalize ['vʌrbə,laɪz] tr exprimer par des mots; (gram) changer en verbe || intr être verbeux

verbatim [vər'betɪm] adj textuel || adv textuellement

verbiage ['vʌrbɪ·ɪdʒ] s verbiage m

verbose [vər'bos] adj verbeux

verdant ['vʌrdənt] adj vert; naïf, candide

verdict ['vʌrdɪkt] s verdict m

verdigris ['vʌrdɪ,gris] s vert-de-gris m

verdure ['vʌrdʒər] s verdure f

verge [vʌrdʒ] s bord m, limite f; on the verge of sur le point de || intr—to verge on or upon toucher à; (bad faith; the age of forty; etc.) friser

verification [,vɛrɪfɪ'keʃən] s vérification f

veri·fy ['vɛrɪ,faɪ] v (pret & pp -fied) tr vérifier

verily ['vɛrɪli] adv en vérité

veritable ['vɛrɪtəbəl] adj véritable

vermilion [vər'mɪljən] adj & s vermillon m

vermin ['vʌrmɪn] s (objectionable person) vermine f || spl (objectionable animals or persons) vermine

vermouth [vər'muθ], ['vʌrmuθ] s vermout m

vernacular [vər'nækjələr] adj vernaculaire || s langue f vernaculaire; (everyday language) langage m vulgaire; (language peculiar to a class or profession) jargon m

versatile ['vʌrsətɪl] adj aux talents variés; (e.g., mind) universel, souple

verse [vʌrs] s vers mpl; (stanza) strophe f; (Bib) verset m

versed [vʌrst] adj—versed in versé dans; spécialiste de

versification [,vʌrsɪfɪ'keʃən] s versification f

versi·fy ['vʌrsɪ,faɪ] v (pret & pp -fied) tr & intr versifier

version ['vʌrʒən] s version f

ver·so ['vʌrso] s (pl -sos) (e.g., of a coin) revers m; (typ) verso m

versus ['vʌrsəs] prep contre

verte·bra ['vʌrtɪbrə] s (pl -brae [,bri] or -bras) vertèbre f

vertebrate ['vʌrtɪ,bret] adj & s vertébré m

ver·tex ['vʌrteks] s (pl -texes or -tices [tɪ,siz]) sommet m

vertical ['vʌrtɪkəl] adj vertical || s verticale f

ver'tical hold' s (telv) commande f de stabilité verticale

ver'tical rud'der s gouvernail m de direction

verti·go ['vʌrtɪ,go] s (pl -gos or -goes) vertige m

very ['vɛri] adj véritable; même, e.g., at this very moment à cet instant même || adv très, e.g., I am very hungry j'ai très faim; bien, e.g., you are very nice vous êtes bien gentil; tout, e.g., the very first le tout premier; e.g., my very best tout mon possible; for my very own pour moi tout seul; very much beaucoup

vesicle ['vɛsɪkəl] s vésicule f

vespers ['vɛspərz] spl vêpres fpl

vessel ['vɛsəl] s bâtiment m, navire m; (container) vase m; (anat, bot, zool) vaisseau m

vest [vest] s gilet m; to play it close to the vest (coll) jouer serré || tr revêtir; to vest with investir de, revêtir de

vest'ed in'terests spl classes fpl dirigeantes

vestibule ['vɛstɪ,bjul] s vestibule m

ves'tibule car' s (rr) wagon m à souf-
flets

vestige ['vɛstɪdʒ] s vestige m

vestment ['vɛstmənt] s vêtement m
sacerdotal

vest'-pock'et adj de poche, de petit
format

ves•try ['vɛstri] s (pl -tries) sacristie f;
(committee) conseil m paroissial

ves'try-man ['vɛstri -mən] marguillier m

Vesuvius [vɪ's(j)uvɪ•əs] s le Vésuve

vetch [vɛtʃ] s vesce f; (Lathyrus sati-
vus) gesse f

veteran ['vɛtərən] s vétéran m

veterinarian [‚vɛtərɪ'nɛrɪ•ən] s vétérinaire mf

veterinar•y ['vɛtərɪ ‚nɛri] adj vétéri-
naire || s (pl -ies) vétérinaire mf

ve•to ['vito] s (pl -toes) veto m || tr
mettre un veto à

vex [vɛks] tr vexer, contrarier

vexation [vɛk'seʃən] s vexation f

via ['vaɪ•ə] prep via

viaduct ['vaɪ•ə ‚dʌkt] s viaduc m

vial ['vaɪ•əl] s fiole f

viand ['vaɪ•ənd] s mets m

vibrate ['vaɪbret] intr vibrer

vibration [vaɪ'breʃən] s vibration f

vicar ['vɪkər] s vicaire m; (in Church
of England) curé m

vicarage ['vɪkərɪdʒ] s presbytère m;
(duties of vicar) cure f

vicarious [vaɪ'kɛrɪ•əs], [vɪ'kɛrɪ•əs] adj
substitut; (punishment) souffert pour
autrui; (power, authority) délégué;
(enjoyment) partagé

vice [vaɪs] s vice m; (device) étau m

vice'-ad'miral s vice-amiral m

vice'-pres'ident s vice-président m

viceroy ['vaɪsrɔɪ] s vice-roi m

vice' squad' s brigade f des mœurs

vice versa ['vaɪsə'vʌrsə], ['vaɪs'vʌrsə]
adv vice versa

vicini•ty [vɪ'sɪnɪti] s (pl -ties) voisinage
m; environs mpl, e.g., **New York and
vicinity** New York et ses environs

vicious ['vɪʃəs] adj vicieux; (mean)
méchant; (ferocious) féroce

vicissitude [vɪ'sɪsɪ ‚t(j)ud] s vicissitude f

victim ['vɪktɪm] s victime f; (e.g., of a
collision, fire) accidenté m

victimize ['vɪktɪ‚maɪz] tr prendre pour
victime; (to swindle) duper

victor ['vɪktər] s vainqueur m

victorious [vɪk'torɪ•əs] adj victorieux

victo•ry ['vɪktəri] s (pl -ries) victoire f

victuals ['vɪtəlz] spl victuailles fpl

vid'eo sig'nal ['vɪdɪ ‚o] s signal m
d'image

vid'eo tape' s bande f magnétique vidéo

vid'eo tape' record'er s magnétoscope
m

vid'eo tape' record'ing s magnétoscope
m

vie [vaɪ] v (pret & pp vied; ger vying)
intr rivaliser, lutter

Vienna [vɪ'ɛnə] s Vienne f

Vien•nese [‚vi•ə'niz] adj viennois || s
(pl -nese) Viennois m

Vietnam [‚vi•ɛt'nɑm] s le Vietnam

Vietnam•ese [vɪ ‚ɛtnə'miz] adj vietna-
mien || s (pl -ese) Vietnamien m

view [vju] s vue f; **in my view** à mon
avis, selon mon opinion; **in view** en
vue; **in view of** étant donné, vu; **on
view** exposé; **with a view to** en vue de
|| tr voir, regarder; considérer, exami-
ner

viewer ['vju•ər] s spectateur m; (for
film, slides, etc.) visionneuse f; (telv)
téléspectateur m

view'find'er s viseur m

view'point' s point m de vue

vigil ['vɪdʒɪl] s veille f; (eccl) vigile f;
to keep a vigil veiller

vigilance ['vɪdʒɪləns] s vigilance f

vigilant ['vɪdʒɪlənt] adj vigilant

vignette [vɪn'jɛt] s vignette f

vigor ['vɪgər] s vigueur f

vigorous ['vɪgərəs] adj vigoureux

vile [vaɪl] adj vil; (smell) infect;
(weather) sale; (disgusting) détestable

vili•fy ['vɪlɪ ‚faɪ] v (pret & pp -fied) tr
diffamer, dénigrer

villa ['vɪlə] s villa f

village ['vɪlɪdʒ] s village m

villager ['vɪlɪdʒər] s villageois m

villain ['vɪlən] s scélérat m; (of a play)
traître m

villainous ['vɪlənəs] adj vil, infame

villain•y ['vɪleni] s (pl -ies) vilenie f,
infamie f

vim [vɪm] s énergie f, vigueur f

vinaigrette' sauce' [‚vɪnə'grɛt] s vinaigrette f

vindicate ['vɪndɪ ‚ket] tr justifier, défendre

vindictive [vɪn'dɪktɪv] adj vindicatif

vine [vaɪn] s plante f grimpante; (grape
plant) vigne f

vinegar ['vɪnɪgər] s vinaigre m

vinegary ['vɪnɪgəri] adj aigre; acariâtre

vine' grow'er [‚gro•ər] s viticulteur m

vine' stock' s cep m

vineyard ['vɪnjərd] s vignoble m, vigne f

vintage ['vɪntɪdʒ] s vendange f; (year)
année f, cru m; (coll) classe f, catégorie f

vin'tage wine' s bon cru m

vin'tage year' s grande année f

vintner ['vɪntnər] s négociant m en
vins; (person who makes wine) vigne-
ron m

vinyl ['vaɪnɪl], ['vɪnɪl] s vinyle m

viola [vɪ'olə], ['vaɪ•ələ] s alto m

violate ['vaɪ•ə ‚let] tr violer

violation [‚vaɪ•ə'leʃən] s violation f

violence ['vaɪ•ələns] s violence f

violent ['vaɪ•ələnt] adj violent

violet ['vaɪ•əlɪt] adj violet || s (color)
violet m; (bot) violette f

violin [‚vaɪ•ə'lɪn] s violon m

violinist [‚vaɪ•ə'lɪnɪst] s violoniste mf

violoncel•lo [‚vaɪ•ələn'tʃɛlo], [‚vi•ələn-
't∫elo] s (pl -los) violoncelle m

viper ['vaɪpər] s vipère f

vira•go [vɪ'rego] s (pl -goes or -gos)
mégère f

virgin ['vʌrdʒɪn] adj vierge || s vierge
f; (male virgin) puceau m

Virgin'ia creep'er [vər'dʒɪnɪ•ə] s vigne
f vierge

virginity [vər'dʒɪnɪtɪ] s virginité f
virility [vɪ'rɪlɪtɪ] s virilité f
virology [vaɪ'rɑlədʒɪ] s virologie f
virtual ['vʌrtʃu-əl] adj véritable, effectif; (mech, opt, phys) virtuel
virtue ['vʌrtʃu] s vertu f; mérite m, avantage m
virtuosi•ty [,vʌrtʃu'ɑsɪtɪ] s (pl -ties) virtuosité f
virtuo•so [,vʌrtʃu'oso] s (pl -sos or -si [si]) virtuose mf
virtuous ['vʌrtʃu-əs] adj vertueux
virulence ['vɪrjələns] s virulence f
virulent ['vɪrjələnt] adj virulent
virus ['vaɪrəs] s virus m
visa ['vizə] s visa m || tr viser
visage ['vɪzɪdʒ] s visage m
vis-à-vis [,vizə'vi] adj face à face || s & adv vis-à-vis m || prep vis-à-vis de, vis-à-vis
viscera ['vɪsərə] spl viscères mpl
viscount ['vaɪkaʊnt] s vicomte m
viscountess ['vaɪkaʊntɪs] s vicomtesse f
viscous ['vɪskəs] adj visqueux
vise [vaɪs] s étau m
visible ['vɪzɪbəl] adj visible
vision ['vɪʒən] s vision f
visionar•y ['vɪʒə,nerɪ] adj visionnaire || s (pl -ies) visionnaire mf
visit ['vɪzɪt] s visite f || tr visiter; (e.g., a person) rendre visite à || intr faire des visites
visitation [,vɪzɪ'teʃən] s visite f; justice f du ciel; clémence f du ciel; (e.g., in a séance) apparition f; Visitation (eccl) Visitation f
vis'iting card' s carte f de visite
vis'iting hours' spl heures fpl de visite
vis'iting nurse' s infirmière f visiteuse
vis'iting profes'sor s visiting m
visitor ['vɪzɪtər] s visiteur m
visor ['vaɪzər] s visière f
vista ['vɪstə] s perspective f
visual ['vɪʒu-əl] adj visuel
visualize ['vɪʒu-ə,laɪz] tr (in one's mind) se faire une image mentale de, se représenter; (to make visible) visualiser
vital ['vaɪtəl] adj vital || vitals spl organes mpl vitaux
vitality [vaɪ'tælɪtɪ] s vitalité f
vitalize ['vaɪtə,laɪz] tr vitaliser
vitamin ['vaɪtəmɪn] s vitamine f
vitiate ['vɪʃɪ,et] tr vicier
vitreous ['vɪtrɪ-əs] adj vitreux
vitriolic [,vɪtrɪ'ɑlɪk] adj (chem) vitriolique; (fig) trempé dans du vitriol
vituperate [vaɪ't(j)upə,ret] tr vitupérer
viva ['vivə] s vivat m || interj vive!
vivacious [vɪ've·əs], [vaɪ've·əs] adj vif, animé
vivaci•ty [vɪ'væsɪtɪ], [vaɪ'væsɪtɪ] s (pl -ties) vivacité f
viva voce ['vaɪvə'vosɪ] adv de vive voix
vivid ['vɪvɪd] adj vif; (description) vivant; (recollection) vivace
vivi•fy ['vɪvɪ,faɪ] v (pret & pp -fied) tr vivifier
vivisection [,vɪvɪ'sɛkʃən] s vivisection f

vixen ['vɪksən] s mégère f; (zool) renarde f
viz. abbr (Lat: videlicet namely, to wit) c.-à-d., à savoir
vizier [vɪ'zɪr], ['vɪzjər] s vizir m
vocabular•y [vo'kæbjə,lerɪ] s (pl -ies) vocabulaire m
vocal ['vokəl] adj vocal; (inclined to express oneself freely) communicatif, démonstratif
vocalist ['vokəlɪst] s chanteur m
vocalize ['vokə,laɪz] tr vocaliser || intr vocaliser; (phonet) se vocaliser
vocation [vo'keʃən] s vocation f; profession f, métier m
voca'tional guid'ance [vo'keʃənəl] s orientation f professionnelle
voca'tional school' s école f professionnelle
vocative ['vakətɪv] s vocatif m
vociferate [vo'sɪfə,ret] intr vociférer
vociferous [vo'sɪfərəs] adj vociférant, criard
vogue [vog] s vogue f; in vogue en vogue
voice [vɔɪs] s voix f; in a loud voice à voix haute; in a low voice à voix basse; with one voice unanimement || tr exprimer; (a consonant) voiser, sonoriser || intr se voiser
voiced adj (phonet) voisé, sonore
voiceless ['vɔɪslɪs] adj sans voix; (consonant) sourd
void [vɔɪd] adj vide; (law) nul; void of dénué de || s vide m || tr vider; (the bowels) évacuer; (law) rendre nul || intr évacuer, excréter
voile [vɔɪl] s voile m
volatile ['valətɪl] adj (solvent) volatil; (disposition) volage; (temper) vif
volatilize ['valətə,laɪz] tr volatiliser || intr se volatiliser
volcanic [val'kænɪk] adj volcanique
volca•no [val'keno] s (pl -noes or -nos) volcan m
volition [və'lɪʃən] s volition f, volonté f; of one's own volition de son propre gré
volley ['valɪ] s volée f || tr lancer à la volée; (sports) reprendre de volée || intr lancer une volée
vol'ley-ball' s volley-ball m
volplane ['val,plen] s vol m plané || intr descendre en vol plané
volt [volt] s volt m
voltage ['voltɪdʒ] s voltage m; high voltage haute tension f
volt'age drop' s perte f de charge
volte-face [volt'fas] s volte-face f
volt'me'ter s voltmètre m
voluble ['valjəbəl] adj volubile
volume ['valjəm] s volume m; to speak volumes en dire long
vol'ume num'ber s tomaison f
voluminous [və'lumɪnəs] adj volumineux
voluntar•y ['valən,terɪ] adj volontaire || s (pl -ies) (mus) morceau m d'orgue improvisé
volunteer [,valən'tɪr] adj & s volontaire mf || tr offrir volontairement ||

intr (mil) s'engager; **to volunteer to** + *inf* s'offrir à + *inf*

voluptuar·y [və'lʌptʃʊ͵ɛri] *adj* voluptuaire ‖ *s* (*pl* **-ies**) voluptueux *m*

voluptuous [və'lʌptʃʊ·əs] *adj* voluptueux

vomit ['vɑmɪt] *s* vomissure *f* ‖ *tr* & *intr* vomir

voodoo ['vudu] *adj* & *s* vaudou *m*

voracious [və're/əs] *adj* vorace

voraci·ty [və'ræsɪti] *s* (*pl* **-ties**) voracité *f*

vor·tex ['vɔrteks] *s* (*pl* **-texes** or **-tices** [tɪ͵siz]) vortex *m*, tourbillon *m*

vota·ry ['votəri] *s* (*pl* **-ries**) fidèle *mf*

vote [vot] *s* vote *m*; **by popular vote** au suffrage universel; **to put to the vote** mettre aux voix; **to tally the votes** dépouiller le scrutin; **vote by show of hands** vote à main levée ‖ *tr* voter; **to vote down** repousser; **to vote in** élire ‖ *intr* voter; **to vote for** voter; **to vote on** passer au vote

voter ['votər] *s* votant *m*, électeur *m*

vot′ing booth′ *s* isoloir *m*

vot′ing machine′ *s* machine *f* électorale

votive ['votɪv] *adj* votif

vouch [vautʃ] *tr* affirmer, garantir ‖ *intr*—**to vouch for** répondre de

voucher ['vautʃər] *s* garant *m*; (*certificate*) récépissé *m*, pièce *f* comptable

vouch·safe′ *tr* octroyer ‖ *intr*—**to vouchsafe to** + *inf* daigner + *inf*

vow [vau] *s* vœu *m*; **to take vows** entrer en religion ‖ *tr* (*e.g.*, *revenge*) jurer ‖ *intr* faire un vœu; **to vow to** faire vœu de

vowel ['vau·əl] *s* voyelle *f*

voyage ['vɔɪ·ɪdʒ] *s* (*by air or sea*) traversée *f*; (*any journey*) voyage *m* ‖ *tr* traverser ‖ *intr* voyager

voyager ['vɔɪ·ɪdʒər] *s* voyageur *m*

vs. *abbr* (**versus**) contre

vulcanize ['vʌlkə͵naɪz] *tr* vulcaniser

vulgar ['vʌlgər] *adj* grossier; (*popular, common; vernacular*) vulgaire

vulgari·ty [vʌl'gærɪti] *s* (*pl* **-ties**) grossièreté *f*, vulgarité *f*

Vul′gar Lat′in *s* latin *m* vulgaire

vulnerable ['vʌlnərəbəl] *adj* vulnérable

vulture ['vʌltʃər] *s* vautour *m*

W

W, w ['dʌbəl͵ju] *s* XXIIIᵉ lettre de l'alphabet

wad [wɑd] *s* (*of cotton*) tampon *m*; (*of papers*) liasse *f*; (*in a gun*) bourre *f* ‖ *v* (*pret* & *pp* **wadded**; *ger* **wadding**) *tr* bourrer

waddle ['wɑdəl] *s* dandinement *m* ‖ *intr* se dandiner

wade [wed] *tr* traverser à gué ‖ *intr* marcher dans l'eau, patauger; **to wade into** (coll) s'attaquer à; **to wade through** (coll) avancer péniblement dans

wad′ing bird′ *s* (orn) échassier *m*

wafer ['wefər] *s* (*thin, crisp cake*) gaufrette *f*; (*pill*) cachet *m*; (*for sealing letters*) pain *m* à cacheter; (eccl) hostie *f*

waffle ['wɑfəl] *s* gaufre *f*

waf′fle i′ron *s* gaufrier *m*

waft [wæft], [wɑft] *tr* porter; (*a kiss*) envoyer ‖ *intr* flotter

wag [wæg] *s* (*of head*) hochement *m*; (*of tail*) frétillement *m*; (*jester*) farceur *m* ‖ *v* (*pret* & *pp* **wagged**; *ger* **wagging**) *tr* (*the head*) hocher; (*the tail*) remuer ‖ *intr* frétiller

wage [wedʒ] *s* salaire *m*; **wages** gages *mpl*, salaire *m*; (fig) salaire, récompense *f* ‖ *tr*—**to wage war** faire la guerre

wage′ earn′er [͵ʌrnər] *s* salarié *m*

wage′-price′ freeze′ *s* blocage *m* des prix et des salaires

wager ['wedʒər] *s* pari *m*; **to lay a wager** faire un pari ‖ *tr* & *intr* parier

wage′ work′er *s* salarié *m*

waggish ['wægɪʃ] *adj* plaisant, facétieux

wagon ['wægən] *s* charrette *f*; (*Conestoga wagon*; *plaything*) chariot *m*; (mil) fourgon *m*; **to be on the wagon** (slang) s'abstenir de boissons alcooliques

wag′tail′ *s* hochequeue *m*, bergeronnette *f*

waif [wef] *s* (*foundling*) enfant *m* trouvé; *animal m* égaré or abandonné; (*stray child*) voyou *m*

wail [wel] *s* lamentation *f*, plainte *f* ‖ *intr* se lamenter, gémir

wain·scot ['wenskət], ['wenskɑt] *s* lambris *m* ‖ *v* (*pret* & *pp* **-scoted** or **-scotted**; *ger* **-scoting** or **-scotting**) *tr* lambrisser

waist [west] *s* (*of human body*; *corresponding part of garment*) taille *f*, ceinture *f*; (*garment*) corsage *m*, blouse *f*

waist′band′ *s* ceinture *f*

waist′cloth′ *s* pagne *m*

waistcoat ['west͵kot], ['weskət] *s* gilet *m*

waist′-deep′ *adj* jusqu'à la ceinture

waist′line′ *s* taille *f*, ceinture *f*; **to keep** or **watch one's waistline** garder or soigner sa ligne

wait [wet] *s* attente *f*; **to lie in wait for** guetter ‖ *tr*—**to wait one's turn** attendre son tour ‖ *intr* attendre; **to wait for** attendre; **to wait on** (*customers*; *dinner guests*) servir

wait′-and-see′ pol′icy *s* attentisme *m*

waiter ['wetər] *s* garçon *m*; (*tray*) plateau *m*

wait′ing list′ *s* liste *f* d'attente

wait'ing room' s salle f d'attente; (of a doctor) antichambre f.

waitress ['wetrɪs] s serveuse f; **waitress!** mademoiselle!

waive [wev] tr renoncer (with dat); (to defer) différer

waiver ['wevər] s renonciation f, abandon m

wake [wek] s (watch by the body of a dead person) veillée f mortuaire; (of a boat or other moving object) sillage m; **in the wake of** dans le sillage de, à la suite de || v (pret waked or woke [wok]; pp waked) tr réveiller || intr —**to wake to** se rendre compte de; **to wake up** se réveiller

wakeful ['wekfəl] adj éveillé

wakefulness ['wekfəlnɪs] s veille f

waken ['wekən] tr éveiller, réveiller || intr s'éveiller, se réveiller

wale [wel] s zébrure f || tr zébrer

Wales [welz] s le pays de Galles

walk [wok] s (act) promenade f; (distance) marche f; (way of walking, bearing) démarche f; (of a garden) allée f; (calling) métier m; **to fall into a walk** (said of horse) se mettre au pas; **to go for a walk** faire une promenade || tr promener; (a horse) promener au pas || intr aller à pied, marcher; (to stroll) se promener; **to walk away** s'en aller à pied; **to walk off with** (a prize) gagner; (a stolen object) décamper avec; **to walk out** sortir, partir subitement; (to go on strike) se mettre en grève; **to walk out on** abandonner; quitter en colère

walk'away' s (coll) victoire f facile

walker ['wokər] s marcheur m, promeneur m; (pedestrian) piéton m; (gocart) chariot m d'enfant

walkie-talkie ['woki'toki] s (rad) émetteur-récepteur m portatif, parle-en-marche m

walk'ing pa'pers spl—**to give s.o. his walking papers** (coll) congédier qn

walk'ing stick' s canne f

walk'-on' s (actor) figurant m, comparse mf; (role) figuration f

walk'out' s (coll) grève f improvisée

walk'o'ver s (coll) victoire f dans un fauteuil

walk'-up' s appartement m sans ascenseur

wall [wol] s mur m; (between rooms; of a pipe, etc.) paroi f; (of a fortification) muraille f; **to go to the wall** succomber; perdre la partie || tr entourer de murs; **to wall up** murer

wall'board' s panneau m or carreau m de revêtement

wall' clock' s pendule f murale

wallet ['walɪt] s portefeuille m

wall'flow'er s (bot) ravenelle f, giroflée f; **to be a wallflower** (coll) faire tapisserie

wall' lamp' s applique f

wall' map' s carte f murale

Walloon [wɑ'lun] adj wallon || s (dialect) wallon m; (person) Wallon m

wallop ['waləp] s (coll) coup m, gnon m; **with a wallop** (fig) à grand fracas || tr (coll) tanner le cuir à, rosser; (a ball) (coll) frapper raide; (to defeat) (coll) battre

wallow ['walo] s souille f || intr se vautrer; (e.g., in wealth) nager

wall'pa'per s papier m peint || tr tapisser

walnut ['wolnət] s noix f; (tree and wood) noyer m

walrus ['wolrəs], ['wolrəs] s morse m

Walter ['woltər] s Gautier m

waltz [wolts] s valse f || tr & intr valser

wan [wan] adj (comp wanner; super wannest) pâle, blême; (weak) faible

wand [wand] s baguette f; (emblem of authority) bâton m, verge f

wander ['wandər] tr vagabonder sur, parcourir || intr errer, vaguer; (said of one's mind) vagabonder

wanderer ['wandərər] s vagabond m

wan'der-lust' s manie f des voyages, bougeotte f

wane [wen] s déclin m; (of moon) décours m || intr décliner; (said of moon) décroître

wangle ['wæŋgəl] tr (to obtain by scheming) (coll) resquiller; (accounts) (coll) cuisiner; (e.g., a leave of absence) (coll) carotter; **to wangle one's way out of** (coll) se débrouiller de || intr (coll) pratiquer le système D

want [want], [wont] s (need; misery) besoin m; (lack) manque m; **for want of** faute de, à défaut de; **to be in want** être dans la gêne || tr vouloir; (to need) avoir besoin de; **to want s.o. to** + inf vouloir que qn + subj; **to want to** + inf avoir envie de + inf, vouloir + inf || intr être dans le besoin; **to be wanting** manquer

want' ads' spl petites annonces fpl

wanton ['wantən] adj déréglé; (e.g., cruelty) gratuit; (e.g., child) espiègle; (e.g., woman) impudique

war [wor] s guerre f; **to go to war** se mettre en guerre; (as a soldier) aller à la guerre; **to wage war** faire la guerre || v (pret & pp warred; ger warring) intr faire la guerre; **to war on** faire la guerre contre

warble ['worbəl] s gazouillement m || intr gazouiller

warbler ['worblər] s (orn) fauvette f

war' cloud' s menace f de guerre

war' correspon'dent s correspondant m de guerre

war' cry' s (pl cries) cri m de guerre

ward [word] s (person, usually a minor under protection of another) pupille mf; (guardianship) tutelle f; (of a city) circonscription f électorale, quartier m; (of a hospital) salle f; (of a lock) gardes fpl || tr—**to ward off** parer

war' dance' s danse f guerrière

warden ['wordən] s gardien m; (of a jail) directeur m; (of a church) marguillier m; (gamekeeper) garde-chasse m

ward' heel'er s politicailleur m servile

ward'robe' s garde-robe f

ward′robe trunk′ s malle-armoire f
ward′room′ s (nav) carré m des officiers
ware [wer] s faïence f; **wares** articles mpl de vente, marchandises fpl
ware′house′ s entrepôt m
ware′house′man s (pl **-men**) garde-magasin m, magasinier m
war′fare′ s guerre f
war′head′ s charge f creuse
war′-horse′ s cheval m de bataille; (coll) vétéran m
warily ['werɪli] adv prudemment
war′like′ adj guerrier
war′ loan′ s emprunt m de guerre
war′ lord′ s seigneur m de la guerre
warm [wɔrm] adj chaud; (welcome, thanks, friend, etc.) chaleureux; (heart) généreux; **it is warm** (said of weather) il fait chaud; **to be warm** (said of person) avoir chaud; **to keep s.th. warm** tenir q.ch. au chaud; **you're getting warm!** (you've almost found it!) vous brûlez! || tr chauffer, faire chauffer; **to warm up** réchauffer || intr se réchauffer; **to warm up** se réchauffer, chauffer, se chauffer; (said of speaker, discussion, etc.) s'animer, s'échauffer
warm′-blood′ed adj passionné, ardent; (animals) à sang chaud
war′ memor′ial s monument m aux morts de la guerre
warmer ['wɔrmər] s (culin) réchaud m
warm′-heart′ed adj au cœur généreux
warm′ing pan′ s bassinoire f
warmonger ['wɔr,mʌŋgər] s belliciste mf
war′ moth′er s marraine f de guerre
warmth [wɔrmθ] s chaleur f
warm′-up′ s exercices mpl d'assouplissement; mise f en condition
warn [wɔrn] tr prévenir; **to warn s.o. to** avertir qn de
warning ['wɔrnɪŋ] s avertissement m; **without warning** par surprise
warn′ing shot′ s coup m de semence
war′ of attri′tion s guerre f d'usure
warp [wɔrp] s (of a fabric) chaîne f; (of a board) gauchissement m; (naut) touée f || tr gauchir; (the mind, judgment, etc.) fausser; (naut) touer || intr se gauchir; (naut) se touer
war′path′ s—**to be on the warpath** être sur le sentier de la guerre; (to be out of sorts) (coll) être d'une humeur de dogue
war′plane′ s avion m de guerre
warrant ['wɔrənt], ['wɔrənt] s garantie f; certificat m; (for arrest) mandat m d'arrêt || tr garantir; certifier; justifier
war′rant of′ficer s (mil) sous-officier m breveté; (nav) premier maître m
warran·ty ['wɔrənti], ['wɔrənti] s (pl **-ties**) garantie f; autorisation f
warren ['wɔrən], ['wɔrən] s garenne f
warrior ['wɔrjər], ['wɔrjər] s guerrier m
Warsaw ['wɔrsə] s Varsovie f
war′ship′ s navire m de guerre

wart [wɔrt] s verrue f
war′time′ s temps m de guerre
war′-torn′ adj dévasté par la guerre
war·y ['weri] adj (comp **-ier**; super **-iest**) prudent, avisé
wash [waʃ], [wɔʃ] s lavage m; (clothes washed or to be washed) lessive f; (dirty water) lavure f; (place where the surf breaks; broken water behind a moving ship) remous m; (aer) souffle m || tr laver; (one's hands, face, etc.) se laver; (dishes, laundry, etc.) faire; (e.g., a seacoast) baigner; **to wash away** enlever; (e.g., a bank) affouiller, ronger || intr se laver; faire la lessive
washable ['waʃəbəl], ['wɔʃəbəl] adj lavable
wash′-and-wear′ adj de repassage superflu, de séchage rapide
wash′ba′sin s (basin) cuvette f; (fixture) lavabo m
wash′bas′ket s corbeille f à linge
wash′board′ s planche f à laver
wash′bowl′ s (basin) cuvette f; (fixture) lavabo m
wash′cloth′ s gant m de toilette
wash′day′ s jour m de lessive
washed′-out′ adj délavé, déteint; (coll) flapi, vanné
washed′-up′ adj (coll) hors de combat, ruiné
washer ['waʃər], ['wɔʃər] s laveur m; (machine) laveuse f, lessiveuse f; (ring of metal) rondelle f; (ring of rubber) rondelle de robinet
wash′er·wom′an s (pl **-wom′en**) blanchisseuse f
wash′ goods′ spl tissus mpl grand teint
washing ['waʃɪŋ], ['wɔʃɪŋ] s lavage m; (act of washing clothes) blanchissage m; (clothes washed or to be washed) lessive f; **washings** lavures fpl
wash′ing machine′ s machine f à laver, laveuse f automatique
wash′ing so′da s cristaux mpl de soude
wash′out′ s affouillement m; (person) (coll) raté m; **to be a washout** (coll) faire fiasco, faire four
wash′rag′ s gant m de toilette, torchon m
wash′room′ s cabinet m de toilette, lavabo m
wash′ sale′ s (com) lavage m des titres
wash′stand′ s lavabo m
wash′tub′ s baquet m, cuvier m
wash′ wa′ter s lavure f
wasp [wasp] s guêpe f
wasp′ waist′ s taille f de guêpe
waste [west] adj (land) inculte; (material) de rebut || s gaspillage m; (garbage) déchets mpl; (wild region) région f inculte; (of time) perte f; (for wiping machinery) chiffons mpl de nettoyage, effiloche f de coton; **to lay waste** dévaster; **wastes** déchets; excrément m || tr gaspiller, perdre || intr—**to waste away** dépérir, maigrir
waste′bas′ket s corbeille f à papier
wasteful ['westfəl] adj gaspilleur
waste′pa′per s papier m de rebut

waste′ pipe′ s tuyau m d'écoulement, vidange f

waste′ prod′ucts spl déchets mpl

wastrel ['westrəl] s gaspilleur m, prodigue mf

watch [wɑtʃ] s montre f; (lookout) garde f, guet m; (naut) quart m; **to be on the watch for** guetter; **to be on watch** (naut) être de quart; **to keep watch over** surveiller || tr (to look at) observer; (to oversee) surveiller || intr être aux aguets; (to keep awake) veiller; **to watch for** guetter; **to watch out** faire attention; **to watch out for** faire attention à; **to watch over** surveiller; **watch out!** attention!, gare!

watch′case′ s boîtier m de montre

watch′ chain′ s chaîne f de montre

watch′ charm′ s breloque f

watch′ crys′tal s verre m de montre

watch′dog′ s chien m de garde; gardien m vigilant

watch′dog′ commit′tee s comité m de surveillance

watchful ['wɑtʃfəl] adj vigilant

watchfulness ['wɑtʃfəlnɪs] s vigilance f

watch′mak′er s horloger m

watch′man s (pl -men) gardien m

watch′ night′ s réveillon m du jour de l'an

watch′ pock′et s gousset m

watch′ strap′ s bracelet m d'une montre

watch′tow′er s tour f de guet

watch′word′ s mot m d'ordre, mot de passe; devise f

water ['wɔtər], ['wɑtər] s eau f; **of the first water** de premier ordre; (diamond) de première eau; **to back water** (naut) culer; reculer; **to be in hot water** (coll) être dans le pétrin; **to fish in troubled waters** pêcher en eau trouble; **to hold water** (coll) tenir debout, être bien fondé; **to make water** (to urinate) uriner; (naut) faire eau; **to pour** or **throw cold water on** (fig) jeter une douche froide sur, refroidir; **to swim under water** nager entre deux eaux; **to tread water** nager debout || tr (e.g., plants) arroser; (horses, cattle, etc.) abreuver; (wine) couper; **to water down** atténuer || intr (said of horses, cattle, etc.) s'abreuver; (said of locomotive, ship, etc.) faire de l'eau; (said of eyes) se mouiller, larmoyer

wa′ter buf′fa·lo s (pl -loes or -los) buffle m

wa′ter car′rier s porteur m d'eau

wa′ter clos′et s water-closet m, waters mpl

wa′ter·col′or s aquarelle f

wa′ter-cooled′ adj à refroidissement d'eau

wa′ter·course′ s cours m d'eau; (of a stream) lit m

wa′ter·cress′ s cresson m de fontaine

wa′ter cure′ s cure f des eaux

wa′ter·fall′ s chute f d'eau

wa′ter·front′ s terrain m sur la rive

wa′ter gap′ s percée f, trouée f, gorge f

wa′ter ham′mer s (in pipe) coup m de bélier

wa′ter heat′er s chauffe-eau m, chauffe-bain m

wa′ter ice′ s boisson f à demi glacée

wa′tering can′ s arrosoir m

wa′tering place′ s (for cattle) abreuvoir m; (for tourists) ville f d'eau

wa′tering pot′ s arrosoir m

wa′tering trough′ s abreuvoir m

wa′ter jack′et s chemise f d'eau

wa′ter lil′y s nénuphar m

wa′ter line′ s ligne f de flottaison; niveau m de l'eau

wa′ter-logged′ adj détrempé

wa′ter main′ s conduite f principale

wa′ter·mark′ s (in paper) filigrane m; (naut) laisse f

wa′ter·mel′on s pastèque f, melon m d'eau

wa′ter me′ter s compteur m à eau

wa′ter pipe′ s conduite f d'eau

wa′ter po′lo s water-polo m

wa′ter pow′er s force f hydraulique, houille f blanche

wa′ter·proof′ adj & s imperméable m

wa′ter rights′ spl droits mpl de captation d'eau, droits d'irrigation

wa′ter·shed′ s ligne f de partage des eaux

wa′ter ski′ing s ski m nautique

wa′ter span′iel s (zool) barbet m

wa′ter·spout′ s descente f d'eau, gouttière f; (funnel of wet air) trombe f

wa′ter-supply sys′tem s service m des eaux; réseau m de conduites d'eau

wa′ter ta′ble s (geol) nappe f phréatique

wa′ter·tight′ adj étanche; (argument) inattaquable; (law) sans clause échappatoire

wa′ter tow′er s château m d'eau

wa′ter wag′on s—**to be on the water wagon** (coll) s'abstenir de boissons alcooliques

wa′ter·way′ s voie f navigable

wa′ter wheel′ s roue f hydraulique; roue à aubes or à palettes; roue-turbine f

wa′ter wings′ spl flotteur m de natation

wa′ter·works′ s (system) canalisations fpl d'eau; (pumping station) usine f de distribution des eaux

watery ['wɔtəri], ['wɑtəri] adj aqueux; (eyes) larmoyant; (food) insipide, fade

watt [wɑt] s watt m

wattage ['wɑtɪdʒ] s puissance f en watts

watt′-hour′ s (pl **watt-hours**) watt-heure m

wattle ['wɑtəl] s (of bird) caroncule f; (of fish) barbillon m

watt′me′ter s wattmètre m

wave [wev] s onde f, vague f; (in hair) ondulation f, geste m de la main; (of heat or cold; of people; of the future) vague f; (phys) onde || tr (a handkerchief) agiter; (the hair) onduler; (a hat, newspaper, cane) brandir; **to wave aside** écarter d'un geste;

to wave good-bye faire un signe d'adieu; **to wave one's hand** faire un geste de la main || *intr* s'agiter; (*said of a flag*) ondoyer; **to wave to** faire signe à

wave′length′ s longueur *f* d'onde

wave′ mo′tion s mouvement *m* ondulatoire

waver ['wevər] *intr* vaciller

wav•y ['wevi] *adj* (*comp* **-ier**; *super* **-iest**) onduleux, ondoyant; (*hair*; *road surface*) ondulé; (*line*) tremblé, onduleux

wax [wæks] s cire *f* || *tr* cirer || *intr*— **to wax and wane** croître et décroître; **to wax indignant** s'indigner

wax′ bean′ s haricot *m* beurre

wax′ pa′per s papier *m* paraffiné

wax′ ta′per s allumette-bougie *f*

wax′wing′ s (orn) jaseur *m*

wax′works′ s musée *m* de cire

way [we] s voie *f*; (*road*) chemin *m*; (*direction*) côté *m*, sens *m*; (*manner*) façon *f*, manière *f*; (*means*) moyen *m*; (*habit, custom*) manière, habitude *f*, usage *m*; **across the way** en face; **all the way** jusqu'au bout; **by the way** à propos; **by way of** par; comme; **get out of the way!** ôter-vous de là!; **in a way** en un certain sens; **in every way** à tous les égards; **in my (his, etc.) own way** à ma (sa, etc.) façon or manière; **in no way** en aucune façon; **in some ways** par certains côtés; **in such a way that** de sorte que; **in that way** de la sorte; **in this way** de cette façon; **on the way** chemin faisant; **on the way to** en route pour; **out of the way** écarté; **that way** par là; **the wrong way** le mauvais sens, la mauvaise route; (*the wrong manner*) la mauvaise façon; (*when brushing hair*) à contre-poil; **this way** par ici; **to be in the way** être encombrant; **to feel one's way** avancer à tâtons; **to get out of the way** s'écarter; **to get (*s.th.* or *s.o.*) out of the way** se débarrasser de (*q.ch.* or *qn*); **to give way** céder; **to go one's own way** faire bande à part; **to go one's way** passer son chemin; **to go out of one's way** faire un détour; (fig) se déranger; **to have one's way** avoir le dernier mot, l'emporter; **to keep out of s.o.'s way** se tenir à l'écart de qn; **to know one's way around** connaître son affaire, être à la coule; **to lead the way** montrer le chemin; **to make one's way** se frayer un chemin; **to make way for** faire place à; **to mend one's ways** s'amender; **to see one's way to** trouver moyen de; **to stand in the way of** barrer le chemin à; **under way** en marche, en cours; **way down** descente *f*; **way in** entrée *f*; **way out** sortie *f*; **ways** (*for launching a ship*) couette *f*, anguilles *fpl*; **way through** passage *m*; **way up** montée *f*; **which way?** par où?

way′bill′ s feuille *f* de route, lettre *f* de voiture

wayfarer ['we ˌfɛrər] s voyageur *m*, vagabond *m*

way′lay′ *v* (*pret & pp* **-laid**) *tr* embusquer; (*to buttonhole*) arrêter au passage

way′ of life′ s manière *f* de vivre, genre *m* de vie, train *m* de vie

way′side′ s bord *m* de la route; **to fall by the wayside** rester en chemin

wayward ['wewərd] *adj* capricieux; rebelle

we [wi] *pron pers* nous §85, §87; nous autres, e.g., **we Americans** nous autres américains

weak [wik] *adj* faible

weaken ['wikən] *tr* affaiblir || *intr* faiblir, s'affaiblir

weakling ['wiklɪŋ] s chétif *m*, malingre *mf*; (*in character*) mou *m*

weak′-mind′ed *adj* irrésolu, d'esprit faible; (*feeble-minded*) débile

weakness ['wiknɪs] s faiblesse *f*

weal [wil] s papule *f*; (*archaic*) bien *m*

wealth [wɛlθ] s richesse *f*

wealth•y ['wɛlθi] *adj* (*comp* **-ier**; *super* **-iest**) riche, opulent

wean [win] *tr* sevrer; **to wean away from** détacher de

weapon ['wepən] s arme *f*

weaponry ['wepənrɪ] s armement *m*

wear [wɛr] s (*use*) usage *m*; (*wasting away from use*) usure *f*; (*clothing*) vêtements *mpl*, articles *mpl* d'habillement; **for evening wear** pour le soir; **for everyday wear** pour tous les jours || *v* (*pret* **wore** [wor]; *pp* **worn** [worn]) *tr* porter; (*to put on*) mettre; **to wear down** or **out** user; (*e.g., one's patience*) épuiser || *intr* s'user; **to wear off** s'effacer; **to wear on** s'écouler, s'avancer; **to wear out** s'user; **to wear well** durer

wearable ['wɛrəbəl] *adj* mettable

wear′ and tear′ [tɛr] s usure *f*

weariness ['wɪrɪnɪs] s lassitude *f*, fatigue *f*; ennui *m*

wear′ing appar′el ['wɛrɪŋ] s vêtements *mpl*, habits *mpl*

wearisome ['wɪrɪsəm] *adj* lassant, ennuyeux

wea•ry ['wɪri] *adj* (*comp* **-rier**; *super* **-riest**) las || *v* (*pret & pp* **-ried**) *tr* lasser || *intr* se lasser

weasel ['wizəl] s (zool) belette *f*; (slang) mouchard *m*

wea′sel words′ *spl* mots *mpl* ambigus

weather ['wɛðər] s temps *m*; **to be under the weather** (coll) se sentir patraque; (*from drinking*) (coll) avoir mal aux cheveux; **what's the weather like?** quel temps fait-il? || *tr* altérer; (*e.g., difficulties*) survivre à, étaler || *intr* s'altérer

weath′er balloon′ s ballon *m* atmosphérique

weath′er-beat′en *adj* usé par les intempéries

weath′er bu′reau s bureau *m* météorologique, météo *f*

weath′er-cock′ s girouette *f*; (fig) girouette, caméléon *m*

weath′er fore′cast *s* bulletin *m* météorologique

weath′er fore′casting *s* prévision *f* du temps

weath′er·man′ *s* (*pl* -men′) météorologue *mf*, météorologiste *mf*

weath′er report′ *s* bulletin *m* de la météo

weath′er strip′ping *s* bourrelet *m*

weath′er vane′ *s* girouette *f*

weave [wiv] *s* armure *f* ‖ *v* (*pret* **wove** [wov] or **weaved**; *pp* **wove** or **woven** [′wovən]) *tr* tisser; **to weave one's way through** se faufiler à travers, se faufiler entre ‖ *intr* tisser; serpenter, zigzaguer

weaver [′wivər] *s* tisserand *m*

web [wɛb] *s* (*piece of cloth*) tissu *m*; (*roll of newsprint*) rouleau *m*; (*of spider*) toile *f*; (*between toes of birds and other animals*) palmure *f*; (*of an iron rail*) âme *f*; (fig) trame *f*

web′-foot′ed *adj* palmé, palmipède

wed [wɛd] *v* (*pret & pp* **wed** or **wedded**; *ger* **wedding**) *tr* (*to join in wedlock*) marier; (*to take in marriage*) épouser ‖ *intr* épouser, se marier

wedding [′wɛdɪŋ] *adj* nuptial ‖ *s* mariage *m*, noces *fpl*

wed′ding ban′quet *s* repas *m* de noce

wed′ding cake′ *s* gâteau *m* de mariage

wed′ding cer′emo·ny *s* (*pl* -nies) cérémonie *f* nuptiale

wed′ding day′ *s* jour *m* des noces; anniversaire *m* du mariage

wed′ding dress′ *s* robe *f* nuptiale, robe de noce

wed′ding march′ *s* marche *f* nuptiale

wed′ding night′ *s* nuit *f* de noces

wed′ding pres′ent *s* cadeau *m* de mariage; **wedding presents** corbeille *f* de mariage

wed′ding ring′ *s* anneau *m* nuptial, alliance *f*

wedge [wɛdʒ] *s* coin *m* ‖ *tr* coincer

wedlock [′wɛdlɑk] *s* mariage *m*

Wednesday [′wɛnzdi] *s* mercredi *m*

wee [wi] *adj* tout petit

weed [wid] *s* mauvaise herbe *f*; **the weed** (coll) le tabac; **weeds** vêtements *mpl* de deuil ‖ *tr & intr* désherber, sarcler; **to weed out** éliminer, extirper

weed′ing hoe′ *s* sarcloir *m*

weed′ kill′er *s* herbicide *m*

week [wik] *s* semaine *f*; **a week from today** d'aujourd'hui en huit; **week in week out** d'un bout de la semaine à l'autre

week′day′ *s* jour *m* de semaine, jour *f* ouvrable

week′end′ *s* fin *f* de semaine, week-end *m* ‖ *intr* passer le week-end

week·ly [′wikli] *adj* hebdomadaire ‖ *s* (*pl* -lies) hebdomadaire *m* ‖ *adv* tous les huit jours

weep [wip] *v* (*pret & pp* **wept** [wɛpt]) *tr* pleurer ‖ *intr* pleurer; (*to drip*) suinter; **to weep for** pleurer; (*joy*) pleurer de

weep′ing wil′low *s* saule *m* pleureur

weep·y [′wipi] *adj* (*comp* -ier; *super* -iest) (coll) pleurnicheur

weevil [′wivəl] *s* charançon *m*

weft [wɛft] *s* (*yarns running across warp*) trame *f*; (*fabric*) tissu *m*

weigh [we] *tr* peser; (*anchor*) lever; **to weigh down** faire pencher; **to weigh in one's hand** soupeser ‖ *intr* peser; **to weigh heavily with** avoir du poids auprès de; **to weigh in** (sports) se faire peser

weight [wet] *s* poids *m*; **to gain weight** prendre du poids; **to lift weights** faire des haltères; **to lose weight** perdre du poids; **to throw one's weight around** (coll) s'imposer ‖ *tr* charger; (*statistically*) pondérer; **to weight down** alourdir

weightless [′wetlɪs] *adj* sans pesanteur

weightlessness [′wetlɪsnɪs] *s* apesanteur *f*

weight′ lift′er [,lɪftər] *s* (sports) haltérophile *m*

weight′ lift′ing *s* poids et haltères *mpl*

weight·y [′weti] *adj* (*comp* -ier; *super* -iest) pesant, lourd; (*troublesome*) grave; important, puissant

weir [wɪr] *s* (*dam*) barrage *m*; (*trap*) filet *m* à poissons

weird [wɪrd] *adj* surnaturel; étrange

welcome [′wɛlkəm] *adj* bienvenu; (*change, news, etc.*) agréable; **to be welcome to** + *inf* être libre de + *inf*; **you are welcome!** (*i.e., gladly received*) soyez le bienvenu!; (*in response to thanks*) de rien!, je vous en prie!, il n'y a pas de quoi!; **you are welcome to it** c'est à votre disposition; (*ironically*) je ne vous envie pas ‖ *s* bienvenue *f*, bon accueil *m* ‖ *tr* souhaiter la bienvenue à, faire bon accueil à, accueillir; **to welcome coldly** faire mauvais accueil à, accueillir froidement

weld [wɛld] *s* soudure *f* autogène; (bot) gaude *f*, réséda *m* ‖ *tr* souder à l'autogène

welder [′wɛldər] *s* soudeur *m*; (mach) soudeuse *f*

welding [′wɛldɪŋ] *s* soudure *f* autogène

welfare [′wɛl,fɛr] *s* bien-être *m*; (*for underprivileged*) aide *f* sociale

wel′fare state′ *s* état-providence *m*

wel′fare work′ *s* assistance *f* sociale

well [wɛl] *adj* bien (*enjoying good health*) bien, bien portant; **all's well** tout est bien; **it would be just as well to** il serait bon de; **to be well** aller bien ‖ *s* puits *m*; (*natural source of water*) source *f*, fontaine *f*; (*of stairway*) cage *f* ‖ *adv* bien; **as well** aussi; **as well as** aussi bien que; **well and good!** à la bonne heure! ‖ *intr*—**to well up** jaillir ‖ *interj* alors!, tiens!

well′-behaved′ *adj* de bonne conduite; (*child*) sage

well′-be′ing *s* bien-être *m*

well′born′ *adj* bien né

well-bred [′wɛl′brɛd] *adj* bien élevé

well′-disposed′ *adj* bien disposé

well-done [′wɛl′dʌn] *adj* bien fait; (culin) bien cuit

well'-dressed' adj bien vêtu

well'-fixed' adj (coll) bien renté, riche

well'-formed' adj bien conformé

well'-found'ed adj bien fondé

well'-groomed' adj paré, soigné

well'-heeled' adj (coll) huppé, riche

well'-informed' adj bien informé

well'-inten'tioned adj bien intentionné

well-kept ['wel'kept] adj bien tenu; (secret) bien gardé

well-known ['wel'non] adj bien connu, notoire

well'-matched' adj bien assorti

well'-mean'ing adj bien intentionné

well'-nigh' adv presque

well'-off' adj fortuné, prospère

well'-preserved' adj bien conservé

well-read ['wel'red] adj qui a beaucoup de lecture

well-spent ['wel'spent] adj bien employé

well'spring' s source f, source intarissable

well' sweep' s chadouf m

well'-thought'-of' adj de bonne réputation

well'-timed' adj opportun

well-to-do ['welte'du] adj aisé, cossu

well-wisher ['wel'wɪ/ər] s partisan m, ami m fidèle

well'-worn' adj usé; (subject) rebattu

Welsh [wel/] adj gallois || s (language) gallois m; **the Welsh** les Gallois mpl || (l.c.) intr (slang) manquer à sa parole, manquer à ses obligations; **to welsh on s.o.** (slang) manquer à qn

Welsh'man s (pl -men) Gallois m

Welsh' rab'bit or **rare'bit** ['rerbɪt] s fondue f au fromage et à la bière sur canapé

welt [welt] s zébrure f; (border) bordure f; (of shoe) trépointe f

welter ['weltər] s confusion f, fouillis m || intr se vautrer

wel'ter-weight' s (boxing) poids m mimoyen

wen [wen] s kyste m sébacé, loupe f

wench [went/] s jeune fille f, jeune femme f

wend [wend] tr—**to wend one's way** (to) diriger ses pas (vers)

west [west] adj & s ouest m || adv à l'ouest, vers l'ouest

western ['western] adj occidental, de l'ouest || s (mov) western m

westerner ['westərnər] s habitant m de l'ouest, Occidental m

West' Ger'many s Allemagne f de l'Ouest; l'Allemagne de l'Ouest

West' In'dies ['ɪndiz] spl Indes fpl occidentales, Antilles fpl

westward ['westwərd] adv vers l'ouest

wet [wet] adj (comp wetter; super wettest) mouillé; (damp) humide; (rainy) pluvieux; (paint) frais; (coll) antiprohibitionniste; **all wet** (slang) fichu, erroné || s antiprohibitionniste mf || v (pret & pp wet or wetted; ger wetting) tr mouiller || intr se mouiller

wet' bat'ter·y s (pl -ies) pile f à liquide

wet' blan'ket s trouble-fête mf, rabat-joie m

wet' nurse' s nourrice f

wet' paint' s peinture f fraîche; (public sign) attention à la peinture

whack [hwæk] s (coll) coup m, gnon m; (try) (coll) tentative f; **to have a whack at** (coll) s'attaquer à || tr (coll) cogner

whale [hwel] s baleine f; (sperm whale) cachalot m; **to have a whale of a time** (coll) s'amuser follement || tr (coll) rosser

whale'bone' s baleine f, fanon m de baleine

whaler ['hwelər] s baleinier m

wharf [hwɔrf] s (pl wharves ['hwɔrvz] or wharfs) quai m, débarcadère m

what [hwɑt] adj interr quel §80, e.g., **what time is it?** quelle heure est-il?; e.g., **what is his occupation?** quel est son métier? || adj rel ce qui, e.g., **I'll give you what water I have left** je vous donnerai ce qui me reste d'eau; ce que, e.g., **I know what drink you want** je sais ce que vous voulez comme boisson || pron interr qu'est-ce qui, e.g., **what happened?** qu'est-ce qui s'est passé?; que, e.g., **what are you doing?** que faites-vous?; qu'est-ce que, e.g., **what are you doing?** qu'est-ce que vous faites?; comment, e.g., **what is he like?** comment est-il?; combien, e.g., **what is two and two?** combien font deux et deux?; **what (did you say)?** comment?; **what else?** quoi d'autre?, quoi encore?; **what for?** pourquoi donc?; **what if,** e.g., **what if I were to die?** si je venais à mourir?; **what if I did?,** **what of it?,** so what? qu'importe?; **what is it?** qu'est-ce que c'est?, qu'est-ce qu'il y a?; **what now?** alors?; **what's that?** qu'est-ce que c'est que cela?; **what then?** et après? || pron rel ce qui, ce que; ce dont §79, e.g., **I have what you need** j'ai ce dont vous avez besoin; ce à quoi, e.g., **I know what you are thinking of** je sais ce à quoi vous pensez; (sometimes untranslated), e.g., **he asked them what time it was** il leur a demandé l'heure; **to know what's what** (coll) s'y connaître, être au courant || interj comment!; **what a que de,** e.g., **what a lot of people!** que de monde!; quel §80, e.g., **what a pity!** quel dommage!

what·ev'er adj quel que §80; moindre or quelconque, e.g., **is there any hope whatever?** y a-t-il le moindre espoir?, y a-t-il un espoir quelconque? || pron tout ce qui; tout ce que, e.g., **tell him whatever you like** dites-lui tout ce que vous voudrez; quoi que, e.g., **whatever you do** quoi que vous fassiez; **whatever comes** à tout hasard

what'not' s étagère f

what's'-his-name' s (coll) Monsieur un tel

wheal [wil] s papule f

wheat [hwit] *s* blé *m*

wheedle ['hwidəl] *tr* enjôler

wheel [hwil] *s* roue *f*; **at the wheel** au volant || *tr* (*to turn*) faire pivoter; (*a wheelbarrow, table, etc.*) rouler || *intr* pivoter; (*said, e.g., of birds in the sky*) tournoyer; **to wheel about** or **around** faire demi-tour

wheelbarrow ['hwil,bæro] *s* brouette *f*

wheel′base′ *s* (aut) empattement *m*

wheel′chair′ *s* fauteuil *m* roulant pour malade, voiture *f* d'infirme

wheel′ horse′ *s* (*horse*) timonier *m*; (*person*) bûcheur *m*

wheelwright ['hwil,rait] *s* charron *m*

wheeze [hwiz] *s* respiration *f* sifflante; (pathol) cornage *m* || *intr* respirer avec peine, souffler

whelp [hwelp] *s* petit *m* || *tr & intr* mettre bas

when [hwen] *adv* quand || *conj* quand, lorsque; (*on which, in which*) où; (*whereas*) alors que

whence [hwens] *adv & conj* d'où

when·ev′er *conj* chaque fois que, quand

where [hwer] *adv & conj* où; **from where** d'où

whereabouts ['hwerə,bauts] *s*—**the whereabouts of** l'endroit où se trouve || *adv & conj* où donc

whereas [hwer′æz] *conj* tandis que, attendu que || *s* considérant *m*

where·by′ *conj* par lequel

wherefore ['hwerfor] *s & adv* pourquoi *m* || *conj* à cause de quoi

where·from′ *adv* d'où

where·in′ *adv* d'où; en quoi || *conj* où

where·of′ *adv* de quoi || *conj* dont §79

where′up·on′ *adv* sur quoi, sur ce

wherever [hwer′evər] *conj* partout où; où que, n'importe où

wherewithal ['hwerwið,əl] *s* ressources *fpl*, moyens *mpl*

whet [hwet] *v* (*pret & pp* **whetted**; *ger* **whetting**) *tr* aiguiser

whet′stone′ *s* pierre *f* à aiguiser

whew [hwju] *interj* ouf!

whey [hwe] *s* petit lait *m*

which [hwitʃ] *adj interr* quel §80, e.g., **which university do you prefer?** quelle université préférez-vous?; **which one?** lequel? || *adj rel* le . . . que, e.g., **choose which road you prefer** choisissez le chemin que vous préférez || *pron interr* lequel §78; **which is which?** lequel des deux est-ce?; **which of them?** lequel d'entre eux? || *pron rel* qui; que; dont §79

which·ev′er *adj rel* n'importe quel || *pron rel* n'importe lequel

whiff [hwif] *s* bouffée *f*; **to get a whiff of** flairer

while [hwail] *s* temps *m*, moment *m*; **a**

long while longtemps; **a (little) while ago** tout à l'heure; **in a little while** sous peu, tout à l'heure || *conj* pendant que; (*as long as*) tant que; (*although*) quoique || *tr*—**to while away** tuer, faire passer

whim [hwim] *s* caprice *m*, lubie *f*

whimper ['hwimpər] *s* pleurnicherie *f* || *tr* dire en pleurnichant || *intr* pleurnicher

whimsical ['hwimzikəl] *adj* capricieux, lunatique

whine [hwain] *s* geignement *m*; (*of siren*) hurlement *m* || *intr* geindre; (*said of siren*) hurler

whin·ny ['hwini] *s* (*pl* **-nies**) hennissement *m* || *v* (*pret & pp* **-nied**) *intr* hennir

whip [hwip] *s* fouet *m* || *v* (*pret & pp* **whipped** or **whipt**; *ger* **whipping**) *tr* fouetter; (*to defeat*) battre; (*the end of a rope*) surlier; **to whip out** (*e.g., a gun*) sortir brusquement; **to whip up** (*e.g., a supper*) (coll) préparer à l'improviste; (*e.g., enthusiasm*) (coll) stimuler

whip′cord′ *s* corde *f* à fouet

whip′ hand′ *s* main *f* du fouet; (*upper hand*) avantage *m*, dessus *m*

whip′lash′ *s* mèche *f* de fouet

whipped′ cream′ *s* crème *f* fouettée, chantilly *m*

whipper-snapper ['hwipər,snæpər] *s* freluquet *m*, paltoquet *m*

whip′ping boy′ *s* tête *f* de Turc

whip′ping post′ *s* poteau *m* des condamnés au fouet

whippoorwill ['hwipər,wil] *s* (*Caprimulgus vociferus*) engoulevent *m* américain

whir [hwʌr] *s* ronflement *m* || *v* (*pret & pp* **whirred**; *ger* **whirring**) *intr* ronfler

whirl [hwʌrl] *s* tourbillon *m*; (*of events, parties, etc.*) succession *f* ininterrompue || *tr* faire tourbillonner || *intr* tourbillonner; **his head whirls** la tête lui tourne

whirligig ['hwʌrli,gig] *s* tourniquet *m*; (ent) gyrin *m*, tourniquet

whirl′pool′ *s* tourbillon *m*, remous *m*

whirl′wind′ *s* tourbillon *m*

whirlybird ['hwʌrli,bʌrd] *s* (coll) hélicoptère *m*

whisk [hwisk] *s* coup *m* léger; (*broom*) époussette *f*; (culin) fouet *m* || *tr* balayer; (culin) fouetter; **to whisk out of sight** escamoter || *intr* aller comme un trait

whisk′ broom′ *s* époussette *f*

whiskers ['hwiskərz] *spl* barbe *f*, poils *mpl* de barbe; (*on side of face*) favoris *mpl*; (*of cat*) moustaches *fpl*

whiskey ['hwiski] *s* whisky *m*

whisper ['hwispər] *s* chuchotement *m* || *tr* chuchoter, dire à l'oreille || *intr* chuchoter

whispering ['hwispəriŋ] *s* chuchotement *m*

whist [hwist] *s* whist *m*

whistle ['hwisəl] *s* (*sound*) sifflement

m; (*device*) sifflet *m*; **to wet one's whistle** (coll) s'humecter le gosier ‖ *tr* siffler, siffloter ‖ *intr* siffler; **to whistle for** siffler; attendre en vain, se voir obligé de se passer de

whis'tle stop' *s* arrêt *m* facultatif

whit [hwɪt] *s*—**not a whit** pas un brin; **to not care a whit** s'en moquer

white [hwaɪt] *adj* blanc ‖ *s* blanc *m*; blanc d'œuf; **whites** (pathol) pertes *fpl* blanches

white'caps' *spl* moutons *mpl*

white' coal' *s* houille *f* blanche

white'-col'lar *adj* de bureau

white' feath'er *s*—**to show the white feather** lâcher pied, flancher, caner

white'fish' *s* poisson *m* blanc, merlan *m*

white' goods' *spl* vêtements *mpl* blancs; tissus *mpl* de coton, cotonnade *f*; (*appliances*) appareils *mpl* électroménagers

white'-haired' *adj* aux cheveux blancs, chenu; (coll) favori

white'-hot' *adj* chauffé à blanc

white' lead' [lɛd] *s* céruse *f*, blanc *m* de céruse

white' lie' *s* mensonge *m* pieux

white' meat' *s* blanc *m*

whiten ['hwaɪtən] *tr* & *intr* blanchir

whiteness ['hwaɪtnɪs] *s* blancheur *f*

white' slav'ery *s* traite *f* des blanches

white' tie' *s* cravate *f* blanche; tenue *f* de soirée

white'wash' *s* blanc *m* de chaux, badigeon *m*; (*cover-up*) couverture *f* ‖ *tr* blanchir à la chaux; (*e.g., a guilty person, a scandal*) blanchir

whither ['hwɪðər] *adv* & *conj* où, là où

whitish ['hwaɪtɪʃ] *adj* blanchâtre

whitlow ['hwɪtlo] *s* panaris *m*

Whitsuntide ['hwɪtsən̩͵taɪd] *s* saison *f* de la Pentecôte

whittle ['hwɪtəl] *tr* tailler au couteau; **to whittle away** or **down** amenuiser

whiz or **whizz** [hwɪz] *s* sifflement *m*; (slang) prodige *m* ‖ *v* (*pret* & *pp* **whizzed**; *ger* **whizzing**) *intr*—**to whiz by** passer en sifflant, passer comme le vent

who [hu] *pron interr* qui; quel §80; **who else?** qui d'autre?; **who is there?** (mil) qui vive? ‖ *pron rel* qui; celui qui §83

whoa [hwo] *interj* holà!, doucement!

who·ev'er *pron rel* quiconque; celui qui §83; qui que, e.g., **whoever you are** qui que vous soyez

whole [hol] *adj* entier ‖ *s* tout *m*, totalité *f*, ensemble *m*; **on the whole** somme toute, à tout prendre

whole'heart'ed *adj* sincère, de bon cœur

whole' note' *s* (mus) ronde *f*

whole' rest' *s* (mus) pause *f*

whole'sale' *adj* & *adv* en gros; (*e.g., slaughter*) en masse ‖ *s* gros *m*, vente *f* en gros ‖ *tr* & *intr* vendre en gros

whole'sale price' *s* prix *m* vendre de gros

wholesaler ['hol͵selər] *s* commerçant *m* en gros, grossiste *mf*

whole'sale trade' *s* commerce *m* de gros

wholesome ['holsəm] *adj* sain

wholly ['holi] *adv* entièrement

whom [hum] *pron interr* qui ‖ *pron rel* que; lequel §78; celui que §83; **of whom** dont, de qui §79

whom·ev'er *pron rel* celui que §83; tous ceux que; (with a preposition) quiconque

whoop [hup], [hwup] *s* huée *f*; (*cough*) quinte *f* ‖ *tr*—**to whoop it up** (slang) pousser des cris ‖ *intr* huer

whoop'ing cough' ['hupɪŋ], ['hwupɪŋ] *s* coqueluche *f*

whopper ['hwapər] *s* (coll) chose *f* énorme; (*lie*) (coll) gros mensonge *m*

whopping ['hwapɪŋ] *adj* (coll) énorme

whore [hor] *s* putain *f* ‖ *intr*—**to whore around** courir la gueuse

whortleber·ry ['hwartəl͵bɛri] *s* (pl **-ries**) myrtille *f*

whose [huz] *pron interr* à qui, e.g., **whose pen is that?** à qui est ce stylo? ‖ *pron rel* dont, de qui §79; duquel §78

why [hwaɪ] *s* (pl **whys** [hwaɪz]) pourquoi *m*; **the why and the wherefore** le pourquoi et le comment ‖ *adv* pourquoi; **why not?** pourquoi pas? ‖ *interj* tiens!; **why, certainly!** mais bien sûr!; **why, yes!** mais oui!

wick [wɪk] *s* mèche *f*

wicked ['wɪkɪd] *adj* méchant, mauvais

wicker ['wɪkər] *adj* en osier ‖ *s* osier *m*

wicket ['wɪkɪt] *s* guichet *m*; (croquet) arceau *m*

wide [waɪd] *adj* large; (*range*) vaste, étendu; (*spread, angle, etc.*) grand; large de, e.g., **eight feet wide** large de huit pieds ‖ *adv* loin, partout; **open wide!** ouvrez bien!

wide'-an'gle *adj* grand-angulaire

wide'-awake' *adj* bien éveillé

widen ['waɪdən] *tr* élargir ‖ *intr* s'élargir

wide'-o'pen *adj* grand ouvert

wide'spread' *adj* (*arms, wings*) étendu; répandu; universel

widow ['wɪdo] *s* veuve *f* ‖ *tr*—**to be widowed** devenir veuf

widower ['wɪdo·ər] *s* veuf *m*

widowhood ['wɪdo͵hud] *s* veuvage *m*

wid'ow's mite' *s* obole *f*

wid'ow's weeds' *spl* deuil *m* de veuve

width [wɪdθ] *s* largeur *f*; (*of cloth*) 16 *m*

wield [wild] *tr* (*sword, pen*) manier; (*power*) exercer

wife [waɪf] *s* (pl **wives** [waɪvz]) femme *f*, épouse *f*

wig [wɪg] *s* perruque *f*

wiggle ['wɪgəl] *s* tortillement *m* ‖ *tr* agiter ‖ *intr* tortiller, se tortiller

wig'wag' *s* télégraphie *f* optique ‖ *v* (*pret* & *pp* **-wagged**; *ger* **-wagging**) *tr* transmettre à bras avec fanions ‖ *intr* signaler à bras avec fanions

wigwam ['wɪgwam] *s* wigwam *m*

wild [waɪld] *adj* sauvage; (*untamed*) sauvage, fauve; (*frantic, mad*) frénétique; (*hair; dance; dream*) échevelé; (*passion; torrent; night*) tumultueux;

(*idea, plan*) insensé, extravagant; (*life*) déréglé; (*blows, bullet, shot*) perdu; **wild about** or **for** fou de || *adv* —**to run wild** dépasser toutes les bornes; (*said of plants*) pousser librement

wild′ boar′ *s* sanglier *m*

wild′ card′ *s* mistigri *m*

wild′cat′ *s* chat *m* sauvage; lynx *m*; (*well*) sondage *m* d'exploration

wild′cat strike′ *s* grève *f* sauvage, grève spontanée

wild′ cher′ry *s* (*pl* -ries) merise *f*; (*tree*) merisier *m*

wilderness ['wɪldərnɪs] *s* désert *m*

wild′fire′ *s* feu *m* grégeois; feu *m* follet; éclairs *mpl* en nappe; **like wildfire** comme une traînée de poudre

wild′ flow′er *s* fleur *f* des champs

wild′ goose′ *s* oie *f* sauvage

wild′-goose′ chase′ *s*—**to go on a wild-goose chase** faire buisson creux

wild′life′ *s* animaux *mpl* sauvages

wild′ oats′ *spl*—**to sow one's wild oats** jeter sa gourme

wile [waɪl] *s* ruse *f* || *tr*—**to wile away** tuer, faire passer

will [wɪl] *s* volonté *f*; (*law*) testament *m*; **against one's will** à contre-cœur; **at will** à volonté; **with a will** de bon cœur || *tr* vouloir; (*to bequeath*) léguer || *intr* vouloir; **do as you will** faites comme vous voudrez || (*pret & cond* **would** [wʊd]) *aux* used to express 1) the future indicative, e.g., **he will arrive early** il arrivera de bonne heure; 2) the future perfect indicative, e.g., **he will have arrived before I leave** il sera arrivé avant que je parte; 3) the present indicative denoting habit or custom, e.g., **after breakfast he will go out for a walk every morning** après le petit déjeuner il fait une promenade tous les matins

willful ['wɪlfəl] *adj* volontaire; (*stubborn*) obstiné

willfulness ['wɪlfəlnɪs] *s* entêtement *m*

William ['wɪljəm] *s* Guillaume *m*

willing ['wɪlɪŋ] *adj* disposé, prêt; **to be willing to** vouloir bien; **willing or unwilling** bon gré mal gré

willingly ['wɪlɪŋli] *adv* volontiers

willingness ['wɪlɪŋnɪs] *s* bonne volonté *f*, consentement *m*

will-o'-the-wisp ['wɪləðə'wɪsp] *s* feu *m* follet; (*fig*) chimère *f*

willow ['wɪlo] *s* saule *m*

willowy ['wɪlo·i] *adj* souple, agile; svelte, élancé; couvert de saules

will′ pow′er *s* force *f* de volonté

willy-nilly ['wɪli'nɪli] *adv* bon gré mal gré

wilt [wɪlt] *tr* flétrir || *intr* se flétrir

wil·y ['waɪli] *adj* (*comp* -ier; *super* -iest) rusé, astucieux

wimple ['wɪmpəl] *s* guimpe *f*

win [wɪn] *s* (coll) victoire *f* || *v* (*pret & pp* **won** [wʌn]; *ger* **winning**) *tr* gagner; (*a victory, a prize*) remporter; **to win back** regagner; **to win over** gagner, convaincre || *intr* gagner; convaincre; **to win out** (coll) réussir

wince [wɪns] *s*—**without a wince** sans sourciller || *intr* tressailler

winch [wɪntʃ] *s* treuil *m*; (*handle, crank*) manivelle *f*

wind [wɪnd] *s* vent *m*; (*breath*) haleine *f*, souffle *m*; **to break wind** lâcher un vent, faire un pet; **to get wind of** avoir vent de; **to sail close to the wind** courir au plus près; **to sail into the wind** aller au lof, venir au lof || *tr* faire perdre le souffle à || *intr* flairer le gibier || [waɪnd] *v* (*pret & pp* **wound** [waʊnd]) *tr* enrouler; (*a timepiece*) remonter; (*yarn, thread, etc.*) pelotonner; **to wind up** enrouler; remonter; (*to finish*) (coll) terminer, régler || *intr* serpenter

windbag ['wɪnd,bæg] *s* (*of bagpipe*) outre *f*; (coll) moulin *m* à paroles

windbreak ['wɪnd,brek] *s* abrivent *m*

wind′ cone′ [wɪnd] *s* (aer) manche *f* à air

winded ['wɪndɪd] *adj* essoufflé

windfall ['wɪnd,fɔl] *s* (fig) aubaine *f*

wind′ing road′ ['waɪndɪŋ] *s* route *f* en lacet

wind′ing sheet′ *s* linceul *m*

wind′ing stairs′ *spl* escalier *m* en colimaçon

wind′ in′strument [wɪnd] *s* (mus) instrument *m* à vent

windlass ['wɪndləs] *s* treuil *m*

windmill ['wɪnd,mɪl] *s* moulin *m* à vent; (*on a modern farm*) aéromoteur *m*; **to tilt at windmills** se battre contre des moulins à vent

window ['wɪndo] *s* fenêtre *f*; (*of ticket office*) guichet *m*; (*of store*) vitrine *f*; (aut) glace *f*

win′dow dress′er *s* étalagiste *mf*

win′dow dress′ing *s* art *m* de l'étalage; (coll) façade *f*

win′dow en′velope *s* enveloppe *f* à fenêtre

win′dow frame′ *s* châssis *m*, dormant *m*

win′dow-pane′ *s* vitre *f*, carreau *m*

win′dow screen′ *s* grillage *m*

win′dow shade′ *s* store *m*

win′dow-shop′ *v* (*pret & pp* -**shopped**; *ger* -**shopping**) *intr* faire du lèche-vitrines, lécher les vitrines

win′dow shut′ter *s* volet *m*

win′dow sill′ *s* rebord *m* de fenêtre

windpipe ['wɪnd,paɪp] *s* trachée-artère *f*

windshield ['wɪnd,ʃild] *s* pare-brise *m*

wind′shield wash′er *s* lave-glace *m*

wind′shield wip′er *s* essuie-glace *m*

windsock ['wɪnd,sak] *s* manche *f* à air

windstorm ['wɪnd,stɔrm] *s* tempête *f* de vent

wind′ tun′nel [wɪnd] *s* tunnel *m* aérodynamique

wind-up ['waɪnd,ʌp] *s* conclusion *f*, fin *f*

windward ['wɪndwərd] *adj & adv* au vent || *s* côté *m* du vent; **to turn to windward** louvoyer

wind·y ['wɪndɪ] *adj* (*comp* **-ier**; *super* **-iest**) venteux; (*verbose*) verbeux; **it is windy** il fait du vent

wine [waɪn] *s* vin *m* ‖ *tr*—**to wine and dine s.o.** fêter qn

wine′ cel′lar *s* cave *f*

wine′ glass′ *s* verre *m* à vin

winegrower ['waɪn,gro·ər] *s* viticulteur *m*

winegrowing ['waɪn,gro·ɪŋ] *s* viticulture *f*

wine′ list′ *s* carte *f* des vins

wine′ press′ *s* pressoir *m*

winer·y ['waɪnərɪ] *s* (*pl* **-ies**) pressoir *m*

wine′ skin′ *s* outre *f* à vin

wine′ stew′ard *s* sommelier *m*; (*of prince, king*) échanson *m*

winetaster ['waɪn,testər] *s* (*person*) dégustateur *m*; (*pipette*) taste-vin *m*

wing [wɪŋ] *s* aile *f*; (*e.g., of hospital*) pavillon *m*; (pol) parti *m*, faction *f*; **in the wings** (theat) dans la coulisse; **on the wing** au vol; **to take wing** prendre son essor ‖ *tr* (*to wound*) blesser; **to wing one's way** voler

wing′ chair′ *s* fauteuil *m* à oreilles

wing′ col′lar *s* col *m* rabattu

wing′ load′ *s* (aer) charge *f* alaire

wing′ nut′ *s* écrou *m* ailé

wing′ spread′ *s* envergure *f*

wink [wɪŋk] *s* clin *m* d'œil; **to not sleep a wink** ne pas fermer l'œil; **to take forty winks** (coll) piquer un roupillon ‖ *tr* cligner ‖ *intr* cligner des yeux; **to wink at** cligner de l'œil à; (*e.g., an abuse*) fermer les yeux sur

winner ['wɪnər] *s* gagnant *m*, vainqueur *m*

winning ['wɪnɪŋ] *adj* gagnant *m*; (*attractive*) séduisant ‖ **winnings** *spl* gains *mpl*

winnow ['wɪno] *tr* vanner, sasser; (*e.g., the evidence*) passer au crible

winsome ['wɪnsəm] *adj* séduisant

winter ['wɪntər] *s* hiver *m* ‖ *intr* passer l'hiver; (*said of animals, troops, etc.*) hiverner

win′ter·green′ *s* (*oil*) wintergreen *m*; (bot) gaulthérie *f*

win·try ['wɪntrɪ] *adj* (*comp* **-trier**; *super* **-triest**) hivernal, froid

wipe [waɪp] *tr* essuyer; **to wipe away** essuyer; **to wipe off** or **out** effacer; (*to annihilate*) anéantir; **to wipe up** nettoyer

wiper ['waɪpər] *s* torchon *m*; (elec) contact *m* glissant; (mach) came *f*

wire [waɪr] *s* fil *m*; télégramme *m*; **hold the wire!** (telp) restez à l'écoute!; **on the wire** (telp) au bout du fil; **reply by wire** réponse *f* télégraphique; **to get in under the wire** arriver juste à temps; terminer juste à temps; **to pull wires** (coll) tirer les ficelles ‖ *tr* attacher avec du fil de fer; (*a message*) télégraphier; (*a house*) canaliser ‖ *intr* télégraphier

wire′ cut′ter *s* coupe-fil *m*

wire′draw′ *v* (*pret* **-drew**; *pp* **-drawn**) *tr* tréfiler

wire′ entan′glement *s* réseau *m* de barbelés

wire′ gauge′ *s* calibre *m* or jauge *f* pour fils métalliques

wire′-haired′ *adj* à poil dur

wireless ['waɪrlɪs] *adj* sans fil

wire′ nail′ *s* clou *m* de Paris

wire′ pho′to *s* (*pl* **-tos**) (trademark) (*device*) bélinographe *m*; (*photo*) bélinogramme *m*

wire′ pull′ing *s* (coll) influences *fpl* secrètes, piston *m*

wire′ record′er *s* magnétophone *m* à fil d'acier

wire′ tap′ *s* (*device*) table *f* d'écoute ‖ *v* (*pret* & *pp* **-tapped**; *ger* **-tapping**) *tr* passer à la table d'écoute

wiring ['waɪrɪŋ] *s* (*e.g., of house*) canalisation *f*; (*e.g., of radio*) montage *m*

wir·y ['waɪrɪ] *adj* (*comp* **-ier**; *super* **-iest**) nerveux; (*hair*) raide

wisdom ['wɪzdəm] *s* sagesse *f*

wis′dom tooth′ *s* dent *f* de sagesse

wise [waɪz] *adj* sage; (*step, decision*) judicieux, prudent; **to be wise to** (slang) voir clair dans le jeu de, percer le jeu de; **to get wise** (coll) se mettre au courant ‖ *s*—**in no wise** en aucune manière ‖ *tr*—**to wise up** (slang) avertir, désabuser

wiseacre ['waɪz,ekər] *s* fat *m*, fierot *m*

wise′ crack′ *s* (coll) blague *f*, plaisanterie *f* ‖ *intr* (coll) blaguer, plaisanter

wise′ guy′ *s* (slang) type *m* goguenard

wish [wɪʃ] *s* souhait *m*, désir *m*; **best wishes** meilleurs vœux *mpl*; (formula used to close a letter) amitiés; **last wishes** dernières volontés *fpl*; **to make a wish** faire un vœu ‖ *tr* souhaiter, désirer; **to wish s.o. s.th.** souhaiter q.ch. à qn; **to wish s.o. to +** *inf* souhaiter que qn + *subj*; **to wish to +** *inf* vouloir + *inf*

wish′ bone′ *s* fourchette *f*

wishful ['wɪʃfəl] *adj* désireux

wish′ful think′ing *s* optimisme *m* à outrance; **to indulge in wishful thinking** se forger des chimères

wish′ing well′ *s* puits *m* aux souhaits

wistful ['wɪstfəl] *adj* pensif, rêveur

wit [wɪt] *s* esprit *m*; (*person*) homme *m* d'esprit; **to be at one's wits' end** ne plus savoir que faire; **to keep one's wits about one** conserver toute sa présence d'esprit; **to live by one's wits** vivre d'expédients

witch [wɪtʃ] *s* sorcière *f*

witch′ craft′ *s* sorcellerie *f*

witch′ doc′tor *s* sorcier *m* guérisseur

witch′es' Sab′bath *s* sabbat *m*

witch′ ha′zel *s* teinture *f* d'hamamélis; (bot) hamamélis *m*

witch′ hunt′ *s* chasse *f* aux sorcières

with [wɪð], [wɪθ] *prep* avec; (*at the home of; in the case of*) chez; (*in spite of*) malgré; à, e.g., **the girl with the blue eyes** la jeune fille aux yeux bleus; e.g., **coffee with milk** café au lait; e.g., **with open arms** à bras ouverts; e.g., **with these words . . .** à ces mots . . . ; de, e.g., **with a loud**

voice d'une voix forte; e.g., **with all his strength** de toutes ses forces; e.g., **to be satisfied with** être satisfait de; e.g., **to fill with** remplir de

with·draw v (pret -drew; pp -drawn) tr retirer || intr se retirer

withdrawal [wɪˈdrɔ·əl], [wɪθˈdrɔ·əl] s retrait m

wither [ˈwɪðər] tr faner || intr se faner

with·hold v (pret & pp -held) tr (money, taxes, etc.) retenir; (permission) refuser; (the truth) cacher

with·hold·ing tax s impôt m retenu à la source

with·in adv à l'intérieur; là-dedans §85A || prep à l'intérieur de; (in less than) en moins de; (within the limits of) dans; (in the bosom of) au sein de; (not exceeding a margin of error of) à . . . près, e.g., **I can tell you what time it is within five minutes** je peux vous dire l'heure à cinq minutes près; à portée de, e.g., **within reach** à portée de la main

with·out adv au-dehors, dehors || prep au dehors de; (lacking, not with) sans; **to do without** se passer de; **without** + ger sans + inf, e.g., **he left without seeing me** il est parti sans me voir; sans que + subj, e.g., **he left without anyone seeing him** il est parti sans que personne ne le vit

with·stand v (pret & pp -stood) tr résister à

witness [ˈwɪtnɪs] s témoin m; **in witness whereof** en foi de quoi; **to bear witness** rendre témoignage || tr (to be present at) être témoin de, assister à; (to attest) témoigner; (e.g., a contract) signer

wit·ness stand s barre f des témoins

witticism [ˈwɪtɪˌsɪzəm] s trait m d'esprit

wittingly [ˈwɪtɪŋli] adv sciemment

wit·ty [ˈwɪti] adj (comp -tier; super -tiest) spirituel

wizard [ˈwɪzərd] s sorcier m

wizardry [ˈwɪzərdri] s sorcellerie f

wizened [ˈwɪzənd] adj desséché

woad [wod] s guède f

wobble [ˈwɑbəl] intr chanceler; (said of table) branler; (said of voice) chevroter; vaciller

wob·bly [ˈwɑbli] adj (comp -blier; super -bliest) vacillant

woe [wo] s malheur m, affliction f; **woe is me!** pauvre de moi!

woebegone [ˈwobɪˌgɔn], [ˈwobɪˌgɑn] adj navré, abattu, désolé

woeful [ˈwofəl] adj triste, désolé; très mauvais

wolf [wʊlf] s (pl wolves [wʊlvz]) loup m; galant m, tombeur m de femmes; **to cry wolf** crier au loup; **to keep the wolf from the door** se mettre à l'abri du besoin, joindre les deux bouts || tr & intr engloutir

wolf' cub' s louveteau m

wolf' hound' s chien-loup m

wolf' pack' s bande f de loups

wolfram [ˈwʊlfrəm] s (element) tungstène m; (mineral) wolfram m

wolf's'-bane' or **wolfs'bane'** s tue-loup m, aconit m, napel m

woman [ˈwʊmən] s (pl women [ˈwɪmɪn]) femme f

wom·an doc·tor s femme f médecin, doctoresse f

womanhood [ˈwʊmənˌhʊd] s le sexe féminin; les femmes fpl

womanish [ˈwʊmənɪʃ] adj féminin; (effeminate) efféminé

wom·an·kin·d s le sexe féminin

wom·an la·bor·er s femme f manœuvre

woman·ly [ˈwʊmənli] adj (comp -lier; super -liest) féminin, femme

wom·an preach·er s femme f pasteur

womb [wum] s utérus m, matrice f; (fig) sein m

wonder [ˈwʌndər] s merveille f; (feeling of surprise) émerveillement m; (something strange) miracle m; **for a wonder** chose étonnante; **no wonder that . . .** rien d'étonnant que . . . ; **to work wonders** faire des merveilles || tr—**to wonder that** s'étonner que; **to wonder why, if, whether** se demander pourquoi, si || intr—**to wonder at** s'émerveiller de, s'étonner de

wonderful [ˈwʌndərfəl] adj merveilleux, étonnant

won·der·land s pays m des merveilles

wonderment [ˈwʌndərmənt] s étonnement m

wont [wʌnt], [wɔnt] adj—**to be wont to** avoir l'habitude de || s—**his wont** son habitude

wonted adj habituel, accoutumé

woo [wu] tr courtiser

wood [wʊd] s bois m; (for wine) fût m; **out of the woods** (coll) hors de danger, hors d'affaire; **to take to the woods** se sauver dans la nature; **woods** bois m or mpl

woodbine [ˈwʊdˌbaɪn] s (honeysuckle) chèvrefeuille m; (Virginia creeper) vigne f vierge

wood' carv'ing s sculpture f sur bois

wood' chuck' s marmotte f d'Amérique

wood' cock' s bécasse f

wood' cut' s (typ) gravure f sur bois

wood' cut'ter s bûcheron m

wooded [ˈwʊdɪd] adj boisé

wooden [ˈwʊdən] adj en bois; (style, manners) guindé, raide

wood' en·grav'ing s (typ) gravure f sur bois

wood'en-head'ed adj (coll) stupide, obtus

wood'en leg' s jambe f en bois

wood'en shoe' s sabot m

wood' grouse' s grand tétras m, grand coq m de bruyère

woodland [ˈwʊdlənd] s pays m boisé || s sylvestre

wood'land scene' s (painting) paysage m boisé

wood'man s (pl -men) bûcheron m

woodpecker [ˈwʊdˌpekər] s pic m; (green woodpecker) pivert m, picvert m

wood' pig'eon s (orn) ramier m

wood'pile' s tas m de bois

wood′ screw′ s vis f à bois
wood′shed′ s bûcher m
woods′man s (pl **-men**) bûcheron m; (trapper) trappeur m, chasseur m
wood′ tick′ s vrillette f
wood′winds′ spl (mus) bois mpl
wood′work′ s (working in wood) menuiserie f; (things made of wood) boiseries fpl
wood′work′er s menuisier m
wood′worm′ s (ent) artison m
wood·y [ˈwʊdi] adj (comp **-ier**; super **-iest**) boisé; (like wood) ligneux
wooer [ˈwuːər] s prétendant m
woof [wuf] s trame f; (fabric) tissu m
woofer [ˈwufər] s (rad) boomer m, woofer m
wool [wʊl] s laine f
woolen [ˈwʊlən] adj de laine ‖ s tissu m de laine; **woolens** tissus m de laine
wool′gath′ering s rêvasserie f
woolgrower [ˈwʊlˌɡroər] s éleveur m des bêtes à laine
wool·ly [ˈwʊli] adj (comp **-lier**; super **-liest**) laineux
word [wʌrd] s mot m; (promise, assurance) parole f; **in other words** autrement dit; **in your own words** en vous propres termes; **my word!** ça alors!; **not a word!** motus!; **the Word** (eccl) le Verbe; **to break one's word** manquer à sa parole; **to have words with** échanger des propos désagréables avec; **to make s.o. eat his words** faire ravaler ses paroles à qn; **to put in a word** placer un mot; **to take s.o. at his word** prendre qn au mot, croire qn sur parole; **upon my word!** ma foi!; **without a word** sans mot dire; **words** (e.g., of song) paroles ‖ tr formuler, rédiger
word′-forma′tion s formation f des mots
wording [ˈwʌrdɪŋ] s langage m
word′ or′der s ordre m des mots
word′-stock′ s vocabulaire m
word·y [ˈwʌrdi] adj (comp **-ier**; super **-iest**) verbeux
work [wʌrk] s travail m, ouvrage m; (production, book) œuvre f, ouvrage m; **at work** en œuvre; (not at home) au travail, au bureau, à l'usine; **out of work** sans travail, en chômage; **to shoot the works** (slang) mettre le paquet; **works** œuvres; mécanisme m; (of clock) mouvement m ‖ tr faire travailler; (to operate) faire fonctionner, faire marcher; (wood, iron) travailler; (mine) exploiter; **to work out** élaborer, résoudre; **to work up** préparer; stimuler ‖ intr travailler; (said of motor, machine, etc.) fonctionner, marcher; (said of remedy) faire de l'effet; (said of wine, beer) fermenter; **how will things work out?** à quoi tout cela aboutira-t-il?; **to work hard** travailler dur; **to work loose** se desserrer; **to work out** (sports) s'entraîner; **to work too hard** se surmener
workable [ˈwʌrkəbəl] adj (feasible)

réalisable; (that can be worked) ouvrable
work′bas′ket s corbeille f à ouvrage
work′bench′ s établi m
work′book′ s manuel m; (notebook) carnet m; (for student) cahier m de devoirs
work′box′ s boîte f à ouvrage; (for needlework) coffret m de travail
work′day′ adj de tous les jours; prosaïque, ordinaire ‖ s jour m ouvrable; (part of day devoted to work) journée f
worked′-up′ adj préparé, ouvré; (excited) agité, emballé
worker [ˈwʌrkər] s travailleur m, ouvrier m, employé m
work′ force′ s main-d'œuvre f; personnel m
work′horse′ s cheval m de charge; (tireless worker) vrai cheval m de labour
work′house′ s maison f de correction; (Brit) asile m des pauvres
work′ing class′ s classe f ouvrière
work′ing day′ s jour m ouvrable; (daily hours for work) journée f
work′ing-girl′ s jeune ouvrière f
work′ing hours′ spl heures fpl de travail
work′ing-man′ s (pl **-men′**) travailleur m
work′ing-wom′an s (pl **-wom′en**) ouvrière f
work′man s (pl **-men**) ouvrier m
workmanship [ˈwʌrkmənˌʃɪp] s habileté f professionnelle, facture f; (work executed) travail m
work′ of art′ s œuvre f d'art
work′out′ s essai m, épreuve f; (physical exercise) séance f d'entraînement
work′room′ s atelier m; (for study) cabinet m de travail, cabinet d'études
work′shop′ s atelier m
work′ stop′page s arrêt m du travail
world [wʌrld] adj mondial ‖ s monde m; **a world of** énormément de; **for all the world** à tous les égards, exactement; **not for all the world** pour rien au monde; **since the world began** depuis que le monde est monde; **the other world** l'autre monde; **to bring into the world** mettre au monde; **to go around the world** faire le tour du monde; **to see the world** voir du pays; **to think the world of** estimer énormément, avoir une très haute opinion de
world′ affairs′ spl affaires fpl internationales
world′-fa′mous adj de renommée mondiale
world′ his′tory s histoire f universelle
world·ly [ˈwʌrldli] adj (comp **-lier**; super **-liest**) mondain
world′ly-wise′ adj—**to be worldly-wise** savoir ce que c'est que la vie
world′ map′ s mappemonde f
World′ Se′ries s championnat m mondial
world′s′ fair′ s exposition f universelle
world′ war′ s guerre f mondiale

world'-wide' adj mondial, universel

worm [wʌrm] s ver m ‖ tr enlever les vers de; (a secret, money, etc.) soutirer; **to worm it out of him** lui tirer les vers du nez ‖ intr se faufiler

worm-eaten ['wʌrm,itən] adj vermoulu

worm' gear' s engrenage m à vis sans fin

worm'wood' s (Artemisia) armoise f; (Artemisia absinthium) armoise absinthe; (something grievous) (fig) absinthe f

worm-y ['wʌrmi] adj (comp **-ier**; super **-iest**) véreux

worn [worn] adj usé, fatigué

worn'-out' adj épuisé, usé; éreinté

worrisome ['wʌrisəm] adj inquiétant; inquiet, anxieux

wor·ry ['wʌri] s (pl **-ries**) souci m, inquiétude f; (cause of anxiety) ennui m, tracas m ‖ v (pret & pp **-ried**) tr inquiéter; (to harass, pester) ennuyer, tracasser; **to be worried** s'inquiéter ‖ intr s'inquiéter; **don't worry!** ne vous en faites pas!

worse [wʌrs] adj comp pire, plus mauvais §91; **and to make matters worse** et par surcroît de malheur; **so much the worse** tant pis; **to make** or **get worse** empirer; **what's worse** qui pis est; **worse and worse** de pis en pis ‖ adv comp pis, plus mal §91

worsen ['wʌrsən] tr & intr empirer

wor·ship ['wʌrʃɪp] s culte m, adoration f ‖ v (pret & pp **-shiped** or **-shipped**; ger **-shiping** or **-shipping**) tr adorer ‖ intr prier; (to go to church) aller au culte

worshiper or **worshipper** ['wʌrʃɪpər] s adorateur m, fidèle mf

worst [wʌrst] adj super pire §91; pis ‖ s (le) pire, (le) pis; **to be hurt the worst** être le plus gravement atteint (blessé, etc.); **to get the worst of it** avoir le dessous ‖ adv super pis §91

worsted ['wʊstɪd] adj de laine peignée ‖ s peigné m, tissu m de laine peignée

wort [wʌrt] s (of beer) moût m

worth [wʌrθ] adj digne de; valant, e.g., **book worth three dollars** livre valant trois dollars; **to be worth** valoir; avoir une fortune de; **to be worth** + ger valoir la peine de + inf; **to be worth while** valoir la peine ‖ s valeur f; **a dollar's worth of** pour un dollar de

worthless ['wʌrθlɪs] adj sans valeur; (person) bon à rien, indigne

worth'while' adj utile, de valeur

wor·thy ['wʌrði] adj (comp **-thier**; super **-thiest**) digne ‖ s (pl **-thies**) notable mf; (hum, ironical) personnage m

would [wʊd] aux used to express 1) the past future, e.g., **he said he would come** il a dit qu'il viendrait; 2) the present conditional, e.g., **he would come if he could** il viendrait s'il pouvait; 3) the past conditional, e.g., **he would have come if he had been able (to)** il serait venu s'il avait pu; 4) the

potential mood, e.g., **would that I knew it!** plût à Dieu que je le sache!, je voudrais le savoir!; 5) the past indicative denoting habit or custom in the past, e.g., **he would visit us every day** il nous visitait tous les jours

would'-be' adj prétendu

wound [wund] s blessure f ‖ tr blesser

wounded ['wundɪd] adj blessé ‖ s— **the wounded** les blessés mpl

wow [waʊ] s (e.g., of phonograph record) distorsion f; (slang) succès m formidable ‖ tr (slang) enthousiasmer ‖ interj (slang) formidable!

wrack [ræk] s vestige m; (ruin) naufrage m; (bot) varech m

wraith [reθ] s apparition f

wrangle ['ræŋgəl] s querelle f ‖ intr se quereller

wrap [ræp] s couverture f; (coat) manteau m ‖ v (pret & pp **wrapped**; ger **wrapping**) tr envelopper, emballer

wrap'around wind'shield s pare-brise m panoramique

wrapper ['ræpər] s saut-de-lit m; (of newspaper or magazine) bande f; (of tobacco) robe f

wrap'ping pa'per s papier m d'emballage

wrath [ræθ], [rɑθ] s colère f

wrathful ['ræθfəl], ['rɑθfəl] adj courroucé, en colère

wreak [rik] tr assouvir

wreath [riθ] s (pl **wreaths** [riðz]) couronne f; (of smoke) volute f, panache m

wreathe [rið] tr enguirlander; (e.g., flowers) entrelacer ‖ intr (said of smoke) s'élever en volutes

wreck [rek] s (shipwreck) naufrage m; (debris at sea or elsewhere) épave f; (of train) déraillement m; (of airplane) écrasement m; (of auto) accident m; (of one's hopes) naufrage; **to be a wreck** être une ruine ‖ tr (a ship, one's hopes) faire échouer; (a train) faire dérailler; (one's health) ruiner

wreckage ['rekɪdʒ] s débris mpl, décombres mpl, ruines fpl

wrecker ['rekər] s (tow truck) dépanneuse f; (person) dépanneur m

wreck'ing car' s voiture f de dépannage

wreck'ing crane' s grue f de dépannage

wren [ren] s (orn) troglodyte m; (kinglet) (orn) roitelet m

wrench [rentʃ] s clef f; (pull) secousse f; (twist of a joint) foulure f ‖ tr (e.g., one's ankle) se fouler; (to twist) tordre

wrest [rest] tr arracher violemment

wrestle ['resəl] s lutte f ‖ intr lutter

wrestling ['reslɪŋ] s (sports) lutte f, catch m

wres'tling match' s rencontre f de catch

wretch [retʃ] s misérable mf

wretched ['retʃɪd] adj misérable

wriggle ['rɪgəl] s tortillement m ‖ tr tortiller ‖ intr se tortiller; **to wriggle out of** esquiver adroitement

wrig·gly ['rɪgli] adj (comp **-glier**; super **-gliest**) frétillant; évasif

wring [rɪŋ] v (pret & pp **wrung** [rʌŋ]) tr tordre; (one's hands) se tordre; (s.o.'s hand) serrer fortement; **to wring out** (clothes) essorer; (money, a secret, etc.) arracher

wringer ['rɪŋər] s essoreuse f

wrinkle ['rɪŋkəl] s (in skin) ride f; (in clothes) pli m, faux pli; (clever idea or trick) (coll) truc m || tr plisser || intr se plisser

wrin·kly ['rɪŋkli] adj (comp **-klier**; super **-kliest**) ridé, chiffonné

wrist [rɪst] s poignet m

wrist′band′ s poignet m

wrist′ watch′ s montre-bracelet f

writ [rɪt] s (eccl) écriture f; (law) acte m judiciaire

write [raɪt] v (pret **wrote** [rot]; pp **written** ['rɪtən]) tr écrire; **to write down** consigner par écrit; baisser le prix de; **to write in** insérer; **to write off** (a debt) passer aux profits et pertes; **to write up** rédiger un compte rendu de; (to ballyhoo) faire l'éloge de || intr écrire; **to write back** répondre par écrit

writer ['raɪtər] s écrivain m

writ′er's cramp′ s crampe f des écrivains

write′-up′ s compte m rendu; (ballyhoo) battage m; (com) surestimation f

writhe [raɪð] intr se tordre

writing ['raɪtɪŋ] s l'écriture f; (something written) écrit m, œuvre f; (profession) métier m d'écrivain; **at this writing** au moment où j'écris; **to put in writing** mettre par écrit

writ′ing desk′ s bureau m, écritoire f; (in schoolroom) pupitre m

writ′ing pa′per s papier m à lettres

wrong [rɔŋ], [rɑŋ] adj (unjust) injuste; (incorrect) erroné; (road, address, side, place, etc.) mauvais; ne pas ... qu'il faut, e.g., **I arrived at the wrong city** je ne suis pas arrivé à la ville qu'il fallait; (word) impropre; qui ne marche pas, e.g., **something is wrong with the motor** il y a quelque chose qui ne marche pas dans le moteur; **to be wrong** (i.e., in error) avoir tort; (i.e., to blame) être le coupable || s mal m; injustice f; **to be in the wrong** être dans son tort, avoir tort; **to do wrong** faire du mal, faire du tort || adv mal; **to go wrong** faire fausse route; (said, e.g., of a plan) ne pas marcher; (said of one falling into evil ways) se dévoyer; **to guess wrong** se tromper || tr faire du tort à, être injuste envers

wrongdoer ['rɔŋ,du·ər], ['rɑŋ,du·ər] s malfaiteur m

wrong′do′ing s mal m, tort m; (misdeeds) méfaits mpl

wrong′ num′ber s (telp) mauvais numéro m; **you have the wrong number** vous vous trompez de numéro

wrong′ side′ s (e.g., of material) revers m, envers m; (of the street) mauvais côté m; **to drive on the wrong side** circuler à contre-voie; **to get out of bed on the wrong side** se lever du pied gauche; **wrong side up** à l'envers; **wrong side up** sens dessus dessous

wrought′ i′ron [rɔt] s fer m forgé

wrought′-up′ adj excité, agité

wry [raɪ] adj (comp **wrier**; super **wriest**) tordu, de travers; forcé, ironique

wry′neck′ s (orn) torcol m; (pathol) torticolis m

X

X, x [eks] s XXIVᵉ lettre de l'alphabet

Xavier ['zævɪ·ər], ['zevɪ·ər] s Xavier m

xenophobe ['zenə,fob] s xénophobe mf

Xerxes ['zɑrksiz] s Xerxès m

Xmas ['krɪsməs] adj de Noël || s Noël m

X′ ray′ s (photograph) radiographie f; **to have an X ray** passer à la radio; **X rays** rayons mpl X

X′-ray′ adj radiographique || **X′-ray′** tr radiographier

X′-ray treat′ment s radiothérapie f

xylophone ['zaɪlə,fon] s xylophone m

Y

Y, y [waɪ] s XXVᵉ lettre de l'alphabet

yacht [jɑt] s yacht m

yacht′ club′ s yacht-club m

yah [jɑ] interj (in disgust) pouah!; (in derision) oh là là!

yam [jæm] s igname f; (sweet potato) patate f douce

yank [jæŋk] s (coll) secousse f || tr (coll) tirer d'un coup sec

Yankee ['jæŋki] adj & s yankee mf

yap [jæp] *s* jappement *m*; (slang) criaillerie *f* || *v* (*pret & pp* **yapped**; *ger* **yapping**) *intr* japper; (slang) criailler; (slang) dégoiser

yard [jɑrd] *s* cour *f*; (*for lumber, for repairs, etc.*) chantier *m*; (*measure*) yard *m*; (naut) vergue *f*; (rr) gare *f* de triage

yard'arm' *s* (naut) bout *m* de vergue

yard'mas'ter *s* (rr) chef *m* de dépôt

yard'stick' *s* yard *m* en bois (en métal, etc.); (fig) unité *f* de comparaison

yarn [jɑrn] *s* fil *m*, filé *m*; (coll) histoire *f*

yarrow ['jæro] *s* mille-feuille *f*

yaw [jɔ] *s* (naut) embardée *f*; **yaws** (pathol) pian *m* || *intr* faire des embardées

yawl [jɔl] *s* yole *f*

yawn [jɔn] *s* bâillement *m* || *intr* bâiller; être béant

ye (old spelling of the [ðə]) *art* le, e.g., **ye olde shoppe** la vieille boutique || [ji] *pron* (obs) vous

yea [je] *s* oui *m*; vote *m* affirmatif || *adv* oui, voire

yeah [jɛ] *adv* (coll) oui; **oh yeah?** (coll) de quoi?; **oh yeah!** (coll) ouais!

yean [jin] *intr* (*said of ewe*) agneler; (*said of goat*) chevreter

year [jɪr] *s* an *m*, année *f*; **to be . . . years old** avoir . . . ans; **year in year out** bon an mal an

year'book' *s* annuaire *m*

yearling ['jɪrlɪŋ] *s* animal *m* d'un an; (*horse*) yearling *m*

yearly ['jɪrli] *adj* annuel || *adv* annuellement

yearn [jɑrn] *intr*—**to yearn for** soupirer après; **to yearn to** brûler de

yearning ['jɑrnɪŋ] *s* désir *m* ardent

yeast [jist] *s* levure *f*

yell [jɛl] *s* hurlement *m*; (school yell) cri *m* de ralliement || *tr & intr* hurler

yellow ['jɛlo] *adj* jaune; (*cowardly*) (coll) froussard; (*e.g., press*) à sensation; **to turn yellow** jaunir; (coll) avoir la frousse || *s* jaune *m* || *tr & intr* jaunir

yel'low-ham'mer *s* (orn) bruant *m* jaune

yellowish ['jɛlo·ɪʃ] *adj* jaunâtre

yel'low-jack'et *s* (ent) frelon *m*

yel'low streak' *s* (coll) trait *m* de lâcheté

yelp [jɛlp] *s* glapissement *m*, jappement *m* || *intr* glapir, japper

yen [jɛn] *s*—**to have a yen to** or **for** (coll) avoir envie de

yeo·man ['joman] *s* (*pl* **-men**) yeoman *m*; (*clerical worker*) (nav) commis *m* aux écritures

yeo'man of the guard' *s* (Brit) hallebardier *m* de la garde du corps

yeo'man's serv'ice *s* effort *m* précieux

yes [jɛs] *s* oui *m* || *adv* oui; (to contradict a negative statement or question) si or pardon, e.g., "You didn't know." "Yes, I did!" "Vous ne le saviez pas." "Si!" || *v* (*pret & pp*

yessed; *ger* **yessing**) *tr* dire oui à || *intr* dire oui

yes' man' *s* (*pl* **men'**) (coll) M. Toujours; **to be a yes man** opiner du bonnet; **yes men** (coll) béni-oui-oui *mpl*

yesterday ['jɛstərdi], ['jɛstər,de] *adj*, *s*, *& adv* hier *m*; **yesterday morning** hier matin

yet [jɛt] *adv* encore; **as yet** jusqu'à présent; **not yet** pas encore || *conj* cependant

yew' tree' [ju] *s* if *m*

Yiddish ['jɪdɪʃ] *adj & s* yiddish *m*

yield [jild] *s* rendement *m*; (crop) produit *m*; (income produced) rapport *m*, revenu *m* || *tr* rendre, produire; (*a profit; a crop*) rapporter; (*to surrender*) céder || *intr* produire, rapporter; céder, se rendre; (public sign) priorité (à droite; à gauche)

YMCA ['waɪ'ɛm'si'e] *s* (letterword) (Young Men's Christian Association) Association *f* des jeunesses chrétiennes

yo·del ['jodəl] *s* tyrolienne *f* || *v* (*pret & pp* **-deled** or **-delled**; *ger* **-deling** or **-delling**) *tr & intr* jodler

yogurt ['jogurt] *s* yogourt *m*

yoke [jok] *s* (*pair of draft animals*) paire *f*; (device to join a pair of draft animals) joug *m*; (*of a shirt*) empiècement *m*; (elec) culasse *f*; (fig) joug; **to throw off the yoke** secouer le joug || *tr* accoupler

yokel ['jokəl] *s* rustaud *m*, manant *m*

yolk [jok] *s* jaune *m* d'œuf

yonder ['jɑndər] *adj* ce . . . -là là-bas || *adv* là-bas

yore [jor] *s*—**of yore** d'antan

you [ju] *pron pers* vous, toi §85; vous, tu §87; vous, te §87 || *pron indef* (coll) on §85, e.g., **you go in this way** on entre par ici

young [jʌŋ] *adj* (comp **younger** ['jʌŋgər]; super **youngest** ['jʌŋgɪst]) jeune || **the young** les jeunes; (of animal) les petits *mpl*; **to be with young** (said of animal) être pleine; **young and old** les grands et les petits

young' la'dy *s* (*pl* **-dies**) jeune fille *f*; (married) jeune femme *f*; **young ladies** jeunes personnes *fpl*

young' man' *s* (*pl* **men'**) jeune homme *m*; **young men** jeunes gens *mpl*

young' peo'ple *spl* jeunes gens *mpl*

youngster ['jʌŋstər] *s* gosse *mf*

your [jur] *adj poss* votre, ton §88

yours [jurz] *pron poss* le vôtre, le tien §89; **a friend of yours** un de vos amis; **cordially yours** (complimentary close) amitiés; **yours truly** or **sincerely yours** (complimentary close) veuillez agréer, Monsieur, l'expression de mes sentiments distingués

your·self [jur'sɛlf] *pron pers* (*pl* **-selves** ['sɛlvz]) vous-même, toi-même §86; vous, te §87; vous, toi §85

youth [juθ] *s* (*pl* **youths** [juθs], [juðz]) jeunesse *f*; (person) jeune homme *m*; **youths** jeunes *mpl*

youthful ['juθfəl] adj jeune, juvénile
yowl [jaʊl] s hurlement m || intr hurler
Yugoslav ['jugo'slav] adj yougoslave
|| s Yougoslave mf

Yugoslavia ['jugo'slavɪ·ə] s Yougo-
slavie f; la Yougoslavie
Yule' log' [jul] s bûche f de Noël
Yule'tide' s les fêtes fpl de Noël

Z

Z, z [zi] or [zed] (Brit) s XXVIᵉ lettre
de l'alphabet
za·ny ['zeni] adj (comp -nier; super
-niest) bouffon, toqué || s (pl -nies)
bouffon m
zeal [zil] s zèle m
zealot ['zɛlət] s zélateur m, adepte mf
zealotry [ˈzɛlətri] s fanatisme m
zealous ['zɛləs] adj zélé
zebra [ˈzibrə] s zèbre m
zenith ['zinɪθ] s zénith m
zephyr ['zɛfər] s zéphyr m
zeppelin [ˈzɛpəlɪn] s zeppelin m
ze·ro ['zɪro] s (pl -ros or -roes) zéro
m || intr—to zero in (mil) régler la
ligne de mire
ze'ro hour' s heure f H
zest [zɛst] s enthousiasme m; (agreeable and piquant flavor) saveur f,
piquant m
Zeus [zus] s Zeus m
zig-zag ['zɪg‚zæg] adj & adv en zigzag
|| s zigzag m || v (pret & pp -zagged;
ger -zagging) intr zigzaguer

zinc [zɪŋk] s zinc m
Zionism ['zaɪ·ə‚nɪzəm] s sionisme m
zip [zɪp] s (coll) sifflement m; (coll)
énergie f || v (pret & pp zipped; ger
zipping) tr fermer à fermeture éclair
|| intr siffler; **to zip by** (coll) passer
comme un éclair
zipper [ˈzɪpər] s fermeture f éclair
zither ['zɪθər] s cithare f
zodiac ['zodɪ‚æk] s zodiaque m
zone [zon] s zone f
zon'ing or'dinance s réglementation f
urbaine
zoo [zu] s zoo m
zoologic(al) [‚zo·ə'lɑdʒɪk(əl)] adj zoologique
zoology [zo'ɑlədʒi] s zoologie f
zoom [zum] s vrombissement m; (aer)
montée f en chandelle || intr vrom-
bir; **to zoom up** monter en chandelle
zoot' suit' [zut] s costume m zazou
Zu·lu ['zulu] adj zoulou || s (pl -lus)
Zoulou m

Speak any language
as easily as you speak your own!

FRENCH

☐ FRENCH STORIES Wallace Fowlie, ed.   10475 • $1.95

☐ THE BANTAM NEW COLLEGE FRENCH & ENGLISH
   DICTIONARY Roger J. Steiner   11692 • $1.95

☐ READ, WRITE, SPEAK FRENCH Mendor Brunetti   2656 • $1.95

HEBREW

☐ THE NEW BANTAM-MEGIDDO HEBREW & ENGLISH
   DICTIONARY Reuben Sivan & Edward A. Levenston   2094 • $1.95

LATIN

☐ THE NEW COLLEGE LATIN & ENGLISH DICTIONARY
   John Traupman   10780 • $1.75

MIDDLE EAST

☐ THE ISRAEL-ARAB READER Walter Laqueur, ed.   2487 • $2.95

SPANISH

☐ SPANISH STORIES Angel Flores, ed.   11231 • $1.95

☐ THE BANTAM NEW COLLEGE SPANISH & ENGLISH DICTIONARY
   Edwin B. Williams   10746 • $1.75

☐ I AM JOAQUIN Rodolfo Gonzales   7230 • $1.25

☐ FIRST SPANISH READER Angel Flores, ed.   6362 • $1.50

☐ GETTING ALONG IN SPANISH Mario Pei   2616 • $1.25

Buy them at your local bookstore or use this handy coupon for ordering:

THE NAMES THAT SPELL GREAT LITERATURE

Choose from today's most renowned world authors—every one an important addition to your personal library.

Hermann Hesse

☐	KNULP	2906	• $1.95
☐	MAGISTER LUDI	2645	• $1.75
☐	DEMIAN	2944	• $1.75
☐	GERTRUDE	10060	• $1.95
☐	THE JOURNEY TO THE EAST	10136	• $1.75
☐	SIDDHARTHA	10266	• $1.75
☐	BENEATH THE WHEEL	10352	• $1.95
☐	NARCISSUS AND GOLDMUND	10466	• $1.95
☐	STEPPENWOLF	11289	• $1.95
☐	ROSSHALDE	11510	• $1.95

Alexander Solzhenitsyn

☐	ONE DAY IN THE LIFE OF IVAN DENISOVICH	2949	• $1.50
☐	AUGUST 1914	2997	• $2.50
☐	STORIES AND PROSE POEMS	7409	• $1.50
☐	THE LOVE-GIRL AND THE INNOCENT	10246	• $1.50
☐	CANCER WARD	11300	• $2.50

Jerzy Kosinski

☐	THE DEVIL TREE	7865	• $1.50
☐	BEING THERE	10625	• $1.75
☐	STEPS	11100	• $1.75
☐	THE PAINTED BIRD	11407	• $1.95

Doris Lessing

☐	THE SUMMER BEFORE THE DARK	2640	• $1.95
☐	THE GOLDEN NOTEBOOK	10425	• $2.25
☐	THE FOUR-GATED CITY	7937	• $1.95

André Schwarz-Bart

☐	THE LAST OF THE JUST	10469	• $1.95

Buy them at your local bookstore or use this handy coupon for ordering:

Bantam Books, Inc., Dépt. EDG, 414 East Golf Road, Des Plaines, Ill. 60016

Please send me the books I have checked above. I am enclosing $_____ (please add 50¢ to cover postage and handling). Send check or money order —no cash or C.O.D.'s please.

Mr/Mrs/Miss_____

Address_____

City_____State/Zip_____

EDG—11/77

Please allow four weeks for delivery. This offer expires 5/78.

Facts at Your Fingertips!

Segovia 94901
8 Evalth in AA

Bantam Book Catalog

Here's your up-to-the-minute listing of every book currently available from Bantam.

This easy-to-use catalog is divided into categories and contains over 1400 titles by your favorite authors.

So don't delay—take advantage of this special opportunity to increase your reading pleasure.

Just send us your name and address and 25¢ (to help defray postage and handling costs).

person	6	7	8	9	10	11
				negative		*negative*
1						
2						
3						
	y—there; to it; to them	en—some; of it; of them	VERB or AUX-ILIARY	pas—not §90B	past participle	personne—no one §90B
4						
5						
6						

present indicative of verbs of the first conjugation is changed to -é, e.g., donné-je? do I give?, but these forms are not in current use in prose. All the forms not used are replaced by the affirmative forms introduced by est-ce que in affirmative interrogative sentences and by n'est-ce pas que in negative interrogatory sentences. And est-ce que and n'est-ce pas que may be thus used in any person of any tense of the indicative. The ending -e of the first singular imperfect subjunctive of some verbs is likewise changed to -é in conditional clauses without si in literary usage, e.g., dussé-je if I should.

In affirmative imperative sentences, the subject pronouns are not expressed and the pronouns in columns 3, 4, 5, 6, and 7 are placed after the verb and attached to it and to each other with hyphens except where elision occurs, and the pronouns in column 4 precede those in column 3. And unless followed by en or y, me is replaced by moi and te is replaced by toi; and moi and toi are stressed.

In negative imperative sentences, the subject pronouns are not expressed either: and columns 2, 3, 4, 5, 6, 7, 8, and 9 have the same order as in negative declarative sentences.

A pronoun of column 5 cannot be used with a pronoun of column 4 but is replaced by a disjunctive pronoun preceded by the preposition à.

§88 The following table shows all the forms of possessive adjectives with their translations into English.

masc sg	fem sg	masc & fem pl	
mon	ma*	mes	my
ton	ta*	tes	your, thy, thine
son	sa*	ses	his, her, its
notre	notre	nos	our
votre	votre	vos	your
leur	leur	leurs	their

* The forms **mon, ton,** and **son** are used instead of **ma, ta,** and **sa** respectively before feminine nouns and adjectives beginning with a vowel or mute h, e.g., **Marie a fait un cadeau à son aïeule** Mary gave a present to her grandmother; e.g., **elle y est venue avec son aimable tante** she came with her nice aunt.

The possessive adjectives:
1) agree in gender and number with the thing possessed rather than with the possessor, e.g., **Marie lit son livre** Mary is reading her book
2) must be repeated before each noun in a series, e.g., **Marie apporte son stylo et son crayon** Mary is bringing her pen and pencil

§89 The following table shows all the forms of possessive pronouns with their translations into English.

	sg	pl	
masc	le mien	les miens	mine
fem	la mienne	les miennes	
masc	le tien	les tiens	yours, thine
fem	la tienne	les tiennes	
masc	le sien	les siens	his, hers, its
fem	la sienne	les siennes	
masc	le nôtre	les nôtres	ours
fem	la nôtre		
masc	le vôtre	les vôtres	yours
fem	la vôtre		
masc	le leur	les leurs	theirs
fem	la leur		

The possessive pronouns:
1) agree in gender and number with the thing possessed rather than with the possessor, e.g., **donnez votre livre à Marie, elle a perdu le sien** give your book to Mary; she has lost hers
2) are preceded by a definite article, e.g., **tu dois obéir à son ordre et au mien** you must obey his order and mine
3) are sometimes used without antecedent: a) **le mien** mine, my own (*i.e., property*); **le sien** his, his own (*i.e., property*); hers, her own (*i.e., property*); etc.; b) **les miens** my folks, my family;

28